AD

EXECUTIVE RECRUITERS ALMANAC

Managing Editor
Steven Graber

Assistant Managing Editor
Jennifer J. Pfalzgraf

Editor
Heidi E. Sampson

Senior Associate Editor
William P. McNeill

Associate Editors
Marcie DiPietro • Michelle Roy Kelly

Editorial Assistants
Michelle Forcier Anderson • Jayna S. Stafford

Editorial Interns
Todd A. Donatello • Kristen M. Gustafson

Adams Media Corporation
HOLBROOK, MASSACHUSETTS

Published by Adams Media Corporation
260 Center Street, Holbrook, MA 02343

ISBN: 1-58062-029-9

Manufactured in the United States of America.

B C D E F G H I J

Because addresses and telephone numbers of smaller companies change rapidly, we recommend you call each company and verify the information before mailing to the employers listed in this book. Mass mailings are not recommended.

While the publisher has made every reasonable effort to obtain and verify accurate information, occasional errors are inevitable due to the magnitude of the database. Should you discover an error, or if a company is missing, please write the editors at the above address so that we may update future editions.

"This publication is designed to provide accurate and authoritative information with regard to the subject matter covered. It is sold with the understanding that the publisher is not engaged in rendering legal, accounting, or other professional advice. If legal advice or other expert assistance is required, the services of a competent professional person should be sought."

—From a *Declaration of Principles* jointly adopted by a Committee of the American Bar Association and a Committee of Publishers and Associations

The appearance of a listing in the book does not constitute an endorsement from the publisher.

This book is available at quantity discounts for bulk purchases.
For information, call 800/872-5627 (in Massachusetts 781/767-8100).

Visit our exciting job and career site at http://www.careercity.com

TABLE OF CONTENTS

SECTION ONE: EMPLOYMENT SERVICES LISTINGS

SECTION TWO: EMPLOYMENT SERVICES INDEXES

INTRODUCTION

Just as more and more companies utilize recruiters and placement agencies to fill their staffing needs, an increasing number of jobseekers turn to executive search firms and other employment services to assist them in their respective job hunts. While it is not advised that you rely on them exclusively, these services can be a valuable resource, offering a wealth of experience and contacts to help you locate suitable job opportunities not otherwise advertised. In short, employment services allow the jobseeker to tap into the hidden job market.

There are several types of employment services you may consider as part of your job search efforts:

EXECUTIVE SEARCH FIRMS

Also known as "headhunters," these firms consist of recruiters who are paid by client companies that hire them specifically to fill a position. The prospective employee is generally not charged a fee.

Companies that do not find it practical to advertise openings in the newspaper or on the Internet often count on executive search firms as an instrumental means to seek out viable candidates. Rather than be inundated with resumes from inexperienced or unqualified candidates, these companies prefer the efficiency of hiring a search firm to help minimize their screening process and find a good match. The recruiters attract and refer qualified candidates, and often approach currently employed candidates directly.

Executive search firms focus on handling higher-salaried technical, executive, and managerial placements. Many firms specialize in particular industries, while generalist firms typically provide placements in a wide range of industries. If you choose to use executive search firms for your job hunt, it is advised that you contact several firms that specialize in your field of interest or expertise, as well as reputable generalist firms in your geographical area.

There are two basic types of executive search firms -- retainer- and contingency-based. Note, however, that some firms conduct searches of both types. Essentially, retainer firms are hired by a client company for a search and paid a fee regardless of whether or not a placement is made. Conversely, contingency firms receive payment only when their candidate is hired. The differences, as well as the advantages and disadvantages of both types of firms, are discussed at greater length in the section titled "Working with Executive Recruiters" (p. 7).

PERMANENT EMPLOYMENT AGENCIES

These are the most common type of placement agencies. They, too, fall into different categories; there are both private agencies and state government agencies. State agencies place a much wider range of individuals. They also work with many low-skill workers, although they do place experienced workers as well and shouldn't be ruled out altogether as a resource. More often, though, jobseekers looking for professional positions will have better luck with private employment agencies. The vast majority of permanent employment agencies listed in this book are private agencies.

Consider choosing an agency that specializes in your profession. Employers in certain high-demand fields depend on specialized employment agencies to find good candidates. Industries that rely heavily on these types of agencies include banking, finance, advertising, data processing, health care, insurance, publishing, retail, and sales, as well as a variety of technical fields. Like executive search firms, most specialized employment agencies aren't as interested in candidates with little or no experience in the particular industry. But since they fill fewer senior-level positions than search firms, a specialized employment agency will still be interested in trying to place you if you're a professional with more than a few years of relevant experience in the industry.

In some states, private employment agencies can charge the jobseeker a fee. However, typically employment agencies charge the employer a fee based on a percentage of the new employee's salary. As a general rule, most employment agencies will never guarantee a job and will not seek payment until after the candidate has been placed. If you're unsure about a particular agency, you may inquire about them with a local chapter of the Better Business Bureau. These agencies must be licensed by the state in which they operate.

TEMPORARY EMPLOYMENT AGENCIES

Temporary agencies are also a viable option. Traditionally, these agencies specialize mainly in clerical and support work, but it's becoming much more common to find temporary assignments in other areas like accounting or computer programming. Some jobseekers opt for temporary assignments to provide additional income during a job search as well as experience for their resume, and even more attractive is the possibility that a temporary assignment may provide valuable business contacts or lead to a permanent job opportunity. There are also some workers in today's market who make their living as temps in very specialized fields. Note that many of the agencies in this book provide both temporary and permanent placements. Generally, your chances at finding a temporary position that evolves into a permanent one will be higher with a temporary agency that is in the business of providing permanent placements as well. You will also find that many temporary agencies classify themselves as "temp-to-perm" or "temp-to-hire" agencies, indicating that they commonly place candidates in temporary jobs which evolve into permanent positions.

Most temporary agencies will require that you send a resume, and this is a good idea even if it is not specifically required. Also, be prepared to take a number of tests at your interview with the agency. The candidate is generally not charged a fee for the agency's services.

CONTRACT SERVICES FIRMS

Firms that place individuals on a contract basis commonly receive job orders from client companies that can last anywhere from a month to over a year. The function of these firms differs from that of a temporary agency in that the candidate has specific, marketable skills they wish to put to work, and the contract recruiter interviews the candidate extensively. Most often, contract services firms specialize in placing technical professionals, though some do specialize in other fields, including clerical and office support. The use of these firms is increasing in popularity, as jobseekers with technical skills recognize the benefit of utilizing and demonstrating their talents at a sampling of different companies, and establishing contacts along the way that could lead to a permanent position, if desired. Most contract services firms do not charge a fee to the candidate.

CAREER/OUTPLACEMENT COUNSELING FIRMS

These firms are very diverse in the services they provide. Many nonprofit organizations -- colleges, universities, private associations -- offer free or very inexpensive counseling services. For-profit career/outplacement counseling services, on the other hand, can charge a broad range of fees, depending on what services they provide. Most of the career/outplacement counseling firms listed in this book are for-profit firms. Services offered include career counseling, outplacement, resume development/writing, interview preparation, assessment testing, and various workshops. Upon contacting one of these firms, you should ask about the specific services that firm provides. Some firms provide career counseling only, teaching you how to conduct your own job search, while others also provide outplacement services. The difference here is that those which provide outplacement will conduct a job search for you, in addition to the counseling services. Firms like these are sometimes referred to as "marketing firms."

According to a representative at Career Ventures Counseling Services in Salem, Massachusetts, fees (paid upfront) for career counseling average about $85 per hour, while counseling firms located in major cities tend to be more expensive. Furthermore, outplacement fees can range from $170 to over $1,000. As with any type of employment service, results are not guaranteed, and you may want to check on a firm's reputation through the local Better Business Bureau.

WORKING WITH EXECUTIVE RECRUITERS

Like all aspects of a job search, you should devise a game plan before you contact an executive recruiter. First and foremost, it is important to distinguish between retainer and contingency search firms and what each has to offer. The fundamental difference is that retainer firms are hired by a client company and paid a fee to perform a search, while contingency firms are paid by the client company only if a placement has been made. Fees are based on the position's first-year salary, usually between 20 and 35 percent, and retainer firm fees tend to be at the higher end of that scale, according to Ivan Samuels, President of Abbott's of Boston, an executive search firm that conducts both types of searches.

Generally, retainer firms are used by companies to fill senior-level positions, with salaries over $60,000. In most cases, a company will hire only one retainer firm to fill a given position, and part of the process is a thorough, on-site visit by the search firm to the client company so that the recruiter may check out the operation. These search firms are recommended for a highly experienced professional seeking a job in his or her current field. Confidentiality is more secure with these firms, since a recruiter may only use your file in consideration for one job at a time, during which you're off-limits to the other recruiters at that firm, and most retainer firms will not freely circulate your resume without permission. This is particularly important to a jobseeker who is currently employed and insists on absolute discretion. If that's the case, however, make sure you don't contact a retainer firm used by your current employer.

Contingency firms make placements that cover a broader salary range, so these firms are more ideal for someone seeking a junior- or mid-level position. Unlike retainer firms, contingency firms may be competing with a few other firms to fill a certain opening. As a result, these firms can be quicker and more responsive to your need to find a job. In addition, a contingency firm will distribute your resume more widely. Some firms require your permission before sending your resume to any given company, while others ask that you trust their discretion. You should inquire about this with your recruiter at the outset, and choose according to your needs.

That said, once you're ready to choose the firms you will contact, keep in mind that recruiters are working for the companies that hire them, not for you, the jobseeker. Attempting to fill a position -- especially amongst fierce competition with other firms -- means your best interests may not be the recruiter's only priority. For this reason, you should contact as many search firms as possible (we recommend a minimum of three), in order to increase your chances of finding your ideal position.

Executive search firms that specialize in your industry of interest are your best bet, and you'll find that many firms have multiple specializations. Generalist firms, however, should not be ruled out. These firms conduct searches in a variety of fields. It is a good idea to contact one or two of these firms as well, particularly the more reputable firms with multiple locations. You should concentrate on firms in your geographical area, but you don't have to limit yourself to these, for some firms operate nationally or internationally.

A phone call is your first step, during which you should speak with a recruiter and exchange all relevant information. Ask lots of questions to determine the firm's credibility, whether they operate on a retainer or contingency basis (or both), and any and all questions you have regarding the firm's procedures. Offer the recruiter information about your employment history, as well as what type of work you are seeking. Make sure you sound enthusiastic, but not pushy. The recruiter will ask that you send a resume and cover letter as soon as possible.

Occasionally, the recruiter will arrange to meet with you, but most often this will not occur until he or she has received your resume and has found a potential match. James E. Slate, President of F-O-R-T-U-N-E Personnel Consultants in Topsfield, Massachusetts, advises that you not expect an abundance of personal attention at the beginning of the relationship with your recruiter, particularly with a large firm that works nationally and does most of its work over the phone. You should, however, use your recruiter's inside knowledge to your best advantage. Some recruiters will help coach you before an interview and most are open about giving you all the facts they know about a client company.

In addition, do your own research on the company before your first interview, although you should never contact a company directly that is considering you for a position through an executive search firm. The recruiter acts as a go-between, including all salary and benefit negotiations.

Additional resources for contacting executive search firms include:

Association of Executive Search Consultants (AESC)
500 Fifth Avenue
Suite 930
New York NY 10110
212/398-9556

American Management Association (AMA)
Management Services Department
135 West 50th Street
New York NY 10020
212/596-8100

EXPLANATION OF LISTINGS

The employment service listings in this book are presented in alphabetical order by state, and by agency type (executive search, permanent, temporary, contract services, and career/outplacement counseling) within each state.

Each listing contains some or all of the following types of information:

- Name of employment service
- Mailing address
- Phone, toll-free phone, and fax number
- Recorded jobline
- Contact person and title or department
- E-mail address
- World Wide Web address
- Employment service profile
- Area(s) of specialization
- Positions commonly filled
- Benefits available
- Corporate headquarters location
- Other area, national, and international locations
- Average salary range of placements
- Number of placements per year

ALABAMA

EXECUTIVE SEARCH FIRMS

ASSOCIATES PERSONNEL INC.
414 East Grove Street, Montgomery AL 36104. 334/269-9675. **Contact:** Manager. **Description:** An executive search firm. **Specializes in the areas of:** Administration; Computer Science/Software; Engineering; Sales.

BREEN PERSONNEL, INC.
P.O. Box 1413, Huntsville AL 35807. 205/536-4431. **Fax:** 205/539-0583. **Contact:** Bill Breen, President. **Description:** An executive search firm operating on both retained and contingency bases. Company pays fee. **Specializes in the areas of:** Computer Science/Software; Engineering; Personnel/Labor Relations. **Positions commonly filled include:** Accountant/Auditor; Buyer; Chief Financial Officer; Computer Programmer; Controller; Credit Manager; Database Manager; Design Engineer; Electrical/Electronics Engineer; Finance Director; Human Resources Manager; Industrial Engineer; Industrial Production Manager; Manufacturing Engineer; Mechanical Engineer; MIS Specialist; Operations/Production Manager; Purchasing Agent/Manager; Quality Control Supervisor; Sales Engineer; Sales Executive; Sales Manager; Software Engineer; Systems Analyst; Telecommunications Manager. **Other U.S. locations:** Nationwide. **Average salary range of placements:** More than $50,000. **Number of placements per year:** 200 - 499.

MARY CHEEK & ASSOCIATES, INC.
11991 Knollwood Road, Northport AL 35475. 205/333-8550. **Fax:** 205/333-9440. **Contact:** Mary Cheek, President. **Description:** An executive search firm operating on both retained and contingency bases. Company pays fee. **Specializes in the areas of:** Accounting/Auditing; Engineering; Industrial; Personnel/Labor Relations; Technical. **Positions commonly filled include:** Accountant/Auditor; Buyer; Chief Financial Officer; Controller; Design Engineer; Draftsperson; Electrical/Electronics Engineer; General Manager; Human Resources Manager; Industrial Engineer; Industrial Production Manager; Management Trainee; Manufacturing Engineer; Mechanical Engineer; Operations/Production Manager; Purchasing Agent/Manager; Quality Control Supervisor; Transportation/Traffic Specialist. **Number of placements per year:** 1 - 49.

CLARK PERSONNEL SERVICE OF MOBILE, INC.
4315 Downtowner Boulevard, Loop North, Mobile AL 36609. 334/342-5511. **Fax:** 334/343-5588. **Contact:** Donna Clark, President. **Description:** An executive search firm operating on a contingency basis. Company pays fee. **Specializes in the areas of:** Accounting/Auditing; Computer Science/Software; Engineering; Industrial; Manufacturing; Personnel/Labor Relations; Sales; Transportation. **Positions commonly filled include:** Accountant/Auditor; Administrative Manager; Aerospace Engineer; Agricultural Engineer; Architect; Bank Officer/Manager; Biological Scientist; Biomedical Engineer; Blue-Collar Worker Supervisor; Branch Manager; Chemical Engineer; Chemist; Civil Engineer; Clerical Supervisor; Computer Programmer; Credit Manager; Draftsperson; Electrical/Electronics Engineer; Human Resources Manager; Industrial Engineer; Manufacturer's/Wholesaler's Sales Rep.; Mechanical Engineer; Metallurgical Engineer; Mining Engineer; Nuclear Engineer; Operations/Production Manager; Petroleum Engineer; Purchasing Agent/Manager; Quality Control Supervisor; Software Engineer; Stationary Engineer; Structural Engineer; Systems Analyst. **Corporate headquarters location:** This Location. **Average salary range of placements:** $30,000 - $50,000. **Number of placements per year:** 200 - 499.

DUNHILL OF SOUTH BIRMINGHAM
2738 18th Street South, Birmingham AL 35209. 205/877-4580. **Toll-free phone:** 800/548-0116. **Fax:** 205/877-4590. **Contact:** Peggy Clarke, President. **Description:** An executive search firm operating on a contingency basis. The firm also provides temporary and contract services. Company pays fee. **Specializes in the areas of:** Accounting/Auditing; Administration; Banking; Computer Science/Software; Finance; Manufacturing; Personnel/Labor Relations; Secretarial; Technical. **Positions commonly filled include:** Accountant/Auditor; Administrative Manager; Bank Officer/Manager; Budget Analyst; Computer Programmer; Credit Manager; Financial Analyst; Health Services Manager; Human Resources Manager; Market Research Analyst; MIS Specialist; Operations/Production Manager; Purchasing Agent/Manager; Quality Control Supervisor; Software Engineer; Systems Analyst; Telecommunications Manager. **Benefits available to temporary workers:** Bonus Award/Plan; Medical Insurance; Paid Holidays; Paid Vacation. **Corporate headquarters location:** Woodbury NY. **Other U.S. locations:** Nationwide. **Number of placements per year:** 50 - 99.

EXECUTIVE PERSONNEL
1612 Highway 78 East, Suite 3, Oxford AL 36203. 205/831-2434. **Contact:** Manager. **Description:** An executive search firm.

F-O-R-T-U-N-E PERSONNEL CONSULTANTS
3311 Bob Wallace Avenue SW, Suite 204, Huntsville AL 35805. 205/534-7282. **Contact:** President. **Description:** An executive search firm operating on a contingency basis. Company pays fee. **Specializes in the areas of:** Accounting/Auditing; Administration; Computer Science/Software; Engineering; Finance; General Management; Industrial; Manufacturing; Personnel/Labor Relations. **Positions commonly filled include:** Accountant/Auditor; Buyer; Ceramics Engineer; Computer Programmer; Design Engineer; Designer; Electrical/Electronics Engineer; Environmental Engineer; Financial Analyst; General Manager; Human Resources Specialist; Industrial Engineer; Industrial Production Manager; Materials Engineer; Mechanical Engineer; Metallurgical Engineer; MIS Specialist; Pharmacist; Quality Control Supervisor; Telecommunications Manager; Transportation/Traffic Specialist. **Corporate headquarters location:** New York NY. **Other U.S. locations:** Nationwide. **Average salary range of placements:** More than $50,000. **Number of placements per year:** 100 - 199.

ROBERT HALF INTERNATIONAL ACCOUNTEMPS
2600A SouthBridge Parkway, Suite 430, Birmingham AL 35209. 205/879-4000. **Contact:** Manager. **World Wide Web address:** http://www.roberthalf.com. **Description:** An executive search firm. Accountemps (also at this location) provides temporary placements. **Specializes in the areas of:** Accounting/Auditing. **Corporate headquarters location:** Menlo Park CA. **Other U.S. locations:** Nationwide.

HEALTHCARE RECRUITERS OF ALABAMA
1945 Hoover Court, Suite 205, Birmingham AL 35226. 205/979-9840. **Fax:** 205/979-5879. **Contact:** Frank Johnson, President. **Description:** An executive search firm operating on both retainer and

contingency bases. The company focuses on the placement of sales, marketing, management, and health care professionals. Company pays fee. **Specializes in the areas of:** Health/Medical; Sales; Technical. **Positions commonly filled include:** Biological Scientist; Biomedical Engineer; Chemist; Clinical Lab Technician; Dental Assistant/Dental Hygienist; Dentist; Dietician/Nutritionist; EEG Technologist; EKG Technician; General Manager; Health Services Manager; Licensed Practical Nurse; Manufacturer's/Wholesaler's Sales Rep.; Market Research Analyst; MIS Specialist; Nuclear Medicine Technologist; Pharmacist; Physical Therapist; Physician; Psychologist; Recreational Therapist; Registered Nurse; Respiratory Therapist; Science Technologist; Software Engineer; Surgical Technician; Veterinarian. **Corporate headquarters location:** Dallas TX. **Other U.S. locations:** Nationwide. **Number of placements per year:** 1 - 49.

HUGHES & ASSOCIATES
3737 Government Boulevard, Suite 304B, Mobile AL 36693. 334/661-8888. **Contact:** Manager. **Description:** An executive search firm. **Specializes in the areas of:** Chemical; Petrochemical.

INFORMATION TECHNOLOGY SERVICES
P.O. Box 7107, Huntsville AL 35807. 205/533-9800. **Contact:** Manager. **Description:** An executive search firm. **Specializes in the areas of:** Computer Science/Software.

LANGFORD SEARCH
2025 Third Avenue North, Suite 301, Birmingham AL 35203. 205/328-5477. **Contact:** Manager. **Description:** An executive search firm. **Specializes in the areas of:** Accounting/Auditing; Finance; Information Technology.

MANAGEMENT RECRUITERS INTERNATIONAL COMPUSEARCH OF MOBILE
3263 Demetropolis Road, Suite 6-C, Mobile AL 36693. 334/602-0104. **Contact:** Mr. R.C. Brock, Manager. **Description:** An executive search firm. **Specializes in the areas of:** Accounting/Auditing; Administration; Advertising; Architecture/Construction; Banking; Chemical; Communications; Computer Hardware/Software; Design; Electrical; Engineering; Food Industry; General Management; Health/Medical; Insurance; Legal; Manufacturing; Operations Management; Personnel/Labor Relations; Procurement; Publishing; Retail; Sales; Technical; Textiles; Transportation. **Positions commonly filled include:** Chemical Engineer; Chemist; Computer Programmer; Electrical/Electronics Engineer; Health Care Administrator; Industrial Engineer; Mechanical Engineer; Registered Nurse; Systems Analyst.

MANAGEMENT RECRUITERS INTERNATIONAL COMPUSEARCH OF BIRMINGHAM
P.O. Box 381626, Birmingham AL 35238-1626. 205/871-3550. **Contact:** Office Manager. **Description:** An executive search firm. **Specializes in the areas of:** Accounting/Auditing; Administration; Advertising; Architecture/Construction; Banking; Chemical; Communications; Computer Hardware/Software; Design; Electrical; Engineering; Food Industry; General Management; Health/Medical; Insurance; Legal; Manufacturing; Operations Management; Personnel/Labor Relations; Procurement; Publishing; Retail; Sales; Technical; Textiles; Transportation.

MILLMAN SEARCH GROUP
28651 U.S. Highway 98, Suite A5, Daphne AL 36526. 334/626-5513. **Contact:** Office Manager. **Description:** An executive search firm. **Specializes in the areas of:** Retail.

NATIONAL LABOR LINE
805 Oakwood Avenue NW, Huntsville AL 35811. 205/535-9541. **Fax:** 205/535-0744. **Contact:** Carol Rouse, Owner. **Description:** An executive search firm that also provides contract services and career/outplacement counseling. Company pays fee. **Specializes in the areas of:** Computer Science/Software; Engineering; Industrial; Technical. **Positions commonly filled include:** Applications Engineer; Blue-Collar Worker Supervisor; Chemical Engineer; Civil Engineer; Computer Programmer; Database Manager; Design Engineer; Draftsperson; Electrical/Electronics Engineer; Environmental Engineer; Industrial Engineer; Internet Services Manager; Manufacturing Engineer; Metallurgical Engineer; MIS Specialist; Online Content Specialist; Physical Therapist; Production Manager; Project Manager; Purchasing Agent/Manager; Quality Control Supervisor; Sales Engineer; Software Engineer; Systems Analyst; Systems Manager; Technical Writer/Editor; Telecommunications Manager; Transportation/Traffic Specialist; Webmaster. **Corporate headquarters location:** This Location. **Other U.S. locations:** Nationwide. **Average salary range of placements:** More than $50,000. **Number of placements per year:** 1 - 49.

SEARCH SOUTH INC.
P.O. Box 2224, Anniston AL 36202. 205/237-1868. **Contact:** Manager. **Description:** An executive search firm.

J.L. SMALL ASSOCIATES
3201 Lovna Road, Birmingham AL 35216. 205/823-4545. **Fax:** 205/824-1430. **Contact:** Jim Small, Owner. **Description:** An executive search firm operating on a contingency basis. Founded in 1989. Company pays fee. **Specializes in the areas of:** Accounting/Auditing; Administration; Engineering; Industrial; Personnel/Labor Relations. **Positions commonly filled include:** Accountant/Auditor; Budget Analyst; Chemical Engineer; Chemist; Chief Financial Officer; Civil Engineer; Computer Programmer; Controller; Environmental Engineer; Financial Analyst; General Manager; Human Resources Manager; Industrial Engineer; Industrial Production Manager; Manufacturing Engineer; Mechanical Engineer; Metallurgical Engineer; MIS Specialist; Operations Manager; Purchasing Agent/Manager; Quality Control Supervisor; Systems Analyst. **Corporate headquarters location:** This Location. **Average salary range of placements:** $30,000 - $50,000. **Number of placements per year:** 1 - 49.

SNELLING SEARCH
400 14th Street SE, Decatur AL 35601. 205/355-5424. **Fax:** 205/355-2298. **Contact:** Jorge Valdes, Manager. **Description:** An executive search firm operating on a contingency basis. Company pays fee. **Specializes in the areas of:** Computer Science/Software; Engineering; Health/Medical; Sales. **Positions commonly filled include:** Applications Engineer; Chemical Engineer; Civil Engineer; Computer Programmer; Database Manager; Design Engineer; Electrical/Electronics Engineer; Environmental Engineer; Industrial Engineer; Manufacturer's/Wholesaler's Sales Rep.; Mechanical Engineer; Metallurgical Engineer; Physical Therapist; Software Engineer; Structural Engineer. **Corporate headquarters location:** Dallas TX. **Other U.S. locations:** Nationwide. **Average salary range of placements:** $30,000 - $50,000. **Number of placements per year:** 1 - 49.

SNELLING SEARCH SNELLING PERSONNEL SERVICES
400 Vestavia Parkway, Suite 221, Vestavia Hills AL 35216-3750. 205/822-7878. **Fax:** 205/979-7663. **Contact:** Manager. **World Wide Web address:**

http://www.snelling.com/birmingham. **Description:** An executive search firm. Snelling Personnel Services (also at this location) provides temporary, temp-to-perm, and permanent placements. Company pays fee. **Specializes in the areas of:** Engineering; Finance; Health/Medical; Manufacturing; Marketing; Sales. **Benefits available to temporary workers:** Medical Insurance; Paid Vacation. **Corporate headquarters location:** Dallas TX. **Other U.S. locations:** Nationwide. **Average salary range of placements:** $30,000 - $150,000. **Number of placements per year:** 200 - 499.

PERMANENT EMPLOYMENT AGENCIES

A-1 EMPLOYMENT SERVICE
1015 Montlamar Drive, Suite 130, Mobile AL 36609-1713. 334/343-9702. **Fax:** 334/343-9706. **Contact:** Dorothy Robney, Owner/Manager. **Description:** A permanent employment agency. Company pays fee. **Specializes in the areas of:** Accounting/Auditing; Administration; Advertising; Banking; Computer Hardware/Software; Finance; Food Industry; General Management; Health/Medical; Industrial; Insurance; Legal; Manufacturing; Nonprofit; Personnel/Labor Relations; Publishing; Retail; Sales; Secretarial; Transportation. **Positions commonly filled include:** Accountant/Auditor; Administrative Assistant; Bookkeeper; Buyer; Chemical Engineer; Chemist; Claim Representative; Clerk; Computer Operator; Computer Programmer; Credit Manager; Customer Service Representative; Data Entry Clerk; Draftsperson; Driver; Editor; EDP Specialist; Electrical/Electronics Engineer; Factory Worker; Hotel Manager; Industrial Designer; Industrial Engineer; Legal Secretary; Light Industrial Worker; Management Trainee; Manufacturing Engineer; Marketing Specialist; Mechanical Engineer; Medical Secretary; Nurse; Operations/Production Manager; Public Relations Specialist; Purchasing Agent/Manager; Quality Control Supervisor; Receptionist; Sales Representative; Secretary; Software Engineer; Systems Analyst; Technical Writer/Editor; Technician; Typist/Word Processor.

AEROTEK, INC.
4910 Corporate Drive, Suite G, Huntsville AL 35805. 205/830-1995. **Toll-free phone:** 800/377-3144. **Fax:** 205/830-2332. **Contact:** Human Resources. **E-mail address:** aerotek.huntsville@internetmci.com. **Description:** A permanent employment agency with divisions concentrating on engineering, telecommunications, laboratory support, and computer applications. **Specializes in the areas of:** Computer Science/Software; Engineering; Industrial; Manufacturing. **Positions commonly filled include:** Aerospace Engineer; Aircraft Mechanic/Engine Specialist; Chemical Engineer; Civil Engineer; Computer Programmer; Cost Estimator; Design Engineer; Designer; Draftsperson; Electrical/Electronics Engineer; Environmental Engineer; Industrial Engineer; Industrial Production Manager; Mechanical Engineer; Metallurgical Engineer; MIS Specialist; Nuclear Engineer; Quality Control Supervisor; Software Engineer; Structural Engineer; Systems Analyst; Technical Writer/Editor. **Corporate headquarters location:** Baltimore MD. **Other U.S. locations:** Nationwide. **Average salary range of placements:** $30,000 - $50,000.

ALABAMA NANNIES, INC.
Office Park Circle, Suite 209-A, Birmingham AL 35223. 205/871-2032. **Contact:** Ginger Dilworth, President. **Description:** A permanent employment agency engaged in the placement of live-in and live-out nannies and governesses. Company pays fee. **Positions commonly filled include:** Nanny. **Number of placements per year:** 1 - 49.

EMPLOYMENT CONSULTANTS INC.
649 South McDonough Street, Montgomery AL 36104. 334/264-0649. **Fax:** 334/263-7413. **Contact:** Janet Hutto, President. **Description:** A permanent employment agency that concentrates on mid-level executive positions in medium-sized firms. The company also places entry-level accounting, engineering, management, and sales professionals, as well as upper-level office and administrative personnel. Company pays fee. **Specializes in the areas of:** Accounting/Auditing; Administration; Computer Science/Software; Engineering; Finance; Health/Medical; Industrial; Legal; Manufacturing; Sales; Secretarial. **Positions commonly filled include:** Accountant/Auditor; Adjuster; Administrative Manager; Agricultural Engineer; Bank Officer/Manager; Biological Scientist; Budget Analyst; Chemist; Civil Engineer; Claim Representative; Clerical Supervisor; Clinical Lab Technician; Computer Programmer; Cost Estimator; Counselor; Credit Manager; Customer Service Representative; Designer; Dietician/Nutritionist; Draftsperson; Economist; Editor; Electrical/Electronics Engineer; Financial Aid Officer; Food Scientist/Technologist; Forester/Conservation Scientist; General Manager; Health Services Manager; Hotel Manager; Human Resources Manager; Industrial Engineer; Industrial Production Manager; Landscape Architect; Management Analyst/Consultant; Management Trainee; Manufacturer's/Wholesaler's Sales Rep.; Mechanical Engineer; Medical Records Technician; Occupational Therapist; Paralegal; Physical Therapist; Property and Real Estate Manager; Public Relations Specialist; Quality Control Supervisor; Radiological Technologist; Registered Nurse; Respiratory Therapist; Restaurant/Food Service Manager; Securities Sales Representative; Social Worker; Speech-Language Pathologist; Structural Engineer; Systems Analyst; Technical Writer/Editor; Transportation/Traffic Specialist; Underwriter/Assistant Underwriter; Urban/Regional Planner. **Average salary range of placements:** $30,000 - $50,000. **Number of placements per year:** 100 - 199.

GENERAL PERSONNEL CORPORATION
616 Gadsden Highway, Suite B, Birmingham AL 35235. 205/833-3467. **Fax:** 205/836-6802. **Contact:** James L. Gilbert, Jr., Recruiter. **Description:** A permanent employment agency. **Specializes in the areas of:** Apparel; Textiles.

MARINE JOBS, INC.
800 Downtowner Boulevard, Suite 111, Mobile AL 36609. 334/380-0765. **Fax:** 334/380-0571. **Contact:** Wendy Sullivan, President. **Description:** A permanent employment agency focusing on both inland and offshore marine industry placements. **Specializes in the areas of:** Maritime. **Corporate headquarters location:** This Location. **Average salary range of placements:** $20,000 - $29,999. **Number of placements per year:** 1000+.

PERFORM STAFFING SERVICE
3107 Independence Drive, Birmingham AL 35209. 205/870-8170. **Contact:** Jerry Sulzby, Vice President/General Manager. **Description:** A permanent employment agency. Company pays fee. **Specializes in the areas of:** Accounting/Auditing; Banking; Computer Hardware/Software. **Positions commonly filled include:** Bookkeeper; Clerk; Data Entry Clerk; EDP Specialist; Factory Worker; Light Industrial Worker; Nurse; Receptionist; Secretary; Stenographer;

Typist/Word Processor. **Number of placements per year:** 50 - 99.

PLACERS, INC.
2475 Hempstead Drive, Birmingham AL 35235. 205/856-0646. **Fax:** 205/856-3387. **Contact:** Gina Wilson, President. **Description:** A permanent employment agency. Company pays fee. **Specializes in the areas of:** Accounting/Auditing; Engineering; Insurance; Manufacturing; Secretarial. **Positions commonly filled include:** Accountant/Auditor; Adjuster; Chemist; Customer Service Representative; Design Engineer; Industrial Engineer; Insurance Agent/Broker; Manufacturer's/Wholesaler's Sales Rep.; Mechanical Engineer; Metallurgical Engineer; Operations/Production Manager; Purchasing Agent/Manager. **Corporate headquarters location:** This Location. **Average salary range of placements:** $30,000 - $50,000. **Number of placements per year:** 1 - 49.

SNELLING PERSONNEL SERVICES
1813 University Drive, Huntsville AL 35801. 205/533-1410. **Fax:** 205/534-6691. **Contact:** George Barnes, Owner/Manager. **Description:** A permanent employment agency. Company pays fee. **Specializes in the areas of:** Computer Science/Software; Engineering; Health/Medical; Sales. **Positions commonly filled include:** Accountant/Auditor; Aerospace Engineer; Civil Engineer; Computer Programmer; Customer Service Representative; Electrical/Electronics Engineer; Industrial Engineer; Manufacturer's/Wholesaler's Sales Rep.; Mechanical Engineer; Nuclear Medicine Technologist; Occupational Therapist; Pharmacist; Physical Therapist; Physicist; Registered Nurse; Software Engineer; Speech-Language Pathologist; Systems Analyst. **Number of placements per year:** 100 - 199.

TALENT TREE STAFFING SERVICES
3075 Highway 150, Birmingham AL 35244. 205/444-8733. **Contact:** Manager. **Description:** A permanent employment agency. **Specializes in the areas of:** Accounting/Auditing; Banking; Secretarial. **Positions commonly filled include:** Claim Representative. **Corporate headquarters location:** Houston TX. **Average salary range of placements:** Less than $20,000. **Number of placements per year:** 1000+.

VIP PERSONNEL, INC.
P.O. Box 361925, Birmingham AL 35236. 205/879-8889. **Fax:** 205/879-8919. **Contact:** Bonnie Wainwright, Owner. **Description:** A permanent employment agency. Founded in 1981. Company pays fee. **Specializes in the areas of:** Accounting/Auditing; Administration; Advertising; Banking; Broadcasting; Computer Science/Software; Finance; General Management; Health/Medical; Industrial; Insurance; Legal; Nonprofit; Personnel/Labor Relations; Sales; Secretarial. **Positions commonly filled include:** Account Manager; Accountant/Auditor; Adjuster; Administrative Assistant; Administrative Manager; Advertising Clerk; Auditor; Bank Officer/Manager; Branch Manager; Budget Analyst; Buyer; Chief Financial Officer; Clerical Supervisor; Computer Programmer; Credit Manager; Customer Service Representative; Database Manager; Finance Director; Financial Analyst; General Manager; Graphic Artist; Graphic Designer; Health Services Manager; Hotel Manager; Human Resources Specialist; Industrial Production Manager; Management Analyst/Consultant; Management Trainee; Manufacturer's/Wholesaler's Sales Rep.; Production Manager; Public Relations Specialist; Purchasing Agent/Manager; Quality Control Supervisor; Sales Engineer; Sales Manager; Sales Representative; Systems Analyst; Typist/Word Processor; Underwriter/Assistant Underwriter. **Corporate headquarters location:** This Location. **Average salary range of placements:** $20,000 - $29,999. **Number of placements per year:** 1000+.

TEMPORARY EMPLOYMENT AGENCIES

LABOR FINDERS
P.O. Box 2843, Tuscaloosa AL 35401. 205/750-0059. **Fax:** 205/752-0056. **Contact:** Manager. **Description:** A temporary agency. **Specializes in the areas of:** Food Industry; Industrial; Manufacturing; Retail; Secretarial; Transportation. **Positions commonly filled include:** Automotive Mechanic; Blue-Collar Worker Supervisor; Branch Manager; Clerical Supervisor; Construction Contractor; Customer Service Representative; Electrician; Landscape Architect; Operations/Production Manager; Typist/Word Processor. **Corporate headquarters location:** Mobile AL. **Other U.S. locations:** FL; LA; MI; TN; TX. **Average salary range of placements:** Less than $20,000. **Number of placements per year:** 500 - 999.

MANPOWER, INC.
235 1/2 Broad Street, Gadsden AL 35901. 205/543-1474. **Contact:** Manager. **Description:** A temporary agency. Founded in 1948. **Specializes in the areas of:** Industrial; Insurance; Sales; Secretarial. **Positions commonly filled include:** Administrative Manager; Advertising Clerk; Clerical Supervisor; Human Resources Specialist; Human Service Worker; Paralegal; Services Sales Representative; Typist/Word Processor. **Corporate headquarters location:** Milwaukee WI. **Average salary range of placements:** Less than $20,000. **Number of placements per year:** 200 - 499.

MEDEX INC.
600 Vestavia Parkway, Suite 200, Birmingham AL 35216. 205/823-5032. **Fax:** 205/823-5232. **Contact:** Tim Smith, Manager. **Description:** A temporary agency that provides clerical and clinical placement for the medical industry. Company pays fee. **Specializes in the areas of:** Health/Medical. **Positions commonly filled include:** Clerical Supervisor; Clinical Lab Technician; Medical Records Technician; Pharmacist; Physician; Registered Nurse. **Corporate headquarters location:** This Location. **Average salary range of placements:** Less than $20,000. **Number of placements per year:** 100 - 199.

SPECIAL COUNSEL
2340 Woodcrest Place, Suite 210, Birmingham AL 35209. 205/870-3330. **Fax:** 205/870-3337. **Contact:** Manager. **World Wide Web address:** http://www.specialcounsel.com. **Description:** A temporary agency that also provides permanent placements. **Specializes in the areas of:** Legal.

WORKFORCE INC.
1355 South Eufaula Avenue, Eufaula AL 36027. 334/687-4222. **Fax:** 334/687-4228. **Contact:** Rachel Britt, Accounts Manager. **Description:** A temporary agency. **Specializes in the areas of:** Accounting/Auditing; Administration; Advertising; Engineering; Food Industry; Industrial; Manufacturing; Personnel/Labor Relations; Retail; Sales; Secretarial. **Positions commonly filled include:** Accountant/Auditor; Administrative Manager; Blue-Collar Worker Supervisor; Buyer; Computer Programmer; Customer Service Representative; Design

Engineer; Draftsperson; Electrician; General Manager; Management Trainee; Manufacturer's/Wholesaler's Sales Rep.; Operations/Production Manager; Purchasing Agent/Manager; Quality Control Supervisor; Services Sales Representative; Typist/Word Processor. **Other U.S. locations:** AR; MS; TN. **Average salary range of placements:** Less than $20,000. **Number of placements per year:** 200 - 499.

CONTRACT SERVICES FIRMS

SEATEC, INC.
P.O. Box 127, Warrior AL 35180. 205/647-4224. **Fax:** 205/647-7677. **Contact:** Richard Phillips, Manager of Recruiting. **E-mail address:** seatecinc@aol.com. **Description:** A contract services firm. Founded in 1979. **Specializes in the areas of:** Architecture/Construction; Computer Science/ Software; Engineering; Manufacturing; Technical. **Positions commonly filled include:** Architect; Chemical Engineer; Chemist; Civil Engineer; Computer Programmer; Cost Estimator; Design Engineer; Designer; Draftsperson; Electrical/Electronics Engineer; Environmental Engineer; Geologist/ Geophysicist; Mechanical Engineer; Metallurgical Engineer; MIS Specialist; Science Technologist; Software Engineer; Structural Engineer; Systems Analyst; Technical Writer/Editor. **Corporate headquarters location:** This Location. **Other U.S. locations:** Huntsville AL; Pensacola FL. **Average salary range of placements:** More than $50,000. **Number of placements per year:** 200 - 499.

CAREER/OUTPLACEMENT COUNSELING FIRMS

WELDTEK TESTING LABORATORY, INC.
2241 Highway 78 West, Oxford AL 36203. 205/835-1155. **Fax:** 205/831-4996. **Contact:** Sherry A. Cable, Human Resource Manager. **E-mail address:** weldtek@quicklink.com. **Description:** A career/ outplacement counseling firm that provides training and certification for welders. Founded in 1988. Company pays fee. **Specializes in the areas of:** Engineering; Industrial; Manufacturing; Personnel/ Labor Relations. **Positions commonly filled include:** Welder. **Average salary range of placements:** Less than $20,000. **Number of placements per year:** 1 - 49.

ALASKA

EXECUTIVE SEARCH FIRMS

ALASKA EXECUTIVE SEARCH (AES)
821 N Street, Suite 204, Anchorage AK 99501. 907/276-5707. **Fax:** 907/279-3731. **Contact:** Manager. **Description:** An executive search firm. **Specializes in the areas of:** Administration; Banking; Clerical; Health/Medical; Professional; Technical.

PERMANENT EMPLOYMENT AGENCIES

ADAMS & ASSOCIATES INC.
3201 C Street, Suite 402, Anchorage AK 99503. 907/561-5161. **Fax:** 907/563-7417. **Contact:** Staffing Specialist. **Description:** A permanent employment agency that also provides temporary placements.

ALASKA EMPLOYMENT SERVICE
10002 Glacier Highway, Suite 200, Juneau AK 99801. 907/465-4562. **Contact:** Recruiter. **World Wide Web address:** http://www.state.ak.us. **Description:** A state employment agency focusing on the seafood industry.

CHUGACH NORTH EMPLOYMENT
3601 C Street, Suite 1414, Anchorage AK 99503. 907/561-4321. **Contact:** Manager. **Description:** A permanent employment agency.

PERSONNEL PLUS EMPLOYMENT AGENCY
3335 Arctic Boulevard, Suite 200, Anchorage AK 99503. 907/563-7587. **Contact:** Manager. **Description:** A permanent employment agency that also provides temporary placements.

TEMPORARY EMPLOYMENT AGENCIES

ELITE EMPLOYMENT SERVICE
1113 West Fireweed Lane, Suite 200, Anchorage AK 99503. 907/276-8367. **Fax:** 907/276-5172. **Contact:** Human Resources. **Description:** A temporary agency that also provides permanent placement. **Specializes in the areas of:** Administration; Clerical; Secretarial.

MANPOWER TEMPORARY SERVICE
4300 B Street, Suite 103, Anchorage AK 99503. 907/562-1440. **Fax:** 907/562-7080. **Contact:** Paula Lindsey, Branch Manager. **World Wide Web address:** http://www.manpower.com. **Description:** A temporary agency. Company pays fee. **Specializes in the areas of:** Clerical; Data Processing; Industrial; Light Industrial; Marketing; Office Support; Technical. **Benefits available to temporary workers:** Computer Training; Paid Holidays; Paid Vacation; Referral Bonus Plan. **Corporate headquarters location:** Milwaukee WI. **Other U.S. locations:** Nationwide. **Number of placements per year:** 1000+.

MANPOWER TEMPORARY SERVICE
714 4th Avenue, Suite 302A, Fairbanks AK 99701. 907/474-8875. **Fax:** 907/479-8272. **Contact:** Paula Lindsey, Branch Manager. **Description:** A temporary agency. **Specializes in the areas of:** Clerical; Light Industrial; Office Support; Technical. **Corporate headquarters location:** Milwaukee WI. **Other U.S. locations:** Nationwide.

OLSTEN STAFFING SERVICES
341 West Tudor Road, Suite 106, Anchorage AK 99503. 907/563-0090. **Toll-free phone:** 800/WORK-NOW. **Fax:** 907/563-1080. **Contact:** Manager. **Description:** A temporary agency offering long-term and short-term assignments. Founded in 1950. **Specializes in the areas of:** Accounting/Auditing; Assembly; Distribution; Engineering; Entry-Level; Finance; Legal Secretarial; Marketing; MIS/EDP; Office Automation; Office Support; Production; Professional; Technical; Telemarketing; Telephone Technical Support. **Positions commonly filled include:** Clerk. **Benefits available to temporary workers:** Bonus Award/Plan; Health Benefits; Paid Holidays; Paid Vacation; Training. **Corporate headquarters location:** Melville NY. **Other U.S. locations:** Nationwide.

PROFESSIONAL BUSINESS SERVICE, INC.
807 G Street, Suite 200, Anchorage AK 99501. 907/279-7679. **Fax:** 907/276-5758. **Contact:** Manager. **Description:** A temporary agency that also provides permanent placements. Company pays fee. **Specializes in the areas of:** Accounting/Auditing; Engineering; Secretarial. **Positions commonly filled include:** Administrative Assistant; Civil Engineer; Computer Operator; Draftsperson; Financial Analyst; Geologist/Geophysicist; Secretary; Technical Writer/Editor; Typist/Word Processor. **Benefits available to temporary workers:** Medical Insurance; Profit Sharing.

CONTRACT SERVICES FIRMS

NORTHWEST TECHNICAL SERVICES
3330 Arctic Boulevard, Suite 201, Anchorage AK 99503. 907/562-1633. **Contact:** Manager. **Description:** A contract services firm.

ARIZONA

EXECUTIVE SEARCH FIRMS

ACCOUNTANTS EXECUTIVE SEARCH
ACCOUNTANTS ON CALL
2111 East Highlands, Suite B420, Phoenix AZ 85016. 602/957-1200. **Contact:** Manager. **Description:** An executive search firm. Accountants on Call (also at this location) is a temporary agency. **Specializes in the areas of:** Accounting/Auditing; Finance.

ACCOUNTING & BOOKKEEPING PERSONNEL, INC.
1702 East Highland Avenue, Suite 200, Phoenix AZ 85016. 602/277-3700. **Fax:** 602/277-8212. **Contact:** Mike Nolan, Recruiter. **Description:** An executive search firm that also provides temporary and permanent placements. Founded in 1990. **Specializes in the areas of:** Accounting/Auditing; Bookkeeping; Finance. **Positions commonly filled include:** Accountant/Auditor; Budget Analyst; Credit Manager; Financial Analyst. **Corporate headquarters location:** This Location. **Other area locations:** Tucson AZ. **Number of placements per year:** 200 - 499.

ACCOUNTING & BOOKKEEPING PERSONNEL, INC.
4400 East Broadway Boulevard, Suite 600, Tucson AZ 85711. 520/323-3600. **Fax:** 520/795-4753. **Contact:** Recruiter. **Description:** An executive search firm that also provides temporary and permanent placements. Company pays fee. **Specializes in the areas of:** Accounting/Auditing; Bookkeeping; Finance. **Positions commonly filled include:** Accountant/ Auditor; Budget Analyst; Credit Manager; Financial Analyst. **Corporate headquarters location:** Phoenix AZ.

AZTECH RECRUITMENT COMPANY
4131 North 24th Street, Suite A122, Phoenix AZ 85016. 602/955-8080. **Contact:** Manager. **Description:** An executive search firm. **Specializes in the areas of:** Computer Science/Software; Engineering; Technical.

BJB MEDICAL ASSOCIATES
10245 East Via Linda, Scottsdale AZ 85258. 602/451-0922. **Contact:** Manager. **Description:** An executive search firm that places physicians. **Specializes in the areas of:** Health/Medical.

BARTHOLDI & COMPANY
10040 East Happy Valley Road, Suite 244, Scottsdale AZ 85255. 602/502-2178. **Contact:** Manager. **Description:** An executive search firm. **Specializes in the areas of:** High-Tech.

THE BREN GROUP
13951 North Scottsdale Road, Scottsdale AZ 85254. 602/951-2736. **Contact:** Michael S. Mudge, Director of Business Development. **Description:** An executive search firm. **Specializes in the areas of:** Hotel/Restaurant; Transportation; Travel. **Positions commonly filled include:** Aircraft Mechanic/Engine Specialist; Computer Programmer; Financial Analyst; General Manager; Hotel Manager; Human Resources Manager; Internet Services Manager; Management Analyst/Consultant; MIS Manager; Quality Control Supervisor; Restaurant/Food Service Manager; Software Engineer; Systems Analyst; Transportation/ Traffic Specialist; Travel Agent. **Average salary range of placements:** $30,000 - $50,000. **Number of placements per year:** 100 - 199.

C.S. ASSOCIATES, LLC
P.O. Box 30926, Tucson AZ 85751-0926. 520/327-7999. **Contact:** J.B. Connelly, Owner. **World Wide Web address:** http://www.csassoc.com. **Description:** An executive search firm. **Specializes in the areas of:** Architecture/Construction; Engineering. **Positions commonly filled include:** Architect; Civil Engineer; Design Engineer; Designer; Draftsperson; Electrical/ Electronics Engineer; Environmental Engineer; Geologist/Geophysicist; Landscape Architect; Mechanical Engineer; Mining Engineer; Structural Engineer; Surveyor; Transportation/Traffic Specialist. **Number of placements per year:** 1 - 49.

CIRCUIT TECHNOLOGY SEARCH INC.
P.O. Box 44168, Tucson AZ 85733. 520/292-9122. **Fax:** 520/292-9221. **Contact:** Rick Greenwald, President. **E-mail address:** circuit@azstarnet.com. **World Wide Web address:** http://www.azstarnet.com/~circuit. **Description:** An executive search firm operating on a contingency basis. Company pays fee. **Specializes in the areas of:** Electronics; Engineering; Manufacturing; Technical. **Positions commonly filled include:** Chemical Engineer; Chemist; Environmental Engineer; Industrial Production Manager; Materials Engineer; Mechanical Engineer; Metallurgical Engineer. **Number of placements per year:** 1 - 49.

CIZEK ASSOCIATES INC.
2390 East Camelback Road, Suite 300, Phoenix AZ 85016. 602/553-1066. **Contact:** Manager. **Description:** A generalist executive search firm.

COMPUTECH CORPORATION
4375 North 75th Street, Scottsdale AZ 85251. 602/947-7534. **Fax:** 602/947-7537. **Contact:** Bob Dirickson, President. **Description:** An executive search firm. Company pays fee. **Specializes in the areas of:** Computer Science/Software. **Positions commonly filled include:** Computer Programmer; Consultant; Software Engineer; Systems Analyst; Technical Writer. **Number of placements per year:** 100 - 199.

CONFIDENTIAL SEARCH INC.
6115 South Kyrene Road, Suite 201, Tempe AZ 85283. 602/820-8663. **Fax:** 602/820-8709. **Contact:** Manager. **Description:** An executive search firm.

CORPORATE DYNAMIX
6619 North Scottsdale Road, Scottsdale AZ 85250. 602/607-0040. **Fax:** 602/607-0054. **Contact:** Manager. **Description:** An executive search firm. **Specializes in the areas of:** High-Tech.

DHR INTERNATIONAL INC.
11811 North Tatum Boulevard, Suite 3031, Phoenix AZ 85028. 602/494-4705. **Contact:** Manager. **Description:** An executive search firm.

THE DORFMAN GROUP
12005 East Mission Lane, Scottsdale AZ 85259. 602/860-8820. **Fax:** 602/860-0888. **Contact:** Mike Flamer, Vice President. **E-mail address:** dorfgrp@getnet.com. **World Wide Web address:** http://www.getnet.com/dorfman. **Description:** An executive search firm operating on both retained and contingency bases. Company pays fee. **Specializes in the areas of:** Engineering; Logistics; Materials; Packaging. **Positions commonly filled include:** Applications Engineer; Civil Engineer; Design Engineer; Electrical/Electronics Engineer; General Manager; Industrial Engineer; Logistics Manager; Manufacturing Engineer; Mechanical Engineer; Project Engineer; Project Manager; Sales Engineer; Sales Executive; Sales Representative; Software Engineer. **Average salary range of placements:** More than $50,000. **Number of placements per year:** 1 - 49.

ELECTRONIC POWER SOURCE
1507 West Loughlin Drive, Chandler AZ 85224. 602/821-1946. **Fax:** 602/821-1941. **Contact:** Garry Moore, Owner. **Description:** A nationwide executive search firm which specializes in analog design, power supplies, ballasts, magnetics, and other high-tech industries. Electronic Power Source operates on both retained and contingency bases. Founded in 1985. Company pays fee. **Specializes in the areas of:** Aerospace; Computer Science/Software; Engineering; Light Industrial. **Positions commonly filled include:** Aerospace Engineer; Applications Engineer; Buyer; Computer Programmer; Database Manager; Designer; Electrical/Electronics Engineer; Industrial Engineer; Manufacturing Engineer; Mechanical Engineer; Software Engineer. **Corporate headquarters location:** This Location. **Other U.S. locations:** Nationwide. **Average salary range of placements:** $30,000 - $50,000. **Number of placements per year:** 1 - 49.

EXECUTEMPS, INC.
7330 North 16th Street, Suite C117, Phoenix AZ 85020. 602/861-1200. **Contact:** Manager. **Description:** An executive search firm. **Specializes in the areas of:** Food Industry.

FISHEL HUMAN RESOURCES ASSOCIATES
5125 North 16th Street, Suite B-125, Phoenix AZ 85016. 602/266-5600. **Fax:** 602/266-5656. **Contact:** Richard A. Fishel, Executive Vice President. **Description:** An executive search firm. Company pays fee. **Specializes in the areas of:** Accounting/Auditing; Administration; Banking; General Management; Human Resources. **Positions commonly filled include:** Accountant; Administrative Manager; Bank Officer/Manager; Buyer; Human Resources Manager. **Number of placements per year:** 200 - 499.

FUSION GROUP
1741 East Morten Avenue, Phoenix AZ 85020. 602/944-8030. **Contact:** Manager. **Description:** An executive search firm that places physicians. **Specializes in the areas of:** Health/Medical.

LYNN GREENBERG ASSOCIATES, INC.
9067 East Evans Drive, Scottsdale AZ 85260. 602/391-9074. **Contact:** Manager. **Description:** An executive search firm that places scientists in areas such as biotechnology and pharmaceuticals. **Specializes in the areas of:** Scientific.

ROBERT HALF INTERNATIONAL/ACCOUNTEMPS
100 West Clarendon Avenue, Phoenix AZ 85013. 602/264-6488. **Contact:** Manager. **World Wide Web address:** http://www.roberthalf.com. **Description:** An executive search firm. Accountemps provides temporary placements. **Specializes in the areas of:** Accounting/Auditing. **Corporate headquarters location:** Menlo Park CA. **Other U.S. locations:** Nationwide.

PHYLLIS HAWKINS & ASSOCIATES
5025 North Central, Suite 611, Phoenix AZ 85012. 602/263-0248. **Fax:** 602/263-1016. **Contact:** Manager. **Description:** An executive search firm. Company pays fee. **Specializes in the areas of:** Legal. **Positions commonly filled include:** Attorney. **Average salary range of placements:** More than $50,000. **Number of placements per year:** 1 - 49.

HOLDAN & ASSOCIATES
P.O. Box 1317, Green Valley AZ 85622. 520/648-3624. **Contact:** Manager. **Description:** An executive search firm. **Specializes in the areas of:** Electronics; Mechanical; Sales.

BETH ISABELLE & ASSOCIATES INC.
P.O. Box 43276, Tucson AZ 85733-3276. 520/319-2500. **Contact:** Manager. **Description:** An executive search firm that focuses on providing placements in Mexico. **Specializes in the areas of:** Banking; Manufacturing.

J.R. PROFESSIONAL SEARCH, INC.
P.O. Box 18356, Tucson AZ 85731. 520/721-1855. **Fax:** 520/721-1855. **Contact:** Ralph B. Steinfeldt, President. **Description:** An executive search firm. **Specializes in the areas of:** Accounting/Auditing; Engineering; Entertainment; Manufacturing; Technical. **Positions commonly filled include:** Aerospace Engineer; Chemical Engineer; Civil Engineer; Computer Programmer; Construction Contractor; Cost Estimator; Credit Manager; Electrical/Electronics Engineer; Industrial Engineer; Mechanical Engineer; Metallurgical Engineer; Meteorologist; Pharmacist; Physician; Quality Control Supervisor; Registered Nurse; Software Engineer; Structural Engineer; Technical Writer/Editor. **Number of placements per year:** 1 - 49.

A.T. KEARNEY EXECUTIVE SEARCH
2141 East Highland Street, Suite 135, Phoenix AZ 85016. 602/994-3032. **Contact:** Manager. **Description:** An executive search firm.

MANAGEMENT RECRUITERS INTERNATIONAL
6262 North Swan Road, Suite 125, Tucson AZ 85718-3600. 520/529-6818. **Fax:** 520/529-6877. **Contact:** Ms. Lorian E. Roethlein, President. **Description:** An executive search firm. **Specializes in the areas of:** Accounting/Auditing; Computer Science/Software; Engineering; Manufacturing. **Positions commonly filled include:** Accountant; Computer Programmer; Design Engineer; Electrical/Electronics Engineer; General Manager; Human Resources Manager; Industrial Engineer; MIS Specialist; Software Engineer; Systems Analyst. **Average salary range of placements:** More than $50,000. **Number of placements per year:** 1 - 49.

MANAGEMENT RECRUITERS INTERNATIONAL
310 South Williams Boulevard, Suite 300, Tucson AZ 85711. **Contact:** Jack DeJong, Managing Member. **Description:** An executive search firm. Company pays fee. **Specializes in the areas of:** Agriculture. **Positions commonly filled include:** Veterinarian. **Number of placements per year:** 50 - 99.

MANAGEMENT RECRUITERS OF SCOTTSDALE
Bank of America Building, 6900 East Camelback Road, Suite 935, Scottsdale AZ 85251-2491. 602/941-1515. **Contact:** Manager. **Description:** An executive search firm. Company pays fee. **Specializes in the areas of:** Accounting/Auditing; Administration; Advertising; Architecture/Construction; Banking; Communications; Computer Hardware/Software; Electrical; Engineering; Finance; Food Industry; General Management; Health/Medical; Insurance; Legal; Manufacturing; Personnel/Labor Relations; Procurement; Publishing; Real Estate; Sales; Technical; Textiles; Transportation.

McEVOY & JOHNSON ASSOCIATES, INC.
10535 North 96th Place, Scottsdale AZ 85258. 602/661-9422. **Contact:** Donna Johnson, President. **E-mail address:** mjassoc@primenet.com. **Description:** An executive search firm. Company pays fee. **Specializes in the areas of:** Computer Science/Software. **Positions commonly filled include:** Computer Programmer; Software Engineer; Systems Analyst. **Average salary range of placements:** More than $50,000. **Number of placements per year:** 50 - 99.

PEARSON & ASSOCIATES
11811 North Tatum Boulevard, Suite P-129, Phoenix AZ 85028-1615. 602/953-9783. **Fax:** 602/996-1261. **Contact:** Bill Haugen, Director of Health Care.

E-mail address: bill@pearson-assoc.com. **World Wide Web address:** http://www.pearson-assoc.com. **Description:** An executive search firm providing nationwide health care placements. Company pays fee. **Specializes in the areas of:** Health/Medical. **Positions commonly filled include:** Accountant/ Auditor; Astronomer; Dietician/ Nutritionist; Health Services Manager; Medical Records Technician; Nuclear Medicine Technologist; Occupational Therapist; Pharmacist; Physical Therapist; Radiological Technologist; Registered Nurse; Respiratory Therapist; Social Worker; Speech-Language Pathologist. **Average salary range of placements:** More than $50,000. **Number of placements per year:** 100 - 199.

PERSONALIZED MANAGEMENT ASSOCIATES
One East Camelback, Suite 550, Phoenix AZ 85012. 602/222-9499. **Fax:** 602/265-0372. **Contact:** David Hottle, CPC, Vice President of Operations. **Description:** An executive search firm operating on both retainer and contingency bases. Company pays fee. **Specializes in the areas of:** Administration; Fashion; Food Industry; Personnel/Labor Relations; Retail. **Positions commonly filled include:** Assistant Manager; Auditor; Branch Manager; Buyer; Database Manager; General Manager; Human Resources Manager; Management Trainee; Marketing Manager; Sales Executive; Sales Manager. **Corporate headquarters location:** Atlanta GA. **Average salary range of placements:** $30,000 - $50,000. **Number of placements per year:** 100 - 199.

PROFESSIONAL EXECUTIVE RESEARCH CONSULTING
P.O. Box 15327, Phoenix AZ 85060-5327. 602/553-9896. **Toll-free phone:** 800/874-7246. **Fax:** 602/553-9897. **Contact:** Gordon Stoa, President. **Description:** An executive search firm operating on a contingency basis. Company pays fee. **Specializes in the areas of:** Engineering; Food Industry; General Management; Manufacturing; Technical. **Positions commonly filled include:** Accountant/Auditor; Administrative Manager; Agricultural Engineer; Bank Officer/Manager; Biochemist; Blue-Collar Worker Supervisor; Buyer; Chemical Engineer; Chemist; Civil Engineer; Construction and Building Inspector; Cost Estimator; Design Engineer; Designer; Draftsperson; Electrical/ Electronics Engineer; Food Scientist/Technologist; General Manager; Industrial Engineer; Industrial Production Manager; Management Trainee; Mechanical Engineer; Mining Engineer; Petroleum Engineer; Property and Real Estate Manager; Structural Engineer; Surveyor. **Average salary range of placements:** $30,000 - $50,000. **Number of placements per year:** 1 - 49.

PROFESSIONAL PLACEMENT INC.
3900 East Camelback Road, Suite 500, Phoenix AZ 85018. 602/955-0870. **Contact:** Manager. **Description:** An executive search firm.

PROFESSIONAL SEARCH
7434 East Stetson Drive, Scottsdale AZ 85251. 602/994-4400. **Contact:** Julie Beauvais, Office Administrator. **Description:** An executive search firm for professionals with AS400 PC client/server mainframe experience. Company pays fee. **Specializes in the areas of:** Computer Science/Software. **Positions commonly filled include:** Computer Programmer; Systems Analyst. **Number of placements per year:** 100 - 199.

SALES CONSULTANTS
4300 North Miller Road, Suite 110, Scottsdale AZ 85251. 602/946-1609. **Fax:** 602/946-6718. **Contact:** Albert Britten, President/General Manager. **Description:** An executive search firm. Company pays fee. **Specializes in the areas of:** Computer Science/ Software; Health/Medical; Medical Technology; Publishing; Sales. **Positions commonly filled include:** Branch Manager; General Manager; Health Services Manager; Product Manager; Sales Manager; Sales Representative; Services Sales Representative. **Number of placements per year:** 50 - 99.

ROBERT SAXON & ASSOCIATES
13430 North Scottsdale Road, Suite 203, Scottsdale AZ 85254. 602/991-4460. **Contact:** Manager. **Description:** An executive search firm. **Specializes in the areas of:** Human Resources; Information Systems; Sales; Secretarial.

SUSAN SCHULTZ & ASSOCIATES
4350 East Camelback Road, Suite B-200, Phoenix AZ 85018. 602/998-1744. **Contact:** Susan Schultz, President. **Description:** An executive search firm. **Number of placements per year:** 1 - 49.

SEARCH MASTERS INTERNATIONAL
500 Foothills South, Suite 2, Sedona AZ 86336. 520/282-3553. **Fax:** 520/282-5881. **Contact:** Manager. **Description:** An executive search firm. **Specializes in the areas of:** Biotechnology; Pharmaceutical.

SEARCHAMERICA INC.
401 North Alma School Road, Suite 14, Chandler AZ 85224. 602/899-8457. **Fax:** 602/899-9757. **Contact:** Steve Jarvis, President. **E-mail address:** info@searchamerica.net. **World Wide Web address:** http://www.searchamerica.net. **Description:** An executive search firm. **Specializes in the areas of:** Computer Science/Software; Engineering; Information Technology. **Positions commonly filled include:** Applications Engineer; Biomedical Engineer; Chemical Engineer; Civil Engineer; Computer Programmer; Database Manager; Design Engineer; Electrical/ Electronics Engineer; Human Resources Manager; Industrial Engineer; Industrial Production Manager; Internet Services Manager; Manufacturing Engineer; Mechanical Engineer; Operations Manager; Production Manager; Project Manager; Sales Engineer; Software Engineer; Systems Analyst. **Average salary range of placements:** More than $50,000. **Number of placements per year:** 50 - 99.

SOURCE SERVICES CORPORATION
5343 North 16th Street, Suite 270, Phoenix AZ 85016. 602/230-0220. **Fax:** 602/248-4204. **Contact:** Manager. **Description:** An executive search firm. The divisions at this location include Source Consulting, Source EDP, and Accountant Source Temps. **Specializes in the areas of:** Accounting/Auditing; Computer Hardware/Software; Information Technology.

SOUTHWEST SEARCH ASSOCIATES
4500 South Lakeshore Drive, Suite 520, Tempe AZ 85282. 602/838-0333. **Fax:** 602/838-0368. **Contact:** Manager. **Description:** An executive search firm. **Specializes in the areas of:** Information Systems.

SPECTRA INTERNATIONAL
6991 East Camelback Road, Suite B-305, Scottsdale AZ 85251. 602/481-0411. **Fax:** 602/481-0525. **Contact:** Sybil Goldberg, President. **Description:** An executive search firm that also provides contract and temporary placements. Company pays fee. **Specializes in the areas of:** Accounting/Auditing; Administration; Computer Science/Software; Engineering; Finance; General Management; Manufacturing; Personnel/Labor Relations; Retail; Sales; Technical; Transportation. **Positions commonly filled include:** Accountant/ Auditor; Administrative Manager; Blue-Collar Worker Supervisor; Branch Manager; Budget Analyst; Buyer; Clerical Supervisor; Computer Programmer; Customer Service Representative; Electrical/Electronics Engineer;

General Manager; Human Resources Manager; Network Engineer; Operations/Production Manager; Purchasing Agent/Manager; Quality Control Supervisor; Retail Manager; Software Engineer. **Number of placements per year:** 200 - 499.

STAFF ONE SEARCH
2800 North 44th Street, Suite 340, Phoenix AZ 85008. 602/952-9060. **Contact:** Maria Savastio, Office Administrator. **Description:** An executive search firm that also provides temporary placements. Company pays fee. **Specializes in the areas of:** Accounting/Auditing; Sales; Secretarial. **Positions commonly filled include:** Accountant/Auditor; Customer Service Representative; Human Resources Specialist; Services Sales Representative; Travel Agent; Typist/Word Processor.

MARJORIE STARR & ASSOCIATES
2266 South Dobson Road, Suite 273, Mesa AZ 85202. 602/730-6050. **Fax:** 602/730-6292. **Contact:** Marjorie Starr, Owner. **E-mail address:** mstarr273@aol.com. **Description:** An executive search firm. Company pays fee. **Specializes in the areas of:** Health/Medical; Industrial Sales and Marketing; Medical Sales and Marketing; Sales. **Positions commonly filled include:** Account Manager; Account Representative; Database Manager; Electrical/Electronics Engineer; Health Services Manager; Home Health Aide; Internet Services Manager; Manufacturer's/Wholesaler's Sales Rep.; Occupational Therapist; Pharmacist; Physical Therapist; Respiratory Therapist; Sales Representative; Services Sales Representative; Telecommunications Manager. **Average salary range of placements:** $30,000 - $50,000. **Number of placements per year:** 200 - 499.

TSS CONSULTING, LTD.
2525 East Camelback Road, Suite 560, Phoenix AZ 85016. 602/955-7000. **Toll-free phone:** 800/489-2425. **Fax:** 602/957-3948. **Contact:** George A. Armes, Senior Consultant. **E-mail address:** mcdjoh@aol.com. **Description:** An executive search firm that provides placements primarily in high-tech industries including telecommunications, aerospace, electronics, petrochemicals, computer systems, semiconductors and microelectronics, and information technology. Company pays fee. **Specializes in the areas of:** Computer Science/Software; Engineering. **Positions commonly filled include:** Electrical/Electronics Engineer; MIS Manager; Software Engineer; Telecommunications Manager. **Number of placements per year:** 1 - 49.

TELE-SOLUTION SEARCH
8655 East Via De Ventura, Suite F-127, Scottsdale AZ 85258. 602/483-1300. **Fax:** 602/483-7221. **Contact:** Carole Wichansky, Manager. **E-mail address:** tele-sol@primenet.com. **Description:** An executive search firm. Company pays fee. **NOTE:** Technical backgrounds, particularly in UNIX and Windows NT applications, are preferred. **Specializes in the areas of:** Computer Hardware/Software; Engineering; Telecommunications. **Positions commonly filled include:** Software Engineer; Telecommunications Manager. **Average salary range of placements:** More than $50,000. **Number of placements per year:** 50 - 99.

TORRANCE RECRUITING, INC.
P.O. Box 1984, Scottsdale AZ 85252-1984. 602/946-9024. **Contact:** Matthew Torrance, Manager. **Description:** An executive search firm. Company pays fee. **Specializes in the areas of:** Publishing. **Positions commonly filled include:** Chief Financial Officer; Cost Estimator; Engineer; General Manager; Production Manager; Quality Control Supervisor; Sales and Marketing Manager. **Average salary range of placements:** More than $50,000. **Number of placements per year:** 1 - 49.

WGI SOLUTIONS
2198 East Camelback Road, Phoenix AZ 85016. 602/957-4799. **Contact:** Manager. **Description:** An executive search firm.

WSA ASSOCIATES
2361 Hyde Park Boulevard, Lake Havasu City AZ 86404. 520/764-2200. **Fax:** 800/489-9192. **Contact:** Jeff Stone, General Manager. **Description:** An executive search firm. Company pays fee. **Specializes in the areas of:** Food Industry; Hotel/Restaurant. **Positions commonly filled include:** Hotel Manager; Human Resources Manager; Restaurant/Food Service Manager. **Average salary range of placements:** $30,000 - $50,000. **Number of placements per year:** 100 - 199.

WEINMAN & ASSOCIATES
7110 East McDonald Drive, Suite B-6, Scottsdale AZ 85253. **Fax:** 602/922-9248. **Contact:** Mary Weinman, President. **Description:** An executive search firm. Founded in 1993. Company pays fee. **Specializes in the areas of:** Food Industry; Hotel/Restaurant; Manufacturing; MIS; Personnel/Labor Relations. **Positions commonly filled include:** Computer Programmer; Hotel Manager; Human Resources Specialist; Purchasing Agent/Manager; Restaurant/Food Service Manager. **Average salary range of placements:** More than $50,000. **Number of placements per year:** 1 - 49.

WITT/KIEFFER, FORD, HADELMAN & LLOYD
432 North 44th Street, Suite 360, Phoenix AZ 85008. 602/267-1370. **Contact:** Manager. **Description:** An executive search firm for upper-level professionals. **Specializes in the areas of:** Health/Medical.

PERMANENT EMPLOYMENT AGENCIES

ACCUSTAFF INC.
1016 East Broadway, Tucson AZ 85719. 520/792-0622. **Contact:** Office Manager. **Description:** A permanent employment agency. **Specializes in the areas of:** Administration; Banking. **Positions commonly filled include:** Accountant/Auditor; Administrator; Clerk; Receptionist; Secretary; Typist/Word Processor. **Number of placements per year:** 500 - 999.

ACCUSTAFF INC.
8027 North Black Canyon Highway, Suite 402, Phoenix AZ 85021. 602/246-7024. **Fax:** 602/864-0021. **Contact:** Manager. **Description:** A permanent employment agency that focuses on accounting placements. **Specializes in the areas of:** Accounting/Auditing; Data Processing; Finance.

AMERICAN CAREER GROUP
2400 East Arizona Biltmore Circle, Phoenix AZ 85016. 602/381-1667. **Fax:** 602/956-6128. **Contact:** Linda J. Baugh, President. **Description:** A permanent employment agency that also provides resume services. **Positions commonly filled include:** Accountant/Auditor; Actuary; Adjuster; Administrative Manager; Agricultural Scientist; Architect; Attorney; Bank Officer/Manager; Biological Scientist; Branch Manager; Chemist; Claim Representative; Clinical Lab Technician; Computer Programmer; Construction Contractor; Cost Estimator; Counselor; Credit

Manager; Customer Service Representative; Designer; Dietician/Nutritionist; Draftsperson; Economist; Editor; Education Administrator; Engineer; Financial Services Sales Representative; Geographer; Health Services Manager; Hotel Manager; Human Resources Manager; Human Service Worker; Industrial Production Manager; Insurance Agent/Broker; Librarian; Licensed Practical Nurse; Management Analyst/Consultant; Management Trainee; Operations/Production Manager; Pharmacist; Physician; Psychologist; Public Relations Specialist; Purchasing Agent/Manager; Quality Control Supervisor; Radio/TV Announcer/Broadcaster; Radio/TV Producer; Real Estate Agent; Recreational Therapist; Registered Nurse; Reporter; Restaurant/Food Service Manager; Science Technologist; Social Worker; Sociologist; Speech-Language Pathologist; Surveyor; Systems Analyst; Teacher/Professor; Technical Writer/Editor; Underwriter/Assistant Underwriter; Urban/Regional Planner; Wholesale and Retail Buyer. **Number of placements per year:** 1 - 49.

ARIZONA MEDICAL EXCHANGE
777 East Missouri, Suite 207, Phoenix AZ 85014. 602/246-4906. **Contact:** Manager. **Description:** A permanent employment agency. Company pays fee. **Specializes in the areas of:** Health/Medical. **Positions commonly filled include:** Claim Representative; Clinical Lab Technician; Credit Manager; Customer Service Representative; EEG Technologist; EKG Technician; Health Services Manager; Licensed Practical Nurse; Medical Records Technician; Physical Therapist; Registered Nurse; Respiratory Therapist; Surgical Technician. **Number of placements per year:** 100 - 199.

CLIFFORD & ASSOCIATES
16042 North 32nd Street, Suite D-14, Phoenix AZ 85032-3852. 602/992-1477. **Fax:** 602/992-7017. **Contact:** Dennis Clifford, Owner. **Description:** A permanent employment agency. Founded in 1992. Company pays fee. **Specializes in the areas of:** Automotive; Finance; Personnel/Labor Relations; Retail; Sales; Secretarial; Transportation. **Positions commonly filled include:** Accountant/Auditor; Administrative Manager; Automotive Mechanic; Blue-Collar Worker Supervisor; Credit Manager; Services Sales Representative. **Average salary range of placements:** $30,000 - $50,000. **Number of placements per year:** 50 - 99.

COMFORCE TECHNICAL SERVICES, INC.
1858 East Southern Avenue, Tempe AZ 85282. 602/897-2479. **Fax:** 602/345-2471. **Contact:** Manager. **Description:** A permanent employment agency that also offers contract placements. **Specializes in the areas of:** Technical.

COMPUTER STRATEGIES, INC.
5620 North Kolb Road, Suite 225, Tucson AZ 85750. 520/721-9544. **Fax:** 520/721-9660. **Contact:** Debbie Brody, Manager. **Description:** A permanent employment agency. **Specializes in the areas of:** Data Processing.

CONSTRUCTION SECRETARIES
1250 East Baseline Road, Suite 104, Tempe AZ 85283. 602/345-1282. **Fax:** 602/530-3546. **Contact:** Susan Sabato, President. **Description:** A permanent employment agency. Company pays fee. **Specializes in the areas of:** Accounting/Auditing; Administration; General Management; Legal; Personnel/Labor Relations; Secretarial. **Positions commonly filled include:** Accountant/Auditor; Administrative Manager; Branch Manager; Clerical Supervisor; Construction Contractor; Credit Manager; Customer Service Representative; Human Resources Specialist; Management Analyst/Consultant; Operations Manager; Purchasing Agent/Manager; Typist/Word Processor; Underwriter/Assistant Underwriter. **Corporate headquarters location:** This Location. **Average salary range of placements:** Less than $20,000. **Number of placements per year:** 500 - 999.

DEALER CONNECTION
7500 East Butherus Drive, Scottsdale AZ 85260. 602/607-6996. **Contact:** Manager. **Description:** A permanent employment agency. Dealer Connection is a national automotive placement service for auto dealers, auto manufacturers, and the heavy-duty truck industry. Founded in 1992. Company pays fee. **Specializes in the areas of:** Automotive; General Management; Personnel/Labor Relations; Retail; Transportation. **Positions commonly filled include:** Accountant/Auditor; Administrative Manager; Automotive Mechanic; Claim Representative; Clerical Supervisor; Cost Estimator; Customer Service Representative; General Manager; Management Analyst/Consultant; Manufacturer's/Wholesaler's Sales Rep.; Public Relations Specialist; Quality Control Supervisor; Services Sales Representative; Transportation/Traffic Specialist. **Corporate headquarters location:** This Location. **Other U.S. locations:** Kansas City MO. **Average salary range of placements:** More than $50,000. **Number of placements per year:** 50 - 99.

ERICKSON AND ASSOCIATES, INC.
HC 32 Box 362-A, Prescott AZ 86303. 520/776-0045. **Fax:** 520/776-0823. **Contact:** Elvin Erickson, President. **E-mail address:** erickson@bslnet.com. **Description:** A permanent employment agency that also provides executive search services. Company pays fee. **Specializes in the areas of:** Computer Hardware/Software; Engineering. **Positions commonly filled include:** Computer Programmer; EDP Specialist; Electrical/Electronics Engineer; Mechanical Engineer; Systems Analyst; Technical Writer/Editor. **Corporate headquarters location:** This Location. **Other U.S. locations:** Nationwide. **Average salary range of placements:** More than $50,000.

GENERAL EMPLOYMENT ENTERPRISES, INC.
100 West Clarendon Avenue, Suite 2240, Phoenix AZ 85013. 602/265-7800. **Fax:** 602/265-1779. **Contact:** Don Cuppy, Manager. **Description:** A permanent employment agency. Company pays fee. **Specializes in the areas of:** Computer Science/Software; Engineering; Manufacturing; Technical. **Positions commonly filled include:** Aerospace Engineer; Biochemist; Biomedical Engineer; Chemical Engineer; Chemist; Civil Engineer; Computer Programmer; Designer; Draftsperson; Electrical/Electronics Engineer; Industrial Engineer; Internet Services Manager; Mechanical Engineer; Metallurgical Engineer; MIS Specialist; Operations; Quality Control Supervisor; Software Engineer; Structural Engineer; Systems Analyst; Technical Writer/Editor; Telecommunications Manager. **Corporate headquarters location:** Oak Brook IL. **Other U.S. locations:** Nationwide. **Average salary range of placements:** $30,000 - $50,000. **Number of placements per year:** 100 - 199.

HUMAN RESOURCE NETWORK, INC.
6045 North Scottsdale Road, Suite 108, Scottsdale AZ 85250. 602/948-1991. **Fax:** 602/948-1667. **Contact:** Diana L. Doss, President. **E-mail address:** hrninc@futureone.com. **World Wide Web address:** http://www.hrninc.com. **Description:** A permanent employment agency that also provides temporary placements. Founded in 1987. Company pays fee. **Specializes in the areas of:** Health/Medical. **Positions commonly filled include:** Licensed Practical Nurse; Medical Assistant; Radiological Technologist; Registered Nurse; Typist/Word Processor. **Benefits available to temporary workers:** Dental Insurance; Medical Insurance; Paid Holidays; Referral Bonus Plan;

Vision Insurance. **Corporate headquarters location:** This Location. **Other area locations:** Tucson AZ. **Average salary range of placements:** $20,000 - $29,999. **Number of placements per year:** 200 - 499.

HUMAN RESOURCE NETWORK, INC.
6369 East Tangue Verde, Suite 180, Tucson AZ 85715. 520/722-8227. **Fax:** 520/722-8188. **Contact:** Manager. **Description:** A permanent employment agency that also provides temporary placements. **Specializes in the areas of:** Health/Medical.

HUNTER TECHNICAL SERVICES
1232 Broadway Road, Suite 202, Tempe AZ 85282. 602/966-7000. **Contact:** Manager. **Description:** A permanent placement agency focusing on technical positions. Hunter Technical Services also offers temporary placement services. **Specializes in the areas of:** Computer Hardware/Software. **Positions commonly filled include:** Mechanical Engineer.

LDS EMPLOYMENT CENTER
4333 North Central Avenue, Phoenix AZ 85012. 602/241-9444. **Fax:** 602/234-3613. **Contact:** Richard Dahl, Employment Coordinator. **Description:** A permanent employment agency. The LDS Employment Center is a nonprofit endeavor operated by full-time missionaries for the Latter-Day-Saints Church. No fee to jobseekers or employers.

PRIORITY STAFFING, INC.
4600 South Mill Avenue, Suite 275, Tempe AZ 85282. 602/491-2191. **Fax:** 602/491-5702. **Contact:** Brenda Ellison, Vice President of Human Resources. **E-mail address:** mail@prioritystaffing.com. **World Wide Web address:** http://www.prioritystaffing.com. **Description:** A permanent employment agency that also provides temporary placements. Founded in 1993. **Specializes in the areas of:** Accounting/Auditing; Administration; Banking; Computer Science/Software; Engineering; Finance; General Management; Health/Medical; Industrial; Insurance; Legal; Manufacturing; Personnel/Labor Relations; Publishing; Sales; Secretarial; Technical. **Positions commonly filled include:** Accountant/Auditor; Administrative Manager; Advertising Clerk; Bank Officer/Manager; Blue-Collar Worker Supervisor; Branch Manager; Chemical Engineer; Claim Representative; Clerical Supervisor; Computer Programmer; Customer Service Representative; Design Engineer; Designer; Financial Analyst; General Manager; Human Resources Specialist; Human Service Worker; Industrial Engineer; Industrial Production Manager; Insurance Agent/Broker; Internet Services Manager; Management Analyst/Consultant; Manufacturer's/Wholesaler's Sales Rep.; Mechanical Engineer; MIS Specialist; Multimedia Designer; Operations Manager; Paralegal; Public Relations Specialist; Quality Control Supervisor; Social Worker; Surveyor; Systems Analyst; Technical Writer/Editor; Typist/Word Processor.

SNELLING PERSONNEL SERVICES
310 South Williams Boulevard, Suite 255, Tucson AZ 85711. **Fax:** 520/790-3901. **Contact:** Recruiter. **Description:** A permanent employment agency. Snelling Personnel Services also provides temporary and contract services. **Specializes in the areas of:** Accounting/Auditing; Administration; Computer Science/Software; Engineering; Sales; Secretarial; Technical. **Positions commonly filled include:** Accountant/Auditor; Ceramics Engineer; Industrial Engineer; Materials Engineer; Metallurgical Engineer; Mining Engineer; Technical Writer/Editor; Typist/Word Processor. **Benefits available to temporary workers:** Medical Insurance; Paid Holidays; Paid Vacation. **Average salary range of placements:** $20,000 - $29,999.

TECH/AID OF ARIZONA
1438 West Broadway, Suite B-225, Tempe AZ 85282. 602/894-6161. **Contact:** Manager. **Description:** A permanent employment agency. Company pays fee. **Specializes in the areas of:** Architecture/Construction; Cable TV; Computer Hardware/Software; Construction; Engineering; Manufacturing; Technical. **Positions commonly filled include:** Aerospace Engineer; Architect; Buyer; Ceramics Engineer; Draftsperson; Electrical/Electronics Engineer; Estimator; Factory Worker; Industrial Engineer; Mechanical Engineer; Metallurgical Engineer; Mining Engineer; Operations/Production Manager; Petroleum Engineer; Purchasing Agent/Manager; Quality Control Supervisor; Technical Writer/Editor; Technician. **Number of placements per year:** 1000+.

TEMPORARY EMPLOYMENT AGENCIES

ACCUSTAFF INC.
4747 North Seventh Street, Suite 140, Phoenix AZ 85014. 602/200-3910. **Contact:** Branch Manager. **Description:** A temporary agency. Company pays fee. **Specializes in the areas of:** Accounting/Auditing; Banking; Personnel/Labor Relations; Secretarial. **Positions commonly filled include:** Accountant/Auditor; Clerical Supervisor; Cost Estimator; Credit Manager; Customer Service Representative; Human Resources Specialist; Management Trainee; Paralegal; Services Sales Representative; Technical Writer/Editor; Typist/Word Processor. **Average salary range of placements:** $20,000 - $29,999. **Number of placements per year:** 500 - 999.

ADECCO
1220 South Alma School Road, Suite 206, Mesa AZ 85210. 602/844-4244. **Contact:** Technical Recruiter. **Description:** A temporary agency. Company pays fee. **Specializes in the areas of:** Art/Design; Computer Science/Software; Engineering. **Positions commonly filled include:** Aerospace Engineer; Architect; Computer Programmer; Designer; Draftsperson; Electrical/Electronics Engineer; Industrial Engineer; Mechanical Engineer; Metallurgical Engineer; Quality Control Supervisor; Sales Representative; Systems Analyst; Technical Writer/Editor.

ADECCO
333 East Osborn, Suite 370, Phoenix AZ 85012. 602/246-1143. **Contact:** Manager. **Description:** A temporary agency. Company pays fee. **Specializes in the areas of:** Clerical; Legal; Manufacturing; Personnel/Labor Relations; Publishing. **Positions commonly filled include:** Administrative Assistant; Bookkeeper; Clerk; Computer Operator; Computer Programmer; Customer Service Representative; Human Resources Manager; Legal Secretary; Quality Control Supervisor; Receptionist; Sales Representative; Secretary; Typist/Word Processor. **Number of placements per year:** 1000+.

DEVAU HUMAN RESOURCES
2131 East Broadway, Suite 34, Tempe AZ 85282. 602/921-3688. **Fax:** 602/968-2396. **Contact:** Terry Wilkey, President. **Description:** A temporary agency and temp-to-hire job placement service focusing on clerical, light industrial, and technical placements. Founded in 1984. **Specializes in the areas of:** Accounting/Auditing; Administration; Industrial; Manufacturing; Retail; Secretarial; Technical. **Average**

salary range of placements: Less than $20,000. **Number of placements per year:** 500 - 999.

EAI HEALTHCARE STAFFING SOLUTIONS
3800 North Central Avenue, Suite 800, Phoenix AZ 85012. 602/266-7400. **Toll-free phone:** 800/736-8066. **Fax:** 602/266-7020. **Contact:** Ellen B. Echales, President. **World Wide Web address:** http://www.eai-healthcare.com. **Description:** EAI Healthcare Staffing is a temporary and temp-to-hire agency. Founded in 1986. Company pays fee. **Specializes in the areas of:** Health/Medical. **Positions commonly filled include:** Administrative Assistant; Biomedical Engineer; Certified Nursing Aide; Clerical Supervisor; Clinical Lab Technician; Computer Programmer; Customer Service Representative; EEG Technologist; EKG Technician; Licensed Practical Nurse; Medical Records Technician; Nuclear Medicine Technologist; Occupational Therapist; Pharmacist; Physical Therapist; Radiological Technologist; Registered Nurse; Respiratory Therapist; Secretary; Software Engineer; Surgical Technician; Typist/Word Processor. **Corporate headquarters location:** This Location. **Other U.S. locations:** Tucson AZ; San Diego CA; Chicago IL; Las Vegas NV; Nashville TN; Dallas TX; Fort Worth TX; Houston TX; San Antonio TX; Seattle WA. **Average salary range of placements:** $20,000 - $29,999. **Number of placements per year:** 100 - 199.

FAVORITE NURSES INC.
727 East Bethany Home Road, Phoenix AZ 85014. 602/265-7440. **Contact:** Manager. **Description:** A temporary agency that places nurses. **Specializes in the areas of:** Health/Medical.

INSURANCE SUPPORT SERVICES
207 West Southern Avenue, Tempe AZ 85282. 602/967-3075. **Fax:** 602/967-0098. **Contact:** Gail Dorks, President. **Description:** A temporary agency which also provides contract services, primarily to property and casualty insurance agents. Founded in 1992. Company pays fee. **Specializes in the areas of:** Insurance; Secretarial. **Positions commonly filled include:** Customer Service Representative. **Number of placements per year:** 1 - 49.

KELLY ASSISTED LIVING SERVICES
3333 East Camelback Road, Suite 167, Phoenix AZ 85018. 602/955-1199. **Contact:** Manager. **Description:** A temporary agency that focuses on home health care staffing. **Specializes in the areas of:** Health/Medical.

KERRY'S REFERRALS
11225 North 28th, Suite B-201, Phoenix AZ 85029-5613. 602/548-8777. **Fax:** 602/548-9453. **Contact:** Ms. Donna Isaacs, Vice President. **Description:** A temporary agency that also provides permanent placements. Founded in 1985. Company pays fee. **Specializes in the areas of:** Accounting/Auditing; Administration; Advertising; Banking; Clerical; Computer Science/Software; General Management; Insurance; Legal; Personnel/Labor Relations; Publishing; Sales; Secretarial. **Positions commonly filled include:** Accountant/Auditor; Administrative Manager; Advertising Clerk; Bank Officer/Manager; Blue-Collar Worker Supervisor; Claim Representative; Clerical Supervisor; Credit Manager; Customer Service Representative; Editor; MIS Specialist; Paralegal; Public Relations Specialist; Securities Sales Representative; Technical Writer/Editor; Typist/Word Processor. **Average salary range of placements:** $30,000 - $50,000. **Number of placements per year:** 1000+.

MANPOWER INTERNATIONAL INC.
645 East Missouri, Suite 260, Phoenix AZ 85012. 602/264-0237. **Contact:** Branch Manager. **Description:** A temporary agency. **Specializes in the areas of:** Data Processing; Industrial; Office Support; Word Processing. **Positions commonly filled include:** Accountant/Auditor; Accounting Clerk; Administrative Assistant; Assembler; Biological Scientist; Bookkeeper; Chemist; Computer Operator; Customer Service Representative; Designer; Desktop Publishing Specialist; Electrical/Electronics Engineer; Inspector/Tester/Grader; Inventory Control Specialist; Machine Operator; Order Clerk; Packaging/Processing Worker; Project Engineer; Proofreader; Receptionist; Records Manager; Research Assistant; Secretary; Software Engineer; Stenographer; Systems Analyst; Technical Writer/Editor; Technician; Telemarketer; Typist/Word Processor. **Benefits available to temporary workers:** Life Insurance; Medical Insurance; Paid Holidays; Paid Vacation. **Number of placements per year:** 1000+.

NORRELL TEMPORARY SERVICES
4350 East Camelback Road, Suite 275-G, Phoenix AZ 85018. 602/956-5844. **Contact:** Branch Manager. **Description:** A temporary agency. Company pays fee. **Specializes in the areas of:** Clerical; Construction; Manufacturing; Sales. **Positions commonly filled include:** Administrative Assistant; Clerk; Computer Operator; Construction Trade Worker; Customer Service Representative; Data Entry Clerk; Draftsperson; Driver; Factory Worker; Legal Secretary; Light Industrial Worker; Receptionist. **Number of placements per year:** 500 - 999.

RETIREE SKILLS INC.
1475 West Prince Road, Tucson AZ 85705. 520/888-8310. **Contact:** Manager. **Description:** A temporary agency. **Specializes in the areas of:** Accounting/Auditing; Engineering; Secretarial. **Positions commonly filled include:** Accountant/Auditor; Civil Engineer; Computer Programmer; Design Engineer; Electrical/Electronics Engineer; Industrial Engineer; Mechanical Engineer; Purchasing Agent/Manager; Technical Writer/Editor; Typist/Word Processor. **Corporate headquarters location:** This Location. **Average salary range of placements:** Less than $20,000. **Number of placements per year:** 100 - 199.

STIVERS TEMPORARY PERSONNEL, INC.
745 East Maryland Avenue, Suite 108, Phoenix AZ 85014. 602/264-4580. **Fax:** 602/264-7688. **Contact:** Christine Goodfarb, Staff Supervisor. **Description:** A temporary agency. Company pays fee. **Specializes in the areas of:** Accounting/Auditing; Administration; Advertising; Banking; Broadcasting; Computer Science/Software; Engineering; Finance; Health/Medical; Industrial; Insurance; Legal; Manufacturing; Nonprofit; Personnel/Labor Relations; Publishing; Retail; Sales; Secretarial; Technical. **Positions commonly filled include:** Accountant/Auditor; Advertising Clerk; Bank Officer/Manager; Branch Manager; Broadcast Technician; Brokerage Clerk; Budget Analyst; Buyer; Claim Representative; Clerical Supervisor; Clinical Lab Technician; Computer Programmer; Credit Manager; Customer Service Representative; Draftsperson; Financial Analyst; General Manager; Health Services Manager; Human Resources Specialist; Human Service Worker; Insurance Agent/Broker; Internet Services Manager; Management Trainee; Market Research Analyst; Medical Records Technician; MIS Specialist; Operations/Production Manager; Paralegal; Property and Real Estate Manager; Purchasing Agent/Manager; Quality Control Supervisor; Real Estate Agent; Restaurant/Food Service Manager; Securities Sales Representative; Services Sales Representative; Software Engineer; Statistician; Surveyor; Systems Analyst; Technical Writer/Editor; Telecommunications Manager; Typist/Word Processor; Underwriter/

Assistant Underwriter. **Benefits available to temporary workers:** Dental Insurance; Medical Insurance; Paid Vacation; Vision Plan. **Corporate headquarters location:** Chicago IL. **Other U.S. locations:** Nationwide. **Average salary range of placements:** Less than $20,000. **Number of placements per year:** 1000+.

TAYLOR DESIGN RECRUITING
6155 East Indian School Road, Suite 100B, Scottsdale AZ 85251. 602/423-5056. **Fax:** 602/423-8595. **Contact:** Steve Tweito, Office Manager. **Description:** A temporary agency that also provides permanent placements. Founded in 1990. Company pays fee. **Specializes in the areas of:** Advertising; Architecture/Construction; Art/Design; Broadcasting; Personnel/Labor Relations; Publishing; Sales; Technical. **Positions commonly filled include:** Advertising Clerk; Architect; Broadcast Technician; Civil Engineer; Computer Programmer; Design Engineer; Designer; Draftsperson; Editor; Landscape Architect; Multimedia Designer; Public Relations Specialist; Systems Analyst; Technical Writer/Editor; Video Production Coordinator. **Corporate headquarters location:** This Location. **Other U.S. locations:** Los Angeles CA; San Francisco CA. **Average salary range of placements:** $20,000 - $29,999. **Number of placements per year:** 500 - 999.

CONTRACT SERVICES FIRMS

ADECCO
P.O. Box 3159, Tempe AZ 85280. 602/267-7254. **Toll-free phone:** 800/238-9141. **Fax:** 602/902-9290. **Contact:** Manager. **Description:** A contract services firm. Founded in 1956. Company pays fee. **Specializes in the areas of:** Architecture/Construction; Computer Science/Software; Engineering; Industrial; Manufacturing; Personnel/Labor Relations; Technical. **Positions commonly filled include:** Aerospace Engineer; Aircraft Mechanic/Engine Specialist; Architect; Blue-Collar Worker Supervisor; Branch Manager; Budget Analyst; Buyer; Chemical Engineer; Civil Engineer; Computer Programmer; Construction Contractor; Design Engineer; Designer; Editor; Electrical/Electronics Engineer; Environmental Engineer; Human Resources Specialist; Industrial Engineer; Industrial Production Manager; Landscape Architect; Mechanical Engineer; Mining Engineer; MIS Specialist; Operations/Production Manager; Petroleum Engineer; Purchasing Agent/Manager; Quality Control Supervisor; Science Technologist; Software Engineer; Structural Engineer; Systems Analyst; Technical Writer/Editor; Telecommunications Manager. **Benefits available to temporary workers:** 401(k); Medical Insurance; Paid Holidays; Paid Vacation. **Corporate headquarters location:** Cambridge MA. **Other U.S. locations:** Nationwide. **International locations:** Worldwide. **Average salary range of placements:** $30,000 - $50,000. **Number of placements per year:** 1000+.

AIDAN GROUP
4110 North Scottsdale Road, Suite 280, Scottsdale AZ 85251. 602/970-9962. **Contact:** Managing Director. **Description:** A contract services firm that focuses on managerial and and accounting placements. **Specializes in the areas of:** Accounting/Auditing; Administration; Banking; Finance; General Management; Manufacturing. **Positions commonly filled include:** Accountant/Auditor; Administrative Manager; Attorney; Economist; Editor; Education Administrator; General Manager; Management Analyst/Consultant; Telecommunications Manager. **Average salary range of placements:** More than $50,000. **Number of placements per year:** 100 - 199.

ANDREWS, STEVENS & ASSOCIATES
4110 North Scottsdale Road, #280, Scottsdale AZ 85251. 602/970-9962. **Contact:** Managing Director. **Description:** A contract services firm. **Specializes in the areas of:** Accounting/Auditing; Administration; Economics; General Management; Legal; Manufacturing; Sales. **Positions commonly filled include:** Accountant/Auditor; Administrative Assistant; Attorney; Bank Officer/Manager; Branch Manager; Financial Analyst; Hotel Manager; Operations/Production Manager. **Corporate headquarters location:** Phoenix AZ. **Average salary range of placements:** More than $50,000. **Number of placements per year:** 100 - 199.

CDI CORPORATION
2323 West 14th Street, Suite 209, Tempe AZ 85281. 602/968-6255. **Toll-free phone:** 800/879-9686. **Fax:** 602/968-1360. **Contact:** Recruiter. **World Wide Web address:** http://www.cdicorp.com. **Description:** A contract services firm. CDI Corporation provides technical and professional staffing services covering a wide range of engineering and computer-related disciplines. **Specializes in the areas of:** Administration; Computer Science/Software; Engineering; Industrial; Manufacturing; Technical. **Positions commonly filled include:** Accountant/Auditor; Aerospace Engineer; Aircraft Mechanic/Engine Specialist; Buyer; Chemical Engineer; Computer Programmer; Cost Estimator; Design Engineer; Designer; Draftsperson; Electrical/Electronics Engineer; Financial Analyst; Industrial Engineer; Internet Services Manager; Mechanical Engineer; MIS Specialist; Purchasing Agent/Manager; Quality Control Supervisor; Software Engineer; Statistician; Structural Engineer; Technical Writer/Editor; Telecommunications Manager. **Corporate headquarters location:** Philadelphia PA. **Other U.S. locations:** Nationwide. **International locations:** Worldwide. **Number of placements per year:** 1000+.

CDI CORPORATION
4400 East Broadway Boulevard, Suite 512, Tucson AZ 85711. 520/795-6900. **Fax:** 520/323-4495. **Contact:** Manager. **World Wide Web address:** http://www.cdicorp.com. **Description:** A contract services firm. **Specializes in the areas of:** Computer Science/Software; Engineering; Manufacturing; Technical. **Positions commonly filled include:** Aerospace Engineer; Agricultural Engineer; Architect; Biomedical Engineer; Budget Analyst; Buyer; Chemical Engineer; Civil Engineer; Clinical Lab Technician; Computer Programmer; Cost Estimator; Design Engineer; Designer; Draftsperson; Electrical/Electronics Engineer; Environmental Engineer; Industrial Engineer; Industrial Production Manager; Internet Services Manager; Landscape Architect; Mechanical Engineer; Metallurgical Engineer; Mining Engineer; MIS Specialist; Software Engineer; Structural Engineer; Systems Analyst; Technical Writer/Editor; Telecommunications Analyst. **Corporate headquarters location:** Philadelphia PA. **Other U.S. locations:** Nationwide. **International locations:** Worldwide. **Average salary range of placements:** $30,000 - $50,000. **Number of placements per year:** 100 - 199.

CROWN TECHNICAL SERVICE
504 East Southern Avenue, Tempe AZ 85282. 602/966-8686. **Contact:** Manager. **Description:** A contract services firm. **Specializes in the areas of:** Construction.

DATATECH SERVICES
1858 East Southern Avenue, Suite 102, Tempe AZ 85282. 602/345-1900. **Contact:** Manager. **Description:** A contract services firm. **Specializes in the areas of:** Technical.

PAUL DICKEN ASSOCIATES, INC.
1930 South Alma School Road, Suite D-207, Mesa AZ 85210. 602/345-2036. **Toll-free phone:** 800/658-5954. **Fax:** 602/345-2997. **Contact:** Jim Hoefer, Manager. **Description:** A contract services firm that also provides temporary placements. Founded in 1985. Company pays fee. **Specializes in the areas of:** Computer Science/Software; Engineering; Manufacturing. **Positions commonly filled include:** Aerospace Engineer; Buyer; Computer Programmer; Customer Service Representative; Design Engineer; Designer; Draftsperson; Electrical/Electronics Engineer; Human Resources Specialist; Mechanical Engineer; MIS Specialist; Quality Control Supervisor; Software Engineer; Technical Writer/Editor; Typist/Word Processor. **Benefits available to temporary workers:** Medical Insurance; Paid Holidays; Paid Vacation. **Corporate headquarters location:** This Location. **Other area locations:** Phoenix AZ. **Number of placements per year:** 1000+.

MEDA TECHNICAL SERVICES, INC.
6263 North Scottsdale Road, Suite 230, Scottsdale AZ 85250. **Toll-free phone:** 800/991-6332. **Fax:** 602/991-3408. **Contact:** Recruiter. **Description:** A contract services firm. Company pays fee. **Specializes in the areas of:** Architecture/Construction; Computer Science/Software; Engineering; Manufacturing; Technical. **Positions commonly filled include:** Aerospace Engineer; Chemical Engineer; Civil Engineer; Computer Programmer; Design Engineer; Designer; Draftsperson; Electrical/Electronics Engineer; Geologist/Geophysicist; Industrial Engineer; Mining Engineer; Software Engineer; Structural Engineer; Systems Analyst; Technical Writer/Editor. **Corporate headquarters location:** Windsor, Ontario. **Other U.S. locations:** Troy MI. **Average salary range of placements:** $30,000 - $50,000. **Number of placements per year:** 200 - 499.

PDS TECHNICAL SERVICE
5150 North 16th Street, Suite C266, Phoenix AZ 85016. 602/280-9777. **Toll-free phone:** 800/456-8644. **Contact:** Peter Janes, Recruiting Manager. **World Wide Web address:** http://www.pdstech.com. **Description:** A contract services firm. Company pays fee. **Specializes in the areas of:** Architecture/Construction; Computer Science/Software; Engineering; Manufacturing; Technical. **Positions commonly filled include:** Aerospace Engineer; Aircraft Mechanic/Engine Specialist; Buyer; Chemical Engineer; Civil Engineer; Computer Programmer; Construction and Building Inspector; Design Engineer; Designer; Draftsperson; Electrical/Electronics Engineer; Industrial Engineer; Landscape Architect; Mechanical Engineer; Metallurgical Engineer; MIS Specialist; Petroleum Engineer; Software Engineer; Structural Engineer; Surveyor; Systems Analyst; Technical Writer/Editor; Urban/Regional Planner. **Corporate headquarters location:** Dallas TX. **Other U.S. locations:** Anchorage AK; Costa Mesa CA; Miami FL; Wichita KS; St. Louis MO; Houston TX; Seattle WA. **Average salary range of placements:** $20,000 - $29,999. **Number of placements per year:** 50 - 99.

PROVISION TECHNOLOGIES
4647 32nd Street, Suite 150, Phoenix AZ 85018. 602/955-8300. **Toll-free phone:** 888/930-8300. **Fax:** 602/955-2614. **Contact:** Manager. **World Wide Web address:** http://www.provisiontech.com. **Description:** A contract services and consulting firm. **Specializes in the areas of:** Computer Science/Software; Information Technology.

DEAN VESLING & ASSOCIATES
6501 East Grant Road, Tucson AZ 85715. 520/886-4766. **Contact:** Manager. **Description:** A contract services firm. **Specializes in the areas of:** Computer Science/Software; High-Tech.

VOLT TECHNICAL SERVICES
3020 East Camelback Road, Suite 365, Phoenix AZ 85016. 602/955-7750. **Contact:** Regional Manager. **Description:** A contract services firm. Company pays fee. **Specializes in the areas of:** Accounting/Auditing; Art/Design; Chemical; Computer Science/Software; Engineering; Personnel/Labor Relations. **Positions commonly filled include:** Accountant/Auditor; Aerospace Engineer; Buyer; Chemical Engineer; Chemist; Civil Engineer; Commercial Artist; Computer Programmer; Draftsperson; Electrical/Electronics Engineer; Human Resources Manager; Industrial Engineer; Mechanical Engineer; Metallurgical Engineer; Physicist; Purchasing Agent/Manager; Quality Control Supervisor; Statistician; Systems Analyst; Technical Writer/Editor. **Corporate headquarters location:** New York NY. **Other U.S. locations:** Nationwide. **International locations:** Worldwide.

H.L. YOH COMPANY
100 West Clarendon, Suite 1450, Phoenix AZ 85013. 602/235-9295. **Contact:** Manager. **Description:** A contract services firm. **Specializes in the areas of:** Computer Science/Software; Information Technology.

H.L. YOH COMPANY
1325 North Wilmot, Suite 320, Tucson AZ 85712. 520/886-2723. **Contact:** Manager. **Description:** A contract services firm. **Specializes in the areas of:** Computer Science/Software; Information Technology.

CAREER/OUTPLACEMENT COUNSELING FIRMS

ALLEN & ASSOCIATES
4725 North Scottsdale Road, Suite 200, Phoenix AZ 85251. **Toll-free phone:** 800/562-7602. **Fax:** 602/423-1661. **Contact:** Manager. **World Wide Web address:** http://www.allenandassociates.com. **Description:** A career/outplacement counseling firm. **Corporate headquarters location:** Maitland FL. **Other U.S. locations:** Nationwide.

FRANKLIN COVEY
7250 North 16th Street, Suite 402, Phoenix AZ 85020. 602/943-4882. **Contact:** Account Executive. **Description:** A career/outplacement counseling firm that provides information to individuals seeking career opportunities in the sports industry. Products offered include an audiocassette tape series, a regular newsletter with job listings, a career enhancement software test, a resume development kit, and a resume bank service. **Positions commonly filled include:** Accountant/Auditor; Administrator; Customer Service Representative; Marketing Specialist; Public Relations Specialist; Services Sales Representative.

BERNARD HALDANE & ASSOCIATES
5151 East Broadway Boulevard, Suite 390, Tucson AZ 85711. 520/790-2767. **Contact:** Manager. **Description:** A career/outplacement counseling firm.

ARKANSAS

EXECUTIVE SEARCH FIRMS

DUNHILL PERSONNEL
P.O. Box 1570, Rogers AR 72757. 501/636-8578. **Fax:** 501/636-1352. **Contact:** Manager. **Description:** An executive search firm operating on a contingency basis. Company pays fee. **Specializes in the areas of:** Accounting/Auditing; Administration; Engineering; Finance; Food Industry; Manufacturing. **Positions commonly filled include:** Accountant/Auditor; Electrical/Electronics Engineer; Mechanical Engineer; Metallurgical Engineer. **Average salary range of placements:** $30,000 - $50,000. **Number of placements per year:** 50 - 99.

EXECUTIVE RECRUITERS OUTPLACEMENT CONSULTANTS
P.O. Box 21810, Little Rock AR 72221-1810. 501/224-7000. **Fax:** 501/224-8534. **Contact:** Greg Downs, Vice President. **Description:** An executive search firm. **Specializes in the areas of:** Accounting/Auditing; Bookkeeping; Computer Programming; Data Processing; Data Security; Engineering; Finance; Sales; Software Engineering.

INTERNATIONAL SEARCH
905 West Alpine, Siloam Springs AR 72761. 501/524-5333. **Fax:** 501/524-8604. **Contact:** W.L. Smith, President. **Description:** An executive search firm operating on a contingency basis. The firm focuses on engineering, construction, and manufacturing industries. Company pays fee. **Specializes in the areas of:** Computer Science/Software; Engineering; General Management; Industrial; Manufacturing; Personnel/Labor Relations. **Positions commonly filled include:** Accountant/Auditor; Aerospace Engineer; Chemical Engineer; Chemist; Civil Engineer; Computer Programmer; Design Engineer; Designer; Draftsperson; Electrical/Electronics Engineer; Environmental Engineer; Geologist/Geophysicist; Human Resources Specialist; Industrial Engineer; Industrial Production Manager; Management Analyst/Consultant; Mechanical Engineer; Metallurgical Engineer; MIS Specialist; Petroleum Engineer; Purchasing Agent/Manager; Quality Control Supervisor; Software Engineer; Structural Engineer; Systems Analyst. **Corporate headquarters location:** This Location. **Average salary range of placements:** $30,000 - $50,000. **Number of placements per year:** 1 - 49.

MDR & ASSOCIATES
11 Ontur Lane, Hot Springs Village AR 71909. **Toll-free phone:** 800/264-9701. **Contact:** Manager. **Description:** An executive search firm.

MANAGEMENT RECRUITERS INTERNATIONAL
2403 Melrose Street, Paragould AR 72450. 870/236-1800. **Contact:** Manager. **Description:** An executive search firm. **Specializes in the areas of:** Chemical Engineering.

MANAGEMENT RECRUITERS OF LITTLE ROCK
Redding Building, Suite 314, 1701 Centerview Drive, Little Rock AR 72211-4313. 501/224-0801. **Fax:** 501/224-0798. **Contact:** Noel K. Hall, Managing Partner. **Description:** An executive search firm operating on a contingency basis. Company pays fee. **Specializes in the areas of:** Accounting/Auditing; Administration; Advertising; Architecture/Construction; Banking; Chemical; Communications; Computer Hardware/Software; Design; Electrical; Engineering; Food Industry; General Management; Health/Medical; Insurance; Legal; Manufacturing; Operations Management; Personnel/Labor Relations; Procurement; Publishing; Retail; Sales; Technical; Textiles; Transportation. **Positions commonly filled include:** Accountant/Auditor; Agricultural Engineer; Computer Programmer; Design Engineer; Electrical/Electronics Engineer; Environmental Engineer; Industrial Engineer; Industrial Production Manager; Mechanical Engineer; MIS Specialist; Physical Therapist; Physician; Quality Control Supervisor; Registered Nurse; Systems Analyst. **Corporate headquarters location:** Cleveland OH. **Average salary range of placements:** More than $50,000. **Number of placements per year:** 50 - 99.

MOORE & ASSOCIATES
5111 Rogers Avenue, Suite 514, Fort Smith AR 72903. 501/478-7052. **Contact:** Manager. **Description:** An executive search firm.

MORRIS & ASSOCIATES
908 Lakeview Drive, #200, Rogers AR 72756-3010. 501/631-4045. **Fax:** 501/631-8984. **Contact:** Dan Morris, President. **Description:** An executive search firm operating on a contingency basis. The firm focuses on recruiting for the pulp and paper industry, including research and development, engineering, sales, marketing, and technical service. Founded in 1989. Company pays fee. **Specializes in the areas of:** Engineering; Technical. **Positions commonly filled include:** Chemical Engineer; Chemist. **Average salary range of placements:** More than $50,000. **Number of placements per year:** 1 - 49.

SEARCH ASSOCIATES
P.O. Box 10703, Fort Smith AR 72917. 501/452-0005. **Contact:** Manager. **Description:** An executive search firm. **Specializes in the areas of:** Health/Medical.

SNELLING SEARCH
3901 Rogers Avenue, Suite B, Fort Smith AR 72903. 501/782-4911. **Fax:** 501/782-4916. **Contact:** Tammy O'Dell, Manager. **Description:** An executive search firm operating on both retainer and contingency bases. Company pays fee. **Specializes in the areas of:** Accounting/Auditing; Administration; Banking; Engineering; Finance; General Management; Insurance; Manufacturing; Personnel/Labor Relations. **Positions commonly filled include:** Accountant/Auditor; Adjuster; Bookkeeper; Claim Representative; Credit Manager; Customer Service Representative; Financial Analyst; General Manager; Industrial Engineer; Industrial Production Manager; Management Trainee; Manufacturer's/Wholesaler's Sales Rep.; Mechanical Engineer; Operations/ Production Manager; Purchasing Agent/Manager; Quality Control Supervisor; Services Sales Representative; Statistician. **Corporate headquarters location:** Dallas TX. **Average salary range of placements:** $30,000 - $50,000. **Number of placements per year:** 200 - 499.

SPENCER CAREERS
212 North 34th Street, Rogers AR 72756. 501/631-1300. **Toll-free phone:** 800/562-7266. **Fax:** 501/631-1551. **Contact:** James Spencer, Manager. **E-mail address:** jspencer@staffing.net. **Description:** An executive search firm operating on a contingency basis. Spencer Careers also provides some contract services. Founded in 1988. Company pays fee. **Specializes in the areas of:** Banking; Computer Science/Software. **Positions commonly filled include:** Computer Programmer; Database Manager; Software Engineer; Systems Analyst; Systems Manager. **Average salary range of placements:** $30,000 - $50,000. **Number of placements per year:** 1 - 49.

TURNAGE EMPLOYMENT SERVICE GROUP
1225 Breckenridge Drive, Suite 206, Little Rock AR 72205. 501/224-6870. **Fax:** 501/224-5709. **Contact:** Office Manager. **Description:** An executive search firm operating on a contingency basis. Company pays fee. **Specializes in the areas of:** Administration; Computer Science/Software; Engineering; General Management; Health/Medical; Industrial; Insurance; Legal; Manufacturing; Personnel/Labor Relations; Sales; Secretarial; Technical. **Positions commonly filled include:** Accountant/Auditor; Administrative Manager; Bank Officer/Manager; Blue-Collar Worker Supervisor; Branch Manager; Buyer; Chemical Engineer; Clerical Supervisor; Computer Programmer; Cost Estimator; Credit Manager; Dental Assistant/Dental Hygienist; Design Engineer; Draftsperson; Electrical/Electronics Engineer; Environmental Engineer; Financial Analyst; General Manager; Health Services Manager; Hotel Manager; Human Resources Specialist; Industrial Production Manager; Licensed Practical Nurse; Management Analyst/Consultant; Management Trainee; Metallurgical Engineer; MIS Specialist; Operations/Production Manager; Paralegal; Property and Real Estate Manager; Public Relations Specialist; Purchasing Agent/Manager; Quality Control Supervisor; Registered Nurse; Restaurant/Food Service Manager; Services Sales Representative; Software Engineer; Systems Analyst; Technical Writer/Editor; Travel Agent; Typist/Word Processor; Underwriter/Assistant Underwriter. **Corporate headquarters location:** This Location. **Other area locations:** Conway AR; Helena AR; Russellville AR. **Average salary range of placements:** $20,000 - $70,000. **Number of placements per year:** 200 - 499.

UTOPIA, INC.
P.O. Box 1010, Melbourne AR 72556. 870/368-3000. **Fax:** 870/368-3010. **Contact:** Steve Miller, President. **Description:** An executive search firm operating on a contingency basis. The firm focuses on management and engineering placement in manufacturing industries. Company pays fee. **Specializes in the areas of:** Engineering; General Management; Industrial; Manufacturing; Personnel/Labor Relations. **Positions commonly filled include:** Buyer; Chemical Engineer; Chemist; Civil Engineer; Computer Programmer; Design Engineer; Electrical/Electronics Engineer; Industrial Designer; Industrial Engineer; Mechanical Engineer; Metallurgical Engineer; MIS Specialist; Operations/Production Manager; Plant Manager; Purchasing Agent/Manager; Quality Control Supervisor; Statistician; Transportation/Traffic Specialist; Vice President. **Corporate headquarters location:** This Location. **Average salary range of placements:** More than $50,000. **Number of placements per year:** 1 - 49.

TEMPORARY EMPLOYMENT AGENCIES

PREMIER STAFFING, INC.
10110 West Markham, Little Rock AR 72205. 501/223-8367. **Fax:** 501/223-8368. **Contact:** Office Manager. **Description:** A temporary agency. **Specializes in the areas of:** Accounting/Auditing; Banking; General Management; Insurance; Personnel/Labor Relations; Sales; Secretarial. **Positions commonly filled include:** Accountant/Auditor; Actuary; Administrative Manager; Advertising Clerk; Bank Officer/Manager; Branch Manager; Brokerage Clerk; Budget Analyst; Buyer; Claim Representative; Clerical Supervisor; Customer Service Representative; Financial Analyst; General Manager; Human Resources Specialist; Operations/Production Manager; Paralegal; Purchasing Agent/Manager; Quality Control Supervisor; Services Sales Representative; Typist/Word Processor; Underwriter. **Corporate headquarters location:** This Location. **Number of placements per year:** 200 - 499.

SEARK BUSINESS SERVICES
205 Fairview Road, Crossett AR 71635. 870/364-6873. **Contact:** Debbie A Barnett, President. **Description:** A temporary agency. Founded in 1983. **Specializes in the areas of:** Accounting/Auditing; Secretarial; Technical. **Positions commonly filled include:** Accountant/Auditor; Clinical Lab Technician; Purchasing Agent/Manager; Typist/Word Processor.

STAFFMARK
2024 Arkansas Valley Drive, Suite 701, Little Rock AR 72212. 501/225-8080. **Contact:** Steve Schulte, President. **Description:** A temporary agency. **Specializes in the areas of:** Computer Hardware/Software; Office Support; Technical. **Positions commonly filled include:** Administrative Assistant; Computer Operator; Computer Programmer; Data Entry Clerk; Secretary; Systems Analyst; Technician.

CALIFORNIA

EXECUTIVE SEARCH FIRMS

AAA McKINSTRY PERSONNEL CONSULTANTS & RESUME SERVICES
1450 North Tustin Road, Suite 130, Santa Ana CA 92705. 714/646-9090. **Contact:** Office Manager. **Description:** A generalist executive search firm that also provides resume writing services.

AAFA (AMERICAN ASSOCIATION OF FINANCE AND ACCOUNTING)
4601 Wilshire Boulevard, Suite 225, Los Angeles CA 90010. 213/938-4768. **Fax:** 213/857-7009. **Contact:** Office Manager. **World Wide Web address:** http://www.aafa.com. **Description:** An executive search firm. **Specializes in the areas of:** Accounting/Auditing; Banking; Personnel/Labor Relations. **Positions commonly filled include:** Accountant/Auditor; Credit Manager; Financial Analyst; Management Analyst/Consultant. **Average salary range of placements:** More than $50,000. **Number of placements per year:** 100 - 199.

ABA STAFFING, INC.
690 Market Street, Suite 800, San Francisco CA 94104. 415/434-4222. **Fax:** 415/434-3958. **Contact:** Staffing Manager. **E-mail address:** info@abastaff.com. **World Wide Web address:** http://www.abastaff.com. **Description:** An executive search firm that focuses on administrative placements in human resource professions. Company pays fee. **Specializes in the areas of:** Accounting/Auditing; Administration; Banking; Computer Science/Software; Finance; Food Industry; General Management; Insurance; Legal; Manufacturing; Personnel/Labor Relations; Retail; Sales; Secretarial. **Positions commonly filled include:** Accountant/Auditor; Attorney; Customer Service Representative; Human Resources Manager; Management Analyst/Consultant; Management Trainee; Manufacturer's/Wholesaler's Sales Rep.; Paralegal; Services Sales Representative. **Number of placements per year:** 50 - 99.

ABA STAFFING, INC.
2121 South El Camino Real, Suite 605, San Mateo CA 94403. 650/349-9200. **Fax:** 650/349-9721. **Contact:** Eva Gonzalez, Employment Specialist. **Description:** An executive search firm that focuses on administrative placements in human resource professions. The firm also offers some temporary placements. Company pays fee. **Specializes in the areas of:** Accounting/Auditing; Advertising; Finance; Health/Medical; Insurance; Legal; Nonprofit; Personnel/Labor Relations; Publishing; Sales; Secretarial; Technical. **Positions commonly filled include:** Accountant/Auditor; Administrative Manager; Branch Manager; Brokerage Clerk; Buyer; Customer Service Representative; Financial Analyst; General Manager; Human Resources Specialist; Internet Services Manager; MIS Specialist; Operations/Production Manager; Paralegal; Public Relations Specialist; Purchasing Agent/Manager; Software Engineer; Technical Writer/Editor; Typist/Word Processor; Underwriter/Assistant Underwriter. **Average salary range of placements:** $30,000 - $50,000. **Number of placements per year:** 1 - 49.

AGA RECRUITING
515 South Figueroa, Suite 325, Los Angeles CA 90071. 310/208-4266. **Contact:** Office Manager. **Description:** An executive search firm. **Specializes in the areas of:** Accounting/Auditing; Finance.

ARI INTERNATIONAL
5199 East Pacific Coast Highway, Suite 212, Long Beach CA 90804. 562/498-7644. **Fax:** 562/498-6466. **Contact:** Ron Curci, President. **E-mail address:** rlcurci@worldnet.att.net. **Description:** An executive search firm. Company pays fee. **Specializes in the areas of:** Health/Medical. **Average salary range of placements:** More than $50,000. **Number of placements per year:** 1 - 49.

AWS INC.
P.O. Box 380, Ross CA 94957. 415/457-8383. **Contact:** Office Manager. **Description:** An executive search firm. **Specializes in the areas of:** Computer Hardware/Software; Food Industry.

ABACUS STAFFING FOR ACCOUNTING
4100 Newport Place, Suite 770, Newport Beach CA 92660. 714/752-7676. **Fax:** 714/752-1447. **Contact:** Todd Peterson, Account Executive. **Description:** An executive search firm that also provides some temporary placements in the accounting and finance industries. **Specializes in the areas of:** Accounting/Auditing; Finance. **Positions commonly filled include:** Accountant/Auditor; Credit Manager; Financial Analyst. **Other area locations:** Brea CA; Long Beach CA. **Average salary range of placements:** $30,000 - $50,000. **Number of placements per year:** 200 - 499.

ACCESS TECHNOLOGY
4000 Barranca Parkway, Suite 250, Irvine CA 92614. 714/850-1000. **Contact:** R.J. Nadel, President. **Description:** An executive search firm that focuses on high-tech placements. **Specializes in the areas of:** Computer Science/Software; Engineering; Manufacturing; Technical. **Positions commonly filled include:** Electrical/Electronics Engineer; Software Engineer; Technical Writer/Editor. **Number of placements per year:** 1 - 49.

ACCOUNTANTS EXECUTIVE SEARCH
3500 West Olive Avenue, Suite 550, Burbank CA 91505. 818/845-6700. **Fax:** 818/845-3237. **Contact:** Susan Hardt, Manager. **Description:** An executive search firm operating on a contingency basis. Company pays fee. **Specializes in the areas of:** Accounting/Auditing; Finance; Tax. **Positions commonly filled include:** Accountant/Auditor; Finance Director; Financial Analyst. **Corporate headquarters location:** Saddle Brook NJ. **Other U.S. locations:** Nationwide. **Number of placements per year:** 100 - 199.

ACCOUNTANTS EXECUTIVE SEARCH ACCOUNTANTS ON CALL
21800 Oxnard Street, Suite 750, Woodland Hills CA 91367. 818/992-7676. **Fax:** 818/992-1360. **Contact:** Area Manager. **Description:** An executive search firm operating on a contingency basis. Accountants On Call (also at this location) provides temporary and permanent placements of accounting, bookkeeping, banking, and financial personnel. Company pays fee. **Specializes in the areas of:** Accounting/Auditing; Finance. **Positions commonly filled include:** Accountant/Auditor; Budget Analyst; Credit Manager; Human Resources Specialist. **Benefits available to temporary workers:** Medical Insurance; Paid Vacation. **Corporate headquarters location:** Saddle Brook NJ. **Other U.S. locations:** Nationwide. **Number of placements per year:** 200 - 499.

ACCOUNTANTS EXECUTIVE SEARCH
ACCOUNTANTS ON CALL
1650 Spruce Street, Suite 412, Riverside CA 92507. 909/686-2100. **Contact:** Manager. **Description:** An executive search firm. Accountants On Call (also at this location) is a temporary and permanent placement agency. **Specializes in the areas of:** Accounting/Auditing; Banking; Finance. **Corporate headquarters location:** Saddle Brook NJ. **International locations:** Worldwide.

ACCOUNTANTS EXECUTIVE SEARCH
ACCOUNTANTS ON CALL
100 Howe Avenue, Suite 210N, Sacramento CA 95825. 916/483-6666. **Contact:** Manager. **Description:** An executive search firm. Accountants On Call (also at this location) is a temporary and permanent placement agency. **Specializes in the areas of:** Accounting/Auditing; Finance. **Corporate headquarters location:** Saddle Brook NJ. **International locations:** Worldwide.

ACCOUNTANTS EXECUTIVE SEARCH
ACCOUNTANTS ON CALL
10960 Wilshire Boulevard, Suite 1115, Los Angeles CA 90024. 310/312-3330. **Fax:** 310/444-0606. **Contact:** Office Manager. **E-mail address:** acctoncall@earthlink.net. **Description:** An executive search firm. Accountants On Call (also at this location) is a temporary and permanent placement agency that focuses on the accounting industry. **Specializes in the areas of:** Accounting/Auditing; Finance. **Positions commonly filled include:** Accountant; Auditor; Budget Analyst; Chief Financial Officer; Controller; Credit Manager; Financial Analyst. **Benefits available to temporary workers:** Medical Insurance; Paid Holidays; Paid Vacation. **Corporate headquarters location:** Saddle Brook NJ. **International locations:** Worldwide. **Average salary range of placements:** $30,000 - $50,000. **Number of placements per year:** 1000+.

ACCOUNTANTS EXECUTIVE SEARCH
ACCOUNTANTS ON CALL
2001 Gateway Place, Suite 200, San Jose CA 95110. 408/437-9779. **Fax:** 408/437-0716. **Contact:** Manager. **Description:** An executive search firm operating on a contingency basis. Accountants On Call (also at this location) is a temporary and permanent placement agency. **Specializes in the areas of:** Accounting/Auditing; Banking; Finance. **Corporate headquarters location:** Saddle Brook NJ. **International locations:** Worldwide.

ACCOUNTANTS EXECUTIVE SEARCH
ACCOUNTANTS ON CALL
One Kaiser Plaza, Suite 1030, Oakland CA 94612. 510/986-1800. **Contact:** Office Manager. **Description:** An executive search firm operating on a contingency basis. Accountants On Call (also at this location) is a temporary and permanent placement agency that focuses on the accounting industry. **Specializes in the areas of:** Accounting/Auditing; Banking; Finance. **Corporate headquarters location:** Saddle Brook NJ. **International locations:** Worldwide.

ACCOUNTANTS EXECUTIVE SEARCH
ACCOUNTANTS ON CALL
6140 Stone Ridge Mall, Suite 360, Pleasanton CA 94588. 510/734-8666. **Contact:** Office Manager. **Description:** An executive search firm operating on a contingency basis. Accountants On Call (also at this location) is a temporary and permanent placement agency that focuses on the accounting industry. **Specializes in the areas of:** Accounting/Auditing; Banking; Finance. **Corporate headquarters location:** Saddle Brook NJ. **International locations:** Worldwide.

ACCOUNTANTS EXECUTIVE SEARCH
ACCOUNTANTS ON CALL
17700 Castleton Street, Suite 265, City of Industry CA 91748. 818/912-0090. **Contact:** Manager. **Description:** An executive search firm. Accountants on Call (also at this location) is a temporary agency. **Specializes in the areas of:** Accounting/Auditing; Finance.

ACCOUNTANTS EXECUTIVE SEARCH
ACCOUNTANTS ON CALL
5000 Birch Street, Suite 550, Newport Beach CA 92660. 714/955-0100. **Contact:** Manager. **Description:** An executive search firm. Accountants on Call (also at this location) is a temporary agency. **Specializes in the areas of:** Accounting/Auditing; Finance.

ACCOUNTANTS EXECUTIVE SEARCH
ACCOUNTANTS ON CALL
44 Montgomery Street, Suite 2310, San Francisco CA 94104. 415/398-3366. **Contact:** Manager. **Description:** An executive search firm. Accountants on Call (also at this location) is a temporary agency. **Specializes in the areas of:** Accounting/Auditing; Finance.

ACCOUNTANTS ON CALL
970 West 190th Street, Suite 420, Torrance CA 90502-1038. 310/527-2777. **Contact:** Karen Young, Branch Manager. **Description:** An executive search firm focusing on accounting and finance placement. The firm operates on a contingency basis. **Specializes in the areas of:** Accounting/Auditing; Finance. **Positions commonly filled include:** Accountant/Auditor; Financial Analyst. **Corporate headquarters location:** Saddle Brook NJ. **Average salary range of placements:** $30,000 - $50,000. **Number of placements per year:** 100 - 199.

ACCOUNTING ADDITIONS
1000 4th Street, Suite 150, San Rafael CA 94901. 415/459-2300. **Fax:** 415/459-2471. **Contact:** Neil Kreuzberger, President. **Description:** An executive search firm operating on both retainer and contingency bases. The firm also offers career/outplacement counseling and contract services. **Specializes in the areas of:** Accounting/Auditing; Finance. **Positions commonly filled include:** Accountant/Auditor; Financial Analyst. **Number of placements per year:** 50 - 99.

ACCOUNTING ADVANTAGE
11601 Wilshire Boulevard, Suite 1820, Los Angeles CA 90025. 310/445-4111. **Fax:** 310/312-8722. **Contact:** Recruiter. **Description:** An executive search firm. Company pays fee. **Specializes in the areas of:** Accounting/Auditing; Finance. **Positions commonly filled include:** Accountant/Auditor; Budget Analyst; Credit Manager; Financial Analyst. **Corporate headquarters location:** Brentwood CA. **Number of placements per year:** 200 - 499.

ACCUSTAFF
39899 Balentine Drive, Suite 265, Newark CA 94560. 510/651-7055. **Fax:** 510/657-6389. **Contact:** Manager. **Description:** An executive search firm that also operates as a temporary and permanent employment agency. Company pays fee. **Specializes in the areas of:** Accounting/Auditing; Administration; Engineering; Industrial; Manufacturing; Personnel/Labor Relations; Sales; Secretarial. **Number of placements per year:** 500 - 999.

ACTIVE SEARCH AND PLACEMENT
2041 Business Center Drive, Suite 102, Irvine CA 92715-1105. 714/833-9900. **Fax:** 714/833-7988. **Contact:** Nada D. Williston, Partner. **Description:** An

executive search firm focusing on investment management, trust, and mutual fund industry placement. The firm operates on both retainer and contingency bases. Company pays fee. **Specializes in the areas of:** Accounting/Auditing; Finance; Sales. **Positions commonly filled include:** Accountant/Auditor; Brokerage Clerk; Customer Service Representative; Financial Analyst; Sales and Marketing Manager. **Corporate headquarters location:** This Location. **Number of placements per year:** 50 - 99.

JEFFREY C. ADAMS & COMPANY
455 Market Street, San Francisco CA 94105. 415/546-4150. **Contact:** Jeffrey Adams, Owner. **Description:** An executive search firm.

ADDLEMAN & JENKINS ASSOCIATES
4460 Redwood Highway, Suite 13, San Rafael CA 94903. 415/491-8980. **Contact:** Manager. **Description:** An executive search firm. **Specializes in the areas of:** Computer Hardware/Software. **Positions commonly filled include:** Hardware Engineer; Software Engineer.

ADLER-BROWN ASSOCIATES
2672 Bayshore Parkway, Suite 524, Mountain View CA 94043. 415/960-7101. **Contact:** Manager. **Description:** An executive search firm. **Specializes in the areas of:** Data Communications.

ADMINISTRATIVE EXECUTIVE SEARCH
3600 Wilshire Boulevard, Suite 2120, Los Angeles CA 90010. 213/368-6960. **Contact:** Manager. **Description:** An executive search firm. **Specializes in the areas of:** Administration.

ADVANCED TECHNOLOGY CONSULTANTS, INC. (ATC)
536 Weddell Drive, Suite 7, Sunnyvale CA 94089. 408/734-0635. **Fax:** 408/734-5833. **Contact:** Reza Vakili, Professional Staffing Manager. **E-mail address:** atci@ix.netcom.com. **Description:** An executive search firm focusing on all areas of the software industry from development to marketing and support. Industry concentrations include software architecture, design and development, quality assurance, technical marketing, product marketing management, customer support, technical writing, and network administration. Company pays fee. **Specializes in the areas of:** Computer Science/Software; Engineering; Sales. **Positions commonly filled include:** Computer Programmer; Design Engineer; Internet Services Manager; Software Engineer; Strategic Relations Manager; Systems Analyst; Technical Writer/Editor. **Corporate headquarters location:** This Location. **Number of placements per year:** 50 - 99.

ADVANCEMENT PERSONNEL SERVICES (APS)
13123 Whistler Avenue, Granada Hills CA 91344. 818/366-2738. **Contact:** Manager. **Description:** An executive search firm. Advancement Personnel Services operates in three divisions: executive search, personnel, and technical recruiting.

THE AFFILIATES
515 South Figueroa, Suite 650, Los Angeles CA 90071. **Contact:** Manager. **Description:** An executive search firm. **Specializes in the areas of:** Legal. **Positions commonly filled include:** Attorney; Legal Secretary; Paralegal.

AFFORDABLE EXECUTIVE RECRUITERS
5518 Lemona Avenue, Sherman Oaks CA 91411. 818/782-8554. **Contact:** Fred Gerson, President. **Description:** An executive search firm. **Specializes in the areas of:** Accounting/Auditing; Banking; Computer Science/Software; Engineering; Finance; General Management; Sales. **Positions commonly filled include:** Accountant/Auditor; Bank Officer/Manager; Computer Programmer; Human Resources Manager; Internet Services Manager; Software Engineer; Systems Analyst; Typist/Word Processor. **Number of placements per year:** 1 - 49.

AGRI SEARCH INTERNATIONAL
P.O. Box 775, Elk Grove CA 95759-0775. 916/689-6400. **Contact:** Ken Yelle, Director. **Description:** An executive search firm. Company pays fee. **Specializes in the areas of:** Agri-Business. **Positions commonly filled include:** Agricultural Engineer; Agricultural Scientist; Veterinarian.

AGRIESTI & ASSOCIATES
16955 Via Del Campo, Suite 240, San Diego CA 92127-7720. 619/451-7766. **Fax:** 619/451-7843. **Contact:** Kay Agriesti, Owner. **Description:** An executive search firm that recruits sales management and marketing professionals nationwide, primarily in the consumer products and medical industries. The firm operates on both retainer and contingency bases. Company pays fee. **Specializes in the areas of:** Sales. **Positions commonly filled include:** Manufacturer's/Wholesaler's Sales Rep. **Corporate headquarters location:** This Location. **Other U.S. locations:** Nationwide. **Number of placements per year:** 50 - 99.

ALEXANDER & COMPANY
3528 Sacramento Street, Suite 103, San Francisco CA 94118-1847. 415/931-7096. **Fax:** 415/206-1525. **Contact:** Penny Alexander, Principal. **Description:** An executive search firm. Company pays fee. **Specializes in the areas of:** Advertising; Computer Hardware/Software; Marketing; Multimedia; Public Relations. **Positions commonly filled include:** Internet Services Manager; Multimedia Designer; Public Relations Specialist; Strategic Relations Manager; Technical Writer/Editor. **Number of placements per year:** 1 - 49.

ALLARD ASSOCIATES
44 Montgomery Street, Suite 500, San Francisco CA 94104. 415/433-0500. **Contact:** Susan Allard, Partner. **Description:** An executive search firm. Company pays fee. **Specializes in the areas of:** Banking; Retail. **Positions commonly filled include:** Credit Manager; Customer Service Manager; Database Manager; Economist; Marketing Manager; Mathematician; Operations/Production Manager; Product Manager; Statistician. **Number of placements per year:** 50 - 99.

ALLARD ASSOCIATES
1059 Court Street, Suite 114, Woodland CA 95695. 530/757-2176. **Contact:** Manager. **Description:** An executive search firm serving the credit card industry nationwide.

ALLIED SEARCH, INC.
8530 Wilshire Boulevard, Suite 404, Beverly Hills CA 90211. 213/680-4040. **Contact:** Office Manager. **Description:** An executive search firm. Company pays fee. **Specializes in the areas of:** Accounting/Auditing; Administration; Banking; Computer Science/Software; Finance; General Management; Health/Medical; Legal; Personnel/Labor Relations; Retail. **Positions commonly filled include:** Accountant/Auditor; Actuary; Attorney; Bank Officer/Manager; Budget Analyst; Buyer; Computer Programmer; Financial Analyst; Hotel Manager; Human Resources Manager; MIS Specialist; Software Engineer; Systems Analyst. **Average salary range of placements:** More than $50,000. **Number of placements per year:** 200 - 499.

ALLIED SEARCH, INC.
2030 Union Street, Suite 206, San Francisco CA 94123. 415/921-2200. **Contact:** Don May, Manager. **Description:** An executive search firm. Company pays fee. **Specializes in the areas of:** Accounting/Auditing; Administration; Banking; Computer Science/Software; Finance; General Management; Health/Medical; Legal; Personnel/Labor Relations; Retail. **Average salary range of placements:** More than $50,000. **Number of placements per year:** 200 - 499.

ALPHA-NET CONSULTING GROUP
3838 Carson Street, 3rd Floor, Torrance CA 90503. 310/792-1994. **Contact:** Miyoko Sasagie, Consultant. **Description:** An executive search firm focusing on the placement of people who are bilingual in Japanese and English. Alpha-Net Consulting Group also places non-bilingual applicants. **Specializes in the areas of:** Accounting/Auditing; Administration; Banking; Computer Science/Software; Engineering; Finance; Food Industry; General Management; Industrial; Manufacturing; Personnel/Labor Relations; Sales; Secretarial; Technical; Transportation.

ALTERNATIVE STAFFING GROUP
1801 Avenue of the Stars, Suite 430, Los Angeles CA 90067. 310/788-0911. **Fax:** 310/788-0736. **Contact:** Carlin Maher, Vice President of Operations. **Description:** An executive search firm that also offers contract services. Company pays fee. **Specializes in the areas of:** Accounting/Auditing; Administration; Banking; Computer Hardware/Software; Finance; Legal; Personnel/Labor Relations; Sales; Secretarial; Technical. **Positions commonly filled include:** Accountant/Auditor; Administrative Manager; Blue-Collar Worker Supervisor; Branch Manager; Brokerage Clerk; Budget Analyst; Computer Programmer; Design Engineer; Financial Analyst; Human Resources Specialist; Internet Services Manager; MIS Specialist; Multimedia Designer; Paralegal; Services Sales Representative; Software Engineer; Typist/Word Processor. **Benefits available to temporary workers:** Dental Insurance; Medical Insurance; Paid Vacation. **Corporate headquarters location:** This Location. **Other area locations:** El Segundo CA; Woodland Hills CA. **Number of placements per year:** 200 - 499.

AMARX SEARCH
9524 Kearny Villa Road, Suite 205, San Diego CA 92126. 619/578-6050. **Contact:** Manager. **Description:** An executive search firm. **Specializes in the areas of:** Computer Hardware/Software.

AMATO & ASSOCIATES OF CALIFORNIA, INC.
388 Market Street, Suite 500, San Francisco CA 94111. 415/781-7664. **Contact:** Joe Amato, President. **Description:** An executive search firm. **Specializes in the areas of:** Insurance. **Number of placements per year:** 100 - 199.

AMERICAN MAGNA SEARCH
P.O. Box 12197, Marina Del Rey CA 90295. 310/306-3973. **Contact:** Manager. **Description:** An executive search firm. **Specializes in the areas of:** Apparel; Fashion.

ANKENBRANDT GROUP
4685 MacArthur Court, Suite 480, Newport Beach CA 92660. 714/955-1455. **Fax:** 714/955-2029. **Contact:** Office Manager. **E-mail address:** ankgrp@ix.netcom.com. **Description:** An executive search firm. Company pays fee. **Specializes in the areas of:** Accounting/Auditing; Administration; Computer Science/Software; Sales; Technical. **Positions commonly filled include:** Accountant/Auditor; Internet Services Manager; Management Analyst/Consultant; Marketing Specialist; Sales Representative; Systems Analyst. **Number of placements per year:** 100 - 199.

JOHN ANTHONY & ASSOCIATES
P.O. Box 12291, La Jolla CA 92039-2291. 619/457-1116. **Contact:** John A. Muller Jr., Principal Recruiter. **Description:** An executive search firm that operates on contingency and retained bases. Company pays fee. **Specializes in the areas of:** Accounting/Auditing; Administration; Biotechnology; Computer Science/Software; Engineering; Finance; General Management; Insurance; Management; Sales; Secretarial; Telecommunications. **Positions commonly filled include:** Accountant; Actuary; Administrative Assistant; Administrative Manager; Auditor; Bank Officer/Manager; Biological Scientist; Biomedical Engineer; Budget Analyst; Chemist; Chief Financial Officer; Computer Programmer; Credit Manager; Database Manager; Finance Director; Financial Analyst; Internet Services Manager; Marketing Manager; Marketing Specialist; Mechanical Engineer; MIS Specialist; Sales Executive; Sales Manager; Science Technologist; Secretary; Software Engineer; Systems Analyst; Systems Manager; Telecommunications Manager; Typist/Word Processor; Underwriter/ Assistant Underwriter. **Average salary range of placements:** More than $50,000. **Number of placements per year:** 1 - 49.

ARBOIT ASSOCIATES
5020 Campus Drive, Newport Beach CA 92660. 714/833-8186. **Contact:** Manager. **Description:** An executive search firm.

ASSOCIATED SOFTWARE CONSULTANTS, INC.
1509 North Sepulveda Boulevard, Manhattan Beach CA 90266-5109. 310/545-5646. **Fax:** 310/546-3433. **Contact:** Marshall Biggs, President. **Description:** An executive search firm. Company pays fee. **Specializes in the areas of:** Administration; Computer Hardware/Software. **Positions commonly filled include:** Computer Operator; Computer Programmer; Data Entry Clerk; EDP Specialist; MIS Specialist; Software Engineer; Systems Analyst; Technical Writer/Editor. **Number of placements per year:** 50 - 99.

AUSTIN ASSOCIATES
215 North Marengo, 2nd Floor, Pasadena CA 91101. 626/793-4807. **Contact:** Manager. **Description:** An executive search firm.

AUTOMOTIVE CAREER PLACEMENT
5776 Stoneridge Mall Road, Suite 126, Pleasanton CA 94588. 510/734-8111. **Fax:** 800/360-8690. **Contact:** Manager. **Description:** An executive search firm that focuses on the automotive industry. Company pays fee. **Specializes in the areas of:** Accounting/Auditing; Automotive; Finance; Sales. **Positions commonly filled include:** Accountant/Auditor; Adjuster; General Manager. **Number of placements per year:** 100 - 199.

THE BADGER GROUP
4125 Blackhawk Plaza Circle, Suite 270, Danville CA 94506. 510/736-5553. **Contact:** Manager. **Description:** An executive search firm for senior-level managers. **Specializes in the areas of:** Administration; High-Tech. **Average salary range of placements:** More than $50,000.

BALLANTYNE ASSOCIATES INC.
P.O. Box 810, Moss Beach CA 94038-0810. 650/634-9464. **Contact:** Della Bernard, Consultant. **Description:** An executive search firm operating on a retainer basis. The firm also offers career counseling services. Company pays fee. **Specializes in the areas of:** Advertising; Food Industry; General Management; Sales. **Positions commonly filled include:** Editor; Food Scientist/Technologist; Market Research Analyst; Reporter. **Number of placements per year:** 1 - 49.

BARNES & ASSOCIATES
1101 Dove Street, Suite 238, Newport Beach CA 92660. 714/253-6750. **Fax:** 714/253-6753. **Contact:** Meredith Schwarz, Managing Partner. **E-mail address:** msbarnes@ix.netcom.com. **Description:** An executive search firm. Founded in 1988. Company pays fee. **Specializes in the areas of:** Computer Hardware/Software; Sales. **Positions commonly filled include:** Computer Programmer; Internet Services Manager; Manufacturer's/Wholesaler's Sales Rep.; Software Engineer; Strategic Relations Manager; Systems Analyst. **Corporate headquarters location:** This Location. **Other U.S. locations:** Nationwide. **Average salary range of placements:** More than $50,000. **Number of placements per year:** 50 - 99.

BAST & ASSOCIATES, INC.
11726 San Vicente Boulevard, Suite 200, Los Angeles CA 90049. 310/207-2100. **Fax:** 310/207-3003. **Contact:** Larry C. Bast, Managing Director. **Description:** An executive search firm focusing on marketing, advertising, and marketing research staffing for consumer goods and service companies. Company pays fee. **Specializes in the areas of:** Advertising; Marketing. **Average salary range of placements:** More than $50,000. **Number of placements per year:** 1 - 49.

BAY RESOURCES INC.
519 17th Street, Suite 510, Oakland CA 94612. 510/465-2781. **Contact:** Sandra Adams, President. **Description:** An executive search firm. **Specializes in the areas of:** Accounting/Auditing; Banking; Finance. **Positions commonly filled include:** Accountant/Auditor; Budget Analyst; Financial Analyst. **Corporate headquarters location:** This Location. **Average salary range of placements:** More than $50,000. **Number of placements per year:** 100 - 199.

THOMAS BECK INC.
P.O. Box 789, Sausalito CA 94966-0789. 415/331-1555. **Fax:** 415/381-1608. **Contact:** Thomas Beck, CEO. **Description:** An executive search firm. Company pays fee. **Specializes in the areas of:** Electronics; Engineering; Sales. **Number of placements per year:** 1 - 49.

RICHARD BECKSTEAD & ASSOCIATES
One First Street, Suite 9, Los Altos CA 94022. 650/949-8138. **Contact:** Richard Beckstead, Owner. **E-mail address:** rbsearch@aol.com. **Description:** An executive search firm that places mid- to upper-level managers. **Specializes in the areas of:** Software Engineering; Telecommunications. **Average salary range of placements:** More than $50,000.

ROBERT BEECH INC.
55 Galley Drive, Novato CA 94949. 415/884-2600. **Contact:** Manager. **Description:** An executive search firm.

ROBERT BEECH WEST INC.
383 South Palm Canyon Drive, Palm Springs CA 92262. 760/864-1380. **Fax:** 760/864-1382. **Contact:** Robert Beech, Director. **Description:** An executive search firm that places sales and marketing professionals in the computer software industry. Company pays fee. **NOTE:** Applicants must have at least four years of experience in a sales or marketing position. **Specializes in the areas of:** Computer Science/Software; Sales. **Positions commonly filled include:** Customer Service Representative; Sales Representative; Software Engineer. **Average salary range of placements:** More than $50,000. **Number of placements per year:** 50 - 99.

EDWARD BELL ASSOCIATES
50 First Street, Suite 320, San Francisco CA 94105. 415/442-0270. **Fax:** 415/442-1862. **Contact:** Professional Recruiter. **E-mail address:** eba@netcom.com. **Description:** An executive search firm operating on both retainer and contingency bases. The firm also provides temporary placement and focuses on accounting, finance, clerical, data processing, and real estate professions. Company pays fee. **Specializes in the areas of:** Accounting/Auditing; Administration; Computer Science/Software; Finance; Secretarial. **Positions commonly filled include:** Accountant/Auditor; Clerical Supervisor; Computer Programmer; Credit Manager; Financial Analyst; Internet Services Manager; Multimedia Designer; Paralegal; Software Engineer; Systems Analyst. **Corporate headquarters location:** This Location. **Average salary range of placements:** More than $50,000. **Number of placements per year:** 100 - 199.

HARVEY BELL & ASSOCIATES
700 Lindsay Avenue, Rohnert Park CA 94928. 707/795-0650. **Contact:** Harvey Bell, Owner. **Description:** An executive search firm. Company pays fee. **Specializes in the areas of:** Administration; Architecture/Construction; Banking; Computer Science/Software; Education; Engineering; Finance; General Management; Health/Medical; Insurance; Legal; Sales. **Positions commonly filled include:** Attorney; Bank Officer/Manager; Biomedical Engineer; Branch Manager; Chiropractor; Computer Programmer; Dentist; Economist; Education Administrator; Electrical/Electronics Engineer; General Manager; Geographer; Geologist/Geophysicist; Health Services Manager; Instrument Engineer; Licensed Practical Nurse; Management Analyst/Consultant; Manufacturer's/Wholesaler's Sales Rep.; Operations/Production Manager; Paralegal; Physician; Quality Control Supervisor; Real Estate Agent; Registered Nurse; Securities Sales Representative; Services Sales Representative; Software Engineer; Systems Analyst; Teacher/Professor; Travel Agent; Veterinarian.

BENCH INTERNATIONAL SEARCH INC.
116 North Robertson Boulevard, Suite 503, Los Angeles CA 90048. 310/854-9900. **Contact:** Manager. **Description:** An executive search firm. **Specializes in the areas of:** Biotechnology; Pharmaceutical.

BENNETT & COMPANY CONSULTING GROUP
2135 Manzanita Drive, Oakland CA 94611-1134. 510/339-3175. **Fax:** 510/339-2162. **Contact:** Linda Bennett, Owner. **E-mail address:** 73542,2504@compuserve.com. **Description:** An executive search firm operating on both retainer and contingency bases. The firm also provides interview coaching. **Specializes in the areas of:** General Management; Human Resources; Nonprofit; Personnel/Labor Relations; Sales. **Positions commonly filled include:** Account Manager; Accountant; Administrative Manager; Applications Engineer; Credit Manager; Database Manager; Human Resources Manager; Management Analyst/Consultant; MIS Specialist; Operations Manager; Project Manager; Public Relations Manager; Quality Control Supervisor; Sales Engineer; Sales Representative; Software Engineer; Systems Analyst; Systems Manager; Technical Writer/Editor. **Average salary range of placements:** More than $50,000. **Number of placements per year:** 1 - 49.

BENTLEY PRICE ASSOCIATES, INC.
3541 West Oak Trail Road, Santa Ynez CA 93460. 805/686-1234. **Contact:** Dennis P. Rizzo, President. **Description:** An executive search firm that places

management consultants in the hospitality industry. **Specializes in the areas of:** Hotel/Restaurant. **Number of placements per year:** 200 - 499.

BIALLA AND ASSOCIATES, INC.
4000 Bridgeway, Suite 201, Sausalito CA 94965. 415/332-7111. **Fax:** 415/332-3964. **Contact:** H. Scott Thomson, Partner and General Manager. **Description:** An executive search firm. Company pays fee. **Specializes in the areas of:** Advertising; General Management; Sales. **Number of placements per year:** 50 - 99.

BILLINGTON & ASSOCIATES, INC.
3250 Wilshire Boulevard, Suite 900, Los Angeles CA 90010. 213/386-7511. **Fax:** 213/386-7025. **Contact:** B.J. Billington, Principal. **Description:** An executive search firm operating on a retained basis. Company pays fee. **Specializes in the areas of:** Accounting/Auditing; Finance. **Positions commonly filled include:** Accountant/Auditor; Administrative Manager; Chief Financial Officer; Clerical Supervisor; Controller; Credit Manager; Customer Service Representative; Economist; Financial Analyst; MIS Specialist. **Average salary range of placements:** More than $50,000. **Number of placements per year:** 1 - 49.

DEBORAH BISHOP & ASSOCIATES
1070 Marina Village Parkway, Suite 203, Alameda CA 94501. 510/523-2305. **Contact:** Manager. **Description:** An executive search firm that provides placements that are director-level or above. **Specializes in the areas of:** Computer Hardware/Software; High-Tech. **Average salary range of placements:** More than $50,000.

THE BLACK LEOPARD
43-695 Skyward Way, La Quinta CA 92253. 760/360-4191. **Toll-free phone:** 800/360-4191. **Fax:** 760/360-4194. **Contact:** Lauren Kurbatoff, Owner. **E-mail address:** tbleopard@aol.com. **Description:** An executive search firm that operates on both retainer and contingency bases. Founded in 1984. Company pays fee. **Specializes in the areas of:** Food Industry; Manufacturing; Personnel/Labor Relations; Publishing; Sales. **Positions commonly filled include:** Accountant/Auditor; Agricultural Engineer; Blue-Collar Worker Supervisor; Buyer; Chemical Engineer; Chemist; Civil Engineer; Computer Programmer; Design Engineer; Electrical/Electronics Engineer; Financial Analyst; Food Scientist/Technologist; Health Services Manager; Manufacturer's/Wholesaler's Sales Rep.; Market Research Analyst; Mechanical Engineer; MIS Specialist; Operations/Production Manager; Purchasing Agent/Manager; Quality Control Supervisor; Services Sales Representative; Software Engineer; Strategic Relations Manager; Systems Analyst; Telecommunications Manager; Transportation/Traffic Specialist. **Average salary range of placements:** $30,000 - $50,000. **Number of placements per year:** 50 - 99.

BLACKHAWK ADVANTAGE, INC.
1100 Irvine Boulevard, Suite 340, Tustin CA 92780. 714/731-9400. **Fax:** 714/731-8400. **Contact:** Phil Andersen, Director. **E-mail address:** phil@blackhawkusa.com. **Description:** An executive search firm that focuses on placement in the financial services industry. **Specializes in the areas of:** Banking; Insurance. **Positions commonly filled include:** Accountant/Auditor; Trust Officer. **Average salary range of placements:** More than $50,000. **Number of placements per year:** 50 - 99.

BLUE, GARNI & COMPANY
Pier One, San Francisco CA 94011. 415/986-1110. **Contact:** Patricia Blue, Principal. **Description:** An executive search firm. Blue, Garni & Company's client businesses include alternative energy and energy finance, distribution and information management, diversified financial services, equipment leasing and management, management consulting, manufacturing portfolio management, project finance, and transportation services. Company pays fee. **Specializes in the areas of:** Accounting/Auditing; Advertising; Banking; Computer Science/Software; Engineering; Finance; General Management; Transportation. **Positions commonly filled include:** Financial Analyst; General Manager; Industrial Engineer; Internet Services Manager; Management Analyst/Consultant; Management Trainee; Mechanical Engineer; Public Relations Specialist; Purchasing Agent/Manager; Strategic Relations Manager; Transportation/Traffic Specialist; Urban/Regional Planner. **Corporate headquarters location:** This Location. **Other area locations:** San Francisco CA. **Average salary range of placements:** More than $50,000. **Number of placements per year:** 1 - 49.

DAN BOLEN & ASSOCIATES
73710 Fred Waring Drive, Suite 116, Palm Desert CA 92260. 760/773-3723. **Contact:** Dan Bolen, Owner. **Description:** An executive search firm focusing on the rotating machinery field. **Specializes in the areas of:** Industrial.

J. BORAGINE & ASSOCIATES
100 Pine Street, Suite 2740, San Francisco CA 94111. 415/433-1143. **Contact:** Manager. **Description:** An executive search firm that places personnel in a variety of industries.

BORDWELL & ASSOCIATES
1400 Quail Street, Suite 100, Newport Beach CA 92660. 714/724-1466. **Contact:** Manager. **Description:** An executive search firm. **Specializes in the areas of:** Legal.

BOWERS THOMAS
11150 West Olympic Boulevard, Suite 805, Los Angeles CA 90064. 310/477-3244. **Fax:** 310/444-1885. **Contact:** Manager. **Description:** An executive search firm focusing on attorney placement at national and international corporations, law firms, and smaller firms. Bowers Thomas offers placement in traditional legal practice areas such as litigation, corporate transactions, and real estate, and also provides expertise in practices such as patient/IP, employment/labor, and tax. The firm operates on both retainer and contingency bases. Company pays fee. **NOTE:** At least one year of practice experience is required for partner and general counsel positions. **Specializes in the areas of:** Legal. **Positions commonly filled include:** Attorney. **Corporate headquarters location:** This Location. **Other area locations:** San Diego CA. **Number of placements per year:** 1 - 49.

BOWMAN ASSOCIATES
1660 South Amphlett Boulevard, Suite 245, San Mateo CA 94402. 415/573-0188. **Contact:** Manager. **Description:** An executive search firm. **Specializes in the areas of:** Hotel/Restaurant.

BOZICH & CRUZ
2540 North First Street, Suite 309, San Jose CA 95131. 408/955-9800. **Contact:** Office Manager. **Description:** An executive search firm. **Specializes in the areas of:** Computer Science/Software.

BRANDENBURG SMITH & ASSOCIATES
4633 Old Ironsides Drive, Suite 400, Santa Clara CA 95054. 408/727-5554. **Contact:** Manager. **Description:** An executive search firm. **Specializes in the areas of:** Engineering; High-Tech.

JAMES BRANDON & ASSOCIATES
509 Capitola Avenue, Capitola CA 95010. 408/475-6131. **Contact:** Manager. **Description:** An executive search firm. **Specializes in the areas of:** Engineering.

BRENNAN ASSOCIATES
19531 Ventura Boulevard, Tarzana CA 91356. 818/881-3046. **Contact:** Mike Brennan, Manager. **Description:** An executive search firm. **Specializes in the areas of:** Real Estate.

BRIDGECREEK PERSONNEL
12792 Valley View Street, Suite 202, Garden Grove CA 92645. 714/891-1771. **Fax:** 714/892-1567. **Contact:** W.A. (Bill) Foster, President. **Description:** An executive search firm. Company pays fee. **Specializes in the areas of:** Distribution; Manufacturing; Plastics. **Positions commonly filled include:** Biological Scientist; Biomedical Engineer; Buyer; Chemical Engineer; Chemist; Civil Engineer; Customer Service Representative; Food Scientist/Technologist; Human Resources Manager; Industrial Engineer; Industrial Production Manager; Management Analyst/Consultant; Management Trainee; Manufacturer's/Wholesaler's Operations/Production Manager; Quality Control Supervisor; Services Sales Representative; Software Engineer. **Number of placements per year:** 50 - 99.

BRIDGEGATE GROUP
18401 Von Karman, Suite 440, Irvine CA 92612. **Contact:** Kevin M. Rosenberg, Managing Director. **Description:** A retained executive search firm focusing on mid- to senior-level placements. BridgeGate Group, a division of SearchWorks L.L.C., features more than 25 specialists in multiple disciplines. Founded in 1967. **Specializes in the areas of:** Accounting/Auditing; Consulting; Finance; Information Systems; Information Technology; Personnel/Labor Relations; Sales; Software Engineering.

BRISTOL ASSOCIATES
5757 West Century Boulevard, Suite 628, Los Angeles CA 90045. 310/670-0525. **Contact:** Manager. **Description:** An executive search firm. **Specializes in the areas of:** Direct Marketing; Food Industry; Health/Medical; Hotel/Restaurant.

BROOK-BLAIR LTD.
15970 High Knoll Road, Encino CA 91436. 818/981-9888. **Fax:** 818/981-9011. **Contact:** Arold Dardik, President. **Description:** An executive search firm operating on both retained and contingency bases. Company pays fee. **Specializes in the areas of:** Banking. **Positions commonly filled include:** Bank Officer/Manager; Financial Analyst. **Average salary range of placements:** More than $50,000. **Number of placements per year:** 1 - 49.

BROOKS ASSOCIATES
610 Anekapa Street, Santa Barbara CA 93101. 805/963-5858. **Fax:** 805/963-2129. **Contact:** President. **Description:** An executive search firm. The firm focuses on the cosmetic industry and operates on both retainer and contingency bases. **Specializes in the areas of:** Advertising; General Management; Sales. **Corporate headquarters location:** This Location. **Other U.S. locations:** Nationwide. **Number of placements per year:** 1 - 49.

A.J. BROWN & ASSOCIATES
2245 East Colorado Boulevard, Suite 335, Pasadena CA 91107. 626/793-1193. **Contact:** Manager. **Description:** An executive search firm. **Specializes in the areas of:** Technical.

DAN BROWN & ASSOCIATES
3620 Northgate Boulevard, Suite 200, Sacramento CA 95834. 916/929-9288. **Fax:** 916/929-5649. **Contact:** Manager. **Description:** An executive search firm. **Specializes in the areas of:** Restaurant.

BROWN VENTURE ASSOCIATES
3000 Sand Hill Road, Building 3, Suite 110, Menlo Park CA 94025. 415/233-0205. **Contact:** Manager. **Description:** An executive search firm that places professionals in vice president and senior-level positions. **Specializes in the areas of:** Computer Science/Software; Electronics.

BRYSON MYERS COMPANY
2083 Old Middlefield Way, Suite 806, Mountain View CA 94043. 650/964-7600. **Fax:** 650/964-7655. **Contact:** Rich Milano, Partner. **E-mail address:** rmilano@hooked.net. **Description:** An executive search firm. Company pays fee. **Specializes in the areas of:** Computer Hardware/Software; Engineering; Health/Medical; Technical. **Positions commonly filled include:** Biomedical Engineer; Ceramics Engineer; Computer Programmer; Electrical/Electronics Engineer; Industrial Designer; Industrial Engineer; Manufacturing Engineer; MIS Specialist; Software Engineer; Technical Writer/Editor. **Number of placements per year:** 50 - 99.

BUFF & ASSOCIATES
21024 Victory Boulevard, Woodland Hills CA 91367. 818/340-6300. **Contact:** Manager. **Description:** An executive search firm. **Specializes in the areas of:** Home Furnishings.

BULLIS & COMPANY, INC.
120 Quintara Street, San Francisco CA 94116-1359. 415/753-6140. **Fax:** 415/753-6653. **Contact:** Richard Bullis, President. **Description:** An executive search firm. Company pays fee. **Specializes in the areas of:** Architecture/Construction; Computer Science/Software; Engineering; Finance; General Management; Manufacturing. **Average salary range of placements:** More than $50,000. **Number of placements per year:** 1 - 49.

BUSINESS AND PROFESSIONAL CONSULTANTS
3255 Wilshire Boulevard, Suite 1732, Los Angeles CA 90010. 213/380-8200. **Contact:** Manager. **Description:** An executive search firm. **Number of placements per year:** 1 - 49.

C&C ASSOCIATES
27001 East La Paz Road, Suite 400, Mission Viejo CA 92691. 714/859-6733. **Contact:** Manager. **Description:** An executive search firm that places sales managers in a variety of industries.

C-E SEARCH
42335 Washington Street, Suite F312, Palm Desert CA 92211. 760/568-3060. **Contact:** Manager. **Description:** An executive search firm. **Specializes in the areas of:** Construction.

CBA
400 Capital Mall, Suite 900, Sacramento CA 95814. 916/449-3922. **Contact:** Manager. **Description:** An executive search firm that places upper-level managers in a variety of fields.

CN ASSOCIATES
4040 Civic Center Drive, Suite 200, San Rafael CA 94903. 415/883-1114. **Fax:** 415/883-3321. **Contact:** Charles Nicolosi, Principal. **E-mail address:** chanic@ix.netcom.com. **Description:** An executive search firm. Company pays fee. **Specializes in the areas of:** Administration; Computer Science/Software; Engineering; Sales; Technical. **Positions commonly filled include:** Branch Manager; Computer Programmer; Internet Services Manager; Management Analyst/Consultant; MIS Specialist; Multimedia Designer;

Radio/TV Announcer/Broadcaster; Software Engineer; Systems Analyst; Telecommunications Manager. **Average salary range of placements:** More than $50,000. **Number of placements per year:** 1 - 49.

C.R. ASSOCIATES
P.O. Box 60998, Palo Alto CA 94306. 650/324-9000. **Contact:** Harold Stephenson, Owner. **Description:** An executive search firm. **Specializes in the areas of:** Banking; Finance.

CRI PROFESSIONAL SEARCH
1784 Leimert Boulevard, Oakland CA 94602-1930. 510/531-1681. **Toll-free phone:** 800/528-1991. **Fax:** 510/531-9599. **Contact:** Chuck Acridge, Owner. **E-mail address:** cri@sirius.com. **Description:** An executive search firm. Company pays fee. **Specializes in the areas of:** Health/Medical; Insurance. **Positions commonly filled include:** Physician. **Average salary range of placements:** More than $50,000. **Number of placements per year:** 1 - 49.

CALIFORNIA MANAGEMENT SEARCH (CMS)
881 11th Street, Suite 117, Lakeport CA 95453. 707/263-6000. **Fax:** 707/263-6800. **Contact:** Randy Marsh, Manager/Owner. **Description:** A contingency executive search firm. Company pays fee. **Specializes in the areas of:** Insurance. **Positions commonly filled include:** Actuary; Adjuster; Branch Manager; Loss Prevention Specialist; Underwriter/Assistant Underwriter. **Corporate headquarters location:** This Location. **Average salary range of placements:** $30,000 - $50,000. **Number of placements per year:** 1 - 49.

CALIFORNIA SEARCH AGENCY, INC.
2603 Main Street, Suite 550, Irvine CA 92614-6232. 714/475-0790. **Fax:** 714/475-0796. **Contact:** Don Crane, President. **E-mail address:** dcrane@jobagency.com. **World Wide Web address:** http://www.jobagency.com. **Description:** An executive search firm focusing on engineering, manufacturing, sales/marketing, research and development, and software/data processing placements. California Search Agency operates on both retainer and contingency bases. Company pays fee. **Specializes in the areas of:** Accounting/Auditing; Administration; Architecture/Construction; Biology; Computer Science/Software; Engineering; Food Industry; General Management; Industrial; Manufacturing; Marketing; Personnel/Labor Relations; Sales; Scientific; Technical; Transportation. **Positions commonly filled include:** Applications Engineer; Biomedical Engineer; Buyer; Chemical Engineer; Chemist; Chief Financial Officer; Civil Engineer; Computer Programmer; Controller; Cost Estimator; Design Engineer; Draftsperson; Electrical/Electronics Engineer; Environmental Engineer; Graphic Artist; Graphic Designer; Human Resources Manager; Industrial Engineer; Industrial Production Manager; Manufacturing Engineer; Marketing Manager; Mechanical Engineer; MIS Specialist; Operations Manager; Project Manager; Quality Control Supervisor; Sales Engineer; Sales Executive; Sales Manager; Sales Representative; Software Engineer; Systems Analyst; Systems Manager; Technical Writer/Editor; Transportation/Traffic Specialist. **Average salary range of placements:** More than $30,000. **Number of placements per year:** 50 - 99.

CALIFORNIA SEARCH CONSULTANTS
2103 El Camino Real, Suite 202, Oceanside CA 92054. 760/439-5511. **Fax:** 760/439-0751. **Contact:** Manager. **Description:** An executive search firm. **Specializes in the areas of:** Electronics; Engineering.

JOHN CAPPELLITTI ASSOCIATES
28047 Dorothy Drive, Suite 200, Agoura Hills CA 91301. 818/841-6670. **Contact:** Manager. **Description:** An executive search and consulting firm. **Specializes in the areas of:** Data Processing.

CAREER ADVANTAGE
1215 East Airport Drive, Suite 125, Ontario CA 91761. 909/466-9232. **Toll-free phone:** 800/576-4620. **Fax:** 909/948-1165. **Contact:** Brynda Woods, President. **E-mail address:** bryndaw@aol.com. **Description:** An executive search firm. Company pays fee. **Specializes in the areas of:** Accounting/Auditing; Administration; Banking; Engineering; Finance; Food Industry; Manufacturing; Personnel/Labor Relations; Sales. **Positions commonly filled include:** Accountant/Auditor; Administrative Manager; Aerospace Engineer; Bank Officer/Manager; Biochemist; Branch Manager; Buyer; Chemical Engineer; Computer Programmer; Design Engineer; Financial Analyst; Human Resources Manager; Industrial Engineer; Industrial Production Manager; Market Research Analyst; Mechanical Engineer; MIS Specialist; Operations/Production Manager; Paralegal; Purchasing Agent/Manager; Software Engineer; Systems Analyst; Telecommunications Manager; Typist/Word Processor. **Corporate headquarters location:** This Location. **Average salary range of placements:** More than $50,000. **Number of placements per year:** 100 - 199.

CARLSON & ASSOCIATES
11400 West Olympic Boulevard, Suite 200, Los Angeles CA 90064. 310/445-1915. **Contact:** Manager. **Description:** An executive search firm. **Specializes in the areas of:** Health/Medical.

J. CARSON & ASSOCIATES
16200 Ventura Boulevard, Suite 228, Encino CA 91326. 818/906-3312. **Fax:** 818/990-2680. **Contact:** Jeannea Nightingale, President. **Description:** An executive search firm. Company pays fee. **Specializes in the areas of:** Market Research. **Positions commonly filled include:** Management Analyst/Consultant; Market Research Analyst; Statistician. **Average salary range of placements:** More than $50,000. **Number of placements per year:** 1 - 49.

CARTER & ASSOCIATES
P.O. Box 21444, El Cajon CA 92021. 619/588-5339. **Contact:** Manager. **Description:** An executive search firm. **Specializes in the areas of:** Publishing.

CARVER DOOLEY ASSOCIATES
2049 Century Park East, Suite 1200, Los Angeles CA 90067. 310/556-0662. **Fax:** 310/556-1767. **Contact:** Kim Carver, Principal. **Description:** An executive search firm. Company pays fee. **Specializes in the areas of:** Accounting/Auditing; Finance. **Positions commonly filled include:** Accountant/Auditor; Credit Manager; EDP Specialist. **Number of placements per year:** 1 - 49.

CERTIFIED EXECUTIVE SEARCH
2846 Lambert Place, Los Angeles CA 90068. 213/388-1143. **Contact:** Manager. **Description:** An executive search firm that provides placements in the construction industry.

CERTIFIED HEALTH AND PERSONNEL
3418 Loma Vista Road, Office G, Ventura CA 93003. 805/339-2968. **Contact:** Manager. **Description:** An executive search firm for health care professionals.

CHAITIN & ASSOCIATES
22543 Ventura Boulevard, Woodland Hills CA 91364. 818/225-8655. **Fax:** 818/225-8660. **Contact:** Chuck Hayes, Sales Manager. **Description:** An executive search firm. **Specializes in the areas of:** Accounting/Auditing; Administration; Broadcasting; Finance; Retail; Sales. **Positions commonly filled**

include: Buyer; Credit Manager; General Manager; Human Resources Manager; Manufacturer's/Wholesaler's Sales Rep. **Average salary range of placements:** More than $50,000. **Number of placements per year:** 50 - 99.

WAYNE CHAMBERLAIN & ASSOCIATES
25835 Narbonne Avenue, Suite 280-C, Lomita CA 90717. 310/534-4840. **Fax:** 310/539-9885. **Contact:** Wayne S. Chamberlain, Owner. **Description:** An executive search firm. Company pays fee. **Specializes in the areas of:** Banking; Engineering; Industrial; Manufacturing. **Positions commonly filled include:** Bank Officer/Manager; Electrical/Electronics Engineer; Mechanical Engineer. **Number of placements per year:** 1 - 49.

ELSIE CHAN & ASSOCIATES INC.
132 North El Camino Real, Suite 514, Encinitas CA 92024. 760/944-9478. **Contact:** Manager. **Description:** An executive search firm. **Specializes in the areas of:** Information Systems.

CHASE MORGAN & ASSOCIATES INC.
1269 Valley High Avenue, Thousand Oaks CA 91362. 805/373-1289. **Contact:** Manager. **Description:** An executive search firm. **Specializes in the areas of:** Insurance.

CLAIMSEARCH/THE SEARCH GROUP
P.O. Box 357, Fort Bragg CA 95437. 707/964-1795. **Fax:** 707/964-1555. **Contact:** Thomas Bayard, Manager. **E-mail address:** tbayard@mcn.org. **Description:** An executive search firm focusing on insurance, claims, and risk management industries. The firm operates on both retainer and contingency bases. Company pays fee. **Specializes in the areas of:** General Management; Insurance; Legal; Risk Management. **Positions commonly filled include:** Account Manager; Adjuster; Attorney; Branch Manager; Claim Representative. **Other U.S. locations:** Nationwide. **Average salary range of placements:** $30,000 - $50,000. **Number of placements per year:** 1 - 49.

CLANCY ASSOCIATES
100 Bush Street, San Francisco CA 94104. 415/931-5743. **Contact:** Manager. **Description:** A retained executive search firm.

COAST TO COAST EXECUTIVE SEARCH
4040 Civic Center Drive, Suite 200, San Rafael CA 94903-1900. 415/492-2870. **Fax:** 415/491-4710. **Contact:** Alan Horowitz, President. **E-mail address:** coast@weo.com. **Description:** An executive search firm focusing on sales, marketing, research/development, and technical staffing in the consumer products, medical, and computer hardware/software industries. Company pays fee. **Specializes in the areas of:** Banking; Computer Science/Software; Food Industry; Health/Medical; Sales; Technical. **Positions commonly filled include:** Food Scientist/Technologist. **Corporate headquarters location:** This Location. **Average salary range of placements:** More than $50,000. **Number of placements per year:** 1 - 49.

THE COELYN GROUP
One Park Plaza, Suite 600, Irvine CA 92614. 714/546-0660. **Contact:** Manager. **Description:** An executive search firm.

COHEN ASSOCIATES
23801 Calabasas Road, Suite 2050, Calabasas CA 91302. 818/222-6600. **Contact:** Nancy Cohen. **Description:** An executive search firm. **Specializes in the areas of:** Wireless Communications.

LARRY COMBS EXECUTIVE SEARCH
4909 Stockdale Highway, Suite 289, Bakersfield CA 93309. 805/831-0149. **Contact:** Manager. **Description:** An executive search firm.

COMPUTER NETWORK RESOURCES INC.
28231 Tinajo, Mission Viejo CA 92692. 714/951-5929. **Fax:** 714/951-6013. **Contact:** Ken Miller, President. **Description:** An executive search firm specializing in information technology for insurance and financial applications. Company pays fee. **Specializes in the areas of:** Computer Science/Software; Insurance; Sales. **Positions commonly filled include:** Systems Analyst; Technical Writer/Editor. **Number of placements per year:** 1 - 49.

COMPUTER PROFESSIONALS UNLIMITED
5942 Edinger Avenue, Suite 113, Huntington Beach CA 92649. 714/891-1244. **Contact:** Manager. **Description:** An executive search firm. **Specializes in the areas of:** Computer Programming; Computer Science/Software.

CONSULTANT SERVICES
12132 Caminito Campana, San Diego CA 92128-2016. 619/673-2000. **Fax:** 619/673-0124. **Contact:** Jerome L. Cohen, President. **Description:** A retained executive search firm that places professionals in mid- and upper-level assignments. Company pays fee. **Specializes in the areas of:** Engineering; Food Industry; General Management; Manufacturing; Sales. **Positions commonly filled include:** Agricultural Engineer; Biological Scientist; Chemical Engineer; Civil Engineer; Dietician/Nutritionist; Electrical/Electronics Engineer; Food Scientist/Technologist; Hotel Manager; Industrial Engineer; Mechanical Engineer; Metallurgical Engineer; Nuclear Engineer; Petroleum Engineer; Restaurant/Food Service Manager; Software Engineer; Stationary Engineer; Structural Engineer. **Average salary range of placements:** More than $50,000.

CORPORATE DYNAMIX
602 Santa Monica Boulevard, Santa Monica CA 90401-2502. 310/260-1390. **Fax:** 310/458-2177. **Contact:** Manager. **E-mail address:** corpdyn@aol.com. **Description:** An executive search firm focusing on the computer hardware/software marketplace. The firm places sales, management, and marketing candidates. **Specializes in the areas of:** Computer Science/Software; Sales. **Positions commonly filled include:** Sales and Marketing Manager; Software Engineer; Systems Analyst. **Average salary range of placements:** More than $50,000. **Number of placements per year:** 100 - 199.

CORPORATE RESOURCES
27281 Las Ramblas, Suite 200, Mission Viejo CA 92691. 714/582-1277. **Contact:** Nigel McClurg. **Description:** An executive search firm. **Specializes in the areas of:** Computer Programming.

CORPORATE SEARCH INC.
6457 Edgemoor Way, San Jose CA 95129. 408/996-3000. **Contact:** Hal Wilson, President. **Description:** An executive search firm. Company pays fee. **Specializes in the areas of:** Computer Science/Software; Design; Engineering; Technical. **Positions commonly filled include:** Aerospace Engineer; Biomedical Engineer; Chemical Engineer; Computer Programmer; Electrical/Electronics Engineer; Financial Analyst; Industrial Engineer; Management Analyst/Consultant; Mechanical Engineer; Metallurgical Engineer; Nuclear Engineer; Systems Analyst; Technical Writer/Editor; Travel Agent. **Number of placements per year:** 1 - 49.

CORPORATE TECHNOLOGY INC.
P.O. Box 70310, Sunnyvale CA 94086. 408/735-1690. **Fax:** 650/949-0448. **Contact:** John Reinhardt,

President. **E-mail address:** corptech@ix.netcom.com. **Description:** An executive search firm that focuses on providing staff in the semiconductor industry. Company pays fee. **Specializes in the areas of:** Engineering. **Positions commonly filled include:** Ceramics Engineer; Chemical Engineer; Design Engineer; Electrical/Electronics Engineer; Mechanical Engineer. **Corporate headquarters location:** This Location. **Average salary range of placements:** More than $50,000. **Number of placements per year:** 1 - 49.

CORY ASSOCIATES
16255 Ventura Boulevard, Suite 710, Encino CA 91436. 818/995-7755. **Contact:** Manager. **Description:** An executive search firm. **Specializes in the areas of:** Sales.

CORY ASSOCIATES AGENCY INC.
1401 Dove Street, Suite 230, Newport Beach CA 92660. 714/261-1988. **Contact:** Candidate Relations Manager. **Description:** A retained executive search firm. **Specializes in the areas of:** Sales.

CREATIVE LEADERSHIP CONSULTANTS
11777 Bernardo Plaza Center, Suite 101, San Diego CA 92128-2405. 619/592-0506. **Fax:** 619/592-0413. **Contact:** Bob Spence, President/CEO. **Description:** An executive search firm operating on a retained basis. Company pays fee. **Positions commonly filled include:** Branch Manager; Education Administrator; General Manager; Health Services Manager; Human Resources Manager; Operations/Production Manager; Software Engineer; Structural Engineer; Technical Writer/Editor. **Other U.S. locations:** Denver CO; Irvine CA. **Average salary range of placements:** More than $50,000. **Number of placements per year:** 50 - 99.

CULVER PERSONNEL SERVICES
226 Airport Parkway, Suite 530, San Jose CA 95110. 408/441-7878. **Fax:** 408/441-7373. **Contact:** Joseph Jackson, Branch Manager. **E-mail address:** culversj@earthlink.net. **Description:** An executive search firm. Culver is one of the largest sales and management recruiting firms in the western U.S., representing over half of the *Fortune* 500 and 1000 companies. Company pays fee. **Specializes in the areas of:** Computer Hardware/Software; Engineering; Health/Medical; Sales; Technical; Transportation. **Positions commonly filled include:** Branch Manager; Management Trainee; Manufacturer's/Wholesaler's Sales Rep.; Real Estate Agent; Services Sales Representative. **Corporate headquarters location:** San Diego CA. **Number of placements per year:** 50 - 99.

CULVER PERSONNEL SERVICES/THE CULVER GROUP
19700 Fairchild Road, Suite 146, Irvine CA 92612. 714/476-3224. **Fax:** 714/476-8725. **Contact:** Michael T. Hobbs, Vice President. **Description:** An executive search firm. **Specializes in the areas of:** Biotechnology; Finance; General Management; Health/Medical; Insurance; Nonprofit; Retail; Sales; Transportation. **Corporate headquarters location:** San Diego CA.

CULVER STAFFING RESOURCES
8885 Rio San Diego Drive, #320, San Diego CA 92108. 619/297-6400. **Fax:** 619/297-5288. **Contact:** Patti Ward, Area Manager. **Description:** An executive search firm that focuses on office support, administration, customer service, and accounting placements. Company pays fee. **Specializes in the areas of:** Accounting/Auditing; Administration; Computer Science/Software; Food Industry; General Management; Health/Medical; Insurance; Secretarial. **Positions commonly filled include:** Administrative Assistant; Administrative Manager; Advertising Clerk; Blue-Collar Worker Supervisor; Branch Manager; Claim Representative; Clerical Supervisor; Computer Operator; Computer Programmer; Credit Manager; Customer Service Representative; Database Manager; General Manager; Graphic Designer; Human Resources Manager; Internet Services Manager; Management Trainee; Secretary; Software Engineer; Technical Writer/Editor; Typist/Word Processor; Underwriter/Assistant Underwriter. **Benefits available to temporary workers:** Medical Insurance; Paid Vacation. **Corporate headquarters location:** This Location. **Other U.S. locations:** Salt Lake City UT. **Average salary range of placements:** $30,000 - $50,000. **Number of placements per year:** 1 - 49.

CURPHEY & MALKIN ASSOCIATES INC.
13011 West Washington Boulevard, Los Angeles CA 90066. 310/822-7555. **Contact:** Manager. **Description:** An executive search firm. **Specializes in the areas of:** Data Processing; Sales; Technical.

DBL ASSOCIATES
11835 West Olympic Boulevard, Suite 835, Los Angeles CA 90064. 310/575-9202. **Fax:** 310/477-9420. **Contact:** David Long, President. **E-mail address:** dlong54673@aol.com. **Description:** An executive search firm. **Specializes in the areas of:** Accounting/Auditing; Administration; Finance; Personnel/Labor Relations. **Positions commonly filled include:** Accountant/Auditor; Chief Financial Officer; Controller; Finance Director; Financial Analyst; General Manager; Human Resources Manager; MIS Manager; Tax Specialist. **Average salary range of placements:** More than $50,000. **Number of placements per year:** 1 - 49.

DNA MEDICAL SEARCH
16133 Ventura Boulevard, Suite 805, Encino CA 91436. 818/774-3646. **Fax:** 818/774-3645. **Contact:** Daniel I. Levy, President. **Description:** An executive search firm. Company pays fee. **Specializes in the areas of:** Administration; Health/Medical. **Positions commonly filled include:** Health Services Manager. **Number of placements per year:** 50 - 99.

D.P. SEARCH
10217 Fair Oaks Boulevard, Fair Oaks CA 95628. 916/863-7138. **Contact:** Manager. **Description:** An executive search firm. **Specializes in the areas of:** Technical.

DACO RECRUITING INC.
9852 West Katella Avenue, Suite 254, Anaheim CA 92804. 714/533-2274. **Contact:** Office Manager. **Description:** An executive search firm. **Specializes in the areas of:** Insurance.

DALEY CONSULTING & SEARCH
1866 Clayton Road, Suite 211, Concord CA 94520. 510/798-3866. **Fax:** 510/798-4475. **Contact:** Mike Daley, Owner. **E-mail address:** mdaley@dpsearch.com. **World Wide Web address:** http://www.dpsearch.com. **Description:** An executive search firm that focuses on the placement of data processing and information systems professionals in the San Francisco Bay Area and Sacramento. Company pays fee. **Specializes in the areas of:** Computer Science/Software; Information Systems; MIS/EDP. **Positions commonly filled include:** Computer Operator; Computer Programmer; MIS Specialist; Software Engineer; Systems Analyst; Systems Manager; Telecommunications Analyst. **Corporate headquarters location:** This Location. **Other area locations:** Sacramento CA. **Average salary range of placements:** More than $50,000. **Number of placements per year:** 1 - 49.

DALEY TECHNICAL SEARCH
4227 Sunrise Boulevard, Fair Oaks CA 95628. 916/863-7111. **Contact:** Manager. **Description:** An

executive search firm. **Specializes in the areas of:** Technical.

DATA CENTER PERSONNEL
24007 Ventura Boulevard, Suite 240, Calabasas CA 91302. 818/225-2830. **Fax:** 818/225-2840. **Contact:** Jim Auld, President. **E-mail address:** datacenter@earthlink.net. **Description:** An executive search firm. Company pays fee. **Specializes in the areas of:** Administration; Computer Science/Software; Information Systems. **Positions commonly filled include:** Computer Programmer; Software Engineer; Systems Analyst. **Average salary range of placements:** More than $50,000. **Number of placements per year:** 50 - 99.

DATA GRAPH EXECUTIVE SEARCH
P.O. Box 1772, Novato CA 94948. 415/898-3171. **Contact:** Manager. **Description:** An executive search firm. **Specializes in the areas of:** Computer Programming; Computer Science/Software.

DAVIDSON & ASSOCIATES
1453 North Benton Way, Los Angeles CA 90026. 213/413-2613. **Contact:** Manager. **Description:** An executive search firm. **Specializes in the areas of:** Communications.

BERT DAVIS EXECUTIVE SEARCH
One Sampson Street, Suite 1900, San Francisco CA 94104. 415/951-4788. **Contact:** Manager. **Description:** An executive search firm. **Specializes in the areas of:** Publishing.

DELTA FINANCIAL SEARCH
9010 Reseda Boulevard, Suite 104, Northridge CA 91324. 818/341-8911. **Contact:** Office Manager. **Description:** An executive search firm that places accounting and financial personnel.

DEMERY ASSOCIATES
201 Wilshire Boulevard, Santa Monica CA 90401. 310/393-3900. **Contact:** Manager. **Description:** An executive search firm. **Specializes in the areas of:** Finance. **Positions commonly filled include:** Financial Analyst; Portfolio Manager.

ROBERT W. DINGMAN COMPANY
650 Hampshire Road, Suite 116, Westlake Village CA 91361. 818/991-5950. **Fax:** 818/778-9288. **Contact:** Manager. **E-mail address:** info@dingman.com. **Description:** A retained executive search firm that places senior-level managers for corporations, nonprofit organizations, and educational institutions. **Specializes in the areas of:** Finance; General Management; Health/Medical; Manufacturing; Sales. **Positions commonly filled include:** General Manager; President.

DIVERSITY SEARCH PARTNERS INC.
Union Station, 800 North Alameda Street, Suite 200, Los Angeles CA 90012. 213/621-2300. **Contact:** Office Manager. **Description:** An executive search firm operating on a retainer basis.

DOMINGUEZ METZ & ASSOCIATES
12 Geary Street, Suite 604, San Francisco CA 94108. 415/765-1505. **Contact:** Office Manager. **Description:** An executive search firm. **Specializes in the areas of:** Distribution; Retail.

DOUGLAS DORFLINGER & ASSOCIATES
9171 Wilshire Boulevard, Suite 510, Beverly Hills CA 90210. 310/276-7091. **Contact:** Office Manager. **Description:** An executive search firm. **Specializes in the areas of:** Construction.

DOUGLAS PERSONNEL ASSOCIATES, INC.
4444 Riverside Drive, Suite 204, Toluca Lake CA 91505. 818/842-2477. **Fax:** 818/842-3874. **Contact:** Leslie Frankel, Owner. **E-mail address:** dpaiwest@aol.com. **Description:** An executive search firm focusing on placement in retail and executive management positions. Company pays fee. **Specializes in the areas of:** Retail. **Positions commonly filled include:** Buyer; Designer; General Manager; Human Resources Manager; Merchandiser; MIS Specialist. **Other U.S. locations:** Paramus NJ. **Average salary range of placements:** More than $50,000. **Number of placements per year:** 100 - 199.

DRUMMER PERSONNEL, INC.
700 South Claremont, Suite 103, San Mateo CA 94402. 650/685-1000. **Fax:** 650/685-1007. **Contact:** Geri Geller, Consultant. **Description:** An executive search firm. Company pays fee. **Specializes in the areas of:** Computer Science/Software; High-Tech; Sales. **Positions commonly filled include:** Computer Programmer; Computer Support Technician; Management Trainee; Manufacturer's/Wholesaler's Sales Rep.; Sales Manager; Systems Manager. **Average salary range of placements:** $30,000 - $50,000. **Number of placements per year:** 50 - 99.

J.H. DUGAN & ASSOCIATES
225 Crossroads Boulevard, Suite 416, Carmel CA 93923. 408/625-5880. **Fax:** 408/625-2504. **Contact:** John Dugan, President. **E-mail address:** plastic-recruiter@jhdugan.com. **World Wide Web address:** http://www.jhdugan.com. **Description:** An executive search firm focusing on market research and acquisitions placement in the plastics industries. Company pays fee. **Specializes in the areas of:** Plastics. **Positions commonly filled include:** Chemical Engineer; Chemist; General Manager; Industrial Engineer; Industrial Production Manager; Manufacturer's/Wholesaler's Sales Rep. **Average salary range of placements:** More than $50,000. **Number of placements per year:** 100 - 199.

DUNHILL PROFESSIONAL SEARCH
1475 South Bascom Avenue, Suite 202, Campbell CA 95008-0629. 408/559-7377. **Fax:** 408/559-7101. **Contact:** Kevin A.P. Keifer, President. **E-mail address:** dunhill@pacbell.net. **Description:** An executive search firm. Company pays fee. **Specializes in the areas of:** Computer Science/Software; Engineering; Industrial; Manufacturing; Sales; Secretarial; Technical. **Positions commonly filled include:** Chemical Engineer; Computer Programmer; Customer Service Representative; Electrical/Electronics Engineer; Manufacturer's/Wholesaler's Sales Rep.; Mechanical Engineer; Operations/Production Manager; Quality Control Supervisor; Software Engineer. **Other U.S. locations:** Nationwide. **Number of placements per year:** 1 - 49.

DUNHILL PROFESSIONAL SEARCH
9 Executive Circle, Suite 240, Irvine CA 92614. 714/474-6666. **Fax:** 714/474-6674. **Contact:** David Vaughan, President. **Description:** An executive search firm. Company pays fee. **Specializes in the areas of:** Engineering; Industrial; Manufacturing; Personnel/Labor Relations; Sales. **Positions commonly filled include:** Computer Programmer; Industrial Engineer; Manufacturer's/Wholesaler's Sales Rep.; Mechanical Engineer; Software Engineer; Systems Analyst. **Other U.S. Locations:** Nationwide. **Number of placements per year:** 50 - 99.

DUNHILL PROFESSIONAL SEARCH OF OAKLAND, INC.
3732 Mount Diablo Boulevard, Suite 375, Lafayette CA 94549. 510/283-5300. **Fax:** 510/283-5310. **Contact:** John Tierney, President. **Description:** An executive search firm that focuses on high-end

engineering and manufacturing management positions in the chemical industry. Searches are conducted on both retainer and contingency bases and candidates are placed throughout the nation. Company pays fee. **Specializes in the areas of:** Engineering; Food Industry; Industrial Sales and Marketing; Manufacturing. **Positions commonly filled include:** Biomedical Engineer; Chemical Engineer; Civil Engineer; Industrial Engineer; Mechanical Engineer; Metallurgical Engineer; Nuclear Engineer; Petroleum Engineer; Software Engineer; Stationary Engineer. **Other U.S. locations:** Nationwide. **Average salary range of placements:** More than $50,000. **Number of placements per year:** 50 - 99.

DUNHILL PROFESSIONAL SEARCH OF SAN FRANCISCO
268 Bush Street, Box 2909, San Francisco CA 94104. 415/956-3700. **Contact:** George Curtiss, President. **Description:** An executive search firm. **Specializes in the areas of:** Banking; Computer Hardware/Software; Electronics; Health/Medical; Paper; Sales. **Other U.S. locations:** Nationwide.

JOANNE DUNN & ASSOCIATES
2001 Wilshire Boulevard, Suite 600, Santa Monica CA 90403. 310/315-2787. **Contact:** Joanne Dunn, Owner. **Description:** An executive search firm.

DUVALL & ASSOCIATES
10 Emerald Glen, Laguna Niguel CA 92677. 714/488-8790. **Fax:** 714/488-8793. **Contact:** Manager. **E-mail address:** karen@duvall.com. **Description:** An executive search firm. **Specializes in the areas of:** Computer Hardware/Software.

DYNAMIC SYNERGY CORPORATION
2730 Wilshire Boulevard, Suite 550, Santa Monica CA 90403-4747. 310/586-1000. **Contact:** Manager. **Description:** An executive search firm. **Specializes in the areas of:** Computer Science/Software; Sales. **Positions commonly filled include:** Computer Programmer; Database Manager; Marketing Manager; Sales Engineer; Software Engineer; Technical Writer/Editor; Webmaster. **Average salary range of placements:** More than $50,000.

ECI
16000 Ventura Boulevard, 5th Floor, Encino CA 91436. **Contact:** Manager. **Description:** An executive search firm specializing in insurance positions at property and casualty insurance companies.

ET SEARCH INC.
1250 Prospect Street, Suite 101, La Jolla CA 92037. 619/459-3443. **Fax:** 619/459-4147. **Contact:** Kathleen Jennings, President. **World Wide Web address:** http://www.etsearch.com. **Description:** An executive search firm that specializes exclusively in placing tax executives with *Fortune* 1000 companies and public accounting firms internationally. The firm operates on a retainer basis.

EAGLE SEARCH ASSOCIATES
336 Bon Air Center, Suite 295, Greenbrae CA 94904. 415/398-6066. **Fax:** 415/456-2313. **Contact:** Mark Gideon, Executive Director. **World Wide Web address:** http://www.eaglesearch.com. **Description:** An executive search firm. Company pays fee. **Specializes in the areas of:** Computer Science/Software; Sales. **Positions commonly filled include:** Account Manager; Account Representative; Sales Engineer; Sales Executive; Sales Representative; Systems Analyst; Systems Engineer. **Average salary range of placements:** More than $50,000. **Number of placements per year:** 50 - 99.

EATON & ASSOCIATES
23161 Lake Center Drive, Suite 201, Lake Forest CA 92630. 714/586-3898. **Contact:** Manager. **Description:** An executive search firm. **Specializes in the areas of:** Health/Medical; Plastics.

EDWARDS & ASSOCIATES
769 Monterey Boulevard, Suite 4, San Francisco CA 94127. 415/585-1900. **Contact:** Manager. **Description:** An executive search firm. **Specializes in the areas of:** Health/Medical; Sales.

ENLOW & ASSOCIATES
775 Baywood Drive, Suite 308, Petaluma CA 94954. 707/778-8100. **Contact:** Manager. **Description:** An executive search firm that places personnel in a variety of industries.

ENSEARCH MANAGEMENT CONSULTANTS
921 Transport Way, Suite 4, Petaluma CA 94954. 707/766-8700. **Toll-free phone:** 800/473-6776. **Fax:** 707/778-1555. **Contact:** Tim Mattis, President. **E-mail address:** headhtr@rpnet.net. **World Wide Web address:** http://www.ensearch.com. **Description:** A nationwide executive search firm specializing in the health care industry. Ensearch works mainly at the administrative level, as well as advanced practice and administrative nursing levels. Company pays fee. **Specializes in the areas of:** Health/Medical. **Positions commonly filled include:** Nurse Practitioner. **Corporate headquarters location:** This Location. **Average salary range of placements:** More than $50,000. **Number of placements per year:** 1 - 49.

ETHOS CONSULTING, INC.
100 Pine Street, Suite 750, San Francisco CA 94111-5208. 415/397-2211. **Fax:** 415/397-0856. **Contact:** Conrad E. Prusak, President. **E-mail address:** conrad@ethos-net.com. **Description:** A senior-level executive search firm. Company pays fee. **Specializes in the areas of:** Banking; Computer Programming; Finance; Food Industry; General Management; Health/Medical; Retail; Sales; Transportation. **Positions commonly filled include:** Bank Officer/Manager; General Manager; Management Analyst/Consultant. **Average salary range of placements:** More than $50,000. **Number of placements per year:** 1 - 49.

EXCEL TECHNICAL SERVICES, INC.
30100 Town Center Drive, Suite 0-129, Laguna Niguel CA 92677. 714/240-0438. **Fax:** 714/240-0817. **Contact:** Bob Langieri, Director. **World Wide Web address:** http://www.excelsearch.com. **Description:** An executive search firm that places programmer analysts, systems analysts, operations, technical support, and communications specialists. This location also places contract programmers on temporary assignments. Founded in 1973. Company pays fee. **Specializes in the areas of:** Administration; Computer Science/Software. **Average salary range of placements:** More than $50,000. **Number of placements per year:** 100 - 199.

EXECUTIVE DIRECTIONS
155 Sansome, Suite 400, San Francisco CA 94104. 415/394-5500. **Contact:** Fred Naderi, President. **E-mail address:** edi@netcom.com. **World Wide Web address:** http://www.edir.com. **Description:** An executive search firm focusing on technical placements. **Specializes in the areas of:** Computer Hardware/Software; Engineering. **Positions commonly filled include:** Computer Programmer; General Manager; Management Analyst/Consultant; MIS Manager; Multimedia Designer; Science Technologist; Software Engineer; Systems Analyst. **Average salary range of placements:** More than $50,000. **Number of placements per year:** 1 - 49.

EXECUTIVE DYNAMICS, INC.
330 Washington Boulevard, Suite 314, Marina del Rey CA 90292. 310/821-6155. **Contact:** Office Manager. **Description:** An executive search firm. **Specializes in the areas of:** Computer Science/Software.

THE EXECUTIVE GROUP
9191 Towne Center Drive, San Diego CA 92122. 619/457-8100. **Contact:** Manager. **Description:** An executive search firm covering a wide range of industries.

EXECUTIVE GROUP WEST
369 San Miguel Drive, Newport Beach CA 92660. 714/759-9000. **Contact:** Manager. **Description:** An executive search firm. **Specializes in the areas of:** Sales.

EXECUTIVE MEDICAL SEARCH
111 Pacifica Street, Suite 250, Irvine CA 92618. 714/753-2718. **Fax:** 714/770-5658. **Contact:** Diana Brewer, President. **Description:** An executive search firm providing placement on a contingency basis in the medical industry, including home health, long-term care, and sub-acute facilities. Company pays fee. **Specializes in the areas of:** Health/Medical. **Positions commonly filled include:** Dietician/Nutritionist; Occupational Therapist; Pharmacist; Physical Therapist; Regional Manager; Registered Nurse; Respiratory Therapist. **Other U.S. locations:** AZ; OR; WA. **Number of placements per year:** 1 - 49.

EXECUTIVE RECRUITERS
P.O. Box 1986, Danville CA 94506. 510/736-1700. **Contact:** Office Manager. **Description:** An executive search firm. **Specializes in the areas of:** Retail.

EXECUTIVE REGISTRY & ASSOCIATES INC.
15315 Magnolia Boulevard, Suite 418, Sherman Oaks CA 91403. 818/501-8088. **Contact:** Manager. **Description:** An executive search firm that focuses on high tech, software, and medical placements.

EXECUTIVE RESOURCE SYSTEMS
27281 Las Ramblas, Suite 200, Mission Viejo CA 92691-6324. 714/367-0777. **Toll-free phone:** 800/366-7029. **Fax:** 714/496-4407. **Contact:** Steve Brody, President. **E-mail address:** ersbrody@pacbell.net. **Description:** An executive search firm focusing on the placement of accounting, finance, engineering, and sales professionals. The company is a charter member of Nationwide Interchange Service. Company pays fee. **Specializes in the areas of:** Accounting/Auditing; Computer Hardware/Software; Engineering; Finance; Personnel/Labor Relations. **Positions commonly filled include:** Accountant/Auditor; Bank Officer/Manager; Bookkeeper; Budget Analyst; Computer Programmer; Credit Manager; EDP Specialist; Financial Analyst; MIS Specialist; Software Engineer; Systems Analyst; Tax Specialist. **Corporate headquarters location:** This Location. **Other U.S. locations:** Boulder CO. **Average salary range of placements:** More than $50,000. **Number of placements per year:** 50 - 99.

EXECUTIVE SEARCH CONSULTANTS
2108 Appaloosa Circle, Petaluma CA 94954-4643. 707/763-0100. **Fax:** 707/765-6983. **Contact:** Peg Iversen, Owner. **E-mail address:** esc@crl.com. **Description:** An executive search firm operating on both retainer and contingency bases. Company pays fee. **Specializes in the areas of:** Computer Science/Software; Engineering; Technical. **Positions commonly filled include:** Computer Programmer; Electrical/Electronics Engineer; Multimedia Designer; Software Engineer. **Average salary range of placements:** More than $50,000. **Number of placements per year:** 1 - 49.

EXECUTIVE SEARCH CONSULTANTS
21241 Ventura Boulevard, Suite 190, Woodland Hills CA 91364. 818/999-9891. **Contact:** Manager. **Description:** An executive search firm that provides placements in New York and Chicago in financial risk management.

EXTRACT & ASSOCIATES
7337 Hyannis Drive, West Hills CA 91307. 818/999-2837. **Contact:** Manager. **Description:** An executive search firm. **Specializes in the areas of:** Manufacturing.

FARGO SEARCH INC.
7801 Mission Center Court, Suite 200, San Diego CA 92108. 619/299-9734. **Contact:** Manager. **Description:** An executive search firm.

LEON A. FARLEY ASSOCIATES
468 Jackson Street, San Francisco CA 94111. 415/989-0989. **Contact:** Manager. **Description:** An executive search firm that provides senior-level placements. **Average salary range of placements:** More than $50,000.

CURTIS FARMER PERSONNEL
6399 Wilshire Boulevard, Suite 712, Los Angeles CA 90048. 213/782-9575. **Contact:** Curtis Farmer, President. **Description:** An executive search firm. Company pays fee. **Specializes in the areas of:** Accounting/Auditing; Administration; Advertising; Computer Science/Software; Engineering; Finance; Legal; Manufacturing; Personnel/Labor Relations; Sales; Technical. **Positions commonly filled include:** Accountant/Auditor; Aerospace Engineer; Attorney; Bank Officer/Manager; Chemical Engineer; Computer Programmer; Economist; Environmental Engineer; Financial Analyst; Human Resources Manager; Industrial Engineer; Market Research Analyst; Mathematician; Mechanical Engineer; MIS Specialist; Multimedia Designer; Nuclear Engineer; Petroleum Engineer; Public Relations Specialist; Quality Control Supervisor; Science Technologist; Securities Sales Representative; Software Engineer; Structural Engineer; Systems Analyst; Telecommunications Manager; Transportation/Traffic Specialist. **Average salary range of placements:** More than $50,000. **Number of placements per year:** 1 - 49.

FERNEBORG & ASSOCIATES
1450 Fashion Island Boulevard, Suite 650, San Mateo CA 94402. 650/577-0100. **Contact:** Manager. **Description:** An executive search firm.

FINESSE PERSONNEL ASSOCIATES
11030 Arrow Route, Rancho Cucamonga CA 91730-4836. 909/980-8765. **Fax:** 909/980-4081. **Contact:** Chrisanne Goodwin, Operations Manager. **Description:** An executive search firm. Company pays fee. **Specializes in the areas of:** Accounting/Auditing; Administration; Computer Hardware/Software; Food Industry; General Management; Insurance; Manufacturing; Personnel/Labor Relations; Sales; Secretarial. **Positions commonly filled include:** Accountant/Auditor; Administrative Manager; Biomedical Engineer; Budget Analyst; Buyer; Computer Programmer; Credit Manager; Draftsperson; Environmental Engineer; Financial Analyst; General Manager; Human Resources Manager; Industrial Engineer; Manufacturer's/Wholesaler's Sales Rep.; Market Research Analyst; MIS Specialist; Operations/Production Manager; Systems Analyst; Typist/Word Processor. **Number of placements per year:** 500 - 999.

NEIL FINK & ASSOCIATES
900 North Point Street, Suite 410, San Francisco CA 94109. 415/441-3777. **Contact:** Office Manager.

Description: An executive search firm that places personnel in companies with interactive audio/visual needs. **Specializes in the areas of:** New Media.

FISHER & ASSOCIATES
1063 Lenor Way, San Jose CA 95128. 408/554-0156. **Fax:** 408/246-7807. **Contact:** Gary Fisher, Owner. **Description:** An executive search firm operating on a retainer basis. Company pays fee. **Specializes in the areas of:** Computer Science/Software; Engineering; General Management; Sales. **Positions commonly filled include:** General Manager; Marketing Manager; Sales Executive. **Average salary range of placements:** More than $50,000. **Number of placements per year:** 1 - 49.

FISHER PERSONNEL MANAGEMENT SERVICES
1219 Morningside Drive, Manhattan Beach CA 90266. 310/546-7507. **Fax:** 310/546-7574. **Contact:** Neal Fisher, President. **Description:** Fisher Personnel Management Services is a generalist firm that offers retained executive recruiting for all industries with manufacturing clients. The firm also provides other related services including career development, compensation planning, management audit, management consulting, organization planning, and succession planning counsel. Founded in 1986. **Specializes in the areas of:** Engineering; Food Industry; General Management; Industrial; Manufacturing; Personnel/Labor Relations; Publishing; Sales; Technical; Transportation. **Positions commonly filled include:** Administrative Manager; Aerospace Engineer; Branch Manager; Chemical Engineer; Computer Programmer; Cost Estimator; Customer Service Representative; Design Engineer; Financial Analyst; Human Resources Specialist; Industrial Engineer; Management Analyst/Consultant; Management Trainee; Market Research Analyst; Mechanical Engineer; MIS Specialist; Multimedia Designer; Nuclear Engineer; Operations/Production Manager; Purchasing Agent/Manager; Quality Control Supervisor; Securities Sales Representative; Software Engineer; Strategic Relations Manager; Structural Engineer; Systems Analyst; Technical Writer/Editor; Telecommunications Manager. **Average salary range of placements:** More than $50,000. **Number of placements per year:** 1 - 49.

GAVIN FORBES & ASSOCIATES
2207 Garnet Avenue, Suite F, San Diego CA 92109. 619/483-6696. **Fax:** 619/483-9560. **Contact:** Manager. **Description:** An executive search firm that places professionals in the banking industry, primarily lending and credit-related positions. Company pays fee. **Specializes in the areas of:** Banking. **Positions commonly filled include:** Bank Officer/Manager. **Other U.S. locations:** Nationwide. **Average salary range of placements:** More than $50,000. **Number of placements per year:** 1 - 49.

F-O-R-T-U-N-E PERSONNEL CONSULTANTS OF BEVERLY HILLS
5300 West Century Boulevard, Suite 208, Los Angeles CA 90045. 310/410-9662. **Fax:** 310/410-0606. **Contact:** Marc Kasten, President. **Description:** An executive search firm focusing on the medical device, pharmaceutical, and biotech industries. The firm operates on both contingency and retainer bases. Company pays fee. **Specializes in the areas of:** Biology; Biotechnology; Engineering; General Management; Health/Medical; Manufacturing; Pharmaceutical. **Positions commonly filled include:** Biological Scientist; Biomedical Engineer; Chemical Engineer; Chemist; Electrical/Electronics Engineer; Industrial Engineer; Industrial Production Manager; Mechanical Engineer; Metallurgical Engineer; Pharmacist; Quality Control Supervisor; Research Scientist. **Corporate headquarters location:** New York NY. **Other U.S. locations:** Nationwide. **Number of placements per year:** 50 - 99.

F-O-R-T-U-N-E PERSONNEL CONSULTANTS
332 Encinitas Boulevard, Suite 200, Encinitas CA 92024. 760/944-8980. **Fax:** 760/944-0075. **Contact:** Mr. Carmine Furioso, President. **Description:** An executive search firm that places professionals in the medical device, pharmaceutical, and biotechnology fields. **Specializes in the areas of:** Health/Medical; Technical. **Positions commonly filled include:** Biomedical Engineer; Quality Control Supervisor; Statistician. **Corporate headquarters location:** New York NY. **Other U.S. locations:** Nationwide. **Average salary range of placements:** More than $50,000.

F-O-R-T-U-N-E PERSONNEL CONSULTANTS
1811 Santa Rita Road, Suite 202, Pleasanton CA 94566. 510/461-0170. **Fax:** 510/461-0270. **Contact:** Manager. **Description:** An executive search firm. **Specializes in the areas of:** Computer Hardware/Software; Engineering; Sales. **Corporate headquarters location:** New York NY. **Other U.S. locations:** Nationwide.

40 PLUS OF SOUTHERN CALIFORNIA
201 South Anita Drive, Suite 203, Orange CA 92868. 714/938-0161. **Contact:** President/Executive. **Description:** An executive search firm. **Specializes in the areas of:** Accounting/Auditing; Administration; Advertising; Architecture/Construction; Art/Design; Banking; Biology; Computer Science/Software; Economics; Engineering; Finance; Food Industry; General Management; Health/Medical; Industrial; Manufacturing; Nonprofit; Personnel/Labor Relations; Sales; Technical; Transportation. **Positions commonly filled include:** Accountant/Auditor; Administrative Manager; Agricultural Engineer; Bank Officer/Manager; Biological Scientist; Biomedical Engineer; Buyer; Chemical Engineer; Civil Engineer; CClinical Lab Technician; Computer Programmer; Construction Contractor; Credit Manager; Economist; Editor; Education Administrator; Financial Analyst; Health Services Manager; Industrial Engineer; Management Analyst/Consultant; Mechanical Engineer; Metallurgical Engineer; Mining Engineer; Operations/ Production Manager; Petroleum Engineer; Software Engineer; Stationary Engineer; Structural Engineer; Systems Analyst. **Number of placements per year:** 100 - 199.

FOX-MORRIS ASSOCIATES
1940 West Orangewood Avenue, Suite 207, Orange CA 92868. 714/634-2600. **Contact:** Office Manager. **Description:** An executive search firm.

CHARLES FRALICK ASSOCIATES
1766 Lacassi, Suite 103, Walnut Creek CA 94596. 510/946-0817. **Contact:** Charles Fralick, Owner. **Description:** An executive search firm. **Specializes in the areas of:** Computer Hardware/Software.

FRESQUEZ AND ASSOCIATES
405 14th Street, Suite 1040, Oakland CA 94612. 510/283-0295. **Fax:** 510/283-0335. **Contact:** Ernesto Fresquez, President. **E-mail address:** efresquez@aol.com. **World Wide Web address:** http://www.fresquez.com. **Description:** An executive search firm that focuses on recruitment of Hispanic and bilingual professionals. Company pays fee. **Specializes in the areas of:** Accounting/Auditing; Administration; Advertising; Engineering; Finance; Food Industry; General Management; Information Systems; Latin America; Manufacturing; Personnel/ Labor Relations; Sales. **Positions commonly filled include:** Accountant/Auditor; Budget Analyst; Civil Engineer; Computer Programmer; Customer Service Representative; Human Resources Manager;

Industrial Engineer; Management Analyst/Consultant; Market Research Analyst; Mechanical Engineer; Operations/Production Manager; Public Relations Specialist; Software Engineer. **Average salary range of placements:** More than $50,000. **Number of placements per year:** 1 - 49.

GCO EXECUTIVE SEARCH
970 West 190th Street, Suite 600, Torrance CA 90502. 310/523-3455. **Contact:** Office Manager. **Description:** An executive search firm. **Specializes in the areas of:** Computer Science/Software.

GM ASSOCIATES
1500 Golden Rain Road, Suite 1, Walnut Creek CA 94595. 510/256-6513. **Fax:** 510/256-6514. **Contact:** George Metz, Owner. **E-mail address:** gfmetz@aol.com. **Description:** An executive search firm operating on a contingency basis. **Specializes in the areas of:** Computer Science/Software; Engineering. **Positions commonly filled include:** Design Engineer; Electrical/Electronics Engineer; MIS Specialist; Quality Control Supervisor; Software Engineer. **Average salary range of placements:** More than $50,000. **Number of placements per year:** 1 - 49.

GM MANAGEMENT
2760-7 Tapo Canyon Road, Suite 120, Simi Valley CA 93063. **Contact:** Office Manager. **Description:** An executive search firm. **Specializes in the areas of:** Insurance.

GPA MANAGEMENT SERVICES, INC.
150 El Camino Real, Suite 120, Tustin CA 92780. 714/550-0778. **Fax:** 714/573-4499. **Contact:** Greg Payne, President. **Description:** An executive search firm. **Positions commonly filled include:** Insurance Agent/Broker. **Number of placements per year:** 50 - 99.

GAGE & ASSOCIATES
5053 Lamart Avenue, Suite 101, Riverside CA 92507. 909/684-4200. **Contact:** Manager. **Description:** An executive search firm.

GAJEK KYLE & ASSOCIATES
17100 Gillette Avenue, Irvine CA 92614. 714/263-8988. **Contact:** Manager. **Description:** An executive search firm. **Specializes in the areas of:** Accounting/Auditing; Finance.

GARB & ASSOCIATES
2001 Wilshire Boulevard, Suite 510, Santa Monica CA 90403. 310/998-3388. **Contact:** Manager. **Description:** An executive search firm. **Specializes in the areas of:** Legal.

GARRISON-RANDALL INC.
One Sansome Street, Suite 2100, San Francisco CA 94104-4432. 415/433-2330. **Contact:** Rita Fornino, Vice President. **Description:** An executive search firm operating on both retainer and contingency bases. Company pays fee. **Specializes in the areas of:** Health/Medical; Nursing Administration. **Positions commonly filled include:** Accountant/Auditor; Clinical Lab Technician; EEG Technologist; EKG Technician; Human Resources Manager; Medical Records Technician; MIS Specialist; Nuclear Medicine Technologist; Occupational Therapist; Physical Therapist; Physician; Psychologist; Registered Nurse; Social Worker; Speech-Language Pathologist; Surgical Technician. **Average salary range of placements:** More than $60,000.

RICHARD GAST & ASSOCIATES
15550-B Rockfield Boulevard, Suite 100, Irvine CA 92618. 714/472-1130. **Contact:** Office Manager. **Description:** An executive search firm. **Specializes in the areas of:** Human Resources.

DIANNE GAUGER & ASSOCIATES
8573 Buena Tierra Place, Buena Park CA 90621-1001. 714/522-4300. **Fax:** 714/522-4338. **Contact:** Dianne Gauger, President. **Description:** An executive search firm focusing on the placement of sales, marketing, engineering, and management professionals in electrical, electronics, and automation industries. Company pays fee. **Specializes in the areas of:** Computer Science/Software; Engineering; General Management; Industrial; Sales; Technical. **Positions commonly filled include:** Computer Programmer; Customer Service Representative; Design Engineer; Electrical/Electronics Engineer; General Manager; Manufacturer's/Wholesaler's Sales Rep.; Mechanical Engineer; Operations/Production Manager; Services Sales Representative; Software Engineer. **Average salary range of placements:** More than $50,000. **Number of placements per year:** 50 - 99.

GLOBAL SEARCH INC.
1285 Stone Drive, Suite 103, San Marcos CA 92069. 760/591-0678. **Contact:** Manager. **Description:** An executive search firm. **Specializes in the areas of:** Engineering.

BARRY GOLDBERG & ASSOCIATES
2049 Century Park East, Suite 1100, Los Angeles CA 90067. 310/277-5800. **Contact:** Manager. **Description:** An executive search firm.

THE GOODMAN GROUP
P.O. Box J, San Rafael CA 94913-3908. 415/472-6500. **Fax:** 415/472-8510. **Contact:** Manager. **Description:** An executive search firm. Company pays fee. **Specializes in the areas of:** Computer Hardware/Software; Engineering; Health/Medical; Insurance; MIS/EDP; Sales. **Positions commonly filled include:** Biomedical Engineer; Civil Engineer; Computer Programmer; EDP Specialist; Electrical/Electronics Engineer; General Manager; Management Analyst/Consultant; Physician; Sales Representative; Systems Analyst. **Number of placements per year:** 50 - 99.

GORELICK & ASSOCIATES
1971 East Fourth Street, Suite 100, Santa Ana CA 92705. 714/660-5050. **Fax:** 714/660-1705. **Contact:** Michael Gorelick, Vice President. **Description:** An executive search firm. **Specializes in the areas of:** Computer Science/Software; Consumer Package Goods; Food Industry; General Management; Sales; Telecommunications. **Positions commonly filled include:** Branch Manager; Management Analyst/Consultant; Manufacturer's/Wholesaler's Sales Rep. **Number of placements per year:** 50 - 99.

GRANT & ASSOCIATES
417 Montgomery Street, Suite 910, San Francisco CA 94104. 415/986-1500. **Fax:** 415/986-1630. **Contact:** Susan Grant, President. **E-mail address:** grantsgg@aol.com. **Description:** A retained executive search firm. **Specializes in the areas of:** Computer Science/Software; Engineering; General Management; Manufacturing; Sales; Technical. **Positions commonly filled include:** Aerospace Engineer; Biochemist; Biomedical Engineer; Branch Manager; Chemical Engineer; Electrical/Electronics Engineer; General Manager; Internet Services Manager; Management Analyst/Consultant; Mechanical Engineer; MIS Specialist; Multimedia Designer; Operations/Production Manager; Services Sales Representative; Software Engineer; Strategic Relations Manager; Systems Analyst; Telecommunications Manager. **Average salary range of placements:** More than $50,000. **Number of placements per year:** 1 - 49.

GREEN ROBERTS & ASSOCIATES
One Sansom Street, Suite 2100, San Francisco CA 94104. 415/951-1012. **Contact:** Manager. **Description:** An executive search firm.

GREGORY & LEIGH
450 San Antonio Road, Suite 20, Palo Alto CA 94306. 650/493-9066. **Contact:** Manager. **Description:** An executive search firm that places personnel in a variety of industries.

GRIFFITH & ASSOCIATES
P.O. Box 5212, Modesto CA 95358. 209/521-2898. **Contact:** Manager. **Description:** An executive search firm that also offers business analysis and motivational speaking services to businesses. **Specializes in the areas of:** Construction; Engineering; Food Industry; Health/Medical; Industrial.

GROENEKAMP & ASSOCIATES
P.O. Box 2308, Beverly Hills CA 90213. 310/855-0119. **Contact:** Manager. **Description:** An executive search firm that places personnel in a variety of industries.

ALICE GUNDERSON ASSOCIATES
5757 West Century Boulevard, Suite 700, Los Angeles CA 90045. 310/216-0157. **Contact:** Office Manager. **Description:** A generalist executive search firm.

HR SPECIALISTS
2255 Watt Avenue, Suite 185, Sacramento CA 95825-0508. 916/488-5300. **Contact:** Peggy Ragland, Director of Operations. **Description:** An executive search firm operating on both retainer and contingency bases.

BERNARD HALDANE & ASSOCIATES
1333 North California, Suite 510, Walnut Creek CA 94596. 510/945-0776. **Contact:** Manager. **Description:** An executive search firm that places personnel in a variety of industries.

HALEY ASSOCIATES
526 Ramona Street, Palo Alto CA 94301. 650/323-0456. **Contact:** Manager. **Description:** An executive search firm. **Specializes in the areas of:** High-Tech.

ROBERT HALF INTERNATIONAL
10877 Wilshire Boulevard, Suite 1605, Los Angeles CA 90024. 310/286-6800. **Contact:** Recruiter. **Description:** An executive search firm. Company pays fee. **Specializes in the areas of:** Accounting/Auditing; Banking; Computer Hardware/Software; Finance; MIS/EDP. **Positions commonly filled include:** Accountant/Auditor; Bank Officer/Manager; Bookkeeper; Computer Programmer; Credit Manager; Data Entry Clerk; EDP Specialist; Financial Analyst; Human Resources Manager; Systems Analyst. **Corporate headquarters location:** Menlo Park CA. **International locations:** Worldwide. **Number of placements per year:** 500 - 999.

HARLEY ASSOCIATES
1370 North Brea Boulevard, Fullerton CA 92835-4125. 714/441-0223. **Fax:** 714/441-0224. **Contact:** Wayne Harley, President. **Description:** An executive search firm that focuses on cellular and wireless industries. **Specializes in the areas of:** Engineering; Technical. **Positions commonly filled include:** Design Engineer; Electrical/Electronics Engineer; Software Engineer; Telecommunications Manager. **Average salary range of placements:** More than $50,000.

HARMELING & ASSOCIATES
3232 Governor Drive, San Diego CA 92122. 619/455-6212. **Contact:** Manager. **Description:** An executive search firm. **Specializes in the areas of:** Architecture/Construction.

HARRISON & HUNT
11400 West Olympic Boulevard, 2nd Floor, Los Angeles CA 90064. 310/445-8815. **Fax:** 310/445-8827. **Contact:** Douglas Grue, President. **E-mail address:** dhgrue@aol.com. **Description:** An executive search firm that operates on a contingency basis. Company pays fee. **Specializes in the areas of:** Tax. **Positions commonly filled include:** Tax Specialist. **Average salary range of placements:** More than $50,000. **Number of placements per year:** 50 - 99.

HARRISON GLENN & ASSOCIATES
801 East Katella Avenue, Suite 210, Anaheim CA 92805. 714/939-2849. **Contact:** Manager. **Description:** An executive search firm.

HAWKINS & ASSOCIATES
2420 University Avenue, San Diego CA 92104. 619/294-2320. **Contact:** Manager. **Description:** An executive search firm.

HEALTHCARE EXECUTIVE RECRUITERS INC.
15300 Ventura Boulevard, Suite 207, Sherman Oaks CA 91403. 818/981-9510. **Fax:** 818/981-9523. **Contact:** Deborah Wilson, Vice President of Operations. **E-mail address:** hcrla@aol.com. **World Wide Web address:** http://www.hcrintl.com. **Description:** An executive search firm. Company pays fee. **Specializes in the areas of:** Engineering; Health/Medical; Technical. **Positions commonly filled include:** Account Representative; Applications Engineer; Biochemist; Chief Financial Officer; Clinical Lab Technician; Computer Programmer; Controller; Database Manager; Design Engineer; Dietician/Nutritionist; Electrical/Electronics Engineer; Industrial Engineer; Industrial Production Manager; Internet Services Manager; Management Analyst/Consultant; MIS Specialist; Online Content Specialist; Pharmacist; Physician; Radiological Technologist; Registered Nurse; Respiratory Therapist; Sales Engineer; Sales Executive; Sales Manager; Sales Representative; Software Engineer; Systems Analyst; Systems Manager; Webmaster. **Corporate headquarters location:** This Location. **Other U.S. locations:** Nationwide. **Average salary range of placements:** More than $50,000. **Number of placements per year:** 1000+.

HEALTHCARE EXECUTIVE RECRUITERS INC.
17003 Ventura Boulevard, Suite E-1, Encino CA 91316. 818/788-0150. **Fax:** 818/788-6549. **Contact:** Susan Fleischer, Chief Operating Officer. **Description:** An executive search firm. Company pays fee. **Specializes in the areas of:** Health/Medical. **Positions commonly filled include:** Health Care Administrator; Health Services Manager; Health Services Worker; Licensed Practical Nurse; Medical Assistant; Medical Records Technician; Occupational Therapist; Physical Therapist; Physician; Registered Nurse; Respiratory Therapist; Surgical Technician. **Corporate headquarters location:** Sherman Oaks CA. **Average salary range of placements:** More than $50,000. **Number of placements per year:** 50 - 99.

HEALTHCARE RECRUITERS INTERNATIONAL
26400 La Alameda Drive, Suite 204, Mission Viejo CA 92691. 714/367-7888. **Fax:** 714/367-7881. **Contact:** Manager. **Description:** An executive search firm. **Specializes in the areas of:** Health/Medical. **Corporate headquarters location:** Sherman Oaks CA.

HEALTHCARE RECRUITERS INTERNATIONAL
1541 Seaside Road SW, Ocean Isle Beach CA 28469. 919/676-4040. **Contact:** Manager. **Description:** An executive search firm. **Specializes in the areas of:**

Health/Medical. **Corporate headquarters location:** Sherman Oaks CA.

HEALTHCARE RECRUITERS OF SAN DIEGO
701 Palomar Airport Road, Suite 300, Carlsbad CA 92009. 760/931-4790. **Fax:** 760/931-9979. **Contact:** Judy Thurmond, Owner. **E-mail address:** judy4hcrsd@aol.com. **Description:** An executive search firm operating on both retained and contingency bases. Company pays fee. **Specializes in the areas of:** Biotechnology; Health/Medical. **Positions commonly filled include:** Account Manager; Account Representative; Applications Engineer; Biochemist; Biomedical Engineer; Branch Manager; Chief Financial Officer; Computer Programmer; Controller; Customer Service Representative; Dietician/Nutritionist; Financial Analyst; General Manager; Health Services Manager; Industrial Production Manager; Manufacturing Engineer; Market Research Analyst; Mechanical Engineer; Medical Records Technician; MIS Specialist; Operations/Production Manager; Pharmacist; Physical Therapist; Physician; Production Manager; Project Manager; Quality Control Supervisor; Registered Nurse; Sales Executive; Sales Representative; Software Engineer; Systems Manager. **Corporate headquarters location:** Sherman Oaks CA. **Average salary range of placements:** More than $50,000. **Number of placements per year:** 50 - 99.

BRUCE HENRY ASSOCIATES
465 California Street, Suite 450, San Francisco CA 94104-1804. 415/398-6540. **Fax:** 415/438-2112. **Contact:** Bruce Henry, Principal. **E-mail address:** brucehenry@earthlink.net. **Description:** A retained executive search firm. Company pays fee. **Specializes in the areas of:** Health/Medical. **Positions commonly filled include:** Administrative Manager; Assistant Manager; Auditor; Biochemist; Branch Manager; Budget Analyst; Buyer; Chief Financial Officer; Computer Programmer; Controller; Database Manager; Dietician/Nutritionist; Finance Director; Financial Analyst; Health Care Risk Consultant; Human Resources Manager; Industrial Engineer; Licensed Practical Nurse; Marketing Manager; Medical Records Technician; MIS Specialist; Operations Manager; Pharmacist; Physical Therapist; Physician; Psychologist; Registered Nurse; Sales Manager; Software Engineer; Systems Analyst; Systems Manager; Technical Writer/Editor; Veterinarian. **Average salary range of placements:** More than $50,000. **Number of placements per year:** 1 - 49.

HERITAGE PACIFIC CORPORATION
15707 Rockfield Boulevard, Irvine CA 92614. 714/768-4501. **Contact:** Gary Draper, Manager. **Description:** An executive search firm focusing on the placement of experienced professionals in the paper industry. **Positions commonly filled include:** Chemical Engineer; Chemist; Civil Engineer; Electrical/Electronics Engineer; Industrial Production Manager; Multimedia Designer; Operations/Production Manager; Quality Control Supervisor. **Average salary range of placements:** More than $50,000. **Number of placements per year:** 1 - 49.

HERRERIAS & ASSOCIATES
P.O. Box 537, Fairfax CA 94978-0537. 415/721-7001. **Contact:** Paul Herrerias, Executive Director. **E-mail address:** recruit@nbn.com. **Description:** A retained executive search firm. **Specializes in the areas of:** Accounting/Auditing; Administration; Advertising; Banking; Finance; General Management; Personnel/Labor Relations; Sales. **Positions commonly filled include:** Accountant/Auditor; Bank Officer/Manager; Financial Analyst; Management Analyst/Consultant; Telecommunications Manager. **Average salary range of placements:** More than $50,000. **Number of placements per year:** 1 - 49.

HEURISTICS SEARCH INC.
2350 Mission College Boulevard, Suite 800, Santa Clara CA 95054. 408/748-1500. **Contact:** Manager. **Description:** An executive search firm. **Specializes in the areas of:** High-Tech.

HILL & ASSOCIATES
860 Via de la Paz, Suite E-2, Pacific Palisades CA 90272. 310/573-1261. **Fax:** 310/573-6290. **Contact:** Tom Hill, President. **Description:** An executive search firm concentrating on the consumer products industry with an emphasis on food and beverages. Most positions are in sales and marketing. Company pays fee. **Specializes in the areas of:** Food Industry; Sales. **Positions commonly filled include:** Market Research Analyst; MIS Specialist. **Average salary range of placements:** More than $50,000. **Number of placements per year:** 1 - 49.

HIRE GROUND
502 Flynn Avenue, Redwood City CA 94063-2927. 650/369-8300. **Fax:** 650/369-4992. **Contact:** Kim Kawar, Owner. **E-mail address:** hireground@aol.com. **Description:** A technical executive search firm for high-tech engineering companies. Company pays fee. **Specializes in the areas of:** Computer Science/Software. **Positions commonly filled include:** Design Engineer; Mining Engineer; MIS Specialist; Multimedia Designer; Software Engineer. **Average salary range of placements:** More than $50,000.

HOCHMAN & ASSOCIATES
1801 Avenue of the Stars, Los Angeles CA 90067. 310/552-0662. **Fax:** 310/552-4650. **Contact:** Judi L. Hochman, President. **Description:** An executive search firm operating on both retainer and contingency bases. The firm provides placements in investment banking and portfolio management. Company pays fee. **Specializes in the areas of:** Banking; Legal; Personnel/Labor Relations. **Positions commonly filled include:** Customer Service Representative; Financial Analyst; Human Service Worker. **Average salary range of placements:** More than $50,000. **Number of placements per year:** 50 - 99.

HOCKETT ASSOCIATES INC.
P.O. Box 1765, Los Altos CA 94023. 415/941-8815. **Contact:** Manager. **Description:** An executive search firm. **Specializes in the areas of:** Biotechnology.

HOLLAND EXECUTIVE SEARCH
P.O. Box 9774, Marina Del Rey CA 90295. 310/459-1802. **Contact:** Robin Holland, President. **Description:** An executive search firm. Company pays fee. **Specializes in the areas of:** Technical. **Positions commonly filled include:** Accountant/Auditor; Attorney; Automotive Mechanic; Design Engineer; General Manager.

HOLLAND McFADZEAN & ASSOCIATES
2901 Tasman Drive, Suite 204, Santa Clara CA 95054. 408/496-0775. **Contact:** Manager. **Description:** An executive search firm. **Specializes in the areas of:** Engineering; Finance; Sales.

HOLLANDER HORIZON INTERNATIONAL
1617 South Pacific Coast Highway, Redondo Beach CA 90277. 310/540-3231. **Fax:** 310/540-4230. **Contact:** Arnold Zimmerman, Senior Partner. **Description:** An executive search firm that recruits scientists and engineers for the food and consumer products industries, primarily for research and development, manufacturing, engineering, and quality control and assurance positions. Company pays fee. **Specializes in the areas of:** Food Industry. **Positions commonly filled include:** Agricultural Engineer; Biological Scientist; Food Scientist/Technologist; Industrial Engineer; Market Research Analyst;

Mechanical Engineer; Operations/Production Manager; Quality Control Supervisor. **Other U.S. locations:** MN; NJ. **Average salary range of placements:** More than $50,000. **Number of placements per year:** 1 - 49.

FRED L. HOOD & ASSOCIATES
23801 Calabasas Road, Suite 2034, Calabasas CA 91302. 818/222-6222. **Contact:** Manager. **Description:** An executive search firm. **Specializes in the areas of:** High-Tech.

R.H. HORTON INTERNATIONAL
24405 Chestnut Street, Suite 107, Santa Clarita CA 91321. 805/222-2272. **Contact:** Manager. **Description:** An executive search firm that places personnel in a variety of industries.

HUGHES PERRY & ASSOCIATES
P.O. Box 384, Sea Ranch CA 95497. 707/785-3083. **Contact:** Manager. **Description:** An executive search firm. **Other area locations:** San Francisco CA. **Specializes in the areas of:** Government.

HUTTON BARNES & ASSOCIATES
5900 Sepulveda Boulevard, Suite 104, Sherman Oaks CA 91411. 818/989-2500. **Contact:** Manager. **Description:** An executive search firm. **Specializes in the areas of:** Computer Hardware/Software; Technical.

IMPACT STAFFING
16787 Bernardo Center Drive, Suite 14, San Diego CA 92128. 619/675-0772. **Contact:** Manager. **Description:** An executive search firm that provides technical placements.

IMPACT, INC.
1000 Fremont Avenue, Suite 210, Los Altos CA 94024. 650/941-9400. **Fax:** 650/917-1424. **Contact:** Mary Voss, President. **Description:** A retained executive search firm. Company pays fee. **Specializes in the areas of:** Computer Science/Software; Engineering; Personnel/Labor Relations. **Positions commonly filled include:** Computer Programmer; Design Engineer; Designer; Electrical/Electronics Engineer; Human Resources Manager; Industrial Engineer; Mathematician; Mechanical Engineer; MIS Specialist; Multimedia Designer; Quality Control Supervisor; Software Engineer; Systems Analyst; Telecommunications Manager. **Benefits available to temporary workers:** 401(k). **Average salary range of placements:** More than $50,000. **Number of placements per year:** 1000+.

INDEPENDENT RESOURCE SYSTEM, INC.
22122 Sherman Way, Suite 209, Canoga Park CA 91303. 818/999-5690. **Fax:** 818/999-5691. **Contact:** Don Speth, President. **Description:** An executive search firm that focuses on providing placement in high-tech industries. The firm operates on both retainer and contingency bases. **Specializes in the areas of:** Administration; Engineering; Sales; Technical. **Positions commonly filled include:** Mechanical Engineer; MIS Specialist; Multimedia Designer; Software Engineer; Technical Writer/Editor; Telecommunications Manager. **Average salary range of placements:** More than $50,000.

INNOVATIVE SEARCH ASSOCIATES
P.O. Box 6955, Laguna Niguel CA 92607. 714/488-0010. **Contact:** Manager. **Description:** An executive search firm. **Specializes in the areas of:** Computer Hardware/Software; High-Tech.

INSURANCE SEARCH GROUP
3323 Watt Avenue, Suite 262, Sacramento CA 95821. 916/488-7871. **Fax:** 916/488-8645. **Contact:** Manager. **Description:** An executive search firm. **Specializes in the areas of:** Insurance.

INTELLEX PERSONNEL SERVICES
28047 Dorothy Drive, Suite 200, Agoura Hills CA 91301. 818/865-0099. **Fax:** 818/865-9153. **Contact:** Gloria Esposito, Account Representative/Recruiter. **Description:** An executive search firm. **Specializes in the areas of:** Computer Science/Software. **Positions commonly filled include:** Computer Programmer; Software Engineer; Systems Analyst; Technical Writer/Editor. **Number of placements per year:** 1 - 49.

INTELLISOURCE COMPUTER CAREERS, LTD.
27921 Via Estancia, San Juan Capistrano CA 92675. 714/496-7927. **Fax:** 714/496-0822. **Contact:** Mark Rinovato, President. **E-mail address:** careers@intellisource.com. **World Wide Web address:** http://www.intellisource.com. **Description:** An executive search firm that focuses on the recruitment and placement of high-technology professionals with software engineering and information technology expertise. IntelliSource works with start-up firms, rapidly growing mid-sized firms, and *Fortune* 500 companies. Company pays fee. **Specializes in the areas of:** Computer Science/Software; Engineering. **Positions commonly filled include:** Computer Programmer; Electrical/Electronics Engineer; Software Engineer; Systems Analyst. **Average salary range of placements:** More than $50,000. **Number of placements per year:** 1 - 49.

INTERACTIVE SEARCH NETWORK
3330 Pierce, Suite 305, San Francisco CA 94123. 415/921-0663. **Contact:** Doug Perlstadt, Manager. **Description:** An executive search firm. **Specializes in the areas of:** Retail.

INTERNATIONAL STAFFING CONSULTANTS
500 Newport Center Drive, Suite 300, Newport Beach CA 92660-7003. 714/721-7990. **Fax:** 714/721-7999. **Contact:** Ian Thomas, Vice President. **E-mail address:** iscinc@iscworld.com. **World Wide Web address:** http://www.iscworld.com. **Description:** An executive search firm operating on a contingency basis. International Staffing Consultants also provides contract services. Company pays fee. **Specializes in the areas of:** Architecture/Construction; Computer Science/Software; Engineering; Industrial; Personnel/Labor Relations; Sales; Technical; Transportation. **Number of placements per year:** 100 - 199.

INTERSTATE RECRUITERS
1336 Moor Park Road, Suite 106, Thousand Oaks CA 91360. 818/706-3737. **Contact:** Manager. **Description:** An executive search firm. **Specializes in the areas of:** Engineering; Health/Medical.

ALAN ISRAEL EXECUTIVE SEARCH
3655 Torrance Boulevard, Suite 316, Torrance CA 90503. 310/370-0144. **Contact:** Alan Israel, Manager. **Description:** An executive search firm specializing in job placements for professionals with applications software experience. **Specializes in the areas of:** Computer Science/Software.

JPM INTERNATIONAL
26060 Acero, Suite 100, Mission Viejo CA 92691. 714/955-2545. **Fax:** 714/757-1320. **Contact:** Trish Ryan, Vice President. **Description:** An executive search firm. Company pays fee. **Specializes in the areas of:** Engineering; Environmental; Health/Medical; Industrial; Insurance; Manufacturing; Sales; Technical; Telecommunications. **Positions commonly filled include:** Biological Scientist; Biomedical Engineer; Chemical Engineer; Electrical/Electronics Engineer; Emergency Medical Technician; Health Services Manager; Manufacturer's/Wholesaler's Sales Rep.;

Mechanical Engineer; Medical Records Technician; Metallurgical Engineer; Nuclear Engineer; Nuclear Medicine Technologist; Occupational Therapist; Pharmacist; Physical Therapist; Radiological Technologist; Registered Nurse; Respiratory Therapist; Services Sales Representative; Software Engineer; Structural Engineer; Systems Analyst. **Corporate headquarters location:** This Location. **Number of placements per year:** 500 - 999.

CINDY JACKSON SEARCH
3031 Tisch Way, San Jose CA 95128. 408/247-6767. **Contact:** Manager. **Description:** An executive search firm. **Specializes in the areas of:** Computer Hardware/Software; Electronics; Sales.

DAVID JAMES SEARCH
27315 Jefferson Avenue, Suite J, Temecula CA 92590. 909/693-2555. **Fax:** 909/693-2881. **Contact:** David James, President. **E-mail address:** letsaudit@aol.com. **World Wide Web address:** http://www.davidjamessearch.com. **Description:** An executive search firm operating on both retainer and contingency bases. The firm places internal auditors with *Fortune* 500 companies. **Positions commonly filled include:** Accountant/Auditor. **Average salary range of placements:** $30,000 - $50,000. **Number of placements per year:** 50 - 99.

THE JAMESON GROUP
1900 Avenue of the Stars, Suite 200, Los Angeles CA 90067-4301. **Contact:** John B. Jameson, President. **E-mail address:** TJG@ix.netcom.com. **Description:** An executive search firm operating on both retainer and contingency bases. Company pays fee. **Specializes in the areas of:** Legal. **Positions commonly filled include:** Attorney. **Average salary range of placements:** More than $50,000. **Number of placements per year:** 50 - 99.

JATINEN & ASSOCIATES
20422 Beach Boulevard, Suite 235, Huntington Beach CA 92646. 714/960-9082. **Fax:** 714/960-1772. **Contact:** Manager. **Description:** An executive search firm focusing on placements in the title insurance industry. **Specializes in the areas of:** Insurance. **Number of placements per year:** 1 - 49.

AARON JENSEN ASSOCIATES INC.
275 North Ola Vista, San Clemente CA 92672. 714/498-6050. **Contact:** Manager. **Description:** An executive search firm. **Specializes in the areas of:** Computer Hardware/Software; Paper.

JEROME & COMPANY
211 Culver Boulevard, Suite R, Playa Del Rey CA 90293. 310/305-1812. **Fax:** 310/305-8678. **Contact:** Gerald E. Jerome, President. **Description:** An executive search firm. Company pays fee. **Specializes in the areas of:** Engineering; General Management; Industrial; Manufacturing. **Positions commonly filled include:** Aerospace Engineer; Electrical/Electronics Engineer; General Manager; Industrial Engineer; Industrial Production Manager; Mechanical Engineer; Operations/Production Manager; Quality Control Supervisor. **Number of placements per year:** 1 - 49.

JOB LINK INC.
7060 Miramar Road, Suite 205, San Diego CA 92121. 619/695-1100. **Contact:** Manager. **Description:** An executive search firm. **Specializes in the areas of:** High-Tech; Manufacturing; Professional; Technical.

JOB SEARCH
137 East Thousand Oaks Boulevard, Suite 203, Thousand Oaks CA 91360. 805/496-9908. **Fax:** 805/496-5512. **Contact:** Peter H. Wolf, President. **E-mail address:** jobsearch@jsearch.com. **World Wide Web address:** http://www.jsearch.com. **Description:** An executive search firm operating on both retainer and contingency bases. Company pays fee. **Positions commonly filled include:** Accountant/Auditor; Aerospace Engineer; Biological Scientist; Biomedical Engineer; Computer Operator; Computer Programmer; Electrical/Electronics Engineer; Industrial Designer; Industrial Engineer; Manufacturing Engineer; MIS Specialist; Operations/Production Manager; Sales Representative; Software Engineer; Systems Analyst. **Average salary range of placements:** More than $50,000. **Number of placements per year:** 500 - 999.

ROYE JOHNSTON & ASSOCIATES
16885 West Bernardo Drive, Suite 270, San Diego CA 92127. 619/487-5200. **Contact:** Manager. **Description:** An executive search firm. **Specializes in the areas of:** Health/Medical. **Positions commonly filled include:** Nurse; Physician.

K&C ASSOCIATES
290A Oakhurst Lane, Arcadia CA 91007. 626/445-1961. **Fax:** 626/445-1961. **Contact:** R.G. Kuhnmuench, President. **Description:** An executive search firm. **Specializes in the areas of:** Construction; Engineering; General Management; Manufacturing; Sales. **Number of placements per year:** 1 - 49.

KABL ABILITY NETWORK
1727 State Street, Santa Barbara CA 93101. 805/563-2398. **Contact:** Brad Naegle, President. **Description:** An executive search firm that focuses on managerial and technical placements. Company pays fee. **Specializes in the areas of:** Computer Science/Software; Executives; General Management; Nonprofit; Personnel/Labor Relations; Telecommunications. **Positions commonly filled include:** Computer Programmer; Electrical/Electronics Engineer; Software Engineer; Systems Analyst. **Average salary range of placements:** More than $50,000. **Number of placements per year:** 1 - 49.

GARY KAPLAN & ASSOCIATES
201 South Lake Avenue, Suite 600, Pasadena CA 91101. 818/796-8100. **Contact:** Gary Kaplan. **Description:** An executive search firm that places personnel in a variety of industries.

HOWARD KARR & ASSOCIATES
1777 Borel Place, Suite 408, San Mateo CA 94402. 415/574-5277. **Contact:** Manager. **Description:** An executive search firm that places personnel in a variety of industries.

KARSCH/CARD
2049 Century Park East, Suite 1200, Los Angeles CA 90067. 310/556-8866. **Contact:** Cris Card, Owner. **Description:** An executive search firm. **Specializes in the areas of:** Advertising; Marketing.

KASS ABELL & ASSOCIATES
10780 Santa Monica Boulevard, Suite 200, Los Angeles CA 90025. 310/475-4666. **Contact:** Manager. **Description:** An executive search firm. **Specializes in the areas of:** Legal.

KAUFMAN DAVIDSON ASSOCIATES
225 Santa Monica Boulevard, Suite 1002, Santa Monica CA 90401. 310/656-3200. **Contact:** Manager. **Description:** An executive search firm. **Specializes in the areas of:** Legal. **Positions commonly filled include:** Attorney.

A.T. KEARNEY EXECUTIVE SEARCH
500 South Grand Avenue, Suite 1780, Los Angeles CA 90071. 213/689-6800. **Contact:** Manager. **Description:** An executive search firm.

A.T. KEARNEY EXECUTIVE SEARCH
3 Lagoon Drive, Suite 160, Redwood City CA 94065. 650/637-6600. **Contact:** Manager. **Description:** An executive search firm. **Specializes in the areas of:** High-Tech.

KEARNEY BOYLE & ASSOCIATES
336 Bon Air Center, Suite 106, Greenbrae CA 94904. 415/925-0397. **Contact:** Manager. **Description:** An executive search firm. **Specializes in the areas of:** Finance; Legal.

E. KEITH & ASSOCIATES
4420 Hotel Circle Court, Suite 250, San Diego CA 92108. 619/294-4294. **Contact:** Office Manager. **Description:** A generalist executive search firm. **Corporate headquarters location:** This Location.

KENNETH, GEORGE, AND ASSOCIATES
6818 Burke Court, Chino CA 91710. 909/591-1980. **Fax:** 909/591-7599. **Contact:** James Kenneth, Managing Partner. **Description:** An executive search firm focusing on the recruitment of accounting and financial personnel. Company pays fee. **Specializes in the areas of:** Accounting/Auditing; Banking; Health/Medical; Manufacturing; Retail. **Positions commonly filled include:** Accountant/Auditor; Budget Analyst; Cost Estimator; Credit Manager; Financial Analyst. **Corporate headquarters location:** This Location. **Other U.S. locations:** Nationwide. **Number of placements per year:** 50 - 99.

KIZER ASHLYN EXECUTIVE SEARCH
21032 Devonshire Street, Suite 207, Chatsworth CA 91311. 818/709-9821. **Contact:** Manager. **Description:** An executive search firm. **Specializes in the areas of:** Finance.

BARRY C. KLEINMAN & ASSOCIATES
2936 Domingo Avenue, Suite 5, Berkeley CA 94705. 510/549-7300. **Contact:** Manager. **Description:** An executive search firm. **Specializes in the areas of:** High-Tech.

KLENIN GROUP
32107 West Lindero Canyon Road, Suite 108, Westlake Village CA 91361. 818/597-3434. **Fax:** 818/597-3438. **Contact:** Larry Klenin, President. **Description:** An executive search firm focusing on the placement of high-tech sales and management personnel. **Specializes in the areas of:** Computer Science/Software; Sales. **Positions commonly filled include:** Systems Analyst. **Average salary range of placements:** More than $50,000. **Number of placements per year:** 50 - 99.

KORN/FERRY INTERNATIONAL
1800 Century Park East, Suite 900, Los Angeles CA 90067. 310/552-1834. **Fax:** 310/553-6452. **Contact:** Office Manager. **Description:** An executive search firm that places upper-level managers in a variety of industries. Company pays fee. **Corporate headquarters location:** This Location. **International locations:** Worldwide. **Average salary range of placements:** More than $50,000.

KORN/FERRY INTERNATIONAL
1300 Dove Street, Suite 300, Newport Beach CA 92660. 714/851-1834. **Contact:** Office Manager. **Description:** An executive search firm that places upper-level managers in a variety of industries. **Corporate headquarters location:** Los Angeles CA. **International locations:** Worldwide. **Average salary range of placements:** More than $50,000.

KORN/FERRY INTERNATIONAL
600 Montgomery Street, 31st Floor, San Francisco CA 94111. 415/956-1834. **Contact:** Office Manager. **Description:** An executive search firm that places upper-level managers in a variety of industries. **Corporate headquarters location:** Los Angeles CA. **International locations:** Worldwide. **Average salary range of placements:** More than $50,000.

KORN/FERRY INTERNATIONAL
2180 Sandhill Road, Menlo Park CA 94025. 650/233-2733. **Contact:** Manager. **Description:** An executive search firm that places upper-level managers in a variety of industries. **Corporate headquarters location:** Los Angeles CA. **International locations:** Worldwide. **Average salary range of placements:** More than $50,000.

EVIE KREISLER & ASSOCIATES
865 South Figueroa Street, Suite 950, Los Angeles CA 90017. 213/622-8994. **Fax:** 213/622-9660. **Contact:** Manager. **Description:** An executive search firm focusing on retail and fashion wholesale/manufacturing placement. Company pays fee. **Specializes in the areas of:** Manufacturing; Retail. **Positions commonly filled include:** Bank Officer/Manager; Computer Programmer; Customer Service Representative; Marketing Specialist; MIS Specialist; Systems Analyst. **Other U.S. locations:** Atlanta GA; Chicago IL; New York NY; Dallas TX. **Average salary range of placements:** More than $50,000. **Number of placements per year:** 100 - 199.

JEFF KROH ASSOCIATES
11400 West Olympic Boulevard, Suite 760, Los Angeles CA 90064. 310/231-0313. **Fax:** 310/231-9232. **Contact:** Manager. **Description:** An executive search firm. **Specializes in the areas of:** Manufacturing; Pharmaceutical.

KUHN MED-TECH
27128-B Paseo Espada, Suite 623, San Juan Capistrano CA 92675. 714/496-3500. **Fax:** 714/496-1716. **Contact:** Larry Kuhn, President. **Description:** An executive search firm. Company pays fee. **Specializes in the areas of:** Engineering; General Management; Health/Medical; Manufacturing; Sales; Technical. **Positions commonly filled include:** Biological Scientist; Biomedical Engineer; Chemical Engineer; Chemist; Electrical/Electronics Engineer; Industrial Engineer; Manufacturing Engineer; Marketing Specialist; Mechanical Engineer; Metallurgical Engineer; Nurse; Operations/Production Manager; Plastics Engineer; Quality Control Supervisor; Sales Representative. **Number of placements per year:** 50 - 99.

JOHN KUROSKY & ASSOCIATES
3 Corporate Park Drive, Suite 210, Irvine CA 92606. 714/851-6370. **Fax:** 714/851-8465. **Contact:** John Kurosky, President. **E-mail address:** jka@ix.netcom.com. **Description:** An executive search firm. Company pays fee. **Specializes in the areas of:** Accounting/Auditing; Administration; Biology; Computer Science/Software; Engineering; Finance; Food Industry; General Management; Health/Medical; Industrial; Legal; Sales; Technical. **Positions commonly filled include:** Abstractor/Indexer; Account Manager; Accountant; Attorney; Biomedical Engineer; Buyer; Chemist; Chief Financial Officer; Civil Engineer; Computer Programmer; Controller; Credit Manager; Database Manager; Design Engineer; Electrical/Electronics Engineer; Finance Director; Food Scientist/Technologist; Industrial Engineer; Industrial Production Manager; Intellectual Property Lawyer; Internet Services Manager; Manufacturing Engineer; Marketing Manager; Mechanical Engineer; Metallurgical Engineer; MIS Manager; Operations Manager; Production Manager; Project Manager; Quality Control Supervisor; Sales Executive; Sales Manager; Software Engineer; Systems Manager; Telecommunications Manager. **Corporate headquarters**

location: This Location. **Other U.S. locations:** Nationwide. **Average salary range of placements:** More than $50,000. **Number of placements per year:** 100 - 199.

MARVIN LABA & ASSOCIATES
6255 West Sunset Boulevard, Suite 617, Los Angeles CA 90028. 213/464-1355. **Fax:** 213/465-0330. **Contact:** Bonnie Milstein, Executive Vice President. **Description:** An executive search firm that focuses on placement in the retail industry. **Specializes in the areas of:** Finance; Human Resources; MIS/EDP; Operations Management; Retail. **Average salary range of placements:** More than $50,000. **Number of placements per year:** 1 - 49.

PAUL LaCOSTA & ASSOCIATES
6727 Flanders Drive, Suite 108, San Diego CA 92121. 619/457-1377. **Fax:** 619/457-0971. **Contact:** Paul LaCosta, President. **Description:** An executive search firm. Company pays fee. **Specializes in the areas of:** Wireless Communications. **Positions commonly filled include:** Accountant/Auditor; Branch Manager; Customer Service Representative; Electrical/Electronics Engineer; Operations/Production Manager; Purchasing Agent/Manager. **Number of placements per year:** 1 - 49.

LANDER INTERNATIONAL
P.O. Box 1370, El Cerrito CA 94530-1370. **Toll-free phone:** 800/548-5318. **Fax:** 510/232-6795. **Contact:** Richard Tuck, President. **E-mail address:** landerint@aol.com. **World Wide Web address:** http://www.landerint.com. **Description:** An executive search firm that focuses on placing audit professionals. Company pays fee. **Specializes in the areas of:** Accounting/Auditing; Computer Science/Software. **Positions commonly filled include:** Auditor; Computer Programmer; EDP Specialist. **Corporate headquarters location:** This Location. **Average salary range of placements:** More than $50,000. **Number of placements per year:** 500 - 999.

LARKIN ASSOCIATES
604 Santa Monica Boulevard, Santa Monica CA 90401. 310/260-0080. **Fax:** 310/260-0090. **Contact:** Managing Director. **Description:** An executive search firm that places personnel in interactive multimedia and software publishing industries. Company pays fee. **Specializes in the areas of:** Art/Design; Computer Science/Software; Sales; Technical. **Positions commonly filled include:** Computer Programmer; Multimedia Designer. **Average salary range of placements:** More than $50,000. **Number of placements per year:** 1 - 49.

LARSEN, WHITNEY, BLECKSMITH, & ZILLIACUS
888 West 6th Street, Suite 500, Los Angeles CA 90071. **Contact:** Sandy Hogan, Director of Research. **E-mail address:** sandy@directnet.com. **World Wide Web address:** http://www.directnet.com~sandy. **Description:** An executive search firm. Company pays fee. **Specializes in the areas of:** Accounting/Auditing; Administration; Banking; Computer Science/Software; Engineering; Finance; Manufacturing; Nonprofit; Personnel/Labor Relations. **Positions commonly filled include:** Accountant/Auditor; Bank Officer/Manager; General Manager; Human Resources Manager; MIS Manager; Software Engineer. **Average salary range of placements:** More than $50,000. **Number of placements per year:** 1 - 49.

LeBLANC & ASSOCIATES
6934 Canby Avenue, Suite 101, Reseda CA 91335. 818/705-5619. **Contact:** Manager. **Description:** An executive search firm. **Specializes in the areas of:** Transportation.

LEFEBER & ASSOCIATES
One Almaden Boulevard, San Jose CA 95113. 408/271-1300. **Contact:** Manager. **Description:** An executive search firm. **Specializes in the areas of:** High-Tech.

LEINOW ASSOCIATES
P.O. Box 154, Woodacre CA 94973. 415/488-4885. **Fax:** 415/488-4886. **Contact:** Leonard Leinow, President. **Description:** An executive search firm focusing on placement in the health care information systems industry. Company pays fee. **Specializes in the areas of:** Health/Medical. **Positions commonly filled include:** Computer Programmer; Design Engineer; MIS Specialist; Software Engineer; Systems Analyst. **Average salary range of placements:** More than $50,000.

LENDING PERSONNEL SERVICES
2938 South Daimler Street, Suite 110, Santa Ana CA 92705. 714/250-8133. **Fax:** 714/250-7180. **Contact:** Carla Bloch, Owner. **Description:** An executive search firm focusing on executive, managerial, and clerical placements in mortgage banking, financial, high-tech, manufacturing, and insurance industries. Company pays fee. **Specializes in the areas of:** Accounting/Auditing; Banking; Computer Science/Software; Finance; General Management; Insurance; Personnel/Labor Relations; Sales. **Positions commonly filled include:** Accountant/Auditor; Adjuster; Bank Officer/Manager; Branch Manager; Budget Analyst; Claim Representative; Computer Programmer; Credit Manager; Customer Service Representative; Financial Analyst; General Manager; Insurance Agent/Broker; Internet Services Manager; MIS Specialist; Operations/Production Manager; Securities Sales Representative; Systems Analyst; Telecommunications Manager; Underwriter/Assistant Underwriter. **Average salary range of placements:** More than $50,000. **Number of placements per year:** 1 - 49.

LIFTER & ASSOCIATES
10918 Lurline Avenue, Chatsworth CA 91311. 818/998-0283. **Fax:** 818/341-7979. **Contact:** Barbara and Jay Lifter, Principals. **E-mail address:** lifters@worldnet.att.net. **Description:** An executive search firm. Company pays fee. **Specializes in the areas of:** Administration; Banking; Computer Science/Software; Consulting; Finance; Information Technology; Insurance; Manufacturing. **Positions commonly filled include:** Computer Programmer; Database Manager; Internet Services Manager; Management Analyst/Consultant; MIS Manager; Multimedia Designer; Project Manager; Software Engineer; Systems Analyst; Systems Manager; Telecommunications Manager; Webmaster. **Average salary range of placements:** More than $50,000. **Number of placements per year:** 1 - 49.

JH LINDELL & COMPANY
560 1st Street East, Sonoma CA 95476. **Contact:** John Lindell, President. **Description:** An executive search firm that places senior management personnel in real estate and construction companies. **Specializes in the areas of:** Architecture/Construction; Real Estate. **Number of placements per year:** 1 - 49.

THE LONDON AGENCY
12424 Wilshire Boulevard, Suite 1270, Los Angeles CA 90025. 310/826-6060. **Fax:** 310/207-4447. **Contact:** Carolyn Gurwich, Manager. **Description:** An executive search firm operating on a contingency basis. Company pays fee. **Specializes in the areas of:** Accounting/Auditing; Advertising; Architecture/Construction; Banking; Broadcasting; Computer Science/Software; Finance; General Management; Health/Medical; Legal; Nonprofit; Retail; Sales; Secretarial. **Positions commonly filled include:**

Administrative Assistant; Advertising Account Executive; Controller; Financial Analyst; Sales Representative; Secretary; Typist/Word Processor. **Average salary range of placements:** $30,000 - $50,000. **Number of placements per year:** 200 - 499.

CL LOVICK & ASSOCIATES
P.O. Box 9402, Inglewood CA 90305. 310/330-3670. **Contact:** Manager. **Description:** An executive search firm that places personnel in a variety of industries.

MIS SEARCH
2099 Gateway Place, Suite 470, San Jose CA 95110. 408/437-0800. **Contact:** Office Manager. **Description:** An executive search firm that focuses on high-tech placements. **Specializes in the areas of:** Administration; Computer Hardware/Software.

KATHY MACDONALD ASSOCIATES
555 California Street, Suite 4490, San Francisco CA 94104. 415/433-0700. **Contact:** Manager. **Description:** An executive search firm. **NOTE:** Please include a cover letter with salary range and industry of interest. **Specializes in the areas of:** Administration. **Positions commonly filled include:** Executive Assistant.

MACIEJEWSKI & ASSOCIATES
348 Broadway, Suite 4, Millbrae CA 94030. 415/692-8803. **Contact:** Manager. **Description:** An executive search firm that places mid- to senior-level executives. **Specializes in the areas of:** High-Tech; Software Development.

MACNAUGHTON ASSOCIATES
3600 Lime Street, Suite 323, Riverside CA 92501-2974. 909/788-4951. **Fax:** 909/788-4953. **Contact:** Sperry MacNaughton, President. **E-mail address:** sperrym@pacbell.net. **Description:** An executive search firm that focuses on higher education placements. Company pays fee. **Specializes in the areas of:** Education; Health/Medical; Human Resources; Nonprofit. **Positions commonly filled include:** Director; President; Vice President. **Average salary range of placements:** More than $50,000. **Number of placements per year:** 1 - 49.

JUDY MADRIGAL & ASSOCIATES
66 Bovet Road, Suite 390, San Mateo CA 94402. 510/795-8121. **Contact:** Manager. **Description:** An executive search firm. **Specializes in the areas of:** Health/Medical.

MAGENTA GROUP
15707 Rockfield Boulevard, Irvine CA 92718. 714/582-0600. **Fax:** 714/457-9136. **Contact:** General Manager. **Description:** An executive search firm that focuses on placement in the commercial printing, business forms, prepress, digital printing, and publishing industries. Company pays fee. **Specializes in the areas of:** Publishing. **Positions commonly filled include:** Sales Manager. **Corporate headquarters location:** Mission Viejo CA. **Average salary range of placements:** $30,000 - $50,000. **Number of placements per year:** 50 - 99.

MAHONEY & BREWER ASSOCIATES
2001 Union Street, Suite 640, San Francisco CA 94123. 415/771-3725. **Contact:** Office Manager. **Description:** An executive search firm. **Specializes in the areas of:** Finance; Government; Health/Medical; High-Tech. **Other U.S. locations:** Atlanta GA. **International locations:** Belgium.

MAJOR, HAGEN & AFRICA
655 Commercial Street, San Francisco CA 94111. 415/956-1010. **Fax:** 415/398-2425. **Contact:** Recruiter. **Description:** An executive search firm. Company pays fee. **Specializes in the areas of:** Legal. **Positions commonly filled include:** Attorney. **Number of placements per year:** 50 - 99.

MALIBU GROUP
770 County Square Drive, Suite 212, Ventura CA 93003. 818/889-9125. **Fax:** 818/889-2054. **Contact:** Bob Woodall, Owner/Manager. **Description:** An executive search firm. Company pays fee. **Specializes in the areas of:** Computer Science/Software; Engineering; Fashion; Finance; Food Industry; Health/Medical; Industrial; Insurance; Manufacturing; Publishing; Retail; Sales; Technical; Transportation. **Positions commonly filled include:** Biomedical Engineer; Buyer; Ceramics Engineer; Chemical Engineer; Chemist; EDP Specialist; Manufacturing Engineer; MIS Specialist; Technical Representative. **Number of placements per year:** 50 - 99.

MANAGEMENT RECRUITERS INTERNATIONAL
494 Alvarado, Suite F, Monterey CA 93940. 408/649-0737. **Contact:** Manager. **Description:** An executive search firm. **Specializes in the areas of:** Health/Medical. **Corporate headquarters location:** Cleveland OH.

MANAGEMENT RECRUITERS INTERNATIONAL
2316 Bell Executive Way, Suite 100, Sacramento CA 95825. 916/565-2700. **Fax:** 916/565-2828. **Contact:** Manager. **Description:** An executive search firm. **Specializes in the areas of:** Banking; Engineering; Information Systems; Manufacturing. **Corporate headquarters location:** Cleveland OH. **Other U.S. locations:** Nationwide.

MANAGEMENT RECRUITERS INTERNATIONAL
2150 Shattuck Avenue, Suite 704, Berkeley CA 94704. 510/486-8100. **Contact:** Manager. **Description:** An executive search firm. **Specializes in the areas of:** Banking; Environmental; Food Industry; Health/Medical. **Corporate headquarters location:** Cleveland OH. **Other U.S. locations:** Nationwide.

MANAGEMENT RECRUITERS INTERNATIONAL
350 Crown Point Circle, Suite 125, Grass Valley CA 95945. 530/273-0200. **Contact:** Manager. **Description:** An executive search firm. **Specializes in the areas of:** Retail. **Corporate headquarters location:** Cleveland OH. **Other U.S. locations:** Nationwide.

MANAGEMENT RECRUITERS INTERNATIONAL
2222 Francisco Drive, Suite 430, El Dorado Hills CA 95762. 916/939-9780. **Contact:** Manager. **Description:** An executive search firm. **Specializes in the areas of:** Food Industry. **Corporate headquarters location:** Cleveland OH. **Other U.S. locations:** Nationwide.

MANAGEMENT RECRUITERS INTERNATIONAL
3001 Douglas Avenue, Suite 230, Roseville CA 95661. 916/781-8110. **Contact:** Manager. **Description:** An executive search firm. **Specializes in the areas of:** High-Tech. **Corporate headquarters location:** Cleveland OH. **Other U.S. locations:** Nationwide.

MANAGEMENT RECRUITERS INTERNATIONAL
7360 El Camino Real, Suite A, Atascadero CA 93422. 805/462-8044. **Contact:** Manager. **Description:** An executive search firm. **Specializes in the areas of:** Biotechnology; Pharmaceutical; Research and Development. **Corporate headquarters location:** Cleveland OH. **Other U.S. locations:** Nationwide.

MANAGEMENT RECRUITERS INTERNATIONAL
2900 Bristol Street, Suite B301, Costa Mesa CA 92626. 408/295-2229. **Fax:** 714/668-0250. **Contact:**

Office Manager. **Description:** An executive search firm. **Specializes in the areas of:** Technical. **Corporate headquarters location:** Cleveland OH. **Other U.S. locations:** Nationwide.

MANAGEMENT RECRUITERS OF BURLINGAME
SALES CONSULTANTS OF BURLINGAME
111 Anza Boulevard, Suite 109, Burlingame CA 94010. 650/548-4800. **Fax:** 650/548-4805. **Contact:** Don Hirschbein, President. **World Wide Web address:** http://www.mrinet.com. **Description:** An executive search firm. Company pays fee. **Specializes in the areas of:** Accounting/Auditing; Administration; Architecture/Construction; Banking; Communications; Computer Hardware/Software; Construction; Electrical; Engineering; Finance; Food Industry; General Management; Health/Medical; Insurance; Manufacturing; Operations Management; Personnel/Labor Relations; Pharmaceutical; Procurement; Publishing; Retail; Sales; Technical; Textiles. **Corporate headquarters location:** Cleveland OH. **Other U.S. locations:** Nationwide. **Number of placements per year:** 100 - 199.

MANAGEMENT RECRUITERS OF CLOVIS
150 Clovis Avenue, Suite 205, Clovis CA 93612-1152. 209/299-7992. **Fax:** 209/299-2167. **Contact:** Gary Hendrickson, Manager. **E-mail address:** food@ix.netcom.com. **World Wide Web address:** http://www.mrinet.com. **Description:** An executive search firm concentrating on the food and beverage processing industry. Company pays fee. **Specializes in the areas of:** Food Industry. **Positions commonly filled include:** Computer Programmer; Electrical/Electronics Engineer; Food Scientist/Technologist; Human Resources Manager; Industrial Engineer; Industrial Production Manager; Manufacturing Engineer; Mechanical Engineer; Production Manager; Quality Control Supervisor; Systems Analyst; Transportation/Traffic Specialist. **Corporate headquarters location:** Cleveland OH. **Other U.S. locations:** Nationwide. **Average salary range of placements:** More than $50,000. **Number of placements per year:** 1 - 49.

MANAGEMENT RECRUITERS OF ENCINO
16027 Ventura Boulevard, Suite 320, Encino CA 91436. 818/906-3155. **Fax:** 818/906-0642. **Contact:** Loren Kaun, Manager. **E-mail address:** consult@MRI-LA.com. **Description:** An executive search firm. Company pays fee. **Specializes in the areas of:** Accounting/Auditing; Administration; Advertising; Architecture/Construction; Banking; Chemical; Communications; Computer Hardware/Software; Construction; Electrical; Engineering; Finance; Food Industry; General Management; Health/Medical; Insurance; Legal; Manufacturing; Operations Management; Personnel/Labor Relations; Pharmaceutical; Procurement; Publishing; Real Estate; Retail; Sales; Technical; Textiles; Transportation. **Positions commonly filled include:** Accountant/Auditor; Administrative Manager; Bank Officer/Manager; Biochemist; Biological Scientist; Biomedical Engineer; Computer Programmer; Cost Estimator; Engineer; Financial Analyst; General Manager; Health Services Manager; Internet Services Manager; MIS Specialist; Occupational Therapist; Operations/Production Manager; Recreational Therapist; Registered Nurse; Respiratory Therapist; Software Engineer; Systems Analyst; Telecommunications Manager. **Corporate headquarters location:** Cleveland OH. **Average salary range of placements:** More than $50,000. **Number of placements per year:** 100 - 199.

MANAGEMENT RECRUITERS OF LAGUNA HILLS
23461 South Pointe Drive, Suite 390, Laguna Hills CA 92653. 714/768-9112. **Fax:** 714/768-6135. **Contact:** Thomas J. Toole, President. **Description:** An executive search firm. Company pays fee. **Specializes in the areas of:** Accounting/Auditing; Advertising; Biology; Computer Science/Software; Engineering; Finance; Food Industry; General Management; Industrial; Manufacturing; Personnel/Labor Relations; Sales; Technical; Transportation. **Positions commonly filled include:** Accountant/Auditor; Attorney; Biological Scientist; Biomedical Engineer; Chemical Engineer; Chemist; Electrical/Electronics Engineer; General Manager; Human Resources Manager; Manufacturer's/Wholesaler's Sales Rep.; Mechanical Engineer; Metallurgical Engineer; Pharmacist; Physical Therapist; Quality Control Supervisor; Restaurant/Food Service Manager; Software Engineer; Systems Analyst. **Corporate headquarters location:** Cleveland OH. **Other U.S. locations:** Nationwide. **Number of placements per year:** 50 - 99.

MANAGEMENT RECRUITERS OF OAKLAND
SALES CONSULTANTS OF OAKLAND
480 Roland Way, Suite 103, Oakland CA 94621. 510/635-7901. **Toll-free phone:** 800/581-7901. **Fax:** 510/562-7237. **Contact:** Tom Thrower, Manager. **E-mail address:** mrsrecruit@internetmci.com. **World Wide Web address:** http://www.mrinet.com. **Description:** An executive search firm. Company pays fee. **Specializes in the areas of:** Administration; Computer Science/Software; Engineering; Finance; Food Industry; General Management; Health/Medical; Industrial; Manufacturing; Sales; Technical. **Positions commonly filled include:** Administrative Manager; Biochemist; Biological Scientist; Biomedical Engineer; Branch Manager; Chemical Engineer; Chemist; Computer Programmer; Construction and Building Inspector; Credit Manager; Design Engineer; Dietician/Nutritionist; EKG Technician; Electrical/Electronics Engineer; Environmental Engineer; Food Scientist/Technologist; Health Services Manager; Human Resources Manager; Industrial Engineer; Industrial Production Manager; Internet Services Manager; Management Analyst/Consultant; Manufacturer's/Wholesaler's Sales Rep.; Mechanical Engineer; Metallurgical Engineer; MIS Specialist; Multimedia Occupational Therapist; Operations/Production Manager; Petroleum Engineer; Pharmacist; Physical Therapist; Physician; Psychologist; Public Relations Specialist; Quality Control Supervisor; Radiological Technologist; Recreational Therapist; Respiratory Therapist; Restaurant/Food Service Manager; Services Sales Representative; Software Engineer; Speech-Language Pathologist; Stationary Engineer; Strategic Relations Manager; Surgical Technician; Systems Analyst; Telecommunications Manager. **Corporate headquarters location:** Cleveland OH. **Other U.S. locations:** Nationwide. **Average salary range of placements:** $30,000 - $50,000. **Number of placements per year:** 500 - 999.

MANAGEMENT RECRUITERS OF ORANGE
One City Boulevard West, Suite 710, Orange CA 92868. 714/978-0500. **Fax:** 714/978-8064. **Contact:** Manager. **Description:** An executive search firm. Company pays fee. **Specializes in the areas of:** Administration; Computer Science/Software; Health/Medical; Publishing; Sales. **Positions commonly filled include:** Computer Programmer; EDP Specialist; Health Services Manager; Insurance Agent/Broker; Nurse; Physician; Software Engineer; Surgical Technician; Systems Analyst; Underwriter/Assistant Underwriter. **Corporate headquarters location:** Cleveland OH. **Other U.S. locations:** Nationwide. **Number of placements per year:** 200 - 499.

MANAGEMENT RECRUITERS OF PLEASANTON
4125 Mohr Avenue, Suite M, Pleasanton CA 94566-4740. 510/462-8579. **Fax:** 510/462-0208. **Contact:** Mike Machi, President. **E-mail address:** mriptown@aol.com. **World Wide Web address:**

http://www.mrinet.com. **Description:** An executive search firm. Company pays fee. **Specializes in the areas of:** Accounting/Auditing; Administration; Architecture/Construction; Banking; Communications; Computer Hardware/Software; Construction; Electrical; Engineering; Finance; Food Industry; General Management; Health/Medical; Personnel/Labor Relations; Pharmaceutical; Procurement; Publishing; Retail; Sales; Technical; Textiles; Transportation. **Corporate headquarters location:** Cleveland OH. **Other U.S. locations:** Nationwide. **Average salary range of placements:** More than $50,000. **Number of placements per year:** 50 - 99.

MANAGEMENT RECRUITERS OF REDLANDS
19 East Citrus, Suite 201, Redlands CA 92373. 909/335-2055. **Fax:** 909/792-4192. **Contact:** M.R. (Maurie) Meyers, Manager. **Description:** An executive search firm. **Specializes in the areas of:** Architecture/Construction; Engineering; Finance; General Management; Manufacturing; Personnel/Labor Relations; Sales; Transportation. **Corporate headquarters location:** Cleveland OH.

MANAGEMENT RECRUITERS OF SAN FRANCISCO
591 Redwood Highway, Suite 2225, Mill Valley CA 94941. 415/981-5950. **Fax:** 415/383-1426. **Contact:** Eric Wheel, Manager. **E-mail address:** ericmri@well.com. **World Wide Web address:** http://www.mrimvca.com. **Description:** An executive search firm. Company pays fee. **Specializes in the areas of:** Administration; Advertising; Banking; Computer Hardware/Software; Construction; Engineering; Legal; Manufacturing; Operations Management; Technical. **Corporate headquarters location:** Cleveland OH. **Other U.S. locations:** Nationwide. **Number of placements per year:** 200 - 499.

MANAGEMENT SEARCH INTERNATIONAL (MSI)
15375 Barranca Parkway, Unit B, Suite 205, Irvine CA 92718. 714/727-4343. **Fax:** 714/753-9110. **Contact:** Recruiter. **Description:** An executive search firm. Founded in 1977. Company pays fee. **Specializes in the areas of:** Accounting/Auditing; Administration; Banking; Finance; Food Industry; Health/Medical; Manufacturing; Personnel/Labor Relations; Retail. **Positions commonly filled include:** Accountant/Auditor; Claim Representative; Computer Programmer; EDP Specialist; Marketing Specialist; MIS Specialist; Systems Analyst. **Number of placements per year:** 1 - 49.

MANAGEMENT SOLUTIONS
99 Almaden Boulevard, Suite 600, San Jose CA 95113. 408/292-6600. **Fax:** 408/298-5714. **Contact:** Rich Williams, President. **World Wide Web address:** http://www.mgmtsolutions.com. **Description:** An executive search firm operating on both retainer and contingency bases. The firm also provides temporary placement and contract services. Company pays fee. **Specializes in the areas of:** Accounting/Auditing; Computer Science/Software; Engineering; Finance; Manufacturing; Personnel/Labor Relations. **Positions commonly filled include:** Accountant/Auditor; Budget Analyst; Computer Programmer; Credit Manager; Design Engineer; Electrical/Electronics Engineer; Environmental Engineer; Financial Analyst; Industrial Engineer; Internet Services Manager; Mechanical Engineer; MIS Specialist; Multimedia Designer; Operations/Production Manager; Quality Control Supervisor; Systems Analyst; Technical Writer/Editor; Telecommunications Manager. **Corporate headquarters location:** This Location. **Other U.S. locations:** Walnut Creek CA; Portland OR. **Number of placements per year:** 1000+.

MARKAR ASSOCIATES
940 South Coast Drive, Suite 175, Costa Mesa CA 92626. 714/433-0100. **Fax:** 714/549-1838. **Contact:** Mike Chitjian, President. **Description:** An executive search firm. Company pays fee. **Specializes in the areas of:** Engineering; Technical. **Positions commonly filled include:** Biomedical Engineer; Chemical Engineer; Chemist; Civil Engineer; Construction Contractor; Cost Estimator; Geological Engineer; Health Services Manager; Mechanical Engineer; Meteorologist; Technical Writer/Editor. **Number of placements per year:** 50 - 99.

MARSEARCH ASSOCIATES
P.O. Box 2002, Thousand Oaks CA 91358. 805/376-2909. **Contact:** Office Manager. **Description:** An executive search firm. **Specializes in the areas of:** Marketing.

MASON CONCEPTS
6380 Wilshire Boulevard, Suite 1000, Los Angeles CA 90048. 213/658-1550. **Fax:** 213/655-1570. **Contact:** Attilio Armeni, President. **E-mail address:** attilio@masonconcepts.com. **World Wide Web address:** http://www.masonconcepts.com. **Description:** An executive search firm. Company pays fee. **Specializes in the areas of:** Computer Science/Software. **Positions commonly filled include:** Computer Programmer; Graphic Artist; Graphic Designer; Internet Services Manager; MIS Specialist; Software Engineer; Systems Analyst; Systems Manager; Technical Writer/Editor; Webmaster. **Average salary range of placements:** More than $50,000. **Number of placements per year:** 500 - 999.

MASTER CONSULTANTS ASSOCIATES
851 Burlway Road, Suite 618, Burlingame CA 94010. 650/340-0416. **Fax:** 650/340-7156. **Contact:** Steven Anderson, President. **Description:** An executive search firm. Company pays fee. **Specializes in the areas of:** Sales. **Positions commonly filled include:** Sales and Marketing Representative. **Average salary range of placements:** $30,000 - $50,000. **Number of placements per year:** 100 - 199.

MASTER SEARCH
P.O. Box 9070, Santa Rosa CA 95405. 707/538-4000. **Fax:** 707/539-4567. **Contact:** Barbara Masters, President. **E-mail address:** gremast@packbell.net. **Description:** An executive search firm. Company pays fee. **Specializes in the areas of:** Computer Science/Software; Engineering. **Positions commonly filled include:** Biological Scientist; Biomedical Engineer; Electrical/Electronics Engineer; Food Scientist/Technologist; Manufacturing Engineer; Mechanical Engineer; Operations/Production Manager; Quality Control Supervisor; Software Engineer. **Other U.S. locations:** Nationwide. **Number of placements per year:** 1 - 49.

MATA & ASSOCIATES
180 Harbor Drive, Suite 208, Sausalito CA 94965. 415/332-2893. **Fax:** 415/332-3916. **Contact:** Dick Mata, Owner. **Description:** An executive search firm for high-tech companies specializing in data processing, computer engineering, software engineering, networking, client/server development, technical support, and telecommunications. Company pays fee. **Specializes in the areas of:** Computer Science/Software. **Positions commonly filled include:** Computer Programmer; Software Engineer; Systems Analyst; Technical Writer/Editor; Telecommunications Manager. **Average salary range of placements:** More than $50,000. **Number of placements per year:** 1 - 49.

K.E. McCARTHY & ASSOCIATES
9800 South Sepulveda Boulevard, Los Angeles CA 90045. 310/568-4070. **Fax:** 310/568-4075. **Contact:** Kevin McCarthy, President. **Description:** A retained executive search firm for financial institutions and technology companies. **Specializes in the areas of:** Accounting/Auditing; Administration; Banking; Computer Science/Software; Finance; General Management. **Positions commonly filled include:** Account Manager; Accountant; Applications Engineer; Bank Officer/Manager; Budget Analyst; Chief Financial Officer; Computer Programmer; Consultant; Controller; Database Manager; Finance Director; Financial Analyst; Management Analyst/Consultant; MIS Specialist; Sales Executive; Software Engineer; Systems Analyst; Systems Manager; Technical Writer/Editor; Telecommunications Manager. **Average salary range of placements:** More than $50,000.

ROBERT McCONNELL & ASSOCIATES
205 East Commonwealth, Suite A, Alhambra CA 91801. 626/289-8764. **Contact:** Robert McConnell, Owner. **Description:** An executive search firm. **Number of placements per year:** 50 - 99.

McCORMACK & ASSOCIATES
5042 Wilshire Boulevard, Suite 505, Los Angeles CA 90036. 213/549-9200. **Contact:** Mr. McCormack, Partner. **Description:** An executive search firm. **Specializes in the areas of:** Nonprofit. **Other area locations:** San Francisco CA.

McCORMACK & ASSOCIATES
353 Sacramento Street, Suite 600, San Francisco CA 94111. 415/421-3300. **Contact:** Adam Forest, Partner. **Description:** An executive search firm. **Specializes in the areas of:** Environmental. **Positions commonly filled include:** Environmental Engineer. **Other area locations:** Los Angeles CA.

McCOY LIMITED
229164 Lyons Avenue, Suite 1C, Newhall CA 91321-2761. **Toll-free phone:** 800/829-6269. **Fax:** 408/734-8441. **Contact:** Joel Burris, Technical Services Manager. **E-mail address:** joel@smartlink.net. **World Wide Web address:** http://www.mccoy.com. **Description:** An executive search firm focusing on the computer industry. Company pays fee. **Specializes in the areas of:** Administration; Computer Science/Software; Engineering; Sales. **Positions commonly filled include:** Computer Programmer; Design Engineer; Designer; Multimedia Designer; Quality Control Supervisor; Software Engineer; Systems Analyst; Technical Writer/Editor. **Average salary range of placements:** More than $50,000. **Number of placements per year:** 100 - 199.

JEFF McDERMOTT & ASSOCIATES
521 West Avenida De Los Lobos M, San Clemente CA 92672. 714/366-1517. **Fax:** 714/366-2422. **Contact:** Jeff McDermott, Owner. **Description:** An executive search firm that places personnel in a variety of industries.

LYNN McINTOSH EXECUTIVE SEARCH
21535 Hawthorne Boulevard, Suite 501, Torrance CA 90503. 310/792-2028. **Contact:** Manager. **Description:** An executive search firm.

McKAVIS & ASSOCIATES
2315 Caringa Way, Suite 52, Carlsbad CA 92009. 760/931-1292. **Contact:** Manager. **Description:** A generalist executive search firm.

SABINE McMANUS & ASSOCIATES
433 North Camden Drive, Suite 1200, Beverly Hills CA 90210. 310/205-2006. **Fax:** 310/559-9883. **Contact:** Sabine McManus, President. **Description:** An executive search firm that places financial and operational candidates in hospitals, managed care companies, and other health care organizations. Company pays fee. **Specializes in the areas of:** Accounting/Auditing; Finance; Health/Medical. **Positions commonly filled include:** Accounting Supervisor; Budget Analyst; Chief Financial Officer; Controller; Financial Analyst; Health Services Manager; Systems Analyst. **Average salary range of placements:** $50,000 - $200,000. **Number of placements per year:** 100 - 199.

MED QUEST
655 Skyway, San Carlos CA 94070-2709. 650/593-3103. **Fax:** 650/593-3104. **Contact:** Lyn Brodhead, President. **E-mail address:** lynmq@ix.netcom.com. **Description:** An executive search firm. **Specializes in the areas of:** Biology; Engineering; Health/Medical; Manufacturing; Pharmaceutical. **Positions commonly filled include:** Biological Scientist; Biomedical Engineer; Chemical Engineer; Chemist; Clinical Lab Technician; Design Engineer; Electrical/Electronics Engineer; Industrial Engineer; Mechanical Engineer; Operations/Production Manager; Quality Control Supervisor; Science Technologist; Statistician. **Average salary range of placements:** More than $50,000. **Number of placements per year:** 1 - 49.

MED-EXEC INTERNATIONAL
100 North Brand Boulevard, Glendale CA 91203-2614. **Toll-free phone:** 800/507-5277. **Fax:** 818/552-5475. **Contact:** Rosemarie Christopher, Principal. **Description:** An executive search firm that operates on a contingency basis. Company pays fee. **Specializes in the areas of:** Biology; Biotechnology; Clinical Research; Diagnostic Imaging; Health/Medical; Medical Device; Pharmaceutical; Quality Assurance; Regulatory Affairs. **Positions commonly filled include:** Auditor; Biochemist; Biological Scientist; Biomedical Engineer; Chemical Engineer; Chemist; Clinical Clinician; Computer Programmer; Electrical/Electronics Engineer; Manufacturing Engineer; Mechanical Engineer; Metallurgical Engineer; Operations/Production Manager; Pharmacist; Production Manager; Project Manager; Quality Assurance Engineer; Quality Control Supervisor; Statistician; Systems Analyst. **Corporate headquarters location:** This Location. **Average salary range of placements:** More than $50,000. **Number of placements per year:** 50 - 99.

MEDICAL EXECUTIVE RECRUITERS
1220 Melody Lane, Suite 106, Roseville CA 95678. 916/786-8615. **Fax:** 916/786-8609. **Contact:** John Cunningham, CEO/President. **E-mail address:** medexec@pacbell.net. **Description:** An executive search firm. Company pays fee. **Specializes in the areas of:** Biology; Biotechnology; Computer Science/Software; Health/Medical; Pharmaceutical. **Positions commonly filled include:** Marketing Manager; Sales Executive; Sales Representative. **Average salary range of placements:** More than $50,000. **Number of placements per year:** 100 - 199.

EDWARD MEISTER EXECUTIVE SEARCH
100 Bush Street, Suite 2309, San Francisco CA 94104. 415/362-6262. **Contact:** Office Manager. **Description:** An executive search firm. **Specializes in the areas of:** Banking.

J.M. MEREDITH & ASSOCIATES
2240 North Rodeo Gulch Road, Soquel CA 95073. 408/479-7522. **Contact:** Manager. **Description:** An executive search firm. **Specializes in the areas of:** Computer Hardware/Software; High-Tech.

MESA INTERNATIONAL
7777 Greenback Lane, Suite 100A, Citrus Heights CA 95610. 916/729-7700. **Fax:** 916/729-1135. **Contact:**

Ken McCollum, President. **E-mail address:** mesa@mesaint.com. **World Wide Web address:** http://www.mesaint.com. **Description:** An executive search firm. Company pays fee. **Specializes in the areas of:** Accounting/Auditing; Administration; Advertising; Architecture/Construction; Banking; Communications; Computer Hardware/Software; Construction; Electrical; Engineering; Finance; Food Industry; General Management; Health/Medical; Insurance; Legal; Manufacturing; Operations Management; Personnel/Labor Relations; Pharmaceutical; Procurement; Publishing; Retail; Sales; Technical; Textiles; Transportation. **Average salary range of placements:** More than $50,000. **Number of placements per year:** 100 - 199.

MILESTONE PROFESSIONAL STAFFING
1474 Kings Lane, Palo Alto CA 94303-2836. 650/321-8994. **Fax:** 650/321-8995. **Contact:** R.B. Parfitt, President. **E-mail address:** parfitts@pacbell.net. **Description:** A retained executive search firm. Company pays fee. **Specializes in the areas of:** Computer Science/Software; Engineering; General Management; Legal; Manufacturing; Personnel/Labor Relations; Sales. **Positions commonly filled include:** Design Engineer; Electrical/Electronics Engineer; General Manager; Human Resources Manager; MIS Specialist; Multimedia Designer; Operations/Production Manager; Purchasing Agent/Manager; Quality Control Supervisor. **Corporate headquarters location:** This Location. **Average salary range of placements:** More than $50,000. **Number of placements per year:** 1 - 49.

CRAIG MILLER ASSOCIATES
1720 East Garry Avenue, Suite 207, Santa Ana CA 92705. 714/261-6246. **Contact:** Manager. **Description:** An executive search firm. **Specializes in the areas of:** High-Tech.

MINDSEED CORPORATION
15 Embarcadero Cove, Brooklyn CA 94606. 510/533-1575. **Contact:** Joanne Anderson, Vice President. **E-mail address:** mindseed@ix.netcom.com. **Description:** A diverse executive search and contract services firm focusing on placement in the entertainment industry including music, television, Internet, CD-ROM, and video game-related areas; and transit projects including buses, trains, and automatic fare collection. Company pays fee. **Specializes in the areas of:** Broadcasting; Manufacturing; Transportation. **Positions commonly filled include:** Automotive Mechanic; Broadcast Technician; Computer Programmer; Electrical/Electronics Engineer; Electrician; Industrial Production Manager; Internet Services Manager; Multimedia Designer; Radio/TV Announcer/Broadcaster; Software Engineer; Systems Analyst; Technical Writer/Editor; Telecommunications Manager; Transportation/Traffic Specialist; Video Production Coordinator. **Corporate headquarters location:** This Location. **Average salary range of placements:** $20,000 - $29,999. **Number of placements per year:** 50 - 99.

MINI-SYSTEMS ASSOCIATES
15373 Innovation Drive, Suite 301, San Diego CA 92128. 619/675-7888. **Fax:** 619/675-7899. **Contact:** Jon Davies, Branch Manager. **Description:** An executive search firm. Company pays fee. **Specializes in the areas of:** Biology; Computer Science/Software; Engineering; Manufacturing; Personnel/Labor Relations; Technical. **Positions commonly filled include:** Biochemist; Biological Scientist; Biomedical Engineer; Buyer; Chemical Engineer; Chemist; Civil Engineer; Clinical Lab Technician; Computer Programmer; Customer Service Representative; Design Engineer; Draftsperson; Electrical/Electronics Engineer; Environmental Engineer; Food Scientist/Technologist; Geologist/Geophysicist; Human Resources Specialist; Industrial Engineer; Internet Services Manager; Management Analyst/Consultant; Mechanical Engineer; Metallurgical Engineer; MIS Specialist; Multimedia Designer; Operations/Production Manager; Petroleum Engineer; Purchasing Agent/Manager; Science Technologist; Software Engineer; Structural Engineer; Technical Writer/Editor; Telecommunications Manager; Veterinarian. **Corporate headquarters location:** Culver City CA. **Other U.S. locations:** Nationwide. **Average salary range of placements:** $30,000 - $50,000. **Number of placements per year:** 200 - 499.

MIXTEC GROUP
31255 Cedar Valley Drive, Suite 327, Westlake Village CA 91362. 818/889-8819. **Contact:** Ward A. Fredericks, Chairman. **Description:** An executive search firm. Company pays fee. **Specializes in the areas of:** Executives; Food Industry; Health/Medical; Manufacturing. **Positions commonly filled include:** Biological Scientist; President; Vice President. **Number of placements per year:** 50 - 99.

JAMES MOORE & ASSOCIATES
90 New Montgomery, Suite 412, San Francisco CA 94105. 415/392-3933. **Fax:** 415/896-0931. **Contact:** Ann Mitchell, Director of Research. **Description:** An executive search firm that focuses on client/server networking, GUI, and object-oriented technology. **Specializes in the areas of:** Computer Hardware/Software. **Positions commonly filled include:** Computer Programmer; Internet Services Manager; Software Engineer; Systems Analyst. **Other area locations:** Mountain View CA. **Average salary range of placements:** More than $50,000.

JAMES MOORE & ASSOCIATES
625 Ellis Street, Mountain View CA 94043. 650/965-2344. **Contact:** Manager. **Description:** An executive search firm. **Specializes in the areas of:** Computer Hardware/Software. **Other area locations:** San Francisco CA.

STEWART MORRIS ASSOCIATES
3868 West Carson Street, Suite 214, Torrance CA 90503. 310/792-1777. **Contact:** Manager. **Description:** An executive search firm.

J.R. MORRISON & ASSOCIATES
2169 Francisco Boulevard East, San Rafael CA 94901. 415/457-4600. **Contact:** Jack Morrison. **Description:** An executive search firm that places personnel in a variety of industries.

MULTISEARCH RECRUITERS
P.O. Box 309, Ballico CA 95303. 209/634-5814. **Fax:** 209/634-2648. **Contact:** Dennis Gallagher, Owner. **Description:** An executive search firm operating on a contingency basis. The firm focuses on the plastics, building materials, and transportation manufacturing industries. Company pays fee. **Specializes in the areas of:** Engineering; Industrial; Sales; Technical. **Positions commonly filled include:** Account Manager; Account Representative; Applications Engineer; Chemical Engineer; Controller; Industrial Engineer; Industrial Production Manager; Manufacturing Engineer; Operations Manager; Production Manager; Quality Control Supervisor; Sales Executive; Sales Manager; Software Engineer. **Other U.S. locations:** Nationwide. **Number of placements per year:** 1 - 49.

MUSICK & ASSOCIATES
2812 Vista Mar Drive, Malibu CA 90265. 310/456-8252. **Fax:** 310/456-5783. **Contact:** Stephen Musick, Owner. **E-mail address:** stevem@professionalplacement.com. **World Wide Web address:** http://www.professionalplacement.com. **Description:**

An executive search firm that also offers contract services. Company pays fee. **Specializes in the areas of:** Accounting/Auditing; Banking; Finance; Food Industry; General Management; Industrial; Insurance; Legal; Manufacturing; Sales. **Positions commonly filled include:** Accountant/Auditor; Budget Analyst; Credit Manager; Financial Analyst; General Manager; Management Analyst/Consultant; Manufacturer's/Wholesaler's Sales Rep.; Multimedia Designer; Software Engineer. **Number of placements per year:** 50 - 99.

J.A. MYRBEN & ASSOCIATES
5334 Marina Pacifica, Long Beach CA 90803. 562/431-2584. **Contact:** Manager. **Description:** An executive search firm. **Specializes in the areas of:** Accounting/Auditing; Finance.

NCC EXECUTIVE SEARCH
1300 Santa Barbara Street, Suite B, Santa Barbara CA 93101. 805/965-0511. **Toll-free phone:** 800/622-0431. **Fax:** 805/730-1694. **Contact:** G. Allan, Recruiter. **E-mail address:** ncc@west.net. **Description:** An executive search firm concentrating on placement in biotech, medical, computer engineering and software, sales, and management positions. The firm is a part of Santa Barbara Placement, a temporary and permanent placement agency. The firm also encompasses Applied Micro Solutions, Inc., which provides contract services. Company pays fee. **Specializes in the areas of:** Administration; Computer Science/Software; Engineering; Finance; General Management; Health/Medical; Personnel/Labor Relations; Technical. **Positions commonly filled include:** Accountant/Auditor; Actuary; Administrative Manager; Advertising Clerk; Aerospace Engineer; Biological Scientist; Biomedical Engineer; Chemical Engineer; Computer Programmer; Electrical/Electronics Engineer; Financial Analyst; General Manager; Manufacturer's/Wholesaler's Sales Rep.; Mechanical Engineer; MIS Specialist; Nuclear Engineer; Nuclear Medicine Technologist; Quality Control Supervisor; Science Technologist; Software Engineer; Strategic Relations Manager; Systems Analyst; Technical Writer/Editor; Telecommunications Manager. **Other area locations:** San Francisco CA; Ventura CA. **Average salary range of placements:** More than $50,000. **Number of placements per year:** 100 - 199.

NATIONAL HOSPITALITY RECRUITERS
1070 Concord Avenue, Suite 267, Concord CA 94590. 510/825-5400. **Toll-free phone:** 888/647-6800. **Fax:** 510/825-5525. **Contact:** Mike Blanchard, Owner. **E-mail address:** jobman2000@msn.com. **Description:** An executive search firm. Company pays fee. **Specializes in the areas of:** Food Industry; Hotel/Restaurant. **Positions commonly filled include:** Chef/Cook/Kitchen Worker; Dietician/ Nutritionist; Food Scientist/Technologist; Hotel Manager; Restaurant/Food Service Manager. **Number of placements per year:** 200 - 499.

NATIONAL RESOURCES
41661 Enterprise Circle North, Suite 117, Temecula CA 92590. 909/694-5577. **Fax:** 909/699-3855. **Contact:** Gene Jenkins, President. **Description:** An executive search firm. Company pays fee. **Specializes in the areas of:** Computer Science/Software. **Positions commonly filled include:** Computer Programmer; Software Engineer; Systems Analyst. **Number of placements per year:** 100 - 199.

NATIONAL SEARCH ASSOCIATES
2035 Corte Del Nogal, Suite 100, Carlsbad CA 92009. 760/431-1115. **Fax:** 760/431-0660. **Contact:** Philip Peluso, President. **Description:** An executive search firm. **Specializes in the areas of:** Biology; Computer Science/Software. **Positions commonly filled include:** Biological Scientist; Biomedical Engineer; Chemist; Software Engineer.

NATIONAL STAFFING BY NOELLE & ASSOCIATES
3518 Cahuenga Boulevard, Suite 314, Los Angeles CA 90068. 213/874-3663. **Fax:** 213/851-8767. **Contact:** Noelle Lea King, Owner. **Description:** An executive search firm. Company pays fee. **Specializes in the areas of:** Health/Medical. **Positions commonly filled include:** Physician; Physician Assistant. **Number of placements per year:** 100 - 199.

NATIONS STAFFING SOLUTIONS/ASSOCIATES RESOURCE INTERNATIONAL
18952 MacArthur Boulevard, Suite 100, Irvine CA 92612. **Toll-free phone:** 888/252-2520. **Recorded jobline:** 714/222-9833. **Contact:** Manager. **Description:** An executive search firm that provides placements in various fields including mortgage banking, financial services, information systems, credit and collections, administrative, technical training, and sales. Company pays fee. **Specializes in the areas of:** Administration; Banking; Computer Science/Software; Credit and Collection; Finance; Insurance. **Positions commonly filled include:** Accountant/Auditor; Bank Officer/Manager; Branch Manager; Clerical Supervisor; Computer Programmer; Credit Manager; Customer Service Representative; MIS Specialist; Securities Sales Representative; Software Engineer; Systems Analyst; Typist/Word Processor; Underwriter/Assistant Underwriter. **Number of placements per year:** 500 - 999.

NETWORK RESOURCE GROUP
P.O. Box 25253, San Mateo CA 94402. 650/344-5550. **Fax:** 650/365-8065. **Contact:** Bob Read, Manager. **Description:** An executive search firm. Company pays fee. **Number of placements per year:** 1 - 49.

NEW VENTURE DEVELOPMENT, INC.
596 Canyon Vista Drive, Thousand Oaks CA 91320. 805/498-8506. **Fax:** 805/498-2735. **Contact:** David R. Du Ket, President. **Description:** An executive search firm. **Specializes in the areas of:** Computer Science/Software; Electronics; Engineering; Sales; Telecommunications. **Positions commonly filled include:** Biological Scientist; Chief Financial Officer; Computer Programmer; Electrical/ Electronics Engineer; Mechanical Engineer; Quality Assurance Engineer; Software Engineer; Structural Engineer; Systems Analyst; Telecommunications Manager. **Number of placements per year:** 50 - 99.

C. NEWELL & ASSOCIATES
18101 Von Karman Avenue, Suite 350, Irvine CA 92612. 714/251-6560. **Contact:** Manager. **Description:** An executive search firm. **Specializes in the areas of:** Legal. **Positions commonly filled include:** Attorney.

NEWPORT STRATEGIC SEARCH
2102 Business Center Drive, Suite 130, Irvine CA 92612. 714/851-1589. **Fax:** 714/851-1198. **Contact:** John Fitzpatrick, President. **Description:** An executive search firm. Company pays fee. **Specializes in the areas of:** Accounting/Auditing; Computer Science/Software; Finance; Telecommunications. **Positions commonly filled include:** Accountant/ Auditor; Financial Analyst; Telecommunications Manager. **Average salary range of placements:** More than $50,000. **Number of placements per year:** 100 - 199.

NICHOLS & ASSOCIATES
1211 West Imperial Highway, Suite 200, Brea CA 92821. 714/680-8380. **Contact:** Office Manager. **Description:** An executive search firm.

NORSELL & ASSOCIATES, INC.
P.O. Box 6686, Auburn CA 95604-6686. 530/269-0121. **Fax:** 530/268-3202. **Contact:** Paul Norsell, President. **Description:** An executive search firm. **Specializes in the areas of:** Biotechnology; General Management; Manufacturing; Pharmaceutical; Sales; Technical. **Positions commonly filled include:** Attorney; Biological Scientist; Biomedical Engineer; Chemical Engineer; Electrical/Electronics Engineer; General Manager; Management Analyst/Consultant; Mechanical Engineer; Operations/ Production Manager; Physician; Science Technologist; Software Engineer.

NYBORG-DOW ASSOCIATES INC.
12781 Woodlake Road, Grass Valley CA 95949. 916/477-7817. **Fax:** 916/477-0745. **Contact:** Marilyn Nyborg, Manager. **E-mail address:** nydow@oro.net. **Description:** An executive search firm operating on a contingency basis. Company pays fee. **Specializes in the areas of:** Engineering. **Positions commonly filled include:** Electrical/Electronics Engineer; Software Engineer. **Average salary range of placements:** More than $50,000. **Number of placements per year:** 1 - 49.

O'CROWLEY & O'TOOLE EXECUTIVE SEARCH
4071 Avenita Sevilla, Cypress CA 90630-3411. 714/816-0286. **Contact:** Manager. **Description:** An executive search firm. **Specializes in the areas of:** Finance; Insurance. **Positions commonly filled include:** Accountant/Auditor; Bank Officer/Manager; Branch Manager; Financial Analyst; Loan Officer; Underwriter/Assistant Underwriter. **Number of placements per year:** 1 - 49.

OMNI SEARCH LTD.
31225 LaBaya, Suite 100, Westlake Village CA 91362. 818/707-4500. **Contact:** Mr. Lory Goldstein, President. **Description:** An executive search firm. **Number of placements per year:** 50 - 99.

OMNI SEARCH LTD.
1291 East Hillsdale Boulevard, Suite 304A, Foster City CA 94404. 650/574-6090. **Fax:** 650/574-4109. **Contact:** David Scardifield, Principal. **Description:** A search firm focusing on high-tech industry placements such as software/hardware engineering, technical support, systems engineering, and sales positions. Company pays fee. **Specializes in the areas of:** Computer Science/Software. **Positions commonly filled include:** Computer Programmer; Electrical/Electronics Engineer; Software Engineer; Systems Analyst; Telecommunications Manager. **Corporate headquarters location:** This Location. **Other U.S. locations:** Nationwide. **Average salary range of placements:** More than $50,000. **Number of placements per year:** 50 - 99.

ONLINE PROFESSIONAL SEARCH
1030 Trellis Lane, Alameda CA 94502-7053. 510/769-7111. **Contact:** Anita Ho, President. **Description:** An executive search firm that recruits and places candidates with a minimum of five years experience in data processing. Online Professional Search focuses on the placement of programmers/analysts, UNIX administrators, Visual Basic programmers, Oracle programmers, and CICS/MVS/IMS systems programmers. **Specializes in the areas of:** Administration; Banking; Computer Science/Software. **Positions commonly filled include:** Computer Programmer; MIS Specialist; Systems Analyst. **Average salary range of placements:** More than $50,000. **Number of placements per year:** 1 - 49.

OPTIMUM EXECUTIVE SEARCH
600 Townsend Street, Suite 410 West, San Francisco CA 94103. 415/863-2700. **Contact:** Manager. **Description:** An executive search firm. **Specializes in the areas of:** Computer Hardware/Software.

ORYX EXECUTIVE SEARCH
3235 Kifer Road, Santa Clara CA 95051. 408/481-0100. **Fax:** 408/481-0123. **Contact:** Manager. **Description:** An executive search firm that focuses on high-tech placements.

DOUGLAS OWEN SEARCH CONSULTANTS
2814 South Court, Palo Alto CA 94306. 650/321-0193. **Contact:** Manager. **Description:** An executive search firm that places senior level management in technological companies. **Specializes in the areas of:** Technical.

PC PERSONNEL
226 Airport Parkway, Suite 625, San Jose CA 95110. 408/452-0500. **Fax:** 408/452-0584. **Contact:** Karl Beckstrand, Technical Recruiter. **E-mail address:** netjobs@aol.com. **World Wide Web address:** http://www.pcpersonnel.com. **Description:** An executive search firm focusing on the placement of computer network experts. The firm also places systems analysts, network administrators, technical support, network engineers, and IS managers on a contract basis. Company pays fee. **Specializes in the areas of:** Computer Science/Software. **Positions commonly filled include:** Internet Services Manager; MIS Specialist; Systems Analyst; Telecommunications Manager. **Benefits available to temporary workers:** Medical Insurance; Paid Holidays; Paid Vacation. **Corporate headquarters location:** San Francisco CA. **Average salary range of placements:** $30,000 - $50,000. **Number of placements per year:** 1 - 49.

PN FINANCIAL RECRUITING
3860 Blackhawk Drive, Suite 130, Danville CA 94506-2163. 510/736-6166. **Fax:** 510/736-6165. **Contact:** Pat Newton, Owner. **World Wide Web address:** http://www.tpi.net/pnfinancial. **Description:** An executive search firm that concentrates on professional placements in accounting, finance, audit, tax, treasury, and credit professions. Company pays fee. **Specializes in the areas of:** Accounting/Auditing; Finance; Personnel/Labor Relations. **Positions commonly filled include:** Accountant/Auditor; Budget Analyst; Chief Financial Officer; Controller; Credit Manager; Financial Analyst; Human Resources Manager. **Average salary range of placements:** More than $50,000. **Number of placements per year:** 200 - 499.

PAAR & ASSOCIATES
17451 Bastanchury Road, Suite 204, Yorba Linda CA 92886. 714/579-1465. **Fax:** 714/579-7921. **Contact:** Fred H. Paar, President. **E-mail address:** fredpaar@msn.com. **World Wide Web address:** http://www.paar.com. **Description:** A retained executive search firm for senior-level managers that also offers outplacement services. **Specializes in the areas of:** Management. **Positions commonly filled include:** Chief Executive Officer; Chief Financial Officer; General Manager; President; Vice President. **Number of placements per year:** 1 - 49.

PACIFIC MEDICAL SEARCH
23441 South Pointe Drive, Suite 90, Laguna Hills CA 92653. 714/581-5977. **Contact:** Manager. **Description:** An executive search firm that provides physician placements.

PACIFIC RECRUITING OFFICES
2102 Business Center Drive, Suite 130, Irvine CA 92612. 714/253-4646. **Contact:** Harvey Dorland, President. **Description:** An executive search firm. Company pays fee. **Specializes in the areas of:** Insurance. **Positions commonly filled include:** Account

Representative; Claim Representative; Management; Sales Representative; Underwriter/Assistant Underwriter. **Number of placements per year:** 50 - 99.

PACIFIC SEARCH GROUP
10100 Santa Monica Boulevard, Suite 700, Los Angeles CA 90067-4011. 310/286-6921. **Fax:** 310/712-0777. **Contact:** Nick Roberts, President. **Description:** Pacific Search Group is an executive search firm that focuses on the placement of financial and accounting personnel. Company pays fee. **Specializes in the areas of:** Accounting/Auditing; Banking; Computer Science/Software; Finance; Food Industry; General Management; Health/Medical; Insurance; Manufacturing; MIS/EDP; Nonprofit; Retail; Sales; Secretarial. **Positions commonly filled include:** Accountant/Auditor; Attorney; Budget Analyst; Credit Manager; Financial Analyst; Management Analyst/Consultant; Purchasing Agent/Manager. **Average salary range of placements:** More than $50,000. **Number of placements per year:** 50 - 99.

PACIFIC SYSTEMS SEARCH
7011 Koll Center Parkway, Suite 270, Pleasanton CA 94566. 510/795-0522. **Fax:** 510/426-9310. **Contact:** Manager. **Description:** An executive search firm. **Specializes in the areas of:** MIS/EDP.

PALERMO & ASSOCIATES
19742 MacArthur Boulevard, Suite 111, Irvine CA 92612. 714/263-9663. **Contact:** Manager. **Description:** An executive search firm that places personnel in a variety of industries.

FRANK PARILLO & ASSOCIATES
1801 East Heim Avenue, Suite 200, Orange CA 92665. 714/921-8008. **Contact:** Manager. **Description:** An executive search firm. **Specializes in the areas of:** Biomedical; Biotechnology.

PARKER & LYNCH EXECUTIVE SEARCH
101 California Street, Suite 1825, San Francisco CA 94111-5821. 415/956-6700. **Fax:** 415/956-5642. **Contact:** Montie Parker, Partner. **Description:** An executive search firm. Company pays fee. **Specializes in the areas of:** Accounting/Auditing; Finance; Personnel/Labor Relations. **Positions commonly filled include:** Accountant/Auditor; Credit Manager; Economist; Financial Analyst; Human Resources Manager; Management Analyst/Consultant; Management Trainee. **Average salary range of placements:** More than $50,000. **Number of placements per year:** 50 - 99.

PASTER & ASSOCIATES
9025 Wilshire Boulevard, Suite 301, Beverly Hills CA 90211. 310/273-5424. **Fax:** 310/273-8378. **Contact:** Steve Paster, President. **Description:** An executive search firm. Company pays fee. **Specializes in the areas of:** Health/Medical; Pharmaceutical; Sales. **Number of placements per year:** 50 - 99.

PEDEN & ASSOCIATES
2000 Broadway Street, Redwood City CA 94063. 650/367-1181. **Fax:** 650/367-7525. **Contact:** Ann Peden, President. **E-mail address:** apeden@pedenassoc.com. **Description:** An executive search firm that places software developers in start-up companies located in the San Francisco Bay Area. Company pays fee. **NOTE:** A minimum of two years experience in the industry is required, as well as experience with various software. **Specializes in the areas of:** Computer Science/Software. **Positions commonly filled include:** Electrical/Electronics Engineer; Software Engineer. **Average salary range of placements:** More than $50,000. **Number of placements per year:** 1 - 49.

PERIN HALL & ASSOCIATES
P.O. Box 232428, Leucadia CA 92023-2428. 760/942-1008. **Contact:** Pat Perin or Sally Hall, Partners. **Description:** An executive search firm. Company pays fee. **Specializes in the areas of:** Manufacturing; Offshore Operations. **Positions commonly filled include:** General Manager; Industrial Engineer; Mechanical Engineer; Operations/Production Manager; Purchasing Agent/Manager. **Number of placements per year:** 50 - 99.

PERKISS & ASSOCIATES
3470 Mount Diablo Boulevard, Lafeyette CA 94549. 510/284-5310. **Contact:** Dave Perkiss, Owner. **Description:** An executive search firm that places sales professionals within high-tech companies. **Specializes in the areas of:** Sales.

PETER JOSEPH ASSOCIATES
25281 Via Piedra Blanca, Laguna Niguel CA 92677. 714/495-1714. **Contact:** Manager. **Description:** An executive search firm. **Specializes in the areas of:** Hotel/Restaurant.

TOM PEZMAN & ASSOCIATES
P.O. Box 3175, San Clemente CA 92674. 714/661-6637. **Fax:** 714/661-6965. **Contact:** Tom Pezman, President. **Description:** An executive search firm. Company pays fee. **Specializes in the areas of:** Broadcasting; Sales; Technical; Telecommunications; Wireless Communications. **Positions commonly filled include:** Computer Programmer; Customer Service Representative; Electrical/Electronics Engineer; Financial Analyst; Software Engineer. **Number of placements per year:** 50 - 99.

PHYSICIANS SEARCH ASSOCIATES
1224 East Katella Avenue, Orange CA 92687. 714/288-8350. **Toll-free phone:** 800/748-6320. **Fax:** 714/288-8345. **Contact:** Manager. **E-mail address:** physsrch@kaiwan.com. **World Wide Web address:** http://www.physrch.com/physrch. **Description:** An executive search firm. Company pays fee. **Specializes in the areas of:** Health/Medical. **Positions commonly filled include:** Physician. **Number of placements per year:** 100 - 199.

PIERCE ASSOCIATES
255 South Grand Avenue, Suite 513, Los Angeles CA 90012. 213/626-6711. **Contact:** Lisa Pierce, Owner. **Description:** An executive search firm. **Specializes in the areas of:** Legal. **Positions commonly filled include:** Attorney. **Other U.S. locations:** Washington DC.

PINSKER & COMPANY
P.O. Box 3269, Saratoga CA 95070. 408/867-5161. **Contact:** Manager. **Description:** An executive search firm. **Specializes in the areas of:** High-Tech; Manufacturing.

PLANTING & ASSOCIATES
220 State Street, Suite H, Los Altos CA 94022. 415/949-2002. **Contact:** Manager. **Description:** An executive search firm. **Specializes in the areas of:** Information Technology.

BOB POLINE ASSOCIATES INC.
12625 High Bluff Drive, Suite 114, San Diego CA 92130. 619/481-3700. **Contact:** Manager. **Description:** An executive search firm. **Specializes in the areas of:** Real Estate.

PREMIER RESOURCES
28202 Cabot Road, Suite 300, Laguna Niguel CA 92677. 714/365-5699. **Contact:** Jerry Thomas, Owner. **Description:** An executive search firm focusing on the information technology industry. Company pays fee. **Specializes in the areas of:** Administration;

Information Technology. **Positions commonly filled include:** Computer Programmer; MIS Specialist; Software Engineer; Systems Analyst. **Average salary range of placements:** More than $50,000. **Number of placements per year:** 1 - 49.

PRINCETON CORPORATE CONSULTANTS
16830 Ventura Boulevard, Suite 346, Encino CA 91436-1707. 818/784-8989. **Contact:** Personnel. **Description:** An executive search firm. **Specializes in the areas of:** Engineering; Health/Medical; Manufacturing; Technical. **Number of placements per year:** 200 - 499.

PRISM GROUP
475 Sansome Street, Suite 1850, San Francisco CA 94111. 415/394-7171. **Contact:** Manager. **Description:** An executive search firm. **Specializes in the areas of:** Information Systems.

PROBUS EXECUTIVE SEARCH
4962 El Camino, Los Altos CA 94022. **Contact:** Manager. **Description:** An executive search firm. **Specializes in the areas of:** Accounting/Auditing; Finance; High-Tech.

PROFESSIONAL DENTAL NETWORK
P.O. Box 84748, San Diego CA 92138. 619/284-2706. **Fax:** 619/284-3405. **Contact:** Linda Turner, Owner. **Description:** Professional Dental Network is an executive search firm that specializes in temporary and permanent placements in dental offices. Company pays fee. **Positions commonly filled include:** Dental Assistant/Dental Hygienist; Office Manager; Receptionist. **Number of placements per year:** 100 - 199.

PROFESSIONAL RECRUITERS INC.
19671 Beach Boulevard, Suite 203, Huntington Beach CA 92648-5901. 714/963-0034. **Fax:** 714/969-0072. **Contact:** Chuck Bechtloff, Owner. **Description:** Professional Recruiters focuses on placing personnel in the paper and packaging industry with an emphasis on companies that manufacture corrugated boxes and folding cartons. Company pays fee. **Specializes in the areas of:** Art/Design; Engineering; General Management; Manufacturing; Publishing; Sales. **Positions commonly filled include:** Buyer; Cost Estimator; Customer Service Representative; Electrical/Electronics Engineer; Electrician; General Manager; Human Resources Manager; Industrial Engineer; Industrial Production Manager; Manufacturer's/Wholesaler's Sales Rep.; Mechanical Engineer; Quality Control Supervisor. **Average salary range of placements:** $30,000 - $50,000. **Number of placements per year:** 1 - 49.

PROFESSIONAL SEARCH ASSOCIATES
3745 West Chapman Avenue, Suite 113, Orange CA 92868-1656. 714/978-9866. **Fax:** 714/978-9868. **Contact:** Mary K. Dowell, Executive Recruiter. **Description:** An executive search firm operating on both retained and contingency bases. Company pays fee. **Specializes in the areas of:** Accounting/Auditing; Administration; Executives; Finance; Food Industry; General Management; MIS/EDP; Operations Management. **Positions commonly filled include:** Account Manager; Account Representative; Accountant/Auditor; Branch Manager; Budget Analyst; Chief Financial Officer; CPA; Credit Manager; Customer Service Representative; Finance Director; Financial Analyst; Financial Manager; Food Scientist/Technologist; Management Analyst/Consultant; Market Research Analyst; MIS Specialist; Operations Manager; Planner; Production Manager; Sales Executive; Sales Manager; Sales Representative; Systems Analyst; Systems Manager; Tax Specialist; Telecommunications Manager. **Average salary range of placements:** More than $50,000. **Number of placements per year:** 1 - 49.

PROFESSIONAL SEARCH INC.
5480 Baltimore Drive, Suite 201, La Mesa CA 91942. 619/697-2138. **Fax:** 619/697-2139. **Contact:** Vernon E. Kleist, President. **E-mail address:** uk@recruitwest.com. **Description:** An executive search firm focusing on the placement of engineering and software professionals. Professional Search operates on both retained and contingency bases. Company pays fee. **Specializes in the areas of:** Engineering; Manufacturing. **Positions commonly filled include:** Computer Programmer; Electrical/Electronics Engineer; Industrial Engineer; Mechanical Engineer; Metallurgical Engineer; Multimedia Designer; Science Technologist; Software Engineer; Systems Analyst. **Number of placements per year:** 1 - 49.

PROFILES EXECUTIVE SEARCH
970 West 190th Street, Suite 600, Torrance CA 90502. 310/523-3400. **Fax:** 310/523-3401. **Contact:** Bari Kaplan, Executive Recruiter. **Description:** An executive search firm. Company pays fee. **Specializes in the areas of:** Computer Science/Software. **Positions commonly filled include:** Software Engineer. **Number of placements per year:** 1 - 49.

PROGRESSIVE SEARCH & CONSULTING
1320 Mt. Diablo Boulevard, Suite D, Walnut Creek CA 94596. 510/930-6340. **Fax:** 510/930-8142. **Contact:** Manager. **Description:** An executive search firm. **Specializes in the areas of:** Consumer Package Goods; Sales.

PROGRESSIVE SEARCH ASSOCIATES
12526 High Bluff Drive, Suite 300, San Diego CA 92130. 619/457-7818. **Contact:** Manager. **Description:** An executive search firm.

PROSEARCH & ASSOCIATES
1500 Quail, Suite 500, Newport Beach CA 92660. 714/452-0630. **Fax:** 714/951-2602. **Contact:** Sharon Dodson, Office Manager. **Description:** An executive search firm operating on both retainer and contingency bases. The firm also offers temporary placements. **Specializes in the areas of:** Accounting/Auditing; Administration; Computer Science/Software; Personnel/Labor Relations; Sales; Secretarial; Technical. **Positions commonly filled include:** Accountant/Auditor; Administrative Manager; Bank Officer/Manager; Branch Manager; Clinical Lab Technician; Computer Programmer; MIS Specialist; Registered Nurse; Software Engineer; Systems Analyst; Technical Writer/Editor. **Average salary range of placements:** $30,000 - $50,000.

PROTOCOL SEARCH & SELECTION
650 Hampshire Road, Suite 100, Westlake Village CA 91361. 805/371-0069. **Fax:** 805/371-0048. **Contact:** Chris Salcido, Branch Manager. **Description:** An executive search firm. Company pays fee. **Specializes in the areas of:** Computer Hardware/Software. **Positions commonly filled include:** Computer Programmer; MIS Specialist; Systems Analyst. **Average salary range of placements:** More than $50,000. **Number of placements per year:** 100 - 199.

PROTOCOL SEARCH & SELECTION
300 North Lake Avenue, Pasadena CA 91101. 626/449-2214. **Fax:** 626/577-0484. **Contact:** Kelly J. Lucas, Vice President/Branch Manager. **Description:** An executive search firm that also provides temporary placements. Company pays fee. **Specializes in the areas of:** Accounting/Auditing; Secretarial. **Positions commonly filled include:** Accountant/Auditor; Administrative Manager; Clerical Supervisor; Data Entry Clerk; Human Resources Manager; Paralegal.

Average salary range of placements: $30,000 - $50,000. **Number of placements per year:** 1000+.

QUEST SEARCH ASSOCIATES INC.
1901 South Bascom Avenue, Suite 1525, Campbell CA 95008. 408/371-8313. **Contact:** Manager. **Description:** An executive search firm that places mid-level and senior-level managers. The firm operates on a retainer basis.

QUEST WORLDWIDE EXECUTIVE SEARCH CORPORATION
5777 West Century Boulevard, Suite 1255, Los Angeles CA 90045. 310/410-7000. **Fax:** 310/410-7000. **Contact:** Manager. **E-mail address:** career@questworldwide.com. **World Wide Web address:** http://www.questworldwide.com. **Description:** An executive search firm that focuses on the placement of technical professionals on both retainer and contingency bases. Founded in 1995. Company pays fee. **Specializes in the areas of:** Computer Science/Software. **Positions commonly filled include:** Computer Programmer; Consultant; MIS Specialist; Software Engineer; Systems Analyst. **Corporate headquarters location:** Hermosa Beach CA. **Average salary range of placements:** More than $50,000. **Number of placements per year:** 50 - 99.

RGA ASSOCIATES
465 California Street, Suite 830, San Francisco CA 94104. 415/397-4646. **Contact:** Manager. **Description:** An executive search firm. **Specializes in the areas of:** Computer Hardware/Software. **Positions commonly filled include:** Computer Programmer.

RJ ASSOCIATES
23730 Canzonet Street, Woodland Hills CA 91367. 818/715-7121. **Fax:** 818/715-9438. **Contact:** Judith Fischer, President. **E-mail address:** rja23730 @ix.netcom.com. **Description:** RJ Associates provides executive search services for middle/upper financial, accounting, and information technology positions. Company pays fee. **Specializes in the areas of:** Accounting/Auditing; Finance; Information Technology. **Positions commonly filled include:** Controller; Finance Director; MIS Specialist. **Average salary range of placements:** More than $50,000. **Number of placements per year:** 50 - 99.

RABER ASSOCIATES
523 West 6th Street, Los Angeles CA 90014. 213/622-0505. **Contact:** Manager. **Description:** An executive search firm.

RADOSEVIC ASSOCIATES
4350 La Jolla Village Drive, Suite 870, San Diego CA 92122-1247. 619/642-0900. **Contact:** Frank Radosevic, Owner. **Description:** A retained executive search firm that places upper-level managers in a variety of industries worldwide. **Average salary range of placements:** More than $50,000.

RALEIGH & COMPANY
611 Washington Street, Suite 2206, San Francisco CA 94111. 415/362-7550. **Contact:** Manager. **Description:** An executive search firm that places personnel in a variety of industries.

RAPHAEL RECRUITMENT
4655 Cherryvale Avenue, Suite 100, Soquel CA 95073. 408/464-2760. **Fax:** 408/479-9046. **Contact:** Kent Halpern, President. **E-mail address:** raphael@cruzio.com. **World Wide Web address:** http://www.raphaelrecruitment.com. **Description:** An executive search firm. Company pays fee. **Specializes in the areas of:** Computer Science/Software; Engineering; Manufacturing. **Positions commonly filled include:** Computer Programmer; Design Engineer; Electrical/Electronics Engineer; Mechanical Engineer; Multimedia Designer; Software Engineer. **Average salary range of placements:** More than $50,000. **Number of placements per year:** 1 - 49.

EDWARD RAST AND COMPANY
235 Montgomery Street, Suite 901, San Francisco CA 94104. 415/986-1710. **Contact:** Edward Rast, Managing Director. **Description:** An executive search firm. Company pays fee. **Specializes in the areas of:** Accounting/Auditing; Administration; Biology; Biotechnology; Computer Science/Software; Finance; General Management; Health/Medical; Multimedia; Nonprofit; Retail; Sales; Technical; Transportation. **Positions commonly filled include:** Accountant/ Auditor; Biological Scientist; Biomedical Engineer; Budget Analyst; Buyer; Clinical Lab Technician; Computer Programmer; Credit Manager; Economist; Financial Analyst; General Manager; Health Services Manager; Management Analyst/Consultant; Operations/Production Manager; Software Engineer; Systems Analyst; Technical Writer/Editor; Wholesale and Retail Buyer. **Number of placements per year:** 50 - 99.

RAYCOR SEARCH
1874 South Pacific Coast Highway, Suite 180, Redondo Beach CA 90277. 310/791-5090. **Toll-free phone:** 800/472-9267. **Fax:** 310/791-5089. **Contact:** R.H. DeFeo, Manager. **E-mail address:** rcsraycor@aol.com. **Description:** An executive search firm. Company pays fee. **Specializes in the areas of:** Accounting/Auditing; Computer Science/Software. **Positions commonly filled include:** Computer Programmer; Consultant; Database Manager; Management Analyst/Consultant; Software Engineer; Systems Analyst; Systems Manager; Technical Writer/Editor; Webmaster. **Corporate headquarters location:** This Location. **Other U.S. locations:** Nationwide. **Average salary range of placements:** More than $50,000. **Number of placements per year:** 1 - 49.

REAL ESTATE EXECUTIVE SEARCH
P.O. Box 40, Santa Rosa CA 95402. 707/525-4591. **Contact:** Manager. **Description:** An executive search firm focusing on placements in the financial sector of the real estate industry, including equity financing and asset management.

RESOURCE PERSPECTIVES, INC.
535 Anton Boulevard, Suite 860, Costa Mesa CA 92626. 714/662-4947. **Fax:** 714/662-4953. **Contact:** Steven Cherney, Ph.D., President. **Description:** A retained executive search firm serving the consumer product industry and specializing in technical and marketing positions. Company pays fee. **Specializes in the areas of:** Engineering; Food Industry; General Management; Industrial; Manufacturing; Sales; Technical. **Positions commonly filled include:** Agricultural Engineer; Agricultural Scientist; Applications Engineer; Biological Scientist; Biomedical Engineer; Chemical Engineer; Chemist; Civil Engineer; Electrical/Electronics Engineer; Environmental Engineer; Food Scientist/Technologist; General Manager; Industrial Engineer; Manufacturing Engineer; Market Research Analyst; Mechanical Engineer; Metallurgical Engineer; Operations Manager; Production Manager; Restaurant/Food Service Manager. **Average salary range of placements:** More than $50,000. **Number of placements per year:** 1 - 49.

RICCI LEE ASSOCIATES, INC.
100 Spear Street, Suite 1810, San Francisco CA 94105. 415/247-2980. **Fax:** 415/247-2985. **Contact:** Carol Ricci Lee, President. **Description:** An executive search firm focusing on marketing, communications,

and advertising placements. **Specializes in the areas of:** Advertising; Sales. **Positions commonly filled include:** Marketing/Public Relations Manager; Public Relations Specialist; Telecommunications Manager. **Number of placements per year:** 100 - 199.

ROBERT RIGGS ASSOCIATES
5100 North 6th Street, Suite 176, Fresno CA 93710. 209/227-2792. **Contact:** Manager. **Description:** An executive search firm that places department managers. **Specializes in the areas of:** Sales.

RICHARD E. RIGLER & ASSOCIATES
23120 Alicia Parkway, Suite 200, Mission Viejo CA 92692-1202. 714/837-6999. **Contact:** Richard E. Rigler, President. **Description:** An executive search firm. Company pays fee. **Specializes in the areas of:** Banking; Engineering; Insurance; Manufacturing; Plastics; Sales. **Positions commonly filled include:** Bank Officer/Manager; Financial Analyst; Industrial Production Manager; Metallurgical Engineer; Quality Control Supervisor. **Number of placements per year:** 1 - 49.

RILEY-COLE RECRUITMENT SPECIALISTS
P.O. Box 10635, Oakland CA 94610-0635. 510/428-2022. **Fax:** 510/428-2072. **Contact:** Jim Riley or Don Cole, Partners. **Description:** An executive search firm operating on a contingency basis that places mid- to senior-level professionals in the food, consumer packaged goods, and retail industries. Company pays fee. **Specializes in the areas of:** Accounting/Auditing; Engineering; Fashion; Finance; Food Industry; General Management; Industrial; Manufacturing; Personnel/Labor Relations; Retail; Sales; Technical. **Positions commonly filled include:** Buyer; Chemical Engineer; Chemist; Customer Service Representative; Electrical/Electronics Engineer; Financial Analyst; Food Scientist/Technologist; Industrial Engineer; Industrial Production Manager; Management Analyst/Consultant; Manufacturer's/Wholesaler's Sales Rep.; Market Research Analyst; Mechanical Engineer; Purchasing Agent/Manager; Quality Control Supervisor; Science Technologist; Wholesale and Retail Buyer. **Average salary range of placements:** More than $50,000. **Number of placements per year:** 1 - 49.

RISHER ASSOCIATES
22865 Lake Forest Drive, Lake Forest CA 92630. 714/455-9777. **Contact:** Manager. **Description:** An executive search firm. **Specializes in the areas of:** Food Industry.

RITTER ASSOCIATES
1190 Saratoga Avenue, Suite 140, San Jose CA 95129. 408/551-6144. **Contact:** Willis Ritter, President. **Description:** An executive search firm. **Specializes in the areas of:** Accounting/Auditing; Administration; Computer Science/Software; Engineering; Finance; General Management; Legal; Manufacturing; Sales. **Positions commonly filled include:** Accountant/Auditor; Administrative Manager; Aerospace Engineer; Attorney; Branch Manager; Electrical/Electronics Engineer; Financial Analyst; General Manager; Industrial Engineer; Management Analyst/Consultant; Software Engineer; Systems Analyst. **Number of placements per year:** 1 - 49.

ROBBINS & SCOTT EXECUTIVE SEARCH
48 Woodward Avenue, Sausalito CA 94965. **Contact:** Manager. **Description:** An executive search firm. **Specializes in the areas of:** Technical.

THE ROGAN GROUP
2900 Bristol Street, Suite H-204, Costa Mesa CA 92626. 714/546-2206. **Fax:** 714/546-1005. **Contact:** Daniel Rogan, Owner. **Description:** An executive search firm. Company pays fee. **Specializes in the areas of:** Insurance. **Positions commonly filled include:** Claim Representative; Insurance Agent/Broker; MIS Specialist; Underwriter/Assistant Underwriter. **Number of placements per year:** 1 - 49.

ROLLINS & ASSOCIATES PERSONNEL SERVICE, INC.
4010 Watson Plaza Drive, Suite 105, Lakewood CA 90712. 562/421-6649. **Contact:** Joan Rollins, President. **Description:** An executive search firm. **Specializes in the areas of:** Import/Export. **Number of placements per year:** 100 - 199.

R. ROLLO ASSOCIATES
725 South Figueroa Street, Suite 3230, Los Angeles CA 90017. 213/688-9444. **Fax:** 213/688-8358. **Contact:** Manager. **Description:** An executive search firm that places personnel in a variety of industries.

ROMAC INTERNATIONAL
101 Metro Drive, Suite 680, San Jose CA 95110. 408/437-2440. **Fax:** 408/437-7534. **Contact:** Manager. **Description:** An executive search firm. **Specializes in the areas of:** Accounting/Auditing; Finance.

ROMAC INTERNATIONAL
3 Lagoon Drive, Redwood City CA 94065. 650/596-1850. **Contact:** Manager. **Description:** An executive search firm. **Specializes in the areas of:** Accounting/Auditing; Finance.

ROMAC INTERNATIONAL
180 Montgomery Street, Suite 1860, San Francisco CA 94104. 415/788-2815. **Contact:** Manager. **Description:** An executive search firm. **Specializes in the areas of:** Accounting/Auditing; Finance.

LARRY ROSENTHAL & ASSOCIATES
2333 Camino del Rio South, Suite 110, San Diego CA 92108. **Contact:** Manager. **Description:** An executive search firm. **Specializes in the areas of:** Computer Hardware/Software; Engineering.

ROWLAND ASSOCIATES
7840 Madison Avenue, Suite 185, Fair Oaks CA 95628. 916/961-3632. **Fax:** 916/962-2938. **Contact:** John R. Rowland, President. **Description:** An executive search firm. Company pays fee. **Specializes in the areas of:** Accounting/Auditing; Architecture/Construction; Banking; Computer Hardware/Software; Engineering; Finance; Manufacturing; Technical. **Positions commonly filled include:** Accountant/Auditor; Architect; Biomedical Engineer; Chemical Engineer; Civil Engineer; Computer Programmer; Electrical/Electronics Engineer; Industrial Engineer; Manufacturing Engineer; Mechanical Engineer; MIS Specialist; Quality Control Supervisor; Software Engineer; Systems Analyst. **Corporate headquarters location:** This Location. **Number of placements per year:** 1 - 49.

ROYAL STAFFING SERVICES
P.O. Box 57528, Sherman Oaks CA 91423. 818/981-1080. **Physical address:** 14011 Ventura Boulevard, Sherman Oaks. **Fax:** 818/981-1338. **Contact:** Rosemarie Wolff, President. **Description:** An executive search firm. **Specializes in the areas of:** Accounting/Auditing; Administration; Advertising; Computer Hardware/Software; Economics; Engineering; Finance; Food Industry; Legal; Manufacturing; Nonprofit; Personnel/Labor Relations; Publishing; Sales; Secretarial; Technical. **Positions commonly filled include:** Accountant/Auditor; Aerospace Engineer; Claim Representative; Clerical Supervisor; Computer Programmer; Design Engineer; Draftsperson; Electrical/Electronics Engineer; Financial Analyst; Health Services Manager; Internet Services Manager; Manufacturer's/Wholesaler's Sales Rep.;

Medical Records Technician; MIS Specialist; Paralegal; Property and Real Estate Manager; Purchasing Agent/Manager; Quality Control Supervisor; Services Sales Representative; Technical Writer/Editor; Telecommunications Manager; Underwriter/Assistant Underwriter. **Benefits available to temporary workers:** Bonus Award/Plan; Medical Insurance; Paid Holidays. **Corporate headquarters location:** This Location. **Number of placements per year:** 50 - 99.

RUSSELL REYNOLDS ASSOCIATES, INC.
333 South Grand Avenue, Suite 3500, Los Angeles CA 90071. 213/489-1520. **Contact:** Manager. **Description:** A generalist executive search firm.

RYAN, MILLER & ASSOCIATES
4601 Wilshire Boulevard, Suite 225, Los Angeles CA 90010. 213/938-4768. **Contact:** Lee Ryan, Partner. **Description:** An executive search firm. **Specializes in the areas of:** Accounting/Auditing; Banking; Finance; Investment; Real Estate. **Number of placements per year:** 100 - 199.

RYAN, MILLER & ASSOCIATES
790 East Colorado Boulevard, Suite 506, Pasadena CA 91101-2113. 626/568-3100. **Fax:** 626/568-3772. **Contact:** Roger Miller, Partner. **E-mail address:** rma11@aol.com. **Description:** An executive search firm specializing in the recruitment and placement of financial professionals. The firm represents the investment banking, investment management, and commercial banking industries and works with entrepreneurial companies placing CFO and treasury positions throughout the United States. **Specializes in the areas of:** Banking; Finance; Personnel/Labor Relations. **Positions commonly filled include:** Accountant/Auditor; Bank Officer/Manager; Budget Analyst; Financial Analyst; Internet Services Manager; Securities Sales Representative. **Average salary range of placements:** More than $50,000. **Number of placements per year:** 100 - 199.

SAI (SLOAN ASSOCIATES INC.)
2855 Mitchell Drive, Suite 117, Walnut Creek CA 94598. 510/932-3000. **Fax:** 510/932-3857. **Contact:** Steve Sloan, President. **Description:** An executive search firm. Company pays fee. **Specializes in the areas of:** Computer Science/Software. **Positions commonly filled include:** Branch Manager; Systems Analyst. **Number of placements per year:** 50 - 99.

SMC GROUP
26772 Vista Terrace, Lake Forest CA 92630-8110. 714/855-4545. **Contact:** Shala Shashani, President. **E-mail address:** hshm59a@prodigy.com. **Description:** An executive search firm focusing on the placement of LAN/WAN professionals. Company pays fee. **Specializes in the areas of:** Computer Hardware/Software. **Positions commonly filled include:** MIS Manager; Software Engineer; Telecommunications Manager. **Number of placements per year:** 50 - 99.

S.R. & ASSOCIATES
5001 Birch Street, Newport Beach CA 92660. 714/756-3271. **Fax:** 714/640-7268. **Contact:** Steve Ross, President. **Description:** An executive search firm that also develops and markets software applications for recruiting industries. Company pays fee. **Specializes in the areas of:** Accounting/Auditing; Computer Science/Software; Sales. **Positions commonly filled include:** Accountant/Auditor; Computer Programmer; Credit Manager; Human Resources Manager; Management Analyst/Consultant; Manufacturer's/Wholesaler's Sales Rep.; Services Sales Representative; Systems Analyst. **Average salary range of placements:** More than $50,000. **Number of placements per year:** 50 - 99.

PENNI SAFFORD & ASSOCIATES
6939 Sunrise Boulevard, Suite 119, Citrus Heights CA 95610. 916/723-5939. **Contact:** Manager. **Description:** An executive search firm. **Specializes in the areas of:** Computer Hardware/Software. **Positions commonly filled include:** Database Manager; Software Engineer.

SAGE TECHNOLOGIES
5190 Harwood Road, San Jose CA 95124-5707. **Contact:** Mitch Leavey, Manager. **Description:** An executive search firm. Company pays fee. **Specializes in the areas of:** Biology; Biotechnology; Pharmaceutical. **Positions commonly filled include:** Biochemist; Biological Scientist; Biomedical Engineer; Chemical Engineer; Chemist; Software Engineer. **Number of placements per year:** 50 - 99.

SALES CONSULTANTS
100 Corporate Pointe, Suite 380, Culver City CA 90230. 310/670-3040. **Fax:** 310/670-2981. **Contact:** Michael Bryant, Branch Manager. **Description:** An executive search firm that focuses on placing sales and sales management personnel, as well as marketing and marketing management. Company pays fee. **Specializes in the areas of:** Sales. **Positions commonly filled include:** Biomedical Engineer; Branch Manager; Electrical/Electronics Engineer; Environmental Engineer; Manufacturer's/Wholesaler's Sales Rep.; Restaurant/Food Service Manager; Software Engineer. **Average salary range of placements:** $30,000 - $50,000. **Number of placements per year:** 100 - 199.

SALES CONSULTANTS OF MODESTO
1101 Sylvan Avenue, Building B, Suite B20, Modesto CA 95350. 209/529-5051. **Fax:** 209/529-5054. **Contact:** Jim Ortman, Owner. **Description:** An executive search firm. Company pays fee. **Specializes in the areas of:** Engineering; Food Industry; Industrial; Manufacturing; Sales; Technical. **Positions commonly filled include:** Biological Scientist; Chemist; Electrical/Electronics Engineer; Food Scientist/Technologist; Industrial Engineer; Wastewater Specialist. **Other U.S. locations:** Nationwide. **Average salary range of placements:** More than $50,000. **Number of placements per year:** 50 - 99.

SALES CONSULTANTS OF SACRAMENTO
4320 Auburn Boulevard, Suite 2100, Sacramento CA 95841. 916/481-7000. **Fax:** 916/481-7099. **Contact:** Ron Whitney, Manager. **E-mail address:** mriscisac@worldnet.att.net. **Description:** An executive search firm operating on both a retainer and contingency basis. **Specializes in the areas of:** Computer Science/Software; Engineering; Industrial; Sales; Technical. **Positions commonly filled include:** Marketing Manager; Marketing Specialist; Sales Engineer; Sales Executive; Sales Manager; Sales Representative. **Other U.S. locations:** Nationwide. **International locations:** Worldwide. **Average salary range of placements:** More than $50,000. **Number of placements per year:** 50 - 99.

SALES PROFESSIONALS PERSONNEL SERVICES
595 Market Street, Suite 2500, San Francisco CA 94105. 415/543-2828. **Contact:** Sheldon Israel, President. **World Wide Web address:** http://www.hamster.org/salespro.html. **Description:** An executive search firm. **Specializes in the areas of:** Sales. **Positions commonly filled include:** Manufacturer's/Wholesaler's Sales Rep.; Marketing Manager; Sales Manager; Services Sales Representative.

SAMPSON MEDICAL SEARCH
22330 Hawthorne Boulevard, Suite 207, Torrance CA 90505. 310/791-1744. **Fax:** 310/791-0684. **Contact:** Judie Sampson, President. **E-mail address:**

sampsonmed@aol.com. **World Wide Web address:** http://www.sampsonmed.com. **Description:** An executive search firm operating on a contingency basis. Company pays fee. **Specializes in the areas of:** Biotechnology; Clinical Research; Health/Medical; Information Systems; Information Technology; Pharmaceutical; Regulatory Affairs. **Positions commonly filled include:** Chief Executive Officer; Clinical Applications Specialist; Computer Programmer; Human Resources Manager; Medical Records Technician; MIS Specialist; Product Manager; Project Manager; Sales Executive; Sales Manager; Sales Representative; Statistician. **Average salary range of placements:** More than $50,000. **Number of placements per year:** 100 - 199.

SANFORD ROSE ASSOCIATES
580 Broadway, Suite 226, Laguna Beach CA 92651. 714/497-5728. **Fax:** 714/497-4086. **Contact:** Bob Dudley, President. **E-mail address:** caorange@aol.com. **World Wide Web address:** http://www.sanfordrose.com. **Description:** An executive search firm focusing on information services. Company pays fee. **Specializes in the areas of:** Computer Science/Software. **Positions commonly filled include:** Computer Programmer; Electrical/Electronics Engineer; MIS Specialist; Purchasing Agent/Manager; Software Engineer; Systems Analyst. **Average salary range of placements:** More than $50,000. **Number of placements per year:** 1 - 49.

SANFORD ROSE ASSOCIATES
13032 St. Thomas Drive, Santa Ana CA 92705. 714/730-5396. **Contact:** Office Manager. **World Wide Web address:** http://www.sanfordrose.com. **Description:** An executive search firm for the semiconductor industry. **Specializes in the areas of:** Electronics.

SANFORD ROSE ASSOCIATES
9471 Florence Circle, Villa Park CA 92861. 714/998-4290. **Contact:** Manager. **World Wide Web address:** http://www.sanfordrose.com. **Description:** An executive search firm for the semiconductor industry. **Specializes in the areas of:** Electronics.

SANFORD ROSE ASSOCIATES
748 Dos Hermanos Road, Santa Barbara CA 93111. 805/966-1846. **Fax:** 805/966-0127. **Contact:** Manager. **World Wide Web address:** http://www.sanfordrose.com. **Description:** An executive search firm. **Specializes in the areas of:** Engineering; High-Tech.

SANFORD ROSE ASSOCIATES
753 East El Camino Real, Suite A, Sunnyvale CA 94087. 408/730-5833. **Fax:** 408/730-5717. **Contact:** Manager. **E-mail address:** sra@ix.netcom.com. **World Wide Web address:** http://www.sanfordrose.com. **Description:** An executive search firm. **Specializes in the areas of:** Data Processing; Engineering; Human Resources.

SANFORD ROSE ASSOCIATES
7919 Pebble Beach Drive, Suite 209, Citrus Heights CA 95610. 916/864-4888. **Fax:** 916/864-4884. **Contact:** Manager. **World Wide Web address:** http://www.sanfordrose.com. **Description:** An executive search firm. **Specializes in the areas of:** Publishing.

SARVER & CARRUTH ASSOCIATES
P.O. Box 1967, Buellton CA 93427-1967. 805/686-4425. **Fax:** 805/686-5941. **Contact:** Catherine Sarver, Principal. **E-mail address:** csarver@silcom.com. **Description:** An executive search firm operating on a contingency basis, specializing in the semiconductor and computer head and disk industries. Company pays fee. **Specializes in the areas of:** Engineering; Scientific; Technical. **Positions commonly filled include:** Design Engineer; Electrical/Electronics Engineer; Manufacturing Engineer; Mechanical Engineer; Systems Analyst. **Corporate headquarters location:** This Location. **Average salary range of placements:** More than $50,000. **Number of placements per year:** 1 - 49.

SASIS CORPORATION
476 B Street, P.O. Box 500, Biggs CA 95917. 530/868-1226. **Toll-free phone:** 800/336-1226. **Fax:** 530/868-1827. **Contact:** Russ Curtis, Chief Information Officer. **E-mail address:** sasis@cncnet.com. **World Wide Web address:** http://www.sasis.com. **Description:** An executive search firm. Company pays fee. **Specializes in the areas of:** Administration; Advertising; Personnel/Labor Relations. **Positions commonly filled include:** Accountant/Auditor; Administrative Manager; Agricultural Engineer; Biochemist; Biomedical Engineer; Budget Analyst; Chemical Engineer; Civil Engineer; Computer Programmer; Electrician; Environmental Engineer; Financial Analyst; Food Scientist/Technologist; Health Services Manager; Internet Services Manager; Management Analyst/Consultant; Operations/Production Manager; Quality Control Supervisor; Radiological Technologist; Registered Nurse; Software Engineer; Stationary Engineer; Surgical Technician; Systems Analyst; Technical Writer/Editor; Urban/Regional Planner; Video Production Coordinator. **Number of placements per year:** 200 - 499.

SCHLATTER & ASSOCIATES
388 Market Street, Suite 500, San Francisco CA 94111. 415/433-8100. **Fax:** 415/421-4176. **Contact:** Craig Schlatter, President. **Description:** An executive search firm. **Specializes in the areas of:** Accounting/Auditing; Finance; MIS/EDP. **Positions commonly filled include:** Accountant/Auditor; Budget Analyst; Chief Financial Officer; Controller; Finance Director; Financial Analyst; Management Analyst/Consultant. **Number of placements per year:** 100 - 199.

AVERY SCHLUETER EXECUTIVE SEARCH
2 Annabel Lane, Suite 260, San Ramon CA 94583. 510/866-8660. **Contact:** Manager. **Description:** An executive search firm that concentrates on the placement of sales professionals in the food processing and packaging machinery industries. **Specializes in the areas of:** Food Industry.

SCOTT-THALER ASSOCIATES, INC.
86 Brookhollow Drive, Santa Ana CA 92705. 714/966-1671. **Fax:** 714/755-7101. **Contact:** Brian D. Thaler, President. **Description:** An executive search firm. **Specializes in the areas of:** Fashion; Logistics; Manufacturing; Retail; Transportation. **Positions commonly filled include:** Buyer; Industrial Engineer; Operations/Production Manager; Purchasing Agent/Manager; Wholesale and Retail Buyer. **Number of placements per year:** 100 - 199.

THE SEARCH GROUP
1328 Sierra Alta Way, Los Angeles CA 90069. 310/550-0292. **Contact:** Manager. **E-mail address:** yardenak@aol.com. **World Wide Web address:** http://www.jobsearch4you.com. **Description:** An executive search firm. **Specializes in the areas of:** Engineering.

THE SEARCH NETWORK
5755 Oberlin Drive, Suite 312, San Diego CA 92121. 619/535-0015. **Fax:** 619/535-0152. **Recorded jobline:** 619/535-8937. **Contact:** Traci Arosta, Manager. **E-mail address:** snetsd@aol.com. **Description:** An

executive search firm that focuses on the placement of high-tech engineering, operations, and mechanical manufacturing professionals. Company pays fee. **Specializes in the areas of:** Engineering; Manufacturing. **Positions commonly filled include:** Design Engineer; Electrical/Electronics Engineer; Internet Services Manager; Mechanical Engineer; MIS Specialist; Multimedia Designer; Nuclear Engineer; Software Engineer. **Average salary range of placements:** More than $50,000. **Number of placements per year:** 50 - 99.

SEARCH WEST
2049 Century Park East, Suite 650, Los Angeles CA 90067. 310/284-8888. **Contact:** General Manager. **Description:** An executive search firm. Company pays fee. **Specializes in the areas of:** Accounting/Auditing; Advertising; Banking; Computer Hardware/Software; Engineering; Finance; Food Industry; Health/Medical; Insurance; MIS/EDP; Real Estate; Sales; Technical. **Positions commonly filled include:** Accountant/Auditor; Administrative Assistant; Aerospace Engineer; Bank Officer/Manager; Biomedical Engineer; Bookkeeper; Chemical Engineer; Civil Engineer; Computer Operator; Computer Programmer; Credit Manager; Customer Service Representative; Draftsperson; Economist; EDP Specialist; Electrical/Electronics Engineer; Financial Analyst; Hotel Manager; Human Resources Manager; Industrial Designer; Industrial Engineer; Insurance Agent/Broker; Marketing Specialist; Nurse; Operations/Production Manager; Purchasing Agent/Manager; Quality Control Supervisor; Sales Representative; Systems Analyst; Technician; Underwriter/Assistant Underwriter. **Number of placements per year:** 1000+.

SEARCH WEST OF ONTARIO
2151 Convention Center Way, Suite 121-B, Ontario CA 91764. 909/937-0100. **Contact:** Nate Reddicks, General Manager. **Description:** An executive search firm. Company pays fee. **Specializes in the areas of:** Accounting/Auditing; Architecture/Construction; Banking; Computer Hardware/Software; Construction; Engineering; Finance; Food Industry; Health/Medical; Insurance; Manufacturing; Personnel/Labor Relations; Publishing; Sales; Technical. **Positions commonly filled include:** Accountant/Auditor; Actuary; Architect; Attorney; Bank Officer/Manager; Biological Scientist; Biomedical Engineer; Buyer; Chemical Engineer; Chemist; Computer Programmer; Draftsperson; Electrical/Electronics Engineer; Financial Analyst; Food Scientist/Technologist; Industrial Designer; Marketing Specialist; Mechanical Engineer; Metallurgical Engineer; MIS Specialist; Petroleum Engineer; Quality Control Supervisor; Sales Representative; Systems Analyst; Technical Writer/Editor; Underwriter/Assistant Underwriter. **Number of placements per year:** 1000+.

SEITCHIK, CORWIN AND SEITCHIK, INC.
3443 Clay Street, San Francisco CA 94118-2008. 415/928-5717. **Contact:** Bill Seitchik, Vice President. **Description:** An executive search firm. **Specializes in the areas of:** Fashion; Manufacturing.

SELTZER FONTAINE BECKWITH
2999 Overland Avenue, Suite 203, Los Angeles CA 90064-4243. 310/839-6000. **Fax:** 310/839-4408. **Contact:** Valerie A. Fontaine, Partner. **E-mail address:** sfbsearch@aol.com. **World Wide Web address:** http://www.sfbsearch.com. **Description:** An executive search firm that places attorneys. The firm operates on both retainer and contingency bases. Company pays fee. **Specializes in the areas of:** Legal. **Positions commonly filled include:** Attorney. **Number of placements per year:** 1 - 49.

THE SEPTEMBER GROUP, INC.
11611 San Vincente Boulevard, Suite 840, Los Angeles CA 90049. 310/207-0444. **Fax:** 310/826-2023. **Contact:** President. **E-mail address:** resumes@septembergroup.com. **Description:** A retained search firm. Company pays fee. **Specializes in the areas of:** Banking; Finance. **Positions commonly filled include:** Bank Officer/Manager; Chief Financial Officer; Economist; Finance Director; Financial Analyst; Fund Manager; Human Resources Manager. **Other U.S. locations:** New York NY; San Francisco CA. **International locations:** London, England; Mexico City, Mexico. **Average salary range of placements:** More than $50,000. **Number of placements per year:** 1 - 49.

SHARP PERSONNEL & SEARCH
1665 East 4th Street, Suite 204, Santa Ana CA 92701. 714/667-6909. **Fax:** 714/667-2916. **Contact:** Manager. **Description:** An executive search firm that also provides temporary placement. Company pays fee. **Specializes in the areas of:** Accounting/Auditing; Banking; Computer Science/Software; Finance; Health/Medical; Insurance; Personnel/Labor Relations; Secretarial. **Positions commonly filled include:** Accountant/Auditor; Bank Officer/Manager; Financial Analyst; Human Resources Manager; Software Engineer; Systems Analyst; Underwriter/Assistant Underwriter. **Benefits available to temporary workers:** Credit Union; Dental Insurance; Paid Holidays; Paid Vacation. **Average salary range of placements:** $30,000 - $50,000. **Number of placements per year:** 100 - 199.

PEGGY SHEA & ASSOCIATES
2660 Town's Gate Road, Suite 800, Westlake Village CA 91361. 818/889-5350. **Contact:** Peggy Shea. **Description:** An executive search firm.

J.W. SILVERIA & COMPANY
1058 Cass Street, Suite A, Monterey CA 93940. **Contact:** James Silveria, Owner. **Description:** An executive search firm. Company pays fee. **Positions commonly filled include:** Accountant/Auditor; Administrative Manager; Agricultural Engineer; Architect; Attorney; Bank Officer/Manager; Biochemist; Branch Manager; Budget Analyst; Buyer; Chemical Engineer; Computer Programmer; Design Engineer; Financial Analyst; Health Services Manager; MIS Specialist; Software Engineer; Systems Analyst. **Average salary range of placements:** $30,000 - $50,000. **Number of placements per year:** 1 - 49.

SINGER STROUSE
1865 California Street, San Francisco CA 94109-4541. 415/781-6444. **Contact:** Pamela Singer, Owner. **Description:** An executive search firm operating on both retained and contingency bases for *Fortune* 500 companies in California. Company pays fee. **Specializes in the areas of:** Accounting/Auditing; Legal; Tax. **Positions commonly filled include:** Accountant; Attorney. **Average salary range of placements:** More than $50,000. **Number of placements per year:** 1 - 49.

CHARLES A. SKORINA & COMPANY
P.O. Box 22556, Carmel CA 93922. 408/624-2330. **Contact:** Charles Skorina, Owner. **Description:** An executive search firm serving financial companies on Wall Street. **Specializes in the areas of:** Finance; High-Tech.

SOURCE SERVICES CORPORATION
879 West 190th Street, Suite 300, Los Angeles CA 90248. 310/323-0808. **Fax:** 310/323-1101. **Contact:** Manager. **Description:** An executive search firm. The divisions at this location include Source EDP, Source Finance, and Accountant Source Temps. **Specializes in**

the areas of: Accounting/Auditing; Computer Hardware/Software; Finance; Information Technology.

SOURCE SERVICES CORPORATION
One Park Plaza, Suite 560, Irvine CA 92614. 714/553-8115. **Fax:** 714/660-1858. **Contact:** Manager. **Description:** An executive search firm. The divisions at this location include Source Consulting, Source EDP, and Source Finance. **Specializes in the areas of:** Computer Hardware/Software; Finance; Information Technology.

SOURCE SERVICES CORPORATION
4510 Executive Drive, Suite 200, San Diego CA 92121. 619/552-0300. **Fax:** 619/452-7011. **Contact:** Manager. **Description:** An executive search firm. The divisions at this location include Source Consulting, Source EDP, Source Engineering, Source Finance, and Accountant Source Temps. **Specializes in the areas of:** Accounting/Auditing; Computer Hardware/Software; Engineering; Finance; Information Technology.

SOURCE SERVICES CORPORATION
425 California Street, Suite 1200, San Francisco CA 94104. 415/434-2410. **Fax:** 415/956-3876. **Contact:** Manager. **Description:** An executive search firm. The divisions at this location include Source EDP, Source Finance, Source Legal, and Accountant Source Temps. **Specializes in the areas of:** Accounting/Auditing; Computer Hardware/Software; Finance; Information Technology; Legal.

SOUTHWEST SEARCH ASSOCIATES
10226 Buena Vista Avenue, Santee CA 92071. 619/562-1103. **Fax:** 619/562-1104. **Contact:** Linda Shaw, Owner. **E-mail address:** shawsearch@msn.com. **Description:** An executive search firm operating on both retainer and contingency bases. **Specializes in the areas of:** Engineering. **Positions commonly filled include:** Chemical Engineer; Design Engineer; Electrical/Electronics Engineer; Environmental Engineer; General Manager; Industrial Engineer; Manufacturing Engineer; Marketing Manager; Marketing Specialist; Mechanical Engineer; MIS Specialist; Product Manager; Project Manager; Quality Control Supervisor; Sales Engineer; Sales Representative; Systems Manager. **Average salary range of placements:** More than $50,000. **Number of placements per year:** 1 - 49.

SPECTRAWEST
39899 Balentine Drive, Suite 218, Newark CA 94560. 510/490-4500. **Fax:** 510/490-6877. **Contact:** Fred Arredondo, Director. **Description:** An executive search firm that places hardware design and software engineers. Clients are predominantly located in the San Francisco Bay Area. Company pays fee. **Specializes in the areas of:** Computer Science/Software; Engineering. **Positions commonly filled include:** Chemical Engineer; Design Engineer; Electrical/Electronics Engineer; Software Engineer. **Average salary range of placements:** More than $50,000. **Number of placements per year:** 1 - 49.

SPECTRUM SEARCH ASSOCIATES, INC.
60 East Highland Avenue, Sierra Madre CA 91024. 213/256-4564. **Contact:** Joe Florence, Employment. **Description:** An executive search firm. Company pays fee. **Specializes in the areas of:** Sales; Telecommunications. **Positions commonly filled include:** Marketing Specialist; Sales Representative. **Number of placements per year:** 1 - 49.

SPLAINE & ASSOCIATES INC.
15951 Los Gatos Boulevard, Los Gatos CA 95032-3488. 408/354-3664. **Fax:** 408/356-6329. **Contact:** Charles Splaine, President. **E-mail address:** cs@exec-search.com. **World Wide Web address:** http://www.exec-search.com. **Description:** An executive search firm. Company pays fee. **Specializes in the areas of:** Computer Hardware/Software; Data Communications; Electronics. **Average salary range of placements:** More than $50,000. **Number of placements per year:** 1 - 49.

M.H. SPRINGER & ASSOCIATES
5855 Topanga Canyon Boulevard, Suite 230, Woodland Hills CA 91367. 818/710-8955. **Contact:** Manager. **Description:** An executive search firm. **Specializes in the areas of:** Finance.

STAFF SEEKERS
18062 Irvine Boulevard, Suite 105, Tustin CA 92780. 714/730-0593. **Fax:** 714/730-3585. **Contact:** Manager. **Description:** An executive search firm that primarily places dental and medical office support staff on retainer and contingency bases. Company pays fee. **Specializes in the areas of:** Health/Medical. **Positions commonly filled include:** Dental Assistant/Dental Hygienist; Licensed Practical Nurse; Medical Assistant; Medical Records Technician; Office Manager. **Average salary range of placements:** $30,000 - $50,000. **Number of placements per year:** 200 - 499.

STEINBRUN, HUGHES AND ASSOCIATES
10940 Wilshire Boulevard, Suite 1600, Los Angeles CA 90024. 310/443-4222. **Fax:** 310/443-4223. **Contact:** Manager. **Description:** An executive search firm operating on a retained basis. Company pays fee. **Specializes in the areas of:** Accounting/Auditing; Administration; Banking; Finance; Food Industry; General Management; Personnel/Labor Relations; Sales. **Positions commonly filled include:** Accountant/Auditor; Budget Analyst; Chief Financial Officer; Controller; Financial Analyst; Fund Manager; Management Analyst/Consultant; Market Research Analyst; MIS Specialist; Operations Manager; Project Manager; Strategy Consultant; Systems Analyst. **Average salary range of placements:** More than $50,000. **Number of placements per year:** 50 - 99.

ADELE STEINMETZ
711 Colorado Avenue, Suite 4, Palo Alto CA 94303. 650/321-3723. **Fax:** 650/321-3703. **Contact:** Adele Steinmetz, Owner. **E-mail address:** astnmetz @ix.netcom. **Description:** An executive search firm. Company pays fee. **Specializes in the areas of:** Computer Science/Software; Engineering; Light Industrial; Manufacturing; Sales; Technical. **Positions commonly filled include:** Chemical Engineer; Chemist; Computer Programmer; Design Engineer; Designer; Draftsperson; Electrical/Electronics Engineer; Environmental Engineer; General Manager; Industrial Engineer; Mathematician; MIS Manager; Operations/Production Manager; Science Technologist; Software Engineer; Systems Analyst; Telecommunications Manager. **Average salary range of placements:** More than $50,000. **Number of placements per year:** 1 - 49.

STONE & ASSOCIATES
10850 Wilshire Boulevard, Suite 800, Los Angeles CA 90024. 310/475-7433. **Contact:** Manager. **Description:** An executive search firm. **Specializes in the areas of:** Insurance.

SUPERIOR SDC
4690 Old Ironside Drive, Suite 450, Santa Clara CA 95054. 408/748-1652. **Contact:** Manager. **Description:** An executive search firm. Superior SDC has divisions at this location that specialize in engineering and computer positions, as well as a division that provides temporary placements.

SYSTEMS CAREERS
211 Sutter Street, Suite 607, San Francisco CA 94108. 415/434-4770. **Contact:** Wayne Sarchett, Principal. **Description:** An executive search firm operating on a contingency basis. Company pays fee. **Specializes in the areas of:** Computer Hardware/Software. **Positions commonly filled include:** Computer Programmer; EDP Specialist; Industrial Engineer; Management Analyst/Consultant; Software Engineer. **Average salary range of placements:** More than $50,000. **Number of placements per year:** 1 - 49.

SYSTEMS RESEARCH GROUP
162 South Rancho Santa Fe Road, Suite B80, Encinitas CA 92024. 760/436-1575. **Fax:** 760/634-3614. **Contact:** Stephen Gebler, President. **World Wide Web address:** http://www.webler.com/srg. **Description:** An executive search firm concentrating on the placement of CAD/CAM/CAE, rapid prototyping, product data management, and computer graphics personnel. Company pays fee. **Specializes in the areas of:** Administration; Computer Science/Software; Engineering; Sales; Technical. **Positions commonly filled include:** Computer Programmer; Design Engineer; Designer; Draftsperson; Electrical/Electronics Engineer; Geographer; Mechanical Engineer; Science Technologist; Software Engineer; Strategic Relations Manager; Systems Analyst. **Average salary range of placements:** More than $50,000. **Number of placements per year:** 50 - 99.

TAX EXECUTIVE SEARCH, INC.
842 South Orange Grove Boulevard, Pasadena CA 91105-1742. 818/403-1522. **Fax:** 818/799-0069. **Contact:** Charles Heil, Principal Recruiter. **Description:** An executive search firm focusing on the placement of tax accountants, tax attorneys, appraisers, and business valuation financial consultants. Company pays fee. **Specializes in the areas of:** Accounting/Auditing; Appraisal; Economics; Finance; Legal; Professional; Sales; Tax; Technical; Valuation. **Positions commonly filled include:** Attorney; Economist; Mathematician; Securities Sales Representative; Services Sales Representative. **Corporate headquarters location:** Pasadena CA. **Number of placements per year:** 1 - 49.

TECHKNOWLEDGE
7700 Irvine Center Drive, Suite 800, Irvine CA 92618. 714/453-1533. **Fax:** 714/456-8323. **Contact:** John Wallin, CEO/Recruiter. **E-mail address:** search@techknowledge.com. **World Wide Web address:** http://www.techknowledge.com. **Description:** A retained executive search firm. Company pays fee. **Specializes in the areas of:** Computer Science/Software; General Management. **Positions commonly filled include:** General Manager; Management Analyst/Consultant; MIS Specialist; Software Engineer. **Average salary range of placements:** More than $50,000. **Number of placements per year:** 1 - 49.

TECHNICAL SEARCH CONSULTANTS
32732 Johnathan Circle, Dana Point CA 92629. 714/493-5488. **Contact:** Manager. **Description:** An executive search firm that focuses on high-tech placements. **Specializes in the areas of:** Computer Science/Software; Electronics; Engineering.

TECHNIQUEST
55 South Market Street, Suite 1001, San Jose CA 95113. 408/293-1122. **Fax:** 408/293-1223. **Contact:** Claudia Lindquist, General Manager. **E-mail address:** c1quest@aol.com. **Description:** An executive search firm focusing on recruitment in biotechnology, medical devices, instrumentation, and electronics industries. Company pays fee. **Specializes in the areas of:** Biology; Engineering. **Positions commonly filled include:** Biochemist; Biological Scientist; Biomedical Engineer; Design Engineer; Electrical/Electronics Engineer; Mechanical Engineer; Metallurgical Engineer; Quality Control Supervisor; Science Technologist; Software Engineer. **Average salary range of placements:** More than $50,000. **Number of placements per year:** 50 - 99.

TECHSTAFF WEST INC.
1200 West Hillcrest Drive, Suite 201, Thousand Oaks CA 91320-2734. 805/376-2250. **Contact:** Sue Duffy, Recruiter. **Description:** An executive search firm. Company pays fee. **Specializes in the areas of:** Technical. **Positions commonly filled include:** Aerospace Engineer; Aircraft Mechanic/Engine Specialist; Biochemist; Biological Scientist; Biomedical Engineer; Chemist; Civil Engineer; Computer Programmer; Draftsperson; Electrical/Electronics Engineer; Environmental Engineer; Industrial Engineer; Internet Services Manager; Mechanical Engineer; Metallurgical Engineer; MIS Specialist; Multimedia Designer; Nuclear Engineer; Software Engineer; Systems Analyst; Technical Writer/Editor; Telecommunications Manager. **Corporate headquarters location:** Milwaukee WI. **Average salary range of placements:** More than $50,000. **Number of placements per year:** 200 - 499.

TELEFORCE INTERNATIONAL
P.O. Box 3175, San Clemente CA 92674-3175. 714/661-3337. **Fax:** 714/661-6965. **Contact:** Joseph Barrigas, President. **Description:** An executive search firm specializing in permanent and leased employee placements in the telecommunications industry. Teleforce International operates on both retainer and contingency bases. Company pays fee. **Specializes in the areas of:** Accounting/Auditing; Administration; Computer Science/Software; Engineering; Finance; General Management; Personnel/Labor Relations; Sales; Telecommunications. **Positions commonly filled include:** Accountant/Auditor; Broadcast Technician; Computer Programmer; Customer Service Representative; Electrical/Electronics Engineer; Financial Analyst; Internet Services Manager; Management Analyst/Consultant; MIS Specialist; Systems Analyst; Telecommunications Manager. **Number of placements per year:** 1 - 49.

TELFORD, ADAMS, & ALEXANDER
402 West Broadway, Suite 900, San Diego CA 92101-3542. 619/238-5686. **Fax:** 619/687-0002. **Contact:** John T. Alexander, Managing Principal. **E-mail address:** jahrstaa@aol.com. **Description:** An executive search firm serving the financial services, accounting, real estate, and electronics industries. **Specializes in the areas of:** Accounting/Auditing; Banking; Computer Science/Software; Finance; General Management; Health/Medical; Insurance; Manufacturing; Personnel/Labor Relations; Retail; Sales. **Positions commonly filled include:** General Manager; Health Services Manager; Human Resources Manager. **Other area locations:** Costa Mesa CA; San Francisco CA. **Average salary range of placements:** More than $50,000. **Number of placements per year:** 50 - 99.

TELFORD, ADAMS, & ALEXANDER
455 Market Street, Suite 1910, San Francisco CA 94105. 415/546-4150. **Fax:** 415/882-3232. **Contact:** Jeffrey C. Adams, Managing Principal. **E-mail address:** jefadams@concentric.net. **Description:** An executive search firm. **Other area locations:** Costa Mesa CA; San Diego CA. **Average salary range of placements:** More than $50,000. **Number of placements per year:** 50 - 99.

TELFORD, ADAMS, & ALEXANDER
650 Town Center Drive, Suite 850, Costa Mesa CA 92626. 714/850-4354. **Fax:** 714/850-4488. **Contact:** John H. Telford, Jr., Managing Principal. **Description:** An executive search firm. **Other area locations:** San Diego CA; San Francisco CA. **Average salary range of placements:** More than $50,000. **Number of placements per year:** 50 - 99.

JUDY THOMPSON & ASSOCIATES
3727 Camino Del Rio South, Suite 200, San Diego CA 92108-4005. 619/281-2626. **Fax:** 619/281-2671. **Contact:** Judy Thompson, President. **Description:** An executive search firm that recruits and places degreed, experienced accounting and financial professionals in permanent positions throughout San Diego County. The firm operates on a retainer and contingency basis. Company pays fee. **Specializes in the areas of:** Accounting/Auditing; Finance. **Positions commonly filled include:** Accountant/Auditor; Accounting Supervisor; Budget Analyst; Chief Financial Officer; Controller; Financial Analyst; Litigation Support Consultant; Vice President of Finance. **Average salary range of placements:** More than $50,000. **Number of placements per year:** 1 - 49.

THORNTON ASSOCIATES
2040 Avenue of the Stars, Los Angeles CA 90067-4703. 310/553-1773. **Fax:** 310/785-0810. **Contact:** Raphaelle Thornton, President. **Description:** A retainer and contingency search firm. Company pays fee. **Specializes in the areas of:** Health/Medical. **Positions commonly filled include:** Human Resources Manager; Registered Nurse. **Average salary range of placements:** More than $50,000. **Number of placements per year:** 1 - 49.

TOD STAFFING
690 Market Street, San Francisco CA 94104. 415/392-0700. **Fax:** 415/392-0752. **Contact:** Pat Hardy, Operations Manager. **E-mail address:** ronfrede@netcom.com. **Description:** An executive search firm. Company pays fee. **Specializes in the areas of:** Accounting/Auditing; Banking; Computer Science/Software; Finance; Insurance; Legal; Manufacturing; Personnel/Labor Relations; Sales; Secretarial. **Positions commonly filled include:** Accountant/Auditor; Administrative Manager; Bank Officer/Manager; Buyer; Claim Representative; Clerical Supervisor; Clinical Lab Technician; Computer Programmer; Counselor; Credit Manager; Customer Service Representative; Draftsperson; Financial Analyst; Human Resources Specialist; Internet Services Manager; Librarian; Market Research Analyst; Medical Records Technician; MIS Specialist; Multimedia Designer; Paralegal; Purchasing Agent/Manager; Quality Control Supervisor; Securities Sales Representative; Services Sales Representative; Software Engineer; Statistician; Systems Analyst; Technical Writer/Editor; Typist/Word Processor; Video Production Coordinator. **Average salary range of placements:** $30,000 - $50,000. **Number of placements per year:** 1000+.

TRIPLE-J SERVICES
1508 18th Street, Suite 302, Bakersfield CA 93301. 805/321-0695. **Fax:** 805/321-0882. **Contact:** Jack Jones, Vice President. **E-mail address:** quack@bak2.lightspeed.net. **Description:** An executive search firm. Company pays fee. **Specializes in the areas of:** Computer Science/Software; Engineering; Food Industry; Oil and Gas; Technical. **Positions commonly filled include:** Agricultural Engineer; Chemical Engineer; Civil Engineer; Computer Programmer; Cost Estimator; Design Engineer; Designer; Draftsperson; Electrical/Electronics Engineer; Environmental Engineer; Industrial Engineer; Mechanical Engineer; MIS Specialist; Petroleum Engineer; Software Engineer; Structural Engineer; Systems Analyst. **Average salary range of placements:** More than $50,000. **Number of placements per year:** 50 - 99.

TRUEX ASSOCIATES
332 Pine Street, 4th Floor, San Francisco CA 94105. 415/433-6222. **Fax:** 415/781-6607. **Contact:** Robert Behney, Manager. **E-mail address:** jobs@sterling-truex.com. **Description:** An executive search firm. Truex Associates also operates as a temporary and permanent employment agency. Company pays fee. **Specializes in the areas of:** Administration; Advertising; Architecture/Construction; Banking; Broadcasting; Finance; General Management; Insurance; Personnel/Labor Relations; Sales; Secretarial. **Positions commonly filled include:** Administrative Assistant; Administrative Manager; Advertising Clerk; Human Resources Manager; Secretary. **Benefits available to temporary workers:** Bonus Award/Plan; Medical Insurance; Paid Vacation. **Corporate headquarters location:** This Location. **Other area locations:** Newport Beach CA; Palo Alto CA; San Jose CA. **Average salary range of placements:** $30,000 - $50,000. **Number of placements per year:** 100 - 199.

UNISEARCH
790 The City Drive South, Suite 150, Orange CA 92868. 714/748-0700. **Fax:** 714/748-7234. **Contact:** James L. Rose, President. **Description:** An executive search firm. Company pays fee. **Specializes in the areas of:** Accounting/Auditing; Administration; Biology; Computer Science/Software; Engineering; Food Industry; Health/Medical; Insurance; Manufacturing; Metals; Plastics; Publishing; Sales; Telecommunications. **Positions commonly filled include:** Accountant/Auditor; Actuary; Biological Scientist; Chiropractor; Clinical Lab Technician; Computer Programmer; Dentist; Dietician/Nutritionist; EEG Technologist; EKG Technician; Emergency Medical Technician; Engineer; Financial Analyst; Food Scientist/Technologist; Health Services Manager; Licensed Practical Nurse; Medical Records Technician; Occupational Therapist; Operations/Production Manager; Pharmacist; Physical Therapist; Physician; Radiological Technologist; Recreational Therapist; Registered Nurse; Respiratory Therapist; Systems Analyst; Underwriter/Assistant Underwriter. **Average salary range of placements:** More than $50,000. **Number of placements per year:** 50 - 99.

UNITED STAFFING SOLUTIONS
P.O. Box 2018, Victorville CA 92392. 619/241-5250. **Toll-free phone:** 800/429-8503. **Fax:** 619/241-5901. **Contact:** Manager. **Description:** An executive search firm focusing on the placement of medical personnel. The firm also provides temporary placement. Company pays fee. **Specializes in the areas of:** Accounting/Auditing; Administration; Advertising; Banking; Biology; Computer Science/Software; Education; Engineering; Finance; Food Industry; General Management; Health/Medical; Industrial; Insurance; Manufacturing; Personnel/Labor Relations; Retail; Sales; Secretarial; Technical. **Positions commonly filled include:** Accountant/Auditor; Administrative Manager; Advertising Clerk; Aerospace Engineer; Architect; Attorney; Bank Officer/Manager; Biochemist; Branch Manager; Broadcast Technician; Chemical Engineer; Chemist; Civil Engineer; Claim Representative; Clinical Lab Technician; Computer Programmer; Customer Service Representative; Electrical/Electronics Engineer; Environmental Engineer; Financial Analyst; Food Scientist/Technologist; Health Services Manager; Industrial Engineer; Management Analyst/Consultant; Medical Records Technician; Multimedia Designer;

Operations/Production Manager; Paralegal; Pharmacist; Registered Nurse; Respiratory Therapist; Securities Sales Representative; Services Sales Representative; Social Worker; Sociologist; Structural Engineer; Systems Analyst; Technical Writer/Editor; Telecommunications Manager; Typist/Word Processor; Underwriter/Assistant Underwriter. **Benefits available to temporary workers:** Dental Insurance; Medical Insurance. **Corporate headquarters location:** This Location. **Other U.S. locations:** Nationwide. **Average salary range of placements:** $30,000 - $50,000. **Number of placements per year:** 1000+.

VALLEY WIDE EMPLOYMENT
2002 North Gateway Boulevard, Suite 118, Fresno CA 93727. 209/252-4002. **Fax:** 209/456-1156. **Contact:** Carole Murray/Wilma Swan, AG Counselors/Owners. **Description:** An executive search firm that focuses on placing management personnel in agricultural fields, including farm/ranch managers, irrigation engineers, and agricultural accountants. Company pays fee. **Specializes in the areas of:** Agri-Business. **Positions commonly filled include:** Accountant/Auditor; Agricultural Engineer. **Average salary range of placements:** $30,000 - $50,000. **Number of placements per year:** 1 - 49.

WGI SOLUTIONS
P.O. Box 3365, Cerritos CA 90703. **Contact:** Manager. **Description:** An executive search firm. **Specializes in the areas of:** Clerical; Industrial; Technical.

LARRY WADE & ASSOCIATES
12526 High Bluff Drive, Suite 240, San Diego CA 92130. 619/481-8300. **Contact:** Manager. **Description:** An executive search firm. **Specializes in the areas of:** Computer Hardware/Software.

WALDORF ASSOCIATES, INC.
11400 West Olympic Boulevard, Suite 200, Los Angeles CA 90064-1507. 310/445-8886. **Fax:** 310/445-8810. **Contact:** Michael Waldorf, President. **E-mail address:** waldorfinc@aol.com. **Description:** An executive search firm operating on both a retainer and a contingency basis. **Specializes in the areas of:** Legal. **Positions commonly filled include:** Attorney; Vice President. **Average salary range of placements:** More than $50,000.

WALKER & TORRENTE
P.O. Box 707, Belvedere CA 94920-0707. 415/435-9178. **Fax:** 415/435-9144. **Contact:** William T. Walker, Partner. **Description:** A retained and contingency executive search firm. Company pays fee. **Specializes in the areas of:** Accounting/Auditing; Administration; Banking; Economics; Finance; General Management; Legal. **Positions commonly filled include:** Accountant/Auditor; Attorney; Bank Officer/Manager; Budget Analyst; Chief Financial Officer; Computer Programmer; Controller; Database Manager; Economist; Financial Analyst; Industrial Engineer; Management Analyst/Consultant; MIS Specialist; Project Manager; Systems Analyst; Underwriter /Assistant Underwriter. **Corporate headquarters location:** This Location. **Average salary range of placements:** More than $50,000. **Number of placements per year:** 1 - 49.

K.K. WALKER PROFESSIONAL RECRUITMENT
P.O. Box 1588, Fair Oaks CA 95628. 916/863-6363. **Fax:** 916/863-3224. **Contact:** Karen Walker, Owner. **Description:** A contingency executive search firm. Company pays fee. **Specializes in the areas of:** Health/Medical. **Positions commonly filled include:** Administrative Manager; Branch Manager; Medical Technologist; Physical Therapist; Registered Nurse; X-ray Technician. **Corporate headquarters location:** This Location. **Average salary range of placements:** More than $50,000. **Number of placements per year:** 1 - 49.

WARREN & MORRIS & MADISON, LTD.
2190 Carmel Valley Road, Del Mar CA 92014. 619/481-3388. **Contact:** Manager. **E-mail address:** info@wmmltd.com. **World Wide Web address:** http://www.wmmltd.com. **Description:** An executive search firm operating on both retainer and contingency bases. Company pays fee. **Specializes in the areas of:** Telecommunications. **Positions commonly filled include:** Account Manager; Account Representative; Advertising Account Executive; Chief Financial Officer; Computer Programmer; ESL Teacher; Finance Director; Financial Analyst; General Manager; Management Analyst/Consultant; Marketing Manager; MIS Specialist; Operations Manager; Purchasing Agent/Manager; Sales Executive; Systems Analyst; Telecommunications Manager. **Corporate headquarters location:** This location. **Other U.S. locations:** Portsmouth NH; Virginia Beach VA. **Average salary range of placements:** More than $50,000. **Number of placements per year:** 100 - 199.

R.J. WATKINS & COMPANY
625 Broadway, Suite 1210, San Diego CA 92101. 619/239-3094. **Contact:** Manager. **Description:** A retained executive search firm. **Specializes in the areas of:** Biotechnology; High-Tech.

D.L. WEAVER & ASSOCIATES
6 Hutton Center Drive, Suite 1150, Santa Ana CA 92707. 714/979-2900. **Contact:** Office Manager. **Description:** An executive search firm. **Specializes in the areas of:** Accounting/Auditing; Computer Hardware/Software; Finance; High-Tech; Real Estate.

WENDELL ASSOCIATES
P.O. Box 7376, San Jose CA 95150-7376. 408/725-1345. **Contact:** Oliver Peeler, Owner. **Description:** An executive search firm. Company pays fee. **Specializes in the areas of:** Computer Hardware/Software; Health/Medical; Sales. **Positions commonly filled include:** Biomedical Engineer; Computer Progra[illegible] Electrical/Electronics Engineer; Mechanical Eng[illegible]eer; Software Engineer.

WENTWORTH COMPANY, INC.
479 West Sixth Street, San Pedro CA 90731-2656. 310/519-0113. **Fax:** 310/519-8402. **Contact:** John Wentworth, President. **Description:** An executive search firm. **Number of placements per year:** 200 - 499.

WESTERN TECHNICAL RESOURCES
451 Los Gatos Boulevard, Suite 102, Los Gatos CA 95032. 408/358-8533. **Toll-free phone:** 800/600-5351. **Fax:** 408/358-8535. **Contact:** Bruce West, Principal. **E-mail address:** wtr@wtrusa.com. **World Wide Web address:** http://www.wtrusa.com. **Description:** An executive search firm that also provides contract placements in a variety of technical disciplines. Company pays fee. **Specializes in the areas of:** Administration; Computer Science/Software; Engineering; Health/Medical; Sales; Technical. **Positions commonly filled include:** Applications Engineer; Biomedical Engineer; Chemical Engineer; Clinical Lab Technician; Computer Operator; Computer Programmer; Database Manager; Design Engineer; Draftsperson; Electrical/Electronics Engineer; Environmental Engineer; Industrial Engineer; Mechanical Engineer; MIS Specialist; Software Engineer; Structural Engineer; Systems Analyst; Technical Writer/Editor. **Benefits available to temporary workers:** Flight Benefits; Medical Insurance; Paid Holidays; Paid Vacation. **Average salary range of**

placements: More than $50,000. **Number of placements per year:** 50 - 99.

WESTPACIFIC NATIONAL SEARCH INC.
23421 South Pointe Drive, Suite 270, Laguna Hills CA 92653. 714/830-8780. **Fax:** 714/830-8781. **Contact:** Glenn Burnett, President. **Description:** An executive search firm serving the insurance, managed care, and health care industries. Company pays fee. **Specializes in the areas of:** Finance; Health/Medical; Sales. **Positions commonly filled include:** Actuary; Claim Representative; Health Services Manager; Market Research Analyst; Nurse; Occupational Therapist; Pharmacist; Physical Therapist; Physician; Quality Control Supervisor; Registered Nurse; Services Sales Representative; Systems Analyst; Underwriter/Assistant Underwriter. **Number of placements per year:** 50 - 99.

DANIEL WIER & ASSOCIATES
333 South Grand Avenue, Suite 2980, Los Angeles CA 90071. 213/628-2580. **Contact:** Manager. **Description:** An executive search firm that places managers in a variety of fields.

WILLIAM-JOHNS COMPANY, INC.
14081 Yorba Street, Suite 202, Tustin CA 92780. 714/544-1222. **Fax:** 714/544-6555. **Contact:** William J. Kresich, President. **Description:** An executive search firm focusing on placements in the hospitality industry. Related areas of operation include franchise sales and operation. Company pays fee. **Specializes in the areas of:** Architecture/Construction; Finance; Legal; Sales. **Positions commonly filled include:** Account Manager; Advertising Account Executive; Architect; Attorney; Financial Analyst; General Manager; Human Resources Manager; Marketing Specialist; Purchasing Agent/Manager. **Average salary range of placements:** More than $50,000. **Number of placements per year:** 50 - 99.

S.R. WILSON INC.
520 Mendicino Avenue, Suite 200, Santa Rosa CA 95401. 707/571-5990. **Contact:** Stoney Wilson, President. **Description:** An executive search firm. **Specializes in the areas of:** Engineering; Legal.

WINSER EXECUTIVE SEARCH
30290 Rancho Viejo Road, Suite 117, San Juan Capistrano CA 92675. 714/443-0225. **Contact:** Manager. **Description:** An executive search firm. **Specializes in the areas of:** Consumer Package Goods; Sales.

WITT/KIEFFER, FORD, HADELMAN & LLOYD
2000 Powell Street, Suite 1645, Emeryville CA 94608. 510/420-1370. **Contact:** Manager. **Description:** An executive search firm for upper-level professionals. **Specializes in the areas of:** Health/Medical.

WORLDWIDE EXECUTIVE SEARCH
620 Newport Center Drive, 11th Floor, Newport Beach CA 92660. 714/721-6603. **Toll-free phone:** 800/807-2622. **Fax:** 714/640-1044. **Contact:** Jim Ginther, President. **Description:** An executive search firm operating on both retained and contingency bases. Company pays fee. **Specializes in the areas of:** Finance; Hotel/Restaurant; Retail. **Positions commonly filled include:** Controller; Credit Manager; Finance Director; Human Resources Manager; Marketing Manager; Sales Executive; Sales Manager. **Corporate headquarters location:** Phoenix AZ. **Average salary range of placements:** More than $50,000. **Number of placements per year:** 50 - 99.

YELVERTON EXECUTIVE SEARCH
2465 East Bayshore Road, Palo Alto CA 94303. 650/354-0231. **Contact:** Manager. **Description:** An executive search firm that focuses on high-tech placements.

DON ZEE ASSOCIATES
6 South Portola, Laguna Beach CA 92677-3315. 714/499-0917. **Fax:** 714/499-0587. **Contact:** Don Zee, President. **Description:** An executive search firm that provides placement in the industrial measurement and control engineering markets worldwide for sales, marketing, engineering, and operations positions. The firm operates on both retainer and contingency bases. Company pays fee. **Specializes in the areas of:** Engineering; Manufacturing; Sales. **Positions commonly filled include:** Chemical Engineer; Civil Engineer; Computer Programmer; Measure and Control Engineer; Mechanical Engineer; Petroleum Engineer; Software Engineer; Systems Analyst. **Average salary range of placements:** More than $50,000. **Number of placements per year:** 1 - 49.

PERMANENT EMPLOYMENT AGENCIES

A PERMANENT SUCCESS EMPLOYMENT SERVICES
12658 Washington Boulevard, Suite 104, Los Angeles CA 90066. 310/305-7376. **Fax:** 310/306-2929. **Contact:** Darrell W. Gurney, Owner. **Description:** A permanent employment agency focusing on nationwide placement of career professionals in sales/marketing, accounting/finance, human resource, and MIS/computer fields. The company also places secretarial and administrative support positions. Company pays fee. **Specializes in the areas of:** Accounting/Auditing; Administration; Computer Science/Software; Finance; Personnel/Labor Relations; Sales; Secretarial. **Positions commonly filled include:** Accountant/Auditor; Administrative Manager; Budget Analyst; Claim Representative; Clerical Supervisor; Computer Programmer; Credit Manager; Customer Service Representative; Financial Analyst; Human Resources Specialist; Manufacturer's/Wholesaler's Sales Rep.; MIS Specialist; Multimedia Designer; Services Sales Representative; Systems Analyst; Technical Writer/Editor; Telecommunications Manager; Typist/Word Processor. **Average salary range of placements:** More than $50,000. **Number of placements per year:** 50 - 99.

AM ENGINEERING
1216 State Street, Suite 310, Santa Barbara CA 93101. **Contact:** Office Manager. **Description:** A permanent employment agency. **Specializes in the areas of:** Engineering.

A.S.A.P. EMPLOYMENT SERVICE
13 Commons Lane, Foster City CA 94404. 650/345-2727. **Fax:** 650/349-1900. **Contact:** Bonnie Marsh, President. **E-mail address:** bonfire95@aol.com. **Description:** A permanent employment agency. Company pays fee. **Specializes in the areas of:** Administration; Art/Design; Banking; Engineering; General Management; Insurance; Legal; Manufacturing; Personnel/Labor Relations; Sales; Technical. **Positions commonly filled include:** Accountant/Auditor; Administrative Manager; Bank Officer/Manager; Budget Analyst; Claim Representative; Cost Estimator; Financial Analyst; General Manager; Industrial Production Manager; Management Analyst/Consultant; Quality Control Supervisor; Services Sales Representative; Software Engineer; Systems Analyst; Technical Writer/Editor; Typist/Word Processor. **Average salary range of**

placements: More than $50,000. **Number of placements per year:** 1 - 49.

AW DATA PROCESSING PERSONNEL
10163 Erie Street, Ventura CA 93004. **Contact:** Manager. **Description:** A permanent employment agency that also provides temporary placements. **Specializes in the areas of:** Computer Hardware/Software; Data Processing; Management.

THE ACCOUNTING GUILD
12400 Wilshire Boulevard, Suite 1275, Los Angeles CA 90025. **Contact:** Manager. **Description:** A permanent employment agency that also provides temporary placements. **Specializes in the areas of:** Accounting/Auditing; Administration; Legal.

ACCOUNTING PARTNERS
2041 Mission College Boulevard, Suite 200, Santa Clara CA 95054. **Contact:** Manager. **Description:** An employment agency offering permanent, temp-to-perm, and temporary positions. **Specializes in the areas of:** Accounting/Auditing.

ACCUSTAFF
16501 Ventura Boulevard, Suite 104, Encino CA 91436-2064. 818/905-5522. **Fax:** 818/905-9411. **Contact:** Patti Taylor, Representative. **Description:** A permanent placement agency which primarily offers positions in office support. The agency also provides temporary placements. Company pays fee. **Specializes in the areas of:** Accounting/Auditing; Computer Science/Software; Finance; Legal; Personnel/Labor Relations; Sales; Secretarial. **Positions commonly filled include:** Accountant/Auditor; Financial Analyst; Human Resources Manager; MIS Specialist; Paralegal; Software Engineer; Typist/Word Processor. **Corporate headquarters location:** This Location. **Other U.S. locations:** Nationwide. **Number of placements per year:** 1000+.

ACT 1 PERSONNEL SERVICES
720 North Archibald Avenue, Ontario CA 91764. 909/987-8679. **Contact:** Manager. **Description:** A permanent employment agency that also does temporary placements. **Specializes in the areas of:** Administration; Clerical.

ACTION PLUS EMPLOYER SERVICES
1211 West Imperial Highway, Suite 100, Brea CA 92821. 714/773-1506. **Fax:** 714/773-9201. **Contact:** Mary Garcia, Vice President. **Description:** A permanent employment agency. Company pays fee. **Specializes in the areas of:** Automotive; General Management; Health/Medical; Manufacturing; Personnel/Labor Relations; Sales. **Positions commonly filled include:** Automotive Mechanic; Biomedical Engineer; Blue-Collar Worker Supervisor; Clinical Lab Technician; Credit Manager; Customer Service Representative; EEG Technologist; Health Services Manager; Human Resources Manager; Licensed Practical Nurse; Operations/Production Manager; Physical Therapist; Physician; Radiological Technologist; Registered Nurse; Services Sales Representative; Surgical Technician. **Corporate headquarters location:** This Location. **Average salary range of placements:** $20,000 - $29,999. **Number of placements per year:** 500 - 999.

ADVANTAGE PERSONNEL INC.
19925 Stevens Creek Boulevard, Suite 141, Cupertino CA 95014. 408/252-0400. **Fax:** 408/252-0101. **Contact:** Cristina Gomez, Owner. **Description:** A permanent employment agency. Company pays fee. **Specializes in the areas of:** Accounting/Auditing; Administration; Advertising; Computer Science/Software; Legal; Manufacturing; Personnel/Labor Relations; Sales; Secretarial. **Positions commonly filled include:** Accountant/Auditor; Administrative Manager; Advertising Clerk; Bank Officer/Manager; Branch Manager; Budget Analyst; Claim Representative; Clerical Supervisor; Credit Manager; Customer Service Representative; Financial Analyst; HManagement Analyst/Consultant; Market Research Analyst; MIS Specialist; Operations/Production Manager; Purchasing Agent/Manager; Quality Control Supervisor; Systems Analyst; Technical Writer/Editor; Typist/Word Processor.

AMTEC ENGINEERING CORPORATION
P.O. Box 1267, Brea CA 92822. 714/993-1900. **Fax:** 714/993-2419. **Contact:** Shawn Byrne, CFO. **E-mail address:** staffing@amtec-eng.com. **World Wide Web address:** http://www.amtec-eng.com. **Description:** A permanent employment agency focusing on high-tech placements. Company pays fee. **Specializes in the areas of:** Computer Science/Software; Engineering; Manufacturing; Technical. **Positions commonly filled include:** Applications Engineer; Biomedical Engineer; Chemical Engineer; Civil Engineer; Computer Operator; Computer Programmer; Consultant; Database Manager; Design Engineer; Designer; Electrical/Electronics Engineer; Electrician; Environmental Engineer; Graphic Designer; Industrial Engineer; Industrial Production Manager; Manufacturing Engineer; Mechanical Engineer; MIS Specialist; Project Manager; Quality Control Supervisor; Sales Engineer; Software Engineer; Structural Engineer; Systems Analyst; Systems Manager; Technical Writer/Editor. **Benefits available to temporary workers:** Dental Insurance; Medical Insurance; Paid Holidays; Paid Vacation. **Average salary range of placements:** $30,000 - $50,000. **Number of placements per year:** 500 - 999.

ANDREW & POTTER, LTD.
1482 East Valley Road, Suite 4, Santa Barbara CA 93150. 805/565-4444. **Toll-free phone:** 800/800-6757. **Fax:** 805/565-4446. **Contact:** Heather Irena Anand, CEO. **World Wide Web address:** http://www.andrewandpotter.com. **Description:** A permanent employment agency. **Specializes in the areas of:** Domestic Help. **Positions commonly filled include:** Domestic Help; Nanny. **Number of placements per year:** 1000+.

APPLE ONE EMPLOYMENT SERVICES
18538 Hawthorne Boulevard, Torrance CA 90504. 310/542-8534. **Contact:** Manager. **Description:** A permanent employment agency. Company pays fee. **Specializes in the areas of:** Accounting/Auditing; Banking; Clerical; Finance; Health/Medical. **Positions commonly filled include:** Administrative Assistant; Bank Officer/Manager; Bookkeeper; Buyer; Clerk; Customer Service Representative; Data Entry Clerk; Human Resources Manager; Legal Secretary; Medical Secretary; Receptionist; Secretary; Typist/Word Processor. **Corporate headquarters location:** Glendale CA. **Other U.S. locations:** Nationwide. **Number of placements per year:** 1000+.

APPLE ONE EMPLOYMENT SERVICES
1295 North Euclid, Anaheim CA 92801. 714/956-5180. **Contact:** Sales Manager. **Description:** A permanent employment agency. Company pays fee. **Specializes in the areas of:** Accounting/Auditing; Clerical; Finance; Personnel/Labor Relations; Sales. **Corporate headquarters location:** Glendale CA. **Other U.S. locations:** Nationwide. **Number of placements per year:** 1000+.

APPLE ONE EMPLOYMENT SERVICES
1970 Broadway, Suite 110, Oakland CA 94612. 510/835-0217. **Contact:** General Manager. **Description:** A permanent employment agency. Company pays fee. **Specializes in the areas of:**

Accounting/Auditing; Clerical; Finance. **Positions commonly filled include:** Accountant/Auditor; Administrative Assistant; Aerospace Engineer; Bank Officer/Manager; Bookkeeper; Buyer; Civil Engineer; Claim Representative; Clerk; Computer Operator; Computer Programmer; Credit Manager; Customer Service Representative; Data Entry Clerk; Draftsperson; Economist; Electrical/Electronics Engineer; Factory Worker; Financial Analyst; Human Resources Manager; Industrial Engineer; Legal Secretary; Marketing Specialist; Mechanical Engineer; Medical Secretary; Operations/Production Manager; Quality Control Supervisor; Receptionist; Sales Representative; Secretary; Stenographer; Typist/Word Processor. **Corporate headquarters location:** Glendale CA. **Other U.S. locations:** Nationwide. **Number of placements per year:** 1000+.

APPLE ONE EMPLOYMENT SERVICES
11352 East 183rd Street, Cerritos CA 90703-5419. 562/924-7009. **Fax:** 562/924-3025. **Contact:** Josee Minero, Branch Manager. **Description:** A permanent employment agency that also provides temporary placements. Company pays fee. **Specializes in the areas of:** Accounting/Auditing; Advertising; Fashion; Food Industry; Health/Medical; Industrial; Manufacturing; Personnel/Labor Relations; Secretarial. **Positions commonly filled include:** Accountant/ Auditor; Computer Programmer; Credit Manager; Customer Service Representative; Electrical/ Electronics Engineer; Financial Analyst; Human Resources Manager; Management Trainee; MIS Specialist; Quality Control Supervisor; Software Engineer; Systems Analyst; Typist/Word Processor. **Corporate headquarters location:** Glendale CA. **Other U.S. locations:** Nationwide. **Number of placements per year:** 1000+.

APPLE ONE EMPLOYMENT SERVICES
44 Montgomery Street, Suite 600, San Francisco CA 94104. 415/397-3201. **Contact:** Amber Ash, Account Executive. **Description:** An employment agency that provides both permanent and temporary placements. Company pays fee. **Specializes in the areas of:** Accounting/Auditing; Administration; Computer Science/Software; General Management; Health/Medical; Legal; Personnel/Labor Relations; Publishing; Sales; Secretarial. **Positions commonly filled include:** Accountant/Auditor; Administrative Manager; Clerical Supervisor; Computer Programmer; Counselor; Customer Service Representative; Internet Services Manager; Management Trainee; Manufacturer's/Wholesaler's Sales Rep.; Market Research Analyst; Medical Records Technician; MIS Specialist; Multimedia Designer; Securities Sales Representative; Services Sales Representative; Telecommunications Manager; Typist/Word Processor. **Corporate headquarters location:** Glendale CA. **Other U.S. locations:** Nationwide. **Average salary range of placements:** $20,000 - $29,999. **Number of placements per year:** 500 - 999.

APPLE ONE EMPLOYMENT SERVICES
225 South Sepulveda Boulevard, Suite 100, Manhattan Beach CA 90266. 310/318-9912. **Fax:** 310/372-8356. **Contact:** Julia English-Dahl, Branch Manager. **Description:** A full-service employment agency offering both permanent and temporary placements. Apple One Employment Services focuses on administrative and clerical positions in the fields of accounting, human resources, marketing, and customer service. Founded in 1964. **Specializes in the areas of:** Sales; Secretarial. **Positions commonly filled include:** Accountant/Auditor; Advertising Clerk; Clerical Supervisor; Customer Service Representative; MIS Specialist; Paralegal; Purchasing Agent/Manager; Technical Writer/Editor; Typist/Word Processor. **Benefits available to temporary workers:** 401(k); Bonus Award/Plan; Dental Insurance; Medical Insurance. **Corporate headquarters location:** Glendale CA. **Other U.S. locations:** Nationwide. **Number of placements per year:** 500 - 999.

APPLE ONE EMPLOYMENT SERVICES
P.O. Box 29048, Glendale CA 91209-9048. 818/240-8688. **Toll-free phone:** 800/564-5644. **Contact:** Manager. **Description:** A permanent employment agency that also provides temporary placements as well as career/outplacement counseling. **Specializes in the areas of:** Accounting/Auditing; Administration; Computer Hardware/Software; Engineering; Industrial; Manufacturing; Personnel/Labor Relations; Sales; Secretarial; Technical. **Positions commonly filled include:** Accountant/Auditor; Administrative Manager; Advertising Clerk; Biomedical Engineer; Blue-Collar Worker Supervisor; Brokerage Clerk; Budget Analyst; Chemical Engineer; Claim Representative; Clinical Lab Technician; Computer Programmer; Credit Manager; Customer Service Representative; Designer; Draftsperson; Electrical/Electronics Engineer; Financial Analyst; Industrial Engineer; Industrial Production Manager; Internet Services Manager; Mechanical Engineer; Medical Records Technician; MIS Specialist; Paralegal; Software Engineer; Technical Writer/Editor; Typist/Word Processor. **Corporate headquarters location:** This Location. **Other U.S. locations:** Nationwide. **Number of placements per year:** 1000+.

APROPOS EMPLOYMENT AGENCY
1850 Mount Diablo Boulevard, Suite 106, Walnut Creek CA 94596. 510/937-3540. **Fax:** 510/945-8385. **Contact:** Dori Val, President. **Description:** A permanent employment agency. Company pays fee. **Specializes in the areas of:** Accounting/Auditing; Administration; Banking; Biology; Computer Science/ Software; Finance; General Management; Health Medical; Industrial; Insurance; Legal; Manufacturing; Personnel/Labor Relations; Sales; Secretarial; Technical; Transportation. **Positions commonly filled include:** Accountant/Auditor; Actuary; Adjuster; Administrative Manager; Attorney; Bank Officer/Manager; Biochemist; Branch Manager; Buyer; Claim Representative; Clerical Supervisor; Computer Programmer; Customer Service Representative; Draftsperson; Financial Analyst; MIS Specialist; Operations/Production Manager; Paralegal; Purchasing Agent/Manager; Quality Control Supervisor; Software Engineer; Systems Analyst; Technical Writer/Editor; Telecommunications Manager; Underwriter/Assistant Underwriter. **Average salary range of placements:** $30,000 - $50,000. **Number of placements per year:** 100 - 199.

BARBARA ARDEN INC.
236 West Portal Avenue, Suite 385, San Francisco CA 94127. 415/585-4900. **Contact:** Manager. **Description:** A permanent employment agency that also provides some executive placements. **Specializes in the areas of:** Legal. **Positions commonly filled include:** Legal Secretary; Paralegal.

ARROWSTAFF SERVICES
2010 North First Street, Suite 300, San Jose CA 95131. 408/437-8989. **Fax:** 408/437-0624. **Contact:** Recruiter. **Description:** A professional management and staffing organization focusing on the placement of engineering, programming, and technical personnel. Founded in 1981. Company pays fee. **Specializes in the areas of:** Administration; Computer Science/ Software; Engineering; Industrial; Manufacturing. **Positions commonly filled include:** Chemical Engineer; Computer Programmer; Design Engineer; Designer; Draftsperson; Electrical/Electronics Engineer; Internet Services Manager; Mechanical Engineer; MIS Specialist; Multimedia Designer; Quality Control Supervisor; Software Engineer; Strategic Relations

Manager; Systems Analyst; Technical Writer/Editor; Telecommunications Manager. **Benefits available to temporary workers:** Dental Insurance; Medical Insurance; Paid Holidays; Paid Vacation. **Average salary range of placements:** $30,000 - $50,000. **Number of placements per year:** 1000+.

ARTLINKS
1450 4th Street, Suite 10, Berkeley CA 94710. 510/528-2668. **Fax:** 510/528-0521. **Contact:** Marti Stites, Owner. **World Wide Web address:** http://www.artlinks-staffing.com. **Description:** A permanent employment agency focusing on the graphic design, multimedia, and publishing industries. The agency also provides temporary placements. Company pays fee. **Specializes in the areas of:** Art/Design. **Positions commonly filled include:** Editor; Editorial Assistant; Graphic Artist; Graphic Designer; Webmaster. **Benefits available to temporary workers:** Direct Deposit. **Corporate headquarters location:** This Location. **Average salary range of placements:** More than $50,000.

ASSURED PERSONNEL SERVICES, INC.
1301 South Beach Boulevard, Suite M, La Habra CA 90631. 562/691-3258. **Contact:** Don Rains, Administrator. **Description:** A permanent employment agency. Company pays fee. **Specializes in the areas of:** Accounting/Auditing; Clerical; Health/Medical; Secretarial. **Positions commonly filled include:** Accountant/Auditor; Administrative Assistant; Advertising Account Executive; Bookkeeper; Clerk; Computer Programmer; Data Entry Clerk; Financial Analyst; Marketing Specialist; Mechanical Engineer; Medical Secretary; Metallurgical Engineer; Nurse; Receptionist; Secretary; Systems Analyst; Technical Writer/Editor; Technician; Typist/Word Processor. **Number of placements per year:** 500 - 999.

BEVERLY HILLS BAR ASSOCIATION PERSONNEL SERVICE
300 South Beverly Drive, Suite 214, Beverly Hills CA 90212. 310/553-4575. **Contact:** Manager. **Description:** A permanent employment agency. Company pays fee. **Specializes in the areas of:** Legal. **Positions commonly filled include:** Attorney; Legal Secretary; Receptionist; Typist/Word Processor. **Number of placements per year:** 50 - 99.

BLAINE & ASSOCIATES
2029 Century Park East, Suite 1080, Los Angeles CA 90067. 310/785-0560. **Fax:** 310/785-9670. **Contact:** Carrie Policella, President. **Description:** A permanent employment agency. Company pays fee. **Specializes in the areas of:** Accounting/Auditing; Administration; Advertising; Computer Science/Software; Finance; Legal; Personnel/Labor Relations; Secretarial. **Positions commonly filled include:** Administrative Manager; Advertising Clerk; Clerical Supervisor; Customer Service Representative; Human Resources Specialist; Paralegal; Typist/Word Processor. **Corporate headquarters location:** This Location. **Other U.S. locations:** Phoenix AZ. **Average salary range of placements:** $30,000 - $50,000. **Number of placements per year:** 100 - 199.

BUSINESS SYSTEMS STAFFING & ASSOCIATES, INC.
10680 West Pico Boulevard, Suite 210, Los Angeles CA 90064. 310/204-6711. **Fax:** 310/204-2941. **Contact:** Vivian Hotchkiss, Owner. **E-mail address:** lajobline@aol.com. **Description:** A permanent employment agency. Company pays fee. **Specializes in the areas of:** Accounting/Auditing; Administration; Advertising; Architecture/Construction; Communications; Computer Science/Software; Engineering; Fashion; General Management; Insurance; Legal; Nonprofit; Personnel/ Labor Relations; Sales; Secretarial; Transportation. **Positions commonly filled include:** Accountant/Auditor; Advertising Clerk; Bank Officer/ Manager; Buyer; Claim Representative; Clinical Lab Technician; Credit Manager; Customer Service Representative; Electrical/Electronics Engineer; Financial Analyst; Human Service Worker; Industrial Engineer; Mechanical Engineer; Metallurgical Engineer; Operations/Production Manager; Paralegal; Social Worker; Software Engineer; Structural Engineer; Systems Analyst. **Benefits available to temporary workers:** Bonus Award/Plan; Credit Union. **Corporate headquarters location:** This Location. **Average salary range of placements:** $30,000 - $50,000. **Number of placements per year:** 200 - 499.

CT PERSONNEL SERVICES
2221 Rosecrans Avenue, Suite 131, El Segundo CA 90245. 310/643-8333. **Fax:** 310/643-7151. **Contact:** Manager. **World Wide Web address:** http://www.cteng.com. **Description:** A permanent employment agency that also provides temporary placements. Company pays fee. **Specializes in the areas of:** Accounting/Auditing; Administration; Architecture/Construction; Clerical; Computer Science/Software; Engineering; Personnel/Labor Relations; Secretarial; Technical. **Positions commonly filled include:** Administrative Assistant; Aerospace Engineer; Clerk; Computer Programmer; Draftsperson; Industrial Engineer; Mechanical Engineer; Physicist; Purchasing Agent/Manager; Receptionist; Secretary; Statistician; Systems Analyst; Technical Writer/Editor; Technician; Typist/Word Processor.

CALIFORNIA JOB CONNECTION
11825 Del Amo Boulevard, Cerritos CA 90703. 562/809-7785. **Toll-free phone:** 800/645-2971. **Fax:** 562/403-3427. **Contact:** Brenda Sanchez, Branch Manager. **Description:** A permanent employment agency. Founded in 1988. Company pays fee. **Specializes in the areas of:** Banking; Computer Science/Software; Industrial; Manufacturing; Personnel/Labor Relations; Sales; Secretarial. **Positions commonly filled include:** Accountant/Auditor; Administrative Manager; Advertising Clerk; Blue-Collar Worker Supervisor; Branch Manager; Buyer; Civil Engineer; Clerical Supervisor; Computer Programmer; Customer Service Representative; Management Trainee; Public Relations Specialist; PQuality Control Supervisor; Technical Writer/Editor; Typist/ Word Processor. **Benefits available to temporary workers:** Medical Insurance; Paid Holidays; Paid Vacation. **Other area locations:** Newport Beach CA. **Average salary range of placements:** $30,000 - $50,000. **Number of placements per year:** 100 - 199.

CANDY STRIPERS MEDICAL PERSONNEL
16531 Bolsa Chica Street, Suite 315, Huntington Beach CA 92649-3596. 714/377-1182. **Fax:** 714/377-1184. **Contact:** Barbara Sue Miller, President. **Description:** A permanent placement agency focusing on the medical, legal, accounting, real estate, and hospitality industries. The agency also provides temporary placements. Company pays fee. **Specializes in the areas of:** Accounting/Auditing; Administration; Advertising; Food Industry; General Management; Health/Medical; Insurance; Legal; Personnel/Labor Relations; Retail; Secretarial. **Positions commonly filled include:** Accountant/ Auditor; Administrative Manager; Branch Manager; Budget Analyst; Buyer; Claim Representative; Clerical Supervisor; Clinical Lab Technician; Computer Programmer; Cost Estimator; Credit Manager; Customer Service Representative; Emergency Medical Technician; Financial Analyst; Human Service Worker; IMedical Records Technician; MIS Specialist; Operations/Production Manager; Paralegal; Physical Therapist; Physician; Property and Real Estate

Manager; Purchasing Agent/Manager; Real Estate Agent; Registered Nurse; Social Worker; Systems Analyst; Technical Writer/Editor; Underwriter/Assistant Underwriter; Veterinarian. **Corporate headquarters location:** This Location. **Other U.S. locations:** Nationwide. **Average salary range of placements:** More than $50,000. **Number of placements per year:** 1000+.

CENTENNIAL ASSOCIATES
1710 South Amphlett Boulevard, San Mateo CA 94402. 650/341-7321. **Contact:** Manager. **Description:** A permanent employment agency. **Specializes in the areas of:** Quality Assurance.

CHOICE PERSONNEL
800 Wilshire Boulevard, Suite 1475, Los Angeles CA 90017. 213/489-3260. **Fax:** 213/624-7318. **Contact:** Donna Callaway, Owner. **Description:** A retained employment agency focusing on permanent and temporary clerical and administrative positions. Company pays fee. **Specializes in the areas of:** Accounting/Auditing; Administration; Banking; Computer Science/Software; Finance; Insurance; Legal; Personnel/Labor Relations; Secretarial. **Positions commonly filled include:** Accountant/Auditor; Computer Programmer; Credit Manager; Customer Service Representative; Human Resources Manager; Paralegal; Systems Analyst; Typist/Word Processor. **Average salary range of placements:** $30,000 - $50,000. **Number of placements per year:** 200 - 499.

CHOSEN FEW PERSONNEL SERVICES
911 Wilshire Boulevard, Suite 1880, Los Angeles CA 90017. 213/689-9400. **Contact:** Kim Walker, Owner. **Description:** A permanent employment agency. Company pays fee. **Specializes in the areas of:** Legal. **Positions commonly filled include:** Accountant/Auditor; Attorney; Bookkeeper; Data Entry Clerk; Legal Secretary; Paralegal; Typist/Word Processor. **Number of placements per year:** 200 - 499.

COLE VOCATIONAL SERVICES
1174 Nevada Street, Redlands CA 92374. 909/307-6584. **Contact:** Manager. **Description:** An employment agency that provides vocational training. **Specializes in the areas of:** Social Services. **Positions commonly filled include:** Human Service Worker. **Average salary range of placements:** Less than $20,000. **Number of placements per year:** 100 - 199.

COLT SYSTEMS PROFESSIONAL PERSONNEL SERVICES
1880 Century Park East, Suite 208, Los Angeles CA 90067. 310/277-4741. **Fax:** 310/277-8317. **Contact:** Sheldon Arons, President. **Description:** A permanent employment agency. **Specializes in the areas of:** Accounting/Auditing; Administration; Clerical; Data Processing; Executives; Finance; Technical. **Positions commonly filled include:** Account Manager; Accountant/Auditor; Administrative Assistant; Bookkeeper; Computer Programmer; Credit Manager; Customer Service Representative; Data Entry Clerk; Engineer; Financial Analyst; Secretary. **Number of placements per year:** 50 - 99.

COMFORCE TECHNICAL SERVICES, INC.
17682 Mitchell North, Suite 100, Irvine CA 92614. 714/660-9544. **Contact:** Manager. **Description:** A permanent employment agency. **Specializes in the areas of:** Light Industrial; Technical.

THE COMPUTER RESOURCES GROUP, INC.
275 Battery Street, Suite 800, San Francisco CA 94111. 415/398-3535. **Contact:** Jackie Autry, Vice President. **Description:** A permanent employment agency. **Specializes in the areas of:** Computer Hardware/Software; MIS/EDP. **Positions commonly filled include:** Computer Programmer; EDP Specialist; MIS Specialist; Systems Analyst. **Number of placements per year:** 1000+.

CORPORATE SOLUTIONS
1173 9th Street, Monterey CA 93940. 408/646-0779. **Contact:** Judy Marra, CPC, Owner. **Description:** A permanent employment agency. Company pays fee. **Specializes in the areas of:** Accounting/Auditing; Finance. **Positions commonly filled include:** Accountant/Auditor; Budget Analyst; Financial Analyst. **Number of placements per year:** 1 - 49.

CREW CALL INC.
28924 South Western Avenue, #107, Rancho Palos Verdes CA 90275. 310/547-1096. **Fax:** 310/547-2334. **Contact:** Office Manager. **Description:** An employment agency focusing on motion picture and television staffing. **Specializes in the areas of:** Film Production. **Positions commonly filled include:** Broadcast Technician; Designer; Editor; Electrician; Film Production Worker; Multimedia Designer; Video Production Coordinator. **Corporate headquarters location:** This Location. **Other U.S. locations:** FL; IL. **Number of placements per year:** 1000+.

MARLENE CRITCHFIELD COMPANY
150 West Gabilan, Suite 2, Salinas CA 93901. 408/753-2466. **Fax:** 408/753-2467. **Contact:** Marlene Critchfield, Owner. **Description:** A permanent employment agency. Company pays fee. **Specializes in the areas of:** Accounting/Auditing; Food Industry; General Management; Manufacturing; Sales. **Positions commonly filled include:** Accountant/Auditor; Aerospace Engineer; Agricultural Scientist; Budget Analyst; Financial Analyst; Food Scientist/Technologist; Industrial Engineer; Mechanical Engineer; Quality Control Supervisor. **Number of placements per year:** 1 - 49.

CULVER PERSONNEL SERVICES
1555 Old Bayshore Highway, Suite 100, Burlingame CA 94010. 650/692-9090. **Fax:** 650/692-6618. **Contact:** Paul Ravetti, Senior Branch Manager. **E-mail address:** culverbg@pacbell.net. **World Wide Web address:** http://www.culvercorp.com. **Description:** An employment agency that focuses on permanent placement of sales, sales management, customer service, management training, and higher level management placements. Company pays fee. **Specializes in the areas of:** Advertising; Broadcasting; Computer Science/Software; Finance; Food Industry; General Management; Health/Medical; Industrial; Insurance; Legal; Personnel/Labor Relations; Publishing; Retail; Sales; Transportation. **Positions commonly filled include:** Account Representative; Advertising Account Executive; Branch Manager; Claim Representative; Internet Services Manager; Management Analyst/Consultant; Management Trainee; Marketing Specialist; Online Content Specialist; Sales Engineer; Sales Representative; Wholesale and Retail Buyer. **Corporate headquarters location:** San Diego CA. **Average salary range of placements:** More than $50,000. **Number of placements per year:** 100 - 199.

CULVER PERSONNEL SERVICES
3900 Kilroy Airport Way, #260, Long Beach CA 90807. 562/427-0069. **Fax:** 562/427-3506. **Contact:** Marti Michalis, Branch Manager. **World Wide Web address:** http://www.culvercorp.com. **Description:** An employment agency that focuses on sales and management staffing. Company pays fee. **Specializes in the areas of:** Advertising; Engineering; Finance; Personnel/Labor Relations; Sales; Transportation. **Positions commonly filled include:** Branch Manager; Customer Service Representative; Securities Sales Representative; Services Sales Representative.

Corporate headquarters location: San Diego CA. **Average salary range of placements:** $30,000 - $50,000. **Number of placements per year:** 50 - 99.

CULVER PERSONNEL SERVICES
3625 Del Amo Boulevard, Suite 185, Torrance CA 90503. 310/793-1164. **Fax:** 310/793-1170. **Contact:** Cathi Charlton, Branch Manager. **Description:** An employment agency focusing on sales and management placements. Company pays fee. **Specializes in the areas of:** Sales. **Positions commonly filled include:** Branch Manager; Management Trainee; Manufacturer's/Wholesaler's Sales Rep.; Services Sales Representative. **Corporate headquarters location:** San Diego CA. **Number of placements per year:** 100 - 199.

CULVER PERSONNEL SERVICES
3 Pointe Drive, Suite 100, Brea CA 92821. 714/990-4459. **Fax:** 714/990-1506. **Contact:** Tamara Sullivan, Vice President. **World Wide Web address:** http://www.culvercorp.com. **Description:** A permanent placement agency. Company pays fee. **Specializes in the areas of:** Sales. **Positions commonly filled include:** Account Manager; Account Representative; Management Trainee; Sales Executive; Sales Manager; Sales Representative. **Corporate headquarters location:** San Diego CA. **Number of placements per year:** 200 - 499.

CULVER PERSONNEL SERVICES
3200 East Inland Empire Boulevard, Suite 150, San Dimas CA 91773. 909/989-3333. **Fax:** 909/989-3962. **Contact:** George Kaszacs, General Manager. **World Wide Web address:** http://www.culvercorp.com. **Description:** A full-service employment agency providing permanent, temporary, and temp-to-hire placements in a wide range of industries. Company pays fee. **Specializes in the areas of:** Sales; Secretarial. **Positions commonly filled include:** Bank Officer/Manager; Branch Manager; Claim Representative; Customer Service Representative; Typist/Word Processor. **Benefits available to temporary workers:** Medical Insurance; Paid Holidays; Paid Vacation. **Corporate headquarters location:** San Diego CA. **Average salary range of placements:** $30,000 - $50,000. **Number of placements per year:** 200 - 499.

DATA CAREERS PERSONNEL SERVICES & SEARCH GROUP
3320 4th Avenue, San Diego CA 92103-5704. 619/291-9994. **Fax:** 619/291-9835. **Contact:** Bob Shelton, Recruiter. **E-mail address:** datacareer@aol.com. **World Wide Web address:** http://members.aol.com/datacareer/data/careers.htm. **Description:** Data Careers Personnel Services & Search Group provides permanent, temporary, and contract placement for the computer industry. Company pays fee. **Specializes in the areas of:** Computer Hardware/Software; Engineering; Finance; MIS/EDP; Software Engineering. **Positions commonly filled include:** Computer Engineer; Computer Operator; Computer Programmer; Customer Service Representative; EDP Specialist; Financial Analyst; Graphic Designer; Internet Services Manager; Operations Manager; Project Manager; Software Engineer; Systems Analyst. **Average salary range of placements:** $30,000 - $50,000. **Number of placements per year:** 50 - 99.

DATA SYSTEMS SEARCH CONSULTANTS
1756 Lacassie Avenue, Suite 202, Walnut Creek CA 94596. 510/256-0635. **Contact:** John R. Martinez, President. **Description:** A permanent employment agency that also provides temporary placements; executive recruitment on a contingency basis; and contract services. Company pays fee. **Specializes in the areas of:** Computer Hardware/Software. **Positions commonly filled include:** Computer Operator; Computer Programmer; MIS Specialist; Network Engineer; Operations/Production Manager; Systems Analyst; Telecommunications Analyst; UNIX System Administrator; Voice/Data Engineer. **Average salary range of placements:** More than $50,000. **Number of placements per year:** 200 - 499.

DECKER & ASSOCIATES PERSONNEL
P.O. Box 5610, Riverside CA 92517. 909/359-1268. **Fax:** 909/369-4012. **Contact:** Dottie Decker, Owner. **Description:** A permanent employment agency. Company pays fee. **Specializes in the areas of:** Advertising; Marketing; Sales. **Positions commonly filled include:** Services Sales Representative. **Average salary range of placements:** $30,000 - $50,000. **Number of placements per year:** 50 - 99.

DENT-ASSIST PERSONNEL SERVICE
725 30th Street, Suite 206, Sacramento CA 95816. 916/443-1113. **Contact:** Lisa Saiia, Director. **Description:** A permanent placement agency for dental professionals. The agency also provides temporary placements. Company pays fee.

DENTAL STATEWIDE STAFFING
P.O. Box 2051, El Cajon CA 92021-0051. 619/443-7252. **Fax:** 619/443-0881. **Contact:** Bonnie Romano, Owner. **Description:** A permanent and temporary placement agency for dental personnel. Company pays fee. **Specializes in the areas of:** Dental. **Corporate headquarters location:** This Location. **Number of placements per year:** 500 - 999.

DEPENDABLE EMPLOYMENT AGENCY NETWORK
9301 Wilshire Boulevard, #403, Beverly Hills CA 90210-5424. 310/274-3434. **Fax:** 310/274-8440. **Contact:** Randy Hudnutt, Account Manager. **Description:** A permanent employment agency that also provides some temporary placements. Company pays fee. **Specializes in the areas of:** Accounting/Auditing; Administration; Banking; Computer Science/Software; Education; Finance; Insurance; Legal; Personnel/Labor Relations; Secretarial. **Positions commonly filled include:** Accountant; Administrative Assistant; Administrative Manager; Advertising Clerk; Brokerage Clerk; Clerical Supervisor; Computer Operator; Computer Programmer; Customer Service Representative; Database Manager; Financial Analyst; Graphic Artist; Market Research Analyst; Marketing Specialist; MIS Specialist; Paralegal; Secretary; Software Engineer; Systems Analyst; Technical Writer/Editor; Typist/Word Processor. **Corporate headquarters location:** This Location. **Average salary range of placements:** $30,000 - $50,000. **Number of placements per year:** 1 - 49.

DESERT PERSONNEL SERVICE, INC.
73350 El Paseo, Suite 205, Palm Desert CA 92260-4240. 619/346-3945. **Fax:** 619/346-2455. **Contact:** Sarah Seils, Owner. **E-mail address:** desertpers@aol.com. **World Wide Web address:** http://www.desertpersonnel.com. **Description:** A full-service staffing agency providing permanent and temporary placements. Company pays fee. **Specializes in the areas of:** Accounting/Auditing; General Management; Personnel/Labor Relations; Secretarial. **Positions commonly filled include:** Accountant/Auditor; Customer Service Representative; Human Resources Specialist; Services Sales Representative; Typist/Word Processor. **Benefits available to temporary workers:** Medical Insurance; Paid Holidays; Paid Vacation; Profit Sharing; Referral Bonus Plan. **Corporate headquarters location:** This Location. **Average salary range of placements:** $30,000 - $50,000. **Number of placements per year:** 50 - 99.

THE DIAL GROUP
14522 East Whittier Boulevard, Whittier CA 90605. 562/945-1071. **Contact:** Doug Lopez, Owner. **Description:** A permanent employment agency. **Specializes in the areas of:** Accounting/Auditing; Banking; Clerical; Finance. **Positions commonly filled include:** Accountant/Auditor; Administrative Assistant; Bookkeeper; Clerk; Computer Operator; Credit Manager; Customer Service Representative; Legal Secretary; Medical Secretary; Sales Representative; Secretary; Stenographer. **Other area locations:** Brea CA; Newport Beach; CA. **Number of placements per year:** 500 - 999.

EASTRIDGE INFOTECH
2355 Northside Drive, Suite 180, San Diego CA 92108. 619/260-2109. **Fax:** 619/280-0843. **Contact:** Joanne Kinsey, Recruiter. **E-mail address:** eastridge@sisna.com. **Description:** An employment agency that also provides temporary placement. Founded in 1971. **Specializes in the areas of:** Computer Science/Software; Technical. **Positions commonly filled include:** Computer Programmer; Draftsperson; Internet Services Manager; Software Engineer; Systems Analyst. **Corporate headquarters location:** This Location. **Other U.S. locations:** Nationwide. **Number of placements per year:** 1 - 49.

EMCO PERSONNEL SERVICE
27575 Via Montoya, San Juan Capistrano CA 92675-5366. 714/487-6870. **Contact:** Dick Tinlin, President. **Description:** A permanent employment agency. Company pays fee. **Specializes in the areas of:** Banking; Finance. **Positions commonly filled include:** Credit Manager. **Number of placements per year:** 50 - 99.

THE EMERALD AGENCY
5230 Pacific Concourse Drive, Suite 200, Los Angeles CA 90045. 310/643-8900. **Fax:** 310/643-8749. **Contact:** Janelle Jenkins, Owner/Manager. **E-mail address:** Emrld1985@aol.com. **World Wide Web address:** http://www.emeraldagency.com. **Description:** An employment agency that offers temporary and permanent placements. The Emerald Agency also offers resume development services. Company pays fee. **Specializes in the areas of:** Legal. **Positions commonly filled include:** Attorney; Engineer; Human Resources Specialist; Legal Secretary; Legal Writer/Editor; MIS Specialist; Systems Analyst. **Corporate headquarters location:** This Location. **Average salary range of placements:** More than $50,000. **Number of placements per year:** 50 - 99.

EMPLOYMENT DEVELOPMENT DEPARTMENT
1325 Pine Street, Redding CA 96001. 530/225-2191. **Fax:** 530/241-4074. **Recorded jobline:** 916/225-2284. **Contact:** Jim Saims, Employment Program Representative. **Description:** The state of California's program for unemployed professionals. The agency also offers career/outplacement counseling. **Specializes in the areas of:** Accounting/Auditing; Administration; Advertising; Banking; Biology; Computer Science/Software; Education; Engineering; Food Industry; General Management; Health/Medical; Industrial; Insurance; Personnel/Labor Relations; Retail; Sales; Secretarial; Technical.

EMPLOYMENT DEVELOPMENT DEPARTMENT
2523 South Mooney Boulevard, Visalia CA 93277-6236. 209/636-7300. **Contact:** Manager. **Description:** A permanent employment agency. **Specializes in the areas of:** Accounting/Auditing; Administration; Art/Design; Banking; Education; Finance; Food Industry; General Management; Health/Medical; Industrial; Insurance; Legal; Manufacturing; Nonprofit; Personnel/Labor Relations; Publishing; Retail; Sales; Transportation. **Positions commonly filled include:** Accountant/Auditor; Administrative Manager; Advertising Clerk; Bank Officer/Manager; Branch Manager; Broadcast Technician; Buyer; Claim Representative; Computer Programmer; Credit Manager; Customer Service Representative; EEG Technologist; Emergency Medical Technician; General Manager; Health Services Manager; Human Resources Specialist; Licensed Practical Nurse; Management Analyst/Consultant; Market Research Analyst; MIS Specialist; Paralegal; Public Relations Specialist; Recreational Therapist; Respiratory Therapist; Typist/Word Processor; Video Production Coordinator. **Corporate headquarters location:** Sacramento CA. **Number of placements per year:** 1000+.

EMPLOYMENT DEVELOPMENT DEPARTMENT
3196 South Higuera Street, San Luis Obispo CA 93401-6928. 805/544-9050. **Contact:** Manager. **Description:** A permanent employment agency.

EMPLOYMENT SERVICE AGENCY
8423 Florence Avenue, Suite C, Downey CA 90240. 562/869-8811. **Fax:** 562/869-7952. **Contact:** Debbie Wallace, Owner. **Description:** A permanent employment agency. Company pays fee. **Specializes in the areas of:** Accounting/Auditing; Food Industry; Health/Medical; Industrial; Manufacturing; Sales; Secretarial. **Positions commonly filled include:** Accountant/Auditor; Adjuster; Clerical Supervisor; Credit Manager; Customer Service Representative; Draftsperson; Management Trainee. **Number of placements per year:** 100 - 199.

FASTEK TECHNICAL SERVICES
4479 Stoneridge Drive, Pleasanton CA 94588. 510/462-1050. **Fax:** 510/462-1139. **Contact:** Holly Quesinberry, Technical Recruiter. **E-mail address:** fastek@sj.bigger.net. **Description:** An employment agency specializing in the placement of workers in the high-tech field. Company pays fee. **Specializes in the areas of:** Accounting/Auditing; Administration; Art/Design; Biology; Computer Science/Software; Engineering; High-Tech; Manufacturing; Sales; Technical. **Positions commonly filled include:** Architect; Biological Scientist; Broadcast Technician; Buyer; Chemical Engineer; Chemist; Civil Engineer; Clinical Lab Technician; Computer Programmer; Cost Estimator; Designer; Draftsperson; Editor; Electrical/Electronics Engineer; Electrician; Industrial Engineer; Internet Services Manager; Landscape Architect; Mechanical Engineer; Software Engineer; Structural Engineer; Systems Analyst; Technical Writer/Editor. **Benefits available to temporary workers:** Medical Insurance. **Corporate headquarters location:** This Location. **Other U.S. locations:** Orange County CA. **Average salary range of placements:** More than $50,000. **Number of placements per year:** 200 - 499.

FAY TECH SERVICES
P.O. Box 1615, Lomita CA 90717. 310/325-8744. **Fax:** 310/547-9373. **Contact:** Nasser Yazdanpanah, Owner. **Description:** A permanent employment agency. **Specializes in the areas of:** Administration; Architecture/Construction; Computer Science/Software; Economics; Engineering; Finance; Manufacturing; Personnel/Labor Relations. **Positions commonly filled include:** Administrative Manager; Chemical Engineer; Civil Engineer; Computer Programmer; Construction and Building Inspector; Cost Estimator; Design Engineer; Electrical/Electronics Engineer; Emergency Medical Technician; Environmental Engineer; Financial Analyst; Industrial Engineer; Industrial Production Manager; Landscape Architect; Mechanical Engineer; Metallurgical Engineer; Operations/Production Manager; Software Engineer; Structural Engineer; Systems Analyst; Technical Writer/Editor; Typist/Word Processor.

FILIPINOS FOR AFFIRMATIVE ACTION
310 8th Street, Suite 306, Oakland CA 94607-4253. 510/465-9876. **Fax:** 510/465-7548. **Contact:** Lillian Galedo, Executive Director. **Description:** A private, nonprofit advocacy organization that provides employment and immigration assistance, information, and other services. Company pays fee. **Specializes in the areas of:** Construction; Health/Medical; Retail; Secretarial. **Average salary range of placements:** Less than $20,000. **Number of placements per year:** 50 - 99.

FIRST CALL STAFFING
1811 Wilshire Boulevard, Suite A, Santa Monica CA 90403. 310/264-9914. **Fax:** 310/998-9217. **Contact:** Rebecca Redyck, Branch Manager. **Description:** A permanent employment agency. Company pays fee. **Specializes in the areas of:** Administration. **Positions commonly filled include:** Administrative Manager; Advertising Clerk; Branch Manager; Brokerage Clerk; Clerical Supervisor; Customer Service Representative; Human Resources Specialist; Purchasing Agent/Manager; Secretary. **Corporate headquarters location:** Torrance CA. **Other area locations:** Glendale CA. **Average salary range of placements:** $20,000 - $29,999. **Number of placements per year:** 1000+.

GPL ENGINEERING
3031 Tisch Way, Suite 810, San Jose CA 95128. 408/243-1077. **Fax:** 408/241-2652. **Contact:** Guy Leo, Owner. **Description:** A permanent employment agency. Company pays fee. **Specializes in the areas of:** Computer Science/Software; Electrical; Engineering. **Positions commonly filled include:** Electrical/Electronics Engineer; Software Engineer. **Number of placements per year:** 1 - 49.

GENERAL EMPLOYMENT ENTERPRISES INC.
21535 Hawthorne Boulevard, Suite 330, Torrance CA 90503. 310/540-9151. **Fax:** 310/316-2095. **Contact:** Agency Manager. **Description:** An employment agency that focuses on placement in the information technology industry including programming, software engineer, and network support technician positions. Company pays fee. **Specializes in the areas of:** Computer Science/Software. **Positions commonly filled include:** Internet Services Manager; MIS Specialist; Multimedia Designer; Software Engineer; Systems Analyst; Technical Writer/Editor; Telecommunications Manager. **Corporate headquarters location:** Oakbrook Terrace IL. **Other U.S. locations:** Nationwide. **Number of placements per year:** 100 - 199.

GENERAL EMPLOYMENT ENTERPRISES INC.
2540 North First Street, Suite 110, San Jose CA 95131. 408/954-9000. **Fax:** 408/943-0404. **Contact:** Albert C. Cato, Agency Manager. **Description:** A permanent employment agency. **Positions commonly filled include:** Aerospace Engineer; Computer Programmer; Design Engineer; Electrical/Electronics Engineer; Human Resources Specialist; Industrial Engineer; Management Analyst/Consultant; Mathematician; Mechanical Engineer; MIS Specialist; Multimedia Designer; Systems Analyst. **Corporate headquarters location:** Oakbrook Terrace IL. **Other U.S. locations:** Nationwide. **Average salary range of placements:** More than $50,000. **Number of placements per year:** 1000+.

GOULD PERSONNEL SERVICES
850 Colorado Boulevard, Suite 104, Los Angeles CA 90041. 213/256-5800. **Fax:** 213/255-0414. **Contact:** Warren Gould, President. **Description:** A permanent employment agency. **Specializes in the areas of:** Accounting/Auditing; Advertising; Architecture/Construction; Banking; Computer Science/Software; Economics; Finance; General Management; Health/Medical; Insurance; Legal; Manufacturing; Nonprofit; Personnel/Labor Relations; Publishing; Sales; Secretarial. **Positions commonly filled include:** Accountant/Auditor; Administrative Manager; Bank Officer/Manager; Branch Manager; Buyer; Chiropractor; Claim Representative; Clerical Supervisor; Computer Programmer; Counselor; Credit Manager; Customer Service Representative; Draftsperson; EKG Technician; Licensed Practical Nurse; Physical Therapist; Registered Nurse. **Average salary range of placements:** $20,000 - $29,999. **Number of placements per year:** 100 - 199.

GREAT 400 GROUP INTERNATIONAL
P.O. Box 5491, Carson CA 90749. 310/518-9627. **Fax:** 310/522-0103. **Contact:** Jules Howard, Manager/Senior Recruiter. **Description:** An employment agency that focuses on placing engineering, computer, and telecommunications professionals. Company pays fee. **Specializes in the areas of:** Computer Hardware/Software; Engineering; Technical. **Positions commonly filled include:** Accountant/Auditor; Administrative Assistant; Chemical Engineer; Chemist; Civil Engineer; Computer Operator; Computer Programmer; EDP Specialist; Electrical/Electronics Engineer; Industrial Engineer; Manufacturing Engineer; Mechanical Engineer; MIS Specialist; Quality Control Supervisor; Software Engineer; Systems Analyst; Technical Writer/Editor; Technician; Typist/Word Processor. **Average salary range of placements:** More than $50,000. **Number of placements per year:** 1 - 49.

INTEGRATED COMMUNITY SERVICES
3020 Kerner Boulevard, San Rafael CA 94901. 415/455-8481. **Fax:** 415/455-8483. **Contact:** Donna Lemmon, Executive Director. **Description:** An employment agency that provides both job placement services and independent living skills training for individuals with disabilities. **Specializes in the areas of:** Education; Nonprofit; Publishing; Retail; Technical. **Positions commonly filled include:** Administrative Manager; Computer Programmer; Customer Service Representative; Human Service Worker; Industrial Production Manager. **Average salary range of placements:** Less than $20,000. **Number of placements per year:** 1 - 49.

INTERIM ACCOUNTING PROFESSIONALS
18500 Von Karman Avenue, Suite 510, Irvine CA 92715. 714/756-1028. **Fax:** 714/756-1225. **Contact:** Kim Bromley, Office Manager. **Description:** A staffing agency for accounting, tax, and finance personnel. Interim Accounting Professionals offers both permanent and temporary placements. Founded in 1946. Company pays fee. **Specializes in the areas of:** Accounting/Auditing; Administration; Banking; Finance. **Positions commonly filled include:** Accountant/Auditor; Chief Financial Officer; Controller; Credit Manager; Financial Analyst. **Corporate headquarters location:** Fort Lauderdale FL. **Other U.S. locations:** Nationwide. **Average salary range of placements:** $30,000 - $50,000. **Number of placements per year:** 500 - 999.

INTERNATIONAL SEARCH CONSULTANTS
30827 Mainmast Drive, Agoura Hills CA 91301. 818/706-2635. **Fax:** 818/706-1358. **Contact:** George Schortz, President. **Description:** An employment agency focusing on sales and marketing placements. The firm operates on a contingency basis. Company pays fee. **Specializes in the areas of:** Engineering; Manufacturing; Sales; Technical. **Positions commonly filled include:** Electrical/Electronics Engineer; Marketing Specialist; Materials Engineer; Mechanical Engineer; Sales Representative. **Corporate headquarters location:** This Location. **Other U.S. locations:** Nationwide. **Average salary range of**

placements: $30,000 - $50,000. **Number of placements per year:** 1 - 49.

INTERTEC DESIGN, INC.
6922 Hollywood Boulevard, Suite 211, Hollywood CA 90028. 213/466-4388. **Fax:** 213/466-4723. **Contact:** George Bryant, Manager. **Description:** A permanent employment agency. Company pays fee. **Specializes in the areas of:** Advertising; Banking; Light Industrial; Nonprofit; Printing; Retail; Sales; Secretarial. **Positions commonly filled include:** Account Representative; Administrative Assistant; Administrative Manager; Editorial Assistant; Graphic Artist; Receptionist; Sales Representative; Secretary. **Corporate headquarters location:** Pennsauken NJ. **Other U.S. locations:** Nationwide. **Average salary range of placements:** $30,000 - $50,000. **Number of placements per year:** 1 - 49.

JAA EMPLOYMENT AGENCY
6404 Wilshire Boulevard, Suite 1230, Los Angeles CA 90048. 213/655-0285. **Fax:** 213/655-0684. **Contact:** Arthur White, President. **Description:** A permanent employment agency. **Specializes in the areas of:** Entry-Level Management; Sales. **Positions commonly filled include:** Bank Officer/Manager; Claim Representative; Customer Service Representative; Management Trainee; Underwriter/Assistant Underwriter.

JACKSON PERSONNEL
717 Market Street, Suite 224, San Francisco CA 94103. 415/546-4500. **Fax:** 415/546-0926. **Contact:** Marilyn Hogan, Manager. **Description:** A permanent employment agency. Company pays fee. **Specializes in the areas of:** Accounting/Auditing; Administration; Computer Science/Software; Insurance; Legal; Manufacturing; Personnel/Labor Relations; Sales; Secretarial; Technical. **Positions commonly filled include:** Accountant/Auditor; Administrative Manager; Advertising Clerk; Bank Officer/Manager; Branch Manager; Claim Representative; Clinical Lab Technician; Computer Programmer; Credit Manager; Designer; Editor; Financial Analyst; Food Scientist/Technologist; Health Services Manager; Management Analyst/Consultant; Medical Records Technician; Paralegal; Quality Control Supervisor; Services Sales Representative; Software Engineer; Typist/Word Processor. **Benefits available to temporary workers:** Bonus Award/Plan. **Average salary range of placements:** $20,000 - $29,999. **Number of placements per year:** 200 - 499.

JOBS PLUS
1720 South Amphlett Boulevard, Suite 123, San Mateo CA 94402. 650/994-2418. **Contact:** Michael Schocket, Job Developer. **Description:** An employment agency for persons with disabilities. Founded in 1992. **Specializes in the areas of:** Retail. **Positions commonly filled include:** Administrative Manager; Customer Service Representative; Medical Records Technician; MIS Specialist; Preschool Worker. **Corporate headquarters location:** San Mateo CA. **Average salary range of placements:** Less than $20,000. **Number of placements per year:** 1 - 49.

JUSTUS PERSONNEL SERVICES
10680 West Pico Boulevard, Suite 210, Los Angeles CA 90064. 310/204-6711. **Fax:** 310/204-2941. **Contact:** Janet Justus, Owner. **Description:** A permanent employment agency. Company pays fee. **Specializes in the areas of:** Computer Operations; Entertainment; Finance; Government; Health/Medical; Legal; Manufacturing; Nonprofit; Real Estate. **Positions commonly filled include:** Accountant/Auditor; Administrative Assistant; Bookkeeper; Clerk; Customer Service Representative; Legal Secretary; Sales and Marketing Manager; Secretary; Systems Analyst; Typist/Word Processor. **Number of placements per year:** 200 - 499.

KELCH & SHEA ASSOCIATES
1717 North California Boulevard, Suite 3B, Walnut Creek CA 94596. 510/932-6011. **Contact:** Manager. **Description:** A permanent employment agency that specializes in staffing automotive dealerships. **Specializes in the areas of:** Automotive Retailing.

LLOYD RITTER & ASSOCIATES
1043 North Shoreline Boulevard, Suite 101, Mountain View CA 94043. 650/964-6644. **Fax:** 650/964-8719. **Contact:** Manager. **Description:** A permanent employment agency. **Specializes in the areas of:** High-Tech. **Positions commonly filled include:** Computer Programmer; MIS Specialist.

MS DATA SERVICE CORPORATION
4030 Birch Street, Suite 101, Newport Beach CA 92660. 714/540-4430. **Contact:** Personnel Manager. **Description:** A permanent employment agency. **Specializes in the areas of:** Computer Hardware/Software; MIS/EDP; Technical. **Positions commonly filled include:** Computer Operator; Computer Programmer; Data Entry Clerk; EDP Specialist; MIS Specialist; Receptionist; Systems Analyst; Typist/Word Processor.

RICHARD MARIES AGENCY
200 West Pondera Avenue, Lancaster CA 93534. 805/942-0466. **Contact:** Office Manager. **Description:** A permanent employment agency. **Specializes in the areas of:** Accounting/Auditing; Clerical; Computer Hardware/Software; Health/Medical; Secretarial. **Positions commonly filled include:** Accountant/uditor; Administrative Assistant; Aerospace Engineer; Bookkeeper; Claim Representative; Customer Service Representative; Data Entry Clerk; General Manager; Hotel Manager; Legal Secretary; Medical Secretary; Receptionist; Secretary; Typist/Word Processor. **Number of placements per year:** 50 - 99.

MARK ASSOCIATES
300 Montgomery Street, Suite 860, San Francisco CA 94104. 415/392-1835. **Fax:** 415/392-7338. **Contact:** Judith Chapman, President. **E-mail address:** markpers @aol.com. **Description:** A permanent employment agency. Company pays fee. **Specializes in the areas of:** Legal. **Positions commonly filled include:** Attorney; Computer Operator; Intellectual Property Lawyer; Legal Secretary; MIS Specialist; Paralegal. **Average salary range of placements:** $30,000 - $50,000. **Number of placements per year:** 100 - 199.

THE MARTIN AGENCIES, INC.
5000 Hopyard Road, Suite 420, Pleasanton CA 94588. 510/225-0900. **Contact:** Peggy Johnston, Administrative Assistant. **Description:** An employment agency that provides both permanent and temporary placement. Company pays fee. **Specializes in the areas of:** Accounting/Auditing; Administration; Computer Science/Software; Personnel/Labor Relations; Sales; Secretarial; Technical. **Positions commonly filled include:** Accountant/Auditor; Administrative Manager; Advertising Clerk; Branch Manager; Buyer; Computer Programmer; Customer Service Representative; Financial Analyst; Internet Services Manager; MIS Specialist; Services Sales Representative; Software Engineer; Systems Analyst; Technical Writer/Editor; Typist/Word Processor. **Benefits available to temporary workers:** 401(k); Paid Holidays. **Other area locations:** Santa Clara CA; Walnut Creek CA. **Average salary range of placements:** $30,000 - $50,000. **Number of placements per year:** 100 - 199.

MAVERICK STAFFING SERVICE, LLC
9640-B Mission Gorge Road, Suite 235, Santee CA 92071. 619/448-7082. **Fax:** 619/448-7083. **Contact:** Elyse Bowers, President/CEO. **Description:** A full-service employment agency that offers contract, executive search, permanent, and temporary placements. The company operates nationwide. Founded in 1991. Company pays fee. **Specializes in the areas of:** Accounting/Auditing; Administration; Advertising; Architecture/Construction; Art/Design; Banking; Computer Science/Software; Engineering; Finance; Food Industry; General Management; Health/Medical; Industrial; Insurance; Legal; Manufacturing; Nonprofit; Personnel/Labor Relations; Sales; Secretarial; Technical; Transportation. **Positions commonly filled include:** Accountant/Auditor; Administrative Manager; Advertising Clerk; Architect; Attorney; Bank Officer/Manager; Branch Manager; Buyer; Civil Engineer; Claim Representative; Clinical Lab Technician; Computer Programmer; Counselor; Financial Analyst; Health Services Manager; Industrial Engineer; Internet Services Manager; Management Analyst/Consultant; Mechanical Engineer; Restaurant/Food Service Manager; Services Sales Representative; Software Engineer; Structural Engineer; Systems Analyst; Technical Writer/Editor; Typist/Word Processor; Wholesale and Retail Buyer. **Number of placements per year:** 200 - 499.

McCALL STAFFING SERVICES
351 California Street, Suite 1200, San Francisco CA 94104. 415/981-3400. **Contact:** Pegi Wheatley, Owner. **Description:** A permanent employment agency. Company pays fee. **Specializes in the areas of:** Clerical; Secretarial. **Positions commonly filled include:** Administrative Assistant; Bookkeeper; Clerk; Data Entry Clerk; Legal Secretary; Receptionist; Secretary; Typist/Word Processor. **Number of placements per year:** 200 - 499.

THE MEDICAL CENTER AGENCY
870 Market Street, Suite 650, San Francisco CA 94102-3014. 415/397-9440. **Fax:** 415/397-9441. **Contact:** Rafael Rey, Owner. **Description:** An employment agency that focuses on the medical and dental fields. Company pays fee. **Specializes in the areas of:** Health/Medical; Insurance. **Positions commonly filled include:** Administrative Manager; Chemist; Claim Representative; Clinical Lab Technician; Dentist; Dietician/Nutritionist; Emergency Medical Technician; Health Services Manager; Licensed Practical Nurse; Medical Records Technician; Nuclear Medicine Technologist; Pharmacist; Physical Therapist; Psychologist; Radiological Technologist; Recreational Therapist; Registered Nurse; Social Worker; Sociologist; Speech-Language Pathologist. **Average salary range of placements:** $20,000 - $29,999. **Number of placements per year:** 100 - 199.

MEDICAL STAFF UNLIMITED
3517 Marconi Avenue, Suite 207, Sacramento CA 95821. 916/485-1986. **Fax:** 916/485-4022. **Contact:** Donna Starr, Director. **E-mail address:** msu20719@tcd.net. **World Wide Web address:** http://www.ally.ins.com/~msu20719. **Description:** An employment agency focusing on the placement of permanent and temporary medical staff. Company pays fee. **Specializes in the areas of:** Health/Medical; Insurance; Secretarial. **Positions commonly filled include:** EEG Technologist; EKG Technician; Medical Records Technician; Medical Secretary; Registered Nurse; Surgical Technician. **Average salary range of placements:** $20,000 - $29,999. **Number of placements per year:** 50 - 99.

JOSEPH MICHAELS
120 Montgomery Street, Suite 1260, San Francisco CA 94104. **Toll-free phone:** 800/786-1099. **Fax:** 415/434-1165. **Contact:** Dennis Billingsley, Vice President. **Description:** A permanent employment agency. Company pays fee. **Specializes in the areas of:** Accounting/Auditing; Finance. **Positions commonly filled include:** Accountant/Auditor; Bookkeeper. **Number of placements per year:** 200 - 499.

MONROE PERSONNEL SERVICES
333 Market Street, Suite 3320, San Francisco CA 94105. 415/882-7100. **Fax:** 415/882-7145. **Contact:** Debra Monroe, Owner. **E-mail address:** monroe333@aol.com. **Description:** A permanent and temporary employment agency whose clients include law firms and international firms. Company pays fee. **Specializes in the areas of:** Engineering; Legal; Printing; Secretarial. **Positions commonly filled include:** Administrative Assistant; Advertising Clerk; Clerical Supervisor; Secretary; Typist/Word Processor. **Benefits available to temporary workers:** Paid Vacation. **Corporate headquarters location:** This Location. **Average salary range of placements:** $30,000 - $50,000. **Number of placements per year:** 50 - 99.

M.O.R.E. EMPLOYMENT SERVICES
261 Placerville Drive, Placerville CA 95667. 530/621-4027. **Fax:** 530/622-0204. **Contact:** Patrick Pettibone, Supported Employment Coordinator. **Description:** A private, nonprofit permanent employment agency that offers counseling, training, and job search assistance for people with developmental disabilities. **Specializes in the areas of:** Food Industry; Health/Medical. **Positions commonly filled include:** Preschool Worker. **Corporate headquarters location:** This Location. **Other area locations:** South Lake Tahoe CA. **Average salary range of placements:** Less than $20,000. **Number of placements per year:** 1 - 49.

MOTHERS-IN-DEED, INC.
TOWN END COUNTRY NANNIES
425 Sherman Avenue, Suite 130, Palo Alto CA 94306. 650/326-8570. **Fax:** 650/326-1556. **Contact:** Recruiter. **Description:** A permanent employment agency. Company pays fee. **Specializes in the areas of:** Child Care, In-Home. **Positions commonly filled include:** Nanny. **Number of placements per year:** 200 - 499.

MULTAX SYSTEMS, INC.
505 North Sepulveda Boulevard, Suite 7, Manhattan Beach CA 90266-6743. 310/379-8398. **Fax:** 310/379-1142. **Contact:** Randy Heinesh, General Manager. **Description:** A permanent employment agency. Company pays fee. **Specializes in the areas of:** Computer Science/Software; Engineering. **Positions commonly filled include:** Computer Programmer; Designer; Draftsperson; Software Engineer; Structural Engineer; Systems Analyst. **Number of placements per year:** 200 - 499.

NATIONAL ASIAN PACIFIC CENTER ON AGING
3407 West 6th Street, Suite 800, Los Angeles CA 90020. 213/365-9005. **Contact:** Project Director. **Description:** A nonprofit, private organization that offers job placements in conjunction with funding from the Older American Act. **Specializes in the areas of:** Retail; Secretarial; Technical; Transportation. **Positions commonly filled include:** Human Service Worker; Licensed Practical Nurse; Market Research Analyst; Registered Nurse; Social Worker; Teacher/Professor; Travel Agent. **Average salary range of placements:** Less than $20,000. **Number of placements per year:** 1 - 49.

NELSON HUMAN RESOURCE SOLUTIONS
19080 Lomita Avenue, Sonoma CA 95476. 707/935-6113. **Fax:** 707/935-6124. **Contact:** Jeff Phelps, Vice

President. **World Wide Web address:** http://www.nelsonjobs.com. **Description:** This location houses administrative offices only. Overall, Nelson Human Resource Solutions provides full-service staffing through four divisions: Nelson Staffing Solutions, Accountants Plus, Nelson Associates, and TechSource. **Specializes in the areas of:** Accounting/Auditing; Administration; Banking; Computer Science/Software; Engineering; Finance; General Management; Industrial; Legal; Light Industrial; Sales; Secretarial; Technical. **Benefits available to temporary workers:** Bonus Award/Plan; Medical Insurance; Paid Holidays. **Corporate headquarters location:** This Location. **Number of placements per year:** 1000+.

NELSON STAFFING SOLUTIONS
ACCOUNTANTS PLUS
3478 Buskirk Avenue, Suite 105, Pleasant Hill CA 94523. 510/933-0505. **Contact:** Office Manager. **Description:** A permanent employment agency that also provides temporary placements. Accountants Plus (also at this location) provides permanent and temporary accounting and finance placements. **Specializes in the areas of:** Administration; Manufacturing; Office Support; Secretarial; Technical. **Corporate headquarters location:** Sonoma CA.

NELSON STAFFING SOLUTIONS
ACCOUNTANTS PLUS
425 California Street, Suite 600, San Francisco CA 94523. 415/989-9911. **Contact:** Office Manager. **Description:** A permanent employment agency that also provides temporary placements. Accountants Plus (also at this location) provides permanent and temporary accounting and finance placements. **Specializes in the areas of:** Administration; Manufacturing; Office Support; Secretarial; Technical. **Corporate headquarters location:** Sonoma CA.

NESCO SERVICE COMPANY
2431 North Tustin Avenue, Suite H, Santa Ana CA 92705-1660. 714/973-1303. **Toll-free phone:** 800/300-9711. **Fax:** 714/972-8947. **Contact:** Nelly Ricti, Branch Manager. **Description:** A permanent employment agency. **Specializes in the areas of:** Accounting/Auditing; Administration; Food Industry; General Management; Manufacturing; Personnel/Labor Relations; Secretarial. **Positions commonly filled include:** Administrative Manager; Blue-Collar Worker Supervisor; Branch Manager; Claim Representative; Clerical Supervisor; Computer Programmer; Restaurant/Food Service Manager; Services Sales Representative; Typist/Word Processor. **Benefits available to temporary workers:** 401(k); Medical Insurance; Paid Holidays; Paid Vacation. **Corporate headquarters location:** Tampa FL. **Other U.S. locations:** Nationwide. **Average salary range of placements:** $20,000 - $29,999. **Number of placements per year:** 1000+.

NURSES INTERNATIONAL
3319 Glendale Boulevard, Suite E, Los Angeles CA 90039. 213/662-1916. **Contact:** Manager. **Description:** A permanent employment agency. **Specializes in the areas of:** Health/Medical. **Positions commonly filled include:** Registered Nurse. **Number of placements per year:** 100 - 199.

OFFICEMATES5
DAYSTAR TEMPORARY SERVICES
3031 Tisch Way, Suite 606, San Jose CA 95128. 408/246-9696. **Fax:** 408/246-2423. **Contact:** Verna File, Regional Manager. **Description:** An employment agency focusing on permanent placement. A division of Management Recruiters International, Officemates5 provides temporary placement through the company's affiliate, Daystar Temporary Services (also at this location). Company pays fee. **Specializes in the areas of:** Accounting/Auditing; Administration; Personnel/Labor Relations; Sales; Secretarial. **Positions commonly filled include:** Accountant/Auditor; Administrative Assistant; Administrative Manager; Advertising Clerk; Branch Manager; Credit Manager; Customer Service Representative; Financial Analyst; Human Resources Specialist; Management Trainee; Marketing Specialist; Typist/Word Processor. **Benefits available to temporary workers:** Dental Insurance; Medical Insurance. **Corporate headquarters location:** Cleveland OH. **Other U.S. locations:** Nationwide. **Average salary range of placements:** $20,000 - $50,000. **Number of placements per year:** 200 - 499.

ONYX PERSONNEL SERVICES
1007 Northlake Avenue, Pasadena CA 91104. 626/798-4528. **Toll-free phone:** 800/838-4669. **Fax:** 626/798-6955. **Contact:** Tina Gallegos, Sales Manager. **Description:** Onyx Personnel focuses on temporary and permanent placement for the following fields: clerical, secretarial, word processing, accounting, sales, management, engineering, and technical. **Specializes in the areas of:** Accounting/Auditing; Finance; General Management; Industrial; Insurance; Sales; Secretarial. **Positions commonly filled include:** Accountant/Auditor; Administrative Manager; Clerical Supervisor; Credit Manager; Customer Service Representative; General Manager; Management Trainee; Quality Control Supervisor; Registered Nurse; Services Sales Representative. **Average salary range of placements:** $20,000 - $29,999. **Number of placements per year:** 200 - 499.

PIPS PERSONNEL SERVICES
5000 East Spring, Long Beach CA 90815. 562/425-8282. **Contact:** Ernie Davis, Owner/General Manager. **Description:** A permanent employment agency. The medical division specializes in mid-level executive management positions nationwide in the homecare, hospital, and long-term care areas. Company pays fee. **Specializes in the areas of:** Accounting/Auditing; Clerical; Finance; Sales. **Positions commonly filled include:** Accountant/Auditor; Administrative Assistant; Bookkeeper; Clerk; Computer Operator; Computer Programmer; Credit Manager; Customer Service Representative; Data Entry Clerk; EDP Specialist; Legal Secretary; Medical Secretary; Receptionist; Sales Representative; Secretary; Support Personnel; Systems Analyst; Technical Writer/Editor; Typist/Word Processor; Underwriter. **Number of placements per year:** 100 - 199.

PREMIER NURSING SERVICE
444 West Ocean Boulevard, Suite 604, Long Beach CA 90802. 562/437-4313. **Fax:** 562/495-1508. **Contact:** Office Manager. **Description:** A permanent employment agency. **Specializes in the areas of:** Health/Medical. **Positions commonly filled include:** Nurse. **Number of placements per year:** 1000+.

PRESTIGE PERSONNEL SERVICE
19071 Colima Road, Rowland Heights CA 91748. 626/964-1082. **Contact:** Ms. Toni Shores, President. **Description:** A permanent employment agency. Company pays fee. **Specializes in the areas of:** Clerical; Manufacturing; Secretarial. **Positions commonly filled include:** Administrative Assistant; Bookkeeper; Clerk; Customer Service Representative; Data Entry Clerk; Human Resources Manager; Legal Secretary; Light Industrial Worker; Sales Representative; Secretary; Stenographer; Typist/Word Processor. **Number of placements per year:** 200 - 499.

PRO FOUND
108 Whispering Pines Drive, Suite 200, Scotts Valley CA 95066. 408/461-7000. **Contact:** Office Manager.

Description: A permanent employment agency. **Specializes in the areas of:** Engineering; Sales.

PRO STAFF PERSONNEL SERVICES
879 West 190th Street, Suite 935, Torrance CA 90248. 310/353-2411. **Fax:** 310/353-2416. **Contact:** Staffing Supervisor. **Description:** A permanent employment agency that also provides temporary placements. **Specializes in the areas of:** Accounting/Auditing; Administration; Computer Science/Software; Industrial; Personnel/Labor Relations. **Positions commonly filled include:** Accountant/Auditor; Administrative Manager; Bank Officer/Manager; Branch Manager; Claim Representative; Computer Programmer; Customer Service Representative; Environmental Engineer; Financial Analyst; Internet Services Manager; MIS Specialist; Services Sales Representative. **Corporate headquarters location:** Minneapolis MN. **Other U.S. locations:** Nationwide. **Number of placements per year:** 1000+.

PRO STAFF PERSONNEL SERVICES
225 West Broadway, Suite 103, Glendale CA 91204-1331. 818/551-9145. **Fax:** 818/551-1284. **Contact:** Manager. **Description:** An employment agency that offers both permanent and temporary placements. **Specializes in the areas of:** Accounting/Auditing; Administration; Banking; Computer Science/Software; Engineering; Finance; Industrial; Insurance; Legal; Manufacturing; Personnel/Labor Relations; Secretarial; Technical. **Positions commonly filled include:** Accountant/Auditor; Administrative Manager; Clerical Supervisor; Computer Programmer; Human Resources Specialist; MIS Specialist; Quality Control Supervisor; Typist/Word Processor. **Benefits available to temporary workers:** 401(k); Dental Insurance; Medical Insurance; Referral Bonus Plan. **Corporate headquarters location:** Minneapolis MN. **Other U.S. locations:** Nationwide. **Average salary range of placements:** $30,000 - $50,000. **Number of placements per year:** 1000+.

PRO STAFF PERSONNEL SERVICES
18300 Von Karman Avenue, Suite 710, Irvine CA 92612. 714/250-8850. **Toll-free phone:** 800/979-2100. **Fax:** 714/250-8862. **Contact:** Deirdre Honner, Recruiter. **E-mail address:** deirdrehonner@prostaff.com. **World Wide Web address:** http://www.prostaff.com. **Description:** A permanent employment agency. Company pays fee. **Specializes in the areas of:** Accounting/Auditing; Administration; Computer Science/Software; Fashion; General Management; Nonprofit; Personnel/Labor Relations. **Positions commonly filled include:** Accountant/Auditor; Administrative Manager; Bank Officer/Manager; Budget Analyst; Buyer; Claim Representative; Computer Programmer; Credit Manager; Customer Service Representative; Electrical/Electronics Engineer; Electrician; Environmental Engineer; Mechanical Engineer; MIS Specialist; Paralegal; Quality Control Supervisor; Software Engineer; Structural Engineer; Technical Writer/Editor; Underwriter/Assistant Underwriter. **Benefits available to temporary workers:** 401(k); Dental Insurance; Medical Insurance; Paid Holidays; Paid Vacation. **Corporate headquarters location:** Minneapolis MN. **Other U.S. locations:** Nationwide. **Number of placements per year:** 500 - 999.

PROFILE PERSONNEL SERVICE
4858 Mercury Street, Suite 212, San Diego CA 92111. 619/593-9292. **Contact:** Timo Masalin, Owner. **Description:** An employment agency that focuses on sales and management positions. Company pays fee. **Specializes in the areas of:** Finance; General Management; Industrial; Manufacturing; Personnel/Labor Relations; Retail; Sales; Transportation. **Positions commonly filled include:** Branch Manager; Credit Manager; Customer Service Representative; General Manager; Manufacturer's/Wholesaler's Sales Rep.; Operations/Production Manager; Services Sales Representative. **Average salary range of placements:** $20,000 - $29,999. **Number of placements per year:** 50 - 99.

PRYOR & ASSOCIATES
90 New Montgomery, Suite 401, San Francisco CA 94105. 415/908-1388. **Contact:** Jo-Ann Pryor, Managing Partner. **Description:** A permanent employment agency. Company pays fee. **Specializes in the areas of:** Insurance. **Positions commonly filled include:** Accountant/Auditor; Actuary; Adjuster; Administrative Manager; Claim Representative; Underwriter. **Number of placements per year:** 50 - 99.

QUORUM/LANIER LEGAL STAFFING
650 Castro Street, Suite 250, Mountain View CA 94041-2056. 650/964-2060. **Fax:** 650/964-2332. **Contact:** Tania Plevel, Staffing Specialist. **E-mail address:** tplevel@qlanier.com. **Description:** A permanent employment agency. Founded in 1993. Company pays fee. **Specializes in the areas of:** Legal. **Positions commonly filled include:** Attorney; Paralegal. **Benefits available to temporary workers:** 401(k); Medical Insurance; Paid Holidays. **Corporate headquarters location:** Bloomington MN. **Other U.S. locations:** Los Angeles CA; San Francisco CA; Chicago IL; Minneapolis MN. **Average salary range of placements:** $30,000 - $50,000. **Number of placements per year:** 200 - 499.

RAND PERSONNEL
1200 Truxtun, Suite 130, Bakersfield CA 93301. 805/325-0751. **Contact:** Sonia Simrin, Owner/Manager. **Description:** A permanent employment agency. Company pays fee. **Positions commonly filled include:** Accountant/Auditor; Administrative Assistant; Bookkeeper; Clerk; Computer Operator; Computer Programmer; Credit Manager; Customer Service Representative; Data Entry Clerk; Draftsperson; EDP Specialist; Legal Secretary; Medical Secretary; Receptionist; Sales Representative; Secretary; Stenographer; Typist/Word Processor. **Number of placements per year:** 100 - 199.

RELIANCE STAFFING SERVICES
201 South Lake Avenue, Suite 507, Pasedena CA 91351. 626/583-4703. **Fax:** 626/583-4760. **Contact:** Renee Dominique, Branch Service Manager. **Description:** An employment agency that specializes in administrative and clerical services, accounting and financial services, manufacturing and assembly support, technical services, and light industrial services. Company pays fee. **Specializes in the areas of:** Computer Science/Software; Manufacturing; Personnel/Labor Relations; Sales; Secretarial; Technical. **Positions commonly filled include:** Computer Programmer; Customer Service Representative; Internet Services Manager; Librarian; MIS Specialist; Operations/Production Manager; Software Engineer; Systems Analyst; Technical Writer/Editor; Typist/Word Processor. **Corporate headquarters location:** Los Angeles CA. **Average salary range of placements:** $20,000 - $29,999. **Number of placements per year:** 100 - 199.

RENOIR STAFFING SERVICES INC.
3710 Grand Avenue, Oakland CA 94610. 510/836-2220. **Fax:** 510/836-0321. **Contact:** Greg Dencker, Vice President. **Description:** A permanent employment agency. **Specializes in the areas of:** Banking; Computer Science/Software; Personnel/Labor Relations; Real Estate. **Positions commonly filled include:** Accountant/Auditor; Administrative Manager; Architect; Computer Programmer; Construction and

Building Inspector; Cost Estimator; Customer Service Representative; Design Engineer; Electrical/Electronics Engineer; Environmental Engineer; General Manager; Human Resources Specialist; Human Service Worker; Management Analyst/Consultant; Mining Engineer; Property and Real Estate Manager; Real Estate Agent; Services Sales Representative; Software Engineer. **Average salary range of placements:** $20,000 - $29,999. **Number of placements per year:** 1000+.

ELIZABETH ROSE AGENCY
1434 6th Street, Suite 3, Santa Monica CA 90401-2527. 310/451-4866. **Fax:** 310/451-3786. **Contact:** Recruiter. **Description:** A full-service domestic employment agency that places nannies, housekeepers, chefs, and personal assistants (often to celebrity clients). **Specializes in the areas of:** Personnel/Labor Relations. **Positions commonly filled include:** Licensed Practical Nurse; Preschool Worker; Registered Nurse; Speech-Language Pathologist; Teacher/Professor. **Number of placements per year:** 100 - 199.

RUSSELL STAFFING RESOURCES, INC.
351 California Street, Suite 850, San Francisco CA 94104. 415/781-1444. **Toll-free phone:** 800/616-5627. **Fax:** 415/986-6003. **Contact:** Carol Russell, President. **E-mail address:** russtaff@sprynet.com. **Description:** A permanent employment agency. Company pays fee. **Specializes in the areas of:** Accounting/Auditing; Administration; Advertising; Banking; Computer Science/Software; Finance; General Management; Insurance; Legal; Manufacturing; Personnel/Labor Relations; Secretarial. **Positions commonly filled include:** Accountant/Auditor; Administrative Manager; Advertising Clerk; Bank Officer/Manager; Branch Manager; Brokerage Clerk; Budget Analyst; Claim Representative; Clerical Supervisor; Computer Programmer; Cost Estimator; Credit Manager; Internet Services Manager; Management Analyst/Consultant; MIS Specialist; Multimedia Designer; Software Engineer; Systems Analyst; Telecommunications Manager; Typist/Word Processor; Underwriter/Assistant Underwriter. **Other area locations:** Petaluma CA. **Average salary range of placements:** $30,000 - $50,000. **Number of placements per year:** 1000+.

SANTA BARBARA PLACEMENT
1300B Santa Barbara Street, Suite B, Santa Barbara CA 93101-2017. 805/965-0511. **Fax:** 805/730-1694. **Contact:** G. Allan, Recruiter. **E-mail address:** ncc@west.net. **Description:** An employment agency operating on both retainer and contingency bases. Santa Barbara Placement offers permanent and temporary placements as well as career/outplacement counseling. **Specializes in the areas of:** Accounting/Auditing; Administration; Advertising; Architecture/Construction; Art/Design; Banking; Biology; Computer Science/Software; Engineering; Finance; General Management; Industrial; Insurance; Legal; Light Industrial; Manufacturing; Nonprofit; Personnel/Labor Relations; Sales; Secretarial; Technical. **Positions commonly filled include:** Account Manager; Account Representative; Accountant; Administrative Assistant; Administrative Manager; Chief Financial Officer; Clinical Lab Technician; Computer Operator; Computer Programmer; Controller; Database Manager; Design Engineer; Electrical/Electronics Engineer; Finance Director; Financial Analyst; Graphic Designer; Internet Services Manager; Marketing Manager; Marketing Specialist; Mechanical Engineer; MIS Specialist; Sales Engineer; Sales Executive; Sales Manager; Sales Representative; Software Engineer; Technical Writer/Editor; Typist /Word Processor. **Corporate headquarters location:** This Location. **Other area locations:** Ventura CA. **Average salary range of placements:** $30,000 - $50,000. **Number of placements per year:** 1000+.

SELECT PERSONNEL SERVICES
1528 Chapala Street, Santa Barbara CA 93101. 805/882-2200. **Fax:** 805/882-2210. **Contact:** Manager. **Description:** An employment agency that provides both permanent and temporary placements. **Benefits available to temporary workers:** Paid Holidays; Paid Vacation. **Average salary range of placements:** $20,000 - $29,999. **Number of placements per year:** 1000+.

SHARF, WOODWARD & ASSOCIATES
5900 Sepulveda Boulevard, Suite 104, Sherman Oaks CA 91411. 818/989-2200. **Fax:** 818/781-5554. **Contact:** Office Manager. **Description:** Sharf, Woodward & Associates is a technical computer contract placement and permanent placement firm. **Specializes in the areas of:** Computer Science/Software. **Positions commonly filled include:** Computer Programmer; MIS Specialist; Software Engineer; Systems Analyst. **Average salary range of placements:** More than $50,000. **Number of placements per year:** 200 - 499.

DAVID SHARP & ASSOCIATES
800 Wilshire Boulevard, Suite 1475, Los Angeles CA 90017-2604. 213/486-9801. **Fax:** 213/486-9874. **Contact:** David Sharp, Owner. **E-mail address:** sharpjobs@earthlink.com. **World Wide Web address:** http://www.sharpjobs.com. **Description:** A full-service permanent employment agency focusing on clerical, finance, and advertising positions. Company pays fee. **Specializes in the areas of:** Accounting/Auditing; Administration; Advertising; Banking; Computer Science/Software; Economics; Finance; General Management; Health/Medical; Legal; Personnel/Labor Relations; Secretarial; Technical. **Positions commonly filled include:** Account Representative; Accountant; Administrative Assistant; Advertising Clerk; Applications Engineer; Bank Officer/Manager; Budget Analyst; Chief Financial Officer; Civil Engineer; Computer Operator; Computer Programmer; EFinancial Analyst; Graphic Artist; Human Resources Manager; Management Analyst/Consultant; MIS Specialist; Paralegal; Secretary; Statistician. **Average salary range of placements:** $30,000 - $50,000. **Number of placements per year:** 500 - 999.

SNELLING PERSONNEL SERVICES
26229 Eden Landing Road, Suite 3, Hayward CA 94545. 510/887-8210. **Fax:** 510/887-8533. **Contact:** Manager. **E-mail address:** haysnell@tdl.com. **World Wide Web address:** http://www.snelling.com/hayward. **Description:** A permanent employment agency. Company pays fee. **Specializes in the areas of:** Accounting/Auditing; Clerical; Legal; Personnel/Labor Relations; Secretarial. **Positions commonly filled include:** Accountant/Auditor; Administrative Assistant; Bookkeeper; Clerical Supervisor; Customer Service Representative; Data Entry Clerk; Human Service Worker; Legal Secretary; Secretary; Typist/Word Processor. **Number of placements per year:** 200 - 499.

SOURCE ENGINEERING
1290 Oakmead Parkway, Suite 318, Sunnyvale CA 94086. 408/738-8440. **Fax:** 408/730-1042. **Contact:** Managing Director. **Description:** A permanent employment agency. Company pays fee. **Specializes in the areas of:** Computer Science/Software; Engineering; Sales; Technical. **Positions commonly filled include:** Branch Manager; Computer Programmer; Electrical/Electronics Engineer; Management Analyst/Consultant; Software Engineer; Systems Analyst. **Number of placements per year:** 50 - 99.

DANIELLE STEVENS & ASSOCIATES
14801 Pacific Avenue, Suite 210, Baldwin Park CA 91706. 626/338-1257. **Contact:** Manager. **Description:** A permanent employment agency that places legal staff. **Specializes in the areas of:** Legal.

FRED STUART PERSONNEL SERVICES
5855 East Naples Plaza, Suite 310, Long Beach CA 90803-5078. 562/439-0921. **Toll-free phone:** 800/298-3021. **Fax:** 562/439-2750. **Contact:** Fred Stuart, Owner. **Description:** An employment agency that also offers contract services. Company pays fee. **Specializes in the areas of:** Administration; Computer Hardware/Software; General Management; Personnel/Labor Relations. **Positions commonly filled include:** Accountant/Auditor; Branch Manager; Chemical Engineer; Civil Engineer; Computer Operator; Computer Programmer; EDP Specialist; Financial Analyst; MIS Specialist; Multimedia Designer; Petroleum Engineer; Software Engineer; Systems Analyst; Technical Writer/Editor; Telecommunications Manager. **Average salary range of placements:** More than $50,000. **Number of placements per year:** 1 - 49.

SUNDAY & ASSOCIATES, INC.
P.O. Box 847, Petaluma CA 94953. 510/644-0440. **Contact:** Michael Sunday, Owner. **Description:** A permanent employment agency. **Specializes in the areas of:** Computer Hardware/Software; Technical. **Positions commonly filled include:** Computer Programmer; Software Engineer; Systems Analyst; Technical Writer/Editor.

SYSTEM ONE
3021 Citrus Circle, Suite 230, Walnut Creek CA 94598. 510/932-8801. **Fax:** 510/932-3651. **Contact:** Dave Doyle, Owner. **E-mail address:** system1search@ccnet.com. **World Wide Web address:** http://www.ccnet.com~system. **Description:** A permanent employment agency. Company pays fee. **Specializes in the areas of:** Computer Science/Software; Engineering; Manufacturing; Technical. **Positions commonly filled include:** Chemical Engineer; Electrical/Electronics Engineer; Industrial Engineer; Manufacturing Engineer; Mechanical Engineer. **Number of placements per year:** 1 - 49.

SYSTEMATICS AGENCY INC.
1448 15th Street, Santa Monica CA 90404. 310/395-4991. **Fax:** 310/395-2254. **Contact:** Peter J. Locke, Owner. **Description:** An employment agency that provides both permanent and temporary placement of computer personnel. Company pays fee. **Specializes in the areas of:** Administration; Computer Science/Software. **Positions commonly filled include:** Computer Programmer; MIS Specialist; Software Engineer; Systems Analyst; Telecommunications Manager. **Average salary range of placements:** $30,000 - $50,000. **Number of placements per year:** 100 - 199.

T.R. EMPLOYMENT AGENCY
2800 28th Street, Suite 330, Santa Monica CA 90405. 310/399-6107. **Contact:** Tel Ramon, Manager. **Description:** A permanent employment agency. Company pays fee. **Specializes in the areas of:** Accounting/Auditing; Administration; Advertising; Bilingual; Engineering; General Management; Industrial; Manufacturing; Sales. **Positions commonly filled include:** Accountant/Auditor; Administrative Assistant; Aerospace Engineer; Architect; Attorney; Biological Scientist; Chemist; Civil Engineer; Computer Programmer; Food Scientist/Technologist; General Manager; Industrial Engineer; Legal Secretary; Purchasing Agent/Manager; Quality Assurance Engineer; Sales Representative; Secretary; Statistician. **Number of placements per year:** 1000+.

TRC STAFFING SERVICES
101 North Brand Boulevard, Suite 920, Glendale CA 91203-2619. 818/548-3597. **Contact:** Nancy Richards, Senior Branch Manager. **World Wide Web address:** http://www.members.gnn.com/gfprbess/com. **Description:** A permanent and temporary staffing service that offers general office, marketing, information processing, accounting/bookkeeping, light industrial, and technical positions. **Specializes in the areas of:** Legal; Personnel/Labor Relations; Secretarial. **Positions commonly filled include:** Human Resources Manager; Paralegal. **Corporate headquarters location:** Atlanta GA. **Other U.S. locations:** Nationwide. **Number of placements per year:** 200 - 499.

TRC STAFFING SERVICES
11300 West Olympic Boulevard, Suite 780, Los Angeles CA 90064. 310/473-4161. **Fax:** 310/445-9243. **Contact:** Branch Manager. **E-mail address:** trcwest@aol.com. **World Wide Web address:** http://www.members.gnn.com/gfprbess/com. **Description:** A permanent and temporary employment agency that provides general office, marketing, information processing, accounting/bookkeeping, light industrial, and technical placements. Founded in 1986. Company pays fee. **Specializes in the areas of:** Accounting/Auditing; Administration; Banking; Computer Science/Software; Education; Finance; Health/Medical; Insurance; Legal; Light Industrial; Nonprofit; Personnel/Labor Relations; Sales; Secretarial. **Positions commonly filled include:** Accountant/Auditor; Administrative Manager; Branch Manager; Computer Programmer; Financial Analyst; General Manager; Human Service Worker; Paralegal; Systems Analyst. **Benefits available to temporary workers:** Medical Insurance; Paid Holidays; Paid Vacation. **Corporate headquarters location:** Atlanta GA. **Other U.S. locations:** Nationwide. **Average salary range of placements:** $20,000 - $29,999. **Number of placements per year:** 500 - 999.

TRC STAFFING SERVICES
1337 East Thousand Oaks Boulevard, Suite 110, Thousand Oaks CA 91360-5713. 805/497-9051. **Fax:** 805/497-4093. **Contact:** Denise Figueiredo, President. **World Wide Web address:** http://www.members.gnn.com/gfprbess/com. **Description:** A permanent employment agency. Company pays fee. **Specializes in the areas of:** Accounting/Auditing; Advertising; Computer Hardware/Software; Engineering; Finance; Health/ Medical; Industrial; Legal; Manufacturing; Nonprofit; Personnel/Labor Relations; Secretarial; Technical. **Positions commonly filled include:** Accountant/Auditor; Biochemist; Branch Manager; Buyer; Clerical Supervisor; Clinical Lab Technician; Cost Estimator; Credit Manager; Customer Service Representative; Electrical/Electronics Engineer; Health Services Manager; Industrial Production Manager; Licensed Practical Nurse; Mechanical Engineer; MIS Specialist; Operations/Production Manager; Typist/Word Processor. **Benefits available to temporary workers:** Medical Insurance; Paid Holidays; Paid Vacation. **Corporate headquarters location:** Atlanta GA. **Other U.S. locations:** Nationwide. **Average salary range of placements:** $30,000 - $50,000. **Number of placements per year:** 1000+.

TAD DATA SERVICES
200 Corporate Pointe, Suite 120, Culver City CA 90230. 310/410-6740. **Contact:** Richard Knorr, Manager. **Description:** A permanent employment agency. **Specializes in the areas of:** Engineering; Technical.

TAD RESOURCES INTERNATIONAL
17621 Irvine Boulevard, Suite 214, Tustin CA 92780-3131. 714/838-4380. **Contact:** Manager. **Description:** An employment agency offering both permanent and

temporary placements. **Specializes in the areas of:** Engineering; Technical. **Positions commonly filled include:** Buyer; Chemical Engineer; Chemist; Civil Engineer; Design Engineer; Designer; Draftsperson; Electrical/Electronics Engineer; Environmental Engineer; Financial Analyst; Industrial Engineer; Market Research Analyst; Mechanical Engineer; MIS Specialist; Multimedia Designer; Nuclear Engineer; Software Engineer; Structural Engineer; Technical Writer/Editor. **Corporate headquarters location:** Cambridge MA. **Other U.S. locations:** Nationwide. **International locations:** Worldwide. **Number of placements per year:** 500 - 999.

TAD RESOURCES INTERNATIONAL
3450 East Spring Street, Suite 103, Long Beach CA 90806. 562/426-0446. **Fax:** 562/426-7876. **Contact:** Ms. Gentle Benjamin, Recruiter. **Description:** A permanent employment agency. Founded in 1956. Company pays fee. **Specializes in the areas of:** Accounting/Auditing; Administration; Computer Science/Software; Engineering; Insurance; Legal; Manufacturing; Secretarial; Technical. **Positions commonly filled include:** Accountant/Auditor; Buyer; Customer Service Representative; Designer; Draftsperson; Electrical/Electronics Engineer; Management Analyst/Consultant; Mechanical Engineer; MIS Specialist; Operations/Production Manager; Paralegal; Quality Control Supervisor; Software Engineer; Structural Engineer; Technical Writer/Editor; Typist/Word Processor. **Benefits available to temporary workers:** 401(k); Dental Insurance; Medical Insurance; Vision Plan. **Corporate headquarters location:** Cambridge MA. **Other U.S. locations:** Nationwide. **International locations:** Worldwide. **Average salary range of placements:** $30,000 - $50,000. **Number of placements per year:** 500 - 999.

TALENT TREE STAFFING SERVICES
11220 Gold Express Drive, Suite 401, Gold River CA 95670. 916/631-1401. **Fax:** 916/631-1406. **Contact:** Jill Zimmerman, Vice President. **World Wide Web address:** http://www.ttree.com. **Description:** An employment agency providing both permanent and temporary placements. Founded in 1976. **Specializes in the areas of:** Banking; Personnel/Labor Relations; Secretarial. **Positions commonly filled include:** Customer Service Representative; Typist/Word Processor. **Benefits available to temporary workers:** 401(k); Dental Insurance; Medical Insurance; Vision Plan. **Corporate headquarters location:** Houston TX. **Other U.S. locations:** Nationwide. **Average salary range of placements:** $30,000 - $50,000. **Number of placements per year:** 50 - 99.

TALENT TREE STAFFING SERVICES
343 Sansome Street, Suite 170, San Francisco CA 94104. 415/391-2333. **Fax:** 415/391-2270. **Contact:** Leigh Shughrou, Service Manager. **World Wide Web address:** http://www.ttree.com. **Description:** An employment agency that provides both permanent and temporary placements. Founded in 1976. Company pays fee. **Specializes in the areas of:** Banking; Finance; Personnel/Labor Relations; Secretarial. **Positions commonly filled include:** Customer Service Representative; Typist/Word Processor. **Benefits available to temporary workers:** 401(k); Dental Insurance; Medical Insurance; Vision Plan. **Corporate headquarters location:** Houston TX. **Other U.S. locations:** Nationwide. **Average salary range of placements:** $30,000 - $50,000. **Number of placements per year:** 50 - 99.

TALENT TREE STAFFING SERVICES
500 Ygnacio Valley Road, Suite 160, Walnut Creek CA 94596. 510/937-4550. **Fax:** 510/937-4552. **Contact:** Leigh Shughrou, Service Manager. **World Wide Web address:** http://www.ttree.com. **Description:** An employment agency that provides both permanent and temporary placements. Founded in 1976. Company pays fee. **Specializes in the areas of:** Banking; Finance; Personnel/Labor Relations; Secretarial. **Positions commonly filled include:** Customer Service Representative; Typist/Word Processor. **Benefits available to temporary workers:** 401(k); Dental Insurance; Medical Insurance; Vision Plan. **Corporate headquarters location:** Houston TX. **Other U.S. locations:** Nationwide. **Average salary range of placements:** $30,000 - $50,000. **Number of placements per year:** 50 - 99.

TALENT TREE STAFFING SERVICES
2600 El Camino Real, Suite 415, Palo Alto CA 94306. 650/813-8310. **Fax:** 650/813-8312. **Contact:** Robin Simpkins, Senior Staffing Consultant. **World Wide Web address:** http://www.ttree.com. **Description:** An employment agency that provides both permanent and temporary placements in administrative, accounting, and customer service positions. Founded in 1976. Company pays fee. **Specializes in the areas of:** Accounting/Auditing; Administration; Banking; Computer Science/Software; Finance; Health/Medical; Personnel/Labor Relations; Sales; Secretarial. **Positions commonly filled include:** Accountant/Auditor; Administrative Manager; Buyer; Clerical Supervisor; Customer Service Representative; Financial Analyst; Human Resources Specialist; Management Trainee; Medical Secretary; Typist/Word Processor. **Benefits available to temporary workers:** 401(k); Dental Insurance; Medical Insurance; Paid Holidays; Referral Bonus Plan; Vision Plan. **Corporate headquarters location:** Houston TX. **Other U.S. locations:** Nationwide. **Average salary range of placements:** $20,000 - $29,999. **Number of placements per year:** 500 - 999.

TECH SEARCH
2015 Bridgeway, Suite 301, Sausalito CA 94965. 415/332-1282. **Toll-free phone:** 800/870-5627. **Fax:** 415/332-1285. **Contact:** Roger M. King, President. **E-mail address:** resume@jobsight.com. **World Wide Web address:** http://www.jobsight.com. **Description:** A permanent employment agency. Company pays fee. **Specializes in the areas of:** Computer Science/Software. **Positions commonly filled include:** Computer Programmer; Software Engineer; Systems Analyst; Technical Writer/Editor. **Other U.S. locations:** Nationwide. **Average salary range of placements:** More than $50,000. **Number of placements per year:** 200 - 499.

TECHNICAL DIRECTIONS, INC. (TDI)
8880 Rio San Diego Drive, Suite 925, San Diego CA 92108. 619/297-5611. **Contact:** Office Manager. **Description:** A permanent employment agency. Company pays fee. **Specializes in the areas of:** Banking; Computer Hardware/Software; Finance; Manufacturing; MIS/EDP; Technical. **Positions commonly filled include:** Computer Programmer; EDP Specialist; Systems Analyst; Technical Writer/Editor. **Number of placements per year:** 50 - 99.

TOD PERSONNEL
20 East 20th Avenue, San Mateo CA 94403. 650/574-8900. **Fax:** 650/574-2636. **Contact:** Manager. **Description:** A permanent employment agency. **Specializes in the areas of:** Legal. **Positions commonly filled include:** Accountant/Auditor; Administrative Manager; Buyer; Claim Representative; Clerical Supervisor; Computer Programmer; Cost Estimator; Credit Manager; Customer Service Representative; Financial Analyst; Management Trainee; Paralegal; Systems Analyst; Technical Writer/Editor. **Number of placements per year:** 500 - 999.

TODAY PERSONNEL SERVICE
98 Battery Street, San Francisco CA 94111. 415/788-2150. **Fax:** 415/788-3197. **Contact:** Pat Hurley, Owner. **E-mail address:** pathurley@todaypersonnel.com. **World Wide Web address:** http://www.todaypersonnel.com. **Description:** A permanent employment agency. Company pays fee. **Specializes in the areas of:** Accounting/Auditing; Administration; Banking; Computer Science/Software; Finance; General Management; Insurance; Legal; Light Industrial; Personnel/Labor Relations; Sales; Secretarial. **Positions commonly filled include:** Accountant/Auditor; Adjuster; Administrative Manager; Advertising Clerk; Bank Officer/Manager; Branch Manager; Brokerage Clerk; Claim Representative; Clerical Supervisor. **Corporate headquarters location:** This Location. **Average salary range of placements:** $30,000 - $50,000. **Number of placements per year:** 1 - 49.

TRANS U.S., INC.
1316 Wilshire Boulevard, Suite 12, Los Angeles CA 90017. 213/483-8388. **Toll-free phone:** 800/998-7888. **Contact:** David Chen, President. **E-mail address:** davidchen@msn.com. **Description:** A permanent employment agency. **Specializes in the areas of:** Accounting/Auditing; Banking; Education; Insurance; Legal; Retail; Secretarial. **Positions commonly filled include:** Accountant/Auditor; Administrative Assistant; Legal Secretary; Marketing Specialist; Medical Secretary; Nurse; Sales Representative. **Average salary range of placements:** $30,000 - $50,000. **Number of placements per year:** 500 - 999.

TRATTNER NETWORK
101 Larkspur Landing Circle, Suite 215, Larkspur CA 94939. 415/380-1199. **Fax:** 415/389-1189. **Contact:** Jim Trattner, President. **E-mail address:** jtrattner@trattnet.com. **World Wide Web address:** http://www.trattnet.com. **Description:** An employment agency that focuses on high-tech placements. **Specializes in the areas of:** Computer Science/Software; Engineering. **Positions commonly filled include:** Computer Programmer; Internet Services Manager; MIS Specialist; Software Engineer; Systems Analyst. **Average salary range of placements:** More than $50,000. **Number of placements per year:** 100 - 199.

THE TRUMAN AGENCY, PERSONNEL SPECIALISTS
13200 Crossroads Parkway North, Suite 470, City of Industry CA 91746. 562/908-1233. **Fax:** 562/908-1238. **Contact:** Robert Truman, Vice President. **Description:** A permanent employment agency. Company pays fee. **Specializes in the areas of:** Accounting/Auditing; Administration; Engineering; Finance; General Management; Manufacturing; Personnel/Labor Relations; Sales; Secretarial; Technical; Transportation. **Positions commonly filled include:** Accountant/Auditor; Actuary; Administrative Manager; Advertising Clerk; Attorney; Blue-Collar Worker Supervisor; Branch Manager; Buyer; Chemical Engineer; Chemist; Clerical Supervisor; Credit Manager; Customer Service Representative; Designer; Draftsperson; Electrical/Electronics Engineer; Financial Analyst; Industrial Engineer; Industrial Production Manager; Mechanical Engineer; Occupational Therapist; Purchasing Agent/Manager; Quality Control Supervisor; Software Engineer; Stationary Engineer; Transportation/Traffic Specialist; Wholesale and Retail Buyer. **Average salary range of placements:** $30,000 - $50,000. **Number of placements per year:** 50 - 99.

TUSTIN PERSONNEL SERVICES, INC.
17702 Irvine Boulevard, Suite 101, Tustin CA 92780. 714/544-6141. **Contact:** JoAnn Manion, Owner. **Description:** A permanent placement agency. Company pays fee. **Specializes in the areas of:** Accounting/Auditing; Clerical; Engineering; Finance; Manufacturing; Personnel/Labor Relations; Technical. **Positions commonly filled include:** Accountant/Auditor; Administrative Assistant; Aerospace Engineer; Bookkeeper; Buyer; Computer Operator; Credit Manager; Draftsperson; Electrical/Electronics Engineer; Factory Worker; Financial Analyst; Industrial Engineer; Light Industrial Worker; Mechanical Engineer; Purchasing Agent/Manager; Receptionist; Secretary; Technical Writer/Editor; Typist/Word Processor. **Number of placements per year:** 100 - 199.

UAW LABOR EMPLOYMENT AND TRAINING CORPORATION
790 East Willow Street, Suite 150, Long Beach CA 90806. 562/989-7700. **Fax:** 562/989-7724. **Contact:** Patricia Williams, President. **Description:** An employment agency and career development center that offers permanent and temporary placements. Founded in 1984. **Specializes in the areas of:** Education; Finance; Health/Medical; Nonprofit; Personnel/Labor Relations; Sales; Secretarial; Technical. **Positions commonly filled include:** Advertising Clerk; Branch Manager; Counselor; Credit Manager; Customer Service Representative; Education Administrator; Financial Analyst; General Manager; MIS Specialist; Multimedia Designer; Teacher/Professor. **Corporate headquarters location:** This Location. **Other U.S. locations:** KY; MI; NY; OH; TN; UT. **Average salary range of placements:** $30,000 - $50,000. **Number of placements per year:** 200 - 499.

UNITED/CORESTAFF STAFFING SERVICES
5000 East Spring Street, Suite 320, Long Beach CA 90815. 562/420-7616. **Contact:** Manager. **Description:** An employment agency that specializes in accounting, legal, technical, industrial, and clerical placement. **Specializes in the areas of:** Accounting/Auditing; Computer Science/Software; Engineering; Legal; Personnel/Labor Relations; Secretarial; Technical. **Positions commonly filled include:** Accountant/Auditor; Aerospace Engineer; Aircraft Mechanic/Engine Specialist; Automotive Mechanic; Civil Engineer; Computer Programmer; Customer Service Representative; Draftsperson; Electrical/Electronics Engineer; Electrician; Human Resources Manager; Mechanical Engineer; MIS Specialist; Quality Control Supervisor; Software Engineer; Structural Engineer; Technical Writer/Editor; Typist/Word Processor. **Corporate headquarters location:** Brea CA. **Other U.S. locations:** Nationwide.

UNITED/CORESTAFF STAFFING SERVICES
275 Saratoga Avenue, Suite 150, Santa Clara CA 95050. 408/984-7203. **Contact:** Manager. **Description:** An employment agency that also offers contract services. Company pays fee. **Specializes in the areas of:** Accounting/Auditing; Administration; Computer Science/Software; Engineering; Finance; General Management; Industrial; Manufacturing; Personnel/Labor Relations; Publishing; Retail; Sales; Technical. **Positions commonly filled include:** Administrative Manager; Blue-Collar Worker Supervisor; Buyer; Claim Representative; Clerical Supervisor; Environmental Engineer; Human Resources Specialist; Management Trainee; Mechanical Engineer; Quality Control Supervisor. **Benefits available to temporary workers:** Bonus Award/Plan; Dental Insurance; Medical Insurance. **Corporate headquarters location:** Brea CA. **Other U.S. locations:** Nationwide. **Average salary range of placements:** $30,000 - $50,000. **Number of placements per year:** 1000+.

VICTOR VALLEY PERSONNEL AGENCY
15000 7th Street, Suite 101, Victorville CA 92392. 619/245-6548. **Fax:** 619/245-7690. **Contact:** Glenda McCormick, Owner. **Description:** A permanent and

temporary employment agency. **Specializes in the areas of:** Accounting/Auditing; Banking; Broadcasting; Engineering; Finance; Health/Medical; Industrial; Insurance; Light Industrial; Printing; Retail; Sales; Secretarial. **Positions commonly filled include:** Account Representative; Accountant/Auditor; Actuary; Adjuster; Administrative Assistant; Advertising Automotive Mechanic; Bank Officer/ Manager; Branch Manager; Broadcast Technician; Brokerage Clerk; Buyer; Certified Nursing Aide; Chemist; Claim Representative; Clerical Supervisor; Computer Operator; Computer Programmer; Construction Contractor; Controller; Cost Estimator; Customer Service Representative; Daycare Worker; Dietician/Nutritionist; Draftsperson; EKG Technician; Electrical/Electronics Engineer; Marketing Manager; Mechanical Engineer; Physician; Real Estate Agent; Registered Nurse; Respiratory Therapist; Secretary; Systems Analyst; Teacher/Professor; Underwriter/ Assistant Underwriter. **Average salary range of placements:** $20,000 - $29,999. **Number of placements per year:** 100 - 199.

VOLT ACCOUNTING SPECIALISTS
3055 Wilshire Boulevard, Suite 100, Los Angeles CA 90010. 213/487-3493. **Fax:** 213/487-0186. **Contact:** Manager. **Description:** A permanent employment agency. Company pays fee. **Specializes in the areas of:** Accounting/Auditing. **Positions commonly filled include:** Accountant/Auditor; Cost Estimator. **Benefits available to temporary workers:** Medical Insurance; Paid Holidays; Paid Vacation; Reimbursement Accounts. **Corporate headquarters location:** Orange CA. **Other U.S. locations:** Nationwide. **Average salary range of placements:** $30,000 - $50,000. **Number of placements per year:** 100 - 199.

THE WINDSOR GROUP
700 South Flower Street, Suite 1100, Los Angeles CA 90017. 213/627-0272. **Contact:** Recruiter. **Description:** A permanent employment agency. Company pays fee. **Specializes in the areas of:** Accounting/Auditing; Administration; Banking; Personnel/Labor Relations; Secretarial. **Positions commonly filled include:** Accountant/Auditor; Administrative Manager; Customer Service Representative; Human Resources Specialist; Internet Services Manager; Services Sales Representative; Typist/Word Processor. **Average salary range of placements:** $30,000 - $50,000. **Number of placements per year:** 50 - 99.

WOLLBORG-MICHELSON PERSONNEL SERVICE
3480 Buskirk, Suite 100, Pleasant Hill CA 94523. 510/946-0200. **Contact:** Tom Bruce, Branch Manager. **Description:** A permanent employment agency. Company pays fee. **Specializes in the areas of:** Clerical; General Labor. **Positions commonly filled include:** Administrative Worker/Clerk; Bookkeeper; Clerk; Data Entry Clerk; Receptionist; Sales Representative; Secretary; Stenographer; Typist/Word Processor.

WOLLBORG-MICHELSON PERSONNEL SERVICE
400 South El Camino Real, Suite 120, San Mateo CA 94402. 650/342-7600. **Contact:** Manager. **Description:** A permanent employment agency. Company pays fee. **Specializes in the areas of:** Administration; General Management; Secretarial; Word Processing. **Positions commonly filled include:** Customer Service Representative. **Average salary range of placements:** $30,000 - $50,000. **Number of placements per year:** 1 - 49.

YOLANDA'S AGENCY
5534 Encino Avenue, Suite 112, Encino CA 91316. 213/872-0083. **Contact:** Daniel A. Guerra, Manager. **Description:** A permanent employment agency. Company pays fee. **Specializes in the areas of:** Domestic Help. **Positions commonly filled include:** Housekeeper; Nanny. **Number of placements per year:** 200 - 499.

YOUR PEOPLE PROFESSIONALS
P.O. Box 5609, Santa Maria CA 93456-5609. 805/928-5725. **Contact:** Tricia Martinez, Personnel Specialist. **Description:** An employment agency that provides both permanent and temporary placements. **Specializes in the areas of:** Accounting/Auditing; Education; Engineering; Finance; Food Industry; General Management; Health/Medical; Industrial; Insurance; Manufacturing; Nonprofit; Personnel/Labor Relations; Publishing; Sales; Technical. **Positions commonly filled include:** Aerospace Engineer; Agricultural Engineer; Branch Manager; Claim Representative; Customer Service Representative; Education Administrator; Electrician; Environmental Engineer; General Manager; Health Services Manager; Hotel Manager; Management Trainee; Medical Records Technician; Preschool Worker; Public Relations Specialist; Quality Control Supervisor; Restaurant/ Food Service Manager; Services Sales Representative; Teacher/Professor; Typist/Word Processor; Underwriter/Assistant Underwriter. **Benefits available to temporary workers:** Paid Vacation. **Number of placements per year:** 500 - 999.

ZEIGER TECHNICAL CAREERS, INC.
20969 Ventura Boulevard, Suite 217, Woodland Hills CA 91364. 818/999-9394. **Fax:** 818/999-5036. **Contact:** Stephen A. Zeiger, President/CEO. **E-mail address:** szeiger147@aol.com. **Description:** A permanent placement agency that focuses on placing technical executives with computer hard disk drive knowledge. Company pays fee. **Specializes in the areas of:** Computer Hardware/Software; General Management; Manufacturing. **Positions commonly filled include:** Biomedical Engineer; Chemical Engineer; Computer Programmer; Design Engineer; Designer; Electrical/Electronics Engineer; General Manager; Human Resources Manager; Industrial Engineer; Industrial Production Manager; Management Analyst/ Consultant; Mechanical Engineer; Metallurgical Engineer; MIS Specialist; Nuclear Engineer; Operations/Production Manager; Physicist; Software Engineer; Statistician; Systems Analyst. **Average salary range of placements:** More than $50,000. **Number of placements per year:** 100 - 199.

AMY ZIMMERMAN & ASSOCIATES
11 North Sepulveda Boulevard, Suite 243, Manhattan Beach CA 90266. 310/798-6979. **Contact:** Manager. **Description:** A permanent employment agency. **Specializes in the areas of:** Accounting/Auditing; Sales; Secretarial.

TEMPORARY EMPLOYMENT AGENCIES

ACCOUNTANTS EXCHANGE
5455 Wilshire Boulevard, Suite 1409, Los Angeles CA 90036. 213/933-7411. **Fax:** 213/857-1075. **Contact:** Gary Sutton, Director. **Description:** A temporary employment agency that also provides permanent placement. Company pays fee. **Specializes in the areas of:** Accounting/Auditing. **Positions commonly filled include:** Accountant/Auditor. **Average salary range of placements:** $30,000 - $50,000. **Number of placements per year:** 200 - 499.

ACCOUNTANTS EXPRESS
4660 La Jolla Drive, Suite 550, San Diego CA 92122. 760/632-1804. **Contact:** Manager. **Description:** A temporary agency. **Specializes in the areas of:** Accounting/Auditing.

ACCOUNTANTS EXPRESS
701 Palomar Airport Road, Suite 300, Carlsbad CA 92009-1025. 760/931-4700. **Contact:** Manager. **Description:** A temporary agency. **Specializes in the areas of:** Accounting/Auditing.

ACCOUNTANTS INC.
111 Anza Boulevard, Suite 400, Burlingame CA 94010. 650/579-1111. **Fax:** 650/579-1927. **Contact:** Rita Moore, Manager of Client Development. **Description:** A provider of both temporary and permanent financial staffing. Founded in 1987. Company pays fee. **Specializes in the areas of:** Accounting/Auditing; Finance. **Positions commonly filled include:** Accountant/Auditor; Budget Analyst; Financial Analyst. **Corporate headquarters location:** This Location. **Other U.S. locations:** Nationwide.

ACCOUNTANTS INC.
2200 Powell Street, Suite 1280, Emeryville CA 94608-1804. 510/601-1111. **Contact:** Manager. **Description:** A temp-to-perm agency. **NOTE:** Applicants should send resumes to 555 Montgomery Street, Suite 811, San Francisco CA 94111-2543. **Specializes in the areas of:** Accounting/Auditing.

ACCOUNTANTS INC.
555 Montgomery Street, Suite 811, San Francisco CA 94111-2543. 415/434-1411. **Contact:** Manager. **Description:** A temp-to-perm agency. **Specializes in the areas of:** Accounting/Auditing.

THE ACCOUNTING GUILD
343 Sansome Street, Suite 170, San Francisco CA 94104. 415/391-3749. **Fax:** 415/391-2270. **Contact:** John St. Germain, Director. **E-mail address:** jhstgerm@ttree.com. **World Wide Web address:** http://www.ttree.com. **Description:** A temporary agency that provides accounting and financial services professionals to client companies. The Accounting Guild is a division of Talent Tree Staffing Services, an employment agency also at this location. Founded in 1976. Company pays fee. **Specializes in the areas of:** Accounting/Auditing; Banking; Finance. **Positions commonly filled include:** Accountant/Auditor; Brokerage Clerk; Credit Manager; Financial Analyst; Securities Sales Representative. **Benefits available to temporary workers:** 401(k); Dental Insurance; Medical Insurance; Paid Holidays. **Corporate headquarters location:** Houston TX. **Other U.S. locations:** Nationwide. **Average salary range of placements:** $30,000 - $50,000.

THE ACCOUNTING GUILD
17800 Castleton Street, Suite 100, City of Industry CA 91748. **Contact:** Manager. **Description:** A temporary and temp-to-perm agency, specializing in a wide range of areas including accounting. **Specializes in the areas of:** Accounting/Auditing. **Corporate headquarters location:** Houston TX. **Other U.S. locations:** Nationwide.

ACCUSTAFF COMPANY
2901 Tasman Drive, Suite 100, Santa Clara CA 95054-1137. 408/727-1782. **Fax:** 408/727-6434. **Contact:** Manager. **Description:** A temporary agency that operates on a contingency basis and focuses on technical and engineering fields. Company pays fee. **Specializes in the areas of:** Accounting/Auditing; Administration; Computer Science/Software; Engineering; Finance; Manufacturing; Technical. **Positions commonly filled include:** Accountant/Auditor; Buyer; Computer Programmer; Design Engineer; Designer; Draftsperson; Electrical/Electronics Engineer; Financial Analyst; Internet Services Manager; Mechanical Engineer; Quality Control Supervisor; Software Engineer; Technical Writer/Editor. **Benefits available to temporary workers:** 401(k); Medical Insurance; Savings Plan. **Average salary range of placements:** More than $50,000. **Number of placements per year:** 1000+.

ACT 1 PERSONNEL SERVICES
647 Main Street, Pleasanton CA 94566. 510/462-8550. **Toll-free phone:** 800/350-4545. **Fax:** 510/426-0689. **Contact:** Manager. **Description:** A temporary agency that also provides permanent placements. Founded in 1978. Company pays fee. **Specializes in the areas of:** Personnel/Labor Relations; Sales; Secretarial. **Positions commonly filled include:** Administrative Assistant; Branch Manager; Claim Representative; Clerical Supervisor; Computer Programmer; Credit Manager; Customer Service Representative; Financial Analyst; Services Sales Representative; Systems Analyst; Typist/Word Processor. **Benefits available to temporary workers:** 401(k); Bonus Award/Plan; Medical Insurance; Vision Insurance. **Corporate headquarters location:** Torrance CA. **Other U.S. locations:** AZ; CO; NC. **Average salary range of placements:** $20,000 - $29,999. **Number of placements per year:** 1000+.

ALEXSYS LEGAL SUPPORT
690 Market Street, Suite 100, San Francisco CA 94104. 415/392-0751. **Fax:** 415/392-0752. **Contact:** Staffing Specialist. **Description:** A temporary agency that provides legal and litigation support placements. Company pays fee. **Specializes in the areas of:** Legal; Personnel/Labor Relations; Secretarial. **Positions commonly filled include:** Accountant/Auditor; Clerical Supervisor; Customer Service Representative; Library Technician; Management Trainee; Typist/Word Processor. **Average salary range of placements:** $20,000 - $29,999. **Number of placements per year:** 500 - 999.

ALFANO TEMPORARY PERSONNEL
11750 Sorrento Valley Road, Suite 154, San Diego CA 92121. 619/453-9580. **Contact:** Vincent Alfano, Manager. **Description:** A temporary agency that focuses on technical, industrial, and office personnel. **Specializes in the areas of:** Engineering; Manufacturing; Technical. **Positions commonly filled include:** Accountant/Auditor; Computer Programmer; Design Engineer; Electrical/Electronics Engineer; Industrial Engineer; Materials Engineer; Mechanical Engineer; Metallurgical Engineer; MIS Specialist; Science Technologist; Software Engineer. **Average salary range of placements:** $30,000 - $50,000. **Number of placements per year:** 500 - 999.

AMERICAN TECHNICAL
4701 Patrick Henry Drive, Suite 2501, Santa Clara CA 95054. 408/727-4653. **Fax:** 408/727-0584. **Contact:** Manager. **Description:** A temporary agency. Company pays fee. **Specializes in the areas of:** Computer Science/Software; Engineering; Manufacturing; Secretarial. **Positions commonly filled include:** Administrative Manager; Buyer; Chemical Engineer; Civil Engineer; Clinical Lab Technician; Computer Programmer; Design Engineer; Designer; Editor; Electrical/Electronics Engineer; Industrial Engineer; Internet Services Manager; Mechanical Engineer; Software Engineer; Systems Analyst; Technical Writer/Editor; Typist/Word Processor. **Benefits available to temporary workers:** 401(k); Dental Insurance; Medical Insurance; Paid Holidays. **Average salary range of placements:** $30,000 - $50,000. **Number of placements per year:** 1000+. **Corporate headquarters location:** This Location.

ANSWERS UNLIMITED
920 South Robertson Boulevard, Los Angeles CA 90035. 310/360-0303. **Contact:** Christine Lieber, President. **Description:** A temporary agency that also operates as a permanent employment agency. Company pays fee. **Specializes in the areas of:** Accounting/Auditing; Administration; Advertising; Art/Design; Computer Science/Software; Finance; General Management; Insurance; Legal; Manufacturing; Nonprofit; Personnel/Labor Relations; Publishing; Secretarial. **Positions commonly filled include:** Accountant/Auditor; Administrative Manager; Advertising Clerk; Attorney; Bank Officer/Manager; Branch Manager; Buyer; Claim Representative; Clerical Supervisor; Computer Programmer; Credit Manager; Customer Service Representative; Editor; Financial Analyst; Internet Services Manager; Multimedia Designer; Operations/Production Manager; Paralegal; Physician; Services Sales Representative; Software Engineer; Technical Writer/Editor; Telecommunications Manager; Travel Agent; Typist/Word Processor. **Number of placements per year:** 200 - 499.

AROSE RECRUITING COMPANY, INC.
P.O. Box 2945, Newport Beach CA 92663. 714/642-2696. **Fax:** 714/642-2694. **Contact:** Deborah Prestia, President. **Description:** A temporary agency focusing on the placement of information technology consultants. **Specializes in the areas of:** Computer Science/Software. **Positions commonly filled include:** Computer Programmer; Internet Services Manager; Management Analyst/Consultant; Multimedia Designer; Software Engineer; Systems Analyst; Technical Writer/Editor; Telecommunications Manager. **Corporate headquarters location:** This Location. **Average salary range of placements:** More than $50,000. **Number of placements per year:** 1 - 49.

BERRA & ASSOCIATES
55 West Sierra Madre Boulevard, Suite Jail, Sierra Madre CA 91024. 626/355-3778. **Contact:** Manager. **Description:** A temporary employment agency for attorneys. **Specializes in the areas of:** Legal.

BEST TEMPORARY SERVICE
1410 3rd Street, Suite 1, Riverside CA 92507. 909/369-1111. **Contact:** Marty Ferguson, Manager. **Description:** A temporary agency. Company pays fee. **Specializes in the areas of:** Accounting/Auditing; Banking; Engineering; Finance; General Management; Industrial; Insurance; Legal; Retail; Secretarial; Transportation. **Positions commonly filled include:** Accountant/Auditor; Administrative Manager; Advertising Clerk; Automotive Mechanic; Bank Officer/Manager; Biochemist; Blue-Collar Worker Supervisor; Branch Manager; Chemical Engineer; Claim Representative; Computer Programmer; Construction and Building Inspector; Customer Service Representative; Electrical/Electronics Engineer; Electrician; Environmental Engineer; Industrial Engineer; Industrial Production Manager; Insurance Agent/Broker; Mechanical Engineer; Software Engineer; Structural Engineer; Systems Analyst; Typist/Word Processor; Underwriter/Assistant Underwriter. **Benefits available to temporary workers:** Bonus Award/Plan; Medical Insurance.

BLUE MOON PERSONNEL INC.
369 Pine Street, Suite 200, San Francisco CA 94104. 415/394-9500. **Fax:** 415/394-9540. **Contact:** Manager. **Description:** A temporary agency focusing on office support placement. Company pays fee. **Specializes in the areas of:** Nonprofit. **Positions commonly filled include:** Administrative Assistant; Typist/Word Processor. **Corporate headquarters location:** This Location. **Average salary range of placements:** $20,000 - $29,999. **Number of placements per year:** 1 - 49.

BRADFORD STAFF, INC.
100 California Street, 14th Floor, San Francisco CA 94111. 415/362-0435. **Toll-free phone:** 800/216-9911. **Fax:** 415/362-4735. **Contact:** Tiffany Ray, Service and Sales Director. **E-mail address:** sf@bradfordstaff.com. **World Wide Web address:** http://www.bradfordstaff.com. **Description:** A temporary employment agency that also provides permanent and temp-to-perm placements. Company pays fee. **Specializes in the areas of:** Accounting/Auditing; Administration; General Management; Legal; Manufacturing; Secretarial; Technical. **Positions commonly filled include:** Account Representative; Accountant; Administrative Manager; Brokerage Clerk; Claim Representative; Clerical Supervisor; Computer Programmer; Customer Service Representative; Database Manager; Design Engineer; Editorial Assistant; Market Research Analyst; Quality Control Supervisor; Secretary; Software Engineer; Systems Analyst; Technical Writer/Editor; Typist/Word Processor; Underwriter/Assistant Underwriter. **Benefits available to temporary workers:** 401(k); Bonus Award/Plan; Credit Union; Dental Insurance; Medical Insurance; Paid Holidays; Profit Sharing. **Corporate headquarters location:** This Location. **Other area locations:** Oakland CA; Palo Alto CA; San Rafael CA; Walnut Creek CA. **Average salary range of placements:** $30,000 - $50,000. **Number of placements per year:** 500 - 999.

CDI CORPORATION
44 Montgomery Street, Suite 2120, San Francisco CA 94104. 415/434-1846. **Contact:** Debra Jaron, Branch Manager. **World Wide Web address:** http://www.cdicorp.com. **Description:** A temporary agency. Company pays fee. **Specializes in the areas of:** Secretarial; Word Processing. **Corporate headquarters location:** Philadelphia PA. **Other U.S. locations:** Nationwide. **International locations:** Worldwide. **Number of placements per year:** 500 - 999.

CDI CORPORATION
3401 West Sunflower Avenue, Suite 225, Santa Ana CA 92704. 714/556-8022. **Fax:** 714/641-0621. **Contact:** Laura Vatcher, Recruiter. **E-mail address:** cdipeople@aol.com. **World Wide Web address:** http://www.cdicorp.com. **Description:** A temporary agency. **Specializes in the areas of:** Administration; Architecture/Construction; Art/Design; Biology; Computer Science/Software; Economics; Engineering; Industrial; Manufacturing; Personnel/Labor Relations; Technical. **Positions commonly filled include:** Aerospace Engineer; Agricultural Engineer; Aircraft Mechanic/Engine Specialist; Architect; Biomedical Engineer; Buyer; Chemical Engineer; Chemist; Civil Engineer; Clinical Lab Technician; Computer Programmer; Construction Contractor; Cost Estimator; Designer; Draftsperson; Editor; Electrical/Electronics Engineer; Financial Analyst; Industrial Production Manager; Internet Services Manager; MIS Specialist; Operations/Production Manager; Quality Control Supervisor; Software Engineer; Stationary Engineer; Statistician; Systems Analyst; Telecommunications Manager; Urban/Regional Planner. **Corporate headquarters location:** Philadelphia PA. **Other U.S. locations:** Nationwide. **International locations:** Worldwide. **Average salary range of placements:** $30,000 - $50,000. **Number of placements per year:** 100 - 199.

CAREER IMAGES
2049 Century Park East, Suite 3730, Los Angeles CA 90067. 310/553-5208. **Fax:** 310/553-8098. **Contact:** Ms. Chris Donaldson, President. **Description:** A temporary agency that also provides permanent placement. The company focuses on entry-level to middle management staffing for law firms, corporations, and the entertainment industry.

Company pays fee. **Specializes in the areas of:** Accounting/Auditing; Clerical; Legal; Secretarial. **Positions commonly filled include:** Accountant/Auditor; Legal Secretary; Management Trainee; Paralegal; Receptionist; Typist/Word Processor. **Average salary range of placements:** $25,000 - $65,000. **Number of placements per year:** 1 - 49.

CHAMPAGNE TEMPORARY HELP
3849 Birch Street, Newport Beach CA 92660. 714/756-1844. **Fax:** 714/756-0904. **Contact:** Pat Hutt, Assignment Supervisor. **Description:** A temporary agency that also provides temp-to-hire and permanent placement for positions in office support, accounting, human resources, and marketing. Company pays fee. **Specializes in the areas of:** Accounting/Auditing; Administration; Banking; Finance; Insurance; Nonprofit; Personnel/Labor Relations; Sales; Secretarial. **Positions commonly filled include:** Accountant/Auditor; Administrative Manager; Advertising Clerk; Clerical Supervisor; Customer Service Representative; Editor; Human Resources Manager; Technical Writer/Editor; Typist/Word Processor. **Average salary range of placements:** $30,000 - $50,000. **Number of placements per year:** 1000+.

CHIPTON-ROSS
1756 Manhattan Beach Boulevard, Manhattan Beach CA 90266. 310/376-8733. **Contact:** Manager. **Description:** A temporary agency. **Specializes in the areas of:** Technical.

COAST PERSONNEL
2295 De La Cruz Boulevard, Santa Clara CA 95050-3020. 408/653-2100. **Fax:** 408/727-4445. **Contact:** Patti Hughes, Recruiting Manager. **Description:** A temporary agency. Company pays fee. **Specializes in the areas of:** Accounting/Auditing; Engineering; Technical. **Positions commonly filled include:** Accountant/Auditor; Chemical Engineer; Chemist; Civil Engineer; Computer Programmer; Design Engineer; Designer; Editor; Electrical/Electronics Engineer; Electrician; Financial Analyst; Mechanical Engineer; MIS Specialist; Software Engineer; Structural Engineer; Typist/Word Processor. **Benefits available to temporary workers:** Dental Insurance; Medical Insurance; Paid Holidays; Paid Vacation. **Corporate headquarters location:** This Location. **Average salary range of placements:** $30,000 - $50,000. **Number of placements per year:** 500 - 999.

COLLIER-YOUNG AGENCY
3345 Wilshire Boulevard, Suite 1007, Los Angeles CA 90010-1810. 213/388-5565. **Fax:** 213/388-1277. **Contact:** Recruiter. **Description:** A temporary agency. **Specializes in the areas of:** Accounting/Auditing; Advertising; Banking; Broadcasting; Finance; Food Industry; General Management; Health/Medical; Insurance; Legal; Publishing; Retail; Sales; Secretarial. **Positions commonly filled include:** Accountant/Auditor; Advertising Clerk; Buyer; Claim Representative; Clerical Supervisor; Customer Service Representative; Medical Records Technician; Secretary; Technical Writer/Editor; Typist/Word Processor. **Average salary range of placements:** $20,000 - $29,999. **Number of placements per year:** 100 - 199.

COMPLIMATE TECHNICAL STAFFING
150 West Iowa Avenue, Suite 203, Sunnyvale CA 94086-6184. 408/773-8994. **Fax:** 408/773-0968. **Contact:** Manager. **E-mail address:** careerdesk@complimate.com. **World Wide Web address:** http://www.complimate.com. **Description:** Provides temporary and permanent personnel for electronic equipment manufacturers and information technology companies. **Specializes in the areas of:** Technical. **Positions commonly filled include:** Computer Programmer; Design Engineer; Internet Services Manager; MIS Specialist; Multimedia Designer; Software Engineer; Systems Analyst; Technical Writer/Editor; Telecommunications Manager. **Average salary range of placements:** $30,000 - $50,000. **Number of placements per year:** 1000+.

CONTRACTORS LABOR POOL
1700 East Lincoln Avenue, Suite 200, Anaheim CA 92805-4323. 714/239-5580. **Contact:** Scott Ingersoll, Manager. **World Wide Web address:** http://www.clp.com. **Description:** A temporary agency that provides construction personnel for licensed contractors. Founded in 1987. Company pays fee. **Specializes in the areas of:** Administration; Construction. **Positions commonly filled include:** Administrative Manager; Construction Contractor; Construction Manager; Electrician. **Benefits available to temporary workers:** Dental Insurance; Medical Insurance. **Corporate headquarters location:** Reno NV. **Other U.S. locations:** Altadena CA; Emeryville CA; Sacramento CA; San Jose CA; Tarzana CA; Everett WA; Seattle WA; Tacoma WA.

CREATIVE ASSETS
562 Mission Street, Suite 601, San Francisco CA 94105. **Contact:** Manager. **Description:** A temporary agency specializing focusing on the placement of free-lance graphic and digital talent in the creative market. **Specializes in the areas of:** Digital Arts; Graphic Arts. **Positions commonly filled include:** Animator; Graphic Designer; Video Editor; Webmaster. **Other U.S. locations:** Seattle WA; Portland OR.

CROSSROADS STAFFING SERVICE
820 Bay Avenue, Suite 144, Capitola CA 95010. 408/476-8367. **Contact:** Trudy Fisher, Branch Manager. **Description:** A temporary agency. **Specializes in the areas of:** Accounting/Auditing; Administration; Computer Science/Software; Engineering; Finance; Food Industry; General Management; Industrial; Insurance; Legal; Manufacturing; Personnel/Labor Relations; Publishing; Secretarial; Technical. **Positions commonly filled include:** Accountant/Auditor; Branch Manager; Buyer; Chemical Engineer; Civil Engineer; Clerical Supervisor; Computer Programmer; Environmental Engineer; Industrial Engineer; Industrial Production Manager; Mechanical Engineer; MIS Specialist; Operations/Production Manager; Typist/Word Processor. **Benefits available to temporary workers:** Medical Insurance; Paid Holidays. **Corporate headquarters location:** San Jose CA.

DEC & ASSOCIATES HEALTHCARE PERSONNEL
1601 East Chapman Avenue, Fullerton CA 92831. 714/447-0826. **Fax:** 714/447-0280. **Contact:** Diane Skullr, Personnel Manager. **Description:** A temporary agency that focuses on the medical and dental fields and also offers contract services. Company pays fee. **Specializes in the areas of:** Health/Medical. **Positions commonly filled include:** Chiropractor; Claim Representative; Clinical Lab Technician; Emergency Medical Technician; Health Services Manager; Human Resources Specialist; Licensed Practical Nurse; Medical Assistant; Medical Records Technician; Nuclear Medicine Technologist; Occupational Therapist; Physical Therapist; Physician Assistant; Radiological Technologist; Registered Nurse; Surgical Technician; Typist/Word Processor. **Number of placements per year:** 500 - 999.

DENTAL PLUS MEDICAL
490 Post Street, Suite 1701, San Francisco CA 94102. 415/677-0961. **Fax:** 415/332-7980. **Contact:** Beverly Davis, Partner. **Description:** A temporary and

permanent employment agency. Company pays fee. **Specializes in the areas of:** Health/Medical. **Positions commonly filled include:** Dental Assistant/Dental Hygienist; Dentist. **Average salary range of placements:** $30,000 - $50,000. **Number of placements per year:** 100 - 199.

DRAKE OFFICE OVERLOAD
17744 Skypark Circle, Suite 290, Irvine CA 92614. 714/474-2974. **Contact:** Office Manager. **Description:** A temporary and permanent placement agency. Company pays fee. **Specializes in the areas of:** Clerical; Data Processing. **Positions commonly filled include:** Bookkeeper; Clerk; Computer Operator; Data Entry Clerk; Legal Secretary; Receptionist; Secretary; Stenographer; Typist/Word Processor. **Number of placements per year:** 500 - 999.

DRAKE OFFICE OVERLOAD
21707 Hawthorne Boulevard, Torrance CA 90503. 310/540-0028. **Fax:** 310/543-2803. **Contact:** Office Manager. **Description:** A temporary agency. Drake Office Overload also provides temp-to-hire clerical, word processing, accounting, customer service, MIS, and light industrial personnel. **Specializes in the areas of:** Accounting/Auditing; Administration; Computer Science/Software; Engineering; General Management; Health/Medical; Industrial; Manufacturing; Personnel/ Labor Relations; Publishing; Sales; Secretarial; Technical; Transportation. **Positions commonly filled include:** Accountant/Auditor; Administrative Manager; Clerical Supervisor; Computer Programmer; Credit Manager; Customer Service Representative; Electrical/ Electronics Engineer; Health Services Manager; MIS Specialist; Operations/Production Manager; Quality Assurance Engineer; Quality Control Supervisor; Services Sales Representative; Software Engineer; Systems Analyst; Technical Writer/Editor; Typist/Word Processor. **Other U.S. locations:** FL; NC; VA; WA. **Number of placements per year:** 1000+.

ELEVENTH HOUR STAFFING SERVICES
15621 Redhill Avenue, Suite 120, Tustin CA 92780. 714/258-2111. **Toll-free phone:** 800/626-7229. **Fax:** 714/258-2025. **Contact:** Lori Kay Tingirides, Area Manager. **Description:** A temporary agency. Company pays fee. **Specializes in the areas of:** Accounting/Auditing; Administration; Advertising; Banking; Engineering; Finance; General Management; Industrial; Insurance; Legal; Manufacturing; Personnel/Labor Relations; Sales; Secretarial; Transportation. **Positions commonly filled include:** Accountant/Auditor; Administrative Manager; Advertising Clerk; Bank Officer/Manager; Brokerage Clerk; Budget Analyst; Buyer; Claim Representative; Computer Programmer; Counselor; Customer Service Representative; Market Research Analyst; Medical Records Technician; MIS Specialist; Paralegal; Purchasing Agent/Manager; Quality Control Supervisor; Restaurant/Food Service Manager; Securities Sales Representative; Services Sales Representative; Systems Analyst; Technical Writer/ Editor; Typist/Word Processor. **Benefits available to temporary workers:** Dental Insurance; Medical Insurance; Paid Holidays. **Corporate headquarters location:** Englewood CO. **Other U.S. locations:** Nationwide. **Average salary range of placements:** $20,000 - $29,999. **Number of placements per year:** 1000+.

ENGINEERING TECHNICAL SERVICE
194 Wikiup Drive, Suite B, Santa Rosa CA 95403-7757. 707/546-4300. **Fax:** 707/546-2644. **Contact:** President. **Description:** A temporary agency that focuses on technical placements for manufacturing industries, mechanical engineering consulting services, and product design and development. Company pays fee. **Specializes in the areas of:** Engineering; Manufacturing; Technical. **Positions commonly filled include:** Biomedical Engineer; Chemical Engineer; Civil Engineer; Design Engineer; Designer; Draftsperson; Electrical/Electronics Engineer; Environmental Engineer; Industrial Engineer; Landscape Architect; Materials Engineer; Mechanical Engineer; Metallurgical Engineer; Software Engineer; Structural Engineer; Technical Writer/Editor. **Average salary range of placements:** $30,000 - $50,000. **Number of placements per year:** 50 - 99.

EXECUTIVE TEMPS
2321 West Olive, Suite F, Burbank CA 91506. 818/563-2939. **Contact:** Office Manager. **Description:** A temporary agency. **Specializes in the areas of:** Entertainment.

EXPRESS PERSONNEL SERVICES
11870 Santa Monica Boulevard, Suite 208, Los Angeles CA 90025. 310/571-2200. **Fax:** 310/571-2200. **Contact:** Manager. **E-mail address:** temps4you@aol.com. **Description:** A temporary agency that also offers permanent placement. **Specializes in the areas of:** Accounting/Auditing; Administration; Finance; General Management; Personnel/Labor Relations; Secretarial. **Positions commonly filled include:** Accountant/Auditor; Brokerage Clerk; Buyer; Clerical Supervisor; Financial Analyst; General Manager; Human Resources Manager; Property and Real Estate Manager; Typist/Word Processor. **Number of placements per year:** 50 - 99.

FAITHFUL SUPPORT SYSTEMS
2245 1st Street, Suite 101, Simi Valley CA 93065-1987. 805/522-8812. **Fax:** 805/522-8826. **Contact:** Manager. **Description:** A temporary agency concentrating on medical billings and collections positions. The firm also provides placement in middle management, accounting, legal, and clerical professions. **Specializes in the areas of:** Health/Medical; Legal; Secretarial. **Positions commonly filled include:** Billing Clerk; Claim Representative; Collections Agent; Financial Analyst; Paralegal. **Number of placements per year:** 1 - 49.

PAT FRANKLYN ASSOCIATES INC.
655 Redwood Highway, Suite 350, Mill Valley CA 94941. 415/388-1894. **Fax:** 415/388-1897. **Contact:** Rhonda Liebof, Partner. **Description:** A temporary agency. Company pays fee. **Specializes in the areas of:** Accounting/Auditing; Administration; Computer Science/Software; Legal; Secretarial. **Positions commonly filled include:** Attorney; Computer Programmer; Credit Manager; Customer Service Representative; Human Resources Specialist; Internet Services Manager; MIS Specialist; Paralegal; Software Engineer; Systems Analyst; Typist/Word Processor. **Average salary range of placements:** $20,000 - $29,999. **Number of placements per year:** 100 - 199.

FULL SERVICE TEMPORARIES
255 North Market Street, Suite 140, San Jose CA 95110. 408/295-6350. **Fax:** 408/295-6355. **Contact:** Operations Manager. **Description:** A temporary agency that also provides permanent placement. Company pays fee. **Specializes in the areas of:** Clerical; Computer Hardware/Software; Design; Light Industrial; Professional; Publishing; Technical. **Positions commonly filled include:** Assembler; Clerical Supervisor; Design Engineer; Draftsperson; Inspector/Tester/Grader; Light Industrial Worker; Purchasing Agent/Manager; Software Engineer; Technician. **Benefits available to temporary workers:** Medical Insurance; Paid Holidays; Paid Vacation. **Number of placements per year:** 1000+.

GARNETT EMPLOYMENT SERVICES INC.
17190 Monterey Road, Suite B, Morgan Hill CA 95037. 408/778-0729. **Fax:** 408/779-9154. **Contact:** Uli Johnson, Manager. **Description:** A temporary agency that also provides permanent placement. Company pays fee. **Specializes in the areas of:** Engineering; Food Industry; General Management; Manufacturing; Sales; Secretarial; Technical; Transportation. **Positions commonly filled include:** Accountant/Auditor; Administrative Manager; Blue-Collar Worker Supervisor; Clerical Supervisor; Customer Service Representative; General Manager; Industrial Production Manager; Restaurant/Food Service Manager; Services Sales Representative; Transportation/Traffic Specialist; Truck Driver; Typist/Word Processor. **Average salary range of placements:** $20,000 - $29,999. **Number of placements per year:** 500 - 999.

GOLDSTEIN & ASSOCIATES
8601 Wilshire Boulevard, Suite 1101, Beverly Hills CA 90211. 310/657-7161. **Fax:** 310/657-7166. **Contact:** David Goldstein, Owner. **E-mail address:** dg90210@aol.com. **Description:** A temporary agency that also provides permanent and contract placements. **Specializes in the areas of:** Accounting/Auditing; Administration; Advertising; Architecture/Construction; Art/Design; Banking; Computer Science/Software; General Management; Health/Medical; Insurance; Legal; Nonprofit; Personnel/Labor Relations; Publishing; Retail; Sales; Secretarial. **Positions commonly filled include:** Accountant/Auditor; Attorney; Branch Manager; Brokerage Clerk; Computer Programmer; Credit Manager; Customer Service Representative; Designer; Financial Analyst; Internet Services Manager; Management Analyst/Consultant; Management Trainee; Medical Records Technician; MIS Specialist; Paralegal; Software Engineer; Systems Analyst; Technical Writer/Editor; Telecommunications Manager; Typist/Word Processor. **Average salary range of placements:** $30,000 - $50,000. **Number of placements per year:** 1 - 49.

INDUSTRIAL SERVICES COMPANY
1070 Concord Avenue, Suite 112, Concord CA 94520. 510/680-4422. **Toll-free phone:** 800/867-2040. **Fax:** 510/680-4482. **Contact:** Jim Stielow, Manager. **World Wide Web address:** http://www.workers.com. **Description:** A temporary agency. Company pays fee. **Specializes in the areas of:** Architecture/Construction; Engineering; Industrial; Manufacturing. **Positions commonly filled include:** Aircraft Mechanic/Engine Specialist; Architect; Automotive Mechanic; Blue-Collar Worker Supervisor; Civil Engineer; Construction and Building Inspector; Design Engineer; Draftsperson; Electrical/Electronics Engineer; Electrician; Environmental Engineer; Industrial Production Manager; Mechanical Engineer; Structural Engineer. **Benefits available to temporary workers:** Paid Holidays. **Average salary range of placements:** $20,000 - $29,999. **Number of placements per year:** 1000+.

INTERIM INDUSTRIAL STAFFING
2862 Arden Way, Suite 225, Sacramento CA 95825. 916/484-1450. **Contact:** Manager. **Description:** A temporary agency. Company pays fee. **Specializes in the areas of:** Clerical; Construction; Food Industry; Health/Medical; Industrial; Insurance; Legal; Manufacturing; MIS/EDP; Sales. **Positions commonly filled include:** Administrative Assistant; Bookkeeper; Clerk; Computer Programmer; Customer Service Representative; Data Entry Clerk; Draftsperson; EDP Specialist; Factory Worker; Food Production Worker; Legal Secretary; Light Industrial Worker; Medical Secretary; Sales Representative; Secretary; Statistician; Typist/Word Processor. **Number of placements per year:** 1000+.

INTERIM PERSONNEL
15260 Ventura Boulevard, Suite 1220, Sherman Oaks CA 91403-5347. 818/789-8211. **Contact:** Kathi Million, Branch Manager. **Description:** A temporary agency. Company pays fee. **Specializes in the areas of:** Industrial; Manufacturing; Personnel/Labor Relations. **Positions commonly filled include:** Administrative Manager; Bookkeeper; Buyer; Clerical Supervisor; Clerk; Computer Operator; Customer Service Representative; Legal Secretary; Medical Secretary; Quality Control Supervisor; Receptionist; Typist/Word Processor. **Benefits available to temporary workers:** Dental Insurance; Medical Insurance. **Corporate headquarters location:** Fort Lauderdale FL. **Other U.S. locations:** Nationwide. **Number of placements per year:** 500 - 999.

INTERIM PERSONNEL
750 West Gonzales Road, Suite 140, Oxnard CA 93030. 805/983-2000. **Contact:** Manager. **Description:** A temporary agency. Company pays fee. **Specializes in the areas of:** Architecture/Construction; Clerical; Food Industry; Health/Medical; Manufacturing; Personnel/Labor Relations; Sales; Technical. **Positions commonly filled include:** Accountant/Auditor; Buyer; Clerk; Computer Operator; Computer Programmer; Data Entry Clerk; Draftsperson; Factory Worker; Human Resources Manager; Nurse; Purchasing Agent/Manager; Receptionist; Secretary; Support Personnel; Systems Analyst; Typist/Word Processor; Waitstaff. **Corporate headquarters location:** Fort Lauderdale FL. **Other U.S. locations:** Nationwide. **Number of placements per year:** 1000+.

INTERIM PERSONNEL
44 Montgomery Street, Suite 1250, San Francisco CA 94104. 415/391-5965. **Contact:** Branch Manager. **Description:** A temporary agency. Company pays fee. **Specializes in the areas of:** Accounting/Auditing; Clerical; MIS/EDP; Sales; Secretarial. **Positions commonly filled include:** Administrative Assistant; Clerk; Human Resources Manager; Legal Secretary; Receptionist; Secretary; Stenographer; Typist/Word Processor. **Corporate headquarters location:** Fort Lauderdale FL. **Other U.S. locations:** Nationwide. **Number of placements per year:** 200 - 499.

INTERIM PERSONNEL
2615 Pacific Coast Highway, Suite 120, Hermosa Beach CA 90254. 310/318-1561. **Fax:** 310/318-1776. **Contact:** Jeri Low, Manager. **Description:** A temporary agency that provides placements for office support and light industrial positions. The agency also provides permanent placements. Company pays fee. **Specializes in the areas of:** Accounting/Auditing; Computer Science/Software. **Positions commonly filled include:** Clerical Supervisor; Human Resources Manager; Typist/Word Processor. **Corporate headquarters location:** Fort Lauderdale FL. **Other U.S. locations:** Nationwide. **Number of placements per year:** 1000+.

INTERIM PERSONNEL
75 South Milpitas Boulevard, Suite 107, Milpitas CA 95035. **Fax:** 408/934-9981. **Contact:** Branch Manager. **Description:** A temporary agency. **Specializes in the areas of:** Administration; Engineering; General Management; Manufacturing; Personnel/Labor Relations; Sales; Technical. **Positions commonly filled include:** Administrative Manager; Branch Manager; Budget Analyst; Buyer; Credit Manager; Customer Service Representative; Editor; Electrician; Environmental Engineer; Human Resources Specialist; Human Service Worker; Internet Services

Manager; Management Trainee; Public Relations Specialist; Purchasing Agent/Manager; Restaurant/Food Service Manager; Software Engineer; Structural Engineer; Technical Writer/Editor; Telecommunications Manager. **Corporate headquarters location:** Fort Lauderdale FL. **Other U.S. locations:** Nationwide. **Number of placements per year:** 200 - 499.

INTERTEC PERSONNEL
1045 East Green Street, Pasadena CA 91106. 626/584-1043. **Fax:** 626/584-1941. **Contact:** Lisa Perez, Branch Manager. **Description:** A temporary agency. Company pays fee. **Specializes in the areas of:** Accounting/Auditing; Industrial; Personnel/Labor Relations; Secretarial. **Positions commonly filled include:** Accountant/Auditor; Administrative Manager; Clerical Supervisor; Customer Service Representative; Human Service Worker; Purchasing Agent/Manager. **Number of placements per year:** 1000+.

ANITA R. JOHNSON & ASSOCIATES
2131 Capital Avenue, Suite 305, Sacramento CA 95816. 916/329-9100. **Contact:** Cordelia R. Kirkland, Associate. **Description:** A temporary agency focusing on the placement of accounting, bookkeeping, and support personnel. **Specializes in the areas of:** Accounting/Auditing; Bookkeeping. **Benefits available to temporary workers:** Paid Vacation. **Number of placements per year:** 1 - 49.

KELLY ASSISTED LIVING SERVICES
4482 Barranca Parkway, Suite 248, Irvine CA 92604. 714/786-7587. **Fax:** 714/786-5047. **Contact:** David Block, Manager. **Description:** A temporary agency that provides home health care aides for senior citizens. **Specializes in the areas of:** Health/Medical. **Positions commonly filled include:** Home Health Aide. **Benefits available to temporary workers:** Medical Insurance; Paid Holidays; Paid Vacation. **Average salary range of placements:** Less than $20,000. **Number of placements per year:** 100 - 199.

KELLY SCIENTIFIC RESOURCES
625 The City Drive, Suite 375, Orange CA 92668. 714/971-0721. **Fax:** 714/971-2443. **Contact:** Branch Manager. **World Wide Web address:** http://www.kellyscientific.com. **Description:** A temporary agency for scientific professionals. **Specializes in the areas of:** Biomedical; Biotechnology; Chemical; Environmental; Food Industry; Petrochemical; Pharmaceutical.

KELLY SERVICES, INC.
1111 Civic Drive, Suite 240, Walnut Creek CA 94596. 510/746-1460. **Contact:** Operations Manager. **Description:** A temporary agency. Company pays fee. **Specializes in the areas of:** Accounting/Auditing; Advertising; Architecture/Construction; Banking; Clerical; Computer Hardware/Software; Engineering; Finance; Food Industry; Health/Medical; Legal; Manufacturing; MIS/EDP; Publishing; Sales; Secretarial; Technical. **Positions commonly filled include:** Accountant/Auditor; Administrative Assistant; Aerospace Engineer; Architect; Biological Scientist; Biomedical Engineer; Bookkeeper; Civil Engineer; Clerk; Commercial Artist; Computer Programmer; Customer Service Representative; Data Entry Clerk; Editor; Electrical/Electronics Engineer; Factory Worker; Financial Analyst; Industrial Designer; Industrial Engineer; Light Industrial Worker; Mechanical Engineer; Receptionist; Sales Representative; Secretary; Systems Analyst; Technical Writer/Editor; Technician; Underwriter/Assistant Underwriter. **Corporate headquarters location:** Troy MI. **Number of placements per year:** 1000+.

KELLY SERVICES, INC.
5950 Canoga Avenue, Suite 415, Woodland Hills CA 91367. 818/999-2050. **Fax:** 818/702-6357. **Contact:** Greg P. Inguagiato, Staffing Specialist. **Description:** A temporary staffing agency that also provides temp-to-hire and permanent placements. Founded in 1946. Company pays fee. **Specializes in the areas of:** Accounting/Auditing; Industrial; Manufacturing; Personnel/Labor Relations; Sales; Secretarial; Technical. **Positions commonly filled include:** Accountant/Auditor; Administrative Manager; Blue-Collar Worker Supervisor; Branch Manager; Claim Representative; Customer Service Representative; Human Resources Specialist; Property and Real Estate Manager; Typist/Word Processor.

KELLY SERVICES, INC.
21250 Hawthorne Boulevard, Suite 750, Torrance CA 90503. 310/543-3589. **Fax:** 310/316-6145. **Contact:** Ms. Pat Georgen, Senior Evaluation Manager. **Description:** A temporary agency. **Specializes in the areas of:** Clerical; Light Industrial; Manufacturing; Office Support; Secretarial; Technical. **Positions commonly filled include:** Accountant/Auditor; Administrative Manager; Biochemist; Branch Manager; Buyer; Chemical Engineer; Clerical Supervisor; Computer Programmer; Industrial Engineer; Internet Services Manager; Management Analyst/Consultant; Software Engineer; Systems Analyst; Technical Writer/Editor; Typist/Word Processor. **Benefits available to temporary workers:** Credit Union; Paid Holidays; Paid Vacation. **Corporate headquarters location:** Troy MI.

KELLY SERVICES, INC.
950 Northgate Drive, Suite 303, San Rafael CA 94901. 415/491-0933. **Fax:** 415/491-4741. **Contact:** Andrea Davis, Employment Specialist. **Description:** A temporary agency. Company pays fee. **Specializes in the areas of:** Administration; Computer Science/Software; Marketing; Secretarial; Technical. **Positions commonly filled include:** Administrative Manager; Aircraft Mechanic/Engine Specialist; Biological Scientist; Biomedical Engineer; Chemist; Civil Engineer; Clerical Supervisor; Customer Service Representative; Design Engineer; Electrical/Electronics Engineer; Management Analyst/Consultant; Mechanical Engineer; MIS Specialist; Nuclear Engineer; Software Engineer; Stationary Engineer; Technical Writer/Editor; Typist/Word Processor. **Benefits available to temporary workers:** Medical Insurance; Paid Vacation. **Corporate headquarters location:** Troy MI.

KELLY TECHNICAL SERVICES
3031 Tisch Way, Suite 300, San Jose CA 95128. 408/557-4900. **Contact:** Chuck Sproat, Manager. **Description:** A temporary agency. **Specializes in the areas of:** Accounting/Auditing; Administration; Biology; Engineering; Finance; Manufacturing; Personnel/Labor Relations; Secretarial; Technical. **Positions commonly filled include:** Accountant/Auditor; Administrative Manager; Agricultural Engineer; Biomedical Engineer; Chemical Engineer; Chemist; Clinical Lab Technician; Computer Programmer; Credit Manager; Design Engineer; Designer; Draftsperson; Electrical/Electronics Engineer; Environmental Engineer; Financial Analyst; Management Analyst/Consultant; MIS Specialist; Multimedia Designer; Software Engineer; Systems Analyst; Technical Writer/Editor; Telecommunications Manager. **Benefits available to temporary workers:** 401(k); Dental Insurance; Medical Insurance; Paid Holidays; Paid Vacation. **Corporate headquarters location:** Troy MI.

KELLY TECHNICAL SERVICES
1400 North Harbor Boulevard, Suite 103, Fullerton CA 92835. 714/879-9763. **Toll-free phone:** 800/659-1401. **Fax:** 714/525-6980. **Contact:** Debbie Mauldin, Senior Technical Recruiter. **Description:** A temporary

agency. Company pays fee. **Specializes in the areas of:** Accounting/Auditing; Administration; Computer Hardware/Software; Engineering; Technical. **Positions commonly filled include:** Accountant/Auditor; Computer Programmer; Draftsperson; Editor; Electrical/Electronics Engineer; Financial Analyst; Human Resources Specialist; Industrial Engineer; Internet Services Manager; Operations/Production Manager; Purchasing Agent/Manager; Quality Control Supervisor. **Corporate headquarters location:** Troy MI. **Average salary range of placements:** More than $50,000. **Number of placements per year:** 500 - 999.

KLEIN & ASSOCIATES
3510 Torrance Boulevard, Suite 112, Torrance CA 90503. 310/540-3140. **Toll-free phone:** 800/475-5346. **Fax:** 310/540-5030. **Contact:** Robert Klein, Owner. **Description:** A temporary agency that places office personnel and computer professionals. The firm also provides permanent placements. Company pays fee. **Specializes in the areas of:** Accounting/Auditing; Administration; Architecture/Construction; Banking; Computer Science/Software; Economics; Engineering; Finance; Industrial; Legal; Light Industrial; Nonprofit; Personnel/Labor Relations; Sales; Secretarial; Technical. **Positions commonly filled include:** Accountant/Auditor; Buyer; Civil Engineer; Clerical Supervisor; Computer Operator; Computer Programmer; Controller; Cost Estimator; Design Engineer; Draftsperson; Economist; Editor; Editorial Assistant; Electrician; Graphic Designer; Human Resources Manager; Industrial Engineer; Internet Services Manager; Purchasing Agent/Manager; Sales Manager; Sales Representative; Secretary; Software Engineer; Statistician; Systems Analyst; Systems Manager; Teacher/Professor; Technical Writer/Editor; Typist/Word Processor; Webmaster. **Benefits available to temporary workers:** Medical Insurance; Paid Holidays; Paid Vacation. **Corporate headquarters location:** This Location. **Average salary range of placements:** $30,000 - $50,000. **Number of placements per year:** 200 - 499.

LAB SUPPORT INC.
7901 Stoneridge Drive, Pleasanton CA 94588-3600. 510/416-0840. **Toll-free phone:** 800/995-7378. **Contact:** Kim Liu, Account Manager. **Description:** A temporary placement agency for scientific professionals. **Specializes in the areas of:** Biology; Health/Medical; Industrial; Manufacturing; Personnel/Labor Relations; Technical. **Positions commonly filled include:** Agricultural Engineer; Biochemist; Biological Scientist; Biomedical Engineer; Chemist; Quality Control Supervisor; Science Technologist. **Benefits available to temporary workers:** 401(k); Bonus Award/Plan; Medical Insurance; Paid Holidays; Stock Purchase. **Corporate headquarters location:** Calabasas CA. **Other U.S. locations:** Nationwide. **Average salary range of placements:** $20,000 - $29,999. **Number of placements per year:** 100 - 199.

LAB SUPPORT INC.
26651 West Agoura Road, Calabasas CA 91302. **Toll-free phone:** 800/475-2958. **Fax:** 818/878-7940. **Contact:** Manager. **World Wide Web address:** http://www.labsupport.com. **Description:** A temporary agency for scientific personnel. Positions typically last for 3 - 4 months. Company pays fee. **Specializes in the areas of:** Biology; Food Industry; Industrial; Manufacturing; Scientific; Technical. **Positions commonly filled include:** Biochemist; Biological Scientist; Ceramics Engineer; Chemical Engineer; Chemist; Environmental Engineer; Food Scientist/Technologist; Materials Engineer; Mechanical Engineer; Metallurgical Engineer; Petroleum Engineer; Quality Control Supervisor; Science Technologist; Technical Writer/Editor. **Benefits available to temporary workers:** 401(k); Medical Insurance; Stock Purchase. **Corporate headquarters location:** This Location. **Other U.S. locations:** Nationwide. **Average salary range of placements:** $20,000 - $29,999. **Number of placements per year:** 200 - 499.

LABOR WORLD
14410 Washington Avenue, Suite 120, San Leandro CA 94578. 510/483-0377. **Fax:** 510/483-9263. **Contact:** Margie Hagen, Branch Manager. **Description:** A temporary agency that focuses on light industrial placements. **Specializes in the areas of:** Food Industry; General Labor; Industrial; Manufacturing; Publishing; Transportation. **Positions commonly filled include:** Blue-Collar Worker Supervisor. **Corporate headquarters location:** Boca Raton FL.

LEGAL RESOURCE PEOPLE
2020 Hurley Way, Suite 410, Sacramento CA 95825-3214. 916/929-6619. **Fax:** 916/929-1311. **Contact:** Kelly Fisher, Administrator. **Description:** A temporary agency that also provides permanent placement. Company pays fee. **Specializes in the areas of:** Health/Medical; Insurance; Legal; Secretarial. **Positions commonly filled include:** Legal Secretary; Paralegal; Receptionist; Typist/Word Processor. **Average salary range of placements:** $30,000 - $50,000. **Number of placements per year:** 500 - 999.

LEIGH & ASSOCIATES LEGAL PERSONNEL PLACEMENT
18552 MacArthur Boulevard, Suite 200, Irvine CA 92612. 714/756-0388. **Fax:** 714/756-0397. **Contact:** Cindy Leigh, President. **Description:** A legal personnel placement firm offering both temporary and permanent placements. Company pays fee. **Specializes in the areas of:** Legal; Secretarial. **Positions commonly filled include:** Attorney; Human Resources Specialist; Legal Secretary; Library Technician; MIS Specialist; Paralegal; Typist/Word Processor. **Corporate headquarters location:** This Location. **Other U.S. locations:** Los Angeles CA.

LEIGH & ASSOCIATES LEGAL PERSONNEL PLACEMENT
444 South Flower Street, Suite 1500, Los Angeles CA 90071. 213/612-4411. **Fax:** 213/612-4433. **Contact:** Recruiter. **Description:** A legal personnel placement firm offering both temporary and permanent placements. Company pays fee. **Specializes in the areas of:** Legal; Secretarial. **Positions commonly filled include:** Attorney; Human Resources Specialist; Legal Secretary; Librarian; MIS Specialist; Paralegal; Typist/Word Processor. **Corporate headquarters location:** Irvine CA.

LINK BUSINESS & PERSONNEL SERVICES
LINK CAREER CENTER
154 East Gobbi, Ukiah CA 95482. 707/468-5465. **Fax:** 707/468-1171. **Contact:** Rachel Peugh, Owner. **Description:** A small, service-oriented agency that offers temporary and temp-to-hire placement services; skills testing; resume services; word processing projects; and bookkeeping. LINK Career Center (also at this location) is a vocational school offering computer training, business courses, and basic skills classes. Company pays fee. **Specializes in the areas of:** Accounting/Auditing; Bookkeeping; Computer Science/Software; Office Support; Secretarial. **Positions commonly filled include:** Clerical Supervisor; Customer Service Representative; Medical Records Technician; Services Sales Representative; Typist/Word Processor. **Average salary range of placements:** $20,000 - $29,999. **Number of placements per year:** 50 - 99.

THE LONDON AGENCY
5670 Wilshire Boulevard, Suite 880, Los Angeles CA 90036. 213/931-9400. **Contact:** Office Manager.

Description: A temporary employment agency. Company pays fee. **Specializes in the areas of:** Accounting/Auditing; Administration; Advertising; Banking; Broadcasting; Computer Hardware/Software; Engineering; Finance; Health/Medical; Insurance; Legal; Nonprofit; Personnel/Labor Relations; Publishing; Secretarial. **Positions commonly filled include:** Accountant/Auditor; Administrative Assistant; Bookkeeper; Clerk; Computer Operator; Computer Programmer; Customer Service Representative; Data Entry Clerk; Legal Secretary; Receptionist; Secretary; Typist/Word Processor. **Number of placements per year:** 200 - 499.

MK TECHNICAL SERVICE
1580 Oakland Road, Suite C104, San Jose CA 95131-2441. 408/453-2562. **Fax:** 408/453-0958. **Contact:** Tony Kuret, Employment. **E-mail address:** mktech1@ix.netcom.com. **World Wide Web address:** http://www.mktech.com. **Description:** A temporary agency focusing on technical placements. **Specializes in the areas of:** Engineering; Industrial; Manufacturing; Technical. **Positions commonly filled include:** Buyer; Computer Programmer; Design Engineer; Designer; Draftsperson; Editor; Electrical/Electronics Engineer; Mechanical Engineer; Software Engineer; Technical Writer/Editor. **Benefits available to temporary workers:** Medical Insurance; Paid Holidays. **Number of placements per year:** 500 - 999.

MACTEMPS
4041 MacArthur Boulevard, Suite 240, Newport Beach CA 92660-2512. 714/476-9900. **Contact:** Sally Kloman, Marketing Manager. **Description:** A temporary agency that focuses on the placement of computer staffing specialists. The agency provides both temporary and permanent placement in computer design and production, technical support, presentation graphics, and multimedia design industries. **Specializes in the areas of:** Administration; Art/Design; Computer Science/Software; Multimedia; Publishing. **Positions commonly filled include:** Computer Programmer; Graphic Designer; Internet Services Manager; MIS Specialist; Multimedia Designer; Software Engineer; Systems Analyst; Typist/Word Processor; Video Production Coordinator. **Benefits available to temporary workers:** 401(k); Dental Insurance; Medical Insurance. **Corporate headquarters location:** Boston MA. **Other U.S. locations:** Nationwide. **Average salary range of placements:** $30,000 - $50,000. **Number of placements per year:** 200 - 499.

MANPOWER, INC.
23 South Hope Avenue, Suite E, Santa Barbara CA 93105. 805/569-2081. **Contact:** Irene Solovij, Branch Manager. **Description:** A temporary agency. Company pays fee. **Specializes in the areas of:** Clerical; Data Security; Industrial; Word Processing. **Positions commonly filled include:** Administrative Assistant; Bookkeeper; Clerk; Computer Operator; Construction Trade Worker; Driver; Factory Worker; Legal Secretary; Light Industrial Worker; Medical Secretary; Receptionist; Secretary; Stenographer; Technical Writer/Editor; Typist/Word Processor. **Corporate headquarters location:** Milwaukee WI. **Number of placements per year:** 1000+.

MANPOWER, INC.
355 South Grand Avenue, Suite 3275, Los Angeles CA 90017. 213/745-6500. **Contact:** Branch Manager. **Description:** A temporary agency. **Specializes in the areas of:** Data Processing; Industrial; Office Support; Word Processing. **Positions commonly filled include:** Accountant/Auditor; Accounting Clerk; Administrative Assistant; Biological Scientist; Bookkeeper; Chemist; Computer Operator; Customer Service Representative; Designer; Desktop Publishing Specialist; Electrician; Inspector/Tester/Grader; Inventory Control Specialist; Machine Operator; Packaging Engineer; Painter; Project Engineer; Proofreader; Receptionist; Records Manager; Research Assistant; Secretary; Software Engineer; Stenographer; Systems Analyst; Technical Writer/Editor; Telemarketer; Transcriptionist; Typist/Word Processor; Welder. **Corporate headquarters location:** Milwaukee WI. **Number of placements per year:** 1000+.

MANPOWER, INC.
One World Trade Center, Suite 208, Long Beach CA 90831-0208. 562/432-8582. **Fax:** 562/432-4482. **Contact:** Jessica Kussman, Branch Supervisor. **Description:** A temporary agency focusing on clerical, industrial, technical, and sales and marketing professions. Company pays fee. **Specializes in the areas of:** Administration; Banking; Industrial; Manufacturing; Personnel/Labor Relations; Sales; Secretarial; Technical. **Positions commonly filled include:** Accountant/Auditor; Customer Service Representative. **Benefits available to temporary workers:** 401(k); Life Insurance; Medical Insurance; Paid Holidays; Paid Vacation; Referral Bonus Plan. **Corporate headquarters location:** Milwaukee WI. **Other U.S. locations:** Nationwide. **Average salary range of placements:** Less than $20,000. **Number of placements per year:** 200 - 499.

MANPOWER, INC.
39650 Liberty Street, Suite 130, Fremont CA 94538. 510/440-9040. **Fax:** 510/440-9048. **Contact:** Service Supervisor. **Description:** A temporary agency that also offers permanent placement. Company pays fee. **Specializes in the areas of:** Accounting/Auditing; Computer Science/Software; Engineering; Finance; General Management; Industrial; Manufacturing; Personnel/Labor Relations; Sales; Technical. **Positions commonly filled include:** Accountant/Auditor; Adjuster; Administrative Manager; Advertising Clerk; Agricultural Engineer; Bank Officer/Manager; Branch Manager; Buyer; Chemical Engineer; Clinical Lab Technician; Computer Programmer; Cost Estimator; Customer Service Representative; Draftsperson; Electrical/Electronics Engineer; General Manager; Geologist/Geophysicist; Human Resources Specialist; Industrial Engineer; Internet Services Manager; Librarian; Management Analyst/Consultant; Mechanical Engineer; MIS Specialist; Multimedia Designer; Operations/Production Manager; Property and Real Estate Manager; Quality Control Supervisor; Radiological Technologist; Securities Sales Representative; Software Engineer; Structural Engineer; Systems Analyst; Technical Writer/Editor; Telecommunications Manager; Typist/Word Processor. **Benefits available to temporary workers:** 401(k); Medical Insurance; Paid Holidays; Paid Vacation; Stock Purchase. **Corporate headquarters location:** Milwaukee WI. **International locations:** Worldwide. **Average salary range of placements:** $20,000 - $29,999. **Number of placements per year:** 1000+.

MANPOWER, INC.
50 California Street, Suite 835, San Francisco CA 94111. 415/781-7171. **Contact:** Branch Manager. **Description:** A temporary agency that also offers some permanent placements. **Specializes in the areas of:** Industrial; Office Support; Telemarketing; Word Processing. **Positions commonly filled include:** Accountant/Auditor; Accounting Clerk; Administrative Assistant; Assembler; Biological Scientist; Bookkeeper; Chemist; Computer Operator; Customer Service Representative; Designer; Desktop Publishing Specialist; Electrician; Inventory Control Specialist; Machine Operator; Materials Manager; Project Engineer; Secretary; Software Engineer; Systems Analyst; Technical Writer/Editor; Telemarketer; Typist/Word Processor. **Benefits available to temporary workers:** Life Insurance; Medical Insurance;

Paid Holidays; Paid Vacation. **Corporate headquarters location:** Milwaukee WI. **International locations:** Worldwide. **Number of placements per year:** 1000+.

MICRO TEMPS SYSTEMS AND PROGRAMMING
17320 Red Hill Avenue, Suite 320, Irvine CA 92614. 714/259-1850. **Contact:** Branch Manager. **Description:** A temporary agency. Company pays fee. **Specializes in the areas of:** Computer Hardware/Software; MIS/EDP; Technical. **Positions commonly filled include:** Aerospace Engineer; Computer Programmer; EDP Specialist; Management Analyst/Consultant; Systems Analyst; Technical Writer/Editor. **Number of placements per year:** 200 - 499.

MICRO TEMPS SYSTEMS AND PROGRAMMING
1733 North First Street, San Jose CA 95112. 408/452-1344. **Fax:** 408/452-1454. **Contact:** Office Manager. **E-mail address:** sanjose@microtemps.com. **World Wide Web address:** http://www.microtemps.com. **Description:** A temporary agency. **Specializes in the areas of:** Computer Science/Software. **Positions commonly filled include:** Software Engineer; Technical Writer/Editor.

MICRO TRACK TEMPORARY SERVICES
4450 California Avenue, #K260, Bakersfield CA 93309. 805/871-9529. **Contact:** Scott Hudbert, President. **E-mail address:** 72040,3702@compuserve.com. **Description:** A temporary agency providing programming technical support services. Company pays fee. **Specializes in the areas of:** Computer Science/Software. **Positions commonly filled include:** Computer Programmer; Systems Analyst. **Benefits available to temporary workers:** Dental Insurance; Medical Insurance; Paid Holidays; Paid Vacation. **Average salary range of placements:** $30,000 - $50,000. **Number of placements per year:** 1 - 49.

MURRAY ENTERPRISES STAFFING SERVICES, INC.
2975 Scott Boulevard, Suite 101, Santa Clara CA 95054. 408/727-9922. **Fax:** 408/727-5666. **Contact:** Tricia Kelly, Office Administrator. **E-mail address:** staffing@murrayent.com. **Description:** A temporary agency. **Specializes in the areas of:** Accounting/Auditing; Administration; Computer Science/Software; Engineering; Industrial; Manufacturing; Personnel/Labor Relations; Sales; Secretarial; Technical. **Positions commonly filled include:** Accountant/Auditor; Administrative Manager; Buyer; Clerical Supervisor; Computer Programmer; Systems Analyst; Technical Writer/Editor; Telecommunications Manager; Typist/Word Processor; Urban/Regional Planner. **Benefits available to temporary workers:** Dental Insurance; Medical Insurance; Paid Holidays. **Average salary range of placements:** $30,000 - $50,000. **Number of placements per year:** 200 - 499.

NORRELL TEMPORARY SERVICES, INC. OF CALIFORNIA
790 East Colorado Boulevard, Suite 102, Pasadena CA 91101. 626/446-8574. **Contact:** Rachel Hirota, Office Manager. **Description:** This location of Norrell provides long-term, temporary assignments. Company pays fee. **Specializes in the areas of:** Bilingual; Clerical; Computer Science/Software; Word Processing. **Positions commonly filled include:** Accountant/Auditor; Administrative Assistant; Clerk; Legal Secretary; Light Industrial Worker; MIS Specialist; Receptionist; Secretary; Stenographer; Support Personnel; Typist/Word Processor. **Corporate headquarters location:** Atlanta GA. **Other U.S. locations:** Nationwide. **Number of placements per year:** 1000+.

NORRELL TEMPORARY SERVICES, INC. OF CALIFORNIA
2377 Crenshaw Boulevard, Suite 156, Torrance CA 90501. 310/782-6436. **Fax:** 310/782-6601. **Contact:** Manager. **Description:** A nationwide leader in temporary and permanent staffing. The company focuses on clerical, technical, industrial, and managerial marketing placement. **Specializes in the areas of:** Accounting/Auditing; Administration; Banking; Industrial; Manufacturing; Personnel/Labor Relations; Sales; Secretarial. **Positions commonly filled include:** Accountant/Auditor; Advertising Clerk; Budget Analyst; Computer Programmer; Customer Service Representative; Editor; Management Trainee; Secretary; Support Personnel; Systems Analyst; Technical Writer/Editor; Transportation/Traffic Specialist; Typist/Word Processor. **Corporate headquarters location:** Atlanta GA. **Other U.S. locations:** Nationwide. **Number of placements per year:** 500 - 999.

NORRELL TEMPORARY SERVICES, INC. OF CALIFORNIA
4525 Wilshire Boulevard, Suite 120, Los Angeles CA 90010. 213/964-9566. **Contact:** Manager. **Description:** A temporary agency. Company pays fee. **Specializes in the areas of:** Bilingual; Clerical; Computer Science/Software; Word Processing. **Positions commonly filled include:** Accountant/Auditor; Administrative Assistant; Clerk; Computer Operator; Customer Service Representative; Data Entry Clerk; Legal Secretary; Light Industrial Worker; MIS Specialist; Receptionist; Secretary; Stenographer; Support Personnel; Typist/Word Processor. **Corporate headquarters location:** Atlanta GA. **Other U.S. locations:** Nationwide. **Number of placements per year:** 1000+.

NORRELL TEMPORARY SERVICES, INC. OF CALIFORNIA
5950 Canoga Avenue, Suite 210, Woodland Hills CA 91367. 818/340-8810. **Contact:** Manager. **Description:** A temporary agency. Company pays fee. **Specializes in the areas of:** Bilingual; Clerical; Computer Science/Software; Word Processing. **Positions commonly filled include:** Accountant/Auditor; Administrative Assistant; Clerk; Computer Operator; Customer Service Representative; Data Entry Clerk; Legal Secretary; Light Industrial Worker; MIS Specialist; Receptionist; Stenographer; Support Personnel; Typist/Word Processor. **Corporate headquarters location:** Atlanta GA. **Other U.S. locations:** Nationwide. **Number of placements per year:** 1000+.

NORRELL TEMPORARY SERVICES, INC. OF CALIFORNIA
2001 Gateway Place, Suite 120, San Jose CA 95110. 408/441-6841. **Fax:** 408/441-6840. **Contact:** Amanda Tubbs, Manager. **Description:** A temporary agency that also provides temp-to-hire and permanent placements. The agency focuses on the placement of computer operators and administrative and technical personnel. Company pays fee. **Specializes in the areas of:** Administration; Computer Science/Software; Personnel/Labor Relations; Secretarial. **Positions commonly filled include:** Administrative Assistant; Clerical Supervisor; Customer Service Representative; Human Resources Specialist; Public Relations Specialist; Purchasing Agent/Manager; Secretary; Systems Analyst; Telecommunications Manager; Typist/Word Processor. **Benefits available to temporary workers:** 401(k); Medical Insurance; Paid Holidays; Paid Vacation. **Average salary range of placements:** $20,000 - $29,999.

O'BRIEN EMPLOYMENT SERVICES
5510 Birdcage Street, Suite 210, Citrus Heights CA 95610. 916/961-2778. **Contact:** Manager. **Description:** A temporary agency. **Specializes in the areas of:** Clerical; Health/Medical. **Positions commonly filled include:** Dental Assistant/Dental Hygienist; Medical Assistant; Secretary.

OLSTEN STAFFING SERVICES
800 East Colorado Boulevard, Suite 120, Pasadena Towers CA 91101. 626/449-1342. **Contact:** Manager. **Description:** A temporary agency. Company pays fee. **Specializes in the areas of:** Accounting/Auditing; Advertising; Banking; Clerical; Finance; Health/Medical; Insurance; Legal; Manufacturing; Real Estate. **Positions commonly filled include:** Accountant/Auditor; Actuary; Administrative Assistant; Administrative Worker/Clerk; Bank Officer/Manager; Bookkeeper; Claim Representative; Clerk; Computer Operator; Computer Programmer; Credit Manager; Customer Service Representative; Data Entry Clerk; Driver; EDP Specialist; Financial Analyst; General Manager; Insurance Agent/Broker; Legal Secretary; Medical Secretary; Purchasing Agent/Manager; Quality Control Supervisor; Receptionist; Sales Representative; Secretary; Statistician; Stenographer; Support Personnel; Typist/Word Processor; Underwriter/Assistant Underwriter. **Number of placements per year:** 1000+.

OLSTEN STAFFING SERVICES
1000 Broadway, Suite 248, Oakland CA 94607. 510/987-7555. **Fax:** 510/987-7553. **Contact:** Cheryl Heinla, Customer Service Manager. **E-mail address:** olsten0032@aol.com. **World Wide Web address:** http://www.olsten.com. **Description:** A temporary agency. Company pays fee. **Specializes in the areas of:** Accounting/Auditing; Clerical; Legal; Secretarial. **Positions commonly filled include:** Administrative Assistant; Bookkeeper; Claim Representative; Clerk; Customer Service Representative; Data Entry Clerk; Driver; Legal Secretary; Light Industrial Worker; Medical Secretary; Receptionist; Secretary; Typist/Word Processor. **Number of placements per year:** 1000+.

OLSTEN STAFFING SERVICES
32990 Alvarado Niles Road, Suite 970, Union City CA 94587-3106. 510/429-8995. **Fax:** 510/429-8909. **Contact:** Ruby Mendoza, Account Representative. **Description:** A temporary agency that also provides permanent placement. Founded in 1950. **Specializes in the areas of:** Accounting/Auditing; Administration; Personnel/Labor Relations; Secretarial. **Positions commonly filled include:** Accountant/Auditor; Blue-Collar Worker Supervisor; Branch Manager; Clerical Supervisor; Customer Service Representative; General Manager; Human Resources Specialist; Typist/Word Processor. **Benefits available to temporary workers:** Dental Insurance; Medical Insurance. **Corporate headquarters location:** Melville NY. **Average salary range of placements:** $20,000 - $29,999. **Number of placements per year:** 200 - 499.

OMNI EXPRESS TEMPS
2185 Faraday Avenue, Suite 120, Carlsbad CA 92008. 760/438-4405. **Fax:** 760/438-4482. **Contact:** Jennifer Mendenhall, Regional Operations Manager. **Description:** A temporary agency. Company pays fee. **Specializes in the areas of:** Accounting/Auditing; Administration; Computer Science/Software; Engineering; Finance; Industrial; Manufacturing; Personnel/Labor Relations; Sales; Technical. **Positions commonly filled include:** Accountant/Auditor; Advertising Clerk; Aerospace Engineer; Aircraft Mechanic/Engine Specialist; Bank Officer/Manager; Blue-Collar Worker Supervisor; Branch Manager; Budget Analyst; Buyer; Chemical Engineer; Chemist; Civil Engineer; Clinical Lab Technician; Computer Programmer; Credit Manager; Design Engineer; Designer; Draftsperson; Electrical/Electronics Engineer; Financial Analyst; Industrial Engineer; Industrial Production Manager; Internet Services Manager; Mechanical Engineer; Metallurgical Engineer; MIS Specialist; Quality Control Supervisor; Software Engineer; Structural Engineer; Systems Analyst; Technical Writer/Editor; Typist/Word Processor. **Benefits available to temporary workers:** 401(k); Dental Insurance; Medical Insurance; Paid Holidays. **Corporate headquarters location:** This Location. **Other U.S. locations:** Escondido CA; San Diego CA; Tustin CA. **Number of placements per year:** 1000+.

ON ASSIGNMENT, INC.
26651 West Agoura Road, Calabasas CA 91302. 818/878-7900. **Fax:** 818/878-7930. **Contact:** Steve Koehler, Training and Recruitment Director. **Description:** A temporary agency that provides placements in laboratories (Lab Support Division) and financial institutions (Finance Support Division). **Specializes in the areas of:** Banking; Finance; Health/Medical. **Positions commonly filled include:** Bank Officer/Manager; Biological Scientist; Biomedical Engineer; Chemical Engineer; Environmental Engineer; Financial Analyst; Food Scientist/Technologist; Lender; Machinist. **Number of placements per year:** 1000+.

PACIFIC PLACEMENT GROUP
20 California Street, 2nd Floor, San Francisco CA 94111-4803. 415/989-0542. **Fax:** 415/391-6325. **Contact:** Jane Groner, President. **E-mail address:** pacificpg@aol.com. **Description:** A temporary agency that also provides permanent placement. **Specializes in the areas of:** Administration; Graphic Arts. **Positions commonly filled include:** Administrative Assistant; Graphic Designer. **Average salary range of placements:** $30,000 - $50,000. **Number of placements per year:** 200 - 499.

PASONA PACIFIC INC.
444 South Flower Street, Main Floor, Los Angeles CA 90071. 213/489-2989. **Fax:** 213/489-4978. **Contact:** Office Manager. **Description:** A temporary agency that also operates as a permanent employment agency and offers career/outplacement counseling. Company pays fee. **Specializes in the areas of:** Accounting/Auditing; Administration; Computer Science/Software; Economics; General Management; Insurance; Sales; Technical. **Positions commonly filled include:** Accountant/Auditor; Administrative Manager; Bank Officer/Manager; Brokerage Clerk; Budget Analyst; Buyer; Clerical Supervisor; Computer Programmer; Cost Estimator; Customer Service Representative; Financial Analyst; Hotel/Motel Clerk; Human Resources Specialist; Industrial Engineer; Internet Services Manager; Manufacturer's/Wholesaler's Sales Rep.; Market Research Analyst; MIS Specialist; Multimedia Designer; Paralegal; Property and Real Estate Manager; Purchasing Agent/Manager; Quality Control Supervisor; Restaurant/Food Service Manager; Services Sales Representative; Software Engineer; Systems Analyst; Technical Writer/Editor; Typist/Word Processor. **Corporate headquarters location:** This Location. **Other U.S. locations:** Newport Beach CA; Torrance CA; New York NY. **Average salary range of placements:** $30,000 - $50,000. **Number of placements per year:** 500 - 999.

PERSONALIZED PLACEMENT AGENCY
746 Villa Street, Mountain View CA 94041. 650/968-4436. **Fax:** 650/968-4436. **Contact:** Gerry Harrison, Human Resources. **Description:** A temporary agency that also offers permanent placements. **Specializes in the areas of:** Accounting/Auditing; Secretarial; Technical. **Positions commonly filled include:** Accountant/Auditor; Administrative Manager;

Advertising Clerk; Biochemist; Buyer; Chemist; Clerical Supervisor; Computer Programmer; Customer Service Representative; Human Resources Specialist; Librarian; MIS Specialist; Operations/Production Manager; Paralegal; Purchasing Agent/Manager; Systems Analyst; Technical Writer/Editor; Typist/Word Processor. **Average salary range of placements:** $20,000 - $29,999. **Number of placements per year:** 500 - 999.

PREMIER PERSONNEL SERVICES
2463 208th Street, Suite 200, Torrance CA 90501. 310/320-1023. **Fax:** 310/320-5456. **Contact:** Anne Kocsis, Owner. **Description:** A temporary agency providing placement in fields including finance, sales, administrative, and clerical. Company pays fee. **Specializes in the areas of:** Accounting/Auditing; Administration; Personnel/Labor Relations; Sales; Secretarial. **Positions commonly filled include:** Accountant/Auditor; Buyer; Customer Service Representative; Human Resources Specialist; Manufacturer's/Wholesaler's Sales Rep.; Purchasing Agent/Manager; Typist/Word Processor. **Number of placements per year:** 200 - 499.

PRESIDIO PERSONNEL SERVICE
3710 State Street, Suite C, Santa Barbara CA 93105. 805/682-2848. **Fax:** 805/682-5211. **Contact:** Gloria Radley, President. **E-mail address:** jobs@presidio-jobs.com. **World Wide Web address:** http://www.presidio-jobs.com. **Description:** A temporary placement agency. Company pays fee. **Specializes in the areas of:** Accounting/Auditing; Administration; Computer Science/Software; General Management; Industrial; Insurance; Legal; Manufacturing; Nonprofit; Personnel/Labor Relations; Retail; Sales; Secretarial. **Positions commonly filled include:** Accountant/Auditor; Administrative Manager; Advertising Clerk; Bank Officer/Manager; Branch Manager; Claim Representative; Clerical Supervisor; Computer Programmer; Credit Manager; Customer Service Representative; Design Engineer; Designer; Editor; Environmental Engineer; Financial Analyst; Industrial Engineer; Industrial Production Manager; Internet Services Manager; Management Analyst/Consultant; Mechanical Engineer; MIS Specialist; Multimedia Designer; Paralegal; Software Engineer; Strategic Relations Manager; Systems Analyst; Telecommunications Manager; Travel Agent; Typist/Word Processor; Underwriter/Assistant Underwriter. **Average salary range of placements:** $20,000 - $29,999. **Number of placements per year:** 1000+.

PRIDESTAFF
3 Point Drive, Suite 305, Brea CA 92821. 714/255-1400. **Fax:** 714/255-9465. **Contact:** Manager. **Description:** A temporary agency focusing on human resource services. Company pays fee. **Specializes in the areas of:** Accounting/Auditing; Clerical; Light Industrial; Office Support; Personnel/Labor Relations; Secretarial. **Positions commonly filled include:** Accountant/Auditor; Buyer; Customer Service Representative; Typist/Word Processor. **Benefits available to temporary workers:** Credit Union; Medical Insurance; Paid Holidays; Paid Vacation; Referral Bonus Plan. **Corporate headquarters location:** Fresno CA. **Other U.S. locations:** AZ; GA. **Number of placements per year:** 100 - 199.

QUESTEMPS
405 Esplanade Drive, #101, Oxnard CA 93030. 805/983-3959. **Fax:** 805/983-6939. **Contact:** Sonia Robles, Operations Manager. **Description:** A temporary employment agency. Company pays fee. **Specializes in the areas of:** Accounting/Auditing; Administration; Engineering; Finance; Industrial; Personnel/Labor Relations; Secretarial. **Positions commonly filled include:** Accountant/Auditor; Buyer; Customer Service Representative; Electrical/Electronics Engineer; Human Resources Specialist; Mechanical Engineer; MIS Specialist; Purchasing Agent/Manager; Quality Control Supervisor; Typist/Word Processor. **Average salary range of placements:** $20,000 - $29,999. **Number of placements per year:** 1000+.

RX RELIEF
1667 South Mission Road, Suite H, Fallbrook CA 92028-4114. 760/723-1143. **Toll-free phone:** 800/797-3543. **Fax:** 760/723-2411. **Contact:** Roy Long, President. **Description:** A temporary agency. Founded in 1978. **Specializes in the areas of:** Health/Medical. **Positions commonly filled include:** Pharmacist. **Benefits available to temporary workers:** Bonus Award/Plan; Medical Insurance. **Average salary range of placements:** More than $50,000. **Number of placements per year:** 100 - 199.

REMEDY INTELLIGENT STAFFING
4371 Glencoe Avenue, Suite B7, Marina Del Rey CA 90292. 310/826-5065. **Fax:** 310/207-4288. **Contact:** Manager. **Description:** A temporary agency. **Specializes in the areas of:** Personnel/Labor Relations; Retail; Sales; Secretarial; Word Processing. **Positions commonly filled include:** Customer Service Representative. **Corporate headquarters location:** San Juan Capistrano CA. **Other U.S. locations:** Nationwide. **Number of placements per year:** 500 - 999.

REMEDY INTELLIGENT STAFFING
820 Myrtle Avenue, Monrovia CA 91016. 626/301-9204. **Fax:** 626/303-2433. **Contact:** Branch Leader. **Description:** A temporary agency focusing on light industrial and technical professions. The agency also provides permanent placements. **Specializes in the areas of:** Engineering; Light Industrial; Manufacturing. **Positions commonly filled include:** Aerospace Engineer; Aircraft Mechanic/Engine Specialist; Automotive Mechanic; Blue-Collar Worker Supervisor; Cost Estimator; Design Engineer; Draftsperson; Electrical/Electronics Engineer; Electrician; Industrial Engineer; Industrial Production Manager; Light Industrial Worker; Mechanical Engineer; Operations/Production Manager. **Corporate headquarters location:** San Juan Capistrano CA. **Other U.S. locations:** Nationwide. **Average salary range of placements:** Less than $20,000. **Number of placements per year:** 500 - 999.

REMEDY INTELLIGENT STAFFING
4300 Stevens Creek Boulevard, Suite 190, San Jose CA 95129-1263. 408/554-8174. **Contact:** Recruiter. **Description:** A temporary agency. Founded in 1965. **Specializes in the areas of:** Administration; Industrial; Manufacturing; Personnel/Labor Relations; Sales; Secretarial. **Positions commonly filled include:** Buyer; Customer Service Representative; Management Trainee. **Benefits available to temporary workers:** Dental Insurance; Medical Insurance; Vision Insurance. **Corporate headquarters location:** San Juan Capistrano CA. **Other U.S. locations:** Nationwide. **Average salary range of placements:** $20,000 - $29,999. **Number of placements per year:** 1000+.

REMEDY INTELLIGENT STAFFING
146 South Main Street, Suite S, Orange CA 92668. 714/938-0800. **Toll-free phone:** 800/338-8367. **Fax:** 714/939-9933. **Contact:** Branch Manager. **Description:** A temporary agency that also offers career and outplacement counseling. **Specializes in the areas of:** Accounting/Auditing; Banking; Computer Hardware/Software; Engineering; Finance; General Management; Health/Medical; Industrial; Insurance; Manufacturing; Publishing; Retail; Sales; Secretarial. **Positions commonly filled include:** Accountant/Auditor; Advertising Clerk; Budget Analyst; Buyer;

Claim Representative; Computer Programmer; Cost Estimator; Credit Manager; Customer Service Representative; Financial Analyst; Human Resources Specialist; MIS Specialist; Operations/Production Manager; Paralegal; Purchasing Agent/Manager; Statistician; Typist/Word Processor; Underwriter/Assistant Underwriter. **Benefits available to temporary workers:** 401(k); Dental Insurance; Medical Insurance; Vision Insurance. **Corporate headquarters location:** San Juan Capistrano CA. **Other U.S. locations:** Nationwide. **Average salary range of placements:** $20,000 - $29,999. **Number of placements per year:** 1000+.

REMEDY INTELLIGENT STAFFING
Emerald Plaza, 402 West Broadway, Suite 2150, San Diego CA 92101. 619/702-0730. **Contact:** Manager. **Description:** A temporary and temp-to-perm employment agency. **Specializes in the areas of:** Administration; Clerical; Secretarial.

RESOURCE PERSONNEL SERVICES
2131 Palomar Airport Road, Suite 300, Carlsbad CA 92009-1436. 760/431-5116. **Fax:** 760/631-2161. **Contact:** Jeff Ullom, President. **Description:** A temporary staffing agency. Company pays fee. **Specializes in the areas of:** Administration; Industrial; Manufacturing; Secretarial; Technical. **Positions commonly filled include:** Administrative Manager; Advertising Clerk; Clerical Supervisor; Customer Service Representative; Draftsperson; Electrical/Electronics Engineer; Electrician; Industrial Engineer; Industrial Production Manager; Mechanical Engineer; MIS Specialist; Technical Writer/Editor; Typist/Word Processor. **Benefits available to temporary workers:** Paid Holidays; Paid Vacation. **Average salary range of placements:** $20,000 - $29,999. **Number of placements per year:** 50 - 99.

RICHMAR ASSOCIATES INC.
283 Brokaw Road, Santa Clara CA 95050. 408/727-6070. **Fax:** 408/727-4465. **Contact:** Manager. **Description:** A temporary and temp-to-perm agency. **Specializes in the areas of:** Administration; Engineering; Manufacturing; Technical.

SAN DIEGO PERSONNEL & EMPLOYMENT
9474 Kearney Villa Road, Suite 105, San Diego CA 92126. 619/689-8500. **Toll-free phone:** 800/685-8500. **Fax:** 619/689-8587. **Contact:** Coordinator. **Description:** A temporary agency. Company pays fee. **Specializes in the areas of:** Accounting/Auditing; Industrial; Manufacturing; Personnel/Labor Relations; Secretarial. **Positions commonly filled include:** Accountant/Auditor; Administrative Manager; Clerical Supervisor; Customer Service Representative; Electrician; Human Resources Specialist; Purchasing Agent/Manager; Quality Control Supervisor; Travel Agent; Typist/Word Processor. **Average salary range of placements:** $20,000 - $29,999. **Number of placements per year:** 1000+.

SELECT PERSONNEL SERVICES
323 North Azusa Avenue, West Covina CA 91791-1146. 626/331-6339. **Fax:** 626/331-7229. **Contact:** Manager. **Description:** A temporary agency. **Specializes in the areas of:** Accounting/Auditing; Manufacturing; Retail; Secretarial. **Positions commonly filled include:** Blue-Collar Worker Supervisor; Typist/Word Processor. **Corporate headquarters location:** This Location. **Other area locations:** Ontario CA. **Average salary range of placements:** Less than $20,000. **Number of placements per year:** 1000+.

SPECTRUM TEMPORARY EMPLOYEES
2130 Geer Road, Suite C, Turlock CA 95380. 209/667-8367. **Fax:** 209/667-4510. **Contact:** Branch Manager. **Description:** A temporary agency that also provides permanent placement. Company pays fee. **Specializes in the areas of:** Accounting/Auditing; Industrial; Manufacturing; Personnel/Labor Relations; Secretarial. **Positions commonly filled include:** Accountant/Auditor; Blue-Collar Worker Supervisor; Clerical Supervisor; Customer Service Representative; Human Resources Specialist; Operations/Production Manager. **Corporate headquarters location:** Campbell CA. **Other area locations:** Hayward CA; Milpitas CA; Newark CA; Sacramento CA.

STAFF CONTROL, INC.
14150 Vine Place, Cerritos CA 90701. 562/407-3700. **Fax:** 562/802-3554. **Contact:** Michael J. Osbourne, Owner. **Description:** A temporary agency. **Specializes in the areas of:** Data Processing. **Corporate headquarters location:** This Location.

STIVERS TEMPORARY PERSONNEL OF CALIFORNIA
55 South Lake Avenue, Suite 100, Pasadena CA 91101. 626/796-8559. **Contact:** Manager. **Description:** A temporary agency. **Specializes in the areas of:** Accounting/Auditing; Banking; Clerical; Finance; Health/Medical; Insurance; Legal. **Positions commonly filled include:** Accountant/Auditor; Actuary; Administrative Assistant; Advertising Clerk; Bookkeeper; Claim Representative; Clerk; Computer Operator; Data Entry Clerk; Legal Secretary.

STIVERS TEMPORARY PERSONNEL OF CALIFORNIA
16601 Ventura Boulevard, Suite 300, Encino CA 91436. 818/906-1145. **Contact:** Manager. **Description:** A temporary agency. **Specializes in the areas of:** Accounting/Auditing; Banking; Clerical; Health/Medical; Insurance; Legal. **Positions commonly filled include:** Account Representative; Actuary; Administrative Assistant; Bookkeeper; Computer Operator; Data Entry Clerk; Legal Secretary; Secretary; Typist/Word Processor; Underwriter/Assistant Underwriter.

STRATEGIC STAFFING
369 Pine Street, San Francisco CA 94104. 415/616-6300. **Fax:** 415/616-6306. **Contact:** Office Manager. **World Wide Web address:** http://www.strategic-staffing.com. **Description:** A temporary agency that also offers temp-to-hire and permanent placements. Company pays fee. **Specializes in the areas of:** Accounting/Auditing; Administration; Advertising; Computer Science/Software; Personnel/Labor Relations; Secretarial; Technical. **Positions commonly filled include:** Accountant/Auditor; Administrative Manager; Advertising Clerk; Branch Manager; Budget Analyst; Claim Representative; Clerical Supervisor; Computer Programmer; Customer Service Representative; Financial Analyst; Management Trainee; Market Research Analyst; MIS Specialist; Software Engineer; Systems Analyst; Technical Writer/Editor; Typist/Word Processor. **Number of placements per year:** 1000+.

STRATEGIC STAFFING PERSONNEL SOLUTIONS, INC. (SSPS)
39159 Paseo Padre Parkway, Suite 106, Fremont CA 94538. 510/744-6800. **Fax:** 510/744-6899. **Contact:** Manager. **Description:** A temporary staffing agency focusing on general labor and technical assignments. **Specializes in the areas of:** Manufacturing; Technical. **Other area locations:** Milpitas CA. **Average salary range of placements:** Less than $20,000. **Number of placements per year:** 1000+.

SUN PERSONNEL SERVICES
915 River Street, Santa Cruz CA 95060. 408/458-5301. **Fax:** 408/458-0950. **Contact:** Richard Huffman, Owner. **Description:** A temporary agency that also provides permanent placement and career/outplacement counseling. **Specializes in the**

areas of: Accounting/Auditing; Computer Science/Software; Engineering; Industrial; Manufacturing; Personnel/Labor Relations; Publishing; Sales; Secretarial. **Positions commonly filled include:** Accountant/Auditor; Administrative Manager; Advertising Clerk; Branch Manager; Budget Analyst; Claim Representative; Clerical Supervisor; Computer Programmer; Credit Manager; Customer Service Representative; Design Engineer; Designer; Draftsperson; Editor; Electrical/Electronics Engineer; Financial Analyst; Management Trainee; Market Research Analyst; Mechanical Engineer; Medical Records Technician; MIS Specialist; Preschool Worker; Quality Control Supervisor; Restaurant/Food Service Manager; Software Engineer; Structural Engineer; Systems Analyst; Telecommunications Manager; Typist/Word Processor. **Benefits available to temporary workers:** Medical Insurance; Paid Vacation. **Average salary range of placements:** $20,000 - $29,999. **Number of placements per year:** 100 - 199.

TLC STAFFING
4820 Mercury Street, Suite D, San Diego CA 92111. 619/569-6260. **Toll-free phone:** 800/834-4576. **Fax:** 619/569-8026. **Contact:** Kay Christian, Vice President of Operations. **E-mail address:** tlc@tlc-staffing. **World Wide Web address:** http://www.dice.com/tlcstaff. **Description:** A temporary agency that also offers contract services. Company pays fee. **Specializes in the areas of:** Administration; Computer Science/Software; Engineering; Human Resources; Sales; Secretarial. **Positions commonly filled include:** Administrative Manager; Buyer; Chemical Engineer; Chemist; Civil Engineer; Clerical Supervisor; Computer Programmer; Customer Service Representative; Draftsperson; Electrical/Electronics Engineer; MIS Specialist; Software Engineer; Systems Analyst; Technical Writer/Editor; Typist/Word Processor. **Benefits available to temporary workers:** 401(k); Direct Deposit; Paid Holidays. **Corporate headquarters location:** This Location. **Other U.S. locations:** Ontario CA. **Average salary range of placements:** $30,000 - $50,000. **Number of placements per year:** 1000+.

TAC STAFFING SERVICES
39159 Paseo Padre Parkway, Suite 107, Fremont CA 94538. 510/797-6444. **Contact:** Manager. **Description:** A temporary agency. **Specializes in the areas of:** Administration. **Other U.S. locations:** Nationwide.

TAC STAFFING SERVICES
2001 Gateway Place, Suite 350, San Jose CA 95110. 408/437-0260. **Contact:** Manager. **Description:** A temporary agency. **Specializes in the areas of:** Administration.

TAC STAFFING SERVICES
1801 California Boulevard, Suite 225, Walnut Creek CA 94596. 510/935-9450. **Contact:** Manager. **Description:** A temporary agency. **Specializes in the areas of:** Administration; Clerical; Light Industrial; Office Support.

TAC STAFFING SERVICES
120 Montgomery Street, Suite 1390, San Francisco CA 94104. 415/391-9933. **Contact:** Manager. **Description:** A temporary agency. **Specializes in the areas of:** Administration; Clerical; Office Support; Secretarial. **Positions commonly filled include:** Administrative Assistant.

TECH/AID OF CALIFORNIA
6345 Balboa Boulevard, Building 4, Suite 186, Encino CA 91316. 818/995-2910. **Contact:** Manager. **Description:** A temporary employment agency. Company pays fee. **Specializes in the areas of:** Computer Hardware/Software; Design; Engineering; Manufacturing. **Positions commonly filled include:** Aerospace Engineer; Architect; Biological Scientist; Chemist; Civil Engineer; Commercial Artist; Draftsperson; Electrical/Electronics Engineer; Industrial Designer; Industrial Engineer; Mechanical Engineer; Physicist; Quality Control Supervisor; Technical Writer/Editor; Technician. **Number of placements per year:** 1000+.

TECH/AID OF CALIFORNIA
1291 East Hillsdale Boulevard, Suite 140, Foster City CA 94404. 650/574-7645. **Contact:** Office Manager. **Description:** A temporary employment agency. Company pays fee. **Specializes in the areas of:** Computer Hardware/Software; Design; Engineering; Manufacturing. **Positions commonly filled include:** Architect; Biological Scientist; Chemist; Civil Engineer; Commercial Artist; Designer; Draftsperson; Electrical/Electronics Engineer; Industrial Designer; Industrial Engineer; Light Industrial Worker; Mechanical Engineer; Technical Writer/Editor; Technician. **Number of placements per year:** 1000+.

TECH/AID OF CALIFORNIA
7700 Edgewater Drive, Suite 543, Oakland CA 94621. 510/577-6700. **Contact:** Office Manager. **Description:** A temporary employment agency. Company pays fee. **Specializes in the areas of:** Computer Hardware/Software; Design; Engineering; Manufacturing. **Positions commonly filled include:** Aerospace Engineer; Architect; Biological Scientist; Chemist; Civil Engineer; Commercial Artist; Designer; Draftsperson; Electrical/Electronics Engineer; Industrial Designer; Industrial Engineer; Light Industrial Worker; Mechanical Engineer; Physicist; Quality Control Supervisor; Technical Writer/Editor; Technician. **Number of placements per year:** 1000+.

TECHNICAL AID CORPORATION
17782 East 17th Street, Suite 103, Tustin CA 92780. 714/573-9111. **Fax:** 714/573-9565. **Contact:** Jerry Gallenson, Branch Manager. **E-mail address:** tustin@techaid.com. **World Wide Web address:** http://www.techaid.com. **Description:** A temporary agency that also offers contract services. **Specializes in the areas of:** Architecture/Construction; Art/Design; Biology; Engineering; Industrial; Manufacturing; Technical. **Positions commonly filled include:** Aerospace Engineer; Aircraft Mechanic/Engine Specialist; Architect; Biochemist; Biological Scientist; Biomedical Engineer; Buyer; Chemical Engineer; Chemist; Civil Engineer; Design Engineer; Designer; Draftsperson; Editor; Electrical/Electronics Engineer; Electrician; Environmental Engineer; Industrial Engineer; Mechanical Engineer; Multimedia Designer; Quality Control Supervisor; Structural Engineer; Technical Writer/Editor; Telecommunications Manager; Urban/Regional Planner. **Corporate headquarters location:** Boston MA. **Other U.S. locations:** Nationwide. **Average salary range of placements:** $30,000 - $50,000. **Number of placements per year:** 1000+.

TECHNICAL AID CORPORATION
1733 North First Street, San Jose CA 95112. 408/434-9800. **Fax:** 408/232-7660. **Contact:** Steve Lion, Branch Manager. **E-mail address:** sanjose@techaid.com. **Description:** A temporary agency. **Specializes in the areas of:** Engineering; Manufacturing; Technical. **Positions commonly filled include:** Aerospace Engineer; Architect; Biochemist; Buyer; Chemical Engineer; Chemist; Civil Engineer; Clinical Lab Technician; Design Engineer; Designer; Draftsperson; Editor; Electrical/Electronics Engineer; Environmental Engineer; Financial Analyst; Industrial Engineer; Industrial Production Manager; Mechanical Engineer; Quality Control Supervisor; Structural Engineer; Technical Writer/Editor; Telecommunications

Manager. **Benefits available to temporary workers:** 401(k); Medical Insurance; Paid Holidays. **Other U.S. locations:** Nationwide. **Average salary range of placements:** $30,000 - $50,000. **Number of placements per year:** 1000+.

TECHNICAL AID CORPORATION
One Civic Plaza Drive, Suite 335, Carson CA 90745. 310/952-9527. **Fax:** 310/952-0728. **Contact:** Liz Allen, Lead Recruiter. **World Wide Web address:** http://www.techaid.com. **Description:** A temporary agency for technical professionals. **Specializes in the areas of:** Art/Design; Engineering; Manufacturing; Technical. **Positions commonly filled include:** Aerospace Engineer; Buyer; Chemical Engineer; Civil Engineer; Design Engineer; Designer; Draftsperson; Electrical/Electronics Engineer; Environmental Engineer; Industrial Engineer; Mechanical Engineer; Nuclear Engineer; Purchasing Agent/Manager; Structural Engineer; Technical Writer/Editor. **Benefits available to temporary workers:** 401(k); Medical Insurance. **Corporate headquarters location:** Boston MA. **International locations:** Worldwide. **Average salary range of placements:** $30,000 - $50,000. **Number of placements per year:** 1000+.

TECHNISKILLS
P.O. Box 51843, Palo Alto CA 94303. 650/494-2261. **Fax:** 650/493-9161. **Contact:** Harold S. Meltzer, President. **Description:** A temporary agency focusing on the placement of engineering and technical personnel. **Specializes in the areas of:** Accounting/Auditing; Computer Science/Software; Engineering; Publishing; Technical. **Positions commonly filled include:** Accountant/Auditor; Aerospace Engineer; Buyer; Chemist; Computer Programmer; Design Engineer; Designer; Draftsperson; Editor; Electrical/Electronics Engineer; Environmental Engineer; Financial Analyst; Industrial Engineer; Internet Services Manager; Mechanical Engineer; Metallurgical Engineer; MIS Specialist; Multimedia Designer; Nuclear Engineer; Software Engineer; Structural Engineer; Systems Analyst; Technical Writer/Editor; Telecommunications Manager; Typist/Word Processor. **Average salary range of placements:** $30,000 - $50,000. **Number of placements per year:** 200 - 499.

TEMPS UNLIMITED, INC.
17411 Chatsworth Street, Granada Hills CA 91344. 818/363-2345. **Fax:** 818/363-3683. **Contact:** Monique Noehles, Manager. **Description:** A temporary employment agency. **Specializes in the areas of:** Industrial; Manufacturing; Personnel/Labor Relations; Secretarial. **Positions commonly filled include:** Cable TV Installer; Customer Service Representative; Receptionist; Typist/Word Processor. **Benefits available to temporary workers:** Paid Holidays. **Average salary range of placements:** $20,000 - $29,999. **Number of placements per year:** 500 - 999.

THOMAS STAFFING
3110 Camino Del Rio South, Suite 314, San Diego CA 92108. 619/285-8114. **Fax:** 619/285-9800. **Contact:** Christy Dok, Account Manager. **E-mail address:** partners@thomas-staffing.com. **World Wide Web address:** http://www.thomas-staffing.com. **Description:** A temporary agency that provides staffing services including temporary, temp-to-perm, and direct hire in administrative, sales, and accounting fields. Founded in 1969. Company pays fee. **Specializes in the areas of:** Retail; Sales; Secretarial. **Positions commonly filled include:** Accountant/Auditor; Administrative Assistant; Customer Service Representative; Management Trainee; Typist/Word Processor. **Benefits available to temporary workers:** 401(k); Medical Insurance; Paid Holidays. **Corporate headquarters location:** Irvine CA. **Average salary range of placements:** $20,000 - $50,000. **Number of placements per year:** 500 - 999.

THOR TEMPORARY SERVICES
4201 Wilshire Boulevard, Suite 410, Los Angeles CA 90010. 310/373-0922. **Contact:** Administration Manager. **Description:** A temporary agency. Company pays fee. **Specializes in the areas of:** Accounting/Auditing; Advertising; Architecture/Construction; Banking; Clerical; Computer Hardware/Software; Finance; Food Industry; Health/Medical; Insurance; Legal; Manufacturing; MIS/EDP; Publishing; Secretarial; Technical; Transportation. **Positions commonly filled include:** Accountant/Auditor; Administrative Assistant; Bookkeeper; Computer Programmer; Credit Manager; Customer Service Representative; Data Entry Clerk; EDP Specialist; Financial Analyst; Legal Secretary; Medical Secretary; Receptionist; Secretary; Stenographer; Systems Analyst; Technical Writer/Editor; Typist/Word Processor. **Number of placements per year:** 1000+.

TREND WESTERN TECHNICAL CORPORATION
4128 West Commonwealth Avenue, Fullerton CA 92833-2536. 714/525-0134. **Contact:** Office Manager. **Description:** A temporary agency. Company pays fee. **Specializes in the areas of:** Computer Hardware/Software; Engineering; Publishing. **Positions commonly filled include:** Aerospace Engineer; Agricultural Engineer; Biological Scientist; Biomedical Engineer; Buyer; Chemical Engineer; Chemist; Civil Engineer; Clerk; Commercial Artist; Computer Operator; Computer Programmer; Data Entry Clerk; Draftsperson; Electrical/Electronics Engineer; Industrial Engineer; Marketing Specialist; Mechanical Engineer; Receptionist; Sales Representative; Systems Analyst; Technical Writer/Editor; Technician; Typist/Word Processor. **Number of placements per year:** 500 - 999.

TRENDTEC INC.
1620 Zanker Road, San Jose CA 95112. 408/436-1200. **Fax:** 408/436-0626. **Contact:** Linda Capiau, Manager. **Description:** A temporary agency. Company pays fee. **Specializes in the areas of:** Computer Science/Software; Engineering; Industrial; Manufacturing. **Positions commonly filled include:** Accountant/Auditor; Architect; Buyer; Chemical Engineer; Civil Engineer; Computer Programmer; Customer Service Representative; Design Engineer; Designer; Draftsperson; Editor; Electrical/Electronics Engineer; Electrician; Environmental Engineer; Financial Analyst; Industrial Engineer; Internet Services Manager; Mechanical Engineer; MIS Specialist; Operations/Production Manager; Purchasing Agent/Manager; Software Engineer; Structural Engineer; Systems Analyst; Technical Writer/Editor; Typist/Word Processor. **Average salary range of placements:** $20,000 - $29,999. **Number of placements per year:** 1000+.

UNITED PERSONNEL SERVICE
1700 South El Camino Real, Suite 410, San Mateo CA 94402. 650/340-6999. **Contact:** Manager. **World Wide Web address:** http://www.directnet.com/united. **Description:** A temporary placement agency. Company pays fee. **Specializes in the areas of:** Administration; Legal; Personnel/Labor Relations; Secretarial. **Positions commonly filled include:** Administrative Manager; Blue-Collar Worker Supervisor; Claim Representative; Clerical Supervisor; Credit Manager; Customer Service Representative; Human Resources Specialist; Paralegal; Quality Control Supervisor; Technical Writer/Editor; Telecommunications Manager; Typist/Word Processor. **Corporate headquarters location:** Brea CA. **Other U.S. locations:** Nationwide. **Average salary range of placements:** $20,000 - $29,999. **Number of placements per year:** 1000+.

VOLT TEMPORARY SERVICES INC.
6140 Stoneridge Mall Road, Suite 145, Pleasanton CA 94588. 510/463-2800. **Fax:** 510/463-2807. **Recorded jobline:** 800/718-4404. **Contact:** Bridget Henry, Branch Manager. **Description:** A temporary agency that also provides permanent placement. Company pays fee. **Specializes in the areas of:** Accounting/Auditing; Computer Science/Software; Industrial; Manufacturing; Personnel/Labor Relations; Publishing; Secretarial. **Positions commonly filled include:** Administrative Assistant; Bookkeeper; Clerk; Customer Service Representative; Data Entry Clerk; Driver; Factory Worker; Legal Secretary; Light Industrial Worker; Medical Secretary; Receptionist; Secretary; Typist/Word Processor. **Corporate headquarters location:** Orange CA. **Other U.S. locations:** Nationwide. **Average salary range of placements:** $20,000 - $29,999. **Number of placements per year:** 1000+.

VOLT TEMPORARY SERVICES INC.
3031 Tisch Way, #600, San Jose CA 95128. 408/247-9777. **Toll-free phone:** 800/718-4404. **Fax:** 408/247-9778. **Contact:** Stephanie Caldwell, Branch Manager. **Description:** A temporary agency. Company pays fee. **Specializes in the areas of:** Accounting/Auditing; Banking; Computer Science/Software; Education; Engineering; Finance; Industrial; Insurance; Legal; Manufacturing; Personnel/Labor Relations; Retail; Sales; Secretarial. **Positions commonly filled include:** Accountant; Administrative Assistant; Customer Service Representative; Secretary; Typist/Word Processor. **Benefits available to temporary workers:** Dental Insurance; Medical Insurance; Referral Bonus Plan. **Corporate headquarters location:** Orange CA. **Other U.S. locations:** Nationwide. **Average salary range of placements:** $20,000 - $29,999.

WESLEY - MEDSTAFF
400 30th Street, Suite 202, Oakland CA 94609. 510/834-8065. **Fax:** 510/834-0760. **Contact:** Manager. **Description:** A temporary staffing agency focusing on the placement of nursing and medical assistants. **Specializes in the areas of:** Health/Medical. **Positions commonly filled include:** Dental Assistant/Dental Hygienist; EKG Technician; Emergency Medical Technician; Registered Nurse; Respiratory Therapist. **Benefits available to temporary workers:** Medical Insurance; Paid Vacation.

WESTERN STAFF SERVICES
1214 Apollo Way, Suite 404-1, Sunnyvale CA 94086. 408/245-4850. **Fax:** 408/245-4858. **Contact:** Patty Pratt, Manager. **Description:** A temporary agency. Company pays fee. **Specializes in the areas of:** Accounting/Auditing; Personnel/Labor Relations; Sales; Secretarial. **Positions commonly filled include:** Human Resources Specialist; Management Trainee; Services Sales Representative; Travel Agent; Typist/Word Processor. **Corporate headquarters location:** Walnut Creek CA. **Average salary range of placements:** $20,000 - $29,999. **Number of placements per year:** 500 - 999.

WESTERN STAFF SERVICES
22672 Lambert Street, Suite 601, Lake Forest CA 92630. 714/855-4011. **Fax:** 714/855-1652. **Contact:** Area Manager. **Description:** A temporary agency. Company pays fee. **Specializes in the areas of:** Accounting/Auditing; Administration; Computer Science/Software; Engineering; Finance; Industrial; Legal; Personnel/Labor Relations; Sales; Secretarial; Technical. **Positions commonly filled include:** Accountant/Auditor; Administrative Manager; Budget Analyst; Buyer; Chemist; Clerical Supervisor; Customer Service Representative; Draftsperson; Electrical/Electronics Engineer; Electrician; Human Resources Specialist; Industrial Production Manager; Insurance Agent/Broker; Management Analyst/Consultant; Management Trainee; MIS Specialist; Paralegal; Software Engineer; Technical Writer/Editor; Telecommunications Manager. **Benefits available to temporary workers:** Dental Insurance; Medical Insurance. **Corporate headquarters location:** Walnut Creek CA. **International locations:** Worldwide. **Number of placements per year:** 1000+.

WESTERN STAFF SERVICES
1213 State Street, Suite L, Santa Barbara CA 93101. 805/962-5229. **Fax:** 805/965-3567. **Contact:** Rebecca Ostrander, Branch Manager. **Description:** A temporary agency that also provides permanent placement. **Specializes in the areas of:** Accounting/Auditing; Administration; Advertising; Architecture/Construction; Computer Science/Software; Engineering; Finance; General Management; Industrial; Legal; Manufacturing; Personnel/Labor Relations; Publishing; Retail; Sales; Secretarial; Technical; Transportation. **Positions commonly filled include:** Accountant/Auditor; Administrative Manager; Advertising Clerk; Aerospace Engineer; Agricultural Engineer; Aircraft Mechanic/Engine Specialist; Architect; Attorney; Automotive Mechanic; Bank Officer/Manager; Blue-Collar Worker Supervisor; Branch Manager; Chemical Engineer; Claim Representative; Clerical Supervisor; Clinical Lab Technician; Computer Programmer; Cost Estimator; Credit Manager; Customer Service Representative; Design Engineer; Draftsperson; Editor; Electrical/Electronics Engineer; Electrician; Environmental Engineer; Financial Analyst; General Manager; Industrial Engineer; Industrial Production Manager; Internet Services Manager; Management Analyst/Consultant; Mechanical Engineer; Metallurgical Engineer; Multimedia Designer; Paralegal; Property and Real Estate Manager; Public Relations Specialist; Quality Control Supervisor; Reporter; Restaurant/Food Service Manager; Services Sales Representative; Software Engineer; Systems Analyst; Technical Writer/Editor; Telecommunications Manager; Travel Agent; Typist/ Word Processor. **Corporate headquarters location:** Walnut Creek CA. **Number of placements per year:** 200 - 499.

WESTERN STAFF SERVICES OF WALNUT CREEK
WESTERN MEDICAL SERVICES
P.O. Box 9280, Walnut Creek CA 94598. 510/930-5300. **Physical address:** 220 North Wiget Lane, Walnut Creek CA. **Contact:** Administrator. **Description:** A temporary agency. Western Medical Services (also at this location) provides health care personnel placements. **Specializes in the areas of:** Accounting/Auditing; Banking; Clerical; Computer Hardware/Software; Health/Medical; MIS/EDP; Sales; Secretarial; Technical. **Positions commonly filled include:** Accountant/Auditor; Actuary; Administrative Assistant; Aerospace Engineer; Agricultural Engineer; Architect; Attorney; Bank Teller; Biological Scientist; Biomedical Engineer; Bookkeeper; Civil Engineer; Claim Representative; Clerk; Clinical Lab Technician; Computer Programmer; Customer Service Representative; Data Entry Clerk; Dietician/Nutritionist; Electrical/Electronics Engineer; Electronics Technician; Emergency Medical Technician; Industrial Designer; Industrial Engineer; Light Industrial Worker; Marketing Specialist; Mechanical Engineer; Medical Records Technician; Medical Secretary; Nurse; Receptionist; Registered Nurse; Respiratory Therapist; Sales Representative; Secretary; Systems Analyst; Technical Writer/Editor; Underwriter/Assistant Underwriter. **Corporate headquarters location:** This Location. **Average salary range of placements:** $30,000 - $50,000. **Number of placements per year:** 1000+.

CONTRACT SERVICES FIRMS

ACCESS TECHNICAL STAFFING
100 Pine Street, Suite 1950, San Francisco CA 94111. 415/788-1200. **Toll-free phone:** 800/287-5977. **Fax:** 415/781-6226. **Contact:** Senior Technical Recruiter. **E-mail address:** alexisd@accstaff.com. **Description:** A contract services firm that places technical consultants with expertise in mainframe and personal computing platforms. The firm also places software engineers, programmers, technical writers, network specialists, and MIS project managers. **Specializes in the areas of:** Administration; Computer Science/Software. **Positions commonly filled include:** Computer Programmer; Internet Services Manager; Management Analyst/Consultant; MIS Specialist; Multimedia Designer; Systems Analyst. **Average salary range of placements:** More than $50,000. **Number of placements per year:** 100 - 199.

ARMSTRONG & ASSOCIATES
P.O. Box 2242, Palm Springs CA 92263. 619/325-0093. **Physical address:** 1199 North Indian Canyon Drive, Palm Springs CA. **Contact:** Recruiter. **Description:** A contract services firm that places medical professionals and office staff. Company pays fee. **Specializes in the areas of:** Health/Medical. **Positions commonly filled include:** Administrative Manager; EEG Technologist; EKG Technician; Health Services Manager; Licensed Practical Nurse; Medical Records Technician; Physical Therapist; Physician; Registered Nurse; Respiratory Therapist. **Number of placements per year:** 1 - 49.

ASSIST TECHNICAL SERVICE
1140 Pedro Street, Suite 2, San Jose CA 95126-3743. 408/287-5544. **Contact:** Larry Coble, Technical Recruiter. **Description:** A contract services firm. **Specializes in the areas of:** Biology; Engineering. **Positions commonly filled include:** Accountant/Auditor; Aerospace Engineer; Architect; Biochemist; Biological Scientist; Biomedical Engineer; Buyer; Chemist; Computer Programmer; Design Engineer; Designer; Draftsperson; Electrical/Electronics Engineer; Financial Analyst; Industrial Engineer; Purchasing Agent/Manager; Quality Control Supervisor; Software Engineer; Systems Analyst; Technical Writer/Editor. **Benefits available to temporary workers:** Paid Holidays. **Average salary range of placements:** $30,000 - $50,000. **Number of placements per year:** 100 - 199.

B&M ASSOCIATES
4180 Ruffis Road, Suite 255, San Diego CA 92123. 619/627-9675. **Contact:** Manager. **Description:** A contract services firm for technical personnel. **Specializes in the areas of:** Computer Science/Software; Engineering; Technical.

B&M ASSOCIATES
3130 South Harbor Boulevard, Suite 360, Santa Ana CA 92704. 714/556-9675. **Contact:** Manager. **Description:** A contract services firm for technical personnel. **Specializes in the areas of:** Computer Science/Software; Engineering; Technical.

BIOSOURCE TECHNICAL SERVICE
333 West El Camino Real, Suite 210, Sunnyvale CA 94087. 408/738-4300. **Fax:** 408/733-3305. **Contact:** Pam Albo, Manager of Business Development. **Description:** A contract services firm. **Specializes in the areas of:** Biology; Food Industry; Pharmaceutical; Technical. **Positions commonly filled include:** Biochemist; Biological Scientist; Biomedical Engineer; Chemical Engineer; Chemist; Clinical Lab Technician; Environmental Engineer; Food Scientist/Technologist; Quality Control Supervisor; Science Technologist; Veterinarian. **Corporate headquarters location:** This Location. **Average salary range of placements:** $30,000 - $50,000. **Number of placements per year:** 100 - 199.

CDS STAFFING SERVICES
604 Mission Street, Suite 450, San Francisco CA 94105. 415/975-3970. **Toll-free phone:** 800/411-4473. **Contact:** Manager. **Description:** A contract services firm. **Specializes in the areas of:** Transportation. **Positions commonly filled include:** Accountant/Auditor; Administrative Manager; Driver; Human Resources Specialist. **Corporate headquarters location:** This Location. **Other U.S. locations:** Seattle WA. **Average salary range of placements:** Less than $20,000. **Number of placements per year:** 100 - 199.

CAREER QUEST
1901 Avenue of the Stars, Suite 920, Los Angeles CA 90067-6001. 310/282-8505. **Fax:** 310/282-0514. **Contact:** Raymond F. Umali, Manager. **E-mail address:** info@careerquest.com. **World Wide Web address:** http://www.careerquest.com. **Description:** A contract services firm that also provides permanent and temporary placements. Company pays fee. **Specializes in the areas of:** Administration; Computer Science/Software; General Management; Industrial; Legal; Personnel/Labor Relations; Sales; Technical. **Positions commonly filled include:** Accountant/Auditor; Administrative Manager; Budget Analyst; Civil Engineer; Computer Programmer; Financial Analyst; Internet Services Manager; Management Analyst/Consultant; MIS Specialist; Software Engineer; Systems Analyst; Typist/Word Processor; Underwriter/Assistant Underwriter.

THE CARL GROUP
21710 Stevens Creek Boulevard, Suite 110, Cupertino CA 95014. 408/255-9171. **Fax:** 408/255-9170. **Contact:** Tim Carl, President. **E-mail address:** jobs@carlgrp.com. **World Wide Web address:** http://www.carlgrp.com. **Description:** A contract services firm that places professionals in engineering, documentation, and multimedia fields. Technical and online documentation are among the areas covered by the firm. Company pays fee. **Positions commonly filled include:** Computer Programmer; Multimedia Designer; Software Engineer; Systems Analyst; Technical Writer/Editor. **Benefits available to temporary workers:** 401(k). **Number of placements per year:** 50 - 99.

CENTENNIAL ASSOCIATES
1340 South DeAnza Boulevard, Suite 206, San Jose CA 95129. 408/973-0646. **Contact:** Manager. **Description:** A contract services firm. **Specializes in the areas of:** Technical.

COMFORCE TECHNICAL SERVICES, INC.
5355 Avenida Encinas, Suite 209, Carlsbad CA 92008. 760/438-8082. **Fax:** 760/931-5883. **Contact:** Manager. **Description:** A contract services firm. **Specializes in the areas of:** Accounting/Auditing; Administration; Manufacturing; Technical.

COMFORCE TECHNICAL SERVICES, INC.
4435 North First Street, Unit 134, Livermore CA 94550. 510/606-3795. **Fax:** 510/606-3799. **Contact:** Manager. **Description:** A contract services firm. **Specializes in the areas of:** Technical.

COMFORCE TECHNICAL SERVICES, INC.
5220 Pacific Concourse Drive, Suite 135, Los Angeles CA 90045. 310/643-2682. **Fax:** 310/643-8656. **Contact:** Manager. **Description:** A contract services firm that also offers some permanent placements. **Specializes in the areas of:** Technical.

COMFORCE TECHNICAL SERVICES, INC.
9449 Balboa Avenue, Suite 202, San Diego CA 92123. 619/565-4992. **Fax:** 619/292-8561. **Contact:** Manager. **Description:** A contract services firm that also offers some temp-to-hire placements. **Specializes in the areas of:** Clerical; Electronics; Light Industrial; Pharmaceutical; Technical.

EDP CONTRACT SERVICES
685 Market Street, Suite 470, San Francisco CA 94105. 650/952-5010. **Contact:** Office Manager. **World Wide Web address:** http://www.edpcs.com. **Description:** A contract services firm. Company pays fee. **Specializes in the areas of:** Accounting/Auditing; Banking; Computer Hardware/Software; Engineering; Finance; Insurance; Manufacturing; MIS/EDP; Nonprofit; Personnel/Labor Relations; Publishing; Technical. **Positions commonly filled include:** Computer Operator; Computer Programmer; EDP Specialist; MIS Specialist; Systems Analyst; Technical Writer/Editor. **Corporate headquarters location:** Newton MA. **Other U.S. locations:** Nationwide. **Number of placements per year:** 1000+.

EDP CONTRACT SERVICES
3180 Crow Canyon Place, Suite 100, San Ramon CA 94583. 510/866-1030. **Toll-free phone:** 888/547-6907. **Contact:** Chris Pankey, Branch Manager. **World Wide Web address:** http://www.edpcs.com. **Description:** A contract services firm. **Specializes in the areas of:** Computer Science/Software; Engineering; Scientific; Technical. **Positions commonly filled include:** Computer Animator; Database Manager; Design Engineer; Electrical/Electronics Engineer; Graphic Designer; Internet Services Manager; MIS Specialist; Online Content Specialist; Software Engineer; Systems Analyst; Technical Writer/Editor; Telecommunications Manager; Video Production Coordinator; Webmaster. **Benefits available to temporary workers:** 401(k); Dental Insurance; Direct Deposit; Medical Insurance. **Corporate headquarters location:** Newton MA. **Other U.S. locations:** Nationwide. **Average salary range of placements:** More than $50,000. **Number of placements per year:** 1000+.

GLOBAL RESOURCES
27520 Hawthorne Boulevard, Suite 150, Rolling Hills Es. CA 90274. 310/544-7145. **Contact:** Don Gertner, Manager. **Description:** A contract services and human resources outsourcing firm. Global Resources also offers management consulting services for a variety of industries.

HALL KINION
1900 McCarthy Boulevard, Suite 420, Milpitas CA 95035. 510/795-1400. **Fax:** 408/428-6484. **Contact:** Linda Fereria, Service Branch Manager. **World Wide Web address:** http://www.hallkinion.com. **Description:** A contract services firm. Founded in 1987. Company pays fee. **Specializes in the areas of:** Accounting/Auditing; Administration; Personnel/Labor Relations; Sales; Secretarial. **Positions commonly filled include:** Accountant/Auditor; Administrative Manager; Buyer; Clerical Supervisor; Computer Programmer; Customer Service Representative; Financial Analyst; Human Resources Specialist; MIS Specialist; Multimedia Designer; Systems Analyst; Typist/Word Processor. **Benefits available to temporary workers:** Dental Insurance; Medical Insurance; Paid Holidays. **Corporate headquarters location:** San Jose CA. **Other U.S. locations:** Nationwide. **Average salary range of placements:** $20,000 - $29,999. **Number of placements per year:** 500 - 999.

MEDICAL FINANCIAL SERVICES
1060 Willow Street, San Jose CA 95125-2350. 408/280-7309. **Fax:** 408/280-6965. **Contact:** Andrew Roberts, Chief Financial Officer. **Description:** A contract services firm focusing on medical accounting. **Specializes in the areas of:** Accounting/Auditing; Health/Medical. **Positions commonly filled include:** Accountant/Auditor; Claim Representative; Clerical Supervisor; Health Services Manager; Human Resources Specialist; Medical Records Technician. **Average salary range of placements:** $20,000 - $29,999. **Number of placements per year:** 200 - 499.

MINDSOURCE SOFTWARE ENGINEERS
2685 Marine Way, Suite 1305, Mountain View CA 94043-1115. 650/254-8909. **Fax:** 650/254-8907. **Contact:** Manager. **E-mail address:** info@mindsrc.com. **World Wide Web address:** http://www.mindsrc.com. **Description:** A contract services firm providing placement in UNIX system administration, Web engineering, and networking. MindSource Software Engineers provides temporary and permanent positions. Company pays fee. **Specializes in the areas of:** Computer Science/Software; Network Administration. **Positions commonly filled include:** Computer Programmer; Internet Services Manager; Software Engineer; Systems Analyst; Telecommunications Manager; Webmaster. **Benefits available to temporary workers:** 401(k); Dental Insurance; Medical Insurance. **Average salary range of placements:** More than $50,000. **Number of placements per year:** 200 - 499.

MORGEN DESIGN INC.
8305 Vickers Street, Suite 110, San Diego CA 92111. 619/279-6300. **Contact:** Manager. **Description:** A contract services firm. **Specializes in the areas of:** Engineering. **Positions commonly filled include:** Biomedical Engineer; Chemical Engineer; Civil Engineer; Clinical Lab Technician; Computer Programmer; Design Engineer; Draftsperson; Electrical/Electronics Engineer; Environmental Engineer; Health Services Manager; Industrial Engineer; Mechanical Engineer; Metallurgical Engineer; MIS Specialist; Registered Nurse; Respiratory Therapist; Software Engineer; Structural Engineer; Systems Analyst; Technical Writer/Editor; Typist/Word Processor. **Corporate headquarters location:** This Location. **Other U.S. locations:** Salt Lake City UT; Seattle WA. **Average salary range of placements:** $30,000 - $50,000. **Number of placements per year:** 50 - 99.

NET WORKERS, INC.
4966 El Camino Real, Suite 213, Los Altos CA 94022-1406. 650/254-2350. **Fax:** 650/254-2355. **Contact:** Senior Recruiter. **E-mail address:** resumes@networkersinc.com. **Description:** A contract services firm that also provides permanent placement. **Specializes in the areas of:** Computer Science/Software; Engineering; Legal; Technical. **Positions commonly filled include:** Attorney; Biological Scientist; Biomedical Engineer; Computer Programmer; Electrical/Electronics Engineer; Human Resources Specialist; Internet Services Manager; MIS Specialist; Multimedia Designer; Paralegal; Public Relations Specialist; Software Engineer; Systems Analyst; Technical Writer/Editor. **Benefits available to temporary workers:** Dental Insurance; Medical Insurance. **Corporate headquarters location:** Incline Village NV. **Average salary range of placements:** More than $50,000. **Number of placements per year:** 100 - 199.

BREN NORRIS ASSOCIATES INC.
150 Post Street, Suite 705, San Francisco CA 94108. 415/693-0355. **Toll-free phone:** 800/765-2736. **Fax:** 415/693-0455. **Contact:** Bren Norris, President. **E-mail address:** bren-bna@ix.netcom.com. **World Wide Web address:** http://www.bren-bna.com. **Description:** A contract services firm that also provides career

outplacement counseling services. Company pays fee. **Specializes in the areas of:** Administration; Computer Science/Software; Technical. **Positions commonly filled include:** Computer Animator; Computer Programmer; Consultant; Database Manager; Design Engineer; Designer; Electrical/Electronics Engineer; Internet Services Manager; Management Analyst/Consultant; Mechanical Engineer; MIS Specialist; Software Engineer; Systems Analyst; Systems Manager; Technical Writer/Editor; Telecommunications Manager; Webmaster. **Benefits available to temporary workers:** Medical Insurance. **Average salary range of placements:** More than $50,000. **Number of placements per year:** 50 - 99.

PC PERSONNEL
101 California Street, Suite 950, San Francisco CA 94111-5866. 415/956-0500. **Fax:** 415/956-1956. **Contact:** Raymond O. Lee, President. **E-mail address:** info@pcpersonnel.com. **World Wide Web address:** http://www.pcpersonnel.com. **Description:** A services firm that provides contract and permanent permanent placements in computer-related fields. The company's divisions include administrative and networking personnel. Company pays fee. **Specializes in the areas of:** Administration; Network Administration. **Positions commonly filled include:** Administrative Assistant; LAN/WAN Designer/Developer; MIS Specialist; Systems Analyst; Technical Support Representative; Typist/Word Processor. **Corporate headquarters location:** This Location. **Other area locations:** San Jose CA. **Average salary range of placements:** $30,000 - $50,000. **Number of placements per year:** 200 - 499.

PEOPLEWARE TECHNICAL RESOURCES, INC.
302 West Grand Avenue, Suite 4, El Segundo CA 90245. 310/640-2406. **Fax:** 310/640-2629. **Contact:** Sheryl Rooker, President. **E-mail address:** peoplew@ix.netcom.com. **World Wide Web address:** http://www.peopleware.com. **Description:** A contract services firm. PeopleWare primarily serves the software development industry. **Specializes in the areas of:** Computer Science/Software; Network Administration; Technical. **Positions commonly filled include:** Computer Programmer; Graphic Artist; Graphic Designer; Internet Services Manager; MIS Specialist; Multimedia Designer; Software Developer; Technical Writer/Editor. **Number of placements per year:** 100 - 199.

PROVISION TECHNOLOGIES
600 Corporate Point, Suite 110, Culver City CA 90230. 310/337-9327. **Fax:** 310/337-7904. **Contact:** Recruiter. **Description:** A contract services and consulting firm. **Specializes in the areas of:** Computer Science/Software; Information Technology.

PROVISION TECHNOLOGIES
22600-C Lambert Street, Suite 902, Lake Forest CA 92630. 714/458-9331. **Fax:** 714/458-0186. **Contact:** Manager. **E-mail address:** resumes@provision-oc.com. **World Wide Web address:** http://www.provision-oc.com. **Description:** A contract services and consulting firm. **Specializes in the areas of:** Computer Science/Software; Information Technology.

PROVISION TECHNOLOGIES
1737 North First Street, Suite 230, San Jose CA 95112. 408/467-3466. **Fax:** 408/467-3463. **Contact:** Manager. **World Wide Web address:** http://www.careerbase.com. **Description:** A contract services and consulting firm. **Specializes in the areas of:** Computer Science/Software; Information Technology.

PROVISION TECHNOLOGIES
3505 El Camino Real, Palo Alto CA 94306. 415/354-8445. **Fax:** 415/354-8456. **Contact:** Office Manager. **World Wide Web address:** http://www.careerbase.com. **Description:** A contract services and consulting firm. **Specializes in the areas of:** Computer Science/Software; Information Technology.

PROVISION TECHNOLOGIES
90 New Montgomery Street, Suite 1020, San Francisco CA 94105. 415/243-3310. **Fax:** 415/243-3317. **Contact:** Manager. **World Wide Web address:** http://www.careerbase.com. **Description:** A contract services and consulting firm. **Specializes in the areas of:** Computer Science/Software; Information Technology.

QUALITY IMAGING SERVICES
P.O. Box 7604, Northridge CA 91327. 818/609-7697. **Fax:** 818/609-7698. **Recorded jobline:** 818/349-7337. **Contact:** Joe Alas, President. **Description:** A contract services firm that provides contract, temporary, and permanent placements for nuclear medicine, ultrasound, and radiology technologist positions. The company also places medical and general clerical personnel. **Specializes in the areas of:** Health/Medical; Personnel/Labor Relations; Secretarial; Technical. **Positions commonly filled include:** Accountant/Auditor; Administrative Manager; Advertising Clerk; Clerical Supervisor; Computer Programmer; General Manager; Medical Records Technician; Nuclear Medicine Technologist; Radiological Technologist; Systems Analyst; Typist/Word Processor. **Average salary range of placements:** $30,000 - $50,000. **Number of placements per year:** 50 - 99.

SIERRA TECHNOLOGY
4141 Manzanita Avenue, Suite 200, Carmichael CA 95608. 916/488-4960. **Fax:** 916/488-7058. **Contact:** Greg Hill, Branch Manager. **E-mail address:** volt_stc@ix.netcom.com. **World Wide Web address:** http://www.volt_tech.com. **Description:** A contract services firm. Sierra Technology is a division of Volt Technical Services. Company pays fee. **Specializes in the areas of:** Computer Science/Software; Engineering; Industrial; Manufacturing; Technical. **Positions commonly filled include:** Aerospace Engineer; Biochemist; Biological Scientist; Biomedical Engineer; Buyer; Chemical Engineer; Chemist; Civil Engineer; Computer Programmer; Construction and Building Inspector; Cost Estimator; Design Engineer; Designer; Electrical/Electronics Engineer; Electrician; Environmental Engineer; Industrial Engineer; Mechanical Engineer; MIS Specialist; Science Technologist; Software Engineer; Structural Engineer; Technical Writer/Editor; Telecommunications Manager. **Benefits available to temporary workers:** 401(k); Dental Insurance; Medical Insurance; Paid Holidays. **Corporate headquarters location:** Orange CA. **Other U.S. locations:** Nationwide. **Average salary range of placements:** $30,000 - $50,000. **Number of placements per year:** 1000+.

SMARTSOURCE INCORPORATED
500 Ygnacio Valley Road, Suite 390, Walnut Creek CA 94596. 510/935-4200. **Fax:** 510/935-0645. **Contact:** Patty Taylor, Partner. **E-mail address:** smartsrce@aol.com. **World Wide Web address:** http://www.smartsourceinc.com. **Description:** A contract services firm. **Specializes in the areas of:** Information Systems; Network Administration; Technical; Telecommunications. **Corporate headquarters location:** This Location. **Other area locations:** Marina Del Rey CA; Sacramento CA. **Number of placements per year:** 200 - 499.

SMARTSOURCE INCORPORATED
2377 Goldmeadow Way, Citrus Heights CA 95670. 916/631-1999. **Fax:** 916/631-1994. **Contact:** Manager. **World Wide Web address:** http://www.

smartsourceinc.com. **Description:** A technical staffing contract services firm. The firm handles project and permanent placements with corporations and large companies in the Sacramento area. Founded in 1992. Company pays fee. **Specializes in the areas of:** Computer Science/Software; Network Administration; Systems Administration. **Positions commonly filled include:** MIS Specialist; Network Administrator; Software Engineer; Systems Analyst; Telecommunications Manager. **Benefits available to temporary workers:** Medical Insurance. **Corporate headquarters location:** Walnut Creek CA. **Other area locations:** Marina Del Rey CA. **Average salary range of placements:** $30,000 - $50,000. **Number of placements per year:** 50 - 99.

SOURCE SERVICES CORPORATION
15260 Ventura Boulevard, Suite 380, Sherman Oaks CA 91403-5307. 818/905-7300. **Fax:** 818/905-8260. **Contact:** Recruiter. **E-mail address:** sors@primenet.com. **Description:** A contract services firm. Company pays fee. **Specializes in the areas of:** Accounting/Auditing; Computer Science/Software; Finance. **Positions commonly filled include:** Accountant/Auditor; Computer Programmer; Credit Manager; Financial Analyst; Internet Services Manager; Licensed Practical Nurse; Registered Nurse; Systems Analyst. **Benefits available to temporary workers:** Medical Insurance. **Corporate headquarters location:** Dallas TX. **Other U.S. locations:** Nationwide. **Average salary range of placements:** More than $50,000. **Number of placements per year:** 100 - 199.

SYNERGY PERSONNEL SERVICES, INC.
66 Bovet Road, San Mateo CA 94402. 650/341-7777. **Fax:** 650/341-7778. **Contact:** Recruiter. **Description:** A contract services firm that also provides temporary and permanent placements in administrative, office automation, and computer technical areas. **Specializes in the areas of:** Administration. **Positions commonly filled include:** Clerical Supervisor; Computer Programmer; MIS Specialist; Systems Analyst; Technical Writer/Editor; Typist/Word Processor. **Average salary range of placements:** $30,000 - $50,000. **Number of placements per year:** 1 - 49.

TAD TECHNICAL SERVICES
3350 Scott Boulevard, Building 2, Santa Clara CA 95054. 408/727-4052. **Fax:** 408/727-4408. **Contact:** Manager. **E-mail address:** jfranks@aol.com. **Description:** A contract services firm. **Specializes in the areas of:** Computer Science/Software; Engineering; Manufacturing; Technical. **Positions commonly filled include:** Accountant/Auditor; Buyer; Computer Programmer; Customer Service Representative; Design Engineer; Designer; Draftsperson; Editor; Electrical/Electronics Engineer; Financial Analyst; Mechanical Engineer; MIS Specialist; Purchasing Agent/Manager; Quality Control Supervisor; Software Engineer; Systems Analyst; Technical Writer/Editor. **Corporate headquarters location:** Cambridge MA. **Other U.S. locations:** Nationwide. **Average salary range of placements:** $30,000 - $50,000. **Number of placements per year:** 100 - 199.

TECHNOLOGY LOCATOR
6480 Weathers Place, Suite 200, San Diego CA 92121-3912. **Toll-free phone:** 800/275-4852. **Fax:** 619/552-6820. **Contact:** Manager. **E-mail address:** jimc@tlcsd.com. **World Wide Web address:** http://www.tlcsd.com. **Description:** A contract services firm focusing on consulting assignments in areas such as engineering, software development, information technology, and network administration. Founded in 1983. **Specializes in the areas of:** Computer Science/Software; Engineering. **Positions commonly filled include:** Computer Programmer; Design Engineer; Electrical/Electronics Engineer; Internet Services Manager; Mechanical Engineer; MIS Specialist; Software Engineer; Systems Analyst. **Benefits available to temporary workers:** 401(k); Cafeteria; Medical Insurance. **Corporate headquarters location:** This Location. **Other area locations:** Mountain View CA. **Average salary range of placements:** More than $50,000. **Number of placements per year:** 200 - 499.

TECHSOURCE
4010 Moorpark Avenue, Suite 209, San Jose CA 95117. 408/345-3077. **Contact:** Manager. **World Wide Web address:** http://www.gonelson.com. **Description:** A contract services firm. **Specializes in the areas of:** Engineering; Information Technology; Technical. **Corporate headquarters location:** Sonoma CA.

TECHSOURCE
11070 White Rock Road, Suite 195, Rancho Cordova CA 95670. 916/853-0402. **Contact:** Manager. **Description:** A contract services firm. **Specializes in the areas of:** Engineering; Information Technology; Technical. **Corporate headquarters location:** Sonoma CA.

VOLT TECHNICAL SERVICES
500 South Douglas Street, El Segundo CA 90245. 310/640-1170. **Fax:** 310/640-1563. **Contact:** Manager. **E-mail address:** voltels@ix.netcom.com. **Description:** A contract services firm. **Specializes in the areas of:** Computer Science/Software; Engineering; Technical. **Positions commonly filled include:** Aerospace Engineer; Architect; Buyer; Chemical Engineer; Computer Programmer; Cost Estimator; Design Engineer; Designer; Draftsperson; Editor; Electrical/Electronics Engineer; Industrial Engineer; Mechanical Engineer; MIS Specialist; Purchasing Agent/Manager; Software Engineer; Structural Engineer; Systems Analyst; Technical Writer/Editor. **Benefits available to temporary workers:** 401(k); Medical Insurance. **Corporate headquarters location:** Orange CA. **Other U.S. locations:** Nationwide. **Average salary range of placements:** $30,000 - $50,000. **Number of placements per year:** 500 - 999.

VOLT TECHNICAL SERVICES
4340 Stevens Creek Boulevard, Suite 180, San Jose CA 95129. 408/556-0555. **Fax:** 408/556-0556. **Contact:** Manager. **E-mail address:** volttech@ix.netcom.com. **Description:** A contract services firm. **Specializes in the areas of:** Computer Science/Software; Engineering; Technical. **Positions commonly filled include:** Buyer; Computer Operator; Computer Programmer; Database Manager; Design Engineer; Draftsperson; Electrical/Electronics Engineer; Electrician; Financial Analyst; Industrial Engineer; Industrial Production Manager; Internet Services Manager; Manufacturing Engineer; Mechanical Engineer; MIS Specialist; Multimedia Designer; Purchasing Agent/Manager; Science Technologist; Software Engineer; Structural Engineer; Technical Writer/Editor; Webmaster. **Benefits available to temporary workers:** 401(k); Direct Deposit; Medical Insurance. **Corporate headquarters location:** Orange CA. **Average salary range of placements:** More than $50,000. **Number of placements per year:** 200 - 499.

H.L. YOH COMPANY
9710 Scranton Street, San Diego CA 92121. 619/622-9005. **Contact:** Manager. **Description:** A contract services firm. **Specializes in the areas of:** Biotechnology.

CAREER/OUTPLACEMENT COUNSELING FIRMS

BROADCAST SKILLS BANK
900 Front Street, San Francisco CA 94111. 415/421-6161. **Fax:** 415/421-6319. **Contact:** Sheryl Mumford, Executive Director. **Description:** A nonprofit career and outplacement counseling service. Company pays fee. **Specializes in the areas of:** Advertising; Broadcasting; Public Relations. **Positions commonly filled include:** Internet Services Manager; Multimedia Designer; Public Relations Manager; Radio/TV Announcer/Broadcaster; Telecommunications Manager. **Corporate headquarters location:** This Location. **Number of placements per year:** 50 - 99.

EFFORTLESS RESUMES
151 Deepstone Drive, San Rafael CA 94903. 415/460-0549. **Contact:** Karen Baird, CPRW. **Description:** A professional resume writing service.

HUMAN RESOURCE MARKETING SERVICES
1717 Rising Glen Road, Los Angeles CA 90069. 310/855-1064. **Contact:** Richard Katz, President. **Description:** A career/outplacement counseling service. **Specializes in the areas of:** Personnel/Labor Relations. **Positions commonly filled include:** Radio/TV Announcer; Video Production Coordinator. **Average salary range of placements:** $30,000 - $50,000. **Number of placements per year:** 50 - 99.

LA WORKS
5200 Irwindale Avenue, Irwindale CA 91706. 626/960-3964. **Fax:** 626/813-2035. **Contact:** Lori Verwiel, Public Relations. **World Wide Web address:** http://www.laworks.org. **Description:** A federally funded, nonprofit government agency offering resume preparation assistance, mock interviews, transition workshops, and outplacement in a variety of fields. **Positions commonly filled include:** Advertising Clerk; Bank Officer/Manager; Blue-Collar Worker Supervisor; Claim Representative; Clerical Supervisor; Customer Service Representative; Draftsperson; Human Service Worker; Preschool Worker. **Number of placements per year:** 100 - 199.

STANLEY, BARBER & ASSOCIATES
10050 North Wolfe Road, Cupertino CA 95014. 408/725-1440. **Fax:** 408/725-1461. **Contact:** Nancy Bergman, Vice President. **E-mail address:** info@stanleyb.com. **World Wide Web address:** http://www.stanleyb.com. **Description:** A career/outplacement counseling firm. **Positions commonly filled include:** Account Manager; Accountant; Administrative Manager; Branch Manager; Civil Engineer; Computer Programmer; Customer Service Representative; Database Manager; General Manager; Industrial Engineer; Internet Services Manager; Management Analyst/Consultant; Manufacturing Engineer; Marketing Manager; Mechanical Engineer; MIS Specialist; Project Manager; Sales Representative; Systems Analyst; Technical Writer/Editor; Webmaster. **Average salary range of placements:** More than $50,000.

COLORADO

EXECUTIVE SEARCH FIRMS

ACCOUNTANTS CHOICE PERSONNEL
5600 Greenwood Plaza Boulevard, Suite 208, Englewood CO 80111. 303/741-6494. **Fax:** 303/741-6499. **Contact:** Ginny Matthes, President/Owner. **Description:** An executive search firm operating on both retained and contingency bases. The firm also provides some temporary placements. Company pays fee. **Specializes in the areas of:** Accounting/Auditing; Administration; Banking; Finance. **Positions commonly filled include:** Accountant/Auditor; Bank Officer/Manager; Budget Analyst; Cost Estimator; Credit Manager; Financial Analyst; Management Analyst/Consultant. **Number of placements per year:** 200 - 499.

ACCOUNTANTS EXECUTIVE SEARCH
1200 17th Street, Suite 2160, Denver CO 80202. 303/571-1116. **Fax:** 303/571-1102. **Contact:** Manager. **Description:** An executive search firm. **Specializes in the areas of:** Accounting/Auditing; Finance.

ALEXANDER GROUP
4575 Hilton Parkway, Suite 102, Colorado Springs CO 80907. 719/528-5700. **Contact:** Manager. **Description:** An executive search firm. **Specializes in the areas of:** Information Technology.

ALPHA GROUP
311 1/2 8th Street, Suite 600, Glenwood Springs CO 81601. 970/945-2336. **Contact:** J. Astrach, President. **Description:** An executive search firm focusing on placement in the area of advanced composite materials. **Specializes in the areas of:** Materials.

AMERICAN MEDICAL RECRUITERS
325 Kremia, Denver CO 80220. 303/393-0791. **Contact:** Manager. **Description:** An executive search firm. **Specializes in the areas of:** Administration; Health/Medical.

THE ARDENT GROUP
3131 South Vaughn Way, Suite 524, Aurora CO 80014. 303/745-6355. **Contact:** Manager. **Description:** An executive search firm. **Specializes in the areas of:** Computer Hardware/Software.

WILLIAM B. ARNOLD ASSOCIATES
Cherry Creek Plaza, 600 South Cherry Street, Suite 1105, Denver CO 80222. 303/393-6662. **Contact:** Manager. **Description:** An executive search firm operating on a retainer basis.

BADER AND COMPANY
1200 17th Street, Suite 1000, Denver CO 80202. 303/572-6028. **Contact:** Geri Bader, Owner. **Description:** An executive recruiting firm. Company pays fee. **Positions commonly filled include:** Attorney; Human Resources Manager. **Average salary range of placements:** More than $50,000. **Number of placements per year:** 1 - 49.

THE BRIDGE
P.O. Box 740297, Arvada CO 80006-0297. 303/422-1900. **Fax:** 303/422-0016. **Contact:** Alex B. Wilcox, Principal. **Description:** A diversified executive search and management consulting firm offering professional search/consulting services. Company pays fee. **Specializes in the areas of:** Accounting/Auditing; Administration; Chemical; Computer Science/Software; Engineering; Environmental; Manufacturing; Personnel/Labor Relations; Sales. **Positions commonly filled include:** Accountant/Auditor; Biological Scientist; Chemist; Computer Programmer; Engineer; Forester/Conservation Scientist; Purchasing Agent/Manager; Quality Control Supervisor; Technical Writer/Editor. **Corporate headquarters location:** This Location. **Average salary range of placements:** More than $50,000. **Number of placements per year:** 1 - 49.

THE BUXTON GROUP LIMITED
707 17th Street, Suite 2800, Denver CO 80202. 303/449-0021. **Contact:** Gary Buxton, CPC. **Description:** An executive search firm. Company pays fee. **Specializes in the areas of:** Banking; Finance. **Number of placements per year:** 100 - 199.

CAREER FORUM, INC.
4350 Wadsworth Boulevard, Suite 300, Wheat Ridge CO 80033. 303/425-8721. **Fax:** 303/425-0535. **Contact:** Stan Grebe, President. **E-mail address:** careerfm@aol.com. **World Wide Web address:** http://www.careerforum.com. **Description:** An executive search firm, operating on both retainer and contingency bases, serving the Rocky Mountain Region. Founded in 1969. Company pays fee. **Specializes in the areas of:** Accounting/Auditing; Administration; Advertising; Architecture/Construction; Computer Science/Software; Engineering; General Management; Industrial; Publishing; Sales; Technical. **Positions commonly filled include:** Account Representative; Administrative Manager; Branch Manager; Buyer; Chemical Engineer; Civil Engineer; Computer Operator; Computer Programmer; Construction Contractor; Electrical/Electronics Engineer; Industrial Engineer; Internet Services Manager; Manufacturing Engineer; Marketing Manager; Mechanical Engineer; MIS Specialist; Operations Manager; Quality Control Supervisor; Sales Engineer; Sales Representative; Software Engineer; Systems Analyst; Telecommunications Manager. **Corporate headquarters location:** This Location. **Other U.S. locations:** Nationwide. **Average salary range of placements:** $30,000 - $50,000. **Number of placements per year:** 200 - 499.

CAREER MARKETING ASSOCIATES
7100 East Belleview Avenue, Suite 102, Greenwood Village CO 80111. 303/779-8890. **Fax:** 303/779-8139. **Contact:** Jan Sather, President. **E-mail address:** cma@cmagroup.com. **World Wide Web address:** http://www.cmagroup.com. **Description:** An executive search firm operating on both retainer and contingency bases. Company pays fee. **Specializes in the areas of:** Computer Science/Software; Engineering; Technical. **Positions commonly filled include:** Biomedical Engineer; Computer Programmer; Database Manager; Electrical/Electronics Engineer; Internet Services Manager; Manufacturing Engineer; Mechanical Engineer; MIS Specialist; Multimedia Designer; Production Manager; Risk Manager; Sales Engineer; Software Engineer; Systems Analyst; Toxicologist. **Benefits available to temporary workers:** Incentive Plan; Medical Insurance; Paid Vacation. **Corporate headquarters location:** This Location. **Average salary range of placements:** More than $50,000. **Number of placements per year:** 100 - 199.

CARLSEN RESOURCES, INC.
800 Belford Avenue, Suite 200, Grand Junction CO 81501. 970/242-9462. **Contact:** Manager. **Description:** An executive search firm. **Specializes in the areas of:** Telecommunications.

CARLSON, BENTLEY ASSOCIATES
3889 Promontory Court, Boulder CO 80304. 303/443-6500. **Contact:** Donald E. Miller, President.

Description: An executive search firm. Company pays fee. **Specializes in the areas of:** Computer Science/Software. **Positions commonly filled include:** Computer Programmer; Systems Analyst. **Number of placements per year:** 1 - 49.

CASEY SERVICES, INC. (CSI)
5300 DTC Parkway, Suite 370, Englewood CO 80111. 303/721-9211. **Fax:** 303/721-9508. **Contact:** Kerrie Hall, Placement Manager. **E-mail address:** csijob@compuserv.com. **Description:** An executive search firm operating on a contingency basis. The firm also provides temporary placements. Casey Services focuses on placing accounting, finance, and information systems personnel. Company pays fee. **Specializes in the areas of:** Accounting/Auditing; Administration; Banking; Computer Science/Software; Finance; General Management; Health/Medical; Sales; Secretarial. **Positions commonly filled include:** Accountant/Auditor; Bank Officer/Manager; Budget Analyst; Computer Programmer; Cost Estimator; Credit Manager; Customer Service Representative; MIS Specialist; Quality Control Supervisor; Software Engineer; Systems Analyst; Telecommunications Manager. **Benefits available to temporary workers:** Dental Insurance; Medical Insurance. **Corporate headquarters location:** Denver CO. **Other U.S. locations:** Chicago IL. **Number of placements per year:** 200 - 499.

CLOCKWISE PARTNERS
P.O. Box 327, Boulder CO 80306. 303/444-3678. **Contact:** Manager. **Description:** An executive search firm. **Specializes in the areas of:** Engineering. **Positions commonly filled include:** Construction Engineer; Hardware Engineer; Sales Engineer; Software Engineer.

COAST TO COAST EXECUTIVE SEARCH
9769 West 119th Drive, Suite 14, Broomfield CO 80021. 303/464-1704. **Fax:** 303/464-1553. **Contact:** Dennis Updyke, Principal. **E-mail address:** exsrch1@aol.com. **Description:** An executive search firm, operating on both retainer and contingency bases, that specializes in the hotel, restaurant, and club industries on a nationwide basis. Company pays fee. **Specializes in the areas of:** Hotel/Restaurant. **Positions commonly filled include:** Hotel Manager; Restaurant/Food Service Manager. **Corporate headquarters location:** This Location. **Average salary range of placements:** More than $50,000. **Number of placements per year:** 1 - 49.

DANIELS & PATTERSON CORPORATE SEARCH, INC.
1732 Marion Street, Denver CO 80218. 303/830-1230. **Fax:** 303/832-6162. **Contact:** Ruby Chavez Patterson, President. **Description:** An executive search firm providing permanent and contract placements. Company pays fee. **Specializes in the areas of:** Computer Hardware/Software; Computer Science/Software; Information Systems; Telecommunications. **Positions commonly filled include:** Administrative Assistant; Computer Programmer; Data Analyst; Data Entry Clerk; MIS Specialist; Software Engineer; Systems Analyst. **Corporate headquarters location:** This Location. **Average salary range of placements:** $30,000 - $50,000. **Number of placements per year:** 1 - 49.

DUNHILL PERSONNEL OF BOULDER
P.O. Box 488, Niwot CO 80544. 303/652-8370. **Fax:** 303/652-8369. **Contact:** Francis Boruff, Owner. **Description:** An executive search firm. **Specializes in the areas of:** Engineering; Food Industry; General Management; Personnel/Labor Relations; Technical.

DUNHILL PERSONNEL OF DENVER (SOUTH)
6909 South Holly Circle, Suite 305, Englewood CO 80112. 303/721-0525. **Fax:** 303/721-0747. **Contact:** Sandra Funt, Vice President. **E-mail address:** dunhillden@aol.com. **Description:** An executive search firm specializing in all areas of health care including clinical, nursing, administration, and allied health, as well as in data processing and information systems. Company pays fee. **Specializes in the areas of:** Computer Science/Software; Health/Medical. **Positions commonly filled include:** Clinical Lab Technician; Computer Programmer; Dietician/Nutritionist; Health Services Manager; MIS Specialist; Occupational Therapist; Pharmacist; Physical Therapist; Physician; Psychologist; Radiological Technologist; Registered Nurse; Respiratory Therapist; Speech-Language Pathologist; Systems Analyst. **Average salary range of placements:** $30,000 - $50,000. **Number of placements per year:** 1 - 49.

DUNHILL PERSONNEL OF FORT COLLINS, INC.
2120 South College Avenue, Suite 3, Fort Collins CO 80525. 970/221-5630. **Fax:** 970/221-5692. **Contact:** Jerold Lyons, President. **E-mail address:** dfc@frii.com. **Description:** An executive search firm that concentrates on agricultural seeds and feeds, microelectronics, wire and cable, and banking. Company pays fee. **Specializes in the areas of:** Banking; Electrical; Engineering; Health/Medical; Sales; Wire and Cable. **Positions commonly filled include:** Bank Officer/Manager; Electrical/Electronics Engineer; Mechanical Engineer; Nurse. **Average salary range of placements:** More than $50,000. **Number of placements per year:** 1 - 49.

EDP RECRUITING SERVICES
10 Inverness Drive East, Suite 240, Englewood CO 80112. 303/694-2222. **Contact:** Manager. **Description:** An executive search firm. **Specializes in the areas of:** Computer Hardware/Software.

EFL ASSOCIATES
7120 East Orchard Road, Suite 240, Englewood CO 80111. 303/779-1724. **Contact:** Manager. **Description:** An executive search firm operating on a retainer basis.

EXECUTIVE CAREER CONSULTANTS
1240 South Parker Road, Suite 203, Denver CO 80224-0145. 303/337-9344. **Fax:** 303/337-0693. **Contact:** Manager. **Description:** An executive search firm offering placement in managerial, technical, sales and marketing, and various administrative and light industrial positions.

EXECUTIVE PERSONNEL
4155 East Jewell Avenue, Denver CO 80222-4504. 303/758-4602. **Fax:** 303/782-4982. **Contact:** Susan MacKey, President. **Description:** An executive search firm. Company pays fee. **Specializes in the areas of:** Sales. **Positions commonly filled include:** Account Manager; Account Representative; Management Trainee; Sales Manager; Sales Representative. **Average salary range of placements:** $30,000 - $50,000. **Number of placements per year:** 1 - 49.

EXECUTIVE SALES SEARCH
6901 South Pierce Street, Suite 100K, Littleton CO 80123. 303/979-4531. **Contact:** Manager. **Description:** An executive search firm that places sales professionals.

EXECUTIVE SEARCH PLACEMENTS
P.O. Box 17403, Boulder CO 80308. 303/776-0094. **Contact:** Manager. **Description:** An executive search firm. **Specializes in the areas of:** Banking.

EXECUTIVES BY STERLING, INC.
1880 South Pierce Street, Suite 16E, Lakewood CO 80232. 303/934-7343. **Fax:** 303/934-8411. **Contact:** Donna Barnhill Brown, Principal. **Description:** An executive search firm focusing on placements in hotels, restaurants, country clubs, and casinos. Founded in 1986. Company pays fee. **Specializes in the areas of:** Food Industry; General Management; Hotel/Restaurant; Sales. **Positions commonly filled include:** Accountant/Auditor; Administrative Manager; Budget Analyst; Customer Service Representative; General Manager; Public Relations Specialist; Restaurant/Food Service Manager; Services Sales Representative. **Corporate headquarters location:** This Location. **International locations:** Worldwide. **Average salary range of placements:** More than $50,000. **Number of placements per year:** 50 - 99.

F-O-R-T-U-N-E PERSONNEL CONSULTANTS
4430 Arapahoe, Suite 165, Boulder CO 80303. 303/541-9840. **Fax:** 303/541-9841. **Contact:** Manager. **Description:** An executive search firm. **Specializes in the areas of:** Computer Science/Software; High-Tech. **Corporate headquarters location:** New York NY. **Other U.S. locations:** Nationwide.

F-O-R-T-U-N-E PERSONNEL CONSULTANTS
6165 Lehman Drive, Suite 202, Colorado Springs CO 80918. 719/599-7353. **Contact:** Manager. **Description:** An executive search firm. **Specializes in the areas of:** Computer Science/Software; Engineering; Manufacturing; Sales. **Corporate headquarters location:** New York NY. **Other U.S. locations:** Nationwide.

F-O-R-T-U-N-E PERSONNEL CONSULTANTS OF DENVER, INC.
7800 South Elati Street, Suite 319, Littleton CO 80120. 303/795-9210. **Fax:** 303/795-9215. **Contact:** Jan L. Dorfman, PE, President. **E-mail address:** fpcdenvr@ix.netcom.com. **Description:** An executive search firm. Company pays fee. **Specializes in the areas of:** Biotechnology; Computer Science/Software; Engineering; Health/Medical; Manufacturing; Medical Technology; Pharmaceutical. **Positions commonly filled include:** Biochemist; Biological Scientist; Biomedical Engineer; Chemical Engineer; Clinical Lab Technician; Computer Programmer; Design Engineer; Designer; Electrical/Electronics Engineer; General Manager; Industrial Engineer; Industrial Production Manager; Materials Engineer; Mathematician; Mechanical Engineer; Metallurgical Engineer; MIS Specialist; Operations/Production Manager; Pharmacist; Quality Control Supervisor; Regulatory Affairs Director; Software Engineer. **Corporate headquarters location:** New York NY. **Other U.S. locations:** Nationwide. **Average salary range of placements:** More than $50,000. **Number of placements per year:** 50 - 99.

GEOSEARCH, INC.
5585 Erindale Drive, Suite 104, Colorado Springs CO 80918-6966. 719/260-7087. **Fax:** 719/260-7389. **Contact:** Richard Serby, President. **E-mail address:** map@usa.net. **World Wide Web address:** http://www.geosearch.com. **Description:** A retainer and contingency executive search firm. **Specializes in the areas of:** Computer Science/Software; Engineering; Technical. **Positions commonly filled include:** Civil Engineer; Computer Programmer; Environmental Engineer; Forester/Conservation Scientist; Geographer; Landscape Architect; Market Research Analyst; Software Engineer; Surveyor; Systems Analyst; Technical Writer/Editor; Urban/Regional Planner. **Average salary range of placements:** $30,000 - $50,000. **Number of placements per year:** 200 - 499.

GIMBLE & NICOL EXECUTIVE SEARCH
1675 Broadway, Suite 1800, Denver CO 80202. 303/892-6400. **Contact:** Manager. **Description:** An executive search firm. **Specializes in the areas of:** Engineering; Legal.

ROBERT HALF INTERNATIONAL
ACCOUNTEMPS
1225 17th Street, Suite 1450, Denver CO 80202. 303/296-1010. **Contact:** Manager. **World Wide Web address:** http://www.roberthalf.com. **Description:** An executive search firm. Accountemps (also at this location) provides temporary placements. **Specializes in the areas of:** Accounting/Auditing. **Corporate headquarters location:** Menlo Park CA. **Other U.S. locations:** Nationwide.

HALLMARK PERSONNEL SYSTEMS, INC.
6825 East Tennessee Avenue, Suite 637, Denver CO 80224. 303/388-6190. **Fax:** 303/355-3760. **Contact:** Joe Sweeney, CPC, General Manager. **Description:** An executive search firm. Company pays fee. **Specializes in the areas of:** Computer Science/Software; Engineering; Food Industry; Personnel/Labor Relations; Technical. **Positions commonly filled include:** Applications Engineer; Biochemist; Biological Scientist; Biomedical Engineer; Chemical Engineer; Computer Programmer; Database Manager; Design Engineer; Electrical/Electronics Engineer; Food Scientist/Technologist; Industrial Engineer; Industrial Production Manager; Mechanical Engineer; MIS Specialist; Operations Manager; Production Manager; Quality Control Supervisor; Software Engineer; Structural Engineer; Systems Analyst; Telecommunications Manager. **Average salary range of placements:** More than $50,000. **Number of placements per year:** 1 - 49.

HEALTH INDUSTRY CONSULTANTS, INC.
MEDQUEST ASSOCIATES
9250 East Costilla Avenue, Suite 600, Englewood CO 80112. 303/790-2009. **Contact:** Jon K. Fitzgerald, President. **Description:** An executive search firm. MedQuest Associates (also at this location) provides medical sales placements. Company pays fee. **Specializes in the areas of:** Medical Sales and Marketing. **Average salary range of placements:** More than $50,000.

HEALTH TECHNOLOGY, INC.
7502 South Willow Circle, Englewood CO 80112. 303/322-6226. **Fax:** 303/721-8173. **Contact:** Karlan Emery, Director/Search Services. **Description:** An executive search firm specializing in marketing and technology-driven positions related to the medical device, biotechnology, and pharmaceutical business sectors. Company pays fee. **Specializes in the areas of:** Biology; Biotechnology; Computer Science/Software; Engineering; Health/Medical; Manufacturing; Medical Technology; Sales; Technical. **Positions commonly filled include:** Biological Scientist; Biomedical Engineer; Ceramics Engineer; Chemist; Design Engineer; Electrical/Electronics Engineer; Materials Engineer; Mechanical Engineer; Metallurgical Engineer; Nuclear Medicine Technologist; Operations/Production Manager; Quality Control Supervisor; Software Engineer. **Average salary range of placements:** More than $50,000. **Number of placements per year:** 1 - 49.

HEALTHCARE RECRUITERS OF THE ROCKIES, INC.
6860 South Yosemite Court, Suite 200, Englewood CO 80112. 303/779-8570. **Fax:** 303/779-7974. **Contact:** Richard Moore, President. **Description:** An executive search firm that places professionals in sales, marketing, field service, management, and engineering positions in the medical device and health care information systems industries. Company pays

fee. **Specializes in the areas of:** Computer Science/Software; Health/Medical; Sales; Technical. **Positions commonly filled include:** Biomedical Engineer; Clinical Lab Technician; Design Engineer; Dietician/Nutritionist; Health Services Manager; Industrial Engineer; Mechanical Engineer; MIS Specialist; Occupational Therapist; Pharmacist; Physical Therapist; Physician; Registered Nurse; Sales Executive; Sales Manager; Sales Representative; Services Sales Representative; Software Engineer; Systems Analyst. **Corporate headquarters location:** Dallas TX. **Average salary range of placements:** More than $50,000. **Number of placements per year:** 50 - 99.

HUMAN RESOURCES SOLUTIONS
1900 Wazee, Suite 260, Denver CO 80202. 303/297-9332. **Contact:** Manager. **Description:** An executive search firm.

I.J. & ASSOCIATES, INC.
2525 South Wadsworth Boulevard, Suite 106, Lakewood CO 80227. 303/984-2585. **Fax:** 303/984-2589. **Contact:** Ila Larson, President. **E-mail address:** ilarson@csn.net. **World Wide Web address:** http://www.ijassoc.com. **Description:** An executive search firm operating on a contingency basis. The firm focuses on the placement of software developers, programmers, and telecommunications professionals. **Specializes in the areas of:** Computer Science/Software. **Positions commonly filled include:** Computer Operator; Computer Programmer; Database Manager; Internet Services Manager; Project Manager; Systems Analyst; Telecommunications Manager; Webmaster. **Average salary range of placements:** More than $50,000. **Number of placements per year:** 1 - 49.

INFORMATION TECHNOLOGIES RESOURCES
370 17th Street, Suite 3170, Denver CO 80202. 303/446-9006. **Fax:** 303/446-9177. **Contact:** Michelle O'Mahoney, President. **Description:** An executive search firm operating on a contingency basis. Company pays fee. **Average salary range of placements:** $30,000 - $50,000. **Number of placements per year:** 100 - 199.

INTEGRITY NETWORK INC.
5445 DTC Parkway, Suite P4, Englewood CO 80111. 303/220-9752. **Contact:** Office Manager. **Description:** An executive search firm. **Specializes in the areas of:** Computer Science/Software; Sales.

JACKSON GROUP INTERNATIONAL
650 South Cherry Street, Suite 610, Denver CO 80246. 303/321-3844. **Fax:** 303/321-3551. **Contact:** Office Manager. **Description:** An executive search firm.

KUTT, INC.
2336 Canyon Boulevard, Suite 202, Boulder CO 80302. 303/440-6111. **Fax:** 303/440-9582. **Contact:** Greg Neighbors, Partner. **Description:** An executive search firm. Company pays fee. **Specializes in the areas of:** Printing; Publishing. **Positions commonly filled include:** Blue-Collar Worker Supervisor; Buyer; Cost Estimator; Customer Service Representative; General Manager; Industrial Engineer; Industrial Production Manager; Manufacturer's/Wholesaler's Sales Rep.; Mechanical Engineer; Quality Control Supervisor; Services Sales Representative. **Average salary range of placements:** $30,000 - $50,000. **Number of placements per year:** 1 - 49.

MDR & ASSOCIATES
387 Monte Vista Road, Golden CO 80401. 303/526-1052. **Contact:** Manager. **Description:** An executive search firm. **Other U.S. locations:** AR; LA.

MANAGEMENT RECRUITERS INTERNATIONAL
1888 Sherman Street, Suite 420, Denver CO 80203. 303/832-5250. **Contact:** Manager. **Description:** An executive search firm. **Specializes in the areas of:** Biotechnology; Chemical; Information Technology; Pharmaceutical; Sales; Telecommunications. **Corporate headquarters location:** Cleveland OH. **Other U.S. locations:** Nationwide.

MANAGEMENT RECRUITERS OF BOULDER
1401 Walnut Street, Boulder CO 80302-5328. 303/447-9900. **Fax:** 303/447-9536. **Contact:** Sandi Gloss, Office Manager. **Description:** A contingency executive search firm. **Specializes in the areas of:** Administration; Banking; Engineering. **Positions commonly filled include:** Electrical/Electronics Engineer; Systems Analyst. **Corporate headquarters location:** Cleveland OH. **Other U.S. locations:** Nationwide. **Average salary range of placements:** More than $50,000. **Number of placements per year:** 50 - 99.

MANAGEMENT RECRUITERS OF COLORADO
8771 Wolff Court, Suite 125, Westminster CO 80030. 303/650-8870. **Fax:** 303/650-8871. **Contact:** Gloria Kellerhals, Managing Partner. **World Wide Web address:** http://www.mrwestminster.com. **Description:** An executive search firm operating on both retained and contingency bases. **Specializes in the areas of:** Health/Medical; Sales. **Positions commonly filled include:** Account Manager; Account Representative; Computer Programmer; Database Manager; Financial Analyst; Fund Manager; Health Services Manager; Management Analyst/Consultant; Registered Nurse; Sales Representative; Systems Analyst; Systems Manager; Technical Writer/Editor. **Corporate headquarters location:** Cleveland OH. **Other U.S. locations:** Nationwide. **Average salary range of placements:** $20,000 - $29,999. **Number of placements per year:** 50 - 99.

MANAGEMENT RECRUITERS OF COLORADO SPRINGS
13 South Tejon, Suite 501, Colorado Springs CO 80903. 719/575-0500. **Contact:** Mark Merriman, Office Manager. **Description:** An executive search firm. **Specializes in the areas of:** Administration; Architecture/Construction; Electrical; Engineering; Finance; Food Industry; General Management; Health/Medical; Manufacturing; Operations Management; Personnel/Labor Relations; Procurement; Sales; Technical.

MANAGEMENT RECRUITERS OF GOLDEN HILL
12600 West Colfax, Suite C440, Lakewood CO 80215. 303/233-8600. **Contact:** Lauri Williams, Coordinator. **Description:** An executive search firm. Company pays fee. **Specializes in the areas of:** Manufacturing. **Positions commonly filled include:** Electrical/Electronics Engineer; Mechanical Engineer. **Number of placements per year:** 50 - 99.

MANAGEMENT WEST
470 22nd Street, Denver CO 80205. 303/388-2888. **Contact:** Manager. **Description:** An executive search firm. **Specializes in the areas of:** Construction.

WILLIAM K. McLAUGHLIN ASSOCIATES
705 North Street, Boulder CO 80304. 303/545-0014. **Contact:** Manager. **Description:** An executive search firm. **Specializes in the areas of:** Legal.

MESA INC. (MANAGEMENT EXECUTIVE SERVICES INC.)
6019 Belmont Way, Parker CO 80134. **Contact:** Manager. **Description:** An executive search firm. **Specializes in the areas of:** Industrial.

MILLER DENVER
P.O. Box 340, Castle Rock CO 80104. 303/688-6630. **Fax:** 303/688-4334. **Contact:** Eric Miller, Owner. **Description:** An executive search firm operating on a contingency basis. Company pays fee. **Specializes in the areas of:** Computer Science/Software; Engineering; Manufacturing; Technical. **Positions commonly filled include:** Applications Engineer; Biomedical Engineer; Buyer; Chemical Engineer; Civil Engineer; Design Engineer; Electrical/Electronics Engineer; Industrial Engineer; Industrial Production Manager; Manufacturing Engineer; Mechanical Engineer; Operations/Production Manager; Quality Control Supervisor; Sales Engineer; Software Engineer; Structural Engineer. **Average salary range of placements:** More than $50,000. **Number of placements per year:** 1 - 49.

NATIONAL AFFIRMATIVE ACTION CAREER NETWORK, INC.
4255 South Buckeye Road, Suite 299, Aurora CO 80013. 303/699-8599. **Fax:** 303/699-8525. **Contact:** Calvin Booker, President. **Description:** An executive search firm offering both retainer and contingency placements nationwide. Company pays fee. **Specializes in the areas of:** Accounting/Auditing; Banking; Engineering; Finance; Food Industry; Manufacturing; Nonprofit; Personnel/Labor Relations. **Positions commonly filled include:** Accountant/Auditor; Attorney; Bank Officer/Manager; Buyer; Chemical Engineer; Chemist; Computer Programmer; Design Engineer; Financial Analyst; Food Scientist/Technologist; Industrial Engineer; Materials Engineer; Mechanical Engineer; Metallurgical Engineer; MIS Specialist; Purchasing Agent/Manager; Reporter; Software Engineer; Technical Writer/Editor; Telecommunications Manager. **Number of placements per year:** 1 - 49.

NATIONAL EXECUTIVE RESOURCES, INC. (NERI)
5445 DTC Parkway, Suite P4, Englewood CO 80111. 303/721-7672. **Contact:** Manager. **Description:** An executive search firm. **Specializes in the areas of:** Technical.

NELSON COULSON & ASSOCIATES INC.
4830 Rusina Road, Suite A, Colorado Springs CO 80907-8126. 719/593-9580. **Toll-free phone:** 800/593-9580. **Fax:** 719/593-9699. **Contact:** Robert Welker, Manager. **Description:** An executive search firm that also operates as a temporary and permanent employment agency. Company pays fee. **Average salary range of placements:** $20,000 - $29,999. **Number of placements per year:** 500 - 999.

NETWORK SEARCH INC.
1651 Yarmouth Avenue, Boulder CO 80304. 303/444-8600. **Contact:** Manager. **Description:** An executive search firm focusing on high-tech placements.

PEAK LTD.
118 North Tejon, Suite 205F, Colorado Springs CO 80903. 719/578-1814. **Fax:** 719/578-1815. **Contact:** Manager. **Description:** An executive search firm that provides placements in property/casualty insurance. **Specializes in the areas of:** Insurance.

PENDLETON RESOURCES
1301 Pennsylvania Street, Suite 240, Denver CO 80203. 303/832-8100. **Contact:** Manager. **Description:** An executive search firm. **Specializes in the areas of:** Computer Science/Software; Construction; Engineering; Information Systems.

PINNACLE SOURCE
4600 South Ulster Street, Suite 975, Denver CO 80237. 303/796-9900. **Contact:** Jordan Greenberg, President. **Description:** A retainer and contingency search firm. Company pays fee. **Specializes in the areas of:** Computer Science/Software; Sales; Technical. **Positions commonly filled include:** Branch Manager; Computer Programmer; MIS Specialist; Services Sales Representative; Software Engineer; Systems Analyst. **Average salary range of placements:** More than $50,000. **Number of placements per year:** 50 - 99.

PLACEMENT PROFESSIONALS INC.
7700 East Arapahoe Road, Suite 200, Englewood CO 80112. 303/721-8308. **Contact:** Manager. **Description:** An executive search firm. **Specializes in the areas of:** Accounting/Auditing; Legal; Sales.

PREMIER CONSULTING
8400 East Prentice Avenue, Suite 1380, Englewood CO 80111. 303/779-1006. **Contact:** Manager. **Description:** An executive search firm. **Specializes in the areas of:** Computer Hardware/Software.

PROFESSIONAL SEARCH AND PLACEMENT
4901 East Dry Creek Road, Littleton CO 80122-4010. 303/779-8004. **Contact:** John Turner, President. **E-mail address:** pspinc@pspjobs.com. **World Wide Web address:** http://www.pspjobs.com. **Description:** An executive search firm specializing in computer technology. The firm recruits nationally and offers permanent and contract assignments. Founded in 1979. **Specializes in the areas of:** Computer Science/Software. **Positions commonly filled include:** Computer Programmer; Software Engineer; Systems Analyst; Technical Writer/Editor. **Benefits available to temporary workers:** Medical Insurance. **Average salary range of placements:** More than $50,000. **Number of placements per year:** 200 - 499.

REAL ESTATE PERSONNEL
1115 Grant Street, Suite 204, Denver CO 80203. 303/832-2380. **Fax:** 303/832-2330. **Contact:** Dan Grantham, Owner. **E-mail address:** dangrant@csn.net. **World Wide Web address:** http://www.csn.net/~dangrant. **Description:** An executive search firm which also operates as a temporary and permanent employment agency. Company pays fee. **Specializes in the areas of:** Accounting/Auditing; Architecture/Construction; Engineering; General Management; Sales. **Positions commonly filled include:** Accountant/Auditor; Administrative Manager; Architect; Civil Engineer; Construction and Building Inspector; Construction Contractor; Cost Estimator; Credit Manager; Draftsperson; Electrical/Electronics Engineer; Financial Analyst; Landscape Architect; Property and Real Estate Manager; Urban/Regional Planner. **Number of placements per year:** 50 - 99.

ROCKY MOUNTAIN RECRUITERS
1801 Broadway, Suite 810, Denver CO 80202. 303/296-2000. **Contact:** Manager. **Description:** An executive search firm. **Specializes in the areas of:** Accounting/Auditing; Finance.

ROTH YOUNG PERSONNEL SERVICES
9725 East Hampden Avenue, Suite 300, Denver CO 80231. 303/755-0075. **Contact:** Office Manager. **Description:** An executive search firm. **Number of placements per year:** 200 - 499.

SALES CONSULTANTS
13111 East Briarwood Avenue, Suite 350, Englewood CO 80112. 303/706-0123. **Contact:** Mr. Terry McManus, Manager. **Description:** An executive search firm. **Specializes in the areas of:** Accounting/Auditing; Administration; Advertising; Architecture/Construction; Banking; Communications; Computer Hardware/Software; Construction; Design; Electrical; Engineering; Finance; Food Industry; General

Management; Health/Medical; Insurance; Legal; Manufacturing; Operations Management; Personnel/ Labor Relations; Pharmaceutical; Procurement; Publishing; Real Estate; Retail; Sales; Technical; Textiles; Transportation. **Corporate headquarters location:**Cleveland OH.

SCHEER & ASSOCIATES
1873 South Bel Aire, Suite 900, Denver CO 80222. 303/757-7357. **Contact:** Manager. **Description:** An executive search firm. **Specializes in the areas of:** Sales.

SNELLING PERSONNEL SERVICES
2460 West 26th Avenue, Suite 360-C, Denver CO 80211. 303/964-8200. **Fax:** 303/964-9312. **Contact:** F. Daryl Gatewood, President. **World Wide Web address:** http://www.snelling.com. **Description:** An executive search firm. Snelling Personnel Services also places temporary personnel and operates on a contingency basis. Company pays fee. **Specializes in the areas of:** Accounting/Auditing; Administration; Computer Science/Software; Engineering; Finance; Personnel/Labor Relations; Sales; Secretarial; Technical. **Positions commonly filled include:** Accountant/Auditor; Bank Officer/Manager; Clerical Supervisor; Computer Programmer; Electrical/ Electronics Engineer; Financial Analyst; Human Resources Manager; Services Sales Representative; Systems Analyst; Typist/Word Processor. **Benefits available to temporary workers:** 401(k); Medical Insurance; Paid Holidays; Paid Vacation. **Corporate headquarters location:** Dallas TX. **International locations:** Worldwide. **Average salary range of placements:** $30,000 - $50,000. **Number of placements per year:** 100 - 199.

SOURCE SERVICES CORPORATION
7730 East Belleview Avenue, Suite 302, Englewood CO 80111. 303/773-3700. **Fax:** 303/773-8201. **Contact:** Office Manager. **Description:** An executive search firm. The divisions at this location include Source Consulting, Source EDP, Source Finance, and Accountant Source Temps. **Specializes in the areas of:** Accounting/Auditing; Computer Hardware/Software; Finance; Information Technology.

STAR PERSONNEL SERVICE
2851 South Parker Road, Aurora CO 80014-2736. 303/695-1161. **Fax:** 303/695-1058. **Contact:** Paul Staffieri, Owner. **Description:** An executive search firm that also operates as a temporary and permanent employment agency. Company pays fee. **Specializes in the areas of:** Accounting/Auditing; Computer Science/Software; Engineering; Finance; General Management; Industrial; Manufacturing; Personnel/ Labor Relations; Retail; Sales. **Positions commonly filled include:** Accountant/Auditor; Computer Programmer; Credit Manager; Draftsperson; General Manager; Health Services Manager; Management Trainee; Mechanical Engineer; Property and Real Estate Manager; Purchasing Agent/Manager; Quality Control Supervisor; Software Engineer; Structural Engineer; Underwriter/Assistant Underwriter. **Average salary range of placements:** $30,000 - $50,000. **Number of placements per year:** 50 - 99.

R.W. SWANSON & ASSOCIATES, INC.
10200 East Girard Avenue, Denver CO 80231. 303/695-0978. **Contact:** Richard Swanson, President. **Description:** An executive search firm. Company pays fee. **Positions commonly filled include:** Accountant/Auditor; Actuary; Adjuster; Administrative Manager; Aerospace Engineer; Agricultural Engineer; Agricultural Scientist; Architect; Attorney; Bank Officer/Manager; Biological Scientist; Branch Manager; Budget Analyst; Buyer; Chemical Engineer; Chemist; Chiropractor; Civil Engineer; Claim Representative; Clinical Lab Technician; Computer Programmer; Construction and Building Inspector; Construction Contractor; Cost Estimator; Credit Manager; Customer Service Representative; Editor; Education Administrator; EKG Technician; Electrical/Electronics Engineer; Financial Analyst; Industrial Production Manager; Insurance Agent; Mechanical Engineer; Operations/Production Manager; Paralegal; Physical Therapist; Physician; Radio/TV Announcer/ Broadcaster; Radiological Technologist; Real Estate Agent; Restaurant/Food Service Manager; Services Sales Representative; Software Engineer; Structural Engineer; Surgical Technician; Surveyor; Systems Analyst; Technical Writer/Editor; Transportation/ Traffic Specialist; Travel Agent; Underwriter/Assistant Underwriter; Urban/ Regional Planner; Wholesale and Retail Buyer. **Average salary range of placements:** More than $50,000. **Number of placements per year:** 100 - 199.

TECHNICAL RECRUITERS OF COLORADO SPRINGS
3322 Water Street, Colorado Springs CO 80904. 719/632-3835. **Contact:** Manager. **Description:** An executive search firm. **Specializes in the areas of:** Engineering.

TRIAD CONSULTANTS
8101 East Prentice Avenue, Suite 610, Englewood CO 80111. 303/220-8516. **Fax:** 303/220-5265. **Contact:** Ronald Burgy, Partner. **E-mail address:** ronburgy@tci-colorado.com. **World Wide Web address:** http://www.tci-colorado.com. **Description:** An executive search firm specializing in the placement of software developers, DBAs, project managers, CIOs, and management consultants, as well as sales and technical support personnel. Company pays fee. **Specializes in the areas of:** Administration; Computer Science/Software; Sales. **Positions commonly filled include:** Computer Programmer; MIS Specialist; Software Engineer; Systems Analyst. **Corporate headquarters location:** This Location. **Average salary range of placements:** More than $50,000. **Number of placements per year:** 100 - 199.

J.Q. TURNER & ASSOCIATES, INC.
200 South Wilcox Street, Unit 217, Castle Rock CO 80104-1913. 303/671-0800. **Fax:** 303/688-0188. **Contact:** Jim Turner, President. **E-mail address:** jqt@jqt.com. **World Wide Web address:** http://jqt.com. **Description:** An executive search firm focusing on the nationwide recruitment of technical professionals for clients in biomedical, industrial, and scientific instrumentation; computers and computer peripherals; robotics; telecommunications; and pyrotechnics. Company pays fee. **Specializes in the areas of:** Computer Hardware/Software; Computer Operations; Computer Science/Software; Engineering; Industrial; Manufacturing; Technical; Telecommunications. **Positions commonly filled include:** Biomedical Engineer; Chemical Engineer; Electrical/Electronics Engineer; Industrial Engineer; Industrial Production Manager; Manufacturing Engineer; Manufacturing Manager; Mechanical Engineer; Optical Engineer; Quality Assurance Engineer; Quality Control Supervisor; Software Engineer. **Average salary range of placements:** More than $50,000. **Number of placements per year:** 1 - 49.

U.S. ENVIROSEARCH
1800 West Littleton Boulevard, Littleton CO 80120. 303/795-9928. **Contact:** Manager. **Description:** An executive search firm that provides placements in the environmental industry.

WELZIG, LOWE & ASSOCIATES
761 West Birch Court, Louisville CO 80027. 303/666-4195. **Contact:** Frank Welzig, President. **Description:** An executive search firm serving a wide range of

industries and disciplines. The firm operates on both retainer and contingency bases. **Specializes in the areas of:** Computer Science/Software; Engineering; Oil and Gas; Technical. **Positions commonly filled include:** Aerospace Engineer; Computer Programmer; Design Engineer; Electrical/Electronics Engineer; MIS Specialist; Software Engineer; Systems Analyst.

JULIE WEST AND ASSOCIATES
4155 East Jewell Avenue, Suite 202, Denver CO 80222. 303/759-1622. **Fax:** 303/691-8069. **Contact:** Julie West, Owner. **Description:** An executive search firm focusing on the placement of sales representatives and sales management professionals for various industries. Company pays fee. **Specializes in the areas of:** General Management; Sales; Sales Promotion. **Positions commonly filled include:** Sales and Marketing Representative; Sales Engineer; Sales Executive; Sales Manager.

WOODMOOR GROUP
P.O. Box 1383, Monument CO 80132-1383. 719/488-8589. **Fax:** 719/488-9043. **Contact:** Ray Bedingfield, President. **E-mail address:** woodmoor@usa.net. **Description:** A technical search firm that focuses on engineering, manufacturing, and product development for food and other packaged goods industries. Company pays fee. **Specializes in the areas of:** Administration; Automotive; Chemical; Engineering; Finance; Food Industry; Heavy Equipment; Industrial; Manufacturing; Oil and Gas; Technical; Transportation. **Positions commonly filled include:** Accountant; Administrative Worker/Clerk; Agricultural Engineer; Biochemist; Biological Scientist; Biomedical Engineer; Budget Analyst; Ceramics Engineer; Chemical Engineer; Chemist; Chief Financial Officer; Computer Programmer; Controller; Corrosion Engineer; Customer Service Representative; Design Engineer; EDP Specialist; Facilities Engineer; Food Scientist/Technologist; General Manager; Industrial Engineer; Industrial Production Manager; Materials Engineer; Mechanical Engineer; Metallurgical Engineer; Mining Engineer; MIS Manager; MIS Specialist; Petroleum Engineer; Software Engineer; Statistician; Structural Engineer; Systems Analyst; Transportation/Traffic Specialist. **Average salary range of placements:** More than $50,000. **Number of placements per year:** 50 - 99.

THE WOODSTONE CONSULTING COMPANY, INC.
43500 Elk River Road, Steamboat Springs CO 80487. 970/879-1079. **Fax:** 970/879-2345. **Contact:** Edward A. Meagher III, President. **Description:** An executive search firm operating on a retainer basis. The Woodstone Consulting Company also offers human resources management consulting, executive coaching, and management development services. **Specializes in the areas of:** Food Industry; Operations Management; Personnel/Labor Relations; Sales. **Average salary range of placements:** More than $50,000. **Number of placements per year:** 1 - 49.

YORK & ASSOCIATES
1019 9th Street, Greeley CO 80631. 970/352-3086. **Fax:** 970/352-3087. **Contact:** Teri F. York, President. **Description:** An executive search firm for the construction industry with a focus on mid-sized construction companies including commercial, industrial, and public works companies nationwide. Company pays fee. **Specializes in the areas of:** Construction. **Positions commonly filled include:** Civil Engineer; Construction Contractor; Construction Manager; Cost Estimator; Environmental Engineer; Industrial Engineer; Mechanical Engineer; Mining Engineer; Operations Manager; Petroleum Engineer; Project Manager; Quality Control Supervisor; Structural Engineer; Vice President of Marketing; Vice President of Operations. **Average salary range of placements:** More than $50,000. **Number of placements per year:** 1 - 49.

YOUNG & THULIN
555 Clover Lane, Boulder CO 80303. 303/499-7242. **Contact:** Manager. **Description:** An executive search firm operating on a retainer basis. **Specializes in the areas of:** High-Tech.

PERMANENT EMPLOYMENT AGENCIES

A TO Z BUSINESS SERVICES
415 East Hyman Avenue, Suite 204, Aspen CO 81611. 970/925-4787. **Fax:** 970/920-1876. **Contact:** Nancy K. Bosshard, Principal. **E-mail address:** atoz@rof.net. **World Wide Web address:** http://www.rof.net/yp/atoz. **Description:** A permanent employment agency which also provides temporary placements. Founded in 1984. Company pays fee. **Specializes in the areas of:** Legal; Nonprofit; Secretarial. **Positions commonly filled include:** Administrative Assistant; Clerical Supervisor; Computer Operator; Computer Programmer; Controller; Database Manager; Paralegal; Real Estate Agent; Secretary; Typist/Word Processor. **Average salary range of placements:** $20,000 - $29,999. **Number of placements per year:** 500 - 999.

ABC NANNIES
50 South Steele Street, Suite 222, Denver CO 80209. 303/321-3866. **Contact:** Ginger Swift, Placement Specialist. **World Wide Web address:** http://www.abcnannies.com. **Description:** A permanent employment agency focusing on placement of nannies with a minimum of two years of child care experience. Founded in 1994. **Specializes in the areas of:** Nannies. **Average salary range of placements:** Less than $20,000. **Number of placements per year:** 100 - 199.

ABSOLUTE EMPLOYMENT SERVICES, INC.
1620 Pennsylvania Street, Denver CO 80203. 303/839-5700. **Contact:** Manager. **Description:** A permanent employment agency. Company pays fee. **Specializes in the areas of:** Clerical; Light Industrial; Manufacturing; Sales; Secretarial. **Positions commonly filled include:** Automotive Mechanic; Clerical Supervisor; Customer Service Representative. **Corporate headquarters location:** This Location. **Number of placements per year:** 1000+.

AHRNSBRAK AND ASSOCIATES, INC.
4155 East Jewell Avenue, Suite 202, Denver CO 80222. 303/758-4119. **Fax:** 303/757-4296. **Contact:** Doris M. Ahrnsbrak, Owner. **Description:** A permanent employment agency. Founded in 1986. Company pays fee. **Specializes in the areas of:** Accounting/Auditing; Administration; Advertising; Banking; Computer Science/Software; Engineering; Finance; General Management; Insurance; Legal; Marketing; Printing; Publishing; Sales; Secretarial. **Positions commonly filled include:** Accountant/Auditor; Administrative Manager; Advertising Clerk; Attorney; Bank Officer/Manager; Branch Manager; Brokerage Clerk; Clerical Supervisor; Computer Programmer; Credit Manager; Customer Service Representative; Financial Analyst; Human Service Worker; Insurance Agent/Broker; Multimedia Designer; Paralegal; Preschool Worker; Public Relations Specialist; Purchasing Agent/Manager; Quality Control Supervisor; Radio/TV Announcer/Broadcaster; Restaurant/Food Service Manager; Technical Writer/Editor; Typist/Word Processor; Underwriter/Assistant Underwriter; Video Production Coordinator.

ASPEN PERSONNEL SERVICES, INC.
1155 South Main Street, Suite 4, Longmont CO 80501. 303/776-9661. **Fax:** 303/776-0195. **Contact:** Muriel Kempf, President/Owner. **Description:** A permanent employment agency which also provides short-term, long-term, and temp-to-hire placement. Founded in 1994. Company pays fee. **Specializes in the areas of:** Clerical; General Labor; Industrial; Manufacturing. **Positions commonly filled include:** Typist/Word Processor. **Average salary range of placements:** Less than $20,000. **Number of placements per year:** 200 - 499.

C.S. BARNES
2900 South Garfield Street, Denver CO 80210. 303/220-1094. **Contact:** Colleen S. Barnes, Owner. **Description:** A permanent employment agency which also provides temporary placement and career/outplacement counseling. Company pays fee. **Specializes in the areas of:** Accounting/Auditing; Architecture/Construction; Finance; Legal. **Positions commonly filled include:** Accountant/Auditor; Administrative Manager; Clerical Supervisor; Cost Estimator; Credit Manager; Customer Service Representative; Environmental Engineer; General Manager; Typist/Word Processor. **Average salary range of placements:** $20,000 - $29,999. **Number of placements per year:** 50 - 99.

CORESTAFF SERVICES
7355 West 88th Avenue, Suite V, Westminster CO 80021. 303/425-6646. **Fax:** 303/425-1101. **Contact:** Maggie Torres, Branch Manager. **World Wide Web address:** http://www.corestaffservices.com. **Description:** A permanent employment agency which also provides temporary placements. Founded in 1983. Company pays fee. **Specializes in the areas of:** Secretarial. **Positions commonly filled include:** Customer Service Representative; Human Resources Specialist; Typist/Word Processor. **Benefits available to temporary workers:** 401(k); Medical Insurance; Paid Holidays; Stock Purchase. **Corporate headquarters location:** Fort Collins CO. **Other U.S. locations:** Nationwide. **Average salary range of placements:** Less than $20,000. **Number of placements per year:** 1000+.

CORESTAFF SERVICES
303 16th Street, Suite 220, Denver CO 80202. 303/825-1500. **Fax:** 303/825-1518. **Contact:** Manager. **Description:** A permanent employment agency which provides both permanent and temporary placement. Company pays fee. **Specializes in the areas of:** Accounting/Auditing; Administration; Manufacturing; Personnel/Labor Relations; Secretarial; Technical. **Positions commonly filled include:** Accountant/Auditor; Claim Representative; Customer Service Representative; Electrician; Human Resources Specialist; Quality Control Supervisor; Technical Writer/Editor; Typist/Word Processor. **Corporate headquarters location:** Fort Collins CO. **Other U.S. locations:** Nationwide. **Number of placements per year:** 1000+.

ELEVENTH HOUR STAFFING SERVICES
8586 East Arapahoe Road, Englewood CO 80112. 303/220-8892. **Fax:** 303/770-8243. **Contact:** Tookie Scherder, Branch Manager. **Description:** A permanent placement agency. The agency provides both permanent and temporary placement, career/outplacement counseling, and contract services. Company pays fee. **Specializes in the areas of:** Accounting/Auditing; Administration; Advertising; Banking; Computer Science/Software; Finance; Food Industry; General Management; Health/Medical; Insurance; Legal; Manufacturing; Retail; Sales; Secretarial; Technical; Transportation. **Positions commonly filled include:** Accountant/Auditor; Administrative Manager; Advertising Clerk; Branch Manager; Brokerage Clerk; Budget Analyst; Computer Programmer; Cost Estimator; Counselor; Credit Manager; Customer Service Representative; Health Services Manager; Human Resources Specialist; Insurance Agent/Broker; Management Analyst/Consultant; Management Trainee; Paralegal; Quality Control Supervisor; Software Engineer; Systems Analyst; Technical Writer/Editor; Telecommunications Manager; Typist/Word Processor. **Corporate headquarters location:** This Location. **Other U.S. locations:** Tustin CA; Kansas City KS. **Number of placements per year:** 500 - 999.

ENSCICON CORPORATION
1775 Sherman Street, Suite 1700, Denver CO 80203. 303/832-8200. **Contact:** Lori Kochevar, Recruiter. **Description:** A permanent employment agency. Enscicon provides permanent placement and consulting services in computer science and engineering fields. Company pays fee. **Specializes in the areas of:** Administration; Computer Science/Software; Engineering; Industrial; Manufacturing; Technical. **Positions commonly filled include:** Aerospace Engineer; Architect; Biomedical Engineer; Chemical Engineer; Chemist; Civil Engineer; Computer Programmer; Design Engineer; Draftsperson; Electrical/Electronics Engineer; Environmental Engineer; Industrial Engineer; Mechanical Engineer; Mining Engineer; MIS Specialist; Nuclear Engineer; Petroleum Engineer; Science Technologist; Software Engineer; Structural Engineer; Technical Writer/Editor. **Benefits available to temporary workers:** 401(k); Dental Insurance; Medical Insurance; Paid Holidays; Paid Vacation. **Number of placements per year:** 200 - 499.

GOODWIN PERSONNEL, INC.
800 Grant Street, Suite 110, Denver CO 80203. 303/863-1500. **Fax:** 303/863-1664. **Contact:** John Wagner, President. **Description:** A permanent placement agency. Founded in 1983. **Specializes in the areas of:** Accounting/Auditing; Administration; Clerical; Consulting; Health/Medical; Legal; Light Industrial; Technical.

MARGARET HOOK'S PERSONNEL
7800 East Union Avenue, Suite 120, Denver CO 80237. 303/770-2100. **Contact:** Margaret Hook, Manager. **Description:** A permanent employment agency. **Specializes in the areas of:** Administration.

JFI (JOBS FOR INDUSTRY)
1888 Sherman Street, Suite 500, Denver CO 80203. 303/831-0048. **Fax:** 303/832-3401. **Contact:** Kevin Courtney, President. **Description:** A permanent employment agency. **Specializes in the areas of:** Distribution; Manufacturing.

JOB STORE STAFFING
7100 East Hampden Avenue, Denver CO 80224-3096. 303/757-7801. **Fax:** 303/757-5604. **Contact:** Dorothy Grandbois, President. **Description:** A permanent employment agency that provides both permanent and temporary staffing of administrative support, accounting, legal, and light industrial personnel. Company pays fee. **Benefits available to temporary workers:** Dental Insurance; Medical Insurance; Paid Holidays; Paid Vacation. **Average salary range of placements:** $20,000 - $30,000. **Number of placements per year:** 1000+.

KELLY SERVICES, INC.
3500 John F. Kennedy Parkway, Suite 206, Fort Collins CO 80525. 970/223-3955. **Fax:** 970/223-0217. **Contact:** Marianne Godwin, Manager. **Description:** A full-service employment agency. Founded in 1946. **Specializes in the areas of:** Clerical;

Light Industrial; Marketing; Technical. **Benefits available to temporary workers:** Medical Insurance; Paid Holidays; Paid Vacation. **Corporate headquarters location:** Troy MI. **Other U.S. locations:** Nationwide. **Average salary range of placements:** $20,000 - $29,999. **Number of placements per year:** 1000+.

LD PLACEMENTS INC.
621 17th Street, Suite 2000, Denver CO 80293. 303/298-7373. **Fax:** 303/298-7732. **Contact:** Manager. **Description:** A permanent employment agency focusing on the placement of administrative support staff. Company pays fee. **Specializes in the areas of:** Accounting/Auditing; Administration; Secretarial. **Positions commonly filled include:** Administrative Manager; Clerical Supervisor; Customer Service Representative; Financial Analyst; Human Resources Specialist; Typist/Word Processor. **Average salary range of placements:** $20,000 - $29,999. **Number of placements per year:** 100 - 199.

LEE MANAGEMENT GROUP
3924 Divot Court, Longmont CO 80503. 303/448-1004. **Contact:** Barbara Lee, President. **Description:** A permanent employment agency focusing on placement of personnel in apparel manufacturing industries. **Specializes in the areas of:** Apparel; Textiles.

MEDICAL PERSONNEL RESOURCES
3333 South Bannock Street, Suite 530, Englewood CO 80110. 303/762-0806. **Fax:** 303/762-0875. **Contact:** Ronald Robacker, President. **Description:** A permanent employment agency that provides personnel for medical clinics and offices in the metro Denver area. Founded in 1981. Company pays fee. **Specializes in the areas of:** Health/Medical. **Positions commonly filled include:** Administrative Manager; Bookkeeper; Claim Representative; Clinical Lab Technician; EEG Technologist; EKG Technician; Health Services Manager; Licensed Practical Nurse; Medical Assistant; Radiological Technologist; Registered Nurse; Surgical Technician. **Average salary range of placements:** Less than $20,000. **Number of placements per year:** 100 - 199.

OFFICE SERVICES UNLIMITED, INC.
PAYROLL PRINCIPALS, INC.
118 West 6th Street, Suite 202, Glenwood Springs CO 81601. 970/945-2433. **Fax:** 970/945-1106. **Contact:** Matilda W. Fischer, President. **Description:** A permanent employment agency that focuses on providing personnel for office positions. The agency also provides temporary placements. Founded in 1979. Company pays fee. **Positions commonly filled include:** Construction Contractor; Construction Manager. **Benefits available to temporary workers:** Medical Insurance; Paid Vacation. **Average salary range of placements:** $20,000 - $29,999. **Number of placements per year:** 50 - 99.

SURGICAL ASSOCIATED SERVICES, INC.
6825 East Tennessee Avenue, Suite 497, Denver CO 80224. 303/322-9111. **Fax:** 303/322-1529. **Contact:** Karyn Songer, Corporate Office Manager. **Description:** A staffing agency. **Specializes in the areas of:** Health/Medical. **Positions commonly filled include:** Registered Nurse; Surgical Assistant; Surgical Technician. **Benefits available to temporary workers:** Dental Insurance; Disability Coverage; Life Insurance; Medical Insurance; Profit Sharing.

TALENT TREE STAFFING SERVICES
183 Inverness Drive West, Englewood CO 80112. 303/643-3439. **Fax:** 303/649-2485. **Contact:** Kori Kautz, Extension Services Coordinator. **Description:** A permanent placement agency specializing in clerical, accounting, and technical positions. The agency also provides some temporary placements. Company pays fee. **Specializes in the areas of:** Accounting/Auditing; Administration; Finance; Secretarial. **Positions commonly filled include:** Accountant/Auditor; Computer Programmer; Financial Analyst; Systems Analyst; Typist/Word Processor. **Corporate headquarters location:** Houston TX. **Other U.S. locations:** Nationwide. **Average salary range of placements:** Less than $20,000. **Number of placements per year:** 100 - 199.

TALENT TREE STAFFING SERVICES
717 17th Street, Suite 140, Denver CO 80202. 303/296-1700. **Fax:** 303/296-1848. **Contact:** Susan Ahrens, Service Manager. **Description:** A permanent employment agency that provides both permanent and temporary placements. **Specializes in the areas of:** Accounting/Auditing; Administration; Banking; Computer Science/Software; Engineering; Finance; Health/Medical; Insurance; Legal; Personnel/Labor Relations; Secretarial. **Positions commonly filled include:** Accountant/Auditor; Human Resources Specialist; MIS Specialist; Technical Writer/Editor; Typist/Word Processor. **Corporate headquarters location:** Houston TX. **Other U.S. locations:** Nationwide. **Average salary range of placements:** $20,000 - $29,999. **Number of placements per year:** 100 - 199.

TERRY PERSONNEL
8958 North Washington Street, Thornton CO 80229. 303/286-8333. **Contact:** Richard Kemp, President. **Description:** A permanent employment agency. **Specializes in the areas of:** Clerical; Construction; Manufacturing; Secretarial. **Positions commonly filled include:** Administrative Assistant; Bookkeeper; Buyer; Civil Engineer; Clerk; Computer Operator; Computer Programmer; Credit Manager; Data Entry Clerk; Draftsperson; EDP Specialist; Factory Worker; Insurance Agent/Broker; Legal Secretary; Light Industrial Worker; Mechanical Engineer; Nurse; Sales Representative; Secretary; Typist/Word Processor. **Number of placements per year:** 200 - 499.

WSI PERSONNEL SERVICE INC.
3400 East Bayaud Avenue, Suite 290, Denver CO 80209. 303/322-8300. **Toll-free phone:** 800/585-2697. **Fax:** 303/322-0233. **Recorded jobline:** 303/322-8300. **Contact:** Shari Donnelly, President. **E-mail address:** sdonne43@aol.com. **Description:** A permanent employment agency which provides both permanent and temporary placement, primarily in health care and clerical positions. Company pays fee. **Specializes in the areas of:** Accounting/Auditing; Administration; Health/Medical. **Positions commonly filled include:** Claim Representative; Clinical Lab Technician; Computer Programmer; Customer Service Representative; EEG Technologist; EKG Technician; Emergency Medical Technician; Health Services Manager; Licensed Practical Nurse; Nuclear Medicine Technologist; Physical Therapist; Radiological Technologist; Registered Nurse; Services Sales Representative; Typist/Word Processor. **Number of placements per year:** 200 - 499.

TEMPORARY EMPLOYMENT AGENCIES

THE ACCOUNTING GUILD
5299 DTC Parkway, Suite 340, Englewood CO 80111. 303/694-4522. **Fax:** 303/796-9651. **Contact:** Accounting Specialist. **Description:** A temporary agency. Company pays fee. **Specializes in the areas of:** Accounting/Auditing; Finance. **Positions commonly filled include:** Accountant/Auditor; Financial Analyst. **Benefits available to temporary workers:** 401(k);

Dental Insurance; Medical Insurance. **Corporate headquarters location:** Houston TX. **Average salary range of placements:** $20,000 - $29,999. **Number of placements per year:** 200 - 499.

ADECCO
44 Cook Street, Suite 110, Denver CO 80206. 303/399-7706. **Contact:** Manager. **Description:** A temporary agency. Company pays fee. **Specializes in the areas of:** Accounting/Auditing; Banking; Clerical; Data Processing; Finance; Insurance; Legal; Secretarial; Technical; Word Processing. **Positions commonly filled include:** Administrative Assistant; Bookkeeper; Claim Representative; Computer Operator; Customer Service Representative; Data Entry Clerk; Factory Worker; Legal Secretary; Light Industrial Worker; Medical Secretary; Public Relations Specialist; Receptionist; Typist/Word Processor. **Number of placements per year:** 50 - 99.

BANKTEMPS, INC.
303 East 17th Avenue, Suite 100, Denver CO 80202. 303/861-4115. **Fax:** 303/861-0377. **Contact:** Steve Angell, Marketing Director. **Description:** A temporary agency that provides personnel services, temporary, and permanent placements to the financial services community, including banks, credit unions, savings and loans, and brokerage and insurance companies. Company pays fee. **Specializes in the areas of:** Banking; Credit and Collection; Personnel/Labor Relations; Secretarial. **Positions commonly filled include:** Bank Officer/Manager; Bank Teller; Branch Manager; Credit Manager; Customer Service Representative; Human Resources Specialist; Management Trainee; Securities Sales Representative; Services Sales Representative; Typist/Word Processor; Underwriter/Assistant Underwriter. **Benefits available to temporary workers:** 401(k); Dental Insurance; Medical Insurance; Paid Holidays; Paid Vacation. **Corporate headquarters location:** This Location. **Other area locations:** Colorado CO. **Other U.S. locations:** Chicago IL. **Average salary range of placements:** Less than $20,000. **Number of placements per year:** 1000+.

EAGLE VALLEY TEMPS
P.O. Box 1469, Avon CO 81620. 970/748-1000. **Contact:** Sandy MacLeod, President. **E-mail address:** evtemps@vail.net. **Description:** A temporary agency. Founded in 1989. **Specializes in the areas of:** Administration; Clerical; Construction; Industrial; Secretarial. **Average salary range of placements:** Less than $20,000. **Number of placements per year:** 500 - 999.

EXECUTEMPS, INC.
8801 East Hampden Avenue, Suite 210, Denver CO 80231. 303/696-6868. **Contact:** Patricia J. Rostvedt, President. **Description:** A temporary agency that also handles permanent placements. Executemps, Inc. focuses on the areas of legal/executive secretaries, office administrators, word processors, receptionists, data entry personnel, and general office support. Company pays fee. **Specializes in the areas of:** Legal; Personnel/Labor Relations; Secretarial. **Positions commonly filled include:** Administrative Assistant; Clerical Supervisor; Legal Secretary; Paralegal; Receptionist; Typist/Word Processor. **Average salary range of placements:** $20,000 - $29,999. **Number of placements per year:** 200 - 499.

THE FIRM
1120 Lincoln Street, Suite 1304, Denver CO 80203. 303/839-9999. **Contact:** Manager. **World Wide Web address:** http://www.thefirm-us.com. **Description:** A temporary and temp-to-perm agency. Company pays fee. **Specializes in the areas of:** Administration. **Positions commonly filled include:** Administrative Assistant; Executive Assistant. **Average salary range of placements:** $30,000 - $50,000.

THE FIRM
5555 DTC Parkway, Suite 3210-C, Englewood CO 80111. 303/889-0000. **Contact:** Manager. **World Wide Web address:** http://www.thefirm-us.com. **Description:** A temporary and temp-to-perm agency. **Specializes in the areas of:** Administration. **Positions commonly filled include:** Administrative Assistant; Executive Assistant. **Average salary range of placements:** $30,000 - $50,000. **Number of placements per year:** 100 - 199.

INTERIM PERSONNEL SERVICES
1901 North Union Boulevard, Suite 105, Colorado Springs CO 80909. 719/636-1606. **Fax:** 719/636-2705. **Contact:** Leasa S. McIntosh, Area Manager. **World Wide Web address:** http://www.interim.com. **Description:** A temporary agency. Founded in 1946. Company pays fee. **Specializes in the areas of:** Administration; Manufacturing; Secretarial. **Positions commonly filled include:** Administrative Manager; Advertising Clerk; Branch Manager; Brokerage Clerk; Buyer; Claim Representative; Clerical Supervisor; Customer Service Representative; Human Resources Specialist; Management Trainee; Medical Records Technician; Public Relations Specialist; Purchasing Agent/Manager; Restaurant/Food Service Manager; Typist/Word Processor. **Corporate headquarters location:** Fort Lauderdale FL. **Average salary range of placements:** $20,000 - $29,999. **Number of placements per year:** 1000+.

INTERIM PERSONNEL SERVICES OF DENVER
8101 East Belleview, Unit W, Denver CO 80237. 303/694-0936. **Fax:** 303/721-8973. **Contact:** Area Manager. **World Wide Web address:** http://www.interim.com. **Description:** A temporary personnel service. Company pays fee. **Specializes in the areas of:** Accounting/Auditing; Banking; Computer Science/Software; Health/Medical; Secretarial. **Positions commonly filled include:** Clerk; Computer Operator; Customer Service Representative; Data Entry Clerk; Driver; Executive Assistant; Legal Secretary; Light Industrial Worker; Receptionist; Secretary; Typist/Word Processor. **Corporate headquarters location:** Fort Lauderdale FL. **Number of placements per year:** 500 - 999.

JOBSEARCH
1107 South Nevada Avenue, Suite 113, Colorado Springs CO 80903. 719/475-9755. **Fax:** 719/575-9585. **Contact:** Michael Bram, President. **Description:** A temporary employment agency which also provides contract services. Founded in 1989. **Specializes in the areas of:** Accounting/Auditing; Administration; Advertising; Architecture/Construction; Banking; Broadcasting; Computer Science/Software; Economics; Education; Engineering; Finance; Food Industry; General Management; Health/Medical; Industrial; Insurance; Legal; Manufacturing; Nonprofit; Personnel/Labor Relations; Publishing; Retail; Sales; Secretarial; Technical; Transportation. **Positions commonly filled include:** Accountant/Auditor; Administrative Manager; Advertising Clerk; Architect; Bank Officer/Manager; Branch Manager; Buyer; Claim Representative; Clerical Supervisor; Clinical Lab Technician; Computer Programmer; Construction Contractor; Editor; EEG Technologist; EKG Technician; Electrical/Electronics Engineer; Environmental Engineer; Health Services Manager; Industrial Engineer; Industrial Production Manager; Internet Services Manager; Licensed Practical Nurse; Management Analyst/Consultant; Mechanical Engineer; Occupational Therapist; Physical Therapist; Radio/TV Announcer/Broadcaster; Registered Nurse; Reporter; Respiratory Therapist; Software Engineer;

Technical Writer/Editor; Telecommunications Manager; Typist/Word Processor. **Number of placements per year:** 1000+.

KELLY SCIENTIFIC RESOURCES
8753 Yates Drive, Suite 105, Westminster CO 80030. 303/427-4140. **Fax:** 303/427-4875. **Contact:** Branch Manager. **World Wide Web address:** http://www.kellyscientific.com. **Description:** A temporary agency for scientific professionals. **Specializes in the areas of:** Biomedical; Biotechnology; Chemical; Environmental; Food Industry; Petrochemical.

KELLY SERVICES, INC.
3025 South Parker Road, Aurora CO 80014. 303/695-9292. **Contact:** Manager. **Description:** A temporary agency. Company pays fee. **Specializes in the areas of:** Accounting/Auditing; Administration; Banking; Computer Science/Software; Education; Engineering; Finance; General Management; Industrial; Legal; Personnel/Labor Relations; Retail; Sales; Secretarial. **Positions commonly filled include:** Claim Representative; Clerical Supervisor; Management Trainee; Quality Control Supervisor. **Corporate headquarters location:** Troy MI. **Other U.S. locations:** Nationwide. **Average salary range of placements:** Less than $20,000. **Number of placements per year:** 1000+.

KELLY TECHNICAL SERVICES
6760 Corporate Drive, Colorado Springs CO 80919-1985. **Toll-free phone:** 800/590-2850. **Fax:** 719/528-5603. **Contact:** Branch Manager. **Description:** A temporary agency which also provides full-time staffing. Company pays fee. **Specializes in the areas of:** Computer Science/Software; Engineering; Manufacturing; Secretarial. **Positions commonly filled include:** Computer Programmer; Customer Service Representative; Design Engineer; Draftsperson; Electrical/Electronics Engineer; Mechanical Engineer; MIS Specialist. **Benefits available to temporary workers:** Paid Holidays; Paid Vacation. **Corporate headquarters location:** Troy MI. **Other U.S. locations:** Nationwide. **Number of placements per year:** 1000+.

LAB SUPPORT INC.
600 South Cherry Street, Suite 1125, Denver CO 80246. 303/964-8870. **Contact:** Linda Gibbons, Account Manager. **Description:** A temporary agency that places chemists, biologists, biochemists, molecular biologists, and microbiologists in industry labs. **Specializes in the areas of:** Biology; Technical. **Positions commonly filled include:** Biochemist; Biological Scientist; Chemist; Food Scientist/Technologist; Microbiologist. **Benefits available to temporary workers:** 401(k); Medical Insurance; Paid Holidays; Stock Purchase. **Corporate headquarters location:** Calabasas CA. **Other U.S. locations:** Nationwide. **Average salary range of placements:** $20,000 - $29,999. **Number of placements per year:** 200 - 499.

LABOR READY, INC.
8490 West Colfax Avenue, Lakewood CO 80215. 303/274-1466. **Contact:** Manager. **Description:** A temporary agency. **Specializes in the areas of:** Industrial; Manufacturing; Personnel/Labor Relations; Publishing; Technical; Transportation. **Positions commonly filled include:** Customer Service Representative; Electrician. **Corporate headquarters location:** Tacoma WA. **Other U.S. locations:** Nationwide. **Number of placements per year:** 1000+.

MANPOWER INTERNATIONAL INC.
5445 DTC Parkway, Suite 925, Englewood CO 80111. 303/740-7310. **Fax:** 303/740-0053. **Contact:** Branch Manager. **Description:** A temporary agency. **Specializes in the areas of:** Administration; Architecture/Construction; Banking; Computer Science/Software; Engineering; Finance; Industrial; Insurance; Legal; Manufacturing; Personnel/Labor Relations; Publishing; Retail; Sales; Secretarial; Technical. **Positions commonly filled include:** Administrative Manager; Aerospace Engineer; Architect; Bank Officer/Manager; Biomedical Engineer; Blue-Collar Worker Supervisor; Branch Manager; Budget Analyst; Civil Engineer; Claim Representative; Clerical Supervisor; Clinical Lab Technician; Computer Programmer; Electrical/Electronics Engineer; Environmental Engineer; Financial Analyst; Human Service Worker; Industrial Engineer; Mechanical Engineer; MIS Specialist; Systems Analyst; Technical Writer/Editor; Telecommunications Manager; Typist/Word Processor. **Corporate headquarters location:** Milwaukee WI. **International locations:** Worldwide. **Average salary range of placements:** $20,000 - $29,999. **Number of placements per year:** 1000+.

MANPOWER INTERNATIONAL INC.
1331 17th Street, Suite 1104, Denver CO 80202. 303/297-9802. **Contact:** Branch Manager. **Description:** A temporary agency. Company pays fee. **Specializes in the areas of:** Office Support; Word Processing. **Positions commonly filled include:** Accountant/Auditor; Accounting Clerk; Administrative Assistant; Assembly Worker; Biological Scientist; Bookkeeper; Chemist; Computer Operator; Customer Service Representative; Design Engineer; Desktop Publishing Specialist; Electrician; Inspector/Tester/Grader; Inventory Control Specialist; Machine Operator; Material Control Specialist; Order Clerk; Packaging/Processing Worker; Painter; Project Engineer; Proofreader; Receptionist; Records Manager; Research Assistant; Secretary; Software Engineer; Systems Analyst; Technical Writer/Editor; Telemarketer; Typist/Word Processor; Welder. **Benefits available to temporary workers:** Life Insurance; Medical Insurance; Paid Holidays; Paid Vacation. **Corporate headquarters location:** Milwaukee WI. **International locations:** Worldwide. **Number of placements per year:** 1000+.

NORRELL TEMPORARY SERVICES
14001 East Iliff Avenue, Suite 216, Aurora CO 80014. 303/337-6306. **Contact:** Recruiter. **Description:** A temporary agency. **Specializes in the areas of:** Accounting/Auditing; Finance; Personnel/Labor Relations; Secretarial. **Positions commonly filled include:** Accountant/Auditor; Budget Analyst; Customer Service Representative; Financial Analyst; Human Resources Specialist; Medical Records Technician; Typist/Word Processor. **Benefits available to temporary workers:** Medical Insurance; Paid Holidays; Paid Vacation. **Other U.S. locations:** Nationwide. **Average salary range of placements:** Less than $20,000. **Number of placements per year:** 1000+.

OFFICE SPECIALISTS INC.
6000 East Evans Avenue, Building 3, Suite 111, Denver CO 80222. 303/757-8840. **Fax:** 303/756-9225. **Recorded jobline:** 303/757-2164. **Contact:** Vicki Steeve, President. **E-mail address:** vsteeve@officespec.com. **World Wide Web address:** http://www.officespec.com. **Description:** A temporary agency. The agency specializes in placement for clerical, graphic arts, and technical positions. Company pays fee. **Specializes in the areas of:** Administration; Art/Design; Computer Science/Software; Secretarial. **Positions commonly filled include:** Civil Engineer; Computer Programmer; Design Engineer; Draftsperson; Electrical/Electronics Engineer; Environmental Engineer; Mechanical Engineer; Software Engineer; Systems Analyst; Technical Writer/Editor; Typist/Word Processor. **Corporate**

headquarters location: Peabody MA. **Average salary range of placements:** $20,000 - $29,999. **Number of placements per year:** 200 - 499.

OFFICE SPECIALISTS INC.
9101 East Kenyan Avenue, Suite 2200, Denver CO 80237. 303/721-8860. **Toll-free phone:** 800/392-JOBS. **Fax:** 303/756-9225. **Contact:** Don Patarino, Branch Manager. **E-mail address:** vsteeve@officespec.com. **World Wide Web address:** http://www.officespec.com. **Description:** A temporary and temp-to-hire agency. **Specializes in the areas of:** Accounting/Auditing; Administration; Health/Medical; Personnel/Labor Relations; Secretarial. **Corporate headquarters location:** Peabody MA. **Average salary range of placements:** $20,000 - $29,999.

OFFICE SPECIALISTS INC.
11990 Grant Street, Northglenn CO 80233. 303/451-0700. **Toll-free phone:** 800/392-JOBS. **Fax:** 303/756-9225. **Contact:** Jim Goodwyn, Branch Manager. **E-mail address:** vsteeve@officespec.com. **World Wide Web address:** http://www.officespec.com. **Description:** A temporary and temp-to-hire agency. **Specializes in the areas of:** Accounting/Auditing; Administration; Health/Medical; Personnel/Labor Relations; Secretarial. **Corporate headquarters location:** Peabody MA. **Average salary range of placements:** $20,000 - $29,999. **Number of placements per year:** 1000+.

OLSTEN STAFFING SERVICES
6025 South Quebec Street, Suite 250, Englewood CO 80111. 303/793-0330. **Fax:** 303/721-6418. **Contact:** Recruitment Specialist. **Description:** A temporary agency which also provides contract services. Company pays fee. **Specializes in the areas of:** Office Support; Personnel/Labor Relations; Secretarial. **Positions commonly filled include:** Administrative Manager; Clerical Supervisor; Customer Service Representative; Human Resources Specialist; Preschool Worker; Purchasing Agent/Manager; Typist/Word Processor. **Corporate headquarters location:** Melville NY. **Other U.S. locations:** Nationwide. **Average salary range of placements:** Less than $20,000. **Number of placements per year:** 1000+.

OLSTEN STAFFING SERVICES
10701 Melody Drive, Suite 425, Northglenn CO 80234. 303/252-8458. **Fax:** 303/252-8511. **Contact:** Kimberly Hauxhurst, Manager. **Description:** A temporary agency. Technical and computer training is available. Founded in 1950. Company pays fee. **Specializes in the areas of:** Administration; Engineering; Industrial; Manufacturing; Secretarial; Technical. **Positions commonly filled include:** Administrative Manager; Blue-Collar Worker Supervisor; Clerical Supervisor; Computer Programmer; Customer Service Representative; Draftsperson; Electrical/Electronics Engineer; Electrician; Mechanical Engineer; MIS Specialist; Software Engineer; Typist/Word Processor. **Benefits available to temporary workers:** Dental Insurance; Medical Insurance; Paid Holidays; Paid Vacation. **Corporate headquarters location:** Melville NY. **Other U.S. locations:** Nationwide. **Average salary range of placements:** Less than $20,000. **Number of placements per year:** 50 - 99.

ON CALL TECHNICAL SERVICES STAFFMARK
3850 North Grant Avenue, Loveland CO 80538. 970/667-3559. **Toll-free phone:** 800/555-8593. **Fax:** 970/667-8966. **Contact:** Larrie Gulden, Technical Division Manager. **E-mail address:** bkjb@csn.net. **World Wide Web address:** http://www.stafftech.com. **Description:** A temporary agency. On Call Technical Services is a division of Staffmark, which has offices nationwide. Company pays fee. **Specializes in the areas of:** Accounting/Auditing; Computer Science/Software; Engineering; Finance; General Management; Industrial; Manufacturing; Technical. **Positions commonly filled include:** Accountant/Auditor; Aerospace Engineer; Architect; Biomedical Engineer; Buyer; Civil Engineer; Clinical Lab Technician; Computer Programmer; Design Engineer; Designer; Draftsperson; Editor; Electrical/Electronics Engineer; Electrician; Environmental Engineer; Financial Analyst; Geologist/Geophysicist; Human Resources Specialist; Industrial Engineer; Internet Services Manager; Market Research Analyst; Mechanical Engineer; MIS Specialist; Operations/Production Manager; Paralegal; Purchasing Agent/Manager; Quality Control Supervisor; Software Engineer; Structural Engineer; Surveyor; Systems Analyst; Technical Writer/Editor; Transportation/Traffic Specialist. **Benefits available to temporary workers:** 401(k); Credit Union; Life Insurance; Medical Insurance; Paid Holidays; Paid Vacation. **Average salary range of placements:** $30,000 - $50,000. **Number of placements per year:** 1000+.

SOS STAFFING SERVICES
11059 East Bethany Road, Cambridge College Building, Suite 20, Aurora CO 80014. 303/329-3776. **Contact:** Sandra Houck, Office Manager. **Description:** A temporary agency. **Specializes in the areas of:** Accounting/Auditing; Banking; Clerical; Computer Hardware/Software; Engineering; Finance; Health/Medical; Insurance; Legal; Personnel/Labor Relations; Publishing; Real Estate; Sales; Technical. **Corporate headquarters location:** Salt Lake City UT. **Other U.S. locations:** AZ; ID; NM; NV; WY. **Number of placements per year:** 200 - 499.

SOS STAFFING SERVICES
1111 West Victory Way, Suite 108, Craig CO 81625. 970/824-0033. **Fax:** 970/824-0034. **Contact:** Manager. **Description:** A temporary agency. **Specializes in the areas of:** Accounting/Auditing; Banking; Food Industry; General Management; Industrial; Insurance; Manufacturing; Retail; Sales; Secretarial; Technical; Transportation. **Positions commonly filled include:** Accountant/Auditor; Automotive Mechanic; Bank Officer/Manager; Customer Service Representative; Geologist/Geophysicist; Medical Records Technician; Typist/Word Processor. **Corporate headquarters location:** Salt Lake City UT. **Other U.S. locations:** AZ; ID; NM; NV; WY. **Average salary range of placements:** Less than $20,000. **Number of placements per year:** 100 - 199.

SOS STAFFING SERVICES
344 East Foothills Parkway, Unit 24E, Fort Collins CO 80525. 970/282-4401. **Contact:** Branch Manager. **Description:** A temporary agency which also provides career/outplacement counseling. Company pays fee. **Specializes in the areas of:** Accounting/Auditing; Food Industry; Industrial; Manufacturing; Personnel/Labor Relations; Publishing; Retail; Secretarial; Technical. **Benefits available to temporary workers:** 401(k); Paid Vacation. **Corporate headquarters location:** Salt Lake City UT. **Other U.S. locations:** AZ; ID; NM; NV; WY. **Average salary range of placements:** $20,000 - $29,999. **Number of placements per year:** 200 - 499.

SENIOR SKILLS
2696 South Colorado Boulevard, Suite 555, Denver CO 80222. 303/756-4440. **Fax:** 303/756-0409. **Contact:** Joan R. Duncan, Owner. **Description:** A temporary employment service providing experienced personnel on a temporary, part-time, or permanent basis. Company pays fee. **Specializes in the areas of:** Clerical; Data Processing; Office Support; Word

Processing. **Average salary range of placements:** $20,000 - $29,999. **Number of placements per year:** 100 - 199.

STIVERS TEMPORARY PERSONNEL
2480 West 26th Avenue, Suite B26, Denver CO 80211. 303/458-1441. **Fax:** 303/477-8069. **Contact:** Sandra Nickerson, District Manager. **Description:** A temporary placement agency specializing in office support. **Specializes in the areas of:** Accounting/Auditing; Administration; Insurance; Legal; Office Support; Personnel/Labor Relations; Secretarial. **Positions commonly filled include:** Customer Service Representative; Typist/Word Processor. **Corporate headquarters location:** Chicago IL. **Other U.S. locations:** Nationwide. **Average salary range of placements:** $20,000 - $29,999. **Number of placements per year:** 1000+.

TPM STAFFING SERVICE
6021 South Syracuse, Suite 210, Englewood CO 80111. 303/771-7208. **Fax:** 303/771-7217. **Contact:** Jody Audet, Vice President. **Description:** A temporary agency. **Specializes in the areas of:** Administration; Food Industry; Light Industrial; Retail; Secretarial. **Positions commonly filled include:** Administrative Assistant; Blue-Collar Worker Supervisor; Claim Representative; Clerical Supervisor; Customer Service Representative; Industrial Engineer; Industrial Production Manager; Operations Manager; Project Manager; Secretary; Typist/Word Processor. **Other U.S. locations:** Phoenix AZ; Anaheim CA; Santa Ana CA. **Average salary range of placements:** $20,000 - $29,999. **Number of placements per year:** 1000+.

TECHNICAL AID CORPORATION
7222 Commerce Center Drive, Colorado Springs CO 80919-2630. 719/592-1133. **Fax:** 719/598-4193. **Contact:** David Landdeck, Branch Manager. **E-mail address:** cdosprings@techaid.com. **World Wide Web address:** http://www.rmii.com/techaid. **Description:** A temporary agency and contract services firm. Founded in 1969. Company pays fee. **Specializes in the areas of:** Administration; Computer Science/Software; Engineering; Industrial; Manufacturing; Personnel/Labor Relations. **Positions commonly filled include:** Administrative Manager; Agricultural Engineer; Architect; Biomedical Engineer; Buyer; Chemical Engineer; Chemist; Civil Engineer; Computer Programmer; Cost Estimator; Design Engineer; Designer; Draftsperson; Electrician; Environmental Engineer; Industrial Engineer; Industrial Production Manager; Management Analyst/Consultant; Mechanical Engineer; MIS Specialist; Multimedia Designer; Operations/Production Manager; Quality Control Supervisor; Software Engineer; Statistician; Structural Engineer; Technical Writer/Editor; Telecommunications Manager; Typist/Word Processor. **Benefits available to temporary workers:** 401(k). **Corporate headquarters location:** Boston MA. **Average salary range of placements:** $30,000 - $50,000. **Number of placements per year:** 500 - 999.

TODAYS TEMPORARY
1099 18th Street, Suite 1820, Denver CO 80202. 303/294-0055. **Fax:** 303/296-6373. **Contact:** Manager. **Description:** A temporary agency specializing in clerical and office support placement. **Specializes in the areas of:** Accounting/Auditing; Administration; Advertising; Architecture/Construction; Banking; Broadcasting; Computer Science/Software; Engineering; Finance; General Management; Industrial; Legal; Manufacturing; Nonprofit; Personnel/Labor Relations; Sales; Secretarial; Technical; Transportation. **Positions commonly filled include:** Administrative Manager; Advertising Clerk; Brokerage Clerk; Clerical Supervisor; Credit Manager; Paralegal; Services Sales Representative; Typist/Word Processor. **Corporate headquarters location:** Dallas TX. **Other U.S. locations:** Nationwide. **Average salary range of placements:** Less than $20,000. **Number of placements per year:** 200 - 499.

WESTERN STAFF SERVICES
6189 Lehman Drive, Suite 205, Colorado Springs CO 80918. 719/522-1200. **Fax:** 719/535-9555. **Contact:** Cheryl Saucedo, Area Manager. **Description:** A temporary agency. Company pays fee. **Specializes in the areas of:** Sales; Secretarial. **Positions commonly filled include:** Accountant/Auditor; Advertising Clerk; Claim Representative; Computer Programmer; Customer Service Representative; Design Engineer; Draftsperson; Electrical/Electronics Engineer; Software Engineer; Systems Analyst; Typist/Word Processor. **Corporate headquarters location:** Walnut Creek CA. **Other U.S. locations:** Nationwide. **Average salary range of placements:** $20,000 - $29,999. **Number of placements per year:** 200 - 499.

WESTERN STAFF SERVICES
2919 Valmont Road, Suite 206, Boulder CO 80301. 303/444-5982. **Fax:** 303/444-5914. **Contact:** Pam Fechuch, Area Manager. **Description:** A temporary agency. Company pays fee. **Specializes in the areas of:** Administration; Industrial; Secretarial; Technical. **Positions commonly filled include:** Electrical/Electronics Engineer; Industrial Production Manager; Purchasing Agent/Manager; Services Sales Representative; Software Engineer; Technical Writer/Editor; Typist/Word Processor. **Benefits available to temporary workers:** Dental Insurance; Medical Insurance; Paid Holidays; Paid Vacation. **Corporate headquarters location:** Walnut Creek CA. **Other U.S. locations:** Nationwide. **Number of placements per year:** 1000+.

CONTRACT SERVICES FIRMS

CDI CORPORATION
1115 Elkton Drive, Suite 101, Colorado Springs CO 80907. 719/592-0890. **Contact:** Manager. **World Wide Web address:** http://www.cdicorp.com. **Description:** A contract services firm that places technical and engineering consultants. **Specializes in the areas of:** Engineering; Technical. **Corporate headquarters location:** Philadelphia PA. **Other U.S. locations:** Nationwide. **International locations:** Worldwide.

CHUCK'S CONTRACT LABOR SERVICE, INC.
707 17th Street, MCI Tower, Suite 100, Denver CO 80201. 303/295-7336. **Contact:** Chuck Harbargh, President. **Description:** A contract services firm.

MARTINEZ & HROMADA ASSOCIATES, INC.
P.O. Box 21876, Denver CO 80221. 303/428-1728. **Fax:** 303/428-1769. **Contact:** Thomas Albert, Technical Support Specialist. **Description:** A contract services firm that provides engineering and technical personnel to a variety of industries. **Specializes in the areas of:** Engineering; Personnel/Labor Relations; Technical. **Positions commonly filled include:** Aerospace Engineer; Architect; Biomedical Engineer; Chemical Engineer; Chemist; Civil Engineer; Computer Programmer; Construction Contractor; Cost Estimator; Design Engineer; Designer; Editor; Electrical/Electronics Engineer; Environmental Engineer; Industrial Engineer; Industrial Production Manager; Mechanical Engineer; Metallurgical Engineer; Mining

Engineer; MIS Specialist; Nuclear Engineer; Petroleum Engineer; Purchasing Agent/Manager; Software Engineer; Stationary Engineer; Structural Engineer; Systems Analyst; Technical Writer/Editor. **Average salary range of placements:** $30,000 - $50,000. **Number of placements per year:** 100 - 199.

OLSTEN HEALTH SERVICES
1660 South Albion, Suite 1110, Denver CO 80222. 303/759-2991. **Fax:** 303/759-3844. **Contact:** Manager. **Description:** A contract services firm that provides in-home health care placements.

H.L. YOH COMPANY
11166 Huron Street, Unit 27, Northglenn CO 80237. 303/280-9000. **Contact:** Manager. **Description:** A contract services firm. **Specializes in the areas of:** Computer Hardware/Software; Engineering. **Positions commonly filled include:** Computer Operator; Computer Programmer; Designer; Draftsperson; Engineer.

CAREER/OUTPLACEMENT COUNSELING FIRMS

A AMERICAN RESUME SERVICE
38th & Washington Street, Wheat Ridge CO 80033. 303/451-1616. **Contact:** Manager. **Description:** A resume writing service.

ABOVE AND BEYOND RESUMES
1660 South Albion Street, Suite 309, Denver CO 80222. 303/512-0102. **Fax:** 303/782-5649. **Contact:** Maria Loewe, President. **Description:** A resume writing service.

ALLEN & ASSOCIATES
2000 South Colorado Boulevard, Suite 3000, Denver CO 80222. **Toll-free phone:** 800/562-7303. **Fax:** 303/691-2662. **Contact:** Office Manager. **World Wide Web address:** http://www.allenandassociates.com. **Description:** A career/outplacement counseling firm. **Corporate headquarters location:** Maitland FL. **Other U.S. locations:** Nationwide.

CREATIVE CAREER CONNECTIONS
2404 Sheffield Circle East, Fort Collins CO 80526. 970/221-3511. **Contact:** Nancy Valentine, Owner. **Description:** A career/outplacement counseling firm. **Specializes in the areas of:** Accounting/Auditing; Advertising; Architecture/Construction; Legal; Retail; Sales; Secretarial. **Positions commonly filled include:** Administrative Manager; Architect; Clerical Supervisor; Construction and Building Inspector; Cost Estimator; Counselor; Customer Service Representative; Draftsperson; Editor; General Manager; Manufacturer's/Wholesaler's Sales Rep.; Paralegal; Public Relations Specialist; Real Estate Agent; Restaurant/Food Service Manager; Securities Sales Representative; Services Sales Representative. **Number of placements per year:** 100 - 199.

40 PLUS OF COLORADO
5800 West Alameda Avenue, Lakewood CO 80226. 303/937-4956. **Fax:** 303/937-4953. **Contact:** Manager. **Description:** A career/outplacement counseling service. **Specializes in the areas of:** Accounting/Auditing; Administration; Advertising; Architecture/Construction; Banking; Broadcasting; Computer Hardware/Software; Education; Engineering; Fashion; Finance; Food Industry; General Management; Health/Medical; Industrial; Insurance; Legal; Manufacturing; Nonprofit; Personnel/Labor Relations; Publishing; Retail; Sales; Secretarial; Technical; Transportation. **Positions commonly filled include:** Accountant/Auditor; Administrative Assistant; Architect; Biological Scientist; Biomedical Engineer; Bookkeeper; Buyer; Ceramics Engineer; Chemical Engineer; Chemist; Civil Engineer; Claim Representative; Clerk; Commercial Artist; Computer Operator; Computer Programmer; Construction Trade Worker; Credit Manager; Customer Service Representative; Data Entry Clerk; Draftsperson; Driver; Editor; EDP Specialist; Electrical/Electronics Engineer; Factory Worker; Hotel Manager; Industrial Designer; Industrial Engineer; Legal Secretary; Light Industrial Worker; Manufacturing Engineer; Marketing Specialist; Mechanical Engineer; Medical Secretary; Metallurgical Engineer; MIS Specialist; Nurse; Operations/Production Manager; Public Relations Specialist; Purchasing Agent/Manager; Quality Control Supervisor; Receptionist; Reporter; Sales Representative; Secretary; Software Engineer; Systems Analyst; Technical Writer/Editor; Technician; Typist/Word Processor. **Number of placements per year:** 100 - 199.

CONNECTICUT

EXECUTIVE SEARCH FIRMS

RYAN ABBOTT SEARCH ASSOCIATES
250 West Main Street, Branford CT 06405. 203/488-7245. **Contact:** Manager. **Description:** An executive search firm. **Specializes in the areas of:** Finance; Pharmaceutical.

ABRAHAM & LONDON, LTD.
7 Old Sherman Turnpike, Suite 209, Danbury CT 06810-4174. 203/730-4000. **Fax:** 203/798-1784. **Contact:** Stuart R. Laub, President. **E-mail address:** stu4jobs@aol.com. **Description:** A worldwide executive search firm operating on a contingency basis that specializes in the placement of sales, marketing, and technical support staff in the telecommunications and computer industries. Company pays fee. **Specializes in the areas of:** Computer Science/Software; Sales. **Positions commonly filled include:** Electrical/Electronics Engineer; Internet Services Manager; Management Analyst/Consultant. **Corporate headquarters location:** This Location. **Other area locations:** Wilton CT.

ACCOUNTANTS EXECUTIVE SEARCH
ACCOUNTANTS ON CALL
2777 Summer Street, Stamford CT 06905. 203/327-5100. **Contact:** Manager. **Description:** An executive search firm. Accountants on Call (also at this location) is a temporary placement agency that focuses on accounting placements. **Specializes in the areas of:** Accounting/Auditing. **Positions commonly filled include:** Accountant.

ACHIEVA GROUP
1216 Farmington Way, West Hartford CT 06107. 860/561-2829. **Contact:** Manager. **Description:** An executive search firm. **Specializes in the areas of:** Finance; Information Systems.

ANDERSON GROUP
741 Boston Post Road, Suite 102, Guilford CT 06437. 203/458-7060. **Fax:** 203/458-7772. **Contact:** James L. Anderson, President. **Description:** An executive search firm. **Specializes in the areas of:** Health/Medical; Manufacturing. **Positions commonly filled include:** Biological Scientist; Biomedical Engineer; Chemical Engineer; Chemist; Designer; Mechanical Engineer; Metallurgical Engineer; Quality Control Supervisor.

ANDREWS & MAHON
P.O. Box 97, East Haddam CT 06423. 860/345-4778. **Fax:** 860/345-3944. **Contact:** Marj Andrews, CPC, Principal. **Description:** An executive search firm. Company pays fee. **Specializes in the areas of:** Insurance; Manufacturing. **Positions commonly filled include:** Accountant/Auditor; Adjuster; Administrative Manager; Budget Analyst; Claim Representative; Computer Programmer; Credit Manager; Financial Analyst; General Manager; Health Services Manager; Human Resources Manager; Insurance Agent/Broker; Mechanical Engineer; MIS Specialist; Quality Control Supervisor; Underwriter/Assistant Underwriter. **Number of placements per year:** 1 - 49.

ATLANTIC SEARCH GROUP
1100 Summer Street, Stamford CT 06905. 203/356-9540. **Contact:** Office Manager. **Description:** An executive search firm. **Specializes in the areas of:** Computer Programming.

BADAL ASSOCIATES INC.
1010 Washington Boulevard, Stamford CT 06901. 203/325-1988. **Contact:** Office Manager. **Description:** A generalist executive search firm.

BALDWIN ASSOCIATES INC.
39 Locust Avenue, Suite 205, New Canaan CT 06480. 203/966-5355. **Contact:** Office Manager. **Description:** A retained executive search firm. **Specializes in the areas of:** Computer Hardware/Software; Telecommunications.

BANKERS SEARCH
P.O. Box 854, Madison CT 06443. 203/245-0694. **Contact:** Manager. **Description:** An executive search firm. **Specializes in the areas of:** Banking.

BARRER LEGAL SEARCH
578 Post Road East, Suite 530, Westport CT 06880. 203/245-0694. **Contact:** Manager. **Description:** An executive search firm. **Specializes in the areas of:** Legal.

BLACKWOOD ASSOCIATES INC.
100 Business Park Drive, Suite 3, New Hartford CT 06057. 860/489-0494. **Contact:** Manager. **Description:** An executive search firm. **Specializes in the areas of:** Accounting/Auditing; Banking; Engineering; Health/Medical.

BOEHMER TOMASCO & ALEXANDER
6527 Main Street, Trumbull CT 06611. 203/452-3660. **Contact:** Manager. **Description:** An executive search firm. **Specializes in the areas of:** Technical.

BOND & COMPANY
10 Saugatuck Avenue, Westport CT 06880. 203/221-3233. **Contact:** Manager. **Description:** An executive search firm.

BONNELL ASSOCIATES LTD.
2960 Post Road, Suite 200, Southport CT 06490. 203/226-2624. **Contact:** Manager. **Description:** An executive search firm. **Specializes in the areas of:** Health/Medical.

BUXBAUM/RINK CONSULTING
P.O. Box 3988, Woodbridge CT 06525. 203/389-5949. **Fax:** 203/397-0615. **Contact:** Sherrie Rink, Partner. **Description:** An executive search firm. Company pays fee. **Specializes in the areas of:** Accounting/Auditing; Finance; General Management; Personnel/Labor Relations; Sales. **Positions commonly filled include:** Accountant/Auditor; Controller; Credit Manager; Human Resources Manager; Marketing Specialist. **Number of placements per year:** 1 - 49.

CAHILL ASSOCIATES
P.O. Box 401, Southington CT 06489-2506. 860/628-3963. **Fax:** 860/628-3966. **Contact:** Peter M. Cahill, President. **Description:** An executive search firm focusing on engineering placements. Company pays fee. **Specializes in the areas of:** Engineering; General Management; Industrial; Manufacturing; Personnel/Labor Relations; Sales; Technical. **Positions commonly filled include:** Buyer; Chemical Engineer; Chemist; Designer; Electrical/ Electronics Engineer; Environmental Engineer; General Manager; Human Resources Manager; Industrial Engineer; Industrial Production Manager; Market Research Analyst; Software Engineer. **Average salary range of placements:** More than $50,000.

THE CAMBRIDGE GROUP, LTD.
1175 Post Road East, Westport CT 06880. 203/226-4243. **Contact:** Manager. **Description:** An executive search firm.

CAREER PROSPECTS
991 Main Street, Suite 3D, East Hartford CT 06108. 860/291-9817. **Contact:** Manager. **Description:** An executive search firm. **Specializes in the areas of:** Data Processing.

CHARTER PERSONNEL SERVICES
P.O. Box 1070, Danbury CT 06813-1070. 203/744-6440. **Physical address:** 52 Federal Road, Danbury CT. **Fax:** 203/748-2122. **Contact:** James T. Fornabaio, President. **Description:** An executive search firm which also provides temporary placements. Company pays fee. **Specializes in the areas of:** Accounting/Auditing; Administration; Biology; Computer Science/Software; Engineering; General Management; Health/Medical; Industrial; Legal; Manufacturing; Secretarial; Technical. **Positions commonly filled include:** Accountant/Auditor; Administrative Manager; Biomedical Engineer; Chemical Engineer; Chemist; Electrical/Electronics Engineer; Industrial Engineer; Mechanical Engineer; Paralegal; Pharmacist; Physician; Quality Control Supervisor; Software Engineer; Statistician; Typist/Word Processor; Veterinarian. **Benefits available to temporary workers:** Medical Insurance. **Number of placements per year:** 200 - 499.

CHAVES & ASSOCIATES
7 Whitney Street Extension, Westport CT 06880. 203/222-2222. **Fax:** 203/222-2223. **Contact:** Victor Chaves, CPC, President. **World Wide Web address:** http://www.chaves.com. **Description:** An executive search firm. Company pays fee. **Specializes in the areas of:** Computer Science/Software. **Positions commonly filled include:** Computer Programmer; Database Manager; Internet Services Manager; MIS Specialist; Multimedia Designer; Software Engineer; Systems Analyst. **Other U.S. locations:** Nationwide. **Average salary range of placements:** More than $50,000. **Number of placements per year:** 200 - 499.

CHENEY ASSOCIATES
3190 Whitney Avenue, Building 1, Hamden CT 06518. 203/281-3736. **Contact:** Manager. **Description:** An executive search firm. **Specializes in the areas of:** Administration; Engineering; Information Technology.

CLIFFORD GARZONE ASSOCIATES
321 Main Street, Farmington CT 06032. 860/675-7054. **Fax:** 860/673-5459. **Contact:** Dawn Garzone, CPC, Search Consultant. **Description:** An executive search firm. Company pays fee. **Specializes in the areas of:** Insurance; Legal. **Positions commonly filled include:** Actuary; Attorney; Claim Representative; Underwriter/Assistant Underwriter. **Number of placements per year:** 1 - 49.

CUPPLES CONSULTING SERVICES
P.O. Box 2526, Stamford CT 06906-0526. 203/327-4406. **Fax:** 203/327-4688. **Contact:** Gerard A. Cupples, Owner. **E-mail address:** gercup@aol.com. **Description:** A worldwide executive search firm operating on a retainer basis that specializes in the medical equipment industry. Company pays fee. **Specializes in the areas of:** Engineering; General Management; Manufacturing; Sales. **Positions commonly filled include:** Biomedical Engineer; Electrical/Electronics Engineer; Nuclear Medicine Technologist; Radiological Technologist. **Corporate headquarters location:** This Location. **Average salary range of placements:** More than $50,000. **Number of placements per year:** 1 - 49.

DATA TRENDS INC.
4133 Whitney Avenue, Hamden CT 06518-1432. 203/287-8485. **Fax:** 203/248-8138. **Contact:** George Flohr, Manager. **E-mail address:** dti2@ix.netcom.com. **Description:** An executive search firm operating on a contingency basis. Data Trends specializes in placing information systems professionals in Connecticut, suburban New York, and western Massachusetts. Company pays fee. **Specializes in the areas of:** Administration; Computer Science/Software. **Positions commonly filled include:** Computer Programmer; Internet Services Manager; MIS Specialist; Software Engineer; Systems Analyst. **Average salary range of placements:** $30,000 - $100,000. **Number of placements per year:** 100 - 199.

DATAPATH SEARCH CORPORATION
32 Sherwood Place, Greenwich CT 06830. 203/869-3536. **Contact:** Manager. **Description:** An executive search firm. **Specializes in the areas of:** Computer Programming; MIS/EDP. **Positions commonly filled include:** Computer Programmer.

DEVELOPMENT SYSTEMS, INC.
The Highland Building, 402 Highland Avenue, Suite 7, Cheshire CT 06410. 203/272-1117. **Contact:** Arnold C. Bernstein, President. **Description:** An executive search firm. Company pays fee. **Specializes in the areas of:** Administration; Computer Hardware/Software; Personnel/Labor Relations; Retail. **Number of placements per year:** 1 - 49.

DIVERSITY RECRUITING SERVICES INC.
621 Farmington Avenue, Hartford CT 06105. 860/231-7786. **Fax:** 860/231-9730. **Contact:** Douglas Dorsey, President. **Description:** An executive search firm. Company pays fee. **Specializes in the areas of:** Accounting/Auditing; Computer Science/Software; Engineering; Finance; Food Industry; General Management; Sales. **Positions commonly filled include:** Accountant/Auditor; Budget Analyst; Chemical Engineer; Civil Engineer; Financial Analyst; Industrial Engineer; Management Trainee; Mechanical Engineer; MIS Specialist; Restaurant/Food Service Manager; Securities Sales Representative; Software Engineer; Systems Analyst; Telecommunications Manager; Underwriter/Assistant Underwriter. **Average salary range of placements:** More than $50,000. **Number of placements per year:** 1 - 49.

DREW PROFESSIONAL RECRUITERS
15 Pepper Ridge Circle, Stratford CT 06497. 203/377-7566. **Contact:** Manager. **Description:** An executive search firm. **Specializes in the areas of:** Health/Medical.

EMMONS ASSOCIATES
226 Lost District Drive, New Canaan CT 06840. 203/966-4584. **Fax:** 203/972-6707. **Contact:** Manager. **Description:** An executive search firm. **Specializes in the areas of:** Computer Hardware/Software.

ENGINEERING RESOURCE RECRUITERS
The Exchange, 270 Farmington Avenue, Suite 306, Farmington CT 06032. 860/674-0366. **Fax:** 860/674-1267. **Contact:** Office Manager. **Description:** An executive search firm. **Specializes in the areas of:** Engineering.

FAIRFAXX CORPORATION
17 High Street, Norwalk CT 06851. 203/838-8300. **Fax:** 203/855-8320. **Contact:** Jeff Thomas, Owner. **Description:** An executive search firm. Fairfaxx Corporation also operates as an employment agency and offers permanent and temporary placements. Company pays fee.

FINANCIAL CAREERS
P.O. Box 125, Rocky Hill CT 06067. 860/563-9991. **Contact:** Manager. **Description:** An executive search

firm. **Specializes in the areas of:** Accounting/Auditing; Banking; Finance.

FINANCIAL EXECUTIVE SEARCH
474 Maple Avenue, Old Saybrook CT 06475. 860/395-5679. **Contact:** Manager. **Description:** An executive search firm that focuses on the placement of bank officers with the occasional placement of other financial professionals. **Specializes in the areas of:** Banking. **Positions commonly filled include:** Bank Officer/Manager.

FLYNN & HANNOCK INC.
1001 Farmington Avenue, West Hartford CT 06107. 860/521-5005. **Contact:** Manager. **Description:** An executive search firm. **Specializes in the areas of:** Personnel/Labor Relations. **Positions commonly filled include:** Human Resources Manager; Human Resources Specialist.

F-O-R-T-U-N-E PERSONNEL CONSULTANTS
36 Mill Plain Road, Suite 308, Danbury CT 06811. 203/798-2700. **Fax:** 203/798-2708. **Contact:** Manager. **Description:** An executive search firm. **Specializes in the areas of:** Health/Medical; Pharmaceutical. **Corporate headquarters location:** New York NY. **Other U.S. locations:** Nationwide.

FRIEDMAN ASSOCIATES
110 Washington Avenue, North Haven CT 06473. 203/234-6303. **Contact:** Manager. **Description:** An executive search firm. **Specializes in the areas of:** Engineering.

GATFIELD GREENWICH & ASSOCIATES
537 Steam Belt Road, 4th Floor, Greenwich CT 06830. 203/622-9191. **Contact:** Manager. **Description:** An executive search firm.

GREY ASSOCIATES
21 Eastwood Road, Norwalk CT 06851. 203/849-9291. **Contact:** Manager. **Description:** An executive search firm. **Specializes in the areas of:** Information Systems.

ALICE GROVES CO.
700 Canal Street, Stamford CT 06902. 203/324-3225. **Contact:** Ken Leavee, President. **Description:** An executive search firm. Company pays fee. **Specializes in the areas of:** Retail. **Positions commonly filled include:** Human Resources Manager; Marketing Specialist; Merchandiser; MIS Specialist; Operations/Production Manager. **Average salary range of placements:** More than $50,000. **Number of placements per year:** 1 - 49.

ROBERT HALF INTERNATIONAL ACCOUNTEMPS
555 Long Wharf Drive, Suite 9H, New Haven CT 06511. 203/562-9262. **Contact:** Manager. **E-mail address:** new_haven@roberthalf.com. **World Wide Web address:** http://www.roberthalf.com. **Description:** An executive search firm. Accountemps (also at this location) provides temporary placements. **Specializes in the areas of:** Accounting/Auditing. **Corporate headquarters location:** Menlo Park CA. **Other U.S. locations:** Nationwide.

ROBERT HALF INTERNATIONAL ACCOUNTEMPS
One Corporate Drive, Suite 118, Shelton CT 06484. 203/929-2600. **Contact:** Manager. **World Wide Web address:** http://www.roberthalf.com. **Description:** An executive search firm. Accountemps (also at this location) provides temporary placements. **Specializes in the areas of:** Accounting/Auditing. **Corporate headquarters location:** Menlo Park CA. **Other U.S. locations:** Nationwide.

ROBERT HALF INTERNATIONAL ACCOUNTEMPS
3001 Summer Street, Stamford CT 06905. 203/324-3399. **Contact:** Manager. **E-mail address:** stamford@roberthalf.com. **World Wide Web address:** http://www.roberthalf.com. **Description:** An executive search firm. Accountemps (also at this location) provides temporary placements. **Specializes in the areas of:** Accounting/Auditing. **Corporate headquarters location:** Menlo Park CA. **Other U.S. locations:** Nationwide.

HARBOR ASSOCIATES
70 New Canaan Avenue, Norwalk CT 06850. 203/849-0863. **Contact:** Manager. **Description:** An executive search firm. **Specializes in the areas of:** Accounting/Auditing; Finance. **Positions commonly filled include:** Accountant/Auditor; Tax Specialist.

HARRIS HEERY AND ASSOCIATES, INC.
40 Richards Avenue, Norwalk CT 06854. 203/857-0808. **Contact:** William Heery, Partner. **Description:** An executive search firm. **Specializes in the areas of:** Food Industry; Sales. **Positions commonly filled include:** Advertising Account Executive; Marketing Specialist. **Number of placements per year:** 50 - 99.

HIGBEE ASSOCIATES
112 Rowayton Avenue, Rowayton CT 06853. 203/853-7600. **Fax:** 203/853-2426. **Contact:** R. Higbee, President. **Description:** An executive search firm operating on a retained basis. Company pays fee. **Specializes in the areas of:** Banking; Health/Medical; Technical; Telecommunications. **Positions commonly filled include:** Human Resources Manager; Market Research Analyst; Marketing Manager; Pharmacist; Physician; Sales Executive; Sales Manager; Software Engineer; Systems Analyst. **Average salary range of placements:** More than $50,000. **Number of placements per year:** 50 - 99.

HIGH-TECH RECRUITERS
30 High Street, Hartford CT 06103. 860/527-4262. **Contact:** Manager. **Description:** An executive search firm. **Specializes in the areas of:** Accounting/Auditing; Engineering; Finance; Information Technology.

HIPP WATERS PROFESSIONAL SEARCH
777 Summer Street, Stamford CT 06901. 203/357-8400. **Contact:** Manager. **Description:** An executive search firm. **Specializes in the areas of:** Accounting/Auditing; Computer Science/Software; Finance; Information Systems; Insurance.

HOBSON ASSOCIATES
293 Spring Street, Southington CT 06489. 860/621-3651. **Contact:** Manager. **Description:** An executive search firm. **Specializes in the areas of:** Sales.

HUMAN RESOURCE CONSULTANTS LTD.
350 Silas Deane Highway, Suite 303, Wethersfield CT 06109. 860/257-7300. **Contact:** Joseph Koneski, CEO. **Description:** An executive search firm. Company pays fee. **Specializes in the areas of:** Engineering; Industrial; Manufacturing; Personnel/Labor Relations; Technical. **Positions commonly filled include:** Biomedical Engineer; Buyer; Chemical Engineer; Chemist; Design Engineer; Designer; Electrical/Electronics Engineer; Environmental Engineer; Health Services Manager; Human Resources Manager; Industrial Engineer; Mechanical Engineer; Pharmacist; Physical Therapist; Physician; Purchasing Agent/Manager; Quality Control Supervisor; Software Engineer; Telecommunications Manager. **Average salary range of placements:** More than $50,000. **Number of placements per year:** 50 - 99.

HUNTINGTON GROUP
6527 Main Street, Trumbull CT 06611. 203/261-1166. **Fax:** 203/452-9153. **Contact:** Rose Rutle, Associate. **World Wide Web address:** http://www.hgllc.com. **Description:** An executive search firm operating on a retained basis. Company pays fee. **Positions commonly filled include:** MIS Specialist. **Average salary range of placements:** More than $50,000. **Number of placements per year:** 100 - 199.

INFONET RESOURCES
10 Columbus Boulevard, Hartford CT 06106. 860/246-3000. **Contact:** Manager. **Description:** An executive search firm. **Specializes in the areas of:** Computer Programming; Computer Science/Software; Information Technology.

JOHNSON & COMPANY
11 Grumman Hill Road, Wilton CT 06897. 203/761-1212. **Contact:** Manager. **Description:** An executive search firm.

KILMAN ADVISORY GROUP
406 Farmington Avenue, Farmington CT 06032-1964. 860/676-7817. **Fax:** 860/676-7839. **Contact:** Paul Kilman, Principal. **Description:** An executive search firm operating on a retainer basis that focuses on the legal field. **Specializes in the areas of:** Legal. **Positions commonly filled include:** Attorney. **Average salary range of placements:** More than $50,000. **Number of placements per year:** 1 - 49.

KORN/FERRY INTERNATIONAL
One Landmark Square, Stamford CT 06901. 203/359-3350. **Contact:** Manager. **Description:** An executive search firm that places upper-level managers in a variety of industries. **Corporate headquarters location:** Los Angeles CA. **International locations:** Worldwide. **Average salary range of placements:** More than $50,000.

LUTZ ASSOCIATES
9 Stephen Street, Manchester CT 06040. 860/647-9338. **Fax:** 860/647-7918. **Contact:** Al Lutz, Owner. **Description:** An executive search firm. Founded in 1987. Company pays fee. **Specializes in the areas of:** Automation/Robotics; Computer Science/Software; Engineering; Industrial; Manufacturing; Technical. **Positions commonly filled include:** Aerospace Engineer; Biomedical Engineer; Computer Programmer; Design Engineer; MIS Specialist; Quality Control Supervisor; Software Engineer; Systems Analyst; Technical Writer/Editor; Telecommunications Manager. **Average salary range of placements:** More than $50,000. **Number of placements per year:** 1 - 49.

MJF ASSOCIATES
P.O. Box 132, Wallingford CT 06492. 203/284-9878. **Fax:** 203/284-9871. **Contact:** Matt Furman, President. **Description:** An executive search firm focusing on professional and technical placements in sales, marketing, engineering, and management. Company pays fee. **Specializes in the areas of:** Engineering; General Management; Industrial; Manufacturing; Sales; Technical. **Positions commonly filled include:** Aerospace Engineer; Branch Manager; Buyer; Chemical Engineer; Computer Programmer; Customer Service Representative; Environmental Engineer; Industrial Engineer; Internet Services Manager; MIS Specialist; Software Engineer; Telecommunications Manager. **Average salary range of placements:** More than $50,000. **Number of placements per year:** 1 - 49.

MRG SEARCH & PLACEMENT INC.
2679 Whitney Avenue, Hamden CT 06518. 203/624-0161. **Contact:** Manager. **Description:** An executive search firm. **Specializes in the areas of:** Computer Programming; Health/Medical. **Positions commonly filled include:** Computer Programmer; Occupational Therapist; Physical Therapist; Physician; Speech-Language Pathologist.

MANAGEMENT RECRUITERS INTERNATIONAL
P.O. Box 1017, Winsted CT 06098-1017. 860/738-5035. **Fax:** 860/738-5039. **Contact:** Jack Bourque, President. **E-mail address:** mriwin@snet.net. **Description:** An executive search firm. Company pays fee. **Specializes in the areas of:** Engineering; Manufacturing; Operations Management; Sales; Scientific; Technical. **Positions commonly filled include:** Chemical Engineer; Electrical/Electronics Engineer; General Manager; Mechanical Engineer; Metallurgical Engineer; Process Engineer; Sales and Marketing Representative. **Corporate headquarters location:** Cleveland OH. **Other U.S. locations:** Nationwide. **Number of placements per year:** 50 - 99.

MANAGEMENT RECRUITERS INTERNATIONAL
57 Danbury Road, Wilton CT 06897-4439. 203/834-1111. **Contact:** Robert Schmidt, Manager. **Description:** An executive search firm. **Specializes in the areas of:** Accounting/Auditing; Administration; Advertising; Architecture/Construction; Banking; Communications; Computer Science/Software; Construction; Electrical; Engineering; Finance; Food Industry; Health/Medical; Insurance; Legal; Manufacturing; MIS/EDP; Operations Management; Personnel/Labor Relations; Procurement; Publishing; Retail; Sales; Technical; Textiles; Transportation. **Corporate headquarters location:** Cleveland OH. **Other U.S. locations:** Nationwide.

MANAGEMENT RECRUITERS INTERNATIONAL
61 Cherry Street, Milford CT 06460. 203/876-8755. **Fax:** 203/877-1281. **Contact:** Sandra Campbell, Senior Partner. **Description:** An executive search firm that focuses on placing executive management, middle management, and technical professional staff. Company pays fee. **Specializes in the areas of:** Biology; Biotechnology; Computer Science/Software; Engineering; Health/Medical; Industrial; Manufacturing; Pharmaceutical; Sales; Technical. **Positions commonly filled include:** Biochemist; Biological Scientist; Biomedical Engineer; Chemical Engineer; Chemist; Clinical Lab Technician; Computer Programmer; Design Engineer; Environmental Engineer; Food Scientist/Technologist; Industrial Engineer; Materials Engineer; Mechanical Engineer; Quality Control Supervisor; Science Technologist; Software Engineer; Statistician. **Corporate headquarters location:** Cleveland OH. **Other U.S. locations:** Nationwide. **Average salary range of placements:** More than $50,000. **Number of placements per year:** 1 - 49.

MANAGEMENT RECRUITERS INTERNATIONAL
100 Melrose Avenue, Greenwich CT 06830. 203/861-2235. **Fax:** 203/861-2245. **Contact:** John Brown, President. **Description:** An executive search firm. **Specializes in the areas of:** Banking; Engineering; Finance. **Positions commonly filled include:** Bank Officer/Manager; Human Resources Manager; Industrial Engineer; Market Research Analyst; MIS Specialist; Radio/TV Announcer/Broadcaster; Systems Analyst. **Corporate headquarters location:** Cleveland OH. **Other U.S. locations:** Nationwide.

MANAGEMENT RECRUITERS INTERNATIONAL
2139 Silas Deane Highway, Rocky Hill CT 06067. 860/563-1268. **Contact:** Manager. **Description:** An executive search firm. **Specializes in the areas of:** Administration; General Management. **Corporate headquarters location:** Cleveland OH. **Other U.S. locations:** Nationwide.

MANAGEMENT RECRUITERS INTERNATIONAL
154 West Street, Building 3, Unit C, Cromwell CT 06146. 860/635-0612. **Contact:** Manager. **Description:** An executive search firm. **Specializes in the areas of:** Sales. **Corporate headquarters location:** Cleveland OH. **Other U.S. locations:** Nationwide.

MANAGEMENT SEARCH
50 Founders Plaza, East Hartford CT 06108. 860/289-1581. **Contact:** Manager. **Description:** An executive search firm. **Specializes in the areas of:** Accounting/Auditing; Engineering; Environmental; Information Systems; Manufacturing.

MAXWELL-MARCUS STAFFING CONSULTANTS
266 Broad Street, Milford CT 06460-0591. 203/874-5424. **Fax:** 203/874-5571. **Contact:** Dan Regan, President. **E-mail address:** maxwell@interserv.com. **World Wide Web address:** http://www.occ.com/mmsc. **Description:** An executive search firm operating on a contingency basis. Company pays fee. **Specializes in the areas of:** Computer Science/Software; Engineering; General Management; Sales; Technical. **Positions commonly filled include:** Administrative Manager; Applications Engineer; Architect; Biochemist; Biological Scientist; Biomedical Engineer; Broadcast Technician; Chemical Engineer; Chemist; Civil Engineer; Computer Operator; Computer Programmer; Database Manager; Design Engineer; Electrical/Electronics Engineer; Environmental Engineer; Industrial Engineer; Industrial Production Manager; Internet Services Manager; Management Analyst/Consultant; Marketing Manager; Mechanical Engineer; MIS Specialist; Multimedia Designer; Sales Executive; Sales Manager; Software Engineer; Systems Analyst; Technical Writer/Editor; Telecommunications Manager; Webmaster. **Average salary range of placements:** More than $50,000. **Number of placements per year:** 50 - 99.

C.A. McINNIS & ASSOCIATES
203 Broad Street, Suite 6, Milford CT 06460. 203/876-7110. **Fax:** 203/783-1230. **Contact:** Carol McInnis, President. **E-mail address:** camcinis@aol.com. **Description:** An executive search firm operating on a retained basis. Company pays fee. **Specializes in the areas of:** Pharmaceutical. **Positions commonly filled include:** Biological Scientist; Chemist; Database Manager; Market Research Analyst; Marketing Manager; Pharmacist; Physician; Project Manager; Registered Nurse; Sales Executive; Statistician. **Average salary range of placements:** More than $50,000. **Number of placements per year:** 50 - 99.

McINTYRE ASSOCIATES
P.O. Box 533, Unionville CT 06085. 860/673-0030. **Contact:** Manager. **Description:** An executive search firm. **Specializes in the areas of:** Computer Hardware/Software; Telecommunications.

THE McKNIGHT GROUP
4 Landmark Square, Suite 201, Stamford CT 06901. 203/357-1891. **Fax:** 203/323-5612. **Contact:** Richard F. McKnight, President. **Description:** An executive search firm. Company pays fee. **Specializes in the areas of:** Accounting/Auditing; Clerical; Finance; Personnel/Labor Relations; Sales; Secretarial; Software Engineering. **Positions commonly filled include:** Accountant/Auditor; Administrative Assistant; Bank Officer/Manager; Bookkeeper; Buyer; Clerk; EDP Specialist; Electrical/Electronics Engineer; Financial Analyst; General Manager; Legal Secretary; Marketing Specialist; Receptionist; Sales Representative; Secretary; Software Engineer; Typist/Word Processor. **Average salary range of placements:** More than $50,000. **Number of placements per year:** 50 - 99.

NLO ASSOCIATES
LA POINTE ASSOCIATES
365 Highland Avenue, Suite 101, Cheshire CT 06410. 203/250-1900. **Contact:** Manager. **Description:** An executive search firm that focuses on health care placements. La Pointe Associates, also at this location, focuses on placements in the engineering industry.

PRH MANAGEMENT, INC.
2777 Summer Street, Stamford CT 06905. 203/327-3900. **Fax:** 203/327-6324. **Contact:** Peter R. Hendelman, President. **Description:** An executive search firm. Company pays fee. **Specializes in the areas of:** Accounting/Auditing; Advertising; Bookkeeping; Computer Science/Software; Engineering; Finance; General Management; Sales; Technical. **Positions commonly filled include:** Accountant/Auditor; Branch Manager; Software Engineer; Telecommunications Manager. **Average salary range of placements:** More than $50,000.

BARRY PERSKY & CO.
256 Post Road East, Westport CT 06880. 203/454-4500. **Fax:** 203/454-3318. **Contact:** Barry Persky, President. **E-mail address:** bpco@pcnet.com. **Description:** An executive search firm. **Specializes in the areas of:** Engineering; Finance; Food Industry; General Management; Health/Medical; Industrial; Manufacturing; Personnel/Labor Relations; Sales; Technical; Transportation. **Positions commonly filled include:** Chemical Engineer; Civil Engineer; Editor; Environmental Engineer; General Manager; Human Resources Manager; Mechanical Engineer; MIS Specialist; Operations/Production Manager; Science Technologist; Structural Engineer; Technical Writer/Editor. **Average salary range of placements:** More than $50,000.

EDWARD J. POSPESIL & COMPANY
44 Long Hill Road, Guilford CT 06437-1870. 203/458-6566. **Fax:** 203/458-6564. **Contact:** Ed Pospesil, Owner/Principal. **E-mail address:** infojobs@ejp.com. **World Wide Web address:** http://www.ejp.com. **Description:** An executive search firm. Company pays fee. **Specializes in the areas of:** Administration; Computer Science/Software; Technical. **Positions commonly filled include:** Computer Programmer; Internet Services Manager; Management Analyst/Consultant; MIS Specialist; Software Engineer; Systems Analyst; Technical Writer/Editor; Telecommunications Manager. **Number of placements per year:** 1 - 49.

QUALITY CONTROL RECRUITERS
P.O. Box 1900, Bristol CT 06011-1900. 203/582-0003. **Fax:** 203/585-7395. **Contact:** Charles V. Urban, President. **Description:** An executive search firm specializing in placing quality control and reliability professionals in a variety of industries. Company pays fee. **Specializes in the areas of:** Engineering; Food Industry; Industrial; Manufacturing; Quality Assurance. **Positions commonly filled include:** Engineer; Food Scientist/Technologist; Quality Control Supervisor; Statistician. **Average salary range of placements:** More than $50,000. **Number of placements per year:** 50 - 99.

RETAIL EXECUTIVES
265 Bic Drive, Milford CT 06460. 203/877-9293. **Contact:** Manager. **Description:** An executive search firm that provides placement in the retail industry.

RETAIL RECRUITERS
2189 Silas Deane Highway, Rocky Hill CT 06067. 860/721-9550. **Contact:** Manager. **Description:** An executive search firm. **Specializes in the areas of:** Retail.

RUSSO ASSOCIATES
P.O. Box 1065, Fairfield CT 06432. 203/333-7761. **Contact:** Manager. **Description:** An executive search firm. **Specializes in the areas of:** Engineering; Technical.

SEDER ASSOCIATES
998 Farmington Avenue, Suite 201, West Hartford CT 06107. 860/236-7511. **Contact:** Manager. **Description:** An executive search firm. **Specializes in the areas of:** Legal.

SIGER & ASSOCIATES
966 Westover Road, Stamford CT 06902. 203/348-0976. **Fax:** 203/348-0698. **Contact:** Ray Milo, President. **E-mail address:** rmilo711@aol.com. **Description:** An executive search firm. Company pays fee. **Specializes in the areas of:** Banking; Computer Science/Software; Consulting; Finance; Health/Medical. **Average salary range of placements:** More than $50,000. **Number of placements per year:** 1 - 49.

HOWARD W. SMITH ASSOCIATES
P.O. Box 230877, Hartford CT 06123-0877. 860/549-2060. **Contact:** Howard Smith, Principal. **Description:** An executive search firm operating on a retainer basis and specializing in the financial services industry. **Specializes in the areas of:** Accounting/Auditing; Banking; Finance; Health/Medical; Insurance; Personnel/Labor Relations. **Positions commonly filled include:** Accountant/Auditor; Actuary; Attorney; Economist; Health Services Manager; Investment Manager; Real Estate Appraiser. **Average salary range of placements:** More than $50,000. **Number of placements per year:** 1 - 49.

SNYDER & COMPANY
35 Old Avon Village, Suite 185, Avon CT 06001-3822. 860/521-9760. **Fax:** 860/521-2495. **Contact:** James F. Snyder, President. **E-mail address:** 74563.3223@compuserve.com. **Description:** An executive search firm. Company pays fee. **Average salary range of placements:** More than $50,000. **Number of placements per year:** 1 - 49.

SOURCE SERVICES CORPORATION
Enterprise Corporate Tower, One Corporate Drive, Suite 215, Shelton CT 06484-6209. 203/944-9001. **Fax:** 203/926-1414. **Contact:** Manager. **Description:** An executive search firm. Company pays fee. **Specializes in the areas of:** Accounting/Auditing; Banking; Computer Science/Software; Engineering; Finance. **Positions commonly filled include:** Accountant/Auditor; Actuary; Bank Officer/Manager; Budget Analyst; Computer Programmer; Credit Manager; Design Engineer; Financial Analyst; Human Resources Manager; Internet Services Manager; MIS Specialist; Multimedia Designer; Operations/Production Manager; Software Engineer; Statistician; Systems Analyst; Technical Writer/Editor; Telecommunications Manager. **Average salary range of placements:** $30,000 - $50,000.

SOURCE SERVICES CORPORATION
111 Founders Plaza, Suite 1501, East Hartford CT 06108. 860/528-0300. **Fax:** 860/291-9497. **Contact:** Manager. **Description:** An executive search firm. The divisions at this location include Source EDP, Source Finance, and Accountant Source Temps. **Specializes in the areas of:** Accounting/Auditing; Computer Hardware/Software; Finance; Information Technology.

STEWART ASSOCIATES
410 Asylum Avenue, Hartford CT 06103. 860/548-1388. **Contact:** Manager. **Description:** An executive search firm. **Specializes in the areas of:** Engineering; Sales.

STRATEGIC EXECUTIVES, INC.
6 Landmark Square, 4th Floor, Stamford CT 06901. 203/359-5757. **Contact:** Manager. **Description:** An executive search firm. **Specializes in the areas of:** Finance; Marketing.

STRATEGIC SEARCH
1344 Silas Deane Highway, Rocky Hill CT 06067. 860/258-1995. **Contact:** Manager. **Description:** An executive search firm. **Specializes in the areas of:** Administration; Engineering; Finance; Insurance.

TECHNICAL SEARCH
304 Main Avenue, Suite 300, Norwalk CT 06851. 203/846-9030. **Contact:** Manager. **Description:** An executive search firm. **Specializes in the areas of:** Computer Science/Software; Engineering. **Positions commonly filled include:** Electrical/Electronics Engineer; Software Developer; Software Engineer.

TUCKER GROUP
111 Reef Road, Fairfield CT 06430. 203/256-3789. **Fax:** 203/256-3790. **Contact:** Brad Hartman, Personnel. **Description:** An executive search firm. Company pays fee. **Specializes in the areas of:** Health/Medical; Sales. **Positions commonly filled include:** Market Research Analyst; Occupational Therapist; Physical Therapist; Speech-Language Pathologist. **Average salary range of placements:** More than $50,000. **Number of placements per year:** 50 - 99.

VEZAN ASSOCIATES
P.O. Box 270753, West Hartford CT 06127-0753. 860/521-8848. **Contact:** Manager. **Description:** An executive search firm operating on a contingency basis. **Specializes in the areas of:** Health/Medical.

WALLACE ASSOCIATES
P.O. Box 11294, Waterbury CT 06703. 203/575-1311. **Fax:** 203/879-2407. **Contact:** Greg Gordon, Principal. **Description:** An executive search firm. Company pays fee. **Specializes in the areas of:** Computer Hardware/Software; Engineering; General Management; Health/Medical; Manufacturing; Packaging; Physician Executive; Technical. **Positions commonly filled include:** Biological Scientist; Biomedical Engineer; Chemical Engineer; Chemist; Computer Programmer; EDP Specialist; Electrical/Electronics Engineer; Industrial Designer; Industrial Engineer; Manufacturing Engineer; Mechanical Engineer; Metallurgical Engineer; MIS Specialist; Operations Research Analyst; Quality Control Supervisor; Software Engineer. **Number of placements per year:** 1 - 49.

WARD LIEBELT ASSOCIATES, INC.
50 Riverside Avenue, Westport CT 06880. 203/454-0414. **Fax:** 203/454-2310. **Contact:** Bert Liebelt, Partner. **Description:** An executive search firm. Company pays fee. **Specializes in the areas of:** Manufacturing. **Positions commonly filled include:** Industrial Production Manager; Operations/Production Manager. **Number of placements per year:** 1 - 49.

WEATHERBY HEALTH CARE
25 Van Zant Street, Norwalk CT 06855-1786. **Toll-free phone:** 800/365-8900. **Contact:** Manager. **Description:** An executive search firm which recruits physicians only. **Specializes in the areas of:** Health/Medical.

THE WESTFIELD GROUP
1010 Washington Boulevard, Stamford CT 06901. 203/406-2300. **Fax:** 203/406-2315. **Contact:** Joanne

Fiala, President. **E-mail address:** info@burkeandassociates.com. **Description:** An executive search firm operating on both retainer and contingency bases. Company pays fee. **Specializes in the areas of:** Accounting/Auditing; Economics; Finance; Personnel/Labor Relations. **Positions commonly filled include:** Accountant/Auditor; Budget Analyst; Computer Programmer; Financial Analyst; HMIS Specialist; Software Engineer; Systems Analyst. **Corporate headquarters location:** This Location. **Other U.S. locations:** One North Broadway, White Plains NY 10601-2310. **Average salary range of placements:** More than $50,000. **Number of placements per year:** 200 - 499.

FRANK WILKINSON & COMPANY
One Selleck Street, Suite 570, Norwalk CT 06855. 203/866-7300. **Fax:** 203/838-7390. **Contact:** Frank M. Wilkinson, President. **E-mail address:** fmw13@aol.com. **Description:** An executive search firm operating on a retainer basis. **Specializes in the areas of:** Marketing; Sales. **Positions commonly filled include:** Fund Manager; Investment Manager; Portfolio Manager. **Average salary range of placements:** More than $50,000. **Number of placements per year:** 1 - 49.

WITTLAN GROUP
181 Post Road West, Westport CT 06880. 203/227-2455. **Contact:** Manager. **Description:** An executive search firm. **Specializes in the areas of:** Marketing; Sales Promotion.

BOB WRIGHT RECRUITING, INC.
56 DeForest Road, Wilton CT 06897. 203/762-9046. **Fax:** 203/762-5807. **Contact:** Bob Wright, President. **World Wide Web address:** http://www.bwr.pair.com. **Description:** An executive search firm operating on a contingency basis. Company pays fee. **Specializes in the areas of:** Advertising; Finance; Food Industry; General Management; Printing; Publishing; Sales. **Positions commonly filled include:** Account Manager; Account Representative; Advertising Clerk; Database Manager; Marketing Specialist; Sales Executive; Sales Manager; Sales Representative; Telecommunications Manager. **Number of placements per year:** 1 - 49.

YANKEE HOSPITALITY SEARCH
406 Farmington Avenue, Farmington CT 06032. 860/738-1900. **Toll-free phone:** 800/YANKEE-1. **Fax:** 860/738-4972. **Contact:** Dan Tolman, President. **Description:** An executive search firm focusing on hospitality industry placements. Company pays fee. **Specializes in the areas of:** Food Industry; Hotel/Restaurant. **Positions commonly filled include:** Food Scientist/Technologist; Hotel Manager; Management Trainee; Restaurant/Food Service Manager. **Number of placements per year:** 50 - 99.

PERMANENT EMPLOYMENT AGENCIES

AVAILABILITY OF HARTFORD INC.
936 Silas Deane Highway, Suite 1T2, Wethersfield CT 06109-4202. 860/529-1688. **Contact:** David Roser, President. **Description:** An employment agency specializing in the placement of engineering, middle management, and production management professionals in the precision metalworking and plastic injection molding industries. Company pays fee. **Specializes in the areas of:** Engineering. **Positions commonly filled include:** Design Engineer; Designer; Industrial Engineer; Industrial Production Manager; Mechanical Engineer. **Average salary range of placements:** $30,000 - $50,000. **Number of placements per year:** 1 - 49.

BA STAFFING, INC.
1208 Main Street, Branford CT 06405. 203/488-2504. **Contact:** Dean Troxell, President. **Description:** A permanent employment agency. Company pays fee. **Specializes in the areas of:** Computer Science/Software. **Positions commonly filled include:** Computer Programmer; Customer Service Representative; Electrical/Electronics Engineer; MIS Specialist; Multimedia Designer; Software Engineer; Systems Analyst. **Average salary range of placements:** More than $50,000. **Number of placements per year:** 200 - 499.

BAILEY EMPLOYMENT SERVICE
20 East Main Street, Waterbury CT 06702. 203/756-8958. **Contact:** Manager. **Description:** A permanent placement agency.

BOHAN & BRADSTREET
34 Park Drive East, Branford CT 06405. 203/488-0068. **Fax:** 203/483-8338. **Contact:** Edward Bradstreet, CPC, President. **E-mail address:** ebb@bohan-bradstreet.com. **World Wide Web address:** http://www.bohan-bradstreet.com. **Description:** A permanent employment agency and executive search firm. **Specializes in the areas of:** Accounting/Auditing; Administration; Computer Science/Software; Data Processing; Engineering; Finance; General Management; Industrial; Personnel/Labor Relations; Sales. **Positions commonly filled include:** Account Manager; Accountant; Administrative Manager; Applications Engineer; Auditor; Budget Analyst; Chief Financial Officer; Computer Programmer; Controller; Credit Manager; Database Manager; Design Engineer; Distribution Manager; Electrical/Electronics Engineer; Environmental Engineer; Finance Director; Financial Analyst; Industrial Engineer; Industrial Production Manager; Internet Services Manager; Management Analyst/Consultant; Manufacturing Engineer; Market Research Analyst; Marketing Manager; Marketing Specialist; Mechanical Engineer; Metallurgical Engineer; MIS Specialist; Operations Manager; Production Manager; Project Manager; Purchasing Agent/Manager; Quality Control Supervisor; Sales Engineer; Sales Executive; Sales Manager; Software Engineer; Systems Analyst; Systems Manager; Vice President of Marketing; Webmaster.

THOMAS BYRNE ASSOCIATES
7 Melrose Drive, Farmington CT 06032-2255. 860/676-2468. **Fax:** 860/676-0272. **Contact:** Tom Byrne, Owner. **Description:** An employment agency focusing on accounting and financial recruitment. Company pays fee. **Specializes in the areas of:** Accounting/Auditing; Finance; Insurance; Manufacturing. **Positions commonly filled include:** Accountant/Auditor; MIS Specialist. **Average salary range of placements:** More than $50,000.

CHARTER PERSONNEL SERVICES
33 Wolcott Road, Suite 6A, Wolcott CT 06716. 203/573-1471. **Contact:** Manager. **Description:** A permanent employment agency that also offers some executive search placements in general business management positions. **Specializes in the areas of:** Biomedical; Clerical; General Management; Light Industrial; Technical.

CHOICE PERSONNEL INC.
733 Summer Street, Suite 406, Stamford CT 06901. 203/324-4744. **Contact:** Manager. **Description:** A permanent employment agency. **Positions commonly filled include:** Administrative Assistant.

DATA PROS
340 Broad Street, Suite 201, Windsor CT 06095-3030. 860/688-0020. **Fax:** 860/683-8903. **Contact:** Len Collyer, President. **Description:** A permanent employment agency. Company pays fee. **Specializes in the areas of:** Computer Science/Software; Engineering; Insurance. **Positions commonly filled include:** Computer Programmer; Electrician; Emergency Medical Technician; Engineer; Systems Analyst. **Number of placements per year:** 100 - 199.

DIVERSIFIED EMPLOYMENT SERVICES, INC.
531 Whalley Avenue, New Haven CT 06511. 203/397-2500. **Fax:** 203/387-5778. **Contact:** D. William DeRosa, Jr., President. **Description:** A permanent employment agency. Founded in 1970. Company pays fee. **Specializes in the areas of:** Accounting/Auditing; Sales; Secretarial. **Positions commonly filled include:** Accountant/Auditor; Draftsperson; Typist/Word Processor. **Average salary range of placements:** $20,000 - $29,999. **Number of placements per year:** 50 - 99.

DIVERSIFIED EMPLOYMENT SERVICES, INC.
63 Center Street, Shelton CT 06484. 203/924-8364. **Contact:** Manager. **Description:** A permanent employment agency. Company pays fee. **Specializes in the areas of:** Accounting/Auditing; Engineering; Manufacturing; Sales; Secretarial. **Positions commonly filled include:** Accountant/Auditor; Blue-Collar Worker Supervisor; Chemist; Clinical Lab Technician; Computer Programmer; Customer Service Representative; Draftsperson; Paralegal; Services Sales Representative; Typist/Word Processor. **Number of placements per year:** 50 - 99.

DUNHILL SEARCH INTERNATIONAL
59 Elm Street, Suite 520, New Haven CT 06510. 203/562-0511. **Fax:** 203/562-2637. **Contact:** Donald Kaiser, President. **E-mail address:** nhdunhill@aol.com. **World Wide Web address:** http://www.internationalsearch.com. **Description:** A permanent employment agency that also places temporary and contract personnel. Dunhill also has a legal staffing division. Founded in 1978. Company pays fee. **Specializes in the areas of:** Accounting/Auditing; Administration; Engineering; Finance; International Executives; Legal; Personnel/Labor Relations; Sales. **Positions commonly filled include:** Account Representative; Accountant; Administrative Assistant; Auditor; Branch Manager; Buyer; Chief Financial Officer; Computer Operator; Computer Programmer; Controller; Customer Service Representative; Design Engineer; Electrical/Electronics Engineer; Financial Analyst; Manufacturing Engineer; Marketing Manager; Marketing Specialist; Mechanical Engineer; MIS Specialist; Paralegal; Purchasing Agent/Manager; Quality Control Supervisor; Sales Engineer; Sales Executive; Sales Manager; Sales Representative; Software Engineer; Systems Analyst; Transportation/Traffic Specialist. **Benefits available to temporary workers:** Paid Holidays; Paid Vacation. **Average salary range of placements:** More than $50,000. **Number of placements per year:** 500 - 999.

EMPLOYMENT OPPORTUNITIES
57 North Street, Suite 320, Danbury CT 06810. 203/797-2653. **Fax:** 203/797-2657. **Contact:** Manager. **Description:** A permanent employment agency. Company pays fee. **Specializes in the areas of:** Accounting/Auditing; Banking; Clerical; Computer Science/Software; Engineering; Food Industry; Health/Medical; Manufacturing; MIS/EDP; Personnel/Labor Relations; Sales; Secretarial; Technical. **Positions commonly filled include:** Accountant/Auditor; Biochemist; Biological Scientist; Biomedical Engineer; Buyer; Chemist; Civil Engineer; Claim Representative; Clerk; Computer Operator; Computer Programmer; Credit Manager; Customer Service Representative; Data Entry Clerk; Draftsperson; Driver; EDP Specialist; Electrical/ Electronics Engineer; Financial Analyst; Food Scientist/Technologist; Human Resources Manager; Industrial Engineer; Insurance Agent/Broker; Internet Services Manager; Legal Secretary; Marketing Specialist; Mechanical Engineer; Medical Secretary; Metallurgical Engineer; MIS Specialist; Operations/Production Manager; Physicist; Purchasing Agent/Manager; Quality Control Supervisor; Receptionist; Secretary; Systems Analyst; Typist/Word Processor. **Number of placements per year:** 1 - 49.

EXECUTIVE REGISTER INC.
34 Mill Plain Road, Danbury CT 06811. 203/743-5542. **Contact:** J. Scott Williams, President. **Description:** An employment agency which also offers executive recruiting services. Company pays fee. **Specializes in the areas of:** Accounting/Auditing; Computer Science/Software; Engineering; Information Systems. **Positions commonly filled include:** Accountant/Auditor; Chemical Engineer; Computer Programmer; Electrical/Electronics Engineer; Financial Analyst; Mechanical Engineer; MIS Specialist; Multimedia Designer; Software Engineer; Systems Analyst. **Number of placements per year:** 50 - 99.

FAIRFIELD TEACHERS AGENCY, INC.
P.O. Box 1141, Fairfield CT 06432. 203/333-0611. **Fax:** 203/334-7224. **Contact:** Mr. Sandy Peterson, Placement Counselor. **Description:** An employment agency that specializes in educational placements in the New York and New England areas. Founded in 1965. **Positions commonly filled include:** Education Administrator; Librarian; Social Worker; Speech-Language Pathologist; Teacher/Professor. **Number of placements per year:** 200 - 499.

GAMBRILL & ASSOCIATES
SOUND TEMPORARIES
One Atlantic Street, 7th Floor, Stamford CT 06901. 203/323-9056. **Toll-free phone:** 800/783-2384. **Fax:** 203/359-3545. **Contact:** Manager. **Description:** A permanent placement agency. Sound Temporaries (also at this location) provides temporary placements in office support positions. Founded in 1983. Company pays fee. **Corporate headquarters location:** Port Chester NY.

GOLDEN DOOR
111 East Avenue, Norwalk CT 06851. 203/853-9242. **Contact:** Manager. **Description:** A permanent placement agency.

HALLMARK TOTALTECH INC.
1090 Elm Street, Rocky Hill CT 06067. 860/529-7500. **Toll-free phone:** 800/876-4255. **Fax:** 860/529-9800. **Contact:** President. **Description:** A permanent employment agency. Company pays fee. **Specializes in the areas of:** Administration; Computer Science/Software; Engineering; Personnel/Labor Relations; Technical. **Positions commonly filled include:** Aircraft Mechanic/Engine Specialist; Blue-Collar Worker Supervisor; Buyer; Clinical Lab Technician; Computer Programmer; Construction and Building Inspector; Cost Estimator; Customer Service Representative; Design Engineer; Designer; Draftsperson; Electrical/Electronics Engineer; Environmental Engineer; Industrial Production Manager; Internet Services Manager; Mechanical Engineer; MIS Specialist; Multimedia Designer; Operations/Production Manager; Property and Real Estate Manager; Quality Control Supervisor; Science Technologist; Services Sales Representative; Software Engineer; Structural Engineer; Systems Analyst; Telecommunications Manager; Typist/Word Processor.

Average salary range of placements: $30,000 - $50,000. **Number of placements per year:** 200 - 499.

HEALTHCARE PROFESSIONAL PLACEMENT
30 Commerce Park Road, Milford CT 06460. 203/882-5500. **Contact:** Placement Office. **Description:** A permanent employment agency. Company pays fee. **Specializes in the areas of:** Health/Medical. **Positions commonly filled include:** Occupational Therapist; Pharmacist; Physical Therapist; Physician; Registered Nurse; Speech-Language Pathologist. **Number of placements per year:** 100 - 199.

J.G. HOOD ASSOCIATES
599 Riverside Avenue, Westport CT 06880. 203/226-1126. **Contact:** Joyce Hood, Owner/President. **E-mail address:** jghood@worldnet.att.net. **Description:** A permanent employment agency. Company pays fee. **Specializes in the areas of:** Administration; Computer Science/Software; Engineering; Industrial; Manufacturing; Personnel/Labor Relations. **Positions commonly filled include:** Accountant/Auditor; Aerospace Engineer; Biomedical Engineer; Chemical Engineer; Chemist; Computer Programmer; Cost Estimator; Designer; Electrical/Electronics Engineer; Industrial Engineer; Industrial Production Manager; Quality Control Supervisor; Science Technologist; Software Engineer; Structural Engineer; Systems Analyst. **Average salary range of placements:** More than $50,000. **Number of placements per year:** 1 - 49.

INDUSTRIAL RECRUITERS ASSOCIATION INC.
20 Hurlbut Street, West Hartford CT 06110. 860/953-3643. **Fax:** 860/953-5684. **Contact:** Len Baron, President. **Description:** A permanent employment agency. Founded in 1979. Company pays fee. **Specializes in the areas of:** Advertising; Engineering; General Management; Industrial; Manufacturing; Publishing; Sales; Technical. **Positions commonly filled include:** Aerospace Engineer; Biochemist; Biological Scientist; Bookkeeper; Buyer; Ceramics Engineer; Chemical Engineer; Civil Engineer; Commercial Artist; Computer Operator; Credit Manager; Customer Service Representative; Draftsperson; Electrical/Electronics Engineer; Factory Worker; Industrial Designer; Industrial Engineer; Manufacturing Engineer; Marketing Specialist; Mechanical Engineer; Metallurgical Engineer; Operations/Production Manager; Purchasing Agent/Manager; Quality Control Supervisor; Sales Representative; Software Engineer; Technical Illustrator; Technical Writer/Editor. **Number of placements per year:** 100 - 199.

JAT, LTD.
P.O. Box 1146, Fairfield CT 06432. 203/371-5877. **Fax:** 203/374-6950. **Contact:** Lois Karni, Counselor. **Description:** A permanent employment agency. Company pays fee. **Specializes in the areas of:** Engineering; Manufacturing; Scientific; Technical. **Positions commonly filled include:** Aerospace Engineer; Aircraft Mechanic/Engine Specialist; Blue-Collar Worker Supervisor; Chemical Engineer; Civil Engineer; Design Engineer; Designer; Draftsperson; Electrical/Electronics Engineer; Environmental Engineer; Industrial Engineer; Industrial Production Manager; Mechanical Engineer; Quality Control Supervisor; Software Engineer; Structural Engineer; Systems Analyst. **Average salary range of placements:** More than $20,000. **Number of placements per year:** 1 - 49.

JOBSHOP
16 Alewives Road, Norwalk CT 06850-2201. 203/853-7927. **Fax:** 203/852-1994. **Contact:** James A. Calka, President. **Description:** A permanent employment agency. Company pays fee. **Specializes in the areas of:** Engineering; Industrial; Scientific; Technical. **Positions commonly filled include:** Applications Engineer; Architect; Biochemist; Biological Scientist; Biomedical Engineer; Broadcast Technician; Buyer; Chemical Engineer; Civil Engineer; Clinical Lab Technician; Computer Operator; Computer Programmer; Database Manager; Design Engineer; Designer; Draftsperson; Electrical/Electronics Engineer; Environmental Engineer; Human Resources Specialist; Industrial Engineer; Internet Services Manager; Manufacturing Engineer; Mechanical Engineer; MIS Specialist; Multimedia Designer; Operations/Production Manager; Quality Control Supervisor; Software Engineer; Systems Analyst; Technical Writer/Editor; Telecommunications Manager. **Average salary range of placements:** $30,000 - $50,000. **Number of placements per year:** 1 - 49.

JOBSOURCE
Two Corporate Drive, Trumbull CT 06611. 203/268-9987. **Fax:** 203/261-2443. **Contact:** Deborah G. Palmieri, President. **Description:** A permanent employment agency. Company pays fee. **Specializes in the areas of:** Accounting/Auditing; Administration; Sales; Secretarial. **Positions commonly filled include:** Accountant/Auditor; Administrative Assistant; Bookkeeper; Budget Analyst; Clerical Supervisor; Computer Programmer; Customer Service Representative; Financial Analyst; Management Trainee; Paralegal; Secretary; Systems Analyst. **Number of placements per year:** 50 - 99.

JUDLIND EMPLOYMENT SERVICES
One Bank Street, Stamford CT 06901. 203/964-8116. **Contact:** Manager. **Description:** A permanent placement agency that also provides some temporary placements.

JULIAN ASSOCIATES INC.
162 Willard Avenue, Newington CT 06111. 860/232-7876. **Fax:** 860/232-8864. **Contact:** Julian Brownstein, President. **Description:** A permanent employment agency. Company pays fee. **Specializes in the areas of:** Advertising; Art/Design. **Number of placements per year:** 1 - 49.

W.R. LAWRY, INC.
P.O. Box 832, Simsbury CT 06070. 860/651-0281. **Physical address:** 6 Wilcox Street, Simsbury CT. **Fax:** 860/651-8324. **Contact:** Bill Lawry, Owner. **Description:** A permanent employment agency. Company pays fee. **Specializes in the areas of:** Computer Science/Software; Engineering; General Management; Technical. **Positions commonly filled include:** Biological Scientist; Engineer; General Manager. **Number of placements per year:** 1 - 49.

LINEAL RECRUITING SERVICES
46 Copper Kettle Road, Trumbull CT 06611. 203/386-1091. **Fax:** 203/386-9788. **Contact:** Lisa Lineal, Owner. **E-mail address:** lineal1@aol.com. **Description:** An employment agency specializing in the electromechanical industry. Company pays fee. **Specializes in the areas of:** Engineering; Sales; Technical. **Positions commonly filled include:** Blue-Collar Worker Supervisor; Customer Service Representative; Design Engineer; Electrical/Electronics Engineer; Electrician; Industrial Production Manager; Mining Engineer; Services Sales Representative. **Number of placements per year:** 1 - 49.

MANAGEMENT SOLUTIONS
36 State Street, North Haven CT 06473. 203/239-7006. **Contact:** Manager. **Description:** A permanent employment agency that also offers some contract services. **Specializes in the areas of:** Computer Programming.

MATRIX SEARCH INC.
495 Route 184, Suite 211, Groton CT 06340. 860/449-0860. **Contact:** Manager. **Description:** A permanent employment agency operating on a contingency basis. **Specializes in the areas of:** Electrical; Electronics; Engineering; Technical.

MERRY EMPLOYMENT GROUP INC.
433 South Main Street, Suite 216, West Hartford CT 06110. 860/678-8891. **Contact:** Manager. **Description:** An employment agency that also provides some executive search services. **Specializes in the areas of:** Finance; MIS/EDP.

NAPOLITANO & WULSTER
311 South Main Street, Cheshire CT 06410. 203/272-2820. **Fax:** 203/250-7207. **Contact:** Tony Napolitano, Owner. **Description:** A permanent employment agency. Company pays fee. **Specializes in the areas of:** Health/Medical. **Positions commonly filled include:** Biochemist; Biomedical Engineer; Chemist; Technical Writer/Editor. **Number of placements per year:** 50 - 99.

NEW ENGLAND PERSONNEL, INC.
Bushnell on the Park, 100 Wells Street, Hartford CT 06103. 860/525-8616. **Contact:** Manager. **Description:** A permanent employment agency placing entry-level through senior-level professionals in a wide range of industries. **Specializes in the areas of:** Administration; Computer Programming; Engineering; Health/Medical.

OFFICE SERVICES OF CONNECTICUT, INC.
940 White Plains Road, Trumbull CT 06611. 203/268-7084. **Fax:** 203/261-0502. **Contact:** Ms. Terry Gates, President. **Description:** A full-service employment agency which provides both permanent and temporary placements. Founded in 1971. Company pays fee. **Specializes in the areas of:** Accounting/Auditing; Administration; Advertising; Banking; Engineering; Finance; Food Industry; General Management; Industrial; Insurance; Legal; Manufacturing; Sales; Secretarial. **Positions commonly filled include:** Accountant/Auditor; Actuary; Administrative Manager; Advertising Clerk; Architect; Chemist; Clinical Lab Technician; Computer Programmer; Customer Service Representative; Environmental Engineer; Financial Analyst; Food Scientist/Technologist; Human Resources Specialist; Industrial Engineer; Manufacturer's/Wholesaler's Sales Rep.; Mechanical Engineer; MIS Specialist; Securities Sales Representative; Services Sales Representative; Software Engineer; Systems Analyst; Typist/Word Processor. **Average salary range of placements:** $30,000 - $50,000. **Number of placements per year:** 200 - 499.

PARAMOUNT RESOURCES
25 Sylvan Road, Suite F, Westport CT 06880. 203/227-4101. **Contact:** Manager. **Description:** A full-service employment agency that places entry-level through senior-level professionals in a wide range of industries. **Specializes in the areas of:** Accounting/Auditing; Computer Graphics; Finance; Secretarial.

PASCALE & LAMORTE, LLC
500 Summer Street, Stamford CT 06901. 203/358-8155. **Fax:** 203/969-3990. **Contact:** Ron Pascale, President. **E-mail address:** pascale@earthlink.net. **World Wide Web address:** http://www.pascale-lamorte.com. **Description:** A permanent employment agency. Company pays fee. **Specializes in the areas of:** Accounting/Auditing; Administration; Computer Science/Software; Finance. **Positions commonly filled include:** Accountant/Auditor; Budget Analyst; Controller; Financial Analyst; Management Analyst/Consultant; Software Engineer; Systems Analyst; Tax Specialist; Treasurer. **Average salary range of placements:** More than $75,000.

PROFESSIONAL EMPLOYMENT
20 South Anguilla Road, Pawcatuck CT 06379. 860/599-8430. **Fax:** 860/599-1779. **Contact:** Joan Kohn, Personnel Consultant. **Description:** A permanent employment agency that also offers temporary placements. Company pays fee. **Positions commonly filled include:** Accountant/Auditor; Biochemist; Blue-Collar Worker Supervisor; Clerical Supervisor; Clinical Lab Technician; Customer Service Representative; Food Scientist/Technologist; Human Resources Specialist; Medical Records Technician; Paralegal; Secretary. **Average salary range of placements:** $20,000 - $29,999. **Number of placements per year:** 100 - 199.

PROFESSIONAL PHARMACY PERSONNEL, INC.
P.O. Box 950, Putnam CT 06260-0950. 860/928-0023. **Fax:** 860/928-1720. **Contact:** Paula J. Kaspar, President. **Description:** A permanent employment agency operating on a contingency basis. The agency focuses on short-term and long-term placements of pharmacists and pharmacy technicians. Founded in 1990. Company pays fee. **Positions commonly filled include:** Pharmacist; Pharmacy Technician. **Average salary range of placements:** More than $50,000. **Number of placements per year:** 1 - 49.

Q.S.I.
P.O Box 5606, Hamden CT 06578. 203/287-8900. **Fax:** 203/248-0911. **Contact:** Kim Feuer, Technical Recruiter. **Description:** A permanent employment agency specializing in MIS technical staffing. Company pays fee. **Specializes in the areas of:** Accounting/Auditing; Computer Science/Software; Finance; Legal. **Positions commonly filled include:** Accountant/Auditor; Attorney; Computer Programmer; Financial Analyst; MIS Specialist; Systems Analyst; Telecommunications Manager. **Average salary range of placements:** More than $50,000. **Number of placements per year:** 1 - 49.

RJS ASSOCIATES, INC.
10 Columbus Boulevard, Hartford CT 06106. 860/278-5840. **Fax:** 860/522-8313. **Contact:** Richard J. Stewart, President. **Description:** A permanent employment agency. Company pays fee. **Positions commonly filled include:** Accountant/Auditor; Actuary; Administrative Manager; Aerospace Engineer; Bank Officer/Manager; Biological Scientist; Biomedical Engineer; Branch Manager; Budget Analyst; Buyer; Chemical Engineer; Claim Representative; Clerical Supervisor; Clinical Lab Technician; Cost Estimator; Credit Manager; Customer Service Representative; EEG Technologist; EKG Technician; Electrical /Electronics Engineer; Electrician; Financial Analyst; General Manager; Geologist/Geophysicist; Health Services Manager; Industrial Engineer; Licensed Practical Nurse; Manufacturer's/Wholesaler's Sales Rep.; Mechanical Engineer; Medical Records Technician; Occupational Therapist; Physical Therapist; Quality Control Supervisor; Recreational Therapist; Respiratory Therapist; Software Engineer; Structural Engineer; Systems Analyst; Technical Writer/Editor; Underwriter/Assistant Underwriter. **Number of placements per year:** 200 - 499.

RKS RESOURCES
22 Fifth Street, Stamford CT 06905. 203/359-9290. **Contact:** Manager. **Description:** A general employment agency.

RESOURCE ASSOCIATES
730 Hopmeadow Street, Simsbury CT 06070. 860/651-4918. **Fax:** 860/651-3137. **Contact:** Eric

Grossman, President. **Description:** A permanent employment agency. **Specializes in the areas of:** Accounting/Auditing; Computer Science/Software; Finance. **Positions commonly filled include:** Accountant/Auditor; Computer Programmer; Financial Analyst; Software Engineer; Systems Analyst.

REYNOLDS TECHNICAL SERVICES INC.
3638 Main Street, Stratford CT 06497. 203/375-1953. **Contact:** Manager. **Description:** A permanent employment agency that also provides some temporary placements. **Specializes in the areas of:** Technical. **Positions commonly filled include:** Computer Programmer; Designer; Draftsperson; Technical Writer/Editor; Tool and Die Maker; Tool Engineer.

SENIOR EMPLOYMENT SERVICE
1642 Bedford Street, Suite 106, Stamford CT 06905. 203/327-4422. **Fax:** 203/327-4098. **Contact:** Peg Mooney, Executive Director. **Description:** A permanent employment agency. Founded in 1975. Company pays fee. **Positions commonly filled include:** Bookkeeper; Clerk; Computer Operator; Customer Service Representative; Data Entry Clerk; Driver; Executive Assistant; Legal Secretary; Medical Secretary; Receptionist; Sales Representative; Secretary; Typist/Word Processor. **Number of placements per year:** 50 - 99.

SNELLING PERSONNEL SERVICES
1 Univac Lane, Windsor CT 06095. 860/688-6226. **Contact:** Manager. **Description:** A full-service employment agency offering both permanent and temporary placements in a wide range of industries.

SNELLING PERSONNEL SERVICES
64 Wall Street, Norwalk CT 06850. 203/853-1281. **Fax:** 203/852-1705. **Contact:** Robert Mouat, Manager. **Description:** A full-service employment agency offering both permanent and temporary placements in a wide range of industries.

STAFFING SOLUTIONS
130 Research Parkway, Meriden CT 06450. 203/237-8633. **Contact:** Manager. **Description:** A permanent employment agency that places all levels of information technology professionals. **Specializes in the areas of:** Information Technology.

SUPER SYSTEMS, INC.
345 North Main Street, Suite 321, West Hartford CT 06117-2508. 860/523-4246. **Fax:** 860/233-6943. **Contact:** Mary Ann Salas, CPC, President. **Description:** A permanent employment agency. **Specializes in the areas of:** Computer Science/Software; Data Processing; Engineering; Health/Medical; Technical. **Positions commonly filled include:** Aerospace Engineer; Agricultural Engineer; Biomedical Engineer; Chemical Engineer; Civil Engineer; Computer Programmer; Electrical/Electronics Engineer; Industrial Engineer; Licensed Practical Nurse; Mechanical Engineer; Occupational Therapist; Physical Therapist; Respiratory Therapist; Software Engineer; Stationary Engineer; Structural Engineer; Systems Analyst. **Number of placements per year:** 50 - 99.

TALENT TREE STAFFING SERVICES
5 Canal Street, Putnam CT 06260. 860/928-2771. **Contact:** Manager. **Description:** A permanent employment agency that provides both permanent and temporary placements. **Specializes in the areas of:** Light Industrial. **Corporate headquarters location:** Houston TX. **Other U.S. locations:** Nationwide.

TURNER ASSOCIATES
P.O. Box 2192, Manchester CT 06430. 860/645-7877. **Contact:** Rubye Banks, Assistant Director. **Description:** A permanent employment agency. **Positions commonly filled include:** Accountant/Auditor; Advertising Clerk; Blue-Collar Worker Supervisor; Buyer; Computer Programmer; Environmental Engineer; General Manager; Industrial Engineer; Industrial Production Manager; Licensed Practical Nurse; Management Trainee; Manufacturer's/Wholesaler's Sales Rep.; MIS Specialist; Recreational Therapist; Registered Nurse; Respiratory Therapist; Services Sales Representative; Software Engineer; Systems Analyst; Typist/Word Processor. **Average salary range of placements:** $30,000 - $50,000. **Number of placements per year:** 1 - 49.

J.R. VAUGHAN & ASSOCIATES
1177 Silas Deane Highway, Wethersfield CT 06109. 860/563-2555. **Contact:** Recruiter. **Description:** A permanent employment agency. Company pays fee. **Specializes in the areas of:** Sales. **Positions commonly filled include:** Manufacturer's/Wholesaler's Sales Rep.; Services Sales Representative. **Number of placements per year:** 100 - 199.

VELEN ASSOCIATES
One Bank Street, Suite 404, Stamford CT 06901. 203/324-5900. **Contact:** Manager. **Description:** A permanent placement agency. **Specializes in the areas of:** Accounting/Auditing; Bookkeeping; Finance.

WESTERN STAFF SERVICES
100 Constitution Plaza, Suite 400, Hartford CT 06103. 860/249-7721. **Contact:** Terri Michaels, Human Resources. **Description:** A permanent and temporary employment agency. **Specializes in the areas of:** Accounting/Auditing; Advertising; Banking; Clerical; Computer Science/Software; Engineering; Finance; Insurance; Legal; Manufacturing; MIS/EDP; Personnel/Labor Relations; Publishing; Sales; Technical. **Positions commonly filled include:** Accountant/Auditor; Administrative Assistant; Advertising Clerk; Aerospace Engineer; Agricultural Engineer; Architect; Attorney; Bank Officer/Manager; Biological Scientist; Biomedical Engineer; Bookkeeper; Buyer; Ceramics Engineer; Chemist; Civil Engineer; Claim Representative; Clerk; Commercial Artist; Computer Programmer; Credit Manager; Customer Service Representative; Data Entry Clerk; Draftsperson; EDP Specialist; Electrical/Electronics Engineer; Financial Analyst; Food Scientist/Technologist; Industrial Designer; Industrial Engineer; Legal Secretary; Marketing Specialist; Mechanical Engineer; Medical Secretary; Metallurgical Engineer; MIS Specialist; Purchasing Agent/Manager; Receptionist; Systems Analyst; Technical Writer/Editor; Underwriter/Assistant Underwriter.

WORKFORCE ONE
235 Interstate Lane, Waterbury CT 06705. 203/759-2180. **Fax:** 203/759-2182. **Contact:** Donald Rulli, President. **E-mail address:** info@workforceone.com. **World Wide Web address:** http://www.workforceone.com. **Description:** A permanent employment agency. **Specializes in the areas of:** Accounting/Auditing; Computer Science/Software; Electronics; Finance; Manufacturing; Personnel/Labor Relations; Secretarial; Technical. **Positions commonly filled include:** Accountant/Auditor; Administrative Manager; Aerospace Engineer; Aircraft Mechanic/Engine Specialist; Bank Officer/Manager; Blue-Collar Worker Supervisor; Branch Manager; Budget Analyst; Buyer; Chemical Engineer; Chemist; Civil Engineer; Clerical Supervisor; Clinical Lab Technician; Computer Programmer; Construction and Building Inspector; Construction Contractor; Cost Estimator; Credit Manager; Customer Service Representative; Design Engineer; Designer; Draftsperson; Electrical/Electronics Engineer;

Environmental Engineer; Financial Analyst; General Manager; Human Resources Specialist; Industrial Engineer; Industrial Production Manager; Management Analyst/Consultant; Mechanical Engineer; Medical Records Technician; MIS Specialist; Purchasing Agent/Manager; Quality Control Supervisor; Software Engineer; Stationary Engineer; Structural Engineer; Systems Analyst; Technical Writer/Editor; Typist/Word Processor. **Average salary range of placements:** $30,000 - $50,000. **Number of placements per year:** 1 - 49.

TEMPORARY EMPLOYMENT AGENCIES

ADMIRAL STAFFING SERVICES
69 Wall Street, Norwalk CT 06850. 203/855-8367. **Contact:** Sally Patrignelli, Personnel Manager. **Description:** A temporary agency. Founded in 1982. **Specializes in the areas of:** Accounting/Auditing; Art/Design; Banking; Education; Engineering; Finance; Food Industry; General Management; Health/Medical; Industrial; Insurance; Legal; Manufacturing; Secretarial; Technical; Transportation. **Positions commonly filled include:** Advertising Clerk; Aircraft Mechanic/Engine Specialist; Bank Officer/Manager; Blue-Collar Worker Supervisor; Budget Analyst; Buyer; Claim Representative; Customer Service Representative; Designer; Draftsperson; Electrical/Electronics Engineer; Electrician; Food Scientist/Technologist; Human Resources Specialist; Quality Control Supervisor; Restaurant/Food Service Manager; Technical Writer/Editor; Typist/Word Processor. **Corporate headquarters location:** This Location. **Other area locations:** Bridgeport CT; Milford CT. **Number of placements per year:** 500 - 999.

ADVANCED PLACEMENT INC.
58 River Street, Milford CT 06460. 203/878-9392. **Toll-free phone:** 800/771-9392. **Fax:** 203/878-9936. **Contact:** Laurie Yontef, Personnel Consultant. **Description:** A temporary agency. Company pays fee. **Specializes in the areas of:** Finance; General Management; Personnel/Labor Relations; Sales; Secretarial. **Positions commonly filled include:** Administrative Manager; Advertising Clerk; Budget Analyst; Buyer; Claim Representative; Clerical Supervisor; Credit Manager; Customer Service Representative; Health Services Manager; Human Resources Specialist; Management Analyst/Consultant; Market Research Analyst; Mechanical Engineer; Operations/Production Manager; Paralegal; Public Relations Specialist; Typist/Word Processor. **Average salary range of placements:** $30,000 - $50,000. **Number of placements per year:** 200 - 499.

CGR STAFFING SERVICES
281 Tresser Boulevard, Stamford CT 06901. 203/316-4642. **Fax:** 203/316-4641. **Contact:** Lisa Topping, Manager. **Description:** A temporary agency specializing in computer graphics placements. Company pays fee. **Specializes in the areas of:** Advertising; Art/Design; Publishing; Sales; Technical. **Positions commonly filled include:** Administrative Manager; Broadcast Technician; Computer Programmer; Customer Service Representative; Designer; Internet Services Manager; MIS Specialist; Multimedia Designer; Technical Writer/Editor; Typist/Word Processor. **Corporate headquarters location:** This Location. **Other U.S. locations:** New York NY. **Average salary range of placements:** $30,000 - $50,000.

CGS STAFFING SERVICES
114 West Main Street, New Britain CT 06051. 860/224-3033. **Fax:** 860/826-1483. **Contact:** Recruiting Coordinator. **World Wide Web address:** http://www.cgs-staffing.com. **Description:** A temporary agency. Founded in 1970. Company pays fee. **Specializes in the areas of:** Administration; Industrial; Manufacturing; Secretarial. **Positions commonly filled include:** Blue-Collar Worker Supervisor; Clerical Supervisor; Customer Service Representative; Human Resources Specialist; Medical Records Technician; Typist/Word Processor. **Corporate headquarters location:** This Location. **Other area locations:** East Hartford CT; New Haven CT; Waterbury CT.

CORPORATE STAFFING SOLUTIONS
98 Mill Plain Road, Danbury CT 06811. 203/744-6020. **Contact:** Office Manager. **Description:** A temporary agency. Company pays fee. **Specializes in the areas of:** Administration; Computer Science/Software; Electronics; General Management; Manufacturing; Personnel/Labor Relations; Sales; Technical. **Corporate headquarters location:** Wallingford CT. **Number of placements per year:** 1000+.

CORPORATE STAFFING SOLUTIONS
433 South Main Street, West Hartford CT 06110. 860/561-1952. **Contact:** Mary Hax, Manager. **Description:** A temporary agency. Company pays fee. **Specializes in the areas of:** Accounting/Auditing; Administration; Advertising; Finance; Industrial; Insurance; Legal; Manufacturing; Personnel/Labor Relations; Sales; Secretarial. **Positions commonly filled include:** Accountant/Auditor; Advertising Clerk; Branch Manager; Claim Representative; Computer Programmer; Customer Service Representative; Human Service Worker; Restaurant/Food Service Manager; Systems Analyst; Telecommunications Manager; Typist/Word Processor. **Benefits available to temporary workers:** Medical Insurance; Paid Holidays; Paid Vacation. **Corporate headquarters location:** Wallingford CT. **Number of placements per year:** 1000+.

CREATIVE SEARCH
50 Washington Street, South Norwalk CT 06854. 203/854-9393. **Fax:** 203/854-0700. **Contact:** Darci Arnold, Manager of Operations. **Description:** A temporary agency specializing in the placement of advertising personnel. Founded in 1988. Company pays fee. **Specializes in the areas of:** Advertising; Publishing. **Positions commonly filled include:** Designer; Editor; Internet Services Manager; Multimedia Designer. **Number of placements per year:** 1 - 49.

FOX RIDGE SERVICES, INC.
624 Village Walk, Guilford CT 06437. 203/458-2000. **Fax:** 203/453-1313. **Contact:** Mary Anne Athanas, President. **Description:** A temporary agency specializing in placements in all areas of engineering. Company pays fee. **Specializes in the areas of:** Engineering; Manufacturing; Technical. **Positions commonly filled include:** Designer; Hardware Engineer; Manufacturing Engineer; Mechanical Engineer; Software Engineer; Technical Illustrator; Technical Writer/Editor. **Average salary range of placements:** More than $50,000. **Number of placements per year:** 1 - 49.

HIRE LOGIC
435 Buckland Road, South Windsor CT 06074. 860/644-8877. **Fax:** 860/644-8801. **Contact:** Suzanne Lingua, Member. **Description:** A temporary agency specializing in the placement of engineering

professionals. Company pays fee. **Specializes in the areas of:** Computer Science/Software; Engineering; Industrial; Manufacturing; Technical. **Positions commonly filled include:** Architect; Biochemist; Biological Scientist; Biomedical Engineer; Broadcast Technician; Buyer; Chemical Engineer; Chemist; Computer Programmer; Cost Estimator; Design Engineer; Designer; Draftsperson; Electrical/Electronics Engineer; Financial Analyst; Human Resources Specialist; Industrial Engineer; Industrial Production Manager; MIS Specialist; Quality Control Supervisor; Radio/TV Announcer/Broadcaster; Software Engineer; Structural Engineer; Systems Analyst; Technical Writer/Editor; Telecommunications Manager. **Average salary range of placements:** More than $50,000. **Number of placements per year:** 100 - 199.

IMPACT PERSONNEL, INC.
40 Richards Avenue, Norwalk CT 06854. 203/866-2444. **Toll-free phone:** 800/283-0087. **Fax:** 203/831-5501. **Contact:** Maryann Donovan, President. **Description:** A temporary agency that also provides permanent placements, primarily office support staffing. Founded in 1989. Company pays fee. **Specializes in the areas of:** Accounting/Auditing; Administration; Advertising; Finance; Personnel/Labor Relations; Sales; Secretarial. **Positions commonly filled include:** Human Resources Specialist; Typist/Word Processor. **Benefits available to temporary workers:** Medical Insurance; Paid Vacation. **Corporate headquarters location:** This Location. **Other area locations:** Fairfield CT.

INTERTEC PERSONNEL
235 Post Road West, Westport CT 06880. 203/222-0050. **Fax:** 203/222-7691. **Contact:** Susan Littman, Director of Personnel. **Description:** A temporary agency. Company pays fee. **Specializes in the areas of:** Accounting/Auditing; Administration; Advertising; Architecture/Construction; Computer Science/Software; Finance; Health/Medical; Legal; Personnel/Labor Relations; Publishing; Sales; Secretarial. **Positions commonly filled include:** Administrative Manager; Clerical Supervisor; Computer Programmer; Services Sales Representative; Typist/Word Processor. **Corporate headquarters location:** Cherry Hill NJ. **Other U.S. locations:** CA; MI. **Average salary range of placements:** $20,000 - $29,999. **Number of placements per year:** 100 - 199.

LAB SUPPORT INC.
6151 West Johnson, Suite 202, Cheshire CT 06410. 203/272-9998. **Toll-free phone:** 800/546-5712. **Contact:** Linda L. Page, Account Manager. **Description:** A temporary agency specializing in the placement of scientists in laboratory positions. Company pays fee. **Specializes in the areas of:** Biology; Food Industry; Technical. **Positions commonly filled include:** Biochemist; Biological Scientist; Chemist; Science Technologist; Technical Writer/Editor. **Corporate headquarters location:** Calabasas CA. **Other U.S. locations:** Nationwide. **Average salary range of placements:** $20,000 - $29,999. **Number of placements per year:** 50 - 99.

MANPOWER, INC.
65 Bank Street, Waterbury CT 06702. 203/756-8303. **Contact:** Office Manager. **Description:** A temporary agency. Company pays fee. **Specializes in the areas of:** Accounting/Auditing; Clerical; Secretarial. **Positions commonly filled include:** Accountant/Auditor; Clerk; Construction Trade Worker; Customer Service Representative; Data Entry Clerk; Draftsperson; Secretary; Stenographer; Technical Writer/Editor; Technician; Typist/Word Processor. **Number of placements per year:** 1000+.

McINTYRE ASSOCIATES
Holly Pond Plaza, 1281 Main Street, Stamford CT 06902. 203/324-0000. **Fax:** 203/324-1102. **Contact:** Diana Burns, Recruiting Coordinator. **Description:** A temporary agency that also provides permanent placements, executive searches, and contract placements. Founded in 1986. Company pays fee. **Specializes in the areas of:** Accounting/Auditing; Administration; Computer Science/Software; Finance; General Management; Legal; Personnel/Labor Relations; Sales; Secretarial. **Positions commonly filled include:** Account Manager; Account Representative; Accountant; Administrative Assistant; Administrative Manager; Advertising Clerk; Computer Programmer; Consultant; Credit Manager; Customer Service Manager; Internet Services Manager; Market Research Analyst; Marketing Specialist; MIS Specialist; Paralegal; Sales Executive; Sales Manager; Sales Representative; Secretary; Systems Analyst; Systems Manager; Typist/Word Processor; Vice President of Finance. **Benefits available to temporary workers:** 401(k); Direct Deposit; Medical Insurance; Paid Vacation; Travel Allowance. **Corporate headquarters location:** This Location. **Other area locations:** Shelton CT. **Average salary range of placements:** More than $50,000. **Number of placements per year:** 1000+.

McLAUGHLIN PERSONNEL
6 Main Street, Chester CT 06412. 860/526-9096. **Fax:** 860/526-1519. **Contact:** Sharon McLaughlin, Principal. **Description:** A temporary agency. Company pays fee. **Specializes in the areas of:** Computer Science/Software. **Positions commonly filled include:** Computer Programmer; MIS Specialist; Systems Analyst. **Other area locations:** Simsbury CT. **Average salary range of placements:** $30,000 - $50,000. **Number of placements per year:** 1 - 49.

NATIONAL STAFFING SERVICES
100 Constitution Plaza, Suite 957, Hartford CT 06103. 860/246-4200. **Contact:** Manager. **Description:** A temporary and temp-to-hire agency. **Specializes in the areas of:** Accounting/Auditing; Clerical. **Positions commonly filled include:** Accountant; Administrative Assistant; Data Entry Clerk.

TECH/AID OF CONNECTICUT
21 New Britain Avenue, Rocky Hill CT 06067. 860/529-5710. **Contact:** Office Manager. **Description:** A temporary agency. Company pays fee. **Specializes in the areas of:** Architecture/Construction; Computer Science/Software; Construction; Engineering; Manufacturing; Technical. **Positions commonly filled include:** Aerospace Engineer; Architectural Engineer; Buyer; Ceramics Engineer; Chemical Engineer; Civil Engineer; Draftsperson; Electrical/Electronics Engineer; Estimator; Industrial Designer; Mechanical Engineer; Metallurgical Engineer; Mining Engineer; Operations/Production Manager; Petroleum Engineer; Purchasing Agent/Manager; Quality Control Supervisor; Technical Writer/Editor; Technician. **Number of placements per year:** 1000+.

TECHNICAL STAFFING SOLUTIONS
919 Stratford Avenue, Suite 2, Stratford CT 06497-6352. 203/381-9700. **Fax:** 203/381-9458. **Contact:** Manager. **E-mail address:** tecstasol@aol.com. **Description:** A temporary agency that also offers permanent placements, primarily in technical fields. Company pays fee. **Specializes in the areas of:** Engineering; Industrial; Manufacturing; Technical. **Positions commonly filled include:** Aerospace Engineer; Biomedical Engineer; Chemical Engineer; Chemist; Civil Engineer; Clinical Lab Technician; Computer Programmer; Design Engineer; Designer; Electrical/Electronics Engineer; Environmental Engineer; Human Resources Specialist; Industrial

Engineer; Materials Engineer; Mechanical Engineer; MIS Specialist; Physicist; Purchasing Agent/Manager; Quality Control Supervisor; Science Technologist; Software Engineer; Structural Engineer; Systems Analyst; Technical Writer/Editor. **Average salary range of placements:** $30,000 - $50,000. **Number of placements per year:** 100 - 199.

UNITED PERSONNEL SERVICES
99 Pratt Street, Suite 603, Hartford CT 06103. 860/560-8009. **Fax:** 860/560-8099. **Contact:** Manager. **Description:** A temporary agency that primarily offers temp-to-hire placements. **Specializes in the areas of:** Administration; Light Industrial; Sales.

WESTERN STAFF SERVICES
14 Hayestown Avenue, Danbury CT 06811. 203/798-8367. **Fax:** 203/744-1878. **Contact:** Jean Palumbo, CPC, Manager. **Description:** A temporary agency. Founded in 1948. Company pays fee. **Specializes in the areas of:** Accounting/Auditing; Administration; Banking; Engineering; Finance; General Management; Industrial; Insurance; Manufacturing; Personnel/Labor Relations; Secretarial; Technical. **Positions commonly filled include:** Bank Officer/Manager; Biochemist; Blue-Collar Worker Supervisor; Branch Manager; Budget Analyst; Chemical Engineer; Chemist; Claim Representative; Clerical Supervisor; Computer Programmer; Design Engineer; Designer; Draftsperson; Electrical/Electronics Engineer; Environmental Engineer; Financial Analyst; Human Resources Specialist; Industrial Engineer; Mechanical Engineer; Medical Records Technician; Purchasing Agent/Manager; Quality Control Supervisor; Software Engineer; Structural Engineer; Systems Analyst; Technical Writer/Editor; Typist/Word Processor; Underwriter/Assistant Underwriter. **Corporate headquarters location:** Walnut Creek CA. **Number of placements per year:** 500 - 999.

CONTRACT SERVICES FIRMS

EDP CONTRACT SERVICES
727 Post Road East, Westport CT 06880. 203/227-2088. **Contact:** Office Manager. **Description:** A contract services firm. Company pays fee. **Specializes in the areas of:** Accounting/Auditing; Banking; Computer Science/Software; Engineering; Finance; Insurance; Manufacturing; MIS/EDP; Nonprofit; Personnel/Labor Relations; Publishing; Technical. **Positions commonly filled include:** Computer Operator; Computer Programmer; EDP Specialist; MIS Specialist; Systems Analyst; Technical Writer/Editor. **Number of placements per year:** 1000+.

PROVISION TECHNOLOGIES
800 Connecticut Boulevard, 6th Floor, East Hartford CT 06108. 860/586-2337. **Fax:** 860/610-0181. **Contact:** Manager. **World Wide Web address:** http://www.careerbase.com. **Description:** A contract services and consulting firm. **Specializes in the areas of:** Computer Science/Software; Information Technology.

TAD TECHNICAL SERVICES
40 Lake Avenue Extension, Danbury CT 06811. 203/794-9665. **Contact:** Manager. **Description:** A contract services firm that also offers some temporary placements. **Specializes in the areas of:** Computer Science/Software; Engineering; Technical. **Positions commonly filled include:** Assembler; Software Engineer.

TAD TECHNICAL SERVICES
553 Plank Road, Waterbury CT 06705. 203/757-0358. **Contact:** Manager. **Description:** A contract services firm that also offers some temporary and permanent placements. **Specializes in the areas of:** Computer Science/Software; Engineering. **Positions commonly filled include:** Design Engineer; Draftsperson.

YOH SCIENTIFIC
1010 Washington Boulevard, Stamford CT 06901. 203/973-0969. **Contact:** Manager. **Description:** A contract services firm. **Specializes in the areas of:** Pharmaceutical; Scientific.

CAREER/OUTPLACEMENT COUNSELING FIRMS

A&A RESUME & PERSONNEL SERVICES
91 Bainton Road, West Hartford CT 06117-2816. 860/549-5262. **Contact:** Lewis Schweitzer, Manager. **Description:** A resume service and employment agency. A&A Resume & Personnel Services prepares, edits, and reproduces resumes for all fields. **Specializes in the areas of:** Accounting/Auditing; Banking; Computer Science/Software; Engineering; Finance; Insurance; Manufacturing; MIS/EDP; Sales; Technical. **Positions commonly filled include:** Accountant/Auditor; Actuary; Attorney; Bank Officer/Manager; Civil Engineer; Claim Representative; Computer Programmer; Credit Manager; Customer Service Representative; EDP Specialist; Electrical/Electronics Engineer; Financial Analyst; Industrial Designer; Industrial Engineer; Mechanical Engineer; Purchasing Agent/Manager; Sales Representative; Statistician; Systems Analyst; Technician; Underwriter/Assistant Underwriter. **Number of placements per year:** 50 - 99.

A&R RESUME SERVICE OF WEST HAVEN
33 Donald Street, West Haven CT 06516. **Contact:** Manager. **Description:** A resume service. Also provides career counseling services.

DELAWARE

EXECUTIVE SEARCH FIRMS

DISCOVERY STAFFING
3519 Silverside Road, Wilmington DE 19810. 302/477-0680. **Contact:** Manager. **Description:** An executive search firm. **Specializes in the areas of:** Finance.

F-O-R-T-U-N-E PERSONNEL CONSULTANTS
254 Chapman Road, Suite 205, Newark DE 19702-5489. 302/453-0404. **Fax:** 302/453-0405. **Contact:** Leonard Weston, President. **Description:** An executive search firm. Company pays fee. **Specializes in the areas of:** Biotechnology; Engineering; General Management; Manufacturing; Petrochemical; Technical. **Positions commonly filled include:** Biochemist; Biological Scientist; Biomedical Engineer; Chemical Engineer; Clinical Lab Technician; Mechanical Engineer; Operations/Production Manager; Quality Control Supervisor; Science Technologist; Technical Writer/Editor. **Corporate headquarters location:** New York NY. **Other U.S. locations:** Nationwide. **Average salary range of placements:** More than $50,000. **Number of placements per year:** 1 - 49.

THE FRANKLIN COMPANY
3801 Kennett Pike, Building C, Suite 109, Wilmington DE 19807. 302/661-4100. **Contact:** Manager. **Description:** An executive search firm. **Specializes in the areas of:** Chemical; Pharmaceutical.

J.B. GRONER EXECUTIVE SEARCH INC.
2803-B Philadelphia Pike, Claymont DE 19703. 302/792-9228. **Fax:** 610/497-5500. **Contact:** James Groner, President. **World Wide Web address:** http://www.execjobsearch.com. **Description:** A small professional search firm that also offers some contract placements in the computer and engineering fields. J.B. Groner Executive Search operates on retainer and contingency bases. Company pays fee. **Specializes in the areas of:** Accounting/Auditing; Administration; Banking; Computer Science/Software; Economics; Engineering; Finance; General Management; Health/Medical; Industrial; Insurance; Legal; Manufacturing; Nonprofit; Personnel/Labor Relations; Sales; Technical. **Positions commonly filled include:** Accountant/Auditor; Administrative Manager; Architect; Attorney; Biological Scientist; Biomedical Engineer; Branch Manager; Civil Engineer; Computer Programmer; Customer Service Representative; Editor; Electrical/Electronics Engineer; Environmental Engineer; Financial Analyst; Health Services Manager; Industrial Engineer; Insurance Agent/Broker; Internet Services Manager; Licensed Practical Nurse; Management Analyst/Consultant; Mechanical Engineer; Physician; Physicist; Restaurant/Food Service Manager; Software Engineer; Speech-Language Pathologist; Structural Engineer; Surgical Technician; Surveyor; Systems Analyst; Teacher/Professor; Technical Writer/Editor; Underwriter/Assistant Underwriter; Urban/Regional Planner. **Average salary range of placements:** More than $50,000. **Number of placements per year:** 1 - 49.

HEALTHCARE NETWORK
P.O. Box 304, New Castle DE 19720. 302/322-9396. **Toll-free phone:** 800/497-4551. **Fax:** 302/322-3586. **Contact:** Judith A. Smith, President. **Description:** An executive search firm specializing in physician recruitment. The firm is part of a national network of physician recruiters and provides placement nationwide. Company pays fee. **Specializes in the areas of:** Health/Medical. **Positions commonly filled include:** Physician. **Corporate headquarters location:** This Location. **Average salary range of placements:** More than $50,000. **Number of placements per year:** 1 - 49.

E.W. HODGES & ASSOCIATES
3 McCormick Drive, Hockessin DE 19707. 302/995-6022. **Contact:** Edward W. Hodges, President. **E-mail address:** ehodges@brahms.udel.edu. **Description:** An executive search firm. Company pays fee. **Specializes in the areas of:** Accounting/Auditing; Administration; Banking; Biology; Engineering; Finance; General Management; Industrial; Legal; Manufacturing; Personnel/Labor Relations; Technical. **Positions commonly filled include:** Accountant/Auditor; Actuary; Administrative Manager; Attorney; Bank Officer/Manager; Branch Manager; Budget Analyst; Buyer; Chemist; Computer Programmer; Construction Contractor; Designer; Economist; Editor; Education Administrator; Engineer; Financial Analyst; General Manager; Health Services Manager; Hotel Manager; Management Analyst/Consultant; Mathematician; Operations/Production Manager; Paralegal; Psychologist; Public Relations Specialist; Purchasing Agent/Manager; Quality Control Supervisor; Systems Analyst; Teacher/Professor; Technical Writer/Editor; Transportation/Traffic Specialist. **Average salary range of placements:** More than $50,000. **Number of placements per year:** 1 - 49.

HORNBERGER MANAGEMENT COMPANY
One Commerce Center, 7th Floor, Wilmington DE 19801. 302/573-2541. **Contact:** Manager. **Description:** An executive search firm. **Specializes in the areas of:** Construction.

INDEPENDENT NATIONAL SEARCH & ASSOCIATES
258 East Camden Avenue, Camden DE 19934. 302/698-1466. **Fax:** 302/698-0659. **Contact:** Manager. **Description:** A consumer manufacturing-oriented search firm. Company pays fee. **Specializes in the areas of:** Accounting/Auditing; Engineering; Finance; Food Industry; General Management; Industrial; Manufacturing; Personnel/Labor Relations. **Positions commonly filled include:** Accountant/Auditor; Biomedical Engineer; Buyer; Chemical Engineer; Chemist; Computer Programmer; Electrical/Electronics Engineer; Environmental Engineer; Financial Analyst; Food Scientist/Technologist; Human Resources Manager; Industrial Engineer; Management Trainee; Operations/Production Manager; Purchasing Agent/Manager; Quality Control Supervisor; Software Engineer; Stationary Engineer; Statistician; Systems Analyst. **Average salary range of placements:** $30,000 - $50,000. **Number of placements per year:** 100 - 199.

JAGER PERSONNEL
P.O. Box 723, Dover DE 19903-0723. 302/736-0111. **Fax:** 302/736-0137. **Contact:** Paula Jager. **Description:** An executive search firm specializing in placing professionals with AS 400, LAN, and WAN experience.

ELLIE MACK ASSOCIATES
2203 Fairfax Boulevard, Talleyville DE 19803. 302/427-9410. **Contact:** Manager. **Description:** An executive search firm.

THE PLACERS, INC.
111 Continental Drive, Suite 201, Christiana DE 19713. 302/456-6800. **Fax:** 302/456-6810. **Contact:** Alan R. Burkhard, CPC, President. **Description:** An executive search firm focusing on accounting, finance, information technology, and various office service

industries. The company also provides temporary and contract services on a contingency basis. Founded in 1972. Company pays fee. **Specializes in the areas of:** Accounting/Auditing; Administration; Banking; Finance; Insurance; Legal; Personnel/Labor Relations; Secretarial. **Positions commonly filled include:** Accountant/Auditor; Administrative Manager; Bank Officer/Manager; Branch Manager; Computer Programmer; Customer Service Representative; Financial Analyst; MIS Specialist; Paralegal; Software Engineer; Systems Analyst; Typist/Word Processor; Underwriter/Assistant Underwriter. **Benefits available to temporary workers:** Paid Holidays; Paid Vacation. **Corporate headquarters location:** Wilmington DE. **Average salary range of placements:** $30,000 - $50,000. **Number of placements per year:** 100 - 199.

PROVIEW RESOURCES INC.
230 Benjamin Boulevard, Bear DE 19701. 302/834-0349. **Contact:** Manager. **Description:** An executive search firm. **Specializes in the areas of:** Computer Hardware/Software.

PERMANENT EMPLOYMENT AGENCIES

CALDWELL STAFFING SERVICES
405 Newark Shopping Center, Newark DE 19711. 302/731-1111. **Fax:** 302/731-5745. **Contact:** Office Manager/Technical Representative. **Description:** An employment agency that provides both permanent and temporary placement. **Specializes in the areas of:** Administration; Banking; Sales. **Positions commonly filled include:** Account Manager; Customer Service Representative; Sales Executive; Sales Representative. **Average salary range of placements:** $30,000 - $50,000. **Number of placements per year:** 50 - 99.

CALDWELL STAFFING SERVICES
3520 Silverside Road, Suite 30, Wilmington DE 19810. 302/478-8700. **Fax:** 302/479-5418. **Contact:** Laurie Pysczynski, Branch Manager. **Description:** An employment agency that provides both permanent and temporary placement. Company pays fee. **Specializes in the areas of:** Accounting/Auditing; Banking; Finance; Insurance; Legal; Sales; Secretarial. **Positions commonly filled include:** Accountant/Auditor; Bookkeeper; Credit Manager; Customer Service Representative; Data Entry Clerk; Legal Secretary; Medical Secretary; Receptionist; Sales Representative; Secretary; Typist/Word Processor. **Number of placements per year:** 50 - 99.

HORIZONS RESOURCES
40 Reads Way, Corporate Commons, New Castle DE 19720. 302/323-1300. **Fax:** 302/323-9373. **Contact:** Manager. **Description:** A permanent employment agency that also provides temporary placements. **Specializes in the areas of:** Banking; Secretarial. **Positions commonly filled include:** Accountant; Administrative Assistant; Bank Officer/Manager; Claim Representative; Paralegal; Sales Executive; Secretary; Typist/Word Processor. **Average salary range of placements:** $20,000 - $50,000.

SUSSEX EMPLOYMENT SERVICES
204-C North Race, Georgetown DE 19947. 302/856-7308. **Contact:** Jeannie Warner, Manager. **Description:** A permanent employment agency. Company pays fee. **Specializes in the areas of:** Clerical. **Positions commonly filled include:** Accountant/Auditor; Administrative Assistant; Administrative Worker/Clerk; Bookkeeper; Clerk; Computer Operator; Computer Programmer; Customer Service Representative; Data Entry Clerk; Draftsperson; EDP Specialist; Legal Secretary; Medical Secretary; Receptionist; Typist/Word Processor. **Number of placements per year:** 100 - 199.

WILMINGTON SENIOR CENTER/EMPLOYMENT SERVICES
1909 North Market Street, Wilmington DE 19802. 302/651-3440. **Contact:** Sandria L. Thompson, Director of Employment Services. **Description:** A permanent employment agency that focuses on assisting people over 50 years of age with gaining unsubsidized employment, job search training, resume preparation, and job counseling. **Specializes in the areas of:** Elderly. **Positions commonly filled include:** Accountant/Auditor; Administrative Worker/Clerk; Bookkeeper; Clerk; Driver; Gardener; Receptionist; Repair Specialist; Sales Representative; Secretary; Typist/Word Processor. **Average salary range of placements:** Less than $20,000. **Number of placements per year:** 200 - 499.

TEMPORARY EMPLOYMENT AGENCIES

INFORMATION TECHNOLOGY SOLUTIONS
2000 Pennsylvania Avenue, Suite 201, Wilmington DE 19806. 302/571-8367. **Contact:** Manager. **Description:** A temporary and temp-to-hire agency. **Specializes in the areas of:** Information Systems.

NETWORK PERSONNEL
P.O. Box 19899, Wilmington DE 19899. 302/656-5555. **Contact:** Manager. **Description:** A temporary and temp-to-perm agency. **Specializes in the areas of:** Customer Service.

THE PLACERS, INC.
2000 Pennsylvania Avenue, Suite 201, Wilmington DE 19806. 302/571-8367. **Contact:** Office Manager. **Description:** A temporary agency that also provides permanent placement. Founded in 1992. **Specializes in the areas of:** Accounting/Auditing; Banking; Food Industry; General Management; Industrial; Manufacturing; Personnel/Labor Relations. **Positions commonly filled include:** Accountant/Auditor; Administrative Manager; Bank Officer/Manager; Branch Manager; Budget Analyst; Civil Engineer; Claim Representative; Clinical Lab Technician; Computer Programmer; Cost Estimator; Credit Manager; Customer Service Representative; Insurance Agent/Broker; Paralegal; Restaurant/Food Service Manager; Underwriter/Assistant Underwriter. **Benefits available to temporary workers:** Paid Holidays; Paid Vacation.

CONTRACT SERVICES FIRMS

H.L. YOH COMPANY
200 Continental Drive, Suite 101, Newark DE 19713. 302/368-6210. **Contact:** Manager. **Description:** A contract services firm. **Specializes in the areas of:** Computer Hardware/Software; Engineering.

DISTRICT OF COLUMBIA

EXECUTIVE SEARCH FIRMS

ABBTECH SERVICES
Dulles International Airport, P.O. Box 20098, Washington DC 20041. 703/450-5252. **Contact:** Manager. **Description:** An executive search firm. **Specializes in the areas of:** Technical.

ACCOUNTANTS EXECUTIVE SEARCH
ACCOUNTANTS ON CALL
1775 K Street NW, Suite 290, Washington DC 20006. 202/829-0003. **Contact:** Manager. **Description:** An executive search firm. Accountants on Call (also at this location) is a temporary agency that focuses on accounting placements. **Specializes in the areas of:** Accounting/Auditing; Finance.

C ASSOCIATES
P.O. Box 73868, Washington DC 20056-3868. 202/518-8595. **Fax:** 202/387-7033. **Contact:** John Capozzi, Jr., President. **E-mail address:** c1assoc @aol.com. **World Wide Web address:** http:// www.cassociates.com. **Description:** An executive search firm that operates on both retained and contingency bases. The firm focuses on technical placements. Company pays fee. **Specializes in the areas of:** Computer Science/Software. **Positions commonly filled include:** Computer Programmer; Software Engineer; Systems Analyst; Webmaster. **International locations:** Canada. **Average salary range of placements:** More than $50,000. **Number of placements per year:** 50 - 99.

CAPITOL SEARCH
1717 K Street NW, Suite 1112, Washington DC 20036. 202/296-8800. **Fax:** 202/296-8820. **Contact:** Office Manager. **Description:** An executive search firm.

FULL SERVICE STAFFING & TECHNOLOGY
3127 Martin Luther King Jr. Avenue SE, Suite 201, Washington DC 20032. 202/561-7525. **Contact:** Manager. **Description:** An executive search firm. **Specializes in the areas of:** Computer Science/Software.

KORN/FERRY INTERNATIONAL
900 19th Street NW, Suite 800, Washington DC 20006. 202/822-9444. **Contact:** Manager. **Description:** An executive search firm that places upper-level managers in a variety of industries. **Corporate headquarters location:** Los Angeles CA. **International locations:** Worldwide. **Average salary range of placements:** More than $50,000.

MAYFAIR ASSOCIATES
1828 L Street, Suite 402, Washington DC 20036. 202/872-0112. **Contact:** Manager. **Description:** An executive search firm.

MEE DERBY & COMPANY
1522 K Street NW, Suite 704, Washington DC 20005-1202. 202/842-8442. **Toll-free phone:** 800/597-8442. **Fax:** 202/842-1900. **Contact:** Robin Mee, President. **E-mail address:** meederby@msn.com. **Description:** An executive search firm that operates on a contingency basis. Company pays fee. **Specializes in the areas of:** Sales. **Positions commonly filled include:** Account Manager; Account Representative; Customer Service Representative; Sales Executive; Sales Manager; Sales Representative. **Average salary range of placements:** $30,000 - $50,000. **Number of placements per year:** 50 - 99.

JOHN MICHAEL ASSOCIATES
Dulles International Airport, P.O. Box 17130, Washington DC 20041. 703/471-6300. **Contact:** Manager. **Description:** An executive search firm. **Specializes in the areas of:** Legal.

MORRISON ASSOCIATES
3907 Harrison Street NW, Washington DC 20015. 202/223-6523. **Contact:** Manager. **Description:** An executive search firm. **Specializes in the areas of:** Nonprofit.

NATIONWIDE ATTORNEY PLACEMENT
1010 Vermont Avenue NW, Suite 408, Washington DC 20005. 202/393-1550. **Contact:** Office Manager. **Description:** An executive search firm that places attorneys. **Specializes in the areas of:** Legal.

NETWORK COMPANIES
1625 K Street NW, Suite 975, Washington DC 20006-1604. 202/463-4900. **Fax:** 202/296-7387. **Contact:** Manager. **Description:** An executive search firm that also offers permanent, temporary, and contract placements. Network Companies also offers seminars and resume consulting sessions. Company pays fee. **Specializes in the areas of:** Accounting/Auditing; Administration; Finance; General Management; Personnel/Labor Relations. **Positions commonly filled include:** Accountant/Auditor; Administrative Manager; Branch Manager; Budget Analyst; Buyer; Clerical Supervisor; Credit Manager; Customer Service Representative; Financial Analyst; General Manager; Human Resources Manager; Management Analyst/Consultant; Typist/Word Processor. **Benefits available to temporary workers:** 401(k); Bonus Award/Plan; Medical Insurance; Paid Holidays; Paid Vacation. **Corporate headquarters location:** Vienna VA. **Average salary range of placements:** $30,000 - $50,000. **Number of placements per year:** 500 - 999.

PIERCE ASSOCIATES
1815 Pennsylvania Avenue NW, Washington DC 20006. 202/835-1776. **Contact:** Office Manager. **Description:** An executive search firm. **Specializes in the areas of:** Legal. **Positions commonly filled include:** Attorney. **Other U.S. locations:** Los Angeles CA.

PREFERRED PLACEMENTS INC.
14150 Columbia Street NW, Washington DC 20001. 202/232-4800. **Contact:** Manager. **Description:** An executive search firm. **Specializes in the areas of:** Legal.

DON RICHARD ASSOCIATES OF WASHINGTON DC
1020 19th Street NW, Washington DC 20036. 202/463-7210. **Fax:** 202/331-9743. **Contact:** Mark Strassman, CEO. **World Wide Web address:** http://www.donrichard.com. **Description:** An executive search firm that also provides temporary placements, contract services, and career counseling. Company pays fee. **Specializes in the areas of:** Accounting/Auditing; Banking; Computer Science/ Software; Finance. **Benefits available to temporary workers:** Medical Insurance; Paid Vacation. **Average salary range of placements:** More than $50,000. **Number of placements per year:** 1000+.

RURAK & ASSOCIATES, INC.
1350 Connecticut Avenue NW, Suite 801, Washington DC 20008. 202/293-7603. **Contact:**

Office Manager. **Description:** A generalist executive search firm.

RUSSELL REYNOLDS ASSOCIATES, INC.
1700 Pennsylvania Avenue NW, Suite 850, Washington DC 20006. 202/628-2150. **Contact:** Manager. **Description:** A generalist executive search firm.

SAVOY PARTNERS LTD.
1620 L Street NW, Suite 801, Washington DC 20036. 202/887-0666. **Contact:** Manager. **Description:** An executive search firm. **Specializes in the areas of:** General Management; Sales; Telecommunications.

TANGENT CORPORATION
1901 L Street NW, Suite 705, Washington DC 20036. 202/331-9484. **Fax:** 202/466-4059. **Contact:** Dana Williams, Marketing Assistant. **E-mail address:** tangent@erols.com. **Description:** An executive search firm operating on a contingency basis that specializes in the permanent placement of administrative professionals. Company pays fee. **Specializes in the areas of:** Accounting/Auditing; Administration; Finance; General Management; Personnel/Labor Relations; Secretarial. **Positions commonly filled include:** Accountant; Administrative Assistant; Administrative Manager; Computer Operator; Customer Service Representative; Editorial Assistant; Financial Analyst; Human Resources Manager; Marketing Specialist; Online Content Specialist; Secretary; Typist/Word Processor. **Corporate headquarters location:** This Location. **Other U.S. locations:** Denver CO. **Average salary range of placements:** $20,000 - $29,999. **Number of placements per year:** 100 - 199.

TRAVAILLE EXECUTIVE SEARCH
1730 Rhode Island Avenue NW, Suite 401, Washington DC 20036. 202/463-6342. **Contact:** Manager. **Description:** An executive search firm. **Specializes in the areas of:** Communications.

PERMANENT EMPLOYMENT AGENCIES

ADMINISTRATIVE ASSISTANCE HIRE STANDARD STAFFING
1350 Connecticut Avenue NW, Suite 1050, Washington DC 20036. 202/496-0300. **Fax:** 202/496-0309. **Contact:** Helen Hopkins, President. **Description:** A permanent and temporary agency that also provides some contract services. Company pays fee. **Specializes in the areas of:** Accounting/Auditing; Legal Secretarial; Nonprofit; Office Support; Sales; Secretarial. **Positions commonly filled include:** Account Manager; Account Representative; Accountant; Administrative Assistant; Administrative Manager; Auditor; Customer Service Representative; Database Manager; Paralegal; Sales Executive; Sales Manager; Sales Representative; Typist/Word Processor. **Benefits available to temporary workers:** Medical Insurance; Paid Holidays. **Corporate headquarters location:** This Location. **Other U.S. locations:** Fort Lauderdale FL; Bethesda MD; McLean VA. **Average salary range of placements:** $20,000 - $29,999. **Number of placements per year:** 100 - 199.

CAREER BLAZERS PERSONNEL SERVICE
1025 Connecticut Avenue NW, Washington DC 20036. 202/467-4222. **Fax:** 202/467-0820. **Contact:** Jeffrey Oxman, President. **World Wide Web address:** http://www.careerblazers.com. **Description:** A full-service professional personnel firm combining full-time placement, temporary placement, and a nationally-accredited computer skills training program. Founded in 1949. Company pays fee. **Specializes in the areas of:** Administration; Finance; General Management; Personnel/Labor Relations; Sales; Secretarial. **Positions commonly filled include:** Accountant/Auditor; Administrative Manager; Advertising Clerk; Branch Manager; Claim Representative; Customer Service Representative; Editor; Human Resources Manager; Human Service Worker; Management Trainee; Manufacturer's/Wholesaler's Sales Rep.; Paralegal; Services Sales Representative; Typist/Word Processor. **Corporate headquarters location:** New York NY. **Other U.S. locations:** Nationwide. **Average salary range of placements:** $30,000 - $50,000. **Number of placements per year:** 1000+.

K.M.S. ASSOCIATES
1620 L Street NW, Suite 801, Washington DC 20036. 202/822-8383. **Fax:** 202/887-4991. **Contact:** Karen Sadowski, President. **Description:** A permanent employment agency that places support and managerial professionals with law firms and corporations. **Specializes in the areas of:** Legal; Nonprofit; Personnel/Labor Relations; Secretarial. **Positions commonly filled include:** Paralegal; Typist/Word Processor. **Average salary range of placements:** $30,000 - $50,000. **Number of placements per year:** 50 - 99.

MEDICAL PERSONNEL SERVICES, INC.
1707 L Street, Suite 250, Washington DC 20036. 202/466-2955. **Contact:** Janet Cline Patrick, President. **Description:** A medical employment agency. **Specializes in the areas of:** Health/Medical. **Positions commonly filled include:** Medical Secretary; Nurse.

PORTFOLIO
1730 K Street NW, Suite 1350, Washington DC 20006. 202/293-5700. **Toll-free phone:** 888/88F-OLIO. **Fax:** 202/293-9025. **Contact:** Manager. **World Wide Web address:** http://www.portfolio skill.com. **Description:** A permanent and temporary agency. **Specializes in the areas of:** Art/Design; Computer Graphics; Multimedia; Technical Writing.

POSITIONS INC.
1730 K Street NW, Suite 907, Washington DC 20006. 202/659-9270. **Fax:** 202/659-9245. **Contact:** Ellen Andrews, Managing Partner. **Description:** A permanent employment agency. **Specializes in the areas of:** Administration; Office Support. **Positions commonly filled include:** Administrative Assistant; Executive Assistant; Receptionist; Secretary.

POTOMAC PERSONNEL
1212 New York Avenue, Suite 250, Washington DC 20005. 202/296-2270. **Fax:** 202/296-2320. **Contact:** Andrea Mignanelli, Quality Service Coordinator. **Description:** A staffing company specializing in permanent and some temporary placements for administrative positions. Potomac Personnel has over 600 offices nationwide. The company also offers career/outplacement counseling. Company pays fee. **Specializes in the areas of:** Accounting/Auditing; Art/Design; Banking; Education; General Management; Health/Medical; Insurance; Legal; Nonprofit; Personnel/Labor Relations; Publishing; Secretarial. **Positions commonly filled include:** Customer Service Representative; Human Resources Manager; MIS Specialist; Paralegal; Telecommunications Manager; Typist/Word Processor. **Benefits available to temporary workers:** 401(k); Dental Insurance; Medical Insurance; Paid Holidays; Paid Vacation. **Corporate headquarters location:** New York NY. **Average salary**

range of placements: $20,000 - $29,999. **Number of placements per year:** 1000+.

SIGMAN & SUMMERFIELD ASSOCIATES, INC.
1120 Connecticut Avenue NW, Suite 270, Washington DC 20036. 202/785-9044. **Fax:** 202/331-0375. **Contact:** Katheleijne Zambrowicz, Partner. **Description:** A permanent employment agency. Company pays fee. **Specializes in the areas of:** Administration; Legal; Nonprofit; Personnel/Labor Relations; Secretarial. **Positions commonly filled include:** Administrative Assistant; Administrative Manager; Clerical Supervisor; Paralegal; Secretary. **Number of placements per year:** 1 - 49.

SNELLING PERSONNEL
1000 16th Street NW, Suite 805, Washington DC 20036. 202/223-3540. **Fax:** 202/872-1967. **Contact:** Recruiter. **Description:** An employment agency that places both permanent and temporary workers. **Specializes in the areas of:** Bookkeeping; Clerical; Hotel/Restaurant; Legal; Office Support. **Positions commonly filled include:** Administrative Worker/Clerk; Clerk; Management; Receptionist; Secretary; Typist/Word Processor.

STAR STAFFING SERVICES
1828 L Street NW, Suite 400, Washington DC 20036-5104. 202/223-5257. **Fax:** 202/833-1943. **Contact:** Recruiter. **Description:** A permanent employment agency. Company pays fee. **Positions commonly filled include:** Accountant/Auditor; Administrative Manager; Clerical Supervisor; Computer Programmer; Librarian; Paralegal; Typist/Word Processor. **Benefits available to temporary workers:** Paid Holidays; Paid Vacation. **Average salary range of placements:** $20,000 - $29,999. **Number of placements per year:** 200 - 499.

TRAK ASSOCIATES
1155 Connecticut Avenue NW, Suite 800, Washington DC 20036. 202/466-8850. **Contact:** Manager. **Description:** A permanent placement agency that also provides some temporary placements. **Specializes in the areas of:** Administration.

TRIFAX CORPORATION
4121 Minnesota Avenue NE, Washington DC 20019. 202/388-6000. **Fax:** 202/388-6001. **Contact:** Ruth Ledbetter, Executive Vice President. **Description:** A permanent employment agency that provides medical placements. **Specializes in the areas of:** Health/Medical; Personnel/Labor Relations. **Positions commonly filled include:** Administrative Assistant; Clerk; Data Entry Clerk; Marketing Specialist; Medical Secretary; Nurse; Social Worker; Typist/Word Processor. **Number of placements per year:** 50 - 99.

WHITMAN ASSOCIATES INC.
1730 K Street NW, Suite 309, Washington DC 20006. 202/659-2111. **Contact:** Manager. **Description:** A permanent employment agency that also provides temporary placements. **Specializes in the areas of:** Secretarial. **Positions commonly filled include:** Administrative Assistant; Legal Secretary; Secretary.

WOODSIDE EMPLOYMENT CONSULTANTS, INC.
1225 Eye Street NW, Suite 401, Washington DC 20005. 202/789-3105. **Contact:** Manager. **Description:** A permanent and temporary employment agency. Company pays fee. **Specializes in the areas of:** Accounting/Auditing; Office Support. **Positions commonly filled include:** Administrative Assistant; Executive Assistant; Legal Secretary; Office Manager; Paralegal; Receptionist.

TEMPORARY EMPLOYMENT AGENCIES

BEST TEMPORARIES, INC.
1101 Connecticut Avenue NW, Suite 801, Washington DC 20036-4303. 202/293-7333. **Fax:** 202/861-0297. **Contact:** Manager. **Description:** A temporary agency. **Specializes in the areas of:** Administration; Nonprofit; Personnel/Labor Relations; Secretarial. **Benefits available to temporary workers:** Paid Holidays; Paid Vacation; Referral Bonus Plan.

GRAPHIC MAC
1301 Connecticut Avenue NW, Lower Level, Washington DC 20036-1815. 202/785-1333. **Fax:** 202/785-5927. **Contact:** Christian Lilley, Operations Manager. **E-mail address:** graphicmac@aol.com. **Description:** A graphic design and publications temporary employment agency. The agency also offers some permanent placements. **Specializes in the areas of:** Art/Design; Printing; Publishing. **Positions commonly filled include:** Designer; Desktop Publishing Specialist; Graphic Designer. **Number of placements per year:** 200 - 499.

LAWCORPS LEGAL STAFFING
1899 L Street NW, 5th Floor, Washington DC 20036. 202/785-5996. **Fax:** 202/785-1118. **Contact:** Ms. Lee E. Arrowood, Administrator. **World Wide Web address:** http://www.lawcorps.com. **Description:** A temporary legal staffing service. The firm places attorneys, law clerks, and paralegals on a temporary, temp-to-hire, and permanent basis. Founded in 1988. Company pays fee. **Specializes in the areas of:** Legal. **Positions commonly filled include:** Attorney; Paralegal. **Benefits available to temporary workers:** Bonus Award/Plan; Medical Insurance; Paid Vacation; Profit Sharing.

MANPOWER
1130 Connecticut Avenue NW, Suite 530, Washington DC 20036. 202/331-8300. **Contact:** Branch Manager. **Description:** A temporary agency. **Specializes in the areas of:** Industrial; Office Support; Telecommunications; Word Processing. **Positions commonly filled include:** Accountant/Auditor; Administrative Assistant; Assembly Worker; Biological Scientist; Bookkeeper; Customer Service Representative; Desktop Publishing Specialist; Electrician; Inspector/Tester/Grader; Inventory Control Specialist; Machine Operator; Packaging/Processing Worker; Painter; Project Engineer; Proofreader; Receptionist; Research Assistant; Software Engineer; Systems Analyst; Typist/Word Processor; Welder. **Benefits available to temporary workers:** Life Insurance; Medical Insurance; Paid Holidays; Paid Vacation. **Number of placements per year:** 1000+.

NRI LEGAL RESOURCES
NRI ACCOUNTING RESOURCES
1015 18th Street NW, Suite 700, Washington DC 20036. 202/659-0200. **Fax:** 202/659-4732. **Contact:** Dori Konopka, General Manager. **E-mail address:** nri@nri-staffing.com. **World Wide Web address:** http://www.nri-staffing.com. **Description:** Provides temporary, temp-to-hire, and permanent placements for administrative and legal professionals. NRI Accounting Resources (also at this location) places accounting professionals. **Specializes in the areas of:** Administration; Legal. **Average salary range of placements:** $30,000 - $50,000. **Number of placements per year:** 500 - 999.

NRI STAFFING RESOURCES
1899 L Street NW, Suite 300, Washington DC 20036. 202/466-4670. **Fax:** 202/466-6593. **Contact:** Robert Mulberger, President. **E-mail address:** nri@nri-staffing.com. **World Wide Web address:** http://www.nri-staffing.com. **Description:** A temporary agency that also offers temp-to-hire and permanent placements. Company pays fee. **Specializes in the areas of:** Administration; General Management. **Positions commonly filled include:** Accountant/Auditor; Actuary; Administrative Manager; Advertising Clerk; Attorney; Financial Analyst; Health Services Manager; Medical Records Technician; Paralegal; Physical Therapist; Typist/Word Processor. **Average salary range of placements:** $20,000 - $29,999. **Number of placements per year:** 500 - 999.

NORRELL SERVICES
4401 Connecticut Avenue NW, Suite 604, Washington DC 20008-2322. 202/686-1199. **Fax:** 202/966-7291. **Contact:** Recruiter. **Description:** A temporary agency that also provides contract placements. **Specializes in the areas of:** Accounting/Auditing; Administration; Banking; Computer Science/Software; Engineering; Finance; Industrial; Insurance; Secretarial; Technical. **Positions commonly filled include:** Accountant/Auditor; Claim Representative; Computer Programmer; Customer Service Representative; Financial Analyst; MIS Specialist; Operations/Production Manager; Software Engineer; Typist/Word Processor. **Benefits available to temporary workers:** 401(k); Dental Insurance; Medical Insurance; Paid Holidays; Paid Vacation; Stock Purchase. **Corporate headquarters location:** Atlanta GA. **International locations:** Worldwide. **Average salary range of placements:** $20,000 - $29,999. **Number of placements per year:** 1000+.

SOURCE SERVICES CORPORATION
1111 19th Street NW, Suite 620, Washington DC 20036. 202/293-9255. **Contact:** Office Manager. **Description:** A temporary agency that also provides temp-to-hire placements. **Specializes in the areas of:** Accounting/Auditing; Finance; Information Technology.

SPECIAL COUNSEL
1001 Connecticut Avenue NW, Washington DC 20036. 202/737-3436. **Fax:** 202/776-0084. **Contact:** Manager. **World Wide Web address:** http://www.specialcounsel.com. **Description:** A temporary and permanent employment agency. **Specializes in the areas of:** Legal.

TEMPORARY STAFFING, INC.
1150 17th Street NW, Suite 202, Washington DC 20036. 202/466-8230. **Fax:** 202/466-8234. **Contact:** Bernadette Gilson, Vice President. **Description:** A temporary agency focusing on administrative secretarial and paralegal placements. Company pays fee. **Specializes in the areas of:** Legal; Secretarial. **Positions commonly filled include:** Paralegal. **Benefits available to temporary workers:** Credit Union; Paid Holidays; Paid Vacation. **Corporate headquarters location:** Annapolis MD. **Average salary range of placements:** $20,000 - $29,999. **Number of placements per year:** 1000+.

TEMPWORLD STAFFING SERVICES
1050 17th Street NW, Suite 750, Washington DC 20036. 202/296-7530. **Contact:** Ilene Rush, Program Manager. **E-mail address:** tempwrld@aol.com. **Description:** A temporary agency. Company pays fee. **Specializes in the areas of:** Accounting/Auditing; Administration; Sales; Secretarial. **Positions commonly filled include:** Administrative Assistant; Computer Operator; Customer Service Representative; Editorial Assistant; Sales Representative; Typist/Word Processor. **Benefits available to temporary workers:** Bonus Award/Plan; Medical Insurance; Paid Holidays; Paid Vacation. **Other U.S. locations:** Nationwide. **Average salary range of placements:** $30,000 - $50,000. **Number of placements per year:** 1000+.

CAREER/OUTPLACEMENT COUNSELING FIRMS

ACCESS: NETWORKING IN THE PUBLIC INTEREST
1001 Connecticut Avenue NW, Suite 838, Washington DC 20036. 202/785-4233. **Fax:** 202/785-4212. **Contact:** Executive Director. **Description:** A national employment clearing house for the nonprofit sector. Products and services include job listing newsletters, over-the-phone career counseling, and civic involvement guides. **Corporate headquarters location:** This Location. **Specializes in the areas of:** Art/Design; Education; Entry-Level; Environmental; Health/Medical; Human Services; International Executives; Liberal Arts; Nonprofit. **Positions commonly filled include:** Customer Service Representative; Editor; General Manager.

BLACKWELL CAREER MANAGEMENT
626 A Street SE, Capitol Hill, Washington DC 20003. 202/546-6835. **Fax:** 202/547-7308. **Contact:** Mary Ann Blackwell, President and Executive Director. **E-mail address:** mbcareer@rsabbs.com. **World Wide Web address:** http://www.bizxp.com. **Description:** An education and career management firm specializing in career transition and advanced marketing services. The firm offers lectures, seminars, workshops, career evaluations, and consultations.

FLORIDA

EXECUTIVE SEARCH FIRMS

ACCOUNTANTS EXECUTIVE SEARCH
ACCOUNTANTS ON CALL
1715 North Westshore Boulevard, Suite 460, Tampa FL 33607. 813/289-0051. **Fax:** 813/289-6004. **Contact:** Jeffrey Waldon, President. **E-mail address:** jwaldon957@aol.com. **Description:** An executive search firm that operates on a contingency basis. Accountants On Call (also at this location) places clerical accounting and bookkeeping personnel in temporary, temp-to-perm, and permanent positions. **Specializes in the areas of:** Accounting/Auditing; Banking; Finance. **Positions commonly filled include:** Accountant; Budget Analyst; Chief Financial Officer; Finance Director; Financial Analyst. **Benefits available to temporary workers:** Medical Insurance; Paid Vacation. **Corporate headquarters location:** Saddle Brook NJ. **International locations:** Worldwide. **Average salary range of placements:** $20,000 - $29,999. **Number of placements per year:** 500 - 999.

ACCOUNTANTS EXECUTIVE SEARCH
ACCOUNTANTS ON CALL
One Alhambra Plaza, Suite 1435, Coral Gables FL 33134. 305/443-9333. **Contact:** Daniel Perron, Manager. **Description:** An executive search firm. Accountants On Call (also at this location) is a temp-to-perm placement agency. **Specializes in the areas of:** Accounting/Auditing; Banking; Finance. **Corporate headquarters location:** Saddle Brook NJ. **International locations:** Worldwide.

ACCOUNTANTS EXECUTIVE SEARCH
ACCOUNTANTS ON CALL
1801 Lee Road, Suite 375, Winter Park FL 32789. 407/629-2999. **Contact:** Manager. **Description:** An executive search firm. Accountants on Call (also at this location) is a temporary agency. **Specializes in the areas of:** Accounting/Auditing; Finance. **Corporate headquarters location:** Saddle Brook NJ. **International locations:** Worldwide.

ACTIVE PROFESSIONALS
2572 Atlantic Boulevard, Suite 1, Jacksonville FL 32207. 904/396-7148. **Fax:** 904/396-6321. **Contact:** Faye Rustin, Owner. **Description:** An executive search firm that also operates as an employment agency. Company pays fee. **Specializes in the areas of:** Accounting/Auditing; Architecture/Construction; Computer Hardware/Software; Engineering; Finance; General Management; Industrial; Insurance; Manufacturing; Personnel/Labor Relations; Sales; Secretarial. **Number of placements per year:** 100 - 199.

AMBIANCE PERSONNEL INC.
7990 SW 117th Avenue, Suite 125, Miami FL 33183-3845. 305/274-7419. **Fax:** 305/598-8071. **Contact:** Eric S. Pollack, Vice President/General Manager. **Description:** An executive search firm that also offers temporary and permanent placements. The company focuses on the international trade and transportation industry, but also provides office support, accounting, information technology, logistics, and materials management personnel. Company pays fee. **Specializes in the areas of:** Accounting/Auditing; Import/Export; Logistics; Sales; Secretarial; Transportation. **Positions commonly filled include:** Accountant/Auditor; Branch Manager; Buyer; Computer Programmer; Credit Manager; Customer Service Representative; Financial Analyst; General Manager; MIS Specialist; Systems Analyst. **Benefits available to temporary workers:** 401(k); Life Insurance; Medical Insurance; Paid Holidays; Paid Vacation. **Number of placements per year:** 200 - 499.

AMERICAN EXECUTIVE SEARCH
AMERICAN RECRUITERS
800 West Cypress Creek Road, Suite 310, Fort Lauderdale FL 33309. 954/771-6663. **Contact:** Manager. **Description:** An executive search firm operating on both retained and contingency bases. Company pays fee. **Specializes in the areas of:** Administration; Clerical; Computer Science/Software; Engineering; Finance; Food Industry; General Management; Health/Medical; Industrial; Insurance; Sales; Secretarial; Technical. **Average salary range of placements:** More than $50,000. **Number of placements per year:** 500 - 999.

AMERICAN RECRUITERS
3900 NW 79th Avenue, Miami FL 33166. 305/592-1455. **Contact:** Manager. **Description:** An executive search firm. **Specializes in the areas of:** Administration; General Management; Sales.

AMERICAN RECRUITERS
800 West Cypress Creek Road, Suite 310, Fort Lauderdale FL 33309. 954/493-9200. **Contact:** Manager. **Description:** An executive search firm. **Specializes in the areas of:** Administration; Clerical; Finance; General Management; Sales.

ASH & ASSOCIATES EXECUTIVE SEARCH
P.O. Box 862, Pompano Beach FL 33061. 954/946-3395. **Contact:** Manager. **Description:** An executive search firm. **Specializes in the areas of:** Information Systems.

ATLANTIC PROFESSIONAL RECRUITERS
3836 Arrow Lakes Drive South, Jacksonville FL 32257. 904/262-3939. **Contact:** Ed Landers, Owner. **Description:** An executive search firm. **Specializes in the areas of:** Engineering; Manufacturing.

A.M. AUSTER ASSOCIATION
283 Northlake Boulevard, Suite 111, Altamonte Springs FL 32701. 407/831-2400. **Contact:** Manager. **Description:** An executive search firm that places personnel in a variety of industries. **Average salary range of placements:** More than $50,000.

BALES-WAUGH GROUP
BALES SALES RECRUITERS, INC.
1301 Riverplace Boulevard, Suite 2016, Jacksonville FL 32207. 904/398-9080. **Fax:** 904/398-8121. **Contact:** Beau Bales, Account Manager. **Description:** An executive search firm specializing in the health care industry and providing executive management searches, sales distribution, and funding/strategic alliance assistance. Bales Sales Recruiters, Inc. (also at this location) is an executive search firm that specializes in sales recruiting in the medical, consumer, business products, and industrial arenas. Company pays fee. **Specializes in the areas of:** Computer Science/Software; General Management; Health/Medical; Sales. **Positions commonly filled include:** Computer Programmer; EEG Technologist; EKG Technician; General Manager; Human Resources Manager; Manufacturer's/Wholesaler's Sales Rep.; MIS Specialist; Radiological Technologist; Registered Nurse; Respiratory Therapist; Surgical Technician; Systems Analyst. **Number of placements per year:** 100 - 199.

BEACH EXECUTIVE SEARCH
10100 West Sample Road, Suite 325, Coral Springs FL 33065. 954/340-7337. **Contact:** Manager. **Description:** An executive search firm.

BENSON AND ASSOCIATES
551 NW 77th Street, Suite 102, Boca Raton FL 33487. 561/997-1600. **Toll-free phone:** 800/275-1221. **Fax:** 561/997-1601. **Contact:** Lou Benson, President. **Description:** An executive search firm that recruits registered representatives for brokerage firms nationwide. Company pays fee. **Specializes in the areas of:** Banking; Brokerage; Sales. **Positions commonly filled include:** Securities Sales Representative; Services Sales Representative. **Average salary range of placements:** More than $50,000. **Number of placements per year:** 1 - 49.

THE BRAND COMPANY, INC.
8402 Red Bay Court, Vero Beach FL 32963. 561/231-1807. **Contact:** Mr. J.B. Spangenberg, President. **Description:** An executive search firm. Company pays fee. **Specializes in the areas of:** Engineering; General Management; Industrial; Manufacturing; Personnel/Labor Relations; Sales. **Positions commonly filled include:** General Manager; Human Resources Manager; Operations Research Analyst; Quality Control Supervisor. **Number of placements per year:** 1 - 49.

BRYAN & ASSOCIATES
WORKNET, ETC.
2931 Plummer Cove Road, Jacksonville FL 32223-6610. 904/880-5275. **Contact:** Bryan Cornwall, President. **Description:** An executive search firm. **Specializes in the areas of:** Accounting/Auditing; Administration; Advertising; Banking; Broadcasting; Computer Science/Software; Economics; Finance; Food Industry; General Management; Health/Medical; Industrial; Insurance; Legal; Manufacturing; Personnel/Labor Relations; Publishing; Retail; Sales; Secretarial; Technical; Transportation. **Positions commonly filled include:** Accountant/Auditor; Adjuster; Administrative Manager; Architect; Attorney; Bank Officer/Manager; Biochemist; Branch Manager; Broadcast Technician; Budget Analyst; Buyer; Claim Representative; Clerical Supervisor; Clinical Lab Technician; Computer Programmer; Customer Service Representative; Editor; Education Administrator; Electrician; Environmental Engineer; Financial Analyst; Health Services Manager; Hotel Manager; Human Service Worker; Industrial Engineer; Insurance Agent/Broker; Management Analyst/Consultant; Occupational Therapist; Paralegal; Quality Control Supervisor; Restaurant/Food Service Manager; Securities Sales Representative; Services Sales Representative; Software Engineer; Strategic Relations Manager; Systems Analyst; Technical Writer/Editor; Typist/Word Processor; Underwriter/Assistant Underwriter; Video Production Coordinator. **Benefits available to temporary workers:** Medical Insurance; Paid Holidays; Paid Vacation. **Average salary range of placements:** $30,000 - $50,000. **Number of placements per year:** 200 - 499.

THE BUTLERS COMPANY
INSURANCE RECRUITERS
2753 State Road 580, Suite 103, Clearwater FL 33761. 813/725-1065. **Fax:** 813/726-7125. **Contact:** Kirby B. Butler, CPC, President. **E-mail address:** kbutler@gte.net. **Description:** An executive search firm. Company pays fee. **Specializes in the areas of:** Insurance; Risk Management; Safety. **Positions commonly filled include:** Actuary; Adjuster; Branch Manager; Claim Representative; Computer Programmer; Customer Service Representative; Insurance Agent/Broker; Loss Prevention Specialist; Marketing Manager; Sales Executive; Systems Analyst; Underwriter/Assistant Underwriter. **Average salary range of placements:** More than $50,000. **Number of placements per year:** 1 - 49.

CANTRELL & ASSOCIATES
433 Harrison Avenue, Suite 1A, Panama City FL 32401. 904/784-1680. **Contact:** Manager. **Description:** An executive search firm. **Specializes in the areas of:** Engineering.

CAPITAL DATA, INC.
P.O. Box 2244, Palm Harbor FL 34682-2244. 813/784-4100. **Toll-free phone:** 800/771-4100. **Fax:** 800/787-4172. **Contact:** Jack Logan, Manager. **E-mail address:** as400cdo@aol.com. **Description:** A full-service executive search firm and employment agency that offers permanent, temporary, and contract placements, as well as career/outplacement counseling. Company pays fee. **Specializes in the areas of:** Computer Science/Software; Technical. **Positions commonly filled include:** Computer Programmer; Software Engineer; Systems Analyst; Technical Writer/Editor; Telecommunications Manager. **Average salary range of placements:** More than $50,000. **Number of placements per year:** 100 - 199.

CAREER CHOICE, INC.
1035 South Semoran Boulevard, Suite 1021-A, Winter Park FL 32792. 407/679-5150. **Fax:** 407/679-0998. **Contact:** C.M. Herrick, President. **Description:** An executive search firm. Company pays fee. **Specializes in the areas of:** Food Industry; Hotel/Restaurant; Sales. **Positions commonly filled include:** Accountant/Auditor; Budget Analyst; Buyer; Chef/Cook/Kitchen Worker; Dietician/Nutritionist; General Manager; Hotel Manager; Human Resources Manager; Insurance Agent/Broker; Physician; Purchasing Agent/Manager; Restaurant/Food Service Manager. **Average salary range of placements:** More than $50,000. **Number of placements per year:** 100 - 199.

CAREER CONCEPTS
1025 South Semoran Boulevard, Suite 1093, Winter Park FL 32792. 407/679-7440. **Fax:** 407/679-9428. **Contact:** Manager. **World Wide Web address:** http://www.ccitech.jobs.com. **Description:** An executive search firm that specializes in placing computer professionals with AS400 or client/server experience. **Specializes in the areas of:** Computer Science/Software; High-Tech. **Positions commonly filled include:** Computer Programmer; Project Manager; Systems Analyst.

CAREERS UNLIMITED, INC.
1515 University Drive, Suite 204B, Coral Springs FL 33071. 954/341-7100. **Toll-free phone:** 800/777-0957. **Fax:** 954/341-7104. **Contact:** John S. Barton, Manager. **E-mail address:** jbcareers@aol.com. **Description:** A contingency executive search firm. Company pays fee. **Specializes in the areas of:** Health/Medical; Insurance. **Corporate headquarters location:** This Location. **Other U.S. locations:** Hendersonville NC. **Average salary range of placements:** More than $50,000. **Number of placements per year:** 1 - 49.

CARTER-EVDEMON & ASSOCIATES
777 South Harbor Island Boulevard, Suite 930, Tampa FL 33602. 813/229-2220. **Contact:** Manager. **Description:** An executive search firm. **Specializes in the areas of:** Insurance.

CENTRAL FLORIDA COMPUTER PLACEMENTS
160 West Evergreen Street, Suite 291, Longwood FL 32750. 407/332-4779. **Contact:** Manager. **Description:** An executive search firm. **Specializes in the areas of:** Computer Science/Software.

THE CHELSEA GROUP
P.O. Box 86647, Madeira Beach FL 33738. 813/397-9905. **Contact:** Office Manager. **Description:** An executive search firm. Company pays fee. **Specializes in the areas of:** Health/Medical. **Positions commonly filled include:** Occupational Therapist; Physical Therapist; Physician; Registered Nurse; Speech-Language Pathologist. **Number of placements per year:** 100 - 199.

COLLI ASSOCIATES OF TAMPA
P.O. Box 2865, Tampa FL 33601. 813/681-2145. **Fax:** 813/661-5217. **Contact:** Carolyn Colli, Manager. **E-mail address:** colli@gte.com. **Description:** An executive search firm. Company pays fee. **Specializes in the areas of:** Computer Science/Software; Engineering; Industrial; Manufacturing. **Positions commonly filled include:** Biomedical Engineer; Buyer; Chemical Engineer; Electrical/Electronics Engineer; Industrial Engineer; Industrial Production Manager; Mechanical Engineer; Operations/Production Manager; Quality Control Supervisor; Software Engineer; Stationary Engineer; Structural Engineer. **Number of placements per year:** 1 - 49.

CONSTRUCTION RESOURCES GROUP, INC.
466 94th Avenue North, St. Petersburg FL 33702. 813/578-1962. **Fax:** 813/578-9982. **Contact:** Cheryl P. Harris, President. **Description:** An executive search firm. Company pays fee. **Specializes in the areas of:** Architecture/Construction. **Positions commonly filled include:** Civil Engineer; Construction Contractor; Construction Manager; Cost Estimator. **Average salary range of placements:** More than $50,000. **Number of placements per year:** 1 - 49.

CORPORATE CONSULTANTS OF AMERICA, INC.
2807 West Busch Boulevard, Suite 202, Tampa FL 33618. 813/932-8804. **Fax:** 813/932-8703. **Contact:** Dana Andrews, President. **Description:** An executive recruiting firm specializing in restaurant management. Company pays fee. **Specializes in the areas of:** Restaurant. **Positions commonly filled include:** Restaurant/Food Service Manager. **Average salary range of placements:** $30,000 - $50,000. **Number of placements per year:** 100 - 199.

CORPORATE SEARCH CONSULTANTS
775 South Kirkman Road, Suite 105, Orlando FL 32811. 407/578-3888. **Contact:** Office Manager. **Description:** An executive search firm. **Specializes in the areas of:** Banking; Finance; Information Systems.

CRITERION EXECUTIVE SEARCH
5420 Bay Center Drive, Suite 101, Tampa FL 33609-3469. 813/286-2000. **Fax:** 813/287-1660. **Contact:** Richard James, President. **Description:** An executive search firm. Company pays fee. **Specializes in the areas of:** Administration; Computer Science/Software; Engineering; Insurance; Legal; Manufacturing; Technical. **Positions commonly filled include:** Accountant/Auditor; Adjuster; Administrative Manager; Agricultural Engineer; Biological Scientist; Biomedical Engineer; Branch Manager; Civil Engineer; Electrical/Electronics Engineer; Human Resources Manager; Industrial Engineer; Industrial Production Manager; Insurance Agent/Broker; Mechanical Engineer; Operations/Production Manager; Purchasing Agent/Manager; Radiological Technologist; Software Engineer; Structural Engineer; Underwriter/Assistant Underwriter. **Number of placements per year:** 100 - 199.

DGA PERSONNEL GROUP, INC.
2691 East Oakland Park Boulevard, Suite 201, Fort Lauderdale FL 33306. 954/561-1771. **Contact:** David Grant, President. **Description:** A contingency search firm and employment agency. **Specializes in the areas of:** Accounting/Auditing; Administration; Architecture/Construction; Banking; Clerical; Computer Hardware/Software; Design; Engineering; Finance; Health/Medical; Industrial; Legal; Manufacturing; Sales; Secretarial; Technical; Transportation. **Positions commonly filled include:** Accountant/Auditor; Adjuster; Administrative Manager; Architect; Bank Officer/Manager; Biological Scientist; Biomedical Engineer; Branch Manager; Buyer; Chemical Engineer; Civil Engineer; Clerical Supervisor; Electrical/Electronics Engineer; Financial Analyst; Industrial Engineer; Industrial Production Manager; Insurance Agent/Broker; Mechanical Engineer; Quality Control Supervisor; Registered Nurse; Software Engineer; Structural Engineer; Technical Writer/Editor; Typist/Word Processor; Underwriter/Assistant Underwriter. **Average salary range of placements:** $30,000 - $50,000.

DHR INTERNATIONAL INC.
2810 East Oakland Park Boulevard, Suite 104, Fort Lauderdale FL 33306. 954/564-6110. **Contact:** Office Manager. **Description:** An executive search firm. **Specializes in the areas of:** Latin America.

DP EXECUTIVE SEARCH
8731 Grey Oaks Avenue, Sarasota FL 34238. 941/925-3503. **Fax:** 941/925-3528. **Contact:** Fred E. Harris, Owner. **Description:** An executive search firm. Company pays fee. **Specializes in the areas of:** Personnel/Labor Relations; Technical. **Positions commonly filled include:** Computer Operator; Computer Programmer; Software Engineer; Systems Analyst. **Number of placements per year:** 1 - 49.

DATA SEARCH NETWORK
21218 St. Andrew's Boulevard, Suite 611, Boca Raton FL 33433. 561/488-8788. **Contact:** Manager. **Description:** An executive search firm. **Specializes in the areas of:** Information Systems.

DELTA SEARCH
10014 North Dale Mabry Highway, Suite 101, Tampa FL 33618. 813/289-0307. **Contact:** Manager. **Description:** An executive search firm.

STEVEN DOUGLAS ASSOCIATES
3040 Universal Boulevard, Suite 190, Weston FL 33331. 954/385-8595. **Contact:** Manager. **Description:** An executive search firm. **Specializes in the areas of:** Accounting/Auditing; Banking; Finance; Information Systems.

DUNHILL OF TAMPA
4350 West Cypress Street, Suite 225, Tampa FL 33607. 813/872-8118. **Contact:** Mona Kramer, Administrative Assistant. **Description:** An executive search firm. **Specializes in the areas of:** Accounting/Auditing; Data Processing; Health/Medical. **Positions commonly filled include:** Accountant/Auditor; EEG Technologist; EKG Technician; Medical Records Technician; Network Administrator; Occupational Therapist; Physical Therapist; Registered Nurse; Respiratory Therapist; Surgical Technician.

DUNHILL STAFFING SERVICES
1915 East Bay Drive, Suite B3, Largo FL 33771. 813/585-0000. **Contact:** Richard Williams, Owner. **Description:** An executive search firm. **Specializes in the areas of:** Technical.

ENVIRONMENTAL HEALTH & SAFETY SEARCH ASSOCIATES
P.O. Box 1325, Palm Harbor FL 34682. 813/787-3225. **Fax:** 813/787-5599. **Contact:** Randy L. Williams, Principal. **Description:** An executive search firm. Company pays fee. **Specializes in the areas of:** Environmental; Industrial; Safety. **Positions commonly**

filled include: Environmental Scientist; Safety Specialist. **Average salary range of placements:** More than $50,000. **Number of placements per year:** 50 - 99.

ETHAN ALLEN PERSONNEL PLACEMENT
5070 Sweetwater Terrace, Cooper City FL 33330. 607/772-1560. **Fax:** 607/772-1564. **Contact:** Michael H. Houlihan, President. **Description:** An executive search firm. Company pays fee. **Specializes in the areas of:** Accounting/Auditing; Administration; Banking; Computer Science/Software; Engineering; Finance; General Management; Industrial; Manufacturing; Personnel/Labor Relations; Sales; Technical. **Positions commonly filled include:** Accountant/Auditor; Bank Officer/Manager; Budget Analyst; Buyer; Computer Programmer; Cost Estimator; Electrical/Electronics Engineer; Environmental Engineer; Financial Analyst; Industrial Engineer; Industrial Production Manager; Internet Services Manager; Management Analyst/Consultant; Mechanical Engineer; MIS Specialist; Quality Control Supervisor; Software Engineer; Systems Analyst; Technical Writer/Editor; Telecommunications Manager. **Number of placements per year:** 100 - 199.

EXECUTIVE CAREER STRATEGIES
7900 North University Drive, Suite 201, Tamarac FL 33321. 954/720-9764. **Contact:** Manager. **Description:** An executive search firm focusing on the placement of insurance and insurance-related professionals. **Specializes in the areas of:** Insurance.

EXECUTIVE EMPLOYMENT SEARCH INC.
4370 South Tamiami Trail, Sarasota FL 34231. 941/921-4744. **Contact:** Manager. **Description:** An executive search firm that focuses on placing managers in a wide variety of fields. **Positions commonly filled include:** Management.

EXECUTIVE MANNING CORPORATION
3000 NE 30th Place, Suite 402, Fort Lauderdale FL 33306. 954/561-5100. **Contact:** Manager. **Description:** An executive search firm covering a wide range of industries.

EXECUTIVE RECRUITING CONSULTANTS
8826 NW 189 Terrace, Miami FL 33018. 305/829-8989. **Contact:** Manager. **Description:** An executive search firm.

EXECUTIVE SALES REGISTRY
14029 North Dale Mabry Highway, Tampa FL 33618. 813/879-1324. **Contact:** Manager. **Description:** An executive search firm. **Specializes in the areas of:** Sales.

EXECUTIVE SEARCH INTERNATIONAL
733 North Magnolia Avenue, Orlando FL 32803. 407/425-6000. **Contact:** Manager. **Description:** An executive search firm. **Specializes in the areas of:** Hotel/Restaurant.

FARWELL GROUP INC.
One Alhambra Plaza, Suite 1425, Coral Gables FL 33134. 305/529-4811. **Contact:** Manager. **Description:** An executive search firm. **Specializes in the areas of:** Banking; Finance.

FIRST EMPLOYMENT CONSULTANTS, INC.
6175 NW 153rd Street, Suite 205, Miami Lakes FL 33014. 305/825-8900. **Fax:** 305/825-8020. **Contact:** Mark Benson, Vice President. **Description:** A search firm that recruits people desiring work in the Middle Eastern nations of Saudi Arabia, United Arab Emirates, and Kuwait. Company pays fee. **Specializes in the areas of:** Architecture/Construction; Banking; Engineering; Finance; Health/Medical; Manufacturing; Technical. **Positions commonly filled include:** Blue-Collar Worker Supervisor; Buyer; Civil Engineer; Construction Contractor; Cost Estimator; Draftsperson; Electrical/Electronics Engineer; Mechanical Engineer; Structural Engineer. **Average salary range of placements:** More than $50,000. **Number of placements per year:** 1000+.

F-O-R-T-U-N-E PERSONNEL CONSULTANTS
98 Sarasota Center Boulevard, Suite C, Sarasota FL 34240. 941/378-5262. **Fax:** 941/379-9233. **Contact:** Arthur R. Grindlinger, President. **E-mail address:** fortune1@gate.net. **Description:** An executive search firm. Company pays fee. **Specializes in the areas of:** Engineering; Industrial; Manufacturing; Materials; Quality Assurance; Transportation. **Positions commonly filled include:** Biomedical Engineer; Chemical Engineer; Electrical/Electronics Engineer; Industrial Engineer; Industrial Production Manager; Mechanical Engineer; Operations/Production Manager; Purchasing Agent/Manager; Quality Control Supervisor; Software Engineer; Transportation/Traffic Specialist. **Corporate headquarters location:** New York NY. **Other U.S. locations:** Nationwide. **Average salary range of placements:** More than $50,000. **Number of placements per year:** 50 - 99.

F-O-R-T-U-N-E PERSONNEL CONSULTANTS OF JACKSONVILLE
3830 Crown Point Road, Suite E, Jacksonville FL 32257. 904/886-2471. **Fax:** 904/886-2472. **Contact:** Bob Pepple, President. **Description:** An executive search firm. Company pays fee. **Specializes in the areas of:** Engineering; Manufacturing; Quality Assurance. **Positions commonly filled include:** Biological Scientist; Biomedical Engineer; Chemist; Engineer; General Manager; Industrial Production Manager; Management Analyst/Consultant; Quality Control Supervisor; Statistician; Telecommunications Manager. **Corporate headquarters location:** New York NY. **Other U.S. locations:** Nationwide. **Number of placements per year:** 50 - 99.

GCA/GULF COAST ASSOCIATES
998 14th Street NE, Winter Haven FL 33881. 941/401-2900. **Contact:** Mr. Chris Gordon, Proprietor. **Description:** An executive search firm. Company pays fee. **Specializes in the areas of:** Engineering; Heating, Air Conditioning, and Refrigeration; Manufacturing. **Positions commonly filled include:** Electrical/Electronics Engineer; Industrial Engineer; Mechanical Engineer; Metallurgical Engineer; Technical Writer/Editor.

GALLIN ASSOCIATES
P.O. Box 1065, Safety Harbor FL 34695. 813/724-8303. **Fax:** 813/724-8503. **Contact:** Office Manager. **Description:** An executive search firm. **Specializes in the areas of:** Chemical; Computer Science/Software; Engineering; MIS/EDP; Personnel/Labor Relations. **Positions commonly filled include:** Chemical Engineer; Chemist; Computer Programmer; Design Engineer; Environmental Engineer; Human Resources Manager; Internet Services Manager; MIS Specialist; Systems Analyst. **Average salary range of placements:** More than $50,000. **Number of placements per year:** 1 - 49.

MICHAEL S. GIMBEL AND ASSOCIATES
201 NE Second Street, Fort Lauderdale FL 33301. 954/525-7000. **Fax:** 954/525-7300. **Contact:** Michael S. Gimbel, President. **Description:** An executive search firm. Founded in 1980. Company pays fee. **Specializes in the areas of:** Accounting/Auditing; Administration; Banking; Computer Science/Software; Consulting; Finance; Health/Medical; Legal. **Positions commonly filled include:** Accountant/Auditor; Attorney; Bank Officer/Manager; Budget Analyst; Computer

Programmer; Credit Manager; Financial Analyst; Management Analyst/Consultant; MIS Specialist; Physician; Systems Analyst. **Average salary range of placements:** More than $50,000. **Number of placements per year:** 100 - 199.

BOB GRAHAM & ASSOCIATES
5401 West Kennedy Boulevard, Suite 1070, Tampa FL 33609. 813/282-4623. **Contact:** Manager. **Description:** An executive search firm. **Specializes in the areas of:** Computer Hardware/Software; Engineering.

ANN GROGAN & ASSOCIATES INC.
1180 Spring Centre South Boulevard, Altamonte Springs FL 32714. 407/788-0303. **Contact:** Manager. **Description:** An executive recruiting firm. **Specializes in the areas of:** Sales.

HR PROFESSIONAL CONSULTANTS, INC.
1975 East Sunrise Boulevard, Suite 604, Fort Lauderdale FL 33304. 954/485-6506. **Fax:** 954/485-6509. **Contact:** Placement Director. **E-mail address:** info@hr-pro.com. **World Wide Web address:** http://www.hr-pro.com. **Description:** An executive search firm operating on both retained and contingency bases. Company pays fee. **Specializes in the areas of:** Accounting/Auditing; Computer Science/Software; Engineering; Personnel/Labor Relations; Secretarial; Technical. **Positions commonly filled include:** Accountant/Auditor; Biochemist; Biomedical Engineer; Chemical Engineer; Chief Financial Officer; Computer Programmer; Electrical/Electronics Engineer; Finance Director; Financial Analyst; Industrial Engineer; Industrial Production Manager; Manufacturing Engineer; Mechanical Engineer; Quality Control Supervisor; Scientist; Secretary; Software Engineer. **Average salary range of placements:** More than $50,000. **Number of placements per year:** 1 - 49.

ROBERT HALF INTERNATIONAL ACCOUNTEMPS
1401 Forum Way, Suite 200, West Palm Beach FL 33401. 561/684-8500. **Fax:** 561/684-9946. **Contact:** Branch Manager. **World Wide Web address:** http://www.roberthalf.com. **Description:** An executive search firm. Accountemps (also at this location) provides temporary placements. Company pays fee. **Specializes in the areas of:** Accounting/Auditing; Finance; Information Systems. **Positions commonly filled include:** Accountant/Auditor; Budget Analyst; Financial Analyst; Market Research Analyst. **Benefits available to temporary workers:** Bonus Award/Plan; Dental Insurance; Medical Insurance; Paid Holidays. **Corporate headquarters location:** Menlo Park CA. **Other U.S. locations:** Nationwide. **Number of placements per year:** 200 - 499.

ROBERT HALF INTERNATIONAL ACCOUNTEMPS
200 East Las Olas Boulevard, Suite 1650, Fort Lauderdale FL 33301. 954/761-3811. **Contact:** Manager. **World Wide Web address:** http://www.roberthalf.com. **Description:** An executive search firm. Accountemps (also at this location) provides temporary placements. **Specializes in the areas of:** Accounting/Auditing. **Corporate headquarters location:** Menlo Park CA. **Other U.S. locations:** Nationwide.

ROBERT HALF INTERNATIONAL ACCOUNTEMPS
225 East Robinson Street, Suite 545, Orlando FL 32801. 407/422-2275. **Contact:** Manager. **E-mail address:** orlando@roberthalf.com. **World Wide Web address:** http://www.roberthalf.com. **Description:** An executive search firm. Accountemps (also at this location) provides temporary placements. **Specializes in the areas of:** Accounting/Auditing. **Corporate headquarters location:** Menlo Park CA. **Other U.S. locations:** Nationwide.

ROBERT HALF INTERNATIONAL ACCOUNTEMPS
500 North WestShore Boulevard, Suite 500, Tampa FL 33609. 813/636-5000. **Contact:** Manager. **World Wide Web address:** http://www.roberthalf.com. **Description:** An executive search firm. Accountemps (also at this location) provides temporary placements. **Specializes in the areas of:** Accounting/Auditing. **Corporate headquarters location:** Menlo Park CA. **Other U.S. locations:** Nationwide.

ROBERT HALF INTERNATIONAL ACCOUNTEMPS
2655 Lejeune Road, Suite A14, Coral Gables FL 33134. 305/447-1757. **Contact:** Manager. **World Wide Web address:** http://www.roberthalf.com. **Description:** An executive search firm. Accountemps (also at this location) provides temporary placements. **Specializes in the areas of:** Accounting/Auditing. **Corporate headquarters location:** Menlo Park CA. **Other U.S. locations:** Nationwide.

HEALTHCARE RECRUITERS INTERNATIONAL
600 Sandtree Drive, Suite 206C, Palm Beach Gardens FL 33403. 561/625-9511. **Contact:** Manager. **Description:** An executive search firm. **Specializes in the areas of:** Health/Medical.

HEALTHCARE RECRUITERS OF CENTRAL FLORIDA
3000 Gulf to Bay Boulevard, Suite 304, Clearwater FL 33759. 813/725-5770. **Fax:** 813/725-9421. **Contact:** Tom Fleury, President. **Description:** An executive search firm. Company pays fee. **Specializes in the areas of:** Health/Medical; Sales. **Positions commonly filled include:** Biological Scientist; Biomedical Engineer; Health Services Manager; Manufacturer's/Wholesaler's Sales Rep.; Occupational Therapist; Pharmacist; Physical Therapist; Respiratory Therapist; Services Sales Representative. **Number of placements per year:** 1 - 49.

THE HILLARY GROUP
6417 Quail Hollow Place, Suite B, Bradenton FL 34210. 941/753-9926. **Contact:** Manager. **Description:** An executive search firm. **Specializes in the areas of:** Medical Device.

HOWARD/WILLIAMS ASSOCIATES
105 South Narcissus Avenue, Suite 806, West Palm Beach FL 33401-5524. 561/833-4888. **Contact:** John Williams, President. **Description:** An executive search firm. **Specializes in the areas of:** Legal. **Positions commonly filled include:** Attorney; Paralegal. **Average salary range of placements:** More than $50,000. **Number of placements per year:** 50 - 99.

INNOTECH GLOBAL RESOURCES
12968 SW 133 Court, Miami FL 33186. 305/232-3432. **Contact:** Manager. **Description:** An executive search firm. **Specializes in the areas of:** Computer Hardware/Software. **Positions commonly filled include:** Computer Programmer.

INTERIM ACCOUNTING PROFESSIONALS
6710 Main Street, Suite 234, Miami Lakes FL 33014. 305/558-1700. **Contact:** Manager. **Description:** An executive search firm. **Specializes in the areas of:** Accounting/Auditing; Human Resources.

INTERNATIONAL INSURANCE CONSULTANTS, INC.
1191 East Newport Center Drive, Suite 206, Deerfield Beach FL 33442. 954/421-0122. **Fax:** 954/421-5751. **Contact:** Glenn A. Wootton, CPC, President. **Description:** An executive search firm operating on

both retained and contingency bases. Company pays fee. **Specializes in the areas of:** Insurance. **Positions commonly filled include:** Actuary; Branch Manager; Broker; Chief Financial Officer; Claim Representative; Environmental Engineer; Finance Director; Financial Analyst; Insurance Agent/Broker; Sales Executive; Underwriter/Assistant Underwriter. **Average salary range of placements:** More than $50,000. **Number of placements per year:** 50 - 99.

JUST MANAGEMENT SERVICES
701 Enterprise Road East, Suite 805, Safety Harbor FL 34695-5342. 813/726-4000. **Fax:** 813/725-4966. **Contact:** Susan Just, President. **Description:** An executive search firm specializing in the apparel and textile industry. Just Management Services fills operational, sales, mechanical/technical, engineering, design, and management positions. Company pays fee. **Specializes in the areas of:** Apparel; Engineering; Fashion; General Management; Manufacturing; Sales. **Positions commonly filled include:** Designer; Industrial Engineer; Quality Control Supervisor. **Average salary range of placements:** $30,000 - $50,000.

KAY HANCOCK APFEL EXECUTIVE SEARCH
777 Brickell, Suite 1130, Miami FL 33131. 305/536-6481. **Contact:** Office Manager. **Description:** An executive search firm focusing on the placement of senior-level positions at financial institutions. The firm operates on a retainer basis. **Specializes in the areas of:** Finance.

A.T. KEARNEY EXECUTIVE SEARCH
200 South Biscayne Boulevard, Suite 3500, Miami FL 33131. 305/577-0046. **Contact:** Manager. **Description:** A generalist executive search firm.

KELLEY & KELLER MANAGEMENT CONSULTANTS
2518 Key Largo Lane, Fort Lauderdale FL 33312. 954/791-4900. **Contact:** Verne Kelley, President. **Description:** An executive search firm that recruits marketing professionals for consumer goods and services firms. Company pays fee. **Specializes in the areas of:** Sales. **Positions commonly filled include:** Marketing Specialist. **Average salary range of placements:** More than $50,000. **Number of placements per year:** 1 - 49.

KEYS EMPLOYMENT AGENCY
P.O. Box 1973, Big Pine Key FL 33043. 305/872-9692. **Fax:** 305/872-9692. **Contact:** Donna Glenn, President. **E-mail address:** dg305@aol.com. **Description:** An executive search firm. Keys Employment Agency recruits computer consultants specializing in SAP. Clients include Big Six accounting firms, top *Fortune* 500 employers, and consulting firms. The agency provides placement nationwide. Company pays fee. **Specializes in the areas of:** Computer Science/Software. **Positions commonly filled include:** Accountant/Auditor; Administrative Manager; Architect; Attorney; Bank Officer/Manager; Branch Manager; Civil Engineer; Computer Programmer; Customer Service Representative; Electrical/Electronics Engineer; Electrician; Emergency Medical Technician; Financial Analyst; Licensed Practical Nurse; Management Analyst/Consultant; Operations/Production Manager; Physical Therapist; Quality Control Supervisor; Restaurant/Food Service Manager; Services Sales Representative; Technical Writer/Editor; Urban/Regional Planner. **Average salary range of placements:** More than $50,000. **Number of placements per year:** 1 - 49.

KOERNER GROUP
9900 West Sample Road, Suite 300, Coral Springs FL 33065. 954/755-6676. **Contact:** Donald S. Koerner, Principal. **E-mail address:** kgroupinc@compuserve.com. **Description:** An executive search firm operating on both retained and contingency bases. Company pays fee. **Specializes in the areas of:** Accounting/Auditing; Banking; Computer Science/Software; Engineering; Finance; General Management; Industrial; Manufacturing; Personnel/Labor Relations. **Positions commonly filled include:** Accountant/Auditor; Biological Scientist; Biomedical Engineer; Budget Analyst; Civil Engineer; Computer Programmer; Credit Manager; Electrical/Electronics Engineer; Financial Analyst; Industrial Engineer; Quality Control Supervisor; Registered Nurse; Software Engineer; Systems Analyst; Technical Writer/Editor. **Number of placements per year:** 50 - 99.

LAMALIE AMROP INTERNATIONAL
3903 Northdale Boulevard, Suite 220, Tampa FL 33624. 813/961-7494. **Contact:** Office Manager. **Description:** A generalist executive search firm.

LaMORTE SEARCH ASSOCIATES, INC.
3003 Yamato Road C8, Suite 1073, Boca Raton FL 33434. 561/997-1100. **Toll-free phone:** 800/422-6306. **Fax:** 561/997-1103. **Contact:** William M. LaMorte, President. **E-mail address:** lsa search@aol.com. **Description:** An executive search firm operating on a contingency basis. Company pays fee. **Specializes in the areas of:** Insurance. **Positions commonly filled include:** Claim Representative; Insurance Agent/Broker; Loss Prevention Specialist; Risk Manager; Underwriter/Assistant Underwriter. **Average salary range of placements:** More than $50,000. **Number of placements per year:** 50 - 99.

R.H. LARSEN & ASSOCIATES, INC.
1401 East Broward Boulevard, Suite 101, Fort Lauderdale FL 33301-2118. 954/763-9000. **Fax:** 954/463-9318. **Contact:** Manager. **Description:** A retained executive search firm. Founded in 1971. **Specializes in the areas of:** Accounting/Auditing; Administration; Architecture/Construction; Banking; Computer Science/Software; Finance; General Management; Manufacturing; Personnel/Labor Relations; Sales. **Average salary range of placements:** More than $75,000. **Number of placements per year:** 1 - 49.

LASHER ASSOCIATES
1200 South Pine Island Road, Suite 370, Fort Lauderdale FL 33324. 954/472-5658. **Contact:** Manager. **Description:** An executive search firm. **Specializes in the areas of:** High-Tech.

LEAR & ASSOCIATES
505 North Park Avenue, Winter Park FL 32789-3268. 407/645-4611. **Fax:** 407/740-8816. **Contact:** Roger Lear, President. **Description:** An executive search firm specializing in property, casualty, life/health, and managed care insurance placements nationwide. Company pays fee. **Specializes in the areas of:** Insurance. **Positions commonly filled include:** Actuary; Adjuster; Claim Representative; Computer Programmer; Insurance Agent/Broker; Loss Prevention Specialist; Underwriter/Assistant Underwriter. **Average salary range of placements:** More than $50,000. **Number of placements per year:** 50 - 99.

THE MAC GROUP
2500 East Hallandale Beach Boulevard, Hallandale FL 33009. 954/454-1399. **Fax:** 954/454-2799. **Contact:** Miriam Domash, Owner. **Description:** An executive search firm. Company pays fee. **Specializes in the areas of:** Chemical; Engineering; Food Industry; Industrial; Manufacturing; Medical Technology; Pharmaceutical. **Positions commonly filled include:** Aerospace Engineer; Biomedical Engineer; Chemist; Civil Engineer; Design Engineer; Draftsperson; Electrical/Electronics Engineer; Food Scientist/Technologist; Industrial Engineer; Materials Engineer;

Mechanical Engineer; Metallurgical Engineer. **Average salary range of placements:** More than $50,000. **Number of placements per year:** 1 - 49.

MANAGEMENT RECRUITERS INTERNATIONAL
3606 Seventh Avenue, Fort Myers FL 33901. 941/939-2223. **Fax:** 941/939-2742. **Contact:** Calvin Beals, Manager. **Description:** An executive search firm. Company pays fee. **Specializes in the areas of:** Banking; Engineering. **Positions commonly filled include:** Actuary; Bank Officer/Manager; Chemical Engineer; Civil Engineer; Electrical/Electronics Engineer; Financial Analyst; Industrial Engineer; Mechanical Engineer; Physical Therapist. **Corporate headquarters location:** Cleveland OH. **Other U.S. locations:** Nationwide. **Number of placements per year:** 50 - 99.

MANAGEMENT RECRUITERS INTERNATIONAL
498 Palm Springs Drive, Suite 100, Altamonte Springs FL 32701. 407/865-7979. **Fax:** 407/865-7670. **Contact:** John Edward Clark, Managing Partner. **Description:** An executive search firm. Company pays fee. **Specializes in the areas of:** Administration; Art/Design; Computer Science/Software; Engineering; Insurance; Publishing; Sales; Telecommunications. **Positions commonly filled include:** Computer Programmer; Electrical/Electronics Engineer; Health Services Manager; Industrial Engineer; Insurance Agent/Broker; Management Analyst/Consultant; Mechanical Engineer; MIS Manager; Operations/Production Manager; Software Engineer; Underwriter/Assistant Underwriter. **Corporate headquarters location:** Cleveland OH. **Other U.S. locations:** Nationwide. **Average salary range of placements:** $30,000 - $50,000. **Number of placements per year:** 1 - 49.

MANAGEMENT RECRUITERS INTERNATIONAL
P.O. Box 7711, Clearwater FL 33758. 813/791-3277. **Contact:** Helen Gleason, Manager. **Description:** An executive search firm. Company pays fee. **Specializes in the areas of:** Health/Medical; Packaging; Sales. **Positions commonly filled include:** Accountant/Auditor; Computer Programmer; Designer; Dietician/Nutritionist; EEG Technologist; EKG Technician; Health Services Manager; Medical Records Technician; Occupational Therapist; Pharmacist; Quality Control Supervisor; Registered Nurse; Respiratory Therapist; Systems Analyst. **Corporate headquarters location:** Cleveland OH. **Other U.S. locations:** Nationwide. **Number of placements per year:** 50 - 99.

MANAGEMENT RECRUITERS INTERNATIONAL
3005 26th Street West, Suite C, Bradenton FL 34205. 941/753-5837. **Contact:** Manager. **Description:** An executive search firm that also provides temporary placements. Company pays fee. **Specializes in the areas of:** Accounting/Auditing; Engineering; Finance; Food Industry; Industrial; Manufacturing; Metals; Paper. **Corporate headquarters location:** Cleveland OH. **Other U.S. locations:** Nationwide. **Number of placements per year:** 1 - 49.

MANAGEMENT RECRUITERS INTERNATIONAL
1700 East Las Olas Boulevard, Fort Lauderdale FL 33301. 954/525-0355. **Fax:** 954/525-0353. **Contact:** Thomas K. Johasky, President. **Description:** An executive search firm. Company pays fee. **Specializes in the areas of:** Health/Medical; Insurance; Sales. **Positions commonly filled include:** Actuary; Adjuster; Biomedical Engineer; Claim Representative; Design Engineer; Industrial Agent/Broker; Mechanical Engineer; Operations/Production Manager; Physician; Underwriter. **Corporate headquarters location:** Cleveland OH. **Other U.S. locations:** Nationwide. **Number of placements per year:** 200 - 499.

MANAGEMENT RECRUITERS INTERNATIONAL
685 Royal Palm Beach Boulevard, Suite 103B, Royal Palm Beach FL 33411. 561/793-8400. **Fax:** 561/793-8471. **Contact:** Manager. **Description:** An executive search firm. **Specializes in the areas of:** Wireless Communications. **Corporate headquarters location:** Cleveland OH. **Other U.S. locations:** Nationwide.

MANAGEMENT RECRUITERS INTERNATIONAL
996B Laguna Drive, Venice FL 34285. 941/484-3900. **Fax:** 941/485-5822. **Contact:** Manager. **Description:** An executive search firm. **Specializes in the areas of:** Information Technology. **Corporate headquarters location:** Cleveland OH. **Other U.S. locations:** Nationwide.

MANAGEMENT RECRUITERS INTERNATIONAL
3332 NE Sugar Hill Avenue, Jensen Beach FL 34957. 561/334-8633. **Fax:** 561/871-1100. **Contact:** Manager. **Description:** An executive search firm. **Specializes in the areas of:** Accounting/Auditing; Finance; High-Tech. **Corporate headquarters location:** Cleveland OH. **Other U.S. locations:** Nationwide.

MANAGEMENT RECRUITERS INTERNATIONAL
370 West Camino Garden Boulevard, Suite 200, Boca Raton FL 33432. 561/393-3991. **Contact:** Manager. **Description:** An executive search firm. **Specializes in the areas of:** Chemical. **Corporate headquarters location:** Cleveland OH. **Other U.S. locations:** Nationwide.

MANAGEMENT RECRUITERS OF BONITA SPRINGS
9240 Bonita Beach Road, Suite 3307, Bonita Springs FL 34135. 941/495-7885. **Fax:** 941/495-7686. **Contact:** Gary F. Shearer, President. **Description:** An executive search firm that provides mid- to senior-level management placements. Company pays fee. **Specializes in the areas of:** Engineering; General Management; Paper. **Positions commonly filled include:** Management Analyst/Consultant; Operations/Production Manager. **Corporate headquarters location:** Cleveland OH. **Other U.S. locations:** Nationwide. **Average salary range of placements:** More than $50,000. **Number of placements per year:** 50 - 99.

MANAGEMENT RECRUITERS OF CORAL GABLES
2121 Ponce de Leon Boulevard, Suite 940, Coral Gables FL 33134. 305/444-1200. **Fax:** 305/444-2266. **Contact:** Stephanie Anderson, Operations Manager. **Description:** An executive search firm. Company pays fee. **Specializes in the areas of:** Biology; Engineering; Manufacturing. **Positions commonly filled include:** Biological Scientist; Biomedical Engineer; Clinical Lab Technician; Electrical/Electronics Engineer; Industrial Production Manager; Quality Control Supervisor; Software Engineer. **Corporate headquarters location:** Cleveland OH. **Other U.S. locations:** Nationwide. **Average salary range of placements:** More than $50,000. **Number of placements per year:** 1 - 49.

MANAGEMENT RECRUITERS OF INDIALANTIC
134 5th Avenue, Suite 208, Indialantic FL 32903-3170. 407/951-7644. **Fax:** 407/951-4235. **Contact:** Lawrence Cinco, General Manager. **World Wide Web address:** http://www.mrirecruiter.com. **Description:** A contingency search firm. Company pays fee. **Specializes in the areas of:** Computer Science/Software; Engineering; Manufacturing; Sales. **Positions commonly filled include:** Agricultural Engineer; Computer Programmer; Design Engineer; Designer; Electrical/Electronics Engineer; Industrial Engineer; Mechanical Engineer; MIS Specialist; Systems Analyst. **Corporate headquarters location:** Cleveland OH. **Other U.S. locations:** Nationwide. **Average salary range of placements:** More than $50,000. **Number of placements per year:** 100 - 199.

MANAGEMENT RECRUITERS OF JACKSONVILLE
4231 Walnut Bend, Jacksonville FL 32257. 904/260-4444. **Fax:** 904/260-4666. **Contact:** Robert Lee, President. **Description:** An executive search firm that provides contingency recruiting for sales and technical design positions within the packaging, material handling, conveying, and automation industries nationwide. Company pays fee. **Specializes in the areas of:** Engineering; Industrial; Sales. **Positions commonly filled include:** Design Engineer; Electrical/Electronics Engineer; Mechanical Engineer; Software Engineer. **Corporate headquarters location:** Cleveland OH. **Other U.S. locations:** Nationwide. **Average salary range of placements:** More than $50,000. **Number of placements per year:** 1 - 49.

MANAGEMENT RECRUITERS OF LAKE COUNTY
1117 North Donnelley Street, Suite 208, Mount Dora FL 32757. 352/383-7101. **Fax:** 352/383-7103. **Contact:** Roger Holloway, President. **Description:** An executive search firm. Company pays fee. **Specializes in the areas of:** Engineering; Food Industry; General Management; Industrial; Manufacturing; Plastics; Sales; Transportation. **Positions commonly filled include:** Agricultural Engineer; Draftsperson; Electrical/Electronics Engineer; Food Scientist/ Technologist; Industrial Engineer; Industrial Production Manager; Mechanical Engineer; Operations/Production Manager; Quality Control Supervisor; Structural Engineer. **Corporate headquarters location:** Cleveland OH. **Other U.S. locations:** Nationwide. **Average salary range of placements:** $30,000 - $50,000. **Number of placements per year:** 1 - 49.

MANAGEMENT RECRUITERS OF MIAMI
815 NW 57th Avenue, Suite 110, Miami FL 33126. 305/264-4212. **Fax:** 305/264-4251. **Contact:** Del Diaz, President. **Description:** An executive search firm. Company pays fee. **Specializes in the areas of:** Accounting/Auditing; Administration; Architecture/ Construction; Computer Science/Software; Engineering; Finance; Health/Medical; Industrial; Manufacturing; Personnel/Labor Relations; Sales. **Positions commonly filled include:** Accountant/ Auditor; Administrative Manager; Branch Manager; Buyer; Chemical Engineer; Civil Engineer; Clinical Lab Technician; Computer Programmer; Customer Service Representative; EKG Technician; Electrical/Electronics Engineer; Financial Analyst; Health Services Manager; Industrial Engineer; Licensed Practical Nurse; Mechanical Engineer; Occupational Therapist; Physical Therapist; Quality Control Supervisor; Radiological Technologist; Registered Nurse; Software Engineer; Systems Analyst; Technical Writer/Editor. **Corporate headquarters location:** Cleveland OH. **Other U.S. locations:** Nationwide. **Number of placements per year:** 50 - 99.

MANAGEMENT RECRUITERS OF PENSACOLA
603-A East Government Street, Pensacola FL 32501. 850/434-6500. **Fax:** 850/434-9911. **Contact:** Ken Kirchgessner, President. **Description:** An executive search firm with a focus on plastics and packaging. Company pays fee. **Specializes in the areas of:** Engineering; Industrial; Manufacturing. **Positions commonly filled include:** Chemical Engineer; Electrical/Electronics Engineer; General Manager; Industrial Engineer; Industrial Production Manager; Mechanical Engineer. **Corporate headquarters location:** Cleveland OH. **Other U.S. locations:** Nationwide. **Average salary range of placements:** More than $50,000. **Number of placements per year:** 1 - 49.

MANAGEMENT RECRUITERS OF PLANT CITY
117 West Alexander Street, Suite 303, Plant City FL 33566. 813/754-6340. **Fax:** 813/754-7557. **Contact:** Office Manager. **Description:** An executive search firm. Company pays fee. **Specializes in the areas of:** Biology; Chemical; Pharmaceutical. **Positions commonly filled include:** Biochemist; Biological Scientist; Chemical Engineer; Chemist. **Corporate headquarters location:** Cleveland OH. **Other U.S. locations:** Nationwide. **Average salary range of placements:** More than $50,000. **Number of placements per year:** 1 - 49.

MANAGEMENT RECRUITERS OF ST. PETERSBURG
9500 Koger Boulevard, Suite 203, St. Petersburg FL 33702. 813/577-2116. **Contact:** Manager. **Description:** An executive search firm. **Specializes in the areas of:** Accounting/Auditing; Administration; Advertising; Architecture/Construction; Banking; Chemical; Communications; Computer Hardware/ Software; Construction; Electrical; Engineering; Finance; Food Industry; General Management; Health/ Medical; Industrial; Insurance; Legal; Manufacturing; Operations Management; Personnel/Labor Relations; Pharmaceutical; Procurement; Publishing; Sales; Technical; Textiles; Transportation. **Corporate headquarters location:** Cleveland OH. **Other U.S. locations:** Nationwide.

MANAGEMENT RECRUITERS OF TALLAHASSEE
1406 Hays Street, Suite 7, Tallahassee FL 32301. 850/656-8444. **Contact:** Kitte Carter, Manager. **Description:** An executive search firm. **Specializes in the areas of:** Accounting/Auditing; Administration; Advertising; Architecture/Construction; Banking; Chemical; Communications; Computer Hardware/ Software; Construction; Design; Electrical; Engineering; Finance; Food Industry; General Management; Health/Medical; Industrial; Insurance; Legal; Manufacturing; Operations Management; Personnel/Labor Relations; Pharmaceutical; Procurement; Publishing; Retail; Sales; Technical; Textiles; Transportation. **Corporate headquarters location:** Cleveland OH. **Other U.S. locations:** Nationwide.

MANAGEMENT RECRUITERS OF TAMPA
500 North Westshore Boulevard, Suite 540, Tampa FL 33609. 813/281-2353. **Contact:** Jim Thomas, General Manager. **Description:** An executive search firm. **Specializes in the areas of:** Accounting/Auditing; Administration; Advertising; Architecture/ Construction; Banking; Chemical; Communications; Computer Hardware/Software; Construction; Design; Electrical; Engineering; Finance; Food Industry; General Management; Health/Medical; Industrial; Insurance; Legal; Manufacturing; Operations Management; Personnel/Labor Relations; Procurement; Publishing; Retail; Sales; Technical; Textiles; Transportation. **Corporate headquarters location:** Cleveland OH. **Other U.S. locations:** Nationwide.

MANKUTA GALLAGHER & ASSOCIATES INC.
8333 West McNab Road, Tamarac FL 33321. 954/720-7357. **Toll-free phone:** 800/797-4276. **Fax:** 954/720-5813. **Contact:** Managing Partner. **Description:** An executive search firm. Company pays fee. **Specializes in the areas of:** Administration; Biology; Computer Science/Software; Engineering; Manufacturing. **Positions commonly filled include:** Biochemist; Biomedical Engineer; Chemical Engineer; Civil Engineer; Computer Programmer; Electrical/ Electronics Engineer; Industrial Engineer; Internet Services Manager; Management Analyst/ Consultant; MIS Specialist; Physical Therapist; Physician; Registered Nurse; Speech-Language Pathologist; Systems Analyst. **Average salary range of placements:** More than $50,000. **Number of placements per year:** 50 - 99.

MARATHON GROUP
2320 South Third Street, Suite 8, Jacksonville Beach FL 32250. 904/270-1107. **Contact:** Office Manager.

Description: An executive search firm that recruits sales, sales management, and production personnel in the label and packaging industry. Company pays fee. **Specializes in the areas of:** Printing; Sales. **Corporate headquarters location:** This Location. **Other U.S. locations:** Atlanta GA. **Average salary range of placements:** More than $50,000. **Number of placements per year:** 1 - 49.

McGUIRE EXECUTIVE SEARCH, INC.
1650 Sand Lake Road, Suite 302, Orlando FL 32809. 407/857-6100. **Fax:** 407/857-8448. **Contact:** Harry McGuire, Manager. **Description:** An executive search firm operating on a contingency basis. Company pays fee. **Specializes in the areas of:** Food Industry; Hotel/Restaurant; Sales. **Positions commonly filled include:** Controller; Human Resources Manager; MIS Specialist; Sales Manager. **Corporate headquarters location:** This Location. **Average salary range of placements:** $30,000 - $50,000. **Number of placements per year:** 1 - 49.

MEADS & ASSOCIATES
6700 South Florida Avenue, Suite 4, Lakeland FL 33813. 941/644-0411. **Contact:** Office Manager. **Description:** An executive search firm. **Specializes in the areas of:** Advertising.

MEDIA MANAGEMENT RESOURCES
31B Gulf Breeze Parkway, Gulf Breeze FL 32561. 904/934-4880. **Contact:** Office Manager. **Description:** An executive search firm. **Specializes in the areas of:** Communications; Telecommunications.

NPF ASSOCIATES LTD., INC.
1999 University Drive, Suite 405, Coral Springs FL 33071. 954/753-8560. **Contact:** Mick Fischler, Research Associate. **Description:** An executive search firm. **Specializes in the areas of:** Personnel/Labor Relations. **Number of placements per year:** 1 - 49.

NATIONAL MEDICAL RECRUITING AND CONSULTING
5051 Castello Drive, Suite 239, Naples FL 33940. 941/417-1848. **Toll-free phone:** 800/755-6954. **Contact:** Jackie Griffin, CEO. **Description:** An executive search firm. **Specializes in the areas of:** Health/Medical. **Positions commonly filled include:** Physician. **Average salary range of placements:** More than $50,000. **Number of placements per year:** 1 - 49.

NATIONWIDE RECRUITERS
5327 Commercial Way, Spring Hill FL 34606. 352/597-5950. **Contact:** Manager. **Description:** An executive search firm. **Specializes in the areas of:** Paper.

NATIONWIDE RECRUITERS
13015 Spring Hill Drive, Spring Hill FL 34609. 352/686-6788. **Contact:** Manager. **Description:** An executive search firm. **Specializes in the areas of:** Paper.

NOLAN & NOLAN
802 Pink Camelia Court, Apopka FL 32712. 407/884-8339. **Contact:** Manager. **Description:** An executive search firm. **Specializes in the areas of:** Health/Medical.

NORRELL TECHNICAL SERVICES
1801 Sarno Road, Suite 1, Melbourne FL 32951. 407/259-8619. **Toll-free phone:** 800/689-8367. **Fax:** 407/255-1930. **Contact:** Jean Lehmann, Division Manager. **World Wide Web address:** http://www.norrelltech.com. **Description:** An executive search firm that offers short-term, long-term, managed, and contract-to-hire staffing opportunities. Company pays fee. **Specializes in the areas of:** Computer Science/Software; Engineering; Industrial; Manufacturing; Personnel/Labor Relations; Technical. **Positions commonly filled include:** Chemical Engineer; Civil Engineer; Computer Programmer; Design Engineer; Electrical/Electronics Engineer; Food Scientist/Technologist; Industrial Engineer; Industrial Production Manager; Internet Services Manager; Mechanical Engineer; MIS Specialist; Multimedia Designer; Software Engineer; Systems Analyst; Technical Writer/Editor. **Benefits available to temporary workers:** 401(k); Dental Insurance; Life Insurance; Medical Insurance. **Corporate headquarters location:** Atlanta GA. **International locations:** Worldwide. **Average salary range of placements:** More than $50,000.

OMNIPARTNERS
7770 West Oakland Park Boulevard, Suite 350, Fort Lauderdale FL 33351. 954/748-9800. **Fax:** 954/747-1130. **Contact:** JoAnn Parrino, Client Services Manager. **Description:** An executive search firm. Company pays fee. **Specializes in the areas of:** Accounting/Auditing; Computer Science/Software; Engineering; Finance; General Management; Insurance; Retail; Sales; Technical; Transportation. **Positions commonly filled include:** Accountant; Applications Engineer; Auditor; Buyer; Chief Financial Officer; Civil Engineer; Computer Programmer; Electrical/Electronics Engineer; Sales Manager; Software Engineer; Typist/Word Processor. **Average salary range of placements:** More than $50,000. **Number of placements per year:** 50 - 99.

OMNISEARCH INC.
3442 East Lake Road, Suite 308, Palm Harbor FL 34685. 813/789-4442. **Fax:** 813/787-7743. **Contact:** Lollie Moyer, President. **E-mail address:** osiflorida@aol.com. **Description:** An executive search firm that focuses on the placement of sales and marketing professionals in the medical, pharmaceutical, food, and consumer packaged goods industries. Company pays fee. **Specializes in the areas of:** Sales. **Average salary range of placements:** More than $50,000. **Number of placements per year:** 50 - 99.

PMR SEARCH CONSULTANTS
428B Osceola Avenue, Jacksonville FL 32250. 904/270-0505. **Contact:** Manager. **Description:** An executive search firm. **Specializes in the areas of:** Legal.

PEARCE & ASSOCIATES
9116 Cypress Green Drive, Suite 201, Jacksonville FL 32256. 904/739-1736. **Fax:** 904/739-1746. **Contact:** Frank Pearce, Owner. **E-mail address:** fpearce@jax-internet.net. **Description:** An executive search firm. Company pays fee. **Specializes in the areas of:** Accounting/Auditing; Real Estate; Sales. **Positions commonly filled include:** Account Representative; Branch Manager; Controller; Sales Executive; Sales Manager; Sales Representative. **Average salary range of placements:** $30,000 - $50,000.

PERFECT SEARCH INC.
1801 Clint Moore Road, #109, Boca Raton FL 33487. 561/995-7533. **Fax:** 561/995-7477. **Contact:** Robin Callicott, President. **Description:** An executive search firm. Company pays fee. **Specializes in the areas of:** Health/Medical; Sales. **Positions commonly filled include:** Manufacturer's/Wholesaler's Sales Rep.; Medical Records Technician. **Number of placements per year:** 50 - 99.

THE PERSONNEL INSTITUTE
725 West Lorraine Drive, Deltona FL 32725-8606. 407/860-1231. **Contact:** Dr. William E. Stuart, President. **Description:** An executive search firm operating on a retainer basis. Company pays fee.

Specializes in the areas of: Computer Hardware/Software; Engineering; Technical. **Positions commonly filled include:** Computer Programmer; Controller; Design Engineer; Environmental Engineer; Marketing Manager; Marketing Specialist; MIS Specialist; Sales Executive; Sales Manager; Software Engineer; Systems Analyst; Systems Manager; Telecommunications Manager. **Number of placements per year:** 200 - 499.

PHYSICIAN EXECUTIVE MANAGEMENT CENTER
4014 Gunn Highway, Tampa FL 33624. 813/963-1800. **Fax:** 813/264-2207. **Contact:** David R. Kirschman, President. **Description:** A retained executive search firm. Company pays fee. **Specializes in the areas of:** Health/Medical; Physician Executive. **Average salary range of placements:** More than $50,000. **Number of placements per year:** 1 - 49.

PRIORITY EXECUTIVE SEARCH
14317 Ravenwood Lane, Tampa FL 33618. 813/933-0082. **Contact:** Manager. **Description:** An executive search firm. **Specializes in the areas of:** Health/Medical.

PRIORITY SEARCH
2600 Maitland Center Parkway, Suite 295, Maitland FL 32751. 407/660-0089. **Fax:** 407/660-2066. **Contact:** Terrie Goodman, Administrative Manager. **E-mail address:** frontdesk@prioritysearch.com. **World Wide Web address:** http://www.prioritysearch.com. **Description:** An executive search firm operating on both retained and contingency bases. **Specializes in the areas of:** Accounting/Auditing; Engineering; Finance; Industrial; Insurance; Marketing; Publishing; Sales; Technical. **Positions commonly filled include:** Account Representative; Accountant/Auditor; Bank Officer/Manager; Chemical Engineer; Chief Financial Officer; Design Engineer; Electrical/Electronics Engineer; Financial Analyst; Industrial Engineer; Industrial Production Manager; Mechanical Engineer; Operations Manager; Quality Control Supervisor; Sales Engineer; Sales Executive; Sales Representative. **Average salary range of placements:** More than $50,000. **Number of placements per year:** 100 - 199.

PULP & PAPER INTERNATIONAL
P.O. Box 540929, Orlando FL 32854. 407/444-9960. **Fax:** 407/444-9964. **Contact:** Philip Riesling, President. **E-mail address:** pulppaper@aol.com. **Description:** An executive search firm providing international placements. Company pays fee. **Specializes in the areas of:** Accounting/Auditing; Engineering; Manufacturing; Technical. **Positions commonly filled include:** Accountant/Auditor; Chemical Engineer; Computer Programmer; Mechanical Engineer; Stationary Engineer; Systems Analyst. **Average salary range of placements:** More than $50,000. **Number of placements per year:** 1 - 49.

R.M.H. ASSOCIATES
2 Hampton Court, Palm Beach Gardens FL 33418. **Toll-free phone:** 800/536-1495. **Contact:** Rosemary Houlihan, President. **Description:** An executive search firm. Company pays fee. **Specializes in the areas of:** Health/Medical; Sales. **Positions commonly filled include:** Nurse; Sales Representative. **Number of placements per year:** 1 - 49.

RETAIL EXECUTIVE SEARCH, INC. (RES)
4260 North State Road 7, Suite 212, Fort Lauderdale FL 33319. 954/731-2300. **Fax:** 954/733-0642. **Contact:** Manuel Kaye, President. **Description:** An executive search firm. Company pays fee. **Specializes in the areas of:** Fashion; Retail. **Positions commonly filled include:** Branch Manager; Budget Analyst; Buyer; General Manager; Human Resources Manager; MIS Specialist; Retail Executive; Retail Manager; Retail Merchandiser. **Number of placements per year:** 200 - 499.

JACK RICHMAN & ASSOCIATES
P.O. Box 25412, Tamarac FL 33320. 305/940-0721. **Fax:** 954/389-9572. **Contact:** Jack Richman, President. **E-mail address:** jrafl@aol.com. **Description:** An executive search firm specializing in the computer industry. Company pays fee. **Specializes in the areas of:** Computer Science/Software; Engineering. **Positions commonly filled include:** Computer Programmer; Systems Analyst; Technical Writer/Editor. **Average salary range of placements:** More than $50,000. **Number of placements per year:** 1 - 49.

ROBINSON & ASSOCIATES
4000 Saint John's Avenue, Suite 35, Jacksonville FL 32205. 904/388-5111. **Contact:** Manager. **Description:** An executive search firm. **Specializes in the areas of:** Administration; Finance; Health/Medical; Information Systems.

GENE ROGERS ASSOCIATES, INC.
13211 SW 32nd Court, Davie FL 33330-4604. 954/476-0221. **Toll-free phone:** 888/333-4589. **Fax:** 954/476-8437. **Contact:** Gene Rogers, President. **E-mail address:** grogers190@aol.com. **Description:** An executive search firm. **Specializes in the areas of:** Banking; Investment. **Positions commonly filled include:** Bank Officer/Manager; Trust Officer. **Average salary range of placements:** More than $50,000. **Number of placements per year:** 1 - 49.

GENE ROGERS ASSOCIATES, INC.
444 Brickell Avenue, Suite J1, Miami FL 33131. 305/476-0221. **Contact:** Manager. **Description:** An executive search firm. **Specializes in the areas of:** Banking; Investment. **Average salary range of placements:** More than $50,000.

ROMAC INTERNATIONAL
500 West Cypress Creek Road, Suite 200, Fort Lauderdale FL 33309. 954/928-0800. **Fax:** 954/771-7649. **Contact:** Manager. **Description:** An executive search firm. **Specializes in the areas of:** Accounting/Auditing; Computer Hardware/Software; Government. **Positions commonly filled include:** Accountant/Auditor; Computer Programmer; EDP Specialist; MIS Specialist; Systems Analyst.

ROMAC INTERNATIONAL
120 West Hyde Park Place, Suite 200, Tampa FL 33606. 813/258-8855. **Toll-free phone:** 800/341-0263. **Contact:** Manager. **Description:** An executive search firm. **Specializes in the areas of:** Accounting/Auditing; Banking; Finance.

ROMAC INTERNATIONAL
111 North Orange Avenue, Suite 1150, Orlando FL 32801. 407/843-0765. **Contact:** Manager. **Description:** An executive search firm. **Specializes in the areas of:** Accounting/Auditing; Finance.

ROTH YOUNG OF TAMPA
5201 West Kennedy Boulevard, Suite 506, Tampa FL 33609. 813/289-6556. **Fax:** 813/289-9118. **Contact:** Barry Cushing, President. **Description:** An executive search firm. Company pays fee. **Specializes in the areas of:** Engineering; Food Industry; Health/Medical; Sales. **Positions commonly filled include:** Buyer; General Manager; Hotel Manager; Medical Doctor. **Number of placements per year:** 50 - 99.

THE RYAN CHARLES GROUP, INC.
2151 West Hillsboro Boulevard, Suite 203, Deerfield FL 33442. 954/421-9112. **Fax:** 954/428-4940. **Contact:** Norman St. Jean, President. **E-mail address:**

ryanc@icanect.net. **World Wide Web address:** http://www.ipcc.com/market/ryancharles. **Description:** An executive search firm. Company pays fee. **Specializes in the areas of:** Accounting/Auditing; Administration; Advertising; Engineering; Finance; General Management; Industrial; Insurance; Manufacturing; Personnel/Labor Relations; Sales. **Positions commonly filled include:** Accountant/ Auditor; Credit Manager; Design Engineer; Electrical/Electronics Engineer; Industrial Engineer; Industrial Production Manager; Mechanical Engineer; MIS Manager; Production Manager; Structural Engineer; Systems Analyst; Telecommunications Manager. **Corporate headquarters:** This Location. **Other U.S. locations:** Oak Brook IL. **Average salary range of placements:** More than $50,000. **Number of placements per year:** 50 - 99.

SAGE CONSULTANTS INC.
10242 NW 47th Street, Fort Lauderdale FL 33351. **Contact:** Office Manager. **Description:** An executive search firm. **Specializes in the areas of:** Construction; Electronics; Pharmaceutical. **Positions commonly filled include:** Construction Manager; Engineer.

SALES CONSULTANTS OF CORAL SPRINGS
9900 West Sample Road, Suite 407, Coral Springs FL 33065. **Contact:** President. **Description:** A contingency search firm specializing in the placement of chemical sales professionals in the pulp and paper industry, as well as product managers and national sales management. Company pays fee. **Specializes in the areas of:** Retail; Sales. **Positions commonly filled include:** Chemical Engineer; Manufacturer's/ Wholesaler's Sales Rep. **Corporate headquarters location:** Cleveland OH. **Other U.S. locations:** Nationwide. **Average salary range of placements:** More than $50,000. **Number of placements per year:** 1 - 49.

SALES CONSULTANTS OF FORT LAUDERDALE
100 West Cypress Creek Road, Suite 880, Fort Lauderdale FL 33309. 954/772-5100. **Fax:** 954/772-0777. **Contact:** Jeff Taylor, Manager. **World Wide Web address:** http://www.mri-sc-usa.com. **Description:** An executive search firm. **Specializes in the areas of:** Accounting/Auditing; Administration; Advertising; Architecture/Construction; Banking; Chemical; Communications; Computer Hardware/S oftware; Construction; Design; Electrical; Engineering; Finance; Food Industry; General Management; Health/ Medical; Industrial; Insurance; Legal; Manufacturing; Operations Management; Personnel/Labor Relations; Procurement; Publishing; Retail; Sales; Technical; Textiles; Transportation. **Corporate headquarters location:** Cleveland OH. **Other U.S. locations:** Nationwide.

SALES CONSULTANTS OF JACKSONVILLE
9471 Baymeadows Road, Suite 204, Jacksonville FL 32256. 904/737-5770. **Contact:** General Manager. **Description:** An executive search firm. **Specializes in the areas of:** Accounting/Auditing; Administration; Advertising; Architecture/Construction; Banking; Chemical; Communications; Computer Hardware/ Software; Construction; Design; Electrical; Engineering; Finance; Food Industry; General Management; Health/Medical; Industrial; Insurance; Legal; Manufacturing; Operations Management; Personnel/Labor Relations; Pharmaceutical; Procurement; Publishing; Retail; Sales; Technical; Textiles; Transportation. **Corporate headquarters location:** Cleveland OH. **Other U.S. locations:** Nationwide.

SALES CONSULTANTS OF SARASOTA
1343 Main Street, Suite 600, Sarasota FL 34236. 941/365-5151. **Fax:** 941/365-1869. **Contact:** Janice Cascio, Administrative Assistant. **Description:** An executive search firm operating on both retained and contingency bases. **Specializes in the areas of:** Computer Hardware/Software; Engineering; Health/ Medical; Industrial; Insurance; Sales. **Positions commonly filled include:** Design Engineer; Industrial Engineer; Industrial Production Manager; Market Research Analyst; Marketing Manager; Mechanical Engineer; Sales Engineer; Sales Executive; Sales Manager; Sales Representative. **Corporate headquarters location:** Cleveland OH. **Other U.S. locations:** Nationwide. **Average salary range of placements:** More than $50,000. **Number of placements per year:** 50 - 99.

SANFORD ROSE ASSOCIATES
2623 McCormick Drive, Suite 104, Clearwater FL 33759. 813/796-2201. **Fax:** 813/669-2942. **Contact:** Manager. **World Wide Web address:** http://www.sanfordrose.com. **Description:** An executive search firm. **Specializes in the areas of:** General Management; Marketing.

SEA-CHANGE, INC.
333 Southern Boulevard, West Palm Beach FL 33405-2654. 561/833-8315. **Fax:** 561/833-8325. **Contact:** Diane McCabe, President. **Description:** An executive search firm that recruits physicians, optometrists, and ophthalmic administrators. **Specializes in the areas of:** Health/Medical. **Positions commonly filled include:** Physician. **Average salary range of placements:** More than $50,000.

SEARCH ENTERPRISES SOUTH, INC.
12358 Wiles Road, Coral Springs FL 33076. 954/755-3121. **Fax:** 954/755-1094. **Contact:** Frank Polacek, President. **E-mail address:** sesi@searchenterprises.com. **World Wide Web address:** http://www.searchenterprises.com. **Description:** An executive search firm. Company pays fee. **Specializes in the areas of:** Engineering; Personnel/Labor Relations; Technical. **Positions commonly filled include:** Biomedical Engineer; Chemical Engineer; Electrical/ Electronics Engineer; Human Resources Manager; Materials Engineer; Metallurgical Engineer. **Average salary range of placements:** More than $50,000. **Number of placements per year:** 100 - 199.

SEARCH MASTERS INTERNATIONAL
4598 Hamlets Grove, Sarasota FL 34235. 941/351-7307. **Contact:** Alex Stevenson, Executive Search Consultant and Founder. **Description:** An executive search firm. Company pays fee. **Specializes in the areas of:** Health/Medical; Sales. **Positions commonly filled include:** Production Manager; Sales and Marketing Manager. **Average salary range of placements:** More than $50,000. **Number of placements per year:** 1 - 49.

SEARCH SPECIALISTS
3319 Powerline Road, Lithia FL 33547. 813/689-1991. **Contact:** Manager. **Description:** An executive search firm that places engineers.

DOUG SEARS & ASSOCIATES (DS&A)
320 Corporate Way, Suite 100, Jacksonville FL 32073. 904/278-9998. **Toll-free phone:** 800/553-5361. **Fax:** 904/278-9995. **Contact:** Melinda Bailey, Vice President of Marketing. **E-mail address:** dsa@d-s-a.com. **World Wide Web address:** http://www.d-s-a.com. **Description:** An executive search firm operating on both retainer and contingency bases. The firm also offers career counseling and resume services. Founded in 1989. Company pays fee. **Specializes in the areas of:** Accounting/Auditing; Administration; Banking; Computer Science/Software; Engineering; Finance; General Management; Health/ Medical; Industrial; Insurance; Legal; Manufacturing;

Personnel/Labor Relations; Sales; Technical. **Positions commonly filled include:** Adjuster; Administrative Manager; Aerospace Engineer; Architect; Attorney; Bank Officer/Manager; Biomedical Engineer; Branch Manager; Chemical Engineer; Civil Engineer; Computer Programmer; Customer Service Representative; Financial Analyst; Industrial Engineer; Insurance Agent/Broker; Internet Services Manager; Management Analyst/Consultant; MIS Specialist; Operations/Production Manager; Physical Therapist; Physician; Registered Nurse; Respiratory Therapist; Software Engineer; Surgical Technician; Systems Analyst; Technical Writer/Editor; Telecommunications Manager. **Corporate headquarters location:** This Location. **International locations:** Worldwide. **Average salary range of placements:** More than $50,000. **Number of placements per year:** 200 - 499.

SKEEGAN & ASSOCIATES
8400 North University Drive, Suite 302, Tamarac FL 33321. 954/722-2151. **Contact:** Manager. **Description:** An executive search firm. **Specializes in the areas of:** Finance.

SNELLING PERSONNEL
9500 Koger Boulevard, St. Petersburg FL 33702. 813/577-9711. **Toll-free phone:** 800/484-5552. **Fax:** 813/577-1071. **Contact:** James Conwell, Manager. **Description:** An executive search firm. **Specializes in the areas of:** Computer Science/Software; Engineering; Manufacturing; Publishing. **Positions commonly filled include:** Aerospace Engineer; Chemical Engineer; Civil Engineer; Computer Programmer; Design Engineer; Designer; Electrical/ Electronics Engineer; Industrial Engineer; Industrial Production Manager; Mechanical Engineer; Software Engineer; Structural Engineer; Systems Analyst. **Average salary range of placements:** $30,000 - $50,000. **Number of placements per year:** 200 - 499.

SOURCE SERVICES CORPORATION
15600 NW 67th Avenue, Suite 201, Miami Lakes FL 33014. 305/556-8000. **Fax:** 305/819-9544. **Contact:** Manager. **Description:** An executive search firm. The divisions at this location include Source EDP, Source Finance, and Accountant Source Temps. **Specializes in the areas of:** Accounting/Auditing; Computer Hardware/Software; Finance.

SOURCE SERVICES CORPORATION
4200 West Cypress Street, Suite 101, Tampa FL 33607. 813/879-2221. **Fax:** 813/879-1095. **Contact:** Manager. **Description:** An executive search firm. The divisions at this location include Source EDP, Source Engineering, and Source Finance. **Specializes in the areas of:** Computer Hardware/Software; Engineering; Finance; Information Technology.

SPECIALIZED SEARCH ASSOCIATES
15200 Carter Road, Suite 201, Delray Beach FL 33446. 561/499-3711. **Fax:** 561/499-3770. **Contact:** Leonard Morris, President. **Description:** An executive search firm operating on a contingency basis. Company pays fee. **Specializes in the areas of:** Construction; Engineering; Sales. **Positions commonly filled include:** Architect; Chemical Engineer; Civil Engineer; Construction and Building Inspector; Construction Contractor; Environmental Engineer; Marketing Manager; Mechanical Engineer; Operations Manager; Sales Engineer; Sales Executive; Sales Manager; Structural Engineer. **Average salary range of placements:** More than $50,000. **Number of placements per year:** 1 - 49.

STERLING CAREER CONSULTANTS, INC.
2240 Palm Beach Lakes Boulevard, Suite 102, West Palm Beach FL 33409. 561/689-8530. **Fax:** 561/689-4557. **Contact:** Yvonne L. DuChene, President. **Description:** An executive search and consulting firm operating on both retained and contingency bases. Sterling Career Consultants also provides temporary and temp-to-perm placements. Company pays fee. **Specializes in the areas of:** Legal. **Positions commonly filled include:** Administrative Assistant; Attorney; Legal Assistant; Legal Secretary; Paralegal; Secretary; Typist/Word Processor. **Benefits available to temporary workers:** Flexible Schedule. **Average salary range of placements:** $30,000 - $50,000. **Number of placements per year:** 100 - 199.

AARON STEWART PERSONNEL INC.
P.O. Box 811690, Boca Raton FL 33481. 954/480-9902. **Contact:** Manager. **Description:** An executive search firm that also operates as a temporary and permanent employment agency. **Specializes in the areas of:** Accounting/Auditing; Banking; Computer Science/Software; Finance; Insurance; Legal; Nonprofit; Personnel/Labor Relations; Publishing; Secretarial. **Number of placements per year:** 200 - 499.

THE STEWART SEARCH GROUP, INC.
P.O. Box 2588, Ponte Vedra Beach FL 32082. 904/285-6622. **Physical address:** 201 ATP Tour Boulevard, Suite 130, Ponte Vedra Beach FL. **Fax:** 904/285-0076. **Contact:** James H. Stewart, President. **E-mail address:** stewgrp@cybermax.net. **Description:** An executive search firm operating on both retained and contingency bases. Company pays fee. **Specializes in the areas of:** Accounting/Auditing; Administration; Advertising; Engineering; Finance; Food Industry; General Management; Health/Medical; Hotel/Restaurant; Marketing; Pharmaceutical; Sales; Telecommunications. **Positions commonly filled include:** Chief Financial Officer; Computer Programmer; Credit Manager; Design Engineer; Electrical/Electronics Engineer; Finance Director; Financial Analyst; Industrial Engineer; Insurance Agent/Broker; Licensed Practical Nurse; Manufacturing Engineer; MIS Specialist; Physician; Quality Control Supervisor; Registered Nurse; Respiratory Therapist; Sales Engineer; Sales Representative; Software Engineer; Systems Analyst; Systems Manager; Technical Writer/Editor; Telecommunications Manager. **Average salary range of placements:** More than $50,000. **Number of placements per year:** 100 - 199.

SUMMIT EXECUTIVE SEARCH CONSULTANTS, INC.
420 Lincoln Road, Suite 265, Miami Beach FL 33139. 305/672-5008. **Fax:** 305/672-5007. **Contact:** Alfred J. Holzman, President. **E-mail address:** summitsearch @compuserve.com. **Description:** A retained executive search firm. Company pays fee. **Specializes in the areas of:** Engineering; Industrial; Manufacturing; Safety. **Positions commonly filled include:** Buyer; Civil Engineer; Design Engineer; Electrical/Electronics Engineer; Environmental Engineer; Human Resources Manager; Industrial Engineer; Industrial Production Manager; Mechanical Engineer; Metallurgical Engineer; Purchasing Agent/Manager; Quality Control Supervisor; Structural Engineer. **Average salary range of placements:** More than $50,000. **Number of placements per year:** 1 - 49.

SUMMIT HEALTH CARE, INC.
7301 NW Fourth Street, Suite 107A, Plantation FL 33317. 954/583-9288. **Contact:** Office Manager. **Description:** An executive search firm offering placements for medical professionals. **Specializes in the areas of:** Health/Medical.

SUMMIT HEALTH CARE, INC.
6950 Phillips Highway, Suite 12, Jacksonville FL 32216. 904/296-6003. **Contact:** Office Manager. **Description:** An executive search firm offering placements for medical and dental professionals.

Positions range from CNAs and dental hygienists to medical billing and clerical personnel. **Specializes in the areas of:** Health/Medical.

SUN PERSONNEL WEST
5444 Bay Center Drive, Suite 215, Tampa FL 33609-3400. 813/286-2009. **Contact:** Recruiter. **E-mail address:** sunwest@primenet.com. **Description:** An executive search firm providing professional placement in sales management positions. **Specializes in the areas of:** Finance; General Management; Health/Medical; Industrial; Manufacturing; Sales. **Average salary range of placements:** $30,000 - $50,000. **Number of placements per year:** 200 - 499.

SYSTEM ONE TECHNICAL STAFFING, INC.
4902 Eisenhower Boulevard, Suite 387, Tampa FL 33634. 813/839-9265. **Fax:** 813/887-3712. **Contact:** Recruiter. **World Wide Web address:** http://www.systemone.com. **Description:** An executive search firm that also provides permanent and temporary placements. Company pays fee. **Specializes in the areas of:** Administration; Computer Science/Software; Engineering; Manufacturing; Technical; Telecommunications. **Benefits available to temporary workers:** 401(k); Paid Vacation. **Corporate headquarters location:** This Location. **Other U.S. locations:** Orlando FL; Atlanta GA; Baltimore MD; Charlotte NC; Raleigh NC; Valley Forge PA; Dallas TX. **Average salary range of placements:** $20,000 - $29,999. **Number of placements per year:** 100 - 199.

SYSTEMS SEARCH, INC.
5200 NW 33rd Avenue, Suite 220, Fort Lauderdale FL 33309. 954/486-5871. **Fax:** 954/733-6444. **Contact:** Manager. **Description:** An executive search firm. **Specializes in the areas of:** Accounting/Auditing.

TECHNISOURCE
1901 West Cypress Creek Road, Fort Lauderdale FL 33309. 954/493-8601. **Contact:** Office Manager. **Description:** An executive search firm. **Specializes in the areas of:** Technical.

WILLIAM M. THOMPSON ASSOCIATES
7069 South Tamiami Trail, Suite A, Sarasota FL 34231. 941/923-7569. **Contact:** William Thompson, President. **Description:** A generalist search firm.

E.G. TODD PHYSICIAN SEARCH
9045 La Fontana, Suite C12, Boca Raton FL 33434. 561/852-0008. **Contact:** Manager. **Description:** An executive search firm that places physicians. **Specializes in the areas of:** Health/Medical.

TOWER CONSULTANTS, LTD.
Central Parkway Professional Plaza, 943 Central Parkway, Stuart FL 34994. 561/225-3595. **Fax:** 561/225-4522. **Contact:** Donna Friedman, President. **E-mail address:** towercons@aol.com. **Description:** A nationwide executive search firm operating on a retainer basis. Tower Consultants specializes in recruiting experienced professionals in the human resources field. Company pays fee. **Specializes in the areas of:** Personnel/Labor Relations. **Positions commonly filled include:** Human Resources Manager. **Average salary range of placements:** More than $50,000. **Number of placements per year:** 50 - 99.

UNIQUEST INTERNATIONAL, INC.
4350 West Cypress Street, Suite 450, Tampa FL 33607. 813/879-1222. **Contact:** Tony Valone, President. **Description:** An executive search firm. Company pays fee. **Specializes in the areas of:** Accounting/Auditing; Administration; Finance; Health/Medical; Insurance; Legal; Telecommunications. **Average salary range of placements:** More than $50,000. **Number of placements per year:** 100 - 199.

UNIVERSAL SEARCH
1460 Brickell Avenue, Suite 204, Miami FL 33131. 305/374-1922. **Contact:** Manager. **Description:** An executive search firm. Company pays fee.

WEATHERBY HEALTH CARE
3230 West Commercial Boulevard, Suite 240, Fort Lauderdale FL 33309. 954/730-3340. **Contact:** Manager. **Description:** An executive search firm offering placements for physicians only.

TERRY M. WEISS & ASSOCIATES
LEGAL AND TAX EXECUTIVE SEARCH
P.O. Box 915656, Longwood FL 32791-5656. 407/774-1212. **Fax:** 407/774-0084. **Contact:** Mr. Terry M. Weiss, Esq., President. **E-mail address:** lawhunter@aol.com. **Description:** An executive search firm. Company pays fee. **Specializes in the areas of:** Accounting/Auditing; Legal; Tax. **Positions commonly filled include:** Accountant; Attorney. **Number of placements per year:** 1 - 49.

THE WITT GROUP
P.O. Box 521281, Longwood FL 32752. 407/324-4137. **Contact:** Manager. **Description:** An executive search firm. **Specializes in the areas of:** Chemical.

WORLD WIDE RECRUITERS
121-1F Rural Park Drive, Oakland Park FL 33309. 954/677-8367. **Contact:** Manager. **Description:** An executive search firm. **Specializes in the areas of:** Insurance.

ZACKRISON ASSOCIATES INC.
P.O. Box 1808, Dunnellon FL 34430. 352/489-2215. **Contact:** Manager. **Description:** An executive search firm. **Specializes in the areas of:** Pharmaceutical.

PERMANENT EMPLOYMENT AGENCIES

A CHOICE NANNY
1413 South Howard Avenue, Suite 201, Tampa FL 33606. 813/254-8687. **Contact:** Eleanor Nesbit, Owner/Manager. **Description:** An employment agency that places permanent and temporary nannies. **Specializes in the areas of:** Nannies. **Number of placements per year:** 100 - 199.

AAA EMPLOYMENT
4035 South Florida Avenue, Lakeland FL 33813. 941/646-9681. **Fax:** 941/646-9683. **Contact:** Trish MacPeek, Franchise Owner. **Description:** A permanent employment agency. Company pays fee. **Specializes in the areas of:** Finance; Health/Medical; Industrial; Insurance; Legal; Manufacturing; Personnel/Labor Relations; Publishing; Retail; Sales; Secretarial; Technical; Transportation. **Positions commonly filled include:** Accountant/Auditor; Administrative Manager; Advertising Clerk; Bank Officer/Manager; Branch Manager; Brokerage Clerk; Budget Analyst; Buyer; Chemist; Civil Engineer; Claim Representative; Clinical Lab Technician; Computer Programmer; Credit Manager; Customer Service Representative; Dental Assistant/Dental Hygienist; Draftsperson; Industrial Production Manager; Insurance Agent/Broker; Licensed Practical Nurse; Mechanical Engineer; Operations/Production Manager; Paralegal; Quality Control Supervisor; Registered Nurse; Restaurant/Food Service Manager; Services Sales Representative; Software Engineer; Systems Analyst; Typist/Word Processor; Underwriter/Assistant Underwriter; Wholesale and Retail Buyer. **Corporate headquarters**

location: St. Petersburg FL. **Other U.S. locations:** GA; IN; MI; NC; SC; TN; VA; WV. **Average salary range of placements:** $20,000 - $29,999. **Number of placements per year:** 100 - 199.

AAA EMPLOYMENT
12995 South Cleveland Avenue, Fort Myers FL 33907-3890. 941/939-7200. **Contact:** V. Jane Kappler, Managing Partner. **Description:** A permanent employment agency. Founded in 1957. **Specializes in the areas of:** Accounting/Auditing; Computer Science/Software; Finance; General Management; Health/Medical; Insurance; Legal; Retail; Sales; Secretarial. **Positions commonly filled include:** Accountant/Auditor; Administrative Manager; Advertising Clerk; Branch Manager; Broadcast Technician; Brokerage Clerk; Clerical Supervisor; Computer Programmer; Construction Contractor; Cost Estimator; Credit Manager; Customer Service Representative; Electrical/Electronics Engineer; Financial Analyst; Health Services Manager; Human Service Worker; Industrial Agent/Broker; Internet Services Manager; Licensed Practical Nurse; Medical Records Technician; MIS Specialist; Operations/Production Manager; Paralegal; Preschool Worker; Registered Nurse; Restaurant/Food Service Manager; Systems Analyst; Telecommunications Manager; Video Production Coordinator. **Corporate headquarters location:** St. Petersburg FL. **Other U.S. locations:** GA; IN; MI; NC; SC; TN; VA; WV. **Average salary range of placements:** $20,000 - $29,999.

AAA EMPLOYMENT
1111 North West Shore Boulevard, Suite 510, Tampa FL 33607. **Contact:** Manager. **Description:** An employment agency focusing on permanent placement in positions from labor to middle management. **Specializes in the areas of:** Accounting/Auditing; Administration; Art/Design; Banking; Biology; Engineering; Food Industry; General Management; Health/Medical; Industrial; Insurance; Legal; Manufacturing; Nonprofit; Personnel/Labor Relations; Publishing; Retail; Sales; Secretarial; Technical. **Positions commonly filled include:** Accountant/Auditor; Adjuster; Administrative Manager; Advertising Clerk; Bank Officer/Manager; Biological Scientist; Biomedical Engineer; Branch Manager; Buyer; Claim Representative; Clerical Supervisor; Clinical Lab Technician; Computer Programmer; Credit Manager; Customer Service Representative; EEG Technologist; EKG Technician; Electrician; Environmental Engineer; Financial Analyst; Health Services Manager; Human Resources Specialist; Industrial Production Manager; Insurance Agent/Broker; Licensed Practical Nurse; Management Analyst/Consultant; Mechanical Engineer; Medical Records Technician; Occupational Therapist; Quality Control Supervisor; Registered Nurse; Respiratory Therapist; Restaurant/Food Service Manager; Systems Analyst; Technical Writer/Editor; Telecommunications Manager; Typist/Word Processor; Underwriter/Assistant Underwriter. **Corporate headquarters location:** St. Petersburg FL. **Other U.S. locations:** GA; IN; MI; NC; SC; TN; VA; WV. **Average salary range of placements:** Less than $20,000. **Number of placements per year:** 100 - 199.

ATS HEALTH SERVICES
5161 Beach Boulevard, Suite 4, Jacksonville FL 32207. 904/398-9098. **Contact:** Manager. **Description:** A permanent employment agency. **Specializes in the areas of:** Health/Medical. **Positions commonly filled include:** Certified Nursing Aide; Licensed Practical Nurse.

ACCOUNTANTS EXPRESS
5200 NW 33rd Avenue, Suite 220, Fort Lauderdale FL 33309. 954/486-8585. **Fax:** 954/733-6444. **Contact:** Steven Sloane, President. **Description:** A permanent employment agency that also provides some temporary placements. Company pays fee. **Specializes in the areas of:** Accounting/Auditing; Finance. **Positions commonly filled include:** Accountant/Auditor; Budget Analyst; Chief Financial Officer; Controller; Credit Manager; Finance Director; Financial Analyst. **Average salary range of placements:** $30,000 - $50,000. **Number of placements per year:** 100 - 199.

ACCUSTAFF INC.
14502 North Dale Mabry Highway, Suite 314, Tampa FL 33618. 813/908-7777. **Fax:** 813/908-7900. **Contact:** Manager. **Description:** A permanent employment agency that also provides some temporary placements. Company pays fee. **Specializes in the areas of:** Clerical; Health/Medical.

AD HOC LAW ASSOCIATES
444 Brickell Avenue, Suite 611, Miami FL 33131. 305/381-9600. **Fax:** 305/381-9396. **Contact:** Suzanne Pallot, President. **Description:** An employment agency handling associate placements and partner placements. Company pays fee. **Specializes in the areas of:** Legal. **Positions commonly filled include:** Attorney; Paralegal. **Average salary range of placements:** More than $50,000. **Number of placements per year:** 1 - 49.

THE ADDSTAFF NETWORK
101 American Center Place, Suite 203, Tampa FL 33619. 813/621-7700. **Fax:** 813/677-4336. **Contact:** Barbara Franchi, Principal. **Description:** A permanent employment agency. Company pays fee. **Specializes in the areas of:** Office Support; Personnel/Labor Relations; Secretarial. **Positions commonly filled include:** Claim Representative; Customer Service Representative; Medical Records Technician; Paralegal. **Number of placements per year:** 1000+.

ALPHA PERSONNEL
ALPHA TEMPS
10707 66th Street, Suite B, Pinellas Park FL 34666-2336. 813/544-5627. **Contact:** Director. **Description:** An employment agency that provides both permanent and temporary placements. Company pays fee. **Specializes in the areas of:** Accounting/Auditing; Banking; Computer Science/Software; Legal; Manufacturing; Nonprofit; Personnel/Labor Relations; Secretarial. **Number of placements per year:** 200 - 499.

AVAILABILITY, INC.
5340 West Kennedy Boulevard, Suite 100, Tampa FL 33609. 813/286-8800. **Fax:** 813/286-0574. **Contact:** Ed Hart, President. **Description:** An employment agency that provides permanent and temporary placements, as well as contract services. **Specializes in the areas of:** Accounting/Auditing; Administration; Banking; Clerical; Computer Science/Software; Engineering; Finance; General Management; Health/Medical; Legal; Personnel/Labor Relations; Publishing; Secretarial. **Positions commonly filled include:** Accountant/Auditor; Administrative Manager; Advertising Clerk; Bank Officer/Manager; Branch Manager; Brokerage Clerk; Claim Representative; Clerical Supervisor; Computer Programmer; Cost Estimator; Credit Manager; Customer Service Representative; Education Administrator; Emergency Medical Technician; Financial Analyst; Health Services Manager; Human Service Worker; Internet Services Manager; Management Analyst/Consultant; Occupational Therapist; Paralegal; Registered Nurse; Respiratory Therapist; Software Engineer; Systems Analyst; Technical Writer/Editor; Telecommunications Manager; Typist/Word Processor; Underwriter/Assistant Underwriter.

B&B PERSONNEL
175 West Granada Boulevard, Ormond Beach FL 32174-7573. 904/672-2632. **Fax:** 904/676-7705. **Contact:** Lauren Brayman, President. **Description:** A full-service employment agency that handles temporary, temp-to-perm, permanent, and executive career placements. The agency also provides referrals and resume services. **Specializes in the areas of:** Accounting/Auditing; Administration; Finance; Food Industry; General Management; Health/Medical; Industrial; Insurance; Legal; Manufacturing; Personnel/Labor Relations; Retail; Sales; Secretarial; Transportation. **Benefits available to temporary workers:** Medical Insurance. **Average salary range of placements:** $20,000 - $29,999.

BELMONT TRAINING & EMPLOYMENT
17800 NW 27th Avenue, Opa-Locka FL 33056. 954/628-3838. **Fax:** 954/628-2331. **Contact:** Steven L. Davis, Center Coordinator. **Description:** A permanent employment agency. **Specializes in the areas of:** Administration; Computer Science/Software; Education; Food Industry; General Management; Retail; Sales; Secretarial. **Positions commonly filled include:** Accountant/Auditor; Administrative Manager; Advertising Clerk; Automotive Mechanic; Blue-Collar Worker Supervisor; Clerical Supervisor; Computer Programmer; Construction Contractor; Customer Service Representative; EKG Technician; Financial Analyst; Human Resources Specialist; Management Trainee; Market Research Analyst; Paralegal; Registered Nurse; Restaurant/Food Service Manager; Teacher/Professor; Typist/Word Processor. **Number of placements per year:** 200 - 499.

CTI GROUP
1535 South 17th Street, Suite 206, Fort Lauderdale FL 33316. 954/728-9975. **Contact:** Manager. **Description:** A permanent employment agency. **Specializes in the areas of:** Maritime.

CAREER PLANNERS, INC.
5730 Corporate Way, Suite 100, West Palm Beach FL 33407. 561/683-8785. **Fax:** 561/683-4047. **Contact:** Deborah M. Finley, President. **Description:** A full-service employment agency offering permanent and temporary placements. Company pays fee. **Specializes in the areas of:** Accounting/Auditing; Administration; Architecture/Construction; Banking; Computer Science/Software; Engineering; Finance; Legal; Manufacturing; Personnel/Labor Relations; Sales; Secretarial. **Positions commonly filled include:** Accountant/Auditor; Administrative Manager; Bank Officer/Manager; Branch Manager; Budget Analyst; Buyer; Civil Engineer; Computer Programmer; Cost Estimator; Credit Manager; Design Engineer; Draftsperson; Environmental Engineer; Financial Analyst; Mechanical Engineer; MIS Specialist; Operations/Production Manager; Paralegal; Property and Real Estate Manager; Purchasing Agent/Manager; Quality Control Supervisor; Securities Sales Representative; Systems Analyst; Technical Writer/Editor; Typist/Word Processor; Underwriter/Assistant Underwriter. **Average salary range of placements:** $30,000 - $50,000. **Number of placements per year:** 200 - 499.

CENTRAL FLORIDA LEGAL-EASE, INC.
2002 East Robinson Street, Orlando FL 32803. 407/895-2565. **Contact:** Jeanna Juliano, Co-Owner. **Description:** An employment agency that offers permanent and temporary placement of support staff to law firms. The company also provides resume assistance and career counseling. Company pays fee. **Specializes in the areas of:** Legal; Secretarial. **Positions commonly filled include:** Attorney; Clerk; Paralegal; Receptionist; Secretary. **Average salary range of placements:** $20,000 - $29,999. **Number of placements per year:** 100 - 199.

COMPU-TECH PERSONNEL
155 Crystal Beach Drive, Destin FL 35248. 904/650-1880. **Contact:** Melanie Castoe, Owner. **Description:** A permanent employment agency.

CREW UNLIMITED INC.
2065 South Federal Highway, Fort Lauderdale FL 33316-3546. 954/462-4624. **Contact:** Ami G. Williams, Manager. **Description:** A professional placement agency for the maritime industry. The firm supplies crew personnel for yachts. Company pays fee. **Specializes in the areas of:** Retail; Sales; Secretarial. **Positions commonly filled include:** Chef/Cook/Kitchen Worker; Electrical/Electronics Engineer; Electrician; Mechanical Engineer; Registered Nurse; Restaurant/Food Service Manager; Ship's Captain; Ship's Mate. **Other U.S. locations:** Newport RI. **Average salary range of placements:** $30,000 - $50,000. **Number of placements per year:** 100 - 199.

DECISION CONSULTANTS
13535 Southern Sound Drive, Suite 220, Clearwater FL 34622. 813/573-2626. **Contact:** Manager. **Description:** A permanent employment agency. **Specializes in the areas of:** Administration; Computer Hardware/Software.

EN-DATA CORPORATION
P.O. Box 2949, Sanford FL 32772-2949. 407/323-0033. **Fax:** 407/323-0685. **Contact:** Virginia Smith, President. **Description:** An employment agency that provides placements in contract programming services and information systems consulting services. Company pays fee. **Specializes in the areas of:** Accounting/Auditing; Computer Science/Software; Data Processing; Information Systems. **Positions commonly filled include:** Computer Operator; Computer Programmer; Database Manager; MIS Specialist; Project Manager; Software Engineer; Systems Analyst; Systems Manager. **Corporate headquarters location:** Orlando FL. **Average salary range of placements:** More than $50,000. **Number of placements per year:** 50 - 99.

EXECUTIVE DIRECTIONS INC.
450 North Park Road, Suite 302, Hollywood FL 33021. 954/962-9444. **Fax:** 954/963-4333. **Contact:** Bob Silverman, Director. **E-mail address:** edifla@shadow.net. **Description:** A permanent employment agency. Company pays fee. **Specializes in the areas of:** Administration; Computer Science/Software. **Positions commonly filled include:** Computer Programmer; Management Analyst/Consultant; Software Engineer; Systems Analyst; Telecommunications Manager. **Average salary range of placements:** $30,000 - $50,000. **Number of placements per year:** 100 - 199.

FIRST RECRUITERS GROUP INC.
1922 Tyler Street, Hollywood FL 33020. 954/922-2912. **Fax:** 954/922-3121. **Contact:** Ginger Cielo, President. **Description:** A permanent placement agency. Company pays fee. **Number of placements per year:** 200 - 499.

FLORAPERSONNEL, INC.
1740 Lake Markham Road, Sanford FL 32771. 407/682-5151. **Fax:** 407/682-2318. **Contact:** Bob Zahra, Manager. **Description:** A permanent employment agency. **Positions commonly filled include:** Horticulturist.

FLORIDA JOBS & BENEFITS CENTER
5729 Manatee Avenue West, Bradenton FL 34209. 941/741-3030. **Fax:** 941/741-3551. **Contact:** Susan

R. Stubbs, Manager. **Description:** A permanent employment agency. **Positions commonly filled include:** Bookkeeper; Clerk; Computer Operator; Construction Trade Worker; Data Entry Clerk; Driver; Factory Worker; Legal Secretary; Light Industrial Worker; Nurse; Receptionist; Secretary; Typist/Word Processor. **Corporate headquarters location:** Tallahassee FL. **Number of placements per year:** 1000+.

FLORIDA JOBS & BENEFITS CENTER
2944 Pennsylvania Avenue, Suite L, Marianna FL 32448. 850/482-9500. **Contact:** B.K. McDonald, Job Service Office Manager. **Description:** A permanent employment agency. **Corporate headquarters location:** Tallahassee FL.

FLORIDA JOBS & BENEFITS CENTER
3550 South Washington Avenue, Suite 23, Titusville FL 32780. 407/383-2735. **Fax:** 407/269-6314. **Contact:** Mike Anderson, Employment Security Manager. **Description:** An employment agency that offers computerized access to job listings, workshops, counseling, and training. **Corporate headquarters location:** Tallahassee FL. **Average salary range of placements:** $20,000 - $29,999. **Number of placements per year:** 1000+.

HALLMARK PERSONNEL INC.
3201 West Commercial Boulevard, Fort Lauderdale FL 33309. 954/739-0600. **Contact:** Manager. **Description:** A permanent employment agency. **Specializes in the areas of:** Administration; Clerical; Office Support.

IMPACT PERSONNEL
1270 Rogers Street, Clearwater FL 33756. 813/447-2288. **Fax:** 813/461-1813. **Contact:** Sheila Sliter, Director. **Description:** A permanent employment agency. **Specializes in the areas of:** Clerical.

JANUS CAREER SERVICE
157 New England Avenue, Suite 240, Winter Park FL 32789. 407/628-1090. **Fax:** 407/628-5115. **Contact:** Jan Leach, President. **Description:** A permanent employment agency. Company pays fee. **Specializes in the areas of:** Administration; Engineering; Finance; Food Industry; General Management; Health/Medical; Personnel/Labor Relations; Sales. **Positions commonly filled include:** Accountant/Auditor; Administrative Manager; Aerospace Engineer; Architect; Attorney; Bank Officer/Manager; Branch Manager; Civil Engineer; Claim Representative; Computer Programmer; Cost Estimator; Customer Service Representative; Designer; Draftsperson; Editor; Electrical/Electronics Engineer; Financial Analyst; Human Resources Manager; Human Service Worker; Industrial Engineer; Insurance Agent/Broker; Management Analyst/Consultant; Mechanical Engineer; Metallurgical Engineer; Mining Engineer; Operations/Production Manager; Quality Control Supervisor; Restaurant/Food Service Manager; Software Engineer; Statistician; Structural Engineer; Systems Analyst; Technical Writer/Editor; Urban/Regional Planner; Wholesale and Retail Buyer. **Number of placements per year:** 100 - 199.

THE JOB PLACE, INC.
428 Julia Street, Titusville FL 32796. 407/268-2250. **Fax:** 407/383-3147. **Contact:** Debra Shuler, President. **Description:** A permanent employment agency that also provides temporary placements. Company pays fee. **Number of placements per year:** 50 - 99.

MADISON TRAVEL CAREERS UNLIMITED
P.O. Box 331052, Miami FL 33233-1052. 305/576-9917. **Fax:** 305/534-3344. **Contact:** Lisa L. Madison, Director/Owner. **E-mail address:** madison@comprel.com. **World Wide Web address:** http://www.comprel.com/madison.htm. **Description:** A permanent employment agency that also provides career/outplacement counseling. Company pays fee. **Specializes in the areas of:** Travel. **Positions commonly filled include:** Reservationist; Sales and Marketing Representative; Travel Agent.

MANPOWER TECHNICAL SERVICES
8181 West Broward Boulevard, Suite 200, Plantation FL 33324. 954/236-0852. **Fax:** 954/236-0688. **Contact:** Michael Zammuto, Technical Manager. **E-mail address:** mptech@earthlink.net. **World Wide Web address:** http://www.manpower.com. **Description:** A permanent employment agency. **Specializes in the areas of:** Engineering; Technical. **Positions commonly filled include:** Biological Scientist; Chemist; Computer Programmer; Electrical/Electronics Engineer; Sales and Marketing Representative; Systems Analyst.

MEDSTAFF
1851 West Colonial Drive, Suite 200, Orlando FL 32804-7019. 407/425-6774. **Fax:** 407/425-6101. **Contact:** Ms. Kim Randall, Placement Director. **Description:** A permanent employment agency that also offers temporary placements. Company pays fee. **Specializes in the areas of:** Health/Medical. **Positions commonly filled include:** Health Services Manager; Licensed Practical Nurse; Medical Assistant; Medical Records Technician; Registered Nurse; Transcriptionist. **Corporate headquarters location:** This Location. **Average salary range of placements:** $20,000 - $29,999. **Number of placements per year:** 100 - 199.

NANNIES 'N MORE, INC.
2700 West Oakland Park Boulevard, Suite 2750-D, Fort Lauderdale FL 33311. 954/735-0902. **Contact:** Marilyn Racow, Owner. **Description:** A permanent placement agency. **Specializes in the areas of:** Domestic Help; Nannies. **Positions commonly filled include:** Chef/Cook/Kitchen Worker; Housekeeper; Nanny. **Average salary range of placements:** Less than $20,000. **Number of placements per year:** 200 - 499.

OFFICEMATES5 PERSONNEL
1500 NW 49th Street, Suite 500, Fort Lauderdale FL 33309-3700. 954/776-4477. **Fax:** 954/776-4488. **Contact:** Personnel Representative. **Description:** A permanent employment agency. Company pays fee. **Specializes in the areas of:** Legal; Office Support; Secretarial. **Positions commonly filled include:** Advertising Clerk; Brokerage Clerk; Customer Service Representative; Paralegal; Typist/Word Processor. **Corporate headquarters location:** Cleveland OH. **Other U.S. locations:** Nationwide. **Average salary range of placements:** $20,000 - $29,999. **Number of placements per year:** 1000+.

PMC&L ASSOCIATES, INC.
328 Banyan Boulevard, Suite K, West Palm Beach FL 33401. 561/659-4523. **Contact:** Manager. **Description:** A permanent employment agency that also offers temporary placements. PMC&L Associates also provides exit and career counseling services. Company pays fee. **Specializes in the areas of:** Accounting/Auditing; Bookkeeping; Chef; Clerical; Data Processing; Engineering; General Management; Office Support; Professional. **Number of placements per year:** 100 - 199.

PASSPORT PLACEMENT SERVICE, INC.
3535 West Fairfield Drive, Pensacola FL 32505. 850/455-8833. **Fax:** 850/455-2700. **Contact:** Johnny M. Smith, President. **Description:** An permanent employment agency that provides placement in the maritime industry. **Specializes in the areas of:** Offshore Operations. **Positions commonly filled**

include: Ship's Captain; Ship's Mate. **Other U.S. locations:** Mobile AL. **Average salary range of placements:** Less than $20,000. **Number of placements per year:** 200 - 499.

PERSONNEL CENTER
P.O. Box 1111, Gainesville FL 32602. 352/372-6377. **Fax:** 352/376-6783. **Contact:** Marion Voyles, Manager. **Description:** A permanent employment agency. **Specializes in the areas of:** Accounting/Auditing; Data Processing; Finance.

PERSONNEL ONE, INC.
1895 West Commercial, Suite 140, Fort Lauderdale FL 33309. 954/491-4100. **Fax:** 954/771-0700. **Contact:** Cary Purre, Area Manager. **Description:** A full-service permanent employment agency. Company pays fee. **Specializes in the areas of:** Administration; Legal; Personnel/Labor Relations; Sales; Secretarial. **Positions commonly filled include:** Accountant/Auditor; Administrative Manager; Administrative Worker/Clerk; Computer Programmer; Customer Service Representative; Human Resources Manager; Paralegal; Systems Analyst; Technical Writer/Editor. **Number of placements per year:** 200 - 499.

PERSONNEL ONE, INC.
770 South Dixie Highway, Coral Gables FL 33146. 305/662-2500. **Fax:** 305/662-6700. **Contact:** Office Manager. **Description:** A permanent employment agency. Company pays fee. **Specializes in the areas of:** Accounting/Auditing; Banking; Computer Science/Software; Engineering; General Management; Legal; Personnel/Labor Relations; Sales; Secretarial; Technical. **Positions commonly filled include:** Accountant/Auditor; Bank Officer/Manager; Biological Scientist; Branch Manager; Chemist; Clerical Supervisor; Clinical Lab Technician; Computer Programmer; Construction and Building Inspector; Construction Contractor; Engineer; Financial Analyst; Human Resources Manager; Human Service Worker; Paralegal; Services Sales Representative; Systems Analyst. **Number of placements per year:** 200 - 499.

PERSONNEL ONE, INC.
3475 Sheridan Street, Hollywood FL 33021. 954/983-4000. **Contact:** Manager. **Description:** A permanent employment agency that also provides temp-to-hire placements. **Positions commonly filled include:** Accountant/Auditor; Administrative Manager; Advertising Clerk; Aerospace Engineer; Agricultural Engineer; Biomedical Engineer; Blue-Collar Worker Supervisor; Chemical Engineer; Civil Engineer; Claim Representative; Clerical Supervisor; Computer Programmer; Cost Estimator; Counselor; Credit Manager; Customer Service Representative; Draftsperson; Electrical/Electronics Engineer; Electrician; Environmental Engineer; Financial Analyst; ndustrial Production Manager; Management Analyst/Consultant; Manufacturer's/Wholesaler's Sales Rep.; MIS Specialist; Operations/Production Manager; Paralegal; Software Engineer; Stationary Engineer; Systems Analyst; Typist/Word Processor; Underwriter/Assistant Underwriter.

SHAVER EMPLOYMENT AGENCY
254 West Tampa Avenue, Venice FL 34285. 941/484-6821. **Fax:** 941/484-6822. **Contact:** Lee Shaver, Owner. **Description:** A permanent employment agency. **Specializes in the areas of:** Accounting/Auditing; Administration; Architecture/Construction; Banking; Computer Science/Software; Food Industry; General Management; Legal; Manufacturing; Retail; Sales. **Positions commonly filled include:** Accountant/Auditor; Administrative Manager; Architect; Attorney; Automotive Mechanic; Bank Officer/Manager; Blue-Collar Worker Supervisor; Branch Manager; Brokerage Clerk; Buyer; Civil Engineer; Computer Programmer; Construction Contractor; Cost Estimator; Counselor; Credit Manager; Customer Service Representative; Dental Assistant/Dental Hygienist; Draftsperson; Electrical/Electronics Engineer; Electrician; Financial Analyst; Food Scientist/Technologist; Health Services Manager; Insurance Agent/Broker; Landscape Architect; Licensed Practical Nurse; Management Trainee; Mechanical Engineer; Medical Records Technician; MIS Specialist; Operations/Production Manager; Paralegal; Real Estate Agent; Registered Nurse; Restaurant/Food Service Manager; Services Sales Representative; Software Engineer; Systems Analyst; Technical Writer/Editor; Travel Agent; Typist/Word Processor. **Number of placements per year:** 200 - 499.

SPALDING'S EMPLOYMENT SERVICE
2880 West Oakland Park Boulevard, Fort Lauderdale FL 33311. 954/730-0910. **Fax:** 954/730-0443. **Contact:** Ferdi Hutchinson, Director. **Description:** A permanent employment agency that offers job search assistance, counseling, resume help, and management training. **Specializes in the areas of:** Accounting/Auditing; Banking; Finance; General Management; Retail; Sales; Secretarial. **Positions commonly filled include:** Accountant/Auditor; Administrative Manager; Advertising Clerk; Automotive Mechanic; Bank Officer/Manager; Blue-Collar Worker Supervisor; Buyer; Claim Representative; Computer Programmer; Cost Estimator; Customer Service Representative; Financial Analyst; Health Services Manager; Human Service Worker; Insurance Agent/Broker; Management Analyst/Consultant; Restaurant/Food Service Manager; Systems Analyst; Typist/Word Processor. **Average salary range of placements:** $20,000 - $29,999. **Number of placements per year:** 500 - 999.

STAFFING SERVICES GROUP
Tri City Plaza, 5186 East Bay Drive, Clearwater FL 33764. 813/524-1554. **Contact:** Debbie Lynch, Branch Manager. **Description:** A permanent employment agency. Company pays fee. **NOTE:** Resumes can also be sent to 15 Bleeker Street, Milburn NJ 07041. **Specializes in the areas of:** Accounting/Auditing; Food Industry; General Management; Health/Medical; Industrial; Insurance; Legal; Manufacturing; Personnel/Labor Relations; Retail; Sales; Secretarial; Technical. **Benefits available to temporary workers:** Medical Insurance; Paid Holidays; Paid Vacation. **Corporate headquarters location:** Milburn NJ. **Average salary range of placements:** Less than $20,000. **Number of placements per year:** 200 - 499.

STAFFING SERVICES GROUP
3137 South Florida Avenue, Lakeland FL 33803. 941/647-1677. **Contact:** Manager. **Description:** A permanent employment agency. **Corporate headquarters location:** Milburn NJ.

STAFFING SERVICES GROUP
5130 Eisenhower Boulevard, Tampa FL 33634. 813/290-9202. **Contact:** Office Manager. **Description:** A permanent employment agency. **Corporate headquarters location:** Milburn NJ.

STAFFING SERVICES GROUP
5011P West Hillsboro Avenue, Tampa FL 33634. 813/249-5155. **Contact:** Manager. **Description:** A permanent employment agency. **Corporate headquarters location:** Milburn NJ.

STAFFING SERVICES GROUP
3014 U.S. Highway 301, Suite 100, Tampa FL 33619. 813/621-2224. **Contact:** Office Manager.

Description: A permanent employment agency. **Corporate headquarters location:** Milburn NJ.

STAFFING SOLUTIONS BY PERSONNEL ONE
6200 North Federal Highway, Boca Raton FL 33487-3248. 561/994-4600. **Fax:** 561/994-9635. **Contact:** Recruiter. **World Wide Web address:** http://www.ssbyp1.com. **Description:** An employment agency that also provides career/outplacement counseling. Company pays fee. **Specializes in the areas of:** Computer Science/Software; Personnel/Labor Relations; Sales; Secretarial. **Positions commonly filled include:** Accountant/Auditor; Administrative Manager; Blue-Collar Worker Supervisor; Brokerage Clerk; Clerical Supervisor; Customer Service Representative; Manufacturer's/Wholesaler's Sales Rep.; Services Sales Representative; Software Engineer. **Average salary range of placements:** $20,000 - $29,999. **Number of placements per year:** 1000+.

STARKE JOBS & BENEFITS CENTER
P.O. Box 1278, Starke FL 32091. 904/964-8092. **Fax:** 904/964-3969. **Contact:** Supervisor. **Description:** An employment agency that provides placements in a variety of industries. **Corporate headquarters location:** Tallahassee FL.

SUNCOAST GROUP
3808 Gunn Highway, Suite 102, Tampa FL 33624. 813/961-1485. **Fax:** 813/961-2038. **Contact:** Michael Loos, Owner. **Description:** An employment agency providing permanent placement services, primarily for recent college graduates and career change applicants. **Specializes in the areas of:** Entry-Level; Entry-Level Management; Finance; General Management; Retail; Sales. **Positions commonly filled include:** Branch Manager; General Manager; Management Trainee; Services Sales Representative. **Average salary range of placements:** $20,000 - $29,999. **Number of placements per year:** 1 - 49.

VELKIN PERSONNEL SERVICES
6405 NW 36th Street, Suite 220, Miami FL 33166. 305/876-9800. **Contact:** Staff Administrator. **Description:** A full-service personnel agency providing permanent and temporary placements, some executive search services, and career/outplacement counseling. Company pays fee. **Specializes in the areas of:** Personnel/Labor Relations. **Positions commonly filled include:** Accountant/Auditor; Adjuster; Administrative Assistant; Administrative Manager; Advertising Clerk; Bank Officer/Manager; Brokerage Clerk; Budget Analyst; Claim Representative; Clerical Supervisor; Computer Programmer; Customer Service Representative; Health Services Manager; Human Resources Specialist; MIS Specialist; Multimedia Designer; Services Sales Representative; Systems Analyst; Typist/Word Processor. **Average salary range of placements:** $20,000 - $29,999. **Number of placements per year:** 200 - 499.

VICTORIA & ASSOCIATES PERSONNEL SERVICE
8181 NW 36th Street, Suite 22, Miami FL 33166. 305/477-2233. **Fax:** 305/477-2149. **Contact:** Odalys Riaseco, Office Manager. **E-mail address:** vicassoc@herald.infi.net. **Description:** A full-service employment agency providing permanent, temp-to-hire, and temporary placements. Company pays fee. **Specializes in the areas of:** Accounting/Auditing; Secretarial. **Positions commonly filled include:** Accountant/Auditor; Bank Officer/Manager; Buyer; Credit Manager; Financial Analyst; Human Resources Specialist; Management Trainee; Typist/Word Processor. **Benefits available to temporary workers:** Medical Insurance; Paid Holidays; Paid Vacation. **Average salary range of placements:** $20,000 - $29,999. **Number of placements per year:** 1000+.

SCOTT WATSON & ASSOCIATES, INC.
100 Second Avenue South, Suite 200-South, St. Petersburg FL 33701-4360. 813/898-2281. **Contact:** Scott Watson, President. **Description:** A permanent employment agency. **Specializes in the areas of:** Banking.

ZANCO PERSONNEL RESOURCES
1900 Main Street, Suite 309, Sarasota FL 34236. 941/955-3844. **Fax:** 941/955-0430. **Contact:** Sharon-Elizabeth Ayers, President. **Description:** A permanent employment agency. Company pays fee. **Specializes in the areas of:** Education; Health/Medical; Personnel/Labor Relations. **Positions commonly filled include:** Human Resources Specialist; Human Service Worker; Registered Nurse; Respiratory Therapist; Speech-Language Pathologist; Teacher/Professor. **Number of placements per year:** 1 - 49.

TEMPORARY EMPLOYMENT AGENCIES

ALS (ALL-WAYS LEGAL SECRETARIES), INC.
150 North Federal Highway, Fort Lauderdale FL 33301. 954/565-6565. **Fax:** 954/522-4659. **Contact:** President/Owner. **Description:** A temporary agency that also provides permanent placements. **Specializes in the areas of:** Legal. **Average salary range of placements:** $20,000 - $29,999. **Number of placements per year:** 200 - 499.

ABLEST STAFFING SERVICES
3101 Maguire Boulevard, Suite 265, Orlando FL 32803-3720. 407/896-1912. **Fax:** 407/898-1015. **Contact:** Brett Benacum, Manager. **Description:** A temporary agency specializing in administrative placements for jobseekers with Word or Excel backgrounds. **Specializes in the areas of:** Administration.

ACCUSTAFF INC.
1875 West Commercial Boulevard, Suite 165, Fort Lauderdale FL 33309. 954/928-0699. **Fax:** 954/772-8343. **Contact:** Branch Manager. **E-mail address:** rosen@accustaff.com. **World Wide Web address:** http://www.accustaff.com. **Description:** A temporary agency. **Specializes in the areas of:** Clerical; Light Industrial; Marketing; Personnel/Labor Relations; Sales. **Positions commonly filled include:** Sales Representative; Secretary. **Benefits available to temporary workers:** 401(k); Paid Holidays; Paid Vacation. **Corporate headquarters location:** Jacksonville FL. **Other U.S. locations:** Nationwide. **Average salary range of placements:** $20,000 - $29,999. **Number of placements per year:** 1000+.

ADECCO
330 South Pineapple Avenue, Suite 101, Sarasota FL 34236-7020. 941/365-5546. **Contact:** Recruiter. **Description:** A temporary agency. Company pays fee. **Specializes in the areas of:** Accounting/Auditing; Administration; Banking; General Management; Industrial; Manufacturing; Sales; Secretarial. **Positions commonly filled include:** Accountant/Auditor; Automotive Mechanic; Blue-Collar Worker Supervisor; Branch Manager; Customer Service Representative; Electrical/Electronics Engineer; Human Resources Specialist; Management Trainee; Public Relations Specialist; Typist/Word Processor. **Benefits available to temporary workers:** 401(k); Medical Insurance; Paid Holidays; Paid Vacation; Tuition Assistance. **Corporate headquarters location:** Redwood City CA. **Other U.S. locations:** Nationwide. **International locations:** Worldwide. **Average salary range of placements:**

$20,000 - $29,999. **Number of placements per year:** 200 - 499.

ALL MEDICAL PERSONNEL
8700 West Flagler Street, Suite 260, Miami FL 33174. **Toll-free phone:** 800/706-2378. **Contact:** Regional Director. **Description:** A temporary employment agency that also offers permanent placements. **Specializes in the areas of:** Health/Medical. **Corporate headquarters location:** Hollywood FL. **Other area locations:** Delray FL; Merritt Island FL; Tampa FL. **Average salary range of placements:** $20,000 - $29,999.

BRICKELL PERSONNEL CONSULTANTS
1110 Brickell Avenue, Miami FL 33131-3132. 305/371-6187. **Contact:** Nidia Torres, President. **Description:** A temporary agency that also provides some permanent and contract placements. Company pays fee. **Specializes in the areas of:** Accounting/Auditing; Administration; Banking; Computer Science/Software; Finance; Legal. **Positions commonly filled include:** Accountant/Auditor; Bank Officer/Manager; Computer Programmer; Credit Manager; Customer Service Representative; Financial Analyst; Internet Services Manager; Management Analyst/Consultant; MIS Specialist; Paralegal; Systems Analyst; Typist/Word Processor. **Number of placements per year:** 200 - 499.

CAREERS USA
4400 North Federal Highway, Boca Raton FL 33431-5187. 561/362-4200. **Fax:** 561/362-9299. **Contact:** Melissa Mowat, Regional Director. **Description:** A temporary agency that also provides temp-to-hire staffing services. **Specializes in the areas of:** Accounting/Auditing; Administration; Data Processing; Light Industrial; Secretarial; Telemarketing. **Benefits available to temporary workers:** Bonus Award/Plan; Medical Insurance; Retirement Plan. **Corporate headquarters location:** Philadelphia PA. **Other U.S. locations:** DC; GA; IL; MD; NJ; PA. **Number of placements per year:** 1000+.

CAREERXCHANGE
220 Miracle Mile, Suite 203, Coral Gables FL 33134. 305/529-0064. **Fax:** 305/529-0122. **Contact:** Elsa Yacques, President. **Description:** A temporary employment agency that also provides permanent placements and training. Company pays fee. **Specializes in the areas of:** Accounting/Auditing; General Management; Legal; Personnel/Labor Relations; Secretarial. **Positions commonly filled include:** Accountant/Auditor; Administrative Manager; Administrator; Advertising Clerk; Blue-Collar Worker Supervisor; Branch Manager; Brokerage Clerk; Budget Analyst; Claim Representative; Clerical Supervisor; Clerk; Construction Contractor; Cost Estimator; Credit Manager; Customer Service Representative; Financial Analyst; Health Services Manager; Human Resources Specialist; Internet Services Manager; Management; Management Trainee; Medical Secretary; Paralegal; Property and Quality Control Supervisor; Real Estate Agent; Receptionist; Technical Writer/Editor; Typist/Word Processor. **Benefits available to temporary workers:** Medical Insurance; Paid Holidays; Paid Vacation. **Number of placements per year:** 200 - 499.

COMPUTEMP INC.
4401 North Federal Highway, Suite 203, Boca Raton FL 33431. 561/750-8745. **Contact:** Manager. **Description:** A temporary and temp-to-hire agency. **Specializes in the areas of:** Computer Science/Software; Technical.

COMPUTER PLUS STAFFING SOLUTIONS, INC.
11300 4th Street North, Suite 115, St. Petersburg FL 33716. 813/578-1121. **Fax:** 813/578-0023. **Contact:** Gary Foddrill, Staffing Specialist. **Description:** A temporary placement agency focusing on placing information systems professionals, particularly computer and network support personnel. **Specializes in the areas of:** Administration; Computer Science/Software; Personnel/Labor Relations. **Positions commonly filled include:** Computer Support Technician; MIS Specialist; Network Support Technician; Operations Engineer; Technical Writer/Editor; Telecommunications Analyst; Typist/Word Processor. **Benefits available to temporary workers:** 401(k); Medical Insurance; Paid Holidays; Paid Vacation. **Other area locations:** Orlando FL; Sarasota FL; Tampa FL. **Average salary range of placements:** $30,000 - $50,000. **Number of placements per year:** 200 - 499.

CUSTOM STAFFING, INC.
2600 Lake Lucien Drive, Suite 205, Maitland FL 32751. 407/667-8755. **Fax:** 407/667-8760. **Contact:** Chas Summers, Client Services Specialist. **Description:** A temporary agency. **Specializes in the areas of:** Accounting/Auditing; Administration; Customer Service; Office Support; Secretarial; Telemarketing; Word Processing. **Other area locations:** Jacksonville FL; Orlando FL.

DENTAL FILL-INS INC.
715 Buchanan Avenue, Lehigh Acres FL 33936-6605. 941/368-2555. **Toll-free phone:** 800/9FILL-IN. **Contact:** Cathy Beresford, Vice President. **Description:** A temporary agency that also provides permanent placements for dental hygienists and dental assistants. Company pays fee. **Specializes in the areas of:** Health/Medical. **Positions commonly filled include:** Dental Assistant/Dental Hygienist.

DONBAR SERVICE CORPORATION
4319 West Kennedy Boulevard, Tampa FL 33609. 813/287-8925. **Fax:** 813/289-4839. **Contact:** Bill Patterson, Account Representative. **Description:** A temporary agency that also provides contract services and permanent placements. Company pays fee. **Specializes in the areas of:** Computer Science/Software; Engineering; Industrial; Manufacturing; Secretarial. **Positions commonly filled include:** Accountant/Auditor; Administrative Manager; Aerospace Engineer; Blue-Collar Worker Supervisor; Civil Engineer; Computer Programmer; Customer Service Representative; Design Engineer; Designer; Draftsperson; Electrical/Electronics Engineer; Electrician; Environmental Engineer; Industrial Engineer; Industrial Production Manager; Materials Engineer; Mechanical Engineer; Metallurgical Engineer; MIS Specialist; Operations/Production Manager; Quality Control Supervisor; Software Engineer; Structural Engineer; Surveyor; Systems Analyst; Typist/Word Processor. **Other area locations:** Largo FL. **Number of placements per year:** 1000+.

EMPLOYERS' ASSISTANT, INC.
25 East Wright Street, Suite 2510, Pensacola FL 32501. 850/432-6311. **Fax:** 850/434-9697. **Contact:** Krissy Box, Staffing Manager. **Description:** A temporary agency. Company pays fee. **Specializes in the areas of:** Accounting/Auditing; Administration; Banking; Education; General Management; Health/Medical; Industrial; Personnel/Labor Relations; Retail; Sales; Secretarial. **Positions commonly filled include:** Accountant/Auditor; Branch Manager; Computer Programmer; Counselor; Health Services Manager; Human Resources Specialist; Medical Records Technician; Pharmacist; Travel Agent; Typist/Word Processor. **Benefits available to temporary workers:** Credit Union; Dental Insurance; Medical Insurance. **Number of placements per year:** 200 - 499.

FIVE STAR TEMPORARY INC.
2943 East Colonial Drive, Orlando FL 32803. 407/898-1125. **Fax:** 407/898-4940. **Contact:** Joseph Carusone, Branch Manager. **Description:** A temporary agency. **Specializes in the areas of:** Administration; Banking; Food Industry; General Management; Health/Medical; Industrial; Legal; Manufacturing; Personnel/Labor Relations; Retail; Sales; Secretarial; Technical. **Positions commonly filled include:** Accountant/Auditor; Administrative Manager; Branch Manager; Buyer; Claim Representative; Clerical Supervisor; Computer Programmer; Cost Estimator; Counselor; Credit Manager; General Manager; Industrial Production Manager; Management Trainee; MIS Specialist; Typist/Word Processor; Underwriter/Assistant Underwriter. **Benefits available to temporary workers:** Medical Insurance; Paid Vacation. **Other area locations:** Longwood FL; Tampa FL. **Average salary range of placements:** $20,000 - $29,999. **Number of placements per year:** 1000+.

FUTURE FORCE PERSONNEL
5705 NW 158th Street, Hialeah FL 33014-6702. **Contact:** Adela Gonzalez, President. **Description:** A temporary agency that also provides permanent, full-time placements. **Specializes in the areas of:** Accounting/Auditing; Administration; Banking; Computer Science/Software; Food Industry; Legal; Manufacturing; Personnel/Labor Relations; Publishing; Retail; Sales; Secretarial. **Benefits available to temporary workers:** Medical Insurance; Paid Holidays; Paid Vacation. **Average salary range of placements:** $20,000 - $29,999. **Number of placements per year:** 1000+.

GIRL FRIDAY PERSONNEL
3876 West Commercial Boulevard, Fort Lauderdale FL 33309. 954/735-5392. **Contact:** Nancy Hollins, Manager. **Description:** A temporary agency. **Specializes in the areas of:** Clerical; Manufacturing; Secretarial. **Corporate headquarters location:** Sarasota FL.

GIRL FRIDAY PERSONNEL
4378 Park Boulevard, Pinellas Park FL 33781. 813/541-5704. **Contact:** Manager. **Description:** A temporary agency. Company pays fee. **Specializes in the areas of:** Accounting/Auditing; Personnel/Labor Relations; Secretarial. **Positions commonly filled include:** Clerical Supervisor; Customer Service Representative; Data Entry Clerk; Human Resources Specialist; Medical Records Technician; Receptionist; Typist/Word Processor. **Corporate headquarters location:** Sarasota FL. **Average salary range of placements:** Less than $20,000. **Number of placements per year:** 500 - 999.

GIRL FRIDAY PERSONNEL
2002 North Lois Avenue, Suite 110, Tampa FL 33607. 813/870-3801. **Toll-free phone:** 800/662-6246. **Fax:** 813/870-3959. **Contact:** Karen Crouse, Branch Manager. **Description:** A temporary agency that also provides permanent placements. The agency places high-level executives, as well as entry-level clerical and medical staff. Company pays fee. **Specializes in the areas of:** Accounting/Auditing; Administration; Advertising; Banking; Computer Science/Software; Finance; General Management; Health/Medical; Industrial; Insurance; Legal; Personnel/Labor Relations; Sales; Secretarial. **Positions commonly filled include:** Accountant/Auditor; Administrative Manager; Advertising Clerk; Bank Officer/Manager; Bookkeeper; Branch Manager; Brokerage Clerk; Clerical Supervisor; Computer Programmer; Credit Manager; Customer Service Representative; Education Administrator; Executive Assistant; General Manager; Human Resources Specialist; Internet Services Manager; Management Trainee; Manufacturer's/Wholesaler's Sales Rep.; Medical Records Technician; MIS Specialist; Paralegal; Preschool Worker; Purchasing Agent/Manager; Services Sales Representative; Strategic Relations Manager; Systems Analyst; Typist/Word Processor. **Benefits available to temporary workers:** Bonus Award/Plan; Medical Insurance; Paid Vacation. **Corporate headquarters location:** Sarasota FL. **Number of placements per year:** 500 - 999.

HASTINGS & HASTINGS PERSONNEL CONSULTANTS
1001 South Brickell Bay Drive, Suite 2902, Miami FL 33131. 305/374-7171. **Contact:** Robin Cox, Executive Vice President. **Description:** A temporary agency that also provides permanent placements. Company pays fee. **Specializes in the areas of:** Accounting/Auditing; Administration; Advertising; Banking; Computer Science/Software; Economics; Finance; Insurance; Legal; Personnel/Labor Relations; Sales; Secretarial. **Positions commonly filled include:** Accountant/Auditor; Adjuster; Administrative Manager; Bank Officer/Manager; Branch Manager; Brokerage Clerk; Budget Analyst; Buyer; Claim Representative; Clerical Supervisor; Computer Programmer; Credit Manager; Customer Service Representative; Financial Analyst; Human Resources Specialist; Insurance Agent/Broker; Internet Services Manager; Management Analyst/Consultant; Market Research Analyst; MIS Specialist; Multimedia Designer; Paralegal; Quality Control Supervisor; Securities Sales Representative; Services Sales Representative; Systems Analyst; Technical Writer/Editor; Typist/Word Processor; Underwriter/Assistant Underwriter. **Benefits available to temporary workers:** Paid Vacation. **Average salary range of placements:** $30,000 - $50,000. **Number of placements per year:** 200 - 499.

INTERIM PERSONNEL
2551 Drew Street, Suite 102, Clearwater FL 33765. 813/797-2171. **Fax:** 813/726-4061. **Contact:** Client Service Supervisor. **Description:** A temporary agency that also provides permanent placements. **Specializes in the areas of:** Accounting/Auditing; Manufacturing; Sales; Secretarial. **Positions commonly filled include:** Accountant/Auditor; Clerical Supervisor; Customer Service Representative; Paralegal; Typist/Word Processor. **Average salary range of placements:** $20,000 - $29,999. **Number of placements per year:** 500 - 999.

KELLY SERVICES, INC.
3300 PGA Boulevard, Suite 800, Palm Beach Gardens FL 33410. 561/694-0116. **Contact:** Branch Manager. **Description:** A temporary agency. **Specializes in the areas of:** Clerical; Manufacturing; Technical. **Corporate headquarters location:** Troy MI. **Other U.S. locations:** Nationwide.

KELLY SERVICES, INC.
1840 West 49th Street, Suite 107, Hialeah FL 33012. 305/822-8210. **Fax:** 305/828-9312. **Contact:** Office Manager. **Description:** A temporary agency. **Specializes in the areas of:** Banking; Industrial; Light Industrial; Sales; Secretarial. **Positions commonly filled include:** Administrative Assistant; Customer Service Representative; Secretary; Typist/Word Processor. **Benefits available to temporary workers:** Medical Insurance; Paid Holidays; Paid Vacation. **Corporate headquarters location:** Troy MI. **Other U.S. locations:** Nationwide. **Average salary range of placements:** $20,000 - $29,999. **Number of placements per year:** 1 - 49.

KELLY SERVICES, INC.
4803 George Road, Suite 300, Tampa FL 33634. 813/243-8855. **Toll-free phone:** 800/46-KELLY. **Fax:** 813/243-9166. **Contact:** Bernadette M. Pello, Service

Recruiter. **Description:** A temporary agency that also provides some permanent, full-time placements. **Specializes in the areas of:** Clerical; Industrial; Light Industrial; Manufacturing; Personnel/Labor Relations; Sales; Secretarial; Technical. **Positions commonly filled include:** Accountant/Auditor; Clerical Supervisor; Customer Service Representative; Human Resources Specialist; Typist/Word Processor. **Benefits available to temporary workers:** Medical Insurance; Paid Holidays; Paid Vacation. **Corporate headquarters location:** Troy MI. **Other U.S. locations:** Nationwide. **Number of placements per year:** 1000+.

KELLY SERVICES, INC.
211 North Ridgewood Avenue, Daytona Beach FL 32114. 904/255-1661. **Toll-free phone:** 800/775-2060. **Fax:** 904/258-9015. **Recorded jobline:** 904/252-4200. **Contact:** Denise Breneman, Area Branch Manager. **Description:** A temporary agency that also provides some temp-to-hire and permanent placements. Company pays fee. **Specializes in the areas of:** Administration; Clerical; Office Support; Retail; Sales; Secretarial; Technical. **Benefits available to temporary workers:** Paid Holidays; Paid Vacation. **Corporate headquarters location:** Troy MI. **Other U.S. locations:** Nationwide. **Average salary range of placements:** Less than $20,000. **Number of placements per year:** 1 - 49.

LEGAL-TO-LEGAL, INC.
112 West Adams Street, Suite 824, Jacksonville FL 32202-3819. 904/356-0883. **Fax:** 904/356-0991. **Contact:** Monica Carter, President. **Description:** A temporary agency that places legal personnel. The agency also offers some permanent placements. Company pays fee. **Specializes in the areas of:** Legal. **Positions commonly filled include:** Legal Secretary; Paralegal. **Average salary range of placements:** $20,000 - $29,999. **Number of placements per year:** 50 - 99.

MANPOWER TEMPORARY SERVICES
10750 North 56th Street, Tampa FL 33617-3643. 813/985-8184. **Contact:** Branch Manager. **Description:** A temporary agency. **Specializes in the areas of:** Clerical; Industrial; Personnel/Labor Relations. **Corporate headquarters location:** Milwaukee WI. **Other U.S. locations:** Nationwide.

MANPOWER TEMPORARY SERVICES
4450 Eau Gallie Boulevard, Suite 104, Melbourne FL 32934. 407/242-2296. **Fax:** 407/242-2217. **Contact:** Sara Pereres, Customer Service Representative. **Description:** A temporary agency. **Specializes in the areas of:** Engineering; General Management; Publishing. **Positions commonly filled include:** Administrative Manager; Advertising Clerk; Blue-Collar Worker Supervisor; Branch Manager; Buyer; Chemical Engineer; Clerical Supervisor; Electrical/Electronics Engineer; Electrician; Mechanical Engineer; Services Sales Representative; Structural Engineer; Technical Writer/Editor; Typist/Word Processor. **Benefits available to temporary workers:** 401(k); Medical Insurance; Paid Vacation. **Corporate headquarters location:** Milwaukee WI. **Other U.S. locations:** Nationwide. **Average salary range of placements:** Less than $20,000. **Number of placements per year:** 200 - 499.

MANPOWER TEMPORARY SERVICES
5200 West Newberry Road, Building D, Suite 6, Gainesville FL 32607-2151. 352/376-5388. **Contact:** Branch Manager. **Description:** A temporary agency. Company pays fee. **Specializes in the areas of:** Data Processing; Light Industrial; Office Support; Technical; Telemarketing; Word Processing. **Positions commonly filled include:** Accountant/Auditor; Accounting Clerk; Administrative Assistant; Assembler; Biological Scientist; Bookkeeper; Chemist; Computer Operator; Customer Service Representative; Designer; Desktop Publishing Specialist; Electrician; Inspector/Tester/Grader; Inventory Control Specialist; Machine Operator; Project Engineer; Proofreader; Receptionist; Research Assistant; Software Engineer; Stenographer; Stock Clerk; Systems Analyst; Technical Writer/Editor; Technician; Telemarketer; Transcriptionist; Typist. **Benefits available to temporary workers:** Life Insurance; Medical Insurance; Paid Holidays; Paid Vacation. **Corporate headquarters location:** Milwaukee WI. **Other U.S. locations:** Nationwide. **Number of placements per year:** 1000+.

NORRELL SERVICES INC.
966 North Cocoa Boulevard, Suite 4, Cocoa FL 32922. 407/633-8028. **Fax:** 407/633-8038. **Contact:** Suzy Mey, Employee Service Specialist. **Description:** A temporary agency. Norrell Services Inc. fills short-term, long-term, and temp-to-hire positions including general labor, clerical, and technical positions. Company pays fee. **Specializes in the areas of:** Accounting/Auditing; Administration; Industrial; Sales; Secretarial. **Positions commonly filled include:** Accountant/Auditor; Blue-Collar Worker Supervisor; Budget Analyst; Clerical Supervisor; Customer Service Representative; Electrician; Human Resources Specialist; Typist/Word Processor. **Benefits available to temporary workers:** Bonus Award/Plan; Daycare Assistance; Medical Insurance. **Corporate headquarters location:** Atlanta GA. **Other U.S. locations:** Nationwide. **Average salary range of placements:** Less than $20,000. **Number of placements per year:** 1000+.

OFFICE OURS
7000 West Palmetto Park Road, Suite 110, Boca Raton FL 33433. 561/392-0202. **Toll-free phone:** 800/925-2955. **Fax:** 561/392-6448. **Contact:** Jeanne Pardo, Office Manager. **Description:** A temporary and temp-to-hire agency. Office Ours is a division of Outsource International, which also owns Labor World. Company pays fee. **Specializes in the areas of:** Accounting/Auditing; Clerical; Legal; Secretarial. **Number of placements per year:** 500 - 999.

OFFICE SPECIALISTS
3400 Lakeside Drive, Suite 100, Miramar FL 33027. 954/437-5074. **Contact:** Valencia McDuffy, Recruiter. **Description:** A temporary agency. **Specializes in the areas of:** Accounting/Auditing; Clerical; Finance; Legal; Word Processing.

OLSTEN PROFESSIONAL STAFFING
One North Dale Mabry Highway, Tampa FL 33609-1845. 813/354-0707. **Contact:** Patti Carr, Branch Manager. **Description:** A temporary agency that also provides permanent placements. Company pays fee. **Specializes in the areas of:** Accounting/Auditing; Computer Science/Software. **Positions commonly filled include:** Accountant/Auditor; Budget Analyst; Cost Estimator; Economist; Financial Analyst. **Benefits available to temporary workers:** Medical Insurance; Paid Vacation. **Corporate headquarters location:** Melville NY. **Other U.S. locations:** Nationwide. **Average salary range of placements:** $20,000 - $29,999. **Number of placements per year:** 200 - 499.

OLSTEN STAFFING SERVICES
801 Brickell Avenue, Miami FL 33131-2951. 305/358-5053. **Contact:** Recruiter. **Description:** A temporary agency. **Specializes in the areas of:** Accounting/Auditing; Banking; Broadcasting; Computer Science/Software; Finance; Health/Medical; Insurance; Legal; Personnel/Labor Relations. **Positions commonly filled include:** Accountant/Auditor; Clerical Supervisor; Computer Programmer; Customer Service Representative; Paralegal; Preschool Worker; Systems

Analyst; Typist/Word Processor. **Corporate headquarters location:** Melville NY. **Other U.S. locations:** Nationwide. **Number of placements per year:** 200 - 499.

OLSTEN STAFFING SERVICES
380-G North Wickham Road, Melbourne FL 32935. 407/255-7777. **Fax:** 407/255-7772. **Contact:** Jennifer Delaney, Personnel. **Description:** A temporary employment agency that also provides temp-to-hire placements. Company pays fee. **Specializes in the areas of:** Computer Science/Software; Engineering; Legal; Manufacturing; Personnel/Labor Relations; Secretarial; Technical. **Positions commonly filled include:** Administrative Manager; Brokerage Clerk; Civil Engineer; Computer Programmer; Customer Service Representative; Design Engineer; Electrical/Electronics Engineer; Electrician; Human Resources Specialist; Industrial Engineer; MIS Specialist; Multimedia Designer; Operations/Production Manager; Paralegal; Quality Control Supervisor; Systems Analyst; Technical Writer/Editor; Typist/Word Processor. **Benefits available to temporary workers:** Medical Insurance; Paid Vacation. **Corporate headquarters location:** Melville NY. **Other U.S. locations:** Nationwide. **Average salary range of placements:** Less than $20,000. **Number of placements per year:** 1000+.

OLSTEN STAFFING SERVICES
8380 Baymeadows Road, Suite 12, Jacksonville FL 32256. 904/737-2400. **Fax:** 904/739-3654. **Recorded jobline:** 904/636-7566. **Contact:** Donna VanDyke, President. **Description:** A temporary agency that also provides permanent placements. Company pays fee. **Specializes in the areas of:** Accounting/Auditing; Administration; Computer Science/Software; Finance; Light Industrial; Secretarial; Technical. **Positions commonly filled include:** Accountant/Auditor; Administrative Manager; Budget Analyst; Buyer; Computer Operator; Computer Programmer; Financial Analyst; Human Resources Manager; Paralegal; Systems Analyst. **Benefits available to temporary workers:** Bonus Award/Plan; Medical Insurance; Paid Vacation. **Corporate headquarters location:** Melville NY. **Other U.S. locations:** Nationwide. **Average salary range of placements:** $20,000 - $29,999. **Number of placements per year:** 1000+.

O'QUIN PERSONNEL
P.O. Box 2263, Lakeland FL 33806. 941/687-2336. **Fax:** 947/687-7321. **Contact:** Manager. **Description:** A temporary employment agency. Company pays fee. **Specializes in the areas of:** Accounting/Auditing; Computer Science/Software; Engineering; Manufacturing; Sales; Secretarial. **Positions commonly filled include:** Accountant/Auditor; Administrative Manager; Advertising Clerk; Bank Officer/Manager; Biochemist; Branch Manager; Buyer; Chemical Engineer; Civil Engineer; Claim Representative; Clerical Supervisor; Clinical Lab Technician; Computer Programmer; Cost Estimator; Customer Service Representative; Environmental Engineer; Financial Analyst; Human Resources Specialist; Industrial Engineer; Industrial Production Manager; Materials Engineer; Metallurgical Engineer; Quality Control Supervisor; Systems Analyst; Travel Agent; Typist/Word Processor; Underwriter/Assistant Underwriter. **Average salary range of placements:** Less than $20,000. **Number of placements per year:** 500 - 999.

PRO STAFF PERSONNEL SERVICES
1101 North Lake Destiny Road, Suite 125, Maitland FL 32751-7114. 407/875-1611. **Fax:** 407/875-1225. **Contact:** Pamie Miller, General Manager. **World Wide Web address:** http://www.prostaff.com. **Description:** A staffing service providing temporary and temp-to-hire placements. Company pays fee. **Specializes in the areas of:** Accounting/Auditing; Administration; Light Industrial; Personnel/Labor Relations; Secretarial; Technical. **Positions commonly filled include:** Computer Programmer; Customer Service Representative; MIS Specialist. **Benefits available to temporary workers:** 401(k); Medical Insurance; Paid Holidays; Paid Vacation. **Corporate headquarters location:** Minneapolis MN. **Other U.S. locations:** Nationwide. **Average salary range of placements:** $20,000 - $29,999. **Number of placements per year:** 1000+.

PROGRESSIVE PERSONNEL
8640 Phillips Avenue, Suite 11, Jacksonville FL 32257. 904/448-6008. **Fax:** 904/448-0809. **Contact:** Dan Wilson, President. **Description:** A temporary agency. **Specializes in the areas of:** Manufacturing; Retail; Secretarial. **Positions commonly filled include:** Computer Programmer. **Benefits available to temporary workers:** Paid Holidays; Paid Vacation. **Corporate headquarters location:** Indianapolis IN. **Average salary range of placements:** $20,000 - $29,999. **Number of placements per year:** 100 - 199.

THE RESERVES NETWORK
6428 West Colonial Drive, Orlando FL 32818. 407/299-0022. **Fax:** 407/299-0089. **Contact:** Manager. **Description:** A temporary agency. **Specializes in the areas of:** Administration; Industrial; Secretarial. **Positions commonly filled include:** Accountant/Auditor; Automotive Mechanic; Blue-Collar Worker Supervisor; Buyer; Customer Service Representative; Electrical/Electronics Engineer; Quality Control Supervisor; Typist/Word Processor. **Benefits available to temporary workers:** 401(k); Medical Insurance; Paid Holidays; Paid Vacation. **Corporate headquarters location:** Cleveland OH. **Average salary range of placements:** Less than $20,000. **Number of placements per year:** 100 - 199.

LINDA ROBINS & ASSOCIATES INC.
10647 SW 88th Street, Suite 6C, Miami FL 33176. 305/598-8848. **Fax:** 305/598-9314. **Contact:** Linda Robins, President. **Description:** A temporary agency that also offers permanent placements. Company pays fee. **Specializes in the areas of:** Accounting/Auditing; Banking; Finance; Health/Medical; Insurance; Manufacturing; Secretarial. **Positions commonly filled include:** Administrative Assistant; Credit Manager; Financial Analyst; Human Resources Manager; Typist/Word Processor. **Benefits available to temporary workers:** 401(k); Credit Union; Medical Insurance; Paid Holidays; Paid Vacation. **Average salary range of placements:** $20,000 - $29,999. **Number of placements per year:** 1000+.

SECRETARIES UNLIMITED, INC.
9428 Baymeadows Road, Suite 120, Jacksonville FL 32256. 904/737-7756. **Fax:** 904/731-1856. **Contact:** Elaine Harris, President. **Description:** A temporary agency that also provides permanent placements. **Specializes in the areas of:** Accounting/Auditing; Secretarial. **Positions commonly filled include:** Administrative Assistant; Computer Programmer; Secretary; Systems Analyst; Typist/Word Processor. **Average salary range of placements:** $20,000 - $50,000. **Number of placements per year:** 200 - 499.

SENIORSTAFF
P.O. Box 48944, Sarasota FL 34230-4944. 941/364-9996. **Fax:** 941/388-2069. **Contact:** Miriam Carpenter, Placement Coordinator. **E-mail address:** blacknsx@usapipeline.com. **Description:** A temporary agency. Company pays fee. **Specializes in the areas of:** Retail; Secretarial. **Positions commonly filled include:** Accountant/Auditor; Adjuster; Restaurant/Food Service Manager; Typist/Word Processor.

Average salary range of placements: $20,000 - $29,999. **Number of placements per year:** 500 - 999.

SNELLING PERSONNEL SERVICES
6555 NW 9th Avenue, Suite 203, Fort Lauderdale FL 33309. 954/771-0090. **Contact:** K. Jerry Philips, Human Resources. **Description:** A temporary agency. **Specializes in the areas of:** Administration; Sales. **Corporate headquarters location:** Dallas TX. **Other U.S. locations:** Nationwide.

SNELLING PERSONNEL SERVICES
2161 Palm Beach Lakes Boulevard, West Palm Beach FL 33409. 561/689-5400. **Fax:** 561/689-5055. **Contact:** Janet Wohlhorn, Manager. **Description:** A temporary employment agency. Company pays fee. **Specializes in the areas of:** Administration; Banking; Sales; Secretarial; Telecommunications. **Positions commonly filled include:** Customer Service Representative; Services Sales Representative; Typist/Word Processor. **Benefits available to temporary workers:** Paid Holidays; Paid Vacation. **Corporate headquarters location:** Dallas TX. **Other U.S. locations:** Nationwide. **Average salary range of placements:** $30,000 - $50,000. **Number of placements per year:** 100 - 199.

SPECIAL COUNSEL
1551 Atlantic Boulevard, Suite 300, Jacksonville FL 32207. 904/737-3436. **Fax:** 904/737-5994. **Contact:** Manager. **World Wide Web address:** http://www.specialcounsel.com. **Description:** Special Counsel is a temporary and permanent employment agency. **Specializes in the areas of:** Legal. **Other U.S. locations:** Nationwide.

TRC STAFFING SERVICES
9770 Baymeadows Road, Suite 123, Jacksonville FL 32256. 904/641-1665. **Fax:** 904/641-1662. **Contact:** Keith Fairchild, President. **E-mail address:** trcjax@aol.com. **World Wide Web address:** http://www.ultimate.org/ajax/trcjobs. **Description:** A temporary agency that also offers temp-to-hire and permanent placement. TRC Staffing focuses on accounting, clerical, managerial, and technical positions. Company pays fee. **Specializes in the areas of:** Accounting/Auditing; Administration; Architecture/Construction; Computer Science/Software; Engineering; General Management; Insurance; Manufacturing; Nonprofit; Personnel/Labor Relations; Secretarial. **Positions commonly filled include:** Accountant/Auditor; Administrative Manager; Architect; Biomedical Engineer; Blue-Collar Worker Supervisor; Branch Manager; Budget Analyst; Buyer; Civil Engineer; Claim Representative; Clerical Supervisor; Computer Programmer; Cost Estimator; Customer Service Representative; Design Engineer; Draftsperson; Financial Analyst; General Manager; Industrial Engineer; Management Analyst/Consultant; Mechanical Engineer; MIS Specialist; Quality Control Supervisor; Software Engineer; Statistician; Systems Analyst; Technical Writer/Editor; Telecommunications Manager; Typist/Word Processor; Underwriter/Assistant Underwriter. **Benefits available to temporary workers:** Medical Insurance; Paid Holidays; Paid Vacation. **Corporate headquarters location:** Atlanta GA. **Other U.S. locations:** Nationwide. **Average salary range of placements:** $20,000 - $29,999. **Number of placements per year:** 200 - 499.

TEMP-ART
P.O. Box 030398, Fort Lauderdale FL 33303-0398. 954/474-7770. **Contact:** Steven Cohen, Owner/President. **E-mail address:** jobs@tempart.com. **World Wide Web address:** http://www.tempart.com. **Description:** A temporary agency. Company pays fee. **Specializes in the areas of:** Advertising; Art/Design. **Positions commonly filled include:** Art Director; Computer Programmer; Designer; Layout Specialist; Multimedia Designer; Systems Analyst. **Average salary range of placements:** $30,000 - $50,000. **Number of placements per year:** 1000+.

TEMPORARY SOLUTIONS
1589 Metropolitan Boulevard, Tallahassee FL 32308. 850/422-0355x210. **Fax:** 850/422-0831. **Contact:** Virginia Rancourt, Manager. **Description:** A temporary agency focusing on office, computer programming, and design placements. **Specializes in the areas of:** Computer Science/Software; Personnel/Labor Relations. **Positions commonly filled include:** Claim Representative; Clerical Supervisor; Computer Programmer; Customer Service Representative; Electrical/Electronics Engineer; Electrician; Typist/Word Processor. **Benefits available to temporary workers:** Medical Insurance; Paid Holidays; Sick Days. **Number of placements per year:** 500 - 999.

TEMPSOLUTIONS, INC.
5118 North 56th Street, Suite 105, Tampa FL 33610. 813/628-4788. **Fax:** 813/628-4836. **Contact:** Sandy Lachs, President. **Description:** A temporary agency that provides professional, technical, and administrative staffing. Temp-to-perm and permanent positions are also offered. **Specializes in the areas of:** Accounting/Auditing; Administration; Art/Design; Computer Science/Software; Publishing. **Positions commonly filled include:** Accountant/Auditor; Administrative Manager; Clerical Supervisor; Computer Programmer; Customer Service Representative; Designer; Draftsperson; Editor; MIS Specialist; Multimedia Designer; Paralegal; Software Engineer; Systems Analyst; Technical Writer/Editor. **Average salary range of placements:** $30,000 - $50,000. **Number of placements per year:** 50 - 99.

TODAYS TEMPORARY
2300 Maitland Center Parkway, Maitland FL 32751-4129. **Fax:** 407/660-5753. **Contact:** Lisa Hart, Operations Manager. **Description:** A temporary agency focusing on clerical placements. Company pays fee. **Specializes in the areas of:** Accounting/Auditing; Finance; Insurance; Legal; Personnel/Labor Relations; Secretarial. **Positions commonly filled include:** Administrative Worker/Clerk; Claim Representative; Clerical Supervisor; Customer Service Representative; Medical Records Technician; Paralegal; Purchasing Agent/Manager; Typist/Word Processor. **Benefits available to temporary workers:** Paid Holidays; Paid Vacation. **Corporate headquarters location:** Dallas TX. **Other U.S. locations:** Nationwide. **Average salary range of placements:** Less than $20,000. **Number of placements per year:** 1000+.

TRANSWORLD CORESTAFF
2699 Lee Road, Suite 310, Winter Park FL 32789. 407/644-9675. **Fax:** 407/644-0028. **Contact:** Lisa Sconyers, Recruiter. **Description:** A temporary agency. **Specializes in the areas of:** Banking; Manufacturing. **Positions commonly filled include:** Blue-Collar Worker Supervisor; Manufacturing Engineer; Production Manager; Typist/Word Processor. **Benefits available to temporary workers:** 401(k); Dental Insurance; Medical Insurance; Paid Vacation; Vision Plan. **Corporate headquarters location:** This Location. **Other U.S. locations:** NJ; OK; SC. **Average salary range of placements:** Less than $20,000. **Number of placements per year:** 1000+.

WESTERN STAFF SERVICES
35180 U.S. Highway 19 North, Suite 104, Palm Harbor FL 34684. 813/787-8367. **Fax:** 813/789-6481. **Contact:** Office Manager. **Description:** A temporary agency that also provides permanent placements. **Specializes in the areas of:** Accounting/

Auditing; Computer Science/Software; Industrial; Manufacturing; Secretarial.

WORKERS OF FLORIDA
511 South Cocoa Boulevard, Cocoa FL 32922-7655. 407/635-8755. **Fax:** 407/690-1263. **Contact:** Branch Manager. **Description:** A temporary agency. **Specializes in the areas of:** Construction; Hotel/Restaurant; Light Industrial. **Average salary range of placements:** $20,000 - $29,999. **Number of placements per year:** 1000+.

CONTRACT SERVICES FIRMS

ACADEMY DESIGN & TECHNICAL SERVICES, INC.
1303 North State Road 7, Margate FL 33063-2887. 954/973-7600. **Fax:** 954/973-4890. **Contact:** Tommy Sholar, Office Manager. **E-mail address:** adts@aol.com. **Description:** A contract services firm that provides temporary, permanent, and contract technical/professional personnel across a wide range of industries. Company pays fee. **Specializes in the areas of:** Architecture/Construction; Computer Science/ Software; Engineering; Industrial; Manufacturing; Technical. **Positions commonly filled include:** Aerospace Engineer; Architect; Buyer; Chemical Engineer; Civil Engineer; Clinical Lab Technician; Computer Programmer; Cost Estimator; Design Engineer; Designer; Draftsperson; Electrical/ Electronics Engineer; Environmental Engineer; Industrial Engineer; Industrial Production Manager; Mechanical Engineer; MIS Specialist; Software Engineer; Structural Engineer; Surveyor; Systems Analyst; Telecommunications Manager. **Benefits available to temporary workers:** Paid Holidays. **Average salary range of placements:** $30,000 - $50,000. **Number of placements per year:** 200 - 499.

ACCUTECH
1551 Atlantic Boulevard, Suite 300, Jacksonville FL 32207. 904/396-4100. **Fax:** 904/398-3819. **Contact:** June Griffin, Account Specialist. **Description:** A contract staffing firm operating commercial, technical, and telecommunications divisions. Company pays fee. **Specializes in the areas of:** Accounting/Auditing; Administration; Banking; Biology; Computer Science/ Software; Engineering; Finance; General Management; Industrial; Legal; Manufacturing; Personnel/Labor Relations; Secretarial; Technical. **Positions commonly filled include:** Accountant/Auditor; Actuary; Adjuster; Administrative Manager; Advertising Clerk; Aerospace Engineer; Agricultural Engineer; Architect; Attorney; Bank Officer/Manager; Branch Manager; Buyer; Chemical Engineer; Claim Representative; Clerical Supervisor; Clinical Lab Technician; Computer Programmer; Credit Manager; Customer Service Representative; Editor; Electrical/Electronics Engineer; Environmental Engineer; Financial Analyst; Food Scientist/Technologist; Health Services Manager; Internet Services Manager; Management Analyst/ Consultant; Market Research Analyst; Mechanical Engineer; MIS Specialist; Multimedia Designer; Operations/Production Manager; Paralegal; Quality Control Supervisor; Software Engineer; Systems Analyst; Technical Writer/Editor; Typist/Word Processor; Urban/Regional Planner; Video Production Coordinator. **Average salary range of placements:** $30,000 - $50,000. **Number of placements per year:** 500 - 999.

ADVANCED R&D, INC.
6704-B Plantation Road, Pensacola FL 32504. 850/484-8662. **Toll-free phone:** 800/477-8662. **Fax:** 850/484-8775. **Contact:** Mike Forster, Regional Sales Manager. **E-mail address:** ardpensa@gulf.net. **World Wide Web address:** http://www.advancedrd.com. **Description:** A contract services firm that places engineers, designers, computer specialists, and other technical professionals on a temporary, contract basis. Founded in 1960. Company pays fee. **Specializes in the areas of:** Engineering; Manufacturing; Technical. **Positions commonly filled include:** Aerospace Engineer; Architect; Ceramics Engineer; Chemical Engineer; Chemist; Civil Engineer; Computer Programmer; Cost Estimator; Design Engineer; Designer; Draftsperson; Electrical/Electronics Engineer; Environmental Engineer; Industrial Engineer; Materials Engineer; Mechanical Engineer; Metallurgical Engineer; Software Engineer; Structural Engineer; Systems Analyst; Technical Writer/Editor. **Benefits available to temporary workers:** 401(k); Bonus Award/Plan; Paid Holidays; Paid Vacation. **Corporate headquarters location:** Orlando FL. **Other U.S. locations:** Huntsville AL; Milwaukee WI. **Number of placements per year:** 200 - 499.

ALL TRADES STAFFING, INC.
1100 North Florida Avenue, Tampa FL 33602. 813/225-1200. **Fax:** 813/223-7580. **Contact:** Kristopher Michie, President. **Description:** A contract services firm for skilled construction and technical workers. **Specializes in the areas of:** Construction; Industrial; Manufacturing; Telecommunications. **Positions commonly filled include:** Automotive Mechanic; Carpenter; Computer Programmer; Construction Contractor; Cost Estimator; Electrician; Systems Analyst; Technician. **Corporate headquarters location:** This Location. **Other U.S. locations:** GA. **Average salary range of placements:** $20,000 - $29,999. **Number of placements per year:** 1000+.

ARCUS STAFFING RESOURCES, INC.
777 South Harbour Island Boulevard, Suite 780, Tampa FL 33602. 813/273-9555. **Fax:** 813/273-9661. **Contact:** Thomas G. Wolf, Vice President. **E-mail address:** wolff@packet.net. **World Wide Web address:** http://www.dpstaff.com/wolf. **Description:** A contract services firm. Company pays fee. **Specializes in the areas of:** Computer Science/Software. **Positions commonly filled include:** Computer Programmer; Internet Services Manager; MIS Specialist; Operations/ Production Manager; Software Engineer; Systems Analyst; Technical Writer/Editor; Telecommunications Manager. **Average salary range of placements:** $30,000 - $50,000. **Number of placements per year:** 100 - 199.

B²D TECHNICAL SERVICES
9455 Koger Boulevard, Suite 114, St. Petersburg FL 33702. 813/570-8008. **Fax:** 813/579-4299. **Contact:** Robert Castor, Account Executive. **Description:** A contract services firm. Founded in 1992. **Specializes in the areas of:** Administration; Computer Science/Software; Design; Engineering; Technical. **Positions commonly filled include:** Aerospace Engineer; Biochemist; Biomedical Engineer; Chemical Engineer; Civil Engineer; Computer Programmer; Cost Estimator; Design Engineer; Designer; Draftsperson; Editor; Electrical/Electronics Engineer; Industrial Engineer; Industrial Production Manager; Mechanical Engineer; Quality Control Supervisor; Software Engineer; Structural Engineer; Systems Analyst; Technical Writer/Editor. **Benefits available to temporary workers:** Paid Holidays; Paid Vacation. **Average salary range of placements:** $30,000 - $50,000. **Number of placements per year:** 50 - 99.

CDI CORPORATION
621 NW 53rd Street, Boca Raton FL 33487. 561/995-1443. **Fax:** 561/995-1442. **Contact:** Office

Manager. **World Wide Web address:** http://www.cdicorp.com. **Description:** A contract services firm. **Specializes in the areas of:** Engineering; Technical. **Corporate headquarters location:** Philadelphia PA. **Other U.S. locations:** Nationwide. **International locations:** Worldwide.

COMFORCE TELECOM, INC.
612 North Indiana Avenue, Tampa FL 34223. 941/475-6600. **Fax:** 941/475-5708. **Contact:** Manager. **Description:** A contract services and consulting firm. **Specializes in the areas of:** Telecommunications.

COMPUTER EXPRESS INTERNATIONAL
3201 West Commercial Boulevard, Suite 200, Fort Lauderdale FL 33309. 954/730-7500. **Contact:** Manager. **Description:** A contract services firm. **Specializes in the areas of:** Computer Science/Software.

CONTRACT HEALTH PROFESSIONALS
7108 Fairway Drive, Suite 290, Palm Beach Gardens FL 33418. 561/624-4334. **Contact:** Manager. **Description:** A contract services firm focusing on the placement of pharmacists and pharmaceutical technicians. **Specializes in the areas of:** Health/Medical.

KELLY ASSISTED LIVING SERVICES
300 31st Street North, Suite 330, St. Petersburg FL 33713-7625. 813/327-5961. **Contact:** Manager. **Description:** A contract services firm focusing on placement of home health aides and homemakers.

NOVACARE EMPLOYEE SERVICES
402 43rd Street West, Bradenton FL 34209. 941/746-0004. **Contact:** Manager. **Description:** A contract services firm. **Specializes in the areas of:** Payroll.

OLSTEN HEALTH SERVICES
1770 NW 64th Street, Suite 620, Fort Lauderdale FL 33309. 954/938-0140. **Contact:** Manager. **Description:** A contract services firm that provides in-home health care placements.

OLSTEN HEALTH SERVICES
4415 Metro Parkway, Suite 308, Fort Meyers FL 33916. 941/275-4443. **Contact:** Manager. **Description:** A contract services firm that provides in-home health care placements.

OLSTEN HEALTH SERVICES
1214 Airport Road, Suite 308, Pensacola FL 32504. 850/244-2403. **Contact:** Manager. **Description:** A contract services firm that provides in-home health care placements.

PROFESSIONAL STAFFING
ABLE BODY TEMPORARY SERVICES, INC.
P.O. Box 4699, Clearwater FL 34618. 813/531-4442. **Toll-free phone:** 800/554-2077. **Fax:** 813/531-5001. **Contact:** Chris Mongelluzzi, Regional Manager. **Description:** A contract services firm that also provides temporary placements. **Specializes in the areas of:** Accounting/Auditing; Administration; Architecture/Construction; Banking; Computer Science/Software; Engineering; Finance; Food Industry; General Labor; General Management; Industrial; Manufacturing; Personnel/Labor Relations; Publishing; Retail; Sales; Secretarial; Technical; Transportation. **Positions commonly filled include:** Administrative Manager; Branch Manager; Construction Contractor; Construction Manager; Credit Manager; Customer Service Representative; Electrical/Electronics Engineer; General Manager; Human Resources Specialist; Industrial Production Manager; Management Analyst/Consultant; Market Research Analyst; Operations/Production Manager; Purchasing Agent/Manager; Quality Control Supervisor; Services Sales Representative; Typist/Word Processor. **Corporate headquarters location:** This Location. **Other U.S. locations:** AL; NC; TN. **Number of placements per year:** 1000+.

STAFF LEASING GROUP
4180 Tamiami Trail, Naples FL 33940-3124. 941/261-4446. **Fax:** 941/261-8707. **Contact:** Richard Foster, Branch Manager. **Description:** An employee leasing company. Company pays fee. **Specializes in the areas of:** Accounting/Auditing; Sales. **Corporate headquarters location:** Bradenton FL. **Other U.S. locations:** AZ; MI; MN. **Average salary range of placements:** $30,000 - $50,000. **Number of placements per year:** 1 - 49.

SUN SOLUTIONS, INC.
5444 Bay Center Drive, Suite 217, Tampa FL 33609. 813/287-2686. **Fax:** 813/286-8162. **Contact:** Recruiter. **E-mail address:** sunwest@primenet.com. **Description:** A contract services firm. Company pays fee. **Specializes in the areas of:** Computer Science/Software. **Positions commonly filled include:** Applications Engineer; Computer Animator; Computer Operator; Computer Programmer; MIS Specialist; Project Manager; Software Engineer; Systems Analyst; Technical Writer/Editor; Webmaster. **Benefits available to temporary workers:** Medical Insurance. **Average salary range of placements:** $30,000 - $50,000. **Number of placements per year:** 50 - 99.

TECHSTAFF
1100 North Florida Avenue, Tampa FL 33602-3302. 813/221-1222. **Fax:** 813/221-6658. **Contact:** Barry Crislip, Recruiter. **World Wide Web address:** http://www.techstaff.com. **Description:** A contract services firm. Company pays fee. **Specializes in the areas of:** Architecture/Construction; Computer Science/Software; Engineering; Manufacturing; Technical. **Positions commonly filled include:** Buyer; Ceramics Engineer; Civil Engineer; Computer Programmer; Design Engineer; Designer; Draftsperson; Electrical/Electronics Engineer; Electrician; Environmental Engineer; Industrial Engineer; Materials Engineer; Mechanical Engineer; MIS Specialist; Software Engineer; Systems Analyst; Technical Writer/Editor; Telecommunications Manager. **Benefits available to temporary workers:** Medical Insurance; Paid Holidays; Paid Vacation. **Corporate headquarters location:** Milwaukee WI. **Other U.S. locations:** CA; IL; IA; MI. **Number of placements per year:** 200 - 499.

UNIFORCE STAFFING SERVICES
14750 NW 77th Court, Suite 305, Miami Lakes FL 33016. 305/820-0531. **Fax:** 305/364-0228. **Contact:** Reina Resnik, Staffing Manager. **E-mail address:** misha2@gate.net. **Description:** A contract services firm. **Positions commonly filled include:** Accountant/Auditor; Administrative Manager; Bank Officer/Manager; Branch Manager; Brokerage Clerk; Budget Analyst; Computer Programmer; Customer Service Representative; Draftsperson; Financial Analyst; Health Services Manager; Operations/Production Manager; Paralegal; Software Engineer; Systems Analyst; Typist/Word Processor; Underwriter/Assistant Underwriter. **Benefits available to temporary workers:** 401(k); Dental Insurance; Medical Insurance; Vision Plan. **Corporate headquarters location:** New Hyde Park NY. **Other U.S. locations:** Nationwide. **Average salary range of placements:** $20,000 - $29,999. **Number of placements per year:** 200 - 499.

CAREER/OUTPLACEMENT COUNSELING FIRMS

ADVANCED CAREER PLANNING (ACP)
P.O. Box 5117, Jacksonville FL 32247-5117. 904/396-4662. **Fax:** 904/396-6611. **Contact:** Libby Sewell, President. **Description:** Provides career counseling and specialized outplacement services to jobseekers.

ALLEN & ASSOCIATES
2601 Maitland Center Parkway, Maitland FL 32751. 407/660-8899. **Toll-free phone:** 800/661-JOBS. **Fax:** 407/661-1294. **Contact:** Office Manager. **World Wide Web address:** http://www.allenandassociates.com. **Description:** A career/outplacement counseling firm. Founded in 1960. **Corporate headquarters location:** This Location. **Other U.S. locations:** Nationwide.

ALLEN & ASSOCIATES
800 West Cypress Creek Road, Suite 280, Ft. Lauderdale FL 33309. 954/772-5600. **Toll-free phone:** 800/562-7705. **Fax:** 954/776-1101. **Contact:** Manager. **World Wide Web address:** http://www.allenandassociates.com. **Description:** A career/outplacement counseling service. **Corporate headquarters location:** Maitland FL. **Other U.S. locations:** Nationwide.

CAREERPRO RESUME & CAREER DEVELOPMENT CENTER, INC.
North Federal Highway, Suite 108, Deerfield Beach FL 33441. 954/428-4935. **Fax:** 954/428-0965. **Contact:** G. William Amme, President. **Description:** A career/outplacement counseling and resume writing service. CareerPro also offers interview skills training and job hunting workshops. **Corporate headquarters location:** This Location. **Other U.S. locations:** Nationwide.

CARRIER'S CAREER SERVICE, INC.
707 Chillingworth Drive, Suite 16, West Palm Beach FL 33409. 561/686-0911. **Fax:** 561/686-7026. **Contact:** Robert Galt, President. **E-mail address:** rbtgalt@aol.com. **Description:** Provides career consulting and resume services. Company pays fee. **Specializes in the areas of:** Accounting/Auditing; Advertising; Banking; Finance; General Management; Health/Medical; Insurance; Marketing; Personnel/Labor Relations; Retail; Sales; Secretarial. **Positions commonly filled include:** Account Representative; Accountant/Auditor; Administrative Assistant; Bank Officer/Manager; Branch Manager; Budget Analyst; Chief Financial Officer; Counselor; Customer Service Representative; Emergency Medical Technician; Licensed Practical Nurse; Registered Nurse; Respiratory Therapist; Typist/Word Processor.

CENTER FOR CAREER DECISIONS
6100 Glades Road, Suite 210, Boca Raton FL 33434. 561/470-9333. **Contact:** Linda Friedman, M.A., Director. **Description:** A career/outplacement counseling firm. **Specializes in the areas of:** Executives; Professional.

ONE STOP CAREER CENTER
900 Central Parkway, Stuart FL 34994. 561/283-8077. **Contact:** Manager. **Description:** A career/outplacement counseling firm. **Number of placements per year:** 100 - 199.

P.H.F. CAREER SERVICES INC.
9900 West Sample Road, Suite 300, Coral Springs FL 33065. 954/344-0004. **Contact:** Paul H. Friedman, Manager. **Description:** A career/outplacement counseling firm. Career Services provides complete resume composition and counseling.

PROFESSIONAL RESUME AND BUSINESS WRITING SERVICE
8306 Mills Drive, Suite 192, Miami FL 33183. 305/274-2813. **Fax:** 305/274-3307. **Contact:** Joseph P. Garbin, President. **E-mail address:** proresum@mindspring.com. **World Wide Web address:** http://www.jobexchange.com/pr. **Description:** A career/outplacement counseling firm.

GEORGIA

EXECUTIVE SEARCH FIRMS

A HIRING ALTERNATIVE
P.O. Box 445, Suwanee GA 30024. 770/513-0226. **Fax:** 770/339-0935. **Contact:** Linda Lenzi-Masters, President. **Description:** An executive search firm. Company pays fee. **Specializes in the areas of:** Accounting/Auditing; Manufacturing; Sales. **Number of placements per year:** 1 - 49.

A.D. & ASSOCIATES EXECUTIVE SEARCH INC.
5589 Woodsong Drive, Suite 104, Dunwoody GA 30338. 770/393-0021. **Fax:** 770/393-9060. **Contact:** A. Dwight Hawksworth, President. **E-mail address:** hawks@mindspring.com. **Description:** An executive search firm that operates on both retainer and contingency bases. Company pays fee. **Specializes in the areas of:** Accounting/Auditing; Administration; Engineering; Finance; General Management; Sales; Technical. **Positions commonly filled include:** Account Manager; Account Representative; Accountant; Attorney; Auditor; Chief Financial Officer; Controller; Finance Director; Financial Analyst; General Manager; Human Resources Manager; Management Analyst/Consultant; Marketing Manager; Sales Executive; Sales Manager; Sales Representative; Systems Analyst; Telecommunications Manager; Vice President. **Corporate headquarters location:** This Location. **Average salary range of placements:** More than $50,000. **Number of placements per year:** 1 - 49.

ACCOUNTANTS & BOOKKEEPERS PERSONNEL
1841 Montreal Road, Suite 212, Tucker GA 30084. 770/938-7730. **Contact:** Manager. **Description:** An executive search firm. **Specializes in the areas of:** Accounting/Auditing; Finance.

ACCOUNTANTS EXECUTIVE SEARCH/ACCOUNTANTS ON CALL
3355 Lennox Road, Suite 530, Atlanta GA 30326. 404/261-4800. **Fax:** 404/237-1853. **Contact:** Beth Herman, Area Vice President. **Description:** An executive search firm. Accountants On Call, also at this location, offers temporary placements in entry-level positions. **Specializes in the areas of:** Accounting/Auditing; Finance. **Positions commonly filled include:** Accountant/Auditor; Budget Analyst; Credit Manager; Financial Analyst. **Benefits available to temporary workers:** Medical Insurance; Paid Vacation; Referral Bonus Plan. **Corporate headquarters location:** Saddlebrook NJ. **Other U.S. locations:** Nationwide. **Average salary range of placements:** More than $50,000. **Number of placements per year:** 100 - 199.

ACCURATE MEDICAL PLACEMENT
THE ACCURATE GROUP
5046 Chestnut Forest Lane, Atlanta GA 30360. 770/452-0443. **Fax:** 770/452-0030. **Contact:** Stephen Blum, President. **Description:** An executive search firm that specializes in the placement of medical professionals. Company pays fee. **Specializes in the areas of:** General Management; Health/Medical; Personnel/Labor Relations; Sales; Secretarial. **Positions commonly filled include:** Customer Service Representative; Dental Assistant/Dental Hygienist; EKG Technician; Health Services Manager; Management Analyst/Consultant; Medical Records Technician; Occupational Therapist; Registered Nurse; Respiratory Therapist; Typist/Word Processor. **Number of placements per year:** 1 - 49.

AGRI-ASSOCIATES
895B McFarland Road, Alpharetta GA 30004. 770/475-2201. **Contact:** Manager. **Description:** An executive search firm. **Specializes in the areas of:** Agri-Business.

AGRI-PERSONNEL
5120 Old Bill Cook Road, Atlanta GA 30349. 404/768-5701. **Fax:** 404/768-5705. **Contact:** D.J. Wicker, General Manager. **Description:** An executive search firm. Company pays fee. **Specializes in the areas of:** Agri-Business. **Positions commonly filled include:** Accountant/Auditor; Agricultural Engineer; Biological Scientist; Chemist; Chief Financial Officer; Civil Engineer; Environmental Engineer; Food Scientist/Technologist; Industrial Engineer; Landscape Architect; Marketing Manager; Mechanical Engineer; Metallurgical Engineer; Quality Control Supervisor; Sales Executive; Sales Manager; Veterinarian. **Average salary range of placements:** More than $50,000.

MICHAEL ALEXANDER GROUP, INC.
333 Sandy Springs Circle, Suite 131, Atlanta GA 30328. 404/256-7848. **Fax:** 404/252-2191. **Contact:** Al Shulhan, President. **Description:** An executive search firm providing permanent placements on a contingency basis. **Specializes in the areas of:** Accounting/Auditing; Banking; Finance. **Positions commonly filled include:** Accountant; Auditor; Budget Analyst; Chief Financial Officer; Controller; Cost Estimator; Credit Manager; Economist; Finance Director; Financial Analyst; Fund Manager; General Manager; Management Analyst/Consultant; MIS Specialist; Systems Analyst.

ANDERSON INDUSTRIAL ASSOCIATES, INC.
P.O. Box 2266, Cumming GA 30128-6501. 770/844-9027. **Fax:** 770/844-9656. **Contact:** Greg Anderson, President. **E-mail address:** aia@atl.mindspring.com. **Description:** An executive search firm that specializes in the placement of technical professionals in both temporary and permanent positions. Company pays fee. **Specializes in the areas of:** Engineering; Industrial; Manufacturing; Technical. **Positions commonly filled include:** Aerospace Engineer; Biomedical Engineer; Chemical Engineer; Civil Engineer; Design Engineer; Draftsperson; Electrical/Electronics Engineer; Environmental Engineer; Industrial Engineer; Mechanical Engineer; Quality Control Supervisor; Structural Engineer. **Average salary range of placements:** More than $50,000. **Number of placements per year:** 1 - 49.

ARJAY & ASSOCIATES
2386 Clower Street, Suite A202, Snellville GA 30078. 770/979-3799. **Fax:** 770/985-7696. **Contact:** David L. Hubert, General Manager. **Description:** An executive search firm. Company pays fee. **Specializes in the areas of:** Computer Science/Software; Engineering; Industrial; Manufacturing. **Positions commonly filled include:** Computer Programmer; EKG Technician; Industrial Engineer; Mechanical Engineer; Metallurgical Engineer; Mining Engineer; Nuclear Engineer; Quality Control Supervisor; Software Engineer; Systems Analyst. **Average salary range of placements:** More than $50,000. **Number of placements per year:** 1 - 49.

ASHFORD MANAGEMENT GROUP
2295 Parklake Drive NE, Atlanta GA 30345. 770/938-6260. **Contact:** Manager. **Description:** An executive search firm. **Specializes in the areas of:** Retail.

ASHLEY-NOLAN INTERNATIONAL, INC.
171 Village Parkway NE, Marietta GA 30067. 770/956-8010. **Fax:** 770/956-1551. **Contact:** Pamela Johns, President. **E-mail address:** ashnol@atlanta.

com. **Description:** An executive search firm. Company pays fee. **Specializes in the areas of:** Accounting/Auditing; Administration; Banking; Computer Science/Software; Engineering; Finance; Manufacturing; Personnel/Labor Relations; Sales; Technical. **Positions commonly filled include:** Accountant/Auditor; Administrative Manager; Budget Analyst; Buyer; Chemical Engineer; Civil Engineer; Construction and Building Inspector; Construction Contractor; Design Engineer; Electrical/Electronics Engineer; Financial Analyst; Industrial Engineer; Mechanical Engineer; Metallurgical Engineer; MIS Specialist; Purchasing Agent/Manager; Software Engineer; Systems Analyst; Telecommunications Manager. **Average salary range of placements:** More than $50,000. **Number of placements per year:** 1 - 49.

BELL OAKS COMPANY, INC.
3390 Peachtree Road NE, Suite 1124, Atlanta GA 30326. 404/261-2170. **Contact:** Mr. Price Harding, President. **Description:** An executive search firm. **Specializes in the areas of:** Accounting/Auditing; Administration; Banking; Engineering; Finance; General Management; Insurance; Manufacturing. **Number of placements per year:** 100 - 199.

CHARLES BERNARD & ASSOCIATES
3951 Snapfinger Parkway, Suite 540, Decatur GA 30035-3203. 404/284-2666. **Toll-free phone:** 800/858-3694. **Fax:** 404/284-8318. **Contact:** Charles B. Courtois, CEO. **E-mail address:** cyberhire@mindspring.com. **World Wide Web address:** http://www.xukor.com/search.html. **Description:** An executive search firm operating on a retainer basis. **Specializes in the areas of:** Food Industry; Sales. **Positions commonly filled include:** Sales Engineer; Sales Executive; Sales Manager; Sales Representative; Vice President of Marketing; Vice President of Operations; Vice President of Sales. **Average salary range of placements:** More than $50,000. **Number of placements per year:** 1 - 49.

BOREHAM INTERNATIONAL
275 Carpenter Drive, Suite 309, Atlanta GA 30328. 404/252-2199. **Fax:** 404/851-9157. **Contact:** Mili Boreham, President. **Description:** Boreham International is an executive search firm that places office support, middle management, and senior-level executive positions. Company pays fee. **Specializes in the areas of:** Accounting/Auditing; Administration; Computer Science/Software; Food Industry; General Management; Import/Export; International Executives; Personnel/Labor Relations; Retail; Sales; Secretarial; Transportation. **Positions commonly filled include:** Accountant/Auditor; Administrative Manager; Claim Representative; Clerical Supervisor; Credit Manager; Customer Service Representative; General Manager; Human Resources Manager; Marketing Specialist; MIS Specialist; Services Sales Representative; Software Engineer; Transportation/Traffic Specialist; Typist/Word Processor. **Number of placements per year:** 1 - 49.

THE BOWERS GROUP, INC.
1850 Parkway Place, Suite 420, Marietta GA 30067-4439. 770/421-1019. **Fax:** 770/509-1095. **Contact:** Brenda Bowers, President. **Description:** An executive search firm. Company pays fee. **Specializes in the areas of:** Computer Hardware/Software. **Positions commonly filled include:** Computer Programmer; MIS Specialist; Systems Analyst. **Average salary range of placements:** More than $50,000. **Number of placements per year:** 1 - 49.

BRADSHAW & ASSOCIATES
1850 Parkway Place, Suite 420, Marietta GA 30067. 770/426-5600. **Fax:** 770/427-1727. **Contact:** Rod Bradshaw, President. **Description:** An executive search firm. Company pays fee. **Specializes in the areas of:** Accounting/Auditing; Biotechnology; Chemical; Computer Hardware/Software; Data Processing; Finance. **Positions commonly filled include:** Accountant/Auditor; Aerospace Engineer; Agricultural Engineer; Bank Officer/Manager; Biochemist; Biological Scientist; Budget Analyst; Chemical Engineer; Civil Engineer; Computer Programmer; Electrical/Electronics Engineer; Environmental Engineer; Financial Analyst; Internet Services Manager; Management Analyst/Consultant; MIS Specialist; Operations/Production Manager; Pharmacist; Physical Therapist; Physician; Registered Nurse; Software Engineer; Systems Analyst; Telecommunications Manager.

BRANNON & TULLY
3690 Holcomb Bridge Road, Norcross GA 30092. 770/447-8773. **Contact:** Manager. **Description:** An executive search firm. **Specializes in the areas of:** Information Technology.

BRIDGES & ASSOCIATES
100 River Hollow Court, Suite 510, Duluth GA 30097. 770/368-9835. **Fax:** 770/368-0822. **Contact:** President. **Description:** An executive search firm. Company pays fee. **Specializes in the areas of:** Insurance. **Number of placements per year:** 1 - 49.

BROWARD-DOBBS INC.
1532 Dunwoody Village Parkway, Suite 200, Atlanta GA 30338. 770/399-0744. **Fax:** 770/395-6881. **Contact:** Luke Greene, President. **Description:** An executive search firm. Company pays fee. **Specializes in the areas of:** Engineering. **Positions commonly filled include:** Architect; Chemical Engineer; Civil Engineer; Designer; Draftsperson; Electrical/Electronics Engineer; Industrial Engineer; Mechanical Engineer; Nuclear Engineer; Software Engineer; Stationary Engineer; Structural Engineer. **Average salary range of placements:** More than $50,000. **Number of placements per year:** 50 - 99.

CMS PERSONNEL SERVICES
205 Smith Street, Vidalia GA 30474-4226. 912/537-2825. **Fax:** 912/537-0264. **Contact:** Virginia Scott, Owner. **Description:** An executive search firm that also provides permanent and temporary placement.

CAREER PLACEMENT ASSOCIATES STAFFING
5901-B Peachtree-Dunwoody Road, Suite 330, Atlanta GA 30328. 770/350-0097. **Contact:** Recruiter. **Description:** An executive search firm. Company pays fee. **Specializes in the areas of:** Accounting/Auditing; Finance. **Positions commonly filled include:** Accountant/Auditor; Bookkeeper; Clerk; Controller; Credit Manager. **Number of placements per year:** 100 - 199.

R.A. CLARK CONSULTING
5 Concourse Parkway, Suite 3100, Atlanta GA 30028. 404/982-0495. **Toll-free phone:** 800/251-0041. **Fax:** 404/982-0499. **Contact:** Richard Clark, President. **E-mail address:** raclarkhrs@aol.com. **World Wide Web address:** http://www.raclark.com. **Description:** An executive search firm that also provides services to corporate human resources departments. Company pays fee. **Specializes in the areas of:** Human Resources; Personnel/Labor Relations. **Positions commonly filled include:** Human Resources Manager; Management Analyst/Consultant. **Average salary range of placements:** More than $50,000. **Number of placements per year:** 50 - 99.

COMMONWEALTH CONSULTANTS
5064 Roswell Road, Suite B101, Atlanta GA 30342. 404/256-0000. **Contact:** Office Manager. **Description:** An executive search firm. **Specializes in the areas of:** Computer Science/Software; Sales.

COMPREHENSIVE SEARCH GROUP
316 South Lewis Street, La Grange GA 30240-3144. 706/884-3232. **Fax:** 706/884-4106. **Contact:** Ms. Merritt Shelton, Researcher/Database Manager. **E-mail address:** compsrch@wp-lag.mindspring.com. **Description:** An executive search firm that specializes in the building products and interior furnishings industries. Company pays fee. **Specializes in the areas of:** Administration; Advertising; Architecture/Construction; Art/Design; Computer Science/Software; Industrial; Manufacturing; Retail; Sales. **Positions commonly filled include:** Administrative Manager; Architect; Computer Programmer; Construction and Building Inspector; Construction Contractor; Design Engineer; Designer; Draftsperson; Industrial Engineer; Industrial Production Manager; Internet Services Manager; Management Trainee; Manufacturer's/Wholesaler's Sales Rep.; MIS Specialist; Services Sales Representative; Software Engineer; Systems Analyst. **Corporate headquarters location:** This Location. **Other area locations:** Atlanta GA. **Other U.S. locations:** Brooklyn NY; New York NY. **Average salary range of placements:** More than $50,000. **Number of placements per year:** 50 - 99.

COMPUTER SEARCH ASSOCIATES
P.O. Box 8403, Atlanta GA 30306. 404/231-0965. **Contact:** Manager. **Description:** An executive search firm. **Specializes in the areas of:** Computer Programming; Computer Science/Software.

COMPUTER TECHNOLOGY SEARCH
3490 Piedmont Road, Suite 310, Atlanta GA 30305. 404/233-6780. **Contact:** Manager. **Description:** An executive search firm. **Specializes in the areas of:** Computer Science/Software; Information Technology. **Corporate headquarters location:** Dallas TX. **Other U.S. locations:** Los Angeles CA; Chicago IL; Kansas City KS.

CORPORATE SEARCH CONSULTANTS
47 Perimeter Center East, Suite 260, Atlanta GA 30346-2001. 770/399-6205. **Fax:** 770/399-6416. **Contact:** Harriet Rothberg, President. **World Wide Web address:** http://www.rothberg.com. **Description:** A nationwide executive search firm. Company pays fee. **Specializes in the areas of:** Accounting/Auditing; Administration; Architecture/Construction; Computer Science/Software; Engineering; Finance; General Management; Health/Medical; Industrial; Manufacturing; Personnel/Labor Relations; Sales; Secretarial; Technical. **Positions commonly filled include:** Accountant/Auditor; Administrative Manager; Architect; Branch Manager; Budget Analyst; Buyer; Civil Engineer; Clerical Supervisor; Clinical Lab Technician; Computer Programmer; Construction Contractor; Cost Estimator; Credit Manager; Customer Service Representative; Design Engineer; Draftsperson; Electrical/Electronics Engineer; Environmental Engineer; Financial Analyst; Health Services Manager; Management Analyst/Consultant; Mechanical Engineer; MIS Specialist; Operations/Production Manager; Physical Therapist; Physician; Quality Control Supervisor; Respiratory Therapist; Software Engineer; Speech-Language Pathologist; Structural Engineer; Systems Analyst; Technical Writer/Editor; Telecommunications Manager; Typist/Word Processor. **Average salary range of placements:** $30,000 - $50,000. **Number of placements per year:** 1000+.

CORPORATE SEARCH INC.
11285 Elkins Road, Suite L3, Roswell GA 30076. 770/442-1030. **Contact:** Manager. **Description:** An executive search firm operating on a retained basis. **Specializes in the areas of:** Telecommunications.

CREATIVE SEARCH
887 West Marietta Street, Suite N-109, Atlanta GA 30309. 404/892-7475. **Contact:** Office Manager. **Description:** An executive search firm. **Specializes in the areas of:** Advertising.

DSA (DIXIE SEARCH ASSOCIATES)
501 Village Trace, Building 9, Marietta GA 30067. 770/850-0250. **Fax:** 770/850-9295. **Contact:** Manager. **E-mail address:** dsa@mindspring.com. **World Wide Web address:** http://www.dsa@mindspring.com/ndsa. **Description:** An executive search firm. Company pays fee. **Specializes in the areas of:** Food Industry; Hotel/Restaurant. **Number of placements per year:** 100 - 199.

DATA MANAGEMENT & STAFF RECRUITERS
3490 Piedmont Road, Suite 310, Atlanta GA 30305. 404/233-0925. **Fax:** 404/231-9778. **Contact:** Manager. **Description:** An executive search firm. **Specializes in the areas of:** Computer Hardware/Software; Information Systems.

DATA PROCESSING SERVICES, INC.
5855 Jimmy Carter Boulevard, Suite 260, Norcross GA 30071. 770/368-1300. **Contact:** Manager. **Description:** An executive search firm. **Specializes in the areas of:** Data Processing; Technical.

DELTA RESOURCE GROUP
P.O. Box 672642, Marietta GA 30006. **Contact:** Manager. **Description:** An executive search firm. **Specializes in the areas of:** Data Communications; Information Technology; Telecommunications.

DUNHILL PROFESSIONAL SEARCH
3340 Peachtree Road NE, Suite 2570, Atlanta GA 30326. 404/261-3751. **Toll-free phone:** 800/536-3751. **Fax:** 404/237-8361. **Contact:** Recruiter. **World Wide Web address:** http://www.avana.net/~dunhill. **Description:** An executive search firm. Company operates on a contingency basis. Company pays fee. **Specializes in the areas of:** Accounting/Auditing; Computer Hardware/Software; Finance; Health/Medical; Marketing; Sales. **Positions commonly filled include:** Accountant; Auditor; Chief Financial Officer; Controller; Financial Analyst; Human Resources Manager; Sales Executive; Sales Manager; Sales Representative. **Corporate headquarters location:** Hauppauge NY. **Other U.S. locations:** Nationwide. **Average salary range of placements:** $30,000 - $50,000. **Number of placements per year:** 50 - 99.

DUNHILL PROFESSIONAL SEARCH
2110 Powers Ferry Road, Suite 110, Atlanta GA 30339-5015. 770/952-0009. **Fax:** 770/952-9422. **Contact:** Jon Harvill, CPC, President. **E-mail address:** dswatlga@mindspring.com. **World Wide Web address:** http://www.dunhillstaff.com. **Description:** An executive search firm that operates on both retainer and contingency bases. Company pays fee. **Specializes in the areas of:** Engineering; Food Industry; Manufacturing; Personnel/Labor Relations; Technical; Transportation. **Positions commonly filled include:** Biomedical Engineer; Buyer; Chemical Engineer; Design Engineer; Designer; Electrical/Electronics Engineer; Environmental Engineer; Industrial Engineer; Mechanical Engineer; Metallurgical Engineer; Operations/Production Manager; Quality Control Supervisor. **Other U.S. locations:** Nationwide. **Average salary range of placements:** More than $50,000. **Number of placements per year:** 1 - 49.

ELLIOT ASSOCIATES
131 Roswell Street, Suite B2-2, Alpharetta GA 30201-1900. 770/664-5354. **Fax:** 770/664-0233. **Contact:** Joan Ray, Senior Vice President. **E-ma**

address: jray@elliotassociates.com. **World Wide Web address:** http://www.elliotassociates.com. **Description:** An executive search firm operating on both retained and contingency bases. Company pays fee. **Specializes in the areas of:** Hotel/Restaurant. **Positions commonly filled include:** Chief Financial Officer; Controller; Market Research Analyst; Marketing Manager; Public Relations Specialist; Purchasing Agent/Manager; Restaurant/Food Service Manager. **Corporate headquarters location:** Tarrytown NY. **Other U.S. locations:** AZ; OH; PA; TX. **Average salary range of placements:** More than $50,000. **Number of placements per year:** 50 - 99.

EMERGING TECHNOLOGY SEARCH
1080 Holcomb Bridge Road, Building 100, Roswell GA 30076. 770/643-4994. **Contact:** Manager. **Description:** An executive search firm and technical recruiter. **Specializes in the areas of:** Data Processing.

EXECU SEARCH
4405 Mall Boulevard, Suite 210, Union City GA 30291. 770/969-8781. **Fax:** 770/969-1259. **Contact:** Manager. **Description:** An executive search firm.

EXECUTIVE FORCE, INC.
2271 Winding Way, Suite 210, Tucker GA 30084. 770/939-0484. **Contact:** Jim Sayers, President. **Description:** An executive search firm. Company pays fee. **Specializes in the areas of:** Banking; Computer Science/Software; Data Processing; Sales. **Positions commonly filled include:** Bank Officer/Manager; Branch Manager; General Manager. **Average salary range of placements:** More than $50,000. **Number of placements per year:** 50 - 99.

EXECUTIVE PERSONNEL SERVICES
7373 Hodgson Memorial Drive, Building 3, Savannah GA 31406. 912/354-3406. **Contact:** Manager. **Description:** An executive search firm.

EXECUTIVE RESOURCE GROUP
127 Peachtree Street, Suite 922, Atlanta GA 30303. 404/522-0888. **Fax:** 404/522-1354. **Contact:** Robert Pauley, Managing Director. **Description:** An executive search firm operating on both retained and contingency bases. Company pays fee. **Specializes in the areas of:** Finance; Health/Medical; Insurance. **Positions commonly filled include:** Chief Executive Officer; Chief Financial Officer; Financial Analyst; Health Services Manager; Management Analyst/Consultant; Sales Executive; Sales Manager; Systems Manager. **Average salary range of placements:** More than $50,000. **Number of placements per year:** 50 - 99.

EXECUTIVE RESOURCE GROUP
2470 Windy Hill Road, Suite 300, Marietta GA 30067. 770/955-1811. **Contact:** Dave Balunas, Manager. **Description:** An executive search firm.

EXECUTIVE SEARCH & PERSONNEL SERVICES, INC.
P.O. Box 3149, Dalton GA 30721. 706/272-4103. **Fax:** 706/226-7785. **Contact:** Nancy Hampton, President. **Description:** An executive search firm operating on both retained and contingency bases. Company pays fee. **Specializes in the areas of:** Textiles. **Positions commonly filled include:** Computer Operator; Electrical/Electronics Engineer; Finance Director; Graphic Artist; Industrial Engineer; Manufacturing Engineer; Production Manager; Quality Control Supervisor; Typist/Word Processor. **Number of placements per year:** 200 - 499.

EXECUTIVE SOURCE INTERNATIONAL
550 Pharr Road, Suite 840, Atlanta GA 30305. 404/231-3783. **Contact:** Manager. **Description:** An executive search firm.

EXPRESS PERSONNEL SERVICE[illegible]
1919 Glynn Avenue, Suite 33, Bru[illegible] 912/265-3777. **Fax:** 912/265-3099. [illegible] Worthington, Owner. **Description:** A[illegible] executive search firm. **Specializes in the** [illegible] Accounting/Auditing; Administration; [illegible] Computer Science/Software; Economics; Engine[illegible] Food Industry; General Management; Health/Medi[illegible] Industrial; Insurance; Legal; Manufacturing; Nonprofit; Personnel/Labor Relations; Retail; Sales; Secretarial; Technical. **Positions commonly filled include:** Accountant/Auditor; Administrative Manager; Bank Officer/Manager; Computer Programmer; Construction Contractor; Credit Manager; Customer Service Representative; Electrical/Electronics Engineer; Electrician; Industrial Engineer; Industrial Production Manager; Landscape Architect; Management Trainee; Manufacturer's/Wholesaler's Sales Rep.; Market Research Analyst; Operations/Production Manager; Paralegal; Purchasing Agent/Manager; Quality Control Supervisor; Radio/TV Announcer/Broadcaster; Registered Nurse; Restaurant/Food Service Manager; Software Engineer; Systems Analyst; Typist/Word Processor. **Benefits available to temporary workers:** 401(k); Medical Insurance. **Corporate headquarters location:** Oklahoma City OK. **Average salary range of placements:** $20,000 - $29,999. **Number of placements per year:** 50 - 99.

F-O-R-T-U-N-E PERSONNEL CONSULTANTS OF ATLANTA
6825 Jimmy Carter Boulevard, Suite 1301, Norcross GA 30071. 770/246-9757. **Fax:** 770/246-0526. **Contact:** James M. Deavours, President. **E-mail address:** search@fpcareers.com. **World Wide Web address:** http://www.fpccareers.com. **Description:** An executive search firm operating on both retainer and contingency bases. Company pays fee. **Specializes in the areas of:** Chemical; Engineering; Food Industry; Manufacturing; Pharmaceutical; Plastics; Quality Assurance; Regulatory Affairs; Research and Development; Technical. **Positions commonly filled include:** Biochemist; Biological Scientist; Biomedical Engineer; Chemical Engineer; Design Engineer; Electrical/Electronics Engineer; Food Scientist/Technologist; Industrial Engineer; Industrial Production Manager; Mechanical Engineer; Operations Manager; Production Manager; Project Manager; Quality Control Supervisor. **Corporate headquarters location:** New York NY. **Other U.S. locations:** Nationwide. **Average salary range of placements:** More than $50,000. **Number of placements per year:** 50 - 99.

FOX-MORRIS ASSOCIATES
9000 Central Park West, Suite 150, Atlanta GA 30328. 770/399-4497. **Fax:** 770/399-4499. **Contact:** Robert Smith, Branch Manager. **Description:** An executive search firm. **Specializes in the areas of:** Accounting/Auditing; Computer Hardware/Software; Engineering; Finance; Manufacturing; MIS/EDP; Personnel/Labor Relations; Sales. **Number of placements per year:** 1000+.

GEORGETOWN DISCOVERIES
P.O. Box 46718, Atlanta GA 31146. 404/256-5583. **Contact:** Lori Quinn, Director. **E-mail address:** 2069378@mcimail.com. **Description:** An executive search firm that provides business management consulting services and outsourcing to companies, associations, and nonprofit organizations. Company pays fee. **Specializes in the areas of:** Telecommunications. **Positions commonly filled include:** Computer Programmer; Design Engineer; Economist; Electrical/Electronics Engineer; Financial Analyst; Management Analyst/Consultant; Operations/Production Manager; Software Engineer; Systems Analyst; Telecommunications Manager. **Corporate headquarters location:** McLean VA. **Average salary**

ge of placements: More than $50,000. Number of placements per year: 50 - 99.

HE HR GROUP, INC.
1000 Circle 75 Parkway, Suite 710, Atlanta GA 30339. 770/984-6711. **Fax:** 770/984-6714. **Contact:** Manager. **Description:** An executive search firm that also provides temporary office support. Company pays fee. **Specializes in the areas of:** Engineering; Personnel/Labor Relations. **Positions commonly filled include:** Electrical/Electronics Engineer; Human Resources Manager; Telecommunications Manager. **Number of placements per year:** 1 - 49.

WILLIAM HALDERSON ASSOCIATES
P.O. Box 566, Dahlonega GA 30533. 706/864-5800. **Contact:** Bill Halderson, President. **Description:** An executive search firm. Company pays fee. **Specializes in the areas of:** Health/Medical. **Positions commonly filled include:** Marketing Specialist; Research Scientist; Sales and Marketing Manager; Sales Representative. **Number of placements per year:** 50 - 99.

ROBERT HALF INTERNATIONAL
ACCOUNTEMPS
3424 Peachtree Road, Suite 2000, Atlanta GA 30326. 770/392-0540. **Contact:** Office Manager. **Description:** An executive search firm. Accountemps (also at this location) provides temporary placements. **Corporate headquarters location:** Menlo Park CA. **Other U.S. locations:** Nationwide.

HALL MANAGEMENT GROUP
736 Green Street, Gainesville GA 30501. 770/534-5568. **Fax:** 770/534-5572. **Contact:** Bill Lennon, President. **World Wide Web address:** http://www.jobconnection.com. **Description:** An executive search firm that places engineers primarily within the automotive, medical device manufacturing, and plastics industries. Company pays fee. **Specializes in the areas of:** Accounting/Auditing; Computer Science/Software; Engineering; Manufacturing; Personnel/Labor Relations; Technical. **Positions commonly filled include:** Accountant/Auditor; Biomedical Engineer; Chemical Engineer; Electrical/Electronics Engineer; Financial Analyst; Human Resources Manager; Mechanical Engineer; Operations/Production Manager; Purchasing Agent/Manager; Systems Analyst. **Benefits available to temporary workers:** Life Insurance; Medical Insurance; Paid Vacation. **Average salary range of placements:** More than $50,000. **Number of placements per year:** 1 - 49.

HARRIS KOVACS ALDERMAN
4170 Ashford Dunwoody Road, Suite 500, Atlanta GA 30319. 404/847-0492. **Toll-free phone:** 800/347-7987. **Contact:** Manager. **Description:** An executive search firm. **Specializes in the areas of:** Health/Medical. **Positions commonly filled include:** Physician.

HEALTHCARE RECRUITERS INTERNATIONAL
2470 Windy Hill Road, Suite 300, Marietta GA 30067. 770/984-0094. **Contact:** Office Manager. **Description:** An executive search firm. **Specializes in the areas of:** Health/Medical.

HINES RECRUITING ASSOCIATION
3580 Habersham Road NW, Atlanta GA 30305. 404/262-7131. **Fax:** 404/842-1815. **Contact:** Bill Harris, Recruiting. **E-mail address:** jobguru@aol.com. **Description:** An executive search firm. **Specializes in the areas of:** Engineering; Manufacturing. **Positions commonly filled include:** Chemical Engineer; Electrical/Electronics Engineer; Human Resources Manager; Industrial Engineer; Mechanical Engineer. **Number of placements per year:** 1 - 49.

HOWIE AND ASSOCIATES, INC.
875 Old Roswell Road, Suite F100, Roswell GA 30076. 770/998-0099. **Fax:** 770/993-7406. **Contact:** Ellen Howie-Brown, President. **E-mail address:** howieinc@ik.netcom.com. **Description:** An executive search firm operating on a contingency basis. Company pays fee. **Specializes in the areas of:** Computer Science/Software; Data Processing. **Positions commonly filled include:** Computer Programmer; Internet Services Manager; Software Engineer; Systems Analyst; Technical Writer/Editor; Telecommunications Manager. **Average salary range of placements:** More than $50,000. **Number of placements per year:** 100 - 199.

ISC OF ATLANTA
INTERNATIONAL CAREER CONTINUATION
4350 Georgetown Square, Suite 707, Atlanta GA 30338. 770/458-4180. **Fax:** 770/458-4131. **Contact:** A. Arthur Kwapisz, President. **Description:** An executive search firm whose clients include *Fortune* 1000 companies as well as privately held national and international, small and mid-sized companies. The firm places professionals in executive and management positions, as well as entry-level positions in a variety of industries. Career transition services are available, along with corporate and individual outplacement and spousal assistance programs. Company pays fee. **Specializes in the areas of:** Accounting/Auditing; Architecture/Construction; Banking; Biology; Engineering; Finance; General Management; Health/Medical; Industrial; Manufacturing; Personnel/Labor Relations; Publishing; Sales. **Positions commonly filled include:** Accountant/Auditor; Administrative Manager; Bank Officer/Manager; Biochemist; Biological Scientist; Biomedical Engineer; Buyer; Chemical Engineer; Civil Engineer; Construction and Building Inspector; Construction Contractor; Designer; Electrical/Electronics Engineer; Environmental Engineer; Human Resources Manager; Industrial Engineer; Industrial Production Manager; Mechanical Engineer; Operations/Production Manager; Pharmacist; Quality Control Supervisor; Restaurant/Food Service Manager; Telecommunications Manager. **Average salary range of placements:** More than $50,000. **Number of placements per year:** 50 - 99.

JES SEARCH FIRM, INC.
3475 Lenox Road, Suite 970, Atlanta GA 30326. 404/262-7222. **Fax:** 404/266-3533. **Contact:** Brenda Evers, President. **Description:** An employment agency engaged in permanent and contract placement. Company pays fee. **Specializes in the areas of:** Computer Science/Software. **Positions commonly filled include:** Software Developer. **Number of placements per year:** 200 - 499.

JJ&H LTD.
JACOBSON ASSOCIATES
1775 The Exchange, Suite 240, Atlanta GA 30339. 770/952-3877. **Fax:** 770/952-0061. **Contact:** Greg Jacobson, Senior Vice President. **E-mail address:** atlanta@jacobson-associates.com. **World Wide Web address:** http://www.jacobson-associates.com. **Description:** An executive search firm operating on both retained and contingency bases. Founded in 1971. Company pays fee. **Specializes in the areas of:** Health/Medical; Insurance. **Positions commonly filled include:** Account Manager; Account Representative; Accountant; Adjuster; Attorney; Chief Financial Officer; Claim Representative; Controller; Insurance Agent/Broker; Marketing Specialist; Occupational Therapist; Pharmacist; Physical Therapist; Physician; Sales Executive; Sales Manager; Systems Manager; Underwriter/Assistant Underwriter. **Corporate headquarters location:** Chicago IL. **Other U.S. locations:** Philadelphia PA. **Average salary range of

placements: More than $50,000. **Number of placements per year:** 100 - 199.

JOB SHOP INC.
218 Oak Street, Suite E, Martinez GA 30907. 706/860-4820. **Fax:** 706/860-4871. **Contact:** President. **Description:** An executive search firm. Founded in 1979. **Specializes in the areas of:** Engineering; Industrial; Manufacturing; Personnel/Labor Relations; Technical. **Positions commonly filled include:** Accountant/Auditor; Blue-Collar Worker Supervisor; Chemical Engineer; Clerical Supervisor; Computer Programmer; Draftsperson; Electrical/Electronics Engineer; Environmental Engineer; Human Resources Specialist; Industrial Engineer; Industrial Production Manager; Mechanical Engineer; Typist/Word Processor. **Average salary range of placements:** $30,000 - $50,000. **Number of placements per year:** 1000+.

A.T. KEARNEY EXECUTIVE SEARCH
1100 Abernathy Road, Suite 900, Atlanta GA 30328. 770/393-9900. **Contact:** Manager. **Description:** A generalist executive search firm.

KENZER CORPORATION OF GEORGIA
1600 Parkwood Circle NW, Suite 310, Atlanta GA 30339-2119. 770/955-7210. **Fax:** 770/955-6504. **Contact:** Marie Powell, Vice President. **Description:** An executive search firm. Company pays fee. **Specializes in the areas of:** Accounting/Auditing; Advertising; Banking; Fashion; Food Industry; General Management; Manufacturing; Personnel/Labor Relations; Retail; Sales. **Positions commonly filled include:** Buyer; General Manager; Human Resources Manager; MIS Specialist; Restaurant/Food Service Manager. **Corporate headquarters location:** New York NY. **Other U.S. locations:** Los Angeles CA; Chicago IL; Minneapolis MN; Dallas TX. **Average salary range of placements:** More than $50,000.

KORN/FERRY INTERNATIONAL
303 Peachtree Street NE, Suite 1600, Atlanta GA 30308. 404/577-7542. **Contact:** Manager. **Description:** An executive search firm that places upper-level managers in a variety of industries. **Corporate headquarters location:** Los Angeles CA. **International locations:** Worldwide. **Average salary range of placements:** More than $50,000.

EVIE KREISLER & ASSOCIATES
2575 Peachtree Road, Suite 300, Atlanta GA 30305. 404/262-0599. **Fax:** 404/262-0699. **Contact:** Debbi Kreisler, President. **Description:** An executive search firm providing middle- and upper-management placement. Company pays fee. **Specializes in the areas of:** Art/Design; Engineering; Fashion; Manufacturing; Retail; Sales. **Positions commonly filled include:** Buyer; Designer; Industrial Engineer; Manufacturer's/Wholesaler's Sales Rep.; Operations/Production Manager; Quality Control Supervisor. **Average salary range of placements:** More than $50,000. **Number of placements per year:** 200 - 499.

LEADER INSTITUTE, INC.
2136 Fox Hound Chase, Suite 250, Atlanta GA 30339. 770/984-2700x100. **Fax:** 770/984-2990. **Contact:** Rick Zabor, President. **E-mail address:** rick@peoplestaff.com. **World Wide Web address:** http://www.peoplestaff.com. **Description:** An executive search firm that provides personnel for permanent and contract needs in information technology markets. Company pays fee. **Specializes in the areas of:** Computer Science/Software; Information Technology. **Positions commonly filled include:** Account Representative; Computer Programmer; Human Resources Manager; Information Systems Consultant; Internet Services Manager; Systems Analyst; Systems Manager. **Average salary range of placements:** More than $50,000. **Number of placements per year:** 50 - 99.

LEGAL PROFESSIONAL STAFFING
2 Ravinia Drive, Suite 380, Atlanta GA 30346. 770/392-7181. **Fax:** 770/392-7175. **Contact:** Manager. **Description:** An executive search firm. **Specializes in the areas of:** Legal.

DOROTHY LONG SEARCH
6065 Roswell Road NE, Sandy Springs GA 30328. 404/252-3787. **Contact:** Manager. **Description:** An executive search firm. **Specializes in the areas of:** Property Management.

LOWDERMAN & HANEY, INC.
3939 Roswell Road NE, Suite 100, Marietta GA 30062. 770/977-3020. **Contact:** Manager. **Description:** An executive search firm for upper-level positions. **Specializes in the areas of:** Health/Medical.

LUCAS FINANCIAL SEARCH
3384 Peachtree Road NE, Suite 710, Atlanta GA 30326. 404/239-5635. **Fax:** 404/239-5692. **Contact:** Jennifer Toole, Administrative Assistant. **E-mail address:** lfsa30326@aol.com. **Description:** An executive search firm. The firm also provides temporary and contract placements. Company pays fee. **Specializes in the areas of:** Accounting/Auditing; Finance; Tax. **Positions commonly filled include:** Accountant/Auditor; Auditor; Bookkeeper; Budget Analyst; Chief Financial Officer; Controller; Financial Analyst; Purchasing Agent/Manager; Systems Analyst. **Benefits available to temporary workers:** Medical Insurance. **Other U.S. locations:** Irvine CA; Chicago IL; Dallas TX; Houston TX. **Average salary range of placements:** $30,000 - $50,000. **Number of placements per year:** 1 - 49.

MIS SEARCH
12 Executive Park Drive, Atlanta GA 30329. 404/325-1132. **Contact:** Manager. **Description:** An executive search firm. **Specializes in the areas of:** Computer Science/Software; MIS/EDP.

MSI INTERNATIONAL
245 Peachtree Center Avenue, Suite 2500, Atlanta GA 30303. 404/659-5050. **Toll-free phone:** 800/511-0383. **Fax:** 404/659-7139. **Contact:** Mike Giuseffi, Vice President. **Description:** An executive search firm. Company pays fee. **Specializes in the areas of:** Banking; Engineering; General Management; Health/Medical.

MSI INTERNATIONAL
1050 Crown Pointe Parkway, Suite 100, Atlanta GA 30338. 770/394-2494. **Toll-free phone:** 800/659-2762. **Fax:** 770/394-2251. **Contact:** James T. Watson, Vice President. **E-mail address:** msimsp@mindspring.com. **World Wide Web address:** http://www.ipa.com/msi. **Description:** An executive search firm operating on both retained and contingency bases. Company pays fee. **Specializes in the areas of:** Architecture/Construction; Banking; Engineering; General Management; Health/Medical; Industrial; Insurance; Sales; Technical. **Positions commonly filled include:** Account Manager; Accountant/Auditor; Administrative Assistant; Applications Engineer; Bank Officer/Manager; Branch Manager; Chief Financial Officer; Civil Engineer; Cost Estimator; Design Engineer; Environmental Engineer; Financial Analyst; Fund Manager; Industrial Engineer; Mechanical Engineer; Operations Manager; Software Engineer; Structural Engineer; Underwriter/Assistant Underwriter. **Other U.S. locations:** CA; LA; TX; VA. **Average salary range of placements:** More than $50,000. **Number of placements per year:** 100 - 199.

BOB MADDOX ASSOCIATES
3134 West Roxboro Road NE, Suite 300, Atlanta GA 30324-2542. 404/231-0558. **Fax:** 404/231-1074. **Contact:** Robert E. Maddox, President. **Description:** A retained executive search firm. Company pays fee. **Specializes in the areas of:** General Management; Nonprofit. **Positions commonly filled include:** Branch Manager; Chief Financial Officer; Development Officer; Executive Director; General Manager. **Other U.S. locations:** Charlotte NC. **Average salary range of placements:** More than $50,000. **Number of placements per year:** 1 - 49.

MAHONEY & BREWER ASSOCIATES
1901 Powers Ferry Road, Suite 280, Atlanta GA 30339. 770/916-0447. **Contact:** Manager. **Description:** An executive search firm. **Specializes in the areas of:** Finance; Government; Health/Medical; High-Tech. **Other U.S. locations:** San Francisco CA. **International locations:** Belgium.

MANAGEMENT RECRUITERS INTERNATIONAL
3700 Crestwood Parkway NW, Suite 320, Duluth GA 30096. 770/925-2266. **Fax:** 770/325-1090. **Contact:** David Riggs, Manager. **E-mail address:** mri.atlanta@internetmci.com. **Description:** An executive search firm. Company pays fee. **Specializes in the areas of:** Biology; Computer Science/Software; Finance; Sales; Technical. **Positions commonly filled include:** Biochemist; Biological Scientist; Biomedical Engineer; Chemical Engineer; Credit Manager; Environmental Engineer; Financial Analyst; Market Research Analyst; Multimedia Designer; Operations/Production Manager; Science Technologist; Securities Sales Representative; Software Engineer. **Corporate headquarters location:** Cleveland OH. **Other U.S. locations:** Nationwide. **Average salary range of placements:** More than $50,000. **Number of placements per year:** 200 - 499.

MANAGEMENT RECRUITERS INTERNATIONAL
21 North Main Street, Alpharetta GA 30201. 770/664-5512. **Fax:** 770/664-5046. **Contact:** John Harvey, President. **Description:** An executive search firm. Company pays fee. **Specializes in the areas of:** Engineering; Food Industry; General Management; Manufacturing; Sales; Technical. **Positions commonly filled include:** Design Engineer; Electrical/Electronics Engineer; Food Scientist/Technologist; Forester/Conservation Scientist; Human Resources Manager; Industrial Engineer; Industrial Production Manager; Management Analyst/Consultant; Mechanical Engineer; Operations/Production Manager; Structural Engineer; Telecommunications Manager. **Corporate headquarters location:** Cleveland OH. **Other U.S. locations:** Nationwide. **Average salary range of placements:** More than $50,000. **Number of placements per year:** 1 - 49.

MANAGEMENT RECRUITERS INTERNATIONAL
600 Peachtree Parkway, Suite 108, Cumming GA 30041. 770/889-5250. **Fax:** 770/889-5257. **Contact:** Manager. **Description:** An executive search firm. **Specializes in the areas of:** Engineering; Logistics. **Corporate headquarters location:** Cleveland OH. **Other U.S. locations:** Nationwide.

MANAGEMENT RECRUITERS INTERNATIONAL
P.O. Box 1455, Perry GA 31069. 912/988-4444. **Contact:** Manager. **Description:** An executive search firm. **Specializes in the areas of:** Apparel; Home Furnishings. **Corporate headquarters location:** Cleveland OH. **Other U.S. locations:** Nationwide.

MANAGEMENT RECRUITERS INTERNATIONAL SALES CONSULTANTS OF COBB COUNTY
P.O. Box 72527, Marietta GA 30007-2527. 770/643-9990. **Contact:** Larry Dougherty, Office Manager. **E-mail address:** mri-cobb@atl.mindspring.com. **Description:** An executive search firm that provides video conferencing, interexecutive placement, and outplacement services. Company pays fee. **Specializes in the areas of:** Computer Science/Software; Engineering; General Management; Logistics; Manufacturing; Technical; Transportation. **Positions commonly filled include:** Branch Manager; Budget Analyst; Computer Programmer; General Manager; Industrial Engineer; Management Analyst/Consultant; Manufacturer's/Wholesaler's Sales Rep.; Marketing/Public Relations Manager; MIS Specialist; Operations/Production Manager; Software Engineer; Systems Analyst; Transportation/Traffic Specialist. **Corporate headquarters location:** Cleveland OH. **Other U.S. locations:** Nationwide. **Average salary range of placements:** More than $50,000. **Number of placements per year:** 100 - 199.

MANAGEMENT RECRUITERS OF ATLANTA
5901 Peachtree-Dunwoody Road NE, Suite 370C, Atlanta GA 30328. **Fax:** 770/698-9384. **Contact:** General Manager. **Description:** An executive search firm. Company pays fee. **Specializes in the areas of:** Accounting/Auditing; Advertising; Banking; Health/Medical; Industrial; Insurance; Pharmaceutical; Transportation. **Positions commonly filled include:** Industrial Engineer; Industrial Production Manager; Sales Representative; Software Engineer; Transportation/Traffic Specialist; Underwriter/Assistant Underwriter. **Corporate headquarters location:** Cleveland OH. **Other U.S. locations:** Nationwide.

MANAGEMENT RECRUITERS OF ATLANTA (NORTH)
30 Woodstock Street, Roswell GA 30075. 770/998-1555. **Contact:** Art Katz, Manager. **Description:** An executive search firm. **Specializes in the areas of:** Accounting/Auditing; Administration; Advertising; Architecture/Construction; Banking; Chemical; Communications; Computer Hardware/Software; Construction; Electrical; Engineering; Finance; Food Industry; General Management; Health/Medical; Insurance; Legal; Manufacturing; Operations Management; Personnel/Labor Relations; Pharmaceutical; Procurement; Publishing; Real Estate; Retail; Sales; Technical; Textiles; Transportation. **Corporate headquarters location:** Cleveland OH. **Other U.S. locations:** Nationwide.

MANAGEMENT RECRUITERS OF ATLANTA (SOUTH)
406 Lime Creek Drive, Suite B, Peachtree City GA 30269. 770/486-0603. **Fax:** 770/631-7684. **Contact:** Ron Wise, Owner. **Description:** An executive search firm. **Specializes in the areas of:** Chemical; Electrical; Engineering; Food Industry; General Management; Manufacturing; Operations Management; Personnel/Labor Relations; Procurement; Sales; Technical; Textiles; Transportation. **Positions commonly filled include:** Branch Manager; Chemical Engineer; Engineer; Mathematician. **Average salary range of placements:** More than $50,000. **Number of placements per year:** 50 - 99. **Corporate headquarters location:** Cleveland OH. **Other U.S. locations:** Nationwide.

MANAGEMENT RECRUITERS OF ATLANTA (WEST)
685 Thornton Way, Suite C, Lithia Springs GA 30021. 770/948-5560. **Fax:** 770/948-5762. **Contact:** Steven Kendall, Owner. **Description:** An executive search firm that specializes in placements for the consumer products and plastic packaging materials industries in the United States and internationally. Company pays fee. **Specializes in the areas of:** Sales. **Positions commonly filled include:** General Manager; Manufacturer's/Wholesaler's Sales Rep.; Sales and Marketing Manager. **Corporate headquarters location:** Cleveland OH. **Other U.S. locations:** Nationwide.

Average salary range of placements: More than $50,000. **Number of placements per year:** 50 - 99.

MANAGEMENT RECRUITERS OF COLUMBUS, INC.
233 12th Street, Suite 818A, Columbus GA 31901-2449. 706/571-9611. **Fax:** 706/571-3288. **Contact:** Michael Silverstein, President. **E-mail address:** michael@mricolumbusga.com. **World Wide Web address:** http://www.mricolumbusga.com. **Description:** An executive search firm operating on both retainer and contingency bases. Company pays fee. **Specializes in the areas of:** Computer Science/Software; Engineering; Information Systems. **Positions commonly filled include:** Applications Engineer; Computer Programmer; Database Manager; Electrical/Electronics Engineer; Industrial Engineer; Manufacturing Engineer; Mechanical Engineer; MIS Specialist; Systems Analyst. **Corporate headquarters location:** Cleveland OH. **Other U.S. locations:** Nationwide. **Average salary range of placements:** More than $50,000.

MANAGEMENT RECRUITERS OF MARIETTA
274 North Marietta Parkway, Suite C, Marietta GA 30060. 770/423-1443. **Fax:** 770/423-1303. **Contact:** James E. Kirby, Managing Principal. **E-mail address:** jkirby@mindspring.com. **Description:** An executive search firm. Company pays fee. **Specializes in the areas of:** Computer Science/Software; Engineering; Fashion; General Management; Industrial; Information Systems; Logistics; Manufacturing; Personnel/Labor Relations; Sales; Transportation. **Positions commonly filled include:** Accountant/Auditor; Aerospace Engineer; Biomedical Engineer; Chemical Engineer; Computer Programmer; Design Engineer; Electrical/Electronics Engineer; General Manager; Human Resources Manager; Industrial Engineer; Management Analyst/Consultant; Mechanical Engineer; MIS Specialist; Quality Control Supervisor; Software Engineer; Systems Analyst; Transportation/Traffic Specialist. **Corporate headquarters location:** Cleveland OH. **Other U.S. locations:** Nationwide. **Average salary range of placements:** More than $50,000. **Number of placements per year:** 50 - 99.

MANAGEMENT RECRUITERS OF SAVANNAH
P.O. Box 22548, Savannah GA 31403. 912/232-0132. **Toll-free phone:** 800/886-0135. **Fax:** 912/232-0136. **Contact:** Ronald W. McElhaney, Managing Partner. **Description:** A contingency and retainer search firm. Company pays fee. **Specializes in the areas of:** Chemical; Engineering; Environmental; Industrial; Plastics; Safety. **Positions commonly filled include:** Chemical Engineer; Chemist; Electrical/Electronics Engineer; Human Resources Manager; Industrial Engineer; Mechanical Engineer; Quality Control Supervisor; Software Engineer. **Corporate headquarters location:** Cleveland OH. **Other U.S. locations:** Nationwide. **Average salary range of placements:** More than $50,000. **Number of placements per year:** 1 - 49.

MED PRO PERSONNEL
1955 Cliff Valley Way, Suite 116, Atlanta GA 30329. 404/633-8280. **Fax:** 404/633-9856. **Contact:** Manager. **Description:** An executive search firm. **Specializes in the areas of:** Health/Medical.

MEDICAL RECRUITMENT SPECIALISTS
449 Pleasant Hill Road, Suite 211, Lilburn GA 30047. 770/495-0575. **Contact:** Carol J. Florey, Owner. **Description:** An executive search firm. **Specializes in the areas of:** Health/Medical. **Positions commonly filled include:** Product Manager; Sales Manager.

MEDICAL SEARCH OF AMERICA, INC.
P.O. Box 1716, Duluth GA 30096. 770/232-0530. **Toll-free phone:** 800/523-1351. **Fax:** 770/232-0610. **Contact:** Charles Sikes, President. **Description:** A multinational health care search firm. **Specializes in the areas of:** Health/Medical. **Positions commonly filled include:** Administrative Manager; Computer Programmer; Counselor; Credit Manager; Dietician/Nutritionist; Education Administrator; Health Services Manager; MIS Specialist; Occupational Therapist; Pharmacist; Physical Therapist; Physician; Psychologist; Radiological Technologist; Registered Nurse; Respiratory Therapist; Social Worker; Speech-Language Pathologist. **Number of placements per year:** 1 - 49.

MEDICAL SEARCH, INC.
100 Crescent Center Parkway, Suite 360, Tucker GA 30084-7039. **Toll-free phone:** 800/849-5502. **Fax:** 770/908-2203. **Contact:** David Alexander, President. **E-mail address:** mednet@mindspring.com. **Description:** An executive search firm that specializes in employer paid mid- to upper-level hospital and biomedical searches. Company pays fee. **Specializes in the areas of:** Engineering; Health/Medical. **Positions commonly filled include:** Biological Scientist; Biomedical Engineer; Chemical Engineer; Chemist; Clinical Lab Technician; Dietician/Nutritionist; Mechanical Engineer; Medical Records Technician; Nuclear Medicine Technologist; Occupational Therapist; Pharmacist; Physical Therapist; Physician; Physician Assistant; Physicist; Psychologist; Quality Control Supervisor; Radiological Technologist; Recreational Therapist; Registered Nurse; Respiratory Therapist; Surgical Technician. **Corporate headquarters location:** This Location. **Other U.S. locations:** Tallahassee FL. **Average salary range of placements:** More than $50,000. **Number of placements per year:** 200 - 499.

MILLARD & ASSOCIATES INC.
2141 Kingston Court, Suite 103, Marietta GA 30067. 770/984-8771. **Fax:** 770/984-8860. **Contact:** Bonnie Millard, President. **Description:** An executive search firm operating on a contingency basis. Company pays fee. **Specializes in the areas of:** Engineering; Manufacturing; Research and Development; Technical; Transportation. **Positions commonly filled include:** Accountant/Auditor; Applications Engineer; Architect; Buyer; Chemical Engineer; Chemist; Civil Engineer; Clinical Lab Technician; Design Engineer; Electrical/Electronics Engineer; Environmental Engineer; Food Scientist/Technologist; Industrial Engineer; Industrial Production Manager; Librarian; Production Manager; Project Manager; Quality Control Supervisor; Sales Engineer; Sales Representative; Software Engineer; Systems Analyst; Transportation/ Traffic Specialist.

NEIS
141 Village Parkway, Building 5, Marietta GA 30067. 770/952-0081. **Fax:** 770/952-0218. **Contact:** Mike Mauldin, President. **Description:** An executive search firm. Company pays fee. **Specializes in the areas of:** Administration; Computer Science/Software; Engineering; Finance; General Management; Health/Medical; Personnel/Labor Relations; Publishing; Retail; Sales; Transportation. **Positions commonly filled include:** Accountant/Auditor; Administrative Manager; Aerospace Engineer; Agricultural Engineer; Branch Manager; Chemical Engineer; Civil Engineer; Clinical Lab Technician; Computer Programmer; Construction Contractor; Credit Manager; Customer Service Representative; Design Engineer; Designer; EKG Technician; Electrical/Electronics Engineer; Emergency Medical Technician; Environmental Engineer; Financial Analyst; Health Services Manager; Industrial Engineer; Internet Services Manager; Licensed Practical Nurse; Management Analyst/Consultant; Manufacturer's/Wholesaler's Sales Rep.; Market Research Analyst; Mechanical Engineer; Medical Records Technician; MIS Specialist; Multimedia Designer; Nuclear Medicine Technologist; Occupational Therapist; Operations/

Production Manager; Paralegal; Petroleum Engineer; Pharmacist; Physical Therapist; Physician; Property and Real Estate Manager; Psychologist; Purchasing Agent/Manager; Radiological Technologist; Registered Nurse; Respiratory Therapist; Restaurant/Food Service Manager; Software Engineer; Structural Engineer; Surgical Technician; Systems Analyst; Technical Writer/Editor; Typist/Word Processor.

NATIONAL PERSONNEL RECRUITERS
6151 Powers Ferry Road, Suite 605, Atlanta GA 30339. 770/955-4221. **Fax:** 770/859-0856. **Contact:** Manager. **Description:** National Personnel Recruiters is an executive search firm for sales professionals. **Specializes in the areas of:** Sales.

NATIONAL RESTAURANT SEARCH INC.
135 Beech Tree Lane, Suite 100, Roswell GA 30075. 770/650-1800. **Contact:** John Chitvanni, President. **Description:** An executive search firm operating on a retainer basis. **Corporate headquarters:** This Location. Company pays fee. **Specializes in the areas of:** Executives; Food Industry; Restaurant. **Positions commonly filled include:** Hotel Manager; Restaurant/Food Service Manager. **Other U.S. locations:** Nationwide. **International locations:** Worldwide. **Average salary range of placements:** More than $50,000. **Number of placements per year:** 100 - 199.

JIM NIXON & ASSOCIATES
P.O. Box 941833, Atlanta GA 31141. 770/458-9963. **Fax:** 770/458-9870. **Contact:** Jim Nixon, Owner. **Description:** An executive search firm. Company pays fee. **Specializes in the areas of:** Banking; Finance; Food Industry; Insurance; Retail; Secretarial. **Positions commonly filled include:** Adjuster; Bank Officer/Manager; Branch Manager; Claim Representative; Credit Manager; Customer Service Representative; Financial Analyst; General Manager; Restaurant/Food Service Manager; Underwriter/Assistant Underwriter. **Number of placements per year:** 1 - 49.

OLIVER SEARCH
P.O. Box 81092, Conyers GA 30208. 770/760-7661. **Contact:** Manager. **Description:** An executive search firm. **Specializes in the areas of:** Food Industry.

OMEGA EXECUTIVE SEARCH
2033 Monroe Drive, Atlanta GA 30324. 404/873-2000. **Contact:** Manager. **Description:** An executive search firm. **Specializes in the areas of:** Hotel/Restaurant.

OMNI RECRUITING
1950 Spectrum Circle, Suite 400, Marietta GA 30067. 770/988-2788. **Fax:** 770/988-2789. **Contact:** Manager. **Description:** An executive search firm. **Specializes in the areas of:** Sales.

PERIMETER PLACEMENT
24 Perimeter Center East, Suite 2417, Atlanta GA 30346. 770/393-0000. **Fax:** 770/393-4370. **Contact:** Manager. **Description:** An executive search firm. **Specializes in the areas of:** Administration; Finance; Sales.

PERSONALIZED MANAGEMENT ASSOCIATES, INC.
1950 Spectrum Circle, Suite B-310, Marietta GA 30067-6059. 770/916-1668. **Toll-free phone:** 800/466-7822. **Fax:** 770/916-1429. **Contact:** Bill Lins, CPC, Director of Operations. **E-mail address:** jobs@pmasearch.com. **Description:** An executive search firm that places recent college graduates through CEOs. Company pays fee. **Specializes in the areas of:** Food Industry; Restaurant; Retail; Sales. **Positions commonly filled include:** Human Resources Manager; Restaurant/Food Service Manager. **Other U.S. locations:** Phoenix AZ. **Average salary range of placements:** More than $50,000. **Number of placements per year:** 500 - 999.

PERSONNEL OPPORTUNITIES INC.
5064 Roswell Road, Suite D-301, Atlanta GA 30342. 404/252-9484. **Fax:** 404/252-9821. **Contact:** President. **Description:** An executive search firm. Founded in 1966. **Specializes in the areas of:** Accounting/Auditing; Computer Hardware/Software; Engineering; Health/Medical; Insurance; Legal; Manufacturing; Sales. **Positions commonly filled include:** Accountant/Auditor; Chemical Engineer; Chemist; Claim Representative; Computer Programmer; Manufacturing Engineer; Mechanical Engineer; Nurse; Sales Representative; Software Engineer; Systems Analyst. **Number of placements per year:** 100 - 199.

PHOENIX PARTNERS
5600 Roswell Road NE, Suite 280, Atlanta GA 30342. 404/250-1133. **Contact:** Office Manager. **Description:** An executive search firm. **Specializes in the areas of:** High-Tech.

PINNACLE CONSULTING GROUP
6621 Bay Circle, Suite 180, Norcross GA 30071. 770/447-3770. **Contact:** Director of Recruiting. **Description:** An executive search firm. Company pays fee. **Specializes in the areas of:** Administration; Computer Science/Software; General Management; Publishing; Retail; Sales. **Positions commonly filled include:** Computer Programmer; General Manager; Services Sales Representative; Software Engineer; Systems Analyst; Wholesale and Retail Buyer. **Number of placements per year:** 1 - 49.

PRO-TECH INC.
P.O. Box 141, Oakwood GA 30566. 770/532-9815. **Fax:** 770/535-6796. **Contact:** Ann Johnson, Plastics Recruiter/Co-Owner. **Description:** A contingency executive search and recruiting firm that focuses on technical, engineering, and manufacturing placements for companies that manufacture plastic products. Company operates on a contingency basis. Company pays fee. **Specializes in the areas of:** Engineering; Manufacturing; Plastics. **Positions commonly filled include:** Chemical Engineer; Chemist; Design Engineer; Designer; General Manager; Industrial Engineer; Mechanical Engineer; Quality Control Supervisor. **Average salary range of placements:** More than $50,000. **Number of placements per year:** 1 - 49.

RIF (RESOURCES IN FOOD)
1627 Peachtree Street NE, Suite 204, Atlanta GA 30309. 404/897-5535. **Fax:** 404/897-5454. **Contact:** Scott Bins, Placement Specialist. **Description:** An executive search firm. Company pays fee. **Specializes in the areas of:** Food Industry; General Management. **Positions commonly filled include:** Branch Manager; Dietician/Nutritionist; General Manager; Hotel Manager; Management Trainee; Restaurant/Food Service Manager. **Corporate headquarters location:** St. Louis MO. **Average salary range of placements:** $30,000 - $50,000. **Number of placements per year:** 1000+.

P.J. REDA & ASSOCIATES, INC.
1955 Cliff Valley Way, Suite 117, Atlanta GA 30329. 404/325-8812. **Fax:** 404/325-8850. **Contact:** Pat Reda, President. **Description:** An executive search firm that also conducts interview skills workshops for supervisors and managers. Company pays fee. **Specializes in the areas of:** Food Industry; General Management; Health/Medical; Personnel/Labor Relations. **Positions commonly filled include:** General Manager; Health Services Manager; Management

Trainee; Restaurant/Food Service Manager. **Number of placements per year:** 175 - 250.

RESOURCE GROUP
P.O. Box 476, Dalton GA 30722. **Contact:** Manager. **Description:** An executive search firm.

DON RICHARD ASSOCIATES
3475 Lenox Road NE, Suite 210, Atlanta GA 30326. 404/231-3688. **Fax:** 404/364-0124. **Contact:** Ed Pease, Co-Owner. **Description:** An executive search firm that provides temporary and permanent placements. Company pays fee. **Specializes in the areas of:** Accounting/Auditing; Bookkeeping; Finance. **Positions commonly filled include:** Accountant/ Auditor; Budget Analyst; Credit Manager; Financial Analyst. **Corporate headquarters location:** Richmond VA. **Other U.S. locations:** Nationwide. **Average salary range of placements:** $30,000 - $50,000. **Number of placements per year:** 200 - 499.

RITA CORPORATION
5505 Interstate North Parkway, Atlanta GA 30328-4603. **Contact:** Manager. **E-mail address:** recruiting@ ilk.com. **Description:** An executive search firm recruiting for a wide variety of industries. **Specializes in the areas of:** Computer Hardware/Software.

ROLLINS SEARCH GROUP
216 Parkway 575, Woodstock GA 30188. 770/516-6042. **Contact:** Manager. **Description:** An executive search firm.

ROMAC INTERNATIONAL
3 Ravinia Drive, Suite 1460, Atlanta GA 30346. 770/604-3880. **Contact:** Manager. **Description:** An executive search firm. **Specializes in the areas of:** Accounting/Auditing; Finance; Information Technology. **Other U.S. locations:** Nationwide.

ROWLAND, MOUNTAIN & ASSOCIATES
4E Executive Park East, Suite 100, Atlanta GA 30329-2202. 404/325-2189. **Fax:** 404/320-0457. **Contact:** Russ Mountain, President. **Description:** An executive search firm operating on both retained and contingency bases. Company pays fee. **Specializes in the areas of:** Sales. **Positions commonly filled include:** Account Manager; Branch Manager; Marketing Manager; Marketing Specialist; Sales Executive; Sales Manager; Sales Representative. **Average salary range of placements:** More than $50,000. **Number of placements per year:** 100 - 199.

RUSSELL REYNOLDS ASSOCIATES, INC.
50 Hurt Plaza, Suite 600, Atlanta GA 30303. 404/577-3000. **Contact:** Manager. **Description:** A generalist executive search firm.

SALES OPPORTUNITIES
6065 Roswell Road, Suite 518, Atlanta GA 30328. 404/256-9314. **Contact:** Manager. **Description:** An executive search firm. **Specializes in the areas of:** Computer Science/Software; Sales.

SANFORD ROSE ASSOCIATES
9650 Ventana Way, Suite 204, Alpharetta GA 30022. 770/232-9900. **Contact:** Mr. Don Patrick, President. **World Wide Web address:** http://www.sanfordrose.com. **Description:** An executive search firm. Company pays fee. **Specializes in the areas of:** Computer Science/Software; Engineering; General Management; Sales; Technical; Wireless Communications. **Positions commonly filled include:** Branch Manager; Electrical/Electronics Engineer; General Manager; Science Technologist; Software Engineer. **Other U.S. locations:** Nationwide. **Number of placements per year:** 1 - 49.

SANFORD ROSE ASSOCIATES
1580 Warsaw Road, Suite 101, Roswell GA 30076. 770/643-4510. **Contact:** Manager. **World Wide Web address:** http://www.sanfordrose.com. **Description:** An executive search firm. **Other U.S. locations:** Nationwide. **Specializes in the areas of:** Banking.

SANFORD ROSE ASSOCIATES
2500 West Broad Street, Suite 106, Athens GA 30606. 706/548-3942. **Contact:** Manager. **World Wide Web address:** http://www.sanfordrose.com. **Description:** An executive search firm. **Specializes in the areas of:** Manufacturing. **Other U.S. locations:** Nationwide.

SEARCH ATLANTA
P.O. Drawer 674899, Marietta GA 30067. 770/984-0880. **Contact:** Manager. **Description:** An executive search firm.

SEARCHAMERICA INC.
180 Plantation Trace, Woodstock GA 30188. 770/751-3920. **Contact:** Manager. **Description:** An executive search firm. Company pays fee. **Specializes in the areas of:** Engineering; Industrial; Manufacturing; Personnel/Labor Relations; Sales; Technical. **Positions commonly filled include:** Buyer; Design Engineer; Designer; Electrical/Electronics Engineer; Human Resources Manager; Industrial Engineer; Industrial Production Manager. **Other U.S. locations:** Nationwide. **Average salary range of placements:** More than $50,000. **Number of placements per year:** 1 - 49.

SELECTIVE SEARCH
7000 Peachtree-Dunwoody Road, Building 4, Suite 100, Atlanta GA 30328. 770/390-9666. **Contact:** Manager. **Description:** An executive search firm. **Specializes in the areas of:** Information Systems.

SNELLING PERSONNEL SERVICES
1337 Canton Road, Suite D-3, Marietta GA 30066-6054. 770/423-1177. **Fax:** 770/423-0558. **Contact:** Manager. **E-mail address:** snelling@cyberatl.net. **World Wide Web address:** http://www.cyberatl.net. **Description:** An executive search firm operating on a contingency basis. The firm also provides some temporary placements. Founded in 1986. Company pays fee. **Specializes in the areas of:** Computer Science/Software; Engineering; Health/Medical; Information Systems; Sales; Secretarial. **Positions commonly filled include:** Chemical Engineer; Clerical Supervisor; Computer Programmer; Credit Manager; Customer Service Representative; Environmental Engineer; Manufacturer's/Wholesaler's Sales Rep.; Mechanical Engineer; Physical Therapist; Services Sales Representative; Software Engineer. **Corporate headquarters location:** Dallas TX. **Other U.S. locations:** Nationwide. **Average salary range of placements:** $30,000 - $50,000. **Number of placements per year:** 100 - 199.

SOFTWARE SEARCH
2163 Northlake Parkway, Suite 100, Tucker GA 30084. 770/934-5138. **Contact:** Larry Okeson, Vice President. **Description:** An executive search firm operating on a contingency basis. The firm also provides contract services. Company pays fee. **Specializes in the areas of:** Administration; Computer Science/Software. **Positions commonly filled include:** Computer Programmer; Database Manager; Software Engineer; Systems Analyst; Systems Manager; Telecommunications Manager. **Other U.S. locations:** Minneapolis MN. **Average salary range of placements:** $30,000 - $50,000. **Number of placements per year:** 200 - 499.

SONDRA SEARCH
P.O. Box 101, Roswell GA 30077. 770/552-1910. **Contact:** Manager. **Description:** An executive search firm. **Specializes in the areas of:** Sales.

SOURCE SERVICES CORPORATION
4170 Ashford Dunwoody Road, Suite 285, Atlanta GA 30319. 404/255-0245. **Contact:** Manager. **Description:** An executive search firm. The divisions at this location include Source Consulting, Source EDP, Source Finance, and Accountant Source Temps. **Specializes in the areas of:** Accounting/Auditing; Computer Hardware/Software; Finance; Information Technology. **Corporate headquarters location:** Dallas TX. **Other U.S. locations:** Nationwide.

SOUTHEASTERN DATA GROUP
100 Galleria Parkway, Suite 400, Atlanta GA 30339. 770/953-0295. **Contact:** Manager. **Description:** An executive search firm. **Specializes in the areas of:** Computer Hardware/Software.

SOUTHERN PROFESSIONAL RECRUITERS
5920 Roswell Road, Suite B107, Atlanta GA 30328. 404/851-9889. **Fax:** 404/843-2984. **Contact:** Manager. **Description:** An executive search firm. **Specializes in the areas of:** Finance; Health/Medical.

STERLING LEGAL SEARCH
5180 Roswell Road, Suite 202, Atlanta GA 30342. 404/250-9766. **Contact:** Manager. **Description:** An executive search firm. **Specializes in the areas of:** Legal.

TPS STAFFING
111 Main Street, Thomson GA 30824. 706/650-3011. **Contact:** Manager. **Description:** An executive search firm.

TAURION CORPORATION
P.O. Box 956716, Duluth GA 30095. 770/449-7155. **Fax:** 770/449-6421. **Contact:** John Puchis, Vice President. **Description:** An executive search firm. Company pays fee. **Specializes in the areas of:** Administration; Computer Science/Software; Data Processing. **Positions commonly filled include:** Computer Programmer; Director; Management; Software Engineer; Systems Analyst. **Number of placements per year:** 1 - 49.

TEAM ONE PARTNERS INC.
3901 Roswell Road NE, Suite 205, Marietta GA 30062. 770/425-6788. **Fax:** 770/425-6886. **Contact:** Manager. **Description:** An executive search firm. Company pays fee. **Specializes in the areas of:** Engineering; General Management; Industrial; Manufacturing; Paper. **Positions commonly filled include:** Chemical Engineer; Electrical/Electronics Engineer; General Manager; Human Resources Manager; Industrial Engineer; Industrial Production Manager; Manufacturer's/Wholesaler's Sales Rep.; Mechanical Engineer; Operations/Production Manager; Purchasing Agent/Manager; Quality Control Supervisor; Transportation/Traffic Specialist. **Number of placements per year:** 1 - 49.

TECH RESOURCE GROUP, INC.
3761 Venture Drive, Duluth GA 30136-5528. 770/418-1051. **Fax:** 770/476-2871. **Contact:** Brian Whitfield, Vice President. **Description:** An executive search firm. Company pays fee. **Specializes in the areas of:** Computer Science/Software. **Positions commonly filled include:** Computer Programmer; MIS Specialist; Systems Analyst; Technical Writer/Editor. **Benefits available to temporary workers:** Medical Insurance. **Average salary range of placements:** More than $50,000. **Number of placements per year:** 100 - 199.

TENNANT & ASSOCIATES
11285 Elkins Road, Roswell GA 30076. 770/740-1609. **Contact:** Office Manager. **Description:** An executive search firm. **Specializes in the areas of:** Computer Science/Software; Telecommunications.

THOMAS EXECUTIVE SEARCH
713 Lanford Springs Drive, Lilburn GA 30047. 770/381-1181. **Fax:** 770/279-0274. **Contact:** Office Manager. **Description:** An executive search firm that focuses on providing placements in the food and beverage industries.

THORNE CONSULTING
4067 Riverlook Parkway, Marietta GA 30067. 770/951-8075. **Toll-free phone:** 800/962-9763. **Fax:** 770/951-1823. **Contact:** Richard Thorne, Search Consultant. **Description:** An executive search firm operating on both retained and contingency bases. Company pays fee. **Specializes in the areas of:** Health/Medical. **Positions commonly filled include:** Chief Financial Officer; Controller; Financial Analyst; Health Care Risk Consultant; Human Resources Manager; Management Analyst/Consultant; Sales Manager; Sales Representative. **Average salary range of placements:** More than $50,000. **Number of placements per year:** 1 - 49.

TOAR CONSULTANTS INC.
1176 Grimes Bridge Road, Suite 200, Roswell GA 30075-3934. 770/993-7663. **Fax:** 770/998-5853. **Contact:** Manager. **E-mail address:** 71521.413@compuserve.com. **Description:** An executive search firm. Company pays fee. **Specializes in the areas of:** Accounting/Auditing; Administration; Banking; Computer Science/Software; Engineering; Finance; General Management; Insurance; Manufacturing; Publishing. **Positions commonly filled include:** Accountant/Auditor; Bank Officer/Manager; Chemical Engineer; Chemist; Civil Engineer; Computer Programmer; Design Engineer; Electrician; Engineer; MIS Manager; Operations/Production Manager; Quality Control Supervisor; Systems Analyst. **Average salary range of placements:** More than $50,000. **Number of placements per year:** 50 - 99.

TYLER & COMPANY
1000 Abernathy Road, Suite 1400, Atlanta GA 30328. 770/396-3939. **Contact:** Office Manager. **Description:** An executive search firm. **Specializes in the areas of:** Health/Medical. **Positions commonly filled include:** Physician.

WHITTAKER & ASSOCIATES
2675 Cumberland Parkway NW, Suite 263, Atlanta GA 30339-3912. 770/434-3779. **Fax:** 770/431-0213. **Contact:** Brad Winkler, President. **Description:** An executive search firm that provides placement of professionals in the food industry both nationally and internationally. Company pays fee. **Specializes in the areas of:** Food Industry. **Positions commonly filled include:** Account Manager; Branch Manager; Buyer; Chemist; Civil Engineer; Credit Manager; Customer Service Representative; Environmental Engineer; Financial Analyst; Food Scientist/Technologist; Industrial Engineer; Manufacturer's/Wholesaler's Sales Rep.; Mechanical Engineer; Operations/Production Manager; Quality Control Supervisor; Services Sales Representative; Systems Analyst. **Average salary range of placements:** $30,000 - $50,000. **Number of placements per year:** 50 - 99.

WORKMAN & ASSOCIATES
223 Brolley Woods Drive, Woodstock GA 30189. 770/926-8892. **Fax:** 770/926-8884. **Contact:** Jim Workman, Owner. **Description:** An executive search firm. Company pays fee. **Specializes in the areas of:**

Banking; Finance; Investment. **Positions commonly filled include:** Financial Services Sales Representative; Securities Sales Representative. **Number of placements per year:** 1 - 49.

STEVE WYMAN & ASSOCIATES
4201 Fairgreen Terrace NE, Marietta GA 30068. 770/977-4410. **Contact:** Manager. **Description:** An executive search firm. **Specializes in the areas of:** Communications.

PERMANENT EMPLOYMENT AGENCIES

A-OK PERSONNEL
P.O. Box 617, Gainesville GA 30503. 770/532-4002. **Physical address:** 200 Main Street, Gainesville GA. **Fax:** 770/287-0852. **Contact:** John O'Kelley, Owner. **Description:** A permanent employment agency. Company pays fee. **Specializes in the areas of:** Accounting/Auditing; Administration; Finance; Health/Medical; Legal; Sales; Secretarial; Transportation. **Positions commonly filled include:** Accountant/Auditor; Clerical Supervisor; Computer Programmer; Dental Assistant/Dental Hygienist; General Manager; Manufacturer's/Wholesaler's Sales Rep.; Paralegal; Services Sales Representative; Typist/Word Processor. **Average salary range of placements:** $20,000 - $29,999. **Number of placements per year:** 50 - 99.

A-1 SERVICE PERSONNEL
1718 Peachtree Street NW, Suite 157, Atlanta GA 30309-2409. 404/885-9675. **Fax:** 404/885-9666. **Contact:** Manager. **Description:** A permanent employment agency. Founded in 1985. **Specializes in the areas of:** Accounting/Auditing; Banking; Finance; Personnel/Labor Relations; Secretarial. **Positions commonly filled include:** Accountant/Auditor; Credit Manager; Customer Service Representative; Human Resources Specialist; Typist/Word Processor; Underwriter/Assistant Underwriter. **Benefits available to temporary workers:** Medical Insurance; Paid Holidays; Paid Vacation. **Number of placements per year:** 500 - 999.

AAA EMPLOYMENT
1512 Gillionville Road, Albany GA 31707-3977. 912/883-4170. **Fax:** 912/883-4172. **Contact:** William H. Andrews, Manager. **Description:** A permanent employment agency. **Specializes in the areas of:** Accounting/Auditing; Finance; Food Industry; General Management; Insurance; Manufacturing; Publishing; Retail; Sales; Secretarial. **Positions commonly filled include:** Accountant/Auditor; Administrative Manager; Advertising Brokerage Clerk; Claim Representative; Computer Programmer; Cost Estimator; Credit Manager; Customer Service Representative; Electrical/Electronics Engineer; Electrician; General Manager; Health Services Manager; Human Service Worker; Insurance Agent/Broker; Operations/Production Manager; Paralegal; Purchasing Agent/Manager; Real Estate Agent; Registered Nurse; Restaurant/Food Service Manager; Services Sales Representative; Telecommunications Manager; Typist/Word Processor; Underwriter/Assistant Underwriter. **Corporate headquarters location:** Clearwater FL. **Average salary range of placements:** $20,000 - $29,999. **Number of placements per year:** 200 - 499.

ACCESS PERSONNEL SERVICES, INC.
200 Galleria Parkway, Suite 420, Atlanta GA 30339-5944. 770/988-8484. **Fax:** 770/988-8522. **Contact:** Renie S. Geller, Recruiter. **Description:** A staffing service. Founded in 1990. **Specializes in the areas of:** Accounting/Auditing; Administration; Banking; Clerical; Customer Service; Secretarial. **Positions commonly filled include:** Accountant/Auditor; Administrative Assistant; Customer Service Representative; Typist/Word Processor. **Benefits available to temporary workers:** Medical Insurance; Paid Holidays; Paid Vacation. **Corporate headquarters:** This Location. **Average salary range of placements:** $21,000 - $30,000. **Number of placements per year:** 200 - 499.

ACCESS PERSONNEL SERVICES, INC.
600 West Peachtree Street, Suite 180, Atlanta GA 30308. 404/872-0888. **Fax:** 404/872-7790. **Contact:** Recruiter. **Description:** A staffing service. Founded in 1990. **Specializes in the areas of:** Accounting/Auditing; Administration; Banking; Clerical; Customer Service; Secretarial. **Positions commonly filled include:** Accountant; Administrative Assistant; Customer Service Representative; Typist/Word Processor. **Benefits available to temporary workers:** Medical Insurance; Paid Holidays; Paid Vacation. **Corporate headquarters:** 200 Galleria Parkway, Suite 420, Atlanta GA 30339-5944.

AD OPTIONS INC.
P.O. Box 7778, Marietta GA 30065. 770/424-7778. **Fax:** 770/919-2254. **Contact:** Alex Wilson, President. **E-mail address:** alexwilson@mindspring.com. **World Wide Web address:** http://www.ad-options.com. **Description:** A permanent employment agency that also provides temporary placements. Founded in 1993. Company pays fee. **Specializes in the areas of:** Advertising; Art/Design; Marketing. **Positions commonly filled include:** Account Manager; Advertising Account Executive; Art Director; Copywriter; Graphic Artist; Graphic Designer; Market Research Analyst; Marketing Manager; Marketing Specialist; Media Buyer; Media Specialist; Public Relations Specialist. **Average salary range of placements:** $30,000 - $50,000. **Number of placements per year:** 50 - 99.

AUGUSTA STAFFING ASSOCIATES
218 Oak Street, Suite E, Martinez GA 30907. 706/860-4820. **Fax:** 706/860-4871. **Contact:** Cynthia Kelly, President. **E-mail address:** asa@jobshopstaffing.com. **Description:** An employment agency providing both permanent and temporary placements. Founded in 1992. Company pays fee. **Specializes in the areas of:** Accounting/Auditing; Administration; Computer Hardware/Software; Engineering; General Management; Industrial; Manufacturing; Personnel/Labor Relations; Retail; Secretarial. **Positions commonly filled include:** Account Manager; Account Representative; Accountant; Administrative Assistant; Administrative Manager; Advertising Account Executive; Assistant Manager; Bank Officer/Manager; Buyer; Chemical Engineer; Chemist; Claim Representative; Computer Operator; Computer Programmer; Controller; Customer Service Representative; Database Manager; Electrical/Electronics Engineer; Graphic Designer; Industrial Engineer; Industrial Production Manager; Manufacturing Engineer; Production Manager; Quality Control Supervisor; Sales Executive; Sales Manager; Sales Representative; Software Engineer; Systems Analyst; Transportation/Traffic Specialist; Typist/Word Processor. **Corporate headquarters location:** This Location. **Average salary range of placements:** $20,000 - $29,999. **Number of placements per year:** 500 - 999.

BUSINESS PROFESSIONAL GROUP, INC.
3490 Piedmont Road, Suite 212, Atlanta GA 30030. 404/262-2577. **Fax:** 770/262-3463. **Contact:** Michelle Abel, Vice President of Operations. **Description:** A

permanent placement agency. **Specializes in the areas of:** Engineering; Entry-Level; MIS/EDP; Technical. **Positions commonly filled include:** Accountant/ Auditor; Buyer; Chemist; Claim Representative; Electrical/Electronics Engineer; Financial Analyst; Industrial Engineer; Management Trainee; Mechanical Engineer; Metallurgical Engineer; Software Engineer; Technical Writer/Editor; Underwriter/Assistant Underwriter. **Number of placements per year:** 100 - 199.

CAREER PLACEMENTS
777 Gloucester Street, Suite 204, Brunswick GA 31520. 912/264-3401. **Fax:** 912/264-3403. **Contact:** Pam McGeachy, President. **Description:** A permanent employment agency. Company pays fee. **Specializes in the areas of:** Accounting/Auditing; Engineering; Sales. **Positions commonly filled include:** Accountant/Auditor; Actuary; Claim Representative; Dietician/Nutritionist; Electrical/Electronics Engineer; Financial Analyst; General Manager; Health Services Manager; Human Resources Manager; Industrial Engineer; Manufacturer's/Wholesaler's Sales Rep.; Mechanical Engineer; Registered Nurse; Software Engineer. **Number of placements per year:** 1 - 49.

CATALINA RESOURCES, INC.
931 Monroe Drive, Suite 102-350, Atlanta GA 30308. 770/220-0770. **Fax:** 770/220-0767. **Contact:** Geri H. Frye, Branch Manager. **E-mail address:** geri@catalinaresources.com. **World Wide Web address:** http://www.catalinaresources.com. **Description:** An employment agency that offers both permanent and temporary placements. Company pays fee. **Specializes in the areas of:** Accounting/Auditing; Administration; Banking; Computer Science/Software; Finance; Health/Medical; Sales; Technical. **Positions commonly filled include:** Accountant/Auditor; Administrative Manager; Bank Officer/Manager; Computer Programmer; Customer Service Representative; Financial Analyst; Financial Services Sales Representative; Internet Services Manager; Management Analyst/Consultant; MIS Specialist; Multimedia Designer; Securities Sales Representative; Systems Analyst; Technical Writer/Editor; Typist/Word Processor. **Corporate headquarters location:** Tampa FL. **Average salary range of placements:** $30,000 - $50,000. **Number of placements per year:** 100 - 199.

CHASE FINANCIAL STAFFING
TYLER TECHNICAL STAFFING
750 Hammond Drive, Building 4, Suite 200, Atlanta GA 30328. 404/250-4448. **Fax:** 404/851-1754. **Contact:** Manager. **Description:** A permanent employment agency that also offers temporary placements and contract services. Tyler Technical Staffing (also at this location) provides permanent, contract, and temporary placements in information technology, electronics, and engineering. Company pays fee. **NOTE:** Resumes for Tyler Technical Staffing should be sent to 750 Hammond Drive, Suite 300, Atlanta GA 30328. **Specializes in the areas of:** Accounting/Auditing; Banking; Finance. **Positions commonly filled include:** Accountant/Auditor; Budget Analyst; Controller; Credit Manager; Finance Director; Financial Analyst; Purchasing Agent/Manager. **Number of placements per year:** 100 - 199.

CLAREMONT-BRANAN, INC.
1298 Rockbridge Road SW, Suite B, Stone Mountain GA 30087. 770/925-2915. **Fax:** 770/925-2601. **Contact:** Phil Collins, President. **Description:** A permanent employment agency. Company pays fee. **Specializes in the areas of:** Architecture/Construction; Design; Engineering. **Positions commonly filled include:** Architect; Civil Engineer; Electrical/Electronics Engineer; Interior Designer; Mechanical Engineer. **Number of placements per year:** 50 - 99.

CoCOUNSEL
1275 Peachtree Street NE, Suite 330, Atlanta GA 30309. 404/885-1993. **Fax:** 404/885-1884. **Contact:** Manager. **Description:** A permanent placement agency. Founded in 1969. **Specializes in the areas of:** Administration; Legal; Secretarial. **Positions commonly filled include:** Administrative Manager; Attorney; Branch Manager; Clerical Supervisor; Human Resources Specialist; Human Service Worker; Legal Secretary; Paralegal; Typist/Word Processor. **Average salary range of placements:** $30,000 - $50,000. **Number of placements per year:** 1000+.

DDS STAFFING RESOURCES INC.
9755 Dogwood Road, Suite 200, Roswell GA 30075. 770/998-7779. **Contact:** Manager. **Description:** A permanent placement agency. Company pays fee. **Specializes in the areas of:** Health/Medical. **Positions commonly filled include:** Claim Representative; Dental Assistant/Dental Hygienist; Dentist; Licensed Practical Nurse; Medical Records Technician; Registered Nurse; Social Worker. **Number of placements per year:** 500 - 999.

DURHAM STAFFING INC.
1343 Canton Road, Suite D2, Marietta GA 30066. 770/499-1665. **Contact:** Brian Durham, Co-Owner. **Description:** A permanent employment agency. Company pays fee. **Specializes in the areas of:** Banking; Distribution; Finance; Manufacturing. **Positions commonly filled include:** Blue-Collar Worker Supervisor; Branch Manager; Customer Service Representative; General Manager. **Number of placements per year:** 1000+.

ELITE STAFFING SERVICES
5881 Glenridge Drive, Suite 260, Atlanta GA 30328. 404/255-7737. **Fax:** 404/303-7736. **Contact:** Natasha Goff, Branch Manager. **Description:** A permanent employment agency. **Specializes in the areas of:** Accounting/Auditing; Administration; Advertising; Banking; Biology; Computer Science/ Software; Economics; Education; Engineering; Finance; General Management; Health/Medical; Industrial; Insurance; Legal; Manufacturing; Nonprofit; Personnel/Labor Relations; Publishing; Retail; Sales; Secretarial; Technical; Transportation. **Positions commonly filled include:** Accountant/Auditor; Administrative Manager; Advertising Clerk; Attorney; Automotive Mechanic; Branch Manager; Broadcast Technician; Budget Analyst; Claim Representative; Clerical Supervisor; Clinical Lab Technician; Computer Programmer; Credit Manager; Customer Service Representative; Electrical/Electronics Engineer; Emergency Medical Technician; General Manager; Health Services Manager; Human Service Worker; Industrial Engineer; Insurance Agent/Broker; Licensed Practical Nurse; Management Analyst/Consultant; Manufacturer's/Wholesaler's Sales Rep.; Mechanical Engineer; Medical Records Technician; MIS Specialist; Paralegal; Pharmacist; Preschool Worker; Property and Real Estate Manager; Quality Control Supervisor; Registered Nurse; Restaurant/Food Service Manager; Securities Sales Representative; Software Engineer; Technical Writer/Editor; Telecommunications Manager; Underwriter/Assistant Underwriter. **Benefits available to temporary workers:** Paid Holidays; Paid Vacation. **Number of placements per year:** 1000+.

EXECUTIVE PLACEMENT SERVICES
5901-C Peachtree-Dunwoody Road, Suite 498, Atlanta GA 30328. 770/396-9114. **Fax:** 770/393-3040. **Contact:** President. **Description:** A permanent employment agency. Founded in 1986. **Specializes in the areas of:** Retail. **Positions commonly filled include:** Buyer; EDP Specialist.

EXPRESS PERSONNEL SERVICES
712 West Taylor Street, Griffin GA 30223. 770/227-9103. **Fax:** 770/227-1139. **Contact:** Phillip Purser, General Manager. **E-mail address:** xpress1134@aol.com. **World Wide Web address:** http://www.monster.com/expresspersonnel. **Description:** A full-service permanent placement agency. Company pays fee. **Specializes in the areas of:** Accounting/Auditing; Administration; Banking; Computer Science/Software; Engineering; Finance; General Management; Industrial; Manufacturing; Personnel/Labor Relations; Sales; Technical. **Positions commonly filled include:** Chemical Engineer; Computer Programmer; Credit Manager; Customer Service Representative; Electrical/Electronics Engineer; Electrician; Industrial Engineer; Industrial Production Manager; Mechanical Engineer; MIS Specialist; Operations/Production Manager; Systems Analyst; Typist/Word Processor. **Number of placements per year:** 1000+.

INTERNATIONAL INSURANCE PERSONNEL, INC.
P.O. Box 28408, Atlanta GA 30358. 404/255-9710. **Fax:** 404/255-9864. **Contact:** Julie B. Dickerson, President. **Description:** A full-service employment agency. Company pays fee. **Specializes in the areas of:** Insurance. **Positions commonly filled include:** Administrative Assistant; Claim Representative; Data Entry Clerk; Insurance Agent/Broker; Management Analyst/Consultant; Sales Representative; Secretary; Stenographer; Typist/Word Processor; Underwriter/Assistant Underwriter. **Benefits available to temporary workers:** Medical Insurance; Paid Vacation. **Average salary range of placements:** $20,000 - $100,000. **Number of placements per year:** 1000+.

MAU, INC.
501 Greene Street, Augusta GA 30901. 706/722-6806. **Contact:** William G. Hatcher, Jr., Vice President. **Description:** A permanent employment agency. Company pays fee. **Specializes in the areas of:** Engineering; Health/Medical; Manufacturing; MIS/EDP. **Positions commonly filled include:** EDP Specialist; Electrical/Electronics Engineer; Industrial Designer; Mechanical Engineer; Physician. **Number of placements per year:** 50 - 99.

THE MALCOLM GROUP, INC.
P.O. Box 178, Marble Hill GA 30148. 770/893-3485. **Fax:** 770/893-3489. **Contact:** Charles Malcolm, President/Owner. **Description:** A permanent placement agency. Company pays fee. **Specializes in the areas of:** Insurance. **Positions commonly filled include:** Actuary; Claim Representative; Insurance Agent/Broker; Underwriter/Assistant Underwriter.

MARATHON CONSULTING
425 East Crossville Road, Suite 115, Roswell GA 30075. 770/640-1595. **Contact:** Office Manager. **Description:** A permanent employment agency. **Specializes in the areas of:** Nuclear Engineering.

MORE PERSONNEL SERVICES INC.
4501 Circle 75 Parkway, Suite A-1190, Atlanta GA 30339. 770/955-0885. **Fax:** 770/955-0767. **Contact:** Linda K. Moore, President. **E-mail address:** morepers@mindspring.com. **World Wide Web address:** http://www.job-morepersonnel.com. **Description:** A permanent employment agency specializing in placing college graduates. Founded in 1988. Company pays fee. **Specializes in the areas of:** Finance; General Management; Insurance; Sales. **Positions commonly filled include:** Account Representative; Accountant; Adjuster; Advertising Account Executive; Assistant Manager; Branch Manager; Claim Representative; Credit Manager; Customer Service Representative; Database Manager; Finance Director; Financial Analyst; Internet Services Manager; Management Analyst/Consultant; Management Trainee; Market Research Analyst; Marketing Manager; Marketing Specialist; Multimedia Designer; Operations Manager; Public Relations Specialist; Sales Engineer; Sales Executive; Sales Manager; Sales Representative. **Corporate headquarters location:** This Location. **Average salary range of placements:** $30,000 - $50,000. **Number of placements per year:** 200 - 499.

NORRED & ASSOCIATES INC.
3420 Norman Berry Drive, Suite 301, Atlanta GA 30354-1324. 404/761-5058. **Fax:** 404/761-1152. **Contact:** Calvin Couch, Human Resources Manager. **Description:** An employment agency that specializes in security services. Founded in 1981. **Specializes in the areas of:** Industrial; Security. **Positions commonly filled include:** Management Trainee; Security Officer. **Average salary range of placements:** Less than $20,000. **Number of placements per year:** 500 - 999.

OFFICEMATES5
DAYSTAR TEMPORARY SERVICES
400 Colony Square, Suite 1001, Atlanta GA 30361. 404/892-1900. **Fax:** 404/892-4792. **Contact:** Kathleen Luck, Manager. **Description:** A permanent employment agency. Company pays fee. **Specializes in the areas of:** Accounting/Auditing; Office Support; Secretarial. **Positions commonly filled include:** Administrative Manager; Advertising Clerk; Clerical Supervisor; Clerk; Customer Service Representative; Human Resources Specialist; Management Trainee; Typist/Word Processor. **Corporate headquarters location:** Cleveland OH. **Other U.S. locations:** Nationwide. **Average salary range of placements:** $20,000 - $29,999. **Number of placements per year:** 500 - 999.

OLSTEN TECHNICAL SERVICES
3424 Peachtree Road NE, Suite 125, Atlanta GA 30326. 404/467-2310. **Toll-free phone:** 800/WOR-KNOW. **Fax:** 404/364-6220. **Contact:** Tim Long, Engineering Design Consultant. **E-mail address:** tim.long@olsten.com. **World Wide Web address:** http://www.olsten.com. **Description:** A permanent employment agency that also provides temporary placements. Company pays fee. **Specializes in the areas of:** Computer Science/Software; Engineering; Technical. **Positions commonly filled include:** Applications Engineer; Architect; Chemical Engineer; Civil Engineer; Computer Operator; Computer Programmer; Design Engineer; Draftsperson; Electrical/Electronics Engineer; Industrial Engineer; Manufacturing Engineer; Mechanical Engineer; Metallurgical Engineer; MIS Specialist; Project Manager; Quality Control Supervisor; Software Engineer; Structural Engineer; Systems Analyst; Technical Writer/Editor; Telecommunications Manager. **Corporate headquarters location:** Melville NY. **International locations:** Worldwide. **Average salary range of placements:** More than $50,000. **Number of placements per year:** 1000+.

PATHFINDERS, INC.
229 Peachtree Street, International Tower, Suite 1500, Atlanta GA 30303. 404/688-5940. **Contact:** Diane Post, President. **Description:** A permanent employment agency. Company pays fee. **Specializes in the areas of:** Secretarial. **Positions commonly filled include:** Administrative Assistant; Administrative Worker/Clerk; Legal Secretary; Secretary. **Number of placements per year:** 500 - 999.

PROFESSIONAL MEDICAL
4350 Georgetown Square, Atlanta GA 30338. 770/458-1648. **Contact:** Manager. **Description:** A permanent employment agency. **Specializes in the areas of:** Accounting/Auditing; General Management; Health/Medical; Sales. **Positions commonly filled include:** Health Services Manager; Licensed Practical

Nurse; Occupational Therapist; Pharmacist; Physical Therapist; Physician; Respiratory Therapist; Services Sales Representative.

QUEST SYSTEMS, INC.
3 Corporate Square, Suite 210, Atlanta GA 30329. 404/636-3000. **Contact:** Manager. **E-mail address:** questsyst@aol.com. **World Wide Web Address:** http://www.questsyst.com. **Description:** A permanent employment agency. **Specializes in the areas of:** Computer Hardware/Software. **Corporate headquarters location:** Bethesda MD. **Other U.S. locations:** Baltimore MD; King of Prussia PA.

RANDSTAD STAFFING SERVICES
1910 Highway 20 South, Suite 275, Conyers GA 30208-2074. 770/922-2888. **Fax:** 770/922-5392. **Contact:** Branch Manager. **Description:** An employment agency that offers permanent and temporary placements and career/outplacement counseling. Founded in 1952. Company pays fee. **Specializes in the areas of:** Accounting/Auditing; Banking; Computer Science/Software; Engineering; Finance; Health/Medical; Industrial; Insurance; Manufacturing; Sales; Secretarial; Technical; Transportation. **Positions commonly filled include:** Accountant/Auditor; Administrative Manager; Blue-Collar Worker Supervisor; Branch Manager; Claim Representative; Computer Programmer; Credit Manager; Electrician; Management Trainee; Manufacturer's/Wholesaler's Sales Rep.; Mechanical Engineer; Quality Control Supervisor; Services Sales Representative; Transportation/Traffic Specialist. **Benefits available to temporary workers:** 401(k); Credit Union; Dental Insurance; Medical Insurance; Vision Insurance. **Corporate headquarters location:** 2015 South Park Place, Atlanta GA 30339. **Other U.S. locations:** AL; MS; SC; TN. **Average salary range of placements:** $20,000 - $29,999. **Number of placements per year:** 500 - 999.

RANDSTAD STAFFING SERVICES
2015 South Park Place, Atlanta GA 30339. 770/937-7000. **Contact:** Eric Vonk, CEO. **Description:** A permanent employment agency. Company pays fee. **Specializes in the areas of:** Accounting/Auditing; Advertising; Banking; Computer Science/Software; Education; General Management; Industrial; Legal; Personnel/Labor Relations; Publishing; Retail; Sales; Secretarial; Technical; Transportation. **Positions commonly filled include:** Accountant/Auditor; Administrative Manager; Advertising Clerk; Brokerage Clerk; Budget Analyst; Buyer; Claim Representative; Computer Programmer; Cost Estimator; Counselor; Credit Manager; Customer Service Representative; Electrician; Financial Analyst; Human Resources Specialist; Industrial Engineer; Paralegal; Teacher/Professor; Travel Agent; Typist/Word Processor; Underwriter/Assistant Underwriter. **Benefits available to temporary workers:** 401(k); Dental Insurance; Disability Coverage; Life Insurance; Medical Insurance; Paid Holidays; Paid Vacation; Vision Plan. **Corporate headquarters location:** This Location. **Other U.S. locations:** AL; MS; SC; TN. **Average salary range of placements:** Less than $20,000. **Number of placements per year:** 100 - 199.

RANDSTAD STAFFING SERVICES
196 Alps Road, Suite 1, Athens GA 30606-4068. 706/548-9590. **Contact:** Vicki Belcher, Manager. **Description:** A permanent employment agency. Founded in 1960. Company pays fee. **Specializes in the areas of:** Administration; Banking; Computer Hardware/Software; Industrial; Manufacturing; Sales. **Positions commonly filled include:** Blue-Collar Worker Supervisor; Computer Programmer; Customer Service Representative; Industrial Production Manager; Quality Control Supervisor; Services Sales Representative; Surveyor; Typist/Word Processor. **Benefits available to temporary workers:** 401(k); Dental Insurance; Medical Insurance. **Corporate headquarters location:** Atlanta GA. **Other U.S. locations:** AL; FL; SC; TN. **Average salary range of placements:** Less than $20,000. **Number of placements per year:** 1000+.

RANDSTAD STAFFING SERVICES
6681 Roswell Road NE, Atlanta GA 30328. 404/250-1008. **Fax:** 404/252-0605. **Contact:** Branch Manager. **Description:** A permanent employment agency. Company pays fee. **Specializes in the areas of:** Accounting/Auditing; Computer Science/Software; Industrial; Manufacturing; Personnel/Labor Relations; Technical. **Positions commonly filled include:** Accountant/Auditor; Administrative Manager; Branch Manager; Claim Representative; Credit Manager; Customer Service Representative; Draftsperson; Financial Analyst; Health Services Manager; Human Resources Specialist; Industrial Engineer; Internet Services Manager; Mechanical Engineer; MIS Specialist; Quality Control Supervisor; Software Engineer; Statistician; Telecommunications Manager; Typist/Word Processor. **Benefits available to temporary workers:** 401(k); Medical Insurance; Paid Holidays; Paid Vacation. **Corporate headquarters location:** Atlanta GA. **Other U.S. locations:** AL; FL; SC; TN. **Average salary range of placements:** $30,000 - $50,000. **Number of placements per year:** 1000+.

SMITH AGENCY
2970 Peachtree Road NW, Suite 820, Atlanta GA 30305. 404/261-4257. **Fax:** 404/261-4259. **Contact:** Cynthia Adams, Personnel Placement Consultant. **Description:** A permanent placement agency. **Specializes in the areas of:** Domestic Help; Nannies. **Positions commonly filled include:** Chauffeur; Chef/Cook/Kitchen Worker; Domestic Help; Housekeeper; Nanny. **Number of placements per year:** 100 - 199.

SNELLING PERSONNEL SERVICES
P.O. Box 2729, Gainesville GA 30503. 770/534-0001. **Fax:** 770/531-0669. **Contact:** Richard Williamson, President. **Description:** A permanent placement agency. **Specializes in the areas of:** Accounting/Auditing; Finance. **Corporate headquarters location:** Dallas TX. **Other U.S. locations:** Nationwide.

SOUTHERN EMPLOYMENT SERVICE
1233 54th Street, Columbus GA 31904. 706/327-6533. **Fax:** 706/323-7920. **Contact:** Manager. **Description:** A permanent employment agency. **Specializes in the areas of:** Accounting/Auditing; Administration; Banking; Computer Hardware/Software; General Management; Industrial; Manufacturing; Personnel/Labor Relations; Sales; Secretarial. **Positions commonly filled include:** Accountant/Auditor; Administrative Assistant; Bookkeeper; Civil Engineer; Clerk; Computer Operator; Computer Programmer; Credit Manager; Customer Service Representative; Data Entry Clerk; Manufacturing Engineer; Mechanical Engineer; MIS Specialist; Operations/Production Manager; Quality Control Supervisor; Sales Manager; Secretary; Systems Analyst; Typist/Word Processor. **Number of placements per year:** 100 - 199.

STAFFING RESOURCES
4275 Shackleford Road, Suite 250, Norcross GA 30093. 770/638-8100. **Contact:** Jeanne Schreider, Manager. **Description:** A permanent employment agency. Founded in 1985. Company pays fee. **Specializes in the areas of:** Accounting/Auditing; Administration; Advertising; Health/Medical; Insurance; Personnel/Labor Relations; Publishing; Sales; Secretarial. **Positions commonly filled include:** Accountant/Auditor; Advertising Clerk; Claim

Representative; Clerical Supervisor; Computer Programmer; Customer Service Representative; Human Resources Specialist; Medical Records Technician; Quality Control Supervisor; Services Sales Representative; Typist/Word Processor. **Benefits available to temporary workers:** 401(k); Medical Insurance; Paid Holidays; Paid Vacation. **Other area locations:** Atlanta GA. **Average salary range of placements:** $20,000 - $29,999. **Number of placements per year:** 1000+.

THOMPSON CONSULTANTS, INC.
P.O. Box 72995, Marietta GA 30007. 770/973-1353. **Fax:** 770/973-1354. **Contact:** Stuart Thompson, President. **Description:** A generalist permanent employment agency. **Positions commonly filled include:** Accountant/Auditor; Administrative Assistant; Administrative Manager; Branch Manager; Buyer; Clerical Supervisor; Customer Service Representative; Financial Analyst; General Manager; Industrial Engineer; Industrial Production Manager; Quality Control Supervisor; Sales Manager; Sales Representative; Secretary. **Average salary range of placements:** $30,000 - $50,000. **Number of placements per year:** 1 - 49.

TODAYS EMPLOYMENT SOLUTIONS
P.O. Box 68, Chatsworth GA 30705-0068. 706/695-7951. **Contact:** Jamie Jones, President. **Description:** A permanent employment agency. Company pays fee. **Specializes in the areas of:** Industrial; Personnel/Labor Relations. **Positions commonly filled include:** Accountant/Auditor; Computer Programmer; Credit Manager; Customer Service Representative; Electrician; Quality Control Supervisor; Typist/Word Processor. **Average salary range of placements:** $20,000 - $29,999. **Number of placements per year:** 500 - 999.

WPPS SOFTWARE STAFFING
230 Peachtree Street NW, Suite 1514, Atlanta GA 30303. 404/588-9100. **Fax:** 404/588-1395. **Contact:** Customer Service Manager. **Description:** A permanent employment agency. **Specializes in the areas of:** Accounting/Auditing; Administration; Advertising; Architecture/Construction; Banking; Computer Science; Finance; Legal; Nonprofit; Personnel/Labor Relations; Publishing; Sales; Secretarial. **Positions commonly filled include:** Accountant; Administrative Manager; Clerical Supervisor; Computer Programmer; Customer Service Representative; Designer; Editor; Human Resources Specialist; Human Service Worker; Paralegal; Software Engineer; Technical Writer; Typist/Word Processor. **Benefits available to temporary workers:** 401(k); Bonus Award/Plan; Medical Insurance; Paid Holidays; Paid Vacation. **Corporate headquarters location:** Charlotte NC. **Average salary range of placements:** $20,000 - $29,999. **Number of placements per year:** 1 - 49.

TEMPORARY EMPLOYMENT AGENCIES

ACCOUNTING RESOURCE TEMPORARIES
1100 Abernathy Road, Suite 625, Atlanta GA 30328. **Contact:** Manager. **Description:** A temporary and temp-to-perm employment agency. **Specializes in the areas of:** Accounting/Auditing.

ALL-STAR TEMPORARY & EMPLOYMENT SERVICES
5848 Bankhead Highway, Suite J, Douglasville GA 30134-2012. 770/942-0264. **Fax:** 770/489-9821. **Contact:** Marlene Van Camp, Owner. **Description:** A temporary agency. Founded in 1978. Company pays fee. **Specializes in the areas of:** Industrial; Secretarial; Transportation. **Positions commonly filled include:** Accountant/Auditor; Blue-Collar Worker Supervisor; Computer Programmer; Quality Control Supervisor. **Benefits available to temporary workers:** Medical Insurance; Paid Holidays; Paid Vacation. **Other area locations:** Atlanta GA; Smyrna GA. **Average salary range of placements:** Less than $20,000. **Number of placements per year:** 1000+.

CALDWELL SERVICES
861 Holcomb Bridge Road, Suite 105, Roswell GA 30076. 770/998-8024. **Fax:** 770/998-0875. **Contact:** Pamela Jones, Coordinator. **Description:** A temporary agency. Founded in 1974. **Specializes in the areas of:** Accounting/Auditing; Personnel/Labor Relations; Secretarial. **Positions commonly filled include:** Accountant/Auditor; Chemist; Customer Service Representative; Typist/Word Processor. **Benefits available to temporary workers:** Bonus Award/Plan; Medical Insurance; Paid Holidays; Paid Vacation. **Other U.S. locations:** AR; IN; NC; SC. **Average salary range of placements:** Less than $20,000. **Number of placements per year:** 500 - 999.

CALDWELL SERVICES
200 Galleria Parkway, Suite 905, Atlanta GA 30339. 770/955-1767. **Fax:** 770/955-0114. **Contact:** Donna Vassil, General Manager. **Description:** A temporary agency. Founded in 1974. Company pays fee. **Specializes in the areas of:** Accounting/Auditing; Administration; Manufacturing; Personnel/Labor Relations; Sales; Secretarial; Technical. **Positions commonly filled include:** Accountant/Auditor; Administrative Manager; Blue-Collar Worker Supervisor; Branch Manager; Claim Representative; Computer Programmer; Customer Service Representative; Electrical/Electronics Engineer; Human Resources Specialist; MIS Specialist; Services Sales Representative; Systems Analyst; Typist/Word Processor. **Benefits available to temporary workers:** Bonus Award/Plan; Medical Insurance; Paid Holidays; Paid Vacation. **Other U.S. locations:** AR; IN; NC; SC. **Average salary range of placements:** $20,000 - $29,999. **Number of placements per year:** 1000+.

COAST TO COAST TECHNICAL SERVICES INC.
6015 Atlantic Boulevard, Suite A, Norcross GA 30071. 770/414-5526. **Toll-free phone:** 800/532-6278. **Fax:** 770/414-5747. **Contact:** Manager. **E-mail address:** coast29@idt.vivid.net. **Description:** A temporary agency that specializes in technical placements and also offers contract services. Founded in 1994. Company pays fee. **Specializes in the areas of:** Computer Science/Software; Engineering; Technical. **Positions commonly filled include:** Architect; Biomedical Engineer; Buyer; Chemical Engineer; Chemist; Civil Engineer; Computer Programmer; Construction Contractor; Cost Estimator; Design Engineer; Draftsperson; Electrical/Electronics Engineer; Environmental Engineer; Industrial Engineer; Internet Services Manager; Landscape Architect; Mechanical Engineer; MIS Specialist; Purchasing Agent/Manager; Quality Control Supervisor; Software Engineer; Structural Engineer; Technical Writer/Editor; Urban/Regional Planner. **Benefits available to temporary workers:** Credit Union; Paid Holidays; Paid Vacation. **Average salary range of placements:** More than $50,000. **Number of placements per year:** 1000+.

DYNAMIC PEOPLE
260 Peachtree Street NW, Suite 800, Atlanta GA 30303-1202. 404/688-1124. **Fax:** 404/688-0268. **Contact:** Linda J. Davis, President. **Description:** A temporary agency. Founded in 1990. **Specializes in the areas of:** Personnel/Labor Relations; Secretarial.

Positions commonly filled include: Administrative Assistant; Customer Service Representative; Secretary; Typist/Word Processor. **Number of placements per year:** 1000+.

EXPRESS PERSONNEL SERVICES
8 Amlajack Boulevard, Newnan GA 30265-1010. 770/253-0133. **Fax:** 770/253-2827. **Contact:** Manager. **Description:** A full-service human resources outsourcing firm primarily offering temporary placements. Company pays fee. **Specializes in the areas of:** Engineering; General Management; Industrial; Manufacturing; Personnel/Labor Relations; Sales; Secretarial; Technical. **Positions commonly filled include:** Administrative Manager; Advertising Clerk; Blue-Collar Worker Supervisor; Branch Manager; Claim Representative; Clerical Supervisor; Computer Programmer; Credit Manager; Customer Service Representative; Electrical/Electronics Engineer; General Manager; Industrial Production Manager; Management Analyst/Consultant; Management Trainee; MIS Specialist; Physical Therapist; Purchasing Agent/ Manager; Quality Control Supervisor; Systems Analyst; Typist/Word Processor. **Benefits available to temporary workers:** 401(k); Medical Insurance; Paid Holidays; Paid Vacation; Scholarship Program. **Corporate headquarters location:** Oklahoma City OK. **International locations:** Worldwide. **Average salary range of placements:** $20,000 - $29,999. **Number of placements per year:** 1000+.

FIRST PRO
3859 Peachtree Road, Atlanta GA 30319. 404/365-8367. **Contact:** Manager. **Description:** A temporary agency. Company pays fee. **Specializes in the areas of:** Administration; General Management; Sales; Secretarial. **Average salary range of placements:** $20,000 - $29,999. **Number of placements per year:** 50 - 99.

HEALTHCARE FINANCIAL STAFFING
2300 Northlake Center Drive, Suite 210, Tucker GA 30084. 770/492-0706. **Toll-free phone:** 800/726-2898. **Fax:** 770/491-0230. **Contact:** Darla David, Certified Account Manager. **Description:** A temporary agency. Company pays fee. **Specializes in the areas of:** Health/Medical. **Positions commonly filled include:** Billing Clerk; Collector; Medical Secretary. **Benefits available to temporary workers:** Dental Insurance; Life Insurance; Medical Insurance. **Corporate headquarters location:** Calabasas CA. **Average salary range of placements:** $20,000 - $29,999. **Number of placements per year:** 200 - 499.

HIRE INTELLECT INC.
1810 Water Place NW, Suite 240, Atlanta GA 30339-2048. 770/850-8502. **Fax:** 770/850-8503. **Contact:** Pamela Craig, Recruiting Manager. **E-mail address:** hireintellect@msn.com. **Description:** A temporary agency. Founded in 1992. Company pays fee. **Specializes in the areas of:** Marketing. **Positions commonly filled include:** Advertising Account Executive; Editor; Graphic Artist; Graphic Designer; Internet Services Manager; Market Research Analyst; Marketing Manager; Marketing Specialist; Public Relations Specialist; Webmaster. **Benefits available to temporary workers:** Paid Holidays; Paid Vacation. **Average salary range of placements:** $30,000 - $50,000.

JORDAN TEMPORARIES
P.O. Box 409, Morrow GA 30260. 770/960-8166. **Contact:** Manager. **Description:** A temporary agency. **Specializes in the areas of:** Accounting/Auditing; Computer Science/Software; Engineering; Personnel/ Labor Relations. **Positions commonly filled include:** Accountant/Auditor; Buyer; Computer Programmer; Engineer; Financial Analyst; Human Resources Manager; Telecommunications Manager. **Average salary range of placements:** $30,000 - $50,000. **Number of placements per year:** 1 - 49.

KELLY SCIENTIFIC RESOURCES
2302 Parklake Drive, Suite 370, Atlanta GA 30345. 770/270-1892. **Fax:** 770/493-9325. **Contact:** Branch Manager. **World Wide Web address:** http://www.kellyscientific.com. **Description:** A temporary agency for scientific professionals. **Specializes in the areas of:** Biomedical; Biotechnology; Chemical; Environmental; Food Industry; Pharmaceutical. **Corporate headquarters location:** Troy MI. **Other U.S. locations:** Nationwide.

KELLY SERVICES, INC.
590 Thornton Road, Suite D, Lithia Springs GA 30057-1591. 770/739-1818. **Contact:** Dee Dickson, Manager. **Description:** A temporary agency. Company pays fee. **Specializes in the areas of:** Accounting/ Auditing; Clerical; Industrial; Light Industrial; Manufacturing. **Positions commonly filled include:** Blue-Collar Worker Supervisor; Buyer; Customer Service Representative. **Benefits available to temporary workers:** Paid Holidays; Paid Vacation. **Corporate headquarters location:** Troy MI. **Other U.S. locations:** Nationwide. **Number of placements per year:** 1000+.

KELLY SERVICES, INC.
211 Broad Street, Suite C, Rome GA 30161-3021. 706/235-9117. **Contact:** Manager. **Description:** A temporary agency. **Specializes in the areas of:** Personnel/Labor Relations; Secretarial; Technical. **Benefits available to temporary workers:** Medical Insurance; Paid Holidays; Paid Vacation. **Corporate headquarters location:** Troy MI. **Other U.S. locations:** Nationwide. **Average salary range of placements:** $20,000 - $29,999. **Number of placements per year:** 1 - 49.

MACTEMPS
999 Peachtree Street NE, Suite 140, Atlanta GA 30309-3964. 404/876-3057. **Fax:** 404/874-9092. **Contact:** Audrie Edison, Market Manager. **Description:** A temporary agency that specializes in the placement of computer professionals experienced in Macintosh and Windows platforms. Company pays fee. **Specializes in the areas of:** Art/Design; Computer Science/Software. **Positions commonly filled include:** Graphic Designer. **Benefits available to temporary workers:** 401(k); Dental Insurance; Disability Coverage; Life Insurance; Medical Insurance. **Corporate headquarters location:** Cambridge MA. **Average salary range of placements:** $30,000 - $40,000. **Number of placements per year:** 500 - 999.

MANPOWER TEMPORARY SERVICES
260 Peachtree Street NW, Suite 900, Atlanta GA 30303. 404/659-3565. **Contact:** Branch Manager. **Description:** A temporary agency. Company pays fee. **Specializes in the areas of:** Data Processing; Light Industrial; Office Support; Technical; Telemarketing. **Positions commonly filled include:** Accounting Clerk; Administrative Assistant; Assembly Worker; Biological Scientist; Bookkeeper; CADD Operator; Chemist; Computer Operator; Customer Service Representative; Electrician; Inspector/Tester/Grader; Inventory Control Specialist; Machine Operator; Material Control Specialist; Packaging/Processing Worker; Project Engineer; Proofreader; Receptionist; Research Assistant; Secretary; Software Engineer; Stock Clerk; Systems Analyst; Technician; Telemarketer; Test Operator; Typist/Word Processor. **Benefits available to temporary workers:** Life Insurance; Medical Insurance; Paid Holidays; Paid Vacation. **Corporate headquarters location:** Milwaukee WI. **Other U.S. locations:** Nationwide. **Number of placements per year:** 1000+.

MANPOWER TEMPORARY SERVICES
187 Robertson Mill Road NE, Milledgeville GA 31061-4960. 912/453-3600. **Contact:** Manager. **Description:** A temporary agency. **Specializes in the areas of:** Accounting/Auditing; Administration; Banking; Computer Hardware/Software; General Management; Manufacturing; Secretarial; Technical. **Positions commonly filled include:** Accountant/Auditor; Administrative Manager; Advertising Clerk; Bank Officer/Manager; Branch Manager; Buyer; Computer Programmer; Credit Manager; Customer Service Representative; Electrician; General Manager; Health Services Manager; Medical Records Technician; Paralegal; Restaurant/Food Service Manager; Services Sales Representative; Typist/Word Processor. **Benefits available to temporary workers:** Medical Insurance; Paid Holidays; Paid Vacation. **Corporate headquarters location:** Milwaukee WI. **Other U.S. locations:** Nationwide. **Average salary range of placements:** $20,000 - $29,999. **Number of placements per year:** 1000+.

MISSION CORPS INTERNATIONAL
HELPING HANDS TEMPORARY SERVICE
975 Memorial Drive, Atlanta GA 30316. 404/584-2304. **Contact:** Manager. **Description:** A temporary agency. Founded in 1993. **Specializes in the areas of:** Administration; Computer Science/Software; Education; Nonprofit; Retail; Sales. **Positions commonly filled include:** Accountant/Auditor; Blue-Collar Worker Supervisor; Counselor; Education Administrator; Financial Analyst; Paralegal; Public Relations Specialist; Services Sales Representative. **Other U.S. locations:** TN; TX. **Average salary range of placements:** Less than $20,000. **Number of placements per year:** 100 - 199.

NORRELL CORPORATION
3535 Piedmont Road NE, Building 14, Atlanta GA 30305. 404/262-2100. **Contact:** Marketing Department. **Description:** A temporary agency. **Specializes in the areas of:** Banking; Clerical. **Positions commonly filled include:** Accountant/Auditor; Bookkeeper; Clerk; Computer Operator; Computer Programmer; Customer Service Representative; Data Entry Clerk; Driver; Factory Worker; Legal Secretary; Medical Secretary; Receptionist; Sales Representative; Secretary; Typist/Word Processor. **Corporate headquarters location:** This Location. **Other U.S. locations:** Nationwide. **Number of placements per year:** 1000+.

NORRELL SERVICES INC.
303 Peachtree Street, Suite 1640, Atlanta GA 30308. 404/577-6683. **Contact:** Beatrice Kelly, Client Service Supervisor. **Description:** A temporary agency. **Specializes in the areas of:** Administration; Data Processing; Secretarial. **Benefits available to temporary workers:** Medical Insurance; Paid Holidays; Paid Vacation. **Corporate headquarters location:** 3535 Piedmont Road NE, Building 14, Atlanta GA 30305. 404/262-2100. **Other U.S. locations:** Nationwide. **Average salary range of placements:** Less than $20,000. **Number of placements per year:** 1000+.

OFFICE SPECIALISTS
3500 Piedmont Road, Atlanta GA 30350. 404/814-9865. **Fax:** 404/814-9866. **Contact:** Christy Huber, Staffing Manager. **Description:** A temporary agency that also provides permanent placements. Founded in 1963. Company pays fee. **Specializes in the areas of:** Accounting/Auditing; Banking; Secretarial. **Positions commonly filled include:** Accountant/Auditor; Customer Service Representative; Medical Records Technician; Typist/Word Processor. **Other U.S. locations:** Nationwide. **Average salary range of placements:** $20,000 - $29,999. **Number of placements per year:** 1000+.

OFFICE SPECIALISTS
1100 Circle 75 Parkway, Suite 1500, Atlanta GA 30339. 770/984-6760. **Fax:** 770/984-6770. **Contact:** Ginger Wallis, Director of Operations. **Description:** A temporary agency. Company pays fee. **Specializes in the areas of:** Administration; Technical. **Other U.S. locations:** Nationwide.

OLSTEN STAFFING SERVICES
2116 Henderson Mill Road, Atlanta GA 30345. 770/938-0212. **Contact:** Connie Bruner, Manager. **Description:** A temporary agency. Company pays fee. **Specializes in the areas of:** Accounting/Auditing; Administration; Finance; Health/Medical; Secretarial; Technical. **Positions commonly filled include:** Accountant/Auditor; Clerical Supervisor; Customer Service Representative; Medical Records Technician; Paralegal; Typist/Word Processor. **Corporate headquarters location:** Melville NY. **Other U.S. locations:** Nationwide. **Average salary range of placements:** $20,000 - $29,999.

OLSTEN STAFFING SERVICES
2131 Pleasant Hill Road, Suite 108, Duluth GA 30096. 770/497-0045. **Fax:** 770/476-5696. **Contact:** Gayle Duffy, Staffing Coordinator. **Description:** A temporary agency. Founded in 1950. **Specializes in the areas of:** Accounting/Auditing; Administration; Banking; Engineering; Finance; Health/Medical; Insurance; Legal; Nonprofit; Personnel/Labor Relations; Retail; Sales; Secretarial. **Positions commonly filled include:** Accountant/Auditor; Claim Representative; Customer Service Representative; Financial Analyst; Human Resources Specialist; Management Trainee; Medical Records Technician; Paralegal; Quality Control Supervisor; Software Engineer; Typist/Word Processor. **Benefits available to temporary workers:** Bonus Award/Plan; Medical Insurance. **Corporate headquarters location:** Melville NY. **Other U.S. locations:** Nationwide. **Average salary range of placements:** $20,000 - $29,999. **Number of placements per year:** 1000+.

PEACHTREE MANAGEMENT & CONSULTING
529 Delphinium Way NW, Acworth GA 30102. 770/926-0838. **Contact:** President. **Description:** A temporary agency. Founded in 1994. Company pays fee. **Specializes in the areas of:** Education; Food Industry. **Positions commonly filled include:** Teacher/Professor. **Corporate headquarters location:** This Location. **Other U.S. locations:** Washington DC. **Average salary range of placements:** Less than $20,000. **Number of placements per year:** 1 - 49.

PERSONNEL AT LAW, INC.
235 Peachtree Street NE, Suite 1707, Atlanta GA 30303. 404/222-9711. **Fax:** 404/222-9714. **Contact:** Judy Wells, President. **E-mail address:** smartpal@atlanta.com. **Description:** A temporary agency focusing on legal placements. Founded in 1978. Company pays fee. **Specializes in the areas of:** Legal; Secretarial. **Positions commonly filled include:** Attorney; Clerical Supervisor; Paralegal; Typist/Word Processor. **Benefits available to temporary workers:** Medical Insurance; Paid Vacation. **Corporate headquarters location:** Southfield MI. **Other U.S. locations:** Nationwide. **Average salary range of placements:** $20,000 - $29,999. **Number of placements per year:** 100 - 199.

PRIORITY 1 STAFFING SERVICES
5805 State Bridge Road, Suite N, Duluth GA 30136. 770/813-1877. **Fax:** 770/813-9422. **Contact:** Lisa George, Staffing Services Manager. **Description:** A temporary agency. **Specializes in the areas of:** Accounting/Auditing; Banking; Computer Science/Software; Finance; Industrial; Insurance; Legal; Personnel/Labor Relations; Sales; Secretarial. **Positions**

commonly filled include: Accountant/Auditor; Credit Manager; Customer Service Representative; Human Resources Specialist; Typist/Word Processor; Underwriter/Assistant Underwriter. **Benefits available to temporary workers:** Medical Insurance. **Corporate headquarters location:** Atlanta GA. **Other U.S. locations:** Baltimore MD. **Number of placements per year:** 1000+.

PROFESSIONAL OPTIONS
5671 Peachtree-Dunwoody Road, Suite 550, Atlanta GA 30342. 404/843-6010. **Contact:** Manager. **Description:** A temporary agency that provides medical placements. **Specializes in the areas of:** Health/Medical.

QUALITY TEMPORARY SERVICE
317 1/2 2nd Street SE, Moultrie GA 31768-4707. 912/891-3458. **Fax:** 912/890-1080. **Contact:** John E. Folds, Owner. **Description:** A temporary agency. **Specializes in the areas of:** Accounting/Auditing; Industrial; Manufacturing; Secretarial. **Positions commonly filled include:** Accountant/Auditor; Advertising Clerk; Automotive Mechanic; Blue-Collar Worker Supervisor; Brokerage Clerk; Buyer; Clerical Supervisor; Customer Service Representative; Draftsperson; Electrician; Human Service Worker; Licensed Practical Nurse; Operations/Production Manager; Purchasing Agent/Manager; Quality Control Supervisor; Registered Nurse; Typist/Word Processor. **Average salary range of placements:** Less than $20,000. **Number of placements per year:** 200 - 499.

RANDSTAD STAFFING SERVICES
420 Crosstown Drive, Peachtree City GA 30269-2915. 770/487-1446. **Toll-free phone:** 800/297-1443. **Fax:** 770/487-1398. **Recorded jobline:** 770/964-0920. **Contact:** Julie K. White, Branch Manager. **Description:** A temporary employment agency. Company pays fee. **Specializes in the areas of:** Manufacturing; Personnel/Labor Relations; Retail; Secretarial. **Positions commonly filled include:** Customer Service Representative; Services Sales Representative; Typist/Word Processor. **Benefits available to temporary workers:** 401(k); Medical Insurance; Paid Holidays; Paid Vacation. **Corporate headquarters location:** Atlanta GA. **Other U.S. locations:** AL; FL; SC; TN. **Average salary range of placements:** Less than $20,000. **Number of placements per year:** 1000+.

RANGER SERVICES
2175 Highpoint Road, Suite 103, Snellville GA 30278-3188. 770/736-5260. **Contact:** Charles Bishop, Manager. **Description:** A temporary agency. Founded in 1990. Company pays fee. **Specializes in the areas of:** Food Industry; Industrial; Personnel/Labor Relations; Publishing; Sales. **Positions commonly filled include:** Accountant/Auditor; Branch Manager; Buyer; Computer Programmer; Construction Contractor; Counselor; Credit Manager; Customer Service Representative; Dental Assistant/Dental Hygienist; General Manager; Hotel Manager; Human Resources Specialist; Insurance Agent/Broker; Typist/Word Processor. **Other U.S. locations:** FL; NC; OH. **Average salary range of placements:** Less than $20,000. **Number of placements per year:** 500 - 999.

RIGHT CHOICE STAFFING
294 South Main, Suite 100, Atlanta GA 30339. 770/664-6909. **Fax:** 770/664-7649. **Contact:** Ray D. Martin, Vice President. **E-mail address:** edmartin@rightchoicestaffing.com. **Description:** A temporary and temp-to-hire agency. Company pays fee. **Specializes in the areas of:** Restaurant. **Positions commonly filled include:** Assistant Manager; Clerical Supervisor; Management Trainee. **Average salary range of placements:** $20,000 - $29,999. **Number of placements per year:** 100 - 199.

SPECIAL COUNSEL
1201 West Peachtree Street, Suite 4830, Atlanta GA 30309. 404/872-6672. **Fax:** 404/892-3180. **Contact:** Manager. **World Wide Web address:** http://www.specialcounsel.com. **Description:** A temporary and permanent employment agency. **Specializes in the areas of:** Legal.

TRC STAFFING SERVICES
7000 Central Parkway, Suite 260, Atlanta GA 30328. 770/399-0092. **Fax:** 770/339-3008. **Contact:** Manager. **Description:** A temporary agency. Founded in 1970. Company pays fee. **Specializes in the areas of:** Administration; Banking; Engineering; Insurance; Personnel/Labor Relations; Sales; Secretarial. **Positions commonly filled include:** Administrative Manager; Advertising Clerk; Claim Representative; Clerical Supervisor; Customer Service Representative; Editor; Human Resources Specialist; Market Research Analyst; Services Sales Representative; Technical Writer/Editor; Typist/Word Processor; Underwriter/Assistant Underwriter. **Benefits available to temporary workers:** Paid Holidays; Paid Vacation. **Average salary range of placements:** $20,000 - $29,999. **Number of placements per year:** 500 - 999.

TAC STAFFING SERVICES
900 Circle 75, Suite 150, Atlanta GA 30339. 770/955-5340. **Contact:** Manager. **Description:** A temporary agency. **Specializes in the areas of:** Customer Service. **Other U.S. locations:** Nationwide.

TEMP RESOURCES
805 Peachtree Street, Suite 565, Atlanta GA 30308. 404/892-1040. **Fax:** 404/892-0038. **Contact:** Regina Dukes, Manager. **Description:** A temporary agency. Company pays fee. **Specializes in the areas of:** Administration; Personnel/Labor Relations. **Positions commonly filled include:** Accountant/Auditor; Administrative Manager; General Manager; Human Resources Specialist; Telecommunications Manager. **Average salary range of placements:** Less than $20,000. **Number of placements per year:** 50 - 99.

TEMPORARY SPECIALTIES
4920 Roswell Road NE, Suite 35, Atlanta GA 30342-2636. 404/303-8611. **Fax:** 404/303-8716. **Contact:** Stephanie Acey, Senior Recruiter. **Description:** A temporary agency. Founded in 1982. **Specializes in the areas of:** Accounting/Auditing; Insurance; Manufacturing; Personnel/Labor Relations; Publishing; Secretarial. **Positions commonly filled include:** Buyer; Clerical Supervisor; Customer Service Representative; Typist/Word Processor. **Benefits available to temporary workers:** Dental Insurance; Life Insurance; Medical Insurance; Paid Holidays; Paid Vacation. **Corporate headquarters location:** Jonesboro GA. **Number of placements per year:** 200 - 499.

TEMPWORLD STAFFING SERVICES
3490 Piedmont Road NE, Suite 422, Atlanta GA 30305-4808. 770/901-5000. **Fax:** 770/233-1468. **Contact:** Diana Haas Ray, Branch Manager. **Description:** A temporary agency that also provides some permanent placements. Company pays fee. **Specializes in the areas of:** Customer Service; Sales; Secretarial; Word Processing. **Positions commonly filled include:** Customer Service Representative; Secretary; Typist/Word Processor. **Benefits available to temporary workers:** 401(k); Scholarship Program.

TODAYS TEMPORARY
1200 Ashwood Parkway, Suite 160, Atlanta GA 30338. 770/396-9224. **Fax:** 770/396-8245. **Contact:** Manager. **Description:** A temporary agency. Company

pays fee. **Specializes in the areas of:** Accounting/Auditing; Administration; Architecture/Construction; Banking; Finance; Insurance; Personnel/Labor Relations; Sales; Secretarial. **Positions commonly filled include:** Administrative Assistant; Administrative Worker/Clerk; Advertising Clerk; Clerical Supervisor; Collector; Customer Service Representative; Data Entry Clerk; Receptionist.

TODAYS TEMPORARY
3333 Peachtree Road, Suite 130, Atlanta GA 30326. 404/237-1113. **Fax:** 404/237-0954. **Contact:** Arni Porson, Operations Manager. **Description:** A temporary agency. Founded in 1970. Company pays fee. **Specializes in the areas of:** Computer Science/Software; Insurance; Secretarial. **Positions commonly filled include:** Accountant/Auditor; Claim Representative; Clerical Supervisor; Typist/Word Processor. **Number of placements per year:** 500 - 999.

WESTERN STAFF SERVICES INC.
537 North Expressway, Griffin GA 30223. 770/229-2411. **Fax:** 770/229-2494. **Contact:** Manager. **Description:** A temporary agency that also offers some permanent placements. Founded in 1948. Company pays fee. **Specializes in the areas of:** Accounting/Auditing; Finance; Industrial; Light Industrial; Manufacturing; Personnel/Labor Relations; Sales; Secretarial. **Positions commonly filled include:** Accountant/Auditor; Branch Manager; Customer Service Representative; Draftsperson; Electrician; Management Trainee; Purchasing Agent/Manager; Quality Control Supervisor. **Benefits available to temporary workers:** 401(k); Paid Holidays; Paid Vacation. **Corporate headquarters location:** Walnut Creek CA. **Other U.S. locations:** Nationwide. **Number of placements per year:** 1000+.

WESTERN STAFF SERVICES INC.
2200 Century Parkway, Suite 3, Atlanta GA 30345. 404/888-0003. **Fax:** 404/873-5291. **Contact:** Alice Chunchick, Area Manager. **Description:** A temporary agency. Founded in 1948. Company pays fee. **Specializes in the areas of:** Accounting/Auditing; Advertising; Computer Science/Software; Industrial; Legal; Manufacturing; Publishing; Secretarial; Technical. **Benefits available to temporary workers:** 401(k); Daycare Assistance; Medical Insurance; Paid Holidays; Paid Vacation. **Corporate headquarters location:** Walnut Creek CA. **Other U.S. locations:** Nationwide. **Average salary range of placements:** $20,000 - $29,999. **Number of placements per year:** 1000+.

WESTERN TECHNICAL SERVICES
7094 Peachtree Industrial Boulevard, Suite 201, Norcross GA 30071. 770/263-6022. **Fax:** 770/449-9291. **Contact:** Senior Recruiting Manager. **Description:** A temporary agency that also offers contract technical services. Founded in 1948. **Specializes in the areas of:** Computer Science/Software; Engineering; Industrial; Manufacturing. **Positions commonly filled include:** Architect; Civil Engineer; Computer Programmer; Design Engineer; Designer; Draftsperson; Electrical/Electronics Engineer; Electrician; Environmental Engineer; Industrial Engineer; Industrial Production Manager; Mechanical Engineer; Metallurgical Engineer; MIS Specialist; Nuclear Engineer; Operations/Production Manager; Quality Control Supervisor; Software Engineer; Structural Engineer; Technical Writer/Editor; Telecommunications Manager. **Corporate headquarters location:** Walnut Creek CA. **Average salary range of placements:** $30,000 - $50,000. **Other U.S. locations:** Nationwide. **Number of placements per year:** 200 - 499.

CONTRACT SERVICES FIRMS

ADECCO TECHNICAL SERVICES
400 Perimeter Center Terrace, Suite 100 North Terrace, Atlanta GA 30346-5326. 770/938-8166. **Fax:** 770/938-5111. **Contact:** Doug Ross, Technical Sales Manager. **E-mail address:** atlanta.tech.center@adecco.com. **World Wide Web address:** http://www.adecco.com. **Description:** A contract services firm formerly known as Adia Technical Services. Founded in 1963. **Specializes in the areas of:** Administration; Architecture/Construction; Art/Design; Computer Science/Software; Engineering; Industrial; Manufacturing; Personnel/Labor Relations; Publishing; Technical. **Positions commonly filled include:** Accountant/Auditor; Biological Scientist; Biomedical Engineer; Chemical Engineer; Civil Engineer; Clinical Lab Technician; Computer Programmer; Electrical/Electronics Engineer; Electrician; Environmental Engineer; Financial Analyst; Industrial Engineer; Internet Services Manager; Management Analyst/Consultant; Mechanical Engineer; MIS Specialist; Multimedia Designer; Operations/Production Manager; Software Engineer; Structural Engineer; Technical Writer/Editor; Telecommunications Manager; Video Production Coordinator. **Benefits available to temporary workers:** 401(k); Medical Insurance; Paid Holidays. **Corporate headquarters location:** Redwood City CA. **Other U.S. locations:** Nationwide. **Average salary range of placements:** $30,000 - $50,000. **Number of placements per year:** 50 - 99.

ADMINISTRATIVE MANAGERS
105 Canton Highway, Cumming GA 30040. **Contact:** Manager. **Description:** A contract services firm. **Specializes in the areas of:** Insurance; Payroll.

ATLANTA TECHNICAL SUPPORT, INC.
One Concourse Parkway, Atlanta GA 30328. 770/390-0963. **Fax:** 770/392-1342. **Contact:** Recruiting Manager. **World Wide Web address:** http://www.atsjobs.com. **Description:** A contract and temp-to-perm placement service. Founded in 1988. Company pays fee. **Specializes in the areas of:** Engineering; Information Technology; Technical; Telecommunications. **Positions commonly filled include:** Agricultural Engineer; Aircraft Mechanic/Engine Specialist; Architect; Biochemist; Biological Scientist; Biomedical Engineer; Clinical Lab Technician; Computer Programmer; Cost Estimator; Design Engineer; Designer; Draftsperson; Electrical/Electronics Engineer; Electrician; Industrial Engineer; Industrial Production Manager; Internet Services Manager; Management Analyst/Consultant; Mechanical Engineer; Metallurgical Engineer; Mining Engineer; MIS Specialist; Multimedia Designer; Nuclear Engineer; Operations/Production Manager; Petroleum Engineer; Purchasing Agent/Manager; Quality Control Supervisor; Science Technologist; Software Engineer; Stationary Engineer; Structural Engineer; Surveyor; Technical Writer/Editor; Telecommunications Manager; Transportation/Traffic Specialist. **Benefits available to temporary workers:** Medical Insurance; Paid Holidays; Paid Vacation. **Average salary range of placements:** More than $50,000. **Number of placements per year:** 500 - 999.

COMFORCE TELECOM, INC.
1950 Spectrum Circle, Suite 400, Atlanta GA 30067. 770/857-4463. **Fax:** 770/857-4388. **Contact:** Manager. **Description:** A contract services firm. **Specializes in the areas of:** Telecommunications.

COMMS PEOPLE
3340 Peachtree Road, Suite 1410, Atlanta GA 30326. 404/812-7600. **Contact:** Office Manager. **Description:** A contract services firm. **Specializes in the areas of:** Information Technology.

COMPAID CONSULTING SERVICES
7840 Roswell Road, Suite 320, Atlanta GA 30350. 770/394-1200. **Fax:** 770/394-4933. **Contact:** Office Manager. **Description:** A contract services firm. **Specializes in the areas of:** Computer Programming; Information Systems. **Positions commonly filled include:** Computer Programmer; Systems Analyst.

COMPREHENSIVE COMPUTER CONSULTING, INC.
7000 Central Parkway, Suite 1000, Atlanta GA 30328. 770/512-0100. **Contact:** Office Manager. **Description:** A contract services firm focusing on computer consulting and technical placements. **Specializes in the areas of:** Computer Science/Software; Technical.

MA&A GROUP INC.
800 Mount Vernon Highway, Suite 250, Atlanta GA 30328. 770/671-0844. **Toll-free phone:** 888/MAA-GROUP. **Fax:** 770/395-7574. **Contact:** Craig Miller, President. **E-mail address:** cmiller@maagroup.com. **World Wide Web address:** http://www.maagroup.com. **Description:** A contract services firm. Company pays fee. **Specializes in the areas of:** Administration; Banking; Computer Science/Software; Technical. **Positions commonly filled include:** Computer Programmer; Database Manager; Information Technology Consultant; Management Consultant; MIS Specialist; Multimedia Designer; Online Content Specialist; Project Manager; Software Engineer; Systems Analyst; Systems Manager; Technical Writer/Editor; Webmaster. **Average salary range of placements:** More than $50,000.

RECRUITMENT SOLUTIONS INC.
2265 Roswell Road, Marietta GA 30062. 770/509-2224. **Contact:** Manager. **Description:** A contract services firm.

SOFTWARE TECHNICAL SERVICES INC.
3020 Holcomb Bridge Road, Norcross GA 30071-1316. 770/449-8966. **Fax:** 770/449-6214. **Contact:** Pundi Narasimhan, President. **E-mail address:** ruby@stscorp.com. **World Wide Web address:** http://www.stscorp.com. **Description:** Provides contract programming services and offshore programming services. Founded in 1983. Company pays fee. **Specializes in the areas of:** Administration; Computer Science/Software; Technical. **Positions commonly filled include:** Computer Programmer; MIS Specialist; Software Engineer; Systems Analyst; Technical Writer/Editor; Technician. **Benefits available to temporary workers:** Bonus Award/Plan; Dental Insurance; Medical Insurance; Paid Vacation; Relocation Assistance. **Corporate headquarters location:** This Location. **Other U.S. locations:** San Francisco CA; Rochester MN; Iselin NJ. **International locations:** Madras, India; Kuala Lumpur, Malaysia. **Average salary range of placements:** $30,000 - $50,000. **Number of placements per year:** 200 - 499.

TECHNICAL ASSOCIATES
P.O. Box 2048, Albany GA 31702. 912/888-6632. **Physical address:** 2423 Westgate Drive, Albany GA. **Toll-free phone:** 800/356-3240x224. **Fax:** 912/435-2826. **Contact:** Ernie Fordham, Technical Services Manager. **Description:** A technical contract services firm. Founded in 1980. **Specializes in the areas of:** Engineering; Technical. **Positions commonly filled include:** Chemical Engineer; Chemist; Civil Engineer; Computer Programmer; Construction Contractor; Database Manager; Designer; Draftsperson; Electrical/Electronics Engineer; Environmental Engineer; Industrial Engineer; Manufacturing Engineer; Mechanical Engineer; MIS Specialist; Project Manager; Sales Engineer; Software Engineer; Structural Engineer; Systems Analyst; Systems Manager; Technical Writer/Editor; Telecommunications Manager. **Benefits available to temporary workers:** 401(k); Paid Holidays; Paid Vacation. **Corporate headquarters location:** This Location. **Other area locations:** Atlanta GA; Macon GA. **Other U.S. locations:** Jackson TN; Memphis TN. **Average salary range of placements:** More than $50,000. **Number of placements per year:** 200 - 499.

H.L. YOH COMPANY
2400 Lake Park Drive, Suite 415, Smyrna GA 30080. 770/432-5200. **Contact:** Manager. **Description:** A contract services firm. **Specializes in the areas of:** Architecture/Construction; Computer Hardware/Software; Engineering; Manufacturing; MIS/EDP; Personnel/Labor Relations; Technical. **Positions commonly filled include:** Aerospace Engineer; Architect; Buyer; Chemical Engineer; Chemist; Civil Engineer; Commercial Artist; Computer Operator; Computer Programmer; Data Entry Clerk; Draftsperson; Driver; EDP Specialist; Electrical/Electronics Engineer; Human Resources Manager; Industrial Designer; Mechanical Engineer; Metallurgical Engineer; MIS Specialist; Operations/Production Manager; Purchasing Agent/Manager; Quality Control Supervisor; Reporter; Software Engineer; Systems Analyst; Technical Writer/Editor; Technician; Typist/Word Processor. **Number of placements per year:** 200 - 499.

CAREER/OUTPLACEMENT COUNSELING FIRMS

ALLEN & ASSOCIATES
100 Circle 75 Parkway, Suite 920, Atlanta GA 30339. 770/916-1999. **Toll-free phone:** 800/562-7404. **Fax:** 770/916-0755. **Contact:** Manager. **World Wide Web address:** http://www.allenandassociates.com. **Description:** Allen & Associates is a career/outplacement counseling firm. **Corporate headquarters location:** Maitland FL. **Other U.S. locations:** Nationwide.

NATIONAL RESUME SERVICE
2660 Holcomb Bridge Road, Suite 224, Alpharetta GA 30022. **Contact:** Manager. **Description:** Offers resume and outplacement services.

HAWAII

EXECUTIVE SEARCH FIRMS

DUNHILL PROFESSIONAL SEARCH OF HAWAII
1164 Bishop Street, Suite 124, Honolulu HI 96813. 808/524-2550. **Fax:** 808/533-2196. **Contact:** Nadine Stollenmaier, President. **E-mail address:** jobsrus@aloha.net. **World Wide Web address:** http://www.dunhillstaff.com. **Description:** An executive search firm. Company pays fee. **Specializes in the areas of:** Accounting/Auditing; Administration; Architecture/Construction; Banking; Computer Science/Software; Engineering; Finance; Food Industry; General Management; Industrial; Manufacturing; Sales; Technical. **Positions commonly filled include:** Accountant/Auditor; Bank Officer/Manager; Computer Operator; Computer Programmer; Data Entry Clerk; Engineer; Insurance Agent/Broker; Secretary. **Other U.S. locations:** Nationwide. **Average salary range of placements:** $30,000 - $50,000. **Number of placements per year:** 1 - 49.

ELLIS & ASSOCIATES
700 Richards Street, Suite 2503, Honolulu HI 96813. 808/526-3812. **Fax:** 808/523-9356. **Contact:** James P. Ellis, President. **E-mail address:** jellis@aloha.net. **Description:** A retained executive search firm that provides placements in a wide variety of industries. The company has experience in placing Japanese and Chinese speakers, as well as those having experience with other languages and cultures. Company pays fee. **Specializes in the areas of:** Accounting/Auditing; Administration; Architecture/Construction; Banking; Computer Science/Software; Engineering; Fashion; Finance; Food Industry; General Management; Health/Medical; Insurance; Personnel/Labor Relations; Retail; Sales; Technical; Transportation. **Positions commonly filled include:** Advertising Account Executive; Bank Officer/Manager; Chief Financial Officer; Controller; Database Manager; Design Engineer; Finance Director; General Manager; Human Resources Manager; Internet Services Manager; Management Analyst/Consultant; Marketing Manager; MIS Specialist; Operations Manager; Project Manager; Sales Executive; Sales Manager; Software Engineer; Systems Manager; Telecommunications Manager; Webmaster. **Corporate headquarters location:** This Location. **Average salary range of placements:** More than $50,000. **Number of placements per year:** 100 - 199.

LAM ASSOCIATES
444 Hobron Lane, Suite 207H, Department AM, Honolulu HI 96815. 808/947-9815. **Contact:** Pat Lam, General Manager/Owner. **Description:** An executive search firm. Company pays fee. **Specializes in the areas of:** Health/Medical. **Positions commonly filled include:** Nurse Practitioner; Pharmacist; Physician; Registered Nurse. **Average salary range of placements:** More than $50,000. **Number of placements per year:** 50 - 99.

MANAGEMENT RECRUITERS INTERNATIONAL
64-1061 Mamalahoa Highway, Suite 10, P.O. Box 2100, Kamuela HI 96743. 808/885-7503. **Contact:** Manager. **Description:** An executive search firm. **Specializes in the areas of:** Computer Science/Software. **Corporate headquarters location:** Cleveland OH. **Other U.S. locations:** Nationwide.

MANAGEMENT SEARCH & CONSULTING, INC.
1001 Bishop Street, Pacific Tower, Suite 2450, Honolulu HI 96813. 808/533-4423. **Fax:** 808/545-2435. **Contact:** Peter S. Glick, President. **E-mail address:** hdhunter@lava.net. **Description:** An executive search firm that places middle, upper-, and senior-level managers. Company pays fee. **Specializes in the areas of:** Accounting/Auditing; Finance; General Management; Health/Medical. **Positions commonly filled include:** Accountant/Auditor; Budget Analyst; Buyer; Chief Executive Officer; Chief Financial Officer; Electrical/Electronics Engineer; Finance Director; Financial Analyst; General Manager; Human Resources Manager; Marketing Manager; President; Project Manager; Systems Analyst; Systems Manager; Vice President of Finance; Vice President of Marketing; Wholesale and Retail Buyer. **Average salary range of placements:** More than $50,000. **Number of placements per year:** 1 - 49.

MARESCA AND ASSOCIATES
98-1961B Kaahumanu Street, Aiea HI 96701. 808/531-0461. **Fax:** 808/521-9993. **Contact:** Shannon Maresca, Owner/Manager. **E-mail address:** smaresca@worldnet.att.net. **Description:** An executive search firm operating on a contingency basis. **Specializes in the areas of:** Computer Science/Software; General Management; Health/Medical; Personnel/Labor Relations. **Positions commonly filled include:** Accountant/Auditor; Administrative Manager; Bank Officer/Manager; Branch Manager; Buyer; Chief Financial Officer; Civil Engineer; Computer Operator; Computer Programmer; Construction Manager; Controller; Cost Estimator; Education Administrator; Electrical/Electronics Engineer; Finance Director; Financial Analyst; General Manager; Health Services Manager; Licensed Practical Nurse; Marketing Manager; Mechanical Engineer; MIS Manager; Paralegal; Physical Therapist; Physician; Registered Nurse; Restaurant/Food Service Manager; Software Engineer; Structural Engineer; Systems Analyst; Technical Writer/Editor; Telecommunications Manager. **Corporate headquarters location:** Honolulu HI. **Average salary range of placements:** More than $50,000. **Number of placements per year:** 1 - 49.

SALES CONSULTANTS OF HONOLULU
810 Richards Street, Suite 800, Honolulu HI 96813. 808/533-3282. **Contact:** Don Bishop, Recruiter. **Description:** An executive search firm. **Specializes in the areas of:** Computer Science/Software; Publishing; Sales; Transportation. **Positions commonly filled include:** Computer Programmer; Hotel Manager; Industrial Engineer; Software Engineer. **Other U.S. locations:** Nationwide. **Average salary range of placements:** $30,000 - $50,000. **Number of placements per year:** 50 - 99.

PERMANENT EMPLOYMENT AGENCIES

EXECUTIVE SUPPORT HAWAII
210 Ward Avenue, Suite 126 Ward Plaza, Honolulu HI 96814. 808/521-5911. **Fax:** 808/536-0352. **Contact:** Manager. **Description:** A permanent employment agency specializing in hotel services, legal, computer technology, and telecommunications.

REMEDY INTELLIGENT STAFFING
98-211 Pali Momi Street, Suite 435-A, Aiea HI 96701. 808/949-3669. **Fax:** 808/949-4022. **Contact:** Janice Lyons, Staffing Coordinator. **Description:** A permanent employment agency. Founded in 1965. Company pays fee. **Positions commonly filled include:** Accountant/Auditor; Bank Officer/Manager; Branch

Manager; Brokerage Clerk; Budget Analyst; Civil Engineer; Claim Representative; Clerical Supervisor; Computer Programmer; Cost Estimator; Counselor; Design Engineer; Editor; Financial Analyst; General Manager; Health Services Manager; Human Resources Specialist; Industrial Production Manager; Management Trainee; Quality Control Supervisor; Real Estate Agent; Systems Analyst; Typist/Word Processor; Underwriter/Assistant Underwriter. **Benefits available to temporary workers:** Medical Insurance; Paid Holidays; Paid Vacation. **Other U.S. locations:** Nationwide. **Average salary range of placements:** $20,000 - $29,999. **Number of placements per year:** 1000+.

REMEDY INTELLIGENT STAFFING
1357 Kapiolani Boulevard, Suite 810, Honolulu HI 96814. **Contact:** Manager. **Description:** A permanent employment agency. Company pays fee. **Positions commonly filled include:** Accountant/Auditor; Administrative Manager; Bank Officer/Manager; Branch Manager; Brokerage Clerk; Budget Analyst; Chemical Engineer; Civil Engineer; Claim Representative; Computer Programmer; Design Engineer; Electrician; Human Resources Specialist; Typist/Word Processor. **Benefits available to temporary workers:** Medical Insurance; Paid Holidays; Paid Vacation. **Other U.S. locations:** Nationwide. **Average salary range of placements:** Less than $20,000. **Number of placements per year:** 500 - 999.

TEMPORARY EMPLOYMENT AGENCIES

ALTRES STAFFING
711 Kapiolani Boulevard, Suite 120, Honolulu HI 96813. 808/591-4940. **Fax:** 808/373-1955. **Contact:** Manager. **E-mail address:** jobs@altres.com. **Description:** A temporary agency that also provides career outplacement counseling. Company pays fee. **Specializes in the areas of:** Accounting/Auditing; Administration; Architecture/Construction; Banking; Computer Science/Software; Health/Medical; Industrial; Legal; Light Industrial; MIS/EDP; Scientific; Secretarial; Technical. **Positions commonly filled include:** Accountant; Administrative Assistant; Bookkeeper; Claim Representative; Clerk; Computer Operator; Customer Service Representative; Data Entry Clerk; Driver; Legal Secretary; Light Industrial Worker; Medical Secretary; MIS Specialist; Paralegal; Receptionist; Secretary; Stenographer; Typist/Word Processor. **Benefits available to temporary workers:** 401(k); Computer Training; Dental Insurance; Medical Insurance; Paid Vacation. **Corporate headquarters location:** This Location. **Average salary range of placements:** $20,000 - $29,999. **Number of placements per year:** 1000+.

KELLY SERVICES, INC.
1100 Ward Avenue, Suite 1020, Honolulu HI 96814. 808/536-9343. **Fax:** 808/545-1506. **Contact:** Larry Welsch, Branch Manager. **Description:** A temporary agency. Company pays fee. **Specializes in the areas of:** Industrial; Sales; Secretarial. **Positions commonly filled include:** Accountant/Auditor; Blue-Collar Worker Supervisor; Computer Programmer; Systems Analyst; Typist/Word Processor. **Benefits available to temporary workers:** Computer Training; Medical Insurance; Paid Holidays; Paid Vacation. **Average salary range of placements:** $18,000 - $30,000. **Number of placements per year:** 1000+.

OLSTEN STAFFING SERVICES
900 Fort Street Mall, Suite 1202, Honolulu HI 96813-3713. 808/523-3313. **Contact:** Signe Godfrey, President/Owner. **Description:** A temporary agency. Olsten handles placements including clerical, secretarial, word processing, and light industrial workers, as well as convention staffing, accounting clerks, computer technicians, draftspeople, and bookkeepers. The agency also offers temp-to-hire positions. Founded in 1987. **Specializes in the areas of:** Accounting/Auditing; Administration; Food Industry; Industrial; Legal; Personnel/Labor Relations; Secretarial; Technical. **Positions commonly filled include:** Accountant/Auditor; Administrative Manager; Brokerage Clerk; Clerical Supervisor; Human Resources Specialist; Services Sales Representative; Software Engineer; Typist/Word Processor. **Benefits available to temporary workers:** Medical Insurance; Paid Holidays; Paid Vacation. **Corporate headquarters location:** Melville NY. **International locations:** Worldwide. **Average salary range of placements:** $20,000 - $29,999. **Number of placements per year:** 1000+.

SELECT STAFFING SERVICES, INC.
550 Paiea Street, Suite 222, Honolulu HI 96819. 808/839-2200. **Fax:** 808/839-4844. **Contact:** President. **Description:** A temporary agency. **Specializes in the areas of:** Accounting/Auditing; Advertising; Computer Hardware/Software. **Positions commonly filled include:** Accountant/Auditor; Administrative Assistant; Bookkeeper; Clerk; Construction Trade Worker; Data Entry Clerk; Driver; Factory Worker; Legal Secretary; Light Industrial Worker; Medical Secretary; Receptionist; Secretary; Stenographer; Typist/Word Processor. **Number of placements per year:** 1000+.

CAREER/OUTPLACEMENT COUNSELING FIRMS

ALU LIKE INC.
3129 Peleke Street, Lihue HI 96766. 808/245-8545. **Contact:** Personnel. **Description:** A career/outplacement agency. Company pays fee. **Specializes in the areas of:** Nonprofit. **Positions commonly filled include:** Accountant; Bank Officer; Bookkeeper; Construction Trade Worker; Customer Service Representative; Data Entry Clerk; Factory Worker; Food and Beverage Service Worker; Hotel Manager; Legal Secretary; Light Industrial Worker; Medical Secretary; Nurse; Public Relations Specialist; Receptionist; Sales Representative; Typist/Word Processor.

THE RESUME PLACE
735 Bishop Street, Suite 238, Honolulu HI 96813. 808/528-1331. **Fax:** 808/521-9901. **Contact:** David Saurer, Manager/Owner. **Description:** A career/outplacement counseling firm and resume writing service. Founded in 1977. **Specializes in the areas of:** Banking; Computer Science/Software; General Management; Nonprofit; Retail; Sales. **Positions commonly filled include:** Buyer; Health Services Manager; Management Trainee; Property and Real Estate Manager; Systems Analyst. **Number of placements per year:** 200 - 499.

IDAHO

EXECUTIVE SEARCH FIRMS

FINNEY & ASSOCIATES
1329 Tamarack Street, Moscow ID 83843. 208/882-3500. **Contact:** Manager. **Description:** An executive search firm. **Specializes in the areas of:** Engineering.

F-O-R-T-U-N-E PERSONNEL CONSULTANTS
960 Broadway Avenue, Suite 540, Boise ID 83706. 208/343-5190. **Fax:** 208/343-6067. **Contact:** Manager. **Description:** An executive search firm. **Specializes in the areas of:** Banking; Finance; Paper. **Corporate headquarters location:** New York NY. **Other U.S. locations:** Nationwide.

HORNE/BROWN INTERNATIONAL
U.S. Bank Plaza, Suite 1200, Boise ID 83702. 208/344-9004. **Fax:** 208/344-0681. **Contact:** Mr. Gene Horne, President. **Description:** An executive search firm. Company pays fee. **Specializes in the areas of:** Accounting/Auditing; Administration; Banking; Engineering; Finance; Food Industry; General Management; Health/Medical; Insurance; Manufacturing; Personnel/Labor Relations; Sales. **Positions commonly filled include:** Accountant/Auditor; Bank Officer/Manager; Biomedical Engineer; Chemical Engineer; Civil Engineer; Electrical/Electronics Engineer; Financial Analyst; Food Scientist/Technologist; General Manager; Health Services Manager; Human Resources Manager; Industrial Engineer; Mechanical Engineer; Metallurgical Engineer; Mining Engineer; Nuclear Engineer; Structural Engineer; Underwriter/Assistant Underwriter.

MANAGEMENT RECRUITERS OF BOISE, INC.
290 Bobwhite Court, Suite 220, Boise ID 83706-3966. 208/336-6770. **Contact:** Craig Alexander, General Manager. **Description:** An executive search firm. Company pays fee. **Specializes in the areas of:** Chemical; Food Industry; Industrial Sales and Marketing; Mining. **Positions commonly filled include:** Chemical Engineer; Chemist; Civil Engineer; Electrical/Electronics Engineer; Food Scientist/Technologist; Mechanical Engineer; Metallurgical Engineer; Mining Engineer; Production Manager; Quality Assurance Engineer. **Number of placements per year:** 50 - 99.

ROBERT WILLIAM JAMES & ASSOCIATES
EXPRESS PERSONNEL
1714 G Street, Lewiston ID 83501. 208/743-6507. **Contact:** Manager. **Description:** An executive search firm. Express Personnel (also at this location) provides temporary and temp-to-hire placements.

WARD-HOFFMAN & ASSOCIATES
2020 Lakewood Drive, Suite 312, Coeur d'Alene ID 83814-2690. 208/667-6095. **Fax:** 208/765-8377. **Contact:** Al Ward, President. **Description:** An executive search firm. Company pays fee. **Specializes in the areas of:** Accounting/Auditing; Administration; Architecture/Construction; Computer Science/Software; Engineering; Food Industry; General Management; Health/Medical; MIS/EDP; Personnel/Labor Relations; Scientific; Technical. **Positions commonly filled include:** Account Manager; Chemical Engineer; Chief Financial Officer; Civil Engineer; Computer Programmer; Controller; Cost Estimator; Database Manager; Design Engineer; Environmental Engineer; Food Scientist/Technologist; General Manager; Industrial Engineer; Manufacturing Engineer; Market Research Analyst; Marketing Manager; Mechanical Engineer; Metallurgical Engineer; MIS Specialist; Physical Therapist; Physician; Project Manager; Purchasing Agent/Manager; Sales Executive; Sales Manager; Software Engineer; Telecommunications Manager; Vice President of Operations. **Average salary range of placements:** More than $50,000. **Number of placements per year:** 100 - 199.

PERMANENT EMPLOYMENT AGENCIES

IDAHO DEPARTMENT OF EMPLOYMENT JOBSERVICE
P.O. Box 1147, Lewiston ID 83501-0430. 208/799-5000. **Fax:** 208/746-5915. **Contact:** Dee Paffile, Consultant. **Description:** A permanent employment agency. **Specializes in the areas of:** General Management; Health/Medical; Insurance; Manufacturing; Retail; Sales. **Positions commonly filled include:** Claim Representative; Clerk; Computer Operator; Data Entry Clerk; Factory Worker; Legal Secretary; Light Industrial Worker; Nurse; Receptionist; Sales Representative; Secretary; Technician; Typist. **Number of placements per year:** 1000+.

INTERMOUNTAIN STAFFING RESOURCES
5400 Franklin Road, Boise ID 83705-1078. 208/345-8200. **Fax:** 208/345-8266. **Contact:** Office Manager. **Description:** Intermountain Staffing Resources is a permanent employment agency. **Specializes in the areas of:** Industrial; Personnel/Labor Relations. **Positions commonly filled include:** Blue-Collar Worker Supervisor; Construction Contractor; Customer Service Representative; Draftsperson; Electrical/Electronics Engineer; Electrician; Quality Control Supervisor. **Corporate headquarters location:** Salt Lake City UT. **Number of placements per year:** 200 - 499.

TEMPORARY EMPLOYMENT AGENCIES

WESTERN STAFF SERVICES
1111 South Orchard Street, Suite 157, Boise ID 83705. 208/345-3828. **Contact:** Davida Corn, Office Manager. **Description:** A temporary employment agency that also provides some permanent placements. **Specializes in the areas of:** Clerical; Computer Hardware/Software; Industrial.

CONTRACT SERVICES FIRMS

VOLT TECHNICAL SERVICES
8100 West Emerald Drive, Suite 120, Boise ID 83704. 208/375-9947. **Contact:** Recruiting. **Description:** A contract services firm for clerical and technical placements. **Specializes in the areas of:** Clerical; Computer Programming; Engineering.

CAREER/OUTPLACEMENT COUNSELING FIRMS

MAGIC VALLEY REHABILITATION SERVICES, INC.
484 Eastland Drive South, Twin Falls ID 83301. 208/734-4112. **Fax:** 208/734-1514. **Contact:** John Bodden, Director of Rehabilitation. **Description:** A career/outplacement counseling and vocational rehabilitation service. Founded in 1973. **Specializes in the areas of:** Education; Nonprofit. **Positions commonly filled include:** Clerical Supervisor; Counselor; General Manager; Human Resources Specialist; Human Service Worker; Operations/Production Manager; Public Relations Specialist; Typist/Word Processor. **Average salary range of placements:** Less than $20,000. **Number of placements per year:** 1 - 49.

ILLINOIS

EXECUTIVE SEARCH FIRMS

ABBOTT SMITH ASSOCIATES
2600 Lexington Street, Broadview IL 60153. 312/664-1976. **Contact:** Manager. **Description:** An executive search firm. **Specializes in the areas of:** Human Resources.

THE ABILITY GROUP
1011 East State Street, Rockford IL 61104. 815/964-0119. **Fax:** 815/964-9965. **Contact:** J. Lowell Hawkinson, Chairman. **Description:** An executive search firm. Company pays fee. **Specializes in the areas of:** Accounting/Auditing; Administration; Computer Science/Software; Engineering; Industrial; Manufacturing; Personnel/Labor Relations; Technical. **Positions commonly filled include:** Accountant/Auditor; Automotive Mechanic; Biomedical Engineer; Buyer; Chemical Engineer; Civil Engineer; Computer Programmer; Customer Service Representative; Design Engineer; Electrical/Electronics Engineer; Electrician; Environmental Engineer; Industrial Engineer; Mechanical Engineer; MIS Specialist; Software Engineer; Structural Engineer; Systems Analyst; Technical Writer/Editor. **Benefits available to temporary workers:** Medical Insurance; Paid Holidays. **Corporate headquarters location:** This Location. **Other U.S. locations:** Oregon IL; Beloit WI. **Average salary range of placements:** $30,000 - $50,000. **Number of placements per year:** 100 - 199.

B.J. ABRAMS & ASSOCIATES INC.
540 Frontage Road, Suite 3040, Northfield IL 60093. 847/446-2966. **Fax:** 847/446-2973. **Contact:** Burt Abrams, President. **Description:** An executive search firm operating on a contingency basis. Company pays fee. **Specializes in the areas of:** Accounting/Auditing; Engineering; General Management; Health/Medical; Human Resources; Manufacturing; Publishing; Sales. **Positions commonly filled include:** Account Manager; Accountant; Auditor; Buyer; Chief Financial Officer; Controller; Customer Service Representative; Financial Analyst; General Manager; Human Resources Manager; Manufacturing Engineer; Mechanical Engineer; Production Manager; Purchasing Agent/Manager; Quality Control Supervisor; Sales Manager; Technical Writer/Editor. **Average salary range of placements:** More than $50,000. **Number of placements per year:** 50 - 99.

ACCORD INC.
10301 West Roosevelt Road, Westchester IL 60154. 708/345-7900. **Contact:** Chester Dombrowski, Manager. **Description:** An executive search firm. Company pays fee. **Specializes in the areas of:** Computer Science/Software; Engineering; Manufacturing; MIS/EDP; Technical. **Positions commonly filled include:** Computer Programmer; Customer Service Representative; Draftsperson; EDP Specialist; Electrical/Electronics Engineer; General Manager; Industrial Engineer; Industrial Production Manager; Mechanical Engineer; MIS Specialist; Quality Control Supervisor; Sales Representative; Software Engineer; Technical Writer/Editor; Technician. **Number of placements per year:** 50 - 99.

ACCOUNT PROS
20 South Clark Street, Suite 820, Chicago IL 60603. 312/263-9300. **Fax:** 312/263-9103. **Contact:** Gerald Jones, Branch Manager. **Description:** An executive search firm focusing on the placement of accounting and finance professionals. Company pays fee. **Specializes in the areas of:** Accounting/Auditing; Banking; Finance. **Positions commonly filled include:** Accountant/Auditor; Budget Analyst; Credit Manager; Customer Service Representative; Financial Analyst. **Benefits available to temporary workers:** 401(k); Dental Insurance; Medical Insurance; Paid Holidays; Paid Vacation. **Corporate headquarters location:** Boston MA. **Other U.S. locations:** Los Angeles CA; Des Plaines IL; Burlington MA. **Average salary range of placements:** $30,000 - $50,000.

ACCOUNT PROS
1700 Higgins Center, Suite 420, Des Plaines IL 60018. 847/298-9400. **Contact:** Branch Manager. **Description:** An executive search firm focusing on accounting and finance placements. **Specializes in the areas of:** Accounting/Auditing; Banking; Finance; Insurance. **Positions commonly filled include:** Accountant/Auditor; Brokerage Clerk; Budget Analyst; Credit Manager; Customer Service Representative; Financial Analyst; Typist/Word Processor. **Corporate headquarters location:** Boston MA. **Other U.S. locations:** Los Angeles CA; Chicago IL; Burlington MA. **Average salary range of placements:** $20,000 - $29,999. **Number of placements per year:** 200 - 499.

ACCOUNTANTS EXECUTIVE SEARCH
ACCOUNTANTS ON CALL
200 North LaSalle, Suite 2830, Chicago IL 60601. 312/782-7711. **Fax:** 312/782-0171. **Contact:** Manager. **Description:** An executive search firm operating on a contingency basis. Accountants On Call (also at this location) is a temporary and permanent placement agency. **Specializes in the areas of:** Accounting/Auditing; Banking; Finance. **Corporate headquarters location:** Saddle Brook NJ. **Other U.S. locations:** Nationwide.

ACCOUNTANTS EXECUTIVE SEARCH
ACCOUNTANTS ON CALL
3400 Dundee Road, Suite 260, Northbrook IL 60062. 847/205-0808. **Contact:** Manager. **Description:** An executive search firm. Accountants On Call (also at this location) provides temporary placements. **Specializes in the areas of:** Accounting/Auditing; Banking; Finance. **Corporate headquarters location:** Saddle Brook NJ. **Other U.S. locations:** Nationwide.

ADAMS & ASSOCIATES INTERNATIONAL
463 West Ruffle Street, Suite D, Barrington IL 60010. 847/304-5300. **Contact:** Manager. **Description:** An executive search firm.

ADVANCED TECHNICAL SEARCH
7728 Sugarbush Lane, Willowbrook IL 60514. 708/387-7200. **Fax:** 630/789-0994. **Contact:** Manager. **Description:** An executive search firm. **Specializes in the areas of:** Engineering; Manufacturing; Technical.

AGRA PLACEMENTS LTD.
2200 North Kickapoo, Suite 2, Lincoln IL 62656. 217/735-4373. **Fax:** 217/732-2041. **Contact:** Perry M. Schneider, President. **E-mail address:** agrail@abelink.com. **World Wide Web address:** http://www.agraplacements.com. **Description:** An executive search firm operating on both retainer and contingency bases. **Specializes in the areas of:** Agri-Business; Agriculture; Food Industry. **Corporate headquarters location:** West Des Moines IA. **Other U.S. locations:** Lincoln IL; Peru IN; Sioux Falls SD.

AMERICAN ENGINEERING COMPANY
188 Industrial Drive, Suite 124, Elmhurst IL 60126. 630/941-7750. **Contact:** Anthony Davero, President. **Description:** A retainer and contingency search firm. Company pays fee. **Specializes in the areas of:** Accounting/Auditing; Computer Science/Software;

Engineering; Finance; Manufacturing; Sales; Secretarial; Technical. **Positions commonly filled include:** Accountant/Auditor; Administrative Manager; Attorney; Budget Analyst; Buyer; Clerical Supervisor; Computer Programmer; Cost Estimator; Counselor; Credit Manager; Customer Service Representative; Design Engineer; Designer; Draftsperson; Electrical/Electronics Engineer; Financial Analyst; Industrial Engineer; Industrial Production Manager; Insurance Agent/Broker; Internet Services Manager; Management Analyst/Consultant; Manufacturer's/ Wholesaler's Sales Rep.; Market Research Analyst; Mechanical Engineer; MIS Specialist; Operations/ Production Manager; Paralegal; Quality Control Supervisor; Software Engineer; Technical Writer/Editor; Telecommunications Manager; Typist/ Word Processor; Underwriter/Assistant Underwriter. **Average salary range of placements:** More than $50,000. **Number of placements per year:** 200 - 499.

AMERICAN MEDICAL SEARCH
555 West Madison Street, Suite 371, Chicago IL 60661. 312/559-7878. **Contact:** Manager. **Description:** An executive search firm that focuses on the placement of physical therapists, occupational therapists, and speech pathologists.

AMERICAN TECHNICAL SEARCH, INC.
2215 York Road, Suite 204, Oak Brook IL 60523. 630/990-1001. **Toll-free phone:** 800/899-7467. **Fax:** 630/990-1009. **Contact:** Raymond Landers, President. **Description:** A full-service technical search firm. Company pays fee. **Specializes in the areas of:** Engineering; Food Industry; General Management; Industrial; Manufacturing; Technical. **Positions commonly filled include:** Aerospace Engineer; Agricultural Engineer; Draftsperson; Electrical/ Electronics Engineer; Electrician; General Manager; Industrial Engineer; Industrial Production Manager; Mechanical Engineer; Metallurgical Engineer; Operations/Production Manager; Software Engineer; Technical Writer/Editor. **Average salary range of placements:** More than $50,000. **Number of placements per year:** 50 - 99.

ARMSTRONG-HAMILTON ASSOCIATES
203 North LaSalle Street, Suite 2100, Chicago IL 60601. 312/558-1461. **Fax:** 312/444-9463. **Contact:** Glenda Peters, President. **E-mail address:** ahapeters@ aol.com. **Description:** An executive search firm. Company pays fee. **Specializes in the areas of:** Accounting/Auditing; Banking; Finance; General Management; Logistics; Office Support; Personnel/Labor Relations; Sales. **Positions commonly filled include:** Account Manager; Accountant; Administrative Assistant; Customer Service Representative; Financial Analyst; Financial Manager; Human Resources Manager; Marketing Specialist; Office Manager; Quality Control Supervisor; Sales Manager; Systems Analyst; Systems Manager; Technical Writer/Editor. **Number of placements per year:** 50 - 99.

B.D.G. SOFTWARE NETWORK
1785 Woodhaven Drive, Crystal Lake IL 60014-1941. 815/477-2334. **Fax:** 815/477-2265. **Contact:** Barry D. Gruner, President. **Description:** An executive search firm operating on both retainer and contingency bases. The firm focuses on the placement of MIS and technical support professionals. Company pays fee. **Specializes in the areas of:** Computer Science/Software. **Positions commonly filled include:** Computer Programmer; Management Analyst/ Consultant; Market Research Analyst; MIS Specialist; Software Engineer; Systems Analyst; Telecommunications Manager. **Average salary range of placements:** More than $50,000. **Number of placements per year:** 1 - 49.

BANKERS GROUP
10 South Riverside Plaza, Chicago IL 60606. 312/930-9456. **Contact:** Manager. **Description:** An executive search firm. **Specializes in the areas of:** Banking; Finance; Insurance.

BARCLAY CONSULTANTS, INC.
155 North Michigan Avenue, 6th Floor, Chicago IL 60601. 312/856-1545. **Contact:** Ms. Daryl Homer, President. **Description:** An executive search firm offering professional, confidential attorney placement services. Company pays fee. **Specializes in the areas of:** Legal. **Positions commonly filled include:** Attorney; Paralegal. **Average salary range of placements:** More than $50,000. **Number of placements per year:** 1 - 49.

BARRETT PARTNERS
100 North LaSalle Street, Suite 1420, Chicago IL 60602. 312/443-8877. **Fax:** 312/443-8866. **Contact:** Joseph Thielman, CPC, President. **World Wide Web address:** http://www.barrettpartners.com. **Description:** An executive search firm. Company pays fee. **Specializes in the areas of:** Accounting/Auditing; Banking; Engineering; Finance. **Positions commonly filled include:** Accountant/Auditor; Bank Officer/Manager; Biomedical Engineer; Budget Analyst; Chemical Engineer; Civil Engineer; Controller; Credit Manager; Electrical/Electronics Engineer; Financial Analyst; Industrial Engineer; Mechanical Engineer; Metallurgical Engineer; Mining Engineer; Software Engineer; Stationary Engineer; Structural Engineer. **Number of placements per year:** 50 - 99.

BETA TECHNOLOGIES
216 South Jefferson Street, Chicago IL 60661. 312/627-1200. **Contact:** Manager. **Description:** An executive search firm. **Specializes in the areas of:** Information Technology.

BEVELLE & ASSOCIATES, INC.
180 North LaSalle, Suite 2010, Chicago IL 60601. 312/807-3852. **Fax:** 312/807-3840. **Contact:** Sadie Bevelle, President. **Description:** An executive search firm. Company pays fee. **Specializes in the areas of:** Accounting/Auditing; Banking; Engineering; General Management; Legal; Personnel/Labor Relations; Secretarial; Transportation. **Positions commonly filled include:** Accountant/Auditor; Administrative Manager; Advertising Clerk; Attorney; Bank Officer/Manager; Blue-Collar Worker Supervisor; Branch Manager; Brokerage Clerk; Civil Engineer; Clerical Supervisor; Computer Programmer; Customer Service Representative; Electrical/Electronics Engineer; General Manager; Human Resources Manager; Mechanical Engineer; Paralegal; Purchasing Agent/Manager; Quality Control Supervisor; Travel Agent; Typist/Word Processor. **Number of placements per year:** 100 - 199.

BICKHAUS & ASSOCIATES
P.O. Box 5083, Bloomington IL 61702. 309/454-2323. **Contact:** Manager. **Description:** An executive search firm that places personnel in a variety of industries.

WILLIAM J. BLENDER & ASSOCIATES
715 Sunset Drive, East Peoria IL 61611. 312/642-7400. **Contact:** William J. Blender. **Description:** An executive search firm. **Specializes in the areas of:** Computer Hardware/Software; Information Technology.

BLOOM, GROSS & ASSOCIATES, INC.
625 North Michigan Avenue, Suite 500, Chicago IL 60611. 312/751-3490. **Fax:** 312/915-0621. **Contact:** Karen Bloom, Principal. **E-mail address:** bloomgross@ aol.com. **Description:** An executive search and

management consulting organization focusing on the recruitment of marketing and communications professionals nationwide. Company pays fee. **Specializes in the areas of:** Art/Design; Market Research; Marketing; Public Relations; Sales Promotion. **Average salary range of placements:** More than $50,000. **Number of placements per year:** 1 - 49.

BONNER & STRICKLIN & ASSOCIATES
8 South Michigan Avenue, Suite 3800, Chicago IL 60602. 312/629-9090. **Contact:** Manager. **Description:** An executive search firm. **Specializes in the areas of:** Telecommunications.

BOULEWARE & ASSOCIATES INC.
175 West Jackson, Suite 1841, Chicago IL 60604. 312/322-0088. **Contact:** Manager. **Description:** An executive search firm that places personnel in a variety of industries.

BRATLAND & ASSOCIATES
5424 Brittany Drive, McHenry IL 60050. 815/344-4335. **Contact:** Manager. **Description:** An executive search firm. **Specializes in the areas of:** Telecommunications.

BRITANNIA
160 East Chicago Street, Elgin IL 60120. 847/697-4600. **Fax:** 847/697-4608. **Contact:** Ellen Gann, Division Coordinator. **Description:** An executive search firm operating on a contingency basis. Company pays fee. **Specializes in the areas of:** Computer Science/Software; Engineering; Industrial; Manufacturing; Sales; Secretarial; Technical. **Positions commonly filled include:** Architect; Biological Scientist; Civil Engineer; Computer Programmer; Customer Service Representative; Design Engineer; Draftsperson; Electrical/Electronics Engineer; Industrial Engineer; Industrial Production Manager; Mechanical Engineer; Operations/Production Manager; Purchasing Agent/Manager; Quality Control Supervisor; Software Engineer; Systems Analyst; Technical Writer/Editor; Telecommunications Manager. **Average salary range of placements:** $30,000 - $50,000. **Number of placements per year:** 50 - 99.

BROOKE CHASE ASSOCIATES, INC.
505 North Lake Shore Drive, Suite 5507, Chicago IL 60611. 312/744-0033. **Fax:** 312/822-0475. **Contact:** Joseph McElmeel, President. **Description:** An executive search firm. Company pays fee. **Specializes in the areas of:** Sales. **Number of placements per year:** 50 - 99.

BURLING GROUP LTD.
333 West Wacker Drive, Suite 2020, Chicago IL 60606-1218. 312/346-0888. **Contact:** Ron Deitch, President. **E-mail address:** tburlinggp@aol.com. **Description:** A retained search firm serving the metropolitan Chicago area. Company pays fee. **Specializes in the areas of:** Accounting/Auditing; Architecture/Construction; Finance; Food Industry; General Management; Health/Medical; Industrial; Insurance; Manufacturing; Personnel/Labor Relations; Publishing; Technical. **Positions commonly filled include:** Accountant/Auditor; Administrative Manager; Branch Manager; Customer Service Representative; Financial Analyst; Industrial Production Manager; Management Analyst/Consultant; Operations/Production Manager; Quality Control Supervisor; Strategic Relations Manager. **Average salary range of placements:** More than $50,000. **Number of placements per year:** 1 - 49.

BURTON ENTERPRISES
3917 East Lincolnway, Sterling IL 61081. 815/626-8168. **Fax:** 815/625-6606. **Contact:** Catherine Sheets, Corporate Manager. **Description:** An executive search firm. **Positions commonly filled include:** Accountant/Auditor; Advertising Clerk; Automotive Mechanic; Bank Officer/Manager; Blue-Collar Worker Supervisor; Branch Manager; Buyer; Clerical Supervisor; Clinical Lab Technician; Computer Programmer; Counselor; Customer Service Representative; General Manager; Health Services Manager; Human Resources Manager; Human Service Worker; Management Trainee; Operations/Production Manager; Public Relations Specialist; Registered Nurse; Systems Analyst. **Benefits available to temporary workers:** Medical Insurance; Paid Vacation. **Corporate headquarters location:** This Location. **Other area locations:** Dixon IL; Oregon IL; Rochelle IL; Sycamore IL. **Other U.S. locations:** Clinton IA.

BURTON PLACEMENT SERVICES
122 May Mart Drive, Rochelle IL 61068. 815/562-5627. **Contact:** Manager. **Description:** An executive search firm. **Corporate headquarters location:** Sterling IL. **Other area locations:** Dixon IL; Oregon IL; Sycamore IL. **Other U.S. locations:** Clinton IA.

BURTON PLACEMENT SERVICES
630 Plaza Drive, Suite 7, Sycamore IL 60178. 815/899-5627. **Contact:** Manager. **Description:** An executive search firm. **Specializes in the areas of:** Engineering; Technical. **Corporate headquarters location:** Sterling IL. **Other area locations:** Dixon IL; Oregon IL; Rochelle IL. **Other U.S. locations:** Clinton IA.

BUSINESS SYSTEMS OF AMERICA, INC.
150 North Wacker Drive, Suite 2970, Chicago IL 60606. 312/849-9222. **Fax:** 312/849-9260. **Contact:** Lou Costabile, Recruiter. **World Wide Web address:** http://www.bussysam.com. **Description:** An executive search firm providing consultants in the areas of LAN and PC technical support. The firm also provides temporary services. Company pays fee. **Specializes in the areas of:** Computer Science/Software. **Positions commonly filled include:** LAN/WAN Designer/Developer; Software Engineer; Systems Analyst; Technical Writer/Editor. **Average salary range of placements:** $30,000 - $50,000. **Number of placements per year:** 50 - 99.

CES, INC.
112 South Grant Street, Hinsdale IL 60521. 630/654-2596. **Fax:** 630/654-2713. **Contact:** James F. Baker, Ph.D., President. **Description:** An executive search firm operating on a retainer basis. CES, Inc. also offers career planning services, training programs, and seminars. Founded in 1973. Company pays fee. **Specializes in the areas of:** Administration; Computer Science/Software; Education; Health/Medical. **Positions commonly filled include:** Biomedical Engineer; Chemical Engineer; Computer Programmer; Education Administrator; Health Services Manager; MIS Specialist; Nuclear Engineer; Software Engineer. **Average salary range of placements:** $30,000 - $50,000. **Number of placements per year:** 1 - 49.

CFR EXECUTIVE SEARCH, INC.
175 West Jackson, Suite A1918, Chicago IL 60604. 312/435-0990. **Fax:** 312/435-1333. **Contact:** Joe Sexton, Vice President. **E-mail address:** cfrexecsearch@msn.com. **Description:** An executive search firm. **Specializes in the areas of:** Accounting/Auditing; Finance. **Positions commonly filled include:** Accountant/Auditor; Budget Analyst; Credit Manager. **Average salary range of placements:** More than $50,000.

C.R.T., INC.
218 South Main Street, Wauconda IL 60084. 847/816-0610. **Fax:** 847/487-0195. **Contact:** William

Mellor, Executive Recruiter. **Description:** An executive search firm. Company pays fee. **Specializes in the areas of:** Computer Science/Software. **Positions commonly filled include:** Computer Programmer; Operations/Production Manager; Software Engineer; Systems Analyst; Technical Writer/Editor. **Number of placements per year:** 1 - 49.

CALLAN & ASSOCIATES
2021 Spring Road, Suite 175, Oak Brook IL 60523. 630/574-9300. **Contact:** Manager. **Description:** A retained executive search firm.

CAPITAL SERVICES GROUP
10 South Riverside Plaza, Chicago IL 60606. 312/930-1106. **Contact:** Manager. **Description:** An executive search firm. **Specializes in the areas of:** Finance; Insurance.

CAPRIO & ASSOCIATES INC.
721 East Madison Avenue, Suite 100, Villa Park IL 60181. 630/832-8825. **Fax:** 630/832-8925. **Contact:** Jerry A. Caprio, President. **Description:** An executive search firm operating on a retainer basis. Caprio & Associates focuses on recruiting senior-level management for the printing, publishing, packaging, and converting industries. Founded in 1975. Company pays fee. **Specializes in the areas of:** Advertising; Packaging; Publishing. **Average salary range of placements:** More than $50,000. **Number of placements per year:** 1 - 49.

NEAL CARDEN ASSOCIATES INC.
620 West Roosevelt Road, Wheaton IL 60187. 630/665-3932. **Contact:** Manager. **Description:** An executive search firm.

CAREER CONSULTANTS
1609 East Golf Avenue, Mahomet IL 61853. 217/586-7020. **Contact:** Kari Sampson, Owner. **Description:** An executive search firm. Company pays fee. **Specializes in the areas of:** Sales. **Number of placements per year:** 1 - 49.

CAREERLINK USA, INC.
4915 East State Street, Rockford IL 61108. 815/227-LINK. **Fax:** 815/227-5482. **Contact:** Ms. Mickey Tyler, President. **E-mail address:** mickey@misha.net. **World Wide Web address:** http://www.career-link.com. **Description:** An executive search firm that also provides human resource consulting and a confidential resume service. Company pays fee. **Positions commonly filled include:** Administrative Manager; Aerospace Engineer; Attorney; Automotive Mechanic; Bank Officer/Manager; Blue-Collar Worker Supervisor; Branch Manager; Civil Engineer; Claim Representative; Computer Programmer; Credit Manager; Customer Service Representative; Design Engineer; Draftsperson; Editor; Electrical/Electronics Engineer; Electrician; Health Services Worker; Industrial Engineer; Insurance Agent/Broker; Licensed Practical Nurse; Management Trainee; Mechanical Engineer; Medical Records Technician; Operations/Production Manager; Paralegal; Quality Control Supervisor; Registered Nurse; Services Sales Representative; Systems Analyst; Technical Writer/Editor; Telecommunications Manager; Typist/Word Processor. **Average salary range of placements:** $30,000 - $50,000. **Number of placements per year:** 50 - 99.

CARLYLE GROUP LTD.
625 North Michigan Avenue, Suite 2100, Chicago IL 60611. 312/587-3030. **Contact:** Office Manager. **Description:** An executive search firm.

CARPENTER ASSOCIATES INC.
20 South Clark Street, Suite 2210, Chicago IL 60603. 312/337-1455. **Contact:** Manager. **Description:** An executive search firm. **Specializes in the areas of:** Direct Marketing.

CARRINGTON & CARRINGTON LTD.
39 South La Salle Street, Chicago IL 60603. 312/606-0015. **Contact:** Manager. **Description:** An executive search firm that places personnel in a variety of industries.

CARTER ASSOCIATES
P.O. Box 310, Matteson IL 60443. 708/503-5020. **Fax:** 708/503-5024. **Contact:** Chuck Carter, President. **Description:** An executive search firm. Company pays fee. **Specializes in the areas of:** Architecture/Construction; Engineering. **Positions commonly filled include:** Architect; Civil Engineer; Construction Contractor; Electrical/Electronics Engineer; Emergency Medical Technician; Landscape Architect; Mechanical Engineer; Mining Engineer; Surveyor. **Average salary range of placements:** More than $50,000. **Number of placements per year:** 50 - 99.

CAST METALS PERSONNEL INC.
512 West Burlington Avenue, La Grange IL 60525. 708/354-0085. **Fax:** 708/354-2490. **Contact:** Chuck Lundeen, President. **Description:** An executive search firm. Company pays fee. **Specializes in the areas of:** Engineering; General Management; Manufacturing. **Positions commonly filled include:** Blue-Collar Worker Supervisor; Electrical/Electronics Engineer; Environmental Engineer; General Manager; Industrial Engineer; Industrial Production Manager; Mechanical Engineer; Metallurgical Engineer; Operations/Production Manager; Quality Control Supervisor. **Average salary range of placements:** $30,000 - $50,000. **Number of placements per year:** 1 - 49.

CEMCO SYSTEMS
2015 Spring Road, Suite 250, Oak Brook IL 60523. 630/573-5050. **Fax:** 630/573-5060. **Contact:** David Gordon, General Manager. **E-mail address:** drgordon@cemcosystems.com. **World Wide Web address:** http://www.cemcosystems.com. **Description:** An executive search firm operating on a contingency basis. **Specializes in the areas of:** Computer Science/Software. **Positions commonly filled include:** Computer Programmer; Database Manager; Information Systems Consultant; Management Analyst/Consultant; MIS Specialist; Software Engineer; Systems Analyst; Systems Manager; Webmaster. **Average salary range of placements:** More than $50,000. **Number of placements per year:** 200 - 499.

CHATTERTON & ASSOCIATES
135 South Wheeling Road, Wheeling IL 60090. 847/537-3830. **Contact:** Manager. **Description:** An executive search firm. **Specializes in the areas of:** Health/Medical.

CHICAGO FINANCIAL SEARCH
125 South Wacker Drive, Suite 300, Chicago IL 60606. 312/207-0400. **Contact:** Mike Kelly, Manager. **Description:** An executive search firm. Company pays fee. **Specializes in the areas of:** Accounting/Auditing; Banking; Brokerage; Computer Science/Software; Finance. **Positions commonly filled include:** Accountant/Auditor; Computer Operator; Computer Programmer; MIS Specialist. **Number of placements per year:** 100 - 199.

CHICAGO LEGAL SEARCH, LTD.
33 North Dearborn Street, Suite 2302, Chicago IL 60602. 312/251-2580. **Fax:** 312/251-0223. **Contact:** Gary D'Alessio, Esq., President. **E-mail address:** chgoleg@interaccess.com. **World Wide Web address:** http://www.chicagolawjobs.com. **Description:** An

executive search firm operating on a retainer basis that places attorneys with law firms and corporations. Company pays fee. **Specializes in the areas of:** Legal. **Positions commonly filled include:** Attorney. **Average salary range of placements:** More than $50,000. **Number of placements per year:** 50 - 99.

CLAREY & ANDREWS INC.
1200 Shermer Road, Suite 108, Northbrook IL 60062. 847/498-2870. **Contact:** Manager. **Description:** A generalist executive search firm.

D. CLESEN COMPANY
9239 Nagle, Morton Grove IL 60053. 847/965-1211. **Fax:** 312/644-0674. **Contact:** Donna M. Clesen, President. **Description:** An executive search firm operating on a contingency basis. Company pays fee. **Specializes in the areas of:** Accounting/Auditing; Finance. **Positions commonly filled include:** Accountant/Auditor; Computer Programmer; Controller; Financial Analyst; Human Resources Manager; Systems Analyst. **Average salary range of placements:** More than $50,000. **Number of placements per year:** 1 - 49.

COGAN & ASSOCIATES
7004 North California Street, Chicago IL 60645. 773/761-1100. **Contact:** Manager. **Description:** An executive search firm. **Specializes in the areas of:** Banking; Finance; Insurance.

COMPUPRO
1117 South Milwaukee Avenue, Suite B9, Libertyville IL 60048. 847/549-8603. **Fax:** 847/549-7429. **Contact:** Doug Baniqued, Human Resources. **Description:** An executive search firm. Company pays fee. **Specializes in the areas of:** Administration; Computer Science/Software. **Positions commonly filled include:** Computer Programmer; Financial Analyst; Management Analyst/Consultant; Software Engineer; Systems Analyst; Technical Writer/Editor. **Number of placements per year:** 1 - 49.

COMPUTER FUTURES EXCHANGE, INC.
1111 Westgate, Oak Park IL 60301. 708/445-8000. **Fax:** 708/445-1498. **Contact:** Corey D. Gimbel, President. **Description:** An executive search firm. Company pays fee. **Specializes in the areas of:** Administration; Banking; Computer Science/Software; Economics; Finance. **Positions commonly filled include:** Computer Programmer; Economist; Mathematician; Securities Sales Representative; Software Engineer; Systems Analyst. **Other area locations:** Chicago IL. **Number of placements per year:** 50 - 99.

COMPUTER FUTURES EXCHANGE, INC.
818 West Daiken, Suite 3, Chicago IL 60601. 773/528-6900. **Contact:** Manager. **Description:** An executive search firm. **Specializes in the areas of:** Computer Science/Software. **Other area locations:** Oak Brook IL.

COMPUTER SEARCH GROUP
20 North Wacker Drive, Suite 2200, Chicago IL 60606. 312/269-9950. **Contact:** Manager. **Description:** An executive search firm. **Specializes in the areas of:** Computer Science/Software; Information Technology.

CONSULTANTS TO EXECUTIVE MANAGEMENT COMPANY LTD.
20 South Clark Street, Suite 610, Chicago IL 60603. 312/855-1500. **Fax:** 312/855-1510. **Contact:** Manager. **Description:** An executive search firm. Company pays fee. **Specializes in the areas of:** Accounting/Auditing; Banking; Finance; Health/Medical; Real Estate. **Positions commonly filled include:** Accountant/Auditor; Actuary; Financial Analyst; Health Services Manager; Property and Real Estate Manager; Registered Nurse; Respiratory Therapist; Speech-Language Pathologist. **Number of placements per year:** 50 - 99.

CONTEMPORARY SERVICES
1701 East Woodfield Road, Suite 1030, Schaumburg IL 60173-5127. 847/619-4000. **Toll-free phone:** 800/252-2190. **Fax:** 847/619-1076. **Contact:** John Westermeier, General Manager. **E-mail address:** csi-chicago@msm.com. **Description:** An executive search firm that focuses on the banking and mortgage, real estate, and finance industries. Company pays fee. **Specializes in the areas of:** Banking; Finance; Mortgage; Real Estate. **Positions commonly filled include:** Bank Officer/Manager; Branch Manager; Credit Manager; Customer Service Representative; Financial Analyst; Property and Real Estate Manager; Quality Control Supervisor; Securities Sales Representative; Underwriter/Assistant Underwriter. **Benefits available to temporary workers:** Paid Holidays; Paid Vacation. **Corporate headquarters location:** This Location. **Other area locations:** Galena IL. **Other U.S. locations:** Indianapolis IN; Troy MI. **Average salary range of placements:** $30,000 - $50,000. **Number of placements per year:** 200 - 499.

CONTINENTAL SYSTEMS ASSOCIATES, INC.
P.O. Box 931, Arlington Heights IL 60006. 847/228-6680. **Fax:** 847/640-6967. **Contact:** David F. Hetzel, President. **Description:** An executive search firm. Company pays fee. **Specializes in the areas of:** MIS/EDP. **Positions commonly filled include:** Manager of Information Systems; MIS Manager; Systems Analyst. **Number of placements per year:** 1 - 49.

CONWAY & ASSOCIATES
1007 Church Street, Evanston IL 60201. 847/866-6832. **Contact:** Manager. **Description:** A generalist executive search firm.

COOK ASSOCIATES, INC.
212 West Kinzie Street, Chicago IL 60610. 312/329-0900. **Fax:** 312/329-1528. **Contact:** Arnie Kins, President. **E-mail address:** akins@cookassociates.com. **Description:** An executive search firm. The firm recruits nationally and internationally for the equipment, food processing, graphic arts, chemical process, metalcasting, retailing, medical products, health care services, vehicle manufacturing, consumer products, packaging, and paper/pulp industries. Company pays fee. **Specializes in the areas of:** Architecture/Construction; Banking; Food Industry; General Management; Industrial; Insurance; Legal; Manufacturing; Publishing; Retail. **Positions commonly filled include:** Executive Assistant; General Manager. **Average salary range of placements:** More than $50,000. **Number of placements per year:** 200 - 499.

CORPORATE CONSULTANTS
480 Central Avenue, Northfield IL 60093-3016. 847/446-5627. **Fax:** 847/446-3536. **Contact:** Allen Arends, President. **Description:** An executive search firm focusing on data/telecommunications and computer-related industries. Company pays fee. **Specializes in the areas of:** Computer Science/Software; Sales. **Positions commonly filled include:** Computer Programmer; Customer Service Representative; Manufacturer's/Wholesaler's Sales Rep.; Market Research Analyst; MIS Specialist; Multimedia Designer; Services Sales Representative; Software Engineer; Strategic Relations Manager; Systems Analyst; Technical Writer/Editor; Telecommunications Manager. **Average salary range of placements:** More than $50,000. **Number of placements per year:** 1 - 49.

CORPORATE ENVIRONMENT, LTD.
P.O. Box 798, Crystal Lake IL 60039-0798. 815/455-6070. **Fax:** 815/455-0124. **Contact:** Thomas P. McDermott, President. **Description:** An executive search firm. **Specializes in the areas of:** Architecture/Construction; Chemical; Engineering; Environmental; Food Industry; General Management; Industrial; Manufacturing; Operations Management; Pharmaceutical; Sales; Technical. **Positions commonly filled include:** Chemical Engineer; Environmental Engineer; Management. **Number of placements per year:** 1 - 49.

CORPORATE SEARCH GROUP
2711 West 183rd Street, Homewood IL 60430. 708/957-4520. **Contact:** Manager. **Description:** An executive search firm that provides placements in the medical diagnostics industry.

CREDENTIA INC.
980 North Michigan Avenue, Suite 1400, Chicago IL 60611. 312/649-0522. **Contact:** Manager. **Description:** An executive search firm that places attorneys. **Specializes in the areas of:** Legal.

CROSLY & ASSOCIATES
707 Skokie Boulevard, Suite 500, Northbrook IL 60062. 847/564-3800. **Contact:** Manager. **Description:** Crosly & Associates is an executive search firm.

CUMBERLAND GROUP
608 South Washington Street, Suite 101, Naperville IL 60540-6663. 630/416-9494. **Fax:** 630/416-3250. **Contact:** Jerry Vogus, Senior Partner. **Description:** An executive search firm. Company pays fee. **Specializes in the areas of:** Engineering; Industrial; Sales. **Positions commonly filled include:** Mechanical Engineer; Metallurgical Engineer; Sales Manager; Sales Representative. **Average salary range of placements:** More than $50,000. **Number of placements per year:** 1 - 49.

DRC & ASSOCIATES
6900 Main Street, Suite 52, Downers Grove IL 60516. 630/810-1411. **Contact:** Manager. **Description:** An executive search firm. **Specializes in the areas of:** Data Processing.

DATA CAREER CENTER, INC.
225 North Michigan Avenue, Suite 930, Chicago IL 60601. 312/565-1060. **Fax:** 312/565-0246. **Contact:** Larry Chaplik, President. **Description:** An executive search firm. Company pays fee. **Specializes in the areas of:** Data Processing; Telecommunications. **Positions commonly filled include:** Administrator; Computer Programmer; Database Manager; LAN/WAN Designer/Developer; Management Analyst/Consultant; Software Engineer; Systems Analyst; Voice/Data Engineer. **Number of placements per year:** 1 - 49.

DATA INTERACTION
1647 West Huron Street, Chicago IL 60622. 312/733-2005. **Contact:** Manager. **Description:** An executive search firm. **Specializes in the areas of:** Computer Science/Software; Information Technology.

DATAQUEST INC.
7105 Virginia Road, Suite 2B, Crystal Lake IL 60014-7985. 815/356-7500. **Fax:** 815/477-2359. **Contact:** Tim Ryan, Senior Recruiter. **E-mail address:** dtaqst@aol.com. **Description:** An executive search firm operating on a contingency basis. Company pays fee. **Specializes in the areas of:** Computer Science/Software. **Positions commonly filled include:** Computer Programmer; Software Engineer. **Average salary range of placements:** $30,000 - $50,000. **Number of placements per year:** 50 - 99.

T.A. DAVIS & ASSOCIATES, INC.
604 Green Bay Road, Kenilworth IL 60043. 847/256-8900. **Fax:** 847/256-8955. **Contact:** Thomas G. Davis, President. **E-mail address:** tadavisinc@aol.com. **Description:** An executive search firm operating on both retained and contingency bases. **Specializes in the areas of:** Hotel/Restaurant. **Average salary range of placements:** More than $50,000. **Number of placements per year:** 1 - 49.

NED DICKEY & ASSOCIATES, INC.
DICKEY STAFFING SOLUTIONS
P.O. Box 15068, Loves Park IL 61132. 815/636-4480. **Fax:** 815/636-4486. **Contact:** Kurt Dickey, President. **Description:** An executive search firm that focuses on technical and professional placements. Dickey Staffing Solutions provides office support and industrial positions in the Rockford area and surrounding communities. Company pays fee. **Specializes in the areas of:** Engineering; Manufacturing; Personnel/Labor Relations. **Positions commonly filled include:** Accountant/Auditor; Advertising Clerk; Architect; Bank Officer/Manager; Branch Manager; Buyer; Chemical Engineer; Chemist; Civil Engineer; Clerical Supervisor; Computer Programmer; Customer Service Representative; Design Engineer; Designer; Electrical/Electronics Engineer; Electrician; Environmental Engineer; Human Resources Manager; Industrial Engineer; Industrial Production Manager; Management Analyst/Consultant; Mechanical Engineer; Medical Records Technician; Paralegal; Quality Control Supervisor; Software Engineer; Strategic Relations Manager; Structural Engineer; Technical Writer/Editor; Typist/Word Processor. **Benefits available to temporary workers:** Credit Union; Paid Holidays; Paid Vacation.

DIECKMANN & ASSOCIATES
2 Prudential Plaza, Suite 5555, 180 Stetson Avenue, Chicago IL 60601. 312/819-5900. **Contact:** Ralph Dieckmann, Owner. **Description:** A generalist executive search firm.

DIENER & ASSOCIATES
4146 Miller Drive, Suite D, Glenview IL 60025-1026. 847/564-3160. **Fax:** 847/564-3818. **Contact:** Joel Diener, President. **Description:** A retainer and contingency search firm. Company pays fee. **Specializes in the areas of:** Accounting/Auditing; Banking; Engineering; Food Industry; General Management; Health/Medical; Manufacturing; Sales; Technical. **Positions commonly filled include:** Accountant/Auditor; Actuary; Attorney; Bank Officer/Manager; Buyer; Chemical Engineer; Chemist; Design Engineer; Designer; Electrical/Electronics Engineer; Food Scientist/Technologist; General Manager; Geologist/Geophysicist; Industrial Engineer; Industrial Production Manager; Mechanical Engineer; Metallurgical Engineer; Mining Engineer; Petroleum Engineer; Physician; Property and Real Estate Manager; Purchasing Agent/Manager; Quality Control Supervisor. **Average salary range of placements:** More than $50,000. **Number of placements per year:** 50 - 99.

DONAHUE BALES ASSOCIATES
303 West Madison, Suite 1150, Chicago IL 60606. 312/732-0999. **Contact:** Manager. **Description:** A generalist executive search firm.

DUNHILL PROFESSIONAL SEARCH OF ROLLING MEADOWS
5005 Newport Drive, Suite 201, Rolling Meadows IL 60008. 847/398-3400. **Contact:** Russ Kunke, Consultant. **Description:** An executive search firm. Company pays fee. **Specializes in the areas of:** Administration; Computer Science/Software; Engineering; Sales. **Positions commonly filled include:** Branch

Manager; Computer Programmer; Electrical/Electronics Engineer; Software Engineer; Systems Analyst. **Number of placements per year:** 1 - 49.

DYNAMIC SEARCH SYSTEMS, INC.
3800 North Wilke Road, Suite 485, Arlington Heights IL 60004. 847/259-3444. **Fax:** 847/259-3480. **Contact:** Michael J. Brindise, President. **E-mail address:** dynamsys@aol.com. **World Wide Web address:** http://www.dssjobs.com. **Description:** An executive search firm that focuses on MIS professional staffing. Company pays fee. **Specializes in the areas of:** Administration; Computer Science/Software; MIS/EDP. **Positions commonly filled include:** Computer Animator; Computer Operator; Computer Programmer; Database Manager; Internet Services Manager; Management Analyst/Consultant; MIS Specialist; Project Manager; Software Engineer; Systems Analyst; Systems Manager; Technical Writer/Editor; Webmaster. **Corporate headquarters location:** This Location. **Average salary range of placements:** More than $50,000. **Number of placements per year:** 200 - 499.

EARLY COCHRAN & OLSON
401 North Michigan Avenue, Suite 515, Chicago IL 60611-4205. **Contact:** Manager. **Description:** An executive search firm for senior-level attorneys. **Specializes in the areas of:** Legal. **Positions commonly filled include:** Attorney.

EASTMAN & ASSOCIATES
1717 North Naper Boulevard, Suite 104, Naperville IL 60563. 630/505-8855. **Fax:** 630/505-8860. **Contact:** Marilyn Wilcox, Recruiter. **Description:** A retained executive search firm focusing on financial services staffing. **Specializes in the areas of:** Accounting/Auditing; Finance; Personnel/Labor Relations; Retail; Sales. **Positions commonly filled include:** Accountant/Auditor; Bank Officer/Manager; Customer Service Representative; Financial Analyst; Human Resources Manager; Industrial Engineer; Securities Sales Representative; Underwriter/Assistant Underwriter. **Corporate headquarters location:** This Location. **Other U.S. locations:** Nationwide. **Average salary range of placements:** $30,000 - $50,000.

THE EASTWOOD GROUP
900 Skokie Boulevard, Suite 116, Northbrook IL 60062. 847/291-8383. **Fax:** 847/291-9753. **Contact:** Bonnie Miller, President. **E-mail address:** eastwoodg@aol.com. **Description:** An executive search firm operating on a contingency basis. Company pays fee. **Specializes in the areas of:** Advertising; Art/Design; Banking; Finance; Health/Medical; Sales. **Positions commonly filled include:** Designer; Editor; Financial Analyst; Market Research Analyst; Public Relations Manager; Technical Writer/Editor; Video Production Coordinator. **Average salary range of placements:** More than $50,000. **Number of placements per year:** 1 - 49.

EFFECTIVE SEARCH INC.
11718 North Main Street, Roscoe IL 61073. 815/623-7400. **Fax:** 815/623-6171. **Contact:** Manager. **Description:** An executive search firm. **Specializes in the areas of:** Engineering.

ELECTRONIC SEARCH
3601 Algonquin Road, Suite 820, Rolling Meadows IL 60008. 847/506-0700. **Contact:** Manager. **Description:** An executive search firm. **Specializes in the areas of:** Technical.

ELLINGTON & ASSOCIATES
1755 Park Street, Suite 200, Naperville IL 60563. 630/305-0088. **Contact:** Manager. **Description:** An executive search firm. **Specializes in the areas of:** Engineering.

ELSKO EXECUTIVE SEARCH
3601 Algonquin, Suite 130, Rolling Meadows IL 60008. 847/394-2400. **Contact:** Training Manager. **Description:** An executive search firm. **Specializes in the areas of:** Accounting/Auditing; Finance. **Number of placements per year:** 100 - 199.

ENGINEERING MANAGEMENT STAFF RECRUITING
35 East Wacker Drive, Suite 1920, Chicago IL 60601. 312/629-1705. **Contact:** Manager. **Description:** An executive search firm. **Specializes in the areas of:** Engineering.

EVERGREENE PARTNERS
635 Elmwood Drive, Wheaton IL 60187. 630/665-4850. **Contact:** Manager. **Description:** An executive search firm. Company pays fee. **Specializes in the areas of:** Food Industry. **Positions commonly filled include:** Chemical Engineer; Electrical/Electronics Engineer; Food Scientist/Technologist; Human Resources Manager; Industrial Engineer; Mechanical Engineer. **Number of placements per year:** 1 - 49.

EXECU SEARCH
14 North Peoria, Chicago IL 60607. 312/432-4000. **Contact:** Manager. **Description:** An executive search firm.

EXECUTIVE CONCEPTS INC.
1000 East Woodfield Road, Schaumburg IL 60173-4728. 847/605-8300. **Fax:** 847/605-8089. **Contact:** Tom Werle, President. **Description:** An executive search firm operating on both retainer and contingency bases that focuses on data processing. Company pays fee. **Specializes in the areas of:** Computer Science/Software. **Positions commonly filled include:** Computer Programmer; Systems Analyst. **Average salary range of placements:** $30,000 - $50,000. **Number of placements per year:** 50 - 99.

EXECUTIVE FINANCIAL CONSULTANTS
6900 Main Street, Suite 169, Downers Grove IL 60515. 630/663-9010. **Contact:** Office Manager. **Description:** An executive search firm. **Specializes in the areas of:** Accounting/Auditing; Finance.

EXECUTIVE INTERVIEWERS
2000 North Racine, Chicago IL 60614. 773/929-3200. **Contact:** Manager. **Description:** An executive search firm covering a wide range of industries.

EXECUTIVE OPTIONS LTD.
910 Skokie Boulevard, Suite 210, Northbrook IL 60062. 847/291-4322. **Contact:** Office Manager. **Description:** An executive search firm focusing on the placement of middle management professionals and above. **Specializes in the areas of:** Finance; Human Resources; Marketing. **Positions commonly filled include:** Human Resources Manager; Marketing Specialist.

EXECUTIVE OPTIONS LTD.
625 North Michigan Avenue, Suite 500, Chicago IL 60611. 312/751-5413. **Contact:** Office Manager. **Description:** An executive search firm.

EXECUTIVE PLACEMENT CONSULTANTS
2700 South River Road, Suite 102, Des Plaines IL 60018. 847/298-6445. **Contact:** Office Manager. **Description:** An executive search firm. **Specializes in the areas of:** Accounting/Auditing; Finance; Information Systems.

EXECUTIVE REFERRAL SERVICES, INC.
8770 West Bryn Mawr, Suite 110, Chicago IL 60631. 773/693-6622. **Fax:** 773/693-8466. **Contact:** Bruce Freier, President. **Description:** An executive search firm. **Specializes in the areas of:** Accounting/Auditing; Architecture/Construction; Fashion; Finance; Food Industry; General Management; Health/Medical; Hotel/Restaurant; Personnel/Labor Relations; Pharmaceutical; Retail; Sales. **Positions commonly filled include:** Accountant; Branch Manager; Buyer; Chief Financial Officer; Construction Contractor; Controller; Finance Director; Financial Analyst; General Manager; Graphic Designer; Human Resources Manager; Marketing Manager; Pharmacist; Physical Therapist; Sales Executive; Sales Manager.

EXECUTIVE SEARCH CONSULTANTS
8 South Michigan, #1205, Chicago IL 60603. 312/251-8400. **Contact:** Manager. **Description:** An executive search firm that focuses on property/casualty insurance placements. **Specializes in the areas of:** Insurance.

EXECUTIVE SEARCH INTERNATIONAL
4300 North Brandywine Drive, Suite 104, Peoria IL 61614-5550. 309/685-6273. **Fax:** 309/685-3757. **Contact:** Robert Vaughan, President. **Description:** An executive search firm operating on both contingency and a retainer bases. Company pays fee. **Specializes in the areas of:** Advertising; Computer Science/Software; Engineering; Industrial; Sales. **Positions commonly filled include:** Account Manager; Account Representative; Accountant; Buyer; Computer Programmer; Customer Service Representative; Design Engineer; Electrical/Electronics Engineer; Financial Analyst; Industrial Engineer; Industrial Production Manager; Manufacturing Engineer; Market Research Analyst; Marketing Specialist; Mechanical Engineer; MIS Specialist; Multimedia Designer; Production Manager; Quality Control Supervisor; Sales Engineer; Sales Executive; Sales Manager; Software Engineer; Systems Analyst; Systems Manager; Technical Writer/Editor; Underwriter/Assistant Underwriter; Vice President. **Corporate headquarters location:** This Location. **Other U.S. locations:** Nationwide. **Average salary range of placements:** More than $50,000. **Number of placements per year:** 100 - 199.

EXECUTIVE SEARCH LTD.
2000 Larkin Avenue, Suite 202, Elgin IL 60123. 847/697-1170. **Contact:** Manager. **Description:** An executive search firm that provides placements for six major corporations in the Midwest in engineering, sales and marketing, accounting and finance, production, and human resources.

EXECUTIVE SEARCH NETWORK
500 North Lake Street, Suite 107, Mundelein IL 60060. 847/837-1460. **Contact:** Mike Tollefson, President. **Description:** An executive search firm. Company pays fee. **Specializes in the areas of:** Computer Hardware/Software; Engineering; Technical. **Positions commonly filled include:** Aerospace Engineer; Buyer; Ceramics Engineer; Chemical Engineer; Computer Programmer; Electrical/Electronics Engineer; Industrial Engineer; Manufacturing Engineer; Marketing Specialist; Mechanical Engineer; Metallurgical Engineer; Purchasing Agent/Manager; Quality Control Supervisor; Software Engineer; Technical Representative; Technical Writer/Editor. **Number of placements per year:** 1 - 49.

FINANCIAL SEARCH CORPORATION
2720 Des Plaines Avenue, Des Plaines IL 60018. 847/297-4900. **Fax:** 847/297-0294. **Contact:** Robert Collins, President. **Description:** An executive search firm. Company pays fee. **Specializes in the areas of:** Accounting/Auditing; Banking; Finance; Insurance. **Positions commonly filled include:** Accountant; Auditor; Budget Analyst; Controller; Cost Estimator; Credit Manager; Finance Director; Financial Analyst. **Corporate headquarters location:** This Location. **Other area locations:** Chicago IL. **Average salary range of placements:** $30,000 - $50,000. **Number of placements per year:** 50 - 99.

FINANCIAL SEARCH CORPORATION
333 West Wacker Drive, Suite 700, Chicago IL 60606. 312/444-2019. **Contact:** Manager. **Description:** An executive search firm. **Specializes in the areas of:** Finance. **Corporate headquarters location:** Des Plaines IL.

FIRST ATTORNEY CONSULTANTS LTD.
P.O. Box 42751, Evergreen Park IL 60805. 708/425-5515. **Contact:** Manager. **Description:** An executive search firm that places attorneys. **Specializes in the areas of:** Legal.

FIRST SEARCH, INC.
6584 Northwest Highway, Chicago IL 60631. 773/774-0001. **Fax:** 773/774-5571. **Contact:** Al Katz, Vice President. **E-mail address:** fsihunter@aol.com. **Description:** An executive search firm. Company pays fee. **Specializes in the areas of:** Computer Science/Software; Engineering; Sales; Technical; Telecommunications. **Positions commonly filled include:** Computer Operator; Computer Programmer; Consultant; Customer Service Representative; Database Manager; Design Engineer; Electrical/Electronics Engineer; Systems Analyst; Systems Manager; Telecommunications Manager; Vice President of Sales. **Benefits available to temporary workers:** 401(k); Life Insurance; Medical Insurance. **Corporate headquarters location:** This Location. **Average salary range of placements:** More than $50,000. **Number of placements per year:** 200 - 499.

F-O-R-T-U-N-E PERSONNEL CONSULTANTS
825 East Golf Road, Suite 1146, Arlington Heights IL 60005. 847/228-7205. **Fax:** 847/228-7206. **Contact:** Manager. **Description:** An executive search firm. **Specializes in the areas of:** Automotive; Insurance; Manufacturing; Quality Assurance. **Corporate headquarters location:** New York NY.

GENERAL COUNSEL CORPORATION
980 North Michigan Avenue, Suite 1400, Chicago IL 60611. 312/649-1959. **Fax:** 312/642-8444. **Contact:** John C. Hoppe, President. **Description:** An executive search firm. Company pays fee. **Specializes in the areas of:** Legal. **Positions commonly filled include:** Attorney. **Number of placements per year:** 1 - 49.

GIFFORD ASSOCIATES
625 North Michigan Avenue, Chicago IL 60611. 312/751-3466. **Contact:** Manager. **Description:** An executive search firm. **Specializes in the areas of:** Design; Health/Medical.

GIOVANNINI ASSOCIATES
4811 Emerson Avenue, Suite 101, Palatine IL 60067. 847/303-1199. **Contact:** Manager. **Description:** An executive search firm. **Specializes in the areas of:** Medical Sales and Marketing.

GIRMAN GROUP
40 Shuman Boulevard, Suite 160, Naperville IL 60563. 630/260-0040. **Fax:** 630/260-0094. **Contact:** Jerrilyn Girman, Partner. **Description:** An executive search firm. **Specializes in the areas of:** Administration; Computer Hardware/Software; Manufacturing; Sales; Technical. **Positions commonly filled include:** Computer Programmer; Consultant; Sales Manager; Sales Representative; Software

Engineer; Systems Analyst. **Number of placements per year:** 50 - 99.

THE GLENWOOD GROUP
6428 Joliet Road, Suite 112, Countryside IL 60525. 708/482-3750. **Contact:** Manager. **Description:** An executive search firm. **Specializes in the areas of:** Engineering; Manufacturing.

GLOBAL SEARCH INC.
875 North Michigan Avenue, Chicago IL 60611. 312/587-9912. **Contact:** Christopher Melillo, President. **Description:** An executive search firm focusing on financial and accounting placements for six *Fortune* 100 companies. **Specializes in the areas of:** Accounting/Auditing; Finance. **Positions commonly filled include:** Accountant/Auditor; Financial Analyst; Management Analyst/Consultant; MIS Specialist. **Number of placements per year:** 50 - 99.

GNODDE ASSOCIATES
128 North Lincoln Street, Hinsdale IL 60521-3439. 630/887-9510. **Fax:** 630/887-9531. **Contact:** Dirk Gnodde, Owner. **Description:** A contingency search firm focusing on financial services. **Specializes in the areas of:** Banking; Finance. **Positions commonly filled include:** Accountant/Auditor; Bank Officer/Manager; Branch Manager; Budget Analyst; Credit Manager; Financial Analyst. **Average salary range of placements:** More than $50,000. **Number of placements per year:** 1 - 49.

GODFREY PERSONNEL INC.
300 West Adams, Suite 612, Chicago IL 60606. 312/236-4455. **Fax:** 312/580-6292. **Contact:** James Godfrey, President. **Description:** An executive search firm that focuses on placement in the insurance industry. Company pays fee. **Specializes in the areas of:** Insurance. **Number of placements per year:** 200 - 499.

DAVID GOMEZ & ASSOCIATES, INC.
20 North Clark Street, Suite 3535, Chicago IL 60602-5002. 312/346-5525. **Fax:** 312/346-1438. **Contact:** Consultant. **World Wide Web address:** http://www.dgai.com. **Description:** An executive search firm. Company pays fee. **Specializes in the areas of:** Accounting/Auditing; Administration; Advertising; Art/Design; Banking; Computer Science/Software; Finance; General Management; Insurance; Manufacturing; Personnel/Labor Relations; Publishing; Sales; Secretarial. **Positions commonly filled include:** Accountant/Auditor; Bank Officer/Manager; Branch Manager; Budget Analyst; Computer Programmer; Credit Manager; Customer Service Representative; Design Engineer; Designer; Financial Analyst; General Manager; Management Analyst/Consultant; Market Research Analyst; MIS Specialist; Operations/Production Manager; Software Engineer; Systems Analyst; Telecommunications Manager; Typist/Word Processor; Underwriter/Assistant Underwriter. **Average salary range of placements:** More than $50,000. **Number of placements per year:** 200 - 499.

GORDON SOTOS & ASSOCIATES
980 North Michigan Avenue, Suite 1400, Chicago IL 60611. 312/943-2800. **Contact:** Manager. **Description:** An executive search firm that places personnel in a variety of industries.

GREYSTONE ASSOCIATES
597 Dunham Road, Gurnee IL 60031. 847/367-2552. **Contact:** Manager. **Description:** An executive search firm. **Specializes in the areas of:** Banking; Finance.

GRICE HOLDENER & ASSOCIATES INC.
39 South Barrington Road, South Barrington IL 60010. 847/382-2950. **Contact:** Office Manager. **Description:** An executive search firm. **Specializes in the areas of:** Computer Programming; Data Processing.

GROSSBERG & ASSOCIATES
1100 Jorie Boulevard, Suite 301, Oak Brook IL 60521. 630/574-0066. **Contact:** Robert Grossberg. **Description:** A retained executive search firm.

HT ASSOCIATES
3030 West Salt Creek Lane, Suite 121, Arlington Heights IL 60005. 847/577-0300. **Contact:** Manager. **Description:** An executive search firm. **Specializes in the areas of:** Technical.

HALE & ASSOCIATES
1010 Jorie Boulevard, Suite 102, Oak Brook IL 60523. 630/990-7750. **Contact:** Office Manager. **Description:** An executive search firm.

ROBERT HALF INTERNATIONAL ACCOUNTEMPS
One Northbrook Place, 5 Revere Drive, Suite 355, Northbrook IL 60062-1561. 847/480-1556. **Fax:** 847/480-1871. **Contact:** Recruiting Manager. **Description:** An executive search firm. Accountemps (also at this location) provides temporary accounting placements. Company pays fee. **Specializes in the areas of:** Accounting/Auditing; Finance. **Positions commonly filled include:** Accountant/Auditor; Bookkeeper; Credit Manager; EDP Specialist. **Corporate headquarters location:** Menlo Park CA. **Other U.S. locations:** Nationwide. **Number of placements per year:** 1000+.

ROBERT HALF INTERNATIONAL ACCOUNTEMPS
2800 West Higgins Road, Suite 180, Hoffman Estates IL 60195-5236. 847/882-7866. **Fax:** 847/885-6387. **Contact:** Branch Manager. **World Wide Web address:** http://www.roberthalf.com. **Description:** An executive search firm. Accountemps (also at this location) provides temporary placements. Company pays fee. **Specializes in the areas of:** Accounting/Auditing; Finance. **Positions commonly filled include:** Accountant/Auditor; Bookkeeper; Credit Manager; EDP Specialist. **Corporate headquarters location:** Menlo Park CA. **Other U.S. locations:** Nationwide. **Number of placements per year:** 1000+.

ROBERT HALF INTERNATIONAL ACCOUNTEMPS
One Oakbrook Terrace, Suite 718, Oakbrook Terrace IL 60181. 630/261-3080. **Fax:** 630/261-3088. **Contact:** Julie West, Staffing Manager. **E-mail address:** oakbrook_terrace@roberthalf.com. **World Wide Web address:** http://www.roberthalf.com. **Description:** An executive search firm. Accountemps (also at this location) provides temporary placements of accounting and finance professionals. Company pays fee. **Specializes in the areas of:** Accounting/Auditing; Banking; Finance. **Positions commonly filled include:** Accountant/Auditor; Adjuster; Administrative Assistant; Bank Officer/Manager; Bookkeeper; Budget Analyst; Chief Financial Officer; Clerk; Computer Operator; Computer Programmer; Controller; Cost Estimator; Credit Manager; Data Entry Clerk; Database Manager; EDP Specialist; Finance Director; Financial Analyst; Software Engineer; Systems Analyst; Technical Writer/Editor; Typist/Word Processor. **Benefits available to temporary workers:** Computer Training; Dental Insurance; Medical Insurance; Paid Holidays; Tuition Assistance; Vision Insurance. **Corporate headquarters location:** Menlo Park CA. **Other U.S. locations:** Nationwide **Average salary range of placements:** $30,000 - $50,000. **Number of placements per year:** 1000+.

ROBERT HALF INTERNATIONAL ACCOUNTEMPS
205 North Michigan Avenue, Suite 3301, Chicago IL 60601. 312/616-8200. **Fax:** 312/616-1155. **Contact:** Placement Manager. **Description:** An executive search firm. Accountemps (also at this location) provides temporary placements. Company pays fee. **Specializes in the areas of:** Accounting/Auditing; Finance. **Positions commonly filled include:** Accountant/ Auditor; Administrative Assistant; Bookkeeper; Credit Manager; EDP Specialist. **Corporate headquarters location:** Menlo Park CA. **Other U.S. locations:** Nationwide. **Number of placements per year:** 1000+.

HAMILTON GREY EXECUTIVE SEARCH, INC.
One South 280 Summitt Avenue, Suite B-3, Oakbrook Terrace IL 60181-3947. 630/932-1114. **Fax:** 630/932-1123. **Contact:** Frank Baron, President. **Description:** An executive search firm that also provides contract placements. The firm operates on a contingency basis. Company pays fee. **Specializes in the areas of:** Information Technology; MIS/EDP. **Positions commonly filled include:** MIS Specialist. **Average salary range of placements:** More than $50,000. **Number of placements per year:** 200 - 499.

HANOVER CROWN & ASSOCIATES
P.O. Box 1606, Oak Brook IL 60522-1606. 630/834-4250. **Contact:** Tony Bonner, President. **Description:** An executive search firm. Company pays fee. **Specializes in the areas of:** Chemical; Engineering; Food Industry. **Positions commonly filled include:** Biological Scientist; Biomedical Engineer; Chemical Engineer; Chemist; Civil Engineer; Electrical/ Electronics Engineer; Food Scientist/Technologist; Mechanical Engineer; Quality Control Supervisor; Science Technologist; Software Engineer. **Average salary range of placements:** More than $50,000. **Number of placements per year:** 1 - 49.

RONALD B. HANSON & ASSOCIATES
22 East Dundee Road, Suite 7, Barrington IL 60010. 847/304-8882. **Fax:** 847/304-8892. **Contact:** Ron Hanson, Owner/President. **Description:** An executive search firm. **Specializes in the areas of:** Executives; Insurance. **Positions commonly filled include:** Actuary; Administrative Manager; General Manager; Insurance Agent/Broker; Management; Management Analyst/ Consultant; Operations/Production Manager; Underwriter/Assistant Underwriter. **Corporate headquarters location:** This Location. **Other U.S. locations:** Nationwide. **Average salary range of placements:** More than $50,000. **Number of placements per year:** 1 - 49.

HEALTH PROFESSIONALS INTERNATIONAL
1601 Sherman Avenue, Suite 400, Evanston IL 60201. 847/328-5262. **Fax:** 847/328-5049. **Contact:** Recruiter. **Description:** An executive search and contract services firm. **Average salary range of placements:** $30,000 - $50,000. **Number of placements per year:** 200 - 499.

HEALTHCARE RECRUITERS INTERNATIONAL
850 North Milwaukee Road, Vernon Hills IL 60061. 847/549-5885. **Contact:** Carolyn Stauner, President. **Description:** An executive search firm. **Specializes in the areas of:** Engineering; Health/Medical; Sales. **Positions commonly filled include:** Biomedical Engineer; Chemical Engineer; Industrial Engineer; Manufacturer's/Wholesaler's Sales Rep.; MIS Specialist; Occupational Therapist; Pharmacist; Physical Therapist; Physician; Registered Nurse; Respiratory Therapist; Software Engineer.

HERSHER & ASSOCIATES
3000 Dundee Road, Suite 314, Northbrook IL 60062. 847/272-4050. **Contact:** Manager. **Description:** An executive search firm. **Specializes in the areas of:** Information Systems.

HIGHLAND GROUP
1639 Highland Avenue, Wilmette IL 60091. 847/251-2900. **Contact:** Manager. **Description:** An executive search firm. **Specializes in the areas of:** Health/Medical.

HOLLINS GROUP INC.
225 West Wacker Drive, Chicago IL 60606. 312/606-8000. **Contact:** Manager. **Description:** An executive search firm operating on a retained basis.

E.A. HOOVER & ASSOCIATES
P.O. Box 37, Villa Park IL 60181. 630/833-2300. **Contact:** Manager. **Description:** An executive search firm. **Specializes in the areas of:** Engineering. **Positions commonly filled include:** Electrical/Electronics Engineer.

ELIZABETH HOWE AND ASSOCIATES
645 North Michigan Avenue, Suite 800, Chicago IL 60611. 312/906-3700. **Fax:** 312/906-3747. **Contact:** Elizabeth Howe, Owner. **Description:** An executive search firm focusing on software companies and mid- to large-size MIS operations. The firm operates on both retainer and contingency bases. **NOTE:** Typical candidates have backgrounds in sales/marketing, management, pre- and post-sales, or project management. Founded in 1991. **Specializes in the areas of:** Computer Science/Software; Finance; Manufacturing; Sales. **Positions commonly filled include:** Computer Programmer; Financial Analyst; MIS Specialist; Services Sales Representative; Software Engineer; Systems Analyst. **Corporate headquarters location:** This Location. **Other U.S. locations:** CA. **Average salary range of placements:** More than $50,000. **Number of placements per year:** 50 - 99.

HUFFORD ASSOCIATES
3 Pembrook Court, Bolingbrook IL 60440. 630/378-0005. **Contact:** Craig Hufford, President. **E-mail address:** hufassoc@xnet.com. **Description:** An executive search firm operating on both retainer and contingency bases that focuses on the voice, data, and wireless communications industries. The firm's clients include both domestic and international companies. **Specializes in the areas of:** Engineering; Marketing; Technical. **Positions commonly filled include:** Software Engineer; Telecommunications Manager. **Average salary range of placements:** More than $50,000. **Number of placements per year:** 1 - 49.

HUMAN RESOURCE TECHNOLOGY
2200 East Devon Avenue, Suite 183, Des Plaines IL 60018. 847/297-8000. **Contact:** Rick Sondhi, President. **E-mail address:** hrtech@mcs.com. **Description:** A retainer-based executive search firm focusing on engineering, marketing, and finance. Company pays fee. **Specializes in the areas of:** Accounting/Auditing; Administration; Computer Science/Software; Engineering; Finance; Food Industry; General Management; Health/Medical; Insurance; Manufacturing; Personnel/Labor Relations; Publishing; Technical. **Positions commonly filled include:** Accountant/Auditor; Actuary; Aerospace Engineer; Agricultural Engineer; Biological Scientist; Biomedical Engineer; Blue-Collar Worker Supervisor; Budget Analyst; Buyer; Chemical Engineer; Chemist; Civil Engineer; Claim Representative; Computer Programmer; Customer Service Representative; Electrical/Electronics Engineer; Financial Analyst; Food Scientist/Technologist; Industrial Engineer; Industrial Production Manager; Maitre d'Hôtel; Materials Engineer; Mechanical Engineer; Metallurgical Engineer; Operations/Production Manager; Petroleum Engineer;

Physical Therapist; Quality Control Supervisor; Software Engineer; Stationary Engineer; Statistician; Structural Engineer; Systems Analyst; Underwriter/ Assistant Underwriter. **Average salary range of placements:** More than $50,000. **Number of placements per year:** 200 - 499.

THE HUNTER RESOURCE GROUP, INC.
One North LaSalle, 24th Floor, Chicago IL 60602. 312/201-0302. **Fax:** 312/201-0402. **Contact:** Frank Scarpelli, President. **E-mail address:** fshunter@ aol.com. **Description:** A search firm focusing on technology, human resources, accounting, and finance. The Hunter Resource Group works with mid-sized to *Fortune* 500 firms throughout North America, Europe, and Asia. Company pays fee. **Specializes in the areas of:** Administration; Computer Science/ Software; General Management; Personnel/Labor Relations. **Positions commonly filled include:** Accountant/Auditor; Computer Programmer; Financial Analyst; General Manager; Human Resources Manager; Internet Services Manager; MIS Specialist; Multimedia Designer; Software Engineer; Systems Analyst. **Average salary range of placements:** More than $50,000.

CATHY HURLESS EXECUTIVE RECRUITING
333 West Wacker Drive, Suite 700, Chicago IL 60606. 312/444-2053. **Contact:** Manager. **Description:** An executive search firm. **Specializes in the areas of:** Advertising.

IZS EXECUTIVE SEARCH
20 North Wacker Drive, Suite 556, Chicago IL 60606. 312/346-6300. **Contact:** Manager. **Description:** An executive search firm. **Specializes in the areas of:** Accounting/Auditing; Finance.

JOHN IMBER ASSOCIATES, LTD.
3601 Algonquin Road, Suite 129, Rolling Meadows IL 60008. 847/506-1700. **Contact:** John Imber, Owner. **Description:** A generalist executive search firm.

INNOVATIVE SYSTEMS GROUP, INC.
799 Roosevelt Road, Building 3, Suite 109, Glen Ellyn IL 60137. 630/858-8500. **Fax:** 630/858-8532. **Contact:** Recruiter. **Description:** An executive search firm. Company pays fee. **Specializes in the areas of:** Administration. **Positions commonly filled include:** Computer Programmer; Software Engineer; Systems Engineer. **Number of placements per year:** 50 - 99.

INSURANCE NATIONAL SEARCH
E.J. ASHTON & ASSOCIATES, LTD.
P.O. Box 1048, Lake Zurich IL 60047-1048. 847/540-9922. **Contact:** Ed Ashton, President. **E-mail address:** ejaltd@aol.com. **World Wide Web address:** http://www.insurancerecruiters.com. **Description:** An executive search firm. Company pays fee. **Specializes in the areas of:** Accounting/Auditing; Administration; Computer Science/Software; Finance; Health/Medical; Insurance; Legal. **Positions commonly filled include:** Accountant/Auditor; Actuary; Adjuster; Attorney; Branch Manager; Budget Analyst; Claim Representative; Computer Programmer; Financial Analyst; Health Services Manager; Human Resources Manager; Internet Services Manager; Management Analyst/Consultant; MIS Specialist; Securities Sales Representative; Software Engineer; Statistician; Systems Analyst; Telecommunications Manager; Underwriter/Assistant Underwriter. **Average salary range of placements:** More than $50,000. **Number of placements per year:** 1 - 49.

IRWIN & WAGNER, INC.
17720 67th Avenue, Tinley Park IL 60477. 708/532-2800. **Fax:** 708/532-2936. **Contact:** Mary Ellen Irwin, President. **Description:** A retained executive search firm. Company pays fee. **Specializes in the areas of:** Food Industry; General Management; Personnel/Labor Relations; Sales. **Positions commonly filled include:** General Manager; Hotel Manager; Human Resources Manager; Restaurant/Food Service Manager. **Average salary range of placements:** More than $50,000. **Number of placements per year:** 1 - 49.

ITEX EXECUTIVE SEARCH
2700 River Road, Des Plaines IL 60018. 847/297-1100. **Contact:** Keith Burgess. **Description:** An executive search firm. **Specializes in the areas of:** Accounting/Auditing; Finance.

JACOBSON ASSOCIATES
INSURANCE STAFFERS
150 North Wacker Drive, Suite 1120, Chicago IL 60606. 312/726-1578. **Contact:** David Jacobson, President. **Description:** An executive search firm. Insurance Staffers (also at this location) is a temporary agency. **Specializes in the areas of:** Health/Medical; Insurance. **Number of placements per year:** 100 - 199.

JOHNSON PERSONNEL COMPANY
861 North Madison Street, Rockford IL 61107. 815/964-0840. **Fax:** 815/964-0855. **Contact:** Darrell Johnson, Owner. **Description:** An executive search firm. Company pays fee. **Specializes in the areas of:** Accounting/Auditing; Computer Science/Software; Engineering; Manufacturing; Personnel/Labor Relations. **Positions commonly filled include:** Accountant/Auditor; Buyer; Ceramics Engineer; Computer Programmer; Electrical/Electronics Engineer; Financial Analyst; Human Resources Manager; Industrial Engineer; Materials Engineer; Mechanical Engineer; Operations/Production Manager; Quality Control Supervisor; Software Engineer; Statistician; Systems Analyst. **Number of placements per year:** 1 - 49.

JERRY L. JUNG CO., INC.
140 Iowa Avenue, Belleville IL 62220-3940. 618/277-8881. **Fax:** 618/277-8386. **Contact:** Jerry Jung, Principal. **E-mail address:** jung8881@aol.com. **Description:** An executive search firm. **Specializes in the areas of:** Computer Science/Software; Engineering; Heating, Air Conditioning, and Refrigeration; Manufacturing. **Positions commonly filled include:** Computer Programmer; Design Engineer; Designer; General Manager; Industrial Engineer; Industrial Mechanical Engineer; Metallurgical Engineer; Operations/Production Manager; Quality Assurance Engineer; Software Engineer. **Average salary range of placements:** More than $50,000. **Number of placements per year:** 1 - 49.

KENNEDY & COMPANY
20 North Wacker Drive, Suite 1745, Chicago IL 60606. 312/372-0099. **Contact:** Office Manager. **Description:** An executive search firm. **Specializes in the areas of:** Banking; Finance.

KENZER CORPORATION
625 North Michigan Avenue, Suite 1244, Chicago IL 60611. 312/266-0976. **Contact:** Office Manager. **Description:** An executive search firm. **Specializes in the areas of:** Finance; Food Industry; Manufacturing; Retail; Wholesaling.

KINDERIS & LOERCHER GROUP
9510 Turnberry Trail, Crystal Lake IL 60014. 815/459-6370. **Fax:** 815/459-6314. **Contact:** Paul Kinderis, President. **Description:** A search firm working exclusively with the insurance industry. Clients include reinsurance companies, mutual insurance companies, major brokers and agencies, risk management companies, and self-insured corporations. **Specializes**

in the areas of: Insurance. **Positions commonly filled include:** Actuary; Adjuster; Claim Representative; Risk Manager; Underwriter/Assistant Underwriter. **Average salary range of placements:** More than $50,000.

KORN/FERRY INTERNATIONAL
233 Wacker Drive, Suite 3300, Chicago IL 60606. 312/466-1834. **Contact:** Manager. **Description:** An executive search firm that places upper-level managers in a variety of industries. **Corporate headquarters location:** Los Angeles CA. **International locations:** Worldwide. **Average salary range of placements:** More than $50,000.

KRECEK & ASSOCIATES LTD.
107 East Front Street, Wheaton IL 60187. 630/653-1300. **Contact:** Manager. **Description:** An executive search firm. **Specializes in the areas of:** Data Processing.

EVIE KREISLER ASSOCIATES INC.
333 North Michigan Avenue, Suite 818, Chicago IL 60601. 312/251-0077. **Contact:** Office Manager. **Description:** An executive search firm. **Specializes in the areas of:** Manufacturing; Retail.

KRESIN WINGARD
333 North Michigan Avenue, Suite 622, Chicago IL 60601. 312/726-8676. **Contact:** Office Manager. **Description:** An executive search firm.

SAMUEL F. KROLL & ASSOCIATES
1804 North Naper Boulevard, Naperville IL 60563-8830. 630/505-5825. **Fax:** 630/505-5826. **Contact:** Sam Kroll, Principal. **E-mail address:** samkroll@soon.com. **Description:** An executive search firm that offers permanent opportunities for information systems professionals ranging from hands-on technical specialists to MIS directors to consultants. Company pays fee. **Specializes in the areas of:** Administration; Computer Science/Software. **Positions commonly filled include:** MIS Manager; MIS Specialist; Project Manager; Systems Analyst; Telecommunications Manager. **Average salary range of placements:** More than $50,000. **Number of placements per year:** 1 - 49.

KUNZER ASSOCIATES, LTD.
1415 West 22nd Street, Suite 1180, Oak Brook IL 60521. 630/574-0010. **Contact:** William Kunzer, President. **Description:** An executive search firm that serves clients in a variety of industries and in all functional areas of senior and middle management. Company pays fee. **Specializes in the areas of:** Accounting/Auditing; Administration; Advertising; Art/Design; Banking; Computer Science/Software; Engineering; Finance; Food Industry; General Management; Health/Medical; Industrial; Manufacturing; Personnel/Labor Relations; Publishing; Retail; Sales; Technical. **Positions commonly filled include:** Administrative Manager; Attorney; Bank Officer/Manager; Chemical Engineer; Chemist; Credit Manager; Design Engineer; Electrical/Electronics Engineer; Health Services Manager; Human Resources Manager; Industrial Engineer; Mechanical Engineer; Metallurgical Engineer; MIS Specialist; Quality Control Supervisor. **Average salary range of placements:** More than $50,000. **Number of placements per year:** 1 - 49.

LMB ASSOCIATES
1468 Sunnyside Avenue, Highland Park IL 60035. 847/831-5990. **Contact:** Lorena Blonsky, Owner. **Description:** An executive search firm.

LAMALIE AMROP INTERNATIONAL
225 West Wacker Drive, Suite 2100, Chicago IL 60606-1129. 312/782-3113. **Fax:** 312/782-1743. **Contact:** Research Department. **Description:** A retained executive search firm that recruits for most major industries.

THE LASO CORPORATION
220 West Huron, Suite 4030, Chicago IL 60610. 312/255-1110. **Contact:** Manager. **Description:** An executive search firm. **Specializes in the areas of:** MIS/EDP.

LAUER SBARBARO ASSOCIATES INC.
30 North LaSalle Street, Suite 4030, Chicago IL 60602. 312/372-7050. **Fax:** 312/704-4393. **Contact:** Manager. **Description:** A generalist executive search firm.

LE BEAU & ASSOCIATES
900 Jorie Boulevard, Oak Brook IL 60521. 630/990-2233. **Contact:** Carl Le Beau, Owner. **Description:** An executive search firm that specializes in placing professionals in the rotating equipment field.

ARLENE LEFF & ASSOCIATES
203 North LaSalle Street, Suite 2100, Chicago IL 60601. 312/558-1350. **Fax:** 312/558-1346. **Contact:** Arlene Leff, Owner. **Description:** An executive search firm. The company has two divisions: Support Level and Executive Search. Company pays fee. **Specializes in the areas of:** Accounting/Auditing; Administration; Advertising; Computer Science/Software; Engineering; Fashion; Finance; General Management; Health/Medical; Industrial; Insurance; Publishing; Retail; Sales; Secretarial. **Positions commonly filled include:** Accountant/Auditor; Administrative Manager; Advertising Clerk; Bank Officer/Manager; Blue-Collar Worker Supervisor; Branch Manager; Buyer; Chemical Engineer; Computer Programmer; Construction Contractor; Cost Estimator; Credit Manager; Design Engineer; Electrical/Electronics Engineer; General Manager; Human Resources Manager; Industrial Engineer; Management Trainee; MIS Specialist; Quality Control Supervisor; Software Engineer; Systems Analyst; Technical Writer/Editor; Typist/Word Processor. **Number of placements per year:** 100 - 199.

LORD & RICHARDS GROUP
1420 Renaissance Drive, Park Ridge IL 60068. 847/298-9010. **Contact:** Manager. **Description:** A generalist executive search firm.

LYNCO MANAGEMENT PERSONNEL
P.O. Box 343, Geneva IL 60134-0343. 630/801-1600. **Contact:** V. Lynn Buehler, CEO. **Description:** A contingency search firm. Company pays fee. **Specializes in the areas of:** Accounting/Auditing; Administration; Banking; Computer Science/Software; Engineering; Finance; Food Industry; General Management; Industrial; Manufacturing; Personnel/Labor Relations; Publishing; Sales; Technical. **Positions commonly filled include:** Accountant/Auditor; Administrative Manager; Agricultural Engineer; Bank Officer/Manager; Biomedical Engineer; Blue-Collar Worker Supervisor; Branch Manager; Budget Analyst; Chemical Engineer; Chemist; Civil Engineer; Computer Programmer; Data Analyst; Design Engineer; Education Administrator; Electrical/Electronics Engineer; Environmental Engineer; Financial Analyst; General Manager; Industrial Engineer; Industrial Production Manager; Insurance Agent/Broker; Internet Services Manager; Management Analyst/Consultant; Mechanical Engineer; Metallurgical Engineer; MIS Specialist; Nuclear Engineer; Operations/Production Manager; Paralegal; Public Relations Specialist; Quality Control Supervisor; Restaurant/Food Service Manager; Services Sales Representative; Software Engineer; Systems Analyst; Technical Writer/Editor; Video Production Coordinator. **Other area locations:** 107 Elm

Avenue, North Aurora IL 60542. **Average salary range of placements:** $30,000 - $50,000. **Number of placements per year:** 100 - 199.

LYNCO MANAGEMENT PERSONNEL
107 Elm Avenue, North Aurora IL 60542. 630/801-1600. **Contact:** Manager. **Description:** An executive search firm. **Specializes in the areas of:** Accounting/Auditing; Administration; Computer Science/Software; Finance.

LYONS & ASSOCIATES
7815 Loch Glen Drive, Crystal Lake IL 60014-3317. 815/477-9292. **Fax:** 815/477-9296. **Contact:** Kent T. Lyons, President. **Description:** An executive search firm focusing on the graphic arts and direct marketing industries for positions ranging from president to manufacturing and sales management. Company pays fee. **Specializes in the areas of:** Publishing; Sales. **Positions commonly filled include:** Cost Estimator; Electrical/Electronics Engineer; General Manager; Human Resources Manager; Industrial Engineer; Industrial Production Manager; Mechanical Engineer; Operations/Production Manager; Services Sales Representative. **Average salary range of placements:** More than $50,000. **Number of placements per year:** 100 - 199.

MBP PERSONNEL
3000 Dundee Road, Suite 411, Northbrook IL 60062. 847/272-3272. **Fax:** 847/272-7398. **Contact:** Alan Cohen, President. **Description:** An executive search firm. Company pays fee. **Specializes in the areas of:** Administration; Banking; Health/Medical; Insurance; Sales; Secretarial; Technical. **Positions commonly filled include:** Account Manager; Account Representative; Administrative Assistant; Bank Officer/Manager; Branch Manager; Certified Nursing Aide; Chief Financial Officer; Claim Representative; Clerical Supervisor; Customer Service Representative; EEG Technologist; EKG Technician; Finance Director; Health Services Manager; Management Analyst/Consultant; Occupational Therapist; Operations Manager; Physical Therapist; Radiological Technologist; Registered Nurse; Respiratory Therapist; Secretary; Surgical Technician; Typist/Word Processor. **Corporate headquarters location:** This Location. **Average salary range of placements:** $30,000 - $50,000. **Number of placements per year:** 100 - 199.

MACRO RESOURCES
68 East Wacker Place, Suite 1600, Chicago IL 60601. 312/554-8900. **Contact:** Frank Roti, President. **Description:** A retainer and contingency search firm. Company pays fee. **Specializes in the areas of:** Banking; Computer Science/Software; Engineering; Finance. **Positions commonly filled include:** Electrical/Electronics Engineer; Mathematician; MIS Specialist; Software Engineer. **Average salary range of placements:** More than $50,000. **Number of placements per year:** 1 - 49.

MAGNUM SEARCH
1000 Golfhurst, Mount Prospect IL 60056. 847/577-0007. **Contact:** Arthur Kristufek, President. **Description:** A generalist firm focusing on the metals manufacturing industry. Company pays fee. **Specializes in the areas of:** Accounting/Auditing; Administration; Engineering; Finance; General Management; Industrial; Manufacturing; Personnel/Labor Relations; Technical. **Positions commonly filled include:** Accountant/Auditor; Administrative Manager; Buyer; Computer Programmer; Credit Manager; Customer Service Representative; Design Engineer; Designer; Draftsperson; Electrical/Electronics Engineer; Financial Analyst; General Manager; Human Resources Manager; Industrial Engineer; Industrial Production Manager; Management Trainee; Market Research Analyst; Mechanical Engineer; Metallurgical Engineer; MIS Specialist; Operations/Production Manager; Quality Control Supervisor; Software Engineer; Systems Analyst; Technical Writer/Editor.

MAJOR HAGEN & AFRICA
35 East Wacker Drive, Suite 2150, Chicago IL 60601. 312/372-1010. **Contact:** Manager. **Description:** An executive search firm. **Specializes in the areas of:** Legal. **Positions commonly filled include:** Attorney.

MANAGEMENT RECRUITERS INTERNATIONAL
7804 West College Drive, Palos Heights IL 60463. 708/361-8778. **Fax:** 708/361-9728. **Contact:** Victor Persico, President. **Description:** An executive search firm. Company pays fee. **Specializes in the areas of:** Banking. **Positions commonly filled include:** Bank Officer/Manager; Commercial Lending Officer. **Corporate headquarters location:** Cleveland OH. **Other U.S. locations:** Nationwide. **Number of placements per year:** 1 - 49.

MANAGEMENT RECRUITERS INTERNATIONAL
211 Landmark Drive, Suite E1, Normal IL 61761. 309/452-1844. **Fax:** 309/452-0403. **Contact:** M. Allan Snedden, Owner/General Manager. **Description:** An executive search firm. **Specializes in the areas of:** Accounting/Auditing; Administration; Computer Programming; Engineering; Finance; Health/Medical; Manufacturing; Personnel/Labor Relations. **Positions commonly filled include:** Accountant/Auditor; Computer Programmer; EDP Specialist; Human Resources Manager; Industrial Engineer; Manufacturing Engineer; MIS Specialist; Systems Analyst. **Corporate headquarters location:** Cleveland OH. **Other U.S. locations:** Nationwide. **Number of placements per year:** 50 - 99.

MANAGEMENT RECRUITERS INTERNATIONAL
2110 North Market Street, Suite D, Champaign IL 61821. 217/398-0050. **Fax:** 217/398-2043. **Contact:** Manager. **Description:** An executive search firm. **Specializes in the areas of:** Administration; Computer Hardware/Software; Engineering. **Corporate headquarters location:** Cleveland OH. **Other U.S. locations:** Nationwide.

MANAGEMENT RECRUITERS INTERNATIONAL
406 North Hough Street, Barrington IL 60010. 847/382-5544. **Contact:** Manager. **Description:** An executive search firm. **Specializes in the areas of:** Heating, Air Conditioning, and Refrigeration. **Corporate headquarters location:** Cleveland OH. **Other U.S. locations:** Nationwide.

MANAGEMENT RECRUITERS OF ALBION
Route 3, Box 138, Albion IL 62806. 618/445-2333. **Fax:** 618/445-3664. **Contact:** Tom Christensen, General Manager. **Description:** An executive search firm. **NOTE:** For November through April, the mailing address is Posada del Sol, Route 3, Box 411, Lot 88, Harlingen TX 78522. **Specializes in the areas of:** Biology; Engineering; Food Industry; General Management; Manufacturing. **Positions commonly filled include:** Agricultural Scientist; Biological Scientist; Buyer; Civil Engineer; Electrical/Electronics Engineer; Food Scientist/Technologist; General Manager; Industrial Engineer; Industrial Mechanical Engineer; Stationary Engineer; Structural Engineer. **Corporate headquarters location:** Cleveland OH. **Other U.S. locations:** Nationwide.

MANAGEMENT RECRUITERS OF ARLINGTON HEIGHTS
SALES CONSULTANTS
3413A North Kennicott Avenue, Arlington Heights IL 60004-1431. 847/590-8880. **Fax:** 847/590-0847.

Contact: Steve Briody, General Manager. **Description:** A contingency search firm focusing on placement in management, marketing, sales, and technical industries. Company pays fee. **Specializes in the areas of:** Food Industry; Industrial; Manufacturing; Personnel/Labor Relations; Sales. **Positions commonly filled include:** Accountant/Auditor; Administrative Manager; Branch Manager; Customer Service Representative; Dietician/Nutritionist; Electrical/ Electronics Engineer; Food Scientist/Technologist; General Manager; Human Resources Manager; Manufacturer's/Wholesaler's Sales Rep.; Services Sales Representative. **Corporate headquarters location:** Cleveland OH. **Other U.S. locations:** Nationwide. **Average salary range of placements:** More than $50,000. **Number of placements per year:** 100 - 199.

MANAGEMENT RECRUITERS OF DES PLAINES, INC.
1400 East Touhy Avenue, Suite 160, Des Plaines IL 60018. 847/297-7102. **Fax:** 847/297-8477. **Contact:** Manager. **Description:** An executive search firm. **Specializes in the areas of:** Accounting/Auditing; Administration; Advertising; Banking; Communications; Computer Science/Software; Design; Electrical; Engineering; Finance; Food Industry; General Management; Health/Medical; Industrial; Manufacturing; Operations Management; Personnel/Labor Relations; Pharmaceutical; Procurement. **Corporate headquarters location:** Cleveland OH. **Other U.S. locations:** Nationwide.

MANAGEMENT RECRUITERS OF ELGIN, INC.
472 North McLean Boulevard, Suite 201, Elgin IL 60123. 847/697-2201. **Fax:** 847/697-0622. **Contact:** Ronald C. Reeves, President. **Description:** An executive search firm. Company pays fee. **Specializes in the areas of:** Art/Design; Engineering; Manufacturing; Publishing; Technical. **Positions commonly filled include:** Customer Service Representative; Design Engineer; Designer; General Manager; Industrial Engineer; Industrial Production Manager; Mechanical Engineer; Quality Control Supervisor; Technical Writer/Editor; Telecommunications Manager. **Corporate headquarters location:** Cleveland OH. **Other U.S. locations:** Nationwide. **Average salary range of placements:** More than $50,000. **Number of placements per year:** 50 - 99.

MANAGEMENT RECRUITERS OF MATTOON
P.O. Box 461, Mattoon IL 61938-9396. 217/235-9393. **Contact:** David Tolle, President. **Description:** An executive search firm. Company pays fee. **Specializes in the areas of:** Food Industry. **Positions commonly filled include:** Chemical Engineer; Chemist; Food Scientist/Technologist; Mechanical Engineer. **Corporate headquarters location:** Cleveland OH. **Other U.S. locations:** Nationwide. **Average salary range of placements:** More than $50,000. **Number of placements per year:** 1 - 49.

MANAGEMENT RECRUITERS OF ROCKFORD, INC.
1463 South Bell School Road, Suite 3, Rockford IL 61108. 815/399-1942. **Contact:** D. Michael Carter, Manager. **Description:** An executive search firm. **Specializes in the areas of:** Accounting/Auditing; Administration; Advertising; Architecture/ Construction; Banking; Chemical; Communications; Computer Science/Software; Design; Electrical; Engineering; Film Production; Food Industry; General Management; Health/Medical; Industrial; Insurance; Legal; Manufacturing; Operations Management; Personnel/Labor Relations; Pharmaceutical; Procurement; Publishing; Retail; Sales; Technical; Textiles; Transportation. **Corporate headquarters location:** Cleveland OH. **Other U.S. locations:** Nationwide.

MANAGEMENT RECRUITERS OF SPRINGFIELD
124 East Laurel Street, Suite B, Springfield IL 62704-3946. 217/544-2051. **Fax:** 217/544-2055. **Contact:** Mark Cobb, General Manager. **E-mail address:** sprfield!mac@mrinet.com. **World Wide Web address:** http://www.mrinet.com. **Description:** A retainer and contingency search firm. Company pays fee. **Specializes in the areas of:** Biotechnology; Engineering; Manufacturing; Pharmaceutical; Technical. **Positions commonly filled include:** Biochemist; Biological Scientist; Biomedical Engineer; Chemical Engineer; Chemist; Clinical Lab Technician; Electrical/Electronics Engineer; Mechanical Engineer; Operations/Production Manager; Purchasing Agent/Manager; Quality Control Supervisor. **Corporate headquarters location:** Cleveland OH. **Other U.S. locations:** Nationwide. **Average salary range of placements:** More than $50,000. **Number of placements per year:** 1 - 49.

MANAGEMENT RECRUITERS OF ST. CHARLES, INC.
10 State Avenue, Suite 201, St. Charles IL 60174. 630/377-6466. **Contact:** Dan Lasse, President. **Description:** A contingency search firm. **Specializes in the areas of:** Manufacturing; Personnel/Labor Relations; Sales. **Positions commonly filled include:** Accountant/Auditor; Biological Scientist; Human Resources Manager; Manufacturing Engineer; Mechanical Engineer; Technical Representative. **Corporate headquarters location:** Cleveland OH. **Other U.S. locations:** Nationwide. **Average salary range of placements:** More than $50,000. **Number of placements per year:** 50 - 99.

MANAGEMENT SUPPORT SERVICES
1865 Bernice Road, Suite 6, Lansing IL 60438-6014. 708/474-8869. **Fax:** 708/474-8782. **Contact:** Mark Hickey, Senior Partner. **Description:** An executive search firm. Company pays fee. **Specializes in the areas of:** Engineering; Finance; General Management; Industrial; Legal; Personnel/Labor Relations; Sales; Technical. **Positions commonly filled include:** Accountant/Auditor; Attorney; Bank Officer/Manager; Blue-Collar Worker Supervisor; Chemical Engineer; Chemist; Civil Engineer; Designer; Electrician; Environmental Engineer; General Manager; Human Resources Manager; Industrial Engineer; Industrial Production Manager; Metallurgical Engineer; Mining Engineer; Nuclear Engineer; Operations/Production Manager; Petroleum Engineer; Purchasing Agent/ Manager; Software Engineer; Structural Engineer; Transportation/Traffic Specialist. **Average salary range of placements:** More than $50,000. **Number of placements per year:** 100 - 199.

MANNING & ASSOCIATES
P.O. Box 666, Belvidere IL 61008. 815/544-0944. **Contact:** John Manning, Owner. **Description:** An executive search firm. **Specializes in the areas of:** Banking.

MANUFACTURING RESOURCES INC.
156 South Prairie Avenue, P.O. Box 262, Bloomingdale IL 60108-1626. 630/529-6200. **Fax:** 630/529-6224. **Contact:** Larry Pemberton, General Manager. **Description:** An executive search firm. Company pays fee. **Specializes in the areas of:** Engineering; Food Industry; Industrial; Manufacturing. **Positions commonly filled include:** Blue-Collar Worker Supervisor; Chemical Engineer; Design Engineer; Designer; Draftsperson; Electrical/Electronics Engineer; Electrician; Food Scientist/Technologist; General Manager; Industrial Engineer; Mechanical Engineer; Quality Control Supervisor; Software Engineer. **Average salary range of placements:** $30,000 - $50,000. **Number of placements per year:** 100 - 199.

MANUFACTURING SEARCH COMPANY
175 Olde Half Bay Road, Lincolnshire IL 60069. 847/634-5518. **Contact:** Manager. **Description:** An executive search firm that provides manufacturing placements.

MANUFACTURING TECHNICAL SEARCH
One Westbrook Road, Corporate Center, Suite 330, Westchester IL 60154. 708/409-9999. **Contact:** Manager. **Description:** An executive search firm. **Specializes in the areas of:** Manufacturing.

MARGESON & ASSOCIATES
P.O. Box 668, West Dundee IL 60118. 847/428-5757. **Contact:** Manager. **Description:** A retained executive search firm.

RICHARD MARKS & ASSOCIATES
2319 Hartzell, Evanston IL 60201. 847/475-7600. **Contact:** Richard Marks. **Description:** An executive search firm. **Specializes in the areas of:** Sales; Systems Design. **Positions commonly filled include:** Systems Engineer.

MARSTELLER WILCOX ASSOCIATES, LTD.
799 Roosevelt Road, Building #3, Suite 108, Glen Ellyn IL 60137. 630/790-4300. **Fax:** 630/790-4495. **Contact:** Mark A. Wilcox, President. **E-mail address:** mark@mwaltd.com. **World Wide Web address:** http://www.mwaltd.com. **Description:** An executive search firm. The firm provides clients with a full range of retained, project-level, contract, and contingency search services. Mark Wilcox Associates also provides on-site recruiting and human resources support services. Company pays fee. **Specializes in the areas of:** Engineering; Food Industry; General Management; Industrial; Manufacturing; Personnel/Labor Relations; Sales; Technical. **Positions commonly filled include:** Account Representative; Accountant/Auditor; Branch Manager; Buyer; Chemical Engineer; Chemist; Chief Financial Officer; Civil Engineer; Computer Programmer; Design Engineer; Environmental Engineer; General Manager; Health Services Manager; Industrial Engineer; Industrial Production Manager; Manufacturing Engineer; Mechanical Engineer; Operations/Production Manager; Public Relations Specialist; Sales Executive; Sales Representative; Structural Engineer; Systems Analyst; Technical Writer/Editor; Vice President of Marketing and Sales. **Benefits available to temporary workers:** Dental Insurance; Medical Insurance; Paid Holidays; Paid Vacation. **Average salary range of placements:** More than $50,000. **Number of placements per year:** 200 - 499.

MASTERS ASSOCIATES
799 Roosevelt Road, Glen Ellyn IL 60137. 630/790-4545. **Contact:** Manager. **Description:** An executive search firm. **Specializes in the areas of:** Insurance; Sales.

MATHEY SERVICES
15170 Bethany Road, Sycamore IL 60178. 815/895-3846. **Fax:** 815/895-1046. **Contact:** Joyce Mathey, President. **Description:** An executive search firm that focuses on placement in the plastics, polymers, petrochemicals, packaging, and chemical industries. Company pays fee. **Specializes in the areas of:** Engineering; Industrial; Manufacturing; Technical. **Positions commonly filled include:** Chemical Engineer; Chemist; Electrical/Electronics Engineer; Industrial Engineer; Mechanical Engineer. **Average salary range of placements:** More than $50,000. **Number of placements per year:** 1 - 49.

PAUL MAY & ASSOCIATES (PMA)
730 North Franklin, Suite 612, Chicago IL 60610-3526. 312/649-8400. **Fax:** 312/649-8999. **Contact:** Paul May, President. **E-mail address:** pma4jobs@aol.com. **Description:** An executive search firm operating on a contingency basis that focuses on recruiting a wide range of information systems professionals. **Specializes in the areas of:** Computer Science/Software; Sales. **Positions commonly filled include:** Computer Programmer; Internet Services Manager; Management Trainee; Systems Analyst. **Average salary range of placements:** $30,000 - $50,000. **Number of placements per year:** 50 - 99.

McCORMICK SEARCH
1111 Plaza Drive, Suite 520, Schaumburg IL 60173. 847/240-0030. **Contact:** Manager. **Description:** An executive search firm. **Specializes in the areas of:** Information Systems.

M.W. McDONALD & ASSOCIATES, INC.
P.O. Box 541, Barrington IL 60010-0541. 630/238-0980. **Fax:** 630/238-0984. **Contact:** Pamela Niedermeier, Director of Research and Operations. **E-mail address:** mwminc@ais.net. **Description:** An executive search firm operating on a retainer basis. **Specializes in the areas of:** Computer Science/Software; Engineering; Sales; Technical. **Positions commonly filled include:** Computer Programmer; Design Engineer; Designer; Draftsperson; Electrical/Electronics Engineer; Industrial Engineer; Mechanical Engineer; Multimedia Designer; Systems Analyst. **Corporate headquarters location:** This Location. **Other U.S. locations:** San Francisco CA. **Average salary range of placements:** More than $50,000. **Number of placements per year:** 50 - 99.

MEDICAL RECRUITERS
351 North Main Street, Carrollton IL 62016. 217/942-9034. **Contact:** Manager. **Description:** An executive search firm. **Specializes in the areas of:** Medical Sales and Marketing.

JUAN MENEFEE & ASSOCIATES
503 South Oak Park Avenue, Oak Park IL 60304. 708/848-7722. **Fax:** 708/848-6008. **Contact:** Juan Menefee, President. **E-mail address:** jmenefee@jmarecruiter.com. **World Wide Web address:** http://www.jmarecruiter.com. **Description:** A retainer and contingency search firm. Company pays fee. **Specializes in the areas of:** Accounting/Auditing; Advertising; Engineering; Personnel/Labor Relations; Sales. **Positions commonly filled include:** Accountant/Auditor; Attorney; Computer Programmer; General Manager; Human Resources Manager; Market Research Analyst; Systems Analyst. **Average salary range of placements:** More than $50,000. **Number of placements per year:** 50 - 99.

R. MICHAELS & ASSOCIATES
P.O. Box 220, Coal Valley IL 61240. 309/234-5062. **Contact:** Manager. **Description:** An executive search firm. **Specializes in the areas of:** Engineering; Manufacturing; Technical.

MIDWEST CONSULTING CORPORATION
1110 Lake Cook Road, Suite 245, Buffalo Grove IL 60089. 847/229-1800. **Contact:** Greg Miller, President. **E-mail address:** midwestco@aol.com. **Description:** A retainer search firm. Company pays fee. **Specializes in the areas of:** Engineering; Sales. **Positions commonly filled include:** Computer Programmer; Electrical/Electronics Engineer; Software Engineer; Systems Analyst; Telecommunications Manager. **Average salary range of placements:** More than $50,000. **Number of placements per year:** 50 - 99.

NATIONAL RESTAURANT SEARCH INC.
617 North Tyler Road, St. Charles IL 60174. 630/584-8448. **Fax:** 630/584-8597. **Contact:** Office

Manager. **Description:** An executive search firm. **Specializes in the areas of:** Hotel/Restaurant.

NATIONAL SEARCH
850 South Lorraine Road, Suite 3M, Wheaton IL 60187. 630/665-8026. **Fax:** 630/665-2992. **Contact:** Walter Pierson III, President. **E-mail address:** walterpierson@alt.net. **Description:** An executive search firm focusing on sales, marketing, engineering, and contracting. The firm operates on both retainer and contingency bases. Company pays fee. **Specializes in the areas of:** Administration; Computer Science/Software; Engineering; Finance; Food Industry; General Management; Health/Medical; Industrial; Insurance; Personnel/Labor Relations; Sales; Technical; Wireless Communications. **Positions commonly filled include:** Account Manager; Account Representative; Administrative Manager; Applications Engineer; Assistant Manager; Biomedical Engineer; Branch Manager; Chemical Engineer; Computer Operator; Computer Programmer; Counselor; Customer Service Representative; Electrical/Electronics Engineer; Financial Analyst; General Manager; Industrial Engineer; Industrial Production Manager; Manufacturing Engineer; Marketing Specialist; MIS Specialist; Operations Manager; Production Manager; Sales Engineer; Sales Manager; Sales Representative; Software Engineer; Systems Analyst; Systems Manager; Telecommunications Manager. **Corporate headquarters location:** This Location. **Other U.S. locations:** Nationwide. **Average salary range of placements:** $30,000 - $50,000. **Number of placements per year:** 1 - 49.

NATIONWIDE COMPUTER SEARCH
60 East Chestnut Street, Suite 390, Chicago IL 60611. 312/944-7563. **Contact:** Office Manager. **Description:** An executive search firm. **Specializes in the areas of:** Computer Hardware/Software.

NETWORK SEARCH INC.
676 St. Claire Street, Suite 2050, Chicago IL 60610. 312/397-8811. **Contact:** Manager. **Description:** An executive search firm. **Specializes in the areas of:** Computer Hardware/Software.

NEW DIRECTIONS, INC.
P.O. Box 88, Wheaton IL 60189. 630/462-1840. **Contact:** Manager. **Description:** An executive search firm. **Specializes in the areas of:** Manufacturing.

KENNETH NICHOLAS & ASSOCIATES
7 Salt Creek Lane, Hinsdale IL 60521. 630/789-0097. **Contact:** Manager. **Description:** An executive search firm. **Specializes in the areas of:** Sales.

NOCEK & ASSOCIATES
433 Eagle's Nest Drive, Darien IL 60561. 630/834-8834. **Contact:** Manager. **Description:** An executive search firm. **Specializes in the areas of:** Accounting/Auditing; Finance.

NORRELL FINANCIAL STAFFING
35 East Wacker Drive, Suite 1545, Chicago IL 60601. 312/460-0417. **Fax:** 312/460-0319. **Contact:** Anthony S. Martorano, Manager. **Description:** An executive search firm that provides professional, outsourcing, and staffing services through a network of more than 400 companies across North America. The firm operates on a contingency basis. Founded in 1961. **Specializes in the areas of:** Accounting/Auditing; Banking; Finance. **Positions commonly filled include:** Accountant/Auditor; Budget Analyst; Credit Manager; Financial Analyst; Management Analyst/Consultant. **Corporate headquarters location:** Atlanta GA. **Average salary range of placements:** $30,000 - $50,000. **Number of placements per year:** 500 - 999.

NU-WAY SEARCH
P.O. Box 494, Lake Zurich IL 60047-0494. 847/726-8444. **Contact:** Steve Riess, Counselor. **Description:** A contingency search firm. Company pays fee. **Specializes in the areas of:** Computer Science/Software. **Positions commonly filled include:** Computer Programmer; Internet Services Manager; Software Engineer; Statistician; Systems Analyst; Technical Writer/Editor; Telecommunications Manager. **Number of placements per year:** 50 - 99.

JOHN R. O'CONNOR & ASSOCIATES
111 West Jackson Boulevard, Suite 1300, Chicago IL 60604-3505. 312/939-1392. **Contact:** John O'Connor, Owner. **Description:** An executive search firm that focuses on the placement of experienced engineers and environmental scientists. Emphasis is placed on infrastructure projects such as highways, bridges, rail/rapid transit, airports, treatment plants, and municipal engineering. Company pays fee. **Specializes in the areas of:** Engineering; Transportation. **Positions commonly filled include:** Civil Engineer; Construction Contractor; Cost Estimator; Design Engineer; Electrical/Electronics Engineer; Environmental Engineer; Environmental Scientist; Mechanical Engineer; Structural Engineer; Surveyor. **Average salary range of placements:** More than $50,000. **Number of placements per year:** 1 - 49.

OFFICEMATES5 OF WHEELING
1400 East Lake Cook Road, Suite 115, Buffalo Grove IL 60089. 847/459-6160. **Contact:** Manager. **Description:** An executive search firm. **Specializes in the areas of:** Accounting/Auditing; Administration; Advertising; Architecture/Construction; Banking; Chemical; Communications; Computer Science/Software; Electrical; Engineering; Finance; Food Industry; General Management; Health/Medical; Legal; Manufacturing; Operations Management; Pharmaceutical; Procurement; Publishing; Retail; Sales; Technical; Textiles; Transportation. **Other U.S. locations:** Nationwide.

OMEGA TECHNICAL CORPORATION
15 Spinning Wheel Road, Suite 120, Hinsdale IL 60521. 630/986-8116. **Fax:** 630/986-0036. **Contact:** Recruiter. **Description:** An executive search firm. Company pays fee. **Specializes in the areas of:** Administration; Computer Science/Software; Engineering; Industrial; Manufacturing; Personnel/Labor Relations; Technical. **Positions commonly filled include:** Aerospace Engineer; Agricultural Engineer; Biomedical Engineer; Chemical Engineer; Civil Engineer; Computer Programmer; Designer; Draftsperson; Electrical/Electronics Engineer; Electrician; Industrial Engineer; Industrial Production Manager; Mechanical Engineer; Metallurgical Engineer; Nuclear Engineer; Purchasing Agent/Manager; Quality Control Supervisor; Software Engineer; Structural Engineer; Systems Analyst; Technical Writer/Editor. **Number of placements per year:** 100 - 199.

OMNI SEARCH LTD.
7400 North Waukegan Road, Suite 1, Niles IL 60714. 847/647-7570. **Contact:** Andrew Kavathas, President. **Description:** An executive search firm. Company pays fee. **Specializes in the areas of:** Engineering; Industrial; Manufacturing; Technical. **Positions commonly filled include:** Designer; Draftsperson; Electrical/Electronics Engineer; Industrial Engineer; Industrial Production Manager; Mechanical Engineer; Operations/Production Manager; Quality Control Supervisor; Stationary Engineer. **Number of placements per year:** 1 - 49.

PAHLMAN, MURPHY AND ATTRIDGE, INC.
8 South Michigan Avenue, Suite 1306, Chicago IL 60603. 312/236-9036. **Fax:** 312/236-4629. **Contact:** Kaye Ruddy, President. **E-mail address:** jobs4you1@

aol.com. **World Wide Web address:** http://www.pmaresources.com. **Description:** An executive search firm that places both executive and clerical professionals. The firm also offers a resume service and career/outplacement counseling. **Specializes in the areas of:** Communications; Market Research; Marketing.

PARKER CROMWELL & ASSOCIATES
122 Calendar Court, La Grange IL 60625. 708/352-8350. **Contact:** Manager. **Description:** A generalist executive search firm.

PELICHEM ASSOCIATES
928 Warren Avenue, Downers Grove IL 60515. 630/960-1940. **Fax:** 630/960-1942. **Contact:** Ken Pelczarski, Owner. **Description:** An executive search firm concentrating on technical, sales/marketing, and operations positions in the chemical, mechanical, and lubrication industries. Company pays fee. **Specializes in the areas of:** Biology; Engineering; General Management; Industrial; Manufacturing; Sales; Technical. **Positions commonly filled include:** Biological Scientist; Chemical Engineer; Chemist; Food Scientist/Technologist; General Manager; Industrial Production Manager; Manufacturer's/Wholesaler's Sales Rep.; Materials Engineer; Metallurgical Engineer; Operations/Production Manager; Quality Control Supervisor; Science Technologist; Services Sales Representative. **Average salary range of placements:** $30,000 - $50,000. **Number of placements per year:** 1 - 49.

POLYTECHNICAL CONSULTANTS, INC.
7213 West Breen, Niles IL 60714. 847/470-9000. **Contact:** Manager. **Description:** An executive search firm. **Specializes in the areas of:** Engineering.

THE PRAIRIE GROUP
One Westbrook Corporation Center, Suite 300, Westchester IL 60154. 708/449-7710. **Contact:** Manager. **Description:** An executive search firm.

PRO-TECH SEARCH INC.
116 West Walnut Street, Chatham IL 62629. 217/483-3565. **Contact:** Manager. **Description:** An executive search firm. **Specializes in the areas of:** Information Technology.

PROFESSIONAL PLACEMENT SERVICES
1100 West Northwest Highway, Arlington Heights IL 60004. 847/253-5300. **Contact:** Patrick M. Latimer, President. **Description:** An executive search firm focusing on the data processing field. Company pays fee. **Specializes in the areas of:** Administration; Computer Science/Software. **Positions commonly filled include:** Computer Programmer; MIS Specialist; Software Engineer; Systems Analyst; Technical Writer/Editor. **Other U.S. locations:** Nationwide. **Average salary range of placements:** $30,000 - $50,000. **Number of placements per year:** 1 - 49.

PROFESSIONAL RESEARCH SERVICES, INC.
1101 Perimeter Drive, Suite 610, Schaumburg IL 60173. 847/995-8800. **Fax:** 847/995-8812. **Contact:** Thomas DeBourcy, President. **E-mail address:** prs1@netwave.net. **World Wide Web address:** http://www.prs1.com. **Description:** An executive search firm. The firm provides recruiting lists, contacts, candidate generation, minority recruiting, and multiple position project hiring. Company pays fee. **Specializes in the areas of:** Accounting/Auditing; Banking; Engineering; General Management; Insurance; Manufacturing; Personnel/Labor Relations; Retail; Sales. **Positions commonly filled include:** Accountant/Auditor; Aerospace Engineer; Agricultural Engineer; Attorney; Bank Officer/Manager; Biological Scientist; Biomedical Engineer; Branch Manager; Budget Analyst; Buyer; Ceramics Engineer; Chemical Engineer; Chemist; Civil Engineer; Computer Programmer; Credit Manager; Customer Service Representative; Economist; Electrical/Electronics Engineer; Financial Analyst; General Manager; Human Resources Manager; Industrial Engineer; Management Analyst/Consultant; Management Trainee; Mechanical Engineer; Public Relations Specialist; Quality Control Supervisor; Restaurant/Food Service Manager; Securities Sales Representative; Software Engineer; Statistician; Structural Engineer; Systems Analyst; Transportation/Traffic Specialist; Underwriter/Assistant Underwriter; Wholesale and Retail Buyer. **Average salary range of placements:** More than $50,000. **Number of placements per year:** 100 - 199.

PROFESSIONAL SEARCH CENTER LIMITED
1450 East American Lane, Suite 1875, Schaumburg IL 60173-6046. 847/330-3250. **Fax:** 847/330-3255. **Contact:** Jerry Hirschel, CPC, President. **E-mail address:** hdhunter1@aol.com. **Description:** An executive search firm operating on both retainer and contingency bases that focuses on the placement of information systems professionals. **Specializes in the areas of:** Computer Science/Software. **Positions commonly filled include:** Computer Programmer; Systems Analyst.

PROSEARCH PLUS
555 East Butterfield Road, Lombard IL 60148. 630/515-0500. **Fax:** 630/515-0500. **Contact:** Don Bogardus, Managing Director. **Description:** An executive search firm operating on both retainer and contingency bases. **Specializes in the areas of:** Accounting/Auditing; Administration; Art/Design; Banking; Finance; Food Industry; Personnel/Labor Relations; Retail; Sales; Secretarial. **Positions commonly filled include:** Accountant/Auditor; Bank Officer/Manager; Buyer; Clerical Supervisor; Computer Programmer; Credit Manager; Customer Service Representative; Financial Analyst; General Manager; Human Resources Manager; MIS Specialist; Services Sales Representative; Software Engineer; Systems Analyst; Technical Writer/Editor; Typist/Word Processor. **Average salary range of placements:** More than $50,000. **Number of placements per year:** 200 - 499.

QUANTUM PROFESSIONAL SEARCH
QUANTUM STAFFING SERVICES
100 West 22nd Street, Suite 115, Lombard IL 60148. 630/916-7300. **Fax:** 630/916-8338. **Contact:** Patrick Brady, President. **E-mail address:** qps@aol.com. **Description:** An executive search firm. Company pays fee. **Specializes in the areas of:** Computer Hardware/Software; Industrial; Light Industrial; Sales; Secretarial. **Positions commonly filled include:** Account Manager; Account Representative; Administrative Assistant; Administrative Manager; Branch Manager; Clerical Supervisor; Consultant; Credit Manager; Customer Service Representative; General Manager; Industrial Engineer; Industrial Production Manager; Management Analyst/Consultant; Manufacturer's/Wholesaler's Sales Rep.; Manufacturing Engineer; Marketing Manager; Operations/Production Manager; Production Manager; Project Manager; Sales Engineer; Sales Executive; Sales Manager; Secretary; Services Sales Representative; Software Engineer; Typist/Word Processor; Vice President of Sales. **Corporate headquarters location:** This Location. **Average salary range of placements:** More than $50,000. **Number of placements per year:** 100 - 199.

THE RALEIGH WARWICK GROUP
1100 Woodfield Road, Schaumburg IL 60173. 847/619-8900. **Fax:** 847/619-9151. **Contact:** Peter McManus, Manager. **Description:** An executive search

firm. Company pays fee. **Specializes in the areas of:** Accounting/Auditing; Administration; Advertising; Banking; Biology; Engineering; Finance; Industrial; Insurance; Manufacturing; Personnel/Labor Relations; Sales. **Positions commonly filled include:** Accountant/Auditor; Actuary; Adjuster; Administrative Manager; Bank Officer/Manager; Biochemist; Biological Scientist; Budget Analyst; Buyer; Chemical Engineer; Chemist; Civil Engineer; Claim Representative; Cost Estimator; Credit Manager; Customer Service Representative; Designer; Electrical/Electronics Engineer; Environmental Engineer; Financial Analyst; Human Resources Manager; Industrial Engineer; Industrial Production Manager; Internet Services Manager; Management Trainee; Market Research Analyst; Mechanical Engineer; Multimedia Designer; Purchasing Agent/ Manager; Quality Control Supervisor; Services Sales Representative; Technical Writer/Editor; Telecommunications Manager; Underwriter/Assistant Underwriter. **Average salary range of placements:** More than $50,000.

VERA L. RAST PARTNERS, INC. (VLRPI)
One South Wacker Drive, Suite 3890, Chicago IL 60606. 312/629-0339. **Fax:** 312/629-0347. **Contact:** Vera Rast, President. **Description:** An executive search firm. Company pays fee. **Specializes in the areas of:** Legal. **Positions commonly filled include:** Attorney. **Number of placements per year:** 1 - 49.

RECRUITMENT NETWORK
10600 Higgins Road, Suite 414, Rosemont IL 60018. 847/298-8830. **Fax:** 847/298-1652. **Contact:** Manager. **Description:** An executive search firm. **Specializes in the areas of:** Information Technology; Sales.

M. RECTOR & ASSOCIATES
40 South Prospect, Suite 200, Roselle IL 60172. 630/894-5060. **Fax:** 630/894-5607. **Contact:** Office Manager. **Description:** An executive search firm that provides placements in shopping centers and beauty salons. **Specializes in the areas of:** Real Estate.

REDELL SEARCH, INC.
P.O. Box 25067, Chicago IL 60625. 773/271-4449. **Fax:** 773/271-9689. **Contact:** John T. Redell, Jr., Managing Partner. **Description:** An executive search firm. Company pays fee. **Specializes in the areas of:** Administration; Computer Science/Software. **Positions commonly filled include:** Computer Programmer; Software Engineer; Systems Analyst; Technical Writer/Editor. **Number of placements per year:** 50 - 99.

REMINGTON GROUP LTD.
111 Lions Drive, Suite 219, Barrington IL 60010. 847/577-2000. **Contact:** Manager. **Description:** An executive search firm. **Specializes in the areas of:** Consumer Package Goods.

RESPONSIVE SEARCH INC.
999 Oakmont Plaza, Suite 535, Westmont IL 60559-5517. 630/789-1300. **Fax:** 630/789-1338. **Contact:** Keith D. Hansel, President. **Description:** An executive search firm operating on both retainer and contingency bases that focuses on placement in the computer industry. **Specializes in the areas of:** Computer Science/Software. **Positions commonly filled include:** Computer Programmer; Systems Analyst. **Average salary range of placements:** More than $50,000. **Number of placements per year:** 50 - 99.

RETAIL RECRUITERS
1400 East Touhy Road, Suite 212, Des Plaines IL 60018. 847/390-6100. **Contact:** Office Manager. **Description:** An executive search firm. **Specializes in the areas of:** Retail.

RETAIL STAFFERS, INC.
150 East Cook Avenue, Libertyville IL 60048. 847/362-6100. **Fax:** 847/362-1826. **Contact:** Kelly L. Anderson, Manager. **Description:** An executive search firm operating on a contingency basis. Company pays fee. **Specializes in the areas of:** General Management; Human Resources; Loss Prevention; Retail; Sales. **Positions commonly filled include:** Assistant Manager; General Manager; Loss Prevention Specialist; Management Trainee. **Number of placements per year:** 100 - 199.

REYMAN & ASSOCIATES
20 North Michigan Avenue, Suite 520, Chicago IL 60602. 312/580-0808. **Contact:** Susan Reyman. **Description:** A generalist executive search firm.

THE RICHARD/ALLEN/WINTER GROUP
102 Wilmont Road, Deerfield IL 60015. 847/948-8222. **Fax:** 847/948-8299. **Contact:** Manager. **Description:** An executive search firm.

RIDENOUR & ASSOCIATES
One East Wacker Drive, Chicago IL 60601. 312/644-1888. **Contact:** Manager. **Description:** An executive search firm. **Specializes in the areas of:** Direct Marketing.

RITT-RITT AND ASSOCIATES
1350 East Touhy Avenue, Des Plaines IL 60018. 847/827-7771. **Fax:** 847/827-9776. **Contact:** Art Ritt, President. **Description:** A retainer and contingency search firm covering all aspects of management in the food and hospitality industries including finance, franchising, marketing, general management, and sales. **Specializes in the areas of:** Food Industry; General Management; Hotel/ Restaurant; Personnel/Labor Relations. **Positions commonly filled include:** Dietician/Nutritionist; Hotel Manager; Human Resources Manager; Restaurant/ Food Service Manager. **Average salary range of placements:** More than $50,000.

THE ROBINSON GROUP
800 East Northwest Highway, Suite 809, Palatine IL 60067. 847/359-0990. **Contact:** Donald Robinson, President. **Description:** An executive search firm focusing on the placement of accounting personnel. Company pays fee. **Specializes in the areas of:** Accounting/Auditing; Consulting; General Management; Manufacturing; Sales; Tax. **Positions commonly filled include:** Auditor; Marketing Manager; Sales Manager; Tax Specialist. **Number of placements per year:** 1 - 49.

ROMAC INTERNATIONAL
20 North Wacker Drive, Suite 1360, Chicago IL 60606. 312/263-0902. **Fax:** 312/263-3023. **Contact:** Rich Cocchiaro, Recruiter. **E-mail address:** lsinger@ romac.com. **Description:** An executive search firm. **Specializes in the areas of:** Accounting/Auditing; Banking; Finance. **Positions commonly filled include:** Accountant/Auditor; Administrative Manager; Bank Officer/Manager; Budget Analyst; Computer Programmer; Customer Service Representative; Financial Analyst; General Manager; Human Resources Manager; Internet Services Manager; MIS Specialist; Property and Real Estate Manager; Services Sales Representative; Software Engineer; Strategic Relations Manager; Technical Writer/Editor. **Benefits available to temporary workers:** Dental Insurance; Medical Insurance; Paid Holidays; Paid Vacation. **Other U.S. locations:** Tampa FL. **Average salary range of placements:** $30,000 - $50,000. **Number of placements per year:** 1000+.

KEITH ROSS & ASSOCIATES, INC.
45 South Park Boulevard, Glen Ellyn IL 60137-6280. 630/858-1000. **Fax:** 630/858-9307. **Contact:** Keith Ross, President. **Description:** A contingency search firm. Company pays fee. **Specializes in the areas of:** Legal. **Positions commonly filled include:** Attorney. **Average salary range of placements:** More than $50,000.

DAVID ROWE & ASSOCIATES INC.
9152 Broadway Avenue, Brookfield IL 60513. 630/323-6166. **Contact:** Manager. **Description:** An executive search firm. **Specializes in the areas of:** Health/Medical.

RUSSELL REYNOLDS ASSOCIATES, INC.
200 South Wacker Drive, Suite 3600, Chicago IL 60606. 312/993-9696. **Contact:** Office Manager. **Description:** A retained executive search firm that mainly places middle and upper-level managers.

THE RYAN CHARLES GROUP, INC.
2021 Midwest Road, Suite 300, Oak Brook IL 60521. 773/233-9111. **Contact:** Manager. **Description:** An executive search firm. **NOTE:** Resumes can also be sent to the corporate office at 2151 West Hillsboro Boulevard, Suite 203, Deerfield FL 33442. 954/421-9112. **Specializes in the areas of:** Accounting/Auditing; Administration; Advertising; Engineering; Finance; General Management; Sales.

SHS, INC.
205 West Wacker Drive, Suite 600, Chicago IL 60606. 312/419-0370. **Fax:** 312/419-8953. **Contact:** Ric Pantaleo, Vice President. **Description:** An executive search firm. Founded in 1988. Company pays fee. **Specializes in the areas of:** Advertising; Broadcasting; General Management; Health/Medical; Sales; Telecommunications. **Positions commonly filled include:** Account Manager; Account Representative; Advertising Account Executive; Biochemist; Branch Manager; Chief Financial Officer; Computer Programmer; Customer Service Representative; Design Engineer; Editor; Editorial Assistant; Graphic Designer; Health Services Manager; Industrial Production Manager; Insurance Agent/Broker; Internet Services Manager; Managing Editor; Marketing Manager; Marketing Specialist; Multimedia Designer; Operations/Production Manager; Sales Engineer; Sales Manager; Technical Writer/Editor; Telecommunications Manager; Vice President of Finance; Video Production Coordinator; Webmaster. **Average salary range of placements:** $30,000 - $50,000. **Number of placements per year:** 1 - 49.

SALES CONSULTANTS
MANAGEMENT RECRUITERS INTERNATIONAL, INC.
3400 Dundee Road, Suite 340, Northbrook IL 60062. 847/509-9000. **Contact:** Manager. **Description:** An executive search firm. **Specializes in the areas of:** Accounting/Auditing; Administration; Advertising; Architecture/Construction; Banking; Chemical; Communications; Computer Science/Software; Design; Electrical; Engineering; Finance; Food Industry; General Management; Health/Medical; Industrial; Insurance; Legal; Manufacturing; Operations Management; Personnel/Labor Relations; Pharmaceutical; Procurement; Publishing; Retail; Sales; Technical; Textiles; Transportation.

SALES CONSULTANTS OF CHICAGO
6420 West 127th Street, Suite 209, Palos Heights IL 60463. 708/371-9677. **Fax:** 708/371-9678. **Contact:** Judy Collins, Manager. **E-mail address:** scstaff@card-recruiter.com. **World Wide Web address:** http://www.card-recruiter.com. **Description:** An executive search firm specializing in the payment services industry. Company pays fee. **Specializes in the areas of:** Administration; Banking; Computer Hardware/Software; Sales; Telecommunications. **Positions commonly filled include:** Auditor; Bank Officer/Manager; Credit Manager; Database Manager; EDP Specialist; Electrical/Electronics Engineer; Financial Analyst; Marketing Manager; Marketing Specialist; MIS Specialist; Sales Manager; Sales Representative; Statistician; Systems Analyst; Systems Manager. **Average salary range of placements:** More than $50,000. **Number of placements per year:** 1 - 49.

SALES CONSULTANTS OF OAK BROOK
1415 West 22nd Street, Suite 725, Oak Brook IL 60523. 630/990-8233. **Fax:** 630/990-2973. **Contact:** Gary Miller, Manager. **Description:** An executive search firm. **Specializes in the areas of:** Accounting/Auditing; Administration; Advertising; Architecture/Construction; Banking; Chemical; Communications; Computer Science/Software; Design; Finance; Food Industry; General Management; Health/Medical; Industrial; Insurance; Legal; Manufacturing; Operations Management; Personnel/Labor Relations; Pharmaceutical; Procurement; Publishing; Regulatory Affairs; Sales; Technical; Textiles; Transportation.

SANFORD ROSE ASSOCIATES
416 East State Street, Rockford IL 61104-1037. 815/964-4080. **Fax:** 815/964-3917. **Contact:** Dennis Wallace, Director. **E-mail address:** srarfi@aol.com. **World Wide Web address:** http://www.sanfordrose.com. **Description:** An executive search firm. **Specializes in the areas of:** Automotive; Engineering. **Positions commonly filled include:** Design Engineer; Industrial Engineer; Manufacturing Engineer; Packaging Engineer; Tool Engineer. **Corporate headquarters location:** Akron OH. **Other U.S. locations:** Nationwide. **International locations:** Singapore. **Average salary range of placements:** More than $50,000. **Number of placements per year:** 50 - 99.

SANFORD ROSE ASSOCIATES
444 South Willow, Suite 11, Effingham IL 62401. 217/342-3928. **Fax:** 217/347-7111. **Contact:** Manager. **World Wide Web address:** http://www.sanfordrose.com. **Description:** An executive search firm. **Specializes in the areas of:** Publishing.

SANFORD ROSE ASSOCIATES
208 South LaSalle, Suite 500, Chicago IL 60604. 312/460-8384. **Fax:** 312/460-8385. **Contact:** Manager. **World Wide Web address:** http://www.sanfordrose.com. **Description:** An executive search firm. **Specializes in the areas of:** Information Technology; Sales.

SANFORD ROSE ASSOCIATES
9405 West Bormet Drive, Suite 1, Mokena IL 60448. 708/479-4854. **Fax:** 708/479-4750. **Contact:** Office Manager. **Description:** An executive search firm. **Specializes in the areas of:** Distribution; Logistics.

DAVID SAXNER & ASSOCIATES
3 First National Plaza, Suite 1400, Chicago IL 60602. 312/214-3360. **Contact:** David Saxner, Owner. **Description:** An executive search firm. David Saxner & Associates also provides management consulting services to the commercial real estate market. **Specializes in the areas of:** Real Estate.

J.R. SCOTT & ASSOCIATES
One South Wacker Drive, Suite 1616, Chicago IL 60606. 312/795-4400. **Contact:** Sherwin J. Fischer, Senior Manager. **Description:** An executive search firm. Company pays fee. **Specializes in the areas of:** Brokerage. **Positions commonly filled include:** Financial Analyst; Management Analyst/Consultant; Securities

Sales Representative. **Number of placements per year:** 50 - 99.

SEARCH CENTRE INC.
1430 Branding Lane, Suite 119, Downers Grove IL 60515. 630/963-3033. **Fax:** 630/963-3170. **Contact:** Scott Rollins, President. **Description:** An executive search firm. Company pays fee. **Specializes in the areas of:** Insurance; Personnel/Labor Relations. **Positions commonly filled include:** Actuary; Human Resources Manager. **Average salary range of placements:** $30,000 - $50,000. **Number of placements per year:** 50 - 99.

SEARCH CONSULTING GROUP
1540 East Dundee Road, Suite 170, Palatine IL 60067. 847/991-4473. **Contact:** Office Manager. **Description:** A generalist executive search firm.

SEARCH DYNAMICS INC.
9420 West Foster Avenue, Suite 200, Chicago IL 60656-1006. 773/992-3900. **Contact:** George Apostle, President. **Description:** A retainer and contingency search firm. **Specializes in the areas of:** Computer Science/Software; Engineering; Manufacturing; Technical. **Positions commonly filled include:** Design Engineer; Designer; Draftsperson; Industrial Engineer; Industrial Production Manager; Metallurgical Engineer; Quality Control Supervisor; Software Engineer. **Number of placements per year:** 50 - 99.

SEARCH ENTERPRISES, INC.
160 Quail Ridge Drive, Westmont IL 60559. 630/654-2300. **Fax:** 630/654-2310. **Contact:** Frank Polacek, President. **E-mail address:** sesi@searchenterprises.com. **World Wide Web address:** http://www.searchenterprises.com. **Description:** An executive search firm operating on a contingency basis. Company pays fee. **Specializes in the areas of:** Engineering; Food Industry; Technical. **Positions commonly filled include:** Biomedical Engineer; Chemical Engineer; Electrical/Electronics Engineer; Industrial Production Manager; Manufacturing Engineer; Mechanical Engineer; Metallurgical Engineer; Production Manager; Project Manager; Quality Control Supervisor. **Average salary range of placements:** More than $50,000. **Number of placements per year:** 100 - 199.

SEARCH SOURCE
2945 Madison Avenue, Granite City IL 62040. 618/876-6060. **Contact:** Manager. **Description:** An executive search firm. **Specializes in the areas of:** Broadcasting; Telecommunications.

SELECT SEARCH INC.
1111 West Dundee Road, 2nd Floor, Wheeling IL 60092. 847/419-8999. **Contact:** Office Manager. **Description:** An executive search firm. **Specializes in the areas of:** Data Processing; Engineering; Technical.

SELLERS & ASSOCIATES
805 Augusta Avenue, Elgin IL 60120. 847/888-1568. **Fax:** 847/888-0028. **Contact:** Steve Sellers, President. **Description:** An executive search firm. Company pays fee. **Specializes in the areas of:** Electronics; Engineering; Manufacturing. **Positions commonly filled include:** Design Engineer; Draftsperson; Electrical/Electronics Engineer; Electrician; Software Engineer; Telecommunications Manager. **Average salary range of placements:** $30,000 - $50,000. **Number of placements per year:** 1 - 49.

SEVCOR INTERNATIONAL, INC.
One Pierce Place, Suite 400E, Itasca IL 60143. 630/250-3088. **Fax:** 630/250-3089. **Contact:** J. Randy Severinsen, President. **Description:** An executive search firm. Company pays fee. **Specializes in the areas of:** Computer Science/Software; Insurance; Technical. **Positions commonly filled include:** Actuary; Computer Programmer; Systems Analyst. **Number of placements per year:** 100 - 199.

SHORR GROUP
500 North Michigan Avenue, Suite 820, Chicago IL 60611. 312/644-5100. **Contact:** Office Manager. **Description:** An executive search firm.

SIEGEL ASSOCIATES
330 West Diversey Parkway, Chicago IL 60657. 773/327-4479. **Contact:** Manager. **Description:** An executive search firm. **NOTE:** The firm places mid- to senior-level executives only with at least 3 years of market research experience. **Specializes in the areas of:** Market Research.

D.W. SIMPSON & CO.
625 North Michigan Avenue, Chicago IL 60611. 312/654-5220. **Fax:** 312/951-8386. **Contact:** Beth Rave, Director of Operations. **E-mail address:** actuaries@aol.com. **Description:** An executive search firm. Company pays fee. **Specializes in the areas of:** Insurance. **Positions commonly filled include:** Actuary. **Average salary range of placements:** More than $50,000. **Number of placements per year:** 100 - 199.

SMITH HANLEY ASSOCIATES, INC.
200 West Madison, Suite 2110, Chicago IL 60606. 312/629-2400. **Fax:** 312/629-0615. **Contact:** Linda Burtch, General Manager. **World Wide Web address:** http://www.smithhanley.com. **Description:** An executive search firm. Company pays fee. **Specializes in the areas of:** Banking; Finance; Food Industry; Health/Medical; Insurance; Market Research; Quantitative Marketing. **Positions commonly filled include:** Credit Manager; Database Manager; Market Research Analyst; Marketing Manager; Statistician; Systems Analyst. **Corporate headquarters location:** New York NY. **Average salary range of placements:** More than $50,000. **Number of placements per year:** 50 - 99.

RALPH SMITH & ASSOCIATES
540 West Frontage Road, Suite 3335, Northfield IL 60093. 847/441-0900. **Fax:** 847/441-0902. **Contact:** Ralph E. Smith, President. **Description:** An executive search firm. Company pays fee. **Specializes in the areas of:** Food Industry; General Management; Industrial; Manufacturing; Personnel/Labor Relations; Sales. **Positions commonly filled include:** Controller; General Manager; Human Resources Manager; Marketing Manager; Operations/Production Manager; Sales Manager. **Average salary range of placements:** More than $50,000. **Number of placements per year:** 1 - 49.

SMITH SCOTT & ASSOCIATES
P.O. Box 941, Lake Forest IL 60045. 847/295-9517. **Fax:** 847/295-9534. **Contact:** Gary J. Smith, Managing Partner. **E-mail address:** gjsmith@smithscott.com. **World Wide Web address:** http://www.smithscott.com. **Description:** An executive search firm. Company pays fee. **Specializes in the areas of:** Computer Science/Software; Information Technology; Personnel/Labor Relations. **Positions commonly filled include:** Human Resources Manager; Systems Analyst. **Average salary range of placements:** More than $50,000. **Number of placements per year:** 1 - 49.

SNELLING PERSONNEL SERVICES
100 North LaSalle Street, Suite 2005, Chicago IL 60602. 312/419-6100. **Fax:** 312/419-6646. **Contact:** Mark Stevens, General Manager. **Description:** An

executive search firm focusing on the recruitment of sales professionals. Company pays fee. **Specializes in the areas of:** Sales; Secretarial. **Corporate headquarters location:** Dallas TX. **Other U.S. locations:** Nationwide. **Average salary range of placements:** $30,000 - $50,000. **Number of placements per year:** 200 - 499.

SNELLING PERSONNEL SERVICES
331 Fulton Street, Peoria IL 61602-1499. 309/676-5581. **Contact:** Sara Zoeller, Manager. **Description:** An executive search firm. Company pays fee. **Specializes in the areas of:** Accounting/Auditing; Engineering; Finance; Sales. **Positions commonly filled include:** Accountant/Auditor; Branch Manager; Budget Analyst; Chemical Engineer; Computer Programmer; Design Engineer; Electrical/Electronics Engineer; General Manager; Hotel Manager; Management Trainee; Mechanical Engineer; MIS Specialist; Restaurant/Food Service Manager; Services Sales Representative; Software Engineer; Systems Analyst; Telecommunications Manager. **Corporate headquarters location:** Dallas TX. **Other U.S. locations:** Nationwide. **Average salary range of placements:** $30,000 - $50,000. **Number of placements per year:** 100 - 199.

SNELLING SEARCH
2201 Fifth Avenue, Suite 5, Moline IL 61265. 309/797-1101. **Fax:** 309/797-7099. **Contact:** James Roeder, Vice President. **E-mail address:** snelling@netexpress.net. **World Wide Web address:** http://www.snellingmoline.com. **Description:** An executive search firm operating on a contingency basis. **Specializes in the areas of:** Accounting/Auditing; Administration; Computer Science/Software; Engineering; Personnel/Labor Relations; Sales. **Positions commonly filled include:** Agricultural Engineer; Buyer; Claim Representative; Computer Programmer; Design Engineer; Electrical/Electronics Engineer; Industrial Engineer; Industrial Production Manager; Internet Services Manager; Management Analyst/Consultant; Materials Engineer; Metallurgical Engineer; Multimedia Designer; Purchasing Agent/Manager; Software Engineer; Systems Analyst. **Corporate headquarters location:** Dallas TX. **Average salary range of placements:** $30,000 - $50,000. **Number of placements per year:** 100 - 199.

SOURCE SERVICES CORPORATION
3701 West Algonquin Road, Suite 380, Rolling Meadows IL 60008. 847/392-0244. **Fax:** 847/577-7693. **Contact:** Manager. **Description:** An executive search firm. The divisions at this location include Source EDP and Accountant Source Temps. **Specializes in the areas of:** Accounting/Auditing; Computer Hardware/Software; Information Technology.

STERLING-GRANT
910 Skokie Highway, Suite 106, Northbrook IL 60062. **Contact:** Manager. **Description:** An executive search firm.

STERN PROFESSIONAL SEARCH & CONSULTANTS, INC.
680 North Lake Shore Drive, Suite 607, Chicago IL 60611. 312/587-7777. **Fax:** 312/587-8907. **Contact:** Janet Grodsky, President. **Description:** An executive search firm that focuses on the furnishings and interior design industries. Company pays fee. **Specializes in the areas of:** Sales. **Positions commonly filled include:** Account Representative; Architect; Branch Manager; CADD Operator; Interior Designer; Project Manager; Sales Executive; Sales Manager; Sales Representative; Vice President of Sales. **Other U.S. locations:** Nationwide. **Average salary range of placements:** $30,000 - $50,000. **Number of placements per year:** 100 - 199.

STONE ENTERPRISES, LTD.
645 North Michigan Avenue, Suite 800, Chicago IL 60611. 773/404-9300. **Fax:** 773/404-9388. **Contact:** Susan L. Stone, President. **Description:** An executive search firm. **Specializes in the areas of:** Accounting/Auditing; Computer Hardware/Software; Distribution; Engineering; Manufacturing; Sales Promotion; Telecommunications.

STRATEGIC RESOURCES UNLIMITED
8410 West Bryn Mawr, 4th Floor, Citicorp Plaza, Chicago IL 60631. 773/380-1250. **Fax:** 773/380-1358. **Contact:** Roberta A. Gilna, President. **E-mail address:** donnz@juno.com. **Description:** An executive search firm operating on both retained and contingency bases. Company pays fee. **Specializes in the areas of:** Accounting/Auditing; Architecture/Construction; Finance; Food Industry; General Management; Personnel/Labor Relations; Sales. **Positions commonly filled include:** Accountant; Auditor; Budget Analyst; Buyer; Chief Financial Officer; Controller; Finance Director; Financial Analyst; General Manager; Human Resources Manager; Market Research Analyst; Marketing Manager; Public Relations Specialist; Purchasing Agent/Manager; Sales Executive. **Corporate headquarters location:** This Location. **Average salary range of placements:** More than $50,000. **Number of placements per year:** 1 - 49.

STRATEGIC SEARCH CORPORATION
645 North Michigan Avenue, Suite 800, Chicago IL 60611. 312/944-4000. **Contact:** Manager. **Description:** An executive search firm.

SYNERGISTICS ASSOCIATES LTD.
400 North State Street, Suite 400, Chicago IL 60610. 312/467-5450. **Fax:** 312/822-0246. **Contact:** Alvin Borenstine, President. **Description:** A retained executive search firm focusing on the placement of chief information officers and computer technology professionals. Company pays fee. **Specializes in the areas of:** Computer Science/Software. **Average salary range of placements:** More than $50,000. **Number of placements per year:** 1 - 49.

SYSTEMS ONE, LTD.
1100 East Woodfield Road, Schaumburg IL 60173-5116. 847/619-9300. **Fax:** 847/619-0071. **Contact:** Ed Hildy, Manager. **Description:** An executive search firm operating on both retainer and contingency bases. Company pays fee. **Specializes in the areas of:** Computer Science/Software. **Positions commonly filled include:** Computer Programmer; Management Analyst/Consultant; MIS Specialist; Software Engineer; Systems Analyst; Telecommunications Manager. **Average salary range of placements:** More than $50,000.

TSC MANAGEMENT SERVICES
P.O. Box 384, Barrington IL 60011. 847/381-0167. **Fax:** 847/381-2169. **Contact:** Robert Stanton, President. **E-mail address:** tscmgtserve@aol.com. **Description:** An executive search firm. Company pays fee. **Specializes in the areas of:** Computer Science/Software; Engineering; Industrial; Interactive Entertainment; Manufacturing; Technical. **Positions commonly filled include:** Computer Programmer; Designer; Electrical/Electronics Engineer; Industrial Engineer; Mechanical Engineer; Quality Control Supervisor; Software Engineer; Statistician; Systems Analyst; Technical Writer/Editor. **Average salary range of placements:** More than $50,000. **Number of placements per year:** 50 - 99.

ROY TALMAN & ASSOCIATES
150 South Wacker Drive, Suite 2250, Chicago IL 60606. 312/425-1300. **Fax:** 312/425-0100. **Contact:**

Ilya Talman, President. **E-mail address:** talman@mcs.com. **World Wide Web address:** http://www.roy-talman.com. **Description:** An executive search firm. Company pays fee. **Specializes in the areas of:** Administration; Banking; Computer Science/Software; Engineering; Finance. **Positions commonly filled include:** Computer Programmer; EDP Specialist; Financial Analyst; Mathematician; MIS Specialist; Software Engineer; Systems Analyst. **Average salary range of placements:** $30,000 - $50,000. **Number of placements per year:** 100 - 199.

TARGET SEARCH INC.
4 Paddock Street, Lemont IL 60439. 630/654-0800. **Contact:** Manager. **Description:** An executive search firm. **Specializes in the areas of:** Data Processing.

TECHNICAL NETWORK SEARCH, INC.
339 West River Road, Suite 203, Elgin IL 60123. 847/888-0875. **Fax:** 847/888-2292. **Contact:** Alan Wera, General Manager. **Description:** An executive search firm. Company pays fee. **Specializes in the areas of:** Engineering; Manufacturing. **Positions commonly filled include:** Designer; Electrical/Electronics Engineer; Industrial Engineer; Mechanical Engineer; Software Engineer; Technical Writer/Editor. **Average salary range of placements:** More than $50,000. **Number of placements per year:** 1 - 49.

TECHNICAL RECRUITING CONSULTANTS
1100 West Northwest Highway, Suite 208, Mt. Prospect IL 60056. 847/394-1101. **Contact:** Dick Latimer, President. **Description:** An executive search firm. Company pays fee. **Specializes in the areas of:** Administration; Computer Science/Software; Engineering; Manufacturing. **Positions commonly filled include:** Civil Engineer; Computer Programmer; EDP Specialist; Electrical/Electronics Engineer; Industrial Engineer; Manufacturing Engineer; Mechanical Engineer; MIS Specialist; Software Engineer; Systems Analyst. **Number of placements per year:** 50 - 99.

TECHNICAL SEARCH
450 East Devon Avenue, Suite 225, Itasca IL 60143-1261. 630/775-0700. **Contact:** Recruiter. **Description:** An engineering search firm. **Specializes in the areas of:** Engineering; Food Industry; Manufacturing. **Positions commonly filled include:** Design Engineer; Designer; Draftsperson; Electrical/Electronics Engineer; Mechanical Engineer; Software Engineer. **Average salary range of placements:** More than $50,000. **Number of placements per year:** 50 - 99.

TUFT & ASSOCIATES
1209 North Astor Street, Chicago IL 60610. 312/642-8889. **Contact:** Manager. **Description:** An executive search firm that focuses on providing placements in professional associations. **Specializes in the areas of:** Nonprofit.

TWIN OAKS TECHNICAL, INC.
12503 South 90th Street, Palos Park IL 60464. 708/923-6040. **Contact:** Manager. **Description:** An executive search firm. **Specializes in the areas of:** Chemical.

K. DAVID UMLAUF EXECUTIVE SEARCH CONSULTANTS
730 North Franklin Street, #612, Chicago IL 60610-3526. 312/649-0304. **Fax:** 312/649-8999. **Contact:** K. David Umlauf, President. **Description:** An executive search firm operating on both retainer and contingency bases that focuses on trust and investment management. The firm represents bank trust departments in search of administrative, investment, and business development executives. Company pays fee. **Specializes in the areas of:** Banking. **Positions commonly filled include:** Bank Officer/Manager. **Average salary range of placements:** More than $50,000. **Number of placements per year:** 1 - 49.

VALENTINE & ASSOCIATES
One Woodfield Lake, Suite 117, Schaumburg IL 60173. 847/605-8090. **Contact:** Janice Book, Recruiter. **Description:** An executive search firm focusing on the placement of material management professionals. Company pays fee. **Specializes in the areas of:** Food Industry; Manufacturing. **Positions commonly filled include:** Buyer; Customer Service Representative; Industrial Production Manager; Operations/Production Manager; Purchasing Agent/Manager; Systems Analyst. **Average salary range of placements:** $30,000 - $50,000.

VERDIN ASSOCIATES
25 East Washington Street, Suite 1500, Chicago IL 60602. 312/855-1055. **Contact:** Office Manager. **Description:** An executive search firm. **Specializes in the areas of:** Legal.

T.I. VINCENT & ASSOCIATES, LTD.
24362 Tanager Court, Barrington IL 60010. 847/540-8440. **Contact:** Tom LuBecky, Vice President. **Description:** An executive search firm. Company pays fee. **Specializes in the areas of:** Brokerage; Finance; Investment. **Positions commonly filled include:** Branch Manager; Broker; Brokerage Clerk; Management; Securities Sales Representative; Support Personnel. **Number of placements per year:** 1 - 49.

ANNE VIOLANTE & ASSOCIATES
770 North Halsted Street, Suite 206, Chicago IL 60622-5972. 312/633-9067. **Contact:** Anne Violante, President. **Description:** An attorney search firm operating on both retainer and contingency bases. **Specializes in the areas of:** Legal. **Positions commonly filled include:** Attorney. **Average salary range of placements:** More than $50,000. **Number of placements per year:** 1 - 49.

VOGRINC & SHORT
429 Phelps Avenue, Rockford IL 61108. 815/394-1001. **Contact:** Manager. **Description:** An executive search firm. **Specializes in the areas of:** Manufacturing.

VOIGT ASSOCIATES
601 Skokie Boulevard, Northbrook IL 60062. 847/564-4152. **Contact:** Raymond Voigt, President. **Description:** An executive search firm operating on a retainer basis that serves the pharmaceutical and biotechnology industries' needs for senior-level scientific, technical, professional, and managerial personnel. Company pays fee. **Specializes in the areas of:** Biology; Technical. **Positions commonly filled include:** Biological Scientist; Biomedical Engineer; Chemical Engineer; Chemist; General Manager. **Other U.S. locations:** Nationwide. **Average salary range of placements:** More than $50,000. **Number of placements per year:** 1 - 49.

WATERFORD EXECUTIVE GROUP
One North 141 County Farm Road, Winfield IL 60190. 630/690-0055. **Contact:** Manager. **Description:** An executive search firm. **Specializes in the areas of:** Insurance.

MICHAEL WAYNE RECRUITERS
1491 Ridge Road, Highland Park IL 60035. 847/831-9344. **Fax:** 847/831-9352. **Contact:** Irwin Goldman, President. **E-mail address:** xecsrch@aol.com. **Description:** A retainer and contingency search firm. Company pays fee. **Specializes in the areas of:** Food Industry. **Positions commonly filled include:** Architect; Buyer; Draftsperson; Food Scientist/Technologist;

Human Resources Manager; Transportation/Traffic Specialist; Wholesale and Retail Buyer. **Average salary range of placements:** More than $50,000. **Number of placements per year:** 1 - 49.

RAY WHITE ASSOCIATES
875 North Michigan Avenue, Chicago IL 60611. 312/266-0100. **Fax:** 312/266-9149. **Contact:** Ray White, President. **Description:** An executive search firm that recruits for various positions in the automotive industry. Company pays fee. **Specializes in the areas of:** Automotive. **Positions commonly filled include:** Account Manager; Applications Engineer; Automotive Mechanic; Branch Manager; Buyer; Controller; Design Engineer; Electrical/Electronics Engineer; Marketing Manager; Project Manager; Quality Control Supervisor; Sales Engineer; Sales Executive; Sales Representative. **Average salary range of placements:** More than $50,000.

ROBERT WHITFIELD & ASSOCIATES
155 North Michigan Avenue, Chicago IL 60601. 312/938-9120. **Contact:** Robert Whitfield. **Description:** An executive search firm. **Specializes in the areas of:** Legal. **Positions commonly filled include:** Attorney.

PHILIP WIELAND & ASSOCIATES
2525 Greenwood Avenue, Wilmette IL 60091. 847/256-8666. **Contact:** Philip J. Wieland, President. **Description:** An executive search firm. **Specializes in the areas of:** Legal.

J. WILLIAMS & ASSOCIATES
151 North Michigan Avenue, Suite 1614, Chicago IL 60601. 312/540-1585. **Contact:** Juanita Williams, Principal. **Description:** An executive search firm that focuses solely on placing patent attorneys. **Specializes in the areas of:** Legal.

WILSON-DOUGLAS-JORDAN
70 West Madison Street, Chicago IL 60602-4205. 312/782-0286. **Contact:** John Wilson, President. **Description:** An executive search firm operating on a retainer basis that concentrates on the information technology industry. Wilson-Douglas-Jordan's clients include several *Fortune* 100 companies and Big Six accounting firms. Company pays fee. **Specializes in the areas of:** Computer Science/Software. **Positions commonly filled include:** Computer Programmer; Management Analyst/Consultant; MIS Specialist; Software Engineer; Systems Analyst; Telecommunications Manager. **Number of placements per year:** 50 - 99.

WINSTON, ROONEY & GREEN
225 West Washington Street, Suite 525, Chicago IL 60606. 312/201-9777. **Fax:** 312/201-9781. **Contact:** David Winston, Recruiter. **Description:** An executive search firm. Company pays fee. **Positions commonly filled include:** Attorney. **Number of placements per year:** 1 - 49.

WITT/KIEFFER, FORD, HADELMAN & LLOYD
2015 Spring Road, Suite 510, Oak Brook IL 60521. 630/990-1370. **Contact:** Manager. **Description:** An executive search firm for upper-level professionals. **Specializes in the areas of:** Health/Medical.

XAGAS & ASSOCIATES
1127 Fargo Boulevard, Geneva IL 60134. 630/232-7044. **Contact:** Steve Xagas, President. **Description:** A retained search firm focusing on the recruitment of quality assurance professionals, operations managers, and automation specialists. The firm also offers career and job search counseling. Company pays fee. **Specializes in the areas of:** Engineering; Food Industry; Industrial; Manufacturing; Technical. **Positions commonly filled include:** Electrical/Electronics Engineer; Mechanical Engineer; Metallurgical Engineer; Operations/Production Manager; Quality Control Supervisor; Software Engineer. **Average salary range of placements:** More than $50,000. **Number of placements per year:** 1 - 49.

PERMANENT EMPLOYMENT AGENCIES

AARP FOUNDATION
SENIOR COMMUNITY SERVICE EMPLOYMENT PROGRAM
P.O. Box 630, 1210 North Main, Edwardsville IL 62025. 618/656-5710. **Contact:** June M. Nealy, Project Director. **Description:** A permanent employment agency for senior citizens. **Specializes in the areas of:** Nonprofit.

A.B.A. PLACEMENTS
A.B.A. TEMPORARIES
1526 Miner Street, Des Plaines IL 60016. 847/297-3535. **Fax:** 847/297-4545. **Contact:** Mic Bennett, Vice President. **World Wide Web address:** http://www.aba-workit.com. **Description:** A permanent employment agency that focuses on office support and industrial placement. Company pays fee. **Specializes in the areas of:** Accounting/Auditing; Administration; Banking; Food Industry; Industrial; Insurance; Legal; Light Industrial; Office Support; Personnel/Labor Relations; Printing; Retail; Sales; Secretarial. **Positions commonly filled include:** Account Manager; Account Representative; Accountant/Auditor; Bank Officer/Manager; Branch Manager; Brokerage Clerk; Buyer; Claim Representative; Computer Operator; Credit Manager; Customer Service Representative; Editorial Assistant; Human Resources Manager; Management Analyst/Consultant; Operations Manager; Paralegal; Production Manager; Quality Control Supervisor; Sales Executive; Sales Manager; Sales Representative; Secretary; Telecommunications Manager; Transportation/Traffic Specialist; Typist/Word Processor. **Benefits available to temporary workers:** Bonus Award/Plan; Medical Insurance; Paid Vacation. **Corporate headquarters location:** This Location. **Other area locations:** Rolling Meadows IL; Wheeling IL. **Average salary range of placements:** $20,000 - $29,999. **Number of placements per year:** 500 - 999.

ASI PERSONNEL SERVICE, INC.
233 North Michigan Avenue, Suite 2306, Chicago IL 60601. 312/819-4690. **Contact:** Clarice Moore, Client Relations. **Description:** A permanent employment agency. Company pays fee. **Specializes in the areas of:** Accounting/Auditing; Banking; General Management; Personnel/Labor Relations; Sales; Secretarial. **Positions commonly filled include:** Accountant/Auditor; Administrative Manager; Advertising Clerk; Bank Officer/Manager; Blue-Collar Worker Supervisor; Branch Manager; Claim Representative; Counselor; Customer Service Representative; Human Resources Specialist; MIS Specialist; Public Relations Specialist; Services Sales Representative; Typist/Word Processor. **Corporate headquarters location:** This Location. **Number of placements per year:** 500 - 999.

ABLEST STAFFING
611 East State Street, Geneva IL 60134. 630/232-1883. **Fax:** 630/232-1904. **Contact:** Carolyn Melka, Office Manager. **Description:** A permanent

employment agency. **Specializes in the areas of:** Computer Science/Software; Health/Medical; Legal; Manufacturing.

ACCURATE PERSONNEL INC.
9 South Fairview Avenue, Park Ridge IL 60068. 847/692-6740. **Fax:** 847/692-6751. **Contact:** Manager. **Description:** A permanent employment agency. Company pays fee. **Specializes in the areas of:** Accounting/Auditing; Banking; Industrial; Secretarial. **Positions commonly filled include:** Accountant/Auditor; Blue-Collar Worker Supervisor; Clerical Supervisor; Counselor; Human Resources Specialist; Quality Control Supervisor; Services Sales Representative; Typist/Word Processor. **Average salary range of placements:** $20,000 - $29,999. **Number of placements per year:** 50 - 99.

ACCURATE RECRUITING INC.
200 West Adams, Suite 2007, Chicago IL 60606. 312/357-2500. **Fax:** 312/630-1165. **Contact:** Manager. **Description:** A permanent employment agency that also provides temporary placements. Company pays fee. **Specializes in the areas of:** Advertising; Economics; Personnel/Labor Relations; Publishing; Sales; Secretarial. **Positions commonly filled include:** Advertising Clerk; Brokerage Clerk; Clerical Supervisor; Customer Service Representative; Editor; General Manager; Human Resources Specialist; Management Trainee; Manufacturer's/Wholesaler's Sales Rep.; Public Relations Specialist; Securities Sales Representative; Services Sales Representative; Telecommunications Manager; Typist/Word Processor. **Average salary range of placements:** $20,000 - $29,999.

ADVANCED PERSONNEL, INC.
1020 Milwaukee Avenue, Suite 105, Deerfield IL 60015. 847/520-9111. **Fax:** 847/520-9489. **Contact:** Gina Sendef, Operations Manager. **Description:** A permanent employment agency that also provides temporary placements and career/outplacement counseling. Founded in 1987. Company pays fee. **Specializes in the areas of:** Office Support. **Positions commonly filled include:** Administrative Assistant; Customer Service Representative; Data Entry Clerk. **Benefits available to temporary workers:** 401(k); Paid Vacation; Referral Bonus Plan. **Corporate headquarters location:** This Location. **Other area locations:** Chicago IL; Gurnee IL; Lombard IL; Rosemont IL; Schaumburg IL. **Average salary range of placements:** $20,000 - $29,999. **Number of placements per year:** 100 - 199.

ADVANCED PERSONNEL, INC.
225 West Washington Street, Suite 500, Chicago IL 60606. 312/422-9333. **Fax:** 312/422-9310. **Contact:** Manager. **Description:** A permanent employment agency. **Specializes in the areas of:** Finance. **Corporate headquarters location:** This Location. **Other area locations:** Gurnee IL; Lombard IL; Rosemont IL; Schaumburg IL.

ADVANTAGE PERSONNEL INC.
1550 North Northwest Highway, Suite 109-C, Park Ridge IL 60068-1458. 847/803-4422. **Fax:** 847/803-4423. **Contact:** Jim Harrison, Owner/Recruiter. **Description:** A permanent placement agency. Company pays fee. **Specializes in the areas of:** Administration; Direct Marketing; Sales. **Positions commonly filled include:** Client Services Representative. **Number of placements per year:** 1 - 49.

AFFILIATED PERSONNEL CONSULTANTS, LTD.
750 West Lake Cook Road, Suite 110, Buffalo Grove IL 60089. 847/520-3200. **Fax:** 847/520-3455. **Contact:** Karen Chern, Owner. **E-mail address:** apc@ais.net. **World Wide Web address:** http://www.apc750@aol.com. **Description:** A permanent employment agency that also provides temporary placements. Company pays fee. **Specializes in the areas of:** Accounting/Auditing; Computer Science/Software; Personnel/Labor Relations; Sales; Secretarial. **Positions commonly filled include:** Account Representative; Administrative Assistant; Clerical Supervisor; Computer Operator; Computer Programmer; Customer Service Representative; Human Resources Manager; Management Trainee; Marketing Specialist; Purchasing Agent/Manager; Sales Executive; Secretary; Typist/Word Processor. **Average salary range of placements:** $20,000 - $29,999.

AMERICAN MEDICAL PERSONNEL INC.
30 East Huron, Suite 4102, Chicago IL 60611-2722. 312/337-4221. **Contact:** Director. **Description:** A permanent employment agency. Company pays fee. **Specializes in the areas of:** Health/Medical; Insurance. **Positions commonly filled include:** Clinical Lab Technician; EEG Technologist; EKG Technician; Health Services Manager; Medical Assistant; Medical Doctor; Nuclear Medicine Technologist; Occupational Therapist; Office Manager; Pharmacist; Physical Therapist; Physician; Radiological Technologist; Registered Nurse; Respiratory Therapist; Surgical Technician; Transcriptionist. **Number of placements per year:** 100 - 199.

AVAILABILITY, INC.
P.O. Box 562, Alton IL 62002. 618/467-6449. **Contact:** Lee J. Hamel, Manager. **Description:** A permanent employment agency. **Specializes in the areas of:** Accounting/Auditing; Administration; Banking; Clerical; Computer Hardware/Software; Engineering; Finance; Sales; Technical.

B-W AND ASSOCIATES, INC.
4415 West Harrison Street, Suite 444, Hillside IL 60162. 708/449-5400. **Fax:** 708/449-5405. **Contact:** Jim Burns, Manager. **E-mail address:** jybbw@aol.com. **Description:** A permanent employment agency. **Specializes in the areas of:** Architecture/Construction; Engineering; Food Industry; Health/Medical; Manufacturing.

BANNER PERSONNEL SERVICE, INC.
122 South Michigan Avenue, Chicago IL 60603. 312/704-6000. **Fax:** 312/580-2515. **Contact:** Laura Long, Vice President. **Description:** A permanent employment agency. Company pays fee. **Specializes in the areas of:** Industrial; Personnel/Labor Relations; Sales; Secretarial. **Positions commonly filled include:** Blue-Collar Worker Supervisor; Clerical Supervisor; Computer Programmer; Customer Service Representative; Human Resources Specialist; Quality Control Supervisor; Typist/Word Processor. **Corporate headquarters location:** This Location. **Average salary range of placements:** $20,000 - $29,999. **Number of placements per year:** 200 - 499.

BANNER PERSONNEL SERVICE, INC.
2215 York Road, Suite 103, Oak Brook IL 60523. 630/574-9499. **Fax:** 630/574-2218. **Contact:** Manager. **Description:** A permanent employment agency. **Specializes in the areas of:** Accounting/Auditing; Consulting; Engineering; Finance; General Management; Industrial; Manufacturing; Office Support; Sales; Secretarial; Technical. **Positions commonly filled include:** Accountant/Auditor; Administrator; Aerospace Engineer; Bookkeeper; Chemical Engineer; Civil Engineer; Computer Programmer; Consultant; Data Entry Clerk; EDP Specialist; Electrical/Electronics Engineer; Environmental Engineer; Financial Analyst; Industrial Engineer; Management Trainee; Mechanical Engineer; Packaging Engineer; Plant Manager; Quality Control

Supervisor; Safety Engineer; Sales Representative; Secretary; Software Engineer; Supervisor; Support Personnel; Systems Analyst; Tax Specialist; Water/Wastewater Engineer. **Corporate headquarters location:** Chicago IL.

BANNER PERSONNEL SERVICE, INC.
1701 East Woodfield Road, Suite 611, Schaumburg IL 60173. 847/706-9180. **Fax:** 847/706-9187. **Contact:** Elaine Ott, Branch Manager. **Description:** A permanent employment agency. Founded in 1970. **Specializes in the areas of:** Accounting/Auditing; Clerical; Consulting; Engineering; Entry-Level Management; Finance; General Management; Industrial; Manufacturing; Office Support; Sales; Secretarial; Technical. **Positions commonly filled include:** Accountant/Auditor; Aerospace Engineer; Bookkeeper; Chemical Engineer; Civil Engineer; Computer Programmer; Consultant; Data Entry Clerk; EDP Specialist; Electrical/Electronics Engineer; Factory Worker; Financial Analyst; Industrial Engineer; Manufacturing Engineer; Mechanical Engineer; Packaging Engineer; Plant Manager; Quality Control Supervisor; Safety Engineer; Sales Representative; Software Engineer; Supervisor; Systems Analyst; Tax Specialist; Water/Wastewater Engineer. **Corporate headquarters location:** Chicago IL.

BANNER PERSONNEL SERVICE, INC.
800 East Diehl Road, Suite 100, Naperville IL 60563. 630/505-8881. **Fax:** 630/505-4566. **Contact:** Ms. Carey Hull, Regional Recruiter. **Description:** A permanent employment agency. Founded in 1970. **Specializes in the areas of:** Accounting/Auditing; Industrial; Sales; Secretarial; Technical; Word Processing. **Corporate headquarters location:** Chicago IL.

BANNER PERSONNEL SERVICE, INC.
1580 South Milwaukee, Suite 102, Libertyville IL 60048. 847/247-2200. **Fax:** 847/247-2202. **Contact:** Melissa Willie, Branch Manager. **Description:** A permanent employment agency. **Specializes in the areas of:** Clerical; Office Support; Secretarial. **Corporate headquarters location:** Chicago IL.

BARRY PERSONNEL RESOURCES, INC.
53 West Jackson Street, Suite 1505, Chicago IL 60603. 312/704-6500. **Fax:** 312/704-4260. **Contact:** Margaret Barry, President. **Description:** A permanent employment agency that also provides temporary placements. **Specializes in the areas of:** Administration; Office Support.

BELL PERSONNEL INC.
5368 West 95th Street, Oak Lawn IL 60453. 708/636-3151. **Fax:** 708/636-9315. **Contact:** Manager. **Description:** A permanent employment agency. Company pays fee. **Specializes in the areas of:** Accounting/Auditing; Administration; Advertising; Banking; Computer Science/Software; Finance; Insurance; Legal; Sales; Secretarial. **Positions commonly filled include:** Accountant/Auditor; Advertising Clerk; Buyer; Clerical Supervisor; Cost Estimator; Credit Manager; Customer Service Representative; General Manager; Human Resources Specialist; Management Trainee; Paralegal; Typist/Word Processor. **Average salary range of placements:** $30,000 - $50,000.

BUSCH EMPLOYMENT AGENCY
185 North Wabash Avenue, Chicago IL 60601. 312/372-7260. **Contact:** Thomas H. Brennan, Owner. **Description:** A permanent employment agency. **Specializes in the areas of:** Food Industry. **Positions commonly filled include:** Assistant Kitchen Manager; Certified Nursing Aide; Chef/Cook/Kitchen Worker; Dietician/Nutritionist; Restaurant/Food Service Manager; Waitstaff. **Average salary range of placements:** $20,000 - $29,999. **Number of placements per year:** 1000+.

CASEY STAFFING SERVICES, INC.
121 South Wilke Road, Suite 600, Arlington Heights IL 60005. 847/253-9030. **Fax:** 847/253-9557. **Recorded jobline:** 847/582-9068. **Contact:** Patricia Casey, Executive Vice President. **Description:** A permanent employment agency that also provides temporary placements. **Specializes in the areas of:** Accounting/Auditing; Banking; Finance; Information Systems. **Positions commonly filled include:** Accountant/Auditor; Accounting Clerk; Accounting Supervisor; Bookkeeper; Collector; Computer Operator; Computer Programmer; Credit Analyst; Data Entry Clerk; Financial Analyst; MIS Specialist; Network Engineer; Payroll Clerk; Systems Analyst. **Corporate headquarters location:** This Location. **Other area locations:** Chicago IL.

CASEY STAFFING SERVICES, INC.
150 North Michigan Avenue, Suite 2815, Chicago IL 60601. 312/332-8367. **Contact:** Office Manager. **Description:** A permanent employment agency that also provides temporary placements. **Specializes in the areas of:** Accounting/Auditing; Finance. **Corporate headquarters location:** Arlington Heights IL.

CHICAGO CAREERS
777 North Michigan Avenue, Chicago IL 60611. 312/440-3397. **Fax:** 312/440-4273. **Contact:** Sue Ellen Erkonen, Owner. **Description:** A permanent employment agency. Company pays fee. **Specializes in the areas of:** Travel. **Positions commonly filled include:** Travel Agent. **Average salary range of placements:** $30,000 - $50,000. **Number of placements per year:** 50 - 99.

CO-COUNSEL, INC.
10 South La Salle Street, Suite 1310, Chicago IL 60603-1002. 312/629-2646. **Fax:** 312/629-2650. **Contact:** Ms. Chris Schlentner, Office Manager. **Description:** A permanent employment agency. **Specializes in the areas of:** Legal. **Corporate headquarters location:** Houston TX. **Other U.S. locations:** Los Angeles CA; Dallas TX.

CORPORATE RESOURCES, LTD.
C.R. TEMPORARIES
300 North Martingale Road, Suite 440, Schaumburg IL 60173. 847/619-1600. **Fax:** 847/619-1554. **Contact:** Ingrid Moore, Co-Owner. **Description:** A permanent employment agency. C.R. Temporaries (also at this location) is a temporary agency. Company pays fee. **Specializes in the areas of:** Secretarial. **Positions commonly filled include:** Administrative Manager; Advertising Clerk; Customer Service Representative; Human Resources Specialist; Paralegal; Typist/Word Processor. **Average salary range of placements:** $20,000 - $29,999. **Number of placements per year:** 500 - 999.

CROWN PERSONNEL
325 West Prospect Avenue, Mount Prospect IL 60056. 847/392-5151. **Fax:** 847/392-0114. **Contact:** Dan Hyland, President. **Description:** A permanent employment agency. **Specializes in the areas of:** Banking; Engineering. **Positions commonly filled include:** Bank Officer/Manager; Electrical/Electronics Engineer; Mechanical Engineer; Typist/Word Processor. **Average salary range of placements:** $30,000 - $50,000. **Number of placements per year:** 1 - 49.

DANNEHL & ASSOCIATES
107 North Second Street, Cissna Park IL 60924. 815/457-2660. **Contact:** Manager. **Description:** A

permanent placement agency. **Specializes in the areas of:** Restaurant.

DENTAL AUXILIARY PLACEMENT SERVICE, INC.
2 Talcott, Suite 32, Park Ridge IL 60068. 847/696-1988. **Fax:** 847/696-4371. **Contact:** Karen Anderson, Director. **Description:** A permanent employment agency specializing in dental staffing. The agency also provides temporary placements. Company pays fee. **Positions commonly filled include:** Dental Assistant/Dental Hygienist; Dentist. **Average salary range of placements:** $30,000 - $50,000. **Number of placements per year:** 1000+.

DESMOND SERVICES INC.
1648 East New York Street, Aurora IL 60505. 630/820-3300. **Contact:** Manager. **Description:** A permanent placement agency.

DUNHILL STAFFING SERVICES OF CHICAGO
68 East Wacker Place, 12th Floor, Chicago IL 60601. 312/346-0933. **Contact:** George Baker, Owner/President. **Description:** A permanent employment agency. **Specializes in the areas of:** Accounting/Auditing; Banking; Computer Science/Software; Finance; Sales.

THE ESQUIRE STAFFING GROUP, LTD.
One South Wacker Drive, Suite 1616, Chicago IL 60606. 312/795-4300. **Fax:** 312/795-4329. **Contact:** Scott J. Fischer, Executive Vice President. **Description:** A permanent employment agency. Company pays fee. **Specializes in the areas of:** Administration; Banking; Clerical; Finance; Insurance; Legal; Retail; Sales; Secretarial. **Positions commonly filled include:** Accountant/Auditor; Administrative Assistant; Broker; Buyer; Claim Representative; Clerk; Customer Service Representative; Data Entry Clerk; Legal Secretary; Marketing Specialist; Receptionist; Retail Executive; Sales Representative; Secretary; Typist/Word Processor. **Benefits available to temporary workers:** Medical Insurance; Pension Plan. **Corporate headquarters location:** This Location. **Other U.S. locations:** Nationwide. **Average salary range of placements:** $20,000 - $29,999. **Number of placements per year:** 200 - 499.

EVE RECRUITERS LTD.
203 North Wabash, Suite 305, Chicago IL 60601. 312/372-7445. **Contact:** Manager. **Description:** A permanent employment agency. **Specializes in the areas of:** Administration; Secretarial.

EXCELL PERSONNEL
33 North Dearborn Street, Suite 400, Chicago IL 60602. 312/372-0014. **Contact:** Manager. **Description:** A permanent employment agency that also provides temporary placements. **Specializes in the areas of:** Office Support.

FIRST STAFFING
P.O. Box 5863, Rockford IL 61125. 815/229-7815. **Contact:** Darlene Furst, President. **Description:** A permanent employment agency. **Specializes in the areas of:** Accounting/Auditing; Banking; Clerical; Computer Science/Software; Engineering; Finance; Health/Medical; Insurance; Manufacturing; MIS/EDP; Secretarial.

GANS, GANS AND ASSOCIATES
175 North Franklin Street, Suite 401, Chicago IL 60606. 312/357-9600. **Contact:** Office Manager. **Description:** A permanent employment agency. **Specializes in the areas of:** Insurance; Legal. **Positions commonly filled include:** Actuary; Attorney; Insurance Agent/Broker; Legal Secretary; Paralegal; Underwriter/Assistant Underwriter.

GENERAL EMPLOYMENT ENTERPRISES, INC.
280 Shuman Boulevard, Suite 185, Naperville IL 60563. 630/983-1233. **Fax:** 630/983-2993. **Contact:** Mike McClintock, Manager. **Description:** A permanent employment agency focusing on placement in information systems and technologies, accounting/finance, and engineering. Company pays fee. **Specializes in the areas of:** Accounting/Auditing; Administration; Computer Science/Software; Engineering; Technical. **Positions commonly filled include:** Accountant/Auditor; Budget Analyst; Chemical Engineer; Computer Programmer; Credit Manager; Customer Service Representative; Design Engineer; Electrical/Electronics Engineer; Financial Analyst; Industrial Engineer; Industrial Production Manager; Mechanical Engineer; MIS Specialist; Multimedia Designer; Purchasing Agent/Manager; Quality Control Supervisor; Software Engineer; Structural Engineer; Systems Analyst; Technical Writer/Editor; Telecommunications Manager. **Average salary range of placements:** More than $50,000. **Number of placements per year:** 1 - 49.

GENERAL EMPLOYMENT ENTERPRISES, INC.
TRIAD PERSONNEL
1101 Perimeter Drive, Suite 735, Schaumburg IL 60173. 847/240-1233. **Fax:** 847/240-1671. **Contact:** Frank Anichini, Branch Manager. **E-mail address:** sch@genp.com. **World Wide Web address:** http://www.genp.com. **Description:** A permanent employment agency and contract services firm. Founded in 1893. Company pays fee. **Specializes in the areas of:** Administration; Computer Hardware/Software. **Positions commonly filled include:** Computer Operator; Computer Programmer; Consultant; Customer Service Representative; Database Manager; Internet Services Manager; MIS Specialist; Software Engineer; Systems Analyst; Systems Manager; Telecommunications Manager; Webmaster. **Corporate headquarters location:** Oakbrook Terrace IL. **Other U.S. locations:** Nationwide. **Average salary range of placements:** $30,000 - $50,000. **Number of placements per year:** 200 - 499.

H/R SEARCH
35 East Wacker Drive, Suite 1052, Chicago IL 60601. 312/658-1400x206. **Fax:** 312/658-1408. **Contact:** Nancy Campbell-Phillips, Manager. **Description:** A permanent employment agency. Company pays fee. **Specializes in the areas of:** Legal; Personnel/Labor Relations; Secretarial. **Positions commonly filled include:** Account Representative; Administrative Assistant; Administrative Manager; Assistant Manager; Computer Operator; Controller; Financial Analyst; Human Resources Manager; Paralegal; Sales Executive; Secretary; Typist/Word Processor. **Corporate headquarters location:** This Location. **Other U.S. locations:** Dallas TX. **Average salary range of placements:** $30,000 - $50,000.

HKA MORTGAGE STAFFING & TRAINING
1500 Waukegan Road, Suite 221, Glenview IL 60025. 847/998-9300. **Toll-free phone:** 800/969-8930. **Fax:** 847/729-6941. **Contact:** Cynthia K. Espinosa, Staffing Consultant. **Description:** A permanent employment agency focusing on the placement of mortgage personnel. The agency also provides temporary placement and contract services. Company pays fee. **Specializes in the areas of:** Banking. **Positions commonly filled include:** Accountant/Auditor; Bank Officer/Manager; Mortgage Banker. **Number of placements per year:** 100 - 199.

HALLMARK PERSONNEL INC.
3158 South River Road, Des Plaines IL 60018. 847/298-1900. **Contact:** Manager. **Description:** A

permanent placement agency. **Specializes in the areas of:** Insurance.

HUMAN RESOURCE CONNECTION, INC.
1900 East Golf Road, Suite M100, Schaumburg IL 60173. 847/995-8090. **Fax:** 847/995-8098. **Contact:** Kim Dooley, Owner. **Description:** A permanent employment agency. Company pays fee. **Specializes in the areas of:** Accounting/Auditing; Administration; Banking; Finance; General Management; Insurance; Legal; Manufacturing; Personnel/Labor Relations; Retail; Sales; Secretarial. **Positions commonly filled include:** Accountant/Auditor; Adjuster; Administrative Manager; Branch Manager; Buyer; Claim Representative; Clerical Supervisor; Credit Manager; Customer Service Representative; Electrical/ Electronics Engineer; Financial Analyst; General Manager; Human Resources Manager; Insurance Agent/Broker; Management Analyst/Consultant; Management Trainee; Paralegal; Securities Sales Representative; Services Sales Representative; Typist/Word Processor. **Number of placements per year:** 200 - 499.

INTERVIEWING CONSULTANTS INC.
19 South LaSalle Street, Suite 900, Chicago IL 60603. 312/263-1710. **Contact:** Ron (Gia) Giambarberee, Owner/Manager. **Description:** Interviewing Consultants is a permanent employment agency that also provides temporary placements. Company pays fee. **Specializes in the areas of:** Accounting/Auditing; Banking; Clerical; Computer Science/Software; Engineering; General Management; Insurance; Legal Secretarial; Office Support; Sales; Secretarial. **Positions commonly filled include:** Accountant/Auditor; Adjuster; Administrative Assistant; Advertising Clerk; Brokerage Clerk; Budget Analyst; Buyer; Claim Representative; Clerical Supervisor; Computer Programmer; Cost Estimator; Customer Service Representative; Electrical/ Electronics Engineer; Financial Analyst; General Manager; Legal Secretary; Management Analyst/ Consultant; Mechanical Engineer; Medical Records Technician; Paralegal; Services Sales Representative; Software Engineer; Systems Analyst; Typist/Word Processor; Underwriter/Assistant Underwriter. **Number of placements per year:** 200 - 499.

J.C.G. LIMITED, INC.
2300 East Higgins Road, Elk Grove Village IL 60007. 847/439-1400. **Contact:** James Greene, President. **Description:** A permanent employment agency. **Specializes in the areas of:** Engineering; Manufacturing; Transportation.

KINGSLEY EMPLOYMENT SERVICE
208 South LaSalle Street, Suite 1877, Chicago IL 60604. 312/726-8190. **Contact:** Edward Friedman, Owner. **Description:** A permanent employment agency. **Specializes in the areas of:** Banking; Finance.

KREZOWSKI & COMPANY
4811 Emerson, Suite 101, Palatine IL 60067. 847/303-0400. **Contact:** Manager. **Description:** A permanent employment agency. **Specializes in the areas of:** Medical Sales and Marketing.

MACINTYRE EMPLOYMENT SERVICE
15 North Arlington Heights Road, Suite 105, Arlington Heights IL 60004. 847/577-8860. **Fax:** 847/577-8863. **Contact:** Elizabeth E. MacIntyre, President. **Description:** A permanent employment agency. **Specializes in the areas of:** Art/Design; Secretarial. **Positions commonly filled include:** Clerical Supervisor; Customer Service Representative; Typist/Word Processor. **Average salary range of placements:** $20,000 - $29,999. **Number of placements per year:** 50 - 99.

MARAMAX PERSONNEL, INC.
5105 Tollview Drive, Suite 101, Rolling Meadows IL 60008. 847/253-0220. **Fax:** 847/253-0463. **Contact:** Maryellen Mackey, Manager. **Description:** A permanent employment agency that focuses on office support placements. Company pays fee. **Specializes in the areas of:** Accounting/Auditing; Administration; Banking; Computer Science/Software; Customer Service; Human Resources; Office Support; Sales; Secretarial. **Number of placements per year:** 100 - 199.

MERIT PERSONNEL INC.
640 Pearson Street, Suite 301, Des Plaines IL 60016. 847/296-2040. **Fax:** 847/296-2051. **Contact:** Manager. **Description:** A permanent employment agency. Company pays fee. **Specializes in the areas of:** Accounting/Auditing; Banking; Personnel/Labor Relations; Secretarial. **Positions commonly filled include:** Customer Service Representative. **Average salary range of placements:** $20,000 - $29,999. **Number of placements per year:** 100 - 199.

MICHAEL DAVID ASSOCIATES, INC.
180 North Michigan Avenue, Suite 1016, Chicago IL 60601. 312/236-4460. **Fax:** 312/236-5401. **Contact:** Director of Administrative Services. **Description:** A permanent employment agency. Company pays fee. **Specializes in the areas of:** Accounting/Auditing; Clerical; Computer Science/Software; Engineering; Finance; Food Industry; Health/Medical; Insurance; Legal; Manufacturing; Personnel/Labor Relations; Sales; Technical. **Number of placements per year:** 200 - 499.

THE MORAN GROUP
18 West Busse Avenue, Suite 10, Mount Prospect IL 60056. 847/506-1050. **Fax:** 847/506-1126. **Contact:** Evan Lysaght, Partner. **Description:** A permanent employment agency. Company pays fee. **Specializes in the areas of:** Retail. **Positions commonly filled include:** Credit Manager. **Number of placements per year:** 1 - 49.

MOUNT PROSPECT EMPLOYMENT SERVICE, LTD.
437 West Prospect Avenue, Mount Prospect IL 60056. 847/394-5660. **Fax:** 847/394-5664. **Contact:** Marilyn Mason, President. **E-mail address:** mpempsvc@aol.com. **Description:** A permanent employment agency focusing on office and clerical placement. Company pays fee. **Specializes in the areas of:** General Management; Secretarial. **Positions commonly filled include:** Administrative Manager; Clerical Supervisor; Customer Service Representative; General Manager; Management Trainee; Typist/Word Processor.

MULLINS & ASSOCIATES, INC.
520 South Northwest Highway, Barrington IL 60010. 847/382-1800. **Fax:** 847/382-1329. **Contact:** Ms. Terri Mullins, Vice President. **Description:** A permanent employment agency. **Specializes in the areas of:** Computer Science/Software; Engineering. **Positions commonly filled include:** Chemical Engineer; Computer Programmer; Design Engineer; Designer; Draftsperson; Industrial Engineer; MIS Specialist; Software Engineer; Systems Analyst. **Number of placements per year:** 200 - 499.

THE MURPHY GROUP
150 East Cook Avenue, Libertyville IL 60048. 847/362-6100. **Fax:** 847/362-1826. **Contact:** Leah Kayle, President. **Description:** A permanent employment agency. Company pays fee. **Specializes in the areas of:** Accounting/Auditing; Clerical; Personnel/Labor Relations; Retail; Sales; Secretarial. **Positions commonly filled include:** Clerical Supervisor; Customer Service Representative; Management

Trainee; Services Sales Representative; Typist/Word Processor. **Number of placements per year:** 100 - 199.

THE MURPHY GROUP
1555 Bond Street, Suite 131, Naperville IL 60563. 630/355-7030. **Fax:** 630/355-8670. **Contact:** Jim Bruno, Director. **E-mail address:** murphygroup@aol.com. **Description:** A permanent employment agency. **Corporate headquarters location:** Oak Brook IL. **Specializes in the areas of:** Administration; General Management; Office Support; Secretarial; Word Processing. **Positions commonly filled include:** Administrator; Clerk; Receptionist; Secretary; Support Personnel. **Average salary range of placements:** \$30,000 - \$50,000.

THE MURPHY GROUP
133 Vine Avenue, Park Ridge IL 60068. 847/825-2136. **Fax:** 847/696-1662. **Contact:** Beth Parsch, Owner. **Description:** A permanent employment agency. **Specializes in the areas of:** Accounting/Auditing; Clerical; Finance; Office Support; Secretarial; Word Processing. **Positions commonly filled include:** Accountant/Auditor; Administrator; Bookkeeper; Budget Analyst; Clerical Supervisor; Clerk; Receptionist; Secretary.

THE MURPHY GROUP
1211 West 22nd Street, Suite 221, Oak Brook IL 60523. 630/574-2840. **Contact:** James R. Bruno, Vice President. **Description:** A permanent employment agency. **Specializes in the areas of:** Accounting/Auditing; Advertising; Banking; Clerical; Computer Science/Software; Engineering; Finance; Food Industry; Insurance; Manufacturing; MIS/EDP; Publishing; Sales; Secretarial; Technical.

NETWORK RESOURCE GROUP INC.
920 South Spring Street, Springfield IL 62704. **Toll-free phone:** 800/519-1000. **Toll-free fax:** 800/519-2425. **Contact:** Martine Davis, Recruiter. **World Wide Web address:** http://www.nrgjobs.com. **Description:** A permanent employment agency. Company pays fee. **Specializes in the areas of:** Computer Science/Software. **Positions commonly filled include:** Computer Programmer; Internet Services Manager; MIS Specialist; Software Engineer; Systems Analyst; Telecommunications Manager. **Average salary range of placements:** \$30,000 - \$50,000. **Number of placements per year:** 1 - 49.

NORRELL HUMAN RESOURCE SERVICES
2 Mid America Plaza, Suite 120, Oakbrook IL 60181. 630/574-0657. **Fax:** 630/574-9028. **Contact:** Shawn VanDerziel, Manager of Recruitment. **Description:** A permanent employment agency. Founded in 1966. Company pays fee. **Specializes in the areas of:** Banking; Retail; Sales. **Positions commonly filled include:** Assistant Manager; Bank Officer/Manager; Branch Manager; Customer Service Representative; Management Trainee; Services Sales Representative. **Corporate headquarters location:** Atlanta GA. **Other U.S. locations:** Nationwide. **Number of placements per year:** 500 - 999.

OFFICEMATES5 OF NORTHFIELD
191 Waukegan Road, Northfield IL 60093. 847/446-7737. **Fax:** 847/446-0090. **Contact:** Lynne Goldberg, President. **Description:** A full-service employment agency. Company pays fee. **Corporate headquarters location:** Cleveland OH. **Average salary range of placements:** \$20,000 - \$29,999. **Number of placements per year:** 100 - 199.

OFFICETEAM
One Oakbrook Terrace, Suite 718, Oakbrook Terrace IL 60181-4476. 630/261-3086. **Fax:** 630/261-9699. **Contact:** Assignment Manager. **Description:** A permanent employment agency. Company pays fee. **Specializes in the areas of:** Administration; Secretarial. **Positions commonly filled include:** Administrative Assistant; Claim Representative; Clerical Supervisor; Clerk; Computer Operator; Legal Secretary; Medical Secretary; Receptionist; Typist/Word Processor. **Number of placements per year:** 1000+.

OFFICETEAM
One Northbrook Place, 5 Revere Drive, Suite 355, Northbrook IL 60062-1561. 847/480-2073. **Fax:** 847/480-1871. **Contact:** Assignment Manager. **Description:** A permanent employment agency. Company pays fee. **Specializes in the areas of:** Administration; Secretarial. **Positions commonly filled include:** Administrative Assistant; Claim Representative; Clerical Supervisor; Clerk; Computer Operator; Legal Secretary; Receptionist; Technician; Typist/Word Processor. **Number of placements per year:** 1000+.

OFFICETEAM
2800 West Higgins Road, Suite 180, Hoffman Estates IL 60195-5236. 847/885-6228. **Fax:** 847/885-6387. **Contact:** Staffing Manager. **Description:** A permanent employment agency. Company pays fee. **Specializes in the areas of:** Administration; Secretarial. **Positions commonly filled include:** Administrative Assistant; Claim Representative; Clerical Supervisor; Clerk; Computer Operator; Customer Service Representative; Data Entry Clerk; Receptionist; Secretary; Typist/Word Processor. **Number of placements per year:** 1000+.

OFFICETEAM
205 North Michigan Avenue, Suite 3301, Chicago IL 60601. 312/616-8258. **Fax:** 312/616-1155. **Contact:** Assignment Manager. **Description:** A permanent employment agency. Company pays fee. **Specializes in the areas of:** Administration; Secretarial. **Positions commonly filled include:** Administrative Assistant; Claim Representative; Clerical Supervisor; Clerk; Computer Operator; Legal Secretary; Medical Secretary; Receptionist; Secretary; Typist/Word Processor. **Number of placements per year:** 1000+.

OLSTEN INFORMATION TECHNOLOGY STAFFING
16 West Ontario, Chicago IL 60610. 312/661-0490. **Fax:** 312/661-0491. **Contact:** Stephanie Bethea, Recruiting Coordinator. **E-mail address:** olsten@xnet.com. **World Wide Web address:** http://www.olsten-chicago.com. **Description:** A permanent employment agency. Company pays fee. **Specializes in the areas of:** Accounting/Auditing; Banking; Computer Science/Software; Industrial; Insurance; Legal; Sales. **Positions commonly filled include:** Computer Programmer; MIS Specialist; Multimedia Designer; Software Engineer; Systems Analyst; Technical Writer/Editor. **Number of placements per year:** 1000+.

OMNI ONE
2200 East Devon Avenue, Suite 246, Des Plaines IL 60018. 847/299-1400. **Fax:** 847/299-4926. **Contact:** Steve Leibovitz, Branch Manager. **E-mail address:** omnione@omnione.com. **World Wide Web address:** http://www.omnione.com. **Description:** A permanent employment agency. **Specializes in the areas of:** Computer Science/Software; Engineering; MIS/EDP; Technical.

THE OPPORTUNITIES GROUP
53 West Jackson Boulevard, Suite 215, Chicago IL 60604. 312/922-5400. **Fax:** 312/347-1206. **Contact:** Manager. **Description:** A permanent employment agency focusing on the placement of office support staff. The agency also provides temporary placements. Company pays fee. **Specializes in the**

areas of: Personnel/Labor Relations; Secretarial. **Positions commonly filled include:** Typist/Word Processor. **Average salary range of placements:** $20,000 - $29,999.

OPPORTUNITY PERSONNEL SERVICE
200 West Adams Street, Suite 1702, Chicago IL 60606. 312/704-9898. **Contact:** Gwen Hudson, President. **Description:** A permanent employment agency. **Specializes in the areas of:** Accounting/Auditing; Clerical; Computer Science/Software; Finance; Insurance; Legal; Manufacturing; Office Support; Personnel/Labor Relations; Sales.

PS INC.
70 West Madison Avenue, Suite 1400, Chicago IL 60602. 312/922-3222. **Fax:** 312/922-2281. **Contact:** Mary Parker, President. **Description:** A permanent employment agency that also provides temporary placement. Company pays fee. **Specializes in the areas of:** Accounting/Auditing; Administration; Computer Science/Software; Finance; Personnel/Labor Relations; Sales; Secretarial. **Positions commonly filled include:** Accountant/Auditor; Administrative Manager; Advertising Clerk; Computer Programmer; Customer Service Representative; Human Resources Specialist; Internet Services Manager; Market Research Analyst; MIS Specialist; Purchasing Agent/Manager; Software Engineer; Systems Analyst; Telecommunications Manager; Typist/Word Processor. **Number of placements per year:** 100 - 199.

PAIGE PERSONNEL
5215 Old Orchard Road, Suite 500A, Skokie IL 60077. 847/966-0700. **Contact:** Office Manager. **Description:** A permanent employment agency. **Specializes in the areas of:** Clerical.

PAIGE PERSONNEL
1175 Corporate Woods Parkway, Suite 110, Vernon Hills IL 60061. 847/634-6606. **Fax:** 847/634-6778. **Contact:** Sharon Murphy, Personnel Manager. **Description:** A permanent employment agency. Company pays fee. **Specializes in the areas of:** Secretarial. **Positions commonly filled include:** Administrative Assistant; Customer Service Representative; Human Resources Specialist; Management Trainee. **Corporate headquarters location:** Skokie IL. **Average salary range of placements:** $20,000 - $29,999. **Number of placements per year:** 50 - 99.

PEAK PROFESSIONAL HEALTH SERVICE
104 East 3rd Street, Rock Falls IL 61071. 815/625-1167. **Contact:** Manager. **Description:** A permanent employment agency that also provides temporary placements. The agency focuses on placements in nursing homes. **Specializes in the areas of:** Health/Medical. **Positions commonly filled include:** Certified Nursing Aide.

PERSONNEL CONNECTION INC.
960 Clocktower Drive, Suite E, Springfield IL 62704. 217/787-9022. **Fax:** 217/787-9231. **Contact:** Carla J. Oller, President. **Description:** A permanent employment agency. Company pays fee. **Specializes in the areas of:** Accounting/Auditing; Administration; Banking; Computer Science/Software; General Management; Insurance; Personnel/Labor Relations; Sales; Secretarial. **Positions commonly filled include:** Accountant/Auditor; Branch Manager; Buyer; Claim Representative; Clerical Supervisor; Computer Programmer; Credit Manager; Customer Service Representative; Industrial Engineer; Mechanical Engineer; Medical Records Technician; Systems Analyst; Underwriter/Assistant Underwriter; Wholesale and Retail Buyer.

PERSONNEL PLACEMENT CONSULTANTS
6841 Cermak Road, Berwyn IL 60402. 708/795-9012. **Fax:** 708/795-9043. **Contact:** Sandra Ihde, President. **Description:** A permanent employment agency. Company pays fee. **Specializes in the areas of:** Accounting/Auditing; Banking; General Management; Legal; Nonprofit; Office Support; Personnel/Labor Relations; Secretarial. **Positions commonly filled include:** Accountant/Auditor; Bank Officer/Manager; Clerical Supervisor; Counselor; Credit Manager; Customer Service Representative; Human Resources Specialist; Insurance Agent/Broker; Operations/Production Manager; Property and Real Estate Manager; Travel Agent; Typist/Word Processor; Underwriter/Assistant Underwriter.

POL-AM EMPLOYMENT AGENCY
3326 North Kildare, Chicago IL 60641. 773/685-6602. **Contact:** Jan Tkaczow, Owner. **Description:** A permanent employment agency. Company pays fee. **Positions commonly filled include:** Domestic Help. **Number of placements per year:** 100 - 199.

PRESTIGE EMPLOYMENT SERVICES, INC.
P.O. Box 160, Flossmoor IL 60422. 708/798-9010. **Fax:** 708/798-9099. **Contact:** Manager. **Description:** A permanent employment agency. **Specializes in the areas of:** Accounting/Auditing; Engineering; Manufacturing; Office Support; Sales; Secretarial; Word Processing. **Positions commonly filled include:** Administrator; Bookkeeper; Civil Engineer; Clerk; Electrical/Electronics Engineer; Factory Worker; Industrial Engineer; Manufacturing Engineer; Mechanical Engineer; Plant Manager; Quality Control Supervisor; Receptionist; Safety Engineer; Secretary; Services Sales Representative; Supervisor; Technician.

SER BUSINESS AND TECHNICAL INSTITUTE
3800 West 26th Street, 2nd Floor, Chicago IL 60623. 773/521-0100. **Contact:** Elba Aranda, Recruiter. **Description:** A permanent employment agency. **Specializes in the areas of:** Clerical; Education; Nonprofit; Secretarial. **Positions commonly filled include:** Advertising Clerk; Brokerage Clerk; Clerical Supervisor; Customer Service Representative; Travel Agent. **Average salary range of placements:** Less than $20,000.

SALEM SERVICES, INC.
2 TransAm Plaza Drive, Suite 170, Oakbrook Terrace IL 60181-4296. 630/932-7000. **Fax:** 630/932-7010. **Contact:** Dori Lorenz, President. **Description:** A permanent employment agency. **Specializes in the areas of:** Office Support.

SELECT STAFFING
8501 West Higgins Road, Suite 740, Chicago IL 60631. 847/699-1147. **Contact:** Danielle Rhode, Personnel Assistant. **Description:** A permanent employment agency. Company pays fee. **Specializes in the areas of:** Accounting/Auditing; General Management; Personnel/Labor Relations; Secretarial. **Positions commonly filled include:** Accountant/Auditor; Advertising Clerk; Branch Manager; Brokerage Clerk; Budget Analyst; Claim Representative; Clerical Supervisor; Computer Programmer; Counselor; Credit Manager; Customer Service Representative; General Manager; Human Resources Specialist; Management Trainee; Manufacturer's/Wholesaler's Sales Rep.; Operations/Production Manager; Property and Real Estate Manager; Quality Control Supervisor; Services Sales Representative; Systems Analyst; Telecommunications Manager; Typist/Word Processor; Underwriter. **Corporate headquarters location:** Schaumburg IL. **Average salary range of placements:** $20,000 - $29,999. **Number of placements per year:** 200 - 499.

SELECTABILITY
1011 East State Street, Rockford IL 61104. 815/964-1777. **Fax:** 815/964-9327. **Contact:** Mark Gallagher, Manager. **Description:** A permanent employment agency. **Specializes in the areas of:** Engineering; General Management; Manufacturing; Technical. **Positions commonly filled include:** Aerospace Engineer; Human Resources Specialist; Industrial Engineer; Mechanical Engineer; Metallurgical Engineer; Software Engineer. **Other U.S. locations:** WI.

STAFFING CONSULTANTS INC.
1701 East Woodfield Road, Suite 903, Schaumburg IL 60173. 847/240-5300. **Toll-free phone:** 800/699-0825. **Fax:** 847/240-5310. **Contact:** Victoria Stumpe, Regional Manager. **E-mail address:** stafconschaum@chicago.avenew.com. **Description:** A permanent employment agency that also provides temporary placements. Company pays fee. **Specializes in the areas of:** Banking; Industrial; Insurance; Light Industrial; Marketing; Nonprofit; Personnel/Labor Relations; Printing; Publishing; Retail; Sales; Secretarial. **Positions commonly filled include:** Account Representative; Administrative Assistant; Assistant Manager; Clerical Supervisor; Customer Service Representative; Sales Executive; Sales Manager; Sales Representative; Systems Analyst; Typist/Word Processor. **Benefits available to temporary workers:** Bonus Award/Plan; Dental Insurance; Medical Insurance. **Corporate headquarters location:** Chicago IL. **Other area locations:** Bloomingdale IL; Crystal Lake IL; Naperville IL; Oak Brook IL. **Average salary range of placements:** \$20,000 - \$29,999. **Number of placements per year:** 100 - 199.

STRAND ASSOCIATES, INC.
2400 West Glenwood Avenue, Suite 226, Joliet IL 60435. 815/744-4200. **Fax:** 815/744-4215. **Contact:** Deirdre F. Egeland, Human Resources Coordinator. **E-mail address:** strand@ais.net. **Description:** A permanent employment agency. **Specializes in the areas of:** Distribution; Engineering; Transportation. **Positions commonly filled include:** Civil Engineer; Consultant; Draftsperson. **Corporate headquarters location:** Madison WI. **Other U.S. locations:** Joliet IL; Lexington KY; Louisville KY. **Average salary range of placements:** \$30,000 - \$50,000. **Number of placements per year:** 1 - 49.

SYSTEMS RESEARCH INC.
1051 Perimeter Drive, Suite 1075, Schaumburg IL 60173. 847/330-1222. **Contact:** Bonnie Albrecht, Office Manager. **Description:** A permanent employment agency. **Specializes in the areas of:** Engineering; Manufacturing; Technical.

TAD TECHNICAL SERVICES
1717 North Naper Boulevard, Suite 101, Naperville IL 60563. 630/505-1913. **Contact:** Office Manager. **Description:** A permanent employment agency.

TALENT TREE OF ILLINOIS
2 North LaSalle, Suite 950, Chicago IL 60602. 312/855-1390. **Contact:** Area Manager. **Description:** A permanent employment agency. **Specializes in the areas of:** Clerical.

TEMPLETON & ASSOCIATES
One East Wacker Drive, Suite 3130, Chicago IL 60601. 312/644-8400. **Contact:** Office Manager. **Description:** A permanent employment agency. **Specializes in the areas of:** Legal. **Positions commonly filled include:** Attorney; Paralegal.

THIRTY THREE PERSONNEL CENTER
33 North Dearborn Street, Suite 1701, Chicago IL 60602. 312/236-2023. **Contact:** Peter Vanes, CPC, President. **Description:** A permanent employment agency. **Specializes in the areas of:** Entry-Level Management; Office Support; Personnel/Labor Relations; Word Processing. **Positions commonly filled include:** Administrator; Clerk; Human Resources Manager; Management Trainee; Receptionist; Secretary; Support Personnel.

U.S. MEDICAL PLACEMENTS INC.
325 West Huron Street, Suite 508, Chicago IL 60610. 312/440-2323. **Contact:** Manager. **Description:** A permanent placement agency. **Specializes in the areas of:** Health/Medical.

VG & ASSOCIATES
9865 West Roosevelt Road, Westchester IL 60154. 708/343-0405. **Fax:** 708/343-1940. **Contact:** Mr. Val T. Grandys, Owner. **Description:** A permanent employment agency. **Specializes in the areas of:** Food Industry; Insurance; Publishing; Sales. **Positions commonly filled include:** Insurance Agent/Broker; Management Trainee; Sales Representative; Services Sales Representative; Underwriter/Assistant Underwriter. **Corporate headquarters location:** This Location. **Average salary range of placements:** \$20,000 - \$29,999. **Number of placements per year:** 1 - 49.

LaDONNA WALLACE & ASSOCIATES
6301 South Cass Avenue, Suite 200, Westmont IL 60559. 630/963-7733. **Contact:** Office Manager. **Description:** A permanent placement agency.

WALSH & COMPANY
731 South Durkin Drive, Springfield IL 62704. 217/793-0200. **Fax:** 217/793-9078. **Contact:** Jack Walsh, Owner. **Description:** A permanent employment agency. Company pays fee. **Specializes in the areas of:** Computer Science/Software; Sales; Secretarial. **Positions commonly filled include:** Computer Programmer; Manufacturer's/Wholesaler's Sales Rep.; MIS Specialist; Software Engineer; Systems Analyst. **Average salary range of placements:** \$30,000 - \$50,000. **Number of placements per year:** 50 - 99.

J.A. WARD ASSOCIATES INC.
One North La Grange Road, La Grange IL 60525. 708/354-7035. **Contact:** Manager. **Description:** A permanent employment agency that also provides temporary placements.

WATTERS & BYRD, INC.
1205 West Oakdale, Chicago IL 60657. 773/883-0250. **Contact:** Kenny Haas, Electrical/Electronics Industry Specialist. **Description:** A permanent employment agency. Company pays fee. **Specializes in the areas of:** Industrial Sales and Marketing; Sales. **Positions commonly filled include:** Electrical/Electronics Engineer; Manufacturer's/Wholesaler's Sales Rep.; Technical Representative. **Number of placements per year:** 1 - 49.

WEB/PACK TECH INC.
3548 South Clinton Avenue, Berwyn IL 60402. 708/795-8755. **Fax:** 708/795-8759. **Contact:** Ed Kavanaugh, President. **Description:** A permanent employment agency that also provides contract services. Company pays fee. **Specializes in the areas of:** Engineering; Food Industry; Sales; Technical. **Positions commonly filled include:** Applications Engineer; Chemical Engineer; Chemist; Design Engineer; Designer; Draftsperson; Electrical/Electronics Engineer; Food Scientist/Technologist; Industrial Engineer; Industrial Production Manager; Manufacturing Engineer; Mechanical Engineer; Sales Engineer; Sales Manager. **Average salary range of placements:** More than \$50,000. **Number of placements per year:** 1 - 49.

WEBB EMPLOYMENT SERVICE
318 Park Avenue, Rockford IL 61101. 815/963-0644. **Fax:** 815/963-0649. **Contact:** Deborah Webb, Owner. **Description:** A permanent employment agency. Company pays fee. **Specializes in the areas of:** Accounting/Auditing; Administration; Architecture/Construction; Computer Science/Software; General Management; Industrial; Manufacturing; Sales; Technical. **Positions commonly filled include:** Accountant/Auditor; Aerospace Engineer; Architect; Bank Officer/Manager; Blue-Collar Worker Supervisor; Broadcast Technician; Budget Analyst; Buyer; Civil Engineer; Computer Programmer; Cost Estimator; Designer; Draftsperson; Electrical/Electronics Engineer; Electrician; General Manager; Industrial Engineer; Industrial Production Manager; Mechanical Engineer; Metallurgical Engineer; MIS Specialist; Purchasing Agent/Manager; Quality Control Supervisor; Services Sales Representative; Software Engineer; Stationary Engineer; Structural Engineer; Surveyor; Systems Analyst; Technical Writer/Editor. **Average salary range of placements:** $30,000 - $50,000. **Number of placements per year:** 1 - 49.

WEST PERSONNEL SERVICE
1100 West Lake Street, Suite 120, Oak Park IL 60301. 708/771-8210. **Contact:** Service Representative. **Description:** A permanent employment agency that also provides temporary placements. Company pays fee. **Specializes in the areas of:** Administration; Office Support; Sales; Secretarial; Word Processing. **Positions commonly filled include:** Administrative Assistant; Sales Representative; Secretary; Typist/Word Processor. **Benefits available to temporary workers:** 401(k); Dental Insurance; Medical Insurance; Paid Holidays; Paid Vacation; Referral Bonus Plan. **Corporate headquarters location:** Charlotte NC.

WEST PERSONNEL SERVICE
1750 East Golf Road, Suite 230, Schaumburg IL 60173. 847/605-0555. **Fax:** 847/605-0568. **Contact:** Pamela Turner, Area Manager. **Description:** A permanent employment agency. Company pays fee. **Specializes in the areas of:** Accounting/Auditing; Personnel/Labor Relations; Secretarial. **Positions commonly filled include:** Administrative Manager; Bank Officer/Manager; Blue-Collar Worker Supervisor; Branch Manager; Brokerage Clerk; Claim Representative; Clerical Supervisor; Computer Programmer; Credit Manager; Customer Service Representative; General Manager; Human Resources Specialist; Management Trainee; Public Relations Specialist; Quality Control Supervisor; Securities Sales Representative; Services Sales Representative; Systems Analyst; Typist/Word Processor; Underwriter/Assistant Underwriter. **Corporate headquarters location:** Charlotte NC. **Average salary range of placements:** $20,000 - $29,999. **Number of placements per year:** 200 - 499.

WEST PERSONNEL SERVICE
1301 West 22nd Street, Oak Brook IL 60523. 630/571-3800. **Contact:** Linda Pawelko, President. **Description:** A permanent employment agency. Company pays fee. **Specializes in the areas of:** Industrial; Sales; Secretarial. **Positions commonly filled include:** Accountant/Auditor; Blue-Collar Worker Supervisor; Buyer; Clerical Supervisor; Customer Service Representative; Human Resources Specialist; Management Trainee; Paralegal; Services Sales Representative; Typist/Word Processor. **Corporate headquarters location:** Charlotte NC. **Average salary range of placements:** $20,000 - $29,999. **Number of placements per year:** 200 - 499.

WILLS & COMPANY, INC.
222 East Wisconsin, Suite 100, Lake Forest IL 60045. 847/735-1622. **Fax:** 847/735-1633. **Contact:** Don Wills, President. **Description:** A permanent employment agency. **Specializes in the areas of:** Computer Hardware/Software; Data Processing.

WORLD EMPLOYMENT SERVICE
1213 Dundee Road, Buffalo Grove IL 60089. 847/870-0900. **Fax:** 847/870-0906. **Contact:** Helga E. Jones, Manager. **Description:** A permanent employment agency. Company pays fee. **Specializes in the areas of:** Accounting/Auditing; Administration; Advertising; Banking; Computer Science/Software; Engineering; Finance; Food Industry; General Management; Health/Medical; Industrial; Insurance; Legal; Manufacturing; Personnel/Labor Relations; Retail; Sales; Technical. **Positions commonly filled include:** Accountant/Auditor; Adjuster; Administrative Manager; Advertising Clerk; Architect; Bank Officer/Manager; Brokerage Clerk; Budget Analyst; Buyer; Chemical Engineer; Claim Representative; Clerical Supervisor; Computer Programmer; Counselor; Credit Manager; Customer Service Representative; Design Engineer; Draftsperson; Electrical/Electronics Engineer; Financial Analyst; Health Services Manager; Hotel Manager; Human Resources Specialist; Industrial Engineer; Industrial Production Manager; Insurance Agent/Broker; Internet Services Manager; Management Analyst/Consultant; Management Trainee; Manufacturer's/Wholesaler's Sales Rep.; Market Research Analyst; Mechanical Engineer; Medical Records Technician; Metallurgical Engineer; MIS Specialist; Operations/Production Manager; Paralegal; Property and Real Estate Manager; Public Relations Specialist; Purchasing Agent/Manager; Restaurant/Food Service Manager; Services Sales Representative; Software Engineer; Statistician; Strategic Relations Manager; Systems Analyst; Technical Writer/Editor; Telecommunications Manager; Transportation/Traffic Specialist; Travel Agent; Typist/Word Processor; Underwriter/Assistant Underwriter. **Average salary range of placements:** $20,000 - $29,999. **Number of placements per year:** 100 - 199.

TEMPORARY EMPLOYMENT AGENCIES

ABLE'S POOL OF TEMPORARIES
180 North Wabash, Suite 802, Chicago IL 60601. 312/580-0380. **Contact:** Jerry Wells, Director. **Description:** A temporary agency. **Specializes in the areas of:** Clerical; Nonprofit; Sales; Technical.

ACCOUNTANT SOURCE TEMPS
150 South Wacker Drive, Chicago IL 60606. 312/629-8000. **Fax:** 312/346-2866. **Contact:** Marianne Volkmar, Branch Manager. **Description:** A temporary agency. Founded in 1960. Company pays fee. **Specializes in the areas of:** Accounting/Auditing; Finance. **Positions commonly filled include:** Accountant/Auditor; Budget Analyst; Credit Manager; Financial Analyst. **Corporate headquarters location:** Dallas TX. **Other U.S. locations:** CA; NY. **Number of placements per year:** 200 - 499.

ACCUSTAFF INCORPORATED
600 Holiday Plaza Drive, Suite 130, Matteson IL 60443. 708/503-9090. **Fax:** 708/503-9095. **Contact:** Priscilla Healy, Branch Manager. **Description:** A temporary agency. **Specializes in the areas of:** Industrial; Manufacturing; Secretarial. **Positions commonly filled include:** Clerical Supervisor; Customer Service Representative; Typist/Word Processor. **Corporate headquarters location:** Woodbury NY. **Other U.S. locations:** Nationwide.

ADECCO
880 South Milwaukee Avenue, Suite 101, Libertyville IL 60048. 847/362-9305. **Fax:** 847/362-9316. **Contact:** Brian Szilagyi, Office Supervisor. **World Wide Web address:** http://www.adecco.com. **Description:** A temp-to-perm agency. Company pays fee. **Specializes in the areas of:** Accounting/Auditing; Industrial; Light Industrial; Manufacturing; Secretarial. **Positions commonly filled include:** Accountant; Administrative Assistant; Customer Service Representative; Secretary; Typist/Word Processor. **Benefits available to temporary workers:** 401(k); Dental Insurance; Direct Deposit; Medical Insurance; Paid Holidays; Paid Vacation; Referral Bonus Plan. **Corporate headquarters location:** Redwood City CA. **Other U.S. locations:** Nationwide. **International locations:** Worldwide. **Average salary range of placements:** $20,000 - $29,999. **Number of placements per year:** 1 - 49.

ADECCO
6340 West 95th Street, Oak Lawn IL 60453. 708/430-5200. **Fax:** 708/430-5435. **Contact:** Erik Halvenson, Office Supervisor. **World Wide Web address:** http://www.adecco.com. **Description:** A temporary agency. Company pays fee. **Specializes in the areas of:** Accounting/Auditing; Banking; Computer Science/Software; Legal; Manufacturing; Personnel/Labor Relations; Sales; Secretarial; Technical. **Positions commonly filled include:** Advertising Clerk; Bank Officer/Manager; Branch Manager; Brokerage Clerk; Clerical Supervisor; Computer Programmer; Credit Manager; Customer Service Representative; Draftsperson; Human Resources Specialist; Systems Analyst; Typist/Word Processor. **Corporate headquarters location:** Redwood City CA. **Other U.S. locations:** Nationwide. **International locations:** Worldwide. **Average salary range of placements:** $20,000 - $29,999. **Number of placements per year:** 1 - 49.

ADECCO
One Mid America Plaza, Suite 120, Oakbrook Terrace IL 60181. 630/368-0211. **Contact:** Kim Wells, Office Manager. **World Wide Web address:** http://www.adecco.com. **Description:** A temporary agency that also provides some permanent placements. **Specializes in the areas of:** Accounting/Auditing; Administration; Banking; Computer Science/Software; Legal; Manufacturing; Personnel/Labor Relations; Sales; Secretarial; Technical. **Positions commonly filled include:** Advertising Clerk; Bank Officer/Manager; Branch Manager; Brokerage Clerk; Clerical Supervisor; Computer Programmer; Credit Manager; Customer Service Representative; Draftsperson; Human Resources Specialist; Systems Analyst; Typist/Word Processor. **Corporate headquarters location:** Redwood City CA. **Other U.S. locations:** Nationwide. **International locations:** Worldwide. **Average salary range of placements:** $20,000 - $29,999. **Number of placements per year:** 1 - 49.

ADECCO
178 Golf Road, Schaumburg IL 60173. 847/310-8230. **Fax:** 847/310-8785. **World Wide Web address:** http://www.adecco.com. **Contact:** Office Manager. **Description:** A temporary agency. Company pays fee. **Specializes in the areas of:** Accounting/Auditing; Administration; Banking; Computer Science/Software; Legal; Manufacturing; Personnel/Labor Relations; Sales; Secretarial; Technical. **Positions commonly filled include:** Advertising Clerk; Bank Officer/Manager; Branch Manager; Brokerage Clerk; Clerical Supervisor; Computer Programmer; Credit Manager; Customer Service Representative; Draftsperson; Human Resources Specialist; Systems Analyst; Typist/Word Processor. **Corporate headquarters location:** Redwood City CA. **Other U.S. locations:** Nationwide. **International locations:** Worldwide. **Average salary range of placements:** $20,000 - $29,999. **Number of placements per year:** 1 - 49.

ADECCO
200 West Madison Avenue, Suite 520, Chicago IL 60606. 312/372-6783. **Contact:** Joyce Johnson, Branch Manager. **World Wide Web address:** http://www.adecco.com. **Description:** A temporary agency. Company pays fee. **Specializes in the areas of:** Accounting/Auditing; Administration; Banking; Computer Science/Software; Legal; Manufacturing; Personnel/Labor Relations; Sales; Secretarial; Technical. **Positions commonly filled include:** Advertising Clerk; Bank Officer/Manager; Branch Manager; Brokerage Clerk; Clerical Supervisor; Computer Programmer; Credit Manager; Customer Service Representative; Draftsperson; Human Resources Specialist; Systems Analyst; Typist/Word Processor. **Corporate headquarters location:** Redwood City CA. **Other U.S. locations:** Nationwide. **International locations:** Worldwide. **Average salary range of placements:** $20,000 - $29,999. **Number of placements per year:** 1 - 49.

ADECCO
1101 West Lake Street, Oak Park IL 60301. 708/848-7800. **Fax:** 708/848-3288. **Contact:** Nancy Stolfe, Branch Manager. **World Wide Web address:** http://www.adecco.com. **Description:** A temporary agency. Company pays fee. **Specializes in the areas of:** Accounting/Auditing; Administration; Banking; Computer Science/Software; Legal; Manufacturing; Personnel/Labor Relations; Sales; Secretarial; Technical. **Positions commonly filled include:** Advertising Clerk; Bank Officer/Manager; Branch Manager; Brokerage Clerk; Clerical Supervisor; Credit Manager; Customer Service Representative; Draftsperson; Human Resources Specialist; Systems Analyst; Typist/Word Processor. **Benefits available to temporary workers:** 401(k); Dental Insurance; Medical Insurance; Paid Holidays; Referral Bonus Plan. **Corporate headquarters location:** Redwood City CA. **Other U.S. locations:** Nationwide. **International locations:** Worldwide. **Average salary range of placements:** $20,000 - $29,999. **Number of placements per year:** 1 - 49.

ADECCO
1560 Sherman Avenue, Evanston IL 60201. 847/328-8300. **Fax:** 847/328-1608. **Contact:** Branch Manager. **World Wide Web address:** http://www.adecco.com. **Description:** A temporary agency. Company pays fee. **Specializes in the areas of:** Accounting/Auditing; Administration; Banking; Computer Science/Software; Legal; Manufacturing; Personnel/Labor Relations; Sales; Secretarial; Technical. **Positions commonly filled include:** Advertising Clerk; Bank Officer/Manager; Branch Manager; Brokerage Clerk; Clerical Supervisor; Computer Programmer; Credit Manager; Customer Service Representative; Draftsperson; Human Resources Specialist; Systems Analyst; Typist/Word Processor. **Corporate headquarters location:** Redwood City CA. **Other U.S. locations:** Nationwide. **International locations:** Worldwide. **Average salary range of placements:** $20,000 - $29,999. **Number of placements per year:** 1 - 49.

ASSURED STAFFING
651 Terra Cotta, Suite 132, Crystal Lake IL 60014. 815/459-8367. **Fax:** 815/459-8450. **Contact:** Donna Kujawa, Branch Manager. **Description:** A temporary agency. Company pays fee. **Specializes in the areas of:** Administration; Industrial; Manufacturing; Personnel/Labor Relations; Secretarial. **Positions commonly filled include:** Account Manager; Account Representative; Accountant; Administrative Assistant; Administrative Manager; Advertising Clerk; Aircraft Mechanic/Engine Specialist; Applications Engineer;

Assistant Manager; Automotive Mechanic; Bank Officer/Manager; Branch Manager; Claim Representative; Clerical Supervisor; Computer Operator; Credit Manager; Customer Service Representative; Database Manager; General Manager; Graphic Artist; Graphic Designer; Human Resources Specialist; Industrial Engineer; Industrial Production Manager; Management Trainee; Marketing Specialist; Purchasing Agent/Manager; Quality Control Supervisor; Sales Executive; Sales Representative; Secretary; Typist/Word Processor. **Benefits available to temporary workers:** Medical Insurance; Paid Holidays. **Corporate headquarters location:** Barrington IL. **Other area locations:** Barrington IL; Marengo IL; Rockford IL; Wheaton IL. **Average salary range of placements:** $20,000 - $29,999. **Number of placements per year:** 500 - 999.

C. BERGER & COMPANY
327 East Gunderson Drive, Carol Stream IL 60188. 630/653-1115. **Contact:** Manager. **Description:** A temporary agency. **Specializes in the areas of:** Library Services. **Positions commonly filled include:** Librarian.

COMPUTEMP INC.
566 West Adams Street, Suite 440, Chicago IL 60661. 312/669-0606. **Contact:** Manager. **Description:** A temporary agency that also provides some permanent placements. **Specializes in the areas of:** Computer Science/Software; Technical.

DAVIS TEMPORARIES INC.
21031 Governors Highway, Olympia Fields IL 60461. 708/747-6100. **Fax:** 708/747-6189. **Contact:** Deborah Davis, Vice President. **Description:** A temporary agency. **Specializes in the areas of:** Banking; Industrial; Manufacturing; Retail. **Positions commonly filled include:** Blue-Collar Worker Supervisor; Clerical Supervisor; Customer Service Representative; Management Trainee; Technical Writer/Editor; Travel Agent; Typist/Word Processor. **Corporate headquarters location:** This Location. **Other U.S. locations:** Chicago Heights IL; Munster IN; Merrillville IN. **Average salary range of placements:** Less than $20,000. **Number of placements per year:** 500 - 999.

DAYSTAR TEMPORARY SERVICES, INC.
191 Waukegan Road, Suite 104, Northfield IL 60093. 847/446-7806. **Fax:** 847/446-0990. **Contact:** Fran Wilkens, Office Manager. **Description:** A temporary agency. Company pays fee. **Specializes in the areas of:** Accounting/Auditing; Administration; Banking; Computer Science/Software; Data Processing; Health/Medical; Insurance; Legal; Office Support; Sales; Secretarial. **Corporate headquarters location:** Cleveland OH. **Average salary range of placements:** $20,000 - $29,999. **Number of placements per year:** 100 - 199.

DYNAMIC PEOPLE
570 Lake Cook Road, Suite 114, Deerfield IL 60015. 847/940-7040. **Fax:** 847/940-4500. **Contact:** Paul M. Duski, Owner. **World Wide Web address:** http://www.dynamic@aol.com. **Description:** A full-service temporary agency that also provides permanent placements. **Specializes in the areas of:** Accounting/Auditing; Health/Medical; Insurance; Legal; Personnel/Labor Relations; Sales; Secretarial. **Positions commonly filled include:** Accountant; Administrative Assistant; Claim Representative; Clerical Supervisor; Computer Operator; Credit Manager; Customer Service Representative; Financial Analyst; Graphic Artist; Human Resources Specialist; Medical Records Technician; Paralegal; Secretary. **Benefits available to temporary workers:** 401(k); Bonus Award/Plan; Daycare Assistance; Medical Insurance; Paid Holidays; Paid Vacation. **Corporate headquarters location:** Atlanta GA. **Other U.S. locations:** Nationwide. **Average salary range of placements:** $20,000 - $29,999. **Number of placements per year:** 500 - 999.

EDP/TEMPS AND CONTRACT SERVICES
2115 Butterfield Road, Suite 101, Oak Brook IL 60523. 630/620-7171. **Fax:** 630/620-6932. **Contact:** Manager. **Description:** A temporary agency. **Specializes in the areas of:** Computer Science/Software. **Positions commonly filled include:** Computer Programmer; Software Engineer; Systems Analyst; Technical Writer/Editor. **Number of placements per year:** 200 - 499.

EXPRESS PERSONNEL SERVICES
977 Lakeview Parkway, Suite 190, Vernon Hills IL 60061. 847/816-8422. **Fax:** 847/816-0888. **Contact:** Cal Rich, Manager. **E-mail address:** express@interaccess.com. **Description:** A temporary agency. Company pays fee. **Specializes in the areas of:** Accounting/Auditing; Administration; Computer Science/Software; Engineering; Finance; General Management; Industrial; Manufacturing; Personnel/Labor Relations; Retail; Sales; Technical. **Positions commonly filled include:** Accountant/Auditor; Adjuster; Administrative Manager; Advertising Clerk; Aerospace Engineer; Automotive Mechanic; Bank Officer/Manager; Biochemist; Biological Scientist; Blue-Collar Worker Supervisor; Branch Manager; Brokerage Clerk; Budget Analyst; Buyer; Chemical Engineer; Chemist; Civil Engineer; Claim Representative; Computer Programmer; Credit Manager; Customer Service Representative; Design Engineer; Electrical/Electronics Engineer; Environmental Engineer; Financial Analyst; General Manager; Hotel Manager; Human Resources Specialist; Industrial Engineer; Management Analyst/Consultant; Mechanical Engineer; Operations/Production Manager; Paralegal; Public Relations Specialist; Quality Control Supervisor; Software Engineer; Systems Analyst; Typist/Word Processor; Underwriter/Assistant Underwriter. **Average salary range of placements:** $20,000 - $29,999. **Number of placements per year:** 1000+.

FELLOWS PLACEMENT
1411 Opus Place, Executive Towers West, Suite 118, Downers Grove IL 60515. 630/968-2771. **Contact:** Ms. Mary Young, CPC, Vice President. **Description:** A temporary agency that also provides permanent placements. **Specializes in the areas of:** Accounting/Auditing; Administration; Banking; Clerical; Entry-Level Management; Finance; Insurance; Office Support; Sales; Secretarial. **Positions commonly filled include:** Accountant; Administrative Assistant; Advertising Clerk; Assistant Manager; Claim Representative; Clerical Supervisor; Computer Operator; Counselor; Credit Manager; Customer Service Representative; Graphic Designer; Management Trainee; Sales Representative; Secretary; Typist/Word Processor. **Benefits available to temporary workers:** Bonus Award/Plan; Medical Insurance; Paid Holidays; Paid Vacation; Profit Sharing; Referral Bonus Plan. **Other area locations:** Buffalo Grove IL; Rosemont IL; Schaumberg IL. **Average salary range of placements:** $30,000 - $50,000.

FELLOWS PLACEMENT
2150 East Lake Cook Road, Suite 180, Buffalo Grove IL 60089. 847/520-7300. **Contact:** Manager. **Description:** A temporary agency that also provides permanent placements. Company pays fee. **Specializes in the areas of:** Food Industry; Health/Medical; Insurance; Manufacturing; Personnel/Labor Relations; Sales; Secretarial. **Positions commonly filled include:** Advertising Clerk; Clerical

Supervisor; Customer Service Representative; Human Resources Specialist; Market Research Analyst; Services Sales Representative; Typist/Word Processor. **Average salary range of placements:** $20,000 - $29,999. **Number of placements per year:** 500 - 999.

FURST STAFFING SERVICES
1111 West 22nd Street, Suite 245, Oak Brook IL 60523. 630/990-0610. **Fax:** 630/990-1143. **Contact:** Jon McKinley, Branch Manager. **Description:** A temporary agency that also provides permanent placement. Company pays fee. **Specializes in the areas of:** Accounting/Auditing; Industrial; Legal; Manufacturing; Personnel/Labor Relations; Secretarial; Technical. **Positions commonly filled include:** Customer Service Representative; Paralegal; Technical Writer/Editor; Typist/Word Processor. **Corporate headquarters location:** Rockford IL. **Average salary range of placements:** $20,000 - $29,999. **Number of placements per year:** 1 - 49.

HEALTHCARE TRAINING & PLACEMENT
260 East Chestnut Street, Chicago IL 60611. 312/787-9028. **Fax:** 312/951-7690. **Contact:** Phyllis Dobrin, Director. **Description:** A temporary agency focusing on medical and dental staffing. The agency also provides permanent placement. **Specializes in the areas of:** Health/Medical. **Positions commonly filled include:** Dental Assistant/Dental Hygienist; Dentist. **Average salary range of placements:** $20,000 - $29,999. **Number of placements per year:** 50 - 99.

INTERIM PERSONNEL
820A Broadway, Mattoon IL 61938. 217/235-2299. **Contact:** Wayne Meinhart, President. **Description:** A temporary agency. Company pays fee. **Specializes in the areas of:** Personnel/Labor Relations. **Positions commonly filled include:** Accountant/Auditor; Advertising Clerk; Bank Officer/Manager; Blue-Collar Worker Supervisor; Claim Representative; Clerical Supervisor; Customer Service Representative; Draftsperson; Electrician; Financial Analyst; General Manager; Human Resources Specialist; Human Service Worker; Industrial Production Manager; Insurance Agent/Broker; Management Trainee; Services Sales Representative; Typist/Word Processor. **Corporate headquarters location:** Fort Lauderdale FL. **Other U.S. locations:** Nationwide. **Average salary range of placements:** Less than $20,000. **Number of placements per year:** 100 - 199.

INTERSTAFF
35 East Wacker Drive, Suite 2350, Chicago IL 60601. 312/551-0777. **Fax:** 312/551-1186. **Contact:** Denny Bennett, President. **Description:** A temporary agency. Interstaff focuses on the placement of recent college graduates in internship-type temporary assignments through its Project Staff program. Company pays fee. **Specializes in the areas of:** Accounting/Auditing; Administration; Advertising; Art/Design; Banking; Economics; Finance; General Management; Insurance; Legal; Nonprofit; Personnel/Labor Relations; Publishing; Sales; Secretarial. **Positions commonly filled include:** Account Manager; Administrative Manager; Advertising Clerk; Bank Officer/Manager; Branch Manager; Brokerage Clerk; Budget Analyst; Cost Estimator; Customer Service Representative; Financial Analyst; General Manager; Human Resources Specialist; Management Trainee; Paralegal; Public Relations Specialist; Securities Sales Representative; Typist/Word Processor. **Average salary range of placements:** $20,000 - $29,999. **Number of placements per year:** 500 - 999.

KELLY SCIENTIFIC RESOURCES
1101 West 31st Street, Suite 120, Downers Grove IL 60515. 630/964-0239. **Fax:** 630/964-0562. **Contact:** Branch Manager. **World Wide Web address:** http://www.kellyscientific.com. **Description:** A temporary agency that provides scientific placements. **Specializes in the areas of:** Biomedical; Chemical; Pharmaceutical.

LAW CORPS LEGAL STAFFING
10 South Riverside Plaza, Suite 1800, Chicago IL 60606. 312/474-6060. **Contact:** Manager. **Description:** A temporary agency that also provides temp-to-perm placements. **Specializes in the areas of:** Legal.

LOMACK AGENCY INC.
1001 South Woodlawn Avenue, Suite 1118G, Chicago IL 60628. 773/264-9110. **Fax:** 773/264-9125. **Contact:** Ms. Sterling, Vice President. **Description:** A temporary agency. **Specializes in the areas of:** Sales; Secretarial. **Positions commonly filled include:** Accountant/Auditor; Administrative Manager; Claim Representative; Clerical Supervisor; Human Resources Specialist; Licensed Practical Nurse; Management Trainee; Medical Records Technician; Typist/Word Processor. **Average salary range of placements:** $30,000 - $50,000. **Number of placements per year:** 50 - 99.

MACK & ASSOCIATES, LTD.
100 North LaSalle Street, Suite 2110, Chicago IL 60602. 312/368-0677. **Fax:** 312/368-1868. **Contact:** Charlene Gorzela, President. **Description:** A temporary agency. Company pays fee. **Specializes in the areas of:** Accounting/Auditing; Banking; Finance; Personnel/Labor Relations; Sales; Secretarial. **Positions commonly filled include:** Administrative Manager; Brokerage Clerk; Human Resources Specialist; Management Trainee; Physical Therapist; Typist/Word Processor. **Number of placements per year:** 200 - 499.

MANPOWER TEMPORARY SERVICES
Citicorp Center, Suite 2950, 500 West Madison Street, Chicago IL 60661-2511. 312/648-4555. **Contact:** Branch Manager. **Description:** A temporary agency. **Specializes in the areas of:** Industrial; Office Support; Telecommunications; Word Processing. **Positions commonly filled include:** Accountant/Auditor; Administrative Assistant; Assembly Worker; Biological Scientist; Bookkeeper; Chemist; Computer Operator; Computer Support Technician; Designer; Desktop Publishing Specialist; Electrician; Inspector/Tester/Grader; Inventory Control Specialist; Machine Operator; Order Clerk; Painter; Proofreader; Secretary; Technical Writer/Editor; Typist/Word Processor; Welder. **Benefits available to temporary workers:** Life Insurance; Medical Insurance; Paid Holidays; Paid Vacation. **Corporate headquarters location:** Milwaukee WI. **Number of placements per year:** 1000+.

MANPOWER TEMPORARY SERVICES
1324 East Empire Street, Bloomington IL 61701. 309/663-1324. **Contact:** Manager. **Description:** A temporary agency. **Specializes in the areas of:** Accounting/Auditing; Banking; Engineering; Industrial; Insurance; Legal; Personnel/Labor Relations. **Positions commonly filled include:** Blue-Collar Worker Supervisor; Computer Programmer; Customer Service Representative; Human Resources Specialist; Market Research Analyst; Mechanical Engineer; Paralegal; Quality Control Supervisor; Systems Analyst. **Corporate headquarters location:** Milwaukee WI. **Number of placements per year:** 1000+.

MANPOWER TEMPORARY SERVICES
735 Main Street, Peoria IL 61602. 309/674-4163. **Fax:** 309/673-0940. **Contact:** John E. Vilberg, Owner. **Description:** A temporary agency. **Specializes in the areas of:** Engineering; Health/Medical; Personnel/Labor Relations. **Positions commonly filled include:**

Administrative Manager; Advertising Clerk; Aerospace Engineer; Chemical Engineer; Civil Engineer; Clerical Supervisor; Customer Service Representative; Design Engineer; Designer; Draftsperson; Electrical/Electronics Engineer; Environmental Engineer; Industrial Engineer; Mechanical Engineer; Quality Control Supervisor; Structural Engineer; Typist/Word Processor. **Corporate headquarters location:** Milwaukee WI. **Average salary range of placements:** $20,000 - $29,999. **Number of placements per year:** 50 - 99.

McCULLUM ASSOCIATES INC.
220 South State Street, Suite 1900, Chicago IL 60604. 312/362-1921. **Fax:** 312/362-1923. **Contact:** Sylvia L. McCullum, President. **Description:** A temporary agency. Company pays fee. **Specializes in the areas of:** Advertising; Architecture/Construction; Engineering; Publishing; Secretarial. **Positions commonly filled include:** Administrative Assistant; Architect; Civil Engineer; Computer Operator; Computer Programmer; Cost Estimator; Database Manager; Draftsperson; Electrical/Electronics Engineer; Graphic Designer; Mechanical Engineer; MIS Specialist; Paralegal; Secretary; Social Worker; Systems Analyst; Technical Writer/Editor; Typist/Word Processor. **Average salary range of placements:** $20,000 - $29,999. **Number of placements per year:** 200 - 499.

MEDICAL TECHNICAL PLACEMENTS, INC.
3340 North Clark Street, Suite 205, Chicago IL 60657. 773/528-6070. **Toll-free phone:** 800/570-4671. **Fax:** 773/528-1226. **Contact:** Manager. **E-mail address:** 103420,1632@compuserve.com. **Description:** A temporary agency. **Specializes in the areas of:** Health/Medical; Personnel/Labor Relations; Technical. **Positions commonly filled include:** EEG Technologist; EKG Technician; Licensed Practical Nurse; Medical Assistant; Medical Technologist; Radiological Technologist. **Average salary range of placements:** Less than $20,000.

NJW & ASSOCIATES, INC.
One East Wacker Drive, Suite 2120, Chicago IL 60601. 312/464-1999. **Fax:** 312/464-1777. **Contact:** Norma Williams, President. **Description:** A temporary agency. **Specializes in the areas of:** Accounting/Auditing; Administration; General Management; Legal; Personnel/Labor Relations; Sales; Secretarial. **Positions commonly filled include:** Customer Service Representative; Health Services Worker; Human Resources Manager; Operations/Production Manager; Paralegal; Services Sales Representative; Software Engineer; Systems Analyst; Technical Writer/Editor; Telecommunications Manager; Typist/Word Processor. **Other U.S. locations:** Skokie IL. **Average salary range of placements:** $30,000 - $50,000.

NORRELL SERVICES
35 East Wacker Drive, Suite 620, Chicago IL 60601. 312/346-9276. **Contact:** David Lee, Branch Manager. **Description:** A temporary agency that also provides contract services. **Specializes in the areas of:** Personnel/Labor Relations; Secretarial. **Positions commonly filled include:** Accountant/Auditor; Administrative Manager; Human Resources Specialist; Typist/Word Processor. **Corporate headquarters location:** Atlanta GA. **Other U.S. locations:** Nationwide. **Number of placements per year:** 1000+.

NORRELL SERVICES
1051 Perimeter Drive, Suite 905, Schaumburg IL 60173. 847/605-1233. **Fax:** 847/605-0801. **Contact:** Carie Mendlik, Customer Service Specialist. **Description:** A temporary agency that also provides temp-to-hire and permanent placement. Company pays fee. **Specializes in the areas of:** Accounting/Auditing; Administration; Industrial; Personnel/Labor Relations; Secretarial. **Positions commonly filled include:** Accountant/Auditor; Adjuster; Administrative Manager; Blue-Collar Worker Supervisor; Branch Manager; Budget Analyst; Claim Representative; Clerical Supervisor; Credit Manager; Customer Service Representative; Financial Analyst; General Manager; Human Resources Specialist. **Corporate headquarters location:** Atlanta GA. **Other U.S. locations:** Nationwide. **Number of placements per year:** 500 - 999.

OFFICE OURS
1111 Plaza Drive, Suite 320, Schaumburg IL 60173. 847/995-1200. **Fax:** 847/619-7255. **Contact:** Michelle Mouhelis, Staffing Coordinator. **Description:** A temporary agency. **Specializes in the areas of:** Accounting/Auditing; Administration; Clerical; Secretarial; Word Processing. **Positions commonly filled include:** Clerical Supervisor; Customer Service Representative; Typist/Word Processor. **Other U.S. locations:** Boca Raton FL; Fort Lauderdale FL. **Average salary range of placements:** $20,000 - $29,999. **Number of placements per year:** 200 - 499.

OLSTEN STAFFING SERVICES
880 West 75th Street, Willowbrook IL 60521. 630/794-9675. **Fax:** 630/794-9725. **Contact:** Lisa Rands, Branch Manager. **Description:** A temporary agency. Company pays fee. **Specializes in the areas of:** Accounting/Auditing; Administration; Computer Science/Software; Legal; Manufacturing; Personnel/Labor Relations. **Positions commonly filled include:** Accountant/Auditor; Administrative Manager; Attorney; Branch Manager; Clerical Supervisor; Computer Programmer; Credit Manager; Customer Service Representative; Financial Analyst; Human Resources Specialist; Paralegal; Systems Analyst. **Average salary range of placements:** $20,000 - $29,999. **Number of placements per year:** 100 - 199.

PRO STAFF PERSONNEL SERVICES
10 South Wacker Drive, Suite 2250, Chicago IL 60606. 312/641-6256. **Contact:** Office Manager. **Description:** A temporary and temp-to-perm agency. **Specializes in the areas of:** Accounting/Auditing; Administration; Information Technology; Office Support.

PROFILE TEMPORARY SERVICE
222 North LaSalle, Suite 900, Chicago IL 60601. 312/541-4141. **Contact:** Manager. **Description:** A temporary agency. **Specializes in the areas of:** Accounting/Auditing; Banking; Finance; Insurance; Manufacturing. **Number of placements per year:** 500 - 999.

RPH ON THE GO, USA, INC.
3330 Old Glenview Road, Wilmette IL 60091. 847/251-9389. **Toll-free phone:** 800/553-7359. **Fax:** 847/251-9690. **Contact:** Kelly Sheridan, Human Resources. **World Wide Web address:** http://www.interaccess.com/rph. **Description:** A temporary agency focusing on the placement of pharmacy professionals. **Specializes in the areas of:** General Management; Health/Medical. **Positions commonly filled include:** Pharmacist. **Average salary range of placements:** More than $50,000.

RELIEF MEDICAL SERVICES, INC.
323 East Ontario, Chicago IL 60611. 312/266-1486. **Fax:** 312/266-0732. **Contact:** Director of Nursing. **Description:** A temporary agency that provides placement in hospitals, nursing homes, and clinics. **Specializes in the areas of:** Health/Medical. **Positions commonly filled include:** Licensed Practical Nurse; Medical Records Technician; Registered Nurse; Surgical Technician. **Other U.S. locations:** Skokie IL.

Average salary range of placements: $20,000 - $29,999. **Number of placements per year:** 1000+.

REMEDY INTELLIGENT STAFFING
6 North Michigan Avenue, Suite 1505, Chicago IL 60602. 312/630-9090. **Fax:** 312/630-9069. **Contact:** Vice President of Operations. **Description:** A temporary agency. Company pays fee. **Specializes in the areas of:** Accounting/Auditing; Administration; Banking; Computer Science/Software; Finance; Food Industry; General Management; Health/Medical; Industrial; Insurance; Legal; Manufacturing; Nonprofit; Personnel/Labor Relations; Publishing; Retail; Sales; Secretarial; Technical. **Positions commonly filled include:** Accountant/Auditor; Administrative Manager; Advertising Clerk; Bank Officer/Manager; Blue-Collar Worker Supervisor; Branch Manager; Brokerage Clerk; Claim Representative; Clerical Supervisor; Computer Programmer; Credit Manager; Customer Service Representative; Editor; Health Services Manager; Human Resources Specialist; Industrial Production Manager; Manufacturer's/Wholesaler's Sales Rep.; Market Research Analyst; Medical Records Technician; MIS Specialist; Operations/Production Manager; Paralegal; Restaurant/Food Service Manager; Services Sales Representative; Systems Analyst; Technical Writer/Editor; Typist/Word Processor; Underwriter/Assistant Underwriter. **Corporate headquarters location:** San Juan Capistrano CA. **Other U.S. locations:** Nationwide.

REP TEMPS, INC.
150 East Huron Avenue, Suite 903, Chicago IL 60611. 312/944-9194. **Fax:** 312/944-9195. **Contact:** Kate Tahaney, Account Manager. **Description:** A temporary agency. Company pays fee. **Specializes in the areas of:** Advertising; Advertising Sales; Media Sales. **Positions commonly filled include:** Administrative Assistant; Advertising Manager; Broadcast Engineer; Buyer; Media Specialist; Promotion Manager; Sales Representative; Transportation/Traffic Specialist.

RIGHT SERVICES INC.
76010 South Kostner Avenue, Chicago IL 60652. 773/581-2100. **Fax:** 773/581-8715. **Contact:** Jean Riley, Manager. **Description:** A temporary agency. **Specializes in the areas of:** Accounting/Auditing; Administration; Banking; Computer Science/Software; Finance; Health/Medical; Insurance; Legal; Manufacturing; Nonprofit; Personnel/Labor Relations; Sales; Secretarial. **Positions commonly filled include:** Financial Analyst; Human Resources Specialist; Medical Records Technician; Public Relations Specialist; Purchasing Agent/Manager; Quality Control Supervisor; Statistician; Typist/Word Processor. **Average salary range of placements:** $20,000 - $29,999. **Number of placements per year:** 500 - 999.

RIGHT SERVICES INC.
2275 Halfday Road, Suite 343, Bannockburn IL 60015. 847/459-1320. **Fax:** 847/459-1365. **Contact:** Kimberly Mescha, Branch Manager. **Description:** A temporary agency that also provides permanent placement. **Specializes in the areas of:** Accounting/Auditing; Banking; Insurance; Personnel/Labor Relations; Sales; Secretarial. **Positions commonly filled include:** Advertising Clerk; Claim Representative; Clerical Supervisor; Customer Service Representative; Typist/Word Processor. **Average salary range of placements:** $20,000 - $29,999.

RIGHT SERVICES INC.
53 West Jackson Boulevard, Suite 1315, Chicago IL 60604. 312/427-4352. **Fax:** 312/427-3145. **Contact:** Karen Pinelli, Client Services Manager. **Description:** A temporary agency that also provides permanent placements. Company pays fee. **Specializes in the areas of:** Accounting/Auditing; Administration; Banking; Finance; General Management; Health/Medical; Nonprofit; Personnel/Labor Relations; Sales; Secretarial. **Positions commonly filled include:** Accountant/Auditor; Clerical Supervisor; Customer Service Representative; Financial Analyst; General Manager; Human Resources Specialist; Human Service Worker; Medical Records Technician; Multimedia Designer; Purchasing Agent/Manager; Typist/Word Processor.

RIGHT SERVICES INC.
477 East Butterfield Road, Suite 100, Lombard IL 60148. 630/969-7010. **Contact:** Sue Murphy, Office Manager. **Description:** A temporary agency. **Specializes in the areas of:** Accounting/Auditing; Banking; Finance; General Management; Health/Medical; Personnel/Labor Relations; Secretarial. **Positions commonly filled include:** Accountant/Auditor; Customer Service Representative; Human Resources Specialist; Paralegal; Typist/Word Processor. **Average salary range of placements:** $20,000 - $29,999. **Number of placements per year:** 1000+.

SEVILLE TEMPORARY SERVICES
180 North Michigan Avenue, Suite 707, Chicago IL 60601. 312/368-1144. **Fax:** 312/368-0207. **Contact:** Matt Bukovy, Operations Manager. **E-mail address:** sevilleinc@aol.com. **Description:** A temporary agency. **Specializes in the areas of:** Legal; Personnel/Labor Relations; Secretarial. **Positions commonly filled include:** Insurance Agent/Broker; Paralegal; Typist/Word Processor; Underwriter/Assistant Underwriter.

SHANNONWOOD STAFFERS, INC.
150 East Cook Avenue, Libertyville IL 60048. 847/362-6100. **Fax:** 847/362-1826. **Contact:** Kelly Webster, Division Manager. **Description:** A temporary agency. Company pays fee. **Specializes in the areas of:** Computer Science/Software; Sales; Secretarial. **Positions commonly filled include:** Claim Representative; Clerical Supervisor; Customer Service Representative; Services Sales Representative; Typist/Word Processor. **Average salary range of placements:** $20,000 - $29,999. **Number of placements per year:** 1 - 49.

SNELLING PERSONNEL SERVICES
999 East Touhy Avenue, Suite 160, Des Plaines IL 60018. 847/296-1026. **Contact:** Manager. **Description:** A temporary agency. **Specializes in the areas of:** Clerical; Food Industry; Sales. **Corporate headquarters location:** Dallas TX. **Other U.S. locations:** Nationwide.

SNELLING PERSONNEL SERVICES
2029 Ogden Avenue, Lisle IL 60532. 630/515-9088. **Fax:** 630/515-9616. **Contact:** Personnel Manager. **Description:** A temporary agency. Company pays fee. **Specializes in the areas of:** Administration. **Positions commonly filled include:** Customer Service Representative; Light Industrial Worker. **Corporate headquarters location:** Dallas TX. **Other U.S. locations:** Nationwide.

SNYDER STAFFING
111 North Sangom, Lincoln IL 62656. 217/732-1108. **Contact:** Manager. **Description:** A temporary agency. **Specializes in the areas of:** Administration; Clerical; Industrial.

STAFFING TEAM INTERNATIONAL
1100 Jorie Boulevard, Suite 132, Oak Brook IL 60523. 630/573-8640. **Fax:** 630/573-8644. **Contact:** Julie Shefcik, Employment Counselor. **Description:** A temporary agency. Company pays fee. **Specializes in the areas of:** Office Support; Sales; Secretarial;

Technical; Transportation. **Positions commonly filled include:** Accountant/Auditor; Administrative Manager; Blue-Collar Worker Supervisor; Branch Manager; Brokerage Clerk; Buyer; Claim Representative; Clerical Supervisor; Computer Programmer; Customer Service Representative; Designer; Draftsperson; Financial Analyst; General Manager; Human Service Worker; Management Trainee; Market Research Analyst; MIS Specialist; Operations/Production Manager; Paralegal; Public Relations Specialist; Purchasing Agent/ Manager; Services Sales Representative; Systems Analyst; Transportation/Traffic Specialist; Typist/Word Processor. **Average salary range of placements:** $20,000 - $29,999. **Number of placements per year:** 500 - 999.

STIVERS TEMPORARY PERSONNEL, INC.
1225 Corporate Boulevard, Suite 100, Aurora IL 60504. 630/851-9330. **Contact:** Office Manager. **Description:** A temporary agency. **Specializes in the areas of:** Accounting/Auditing; Banking; Clerical; Engineering; Finance; Health/Medical; Insurance; Legal; Manufacturing; MIS/EDP; Personnel/Labor Relations; Real Estate; Transportation.

TEMPFLEET
8 South Michigan Avenue, Suite 1306, Chicago IL 60603. 312/236-0155. **Fax:** 312/236-4629. **Contact:** Kaye Ruddy, President. **Description:** A temporary agency. **Specializes in the areas of:** Accounting/Auditing; Secretarial; Word Processing.

TEMPORARY ASSOCIATES
400 Lake Street, Suite 320, Roselle IL 60172. 630/893-7336. **Contact:** Manager. **Description:** A temporary agency. Company pays fee. **Specializes in the areas of:** Administration; Banking; Food Industry; Industrial; Sales; Secretarial. **Positions commonly filled include:** Accountant/Auditor; Blue-Collar Worker Supervisor; Claim Representative; Clerical Supervisor; Customer Service Representative; Operations/ Production Manager; Quality Control Supervisor; Services Sales Representative; Telecommunications Manager; Transportation/Traffic Specialist; Typist/ Word Processor; Video Production Coordinator. **Average salary range of placements:** $20,000 - $29,999. **Number of placements per year:** 100 - 199.

UNIFORCE STAFFING SERVICES
1500 Waukegan Road, Suite 221, Glen View IL 60025. 847/998-9300. **Contact:** Manager. **Description:** A temporary, temp-to-perm, and permanent employment agency. **Specializes in the areas of:** Mortgage.

WORKING WORLD INC.
P.O. Box 58, Richmond IL 60071. 815/678-2442. **Fax:** 815/678-2616. **Contact:** Monica Hayes, Branch Manager. **Description:** A temporary agency. Company pays fee. **Specializes in the areas of:** Accounting/ Auditing; Administration; Computer Science/Software; Finance; General Management; Industrial; Insurance; Legal; Manufacturing; Personnel/Labor Relations; Sales; Secretarial; Technical. **Positions commonly filled include:** Accountant/Auditor; Blue-Collar Worker Supervisor; Customer Service Representative; Industrial Production Manager; Management Trainee; Manufacturer's/Wholesaler's Sales Rep.; Medical Records Technician; MIS Specialist; Operations/ Production Manager; Quality Control Supervisor; Typist/Word Processor; Underwriter/Assistant Underwriter. **Corporate headquarters location:** Crystal Lake IL. **Number of placements per year:** 200 - 499.

CONTRACT SERVICES FIRMS

ADVANCED RESOURCES
ADVANCED CLINICAL
1300 East Woodfield Road, Suite 506, Schaumburg IL 60173. 847/995-9222. **Fax:** 847/995-9290. **Contact:** Krista Harris, Staffing Coordinator. **E-mail address:** kharris@advancedgroup.com. **Description:** A contract services firm that also provides consulting services. Advanced Clinical (also at this location) is a contract services firm that focuses on placement in biology fields and health/medical areas. The firm places physicians, pharmacists, registered nurses, emergency medical technicians, medical records technicians, and respiratory therapists. Founded in 1993. **Specializes in the areas of:** Computer Science/Software. **Positions commonly filled include:** Computer Programmer; MIS Specialist; Systems Analyst. **Benefits available to temporary workers:** 401(k). **Corporate headquarters location:** This Location. **Other U.S. locations:** San Francisco CA; Atlanta GA. **Average salary range of placements:** More than $50,000. **Number of placements per year:** 50 - 99.

ALTERNATIVE RESOURCES CORPORATION
222 South Riverside Plaza, Suite 830, Chicago IL 60606. 312/474-9200. **Contact:** Mary Beth Canfield, Marketing Specialist. **Description:** A contract services firm that focuses on mainframes and networking. **Specializes in the areas of:** Computer Science/Software; Information Technology; Technical. **Positions commonly filled include:** Computer Operator; Consultant; Database Manager; MIS Manager; Software Engineer; Systems Analyst; Systems Manager; Technical Writer/Editor; Telecommunications Manager; Vice President; Webmaster. **Corporate headquarters location:** Lincolnshire IL. **Other U.S. locations:** Nationwide.

AMERICAN CONTRACT SERVICES, INC.
2215 York Road, Oak Brook IL 60523. 630/571-4100. **Toll-free phone:** 800/899-7467. **Fax:** 630/990-1009. **Contact:** Denise Lipskis, Operations Manager. **Description:** A contract services firm focusing on engineering. **Specializes in the areas of:** Architecture/Construction; Engineering; Food Industry; Industrial; Technical. **Positions commonly filled include:** Architect; Chemical Engineer; Civil Engineer; Cost Estimator; Draftsperson; Environmental Engineer; Mining Engineer; Structural Engineer. **Average salary range of placements:** $30,000 - $50,000. **Number of placements per year:** 100 - 199.

CDI CORPORATION
2485 Federal Drive, Building 3, Decatur IL 62526. 217/875-0393. **Contact:** Manager. **World Wide Web address:** http://www.cdicorp.com. **Description:** A contract services firm. **Specializes in the areas of:** Engineering; Technical. **Corporate headquarters location:** Philadelphia PA. **Other U.S. locations:** Nationwide. **International locations:** Worldwide.

CARSON MANAGEMENT ASSOCIATES
456 Fulton, Suite 394, Peoria IL 61602. 309/637-7800. **Fax:** 309/637-7836. **Contact:** James Carson, Owner. **Description:** A contract services firm. Company pays fee. **Specializes in the areas of:** Accounting/Auditing; Administration; Art/Design; Computer Science/Software; Engineering; Finance; General Management; Manufacturing; Personnel/Labor Relations; Publishing; Sales; Technical. **Positions commonly filled include:** Accountant/Auditor; Aerospace Engineer; Agricultural Engineer; Blue-Collar Worker Supervisor; Branch Manager; Chemical Engineer; Civil Engineer; Computer Programmer; Cost Estimator; Customer Service Representative; Design

Engineer; Designer; Draftsperson; Electrical/Electronics Engineer; Electrician; Environmental Engineer; Financial Analyst; General Manager; Health Services Manager; Human Resources Manager; Industrial Engineer; Manufacturer's/Wholesaler's Sales Rep.; Mechanical Engineer; MIS Specialist; Multimedia Designer; Operations/Production Manager; Purchasing Agent/Manager; Quality Control Supervisor; Software Engineer; Systems Analyst; Technical Writer/Editor; Transportation/Traffic Specialist. **Average salary range of placements:** $30,000 - $50,000. **Number of placements per year:** 1 - 49.

COMFORCE TELECOM, INC.
110 East Schiller Street, Suite 302, Elmhurst IL 60123. 630/279-9200. **Fax:** 630/279-9310. **Contact:** Manager. **Description:** A contract services firm that also provides permanent placements. **Specializes in the areas of:** Telecommunications.

JENDER & COMPANY
800 West 5th Street, Naperville IL 60563. 630/355-7797. **Contact:** Manager. **Description:** A contract services firm. **Specializes in the areas of:** Administration; Computer Science/Software; Engineering; General Management; Industrial; Manufacturing. **Average salary range of placements:** More than $50,000. **Number of placements per year:** 1 - 49.

POLLAK AND SKAN, INC.
25 Northwest Point Boulevard, Suite 900, Elk Grove Village IL 60007. 847/437-8888. **Toll-free phone:** 800/544-7817. **Fax:** 847/437-9073. **Contact:** Gary Krebs, Account Executive. **World Wide Web address:** http://www.pscts.com. **Description:** A contract services firm. **Specializes in the areas of:** Computer Science/Software; Engineering; Industrial; Manufacturing; Technical. **Positions commonly filled include:** Aerospace Engineer; Aircraft Mechanic/Engine Specialist; Architect; Biomedical Engineer; Chemical Engineer; Chemist; Civil Engineer; Clinical Lab Technician; Computer Programmer; Cost Estimator; Design Engineer; Designer; Draftsperson; Electrical/Electronics Engineer; Electrician; Environmental Engineer; Food Scientist/Technologist; Industrial Engineer; Mechanical Engineer; Metallurgical Engineer; MIS Specialist; Multimedia Designer; Nuclear Engineer; Petroleum Engineer; Quality Control Supervisor; Software Engineer; Stationary Engineer; Structural Engineer; Systems Analyst; Technical Writer/Editor. **Corporate headquarters location:** Chicago IL. **Other U.S. locations:** Nationwide.

PROVISION TECHNOLOGIES
223 West Jackson, Suite 1008, Chicago IL 60606. 312/986-9640. **Fax:** 312/986-9645. **Contact:** Recruiter. **E-mail address:** tadata@ziplink.net. **World Wide Web address:** http://www.careerbase.com. **Description:** A contract services firm. Company pays fee. **Specializes in the areas of:** Computer Science/Software. **Positions commonly filled include:** Computer Programmer; Database Manager; Internet Services Manager; Network Engineer; Project Manager; Software Engineer; Systems Analyst; Systems Engineer; Technical Support Engineer; Telecommunications Manager; Webmaster. **Benefits available to temporary workers:** 401(k); Medical Insurance. **Corporate headquarters location:** Cambridge MA. **Other U.S. locations:** Nationwide. **Average salary range of placements:** $30,000 - $50,000. **Number of placements per year:** 50 - 99.

TDF CORPORATION
1717 Park Street, Suite 301, Naperville IL 60563-8478. 630/355-1800. **Fax:** 630/355-1338. **Contact:** Nick Dragisic, Vice President/Operations. **E-mail address:** tdf95@aol.com. **Description:** A contract services firm that focuses on technical computer placements. **Specializes in the areas of:** Administration; Computer Science/Software; Engineering. **Positions commonly filled include:** Computer Programmer; Design Engineer; Electrical/Electronics Engineer; Human Resources Manager; Management Analyst/Consultant; MIS Specialist; Services Sales Representative; Software Engineer; Systems Analyst; Technical Writer/Editor. **Average salary range of placements:** $30,000 - $50,000. **Number of placements per year:** 1 - 49.

H.L. YOH COMPANY
1200 Jorie Boulevard, Oak Brook IL 60523. 630/990-8800. **Contact:** Manager. **Description:** A contract services firm. **Specializes in the areas of:** Engineering; Scientific. **Other U.S. locations:** Nationwide.

CAREER/OUTPLACEMENT COUNSELING FIRMS

A ADVANCED RESUME SERVICE, INC.
1900 East Golf Road, Suite M100, Schaumburg IL 60173. 847/517-1088. **Fax:** 847/517-1126. **Contact:** Steven Provenzano, President/CPRW. **E-mail address:** advresumes@aol.com. **World Wide Web address:** http://www.amsquare.com/america/advanced.html. **Description:** A resume writing and career/outplacement service. The firm provides free resume analysis, writing, and printing; personal interviews; and career marketing seminars for large corporations. **Corporate headquarters location:** Streamwood IL.

A ADVANCED RESUME SERVICE, INC.
701 East Irving Park Road, Suite 201, Roselle IL 60172. 630/582-1088. **Contact:** Manager. **World Wide Web address:** http://www.amsquare.com/america/advanced.html. **Description:** A resume writing and career/ outplacement service. The firm provides free resume analysis, writing, and printing; personal interviews; and career marketing seminars for large corporations. **Corporate headquarters location:** Streamwood IL.

ABSOLUTE CAREER SERVICES
1122 Westgate, Suite 201, Oak Park IL 60301. **Toll-free phone:** 800/747-2987. **Contact:** Robert Meier, Owner/Founder. **E-mail address:** wmmeier@aol.com. **Description:** A career/outplacement counseling firm that also provides resume writing services. **Corporate headquarters location:** Chicago IL.

ABSOLUTE CAREER SERVICES
WILLIAM MEIER & ASSOCIATES
333 North Michigan Avenue, Suite 2032, Chicago IL 60601. 312/726-2350. **Toll-free phone:** 800/747-2987. **Contact:** Robert Meier, Owner/Founder. **E-mail address:** wmmeier@aol.com. **Description:** A career/outplacement counseling firm that also provides resume writing services. **Corporate headquarters location:** This Location.

ALL WRITE RESUMES, INC.
287 Peterson Road, Libertyville IL 60048. 847/816-1800. **Fax:** 847/816-1822. **Contact:** Alice Jorgensen, Chief Writer. **Description:** A resume writing service.

CORPORATE ORGANIZING AND RESEARCH SERVICES, INC.
One Pierce Place, Suite 300 East, Itasca IL 60143. 630/250-8677. **Contact:** Manager. **Description:** A career/outplacement counseling firm.

HARVARD OAKS ENTERPRISES, INC.
208 South LaSalle, Suite 1681, Chicago IL 60604. 312/372-3050. **Contact:** Ms. Leslie Fischer, President. **Description:** A career/outplacement counseling firm.

ILLINOIS VETERANS LEADERSHIP PROGRAM
725 North Grand Avenue East, Springfield IL 62702. 217/523-5105. **Fax:** 217/523-5164. **Contact:** Sheila Cutright, Veterans Employment Counselor. **E-mail address:** hireavet@aol.com. **Description:** A career/outplacement counseling firm for former military members only. This location focuses on state job opportunities. **Specializes in the areas of:** Accounting/Auditing; Administration; Biology; Computer Science/Software; Finance; General Management; Manufacturing; Personnel/Labor Relations; Secretarial. **Positions commonly filled include:** Accountant/Auditor; Actuary; Administrative Manager; Automotive Mechanic; Bank Officer/Manager; Civil Engineer; Claim Representative; Clerical Supervisor; Clinical Lab Technician; Computer Programmer; Customer Service Representative; Electrical/Electronics Engineer; Emergency Medical Technician; Health Services Manager; Human Resources Manager; Human Service Worker; Industrial Production Manager; Management Trainee; Medical Records Technician; MIS Specialist; Operations/Production Manager; Quality Control Supervisor; Radiation Therapist; Securities Sales Representative; Systems Analyst. **Corporate headquarters location:** Chicago IL. **Other area locations:** Belleville IL; Decatur IL; Peoria IL.

SHEA ASSOCIATES
800 Enterprise Drive, Suite 128, Oak Brook IL 60521. 630/573-4266. **Contact:** Manager. **Description:** A career/outplacement counseling firm.

UNITED WORKFORCE DEVELOPMENT
700 East Oak Street, Canton IL 61520-3168. 309/647-5680. **Fax:** 309/647-5688. **Contact:** Liz Hayman, Manager. **Description:** A career/outplacement counseling firm that provides skill enhancement training.

INDIANA

EXECUTIVE SEARCH FIRMS

ABS-AARON BUSINESS SYSTEMS
911 East 86th Street, Suite 103, Indianapolis IN 46240. 317/251-0125. **Contact:** Office Manager. **Description:** An executive search firm providing low- to middle-management placements. **Specializes in the areas of:** Sales.

ALEXANDER & ASSOCIATES
P.O. Box 335, Granger IN 46530. 219/271-0594. **Contact:** Manager. **Description:** An executive search firm. **Specializes in the areas of:** Manufacturing. **Positions commonly filled include:** General Manager; Human Resources Specialist; Product Engineer. **Average salary range of placements:** $30,000 - $50,000.

ALLIED HEALTH RECRUITERS
8081 South Madison Avenue, Suite 273, Indianapolis IN 46227-6001. 317/780-6788. **Fax:** 317/780-5888. **Contact:** Manager. **Description:** An executive search firm that focuses on occupational, physical, and speech therapy. **Specializes in the areas of:** Health/Medical.

THE BENNETT GROUP
5640 Professional Circle, Indianapolis IN 46241. 317/247-1240. **Contact:** Manager. **Description:** An executive search firm. **Specializes in the areas of:** Electronics; Engineering; High-Tech.

BINDLEY ASSOCIATES
320 North Meridian Street, Suite 612, Indianapolis IN 46204. 317/464-8144. **Contact:** Manager. **Description:** An executive search firm. **Specializes in the areas of:** Legal.

CANIS MAJOR, INC.
HR QUEST
P.O. Box 742, Carmel IN 46032-0742. 317/581-8880. **Toll-free phone:** 800/536-4276. **Fax:** 317/581-8856. **Contact:** Carol Albright, President. **Description:** A contingency search firm specializing in insurance, occupational health/safety, human resources, manufacturing control technicians, and MIS/EDP. Company pays fee. **Specializes in the areas of:** Administration; Computer Science/Software; Engineering; Industrial; Insurance; Manufacturing; MIS/EDP; Personnel/Labor Relations; Safety. **Positions commonly filled include:** Adjuster; Claim Representative; Electrical/Electronics Engineer; Human Resources Manager; Industrial Engineer; Licensed Practical Nurse; Registered Nurse; Underwriter/Assistant Underwriter. **Average salary range of placements:** $30,000 - $50,000. **Number of placements per year:** 1 - 49.

CAREERS UNLIMITED INC.
1238 South Main Street, Elkhart IN 46516. 219/293-0659. **Fax:** 219/294-1254. **Contact:** Steve Berger, President/Owner. **Description:** An executive search firm operating on a contingency basis. The firm also provides some contract services. Company pays fee. **Specializes in the areas of:** Computer Science/Software; Engineering; General Management; Industrial; Manufacturing. **Positions commonly filled include:** Computer Programmer; Electrical/Electronics Engineer; Industrial Engineer; Industrial Production Manager; Manufacturing Engineer; Mechanical Engineer; Production Manager; Systems Analyst. **Number of placements per year:** 1 - 49.

CHEVIGNY PERSONNEL AGENCY
P.O. Box 11342, Gary IN 46411-1342. 219/663-7801. **Fax:** 219/663-7819. **Contact:** Jule Chevigny, President. **Description:** A contingency search firm. Company pays fee. **Specializes in the areas of:** Engineering; Industrial; Manufacturing; MIS/EDP. **Positions commonly filled include:** Accountant/Auditor; Bank Officer/Manager; Chemical Engineer; Civil Engineer; Computer Programmer; Design Engineer; Electrical/Electronics Engineer; Environmental Engineer; Industrial Engineer; Industrial Production Manager; Mechanical Engineer; Metallurgical Engineer; MIS Specialist; Purchasing Agent/Manager; Quality Control Supervisor; Restaurant/Food Service Manager; Structural Engineer; Systems Analyst.

COMPUSEARCH
1657 Commerce Drive, Suite 15B, South Bend IN 46628. 219/239-2970. **Contact:** Office Manager. **Description:** An executive search firm for computer professionals. **Specializes in the areas of:** Computer Hardware/Software.

THE CONSULTING FORUM, INC.
9200 Keystone Crossing, Suite 700, Indianapolis IN 46240. 317/580-4800. **Fax:** 317/580-4801. **Contact:** Don Kellner, President. **E-mail address:** admin@consultingforum.com. **Description:** An executive search firm operating on both retainer and contingency bases. The firm specializes in the recruitment of information systems professionals, software engineers, and computer specialists. Company pays fee. **Specializes in the areas of:** Administration; Computer Science/Software; Information Systems. **Positions commonly filled include:** Computer Programmer; MIS Specialist; Software Engineer; Systems Analyst; Technical Writer/Editor. **Average salary range of placements:** $30,000 - $50,000. **Number of placements per year:** 100 - 199.

CREATIVE FINANCIAL STAFFING
330 East Jefferson Boulevard, South Bend IN 46601. 219/236-7600. **Contact:** Manager. **Description:** An executive search firm. **Specializes in the areas of:** Finance.

THE CURARE GROUP, INC.
4001 East Third Street, Suite B, Bloomington IN 47401. 812/331-0645. **Fax:** 812/331-0659. **Contact:** David Witte, Senior Consultant. **Description:** An executive search firm focusing on contingency recruitment of primary care physicians, including family practice, internal medicine, pediatrics, and OB/GYN. Founded in 1991. Company pays fee. **Specializes in the areas of:** Health/Medical. **Positions commonly filled include:** Physician. **Other U.S. locations:** New Orleans LA. **Average salary range of placements:** More than $50,000.

DATA FORCE
715 North Park Avenue, Indianapolis IN 46202. 317/636-9900. **Contact:** Manager. **Description:** An executive search firm. **Specializes in the areas of:** Information Systems.

DOBIAS GROUP
130 West Main Street, Fort Wayne IN 46802. 219/436-6570. **Contact:** Manager. **Description:** An executive search firm. **Specializes in the areas of:** Hotel/Restaurant.

DUNHILL OF BROWN COUNTY
P.O. Box 1068, Nashville IN 47448. 812/988-1944. **Contact:** George W. Rogers, President. **Description:** An executive search firm. Company pays fee.

Specializes in the areas of: Engineering; Health/Medical; Industrial; Manufacturing; Personnel/Labor Relations; Technical. **Positions commonly filled include:** Aerospace Engineer; Agricultural Engineer; Biomedical Engineer; Chemical Engineer; Chemist; Civil Engineer; Designer; Electrical/Electronics Engineer; Health Services Manager; Industrial Engineer; Industrial Production Manager; Mechanical Engineer; Metallurgical Engineer. **Number of placements per year:** 100 - 199.

DUNHILL PROFESSIONAL SEARCH
9918 Coldwater Road, Fort Wayne IN 46825-2040. 219/489-5966. **Fax:** 219/489-6120. **Contact:** Office Manager. **E-mail address:** dunftwin@aol.com. **Description:** An executive search firm operating on a contingency basis. Company pays fee. **Specializes in the areas of:** Engineering; Industrial; Manufacturing; Technical. **Positions commonly filled include:** Chemical Engineer; Chemist; Design Engineer; General Manager; Industrial Engineer; Industrial Production Manager; Mechanical Engineer; Metallurgical Engineer; Operations/Production Manager; Quality Control Supervisor; Statistician. **Other U.S. locations:** Nationwide. **Average salary range of placements:** $30,000 - $50,000.

EXCELLENCE IN SEARCH
10499 North College Avenue, Suite 100, Indianapolis IN 46280. 317/573-5222. **Fax:** 317/573-5223. **Contact:** Manager. **Description:** An executive search firm. **Specializes in the areas of:** Data Processing; Health/Medical.

EXECUSEARCH
5732 Coventry Lane, Fort Wayne IN 46804. 219/436-7470. **Contact:** Manager. **Description:** An executive search firm.

EXECUSEARCH
105 East Jefferson Boulevard, Suite 800, South Bend IN 46601-1811. 219/233-9353. **Contact:** Manager. **Description:** An executive search firm. **Specializes in the areas of:** Accounting/Auditing; Administration; Advertising; Architecture/Construction; Banking; Chemical; Communications; Computer Hardware/Software; Construction; Electrical; Engineering; Finance; Food Industry; General Management; Health/Medical; Insurance; Legal; Manufacturing; Personnel/Labor Relations; Pharmaceutical; Procurement; Publishing; Real Estate; Retail; Sales; Technical; Textiles; Transportation.

EXECUTEC PERSONNEL SERVICES, INC.
8900 Keystone Crossing, Suite 1275, Indianapolis IN 46240. 317/571-0001. **Contact:** Office Manager. **Description:** An executive search firm for individuals with experience in technical fields. **Specializes in the areas of:** Computer Science/Software; Engineering; Industrial Sales and Marketing; Information Systems.

FLEXIBLE TECHNICALS
1010 West Coliseum Boulevard, Fort Wayne IN 46808. 219/436-3868. **Contact:** Manager. **Description:** An executive search firm. **Specializes in the areas of:** Technical.

F-O-R-T-U-N-E PERSONNEL CONSULTANTS
347 West Berry Street, Fort Wayne IN 46802. 219/424-5159. **Fax:** 219/424-4201. **Contact:** Manager. **Description:** An executive search firm. **Specializes in the areas of:** Electronics; Plastics; Rubber. **Corporate headquarters location:** New York NY. **Other U.S. locations:** Nationwide.

FRANKLIN EMPLOYMENT SERVICES
P.O. Box 1391, South Bend IN 46624. 219/289-7128. **Fax:** 219/287-2270. **Contact:** Phil Niswonger, Director. **E-mail address:** franklinot@aol.com. **Description:** An executive search firm. **Average salary range of placements:** $20,000 - $29,999. **Number of placements per year:** 1 - 49.

GREAT LAKES SEARCH
1010 West Coliseum Boulevard, Fort Wayne IN 46808. 219/436-2534. **Contact:** Office Manager. **Description:** An executive search firm. **Specializes in the areas of:** Engineering; Finance; Manufacturing.

HMO EXECUTIVE SEARCH
8910 Purdue Road, Suite 200, Indianapolis IN 46268-1155. 317/872-1056. **Fax:** 317/879-1233. **Contact:** Dick Carroll, CPC, President. **Description:** An executive search firm. Company pays fee. **Specializes in the areas of:** Health/Medical. **Positions commonly filled include:** Registered Nurse. **Number of placements per year:** 50 - 99.

ROBERT HALF INTERNATIONAL
OFFICETEAM
135 North Pennsylvania Avenue, Suite 2300, Indianapolis IN 46204. 317/687-3270. **Contact:** Manager. **World Wide Web address:** http://www.roberthalf.com. **Description:** An executive search firm. OfficeTeam (also at this location) provides temporary and permanent administrative placements. Accountemps (also at this location) provides temporary placements. **Specializes in the areas of:** Accounting/Auditing. **Corporate headquarters location:** Menlo Park CA. **Other U.S. locations:** Nationwide.

THE HART LINE INC.
P.O. Box 39, Brazil IN 47834. 812/448-3490. **Fax:** 812/442-5227. **Contact:** Eric V. Stearley, CPC, President. **Description:** An executive search firm. Company pays fee. **Specializes in the areas of:** Engineering; Manufacturing. **Positions commonly filled include:** Electrical/Electronics Engineer; Industrial Engineer; Mechanical Engineer; Software Engineer. **Average salary range of placements:** $30,000 - $50,000. **Number of placements per year:** 50 - 99.

KEITH HAYES & ASSOCIATES
8420 Galley Court, Indianapolis IN 46236. 317/823-7100. **Contact:** Manager. **Description:** An executive search firm. **Specializes in the areas of:** Health/Medical; Pharmaceutical.

HEALTH LINK
EXECUTIVE PLACEMENT SERVICES
1321 North Meridian Street, Suite 209, Indianapolis IN 46202. 317/321-0200. **Contact:** Manager. **Description:** An executive search firm. Executive Placement Services (also at this location) provides computer and information technology placements. **Specializes in the areas of:** Health/Medical.

INSURANCE PEOPLE
4755 Kingsway Drive, Suite 300, Indianapolis IN 46205. 317/253-2128. **Contact:** Office Manager. **Description:** An executive search firm. **Specializes in the areas of:** Insurance.

JOHNSON BROWN ASSOCIATES
55 Monument Circle, Suite 1214, Indianapolis IN 46204. 317/237-4328. **Fax:** 317/237-4335. **Contact:** Dan Brown/Kim Johnson, Principals. **Description:** An executive search firm that operates on both retainer and contingency bases. Company pays fee. **Specializes in the areas of:** Accounting/Auditing; Engineering; Industrial; Information Technology; Investment; Personnel/Labor Relations; Sales; Technical. **Positions commonly filled include:** Account Manager; Account Representative; Accountant; Administrative Assistant; Applications Engineer;

Architect; Auditor; Budget Analyst; Buyer; Chief Financial Officer; Controller; Customer Service Representative; Design Engineer; Education Administrator; Financial Analyst; Fund Manager; General Manager; Human Resources Manager; Industrial Engineer; Industrial Production Manager; Manufacturing Engineer; Market Research Analyst; Marketing Manager; Marketing Specialist; Mechanical Engineer; Metallurgical Engineer; Operations Manager; Project Manager; Public Relations Specialist; Purchasing Agent/Manager; Quality Control Supervisor; Sales Engineer; Sales Executive; Sales Manager; Sales Representative; Systems Manager. **Corporate headquarters location:** This Location. **Average salary range of placements:** More than $50,000. **Number of placements per year:** 1 - 49.

MARY KENNEDY & ASSOCIATES
5987 East 71st Street, Suite 210, Indianapolis IN 46220. 317/579-6942. **Contact:** Mary Kennedy, Owner. **Description:** An executive search firm.

KEY SALES PERSONNEL
312 NW Martin Luther King Boulevard, Suite 100, Evansville IN 47708. 812/426-2244. **Contact:** George Krauss, Vice President. **Description:** An executive search firm. **Specializes in the areas of:** Sales. **Positions commonly filled include:** Manufacturer's/ Wholesaler's Sales Rep.; Sales Engineer; Services Sales Representative.

LANGE & ASSOCIATES, INC.
107 West Market Street, Wabash IN 46992. 219/563-7402. **Fax:** 219/563-3897. **Contact:** Jim Lange, President. **Description:** An executive search firm that also operates as a contract services firm. Company pays fee. **Specializes in the areas of:** Accounting/Auditing; Engineering; General Management; Manufacturing; Personnel/Labor Relations; Sales. **Positions commonly filled include:** Accountant/Auditor; Blue-Collar Worker Supervisor; Buyer; Chemical Engineer; Chemist; Cost Estimator; Design Engineer; Electrical/Electronics Engineer; Environmental Engineer; General Manager; Human Resources Manager; Industrial Engineer; Industrial Production Manager; Materials Engineer; Mechanical Engineer; Operations/Production Manager; Purchasing Agent/Manager; Quality Control Supervisor. **Number of placements per year:** 1 - 49.

THE MALLARD GROUP
3322 Oak Borough, Fort Wayne IN 46804. 219/436-3970. **Fax:** 219/436-7012. **Contact:** Robert Hoffman, Director. **Description:** An executive search firm operating on a contingency basis. Company pays fee. **Specializes in the areas of:** Computer Science/Software; Engineering; Manufacturing; Sales. **Positions commonly filled include:** Design Engineer; Electrical/Electronics Engineer; Human Resources Manager; Industrial Engineer; Mechanical Engineer; Metallurgical Engineer; Purchasing Agent/Manager; Software Engineer. **Number of placements per year:** 1 - 49.

MANAGEMENT RECRUITERS INTERNATIONAL
15209 Herriman Boulevard, Noblesville IN 46060. 317/773-4323. **Fax:** 317/773-9744. **Contact:** H. Peter Isenberg, President. **Description:** An executive search firm. Company pays fee. **Specializes in the areas of:** Administration; Computer Science/Software; Engineering; General Management; Industrial; Manufacturing; Sales. **Positions commonly filled include:** Computer Programmer; Designer; Draftsperson; Electrical/Electronics Engineer; Food Scientist/Technologist; Industrial Engineer; Industrial Production Manager; Manufacturer's/Wholesaler's Sales Rep.; Mechanical Engineer; Metallurgical Engineer; Pharmacist; Software Engineer; Systems Analyst. **Corporate headquarters location:** Cleveland OH. **Other U.S. locations:** Nationwide. **Average salary range of placements:** More than $50,000. **Number of placements per year:** 1 - 49.

MANAGEMENT RECRUITERS INTERNATIONAL
P.O. Box 2234, Columbus IN 47202. 812/372-5500. **Fax:** 812/372-8292. **Contact:** Manager. **Description:** An executive search firm. **Specializes in the areas of:** Banking; Computer Programming; Engineering. **Corporate headquarters location:** Cleveland OH. **Other U.S. locations:** Nationwide.

MANAGEMENT RECRUITERS INTERNATIONAL SALES CONSULTANTS
8200 Haverstick Road, Suite 240, Indianapolis IN 46240. 317/257-5411. **Contact:** Office Manager. **Description:** An executive search firm. **Specializes in the areas of:** Marketing; Sales; Technical. **Corporate headquarters location:** Cleveland OH. **Other U.S. locations:** Nationwide.

MANAGEMENT RECRUITERS OF EVANSVILLE
Riverside 1 Building, Suite 209, 101 Court Street, Evansville IN 47708. 812/464-9155. **Fax:** 812/422-6718. **Contact:** Manager. **Description:** An executive search firm. **Specializes in the areas of:** Accounting/Auditing; Administration; Advertising; Architecture/Construction; Banking; Chemical; Communications; Computer Hardware/Software; Construction; Electrical; Engineering; Finance; Food Industry; General Management; Health/Medical; Insurance; Legal; Manufacturing; Personnel/Labor Relations; Pharmaceutical; Procurement; Publishing; Real Estate; Retail; Sales; Technical; Textiles; Transportation. **Corporate headquarters location:** Cleveland OH. **Other U.S. locations:** Nationwide.

MANAGEMENT RECRUITERS OF INDIANAPOLIS
3905 Vincennes Road, Suite 202, Indianapolis IN 46268. 317/228-3300. **Fax:** 317/228-3317. **Contact:** Jodi Pope, Administrative Manager. **Description:** An executive search firm. **Specializes in the areas of:** Accounting/Auditing; Administration; Advertising; Architecture/Construction; Banking; Chemical; Communications; Computer Hardware/Software; Construction; Electrical; Engineering; Finance; Food Industry; General Management; Health/Medical; Insurance; Legal; Manufacturing; Operations Management; Personnel/Labor Relations; Pharmaceutical; Procurement; Publishing; Real Estate; Retail; Sales; Technical; Textiles; Transportation. **Positions commonly filled include:** Account Manager; Accountant; Adjuster; Applications Engineer; Branch Manager; Buyer; Chemical Engineer; Civil Engineer; Claim Representative; Clinical Lab Technician; Computer Operator; Computer Programmer; Controller; Database Manager; Design Engineer; Editor; Electrical/Electronics Engineer; Environmental Engineer; Financial Analyst; Graphic Artist; Industrial Engineer; Industrial Insurance Agent/Broker; Management Analyst/Consultant; Manufacturing Engineer; Marketing Specialist; Mechanical Engineer; MIS Specialist; Operations Manager; Production Manager; Project Manager; Public Relations Specialist; Quality Control Supervisor; Sales Engineer; Sales Executive; Sales Manager; Sales Representative; Software Engineer; Systems Analyst; Systems Manager; Underwriter/Assistant Underwriter. **Corporate headquarters location:** Cleveland OH. **Other U.S. locations:** Nationwide. **Average salary range of placements:** $30,000 - $50,000. **Number of placements per year:** 50 - 99.

MANAGEMENT RECRUITERS OF RICHMOND STAFFING SOLUTIONS OF RICHMOND
2519 East Main Street, Suite 101, Richmond IN 47374-5864. 765/935-3356. **Contact:** Mr. Rande

Martin, Manager. **Description:** An executive search firm. **Specializes in the areas of:** Accounting/Auditing; Administration; Advertising; Architecture/ Construction; Banking; Chemical; Communications; Computer Hardware/Software; Construction; Electrical; Engineering; Finance; Food Industry; General Management; Health/Medical; Insurance; Legal; Manufacturing; Operations Management; Personnel/Labor Relations; Pharmaceutical; Procurement; Publishing; Real Estate; Retail; Sales; Technical; Textiles; Transportation. **Corporate headquarters location:** Cleveland OH. **Other U.S. locations:** Nationwide.

MANAGEMENT SERVICES
P.O. Box 830, Middlebury IN 46540-0830. 219/825-3909. **Fax:** 219/825-7115. **Contact:** Office Manager. **Description:** An executive search firm operating on a contingency basis. The firm focuses on administrative, technical, and executive management placements. Company pays fee. **Specializes in the areas of:** Computer Science/Software; Engineering; Manufacturing; Personnel/Labor Relations; Sales. **Positions commonly filled include:** Accountant/ Auditor; Buyer; Chemical Engineer; Computer Programmer; Electrical/Electronics Engineer; Financial Analyst; General Manager; Human Resources Manager; Industrial Engineer; Industrial Production Manager; Mechanical Engineer; Metallurgical Engineer; MIS Specialist; Operations/Production Manager; Quality Control Supervisor; Software Engineer; Systems Analyst; Transportation/Traffic Specialist. **Number of placements per year:** 1 - 49.

MAYHALL SEARCH GROUP INC.
4410 Executive Boulevard, Suite 1A, Fort Wayne IN 46808. 219/484-7770. **Contact:** Office Manager. **Description:** An executive search firm. **Specializes in the areas of:** Accounting/Auditing; Manufacturing; Sales.

McNERNEY & ASSOCIATES
25416 CR 6E, Suite 206, Elkhart IN 46514. 219/262-2229. **Contact:** Manager. **E-mail address:** mcnsearch@aol.com. **Description:** An executive search firm. **Specializes in the areas of:** Computer Programming; Data Processing; Engineering.

MEDICAL RECRUITMENT SPECIALISTS
8910 Purdue Road, Indianapolis IN 46268. 317/875-6080. **Contact:** Manager. **Description:** An executive search firm. **Specializes in the areas of:** Health/Medical. **Positions commonly filled include:** Product Manager; Sales Manager.

MICHIANA PERSONNEL SERVICE
1441 Northside Boulevard, South Bend IN 46615. 219/232-3364. **Contact:** Manager. **Description:** An executive search firm.

MILLER PERSONNEL CONSULTANTS
931 East 86th Street, Suite 103, Indianapolis IN 46240. 317/251-5938. **Toll-free phone:** 800/851-5938. **Fax:** 317/251-5762. **Contact:** Mark Miller, Owner/Manager. **Description:** An executive search firm operating on a contingency basis. Company pays fee. **Specializes in the areas of:** Engineering; Manufacturing. **Positions commonly filled include:** Applications Engineer; Design Engineer; Electrical/Electronics Engineer; Industrial Engineer; Industrial Production Manager; Manufacturing Engineer; Mechanical Engineer; Operations Manager; Production Manager; Purchasing Agent/Manager; Quality Control Supervisor; Sales Engineer; Software Engineer. **Other U.S. locations:** Nationwide. **Average salary range of placements:** More than $50,000. **Number of placements per year:** 50 - 99.

MONTE DENBO ASSOCIATES
127 North Front Street, Rising Sun IN 47040. 812/438-2400. **Contact:** Manager. **Description:** An executive search firm that places senior-level managers. **Specializes in the areas of:** Engineering.

MORLEY GROUP
8910 Purdue Road, Suite 670, Indianapolis IN 46268. 317/879-4770. **Contact:** Manager. **Description:** An executive search firm that also provides some contract and temporary placements. **Specializes in the areas of:** Banking; Clerical; Engineering; Finance; Health/Medical; Human Resources; Information Systems; Manufacturing.

NATIONAL CORPORATE CONSULTANTS, INC.
ADVANTAGE SERVICES, INC.
409 East Cook Road, Suite 200, Fort Wayne IN 46825. 219/493-4506. **Contact:** Office Manager. **Description:** An executive search firm. **Specializes in the areas of:** Accounting/Auditing; Administration; Banking; Chemical; Computer Hardware/Software; Engineering; Finance; Food Industry; Manufacturing; Pharmaceutical; Technical; Transportation. **Number of placements per year:** 50 - 99.

NATIONAL RECRUITING SERVICE
P.O. Box 218, Dyer IN 46311. 219/865-2373. **Contact:** Stanley M. Hendricks, II, Owner. **Description:** An executive search firm operating on both retained and contingency bases. Company pays fee. **Specializes in the areas of:** Metals; Plastics. **Positions commonly filled include:** General Manager; Industrial Engineer; Industrial Production Manager; Manufacturing Engineer; Marketing Manager; Mechanical Engineer; Operations/Production Manager; Sales Engineer; Sales Executive; Sales Representative. **Average salary range of placements:** More than $50,000. **Number of placements per year:** 1 - 49.

OAKWOOD INTERNATIONAL INC.
3935 Lincoln Way East, Suite A, Mishawaka IN 46544. 219/255-9861. **Fax:** 219/257-8914. **Contact:** Scott Null, President. **E-mail address:** brent@mvillage.com. **World Wide Web address:** http://www.interact.withus.com/oakwood. **Description:** A contingency search firm. Company pays fee. **Specializes in the areas of:** Administration; Computer Science/Software; Engineering; General Management; Manufacturing; Sales; Technical. **Positions commonly filled include:** Aerospace Engineer; Biomedical Engineer; Branch Manager; Chemical Engineer; Chemist; Civil Engineer; Computer Programmer; Design Engineer; Designer; Draftsperson; Electrical/Electronics Engineer; Industrial Engineer; Internet Services Manager; Mechanical Engineer; Metallurgical Engineer; MIS Specialist; Multimedia Designer; Quality Control Supervisor; Software Engineer; Structural Engineer; Systems Analyst; Technical Writer/Editor; Telecommunications Manager. **Average salary range of placements:** More than $50,000. **Number of placements per year:** 1 - 49.

OFFICEMATES5 OF INDIANAPOLIS
1099 North Meridian Street, Landmark Building, Suite 640, Indianapolis IN 46204. 317/237-2787. **Contact:** Manager. **Description:** An executive search firm. **Specializes in the areas of:** Accounting/Auditing; Administration; Advertising; Architecture/ Construction; Banking; Chemical; Communications; Computer Hardware/Software; Construction; Electrical; Engineering; Finance; Food Industry; General Management; Health/Medical; Insurance; Legal; Manufacturing; Personnel/Labor Relations; Pharmaceutical; Procurement; Publishing; Real Estate; Retail; Sales; Technical; Textiles; Transportation.

OFFICEMATES5 OF INDIANAPOLIS (NORTH)
8888 Keystone Crossing Boulevard, Suite 1420, Indianapolis IN 46240. 317/843-2512. **Contact:** Manager. **Description:** An executive search firm. **Specializes in the areas of:** Accounting/Auditing; Administration; Advertising; Architecture/Construction; Banking; Chemical; Communications; Computer Hardware/Software; Construction; Electrical; Engineering; Finance; Food Industry; General Management; Health/Medical; Legal; Manufacturing; Personnel/Labor Relations; Pharmaceutical; Procurement; Publishing; Real Estate; Retail; Sales; Technical; Textiles; Transportation.

PERSONNEL PLUS, INC.
300 West Jefferson Street, Plymouth IN 46563. 219/935-5727. **Fax:** 219/935-4521. **Contact:** Marcy Eckhoff, CPC, President. **Description:** An executive search firm focusing on placements in the automotive, HVAC, and engine cooling industries. The firm operates on both retainer and contingency bases. Founded in 1976. Company pays fee. **Specializes in the areas of:** Engineering; Technical; Transportation. **Positions commonly filled include:** Electrical/Electronics Engineer; Mechanical Engineer.

PERSONNEL RECRUITERS
3077 East 98th Street, Suite 210, Indianapolis IN 46280. 317/580-5730. **Contact:** Manager. **Description:** An executive search firm. **Specializes in the areas of:** Administration; Engineering.

QUIRING ASSOCIATES HUMAN RESOURCE CONSULTING GROUP
7321 Shadeland Station Way, Suite 150, Indianapolis IN 46256-3935. 317/841-7575. **Fax:** 317/577-8240. **Contact:** Patti Quiring, CPC, President. **World Wide Web address:** http://www.iquest.net/quiring. **Description:** An executive search firm. Company pays fee. **Specializes in the areas of:** Accounting/Auditing; Administration; Banking; Computer Science/Software; Engineering; Finance; Health/Medical; Industrial; Insurance; Manufacturing; Nonprofit; Personnel/Labor Relations; Sales; Technical. **Positions commonly filled include:** Accountant/Auditor; Bank Officer/Manager; Computer Programmer; Computer Scientist; Engineer; Financial Consultant; Manufacturing Engineer; Scientist. **Average salary range of placements:** $30,000 - $50,000. **Number of placements per year:** 50 - 99.

RDN SERVICES
P.O. Box 1531, Warsaw IN 46581-1531. 219/269-9042. **Fax:** 219/269-9742. **Contact:** Richard Neff, President. **Description:** An executive search firm operating on a retainer basis. Company pays fee. **Specializes in the areas of:** Manufacturing; Personnel/Labor Relations; Technical. **Positions commonly filled include:** Design Engineer; Electrical/Electronics Engineer; Environmental Engineer; General Manager; Industrial Engineer; Industrial Production Manager; Mechanical Engineer; Purchasing Agent/Manager; Quality Control Supervisor. **Average salary range of placements:** More than $50,000. **Number of placements per year:** 1 - 49.

SALES SEARCH
2420 North Coliseum Boulevard, Suite 220, Fort Wayne IN 46805. 219/485-0850. **Fax:** 219/482-1943. **Contact:** Manager. **Description:** An executive search firm that provides sales placements.

SANFORD ROSE ASSOCIATES
P.O. Box 1106, Newburgh IN 47629. 812/853-9325. **Fax:** 812/853-1953. **Contact:** Ken Forbes, Director. **E-mail address:** kforbes@aol.com. **World Wide Web address:** http://www.sanfordrose.com. **Description:** A retained and contingency search firm. Company pays fee. **Positions commonly filled include:** Account Manager; Account Representative; Advertising Account Executive; Advertising Clerk; Graphic Artist; Graphic Designer; Human Resources Manager; Market Research Analyst; Marketing Manager; Marketing Specialist; Multimedia Designer; Operations Manager; Public Relations Specialist; Sales Executive; Sales Manager; Sales Representative. **Average salary range of placements:** $30,000 - $50,000. **Number of placements per year:** 1 - 49.

SANFORD ROSE ASSOCIATES
650 East Carmel Drive, Suite 450, Carmel IN 46032. 317/848-9987. **Fax:** 317/848-9979. **Contact:** Manager. **World Wide Web address:** http://www.sanfordrose.com. **Description:** An executive search firm. **Specializes in the areas of:** Finance; Insurance.

SMITH & SYBERG INC.
825 Washington Street, Suite 2A, Columbus IN 47201. 812/372-7254. **Contact:** Manager. **Description:** An executive search firm.

SOURCE SERVICES CORPORATION
111 Monument Circle, Suite 3930, Indianapolis IN 46204-5139. 317/631-2900. **Fax:** 317/682-6100. **Contact:** Manager. **Description:** An executive search firm. The divisions at this location include Source Consulting, Source EDP, Source Healthcare Staffing, and Accountant Source Temps. **Specializes in the areas of:** Accounting/Auditing; Computer Hardware/Software; Health/Medical; Information Technology.

J. SPAHN & ASSOCIATES
13819 Stone Drive, Carmel IN 46032. 317/580-0925. **Contact:** Manager. **Description:** An executive search firm. **Specializes in the areas of:** Hotel/Restaurant.

STRATEGIC RESOURCE MANAGEMENT
3500 DePauw Boulevard, Suite 1034, Indianapolis IN 46268. 317/872-8900. **Contact:** Office Manager. **Description:** An executive search firm. **Specializes in the areas of:** Health/Medical. **Positions commonly filled include:** Certified Nursing Aide; Physical Therapist; Physician.

TECHNICAL SEARCH & RECRUITERS
P.O. Box 2088, Clarksville IN 47131. 812/284-3012. **Fax:** 812/284-4536. **Contact:** Manager. **Description:** An executive search firm. **Specializes in the areas of:** Engineering; Human Resources.

UNIQUE, INC.
9850 North Michigan Avenue, Carmel IN 46032. 317/875-8281. **Fax:** 317/875-3127. **Contact:** Jennifer Flora, President. **Description:** An executive search firm specializing in sales, data processing, telecommunications, office support, and high-technology staffing. Company pays fee. **Specializes in the areas of:** Computer Science/Software; Food Industry; General Management; Legal; Personnel/Labor Relations; Publishing; Sales; Secretarial. **Positions commonly filled include:** Branch Manager; Clerical Supervisor; Computer Programmer; Customer Service Representative; General Manager; Hotel Manager; Human Resources Manager; Management Trainee; Paralegal; Restaurant/Food Service Manager; Services Sales Representative; Software Engineer; Systems Analyst; Telecommunications Manager; Typist/Word Processor. **Number of placements per year:** 500 - 999.

PERMANENT EMPLOYMENT AGENCIES

ACCOUNTANTS ON CALL
111 Monument Circle, Bank One Tower, Indianapolis IN 46204. 317/686-0001. **Contact:** Manager. **Description:** A permanent employment agency that also provides some temporary placements. **Specializes in the areas of:** Accounting/Auditing.

ADECCO
1417 West Coliseum Boulevard, Fort Wayne IN 46808. 219/482-2390. **Contact:** Branch Manager. **Description:** A permanent employment agency that also provides some temporary placements. **Specializes in the areas of:** Clerical.

AGRA PLACEMENTS, LTD.
16 East Fifth Street, Peru IN 46970. 765/472-1988. **Fax:** 765/472-7568. **Contact:** Doug Rice, Manager. **Description:** A permanent employment agency. **Specializes in the areas of:** Agri-Business; Chemical.

ALPHA RAE PERSONNEL, INC.
127 West Berry Street, Suite 200, Fort Wayne IN 46802. 219/426-8227. **Fax:** 219/426-1152. **Contact:** Rae Pearson, President. **Description:** A permanent employment agency. **Specializes in the areas of:** Computer Science/Software; Data Processing; Engineering; Legal; Sales; Software Engineering.

AMERICA WORKS
2021 North Meridian Street, Indianapolis IN 46208. 317/923-3600. **Contact:** Manager. **Description:** A permanent employment agency.

ANGOLA PERSONNEL SERVICES, INC.
901 North Wayne Street, Suite B, Angola IN 46703. 219/665-1162. **Fax:** 219/665-6997. **Contact:** Jeff Peters, President/Owner. **Description:** A permanent employment agency focusing on clerical, secretarial, light industrial, word processing, and technical placements. Company pays fee. **Specializes in the areas of:** Engineering; Industrial; Manufacturing; Personnel/Labor Relations; Secretarial. **Positions commonly filled include:** Blue-Collar Worker Supervisor; Clerical Supervisor; Customer Service Representative; Design Engineer; Designer; General Manager; Human Resources Specialist; Industrial Engineer; Industrial Production Manager; Mechanical Engineer; Quality Control Supervisor. **Benefits available to temporary workers:** Paid Holidays; Paid Vacation. **Other U.S. locations:** Auburn IN; Archbold OH. **Average salary range of placements:** $20,000 - $29,999. **Number of placements per year:** 1000+.

BANE & ASSOCIATES
19 1/2 South Eighth Street, Richmond IN 47374. 765/966-5512. **Contact:** David Bane, Owner/CEO. **Description:** A permanent employment agency that also conducts some executive searches. **Specializes in the areas of:** Industrial.

BARRISTER PERSONNEL
155 East Market Street, Suite 701, Indianapolis IN 46204. 317/637-0123. **Contact:** Office Manager. **Description:** A permanent employment agency that also provides some temporary placements. **Specializes in the areas of:** Legal Secretarial.

BONE PERSONNEL, INC.
6424 Lima Road, Fort Wayne IN 46818. 219/489-3350. **Fax:** 219/489-0556. **Contact:** Manager. **Description:** A permanent employment agency. Company pays fee. **Positions commonly filled include:** Accountant/Auditor; Administrative Manager; Advertising Clerk; Biomedical Engineer; Branch Manager; Budget Analyst; Buyer; Chemical Engineer; Chemist; Civil Engineer; Clerical Supervisor; Computer Programmer; Construction Contractor; Cost Estimator; Credit Manager; Designer; Draftsperson; Electrical/Electronics Engineer; Electrician; Financial Analyst; General Manager; Health Services Manager; Hotel Manager; Industrial Engineer; Industrial Production Manager; Manufacturer's/Wholesaler's Sales Rep.; Mechanical Engineer; Metallurgical Engineer; Paralegal; Quality Control Supervisor; Restaurant/Food Service Manager; Science Technologist; Services Sales Representative; Software Engineer; Stationary Engineer; Structural Engineer; Systems Analyst. **Number of placements per year:** 1000+.

BILL CALDWELL EMPLOYMENT SERVICE
123 Main Street, Suite 307, Evansville IN 47708. 812/423-8006. **Fax:** 812/423-8008. **Contact:** Carmen M. Caldwell, Manager. **Description:** A permanent employment agency. **Specializes in the areas of:** Accounting/Auditing; Banking; Computer Science/Software; Engineering; Finance; General Management; Health/Medical; Industrial; Manufacturing; Retail; Sales. **Positions commonly filled include:** Accountant/Auditor; Actuary; Adjuster; Administrative Manager; Advertising Clerk; Agricultural Engineer; Architect; Attorney; Automotive Mechanic; Bank Officer/Manager; Biochemist; Biological Scientist; Biomedical Engineer; Branch Manager; Budget Analyst; Buyer; Chemical Engineer; Chemist; Civil Engineer; Claim Representative; Clerical Supervisor; Clinical Lab Technician; Computer Programmer; Cost Estimator; Customer Service Representative; Design Engineer; Designer; Editor; EEG Technologist; Electrical/Electronics Engineer; Electrician; Financial Analyst; Food Scientist/Technologist; General Manager; Health Services Manager; Human Resources Specialist; Industrial Engineer; Internet Services Manager; Management Analyst/Consultant; Market Research Analyst; Materials Engineer; Mechanical Engineer; Metallurgical Engineer; Mining Engineer; Operations/Production Manager; Pharmacist; Physical Therapist; Public Relations Specialist; Quality Control Supervisor; Radio/TV Announcer/Broadcaster; Radiological Technologist; Real Estate Agent; Restaurant/Food Service Manager; Services Sales Representative; Software Engineer; Statistician; Systems Analyst; Typist/Word Processor; Underwriter/Assistant Underwriter.

CAREER CONSULTANTS, INC.
107 North Pennsylvania, Suite 400, Indianapolis IN 46204. 317/639-5601. **Contact:** Manager. **Description:** A permanent employment agency. Company pays fee. **Specializes in the areas of:** Accounting/Auditing; Computer Science/Software; Engineering; Food Industry; Industrial; Information Systems; Manufacturing; Technical. **Positions commonly filled include:** Accountant/Auditor; Computer Programmer; Electrical/Electronics Engineer; Financial Analyst; Human Resources Manager; Industrial Engineer; Industrial Production Manager; Mechanical Engineer; Metallurgical Engineer; Purchasing Agent/Manager; Quality Control Supervisor; Software Engineer; Statistician; Systems Analyst; Technical Writer/Editor. **Number of placements per year:** 50 - 99.

CENTURY PERSONNEL INC.
11590 North Meridian Street, Suite 500, Carmel IN 46032. 317/580-8500. **Contact:** Office Manager. **Description:** A permanent employment agency. **Specializes in the areas of:** Accounting/Auditing; Data Processing; Engineering; Health/Medical; Technical.

CROWE, CHIZEK AND COMPANY
330 East Jefferson Boulevard, P.O. Box 7, South Bend IN 46624. 219/232-3992. **Fax:** 219/236-8692.

Contact: Janet Racht, Senior Manager. **Description:** A permanent employment agency. **Specializes in the areas of:** Accounting/Auditing; Banking; Finance; Manufacturing.

DATA ACCESS
5420 West Southern Avenue, Suite 201, Indianapolis IN 46241. 317/545-5882. **Contact:** Manager. **Description:** A permanent employment agency. **Specializes in the areas of:** Clerical; Engineering.

PAT DAY PERSONNEL INC.
6100 North Keystone, Suite 222, Indianapolis IN 46220. 317/257-1411. **Contact:** Manager. **Description:** A permanent employment agency. **Specializes in the areas of:** Clerical; Office Support; Restaurant; Retail; Sales. **Positions commonly filled include:** Restaurant/Food Service Manager; Retail Manager; Sales Representative.

DENTAL MEDICAL POWER INC.
5249 Southeast Street, Suite B, Indianapolis IN 46227. 317/337-1312. **Contact:** Office Manager. **Description:** A permanent employment agency that also provides some temporary placements. **Specializes in the areas of:** Health/Medical.

EMPLOYMENT MART INC.
7002 Graham Road, Indianapolis IN 46220. 317/842-8890. **Contact:** Manager. **Description:** A permanent employment agency. **Specializes in the areas of:** Engineering.

EMPLOYMENT RECRUITERS INC.
P.O. Box 1624, Elkhart IN 46515-1624. 219/262-2654. **Fax:** 219/262-0095. **Contact:** Suzanne Pedler, President. **Description:** A permanent employment agency that places professionals with manufacturers throughout the Midwest. Founded in 1982. Company pays fee. **Specializes in the areas of:** Computer Science/Software; Engineering; General Management; Industrial; Manufacturing; Sales. **Positions commonly filled include:** Chemical Engineer; Chemist; Computer Programmer; Credit Manager; Customer Service Manager; Customer Service Representative; Design Engineer; Designer; Draftsperson; Electrical/Electronics Engineer; Environmental Engineer; Food Scientist/Technologist; General Manager; Industrial Engineer; Industrial Production Manager; Manufacturer's/Wholesaler's Sales Rep.; Market Research Analyst; Mathematician; Metallurgical Engineer; Mining Engineer; MIS Specialist; Operations/Production Manager; Purchasing Agent/Manager; Quality Control Supervisor; Safety Engineer; Science Technologist; Software Engineer; Stationary Engineer; Statistician; Strategic Relations Manager; Structural Engineer; Systems Analyst; Technical Writer/Editor. **Average salary range of placements:** $30,000 - $50,000. **Number of placements per year:** 1 - 49.

FLEXIBLE ACCOUNTANTS
1010 West Coliseum Boulevard, Fort Wayne IN 46808. 219/484-2903. **Toll-free phone:** 888/777-7129. **Fax:** 219/471-8101. **Contact:** Janet Hambrock, Branch Manager. **E-mail address:** flexacc@fwi.com. **World Wide Web address:** http://www.flexgrp.com. **Description:** A permanent employment agency that also provides some temporary placements. Company pays fee. **Specializes in the areas of:** Accounting/Auditing; Finance. **Positions commonly filled include:** Accountant; Auditor; Budget Analyst; Controller; Credit Manager; Finance Director; Financial Analyst. **Benefits available to temporary workers:** Paid Holidays; Paid Vacation; Referral Bonus Plan. **Corporate headquarters location:** Little Rock AR. **Other U.S. locations:** Nationwide. **Number of placements per year:** 100 - 199.

HOBART EMPLOYMENT AGENCY
58 Jefferson Street, Valparaiso IN 46383. 219/462-3488. **Contact:** Manager. **Description:** A permanent employment agency. **Specializes in the areas of:** Accounting/Auditing; Administration; Banking; Engineering; Finance; Industrial; Insurance; Legal. **Positions commonly filled include:** Accountant/Auditor; Adjuster; Administrative Manager; Attorney; Automotive Mechanic; Bank Officer/Manager; Blue-Collar Worker Supervisor; Branch Manager; Civil Engineer; Claim Representative; Clerical Supervisor; Computer Programmer; Construction Contractor; Cost Estimator; Electrical/Electronics Engineer; Electrician; Environmental Engineer; Financial Analyst; Health Services Manager; Industrial Engineer; Industrial Production Manager; Insurance Agent/Broker; Licensed Practical Nurse; Management Analyst/Consultant; Mechanical Engineer; Paralegal; Registered Nurse; Restaurant/Food Service Manager; Software Engineer; Structural Engineer; Systems Analyst; Typist/Word Processor; Underwriter/ Assistant Underwriter. **Average salary range of placements:** $20,000 - $29,999.

HUNTER-LAWYER PERSONNEL
70 East 91st Street, Suite 101, Indianapolis IN 46240. 317/848-1948. **Contact:** Office Manager. **Description:** A permanent employment agency. **Specializes in the areas of:** Clerical; Management; Secretarial.

INDIANA WORKFORCE DEVELOPMENT SERVICES
1776 West 37th Avenue, Gary IN 46408-2000. 219/981-1520. **Fax:** 219/884-5148. **Contact:** Job Desk. **Description:** An Indiana state employment office that offers permanent placement, individual skill/needs assessment, counseling, skills training, unemployment insurance protection, and labor market information. **Corporate headquarters location:** Indianapolis IN.

JOB PLACEMENT SERVICE INC.
5404 North Calumet Avenue, Valparaiso IN 46383. 219/462-7894. **Contact:** James S. Holycross, Vice President. **Description:** A permanent employment agency. **Specializes in the areas of:** Accounting/Auditing; Administration; Advertising; Architecture/Construction; Computer Science/Software; Engineering; Finance; General Management; Industrial; Insurance; Legal; Manufacturing; Nonprofit; Personnel/Labor Relations; Retail; Sales; Secretarial. **Positions commonly filled include:** Accountant/Auditor; Advertising Clerk; Architect; Automotive Mechanic; Branch Manager; Buyer; Chemist; Claim Representative; Clerical Supervisor; Clinical Lab Technician; Computer Programmer; Cost Estimator; Counselor; Credit Manager; Customer Service Representative; Design Engineer; Designer; Draftsperson; Editor; Electrical/Electronics Engineer; Electrician; Financial Analyst; Industrial Engineer; Industrial Insurance Agent/Broker; Operations/Production Manager; Software Engineer; Systems Analyst; Typist/Word Processor. **Average salary range of placements:** Less than $20,000. **Number of placements per year:** 500 - 999.

KENDALL & DAVIS, INC.
415 East Cook Road, Suite 200, Fort Wayne IN 46825. 219/489-8014. **Toll-free phone:** 800/860-8014. **Fax:** 800/860-2982. **Contact:** Manager. **Description:** A permanent placement agency that also provides some contract services. Company pays fee. **Specializes in the areas of:** Computer Science/Software. **Positions commonly filled include:** Computer Operator; Computer Programmer; MIS Specialist; Systems Analyst; Technical Writer/Editor; Telecommunications Manager. **Benefits available to temporary workers:** 401(k); Dental Insurance; Disability Coverage; Life Insurance; Medical Insurance;

Profit Sharing. **Corporate headquarters location:** This Location. **Other U.S. locations:** Detroit MI. **Average salary range of placements:** More than $50,000. **Number of placements per year:** 200 - 499.

KRISE PROFESSIONAL PERSONNEL SERVICES
P.O. Box 53136, Indianapolis IN 46253. 317/299-3882. **Contact:** Randy Krise CPC, Owner. **Description:** A permanent employment agency focusing on engineering and technical manufacturing management. Company pays fee. **Specializes in the areas of:** Engineering; Manufacturing; Personnel/Labor Relations. **Positions commonly filled include:** Aerospace Engineer; Agricultural Engineer; Biomedical Engineer; Chemical Engineer; Civil Engineer; Electrical/Electronics Engineer; Human Resources Manager; Industrial Engineer; Industrial Production Manager; Mechanical Engineer; Metallurgical Engineer; Purchasing Agent/Manager; Quality Control Supervisor; Software Engineer; Stationary Engineer; Structural Engineer. **Average salary range of placements:** $30,000 - $50,000. **Number of placements per year:** 1 - 49.

DAN LANE PERSONNEL
8395 Keystone Crossing, Suite 213, Indianapolis IN 46240. 317/255-9632. **Contact:** Office Manager. **Description:** A permanent employment agency.

LIFE EMPLOYMENT SERVICE
710 Life Building, 300 Main Street, Lafayette IN 47901. 765/742-0278. **Fax:** 765/742-0270. **Contact:** Charles A. Hoovler, Manager. **E-mail address:** charlie@life-employment.com. **Description:** A permanent employment agency. Company pays fee. **Specializes in the areas of:** Accounting/Auditing; Banking; Fashion; Finance; Food Industry; General Management; Retail; Sales; Secretarial. **Positions commonly filled include:** Branch Manager; Buyer; Clerical Supervisor; Credit Manager; General Manager; Hotel Manager; Management Trainee; Manufacturer's/Wholesaler's Sales Rep.; Purchasing Agent/Manager; Restaurant/Food Service Manager; Securities Sales Representative; Services Sales Representative; Typist/Word Processor. **Average salary range of placements:** $30,000 - $50,000. **Number of placements per year:** 100 - 199.

MAYS & ASSOCIATES INC.
941 East 86th Street, Suite 109, Indianapolis IN 46240. 317/253-9999. **Fax:** 317/253-2749. **Contact:** Roger R. Mays, President. **Description:** A permanent employment agency. Company pays fee. **Specializes in the areas of:** Computer Science/Software; Engineering; Manufacturing. **Positions commonly filled include:** Aerospace Engineer; Biomedical Engineer; Chemical Engineer; Computer Programmer; Designer; Electrical/Electronics Engineer; Human Resources Manager; Industrial Engineer; Mechanical Engineer; Metallurgical Engineer; Quality Control Supervisor; Software Engineer; Structural Engineer; Systems Analyst. **Number of placements per year:** 50 - 99.

MID WEST PERSONNEL
P.O. Box 5325, Evansville IN 47716. 812/477-5531. **Contact:** Manager. **Description:** A permanent employment agency. **Specializes in the areas of:** Design; Engineering; Manufacturing.

NATIONAL EXECUTIVE CONSULTANTS, INC.
2621 West Lincoln Highway, Suite B, Merrillville IN 46410. 219/736-0406. **Contact:** Morrie Stilley, President. **Description:** A permanent employment agency. **Specializes in the areas of:** Metals.

P.R. PERSONNEL
537 West Jefferson, Fort Wayne IN 46802. 219/422-4671. **Contact:** Manager. **Description:** A permanent employment agency that places personnel in most major industries.

PERRY PERSONNEL PLUS
200 West Pike Street, Goshen IN 46526. 219/533-7330. **Fax:** 219/533-1417. **Contact:** Manager. **Description:** A permanent employment agency. **Specializes in the areas of:** Accounting/Auditing; Banking; Industrial; Manufacturing; Personnel/Labor Relations; Sales; Secretarial. **Positions commonly filled include:** Accountant/Auditor; Bank Officer/Manager; Blue-Collar Worker Supervisor; Branch Manager; Buyer; Clerical Supervisor; Computer Programmer; Credit Manager; Customer Service Representative; General Manager; Human Resources Specialist; Industrial Engineer; Industrial Production Manager; Mechanical Engineer; MIS Specialist; Operations/Production Manager; Quality Control Supervisor; Systems Analyst. **Corporate headquarters location:** Sturgis MI. **Other U.S. locations:** Goshen IN; Coldwater MI; Three Rivers MI.

PERSONNEL PARTNERS
828 East Jefferson, Suite 200, South Bend IN 46617. 219/234-2115. **Contact:** Manager. **Description:** A permanent employment agency. **Specializes in the areas of:** Light Industrial.

PRO RESOURCES
1728 Spy Run Avenue, Fort Wayne IN 46805. 219/420-2117. **Contact:** Manager. **Description:** A permanent employment agency that also provides some temporary placements. **Specializes in the areas of:** Light Industrial.

PYRAMIDS PERSONNEL
8910 Purdue Road, Suite 200, Indianapolis IN 46268-1155. 317/872-4960. **Contact:** Manager. **Description:** A permanent employment agency. **Specializes in the areas of:** Clerical; Office Support.

QUALITY SEARCH
1100 South Calumet Road, Suite One, Chesterton IN 46304. 219/926-8202. **Fax:** 219/926-3834. **Contact:** James L. Jeselnick, President. **E-mail address:** quality@staffing.net. **World Wide Web address:** http://www.niia.net/biz/quality. **Description:** A technical engineering recruiting firm that focuses on the placement of packaging professionals. Company pays fee. **Specializes in the areas of:** Engineering; Food Industry; General Management; Technical. **Positions commonly filled include:** Buyer; Chemical Engineer; Design Engineer; Designer; Industrial Engineer; Manufacturing Engineer; Mechanical Engineer; Quality Control Supervisor. **Corporate headquarters location:** This Location. **Other U.S. locations:** Show Low AZ; Grand Rapids MI. **Average salary range of placements:** More than $50,000. **Number of placements per year:** 50 - 99.

THE REGISTRY INC.
600 King Cole Building, 7 North Meridian Street, Indianapolis IN 46204-3033. 317/634-1200. **Fax:** 317/263-3845. **Contact:** Director of Operations. **Description:** A permanent employment agency. **Specializes in the areas of:** Accounting/Auditing; Administration; Bookkeeping; Clerical; Computer Science/Software; Health/Medical; Legal; Real Estate.

RELIABLE TECHNICAL SERVICES
P.O. Box 2126, Muncie IN 47307. 765/282-6907. **Contact:** Manager. **Description:** A permanent employment agency. **Specializes in the areas of:** Technical.

SNELLING & SNELLING
1000 East 80th Place, Merrillville IN 46410-5644. 219/769-2922. **Fax:** 219/755-0557. **Contact:** Cheri

K. Elser, General Manager. **Description:** A permanent placement agency. Founded in 1985. Company pays fee. **Specializes in the areas of:** Accounting/Auditing; Sales; Secretarial. **Positions commonly filled include:** Bookkeeper; Restaurant/Food Service Manager; Secretary; Services Sales Representative. **Number of placements per year:** 100 - 199.

TIME SERVICES, INC.
P.O. Box 784, Kendallville IN 46755-0784. 219/347-3940. **Toll-free phone:** 800/837-8463. **Fax:** 219/347-9619. **Contact:** Melissa Carpenter, Branch Manager. **Description:** A permanent employment agency providing clerical, industrial, and technical placements. Company pays fee. **Specializes in the areas of:** Industrial; Manufacturing; Secretarial. **Positions commonly filled include:** Blue-Collar Worker Supervisor; Customer Service Representative. **Benefits available to temporary workers:** Medical Insurance; Paid Holidays; Paid Vacation. **Corporate headquarters location:** Fort Wayne IN. **Other area locations:** Auburn IN. **Average salary range of placements:** Less than $20,000. **Number of placements per year:** 200 - 499.

TEMPORARY EMPLOYMENT AGENCIES

ACCUSTAFF
7863 Broadway, Suite 112, Merrillville IN 46410. 219/769-3448. **Contact:** Georgina Segan, Manager. **Description:** A temporary agency. **Positions commonly filled include:** Accountant/Auditor; Bookkeeper; Clerk; Computer Operator; Computer Programmer; Customer Service Representative; Data Entry Clerk; Driver; Factory Worker; Legal Secretary; Light Industrial Worker; Medical Secretary; Purchasing Agent/Manager; Receptionist; Secretary; Statistician; Stenographer; Typist/Word Processor.

ACCUSTAFF
600 North Alabama Street, Suite 600A, Indianapolis IN 46204. 317/488-8367. **Fax:** 317/488-8403. **Contact:** Steve Frankovitz, Owner. **Description:** A temporary agency. Company pays fee. **Specializes in the areas of:** Food Industry; Industrial; Manufacturing; Publishing; Sales; Secretarial; Technical. **Positions commonly filled include:** Customer Service Representative; Typist/Word Processor.

ADECCO
3500 West Depauw Boulevard, Suite 2041, Indianapolis IN 46268. 317/872-8091. **Contact:** Branch Manager. **Description:** A temporary agency that also offers some temp-to-perm placements. **Specializes in the areas of:** Administration; Secretarial; Word Processing.

CORPORATE STAFFING RESOURCES
820 North Baldwin Avenue, Marion IN 46952. **Contact:** Carla Poole, Branch Manager. **World Wide Web address:** http://www.csronline.com. **Description:** A short- and long-term temporary placement firm. Founded in 1985. **Specializes in the areas of:** Personnel/Labor Relations. **Positions commonly filled include:** Blue-Collar Worker Supervisor; Branch Manager; Clerical Supervisor; Computer Programmer; Credit Manager; Customer Service Representative; Draftsperson; Financial Analyst; General Manager; Human Resources Manager; Human Service Worker; Industrial Engineer; Industrial Production Manager; Insurance Agent/Broker; Operations/Production Manager; Quality Control Supervisor; Securities Sales Representative; Systems Analyst; Typist/Word Processor; Underwriter/Assistant Underwriter. **Corporate headquarters location:** South Bend IN. **Average salary range of placements:** Less than $20,000. **Number of placements per year:** 200 - 499.

CORPORATE STAFFING RESOURCES
100 East Wayne Street, Suite 100, South Bend IN 46601. 219/233-8209. **Fax:** 219/280-2653. **Contact:** Gail Daley, Recruiting Assistant. **World Wide Web address:** http://www.csronline.com. **Description:** A temporary agency that also provides contract technical placements. Founded in 1987. Company pays fee. **Specializes in the areas of:** Accounting/Auditing; Administration; Computer Science/Software; Engineering; Industrial; Manufacturing; Technical. **Positions commonly filled include:** Accountant/Auditor; Administrative Manager; Architect; Biological Scientist; Buyer; Chemical Engineer; Chemist; Civil Engineer; Computer Programmer; Credit Manager; Customer Service Representative; Designer; Electrical/Electronics Engineer; Electrician; Environmental Engineer; Financial Analyst; Industrial Engineer; Industrial Production Manager; Laboratory Technician; Mechanical Engineer; MIS Specialist; Operations/Production Manager; Purchasing Agent/Manager; Quality Control Supervisor; Software Engineer; Structural Engineer; Systems Analyst; Technical Writer/Editor. **Corporate headquarters location:** This Location. **Other U.S. locations:** MI; MO; OH. **Number of placements per year:** 1000+.

CORPORATE STAFFING RESOURCES
3552 Commerce Drive, Warsaw IN 46580. 219/269-2149. **Fax:** 219/269-3465. **Recorded jobline:** 219/237-9675. **Contact:** Mary Joyner, Branch Manager. **World Wide Web address:** http://www.csronline.com. **Description:** A temporary agency that also provides career/outplacement counseling. Company pays fee. **Specializes in the areas of:** Administration; Computer Science/Software; Engineering; General Management; Industrial; Manufacturing; Sales; Technical. **Positions commonly filled include:** Biomedical Engineer; Blue-Collar Worker Supervisor; Buyer; Chemical Engineer; Chemist; Civil Engineer; Claim Representative; Clerical Supervisor; Computer Programmer; Customer Service Representative; Design Engineer; Editor; Electrical/Electronics Engineer; Environmental Engineer; Financial Analyst; General Manager; Industrial Engineer; Industrial Production Manager; Mechanical Engineer; Operations/Production Manager; Quality Control Supervisor; Services Sales Representative; Software Engineer; Systems Analyst; Technical Writer/Editor; Typist/Word Processor. **Corporate headquarters location:** South Bend IN. **Average salary range of placements:** Less than $20,000. **Number of placements per year:** 1000+.

CROWN TEMPORARY SERVICES OF INDIANAPOLIS
3901 North Meridian Street, Suite 12, Indianapolis IN 46208. 317/924-5554. **Contact:** Office Manager. **Description:** A temporary agency. Company pays fee. **Specializes in the areas of:** Accounting/Auditing; Banking; Clerical; Engineering; Finance; Insurance; Legal; Manufacturing; Personnel/Labor Relations. **Positions commonly filled include:** Accountant/Auditor; Administrative Assistant; Advertising Clerk; Bookkeeper; Claim Representative; Clerk; Computer Operator; Computer Programmer; Construction Trade Worker; Customer Service Representative; Data Entry Clerk; Driver; Factory Worker; Legal Secretary; Light Industrial Worker; Marketing Specialist; Medical Secretary; Receptionist; Sales Representative; Typist/Word Processor. **Number of placements per year:** 1000+.

DUNHILL STAFFING SYSTEMS
5420 Southern Avenue, Suite 103, Indianapolis IN 46241. 317/247-1775. **Fax:** 317/241-4029. **Contact:** Manager. **Description:** A temporary agency that also provides permanent placements. **Specializes in the areas of:** Computer Science/Software; Industrial; Manufacturing; Secretarial; Technical. **Positions commonly filled include:** Blue-Collar Worker Supervisor; Branch Manager; Claim Representative; Clerical Supervisor; Computer Programmer; Customer Service Representative; Mechanical Engineer; Medical Records Technician; Systems Analyst. **Other U.S. locations:** Nationwide. **Number of placements per year:** 1000+.

EMPLOYMENT PLUS
4629 East Morningside Drive, Bloomington IN 47408. 812/333-1070. **Contact:** Manager. **Description:** A temporary agency that also provides temp-to-perm and permanent placements. **Specializes in the areas of:** Clerical; Light Industrial; Technical.

EXPRESS PERSONNEL
268 West U.S. Highway 30, Valparaiso IN 46385. 219/465-1868. **Contact:** Manager. **Description:** A temporary agency. **Specializes in the areas of:** Accounting/Auditing; Clerical; Finance; Industrial.

FIRST CALL TEMPORARY SERVICES INC.
3 Glen Miller Parkway, Richmond IN 47374. 219/726-3667. **Contact:** Office Manager. **Description:** A temporary agency. **Specializes in the areas of:** Industrial; Sales; Secretarial. **Positions commonly filled include:** Typist/Word Processor. **Corporate headquarters location:** Indianapolis IN. **Number of placements per year:** 500 - 999.

FLEXIBLE PERSONNEL
STAFFMARK MEDICAL STAFFING
1010 West Coliseum Boulevard, Suite E, Fort Wayne IN 46808. 219/482-3532. **Contact:** Manager. **Description:** A temporary agency that also offers temp-to-perm and permanent placements. **Specializes in the areas of:** Clerical; Health/Medical; Industrial.

INTERIM PERSONNEL
52 Girls School Road, Indianapolis IN 46231. 317/273-4444. **Contact:** Manager. **World Wide Web address:** http://www.interim.com. **Description:** A temporary agency. **Specializes in the areas of:** Administration; Industrial; Office Support; Word Processing. **Corporate headquarters location:** Fort Lauderdale FL. **Other U.S. locations:** Nationwide.

KELLY SERVICES, INC.
3413 North Briarwood Lane, Muncie IN 47304-5210. 765/284-0897. **Contact:** Supervisor. **Description:** A temporary agency. **Specializes in the areas of:** Secretarial; Technical. **Positions commonly filled include:** Customer Service Representative; Typist/Word Processor. **Corporate headquarters location:** Troy MI. **International locations:** Worldwide.

MAC STAFFING
3500 De Pauw Boulevard, Suite 1076, Indianapolis IN 46268. 317/872-5153. **Contact:** Ken Wetzel, President. **Description:** A temporary agency. Company pays fee. **Specializes in the areas of:** Administration; Advertising; Art/Design; Computer Science/Software; Publishing. **Positions commonly filled include:** Designer; Draftsperson; Editor; Multimedia Designer; Technical Writer/Editor; Typist/Word Processor; Video Production Coordinator. **Number of placements per year:** 200 - 499.

MANPOWER TECHNICAL SERVICES
205 East New York Street, Indianapolis IN 46204. 317/262-2020. **Toll-free phone:** 800/366-0557. **Fax:** 317/269-0515. **Contact:** Connie Whisner, Technical Services Manager. **Description:** A temporary agency. **Specializes in the areas of:** Computer Science/Software; Engineering; Technical. **Positions commonly filled include:** Chemical Engineer; Civil Engineer; Computer Programmer; Design Engineer; Electrical/Electronics Engineer; Industrial Engineer; Mechanical Engineer; Metallurgical Engineer; MIS Specialist; Quality Control Supervisor; Software Engineer; Structural Engineer; Systems Analyst. **Corporate headquarters location:** Milwaukee WI. **Average salary range of placements:** $30,000 - $50,000. **Number of placements per year:** 200 - 499.

NORRELL STAFFING SERVICES
201 South Emerson Avenue, Suite 140, Greenwood IN 46143. 317/885-9599. **Contact:** Manager. **Description:** A temporary agency. **Specializes in the areas of:** Industrial; Manufacturing; Personnel/Labor Relations; Secretarial. **Positions commonly filled include:** Accountant/Auditor; Administrative Manager; Advertising Clerk; Blue-Collar Worker Supervisor; Claim Representative; Clerical Supervisor; Clinical Lab Technician; Customer Service Representative; Human Resources Specialist; Librarian; Manufacturer's/Wholesaler's Sales Rep.; Purchasing Agent/Manager; Systems Analyst; Typist/Word Processor. **Corporate headquarters location:** Atlanta GA. **Other U.S. locations:** Nationwide. **Average salary range of placements:** Less than $20,000. **Number of placements per year:** 1000+.

NORRELL STAFFING SERVICES OF EVANSVILLE
500 North Congress Avenue, Evansville IN 47715. 812/473-3838. **Contact:** Manager. **Description:** A temporary agency. Company pays fee. **Specializes in the areas of:** Clerical; Manufacturing. **Positions commonly filled include:** Bookkeeper; Clerk; Computer Operator; Draftsperson; Factory Worker; Legal Secretary; Light Industrial Worker; Medical Secretary; Receptionist; Secretary; Stenographer; Typist/Word Processor. **Corporate headquarters location:** Atlanta GA. **Other U.S. locations:** Nationwide.

OLSTEN STAFFING SERVICES
3005 25th Street, Columbus IN 47203. 812/372-2722. **Toll-free phone:** 800/789-1100. **Fax:** 812/372-2999. **Contact:** Tammy Finley, Branch Manager. **Description:** A temporary agency. Company pays fee. **Specializes in the areas of:** Accounting/Auditing; Industrial; Legal; Manufacturing; Personnel/Labor Relations; Secretarial. **Positions commonly filled include:** Accountant/Auditor; Administrative Manager; Advertising Clerk; Blue-Collar Worker Supervisor; Clerical Supervisor; Computer Programmer; Customer Service Representative; Industrial Production Manager; Paralegal; Quality Control Supervisor; Restaurant/Food Service Manager; Systems Analyst; Typist/Word Processor. **Corporate headquarters location:** Melville NY. **Average salary range of placements:** Less than $20,000. **Number of placements per year:** 1000+.

PERSONNEL MANAGEMENT INC.
P.O. Box 322, Jeffersonville IN 47131. 812/284-3223. **Fax:** 812/285-6506. **Contact:** Office Manager. **Description:** A temporary agency. Company pays fee. **Specializes in the areas of:** Industrial; Light Industrial; Retail; Secretarial. **Positions commonly filled include:** Account Representative; Administrative Assistant; Blue-Collar Worker Supervisor; Customer Service Representative; Secretary. **Benefits available to temporary workers:** 401(k); Life Insurance; Medical Insurance; Paid Holidays; Paid Vacation. **Corporate headquarters location:** Greenwood IN. **Other U.S. locations:** FL; GA; KY. **Average salary range of placements:** Less than $20,000. **Number of placements per year:** 1000+.

RUSH TEMPORARIES
3610 Westview Boulevard, Muncie IN 47304. 765/529-3116. **Fax:** 765/529-3519. **Contact:** Office Manager. **Description:** A temporary agency. Company pays fee. **Specializes in the areas of:** Accounting/Auditing; Advertising; Banking; Computer Science/Software; Engineering; Finance; General Management; Industrial; Insurance; Manufacturing; Personnel/Labor Relations; Retail; Sales; Transportation. **Positions commonly filled include:** Automotive Mechanic; Bank Officer/Manager; Blue-Collar Worker Supervisor; Branch Manager; Claim Representative; Clerical Supervisor; Computer Programmer; Construction Contractor; Credit Manager; Customer Service Representative; Draftsperson; Electrician; Human Resources Manager; Industrial Engineer; Industrial Production Manager; Preschool Worker; Quality Control Supervisor; Restaurant/Food Service Manager; Securities Sales Representative. **Corporate headquarters location:** Anderson IN. **Other area locations:** Carmel IN; Indianapolis IN; Muncie IN; Richmond IN; Seymour IN. **Average salary range of placements:** Less than $20,000. **Number of placements per year:** 1 - 49.

STAR STAFFING
332 Third Avenue, Suite 5, Jasper IN 47546. 812/482-6836. **Toll-free phone:** 800/551-6823. **Fax:** 812/482-2490. **Contact:** Tricia Neukam, Service Representative. **Description:** A temporary agency. Founded in 1961. Company pays fee. **Specializes in the areas of:** Industrial; Manufacturing; Secretarial. **Positions commonly filled include:** Clerical Supervisor; Computer Programmer; Customer Service Representative; Management Trainee; MIS Specialist; Services Sales Representative; Software Engineer; Typist/Word Processor. **Benefits available to temporary workers:** Medical Insurance; Paid Holidays; Paid Vacation. **Corporate headquarters location:** South Bend IN. **Average salary range of placements:** Less than $20,000. **Number of placements per year:** 1000+.

TRC STAFFING SERVICES
8720 Castle Creek Parkway, Suite 112, Indianapolis IN 46250. 317/842-7779. **Fax:** 317/849-3166. **Contact:** Meri Robins, Manager. **Description:** A temporary agency. **Specializes in the areas of:** Computer Science/Software; Industrial; Secretarial; Technical. **Positions commonly filled include:** Administrative Assistant; Computer Operator; Customer Service Representative; MIS Specialist; Secretary; Software Engineer; Systems Analyst; Typist/Word Processor. **Benefits available to temporary workers:** 401(k); Paid Holidays; Paid Vacation; Referral Bonus Plan. **Corporate headquarters location:** Atlanta GA. **Other U.S. locations:** Nationwide. **Number of placements per year:** 200 - 499.

TRY TEMPS INC.
P.O. Box 339, Chandler IN 47610. 812/925-3903. **Fax:** 812/925-3920. **Contact:** R.L. Guy, Owner. **Description:** A temporary agency that also provides some permanents. Company pays fee. **Specializes in the areas of:** Engineering; Industrial; Technical. **Positions commonly filled include:** Aerospace Engineer; Agricultural Engineer; Architect; Biological Scientist; Biomedical Engineer; Ceramics Engineer; Chemist; Civil Engineer; Draftsperson; Electrical/Electronics Engineer; Industrial Designer; Industrial Engineer; Management Analyst/Consultant; Mechanical Engineer; Technical Writer/Editor. **Benefits available to temporary workers:** Medical Insurance; Paid Holidays; Paid Vacation. **Average salary range of placements:** $30,000 - $50,000. **Number of placements per year:** 1 - 49.

WESTERN STAFF SERVICES
512 Noble Drive, Fort Wayne IN 46825. 219/486-5649. **Fax:** 219/484-8877. **Contact:** Kevin Snyder, Manager. **Description:** A temporary agency that also provides permanent placement. **Specializes in the areas of:** Manufacturing; Secretarial. **Positions commonly filled include:** Accountant/Auditor; Blue-Collar Worker Supervisor; Clerical Supervisor; Computer Programmer; Customer Service Representative; Dental Assistant/Dental Hygienist; Electrical/Electronics Engineer; Mechanical Engineer; MIS Specialist; Paralegal; Systems Analyst; Typist/Word Processor. **Corporate headquarters location:** Walnut Creek CA. **Average salary range of placements:** Less than $20,000. **Number of placements per year:** 200 - 499.

WIMMER TEMPORARIES AND DIRECT PLACEMENT
1415 West Jeffras Avenue, Marion IN 46952. 765/664-9550. **Fax:** 765/664-9553. **Contact:** Bill Wimmer, President. **E-mail address:** wimmer@comteck.com. **Description:** A temporary agency for professionals, engineers, and general management. Company pays fee. **Specializes in the areas of:** Computer Science/Software; Engineering; General Management; Industrial; Manufacturing; Personnel/Labor Relations; Technical. **Positions commonly filled include:** Accountant/Auditor; Administrative Manager; Agricultural Engineer; Chemical Engineer; Customer Service Representative; Design Engineer; Draftsperson; Electrical/Electronics Engineer; Electrician; Human Resources Manager; Industrial Engineer; Licensed Practical Nurse; Mechanical Engineer; Operations/Production Manager; Paralegal; Quality Control Supervisor; Registered Nurse; Typist/Word Processor. **Benefits available to temporary workers:** Life Insurance; Medical Insurance; Paid Holidays; Paid Vacation; Tuition Assistance. **Other area locations:** Highland IN. **Average salary range of placements:** $20,000 - $29,999. **Number of placements per year:** 200 - 499.

CONTRACT SERVICES FIRMS

ACA CALUMET INC.
8252 Virginia Street, Merrillville IN 46410. 219/736-3855. **Contact:** Manager. **Description:** A contract services firm. **Specializes in the areas of:** Engineering; Technical.

ACA CALUMET INC.
911 Broadripple Avenue, Suite B, Indianapolis IN 46220. 317/254-8285. **Contact:** Office Manager. **Description:** A contract services firm. **Specializes in the areas of:** Engineering; Technical.

ACA KOKOMO INC.
P.O. Box 2314, Kokomo IN 46904-2314. 765/459-3931. **Contact:** Manager. **Description:** A contract services firm. **Specializes in the areas of:** Engineering; Technical. **Positions commonly filled include:** Engineer; Technician.

BELCAN TECHNICAL SERVICES
8355 Rockville Road, Suite 100, Indianapolis IN 46234. 317/273-6700. **Toll-free phone:** 800/967-5287. **Fax:** 317/273-6707. **Contact:** Michael G. Tribul, Branch Manager. **E-mail address:** techind@tech.belcan.com. **World Wide Web address:** http://www.belcan.com. **Description:** A contract services firm. Company pays fee. **Specializes in the areas of:** Engineering; Industrial; Technical. **Positions commonly filled include:** Chemical Engineer; Chemist; Civil Engineer; Computer Operator; Database Manager;

Design Engineer; Draftsperson; Electrical/Electronics Engineer; Environmental Engineer; Geologist/ Geophysicist; Industrial Engineer; Internet Services Manager; Manufacturing Engineer; Mechanical Engineer; Metallurgical Engineer; MIS Specialist; Production Manager; Purchasing Agent/Manager; Quality Control Supervisor; Registered Nurse; Software Engineer; Systems Analyst; Systems Manager; Technical Writer/Editor; Telecommunications Manager. **Corporate headquarters location:** Cincinnati OH. **Other U.S. locations:** Nationwide. **Average salary range of placements:** $30,000 - $50,000. **Number of placements per year:** 200 - 499.

CMS MANAGEMENT SERVICES
5920 Castle Way West Drive, Suite 120, Indianapolis IN 46250. 317/842-5777. **Contact:** Manager. **Description:** A contract services firm that also offers some contract-to-hire and permanent placements. **Specializes in the areas of:** Accounting/Auditing; Engineering; Finance.

CONTINENTAL DESIGN COMPANY
2710 Enterprise Drive, Anderson IN 46013. 765/778-9999. **Toll-free phone:** 800/875-4557. **Contact:** Cathy Mellinger, Director of Human Resources. **Description:** A contract services firm. **Specializes in the areas of:** Automotive; Design; Engineering; Manufacturing; Technical. **Positions commonly filled include:** Chemical Engineer; Computer Programmer; Design Engineer; Designer; Draftsperson; Electrical/Electronics Engineer; Industrial Engineer; Mechanical Engineer; Metallurgical Engineer; Systems Analyst; Technical Writer/Editor. **Corporate headquarters location:** This Location. **Other U.S. locations:** Troy MI. **Average salary range of placements:** $30,000 - $50,000. **Number of placements per year:** 50 - 99.

POLLAK AND SKAN, INC.
9143 Indianapolis Boulevard, Highland IN 46322. 219/838-0004. **Contact:** Manager. **Description:** A contract services firm. **Specializes in the areas of:** Computer Hardware/Software; Engineering.

QCI TECHNICAL STAFFING
4705 Illinois Road, Suite 113, Fort Wayne IN 46804. 219/436-9797. **Fax:** 219/436-6228. **Contact:** William E. Quackenbush, President. **World Wide Web address:** http://www.qcitechstaffing.com. **Description:** A contract services firm. Company pays fee. **Specializes in the areas of:** Administration; Computer Science/ Software; Engineering; Technical. **Positions commonly filled include:** Computer Programmer; Design Engineer; Draftsperson; Electrical/Electronics Engineer; Electrician; Industrial Engineer; Manufacturing Engineer; Mechanical Engineer; MIS Specialist; Project Manager; Software Engineer; Systems Analyst. **Benefits available to temporary workers:** Holiday Bonus; Paid Vacation. **Average salary range of placements:** $30,000 - $50,000. **Number of placements per year:** 100 - 199.

TAD TECHNICAL SERVICES
7007 Graham Road, Suite 207, Indianapolis IN 46220. 317/842-2870. **Fax:** 317/842-3085. **Contact:** Chris Ponsler, Branch Manager. **E-mail address:** dmcdonald@iquest.net. **World Wide Web address:** http://www.tadresources.com. **Description:** A contract services firm. Company pays fee. **Specializes in the areas of:** Administration; Architecture/ Construction; Computer Science/Software; Engineering; Manufacturing; Technical. **Positions commonly filled include:** Architect; Biochemist; Biomedical Engineer; Chemical Engineer; Civil Engineer; Clinical Lab Technician; Computer Programmer; Design Engineer; Draftsperson; Electrical/Electronics Engineer; Industrial Engineer; Industrial Production Manager; Internet Services Manager; Mechanical Engineer; MIS Specialist; Multimedia Designer; Software Engineer; Structural Engineer; Systems Analyst; Technical Writer/Editor. **Corporate headquarters location:** Cambridge MA. **Average salary range of placements:** $30,000 - $50,000. **Number of placements per year:** 200 - 499.

TECHNETICS CORPORATION
6408 Castleplace Drive, Indianapolis IN 46250. 317/842-5377. **Toll-free phone:** 800/467-8324. **Fax:** 317/842-6992. **Contact:** Recruiter. **Description:** A contract services firm. Company pays fee. **Specializes in the areas of:** Architecture/Construction; Computer Science/Software; Engineering; Industrial; Manufacturing; Technical. **Positions commonly filled include:** Architect; Biomedical Engineer; Chemical Engineer; Civil Engineer; Computer Programmer; Design Engineer; Designer; Draftsperson; Editor; Electrical/Electronics Engineer; Electrician; Environmental Engineer; Industrial Engineer; Industrial Production Manager; Internet Services Manager; Mechanical Engineer; Metallurgical Engineer; MIS Specialist; Multimedia Designer; Operations/Production Manager; Purchasing Agent/Manager; Quality Control Supervisor; Science Technologist; Software Engineer; Structural Engineer; Systems Analyst; Technical Writer/Editor. **Average salary range of placements:** $30,000 - $50,000. **Number of placements per year:** 100 - 199.

H.L. YOH COMPANY
2345 South Lynhurst Drive, Suite 111, Indianapolis IN 46241. 317/381-7000. **Contact:** Manager. **Description:** A contract services firm that also provides some temporary and temp-to-hire placements. **Specializes in the areas of:** Administration; Computer Hardware/Software; Engineering; Technical.

CAREER/OUTPLACEMENT COUNSELING FIRMS

GREEN THUMB INC.
P.O. Box 687, Seymour IN 47274. 812/522-7930. **Contact:** Manager. **Description:** Provides job training and skills training to individuals aged 55 or over.

JOB CORPS
504 Broadway, Suite 727, Gary IN 46402-1921. 219/882-2677. **Toll-free phone:** 800/624-9192. **Fax:** 219/882-6718. **Contact:** Winoy R. Spencer, Counselor. **Description:** A career/outplacement counseling firm. Company pays fee. **Positions commonly filled include:** Claim Representative; Clinical Lab Technician; Computer Programmer; Customer Service Representative; Electrical/Electronics Engineer; Electrician; Licensed Practical Nurse; Restaurant/Food Service Manager; Services Sales Representative; Typist/Word Processor. **Number of placements per year:** 1000+.

WARRICK COUNTY EMPLOYMENT & TRAINING CENTER
224 West Main Street, Boonville IN 47601. 812/897-4700. **Fax:** 812/897-6352. **Contact:** Paul K. Wright, Executive Director. **Description:** A career/ outplacement agency and training center. **NOTE:** Clients must be JTPA (Job Training Partnership Act) eligible. **Specializes in the areas of:** Industrial; Manufacturing; Retail; Sales; Secretarial; Transportation. **Positions commonly filled include:** Draftsperson; Electrician; Maintenance Technician. **Average salary range of placements:** $20,000 - $29,999. **Number of placements per year:** 50 - 99.

IOWA

EXECUTIVE SEARCH FIRMS

ATKINSON SEARCH & PLACEMENT INC.
P.O. Box 493, Fairfield IA 52556. 515/472-3666. **Fax:** 515/472-7270. **Contact:** Arthur Atkinson, President. **Description:** An executive search firm. Company pays fee. **Specializes in the areas of:** Computer Science/Software. **Positions commonly filled include:** Engineer; Marketing Specialist; Sales Representative; Software Engineer; Technical Writer/Editor. **Number of placements per year:** 1 - 49.

BRYANT BUREAU SALES RECRUITERS
2435 Kimberly Road, Suite 110 North, Bettendorf IA 52722. 319/355-4411. **Fax:** 319/355-3635. **Contact:** Doug Ryan, CPC, President. **Description:** An executive search firm operating on a contingency basis. Company pays fee. **Specializes in the areas of:** Sales. **Positions commonly filled include:** Insurance Agent/Broker; Manufacturer's/Wholesaler's Sales Rep.; Services Sales Representative. **Average salary range of placements:** $30,000 - $50,000. **Number of placements per year:** 50 - 99.

BURTON PLACEMENT SERVICES
1651 Lincolnway, Clinton IA 52732. 319/243-6791. **Fax:** 319/243-6895. **Contact:** Karen L. Schoen, Sales/Staffing Consultant. **Description:** An executive search firm that provides placement for computer, human resource, management, and technical professionals. Burton also places industrial and clerical professionals in temporary assignments. **Specializes in the areas of:** Accounting/Auditing; Administration; Banking; Computer Science/Software; Engineering; Finance; General Management; Industrial; Legal; Manufacturing; Personnel/Labor Relations; Publishing; Retail; Sales; Secretarial; Technical. **Positions commonly filled include:** Accountant/Auditor; Administrative Manager; Advertising Clerk; Aircraft Mechanic/Engine Specialist; Bank Officer/Manager; Claim Representative; Clerical Supervisor; Computer Programmer; Counselor; Credit Manager; General Manager; Health Services Manager; Health Services Worker; Hotel Manager; Human Resources Manager; Industrial Engineer; Management Trainee; Medical Records Technician; Public Relations Specialist; Quality Control Supervisor; Systems Analyst; Telecommunications Manager; Underwriter/Assistant Underwriter. **Corporate headquarters location:** Sterling IL. **Other U.S. locations:** Dixon IL; Oregon IL; Rochelle IL; Sycamore IL.

BYRNES & RUPKEY, INC.
3356 Kimball Avenue, Waterloo IA 50702. 319/234-6201. **Fax:** 319/234-6360. **Contact:** Lois Rupkey, Executive Vice President. **E-mail address:** weplace@forbin.com. **World Wide Web address:** http://www.forbin.com/weplace. **Description:** An executive search firm. **Specializes in the areas of:** Administration; Architecture/Construction; Banking; Computer Science/Software; Engineering; Finance; General Management; Health/Medical; Industrial; Insurance; Manufacturing; Personnel/Labor Relations; Retail; Sales; Secretarial; Technical. **Positions commonly filled include:** Civil Engineer; Computer Programmer; Draftsperson; Electrical/Electronics Engineer; Human Resources Manager; Mechanical Engineer; Occupational Therapist; Physical Therapist; Physician; Restaurant/Food Service Manager; Software Engineer. **Other U.S. locations:** Warwick RI.

CSI EMPLOYMENT
P.O. Box 1127, 319 North Main, Burlington IA 52601. 319/753-0223. **Toll-free phone:** 800/615-2850. **Fax:** 319/753-5268. **Contact:** Liz Wilcox, Vice President. **Description:** An executive search firm that also provides some contract, permanent, and temporary placements. Company pays fee. **Specializes in the areas of:** Administration; Engineering; General Management; Industrial; Light Industrial; Personnel/Labor Relations; Secretarial. **Positions commonly filled include:** Account Manager; Accountant; Administrative Assistant; Chemical Engineer; Chemist; Civil Engineer; Clerical Supervisor; Computer Operator; Computer Programmer; Customer Service Representative; Design Engineer; Electrical/ Electronics Engineer; Electrician; Environmental Engineer; Industrial Engineer; Industrial Production Manager; Manufacturing Engineer; Mechanical Engineer; Operations Manager; Production Manager; Project Manager; Quality Control Supervisor; Sales and Marketing Representative; Typist/Word Processor. **Benefits available to temporary workers:** Life Insurance; Medical Insurance; Paid Holidays; Paid Vacation. **Other area locations:** Ft. Madison IA; Mount Pleasant IA. **Corporate headquarters location:** This Location. **Average salary range of placements:** Less than $20,000. **Number of placements per year:** 1000+.

CAREER SEARCH ASSOCIATES
Regency West One, 1501 50th Street, Suite 381, West Des Moines IA 50266. 515/224-2183. **Contact:** Manager. **Description:** An executive search firm. **Specializes in the areas of:** Accounting/Auditing; Administration; Engineering; Information Systems.

DRAKE-BRENNAN, INC.
dba SNELLING PERSONNEL
2423 Ingersoll, West Des Moines IA 50312. 515/244-9999. **Contact:** Charles Drake, President. **Description:** An executive search firm that also provides temporary placements. Company pays fee. **Specializes in the areas of:** Engineering; Finance; Insurance; Sales; Technical. **Positions commonly filled include:** Accountant/Auditor; Actuary; Agricultural Engineer; Bank Officer/Manager; Chemical Engineer; Civil Engineer; Computer Programmer; Electrical/Electronics Engineer; Financial Analyst; Health Services Manager; Industrial Engineer; Insurance Agent/Broker; Mechanical Engineer; Operations/Production Manager; Securities Sales Representative; Software Engineer; Structural Engineer; Underwriter/Assistant Underwriter. **Benefits available to temporary workers:** 401(k); Paid Holidays; Paid Vacation. **Number of placements per year:** 200 - 499.

EXECUTIVE ENGINEERING SEARCH
911 Oakbrook Drive, Mount Pleasant IA 52641-2717. 319/986-5254. **Contact:** Gary Warner, Account Executive. **Description:** An executive search firm focusing on engineering and upper level management positions. Company pays fee. **Specializes in the areas of:** Engineering; General Management; Manufacturing. **Positions commonly filled include:** Aerospace Engineer; Chemical Engineer; Design Engineer; Electrical/Electronics Engineer; Environmental Engineer; Industrial Engineer; Management Analyst/ Consultant; Mechanical Engineer; Quality Control Supervisor. **Other area locations:** Iowa City IA. **Average salary range of placements:** More than $50,000. **Number of placements per year:** 1 - 49.

EXECUTIVE SEARCH ASSOCIATES
701 Pierce Street, Suite 300, Pioneer Bank Building, Sioux City IA 51102. 712/277-8103. **Contact:** Office Manager. **Description:** An executive search firm. Company pays fee. **Specializes in the areas of:** Accounting/Auditing; Administration; Computer Science/Software; Engineering; Finance; Food

Industry; General Management; Health/Medical; Insurance; Legal; Manufacturing; Personnel/Labor Relations; Retail; Sales; Secretarial; Telecommunications. **Positions commonly filled include:** Accountant/Auditor; Bank Officer/Manager; Branch Manager; Brokerage Clerk; Budget Analyst; Civil Engineer; Claim Representative; Clerical Supervisor; Computer Programmer; Cost Estimator; Counselor; Customer Service Representative; Electrical/Electronics Engineer; Financial Analyst; Health Services Manager; Hotel Manager; Human Resources Manager; Industrial Engineer; Industrial Production Manager; Insurance Agent/Broker; Internet Services Manager; Librarian; Licensed Practical Nurse; Management Trainee; Market Research Analyst; Metallurgical Engineer; MIS Specialist; Multimedia Designer; Operations/Production Manager; Paralegal; Pharmacist; Physical Therapist; Quality Control Supervisor; Restaurant/Food Service Manager; Securities Sales Representative; Services Sales Representative; Software Engineer; Systems Analyst; Telecommunications Manager; Typist/Word Processor; Underwriter/Assistant Underwriter. **Average salary range of placements:** $20,000 - $29,999. **Number of placements per year:** 100 - 199.

FRANCIS & ASSOCIATES
6923 Vista Drive, West Des Moines IA 50266. 515/221-9800. **Contact:** Manager. **Description:** An executive search firm.

ROBERT HALF INTERNATIONAL
317 6th Avenue, Suite 700, Des Moines IA 50309. 515/244-4414. **Contact:** Manager. **Description:** An executive search firm.

ROBERT HALF INTERNATIONAL
ACCOUNTEMPS
1200 35th Street, Suite 600, West Des Moines IA 50266. 515/226-1700. **Contact:** Manager. **World Wide Web address:** http://www.roberthalf.com. **Description:** An executive search firm. Accountemps (also at this location) provides temporary placements. **Specializes in the areas of:** Accounting/Auditing. **Corporate headquarters location:** Menlo Park CA. **Other U.S. locations:** Nationwide.

THE HUMAN RESOURCE GROUP
808 Fifth Avenue, Des Moines IA 50309. 515/243-8855. **Fax:** 515/243-8866. **Contact:** Will Canine, President. **Description:** An executive search firm operating on a contingency basis. **Specializes in the areas of:** Architecture/Construction; Banking; Engineering; Finance; General Management. **Positions commonly filled include:** Civil Engineer; Construction Trade Worker; Electrical/Electronics Engineer; Mechanical Engineer; MIS Specialist. **Average salary range of placements:** $30,000 - $50,000. **Number of placements per year:** 1 - 49.

MANAGEMENT RECRUITERS INTERNATIONAL
1312 Fourth Street SW, Suite 102, Mason City IA 50401. 515/424-1680. **Fax:** 515/424-6868. **Contact:** Cheryl Plagge, President. **E-mail address:** cplagge@willowtree.com. **Description:** An executive search firm that focuses on information systems positions. Company pays fee. **Specializes in the areas of:** Administration; Computer Science/Software; Food Industry; Insurance; Manufacturing; Technical. **Positions commonly filled include:** Computer Programmer; Management Analyst/Consultant; MIS Specialist; Software Engineer; Systems Analyst; Telecommunications Manager. **Corporate headquarters location:** Cleveland OH. **Other U.S. locations:** Nationwide. **Average salary range of placements:** More than $50,000. **Number of placements per year:** 1 - 49.

MANAGEMENT RECRUITERS INTERNATIONAL
150 First Avenue NE, Suite 400, Cedar Rapids IA 52401. 319/366-8441. **Fax:** 319/366-1103. **Contact:** Office Manager. **World Wide Web address:** http://www.mricr.com. **Description:** An executive search firm. **Specializes in the areas of:** Accounting/Auditing; Administration; Advertising; Architecture/Construction; Banking; Chemical; Communications; Computer Software; Design; Electrical; Engineering; Food Industry; General Management; Insurance; Legal; Manufacturing; Operations Management; Personnel; Procurement; Publishing; Retail; Sales; Technical; Transportation. **Corporate headquarters location:** Cleveland OH. **Other U.S. locations:** Nationwide.

MANAGEMENT RECRUITERS INTERNATIONAL
806 Fifth Street, Suite 209, Coralville IA 52241. 319/354-4320. **Contact:** John Sims, Manager. **Description:** An executive search firm. **Specializes in the areas of:** Accounting/Auditing; Administration; Advertising; Architecture/Construction; Banking; Chemical; Communications; Computer Hardware/Software; Design; Electrical; Engineering; Food Industry; General Management; Health/Medical; Insurance; Legal; Manufacturing; Operations Management; Personnel/Labor Relations; Procurement; Publishing; Retail; Sales; Technical; Textiles; Transportation. **Corporate headquarters location:** Cleveland OH. **Other U.S. locations:** Nationwide.

MANAGEMENT RECRUITERS INTERNATIONAL
P.O. Box 1400, Spencer IA 51301. 712/262-2701. **Fax:** 712/262-4005. **Contact:** Manager. **Description:** An executive search firm. **Specializes in the areas of:** Computer Hardware/Software; Engineering; Manufacturing; Technical. **Corporate headquarters location:** Cleveland OH. **Other U.S. locations:** Nationwide.

MANAGEMENT RECRUITERS INTERNATIONAL
106 West Lowe, Fairfield IA 52556. 515/469-5811. **Contact:** Manager. **Description:** An executive search firm. **Specializes in the areas of:** Administration; Health/Medical; Human Resources; Information Technology. **Corporate headquarters location:** Cleveland OH. **Other U.S. locations:** Nationwide.

MANAGEMENT RECRUITERS INTERNATIONAL
7400 University, Suite D, Clive IA 50325. 515/255-1242. **Contact:** Manager. **Description:** An executive search firm. **Corporate headquarters location:** Cleveland OH. **Other U.S. locations:** Nationwide.

MANAGEMENT RECRUITERS INTERNATIONAL
COMPUSEARCH
Alpine Centre South, Penthouse, 2435 Kimberly Road, Bettendorf IA 52722. 319/359-3503. **Contact:** Jerry Herrmann, Manager. **Description:** An executive search firm. **Specializes in the areas of:** Accounting/Auditing; Administration; Advertising; Architecture/Construction; Banking; Communications; Computer Hardware/Software; Design; Electrical; Engineering; Food Industry; General Management; Health/Medical; Insurance; Legal; Manufacturing; Operations Management; Personnel/Labor Relations; Procurement; Publishing; Retail; Sales; Technical; Textiles; Transportation. **Corporate headquarters location:** Cleveland OH. **Other U.S. locations:** Nationwide.

McGLADREY SEARCH GROUP
400 Locust Street, Suite 640, Des Moines IA 50309. 515/281-9200. **Fax:** 515/284-1545. **Contact:** Thomas Hamilton, Manager. **Description:** A retained executive search firm. Company pays fee. **Specializes in the areas of:** Accounting/Auditing; Administration; Banking; Data Processing; Engineering; General Management; Manufacturing; Personnel/Labor Relations; Sales. **Positions commonly filled include:**

Chief Financial Officer; Controller; Human Resources Manager; Industrial Production Manager; Manufacturing Engineer; Marketing Manager; Mechanical Engineer; MIS Specialist; Production Manager; Sales Engineer; Sales Executive; Sales Manager; Sales Representative; Secretary. **Corporate headquarters location:** Minneapolis MN. **Other U.S. locations:** Nationwide. **Average salary range of placements:** More than $50,000. **Number of placements per year:** 50 - 99.

MID AMERICA SEARCH
4401 Westown Parkway, Suite 226, West Des Moines IA 50266. 515/225-1942. **Fax:** 515/225-3941. **Contact:** Manager. **Description:** An executive search firm. **Specializes in the areas of:** Insurance.

PERSONNEL, INC.
604 Locust Street, Suite 516, Des Moines IA 50309-3720. 515/243-7687. **Fax:** 515/243-3350. **Contact:** Diane Wright, Vice President. **Description:** An executive search firm that also offers career/outplacement services, testing services, and temporary placements. Company pays fee. **Specializes in the areas of:** Banking; Clerical; Computer Hardware/Software; Finance; Food Industry; General Management; Legal; Sales; Secretarial; Technical. **Positions commonly filled include:** Bookkeeper; Data Entry Clerk; Legal Secretary; Medical Secretary; Receptionist; Sales Representative; Secretary; Typist/Word Processor. **Number of placements per year:** 100 - 199.

PREMIER SEARCH GROUP
417 First Avenue SE, Cedar Rapids IA 52401. 319/362-2300. **Fax:** 319/362-2333. **Contact:** Manager. **Description:** An executive search firm. **Specializes in the areas of:** Accounting/Auditing; Engineering; Human Resources; Manufacturing; Technical.

QUALITY RECRUITERS INC.
908 First Avenue South, M-27, Fort Dodge IA 50501. 515/573-2400. **Contact:** Manager. **Description:** An executive search firm. **Specializes in the areas of:** Automotive; Health/Medical.

SANFORD ROSE ASSOCIATES
3343 Southgate Court SW, Suite 205, Cedar Rapids IA 52404. 319/286-2969. **Fax:** 319/286-2971. **Contact:** Manager. **World Wide Web address:** http://www.sanfordrose.com. **Description:** An executive search firm. **Specializes in the areas of:** General Management; Transportation. **Other U.S. locations:** Nationwide.

SEDONA STAFFING SERVICES, INC.
3392 Hillcrest Road, Dubuque IA 52001. 319/556-3040. **Toll-free phone:** 800/383-7641. **Contact:** James Townsend, President. **Description:** An executive search firm that also provides temporary placements. Company pays fee. **Specializes in the areas of:** Accounting/Auditing; Banking; Clerical; Manufacturing; Secretarial. **Positions commonly filled include:** Accountant/Auditor; Administrative Assistant; Bank Officer/Manager; Bookkeeper; Claim Representative; Computer Programmer; Credit Manager; Customer Service Representative; Electrical/Electronics Engineer; Legal Secretary; Marketing Specialist; Mechanical Engineer; Medical Secretary; Purchasing Agent/Manager; Receptionist; Sales Representative; Secretary; Stenographer; Systems Analyst; Typist/Word Processor. **Benefits available to temporary workers:** 401(k); Bonus Award/Plan; Medical Insurance. **Average salary range of placements:** $30,000 - $50,000. **Number of placements per year:** 1 - 49.

LEE SMITH & ASSOCIATES
7177 Hickman Road, Suite 10, Des Moines IA 30222. 515/270-2791. **Contact:** Manager. **Description:** An executive search firm.

TUCKER PERSONNEL CONSULTANTS
1728 34th Street NE, Cedar Rapids IA 52402. 319/362-2936. **Contact:** Manager. **Description:** An executive search firm. **Specializes in the areas of:** Engineering.

PERMANENT EMPLOYMENT AGENCIES

AGRA PLACEMENTS, LTD.
4949 Pleasant Street, Suite 1, West Des Moines IA 50266. 515/225-6562. **Fax:** 515/225-7733. **Contact:** Manager. **Description:** An executive search firm. **Specializes in the areas of:** Agri-Business; Chemical; Engineering; Manufacturing.

BREI & ASSOCIATES, INC.
2598 28th Avenue, Marion IA 52302. 319/377-9196. **Fax:** 319/377-9219. **Contact:** Randy Brei, President. **E-mail address:** rbrei@netins.net. **World Wide Web address:** http://www.netins.net/showcase/rdbrei. **Description:** A permanent employment agency that focuses on placement of electronics engineers and software developers. Areas covered include software design, hardware design, and systems engineering. Company pays fee. **Specializes in the areas of:** Computer Science/Software; Engineering. **Positions commonly filled include:** Computer Programmer; Design Engineer; Electrical/Electronics Engineer; Mechanical Engineer; Software Engineer; Systems Analyst; Technical Writer/Editor. **Average salary range of placements:** More than $50,000. **Number of placements per year:** 1 - 49.

CAMBRIDGE STAFFING
610 32nd Avenue SW, Suite A, Cedar Rapids IA 52404-3910. 319/366-7771. **Contact:** Office Manager. **Description:** A permanent employment agency. Company pays fee. **Specializes in the areas of:** Accounting/Auditing; Clerical; Computer Science/Software; Engineering; Health/Medical; Manufacturing; Sales; Secretarial. **Positions commonly filled include:** Accountant/Auditor; Architect; Bank Officer/Manager; Blue-Collar Worker Supervisor; Clerical Supervisor; Computer Programmer; Design Engineer; Human Resources Manager; Industrial Designer; Industrial Engineer; Mechanical Engineer; MIS Specialist; Physical Therapist; Physician; Purchasing Agent/Manager; Respiratory Therapist; Sales Representative; Secretary; Typist/Word Processor. **Benefits available to temporary workers:** 401(k); Bonus Award/Plan; Dental Insurance; Medical Insurance; Paid Holidays; Paid Vacation. **Corporate headquarters location:** This Location. **Other U.S. locations:** Nationwide. **Average salary range of placements:** More than $50,000. **Number of placements per year:** 100 - 199.

CAREER FINDERS
7517 Douglas Avenue, Suite 7, Urbandale IA 50322. 515/278-9467. **Contact:** Manager. **Description:** A permanent employment agency that also provides some temporary placements.

CAREERNET, INC.
2120 Grand Avenue, Des Moines IA 50312. 515/244-3902. **Fax:** 515/244-5119. **Contact:** Recruiter. **Description:** A permanent employment agency that also offers career/outplacement counseling. Company

pays fee. **Specializes in the areas of:** Office Support. **Positions commonly filled include:** Accountant/Auditor; Administrative Manager; Advertising Clerk; Brokerage Clerk; Claim Representative; Customer Service Representative; General Manager; Operations/Production Manager; Services Sales Representative; Technical Writer/Editor; Typist/Word Processor. **Average salary range of placements:** Less than $20,000. **Number of placements per year:** 100 - 199.

CITY & NATIONAL EMPLOYMENT INC./RECRUITING COMPANY
P.O. Box 83, Waterloo IA 50702. 319/232-6641. **Fax:** 319/232-5700. **Contact:** Michael C. Grillo, Manager of Engineering/Recruitment. **E-mail address:** michaelgrillo@wordnet.alt.net. **Description:** A permanent employment agency. Company pays fee. **Specializes in the areas of:** Data Processing; Engineering. **Positions commonly filled include:** Aerospace Engineer; Biomedical Engineer; Ceramics Engineer; Chemical Engineer; Civil Engineer; Electrical/Electronics Engineer; Manufacturing Engineer; Mechanical Engineer; Metallurgical Engineer; Software Engineer; Structural Engineer. **Number of placements per year:** 200 - 499.

EXECUTIVE RESOURCES
3816 Ingersoll Avenue, Des Moines IA 50312. 515/287-6880. **Fax:** 515/255-9445. **Contact:** Ms. Gerry Mullane, President. **Description:** A permanent employment agency. **Specializes in the areas of:** Computer Hardware/Software; Data Processing; Insurance; Sales.

IOWA WORKFORCE DEVELOPMENT CENTER
2700 First Avenue South, Fort Dodge IA 50501. 515/576-3131. **Fax:** 515/955-1420. **Contact:** Terry Augustus, Recruiter. **World Wide Web address:** http://www.state.ia.us/government/wd/index.htm. **Description:** A state-operated permanent employment agency. **Specializes in the areas of:** Nonprofit. **Positions commonly filled include:** Accountant/Auditor; Administrative Assistant; Aerospace Engineer; Architect; Biomedical Engineer; Bookkeeper; Civil Engineer; Claim Representative; Clerk; Computer Operator; Computer Programmer; Credit Manager; Customer Service Representative; Data Entry Clerk; Editor; EDP Specialist; Electrical/Electronics Engineer; Industrial Designer; Industrial Engineer; Legal Manufacturing Engineer; Mechanical Engineer; MIS Specialist; Nurse; Sales Representative; Software Engineer; Systems Analyst; Technical Writer/Editor; Technician; Typist/Word Processor. **Number of placements per year:** 1000+.

IOWA WORKFORCE DEVELOPMENT CENTER
321 Stevens Street, Iowa Falls IA 50126-2212. 515/648-4781. **Contact:** Norman Bissell, Job Service Interviewer. **Description:** A state-operated employment agency. **Positions commonly filled include:** Blue-Collar Worker Supervisor; Branch Manager; Clerical Supervisor; Construction Contractor; General Manager; Insurance Agent/Broker; Management Trainee; Registered Nurse. **Number of placements per year:** 200 - 499.

PRATT-YOUNGLOVE, INC.
504 Nebraska Street, Sioux City IA 51101. 712/255-7961. **Contact:** E. David Pratt III, Manager. **Description:** A permanent employment agency. Company pays fee. **Specializes in the areas of:** Accounting/Auditing; Banking; Food Industry; Manufacturing. **Positions commonly filled include:** Accountant/Auditor; Administrative Assistant; Attorney; Bank Officer/Manager; Biological Scientist; Bookkeeper; Chemical Engineer; Chemist; Civil Engineer; Clerk; Computer Operator; Credit Manager; Customer Service Representative; Data Entry Clerk; Draftsperson; EDP Specialist; Electrical/Electronics Engineer; Financial Analyst; Food Scientist/Technologist; Industrial Engineer; Legal Secretary; Mechanical Engineer; Medical Secretary; MIS Specialist; Nurse; Operations/Production Manager; Receptionist; Sales Representative; Systems Analyst; Technician; Typist/Word Processor; Underwriter/Assistant Underwriter. **Number of placements per year:** 100 - 199.

DEE SPRINGER PERSONNEL
2435 Kimberly Road, Suite 140S, Bettendorf IA 52722. 319/355-0241. **Contact:** Office Manager. **Description:** A permanent placement agency.

STAFFING EDGE
1001 Office Park Road, Suite 320, West Des Moines IA 50265. 515/224-0446. **Fax:** 515/224-6599. **Contact:** Manager. **Description:** A permanent employment agency. **Specializes in the areas of:** Accounting/Auditing; Data Processing; Engineering; Finance; Insurance; Personnel/Labor Relations; Sales; Software Engineering.

NATE VIALL & ASSOCIATES
P.O. Box 12238, Des Moines IA 50312. 515/274-1729. **Fax:** 515/274-5646. **Contact:** Nate Viall, President. **Description:** A permanent employment agency. Company pays fee. **Specializes in the areas of:** Administration; Computer Science/Software. **Positions commonly filled include:** Computer Programmer; Systems Analyst.

TEMPORARY EMPLOYMENT AGENCIES

BLANCHARD SERVICES
617 North Adams, Carroll IA 51401. 712/792-5956. **Fax:** 712/792-5973. **Contact:** Phyllis C. Blanchard, Owner. **Description:** A temporary agency. Company pays fee. **Specializes in the areas of:** Accounting/Auditing; Food Industry; Manufacturing; Secretarial. **Positions commonly filled include:** Accountant/Auditor; Administrative Manager; Advertising Bank Officer/Manager; Branch Manager; Chemical Engineer; Civil Engineer; Customer Service Representative; Electrician; Health Services Manager; Mechanical Engineer; Restaurant/Food Service Manager; Stationary Engineer; Typist/Word Processor. **Average salary range of placements:** Less than $20,000. **Number of placements per year:** 50 - 99.

HELPING HANDS TEMPORARY SERVICE
27 North Center Street, Marshalltown IA 50158-4912. 515/752-5040. **Fax:** 515/753-2165. **Contact:** Arlene Wenzel, Owner/Operator. **Description:** A temporary agency. **Specializes in the areas of:** Accounting/Auditing; Administration; Architecture/Construction; Banking; Computer Science/Software; Education; Engineering; Fashion; Finance; Food Industry; General Management; Health/Medical; Industrial; Insurance; Legal; Manufacturing; Nonprofit; Personnel/Labor Relations; Publishing; Retail; Sales; Secretarial. **Positions commonly filled include:** Administrative Manager; Advertising Clerk; Architect; Blue-Collar Worker Supervisor; Buyer; Claim Representative; Clerical Supervisor; Computer Programmer; Credit Manager; Customer Service Representative; Draftsperson; Human Service Worker; Paralegal; Systems Analyst; Typist/Word Processor. **Benefits available to temporary workers:** Medical Insurance; Paid Holidays; Paid Vacation. **Number of placements per year:** 500 - 999.

KELLY SERVICES, INC.
400 Locust Street, Suite 250, Des Moines IA 50309-2331. 515/282-0264. **Fax:** 515/243-6948. **Contact:** Laura Williams, Supervisor. **Description:** A temporary agency. Founded in 1946. Company pays fee. **Specializes in the areas of:** Accounting/Auditing; Administration; Computer Science/Software; Light Industrial; Personnel/Labor Relations; Sales; Secretarial. **Positions commonly filled include:** Accountant/Auditor; Clerical Supervisor; Computer Programmer; Customer Service Representative; Human Resources Specialist; MIS Specialist; Services Sales Representative; Systems Analyst; Typist/Word Processor. **Benefits available to temporary workers:** Medical Insurance; Paid Holidays; Paid Vacation. **Corporate headquarters location:** Troy MI. **Average salary range of placements:** Less than $20,000. **Number of placements per year:** 1000+.

KELLY SERVICES, INC.
10101 University Avenue, Clive IA 50325. 515/223-6599. **Fax:** 515/222-0560. **Contact:** Supervisor. **Description:** A temporary agency. **Specializes in the areas of:** Sales; Secretarial. **Positions commonly filled include:** Claim Representative; Customer Service Representative; Typist/Word Processor. **Benefits available to temporary workers:** Medical Insurance; Paid Holidays; Paid Vacation. **Corporate headquarters location:** Troy MI. **Average salary range of placements:** Less than $20,000. **Number of placements per year:** 200 - 499.

MID-STATES TECHNICAL STAFFING SERVICES, INC.
5309 Victoria Avenue, Davenport IA 52807-2989. 319/359-7042. **Fax:** 319/359-6331. **Contact:** Connie Whitcomb, Recruiting Specialist. **E-mail address:** midstatestech@accustaff.com. **Description:** A temporary agency and contract services firm. Company pays fee. **Specializes in the areas of:** Engineering. **Positions commonly filled include:** Chemical Engineer; Civil Engineer; Computer Programmer; Electrical/Electronics Engineer; Electrician; Environmental Engineer; Industrial Engineer; Industrial Production Manager; Manufacturing Engineer; Mechanical Engineer; MIS Specialist; Software Engineer; Systems Analyst; Systems Manager; Technical Writer/Editor. **Benefits available to temporary workers:** 401(k); Medical Insurance. **Corporate headquarters location:** This Location. **Other U.S. locations:** Louisville KY. **Average salary range of placements:** $30,000 - $50,000. **Number of placements per year:** 200 - 499.

SALEM MANAGEMENT INC.
dba RUDY SALEM STAFFING SERVICES
319 Grand Avenue, Spencer IA 51301. 712/262-5990. **Toll-free phone:** 800/517-2536. **Fax:** 712/262-4383. **Contact:** Lori Scheid, Office Manager. **Description:** A temporary agency focusing on clerical and light industrial placements. The agency also offers permanent positions. Founded in 1994. Company pays fee. **Specializes in the areas of:** Accounting/Auditing; Administration; Industrial; Manufacturing; Secretarial. **Positions commonly filled include:** Accountant/Auditor; Administrative Manager; Branch Manager; Brokerage Clerk; Claim Representative; Credit Manager; Customer Service Representative; Health Services Manager; Industrial Production Manager; MIS Specialist; Restaurant/Food Service Manager; Systems Analyst; Typist/Word Processor. **Benefits available to temporary workers:** Paid Holidays; Referral Bonus Plan. **Corporate headquarters location:** Sioux City IA. **Average salary range of placements:** Less than $20,000. **Number of placements per year:** 100 - 199.

SALEM MANAGEMENT INC.
dba RUDY SALEM STAFFING SERVICES
P.O. Box 3124, Sioux City IA 51102-3124. 712/277-4204. **Fax:** 712/277-1512. **Contact:** Steve Salem, President. **E-mail address:** staffing@salemmgmt.com. **Description:** A temporary employment agency that also provides permanent placements and contract services. The agency focuses on clerical and light industrial positions. Founded in 1983. Company pays fee. **Specializes in the areas of:** Accounting/Auditing; Engineering; Finance; General Management; Industrial; Light Industrial; Manufacturing; Personnel/Labor Relations; Sales; Secretarial. **Positions commonly filled include:** Account Representative; Accountant/Auditor; Adjuster; Administrative Assistant; Administrative Manager; Bank Officer/Manager; Branch Manager; Brokerage Chemical Engineer; Chief Financial Officer; Civil Engineer; Clinical Lab Technician; Computer Programmer; Credit Manager; Customer Service Representative; Electrical/Electronics Engineer; Financial Analyst; Industrial Engineer; Industrial Production Manager; Insurance Agent/Broker; Mechanical Engineer; MIS Specialist; Paralegal; Restaurant/Food Service Manager; Typist/Word Processor. **Benefits available to temporary workers:** Medical Insurance; Paid Holidays. **Corporate headquarters location:** This Location. **Other area locations:** Spencer IA. **Average salary range of placements:** $20,000 - $29,999. **Number of placements per year:** 1000+.

TECHSTAFF, INC.
2828 18th Street, Suite 2, Bettendorf IA 52722. 319/355-4400. **Fax:** 319/355-0694. **Contact:** Steven Nord, Sales Manager. **Description:** A temporary agency that also provides permanent placements. TechStaff focuses on engineering and technical placement. **Specializes in the areas of:** Computer Science/Software; Engineering; Manufacturing. **Positions commonly filled include:** Aerospace Engineer; Biomedical Engineer; Chemical Engineer; Chemist; Civil Engineer; Computer Programmer; Electrical/Electronics Engineer; Electrician; Environmental Engineer; Industrial Engineer; Mechanical Engineer; MIS Specialist; Operations/Production Manager; Software Engineer; Systems Analyst. **Number of placements per year:** 100 - 199. **Corporate headquarters location:** Milwaukee WI. **Other U.S. locations:** Oxnard CA; Tampa FL; Chicago IL; Grand Rapids MI; Green Bay WI.

TRI-STATE NURSING ENTERPRISES, INC.
1408 Nebraska Street, Sioux City IA 51105-1237. 712/277-4442. **Toll-free phone:** 800/727-1912. **Contact:** Bridget Hoefling, President. **Description:** A temporary agency. **Specializes in the areas of:** Health/Medical. **Positions commonly filled include:** Certified Nursing Aide; Clinical Lab Technician; Dental Assistant/Dental Hygienist; Licensed Practical Nurse; Occupational Therapist; Physical Therapist; Recreational Therapist; Registered Nurse; Respiratory Therapist; Social Worker. **Average salary range of placements:** $20,000 - $60,000. **Number of placements per year:** 50 - 99.

CONTRACT SERVICES FIRMS

CDI CORPORATION
P.O. Box 854, Bettendorf IA 52722. 319/359-8233. **Fax:** 319/359-5817. **Contact:** Manager. **World Wide Web address:** http://www.cdicorp.com. **Description:** A contract services firm. **Specializes in the areas of:** Engineering; Technical. **Corporate headquarters location:** Philadelphia PA. **Other U.S. locations:** Nationwide. **International locations:** Worldwide.

MANPOWER TECHNICAL SERVICES
1113 Second Avenue SE, Cedar Rapids IA 52403. 319/366-1660. **Fax:** 319/366-6536. **Contact:** Scott M. Griffin, Manager. **Description:** A contract services firm. Founded in 1969. **Specializes in the areas of:** Computer Science/Software; Engineering. **Positions commonly filled include:** Agricultural Engineer; Biological Scientist; Biomedical Engineer; Chemical Engineer; Civil Engineer; Computer Programmer; Draftsperson; Electrical/Electronics Engineer; Industrial Engineer; Mechanical Engineer; MIS Specialist; Software Engineer; Systems Analyst; Technical Writer/Editor. **Benefits available to temporary workers:** 401(k); Dental Insurance; Medical Insurance; Paid Vacation. **Number of placements per year:** 200 - 499.

NATIONJOB INC.
601 SW 9th Street, Suite J, Des Moines IA 50309. 515/964-6718. **Fax:** 515/964-6737. **Contact:** R.J. Hejlik, President. **E-mail address:** nationj@worf.netins.net. **World Wide Web address:** http://www.nationjob.com. **Description:** A contract services firm. NationJob offers an electronic database of employment opportunities and company information accessible on the Internet. Company pays fee.

STAFF MANAGEMENT, INC.
2712 Orchard Drive, Suite A, Cedar Falls IA 50613. 319/266-1320. **Fax:** 319/266-1616. **Contact:** Patience Frankl, Human Resource Representative. **Description:** A contract services firm. Company pays fee. **Specializes in the areas of:** Accounting/Auditing; Administration; Computer Science/Software; Engineering; Health/Medical; Industrial; Insurance; Manufacturing; Personnel/Labor Relations; Secretarial; Technical. **Positions commonly filled include:** Accountant/Auditor; Buyer; Claim Representative; Computer Programmer; Design Engineer; Designer; Draftsperson; Human Resources Specialist; Industrial Engineer; Licensed Practical Nurse; Mechanical Engineer; MIS Specialist; Purchasing Agent/Manager; Registered Nurse; Software Engineer; Systems Analyst; Technical Writer/Editor; Typist/Word Processor. **Benefits available to temporary workers:** 401(k); Dental Insurance; Life Insurance; Medical Insurance.

TAD TECHNICAL SERVICES
2705 Kimberly Road, Bettendorf IA 52722-3506. 319/359-1500. **Fax:** 319/359-9497. **Contact:** Becky Mathis, Sales Manager. **Description:** A contract services firm. Founded in 1956. Company pays fee. **Specializes in the areas of:** Computer Science/Software; Engineering. **Positions commonly filled include:** Chemical Engineer; Chemist; Civil Engineer; Computer Programmer; Design Engineer; Designer; Draftsperson; Geographer; Geologist/Geophysicist; Industrial Engineer; Landscape Architect; Mechanical Engineer; Metallurgical Engineer; Mining Engineer; MIS Specialist; Nuclear Engineer; Petroleum Engineer; Software Engineer; Stationary Engineer; Structural Engineer; Surveyor; Systems Analyst; Technical Writer/Editor. **Benefits available to temporary workers:** 401(k); Life Insurance; Medical Insurance. **Corporate headquarters location:** Cambridge MA. **Average salary range of placements:** $30,000 - $50,000. **Number of placements per year:** 1 - 49.

KANSAS

EXECUTIVE SEARCH FIRMS

ACCOUNTING EDGE
8500 College Boulevard, Shawnee Mission KS 66210. 913/722-4200. **Contact:** Manager. **Description:** An executive search firm. **NOTE:** Resumes should be sent to 4220 Shawnee Mission Parkway, Suite 101B, Fairway KS 66205. **Specializes in the areas of:** Accounting/Auditing.

DAVID J. BAEHR & ASSOCIATES
6301 West 126th Terrace, Shawnee Mission KS 66209. 913/491-4096. **Fax:** 913/491-3808. **Contact:** David Baehr, President. **Description:** A contingency executive search firm that focuses on grain processing and allied industries. **Specializes in the areas of:** Food Industry. **Positions commonly filled include:** Agricultural Scientist; Chemist; Draftsperson; Food Scientist/Technologist; Mechanical Engineer; Plant Manager. **Average salary range of placements:** $30,000 - $75,000. **Number of placements per year:** 1 - 49.

CAREERS UNLIMITED, INC.
P.O. Box 12111, Shawnee Mission KS 66282-2111. 913/469-1709. **Fax:** 913/469-5568. **Contact:** Bud Burris, President. **Description:** An executive search firm. Company pays fee. **Average salary range of placements:** More than $75,000. **Number of placements per year:** 100 - 199.

CENTURY
5300 College Boulevard, Suite A, Overland Park KS 66211. 913/451-8333. **Contact:** Tim Thornton, Vice President. **Description:** An executive search firm. **Specializes in the areas of:** Banking; Health/Medical. **Positions commonly filled include:** Chief Financial Officer; Laboratory Technician; Lender; Nurse; Occupational Therapist; Physical Therapist; Trust Officer.

CHARLTON & ASSOCIATES
7300 College Boulevard, Suite 301, Overland Park KS 66210. 913/338-4560. **Contact:** Manager. **Description:** An executive search firm. **Specializes in the areas of:** Information Systems.

THE CHASE GROUP
7300 West 110th Street, Suite 560, Overland Park KS 66210. 913/663-3100. **Fax:** 913/663-3131. **Contact:** Manager. **Description:** An executive search firm. **Specializes in the areas of:** Biotechnology; Pharmaceutical.

CONTINENTAL BUSINESS SYSTEMS
5845 Horton Street, Suite 202, Shawnee Mission KS 66202. 913/677-0200. **Fax:** 913/677-0760. **Contact:** Larry McWilliams, President. **Description:** An executive search firm that concentrates on the placement of data processing professionals. Company pays fee. **Specializes in the areas of:** Computer Science/Software. **Positions commonly filled include:** Computer Operator; Computer Programmer; Database Manager; Operations Manager; Software Engineer; Systems Analyst; Systems Manager; Technical Writer/Editor; Webmaster. **Average salary range of placements**

DUNHILL PERSONNEL
3706 SW Topeka Boulevard, Topeka KS 66609-1239. 785/267-2773. **Contact:** Bob Washatka, President/ Owner. **Description:** An executive search firm operating on a contingency basis that also provides temporary placements. Company pays fee. **Specializes in the areas of:** Accounting/Auditing; Administration; Computer Hardware/Software; Finance; Office Support; Secretarial. **Positions commonly filled include:** Accountant; Administrative Assistant; Applications Engineer; Computer Programmer; Secretary. **Benefits available to temporary workers:** Paid Holidays; Paid Vacation. **Average salary range of placements:** $30,000 - $50,000. **Number of placements per year:** 50 - 99.

EFFECTIVE SEARCH INC.
301 North Main Street, Suite 1320, Wichita KS 67202. 316/267-9180. **Fax:** 316/267-9187. **Contact:** Manager. **Description:** An executive search firm. **Specializes in the areas of:** Information Systems.

EXECU-SEARCH INTERNATIONAL
250 North Rock Road, Suite 300, Wichita KS 67206. 316/683-3525. **Contact:** Manager. **Description:** An executive search firm specializing in manufacturing and sales.

ROBERT HALF INTERNATIONAL
ACCOUNTEMPS
10955 Lowell Avenue, Suite 490, Overland Park KS 66210. 913/451-7600. **Contact:** Manager. **Description:** An executive search firm. Accountemps (also at this location) provides temporary placements. **Corporate headquarters location:** Menlo Park CA. **Other U.S. locations:** Nationwide.

HENSLER & ASSOCIATES
9300 West 110th Street, Suite 160, Overland Park KS 66210. 913/451-9460. **Contact:** Manager. **Description:** An executive search firm. **Specializes in the areas of:** Data Processing.

JAG & ASSOCIATES ATTORNEY SEARCH
7299 West 98th Terrace, Building 6, Overland Park KS 66212. 913/648-6627. **Contact:** Manager. **Description:** An executive search firm. **Specializes in the areas of:** Legal. **Positions commonly filled include:** Attorney.

KAPLAN & ASSOCIATES
4550 West 109th Street, Suite 312, Overland Park KS 66211. 913/498-3900. **Contact:** Manager. **Description:** An executive search firm. **Specializes in the areas of:** Accounting/Auditing; Finance.

LEGAL SEARCH ASSOCIATES
6701 West 64th Street, Suite 210, Overland Park KS 66202. 913/722-3500. **Contact:** Manager. **Description:** An executive search firm. **Specializes in the areas of:** Legal.

MANAGEMENT RECRUITERS INTERNATIONAL
8100 East 22nd Street North, Building 1500, Suite B, Wichita KS 67226. 316/682-8239. **Contact:** Office Manager. **Description:** An executive search firm.

MANAGEMENT RECRUITERS INTERNATIONAL
7600 West 105th Street, Suite 204, Overland Park KS 66210. 913/663-2323. **Contact:** Manager. **Description:** An executive search firm. **Specializes in the areas of:** Insurance.

MANAGEMENT RECRUITERS OF OVERLAND PARK
SALES CONSULTANTS
OFFICEMATES5
9401 Indian Creek Parkway, Suite 920, Overland Park KS 66210. 913/661-9300. **Fax:** 913/661-9030. **Contact:** Office Manager. **Description:** An executive search firm. **Specializes in the areas of:** Accounting/Auditing; Administration; Advertising; Architecture/Construction; Banking; Chemical;

Communications; Computer Hardware/Software; Design; Electrical; Engineering; Food Industry; General Management; Health/Medical; Insurance; Legal; Manufacturing; Operations Management; Personnel/ Labor Relations; Procurement; Publishing; Retail; Sales; Technical; Textiles; Transportation.

MANAGEMENT RECRUITERS OF TOPEKA
3400 SW Van Buren, Topeka KS 66611. 785/267-5430. **Fax:** 785/267-0513. **Contact:** Kirk Hawkins, President. **Description:** An executive search firm operating on both contingency and retained bases. Company pays fee. **Specializes in the areas of:** Accounting/Auditing; Agriculture; Engineering; Finance; Health/Medical; Industrial. **Positions commonly filled include:** Accountant; Administrative Assistant; Auditor; Chief Financial Officer; Civil Engineer; Clerical Supervisor; Clinical Lab Technician; EEG Technologist; EKG Technician; Electrical/Electronics Engineer; Finance Director; Financial Analyst; Industrial Engineer; Manufacturing Engineer; Occupational Therapist; Paralegal; Pharmacist; Physical Therapist; Registered Nurse; Respiratory Therapist; Secretary; Surgical Technician. **Average salary range of placements:** More than $50,000. **Number of placements per year:** 50 - 99.

MIDWEST SEARCH GROUP
P.O. Box 26423, Shawnee Mission KS 66225. 913/681-8228. **Contact:** Manager. **Description:** An executive search firm. **Specializes in the areas of:** Accounting/Auditing; Finance.

NETWORK OF EXCELLENCE
P.O. Box 25203, Overland Park KS 66225. 913/897-2177. **Fax:** 913/897-2178. **Contact:** Henri Boucard, President. **Description:** An executive search firm. Company pays fee. **Specializes in the areas of:** Advertising; Broadcasting; Business Services; Education; Engineering; Food Industry; General Management; Health/Medical; Industrial; Sales; Textiles; Transportation. **Positions commonly filled include:** Attorney; Branch Manager; Chemist; Dentist; General Manager; Health Services Manager; Industrial Engineer; Industrial Production Manager; Mechanical Engineer; Operations/Production Manager; Physician; Radio/TV Announcer/Broadcaster; Registered Nurse; Restaurant/Food Service Manager; Services Sales Representative; Teacher/Professor; Veterinarian. **Number of placements per year:** 1 - 49.

PERSONNEL MANAGEMENT RESOURCES
P.O. Box 67513, Topeka KS 66667. 785/478-0002. **Fax:** 785/478-3195. **Contact:** Clay M. Zapletal, President. **Description:** An executive search firm. Company pays fee. **Specializes in the areas of:** Health/Medical. **Positions commonly filled include:** Management; Nurse; Occupational Therapist; Pharmacist; Physical Therapist; Physician; Registered Nurse; Speech-Language Pathologist. **Number of placements per year:** 1 - 49.

PETERSON GROUP
14351 West 81st Place, Shawnee Mission KS 66215. 913/599-4804. **Contact:** Manager. **Description:** An executive search firm that places physicians. **Specializes in the areas of:** Health/Medical.

SEARCH CONSULTANTS, INC.
P.O. Box 780932, Wichita KS 67278. 316/684-0615. **Contact:** Manager. **Description:** An executive search firm. **Specializes in the areas of:** Data Processing.

SEARCH ONE INC.
10800 Farley Road, Suite 320, Overland Park KS 66210. 913/451-2408. **Contact:** Office Manager. **Description:** An executive search firm. **Specializes in the areas of:** Information Technology.

SHERRIFF & ASSOCIATES
10983 Granada, Suite 202, Overland Park KS 66211. 913/451-2112. **Fax:** 913/451-3931. **Contact:** Julie A. Sherriff, President. **Description:** A retainer and contingency executive search firm. **Specializes in the areas of:** Health/Medical. **Positions commonly filled include:** Physician. **Average salary range of placements:** More than $50,000. **Number of placements per year:** 1 - 49.

B.E. SMITH ASSOCIATES
10100 Santa Fe Drive, Shawnee Mission KS 66206. 913/341-9116. **Contact:** Manager. **Description:** An executive search firm. **Specializes in the areas of:** Health/Medical.

SMITH BROWN & JONES
Box 6513, Shawnee Mission KS 66206. 816/531-4770. **Fax:** 816/531-5010. **Contact:** Don Smith, President. **E-mail address:** dlsmith@streek.com. **World Wide Web address:** http://www.streek.com/sbj. **Description:** A retainer and contingency search firm. Company pays fee. **Specializes in the areas of:** Architecture/Construction; Banking; Biology; Engineering; Food Industry; Manufacturing; Personnel/ Labor Relations; Sales; Transportation. **Positions commonly filled include:** Accountant/Auditor; Agricultural Scientist; Bank Officer/Manager; Biological Scientist; Buyer; Chemist; Dietician/Nutritionist; Economist; Engineer; Food Scientist/Technologist; General Manager; Occupational Therapist; Pharmacist; Physical Therapist; Property and Real Estate Manager; Quality Control Supervisor; Transportation/Traffic Specialist; Veterinarian. **Other U.S. locations:** Naples FL. **Average salary range of placements:** More than $50,000. **Number of placements per year:** 50 - 99.

SOURCE EDP
10300 West 103rd Street, Suite 101, Overland Park KS 66214. 816/474-3393. **Contact:** Manager. **Description:** An executive recruiter. **Specializes in the areas of:** Accounting/Auditing; Finance; Information Technology.

SOURCE SERVICES CORPORATION
10300 West 103rd Street, Suite 101, Overland Park KS 66214. 913/888-8885. **Contact:** Manager. **Description:** An executive search firm. The divisions at this location include Source EDP and Source Finance. **Specializes in the areas of:** Computer Hardware/Software; Data Processing; Finance; Information Technology.

STONEBURNER ASSOCIATES, INC.
10000 West 75th Street, Suite 102, Shawnee Mission KS 66204. 913/432-0055. **Fax:** 913/432-0056. **Contact:** Dwight Stoneburner, Owner. **Description:** An executive search firm. Company pays fee. **Specializes in the areas of:** Accounting/Auditing; Computer Science/Software; Engineering; Food Industry; General Management; Health/Medical; Industrial; Manufacturing; Personnel/Labor Relations; Publishing; Sales; Technical. **Positions commonly filled include:** Biological Scientist; Biomedical Engineer; Buyer; Chemical Engineer; Chemist; Civil Engineer; Computer Programmer; Electrical/Electronics Engineer; Food Scientist/Technologist; Industrial Engineer; Mechanical Engineer; Operations/Production Manager; Physical Therapist; Physician; Quality Control Supervisor; Software Engineer; Systems Analyst. **Average salary range of placements:** $30,000 - $50,000. **Number of placements per year:** 100 - 199.

WINN GROUP
501 Lawrence Avenue, Lawrence KS 66049. 913/842-7111. **Contact:** Manager. **Description:** An executive search firm that places property and casualty insurance actuaries.

PERMANENT EMPLOYMENT AGENCIES

BOSSLER-HIX FINANCIAL CAREERS
6405 Metcalf, Suite 418, Overland Park KS 66202. 913/262-8635. **Contact:** Jennifer Bryant, Manager. **Description:** A permanent employment agency. They also provide temporary placements. **Specializes in the areas of:** Banking. **Benefits available to temporary workers:** Paid Holidays; Paid Vacation. **Average salary range of placements:** Less than $30,000.

BOWMAN & MARSHALL
P.O. Box 25503, Overland Park KS 66225-5503. 913/648-3332. **Fax:** 913/341-9596. **Contact:** Peter O. Grassl, President. **E-mail address:** bowmarsh@aol.com. **World Wide Web address:** http://www.bowmarsh.com. **Description:** A permanent employment agency. Company pays fee. **Specializes in the areas of:** Accounting/Auditing; Finance. **Positions commonly filled include:** Accountant; Auditor; Budget Analyst; Controller; Finance Director; Financial Analyst.

BUSINESS SPECIALISTS
105 South Broadway Street, Suite 200, Wichita KS 67202-4217. 316/267-7375. **Fax:** 316/267-1085. **Contact:** Bim Heineman, Vice President. **Description:** A permanent employment agency. Company pays fee. **Specializes in the areas of:** Accounting/Auditing; Administration; Advertising; Architecture/Construction; Banking; Computer Science/Software; Engineering; Finance; Food Industry; General Management; Health/Medical; Industrial; Insurance; Legal; Manufacturing; Nonprofit; Personnel/Labor Relations; Publishing; Retail; Sales; Secretarial; Technical. **Corporate headquarters location:** This Location. **Other U.S. locations:** San Francisco CA; Denver CO. **Number of placements per year:** 1000+.

DUNHILL OF WICHITA
317 South Hydraulic, Wichita KS 67211. 316/265-9541. **Contact:** Harold Wood, President. **Description:** A permanent employment agency. **Specializes in the areas of:** Accounting/Auditing; Banking; Computer Hardware/Software; Engineering; Manufacturing; Technical. **Positions commonly filled include:** Accountant/Auditor; Bank Officer/Manager; Computer Operator; Computer Programmer; General Manager; Industrial Designer; Industrial Engineer; Purchasing Agent/Manager; Technician. **Other U.S. locations:** Nationwide.

FLAMING AND ASSOCIATES
120 West Sixth, Suite 120, Newton KS 67114. 316/283-3851. **Contact:** Don Stucky. **Description:** A permanent employment agency. **Specializes in the areas of:** Engineering; Manufacturing.

MORGAN HUNTER CORPORATE SEARCH
6800 College Boulevard, Suite 550, Overland Park KS 66211. 913/491-3434. **Contact:** Jerry Hellebusch, President/Owner. **Description:** A permanent employment agency. Company pays fee. **Specializes in the areas of:** Accounting/Auditing; Administration; Computer Science/Software; Finance; Insurance; Secretarial. **Positions commonly filled include:** Accountant/Auditor; Administrative Manager; Budget Analyst; Claim Representative; Clerical Supervisor; Computer Programmer; Credit Manager; Customer Service Representative; Financial Analyst; Systems Analyst; Underwriter/Assistant Underwriter. **Number of placements per year:** 200 - 499.

J.T. NELSON & ASSOCIATES
7700 West 63rd Street, Suite 201, Overland Park KS 66202. 913/236-9433. **Fax:** 913/236-9491. **Contact:** J.T. Nelson, President. **Description:** A permanent employment agency. Company pays fee. **Specializes in the areas of:** Engineering; Manufacturing; Technical. **Positions commonly filled include:** Chemical Engineer; Chemist; Electrical/Electronics Engineer; Maintenance Supervisor; Mechanical Engineer. **Number of placements per year:** 1 - 49.

PARR & ASSOCIATES
P.O. Box 40461, Overland Park KS 66204. 913/888-3888. **Contact:** Manager. **Description:** A permanent employment agency. Company pays fee. **Specializes in the areas of:** Engineering; Health/Medical; Industrial; Manufacturing; Sales; Technical. **Positions commonly filled include:** Agricultural Engineer; Agricultural Scientist; Biomedical Engineer; Chemical Engineer; Chemist; Civil Engineer; Cost Estimator; Designer; Electrical/Electronics Engineer; Electrician; Industrial Engineer; Industrial Production Manager; Licensed Practical Nurse; Mechanical Engineer; Metallurgical Engineer; Operations/Production Manager; Quality Control Supervisor; Registered Nurse; Services Sales Representative; Structural Engineer; Teacher/Professor. **Number of placements per year:** 50 - 99.

PREFERRED MEDICAL PLACEMENT
125 South Clairborne, Olathe KS 66062. 913/780-6845. **Contact:** Manager. **Description:** A permanent placement agency. **Specializes in the areas of:** Health/Medical.

ROLLHEISER & ASSOCIATES
9393 West 110th Street, Suite 500, Overland Park KS 66210. 913/681-8060. **Contact:** Manager. **Description:** A permanent placement agency. **Specializes in the areas of:** Computer Science/Software.

TECHNICAL JOB SERVICE
6916 West Harry Street, Wichita KS 67209. 316/946-0705. **Contact:** Manager. **Description:** A permanent placement agency. **Specializes in the areas of:** Engineering.

WICHITA BAR ASSOCIATION LEGAL PLACEMENT SERVICE
301 North Main Street, Suite 700, Wichita KS 67202. 316/263-2251. **Fax:** 316/263-0629. **Contact:** Linda Fuson, Placement Director. **Description:** A permanent employment agency that focuses on staff placements for attorneys' offices. Company pays fee. **Specializes in the areas of:** Legal; Secretarial. **Positions commonly filled include:** Legal Assistant; Legal Secretary; Office Manager; Paralegal; Receptionist; Secretary; Stenographer; Typist/Word Processor. **Average salary range of placements:** $20,000 - $29,999. **Number of placements per year:** 50 - 99.

WILLIAM LAWRENCE & ASSOCIATES
125 North Market Street, Suite 1250, Wichita KS 67202. 316/269-4010. **Contact:** Larry Coons, President. **Description:** A permanent employment agency. Company pays fee. **Positions commonly filled include:** Accountant/Auditor; Administrative Assistant; Advertising Account Executive; Bank Officer/Manager; Bookkeeper; Claim Representative; Computer Programmer; Customer Service Representative; Data Entry Clerk; EDP Specialist; Electrical/Electronics Engineer; Financial Analyst; Industrial Designer; Industrial Engineer; Insurance Agent/Broker; Interior Designer; Legal Secretary; Marketing Specialist; Mechanical Engineer; Medical Secretary; Nurse; Receptionist; Sales Representative; Systems Analyst; Technical Writer/Editor; Typist/Word Processor; Underwriter/Assistant Underwriter. **Number of placements per year:** 500 - 999.

TEMPORARY EMPLOYMENT AGENCIES

ALTERNATIVE STAFFING AND PERSONNEL, INC.
P.O. Box 12222, Overland Park KS 66282. 913/338-2772. **Fax:** 913/338-2830. **Contact:** Joyce McNeely, Vice President. **Description:** A temporary agency. Company pays fee. **Specializes in the areas of:** Accounting/Auditing; Administration; Health/Medical; Insurance; Secretarial. **Positions commonly filled include:** Accountant/Auditor; Automotive Mechanic; Clerical Supervisor; Clinical Lab Technician; Customer Service Representative; Dental Assistant/Dental Hygienist; Medical Records Technician; Physical Therapist; Recreational Therapist; Registered Nurse; Typist/Word Processor; Underwriter/Assistant Underwriter. **Average salary range of placements:** Less than $20,000. **Number of placements per year:** 100 - 199.

ELEVENTH HOUR STAFFING SERVICES
7203 West 110th Street, Overland Park KS 66210. 913/451-7777. **Toll-free phone:** 800/860-8424. **Fax:** 913/451-7890. **Contact:** Julie Davidson, Area Manager. **Description:** A temporary agency that also provides permanent employment in secretarial, clerical, administrative, and technical positions. Founded in 1988. Company pays fee. **Specializes in the areas of:** Accounting/Auditing; Administration; Advertising; Banking; Computer Science/Software; Engineering; Finance; Food Industry; General Labor; Health/Medical; Insurance; Legal; Manufacturing; Personnel/Labor Relations; Retail; Sales; Secretarial; Technical; Transportation. **Positions commonly filled include:** Accountant/Auditor; Administrative Manager; Bank Officer/Manager; Branch Manager; Brokerage Clerk; Budget Analyst; Computer Programmer; Cost Estimator; Credit Manager; Customer Service Representative; Health Services Manager; Insurance Agent/Broker; Management Analyst/Consultant; Medical Records Technician; MIS Specialist; Paralegal; Quality Control Supervisor; Restaurant/Food Service Manager; Systems Analyst; Technical Writer/Editor; Typist/Word Processor. **Benefits available to temporary workers:** Bonus Award/Plan; Dental Insurance; Medical Insurance; Paid Holidays. **Number of placements per year:** 500 - 999.

KANSAS WORKFORCE, INC.
P.O. Box 708, El Dorado KS 67042. 316/320-5288. **Fax:** 316/320-3525. **Contact:** Cyle Moon, Office Manager. **Description:** A temporary agency that also provides permanent placements. Company pays fee. **Specializes in the areas of:** Industrial; Manufacturing; Secretarial. **Positions commonly filled include:** Computer Operator; Secretary; Typist/Word Processor. **Average salary range of placements:** Less than $20,000. **Number of placements per year:** 200 - 499.

KELLY ASSISTED LIVING SERVICES
1047 SW Gage Boulevard, Topeka KS 66604-1780. **Contact:** Recruiter. **Description:** A temporary agency. **Specializes in the areas of:** Health/Medical. **Positions commonly filled include:** Branch Manager; Licensed Practical Nurse; Registered Nurse. **Benefits available to temporary workers:** Paid Holidays; Paid Vacation. **Corporate headquarters location:** Detroit MI. **Other U.S. locations:** Nationwide.

KEY STAFFING
400 SW Croix, Topeka KS 66611. 785/267-9999. **Fax:** 785/267-9905. **Contact:** Patti Bossert, President. **E-mail address:** keystaffing@mail.cjnetworks.com. **World Wide Web address:** http://www.cjnetworks.com/~keystaffing. **Description:** A temporary agency focusing on clerical, sales, and light industrial positions. Key Staffing also provides permanent placements. Company pays fee. **Specializes in the areas of:** Computer Science/Software; Industrial; Manufacturing; Nonprofit; Publishing; Retail; Sales; Secretarial. **Positions commonly filled include:** Accountant/Auditor; Blue-Collar Worker Supervisor; Branch Manager; Clerical Supervisor; Computer Operator; Computer Programmer; Credit Manager; Customer Service Representative; Industrial Production Manager; Operations/Production Manager; Purchasing Agent/Manager; Services Sales Representative; Typist/Word Processor. **Average salary range of placements:** $30,000 - $50,000. **Number of placements per year:** 1000+.

MANPOWER, INC.
555 Poyntz Avenue, Suite 245, Manhattan KS 66502. 785/776-1094. **Contact:** Office Manager. **Description:** A temporary agency. Company pays fee. **Specializes in the areas of:** Clerical; Computer Hardware/Software; Construction; Legal; Manufacturing; Personnel/Labor Relations. **Positions commonly filled include:** Administrative Assistant; Advertising Clerk; Bookkeeper; Buyer; Clerk; Computer Operator; Computer Programmer; Construction Trade Worker; Data Entry Clerk; Driver; Factory Worker; Legal Secretary; Light Industrial Worker; Medical Secretary; Public Relations Specialist; Receptionist; Typist/Word Processor. **Corporate headquarters location:** Milwaukee WI.

MANPOWER, INC.
335 North Washington Street, Suite 160, Hutchinson KS 67501-4861. 316/665-5213. **Toll-free phone:** 800/962-5580. **Fax:** 316/665-6089. **Contact:** Charlotte Summers, Manager. **Description:** A temporary agency. Founded in 1947. **Specializes in the areas of:** Industrial; Technical. **Positions commonly filled include:** Accountant/Auditor; Administrative Manager; Aerospace Engineer; Clerical Supervisor; Electrician. **Benefits available to temporary workers:** Medical Insurance; Paid Holidays; Paid Vacation. **Corporate headquarters location:** Milwaukee WI. **Average salary range of placements:** Less than $20,000. **Number of placements per year:** 200 - 499.

UNIFORCE STAFFING SERVICES
10551 Barkley, Suite 140, Overland Park KS 66212. 913/341-3300. **Fax:** 913/341-5256. **Contact:** Cathy Vollmer, Sales Director. **Description:** A temporary and temp-to-perm agency for general office, office automation, medical office, customer service, and market research clients. **Specializes in the areas of:** Accounting/Auditing; Clerical; Data Processing; Health/Medical; Legal; Sales; Secretarial; Word Processing. **Positions commonly filled include:** Administrative Assistant; Claim Representative; Clerk; Computer Operator; Computer Programmer; Customer Service Representative; Data Entry Clerk; Financial Analyst; Management Analyst/Consultant; Medical Secretary; Receptionist; Typist/Word Processor. **Benefits available to temporary workers:** Paid Holidays; Paid Vacation. **Corporate headquarters location:** Woodbury NY. **Other U.S. locations:** Nationwide. **Number of placements per year:** 1000+.

WESTERN STAFF SERVICES
1031 SW Gage Boulevard, Topeka KS 66604-1758. 785/273-3939. **Fax:** 785/273-4078. **Contact:** Alan Mayfield, Branch Manager. **Description:** A temporary agency that also provides some permanent placements. Company pays fee. **Specializes in the areas of:** Accounting/Auditing; Finance; Industrial; Legal; Personnel/Labor Relations; Publishing; Secretarial. **Positions commonly filled include:** Accountant/Auditor; Administrative Manager; Architect; Computer Programmer; Customer Service

Representative; Draftsperson; Human Resources Specialist; Medical Records Technician; Paralegal; Services Sales Representative; Typist/Word Processor. **Average salary range of placements:** $20,000 - $29,999. **Number of placements per year:** 1 - 49.

CONTRACT SERVICES FIRMS

CDI CORPORATION
505 South Broadway, Suite 222, Wichita KS 67202. 316/267-3434. **Fax:** 316/267-3311. **Contact:** Manager. **World Wide Web address:** http://www.cdicorp.com. **Description:** A contract services firm. **Specializes in the areas of:** Engineering; Technical. **Corporate headquarters location:** Philadelphia PA. **Other U.S. locations:** Nationwide. **International locations:** Worldwide.

COMPUTER PROFESSIONALS
P.O. Box 2184, Shawnee Mission KS 66201-1184. 913/384-3056. **Fax:** 913/384-9516. **Contact:** Norm Capps, Account Executive. **World Wide Web address:** http://www.cpnotes.com. **Description:** A contract services firm that focuses on placing implementors of SAP, Baan, and PeopleSoft. Company pays fee. **Specializes in the areas of:** Computer Science/Software. **Positions commonly filled include:** Computer Programmer; Project Manager; Software Engineer; Systems Analyst; Systems Manager; Telecommunications Manager. **Benefits available to temporary workers:** 401(k); Medical Insurance. **Corporate headquarters location:** This Location. **Average salary range of placements:** More than $50,000. **Number of placements per year:** 50 - 99.

FOSTER DESIGN COMPANY
P.O. Box 47280, Wichita KS 67201-7280. **Toll-free phone:** 800/345-3394. **Fax:** 316/832-9357. **Contact:** Barbara Taggart, Vice President of Contract Staffing. **Description:** A contract services firm. **Specializes in the areas of:** Computer Science/Software; Engineering; Industrial; Manufacturing; Technical. **Positions commonly filled include:** Aerospace Engineer; Biochemist; Biological Scientist; Biomedical Engineer; Chemical Engineer; Chemist; Civil Engineer; Computer Programmer; Design Engineer; Electrical/Electronics Engineer; Environmental Engineer; Mechanical Engineer; Metallurgical Engineer; MIS Specialist; Quality Control Supervisor; Software Engineer; Systems Analyst; Technical Writer/Editor; Telecommunications Manager. **Benefits available to temporary workers:** 401(k); Paid Holidays; Paid Vacation. **Number of placements per year:** 200 - 499.

LEGALTEMPS OF KANSAS, INC.
154 North Emporia Street, Suite 100, Wichita KS 67202-2515. 316/267-8677. **Fax:** 316/267-8069. **Contact:** Dana M. Milby, President. **Description:** A contract services firm that provides temporary, contract, and permanent help to law firms and corporate legal departments. The firm also places attorneys for research and writing projects. Founded in 1994. Company pays fee. **Specializes in the areas of:** Legal. **Positions commonly filled include:** Attorney; Legal Secretary; Paralegal. **Benefits available to temporary workers:** Bonus Award/Plan; Medical Insurance; Paid Vacation. **Average salary range of placements:** $20,000 - $29,999. **Number of placements per year:** 1 - 49.

MEGAFORCE LTD.
5401 College Boulevard, Suite 110, Leawood KS 66211. 913/491-6625x309. **Toll-free phone:** 800/676-6625x309. **Fax:** 913/491-9846. **Contact:** Ryan MacDonald, Director of Marketing. **World Wide Web address:** http://www.megaforceusa.com. **Description:** A contract services firm that focuses on computer and information technology areas including mainframe, client/server, and computer software. **Specializes in the areas of:** Computer Science/Software. **Positions commonly filled include:** Computer Operator; Computer Programmer; Technical Writer/Editor. **Benefits available to temporary workers:** 401(k); Dental Insurance; Medical Insurance; Tuition Assistance. **Corporate headquarters location:** This Location. **Other U.S. locations:** Colorado Springs CO; Springfield IL. **Average salary range of placements:** $30,000 - $50,000.

METRO INFORMATION SERVICES
6405 Metcalf, Suite 425, Shawnee Mission KS 66202. 913/236-8288. **Contact:** Office Manager. **Description:** A contract services firm. Company pays fee. **Specializes in the areas of:** Data Processing. **Positions commonly filled include:** Computer Operator; Computer Programmer; Customer Service Representative; Data Entry Clerk; EDP Specialist; Marketing Specialist; MIS Specialist; Systems Analyst; Technical Writer/Editor; Technician; Typist/Word Processor. **Number of placements per year:** 100 - 199.

TEMTECH
10000 West 75th Street, Suite 118, Shawnee Mission KS 66204-2241. 913/831-1821. **Fax:** 913/831-1834. **Contact:** Carlene White, President. **Description:** A contract services firm providing technical, engineering, and manufacturing executives for both temporary and permanent assignments. **Specializes in the areas of:** Architecture/Construction; Art/Design; Computer Science/Software; Engineering; Food Industry; General Management; Health/Medical; Manufacturing; Personnel/Labor Relations; Sales; Technical. **Positions commonly filled include:** Accountant/Auditor; Administrative Manager; Architect; Biomedical Engineer; Branch Manager; Buyer; Chemical Engineer; Civil Engineer; Clerical Supervisor; Customer Service Representative; Design Engineer; EEG Technologist; EKG Technician; Electrical/Electronics Engineer; Emergency Medical Technician; Environmental Engineer; Financial Analyst; Industrial Engineer; Industrial Production Manager; Licensed Practical Nurse; Mechanical Engineer; Medical Records Technician; MIS Specialist; Occupational Therapist; Operations/Production Manager; Physical Therapist; Purchasing Agent/Manager; Quality Control Supervisor; Registered Nurse; Services Sales Representative; Software Engineer; Systems Analyst; Technical Writer/Editor; Typist/Word Processor. **Benefits available to temporary workers:** Paid Holidays; Paid Vacation. **Average salary range of placements:** More than $50,000. **Number of placements per year:** 100 - 199.

WYATT & ASSOCIATES INC.
9235 East Harry Street, Wichita KS 67207. 316/682-6740. **Contact:** Manager. **Description:** A contract services firm. **Specializes in the areas of:** Engineering.

H.L. YOH COMPANY
7133 West 95th Street, Suite 205, Overland Park KS 66212. 913/648-4004. **Contact:** Office Manager. **Description:** A contract services firm. **Specializes in the areas of:** Technical.

KENTUCKY

EXECUTIVE SEARCH FIRMS

ANGEL GROUP INTERNATIONAL
4360 Brownsboro Road, Suite 240, Louisville KY 40207. 502/897-0333. **Fax:** 502/897-0496. **Contact:** Beth Enyeart, Manager. **E-mail address:** info@angel-group.com. **World Wide Web address:** http://www.angel-group.com. **Description:** An executive search firm. **Specializes in the areas of:** Accounting/Auditing; Administration; Advertising; Architecture/Construction; Banking; Chemical; Communications; Computer Hardware/Software; Design; Electrical; Engineering; Food Industry; General Management; Health/Medical; Insurance; Legal; Manufacturing; Operations Management; Personnel/ Labor Relations; Procurement; Publishing; Retail; Sales; Technical; Textiles; Transportation.

CAREER COUNSELING EXECUTIVE
1401 Spring Bank Drive, Building C, Suite 4, Owensboro KY 42303. 502/686-7766. **Contact:** Manager. **Description:** An executive search firm operating on a contingency basis.

ENGINEERING & EXECUTIVE SEARCH INC.
141 North Sherrin Avenue, Suite 221, Louisville KY 40207. 502/895-3055. **Fax:** 502/895-3055. **Contact:** Patrick A. Thomas, President. **Description:** An executive search firm. Company pays fee. **Specializes in the areas of:** Banking; Communications; Finance; Food Industry; Health/Medical. **Positions commonly filled include:** Accountant/Auditor; Attorney; Buyer; Computer Programmer; Cost Estimator; Electrical/ Electronics Engineer; Financial Analyst; Food Scientist/Technologist; Human Resources Manager; Industrial Engineer; Industrial Production Manager; Mechanical Engineer; Metallurgical Engineer; Public Relations Specialist; Purchasing Agent/Manager; Quality Control Supervisor; Science Technologist; Structural Engineer; Systems Analyst. **Number of placements per year:** 1 - 49.

THE EXECUTIVE ADVANTAGE
P.O. Box 1176, Bowling Green KY 42102-1176. 502/781-0234. **Fax:** 502/842-9116. **Contact:** Pam Witcher, Recruiter/Manager. **Description:** An executive search firm that focuses on the recruitment of personnel in all areas of industrial, sales and marketing, direct marketing, and customer service. Company pays fee. **Specializes in the areas of:** Industrial; Sales. **Positions commonly filled include:** Cost Estimator; Credit Manager; Manufacturer's/ Wholesaler's Sales Rep.; MIS Specialist; Operations/ Production Manager; Services Sales Representative; Software Engineer; Systems Analyst. **Average salary range of placements:** $30,000 - $80,000. **Number of placements per year:** 1 - 49.

EXECUTIVE SEARCH LINK, LTD.
3207 Running Deer Circle, Louisville KY 40241. 217/687-2888. **Contact:** Manager. **Description:** An executive search firm specializing in engineering and operations management. **Corporate headquarters location:** Seymour IL.

FIRST CHOICE SERVICES
1711 Ashley Circle, Suite 6, Bowling Green KY 42104. 502/782-9152. **Contact:** Bob Toth, President. **Description:** An executive search firm. **Specializes in the areas of:** Health/Medical. **Positions commonly filled include:** Physician.

F-O-R-T-U-N-E PERSONNEL CONSULTANTS OF OWENSBORO
620 Carlton Drive, Owensboro KY 42303. 502/686-7277. **Fax:** 502/686-7215. **Contact:** Joe Vance, President. **E-mail address:** jev022039@aol.com. **Description:** An executive search firm operating on a contingency basis. Company pays fee. **Positions commonly filled include:** Accountant/Auditor; Buyer; Chemical Engineer; Civil Engineer; Computer Programmer; Cost Estimator; Design Engineer; Electrical/Electronics Engineer; Financial Analyst; Industrial Designer; Industrial Engineer; Mechanical Engineer; Metallurgical Engineer; Operations/ Production Manager; Quality Control Supervisor; Systems Analyst. **Corporate headquarters location:** New York NY. **Other U.S. locations:** Nationwide. **Average salary range of placements:** $30,000 - $50,000. **Number of placements per year:** 1 - 49.

ROBERT HALF INTERNATIONAL ACCOUNTEMPS
220 Lexington Green Circle, Suite 510, Lexington KY 40503. 606/245-1800. **Contact:** Manager. **World Wide Web address:** http://www.roberthalf.com. **Description:** An executive search firm. Accountemps (also at this location) provides temporary placements. **Specializes in the areas of:** Accounting/Auditing. **Corporate headquarters location:** Menlo Park CA. **Other U.S. locations:** Nationwide.

ROBERT HALF INTERNATIONAL ACCOUNTEMPS
6060 Dutchman's Lane, Suite 240, Louisville KY 40205. 502/456-4253. **Contact:** Office Manager. **Description:** An executive search firm. Accountemps (also at this location) provides temporary placements. **Specializes in the areas of:** Accounting/Auditing. **Corporate headquarters location:** Menlo Park CA. **Other U.S. locations:** Nationwide.

HEALTHCARE RECRUITERS INTERNATIONAL
101 North Seventh Street, Louisville KY 40206. 502/561-3484. **Fax:** 502/561-3444. **Contact:** Manager. **Description:** An executive search firm. **Specializes in the areas of:** Health/Medical.

THE HINDMAN COMPANY
Browenton Place, Suite 110, 2000 Warrington Way, Louisville KY 40222. 502/426-4040. **Contact:** Manager. **Description:** An executive search firm. **Specializes in the areas of:** High-Tech.

DON KESTLER & ASSOCIATES
231 Buster Pike, Harrodsburg KY 40330. 606/748-9516. **Contact:** Manager. **Description:** An executive search firm. **Specializes in the areas of:** Manufacturing.

KOLOK ENTERPRISES
P.O. Box 582, Owensboro KY 42302. 502/685-3676. **Fax:** 502/683-8897. **Contact:** Joan Kolok, Personnel Consultant. **Description:** An executive search firm operating on a contingency basis. Company pays fee. **Specializes in the areas of:** Engineering; Manufacturing. **Positions commonly filled include:** Chemical Engineer; Electrical/Electronics Engineer; Industrial Engineer; Mechanical Engineer; Metallurgical Engineer; MIS Specialist. **Average salary range of placements:** $30,000 - $50,000. **Number of placements per year:** 1 - 49.

KOVAC BERRINS AG INC.
2057 Regency Circle, Suite D, Lexington KY 40503. 606/278-0482. **Contact:** David Dryden, Managing Partner. **Description:** An executive search firm operating on both retainer and contingency bases. Company pays fee. **Specializes in the areas of:** Engineering; General Management; Sales. **Positions**

commonly filled include: Accountant/Auditor; Branch Manager; Buyer; Chemical Engineer; Chemist; Civil Engineer; Computer Programmer; Construction Contractor; Cost Estimator; General Manager; Industrial Engineer; Mechanical Engineer; Metallurgical Engineer; Mining Engineer; Software Engineer. **Average salary range of placements:** $30,000 - $50,000.

J.C. MALONE ASSOCIATES
1941 Bishop Lane, Louisville KY 40210. 502/456-2380. **Contact:** Manager. **Description:** An executive search firm.

MANAGEMENT RECRUITERS INTERNATIONAL
2350 Sterlington Road, Lexington KY 40517. 606/273-5665. **Fax:** 606/273-9106. **Contact:** Manager. **Description:** An executive search firm. **Specializes in the areas of:** Engineering; Information Systems; Insurance; Manufacturing.

MANAGEMENT RECRUITERS INTERNATIONAL
105 Citation Drive, Suite A, Danville KY 40422. 606/236-0505. **Contact:** Manager. **Description:** An executive search firm. **Specializes in the areas of:** Manufacturing.

MANAGEMENT RECRUITERS OF RICHMOND
P.O. Box 263, Richmond KY 40476. 606/624-3535. **Fax:** 606/624-3539. **Contact:** Ron Lawson, General Manager. **Description:** An executive search firm. Company pays fee. **Specializes in the areas of:** Engineering; General Management; Manufacturing. **Positions commonly filled include:** Chemical Engineer; Electrical/Electronics Engineer; Industrial Engineer; Mechanical Engineer; Quality Control Supervisor. **Number of placements per year:** 1 - 49.

KAREN MARSHALL ASSOCIATES
6304 Deep Creek Drive, Prospect KY 40059. 502/228-0800. **Fax:** 502/228-0663. **Contact:** Karen Marshall, Systems Recruiter. **Description:** A contingency executive search firm. Company pays fee. **Specializes in the areas of:** Administration; Computer Science/Software. **Positions commonly filled include:** Computer Programmer; Internet Services Manager; MIS Specialist; Software Engineer; Statistician; Systems Analyst; Telecommunications Manager. **Corporate headquarters location:** Louisville KY. **Average salary range of placements:** $30,000 - $50,000. **Number of placements per year:** 1 - 49.

NEESSEN PROFESSIONAL SEARCH
P.O. Box 862, Versailles KY 40383. 606/873-0033. **Contact:** James R. Neessen, Owner/President. **E-mail address:** jamerneessen@msn.com. **Description:** An executive search that operates on both retainer and contincency bases.firm. Company operates on a retainer basis. Company operates on a contingency basis. **Specializes in the areas of:** Accounting/Auditing; Engineering; General Management; Manufacturing; Personnel/Labor Relations. **Positions commonly filled include:** Applications Engineer; Buyer; Chief Financial Officer; Design Engineer; Electrical/Electronics Engineer; Industrial Engineer; Industrial Production Manager; Manufacturing Engineer; Operations Manager; Production Manager; Project Manager; Quality Control Supervisor. **Average salary range of placements:** $30,000 - $50,000. **Number of placements per year:** 1 - 49.

PROFESSIONAL SEARCH
P.O. Box 22236, Louisville KY 40252. 502/222-1860. **Contact:** Barry R. Wilhelm, Principal Consultant. **Description:** An executive search firm. Professional Search has over 15 years of experience in placing experienced engineers, manufacturing managers, human resource professionals, and chemists. Company pays fee. **Specializes in the areas of:** Engineering; Manufacturing; Personnel/Labor Relations; Technical. **Positions commonly filled include:** Chemical Engineer; Chemist; Civil Engineer; Electrical/Electronics Engineer; Human Resources Manager; Industrial Engineer; Industrial Production Manager; Mechanical Engineer; Operations/Production Manager; Quality Control Supervisor. **Average salary range of placements:** $30,000 - $50,000. **Number of placements per year:** 1 - 49.

PROFESSIONAL SEARCH CONSULTANTS
2500 Meibinger Tower, Louisville KY 40202. 502/583-1530. **Contact:** Manager. **Description:** An executive search firm. **Specializes in the areas of:** Legal.

ROMAC INTERNATIONAL
4965 U.S. Highway 42, Suite 2900, Louisville KY 40222. 502/339-2900. **Fax:** 502/339-2888. **Contact:** Office Manager. **Description:** An executive search firm. **Specializes in the areas of:** Information Technology.

SANFORD ROSE ASSOCIATES
2100 Gardener Lane, Suite 107, Louisville KY 40205. 502/451-4444. **Fax:** 502/459-8377. **Contact:** Manager. **World Wide Web address:** http://www.sanfordrose.com. **Description:** An executive search firm. **Specializes in the areas of:** Engineering; Medical Technology.

SHARROW & ASSOCIATES
8100 Burlington Pike, Suite 336, Florence KY 41042. 606/282-0111. **Fax:** 606/282-0916. **Contact:** Steven G. Stoll, Managing Partner. **Description:** An executive search firm focusing on accounting, engineering, and commercial and residential real estate. Company pays fee. **Specializes in the areas of:** Banking; Engineering; Finance; Sales. **Positions commonly filled include:** Accountant/Auditor; Attorney; Automotive Mechanic; Bank Officer/Manager; Civil Engineer; Construction Engineer; Credit Manager; Financial Analyst; Mechanical Engineer; Occupational Therapist; Physical Therapist; Property and Real Estate Manager; Structural Engineer. **Corporate headquarters location:** Detroit MI. **Other U.S. locations:** Angola IN; Cincinnati OH. **Average salary range of placements:** More than $50,000. **Number of placements per year:** 50 - 99.

SNELLING PERSONNEL SERVICES
4010 DuPont Circle, Professional Tower Building, Suite 419, Louisville KY 40207. 502/895-9494. **Contact:** Steve Steinmetz, President. **Description:** An executive search firm. **Specializes in the areas of:** Administration; Computer Hardware/Software; Engineering; Manufacturing; Sales; Technical.

SOURCE SERVICES CORPORATION
2850 National City Tower, Louisville KY 40202. 502/581-9900. **Contact:** Manager. **Description:** An executive search firm. **Specializes in the areas of:** Administration; Information Technology.

STAFFING ALTERNATIVES
1733 Campus Plaza Court, Suite 10, Bowling Green KY 42101. 502/796-2040. **Contact:** Michael Riggs, Branch Manager. **Description:** An executive search firm operating on a contingency basis. **Average salary range of placements:** $20,000 - $29,999. **Number of placements per year:** 50 - 99.

VERSA-TECH EMPLOYMENT SERVICES
7400 New LaGrange, Suite 200, Louisville KY 40222. 502/425-8058. **Contact:** Manager. **Description:** An executive search firm. **Specializes in the areas of:** Technical.

WELLER-WOOLEY & ASSOCIATES
P.O. Box 892, Covington KY 41012. 606/491-1891. **Fax:** 606/655-2952. **Contact:** R. Vernon Weller, Partner. **Description:** An executive search firm focusing on technical recruitment. **Specializes in the areas of:** Industrial; Manufacturing. **Positions commonly filled include:** Biomedical Engineer; Buyer; Designer; Draftsperson; Electrical/Electronics Engineer; Industrial Engineer; Mechanical Engineer; Metallurgical Engineer; Purchasing Agent/Manager; Quality Control Supervisor; Software Engineer. **Average salary range of placements:** $30,000 - $50,000.

PERMANENT EMPLOYMENT AGENCIES

ACCESS COMPUTER CAREERS
404 Republic Building, Louisville KY 40202. 502/569-2810. **Contact:** Manager. **Description:** A permanent employment agency. **Specializes in the areas of:** Computer Hardware/Software; Computer Science/Software.

BELCAN STAFFING SERVICES
6895 Burlington Pike, Suite 100, Florence KY 41042. 606/282-8533. **Fax:** 606/282-3641. **Contact:** Manager. **E-mail address:** mbp@belrs.belcan. **World Wide Web address:** http://www.belcan.com. **Description:** A permanant employment agency that also provides temp-to-hire and temporary placements. **Specializes in the areas of:** Accounting/Auditing; Banking; Food Industry; General Management; Health/Medical; Industrial; Legal; Light Industrial; Secretarial. **Average salary range of placements:** Less than $20,000. **Number of placements per year:** 1000+.

C.M. MANAGEMENT SERVICES
698 Perimeter Drive, Suite 200, Lexington KY 40517. 606/266-5000. **Contact:** Office Manager. **Description:** A permanent employment agency. Company pays fee. **Specializes in the areas of:** Accounting/Auditing; Banking; Clerical; Computer Hardware/Software; Engineering; Food Industry; Manufacturing; Sales; Secretarial; Technical. **Positions commonly filled include:** Accountant/Auditor; Administrative Assistant; Bank Officer/Manager; Biological Scientist; Bookkeeper; Computer Programmer; Customer Service Representative; EDP Specialist; Electrical/Electronics Engineer; Factory Worker; Financial Analyst; Human Resources Manager; Industrial Engineer; Legal Secretary; Light Industrial Worker; Marketing Specialist; Mechanical Engineer; Metallurgical Engineer; Receptionist; Sales Representative; Systems Analyst; Typist/Word Processor. **Number of placements per year:** 50 - 99.

COMPUTER CAREER CONSULTANTS
P.O. Box 22426, Louisville KY 40252. 502/394-0388. **Fax:** 502/394-9443. **Contact:** Recruiter. **Description:** A permanent employment agency. Company pays fee. **Specializes in the areas of:** Computer Hardware/Software; MIS/EDP. **Positions commonly filled include:** Computer Programmer; EDP Specialist; MIS Specialist; Sales Representative; Systems Analyst.

CROWN PERSONNEL SERVICES
2100 Gardiner Lane, Suite 215, Louisville KY 40205. 502/454-5500. **Fax:** 502/473-0140. **Contact:** Jay Hodge, Manager. **Description:** A full-service employment agency. Company pays fee. **Positions commonly filled include:** Claim Representative; Clerical Supervisor; Computer Programmer; Construction Contractor; Credit Manager; Customer Service Representative; Data Entry Clerk; Draftsperson; Electrician; Factory Worker; Legal Secretary; Light Industrial Worker; Marketing Specialist; Medical Secretary; Paralegal; Quality Control Supervisor; Receptionist; Typist/Word Processor. **Corporate headquarters location:** Columbus OH. **Average salary range of placements:** Less than $20,000. **Number of placements per year:** 1000+.

HOUCK CAREER CONSULTANTS (HCC)
7404 Old Coach Road, Suite 110, Crestwood KY 40014-9787. 502/241-2882. **Fax:** 502/241-6411. **Contact:** Recruiter. **Description:** A permanent employment agency. Company pays fee. **Specializes in the areas of:** Computer Hardware/Software. **Positions commonly filled include:** Computer Programmer; EDP Specialist; MIS Specialist; Software Engineer; Systems Analyst. **Number of placements per year:** 1 - 49.

OLSTEN KIMBERLY QUALITY CARE
710 Executive Park, Louisville KY 40207. 502/895-4213. **Contact:** Jeannie Cundiss, Branch Director. **Description:** A permanent employment agency. **Specializes in the areas of:** Health/Medical. **Positions commonly filled include:** Nurse.

PERSONNEL SOLUTIONS, INC.
P.O. Box 34484, Louisville KY 40232. 502/485-1140. **Fax:** 502/485-1242. **Contact:** Brenda Schissler, President. **Description:** A permanent employment agency. Company pays fee. **Specializes in the areas of:** Architecture/Construction; Banking; Engineering; Finance; Industrial; Manufacturing. **Positions commonly filled include:** Administrative Assistant; Bookkeeper; Chemical Engineer; Civil Engineer; Clerk; Computer Operator; Computer Programmer; Construction Trade Worker; Customer Service Representative; Data Entry Clerk; Draftsperson; Driver; Electrical/Electronics Engineer; Factory Worker; Industrial Designer; Industrial Engineer; Light Industrial Worker; Manufacturing Engineer; Mechanical Engineer; Metallurgical Engineer; Operations/Production Manager; Quality Control Supervisor; Receptionist; Sales Representative; Secretary; Software Engineer; Systems Analyst; Typist/Word Processor. **Number of placements per year:** 1 - 49.

PRECISION STAFFING, INC.
113 Consumer Lane, Frankfort KY 40601-8489. 502/227-7000. **Fax:** 502/227-2929. **Contact:** Carol Smith, Branch Manager. **Description:** A permanent employment agency. Company pays fee. **Specializes in the areas of:** Accounting/Auditing; Administration; Banking; Clerical; Food Industry; Health/Medical; Industrial; Insurance; Legal; Light Industrial; Manufacturing; Personnel/Labor Relations; Secretarial. **Benefits available to temporary workers:** Medical Insurance; Paid Holidays; Paid Vacation. **Corporate headquarters location:** Lexington KY. **Other area locations:** Mount Sterling KY; Shelbyville KY. **Average salary range of placements:** $20,000 - $29,999. **Number of placements per year:** 500 - 999.

TLI TECHNICAL STAFFING
7400 New LaGrange Road, Suite 200, Louisville KY 40222. 502/425-8384. **Fax:** 502/425-2924. **Contact:** Jim MacLeod, President. **Description:** A permanent and temporary technical placement service. Company pays fee. **Specializes in the areas of:** Engineering; Industrial; Manufacturing; Technical. **Positions commonly filled include:** Architect; Chemical Engineer; Civil Engineer; Computer Programmer; Computer Scientist; Cost Estimator; Design Engineer; Designer; Draftsperson; Electrical/Electronics Engineer; Environmental Engineer; Industrial Engineer; Industrial

Production Manager; Mechanical Engineer; Software Engineer; Structural Engineer. **Benefits available to temporary workers:** Dental Insurance; Medical Insurance; Paid Holidays; Paid Vacation. **Average salary range of placements:** $20,000 - $29,999. **Number of placements per year:** 1 - 49.

TEMPORARY HORSE CARE & EMPLOYMENT SERVICES, INC.
2189 Ballard Road, Lawrenceburg KY 40342. 502/839-1015. **Contact:** Michele Oren, Owner. **Description:** An employment service for horse farms, providing permanent and temporary placements for positions in the office, barn, and field. Company pays fee. **Positions commonly filled include:** General Manager; Sales Representative; Secretary; Training Specialist. **Corporate headquarters location:** This Location. **Other U.S. locations:** Ocala FL. **Average salary range of placements:** $20,000 - $29,999. **Number of placements per year:** 200 - 499.

TEMPORARY EMPLOYMENT AGENCIES

J.E.M. & ASSOCIATES, INC.
306 Preachersville Road, Stanford KY 40484. 606/365-2900. **Fax:** 606/365-1449. **Contact:** John Marcum, President. **Description:** A temporary agency. Founded in 1991. Company pays fee. **Specializes in the areas of:** Accounting/Auditing; Engineering; Manufacturing; Personnel/Labor Relations. **Positions commonly filled include:** Accountant/Auditor; Blue-Collar Worker Supervisor; Civil Engineer; Clerical Supervisor; Computer Programmer; Cost Estimator; Design Engineer; Electrical/Electronics Engineer; Environmental Engineer; Financial Analyst; Industrial Engineer; Management Analyst/Consultant; Mechanical Engineer; Operations/Production Manager; Quality Control Supervisor; Structural Engineer; Systems Analyst; Technical Writer/Editor. **Benefits available to temporary workers:** Paid Holidays; Paid Vacation. **Average salary range of placements:** $15,000 - $29,999. **Number of placements per year:** 100 - 199.

THE LEGAL EDGE, INC.
THE PROFESSIONAL EDGE, INC.
565 Starks Building, Louisville KY 40202. 502/581-9861. **Fax:** 502/581-0587. **Contact:** Donna Walters, Placement Specialist. **Description:** A temporary agency that focuses on temporary and permanent placements of legal secretaries, paralegals, attorneys, receptionists, runners, and executive secretaries. The Legal Edge offers legal administrative support, while The Professional Edge offers general administrative support. Company pays fee. **Specializes in the areas of:** Legal. **Positions commonly filled include:** Paralegal; Typist/Word Processor. **Benefits available to temporary workers:** Medical Insurance; Paid Vacation. **Average salary range of placements:** $20,000 - $29,999. **Number of placements per year:** 200 - 499.

MANPOWER INC.
600 Perimeter Drive, Lexington KY 40517-4119. 606/268-1331. **Contact:** Maggie Coats, Area Manager. **E-mail address:** manprlex@mis.net. **World Wide Web address:** http://www.manpower.com. **Description:** A temporary agency. **Specializes in the areas of:** Accounting/Auditing; Administration; Computer Science/Software; Engineering; Industrial; Light Industrial; MIS/EDP; Scientific; Secretarial; Technical. **Positions commonly filled include:** Accountant/Auditor; Administrative Assistant; Buyer; Chemical Engineer; Clinical Lab Technician; Computer Programmer; Database Manager; Design Engineer; Draftsperson; Electrical/Electronics Engineer; Environmental Engineer; Financial Analyst; Graphic Artist; Industrial Engineer; Industrial Production Manager; Manufacturing Engineer; Mechanical Engineer; MIS Specialist; Online Content Specialist; Operations/Production Manager; Software Engineer; Systems Analyst; Technical Writer/Editor; Typist/Word Processor; Webmaster. **Benefits available to temporary workers:** 401(k); Franchise Program; Life Insurance; Medical Insurance; Paid Holidays; Paid Vacation; Referral Bonus Plan. **Corporate headquarters location:** Milwaukee WI. **Other U.S. locations:** Nationwide. **International locations:** Worldwide. **Number of placements per year:** 1000+.

OFFICETEAM
6060 Dutchmans Lane, Suite 240, Louisville KY 40205-3277. 502/473-7009. **Fax:** 502/456-1631. **Contact:** April Graber, Division Director. **World Wide Web address:** http://www.officeteam.com. **Description:** A temporary agency. Company pays fee. **Specializes in the areas of:** Administration; Secretarial. **Positions commonly filled include:** Administrative Assistant; Human Resources Manager; Paralegal; Typist/Word Processor. **Corporate headquarters location:** Menlo Park CA. **Other U.S. locations:** Nationwide. **Average salary range of placements:** $20,000 - $29,999. **Number of placements per year:** 1000+.

PRECISION STAFFING, INC.
2358 Sterlington Road, Lexington KY 40517. 606/272-2030. **Contact:** Manager. **Description:** A temporary and temp-to-perm agency. **Specializes in the areas of:** Clerical; Industrial; Technical.

STAFFING ALTERNATIVES
200 High Rise Drive, Suite 147, Louisville KY 40213. 502/962-4100. **Fax:** 502/962-4105. **Contact:** Michael Seiler, Manager. **World Wide Web address:** http://www.ka.net/mseiler. **Description:** A temporary agency. **Specializes in the areas of:** Industrial; Light Industrial; Manufacturing. **Benefits available to temporary workers:** Medical Insurance; Paid Holidays; Paid Vacation; Referral Bonus Plan. **Average salary range of placements:** Less than $20,000. **Number of placements per year:** 1000+.

TEMPORARY PROFESSIONALS INC.
1402 East 4th Street, Owensboro KY 42303. 502/685-2090. **Contact:** Gary Boswell, President. **Description:** A temporary agency. Company pays fee. **Specializes in the areas of:** Accounting/Auditing; Clerical; Construction; Insurance. **Positions commonly filled include:** Accountant/Auditor; Administrative Worker/Clerk; Bookkeeper; Clerk; Computer Operator; Computer Programmer; Data Entry Clerk; Factory Worker; Legal Secretary; Medical Secretary; Nurse; Receptionist; Secretary; Stenographer; Typist/Word Processor. **Average salary range of placements:** Less than $20,000. **Number of placements per year:** 1000+.

TEMPS PLUS OF PADUCAH
819 Broadway Street, Paducah KY 42001-6807. 502/444-0030. **Fax:** 502/442-6679. **Contact:** Manager. **E-mail address:** tempsplus@sunsixinsi.net. **Description:** A temporary agency that also provides permanent placements.

CONTRACT SERVICES FIRMS

PROVISION TECHNOLOGIES
4010 DuPont Circle, Suite 475, Louisville KY 40207. 502/893-2200. **Fax:** 502/893-0037. **Contact:** Manager. **World Wide Web address:** http://www.careerbase.com. **Description:** A contract services and consulting firm. **Specializes in the areas of:** Computer Science/Software; Information Technology.

CAREER/OUTPLACEMENT COUNSELING FIRMS

RESUMES, ETC.
366 Waller Avenue, Suite 209, Lexington KY 40504-2921. 606/273-7863. **Contact:** Bruce Koenig, Owner. **Description:** A full-service agency providing writing, design, layout, and printing of entry-level to executive resumes and related items. **Average salary range of placements:** $30,000 - $50,000. **Number of placements per year:** 1000+.

LOUISIANA

EXECUTIVE SEARCH FIRMS

ASTRO EXECUTIVE SEARCH FIRM
11219 Muriel Avenue, Suite 418, Baton Rouge LA 70816. 504/292-7363. **Fax:** 504/292-7364. **Contact:** Annemarie T. Danielsen, Owner/National Recruiter. **E-mail address:** astroexec@linknet.net. **Description:** An executive search firm that handles permanent placement of engineering and computer science professionals. Company pays fee. **NOTE:** Clients must have a degree and three years experience in a focused field. **Specializes in the areas of:** Computer Science/Software; Engineering. **Positions commonly filled include:** Chemical Engineer; Civil Engineer; Computer Programmer; Database Manager; Design Engineer; Electrical/Electronics Engineer; Environmental Engineer; Industrial Engineer; Industrial Production Manager; Manufacturing Engineer; Mechanical Engineer; MIS Specialist; Operations Manager; Quality Control Supervisor; Sales Engineer; Software Engineer; Systems Analyst; Systems Manager. **Average salary range of placements:** More than $50,000. **Number of placements per year:** 1 - 49.

CAREER PERSONNEL CONSULTANTS
4640 South Carrollton Avenue, New Orleans LA 70119-6051. **Contact:** Henry LaRoche, President. **Description:** A retainer and contingency search firm. Company pays fee. **Specializes in the areas of:** Accounting/Auditing; Finance; Industrial; Manufacturing; Personnel/Labor Relations; Technical. **Positions commonly filled include:** Accountant/Auditor; Administrative Manager; Bank Officer/Manager; Chemical Engineer; Chemist; Civil Engineer; Design Engineer; Electrical/Electronics Engineer; Environmental Engineer; Financial Analyst; Industrial Engineer; Management Analyst/Consultant; Mechanical Engineer; Surveyor. **Average salary range of placements:** More than $50,000. **Number of placements per year:** 1 - 49.

CLERTECH GROUP, INC.
P.O. Box 19344, New Orleans LA 70179. 504/486-9733. **Physical address:** 7029 Canal Boulevard, New Orleans LA. **Fax:** 504/482-1475. **Contact:** George Dorko, Director of Technical Recruiting. **Description:** A retainer and contingency search firm. Company pays fee. **Specializes in the areas of:** Computer Science/Software; Economics; Electrical; Engineering; Technical. **Positions commonly filled include:** Computer Programmer; Cost Estimator; Design Engineer; Economist; Electrical/Electronics Engineer; Mechanical Engineer; MIS Specialist; Nuclear Engineer; Operations/Production Manager; Software Engineer; Structural Engineer; Systems Analyst; Telecommunications Manager. **Average salary range of placements:** More than $50,000. **Number of placements per year:** 1 - 49.

DUNHILL OF BATON ROUGE
5723 Superior Drive, Suite B-4, Baton Rouge LA 70816-6086. 504/291-0450. **Contact:** Mr. E.H. Falcon, Owner. **Description:** An executive search firm. **Specializes in the areas of:** Chemical; Engineering; Paper; Petrochemical; Technical. **Other U.S. locations:** Nationwide. **Number of placements per year:** 50 - 99.

DUNHILL PERSONNEL SYSTEM OF LOUISIANA
2920 Knight Street, Suite 140, Shreveport LA 71105-2412. 318/861-3576. **Contact:** Don Richards, President. **Description:** An executive search firm. **Specializes in the areas of:** Engineering; Information Technology; Technical. **Other U.S. locations:** Nationwide.

GELPI & ASSOCIATES
P.O. Box 231187, Harahan LA 70183. 504/737-6086. **Contact:** Manager. **Description:** An executive search firm. **Specializes in the areas of:** Insurance.

HEALTHCARE RECRUITERS INTERNATIONAL
3500 North Causeway Boulevard, Suite 160, Metairie LA 70002. 504/838-8875. **Contact:** Manager. **Description:** An executive search firm. **Specializes in the areas of:** Health/Medical.

HOWARD ENTERPRISES
3925 North I-10 Service Road, Suite 117, Metairie LA 70002. 504/830-2935. **Contact:** Office Manager. **Description:** An executive search firm.

MDR & ASSOCIATES
436 Metairie Lawn Drive, Metairie LA 70001. 504/828-7637. **Contact:** Manager. **Description:** An executive search firm. **Specializes in the areas of:** Personnel/Labor Relations; Sales. **Other U.S. locations:** AR; CO.

MSI PHYSICIAN RECRUITERS
701 Poydras Street, Suite 3880, New Orleans LA 70139. 504/522-6700. **Contact:** Office Manager. **Description:** An executive search firm that places physicians. **Specializes in the areas of:** Health/Medical.

MANAGEMENT RECRUITERS INTERNATIONAL
1401 Hudson Lane, Suite 135, Monroe LA 71201. 318/322-2200. **Contact:** Manager. **Description:** An executive search firm. **Specializes in the areas of:** Engineering. **Corporate headquarters location:** Cleveland OH. **Other U.S. locations:** Nationwide.

MANAGEMENT RECRUITERS INTERNATIONAL
920 Pierremont, Suite 112, Shreveport LA 71106. 318/865-8411. **Contact:** Manager. **Description:** An executive search firm. **Specializes in the areas of:** Health/Medical; Information Systems; Manufacturing. **Corporate headquarters location:** Cleveland OH. **Other U.S. locations:** Nationwide.

MANAGEMENT RECRUITERS INTERNATIONAL
106 Village Street, Slidell LA 70458. 504/847-1900. **Fax:** 504/847-1984. **Contact:** Manager. **Description:** An executive search firm. **Specializes in the areas of:** Information Systems. **Corporate headquarters location:** Cleveland OH. **Other U.S. locations:** Nationwide.

MANAGEMENT RECRUITERS INTERNATIONAL
1408 Energy Center, 1100 Poydras Street, New Orleans LA 70163. 504/525-3888. **Contact:** Manager. **Description:** An executive search firm. **Corporate headquarters location:** Cleveland OH. **Other U.S. locations:** Nationwide.

MANAGEMENT RECRUITERS OF BATON ROUGE
P.O. Box 3553, Baton Rouge LA 70821-3553. 504/383-1234. **Contact:** Manager. **Description:** An executive search firm. **Specializes in the areas of:** Accounting/Auditing; Administration; Advertising; Architecture/Construction; Banking; Chemical; Communications; Computer Hardware/Software; Design; Electrical; Engineering; Food Industry; General Management; Health/Medical; Insurance; Legal; Manufacturing; Operations Management; Personnel/Labor Relations; Procurement; Publishing; Retail; Sales; Technical; Textiles; Transportation. **Corporate headquarters location:** Cleveland OH. **Other U.S. locations:** Nationwide.

MANAGEMENT RECRUITERS OF BATON ROUGE
SALES CONSULTANTS OF BATON ROUGE
2237 South Acadian Thruway, Suite 707, Baton Rouge LA 70808. 504/928-2212. **Fax:** 504/928-1109. **Contact:** Manager. **Description:** An executive search firm. **Specializes in the areas of:** Accounting/Auditing; Administration; Advertising; Architecture/Construction; Banking; Chemical; Communications; Computer Hardware/Software; Design; Electrical; Engineering; Food Industry; General Management; Health/Medical; Insurance; Legal; Manufacturing; Operations Management; Personnel/Labor Relations; Procurement; Publishing; Retail; Sales; Technical; Textiles; Transportation. **Corporate headquarters location:** Cleveland OH. **Other U.S. locations:** Nationwide.

MANAGEMENT RECRUITERS OF METAIRIE
SALES CONSULTANTS OF METAIRIE
P.O. Box 6605, Metairie LA 70009. 504/831-7333. **Contact:** Office Manager. **Description:** An executive search firm. Another division of Management Recruiters, CompuSearch, also operates at this location. **Specializes in the areas of:** Accounting/Auditing; Administration; Advertising; Architecture/Construction; Banking; Chemical; Communications; Computer Hardware/Software; Design; Electrical; Engineering; Food Industry; General Management; Health/Medical; Insurance; Legal; Manufacturing; Operations Management; Personnel/Labor Relations; Procurement; Publishing; Retail; Sales; Technical; Textiles; Transportation. **Corporate headquarters location:** Cleveland OH. **Other U.S. locations:** Nationwide.

RHEMA EMPLOYMENT AGENCY
1304 Bertrand Drive, Suite D5, Lafayette LA 70506. 318/234-8880. **Contact:** Manager. **Description:** An executive search firm. **Specializes in the areas of:** Maritime.

RIVER REGION PERSONNEL, INC.
1537 Metairie Road, Metairie LA 70005. 504/831-4746. **Fax:** 504/831-9916. **Contact:** Chuck Zamjohn, President. **Description:** A retainer and contingency search firm placing technical and professional candidates. **Specializes in the areas of:** Engineering; Personnel/Labor Relations. **Positions commonly filled include:** Buyer; Chemical Engineer; Civil Engineer; Electrical/Electronics Engineer; Industrial Engineer; Mechanical Engineer; Metallurgical Engineer; Petroleum Engineer. **Average salary range of placements:** More than $50,000. **Number of placements per year:** 1 - 49.

SANFORD ROSE ASSOCIATES
300 Mariners Plaza, Suite 321A, Mandeville LA 70448. 504/674-5050. **Fax:** 504/674-6670. **Contact:** Manager. **World Wide Web address:** http://www.sanfordrose.com. **Description:** An executive search firm. **Specializes in the areas of:** General Management; Medical Sales and Marketing. **Other U.S. locations:** Nationwide.

SNELLING PERSONNEL SERVICES
1500 Louisville Avenue, Monroe LA 71201. 318/387-6090. **Fax:** 318/361-6097. **Contact:** Wayne Williamson, President. **Description:** An executive search firm. Company pays fee. **Specializes in the areas of:** Accounting/Auditing; Administration; Banking; Computer Science/Software; Engineering; Health/Medical; Manufacturing; Personnel/Labor Relations; Sales. **Positions commonly filled include:** Accountant/Auditor; Bank Officer/Manager; Biological Scientist; Chemical Engineer; Chemist; Civil Engineer; Claim Representative; Computer Programmer; Draftsperson; Electrical/Electronics Engineer; Human Resources Manager; Industrial Engineer; Mechanical Engineer; Occupational Therapist; Paralegal; Pharmacist; Physical Therapist; Physician; Quality Control Supervisor; Registered Nurse; Respiratory Therapist; Restaurant/Food Service Manager; Systems Analyst. **Other U.S. locations:** Nationwide. **Number of placements per year:** 200 - 499.

SNELLING PERSONNEL SERVICES
7809 Jefferson Highway, Suite C-1, Baton Rouge LA 70809. 504/927-0096. **Contact:** Office Manager. **Description:** An executive search firm. **Specializes in the areas of:** Accounting/Auditing; Banking; Computer Hardware/Software; Engineering; Sales. **Other U.S. locations:** Nationwide. **Number of placements per year:** 50 - 99.

TALLEY & ASSOCIATES, INC.
TALLEY TEMPORARIES
1105 West Prien Lake Road, Suite D, Lake Charles LA 70601. 318/474-JOBS. **Fax:** 318/474-0885. **Contact:** Burt Bollotte, Manager. **Description:** A full-service executive search firm. **Specializes in the areas of:** Accounting/Auditing; Administration; Advertising; Architecture/Construction; Banking; Biology; Computer Science/Software; Engineering; Fashion; Finance; Food Industry; General Management; Health/Medical; Legal; Manufacturing; Personnel/Labor Relations; Publishing; Retail; Sales; Secretarial; Technical; Transportation. **Positions commonly filled include:** Accountant/Auditor; Adjuster; Administrative Manager; Advertising Clerk; Architect; Attorney; Bank Officer/Manager; Branch Manager; Broadcast Technician; Chemical Engineer; Chemist; Civil Engineer; Clerical Supervisor; Computer Programmer; Cost Estimator; Credit Manager; Customer Service Representative; Electrical/Electronics Engineer; Environmental Engineer; Financial Analyst; Industrial Engineer; Industrial Production Manager; Insurance Agent/Broker; Licensed Practical Nurse; Mechanical Engineer; MIS Specialist; Occupational Therapist; Paralegal; Pharmacist; Physical Therapist; Physician; Quality Control Supervisor; Radiological Technologist; Registered Nurse; Restaurant/Food Service Manager; Systems Analyst; Technical Writer/Editor; Typist/Word Processor; Video Maintenance Engineer.

TECHNICAL & PROFESSIONAL SOURCES
14726 Avalon Avenue, Baton Rouge LA 70816. 504/273-4001. **Fax:** 504/275-5807. **Contact:** Dennis Harris, Process Industry Specialist. **Description:** A retainer and contingency search firm. Company pays fee. **Specializes in the areas of:** Engineering; Industrial; Manufacturing; Sales. **Positions commonly filled include:** Aerospace Engineer; Chemical Engineer; Chemist; Electrical/Electronics Engineer; Industrial Engineer; Industrial Production Manager; Mechanical Engineer; Operations/Production Manager; Quality Control Supervisor; Services Sales Representative; Structural Engineer. **Average salary range of placements:** More than $50,000. **Number of placements per year:** 1 - 49.

PERMANENT EMPLOYMENT AGENCIES

ACCOUNTING PERSONNEL CONSULTANTS
STAT RESOURCES
210 Baronne Street, Suite 922, New Orleans LA 70112. 504/581-7800. **Contact:** Office Manager. **Description:** A permanent placement agency. **Specializes in the areas of:** Accounting/Auditing; Engineering.

ADVANTAGE PERSONNEL INC.
11224 Boardwalk Drive, Suite E1-1, Baton Rouge LA 70816. 504/273-8900. **Contact:** Office Manager. **Description:** A permanent placement agency.

CORPORATE CONNECTION INC.
201 St. Charles Avenue, New Orleans LA 70170. 504/582-1315. **Contact:** Manager. **Description:** A permanent employment agency that also provides some temporary placements.

DELTA PERSONNEL
111 Veterans Boulevard, Suite 1400, Metairie LA 70005. 504/833-5200. **Fax:** 504/833-5296. **Contact:** David Lawrence, President. **Description:** A permanent employment agency. Company pays fee. **Specializes in the areas of:** Engineering; General Management; Sales. **Positions commonly filled include:** Branch Manager; Chemical Engineer; Chemist; Civil Engineer; Customer Service Representative; Draftsperson; Electrical/Electronics Engineer; Industrial Engineer; Industrial Production Manager; Mechanical Engineer; Operations/Production Manager; Restaurant/Food Service Manager; Securities Sales Representative; Services Sales Representative; Structural Engineer. **Number of placements per year:** 1 - 49.

DRIGGERS & BLACKWELL PERSONNEL
1440 Goodwin Road, Ruston LA 71270. 318/251-0244. **Contact:** Manager. **Description:** A permanent placement agency.

LOUISIANA OFFICE OF EMPLOYMENT SECURITY
P.O. Box 271, Alexandria LA 71309. 318/487-5532. **Contact:** Office Manager. **Description:** A permanent employment agency. **Number of placements per year:** 1000+.

MEDFORCE PHYSICIAN SERVICES
3421 North Causeway Boulevard, Suite 503, Metairie LA 70002. 504/837-2002. **Fax:** 504/836-2831. **Contact:** Office Manager. **Description:** A permanent employment agency. Company pays fee. **Specializes in the areas of:** Health/Medical. **Positions commonly filled include:** Physician. **Number of placements per year:** 50 - 99.

MEDI-LEND NURSING SERVICES, INC.
6305 Allegiance Field, Suite 400, New Orleans LA 70122. 504/283-3767. **Fax:** 504/283-6004. **Contact:** Manager. **Description:** A permanent employment agency. **Specializes in the areas of:** Health/Medical. **Positions commonly filled include:** Licensed Practical Nurse; Registered Nurse. **Other U.S. locations:** FL; TX. **Average salary range of placements:** $30,000 - $50,000. **Number of placements per year:** 500 - 999.

OLSTEN PERSONNEL
BRIGGS LEGAL STAFFING
1555 Poydras Street, Suite 140, New Orleans LA 70116. 504/581-9401. **Contact:** Manager. **Description:** A permanent employment agency. Briggs Legal Staffing (also at this location) provides permanent placements for the legal industry. Company pays fee. **Specializes in the areas of:** Industrial; Legal; Secretarial. **Positions commonly filled include:** Accountant/Auditor; Blue-Collar Worker Supervisor; Clerical Supervisor; Computer Programmer; Credit Manager; Customer Service Representative; Human Resources Specialist; Paralegal; Typist/Word Processor. **Benefits available to temporary workers:** 401(k); Paid Holidays; Paid Vacation. **Average salary range of placements:** $20,000 - $29,999. **Number of placements per year:** 100 - 199.

SHIELL PERSONNEL
2040 North Causeway Boulevard, Mandeville LA 70471. 504/674-1616. **Contact:** Donald M. Shiell, Owner. **Description:** A permanent employment agency and executive search firm. Company pays fee. **Specializes in the areas of:** Health/Medical; Medical Device; Pharmaceutical; Sales. **Positions commonly filled include:** Accountant/Auditor; Chemical Engineer; Chemist; Environmental Engineer; Human Resources Manager; Marketing Manager; Mechanical Engineer; Sales Executive; Sales Manager; Services Sales Representative. **Corporate headquarters location:** New Orleans LA. **Average salary range of placements:** More than $50,000. **Number of placements per year:** 200 - 499.

TEMPORARY EMPLOYMENT AGENCIES

ASCENT CONSULTING GROUP
650 Poydras Street, Suite 2523, New Orleans LA 70130. 504/522-6611. **Toll-free phone:** 888/347-6622. **Fax:** 504/524-5701. **Contact:** Manager. **E-mail address:** ascent@cmq.com. **Description:** A temporary agency. Company pays fee. **Specializes in the areas of:** Accounting/Auditing; Administration; Computer Science/Software; Finance; Sales. **Positions commonly filled include:** Account Manager; Account Representative; Accountant; Administrative Assistant; Administrative Manager; Chief Financial Officer; Computer Operator; Computer Programmer; Controller; Cost Estimator; Credit Manager; Customer Service Representative; Database Manager; Finance Director; Financial Analyst; Human Resources Manager; Internet Services Manager; Management Analyst/Consultant; Market Research Analyst; MIS Specialist; Systems Analyst; Systems Manager; Technical Writer/Editor; Webmaster. **Average salary range of placements:** $30,000 - $50,000. **Number of placements per year:** 100 - 199.

INTERIM PERSONNEL
9634 Airline Highway, Suite 1A, Baton Rouge LA 70815. 504/925-5686. **Contact:** Paulette Scott, Operations Manager. **World Wide Web address:** http://www.interim.com. **Description:** A temporary agency. Company pays fee. **Specializes in the areas of:** Clerical; Engineering; Industrial; Technical. **Positions commonly filled include:** Accountant/Auditor; Administrative Assistant; Advertising Clerk; Bookkeeper; Chemical Engineer; Chemist; Clerk; Computer Operator; Computer Programmer; Construction Trade Worker; Customer Service Representative; Data Entry Clerk; Draftsperson; Driver; EDP Specialist; Electrical/Electronics Engineer; Factory Worker; Food Scientist/Technologist; Industrial Designer; Industrial Engineer; Legal Secretary; Light Industrial Worker; Mechanical Engineer; Medical Secretary; Receptionist; Systems Analyst; Technician; Typist/Word Processor. **Number of placements per year:** 1000+.

KEENAN STAFFING INC.
2800 Veterans Memorial Boulevard, Suite 213, Metairie LA 70002. 504/834-0511. **Fax:** 504/834-1301. **Contact:** Thomas Keenan, President. **Description:** A temporary agency. Company pays fee. **Specializes in the areas of:** Accounting/Auditing; Art/Design; Banking; Finance; Health/Medical; Insurance; Personnel/Labor Relations; Sales; Secretarial. **Positions commonly filled include:** Accountant/Auditor; Administrative Manager; Advertising Clerk; Branch Manager; Brokerage Clerk; Budget Analyst; Claim Representative; Clerical Supervisor; Credit Manager; Customer Service

Representative; Draftsperson; Financial Analyst; Geographer; Human Resources Specialist; Insurance Agent/Broker; Librarian; Management Trainee; Market Research Analyst; Medical Records Technician; Operations/Production Manager; Paralegal; Public Relations Specialist; Services Sales Representative; Typist/Word Processor. **Average salary range of placements:** $20,000 - $29,999. **Number of placements per year:** 500 - 999.

MANPOWER, INC.
100 Parkview Drive, Suite 30, New Iberia LA 70563. 318/367-7173. **Fax:** 318/367-7176. **Contact:** Rachelle Migues, Branch Manager. **Description:** A temporary service offering placements in industrial, clerical, and technical areas. Computer training courses are offered. **Specializes in the areas of:** Clerical; Computer Science/Software; Industrial; Technical. **Benefits available to temporary workers:** Medical Insurance; Paid Vacation.

NORRELL STAFFING SERVICES
3929 Veterans Memorial Boulevard, Suite 101, Metairie LA 70002-5613. 504/833-1868. **Fax:** 504/834-3839. **Contact:** Kathryn Paddack, Administrator. **Description:** A temporary agency. Founded in 1970. Company pays fee. **Specializes in the areas of:** Personnel/Labor Relations. **Positions commonly filled include:** Customer Service Representative; Typist/Word Processor. **Corporate headquarters location:** Atlanta GA. **Other U.S. locations:** Nationwide. **Average salary range of placements:** Less than $20,000. **Number of placements per year:** 500 - 999.

PREMIER STAFFING, INC.
P.O. Box 91107, Lafayette LA 70509. 318/896-4140. **Toll-free phone:** 800/349-4140. **Fax:** 318/896-9278. **Contact:** Manager. **Description:** A temporary agency which also provides permanent placement. Founded in 1990. Company pays fee. **Specializes in the areas of:** Architecture/Construction; Health/Medical. **Positions commonly filled include:** Construction Contractor; Construction Manager; Electrician; Landscape Architect; Licensed Practical Nurse; Occupational Therapist; Physical Therapist; Registered Nurse. **Corporate headquarters location:** This Location. **Other area locations:** New Iberia LA. **Average salary range of placements:** $20,000 - $29,999. **Number of placements per year:** 1 - 49.

PROFESSIONAL TEMPORARIES
1515 Poydras Street, Suite 1845, New Orleans LA 70112. 504/522-5665. **Fax:** 504/524-3248. **Contact:** Edgar Higginbotham, President. **Description:** A temporary agency. Company pays fee. **Specializes in the areas of:** Clerical; Light Industrial; Technical. **Positions commonly filled include:** Accountant/Auditor; Blue-Collar Worker Supervisor; Buyer; Customer Service Representative; Dental Assistant/Dental Hygienist; Draftsperson; Electrician; Landscape Architect; Management Trainee; Paralegal; Purchasing Agent/Manager; Services Sales Representative; Typist/Word Processor. **Average salary range of placements:** Less than $20,000. **Number of placements per year:** 200 - 499.

SPECIAL COUNSEL
1100 Poydras Street, Suite 1260, New Orleans LA 70163. 504/522-0133. **Fax:** 504/522-0195. **Contact:** Manager. **World Wide Web address:** http://www.specialcounsel.com. **Description:** A temporary and permanent employment agency. **Specializes in the areas of:** Legal.

TECH 2000 SERVICES & STAFFING, INC.
11715 Bricksome Avenue, Suite B2, Baton Rouge LA 70816. 504/293-9908. **Fax:** 504/293-9367. **Contact:** Julia J. Collins, Chief Operating Officer. **Description:** A temporary agency. Founded in 1994. Company pays fee. **Specializes in the areas of:** Technical. **Positions commonly filled include:** Biochemist; Biological Scientist; Chemical Engineer; Chemist; Clinical Lab Technician; Design Engineer; Designer; Draftsperson; Environmental Engineer; Food Scientist/Technologist; Geologist/Geophysicist; Laboratory Technician; Mechanical Engineer; Quality Control Supervisor. **Benefits available to temporary workers:** Dental Insurance; Life Insurance; Medical Insurance; Paid Holidays; Vision Insurance. **Corporate headquarters location:** This Location. **Other U.S. locations:** Pasadena TX. **Average salary range of placements:** $30,000 - $50,000. **Number of placements per year:** 50 - 99.

TECHNICAL RESOURCE STAFFING SERVICES
11715 Brookson Avenue, Suite A6, Baton Rouge LA 70816. 504/296-8000. **Fax:** 504/291-6800. **Contact:** Branch Manager. **Description:** A temporary agency. **Specializes in the areas of:** Accounting/Auditing; Computer Science/Software; Food Industry; General Management; Industrial; Manufacturing; Retail; Secretarial. **Positions commonly filled include:** Accountant/Auditor; Administrative Manager; Advertising Clerk; Bank Officer/Manager; Branch Manager; Claim Representative; Clerical Supervisor; Clinical Lab Technician; Computer Programmer; Cost Estimator; Credit Manager; Customer Service Representative; Draftsperson; Health Services Manager; Industrial Production Manager; Management Trainee; Operations/Production Manager; Quality Control Supervisor; Restaurant/Food Service Manager; Software Engineer; Systems Analyst; Typist/Word Processor. **Corporate headquarters location:** Orange TX. **Number of placements per year:** 500 - 999.

WESTERN STAFF SERVICES
2015 Gus Kaplan Drive, Alexandria LA 71301. 318/487-0416. **Fax:** 318/442-5704. **Contact:** Kathy Littlepage, Recruiter. **E-mail address:** westaff@centuryinter.net. **World Wide Web address:** http://www.ax.centuryinter.net/. **Description:** A temporary agency. Company pays fee. **Specializes in the areas of:** Clerical; Health/Medical; Light Industrial; Personnel/Labor Relations; Secretarial; Technical. **Positions commonly filled include:** Carpenter; Medical Records Technician; Operations/Production Manager; Paralegal; Typist/Word Processor. **Benefits available to temporary workers:** Medical Insurance. **Corporate headquarters location:** Walnut Creek CA. **Other U.S. locations:** Nationwide. **Average salary range of placements:** Less than $20,000. **Number of placements per year:** 200 - 499.

WESTERN STAFF SERVICES
601 Poydras Street, Suite 2425, New Orleans LA 70130. 504/529-2338. **Contact:** Allison Thomas, Manager. **Description:** A temporary agency. Company pays fee. **Specializes in the areas of:** Accounting/Auditing; Administration; Computer Science/Software; Food Industry; Insurance; Legal; Personnel/Labor Relations; Secretarial. **Positions commonly filled include:** Accountant/Auditor; Claim Representative; Clerical Supervisor; Computer Programmer; Customer Service Representative; Draftsperson; Human Resources Specialist; Medical Records Technician; Paralegal; Systems Analyst; Technical Writer/Editor; Typist/Word Processor. **Corporate headquarters location:** Walnut Creek CA. **Other U.S. locations:** Nationwide. **Average salary range of placements:** $20,000 - $29,999.

X TECHS
4829 Prytania Street, Suite 102, New Orleans LA 70115. 504/895-8324. **Fax:** 504/895-8353. **Contact:** Patricia Hamilton, President. **Description:** A temporary

agency. **Specializes in the areas of:** Health/Medical. **Positions commonly filled include:** Clinical Lab Technician; Occupational Therapist; Physical Therapist; Radiological Technologist; Surgical Technician. **Average salary range of placements:** $30,000 - $50,000. **Number of placements per year:** 50 - 99.

CONTRACT SERVICES FIRMS

CDI ENGINEERING
One Lakeside Place, Suite 608, Lake Charles LA 70601. 318/439-1659. **Contact:** Manager. **World Wide Web address:** http://www.cdicorp.com. **Description:** A contract services firm. **Corporate headquarters location:** Philadelphia PA. **Other U.S. locations:** Nationwide. **International locations:** Worldwide. **Specializes in the areas of:** Engineering.

CONCRETE SOLUTIONS INC.
9151 Interline Road, Baton Rouge LA 70809. 504/923-2026. **Contact:** Manager. **Description:** A contract services firm.

UNIVERSAL PERSONNEL
4949 Bullard Avenue, Suite 190, New Orleans LA 70128. 504/241-1724. **Toll-free phone:** 800/245-8274. **Fax:** 504/246-1815. **Contact:** Ron Leonard, General Sales Manager. **E-mail address:** jobsearch @universalpersonnel.com. **Description:** A contract services firm that also provides permanent placements. **Specializes in the areas of:** Engineering; Technical. **Positions commonly filled include:** Applications Engineer; Architect; Biomedical Engineer; Chemical Engineer; Civil Engineer; Computer Animator; Computer Operator; Computer Programmer; Construction and Building Inspector; Cost Estimator; Database Manager; Design Engineer; Draftsperson; Electrical/Electronics Engineer; Environmental Engineer; Industrial Engineer; Internet Services Manager; Licensed Practical Nurse; Mechanical Engineer; Physical Therapist; Project Manager; Registered Nurse; Respiratory Therapist; Sales Engineer; Software Engineer; Structural Engineer; Systems Analyst; Technical Writer/Editor. **Benefits available to temporary workers:** 401(k); Life Insurance; Medical Insurance; Paid Holidays; Paid Vacation. **Corporate headquarters location:** This Location. **Other U.S. locations:** Fort Walton FL; Biloxi MS. **Average salary range of placements:** $30,000 - $50,000. **Number of placements per year:** 200 - 499.

CAREER/OUTPLACEMENT COUNSELING FIRMS

CAREERPRO RESUME SERVICE
1320 South Carollton Avenue, New Orleans LA 70118. 504/524-1335. **Contact:** Office Manager. **Description:** A career/outplacement counseling and resume writing service.

PORT CITY ENTERPRISES
P.O. Box 113, Port Allen LA 70767. 504/344-1142. **Fax:** 504/344-1192. **Contact:** Regina L. Slaton, Executive Director. **Description:** A career/outplacement counseling agency that provides supported employment and shelter employment to persons with severe disabilities. **Specializes in the areas of:** Nonprofit; Personnel/Labor Relations. **Positions commonly filled include:** Accountant/Auditor; Administrative Manager; Employment Interviewer. **Number of placements per year:** 1 - 49.

SUCCESS IMAGES
7330 Highland Road, Suite 120, Baton Rouge LA 70808. 504/769-2307. **Contact:** Shirley White, Ed.D., President. **Description:** A career/outplacement counseling agency.

MAINE

EXECUTIVE SEARCH FIRMS

ACORN FINANCIAL GROUP
P.O. Box 450, Kennebunk ME 04083. 207/985-8776. **Contact:** Manager. **Description:** An executive search firm. **Specializes in the areas of:** Accounting/Auditing.

ALL STAFF PLACEMENT SERVICES
AMERICAN PERSONNEL
550 Forest Avenue, Portland ME 04104. 207/774-0114. **Contact:** Manager. **Description:** All Staff Placement Services is an executive search firm that provides permanent placements in all fields. American Personnel (also at this location) is a contract services agency.

CAREER MANAGEMENT ASSOCIATES
72 Pine Street, Portland ME 04102-3736. 207/780-1125. **Fax:** 207/780-1253. **Contact:** Mark Rajotte, President. **Description:** An executive search and career development firm. Company pays fee. **Specializes in the areas of:** Accounting/Auditing; Administration; Advertising; Banking; Engineering; Finance; General Management; Health/Medical; Insurance; Manufacturing; Nonprofit; Publishing; Retail; Sales. **Positions commonly filled include:** Accountant/Auditor; Actuary; Budget Analyst; Chemical Engineer; Civil Engineer; Claim Representative; Computer Programmer; Credit Manager; Customer Service Representative; Financial Analyst; MIS Specialist; Sales Manager; Services Sales Representative; Software Engineer; Systems Analyst; Underwriter/Assistant Underwriter. **Average salary range of placements:** $30,000 - $85,000. **Number of placements per year:** 1 - 49.

COLEMAN & PATRICK, INC.
P.O. Box 543, West Boothbay Harbor ME 04575. 207/633-5655. **Contact:** Manager. **Description:** An executive search firm that specializes in the retail and service industries.

COMPUSOURCE
56 Industrial Park Road, Suite 6, Saco ME 04072. 207/284-1188. **Contact:** Lincoln Page, President. **Description:** An executive search firm. **Specializes in the areas of:** Computer Hardware/Software; Computer Operations; Computer Programming.

EXECUTIVE SEARCH OF NEW ENGLAND
131 Ocean Street, South Portland ME 04106. 207/741-4100. **Fax:** 207/741-4110. **Contact:** Charles Kimball, Systems Specialist. **World Wide Web address:** http://www.nationaljobbank.com. **Description:** An executive search firm and one of the largest professional temporary placement firms in Maine. Company pays fee. **Specializes in the areas of:** Accounting/Auditing; Administration; Banking; Computer Science/Software; Finance; General Management; Manufacturing; Personnel/Labor Relations; Sales. **Positions commonly filled include:** Accountant/Auditor; Adjuster; Bank Officer/Manager; Branch Manager; Budget Analyst; Claim Representative; Computer Programmer; Credit Manager; Industrial Production Manager; Insurance Agent/Broker; Mechanical Engineer; Physical Therapist; Physician; Registered Nurse; Systems Analyst. **Average salary range of placements:** $30,000 - $50,000.

GOODRICH CONSULTING
P.O. Box 4534, Portland ME 04112. 207/799-6192. **Contact:** Wayne Goodrich, President. **Description:** An executive search firm. **Specializes in the areas of:** Engineering; Industrial; Manufacturing; Personnel/Labor Relations; Sales. **Positions commonly filled include:** Accountant/Auditor; Buyer; Ceramics Engineer; Electrical/Electronics Engineer; Industrial Engineer; Manufacturing Engineer; Mechanical Engineer; Operations/Production Manager; Purchasing Agent/Manager; Sales Representative. **Number of placements per year:** 1 - 49.

GREAT MOOSE LAKE CORPORATION
605 U.S. Route 1, Scarborough ME 04074. 207/883-6561. **Toll-free phone:** 800/434-6561. **Fax:** 207/883-2964. **Contact:** Chris Griffith, President. **E-mail address:** chrisg@selectech.com. **World Wide Web address:** http://www.selectech.com. **Description:** A high-tech recruiting and placement firm. Great Moose Lake Corporation focuses on permanent placements in information technology for Maine only. **Specializes in the areas of:** Information Technology. **Positions commonly filled include:** Computer Programmer; MIS Specialist; Multimedia Designer; Software Engineer; Systems Analyst; Technical Writer/Editor; Telecommunications Manager. **Average salary range of placements:** More than $50,000. **Number of placements per year:** 1 - 49.

JOHN JAY & COMPANY
44 Exchange Street, Suite 305, Portland ME 04101. 207/772-6951. **Fax:** 207/772-0159. **Contact:** Jay Hotchkiss, SPHR, President. **Description:** A small, consulting-focused executive search firm. Company pays fee. **Specializes in the areas of:** Biology; Engineering; General Management; Health/Medical; Industrial; Manufacturing; Personnel/Labor Relations; Sales; Technical. **Positions commonly filled include:** Accountant/Auditor; Administrative Manager; Attorney; Bank Officer/Manager; Biochemist; Biological Scientist; Biomedical Engineer; Branch Manager; Credit Manager; Design Engineer; Electrical/Electronics Engineer; Human Resources Manager; Industrial Engineer; Management Analyst/Consultant; Mechanical Engineer; Physician; Quality Control Supervisor; Restaurant/Food Service Manager; Strategic Relations Manager; Structural Engineer. **Average salary range of placements:** More than $50,000. **Number of placements per year:** 1 - 49.

LAKE MEDICAL ASSOCIATES
12 Elm Street, Gorham ME 04038. 207/839-4004. **Fax:** 207/839-2118. **Contact:** Jack Schraeter, CEO. **E-mail address:** lakemed@aol.com. **Description:** A retainer and contingency search firm specializing in health care placements. Company pays fee. **Specializes in the areas of:** Health/Medical. **Positions commonly filled include:** Physical Therapist; Physician. **Average salary range of placements:** More than $50,000. **Number of placements per year:** 1 - 49.

NATIONAL RECRUITERS OF MAINE, INC.
P.O. Box 8257, Portland ME 04104. 207/774-0366. **Fax:** 207/774-0370. **Contact:** Warren Mahan, President. **Description:** An executive search firm. Company pays fee. **Specializes in the areas of:** Engineering; Industrial; Manufacturing; Paper; Sales; Technical. **Positions commonly filled include:** Biological Scientist; Chemical Engineer; Chemist; Designer; Development Manager; Electrical/Electronics Engineer; Mechanical Engineer; Project Engineer; Sales Manager; Services Sales Representative; Stationary Engineer. **Number of placements per year:** 1 - 49.

NORTHERN CONSULTANTS
P.O. Box 220, Hampden ME 04444. 207/862-2323. **Contact:** James D. Brown, SPE, President. **Description:** An executive search firm.

PEMBERTON & ASSOCIATES
193 Exchange Street, Portland ME 04104. 207/775-1772. **Contact:** Manager. **Description:** An executive search firm.

THE PORTER HAMEL GROUP, INC.
295 Forest Avenue, Suite 140, Portland ME 04101. 207/828-1134. **Fax:** 207/828-1540. **Contact:** Jeff Porter, President. **E-mail address:** phgroup@ix.netcom.com. **Description:** A retainer and contingency search firm focusing on the placement of operations and technical professionals in the food manufacturing industry. Company pays fee. **Specializes in the areas of:** Engineering; Food Industry; Manufacturing; Personnel/Labor Relations. **Positions commonly filled include:** Food Scientist/Technologist; Industrial Engineer; Operations/ Production Manager; Quality Control Supervisor. **Corporate headquarters location:** This location. **Other U.S. locations:** Lansdale PA. **Average salary range of placements:** More than $50,000. **Number of placements per year:** 1 - 49.

PRO SEARCH, INC.
P.O. Box 7489, Portland ME 04112. 207/775-7600. **Contact:** Manager. **Description:** An executive search firm. **Specializes in the areas of:** Accounting/Auditing; Customer Service; Information Systems; Sales.

RAND ASSOCIATES
204 Lafayette Center, Kennebunk ME 04043. 207/985-7700. **Contact:** Manager. **Description:** An executive search firm with an emphasis on the manufacturing and financial services industries.

PERMANENT EMPLOYMENT AGENCIES

BONNEY PERSONNEL SERVICES
37 Park Street, Lewiston ME 04240. 207/783-7000. **Contact:** Manager. **Description:** A permanent employment agency that also offers temp-to-perm placements. **Other area locations:** Portland ME.

BONNEY STAFFING & TRAINING
477 Congress Street, Portland ME 04101. 207/773-3829. **Fax:** 207/773-1864. **Contact:** Joel Gratwick, CPC, Owner. **Description:** A permanent employment agency. **Specializes in the areas of:** Accounting/Auditing; Finance. **Other area locations:** Lewiston ME.

CREATIVE WORK SYSTEMS
168 Lisbon Street, Lewiston ME 04240. 207/795-6737. **Contact:** Manager. **Description:** A nonprofit, permanent employment agency that provides employment for the disabled.

EMPLOYMENT TRUST INC. (ETI)
470 Forest Avenue, Suite 301, Portland ME 04101. 207/775-1924. **Fax:** 207/775-2505. **Contact:** Richard C. Petersen, President. **Description:** A permanent employment agency providing employment for disadvantaged workers.

GOODWILL PROFESSIONAL SERVICES
347 Leighton Road, Augusta ME 04330. 207/626-0170. **Contact:** Manager. **Description:** A permanent employment agency.

INITIAL STAFFING SERVICES
11 Free Street, Portland ME 04101. 207/774-5300. **Contact:** Office Manager. **Description:** A permanent employment agency.

JOBS UNLIMITED/IDEAL SOLUTIONS
P.O. Box 334, Moody ME 04054. 207/646-9595. **Contact:** Manager. **Description:** A permanent employment agency. **Specializes in the areas of:** Hotel/Restaurant.

LEBEL PERSONNEL
99 Larrabee Road, Westbrook ME 04092. 207/854-2422. **Contact:** Manager. **Description:** A permanent employment agency.

PAGEMPLOYMENT
193 Exchange Street, Bangor ME 04401. 207/945-3301. **Contact:** Manager. **Description:** A permanent employment agency.

PAPER INDUSTRY RECRUITMENT (PIR)
36 Main Street, Gorham ME 04038. 207/839-2633. **Fax:** 207/839-2634. **Contact:** Maynard Charron, Owner. **E-mail address:** pir@gwi.net. **World Wide Web address:** http://www.ccsme.com/pir/. **Description:** A permanent employment agency. Company pays fee. **Specializes in the areas of:** Engineering; Industrial; Manufacturing; Paper. **Positions commonly filled include:** Chemical Engineer; Chemist; Designer; Electrical/Electronics Engineer; General Manager; Human Resources Manager; Mechanical Engineer; Quality Control Supervisor. **Number of placements per year:** 1 - 49.

PHOENIX INDUSTRIES
230 Bomarc Road, Bangor ME 04401. 207/941-2895. **Contact:** Manager. **Description:** Provides employment for people with mental and physical disabilities.

PORTLAND NANNIES
P.O. Box 9739-1148, Portland ME 04104. 207/871-0665. **Contact:** Manager. **Description:** A nanny placement agency. **Specializes in the areas of:** Child Care, In-Home.

RO-LAN ASSOCIATES, INC.
86 Main Street, Auburn ME 04210. 207/784-1010. **Fax:** 207/782-3446. **Contact:** Rolande L. LaPointe, President. **Description:** An employment agency that provides permanent, temp-to-perm, and temporary placements, as well as resume writing services. Company pays fee. **Positions commonly filled include:** Account Representative; Accountant; Administrative Assistant; Computer Operator; Computer Programmer; Customer Service Representative; Database Manager; Electrician; Graphic Artist; Health Services Manager; Industrial Engineer; Industrial Production Manager; Licensed Practical Nurse; Mechanical Engineer; MIS Specialist; Paralegal; Production Manager; Registered Nurse; Restaurant/Food Service Manager; Sales Executive; Software Engineer; Systems Analyst; Typist/Word Processor. **Number of placements per year:** 1000+.

SPRINGBORN STAFFING SERVICE
130 Middle Street, Portland ME 04101. 207/761-8367. **Contact:** Manager. **Description:** A permanent employment agency.

TAD RESOURCES INTERNATIONAL
400 Riverside Street, Portland ME 04103. 207/797-8600. **Contact:** Manager. **Description:** A permanent employment agency. **Specializes in the areas of:** Technical.

TWIN CITY EMPLOYMENT SERVICE
159 State Street, Bangor ME 04401. 207/942-0977. **Contact:** Manager. **Description:** A permanent employment agency.

TEMPORARY EMPLOYMENT AGENCIES

ACCOMPLISHED PROFESSIONALS
P.O. Box 7040, Portland ME 04112. 207/773-4749. **Fax:** 207/773-2645. **Contact:** Louis LaPierre, President. **Description:** A temporary employment agency. Company pays fee. **Specializes in the areas of:** Accounting/Auditing; Administration; Banking; Computer Science/Software; Finance; General Management; Insurance; Manufacturing; Personnel/ Labor Relations; Secretarial. **Positions commonly filled include:** Accountant/Auditor; Actuary; Adjuster; Administrative Manager; Bank Officer/Manager; Branch Manager; Computer Programmer; Cost Estimator; Credit Manager; Customer Service Representative; Financial Analyst; General Manager; Health Services Worker; Insurance Agent/Broker; MIS Specialist; Paralegal; Quality Control Supervisor; Software Engineer; Systems Analyst; Technical Writer/Editor; Typist/Word Processor; Underwriter/ Assistant Underwriter. **Average salary range of placements:** $30,000 - $50,000. **Number of placements per year:** 50 - 99.

ASK, INC.
11 Union Street, Rockland ME 04841. 207/594-8418. **Fax:** 207/594-9090. **Contact:** Joanne Miller, President. **Description:** A temporary agency focusing on clerical positions. Ask, Inc. also provides permanent placement. **Specializes in the areas of:** Accounting/Auditing; General Management; Legal; Publishing; Sales; Secretarial. **Positions commonly filled include:** Accountant/Auditor; Administrative Manager; Advertising Clerk; Bank Officer/Manager; Branch Manager; Claim Representative; Clerical Supervisor; Computer Programmer; General Manager; Paralegal; Public Relations Specialist; Systems Analyst; Typist/Word Processor. **Number of placements per year:** 100 - 199.

AT WORK PERSONNEL SERVICE
43 Acme Road, Brewer ME 04412. 207/989-0824. **Toll-free phone:** 800/947-2166. **Contact:** Roni White, Service Coordinator. **Description:** A temporary agency that places candidates on temporary and temporary-to-permanent assignments. Company pays fee. **Specializes in the areas of:** Accounting/Auditing; Architecture/Construction; Education; Finance; Food Industry; General Management; Health/Medical; Industrial; Insurance; Legal; Manufacturing; Retail; Sales; Secretarial; Transportation. **Positions commonly filled include:** Accountant/Auditor; Actuary; Adjuster; Administrative Manager; Bank Officer/Manager; Branch Manager; Claim Representative; Clinical Lab Technician; Computer Programmer; Construction and Building Inspector; Construction Contractor; Cost Estimator; Credit Manager; Customer Service Representative; Draftsperson; Editor; Education Administrator; EEG Technologist; EKG Technician; Electrician; Emergency Medical Technician; Financial Analyst; Food Scientist/Technologist; Human Service Worker; Industrial Production Manager; Insurance Agent/Broker; Internet Services Manager; Librarian; Licensed Practical Nurse; Management Analyst/ Consultant; Manufacturer's/Wholesaler's Sales Rep.; Medical Records Technician; MIS Specialist; Paralegal; Physical Therapist; Quality Control Supervisor; Radiological Technologist; Real Estate Agent; Registered Nurse; Respiratory Therapist; Restaurant/ Food Service Manager; Services Sales Representative; Systems Analyst; Telecommunications Manager; Typist/Word Processor; Video Production Coordinator. **Benefits available to temporary workers:** Medical Insurance. **Corporate headquarters location:** Brooks ME. **Average salary range of placements:** Less than $20,000. **Number of placements per year:** 200 - 499.

TECHNICAL AID CORPORATION
71 Hospital Street, Augusta ME 04330. 207/622-5352. **Contact:** Manager. **Description:** A temporary agency. **Other U.S. locations:** Nationwide. **Specializes in the areas of:** Technical.

TEMPO EMPLOYMENT SERVICE
P.O. Box 31, Presque Isle ME 04769. 207/764-0772. **Fax:** 207/764-2620. **Contact:** Recruiter. **Description:** A temporary employment agency. **Specializes in the areas of:** Retail; Secretarial. **Positions commonly filled include:** Accountant/Auditor; Automotive Mechanic; Broadcast Technician; Budget Analyst; Construction and Building Inspector; Construction Contractor; Customer Service Representative; Health Services Manager; Human Resources Specialist; Typist/Word Processor. **Average salary range of placements:** Less than $20,000. **Number of placements per year:** 200 - 499.

CONTRACT SERVICES FIRMS

COMBINED RESOURCES INC.
67 Minot Avenue, Auburn ME 04210. 207/782-8246. **Contact:** Manager. **Description:** A contract services firm. **Specializes in the areas of:** Human Services.

GLOBAL ENGINEERS, INC.
P.O. Box 72, Bailey Island ME 04003-0782. 207/833-2800. **Fax:** 207/833-0021. **Contact:** Candice Wright, Manager. **E-mail address:** jobs@globalengineers.com. **World Wide Web address:** http://www.globalengineers.com. **Description:** A contract services firm that provides technical personnel for short-term and permanent positions. Company pays fee. **Specializes in the areas of:** Engineering; Technical. **Positions commonly filled include:** Biomedical Engineer; Chemical Engineer; Civil Engineer; Design Engineer; Draftsperson; Electrical/Electronics Engineer; Environmental Engineer; Industrial Engineer; Mechanical Engineer; Petroleum Engineer; Software Engineer; Stationary Engineer; Structural Engineer. **Benefits available to temporary workers:** Housing Allowance; Travel Allowance. **Average salary range of placements:** $30,000 - $50,000.

NEW ENGLAND HOME HEALTH CARE
P.O. Box 722, Bangor ME 04402-0722. 207/945-3374. **Toll-free phone:** 800/287-0338. **Fax:** 207/942-1022. **Contact:** Brenda Gore, Human Resource Manager. **Description:** A contract services firm. **Specializes in the areas of:** Health/Medical. **Positions commonly filled include:** Certified Nursing Aide; Data Entry Clerk; Human Resources Manager; Licensed Practical Nurse; Registered Nurse; Secretary. **Average salary range of placements:** Less than $20,000. **Number of placements per year:** 50 - 99.

MARYLAND

EXECUTIVE SEARCH FIRMS

ACCESS ASSOCIATES INC.
1107 Kenilworth Drive, Suite 307, Towson MD 20874. 410/821-7190. **Contact:** Manager. **Description:** An executive search firm.

ACCOUNTANTS EXECUTIVE SEARCH
ACCOUNTANTS ON CALL
201 North Charles Street, Suite 1106, Baltimore MD 21202. 410/685-5700. **Fax:** 410/685-5736. **Contact:** Manager. **Description:** An executive search firm. Accountants On Call (also at this location) is a temporary agency. **Specializes in the areas of:** Accounting/Auditing; Banking; Finance.

AUTO CAREERS
11700 Rutledge Road, Timonium MD 21093-2021. 410/561-1818. **Fax:** 410/561-5923. **Contact:** John O'Hare, President. **Description:** An executive search firm operating on a retainer basis that focuses on the retail automotive industry. **Specializes in the areas of:** Automotive; Sales. **Positions commonly filled include:** Accountant/Auditor; Automotive Mechanic. **Average salary range of placements:** More than $50,000. **Number of placements per year:** 50 - 99.

D.W. BAIRD & ASSOCIATES
10751 Falls Road, Suite 250, Lutherville MD 21093. 410/339-7670. **Contact:** David Baird, President. **Description:** An executive search firm. Company pays fee. **Specializes in the areas of:** Engineering; General Management; Industrial; Manufacturing; Sales; Technical. **Positions commonly filled include:** Chemical Engineer; Chemist; Electrical/Electronics Engineer; Environmental Engineer; General Manager; Industrial Engineer; Mechanical Engineer; Plant Manager; Quality Control Supervisor. **Average salary range of placements:** More than $50,000. **Number of placements per year:** 1 - 49.

BEAR TREES CONSULTING INC.
249 Blaze Climber Way, Rockville MD 20852. 301/217-5976. **Fax:** 301/309-8769. **Contact:** Brad Lewis, President. **E-mail address:** blewis5950 @aol.com. **Description:** An executive search firm operating on both retainer and contingency bases. Company pays fee. **Specializes in the areas of:** Computer Science/Software; Sales; Technical. **Positions commonly filled include:** Computer Programmer; MIS Specialist; Multimedia Designer; Software Engineer; Systems Analyst; Technical Writer/Editor; Telecommunications Manager. **Average salary range of placements:** More than $50,000. **Number of placements per year:** 100 - 199.

BLUE CHIP STAFFING SERVICE
120 East Baltimore Street, Suite 2220, Baltimore MD 21202. 410/752-8367. **Contact:** Office Manager. **Description:** An executive search firm.

BRANDJES ASSOCIATES
16 South Calvert Street, Suite 500, Baltimore MD 21202. 410/547-6887. **Fax:** 410/727-2489. **Contact:** Michael Brandjes, President. **Description:** An executive search firm. **Specializes in the areas of:** Finance.

BRINDISI SEARCH
10751 Falls Road, Suite 250, Lutherville MD 21093. 410/339-7673. **Contact:** Manager. **Description:** An executive search firm. **Specializes in the areas of:** Human Resources.

CAPLAN ASSOCIATES
28 Allegheny Avenue, Suite 600, Baltimore MD 21204. 410/821-9351. **Fax:** 410/583-1901. **Contact:** Robert Caplan, President. **Description:** An executive search firm. Company pays fee. **Specializes in the areas of:** Accounting/Auditing; Finance; Health/Medical; Manufacturing; Personnel/Labor Relations; Retail; Sales. **Positions commonly filled include:** Accountant/Auditor; Budget Analyst; Buyer; Credit Manager; Health Services Manager; Marketing Specialist; Purchasing Agent/Manager; Services Sales Representative. **Average salary range of placements:** $30,000 - $50,000. **Number of placements per year:** 50 - 99.

COLUMBIA CONSULTING
8323 Cherry Lane, Suite A13, Laurel MD 20707. 301/470-1555. **Contact:** Manager. **Description:** An executive search firm. **Specializes in the areas of:** Computer Hardware/Software; Information Systems; Information Technology.

COMPREHENSIVE SEARCH GROUP
201 West Padonia Road, Suite 101, Timonium MD 21093. 410/252-8911. **Contact:** Manager. **Description:** An executive search firm. **Specializes in the areas of:** Sales.

COMPUTER MANAGEMENT INC.
809 Glen Eagle Court, Suite 205, Towson MD 21286. 410/583-0050. **Fax:** 410/494-9410. **Contact:** Janet Miller, President. **Description:** An executive search firm that focuses on the placement of technical professionals. Company pays fee. **Specializes in the areas of:** Computer Operations; Information Systems. **Positions commonly filled include:** Computer Programmer; Network Engineer; Software Engineer; Systems Analyst. **Number of placements per year:** 1 - 49.

COMPUTRADE, INC.
51 Monroe Street, Suite 1210, Rockville MD 20850. 301/309-6800. **Contact:** George Schnabel, Managing Director. **Description:**An executive search firm that focuses on financial and investment management staffing. Company pays fee. **Specializes in the areas of:** Finance. **Positions commonly filled include:** Financial Analyst. **Average salary range of placements:** More than $50,000. **Number of placements per year:** 50 - 99.

COMTEX, INC.
12024 Blackberry Terrace, North Potomac MD 20878. 301/340-6963. **Fax:** 301/340-7008. **Contact:** Lynn Argain, Principal. **E-mail address:** comtex@ erols.com. **Description:** An executive search firm operating on both retained and contingency bases. Company pays fee. **Specializes in the areas of:** Computer Hardware/Software; Sales; Technical. **Positions commonly filled include:** Account Manager; Account Representative; Applications Engineer; Branch Manager; Database Manager; Design Engineer; Internet Services Manager; Sales Engineer; Sales Executive; Sales Representative; Software Engineer; Systems Engineer; Webmaster. **Average salary range of placements:** More than $50,000. **Number of placements per year:** 100 - 199.

CROSS COUNTRY CONSULTANTS, INC.
FALLSTAFF SEARCH
111 Warren Road, Suite 4B, Hunt Valley MD 21030. 410/666-1100. **Contact:** Sheldon Gottesfeld, President. **Description:** An executive search firm. Fallstaff Search (also at this location) is an executive search firm that specializes in health care, sales, and industrial positions. **NOTE:** Resumes for Fallstaff Search should be addressed to Robert Chertkof,

President. **Specializes in the areas of:** Accounting/Auditing; Engineering; Finance. **Number of placements per year:** 50 - 99.

EMPLOYER EMPLOYEE EXCHANGE, INC.
200 East Joppa Road, Suite 304, Towson MD 21286. 410/821-1900. **Toll-free phone:** 800/821-1902. **Fax:** 410/821-1904. **Contact:** Mike Worrell, Technical Recruiter. **E-mail address:** eee11@aol.com. **Description:** An executive search firm. Company pays fee. **Specializes in the areas of:** Administration; Computer Science/Software; Engineering; Sales; Secretarial; Technical. **Positions commonly filled include:** Accountant/Auditor; Chemical Engineer; Chemist; Civil Engineer; Computer Programmer; Customer Service Representative; Draftsperson; Electrical/Electronics Engineer; Industrial Engineer; MIS Specialist; Software Engineer; Structural Engineer; Systems Analyst; Technical Writer/Editor; Typist/Word Processor. **Benefits available to temporary workers:** Bonus Award/Plan; Medical Insurance; Paid Holidays; Paid Vacation. **Average salary range of placements:** $30,000 - $50,000. **Number of placements per year:** 100 - 199.

EXECUTIVE DYNAMICS, INC.
1107 Kenilworth Drive, Suite 208, Towson MD 21204. 410/494-1400. **Contact:** Office Manager. **Description:** An executive search firm operating on a contingency basis.

EXECUTIVE PLACEMENT ASSOCIATES
6001 Montrose Road, Suite 702, Rockville MD 20852. 301/231-8150. **Fax:** 301/881-2918. **Contact:** Mark Suss, President. **Description:** An executive search firm. Company pays fee. **Specializes in the areas of:** Advertising; Retail. **Positions commonly filled include:** Branch Manager; Buyer; District Manager; General Manager; Human Resources Manager; Operations/Production Manager; Store Manager; Wholesale and Retail Buyer. **Number of placements per year:** 50 - 99.

EXECUTIVE RECRUITERS
7315 Wisconsin Avenue, Suite 333E, Bethesda MD 20814. 301/469-3100. **Contact:** Office Manager. **Description:** An executive search firm specializing in retail management.

FALLSTAFF SEARCH
111 Warren Road, Suite 4B, Hunt Valley MD 21030. 410/666-1100. **Fax:** 410/666-1119. **Contact:** Office Manager. **Description:** An executive search firm. **Specializes in the areas of:** Health/Medical; Sales. **Positions commonly filled include:** Biomedical Engineer; Chemical Engineer; Civil Engineer; Property and Real Estate Manager. **Number of placements per year:** 100 - 199.

A.G. FISHKIN AND ASSOCIATES, INC.
P.O. Box 34413, Bethesda MD 20827. 301/770-4944. **Fax:** 301/983-0415. **Contact:** Anita Fishkin, President. **E-mail address:** afishkin@us.net. **Description:** An executive search firm operating on both retained and contingency bases. Company pays fee. **Specializes in the areas of:** Computer Hardware/Software; Data Communications; Information Technology; Sales; Technical; Telecommunications; Wireless Communications. **Positions commonly filled include:** Computer Programmer; Electrical/Electronics Engineer; Management Analyst/Consultant; Sales Representative; Systems Analyst. **Average salary range of placements:** More than $50,000. **Number of placements per year:** 1 - 49.

F-O-R-T-U-N-E PERSONNEL CONSULTANTS
Fortune Center, 42 Idlewild Street, Bel Air MD 21014. 410/893-0450. **Fax:** 410/893-1121. **Contact:** Office Manager. **Description:** An executive search firm. Company pays fee. **Specializes in the areas of:** Engineering; Manufacturing. **Positions commonly filled include:** Chemical Engineer; Electrical/Electronics Engineer; Environmental Engineer; Industrial Engineer; Mechanical Engineer. **Corporate headquarters location:** New York NY. **Other U.S. locations:** Nationwide. **Average salary range of placements:** More than $50,000. **Number of placements per year:** 50 - 99.

FUTURES, INC.
8600 LaSalle Road, Suite 315, Baltimore MD 21286. 410/337-2001. **Contact:** Daniel Otakie, CPC, President. **Description:** An executive search firm. Company pays fee. **Specializes in the areas of:** Accounting/Auditing; Administration; Architecture/Construction; Banking; Computer Hardware/Software; Engineering; Fashion; Finance; Food Industry; General Management; Health/Medical; Insurance; Legal; Manufacturing; Personnel/Labor Relations; Retail; Sales; Technical; Transportation. **Positions commonly filled include:** Accountant/Auditor; Administrative Assistant; Architect; Biological Scientist; Biomedical Engineer; Bookkeeper; Chemical Engineer; Chemist; Civil Engineer; Claim Representative; Computer Programmer; Customer Service Representative; EDP Specialist; Electrical/Electronics Engineer; Industrial Designer; Industrial Engineer; Legal Secretary; Manufacturing Engineer; Mechanical Engineer; Medical Secretary; MIS Specialist; Nurse; Quality Control Supervisor; Sales Representative; Software Engineer; Systems Analyst; Technical Writer/Editor; Typist/Word Processor.

GRANT/MORGAN ASSOCIATES
7500 Old Georgetown Road, Suite 710, Bethesda MD 20814. 301/718-8888. **Contact:** Office Manager. **Description:** An executive search firm. **Specializes in the areas of:** Finance.

L.S. GROSS & ASSOCIATES
28 Allegheny Avenue, Baltimore MD 21204. 410/821-9351. **Fax:** 410/583-1901. **Contact:** Linda Gross, President. **Description:** A retainer and contingency search firm. **Specializes in the areas of:** Administration; Advertising; Biology; Computer Science/Software; Engineering; Finance; Food Industry; General Management; Health/Medical; Industrial; Legal; Manufacturing; Personnel/Labor Relations; Publishing. **Positions commonly filled include:** Administrative Manager; Attorney; Biochemist; Biomedical Engineer; Chemical Engineer; Computer Programmer; Economist; Electrical/Electronics Engineer; Environmental Engineer; Food Scientist/Technologist; Health Services Manager; Industrial Engineer; Internet Services Manager; Management Analyst/Consultant; MIS Specialist; Paralegal; Physical Therapist; Physician; Registered Nurse; Software Engineer; Structural Engineer; Surgical Technician; Systems Analyst. **Average salary range of placements:** More than $50,000. **Number of placements per year:** 1 - 49.

HRM SEARCH TEAM INC.
P.O. Box 43122, Baltimore MD 21236. 410/592-3488. **Contact:** Manager. **Description:** An executive search firm. **Specializes in the areas of:** Hotel/Restaurant.

ROBERT HALF INTERNATIONAL ACCOUNTEMPS
100 East Pratt Street, Suite 310, Baltimore MD 21202. 410/385-1600. **Contact:** Office Manager. **Description:** An executive search firm. Accountemps (also at this location) provides temporary placements. **Corporate headquarters location:** Menlo Park CA. **Other U.S. locations:** Nationwide.

THE HANOVER GROUP
11707 Hunters Run Drive, Hunt Valley MD 21030. 410/785-1912. **Fax:** 410/785-1913. **Contact:** Tom Graff, President. **Description:** An executive search firm operating on a contingency basis. Company pays fee. **Specializes in the areas of:** Banking; Finance. **Positions commonly filled include:** Bank Officer/Manager. **Corporate headquarters location:** This Location. **Other area locations:** Baltimore MD. **Average salary range of placements:** More than $50,000. **Number of placements per year:** 1 - 49.

HEALTHCARE RECRUITERS INTERNATIONAL
4500 Black Rock Road, Suite 102, Hampstead MD 21074. 410/239-6464. **Contact:** Manager. **Description:** An executive search firm. **Specializes in the areas of:** Health/Medical.

JDG ASSOCIATES LIMITED
1700 Research Boulevard, Rockville MD 20850. 301/340-2210. **Fax:** 301/762-3117. **Contact:** Joseph DeGioia, President. **E-mail address:** degioia@jdgsearch.com. **Description:** An executive search firm serving the fields of information technology, engineering, management consulting, quantitative science, and association management. The firm operates on both retainer and contingency bases. Company pays fee. **Specializes in the areas of:** Administration; Computer Science/Software; Economics; Engineering; Nonprofit. **Positions commonly filled include:** Budget Analyst; Computer Programmer; Economist; Electrical/Electronics Engineer; Financial Analyst; Industrial Engineer; Management Analyst/Consultant; Mathematician; MIS Specialist; Multimedia Designer; Science Technologist; Software Engineer; Systems Analyst; Telecommunications Manager. **Average salary range of placements:** More than $50,000. **Number of placements per year:** 200 - 499.

A.T. KEARNEY INC.
300 West Pratt Street, Suite 500, Baltimore MD 21201. 410/625-2995. **Contact:** Office Manager. **Description:** An executive search firm. **Specializes in the areas of:** Finance.

KRAUTHAMER & ASSOCIATES
5530 Wisconsin Avenue, Chevy Chase MD 20815. 301/654-7533. **Contact:** Manager. **Description:** An executive search firm placing personnel in a wide range of industries.

KEN LEINER ASSOCIATES, INC.
11510 Georgia Avenue, Suite 105, Wheaton MD 20902. 301/933-8800. **Contact:** Office Manager. **Description:** An executive search firm. **Specializes in the areas of:** Technical.

MANAGEMENT RECRUITERS INTERNATIONAL
132 East Main Street, Suite 300, Salisbury MD 21801. 410/548-4473. **Contact:** Manager. **Description:** An executive search firm. **Corporate headquarters location:** Cleaveland OH. **Other U.S. locations:** Natonwide.

MANAGEMENT RECRUITERS INTERNATIONAL
5550 Sperrett Place, Suite 314, Columbia MD 21044. 410/715-1141. **Contact:** Manager. **Description:** An executive search firm. **Specializes in the areas of:** Manufacturing; Plastics. **Corporate headquarters location:** Cleaveland OH. **Other U.S. locations:** Natonwide.

MANAGEMENT RECRUITERS OF ANNAPOLIS
2083 West Street, Suite 5A, Annapolis MD 21401. 410/841-6600. **Contact:** John Czajkowski, Manager. **Description:** An executive search firm. **Specializes in the areas of:** Accounting/Auditing; Administration; Advertising; Architecture/Construction; Banking; Chemical; Communications; Computer Hardware/Software; Design; Electrical; Engineering; Finance; Food Industry; General Management; Health/Medical; Insurance; Legal; Manufacturing; Operations Management; Personnel/Labor Relations; Pharmaceutical; Procurement; Publishing; Retail; Sales; Technical; Textiles; Transportation.. **Corporate headquarters location:** Cleaveland OH. **Other U.S. locations:** Natonwide.

MANAGEMENT RECRUITERS OF BALTIMORE
SALES CONSULTANTS OF BALTIMORE
9515 Deereco Road, Suite 900, Timonium MD 21093. 410/252-6616. **Fax:** 410/252-7076. **Contact:** Ken Davis, President. **Description:** An executive search firm. Company pays fee. **Specializes in the areas of:** Accounting/Auditing; Administration; Advertising; Architecture/Construction; Banking; Chemical; Communications; Computer Hardware/Software; Design; Electrical; Engineering; Finance; Food Industry; General Management; Health/Medical; Insurance; Legal; Manufacturing; Operations Management; Personnel/Labor Relations; Pharmaceutical; Procurement; Publishing; Retail; Sales; Technical; Textiles; Transportation. **Positions commonly filled include:** Accountant/Auditor; Bank Officer/Manager; Biological Scientist; Biomedical Engineer; Chemical Engineer; Civil Engineer; Claim Representative; Computer Programmer; Credit Manager; Customer Service Representative; Electrical/Electronics Engineer; Financial Analyst; Industrial Engineer; Insurance Agent/Broker; Mechanical Engineer; Operations/Production Manager; Paralegal; Quality Control Supervisor; Software Engineer; Systems Analyst; Typist/Word Processor; Underwriter/Assistant Underwriter. **Corporate headquarters location:** Cleveland OH. **Other U.S. locations:** Nationwide. **Average salary range of placements:** More than $50,000. **Number of placements per year:** 200 - 499.

MANAGEMENT RECRUITERS OF BETHESDA
COMPUSEARCH OF BETHESDA
8710 Preston Place, Chevy Chase MD 20815. 301/654-9282. **Fax:** 301/320-1877. **Contact:** Office Manager. **E-mail address:** mrbethesda@aol.com. **Description:** An executive search firm focusing on the data communications and retail specialty industries. **Specializes in the areas of:** Accounting/Auditing; Administration; Advertising; Architecture/Construction; Banking; Communications; Computer Hardware/Software; Design; Electrical; Engineering; Finance; Food Industry; General Management; Health/Medical; Insurance; Legal; Manufacturing; Operations Management; Personnel/Labor Relations; Procurement; Publishing; Retail; Sales; Technical; Textiles; Transportation. **Corporate headquarters location:** Cleaveland OH. **Other U.S. locations:** Natonwide.

MANAGEMENT RECRUITERS OF FREDERICK
201 Thomas Johnson Drive, Suite 202, Frederick MD 21702. 301/663-0600. **Fax:** 301/663-0454. **Contact:** Ms. Pat Webb, Owner/Manager. **Description:** An executive search firm. **Specializes in the areas of:** Accounting/Auditing; Administration; Advertising; Architecture/Construction; Banking; Chemical; Communications; Computer Hardware/Software; Design; Electrical; Engineering; Finance; Food Industry; General Management; Health/Medical; Insurance; Legal; Manufacturing; Operations Management; Personnel/Labor Relations; Pharmaceutical; Procurement; Publishing; Retail; Sales; Technical; Textiles; Transportation. **Corporate headquarters location:** Cleaveland OH. **Other U.S. locations:** Natonwide.

MANAGEMENT RECRUITERS OF WASHINGTON, D.C.
1100 Wayne Avenue, Suite 1080, Silver Spring MD 20910. 301/589-5400. **Fax:** 301/589-3033. **Contact:** Manager. **Description:** An executive search firm. **Specializes in the areas of:** Accounting/Auditing; Computer Hardware/Software; Design; Finance; Health/Medical; Market Research. **Corporate headquarters location:** Cleaveland OH. **Other U.S. locations:** Natonwide.

NETWORK SEARCH INC.
14609 Settlers Landing Way, Potomac MD 20878. 301/762-7960. **Fax:** 301/762-7959. **Contact:** Office Manager. **Description:** An executive search firm. **Specializes in the areas of:** Accounting/Auditing; Finance.

PLACEMENT ASSOCIATES
6001 Montrose Road, Suite 702, Rockville MD 20852. 301/231-8150. **Fax:** 301/881-2918. **Contact:** Manager. **Description:** An executive search firm. **Specializes in the areas of:** Advertising; Marketing; Retail.

PORTER GROUP INC.
10320 Little Patuxent Parkway, Suite 1100, Columbia MD 21044. 410/992-7776. **Fax:** 410/992-7796. **Contact:** Lynn Dobson, Administrator. **Description:** An executive search firm that provides placement for entry-level to upper-level sales professionals. Company pays fee. **Specializes in the areas of:** Sales. **Average salary range of placements:** More than $50,000. **Number of placements per year:** 200 - 499.

DON RICHARD ASSOCIATES
5 Choke Cherry Road, Suite 378, Rockville MD 20850. 301/590-9800. **Contact:** Office Manager. **Description:** An executive search firm. **Specializes in the areas of:** Accounting/Auditing; Bookkeeping; Finance. **Other U.S. locations:** Nationwide.

SALES CONSULTANTS OF BALTIMORE CITY
575 South Charles Street, Suite 401, Baltimore MD 21201. 410/727-5750. **Fax:** 410/727-1253. **Contact:** Steven Braun, President. **E-mail address:** resume @aol.com. **Description:** An executive search firm. Company pays fee. **Specializes in the areas of:** Advertising; Computer Hardware/Software; Education; Fashion; Food Industry; General Management; Health/Medical; Industrial; Insurance; Manufacturing; Personnel/Labor Relations; Publishing; Retail; Sales. **Positions commonly filled include:** Administrative Assistant; Bookkeeper; Buyer; Claim Representative; Credit Manager; Customer Service Representative; Data Entry Clerk; EDP Specialist; Electrical/Electronics Engineer; Legal Secretary; Marketing Specialist; Medical Secretary; MIS Specialist; Nurse; Receptionist; Recruiter; Sales Representative; Software Engineer; Systems Analyst; Typist/Word Processor. **Corporate headquarters location:** Cleveland OH. **Other U.S. locations:** Nationwide. **International locations:** Worldwide. **Average salary range of placements:** More than $50,000. **Number of placements per year:** 200 - 499.

SALES CONSULTANTS OF COLUMBIA
10320 Little Patuxent Parkway, Suite 511, Columbia MD 21044. 410/992-4900. **Fax:** 410/992-4905. **Contact:** David Rubin, General Manager. **Description:** An executive search firm. Company pays fee. **Specializes in the areas of:** Computer Hardware/Software; Data Communications; Engineering; Sales; Telecommunications. **Positions commonly filled include:** Sales Representative; Telecommunications Analyst. **Corporate headquarters location:** Cleveland OH. **Other U.S. locations:** Nationwide. **International locations:** Worldwide. **Number of placements per year:** 1 - 49.

SALES CONSULTANTS OF PRINCE GEORGES COUNTY
7515 Annapolis Road, Suite 304, Hyattsville MD 20784. 301/731-4201. **Contact:** Tom Hummel, Manager. **Description:** An executive search firm. **Specializes in the areas of:** Accounting/Auditing; Administration; Advertising; Architecture/Construction; Banking; Chemical; Communications; Computer Hardware/Software; Design; Electrical; Engineering; Finance; Food Industry; General Management; Health/Medical; Insurance; Legal; Manufacturing; Operations Management; Personnel/Labor Relations; Pharmaceutical; Procurement; Publishing; Retail; Sales; Technical; Textiles; Transportation. **Corporate headquarters location:** Cleveland OH. **Other U.S. locations:** Nationwide. **International locations:** Worldwide.

SALES CONSULTANTS OF ROCKVILLE, INC.
51 Monroe Street, Suite 1405, Rockville MD 20850. 301/610-7300. **Toll-free phone:** 800/875-9630. **Fax:** 301/610-0100. **Contact:** Brian Hoffman, General Manager. **E-mail address:** mrisc@access.digex.net. **Description:** An executive search firm operating on both retainer and contingency bases. This location specializes in recruiting hard-to-find professionals in the high-tech arena from sales professionals to technical support specialists to executive level management. This location also provides videoconferencing, compatibility assessments, and outplacement services. Company pays fee. **Specializes in the areas of:** Computer Science/Software; General Management; Sales; Telecommunications. **Positions commonly filled include:** Computer Programmer; Internet Services Manager; Online Content Specialist; Operations Manager; Project Manager; Sales Engineer; Sales Executive; Sales Representative; Software Engineer; Systems Analyst; Systems Manager; Telecommunications Manager. **Corporate headquarters location:** Cleveland OH. **Other U.S. locations:** Nationwide. **International locations:** Worldwide. **Average salary range of placements:** More than $50,000. **Number of placements per year:** 100 - 199.

SANFORD ROSE ASSOCIATES
10630 Little Patuxent Parkway, Suite 309, Columbia MD 21044. 301/596-4000. **Fax:** 301/596-4001. **Contact:** Manager. **World Wide Web address:** http://www.sanfordrose.com. **Description:** An executive search firm. **Specializes in the areas of:** Engineering; Research and Development. **Other U.S. locations:** Nationwide.

SANFORD ROSE ASSOCIATES
51 Monroe Street, Suite 700, Rockville MD 20850. 301/762-1800. **Fax:** 307/762-3688. **Contact:** Office Manager. **World Wide Web address:** http://www.sanfordrose.com. **Description:** An executive search firm. **Specializes in the areas of:** Engineering; Food Industry; Paper. **Other U.S. locations:** Nationwide.

SEARCH CONSULTANTS, INC.
10400 Little Patuxent Parkway, Columbia MD 21044. 410/715-0900. **Fax:** 410/715-1137. **Contact:** David Hall, Partner. **E-mail address:** dhall001@interser.com. **Description:** An executive search firm that provides placement in the financial, data processing, and health care industries. Company pays fee. **Specializes in the areas of:** Accounting/Auditing; Computer Hardware/Software. **Positions commonly filled include:** Accountant/Auditor; Budget Analyst; Computer Programmer; Financial Analyst; Management Analyst/Consultant; MIS Specialist; Multimedia Designer; Software Engineer; Systems Analyst. **Average salary range of placements:** $30,000 - $50,000. **Number of placements per year:** 50 - 99.

THE SEARCH GROUP
9405 Hickory Limb, Columbia MD 21045. 410/381-3940. **Contact:** Manager. **Description:** An executive search firm. **Specializes in the areas of:** Insurance.

SEEK INTERNATIONAL, INC.
15 Stablemere Court, Baltimore MD 21209-1062. 410/653-9680. **Fax:** 410/653-9682. **Contact:** Heather Finley, Account Executive. **E-mail address:** seekint@seekint.com. **World Wide Web address:** http://www.seekint.com. **Description:** An executive search firm that works primarily with major corporations. Company pays fee. **Specializes in the areas of:** Computer Science/Software; High-Tech; Sales. **Positions commonly filled include:** Account Manager; Account Representative; Sales Executive; Sales Manager; Sales Representative; Software Engineer; Systems Analyst. **Corporate headquarters location:** This Location. **Average salary range of placements:** More than $50,000. **Number of placements per year:** 1 - 49.

SOURCE SERVICES CORPORATION
120 East Baltimore Street, Suite 1950, Baltimore MD 21202. 410/727-4050. **Fax:** 410/727-6808. **Contact:** Manager. **Description:** An executive search firm. The divisions at this location include Source Consulting and Source Finance. **Specializes in the areas of:** Computer Hardware/Software; Finance. **Other U.S. locations:** Nationwide.

SUDINA SEARCH INC.
375 West Padonia Road, Suite 235, Timonium MD 21093-2100. 410/252-6900. **Fax:** 410/252-8033. **Contact:** Chuck Sudina, President. **E-mail address:** sudina@access.digex.net. **World Wide Web address:** http://www.sudinasearch.com. **Description:** An executive search firm. Company pays fee. **Specializes in the areas of:** Accounting/Auditing; Computer Science/Software; Finance; Health/Medical. **Positions commonly filled include:** Accountant/Auditor; Computer Programmer; Financial Analyst; Health Services Manager; MIS Specialist; Multimedia Designer; Software Engineer; Systems Analyst; Telecommunications Manager. **Corporate headquarters location:** Baltimore MD. **Other U.S. locations:** Nationwide. **Average salary range of placements:** More than $50,000. **Number of placements per year:** 200 - 499.

TCM ENTERPRISES
57 West Timonium Road, Suite 310, Timonium MD 21093. 410/561-5244. **Fax:** 410/561-5248. **Contact:** Tom McPoyle, Director. **E-mail address:** tmcpoyle@erols.com. **Description:** An executive and high-tech recruiter. Company pays fee. **Specializes in the areas of:** Computer Science/Software; Engineering; General Management; Sales; Technical. **Positions commonly filled include:** Aerospace Engineer; Biochemist; Biomedical Engineer; Chemical Engineer; Civil Engineer; Computer Programmer; Design Engineer; Electrical/Electronics Engineer; Environmental Engineer; Industrial Engineer; Industrial Production Manager; Mechanical Engineer; Metallurgical Engineer; Software Engineer; Structural Engineer; Systems Analyst. **Other U.S. locations:** Nationwide. **Average salary range of placements:** More than $50,000. **Number of placements per year:** 1 - 49.

THOROUGHBRED EXECUTIVE SEARCH
9722 Groffs Mill Drive, Suite 224, Owings Mills MD 21117. 410/581-1124. **Contact:** Office Manager. **Description:** An executive search firm. **Specializes in the areas of:** Management Consulting.

UNIVERSAL HEALTH CARE PLACEMENTS
5602 Baltimore National Pike, Suite 508, Baltimore MD 21228. 410/719-7800. **Contact:** Manager. **Description:** A placement agency for medical administrative personnel, with heavy emphasis on the billing and collection practices within the industry. **Specializes in the areas of:** Health/Medical.

VEY MARK ASSOCIATES, INC.
8753 Ruppert Court, Ellicott City MD 21043-5451. 410/992-8422. **Fax:** 410/992-8934. **Contact:** Harvey M. Weisberg, President. **Description:** An executive search firm operating on both retainer and contingency bases. Company pays fee. **Specializes in the areas of:** Computer Science/Software; Engineering. **Positions commonly filled include:** Computer Programmer; Electrical/Electronics Engineer; Mathematician; Software Engineer; Systems Analyst. **Average salary range of placements:** More than $50,000. **Number of placements per year:** 1 - 49.

WALLACH ASSOCIATES, INC.
P.O. Box 6016, Rockville MD 20849-6016. 301/231-9000. **Contact:** Manager. **Description:** An executive search firm. Company pays fee. **Specializes in the areas of:** Aerospace; Defense Industry; Electronics; Research and Development.

WINSTON SEARCH, INC.
16 Greenmeadow Drive, Suite 305, Timonium MD 21093. 410/560-1111. **Fax:** 410/560-0112. **Contact:** Tom Winston, President. **Description:** A retained search company that also offers career/outplacement counseling. Company pays fee. **Specializes in the areas of:** Accounting/Auditing; Administration; Advertising; Computer Science/Software; Engineering; Finance; General Management; Industrial; Manufacturing; Personnel/Labor Relations; Sales. **Positions commonly filled include:** Accountant/Auditor; Biomedical Engineer; Branch Manager; Chemical Engineer; Chemist; Civil Engineer; Design Engineer; Electrical/Electronics Engineer; Financial Analyst; Industrial Engineer; Industrial Production Manager; Management Analyst/Consultant; Market Research Analyst; Mechanical Engineer; MIS Specialist; Operations/Production Manager; Software Engineer; Systems Analyst; Telecommunications Manager. **Average salary range of placements:** More than $50,000. **Number of placements per year:** 100 - 199.

WITT/KIEFFER, FORD, HADELMAN & LLOYD
4550 Montgomery Avenue, Suite 615N, Bethesda MD 20814. 301/654-5070. **Contact:** Manager. **Description:** An executive search firm for upper-level professionals. **Specializes in the areas of:** Health/Medical.

PERMANENT EMPLOYMENT AGENCIES

AAA EMPLOYMENT
1501 Edgemore Avenue, Suite A, Salisbury MD 21801. 410/546-5955. **Contact:** Office Manager. **Description:** A permanent employment agency. Company pays fee. **Positions commonly filled include:** Accountant/Auditor; Administrative Manager; Bank Officer/Manager; Chemist; Computer Programmer; Construction and Building Inspector; Cost Estimator; Counselor; Customer Service Representative; Designer; Draftsperson; Editor; Electrician; Food Scientist/Technologist; Industrial Designer; Industrial Engineer; Mechanical Engineer; MIS Specialist; Operations/Production Manager; Quality Control Supervisor; Registered Nurse; Restaurant/Food Service Manager; Securities Sales Representative. **Number of placements per year:** 100 - 199.

ADMIN PERSONNEL SERVICES
1112 Wayne Avenue, Silver Spring MD 20910. 301/565-3900. **Fax:** 301/588-9044. **Contact:** Robert L. McDermott, Owner. **Description:** A permanent employment agency. Company pays fee. **Specializes in the areas of:** Accounting/Auditing; Administration; Banking; Clerical; Computer Hardware/Software; Finance; Mortgage; Sales. **Positions commonly filled include:** Accountant/Auditor; Administrative Assistant; Administrative Worker/Clerk; Bank Officer/Manager; Bookkeeper; Clerk; Computer Operator; Computer Programmer; Credit Manager; Customer Service Representative; Data Entry Clerk; EDP Specialist; Legal Secretary; Medical Secretary; Receptionist; Sales Executive; Sales Representative; Secretary; Typist/Word Processor. **Other U.S. locations:** DC; VA. **Number of placements per year:** 1000+.

ATLAS PERSONNEL AGENCY
11820 Parklawn Drive, Suite 330, Rockville MD 20852. 301/984-8075. **Contact:** Office Manager. **Description:** A permanent employment agency. Company pays fee. **Specializes in the areas of:** Accounting/Auditing; Banking; Computer Science/Software; Finance; Office Support. **Positions commonly filled include:** Accountant/Auditor; Administrative Assistant; Bookkeeper; Financial Analyst; Secretary. **Number of placements per year:** 200 - 499.

CAREER NETWORK SERVICE INC.
9175 Guilford Road, Suite 205, Columbia MD 21046. 410/880-4800. **Contact:** Manager. **Description:** A permanent placement agency. **Specializes in the areas of:** Computer Hardware/Software; High-Tech.

CAREERS III, INC.
9039 Shady Grove Court, Gaithersburg MD 20877. 301/977-7000. **Contact:** Mr. Pat Busbice, President. **Description:** A permanent employment agency. Company pays fee. **Specializes in the areas of:** Clerical. **Positions commonly filled include:** Administrative Assistant; Bookkeeper; Clerk; Customer Service Representative; Data Entry Clerk; Legal Secretary; Medical Secretary; Receptionist; Secretary; Stenographer; Technical Writer/Editor; Typist/Word Processor. **Number of placements per year:** 200 - 499.

CEMCON INTERNATIONAL INC.
1517 Reisterstown Road, Suite 205, Pikesville MD 21208. 410/653-9121. **Fax:** 410/653-8864. **Contact:** Mr. Lee Rudolph, General Manager. **Description:** A permanent employment agency serving the Portland cement and concrete industry. **Specializes in the areas of:** Engineering; Manufacturing. **Positions commonly filled include:** Chemical Engineer; Civil Engineer; Electrical/Electronics Engineer; Mechanical Engineer; Mining Engineer. **Average salary range of placements:** More than $50,000. **Number of placements per year:** 50 - 99.

DUNHILL OF ROCKVILLE, INC.
414 Hungerford Drive, Suite 252, Rockville MD 20850. 301/654-2115. **Contact:** Gordon Powers, President. **Description:** A permanent employment agency. Company pays fee. **Specializes in the areas of:** Accounting/Auditing; Banking; Clerical; Finance. **Positions commonly filled include:** Accountant/Auditor; Bank Officer/Manager; Bookkeeper; Financial Analyst; Legal Secretary; Medical Secretary; Purchasing Agent/Manager; Receptionist; Secretary; Statistician; Stenographer; Typist/Word Processor. **Number of placements per year:** 1 - 49.

J.R. ASSOCIATES
152 Rollins Avenue, Suite 200, Rockville MD 20852. 301/984-8885. **Contact:** Daniel Keller, President. **Description:** A permanent employment agency. Company pays fee. **Specializes in the areas of:** Administration; Computer Hardware/Software; Engineering; Sales; Technical. **Positions commonly filled include:** Computer Programmer; Data Analyst; EDP Specialist; Financial Analyst; Marketing Specialist; MIS Specialist; Sales Engineer; Sales Representative; Systems Analyst; Telecommunications Analyst. **Number of placements per year:** 50 - 99.

THE JONATHAN LADD COMPANY
14504 Greenview Drive, Suite 204, Laurel MD 20708-3290. 301/470-4100. **Fax:** 301/470-2805. **Contact:** Stephen Garafalo, Candidate Sourcing Manager. **E-mail address:** sgarofalo@jonathanladd.org. **World Wide Web address:** http://www.inc.com/users/salesmeeting.html. **Description:** A permanent employment agency that organizes sales recruitment fairs nationwide. Company pays fee. **Specializes in the areas of:** Sales. **Positions commonly filled include:** Account Manager; Account Representative; Real Estate Agent; Registered Nurse; Sales Engineer; Sales Executive; Sales Manager; Sales Representative. **Corporate headquarters location:** This Location. **Other U.S. locations:** Atlanta GA. **Average salary range of placements:** $30,000 - $50,000. **Number of placements per year:** 500 - 999.

TOM McCALL & ASSOCIATES
10 North Calvert Street, Suite 506, Baltimore MD 21202. 410/539-0700. **Toll-free phone:** 800/676-1502. **Contact:** Charley Greene, Manager. **Description:** A permanent employment agency. Founded in 1948. Company pays fee. **Specializes in the areas of:** General Management; Sales. **Positions commonly filled include:** Account Manager; General Manager; Management Trainee; Marketing Manager; Marketing Specialist; Sales Executive; Sales Representative. **Average salary range of placements:** $30,000 - $50,000. **Number of placements per year:** 100 - 199.

MERIT EMPLOYMENT AGENCY
414 Hungerford Drive, Suite 252, Rockville MD 20850-4125. 301/738-1600. **Fax:** 301/762-4694. **Contact:** Stephanie Godwin, CPC, President. **Description:** A permanent employment agency specializing in placing all levels of accounting positions and all levels of administrative positions. Company pays fee. **Specializes in the areas of:** Accounting/Auditing; Administration; Finance; Secretarial. **Positions commonly filled include:** Accountant/Auditor; Administrative Assistant; Chief Executive Officer; Clerical Supervisor; Computer Programmer; Customer Service Representative; Editor; Financial Analyst; Human Resources Manager; MIS Specialist; Secretary; Software Engineer; Systems Analyst; Typist/Word Processor. **Average salary range of placements:** $30,000 - $50,000. **Number of placements per year:** 1 - 49.

MOTHERS WORLD, INC.
P.O. Box 11066, Takoma Park MD 20913. 301/270-8804. **Contact:** Regina Williams, President. **Description:** A permanent employment agency that provides nanny placement and also places nurses in hospitals and nursing homes. **Positions commonly filled include:** Health Services Manager; Licensed Practical Nurse; Medical Records Technician; Registered Nurse; Social Worker.

ONSITE COMMERCIAL STAFFING
201 South Cleveland Avenue, Hagerstown MD 21740. 301/797-2905. **Fax:** 301/739-3948. **Contact:** Tina Roach, Manager of Administration. **Description:** A full-service permanent employment agency which also provides temporary placements. Company pays fee. **Specializes in the areas of:** Accounting/Auditing; Administration; Banking; Engineering; Industrial;

Secretarial. **Positions commonly filled include:** Accountant/Auditor; Administrative Assistant; Blue-Collar Worker Supervisor; Computer Programmer; Customer Service Representative; Data Entry Clerk; Design Engineer; Designer; Draftsperson; Electrician; Financial Analyst; Human Resources Specialist; Industrial Engineer; Market Research Analyst; Mechanical Engineer; MIS Specialist; Purchasing Agent/Manager; Quality Control Supervisor; Systems Analyst; Typist/Word Processor. **Benefits available to temporary workers:** Paid Holidays; Paid Vacation. **Corporate headquarters location:** Baltimore MD. **Number of placements per year:** 1000+.

OPPORTUNITY SEARCH INC.
P.O. Box 751, Olney MD 20830. 301/924-4741. **Fax:** 301/924-1318. **Contact:** Marc Tappis, President. **Description:** A permanent employment agency that also provides some executive searches. Company pays fee. **Specializes in the areas of:** Computer Science/Software. **Positions commonly filled include:** Computer Programmer; Electrical/Electronics Engineer; Systems Analyst. **Average salary range of placements:** More than $50,000. **Number of placements per year:** 1 - 49.

PROFESSIONAL PERSONNEL SERVICES
1420 East Joppa Road, Towson MD 21286. 410/823-5630. **Fax:** 410/821-9423. **Contact:** Neal Fisher, President. **Description:** A permanent and temporary employment agency. Company pays fee. **Specializes in the areas of:** Computer Science/Software. **Positions commonly filled include:** Computer Operator; Computer Programmer; Database Manager; MIS Specialist; Operations Manager; Software Engineer; Systems Analyst; Systems Manager; Telecommunications Manager. **Benefits available to temporary workers:** Paid Holidays; Paid Vacation. **Number of placements per year:** 1 - 49.

QUEST SYSTEMS, INC.
4701 Sangamore Road, Suite 260N, Bethesda MD 20816. 301/229-4200. **Fax:** 301/229-0965. **Contact:** Tom Carter, Manager. **E-mail address:** questsyst@aol.com. **World Wide Web address:** http://www.questsyst.com. **Description:** A permanent employment agency specializing in computer technologies and information systems. Company pays fee. **Specializes in the areas of:** Computer Science/Software; MIS/EDP. **Positions commonly filled include:** Computer Programmer; MIS Specialist; Software Engineer; Systems Analyst. **Corporate headquarters location:** This Location. **Other U.S. locations:** Atlanta GA; Philadelphia PA. **Other area locations:** Baltimore MD. **Average salary range of placements:** $30,000 - $50,000. **Number of placements per year:** 1000+.

QUEST SYSTEMS, INC.
11350 McCormick Road, Executive Plaza One, Suite 408, Hunt Valley MD 21031. 410/771-6600. **Fax:** 410/771-1907. **Contact:** Barry Bollinger, Manager. **E-mail address:** questsyst@aol.com. **World Wide Web address:** http://www.questsyst.com. **Description:** A permanent employment agency focusing on computer technologies and information systems. Company pays fee. **Specializes in the areas of:** Administration; Computer Science/Software. **Positions commonly filled include:** Computer Programmer; MIS Specialist; Software Engineer; Systems Analyst. **Corporate headquarters location:** Bethesda MD. **Other U.S. locations:** Atlanta GA; Philadelphia PA. **Other area locations:** Baltimore MD. **Average salary range of placements:** $30,000 - $50,000. **Number of placements per year:** 1000+.

SNELLING PERSONNEL SERVICES
20 South Charles Street, 4th Floor, Baltimore MD 21201. 410/528-9400. **Contact:** Office Manager. **Description:** A full-service placement agency that places both permanent and temporary workers. Company pays fee. **Positions commonly filled include:** Accountant/Auditor; Administrative Assistant; Architect; Bank Officer/Manager; Biomedical Engineer; Bookkeeper; Chemical Engineer; Claim Representative; Credit Manager; Customer Service Representative; Data Entry Clerk; Electrical/Electronics Engineer; Electronics Technician; Financial Analyst; Industrial Engineer; Insurance Agent/Broker; Legal Secretary; Marketing Specialist; Mechanical Engineer; Medical Secretary; Operations/Production Manager; Quality Control Supervisor; Receptionist; Sales Manager; Sales Representative; Secretary; Technical Writer/Editor; Technician; Typist/Word Processor. **Number of placements per year:** 50 - 99.

TECHNICAL PROFESSIONAL SEARCH GROUP
1305 Warwick Drive, Lutherville MD 21093. 410/296-4944. **Fax:** 410/321-4834. **Contact:** Dan Jones, Senior Consultant. **E-mail address:** 105326,2522@compuserve.com. **Description:** A permanent employment agency operating on a contingency basis. Company pays fee. **Specializes in the areas of:** Computer Graphics; Computer Hardware/Software; Computer Operations; Computer Programming; Computer Science/Software; Engineering. **Positions commonly filled include:** Chemical Engineer; Civil Engineer; Computer Programmer; Design Engineer; Electrical/Electronics Engineer; Manufacturing Engineer; Mechanical Engineer; Software Engineer. **Corporate headquarters location:** This location. **Average salary range of placements:** More than $30,000. **Number of placements per year:** 1 - 49.

TECHNICAL TALENT LOCATORS, LTD.
8850 Stanford Boulevard, Suite 1850, Columbia MD 21045-4753. 410/995-6051. **Fax:** 410/995-6281. **Contact:** Stephen Horn, President. **Description:** A permanent employment agency. Company pays fee. **Specializes in the areas of:** Computer Science/Software; Engineering; Technical. **Positions commonly filled include:** Computer Programmer; Design Engineer; Software Engineer; Systems Analyst. **Average salary range of placements:** More than $50,000. **Number of placements per year:** 50 - 99.

TRI-SERV INC.
22 West Padonia Road, Suite C-353, Timonium MD 21093. 410/561-1740. **Fax:** 410/252-7417. **Contact:** Walter J. Braczynski, President. **Description:** Provides permanent placement for all levels of technical personnel. Company pays fee. **Specializes in the areas of:** Computer Hardware/Software; Engineering; Manufacturing; Technical. **Positions commonly filled include:** Aerospace Engineer; Ceramics Engineer; Chemical Engineer; Chemist; Civil Engineer; Computer Operator; Computer Programmer; Draftsperson; Electrical/Electronics Engineer; Industrial Engineer; Mechanical Engineer; Operations/Production Manager; Quality Control Supervisor; Systems Analyst; Technical Writer/Editor; Technician. **Average salary range of placements:** $30,000 - $50,000. **Number of placements per year:** 200 - 499.

VIRTUAL STAFFING SERVICES
P.O. Box 757, Lexington Park MD 20653. 301/862-5388. **Physical address:** 216155 South Essex Drive, Suite 50, Lexington Park MD. **Toll-free phone:** 800/439-9402. **Fax:** 301/862-9189. **Contact:** Ann Gallagher, Database Administrator. **Description:** A permanent employment agency that also provides temporary placements. Company pays fee. **Specializes in the areas of:** Administration; Computer Science/Software; Engineering; Secretarial; Technical. **Positions commonly filled include:** Accountant/Auditor; Administrative Assistant; Administrative

Manager; Computer Programmer; Cost Estimator; Customer Service Representative; Electrical/ Electronics Engineer; Financial Analyst; Insurance Agent/Broker; Management Analyst/Consultant; Mechanical Engineer; MIS Specialist; Multimedia Designer; Physical Therapist; Registered Nurse; Restaurant/Food Service Manager; Software Engineer; Systems Analyst; Technical Writer/Editor; Typist/Word Processor. **Benefits available to temporary workers:** Medical Insurance; Paid Holidays; Paid Vacation. **Corporate headquarters location:** Eatontown NJ. **Average salary range of placements:** $20,000 - $29,999. **Number of placements per year:** 500 - 999.

TEMPORARY EMPLOYMENT AGENCIES

ADECCO
300 East Lombard Street, Suite 935, Baltimore MD 21202. 410/837-2444. **Contact:** Branch Manager. **Description:** A temporary agency. Company pays fee. **Specializes in the areas of:** Accounting/Auditing; Communications; Data Processing; General Labor; Secretarial; Word Processing.

ADECCO
6303 Ivy Lane, Suite 140, Greenbelt MD 20770-6326. 301/220-1191. **Fax:** 301/220-1339. **Contact:** Office Supervisor. **Description:** A temporary agency. Company pays fee. **Specializes in the areas of:** Light Industrial; Office Support; Retail; Sales; Secretarial. **Positions commonly filled include:** Customer Service Representative; Paralegal; Typist/Word Processor. **Benefits available to temporary workers:** Medical Insurance; Paid Holidays; Paid Vacation; Tuition Assistance. **Corporate headquarters location:** Redwood City CA. **Average salary range of placements:** $20,000 - $29,999.

CAPITOL STAFFING SOLUTIONS
6256 Montrose Road, Rockville MD 20852. 301/816-0130. **Fax:** 301/816-0132. **Contact:** Office Manager. **Description:** A temporary agency that also provides some permanent placements. **Specializes in the areas of:** Administration; Technical.

COMPUTER TEMPORARIES
8100 Professional Place, Suite 200, Lanham MD 20785. 202/408-7042. **Contact:** Office Manager. **Description:** A temporary agency. **Specializes in the areas of:** Computer Programming; Computer Science/Software.

CONTEMPORARIES, INC.
1010 Wayne Avenue, Silver Spring MD 20910-5600. 301/565-0445. **Fax:** 301/565-0452. **Contact:** Recruiter. **E-mail address:** contemps@cs.com. **World Wide Web address:** http://www.cs.com/contemps. **Description:** A temporary agency. **Specializes in the areas of:** Administration; Secretarial. **Positions commonly filled include:** Accountant/Auditor; Administrative Manager; Paralegal. **Average salary range of placements:** Less than $20,000. **Number of placements per year:** 500 - 999.

EXCEL TEMPORARY SERVICES
7701 Greenbelt Road, Suite 212, Greenbelt MD 20770. 301/982-5566. **Fax:** 301/982-3393. **Contact:** Christine Hardy, Operations Manager. **Description:** A temporary agency. Founded in 1990. **Specializes in the areas of:** Banking; Personnel/Labor Relations; Secretarial. **Positions commonly filled include:** Accountant/Auditor; Claim Representative; Customer Service Representative; Human Resources Specialist; Technical Writer/Editor; Typist/Word Processor. **Benefits available to temporary workers:** Bonus Award/Plan; Medical Insurance; Paid Holidays; Paid Vacation. **Corporate headquarters location:** Atlanta GA. **Average salary range of placements:** Less than $20,000. **Number of placements per year:** 200 - 499.

MARGE FOX PERSONNEL SERVICES
40 York Road, Suite 210, Baltimore MD 21204-5243. 410/296-5044. **Fax:** 410/339-7937. **Contact:** Thomas Fox, Vice President. **Description:** A temporary and permanent staffing service for computer and administrative support. Founded in 1974. Company pays fee. **Specializes in the areas of:** Computer Science/Software; Secretarial. **Positions commonly filled include:** Computer Programmer; Customer Service Representative; Systems Analyst; Typist/Word Processor. **Benefits available to temporary workers:** Medical Insurance; Paid Holidays; Paid Vacation. **Average salary range of placements:** $20,000 - $29,999. **Number of placements per year:** 200 - 499.

INTERIM PERSONNEL
102 West Pennsylvania Avenue, Suite 204, Towson MD 21204. 410/828-8071. **Fax:** 410/828-6394. **Contact:** Mike Phillips, Branch Manager. **World Wide Web address:** http://www.interim.com. **Description:** A temporary agency that also provides permanent placements and some career/outplacement and consulting services. Company pays fee. **Specializes in the areas of:** Administration; Food Industry; Light Industrial; Personnel/Labor Relations; Retail; Secretarial. **Positions commonly filled include:** Assembly Worker; Bookkeeper; Clerk; Computer Operator; Customer Service Representative; Data Entry Clerk; Draftsperson; Factory Worker; Legal Secretary; Light Industrial Worker; Medical Secretary; Receptionist; Typist/Word Processor. **Corporate headquarters location:** Fort Lauderdale FL. **Other U.S. locations:** Nationwide. **Average salary range of placements:** $20,000 - $29,999. **Number of placements per year:** 1000+.

KELLY SCIENTIFIC RESOURCES
One Church Street, Suite 304, Rockville MD 20850. 301/424-6484. **Fax:** 301/424-6977. **Contact:** Branch Manager. **World Wide Web address:** http://www.kellyscientific.com. **Description:** A temporary agency for scientific professionals. **Specializes in the areas of:** Biomedical; Biotechnology; Chemical; Environmental; Food Industry; Petrochemical.

MICRO TEMPS
7500 Greenway Center Drive, Suite 400, Greenbelt MD 20770. 301/474-9063. **Contact:** Manager. **Description:** A temporary agency. Company pays fee. **Specializes in the areas of:** Administration; Computer Science/Software; Engineering; Technical. **Positions commonly filled include:** Communications Engineer; Computer Operator; Computer Programmer; Design Engineer; EDP Specialist; MIS Specialist; Software Engineer; Systems Analyst; Systems Engineer; Technical Writer/Editor. **Number of placements per year:** 1000+.

NRI HEALTHCARE
11400 Rockville Pike, Suite 820, Rockville MD 20852. 301/230-0444. **Fax:** 301/230-0451. **Contact:** Wanda Smith, General Manager. **World Wide Web address:** http://www.nri-staffing.com. **Description:** A temporary and permanent placement agency. Company pays fee. **Specializes in the areas of:** Health/Medical. **Positions commonly filled include:** Certified Nursing Aide; Licensed Practical Nurse; Pharmacist; Physical Therapist; Speech-Language Pathologist. **Average salary range of placements:**

$30,000 - $50,000. **Number of placements per year:** 200 - 499.

SALSBURY & ASSOCIATES PERSONNEL, INC.
102 West Pennsylvania Avenue, Suite 301, Towson MD 21204. 410/321-8310. **Fax:** 410/321-8312. **Contact:** Marshall Salsbury, CPA, President. **Description:** A temporary agency focusing on the financial field. The firm also provides permanent placement. Company pays fee. **Specializes in the areas of:** Accounting/Auditing; Bookkeeping. **Positions commonly filled include:** Accountant/Auditor; Bookkeeper; Controller; Credit Manager; Finance Director; Financial Analyst. **Other area locations:** Columbia MD.

SPARKS PERSONNEL SERVICES
15825 Shady Grove Road, Rockville MD 20850. 301/926-7800. **Fax:** 301/948-5890. **Contact:** Amy Shirilla, Branch Manager. **Description:** A temporary agency focusing on office support, customer service, administrative, and clerical placement. **Specializes in the areas of:** Personnel/Labor Relations; Sales; Secretarial. **Positions commonly filled include:** Administrative Manager; Typist/Word Processor. **Benefits available to temporary workers:** Medical Insurance; Paid Holidays; Paid Vacation. **Number of placements per year:** 1000+.

SPECIAL COUNSEL
16 South Calvert Street, Suite 501, Baltimore MD 21202. 410/385-5350. **Fax:** 410/385-5352. **Contact:** Vice President of Operations. **World Wide Web address:** http://www.specialcounsel.com. **Description:** A temporary agency that places legal practitioners in law firms and corporate legal departments on both temporary and direct hire bases. **Specializes in the areas of:** Legal. **Benefits available to temporary workers:** 401(k); Bonus Award/Plan; Paid Holidays; Paid Vacation. **Other U.S. locations:** Nationwide. **Average salary range of placements:** $30,000 - $50,000. **Number of placements per year:** 500 - 999.

TAC STAFFING SERVICES
7500 Greenway Center Drive, Suite 330, Greenville MD 20770. 301/963-9590. **Contact:** Manager. **Description:** A temporary agency. Company pays fee. **Specializes in the areas of:** Accounting/Auditing; Advertising; Banking; Clerical; Education; Finance; Health/Medical; Insurance; Legal; Manufacturing; Nonprofit; Personnel/Labor Relations; Publishing; Sales; Transportation. **Positions commonly filled include:** Bookkeeper; Clerk; Data Entry Clerk; Factory Worker; Legal Secretary; Light Industrial Worker; Medical Secretary; Receptionist; Typist/Word Processor. **Corporate headquarters location:** Newton MA. **Other U.S. locations:** Nationwide. **Number of placements per year:** 1000+.

TAD STAFFING SERVICES
8600 LaSalle Road, 103 Potomac Building, Towson MD 21286. 410/821-0900. **Fax:** 410/821-7067. **Contact:** Manager. **Description:** A temporary agency. Founded in 1956. Company pays fee. **Specializes in the areas of:** Accounting/Auditing; Administration; Architecture/Construction; Art/Design; Banking; Biology; Computer Science/Software; Education; Engineering; Finance; Food Industry; General Management; Health/Medical; Industrial; Insurance; Legal; Manufacturing; Personnel/Labor Relations; Publishing; Sales; Secretarial; Technical; Transportation. **Positions commonly filled include:** Accountant/Auditor; Administrative Manager; Advertising Clerk; Claim Representative; Computer Programmer; Customer Service Representative; Electrical/Electronics Engineer; MIS Specialist; Operations/Production Manager; Quality Control Supervisor; Systems Analyst; Technical Writer/Editor; Typist/Word Processor. **Benefits available to temporary workers:** 401(k); Bonus Award/Plan; Medical Insurance; Paid Holidays; Paid Vacation. **Corporate headquarters location:** Cambridge MA. **Other U.S. locations:** Nationwide. **Average salary range of placements:** $20,000 - $29,999. **Number of placements per year:** 1000+.

TECH/AID OF MARYLAND
7000 Security Boulevard, Suite 108, Baltimore MD 21244. 410/597-9550. **Contact:** Office Manager. **Description:** A temporary agency. Company pays fee. **Specializes in the areas of:** Architecture/Construction; Cable TV; Computer Hardware/Software; Engineering; Manufacturing; Technical. **Positions commonly filled include:** Architect; Buyer; Ceramics Engineer; Civil Engineer; Electrical/Electronics Engineer; Estimator; Industrial Designer; Industrial Engineer; Mechanical Engineer; Operations/Production Manager; Technical Writer/Editor. **Other U.S. locations:** Nationwide. **Number of placements per year:** 1000+.

TECHNICAL SOFTWARE SOLUTIONS, INC.
7901 Sandy Spring Road, Suite 505, Laurel MD 20707. 301/369-0040. **Toll-free phone:** 888/369-0040. **Fax:** 301/369-0045. **Contact:** Tom Mavrikes, Recruiter. **E-mail address:** md@solutions1.com. **World Wide Web address:** http://www.solutions1.com. **Description:** A temporary and permanent employment agency that places technical professionals. **Specializes in the areas of:** Computer Programming; Technical. **Positions commonly filled include:** Computer Programmer; Systems Analyst; Technical Writer/Editor. **Benefits available to temporary workers:** 401(k); Dental Insurance; Life Insurance; Medical Insurance.

TELESEC STAFFING SERVICES, INC.
10408 Montgomery Avenue, Kensington MD 20895. 301/949-3110. **Contact:** Recruiting Coordinator. **Description:** A temporary agency. **Specializes in the areas of:** Construction; Engineering; Health/Medical. **Positions commonly filled include:** Administrative Assistant; Bookkeeper; Claim Representative; Clerk; Customer Service Representative; Legal Secretary; Librarian; Light Industrial Worker; Medical Secretary; Receptionist; Typist/Word Processor.

TEMPS & COMPANY
10320 Little Patuxent Parkway, Columbia MD 21044. 410/740-4311. **Fax:** 410/997-5030. **Contact:** Lisa Miller, Manager. **Description:** A temporary agency. Founded in 1981. Company pays fee. **Specializes in the areas of:** Administration; Secretarial. **Positions commonly filled include:** Administrative Manager; Brokerage Clerk; Clerical Supervisor; Customer Service Representative. **Benefits available to temporary workers:** Dental Insurance; Life Insurance; Medical Insurance. **Average salary range of placements:** $20,000 - $29,999. **Number of placements per year:** 100 - 199.

CONTRACT SERVICES FIRMS

A CHOICE NANNY
5110 Ridgefield Road, Suite 403, Bethesda MD 20816. 301/652-2229. **Toll-free phone:** 800/736-2669. **Fax:** 301/652-0069. **Contact:** Manager. **Description:** A contract services firm that matches nannies, daycare workers, students, and babysitters with families wanting in-home child care. **Specializes in the areas of:** Child Care, In-Home; Nannies.

Positions commonly filled include: Nanny; Teacher/Professor. **Corporate headquarters location:** This Location. **Other U.S. locations:** Nationwide.

AMERICAN SERVICE TECHNOLOGY, INC.
Route 2, Box 173, Leonardtown MD 20650. 301/737-0010. **Fax:** 301/737-0011. **Contact:** John A. Mason, President. **Description:** A contract services firm. **Specializes in the areas of:** Education; Transportation. **Positions commonly filled include:** Marine Scientist; Teacher/Professor. **Average salary range of placements:** $30,000 - $50,000. **Number of placements per year:** 1 - 49.

DANSOURCES TECHNICAL SERVICES, INC.
1010 Rockville Pike, Suite 405, Rockville MD 20852-1419. 301/217-0425. **Fax:** 301/217-0508. **Contact:** John Kim, Vice President. **E-mail address:** dansources@nmaa.org. **Description:** A contract services firm. Company pays fee. **Specializes in the areas of:** Computer Science/Software; Technical. **Positions commonly filled include:** Computer Programmer; Internet Services Manager; Multimedia Designer; Software Engineer; Systems Analyst. **Benefits available to temporary workers:** Medical Insurance. **Average salary range of placements:** More than $50,000. **Number of placements per year:** 50 - 99.

ECHELON SERVICE COMPANY
7400 York Road, Suite 302, Towson MD 21204. 410/321-8254. **Fax:** 410/321-8385. **Contact:** Gordon Barclay, Personnel Manager. **E-mail address:** recruit@the-hermes.net. **Description:** A contract services firm that provides contract and permanent staffing services for engineers, computer hardware/software professionals, and associated support staff. Founded in 1982. Company pays fee. **Specializes in the areas of:** Computer Science/Software; Engineering; Industrial; Manufacturing; Technical. **Positions commonly filled include:** Aerospace Engineer; Aircraft Mechanic/Engine Specialist; Biomedical Engineer; Buyer; Ceramics Engineer; Chemical Engineer; Computer Programmer; Design Engineer; Draftsperson; Electrical/Electronics Engineer; Environmental Engineer; Industrial Engineer; Industrial Production Manager; Mechanical Engineer; Metallurgical Engineer; MIS Specialist; Multimedia Designer; Software Engineer; Stationary Engineer; Structural Engineer; Systems Analyst; Technical Writer/Editor; Telecommunications Manager; Typist/Word Processor. **Benefits available to temporary workers:** 401(k); Bonus Award/Plan; Medical Insurance; Paid Holidays; Paid Vacation. **Average salary range of placements:** More than $50,000. **Number of placements per year:** 100 - 199.

PROVISION TECHNOLOGIES
NATIONAL RECRUITING CENTER
444 North Frederick Avenue, Suite 305, Gaithersburg MD 20879. 301/519-1250. **Toll-free phone:** 800/573-2789. **Fax:** 301/519-1265. **Contact:** Manager. **World Wide Web address:** http://www.careerbase.com. **Description:** This location is the national recruiting center. Overall, ProVision is a contract services and consulting firm. **Specializes in the areas of:** Computer Science/Software; Information Technology.

CAREER/OUTPLACEMENT COUNSELING FIRMS

SAMUEL R. BLATE ASSOCIATES
10331 Watkins Mill Drive, Montgomery Village MD 20886. 301/840-2248. **Fax:** 301/990-0707. **Contact:** Samuel R. Blate, President. **E-mail address:** samblate@bellatlantic.net. **World Wide Web address:** http://www.members/aol/samblate/index.html. **Description:** A career/outplacement counseling service that assists candidates with resume and cover letter development. **Average salary range of placements:** More than $50,000. **Number of placements per year:** 100 - 199.

CAREER COUNSELING
7100 Baltimore Avenue, Suite 208, College Park MD 20740. 301/779-1917. **Contact:** Anne S. Headley, M.A., Owner. **E-mail address:** asheadley@aol.com. **Description:** A career/outplacement counseling firm specializing in assessment, career decision-making, and job search strategies.

CAREER PERSPECTIVES
510 Sixth Street, Annapolis MD 21403. 410/280-2299. **Fax:** 410/280-1406. **Contact:** Jeanne Slawson, Owner. **Description:** A career counseling firm that provides a variety of services including career planning and development, job search techniques and strategies, information on workplace issues, and career management. **Corporate headquarters location:** This location.

KAREN KING CAREER CHANGERS
7315 Wisconsin Avenue, Bethesda MD 20814. 301/654-5155. **Contact:** Manager. **Description:** A career counseling and resume service.

THE RESUME PLACE
310 Frederick Road, Baltimore MD 21228. 410/744-4324. **Contact:** Kathy Troutman, Owner. **Description:** A resume assistance and career counseling service.

WHITE RIDGELY ASSOCIATES, INC.
2201 Old Court Road, Baltimore MD 21208. 410/296-1900. **Contact:** Manager. **Description:** A career/outplacement counseling firm. **Specializes in the areas of:** Accounting/Auditing; Administration; Banking; Finance; Health/Medical; Insurance; Personnel/Labor Relations; Sales. **Number of placements per year:** 50 - 99.

MASSACHUSETTS

EXECUTIVE SEARCH FIRMS

AKS ASSOCIATES LTD.
175 Derby Street, Suite 9, Hingham MA 02043. 781/740-1704. **Contact:** Manager. **Description:** An executive search firm.

AARDVARK SYSTEMS & PROGRAMMING
129 South Street, Boston MA 02111. 617/367-8081. **Fax:** 617/367-2334. **Contact:** Manager. **Description:** An executive search firm that places computer consultants.

ABBOTT'S OF BOSTON, INC.
P.O. Box 588, Waltham MA 02254. 617/332-1100. **Fax:** 617/558-7771. **Contact:** Ivan Samuels, President. **Description:** An executive search firm operating on a contingency basis. Company pays fee. **Specializes in the areas of:** Computer Science/Software; Engineering; Health/Medical; Industrial; Manufacturing; Personnel/Labor Relations; Technical. **Positions commonly filled include:** Biological Scientist; Biomedical Engineer; Computer Programmer; Design Engineer; Electrical/Electronics Engineer; Health Services Manager; Human Resources Manager; Internet Services Manager; Mechanical Engineer; MIS Specialist; Multimedia Designer; Software Engineer; Statistician; Systems Analyst. **Corporate headquarters location:** Newton MA. **Average salary range of placements:** More than $50,000. **Number of placements per year:** 1 - 49.

ABLE ASSOCIATES
1504 Pleasant Street, Fall River MA 02723. 508/999-0212. **Contact:** Manager. **Description:** An executive search firm.

ACCOUNT PROS
8 New England Executive Park East, 3rd Floor, Burlington MA 01803. 781/229-2288. **Contact:** Manager. **Description:** An executive search firm. **Specializes in the areas of:** Accounting/Auditing; Finance. **Corporate headquarters location:** Boston MA. **Other U.S. locations:** Los Angeles CA; Chicago IL.

ACCOUNTANTS ON CALL
99 Summer Street, Suite 1240, Boston MA 02110. 617/345-0440. **Fax:** 617/345-0423. **Contact:** Joanne Hogan, Executive Search Manager. **Description:** An executive search firm focusing on accounting recruitment and placement. Company pays fee. **Specializes in the areas of:** Accounting/Auditing. **Positions commonly filled include:** Accountant/Auditor. **Corporate headquarters location:** Saddlebrook NJ. **Other U.S. locations:** Nationwide. **Average salary range of placements:** $30,000 - $50,000. **Number of placements per year:** 50 - 99.

ACCOUNTING RESOURCE
3 Edgewater Drive, Norwood MA 02062. 781/255-0300. **Fax:** 781/255-0029. **Contact:** Manager. **Description:** An executive search firm. **Specializes in the areas of:** Accounting/Auditing.

ACCURATE SEARCH CONSULTANTS
390 Main Street, Suite 830, Worcester MA 01608. 508/799-9599. **Contact:** Manager. **Description:** An executive search firm. **Specializes in the areas of:** Accounting/Auditing; Customer Service; Office Support; Sales.

AMERICAN INSURANCE EXECUTIVES
148 State Street, Suite 405, Boston MA 02109. 617/248-6883. **Fax:** 617/248-8650. **Contact:** Manager. **Description:** An executive search firm that provides placement in the insurance industry.

ANSARA, BICKFORD, & FISKE
P.O. Box 239, West Springfield MA 01090. 413/733-0791. **Fax:** 413/731-1486. **Contact:** Manager. **Description:** An executive search firm operating on both retained and contingency bases. **Specializes in the areas of:** Engineering. **Positions commonly filled include:** Biomedical Engineer; Civil Engineer; Communications Engineer; Design Engineer; Electrical/Electronics Engineer; Industrial Engineer; Manufacturing Engineer; Mechanical Engineer; Sales Engineer; Software Engineer; Structural Engineer; Systems Manager; Technical Writer/Editor. **Average salary range of placements:** More than $50,000. **Number of placements per year:** 100 - 199.

MICHAEL ANTHONY ASSOCIATES
42 Washington Street, Wellesley MA 02181. 781/237-4950. **Contact:** Manager. **Description:** An executive search firm. **Specializes in the areas of:** Environmental; Health/Medical; Information Technology.

ANTHONY MICHAEL & COMPANY
800 Hingham Street, Rockland MA 02370. 781/871-9600. **Contact:** Manager. **Description:** An executive search firm. **Specializes in the areas of:** Banking; Finance.

APPLIED RESOURCES INC.
42 High Street, Suite 2, Medford MA 02153. 781/391-1202. **Contact:** Manager. **Description:** An executive search firm operating on a contingency basis. **Specializes in the areas of:** Engineering.

ARCHITECHS
2 Electronics Avenue, Danvers MA 01923. 978/777-8500. **Fax:** 978/774-5620. **Contact:** Bob Jones, Principal. **E-mail address:** bjones@architechs.com. **Description:** An executive search firm operating on both retained and contingency bases. Company pays fee. **Specializes in the areas of:** Computer Science/Software; Engineering; Information Systems. **Positions commonly filled include:** Computer Programmer; Internet Services Manager; MIS Specialist; Multimedia Designer; Science Technologist; Software Engineer; Systems Analyst. **Average salary range of placements:** More than $50,000. **Number of placements per year:** 100 - 199.

ARNOLD ASSOCIATES
10 Post Office Square, Suite 600 South, Boston MA 02109. 617/988-0403. **Contact:** Office Manager. **Description:** An executive search firm. **Specializes in the areas of:** Finance.

NANCY ATKINS ASSOCIATES
199 Sudbury Road, Concord MA 01742. 978/371-9794. **Contact:** Manager. **Description:** An executive search firm. **Specializes in the areas of:** Retail.

ATLANTIC SEARCH GROUP INC.
One Liberty Square, Boston MA 02109-4825. 617/426-9700. **Contact:** Manager. **Description:** An executive search firm operating on a contingency basis. Company pays fee. **Specializes in the areas of:** Accounting/Auditing; Finance. **Positions commonly filled include:** Accountant/Auditor; Budget Analyst; Credit Manager; Financial Analyst. **Average salary range of placements:** $30,000 - $50,000. **Number of placements per year:** 100 - 199.

AUERBACH ASSOCIATES
30 Winter Street, Boston MA 02108. 617/451-0095. **Contact:** Manager. **Description:** An executive search

firm. **Specializes in the areas of:** Education; Health/Medical; Nonprofit.

NATHAN BARRY & ASSOCIATES
301 Union Wharf, Boston MA 02109. 617/227-6067. **Contact:** Manager. **Description:** An executive search firm. **Specializes in the areas of:** Biotechnology; Health/Medical.

BASKIND CONSULTING & PLACEMENT
150 Speen Street, Framingham MA 01701. 508/620-0610. **Contact:** Manager. **Description:** An executive search firm. **Specializes in the areas of:** Accounting/Auditing; Finance.

BEACON SEARCH PROFESSIONALS
146 North Main Street, Leominster MA 01453. 978/534-8400. **Fax:** 978/534-4313. **Contact:** Gary Safer, President. **Description:** An executive search firm operating on both retainer and contingency bases. Clients range from *Fortune* 500 restaurant chains to independent restaurants. Company pays fee. **Specializes in the areas of:** Food Industry; Hotel/Restaurant. **Positions commonly filled include:** Hotel Manager; Human Resources Manager; Management Trainee; Restaurant/Food Service Manager. **Other U.S. locations:** Nationwide. **Average salary range of placements:** $30,000 - $50,000. **Number of placements per year:** 200 - 499.

BERKSHIRE SEARCH ASSOCIATES
P.O. Box 459, Becket MA 01223. 413/623-8855. **Fax:** 413/623-8858. **Contact:** Donald Munger, CPC, President. **Description:** An executive search firm operating on a contingency basis. The firm focuses on engineering, construction, and manufacturing as well as HVAC and OEM sales and marketing. Company pays fee. **Specializes in the areas of:** Architecture/Construction; Construction; Design; Engineering; Manufacturing. **Positions commonly filled include:** Architect; Branch Manager; Chemical Engineer; Civil Engineer; Construction Contractor; Cost Estimator; Design Engineer; Designer; Draftsperson; Electrical/Electronics Engineer; Environmental Engineer; Industrial Engineer; Industrial Production Manager; Landscape Architect; Mechanical Engineer; Metallurgical Engineer; Mining Engineer; Operations/Production Manager; Purchasing Agent/Manager; Sales Manager; Software Engineer; Stationary Engineer; Structural Engineer; Surveyor. **Number of placements per year:** 1 - 49.

BIOWORKS INC.
7 Harris Avenue, Boston MA 02131. 617/522-8618. **Fax:** 617/983-0624. **Contact:** Elena Cervone, President. **Description:** An executive search firm operating on both retainer and contingency bases. The firm focuses on biotechnology and biomedical placement. Company pays fee. **Specializes in the areas of:** Biotechnology. **Positions commonly filled include:** Biological Scientist; Biomedical Engineer; Chemical Engineer; Chemist; Food Scientist/Technologist; Metallurgical Engineer; Quality Control Supervisor. **Average salary range of placements:** $30,000 - $50,000. **Number of placements per year:** 1 - 49.

BLANEY EXECUTIVE SEARCH
Damon Mill Square, Concord MA 01742. 978/371-2192. **Contact:** Manager. **Description:** An executive search firm. **Specializes in the areas of:** Computer Hardware/Software; High-Tech.

BOSTON ASSOCIATES
MINUTEMAN TECHNICAL SERVICE
35 Bedford Street, Lexington MA 02173. 781/861-7493. **Contact:** Manager. **Description:** An executive search firm. Minutemen Technical Service (also at this location) is a contract services firm that provides technical placements.

BOWDOIN GROUP
40 Williams Street, Wellesley MA 02181. 781/239-9933. **Contact:** Office Manager. **Description:** An executive search firm. **Specializes in the areas of:** Data Communications; Health/Medical; Telecommunications.

BRADFORD BARNES ASSOCIATES
100 Franklin Street, Boston MA 02110. 617/451-1100. **Contact:** Manager. **Description:** An executive search firm. **Specializes in the areas of:** Administration; Biotechnology; Health/Medical; High-Tech.

BREITNER CLARK & HALL
63 South Main Street, Randolph MA 02368. 781/986-0011. **Contact:** Manager. **Description:** An executive search firm. **Specializes in the areas of:** Health/Medical. **Positions commonly filled include:** Physician; Physician Assistant.

CEC ASSOCIATES
52 Accord Park Drive, Norwell MA 02061. 781/982-0205. **Contact:** Manager. **Description:** An executive search firm. **Specializes in the areas of:** Health/Medical.

CAMPBELL ASSOCIATES
18 Tremont Street, Boston MA 02108. 617/227-2028. **Contact:** Joan Campbell, President. **Description:** An executive search firm operating on a contingency basis. The firm focuses on financial services, marketing, and advertising placement. **Specializes in the areas of:** Administration; Advertising; Banking; Computer Science/Software; Finance; Sales; Word Processing. **Positions commonly filled include:** Financial Analyst; Human Resources Manager; Market Research Analyst; Public Relations Specialist; Securities Sales Representative.

MICHAEL CANTOR ASSOCIATES
P.O. Box 977, Middleton MA 01949. 978/777-9855. **Contact:** Manager. **Description:** An executive search firm. **Specializes in the areas of:** Computer Science/Software.

CAREER SUCCESS INTERNATIONAL
9 Pickerel Road, Suite 1201-32, Wellesley MA 02181. 617/928-3659. **Contact:** Manager. **Description:** An executive search firm. **Specializes in the areas of:** Marketing; Public Relations.

CAREERFILE
P.O. Box 3331, Pittsfield MA 01202. 413/499-2498. **Fax:** 413/448-5673. **Contact:** C. Welch, President. **E-mail address:** resume@careerfile.com. **World Wide Web address:** http://www.careerfile.com. **Description:** An executive search firm operating on both retainer and contingency bases. Careerfile is primarily involved in the placement of executive, managerial, and technical talent. Company pays fee. **Positions commonly filled include:** Accountant/Auditor; Actuary; Adjuster; Administrative Manager; Advertising Clerk; Aerospace Engineer; Architect; Bank Officer/Manager; Biochemist; Biomedical Engineer; Branch Manager; Buyer; Chemical Engineer; Civil Engineer; Clinical Lab Technician; Computer Programmer; Construction Contractor; Cost Estimator; Credit Manager; Electrical/Electronics Engineer; Electrician; Financial Analyst; Health Services Manager; Industrial Engineer; Industrial Production Manager; Insurance Agent/Broker; Management Analyst/Consultant; Market Research Analyst; MIS Specialist; Operations/Production Manager; Pharmacist; Quality Control Supervisor; Real Estate Agent; Restaurant/Food Service Manager; Securities Sales Representative;

Services Sales Representative; Social Worker; Software Engineer; Structural Engineer; Surveyor; Systems Analyst; Technical Writer/Editor; Underwriter/Assistant Underwriter. **Other U.S. locations:** Nationwide. **Average salary range of placements:** More than $50,000.

CARNEY, SANDOE AND ASSOCIATES
136 Boylston Street, Boston MA 02116. 617/542-0260. **Toll-free phone:** 800/225-7986. **Fax:** 617/542-9400. **Contact:** Sarah Wheeler, Director of Recruitment. **World Wide Web address:** http://www.csa-teach.com. **Description:** A retained executive search firm that places teachers and education administrators in independent schools. Company pays fee. **Specializes in the areas of:** Education. **Positions commonly filled include:** Education Administrator; Teacher/Professor. **Number of placements per year:** 500 - 999.

CARTER/MACKAY OF FRAMINGHAM
111 Speen Street, Framingham MA 01701. 508/626-2240. **Fax:** 508/879-2327. **Contact:** Michael Rowell, Vice President. **E-mail address:** carmac@tiac.net. **World Wide Web address:** http://www.cartermackay.com. **Description:** An executive search firm operating on a contingency basis. Company pays fee. **Specializes in the areas of:** Biotechnology; Computer Science/Software; Data Communications; Industrial; Medical Technology; Pharmaceutical; Sales; Telecommunications. **Positions commonly filled include:** Product Manager; Sales and Marketing Manager; Technical Support Manager. **Corporate headquarters location:** This Location. **Other U.S. locations:** Hasbrouck Heights NJ; Great Neck NY; Cary NC. **Average salary range of placements:** More than $50,000.

CHALONER ASSOCIATES
P.O. Box 1097, Back Bay Station, Boston MA 02117. 617/451-5170. **Contact:** Manager. **Description:** An executive search firm. **Specializes in the areas of:** Communications; Public Relations.

CIAK ASSOCIATES
227 Gore Road, Webster MA 01570. 508/943-3126. **Fax:** 508/943-5351. **Contact:** Kenneth R. Ciak, President. **Description:** An executive search firm for computer and other high-tech professionals. Company pays fee. **Specializes in the areas of:** Administration. **Positions commonly filled include:** Computer Programmer; Systems Analyst. **Number of placements per year:** 1 - 49.

CLAYMAN & COMPANY INC.
20 Park Plaza, Suite 483, Boston MA 02110. 617/578-9999. **Fax:** 617/578-9929. **Contact:** S.G. Clayman, President. **Description:** An executive search firm operating on a retained basis. Company pays fee. **Specializes in the areas of:** Sales. **Positions commonly filled include:** Public Relations Specialist. **Average salary range of placements:** More than $50,000. **Number of placements per year:** 50 - 99.

CLEAR POINT CONSULTANTS
3 Centennial Drive, Peabody MA 01960. 978/532-6400. **Toll-free phone:** 888/542-4004. **Fax:** 978/532-6292. **Contact:** Cynthia A. Thornton, Vice President. **E-mail address:** cthorn@clearpnt.com. **World Wide Web address:** http://www.clearpnt.com. **Description:** An executive search firm operating on a contingency basis. The firm focuses on the placement of technical writers, editors, course developers, user interface designers, and production specialists in software companies. The firm also provides contract placements. Company pays fee. **Specializes in the areas of:** Computer Science/Software; Publishing; Technical. **Positions commonly filled include:** Editor; Instructional Designer; Internet Services Manager; Multimedia Designer; Online Content Specialist; Technical Writer/Editor; Webmaster. **Average salary range of placements:** More than $50,000. **Number of placements per year:** 200 - 499.

THE CLIENT SERVER GROUP, INC.
10 West Central Street, Natick MA 01760. 508/653-2900. **Fax:** 508/653-2977. **Contact:** John Plugis, President. **Description:** An executive search firm operating on a contingency basis. Positions are primarily in the information management and software development areas of the financial, consulting, and software development industries. **NOTE:** A minimum of three years of commercial, post-academic experience is required for most positions. **Specializes in the areas of:** Banking; Computer Science/Software; Insurance. **Positions commonly filled include:** Computer Programmer; Internet Services Manager; Quality Assurance Engineer; Software Engineer; Systems Analyst; Telecommunications Manager. **Average salary range of placements:** More than $50,000. **Number of placements per year:** 1 - 49.

COAST TO COAST SALES RECRUITERS
6 Yorkshire Circle, Westborough MA 01581. 508/366-2400. **Contact:** Manager. **Description:** An executive search firm. **Specializes in the areas of:** Sales.

COMPUTER SECURITY PLACEMENT
P.O. Box 204-B, Northborough MA 01532. 508/393-7803. **Fax:** 508/393-6802. **Contact:** Cameron Carey, President. **Description:** An executive search firm operating on a contingency basis. The firm focuses on placing high-level professionals in the fields of data security and disaster recovery planning. Company pays fee. **Specializes in the areas of:** Banking; Computer Science/Software; Finance; Food Industry; Insurance. **Positions commonly filled include:** Systems Analyst. **Average salary range of placements:** More than $50,000. **Number of placements per year:** 1 - 49.

CORPORATE GROWTH RESOURCES
550 Worcester Road, Framingham MA 01701. 508/879-8200. **Contact:** Manager. **Description:** An executive search firm. **Specializes in the areas of:** Technical.

CYR ASSOCIATES, INC.
177 Worcester Street, Suite 303, Wellesley Hills MA 02181. 781/235-5900. **Fax:** 781/239-0140. **Contact:** Maury N. Cyr, President. **E-mail address:** cyrinc@mindspring.com. **World Wide Web address:** http://www.mindspring.com/~cyrinc. **Description:** An executive search firm operating on both retained and contingency bases. The firm concentrates on the areas of consumer products and direct marketing. Company pays fee. **Specializes in the areas of:** Art/Design; Biology; Engineering; Fashion; Food Industry; General Management; Industrial; Manufacturing; Materials; Nonprofit; Personnel/Labor Relations; Sales; Technical; Textiles; Transportation. **Positions commonly filled include:** Buyer; Chemical Engineer; Chemist; Designer; Food Scientist/Technologist; Industrial Engineer; Manufacturer's/Wholesaler's Sales Rep.; Metallurgical Engineer; Operations/Production Manager; Purchasing Agent/Manager; Quality Control Supervisor. **Average salary range of placements:** $30,000 - $50,000. **Number of placements per year:** 1 - 49.

DANA ASSOCIATES INC.
353 Huron Avenue, Cambridge MA 02138. 617/661-0779. **Contact:** Manager. **Description:** An executive search firm. **Specializes in the areas of:** Marketing; Sales.

ROBERT H. DAVIDSON ASSOCIATES, INC.
EXECUTIVE AND PROFESSIONAL RESUME SERVICE
1410 Providence Highway, Norwood MA 02062. 781/769-8350. **Fax:** 781/769-8391. **Contact:** Robert H. Davidson, President. **E-mail address:** rdjobs@gis.net. **World Wide Web address:** http://www.gis.net/~rdjobs. **Description:** An executive search and consulting firm. Robert H. Davidson Associates also provides resume services through its Executive and Professional Resume Service division. Company pays fee. **Specializes in the areas of:** Accounting/Auditing; Automotive; Computer Science/Software; Electronics; Engineering; Environmental; Finance; Health/Medical; Manufacturing; Sales. **Positions commonly filled include:** Biological Scientist; Budget Analyst; Buyer; Chemist; Computer Programmer; Electrical/Electronics Engineer; Industrial Engineer; Mechanical Engineer; Metallurgical Engineer; Purchasing Agent/Manager; Software Engineer; Technical Writer/Editor. **Number of placements per year:** 1 - 49.

DELUCA & ASSOCIATES
15 Simpson Lane, Falmouth MA 02540. 508/457-1122. **Contact:** Manager. **Description:** An executive search firm that places physicians. **Specializes in the areas of:** Health/Medical.

DEREK ASSOCIATES
P.O. Box 13, Mendon MA 01765. 508/883-2289. **Fax:** 508/883-2264. **Contact:** Joren Fishback, President. **E-mail address:** joren@kersur.net. **Description:** An executive search firm operating on a contingency basis. The firm also provides contract placements. **Specializes in the areas of:** Computer Science/Software; Environmental; Transportation. **Positions commonly filled include:** Chemical Engineer; Civil Engineer; Computer Programmer; Database Manager; Design Engineer; Environmental Engineer; MIS Specialist; Software Engineer; Systems Analyst; Systems Manager; Transportation/Traffic Specialist; Webmaster. **Average salary range of placements:** More than $50,000. **Number of placements per year:** 1 - 49.

DIRECTIONS MEDICAL GROUP
1661 Worcester Road, Suite 207, Framingham MA 01701. 508/620-1300. **Contact:** Office Manager. **Description:** An executive search firm. **Specializes in the areas of:** Health/Medical.

DIVERSIFIED MANAGEMENT RESOURCES
10 Post Office Square, Boston MA 02109. 617/338-3040. **Contact:** Manager. **Description:** An executive search firm. **Specializes in the areas of:** Investment.

DIVERSITY ASSOCIATES
281 Andover Street, North Andover MA 01845. 978/689-0036. **Fax:** 978/688-7310. **Contact:** Mary Mascola, President. **E-mail address:** diversity@mdc.net. **World Wide Web address:** http://www.diversityassociates.com. **Description:** An executive search firm operating on both retainer and a contingency bases. Company pays fee. **Specializes in the areas of:** Computer Science/Software; Engineering; Manufacturing; Sales; Scientific; Technical. **Positions commonly filled include:** Account Manager; Aerospace Engineer; Database Manager; Design Engineer; Electrical/Electronics Engineer; Industrial Engineer; Mechanical Engineer; Sales Engineer; Software Engineer. **Average salary range of placements:** More than $50,000. **Number of placements per year:** 1 - 49.

DIVERSITY SEARCH SPECIALISTS
10 Winthrop Square, 4th Floor, Boston MA 02110. 617/426-5110. **Fax:** 617/426-2298. **Contact:** Office Manager. **Description:** An executive search firm. Company pays fee. **Specializes in the areas of:** Accounting/Auditing; Administration; Engineering; Legal; Personnel/Labor Relations; Technical. **Average salary range of placements:** More than $50,000.

DOUGLAS-ALLEN, INC.
1500 Main Street, Suite 2408, Springfield MA 01115. 413/739-0900. **Contact:** Manager. **Description:** An executive search firm. **Specializes in the areas of:** Finance.

EASTWOOD PERSONNEL ASSOCIATES, INC.
P.O. Box 462, Franklin MA 02038. 508/528-8111. **Fax:** 508/528-1221. **Contact:** Rick Hohenberger, President. **Description:** An executive search firm operating on a contingency basis. The firm focuses on financial and computer software placement. Company pays fee. **Specializes in the areas of:** Banking; Computer Science/Software. **Positions commonly filled include:** Bank Officer/Manager; Computer Programmer; Financial Analyst; MIS Specialist; Software Engineer; Systems Analyst. **Number of placements per year:** 1 - 49.

EDUCATIONAL MANAGEMENT NETWORK
98 Old South Road, Nantucket MA 02554. 508/228-6700. **Contact:** Manager. **Description:** An executive search firm. **Specializes in the areas of:** Education; Nonprofit.

HENRY ELLIOTT & COMPANY INC.
One Washington Street, Suite 208, Wellesley MA 02181. **Toll-free phone:** 800/417-7000. **Contact:** Manager. **Description:** An executive search firm. **Specializes in the areas of:** Computer Programming.

ENGINUITY SEARCH
76 Bedford Street, Suite 30, Lexington MA 02173. 781/862-6300. **Contact:** Manager. **Description:** An executive search firm. **Specializes in the areas of:** Computer Hardware/Software; Engineering.

EXCALIBUR ASSOCIATES
One Pond Park Road, Hingham MA 02043. 617/261-4936. **Contact:** Manager. **Description:** An executive search firm. **Specializes in the areas of:** Finance.

EXECU SOURCE
162 Boylston Street, Suite 61, Boston MA 02116. **Toll-free phone:** 800/903-9328. **Fax:** 800/440-5483. **Contact:** Manager. **Description:** An executive search firm focusing on the insurance industry. **Specializes in the areas of:** Insurance.

EXECUTIVE SEARCH INTERNATIONAL
60 Walnut Street, Wellesley MA 02181. 781/239-0303. **Contact:** Manager. **Description:** A generalist executive search firm.

EXECUTIVE SEARCH NORTHEAST, INC.
800 Hingham Street, 204-S, Rockland MA 02370. 781/871-6010. **Fax:** 781/871-6030. **Contact:** Michael A. Arieta, President and CEO. **E-mail address:** marieta@esni.com. **World Wide Web address:** http://www.esni.com. **Description:** A retained executive search firm placing senior- and executive-level construction and environmental consulting executives. Company pays fee. **Specializes in the areas of:** Construction; Environmental. **Positions commonly filled include:** Civil Engineer; Construction and Building Inspector; Construction Contractor; Cost Estimator. **Average salary range of placements:** More than $50,000. **Number of placements per year:** 1 - 49.

FENWICK PARTNERS
57 Bedford Street, Suite 101, Lexington MA 02173. 781/862-3370. **Contact:** Manager. **Description:** An

executive search firm. **Specializes in the areas of:** High-Tech.

FINANCIAL SEARCH GROUP
800 Turnpike Street, Suite 300, North Andover MA 01845. 978/682-4123. **Fax:** 978/685-1048. **Contact:** Manager. **Description:** An executive search firm that provides placements in the finance industry.

FITZGERALD ASSOCIATES
21 Muzzey Street, Lexington MA 02173. 781/863-1945. **Fax:** 781/863-8872. **Contact:** Manager. **Description:** An executive search firm operating on a retainer basis. The firm focuses on placing managed care and health care information management professionals. Company pays fee. **Specializes in the areas of:** Health/Medical; Insurance. **Positions commonly filled include:** Marketing Specialist; MIS Specialist; Physician; Registered Nurse; Sales Executive; Software Engineer. **Other U.S. locations:** Nationwide. **Average salary range of placements:** More than $50,000. **Number of placements per year:** 1 - 49.

FORD & FORD EXECUTIVE SEARCH
105 Chestnut Street, Needham MA 02192. 781/449-8200. **Fax:** 781/444-7335. **Contact:** Bernard Ford, Principal. **Description:** An executive search firm operating on both retainer and contingency bases. Company pays fee. **Specializes in the areas of:** Accounting/Auditing; Administration; Advertising; Art/Design; Computer Science/Software; Fashion; Personnel/Labor Relations; Publishing; Retail; Sales. **Positions commonly filled include:** Branch Manager; Environmental Engineer; General Manager; Human Resources Manager; Internet Services Manager; Market Research Analyst; MIS Specialist; Multimedia Designer; Public Relations Specialist; Technical Writer/Editor.

F-O-R-T-U-N-E PERSONNEL CONSULTANTS
100 Corporate Place, Suite 200, Peabody MA 01960. 978/535-9920. **Fax:** 978/535-4482. **Contact:** Office Manager. **Description:** An executive search firm. **Specializes in the areas of:** Biotechnology; Pharmaceutical. **Corporate headquarters location:** New York NY. **Other U.S. locations:** Nationwide.

F-O-R-T-U-N-E PERSONNEL CONSULTANTS
180 Denslow Road, Unit 4, East Longmeadow MA 01028. 413/525-3800. **Fax:** 413/525-2971. **Contact:** Manager. **Description:** An executive search firm. **Specializes in the areas of:** Health/Medical; Medical Technology; Pharmaceutical. **Corporate headquarters location:** New York NY. **Other U.S. locations:** Nationwide.

F-O-R-T-U-N-E PERSONNEL CONSULTANTS OF TOPSFIELD
458 Boston Street, Topsfield MA 01983. 978/887-2032. **Fax:** 978/887-2336. **Contact:** James E. Slate, President. **E-mail address:** plastics@topsfpc.com. **World Wide Web address:** http://www.topsfpc.com. **Description:** An executive search firm operating on both retainer and contingency bases. Company pays fee. **Specializes in the areas of:** Engineering; General Management; Manufacturing; Plastics; Sales. **Positions commonly filled include:** Chemical Engineer; Electrical/Electronics Engineer; Industrial Engineer; Industrial Production Manager; Mechanical Engineer; Plastics Engineer. **Corporate headquarters location:** New York NY. **Other U.S. locations:** Nationwide. **Average salary range of placements:** More than $50,000. **Number of placements per year:** 1 - 49.

FRANKLIN INTERNATIONAL SEARCH, INC.
4 Franklin Commons, Framingham MA 01702. 508/872-1133. **Contact:** Manager. **Description:** An executive search firm. **Specializes in the areas of:** Communications; Data Communications; Telecommunications.

FUTURES, INC.
55 Old Bedford Road, Lincoln MA 01773. 781/259-4500. **Fax:** 781/259-4508. **Contact:** Thomas P. Colacchio, President. **Description:** An executive search firm that also provides some contract placements. Company pays fee. **Specializes in the areas of:** Food Industry; Sales; Transportation. **Positions commonly filled include:** Account Manager; Account Representative; Assistant Manager; Buyer; Food and Beverage Service Worker; General Manager; Human Resources Manager; Sales and Marketing Representative; Sales Executive; Sales Manager; Sales Representative. **Average salary range of placements:** More than $50,000. **Number of placements per year:** 100 - 199.

GATTI & ASSOCIATES
266 Main Street, Suite 21, Medfield MA 02052. 508/359-4153. **Fax:** 508/359-5902. **Contact:** Mike Fitzgerald, Associate. **Description:** An executive search firm operating on both retainer and contingency bases. The company focuses on the search and placement of human resources professionals. Company pays fee. **Specializes in the areas of:** Personnel/Labor Relations. **Positions commonly filled include:** Human Resources Manager. **Average salary range of placements:** More than $50,000. **Number of placements per year:** 100 - 199.

DELORES F. GEORGE, CPC
269 Hamilton Street, Worcester MA 01604. 508/754-3451. **Fax:** 508/754-1367. **Contact:** Delores F. George, Employment Specialist. **E-mail address:** deloesg@ultranet.com. **Description:** An executive search firm that also provides temporary placements. Company pays fee. **Specializes in the areas of:** Information Technology. **Positions commonly filled include:** Chemical Engineer; Computer Operator; Computer Programmer; Consultant; Database Manager; Design Engineer; Electrical/Electronics Engineer; Internet Services Manager; Manufacturing Engineer; MIS Specialist; Software Engineer; Systems Analyst; Systems Manager; Telecommunications Manager; Webmaster. **Corporate headquarters location:** This Location. **Other U.S. locations:** Nationwide. **International locations:** Worldwide. **Average salary range of placements:** More than $50,000. **Number of placements per year:** 50 - 99.

GILREATH WEATHERBY INC.
P.O. Box 1483, Manchester MA 01944. 978/526-8771. **Contact:** Jim Gilreath, President. **Description:** An executive search firm operating on a retainer basis. The firm specializes in the recruitment and placement of executive and management professionals in manufacturing industries. Company pays fee. **Specializes in the areas of:** Accounting/Auditing; Consumer Package Goods; Engineering; General Management; Industrial; Manufacturing; Personnel/Labor Relations; Quality Assurance; Sales. **Positions commonly filled include:** General Manager. **Average salary range of placements:** More than $50,000. **Number of placements per year:** 1 - 49.

GILVAR & ASSOCIATES
29 Concord Square, Boston MA 02118. 617/437-0850. **Contact:** Manager. **Description:** An executive search firm. **Specializes in the areas of:** Education.

GLOU INTERNATIONAL
687 Highland Avenue, Needham MA 02194. 781/449-3310. **Contact:** Office Manager. **Description:** An executive search firm.

L.J. GONZER ASSOCIATES
274 Main Street, Reading MA 01867. 781/942-0450. **Toll-free phone:** 888/639-6945. **Fax:** 781/942-0164. **Contact:** Hank Bardol, New England Regional Manager. **World Wide Web address:** http://www.gonzer.com. **Description:** An executive search firm that focuses on technical positions including engineering and drafting professionals. L.J. Gonzer Associates also provides temporary placements. **Specializes in the areas of:** Art/Design; Engineering; Industrial; Scientific; Technical. **Positions commonly filled include:** Applications Engineer; Draftsperson; Electrical/Electronics Engineer; Electrician; Environmental Engineer; Graphic Designer; Industrial Engineer; Industrial Production Manager; Internet Services Manager; Manufacturing Engineer; Mechanical Engineer; MIS Specialist; Multimedia Designer; Production Manager; Software Developer; Systems Analyst; Systems Manager; Technical Writer/Editor; Webmaster. **Benefits available to temporary workers:** 401(k); Medical Insurance; Paid Holidays; Paid Vacation. **Average salary range of placements:** $30,000-$50,000. **Number of placements per year:** 200 - 499.

MARTIN GRANT ASSOCIATES, INC.
65 Franklin Street, Boston MA 02110. 617/357-5380. **Fax:** 617/482-6581. **Contact:** Barry Davis, Manager. **Description:** An executive search firm operating on both retainer and contingency bases. The firm focuses on property/casualty insurance positions. Company pays fee. **Specializes in the areas of:** Insurance. **Positions commonly filled include:** Account Manager; Account Representative; Adjuster; Claim Representative; Insurance Agent/Broker; Marketing Specialist; Sales Representative; Underwriter/Assistant Underwriter. **Number of placements per year:** 1 - 49.

GREENE & COMPANY
5 Powderhouse Lane, Sherborn MA 01770. 508/655-1210. **Fax:** 508/655-2139. **Contact:** Timothy G. Greene, President. **Description:** An executive search firm operating on a retained basis. The firm focuses on placing professionals in senior-level management positions at banks and financial institutions in New England. Company pays fee. **Specializes in the areas of:** Banking; Finance. **Positions commonly filled include:** Bank Officer/Manager; Branch Manager; Credit Manager; Financial Analyst; Market Research Analyst. **Average salary range of placements:** More than $50,000. **Number of placements per year:** 1 - 49.

A. GREENSTEIN & COMPANY
20 Vernon Street, Norwood MA 02062. 781/769-4966. **Fax:** 781/769-9269. **Contact:** Arlene C. Greenstein, President. **Description:** An executive search firm operating on a retained basis. The firm focuses on management placements at high-technology corporations. Company pays fee. **Specializes in the areas of:** Engineering; Sales. **Average salary range of placements:** $80,000 - $150,000. **Number of placements per year:** 100 - 199.

GUSTIN PARTNERS LTD.
2276 Washington Street, Newton MA 02162. 617/332-0800. **Contact:** Manager. **Description:** An executive search firm. **Specializes in the areas of:** High-Tech; Information Technology.

H&G ASSOCIATES INC.
160 Speen Street, Suite 310, Framingham MA 01701. 508/820-0048. **Fax:** 508/820-0104. **Contact:** Marilyn Lee, President. **Description:** An executive search firm operating on a contingency basis. The firm focuses on the recruitment and placement of marketing, sales, technical support, and customer support professionals in small, start-up software companies. Company pays fee. **Specializes in the areas of:** Sales. **Average salary range of placements:** More than $50,000.

HM ASSOCIATES
2 Electronics Avenue, Danvers MA 01923. 978/762-7474. **Fax:** 978/739-9071. **Contact:** Hugh MacKenzie, CPC, President. **E-mail address:** hmassc@aol.com. **Description:** An executive search firm operating on a contingency basis. Company pays fee. **Specializes in the areas of:** Computer Science/Software; Engineering; Information Technology; Technical; Telecommunications. **Positions commonly filled include:** Design Engineer; Electrical/Electronics Engineer; Manufacturing Engineer; Marketing Manager; Mechanical Engineer; MIS Specialist; Online Content Specialist; Sales Manager; Software Engineer; Systems Manager; Telecommunications Manager. **Average salary range of placements:** More than $50,000. **Number of placements per year:** 1 - 49.

H.R.I. SERVICES INC.
1200 East Street, Dedham MA 02026. 781/251-9188. **Contact:** Paul R. Tallino, President. **Description:** An executive search firm. Company pays fee. **Specializes in the areas of:** Food Industry. **Positions commonly filled include:** Food Scientist/Technologist; Hotel Manager; Restaurant/Food Service Manager. **Number of placements per year:** 100 - 199.

ROBERT HALF INTERNATIONAL ACCOUNTEMPS
5 Cherry Hill Drive, Danvers MA 01923. 978/774-8110. **Contact:** Manager. **Description:** An executive search firm. Accountemps (also at this location) provides temporary placements. **Specializes in the areas of:** Accounting/Auditing. **Corporate headquarters location:** Menlo Park CA. **Other U.S. locations:** Nationwide.

ROBERT HALF INTERNATIONAL ACCOUNTEMPS
P.O. Box 2000, Boston MA 02110. 617/951-4000. **Contact:** Manager. **Description:** An executive search firm. Accountemps (also at this location) provides temporary placements. **Specializes in the areas of:** Accounting/Auditing. **Corporate headquarters location:** Menlo Park CA. **Other U.S. locations:** Nationwide.

ROBERT HALF INTERNATIONAL ACCOUNTEMPS
One Monarch Place, Springfield MA 01144. 413/734-7752. **Contact:** Manager. **Description:** An executive search firm. Accountemps (also at this location) provides temporary placements. **Specializes in the areas of:** Accounting/Auditing. **Corporate headquarters location:** Menlo Park CA. **Other U.S. locations:** Nationwide.

ROBERT HALF INTERNATIONAL ACCOUNTEMPS
2 Westborough Business Park, 200 Friberg Parkway, Suite 3000, Westborough MA 01581. 508/898-0900. **Contact:** Manager. **World Wide Web address:** http://www.roberthalf.com. **Description:** An executive search firm. Accountemps (also at this location) provides temporary placements. **Specializes in the areas of:** Accounting/Auditing. **Corporate headquarters location:** Menlo Park CA. **Other U.S. locations:** Nationwide.

HAMBLIN GROUP
526 Boston Post Road, Wayland MA 01778. 508/358-0191. **Fax:** 508/358-0193. **Contact:** Karen Curley, President. **Description:** An executive search

firm operating on a contingency basis. The firm focuses on high-tech sales and marketing placement. Company pays fee. **Specializes in the areas of:** Sales. **Average salary range of placements:** More than $50,000. **Number of placements per year:** 50 - 99.

HARBOR CONSULTING CORPORATION
10 State Street, Woburn MA 01801. 781/938-6886. **Fax:** 781/932-0421. **Contact:** Mike Moore, President. **Description:** An executive search firm operating on a retainer basis. The firm focuses on the computer software and electronics industries. Company pays fee. **Specializes in the areas of:** Computer Science/Software; Engineering. **Positions commonly filled include:** Computer Programmer; Internet Services Manager; Software Engineer; Systems Analyst; Telecommunications Manager. **Average salary range of placements:** More than $50,000. **Number of placements per year:** 50 - 99.

HARVEST PERSONNEL
65 James Street, Worcester MA 01603. 508/792-4545. **Contact:** Gina Palumbo, Internet Coordinator. **E-mail address:** resumes@harvestpersonnel.com. **World Wide Web address:** http://www.harvestpersonnel.com. **Description:** An executive search firm operating on a contingency basis. **Specializes in the areas of:** Accounting/Auditing; Administration; Banking; Biology; Computer Science/Software; Engineering; Finance; General Management; Health/Medical; Insurance; Legal; Secretarial; Technical. **Positions commonly filled include:** Accountant/Auditor; Aerospace Engineer; Attorney; Bank Officer/Manager; Biological Scientist; Biomedical Engineer; Budget Analyst; Claim Representative; Clinical Lab Technician; Computer Programmer; EEG Technologist; EKG Technician; Electrical/Electronics Engineer; Environmental Engineer; Financial Analyst; Health Services Manager; Industrial Engineer; Industrial Production Manager; Internet Services Manager; Licensed Practical Nurse; Mechanical Engineer; MIS Specialist; Multimedia Designer; Occupational Therapist; Operations/Production Manager; Physical Therapist; Registered Nurse; Respiratory Therapist; Science Technologist; Software Engineer; Surgical Technician; Technical Writer/Editor; Typist/Word Processor; Underwriter/Assistant Underwriter. **Corporate headquarters location:** Ware MA. **Other area locations:** Marlborough MA. **Other U.S. locations:** Hartford CT. **Average salary range of placements:** $30,000 - $50,000. **Number of placements per year:** 1000+.

HEALTHCARE RECRUITERS INTERNATIONAL
100 Corporate Place, Suite 401, Peabody MA 01960. 978/535-3302. **Contact:** Manager. **Description:** An executive search firm. **Specializes in the areas of:** Health/Medical.

HIGH TECH VENTURES
55 Old Bedford Road, Lincoln MA 01733. 781/259-4444. **Fax:** 781/259-1361. **Contact:** Manager. **Description:** An executive search firm that provides placements in computer software start-up companies. **Specializes in the areas of:** Computer Science/Software.

HOSPITALITY EXECUTIVE SEARCH
729 Boylston Street, Boston MA 02116-2639. 617/266-7700. **Fax:** 617/267-2033. **Contact:** Jonathan M. Spatt, President. **Description:** An executive search firm operating on a retainer basis. The firm focuses on the food and hospitality industries. Company pays fee. **Specializes in the areas of:** Food Industry. **Positions commonly filled include:** Hotel Manager; Restaurant/Food Service Manager. **Average salary range of placements:** More than $50,000. **Number of placements per year:** 50 - 99.

INTERACTIVE SOFTWARE PLACEMENT
465 Auburn Street, Newton MA 02162. 617/527-2700. **Contact:** Manager. **Description:** An executive search firm. **Specializes in the areas of:** Computer Hardware/Software; Software Development.

JNB ASSOCIATES, INC.
990 Washington Street, Suite 200, Dedham MA 02026. 617/451-0355. **Contact:** Office Manager. **Description:** An executive search firm. **Specializes in the areas of:** Banking; Finance.

JUDGE TECHNICAL SERVICES
200 Foxboro Boulevard, Suite 700, Foxboro MA 02035. **Toll-free phone:** 800/765-5874. **Fax:** 508/698-2122. **Contact:** Michael Cooper, Branch Manager. **E-mail address:** careers@tiac.net. **World Wide Web address:** http://www.brainiac.com/tsnetwork. **Description:** An executive search firm. Company pays fee. **Specializes in the areas of:** Banking; Computer Science/Software; Engineering; Information Systems; Information Technology. **Positions commonly filled include:** Architect; Biochemist; Biological Scientist; Biomedical Engineer; Chemical Engineer; Chemist; Computer Animator; Computer Operator; Computer Programmer; Construction Contractor; Database Manager; Design Engineer; Draftsperson; Electrical/Electronics Engineer; Environmental Engineer; Industrial Engineer; Manufacturing Engineer; Mechanical Engineer; Sales Engineer; Software Engineer; Telecommunications Manager. **Benefits available to temporary workers:** 401(k); Medical Insurance. **Corporate headquarters location:** Bala Cynwyd PA. **Other area locations:** Foxboro MA. **Other U.S. locations:** Edison NJ; New York NY; Alexandria VA. **Average salary range of placements:** $30,000 - $50,000. **Number of placements per year:** 1000+.

S.D. KELLY & ASSOCIATES
990 Washington Street, Suite 314, Dedham MA 02026. 781/326-8038. **Fax:** 781/326-6123. **Contact:** Nancy Landry, Office Manager. **World Wide Web address:** http://www.sdkelly.com. **Description:** An executive search firm specializing in the areas of sales, marketing, engineering, manufacturing, and general management. The firm operates on a contingency basis. **Positions commonly filled include:** Biological Scientist; Biomedical Engineer; Chemical Engineer; Chemist; Customer Service Representative; Design Engineer; Designer; Electrical/Electronics Engineer; General Manager; Industrial Production Manager; Manufacturer's/Wholesaler's Sales Rep.; Market Research Analyst; Marketing Manager; Mechanical Engineer; Metallurgical Engineer. **Average salary range of placements:** More than $50,000. **Number of placements per year:** 100-199.

JOHN J. KENNEDY ASSOCIATES, INC.
35 Bedford Street, Suite 4, Lexington MA 02173. 781/863-8860. **Contact:** Manager. **Description:** An executive search firm. **Specializes in the areas of:** High-Tech.

KINGSBURY WAX BOVA
501 Cambridge Street, Cambridge MA 02141. 617/868-6166. **Fax:** 617/868-0817. **Contact:** Robert M. Wax, President. **E-mail address:** rowax@kwb.com. **Description:** An executive search firm operating on a retainer basis. Company pays fee. **Specializes in the areas of:** Accounting/Auditing; Publishing. **Positions commonly filled include:** Budget Analyst; Financial Analyst; Sales Manager. **Corporate headquarters location:** This Location. **Other U.S. locations:** New York NY. **Average salary range of placements:** More than $50,000. **Number of placements per year:** 50 - 99.

THE KINLIN COMPANY
749 Main Street, Osterville MA 02655. 508/420-1165. **Contact:** Manager. **Description:** An executive search firm. **Specializes in the areas of:** Finance.

THE KLEVEN GROUP
P.O. Box 636, Lexington MA 02173. 781/861-1020. **Contact:** Manager. **Description:** An executive search firm.

KORN/FERRY INTERNATIONAL
One International Place, 11th Floor, Boston MA 02110. 617/345-0200. **Contact:** Office Manager. **Description:** An executive search firm that places upper-level managers in a variety of industries. **Corporate headquarters location:** Los Angeles CA. **International locations:** Worldwide. **Average salary range of placements:** More than $50,000.

THE KOTEEN ASSOCIATES
70 Walnut Street, Wellesley MA 02181. 781/239-0011. **Fax:** 781/239-0607. **Contact:** Anne Koteen, President. **E-mail address:** recruit@koteenassoc.com. **Description:** An executive search firm. Company pays fee. **Specializes in the areas of:** Computer Science/Software. **Positions commonly filled include:** Computer Programmer; Development Manager; Internet Services Manager; Management Analyst/Consultant; MIS Specialist; Software Engineer; Systems Analyst; Telecommunications Manager. **Average salary range of placements:** More than $50,000. **Number of placements per year:** 50 - 99.

LAKE & MANNING
4 Evergreen Lane, Hopedale MA 01747. 508/473-6955. **Fax:** 508/473-6956. **Contact:** Audrey Lake, Partner. **E-mail address:** lakemannin@aol.com. **Description:** An executive search firm. Company pays fee. **Specializes in the areas of:** Advertising; Computer Hardware/Software; Engineering; General Management; Publishing; Sales; Technical. **Positions commonly filled include:** Commercial Artist; Computer Programmer; Editor; Electrical/Electronics Engineer; Industrial Designer; Marketing Specialist; Operations/Production Manager; Public Relations Specialist; Reporter; Sales Representative; Software Engineer; Systems Analyst; Technical Illustrator; Technical Writer/Editor; Typist/Word Processor.

ALAN LEVINE ASSOCIATES
275 Turnpike Street, Canton MA 02021. 781/821-1133. **Contact:** Manager. **Description:** An executive search firm. **Specializes in the areas of:** Retail.

THE LITTLETON GROUP
136 Main Street, Acton MA 01720. 978/263-7221. **Fax:** 978/263-7740. **Contact:** Carl Tomforde, President. **Description:** An executive search firm operating on a contingency basis. The Littleton Group recruits and places high-technology professionals in various disciplines, primarily in the New England area. Company pays fee. **Specializes in the areas of:** Accounting/Auditing; Computer Hardware/Software; Engineering; General Management; Manufacturing; Personnel/Labor Relations; Sales; Technical. **Positions commonly filled include:** Accountant/Auditor; Buyer; Computer Programmer; Draftsperson; Electrical/Electronics Engineer; Industrial Engineer; Manufacturing Engineer; Marketing Specialist; Mechanical Engineer; Operations/Production Manager; Purchasing Agent/Manager; Quality Control Supervisor; Sales Representative; Software Engineer. **Average salary range of placements:** More than $50,000. **Number of placements per year:** 1 - 49.

LOCKE ASSOCIATES
500 East Washington Street, North Attleboro MA 02760. 508/643-0444. **Fax:** 508/643-1443. **Contact:** John A. Locke, President. **Description:** An executive search firm. **Specializes in the areas of:** Computer Science/Software; Engineering; Environmental. **Positions commonly filled include:** Biological Scientist; Chemical Engineer; Chemist; Civil Engineer; Hydrogeologist; Sales Representative. **Corporate headquarters location:** This Location. **Other U.S. locations:** Charlotte NC. **Average salary range of placements:** More than $50,000. **Number of placements per year:** 1 - 49.

LOGIX INC.
1601 Trapelo Road, Waltham MA 02154. 781/890-0500. **Fax:** 781/890-3535. **Contact:** David M. Zell, President/CEO. **Description:** An executive search firm. Company pays fee. **Specializes in the areas of:** Administration; Biology; Computer Science/Software; Engineering; Technical. **Positions commonly filled include:** Biological Scientist; Biomedical Engineer; Chemist; Computer Programmer; Electrical/Electronics Engineer; Software Engineer; Systems Analyst. **Number of placements per year:** 200 - 499.

MADISON GROUP
92 Hayden Avenue, Lexington MA 02173. 781/862-7717. **Contact:** Manager. **Description:** A generalist executive search firm.

MANAGEMENT DEVELOPERS INC.
687 Highland Avenue, Needham MA 02194. 781/449-8400. **Contact:** Dale Boch, Owner. **Description:** An executive search firm operating on both retainer and contingency bases. The firm focuses on automotive industry placement and also provides consultation services and short-term financing for small businesses. Company pays fee. **Specializes in the areas of:** Automotive. **Positions commonly filled include:** Automotive Mechanic; Financial Analyst; Human Resources Manager. **Average salary range of placements:** $30,000 - $50,000. **Number of placements per year:** 50 - 99.

MANAGEMENT RECRUITERS INTERNATIONAL
607 Boylston Street, Suite 700, Boston MA 02116. 617/262-5050. **Contact:** Jack Nehiley, General Manager. **Description:** An executive search firm. **Specializes in the areas of:** Accounting/Auditing; Administration; Advertising; Architecture/Construction; Banking; Communications; Computer Hardware/Software; Construction; Electrical; Engineering; Finance; Food Industry; General Management; Health/Medical; Industrial; Insurance; Manufacturing; MIS/EDP; Operations Management; Personnel/Labor Relations; Pharmaceutical; Procurement; Publishing; Retail; Sales; Technical; Transportation.

MANAGEMENT RECRUITERS INTERNATIONAL OF BRAINTREE
639 Granite Street, Braintree MA 02184. 781/848-1666. **Contact:** Steve Morse, Manager. **Description:** An executive search firm. **Specializes in the areas of:** Accounting/Auditing; Administration; Advertising; Architecture/Construction; Banking; Communications; Computer Hardware/Software; Construction; Electrical; Engineering; Finance; Food Industry; General Management; Health/Medical; Insurance; Legal; Manufacturing; Operations Management; Personnel/Labor Relations; Pharmaceutical; Procurement; Publishing; Retail; Sales; Technical; Textiles; Transportation.

MANAGEMENT RECRUITERS INTERNATIONAL OF SPRINGFIELD
1500 Main Street, Suite 1822, Springfield MA 01115. 413/781-1550. **Contact:** Manager. **Description:** An executive search firm. **Specializes in the areas of:** Accounting/Auditing; Administration; Advertising;

Architecture/Construction; Banking; Communications; Computer Hardware/Software; Electrical; Engineering; Finance; Food Industry; General Management; Health/Medical; Personnel/Labor Relations; Pharmaceutical; Procurement; Publishing; Sales; Technical; Textiles; Transportation.

MANAGEMENT RECRUITERS INTERNATIONAL OF WESTBOROUGH
Westborough Office Park, 2000 West Park Drive, Westborough MA 01581. 508/366-9900. **Contact:** Irene Garrity, Manager. **Description:** An executive search firm. **Specializes in the areas of:** Accounting/Auditing; Administration; Advertising; Architecture/Construction; Banking; Communications; Computer Hardware/Software; Construction; Electrical; Engineering; Finance; Food Industry; General Management; Health/Medical; Insurance; Legal; Personnel/Labor Relations; Pharmaceutical; Procurement; Retail; Sales; Technical; Textiles; Transportation.

MANAGEMENT SEARCH, INC.
201 Park Avenue, West Springfield MA 01089. 413/732-2384. **Contact:** Manager. **Description:** An executive search firm. **Specializes in the areas of:** Engineering; Finance; Information Systems.

F.L. MANNIX & COMPANY
10 Village Road, Weston MA 02193. 781/894-9660. **Contact:** F.L. Mannix, President. **Description:** An executive search firm that places professionals in the high-technology, broadcast, and various other industries. **Specializes in the areas of:** Administration; Broadcasting; Computer Science/Software; Engineering. **Positions commonly filled include:** Computer Programmer; Electrical/Electronics Engineer; Internet Services Manager; MIS Specialist; Systems Analyst; Telecommunications Manager. **Other U.S. locations:** Nationwide. **Average salary range of placements:** $30,000 - $50,000.

MARLETTE PERSONNEL SEARCH
380 Union Street, West Springfield MA 01089. 413/781-0240. **Contact:** Manager. **Description:** An executive search firm. **Specializes in the areas of:** Engineering; Scientific.

MASTER SEARCH
531 Pleasant Street, Southbridge MA 01550. 508/765-2633. **Contact:** George R. Downing, Technical Services Manager. **Description:** An executive search firm. **Specializes in the areas of:** Accounting/Auditing; Art/Design; Biology; Engineering; Finance; General Management; Industrial; Manufacturing; Plastics; Technical. **Positions commonly filled include:** Accountant/Auditor; Automotive Mechanic; Biological Scientist; Buyer; Chemist; Cost Estimator; Customer Service Representative; Designer; Electrician; Engineer; Financial Analyst; Food Scientist/Technologist; Industrial Production Manager; Purchasing Agent/Manager; Quality Control Supervisor; Technical Writer/Editor. **Number of placements per year:** 1 - 49.

McDEVITT ASSOCIATES
90 Madison Street, Suite 403, Worcester MA 01608-2030. 508/752-5226. **Fax:** 508/755-2940. **Contact:** Larry McDevitt, Executive Recruiter. **E-mail address:** mcdassoc@ultranet.com. **Description:** An executive search firm. The company is online nationwide with over 650 smaller agencies via Nationwide Interchange Service, Recruiter's Exchange and Recruiters On Line, and Staffing Interchange. McDevitt Associates also places professionals in long-term contracting assignments. Company pays fee. **Specializes in the areas of:** Accounting/Auditing; Administration; Computer Science/Software; Engineering; Finance; General Management; Insurance; Manufacturing; Personnel/Labor Relations; Sales. **Positions commonly filled include:** Accountant/Auditor; Claim Representative; Computer Programmer; Customer Service Representative; Design Engineer; Draftsperson; Internet Services Manager; MIS Specialist; Quality Control Supervisor; Systems Analyst. **Average salary range of placements:** $30,000 - $50,000. **Number of placements per year:** 50 - 99.

MEDICAL BUREAU
101 Tremont Street, Boston MA 02108. 617/482-2400. **Fax:** 617/482-7290. **Contact:** Bill Cass, Manager. **Description:** An executive search firm operating on both retained and contingency bases. Company pays fee. **Specializes in the areas of:** Health/Medical. **Positions commonly filled include:** Biological Scientist; Biomedical Engineer; Clinical Lab Technician; Dental Assistant/Dental Hygienist; Dentist; Dietician/Nutritionist; EEG Technologist; EKG Technician; Health Services Manager; Medical Records Technician; Occupational Therapist; Pharmacist; Physical Therapist; Physician; Recreational Therapist; Registered Nurse; Respiratory Therapist; Stationary Engineer. **Number of placements per year:** 100 - 199.

MICRO-COMM EXECUTIVE SEARCH
800 Turnpike Street, North Andover MA 01845. 978/685-2272. **Contact:** Manager. **Description:** An executive search firm. **Specializes in the areas of:** Communications; Technical.

MORENCY ASSOCIATES
301 Newbury Street, Suite 242, Danvers MA 01923. 978/750-4460. **Fax:** 978/750-4465. **Contact:** Marcia Morency, President. **Description:** An executive search firm. Company pays fee. **Specializes in the areas of:** Accounting/Auditing; Administration; Computer Hardware/Software; Finance; Publishing; Sales; Technical. **Positions commonly filled include:** Accountant/Auditor; Buyer; Claim Representative; Computer Programmer; Contract/Grant Administrator; EDP Specialist; Marketing Specialist; MIS Specialist; Sales Representative; Software Engineer. **Number of placements per year:** 1 - 49.

MORGAN & ASSOCIATES
P.O. Box 379, Granby MA 01033. 413/467-9156. **Fax:** 413/467-3003. **Contact:** Diane R. Morgan, Owner. **E-mail address:** morgan.assoc@the-spa.com. **Description:** An executive search firm operating on both retainer and contingency bases. Company pays fee. **Specializes in the areas of:** Automation/Robotics; Computer Science/Software; Engineering; Manufacturing. **Positions commonly filled include:** Aerospace Engineer; Computer Programmer; Design Engineer; Electrical/Electronics Engineer; Engineer; Mechanical Engineer; Operations/Production Manager; Physical Therapist; Software Engineer; Systems Analyst. **Average salary range of placements:** $30,000 - $50,000. **Number of placements per year:** 50 - 99.

MURPHY ASSOCIATES
1550 Worcester Road, Suite 124W, Framingham MA 01702. 508/460-0336. **Contact:** Office Manager. **Description:** An executive search firm. **Specializes in the areas of:** Sales.

NACHMAN BIOMEDICAL
50 Church Street, Cambridge MA 02138. 617/492-8911. **Contact:** Manager. **Description:** An executive search firm. **Specializes in the areas of:** Biomedical.

NAGLER, ROBBINS AND POE
65 William Street, Wellesley Hills MA 02181. 781/431-1330. **Contact:** Leon G. Nagler, President.

Description: An executive search firm. **Number of placements per year:** 1 - 49.

NAVIN GROUP
80 Washington Street, Norwell MA 02061. 781/871-6770. **Contact:** Manager. **Description:** An executive search firm. **Specializes in the areas of:** Health/Medical.

NELSON ASSOCIATES
90 Madison Street, Suite 403, Worcester MA 01608-2030. 508/754-1600. **Contact:** Manager. **Description:** An executive search firm. **Specializes in the areas of:** Insurance.

NEW AMERICAN SEARCH
P.O. Box 451, Hingham MA 02043. 781/740-8141. **Contact:** Manager. **Description:** An executive search firm. **Specializes in the areas of:** Hotel/Restaurant.

NEW BOSTON SELECT GROUP, INC.
50 Milk Street, Boston MA 02109. 617/482-3900. **Toll-free phone:** 800/648-2469. **Fax:** 617/375-0831. **Contact:** C. Scott Bevins, Vice President/Business Development. **E-mail address:** scott.bevins@nbsg.com. **World Wide Web address:** http://www.nbsg.com. **Description:** An executive search firm. Company pays fee. **Specializes in the areas of:** Accounting/Auditing; Banking; Computer Hardware/Software; Engineering; Finance; MIS/EDP. **Positions commonly filled include:** Accountant/Auditor; Computer Programmer; EDP Specialist; Electrical/Electronics Engineer; Financial Analyst; Systems Analyst. **Benefits available to temporary workers:** 401(k); Medical Insurance. **Corporate headquarters location:** This Location. **Other U.S. locations:** Nationwide. **International locations:** Worldwide. **Average salary range of placements:** More than $50,000. **Number of placements per year:** 1000+.

NEW DIMENSIONS IN TECHNOLOGY, INC.
74 Atlantic Avenue, Suite 101, Marblehead MA 01945. 781/639-0866. **Fax:** 781/639-0863. **Contact:** Beverly A. Kahn, President. **E-mail address:** ndt@ndt.com. **World Wide Web address:** http://www.ndt.com. **Description:** An executive search firm operating on both retainer and contingency bases. The firm focuses on senior level searches as well as recruitment of professionals for advanced development, information technology, consumer electronics, and consulting. Company pays fee. **Specializes in the areas of:** Computer Hardware/Software; Computer Science/Software; Consulting; Engineering; Finance; General Management; Information Technology; Insurance; Marketing; Multimedia; Network Administration; Software Engineering; Start-up Organizations; Telecommunications. **Positions commonly filled include:** Computer Programmer; Consultant; Electrical/Electronics Engineer; Financial Analyst; Information Systems Consultant; Management Analyst/Consultant; Software Engineer; Systems Analyst. **Corporate headquarters location:** This Location. **Other U.S. location:** Seattle WA. **Average salary range of placements:** More than $50,000. **Number of placements per year:** 500 - 999.

NEW ENGLAND LEGAL SEARCH
280 Commonwealth Avenue, Suite G5, Boston MA 02116. 617/266-6068. **Fax:** 617/266-8510. **Contact:** Dee B. McMeekan, Esq., President. **Description:** An executive search firm operating on a contingency basis. New England Legal Search places experienced attorneys with major law firms and corporations. Company pays fee. **Specializes in the areas of:** Legal. **Positions commonly filled include:** Attorney. **Average salary range of placements:** More than $50,000.

NEW ENGLAND RECRUITERS
809 Turnpike Street, Suite 204, North Andover MA 01845. 978/681-5627. **Fax:** 978/681-6442. **Contact:** Manager. **Description:** An executive search firm. **Specializes in the areas of:** Accounting/Auditing; Engineering; Manufacturing; Sales.

NEW ENGLAND SEARCH, INC.
P.O. Box 1248, Mill Street, Webster MA 01570. 508/943-3000. **Fax:** 508/943-9958. **Contact:** Maureen V. Duso, CPC, President. **E-mail address:** nesars@ziplink.net. **Description:** An executive search firm operating on both retainer and contingency bases. Founded in 1984. Company pays fee. **Specializes in the areas of:** Accounting/Auditing; Administration; Computer Science/Software; Engineering; Finance; Manufacturing; Personnel/Labor Relations. **Positions commonly filled include:** Accountant/Auditor; Administrative Manager; Computer Programmer; Design Engineer; Electrical/Electronics Engineer; Financial Analyst; General Manager; Human Resources Manager; Industrial Engineer; Industrial Production Manager; Mechanical Engineer; MIS Specialist; Quality Control Supervisor; Software Engineer; Systems Analyst; Telecommunications Manager. **Corporate headquarters location:** This Location. **Average salary range of placements:** More than $50,000. **Number of placements per year:** 50 - 99.

NORTHEAST SEARCH
310 Franklin Street, Suite 545, Boston MA 02110. 617/292-0152. **Contact:** Office Manager. **Description:** An executive search firm. Company pays fee. **Specializes in the areas of:** Health/Medical. **Positions commonly filled include:** Occupational Therapist; Physical Therapist. **Number of placements per year:** 1 - 49.

OLSTEN PROFESSIONAL ACCOUNTING SERVICES
100 Summer Street, Suite 3210, Boston MA 02110. 617/542-1480. **Fax:** 617/542-1484. **Contact:** Kristen Bak, Manager. **Description:** An executive search firm operating on both retainer and contingency bases. Olsten Professional Accounting Services focuses on the placement of accounting and financial personnel. Company pays fee. **Specializes in the areas of:** Accounting/Auditing; Administration; Banking; Economics; Finance; Personnel/Labor Relations. **Positions commonly filled include:** Accountant/Auditor; Adjuster; Administrative Manager; Bank Officer/Manager; Budget Analyst; Buyer; Clerical Supervisor; Cost Estimator; Customer Service Representative; Economist; Financial Analyst; General Manager; Management Analyst/Consultant; Operations/Production Manager; Secretary. **Corporate headquarters location:** Melville NY. **Number of placements per year:** 200 - 499.

THE ONSTOTT GROUP
60 William Street, Wellesley MA 02181. 781/235-3050. **Contact:** Manager. **Description:** A generalist executive search firm.

ORGANIZATION RESOURCES INC.
63 Atlantic Avenue, Boston Harbor, Boston MA 02110. 617/742-8970. **Contact:** Office Manager. **Description:** An executive search firm.

THE ORIGINAL RESUME COMPANY
1105 Lakeview Avenue, Dracut MA 01826. 978/957-6600. **Fax:** 978/957-6605. **Contact:** Thomas P. Gove, President. **E-mail address:** origresume@aol.com. **World Wide Web address:** http://www.bestrecruiters.com. **Description:** An executive search firm that places entry-level applicants to CEOs in a wide variety of industries. The Original Resume Company also provides resume and cover letter services. Company pays fee. **Average salary range of placements:**

$30,000 - $50,000. **Number of placements per year:** 200 - 499.

P.A.R. ASSOCIATES INC.
60 State Street, Suite 1040, Boston MA 02109. 617/367-0320. **Contact:** Peter A. Rabinowitz, President. **Description:** An executive search firm. **Specializes in the areas of:** Health/Medical. **Number of placements per year:** 50 - 99.

PALADIN PERSONNEL CONSULTANTS
3 Bridle Path, Sherborn MA 01770. 508/651-1909. **Fax:** 508/651-1908. **Contact:** Andrew Sideman, Principal. **Description:** An executive search firm. **Specializes in the areas of:** Computer Science/Software; Engineering; Sales; Technical. **Positions commonly filled include:** Computer Programmer; Electrical/Electronics Engineer; Systems Analyst; Technical Writer/Editor.

D.P. PARKER & ASSOCIATES INC.
372 Washington Street, Wellesley MA 02181. 781/237-1220. **Fax:** 781/237-4702. **Contact:** Dr. David P. Parker, President. **E-mail address:** information@dpparker.com. **World Wide Web address:** http://www.dpparker.com. **Description:** An executive search firm operating on a retainer basis. Company pays fee. **Specializes in the areas of:** Engineering; General Management; Manufacturing. **Positions commonly filled include:** Biological Scientist; Chemical Engineer; Chemist; Electrical/Electronics Engineer; General Manager; Mechanical Engineer; Metallurgical Engineer; Nuclear Engineer; Operations/Production Manager. **Average salary range of placements:** More than $50,000.

PARTRIDGE ASSOCIATES, INC.
1200 Providence Highway, Sharon MA 02067. 781/784-4144. **Contact:** Manager. **Description:** An executive search firm. **Specializes in the areas of:** Hotel/Restaurant.

PHILLIPS & ASSOCIATES
62 Derby Street, Hingham MA 02043. 781/740-9699. **Fax:** 781/740-9064. **Contact:** Manager. **Description:** An executive search firm operating on both retainer and contingency bases. Company pays fee. **Specializes in the areas of:** Accounting/Auditing; Administration; Health/Medical; Nonprofit; Sales. **Positions commonly filled include:** Accountant/Auditor; Budget Analyst; Financial Analyst; Health Services Manager; Human Resources Manager; Licensed Practical Nurse; Management Analyst/Consultant; MIS Specialist; Occupational Therapist; Pharmacist; Physical Therapist; Physician; Registered Nurse; Respiratory Therapist; Speech-Language Pathologist. **Average salary range of placements:** More than $50,000. **Number of placements per year:** 100 - 199.

THE PICKWICK GROUP, INC.
36 Washington Street, Suite 240, Wellesley MA 02181. 781/235-6222. **Contact:** Cecile J. Klavens, President. **Description:** An executive search firm operating on a contingency basis. The firm also provides contract services. Company pays fee. **Specializes in the areas of:** Accounting/Auditing; Computer Science/Software; Finance; Health/Medical; Nonprofit; Personnel/Labor Relations. **Positions commonly filled include:** Account Manager; Accountant/Auditor; Budget Analyst; Chief Financial Officer; Controller; Credit Manager; Finance Director; Financial Analyst; Graphic Designer; Human Resources Manager; Internet Services Manager; Management Analyst/Consultant; Market Research Analyst; Project Manager; Sales Manager; Software Engineer; Systems Analyst; Systems Manager; Technical Writer/Editor; Webmaster. **Benefits available to temporary workers:** Medical Insurance. **Average salary range of placements:** More than $50,000. **Number of placements per year:** 50 - 99.

PILE AND COMPANY
535 Boylston Street, Boston MA 02116. 617/267-5000. **Fax:** 617/421-1899. **Contact:** Manager. **Description:** An executive search and management consulting firm. **Specializes in the areas of:** Advertising. **Average salary range of placements:** More than $50,000. **Number of placements per year:** 100 - 199.

NORMAN POWERS ASSOCIATES
P.O. Box 3221, Framingham MA 01705. 508/877-2025. **Contact:** Manager. **Description:** An executive search firm operating on both retainer and contingency bases. The firm focuses on the placement of professionals in the commercial and military electronics industry, from high-tech research and development companies to manufacturers of technical products such as networking and communications equipment. Company pays fee. **Specializes in the areas of:** Computer Science/Software; Engineering; Manufacturing. **Positions commonly filled include:** Computer Programmer; Design Engineer; Electrical/Electronics Engineer; Mechanical Engineer; Software Engineer; Systems Analyst.

PRESTONWOOD ASSOCIATES
266 Main Street, Suite 12A, Medfield MA 02052. 508/359-7100. **Contact:** Manager. **Description:** An executive search firm. **Specializes in the areas of:** Marketing; Sales.

PROFESSIONAL PLACEMENT CONSULTING GROUP
P.O. Box 462, Whitinsville MA 01588. 508/234-6674. **Contact:** Manager. **Description:** An executive search firm. **Specializes in the areas of:** Computer Science/Software; High-Tech; Telecommunications.

PROGRESSIVE SEARCH ASSOCIATES, INC. (PSA)
465 Auburn Street, Auburndale MA 02166. 617/244-1250. **Contact:** David J. Abrams, President. **E-mail address:** djab@ix.netcom.com. **Description:** An executive search firm operating on both retainer and contingency bases. Company pays fee. **Specializes in the areas of:** Computer Science/Software; Sales; Technical. **Positions commonly filled include:** Internet Services Manager; MIS Specialist; Software Engineer; Technical Writer/Editor; Telecommunications Manager. **Average salary range of placements:** More than $50,000. **Number of placements per year:** 50 - 99.

PROQUEST
5 Alexander Road, Billerica MA 01821. 978/670-9118. **Fax:** 978/670-2356. **Contact:** Daniel Casey, President. **World Wide Web address:** http://www.members.aol.com/prqust/proquest.html. **Description:** An executive search firm operating on both retained and contingency bases. The firm focuses on the financial investment and retirement services industries. Company pays fee. **Specializes in the areas of:** Finance; Insurance. **Positions commonly filled include:** Account Manager; Administrator; Investment Manager. **Average salary range of placements:** $30,000 - $50,000.

PROSEARCH, INC.
599 North Avenue, Wakefield MA 01880. 781/245-2224. **Fax:** 781/224-4252. **Contact:** Mr. Patrick Cresse, Senior Technical Recruiter. **E-mail address:** search@share.net. **Description:** An executive search firm that operates on a contingency basis. The firm focuses on professional MIS placement in the financial services and software industries. **Specializes in the areas of:** Administration; Computer Science/Software. **Positions commonly filled include:** Computer

Programmer; Internet Services Manager; MIS Specialist; Systems Analyst. **Average salary range of placements:** More than $50,000. **Number of placements per year:** 1 - 49.

QUALITY SEARCH
314 Liberty Square, Danvers MA 01923. 978/777-0220. **Fax:** 978/777-9110. **Contact:** Manager. **Description:** An executive search firm. **Specializes in the areas of:** Software Quality Assurance.

BRUCE RAFEY ASSOCIATES
P.O. Box 510, Lynn MA 01903. 781/581-3373. **Toll-free phone:** 800/44-RAFEY. **Fax:** 781/599-6849. **Contact:** Bruce Rafey, President. **Description:** An executive search firm. **Specializes in the areas of:** Electronics.

J.E. RANTA ASSOCIATES
112 Washington Street, Marblehead MA 01945. 781/639-0788. **Fax:** 781/631-9828. **Contact:** Ed Ranta, Owner/President. **Description:** An executive search firm operating on both retained and contingency bases. Founded in 1985. Company pays fee. **Specializes in the areas of:** Administration; Computer Science/Software; Data Processing; Finance; MIS/EDP; Technical. **Positions commonly filled include:** Computer Programmer; Internet Services Manager; Management Analyst/Consultant; MIS Specialist; Systems Analyst; Telecommunications Manager. **Average salary range of placements:** More than $50,000. **Number of placements per year:** 1 - 49.

RAYMOND KARSAN ASSOCIATES
18 Commerce Way, 7th Floor, Woburn MA 01801. 781/932-0400. **Contact:** William Docker, Principal. **Description:** An executive search firm operating on a retainer basis. Company pays fee. **Positions commonly filled include:** Biomedical Engineer; Design Engineer; Electrical/Electronics Engineer; General Manager; Human Resources Manager; Mechanical Engineer; MIS Specialist; Multimedia Designer; Quality Control Supervisor; Software Engineer; Telecommunications Manager. **Average salary range of placements:** More than $50,000. **Number of placements per year:** 50 - 99.

RECRUITING SPECIALISTS
P.O. Box 572, Dedham MA 02027-0572. 781/329-5850. **Fax:** 781/329-5840. **Contact:** Cindy Laughlin, President. **Description:** An executive search firm that recruits nationwide for the retail and food/hospitality industries. Recruiting Specialists operates on a contingency basis. Company pays fee. **Specializes in the areas of:** Food Industry; Retail. **Other U.S. locations:** Nationwide. **Average salary range of placements:** $30,000 - $50,000. **Number of placements per year:** 100 - 199.

RESOURCES OBJECTIVES INC.
185 Devonshire Street, Boston MA 02110. 617/338-5500. **Fax:** 617/338-5558. **Contact:** D.W. Dacosta, Director. **E-mail address:** mtemp@tiac.net. **Description:** An executive search firm operating on a retainer basis. Company pays fee. **Specializes in the areas of:** Banking; Computer Science/Software; Legal; Sales. **Positions commonly filled include:** Accountant/Auditor; Attorney; Bank Officer/Manager; Branch Manager; Physician; Software Engineer; Technical Writer/Editor. **Other U.S. locations:** Nationwide. **Number of placements per year:** 50 - 99.

THE RETAIL NETWORK
161 Forbes Road, Braintree MA 02184. 781/380-8830. **Fax:** 781/380-7656. **Contact:** Gary Belastock, Vice President. **Description:** An executive search firm operating on both retainer and contingency bases. The firm focuses on retail industry placement. Company pays fee. **Specializes in the areas of:** Retail. **Positions commonly filled include:** Buyer; Retail Executive; Retail Manager; Retail Merchandiser; Wholesale and Retail Buyer. **Corporate headquarters location:** Boynton Beach FL. **Other U.S. locations:** Nationwide. **Average salary range of placements:** $30,000 - $50,000. **Number of placements per year:** 100 - 199.

RETAIL SEARCH OF NEW ENGLAND
194 Forbes Road, Braintree MA 02184. 781/849-9909. **Contact:** Manager. **Description:** An executive search firm that provides retail placements.

ROBSHAM ASSOCIATES
4 Faneuil Hall Marketplace, Boston MA 02109. 617/742-2944. **Contact:** Manager. **Description:** An executive search firm. **Specializes in the areas of:** Finance; Marketing.

ROSTIE & ASSOCIATES
25 Burlington Mall Road, Suite 300, Burlington MA 01803. 617/270-0673. **Contact:** Office Manager. **Description:** An executive search firm. **Specializes in the areas of:** Computer Operations.

LOUIS RUDZINSKY ASSOCIATES, INC.
394 Lowell Street, Suite 17, P.O. Box 640, Lexington MA 02173. 781/862-6727. **Contact:** Howard Rudzinsky, Vice President. **Description:** An executive search firm. **Specializes in the areas of:** Computer Hardware/Software; Engineering; Sales; Technical. **Number of placements per year:** 50 - 99.

RUSSELL REYNOLDS ASSOCIATES, INC.
45 School Street, Boston MA 02108. 617/523-1111. **Contact:** Manager. **Description:** An executive search firm. **Specializes in the areas of:** Finance; Health/Medical; High-Tech; Industrial.

SALES & MARKETING SEARCH INC.
100 Conifer Hill Drive, Suite 108, Danvers MA 01923. 978/777-9997. **Fax:** 978/777-9998. **Contact:** Russell Smith, Managing Partner. **E-mail address:** russ@smsearch.com. **World Wide Web address:** http://www.smsearch.com. **Description:** An executive search firm operating on both retainer and contingency bases. The firm focuses on the recruitment and placement of sales and marketing professionals in the computer, data communications, and telecommunications industries. Company pays fee. **Specializes in the areas of:** Sales. **Positions commonly filled include:** Marketing Manager; Sales Manager; Sales Representative. **Average salary range of placements:** More than $50,000. **Number of placements per year:** 50 - 99.

SALES CONSULTANTS OF CAPE COD
P.O. Box 420, Sagamore Beach MA 02562. 508/888-8704. **Contact:** Ed Cahan, Manager. **Description:** An executive search firm. **Specializes in the areas of:** Accounting/Auditing; Administration; Advertising; Architecture/Construction; Banking; Communications; Computer Hardware/Software; Construction; Electrical; Engineering; Finance; Food Industry; General Management; Health/Medical; Operations Management; Personnel/Labor Relations; Pharmaceutical; Procurement; Publishing; Real Estate; Retail; Sales; Technical; Textiles; Transportation. **Corporate headquarters location:** Cleveland OH. **Other U.S. locations:** Nationwide.

SALES CONSULTANTS OF MANSFIELD
272 Chauncy Street, Mansfield MA 02048. 508/339-1924. **Contact:** James L. Noyes, Manager. **Description:** An executive search firm operating on a contingency basis. The firm places marketing, sales, management, and technical personnel and works with

suppliers of chemicals used in the electronics industry. **Specializes in the areas of:** General Management; Operations Management; Sales; Technical. **Positions commonly filled include:** General Manager; Market Research Analyst; Services Sales Representative. **Corporate headquarters location:** Cleveland OH. **Other U.S. locations:** Nationwide. **Average salary range of placements:** More than $50,000. **Number of placements per year:** 1 - 49.

SALES CONSULTANTS OF PLYMOUTH COUNTY
567 Pleasant Street, Suite 8, Brockton MA 02401. 508/587-2030. **Fax:** 508/587-9261. **Contact:** Milt Feinson, President. **Description:** An executive search firm. **Specializes in the areas of:** Accounting/Auditing; Administration; Advertising; Architecture/Construction; Banking; Communications; Computer Hardware/Software; Electrical; Engineering; Finance; Food Industry; General Management; Health/Medical; Insurance; Legal; Manufacturing; Operations Management; Personnel/Labor Relations; Pharmaceutical; Procurement; Publishing; Retail; Sales; Technical; Textiles; Transportation. **Corporate headquarters location:** Cleveland OH. **Other U.S. locations:** Nationwide. **Average salary range of placements:** $30,000 - $50,000.

SALES CONSULTANTS OF WELLESLEY
888 Worcester Street, Suite 95, Wellesley MA 02181. 781/235-7700. **Fax:** 781/237-7207. **Contact:** Arthur J. Durante, General Manager. **Description:** An executive search firm. **Specializes in the areas of:** Accounting/Auditing; Administration; Advertising; Architecture/Construction; Banking; Communications; Computer Hardware/Software; Construction; Electrical; Engineering; Finance; Food Industry; General Management; Health/Medical; Insurance; Legal; Manufacturing; Operations Management; Personnel/Labor Relations; Pharmaceutical; Procurement; Publishing; Retail; Sales; Technical; Textiles; Transportation. **Corporate headquarters location:** Cleveland OH. **Other U.S. locations:** Nationwide.

SCIENTIFIC RESOURCES
214 Garden Street, Needham MA 02192. 781/449-8760. **Contact:** Manager. **Description:** An executive search firm. **Specializes in the areas of:** Biotechnology; Medical Technology; Pharmaceutical.

SEARCH & PLACEMENT SERVICES, INC.
P.O. Box 3331, Pittsfield MA 01202. 413/499-2498. **Contact:** Manager. **Description:** A generalist executive search firm.

SEARCH INTERNATIONAL
P.O. Box 81, Newburyport MA 01950. 978/465-4000. **Fax:** 978/465-4069. **Contact:** Brian E. Eagar, President. **Description:** An executive search firm. Company pays fee. **Specializes in the areas of:** Hotel/Restaurant. **Positions commonly filled include:** General Manager; Hotel Manager; Restaurant/Food Service Manager. **Number of placements per year:** 50 - 99.

SEARCH PROFESSIONALS
150 Wood Road, Braintree MA 02184. 781/843-0700. **Fax:** 781/848-8634. **Contact:** Richard Barzelay, President. **Description:** An executive search firm. Company pays fee. **Specializes in the areas of:** Personnel/Labor Relations; Retail. **Positions commonly filled include:** Human Resources Manager; Purchasing Agent/Manager; Wholesale and Retail Buyer. **Number of placements per year:** 100 - 199.

SEARCHNET
P.O. Box 252, Stow MA 01775. 978/897-9193. **Contact:** Linda Rogers, Owner. **Description:** An executive search firm operating on a retainer basis. **Specializes in the areas of:** Fashion; Retail. **Positions commonly filled include:** Architect; Branch Manager; Buyer; Construction Contractor; Customer Service Representative; Designer; General Manager; Human Resources Manager; Management Analyst/Consultant; Management Trainee; MIS Specialist; Operations/Production Manager; Systems Analyst. **Average salary range of placements:** More than $50,000. **Number of placements per year:** 50 - 99.

SELECTED EXECUTIVES INC.
76 Winn Street, Woburn MA 01801. 781/933-1500. **Fax:** 781/933-4145. **Contact:** Mr. Lee R. Sanborn, Jr., Manager. **Description:** An executive search firm operating on both retainer and contingency bases. Company pays fee. **Specializes in the areas of:** Accounting/Auditing; Computer Science/Software; Engineering; Finance; Manufacturing; Personnel/Labor Relations; Sales. **Positions commonly filled include:** Accountant/Auditor; Actuary; Administrative Manager; Aerospace Engineer; Attorney; Automotive Mechanic; Bank Officer/Manager; Budget Analyst; Civil Engineer; Claim Representative; Clinical Lab Technician; Computer Programmer; Credit Manager; Customer Service Representative; Design Engineer; Electrical/Electronics Engineer; Environmental Engineer; Financial Analyst; Industrial Engineer; Management Analyst/Consultant; Mechanical Engineer; MIS Specialist; Quality Control Supervisor; Registered Nurse; Software Engineer; Systems Analyst; Technical Writer/Editor; Underwriter/Assistant Underwriter. **Average salary range of placements:** More than $50,000. **Number of placements per year:** 200 - 499.

SETFORD-SHAW-NAJARIAN ASSOCIATES
10 High Street, 6th Floor, Boston MA 02110. 617/422-0441. **Fax:** 617/422-0487. **Contact:** Matthew Malvese, Manager. **E-mail address:** mmalvese@tisny.com. **World Wide Web address:** http://www.tisny.com. **Description:** An executive search firm that also offers some contract placements. **Specializes in the areas of:** Information Technology. **Positions commonly filled include:** Computer Programmer; Database Manager; Human Resources Manager; MIS Specialist; Software Engineer; Systems Analyst; Webmaster. **Corporate headquarters location:** New York NY. **Number of placements per year:** 100-199.

L.A. SILVER ASSOCIATES
463 Worcester Road, Framingham MA 01701. 508/879-2603. **Fax:** 508/879-8425. **Contact:** Mr. Lee Silver, President. **Description:** A retained executive search firm. Company pays fee. **Specializes in the areas of:** Computer Science/Software; Telecommunications. **Corporate headquarters location:** This Location. **Average salary range of placements:** More than $50,000. **Number of placements per year:** 100 - 199.

CHRISTOPHER SMALLHORN EXECUTIVE RECRUITING
One Boston Place, 18th Floor, Boston MA 02108. 617/723-8180. **Contact:** Manager. **Description:** An executive search firm.

SNELLING & SNELLING
545 Boylston Street, Boston MA 02116. 617/262-5151. **Fax:** 617/262-9789. **Contact:** Ed Diamond, President. **Description:** An executive search firm operating on a contingency basis.

STEPHEN M. SONIS ASSOCIATES
275 Turnpike Street, Suite 202, Canton MA 02021. 781/821-0303. **Contact:** Manager. **Description:** An executive search firm. **Specializes in the areas of:** Retail.

SOURCE SERVICES CORPORATION
20 Burlington Mall Road, Suite 305, Burlington MA 01803. 781/272-5000. **Fax:** 781/273-4969. **Contact:** Manager. **Description:** An executive search firm. The divisions at this location include Source Consulting, Source Engineering, and Accountant Source Temps. **Specializes in the areas of:** Accounting/Auditing; Computer Hardware/Software; Engineering.

SOURCE SERVICES CORPORATION
1500 West Park Drive, Suite 390, Westborough MA 01581. 508/366-2600. **Fax:** 508/898-0115. **Contact:** Manager. **Description:** An executive search firm. The divisions at this location include Source EDP and Source Engineering. **Specializes in the areas of:** Computer Hardware/Software; Engineering; Information Technology.

STONE & YOUNGBLOOD
304 Newbury Street, Boston MA 02115. 781/647-0070. **Fax:** 781/647-0460. **Contact:** Stephen Sarkis, Vice President. **Description:** An executive search firm operating on retained and contingency bases. Company pays fee. **Specializes in the areas of:** Advertising; Architecture/Construction; Art/Design; Broadcasting; Computer Science/Software; Finance; Food Industry; General Management; Health/Medical; Insurance; Publishing; Retail; Sales. **Positions commonly filled include:** Account Manager; Account Representative; Advertising Account Executive; Assistant Manager; Broadcast Technician; Buyer; Chief Financial Officer; Editor; Food Scientist/Technologist; Graphic Artist; Graphic Designer; Insurance Agent/Broker; Internet Services Manager; Managing Editor; Online Content Specialist; Operations Engineer; Sales Executive; Sales Representative; Vice President of Marketing; Vice President of Operations. **Average salary range of placements:** More than $50,000.

STONE CONSULTING GROUP & LEGAL SEARCH SPECIALISTS
10 Winthrop Square, 4th Floor, Boston MA 02110. 617/426-2992. **Fax:** 617/426-2298. **Contact:** Jonathan Stone, Principal. **Description:** An executive search firm operating on a retained basis. Company pays fee. **Specializes in the areas of:** Administration; Biology; Computer Science/Software; Engineering; Personnel/Labor Relations; Technical. **Positions commonly filled include:** Attorney; Bank Officer/Manager; Biological Scientist; Biomedical Engineer; Chief Financial Officer; Client Services Representative; Computer Programmer; Controller; Economist; Fundraising Specialist; Human Resources Manager; Intellectual Property Lawyer; MIS Specialist; Paralegal.

STONE GROUP INC.
715 Boylston Street, Boston MA 02116. 617/262-2700. **Fax:** 617/262-0722. **Contact:** Terrence O'Neil, President. **Description:** An executive search firm operating on both retainer and contingency bases. The firm focuses on the placement of professionals in the insurance and risk management industries. Company pays fee. **Specializes in the areas of:** Insurance. **Positions commonly filled include:** Insurance Agent/Broker; Underwriter/Assistant Underwriter. **Average salary range of placements:** More than $50,000.

STRAUBE ASSOCIATES
855 Turnpike Street, North Andover MA 01845. 978/687-1993. **Fax:** 978/687-1886. **Contact:** Stanley H. Straube, President. **Description:** An executive search firm. Company pays fee. **Specializes in the areas of:** Banking; Computer Science/Software; Engineering; General Management; Health/Medical; Manufacturing; Personnel/Labor Relations; Sales; Technical. **Number of placements per year:** 1 - 49.

SULLIVAN ASSOCIATES
175 Derby Street, Suite 7, Hingham MA 02043. 781/749-2242. **Contact:** Manager. **Description:** An executive search firm. **Specializes in the areas of:** Finance; High-Tech; Manufacturing; Sales.

T.F.S. HUMAN RESOURCE SOLUTIONS, INC.
205 Broadway, Cambridge MA 02139-1901. 617/864-6330. **Contact:** Burton Bartzoff, Principal. **Description:** An executive search firm. **Specializes in the areas of:** Accounting/Auditing; Finance; General Management; Personnel/Labor Relations; Sales. **Number of placements per year:** 50 - 99.

THE TOWER GROUP
8 Hunton Circle, Attleboro MA 02703. 508/226-6735. **Contact:** Jim Tower, President. **Description:** An executive search firm operating on both retainer and contingency bases. The firm focuses on the placement of sales personnel in the medical industry. Company pays fee. **Specializes in the areas of:** Sales.

UNITED PROFESSIONAL PLACEMENT
3 East Mountain Street, Worcester MA 01606. 508/853-9000. **Fax:** 508/853-0311. **Contact:** Mr. Patrick Kelley, President. **Description:** An executive search firm operating on both retainer and contingency bases. **NOTE:** A college degree is required. **Specializes in the areas of:** Communications; Engineering; Food Industry; Industrial; Manufacturing; Plastics; Sales. **Positions commonly filled include:** Accountant/Auditor; Branch Manager; Customer Service Representative; Design Engineer; Draftsperson; Electrical/Electronics Engineer; Industrial Engineer; Management Trainee; Mechanical Engineer; Restaurant/Food Service Manager. **Number of placements per year:** 100 - 199.

VAN/GRACE ASSOCIATES, INC.
276 West Main Street, Northborough MA 01532. 508/393-1700. **Fax:** 508/393-1780. **Contact:** Stephen J. Morris, President. **E-mail address:** vangrace@vangrace.com. **Description:** An executive search firm. Van/Grace Associates focuses on the plastic, rubber, polymer, coating, converting, biomedical, and adhesive industries. Founded in 1962. Company pays fee. **Specializes in the areas of:** Engineering. **Positions commonly filled include:** Chemical Engineer; Chemist. **Average salary range of placements:** More than $50,000. **Number of placements per year:** 50 - 99.

VANGUARD EXECUTIVE SERVICES
512 West Main Street, Shrewsbury MA 01545. 508/842-5600. **Fax:** 508/842-4959. **Contact:** Irene Maloney, Office Manager. **Description:** An executive search firm operating on a retained basis. Company pays fee. **Specializes in the areas of:** Engineering; Manufacturing.

VERSION 2.0 CORPORATION
60 State Street, Suite 700, Boston MA 02109. 617/742-3802. **Fax:** 617/742-3805. **Contact:** Michael J. Hogarty, Managing Partner. **E-mail address:** hogarty@v20.com. **Description:** An executive search firm. Company pays fee. **Positions commonly filled include:** Computer Programmer; Systems Analyst.

THE WARD GROUP
8 Cedar Street, Woburn MA 01801. 781/938-4000. **Fax:** 781/938-4100. **Contact:** Jim Ward, President. **E-mail address:** thewardgroup@aol.com. **Description:** An executive search firm operating on a retainer basis. The Ward Group focuses on marketing and communications staffing. Company pays fee. **Specializes in the areas of:** Advertising; Communications; Public Relations; Sales. **Average**

salary range of placements: More than $50,000. **Number of placements per year:** 50 - 99.

S.B. WEBSTER & ASSOCIATES, INC.
P.O. Box 1007, Duxbury MA 02331. 781/934-6603. **Fax:** 781/934-9181. **Contact:** William L. Webster, President. **Description:** An executive search firm operating on a retainer basis. Company pays fee. **Specializes in the areas of:** Administration; Computer Science/Software; General Management; Manufacturing. **Positions commonly filled include:** MIS Specialist; Software Engineer. **Average salary range of placements:** More than $50,000. **Number of placements per year:** 1 - 49.

WILLMOTT & ASSOCIATES
922 Waltham Street, Suite 103, Lexington MA 02173. 781/863-5400. **Contact:** Office Manager. **Description:** An executive search firm. **Specializes in the areas of:** Human Resources.

WINFIELD ASSOCIATES
53 Winter Street, Weymouth MA 02189. 781/337-1010. **Fax:** 781/335-0089. **Contact:** Carl W. Siegel, Principal. **Description:** An executive search firm operating on a contingency basis. Company pays fee. **Specializes in the areas of:** Biology; Engineering; Health/Medical. **Positions commonly filled include:** Biological Scientist; Biomedical Engineer; Electrical/Electronics Engineer; Mechanical Engineer. **Number of placements per year:** 1 - 49.

WRIGHT ASSOCIATES
929 Main Street, Millis MA 02054. 508/376-0000. **Contact:** Manager. **Description:** An executive search firm. **Specializes in the areas of:** Administration.

XAVIER ASSOCIATES, INC.
1350 Belmont Street, Brockton MA 02401. 508/584-9414. **Contact:** Manager. **Description:** An executive search firm. **Specializes in the areas of:** Consumer Products; Finance; High-Tech.

PERMANENT EMPLOYMENT AGENCIES

AARP SENIOR EMPLOYMENT PROGRAM
P.O. Box 2065, Danvers MA 01923. 978/777-7582. **Contact:** Harold O'Connell, Project Director. **Description:** A permanent employment agency that provides permanent placement for older adults.

AARP SENIOR EMPLOYMENT PROGRAM
27 Water Street, Suite 104, Wakefield MA 01880. 781/246-5307. **Fax:** 781/246-5355. **Contact:** Liane H. Gould, Project Director. **Description:** A permanent employment agency that provides placements for older workers. **Average salary range of placements:** $20,000 - $29,999. **Number of placements per year:** 1 - 49.

ABBOT PERSONNEL CONSULTING SERVICES, INC.
4 Faneuil Hall Marketplace, South Market, 4th Floor, Boston MA 02109. 617/423-0202. **Fax:** 617/227-7915. **Contact:** Personnel. **Description:** A permanent employment agency. **Specializes in the areas of:** Administration; Clerical; Office Support; Personnel/Labor Relations.

ABILITY SEARCH OF NEW ENGLAND
P.O. Box 883, Framingham MA 01701. 508/872-2060. **Fax:** 508/872-2345. **Contact:** Jerry Vengrow, President. **Description:** A permanent employment agency. Company pays fee. **Specializes in the areas of:** Accounting/Auditing; Administration; Biology; Computer Science/Software; Engineering; Finance; General Management; Industrial; Legal; Manufacturing; Personnel/Labor Relations; Publishing; Sales; Secretarial; Technical. **Positions commonly filled include:** Accountant/Auditor; Aerospace Engineer; Architect; Attorney; Biological Scientist; Biomedical Engineer; Budget Analyst; Buyer; Chemical Engineer; Chemist; Civil Engineer; Clinical Lab Technician; Computer Engineer; Computer Programmer; Customer Service Representative; Draftsperson; EEG Technologist; EKG Technician; Electrical/Electronics Engineer; Electrician; Financial Analyst; Industrial Engineer; Industrial Production Manager; Management Analyst/Consultant; Mechanical Engineer; Physician; Physicist; Quality Control Supervisor; Radiological Technologist; Software Engineer; Structural Engineer; Systems Analyst; Technical Writer/Editor. **Number of placements per year:** 50 - 99.

ACTIVE EMPLOYMENT SERVICE
108 Grove Street, Worcester MA 01605-2651. 508/756-6550. **Contact:** Recruiter. **Description:** A permanent employment agency that also provides resume writing services and temporary placements.

ADDITIONAL TECHNICAL SUPPORT SERVICES
1466 Main Street, Waltham MA 02154. 781/893-5600. **Contact:** Office Manager. **Description:** A permanent employment agency. Company pays fee. **Specializes in the areas of:** Computer Hardware/Software; Engineering; Manufacturing; MIS/EDP; Technical. **Positions commonly filled include:** Aerospace Engineer; Civil Engineer; Computer Programmer; Draftsperson; Electrical/Electronics Engineer; Industrial Engineer; Mechanical Engineer; MIS Specialist; Purchasing Agent/Manager; Quality Control Supervisor; Sales Representative; Secretary; Systems Analyst; Technical Writer/Editor; Technician. **Number of placements per year:** 500 - 999.

ADVANCE PERSONNEL
P.O. Box 3009, 60 Mall Road, Burlington MA 01803. 781/273-4250. **Fax:** 781/273-2369. **Contact:** Branch Manager. **Description:** A permanent employment agency that also provides some temporary placements. Advance Personnel is a division of Robert Half International. Company pays fee. **Specializes in the areas of:** Advertising; Art/Design; Computer Hardware/Software; Engineering; Publishing; Sales; Technical. **Positions commonly filled include:** Commercial Artist; Editor; Graphic Designer; Marketing Specialist; Multimedia Designer; Technical Writer/Editor. **Corporate headquarters location:** Menlo Park CA. **Other U.S. locations:** Nationwide. **Number of placements per year:** 500 - 999.

ALL PRO PERSONNEL
18 Tremont Street, Boston MA 02108. 617/742-5585. **Contact:** Manager. **Description:** A permanent and temp-to-perm placement agency.

ALPHA PERSONNEL
P.O. Box 67, Mansfield MA 02048. 978/282-8500. **Contact:** Manager. **Description:** A permanent placement agency that also provides temporary and temp-to-perm placements.

AMERICAN NANNY COMPANY
P.O. Box 97, New Town MA 02258. 617/244-5154. **Contact:** Manager. **Description:** A permanent employment agency. Company pays fee. **Specializes in the areas of:** Child Care, In-Home. **Positions commonly filled include:** Nanny. **Average salary range of placements:** Less than $20,000. **Number of placements per year:** 100 - 199.

AMERICAN PERSONNEL SERVICE
185 Devonshire Street, Boston MA 02110. 617/350-0080. **Contact:** Manager. **Description:** A permanent placement agency.

ARTHUR-BLAIR ASSOCIATES INC.
One Court Street, Suite 500, Boston MA 02108. 617/723-8135. **Fax:** 617/723-8140. **Contact:** Tom Phinney, Owner. **Description:** A permanent and temporary placement agency. Company pays fee. **Specializes in the areas of:** Banking; Finance; Mortgage; Personnel/Labor Relations; Secretarial. **Positions commonly filled include:** Branch Manager; Brokerage Clerk; Clerical Supervisor; Underwriter/Assistant Underwriter. **Number of placements per year:** 100 - 199.

ASSOCIATED CAREER NETWORK
355 Union Street, New Bedford MA 02740. 508/990-1118. **Contact:** Manager. **Description:** A permanent employment agency that also provides temporary placements. **Specializes in the areas of:** Manufacturing.

BOSTONIAN PERSONNEL
P.O. Box 95, South Weymouth MA 02190. 781/340-3300. **Contact:** Manager. **Description:** A permanent placement agency. **Specializes in the areas of:** Legal.

BRADY EMPLOYMENT SERVICE
44 Bromfield Street, Boston MA 02108. 617/422-0488. **Fax:** 617/422-0490. **Contact:** George J. Brady, Owner/Manager. **Description:** A permanent employment agency. Company pays fee. **Specializes in the areas of:** Electrical; Engineering; General Management; Industrial; Manufacturing; Personnel/Labor Relations. **Positions commonly filled include:** Buyer; Chemical Engineer; Designer; Draftsperson; Electrical/Electronics Engineer; Electrician; Industrial Engineer; Industrial Production Manager; Manufacturing Engineer; Mechanical Engineer; Quality Control Supervisor.

BRENTWOOD PERSONNEL
1408 Providence Highway, Suite 322, Norwood MA 02062. 781/848-6330. **Contact:** Jeff Kurtz, President. **Description:** A permanent employment agency. **Specializes in the areas of:** Computer Hardware/Software; Engineering; MIS/EDP. **Positions commonly filled include:** Aerospace Engineer; Computer Programmer; Electrical/Electronics Engineer; Physicist. **Number of placements per year:** 50 - 99.

BUCKINGHAM PERSONNEL SERVICE
470 Washington Street, Suite 23, Norwood MA 02062. 781/762-7888. **Contact:** Office Manager. **Description:** A permanent placement agency.

CQ PERSONNEL
76 Canal Street, Boston MA 02114. 617/248-8688. **Contact:** Manager. **Description:** A permanent employment agency that also provides temporary placements.

C.R.W. & ASSOCIATES
P.O. Box 66126, Newton MA 02166. 617/928-0408. **Contact:** Charles R. Watt, Managing Director. **Description:** A permanent employment agency. Company pays fee. **Specializes in the areas of:** Administration; Computer Science/Software. **Positions commonly filled include:** Computer Programmer; Software Engineer; Systems Analyst. **Number of placements per year:** 100 - 199.

CAREER CENTER, INC.
1253 Highland Avenue, Needham MA 02192. 781/444-0650. **Contact:** Manager. **Description:** A permanent placement agency.

CENTOR PERSONNEL
185 New Boston Street, Woburn MA 01801. 781/935-2955. **Fax:** 781/935-2954. **Contact:** Paulette Centor, President. **E-mail address:** pcentor@tiac.net. **World Wide Web address:** http://www.tiac.net/users/pcentor. **Description:** A permanent placement agency. Company pays fee. **Specializes in the areas of:** Computer Science/Software; Sales. **Positions commonly filled include:** Account Manager; Account Representative; Marketing Manager; Marketing Specialist; Sales Executive; Sales Manager; Sales Representative. **Average salary range of placements:** More than $50,000. **Number of placements per year:** 1 - 49.

CLEARY CONSULTANTS INC.
21 Merchants Row, Boston MA 02109. 617/367-7189. **Fax:** 617/367-3202. **Contact:** Mary Cleary, President. **Description:** A permanent employment agency. Company pays fee. **Specializes in the areas of:** Accounting/Auditing; Administration; Advertising; Banking; Computer Science/Software; Finance; Health/Medical; Legal; Personnel/Labor Relations; Sales; Secretarial. **Positions commonly filled include:** Accountant/Auditor; Actuary; Administrative Manager; Advertising Clerk; Attorney; Bank Officer/Manager; Branch Manager; Brokerage Clerk; Clerical Supervisor; Customer Service Representative; Financial Analyst; Health Services Manager; Licensed Practical Nurse; Medical Records Technician; Paralegal; Pharmacist; Physician; Quality Control Supervisor; Registered Nurse; Software Engineer; Systems Analyst; Travel Agent. **Number of placements per year:** 500 - 999.

CONSTRUCTION DIRECTORY
850 Bridge Road, Eastham MA 02642. 508/255-9082. **Fax:** 508/255-9107. **Contact:** Dave Toms, President. **Description:** A permanent employment agency that places professionals in the building contracting industry. Company pays fee. **Specializes in the areas of:** Construction; Engineering. **Positions commonly filled include:** Civil Engineer; Construction Contractor; Surveyor. **Number of placements per year:** 1 - 49.

DERBY ASSOCIATES INC.
420 Washington Street, Braintree MA 02184-4755. 781/848-6969. **Fax:** 781/848-6984. **Contact:** Ann Marie Briggs, President. **Description:** A permanent employment agency that focuses on the permanent placement of office support personnel. Company pays fee. **Specializes in the areas of:** Accounting/Auditing; Administration; Advertising; Architecture/Construction; Art/Design; Banking; Computer Science/Software; Engineering; Fashion; Finance; Sales. **Positions commonly filled include:** Accountant/Auditor; Advertising Clerk; Bank Officer/Manager; Branch Manager; Brokerage Clerk; Budget Analyst; Clerical Supervisor; Computer Programmer; Credit Manager; Customer Service Representative; Typist/Word Processor. **Average salary range of placements:** $30,000 - $50,000. **Number of placements per year:** 500 - 999.

DISCOVERY PERSONNEL INC.
150 Speen Street, Suite 303, Framingham MA 01701-2004. 508/872-5100. **Contact:** Janet Brouthers, Manager. **Description:** A permanent employment agency. Company pays fee. **Specializes in the areas of:** Administration; Banking; Sales; Secretarial. **Positions commonly filled include:** Accountant/Auditor; Bank Officer/Manager; Branch Manager; Brokerage Clerk; Budget Analyst; Buyer; Clerical Supervisor; Credit Manager; Customer Service Representative; Financial Analyst; Human Resources Specialist; Typist/Word Processor; Underwriter/Assistant Underwriter. **Average salary range of

placements: $30,000 - $50,000. **Number of placements per year:** 100 - 199.

EF TECHNICAL RESOURCES
1218 Boylston Street, Newton MA 02164-1017. 617/969-7850. **Fax:** 617/969-9429. **Contact:** Elli Freihofer, Owner. **Description:** A permanent employment agency. Company pays fee. **Specializes in the areas of:** Administration; Computer Science/Software; Technical. **Positions commonly filled include:** Computer Programmer; MIS Specialist; Software Engineer; Systems Analyst. **Number of placements per year:** 1 - 49.

FRANKLIN-PIERCE ASSOCIATES
One Liberty Square, Boston MA 02109-4825. 617/695-1700. **Fax:** 617/695-0683. **Contact:** Edward A. Blum, Vice President/General Manager. **Description:** A permanent employment agency. Company pays fee. **Specializes in the areas of:** Office Support; Secretarial. **Positions commonly filled include:** Administrative Assistant; Customer Service Representative; Human Resources Specialist; Secretary; Typist/Word Processor. **Number of placements per year:** 500 - 999.

GILLARD ASSOCIATES
75 McNeil Way, Dedham MA 02026. 781/329-4731. **Fax:** 781/329-1357. **Contact:** Elizabeth Gillard, President. **E-mail address:** gillardlgl@aol.com. **Description:** A permanent employment agency. Company pays fee. **Specializes in the areas of:** Legal. **Positions commonly filled include:** Attorney; Legal Secretary; Paralegal. **Number of placements per year:** 1 - 49.

HILTON ASSOCIATES
321 Cabot Street, Beverly MA 01915. 978/921-0840. **Contact:** Executive Vice President. **Description:** A permanent employment agency. Company pays fee. **Specializes in the areas of:** Health/Medical; MIS/EDP; Sales. **Positions commonly filled include:** Biological Scientist; Computer Programmer; Customer Service Representative; MIS Specialist; Nurse; Sales Rep. **Number of placements per year:** 200 - 499.

HUMAN RESOURCE CONSULTANTS
1252 Elm Street, West Springfield MA 01089. 413/737-7563. **Fax:** 413/731-9897. **Contact:** John M. Turner, President. **Description:** A permanent employment agency. Company pays fee. **Specializes in the areas of:** Biology; Computer Science/Software; Engineering; Health/Medical. **Positions commonly filled include:** Biomedical Engineer; Computer Programmer; Industrial Engineer; Physical Therapist; Respiratory Therapist; Software Engineer; Systems Analyst. **Number of placements per year:** 50 - 99.

HUNTER ASSOCIATES
181 Park Avenue, West Springfield MA 01089-3365. 413/737-6560. **Fax:** 413/785-1295. **Contact:** Daniel M. Shooshan, Principal. **E-mail address:** hunter@hunterworldwide.com. **World Wide Web address:** http://www.hunterworldwide.com/~hunter. **Description:** A permanent employment agency. Hunter Associates focuses on the placement of management and technical professionals worldwide. Company pays fee. **Specializes in the areas of:** Engineering; Manufacturing. **Positions commonly filled include:** Design Engineer; Electrical/Electronics Engineer; Industrial Engineer; Mechanical Engineer; Software Engineer. **Average salary range of placements:** $30,000 - $50,000. **Number of placements per year:** 1 - 49.

I.T. RESOURCES
6 Summit Road, Lexington MA 02173-6004. 781/863-2661. **Fax:** 781/863-2686. **Contact:** Ken Loomis, President. **World Wide Web address:** http://www.ourworld.compuserve.com/homepages/kloomis. **Description:** A permanent employment agency. Company pays fee. **Specializes in the areas of:** Administration; Computer Science/Software. **Positions commonly filled include:** Computer Programmer; MIS Specialist; Software Engineer; Systems Analyst; Telecommunications Manager. **Average salary range of placements:** More than $50,000. **Number of placements per year:** 50 - 99.

IN SEARCH OF NANNY INC.
5 Cherry Hill Drive, Danvers MA 01923-2500. 978/777-9891. **Fax:** 978/762-6255. **Contact:** Betty Davis, President. **Description:** A permanent employment agency that places nannies for in-home child care. **Specializes in the areas of:** Education; Nannies; Social Services. **Number of placements per year:** 200 - 499.

INSURANCE PERSONNEL RECRUITERS
20 Pulsifer Street, P.O. Box 292, Newtonville MA 02160. 617/969-2192. **Fax:** 617/439-3253. **Contact:** Robert P. Whitten, President. **E-mail address:** ipr1@juno.com. **Description:** A permanent employment agency. Company pays fee. **Specializes in the areas of:** Insurance. **Positions commonly filled include:** Accountant/Auditor; Actuary; Adjuster; Administrative Manager; Attorney; Claim Representative; Claims Investigator; Customer Service Representative; Insurance Agent/Broker; Underwriter/Assistant Underwriter. **Number of placements per year:** 1 - 49.

INSURANCE STAFFING SERVICES
50 Salem Street, Building B, Lynnfield MA 01940. 781/246-6786. **Toll-free phone:** 800/601-1113. **Fax:** 781/246-6788. **Contact:** Annis Legrow, Placement Manager. **E-mail address:** instemps@aol.com. **Description:** A permanent employment agency that provides both permanent and temporary placement of insurance professionals. Company pays fee. **Specializes in the areas of:** Insurance. **Positions commonly filled include:** Adjuster; Brokerage Clerk; Claim Representative; Clerical Supervisor; Customer Service Representative; Insurance Agent/Broker; Operations/Production Manager; Underwriter/Assistant Underwriter. **Average salary range of placements:** $30,000 - $50,000. **Number of placements per year:** 50 - 99.

INTERACTIVE SOFTWARE PLACEMENT, INC. (ISPI)
465 Auburn Street, Newton MA 02166. 617/527-2700. **Fax:** 617/965-7998. **Contact:** Sean Leary, President. **Description:** A permanent employment agency. **Specializes in the areas of:** Software Development; Software Engineering; Software Quality Assurance.

WILLIAM JAMES ASSOCIATES
800 Turnpike Street, Suite 300, North Andover MA 01845-6156. 978/685-0700. **Fax:** 978/685-7113. **Contact:** Bill Josephson, President. **Description:** A permanent employment agency. **Specializes in the areas of:** Computer Science/Software. **Positions commonly filled include:** Computer Programmer; Software Engineer; Systems Analyst.

KNF&T INC.
84 State Street, Boston MA 02109. 617/227-0677. **Fax:** 617/227-8309. **Contact:** Personnel Consultant. **E-mail address:** info@knft.com. **World Wide Web address:** http://www.knft.com. **Description:** A permanent and temporary staffing agency. Founded in 1983. Company pays fee. **Specializes in the areas of:** Administration. **Positions commonly filled include:** Accountant; Administrative Assistant; Administrative Manager; Clerical Supervisor; Customer Service

Representative; Data Entry Clerk; Editorial Assistant; Graphic Artist; Graphic Designer; Human Resources Assistant; Marketing Assistant; Receptionist; Sales Representative; Secretary; Typist/Word Processor. **Benefits available to temporary workers:** Medical Insurance; Paid Holidays; Paid Vacation. **Corporate headquarters location:** This Location. **Other area locations:** Westborough MA. **Average salary range of placements:** $30,000 - $50,000. **Number of placements per year:** 1000+.

KINGSTON-DWIGHT ASSOCIATES
100 Franklin Street, Suite 300, Boston MA 02110. 617/350-8811. **Contact:** Joseph J. Hyde, Jr., Partner. **Description:** A permanent employment agency. Company pays fee. **Specializes in the areas of:** Accounting/Auditing; Banking; Finance. **Positions commonly filled include:** Account Representative; Bookkeeper; Controller; Credit Manager; EDP Specialist; Financial Analyst. **Number of placements per year:** 100 - 199.

LANE EMPLOYMENT SERVICE, INC.
370 Main Street, Suite 820, Worcester MA 01608. 508/757-5678. **Contact:** Richard Lane, CPC/President. **Description:** A permanent employment agency. Company pays fee. **Specializes in the areas of:** Accounting/Auditing; Banking; Clerical; Computer Hardware/Software; Engineering; Finance; Insurance; Manufacturing; MIS/EDP; Secretarial. **Positions commonly filled include:** Accountant/Auditor; Actuary; Administrative Assistant; Bank Officer/Manager; Biological Scientist; Bookkeeper; Claim Representative; Computer Programmer; Credit Manager; Data Entry Clerk; EDP Specialist; Electrical/Electronics Engineer; Financial Analyst; General Manager; Human Resources Manager; Industrial Designer; Industrial Engineer; Legal Secretary; Marketing Specialist; Mechanical Engineer; Medical Secretary; Metallurgical Engineer; Purchasing Agent/Manager; Receptionist; Systems Analyst; Typist/Word Processor.

JOHN LEONARD PERSONNEL ASSOCIATES
One Post Office Square, Boston MA 02109. 617/423-6800. **Fax:** 617/451-0384. **Contact:** Linda J. Poldoian, President. **Description:** A permanent and temporary placement agency. Company pays fee. **Specializes in the areas of:** Advertising; Architecture/Construction; Biotechnology; Engineering; Finance; Health/Medical; Legal; Personnel/Labor Relations; Secretarial. **Positions commonly filled include:** Administrative Assistant; Bookkeeper; Computer Operator; Customer Service Representative; Data Entry Clerk; Human Resources Specialist; Internet Services Manager; Legal Secretary; Medical Secretary; MIS Specialist; Paralegal; Sales Representative; Typist/Word Processor. **Other area locations:** Cambridge MA; Wellesley MA; Westborough MA. **Number of placements per year:** 500 - 999.

JOHN LEONARD PERSONNEL ASSOCIATES
70 Walnut Street, Wellesley MA 02181. 781/431-5948. **Contact:** Lisa McPhee, Manager. **Description:** A permanent employment agency. Company pays fee. **Specializes in the areas of:** Advertising; Architecture/Construction; Banking; Biotechnology; Computer Hardware/Software; Engineering; Finance; Health/Medical; Legal; Personnel/Labor Relations; Secretarial. **Positions commonly filled include:** Administrative Assistant; Bookkeeper; Clerk; Computer Operator; Customer Service Representative; Data Entry Clerk; Legal Secretary; Medical Secretary; Typist/Word Processor.

JOHN LEONARD PERSONNEL ASSOCIATES
50 Church Street, Cambridge MA 02138. 617/864-7200. **Contact:** Manager. **Description:** A permanent and temporary employment agency. **Specializes in the areas of:** Administration.

NATIONWIDE BUSINESS SERVICE
P.O. Box 457, Westfield MA 01086. 413/568-9568. **Fax:** 413/568-9607. **Contact:** Alan Cheika, President/Technical Recruiter. **Description:** A permanent employment agency. Company pays fee. **Specializes in the areas of:** Engineering; Manufacturing; Technical. **Positions commonly filled include:** Chemical Engineer; Computer Programmer; Electrical/Electronics Engineer; Industrial Engineer; Mechanical Engineer; Structural Engineer; Systems Analyst. **Number of placements per year:** 1 - 49.

NEW BOSTON SELECT STAFFING
146 Bowdoin Street, Boston MA 02108. 617/720-0990. **Toll-free phone:** 800/833-9080. **Fax:** 617/723-8822. **Contact:** Ann E. Merlini, Director of Sales and Training. **Description:** A permanent employment agency. Company pays fee. **Specializes in the areas of:** Sales; Secretarial. **Positions commonly filled include:** Administrative Assistant; Bookkeeper; Clerk; Customer Service Representative; Data Entry Clerk; Legal Secretary; Medical Secretary; Receptionist; Sales Representative; Secretary; Typist/Word Processor. **Corporate headquarters location:** Woburn MA. **Other U.S. locations:** Atlanta GA. **Number of placements per year:** 500 - 999.

NEW ENGLAND JOB PLACEMENT
1634 Westover Road, Chicopee MA 01020-2818. 413/593-1060. **Fax:** 413/593-5277. **Contact:** Mike Grimes, Owner. **Description:** A permanent employment agency that focuses on the restaurant industry. Company pays fee. **Specializes in the areas of:** Food Industry. **Positions commonly filled include:** Restaurant/Food Service Manager. **Number of placements per year:** 1 - 49.

NEW ENGLAND PERSONNEL, INC.
2 Oliver Street, 9th Floor, Boston MA 02109. 617/542-3500. **Fax:** 617/542-3501. **Contact:** Kim Gonsalves, President. **Description:** A permanent employment agency that provides both permanent and temporary placements. Company pays fee. **Specializes in the areas of:** Administration; Industrial; Legal; Personnel/Labor Relations; Sales; Secretarial. **Positions commonly filled include:** Administrative Manager; Clerical Supervisor; Customer Service Representative; Paralegal; Services Sales Representative; Typist/Word Processor. **Number of placements per year:** 50 - 99.

THE ORIGINAL NANNY SERVICE
172 Institute Road, Worcester MA 01602-2136. 508/755-9284. **Contact:** Judy Flynn, President. **Description:** A nanny placement agency. **Specializes in the areas of:** Child Care, In-Home; Nannies. **Positions commonly filled include:** Nanny. **Average salary range of placements:** Less than $20,000.

PARENTS IN A PINCH
45 Bartlett Crescent, Brookline MA 02146-2208. 617/739-5437. **Fax:** 617/739-1939. **Contact:** Joy Manon, Recruitment Specialist. **Description:** A permanent employment agency that offers placement of child care providers in parents' homes, both temporary and long-term. **Specializes in the areas of:** Child Care, In-Home. **Average salary range of placements:** Less than $20,000. **Number of placements per year:** 1000+.

PARITY AND ASSOCIATES
313 Adams Street, Abington MA 02351. 781/878-5556. **Fax:** 781/878-6465. **Contact:** George Thompson, Staffing. **Description:** A permanent employment agency that places telemarketers. **Positions commonly filled include:** Telemarketer.

PLACEMENT COMPANY
7 Faneuil Hall Marketplace, Boston MA 02109. 617/723-9098. **Contact:** Manager. **Description:** A permanent placement agency. **Specializes in the areas of:** Accounting/Auditing; Finance.

PRESTIGE PLACEMENT CONSULTANTS
25 Storey Avenue, Suite 330, Newburyport MA 01950-1869. 978/462-5037. **Contact:** Jill Healey, President. **Description:** A permanent employment agency focusing on the placement of experienced insurance personnel. Company pays fee. **Specializes in the areas of:** Insurance. **Positions commonly filled include:** Claim Representative; Customer Service Representative; Insurance Services Manager; Sales Representative.

PROPOS ASSOCIATES, INC.
South End Bridge Circle, Agawam MA 01001. 413/789-3750. **Fax:** 413/789-3755. **Contact:** David Anable, President. **Description:** A permanent employment agency that provides both permanent and temporary placements. Company pays fee. **Specializes in the areas of:** Engineering; Insurance; Secretarial; Technical. **Positions commonly filled include:** Bookkeeper; Claim Representative; Customer Service Representative; Data Entry Clerk; Electrical/Electronics Engineer; Factory Worker; Legal Secretary; Light Industrial Worker; Manufacturing Engineer; Mechanical Engineer; Medical Secretary; Receptionist; Secretary; Technician; Typist/Word Processor. **Number of placements per year:** 1 - 49.

QUALITY PERSONNEL INC.
623 Pleasant Street, Brockton MA 02401-2511. 508/588-0500. **Contact:** Richard Hirsch, President. **Description:** A permanent employment agency that also provides temporary placements. Company pays fee. **Specializes in the areas of:** General Management; Light Industrial; Personnel/Labor Relations; Secretarial. **Positions commonly filled include:** General Manager; Human Resources Specialist; MIS Specialist; Services Sales Representative; Typist/Word Processor. **Average salary range of placements:** $20,000 - $29,999. **Number of placements per year:** 100 - 199.

E.S. RANDO ASSOCIATES, INC.
P.O. Box 654, Wilmington MA 01887. 978/657-4730. **Fax:** 978/658-4650. **Contact:** Lisa (TSI) or Grace (SAS), Recruiters. **E-mail address:** jobs@rando.com. **World Wide Web address:** http://www.rando.com. **Description:** A permanent employment agency specializing in permanent, temporary, and contract placements for professionals with a background in Model 204, SAS, and TSI. Founded in 1970. Company pays fee. **Specializes in the areas of:** Computer Hardware/Software; Health/Medical; Information Systems; MIS/EDP; Software Engineering. **Positions commonly filled include:** Computer Programmer; Database Manager; EDP Specialist; Finance Director; Financial Analyst; Management Analyst/Consultant; MIS Specialist; Project Manager; Software Engineer; Statistician; Systems Analyst. **Average salary range of placements:** More than $50,000. **Number of placements per year:** 50 - 99.

REARDON ASSOCIATES, INC.
990 Washington Street, Dedham MA 02026. 781/329-2660. **Fax:** 781/329-9918. **Contact:** Donald B. Tule, President. **Description:** A permanent employment agency. Company pays fee. **Specializes in the areas of:** Accounting/Auditing; Administration; Finance; Manufacturing; Personnel/Labor Relations; Secretarial. **Positions commonly filled include:** Accountant/Auditor; Budget Analyst; Buyer; Computer Programmer; Credit Manager; Financial Analyst; Human Resources Manager; Industrial Engineer; Purchasing Agent/Manager; Quality Control Supervisor; Systems Analyst. **Corporate headquarters location:** This Location. **Number of placements per year:** 200 - 499.

REARDON ASSOCIATES, INC.
27 Cambridge Street, Burlington MA 01803. 781/270-4400. **Fax:** 781/229-6814. **Contact:** Michelle Kramer, Division Manager. **E-mail address:** reardon@tiac.net. **World Wide Web address:** http://www.reardonassoc.com. **Description:** A permanent employment agency focusing on human resources, manufacturing, operations, finance, and MIS personnel. Company pays fee. **Specializes in the areas of:** Accounting/Auditing; Computer Science/Software; Manufacturing; Personnel/Labor Relations; Secretarial. **Positions commonly filled include:** Accountant/Auditor; Administrative Assistant; Bookkeeper; Clerk; Customer Service Representative; Human Resources Specialist; MIS Specialist; Operations/Production Manager; Purchasing Agent/Manager; Receptionist; Secretary; Typist/Word Processor. **Benefits available to temporary workers:** Medical Insurance; Paid Holidays; Paid Vacation. **Corporate headquarters location:** Dedham MA. **Average salary range of placements:** $30,000 - $50,000. **Number of placements per year:** 500 - 999.

THE RESOURCE PARTNERSHIP
20 Park Plaza, Suite 605, Boston MA 02116. 617/350-8921. **Fax:** 617/542-2474. **Contact:** Kathy Petkauskos, Office Manager. **Description:** A permanent employment agency. **Specializes in the areas of:** Disabled Applicants. **Number of placements per year:** 200 - 499.

ROMAC INTERNATIONAL
133 Federal Street, Suite 300, Boston MA 02110. 617/350-0945. **Fax:** 617/542-8570. **Contact:** Brian C. Cuddy, Division President. **Description:** A full-service staffing firm placing candidates on temporary, contract, and permanent assignments. The agency also provides career/outplacement counseling and executive searches. Company pays fee. **Specializes in the areas of:** Accounting/Auditing; Finance; Insurance. **Positions commonly filled include:** Accountant/Auditor; Actuary; Bookkeeper; Budget Analyst; Chief Financial Officer; Clerk; Computer Programmer; Controller; Credit Manager; Data Entry Clerk; Database Manager; EDP Specialist; Finance Director; Financial Analyst; Human Resources Specialist; Internet Services Manager; MIS Specialist; Operations Manager; Systems Analyst; Systems Manager. **Corporate headquarters location:** Tampa FL.

ROUTHIER PLACEMENT SPECIALISTS
160 State Street, Boston MA 02109. 617/742-2747. **Fax:** 617/742-3374. **Contact:** Tom Routhier, President. **E-mail address:** recept414@aol.com. **Description:** A permanent employment agency that also provides temporary placements. Company pays fee. **Specializes in the areas of:** Administration; Legal; Secretarial. **Positions commonly filled include:** Administrative Assistant; Data Entry Clerk; Secretary; Typist/Word Processor. **Average salary range of placements:** $30,000 - $50,000. **Number of placements per year:** 100 - 199.

GEORGE D. SANDEL ASSOCIATES
P.O. Box 588, Waltham MA 02254. 617/558-7770. **Fax:** 617/558-7771. **Contact:** Ivan Samuels, President. **E-mail address:** irsxgdsa@erols.com. **Description:** A permanent employment agency. Company pays fee. **Specializes in the areas of:** Administration; Computer Science/Software; Engineering; Health/Medical; Industrial; Manufacturing; Personnel/Labor Relations; Sales; Technical. **Positions commonly filled include:** Aerospace Engineer;

Biological Scientist; Biomedical Engineer; Computer Programmer; Electrical/Electronics Engineer; Health Services Manager; Human Resources Manager; Industrial Engineer; Mechanical Engineer; Physical Therapist; Physicist; Registered Nurse; Software Engineer; Systems Analyst. **Number of placements per year:** 1 - 49.

SCOTT-WAYNE ASSOCIATES
425 Boylston Street, 4th Floor, Boston MA 02116. 617/587-3000. **Fax:** 617/587-3030. **Contact:** R. Steven Dow, Executive Vice President. **E-mail address:** swa@gte.net. **Description:** A permanent employment agency. **Specializes in the areas of:** Accounting/Auditing; Banking; Finance. **Positions commonly filled include:** Accountant/Auditor; Budget Analyst; Credit Manager; Customer Service Representative; Financial Analyst. **Corporate headquarters location:** Topsfield MA. **Average salary range of placements:** More than $50,000. **Number of placements per year:** 50 - 99.

SELECTIVE OFFICE STAFFING
218 Boston Street, Topsfield MA 01983-2200. 978/887-0200. **Toll-free phone:** 800/427-0204. **Fax:** 978/887-0286. **Contact:** Sheila Burke, President. **Description:** A permanent employment agency that also provides temporary placements. Company pays fee. **Specializes in the areas of:** Accounting/Auditing; Personnel/Labor Relations; Sales; Secretarial. **Positions commonly filled include:** Accountant/Auditor; Administrative Manager; Buyer; Clerical Supervisor; Credit Manager; Customer Service Representative; Financial Analyst; Human Resources Specialist; Operations/Production Manager; Paralegal; Technical Writer/Editor; Typist/Word Processor. **Average salary range of placements:** $20,000 - $29,999. **Number of placements per year:** 50 - 99.

THE SKILL BUREAU, INC.
129 Tremont Street, Boston MA 02108. 617/423-2986. **Fax:** 617/423-9183. **Contact:** Jean McCarty, Vice President. **E-mail address:** tsb@skillbureau.com. **World Wide Web address:** http://www.skillbureau.com. **Description:** A permanent employment agency that provides both permanent and temporary placements. Founded in 1966. Company pays fee. **Specializes in the areas of:** Secretarial; Word Processing. **Positions commonly filled include:** Administrative Assistant; Administrative Manager; Clerical Supervisor; Computer Operator; Customer Service Representative; Secretary; Typist/Word Processor. **Benefits available to temporary workers:** Medical Insurance; Paid Holidays; Paid Vacation; Profit Sharing; Referral Bonus Plan. **Corporate headquarters location:** This Location. **Average salary range of placements:** $30,000 - $50,000.

SNELLING PERSONNEL SERVICES
3 Courthouse Lane, Chelmsford MA 01824. 978/970-3434. **Fax:** 978/970-3637. **Contact:** Manager. **Description:** A permanent employment agency that also provides temporary placements. Company pays fee. **Specializes in the areas of:** Accounting/Auditing; Administration; Advertising; Computer Science/Software; Manufacturing; Personnel/Labor Relations; Publishing; Sales; Secretarial. **Positions commonly filled include:** Accountant/Auditor; Adjuster; Administrative Manager; Chemist; Claim Representative; Clerical Supervisor; Clinical Lab Technician; Computer Programmer; Cost Estimator; Counselor; Credit Manager; Customer Service Representative; Designer; Insurance Agent/Broker; Management Trainee; Paralegal; Purchasing Agent/Manager; Quality Control Supervisor; Services Sales Representative; Software Engineer; Systems Analyst. **Corporate headquarters location:** Dallas TX. **Other U.S. locations:** Nationwide. **Number of placements per year:** 200 - 499.

SOURCE EDP
155 Federal Street, Suite 410, Boston MA 02110. 617/482-8211. **Fax:** 617/482-9084. **Contact:** Steve McMahan, Branch Manager. **Description:** A permanent employment agency. Company pays fee. **Specializes in the areas of:** Computer Hardware/Software; MIS/EDP; Sales. **Positions commonly filled include:** Computer Operator; Computer Programmer; EDP Specialist; MIS Specialist; Sales Representative; Systems Analyst; Technical Writer/Editor. **Other U.S. locations:** Nationwide. **Number of placements per year:** 1000+.

SPECTRA PROFESSIONAL SEARCH
SPECTRA TEMPS
Faneuil Hall Marketplace, 2 South Building, 4th Floor, Boston MA 02109. 617/720-0010. **Fax:** 617/720-1483. **Contact:** Rick Ryan, Director of Temporary Services. **Description:** A permanent employment agency concentrating on administrative and legal support staffing. Spectra Temps (also at this location) provides temporary placements. Company pays fee. **Specializes in the areas of:** Advertising; Banking; Finance; Legal; Secretarial. **Positions commonly filled include:** Administrative Assistant; Administrative Worker/Clerk; Paralegal; Secretary. **Benefits available to temporary workers:** Dental Insurance; Medical Insurance. **Other U.S. locations:** Providence RI. **Average salary range of placements:** $20,000 - $29,000. **Number of placements per year:** 100-199.

TECHNICAL PERSONNEL SERVICES INC.
867 Turnpike Street, Suite 213, North Andover MA 01845. 978/794-3347. **Fax:** 978/794-9291. **Contact:** Paul Donatio, General Manager. **E-mail address:** techpers@tpsjobs.com. **World Wide Web address:** http://www.tpsjobs.com. **Description:** A permanent employment agency that places both permanent and temporary personnel and offers some contract services. Company pays fee. **Specializes in the areas of:** Architecture/Construction; Banking; Computer Science/Software; Engineering; Industrial; Manufacturing; Technical. **Positions commonly filled include:** Biomedical Engineer; Chemical Engineer; Civil Engineer; Computer Programmer; Designer; Electrical/Electronics Engineer; Industrial Engineer; Mechanical Engineer; Metallurgical Engineer; Nuclear Engineer; Structural Engineer. **Number of placements per year:** 100 - 199.

TESMER ALLEN ASSOCIATES
P.O. Box 1491, Westborough MA 01581. 508/366-1160. **Fax:** 508/366-6419. **Contact:** John B. Allen, Vice President. **E-mail address:** jballen@tiac.net. **Description:** A permanent employment agency focusing on the recruitment and placement of engineering and MIS personnel. Company pays fee. **Specializes in the areas of:** Computer Hardware/Software; Engineering. **Positions commonly filled include:** Ceramics Engineer; Chemical Engineer; Chemist; Computer Programmer; EDP Specialist; Electrical/Electronics Engineer; Environmental Engineer; Industrial Engineer; Manufacturing Engineer; Mechanical Engineer; MIS Specialist; Multimedia Designer; Software Engineer; Systems Analyst. **Average salary range of placements:** $30,000 - $50,000. **Number of placements per year:** 50 - 99.

TIMELY SOLUTIONS, INC.
187 Ballardvale Street, Wilmington MA 01887. 978/988-8880. **Toll-free phone:** 888/633-8880. **Fax:** 978/988-2252. **Contact:** William E. Chetwynd, President. **Description:** A permanent employment agency that offers both permanent and contract software placements. Areas of focus include

information systems, software engineering, quality assurance, and technical writing. Company pays fee. **Specializes in the areas of:** Administration; Computer Science/Software. **Positions commonly filled include:** Computer Programmer; MIS Specialist; Systems Analyst; Technical Writer/Editor. **Average salary range of placements:** More than $50,000. **Number of placements per year:** 100 - 199.

TOTAL TECHNICAL SERVICES, INC.
167 Pleasant Street, Attleboro MA 02703. 508/226-3880. **Toll-free phone:** 800/342-2364. **Fax:** 508/226-4363. **Contact:** Karl E. Whelan, Branch Manager. **Description:** A permanent employment agency focusing on technical placements. Company pays fee. **Specializes in the areas of:** Administration; Computer Science/Software; Engineering; Industrial; Manufacturing; Personnel/Labor Relations; Secretarial; Technical. **Positions commonly filled include:** Administrative Manager; Chemical Engineer; Civil Engineer; Computer Programmer; Electrical/Electronics Engineer; Electrician; Environmental Engineer; Industrial Engineer; Mechanical Engineer; MIS Specialist; Multimedia Designer; Software Engineer; Systems Analyst; Technical Writer/Editor; Typist/Word Processor; Urban/Regional Planner. **Benefits available to temporary workers:** Medical Insurance; Paid Vacation. **Corporate headquarters location:** Waltham MA. **Other area locations:** Boston MA. **Other U.S. locations:** Atlanta GA; Dallas TX. **Average salary range of placements:** $20,000 - $29,999. **Number of placements per year:** 200 - 499.

TRAVEL CAREER NETWORK, LTD.
44 School Street, Suite 705, Boston MA 02108. 617/722-0079. **Fax:** 617/722-4063. **Contact:** Ms. Marty Robinson, President. **Description:** A permanent employment agency. Company pays fee. **Specializes in the areas of:** Travel. **Positions commonly filled include:** Accountant/Auditor; Customer Service Representative; General Manager; Travel Agent. **Number of placements per year:** 50 - 99.

TRAVEL INDUSTRY CONSULTANTS
404 East Street, Hingham MA 02043. 781/749-8344. **Toll-free phone:** 800/343-5350. **Fax:** 781/749-7080. **Contact:** Cheryl M. Cormier, President. **E-mail address:** ccorm0180@aol.com. **Description:** A permanent and temporary employment agency. Company pays fee. **Specializes in the areas of:** Travel. **Positions commonly filled include:** Travel Agent.

MICHAEL WARD ASSOCIATES
P.O. Box 740, Boston MA 02117-0740. 617/232-1950. **Physical address:** 396 Commonwealth Avenue, Boston MA. **Contact:** Manager. **Description:** A permanent employment agency. Company pays fee. **Specializes in the areas of:** Health/Medical. **Positions commonly filled include:** Nurse. **Number of placements per year:** 50 - 99.

YANKEE SITTERS NANNY AGENCY
P.O. Box 392, Webster MA 01570-0392. 508/949-6244. **Fax:** 508/949-6244. **Contact:** Beulah Seitz, Director/Owner. **Description:** A permanent employment agency that places nannies in full-time positions for a minimum of one year. Company pays fee. **Specializes in the areas of:** Child Care, In-Home; Nannies. **Average salary range of placements:** Less than $20,000. **Number of placements per year:** 50 - 99.

TEMPORARY EMPLOYMENT AGENCIES

ABA PERSONNEL
25 Pleasant Street, Newburyport MA 01950. 978/462-4600. **Contact:** Manager. **Description:** A temporary and temp-to-perm agency that also provides permanent placements. **Specializes in the areas of:** Administration; Light Industrial; Office Support.

A.S.I. TEMPS
P.O. Box 740, Boston MA 02117-0740. 617/262-4900. **Physical address:** 396 Commonwealth Avenue, Boston MA. **Contact:** Keith D. Alter, President. **Description:** A temporary agency. **Specializes in the areas of:** Health/Medical; Insurance; Legal. **Positions commonly filled include:** Insurance Agent/Broker; Medical Records Technician; Physical Therapist. **Benefits available to temporary workers:** Dental Insurance; Medical Insurance; Paid Vacation. **Other area locations:** Springfield MA. **Other U.S. locations:** Hartford CT. **Number of placements per year:** 1 - 49.

ACCOUNTEMPS
10 Forbes Road, West Wing, Braintree MA 02184-2605. 781/848-9800. **Fax:** 781/848-9866. **Contact:** Nancy Doyle, Branch Manager. **Description:** A temporary agency that focuses on accounting, finance, and bookkeeping. Company pays fee. **Specializes in the areas of:** Accounting/Auditing; Banking; Finance. **Positions commonly filled include:** Accountant/Auditor; Bank Officer/Manager; Credit Manager; Financial Analyst. **Corporate headquarters location:** Menlo Park CA. **Other U.S. locations:** Nationwide.

ADECCO
1250 Hancock Street, Quincy MA 02169. 617/773-6226. **Fax:** 617/770-3624. **Contact:** Mike Bowen, Office Manager. **E-mail address:** quincy.ma.office@adecco.com. **World Wide Web address:** http://www.adecco.com. **Description:** A temporary employment agency that also provides permanent placements. **Specializes in the areas of:** Administration; Banking; Fashion; Light Industrial; Retail; Secretarial. **Positions commonly filled include:** Administrative Assistant; Clerical Supervisor; Secretary; Typist/Word Processor. **Benefits available to temporary workers:** 401(k); Dental Insurance; Medical Insurance; Paid Holidays; Paid Vacation; Tuition Assistance. **Corporate headquarters location:** Redwood City CA. **Other U.S. locations:** Nationwide. **International locations:** Worldwide. **Average salary range of placements:** $20,000 - $29,999. **Number of placements per year:** 500 - 999.

ALDEN AND CLARK, INC.
P.O. Box 180177, Boston MA 02118. 617/247-1147. **Contact:** Alden Thatcher, Vice President of Recruitment. **Description:** A temporary agency that focuses on the placement of freelance graphic designers. Company pays fee. **Specializes in the areas of:** Advertising; Art/Design; Publishing. **Positions commonly filled include:** Artist; Graphic Artist; Mechanical Artist. **Number of placements per year:** 200 - 499.

ARBOR ASSOCIATES
15 Court Square, Suite 1050, Boston MA 02108. 617/227-8829. **Contact:** Lori Bass, Director of Child Care. **Description:** A temporary agency/staffing service that places behavioral health, human services, and child care professionals in residential, hospital, and day care center settings. Company pays fee. **Specializes in the areas of:** Eldercare, In-Home; Human Services. **Positions commonly filled include:** Counselor; Daycare Teacher; Social Worker; Teacher Aide. **Number of placements per year:** 1000+.

ATTORNEY SPECIAL ASSIGNMENT PLACEMENT
4 Faneuil Hall Market Place, 4th Floor, Boston MA 02109-1647. 617/742-0112. **Fax:** 617/742-1417. **Contact:** Shelley Widoff, President. **Description:** A temporary agency that provides temporary and permanent placement of attorneys and paralegals in the greater Boston area. Company pays fee. **Specializes in the areas of:** Banking; Finance; Insurance; Legal. **Positions commonly filled include:** Attorney; Paralegal. **Average salary range of placements:** $30,000 - $50,000. **Number of placements per year:** 100 - 199.

BRATTLE TEMPS
176 Federal Street, 5th Floor, Boston MA 02110. 617/345-9900. **Contact:** Recruiter. **Description:** A temporary agency that focuses on administrative support positions in academic settings. Company pays fee. **Specializes in the areas of:** Advertising; Architecture/Construction; Education; Health/Medical; Nonprofit; Publishing; Secretarial. **Positions commonly filled include:** Administrative Assistant; Customer Service Representative; Editor; Education Administrator; Human Resources Specialist; Human Service Worker; Librarian; Typist/Word Processor. **Average salary range of placements:** $20,000 - $29,999. **Number of placements per year:** 1000+.

CORPORATE STAFFING SOLUTIONS
180 Westfield Street, West Springfield MA 01089. 413/739-4100. **Fax:** 413/739-5584. **Contact:** Jeffrey N. Schneider, Vice President. **Description:** A temporary agency. Company pays fee. **Specializes in the areas of:** Accounting/Auditing; Administration; Advertising; Finance; Industrial; Insurance; Legal; Manufacturing; Marketing; MIS/EDP; Personnel/Labor Relations; Sales; Secretarial. **Positions commonly filled include:** Accountant; Auditor; Branch Manager; Claim Representative; Computer Programmer; Customer Service Representative; Human Service Worker; Paralegal; Restaurant/Food Service Manager; Services Sales Representative; Systems Analyst; Typist/Word Processor. **Benefits available to temporary workers:** Medical Insurance; Paid Holidays; Paid Vacation. **Corporate headquarters location:** Wallingford CT. **Number of placements per year:** 1000+.

DAVIS COMPANIES
33 Boston Post Road West, Marlborough MA 01752. 508/480-9500. **Fax:** 508/481-8519. **Contact:** Andrea Pion, Vice President. **Description:** A temporary agency that provides both temporary and permanent staffing to accounting, banking, finance, and insurance companies. **Specializes in the areas of:** Accounting/Auditing; Banking; Finance; Insurance. **Positions commonly filled include:** Bank Officer/Manager; Branch Manager; Brokerage Clerk; Budget Analyst; Cost Estimator; Credit Manager; Financial Analyst; Insurance Agent/Broker; Securities Sales Representative. **Average salary range of placements:** $30,000 - $50,000. **Number of placements per year:** 1000+.

DUNHILL STAFFING SYSTEMS
138 Memorial Avenue, West Springfield MA 01089. 413/733-5147. **Contact:** Manager. **Description:** A temporary agency. Company pays fee. **Specializes in the areas of:** Accounting/Auditing; Administration; Computer Science/Software; Engineering; Health/ Medical; Industrial; Legal; Manufacturing; Personnel/Labor Relations; Sales; Secretarial. **Positions commonly filled include:** Accountant/Auditor; Administrative Manager; Bank Officer/Manager; Biochemist; Biological Scientist; Biomedical Engineer; Blue-Collar Worker Supervisor; Branch Manager; Buyer; Chemical Engineer; Civil Engineer; Claim Representative; Computer Programmer; Counselor; Customer Service Representative; Design Engineer; Draftsperson; Electrical/Electronics Engineer; Environmental Engineer; Human Resources Specialist; Industrial Engineer; Industrial Production Manager; Manufacturer's/Wholesaler's Sales Rep.; Market Research Analyst; Medical Records Technician; MIS Specialist; Nuclear Engineer; Operations/Production Manager; Paralegal; Property and Real Estate Manager; Software Engineer; Systems Analyst; Telecommunications Manager; Typist/Word Processor; Underwriter/Assistant Underwriter. **Benefits available to temporary workers:** Medical Insurance; Paid Holidays; Paid Vacation. **Corporate headquarters location:** Long Island NY. **Other U.S. locations:** Nationwide. **Average salary range of placements:** $20,000 - $29,999. **Number of placements per year:** 100 - 199.

EDITORIAL SERVICES OF NEW ENGLAND
10 Fawcett Street, Cambridge MA 02138. 617/354-2828. **Fax:** 617/354-8328. **Contact:** Charissa Westerlund, Staffing Coordinator. **E-mail address:** admin@esne.com. **World Wide Web address:** http://www.esne.com. **Description:** A temporary and permanent employment agency. Company pays fee. **Specializes in the areas of:** Computer Hardware/ Software; Education; Finance; Health/ Medical; Publishing. **Positions commonly filled include:** Editor; Editorial Assistant; Graphic Artist; Graphic Designer; Managing Editor; Production Manager; Project Manager; Public Relations Manager; Technical Writer/Editor; Webmaster. **Benefits available to temporary workers:** 401(k); Direct Deposit; Medical Insurance. **Corporate headquarters location:** This Location. **Average salary range of placements:** $30,000 - $50,000. **Number of placements per year:** 200 - 499.

ENGINEERING MANAGEMENT SUPPORT, INC. (EMSI)
P.O. Box 5043, 330 Boston Road, Billerica MA 01821. 978/667-0896. **Toll-free phone:** 800/661-8268. **Fax:** 978/667-1630. **Contact:** Valerie Wrenn, Recruiter. **E-mail address:** emsi@tiac.net. **World Wide Web address:** http://www.tiac.net/users/emsi. **Description:** A temporary agency focusing on placing high-tech personnel. The agency also provides permanent placement. Company pays fee. **Specializes in the areas of:** Engineering; Industrial; Manufacturing; Technical. **Positions commonly filled include:** Administrative Assistant; Computer Programmer; Design Engineer; Designer; Electrical/Electronics Engineer; Electrician; Industrial Engineer; Mechanical Engineer; MIS Specialist; Purchasing Agent/Manager; Secretary; Software Engineer; Systems Analyst; Transportation/Traffic Specialist. **Average salary range of placements:** $20,000 - $29,999. **Number of placements per year:** 100 - 199.

GENERAL COMPUTER RESOURCES
24 Ray Avenue, Suite 105, Burlington MA 01803. 781/270-7020. **Contact:** Manager. **Description:** A temporary agency. **Specializes in the areas of:** Computer Hardware/Software; Computer Programming; Computer Science/Software.

HUMAN SERVICE OPTIONS, INC.
35 Braintree Hill Office Park, Suite 307, Braintree MA 02184. 781/356-0710. **Fax:** 781/356-0748. **Contact:** Joe Donahue, Director of Temporary Employment. **Description:** A temporary agency that provides direct care to schools, group homes, and workshops. The firm also provides a home care service for elderly and homebound individuals and community residences for developmentally disabled adults. **Specializes in the areas of:** Health/Medical; Human Services. **Positions commonly filled include:** Human Service Worker; Physical Therapist; Registered Nurse; Social Worker; Teacher/Professor. **Benefits available to temporary workers:** 401(k); Dental Insurance; Medical Insurance;

Tuition Assistance. **Average salary range of placements:** Less than $20,000. **Number of placements per year:** 100 - 199.

INTERIM PERSONNEL
One State Street, Suite 550, Boston MA 02109-3507. 617/248-8855. **Fax:** 617/248-1991. **Contact:** Branch Manager. **Description:** A temporary agency. Company pays fee. **Specializes in the areas of:** Accounting/Auditing; Legal; Sales; Secretarial. **Positions commonly filled include:** Accountant/Auditor; Claim Representative; Customer Service Representative; Paralegal; Typist/Word Processor. **Corporate headquarters location:** Fort Lauderdale FL. **Other U.S. locations:** Nationwide. **Number of placements per year:** 1000+.

INTERIM PERSONNEL
68 Westfield Street, West Springfield MA 01089. 413/781-4120. **Fax:** 413/747-9347. **Contact:** David Stickles, Manager. **Description:** A temporary agency that focuses on accounting, clerical, light industrial, and technical positions. Company pays fee. **Specializes in the areas of:** Accounting/Auditing; Industrial; Secretarial. **Positions commonly filled include:** Accountant/Auditor; Administrative Manager; Blue-Collar Worker Supervisor; Branch Manager; Claim Representative; Clerical Supervisor; Customer Service Representative; Hotel Manager; Management Trainee; Restaurant/Food Service Manager; Services Sales Representative; Systems Analyst; Typist/Word Processor. **Benefits available to temporary workers:** Medical Insurance; Paid Vacation. **Corporate headquarters location:** Fort Lauderdale FL. **Other U.S. locations:** Nationwide. **Average salary range of placements:** $20,000 - $29,999. **Number of placements per year:** 1000+.

JOHNSON & HILL STAFFING SERVICE
95 State Street, Springfield MA 01103-2005. 413/746-3535. **Contact:** Andrea Hill, Vice President of Operations. **Description:** A temporary and permanent employment agency that places administrative, clerical, marketing, professional, accounting, and light industrial workers. Company pays fee. **Specializes in the areas of:** Banking; Education; Finance; General Management; Health/Medical; Industrial; Insurance; Legal; Manufacturing; Personnel/Labor Relations; Secretarial. **Positions commonly filled include:** Accountant/Auditor; Computer Programmer; Customer Service Representative; Human Resources Specialist; Market Research Analyst; Paralegal; Quality Control Supervisor; Technical Writer/Editor; Typist/Word Processor. **Benefits available to temporary workers:** Medical Insurance; Paid Holidays; Paid Vacation. **Other area locations:** Northampton MA. **Average salary range of placements:** $20,000 - $29,999. **Number of placements per year:** 500 - 999.

KELLY SERVICES, INC.
250 Commercial Street, Worcester MA 01608. 508/753-2954. **Contact:** Office Manager. **Description:** A temporary agency. Company pays fee. **Specializes in the areas of:** Clerical; Industrial; Sales; Technical. **Positions commonly filled include:** Administrative Assistant; Bookkeeper; Clerk; Factory Worker; Legal Secretary; Light Industrial Worker; Receptionist; Secretary; Typist/Word Processor. **Corporate headquarters location:** Troy MI. **Number of placements per year:** 1000+.

KELLY SERVICES, INC.
40 Speen Street, Framingham MA 01701. 508/370-0238. **Contact:** Office Manager. **Description:** A temporary agency. Company pays fee. **Specializes in the areas of:** Clerical; Industrial; Sales; Technical. **Positions commonly filled include:** Administrative Assistant; Bookkeeper; Clerical Supervisor; Factory Worker; Legal Secretary; Light Industrial Worker; Receptionist; Secretary; Typist/Word Processor. **Number of placements per year:** 1000+.

KELLY SERVICES, INC.
75 South Church Street, Pittsfield MA 01201-6132. 413/445-4528. **Contact:** Christine MacNew, Supervisor/Account Representative. **Description:** A temporary agency. **Specializes in the areas of:** Accounting/Auditing; Personnel/Labor Relations; Secretarial; Technical. **Positions commonly filled include:** Accountant/Auditor; Medical Records Technician; Secretary; Typist/Word Processor. **Corporate headquarters location:** Troy MI. **Other U.S. locations:** Nationwide. **Average salary range of placements:** Less than $20,000. **Number of placements per year:** 500 - 999.

KENNISON & ASSOCIATES, INC.
21 Custom House Street, Boston MA 02110. 617/478-2888. **Fax:** 617/478-2887. **Contact:** Recruiter. **Description:** A temporary and permanent placement agency focusing on office support positions. Company pays fee. **Specializes in the areas of:** Finance; Legal; Secretarial. **Positions commonly filled include:** Administrative Manager; Brokerage Clerk; Budget Analyst; Clerical Supervisor; Customer Service Representative; Financial Analyst; Technical Writer/Editor; Typist/Word Processor. **Benefits available to temporary workers:** Paid Holidays. **Average salary range of placements:** $30,000 - $50,000. **Number of placements per year:** 200 - 499.

L&L TEMPORARIES
101 Tremont Street, Boston MA 02108-5004. 617/423-4455. **Fax:** 617/423-4955. **Contact:** Susan Yerdon, Director. **Description:** A temporary agency that also provides permanent placement. Company pays fee. **Specializes in the areas of:** Accounting/Auditing; Banking; Health/Medical; Industrial; Insurance; Legal; Light Industrial; Manufacturing; Secretarial. **Positions commonly filled include:** Accountant/Auditor; Advertising Clerk; Blue-Collar Worker Supervisor; Buyer; Clerical Supervisor; Credit Manager; Customer Service Representative; Medical Records Technician; Paralegal; Typist/Word Processor. **Benefits available to temporary workers:** Medical Insurance; Paid Holidays; Paid Vacation. **Average salary range of placements:** $20,000 - $29,999. **Number of placements per year:** 50 - 99.

LAB SUPPORT INC.
One New England Executive Park, Burlington MA 01803. 781/229-2505. **Fax:** 781/229-1902. **Contact:** Account Manager. **Description:** A temporary agency focusing on providing placement in scientific industries. **Specializes in the areas of:** Biology; Chemical; Food Industry; Manufacturing. **Positions commonly filled include:** Biochemist; Biological Scientist; Chemical Engineer; Chemist; Clinical Lab Technician; Food Scientist/Technologist; Quality Control Supervisor; Science Technologist. **Benefits available to temporary workers:** 401(k); Medical Insurance. **Corporate headquarters location:** CA. **Other U.S. locations:** Nationwide. **Average salary range of placements:** $20,000 - $29,999. **Number of placements per year:** 200 - 499.

MANPOWER TEMPORARY SERVICES
25 Burlington Mall Road, Burlington MA 01803. 781/270-4101. **Fax:** 781/270-0459. **Contact:** Joan Kotronis, Branch Manager. **Description:** A temporary agency. Company pays fee. **Specializes in the areas of:** Administration; Industrial; Personnel/Labor Relations. **Positions commonly filled include:** Administrative Assistant; Graphic Designer; Human Resources Manager. **Benefits available to temporary**

workers: Medical Insurance; Paid Holidays; Paid Vacation; Stock Option. **Corporate headquarters location:** Milwaukee WI. **Other U.S. locations:** Nationwide. **Number of placements per year:** 500 - 999.

MANPOWER TEMPORARY SERVICES
10 New England Business Center, Andover MA 01810. 978/685-7778. **Fax:** 978/682-0470. **Contact:** Brad Schulte, Manager. **Description:** A temporary agency that also provides some permanent placements. **Specializes in the areas of:** Accounting/Auditing; Administration; Banking; Computer Science/Software; Fashion; Finance; Food Industry; Health/Medical; Industrial; Insurance; Manufacturing; Secretarial. **Positions commonly filled include:** Accountant/Auditor; Advertising Clerk; Blue-Collar Worker Supervisor; Buyer; Claim Representative; Computer Operator; Computer Programmer; Customer Service Representative; Database Manager; Human Service Worker; Insurance Agent/Broker; Secretary; Software Engineer; Systems Analyst; Typist/Word Processor. **Benefits available to temporary workers:** 401(k); Medical Insurance. **Corporate headquarters location:** Milwaukee WI. **Number of placements per year:** 1000+.

MANPOWER TEMPORARY SERVICES
9 Hillside Avenue, Waltham MA 02154. 781/487-9870. **Fax:** 781/487-9875. **Contact:** Branch Manager. **Description:** A temporary agency. Company pays fee. **Specializes in the areas of:** Clerical; Data Processing; Secretarial. **Positions commonly filled include:** Administrative Assistant; Customer Service Representative; Data Entry Clerk; Receptionist; Typist/Word Processor. **Benefits available to temporary workers:** Medical Insurance; Paid Holidays; Paid Vacation. **Corporate headquarters location:** Milwaukee WI. **Other U.S. locations:** Nationwide. **Average salary range of placements:** Less than $20,000. **Number of placements per year:** 1000+.

MANPOWER TEMPORARY SERVICES
110 Turnpike Road, Westborough MA 01581-2864. 508/870-0900. **Fax:** 508/870-0707. **Contact:** Denise Gillespie, Branch Supervisor. **Description:** A temporary agency that focuses on office and light industrial placements. Company pays fee. **Specializes in the areas of:** Industrial; Manufacturing; Secretarial. **Corporate headquarters location:** Milwaukee WI. **Other U.S. locations:** Nationwide. **Average salary range of placements:** Less than $20,000.

MANPOWER TEMPORARY SERVICES
15 Midstate Drive, Suite 210, Auburn MA 01501-1856. 508/832-8760. **Fax:** 508/832-8763. **Contact:** Michelle McCarthy, Service Representative. **Description:** A temporary agency. **Specializes in the areas of:** Banking; Industrial; Sales. **Positions commonly filled include:** Accountant/Auditor; Customer Service Representative; Receptionist; Typist/Word Processor. **Benefits available to temporary workers:** Bonus Award/Plan; Medical Insurance; Paid Vacation. **Corporate headquarters location:** Milwaukee WI. **Other U.S. locations:** Nationwide. **Average salary range of placements:** Less than $20,000. **Number of placements per year:** 500 - 999.

MANPOWER TEMPORARY SERVICES
101 Federal Street, Boston MA 02110. 617/443-4100. **Contact:** Branch Manager. **Description:** A temporary agency. Company pays fee. **Specializes in the areas of:** Light Industrial; Office Support; Technical; Telemarketing; Word Processing. **Positions commonly filled include:** Accountant/Auditor; Accounting Clerk; Administrative Assistant; Assembler; Biological Scientist; Bookkeeper; Chemist; Computer Operator; Customer Service Representative; Designer; Desktop Publishing Specialist; Electrician; Machine Operator; Material Control Specialist; Order Clerk; Packaging/Processing Worker; Painter; Project Engineer; Proofreader; Receptionist; Research Assistant; Secretary; Software Engineer; Systems Analyst; Technical Writer/Editor; Typist/Word Processor. **Benefits available to temporary workers:** Life Insurance; Medical Insurance; Paid Holidays; Paid Vacation. **Corporate headquarters location:** Milwaukee WI. **Number of placements per year:** 1000+.

MANPOWER, INC.
7 Essex Green Drive, Peabody MA 01960-2920. 978/977-9000. **Fax:** 978/977-9868. **Contact:** Service Representative. **Description:** A temporary agency. **Specializes in the areas of:** Administration; Health/Medical; Industrial; Insurance; Legal; Manufacturing; Personnel/Labor Relations; Sales; Secretarial. **Positions commonly filled include:** Accountant/Auditor; Claim Representative; Computer Programmer; Customer Service Representative; Human Resources Specialist; Operations/Production Manager; Paralegal; Quality Control Supervisor; Systems Analyst; Technical Writer/Editor; Typist/Word Processor; Video Production Coordinator. **Benefits available to temporary workers:** Life Insurance; Medical Insurance; Paid Holidays; Paid Vacation. **Corporate headquarters location:** Milwaukee WI. **Number of placements per year:** 1000+.

MASS TEMPS INC.
P.O. Box 6111, Haverhill MA 01831. 978/469-9004. **Fax:** 978/469-9006. **Contact:** Joseph Cross, Manager. **Description:** A temporary agency. Company pays fee. **Specializes in the areas of:** Industrial; Manufacturing; Nonprofit; Publishing; Retail; Secretarial. **Positions commonly filled include:** Accountant/Auditor; Typist/Word Processor. **Average salary range of placements:** Less than $20,000. **Number of placements per year:** 200 - 499.

MICRO TECH CONSULTANTS INC.
42 Weston Street, Waltham MA 02154. 781/891-4870. **Contact:** Manager. **Description:** A temporary agency that also provides permanent placement. **Specializes in the areas of:** Engineering; Manufacturing. **Positions commonly filled include:** Buyer; Design Engineer; Designer; Editor; Electrical/Electronics Engineer; Industrial Engineer; Mechanical Engineer; Purchasing Agent/Manager; Quality Control Supervisor; Technical Writer/Editor. **Number of placements per year:** 1000+.

MICRO TECH PROFESSIONALS, INC.
P.O. Box 496, Waltham MA 02254-0496. 781/890-6444. **Fax:** 781/890-3355. **Contact:** Denise Dunne, President. **E-mail address:** microtec@ix.netcom.com. **Description:** A temporary agency. **Specializes in the areas of:** Computer Science/Software; Engineering. **Positions commonly filled include:** MIS Specialist; Multimedia Designer; Software Engineer; Technical Writer/Editor. **Benefits available to temporary workers:** 401(k). **Number of placements per year:** 200 - 499.

MOLARI, INC.
80 Center Street, Pittsfield MA 01201. 413/499-4546. **Toll-free phone:** 800/649-4562. **Fax:** 413/442-6519. **Contact:** Jennifer Casey, Director of Personnel. **World Wide Web address:** http://www.molaripeople.com. **Description:** A temporary agency that also provides permanent placements. Company pays fee. **Specializes in the areas of:** Clerical; Health/Medical; Industrial; Office Support. **Positions commonly filled include:** Accountant/Auditor; Administrative Assistant; Blue-Collar Worker Supervisor; Buyer; Certified Nursing Aide; Claim Representative; Clerical Supervisor; Computer

Operator; Computer Programmer; Customer Service Representative; Licensed Practical Nurse; Market Research Analyst; Marketing Specialist; MIS Specialist; Physical Therapist; Purchasing Agent/ Manager; Quality Control Supervisor; Recreational Therapist; Registered Nurse; Secretary; Systems Analyst; Technical Writer/Editor; Typist/Word Processor. **Benefits available to temporary workers:** Paid Holidays; Paid Vacation. **Average salary range of placements:** Less than $20,000. **Number of placements per year:** 500 - 999.

NEED PERSONNEL PLACEMENT
151 Providence Highway, Norwood MA 02062. 781/769-4390. **Fax:** 781/769-1245. **Contact:** Larry Cedrone, Vice President. **E-mail address:** needjobs@needjobs.com. **World Wide Web address:** http://www.needjobs.com. **Description:** A temporary agency that also provides permanent placement. Company pays fee. **Specializes in the areas of:** Accounting/Auditing; Administration; Architecture/ Construction; Art/Design; Biology; Computer Science/ Software; Economics; Engineering; General Management; Industrial; Manufacturing; Personnel/ Labor Relations; Publishing; Sales; Secretarial; Technical. **Positions commonly filled include:** Accountant/Auditor; Architect; Biochemist; Biological Scientist; Biomedical Engineer; Civil Engineer; Clerical Supervisor; Clinical Lab Technician; Computer Programmer; Cost Estimator; Customer Service Representative; Draftsperson; Electrical/Electronics Engineer; Electrician; Environmental Engineer; Financial Analyst; Health Services Manager; Industrial Engineer; Management Analyst/Consultant; Market Research Analyst; Mechanical Engineer; Medical Records Technician; MIS Specialist; Occupational Therapist; Physical Therapist; Quality Control Supervisor; Services Sales Representative; Sociologist; Software Engineer; Structural Engineer; Surveyor; Systems Analyst; Technical Writer/Editor; Typist/Word Processor; Video Production Coordinator. **Number of placements per year:** 500 - 999.

NEW BOSTON SELECT STAFFING
45 Braintree Hill Office Park, Suite 101, Braintree MA 02184. 781/848-2211. **Fax:** 781/849-1758. **Contact:** Manager. **Description:** A temporary and temp-to-perm agency. **Specializes in the areas of:** Administration; Clerical; Light Industrial; Office Support.

NEW PERSPECTIVES PERSONNEL
600 West Cummings Park, Woburn MA 01904. 781/938-8247. **Fax:** 781/932-8622. **Contact:** Ms. Noelle Aiken, Consultant. **Description:** A temporary agency that also provides permanent placement in office support areas. Company pays fee. **Specializes in the areas of:** Accounting/Auditing; Clerical; Personnel/Labor Relations; Secretarial. **Positions commonly filled include:** Account Representative; Administrative Assistant; Customer Service Representative; Secretary; Typist/Word Processor. **Benefits available to temporary workers:** Bonus Award/Plan; Dental Insurance; Medical Insurance; Paid Vacation; Referral Bonus Plan. **Corporate headquarters location:** Beverly MA. **Average salary range of placements:** $20,000 - $29,999. **Number of placements per year:** 100 - 199.

OFFICE SPECIALISTS
1256 Park Street, Stoughton MA 02072-3745. 781/341-6070. **Toll-free phone:** 800/750-0449. **Fax:** 781/341-6072. **Contact:** Kim Chestnut, Staffing Manager. **Description:** A temporary and temp-to-perm agency. **Specializes in the areas of:** Accounting/Auditing; Clerical; Office Support; Secretarial; Word Processing. **Positions commonly filled include:** Customer Service Representative; Desktop Publishing Specialist; Typist/Word Processor. **Benefits available to temporary workers:** Medical Insurance; Paid Vacation. **Corporate headquarters location:** Peabody MA. **Average salary range of placements:** Less than $20,000. **Number of placements per year:** 1000+.

OFFICE SPECIALISTS
1253 Worcester Road, Framingham MA 01701-5250. 508/879-6332. **Toll-free phone:** 800/392-5627. **Contact:** Nancy Sherman, Staffing Manager. **Description:** A temporary agency. **Specializes in the areas of:** Accounting/Auditing; Secretarial. **Positions commonly filled include:** Accounting Clerk; Administrative Assistant; Bookkeeper; Customer Service Representative; Data Entry Clerk; Receptionist; Secretary. **Corporate headquarters location:** Peabody MA. **Other U.S. locations:** Nationwide. **Average salary range of placements:** $20,000 - $29,999. **Number of placements per year:** 1000+.

OFFICETEAM
14 Story Street, Cambridge MA 02138. 617/876-9000. **Fax:** 617/354-7025. **Contact:** Jill Pappalardo, Division Director. **Description:** A temporary agency. Company pays fee. **Specializes in the areas of:** Administration; Data Processing; Secretarial. **Positions commonly filled include:** Advertising Clerk; Clerical Supervisor. **Benefits available to temporary workers:** Medical Insurance; Referral Bonus Plan. **Corporate headquarters location:** Menlo Park CA. **Other U.S. locations:** Nationwide. **Average salary range of placements:** $20,000 - $29,999. **Number of placements per year:** 1000+.

OLSTEN STAFFING SERVICES
20 Burlington Mall Road, Suite 251, Burlington MA 01803-4123. 781/270-9490. **Fax:** 781/270-9294. **Contact:** Scott Ragusa, Branch Manager. **Description:** A temporary agency that focuses on office automation, office services, technical and production, and assembly placements. Company pays fee. **Specializes in the areas of:** Administration; Manufacturing; Personnel/Labor Relations; Secretarial. **Positions commonly filled include:** Administrative Manager; Clerical Supervisor; Customer Service Representative; Quality Control Supervisor; Typist/Word Processor. **Benefits available to temporary workers:** Medical Insurance; Paid Vacation. **Corporate headquarters location:** Melville NY. **Other U.S. locations:** Nationwide. **International locations:** Worldwide. **Average salary range of placements:** $20,000 - $29,999. **Number of placements per year:** 500 - 999.

OLSTEN STAFFING SERVICES
111 Speen Street, Suite 304, Framingham MA 01701. 508/875-1970. **Fax:** 508/875-7779. **Contact:** Katherine M. Connors, Personnel Supervisor. **World Wide Web address:** http://www.worknow.com. **Description:** A temporary agency. Founded in 1950. **Specializes in the areas of:** Customer Service; Secretarial. **Positions commonly filled include:** Administrative Assistant; Clerical Supervisor; Customer Service Representative; Secretary; Typist/Word Processor. **Benefits available to temporary workers:** Medical Insurance; Paid Vacation. **Corporate headquarters location:** Melville NY. **Other U.S. locations:** Nationwide. **International locations:** Worldwide. **Average salary range of placements:** $20,000 - $29,999. **Number of placements per year:** 1000+.

PRO STAFF
790 Boston Road, Billerica MA 01821. 978/663-5378. **Toll-free phone:** 800/938-9675. **Fax:** 978/670-2103. **Contact:** Terry Ryan, Staffing Manager. **Description:** A temporary agency that also places

temp-to-perm positions. Company pays fee. **Specializes in the areas of:** Accounting/Auditing; Administration; Advertising; Computer Science/ Software; General Management; Health/Medical; Industrial; Personnel/Labor Relations; Publishing; Retail; Sales; Secretarial; Technical. **Positions commonly filled include:** Accountant/Auditor; Administrative Assistant; Bank Officer/Manager; Bookkeeper; Buyer; Customer Service Representative; Draftsperson; EDP Specialist; Factory Worker; Legal Secretary; Light Industrial Worker; Medical Secretary; Nurse; Operations/Production Manager; Quality Control Supervisor; Sales Representative; Technical Illustrator; Technical Representative; Technical Writer/ Editor; Technician; Typist/Word Processor. **Benefits available to temporary workers:** 401(k); Medical Insurance; Paid Holidays; Paid Vacation. **Other U.S. locations:** Nationwide. **Average salary range of placements:** $20,000 - $29,999. **Number of placements per year:** 200 - 499.

PRO STAFF
1661 Worcester Road, Suite 101, Framingham MA 01701. 508/879-9251. **Contact:** Manager. **Description:** A temporary agency. Company pays fee. **Specializes in the areas of:** Accounting/Auditing; Finance; Human Services; Manufacturing; Office Support. **Positions commonly filled include:** Accountant/Auditor; Administrative Assistant; Bookkeeper; Customer Service Representative; Data Entry Clerk; Factory Worker; Legal Secretary; Medical Secretary; Quality Control Supervisor; Sales Representative; Technical Writer/Editor; Typist/Word Processor; Warehouse/Distribution Worker. **Other U.S. locations:** Nationwide.

PRO STAFF
7 Alfred Street, Suite 205, Woburn MA 01801. 617/937-0111. **Contact:** Manager. **Description:** A temporary agency that also provides permanent placements. **Specializes in the areas of:** Graphic Arts; Multimedia.

PRO STAFF ACCOUNTING
535 Boylston Street, 11th Floor, Boston MA 02116. 617/357-0330. **Contact:** Manager. **Description:** A temporary agency. **Specializes in the areas of:** Accounting/Auditing.

RELIEF RESOURCES INC.
P.O. Box 538, Hadley MA 01035-0538. 413/584-7667. **Toll-free phone:** 800/639-5094. **Contact:** Dale Jones, Recruiter. **Description:** A temporary agency that focuses on human service placements. **Specializes in the areas of:** Nonprofit. **Positions commonly filled include:** Counselor; Human Service Worker; Preschool Worker; Social Worker; Teacher/Professor. **Benefits available to temporary workers:** Paid Vacation. **Other area locations:** Cambridge MA; Worcester MA. **Other U.S. locations:** Hartford CT; Providence RI. **Average salary range of placements:** Less than $20,000. **Number of placements per year:** 1000+.

SALES TEMPS INC.
49 Winchester Street, Newton MA 02161. 617/964-8828. **Fax:** 617/332-0365. **Contact:** Ed Katzenberg, President. **E-mail address:** katzed@salestemps.com. **World Wide Web address:** http://www.salestemps.com. **Description:** A temporary agency that focuses on placing sales and marketing professionals in temporary and permanent positions in a variety of industries. Company pays fee. **Specializes in the areas of:** Sales. **Positions commonly filled include:** Account Manager; Account Representative; Applications Engineer; Customer Service Representative; Marketing Manager; Sales Engineer; Sales Executive; Sales Manager; Sales Representative; Securities Sales Representative; Services Sales Representative; Vice President of Marketing and Sales. **Average salary range of placements:** $30,000 - $50,000. **Number of placements per year:** 50 - 99.

SELECTEMPS
50 Franklin Street, Worcester MA 01608-1914. 508/792-1212. **Fax:** 508/792-5944. **Contact:** Branch Manager. **Description:** A temporary agency. **Specializes in the areas of:** Advertising; Architecture/ Construction; Banking; Biology; Broadcasting; Computer Science/Software; Electronics; Industrial; Insurance; Legal; Light Industrial; Publishing; Sales; Secretarial; Technical. **Positions commonly filled include:** Typist/Word Processor. **Benefits available to temporary workers:** Medical Insurance; Paid Vacation. **Corporate headquarters location:** Framingham MA. **Average salary range of placements:** $20,000 - $29,999. **Number of placements per year:** 1000+.

SPECIAL COUNSEL
40 Broad Street, 2nd Floor, Boston MA 02109. 617/338-7700. **Fax:** 617/338-1777. **Contact:** Manager. **World Wide Web address:** http://www.specialcounsel.com. **Description:** A temporary employment agency that also provides permanent placements. **Specializes in the areas of:** Legal.

SUMMIT TECHNICAL SERVICES INC.
50 Braintree Hill Park, Suite 201, Braintree MA 02184-8724. 781/848-4321. **Fax:** 781/848-2306. **Contact:** Roseanne Venezia, Recruiting Manager. **E-mail address:** rvenezia@summit-technical.com. **World Wide Web address:** http://www.summit-technical.com. **Description:** A temporary and permanent employment agency. Company pays fee. **Specializes in the areas of:** Architecture/Construction; Art/Design; Computer Science/Software; Engineering; Manufacturing. **Positions commonly filled include:** Buyer; Chemical Engineer; Chemist; Computer Programmer; Design Engineer; Designer; Draftsperson; Electrician; Graphic Artist; Graphic Designer; Industrial Engineer; Manufacturing Engineer; Materials Engineer; Mechanical Engineer; Purchasing Agent/Manager; Quality Control Supervisor; Software Engineer; Technical Writer/Editor; Webmaster. **Benefits available to temporary workers:** 401(k). **Corporate headquarters location:** Warwick RI. **Other U.S. locations:** Nationwide. **Average salary range of placements:** $30,000 - $50,000. **Number of placements per year:** 200 - 499.

TAC STAFFING SERVICES
175 Highland Avenue, Needham MA 02194. 781/449-8005. **Fax:** 781/449-9310. **Contact:** Manager. **Description:** A temporary agency. **Specializes in the areas of:** Advertising; Education; Insurance; Nonprofit; Personnel/Labor Relations; Publishing; Secretarial. **Corporate headquarters location:** Newton MA.

TAC STAFFING SERVICES
291 Main Street, Milford MA 01757. 508/478-5851. **Fax:** 508/478-5856. **Contact:** Personnel Recruiter. **Description:** A temporary agency. **Specializes in the areas of:** Accounting/Auditing; Secretarial. **Positions commonly filled include:** Assembler; Customer Service Representative; Receptionist; Secretary; Typist/Word Processor. **Benefits available to temporary workers:** Bonus Award/Plan; Computer Training; Medical Insurance. **Corporate headquarters location:** Newton MA. **Other U.S. locations:** Nationwide. **Number of placements per year:** 1000+.

TAD STAFFING SERVICES
221 Chelmsford Street, Suite 2, Chelmsford MA 01824. 978/256-5244. **Contact:** Susan Fuller, Area Manager. **Description:** A temporary agency. Company

pays fee. **Specializes in the areas of:** Accounting/Auditing; Clerical; Computer Hardware/ Software; Engineering; Finance; Food Industry; Health/Medical; Insurance; Manufacturing; Personnel/Labor Relations; Publishing. **Positions commonly filled include:** Accountant/Auditor; Administrative Assistant; Clerk; Computer Operator; Customer Service Representative; Data Entry Factory Worker; Financial Analyst; Legal Secretary; Light Industrial Worker; Secretary; Stenographer; Technician; Typist/Word Processor. **Corporate headquarters location:** Cambridge MA. **Other U.S. locations:** Nationwide. **Number of placements per year:** 1000+.

TAD STAFFING SERVICES
1212 Hancock Street, Quincy MA 02169. 617/471-8008. **Contact:** Heather Rice, Staffing Supervisor. **Description:** A temporary agency that places both temporary and permanent personnel in accounting, secretarial, and word processing positions. Company pays fee. **Specializes in the areas of:** Accounting/Auditing; Secretarial. **Positions commonly filled include:** Accountant/Auditor; Typist/Word Processor. **Benefits available to temporary workers:** Medical Insurance; Paid Vacation. **Corporate headquarters location:** Cambridge MA. **Other U.S. locations:** Nationwide. **Average salary range of placements:** $20,000 - $29,999. **Number of placements per year:** 1000+.

TRAVCORPS, INC.
40 Eastern Avenue, Malden MA 02148. 781/322-2600. **Contact:** Sheri Johanson, Contract Manager. **Description:** A temporary agency. Company pays fee. **Specializes in the areas of:** Health/Medical. **Positions commonly filled include:** Nurse; Physical Therapist; Respiratory Therapist; X-ray Technician.

TRICOR ASSOCIATES
50 North Street, Medfield MA 02052-1624. 508/359-4455. **Fax:** 508/359-7965. **Contact:** Dotti Cohen, Partner. **Description:** A temporary agency that also provides permanent placement. The agency focuses on office support positions. **Specializes in the areas of:** Accounting/Auditing; Administration; Advertising; Sales; Secretarial. **Positions commonly filled include:** Accountant/Auditor; Administrative Manager; Advertising Clerk; Buyer; Claim Representative; Customer Service Representative; Medical Records Technician.

UNLIMITED OPPORTUNITIES
209 West Central Street, Natick MA 01760-3716. 508/650-3612. **Fax:** 508/652-0748. **Contact:** Recruiter. **Description:** A temporary agency that also provides permanent placements. Company pays fee. **Specializes in the areas of:** Sales; Secretarial. **Positions commonly filled include:** Accountant/ Auditor; Administrative Manager; Advertising Clerk; Blue-Collar Worker Supervisor; Buyer; Claim Representative; Clerical Supervisor; Credit Manager; Customer Service Representative; Typist/Word Processor. **Benefits available to temporary workers:** Bonus Award/Plan; Paid Holidays. **Corporate headquarters location:** This Location. **Average salary range of placements:** $30,000 - $50,000. **Number of placements per year:** 1000+.

VOLT SERVICES GROUP
400 West Cummings Park, Woburn MA 01801. 781/938-6969. **Fax:** 781/932-9298. **Contact:** Stephanie Gerard, Branch Manager. **Description:** A temporary agency. Company pays fee. **Specializes in the areas of:** Administration; General Management; Industrial; Legal; Light Industrial; MIS/EDP; Office Support; Personnel/Labor Relations; Sales; Secretarial. **Positions commonly filled include:** Administrative Assistant; Administrative Manager; Claim Representative; Computer Operator; Customer Service Representative; Manufacturing Engineer; Marketing Manager; Operations Manager; Paralegal; Production Manager; Project Manager; Purchasing Agent/Manager; Quality Control Supervisor; Sales Executive; Sales Manager; Sales Representative; Secretary; Typist/Word Processor. **Benefits available to temporary workers:** Daycare Assistance; Dental Insurance; Medical Insurance; Paid Holidays; Paid Vacation. **Corporate headquarters location:** Orange CA. **Other U.S. locations:** Nationwide. **Average salary range of placements:** $30,000-$50,000. **Number of placements per year:** 1000+.

THE WALLACE LAW REGISTRY
31 St. James Avenue, Suite 910, Boston MA 02116. 617/482-8052. **Toll-free phone:** 800/248-4529. **Fax:** 617/482-8054. **Contact:** Marciann Dunnagan, Managing Director. **Description:** A temporary agency. Company pays fee. **Specializes in the areas of:** Legal. **Positions commonly filled include:** Attorney; Paralegal. **Corporate headquarters location:** Hartford CT. **Average salary range of placements:** More than $50,000. **Number of placements per year:** 100 - 199.

CONTRACT SERVICES FIRMS

APOLLO DESIGN SERVICE
P.O. Box 1883, 160 Main Street, Suite 8, Haverhill MA 01831. **Contact:** Manager. **Description:** A contract services firm. **Specializes in the areas of:** Construction; Design; Engineering; Manufacturing. **Positions commonly filled include:** Construction Contractor; Engineer. **Other U.S. locations:** Nashua NH.

ARBOR ASSOCIATES, INC.
15 Court Square, Suite 1050, Boston MA 02860. 617/227-8829. **Contact:** Manager. **Description:** A contract services firm providing placements in mental health, social work, and daycare. **Other area locations:** Framingham MA; Lawrence MA; Worcester MA. **Other U.S. locations:** Providence RI.

B&M ASSOCIATES
18 Commerce Way, Suite 5000, Woburn MA 01801. 781/938-9120. **Contact:** Staffing Services. **Description:** A contract services firm that focuses on technical placements. Company pays fee. **Specializes in the areas of:** Engineering; Manufacturing; Personnel/Labor Relations; Sales. **Positions commonly filled include:** Aerospace Engineer; Aircraft Mechanic/Engine Specialist; Buyer; Chemical Engineer; Civil Engineer; Computer Programmer; Cost Estimator; Design Engineer; Draftsperson; Editor; Electrical/Electronics Engineer; Industrial Engineer; Mechanical Engineer; MIS Specialist; Purchasing Agent/Manager; Quality Control Supervisor; Software Engineer; Systems Analyst. **Other U.S. locations:** San Diego CA; Santa Ana CA; Manchester NH; Dallas TX; Vienna VA. **Average salary range of placements:** $30,000 - $50,000. **Number of placements per year:** 200 - 499.

CDI CORPORATION
492 Old Connecticut Path, 1st Floor, Framingham MA 01701. 508/628-1700. **Fax:** 508/628-1711. **Contact:** Manager. **World Wide Web address:** http://www.cdicorp.com. **Description:** A contract services firm. **Specializes in the areas of:** Design; Engineering; Information Systems; Manufacturing; Technical. **Corporate headquarters location:**

Philadelphia PA. **Other U.S. locations:** Nationwide. **International locations:** Worldwide.

COMPUTER EXPRESS INTERNATIONAL
301 North Avenue, Wakefield MA 01880. 781/246-4477. **Contact:** Manager. **Description:** A contract services firm. **Specializes in the areas of:** Computer Operations; Computer Science/Software.

CONTRACT SOLUTIONS, INC.
4 Faneuil Hall Marketplace, 4th Floor, Boston MA 02109. 617/367-2990. **Contact:** Manager. **Description:** A contract services company that provides some permanent placements for professionals with AS400 or LAN/WAN experience. **Specializes in the areas of:** Computer Hardware/Software. **Positions commonly filled include:** LAN/WAN Designer/Developer.

DIGITAL ARTS GROUP
279 Cambridge Street, Burlington MA 01803-2530. 781/273-2780. **Fax:** 781/273-5592. **Contact:** Robert Melillo, President. **Description:** A computer consulting contract services firm. **Specializes in the areas of:** Computer Science/Software; Engineering; Technical. **Positions commonly filled include:** Computer Programmer; Customer Service Representative; Design Engineer; Designer; Draftsperson; Editor; Electrical/Electronics Engineer; Financial Analyst; Internet Services Manager; Mechanical Engineer; MIS Specialist; Multimedia Designer; Software Engineer; Statistician; Systems Analyst; Technical Writer/Editor; Telecommunications Manager. **Other U.S. locations:** Washington DC; Orlando FL. **Number of placements per year:** 200 - 499.

EDI SPECIALISTS, INC.
P.O. Box 116, Raynham MA 02767-1799. **Toll-free phone:** 800/821-4644. **Fax:** 508/822-7375. **Contact:** Joe Gilbody, President. **E-mail address:** info@edispecialists.com. **World Wide Web address:** http://www.edispecialists.com. **Description:** A contract services firm that focuses on EDI human resource placements. Company pays fee. **Specializes in the areas of:** Computer Science/Software. **Positions commonly filled include:** Computer Programmer; Management Analyst/Consultant; MIS Specialist; Software Engineer; Strategic Relations Manager; Systems Analyst; Telecommunications Manager. **Other U.S. locations:** Nationwide. **Average salary range of placements:** More than $50,000. **Number of placements per year:** 200 - 499.

THE ENVIRONMENTAL CAREERS ORGANIZATION
179 South Street, Boston MA 02111. 617/426-4375. **Contact:** Manager. **World Wide Web address:** http://www.eco.org. **Description:** A contract services firm. Company pays fee. **Specializes in the areas of:** Biology; Computer Science/Software; Engineering; Technical. **Positions commonly filled include:** Biological Scientist; Chemical Engineer; Chemist; Civil Engineer; Computer Programmer; Environmental Engineer; Forester/Conservation Scientist; Geographer; Geologist/Geophysicist; Science Technologist; Surveyor; Systems Analyst; Technical Writer/Editor. **Corporate headquarters location:** This location. **Other U.S. locations:** San Francisco CA; Cleveland OH; Seattle WA. **Average salary range of placements:** $20,000 - $29,999. **Number of placements per year:** 500 - 999.

INTERIM TECHNOLOGY
31 St. James Avenue, Suite 210, Boston MA 02116. 617/542-1700. **Fax:** 617/956-4080. **Contact:** Technical Staffing Specialist. **E-mail address:** 104436.2506@compuserve.com. **World Wide Web address:** http://www.interim.com. **Description:** A contract services firm. Company pays fee. **Specializes in the areas of:** Technical. **Positions commonly filled include:** Computer Operator; Database Manager; MIS Specialist; Systems Analyst; Systems Manager; Technical Support Representative; Technician. **Benefits available to temporary workers:** 401(k); Dental Insurance; Flexible Schedule; Medical Insurance; Stock Purchase. **Corporate headquarters location:** NJ. **Average salary range of placements:** $30,000 - $50,000. **Number of placements per year:** 50 - 99.

LYNX INC.
420 Bedford Street, Suite 200, Lexington MA 02173. 781/274-6400. **Fax:** 781/274-6300. **Contact:** Philip J. Hurd, President. **E-mail address:** discover@lynxinc.com. **World Wide Web address:** http://www.lynxinc.com. **Description:** A contract services firm. Company pays fee. **Specializes in the areas of:** Accounting/Auditing; Administration; Computer Science/Software; Finance; MIS/EDP; Scientific; Software Engineering; Technical. **Positions commonly filled include:** Accountant; Applications Engineer; Auditor; Budget Analyst; Chief Financial Officer; Computer Animator; Computer Programmer; Controller; Cost Estimator; Credit Manager; Database Manager; Financial Analyst; Internet Services Manager; MIS Specialist; Multimedia Designer; Online Content Specialist; Software Engineer; Systems Analyst; Systems Manager; Vice President; Webmaster. **Average salary range of placements:** $30,000 - $50,000. **Number of placements per year:** 200 - 499.

NATIONAL ENGINEERING SERVICE
10 Cedar Street, Suite 27, Woburn MA 01801. 508/261-1166. **Contact:** Manager. **Description:** A contract services firm. **Specializes in the areas of:** Engineering; Technical.

NORRELL STAFFING SERVICES
107 Audubon Road, Suite 210, Wakefield MA 01880-1245. 781/246-1560. **Fax:** 781/246-4988. **Contact:** General Manager. **World Wide Web address:** http://www.norrell.com. **Description:** A contract services firm providing long- and short-term staffing assignments. Company pays fee. **Specializes in the areas of:** Administration; Computer Science/Software; Industrial; Manufacturing; Personnel/Labor Relations; Sales; Secretarial; Technical. **Positions commonly filled include:** Accountant/Auditor; Administrative Manager; Advertising Clerk; Clerical Supervisor; Construction Contractor; Customer Service Representative; Human Resources Specialist; Manufacturer's/Wholesaler's Sales Rep.; Services Sales Representative; Software Engineer; Typist/Word Processor. **Benefits available to temporary workers:** 401(k); Medical Insurance; Paid Holidays; Paid Vacation. **Corporate headquarters location:** Atlanta GA. **Other U.S. locations:** Nationwide. **Average salary range of placements:** $20,000 - $29,999. **Number of placements per year:** 1000+.

PROVISION TECHNOLOGIES
2000 West Park Drive, Suite 160, Westborough MA 01581. 508/616-9200. **Fax:** 508/616-9208. **Contact:** Manager. **World Wide Web address:** http://www.careerbase.com. **Description:** A contract services and consulting firm. **Specializes in the areas of:** Computer Science/Software; Information Technology.

RESOURCE MANAGEMENT INTERNATIONAL
281 Main Street, Fitchburg MA 01420. 978/343-0048. **Contact:** Rey Lopez, Operations Manager. **Description:** A contract services firm. **Specializes in the areas of:** Human Resources; Personnel/Labor Relations. **Positions commonly filled include:** Accountant/Auditor; Human Resources Specialist.

ROMAC INTERNATIONAL
8 New England Executive Park, Burlington MA 01803. 781/270-4441. **Fax:** 781/270-4443. **Contact:** Manager. **Description:** A contract services firm for computer specialists. **Positions commonly filled include:** Internet Specialist; MIS Specialist; Software Engineer. **Average salary range of placements:** More than $50,000.

TECH/AID
P.O. Box 670, Waltham MA 02154. 781/891-0800. **Physical address:** 295 Weston Street, Waltham MA. **Contact:** Office Manager. **Description:** A contract services firm. Company pays fee. **Specializes in the areas of:** Architecture/Construction; Cable TV; Computer Hardware/Software; Construction; Engineering; Manufacturing; Technical. **Positions commonly filled include:** Architect; Chemical Engineer; Civil Engineer; Draftsperson; Electrical/Electronics Engineer; Estimator; Industrial Designer; Industrial Engineer; Mechanical Engineer; Quality Control Supervisor. **Number of placements per year:** 1000+.

TECH/AID
400 Grove Street, Worcester MA 01605. 508/792-6255. **Toll-free phone:** 800/645-0045. **Fax:** 508/792-2903. **Contact:** Office Manager. **World Wide Web address:** http://www.techaid.com. **Description:** A contract services firm and temporary employment agency. Company pays fee. **Specializes in the areas of:** Engineering; Industrial; Manufacturing; Personnel/Labor Relations; Scientific; Technical. **Positions commonly filled include:** Architect; Buyer; Chemical Engineer; Electrical/Electronics Engineer; Industrial Engineer; Mechanical Engineer; Technical Writer/Editor. **Corporate headquarters location:** Upper Newton Falls MA. **Number of placements per year:** 1000+.

TECH RESOURCE INC.
639 Washington Street, Norwood MA 02062-3547. 781/769-2115. **Contact:** Recruiter. **Description:** A contract services firm. Company pays fee. **Specializes in the areas of:** Administration; Computer Science/Software; Secretarial; Technical. **Positions commonly filled include:** Claim Representative; Clerical Supervisor; Computer Programmer; Electrical/Electronics Engineer; Management Analyst/Consultant; MIS Specialist; Services Sales Representative; Software Engineer; Systems Analyst; Typist/Word Processor. **Benefits available to temporary workers:** Paid Holidays; Paid Vacation. **Number of placements per year:** 200 - 499.

H.L. YOH COMPANY
135 Beaver Street, Waltham MA 02154. 781/273-5151. **Contact:** Carol Clark, New England Branch Manager. **Description:** A contract services firm. **Specializes in the areas of:** Architecture/Construction; Computer Hardware/Software; Engineering; Manufacturing; MIS/EDP; Personnel/Labor Relations; Technical. **Positions commonly filled include:** Architect; Chemical Engineer; Civil Engineer; Commercial Artist; Computer Programmer; Data Entry Clerk; Draftsperson; Editor; EDP Specialist; Electrical/Electronics Engineer; Industrial Designer; Industrial Engineer; Manufacturing Engineer; MIS Specialist; Operations/Production Manager; Software Engineer; Systems Analyst; Technical Illustrator; Technical Writer/Editor; Technician; Typist/Word Processor. **Number of placements per year:** 200 - 499.

CAREER/OUTPLACEMENT COUNSELING FIRMS

ACTION CAREER MANAGEMENT
25 Whaler Lane, North Quincy MA 02171-1553. 617/479-5665. **Fax:** 617/479-5431. **Contact:** R. Scott Gledhill, President. **Description:** A career/outplacement counseling firm.

BERKE & PRICE ASSOCIATES
6 New Town Way, Chelmsford MA 01824. 978/256-0482. **Toll-free phone:** 800/552-3753. **Fax:** 978/250-0787. **Contact:** Judit E. Price, Principal. **Description:** A career/outplacement counseling firm that also offers resume writing services. Founded in 1980.

THE BOSTON CAREER LINK
281 Huntington Avenue, Boston MA 02115. 617/536-1888. **Contact:** Manager. **Description:** A career/outplacement counseling firm.

THE CAREER COUNSELING NETWORK
140 Vine Street, Chestnut Hill MA 02167. 617/332-1670. **Contact:** John Decker, President. **Description:** A career/outplacement counseling firm.

THE CAREER PLACE
Trade Center Park, 100 Sylvan Road, Suite G100, Woburn MA 01810-1891. **Toll-free phone:** 888/273-WORK. **Fax:** 781/932-5566. **Contact:** Vicki Litzinger, Manager, Career Resource Library. **Description:** A nonprofit career/outplacement counseling agency whose services include an on-line service and on-site listing of job openings; re-employment services; employment workshops; and self-assessment services.

CAREER POINT
850 High Street, Holyoke MA 01040. 413/532-4900. **Contact:** Employee Services. **Description:** A career/outplacement counseling firm.

CAREER SOURCE
185 Alewife Brook Parkway, Cambridge MA 02138. 617/661-7867. **Toll-free phone:** 888/454-9675. **Contact:** Manager. **Description:** A career/outplacement counseling firm.

CAREER VENTURES COUNSELING SERVICES
60 Washington Street, Suite 2, Salem MA 01970. 978/744-1012. **Contact:** Andrew S. Brown, President. **Description:** A career/outplacement counseling firm that also provides testing and assessment, pre-retirement planning, resume development, interview preparation, and job search assistance. Founded in 1993. **Other area locations:** Boston MA.

CAREER VENTURES COUNSELING SERVICES
3 School Street, Boston MA 02108. 617/263-7744. **Contact:** Manager. **Description:** A career/outplacement firm.

CAREERPRO CAREER DEVELOPMENT CENTER
50 Beacon Street, Boston MA 02108. 617/523-7660. **Fax:** 617/523-8622. **Contact:** Lynn G. Lieberman, Manager. **Description:** Provides comprehensive career management, employment counseling, outplacement, and job search assistance, including resume development, cover letters, and interviewing techniques.

CAREERPRO CAREER DEVELOPMENT CENTER
950 Watertown Street, Suite 9, West Newton MA 02165. 617/965-7760. **Fax:** 617/964-2323. **Contact:** Michael Kaye, Manager. **Description:** CareerPro Career Development Center provides broad-based career management, outplacement, employment counseling, and job search assistance, including the development of resumes and related documentation.

CAREERPRO CAREER DEVELOPMENT CENTER
6 Pleasant Street, Suite 602, Malden MA 02148. 781/324-7890. **Contact:** Steve Dionne, Manager. **Description:** CareerPro Career Development Center provides comprehensive career management, outplacement, employment counseling, job search assistance, Internet access, and resume development services.

THE CENTER FOR PROFESSIONAL DEVELOPMENT IN THE LAW
955 Massachusetts Avenue, Cambridge MA 02139. 617/868-6669. **Fax:** 617/876-0203. **Contact:** Ronald W. Fox, Managing Partner. **World Wide Web address:** http://www.shore.net/~cpdl. **Description:** A career counseling firm that works with law students and lawyers in transition. **Specializes in the areas of:** Legal.

THE COMPETITIVE EDGE
P.O. Box 311, Woburn MA 01801. 781/932-3232. **Contact:** Anne Savas, Principal. **E-mail address:** asavas@ix.netcom.com. **Description:** A resume writing and career/outplacement counseling firm.

FUTUREWORKS
One Federal Street, Building 103-3, Springfield MA 01105. 413/858-2800. **Contact:** Manager. **Description:** A career/outplacement counseling firm.

JEWISH VOCATIONAL SERVICE
105 Chauncy Street, 6th Floor, Boston MA 02111. 617/451-8147. **Contact:** George Zeller, Employment Specialist. **Description:** A career/outplacement counseling agency that also provides resume writing services. **Positions commonly filled include:** Accountant/Auditor; Administrative Assistant; Computer Support Technician; Data Entry Clerk; Human Resources Specialist; Human Service Worker; Marketing Specialist; Services Sales Representative; Technical Support Representative. **Number of placements per year:** 100 - 199.

JEWISH VOCATIONAL SERVICE
26 West Street, 3rd Floor, Boston MA 02111. 617/542-1993. **Fax:** 617/423-8711. **Contact:** Deborah Burwick, Employment Specialist. **Description:** A career/outplacement counseling firm.

JOBNET
210 South Street, Boston MA 02111. 617/338-0809. **Toll-free phone:** 800/5-JOBNET. **Contact:** Manager. **Description:** A career/outplacement counseling firm.

METRO SOUTHWEST EMPLOYMENT & TRAINING CAREER CENTER
P.O. Box 740, Norwood MA 02062. **Contact:** Manager. **Description:** A career/outplacement service and training facility for displaced and laid-off workers. **NOTE:** Job openings are posted at the center.

PERSONAL AND CAREER COUNSELING
34 Follen Street, Cambridge MA 02138. 617/864-9097. **Contact:** Sheila G. Cook, Counselor. **Description:** A career/outplacement counseling firm.

WIND JOB CENTER
P.O. Box 4174, Andover MA 01810. 978/475-2742. **Fax:** 978/887-9298. **Contact:** Fred Nothnagel, Director. **E-mail address:** fmn@shore.net. **Description:** A career/outplacement counseling firm. Company pays fee. **Specializes in the areas of:** Accounting/Auditing; Administration; Advertising; Banking; Computer Science/Software; Engineering; Finance; General Management; Health/Medical; Manufacturing; Nonprofit; Personnel/Labor Relations; Publishing; Sales; Technical. **Number of placements per year:** 200 - 499.

THE WORK PLACE
75-101 Federal Street, 3rd Floor, Boston MA 02110. 617/737-0093. **Toll-free phone:** 800/436-WORK. **Fax:** 617/428-0380. **Contact:** Judith Lorei, Assistant Director. **World Wide Web address:** http://www.masscareers.state.ma.us. **Description:** A career/outplacement counseling firm that also offers a career resource library, job listings, and workshops. **Specializes in the areas of:** Accounting/Auditing; Administration; Food Industry; Light Industrial; Nonprofit; Secretarial. **Positions commonly filled include:** Administrative Assistant; Administrative Manager; Certified Nursing Aide; Computer Operator; Computer Programmer; Customer Service Representative; Database Manager; Electrical/Electronics Engineer; Human Resources Manager; Sales Representative; Typist/Word Processor. **Number of placements per year:** 200 - 499.

MICHIGAN

EXECUTIVE SEARCH FIRMS

AJM PROFESSIONAL SERVICES
803 West Big Beaver Road, Suite 357, Troy MI 48084-4734. 248/244-2222. **Fax:** 248/244-2233. **Contact:** Jeffrey Jones, Principal. **E-mail address:** ajmps@aol.com. **World Wide Web address:** http://www.ajmps.com. **Description:** An executive search firm focusing on information systems staffing. Company pays fee. **Specializes in the areas of:** Administration; Computer Science/Software. **Positions commonly filled include:** Computer Programmer; Management Analyst/Consultant; MIS Specialist; Software Engineer; Systems Analyst. **Average salary range of placements:** More than $50,000. **Number of placements per year:** 100 - 199.

ABILITY SEARCH GROUP
30400 Telegraph Road, Suite 474, Bingham Farms MI 48025. 248/594-2100. **Fax:** 248/594-2121. **Contact:** Manager. **Description:** An executive search firm that provides data processing placements.

ACCENT ON ACHIEVEMENT
3190 Rochester Road, Suite 104, Troy MI 48083. 248/528-1390. **Toll-free phone:** 800/828-5340. **Fax:** 248/528-9335. **Contact:** Charlene Brown, CPA, President. **E-mail address:** achieve@home.msen.com. **World Wide Web address:** http://www.accent-on-achievement.com. **Description:** An executive search firm that also provides temporary placements. Company pays fee. **Specializes in the areas of:** Accounting/Auditing; Finance. **Positions commonly filled include:** Accountant/Auditor; Actuary; Budget Analyst; Controller; Finance Director; Financial Analyst. **Benefits available to temporary workers:** Paid Holidays; Paid Vacation. **Other area locations:** Southfield MI. **Average salary range of placements:** More than $50,000. **Number of placements per year:** 50 - 99.

ACCOUNTANTS CONNECTION INC.
32540 Schoolcraft Road, Suite 100, Livonia MI 48150. 313/513-7800. **Contact:** Office Manager. **Description:** An executive search firm. **Specializes in the areas of:** Accounting/Auditing; Bookkeeping.

ACCOUNTANTS EXECUTIVE SEARCH
ACCOUNTANTS ON CALL
28411 Northwestern Highway, Suite 910, Southfield MI 48034. 810/356-0660. **Contact:** Manager. **Description:** An executive search firm. Accountants on Call (also at this location) is a temporary agency. **Specializes in the areas of:** Accounting/Auditing; Finance.

ACTION SELL ASSOCIATES
24333 Southfield Road, Suite 201, Southfield MI 48075. 248/569-5460. **Contact:** Manager. **Description:** An executive search firm. **Specializes in the areas of:** Health/Medical. **Positions commonly filled include:** Physician.

ADVANCE ASSOCIATES
3680 Edgemont, Troy MI 48084. 248/649-2456. **Contact:** Manager. **Description:** An executive search firm. **Specializes in the areas of:** Engineering; Manufacturing; Technical.

ADVANCE EMPLOYMENT
1711 North West Avenue, Jackson MI 49202. 517/787-3333. **Fax:** 517/787-3380. **Contact:** Recruiter. **E-mail address:** ddodge@advanceteam.com. **World Wide Web address:** http://www.advanceteam.com. **Description:** An executive search firm placing light industrial, clerical, and technical personnel. Company pays fee. **Specializes in the areas of:** Accounting/Auditing; Administration; Banking; Computer Science/Software; Engineering; Industrial; Personnel/Labor Relations; Publishing; Sales. **Positions commonly filled include:** Accountant/Auditor; Adjuster; Automotive Mechanic; Branch Manager; Buyer; Chemical Engineer; Computer Programmer; Human Resources Specialist; Industrial Engineer; Internet Services Manager; Management Analyst/Consultant; Management Trainee; Mechanical Engineer; Public Relations Specialist; Typist/Word Processor. **Benefits available to temporary workers:** Paid Holidays; Paid Vacation; Tuition Assistance. **Number of placements per year:** 100 - 199.

ADVANCE PERSONNEL OF MICHIGAN
251 106th Avenue, Plainwell MI 49080-9302. 616/685-8505. **Toll-free phone:** 888/685-8566. **Fax:** 616/685-5857. **Contact:** Arthur Flanders, Owner. **Description:** An executive search firm providing personnel for manufacturers. **Specializes in the areas of:** Engineering; Personnel/Labor Relations. **Positions commonly filled include:** Accountant; Blue-Collar Worker Supervisor; Controller; Design Engineer; Draftsperson; Electrical/Electronics Engineer; Electrician; Graphic Artist; Graphic Designer; Human Resources Manager; Manufacturing Engineer; Mechanical Engineer; Metallurgical Engineer; MIS Specialist; Operations Manager; Production Manager; Public Relations Manager; Purchasing Agent/Manager; Quality Control Supervisor; Sales Engineer; Sales Manager; Sales Representative; Software Engineer. **Corporate headquarters location:** This Location. **Average salary range of placements:** More than $50,000. **Number of placements per year:** 100 - 199.

ADVANCED EXECUTIVE RESOURCES
3040 Charlevoix Drive, Grand Rapids MI 49546. 616/942-4030. **Fax:** 616/942-9950. **Contact:** Office Manager. **Description:** An executive search firm.

ADVANCED TECHNICAL RESOURCES
888 West Big Beaver Road, Suite 720, Troy MI 48084. 248/269-1111. **Toll-free phone:** 800/464-4449. **Fax:** 248/643-8609. **Contact:** Vincent Vizzaccaro, President. **E-mail address:** 75352,2753@compuserve.com. **Description:** An executive search firm operating on a contingency basis and focusing on the placement of data processing and engineering professionals. Company pays fee. **Specializes in the areas of:** Administration; Art/Design; Computer Science/Software; Engineering; Manufacturing; Personnel/Labor Relations; Sales. **Positions commonly filled include:** Chemical Engineer; Computer Programmer; Design Engineer; Designer; Draftsperson; Electrical/Electronics Engineer; Environmental Engineer; Human Resources Manager; Industrial Engineer; Industrial Production Manager; Internet Services Manager; Management Analyst/Consultant; Manufacturer's/Wholesaler's Sales Rep.; Market Research Analyst; Mechanical Engineer; Metallurgical Engineer; MIS Specialist; Multimedia Designer; Services Sales Representative; Software Engineer; Systems Analyst; Technical Writer/Editor; Telecommunications Manager. **Benefits available to temporary workers:** Medical Insurance. **Other U.S. locations:** Nationwide. **Average salary range of placements:** $30,000 - $50,000. **Number of placements per year:** 50 - 99.

THE ADVANTAGE GROUP
2690 Crooks Road, Suite 414, Troy MI 48084. 248/362-1500. **Fax:** 248/362-2880. **Contact:** Anthony C. Fontana, CPA, Senior Partner. **E-mail**

address: advntgrp@aol.com. **Description:** An executive search firm that also provides contract positions. Company pays fee. **Specializes in the areas of:** Accounting/Auditing; Banking; Finance. **Positions commonly filled include:** Accountant/Auditor; Budget Analyst; Cost Estimator; Financial Analyst. **Average salary range of placements:** $30,000 - $50,000. **Number of placements per year:** 1 - 49.

AEGIS GROUP
23875 Novi Road, Novi MI 48375-3243. 248/344-1450. **Fax:** 248/347-2231. **Contact:** Tim Ignash, President. **E-mail address:** resume@aegis-group.com. **Description:** An executive search firm focusing on the recruitment of health care executives and physicians for health care systems, insurer groups, managed care organizations, and hospitals. Company pays fee. **Specializes in the areas of:** Health/Medical. **Positions commonly filled include:** Accountant/Auditor; Financial Analyst; General Manager; Health Services Manager; Human Resources Manager; Medical Records Technician; MIS Specialist; Occupational Therapist; Physical Therapist; Registered Nurse; Respiratory Therapist; Surgical Technician. **Other U.S. locations:** Nationwide. **Average salary range of placements:** More than $50,000. **Number of placements per year:** 1 - 49.

ALDEN GROUP INC.
74 West Long Lake Road, Suite 102, Bloomfield Hills MI 48304. 248/644-0210. **Contact:** Office Manager. **Description:** An executive search firm.

ALLEGHENY SEARCH ASSOCIATES
846 Dahlia Street, Rochester Hills MI 48307. 248/651-9550. **Contact:** Manager. **Description:** An executive search firm. **Specializes in the areas of:** Engineering.

ALLIANCE INDUSTRIES
33117 Hamilton Court, Suite 125, Farmington Hills MI 48334-3355. 248/489-9100. **Fax:** 248/489-9196. **Contact:** Manager. **Description:** An executive search firm. **Specializes in the areas of:** Automotive.

AMERICAN COMPUTER SERVICE
29777 Telegraph Road, Southfield MI 48034-1303. 248/827-1200. **Fax:** 248/827-4644. **Contact:** Dan Corp, President. **Description:** A contingency search firm. **Specializes in the areas of:** Computer Science/Software; Sales. **Positions commonly filled include:** Sales Manager; Sales Representative; Software Engineer. **Average salary range of placements:** More than $50,000. **Number of placements per year:** 50 - 99.

ASSOCIATES
222 Franklin Street, Grand Haven MI 49417. 616/842-8596. **Fax:** 616/842-6647. **Contact:** Bob Clark, President. **Description:** An executive search firm that focuses on the automotive supply industry. Company pays fee. **Specializes in the areas of:** Automotive; Engineering; General Management; Manufacturing; Transportation. **Positions commonly filled include:** Account Representative; Applications Engineer; Chemical Engineer; Design Engineer; Environmental Engineer; General Manager; Human Resources Manager; Industrial Engineer; Manufacturing Engineer; Mechanical Engineer; Operations Manager; Production Manager; Project Manager; Quality Control Supervisor; Sales Engineer; Sales Manager; Vice President of Operations. **Average salary range of placements:** More than $50,000. **Number of placements per year:** 1 - 49.

THE AUCON COMPANY
3779 High Gate Road, Muskegon MI 49441. 616/798-4883. **Fax:** 616/798-4087. **Contact:** Raymond B. Audo, President. **Description:** An executive search firm operating on both retainer and contingency bases. Company pays fee. **Specializes in the areas of:** Accounting/Auditing; Administration; Computer Science/Software; Engineering; General Management; Industrial; Manufacturing; Technical. **Average salary range of placements:** More than $50,000. **Number of placements per year:** 1 - 49.

AUTOMOTIVE CAREERS
2959 Lucerne Drive SE, Grand Rapids MI 49546-7173. 616/942-5700. **Fax:** 616/942-5214. **Contact:** C. Thomas Conrad, President. **Description:** A search firm for automotive dealership managers. Company pays fee. **Specializes in the areas of:** Accounting/Auditing; Finance; Retail; Sales. **Positions commonly filled include:** Accountant/Auditor; General Manager; Manufacturer's/Wholesaler's Sales Rep. **Number of placements per year:** 1 - 49.

BEACON SERVICES INC.
4595 Broadmoor Avenue SE, Grand Rapids MI 49512. 616/698-7979. **Fax:** 616/698-0838. **Contact:** Gordon Nellis, Division Manager. **World Wide Web address:** http://www.beaconweb.com. **Description:** An executive search firm. **Specializes in the areas of:** Administration; Engineering; General Management; Industrial; Manufacturing; Transportation. **Positions commonly filled include:** Design Engineer; Designer; Electrical/Electronics Engineer; Industrial Engineer; Mechanical Engineer; MIS Specialist; Operations/Production Manager; Quality Control Supervisor. **Average salary range of placements:** More than $50,000.

BENFORD ASSOCIATES
3000 Town Center, Suite 1333, Southfield MI 48075. 248/351-0250. **Fax:** 248/351-8698. **Contact:** Edward Benford, Manager. **Description:** An executive search firm that operates on both retainer and contingency bases. Company pays fee. **Specializes in the areas of:** Accounting/Auditing; Banking; Engineering; Food Industry; Industrial; Manufacturing; Personnel/Labor Relations. **Positions commonly filled include:** Automotive Mechanic; Bank Officer/Manager; Budget Analyst; Buyer; Chemical Engineer; Financial Analyst; Human Resources Manager; Industrial Engineer; Mechanical Engineer; Metallurgical Engineer; Operations/Production Manager; Purchasing Agent/Manager; Quality Control Supervisor. **Average salary range of placements:** More than $50,000. **Number of placements per year:** 50 - 99.

BRABOY & ASSOCIATES, INC.
P.O. Box 250134, Franklin MI 48025. 248/350-8770. **Fax:** 248/350-8771. **Contact:** Jay Braboy, President. **Description:** A retained executive search firm for the automotive plastic industry. Company pays fee. **Specializes in the areas of:** Executives; Sales. **Positions commonly filled include:** Manufacturer's/Wholesaler's Sales Rep. **Average salary range of placements:** More than $50,000. **Number of placements per year:** 1 - 49.

BRYANT BUREAU
18600 Florence Street, Roseville MI 48066. 810/772-6452. **Fax:** 810/772-6788. **Contact:** Jacqueline Nabat, Director of Engineering and Recruitment. **E-mail address:** bbsearch@flash.net. **World Wide Web address:** http://www.bryantjobsearch.com. **Description:** An executive search firm. Company pays fee. **Specializes in the areas of:** Engineering; Sales. **Positions commonly filled include:** Electrical/Electronics Engineer; Mechanical Engineer; Plastics Engineer. **Corporate headquarters location:** Dallas TX. **Other U.S. locations:** Nationwide. **Average salary range of placements:** More than $50,000. **Number of placements per year:** 100 - 199.

CAREER SEARCH INC.
33117 Hamilton Court, Suite 200, Farmington Hills MI 48334. 248/553-8200. **Contact:** Office Manager. **Description:** An executive search firm. **Specializes in the areas of:** Computer Hardware/Software.

CARMAC EXECUTIVE RECRUITING
32401 West Eight Mile Road, Livonia MI 48152. 248/478-5550. **Fax:** 248/478-5552. **Contact:** Thomas McInnes, Owner. **Description:** An executive search firm that provides placement in the automotive industry on a nationwide basis. **Specializes in the areas of:** Engineering; Manufacturing; Sales. **Positions commonly filled include:** Design Engineer; Designer; Mechanical Engineer; Operations/Production Manager; Quality Control Supervisor. **Number of placements per year:** 1 - 49.

CASE & COMPANY
15008 Kercheval Street, Grosse Pointe Park MI 48230. 313/331-6095. **Fax:** 313/823-2439. **Contact:** David R. Case, President. **Description:** An executive search firm that operates on a contingency basis and focuses on the automotive engineering industry. Company pays fee. **Specializes in the areas of:** Engineering; General Management; Manufacturing. **Positions commonly filled include:** Buyer; Design Engineer; Designer; Human Resources Manager; Industrial Engineer; Industrial Production Manager; Manufacturing Engineer; Mechanical Engineer; Metallurgical Engineer; Production Manager; Purchasing Agent/Manager; Quality Control Supervisor; Sales Engineer. **Number of placements per year:** 1 - 49.

CATALYST HEALTH CARE GROUP
2710 West Court Street, Suite 1, Flint MI 48503. 810/762-6900. **Contact:** Manager. **Description:** An executive search firm that places experienced personnel in medical centers and hospitals. **Specializes in the areas of:** Health/Medical.

CHRISTOPHER & ASSOCIATES
292 South Main Street, Plymouth MI 48170. 734/453-5656. **Contact:** Manager. **Description:** An executive search firm for automotive supply companies. **Specializes in the areas of:** Operations Management; Technical.

CIRCLEWOOD SEARCH GROUP, INC.
3307 East Kilgore, Suite 2, Kalamazoo MI 49001. 616/383-9520. **Toll-free phone:** 800/968-9520. **Fax:** 616/383-9530. **Contact:** Melissa Webb, President. **E-mail address:** circlewd@net-link.net. **World Wide Web address:** http://www.circlewood.com. **Description:** An executive search firm that places medical professionals in hospitals, health care systems, and private practices nationwide. Company pays fee. **Specializes in the areas of:** Health/Medical. **Positions commonly filled include:** Health Care Administrator; Nurse Practitioner; Occupational Therapist; Physical Therapist; Physician; Physician Assistant; Registered Nurse. **Average salary range of placements:** More than $50,000. **Number of placements per year:** 50 - 99.

COLLINS & ASSOCIATES
10188 West H Avenue, Kalamazoo MI 49009-8506. 616/372-4300. **Fax:** 616/372-3921. **Contact:** Phil Collins, Principal. **E-mail address:** pcollins@collins-associates.com. **World Wide Web address:** http://www.collins-associates.com. **Description:** An executive search firm operating on both retainer and contingency bases and providing technical placements in the computer industry. Company pays fee. **Specializes in the areas of:** Computer Science/Software. **Positions commonly filled include:** Computer Programmer; Internet Services Manager; MIS Specialist; Software Engineer; Systems Analyst; Telecommunications Manager. **Average salary range of placements:** $30,000 - $50,000. **Number of placements per year:** 1 - 49.

COMPASS GROUP LTD.
401 South Old Woodward Avenue, Suite 460, Birmingham MI 48009. 248/540-9110. **Fax:** 248/540-2944. **Contact:** Manager. **Description:** A generalist executive search firm.

CONTINENTAL SEARCH ASSOCIATES
P.O. Box 413, Birmingham MI 48012. 248/644-4506. **Contact:** Manager. **Description:** An executive search firm. **Specializes in the areas of:** Construction; Engineering.

CORPORATE AMERICA PERSONNEL CONSULTANTS
5310 Hertford Drive, Troy MI 48098. 248/879-1804. **Contact:** Manager. **Description:** An executive search firm.

CORPORATE BUSINESS SERVICES LTD.
913 West Holems Road, Suite 100, Lansing MI 48910-0411. 517/394-1800. **Fax:** 517/394-2033. **Contact:** Michael Keen, President. **Description:** An executive search firm. Company pays fee. **Specializes in the areas of:** Computer Science/Software; Engineering; Food Industry; General Management; Sales. **Positions commonly filled include:** Computer Programmer; General Manager; Management Trainee; Manufacturer's/Wholesaler's Sales Rep.; Restaurant /Food Service Manager; Systems Analyst. **Average salary range of placements:** $30,000 - $50,000. **Number of placements per year:** 200 - 499.

CORPORATE SOLUTIONS
77 East Long Lake Road, Bloomfield Hills MI 48304. 248/647-6370. **Fax:** 248/647-6383. **Contact:** Jim Bryant, President. **Description:** A contingency search firm for data processing professionals with a minimum of one year work experience. This location also provides contract personnel for all levels of data processing. **Specializes in the areas of:** Computer Science/Software. **Positions commonly filled include:** Computer Programmer; Project Manager; Systems Analyst. **Average salary range of placements:** $30,000 - $50,000. **Number of placements per year:** 1 - 49.

DAVIDSON, LAIRD & ASSOCIATES
29260 Franklin, Suite 110, Southfield MI 48034. 248/358-2160. **Fax:** 248/358-1225. **Contact:** Meri Laird, President. **E-mail address:** mlaird@rust.net. **Description:** An executive search firm that focuses on the automotive and plastics industries. Davidson, Laird & Associates also places secretarial and administrative candidates. Company pays fee. **Specializes in the areas of:** Accounting/Auditing; Engineering; Manufacturing; Personnel/Labor Relations; Secretarial. **Positions commonly filled include:** Buyer; Chemical Engineer; Cost Estimator; Design Engineer; Designer; Electrical/Electronics Engineer; Industrial Engineer; Industrial Production Manager; Mechanical Engineer; Metallurgical Engineer; Typist/Word Processor. **Average salary range of placements:** $30,000 - $50,000. **Number of placements per year:** 50 - 99.

DICKSON ASSOCIATES INC.
3001 West Big Beaver Road, Troy MI 48084. 248/643-9480. **Contact:** Manager. **Description:** An executive search firm. **Specializes in the areas of:** Accounting/Auditing; Engineering; Finance; Information Systems.

DURHAM ASSOCIATES INC.
11678 Doane Road, South Lyon MI 48718. 248/486-3888. **Contact:** Manager. **Description:** An executive search firm. **Specializes in the areas of:** Chemical.

G.L. DYKSTRA ASSOCIATES
P.O. Box 141546, Grand Rapids MI 49514. 616/791-9651. **Contact:** Manager. **Description:** An executive search firm.

GENE ELLEFSON & ASSOCIATES INC.
30100 Telegraph Road, Suite 422, Bingham Farms MI 48025. 248/642-3456. **Fax:** 248/642-3978. **Contact:** Gene Ellefson, President. **E-mail address:** gellefson@advdata.net. **Description:** An executive search firm that focuses on the placement of sales and engineering personnel with automotive manufacturers and suppliers. Company pays fee. **Specializes in the areas of:** Accounting/Auditing; Engineering; Manufacturing; Sales. **Positions commonly filled include:** Account Manager; Account Representative; Accountant; Controller; Cost Estimator; Design Engineer; Electrical/Electronics Engineer; Finance Director; Industrial Engineer; Mechanical Engineer; Sales Engineer; Sales Executive; Sales Manager. **Average salary range of placements:** More than $50,000. **Number of placements per year:** 1 - 49.

ELWELL & ASSOCIATES
301 East Liberty, Suite 535, Ann Arbor MI 48104. 734/662-8775. **Contact:** Manager. **Description:** An executive search firm. **Specializes in the areas of:** Manufacturing.

EMPLEX CORPORATION
25160 Lahser Road, Southfield MI 48034-2752. 248/352-2361. **Fax:** 248/352-6639. **Contact:** George Hayes, President. **Description:** An executive search and human resources consulting firm for mid-sized manufacturers and distributors. Company pays fee. **Positions commonly filled include:** Accountant/Auditor; Design Engineer; General Manager; Industrial Production Manager; Mechanical Engineer; Metallurgical Engineer; MIS Specialist; Purchasing Agent/Manager; Sales Manager. **Average salary range of placements:** More than $50,000. **Number of placements per year:** 1 - 49.

EXEC-TECH CORPORATION
P.O. Box 661, Highland MI 48357. 248/685-8798. **Fax:** 248/685-3427. **Contact:** Gilbert Lambrecht, President. **Description:** An executive search firm. Company pays fee. **Specializes in the areas of:** Engineering; Manufacturing; Sales. **Positions commonly filled include:** Chemical Engineer; Electrical/Electronics Engineer; Industrial Engineer; Manufacturer's/Wholesaler's Sales Rep.; Mechanical Engineer. **Number of placements per year:** 1 - 49.

EXECUQUEST, INC.
2050 Breton Road SE, Suite 103, Grand Rapids MI 49546-5547. 616/949-1800. **Fax:** 616/949-0561. **Contact:** William L. Waanders, President. **E-mail address:** execuquest@aol.com. **Description:** An executive search firm operating on a retainer basis that focuses on mid-level and senior-level management positions in manufacturing and banking. Company pays fee. **Specializes in the areas of:** Accounting/Auditing; Banking; Finance; General Management; Manufacturing; Personnel/Labor Relations. **Positions commonly filled include:** Accountant/Auditor; Bank Officer/Manager; Financial Analyst; Human Resources Manager. **Average salary range of placements:** More than $50,000. **Number of placements per year:** 1 - 49.

EXECUTECH, INC.
2002 Hogback Road, Suite 9, Ann Arbor MI 48105-9732. 734/483-8454. **Fax:** 734/483-0740. **Contact:** Donald Frederick, CEO. **E-mail address:** extinc@aol.com. **Description:** A retainer and contingency search firm. Company pays fee. **Specializes in the areas of:** Computer Science/Software. **Positions commonly filled include:** Computer Programmer; Internet Services Manager; Metallurgical Engineer; MIS Specialist; Multimedia Designer; Quality Control Supervisor; Systems Analyst; Telecommunications Manager. **Average salary range of placements:** More than $50,000. **Number of placements per year:** 1 - 49.

EXECUTIVE AND TECHNICAL PERSONNEL
5409 Kelly Road, Flint MI 48504. 810/732-8390. **Fax:** 810/732-7463. **Contact:** John I. Lutz, President/Owner. **Description:** An executive search firm. Company pays fee. **Specializes in the areas of:** Engineering; General Management; Industrial; Manufacturing; Technical. **Positions commonly filled include:** Chemical Engineer; Design Engineer; Electrical/Electronics Engineer; General Manager; Human Resources Specialist; Industrial Engineer; Industrial Production Manager; Materials Engineer; Mechanical Engineer; Metallurgical Engineer; Operations/Production Manager; Purchasing Agent/Manager; Quality Control Supervisor. **Average salary range of placements:** More than $50,000. **Number of placements per year:** 1 - 49.

EXECUTIVE GOLF SEARCH, INC.
669 Westchester Road, Saginaw MI 48603. 517/797-0677. **Contact:** Manager. **Description:** An executive search firm.

EXECUTIVE MANAGEMENT SEARCH
17496 Meadow Wood, Spring Lake MI 49456. 616/846-3051. **Fax:** 616/846-3085. **Contact:** Arthur F. Schwartz, General Manager. **Description:** A contingency search firm. Company pays fee. **Specializes in the areas of:** Administration; Biology; Engineering; General Management; Health/Medical; Industrial; Manufacturing; Personnel/Labor Relations; Sales; Technical; Transportation. **Positions commonly filled include:** Accountant/Auditor; Administrative Manager; Aerospace Engineer; Agricultural Engineer; Biological Scientist; Biomedical Engineer; Branch Manager; Chemical Engineer; Chemist; Civil Engineer; Construction Contractor; Credit Manager; Customer Service Representative; Designer; Electrical/Electronics Engineer; General Manager; Geologist/Geophysicist; Human Resources Manager; Industrial Engineer; Industrial Production Manager; Management Analyst/Consultant; Mechanical Engineer; Metallurgical Engineer; Operations/Production Manager; Petroleum Engineer; Purchasing Agent/Manager; Quality Control Supervisor; Science Technologist; Transportation/Traffic Specialist. **Average salary range of placements:** More than $50,000. **Number of placements per year:** 1 - 49.

EXECUTIVE PERSONNEL
5409 Kelly Road, Flint MI 48504. 810/732-8390. **Contact:** Manager. **Description:** An executive search firm. **Specializes in the areas of:** Manufacturing.

EXECUTIVE RECRUITERS
21751 West Nine Mile Road, Suite 202, Southfield MI 48075. 248/357-5373. **Contact:** Office Manager. **Description:** An executive search firm with various areas of specialization including medical sales, electronics, automotive engineering, and computers.

EXECUTIVE RECRUITERS INTERNATIONAL
1150 Griswold, Suite 3000, Detroit MI 48226-1900. 313/961-6200. **Fax:** 313/963-1826. **Contact:** Kathleen A. Sinclair, President. **Description:** An executive search firm. Company pays fee. **Specializes in the areas of:** Administration; Architecture/Construction; Automotive; Computer Science/Software; Engineering; Environmental; General Management; Industrial; Manufacturing; Personnel/Labor Relations; Publishing; Real Estate; Sales;

Technical; Transportation. **Positions commonly filled include:** Accountant/Auditor; Administrative Manager; Architect; Automotive Mechanic; Biological Scientist; Biomedical Engineer; Blue-Collar Worker Supervisor; Buyer; Chemical Engineer; Chemist; Civil Engineer; Computer Programmer; Construction and Building Inspector; Construction Contractor; Cost Estimator; Customer Service Representative; Designer; Draftsperson; Electrical/Electronics Engineer; Electrician; Environmental Engineer; General Manager; Geologist/Geophysicist; Human Resources Manager; Industrial Engineer; Industrial Production Manager; Landscape Architect; Management Analyst/ Consultant; Manufacturer's/Wholesaler's Sales Rep.; Mechanical Engineer; Metallurgical Engineer; Mining Engineer; Nuclear Engineer; Operations/Production Manager; Petroleum Engineer; Public Relations Specialist; Purchasing Agent/Manager; Quality Control Supervisor; Services Sales Representative; Software Engineer; Stationary Engineer; Structural Engineer; Surveyor; Systems Analyst; Technical Writer/Editor; Urban/Regional Planner; Water Transportation Specialist. **International locations:** Worldwide. **Number of placements per year:** 1 - 49.

F-O-R-T-U-N-E PERSONNEL CONSULTANTS
800 West Long Lake Road, Bloomfield Hills MI 48302-2056. 248/642-9383. **Fax:** 248/642-9575. **Contact:** Karl Zimmermann, President. **Description:** An executive search firm. Company pays fee. **Specializes in the areas of:** General Management; Materials; Purchasing; Quality Assurance. **Positions commonly filled include:** General Manager; Materials Manager; Purchasing Agent/Manager; Quality Control Supervisor. **Corporate headquarters location:** New York NY. **Other U.S. locations:** Nationwide. **Average salary range of placements:** More than $50,000. **Number of placements per year:** 1 - 49.

F-O-R-T-U-N-E PERSONNEL CONSULTANTS OF FARMINGTON
31800 Northwestern Highway, Suite 207, Farmington Hills MI 48334-1664. 248/932-8870. **Fax:** 248/932-8875. **Contact:** Gary Snyder, President. **Description:** An executive search firm operating on both retained and contingency bases. **Specializes in the areas of:** Accounting/Auditing; Engineering. **Positions commonly filled include:** Biomedical Engineer; Chemical Engineer; Design Engineer; Mechanical Engineer; MIS Specialist; Physician; Software Engineer. **Corporate headquarters location:** New York NY. **Other U.S. locations:** Nationwide. **Average salary range of placements:** More than $50,000. **Number of placements per year:** 1 - 49.

F-O-R-T-U-N-E PERSONNEL CONSULTANTS OF TROY, INC.
560 Kirts Boulevard, Suite 102, Troy MI 48084. 248/244-9646. **Fax:** 248/244-8568. **Contact:** Robert Tell, President. **Description:** An executive search firm operating on both retained and contingency bases. Company pays fee. **Specializes in the areas of:** Engineering; General Management; Health/Medical; Manufacturing. **Positions commonly filled include:** Administrative Manager; Biomedical Engineer; Chemical Engineer; Design Engineer; Designer; Electrical/Electronics Engineer; Environmental Engineer; General Manager; Health Services Manager; Mechanical Engineer; Metallurgical Engineer; Occupational Therapist; Physical Therapist; Physician. **Corporate headquarters location:** New York NY. **Other U.S. locations:** Nationwide. **Average salary range of placements:** More than $50,000. **Number of placements per year:** 1 - 49.

DAVID FRANKLIN ASSOCIATES, INC.
909 Pleasant Drive, Ypsilanti MI 48197. 734/459-5966. **Fax:** 734/451-0964. **Contact:** David Germon, President. **E-mail address:** dgermon@grfn.org. **Description:** An executive search firm that focuses on technical and automotive placements. Company pays fee. **Specializes in the areas of:** Engineering; General Management; Manufacturing; Personnel/Labor Relations; Technical. **Positions commonly filled include:** Buyer; Chemical Engineer; Design Engineer; Electrical/Electronics Engineer; Human Resources Specialist; Industrial Designer; Industrial Engineer; Manufacturing Engineer; Materials Engineer; Mechanical Engineer; Metallurgical Engineer; Quality Control Supervisor. **Average salary range of placements:** More than $50,000. **Number of placements per year:** 1 - 49.

GAM EXECUTIVE SEARCH
30400 Telegraph Road, Suite 358, Bingham Farms MI 48025. **Contact:** Manager. **Description:** An executive search firm. **Specializes in the areas of:** Automotive.

GBL ASSOCIATES INC.
6966 Crooks Road, Suite 20, Troy MI 48098. 248/813-9595. **Contact:** Manager. **Description:** An executive search firm. **Specializes in the areas of:** Engineering.

GRS
934 West Fulton, Grand Rapids MI 49504. 616/242-7700. **Contact:** Bill Fischer, Senior Consultant. **Description:** A retainer and contingency search firm. Company pays fee. **Specializes in the areas of:** Accounting/Auditing; Administration; Computer Science/Software; Engineering; Finance; General Management; Manufacturing; Personnel/Labor Relations; Technical. **Positions commonly filled include:** Blue-Collar Worker Supervisor; Branch Manager; Buyer; Chemical Engineer; Claim Representative; Computer Programmer; Design Engineer; Designer; Draftsperson; Electrical/Electronics Engineer; Financial Analyst; General Manager; Human Resources Manager; Industrial Engineer; Industrial Production Manager; Mechanical Engineer; Metallurgical Engineer; MIS Specialist; Purchasing Agent/Manager; Quality Control Supervisor; Software Engineer; Systems Analyst. **Average salary range of placements:** $30,000 - $50,000. **Number of placements per year:** 1 - 49.

GENESYS HEALTH PERSONNEL
112 South Dort Highway, Suite A, Flint MI 48503. 810/238-8700. **Contact:** Manager. **Description:** An executive search firm focusing on the placement of medical receptionists, medical assistants, home health aides, and CNAs. RNs are also placed at local hospitals on an as-needed, contingency fee basis. **Specializes in the areas of:** Health/Medical.

GIACOMIN GROUP INC.
3000 Town Center, Suite 2237, Southfield MI 48075. 248/352-1470. **Fax:** 248/358-4499. **Contact:** Manager. **Description:** An executive search firm that operates on both retainer and contingency bases. Company pays fee. **Specializes in the areas of:** Engineering; General Management; Manufacturing; Sales. **Positions commonly filled include:** Electrical/Electronics Engineer; Mechanical Engineer. **Average salary range of placements:** More than $50,000.

JOSEPH GOLDRING & ASSOCIATES
31500 West Thirteen Mile Road, Suite 200, Farmington Hills MI 48334. 248/539-2660. **Fax:** 248/539-2667. **Contact:** Joe Goldring, President. **Description:** An executive search firm . Company pays fee. **Specializes in the areas of:** Accounting/Auditing; Administration; Computer Science/Software; Engineering; Finance; General Management; Health/ Medical; Industrial; Manufacturing; Personnel/Labor

Relations; Sales. **Positions commonly filled include:** Account Manager; Actuary; Aerospace Engineer; Attorney; Budget Analyst; Buyer; Chemical Engineer; Civil Engineer; Computer Programmer; Cost Estimator; Design Engineer; EEG Technologist; EKG Technician; Electrical/Electronics Engineer; Environmental Engineer; Financial Analyst; Health Services Manager; Human Resources Specialist; Industrial Engineer; Manufacturer's/Wholesaler's Sales Rep.; Mechanical Engineer; Medical Records Technician; Metallurgical Engineer; MIS Specialist; Occupational Therapist; Paralegal; Physical Therapist; Physician; Purchasing Agent/Manager; Registered Nurse; Respiratory Therapist; Software Engineer; Speech-Language Pathologist; Surgical Technician; Systems Analyst. **Average salary range of placements:** $30,000 - $50,000. **Number of placements per year:** 50 - 99.

GRAPHIC ARTS MARKETING ASSOCIATES
3533 Deepwood Drive, Lambertville MI 48144. 734/854-5225. **Fax:** 734/854-5224. **Contact:** Jacqueline Crawford, President. **E-mail address:** graphicama@aol.com. **Description:** An executive search firm. Company pays fee. **Specializes in the areas of:** Advertising; Art/Design; Broadcasting; Market Research; Marketing; Printing. **Positions commonly filled include:** Account Representative; Copywriter; Customer Service Representative; Designer; Graphic Artist; Multimedia Designer; Public Relations Specialist; Sales Representative; Technical Writer/Editor; Video Production Coordinator. **Number of placements per year:** 50 - 99.

GUIDARELLI ASSOCIATES, INC.
2933 West John Beers Road, Stevensville MI 49127-1113. 616/429-7001. **Fax:** 616/429-7003. **Contact:** Shelly Guidarelli, President/Owner. **Description:** An executive search firm. Company pays fee. **Specializes in the areas of:** Personnel/Labor Relations; Sales. **Positions commonly filled include:** Human Resources Manager. **Average salary range of placements:** More than $50,000. **Number of placements per year:** 1 - 49.

ROBERT HALF INTERNATIONAL
One Towne Square, Suite 1050, Southfield MI 48076. 248/524-3100. **Fax:** 248/524-3115. **Contact:** George Corser, Division Director. **World Wide Web address:** http://www.roberthalf.com. **Description:** An executive search firm. Company pays fee. **Specializes in the areas of:** Accounting/Auditing; Administration; Banking; Computer Science/Software; Finance. **Positions commonly filled include:** Accountant/Auditor; Bank Officer/Manager; Budget Analyst; Computer Programmer; Cost Estimator; Credit Manager; Financial Analyst; Internet Services Manager; Management Analyst/Consultant; MIS Specialist; Software Engineer; Systems Analyst; Technical Writer/Editor. **Corporate headquarters location:** Menlo Park CA. **Other U.S. locations:** Nationwide. **Average salary range of placements:** $30,000 - $50,000. **Number of placements per year:** 500 - 999.

ROBERT HALF INTERNATIONAL ACCOUNTEMPS
333 Bridge Street NW, Suite 830, Grand Rapids MI 49504. 616/454-9444. **Contact:** Manager. **World Wide Web address:** http://www.roberthalf.com. **Description:** An executive search firm. Accountemps (also at this location) provides temporary placements. **Corporate headquarters location:** Menlo Park CA. **Other U.S. locations:** Nationwide.

THE HALLMAN GROUP INC.
7901 Sprinkle Road, Portage MI 49002. 616/324-3990. **Fax:** 616/324-3590. **Contact:** Ken Killman, Owner. **Description:** An executive search firm. Company pays fee. **Specializes in the areas of:** Administration; Computer Science/Software; Engineering; Manufacturing. **Positions commonly filled include:** Accountant/Auditor; Chemical Engineer; Computer Programmer; Design Engineer; Electrical/Electronics Engineer; Industrial Engineer; Mechanical Engineer; Metallurgical Engineer; MIS Specialist; Software Engineer; Systems Analyst. **Average salary range of placements:** $30,000 - $50,000. **Number of placements per year:** 50 - 99.

HARPER ASSOCIATES
29870 Middlebelt Road, Farmington Hills MI 48334. 248/932-1170. **Fax:** 248/932-4214. **Contact:** Office Manager. **Description:** A contingency search firm. Company pays fee. **Specializes in the areas of:** Architecture/Construction; Finance; Food Industry; Health/Medical. **Positions commonly filled include:** Accountant/Auditor; Architect; Biomedical Engineer; Dietician/Nutritionist; Food Scientist/Technologist; Medical Records Technician; Nurse; Physical Therapist; Physician. **Average salary range of placements:** $30,000 - $50,000. **Number of placements per year:** 100 - 199.

HEALTHCARE RECRUITERS INTERNATIONAL
10327 East Grand River, Suite 409, Brighton MI 48116. 810/227-7055. **Fax:** 810/227-7307. **Contact:** Gayle Amlie, President. **Description:** An executive search firm. Company pays fee. **Specializes in the areas of:** Administration; Biology; Computer Science/Software; Engineering; Finance; Health/Medical; Manufacturing; Sales. **Positions commonly filled include:** Accountant/Auditor; Administrative Manager; Attorney; Biological Scientist; Biomedical Engineer; Branch Manager; Budget Analyst; Buyer; Chemical Engineer; Chemist; Claim Representative; Clinical Lab Technician; Computer Programmer; Computer Scientist; Customer Service Representative; Design Engineer; Dietician/Nutritionist; EEG Technologist; EKG Technician; Electrical/Electronics Engineer; Financial Analyst; General Manager; Health Services Manager; Industrial Engineer; Industrial Production Manager; Management Analyst/Consultant; Manufacturer's/Wholesaler's Sales Rep.; Market Research Analyst; Mechanical Engineer; Medical Records Technician; MIS Specialist; Nuclear Medicine Technologist; Occupational Therapist; Operations Engineer; Pharmacist; Physical Therapist; Physician; Registered Nurse; Respiratory Therapist; Science Technologist; Services Sales Representative; Software Engineer; Speech-Language Pathologist; Technical Writer/Editor; Telecommunications Manager. **Other U.S. locations:** Nationwide. **Average salary range of placements:** $30,000 - $50,000. **Number of placements per year:** 50 - 99.

HARVEY HOHAUSER & ASSOCIATES
5600 New King Street, Suite 355, Troy MI 48098-2652. **Contact:** Harvey Hohauser, President. **Description:** A retainer search firm. Company pays fee. **Specializes in the areas of:** Administration; Banking; Engineering; Finance; Manufacturing. **Positions commonly filled include:** Management. **Average salary range of placements:** More than $50,000. **Number of placements per year:** 50 - 99.

IBA SEARCH CONSULTANTS
8300 Thornapple River Drive, Caledonia MI 49316. 616/891-2160. **Fax:** 616/891-1180. **Contact:** Jim Lakatos, President. **E-mail address:** ibahunter@wingsisp.com. **World Wide Web address:** http://www.wingsisp.com/ibaresearch. **Description:** An executive search firm operating on a contingency basis. Company pays fee. **Specializes in the areas of:** Computer Science/Software; Engineering; Manufacturing; Technical. **Positions commonly filled include:** Aerospace Engineer; Agricultural Engineer;

Biological Scientist; Biomedical Engineer; Chemical Engineer; Chemist; Civil Engineer; Computer Programmer; Designer; Draftsperson; Electrical/Electronics Engineer; General Manager; Industrial Engineer; Industrial Production Manager; Mechanical Engineer; Metallurgical Engineer; Nuclear Engineer; Operations/Production Manager; Quality Control Supervisor; Science Technologist; Software Engineer; Stationary Engineer; Structural Engineer; Systems Analyst; Technical Writer/Editor; Telecommunications Manager. **Average salary range of placements:** $30,000 - $50,000. **Number of placements per year:** 1 - 49.

INFORMATION SYSTEMS EXECUTIVE RECRUITERS
600 South Adams, Suite 210, Birmingham MI 48009. 248/647-0850. **Contact:** Manager. **Description:** An executive search firm. **Specializes in the areas of:** Information Systems.

LAKE ASSOCIATES
105 South Cochran Avenue, Charlotte MI 48813. 517/543-1340. **Fax:** 517/543-1343. **Contact:** Richard Dowling, Owner. **Description:** An executive search firm operating on both retained and contingency bases for hotels, clubs, and resorts. Company pays fee. **Specializes in the areas of:** Hotel/Restaurant; Sales. **Positions commonly filled include:** Controller; Food Service Manager; General Manager; Hotel Manager. **Average salary range of placements:** $30,000 - $50,000. **Number of placements per year:** 1 - 49.

LAMBERT INTERNATIONAL
P.O. Box 867, Jenison MI 49429. 616/261-0753. **Contact:** Manager. **Description:** An executive search firm. **Specializes in the areas of:** General Management; Technical.

JOHN LAWRENCE GROUP
26111 West 14 Mile Road, Suite LL1, Franklin MI 48025-1169. 248/932-7770. **Toll-free phone:** 800/218-9135. **Fax:** 248/932-7774. **Contact:** Office Manager. **E-mail address:** jlgcareer@aol.com. **World Wide Web address:** http://www.johnlawrencegroup.com. **Description:** An executive search firm for a variety of printing/publishing fields including commercial printing, books, direct mail, prepress, catalogs, newspapers, bank check printing, and other specialty printing areas. Company pays fee. **Specializes in the areas of:** Publishing. **Positions commonly filled include:** Chief Financial Officer; Controller; Cost Estimator; Customer Service Representative; Financial Manager; General Manager; Multimedia Designer; Operations Manager; President; Production Manager; Sales Executive; Sales Manager; Sales Representative. **Average salary range of placements:** More than $50,000. **Number of placements per year:** 1 - 49.

LEGAL SEARCH & MANAGEMENT
22821 Violet Street, Suite 100, Farmington MI 48336. 248/471-3443. **Contact:** Office Manager. **Description:** An executive search firm that provides legal placements.

DAVID LINDEMER ASSOCIATES
206 South Fifth Avenue, Suite 250, Ann Arbor MI 48104. 734/761-3999. **Fax:** 734/761-3010. **Contact:** David Lindemer, President. **Description:** An executive search firm operating on both retainer and contingency bases. Company pays fee. **Specializes in the areas of:** Administration; General Management; Manufacturing; Personnel/Labor Relations. **Positions commonly filled include:** Design Engineer; General Manager; Human Resources Manager. **Average salary range of placements:** More than $50,000. **Number of placements per year:** 1 - 49.

MGM EXECUTIVE SEARCH
32255 Northwestern Highway, Suite 190, Farmington Hills MI 48334. 248/932-9770. **Contact:** Manager. **Description:** An executive search firm. **Positions commonly filled include:** Chief Financial Officer; Human Resources Specialist.

MANAGEMENT RECRUITERS INTERNATIONAL
550 Stephenson Highway, Suite 407, Troy MI 48083. 248/585-4200. **Contact:** Ed Moelle, Manager. **Description:** An executive search firm. **Specializes in the areas of:** Accounting/Auditing; Administration; Advertising; Architecture/Construction; Automotive; Banking; Chemical; Communications; Computer Hardware/Software; Design; Electrical; Engineering; Food Industry; General Management Health/Medical; Industrial; Insurance; Legal; Manufacturing; Operations Management; Personnel/Labor Relations; Procurement; Publishing; Quality Assurance; Retail Sales; Sales; Technical; Textiles; Transportation. **Corporate headquarters location:** Cleveland OH. **Other U.S. locations:** Nationwide.

MANAGEMENT RECRUITERS INTERNATIONAL
2929 Plymouth Road, Suite 209, Ann Arbor MI 48105. 734/769-1720. **Contact:** Office Manager. **Description:** An executive search firm. **Specializes in the areas of:** Accounting/Auditing; Banking; Data Processing; Insurance. **Corporate headquarters location:** Cleveland OH. **Other U.S. locations:** Nationwide.

MANAGEMENT RECRUITERS INTERNATIONAL
124 North Division Street, Traverse City MI 49684. 616/947-8000. **Contact:** Manager. **Description:** An executive search firm. **Specializes in the areas of:** Engineering; Information Technology. **Corporate headquarters location:** Cleveland OH. **Other U.S. locations:** Nationwide.

MANAGEMENT RECRUITERS INTERNATIONAL
300 River Place, Suite 3000, Detroit MI 48207. 313/568-4300. **Contact:** Manager. **Description:** An executive search firm. **Corporate headquarters location:** Cleveland OH. **Other U.S. locations:** Nationwide.

MANAGEMENT RECRUITERS INTERNATIONAL
400 136th Avenue, Holland MI 49424. 616/396-2620. **Contact:** Manager. **Description:** An executive search firm. **Specializes in the areas of:** Manufacturing; Technical. **Corporate headquarters location:** Cleveland OH. **Other U.S. locations:** Nationwide.

MANAGEMENT RECRUITERS OF BATTLE CREEK
67 West Michigan Avenue, Suite 401C, Battle Creek MI 49017. 616/968-5959. **Contact:** Manager. **Description:** An executive search firm. Company pays fee. **Specializes in the areas of:** Accounting/Auditing; Administration; Advertising; Computer Science/Software; Engineering; Finance; Health/Medical; Industrial; Manufacturing. **Positions commonly filled include:** Buyer; Chemical Engineer; Computer Programmer; Cost Estimator; Design Engineer; Designer; Financial Analyst; Health Services Manager; Industrial Engineer; Industrial Production Manager; Mechanical Engineer; Medical Records Technician; Metallurgical Engineer; MIS Specialist; Operations/Production Manager; Quality Control Supervisor; Software Engineer; Systems Analyst. **Corporate headquarters location:** Cleveland OH. **Other U.S. locations:** Nationwide. **Average salary range of placements:** $30,000 - $50,000. **Number of placements per year:** 100 - 199.

MANAGEMENT RECRUITERS OF BINGHAM FARMS
30700 Telegraph Road, Suite 3650, Bingham Farms MI 48025. 248/647-2828. **Contact:** Manager. **Description:** An executive search firm. **Specializes in the areas of:** Accounting/Auditing; Administration; Advertising; Architecture/Construction; Banking; Chemical; Communications; Computer Hardware/Software; Design; Electrical; Engineering; Food Industry; General Management; Health/Medical; Insurance; Legal; Manufacturing; Operations Management; Personnel/Labor Relations; Procurement; Publishing; Real Estate; Retail; Sales; Technical; Textiles; Transportation. **Corporate headquarters location:** Cleveland OH. **Other U.S. locations:** Nationwide.

MANAGEMENT RECRUITERS OF DEARBORN
Parklane Towers West, Suite 1224, Three Parklane Boulevard, Dearborn MI 48126-2591. 313/336-6650. **Contact:** Elaine Kozlowski, Manager. **Description:** An executive search firm. **Specializes in the areas of:** Accounting/Auditing; Administration; Architecture/Construction; Banking; Chemical; Communications; Computer Hardware/Software; Design; Electrical; Engineering; Food Industry; General Management; Health/Medical; Insurance; Manufacturing; Operations Management; Personnel/Labor Relations; Procurement; Publishing; Sales; Technical; Transportation. **Corporate headquarters location:** Cleveland OH. **Other U.S. locations:** Nationwide.

MANAGEMENT RECRUITERS OF FLINT
5524 South Saginaw Street, Flint MI 48507. 810/695-0120. **Fax:** 810/695-0522. **Contact:** Rick Reed, Co-Owner. **Description:** An executive search firm operating on both contingency and retained bases. Company pays fee. **Specializes in the areas of:** Accounting/Auditing; Administration; Architecture/Construction; Chemical; Communications; Computer Hardware/Software; Computer Science/Software; Design; Electrical; Engineering; Food Industry; General Management; Health/Medical; Industrial; Insurance; Legal; Light Industrial; Manufacturing; Operations Management; Personnel/Labor Relations; Procurement; Retail; Sales; Scientific; Technical; Textiles; Transportation. **Positions commonly filled include:** Applications Engineer; Blue-Collar Worker Supervisor; Buyer; Chemical Engineer; Civil Engineer; Computer Programmer; Cost Estimator; Database Manager; Design Engineer; Designer; Draftsperson; Electrical/Electronics Engineer; Electrician; Industrial Engineer; Industrial Production Manager; Manufacturing Engineer; Mechanical Engineer; Metallurgical Engineer; MIS Specialist; Operations Manager; Production Manager; Project Manager; Purchasing Agent/Manager; Quality Control Supervisor; Sales Engineer; Software Engineer; Systems Analyst; Systems Manager. **Corporate headquarters location:** Cleveland OH. **Other U.S. locations:** Nationwide. **Average salary range of placements:** $30,000 - $50,000. **Number of placements per year:** 50 - 99.

MANAGEMENT RECRUITERS OF GRAND RAPIDS
146 Monroe Center, Suite 1126, Grand Rapids MI 49503. 616/336-8484. **Contact:** Office Manager. **Description:** An executive search firm. **Specializes in the areas of:** Banking; Chemical; Finance; Health/Medical; Metals; Sales.**Corporate headquarters location:** Cleveland OH. **Other U.S. locations:** Nationwide.

MANAGEMENT RECRUITERS OF KALAMAZOO
4021 West Main Street, Suite 200, Kalamazoo MI 49006-2746. 616/381-1153. **Fax:** 616/381-8031. **Contact:** Manager. **Description:** An executive search firm. **Specializes in the areas of:** Accounting/Auditing; Administration; Advertising; Architecture/Construction; Banking; Chemical; Communications; Computer Hardware/Software; Design; Electrical; Engineering; Food Industry; General Management; Health/Medical; Insurance; Legal; Manufacturing; Operations Management; Personnel/Labor Relations; Procurement; Publishing; Retail; Sales; Technical; Textiles; Transportation. **Corporate headquarters location:** Cleveland OH. **Other U.S. locations:** Nationwide.

MANAGEMENT RECRUITERS OF LANSING
2491 Cedar Park Drive, Holt MI 48842-2184. 517/694-1153. **Contact:** John Peterson, Manager. **Description:** An executive search firm. **Specializes in the areas of:** Accounting/Auditing; Administration; Advertising; Architecture/Construction; Banking; Chemical; Communications; Computer Hardware/Software; Design; Electrical; Engineering; Food Industry; General Management; Health/Medical; Insurance; Legal; Manufacturing; Operations Management; Personnel/Labor Relations; Procurement; Publishing; Retail; Sales; Technical; Textiles; Transportation. **Corporate headquarters location:** Cleveland OH. **Other U.S. locations:** Nationwide.

MANAGEMENT RECRUITERS OF LIVONIA
37677 Professional Center Drive, Suite 100-C, Livonia MI 48154-1138. 734/953-9590. **Fax:** 734/953-0566. **Contact:** Don Eden, President. **Description:** A contingency search firm. **Specializes in the areas of:** Accounting/Auditing; Administration; Engineering; Finance; General Management; Industrial; Sales. **Positions commonly filled include:** Accountant/Auditor; Branch Manager; Buyer; Chemical Engineer; Customer Service Representative; Designer; Electrical/Electronics Engineer; Electrician; Financial Analyst; General Manager; Industrial Engineer; Industrial Production Manager; Manufacturer's/Wholesaler's Sales Rep.; Mechanical Engineer; Metallurgical Engineer; Purchasing Agent/Manager; Quality Control Supervisor; Transportation/Traffic Specialist; Wholesale and Retail Buyer. **Corporate headquarters location:** Cleveland OH. **Other U.S. locations:** Nationwide. **Average salary range of placements:** $30,000 - $50,000. **Number of placements per year:** 1 - 49.

MANAGEMENT RECRUITERS OF MUSKEGON
3145 Henry Street, Suite 203, Muskegon MI 49441. 616/755-6486. **Fax:** 616/759-8041. **Contact:** John R. Mitchell, Jr., Manager. **Description:** An executive search firm. **Specializes in the areas of:** Accounting/Auditing; Administration; Advertising; Architecture/Construction; Banking; Chemical; Communications; Computer Hardware/Software; Design; Electrical; Engineering; Food Industry; General Management; Health/Medical; Insurance; Legal; Manufacturing; Operations Management; Personnel/Labor Relations; Procurement; Publishing; Retail; Sales; Technical; Textiles; Transportation. **Corporate headquarters location:** Cleveland OH. **Other U.S. locations:** Nationwide.

MANAGEMENT RECRUITERS OF ROCHESTER
2530 South Rochester Road, Rochester Hills MI 48307. 248/299-1900. **Fax:** 248/299-5681. **Contact:** Manager. **E-mail address:** mrnocmi@mrnoc. **Description:** An executive search firm operating on both retained and contingency bases. **Specializes in the areas of:** Accounting/Auditing; Administration; Banking; Chemical; Communications; Computer Hardware/Software; Design; Electrical; Engineering; Finance; General Management; Health/Medical; Insurance; Legal; Manufacturing; Nonprofit; Operations Management; Personnel/Labor Relations; Procurement; Retail; Sales; Technical; Textiles; Transportation. **Corporate headquarters location:** Cleveland OH. **Other U.S. locations:** Nationwide. **International locations:** Worldwide. **Average salary**

range of placements: More than $50,000. **Number of placements per year:** 100 - 199.

MANAGEMENT RECRUITERS OF SOUTHEASTERN MICHIGAN
P.O. Box 3, Blissfield MI 49228-0003. 517/486-2167. **Fax:** 517/486-2324. **Contact:** Mary W. Snellbaker, Owner/Manager. **Description:** An executive search firm. Company pays fee. **Specializes in the areas of:** Accounting/Auditing; Engineering; General Management; Industrial; Manufacturing; Personnel/Labor Relations; Technical. **Positions commonly filled include:** Design Engineer; Environmental Engineer; General Manager; Human Resources Manager; Industrial Engineer; Industrial Production Manager; Mechanical Engineer; Metallurgical Engineer; Purchasing Agent/Manager; Quality Control Supervisor; Stationary Engineer. **Corporate headquarters location:** Cleveland OH. **Other U.S. locations:** Nationwide. **Number of placements per year:** 1 - 49.

MEDMATCH
441 South Livernois Road, Suite 175, Rochester Hills MI 48307. 248/651-0652. **Fax:** 248/651-2748. **Contact:** Manager. **Description:** An executive search firm. **Specializes in the areas of:** Health/Medical.

MEDSEARCH INC.
530 Pine Street, Suite D, Rochester MI 48307-1482. 248/656-8450. **Contact:** Manager. **Description:** An executive search firm that operates on a contingency basis. Company pays fee. **Specializes in the areas of:** Health/Medical. **Positions commonly filled include:** Health Services Manager; Occupational Therapist; Physical Therapist; Physician. **Number of placements per year:** 1 - 49.

METROSTAFF
26261 Evergreen Road, Suite 500, Southfield MI 48076. 248/557-8700. **Fax:** 248/557-8507. **Contact:** Michael Callaway, President. **Description:** An executive search firm. Company pays fee. **Specializes in the areas of:** Computer Science/Software; Engineering; Health/Medical; Industrial; Secretarial; Transportation. **Positions commonly filled include:** Computer Programmer; Design Engineer; EEG Technologist; EKG Technician; Electrical/Electronics Engineer; Industrial Engineer; Industrial Production Manager; Licensed Practical Nurse; Mechanical Engineer; MIS Specialist; Occupational Therapist; Operations/Production Manager; Physical Therapist; Quality Control Supervisor; Registered Nurse; Software Engineer; Systems Analyst; Technical Writer/Editor; Typist/Word Processor. **Number of placements per year:** 1000+.

MICHIGAN SEARCH PLUS
25882 Orchard Lake Road, Suite 207, Farmington Hills MI 48336. 248/471-6110. **Contact:** Christy Greeneisen, President. **World Wide Web address:** http://www.michsrchpl@gnn.com. **Description:** An executive search firm. Company pays fee. **Specializes in the areas of:** Administration; Computer Science/Software; Engineering; Finance; General Management; Industrial; Manufacturing; Personnel/Labor Relations; Sales; Secretarial. **Positions commonly filled include:** Automotive Engineer; Biomedical Engineer; Buyer; Chemical Engineer; Chemist; Computer Programmer; Cost Estimator; Design Engineer; Designer; Draftsperson; Electrical/Electronics Engineer; Electrician; Environmental Engineer; Financial Analyst; Food Scientist/Technologist; Human Resources Manager; Industrial Engineer; Industrial Production Manager; Manufacturer's/Wholesaler's Sales Rep.; Mechanical Engineer; MIS Specialist; Operations/Production Manager; Paralegal; Purchasing Agent/Manager; Quality Control Supervisor; Science Technologist; Software Engineer; Systems Analyst; Transportation/Traffic Specialist. **Number of placements per year:** 50 - 99.

DARNELL MITCHELL & ASSOCIATES
25330 Telegraph, Southfield MI 48034. 248/357-5300. **Contact:** Manager. **Description:** An executive search firm. **Specializes in the areas of:** Engineering.

C.A. MOORE & ASSOCIATES, INC.
15500 Wayzata Boulevard, Suite 803C, Wayzata MI 55391. 612/473-0990. **Contact:** Connie Moore, President. **E-mail address:** camoore@mcg.net. **Description:** An executive search firm operating on both retained and contingency bases. Company pays fee. **Specializes in the areas of:** Accounting/Auditing; Direct Marketing; Finance; Insurance; Legal; Risk Management. **Positions commonly filled include:** Accountant/Auditor; Adjuster; Administrative Worker/Clerk; Attorney; Controller; Finance Director; Financial Analyst; General Manager; Human Resources Manager; Insurance Agent/Broker; Operations/Production Manager; Sales Executive; Sales Manager; Sales Representative; Underwriter/Assistant Underwriter. **Number of placements per year:** 1 - 49.

OFFICE STAFFING RECRUITING
4234 Cascade Road, Grand Rapids MI 49546. 616/949-2525. **Fax:** 616/949-2982. **Contact:** Pam McMaster, Team Manager. **Description:** An executive search firm. **Specializes in the areas of:** Accounting/Auditing; Administration; Banking; Computer Science/Software; Engineering; Finance; General Management; Industrial; Insurance; Manufacturing; Personnel/Labor Relations; Sales; Secretarial. **Positions commonly filled include:** Accountant/Auditor; Administrative Manager; Branch Manager; Brokerage Clerk; Buyer; Claim Representative; Clerical Supervisor; Computer Programmer; Design Engineer; General Manager; Human Resources Specialist; Human Service Worker; Industrial Production Manager; Insurance Agent/Broker; Manufacturer's/Wholesaler's Sales Rep.; Mechanical Engineer; Operations/Production Manager; Purchasing Agent/Manager; Quality Control Supervisor; Securities Sales Representative; Software Engineer; Systems Analyst; Telecommunications Manager; Underwriter/Assistant Underwriter. **Average salary range of placements:** $30,000 - $50,000. **Number of placements per year:** 50 - 99.

OPEN PAGE SEARCH SERVICES
1354 Ardmoor Avenue, Ann Arbor MI 48103-5348. 734/761-3556. **Fax:** 734/761-1554. **Contact:** Frederick Page, Principal. **Description:** An executive search firm that focuses on placement of actuaries. Company pays fee. **Specializes in the areas of:** Administration; Computer Science/Software; Insurance. **Positions commonly filled include:** Actuary; Computer Programmer; Financial Analyst; Management Analyst/Consultant; Mathematician; MIS Specialist; Securities Sales Representative; Software Engineer; Systems Analyst; Underwriter/Assistant Underwriter. **Number of placements per year:** 1 - 49.

OPPORTUNITY KNOCKING, INC.
9677 Peer Road, South Lyon MI 48178. 248/437-3700. **Fax:** 248/437-0939. **Contact:** Calvin Weaver, Executive Placement Manager. **E-mail address:** hobbes9@idt.net. **Description:** An executive search firm focusing on computer personnel. Company pays fee. **Specializes in the areas of:** Computer Science/Software. **Positions commonly filled include:** Database Manager; Internet Services Manager; MIS Manager; Software Engineer; Systems Analyst; Systems Manager. **Average salary range of**

placements: More than $50,000. **Number of placements per year:** 1 - 49.

PARR SEARCH
385 Bay Pointe Road, Lake Orion MI 48362. **Contact:** Mauro Nobili, President. **Description:** A contingency and retainer search firm focusing on engineering and technical fields. Company pays fee. **Specializes in the areas of:** Engineering; Industrial; Manufacturing. **Positions commonly filled include:** Chemical Engineer; Cost Estimator; Design Engineer; Designer; Electrical/Electronics Engineer; Environmental Engineer; General Manager; Human Resources Manager; Industrial Engineer; Industrial Production Manager; Mechanical Engineer; Metallurgical Engineer; Operations/Production Manager; Purchasing Agent/Manager; Stationary Engineer; Structural Engineer; Technical Writer/Editor. **Average salary range of placements:** More than $50,000. **Number of placements per year:** 1 - 49.

PREMIER HEALTHCARE RECRUITERS
3744 Campbell Street, Dearborn MI 48124. 313/277-0821. **Fax:** 313/277-0832. **Contact:** Diana L. Watson, CPC, President. **E-mail address:** dianalynn4@aol.com. **Description:** An executive search firm operating on a contingency basis. Premier Healthcare Recruiters places physicians in both clinical and administrative positions. Company pays fee. **Specializes in the areas of:** Health/Medical. **Positions commonly filled include:** Physician. **Average salary range of placements:** More than $50,000. **Number of placements per year:** 1 - 49.

PROFESSIONAL ADVANCEMENT INSTITUTE
28422 Tavistock Trail, Southfield MI 48034. 248/356-6660. **Fax:** 248/356-6662. **Contact:** Erwin Posner, President. **Description:** An executive search firm focusing on the pharmaceutical, biotech, and health care industries and professionals with SAS or COBOL programming experience. Company pays fee. **Specializes in the areas of:** Biology; Engineering; Health/Medical. **Positions commonly filled include:** Biochemist; Biological Scientist; Chemical Engineer; Chemist; Computer Programmer; Health Services Manager; Industrial Engineer; Mechanical Engineer; Occupational Therapist; Pharmacist; Physical Therapist; Physician. **Average salary range of placements:** More than $50,000. **Number of placements per year:** 100 - 199.

PROFESSIONAL CAREER SEARCH
1680 Viewpond Drive SE, Grand Rapids MI 49508. 616/281-3110. **Contact:** Manager. **Description:** An executive search firm. **Specializes in the areas of:** Administration; Sales; Technical.

PROFESSIONAL CAREER SEARCH
5464 Holiday Terrace, Kalamazoo MI 49009. 616/372-3339. **Fax:** 616/372-3363. **Contact:** Manager. **Description:** An executive search firm. **Specializes in the areas of:** Administration; Sales; Technical.

PROFESSIONAL PERSONNEL CONSULTANTS INTERNATIONAL
28200 Orchard Lake Road, Farmington Hills MI 48334. 248/737-1750. **Fax:** 248/737-5886. **Contact:** Dan Mistura, President. **Description:** A management and executive search firm. Company pays fee. **Specializes in the areas of:** Accounting/Auditing; Administration; Computer Science/Software; Engineering; Finance; Health/Medical; Manufacturing; Personnel/Labor Relations; Sales; Secretarial; Technical. **Positions commonly filled include:** Accountant/Auditor; Budget Analyst; Buyer; Chemist; Computer Programmer; Credit Manager; Designer; Electrical/Electronics Engineer; Financial Analyst; General Manager; Human Resources Manager; Industrial Engineer; Mechanical Engineer; Metallurgical Engineer; Nuclear Engineer; Occupational Therapist; Pharmacist; Physical Therapist; Physician; Purchasing Agent/Manager; Quality Control Supervisor; Software Engineer; Structural Engineer; Systems Analyst. **Other U.S. locations:** Nationwide. **Average salary range of placements:** More than $50,000. **Number of placements per year:** 200 - 499.

PROSEARCH, INC.
34405 West 12 Mile Road, Suite 196, Farmington Hills MI 48331. 248/488-3330. **Fax:** 248/488-1015. **Contact:** Robert Eberline, Vice President. **E-mail address:** psimsi@compuserve.com. **Description:** An executive search firm operating on both retainer and contingency bases. ProSearch, Inc. provides contract professionals, temp-to-perm staffing, permanent staff recruitment, and outsourcing services. Founded in 1991. Company pays fee. **Specializes in the areas of:** Accounting/Auditing; Administration; Banking; Computer Science/Software; Finance; Manufacturing. **Positions commonly filled include:** Accountant/Auditor; Bank Officer/Manager; Budget Analyst; Computer Programmer; Credit Manager; Financial Analyst; MIS Specialist; Software Engineer; Systems Analyst. **Corporate headquarters location:** This Location.

RECRUITING SOLUTIONS
6260 Nicholas Drive, West Bloomfield MI 48322. 248/737-9022. **Fax:** 248/737-9165. **Contact:** Manager. **Description:** A retained executive search firm.

REHABILITATION THERAPY RESOURCES
32854 Five Mile Road, Livonia MI 48154. 734/522-3334. **Fax:** 734/762-2001. **Contact:** Lisa A. Keefer, President. **E-mail address:** physther@wwnet.com. **World Wide Web address:** http://www.net~physther.com. **Description:** An executive search firm that focuses on rehabilitation professional placement. Company pays fee. **Specializes in the areas of:** Health/Medical. **Positions commonly filled include:** Occupational Therapist; Physical Therapist. **Corporate headquarters location:** This Location. **Average salary range of placements:** $30,000 - $50,000. **Number of placements per year:** 1 - 49.

ROONEY PERSONNEL COMPANY
159 Pierce Street, Suite 203, Birmingham MI 48009. 248/258-5533. **Toll-free phone:** 800/755-5888. **Fax:** 248/258-5671. **Contact:** Michael Rooney, President. **World Wide Web address:** http://www.motor-city.com/rooney. **Description:** An executive search firm operating on a contingency basis for restaurants, hotels, and country clubs. Company pays fee. **Specializes in the areas of:** Hotel/Restaurant; Retail. **Positions commonly filled include:** Restaurant/Food Service Manager. **Average salary range of placements:** $30,000 - $50,000. **Number of placements per year:** 100 - 199.

ROTH YOUNG PERSONNEL SERVICES OF DETROIT, INC.
31275 Northwestern Highway, Suite 116, Farmington Hills MI 48334. 248/626-6033. **Fax:** 248/626-7079. **Contact:** Sam Skeegan, President. **Description:** An executive search firm. Company pays fee. **Specializes in the areas of:** Advertising; Engineering; Food Industry; Health/Medical; Manufacturing; Pharmaceuticals; Retail; Sales. **Positions commonly filled include:** Biological Scientist; Biomedical Engineer; Chemical Engineer; Chemist; Hotel Manager; Industrial Designer; Industrial Engineer; Marketing Specialist; Nurse; Quality Control Supervisor; Sales Representative. **Corporate headquarters location:** New York NY. **Other U.S. locations:** Nationwide. **Average**

salary range of placements: More than $50,000. **Number of placements per year:** 100 - 199.

SALES CONSULTANTS OF AUBURN HILLS
2701 University Drive, Suite 205, Auburn Hills MI 48326. 248/373-7177. **Fax:** 248/373-7759. **Contact:** Boe Embrey, Owner/President. **Description:** An executive search firm. Company pays fee. **Specializes in the areas of:** Computer Science/Software; Engineering; Health/Medical; Industrial; Manufacturing; Sales. **Positions commonly filled include:** Biomedical Engineer; Branch Manager; Chemical Engineer; Civil Engineer; Electrical/Electronics Engineer; Manufacturer's/Wholesaler's Sales Rep.; Mechanical Engineer; Mining Engineer; Software Engineer. **Corporate headquarters location:** Cleveland OH. **Other U.S. locations:** Nationwide. **Number of placements per year:** 50 - 99.

SALES CONSULTANTS OF DETROIT
29777 Telegraph Road, Suite 2260, Southfield MI 48034. 248/352-9200. **Fax:** 248/352-9374. **Contact:** Thomas J. Hoy, Manager. **Description:** An executive search firm operating on a contingency basis that focuses on placing sales professionals. Company pays fee. **Specializes in the areas of:** Accounting/Auditing; Administration; Advertising; Architecture/ Construction; Banking; Chemical; Communications; Computer Hardware/Software; Design; Electrical; Engineering; Food Industry; Health/Medical; Insurance; Legal; Manufacturing; Operations Management; Personnel/Labor Relations; Procurement; Publishing; Retail; Technical; Textiles; Transportation.**Corporate headquarters location:** Cleveland OH. **Other U.S. locations:** Nationwide. **Average salary range of placements:** $30,000 - $50,000. **Number of placements per year:** 1 - 49.

SALES CONSULTANTS OF FARMINGTON HILLS
30445 Northwestern Highway, Suite 360, Farmington Hills MI 48334. 248/626-6600. **Fax:** 248/626-7542. **Contact:** Mark Gilbert, Manager. **E-mail address:** salcon@careers-usa.com. **World Wide Web address:** http://www.careers-usa.com. **Description:** An executive search firm. Company pays fee. **Specializes in the areas of:** Communications; Computer Hardware/Software; Design; Electrical; Engineering; General Management; Health/Medical; Manufacturing; Operations Management; Procurement; Retail; Sales; Technical; Telecommunications; Textiles. **Corporate headquarters location:** Cleveland OH. **Other U.S. locations:** Nationwide. **Average salary range of placements:** More than $50,000. **Number of placements per year:** 200 - 499.

SALES CONSULTANTS OF GENESEE, INC.
10801 South Saginaw Street, Suite G, Grand Blanc MI 48439-8126. 810/603-0452. **Toll-free phone:** 800/976-1972. **Fax:** 810/603-0751. **Contact:** Rebecca Leinen, President. **Description:** An executive search firm operating on a contingency basis. Company pays fee. **Specializes in the areas of:** Health/Medical; Pharmaceutical. **Positions commonly filled include:** Account Manager; Account Representative; Marketing Manager; Marketing Specialist; Sales Executive; Sales Manager; Sales Representative. **Corporate headquarters location:** Cleveland OH. **Other U.S. locations:** Nationwide. **Average salary range of placements:** More than $50,000. **Number of placements per year:** 1 - 49.

SALES CONSULTANTS OF LANSING
912 Centennial Way, Suite 340, Lansing MI 48917. 517/323-4404. **Fax:** 517/323-8083. **Contact:** Jeffrey A. Yeager, Manager. **Description:** An executive search firm focusing on sales and upper management placement in the chemicals, plastics, and automotive industries. Company pays fee. **Specializes in the areas of:** Automotive; Chemical; Electrical; Engineering; General Management; Plastics; Sales; Technical; Transportation. **Corporate headquarters location:** Cleveland OH. **Other U.S. locations:** Nationwide. **Average salary range of placements:** More than $50,000. **Number of placements per year:** 1 - 49.

SANFORD ROSE ASSOCIATES
25900 Greenfield Road, Suite 236, Oak Park MI 48237. 248/968-3210. **Fax:** 248/968-2908. **Contact:** Martin Rosenfeld, President. **World Wide Web address:** http://www.sanfordrose.com. **Description:** An executive search firm that operates on both retained and contingency bases. Company pays fee. **Specializes in the areas of:** Legal. **Positions commonly filled include:** Attorney; Finance Director; Intellectual Property Lawyer; Operations Manager. **Average salary range of placements:** More than $50,000. **Number of placements per year:** 1 - 49.

SANFORD ROSE ASSOCIATES
1000 West University Drive, Suite 203, Rochester MI 48307. 248/608-9005. **Fax:** 248/608-9010. **Contact:** Manager. **World Wide Web address:** http://www.sanfordrose.com. **Description:** An executive search firm. **Specializes in the areas of:** Engineering; General Management; Logistics.

SEARCH SOLUTIONS
P.O. Box 125, Three Oaks MI 49128. 616/756-6830. **Contact:** Manager. **Description:** An executive search firm. **Specializes in the areas of:** Consumer Package Goods.

SELECTIVE RECRUITING ASSOCIATES, INC.
P.O. Box 130287, Ann Arbor MI 48113-0287. 734/994-5632. **Fax:** 734/996-8181. **Contact:** David Calhoun, President. **E-mail address:** recruiter@selective.com. **World Wide Web address:** http://www.selective.com. **Description:** An executive search and technical recruiting firm serving the automotive industry. Company pays fee. **Specializes in the areas of:** Accounting/Auditing; Engineering; Industrial; Manufacturing; Technical. **Positions commonly filled include:** Chemical Engineer; Design Engineer; Designer; Electrical/Electronics Engineer; Industrial Engineer; Manufacturer's/Wholesaler's Sales Rep.; Operations/Production Manager; Purchasing Agent/Manager; Quality Control Supervisor; Software Engineer. **Other U.S. locations:** Nationwide. **Average salary range of placements:** More than $50,000. **Number of placements per year:** 50 - 99.

SHARROW & ASSOCIATES INC.
24735 Van Dyke Avenue, Center Line MI 48015. 810/759-6910. **Toll-free phone:** 800/344-5032. **Fax:** 810/759-6914. **Contact:** Douglas Sharrow, President. **E-mail address:** david@access.digex.net. **World Wide Web address:** http://www.access.digex.net/~david/saph.html. **Description:** An executive search firm. Company pays fee. **Specializes in the areas of:** Architecture/Construction; Computer Science/ Software; Engineering; Health/Medical; Insurance; Legal. **Positions commonly filled include:** Chemical Engineer; Chemist; Computer Programmer; Construction and Building Inspector; Construction Contractor; Electrical/Electronics Engineer; Industrial Engineer; Mechanical Engineer; Occupational Therapist; Patent Examiner; Physical Therapist; Property and Real Estate Manager; Systems Analyst. **Other U.S. locations:** Florence KY. **Average salary range of placements:** More than $50,000. **Number of placements per year:** 50 - 99.

SMITH PROFESSIONAL SEARCH
600 South Adams Street, Suite 210, Birmingham MI 48009. 248/540-8580. **Contact:** Office Manager.

Description: An executive search firm. **Specializes in the areas of:** Accounting/Auditing; Human Resources.

SOURCE TECHNOLOGY
3155 West Big Beaver Road, Suite 119, Troy MI 48084. 248/816-8484. **Fax:** 248/816-3111. **Contact:** Greg Stephens, President. **E-mail address:** janiss4535@aol.com. **Description:** A professional search firm. Company pays fee. **Specializes in the areas of:** Computer Science/Software; Engineering; General Management; Industrial; Technical. **Positions commonly filled include:** Chemical Engineer; Design Engineer; Designer; Electrical/Electronics Engineer; Industrial Engineer; Mechanical Engineer; Metallurgical Engineer; Structural Engineer. **Number of placements per year:** 100 - 199.

STERLING FIELD ASSOCIATES, INC.
697 Bridge Park Drive, Troy MI 48098. 248/879-7490. **Fax:** 248/879-2530. **Contact:** Steve Walmsley, President. **Description:** An executive search firm. The firm's clients include hospitals, physician groups, managed care companies, and consulting firms throughout the country. Company pays fee. **Specializes in the areas of:** Computer Science/Software; Finance; Health/Medical. **Positions commonly filled include:** Accountant/Auditor; Computer Programmer; Health Services Manager; Management Analyst/Consultant; Medical Records Technician; MIS Specialist; Physical Therapist; Physician; Registered Nurse; Software Engineer; Systems Analyst. **Other U.S. locations:** Nationwide. **Average salary range of placements:** More than $50,000. **Number of placements per year:** 1 - 49.

T.M.S. ASSOCIATES
3964 Old Creek, Birmingham MI 48084. 248/244-9406. **Contact:** Thomas Spada, President. **Description:** An executive search firm. Company pays fee. **Specializes in the areas of:** Legal. **Positions commonly filled include:** Attorney; Legal Secretary. **Number of placements per year:** 1 - 49.

THOMAS & ASSOCIATES OF MICHIGAN
16283 Red Arrow Highway, P.O. Box 366, Union Pier MI 49129. 616/469-5760. **Fax:** 616/469-5774. **Contact:** Thomas Zonka, President. **E-mail address:** tzonka@hc.cns.net. **Description:** An executive search firm that also provides contract and temp-to-perm placements. Company pays fee. **Specializes in the areas of:** Computer Science/Software; Engineering; General Management; Industrial; Manufacturing; Personnel/Labor Relations; Sales; Transportation. **Positions commonly filled include:** Buyer; Chemical Engineer; Computer Programmer; Designer; Electrical/Electronics Engineer; General Manager; Human Resources Manager; Industrial Engineer; Industrial Production Manager; Manufacturer's/Wholesaler's Sales Rep.; Mechanical Engineer; Metallurgical Engineer; Operations/Production Manager; Purchasing Agent/Manager; Quality Control Supervisor; Software Engineer; Structural Engineer; Systems Analyst; Transportation/Traffic Specialist. **Average salary range of placements:** More than $50,000. **Number of placements per year:** 200 - 499.

TOTAL RECRUITMENT SERVICES
3680 44th Street SE, Grand Rapids MI 49512. 616/554-3344. **Contact:** Rich Gotch, General Manager. **Description:** An executive search firm. Company pays fee. **Specializes in the areas of:** Sales. **Positions commonly filled include:** Computer Programmer; Systems Analyst. **Number of placements per year:** 1 - 49.

TROY TECH SERVICES
1000 Three Mile Road NW, Grand Rapids MI 49544. 616/784-9100. **Toll-free phone:** 800/345-5710. **Fax:** 616/784-9705. **Contact:** Rita Cribbs, Manager. **Description:** An executive search firm and employment agency. **Specializes in the areas of:** Engineering. **Positions commonly filled include:** Computer Programmer; Design Engineer; Designer; Draftsperson; MIS Specialist; Software Engineer; Systems Analyst; Technical Writer/Editor. **Other U.S. locations:** Nationwide. **Average salary range of placements:** $30,000 - $50,000. **Number of placements per year:** 1000+.

VENTURE MANAGEMENT & STAFFING
3163 Flushing Road, Suite 110, Flint MI 48504. 810/233-0776. **Fax:** 810/233-4469. **Contact:** Jeffrey Balentodic, General Manager. **Description:** An executive search firm that focuses on industrial, medical, and business positions. Company pays fee. **Specializes in the areas of:** Accounting/Auditing; Engineering; General Management; Health/Medical; Industrial; Manufacturing; Personnel/Labor Relations; Retail; Sales; Secretarial; Technical. **Positions commonly filled include:** Accountant/Auditor; Architect; Attorney; Automotive Mechanic; Bank Officer/Manager; Biomedical Engineer; Blue-Collar Worker Supervisor; Branch Manager; Chemical Engineer; Claim Representative; Clinical Lab Technician; Computer Programmer; EEG Technologist; EKG Technician; Electrical/Electronics Engineer; Electrician; Financial Analyst; General Manager; Health Services Manager; Human Resources Manager; Industrial Engineer; Industrial Production Manager; Landscape Architect; Management Trainee; Occupational Therapist; Operations/Production Manager; Purchasing Agent/Manager; Quality Control Supervisor; Registered Nurse; Surgical Technician; Systems Analyst; Telecommunications Manager; Typist/Word Processor. **Average salary range of placements:** $30,000 - $50,000. **Number of placements per year:** 200 - 499.

GENE WAGNER ASSOCIATES
30400 Telegraph Road, Suite 358, Bingham Farms MI 48025. **Contact:** Manager. **Description:** An executive search firm. **Specializes in the areas of:** Chemical.

WELIVER & ASSOCIATES
5340 Plymouth Road, Suite 108, Ann Arbor MI 48105. 734/913-0070. **Fax:** 734/913-0079. **Contact:** Billie Weliver, President. **E-mail address:** edweliver@worldnet.att.net. **Description:** An executive search firm. Company pays fee. **Specializes in the areas of:** Engineering; Human Resources; MIS/EDP. **Positions commonly filled include:** Engineer; Human Resources Manager; Human Resources Specialist; MIS Manager; MIS Specialist. **Average salary range of placements:** $30,000 - $50,000. **Number of placements per year:** 50 - 99.

DUANE WILSON ASSOCIATES
3133 Myddleton Drive, Troy MI 48084. 810/647-3234. **Contact:** Duane Wilson. **Description:** An executive search firm for small to mid-sized automotive supply companies. **Specializes in the areas of:** Automotive; Technical.

WING TIPS AND PUMPS, INC.
P.O. Box 99580, Troy MI 48099-9580. 248/641-0980. **Fax:** 248/641-0895. **Contact:** Mr. Verba Edwards, CEO. **Description:** A retainer and contingency search firm. Company pays fee. **Specializes in the areas of:** Accounting/Auditing; Banking; Computer Science/Software; Engineering; Finance; Health/Medical; Insurance; Legal; Manufacturing; Personnel/Labor Relations; Sales; Technical. **Positions commonly filled include:** Accountant/Auditor; Aerospace Engineer; Attorney; Automotive Mechanic; Buyer; Chemical Engineer; Computer Programmer; Cost Estimator; Design

Engineer; Designer; Electrical/Electronics Engineer; Electrician; Environmental Engineer; Health Services Manager; Industrial Engineer; Insurance Agent/Broker; Licensed Practical Nurse; Mechanical Engineer; MIS Specialist; Physician; Registered Nurse; Software Engineer; Systems Analyst; Underwriter/Assistant Underwriter. **Other U.S. locations:** Nationwide. **Average salary range of placements:** More than $50,000. **Number of placements per year:** 1 - 49.

JIM WOODSON AND ASSOCIATES
1080 River Oaks Drive, Suite B-102, Jackson MI 39208. 601/936-4037. **Fax:** 601/936-4041. **Contact:** Jim Woodson, President. **Description:** A contingency search firm that focuses on the placement of engineering and manufacturing professionals. Company pays fee. **Specializes in the areas of:** Accounting/Auditing; Engineering; Manufacturing. **Positions commonly filled include:** Accountant/ Auditor; Chemical Engineer; Chemist; Design Engineer; Electrical/Electronics Engineer; General Manager; Human Resources Manager; Industrial Engineer; Industrial Production Manager; Mechanical Engineer; Metallurgical Engineer; Purchasing Agent/Manager; Quality Control Supervisor; Software Engineer.

PERMANENT EMPLOYMENT AGENCIES

AE EMPLOYMENT SERVICES
2922 Fuller Avenue NE, Suite 205, Grand Rapids MI 49505. 616/831-5323. **Fax:** 616/831-5324. **Contact:** Deb Laakso, President. **Description:** An employment agency. **Specializes in the areas of:** Architecture/ Construction; Art/Design; Computer Science/ Software; Engineering. **Positions commonly filled include:** Architect; Chemical Engineer; Civil Engineer; Computer Programmer; Construction and Building Inspector; Design Engineer; Designer; Draftsperson; Electrical/Electronics Engineer; Environmental Engineer; Landscape Architect; Mechanical Engineer; MIS Specialist; Multimedia Designer; Software Engineer; Structural Engineer; Surveyor; Systems Analyst; Transportation/Traffic Specialist. **Benefits available to temporary workers:** Medical Insurance; Paid Holidays. **Average salary range of placements:** $30,000 - $50,000. **Number of placements per year:** 1 - 49.

ACCOUNT ABILITY NOW
P.O. Box 1149, Grand Rapids MI 49501. 616/235-1149. **Contact:** Manager. **Description:** A permanent employment agency. **Specializes in the areas of:** Accounting/Auditing; Information Systems.

ACCOUNTANTS ONE INC.
24901 Northwestern Highway, Suite 516, Southfield MI 48075-2598. 248/354-2410. **Contact:** Linda Hoffman, President. **Description:** A permanent employment agency. Company pays fee. **Specializes in the areas of:** Accounting/Auditing; Banking; Finance. **Positions commonly filled include:** Accountant/Auditor; Bookkeeper; Credit Manager; Data Entry Clerk; Financial Analyst. **Number of placements per year:** 1 - 49.

ACTION ASSOCIATES
P.O. Box 570, Brighton MI 48116. 810/227-4868. **Contact:** Manager. **Description:** A permanent employment agency and training center.

ACTION MANAGEMENT CORPORATION
915 South Grand Traverse Street, Flint MI 48502. 810/234-2828. **Fax:** 810/234-5159. **Contact:** Valerie June, Executive Search Coordinator. **E-mail address:** action1@tir.com. **World Wide Web address:** http://www.action-mgmt.com. **Description:** A permanent employment agency. Company pays fee. **Specializes in the areas of:** Computer Science/Software; Engineering; General Management; Personnel/Labor Relations; Sales; Technical. **Positions commonly filled include:** Account Representative; Advertising Account Executive; Blue-Collar Worker Supervisor; Branch Manager; Claim Representative; Clerical Supervisor; Computer Programmer; Counselor; Customer Service Representative; Draftsperson; Education Administrator; Electrical/Electronics Engineer; Financial Analyst; General Manager; Hotel Manager; Human Resources Manager; Human Resources Specialist; Human Service Worker; Industrial Engineer; Manufacturer's/Wholesaler's Sales Rep.; Manufacturing Engineer; Marketing Specialist; Mechanical Engineer; MIS Specialist; Production Manager; Public Relations Specialist; Quality Control Supervisor; Restaurant/Food Service Manager; Sales Engineer; Sales Executive; Services Sales Representative; Software Engineer; Systems Analyst; Telecommunications Manager; Typist/Word Processor. **Corporate headquarters location:** This Location. **Other area locations:** Detroit MI. **Other U.S. locations:** Arlington VA. **Average salary range of placements:** $30,000 - $70,000. **Number of placements per year:** 100 - 199.

ARKAY, INC.
23651 Goddard, Taylor MI 48180. 734/374-2929. **Fax:** 734/374-2453. **Contact:** Eric Esau, Business Manager. **Description:** A permanent employment agency. **Specializes in the areas of:** Nonprofit. **Positions commonly filled include:** Job Coach/Developer. **Number of placements per year:** 1 - 49.

ASSISTING PROFESSIONALS INC.
2000 North Woodward Avenue, Suite 250, Bloomfield Hills MI 48304. 248/647-9800. **Fax:** 248/647-2240. **Contact:** Nancy Black, Owner. **Description:** A permanent employment agency that provides both permanent and temporary placement. **Positions commonly filled include:** Accountant/Auditor; Actuary; Administrative Manager; Aerospace Engineer; Architect; Bank Officer/Manager; Biochemist; Branch Manager; Budget Analyst; Chemical Engineer; Civil Engineer; Claim Representative; Clerical Supervisor; Computer Programmer; Cost Estimator; Credit Manager; Customer Service Representative; Design Engineer; Designer; Editor; Electrical/Electronics Engineer; Environmental Engineer; Financial Analyst; General Manager; Geologist/Geophysicist; Human Resources Specialist; Industrial Engineer; Industrial Production Manager; Management Analyst/Consultant; Manufacturer's/Wholesaler's Sales Rep.; Market Research Analyst; Mechanical Engineer; MIS Specialist; Operations/Production Manager; Property and Real Estate Manager; Public Relations Specialist; Quality Control Supervisor; Systems Analyst; Technical Writer/Editor. **Average salary range of placements:** More than $50,000. **Number of placements per year:** 1 - 49.

BARMAN STAFFING SOLUTIONS
BARMAN PERSONNEL
2976 Ivanrest, Grandville MI 49418. 616/531-4122. **Contact:** Paul Barman, President. **Description:** A permanent employment agency. Company pays fee. **Specializes in the areas of:** Accounting/Auditing; Architecture/Construction; Computer Science/ Software; Design; Engineering; Food Industry; Health/Medical; Industrial; Manufacturing; MIS/EDP. **Positions commonly filled include:** Accountant/ Auditor; Aerospace Engineer; Agricultural Engineer;

Architect; Ceramics Engineer; Electrical/Electronics Engineer; Financial Analyst; General Manager; Human Resources Manager; Industrial Designer; Industrial Engineer; Interior Designer; Mechanical Engineer; Metallurgical Engineer; Purchasing Agent/Manager. **Number of placements per year:** 1 - 49.

BUSINESS TRENDS, INC.
5455 Corporate Drive, Suite 210, Troy MI 48098. 248/952-0070. **Fax:** 248/952-0089. **Contact:** Brad Carson, Vice President. **Description:** A permanent and temporary employment agency. **Specializes in the areas of:** Telecommunications.

CALVERT ASSOCIATES INC.
202 East Washington Street, Suite 304, Ann Arbor MI 48104-2017. 734/769-5413. **Contact:** Peter Calvert Cokinos, President. **Description:** A permanent employment agency focusing on sales, editorial, and management positions in college publishing. Company pays fee. **Specializes in the areas of:** Publishing; Sales. **Positions commonly filled include:** Editor; Manufacturer's/Wholesaler's Sales Rep.; Sales Manager; Technical Writer/Editor. **Average salary range of placements:** $30,000 - $50,000. **Number of placements per year:** 1 - 49.

CAREER QUEST, INC.
1760 Grand River Avenue, East Lansing MI 48823. 517/485-3330. **Fax:** 517/485-8821. **Contact:** Manager. **Description:** A permanent employment agency that also provides career/outplacement counseling. Company pays fee. **Specializes in the areas of:** Accounting/Auditing; Administration; Art/Design; Banking; Computer Science/Software; Economics; Finance; General Management; Insurance; Manufacturing; Sales; Secretarial. **Positions commonly filled include:** Accountant/Auditor; Administrative Manager; Bank Officer/Manager; Blue-Collar Worker Supervisor; Branch Manager; Brokerage Clerk; Budget Analyst; Buyer; Claim Representative; Clerical Supervisor; Clinical Lab Technician; Computer Programmer; Customer Service Representative; Design Engineer; Designer; Draftsperson; Electrical/Electronics Engineer; Electrician; Financial Analyst; General Manager; Health Services Manager; Human Resources Specialist; Insurance Agent/Broker; Management Analyst/Consultant; Management Trainee; MIS Specialist; Property and Real Estate Manager; Public Relations Specialist; Quality Control Supervisor; Real Estate Agent; Services Sales Representative; Software Engineer; Systems Analyst; Typist/Word Processor. **Benefits available to temporary workers:** Bonus Award/Plan; Paid Vacation. **Corporate headquarters location:** Lansing MI. **Average salary range of placements:** $20,000 - $29,999. **Number of placements per year:** 50 - 99.

CLARK & HARTMAN PROFESSIONAL SEARCH INC.
1829 West Stadium Boulevard, Suite 100, Ann Arbor MI 48103. 734/996-3100. **Contact:** Lewis Clark, President. **Description:** A permanent employment agency. **Specializes in the areas of:** Computer Hardware/Software. **Positions commonly filled include:** Computer Operator; Computer Programmer; Data Entry Clerk; Systems Analyst.

CONTRACT PROFESSIONALS, INC.
4141 West Walton Boulevard, Waterford MI 48329. 248/673-3800. **Toll-free phone:** 800/228-4803. **Fax:** 248/673-5992. **Contact:** Tina York, Technical Recruiter. **E-mail address:** cpi@cpijobs.com. **Description:** A permanent employment agency. Company pays fee. **Specializes in the areas of:** Data Processing; Engineering. **Positions commonly filled include:** Aerospace Engineer; Ceramics Engineer; Chemical Engineer; Civil Engineer; Computer Programmer; Design Engineer; Draftsperson; EDP Specialist; Electrical/Electronics Engineer; Financial Analyst; Industrial Designer; Industrial Engineer; Interior Designer; Mechanical Engineer; Metallurgical Engineer; Mining Engineer; Petroleum Engineer; Services Sales Representative; Software Engineer; Structural Engineer; Systems Analyst; Technical Writer/Editor; Technician; Telecommunications Manager. **Benefits available to temporary workers:** 401(k); Dental Insurance; Life Insurance; Medical Insurance. **Other area locations:** Dearborn MI. **Other U.S. locations:** Cleveland OH. **Average salary range of placements:** More than $50,000. **Number of placements per year:** 500 - 999.

CORPORATE STAFFING RESOURCES
815 Main Street, Joseph MI 49085. 616/983-5803. **Fax:** 616/983-5827. **Recorded jobline:** 219/233-8209. **Contact:** Linda McGlothlen, Branch Manager. **Description:** A permanent employment agency. Company pays fee. **Specializes in the areas of:** Accounting/Auditing; Administration; Computer Science/Software; Engineering; General Management; Manufacturing; Personnel/Labor Relations; Sales; Technical. **Positions commonly filled include:** Accountant/Auditor; Administrative Manager; Advertising Clerk; Aerospace Engineer; Agricultural Engineer; Aircraft Mechanic/Engine Specialist; Biochemist; Biological Scientist; Biomedical Engineer; Blue-Collar Worker Supervisor; Branch Manager; Chemical Engineer; Chemist; Civil Engineer; Clerical Supervisor; Computer Programmer; Cost Estimator; Credit Manager; Customer Service Representative; Design Engineer; Designer; Draftsperson; Electrical/Electronics Engineer; Environmental Engineer; Financial Analyst; General Manager; Health Services Manager; Human Resources Specialist; Industrial Engineer; Industrial Production Manager; Internet Services Manager; Management Analyst/Consultant; Market Research Analyst; MIS Specialist; Multimedia Designer; Operations/Production Manager; Science Technologist; Software Engineer; Statistician; Structural Engineer; Systems Analyst; Technical Writer/Editor; Telecommunications Manager; Typist/Word Processor. **Benefits available to temporary workers:** 401(k); Paid Holidays; Paid Vacation. **Corporate headquarters location:** South Bend IN. **Other U.S. locations:** Nationwide. **Number of placements per year:** 500 - 999.

DAVIS-SMITH MEDICAL EMPLOYMENT SERVICE INC.
27656 Franklin Road, Southfield MI 48034. 248/354-4100. **Contact:** Charles C. Corbert, CPC, President. **Description:** A permanent employment agency. Company pays fee. **Specializes in the areas of:** Clerical. **Positions commonly filled include:** Administrative Worker/Clerk; Bookkeeper; Medical Secretary; Nurse; Receptionist; Secretary; Technician; Typist/Word Processor. **Number of placements per year:** 50 - 99.

DAY PERSONNEL, INC.
dba DOROTHY DAY PERSONNEL OF MICHIGAN, INC.
3001 West Big Beaver Road, Suite 119, Troy MI 48084. 248/649-6797. **Fax:** 248/649-2496. **Contact:** Diane York, CPC, Office Manager. **World Wide Web address:** http://www.niteline.com/dayinc. **Description:** A permanent and temporary employment agency. Founded in 1953. Company pays fee. **Specializes in the areas of:** Retail; Sales; Secretarial; Technical; Transportation. **Positions commonly filled include:** Accountant/Auditor; Adjuster; Administrative Manager; Advertising Clerk; Branch Manager; Chemical Engineer; Civil Engineer; Clerical Supervisor; Computer Programmer; Cost Estimator; Counselor; Credit Manager; Customer Service Representative; Design Engineer; Systems Analyst. **Corporate headquarters location:** This Location. **Other area locations:** 17199 Laurel Park Drive North, Suite 40,

Livonia MI 48152. 313/591-6700. **Number of placements per year:** 50 - 99.

DAY PERSONNEL, INC.
dba DOROTHY DAY PERSONNEL OF MICHIGAN, INC.
17199 Laurel Park Drive North, Suite 40, Livonia MI 48152. 313/591-6700. **Contact:** Office Manager. **Description:** A permanent and Temporary employment agency. founded in 1953. Company pays fee. **Specializes in the areas of:** Accounting; Bookkeeping; Secretarial; Sales; Technical; Engineering; Management. **Corporate headquarters location:** Troy MI. **Other area locations:** Livonia MI.

DEVLAN, INC.
24543 Indoplex Circle, Farmington MI 48335-2529. 248/442-2960. **Fax:** 248/442-7356. **Contact:** Kathleen Schweiger, Human Resources Manager. **Description:** A permanent employment agency focusing on the pharmaceutical industry. Company pays fee. **Specializes in the areas of:** Engineering; Health/Medical; Pharmaceutical. **Positions commonly filled include:** Biochemist; Biomedical Engineer; Chemical Engineer; Chemist; Computer Programmer; Construction Contractor; Design Engineer; Electrical/ Electronics Engineer; Environmental Engineer; Mechanical Engineer; MIS Specialist; Pharmacist; Software Engineer; Systems Analyst. **Average salary range of placements:** $20,000 - $29,999. **Number of placements per year:** 1 - 49.

DIVERSIFIED RECRUITERS
27400 Meadowbrook Road, Novi MI 48377. 248/344-6700. **Contact:** Manager. **Description:** A permanent employment agency. **Specializes in the areas of:** Clerical; Engineering; Office Support; Technical.

ELECTRONIC SYSTEMS PERSONNEL
3 Parklane Boulevard, Suite 521 West, Dearborn MI 48126. 313/336-3400. **Contact:** Office Manager. **Description:** A permanent placement agency that also provides contract services. **Specializes in the areas of:** Data Processing.

ENGINEERING PROFESSIONALS INC.
38869 Plumbrook Drive, Farmington Hills MI 48331. 248/489-9598. **Contact:** Manager. **Description:** A permanent placement agency that also provides contract services. **Specializes in the areas of:** Engineering.

EXECUSEARCH OF SOUTHWEST MICHIGAN
4615 West Main Street, Kalamazoo MI 49006. 616/342-5050. **Fax:** 616/342-5084. **Contact:** John Compere, CEO, Co-owner. **Description:** A permanent employment agency. **Specializes in the areas of:** Engineering; Industrial; Manufacturing; Personnel/ Labor Relations. **Positions commonly filled include:** Civil Engineer; Electrical/Electronics Engineer; Human Resources Manager; Industrial Production Manager; Mechanical Engineer; Metallurgical Engineer; Purchasing Agent/Manager.

EXECUTECH RESOURCE CONSULTANTS
5700 Crooks Road, Suite 105, Troy MI 48098. 248/828-3000. **Fax:** 248/828-3333. **Contact:** Jeff Bagnasco, Office Manager. **Description:** A permanent employment agency. **Specializes in the areas of:** Automotive; Computer Programming; Office Support; Plastics; Sales. **Positions commonly filled include:** Administrative Worker/Clerk; Automotive Engineer; Computer Programmer; Manufacturing Engineer; Plastics Engineer.

JOE L. GILES AND ASSOCIATES, INC.
18105 Parkside Street, Suite 14, Detroit MI 48221. 313/864-0022. **Fax:** 313/864-8351. **Contact:** Joe L. Giles, Owner/President. **Description:** A permanent employment agency. Company pays fee. **Specializes in the areas of:** Computer Hardware/Software; Engineering; MIS/EDP. **Positions commonly filled include:** EDP Specialist; Electrical/Electronics Engineer; Mechanical Engineer; MIS Specialist; Systems Analyst. **Number of placements per year:** 50 - 99.

STEVEN J. GREENE & ASSOCIATES
29200 Vassar Street, Suite 545, Livonia MI 48152-2116. 248/473-7210. **Fax:** 248/473-4548. **Contact:** Steven Greene, Owner/Manager. **Description:** A permanent employment agency. Company pays fee. **Specializes in the areas of:** Industrial; Manufacturing; Office Support; Sales. **Positions commonly filled include:** Account Manager; Account Representative; Administrative Assistant; Management Trainee; Manufacturer's/Wholesaler's Sales Rep.; Quality Control Supervisor; Sales Engineer; Sales Manager; Sales Representative; Services Sales Representative. **Average salary range of placements:** $30,000 - $50,000. **Number of placements per year:** 100 - 199.

GROSSE POINTE EMPLOYMENT
18514 Mack Avenue, Grosse Pointe Farms MI 48236. 313/885-4576. **Contact:** Flo Wise, Owner. **Description:** A permanent employment agency. **Specializes in the areas of:** Clerical; Domestic Help; General Management; Health/Medical; Secretarial. **Positions commonly filled include:** Chauffeur; Chef/Cook/Kitchen Worker; Daycare Worker; Groundskeeper; Housekeeper; Licensed Practical Nurse; Nanny; Paralegal; Secretary; Typist/Word Processor. **Number of placements per year:** 50 - 99.

HEALTH CARE PROFESSIONALS
25899 West 12 Mile Road, Suite 380, Southfield MI 48034-8343. 248/357-7080. **Fax:** 248/357-4606. **Contact:** Don Dezenski, Vice President. **Description:** A staffing agency that provides permanent and temporary staffing to health care facilities and health insurance organizations throughout the metropolitan Detroit area. **Specializes in the areas of:** Health/Medical. **Positions commonly filled include:** Clinical Lab Technician; Data Entry Clerk; EEG Technologist; EKG Technician; Medical Assistant; Medical Records Technician; Nuclear Medicine Technologist; Radiological Technologist; Receptionist; Registered Nurse; Respiratory Therapist; Surgical Technician. **Number of placements per year:** 200 - 499.

WILLIAM HOWARD AGENCY
38701 Seven Mile Road, Suite 445, Livonia MI 48152. 734/464-6777. **Contact:** Christina Fortucci, Administrator. **Description:** A permanent employment agency that also offers career counseling services. **Specializes in the areas of:** Accounting/Auditing; Advertising; Architecture/Construction; Banking; Computer Hardware/Software; Construction; Design; Education; Engineering; Food Industry; Health/Medical; Insurance; Legal; Manufacturing; MIS/EDP; Nonprofit; Publishing; Real Estate; Sales; Secretarial; Technical; Transportation. **Positions commonly filled include:** Accountant/Auditor; Administrative Assistant; Advertising Account Executive; Agricultural Engineer; Architect; Attorney; Bank Officer/Manager; Biological Scientist; Biomedical Engineer; Bookkeeper; Ceramics Engineer; Civil Engineer; Claim Representative; Clerk; Commercial Artist; Computer Programmer; Credit Manager; Customer Service Representative; Data Entry Clerk; Draftsperson; Economist; EDP Specialist; Electrical/Electronics Engineer; Financial Analyst; General Manager; Hotel Manager; Human Resources Manager; Industrial Designer; Industrial Engineer; Insurance Agent/Broker; Interior Designer; Legal Secretary; Management Analyst/Consultant; Marketing Specialist; Mechanical Engineer; Medical

Secretary; Metallurgical Engineer; Mining Engineer; Nurse; Petroleum Engineer; Physicist; Public Relations Specialist; Purchasing Agent/Manager; Receptionist; Secretary; Statistician; Stenographer; Systems Analyst; Technical Writer/Editor; Technician; Typist/Word Processor; Underwriter/Assistant Underwriter. **Number of placements per year:** 100 - 199.

HUMAN RESOURCES EMPLOYMENT SERVICES
31 Oakland Avenue, Suite A, Pontiac MI 48342. 248/338-8880. **Fax:** 248/338-9434. **Contact:** Cherie Hunter, Accounts Coordinator. **Description:** A permanent employment agency. Company pays fee. **Specializes in the areas of:** General Management; Industrial; Manufacturing; Personnel/Labor Relations; Sales; Secretarial. **Positions commonly filled include:** Blue-Collar Worker Supervisor; Clerical Supervisor; Customer Service Representative; Draftsperson; Human Resources Specialist; Industrial Production Manager; Quality Control Supervisor; Services Sales Representative; Typist/Word Processor. **Average salary range of placements:** $20,000 - $29,999. **Number of placements per year:** 1000+.

JOB FAIR NETWORK OF MICHIGAN
10823 Melbourne, Allen Park MI 48101. 313/381-0093. **Fax:** 313/381-0099. **Contact:** Chuck Vincent, President. **World Wide Web address:** http://www.careercentermich.com. **Description:** A permanent employment agency that also organizes technical job fairs, as well as multi-industry job fairs. Company pays fee. **Specializes in the areas of:** Administration; Architecture/Construction; Computer Science/Software; Engineering; Industrial; Manufacturing; Personnel/Labor Relations; Technical; Transportation. **Positions commonly filled include:** Aerospace Engineer; Agricultural Engineer; Aircraft Mechanic/Engine Specialist; Architect; Biological Scientist; Biomedical Engineer; Broadcast Technician; Budget Analyst; Chemical Engineer; Chemist; Civil Engineer; Computer Programmer; Construction Contractor; Construction Manager; Cost Estimator; Design Engineer; Designer; Draftsperson; Electrical/Electronics Engineer; Electrician; Environmental Engineer; Financial Analyst; Food Scientist/T echnologist; Food Service Manager; Industrial Engineer; Industrial Production Manager; Internet Services Manager; Landscape Architect; Management Analyst/Consultant; Market Research Analyst; Mechanical Engineer; Metallurgical Engineer; Mining Engineer; MIS Specialist; Multimedia Designer; Nuclear Engineer; Quality Control Supervisor; Software Engineer; Stationary Engineer; Statistician; Structural Engineer; Systems Analyst; Technical Writer/Editor; Telecommunications Manager. **Average salary range of placements:** $30,000 - $50,000. **Number of placements per year:** 500 - 999.

JOB LINE
660 Cascade West Parkway SE, Grand Rapids MI 49546. 616/949-2424. **Fax:** 616/949-4112. **Contact:** Rudy Sterrett, President. **Description:** A permanent employment agency. **Positions commonly filled include:** Accountant/Auditor; Adjuster; Administrative Manager; Advertising Clerk; Agricultural Engineer; Aircraft Mechanic/Engine Specialist; Architect; Automotive Mechanic; Bank Officer/Manager; Biochemist; Biological Scientist; Blue-Collar Worker Supervisor; Branch Manager; Budget Analyst; Chemical Engineer; Computer Programmer; Draftsperson; Electrician; Financial Analyst; General Manager; Human Resources Specialist; Industrial Production Manager; Management Analyst/Consultant; Occupational Therapist; Public Relations Specialist; Quality Control Supervisor; Real Estate Agent; Restaurant/Food Service Manager; Social Worker; Software Engineer; Systems Analyst; Technical Writer/Editor; Underwriter/Assistant Underwriter. **Average salary range of placements:** $20,000 - $50,000. **Number of placements per year:** 500 - 999.

KEY PERSONNEL
570 East 16th Street, Holland MI 49424. 616/396-7575. **Fax:** 616/396-3327. **Contact:** Manager. **Description:** A permanent employment agency. Company pays fee. **Specializes in the areas of:** Accounting/Auditing; Administration; Art/Design; Computer Science/Software; Engineering; Industrial; Manufacturing; Personnel/Labor Relations. **Positions commonly filled include:** Accountant/Auditor; Administrative Manager; Designer; Draftsperson; Electrical/Electronics Engineer; Human Resources Manager; Industrial Engineer; Purchasing Agent/Manager; Quality Control Supervisor; Software Engineer. **Number of placements per year:** 500 - 999.

HENRY LABUS PERSONNEL INC.
P.O. Box 458, Eastpointe MI 48021-0458. 810/772-1150. **Fax:** 810/772-1446. **Contact:** Henry Labus, President. **Description:** A permanent employment agency. Company pays fee. **Specializes in the areas of:** Accounting/Auditing; Banking. **Positions commonly filled include:** Accountant/Auditor; Budget Analyst; Credit Manager; Financial Analyst. **Average salary range of placements:** More than $50,000. **Number of placements per year:** 1 - 49.

LUDOT PERSONNEL
6056 North Sheldon Road, Canton MI 48187. 248/353-9720. **Contact:** Michael Morton, Vice President. **Description:** A permanent employment agency. Company pays fee. **Specializes in the areas of:** Automotive; Computer Hardware/Software; Engineering; Manufacturing; MIS/EDP. **Positions commonly filled include:** Accountant/Auditor; Aerospace Engineer; Economist; Electrical/Electronics Engineer; Industrial Engineer; Mechanical Engineer; Metallurgical Engineer; MIS Specialist; Quality Control Supervisor; Systems Analyst. **Number of placements per year:** 50 - 99.

MASTERSON PERSONNEL OF MICHIGAN, INC.
2020 Hogback Road, Suite 9, Ann Arbor MI 48105. 734/677-2600. **Fax:** 734/677-4730. **Contact:** Harold Breitkreutz, Account Manager. **Description:** A permanent employment agency. Company pays fee. **Positions commonly filled include:** Administrative Assistant; Assembly Worker; Clerical Supervisor; Customer Service Representative; Maintenance Technician; Receptionist; Shipping and Receiving Clerk; Typist/Word Processor. **Benefits available to temporary workers:** 401(k); Medical Insurance. **Corporate headquarters location:** Minneapolis MN. **Other U.S. locations:** Edina MN; St. Paul MN. **Average salary range of placements:** Less than $20,000.

MICHIGAN EMPLOYMENT SECURITY AGENCY
401 East 13 Mile Road, Madison Heights MI 48071. 248/589-1600. **Contact:** Office Manager. **Description:** A permanent employment agency.

MICHIGAN EMPLOYMENT SECURITY AGENCY WESTERN MICHIGAN DIVISION
3391 Plainfield NE, Grand Rapids MI 49505. 616/361-3200. **Fax:** 616/361-3223. **Contact:** Office Manager. **Description:** A permanent employment agency.

MICHIGAN INDIAN EMPLOYMENT AND TRAINING SERVICES
325 East Lake Street, Petoskey MI 49770. 616/347-9330. **Fax:** 616/347-9339. **Contact:** Quintin Walker, Regional Manager. **Description:** A permanent employment and training services agency for Native Americans. Services include resume assistance, job

referrals, and support services. **Specializes in the areas of:** Education. **Positions commonly filled include:** Assembly Worker; Bookkeeper; Carpenter; Clerk; Construction Trade Worker; Light Industrial Worker; Receptionist; Reporter; Secretary; Typist/Word Processor. **Corporate headquarters location:** Lansing MI. **Other area locations:** Ann Arbor MI; Flint MI; Iron Mountain MI; Mount Pleasant MI; Portage MI. **Average salary range of placements:** Less than $20,000. **Number of placements per year:** 1 - 49.

MONROE COUNTY EMPLOYMENT & TRAINING
1531 North Telegraph Road, Monroe MI 48161. 734/243-7100. **Fax:** 734/243-7017. **Contact:** Jerry Spence, Training Coordinator. **Description:** A federally funded permanent employment agency that also provides job training programs for economically disadvantaged workers. The firm also participates in Michigan's welfare to work program. **Positions commonly filled include:** Advertising Clerk; Automotive Mechanic; Bank Officer/Manager; Blue-Collar Worker Supervisor; Branch Manager; Buyer; Claim Representative; Clerical Supervisor; Computer Programmer; Customer Service Representative; Dental Assistant/Dental Hygienist; EKG Technician; Electrician; Emergency Medical Technician; Human Service Worker; Industrial Production Manager; Licensed Practical Nurse; Management Trainee; Medical Records Technician; MIS Specialist; Operations/Production Manager; Paralegal; Physical Therapist; Preschool Worker; Respiratory Therapist; Restaurant/Food Service Manager; Services Sales Representative; Social Worker; Travel Agent. **Average salary range of placements:** Less than $20,000. **Number of placements per year:** 500 - 999.

NANNY ATTACHMENT SERVICE
P.O. Box 382, Whitehall MI 49461. 616/893-6908. **Toll-free phone:** 800/528-2498. **Contact:** Teresa Grey, Owner/President. **Description:** A permanent employment agency. A professional recruiter of nannies for family in-home child care. Company pays fee. **Specializes in the areas of:** Child Care, In-Home; Nannies. **Average salary range of placements:** Less than $20,000. **Number of placements per year:** 50 - 99.

THE NANNY NETWORK
47505 Van Dyke, Utica MI 48317. 810/739-2100. **Fax:** 810/739-4217. **Contact:** Linda Guastella, President. **Description:** A permanent employment agency focusing on nanny placement on a permanent or temporary basis. Company pays fee. **Specializes in the areas of:** Child Care, In-Home; Nannies. **Positions commonly filled include:** Nanny. **Average salary range of placements:** Less than $20,000. **Number of placements per year:** 200 - 499.

NATIONWIDE CAREER NETWORK
5445 Corporate Drive, Suite 160, Troy MI 48098-2683. 248/641-7779. **Fax:** 248/641-7778. **Contact:** Carol Peters, President. **Description:** A permanent and temporary employment agency. Company pays fee. **Specializes in the areas of:** Computer Science/Software; Engineering; Finance; Health/Medical; Sales; Secretarial; Technical. **Positions commonly filled include:** Applications Engineer; Biomedical Engineer; Certified Nursing Aide; Chemical Engineer; Chemist; Civil Engineer; Clerical Supervisor; Clinical Lab Technician; Computer Operator; Computer Programmer; Cost Estimator; Customer Service Representative; Database Manager; Design Engineer; EKG Technician; Industrial Engineer; Industrial Production Manager; Licensed Practical Nurse; Management Analyst/Consultant; MIS Specialist; Physical Therapist; Physician; Purchasing Agent/Manager; Registered Nurse; Sales Engineer; Sales Manager; Sales Representative; Secretary; Software Engineer; Surgical Technician; Systems Analyst; Systems Manager; Technical Writer/Editor; Typist/Word Processor. **Average salary range of placements:** $30,000 - $50,000. **Number of placements per year:** 500 - 999.

OAKLAND RESOURCES
27600 Northwest Highway, Suite 120, Southfield MI 48034. 248/799-3022. **Fax:** 248/799-3023. **Contact:** Gordon Nyquist, General Manager. **Description:** A permanent employment agency. Company pays fee. **Positions commonly filled include:** Computer Programmer; Management Analyst/Consultant; Systems Analyst. **Number of placements per year:** 1 - 49.

PERMANENT STAFF COMPANY
850 Stephenson Highway, Suite 303, Troy MI 48083-1160. 248/585-2720. **Contact:** Recruiter. **Description:** A permanent employment agency focusing on office support to middle management positions. The agency also provides temporary help. **Specializes in the areas of:** Secretarial. **Positions commonly filled include:** Administrative Assistant; Administrative Manager; Advertising Clerk; Customer Service Representative; Human Resources Specialist; Management Trainee; Paralegal; Receptionist; Secretary; Services Sales Representative. **Average salary range of placements:** $20,000 - $29,999. **Number of placements per year:** 100 - 199.

PREFERRED EMPLOYMENT PLANNING
1479 West Bristol Road, Flint MI 48507-5523. 810/233-7200. **Fax:** 810/233-3095. **Contact:** Dan LePard, Manager. **Description:** A permanent employment agency. **Specializes in the areas of:** Administration; Computer Science/Software; Engineering; Finance; Food Industry; General Management; Industrial; Manufacturing; Personnel/Labor Relations; Retail; Sales; Secretarial; Technical. **Positions commonly filled include:** Accountant/Auditor; Administrative Manager; Advertising Clerk; Blue-Collar Worker Supervisor; Branch Manager; Ceramics Engineer; Chemical Engineer; Clerical Supervisor; Computer Programmer; Counselor; Credit Manager; Customer Service Representative; Design Engineer; Electrical/Electronics Engineer; Environmental Engineer; Human Service Worker; Industrial Engineer; Industrial Production Manager; Materials Engineer; Mechanical Engineer; MIS Specialist; Operations/Production Manager; Pharmacist; Purchasing Agent/Manager; Quality Control Supervisor; Radio/TV Announcer/Broadcaster; Reporter; Restaurant/Food Service Manager; Securities Sales Representative; Services Sales Representative; Social Worker; Software Engineer; Speech-Language Pathologist; Systems Analyst; Technical Writer/Editor; Typist/Word Processor. **Average salary range of placements:** $20,000 - $100,000. **Number of placements per year:** 100 - 199.

RESOURCE TECHNOLOGIES CORPORATION
431 Stephenson Highway, Troy MI 48083. 248/585-4750. **Contact:** Manager. **Description:** A permanent employment agency that focuses on placement in computer industries. **Specializes in the areas of:** Computer Science/Software; Design; Engineering.

SALES EXECUTIVES INC.
755 West Big Beaver Road, Suite 2107, Troy MI 48084. 248/362-1900. **Fax:** 248/362-0253. **Contact:** Mr. Dale Statson, President. **Description:** A permanent employment agency. Company pays fee. **Specializes in the areas of:** Chemical; Computer Hardware/Software; Finance; General Management; Health/Medical; Plastics; Sales. **Positions commonly filled include:** Marketing Specialist; Sales Manager;

Sales Representative. **Number of placements per year:** 200 - 499.

SKILL TECH EMPLOYMENT
4500 North Grand River Avenue, Lansing MI 48906. 517/321-2332. **Fax:** 517/321-6526. **Contact:** Office Manager. **Description:** A permanent employment agency. **Specializes in the areas of:** Industrial; Manufacturing. **Positions commonly filled include:** Industrial Engineer.

SNELLING PERSONNEL SERVICES
18600 Florence Street, Roseville MI 48066. 810/772-6760. **Contact:** Ron Daiza, Manager. **Description:** A full-service employment agency that provides permanent and temporary placements. Company pays fee. **Specializes in the areas of:** Legal; Publishing; Secretarial. **Positions commonly filled include:** Administrative Worker/Clerk; Bookkeeper; Brokerage Clerk; Paralegal; Receptionist; Secretary; Typist/Word Processor. **Corporate headquarters location:** Dallas TX. **Other area locations:** Bingham Farm MI; Royal Oak MI. **Number of placements per year:** 100 - 199.

SNELLING PERSONNEL SERVICES
30100 Telegraph Road, Suite 474, Bingham Farms MI 48025. 248/644-4600. **Fax:** 248/644-4739. **Contact:** Jacqueline Dombroski, President. **Description:** A permanent employment agency. Company pays fee. **Specializes in the areas of:** Engineering; Health/Medical; Manufacturing; Secretarial. **Positions commonly filled include:** Administrative Assistant; Bookkeeper; Chemical Engineer; Chemist; Clerk; Data Entry Clerk; Electrical/Electronics Engineer; Manufacturing Engineer; Mechanical Engineer; Quality Control Supervisor; Receptionist; Secretary; Typist/Word Processor. **Benefits available to temporary workers:** 401(k). **Corporate headquarters location:** Dallas TX. **Other area locations:** Roseville MI; Royal Oak MI. **Average salary range of placements:** More than $50,000. **Number of placements per year:** 200 - 499.

SOURCE EDP
2000 Town Center, Suite 850, Southfield MI 48075. 248/352-6520. **Fax:** 248/352-7514. **Contact:** Brad Foster, Director. **Description:** A permanent employment agency. Company pays fee. **Specializes in the areas of:** Administration; Computer Science/Software. **Positions commonly filled include:** Computer Programmer; Software Engineer; Systems Analyst; Technical Writer/Editor. **Number of placements per year:** 100 - 199.

SOURCE SERVICES CORPORATION
161 Ottawa NW, Suite 409-D, Grand Rapids MI 49503. 616/459-3600. **Fax:** 616/459-3670. **Contact:** Director. **Description:** A permanent employment agency. Company pays fee. **Specializes in the areas of:** Accounting/Auditing; Computer Science/Software; Engineering; Finance; Manufacturing. **Positions commonly filled include:** Accountant/Auditor; Budget Analyst; Computer Programmer; Financial Analyst; MIS Specialist; Software Engineer; Systems Analyst. **Benefits available to temporary workers:** Medical Insurance. **Corporate headquarters location:** Dallas TX. **Other U.S. locations:** Nationwide. **Average salary range of placements:** $30,000 - $50,000. **Number of placements per year:** 200 - 499.

SOUTHEAST MICHIGAN CAREER SERVICE
29444 Northwestern Highway, Suite 500, Southfield MI 48034. 248/827-2502. **Fax:** 248/827-9936. **Contact:** Jodi Blain, President. **Description:** A permanent employment agency. Company pays fee. **Positions commonly filled include:** Accountant/Auditor; Advertising Clerk; Attorney; Bank Officer/Manager; Biochemist; Biological Scientist; Biomedical Engineer; Branch Manager; Broadcast Technician; Budget Analyst; Buyer; Chemical Engineer; Chemist; Civil Engineer; Counselor; Credit Manager; Customer Service Representative; Design Engineer; Economist; Editor; Electrical/Electronics Engineer; Environmental Engineer; Financial Analyst; General Manager; Health Services Manager; Hotel Manager; Human Resources Specialist; Industrial Engineer; Management Analyst/Consultant; Market Research Analyst; Mechanical Engineer; Operations/Production Manager; Public Relations Specialist; Quality Control Supervisor; Reporter; Restaurant/Food Service Manager; Services Sales Representative; Sociologist; Technical Writer/Editor; Telecommunications Manager. **Number of placements per year:** 100 - 199.

TEA INC.
161 Ottawa Avenue NW, Suite 309H, Grand Rapids MI 49503-2704. 616/451-9891. **Fax:** 616/451-8899. **Contact:** Larry Wesholski, President. **Description:** A permanent employment agency. Company pays fee. **Specializes in the areas of:** Accounting/Auditing; Banking; Manufacturing; Secretarial. **Positions commonly filled include:** Accountant/Auditor; Administrative Manager; Attorney; Bank Officer/Manager; Blue-Collar Worker Supervisor; Branch Manager; Clerical Supervisor; Computer Programmer; Credit Manager; Electrical/Electronics Engineer; Human Resources Manager; Industrial Engineer; Industrial Production Manager; MIS Specialist; Paralegal; Quality Control Supervisor; Systems Analyst; Typist/Word Processor; Underwriter/Assistant Underwriter. **Average salary range of placements:** $30,000 - $50,000. **Number of placements per year:** 1 - 49.

TECHNICAL PROFESSIONAL SERVICE INC.
1405 South Yankee Springs Road, Middleville MI 49333. 616/891-9261. **Toll-free phone:** 888/228-3600. **Fax:** 616/891-9263. **Contact:** Arnaldo R. Rodriguez, President. **E-mail address:** tps83@aol.com. **Description:** A permanent employment agency. Company pays fee. **Specializes in the areas of:** Architecture/Construction; Art/Design; Computer Science/Software; Engineering; General Management; Industrial; Manufacturing; MIS/EDP; Personnel/Labor Relations; Technical. **Positions commonly filled include:** Administrative Manager; Aerospace Engineer; Agricultural Engineer; Aircraft Mechanic/Engine Specialist; Architect; Blue-Collar Worker Supervisor; Branch Manager; Buyer; Chemical Engineer; Civil Engineer; Claim Representative; Clerical Supervisor; Clinical Lab Technician; Computer Programmer; Cost Estimator; Customer Service Representative; Design Engineer; Draftsperson; Electrical/Electronics Engineer; Environmental Engineer; Financial Analyst; General Manager; Geologist/Geophysicist; Human Resources Specialist; Industrial Production Manager; Management Analyst/Consultant; Market Research Analyst; Mechanical Engineer; Mining Engineer; Quality Control Supervisor; Software Engineer; Statistician; Systems Analyst; Technical Writer/Editor. **Benefits available to temporary workers:** Medical Insurance; Paid Holidays; Paid Vacation. **Number of placements per year:** 100 - 199.

HENRY WELKER & ASSOCIATES
P.O. Box 530846, Livonia MI 48153-0846. 734/953-4900. **Fax:** 734/953-5918. **Contact:** William Harvey, Account Manager. **E-mail address:** welker@aol.com. **Description:** A permanent employment agency. Company pays fee. **Specializes in the areas of:** Computer Science/Software; Engineering; General Management; Information Technology; Manufacturing; Sales. **Positions commonly filled include:** Chemical Engineer; Computer Programmer; Cost Estimator; Electrical/Electronics Engineer; General Manager; Industrial Engineer; Mechanical Engineer; Metallurgical

Engineer; Purchasing Agent/Manager; Quality Control Supervisor; Software Engineer; Systems Analyst. **Average salary range of placements:** More than $50,000. **Number of placements per year:** 1 - 49.

WISE PERSONNEL SERVICES, INC.
200 Admiral Avenue, Kalamazoo MI 49002-3503. 616/323-2300. **Toll-free phone:** 800/842-2136. **Fax:** 616/323-8588. **Contact:** Manager. **Description:** A permanent employment agency. Company pays fee. **Specializes in the areas of:** Accounting/Auditing; Administration; Computer Science/Software; Engineering; Sales; Technical. **Positions commonly filled include:** Accountant/Auditor; Administrative Manager; Architect; Chemical Engineer; Clerical Supervisor; Computer Programmer; Customer Service Representative; Design Engineer; Designer; Draftsperson; Electrical/Electronics Engineer; Electrician; Industrial Engineer; Industrial Production Manager; Internet Services Manager; Mechanical Engineer; Quality Control Supervisor; Services Sales Representative; Software Engineer; Surveyor; Systems Analyst. **Benefits available to temporary workers:** Dental Insurance; Medical Insurance; Paid Holidays; Paid Vacation. **Number of placements per year:** 50 - 99.

WOOD PERSONNEL SERVICES
WOOD TEMPORARY STAFFING
P.O. Box 196, St. Joseph MI 49085. 616/983-6767. **Fax:** 616/983-0901. **Contact:** Recruiter. **Description:** A permanent employment agency that focuses on engineering, information systems, and agriculture. The temporary division focuses on clerical, light industrial, and technical placements. Company pays fee. **Specializes in the areas of:** Accounting/Auditing; Computer Science/Software; Engineering; Industrial; Manufacturing; Personnel/Labor Relations. **Positions commonly filled include:** Advertising Clerk; Agricultural Engineer; Buyer; Computer Programmer; Credit Manager; Design Engineer; Draftsperson; Electrical/Electronics Engineer; Environmental Engineer; Financial Analyst; General Manager; Industrial Engineer; Mechanical Engineer; MIS Specialist; Quality Control Supervisor; Systems Analyst. **Average salary range of placements:** $30,000 - $50,000. **Number of placements per year:** 50 - 99.

YOUR PREFERENCE REFERRAL NETWORK
17336 Harper Avenue, Suite 24, Detroit MI 48224. 313/886-3227. **Fax:** 313/259-0975. **Contact:** Manager. **Description:** A permanent employment agency. **Specializes in the areas of:** Administration; Art/Design; Computer Science/Software; General Management; Secretarial; Technical. **Positions commonly filled include:** Computer Programmer; Electrical/Electronics Engineer; Electrician; General Manager; Graphic Artist; Management Trainee; Respiratory Therapist; Systems Analyst; Typist/Word Processor. **Number of placements per year:** 50 - 99.

TEMPORARY EMPLOYMENT AGENCIES

ACCOUNTEMPS
OFFICETEAM
201 West Big Beaver Road, Suite 310, Troy MI 48084. 248/524-9050. **Toll-free phone:** 800/803-8367. **Fax:** 248/524-3115. **Contact:** Manager. **Description:** A temporary service focusing on accounting, finance, and banking. OfficeTeam, also at this location, provides temporary and permanent placements for office and administrative professionals. Company pays fee. **Specializes in the areas of:** Accounting/Auditing; Administration; Banking; Finance; Secretarial. **Positions commonly filled include:** Accountant/Auditor; Administrative Manager; Advertising Clerk; Bank Officer/Manager; Budget Analyst; Claim Representative; Cost Estimator; Credit Manager; Financial Analyst; Services Sales Representative; Typist/Word Processor. **Benefits available to temporary workers:** Medical Insurance; Paid Holidays; Paid Vacation; Tuition Assistance. **Corporate headquarters location:** Menlo Park CA. **Other U.S. locations:** Nationwide. **Number of placements per year:** 1000+.

ALTERNATIVE STAFF, INC.
1000 John R. Road, Suite 102, Troy MI 48083. 248/589-3830. **Fax:** 248/589-3239. **Contact:** Sara Osman, President. **Description:** A temporary agency that focuses on office support, technical, and light technical placements. Company pays fee. **Specializes in the areas of:** Accounting/Auditing; Industrial; Insurance; Manufacturing; Personnel/Labor Relations; Secretarial. **Positions commonly filled include:** Customer Service Representative; Typist/Word Processor. **Benefits available to temporary workers:** Dental Insurance; Life Insurance; Medical Insurance; Paid Holidays; Paid Vacation; Vision Insurance. **Average salary range of placements:** Less than $20,000. **Number of placements per year:** 200 - 499.

BEACON SERVICES INC.
42 West 10th Street, Holland MI 49423. 616/639-1332. **Contact:** Manager. **Description:** A temporary and permanent employment agency. **Specializes in the areas of:** Clerical; Health/Medical; Industrial; Legal.

DENTAL MEDICAL SERVICES INC.
2025 East Beltline SE, Suite 502, Grand Rapids MI 49546. **Contact:** Recruiter. **Description:** A temporary agency focusing on the placement of medical and dental personnel. Company pays fee. **Specializes in the areas of:** Health/Medical; Personnel/Labor Relations. **Positions commonly filled include:** Dental Assistant/Dental Hygienist; EEG Technologist; EKG Technician; Emergency Medical Technician; Health Services Manager; Licensed Practical Nurse; Medical Records Technician; Pharmacist; Physical Therapist; Radiological Technologist; Registered Nurse. **Average salary range of placements:** $20,000 - $29,999. **Number of placements per year:** 200 - 499.

DESIGN & ENGINEERING SERVICE
14220 Camelot Drive, Sterling Heights MI 48312. 810/268-0481. **Contact:** Manager. **Description:** A temporary and temp-to-perm agency. **Specializes in the areas of:** Design; Engineering.

DYNAMIC PEOPLE
100 East Big Beaver Road, Suite 826, Troy MI 48083-1249. 248/680-9760. **Fax:** 248/680-1409. **Contact:** Mary Fayerweather, Owner. **Description:** A temporary agency that also offers contract services. **Specializes in the areas of:** Accounting/Auditing; Administration; Secretarial. **Positions commonly filled include:** Advertising Clerk; Claim Representative; Customer Service Representative; Human Resources Manager; Market Research Analyst; Systems Analyst; Typist/Word Processor. **Corporate headquarters location:** Atlanta GA. **Other U.S. locations:** Nationwide. **Number of placements per year:** 500 - 999.

ENTECH SERVICES INC.
363 West Big Beaver Road, Troy MI 48084. 248/528-8090. **Contact:** Manager. **Description:** A temporary

agency. **Specializes in the areas of:** Clerical; Health/Medical; Light Industrial; Technical.

EXPRESS PERSONNEL SERVICES
1740 West Big Beaver Road, Suite 220, Troy MI 48084. 248/643-8590. **Fax:** 248/643-4362. **Contact:** John Bower, Owner. **Description:** A temporary agency. Founded in 1983. Company pays fee. **Specializes in the areas of:** Accounting/Auditing; Banking; Engineering; Food Industry; Industrial; Insurance; Legal; Manufacturing; Personnel/Labor Relations; Publishing; Retail; Secretarial. **Positions commonly filled include:** Accountant/Auditor; Advertising Clerk; Blue-Collar Worker Supervisor; Clerical Supervisor; Customer Service Representative; Human Resources Manager; Management Trainee; Mechanical Engineer; Operations/Production Manager; Paralegal; Purchasing Agent/Manager; Quality Control Supervisor; Restaurant/Food Service Manager; Software Engineer; Technical Writer/Editor; Typist/Word Processor. **Benefits available to temporary workers:** Life Insurance; Medical Insurance; Paid Holidays; Paid Vacation; Scholarship Program. **Corporate headquarters location:** Oklahoma City OK. **Number of placements per year:** 200 - 499.

EXPRESS PERSONNEL SERVICES
38215 West 10 Mile Road, Farmington Hills MI 48335. 248/474-5000. **Fax:** 248/474-6833. **Contact:** Manager. **Description:** A temporary agency. Services include temporary assignments, full-time placements, contract staffing, human resource services, and facility staffing and management. Company pays fee. **Specializes in the areas of:** Accounting/Auditing; Banking; Food Industry; Industrial; Insurance; Legal; Manufacturing; Personnel/Labor Relations; Publishing; Retail; Secretarial. **Positions commonly filled include:** Accountant/Auditor; Blue-Collar Worker Supervisor; Clerical Supervisor; Customer Service Representative; Human Resources Specialist; Management Trainee; Mechanical Engineer; Operations/Production Manager; Paralegal; Purchasing Agent/Manager; Quality Control Supervisor; Restaurant/Food Service Manager; Software Engineer; Technical Writer/Editor; Typist/Word Processor. **Benefits available to temporary workers:** 401(k); Life Insurance; Medical Insurance. **Corporate headquarters location:** Oklahoma City OK. **Average salary range of placements:** $30,000 - $50,000.

EXPRESS PERSONNEL SERVICES
3061 Walton Boulevard, Auburn Hills MI 48326. 248/373-0080. **Fax:** 248/373-7192. **Contact:** John Bower, Owner/Operator. **Description:** A temporary agency. Services include temporary assignments, full-time placements, and contract staffing. Company pays fee. **Specializes in the areas of:** Accounting/Auditing; Advertising; Banking; Food Industry; Health/Medical; Industrial; Insurance; Manufacturing; Personnel/Labor Relations; Publishing; Retail; Secretarial. **Positions commonly filled include:** Accountant/Auditor; Blue-Collar Worker Supervisor; Clerical Supervisor; Customer Service Representative; Human Resources Specialist; Management Trainee; Market Research Analyst; Operations/Production Manager; Paralegal; Purchasing Agent/Manager; Quality Control Supervisor; Services Sales Representative; Surveyor; Technical Writer/Editor; Typist/Word Processor; Underwriter/Assistant Underwriter. **Benefits available to temporary workers:** Life Insurance; Medical Insurance; Paid Holidays; Paid Vacation; Scholarship Program. **Corporate headquarters location:** Oklahoma City OK.

EXPRESS PERSONNEL SERVICES
16250 East 13 Mile Road, Roseville MI 48066-1524. 810/779-5090. **Fax:** 810/779-5453. **Contact:** Annette Sherman, Manager. **Description:** A temporary agency. Company pays fee. **Specializes in the areas of:** Accounting/Auditing; Engineering; General Management; Industrial; Manufacturing; Personnel/Labor Relations; Sales; Secretarial. **Positions commonly filled include:** Accountant/Auditor; Adjuster; Administrative Manager; Advertising Clerk; Branch Manager; Buyer; Claim Representative; Clerical Supervisor; Computer Programmer; Customer Service Representative; Electrical/Electronics Engineer; Electrician; Industrial Engineer; Industrial Production Manager; Mechanical Engineer; Operations/Production Manager; Quality Control Supervisor; Services Sales Representative; Software Engineer; Systems Analyst. **Corporate headquarters location:** Oklahoma City OK. **Number of placements per year:** 50 - 99.

INTERIM PERSONNEL
31509 Plymouth Road, Livonia MI 48150. 313/261-3830. **Contact:** Area Manager. **Description:** A temporary agency. Company pays fee. **Specializes in the areas of:** Manufacturing; Secretarial. **Positions commonly filled include:** Bookkeeper; Clerical Supervisor; Computer Operator; Customer Service Representative; Data Entry Clerk; Electronics Technician; Factory Worker; Legal Secretary; Light Industrial Worker; Medical Secretary; Receptionist; Secretary; Stenographer; Technician; Typist/Word Processor. **Benefits available to temporary workers:** Paid Holidays; Paid Vacation. **Other U.S. locations:** Nationwide. **Average salary range of placements:** Less than $20,000. **Number of placements per year:** 500 - 999.

INTERIM PERSONNEL
131 Columbia Avenue East, Battle Creek MI 49015. 616/963-6768. **Fax:** 616/963-6860. **Contact:** Kelly Witt, Customer Service Assistant. **Description:** A temporary agency. **Specializes in the areas of:** Industrial; Manufacturing; Personnel/Labor Relations; Secretarial. **Positions commonly filled include:** Blue-Collar Worker Supervisor; Draftsperson; Human Resources Specialist; Typist/Word Processor. **Other U.S. locations:** Nationwide.

KELLY ASSISTED LIVING SERVICES
999 West Big Beaver Road, Troy MI 48084-4716. 248/353-0920. **Toll-free phone:** 800/541-9819. **Contact:** Manager. **Description:** A temporary employment agency. **Specializes in the areas of:** Health/Medical. **Corporate headquarters location:** This Location.

KELLY SCIENTIFIC RESOURCES
33533 West Twelve Mile Road, Suite 140, Farmington Hills MI 48331. 248/848-9360. **Fax:** 248/848-9315. **Contact:** Branch Manager. **World Wide Web address:** http://www.kellyscientific.com. **Description:** A temporary agency. **Specializes in the areas of:** Automotive; Biotechnology; Chemical; Environmental; Food Industry; Pharmaceutical.

KELLY SERVICES, INC.
3200 Greenfield Road, Suite 303, Dearborn MI 48120. 313/271-5300. **Fax:** 313/336-3112. **Contact:** Catina Kristofik, Branch Manager. **Description:** A temporary agency. Company pays fee. **Specializes in the areas of:** Personnel/Labor Relations; Sales; Secretarial. **Positions commonly filled include:** Administrative Manager; Human Resources Specialist. **Number of placements per year:** 1000+.

MANPOWER, INC.
3011 West Grand Boulevard, Suite 412, Detroit MI 48202. 313/871-1010. **Contact:** Manager. **Description:** A temporary agency. Company pays fee. **Specializes in the areas of:** Clerical; Light Industrial; Office Support; Technical; Telemarketing; Word Processing. **Positions commonly filled include:**

Accountant/Auditor; Accounting Clerk; Administrative Assistant; Assembler; Biological Scientist; Bookkeeper; Chemist; Computer Operator; Customer Service Representative; Design Engineer; Desktop Publishing Specialist; Electrician; Machine Operator; Material Control Specialist; Order Clerk; Packaging/Processing Worker; Painter; Project Engineer; Proofreader; Receptionist; Records Manager; Research Assistant; Secretary; Software Engineer; Stenographer; Systems Analyst; Technical Writer/Editor; Technician; Transcriptionist; Typist/Word Processor; Welder. **Benefits available to temporary workers:** 401(k); Life Insurance; Medical Insurance; Paid Holidays; Paid Vacation. **Corporate headquarters location:** Milwaukee WI. **Other U.S. locations:** Nationwide. **Average salary range of placements:** Less than $20,000. **Number of placements per year:** 1000+.

MANPOWER, INC.
2341 Stone Bridge Drive, Flint MI 48532. 810/733-1520. **Fax:** 810/733-0240. **Contact:** Meichelle Hoyt, District Manager. **Description:** A temporary employment agency. Company pays fee. **Specializes in the areas of:** Personnel/Labor Relations. **Positions commonly filled include:** Accountant/Auditor; Blue-Collar Worker Supervisor; Clerical Supervisor; Medical Records Technician; Paralegal; Typist/Word Processor. **Benefits available to temporary workers:** Dental Insurance; Life Insurance; Medical Insurance. **Corporate headquarters location:** Milwaukee WI. **Other U.S. locations:** Nationwide. **Average salary range of placements:** Less than $20,000. **Number of placements per year:** 1000+.

NUSTAR TEMPORARY SERVICES
P.O. Box 342, Iron Mountain MI 49801. 906/779-1512. **Fax:** 906/779-2910. **Contact:** Jim Sliek, President. **Description:** A temporary agency that also provides permanent home health care placement. **Specializes in the areas of:** Health/Medical; Manufacturing; Secretarial; Transportation. **Positions commonly filled include:** Blue-Collar Worker Supervisor; Buyer; Cost Estimator; Customer Service Representative; Dental Assistant/Dental Hygienist; Draftsperson; Electrician; Health Services Manager; Licensed Practical Nurse; Management Trainee; MIS Specialist; Recreational Therapist; Registered Nurse; Technical Writer/Editor; Typist/Word Processor. **Benefits available to temporary workers:** Life Insurance; Medical Insurance. **Other area locations:** Houghton MI; Jackson MI. **Average salary range of placements:** $20,000 - $29,999. **Number of placements per year:** 100 - 199.

OLSTEN PROFESSIONAL ACCOUNTING SERVICES
2935 Buchanan SW, Grand Rapids MI 49548. 616/247-0004. **Fax:** 616/452-7207. **Contact:** Placement Specialist. **Description:** A temporary and permanent employment agency. Company pays fee. **Specializes in the areas of:** Accounting/Auditing; Banking; Finance; Health/Medical; Manufacturing. **Positions commonly filled include:** Accountant/Auditor; Bank Officer/Manager; Brokerage Clerk; Budget Analyst; Buyer; Cost Estimator; Credit Manager; Financial Analyst; Securities Sales Representative. **Corporate headquarters location:** Melville NY. **Number of placements per year:** 500 - 999.

PERSONNEL AT LAW, INC.
3000 Town Center, Suite 2030, Southfield MI 48075. 248/358-0060. **Toll-free phone:** 888/THE-TEMP. **Fax:** 248/358-0235. **Contact:** Judy Wells, President. **E-mail address:** smartpal@tir.com. **Description:** A temporary and permanent employment agency providing placement of experienced legal professionals. The company created two new divisions in 1997, Secretaries EtCetera and Net Staffing. Company pays fee. **Specializes in the areas of:** Information Technology; Legal; Secretarial. **Positions commonly filled include:** Attorney; Clerical Supervisor; Paralegal; Typist/Word Processor. **Benefits available to temporary workers:** Bonus Award/Plan; Medical Insurance; Paid Vacation. **Corporate headquarters location:** This Location. **Other U.S. locations:** Atlanta GA. **Average salary range of placements:** $20,000 - $29,999. **Number of placements per year:** 1000+.

THE SUMMIT GROUP OF MICHIGAN, INC.
19218 Livernois, Detroit MI 48221. 313/863-6100. **Fax:** 313/861-2050. **Contact:** Samuel C. Rucker, General Manager. **Description:** A temporary employment agency. **Specializes in the areas of:** Accounting/Auditing; Computer Science/Software; Telecommunications. **Positions commonly filled include:** Accountant/Auditor; Administrative Manager; Attorney; Clerical Supervisor; General Manager; Property and Real Estate Manager; Real Estate Agent; Registered Nurse; Telecommunications Manager; Travel Agent; Typist/Word Processor. **Average salary range of placements:** $30,000 - $50,000. **Number of placements per year:** 50 - 99.

SYGNETICS INC.
570 Kirts Boulevard, Suite 237, Troy MI 48084. 248/244-9595. **Fax:** 248/244-9726. **Contact:** President. **E-mail address:** eagle@mich.com. **Description:** A temporary and permanent staffing firm. Company pays fee. **Specializes in the areas of:** Computer Science/Software; Engineering; Manufacturing; Secretarial. **Positions commonly filled include:** Buyer; Computer Programmer; Customer Service Representative; Design Engineer; Designer; Electrical/Electronics Engineer; MIS Specialist; Software Engineer; Systems Analyst; Typist/Word Processor. **Benefits available to temporary workers:** Medical Insurance; Paid Holidays; Paid Vacation. **Average salary range of placements:** $30,000 - $50,000. **Number of placements per year:** 200 - 499.

TRC STAFFING SERVICES
2110 15 Mile Road, Sterling Heights MI 48310-4806. 810/939-3210. **Fax:** 810/978-0572. **Contact:** Delores Patouhas, Vice President. **Description:** A temporary agency. Founded in 1980. Company pays fee. **Specializes in the areas of:** Sales; Secretarial. **Positions commonly filled include:** Customer Service Representative; Human Resources Specialist; Services Sales Representative; Typist/Word Processor. **Corporate headquarters location:** Atlanta GA. **Other U.S. locations:** Nationwide. **Benefits available to temporary workers:** Paid Holidays; Paid Vacation; Referral Bonus Plan. **Number of placements per year:** 1000+.

TEMPORARY TECHNICAL SERVICES, INC.
2921 Wildwood Avenue, Jackson MI 49202. 517/784-7006. **Fax:** 517/784-5082. **Contact:** Nicole Daniels, Recruiter. **Description:** A temporary agency that also provides contract services. Founded in 1994. **Specializes in the areas of:** Engineering; Industrial; Manufacturing; Personnel/Labor Relations; Technical. **Positions commonly filled include:** Architect; Chemical Engineer; Chemist; Civil Engineer; Computer Programmer; Construction Contractor; Cost Estimator; Design Engineer; Designer; Draftsperson; Electrical/Electronics Engineer; Environmental Engineer; Food Scientist/Technologist; General Manager; Industrial Engineer; Industrial Production Manager; Mechanical Engineer; Metallurgical Engineer; Mining Engineer; Operations/Production Manager; Petroleum Engineer; Quality Control Supervisor; Science Technologist; Structural Engineer; Systems Analyst; Technical Writer/Editor. **Benefits available to temporary workers:** 401(k); Medical Insurance; Paid Holidays; Paid

Vacation. **Other area locations:** Southfield MI. **Average salary range of placements:** $30,000 - $50,000. **Number of placements per year:** 50 - 99.

TOTAL EMPLOYEE MANAGEMENT
28800 Van Dyke Avenue, Warren MI 48093-2748. 810/573-6327. **Contact:** Jamie Smith, Office Manager. **Description:** A temporary agency that also provides permanent placement and career counseling. **Specializes in the areas of:** Insurance; Personnel/Labor Relations; Secretarial. **Positions commonly filled include:** Accountant/Auditor; Administrative Manager; Clerical Supervisor; Computer Programmer; Financial Analyst; Insurance Agent/Broker; Public Relations Specialist; Service Manager; Systems Analyst. **Benefits available to temporary workers:** Life Insurance; Medical Insurance. **Average salary range of placements:** $30,000 - $50,000. **Number of placements per year:** 200 - 499.

TRILLIUM STAFFING
2222 South Linden Road, Flint MI 48532-5413. 810/733-7180. **Fax:** 810/733-2560. **Contact:** Anne Magalski, Area Manager. **Description:** A temporary agency. Company pays fee. **Specializes in the areas of:** Accounting/Auditing; Administration; Banking; Computer Science/Software; Engineering; General Management; Industrial; Manufacturing; Personnel/Labor Relations; Sales; Secretarial; Technical. **Positions commonly filled include:** Accountant/Auditor; Administrative Manager; Blue-Collar Worker Supervisor; Bookkeeper; Branch Manager; Clerical Supervisor; Computer Operator; Customer Service Representative; Data Entry Clerk; Design Engineer; Draftsperson; Factory Worker; General Manager; Human Resources Specialist; Industrial Engineer; Industrial Production Manager; Light Industrial Worker; Medical Secretary; MIS Specialist; Operations/Production Manager; Purchasing Agent/Manager; Quality Control Supervisor; Receptionist; Secretary; Services Sales Representative; Stenographer; Systems Analyst; Technician; Typist/Word Processor. **Benefits available to temporary workers:** 401(k); Medical Insurance; Paid Holidays; Paid Vacation. **Corporate headquarters location:** Kalamazoo MI. **Other area locations:** East Tawas MI; Saginaw MI. **Other U.S. locations:** IN; WI. **Average salary range of placements:** $20,000 - $29,999. **Number of placements per year:** 500 - 999.

TRILLIUM STAFFING
4800 Fashion Square Boulevard, Suite 120, Saginaw MI 48604. 517/799-5960. **Fax:** 517/799-8570. **Contact:** Yvette M. Serrato, Area Manager. **Description:** A temporary agency. Company pays fee. **Specializes in the areas of:** Accounting/Auditing; Architecture/Construction; Computer Science/Software; Engineering; General Management; Sales; Secretarial. **Positions commonly filled include:** Bank Officer/Manager; Bookkeeper; Branch Manager; Clerk; Computer Operator; Customer Service Representative; Data Entry Clerk; Draftsperson; Electronics Technician; Factory Worker; Human Resources Manager; Industrial Engineer; Legal Secretary; Light Industrial Worker; Mechanical Engineer; Medical Secretary; MIS Specialist; Purchasing Agent/Manager; Receptionist; Secretary; Services Sales Representative; Stenographer; Technician; Typist/Word Processor. **Corporate headquarters location:** Kalamazoo MI. **Other area locations:** East Tawas MI; Flint MI. **Other U.S. locations:** IN; WI. **Number of placements per year:** 1000+.

TRILLIUM STAFFING
836 East Bay Street, East Tawas MI 48730-0504. 517/362-3452. **Fax:** 517/362-6444. **Contact:** Bob Lee, Branch Manager. **E-mail address:** llee@voyager.net. **Description:** A temporary agency. Founded in 1984. **Specializes in the areas of:** Accounting/Auditing; Administration; Banking; Computer Science/Software; Engineering; Finance; Food Industry; General Management; Industrial; Legal; Manufacturing; Personnel/Labor Relations; Publishing; Retail; Sales; Secretarial; Technical. **Positions commonly filled include:** Accountant/Auditor; Adjuster; Administrative Manager; Automotive Mechanic; Bank Officer/Manager; Blue-Collar Worker Supervisor; Branch Manager; Brokerage Clerk; Budget Analyst; Buyer; Chemical Engineer; Chemist; Claim Representative; Computer Programmer; Construction Contractor; Credit Manager; Customer Service Manager; Designer; Draftsperson; Electrical/Electronics Engineer; Electrician; Financial Analyst; Industrial Engineer; Industrial Production Manager; Market Research Analyst; Mechanical Engineer; Medical Records Technician; MIS Specialist; Operations/Production Manager; Paralegal; Property and Real Estate Manager; Public Relations Specialist; Purchasing Agent/Manager; Quality Control Supervisor; Restaurant/Food Service Manager; Services Sales Representative; Software Engineer; Statistician; Structural Engineer; Systems Analyst; Technical Writer/Editor; Transportation/ Traffic Specialist; Travel Agent; Typist/Word Processor. **Benefits available to temporary workers:** 401(k); Paid Holidays; Paid Vacation. **Corporate headquarters location:** Kalamazoo MI. **Other area locations:** Flint MI; Saginaw MI. **Other U.S. locations:** IN; WI. **Number of placements per year:** 200 - 499.

WORKFORCE, INC.
334 South Broadway, Lake Orion MI 48362. 248/693-3232. **Toll-free phone:** 800/974-1107. **Fax:** 248/693-3234. **Contact:** Pamela Boyd, President. **Description:** A temporary agency that provides human resource recruiting and placement as well as consulting services. Company pays fee. **Specializes in the areas of:** Accounting/Auditing; Computer Science/Software; Engineering; General Management; Industrial; Insurance; Manufacturing; Nonprofit; Publishing; Sales; Secretarial. **Positions commonly filled include:** Accountant/Auditor; Adjuster; Administrative Manager; Buyer; Claim Representative; Clerical Supervisor; Customer Service Representative; Draftsperson; Manufacturer's/Wholesaler's Sales Rep.; Purchasing Agent/Manager; Services Sales Representative; Software Engineer; Systems Analyst; Travel Agent; Typist/Word Processor. **Benefits available to temporary workers:** Medical Insurance; Paid Vacation. **Other area locations:** Chesterfield MI. **Number of placements per year:** 500 - 999.

CONTRACT SERVICES FIRMS

ACRO SERVICE CORPORATION
17187 North Laurel Park Drive, Suite 165, Livonia MI 48152-2600. 734/591-1100. **Toll-free phone:** 800/886-7800. **Fax:** 734/591-1217. **Contact:** Dave Gaspard, Recruiting Manager. **E-mail address:** acro@oeonline. **World Wide Web address:** http://www.oeonline.com/~acro/acro.html. **Description:** A contract services firm. Company pays fee. **Specializes in the areas of:** Computer Science/Software; Engineering. **Positions commonly filled include:** Aerospace Engineer; Chemical Engineer; Chemist; Civil Engineer; Computer Programmer; Cost Estimator; Design Engineer; Designer; Electrical/Electronics Engineer; Industrial Engineer; Internet Services Manager; Mechanical Engineer; MIS Specialist; Software Engineer; Structural Engineer; Systems

Analyst; Technical Writer/Editor. **Average salary range of placements:** $20,000 - $29,999. **Number of placements per year:** 500 - 999.

ADVANCED RESOURCES OF MICHIGAN, INC.
32300 Northwestern Highway, Suite 225, Farmington Hills MI 48334. 248/539-2280. **Fax:** 248/539-2288. **Contact:** Recruiter. **Description:** A contract services firm. Founded in 1985. Company pays fee. **Specializes in the areas of:** Administration; Computer Science/Software; Telecommunications. **Positions commonly filled include:** Computer Programmer; Internet Services Manager; MIS Specialist; Software Engineer; Systems Analyst; Technical Writer/Editor; Telecommunications Manager. **Benefits available to temporary workers:** Life Insurance; Paid Vacation; Tuition Assistance. **Other U.S. locations:** Chicago IL. **Average salary range of placements:** $30,000 - $50,000. **Number of placements per year:** 100 - 199.

ALLIED TECHNICAL SERVICE
2968 Venture Drive, Midland MI 48640. 517/832-9063. **Fax:** 517/832-9069. **Contact:** Garrett L. Chaney, Director of Marketing. **E-mail address:** chaneygl@tm.net. **World Wide Web address:** http://www.alliedtechservice.com. **Description:** A contract services firm placing people in contract or direct hire positions. Company pays fee. **Specializes in the areas of:** Architecture/Construction; Art/Design; Engineering; General Management; Industrial; Sales; Technical. **Positions commonly filled include:** Account Manager; Account Representative; Administrative Assistant; Applications Engineer; Architect; Assistant Manager; Biochemist; Branch Manager; Buyer; Chemical Engineer; Computer Operator; Computer Programmer; Design Engineer; Electrical/Electronics Engineer; Electrician; Environmental Engineer; Graphic Artist; Graphic Designer; Industrial Production Manager; Manufacturing Engineer; Marketing Manager; Mechanical Engineer; Metallurgical Engineer; Operations Manager; Production Manager; Purchasing Agent/Manager; Sales Engineer; Sales Executive; Sales Representative; Secretary; Software Engineer; Structural Engineer; Systems Analyst; Systems Manager. **Corporate headquarters location:** This Location. **Average salary range of placements:** $30,000 - $50,000. **Number of placements per year:** 50 - 99.

ARGUS & ASSOCIATES
28064 Center Oak Court, Suite B, Wixom MI 48393. 248/344-8700. **Contact:** Manager. **Description:** A contract services firm. **Specializes in the areas of:** Engineering.

CDI CORPORATION
2627 East Beltline SE, Grand Rapids MI 49546. 616/942-0604. **Contact:** Manager. **World Wide Web address:** http://www.cdicorp.com. **Description:** A contract services firm. **Specializes in the areas of:** Engineering; Technical. **Corporate headquarters location:** Philadelphia PA. **Other U.S. locations:** Nationwide. **International locations:** Worldwide.

CAREER ASSOCIATES INC.
25160 Lahser Road, Suite 201, Southfield MI 48034. 810/208-0098. **Toll-free phone:** 800/670-8864. **Contact:** William Mauer, Manager of Technical Services. **Description:** A contract services firm that also provides temporary placements. Company pays fee. **Specializes in the areas of:** Computer Science/Software; Engineering; Industrial; Manufacturing; Technical. **Positions commonly filled include:** Automotive Mechanic; Buyer; Ceramics Engineer; Chemist; Computer Programmer; Design Engineer; Designer; Draftsperson; Electrical/Electronics Engineer; Electrician; Environmental Engineer; Industrial Engineer; Industrial Production Manager; Materials Engineer; Mechanical Engineer; Metallurgical Engineer; Purchasing Agent/Manager; Quality Control Supervisor; Software Engineer; Systems Analyst; Technical Writer/Editor. **Benefits available to temporary workers:** Paid Holidays; Paid Vacation; Retirement Plan. **Number of placements per year:** 50 - 99.

CIBER, INC.
4 Parklane Boulevard, Suite 323, Dearborn MI 48126-2660. 313/271-1221. **Toll-free phone:** 800/800-0271. **Fax:** 313/271-3416. **Contact:** Henry Welker, Human Resources. **World Wide Web address:** http://www.ciber.com. **Description:** A contract services firm. **Specializes in the areas of:** Administration; Computer Science/Software; Technical. **Positions commonly filled include:** Computer Programmer; MIS Specialist; Software Engineer; Systems Analyst; Telecommunications Manager. **Corporate headquarters location:** Denver CO. **Other U.S. locations:** Nationwide. **Average salary range of placements:** $30,000 - $50,000. **Number of placements per year:** 100 - 199.

DYNAMIC PERSONNEL
2565 Van Omen Drive, Holland MI 49424-8208. 616/399-5220. **Contact:** Manager. **Description:** A contract services firm. Company pays fee. **Specializes in the areas of:** Accounting/Auditing; Art/Design; Computer Science/Software; Engineering; Industrial; Manufacturing; Personnel/Labor Relations. **Positions commonly filled include:** Accountant/Auditor; Bank Officer/Manager; Budget Analyst; Buyer; Ceramics Engineer; Civil Engineer; Computer Programmer; Design Engineer; Electrical/Electronics Engineer; Human Resources Specialist; Industrial Engineer; Materials Engineer; Metallurgical Engineer; Quality Control Supervisor; Systems Analyst; Technical Writer/Editor. **Number of placements per year:** 200 - 499.

INTERTEC DESIGN INC.
713 Ashman Street, Suite 4, Midland MI 48640-4906. 517/832-3300. **Contact:** Shawn Loachridge, Personnel/Marketing Manager. **Description:** A contract services firm. **Specializes in the areas of:** Biology; Engineering. **Positions commonly filled include:** Buyer; Ceramics Engineer; Chemist; Civil Engineer; Construction and Building Inspector; Construction Contractor; Cost Estimator; Design Engineer; Designer; Draftsperson; Electrical/Electronics Engineer; Environmental Engineer; Industrial Engineer; Materials Engineer; Mechanical Engineer; Metallurgical Engineer. **Number of placements per year:** 50 - 99.

KELLY TECHNICAL SERVICES
4400 South Saginaw Street, Suite 1335, Flint MI 48507. 810/232-2585. **Fax:** 810/232-2521. **Contact:** Cindi Gay, Technical Recruiter. **Description:** A contract services firm. **Specializes in the areas of:** Accounting/Auditing; Administration; Art/Design; Biology; Computer Science/Software; Engineering; Industrial; Manufacturing; Personnel/Labor Relations; Publishing; Technical. **Positions commonly filled include:** Accountant/Auditor; Administrative Manager; Biochemist; Biological Scientist; Biomedical Engineer; Blue-Collar Worker Supervisor; Branch Manager; Budget Analyst; Chemical Engineer; Civil Engineer; Computer Programmer; Electrical/Electronics Engineer; Environmental Engineer; Financial Analyst; General Manager; Industrial Engineer; Internet Services Manager; Mechanical Engineer; MIS Specialist; Multimedia Designer; Operations/Production Manager; Quality Control Supervisor; Software Engineer; Systems Analyst; Technical Writer/Editor; Telecommunications Manager. **Benefits available to temporary workers:** Dental Insurance; Life Insurance; Medical Insurance; Paid Holidays; Paid Vacation.

Corporate headquarters location: Troy MI. **Number of placements per year:** 100 - 199.

MANPOWER TECHNICAL SERVICES
25300 Telegraph Road, Southfield MI 48034-7402. 248/351-0416. **Fax:** 248/351-3296. **Contact:** Pam Marx, Manager. **Description:** A contract services firm focusing on technical placements.Company pays fee. **Specializes in the areas of:** Accounting/Auditing; Administration; Computer Science/Software; Engineering; Finance; Manufacturing; Personnel/Labor Relations; Technical. **Positions commonly filled include:** Accountant/Auditor; Administrative Manager; Biochemist; Chemical Engineer; Chemist; Computer Programmer; Designer; Electrical/Electronics Engineer; Electrician; Financial Analyst; Human Resources Specialist; Internet Services Manager; Management Analyst/Consultant; Market Research Analyst; Mechanical Engineer; MIS Specialist; Paralegal; Quality Control Supervisor; Software Engineer; Systems Analyst. **Benefits available to temporary workers:** Dental Insurance; Medical Insurance; Paid Holidays; Paid Vacation; Vision Insurance. **International locations:** Worldwide. **Average salary range of placements:** $30,000 - $50,000. **Number of placements per year:** 500 - 999.

MODERN ENGINEERING
3 Parklane Boulevard, Dearborn MI 48120. 313/336-6987. **Fax:** 313/336-5265. **Contact:** Recruiting Executive Manager. **Description:** Places contract workers for other companies. **Specializes in the areas of:** Automotive. **Positions commonly filled include:** Automotive Mechanic; Cost Estimator; Designer; Draftsperson; Electrical/Electronics Engineer; Industrial Engineer; Mechanical Engineer; Metallurgical Engineer; Quality Control Supervisor; Structural Engineer; Technical Writer/Editor; Transportation/Traffic Specialist. **Corporate headquarters location:** Warren MI.

PROFESSIONAL RESOURCE ASSOCIATES
201 Broadway, Marine City MI 48039. 810/765-1181. **Fax:** 810/765-1182. **Contact:** Jim Petitpren, Vice President. **E-mail address:** jim@pra-usa.com. **World Wide Web address:** http://www.pra-usa.com. **Description:** A contract services firm and permanent employment agency for technical professionals. Company pays fee. **Specializes in the areas of:** Administration; Computer Science/Software; Engineering; Industrial; Manufacturing; Technical. **Positions commonly filled include:** Ceramics Engineer; Computer Programmer; Design Engineer; Draftsperson; Editor; Electrical/Electronics Engineer; Industrial Engineer; Materials Engineer; Mechanical Engineer; Metallurgical Engineer; MIS Specialist; Quality Control Supervisor; Software Engineer; Systems Analyst; Technical Writer/Editor; Video Production Coordinator. **Benefits available to temporary workers:** 401(k); Cafeteria; Medical Insurance; Paid Holidays; Paid Vacation. **Average salary range of placements:** $30,000 - $50,000. **Number of placements per year:** 50 - 99.

PROVISION TECHNOLOGIES
26877 Northwestern Highway, Suite 311, Southfield MI 48034. 248/386-0895. **Fax:** 248/386-0855. **Contact:** Manager. **World Wide Web address:** http://www.careerbase.com. **Description:** A contract services and consulting firm. **Specializes in the areas of:** Computer Science/Software; Information Technology.

RC ENGINEERING AND MANAGEMENT SERVICES, INC.
10801 South Saginaw Street, Suite E, Grand Blanc MI 48439. 810/695-3381. **Toll-free phone:** 800/525-4118. **Fax:** 810/695-7904. **Contact:** Laura Wirth, Technical Recruiter. **World Wide Web address:** http://www.rcengineering.com. **Description:** A contract services firm. Company pays fee. **Specializes in the areas of:** Engineering. **Positions commonly filled include:** Administrative Assistant; Civil Engineer; Design Engineer; Draftsperson; Industrial Engineer; Manufacturing Engineer; Mechanical Engineer; Software Engineer; Technical Writer/Editor. **Number of placements per year:** 1 - 49.

RHI CONSULTING
201 West Big Beaver Road, Suite 310, Troy MI 48084. 248/524-3698. **Fax:** 248/524-3113. **Contact:** Robert Prosser, Division Director. **E-mail address:** rhictroy@aol.com. **Description:** A contract services firm that provides consultants for projects ranging from personal computing to multiple platform integration. Company pays fee. **Specializes in the areas of:** Administration; Computer Science/Software; Technical. **Positions commonly filled include:** Computer Programmer; Internet Services Manager; Management Analyst/Consultant; MIS Specialist; Software Engineer; Systems Analyst; Technical Writer/Editor. **Benefits available to temporary workers:** Medical Insurance; Paid Holidays; Paid Vacation. **Corporate headquarters location:** Menlo Park CA. **Other U.S. locations:** Nationwide. **Number of placements per year:** 200 - 499.

SOFTWARE SERVICES CORPORATION
650 Avis Drive, Suite 100, Ann Arbor MI 48108. 734/996-3636. **Toll-free phone:** 800/448-1568. **Fax:** 734/669-2330. **Contact:** Dave Cortright, Director of Technical Recruiting. **World Wide Web address:** http://www.software-services.com. **Description:** A contract services firm that focuses on custom software development, network integration, and consulting services. Company pays fee. **Specializes in the areas of:** Computer Hardware/Software; Engineering; Manufacturing; MIS/EDP; Technical. **Positions commonly filled include:** Computer Programmer; Database Manager; EDP Specialist; Electrical/Electronics Engineer; Industrial Engineer; Internet Services Manager; Mechanical Engineer; MIS Specialist; Project Manager; Software Engineer; Systems Analyst; Technical Writer/Editor; Telecommunications Manager; Webmaster. **Benefits available to temporary workers:** 401(k); Dental Insurance; Medical Insurance; Paid Holidays; Paid Vacation; Sick Days; STD/LTD Coverage; Tuition Assistance; Vision Insurance. **Number of placements per year:** 100 - 199.

TAD TECHNICAL SERVICES
3131 South Saginaw Road, Midland MI 48640. 517/496-9377. **Fax:** 517/496-2649. **Contact:** Bob DeJong, Branch Manager. **World Wide Web address:** http://www.tad.resources.com. **Description:** A contract services firm. **Specializes in the areas of:** Computer Science/Software; Engineering; Industrial; Scientific; Technical. **Positions commonly filled include:** Applications Engineer; Biochemist; Buyer; Chemical Engineer; Chemist; Civil Engineer; Clinical Lab Technician; Computer Operator; Computer Programmer; Cost Estimator; Customer Service Representative; Design Engineer; Draftsperson; Electrical/Electronics Engineer; Graphic Artist; Graphic Designer; Human Resources Manager; Industrial Engineer; Manufacturing Engineer; Mechanical Engineer; Metallurgical Engineer; MIS Specialist; Purchasing Agent/Manager; Software Engineer; Systems Analyst; Systems Manager. **Benefits available to temporary workers:** 401(k); Dental Insurance; Medical Insurance; Paid Holidays; Paid Vacation. **Corporate headquarters location:** Cambridge MA. **Average salary range of placements:** $30,000 - $50,000. **Number of placements per year:** 200 - 499.

TECHNICAL AID CORPORATION
16800 Executive Plaza, Suite 795, Dearborn MI 48126. 313/271-3600. **Contact:** Office Manager. **Description:** A contract services firm. **Specializes in the areas of:** Computer Hardware/Software; Engineering; Information Technology.

UNLIMITED STAFFING SOLUTIONS, INC.
4111 Andover Road, Suite 140, Bloomfield Hills MI 48302. 248/258-5111. **Fax:** 248/258-8895. **Contact:** Caleene Jones, President. **E-mail address:** ussi@flash.net. **World Wide Web address:** http://www.unlimitedstaffing.com. **Description:** A contract technical services firm focusing on data processing and engineering. Company pays fee. **Specializes in the areas of:** Accounting/Auditing; Administration; Computer Science/Software; Engineering; Finance; Personnel/Labor Relations; Publishing; Secretarial; Technical; Transportation. **Positions commonly filled include:** Accountant/ Auditor; Administrative Manager; Aerospace Engineer; Agricultural Engineer; Aircraft Mechanic/Engine Specialist; Architect; Chemical Engineer; Chemist; Civil Engineer; Clerical Supervisor; Computer Programmer; Customer Service Representative; Design Engineer; Designer; Draftsperson; Electrical/Electronics Engineer; Financial Analyst; Industrial Engineer; Industrial Production Manager; Mechanical Engineer; MIS Specialist; Nuclear Engineer; Science Technologist; Software Engineer; Systems Analyst; Telecommunications Manager; Typist/Word Processor. **Benefits available to temporary workers:** 401(k); Dental Insurance; Medical Insurance. **Average salary range of placements:** $30,000 - $50,000. **Number of placements per year:** 200 - 499.

H.L. YOH COMPANY
755 West Big Beaver Road, Suite 419, Troy MI 48084. 248/362-0099. **Contact:** Office Manager. **Description:** A contract services firm. **Specializes in the areas of:** Automotive; Computer Science/ Software; Information Technology; Technical.

CAREER/OUTPLACEMENT COUNSELING FIRMS

CAREER DIRECTIONS
300 North 5th Avenue, Suite 120, Ann Arbor MI 48104. 734/663-0677. **Fax:** 734/663-8728. **Contact:** David Gruner, Principal. **Description:** A career/ outplacement counseling service that offers hiring/promotion evaluations, performance coaching, career development, and outplacement services.

THE LETTER WRITER
9437 Hagerty Road, Plymouth MI 48170. 734/455-8892. **Contact:** Ginny Eades, Owner. **Description:** A career/outplacement counseling service.

MINNESOTA

EXECUTIVE SEARCH FIRMS

ACCOUNTANTS EXCHANGE, INC.
2233 Hamline Avenue North, Roseville Professional Center, Suite 420, Roseville MN 55113. 612/636-5490. **Contact:** Chuck McBride, President. **Description:** An executive search firm. **Specializes in the areas of:** Accounting/Auditing; Finance. **Number of placements per year:** 1 - 49.

ACCOUNTANTS EXECUTIVE SEARCH
ACCOUNTANTS ON CALL
45 South 7th Street, Suite 3004, Minneapolis MN 55402. 612/341-9900. **Contact:** Office Manager. **Description:** An executive search firm. Accountants on Call (also at this location) is a temporary agency. **Specializes in the areas of:** Accounting/Auditing; Finance. **Corporate headquarters location:** Saddlebrook NJ. **Other U.S. locations:** Nationwide.

ACCOUNTANTS PLACEMENT REGISTRY, INC.
1705 Cope Avenue, Suite A, Maplewood MN 55109. 612/773-9018. **Fax:** 612/770-8071. **Recorded jobline:** 612/773-0648. **Contact:** Robert S. Culver, President. **Description:** An executive search firm that focuses on the financial industry. Company pays fee. **Specializes in the areas of:** Accounting/Auditing; Finance. **Positions commonly filled include:** Accountant/Auditor; Bank Officer/Manager; Budget Analyst; Cost Estimator; Credit Manager; Financial Analyst. **Average salary range of placements:** $30,000 - $50,000. **Number of placements per year:** 50 - 99.

ADD ON HUMAN RESOURCE SPECIALTIES, INC.
255 East Roselawn Avenue, Suite 49, St. Paul MN 55117. 612/488-1000. **Toll-free phone:** 800/305-7761. **Fax:** 612/488-9585. **Contact:** Linda Longlet, President. **E-mail address:** addon@onecalltelcom.com. **World Wide Web address:** http://www.interpage.com/addon.htm. **Description:** An executive search firm. Company pays fee. **Specializes in the areas of:** Telecommunications. **Positions commonly filled include:** Customer Service Representative; Sales Executive; Sales Manager; Sales Representative; Software Engineer; Telecommunications Manager. **Average salary range of placements:** $30,000 - $50,000. **Number of placements per year:** 1 - 49.

ADVANCE PERSONNEL RESOURCES
715 Florida Avenue South, Suite 301, Golden Valley MN 55426-1729. 612/546-6779. **Fax:** 612/546-2523. **Contact:** Larry Happe, CPC, Owner. **Description:** An executive search firm. Company pays fee. **Specializes in the areas of:** Accounting/Auditing; Finance; General Management; Manufacturing; Personnel/Labor Relations; Publishing; Sales; Transportation. **Positions commonly filled include:** Accountant/Auditor; Attorney; Management Analyst/Consultant; Market Research Analyst; Operations/Production Manager; Quality Control Supervisor; Services Sales Representative; Strategic Relations Manager; Telecommunications Manager. **Average salary range of placements:** $30,000 - $80,000. **Number of placements per year:** 1 - 49.

AGRI CONSULTANTS
18353 Heathcote Lane, Wayzata MN 55391. 612/542-8550. **Fax:** 612/544-1850. **Contact:** Mark Parsons, President. **Description:** An executive search firm. Company pays fee. **Specializes in the areas of:** Sales; Technical. **Positions commonly filled include:** Agricultural Engineer; Agricultural Scientist; Manufacturer's/Wholesaler's Sales Rep.; Operations/Production Manager; Veterinarian. **Number of placements per year:** 1 - 49.

AGRI-BUSINESS SERVICES, INC.
P.O. Box 1237, Lakeville MN 55044. 612/469-6767. **Fax:** 612/469-6768. **Contact:** Michael J. Morrison, President. **Description:** An executive search firm operating on a contingency basis. The firm focuses on food processing and agri-business industries. Company pays fee. **Specializes in the areas of:** Biology; Engineering; Food Industry; General Management; Manufacturing; Sales; Technical. **Positions commonly filled include:** Biochemist; Biological Scientist; Blue-Collar Worker Supervisor; Branch Manager; Chemical Engineer; Chemist; Civil Engineer; Customer Service Representative; Design Engineer; Dietician/Nutritionist; Food Scientist/Technologist; Forester/Conservation Scientist; General Manager; Manufacturer's/Wholesaler's Sales Rep.; Quality Control Supervisor; Services Sales Representative; Veterinarian.

ALTERNATIVE CHOICE HEALTH SERVICES
2021 East Hennepin Street, Suite 135, Minneapolis MN 55413. 612/378-1474. **Contact:** Manager. **Description:** An executive search firm that places home health care professionals. **Specializes in the areas of:** Health/Medical.

ARCHAMBAULT GROUP
5831 Cedar Lake Road South, St. Louis Park MN 55416. 612/545-6296. **Contact:** Office Manager. **Description:** An executive search firm. **Specializes in the areas of:** Finance.

BRADLEY & ASSOCIATES
5341 River Bluff Curve, Suite 116, Minneapolis MN 55437. 612/884-2607. **Fax:** 612/884-2019. **Contact:** John Bradley, President. **Description:** An executive search firm. **Specializes in the areas of:** Accounting/Auditing; Engineering; Food Industry; Manufacturing. **Positions commonly filled include:** Account Manager; Biological Scientist; Chemical Engineer; Controller; Electrical/Electronics Engineer; Mechanical Engineer.

BRIGHT SEARCH/PROFESSIONAL STAFFING
8120 Penn Avenue South, Suite 167, Minneapolis MN 55431-1326. 612/884-8111. **Fax:** 612/881-9197. **Contact:** Leo Bright, Owner/President. **Description:** An executive search firm operating on both retained and contingency bases. Company pays fee. **Specializes in the areas of:** Consulting; Engineering; General Management; Health/Medical; Industrial; Legal; Manufacturing; Personnel/Labor Relations; Sales; Technical. **Positions commonly filled include:** Attorney; Chemical Engineer; Design Engineer; Electrical/Electronics Engineer; General Manager; Human Resources Specialist; Industrial Engineer; Industrial Production Manager; Management Analyst/Consultant; Mechanical Engineer; Metallurgical Engineer; Purchasing Agent/Manager; Quality Control Supervisor; Services Sales Representative; Software Engineer; Systems Analyst; Technical Writer/Editor; Transportation/Traffic Specialist.

BRINK INTERNATIONAL ASSOCIATES
5780 Lincoln Drive, Edina MN 55436. 612/931-9622. **Contact:** Manager. **Description:** An executive search firm. **Specializes in the areas of:** Hotel/Restaurant.

CERTIFIED ACCOUNTING PROS
333 Washington Avenue North, Minneapolis MN 55401. 612/373-9495. **Contact:** Office Manager. **Description:** An executive search firm. **Specializes in the areas of:** Accounting/Auditing.

COMPUTER EMPLOYMENT
5151 Edina Industrial Boulevard, Suite 299, Edina MN 55439. 612/831-4566. **Fax:** 612/831-4684. **Contact:** Marty Koepp, Owner. **E-mail address:** mkoepp@computeremployment.com. **Description:** An executive search firm operating on a contingency basis and focusing on the computer industry. Company pays fee. **Specializes in the areas of:** Administration; Computer Science/Software. **Positions commonly filled include:** Computer Programmer; Management Analyst/Consultant; MIS Specialist; Software Engineer; Systems Analyst; Telecommunications Manager. **Average salary range of placements:** $50,000 - $75,000. **Number of placements per year:** 50 - 99.

COMPUTER PERSONNEL
5353 Wayzata Boulevard, Suite 604, Minneapolis MN 55416. 612/542-8053. **Contact:** Office Manager. **Description:** An executive search firm. **Specializes in the areas of:** Computer Science/Software. **Other U.S. locations:** Seattle WA.

ROBERT CONNELLY AND ASSOCIATES INC.
P.O. Box 24028, Minneapolis MN 55424. 612/925-3039. **Contact:** Robert F. Olsen, President. **Description:** An executive search firm. **Number of placements per year:** 50 - 99.

CUSTOM SEARCH INC.
9800 Shelard Parkway, Suite 104, Plymouth MN 55441. 612/591-6111. **Contact:** Office Manager. **Description:** An executive search firm. **Specializes in the areas of:** Software Engineering; Technical.

CHARLES DAHL & ASSOCIATES
77 13th Avenue NE, Minneapolis MN 55143-1001. 612/331-7777. **Contact:** Manager. **Description:** An executive search firm. **Specializes in the areas of:** Engineering; Finance; Information Technology.

DEVELOPMENT SEARCH SPECIALISTS
W-3072 First National Bank Building, St. Paul MN 55101-1312. 612/224-3750. **Contact:** Fred J. Lauerman, Principal. **Description:** An executive search firm. Company pays fee. **Specializes in the areas of:** Nonprofit. **Positions commonly filled include:** Fundraising Specialist; General Manager; Public Relations Specialist. **Number of placements per year:** 1 - 49.

DIETRICH & ASSOCIATES
5775 Wayzata Boulevard, Suite 700, Minneapolis MN 55416. 612/525-2205. **Fax:** 612/545-0856. **Contact:** Marilyn Dietrich, Owner. **Description:** An executive search firm. Company pays fee. **Specializes in the areas of:** Engineering; Manufacturing. **Positions commonly filled include:** Design Engineer; Electrical/Electronics Engineer; Industrial Engineer; Industrial Production Manager; Mechanical Engineer; Operations/Production Manager; Purchasing Agent/Manager; Quality Control Supervisor; Transportation/Traffic Specialist. **Average salary range of placements:** More than $50,000. **Number of placements per year:** 1 - 49.

EHS & ASSOCIATES, INC.
1516 West Lake Street, Suite 102, Minneapolis MN 55408. 612/824-3993. **Fax:** 612/824-4843. **Contact:** Brian Hirt, Vice President. **Description:** An executive search firm. Company pays fee. **Specializes in the areas of:** Administration; Art/Design; Computer Science/Software; Food Industry; Health/Medical. **Positions commonly filled include:** Computer Programmer; Dental Assistant/Dental Hygienist; Dentist; Hotel Manager; Pharmacist; Physical Therapist; Physician; Purchasing Agent/Manager; Registered Nurse; Restaurant/Food Service Manager; Software Engineer; Systems Analyst. **Number of placements per year:** 200 - 499.

ESP SYSTEMS PROFESSIONALS
701 4th Avenue South, Suite 1800, Minneapolis MN 55415-1819. 612/337-3000. **Fax:** 612/337-9199. **Contact:** Robert R. Hildreth, President. **E-mail address:** careers@esp.com. **World Wide Web address:** http://www.esp.com. **Description:** An executive search firm that focuses on placing information systems professionals, from programmers to senior managers. Company pays fee. **Specializes in the areas of:** Computer Science/Software. **Positions commonly filled include:** Computer Programmer; Internet Services Manager; MIS Specialist; Software Engineer; Systems Analyst. **Average salary range of placements:** $35,000 - $60,000. **Number of placements per year:** 500 - 999.

ELLS PERSONNEL SYSTEMS, INC.
9900 East Bren Road, Suite 105, Minnetonka MN 55343. 612/338-4570. **Contact:** President. **Description:** An executive search firm. Founded in 1912. Company pays fee. **Specializes in the areas of:** Accounting/Auditing; Administration; Advertising; Banking; Clerical; Engineering; Finance; General Management; Health/Medical; Manufacturing; Nonprofit; Personnel/Labor Relations; Publishing; Sales; Secretarial. **Positions commonly filled include:** Accountant/Auditor; Administrative Assistant; Bank Officer/Manager; Biomedical Engineer; Bookkeeper; Civil Engineer; Clerk; Credit Manager; Customer Service Representative; Data Entry Clerk; Draftsperson; Electrical/Electronics Engineer; General Manager; Industrial Designer; Industrial Engineer; Legal Secretary; Marketing Specialist; Mechanical Engineer; Medical Secretary; Quality Control Supervisor; Sales Representative; Secretary; Systems Analyst; Typist/Word Processor. **Number of placements per year:** 100 - 199.

EMERGING TECHNOLOGY SERVICES
572 Highland Road, Minnetonka MN 55345. 612/937-2200. **Contact:** Manager. **Description:** An executive search firm. **Specializes in the areas of:** Information Systems.

ENTERPRISE SEARCH SERVICE
3639 Admiral Lane, Minneapolis MN 55429. 612/537-7310. **Contact:** Manager. **Description:** An executive search firm. **Specializes in the areas of:** Computer Science/Software.

ERSPAMER ASSOCIATES
4010 West 65th Street, Suite 100, Edina MN 55435. 612/925-3747. **Fax:** 612/925-4022. **Contact:** Roy C. Erspamer, Principal. **Description:** An executive search firm. Company pays fee. **Specializes in the areas of:** Health/Medical; Medical Technology. **Positions commonly filled include:** Biochemist; Biomedical Engineer; Chemical Engineer; Chemist; Design Engineer; Electrical/Electronics Engineer; Manufacturing Engineer; Mechanical Engineer; Metallurgical Engineer; Quality Control Supervisor; Regulatory Affairs Director; Software Engineer; Statistician. **Number of placements per year:** 1 - 49.

ESQUIRE SEARCH, LTD.
105 South Fifth Street, Suite 1800, Minneapolis MN 55402. 612/340-9068. **Fax:** 612/340-1218. **Contact:** Patricia A. Comeford, President. **Description:** An executive search firm. Company pays fee. **Specializes in the areas of:** Legal. **Positions commonly filled include:** Attorney.

EXECU-TECH SEARCH INC.
3500 West 80th Street, Suite 20, Bloomington MN 55431. 612/893-6915. **Contact:** Office Manager.

Description: An executive search firm focusing on the placement of chemical, electrical, and mechanical engineering professionals. **Specializes in the areas of:** Engineering.

EXECUTIVE SEARCH INC.
5401 Gamble Drive, Suite 275, Minneapolis MN 55416. 612/541-9153. **Contact:** Office Manager. **Description:** An executive search firm.

FAIRFAX GROUP
9800 Sheland Parkway, Suite 110, Plymouth MN 55441. 612/541-9898. **Fax:** 612/541-9124. **Contact:** Manager. **Description:** An executive search firm. **Specializes in the areas of:** Information Systems; Logistics; Manufacturing.

FALLS MEDICAL SEARCH
34 Forest Dale Road, Minneapolis MN 55410. 612/922-0207. **Contact:** Manager. **Description:** An executive search firm that places physicians.

FOCUS EXECUTIVE SEARCH
431 South 7th Street, Suite 2475, Minneapolis MN 55415-1821. 612/334-5858. **Contact:** Tim McLafferty, President. **Description:** An executive search firm that places mid- to executive-level professionals in the food and pharmacy industries. Company pays fee. **Specializes in the areas of:** Food Industry; Pharmaceutical. **Positions commonly filled include:** Agricultural Engineer; Biological Scientist; Chemical Engineer; Dietician/Nutritionist; Food Scientist/Technologist; Human Resources Manager; Pharmacist. **Average salary range of placements:** More than $50,000. **Number of placements per year:** 100 - 199.

FOGARTY & ASSOCIATES
6600 France Street, Suite 210, Edina MN 55435. 612/831-2828. **Contact:** Manager. **Description:** An executive search firm. **Specializes in the areas of:** Health/Medical.

GATEWAY SEARCH INC.
15500 Wayzata Boulevard, Suite 221, Wayzata MN 55391-1438. 612/473-3137. **Fax:** 612/473-3276. **Contact:** James Bortolussi, President. **Description:** An executive search firm operating on a contingency basis. Company pays fee. **Specializes in the areas of:** Computer Science/Software. **Positions commonly filled include:** Client/Server Specialist; Computer Programmer; Database Manager; Network Administrator; Software Engineer; Systems Analyst; UNIX System Administrator. **Average salary range of placements:** More than $50,000. **Number of placements per year:** 1 - 49.

GERDES SINGER & ASSOCIATES INC.
120 South 6th Street, Suite 2480, Minneapolis MN 55402. 612/335-3553. **Contact:** Office Manager. **Description:** An executive search firm that focuses primarily on the creative end of advertising. **Specializes in the areas of:** Advertising.

ROGER G. GILMER AND ASSOCIATES
14581 Grand Avenue South, Burnsville MN 55306. 612/435-6565. **Contact:** Roger Gilmer, Owner. **Description:** An executive search firm. Company pays fee. **Specializes in the areas of:** Engineering; Manufacturing. **Positions commonly filled include:** Biomedical Engineer; Electrical/Electronics Engineer; Mechanical Engineer; Quality Control Supervisor. **Number of placements per year:** 1 - 49.

GLEASON DALE KEENE & ASSOCIATES, INC.
7401 Metro Boulevard, Suite 460, Minneapolis MN 55439. 612/844-0121. **Contact:** Office Manager. **Description:** An executive search firm.

HR SERVICES OF PLYMOUTH
P.O. Box 564, Rockford MN 55373. 612/477-6595. **Fax:** 612/477-6609. **Contact:** Manager. **Description:** An executive search firm. Company pays fee. **Specializes in the areas of:** Architecture/Construction; Engineering; Food Industry; Industrial; Manufacturing; Personnel/Labor Relations. **Positions commonly filled include:** Blue-Collar Worker Supervisor; Ceramics Engineer; Chemical Engineer; Chemist; Civil Engineer; Construction Trade Worker; Electrical/Electronics Engineer; Industrial Engineer; Manufacturing Engineer; Mechanical Engineer; Metallurgical Engineer; Operations/Production Manager; Purchasing Agent/Manager; Quality Control Supervisor; Structural Engineer; Technical Illustrator. **Average salary range of placements:** $30,000 - $50,000. **Number of placements per year:** 50 - 99.

ROBERT HALF INTERNATIONAL ACCOUNTEMPS
80 South 8th Street, Suite 2850, Minneapolis MN 55402. 612/339-9001. **Contact:** Manager. **World Wide Web address:** http://www.roberthalf.com. **Description:** An executive search firm. Accountemps (also at this location) provides temporary placements. **Specializes in the areas of:** Accounting/Auditing. **Corporate headquarters location:** Menlo Park CA. **Other U.S. locations:** Nationwide.

ROBERT HALF INTERNATIONAL ACCOUNTEMPS
10405 6th Avenue North, Suite 220, Plymouth MN 55441. 612/545-0911. **Contact:** Manager. **World Wide Web address:** http://www.roberthalf.com. **Description:** An executive search firm. Accountemps (also at this location) provides temporary placements. **Specializes in the areas of:** Accounting/Auditing. **Corporate headquarters location:** Menlo Park CA. **Other U.S. locations:** Nationwide.

HAYDEN & ASSOCIATES
7825 Washington Avenue South, Suite 120, Bloomington MN 55439. 612/941-6300. **Contact:** Manager. **Description:** An executive search firm. **Specializes in the areas of:** Advertising; Data Processing; Finance; Medical Sales and Marketing; Sales.

HAYDEN SEARCH GROUP
505 North Highway 169, Suite 275, Plymouth MN 55441. 612/553-0523. **Fax:** 612/553-0618. **Contact:** Todd Hayden, President. **Description:** An executive search firm that places accounting and finance professionals. Company pays fee. **Specializes in the areas of:** Accounting/Auditing; Finance. **Positions commonly filled include:** Accountant/Auditor; Administrative Manager; Budget Analyst; Cost Estimator; Credit Manager; Economist; Financial Analyst; MIS Specialist; Property and Real Estate Manager. **Number of placements per year:** 50 - 99.

HEALTHCARE RECRUITERS OF MINNESOTA
6442 City West Parkway, Suite 303, Eden Prairie MN 55344. 612/942-5424. **Fax:** 612/942-5452. **Contact:** Steven J. Yungner, President. **World Wide Web address:** http://www.hcrintl.com/minnesot.html. **Description:** An executive search firm that places sales, sales management, marketing, and executive professionals in the health care industry. Company pays fee. **Specializes in the areas of:** Health/Medical; Medical Sales and Marketing; Sales. **Positions commonly filled include:** Branch Manager; General Manager; Health Services Manager; Marketing Manager; Medical Sales; Pharmacist; Physical Therapist; Physician; Product Manager; Regulatory Affairs Director; Sales Manager; Sales Representative. **Corporate headquarters location:** Minneapolis MN. **Other U.S. locations:** Nationwide. **Average salary**

range of placements: $30,000 - $50,000. **Number of placements per year:** 50 - 99.

HEINZE & ASSOCIATES
6125 Blue Circle Drive, Suite 218, Minnetonka MN 55343. 612/938-2828. **Contact:** Office Manager. **Description:** An executive search firm. **Specializes in the areas of:** General Management. **Average salary range of placements:** $100,000 +.

HILLEREN & ASSOCIATES
1600 West 82nd Street, Suite 180, Bloomington MN 55431. 612/888-4680. **Fax:** 612/888-5053. **Contact:** Jerry Hilleren, Owner. **Description:** An executive search firm that focuses on the placement of medical industry and medical sales professionals. Company pays fee. **Specializes in the areas of:** Health/Medical; Sales. **Positions commonly filled include:** Health Services Manager; Radiological Technologist; Services Sales Representative. **Average salary range of placements:** More than $50,000. **Number of placements per year:** 50 - 99.

T.H. HUNTER, INC.
526 Nicollet Mall, Suite 310, Minneapolis MN 55402. 612/339-0530. **Fax:** 612/338-4757. **Contact:** Martin Conroy, Executive Recruiter. **Description:** An executive search firm. Company pays fee. **Specializes in the areas of:** Accounting/Auditing; Administration; Advertising; Banking; Biology; Computer Science/Software; Economics; Engineering; Finance; Food Industry; Health/Medical; Insurance; Legal; Manufacturing; Nonprofit; Personnel/Labor Relations; Publishing; Retail; Sales; Technical. **Positions commonly filled include:** Accountant/Auditor; Actuary; Attorney; Bank Officer/Manager; Biomedical Engineer; Branch Manager; Computer Programmer; Credit Manager; Economist; Financial Analyst; General Manager; Health Services Manager; Internet Services Manager; Licensed Practical Nurse; Management Analyst/Consultant; Mechanical Engineer; Occupational Therapist; Physical Therapist; Physician; Quality Control Supervisor; Registered Nurse; Software Engineer; Speech-Language Pathologist; Systems Analyst; Technical Writer/Editor; Urban/Regional Planner. **Average salary range of placements:** More than $50,000. **Number of placements per year:** 50 - 99.

JFK SEARCH
10 South Fifth Street, Minneapolis MN 55402. 612/332-8082. **Contact:** Manager. **Description:** An executive search firm. **Specializes in the areas of:** Advertising.

JACKLEY SEARCH CONSULTANTS
14581 Grand Avenue South, Burnsville MN 55306. 612/831-2344. **Contact:** Manager. **Description:** An executive search firm. **Specializes in the areas of:** Engineering; High-Tech.

ERIC KERCHEVAL & ASSOCIATES, EXECUTIVE RECRUITERS
15 South First Street, Suite A4, Minneapolis MN 55401. 612/338-7944. **Contact:** Office Manager. **Description:** An executive search firm. **Specializes in the areas of:** Advertising; Hotel/Restaurant.

GEORGE KONIK ASSOCIATES INC.
7242 Metro Boulevard, Minneapolis MN 55439. 612/835-5550. **Contact:** Manager. **Description:** An executive search firm. **Specializes in the areas of:** Human Resources; Technical.

KORN/FERRY INTERNATIONAL
4816 IDS Center, Minneapolis MN 55402. 612/333-1834. **Contact:** Manager. **Description:** An executive search firm that places upper-level managers in a variety of industries. **Corporate headquarters location:** Los Angeles CA. **International locations:** Worldwide. **Average salary range of placements:** More than $50,000.

La BREE & ASSOCIATES
6440 Flying Cloud Drive, Suite 115, Eden Prairie MN 55344. 612/941-4525. **Contact:** Office Manager. **Description:** An executive placement firm. **Specializes in the areas of:** Construction; Finance; Insurance.

SUSAN LEE & ASSOCIATES
4300 West 70th Street, Edina MN 55435. 612/929-1039. **Contact:** Manager. **Description:** An executive search firm. **Specializes in the areas of:** Printing; Publishing.

HOWARD LIEBERMAN & ASSOCIATES INC.
311 First Avenue North, Suite 503, Minneapolis MN 55401. 612/338-2432. **Fax:** 612/332-8860. **Contact:** Howard Lieberman, President. **E-mail address:** hla503@aol.com. **World Wide Web address:** http://www.member.aol.com/hlassist/hla.html. **Description:** An executive search firm focusing on the placement of attorneys in law firms and corporations. Company pays fee. **Specializes in the areas of:** Legal. **Positions commonly filled include:** Attorney. **Number of placements per year:** 1 - 49.

MANAGEMENT RECRUITERS OF MINNEAPOLIS
SALES CONSULTANTS OF MINNEAPOLIS
7550 France Avenue South, Suite 180, Edina MN 55435. 612/835-4466. **Contact:** Office Manager. **Description:** An executive search firm operating on a contingency basis. **Specializes in the areas of:** Accounting/Auditing; Administration; Advertising; Architecture/Construction; Banking; Chemical; Communications; Computer Hardware/Software; Construction; Design; Electrical; Engineering; Finance; Food Industry; General Management; Health/Medical; Industrial; Insurance; Legal; Manufacturing; Operations Management; Personnel/Labor Relations; Pharmaceutical; Procurement; Publishing; Real Estate; Retail; Sales; Technical; Textiles; Transportation.

MANAGEMENT RECRUITERS OF ROCHESTER
1903 South Broadway, Rochester MN 55904. 507/282-2400. **Contact:** Nona Vierkant, Office Manager. **Description:** An executive search firm operating on a contingency basis. Company pays fee. **Specializes in the areas of:** Computer Science/Software. **Positions commonly filled include:** Computer Programmer; Systems Analyst. **Average salary range of placements:** $30,000 - $50,000. **Number of placements per year:** 1 - 49.

LEE MARSH & ASSOCIATES
1469 Highview Avenue, Eagan MN 55121. 612/452-5412. **Fax:** 612/452-9051. **Contact:** Lee Marsh, Owner. **E-mail address:** marsh042@gold.tc.umn.edu. **Description:** A technical executive search firm focusing on software engineering. Company pays fee. **Specializes in the areas of:** Engineering; Technical. **Positions commonly filled include:** Computer Programmer; Design Engineer; Electrical/Electronics Engineer; Sales Representative; Software Engineer; Systems Analyst. **Number of placements per year:** 50 - 99.

BRAD MARTIN & ASSOCIATES
5353 Wayzata Boulevard, Minneapolis MN 55416. 612/544-4130. **Contact:** Manager. **Description:** An executive search firm. **Specializes in the areas of:** Manufacturing.

MARY L. MAYER, LTD.
P.O. Box 250, Medina MN 55340-0250. 612/473-7700. **Fax:** 612/449-0772. **Contact:** Mary Mayer,

President. **Description:** An executive search firm focusing on the property/casualty insurance industry. Company pays fee. **Specializes in the areas of:** Insurance; Sales. **Positions commonly filled include:** Actuary; Adjuster; Administrative Manager; Branch Manager; Claim Representative; Clerical Supervisor; Customer Service Representative; General Manager; Human Resources Specialist; Insurance Agent/Broker; MIS Specialist; Systems Analyst; Underwriter/Assistant Underwriter. **Average salary range of placements:** More than $50,000. **Number of placements per year:** 1 - 49.

McGLADREY & PULLEN
227 West First Street, Suite 700, Duluth MN 55802-1913. 218/727-5025. **Fax:** 218/727-1438. **Contact:** Karen S. Andresan, Recruiter. **Description:** An executive search firm. Company pays fee. **Specializes in the areas of:** Accounting/Auditing; Economics; General Management; Nonprofit; Personnel/Labor Relations. **Positions commonly filled include:** Accountant/Auditor; Bank Officer/Manager; Branch Manager; Chemist; Civil Engineer; Clerical Supervisor; Computer Programmer; Credit Manager; Customer Service Representative; Financial Analyst; General Manager; Health Services Manager; Hotel Manager; Human Resources Specialist; Management Analyst/Consultant; Manufacturer's/Wholesaler's Sales Rep.; MIS Specialist; Operations/Production Manager; Paralegal; Property and Real Estate Manager; Purchasing Agent/Manager; Quality Control Supervisor; Systems Analyst; Telecommunications Manager; Typist/Word Processor. **Corporate headquarters location:** Minneapolis MN. **Other U.S. locations:** Nationwide. **Average salary range of placements:** $30,000 - $50,000. **Number of placements per year:** 50 - 99.

MEDSEARCH CORPORATION
6545 France Avenue South, Edina MN 55435. 612/926-6584. **Contact:** Manager. **Description:** An executive search firm. **Specializes in the areas of:** Health/Medical. **Positions commonly filled include:** Physician.

METRO HOSPITALITY CONSULTANTS
9448 Lyndale Avenue South, Suite 223, Bloomington MN 55420. 612/884-4299. **Contact:** Debra Kiefat, President. **Description:** An executive search firm that focuses on placing professionals in the hospitality industry. Company pays fee. **Specializes in the areas of:** Food Industry. **Positions commonly filled include:** Restaurant/Food Service Manager. **Corporate headquarters location:** Minneapolis MN. **Number of placements per year:** 1 - 49.

C.A. MOORE & ASSOCIATES INC.
15500 Wayzata Boulevard, Suite 803C, Wayzata MN 55391. 612/473-0990. **Contact:** Office Manager. **Description:** An executive search firm. **Specializes in the areas of:** Finance; Insurance.

NER, INC. (NATIONAL ENGINEERING RESOURCES)
6200 Shingle Creek Parkway, Suite 160, Brooklyn Center MN 55430. 612/561-7610. **Toll-free phone:** 800/665-7610. **Fax:** 612/561-7675. **Contact:** Technical Recruiter. **E-mail address:** nerinc@sprynet.com. **World Wide Web address:** http://www.occ.com/ner. **Description:** An executive search firm focusing on the placement of engineering, technical, and scientific personnel. **Specializes in the areas of:** Administration; Clerical; Computer Hardware/Software; Engineering; Industrial; Medical Technology; Oil and Gas; Petrochemical; Publishing; Technical. **Positions commonly filled include:** Administrative Manager; Agricultural Engineer; Aircraft Mechanic/Engine Specialist; Ceramics Engineer; Computer Programmer; Materials Engineer; Medical Assistant; Metallurgical Engineer; Nuclear Engineer; Quality Control Supervisor; Software Engineer; Structural Engineer; Systems Analyst. **Number of placements per year:** 1 - 49.

NESS GROUP INC.
762 Pillsbury Court, 200 South 6th Street, Minneapolis MN 55406. 612/344-1100. **Fax:** 612/344-1105. **Contact:** Manager. **Description:** An executive search firm.

G.J. NIENHAUS & ASSOCIATES
2800 East Cliff Raod, Suite 260, Burnsville MN 55337. 612/890-5702. **Contact:** Office Manager. **Description:** An executive search firm. **Specializes in the areas of:** Packaging.

NORTH AMERICAN RECRUITERS
4725 Olson Memorial Highway, Suite 100, Golden Valley MN 55422. 612/591-1951. **Toll-free phone:** 800/886-7598. **Fax:** 612/591-5850. **Contact:** David Knutson, President. **Description:** An executive search firm operating on a retainer basis. Company pays fee. **Specializes in the areas of:** Accounting/Auditing; Administration; Computer Science/Software; Engineering; Finance; General Management; Health/Medical; Industrial; Manufacturing; Sales; Technical. **Positions commonly filled include:** Accountant/Auditor; Computer Programmer; Customer Service Representative; Electrical/Electronics Engineer; Financial Analyst; General Manager; Industrial Engineer; Industrial Production Manager; Mechanical Engineer; Operations/Production Manager; Purchasing Agent/Manager; Services Sales Representative; Software Engineer; Systems Analyst; Telecommunications Manager. **Average salary range of placements:** More than $50,000. **Number of placements per year:** 100 - 199.

NORTHLAND EMPLOYMENT SERVICES INC.
10801 Wayzata Boulevard, Suite 325, Minnetonka MN 55305. 612/541-1060. **Fax:** 612/595-9878. **Contact:** David Gavin, President. **World Wide Web address:** http://www.jobsmn.com. **Description:** An executive search firm operating on both retained and contingency bases. Company pays fee. **Specializes in the areas of:** Architecture/Construction; Biology; Computer Science/Software; Engineering; Technical. **Positions commonly filled include:** Biochemist; Biological Scientist; Biomedical Engineer; Chemical Engineer; Chemist; Civil Engineer; Computer Animator; Computer Operator; Construction Contractor; Database Manager; Design Engineer; Electrical/Electronics Engineer; Environmental Engineer; Geologist/Geophysicist; Industrial Engineer; Manufacturing Engineer; Mechanical Engineer; MIS Specialist; Project Manager; Quality Control Supervisor; Software Engineer; Systems Analyst; Systems Manager; Webmaster. **Average salary range of placements:** More than $50,000. **Number of placements per year:** 200 - 499.

NYCOR SEARCH INC.
4930 West 77th Street, Suite 300, Minneapolis MN 55435-4809. 612/831-6444. **Fax:** 612/835-2883. **Contact:** Mark Cline, Operations Manager. **E-mail address:** jobs@nycor.com. **World Wide Web address:** http://www.nycor.com. **Description:** An executive search firm that focuses on permanent and contract placement of experienced professionals in engineering and other technical disciplines. Company pays fee. **Specializes in the areas of:** Architecture/Construction; Computer Science/Software; Engineering; General Management; Industrial; Manufacturing; Technical. **Positions commonly filled include:** Biomedical Engineer; Chemical Engineer; Chemist; Civil Engineer; Clinical Lab Technician; Computer Programmer; Design Engineer; Designer; Draftsperson;

Electrical/Electronics Engineer; Food Scientist/ Technologist; General Manager; Industrial Engineer; Internet Services Manager; Materials Engineer; Mathematician; Mechanical Engineer; Metallurgical Engineer; MIS Specialist; Multimedia Designer; Operations/Production Manager; Petroleum Engineer; Purchasing Agent/Manager; Quality Control Supervisor; Science Technologist; Software Engineer; Systems Analyst; Technical Writer/Editor; Telecommunications Manager. **Benefits available to temporary workers:** Medical Insurance; Paid Holidays; Paid Vacation. **Average salary range of placements:** More than $50,000. **Number of placements per year:** 200 - 499.

PERSONNEL ASSISTANCE CORPORATION
1242 Homestead Trail, Long Lake MN 55356. 612/476-0674. **Contact:** Donald E. Pearson, President. **Description:** An executive search firm operating on a contingency basis. Company pays fee. **Specializes in the areas of:** Engineering; Industrial; Manufacturing; Technical. **Positions commonly filled include:** Agricultural Engineer; Design Engineer; Designer; General Manager; Industrial Production Manager; Mechanical Engineer; Operations/Production Manager. **Average salary range of placements:** $30,000 - $100,000. **Number of placements per year:** 1 - 49.

PIONEER SEARCH, INC.
P.O. Box 277, Center City MN 55012. 612/257-3957. **Contact:** Manager. **Description:** An executive search firm. **Specializes in the areas of:** Computer Hardware/Software; Engineering.

PROFESSIONAL RECRUITERS INC.
17641 Kettering Trail, Lakeville MN 55044-9344. 612/892-3700. **Fax:** 612/892-3711. **Contact:** Robert Reinitz, President. **E-mail address:** headhunt@primenet.com. **World Wide Web address:** http://www.professionalrecruiters.com. **Description:** An executive search firm operating on both retainer and contingency bases that focuses on the placement of electrical, electronic, high-tech, and sales and marketing professionals. Company pays fee. **Specializes in the areas of:** High-Tech; Industrial; Management; Marketing; Sales. **Positions commonly filled include:** Account Representative; Applications Engineer; Marketing Manager; Product Manager; Sales Engineer; Sales Manager; Vice President of Marketing; Vice President of Sales. **Average salary range of placements:** More than $50,000. **Number of placements per year:** 1 - 49.

PROGRAMMING ALTERNATIVES OF MINNESOTA, INC.
7701 France Avenue South, Suite 100, Edina MN 55435. 612/922-7879. **Fax:** 612/922-3726. **Contact:** Kenneth Rosaro, Divisional Manager. **Description:** An executive search firm that focuses on information technology staffing and consulting. Company pays fee. **Specializes in the areas of:** Biotechnology; Computer Science/Software; Data Processing; Engineering; Industrial; Manufacturing; Technical. **Positions commonly filled include:** Aerospace Engineer; Biomedical Engineer; Chemical Engineer; Computer Programmer; Design Engineer; Electrical/ Electronics Engineer; Industrial Designer; Mechanical Engineer; MIS Specialist; Physicist; Software Engineer; Systems Analyst; Technical Writer/Editor; Telecommunications Manager. **Corporate headquarters location:** Minneapolis MN. **Average salary range of placements:** More than $50,000. **Number of placements per year:** 50 - 99.

QUANTUM CONSULTING & PLACEMENT
6600 City West Parkway, Suite 310, Eden Prairie MN 55344. 612/829-5950. **Fax:** 612/829-5988. **Contact:** Doug Berg, President/Recruiter. **Description:** An executive search firm. Company pays fee. **Specializes in the areas of:** Computer Science/Software. **Positions commonly filled include:** Computer Programmer; Systems Analyst. **Number of placements per year:** 1 - 49.

RAUENHORST RECRUITING COMPANY
7600 Parklawn Avenue, Suite 215, Edina MN 55435. 612/897-1420. **Contact:** Manager. **Description:** A generalist executive search firm.

REGENCY RECRUITERS, INC.
7101 York Avenue South, Suite 248, Edina MN 55435-4450. 612/921-3377. **Contact:** David Tetzloff, President. **Description:** An executive search firm focusing on engineering positions, including electrical and mechanical design, software, and manufacturing. Company pays fee. **Specializes in the areas of:** Computer Science/Software; Engineering; Industrial; Manufacturing; Technical. **Positions commonly filled include:** Aerospace Engineer; Biomedical Engineer; Chemical Engineer; Computer Programmer; Draftsperson; Electrical/Electronics Engineer; Mechanical Engineer; Metallurgical Engineer; Quality Control Supervisor; Software Engineer. **Average salary range of placements:** More than $50,000.

RESOURCE SEARCH
1660 South Highway 100, Suite 145, St. Louis Park MN 55416. 612/546-0099. **Fax:** 612/546-4102. **Contact:** John Breczinski, President. **Description:** An executive search firm. Company pays fee. **Specializes in the areas of:** Advertising; Art/Design; Engineering; Food Industry; General Management; Health/Medical; Industrial; Manufacturing; Sales. **Positions commonly filled include:** Design Engineer; Designer; Electrical/Electronics Engineer; General Manager; Manufacturer's/Wholesaler's Sales Rep.; Market Research Analyst; Mechanical Engineer; Operations/ Production Manager; Public Relations Specialist; Services Sales Representative. **Average salary range of placements:** More than $50,000. **Number of placements per year:** 1 - 49.

ROTH YOUNG EXECUTIVE RECRUITERS
4620 West 77th Street, Suite 290, Edina MN 55435-4924. 612/831-6655. **Fax:** 612/831-7413. **Contact:** Donald Spahr, President. **Description:** An executive search firm. Company pays fee. **Specializes in the areas of:** Fashion; Food Industry; Health/Medical; Hotel/Restaurant; Personnel/Labor Relations; Retail; Sales. **Positions commonly filled include:** Buyer; Food Scientist/Technologist; Hotel Manager; Human Resources Manager; Manufacturer's/Wholesaler's Sales Rep.; Occupational Therapist; Physical Therapist; Quality Control Supervisor; Recreational Therapist; Restaurant/Food Service Manager; Retail Manager; Sales Representative; Speech-Language Pathologist. **Number of placements per year:** 50 - 99.

RUSSELL REYNOLDS ASSOCIATES, INC.
90 South Seventh Street, Suite 3050, Minneapolis MN 55402. 612/332-6966. **Contact:** Office Manager. **Description:** A generalist executive search firm.

SATHE & ASSOCIATES EXECUTIVE SEARCH
5821 Cedar Lake Road, St. Louis Park MN 55416. 612/546-2100. **Fax:** 612/546-6930. **Contact:** Mark Sathe, President. **Description:** An executive search firm. Company pays fee. **Specializes in the areas of:** Accounting/Auditing; Administration; Architecture/ Construction; Banking; Engineering; Finance; Food Industry; General Management; Industrial; Manufacturing; Nonprofit; Personnel/Labor Relations; Sales. **Positions commonly filled include:** Accountant/Auditor; Bank Officer/Manager; Buyer; Electrical/Electronics Engineer; Hotel Manager;

Industrial Engineer; Mechanical Engineer; Purchasing Agent/Manager; Quality Control Supervisor. **Number of placements per year:** 1 - 49.

SCHALEKAMP & ASSOCIATES, INC.
2608 West 102nd Street, Minneapolis MN 55431-3346. 612/948-1948. **Fax:** 612/948-9677. **Contact:** Paul D. Schalekamp, President. **E-mail address:** schalekamp@aol.com. **Description:** An executive search firm that focuses on placing property and casualty insurance professionals. Company pays fee. **Specializes in the areas of:** Insurance. **Positions commonly filled include:** Claim Representative; Insurance Agent/Broker; Loss Prevention Specialist; MIS Specialist; Risk Manager. **Average salary range of placements:** More than $50,000. **Number of placements per year:** 1 - 49.

SEARCH SPECIALISTS
2655 North Shore Drive, Wayzata MN 55391. 612/449-8990. **Fax:** 612/449-0369. **Contact:** Craig Lindell, President. **E-mail address:** clindell@sprynet.com. **World Wide Web address:** http://www.cities~online.com/search. **Description:** An executive search firm focusing on architectural, engineering, data processing, software development, and sales and marketing industries. Company pays fee. **Specializes in the areas of:** Architecture/Construction; Computer Science/Software; Engineering; Sales. **Positions commonly filled include:** Architect; Civil Engineer; Design Engineer; Electrical/Electronics Engineer; Mechanical Engineer; Software Engineer; Structural Engineer. **Average salary range of placements:** $20,000 - $29,999. **Number of placements per year:** 1 - 49.

SEARCHTEK
4900 Highway 169, Suite 309, Minneapolis MN 55428. 612/531-0766. **Fax:** 612/531-0667. **Contact:** Gerald Otten, President. **Description:** An executive search firm focusing on engineering placement. Company pays fee. **Specializes in the areas of:** Engineering; High-Tech. **Positions commonly filled include:** Biomedical Engineer; Electrical/Electronics Engineer; Software Engineer. **Average salary range of placements:** More than $50,000. **Number of placements per year:** 1 - 49.

SOURCE SERVICES CORPORATION
Pillsbury Center South, 220 South Sixth Street, Suite 810, Minneapolis MN 55402. 612/332-6460. **Contact:** Manager. **Description:** An executive search firm. The divisions at this location include Source EDP and Accountant Source Temps. **Specializes in the areas of:** Accounting/Auditing; Computer Hardware/Software; Information Technology.

STAFF CONNECTION, INC.
1000 Shelard Parkway, Suite 101, St. Louis Park MN 55426-4917. 612/545-2228. **Fax:** 612/545-3699. **Contact:** Craig Lyon, Secretary/Treasurer. **E-mail address:** sci@mm.com. **Description:** An executive search firm operating on a contingency basis. **Specializes in the areas of:** Computer Science/Software; Engineering; Technical. **Positions commonly filled include:** Computer Programmer; Internet Services Manager; MIS Specialist; Software Engineer; Systems Analyst. **Corporate headquarters location:** Minneapolis MN. **Other U.S. locations:** Phoenix AZ; Las Vegas NV. **Average salary range of placements:** $30,000 - $90,000.

SYSTEMS SEARCH, INC.
P.O. Box 600, Anoka MN 55303. 612/323-9690. **Contact:** Mike Fitzpatrick, President. **E-mail address:** 74352.3305@compuserve.com. **Description:** An executive search firm that recruits and places computer professionals including systems analysts, consultants, engineers, administrators, and programmers. Company pays fee. **Specializes in the areas of:** Administration; Computer Science/Software. **Positions commonly filled include:** Computer Programmer; Internet Services Manager; Management Analyst/Consultant; MIS Specialist; Multimedia Designer; Software Engineer; Systems Analyst; Telecommunications Manager. **Average salary range of placements:** $30,000 - $50,000. **Number of placements per year:** 1 - 49.

RICHARD THOMPSON ASSOCIATES
701 Fourth Avenue South, Minneapolis MN 55415. 612/339-6060. **Contact:** Manager. **Description:** An executive search firm.

TOTAL SEARCH
1541 Berne Road, Fridley MN 55421. 612/571-0247. **Contact:** Tom Harrington, President. **Description:** An executive search firm operating on a contingency basis that focuses on placing food management, retail management, and computer science professionals. Company pays fee. **Specializes in the areas of:** Computer Science/Software; Food Industry; Publishing; Retail. **Positions commonly filled include:** Computer Programmer; Restaurant/Food Service Manager; Systems Analyst. **Number of placements per year:** 50 - 99.

TWIN CITY SEARCH
3989 Central Avenue North, Suite 215, Minneapolis MN 55421. 612/789-4537. **Contact:** Office Manager. **Description:** An executive search firm. **Specializes in the areas of:** Computer Hardware/Software; Technical.

WILLIAMS EXECUTIVE SEARCH
4200 Norwest Center, 90 South 7th Street, Minneapolis MN 55402. 612/339-2900. **Contact:** Office Manager. **Description:** An executive search firm.

PERMANENT EMPLOYMENT AGENCIES

A&B PERSONNEL, INC.
101 East 5th Street, Suite 2206, St. Paul MN 55101-1808. 612/292-8519. **Fax:** 612/297-6454. **Contact:** Denise Reuss, President. **Description:** A permanent employment agency that places clerical and light industrial workers in temporary and permanent positions. Company pays fee. **Specializes in the areas of:** Industrial; Manufacturing; Secretarial. **Positions commonly filled include:** Blue-Collar Worker Supervisor; Brokerage Clerk; Buyer; Clerical Supervisor; Customer Service Representative; Machine Operator; Purchasing Agent/Manager; Typist/Word Processor; Warehouse/Distribution Worker. **Average salary range of placements:** $20,000 - $29,000.

ADVANTAGE PERSONNEL INC.
408 West 65th Street, Richfield MN 55423-1402. 612/861-9930. **Fax:** 612/861-9543. **Contact:** W. John Knopf II, General Manager. **Description:** A permanent employment agency focusing on the placement of light industrial workers. **Specializes in the areas of:** Industrial; Light Industrial. **Average salary range of placements:** Less than $20,000. **Number of placements per year:** 50 - 99.

AGRO QUALITY SEARCH INC.
7260 University Avenue NE, Suite 305, Fridley MN 55432-3129. 612/572-3737. **Fax:** 612/572-3738. **Contact:** Jerry L. Olson, President. **Description:** A permanent placement agency focusing on placements in agriculture and food industries. Company pays fee. **Specializes in the areas of:** Agriculture; Sales; Technical. **Positions commonly filled include:** Agricultural Engineer; Design Engineer; Food Scientist/Technologist; General Manager; Human Resources Specialist; Industrial Engineer; Manufacturer's/Wholesaler's Sales Rep.; Mechanical Engineer; Purchasing Agent/Manager; Transportation/ Traffic Specialist. **Average salary range of placements:** $30,000 - $50,000. **Number of placements per year:** 1 - 49.

ALTERNATIVE STAFFING, INC.
8120 Penn Avenue South, Suite 570, Bloomington MN 55431-1326. 612/888-6077. **Contact:** Kim Howard, President. **Description:** A permanent employment agency. Company pays fee. **Specializes in the areas of:** Accounting/Auditing; Clerical; Computer Hardware/Software; Legal; Manufacturing; Publishing; Sales; Secretarial. **Positions commonly filled include:** Accountant/Auditor; Administrative Assistant; Bookkeeper; Claim Representative; Clerk; Computer Programmer; Credit Manager; Customer Service Representative; Data Entry Clerk; Draftsperson; Factory Worker; Financial Analyst; Human Resources Manager; Legal Secretary; Light Industrial Worker; Marketing Specialist; Medical Secretary; Purchasing Agent/Manager; Receptionist; Sales Representative; Secretary; Stenographer; Typist/Word Processor. **Number of placements per year:** 1000+.

BARTZ ROGERS & PARTNERS
6465 Wayzata Boulevard, Minneapolis MN 55426. 612/936-0657. **Fax:** 612/936-0142. **Contact:** Douglas Bartz, Partner. **Description:** A permanent employment agency. Company pays fee. **Specializes in the areas of:** Computer Science/Software. **Positions commonly filled include:** Computer Programmer; Systems Analyst. **Number of placements per year:** 100 - 199.

DIVERSIFIED EMPLOYMENT INC.
5801 Duluth Street, Golden Valley MN 55422. 612/546-8255. **Fax:** 612/546-4106. **Contact:** Recruiter. **Description:** A permanent employment agency that also provides contract services and career counseling. Company pays fee. **Specializes in the areas of:** Accounting/Auditing; Administration; Advertising; Art/Design; Engineering; General Management; Industrial; Manufacturing; Publishing; Sales; Secretarial; Technical. **Positions commonly filled include:** Accountant/Auditor; Administrative Manager; Advertising Clerk; Automotive Mechanic; Blue-Collar Worker Supervisor; Buyer; Clerical Supervisor; Construction and Building Inspector; Counselor; Customer Service Representative; Design Engineer; Designer; Draftsperson; Electrical/Electronics Engineer; Electrician; Industrial Engineer; Industrial Production Manager; Mechanical Engineer; Multimedia Designer; Operations/Production Manager; Quality Control Supervisor; Restaurant/Food Service Manager; Software Engineer; Structural Engineer; Systems Analyst; Technical Writer/Editor; Typist/Word Processor; Underwriter/Assistant Underwriter. **Average salary range of placements:** $20,000 - $29,999. **Number of placements per year:** 200 - 499.

EMPLOYMENT ADVISORS
6600 France Avenue South, Suite 515, Edina MN 55435. 612/925-3666. **Toll-free phone:** 800/488-8634. **Fax:** 612/924-0111. **Contact:** Manager. **Description:** A permanent employment agency. **Specializes in the areas of:** Banking; Customer Service; General Management; Sales. **Number of placements per year:** 500 - 999.

EMPLOYMENT ADVISORS
526 Nicollet Mall, Suite 300, Minneapolis MN 55402-1008. 612/339-0521. **Toll-free phone:** 800/959-0521. **Fax:** 612/338-4757. **Contact:** Vicky Sherman, General Manager. **Description:** A permanent employment agency that focuses on the placement of college graduates in entry-level and mid-level business positions. **Specializes in the areas of:** Customer Service; Finance; General Management; Retail; Sales. **Positions commonly filled include:** Credit Manager; Customer Service Representative; Management Trainee; Public Relations Specialist; Restaurant/Food Service Manager; Sales Representative. **Average salary range of placements:** $20,000 - $29,999. **Number of placements per year:** 200 - 499.

EXPRESS PERSONNEL SERVICES
7101 France Avenue South, Edina MN 55435. 612/915-2000. **Contact:** Jim Johnson, Owner. **Description:** A permanent employment agency that places both temporary and permanent workers. Company pays fee. **Specializes in the areas of:** Industrial; Manufacturing; Personnel/Labor Relations; Secretarial. **Positions commonly filled include:** Accountant/Auditor; Administrative Manager; Blue-Collar Worker Supervisor; Branch Manager; Brokerage Clerk; Buyer; Claim Representative; Clerical Supervisor; Credit Manager; Customer Service Representative; General Manager; Human Resources Manager; MIS Specialist; Purchasing Agent/Manager; Quality Control Supervisor; Services Sales Representative; Technical Writer/Editor; Typist/Word Processor. **Benefits available to temporary workers:** Paid Holidays; Paid Vacation. **Corporate headquarters location:** Oklahoma City OK. **Average salary range of placements:** $20,000 - $29,999.

FINANCIAL STAFF RECRUITERS
1600 West 82nd Avenue, Bloomington MN 55431. 612/885-3040. **Contact:** Manager. **Description:** A permanent employment agency. **Specializes in the areas of:** Accounting/Auditing; Finance.

FIRSTAFF, INC.
3800 West 80th Street, Suite 1155, Bloomington MN 55431. 612/893-7555. **Fax:** 612/893-7550. **Contact:** Recruiter. **Description:** A permanent employment agency that also offers computer training courses. Company pays fee. **Specializes in the areas of:** Administration; Legal; Secretarial. **Positions commonly filled include:** Administrative Assistant; Bookkeeper; Claim Representative; Clerk; Customer Service Representative; Data Entry Clerk; Executive Assistant; Legal Secretary; Medical Secretary; Receptionist; Secretary; Typist/Word Processor. **Number of placements per year:** 1000+.

HEALTH PERSONNEL OPTIONS CORPORATION
2550 University Avenue West, Suite 315N, St. Paul MN 55114. 612/647-1160. **Fax:** 612/647-1903. **Contact:** Martin Kieffer, President. **Description:** A permanent employment agency focusing on the placement of health care professionals. Company pays fee. **Specializes in the areas of:** Health/Medical. **Positions commonly filled include:** Dental Assistant/Dental Hygienist; Dentist; EEG Technologist; EKG Technician; Health Services Manager; Licensed Practical Nurse; Medical Records Technician; Nuclear Medicine Technologist; Occupational Therapist; Physical Therapist; Physician; Radiological Technologist; Registered Nurse; Respiratory Therapist; Social Worker; Speech-Language Pathologist; Surgical Technician. **Other U.S. locations:** Nationwide. **Number of placements per year:** 100 - 199.

HUMAN RESOURCES PERSONNEL SERVICES
6800 France Avenue South, Suite 173, Edina MN 55435-2007. 612/929-3000. **Fax:** 612/927-4313. **Contact:** Susan Miller, Manager. **E-mail address:** hrps@hrsearch.com. **World Wide Web address:** http://www.hrsearch.com. **Description:** A permanent employment agency that focuses on the placement of human resources professionals. The agency also provides temporary placements. Company pays fee. **Specializes in the areas of:** Personnel/Labor Relations. **Positions commonly filled include:** Human Resources Manager.

KAPOSIA, INC.
380 East Lafayette Frontage Road South, St. Paul MN 55107-1216. 612/224-6974. **Fax:** 612/224-7249. **Contact:** Peg Ring, Human Resources/Administrative Assistant. **Description:** A permanent employment agency for individuals with developmental disabilities. **Specializes in the areas of:** Human Services; Nonprofit; Social Services. **Positions commonly filled include:** Accountant/Auditor; Counselor; Human Service Worker; Services Sales Representative. **Benefits available to temporary workers:** Paid Vacation. **Number of placements per year:** 1 - 49.

MANPOWER TECHNICAL SERVICES
3601 Minnesota Drive, Suite 450, Bloomington MN 55435. 612/820-0365. **Fax:** 612/820-0350. **Contact:** Manager. **Description:** A permanent employment agency. Company pays fee. **Specializes in the areas of:** Administration; Computer Science/Software; Engineering; Finance; Industrial; Manufacturing; Personnel/Labor Relations; Publishing; Technical. **Positions commonly filled include:** Accountant/Auditor; Administrative Manager; Bank Officer/Manager; Biochemist; Biological Scientist; Biomedical Engineer; Branch Manager; Broadcast Technician; Chemical Engineer; Computer Programmer; Credit Manager; Customer Service Representative; Design Engineer; Draftsperson; Editor; Electrical/Electronics Engineer; Environmental Engineer; Financial Analyst; Food Scientist/Technologist; Industrial Engineer; Industrial Production Manager; Insurance Agent/Broker; Internet Services Manager; Management Analyst/Consultant; Materials Engineer; Mechanical Engineer; MIS Specialist; Multimedia Designer; Operations/Production Manager; Paralegal; Physicist; Quality Control Supervisor; Software Engineer; Structural Engineer; Systems Analyst; Technical Writer/Editor; Typist/Word Processor; Underwriter/Assistant Underwriter; Video Production Coordinator. **Benefits available to temporary workers:** 401(k); Medical Insurance. **Corporate headquarters location:** Milwaukee WI. **Other U.S. locations:** Nationwide. **Average salary range of placements:** More than $50,000. **Number of placements per year:** 500 - 999.

MIDWEST FARM WORKERS EMPLOYMENT & TRAINING
P.O. Box 1231, St. Cloud MN 56302. 320/253-7010. **Contact:** Manager. **Description:** An employment agency that provides seasonal placements and training services for farm workers.

PALESCH & ASSOCIATES, INC.
530 Kristen Lane, Maple Plain MN 55359. 612/955-3390. **Contact:** Tom Palesch, President. **Description:** A permanent employment agency. Company pays fee. **Specializes in the areas of:** Metals. **Positions commonly filled include:** Operations/Production Manager. **Number of placements per year:** 50 - 99.

PROFESSIONAL ALTERNATIVES, INC.
15500 Wayzata Boulevard, Suite 819, Wayzata MN 55391. 612/404-2600. **Contact:** Vice President. **Description:** A full-service permanent employment agency focusing on placing mid- and upper-level professionals. Company pays fee. **Specializes in the areas of:** Accounting/Auditing; Advertising; Finance; General Management; Personnel/Labor Relations; Sales. **Positions commonly filled include:** Accountant/Auditor; Administrative Manager; Advertising Clerk; Bank Officer/Manager; Blue-Collar Worker Supervisor; Branch Manager; Buyer; Claim Representative; Clerical Supervisor; Computer Programmer; Credit Manager; Customer Service Representative; Financial Analyst; Financial Services Sales Representative; General Manager; Human Resources Manager; Management Analyst/Consultant; Manufacturer's/Wholesaler's Sales Rep.; Market Research Analyst; MIS Specialist; Operations/Production Manager; Property and Real Estate Manager; Public Relations Specialist; Purchasing Agent/Manager; Quality Control Supervisor; Securities Sales Representative; Services Sales Representative; Strategic Relations Manager; Systems Analyst; Telecommunications Manager. **Average salary range of placements:** $30,000 - $50,000. **Number of placements per year:** 50 - 99.

SECRETARY & ACCOUNTING SERVICE
50 West 2nd Street, Winona MN 55987-3440. 507/454-5804. **Fax:** 507/454-5804. **Contact:** Lucia Bartsh, Owner. **Description:** A permanent employment agency that places professionals for both permanent and temporary positions. Company pays fee. **Specializes in the areas of:** Accounting/Auditing; Secretarial. **Positions commonly filled include:** Accountant/Auditor; Administrative Manager; Clerical Supervisor; Computer Programmer; Draftsperson; General Manager; Human Resources Manager; Management Trainee; Medical Records Technician; MIS Specialist; Paralegal; Purchasing Agent/Manager; Software Engineer; Systems Analyst; Technical Writer/Editor; Typist/Word Processor. **Average salary range of placements:** $20,000 - $29,999. **Number of placements per year:** 50 - 99.

TECHNICAL RESOURCES, INC.
7460 Market Place Drive, Eden Prairie MN 55344-3634. 612/941-9441. **Toll-free phone:** 800/298-5627. **Fax:** 612/941-9440. **Contact:** Alice E. Riggs, Account Executive. **E-mail address:** tri@rsgi.com. **Description:** A permanent employment agency. Company pays fee. **Specializes in the areas of:** Computer Science/Software; Engineering; Food Industry; Industrial; Manufacturing; Technical. **Positions commonly filled include:** Aerospace Engineer; Architect; Buyer; Ceramics Engineer; Chemical Engineer; Chemist; Civil Engineer; Computer Programmer; Design Engineer; Designer; Draftsperson; Editor; Electrical/Electronics Engineer; Industrial Engineer; Industrial Production Manager; Materials Engineer; Mechanical Engineer; Metallurgical Engineer; MIS Specialist; Operations/Production Manager; Software Engineer; Statistician; Structural Engineer; Systems Analyst; Technical Writer/Editor. **Benefits available to temporary workers:** 401(k); Medical Insurance; Paid Vacation. **Average salary range of placements:** More than $50,000. **Number of placements per year:** 100 - 199.

ULTIMATE SEARCH UNLIMITED
TEMPS UNLIMITED
2233 University Avenue West, St. Paul MN 55114-1629. 612/649-3131. **Fax:** 612/649-3041. **Contact:** Robert H. Draack, Vice President/General Manager. **Description:** A permanent employment agency. Temps Unlimited (also at this location) provides temporary placements. Company pays fee. **Specializes in the areas of:** Administration; Banking; Engineering; Finance; Food Industry; General Management; Health/Medical; Legal; MIS/EDP; Sales; Secretarial. **Positions commonly filled include:** Account Manager;

Account Representative; Administrative Manager; Attorney; Bank Officer/Manager; Branch Manager; Certified Nursing Aide; Chief Financial Officer; Claim Representative; Computer Operator; Computer Programmer; Credit Manager; Customer Service Representative; Database Manager; Design Engineer; EEG Technologist; Electrical/Electronics Engineer; Emergency Medical Technician; Finance Director; Financial Analyst; Industrial Engineer; Industrial Production Manager; Insurance Agent/Broker; Licensed Practical Nurse; Occupational Therapist; Operations Manager; Paralegal; Pharmacist; Physical Therapist; Physician; Quality Control Supervisor; Registered Nurse; Respiratory Therapist; Sales Representative; Software Engineer; Speech-Language Pathologist; Surgical Technician; Telecommunications Manager; Typist/Word Processor. **Benefits available to temporary workers:** Paid Holidays; Paid Vacation. **Average salary range of placements:** $30,000 - $50,000. **Number of placements per year:** 200 - 499.

WEST EMPLOYMENT SOLUTIONS
112 North Third Street, Suite 201, Minneapolis MN 55401-1650. 612/338-8035. **Fax:** 612/338-8057. **Contact:** Don Westrum, President. **Description:** A permanent employment agency that focuses on the placement of recent college graduates in entry-level business trainee positions. Company pays fee. **Specializes in the areas of:** Banking; Finance; Food Industry; Retail; Sales; Secretarial; Transportation. **Positions commonly filled include:** Bank Officer/Manager; Branch Manager; Credit Manager; Customer Service Representative; Hotel Manager; Restaurant/Food Service Manager; Services Sales Representative. **Average salary range of placements:** $20,000 - $29,999. **Number of placements per year:** 200 - 499.

WHITNEY & ASSOCIATES, INC.
625 Kinnard Financial Center, 920 2nd Avenue South, Minneapolis MN 55402-4035. 612/338-5600. **Fax:** 612/349-6129. **Contact:** David L. Whitney, President. **E-mail address:** wa625@aol.com. **World Wide Web address:** http://www.whitneyinc.com. **Description:** A permanent employment agency focusing on the placement of accounting, financial, and bookkeeping professionals. Company pays fee. **Specializes in the areas of:** Accounting/Auditing; Bookkeeping; Finance; Tax. **Positions commonly filled include:** Accountant/Auditor; Accounting Clerk; Bookkeeper; Chief Financial Officer; Controller; Credit Manager; Financial Analyst. **Average salary range of placements:** $30,000 - $50,000. **Number of placements per year:** 200 - 499.

WORKING RELATIONSHIPS INC.
1405 Lilac Drive, Suite 150, Minneapolis MN 55422. 612/546-2999. **Fax:** 612/546-2898. **Contact:** Steven Bobzin, Recruiter. **World Wide Web address:** http://www.workingrelationships.com. **Description:** A permanent placement agency. Company pays fee. **Specializes in the areas of:** Accounting/Auditing; Administration; General Management; Sales; Secretarial. **Positions commonly filled include:** Administrative Assistant; Buyer; Customer Service Representative; Operations/Production Manager; Project Manager; Sales Representative; Secretary; Typist/Word Processor. **Average salary range of placements:** $20,000 - $29,999. **Number of placements per year:** 100 - 199.

YOUTH EMPLOYMENT PROJECT, INC.
Civic Drive Plaza, 300 11th Avenue NW, Suite 120, Rochester MN 55901. 507/252-2442. **Contact:** Nancy Wehseler, Executive Director. **Description:** A permanent employment agency. **Specializes in the areas of:** Agri-Business; Child Care, In-Home; Hotel/Restaurant; Office Support; Retail. **Positions commonly filled include:** Child Care Director; Retail Sales Worker. **Number of placements per year:** 1000+.

TEMPORARY EMPLOYMENT AGENCIES

ABBY BLU INC.
515 Foshay Tower, 821 Marquette Avenue, Minneapolis MN 55402. 612/338-3200. **Fax:** 612/349-2983. **Contact:** Manager. **Description:** A temporary and permanent placement agency that focuses on office support. Company pays fee. **Specializes in the areas of:** Accounting/Auditing; Advertising; Architecture/Construction; Banking; Computer Science/Software; General Management; Insurance; Legal; Manufacturing; Nonprofit; Personnel/Labor Relations; Secretarial. **Positions commonly filled include:** Accountant/Auditor; Claim Representative; Clerical Supervisor; Credit Manager; Customer Service Representative; Financial Analyst; Human Resources Specialist; Market Research Analyst; Medical Records Technician; Paralegal; Typist/Word Processor. **Benefits available to temporary workers:** 401(k); Paid Holidays; Paid Vacation. **Number of placements per year:** 1000+.

ADD ON STAFFING SOLUTIONS INC.
255 East Roselawn Avenue, Suite 50, St. Paul MN 55117. 612/488-1000. **Fax:** 612/488-9585. **Contact:** Sharon Murphy, President. **E-mail address:** skmurphy@mn.state.net. **Description:** A temporary agency that also provides contract services. Company pays fee. **Specializes in the areas of:** Accounting/Auditing; Administration; Banking; Finance; Light Industrial; Personnel/Labor Relations; Sales; Secretarial. **Positions commonly filled include:** Account Representative; Accountant/Auditor; Administrative Assistant; Advertising Clerk; Claim Representative; Clerical Supervisor; Computer Operator; Computer Programmer; Credit Manager; Customer Service Representative; Draftsperson; Electrical/Electronics Engineer; Electronics Technician; Medical Records Technician; Sales Representative; Software Engineer; Systems Analyst; Typist/Word Processor. **Benefits available to temporary workers:** Dental Insurance; Medical Insurance; Paid Holidays; Paid Vacation. **Number of placements per year:** 1000+.

ANSWER PERSONNEL SERVICE, INC.
220 Robert Street South, Suite 208, St. Paul MN 55107-1626. 612/293-1887. **Contact:** Bruce Labelle, Coordinator. **Description:** A temporary agency. **Specializes in the areas of:** Engineering; Food Industry; Industrial; Manufacturing. **Positions commonly filled include:** Clerical Supervisor; Computer Programmer. **Average salary range of placements:** $20,000 - $29,999. **Number of placements per year:** 500 - 999.

AWARD TEMPORARY SERVICES
6800 France Avenue South, Suite 173, Edina MN 55435-2004. 612/561-5444. **Contact:** Staffing Manager. **Description:** A temporary agency that also provides some permanent placements. **Specializes in the areas of:** Accounting/Auditing; Clerical; Data Entry; Industrial; Light Industrial; Office Support; Word Processing. **Positions commonly filled include:** Accounting Clerk.

DESIGN PERSONNEL RESOURCES INC.
3508 Lexington Avenue North, St. Paul MN 55126. 612/482-0075. **Contact:** Manager. **Description:** A

temporary and temp-to-hire agency. **Specializes in the areas of:** Architecture/Construction; Design.

ENVIROSTAFF, INC.
151 West Burnsville Parkway, Burnsville MN 55337. 612/894-6440. **Contact:** Manager. **Description:** A temporary agency. **Specializes in the areas of:** Environmental.

FLATLEY TECHNICAL SERVICES, INC.
3600 West 80th Street, Suite 535, Bloomington MN 55431. 612/896-3435. **Contact:** Ron Edlund, General Manager. **Description:** A temporary agency. **Specializes in the areas of:** Architecture/Construction; Consulting; Engineering; Manufacturing; Materials; Publishing; Technical. **Positions commonly filled include:** Architect; Architectural Engineer; Civil Engineer; Designer; Draftsperson; Electrical/Electronics Engineer; Industrial Engineer; Manufacturing Engineer; Mechanical Engineer; Production Manager; Purchasing Agent/Manager; Quality Control Supervisor; Software Engineer; Structural Engineer; Technical Illustrator; Technical Writer/Editor; Technician. **Number of placements per year:** 500 - 999.

GRAPHIC STAFFING INC.
5801 Duluth Street, Suite 104, Minneapolis MN 55422. 612/546-1292. **Fax:** 612/546-7822. **Contact:** Wayne Gorian, President. **E-mail address:** cptgraphic@aol.com. **World Wide Web address:** http://www.graphicstaffing.com. **Description:** A temporary and temp-to-perm agency. **Specializes in the areas of:** Advertising; Art/Design; Publishing. **Positions commonly filled include:** Advertising Clerk; Computer Animator; Graphic Artist; Graphic Designer; Video Production Coordinator; Webmaster. **Other U.S. locations:** Chicago IL. **Average salary range of placements:** $30,000 - $50,000. **Number of placements per year:** 100 - 199.

INTERIM LEGAL PROFESSIONALS
80 South 8th Street, Suite 3630, Minneapolis MN 55402. 612/339-7663. **Fax:** 612/339-9274. **Contact:** Pamela Lynch, Branch Manager. **Description:** A temporary agency that places legal professionals. Company pays fee. **Specializes in the areas of:** Legal. **Positions commonly filled include:** Attorney; Paralegal. **Benefits available to temporary workers:** Dental Insurance; Medical Insurance; Vision Insurance. **Corporate headquarters location:** Fort Lauderdale FL. **Average salary range of placements:** $30,000 - $50,000. **Number of placements per year:** 500 - 999.

JOHNSON TEMPORARIES, INC.
1396 White Bear Avenue North, Suite A, St. Paul MN 55106. 612/774-5843. **Contact:** Dana Johnson, Director. **Description:** A temporary agency that also provides some permanent placements of health care workers. Company pays fee. **Specializes in the areas of:** Health/Medical. **Positions commonly filled include:** Counselor; Human Service Worker; Psychologist; Recreational Therapist; Registered Nurse; Social Worker. **Average salary range of placements:** $20,000 - $29,999. **Number of placements per year:** 200 - 499.

KELLY SCIENTIFIC RESOURCES
6464 Wayzata Boulevard, Suite 155, St. Louis Park MN 55426. 612/797-0500. **Fax:** 612/797-0611. **Contact:** Branch Manager. **World Wide Web address:** http://www.kellyscientific.com. **Description:** A temporary agency for scientific professionals. **Specializes in the areas of:** Biomedical; Chemical; Food Industry; Pharmaceutical.

LYNN TEMPORARY
1821 University Avenue West, Suite 106S, St. Paul MN 55104-2801. 612/645-9233. **Contact:** Carol Glewwe, President. **Description:** A temporary agency that focuses on clerical, technical, and professional placements. **Specializes in the areas of:** Computer Science/Software; Engineering; Nonprofit; Personnel/Labor Relations; Publishing; Secretarial; Technical. **Positions commonly filled include:** Accountant/Auditor; Administrative Manager; Architect; Biomedical Engineer; Chemical Engineer; Clerical Supervisor; Computer Programmer; Customer Service Representative; Design Engineer; Designer; Draftsperson; Editor; Electrical/Electronics Engineer; Library Technician; Mechanical Engineer; Medical Records Technician; MIS Specialist; Software Engineer; Systems Analyst; Technical Writer/Editor; Typist/Word Processor; Video Production Coordinator. **Average salary range of placements:** $20,000 - $29,999. **Number of placements per year:** 200 - 499.

MANPOWER TEMPORARY SERVICES
150 South Fifth Street, Suite 336, Minneapolis MN 55401. 612/375-9200. **Contact:** Branch Manager. **Description:** A temporary agency. Company pays fee. **Specializes in the areas of:** Data Processing; Industrial; Secretarial; Technical; Telephone Technical Support; Word Processing. **Positions commonly filled include:** Accountant/Auditor; Accounting Clerk; Administrative Assistant; Assembly Worker; Biological Scientist; Bookkeeper; Customer Service Manager; Desktop Publishing Specialist; Electrician; Inspector/Tester/Grader; Inventory Control Specialist; Packaging/Processing Worker; Painter; Project Engineer; Proofreader; Receptionist; Research Assistant; Secretary; Software Engineer; Systems Analyst; Technical Writer/Editor; Telemarketer; Transcriptionist; Typist/Word Processor; Welder. **Benefits available to temporary workers:** Life Insurance; Medical Insurance; Paid Holidays; Paid Vacation.

MIDWEST STAFFING SERVICES
7900 Xerxes Avenue South, Suite 910, Bloomington MN 55431-1106. 612/896-2055. **Fax:** 612/896-2059. **Contact:** Director of Operations. **Description:** A temporary agency. **Specializes in the areas of:** Accounting/Auditing; Legal; Manufacturing; Personnel/Labor Relations; Secretarial. **Positions commonly filled include:** Claim Representative; Clerical Supervisor; Customer Service Representative; General Manager; Human Resources Manager; Librarian; Medical Records Technician; Paralegal; Public Relations Specialist; Typist/Word Processor. **Average salary range of placements:** $20,000 - $29,999.

THOMAS MOORE INC.
608 2nd Avenue South, Suite 465, Minneapolis MN 55402-1907. 612/338-4884. **Contact:** Recruiter. **Description:** A temporary agency. Company pays fee. **Specializes in the areas of:** Accounting/Auditing; Banking; Finance. **Positions commonly filled include:** Accountant/Auditor; Budget Analyst; Credit Manager; Financial Analyst. **Benefits available to temporary workers:** Paid Holidays; Paid Vacation.

STAFF IT PERSONNEL SERVICES
526 Nicollet Mall, Minneapolis MN 55402. 612/339-7085. **Fax:** 612/338-4757. **Contact:** Alison Riedel, Manager. **Description:** A temporary agency that also provides temp-to-perm and permanent placements. Company pays fee. **Specializes in the areas of:** Accounting/Auditing; Finance; Retail; Secretarial. **Positions commonly filled include:** Accountant/Auditor; Administrative Assistant; Clerical Supervisor; Customer Service Representative; Secretary; Typist/Word Processor. **Benefits available to temporary workers:** Bonus Award/Plan; Medical Insurance; Paid Vacation. **Average salary range of placements:** $20,000 - $29,999. **Number of placements per year:** 200 - 499.

TEMP FORCE
6550 York Avenue South, Suite 640, Edina MN 55435. 612/920-9119. **Contact:** Office Manager. **Description:** A temporary agency. Company pays fee. **Specializes in the areas of:** Industrial; Secretarial; Technical.

JEAN THORNE INC.
336 North Robert Street, Suite 100, St. Paul MN 55101. 612/298-0400. **Fax:** 612/298-0448. **Contact:** Christine Kelleher, Recruitment Manager. **Description:** A temporary agency. **Specializes in the areas of:** Accounting/Auditing; Banking; Office Support; Secretarial. **Positions commonly filled include:** Accountant; Administrative Assistant; Customer Service Representative. **Benefits available to temporary workers:** Dental Insurance; Life Insurance; Medical Insurance; Referral Bonus Plan. **Other area locations:** Mankato MN. **Other U.S. locations:** Fargo ND.

CONTRACT SERVICES FIRMS

CDI CORPORATION
5775 Wayzata Boulevard, Suite 875, St. Louis Park MN 55416. 612/541-9967. **Fax:** 612/541-9605. **Contact:** Manager. **World Wide Web address:** http://www.cdicorp.com. **Description:** A contract services firm. **Specializes in the areas of:** Technical. **Corporate headquarters location:** Philadelphia PA. **Other U.S. locations:** Nationwide. **International locations:** Worldwide.

CDI CORPORATION
1915 Highway 52 North, Suite 222-B, Rochester MN 55901. **Toll-free phone:** 888/686-8979. **Contact:** Manager. **World Wide Web address:** http://www.cdicorp.com. **Description:** A contract services firm. **Specializes in the areas of:** Engineering; Technical. **Corporate headquarters location:** Philadelphia PA. **Other U.S. locations:** Nationwide. **International locations:** Worldwide.

COMPUTEMP, INC.
8500 Normandale Lake Boulevard, Suite 1670, Bloomington MN 55437. 612/921-8866. **Contact:** Manager. **Description:** A contract services firm. **Specializes in the areas of:** Information Technology.

HUMAN RESOURCE STAFFING, INC.
7242 Metro Boulevard, Minneapolis MN 55439. 612/835-5550. **Fax:** 612/835-7294. **Contact:** Cindy Ridley, Recruiter. **Description:** A contract services firm that places human resource consultants and professionals. Company pays fee. **Specializes in the areas of:** Personnel/Labor Relations. **Positions commonly filled include:** Human Resources Manager; Recruiter. **Benefits available to temporary workers:** 401(k); Dental Insurance; Medical Insurance; Paid Holidays; Paid Vacation. **Average salary range of placements:** $30,000 - $50,000. **Number of placements per year:** 1 - 49.

LABORATORY RESOURCES INC.
7460 Market Place Drive, Eden Prairie MN 55344. 612/941-9441. **Toll-free phone:** 800/298-5627. **Fax:** 612/941-9440. **Contact:** Account Manager. **E-mail address:** lri@rsgi.com. **Description:** A contract services firm. Company pays fee. **Specializes in the areas of:** Biology; Technical. **Positions commonly filled include:** Biological Scientist; Biomedical Engineer; Chemical Engineer; Chemist; Clinical Lab Technician; Food Scientist/Technologist; Forester/Conservation Scientist; Geologist/Geophysicist; Quality Control Supervisor; Science Technologist. **Benefits available to temporary workers:** 401(k); Dental Insurance; Medical Insurance; Paid Holidays; Paid Vacation. **Average salary range of placements:** $30,000 - $50,000. **Number of placements per year:** 50 - 99.

PRECISION DESIGN, INC.
15-10th Avenue South, Suite 102, Hopkins MN 55343-7561. 612/933-6550. **Fax:** 612/933-0344. **Contact:** Larry Helgerson, President. **World Wide Web address:** http://www.mn-job.com/precisiondecision/index.html. **Description:** A contract services firm. Company pays fee. **Specializes in the areas of:** Engineering. **Positions commonly filled include:** Design Engineer; Draftsperson; Electrical/Electronics Engineer; Industrial Engineer; Manufacturing Engineer; Mechanical Engineer; Software Engineer; Technical Writer/Editor. **Benefits available to temporary workers:** 401(k); Medical Insurance; Paid Holidays; Paid Vacation. **Average salary range of placements:** More than $50,000. **Number of placements per year:** 100 - 199.

PROVISION TECHNOLOGIES
4550 West 77th Street, Suite 224, Minneapolis MN 55435. 612/806-0700. **Fax:** 612/806-0678. **Contact:** Manager. **World Wide Web address:** http://www.careerbase.com. **Description:** A contract services firm. **Specializes in the areas of:** Computer Science/Software; Information Technology.

SOURCE SERVICES CORPORATION
8500 Normandale Lake Boulevard, Suite 2160, Bloomington MN 55437-3833. 612/835-5100. **Fax:** 612/835-1548. **Contact:** Recruiter. **E-mail address:** weibyek@sourcesvc.com. **World Wide Web address:** http://www.dlinc.com. **Description:** A contract services firm that also offers temporary placements. The firm focuses on placing accountants and computer professionals. Company pays fee. **Specializes in the areas of:** Accounting/Auditing; Computer Science/Software; Secretarial. **Positions commonly filled include:** Accountant/Auditor; Budget Analyst; Computer Programmer; Financial Analyst; MIS Specialist; Software Engineer; Systems Analyst; Telecommunications Manager; Typist/Word Processor. **Benefits available to temporary workers:** Medical Insurance; Paid Vacation; Profit Sharing. **Corporate headquarters location:** Dallas TX. **Other U.S. locations:** Nationwide. **Average salary range of placements:** $30,000 - $50,000. **Number of placements per year:** 200 - 499.

STROM AVIATION
10501 Wayzata Boulevard, Minnetonka MN 55305. 612/544-3611. **Toll-free phone:** 800/743-8988. **Fax:** 612/544-3948. **Contact:** Lead Recruiter. **Description:** A contract services firm that provides experienced aircraft maintenance personnel to heavy maintenance overhaul repair stations for all types of aircraft. Company pays fee. **Positions commonly filled include:** Aircraft Mechanic/Engine Specialist. **Benefits available to temporary workers:** Paid Holidays; Paid Vacation. **Corporate headquarters location:** Minneapolis MN. **Other U.S. locations:** Tempe AZ; Dallas TX. **Average salary range of placements:** $20,000 - $29,999.

SYSDYNE CORPORATION
1660 South Highway 100, Suite 424, Minneapolis MN 55416-1533. 612/541-9889. **Toll-free phone:** 888/797-3963. **Fax:** 612/541-9887. **Contact:** Jannie Crabtree Higgins, Recruiter. **E-mail address:** techjobs@sysdyne.com. **World Wide Web address:** http://www.sysdyne.com. **Description:** A contract services firm that provides professional technical staffing. **Specializes in the areas of:** Computer Science/Software; Engineering. **Positions commonly**

filled include: Biomedical Engineer; Computer Programmer; Design Engineer; Draftsperson; Electrical/Electronics Engineer; Mechanical Engineer; MIS Specialist; Sales Engineer; Software Engineer; Technical Writer/Editor. **Benefits available to temporary workers:** 401(k); Cafeteria; Savings Plan. **Average salary range of placements:** $30,000 - $50,000. **Number of placements per year:** 50 - 99.

WORK PLACE SOLUTIONS
7900 Xerxes Avenue South, Suite 910, Bloomington MN 55431-1123. **Contact:** Mr. Kelly Hester, General Manager. **Description:** A contract services firm. Company pays fee. **Specializes in the areas of:** Computer Science/Software; Engineering; Manufacturing. **Positions commonly filled include:** Architect; Civil Engineer; Computer Programmer; Draftsperson; Electrical/Electronics Engineer; Industrial Engineer; Quality Control Supervisor; Software Engineer; Structural Engineer; Systems Analyst. **Average salary range of placements:** $30,000 - $50,000. **Number of placements per year:** 100 - 199.

H.L. YOH COMPANY
2626 East 82nd Street, Suite 355, Bloomington MN 55425. 612/854-2400. **Toll-free phone:** 888/243-3557. **Fax:** 612/854-0512. **Contact:** Linda Eisenzimmer, Technical Recruiter. **E-mail address:** lindayoh@skypoint.com. **Description:** A contract services firm. **Specializes in the areas of:** Computer Science/Software; Engineering; Industrial; Technical. **Positions commonly filled include:** Administrative Assistant; Buyer; Chemical Engineer; Chemist; Computer Operator; Computer Programmer; Database Manager; Design Engineer; Draftsperson; Electrical/Electronics Engineer; Environmental Engineer; Graphic Artist; Graphic Designer; Industrial Engineer; Industrial Production Manager; Manufacturing Engineer; Mechanical Engineer; Metallurgical Engineer; Operations Manager; Project Manager; Purchasing Agent/Manager; Quality Control Supervisor; Secretary; Software Engineer; Systems Analyst; Systems Manager; Technical Writer/Editor; Typist/Word Processor. **Benefits available to temporary workers:** 401(k); Credit Union; Disability Coverage; Medical Insurance. **Corporate headquarters location:** Philadelphia PA. **Other U.S. locations:** Nationwide. **International locations:** China. **Average salary range of placements:** $30,000 - $50,000. **Number of placements per year:** 200 - 499.

CAREER/OUTPLACEMENT COUNSELING FIRMS

ALLEN & ASSOCIATES
6600 France Avenue South, Suite 615, Minneapolis MN 55435. 612/925-9646. **Toll-free phone:** 800/562-7925. **Fax:** 612/925-9662. **Contact:** Manager. **World Wide Web address:** http://www.allenandassociates.com. **Description:** A career/outplacement counseling firm. **Corporate headquarters location:** Maitland FL. **Other U.S. locations:** Nationwide.

QUALITY OFFICE SERVICES
12710 Falcon Court North, White Bear Lake MN 55110. 612/426-2516. **Contact:** Mrs. Lois M. Rather, Owner. **Description:** A professional resume writing service.

WORKING OPPORTUNITIES FOR WOMEN
2700 University Avenue West, Suite 12, St. Paul MN 55114. 612/647-9961. **Contact:** Yvette Oldendorf, Executive Director. **Description:** A career/outplacement counseling firm for women.

MISSISSIPPI

EXECUTIVE SEARCH FIRMS

DUNHILL OF MADISON
P.O. Box 1218, Madison MS 39130. 228/865-4095. **Contact:** Manager. **Description:** An executive search firm.

DUNHILL PROFESSIONAL SEARCH OF JACKSON
13 North Town Drive, Suite 220, Jackson MS 39211. 601/956-1060. **Contact:** Manager. **Description:** An executive search firm. **Specializes in the areas of:** Accounting/Auditing; Computer Hardware/Software; Engineering.

IMPACT PERSONNEL SERVICES
212 Haddon Circle, Brandon MS 39042-8046. 601/992-1591. **Fax:** 601/992-5037. **Contact:** Jan Prystupa, Owner. **Description:** A service-oriented executive search firm offering nationwide and worldwide placements. Company pays fee. **Specializes in the areas of:** Administration; Computer Science/Software; Engineering; General Management; Industrial; Manufacturing; Personnel/Labor Relations. **Positions commonly filled include:** Chemical Engineer; Civil Engineer; Computer Programmer; Design Engineer; Designer; Draftsperson; Electrical/Electronics Engineer; General Manager; Human Resources Manager; Industrial Engineer; Industrial Production Manager; Internet Services Manager; Mechanical Engineer; Metallurgical Engineer; MIS Specialist; Petroleum Engineer; Physical Therapist; Physician; Quality Control Supervisor; Structural Engineer; Systems Analyst; Technical Writer/Editor; Telecommunications Manager. **Number of placements per year:** 50 - 99.

MANAGEMENT RECRUITERS INTERNATIONAL
1755 Clelia Drive, Suite 102, Jackson MS 39216. 601/366-4488. **Contact:** Manager. **Description:** An executive search firm. **Specializes in the areas of:** Accounting/Auditing; Data Processing; Engineering.

MANAGEMENT RECRUITERS OF JACKSON
2506 Lakeland Drive, Suite 408, Jackson MS 39208-9752. 601/936-7900. **Fax:** 601/936-9004. **Contact:** Mike Van Wick, President. **Description:** An executive search firm focusing on providing human resource solutions. The firm focuses on in technical and operations recruitment. Company pays fee. **Specializes in the areas of:** Food Industry. **Positions commonly filled include:** Biochemist; Chemical Engineer; Chemist; Design Engineer; Draftsperson; Electrical/Electronics Engineer; Environmental Engineer; Food Scientist/Technologist; General Manager; Human Resources Specialist; Industrial Engineer; Industrial Production Manager; Mechanical Engineer; Operations/Production Manager; Quality Control Supervisor. **Corporate headquarters location:** Cleveland OH. **Other U.S. locations:** Nationwide. **Average salary range of placements:** More than $50,000. **Number of placements per year:** 50 - 99.

PERSONNEL UNLIMITED
P.O. Box 686, Amory MS 38821-0686. 601/256-1462. **Contact:** Ken Lawrence, President. **Description:** An executive search firm. Company pays fee. **Specializes in the areas of:** Accounting/Auditing; Engineering; Industrial; Manufacturing; Personnel/Labor Relations. **Positions commonly filled include:** Accountant/Auditor; Clerical Supervisor; Clinical Lab Technician; Computer Programmer; Credit Manager; Customer Service Representative; Design Engineer; Draftsperson; Environmental Engineer; Human Resources Specialist; Industrial Engineer; Industrial Production Manager; Mechanical Engineer; Metallurgical Engineer; Purchasing Agent/Manager; Software Engineer; Systems Analyst; Typist/Word Processor. **Average salary range of placements:** $30,000 - $50,000. **Number of placements per year:** 50 - 99.

JIM WOODSON & ASSOCIATES
1080 River Oaks Drive, Suite B-102, Jackson MS 39208. 601/936-4037. **Contact:** Jim Woodson, President. **Description:** An executive search firm. Company pays fee. **Specializes in the areas of:** Accounting/Auditing; Engineering; Manufacturing. **Positions commonly filled include:** Accountant/Auditor; Chemist; Construction Contractor; Cost Estimator; Electrical/Electronics Engineer; Industrial Engineer; Mechanical Engineer; Metallurgical Engineer. **Number of placements per year:** 1 - 49.

PERMANENT EMPLOYMENT AGENCIES

AAA EMPLOYMENT
1775 Lelia Drive, Suite B, Jackson MS 39216-4836. 601/362-5423. **Contact:** Gwen Hatton, Administrator/Consultant. **Description:** A full-service permanent employment agency that handles permanent and temporary placements in a wide variety of fields. Founded in 1957. **Corporate headquarters location:** Clearwater FL. **Average salary range of placements:** $20,000 - $40,000. **Number of placements per year:** 1000+.

ANDRUS ASSOCIATES INC.
dba SERVICE SPECIALISTS LTD.
500 Greymont Avenue, Suite A, Jackson MS 39202-3446. 601/948-8980. **Fax:** 601/948-8983. **Contact:** Elva Giddings, President. **Description:** A full-service permanent employment agency offering permanent, temporary, and temp-to-hire placements. The firm also provides career/outplacement counseling. Company pays fee. **Specializes in the areas of:** Accounting/Auditing; Administration; Banking; Computer Science/Software; Engineering; Finance; Industrial; Manufacturing; Personnel/Labor Relations; Sales; Secretarial. **Positions commonly filled include:** Accountant/Auditor; Adjuster; Administrative Manager; Blue-Collar Worker Supervisor; Buyer; Chemical Engineer; Computer Programmer; Design Engineer; Draftsperson; Environmental Engineer; Financial Analyst; Human Resources Specialist; Industrial Engineer; Industrial Production Manager; Management Trainee; Mechanical Engineer; Purchasing Agent/Manager; Services Sales Representative; Typist/Word Processor. **Average salary range of placements:** $30,000 - $50,000. **Number of placements per year:** 100 - 199.

CAPITOL STAFFING SOLUTIONS
460 Briarwood Drive, Suite 100, Jackson MS 39206. 601/957-1755. **Fax:** 601/957-3880. **Contact:** Carolyn Harrison, Certified Personnel Consultant. **Description:** A permanent employment agency that also offers temporary and temp-to-perm placements. Company pays fee. **Specializes in the areas of:** Accounting/Auditing; Clerical; Insurance; Legal; Office Support; Sales; Secretarial. **Positions commonly filled include:** Accountant/Auditor; Administrative Assistant; Bank Officer/Manager; Bookkeeper; Claim Representative; Clerk; Computer Programmer; Credit

Manager; Customer Service Representative; Data Entry Clerk; General Manager; Human Resources Manager; Legal Secretary; Marketing Specialist; Medical Secretary; Paralegal; Public Relations Specialist; Purchasing Agent/Manager; Secretary; Stenographer; Systems Analyst; Technical Writer/Editor; Typist/Word Processor; Underwriter/ Assistant Underwriter. **Average salary range of placements:** Less than $20,000. **Number of placements per year:** 200 - 499.

COATS & COATS PERSONNEL
P.O. Box 1009, Meridian MS 39302. 601/693-2991. **Fax:** 601/693-9983. **Contact:** Tom Coats, Owner. **Description:** A permanent employment agency that focuses on technical placements in aerospace, industrial, and professional areas. Founded in 1968. Company pays fee. **Specializes in the areas of:** Accounting/Auditing; Computer Science/Software; Engineering; Food Industry; General Management; Industrial; Manufacturing; Personnel/Labor Relations; Retail; Sales; Secretarial; Technical. **Positions commonly filled include:** Accountant/Auditor; Aerospace Engineer; Blue-Collar Worker Supervisor; Branch Manager; Chemical Engineer; Civil Engineer; Computer Programmer; Counselor; Credit Manager; Design Engineer; Draftsperson; Electrical/Electronics Engineer; Environmental Engineer; General Manager; Human Resources Specialist; Industrial Engineer; Industrial Production Manager; Internet Services Manager; Management Trainee; Manufacturer's/ Wholesaler's Sales Rep.; Mechanical Engineer; Medical Records Technician; MIS Specialist; Paralegal; Registered Nurse; Restaurant/Food Service Manager; Software Engineer; Speech-Language Pathologist; Typist/Word Processor. **Average salary range of placements:** Over $25,000. **Number of placements per year:** 500 - 999.

LABORCHEX COMPANIES
1985 Lakeland Drive, Jackson MS 39216. 601/362-0366. **Toll-free phone:** 800/880-0366. **Fax:** 601/981-2722. **Toll-free fax:** 800/844-2722. **Contact:** Steven J. Austin, Director of Communications. **Description:** A permanent employment agency. Founded in 1985. **Specializes in the areas of:** Manufacturing; Secretarial. **Positions commonly filled include:** Administrative Manager; Credit Manager; Customer Service Representative; General Manager; Human Resources Specialist; Industrial Production Manager; Purchasing Agent/Manager; Quality Control Supervisor; Restaurant/Food Service Manager; Typist/Word Processor. **Average salary range of placements:** $20,000 - $29,999. **Number of placements per year:** 200 - 499.

MISSISSIPPI STATE EMPLOYMENT SERVICES
P.O. Box 640, Clarksdale MS 38614. 601/627-1842. **Physical address:** 620 South State Street, Clarksdale MS. **Contact:** Alfred Jones, Office Manager. **Description:** Operates the state job program. **Specializes in the areas of:** Advertising; Education; Nonprofit; Personnel/Labor Relations. **Positions commonly filled include:** Blue-Collar Worker Supervisor; Claim Representative; Electrician; Human Service Worker; Management Trainee; Social Worker; Teacher/ Professor. **Corporate headquarters location:** Jackson MS. **Average salary range of placements:** $20,000 - $29,999. **Number of placements per year:** 1000+.

OPPORTUNITIES UNLIMITED
P.O. Box 1518, Pascagoula MS 39568. 228/762-8068. **Physical address:** 3903 Market Street, Pascagoula MS. **Contact:** Bob Dubose, Manager. **Description:** A permanent employment agency. **Specializes in the areas of:** Accounting/Auditing; Clerical; Computer Hardware/Software; Engineering; Finance; Manufacturing; Technical. **Positions commonly filled include:** Aerospace Engineer; Buyer; Chemical Engineer; Civil Engineer; Computer Programmer; EDP Specialist; Electrical/Electronics Engineer; Financial Analyst; Human Resources Manager; Industrial Engineer; Legal Secretary; Mechanical Engineer; Metallurgical Engineer; MIS Specialist; Nurse; Occupational Therapist; Petroleum Engineer; Physician; Physicist; Quality Control Supervisor; Receptionist; Secretary; Systems Analyst; Technical Writer/Editor; Typist/Word Processor. **Number of placements per year:** 50 - 99.

RECRUITMENT & TRAINING OF MISSISSIPPI, INC.
P.O. Box 1461, Columbus MS 39703. 601/328-8037. **Fax:** 601/328-8037. **Contact:** Kelly Floyd, Vice President. **Description:** A permanent employment agency. Founded in 1988. **Specializes in the areas of:** Administration; Broadcasting; Education; General Management; Health/Medical; Legal; Manufacturing; Nonprofit; Personnel/Labor Relations; Retail; Sales; Secretarial; Technical; Transportation. **Positions commonly filled include:** Administrative Manager; Broadcast Technician; Claim Representative; Clerical Supervisor; Computer Programmer; Customer Service Representative; Education Administrator; Electrician; Financial Analyst; Food Scientist/Technologist; General Manager; Health Services Manager; Hotel Manager; Human Resources Specialist; Human Service Worker; Librarian; Management Trainee; Occupational Therapist; Paralegal; Physical Therapist; Purchasing Agent/Manager; Services Sales Representative; Social Worker; Systems Analyst; Teacher/Professor; Technical Writer/Editor; Telecommunications Manager; Transportation/Traffic Specialist; Typist/Word Processor. **Average salary range of placements:** Less than $20,000. **Number of placements per year:** 100 - 199.

TATUM PERSONNEL INC.
293 Highland Village, Jackson MS 39211. 601/362-3135. **Fax:** 601/981-5995. **Contact:** Lauren Thigpen, Office Manager. **Description:** A permanent employment agency offering permanent and temporary placements. **Specializes in the areas of:** Administration; Computer Science/Software; Engineering; Insurance; Manufacturing; Sales; Secretarial. **Positions commonly filled include:** Accountant/Auditor; Bank Officer/Manager; Buyer; Chemical Engineer; Civil Engineer; Claim Representative; Clerical Supervisor; Computer Programmer; Cost Estimator; Credit Manager; Customer Service Representative; Draftsperson; Electrical/Electronics Engineer; Human Resources Manager; Industrial Engineer; Industrial Production Manager; Management Trainee; Manufacturer's/ Wholesaler's Sales Rep.; Mechanical Engineer; Operations/Production Manager; Paralegal; Purchasing Agent/Manager; Quality Control Supervisor; Restaurant/Food Service Manager; Securities Sales Representative; Services Sales Representative; Software Engineer; Structural Engineer; Systems Analyst; Underwriter/Assistant Underwriter.

TEMPORARY EMPLOYMENT AGENCIES

COLUMBUS PERSONNEL INC.
105 5th Street North, Suite 201, Columbus MS 39701-4551. 601/328-1042. **Contact:** Mark A. Smith, Vice President. **Description:** A temporary agency that also provides temp-to-perm, planned staffing programs, and permanent placements. Company pays fee. **Specializes in the areas of:** Industrial; Manufacturing; Secretarial. **Positions**

commonly filled include: Blue-Collar Worker Supervisor; Customer Service Representative; Typist/Word Processor. **Benefits available to temporary workers:** Life Insurance; Medical Insurance; Paid Holidays; Paid Vacation. **Average salary range of placements:** $20,000 - $29,999. **Number of placements per year:** 1000+.

EPSCO PERSONNEL SERVICE, INC.
P.O. Box 5172, Columbus MS 39704. 601/327-2505. **Contact:** Cora Perkins, Manager. **Description:** A temporary agency. EPSCO provides temporary, temp-to-hire, and permanent placements. Founded in 1987. Company pays fee. **Specializes in the areas of:** Accounting/Auditing; Banking; Computer Science/Software; Engineering; Food Industry; Industrial; Legal; Light Industrial; Manufacturing; Personnel/Labor Relations; Sales; Secretarial; Technical. **Positions commonly filled include:** Accountant/Auditor; Blue-Collar Worker Supervisor; Customer Service Representative; Electrician; Human Resources Specialist; Industrial Engineer; Industrial Production Manager; Operations/Production Manager; Quality Control Supervisor; Restaurant/Food Service Manager; Services Sales Representative; Surveyor; Transportation/Traffic Specialist; Typist/Word Processor. **Benefits available to temporary workers:** Medical Insurance. **Corporate headquarters location:** Tupelo MS. **Other U.S. locations:** AL; GA; TN. **Average salary range of placements:** Less than $20,000. **Number of placements per year:** 500 - 999.

EPSCO PERSONNEL SERVICE, INC.
2944 Terry Road, Jackson MS 39212-3055. 601/372-3787. **Fax:** 601/372-1199. **Contact:** Linda Edwards, Manager. **Description:** A temporary agency. Founded in 1987. **Specializes in the areas of:** Accounting/Auditing; Engineering; General Management; Industrial; Manufacturing; Personnel/Labor Relations; Sales; Secretarial. **Positions commonly filled include:** Accountant/Auditor; Administrative Manager; Blue-Collar Worker Supervisor; Branch Manager; Buyer; Chemical Engineer; Computer Programmer; Customer Service Representative; Electrical/Electronics Engineer; Financial Analyst; General Manager; Hotel Manager; Human Resources Specialist; Industrial Engineer; Industrial Production Manager; Management Analyst/Consultant; Management Trainee; Mechanical Engineer; Operations/Production Manager; Purchasing Agent/Manager; Quality Control Supervisor; Restaurant/Food Service Manager; Typist/Word Processor. **Benefits available to temporary workers:** 401(k); Dental Insurance; Medical Insurance; Paid Holidays; Paid Vacation. **Corporate headquarters location:** Tupelo MS. **Other U.S. locations:** AL; GA; TN. **Number of placements per year:** 100 - 199.

EPSCO PERSONNEL SERVICE, INC.
806 East Waldron Street, Suite B, Corinth MS 38834-4951. 601/286-8066. **Fax:** 601/286-8042. **Contact:** Manager. **Description:** A temporary employment agency. Founded in 1987. Company pays fee. **Specializes in the areas of:** Personnel/Labor Relations. **Positions commonly filled include:** Clerical Supervisor; Clinical Lab Technician; Computer Programmer; Industrial Production Manager; Purchasing Agent/Manager; Real Estate Agent; Restaurant/Food Service Manager; Systems Analyst; Technical Writer/Editor; Typist/Word Processor. **Corporate headquarters location:** Tupelo MS. **Other U.S. locations:** AL; GA; TN. **Average salary range of placements:** Less than $20,000. **Number of placements per year:** 200 - 499.

NORRELL STAFFING SERVICES
8912 Mid South Avenue, Olive Branch MS 38654. 601/895-5500. **Fax:** 601/895-8443. **Contact:** Customer Service Manager. **Description:** A temporary agency. **Specializes in the areas of:** Accounting/Auditing; Distribution; Manufacturing; Personnel/Labor Relations. **Benefits available to temporary workers:** Medical Insurance; Paid Holidays; Paid Vacation. **Corporate headquarters location:** Atlanta GA. **Other U.S. locations:** Nationwide. **Average salary range of placements:** Less than $20,000. **Number of placements per year:** 1000+.

SPECIAL COUNSEL
633 North State Street, Suite 608, Jackson MS 39202. 601/949-3000. **Fax:** 601/949-3001. **Contact:** Manager. **World Wide Web address:** http://www.specialcounsel.com. **Description:** A temporary and permanent employment agency. **Specializes in the areas of:** Legal.

MISSOURI

EXECUTIVE SEARCH FIRMS

AARON CONSULTING, INC.
P.O. Box 9436, St. Louis MO 63117. 314/367-2627. **Fax:** 314/367-2919. **Contact:** Aaron Williams, CPC, President. **World Wide Web address:** http://www.aaronlaw.com. **Description:** An executive search firm operating on a contingency basis. Company pays fee. **Specializes in the areas of:** Legal. **Positions commonly filled include:** Attorney. **Average salary range of placements:** More than $50,000. **Number of placements per year:** 1 - 49.

ACCOUNTANTS EXECUTIVE SEARCH
911 Main Street, Suite 620, Kansas City MO 64105. 816/421-7774. **Contact:** Manager. **Description:** An executive search firm that focuses on accounting placements. **Corporate headquarters location:** Saddle Brook NJ. **Other U.S. locations:** Nationwide.

ACCOUNTANTS EXECUTIVE SEARCH
ACCOUNTANTS ON CALL
One City Center, 515 North 6th Street, Suite 1340, St. Louis MO 63101. 314/436-0500. **Contact:** Manager. **Description:** An executive search firm. Accountants on Call (also at this location) is a temporary agency. **Specializes in the areas of:** Accounting/Auditing; Finance.

ACCOUNTANTS EXECUTIVE SEARCH
ACCOUNTANTS ON CALL
111 Westport Plaza, Suite 512, St. Louis MO 63146. 314/576-0006. **Contact:** Manager. **Description:** An executive search firm. Accountants on Call (also at this location) is a temporary agency. **Specializes in the areas of:** Accounting/Auditing; Finance.

ACCOUNTING CAREER CONSULTANTS
1001 Craig Road, Suite 429, St. Louis MO 63146. 317/569-9898. **Contact:** Manager. **Description:** An executive search firm. **Specializes in the areas of:** Accounting/Auditing; Finance.

ADVANCED CAREERS OF KANSAS CITY, INC.
6528 Raytown Road, Kansas City MO 64133. 816/358-3553. **Fax:** 816/358-3566. **Contact:** Hal Willis, Vice President. **E-mail address:** hwillis711@aol.com. **Description:** An executive search firm operating on a contingency basis. Company pays fee. **Specializes in the areas of:** Accounting/Auditing; Engineering; Finance; General Management; Manufacturing; Personnel/Labor Relations; Sales; Technical. **Positions commonly filled include:** Accountant/Auditor; Chemical Engineer; Civil Engineer; Electrical/Electronics Engineer; Manufacturing Engineer; Mechanical Engineer; Sales Representative. **Number of placements per year:** 1 - 49.

AGRI-ASSOCIATES
500 Nichols Road, Kansas City MO 64112. 816/531-7980. **Contact:** Manager. **Description:** An executive search firm. **Specializes in the areas of:** Agriculture.

AGRI-TECH PERSONNEL, INC.
3113 Northeast 69th Street, Kansas City MO 64119. 816/453-7200. **Fax:** 816/453-6001. **Contact:** Dale Pickering, President. **Description:** An executive search firm operating on a contingency basis. The firm focuses on agricultural and food industry placement. Areas of concentration include administration, engineering, human resources, manufacturing, marketing, sales, and transportation. Positions range from entry-level to management. Company pays fee. **Specializes in the areas of:** Agriculture; Engineering; Food Industry; Manufacturing; Personnel/Labor Relations; Technical; Transportation. **Positions commonly filled include:** Agricultural Engineer; Buyer; Chemical Engineer; Chemist; Credit Manager; Design Engineer; Draftsperson; Electrical/Electronics Engineer; Environmental Engineer; Food Scientist/Technologist; General Manager; Human Resources Specialist; Industrial Engineer; Mechanical Engineer; Operations/Production Manager; Purchasing Agent/Manager; Quality Control Supervisor; Structural Engineer; Transportation/Traffic Specialist; Veterinarian.

ALLAN-JAMES ASSOCIATES
P.O. Box 11370, Springfield MO 65808. 417/881-6767. **Fax:** 417/881-0366. **Contact:** Roger A. Aistrup, President. **E-mail address:** aja@getonthe.net. **World Wide Web address:** http://www.jobsinplastics.com. **Description:** An executive search firm that focuses on the recruitment of management, engineering, administrative, and technical personnel for the plastics industry. **Specializes in the areas of:** Plastics. **Positions commonly filled include:** Applications Engineer; Biomedical Engineer; Buyer; Chemical Engineer; Chemist; Chief Financial Officer; Computer Programmer; Controller; Design Engineer; General Manager; Human Resources Manager; Industrial Engineer; Industrial Production Manager; Manufacturing Engineer; MIS Specialist; Operations Manager; Production Manager; Project Manager; Purchasing Agent/Manager; Quality Control Supervisor; Software Engineer; Systems Analyst. **Average salary range of placements:** $40,000 - $80,000. **Number of placements per year:** 1 - 49.

AMERICAN AUTOMOTIVE PERSONNEL CONSULTANTS, INC.
P.O. Box 1957, Maryland Heights MO 63043. 314/569-5959. **Fax:** 314/441-2272. **Contact:** A. H. (Buzz) Burling, President. **Description:** An executive search firm operating on both retainer and contingency bases. Company pays fee. **Specializes in the areas of:** Automotive; Manufacturing; Retail; Sales. **Positions commonly filled include:** Accountant/Auditor; Automotive Engineer; Automotive Mechanic; Customer Service Representative; Design Engineer; Designer; Financial Analyst; General Manager; Industrial Engineer; Industrial Production Manager; Management Analyst/Consultant; Manufacturer's/Wholesaler's Sales Rep.; Mechanical Engineer; Operations/Production Manager; Quality Control Supervisor; Sales Manager; Service Manager; Services Sales Representative; Technical Writer/Editor. **Number of placements per year:** 50 - 99.

ANDERSON HEALTHCARE INC.
1715 Wilmington Court, Ballwin MO 63021. 314/394-0100. **Contact:** Manager. **Description:** An executive search firm that places physicians. **Specializes in the areas of:** Health/Medical. **Positions commonly filled include:** Physician.

KEN BROWN & COMPANY
1036B West Battlefield, Springfield MO 65807. 417/883-9444. **Fax:** 417/883-9947. **Contact:** Ken Brown, President. **E-mail address:** bbrown@kenbrown.com. **World Wide Web address:** http://www.kenbrown.com. **Description:** An executive search firm operating on both retained and contingency bases. Company pays fee. **Specializes in the areas of:** Engineering; Food Industry; Manufacturing. **Positions commonly filled include:** Chemical Engineer; Electrical/Electronics Engineer; Food Scientist/Technologist; Human Resources Manager; Industrial Engineer; Industrial Production Manager; Manufacturing Engineer; Mechanical

Engineer; Operations Manager; Project Manager; Quality Control Supervisor; Transportation/Traffic Specialist. **Average salary range of placements:** More than $50,000. **Number of placements per year:** 50 - 99.

BURNS EMPLOYMENT SERVICE, INC.
9229 Ward Parkway, Kansas City MO 64114-3335. 816/361-6444. **Fax:** 816/361-7747. **Contact:** Kevin Burns, President. **Description:** An executive search firm. Company pays fee. **Specializes in the areas of:** Accounting/Auditing; Advertising; Architecture/Construction; Banking; Biology; Computer Science/Software; Education; Engineering; Finance; Food Industry; General Management; Industrial; Insurance; Manufacturing; Sales; Technical. **Positions commonly filled include:** Accountant/Auditor; Administrative Manager; Architect; Attorney; Bank Officer/Manager; Biochemist; Biological Scientist; Biomedical Engineer; Branch Manager; Budget Analyst; Buyer; Chemical Engineer; Chemist; Civil Engineer; Claim Representative; Clerical Supervisor; Computer Programmer; Cost Estimator; Credit Manager; Customer Service Representative; Design Engineer; Designer; Draftsperson; Economist; Education Administrator; Electrical/Electronics Engineer; Environmental Engineer; Financial Analyst; Food Scientist/Technologist; General Manager; Geologist/Geophysicist; Industrial Engineer; Industrial Production Manager; Management Trainee; Market Research Analyst; Materials Engineer; Mechanical Engineer; Metallurgical Engineer; MIS Specialist; Operations/Production Manager; Petroleum Engineer; Public Relations Specialist; Purchasing Agent/Manager; Quality Control Supervisor; Science Technologist; Services Sales Representative; Software Engineer; Structural Engineer; Surveyor; Systems Analyst; Technical Writer/Editor; Telecommunications Manager; Transportation/Traffic Specialist; Underwriter/Assistant Underwriter. **Number of placements per year:** 500 - 999.

CAREER SERVICES, INC.
4339 West William Street, Brookline Station MO 65619-9277. 417/881-3554. **Contact:** Lynne Haggerman, President. **Description:** An executive search firm and employment agency. Company pays fee. **Positions commonly filled include:** Accountant/Auditor; Actuary; Administrative Manager; Advertising Clerk; Bank Officer/Manager; Blue-Collar Worker Supervisor; Branch Manager; Brokerage Clerk; Budget Analyst; Buyer; Claim Representative; Clerical Supervisor; Clinical Lab Technician; Computer Programmer; Construction and Building Inspector; Construction Contractor; Cost Estimator; Counselor; Credit Manager; Customer Service Representative; Dental Assistant/Dental Hygienist; Designer; Dietician/Nutritionist; Draftsperson; Editor; Education Administrator; EEG Technologist; EKG Technician; Electrician; Emergency Medical Technician; Financial Analyst; General Manager; Health Services Worker; Hotel Manager; Human Resources Specialist; Human Service Worker; Industrial Production Manager; Insurance Agent/Broker; Librarian; Licensed Practical Nurse; Management Analyst/Consultant; Management Trainee; Manufacturer's/Wholesaler's Sales Rep.; Market Research Analyst; Mathematician; Medical Records Technician; MIS Specialist; Nuclear Medicine Technologist; Occupational Therapist; Operations/Production Manager; Paralegal; Pharmacist; Physical Therapist; Preschool Worker; Psychologist; Public Relations Specialist; Quality Control Supervisor; Radio/TV Announcer/Broadcaster; Radiological Technologist; Real Estate Agent; Recreational Therapist; Registered Nurse; Reporter; Respiratory Therapist; Restaurant/Food Service Manager; Securities Sales Representative; Social Worker; Speech-Language Pathologist; Surgical Technician; Surveyor; Teacher/Professor; Technical Writer/Editor; Telecommunications Manager; Transportation/Traffic Specialist; Travel Agent; Underwriter/Assistant Underwriter; Video Production Coordinator. **Number of placements per year:** 1 - 49.

THE CHRISTIANSEN GROUP
2101 West Chesterfield Boulevard, Suite B202, Springfield MO 65807. 417/889-9696. **Fax:** 417/889-8960. **Contact:** Scott Christiansen, Principal. **E-mail address:** cgroup1@aol.com. **Description:** An executive search firm. Company pays fee. **Specializes in the areas of:** Engineering; Food Industry; Industrial; Manufacturing; Technical; Transportation. **Positions commonly filled include:** Agricultural Engineer; Biochemist; Buyer; Chemical Engineer; Chemist; Clinical Lab Technician; Design Engineer; Electrical/Electronics Engineer; Environmental Engineer; Food Scientist/Technologist; General Manager; Human Resources Specialist; Industrial Engineer; Industrial Production Manager; Management Trainee; Mechanical Engineer; Operations/Production Manager; Quality Control Supervisor; Stationary Engineer; Transportation/Traffic Specialist. **Average salary range of placements:** More than $50,000. **Number of placements per year:** 1 - 49.

GRANT COOPER & ASSOCIATES
795 Office Parkway, Suite 117, St. Louis MO 63141. 314/567-4690. **Fax:** 314/567-4697. **Contact:** Manager. **Description:** An executive search firm.

CORPORATE PERSONNEL & ASSOCIATES
851 Northwest 45th Street, Gladstone MO 64116-4612. 816/454-4080. **Contact:** Recruiter. **Description:** An executive search firm. Company pays fee. **Specializes in the areas of:** Sales. **Positions commonly filled include:** Branch Manager; Computer Programmer; General Manager; Management Trainee; Manufacturer's/Wholesaler's Sales Rep.; Services Sales Representative; Systems Analyst. **Number of placements per year:** 100 - 199.

JIM CRUMPLEY & ASSOCIATES
1200 East Woodhurst Drive, Suite B400, Springfield MO 65804. 417/882-7555. **Fax:** 417/882-8555. **Contact:** Jim Crumpley, Owner. **Description:** An executive search firm. Company pays fee. **Specializes in the areas of:** Biology; Engineering; Health/Medical; Pharmaceutical. **Positions commonly filled include:** Biological Scientist; Biomedical Engineer; Chemical Engineer; Chemist; Electrical/Electronics Engineer; Industrial Engineer; Mechanical Engineer; Purchasing Agent/Manager; Registered Nurse; Veterinarian. **Number of placements per year:** 1 - 49.

DEBBON RECRUITING GROUP
P.O. Box 510323, St. Louis MO 63151. 314/846-9101. **Contact:** John Zipfel, President. **E-mail address:** debbongrp@aol.com. **Description:** An executive search firm operating on both retainer and contingency bases. Company pays fee. **Specializes in the areas of:** Engineering; Food Industry; General Management; Personnel/Labor Relations; Pharmaceutical. **Positions commonly filled include:** Biochemist; Biological Scientist; Chemical Engineer; Chemist; Food Scientist/Technologist; Human Resources Manager; Industrial Engineer; Industrial Production Manager; Mechanical Engineer; Operations/Production Manager; Plant Engineer; Production Manager; Project Manager; Quality Control Supervisor. **Other U.S. locations:** Nationwide. **Average salary range of placements:** $30,000 - $50,000. **Number of placements per year:** 1 - 49.

DUNHILL PERSONNEL SYSTEM OF MISSOURI
1350 Rustic View Drive, Ballwin MO 63011. 314/394-0602. **Fax:** 314/394-2802. **Contact:** Don

Vogel, Manager. **E-mail address:** dschdmo@dunhillstaff.com. **Description:** An executive search firm operating on a contingency basis. Company pays fee. **Specializes in the areas of:** Engineering; Industrial; Metals. **Positions commonly filled include:** Accountant/Auditor; Electrical/Electronics Engineer; Environmental Engineer; General Manager; Human Resources Manager; Industrial Engineer; Industrial Production Manager; Manufacturing Engineer; Mechanical Engineer; Metallurgical Engineer; MIS Specialist; Operations Manager; Production Manager; Project Manager; Purchasing Agent/Manager; Quality Control Supervisor; Sales Manager; Sales Representative. **Number of placements per year:** 1 - 49.

DUNHILL PERSONNEL SYSTEM OF MISSOURI
400 East Red Bridge Road, Suite 203, Kansas City MO 64131. 816/942-8620. **Contact:** Don Phillips, President. **Description:** An executive search firm. **Specializes in the areas of:** Electronics; Engineering.

EMPLOYER ADVANTAGE
705 Illinois Avenue, Joplin MO 64801. 417/782-3909. **Toll-free phone:** 800/467-3909. **Fax:** 417/782-3802. **Contact:** Dr. Lee Allphin, President. **Description:** An executive search firm. Company pays fee. **Specializes in the areas of:** Accounting/Auditing; Administration; Architecture/Construction; Banking; Computer Science/Software; Education; Engineering; Finance; General Management; Health/Medical; Industrial; Insurance; Manufacturing; Nonprofit; Personnel/Labor Relations; Publishing; Sales; Secretarial; Technical; Transportation. **Positions commonly filled include:** Accountant/Auditor; Administrative Manager; Bank Officer/Manager; Blue-Collar Worker Supervisor; Chemist; Clerical Supervisor; Computer Programmer; Construction and Building Inspector; Construction Contractor; Cost Estimator; Counselor; Credit Manager; Customer Service Manager; Dental Assistant/Dental Hygienist; Dentist; Draftsperson; Education Administrator; Electrical/Electronics Engineer; Electrician; Emergency Medical Technician; Environmental Engineer; Financial Analyst; General Manager; Health Services Manager; Hotel Manager; Human Resources Specialist; Human Service Worker; Industrial Engineer; Industrial Production Manager; Insurance Agent/Broker; Internet Services Manager; Landscape Architect; Librarian; Licensed Practical Nurse; Management Analyst/Consultant; Manufacturer's/Wholesaler's Sales Rep.; Market Research Analyst; Mechanical Engineer; Medical Records Technician; Metallurgical Engineer; MIS Specialist; Multimedia Designer; Occupational Therapist; Operations/Production Manager; Paralegal; Petroleum Engineer; Physical Therapist; Physician; Preschool Worker; Property and Real Estate Manager; Psychologist; Public Relations Specialist; Purchasing Agent/Manager; Quality Control Supervisor; Recreational Therapist; Registered Nurse; Respiratory Therapist; Restaurant/Food Service Manager; Sales Representative; Science Technologist; Securities Sales Representative; Social Worker; Sociologist; Software Engineer; Stationary Engineer; Surveyor; Systems Analyst; Teacher/Professor; Technical Writer/Editor; Telecommunications Manager; Transportation/Traffic Specialist; Typist/Word Processor; Underwriter/Assistant Underwriter; Veterinarian; Video Production Coordinator. **Other U.S. locations:** Phoenix AZ; Atlanta GA. **Average salary range of placements:** $20,000 - $29,999. **Number of placements per year:** 200 - 499.

EXECUSEARCH, INC.
12977 North Outer Forty Road, Suite 315, St. Louis MO 63141. 314/878-2090. **Fax:** 314/878-1337. **Contact:** Ronald G. Theby, CPA, President. **Description:** An executive search firm operating on a contingency basis. The firm focuses on the placement of accounting and finance professionals. Company pays fee. **Specializes in the areas of:** Accounting/Auditing; Finance. **Positions commonly filled include:** Accountant/Auditor; Budget Analyst; Financial Analyst. **Average salary range of placements:** $30,000 - $50,000. **Number of placements per year:** 100 - 199.

EXECUTIVE CAREER CONSULTANTS, INC.
2258 Schuetz Road, St. Louis MO 63146. 314/994-3737. **Fax:** 314/994-3742. **Contact:** Bruce Bauer, President. **Description:** An executive search firm. **Positions commonly filled include:** Accountant/Auditor; Computer Programmer; Systems Analyst. **Other U.S. locations:** Nationwide. **Average salary range of placements:** $30,000 - $50,000. **Number of placements per year:** 50 - 99.

EXECUTIVE MARKETING GROUP
11861 West Line Industrial Drive, Suite 500, St. Louis MO 63146. 314/569-2900. **Contact:** Manager. **Description:** An executive search firm.

EXECUTIVE RECRUITERS
2700 Rockcreek Parkway, Suite 303, North Kansas City MO 64117-2519. 816/471-0774. **Contact:** Manager. **Description:** An executive search firm covering a wide range of industries. **Specializes in the areas of:** Data Processing; Engineering; Manufacturing; Telecommunications.

F-O-R-T-U-N-E PERSONNEL CONSULTANTS
1736 East Sunshine, Suite 707, Springfield MO 65804. 417/887-6737. **Fax:** 417/887-6955. **Contact:** Bill Belle Isle, President. **Description:** An executive search firm operating on both retainer and contingency bases. The firm focuses on the placement of management and engineering professionals. Company pays fee. **Specializes in the areas of:** Accounting/Auditing; Engineering; General Management; Industrial; Manufacturing; Publishing. **Positions commonly filled include:** Accountant/Auditor; Agricultural Engineer; Designer; Electrical/Electronics Engineer; Environmental Engineer; General Manager; Industrial Engineer; Industrial Production Manager; Mechanical Engineer; Metallurgical Engineer; Operations/Production Manager; Purchasing Agent/Manager; Quality Control Supervisor; Software Engineer; Structural Engineer. **Corporate headquarters location:** New York NY. **Other U.S. locations:** Nationwide. **Average salary range of placements:** More than $50,000. **Number of placements per year:** 1 - 49.

GIBSON & ASSOCIATES
2345 East Grand Avenue, Springfield MO 65804. 417/886-3534. **Fax:** 417/886-6963. **Contact:** Gary Gibson, President/Owner. **Description:** An executive search firm. **Specializes in the areas of:** Manufacturing. **Positions commonly filled include:** Accountant/Auditor; Attorney; Automotive Mechanic; Biological Scientist; Blue-Collar Worker Supervisor; Buyer; Chemist; Computer Programmer; Construction Contractor; Customer Service Representative; Designer; Draftsperson; Electrical/Electronics Engineer; Electrician; Financial Analyst; Food Scientist/Technologist; General Manager; Human Resources Manager; Human Service Worker; Industrial Engineer; Licensed Practical Nurse; Manufacturer's/Wholesaler's Sales Rep.; Mechanical Engineer; Operations/Production Manager; Physician; Public Relations Specialist; Purchasing Agent/Manager; Quality Control Supervisor; Registered Nurse; Securities Sales Representative; Systems Analyst; Transportation/Traffic Specialist. **Number of placements per year:** 1 - 49.

ANNIE GRAY ASSOCIATES INC.
12400 Olive Boulevard, Saint Louis MO 63141. 314/275-4405. **Fax:** 314/523-4523. **Contact:** Annie Gray, President. **E-mail address:** xxsrch@aol.com. **Description:** An executive search firm that focuses on recruiting CEOs, presidents, and vice presidents for supermarkets nationwide. **Specializes in the areas of:** Food Industry; Retail. **Average salary range of placements:** More than $50,000. **Number of placements per year:** 1 - 49.

GRUEN & ASSOCIATES, INC.
9270 Olive Boulevard, St. Louis MO 63134. 314/567-1478. **Fax:** 314/567-0567. **Contact:** Brian Gruen, Director of Recruitment. **E-mail address:** bgruen@aol.com. **Description:** An executive search firm that focuses on placement in the information systems industry. The company operates on both retainer and contingency bases. Company pays fee. **Specializes in the areas of:** Computer Science/Software; Information Systems; Market Research. **Positions commonly filled include:** Account Manager; Computer Programmer; Database Manager; Internet Services Manager; Market Research Analyst; MIS Manager; MIS Specialist; Software Engineer; Statistician; Systems Analyst; Systems Manager; Webmaster. **Corporate headquarters location:** Medora IL. **Other U.S. locations:** Nationwide. **Average salary range of placements:** More than $50,000. **Number of placements per year:** 50 - 99.

ROBERT HALF INTERNATIONAL
One Metropolitan Square, Suite 2130, St. Louis MO 63102. 314/621-0500. **Contact:** Manager. **World Wide Web address:** http://www.roberthalf.com. **Description:** An executive search firm. Accountemps (also at this location) provides temporary placements. **Specializes in the areas of:** Accounting/Auditing. **Corporate headquarters location:** Menlo Park CA. **Other U.S. locations:** Nationwide.

ROBERT HALF INTERNATIONAL ACCOUNTEMPS
127 West 10th Street, Suite 956, Kansas City MO 64105. 816/474-4583. **Contact:** Manager. **World Wide Web address:** http://www.roberthalf.com. **Description:** An executive search firm. Accountemps (also at this location) provides temporary placements. **Specializes in the areas of:** Accounting/Auditing. **Corporate headquarters location:** Menlo Park CA. **Other U.S. locations:** Nationwide.

ROBERT HALF INTERNATIONAL ACCOUNTEMPS
12655 Olive Boulevard, Suite 410, St. Louis MO 63141. 314/205-1850. **Contact:** Manager. **World Wide Web address:** http://www.roberthalf.com. **Description:** An executive search firm. Accountemps (also at this location) provides temporary placements. **Specializes in the areas of:** Accounting/Auditing. **Corporate headquarters location:** Menlo Park CA. **Other U.S. locations:** Nationwide.

HASKELL ASSOCIATES, INC.
P.O. Box 31547, St. Louis MO 63131. 314/966-0745. **Fax:** 314/227-1567. **Contact:** Jerry Haskell, President/Owner. **Description:** An executive search firm operating on both retainer and contingency bases. The firm focuses on metalworking industries. Company pays fee. **Specializes in the areas of:** Engineering; General Management; Industrial; Manufacturing. **Positions commonly filled include:** General Manager; Industrial Engineer; Industrial Production Manager; Materials Engineer; Mechanical Engineer; Metallurgical Engineer; Purchasing Agent/Manager; Quality Control Supervisor. **Average salary range of placements:** More than $50,000. **Number of placements per year:** 1 - 49.

HEALTHCARE RECRUITERS INTERNATIONAL
15400 South Outer 40, Suite 100, Chesterfield MO 63017. 314/530-1030. **Fax:** 314/530-1039. **Contact:** Manager. **Description:** An executive search firm. **Specializes in the areas of:** Health/Medical; Sales.

HUEY ENTERPRISES
273 Clarkson Executive Park, Ballwin MO 63011. 314/394-9393. **Fax:** 314/394-2569. **Contact:** Arthur T. Huey, President. **Description:** An executive search firm. Company pays fee. **Specializes in the areas of:** Accounting/Auditing; Legal; Retail; Sales. **Positions commonly filled include:** Accountant/Auditor; Architect; Attorney; Civil Engineer; Construction Contractor; Cost Estimator; Economist; Electrical/Electronics Engineer; Financial Analyst; General Manager; Geologist/Geophysicist; Mechanical Engineer; Planner; Property and Real Estate Manager; Real Estate Agent. **Number of placements per year:** 1 - 49.

HUNTRESS REAL ESTATE EXECUTIVE SEARCH
P.O. Box 8667, Kansas City MO 64114. 913/383-8180. **Fax:** 913/383-8184. **Contact:** Stan Stanton, President. **Description:** An executive search firm. Company pays fee. **Specializes in the areas of:** Architecture/Construction; Retail. **Positions commonly filled include:** Architect.

J.M. GROUP
P.O. Box 1128, Ballwin MO 63022. 314/227-3838. **Contact:** Manager. **Description:** An executive search firm. **Specializes in the areas of:** Engineering.

JRL EXECUTIVE RECRUITERS
2700 Rockcreek Parkway, Suite 303, North Kansas City MO 64117. 816/471-4022. **Fax:** 816/471-8634. **Contact:** Larry Eason, President. **Description:** An executive search firm that focuses on placing technical and senior-level management personnel in various industries including automotive, manufacturing, utilities, plastics, food processing, medical, pharmaceutical, electronics, and information technology. Company pays fee. **Specializes in the areas of:** Administration; Architecture/Construction; Computer Science/Software; Engineering; Food Industry; General Management; Personnel/Labor Relations; Publishing; Technical; Transportation. **Positions commonly filled include:** Biomedical Engineer; Chemical Engineer; Chemist; Civil Engineer; Construction Manager; Cost Estimator; Design Engineer; Designer; Environmental Engineer; Food Scientist/Technologist; General Manager; Human Resources Specialist; Industrial Engineer; Industrial Production Manager; Landscape Architect; Mechanical Engineer; Metallurgical Engineer; Mining Engineer; Nuclear Engineer; Operations/Production Manager; Petroleum Engineer; Property and Real Estate Manager; Quality Control Supervisor; Software Engineer; Stationary Engineer; Structural Engineer; Surveyor; Technical Writer/Editor; Telecommunications Manager. **Average salary range of placements:** More than $50,000. **Number of placements per year:** 50 - 99.

JOB FINDERS EMPLOYMENT SERVICES
311 Bernadette Drive, Suite C, Columbia MO 65203. 573/446-4250. **Fax:** 573/446-4257. **Contact:** Anne Williams, Manager. **Description:** An executive search firm that also offers career and outplacement counseling. The firm operates on a contingency basis. **Positions commonly filled include:** Accountant/Auditor; Advertising Clerk; Bank Officer/Manager; Buyer; Chemist; Cost Estimator; Credit Manager; Customer Service Representative; Electrical/Electronics Engineer; Environmental Engineer; General Manager; Hotel Manager; Human Resources Specialist; Industrial Engineer; Management Trainee;

Manufacturer's/Wholesaler's Sales Rep.; Pharmacist; Restaurant/Food Service Manager; Services Sales Representative. **Benefits available to temporary workers:** Bonus Award/Plan; Dental Insurance; Medical Insurance. **Number of placements per year:** 50 - 99.

KEYSTONE PARTNERSHIP
231 South Bemiston Road, Clayton MO 63105. 314/721-7200. **Contact:** Manager. **Description:** An executive search firm.

J.B. LINDE & ASSOCIATES
16100 Chesterfield Parkway South, Suite 385, Chesterfield MO 63017. 314/532-8040. **Contact:** Manager. **Description:** An executive search firm. **Specializes in the areas of:** Manufacturing.

LLOYD, MARTIN & ASSOCIATES
2258 Schuetz Road, Suite 108, St. Louis MO 63146. 314/991-8500. **Fax:** 314/991-8055. **Contact:** Fred Lloyd, Owner. **Description:** An executive search firm operating on a contingency basis. The firm focuses on the placement of information systems professionals. Company pays fee. **Specializes in the areas of:** Administration; Computer Science/Software. **Positions commonly filled include:** Computer Programmer; Internet Services Manager; Management Analyst/ Consultant; MIS Specialist; Multimedia Designer; Software Engineer; Systems Analyst; Technical Writer/Editor; Telecommunications Manager. **Average salary range of placements:** More than $50,000. **Number of placements per year:** 50 - 99.

CHARLES LUNTZ & ASSOCIATES, INC.
14323 South Outer 40 Road, Suite 400 South, Chesterfield MO 63017. 314/275-7992. **Fax:** 314/275-7063. **Contact:** Charles Luntz, President. **Description:** An executive search firm. Company pays fee. **Specializes in the areas of:** Advertising; Architecture/Construction; Banking; General Management; Manufacturing; Personnel/Labor Relations; Publishing; Sales; Technical. **Positions commonly filled include:** Accountant/Auditor; Administrative Manager; Architect; Attorney; Bank Officer/Manager; Biological Scientist; Branch Manager; Chemist; Clinical Lab Technician; Construction Contractor; Credit Manager; Customer Service Representative; Designer; Engineer; Food Scientist/ Technologist; General Manager; Health Services Manager; Human Resources Manager; Industrial Production Manager; Licensed Practical Nurse; Occupational Therapist; Operations/Production Manager; Pharmacist; Physical Therapist; Physician; Physicist; President; Public Relations Specialist; Quality Control Supervisor; Recreational Therapist; Registered Nurse; Respiratory Therapist; Securities Sales Representative; Vice President.

MANAGEMENT RECRUITERS INTERNATIONAL
3301 Rider Trail South, Suite 100, St. Louis MO 63045. 314/344-0959. **Fax:** 314/298-7706. **Contact:** Patrick Hoene, Manager. **World Wide Web address:** http://www.htinfo.com/mristl.htm. **Description:** An executive search firm. Company pays fee. **Specializes in the areas of:** Accounting/Auditing; Banking; Engineering; Finance; Industrial; Sales; Transportation. **Positions commonly filled include:** Account Manager; Accountant/Auditor; Chief Financial Officer; Computer Programmer; Controller; Database Manager; Financial Analyst; Industrial Engineer; Management Analyst/ Consultant; MIS Specialist; Sales Executive; Sales Manager; Software Engineer; Systems Analyst. **Corporate headquarters location:** Cleveland OH. **Other U.S. locations:** Nationwide. **Average salary range of placements:** More than $50,000. **Number of placements per year:** 50 - 99.

MANAGEMENT RECRUITERS INTERNATIONAL
P.O. Box 1197, Camdenton MO 65020. 573/346-4833. **Contact:** Manager. **Description:** An executive search firm. **Specializes in the areas of:** Computer Science/Software; Health/Medical. **Corporate headquarters location:** Cleveland OH. **Other U.S. locations:** Nationwide.

MANAGEMENT RECRUITERS OF KANSAS CITY
712 Broadway, Suite 500, Kansas City MO 64105. 816/221-2377. **Contact:** Steve Orr, Manager. **Description:** An executive search firm. **Specializes in the areas of:** Accounting/Auditing; Administration; Advertising; Architecture/Construction; Banking; Chemical; Communications; Computer Hardware/ Software; Design; Electrical; Engineering; Finance; Food Industry; General Management; Health/Medical; Industrial; Insurance; Legal; Manufacturing; Operations Management; Personnel/Labor Relations; Pharmaceutical; Procurement; Publishing; Real Estate; Retail; Sales; Technical; Textiles; Transportation. **Corporate headquarters location:** Cleveland OH. **Other U.S. locations:** Nationwide.

MANAGEMENT RECRUITERS OF SPRINGFIELD
1807 East Edgewood, Suite B, Springfield MO 65804. 417/882-6220. **Contact:** Manager. **Description:** An executive search firm. **Specializes in the areas of:** Accounting/Auditing; Administration; Advertising; Architecture/Construction; Banking; Chemical; Communications; Computer Hardware/Software; Design; Electrical; Engineering; Finance; Food Industry; General Management; Health/Medical; Industrial; Insurance; Legal; Manufacturing; Operations Management; Personnel/Labor Relations; Pharmaceutical; Procurement; Publishing; Real Estate; Retail; Sales; Technical; Textiles; Transportation. **Corporate headquarters location:** Cleveland OH. **Other U.S. locations:** Nationwide.

MANAGEMENT RECRUITERS OF ST. LOUIS (CLAYTON)
11701 Borman Drive, Suite 250, St. Louis MO 63146. 314/991-4355. **Contact:** Phil Bertsch, Manager. **Description:** An executive search firm. **Specializes in the areas of:** Accounting/Auditing; Administration; Advertising; Architecture/ Construction; Banking; Chemical; Communications; Computer Hardware/Software; Design; Electrical; Engineering; Finance; Food Industry; General Management; Health/Medical; Industrial; Insurance; Legal; Manufacturing; Operations Management; Personnel/Labor Relations; Pharmaceutical; Procurement; Publishing; Real Estate; Retail; Sales; Technical; Textiles; Transportation. **Corporate headquarters location:** Cleveland OH. **Other U.S. locations:** Nationwide.

MANAGEMENT RECRUITERS OF ST. LOUIS (WEST COUNTY)
200 Fabricator Drive, Fenton MO 63026. 314/349-4455. **Contact:** J. Edward Travis, General Manager. **Description:** An executive search firm. **Specializes in the areas of:** Accounting/Auditing; Administration; Advertising; Architecture/Construction; Banking; Chemical; Communications; Computer Hardware/ Software; Design; Electrical; Engineering; Finance; Food Industry; General Management; Health/Medical; Industrial; Insurance; Legal; Manufacturing; Operations Management; Personnel/Labor Relations; Pharmaceutical; Procurement; Publishing; Real Estate; Sales; Technical; Textiles; Transportation. **Corporate headquarters location:** Cleveland OH. **Other U.S. locations:** Nationwide.

MEDICAL RESOURCES & ASSOCIATES
9523 32nd Street, Independence MO 64052. 816/461-1960. **Fax:** 816/461-1936. **Contact:** Sheri

Scott, CPC, Recruiter. **Description:** An executive search firm operating on both retainer and contingency bases. Company pays fee. **Specializes in the areas of:** Health/Medical. **Positions commonly filled include:** Administrative Manager; Dental Lab Technician; Dentist; Dietician/Nutritionist; Emergency Medical Technician; Health Services Manager; Licensed Practical Nurse; Management Analyst/Consultant; Medical Records Technician; Occupational Therapist; Pharmacist; Physical Therapist; Physician; Registered Nurse; Respiratory Therapist; Social Worker; Speech-Language Pathologist; Strategic Relations Manager; Surgical Technician; Systems Analyst. **Average salary range of placements:** More than $50,000. **Number of placements per year:** 1 - 49.

J. MILES PERSONNEL SERVICES
3029 East Sunshine Street, Suite A, Springfield MO 65804. 417/882-5585. **Fax:** 417/882-0656. **Contact:** Jean Miles, Owner. **Description:** An executive search firm operating on a contingency basis. Company pays fee. **Specializes in the areas of:** Engineering; Food Industry; Industrial; Manufacturing; Personnel/Labor Relations; Transportation. **Positions commonly filled include:** Accountant/Auditor; Agricultural Engineer; Buyer; Chemical Engineer; Chemist; Design Engineer; Electrical/Electronics Engineer; Environmental Engineer; Food Scientist/Technologist; General Manager; Human Resources Specialist; Industrial Engineer; Industrial Production Manager; Mechanical Engineer; Operations/Production Manager; Purchasing Agent/Manager; Quality Control Supervisor; Transportation/Traffic Specialist. **Number of placements per year:** 1 - 49.

NATIONAL PHYSICIAN PLACEMENT SERVICES
1515 North Warson Road, Suite 205, St. Louis MO 63132. 314/426-6777. **Fax:** 314/426-0707. **Contact:** Michael J. Brenner, President. **Description:** An executive search firm operating on both retainer and contingency bases. The firm focuses on the placement of physicians. This location also houses National Personnel Placement Services, a permanent and contract placement firm specializing in print, chemicals, packaging, and financial industries; and National Temporaries, a temporary placement agency for banking, credit, finance, and insurance industries. Company pays fee. **Specializes in the areas of:** Banking; Finance; Health/Medical; Industrial; Insurance; Publishing; Sales; Secretarial. **Positions commonly filled include:** Actuary; Adjuster; Bank Officer/Manager; Biochemist; Branch Manager; Budget Analyst; Chemical Engineer; Chemist; Claim Representative; Credit Manager; Customer Service Representative; Electrical/Electronics Engineer; Environmental Engineer; General Manager; Health Services Manager; Industrial Engineer; Manufacturer's/Wholesaler's Sales Rep.; Operations/Production Manager; Physician; Quality Control Supervisor; Securities Sales Representative; Services Sales Representative; Typist/Word Processor. **Other U.S. locations:** Nationwide. **Number of placements per year:** 50 - 99.

OFFICEMATES5 OF ST. LOUIS (DOWNTOWN)
211 North Broadway, Suite 2360, St. Louis MO 63102. 314/241-5866. **Contact:** Carol Zagarri, General Manager. **Description:** An executive search firm. **Specializes in the areas of:** Accounting/Auditing; Administration; Advertising; Architecture/Construction; Banking; Chemical; Communications; Computer Hardware/Software; Design; Electrical; Engineering; Finance; Food Industry; General Management; Health/Medical; Industrial; Insurance; Legal; Manufacturing; Operations Management; Personnel/Labor Relations; Procurement; Publishing; Real Estate; Sales; Technical; Textiles; Transportation.

OLDFIELD GROUP
701 Emerson Road, Suite 475, St. Louis MO 63141. 314/569-2000. **Contact:** Manager. **Description:** An executive search firm. **Specializes in the areas of:** Engineering.

PARTNERS GROUP
P.O. Box 339, Blue Springs MO 64013. 913/676-5010. **Contact:** Manager. **Description:** An executive search firm. **Specializes in the areas of:** Insurance.

PINNACLE EXECUTIVE GROUP
11907 East 64th Street, Kansas City MO 64133. 816/356-5302. **Fax:** 816/356-5747. **Contact:** Scott Eckley, Managing Partner. **E-mail address:** pinnacle@pinnaclexec.com. **Description:** An executive search firm. Company pays fee. **Specializes in the areas of:** Computer Science/Software; Finance; Information Systems; Scientific; Technical. **Positions commonly filled include:** Agricultural Engineer; Biochemist; Biomedical Engineer; Chemical Engineer; Chemist; Computer Programmer; Electrical/Electronics Engineer; Financial Analyst; General Manager; Industrial Engineer; Industrial Production Manager; Mechanical Engineer; Operations/Production Manager; Software Engineer; Systems Analyst. **Average salary range of placements:** $30,000 - $50,000. **Number of placements per year:** 50 - 99.

RAICHE & ASSOCIATES, INC.
11021 Natural Bridge Road, Bridgeton MO 63044-2317. 314/895-4554. **Contact:** Donald L. Raiche, President. **Description:** An executive search firm. Company pays fee. **Specializes in the areas of:** Computer Hardware/Software. **Positions commonly filled include:** Computer Programmer; MIS Manager; Program Manager; Project Manager; Systems Analyst; Systems Manager; Technical Support Manager. **Number of placements per year:** 1 - 49.

THE RIVER BEND GROUP
36 Four Seasons Shopping Center, Suite 343, Chesterfield MO 63017. 314/579-9729. **Fax:** 314/469-8592. **Contact:** John M. Sroka, Owner. **E-mail address:** jsroka@aol.com. **Description:** An executive search firm that focuses on placing technical professionals. Company pays fee. **Specializes in the areas of:** Computer Science/Software; Technical. **Positions commonly filled include:** Computer Programmer; Internet Services Manager; MIS Specialist; Software Engineer; Systems Analyst. **Average salary range of placements:** More than $50,000. **Number of placements per year:** 50 - 99.

J.D. RUHMANN & ASSOCIATES
142 North Main Street, Suite 100, St. Charles MO 63301. 314/723-2200. **Fax:** 314/723-0440. **Contact:** John D. Ruhmann, President. **Description:** An executive search firm that focuses on professional recruiting for the life sciences field. **Specializes in the areas of:** Biology. **Positions commonly filled include:** Biochemist; Biological Scientist; Biomedical Engineer; Chemist; Industrial Engineer; Quality Control Supervisor; Science Technologist. **Average salary range of placements:** More than $50,000. **Number of placements per year:** 1 - 49.

SALES RECRUITERS INC.
P.O. Box 326, Grandview MO 64030. 816/767-9229. **Contact:** Manager. **Description:** An executive search firm. **Specializes in the areas of:** Data Processing; Engineering; Sales.

SANFORD ROSE ASSOCIATES
5407 East Riverview, Springfield MO 65809. 417/887-0484. **Fax:** 417/887-4677. **Contact:** Manager. **World Wide Web address:** http://www.

sanfordrose.com. **Description:** An executive search firm. **Specializes in the areas of:** Banking; MIS/EDP.

SEARCH PROFESSIONALS
2055 Craigshire, Suite 300, St. Louis MO 63146. 314/434-0230. **Fax:** 314/434-0890. **Contact:** Ronald S. Silverstein, President. **Description:** An executive search firm focusing on the placement of accounting and financial personnel at the professional level. Company pays fee. **Specializes in the areas of:** Accounting/Auditing; Finance. **Positions commonly filled include:** Accountant/Auditor; Budget Analyst; Credit Manager; Financial Analyst. **Average salary range of placements:** $30,000 - $50,000. **Number of placements per year:** 1 - 49.

GORDON A. SMITH & ASSOCIATES
330 South 6th Street, Saint Charles MO 63301-2637. 314/947-3019. **Fax:** 314/723-7226. **Contact:** Recruiter. **Description:** An executive search firm focusing on engineering placements. Company pays fee. **Specializes in the areas of:** Engineering; Manufacturing; Technical. **Positions commonly filled include:** Aerospace Engineer; Agricultural Engineer; Chemical Engineer; Chemist; Civil Engineer; Designer; Electrical/Electronics Engineer; General Manager; Industrial Engineer; Mechanical Engineer; Metallurgical Engineer; Mining Engineer; Software Engineer; Telecommunications Manager. **Other U.S. locations:** Nationwide. **Number of placements per year:** 1 - 49.

SOURCE SERVICES CORPORATION
One City Place Drive, Suite 170, St. Louis MO 63141. 314/432-4500. **Fax:** 314/995-5311. **Contact:** Kathleen Paul, Recruiter. **E-mail address:** sscslm@sourcesvc.com. **World Wide Web address:** http://www.sourceslm.com. **Description:** An executive search firm. Company pays fee. **Specializes in the areas of:** Accounting/Auditing; Administration; Computer Science/Software; Finance; Technical. **Positions commonly filled include:** Accountant; Administrative Assistant; Administrative Manager; Auditor; Bank Officer/Manager; Budget Analyst; Buyer; Chief Financial Officer; Clerical Supervisor; Computer Operator; Computer Programmer; Controller; Cost Estimator; Credit Manager; Customer Service Representative; Database Manager; Finance Director; Financial Analyst; Human Resources Manager; Internet Services Manager; Management Analyst/Consultant; MIS Specialist; Operations Manager; Project Manager; Secretary; Software Engineer; Systems Analyst; Systems Manager; Technical Writer/Editor; Telecommunications Manager; Typist/Word Processor. **Benefits available to temporary workers:** Medical Insurance; Paid Vacation. **Other U.S. locations:** Nationwide. **Average salary range of placements:** $30,000 - $50,000. **Number of placements per year:** 200 - 499.

TECHNICAL RESOURCES INTERNATIONAL
968 Chestnut Ridge Road, Ballwin MO 63021. 314/861-2059. **Toll-free phone:** 800/549-2059. **Fax:** 314/861-2269. **Contact:** Tony Montane, President. **Description:** An executive search firm focusing on engineering and information systems placement. The firm also operates as a temporary agency. Company pays fee. **Specializes in the areas of:** Computer Science/Software; Engineering. **Positions commonly filled include:** Computer Programmer; Design Engineer; Electrical/Electronics Engineer; Industrial Engineer; Mechanical Engineer; MIS Specialist; Software Engineer; Structural Engineer; Systems Analyst. **Benefits available to temporary workers:** Medical Insurance; Paid Vacation. **Number of placements per year:** 1 - 49.

J.E. WOTTOWA & ASSOCIATES
700 St. Louis Union Station, Suite 210, St. Louis MO 63103. 314/621-4900. **Contact:** Manager. **Description:** An executive search firm.

PERMANENT EMPLOYMENT AGENCIES

ABC EMPLOYMENT SERVICE
7730 Carondelet, Suite 116, St. Louis MO 63105-3325. 314/725-3140. **Contact:** General Manager. **Description:** A permanent employment agency focusing on manufacturing, construction, and mining industries. Company pays fee. **Specializes in the areas of:** Accounting/Auditing; Architecture/Construction; Biology; Engineering; Finance; General Management; Industrial; Manufacturing; Personnel/Labor Relations; Sales; Technical. **Positions commonly filled include:** Accountant/Auditor; Aerospace Engineer; Agricultural Engineer; Biochemist; Biological Scientist; Biomedical Engineer; Budget Analyst; Buyer; Ceramics Engineer; Chemical Engineer; Chemist; Civil Engineer; Computer Programmer; Credit Manager; Draftsperson; Electrical/Electronics Engineer; Environmental Engineer; Financial Analyst; General Manager; Geologist/Geophysicist; Industrial Engineer; Industrial Production Manager; Marketing Specialist; Mechanical Engineer; Metallurgical Engineer; Purchasing Agent/Manager; Quality Control Supervisor; Software Engineer; Strategic Relations Manager; Structural Engineer.

JAY ALEXANDER & ASSOCIATES
dba KIRDONN GROUP
106 West 11th Street, Suite 1250, Kansas City MO 64105-1806. 816/474-0700. **Fax:** 816/474-0702. **Contact:** Jim Panus, President. **Description:** A permanent employment agency that focuses on sales recruiting. Company pays fee. **Specializes in the areas of:** Advertising; Broadcasting; Computer Science/Software; Food Industry; Industrial; Manufacturing; Publishing; Sales. **Positions commonly filled include:** Management Trainee; Manufacturer's/Wholesaler's Sales Rep.; Sales Manager; Securities Sales Representative; Services Sales Representative. **Number of placements per year:** 200 - 499.

L.P. BANNING, INC.
782 Ambois Drive, Suite 302, Clayton MO 63105-3506. 314/863-1770. **Fax:** 314/863-5865. **Contact:** John Speno, Vice President. **Description:** A permanent employment agency. Company pays fee. **Specializes in the areas of:** Accounting/Auditing; Architecture/Construction; Computer Science/Software; Engineering; Finance; Food Industry; General Management; Health/Medical; Insurance; Legal; Personnel/Labor Relations; Sales; Secretarial; Technical. **Positions commonly filled include:** Accountant/Auditor; Administrative Assistant; Attorney; Branch Manager; Buyer; Chemical Engineer; Chemist; Civil Engineer; Computer Programmer; Controller; Customer Service Rep.; Database Manager; Draftsperson; Electrical/Electronics Engineer; Environmental Engineer; Financial Analyst; Human Resources Manager; Industrial Engineer; Management Trainee; Mechanical Engineer; MIS Specialist; Occupational Therapist; Operations Manager; Paralegal; Purchasing Agent/Manager; Quality Control Supervisor; Receptionist; Sales Rep.; Secretary; Systems Analyst; Systems Manager; Typist/Word Processor; Underwriter/Assistant Underwriter. **Average salary range of placements:** $30,000 - $50,000. **Number of placements per year:** 200 - 499.

BESTEMPS INC.
3675 South Noland Road, Independence MO 64055-6505. 816/254-8844. **Fax:** 816/254-4225. **Contact:**

Recruiter. **E-mail address:** contact@bestemps.com. **World Wide Web address:** http://www.bestemps.com. **Description:** A permanent employment agency that also provides temporary placements. Company pays fee. **Specializes in the areas of:** Accounting/Auditing; Industrial; Secretarial. **Positions commonly filled include:** Blue-Collar Worker Supervisor; Buyer; Clerical Supervisor; Computer Operator; Computer Programmer; Human Resources Manager; Production Manager; Project Manager; Secretary; Typist/Word Processor. **Benefits available to temporary workers:** Paid Holidays; Paid Vacation; Profit Sharing.

BRADFORD & GALT CONSULTING SERVICES
12400 Olive Boulevard, Suite 430, St. Louis MO 63141. 314/434-9200. **Fax:** 314/434-9266. **Contact:** Staff Manager. **Description:** A permanent placement agency. Company pays fee. **Specializes in the areas of:** Computer Science/Software; Information Technology. **Positions commonly filled include:** Computer Programmer; Systems Analyst. **Other U.S. locations:** Chicago IL; Peoria IL; Kansas City KS; Dallas TX. **Number of placements per year:** 200 - 499.

CRIDER & ASSOCIATES
699 West Woodbine Avenue, St. Louis MO 63122. 314/965-6665. **Fax:** 314/965-2701. **Contact:** Patrick Crider, President. **Description:** A permanent employment agency. Company pays fee. **Specializes in the areas of:** Engineering; Industrial; Manufacturing; Personnel/Labor Relations. **Positions commonly filled include:** Electrical/Electronics Engineer; Human Resources Manager; Industrial Engineer; Mechanical Engineer; Metallurgical Engineer; Purchasing Agent/Manager; Quality Control Supervisor. **Number of placements per year:** 50 - 99.

DECK & DECKER EMPLOYMENT SERVICE
715 West McCarty Street, Jefferson City MO 65101. 573/636-2161. **Toll-free phone:** 800/226-2530. **Fax:** 573/636-2162. **Contact:** Kevin Honeycutt, Manager. **Description:** A full-service permanent employment agency. **Specializes in the areas of:** Accounting/Auditing; Administration; Banking; Engineering; Finance; Food Industry; General Management; Health/Medical; Industrial; Insurance; Legal; Manufacturing; Retail; Sales; Secretarial. **Positions commonly filled include:** Accountant/Auditor; Adjuster; Administrative Manager; Advertising Clerk; Bank Officer/Manager; Blue-Collar Worker Supervisor; Computer Programmer; Credit Manager; Customer Service Rep.; General Manager; Hotel Manager; Insurance Agent/Broker; Management Trainee; Manufacturer's/Wholesaler's Sales Rep.; Medical Records Technician; Paralegal; Restaurant/Food Service Manager; Services Sales Rep.; Software Engineer; Travel Agent; Typist/Word Processor. **Average salary range of placements:** Less than $20,000. **Number of placements per year:** 50 - 99.

DECKER PERSONNEL
1900 North Providence Road, Suite 207, Columbia MO 65202-3710. 573/449-0876. **Toll-free phone:** 888/562-4625. **Fax:** 573/449-0878. **Recorded jobline:** 573/449-0890. **Contact:** Jack W. Rogers, MA Ed., President. **E-mail address:** deckerjobs@aol.com. **World Wide Web address:** http://www.deckerjobs.com. **Description:** A permanent employment agency that also offers contract services and career counseling. Company pays fee. **Specializes in the areas of:** Accounting/Auditing; Administration; Computer Science/Software; Engineering; Finance; Food Industry; General Management; Health/Medical; Hotel/Restaurant; Industrial; Light Industrial; Manufacturing; Personnel/Labor Relations; Retail; Sales; Technical. **Positions commonly filled include:** Account Manager; Account Rep.; Adjuster; Administrative Assistant; Administrative Manager; Applications Engineer; Assistant Manager; Auditor; Bank Officer/Manager; Branch Manager; Budget Analyst; Buyer; Chemical Engineer; Chief Financial Officer; Civil Engineer; Claim Rep.; Clerical Supervisor; Computer Programmer; Controller; Cost Estimator; Credit Manager; Customer Service Rep.; Database Manager; Design Engineer; Draftsperson; Environmental Engineer; Finance Director; Financial Analyst; Fund Manager; General Manager; Human Resources Manager; Industrial Engineer; Industrial Production Manager; Internet Services Manager; Licensed Practical Nurse; Management Trainee; Managing Editor; Manufacturing Engineer; Market Research Analyst; Marketing Manager; Marketing Specialist; Mechanical Engineer; Medical Records Technician; MIS Specialist; Online Content Specialist; Operations/Production Manager; Purchasing Agent/Manager; Quality Control Supervisor; Registered Nurse; Sales Engineer; Sales Executive; Sales Manager; Sales Rep.; Secretary; Software Engineer; Surgical Technician; Systems Analyst; Systems Manager; Telecommunications Manager; Transportation/Traffic Specialist; Typist/Word Processor; Webmaster. **Corporate headquarters location:** This Location. **Other U.S. locations:** Nationwide. **International locations:** Worldwide. **Average salary range of placements:** $30,000 - $50,000. **Number of placements per year:** 100 - 199.

DESIGN ALTERNATIVES
15 South Florissant Road, Ferguson MO 63135. 314/521-9988. **Toll-free phone:** 800/678-7194. **Fax:** 314/521-1088. **Contact:** Charles Henson, President. **Description:** A permanent employment agency that also provides temporary placements. Company pays fee. **Specializes in the areas of:** Architecture/Construction; Engineering; Technical. **Positions commonly filled include:** Architect; Biochemist; Chemical Engineer; Chemist; Civil Engineer; Computer Operator; Computer Programmer; Design Engineer; Draftsperson; Electrical/Electronics Engineer; Environmental Engineer; Graphic Artist; Graphic Designer; Industrial Engineer; Mechanical Engineer; MIS Specialist; Software Engineer; Technical Writer/Editor. **Benefits available to temporary workers:** Medical Insurance; Paid Vacation. **Average salary range of placements:** $30,000 - $50,000. **Number of placements per year:** 100 - 199.

EDUCATIONAL PLACEMENT SERVICE
1001 Craig Road, Suite 170, St. Louis MO 63146. 314/991-5855. **Fax:** 314/991-5295. **Contact:** Gary Loup, CTC, Placement Director. **Description:** A permanent employment agency focusing on education placements in public, private, and parochial schools. **Specializes in the areas of:** Education. **Positions commonly filled include:** Counselor; Education Administrator; Librarian; Registered Nurse; Speech-Language Pathologist; Teacher/Professor. **Average salary range of placements:** $20,000 - $29,999. **Number of placements per year:** 50 - 99.

FIRST PLACE INC.
4925 West Spinnaker Lane, Willard MO 65781. 417/883-7353. **Contact:** Manager. **Description:** A permanent employment agency for most major industries.

HDB INCORPORATED
301 Baxter Acres Drive, St. Louis MO 63011-3939. 314/391-7799. **Fax:** 314/391-1224. **Contact:** Kathryn Davis-Wolfe, President. **E-mail address:** kwolfe@hdbinc.com. **Description:** A permanent employment agency. Company pays fee. **Specializes in the areas of:** Administration; Computer Science/Software; Consulting. **Positions commonly filled include:** Computer Programmer; Systems Analyst. **Number of placements per year:** 50 - 99.

JACKSON EMPLOYMENT AGENCY
3450 Prospect Avenue, Kansas City MO 64128. 816/921-0181. **Contact:** Charles H. Jackson Sr., President. **Description:** A permanent employment agency. **Specializes in the areas of:** Biology; Computer Science/Software; Engineering; Finance; Food Industry; Personnel/Labor Relations. **Positions commonly filled include:** Accountant/Auditor; Aerospace Engineer; Agricultural Engineer; Agricultural Scientist; Architect; Attorney; Biological Scientist; Biomedical Engineer; Chemical Engineer; Chemist; Civil Engineer; Computer Programmer; Cost Estimator; Credit Manager; Electrical/Electronics Engineer; Electrician; Financial Analyst; Food Scientist/Technologist; Human Resources Manager; Industrial Engineer; Mathematician; Mechanical Engineer; Metallurgical Engineer; Meteorologist; Mining Engineer; Nuclear Engineer; Petroleum Engineer; Purchasing Agent/Manager; Software Engineer; Stationary Engineer; Statistician; Structural Engineer; Systems Analyst; Telecommunications Manager; Transportation/Traffic Specialist. **Number of placements per year:** 50 - 99.

KENNISON & ASSOCIATES INC.
3101 Broadway, Suite 280, Kansas City MO 64111. 816/753-4401. **Fax:** 816/753-3430. **Contact:** Gary S. Fawkes, Managing Partner. **Description:** A permanent employment agency. Company pays fee. **Specializes in the areas of:** Computer Science/Software; Health/Medical. **Positions commonly filled include:** Computer Programmer; Management Analyst/Consultant; Occupational Therapist; Physical Therapist; Recreational Therapist; Respiratory Therapist; Speech-Language Pathologist; Systems Analyst; Technical Writer/Editor.

LANDAJOB
6300 Walnut Street, Kansas City MO 64113. 816/523-1881. **Contact:** Mary Crissman, Partner. **Description:** A permanent employment agency. **Specializes in the areas of:** Advertising; Clerical; Insurance; Publishing; Secretarial. **Positions commonly filled include:** Accountant/Auditor; Administrative Assistant; Advertising Executive; Bookkeeper; Commercial Artist; Factory Worker; Marketing Specialist; Public Relations Specialist; Receptionist; Sales Rep.; Secretary; Technical Writer/Editor; Typist/Word Processor. **Number of placements per year:** 50 - 99.

LINDE GROUP
220 North 4th Street, Suite 302, 220 Mansion House Center, St. Louis MO 63102. 314/621-2950. **Contact:** Manager. **Description:** A permanent employment agency that also provides some temporary placements. **Specializes in the areas of:** Accounting/Auditing; Administration; Office Support. **Other area locations:** Kansas City MO.

MISSOURI DIVISION OF EMPLOYMENT SERVICES
505 Washington Avenue, St. Louis MO 63101. 314/340-4700. **Fax:** 314/340-4910. **Contact:** Employment Services. **Description:** A permanent employment agency. **Number of placements per year:** 1000+.

PREFERRED RESOURCES
701 Emerson Road, Suite 475, Saint Louis MO 63141-6754. 314/567-7600. **Contact:** Michael Honer, Manager. **Description:** A permanent employment agency. **Specializes in the areas of:** MIS/EDP.

PROFESSIONAL RECRUITERS INC.
625 North Euclid, St. Louis MO 63108. 314/367-0052. **Contact:** Manager. **Description:** A permanent employment agency that also provides temporary placements.

ST. PATRICK EMPLOYMENT SERVICE
711 North 11th Street, St. Louis MO 63101. 314/421-4013. **Contact:** Employment Counselor. **Description:** A permanent employment agency. **Specializes in the areas of:** Nonprofit. **Positions commonly filled include:** Clerk; Computer Operator; Customer Service Rep.; Data Entry Clerk; Driver; Factory Worker; Housekeeper; Light Industrial Worker; Receptionist; Secretary; Typist/Word Processor.

SNELLING PERSONNEL SERVICES
16100 Chesterfield Parkway South, Suite 285, Chesterfield MO 63017. 314/532-1004. **Contact:** A.H. Harter, Jr., President. **Description:** A permanent employment agency that also offers some temporary placements. Company pays fee. **Specializes in the areas of:** Accounting/Auditing; Administration; Advertising; Banking; Computer Hardware/Software; Engineering; Finance; Food Industry; General Management; Industrial; Insurance; Legal; Manufacturing; Retail; Sales; Secretarial; Technical. **Positions commonly filled include:** Accountant/Auditor; Administrative Assistant; Aerospace Engineer; Architect; Attorney; Biological Scientist; Biomedical Engineer; Bookkeeper; Buyer; Ceramics Engineer; Chemical Engineer; Chemist; Civil Engineer; Claim Rep.; Clerk; Computer Programmer; Credit Manager; Customer Service Rep.; Data Entry Clerk; Draftsperson; EDP Specialist; Electrical/ Electronics Engineer; Hotel Manager; Industrial Designer; Industrial Engineer; Legal Secretary; Manufacturing Engineer; Marketing Specialist; Mechanical Engineer; Medical Secretary; Metallurgical Engineer; MIS Specialist; Operations/Production Manager; Public Relations Specialist; Purchasing Agent/Manager; Quality Control Supervisor; Receptionist; Recruiter; Sales Rep.; Secretary; Software Engineer; Systems Analyst; Systems Engineer; Technical Illustrator; Technical Writer/Editor; Technician; Typist/Word Processor; Underwriter/ Assistant Underwriter. **Corporate headquarters location:** Dallas TX. **Other U.S. locations:** Nationwide. **Number of placements per year:** 500 - 999.

TLC CAREGIVERS
8080 Ward Parkway, Suite 104, Kansas City MO 64114. 816/444-6400. **Toll-free phone:** 800/707-4852. **Fax:** 816/444-6499. **Contact:** Shanna Mundell, President. **Description:** A permanent employment agency providing both permanent and temporary placements. Company pays fee. **Specializes in the areas of:** Child Care, In-Home. **Positions commonly filled include:** Daycare Teacher; Nanny. **Number of placements per year:** 1000+.

TOBERSON GROUP
1034 South Brentwood, Suite 1515, St. Louis MO 63117. 314/726-0500. **Contact:** James C. Anderson, President. **Description:** A permanent employment agency. Company pays fee. **Specializes in the areas of:** Food Industry; Health/Medical; Hotel/Restaurant; Retail; Sales. **Number of placements per year:** 50 - 99.

TEMPORARY EMPLOYMENT AGENCIES

ACCOUNTANT SOURCE TEMPS
One Cityplace Drive, Suite 170, St. Louis MO 63141. 314/432-4500. **Fax:** 314/432-6668. **Contact:** Ms. Julie Henrich, Placement Specialist. **Description:** A temporary agency that focuses on accounting, computer, clerical, and administrative positions.

Company pays fee. **Specializes in the areas of:** Accounting/Auditing; Finance; Secretarial. **Positions commonly filled include:** Accountant/Auditor; Budget Analyst; Clerical Supervisor; Credit Manager; Customer Service Representative; Financial Analyst; Typist/Word Processor. **Benefits available to temporary workers:** Medical Insurance; Paid Holidays. **Corporate headquarters location:** Dallas TX. **Other U.S. locations:** Nationwide. **Average salary range of placements:** $20,000 - $29,999. **Number of placements per year:** 200 - 499.

ACCOUNTEMPS
One Metropolitan Square, Suite 2130, St. Louis MO 63102-2733. 314/621-8367. **Fax:** 314/621-4967. **Contact:** Recruiter. **World Wide Web address:** http://www.rhic.com. **Description:** A temporary agency focusing on placements in accounting and finance industries. Accountemps is a division of Robert Half International. Company pays fee. **Specializes in the areas of:** Accounting/Auditing; Computer Science/Software; Finance. **Positions commonly filled include:** Accountant/Auditor; Budget Analyst; Credit Manager; Financial Analyst; MIS Specialist. **Benefits available to temporary workers:** Life Insurance; Medical Insurance; Paid Holidays. **Corporate headquarters location:** Menlo Park CA. **Other U.S. locations:** Nationwide. **Average salary range of placements:** $20,000 - $29,999. **Number of placements per year:** 50 - 99.

ADECCO
2639 East 32nd Street, Suite W, Joplin MO 64804. 417/624-1911. **Fax:** 417/624-2120. **Contact:** Karol Bowman, Branch Manager. **Description:** A temporary agency. Company pays fee. **Specializes in the areas of:** Manufacturing; Retail; Sales; Secretarial. **Positions commonly filled include:** Buyer; Claim Representative; Customer Service Representative; Dental Assistant/Dental Hygienist; Electrician; Human Resources Specialist; Manufacturer's/Wholesaler's Sales Rep.; Typist/Word Processor. **Benefits available to temporary workers:** Life Insurance; Medical Insurance. **Corporate headquarters location:** Redwood City CA. **Other U.S. locations:** Nationwide. **International locations:** Worldwide. **Average salary range of placements:** Less than $20,000. **Number of placements per year:** 500 - 999.

AMERICAN HEALTH CARE, INC.
75 Worthington Street, Suite 105, Maryland Heights MO 63043. 314/576-4000. **Contact:** Director of Operations. **Description:** A temporary agency. **Specializes in the areas of:** Health/Medical. **Positions commonly filled include:** Home Health Aide. **Number of placements per year:** 200 - 499.

ANESTEMPS, INC.
4096 Fox Island Drive, Florissant MO 63034-2014. 314/839-8004. **Toll-free phone:** 800/344-2882. **Fax:** 314/839-2345. **Contact:** Robert McCoy, President. **Description:** A temporary employment agency that focuses on providing anesthesia personnel on a temporary, per diem, or permanent basis. **Specializes in the areas of:** Health/Medical.

AUSTIN NICHOLS TECHNICAL TEMPORARIES
1100 Main Street, Suite 1560, Kansas City MO 64105. 816/471-5575. **Fax:** 816/471-6690. **Contact:** Lori Thompson, Staffing Manager. **Description:** A temporary agency. Company pays fee. **Specializes in the areas of:** Engineering; Manufacturing. **Positions commonly filled include:** Aerospace Engineer; Agricultural Engineer; Architect; Biochemist; Biomedical Engineer; Buyer; Chemical Engineer; Chemist; Civil Engineer; Computer Programmer; Cost Estimator; Design Engineer; Designer; Draftsperson; Electrical/Electronics Engineer; Electrician; Environmental Engineer; Geologist/Geophysicist; Industrial Engineer; Industrial Production Manager; Mechanical Engineer; MIS Specialist; Purchasing Agent/Manager; Quality Control Supervisor; Software Engineer; Structural Engineer; Surveyor; Systems Analyst; Technical Writer/Editor; Telecommunications Manager. **Benefits available to temporary workers:** Paid Holidays; Paid Vacation. **Average salary range of placements:** $30,000 - $50,000. **Number of placements per year:** 100 - 199.

BUSINESS PERSONNEL SERVICES, INC.
7604 East 87th Street, Kansas City MO 64138. 816/356-7666. **Fax:** 816/356-0069. **Contact:** Office Manager. **Description:** A temporary agency that also provides permanent and contract placements. The firm focuses on clerical, administrative, data processing, and office support. Company pays fee. **Specializes in the areas of:** Accounting/Auditing; Administration; Advertising; Banking; Computer Science/Software; Education; Engineering; Finance; Food Industry; General Management; Health/Medical; Industrial; Insurance; Legal; Manufacturing; Personnel/Labor Relations; Publishing; Sales; Secretarial; Transportation. **Number of placements per year:** 200 - 499.

CROWN SERVICES, INC.
9666 Olive Street, Suite 100, Olivette MO 63132. 314/993-5333. **Contact:** Manager. **Description:** A temporary agency. Company pays fee. **Specializes in the areas of:** Accounting/Auditing; Banking; Clerical; Engineering; Insurance; Legal; Manufacturing; Personnel/Labor Relations. **Positions commonly filled include:** Accountant/Auditor; Administrative Assistant; Advertising Clerk; Bookkeeper; Claim Representative; Clerk; Computer Operator; Computer Programmer; Construction Trade Worker; Customer Service Representative; Data Entry Clerk; Driver; Factory Worker; Legal Secretary; Light Industrial Worker; Marketing Specialist; Medical Secretary; Receptionist; Sales Representative; Secretary; Typist/Word Processor. **Number of placements per year:** 1000+.

CROWN SERVICES, INC.
3316 Broadway Street, Kansas City MO 64111-2402. 816/931-3222. **Fax:** 816/931-3380. **Contact:** Judy Mertz, Branch Manager. **Description:** A temporary agency. **Specializes in the areas of:** Industrial; Manufacturing. **Benefits available to temporary workers:** Medical Insurance; Paid Vacation. **Corporate headquarters location:** Columbus OH. **Average salary range of placements:** Less than $20,000. **Number of placements per year:** 200 - 499.

ENVIROSTAFF, INC.
17600 Chesterfield Airport Road, Suite 101, Chesterfield MO 63005. 314/530-7120. **Fax:** 314/530-7195. **Contact:** Damien R. Flaherty, Area Manager. **Description:** A temporary agency. **Specializes in the areas of:** Environmental. **Positions commonly filled include:** Biological Scientist; Chemical Engineer; Chemist; Civil Engineer; Construction and Building Inspector; Construction Contractor; Design Engineer; Draftsperson; Environmental Engineer; Geologist/Geophysicist; Radiological Technologist; Surveyor; Technical Writer/Editor. **Benefits available to temporary workers:** Medical Insurance; Paid Holidays; Paid Vacation. **Corporate headquarters location:** Burnsville MN. **Other U.S. locations:** Nationwide.

EXECUTEMPS, INC.
307 East 63rd Street, Kansas City MO 64112. 816/363-8367. **Fax:** 816/523-0905. **Contact:** Michael Jack, President. **Description:** A temporary agency. **Specializes in the areas of:** Accounting/Auditing; Computer Science/Software; Legal; Secretarial. **Positions commonly filled include:** Accountant/

Auditor; Attorney; Computer Programmer; MIS Specialist; Paralegal; Systems Analyst; Typist/Word Processor.

INSURANCE OVERLOAD SYSTEMS
1807 Park 270 Drive, Building 1, Suite 470, St. Louis MO 63146-4021. 314/434-0909. **Toll-free phone:** 800/822-5848. **Fax:** 314/434-8820. **Contact:** Ms. Tracy Davis, Assistant Vice President. **World Wide Web address:** http://www.iostemps.com. **Description:** A temporary agency that also provides contract services. Company pays fee. **Specializes in the areas of:** Health/Medical; Insurance. **Positions commonly filled include:** Account Representative; Adjuster; Administrative Assistant; Auditor; Claim Representative; Customer Service Representative; Insurance Agent/Broker; Licensed Practical Nurse; Paralegal; Registered Nurse; Typist/Word Processor; Underwriter/Assistant Underwriter. **Benefits available to temporary workers:** Credit Union; Dental Insurance; Life Insurance; Medical Insurance; Vision Insurance. **Corporate headquarters location:** Dallas TX. **Other U.S. locations:** Nationwide. **Average salary range of placements:** $30,000 - $50,000. **Number of placements per year:** 200 - 499.

JODOC ENTERPRISES
655 East Springfield Avenue, Sullivan MO 63080. 573/468-5269. **Fax:** 573/468-5270. **Contact:** Damon D. Berti, President. **Description:** A temporary and permanent employment agency. Company pays fee. **Specializes in the areas of:** Accounting/Auditing; Administration; Engineering; Food Industry; General Management; Industrial; Legal; Light Industrial; Manufacturing; Personnel/Labor Relations; Retail; Secretarial. **Positions commonly filled include:** Accountant/Auditor; Blue-Collar Worker Supervisor; Buyer; Computer Programmer; Customer Service Representative; Design Engineer; Designer; Draftsperson; Electrician; Forester/Conservation Scientist; Human Resources Specialist; Licensed Practical Nurse; Medical Records Technician; Purchasing Agent/Manager; Typist/Word Processor. **Benefits available to temporary workers:** Medical Insurance; Paid Holidays; Paid Vacation. **Other area locations:** Sunrise Beach MO. **Average salary range of placements:** $20,000 - $29,999. **Number of placements per year:** 500 - 999.

KELLY SCIENTIFIC RESOURCES
55 West Port Plaza Drive, Suite 412, St. Louis MO 63146. 314/514-0179. **Fax:** 314/514-1589. **Contact:** Branch Manager. **World Wide Web address:** http://www.kellyscientific.com. **Description:** A temporary agency for scientific professionals. **Specializes in the areas of:** Chemical; Environmental; Food Industry; Health/Medical; Pharmaceutical.

KENDALLWOOD/ARCADIA HEALTH CARE SERVICES
One West Armour Boulevard, Suite 305, Kansas City MO 64111. 816/531-3550. **Toll-free phone:** 800/757-7501. **Fax:** 816/531-3010. **Contact:** Manager. **Description:** A temporary agency that focuses on home health placements. **Specializes in the areas of:** Health/Medical. **Positions commonly filled include:** Licensed Practical Nurse; Registered Nurse. **Benefits available to temporary workers:** Dental Insurance; Medical Insurance. **Average salary range of placements:** $20,000 - $29,999. **Number of placements per year:** 50 - 99.

B. LOEHR TEMPORARIES
P.O. Box 21530, St. Louis MO 63132-0530. 314/567-6500. **Contact:** John Hayes, President. **Description:** A temporary agency. **Specializes in the areas of:** Clerical; Industrial; Technical. **Positions commonly filled include:** Administrative Assistant; Bookkeeper; Chemist; Clerk; Data Entry Clerk; Draftsperson; Factory Worker; Legal Secretary; Light Industrial Worker; Medical Secretary; Receptionist; Secretary; Statistician; Stenographer; Technician; Typist/Word Processor.

MANPOWER TEMPORARY SERVICES
4473 Forest Park Boulevard, St. Louis MO 63108. 314/534-5211. **Contact:** Branch Manager. **Description:** A temporary agency. Company pays fee. **Specializes in the areas of:** Light Industrial; Office Support; Technical; Word Processing. **Positions commonly filled include:** Accountant/Auditor; Accounting Clerk; Administrative Assistant; Assembler; Biological Scientist; Bookkeeper; Chemist; Computer Operator; Customer Service Representative; Designer; Desktop Publishing Specialist; Electrician; Inspector/Tester/Grader; Inventory Control Specialist; Librarian; Machine Operator; Material Control Specialist; Order Clerk; Packaging/Processing Worker; Painter; Project Engineer; Proofreader; Receptionist; Research Technician; Software Engineer; Systems Analyst; Technical Writer/Editor; Telemarketer; Typist/Word Processor. **Benefits available to temporary workers:** Life Insurance; Medical Insurance; Paid Holidays; Paid Vacation. **Number of placements per year:** 1000+.

MANPOWER TEMPORARY SERVICES
820 North Main Street, Suite B, Sikeston MO 63801. 573/472-3800. **Toll-free phone:** 800/889-1827. **Fax:** 573/472-4669. **Contact:** Manager. **Description:** A temporary agency. Company pays fee. **Specializes in the areas of:** Computer Science/Software; Industrial; Personnel/Labor Relations; Sales; Secretarial. **Positions commonly filled include:** Blue-Collar Worker Supervisor; Clerical Supervisor; Machine Operator; Secretary. **Benefits available to temporary workers:** Medical Insurance; Paid Holidays; Paid Vacation. **Corporate headquarters location:** Milwaukee WI. **Other U.S. locations:** Nationwide. **Average salary range of placements:** Less than $20,000. **Number of placements per year:** 200 - 499.

MANPOWER TEMPORARY SERVICES
3630 South Geyer Road, St. Louis MO 63127-1230. 314/966-5747. **Fax:** 314/966-5819. **Contact:** Branch Manager. **Description:** A temporary agency that also provides career/outplacement counseling. **Specializes in the areas of:** Accounting/Auditing; Banking; Computer Science/Software; Engineering; Finance; General Management; Industrial; Insurance; Legal; Manufacturing; Nonprofit; Personnel/Labor Relations; Publishing; Retail; Secretarial; Technical; Transportation. **Positions commonly filled include:** Accountant/Auditor; Chemical Engineer; Chemist; Claim Representative; Clerical Supervisor; Computer Programmer; Credit Manager; Customer Service Representative; Draftsperson; Electrical/Electronics Engineer; Electrician; Financial Analyst; Health Services Manager; Human Resources Specialist; Industrial Engineer; Management Trainee; Mechanical Engineer; Mining Engineer; MIS Specialist; Systems Analyst. **Benefits available to temporary workers:** Life Insurance; Medical Insurance; Paid Vacation. **Corporate headquarters location:** Milwaukee WI. **Other U.S. locations:** Nationwide. **Number of placements per year:** 1000+.

NORRELL SERVICES INC.
11330 Olive Street, Suite 317, St. Louis MO 63146. 314/432-8880. **Fax:** 314/432-1393. **Contact:** Manager. **Description:** A temporary employment agency. Company pays fee. **Specializes in the areas of:** Manufacturing; Secretarial; Technical. **Positions commonly filled include:** Clinical Lab Technician; Typist/Word Processor. **Benefits available to temporary workers:** 401(k); Medical Insurance; Paid Holidays; Paid Vacation. **Average salary range of**

placements: Less than $20,000. **Number of placements per year:** 200 - 499.

OLSTEN STAFFING SERVICES
2025 Craigshire Drive, St. Louis MO 63146. 314/434-2800. **Contact:** William C. Young, Area Manager. **Description:** A temporary agency. Company pays fee. **Specializes in the areas of:** Accounting/Auditing; Clerical; Health/Medical; Legal; Manufacturing; MIS/EDP; Secretarial. **Positions commonly filled include:** Accountant/Auditor; Administrative Assistant; Aerospace Engineer; Biomedical Engineer; Bookkeeper; Civil Engineer; Clerk; Data Entry Clerk; Draftsperson; EDP Specialist; Electrical/Electronics Engineer; Factory Worker; Human Resources Manager; Industrial Engineer; Legal Secretary; Light Industrial Worker; Medical Secretary; Metallurgical Engineer; Nurse; Petroleum Engineer; Receptionist; Secretary; Stenographer; Technician; Typist/Word Processor. **Corporate headquarters location:** Melville NY. **Other U.S. locations:** Nationwide. **Number of placements per year:** 1000+.

OLSTEN STAFFING SERVICES
1201 East 15th Street, Joplin MO 64804-0812. 417/623-1212. **Fax:** 417/623-8966. **Contact:** William C. Scearce, Area Representative. **Description:** A temporary agency. Company pays fee. **Specializes in the areas of:** General Management; Industrial; Personnel/Labor Relations; Secretarial; Technical. **Positions commonly filled include:** Accountant/Auditor; Advertising Clerk; Blue-Collar Worker Supervisor; Clerical Supervisor; Clinical Lab Technician; Customer Service Representative; Human Resources Specialist; Human Service Worker; Industrial Production Manager; Management Trainee; Manufacturer's/Wholesaler's Sales Rep.; MIS Specialist; Paralegal; Purchasing Agent/Manager; Typist/Word Processor. **Corporate headquarters location:** Melville NY. **Other U.S. locations:** Nationwide. **Average salary range of placements:** $20,000 - $29,999. **Number of placements per year:** 500 - 999.

SNELLING PERSONNEL SERVICES
12400 Olive Boulevard, Suite 325, Creve Coeur MO 63141-5437. 314/576-1466. **Contact:** Beth Kreminski, Owner. **Description:** A full-service temporary agency specializing in temporary and temp-to-hire positions. Also provides career counseling services. **Specializes in the areas of:** Administration; Secretarial. **Number of placements per year:** 1 - 49.

WORKFORCE, INC.
119 East Columbia Street, Farmington MO 63640. 573/756-6700. **Contact:** David Braun, Owner. **Description:** A temporary agency. Company pays fee. **Specializes in the areas of:** Industrial; Manufacturing; Secretarial. **Positions commonly filled include:** Accountant/Auditor; Administrative Manager; Blue-Collar Worker Supervisor; Chemical Engineer; Clerical Supervisor; Customer Service Representative; Electrician; Human Resources Specialist; Industrial Production Manager; Management Trainee; Manufacturer's/Wholesaler's Sales Rep.; Mining Engineer; Operations/Production Manager; Quality Control Supervisor; Typist/Word Processor. **Benefits available to temporary workers:** Paid Vacation. **Average salary range of placements:** Less than $20,000. **Number of placements per year:** 1000+.

CONTRACT SERVICES FIRMS

ADVANTAGE FINANCIAL GROUP
P.O. Box 1445, Columbia MO 65205. **Contact:** Manager. **Description:** A contract services firm. **Specializes in the areas of:** Payroll; Tax.

BOTTOM LINE PROFESSIONAL SERVICES
320 Brookes Drive, Hazelwood MO 63042-2736. 314/367-5691. **Fax:** 314/895-5925. **Contact:** Bob Frank, Vice President. **Description:** A contract services firm. **Specializes in the areas of:** Accounting/Auditing; Administration; Biology; Computer Science/Software; Engineering; Finance; General Management; Legal; Personnel/Labor Relations; Technical. **Positions commonly filled include:** Accountant/Auditor; Aerospace Engineer; Architect; Attorney; Bank Officer/Manager; Biochemist; Biological Scientist; Biomedical Engineer; Budget Analyst; Buyer; Chemical Engineer; Chemist; Civil Engineer; Clinical Lab Technician; Computer Programmer; Construction Contractor; Cost Estimator; Customer Service Rep.; Dentist; Design Engineer; Designer; Electrical/Electronics Engineer; Environmental Engineer; Financial Analyst; Forester/Conservation Scientist; General Manager; Health Services Manager; Human Resources Specialist; Industrial Engineer; Library Technician; Management Analyst/Consultant; Mathematician; Mechanical Engineer; Mining Engineer; MIS Specialist; Nuclear Engineer; Petroleum Engineer; Purchasing Agent/Manager; Registered Nurse; Social Worker; Software Engineer; Stationary Engineer; Structural Engineer; Systems Analyst; Telecommunications Manager; Veterinarian. **Average salary range of placements:** More than $50,000. **Number of placements per year:** 100 - 199.

CDI CORPORATION
800 West 47th Street, Suite 403, Kansas City MO 64112. 816/960-0450. **Contact:** Manager. **World Wide Web address:** http://www.cdicorp.com. **Description:** A contract services firm. **Specializes in the areas of:** Engineering; Technical. **Corporate headquarters location:** Philadelphia PA. **Other U.S. locations:** Nationwide.

COMFORCE TECHNICAL SERVICES, INC.
5976 Howdershell Road, Suite 106, Hazelwood MO 63042. 314/731-8450. **Contact:** Manager. **Description:** A contract services firm. **Specializes in the areas of:** Engineering; Technical.

KENDALL & DAVIS COMPANY
11325 Concord Village Avenue, St. Louis MO 63123. 314/843-8838. **Toll-free phone:** 800/950-1551. **Fax:** 314/843-2262. **Contact:** Judi Phillips, Administrative Assistant. **E-mail address:** kendall@theonramp.net. **World Wide Web address:** http://www.kendallanddavis.com. **Description:** A contract services firm. Company pays fee. **Specializes in the areas of:** Health/Medical. **Positions commonly filled include:** Physician. **Number of placements per year:** 1 - 49.

KNOCHE CONNECTION
621 Duncan Road, Blue Springs MO 64014. 816/224-3600. **Fax:** 816/224-3602. **Contact:** Jim Knoche, Consultant. **E-mail address:** knoche@qni.com. **Description:** A contract services firm that also offers permanent placements. Company pays fee. **Specializes in the areas of:** Computer Science/Software. **Positions commonly filled include:** Computer Programmer; Operations/Production Manager; Systems Analyst; Telecommunications Manager. **Average salary range of placements:** $30,000 - $50,000. **Number of placements per year:** 50 - 99.

REHABCARE GROUP
7733 Forsyth Boulevard, Suite 1700, St. Louis MO 63105. 314/863-7422. **Toll-free phone:** 800/677

1238. **Fax:** 314/863-0769. **Contact:** Ms. Sean Mahoney, Vice President of Recruiting. **Description:** RehabCare Group is a leading provider of acute rehabilitation, subacute, outpatient, and temporary therapist staffing services on a contract basis in conjunction with over 750 hospitals, nursing homes, and contract therapy companies in all 50 states. **Specializes in the areas of:** Health/Medical. **Positions commonly filled include:** Occupational Therapist; Physical Therapist; Recreational Therapist; Social Worker; Speech-Language Pathologist. **Benefits available to temporary workers:** 401(k); Dental Insurance; Life Insurance; Medical Insurance; Tuition Assistance. **Corporate headquarters location:** This Location. **Other U.S. locations:** Nationwide. **Listed on:** NASDAQ.

REHABWORKS
12825 Flushing Meadows Drive, St. Louis MO 63131. 314/821-0008. **Contact:** Manager. **Description:** RehabWorks is one of two contract rehabilitation companies owned by Horizon Healthcare Corporation. Together, Community Rehabilitation Center and RehabWorks provide occupational, speech, and physical therapy services to patients in nursing homes and geriatric units at hospitals through 276 contracts, covering approximately 31,000 beds. **Specializes in the areas of:** Health/Medical.

TEAM INTERNATIONAL INC.
P.O. Box 18157, Raytown MO 64133-0057. **Toll-free phone:** 800/786-7140. **Fax:** 816/737-1451. **Contact:** Sherry Kyle, Account Executive. **Description:** A contract services firm that focuses on placement of technical personnel, including engineers, designers, and drafters. **Specializes in the areas of:** Engineering. **Positions commonly filled include:** Chemical Engineer; Civil Engineer; Design Engineer; Designer; Draftsperson; Industrial Engineer; Petroleum Engineer; Structural Engineer. **Benefits available to temporary workers:** Paid Holidays; Paid Vacation. **Corporate headquarters location:** Kansas City MO. **Average salary range of placements:** $30,000 - $50,000. **Number of placements per year:** 200 - 499.

WESTERN TECHNICAL SERVICES
763 South New Ballas Road, Suite 300, St. Louis MO 63141. 314/994-3950. **Fax:** 314/994-3940. **Contact:** Greg Hill, Vice President. **Description:** A contract services firm. **Specializes in the areas of:** Accounting/Auditing; Architecture/Construction; Biology; Computer Science/Software; Engineering; Food Industry; Technical. **Positions commonly filled include:** Accountant/Auditor; Architect; Biochemist; Chemist; Computer Programmer; Draftsperson; Environmental Engineer; Industrial Engineer; Mechanical Engineer; MIS Specialist; Systems Analyst. **Average salary range of placements:** $20,000 - $29,999. **Number of placements per year:** 1000+.

H.L. YOH COMPANY
14323 South Outer 40, Suite 484 South, St. Louis MO 63017. 314/878-0666. **Contact:** Manager. **Description:** A contract services firm. **Specializes in the areas of:** Engineering; High-Tech.

CAREER/OUTPLACEMENT COUNSELING FIRMS

THOMAS E. BROWN CAREER PLANNING
225 South Meramec Avenue, Suite 728, St. Louis MO 63105. 314/725-8122. **Fax:** 314/725-3470. **Contact:** Thomas E. Brown, LPC, Owner. **E-mail address:** tbrown10@ix.netcom.com. **Description:** A career/outplacement counseling firm.

BERNARD HALDANE ASSOCIATES
680 Craig Road, Suite 400, St. Louis MO 63141. 314/991-5444. **Toll-free phone:** 800/264-8898. **Fax:** 314/991-5207. **Contact:** Alan. R. Ludmer, President. **E-mail address:** careers@haldanestl.com. **Description:** A career/outplacement counseling service. **Number of placements per year:** 200 - 499.

MONTANA

EXECUTIVE SEARCH FIRMS

FINN'S EMPLOYMENT
P.O. Box 30356, Billings MT 59107. 406/259-1548. **Contact:** Jim Finnerty, President. **Description:** An executive search firm that operates on a contingency basis. Company pays fee. **Specializes in the areas of:** Health/Medical. **Positions commonly filled include:** Nurse Practitioner; Occupational Therapist; Pharmacist; Physical Therapist; Physician; Physician Assistant; Registered Nurse. **Number of placements per year:** 1 - 49.

F-O-R-T-U-N-E PERSONNEL CONSULTANTS
104 East Main Street, Suite 302, Bozeman MT 59715. 406/585-1332. **Fax:** 406/585-2255. **Contact:** Manager. **Description:** An executive search firm. Company pays fee. **Specializes in the areas of:** Biology; Biotechnology; Engineering; Medical Technology; Pharmaceutical. **Positions commonly filled include:** Agricultural Scientist; Biological Scientist; Biomedical Engineer; Chemical Engineer; Chemist; Clinical Lab Technician; Mechanical Engineer; Quality Control Supervisor; Statistician. **Corporate headquarters location:** New York NY. **Other U.S. locations:** Nationwide. **Number of placements per year:** 1 - 49.

W.R. KNAPP AND ASSOCIATES
4290 Wild Fox, Suite 200, Missoula MT 59802. 406/721-2221. **Fax:** 406/721-2227. **Contact:** Bob Knapp, Principal. **E-mail address:** wrknapp@montana.com. **Description:** An executive search firm. Company pays fee. **Specializes in the areas of:** Engineering; Technical; Transportation. **Positions commonly filled include:** Branch Manager; Chemical Engineer; Civil Engineer; Design Engineer; Economist; Environmental Engineer; General Manager; Geologist/Geophysicist; Geotechnical Engineer; Structural Engineer; Transportation/Traffic Specialist; Urban/Regional Planner. **Average salary range of placements:** More than $50,000. **Number of placements per year:** 1 - 49.

NELSON PERSONNEL
3700 South Russell Street, Suite B110, Missoula MT 59801. 406/543-6033. **Contact:** Manager. **Description:** An executive search firm.

PERMANENT EMPLOYMENT AGENCIES

CAREER CONCEPTS, INC.
220 East Center Street, Kalispell MT 59901. 406/755-0533. **Contact:** Manager. **Description:** A permanent placement agency.

EXPRESS PERSONNEL
3709 Brooks, Missoula MT 59801. 406/542-0323. **Contact:** Jay Olson, Owner. **Description:** A permanent employment agency. Company pays fee. **Specializes in the areas of:** Accounting/Auditing; Banking; Clerical; Engineering; Health/Medical; Legal; Sales; Secretarial. **Positions commonly filled include:** Accountant/Auditor; Architect; Bank Officer/Manager; Bookkeeper; Ceramics Engineer; Civil Engineer; Clerk; Computer Programmer; Construction Trade Worker; Credit Manager; Customer Service Representative; Data Entry Clerk; Dietician/Nutritionist; Draftsperson; Driver; Electrical/Electronics Engineer; General Manager; Hotel Manager; Human Resources Manager; Legal Secretary; Light Industrial Worker; Marketing Specialist; Mechanical Engineer; Medical Secretary; Mining Engineer; Public Relations Specialist; Receptionist; Sales Representative; Secretary; Typist/Word Processor; Underwriter/Assistant Underwriter. **Corporate headquarters location:** Oklahoma City OK. **Other U.S. locations:** Nationwide. **Number of placements per year:** 200 - 499.

LABOR CONTRACTING STAFFING SERVICES
275 Corporate Drive, Suite J, Kalispell MT 59901. 406/752-0191. **Toll-free phone:** 800/477-2718. **Fax:** 406/752-4708. **Contact:** Kristen Heck, Manager. **Description:** A permanent employment agency located in the Rocky Mountains of Montana. Areas of focus include skilled industrial and professional placement. Founded in 1985. Company pays fee. **Specializes in the areas of:** Engineering; Manufacturing; Personnel/Labor Relations; Sales. **Benefits available to temporary workers:** Paid Vacation. **Corporate headquarters location:** This Location. **Other area locations:** Bozeman MT; Missoula MT. **Number of placements per year:** 1000+.

NANNIES PREFERRED
1313 2nd West Hill Drive, Great Falls MT 59404-3029. 406/727-9897. **Contact:** Sandra Goff, President. **Description:** A permanent employment agency that focuses on placement of nannies. Nannies Preferred also works with other agencies around the United States in a referral capacity. Founded in 1986. **Specializes in the areas of:** Child Care, In-Home. **Positions commonly filled include:** Nanny. **Average salary range of placements:** Less than $20,000. **Number of placements per year:** 1 - 49.

TEMPORARY EMPLOYMENT AGENCIES

KELLY SERVICES, INC.
2070 Overland Avenue, Suite 102, Billings MT 59102. 406/652-2070. **Fax:** 406/652-3468. **Contact:** Human Resources. **Description:** A temporary agency that also provides permanent placements. Company pays fee. **Specializes in the areas of:** Clerical; Health/Medical; Insurance; Legal; Light Industrial; Office Support; Sales; Secretarial. **Corporate headquarters location:** Troy MI. **Other U.S. locations:** Nationwide. **Average salary range of placements:** $20,000 - $29,999. **Number of placements per year:** 1 - 49.

MANPOWER TEMPORARY SERVICES
2101 Overland Avenue, Suite 101, Billings MT 59102. 406/652-9401. **Fax:** 406/652-6763. **Contact:** Branch Manager. **Description:** A temporary agency. **Specializes in the areas of:** Clerical; Light Industrial; Technical. **Corporate headquarters location:** Milwaukee WI. **Other U.S. locations:** Nationwide. **International locations:** Worldwide.

CONTRACT SERVICES FIRMS

HEARTLAND NANNIES & COMPANIONS
HEARTLAND CAREGIVERS
5500 Grant Creek Road, Missoula MT 59802. 406/542-0241. **Fax:** 406/549-7304. **Contact:** Karen Ryan, Owner. **Description:** A contract services firm. Employer pays fee. Positions commonly filled include: Couples for estates; Human Service Worker; Nanny. **Specializes in the areas of:** Domestic Help; Eldercare, In-Home; Nannies. **Number of placements per year:** 200 - 499.

NEBRASKA

EXECUTIVE SEARCH FIRMS

ADAMS, INC.
13906 Gold Circle, Suite 101, Omaha NE 68144. 402/333-3009. **Fax:** 402/333-3448. **Contact:** Jay B. Adams, President. **Description:** An executive search firm. **Specializes in the areas of:** Banking. **Positions commonly filled include:** Loan Officer; Trust Officer. **Number of placements per year:** 50 - 99.

APEX SYSTEMS INC.
1820 Hillcrest Drive, Suite F, Bellevue NE 68005. 402/291-1200. **Contact:** Manager. **Description:** An executive search firm. **Specializes in the areas of:** Data Processing.

AUREUS GROUP
11825 Q Street, Omaha NE 68137-3503. 402/891-1118. **Toll-free phone:** 800/456-5857. **Fax:** 402/895-7812. **Contact:** Craig Wolf, Division Manager. **E-mail address:** aureusmed@aol.com. **Description:** An executive search firm. The firm also offers some temporary placements. **Specializes in the areas of:** Health/Medical.

CHOICE ENTERPRISES
6653 Sorenson Parkway, Omaha NE 68152. 402/571-8140. **Fax:** 402/571-5027. **Contact:** Jack L. Choice, Owner. **E-mail address:** cbc.execsearch@worldnet.att.net. **Description:** An executive search firm. Choice Enterprises operates through three divisions. Careers by Choice handles executive search services in data processing, engineering, finance, and accounting; CBC Temporaries is a temporary agency and contract services firm that provides temporary staffing, project management, and payroll services; and CBC Construction Services offers general and electrical contracting services. Founded in 1979. Company pays fee. **Specializes in the areas of:** Accounting/Auditing; Administration; Computer Science/Software; Engineering; Finance; Health/Medical; Manufacturing; Secretarial. **Average salary range of placements:** More than $50,000. **Number of placements per year:** 50 - 99.

COMPUSEARCH OF LINCOLN
210 Gateway, Suite 434, Lincoln NE 68505-2438. 402/467-5549. **Fax:** 402/467-1150. **Contact:** Bill Elam, Manager. **Description:** An executive search firm. **Specializes in the areas of:** Accounting/Auditing; Administration; Advertising; Architecture/Construction; Banking; Chemical; Communications; Computer Hardware/Software; Design; Electrical; Engineering; Food Industry; General Management; Health/Medical; Insurance; Legal; Manufacturing; Operations Management; Personnel/Labor Relations; Procurement; Publishing; Real Estate; Retail; Sales; Technical; Textiles; Transportation.

CORPORATE RECRUITERS, LTD.
4780 South 131st Street, Suite D, Omaha NE 68137. 402/896-3881. **Contact:** Linda Malerbi, Vice President. **Description:** An executive search firm. Company pays fee. **Specializes in the areas of:** Accounting/Auditing; Administration; Banking; Computer Science/Software; Food Industry; General Management; Health/Medical; Industrial; Legal; Manufacturing; Personnel/Labor Relations; Sales; Secretarial; Transportation. **Number of placements per year:** 50 - 99.

ROSE CRUM ASSOCIATES
1941 South 42nd Street, Suite 318, Cherrywood Mall, Omaha NE 68105. 402/341-1475. **Toll-free phone:** 800/243-3613. **Fax:** 402/346-5305. **Contact:** Rose Crum, President. **Description:** An executive search firm. Company pays fee. **Specializes in the areas of:** Apparel; Fashion; Health/Medical; Personnel/Labor Relations; Retail; Sales. **Positions commonly filled include:** Buyer; Occupational Therapist; Physical Therapist; Physician; Speech-Language Pathologist. **Average salary range of placements:** More than $50,000. **Number of placements per year:** 100 - 199.

DHR INTERNATIONAL INC.
5000 Central Park Drive, Suite 204, Lincoln NE 68504. 402/464-0566. **Contact:** Manager. **Description:** A generalist executive search firm.

DUNHILL PROFESSIONAL SEARCH
13709 B Street, Omaha NE 68144. 402/334-1233. **Fax:** 402/334-0290. **Contact:** Ken Jaspersen, President. **Description:** An executive search firm that focuses on industries including credit cards, trust banking, commercial lending, and agri-business. Company pays fee. **Specializes in the areas of:** Agri-Business; Banking; Credit and Collection. **Positions commonly filled include:** Accountant/Auditor; Agricultural Engineer; Agricultural Scientist; Bank Officer/Manager; Branch Manager; Credit Manager; Financial Analyst; Services Sales Representative. **Average salary range of placements:** $30,000 - $50,000. **Number of placements per year:** 1 - 49.

EXPRESS PERSONNEL
12119 Pacific Street, Omaha NE 68154. 402/333-5353. **Contact:** Larry Humberstone, Owner. **Description:** An executive search firm that also operates as a temporary and permanent employment agency. Company pays fee. **Specializes in the areas of:** Administration; Computer Science/Software; Engineering; Finance; Food Industry; General Management; Industrial; Insurance; Manufacturing; Personnel/Labor Relations; Sales; Secretarial; Technical; Transportation. **Positions commonly filled include:** Administrative Manager; Agricultural Engineer; Attorney; Bank Officer/Manager; Branch Manager; Buyer; Computer Programmer; Credit Manager; Dietician/Nutritionist; Electrical/Electronics Engineer; Environmental Engineer; Financial Analyst; General Manager; Human Resources Specialist; Management Trainee; MIS Specialist; Multimedia Designer; Operations/Production Manager; Public Relations Specialist; Purchasing Agent/Manager; Quality Control Supervisor; Restaurant/Food Service Manager; Software Engineer; Systems Analyst; Telecommunications Manager; Transportation/Traffic Specialist; Travel Agent; Underwriter/Assistant Underwriter; Urban/Regional Planner; Video Production Coordinator. **Average salary range of placements:** $30,000 - $50,000. **Number of placements per year:** 100 - 199.

HAHN TECHNICAL STAFFING
1517 Broadway, Suite 125, Scott's Bluff NE 69361. 812/372-0125. **Contact:** Gary Hahn, President. **Description:** An executive search firm. **Specializes in the areas of:** Engineering; Manufacturing.

ROBERT HALF INTERNATIONAL/ACCOUNTEMPS
1125 South 103rd Street, Suite 100, Omaha NE 68124. 402/397-8107. **Contact:** Manager. **World Wide Web address:** http://www.roberthalf.com. **Description:** An executive search firm. Accountemps (also at this location) provides temporary placements. **Specializes in the areas of:** Accounting/Auditing. **Corporate headquarters location:** Menlo Park CA. **Other U.S. locations:** Nationwide.

HARRISON MOORE INC.
7638 Pierce Street, Omaha NE 68124. 402/391-5494. **Contact:** Manager. **Description:** An executive search firm that focuses on the foundry industry. **Specializes in the areas of:** Metals.

MANAGEMENT RECRUITERS OF OMAHA
OFFICEMATES5 OF OMAHA
7171 West Mercy Road, Suite 252, Omaha NE 68106. 402/397-8320. **Fax:** 402/397-6322. **Contact:** Les Zanotti, Manager. **Description:** An executive search firm. **Specializes in the areas of:** Accounting/Auditing; Administration; Advertising; Architecture/Construction; Banking; Chemical; Communications; Computer Hardware/Software; Design; Electrical; Engineering; Food Industry; General Management; Health/Medical; Insurance; Legal; Manufacturing; Operations Management; Personnel/Labor Relations; Procurement; Publishing; Retail; Sales; Technical; Textiles; Transportation.

NOLL HUMAN RESOURCE SERVICES
12905 West Dodge Road, Omaha NE 68154. 402/391-7736. **Toll-free phone:** 800/536-7600. **Fax:** 402/391-6748. **Contact:** Recruiter. **Description:** An executive search firm. **Specializes in the areas of:** Administration; Banking; Computer Science/Software; General Management; Health/Medical; Secretarial; Transportation. **Positions commonly filled include:** Actuary; Bank Officer/Manager; Clerical Supervisor; Computer Programmer; Financial Analyst; General Manager; Health Services Manager; Licensed Practical Nurse; Management Analyst/Consultant; Occupational Therapist; Operations/Production Manager; Paralegal; Physical Therapist; Physician; Radiological Technologist; Registered Nurse; Respiratory Therapist; Surgical Technician; Transportation/Traffic Specialist. **Other U.S. locations:** Dallas TX. **Number of placements per year:** 200 - 499.

ODYSSEY GROUP
1104 South 76th Avenue, Suite B, Omaha NE 68124. 402/391-2065. **Contact:** Manager. **Description:** An executive search firm. **Specializes in the areas of:** Clerical.

DON PARISET ASSOCIATES
1525 South 106th Street, Omaha NE 68124. 402/397-7092. **Contact:** Don Pariset. **Description:** An executive search firm. **Specializes in the areas of:** Engineering.

PROFESSIONS
501 Olson Drive, Suite 2, Papillion NE 68046-5752. 402/331-6440. **Toll-free phone:** 888/434-6877. **Fax:** 402/331-8826. **Contact:** David Hawkins, President. **E-mail address:** jobsarus@neonramp.com. **World Wide Web address:** http://www.jobsarus.com. **Description:** An executive search firm. Company pays fee. **Specializes in the areas of:** Computer Science/Software. **Positions commonly filled include:** Applications Engineer; Computer Animator; Computer Operator; Computer Programmer; Database Manager; Internet Services Manager; MIS Specialist; Online Content Specialist; Operations Manager; Project Manager; Software Engineer; Systems Analyst; Systems Manager; Technical Writer/Editor; Telecommunications Manager; Webmaster. **Average salary range of placements:** More than $50,000. **Number of placements per year:** 100 - 199.

RECRUITERS INTERNATIONAL, INC.
11330 Q Street, Suite 218, Omaha NE 68137. 402/339-9839. **Fax:** 402/339-4024. **Contact:** Kenneth H. Mertins, President. **Description:** An executive search firm. Company pays fee. **Specializes in the areas of:** Sales. **Corporate headquarters:** This location. **Average salary range of placements:** More than $20,000.

THE REGENCY GROUP, LTD.
256 North 115th Street, Suite 1, Omaha NE 68154-2521. 402/334-7255. **Fax:** 402/334-7148. **Contact:** Dan J. Barrow, CPC, General Manager. **E-mail address:** info@regencygroup.com. **World Wide Web address:** http://www.regencygroup.com. **Description:** An executive search firm operating on a contingency basis. Company pays fee. **Specializes in the areas of:** Administration; Computer Science/Software; Telecommunications. **Positions commonly filled include:** Computer Programmer; Design Engineer; MIS Specialist; Multimedia Designer; Operations/Production Manager; Software Engineer; Systems Analyst; Technical Writer/Editor; Telecommunications Manager. **Average salary range of placements:** More than $50,000. **Number of placements per year:** 50 - 99.

RELIABLE NATIONAL PERSONNEL CONSULTANTS
Atrium Plaza, 11318 Davenport Street, Omaha NE 68154. 402/330-2814. **Fax:** 402/330-8164. **Contact:** Harlan Rohmberg, CPC, President. **Description:** A national executive search firm with 300 affiliated offices. Company pays fee. **Specializes in the areas of:** Architecture/Construction; Computer Hardware/Software; Executives; Finance. **Positions commonly filled include:** Accountant/Auditor; Administrator; Architect; Data Processor; Engineer; Management. **Number of placements per year:** 50 - 99.

SALES CONSULTANTS OF OMAHA
3568 Dodge Street, Omaha NE 68131. **Contact:** Manager. **Description:** An executive search firm. Company pays fee. **Specializes in the areas of:** Agriculture; Banking; Finance; Health/Medical; Industrial; Publishing; Sales; Telecommunications; Transportation. **Positions commonly filled include:** Accountant/Auditor; Actuary; Agricultural Engineer; Bank Officer/Manager; Branch Manager; Clerical Supervisor; Computer Programmer; Credit Manager; Dietician/Nutritionist; EKG Technician; Emergency Medical Technician; General Manager; Health Services Manager; Licensed Practical Nurse; Pharmacist; Physician; Recreational Therapist; Registered Nurse; Respiratory Therapist; Telecommunications Manager; Transportation/Traffic Specialist; Travel Agent. **Number of placements per year:** 1 - 49.

PERMANENT EMPLOYMENT AGENCIES

ACCOUNTING RESOURCES INC.
770 North Cotner Boulevard, Suite 325, Lincoln NE 68505. 402/464-4488. **Contact:** Manager. **Description:** A permanent employment agency that also provides some temporary placements. **Specializes in the areas of:** Accounting/Auditing.

AMERI SEARCH INC.
3710 Central Avenue, Suite 13, Kearney NE 68847. 308/237-2422. **Contact:** Manager. **Description:** A permanent and temporary employment agency that also provides some executive recruiting. **Specializes in the areas of:** Clerical; Data Processing; Sales.

ARCADIA HEALTH CARE
111 South 56th Street, Suite 100, Lincoln NE 68504-3511. 402/464-2220. **Contact:** Manager. **Description:** A permanent employment agency. Arcadia Health Care provides skilled and unskilled nursing placements for both in-home patients and health care facilities. **Specializes in the areas of:** Health/Medical.

BUSINESS PROFESSIONS, INC.
11128 John Galt Boulevard, Suite 595, Omaha NE 68137. 402/593-0404. **Fax:** 402/593-0505. **Contact:** John Howard, Executive Recruiter. **E-mail address:** bpinc@radiks.net. **Description:** A permanent employment agency. Founded in 1994. Company pays fee. **Specializes in the areas of:** General Management. **Positions commonly filled include:** Bank Officer/Manager; Hotel Manager; Restaurant/Food Service Manager; Retail Manager.

EGGERS COMPANY
11272 Elm Street, Omaha NE 68144. 402/333-3480. **Fax:** 402/333-9759. **Contact:** James W. Eggers, CPC, President. **Description:** A permanent employment agency. **Specializes in the areas of:** Accounting/Auditing; Banking; Computer Science/Software; Insurance; Manufacturing; Retail; Sales.

HANSEN AGRI-PLACEMENT
P.O. Box 1172, Grand Island NE 68802. 308/382-7350. **Fax:** 308/382-7427. **Contact:** Jack Hansen, Owner. **E-mail address:** hansenag@kdsi.net. **Description:** An employment agency. Company pays fee. **Specializes in the areas of:** Accounting/Auditing; Engineering; Finance; Food Industry; General Management; Manufacturing; Sales. **Positions commonly filled include:** Accountant/Auditor; Actuary; Advertising Clerk; Agricultural Engineer; Architect; Attorney; Bank Officer/Manager; Bookkeeper; Buyer; Chemist; Civil Engineer; Claim Representative; Clerk; Commercial Artist; Computer Operator; Computer Programmer; Credit Manager; Customer Service Representative; Data Entry Clerk; Draftsperson; EDP Specialist; Electrical/Electronics Engineer; Financial Analyst; General Manager; Hotel Manager; Human Resources Manager; Industrial Engineer; Insurance Agent/Broker; Legal Secretary; Manufacturing Engineer; Marketing Specialist; Mechanical Engineer; Medical Secretary; MIS Specialist; Operations/Production Manager; Purchasing Agent/Manager; Quality Control Supervisor; Receptionist; Sales Representative; Secretary; Stenographer; Systems Analyst; Technician; Typist/Word Processor. **Number of placements per year:** 1000+.

PROFESSIONAL PERSONNEL SERVICE
3201 Pioneers Boulevard, Suite 222, Lincoln NE 68502. 402/483-7821. **Contact:** Manager. **Description:** A permanent placement agency. **Specializes in the areas of:** Administration; Technical.

PROFESSIONAL RECRUITERS INC.
P.O. Box 24227, Omaha NE 68124. 402/397-2885. **Physical address:** 7253 Grover Street, Omaha NE. **Fax:** 402/397-7357. **Contact:** Wayne L. Smith, President. **Description:** A permanent employment agency. Company pays fee. **Specializes in the areas of:** Computer Science/Software; Engineering; Manufacturing; Personnel/Labor Relations. **Positions commonly filled include:** Agricultural Engineer; Ceramics Engineer; Chemical Engineer; Computer Programmer; Electrical/Electronics Engineer; Human Resources Manager; Industrial Engineer; Industrial Production Manager; Materials Engineer; Mechanical Engineer; Metallurgical Engineer; Purchasing Agent/Manager; Quality Control Supervisor; Software Engineer; Statistician; Systems Analyst. **Number of placements per year:** 200 - 499.

TEMPORARY EMPLOYMENT AGENCIES

ADECCO
1941 South 42nd Street, Suite 304, Omaha NE 68105. 402/346-7500. **Fax:** 402/393-5606. **Contact:** Lynn Wartinger, Office Supervisor. **Description:** A temporary agency. Adecco also offers temp-to-hire and permanent placement. Founded in 1957. Company pays fee. **Specializes in the areas of:** Accounting/Auditing; Industrial; Secretarial; Technical. **Positions commonly filled include:** Customer Service Representative; Human Resources Specialist; Medical Records Technician; Paralegal. **Benefits available to temporary workers:** 401(k); Dental Insurance; Medical Insurance; Paid Holidays; Paid Vacation. **Corporate headquarters location:** Redwood City CA. **Other U.S. locations:** Nationwide. **Average salary range of placements:** Less than $20,000. **Number of placements per year:** 200 - 499.

KELLY SERVICES, INC.
9140 West Dodge Road, Suite 230, Omaha NE 68114. 402/393-5000. **Fax:** 402/393-2140. **Contact:** Ms. Dee Felici, Branch Manager. **Description:** A temporary agency. Founded in 1946. Company pays fee. **Specializes in the areas of:** Accounting/Auditing; Banking; Clerical; Health/Medical; Industrial; Manufacturing; Personnel/Labor Relations; Retail; Sales; Secretarial. **Positions commonly filled include:** Administrative Manager; Advertising Clerk; Bank Officer/Manager; Blue-Collar Worker Supervisor; Branch Manager; Clerical Supervisor; Computer Programmer; Credit Manager; Customer Service Representative; Food Scientist/Technologist; Human Resources Specialist; Human Service Worker; Management Trainee; Medical Records Technician; Quality Control Supervisor; Services Sales Representative; Telecommunications Manager; Typist/Word Processor. **Benefits available to temporary workers:** Paid Holidays; Paid Vacation. **Corporate headquarters location:** Troy MI. **Other U.S. locations:** Nationwide. **Average salary range of placements:** $20,000 - $29,999. **Number of placements per year:** 1000+.

OUTSOURCE II, INC.
4315 South 90th Street, Omaha NE 68127. 402/331-7300. **Toll-free phone:** 800/259-7269. **Contact:** Manager. **Description:** A temporary agency that also provides contract services. Company pays fee. **Specializes in the areas of:** Computer Science/Software; Finance; General Management; Personnel/Labor Relations; Sales; Secretarial. **Positions commonly filled include:** Accountant/Auditor; Administrative Manager; Advertising Clerk; Bank Officer/Manager; Blue-Collar Worker Supervisor; Buyer; Claim Representative; Clerical Supervisor; Computer Programmer; Construction Contractor; Cost Estimator; Counselor; Credit Manager; Customer Service Representative; Draftsperson; Editor; Environmental Engineer; Financial Analyst; General Manager; Human Resources Specialist; Industrial Production Manager; Insurance Agent/Broker; Internet Services Manager; Management Analyst/Consultant; Management Trainee; Manufacturer's/Wholesaler's Sales Rep.; Market Research Analyst; MIS Specialist; Multimedia Designer; Operations/Production Manager; Paralegal; Public Relations Specialist; Quality Control Supervisor; Real Estate Agent; Securities Sales Representative; Services Sales Representative; Technical Writer/Editor; Telecommunications Manager; Transportation/Traffic Specialist; Typist/Word Processor; Underwriter/Assistant Underwriter; Video Production Coordinator.

SHARP PERSONNEL
719 North 48th Street, Lincoln NE 68504. 402/466-1980. **Fax:** 402/466-2165. **Contact:** Shari Vermeer, Branch Manager. **Description:** A temporary agency. Company pays fee. **Specializes in the areas of:**

Administration; General Management; Industrial; Light Industrial; Manufacturing; Personnel/Labor Relations; Publishing; Sales; Secretarial; Technical. **Positions commonly filled include:** Accountant/Auditor; Administrative Manager; Blue-Collar Worker Supervisor; Branch Manager; Clerical Supervisor; Clinical Lab Technician; Computer Programmer; Customer Service Representative; Electrical/ Electronics Engineer; General Manager; Human Resources Specialist; Industrial Production Manager; Mechanical Engineer; Operations/Production Manager; Quality Control Supervisor; Travel Agent; Typist/Word Processor. **Benefits available to temporary workers:** Medical Insurance; Paid Holidays; Paid Vacation. **Other U.S. locations:** KS; MO; OK. **Average salary range of placements:** Less than $20,000. **Number of placements per year:** 1000+.

CONTRACT SERVICES FIRMS

DONNA'S OFFICE SERVICE
221 South Jeffers Street, Suite 1, North Platte NE 69101-5371. 308/532-9236. **Contact:** Donna Fair, Owner. **Description:** A contract services firm that provides a variety of office services. Founded in 1994. **Specializes in the areas of:** Accounting/Auditing; Clerical; Legal; Personnel/Labor Relations; Retail; Secretarial. **Positions commonly filled include:** Accountant/Auditor; Customer Service Representative; Human Service Worker; Legal Secretary; Typist/Word Processor. **Average salary range of placements:** $20,000 - $29,999. **Number of placements per year:** 1 - 49.

PROVISION TECHNOLOGIES
8630 Cass, Suite 203, Omaha NE 68154. 402/393-4990. **Contact:** Manager. **World Wide Web address:** http://www.careerbase.com. **Description:** A contract services and consulting firm. **Specializes in the areas of:** Computer Science/Software; Information Technology.

NEVADA

EXECUTIVE SEARCH FIRMS

EXECUTIVE MANAGEMENT RESOURCES
3885 South Decatur, Suite 3000, Las Vegas NV 89103. 702/220-3000. **Contact:** Manager. **Description:** An executive search firm. Executive Management Resources does not specialize but does place a large portion of its clients in the gaming sector. **Specializes in the areas of:** Casinos.

ROBERT HALF INTERNATIONAL ACCOUNTEMPS/OFFICETEAM
5310 Kietzke Lane, Suite 205, Reno NV 89511. 702/739-9797. **Contact:** Manager. **Description:** An executive search firm. Accountemps provides temporary placements. OfficeTeam provides temporary clerical and office support placements. **Specializes in the areas of:** Accounting/Auditing. **Corporate headquarters location:** Menlo Park CA. **Other U.S. locations:** Nationwide.

MANAGEMENT RECRUITERS INTERNATIONAL
4530 Southeastern, Suite A12, Las Vegas NV 89119. 702/733-1818. **Contact:** Manager. **Description:** An executive search firm. **Specializes in the areas of:** Construction; Engineering. **Corporate headquarters location:** Cleveland OH. **Other U.S. locations:** Nationwide.

MANAGEMENT RECRUITERS OF RENO
1025 Ridgeview Drive, Suite 100, Reno NV 89509. 702/826-5243. **Fax:** 702/826-8329. **Contact:** J. Edward Trapp, Owner/Manager. **Description:** An executive search firm operating on a contingency basis. Founded in 1979. Company pays fee. **Specializes in the areas of:** Accounting/Auditing; Administration; Computer Hardware/Software; Engineering; Health/Medical; Insurance; Manufacturing; Sales; Transportation. **Positions commonly filled include:** Accountant/Auditor; Actuary; Buyer; Chemical Engineer; Computer Programmer; Cost Estimator; EEG Technologist; EKG Technician; Electrical/Electronics Engineer; General Manager; Hotel Manager; Mechanical Engineer; MIS Specialist; Operations/Production Manager; Pharmacist; Physician; Software Engineer; Systems Analyst; Underwriter/Assistant Underwriter. **Average salary range of placements:** $30,000 - $50,000. **Number of placements per year:** 1 - 49.

MATRIX GROUP
501 South Rancho Drive, Suite G46, Las Vegas NV 89106. 702/598-0070. **Contact:** Manager. **Description:** An executive search firm. **Specializes in the areas of:** Clerical; Engineering; MIS/EDP; Mortgage.

RESOURCE NETWORK
2001 East Flamingo Road, Suite 100T, Las Vegas NV 89119. 702/796-0111. **Contact:** Manager. **Description:** An executive search firm.

DOUG STUMPF ASSOCIATES
1301 East Sunset Road, Box 8115, Las Vegas NV 89119. 702/597-2554. **Toll-free phone:** 800/405-8077. **Fax:** 702/597-2554. **Contact:** Helene Stumpf, Principal. **Description:** An executive search firm operating on a contingency basis. Company pays fee. **Specializes in the areas of:** Fire Protection Engineering; Safety. **Positions commonly filled include:** Cost Estimator; Design Engineer; Designer; Draftsperson; Electrical/Electronics Engineer; Fire Science/Protection Engineer; Operations Manager; Safety Engineer; Sales Engineer; Sales Executive; Sales Rep.; Services Sales Rep. **Average salary range of placements:** $30,000 - $50,000.

PERMANENT EMPLOYMENT AGENCIES

ACUMEN PERSONNEL
2909 West Charleston Boulevard, Las Vegas NV 89102. 702/877-6775. **Fax:** 702/878-9297. **Contact:** Lynn Murray, Owner. **Description:** An employment agency offering both permanent and temporary positions. **Specializes in the areas of:** Accounting/Auditing; Computer Hardware/Software.

CHARM UNLIMITED INC.
1712 Kasabian Avenue, Las Vegas NV 89104. 702/735-2335. **Contact:** Marcel P. LeBon, President. **Description:** An employment agency. **Specializes in the areas of:** Advertising; Fashion. **Positions commonly filled include:** Advertising Clerk; Operations/Production Manager.

INTERIM PERSONNEL
808 East College Parkway, Suite 104, Carson City NV 89706. 702/885-0809. **Fax:** 702/885-0858. **Contact:** Jan Johnson, Personnel Coordinator. **Description:** An employment agency that concentrates on temporary, direct hire, and leased employees. Founded in 1976. **Positions commonly filled include:** Accountant; Architect; Blue-Collar Worker Supervisor; Buyer; Chemical Engineer; Civil Engineer; Claim Rep.; Clerical Supervisor; Customer Service Rep.; Dental Assistant/Hygienist; Design Engineer; Designer; Draftsperson; Electrical/Electronics Engineer; Industrial Engineer; Industrial Production Manager; Insurance Agent/Broker; Licensed Practical Nurse; Manufacturer's/Wholesaler's Sales Rep.; Mechanical Engineer; Paralegal; Quality Control Supervisor; Teacher/Professor; Travel Agent; Typist/Word Processor. **Average salary range of placements:** Less than $20,000. **Number of placements per year:** 200 - 499.

KIDS CARE CONNECTION
2441 Tech Center Court, Suite 112, Las Vegas NV 89128. 702/255-0003. **Fax:** 702/255-0779. **Recorded jobline:** 702/226-5538. **Contact:** Shari Kermer, President. **Description:** An employment agency focusing on nanny placement and babysitting. Kids Care Connection provides live out, live in, permanent, and temporary child care. **Specializes in the areas of:** Child Care, In-Home; Nannies. **Positions commonly filled include:** Nanny; Teacher/Professor. **Average salary range of placements:** Less than $20,000. **Number of placements per year:** 100 - 199.

NANNY PLACEMENT AGENCY
P.O. Box 33580, Reno NV 89533-3580. 702/334-4725. **Contact:** Manager. **Description:** A permanent employment agency. **NOTE:** Nannies must be at least 21 years old. U.S. citizenship or a work permit is necessary. References and criminal, credit, and driving reports are also required. Company pays fee. **Specializes in the areas of:** Child Care, In-Home; Nannies. **Positions commonly filled include:** Nanny. **Average salary range of placements:** Less than $20,000. **Number of placements per year:** 1 - 49.

SALES STAFFING SPECIALISTS
2685 South Rainbow Boulevard, Suite 109, Las Vegas NV 89102. 702/257-3835. **Fax:** 702/257-3859.

Contact: Susan Daum, Manager. **Description:** A permanent employment agency and executive search firm that places sales professionals in a variety of industries including advertising, chemicals, computers, construction, retail, electronics, finance, health care, and telecommunications. Company pays fee. **Specializes in the areas of:** Sales. **Positions commonly filled include:** Sales Engineer; Sales Executive; Sales Manager; Sales Rep. **Corporate headquarters location:** San Diego CA. **Average salary range of placements:** $30,000 - $50,000. **Number of placements per year:** 200 - 499.

TALENT TREE STAFFING SERVICES
2920 South Jones Boulevard, Suite 220, Las Vegas NV 89102-5310. 702/362-8600. **Fax:** 702/362-3724. **Contact:** Ms. Janice Wesen, President. **Description:** A temporary and permanent employment service. Company pays fee. **Specializes in the areas of:** Accounting/Auditing; Administration; Advertising; Banking; Education; Engineering; Finance; Insurance; Legal; Manufacturing; Personnel/Labor Relations; Publishing; Secretarial. **Positions commonly filled include:** Customer Service Rep.; MIS Specialist; Paralegal; Typist/Word Processor. **Benefits available to temporary workers:** 401(k); Dental Insurance; Medical Insurance. **Corporate headquarters location:** Houston TX. **Other U.S. locations:** Nationwide. **Average salary range of placements:** $20,000 - $29,999. **Number of placements per year:** 1000+.

TEMPORARY EMPLOYMENT AGENCIES

LABOR FINDERS
P.O. Box 20292, Carson City NV 89721-0292. 702/884-4645. **Physical address:** 933 Woodside, Carson City NV. **Fax:** 702/884-2989. **Contact:** Manager. **Description:** A temporary agency providing day labor that focuses on the construction industry. Company pays fee. **Specializes in the areas of:** Construction; Food Industry; Heavy Equipment; Industrial; Publishing. **Positions commonly filled include:** Blue-Collar Worker Supervisor; Electrical/Electronics Engineer; Electrician; Production Worker; Truck Driver. **Corporate headquarters location:** Palm Beach Gardens FL. **Other U.S. locations:** Nationwide. **Average salary range of placements:** $20,000 - $29,999. **Number of placements per year:** 50 - 99.

MANPOWER TEMPORARY SERVICES
1755 Vassar Street, Reno NV 89502. 702/322-2000. **Contact:** Branch Manager. **Description:** A temporary agency. **Specializes in the areas of:** Clerical; Computer Hardware/Software; Construction; Engineering; Secretarial; Technical. **Positions commonly filled include:** Accountant/Auditor; Aerospace Engineer; Agricultural Engineer; Biomedical Engineer; Bookkeeper; Civil Engineer; Clerk; Computer Programmer; Construction Trade Worker; Customer Service Representative; Data Entry Clerk; Draftsperson; Driver; Electrical/Electronics Engineer; Financial Analyst; Industrial Designer; Industrial Engineer; Legal Secretary; Light Industrial Worker; Medical Secretary; Metallurgical Engineer; Receptionist; Secretary; Statistician; Stenographer; Technical Writer/Editor; Technician; Typist/Word Processor. **Number of placements per year:** 200 - 499.

MANPOWER TEMPORARY SERVICES
314 Las Vegas Boulevard North, Las Vegas NV 89101. 702/384-3168. **Contact:** Branch Manager. **Description:** A temporary agency. Company pays fee. **Specializes in the areas of:** Data Processing; Industrial; Office Support; Professional; Technical; Word Processing. **Positions commonly filled include:** Accountant/Auditor; Accounting Supervisor; Administrative Assistant; Assembly Worker; Bookkeeper; Chemist; Computer Operator; Customer Service Representative; Desktop Publishing Specialist; Electrician; Inspector/Tester/Grader; Machine Operator; Packaging/Processing Worker; Painter; Project Engineer; Proofreader; Receptionist; Research Assistant; Secretary; Software Engineer; Stenographer; Systems Analyst; Technical Writer/Editor; Technician; Typist/Word Processor; Welder. **Benefits available to temporary workers:** Life Insurance; Medical Insurance; Paid Holidays; Paid Vacation. **Number of placements per year:** 1000+.

CONTRACT SERVICES FIRMS

REHABWORKS
1755 East Plum Lane, Suite 258, Reno NV 89502. 702/323-2332. **Contact:** Manager. **Description:** RehabWorks (formerly Nevada Rehabilitation Services Corporation) is one of two contract rehabilitation companies owned by Horizon Healthcare Corporation. Together, Community Rehabilitation Center and RehabWorks provide occupational, speech, and physical therapy services to patients in nursing homes and geriatric units at hospitals through 276 contracts, covering approximately 31,000 beds. **Specializes in the areas of:** Health/Medical.

CAREER/OUTPLACEMENT COUNSELING FIRMS

NEVADA BUSINESS SERVICES (NBS)
940 West Owens, Las Vegas NV 89106. 702/646-7675. **Fax:** 702/646-7812. **Contact:** Bill Murphy, Program Manager. **Description:** A federally funded employment/training program available to eligible individuals. NBS offers career counseling, employment workshops, and classroom training in a wide variety of areas to increase job skills. NBS also arranges on-the-job training and job placement with employers. **Specializes in the areas of:** Administration; Clerical; Education; General Management; Nonprofit.
Other area locations:

- 109 Military Circle, P.O. Box 3288, Tonopah NV 89049. 702/482-6909x6038. (Administration; Education; General Management; Nonprofit; Secretarial)
- P.O. Box 26, Caliente NV 89008. 702/726-3154. (Administration; Education; General Management; Nonprofit; Secretarial)

NEW HAMPSHIRE

EXECUTIVE SEARCH FIRMS

ABLE 1 STAFFING
126 Daniel Street, Portsmouth NH 03801. 603/436-1151. **Fax:** 603/436-0285. **Contact:** Laura Montville, President. **E-mail address:** staffing@able1.com. **World Wide Web address:** http://www.bluefin.net/~able1. **Description:** An executive search firm. Company pays fee. **Specializes in the areas of:** Accounting/Auditing; Banking; Clerical; Computer Hardware/Software; Engineering; Finance; Health/Medical; Insurance; Legal; Publishing; Sales; Secretarial; Technical; Transportation. **Positions commonly filled include:** Accountant/Auditor; Actuary; Administrative Assistant; Aerospace Engineer; Agricultural Engineer; Attorney; Bank Officer/Manager; Biological Scientist; Biomedical Engineer; Bookkeeper; Civil Engineer; Claim Representative; Clerk; Computer Programmer; Credit Manager; Data Entry Clerk; Draftsperson; EDP Specialist; Electrical/Electronics Engineer; Financial Analyst; Industrial Designer; Industrial Engineer; Insurance Agent/Broker; Legal Secretary; Management Analyst/Consultant; Marketing Specialist; Mechanical Engineer; Medical Secretary; Nurse; Purchasing Agent/Manager; Receptionist; Secretary; Systems Analyst; Technical Writer/Editor; Technician; Typist/Word Processor; Underwriter/Assistant Underwriter. **Number of placements per year:** 1 - 49.

ACCESS DATA PERSONNEL, INC.
649 2nd Street, Manchester NH 03102. 603/641-6300. **Contact:** Manager. **Description:** An executive search firm. **Specializes in the areas of:** Information Systems; Information Technology.

ADVANCED RECRUITING & CONSULTING
75 Gilcreast Road, Londonderry NH 03053. 603/425-2488. **Fax:** 603/432-2533. **Contact:** Kim C. Scoggins, Senior Partner. **Description:** An executive search firm operating on a contingency basis. Company pays fee. **Specializes in the areas of:** Accounting/Auditing; Finance. **Positions commonly filled include:** Accountant/Auditor; Budget Analyst; Chief Financial Officer; Financial Analyst. **Other U.S. locations:** Boston MA. **Number of placements per year:** 50 - 99.

SHAWN ALEXANDER ASSOCIATES
P.O. Box 417, Amherst NH 03031. 603/672-6116. **Contact:** Manager. **Description:** An executive search firm. **Specializes in the areas of:** High-Tech.

ANTHONY EXECUTIVE SEARCH
P.O. Box 320, Dublin NH 03444. 603/563-8222. **Fax:** 603/563-7118. **Contact:** Manager. **Description:** An executive search firm. **Specializes in the areas of:** Insurance.

ARC-PROFILES
75 Gilcreast Road, Suite 305, Londonderry NH 03053. 603/437-5555. **Contact:** John Peterson, Recruiter. **Description:** An executive search firm operating on both retainer and contingency bases. Company pays fee. **Specializes in the areas of:** Accounting/Auditing; Banking; Finance. **Positions commonly filled include:** Accountant/Auditor; Bank Officer/Manager; Branch Manager; Budget Analyst; Credit Manager; Financial Analyst; Systems Analyst. **Other U.S. locations:** Boston MA. **Average salary range of placements:** $30,000 - $50,000. **Number of placements per year:** 1 - 49.

ASSOCIATED EXECUTIVE MANAGEMENT
P.O. Box 4783, Portsmouth NH 03801. 603/430-7537. **Contact:** Manager. **Description:** An executive search firm.

BARCLAY PERSONNEL SYSTEMS, INC.
One Executive Park Drive, Bedford NH 03110. 603/669-2011. **Contact:** Manager. **Description:** An executive search firm operating on a contingency basis. **Specializes in the areas of:** Accounting/Auditing; Engineering; Food Industry; Industrial; Insurance; Legal; Marketing; Retail; Sales; Secretarial; Technical. **Positions commonly filled include:** Account Manager; Account Representative; Adjuster; Administrative Assistant; Buyer; Claim Representative; Credit Manager; Customer Service Representative; Design Engineer; Draftsperson; Finance Director; Fund Manager; General Manager; Manufacturing Engineer; Marketing Manager; Production Manager; Purchasing Agent/Manager; Sales Engineer; Sales Executive; Secretary. **Average salary range of placements:** $30,000 - $50,000. **Number of placements per year:** 200 - 499.

BARRETT & COMPANY
59 Stiles Road, Suite 105, Salem NH 03079. 603/890-1111. **Fax:** 603/890-1118. **Contact:** LeeAnne Martino, Office Manager. **E-mail address:** headhunt@iname.com. **Description:** An executive search firm. Company pays fee. **Specializes in the areas of:** Advertising; Engineering; General Management; Health/Medical; Sales. **Positions commonly filled include:** General Manager; Health Services Manager; Human Resources Specialist; Management Trainee; Operations/Production Manager; Sales Rep. **Number of placements per year:** 50 - 99.

BARTHOLDI & COMPANY
14 Douglas Way, Exeter NH 03833. 603/772-4228. **Contact:** Manager. **Description:** An executive search firm. **Specializes in the areas of:** High-Tech.

CAREER PROFILES
P.O. Box 4430, Portsmouth NH 03802. 603/433-3355. **Fax:** 603/433-8678. **Contact:** Norm Gray, Owner. **E-mail address:** normgray@careerprofiles.net. **World Wide Web address:** http://www.careerprofiles.net. **Description:** An executive search firm operating on a contingency basis. The firm focuses on the placement of sales representatives and medical professionals. **Specializes in the areas of:** Health/Medical; Publishing; Sales. **Positions commonly filled include:** Licensed Practical Nurse; Physical Therapist; Physician; Registered Nurse.

CHAUCER GROUP
55 Morrill Road, Canterbury NH 03224. 603/783-9500. **Fax:** 603/783-9229. **Contact:** Robert J. Thompson, CPC, President. **E-mail address:** info@chaucer.com. **World Wide Web address:** http://www.chaucer.com. **Description:** An executive search firm operating on both retained and contingency bases. Company pays fee. **Specializes in the areas of:** Computer Science/Software; Engineering; Industrial; Manufacturing; Marketing; Sales; Technical. **Positions commonly filled include:** Applications Engineer; Biochemist; Biomedical Engineer; Chemical Engineer; Chemist; Database Manager; Design Engineer; Draftsperson; Electrical/Electronics Engineer; Industrial Engineer; Industrial Production Manager; Internet Services Manager; Management Analyst/Consultant; Manufacturing Engineer; Mechanical Engineer; Online Content Specialist; Operations Manager; Public Relations Specialist; Quality Control Supervisor; Sales Engineer; Sales Representative; Software Engineer; Systems Analyst; Technical Writer/Editor; Telecommunications Manager. **Corporate headquarters location:** This Location. **Other area locations:** Jaffrey NH;

Manchester NH; Windham NH. **Average salary range of placements:** $20,000 - $29,999. **Number of placements per year:** 100 - 199.

CLAYMAN MANAGEMENT SERVICE
500 North Commercial Street, Manchester NH 03101. 603/644-7800. **Fax:** 603/644-5560. **Contact:** Stan Clayman, President. **Description:** An executive search firm. Company pays fee. **Specializes in the areas of:** Fashion; Footwear; Health/Medical; Sporting Goods. **Positions commonly filled include:** Chief Executive Officer; Chief Financial Officer; Designer; Emergency Medical Technician; Health Services Manager; Industrial Engineer; Licensed Practical Nurse; Market Research Analyst; Marketing Manager; Medical Records Technician; MIS Specialist; Occupational Therapist; Operations/Production Manager; Physical Therapist; Physician; Purchasing Agent/Manager; Quality Control Supervisor; Registered Nurse; Respiratory Therapist; Sales Executive; Sales Manager; Surgical Technician. **Number of placements per year:** 50 - 99.

CURTIS ASSOCIATES
P.O. Box 1543, Portsmouth NH 03802-1543. 603/749-9700. **Contact:** Steve Curtis, Manager. **Description:** An executive search firm. **Specializes in the areas of:** Accounting/Auditing. **Other U.S. locations:** Boston MA; Portland ME.

DUBOIS & COMPANY
14 Birch Drive, Newmarket NH 03857. 603/659-6001. **Contact:** Paulette Dubois, Principal/Owner. **Description:** An executive search firm operating on both retainer and contingency bases. **Specializes in the areas of:** Accounting/Auditing; Administration; Banking; Biology; Computer Science/Software; Engineering; General Management; Health/Medical; Manufacturing; Personnel/Labor Relations; Publishing; Retail; Sales; Technical. **Positions commonly filled include:** Accountant/Auditor; Administrative Manager; Architect; Bank Officer/Manager; Biochemist; Biological Scientist; Biomedical Engineer; Budget Analyst; Buyer; Chemical Engineer; Chemist; Civil Engineer; Clerical Supervisor; Clinical Lab Technician; Computer Programmer; Credit Manager; Customer Service Representative; Design Engineer; Designer; Electrical/Electronics Engineer; Electrician; Emergency Medical Technician; Environmental Engineer; Financial Analyst; Health Services Manager; Human Resources Specialist; Industrial Engineer; Industrial Production Manager; Internet Services Manager; Manufacturer's/Wholesaler's Sales Rep.; Market Research Analyst; Mechanical Engineer; Medical Records Technician; MIS Specialist; Multimedia Designer; Operations Manager; Public Relations Specialist; Purchasing Agent/Manager; Quality Control Supervisor; Science Technologist; Software Engineer; Structural Engineer; Systems Analyst; Telecommunications Manager; Transportation/Traffic Specialist. **Average salary range of placements:** More than $50,000. **Number of placements per year:** 1 - 49.

ENTERPRISE TECHNOLOGIES
130 Main Street, Suite 201, Salem NH 03079. 603/890-3700. **Fax:** 603/890-8701. **Contact:** Linda Bonvie, Executive Director. **E-mail address:** ent@inc-net.com. **Description:** An executive search firm. **Specializes in the areas of:** Computer Science/Software; Engineering; Manufacturing; Personnel/Labor Relations; Technical. **Positions commonly filled include:** Computer Programmer; Design Engineer; Electrical/Electronics Engineer; MIS Specialist; Quality Control Supervisor; Software Engineer; Systems Analyst; Technical Writer/Editor; Telecommunications Manager. **Average salary range of placements:** More than $50,000. **Number of placements per year:** 1 - 49.

F-O-R-T-U-N-E PERSONNEL CONSULTANTS
505 Hollis Street, Nashua NH 03062. 603/880-4900. **Contact:** Norman J. Oppenheim, President. **Description:** An executive search firm operating on a contingency basis. Company pays fee. **Specializes in the areas of:** Biomedical; Biotechnology; Medical Technology; Pharmaceutical. **Corporate headquarters location:** New York NY. **Other U.S. locations:** Nationwide. **Average salary range of placements:** More than $50,000. **Number of placements per year:** 50 - 99.

ROBERT HALF INTERNATIONAL/ACCOUNTEMPS
1155 Elm Street, 8th Floor, Manchester NH 03101. 603/641-9400. **Contact:** Manager. **Description:** An executive search firm. Accountemps (also at this location) provides temporary placements. **Corporate headquarters location:** Menlo Park CA. **Other U.S. locations:** Nationwide.

HART, HAWKINS & COMPANY
501 Islington Street, Portsmouth NH 03801. 603/431-1200. **Fax:** 603/431-1878. **Contact:** William G. Hawkins Jr., President. **E-mail address:** hawksearch@aol.com. **Description:** An executive search firm. **Specializes in the areas of:** Computer Science/Software; Multimedia; Publishing. **Positions commonly filled include:** Account Representative; Computer Programmer; Production Manager; Sales Executive; Sales Manager; Sales Representative; Software Engineer; Systems Analyst. **Average salary range of placements:** More than $50,000. **Number of placements per year:** 50 - 99.

HIGH TECH OPPORTUNITIES INC.
264B North Broadway, Suite 206, Salem NH 03079-2160. 603/893-9486. **Fax:** 603/893-9492. **Contact:** Manager. **Description:** An executive search firm operating on both retainer and contingency bases. The firm focuses on the semiconductor, computer hardware and software, and satellite and communications fields. Company pays fee. **Specializes in the areas of:** Engineering. **Positions commonly filled include:** Broadcast Technician; Design Engineer; Electrical/Electronics Engineer. **Average salary range of placements:** More than $50,000. **Number of placements per year:** 1 - 49.

HILLSBOROUGH RECRUITERS
12 Bel Aire Avenue, Merrimack NH 03054. 603/429-2787. **Contact:** Manager. **Description:** An executive search firm. **Specializes in the areas of:** Health/Medical.

LLOYD PERSONNEL CONSULTANTS
7 Medallion Center, Merrimack NH 03054. 603/424-0020. **Fax:** 603/424-8207. **Contact:** Paul D. Smith, President. **Description:** An executive search firm operating on both retainer and contingency bases. Company pays fee. **Specializes in the areas of:** Computer Science/Software; Manufacturing; Personnel/Labor Relations; Sales; Technical. **Positions commonly filled include:** Customer Service Representative; Internet Services Manager; Operations Manager; Public Relations Specialist; Quality Control Supervisor; Services Sales Representative; Software Engineer; Systems Analyst. **Other U.S. locations:** NJ; NY. **Average salary range of placements:** More than $50,000. **Number of placements per year:** 50 - 99.

MANAGEMENT RECRUITERS INTERNATIONAL OF BEDFORD
Cold Stream Office Park, 116-C South River Road, Bedford NH 03110. 603/669-9800. **Fax:** 603/623-8609. **Contact:** Mike Bacon, Manager. **Description:** An executive search firm. **Specializes in the areas of:** Accounting/Auditing; Administration; Advertising; Banking; Communications; Computer Hardware/

Software; Construction; Electrical; Engineering; Finance; Food Industry; General Management; Health/Medical; Insurance; Legal; Manufacturing; Operations Management; Personnel/Labor Relations; Procurement; Publishing; Sales; Technical; Transportation.

PAMELA L. MULLIGAN INC.
56 Hopkins Green Road, Hopkinton NH 03229. 603/226-2262. **Fax:** 603/226-2212. **Contact:** Pamela L. Mulligan, President. **Description:** An executive search firm operating on a retainer basis. Company pays fee. **Specializes in the areas of:** Health/Medical. **Positions commonly filled include:** Chief Executive Officer; Chief Financial Officer; Claim Representative; Information Specialist; Marketing Specialist; Registered Nurse; Sales and Marketing Representative. **Number of placements per year:** 1 - 49.

PACIFIC SEARCH CONSULTANTS
5 Lafayette Place, Unit 4A, Hampton Falls NH 03844. 603/929-0100. **Contact:** Manager. **Description:** An executive search firm. **Specializes in the areas of:** Telecommunications.

POWER SEARCH INC.
472 State Route 111, Unit B, Hampstead NH 03841. 603/329-1144. **Contact:** Edward Murphy, President. **Description:** An executive search firm.

PREFERRED RESOURCES GROUP
P.O. Box 6370, Nashua NH 03063. 603/889-0112. **Fax:** 603/598-4915. **Contact:** Thomas Shiber, Principal. **E-mail address:** t-shiber@aol.com. **Description:** An executive search firm operating on both retainer and contingency bases. Company pays fee. **Specializes in the areas of:** Administration; Computer Science/Software; Engineering; General Management; Industrial; Manufacturing; Technical. **Positions commonly filled include:** Buyer; Chemical Engineer; Computer Programmer; Design Engineer; Electrical/Electronics Engineer; General Manager; Industrial Engineer; Industrial Production Manager; Internet Services Manager; Mechanical Engineer; Metallurgical Engineer; MIS Specialist; Multimedia Designer; Operations/Production Manager; Purchasing Agent/Manager; Quality Control Supervisor; Software Engineer; Structural Engineer; Systems Analyst; Technical Writer/Editor; Telecommunications Manager. **Average salary range of placements:** More than $50,000. **Number of placements per year:** 1 - 49.

R.G.T. ASSOCIATES, INC.
P.O. Box 1032, Portsmouth NH 03802-1032. 603/431-9500. **Fax:** 603/431-6984. **Contact:** Bob Thiboutot, CPC, President. **Description:** An executive search firm. Company pays fee. **Specializes in the areas of:** Accounting/Auditing; Administration; Banking; Clerical; Computer Hardware/Software; Engineering; Finance; Manufacturing; Sales; Technical. **Positions commonly filled include:** Accountant/Auditor; Administrative Assistant; Aerospace Engineer; Bank Officer/Manager; Bookkeeper; Computer Programmer; Credit Manager; Customer Service Representative; Data Entry Clerk; Draftsperson; EDP Specialist; Electrical/Electronics Engineer; Financial Analyst; Industrial Engineer; Legal Secretary; Marketing Specialist; Mechanical Engineer; Medical Secretary; MIS Specialist; Operations Manager; Purchasing Agent/Manager; Quality Control Supervisor; Receptionist; Sales Representative; Secretary; Systems Analyst; Typist/Word Processor. **Average salary range of placements:** More than $50,000. **Number of placements per year:** 1 - 49.

SALES CONSULTANTS
1106 Hooksett Road, Hooksett NH 03106. 603/626-8400. **Contact:** Manager. **Description:** An executive search firm operating on both retainer and contingency bases. **Specializes in the areas of:** Advertising; Art/Design; Fashion; Food Industry; General Management; Health/Medical; Sales. **Positions commonly filled include:** Customer Service Representative; Design Engineer; Designer; Food Scientist/Technologist; General Manager; Management Analyst/Consultant; Market Research Analyst; Occupational Therapist; Physical Therapist; Physician. **Average salary range of placements:** More than $50,000. **Number of placements per year:** 1 - 49.

SALES CONSULTANTS OF NASHUA-MANCHESTER
6 Medallion Center, Merrimack NH 03054. 603/424-3282. **Fax:** 603/424-3286. **Contact:** Sheldon Baron, Manager/Owner. **Description:** An executive search firm that also operates as an employment agency. Company pays fee. **Specializes in the areas of:** Advertising; Banking; Biology; Computer Science/Software; Engineering; Fashion; Finance; Health/Medical; Industrial; Insurance; Operations Management; Procurement; Retail; Sales; Technical. **Positions commonly filled include:** Bank Officer/Manager; Biological Scientist; Chemical Engineer; Design Engineer; Dietician/Nutritionist; Electrical/Electronics Engineer; Environmental Engineer; Financial Analyst; Health Services Manager; Industrial Engineer; Industrial Production Manager; Insurance Agent/Broker; Mechanical Engineer; Pharmacist; Physical Therapist; Physician; Registered Nurse; Respiratory Therapist; Science Technologist; Software Engineer; Telecommunications Manager. **Average salary range of placements:** $30,000 - $50,000. **Number of placements per year:** 50 - 99.

SALES RECRUITERS INC.
12 St. James Place, Nashua NH 03062. 603/888-3700. **Fax:** 603/888-3768. **Contact:** Henry Glickel, President. **Description:** An executive search firm operating on a contingency basis. Company pays fee. **Specializes in the areas of:** Marketing; Sales. **Positions commonly filled include:** Account Manager; Account Representative; Management Trainee; Sales Engineer; Sales Executive; Sales Manager; Sales Representative. **Average salary range of placements:** More than $50,000. **Number of placements per year:** 50 - 99.

SNOWDEN ASSOCIATES
400 The Hill, Portsmouth NH 03801. 603/431-1553. **Contact:** Manager. **Description:** A generalist executive search firm.

SOURCE SERVICES CORP./SOURCE ENGINEERING
71 Spit Brook Road, Suite 305, Nashua NH 03060. 603/888-1700. **Fax:** 603/888-7826. **Contact:** Manager. **Description:** An executive search firm. **Specializes in the areas of:** Engineering.

SPECTRUM MEDICAL SEARCH
76 Northeastern Boulevard, Nashua NH 03062. 603/883-1900. **Toll-free phone:** 800/639-1919. **Contact:** Manager. **Description:** An executive search firm operating on a contingency basis. **Specializes in the areas of:** Health/Medical. **Positions commonly filled include:** Occupational Therapist; Physical Therapist; Speech-Language Pathologist. **Average salary range of placements:** $30,000 - $50,000. **Number of placements per year:** 50 - 99.

SPROUT/STANDISH, INC.
82 Palomino Lane, Suite 503, Bedford NH 03110. 603/622-0700. **Fax:** 603/622-4172. **Contact:** David A. Clark, President. **E-mail address:** ssi@printquest.com. **World Wide Web address:** http://www.printquest.com. **Description:** An executive search firm. Company pays fee. **Specializes in the areas of:** Electronics; Packaging; Publishing. **Number of placements per year:** 50 - 99.

STAT SEARCH
7 Colby Court, Unit 4-204, Bedford NH 03110. 603/666-5500. **Fax:** 603/623-5322. **Contact:** Dale Pouklemba, President. **Description:** An executive search firm operating on both retainer and contingency bases. The firm focuses on the placement of health care professionals in mid-management to top executive-level positions. Company pays fee. **Specializes in the areas of:** Finance; Health/Medical; Managed Care; Sales. **Positions commonly filled include:** General Manager; Sales Manager; Vice President. **Corporate headquarters location:** This Location. **Other U.S. locations:** Nationwide. **Average salary range of placements:** More than $50,000. **Number of placements per year:** 1 - 49.

TECHNICAL NEEDS
18 Pelham Road, Salem NH 03079. 603/893-3033. **Fax:** 603/893-7154. **Contact:** Stephen Gudek, Jr., President. **Description:** An executive search firm focusing on the placement of engineering professionals. Company pays fee. **Specializes in the areas of:** Engineering; Manufacturing; Technical. **Positions commonly filled include:** Design Engineer; Designer; Draftsperson; Electrical/Electronics Engineer; Industrial Engineer; Mechanical Engineer; MIS Specialist; Purchasing Agent/Manager; Quality Control Supervisor; Software Engineer; Technical Writer/Editor. **Number of placements per year:** 100 - 199.

ZYMAC INC.
EDA PLUS
46B Nashua Road, Suite 8B, Londonderry NH 03053. 603/625-4411. **Contact:** Manager. **Description:** An executive search firm. **Specializes in the areas of:** Software Development.

PERMANENT EMPLOYMENT AGENCIES

ACCESS CONSULTING, INC.
54A Oyster River Road, Durham NH 03824-3029. 603/868-7884. **Contact:** Consultant. **Description:** A permanent employment agency. Company pays fee. **Specializes in the areas of:** Administration; Communications; Computer Operations; Computer Science/Software; Data Processing; Engineering; Technical. **Positions commonly filled include:** Computer Programmer; Designer; Electrical/Electronics Engineer; Management Analyst/Consultant; Software Engineer; Systems Analyst; Technical Writer/Editor. **Number of placements per year:** 50 - 99.

ALLSTAFF CONTRACT SERVICES, INC.
P.O. Box 385, North Hampton NH 03862. 603/964-1780. **Toll-free phone:** 800/854-4290. **Contact:** Kris Day, Office Manager. **Description:** A permanent employment agency that also provides temporary placements. Company pays fee. **Specializes in the areas of:** Accounting/Auditing; Administration; Art/Design; Biology; Clerical; Computer Science/Software; Education; Engineering; Finance; Food Industry; General Management; Health/Medical; Legal; Light Industrial; Personnel/Labor Relations; Sales; Technical. **Positions commonly filled include:** Accountant/Auditor; Budget Analyst; Claim Representative; Clerical Supervisor; Computer Programmer; Customer Service Representative; Design Engineer; Electrical/Electronics Engineer; Environmental Engineer; Financial Analyst; Human Resources Specialist; Industrial Engineer; Industrial Production Manager; Internet Services Manager; Management Analyst/Consultant; Mechanical Engineer; Medical Records Technician; MIS Specialist; Operations/Production Manager; Public Relations Specialist; Purchasing Agent/Manager; Quality Control Supervisor; Restaurant/Food Service Manager; Software Engineer; Systems Analyst; Teacher/Professor; Technical Writer/Editor; Telecommunications Manager; Typist/Word Processor. **Other U.S. locations:** Portland ME.

BARROS ASSOCIATES
16 Route 111, Unit 4, Derry NH 03038. 603/894-0055. **Fax:** 603/894-0066. **Contact:** Daniel Barros, President. **Description:** A permanent employment agency. Company pays fee. **Specializes in the areas of:** Communications; Computer Science/Software; Network Administration. **Positions commonly filled include:** Software Engineer. **Number of placements per year:** 1 - 49.

CAREER CONNECTIONS, INC.
74 Northeastern Boulevard, Unit 17, Nashua NH 03062. 603/880-7184. **Fax:** 603/880-5460. **Contact:** Linda Piper, CPC, President. **Description:** A permanent employment agency. Company pays fee. **Specializes in the areas of:** Accounting/Auditing; Legal; Marketing; Personnel/Labor Relations; Sales; Secretarial. **Positions commonly filled include:** Account Representative; Accountant; Administrative Assistant; Human Resources Manager; Sales Manager; Sales Representative; Secretary; Typist/Word Processor; Underwriter/Assistant Underwriter.

CENTRAL NEW HAMPSHIRE EMPLOYMENT SERVICES
25 Beacon Street East, Suite 201, Laconia NH 03246. 603/528-2828. **Toll-free phone:** 800/256-2482. **Fax:** 603/528-6625. **Contact:** Christine St. Cyr, General Manager. **Description:** A permanent employment agency that also provides temporary placements. Company pays fee. **Specializes in the areas of:** Accounting/Auditing; Administration; Banking; Computer Science/Software; Engineering; Finance; Health/Medical; Insurance; Legal; Manufacturing; Personnel/Labor Relations; Sales; Secretarial. **Positions commonly filled include:** Accountant/Auditor; Aerospace Engineer; Architect; Bank Officer/Manager; Bookkeeper; Civil Engineer; Clerk; Computer Programmer; Credit Manager; Customer Service Representative; Data Entry Clerk; Draftsperson; EDP Specialist; Electrical/Electronics Engineer; Human Resources Manager; Industrial Designer; Legal Secretary; Mechanical Engineer; Medical Secretary; Metallurgical Engineer; Receptionist; Sales Representative; Secretary; Systems Analyst; Typist/Word Processor; Underwriter/Assistant Underwriter. **Other area locations:** Concord NH. **Average salary range of placements:** $20,000 - $29,999. **Number of placements per year:** 500 - 999.

CHAUCER GROUP
P.O. Box 368, Jaffrey NH 03452. 603/532-5800. **Fax:** 603/532-5800. **Contact:** Hobie Harmon, Principal. **E-mail address:** hobie@chaucer.mv.com. **Description:** A permanent employment agency. Company pays fee. **Specializes in the areas of:** Engineering; Industrial; Manufacturing; Technical. **Positions commonly filled include:** Biomedical Engineer; Chemical Engineer; Electrical/Electronics Engineer; General Manager; Industrial Engineer; Mechanical Engineer; Metallurgical Engineer; Purchasing Agent/Manager; Quality Control Supervisor. **Corporate headquarters location:** Canterbury NH. **Average salary range of placements:** $30,000 - $50,000. **Number of placements per year:** 1 - 49.

EXETER 2100
Computer Park, P.O. Box 2120, Hampton NH 03842. 603/926-6712. **Fax:** 603/926-0536. **Contact:** Bruce Montville, Managing Partner. **Description:** A permanent employment agency. Company pays fee.

Specializes in the areas of: Computer Science/Software; Information Systems. **Positions commonly filled include:** Computer Programmer; EDP Specialist; Software Engineer.

KENDA SYSTEMS
One Stiles Road, Suite 106, Salem NH 03079. 603/898-7884. **Contact:** Manager. **Description:** A permanent and temporary employment agency that focuses on the placement of computer consultants and software engineers. **Specializes in the areas of:** Computer Science/Software.

KEY PERSONNEL, INC.
216 Lafayette Road, North Hampton NH 03862. 603/964-9495. **Fax:** 603/964-2271. **Contact:** Marilyn C. Jackson, Corporate Manager. **E-mail address:** mcb@keycomp.com. **Description:** A permanent employment agency that also provides temporary placements. Company pays fee. **Specializes in the areas of:** Accounting/Auditing; Administration; Computer Science/Software; Secretarial; Technical. **Positions commonly filled include:** Account Manager; Account Representative; Accountant; Administrative Assistant; Administrative Manager; Applications Engineer; Assistant Manager; Branch Manager; Budget Analyst; Buyer; Chemical Engineer; Chemist; Chief Financial Officer; Claim Representative; Clerical Supervisor; Clinical Lab Technician; Computer Operator; Computer Programmer; Controller; Credit Manager; Customer Service Representative; Database Manager; Project Manager; Secretary; Software Engineer; Systems Analyst; Systems Manager; Typist/Word Processor. **Benefits available to temporary workers:** Computer Training; Medical Insurance; Paid Holidays; Paid Vacation; Retirement Plan.

NATIONAL EMPLOYMENT SERVICE CORPORATION
95 Albany Street, Suite 3, Portsmouth NH 03801. 603/427-0125. **Toll-free phone:** 800/EMPLOYMENT. **Fax:** 603/427-1411. **Contact:** Contract Manager. **World Wide Web address:** http://www.nationalemployment.com. **Description:** A permanent and temporary employment agency. Founded in 1992. Company pays fee. **Specializes in the areas of:** Accounting/Auditing; Administration; Architecture/Construction; Banking; Computer Science/Software; Economics; Engineering; Finance; Food Industry; General Management; Health/Medical; Industrial; Manufacturing; Personnel/Labor Relations; Retail; Sales; Transportation. **Corporate headquarters location:** This Location. **Other area locations:** Nashua NH. **Average salary range of placements:** $30,000 - $50,000. **Number of placements per year:** 1000+.

NATIONAL EMPLOYMENT SERVICE CORPORATION
402 Amherst Street, Nashua NH 03063. **Toll-free phone:** 800/598-0255. **Contact:** Contract Manager. **World Wide Web address:** http://www.nationalemployment.com. **Description:** A permanent and temporary employment agency. **Specializes in the areas of:** Engineering; Finance; Information Technology. **Corporate headquarters location:** Portsmouth NH.

PROFESSIONAL RECRUITERS INC.
5 Coliseum Avenue, Nashua NH 03063. 603/886-3909x316. **Fax:** 603/886-4205. **Recorded jobline:** 603/886-3909x304. **Contact:** Timothy E. Moran, CPC/CEO. **Description:** A permanent employment agency. Company pays fee. **Specializes in the areas of:** Accounting/Auditing; Banking; Computer Science/Software; Network Administration; Personnel/Labor Relations; Technical. **Positions commonly filled include:** Accountant/Auditor; Bank Officer/Manager; Branch Manager; Budget Analyst; Computer Programmer; Credit Manager; Financial Analyst; Software Engineer; Systems Analyst. **Average salary range of placements:** More than $50,000. **Number of placements per year:** 1000+.

RESOURCE RECRUITING
CONTEMPORARY ACCOUNTANTS
547 Amherst Street, Nashua NH 03063. 603/595-2822. **Fax:** 603/889-0259. **Contact:** Robert C. Harrington, Executive Vice President. **Description:** A permanent employment agency. Company pays fee. **Specializes in the areas of:** Accounting/Auditing; Administration; Banking; Computer Science/Software; Legal; Manufacturing; Operations Management; Sales; Secretarial. **Positions commonly filled include:** Accountant/Auditor; Bookkeeper; Chief Financial Officer; Clerk; Collections Agent; Controller; Credit Manager; Manager of Information Systems; Payroll Clerk; Secretary. **Average salary range of placements:** $30,000 - $50,000. **Number of placements per year:** 50 - 99.

SOFTWARE NETWORKS INC.
125 Main Street, Suite A, Newmarket NH 03857. 603/659-1000. **Fax:** 603/359-1005. **Contact:** Dan Craig, President. **Description:** An employment agency that focuses on permanent placement in the software development and communications industries. Founded in 1990. Company pays fee. **Specializes in the areas of:** Computer Science/Software. **Positions commonly filled include:** Computer Programmer; Design Engineer; Electrical/Electronics Engineer; Software Engineer. **Average salary range of placements:** More than $50,000. **Number of placements per year:** 50 - 99.

TECH/AID OF NEW HAMPSHIRE
71 Spit Brook Road, Suite 102, Nashua NH 03060. 603/891-4100. **Contact:** Recruiter. **Description:** A permanent employment agency. Company pays fee. **Specializes in the areas of:** Architecture/Construction; Cable TV; Computer Hardware/Software; Construction; Engineering; Manufacturing; Technical. **Positions commonly filled include:** Aerospace Engineer; Architectural Engineer; Buyer; Ceramics Engineer; Chemical Engineer; Civil Engineer; Draftsperson; Electrical/Electronics Engineer; Estimator; Industrial Designer; Mechanical Engineer; Metallurgical Engineer; Mining Engineer; Operations/Production Manager; Petroleum Engineer; Purchasing Agent/Manager; Quality Control Supervisor; Technical Writer/Editor; Technician. **Number of placements per year:** 1000+.

TECHNICAL DIRECTIONS, INC. (TDI)
78 Northeastern Boulevard, Suite 2B, Nashua NH 03062. 603/880-6720. **Fax:** 603/880-7859. **Contact:** Jeff Barsanti, Recruiter. **Description:** A permanent employment agency. Company pays fee. **Specializes in the areas of:** Administration; Computer Hardware/Software; Engineering; Sales; Technical. **Positions commonly filled include:** Aerospace Engineer; Biomedical Engineer; Computer Programmer; EDP Specialist; Electrical/Electronics Engineer; Industrial Engineer; Marketing Specialist; Mechanical Engineer; Metallurgical Engineer; MIS Specialist; Systems Analyst; Technical Writer/Editor.

THOMAS & KAVANAUGH
277 Harmony Road, Northwood NH 03261. 603/942-5800. **Fax:** 603/225-5516. **Contact:** Robert Thomas, President. **Description:** A permanent employment agency. Company pays fee. **Specializes in the areas of:** Accounting/Auditing; Banking. **Positions commonly filled include:** Account Representative; Construction Contractor; Structural Engineer. **Number of placements per year:** 1 - 49.

TEMPORARY EMPLOYMENT AGENCIES

BENETEMPS INC.
88 Stiles Road, Suite 203, Salem NH 03079. 603/893-7472. **Contact:** Robert Spiegelman, President/Owner. **Description:** A temporary agency. Company pays fee. **Specializes in the areas of:** Consulting; Personnel/Labor Relations. **Positions commonly filled include:** Actuary; Human Resources Specialist. **Benefits available to temporary workers:** 401(k); Life Insurance; Medical Insurance. **Average salary range of placements:** $30,000 - $50,000. **Number of placements per year:** 50 - 99.

CHESHIRE EMPLOYMENT SERVICE
800 Park Avenue, Keene NH 03431. 603/357-3400. **Fax:** 603/357-3406. **Contact:** Office Manager. **Description:** A temporary agency that also provides permanent placement. Company pays fee. **Specializes in the areas of:** Accounting/Auditing; Administration; Advertising; Banking; Computer Science/Software; Engineering; Finance; General Management; Manufacturing; Personnel/Labor Relations; Publishing; Secretarial. **Average salary range of placements:** $20,000 - $29,999. **Number of placements per year:** 50 - 99.

CONTACT RECRUITERS, INC.
90 Stiles Road, Suite 202, Salem NH 03079. 603/898-2266. **Fax:** 603/898-1822. **Contact:** D.W. Monroe, Recruiter. **E-mail address:** info@gator.mv.com. **World Wide Web address:** http://www.resourcecenter.com/gator.software. **Description:** A temporary agency that provides temporary, contract, and permanent placements of hardware and software engineers. Company pays fee. **Specializes in the areas of:** Computer Science/Software; Engineering; Technical. **Positions commonly filled include:** Software Engineer. **Average salary range of placements:** More than $50,000.

KELLY SERVICES, INC.
6 Bedford Farms, Bedford NH 03110. 603/625-6457. **Contact:** Melissa Finnegan, Supervisor. **Description:** A temporary agency. **Specializes in the areas of:** Clerical; Industrial; Sales; Technical.

KELLY SERVICES, INC.
One Tara Boulevard, Nashua NH 03062. 603/888-8180. **Contact:** Mercedes Cernuda, Supervisor. **Description:** A temporary agency. **Specializes in the areas of:** Clerical; Industrial; Sales; Technical.

MANPOWER TEMPORARY SERVICES
410 Amherst Street, Suite 175, Nashua NH 03063. 603/882-0015. **Contact:** Susan Martin, Manager. **Description:** A temporary agency. **Specializes in the areas of:** Accounting/Auditing; Banking; Food Industry; General Management; Industrial; Insurance; Legal; Light Industrial; Marketing; Nonprofit; Retail; Sales; Secretarial; Technical. **Positions commonly filled include:** Administrative Assistant; Clerical Supervisor; Computer Operator; Customer Service Representative; Graphic Artist; Secretary; Typist/Word Processor. **Benefits available to temporary workers:** Life Insurance; Medical Insurance; Paid Holidays; Paid Vacation. **Corporate headquarters location:** Milwaukee WI.

MANPOWER TEMPORARY SERVICES
18 North Main Street, Concord NH 03301. 603/224-7115. **Contact:** Branch Manager. **Description:** A temporary agency. Company pays fee. **Specializes in the areas of:** Data Processing; Light Industrial; Office Support; Technical; Word Processing. **Positions commonly filled include:** Accountant/Auditor; Accounting Clerk; Administrative Assistant; Assembler; Biological Scientist; Bookkeeper; Chemist; Computer Operator; Customer Service Representative; Designer; Desktop Publishing Specialist; Electrician; Inspector/Tester/Grader; Inventory Control Specialist; Machine Operator; Material Control Specialist; Packaging/Processing Worker; Painter; Project Engineer; Proofreader; Receptionist; Records Manager; Research Assistant; Secretary; Software Engineer; Stenographer; Systems Analyst; Technical Writer/Editor; Technician; Telemarketer; Typist/Word Processor. **Benefits available to temporary workers:** Life Insurance; Medical Insurance; Paid Holidays; Paid Vacation. **Corporate headquarters location:** Milwaukee WI. **Number of placements per year:** 1000+.

PELHAM PROFESSIONAL GROUP, INC.
339 Main Street, Nashua NH 03060. 603/882-6433. **Fax:** 603/882-5045. **Contact:** Joan Sullivan, Office Manager. **Description:** A temporary agency. **Specializes in the areas of:** Administration; Food Industry; Manufacturing; Retail; Secretarial; Technical. **Positions commonly filled include:** Clerical Supervisor; Customer Service Representative; Draftsperson; Electrical/Electronics Engineer; Industrial Production Manager; Mechanical Engineer; Purchasing Agent/Manager; Quality Control Supervisor; Typist/Word Processor. **Corporate headquarters location:** North Andover MA. **Number of placements per year:** 500 - 999.

TAC STAFFING SERVICES
One Trafalgar Square, Nashua NH 03063. 603/882-4200. **Fax:** 603/889-3572. **Contact:** Pamela Noble, Office Manager. **Description:** A temporary agency. Company pays fee. **Specializes in the areas of:** Accounting/Auditing; Banking; Clerical; Finance; Insurance; Light Industrial; Manufacturing; Retail; Sales; Secretarial; Transportation. **Positions commonly filled include:** Bookkeeper; Clerk; Data Entry Clerk; Driver; Factory Worker; Legal Secretary; Light Industrial Worker; Medical Secretary; Receptionist; Typist/Word Processor. **Corporate headquarters location:** Newton MA. **Average salary range of placements:** $20,000 - $29,999. **Number of placements per year:** 1000+.

TRI-STATE PROFESSIONALS
P.O. Box 958, Keene NH 03431. 603/352-4155. **Toll-free phone:** 800/227-3577. **Fax:** 603/357-7701. **Contact:** Recruiter. **E-mail address:** tristateprofess@monad.net. **Description:** A temporary agency. Founded in 1987. **Specializes in the areas of:** Engineering; Technical. **Positions commonly filled include:** Certified Nursing Aide; Design Engineer; Draftsperson; Electrical/Electronics Engineer; Electrician; Industrial Engineer; Licensed Practical Nurse; Mechanical Engineer; Registered Nurse; Secretary; Technical Writer/Editor; Typist/Word Processor.

WESTERN STAFF SERVICES
507 State Street, Portsmouth NH 03801. 603/427-0666. **Fax:** 603/431-6984. **Contact:** Ginette Thiboutot, Affiliate Owner. **Description:** A temporary agency. Founded in 1948. Company pays fee. **Specializes in the areas of:** Accounting/Auditing; Secretarial. **Positions commonly filled include:** Buyer; Customer Service Representative; Paralegal; Typist/Word Processor. **Benefits available to temporary workers:** Medical Insurance; Paid Holidays; Paid Vacation. **Corporate headquarters location:** Walnut Creek CA. **Other U.S. locations:** Nationwide. **Average salary range of placements:** Less than $20,000. **Number of placements per year:** 200 - 499.

CONTRACT SERVICES FIRMS

AFFORDABLE SOLUTIONS
114 Perimeter Road, Nashua NH 03063-1301. 603/880-4300. **Fax:** 603/880-0639. **Contact:** Thomas M. Tate, Vice President. **Description:** A contract services firm. **Specializes in the areas of:** Engineering; Industrial; Manufacturing; Sales. **Positions commonly filled include:** Buyer; Computer Programmer; Design Engineer; Designer; Draftsperson; Electrical/Electronics Engineer; Electrician; Mechanical Engineer; Purchasing Agent/Manager; Quality Control Supervisor; Software Engineer; Structural Engineer; Technical Writer/Editor; Telecommunications Manager. **Number of placements per year:** 200 - 499.

CDI CORPORATION
Northridge Business Center, 74 Northeastern Boulevard, Suite 21A, Nashua NH 03062. 603/883-0705. **Fax:** 603/883-9973. **Contact:** Manager. **World Wide Web address:** http://www.cdicorp.com. **Description:** A contract services firm. **Specializes in the areas of:** Engineering; Technical. **Corporate headquarters location:** Philadelphia PA. **Other U.S. locations:** Nationwide. **International locations:** Worldwide.

CONTRACT SOLUTIONS, INC.
2 Keewaydin Drive, Salem NH 03079. 603/893-6776. **Fax:** 603/893-4208. **Contact:** Recruiter. **Description:** A contract services firm. Company pays fee. **Specializes in the areas of:** Computer Science/Software; Engineering; Information Technology. **Positions commonly filled include:** Computer Programmer; Internet Services Manager; Mining Engineer; MIS Specialist; Multimedia Designer; Nuclear Engineer; Quality Control Supervisor; Software Engineer; Systems Analyst; Technical Writer/Editor; Telecommunications Manager. **Other area locations:** Rye NH. **Other U.S. locations:** Boston MA; Cincinnati OH. **Number of placements per year:** 1000+.

THE CUSHING GROUP
P.O. Box 3210, Nashua NH 03061-3210. 603/883-0130. **Toll-free phone:** 800/392-9971. **Fax:** 603/883-1516. **Contact:** Craig Pagelow, Business Development Manager. **E-mail address:** info@cushing.com. **World Wide Web address:** http://www.cushing.com. **Description:** A contract services firm. The Cushing Group provides training and consulting services and focuses on distributed object computing. **Specializes in the areas of:** Computer Science/Software. **Positions commonly filled include:** Computer Programmer; Systems Analyst. **Average salary range of placements:** More than $50,000. **Number of placements per year:** 1 - 49.

CUSTOM SOFTWARE SERVICES, INC.
One Indian Head Plaza, Suite 600, Nashua NH 03060. 603/595-2542. **Fax:** 603/595-0009. **Contact:** Manager. **Description:** A contract services firm. **Positions commonly filled include:** Computer Programmer; Electrical/Electronics Engineer; Systems Analyst. **Average salary range of placements:** $30,000 - $50,000. **Number of placements per year:** 1 - 49.

NORRELL SERVICES
500 Harvey Road, Manchester NH 03103. 603/624-4220. **Fax:** 603/625-2980. **Contact:** Jennifer Hall, Lead Customer Service Specialist. **Description:** A contract services firm that also provides temporary placements. Company pays fee. **Benefits available to temporary workers:** Dental Insurance; Medical Insurance; Paid Holidays; Paid Vacation. **Corporate headquarters location:** Atlanta GA. **Other U.S. locations:** Nationwide. **Average salary range of placements:** Less than $20,000. **Number of placements per year:** 200 - 499.

SURGE RESOURCES INC.
136 Harvey Road, Londonderry NH 03053-7401. 603/623-0007. **Toll-free phone:** 800/SURGE-USA. **Fax:** 603/624-7007. **Contact:** Lou Panico, Recruiter. **Description:** A contract services firm that provides temporary, contract, and permanent job placements. Company pays fee. **Specializes in the areas of:** Accounting/Auditing; Administration; Architecture/Construction; Art/Design; Computer Science/Software; Economics; Education; Engineering; Finance; General Management; Industrial; Manufacturing; Nonprofit; Personnel/Labor Relations; Retail; Sales. **Positions commonly filled include:** Accountant/Auditor; Aerospace Engineer; Architect; Bank Officer/Manager; Blue-Collar Worker Supervisor; Civil Engineer; Clerical Supervisor; Computer Programmer; Construction and Building Inspector; Cost Estimator; Customer Service Representative; Design Engineer; Editor; Insurance Agent/Broker; Mechanical Engineer; MIS Specialist; Paralegal; Purchasing Agent/Manager; Quality Control Supervisor; Services Sales Representative; Software Engineer; Systems Analyst; Telecommunications Manager; Typist/Word Processor. **Benefits available to temporary workers:** 401(k); Dental Insurance; Medical Insurance. **Average salary range of placements:** $30,000 - $50,000. **Number of placements per year:** 1000+.

TECHNICAL EMPLOYMENT SERVICES INC.
127 Main Street, Suite 16, Nashua NH 03060. 603/881-8622. **Fax:** 603/881-8647. **Contact:** Dan Duncanson, President. **Description:** A contract services firm. Founded in 1992. Company pays fee. **Specializes in the areas of:** Design; Engineering. **Positions commonly filled include:** Aerospace Engineer; Blue-Collar Worker Supervisor; Chemical Engineer; Civil Engineer; Computer Programmer; Design Engineer; Designer; Draftsperson; Electrical/Electronics Engineer; Environmental Engineer; Industrial Engineer; Industrial Production Manager; Internet Services Manager; Machinist; Mechanical Engineer; MIS Specialist; Operations/Production Manager; Petroleum Engineer; Science Technologist; Software Engineer; Structural Engineer; Systems Analyst; Technical Writer/Editor; Telecommunications Manager. **Benefits available to temporary workers:** Medical Insurance; Paid Holidays. **Average salary range of placements:** $30,000 - $50,000. **Number of placements per year:** 100 - 199.

CAREER/OUTPLACEMENT COUNSELING FIRMS

CAREERPRO
76 Jenkins Road, Bedford NH 03110. 603/668-9249. **Contact:** Office Manager. **Description:** A career/outplacement counseling service.

NEW JERSEY

EXECUTIVE SEARCH FIRMS

AV SEARCH CONSULTANTS
674 Route 202/206, Bridgewater NJ 08807. 908/429-7800. **Contact:** Manager. **Description:** An executive search firm that provides legal placements.

ABBOTT ASSOCIATES INC.
1099 Wall Street West, Lyndhurst NJ 07071. 201/804-8100. **Contact:** Manager. **Description:** An executive search firm. **Specializes in the areas of:** Accounting/Auditing; Finance.

ABLE CAREERS
240 West Passaic Street, Maywood NJ 07607. 201/845-7771. **Contact:** Manager. **Description:** An executive search firm.

ACCESS SYSTEMS
101 Gibraltar Drive, Suite 2F, Morris Plains NJ 07950-1287. 973/984-7960. **Fax:** 973/984-7963. **Contact:** Joanne Palzer, President. **Description:** An executive search firm operating on a contingency basis that focuses on the placement of high-level sales and technical sales support professionals in computer, software, and data communications fields. Company pays fee. **Specializes in the areas of:** Computer Science/Software; Data Communications; Sales. **Positions commonly filled include:** Manufacturer's/Wholesaler's Sales Rep.; Services Sales Representative. **Average salary range of placements:** More than $50,000. **Number of placements per year:** 1 - 49.

ACCOUNTANTS EXECUTIVE SEARCH
ACCOUNTANTS ON CALL
80 Route 4 East, Suite 230, Paramus NJ 07652. 201/368-9200. **Contact:** Manager. **Description:** An executive search firm. Accountants On Call (also at this location) offers temporary placements. **Specializes in the areas of:** Accounting/Auditing; Banking; Finance.

ACCOUNTANTS EXECUTIVE SEARCH
ACCOUNTANTS ON CALL
379 Thornall Street, Edison NJ 08837. 732/906-1100. **Contact:** Manager. **Description:** An executive search firm. Accountants On Call (also at this location) offers temporary placements. **Specializes in the areas of:** Accounting/Auditing; Finance.

ACCOUNTANTS EXECUTIVE SEARCH
ACCOUNTANTS ON CALL
354 Eisenhower Parkway, Plaza One, 2nd Floor, Livingston NJ 07039. 973/533-0600. **Contact:** Manager. **Description:** An executive search firm. Accountants On Call (also at this location) offers temporary placements. **Specializes in the areas of:** Accounting/Auditing; Finance.

ACCOUNTANTS PROFESSIONAL SEARCH
P.O. Box 1734, Englewood Cliffs NJ 07632. 201/288-2888. **Contact:** Manager. **Description:** An executive search firm. **Specializes in the areas of:** Accounting/Auditing.

ADEL-LAWRENCE ASSOCIATES
1208 Highway 34, Suite 18, Aberdeen NJ 07747. 702/566-4914. **Fax:** 702/566-9326. **Contact:** Larry Radzely, President. **Description:** An executive search firm. Company pays fee. **Specializes in the areas of:** Computer Science/Software; Engineering; Health/Medical; Technical. **Positions commonly filled include:** Biomedical Engineer; Clinical Lab Technician; Design Engineer; Electrical/Electronics Engineer; Mechanical Engineer; MIS Specialist; Software Engineer; Systems Analyst; Telecommunications Manager. **Average salary range of placements:** More than $50,000. **Number of placements per year:** 200 - 499.

ADVANCE POSITIONS INC.
9 South Main Street, Marlboro NJ 07746. 732/577-1122. **Contact:** President. **Description:** An executive search firm. **Specializes in the areas of:** Food Industry; General Management; Logistics; Retail; Transportation. **Positions commonly filled include:** Buyer; Distribution Manager; Industrial Engineer; Logistics Manager; Operations/Production Manager; Purchasing Agent/Manager; Transportation/Traffic Specialist. **Number of placements per year:** 1 - 49.

ADVANCED TECHNICAL SEARCH
168 Walker Road, West Orange NJ 07052. 973/669-0400. **Contact:** Manager. **Description:** An executive search firm. **Specializes in the areas of:** Wireless Communications.

ALLEN ASSOCIATES
128 Elliot Place, South Plainfield NJ 07080. 908/753-3751. **Contact:** Manager. **Description:** An executive search firm that places personnel in a range of fields.

DAVID ALLEN ASSOCIATES
P.O. Box 56, Haddonfield NJ 08033-0048. 609/795-6470. **Fax:** 609/795-0175. **Contact:** David Ritchings, Partner. **E-mail address:** david.allen.search@worldnet.att.net. **World Wide Web address:** http://www.quikpage.com/a/allendavid. **Description:** An executive search firm operating on both retained and contingency bases. Founded in 1980. Company pays fee. **Specializes in the areas of:** Banking; Food Industry; General Management. **Positions commonly filled include:** Account Manager; Account Rep.; Bank Officer/Manager; Budget Analyst; Chemical Engineer; Chief Financial Officer; Controller; Credit Manager; Economist; Finance Director; Financial Analyst; Fund Manager; General Manager; Human Resources Manager; Management Analyst/Consultant; Market Research Analyst; Marketing Manager; Marketing Specialist; Sales Representative; Securities Sales Representative. **Corporate headquarters location:** This Location. **Other U.S. locations:** Nationwide. **Average salary range of placements:** More than $50,000. **Number of placements per year:** 50 - 99.

FRANK ALLEN & ASSOCIATES
15 James Street, Florham Park NJ 07932. 973/966-1606. **Contact:** Manager. **Description:** An executive search firm. **Specializes in the areas of:** Human Resources.

ALTA ASSOCIATES, INC.
8 Bartles Corner Road, Suite 21, Flemington NJ 08822. 908/806-8442. **Fax:** 908/806-8443. **Contact:** Joyce Brocaglia, Vice President. **Description:** An executive search firm. Company pays fee. **Specializes in the areas of:** Computer Hardware/Software. **Positions commonly filled include:** Computer Programmer; Database Manager; EDP Specialist; MIS Specialist. **Number of placements per year:** 50 - 99.

ANDERSON WRIGHT ASSOCIATES
375 Johnson Avenue Annex, Englewood NJ 07631. 201/567-8080. **Contact:** Manager. **Description:** An executive search firm. **Specializes in the areas of:** Finance; Pharmaceutical.

ANDOS ASSOCIATES INC.
2 Stone House Road, Mendham NJ 07945. 201/934-7766. **Contact:** Manager. **Description:** An executive

search firm. **Specializes in the areas of:** Pharmaceutical.

R.W. APPLE & ASSOCIATES
200 Atlantic Avenue, Box 200, Manasquan NJ 08736-1352. 732/223-4305. **Fax:** 732/223-4325. **Contact:** Richard Apple, Owner. **Description:** An executive search firm operating on a retainer basis and focusing on environmental science and engineering consulting industries. Company pays fee. **Specializes in the areas of:** Environmental. **Positions commonly filled include:** Chemical Engineer; Civil Engineer; Environmental Engineer; Geologist/Geophysicist. **Average salary range of placements:** More than $50,000. **Number of placements per year:** 1 - 49.

THE ASCHER GROUP
7 Becker Farm Road, Roseland NJ 07068. 973/597-1900. **Contact:** Personnel. **Description:** An executive search firm that also operates as a temporary agency. Company pays fee. **Specializes in the areas of:** Accounting/Auditing; Finance; Personnel/Labor Relations; Secretarial. **Positions commonly filled include:** Accountant/Auditor; Bank Officer/Manager; Budget Analyst; Credit Manager; EKG Technician; Financial Analyst; Human Resources Specialist; Purchasing Agent/Manager; Typist/Word Processor. **Number of placements per year:** 1000+.

ASSURANCE HEALTH CARE SERVICES
25 East Spring Valley Avenue, Maywood NJ 07607. 201/845-4461. **Contact:** Manager. **Description:** An executive search firm that places nurses. **Specializes in the areas of:** Health/Medical.

ASSURANCE HEALTH CARE SERVICES
P.O. Box 465, Morris Plains NJ 07950. 973/538-7594. **Contact:** Manager. **Description:** An executive search firm for health care professionals. **Specializes in the areas of:** Health/Medical.

BALCOR ASSOCIATES
P.O. Box 873, Union City NJ 07087. 201/854-2525. **Contact:** Manager. **Description:** An executive search firm. **Specializes in the areas of:** Accounting/Auditing; Consumer Package Goods; Finance; Human Resources; Manufacturing.

BARCLAY CONSULTANTS
201 Union Lane, Brielle NJ 08730. 732/223-1131. **Contact:** Manager. **Description:** An executive search firm that specializes in placing computer sales professionals. **Specializes in the areas of:** Sales.

R.P. BARONE ASSOCIATES
3121 Atlantic Avenue, P.O. Box 706, Allenwood NJ 08720. 732/292-0900. **Contact:** L. Donald Rizzo, President. **Description:** An executive search firm operating on both retainer and contingency bases. The firm focuses on the placement of engineering, marketing, and manufacturing personnel in the industrial marketplace. Company pays fee. **Specializes in the areas of:** Engineering; Manufacturing; Sales. **Positions commonly filled include:** Architect; Biochemist; Biomedical Engineer; Chemical Engineer; Chemist; Civil Engineer; Construction and Building Inspector; Cost Estimator; Design Engineer; Draftsperson; Electrical/Electronics Engineer; Environmental Engineer; Food Scientist/Technologist; General Manager; Industrial Engineer; Industrial Production Manager; Market Research Analyst; Mechanical Engineer; Metallurgical Engineer; Operations/Production Manager; Purchasing Agent/Manager; Science Technologist; Structural Engineer. **Average salary range of placements:** More than $50,000. **Number of placements per year:** 1 - 49.

GARY S. BELL ASSOCIATES, INC.
55 Harristown Road, Glen Rock NJ 07452. 201/670-4900. **Fax:** 201/670-4940. **Contact:** Gary S. Bell, President. **E-mail address:** gsbassoc@aol.com. **World Wide Web address:** http://www.mindspring.com/careerdr/garbell.html. **Description:** An executive search firm. Company pays fee. **Specializes in the areas of:** Biology; Biotechnology; Chemical; Clinical Research; Engineering; Environmental; General Management; Health/Medical; Manufacturing; Pharmaceutical. **Positions commonly filled include:** Biochemist; Biological Scientist; Biomedical Engineer; Chemical Engineer; Chemist; Computer Programmer; Design Engineer; Electrical/Electronics Engineer; Licensed Practical Nurse; Market Research Analyst; Mechanical Engineer; MIS Specialist; Pharmacist; Physician; Purchasing Agent/Manager; Quality Control Supervisor; Registered Nurse; Respiratory Therapist; Software Engineer; Statistician; Systems Analyst. **Average salary range of placements:** More than $50,000. **Number of placements per year:** 50 - 99.

BESEN ASSOCIATES
115 Route 46 West, Suite 25, Mountain Lakes NJ 07046. 973/334-5533. **Contact:** Manager. **Description:** An executive search firm. **Specializes in the areas of:** Pharmaceutical.

BLAIR ASSOCIATES
210 Summit Avenue, Montvale NJ 07645. 201/573-0900. **Contact:** Manager. **Description:** An executive search firm that places personnel in various industries.

BLAKE & ASSOCIATES EXECUTIVE SEARCH
P.O. Box 1425, Pleasantville NJ 08232. 609/645-3330. **Fax:** 609/383-0320. **Contact:** Ed Blake, President. **Description:** An executive search firm. Company pays fee. **Specializes in the areas of:** Accounting/Auditing; Administration; Advertising; Architecture/Construction; Art/Design; Banking; Biology; Computer Science/Software; Economics; Engineering; Finance; Food Industry; General Management; Health/Medical; Industrial; Insurance; Legal; Manufacturing; Personnel/Labor Relations; Publishing; Retail; Sales; Secretarial. **Positions commonly filled include:** Accountant/Auditor; Adjuster; Administrative Manager; Agricultural Engineer; Agricultural Scientist; Architect; Attorney; Bank Officer/Manager; Biological Scientist; Biomedical Engineer; Brokerage Clerk; Budget Analyst; Buyer; Chemical Engineer; Chemist; Civil Engineer; Claim Representative; Clerical Supervisor; Computer Programmer; Construction and Building Inspector; Construction Contractor; Cost Estimator; Credit Manager; Customer Service Representative; Dental Lab Technician; Dentist; Dietician/Nutritionist; Draftsperson; EEG Technologist; EKG Technician; Electrical/Electronics Engineer; Electrician; Financial Analyst; Food Scientist/Technologist; General Manager; Health Services Manager; Human Resources Manager; Human Service Worker; Industrial Engineer; Industrial Production Manager; Insurance Agent/Broker; Management Trainee; Materials Engineer; Mechanical Engineer; Medical Records Technician; Nuclear Medicine Technologist; Occupational Therapist; Paralegal; Physical Therapist; Public Relations Specialist; Purchasing Agent/Manager; Quality Control Supervisor; Radiological Technologist; Recreational Therapist; Respiratory Therapist; Restaurant/Food Service Manager; Science Technologist; Securities Sales Representative; Software Engineer; Speech-Language Pathologist; Structural Engineer; Surgical Technician; Surveyor; Systems Analyst; Technical Writer/Editor; Underwriter/Assistant Underwriter; Urban/Regional Planner; Wholesale and Retail Buyer. **Number of placements per year:** 50 - 99.

BONIFIELD ASSOCIATES
3003-E Lincoln Drive West, Marlton NJ 08053. 609/596-3300. **Fax:** 609/596-8866. **Contact:** Richard Tyson, President. **E-mail address:** info@bonifield.com. **World Wide Web address:** http://www.bonifield.com. **Description:** An executive search firm operating on a contingency basis. Company pays fee. **Specializes in the areas of:** Banking; Insurance. **Positions commonly filled include:** Accountant/Auditor; Actuary; Attorney; Bank Officer/Manager; Claim Representative; Insurance Agent/Broker; Underwriter/Assistant Underwriter. **Average salary range of placements:** More than $50,000. **Number of placements per year:** 50 - 99.

BRETT ASSOCIATES
2184 Morris Avenue, Union NJ 07083. 908/687-7772. **Contact:** Manager. **Description:** An executive search firm. **Specializes in the areas of:** Manufacturing.

BROAD WAVERLY & ASSOCIATES
P.O. Box 741, Red Bank NJ 07701. 732/747-4400. **Contact:** Manager. **Description:** An executive search firm. **Specializes in the areas of:** Accounting/Auditing; Insurance; Light Industrial; Technical.

BROOKDALE SEARCH ASSOCIATES
P.O. Box 1293, Bloomfield NJ 07003. 973/338-0515. **Fax:** 973/338-1242. **Contact:** Manager. **Description:** An executive search firm. **Specializes in the areas of:** Electrical; Electronics; Heating, Air Conditioning, and Refrigeration; Technical.

BUTTERFASS PEPE & McCALLAN
P.O. Box 721, Mahwah NJ 07430. 201/512-3330. **Contact:** Manager. **Description:** An executive search firm. **Specializes in the areas of:** Investment.

CFB ASSOCIATES
94 Washington Street, Paterson NJ 07505. 973/881-8284. **Contact:** Manager. **Description:** An executive search firm. **Positions commonly filled include:** Biochemist.

CAPITAL FINANCE RECRUITING
321 Commercial Avenue, Suite 220, Palisades Park NJ 07650. 201/585-8444. **Contact:** Manager. **Description:** An executive search firm. **Specializes in the areas of:** Administration; Data Processing.

CAPSTONE ASSOCIATES
33 Wood Avenue South, 5th Floor, Iselin NJ 08830. 732/906-1300. **Contact:** Manager. **Description:** An executive search firm. **Specializes in the areas of:** Computer Hardware/Software.

CAREER MANAGEMENT INTERNATIONAL
197 Route 18, Suite 102, East Brunswick NJ 08816. 732/937-4800. **Fax:** 732/937-4770. **Contact:** Karen Geipel, Assistant to the President. **Description:** An executive search firm that recruits middle- and senior-level executives for the fashion and retail industries. The firm operates on a retainer basis. Company pays fee. **Specializes in the areas of:** Fashion; Finance; General Management; Personnel/Labor Relations; Retail; Sales. **Positions commonly filled include:** Administrative Manager; Buyer; Credit Manager; Designer; Human Resources Manager; Management Analyst/Consultant; MIS Specialist; Operations/Production Manager. **Average salary range of placements:** More than $50,000. **Number of placements per year:** 50 - 99.

CAREER SEARCH ASSOCIATES
1090 Broadway, Suite 204, West Long Branch NJ 07764. 732/222-5333. **Fax:** 732/222-2332. **Contact:** Bruce Rovinsky, President. **Description:** An executive search firm. Company pays fee. **Specializes in the areas of:** Accounting/Auditing; Advertising; Distribution; Engineering; Finance; Food Industry; General Management; Industrial; Manufacturing; Personnel/Labor Relations; Retail; Sales; Transportation. **Positions commonly filled include:** Accountant/Auditor; Buyer; Computer Programmer; Credit Manager; Customer Service Rep.; Engineer; Financial Analyst; General Manager; Manufacturer's/Wholesaler's Sales Rep.; Restaurant/Food Service Manager; Retail Manager; Systems Analyst; Transportation/Traffic Specialist; Wholesale and Retail Buyer. **Number of placements per year:** 50 - 99.

CAREERS ON TRACK
150 County Road, Box 222, Tenafly NJ 07670. 201/894-0600. **Fax:** 201/853-7940. **Contact:** Gary Tabor, Owner. **E-mail address:** tabortrak@aol.com. **Description:** An executive search firm. **Specializes in the areas of:** Sales. **Positions commonly filled include:** General Manager; Management Analyst/Consultant; Marketing Manager. **Average salary range of placements:** More than $50,000. **Number of placements per year:** 1 - 49.

CAREERWORKS
520 Main Street, Suite 302, Fort Lee NJ 07024-4501. 201/592-1460. **Contact:** Mark Raskin, President. **E-mail address:** careerw@aol.com. **Description:** An executive search firm operating on a contingency basis. Company pays fee. **Specializes in the areas of:** Accounting/Auditing; Administration; Engineering; Finance; General Management; Manufacturing; Personnel/Labor Relations; Sales. **Positions commonly filled include:** Accountant/Auditor; Financial Analyst; General Manager; Hotel Manager; Operations/Production Manager; Restaurant/Food Service Manager; Transportation/Traffic Specialist. **Number of placements per year:** 50 - 99.

CARTER McKENZIE INC.
300 Executive Drive, Suite 250, West Orange NJ 07052-3303. 973/736-7100. **Fax:** 973/736-9416. **Contact:** John Capo, Vice President. **E-mail address:** jcapo@carter-mckenzie.com. **World Wide Web address:** http://www.carter-mckenzie.com. **Description:** An executive search firm operating on both retainer and contingency bases that focuses on the placement of MIS professionals. Company pays fee. **Specializes in the areas of:** Administration; Computer Science/Software. **Positions commonly filled include:** Computer Programmer; MIS Specialist; Software Engineer; Systems Analyst; Telecommunications Manager. **Average salary range of placements:** More than $50,000. **Number of placements per year:** 100 - 199.

CARTER/MACKAY PERSONNEL INC.
777 Terrace Avenue, Hasbrouck Heights NJ 07604. 201/288-5100. **Fax:** 201/288-2660. **Contact:** Bruce Green, Vice President. **E-mail address:** cartmackay@aol.com. **World Wide Web address:** http://www.cartermackay.com. **Description:** An executive search firm. Company pays fee. **Specializes in the areas of:** Computer Hardware/Software; Computer Science/Software; Data Communications; Health/Medical; Pharmaceutical; Sales; Technical. **Positions commonly filled include:** General Manager; Manufacturer's/Wholesaler's Sales Rep.; Marketing Manager; Sales Manager; Systems Analyst. **Other U.S. locations:** Framingham MA; Cary NC; Great Neck NY. **Average salary range of placements:** More than $50,000.

L. CAVALIERE & ASSOCIATES
2300 State Route 27, North Brunswick NJ 08902. 732/940-3100. **Fax:** 732/940-2266. **Contact:** Louis Cavaliere, Managing Director. **Description:** An executive search firm operating on both retainer and

contingency bases. Company pays fee. **Specializes in the areas of:** Computer Science/Software. **Positions commonly filled include:** Computer Programmer; Management Analyst/Consultant; Software Engineer; Systems Analyst. **Average salary range of placements:** More than $50,000. **Number of placements per year:** 1 - 49.

CERTIFIED PERSONNEL CORPORATION
P.O. Box 36, Berkeley Heights NJ 07922. 908/322-0404. **Fax:** 908/322-1738. **Contact:** Peter Gilbert, Managing Partner. **E-mail address:** peter_gilbert@notes.interliant.com. **World Wide Web address:** http://www.certifiedpersonnel.com. **Description:** An executive search firm operating on a contingency basis and focusing on the placement of Lotus Notes developers and administrators. Clients include international banks and financial institutions, large insurance companies, consulting organizations, Big Six CPA firms, and *Fortune* 500 companies. **Positions commonly filled include:** Computer Programmer; MIS Specialist; Systems Analyst. **Average salary range of placements:** More than $50,000.

CHRISTENSON & HUTCHISON
466 Southern Boulevard, Chatham NJ 07928. 973/966-1600. **Contact:** Manager. **Description:** An executive search firm.

CHURCHILL & HARRIMAN, INC.
601 Ewing Street, Suite B7, Princeton NJ 08540. 609/921-3551. **Fax:** 609/921-1061. **Contact:** Kenneth J. Peterson, President. **Description:** An executive search firm that also provides per diem information technology consulting services. Company pays fee. **Specializes in the areas of:** Administration; Computer Science/Software. **Positions commonly filled include:** Computer Programmer; Systems Analyst. **Average salary range of placements:** More than $50,000. **Number of placements per year:** 50 - 99.

COMPUTER EASE
1301 Monmouth Avenue, Lakewood NJ 08701. 732/370-7148. **Contact:** Manager. **Description:** An executive search firm that places computer professionals. **Positions commonly filled include:** Computer Programmer; Systems Analyst.

CORPORATE INFORMATION SEARCH
71 Union Avenue, Rutherford NJ 07070. 201/896-0600. **Contact:** Manager. **Description:** An executive search firm. **Specializes in the areas of:** Information Technology.

CORPORATE ONE, INC.
350 West Passaic Street, Rochelle Park NJ 07662. 201/368-0088. **Fax:** 201/368-3566. **Contact:** Ron Kolman, President. **Description:** An executive search firm. Company pays fee. **Specializes in the areas of:** Accounting/Auditing; Consumer Package Goods; Finance; Food Industry; International Executives; Manufacturing. **Positions commonly filled include:** Accounting Supervisor; Vice President of Finance. **Number of placements per year:** 1 - 49.

COX DARROW & OWENS, INC.
6 Clementon Road East, Suite E4, Gibbsboro NJ 08026-1199. 609/782-1300. **Fax:** 609/782-7277. **Contact:** Bob Darrow, Vice President/Partner. **Description:** An executive search firm operating on a contingency basis. Company pays fee. **Specializes in the areas of:** Banking; Engineering; Industrial; Manufacturing; Mortgage; Personnel/Labor Relations; Sales; Technical. **Positions commonly filled include:** Chemical Engineer; Electrical/Electronics Engineer; Human Resources Manager; Mechanical Engineer; Purchasing Agent/Manager; Quality Control Supervisor; Telecommunications Manager. **Other U.S. locations:** Nationwide. **Average salary range of placements:** $30,000 - $50,000. **Number of placements per year:** 50 - 99.

D'ANDREA ASSOCIATES INC.
296 Amboy Avenue, Metuchen NJ 08840. 732/906-0110. **Fax:** 732/906-0116. **Contact:** Nick D'Andrea, President. **Description:** An executive search firm. Company pays fee. **Specializes in the areas of:** Banking; General Management. **Positions commonly filled include:** Bank Officer/Manager; Financial Analyst; Fund Manager; General Manager; Human Resources Manager; Sales Executive; Sales Manager; Sales Rep. **Average salary range of placements:** More than $50,000. **Number of placements per year:** 1 - 49.

DATA HUNTERS, INC.
P.O. Box 884, Ramsey NJ 07446-0884. 201/825-1368. **Fax:** 201/327-4234. **Contact:** Bette Rosenfeld, President. **E-mail address:** datahunt@nis.net. **Description:** An executive search firm and employment agency. Company pays fee. **Specializes in the areas of:** Computer Science/Software; Data Processing. **Positions commonly filled include:** Computer Programmer; Internet Services Manager; MIS Specialist; Software Engineer; Systems Analyst; Telecommunications Manager. **Number of placements per year:** 1 - 49.

DATA PROFESSIONALS UNLIMITED
50 Heights Road, Clifton NJ 07012-1215. 973/779-3942. **Fax:** 973/779-2063. **Contact:** Jerry Wallace, President. **Description:** An executive search firm. Company pays fee. **Specializes in the areas of:** Food Industry. **Positions commonly filled include:** Biological Scientist; Chemical Engineer; Chemist; Food Scientist/Technologist; Purchasing Agent/Manager; Quality Control Supervisor. **Number of placements per year:** 50 - 99.

DATA SEARCH NETWORK
P.O. Box 305, Emerson NJ 07630. 201/967-8600. **Contact:** Manager. **Description:** An executive search firm. **Specializes in the areas of:** Information Systems.

THE DATAFINDERS GROUP, INC.
25 East Spring Valley Avenue, Maywood NJ 07607. 201/845-7700. **Fax:** 201/845-7365. **Contact:** Thomas J. Credidio, Vice President. **E-mail address:** postmaster@data-finders.com. **World Wide Web address:** http://www.data-finders.com. **Description:** An executive search firm. Company pays fee. **Specializes in the areas of:** Computer Science/Software; MIS/EDP; Sales. **Positions commonly filled include:** Computer Programmer; EDP Specialist; Manufacturer's/Wholesaler's Sales Rep.; Services Sales Representative; Software Engineer; Systems Analyst. **Number of placements per year:** 200 - 499.

CLARK DAVIS ASSOCIATES
7 Century Drive, Parsippany NJ 07054. 973/267-5511. **Contact:** Manager. **Description:** An executive search firm. **Specializes in the areas of:** Accounting/Auditing; Engineering; Information Systems.

DEAN-WHARTON ASSOCIATES
166 Westend Avenue, Somerville NJ 08876. 908/231-1818. **Contact:** Manager. **Description:** An executive search firm. **Specializes in the areas of:** Human Resources.

M.T. DONALDSON ASSOCIATES, INC.
4400 Route 9 South, Suite 1000, Freehold NJ 07728. 732/303-7890. **Fax:** 732/462-9149. **Contact:** Sol Premisler, President. **Description:** An executive search firm. **Specializes in the areas of:** Engineering; Food Industry; Health/Medical; Industrial; Manufacturing;

Personnel/Labor Relations. **Positions commonly filled include:** Chemical Engineer; Chemist; Food Scientist/ Technologist; Industrial Engineer; Industrial Production Manager; Mechanical Engineer; Pharmacist; Purchasing Agent/Manager; Quality Control Supervisor. **Average salary range of placements:** More than $50,000. **Number of placements per year:** 1 - 49.

DOUGLAS PERSONNEL ASSOCIATES INC.
12 Route 17 North, Paramus NJ 07652-2644. **Fax:** 201/368-3881. **Contact:** Ms. Tobey Klein, President. **Description:** An executive search and recruitment firm for the retail industry. Company pays fee. **Specializes in the areas of:** Retail. **Positions commonly filled include:** Buyer; Human Resources Specialist. **Average salary range of placements:** $30,000 - $50,000. **Number of placements per year:** 50 - 99.

DOW-TECH
1700 Route 23 North, Suite 330, Wayne NJ 07470. 973/696-8000. **Fax:** 973/696-1964. **Contact:** Chris Dowling, President. **Description:** An executive search firm. Company pays fee. **Specializes in the areas of:** Electrical; Electronics; Sales. **Positions commonly filled include:** Electrical/Electronics Engineer; Marketing Manager; Marketing Specialist; Sales and Marketing Manager; Sales Engineer; Sales Manager; Sales Rep. **Number of placements per year:** 50 - 99.

DREIER CONSULTING
P.O. Box 356, Ramsey NJ 07446. 201/327-1113. **Fax:** 201/327-0816. **Contact:** Jennifer Hernandez, Administrative Assistant. **E-mail address:** dreiercslt@mindspring.com. **World Wide Web address:** http://www.dreierconsulting.com. **Description:** An executive search firm operating on a contingency basis and focusing on the medical, electronics, and telecommunications industries. Company pays fee. **Specializes in the areas of:** Computer Science/Software; Engineering; Manufacturing; Sales. **Positions commonly filled include:** Biomedical Engineer; Computer Programmer; Design Engineer; Electrical/Electronics Engineer; General Manager; Mechanical Engineer; Software Engineer. **Other U.S. locations:** Nationwide. **Average salary range of placements:** More than $50,000. **Number of placements per year:** 1 - 49.

DREW ASSOCIATES INTERNATIONAL
77 Park Street, Montclair NJ 07042. 973/746-8877. **Contact:** Manager. **Description:** An executive search firm. **Specializes in the areas of:** Health/Medical.

DUNHILL PERSONNEL OF CHERRY HILL, INC.
1040 Kings Highway North, Suite 400, Cherry Hill NJ 08034. 609/667-9180. **Contact:** Bill Emerson, Owner. **Description:** An executive search firm.

DUNHILL PROFESSIONAL SEARCH
303 West Main Street, Freehold NJ 07728. 732/431-2700. **Fax:** 732/431-0329. **Contact:** Rich Hanson, President. **Description:** An executive search firm. Company pays fee. **Specializes in the areas of:** Accounting/Auditing; Banking; Finance; Secretarial. **Positions commonly filled include:** Accountant/ Auditor; Administrative Assistant; Bookkeeper; Budget Analyst; Economist; EDP Specialist; Executive Assistant; Financial Analyst; Legal Secretary; Receptionist; Secretary; Typist/Word Processor. **Number of placements per year:** 1 - 49.

DUNHILL PROFESSIONAL SEARCH OF RAMSEY
393 State Route 202, Oakland NJ 07436-2744. 201/337-2200. **Fax:** 201/337-3445. **Contact:** Roger Lippincott, President. **E-mail address:** dsramnj@ dunhillstaff.com. **Description:** An executive search firm. Company pays fee. **Specializes in the areas of:** Personnel/Labor Relations; Sales. **Positions commonly filled include:** Human Resources Specialist; Manufacturer's/Wholesaler's Sales Rep.; Sales Rep.; Training Manager. **Average salary range of placements:** More than $50,000. **Number of placements per year:** 50 - 99.

DYNAMIC RECRUITERS INC.
59 East Mill Road, Box 16, Long Valley NJ 07853. 908/876-8420. **Contact:** Manager. **Description:** An executive search firm. **Specializes in the areas of:** Aerospace; Industrial; Pharmaceutical; Plastics. **Benefits available to temporary workers:** Accident/Emergency Insurance.

EAGLE RESEARCH INC.
373-D Route 46 West, Fairfield NJ 07004. 973/244-0992. **Fax:** 973/244-1239. **Contact:** Annette S. Baron, PA, President. **E-mail address:** asbaron@aol. com. **Description:** An executive search firm operating on both retainer and contingency bases. Company pays fee. **Specializes in the areas of:** Biotechnology; Pharmaceutical. **Positions commonly filled include:** Physician. **International locations:** Worldwide. **Average salary range of placements:** More than $50,000. **Number of placements per year:** 1 - 49.

ELECTRONIC SEARCH INC.
P.O. Box 506, Bradley Beach NJ 07720. 732/775-5017. **Fax:** 732/775-5035. **Contact:** Tom Manni, Regional Manager. **World Wide Web address:** http://www.electronicsearch.com. **Description:** An executive search firm operating on both retained and contingency bases. Company pays fee. **Specializes in the areas of:** Engineering; Wireless Communications. **Positions commonly filled include:** Applications Engineer; Electrical/Electronics Engineer; Sales Engineer; Software Engineer; Telecommunications Manager. **Corporate headquarters location:** Rolling Meadows CA. **Other U.S. locations:** San Diego CA. **Average salary range of placements:** More than $50,000. **Number of placements per year:** 100 - 199.

ELIAS ASSOCIATES
P.O. Box 396, East Brunswick NJ 08816. 732/390-4600. **Contact:** Manager. **Description:** A generalist executive search firm.

EXECUTIVE EXCHANGE CORPORATION
2517 Highway 35, Suite G-103, Manasquan NJ 08736. 732/223-6655. **Fax:** 732/223-1162. **Contact:** Elizabeth B. Glosser, Owner. **Description:** An executive search firm that operates on a contingency basis and focuses on the placement of computer-related sales professionals. Executive Exchange Corporation is also a member of Nationwide Interchange, a national job search network of recruiters. Company pays fee. **Specializes in the areas of:** Sales. **Positions commonly filled include:** Account Manager; Marketing Manager; Services Sales Rep. **Average salary range of placements:** $30,000 - $50,000. **Number of placements per year:** 100 - 199.

EXECUTIVE NETWORK, INC.
147 Columbia Turnpike, Suite 307, Florham Park NJ 07932-2145. 973/966-5400. **Fax:** 973/966-0304. **Contact:** Elissa Marcus, President. **Description:** An executive search firm. Company pays fee. **Specializes in the areas of:** Accounting/Auditing; Administration; Computer Science/Software; Finance; Insurance; Personnel/Labor Relations; Retail; Sales; Secretarial; Technical. **Positions commonly filled include:** Accountant/Auditor; Administrative Manager; Advertising Clerk; Budget Analyst; Claim Rep.; Clerical Supervisor; Computer Programmer; Customer Service Rep.; Financial Analyst; Human Resources Specialist; Management Trainee; MIS Specialist; Purchasing Agent/Manager; Services Sales Rep.; Software

Engineer; Systems Analyst; Underwriter/Assistant Underwriter. **Number of placements per year:** 50 - 99.

EXECUTIVE RECRUITERS, INC.
855 Valley Road, Clifton NJ 07013-2441. 973/471-7878. **Contact:** Manager. **Description:** An executive search firm specializing in insurance placements.

EXECUTIVE REGISTRY INC.
12 Route 17 North, Paramus NJ 07652. 201/587-1010. **Contact:** Manager. **Description:** An executive search firm specializing. **Specializes in the areas of:** Information Systems; Retail.

EXECUTIVE SEARCH, INC.
48 Headquarters Plaza, Morristown NJ 07960. 973/538-2300. **Contact:** Recruitment Coordinator. **Description:** An executive search firm. Company pays fee. **Specializes in the areas of:** Accounting/Auditing; Administration; Banking; Finance; General Management; Insurance; Legal; Personnel/Labor Relations; Sales; Secretarial. **Positions commonly filled include:** Accountant/Auditor; Administrative Manager; Attorney; Bank Officer/Manager; Claim Rep.; Clerical Supervisor; Credit Manager; Customer Service Rep.; Financial Analyst; Health Services Manager; Human Resources Manager; Insurance Agent/Broker; Management Analyst/Consultant; Management Trainee; Manufacturer's/Wholesaler's Sales Rep.; Operations Manager; Paralegal; Public Relations Specialist; Purchasing Agent/Manager; Securities Sales Rep.; Technical Writer/Editor; Underwriter/Assistant Underwriter; Wholesale/Retail Buyer.

FAB ASSOCIATES
146 Lakeview Drive South, Suite 200, Gibbsboro NJ 08026. 609/783-7361. **Contact:** Manager. **Description:** An executive search firm. **Specializes in the areas of:** Insurance.

FOLEY PROCTOR YOSKOWITZ
One Cattano Avenue, Morristown NJ 07960. 973/605-1000. **Fax:** 973/605-1020. **Contact:** Richard W. Proctor, Partner. **Description:** An executive search firm. Company pays fee. **Specializes in the areas of:** Health/Medical; Physician Executive. **Positions commonly filled include:** Administrator; Chief Executive Officer; Physician; Physician Assistant. **Other U.S. locations:** New York NY. **Average salary range of placements:** More than $50,000. **Number of placements per year:** 50 - 99.

F-O-R-T-U-N-E PERSONNEL CONSULTANTS
350 West Passaic Street, Rochelle Park NJ 07662. 201/843-7621. **Fax:** 201/843-8189. **Contact:** Manager. **Description:** An executive search firm operating on both retained and contingency bases. **Specializes in the areas of:** Biotechnology; General Management; Materials; Medical Technology; Pharmaceutical. **Corporate headquarters location:** New York NY. **Other U.S. locations:** Nationwide.

F-O-R-T-U-N-E PERSONNEL CONSULTANTS OF MENLO PARK
16 Bridge Street, Metuchen NJ 08840. 732/494-6266. **Fax:** 732/494-5669. **Contact:** Peter Provda, President. **Description:** An executive search firm. Company pays fee. **Specializes in the areas of:** Engineering; Food Industry; Manufacturing; Personnel/Labor Relations; Technical. **Positions commonly filled include:** Biochemist; Biological Scientist; Biomedical Engineer; Chemical Engineer; Computer Programmer; Designer; Electrical/Electronics Engineer; Food Scientist/Technologist; Human Resources Manager; Industrial Engineer; Mechanical Engineer; Operations/Production Manager; Purchasing Agent/Manager; Quality Control Supervisor; Science Technologist; Software Engineer; Systems Analyst. **Corporate headquarters location:** New York NY. **Other U.S. locations:** Nationwide. **Number of placements per year:** 1 - 49.

FOSTER ASSOCIATES
The Livery, 209 Cooper Avenue, Upper Montclair NJ 07043. 973/746-2800. **Contact:** Manager. **Description:** An executive search firm. **Specializes in the areas of:** Accounting/Auditing; Consulting; Finance; Legal.

THE FOSTER McKAY GROUP
30 Vreeland Road, Florham Park NJ 07932. 973/966-0909. **Fax:** 973/966-6925. **Contact:** Allen Galorenzo, Partner. **World Wide Web address:** http://www.hrm-inc.com. **Description:** An executive search firm operating on both retained and contingency bases. Company pays fee. **Specializes in the areas of:** Accounting/Auditing; Finance. **Positions commonly filled include:** Accountant/Auditor; Budget Analyst; Chief Financial Officer; Controller; Finance Director; Financial Analyst. **Average salary range of placements:** More than $50,000. **Number of placements per year:** 100 - 199.

FOX-MORRIS ASSOCIATES
1050 Wall Street West, Suite 410, Lyndhurst NJ 07071. 201/933-8900. **Contact:** Manager. **Description:** An executive search firm. **Specializes in the areas of:** Human Resources.

GARRETT GROUP
342 Parsippany Road, Parsippany NJ 07054. 973/884-0711. **Fax:** 973/884-1307. **Contact:** Mr. Bernd Stecker, Recruiting. **Description:** An executive search firm. **Specializes in the areas of:** Electronics; Engineering; Marketing. **Average salary range of placements:** More than $50,000.

GIBSON MARTIN CONSULTING
694 Route 15 South, Suite 205B, Lake Hopatcong NJ 07849. 973/663-3300. **Fax:** 973/663-3316. **Contact:** Robert Lee, Principal. **E-mail address:** gmcboblee@careergoals.com. **World Wide Web address:** http://www.careergoals.com. **Description:** An executive search firm. Company pays fee. **Specializes in the areas of:** Accounting/Auditing; Administration; Computer Science/Software; Finance. **Positions commonly filled include:** Accountant/Auditor; Architect; Budget Analyst; Chemist; Computer Programmer; Financial Analyst; Systems Analyst.

GILBERT & VAN CAMPEN INTERNATIONAL
393 Lake Shore Drive, Belvidere NJ 07823. 908/475-2222. **Contact:** Manager. **Description:** An executive search firm that places high-level executives.

GILBERT TWEED ASSOCIATES INC.
155 Prospect Street, Suite 100, West Orange NJ 07052. 973/731-3033. **Contact:** Manager. **Description:** An executive search firm.

LAWRENCE GLASER ASSOCIATES INC.
505 South Lenola Road, Moorestown NJ 08057. 609/778-9500. **Fax:** 609/778-4390. **Contact:** Lawrence Glaser, President. **Description:** An executive search firm. **Specializes in the areas of:** Food Industry; Sales. **Average salary range of placements:** More than $50,000. **Number of placements per year:** 50 - 99.

GLOBAL SEARCH, INC.
41 Vreeland Avenue, Totowa NJ 07512. 201/890-1025. **Contact:** Manager. **Description:** An executive search firm.

L.J. GONZER ASSOCIATES
1225 Raymond Boulevard, Newark NJ 07102.

973/624-5600. **Contact:** Manager. **Description:** An executive search firm.

GRANT FRANKS & ASSOCIATES
929 North Kings Highway, Cherry Hill NJ 08034. 609/779-9030. **Fax:** 609/779-0898. **Contact:** Lou Franks, Owner. **Description:** An executive search firm operating on a contingency basis. Company pays fee. **Specializes in the areas of:** Accounting/Auditing; Engineering; Manufacturing. **Positions commonly filled include:** Accountant/Auditor; Biomedical Engineer; Chemical Engineer; Chemist; Claim Representative; Credit Manager; Customer Service Representative; Electrical/Electronics Engineer; Financial Analyst; Food Scientist/Technologist; Human Resources Manager; Mechanical Engineer; Operations/Production Manager; Physical Therapist; Quality Control Supervisor; Underwriter/Assistant Underwriter.

HADLEY ASSOCIATES
147 Columbia Turnpike, Suite 104, Florham Park NJ 07932-2145. 973/377-9177. **Fax:** 973/377-9223. **Contact:** Thomas Hadley, President. **Description:** An executive search firm operating on both retainer and contingency bases. **Specializes in the areas of:** Health/Medical. **Positions commonly filled include:** Biological Scientist; Biomedical Engineer; Chemical Engineer; Chemist; Clinical Lab Technician; Environmental Engineer; Pharmacist; Quality Control Supervisor; Radiological Technologist; Statistician. **Average salary range of placements:** More than $50,000. **Number of placements per year:** 1 - 49.

ROBERT HALF INTERNATIONAL/ACCOUNTEMPS
70 Wood Avenue South, Iselin NJ 08830. 732/634-7200. **Contact:** Manager. **Description:** An executive search firm. Accountemps (also at this location) provides temporary placements. **Specializes in the areas of:** Accounting/Auditing. **Corporate headquarters location:** Menlo Park CA. **Other U.S. locations:** Nationwide. **International locations:** Worldwide.

ROBERT HALF INTERNATIONAL/ACCOUNTEMPS
959 Route 46 East, 4th Floor, Parsippany NJ 07054. 973/455-7300. **Contact:** Manager. **Description:** An executive search firm. Accountemps (also at this location) provides temporary placements. **Specializes in the areas of:** Accounting/Auditing. **Corporate headquarters location:** Menlo Park CA. **Other U.S. locations:** Nationwide. **International locations:** Worldwide.

HARRIS EXECUTIVE SEARCH
1800 Fairlawn Avenue, Fairlawn NJ 07410. 201/703-1414. **Contact:** Manager. **Description:** An executive search firm. **Specializes in the areas of:** Engineering; Manufacturing.

HEADHUNTERS EXECUTIVE SEARCH
25 River Road, Suite C26, Nutley NJ 07110. 973/667-2799. **Fax:** 973/667-3609. **Contact:** Elaine Jones, Vice President. **Description:** An executive search firm. Company pays fee. **Specializes in the areas of:** Health/Medical; Sales. **Number of placements per year:** 200 - 499.

HEALTHCARE RECRUITERS INTERNATIONAL
3 Eves Drive, Suite 303, Marlton NJ 08053. 609/596-7179. **Fax:** 609/596-6895. **Contact:** Diane Rosamelea, General Manager. **Description:** An executive search firm. Company pays fee. **Specializes in the areas of:** Health/Medical. **Positions commonly filled include:** Biological Scientist; Biomedical Engineer; Marketing Manager; MIS Specialist; Recruiter; Software Engineer. **Other U.S. locations:** Dallas TX. **Average salary range of placements:** $30,000 - $50,000. **Number of placements per year:** 50 - 99.

HEALTHCARE RECRUITERS INTERNATIONAL
55 Harristown Road, Glen Rock NJ 07452. 201/670-9800. **Contact:** Manager. **Description:** An executive search firm. **Specializes in the areas of:** Health/Medical.

HOLM PERSONNEL CONSULTANTS
333-B Route 46 West, Suite 202, Fairfield NJ 07004. 973/808-1933. **Contact:** Personnel. **Description:** An executive search firm that also operates as an employment agency. Company pays fee. **Specializes in the areas of:** Accounting/Auditing; Administration; Computer Science/Software; General Management; Personnel/Labor Relations; Sales; Secretarial. **Positions commonly filled include:** Accountant/Auditor; Administrative Manager; Budget Analyst; Buyer; Computer Programmer; Credit Manager; Financial Analyst; Human Resources Specialist; Management Trainee; MIS Specialist; Purchasing Agent/Manager; Software Engineer; Systems Analyst; Telecommunications Manager; Transportation/Traffic Specialist. **Average salary range of placements:** $30,000 - $50,000. **Number of placements per year:** 50 - 99.

HRESHKO CONSULTING GROUP
850 U.S. Highway 1, North Brunswick NJ 08902. 732/545-9000. **Fax:** 732/545-0800. **Contact:** Frank Hreshko, Managing Director. **Description:** An executive search firm. Company pays fee. **Specializes in the areas of:** Accounting/Auditing; Banking; Computer Science/Software; Finance; General Management; Insurance; Manufacturing; Personnel/Labor Relations; Sales. **Positions commonly filled include:** Accountant/Auditor; Computer Programmer; Financial Analyst; General Manager; Human Resources Specialist; Management Analyst/Consultant; MIS Specialist; Software Engineer; Systems Analyst; Telecommunications Manager. **Average salary range of placements:** More than $50,000. **Number of placements per year:** 100 - 199.

HUFF ASSOCIATES
95 Reef Drive, Ocean City NJ 08226. 609/399-2867. **Contact:** W.Z. Huff, President. **Description:** An executive search firm. Company pays fee. **Specializes in the areas of:** Health/Medical; Manufacturing; Technical. **Positions commonly filled include:** Biomedical Engineer; Ceramics Engineer; Chemical Engineer; Chemist; Civil Engineer; Electrical/Electronics Engineer; Manufacturing Engineer; Mechanical Engineer; Metallurgical Engineer; Nurse; Physician. **Number of placements per year:** 1 - 49.

INSEARCH INC.
231 South White Horse Pike, Audubon NJ 08106. **Contact:** Dawn Sadlowski, Assistant. **E-mail address:** insearch@aol.com. **World Wide Web address:** http://www.qwikpages.com/l/insearch. **Description:** An executive search firm. **Specializes in the areas of:** Food Industry; Hotel/Restaurant; Insurance. **Positions commonly filled include:** Actuary; Food Scientist/Technologist; Hotel Manager; Insurance Agent/Broker. **Average salary range of placements:** $30,000 - $50,000. **Number of placements per year:** 200 - 499.

INTER-REGIONAL EXECUTIVE SEARCH, INC.
191 Hamburg Turnpike, Pompton Lakes NJ 07441-2332. 973/616-8800. **Fax:** 973/616-8115. **Contact:** Frank Risalvato, Managing Partner. **E-mail address:** ires@msn.com. **World Wide Web address:** http://www.dfx.com/ires. **Description:** An executive search firm. Company pays fee. **Specializes in the areas of:** Accounting/Auditing; Engineering; Finance; Insurance; Sales. **Positions commonly filled include:** Accountant/Auditor; Administrative Manager; Bank Officer/Manager; Budget Analyst; Chemical Engineer; Chemist; Claim Rep.; Credit Manager; Customer

Service Rep.; Design Engineer; Designer; Economist; Financial Analyst; Industrial Engineer; Industrial Production Manager; Insurance Agent/Broker; Market Research Analyst; Mechanical Engineer; MIS Specialist; Nuclear Engineer; Pharmacist; Purchasing Agent/Manager; Telecommunications Manager; Underwriter/Assistant Underwriter. **Average salary range of placements:** $50,000 - $100,000. **Number of placements per year:** 100 - 199.

J.M. JOSEPH ASSOCIATES
P.O. Box 104, High Bridge NJ 08829-0104. 908/638-6877. **Fax:** 908/638-8220. **Contact:** C. Russell Ditzel, Managing Director. **E-mail address:** cditzel@vcx.net. **Description:** An executive search firm. Company pays fee. **Specializes in the areas of:** Administration; Computer Science/Software; Engineering; Food Industry; Health/Medical; Manufacturing; Personnel/Labor Relations; Sales; Technical. **Positions commonly filled include:** Financial Analyst; Food Scientist/Technologist; Human Resources Specialist; Industrial Engineer; Industrial Production Manager; MIS Specialist; Operations/Production Manager. **Average salary range of placements:** More than $50,000. **Number of placements per year:** 1 - 49.

KANE ASSOCIATES
41 Vreeland Avenue, Totowa NJ 07512. 201/890-9110. **Contact:** Manager. **Description:** An executive search firm operating on a contingency basis.

KARRAS PERSONNEL INC.
2 Central Avenue, Madison NJ 07940. 973/966-6800. **Contact:** Bill Karras, Recruiter. **Description:** An executive search firm. Company pays fee. **Specializes in the areas of:** Human Resources. **Average salary range of placements:** More than $50,000.

THE KELLER GROUP/CAREERS INC.
P.O. Box 520, Suite 172, Wyckoff NJ 07481. 201/837-6612. **Fax:** 201/837-8783. **Contact:** Keith Eller, President. **E-mail address:** keller520@msn.com. **Description:** An executive search firm operating on a contingency basis. Careers Inc. specializes in marketing placements. **Specializes in the areas of:** Biology; Chemistry; Food Science; Information Systems; Pharmaceutical; Technical and Scientific. **Average salary range of placements:** More than $50,000. **Number of placements per year:** 1 - 49.

KEY EMPLOYMENT
1014 Livingston Avenue, North Brunswick NJ 08902. 732/249-2454. **Fax:** 732/249-2521. **Contact:** Gary Silberger, President. **Description:** An executive search firm. **Specializes in the areas of:** Accounting/Auditing; Administration; Advertising; Engineering; Sales; Technical; Transportation. **Positions commonly filled include:** Chemical Engineer; Civil Engineer; Computer Programmer; Design Engineer; Designer; Electrical/Electronics Engineer; Environmental Engineer; Financial Analyst; Industrial Engineer; Industrial Production Manager; Market Research Analyst; Mechanical Engineer; MIS Specialist; Purchasing Agent/Manager; Software Engineer; Structural Engineer; Systems Analyst; Telecommunications Manager. **Average salary range of placements:** More than $50,000. **Number of placements per year:** 1 - 49.

T.J. KOELLHOFFER & ASSOCIATES
250 State Route 28, Suite 206, Bridgewater NJ 08807. 908/526-6880. **Fax:** 908/725-2653. **Contact:** Tom Koellhoffer, Principal. **E-mail address:** tomkoell@aol.com. **Description:** An executive search firm. Company pays fee. **Specializes in the areas of:** Broadcasting; Computer Science/Software; Engineering; Manufacturing; Technical. **Positions commonly filled include:** Aerospace Engineer; Biomedical Engineer; Electrical/Electronics Engineer; Materials Engineer; Mechanical Engineer; Multimedia Designer; Physicist; Software Engineer. **Average salary range of placements:** More than $50,000. **Number of placements per year:** 1 - 49.

KORN/FERRY INTERNATIONAL
One Palmer Square, Suite 330, Princeton NJ 08542. 609/921-8811. **Contact:** Manager. **Description:** An executive search firm that places upper-level managers in a variety of industries. **Corporate headquarters location:** Los Angeles CA. **International locations:** Worldwide. **Average salary range of placements:** More than $50,000.

PAUL KULL & COMPANY
18 Meadowbrook Road, Randolph NJ 07869. 973/361-7440. **Contact:** Paul Kull, Owner. **Description:** An executive search firm. Company pays fee. **Specializes in the areas of:** Computer Hardware/Software; Engineering; General Management; Manufacturing; Sales; Technical. **Positions commonly filled include:** Aerospace Engineer; Biochemist; Biomedical Engineer; Chemical Engineer; Computer Programmer; Electrical/Electronics Engineer; Industrial Engineer; Manufacturing Engineer; Marketing Specialist; Mechanical Engineer; Software Engineer. **Number of placements per year:** 1 - 49.

L&K ASSOCIATES
179 West Broadway, P.O. Box 202, Salem NJ 08079-1328. 609/935-3070. **Contact:** Gene Lank, President. **Description:** An executive search firm operating on both retained and contingency bases. Company pays fee. **Specializes in the areas of:** Computer Science/Software; Legal; Technical; Telecommunications. **Positions commonly filled include:** Attorney; Computer Programmer; MIS Specialist; Systems Analyst; Telecommunications Manager. **Average salary range of placements:** More than $50,000. **Number of placements per year:** 1 - 49.

LANCASTER ASSOCIATES/THE SWAN GROUP
94 Grove Street, Somerville NJ 08876. 908/526-5440. **Fax:** 908/526-1992. **Contact:** Ray Lancaster, President. **Description:** A retainer and contingency search firm. Company pays fee. **Specializes in the areas of:** Computer Science/Software; Technical. **Positions commonly filled include:** MIS Specialist; Telecommunications Manager. **Average salary range of placements:** More than $50,000. **Number of placements per year:** 1 - 49.

LAW PROS LEGAL PLACEMENT SERVICES, INC.
107 East Mount Pleasant Avenue, Livingston NJ 07039. 973/535-8446. **Fax:** 973/535-1860. **Contact:** Beth Fleischer, Principal. **Description:** An executive search firm. Company pays fee. **Specializes in the areas of:** Legal. **Positions commonly filled include:** Attorney; Paralegal. **Average salary range of placements:** $30,000 - $50,000. **Number of placements per year:** 100 - 199.

JONATHAN LAWRENCE ASSOCIATES
103 Washington Avenue, Morristown NJ 07960. 973/285-1988. **Contact:** Manager. **Description:** An executive search firm. Company pays fee. **Specializes in the areas of:** Administration; Computer Science/Software.

ALAN LERNER ASSOCIATES
400 Lakeview Commons, Gibbsboro NJ 08026. 609/435-1600. **Contact:** Manager. **Description:** An executive search firm.

MIS SEARCH
450 Harmon Meadow Boulevard, 1st Floor, Secaucus NJ 07094. 201/330-0080. **Fax:** 201/330-8729.

Contact: Maryanne McGuire, Technical Recruiter. **Description:** An executive search firm. Company pays fee. **Specializes in the areas of:** Administration; Computer Science/Software. **Positions commonly filled include:** Computer Programmer; Systems Analyst.

MJE RECRUITERS, INC.
12 Furler Street, Totowa NJ 07512. 973/785-0885. **Fax:** 973/785-4494. **Contact:** Barry Emen, President. **E-mail address:** barry@mjerecruiters.com. **World Wide Web address:** http://www.mjerecruiters.com. **Description:** An executive search firm. Company pays fee. **Specializes in the areas of:** Accounting/Auditing; Banking; Finance; Insurance; Investment. **Positions commonly filled include:** Accountant/Auditor; Bank Officer/Manager; Budget Analyst; Finance Director; Financial Analyst; Fund Manager. **Number of placements per year:** 50 - 99.

MAJOR SEARCH
500 North Franklin Turnpike, Suite 17, Ramsey NJ 07446. 201/934-9666. **Fax:** 201/818-0339. **Contact:** Pam Ericson, Consultant. **E-mail address:** recruiter@majorinc.com. **World Wide Web address:** http://www.majorinc.com. **Description:** An executive search firm. **Specializes in the areas of:** General Management; Personnel/Labor Relations; Sales. **Positions commonly filled include:** General Manager; Human Resources Specialist; Operations/Production Manager; Software Engineer; Systems Analyst; Telecommunications Manager. **Average salary range of placements:** More than $50,000. **Number of placements per year:** 1 - 49.

MANAGEMENT CATALYSTS
P.O. Box 70, Ship Bottom NJ 08008. 609/597-0079. **Fax:** 609/597-2860. **Contact:** Dr. J.R. Stockton, President. **Description:** An executive search firm. Company pays fee. **Specializes in the areas of:** Food Industry; Research and Development; Technical. **Positions commonly filled include:** Agricultural Engineer; Agricultural Scientist; Biochemist; Biological Scientist; Biomedical Engineer; Chemical Engineer; Chemist; Clinical Lab Technician; Dietician/Nutritionist; Environmental Engineer; Food Scientist/Technologist; Quality Control Supervisor; Science Technologist. **Average salary range of placements:** More than $50,000. **Number of placements per year:** 1 - 49.

MANAGEMENT GROUP OF AMERICA, INC.
250 Passaic Avenue, Suite 210, Fairfield NJ 07004. 973/808-3300. **Fax:** 973/882-9284. **Contact:** James W. Byrne, President. **Description:** An executive search firm that also provides some temporary and contract placements. Company pays fee. **Specializes in the areas of:** Insurance. **Positions commonly filled include:** Customer Service Rep.; Insurance Agent/Broker; Sales Rep. **Average salary range of placements:** $30,000 - $50,000. **Number of placements per year:** 100 - 199.

MANAGEMENT RECRUITERS INTERNATIONAL
P.O. Box 244, Hope NJ 07844. 908/459-5798. **Contact:** Manager. **Description:** An executive search firm. **Specializes in the areas of:** Human Resources.
Other area locations:
- 10 Anderson Road, Bernardsville NJ 07924. 908/204-0070. (Computer Hardware/Software)
- 440 County Road 513, Califon NJ 07830. 908/832-6455. (Insurance)
- 1040 North Kings Highway, Suite 705, Cherry Hill NJ 08034. 609/667-3381.
- 17 Hanover Road, Suite 450, Florham Park NJ 07932. 973/593-0400. (Data Communications; Sales; Telecommunications)
- 24 Lackawanna Plaza, Millburn NJ 07041. 973/379-4020. (Computer Hardware/Software; Computer Programming; Engineering; Sales)
- 1104 Springfield Avenue, Mountainside NJ 07092. 908/789-9400. (Office Support; Sales)
- 150 Floral Avenue, New Providence NJ 07974. 908/771-0600. (Information Systems; Sales)
- 4 Waterloo Road, Stanhope NJ 07874. 973/691-2020. (Computer Hardware/Software)

MANAGEMENT RECRUITERS OF BAY HEAD
106 Bridge Avenue, Bay Head NJ 08742. 732/714-1300. **Fax:** 732/714-1311. **Contact:** Bob Ceresi, General Manager. **E-mail address:** recruiter@mrielectrical.com. **World Wide Web address:** http://www.mrielectrical.com. **Description:** An executive search firm. Company pays fee. **Specializes in the areas of:** Computer Science/Software; Electrical; Electronics; Engineering; Industrial; Manufacturing; Sales; Technical. **Positions commonly filled include:** Buyer; Chemical Engineer; Computer Programmer; Customer Service Representative; Draftsperson; Electrical/Electronics Engineer; Industrial Engineer; Industrial Production Manager; Management Trainee; Manufacturer's/Wholesaler's Sales Rep.; Mechanical Engineer; Metallurgical Engineer; Purchasing Agent/Manager; Quality Control Supervisor; Services Sales Representative; Software Engineer; Systems Analyst; Wholesale and Retail Buyer. **Corporate headquarters location:** Cleveland OH. **Other U.S. locations:** Nationwide. **Average salary range of placements:** More than $50,000. **Number of placements per year:** 50 - 99.

MANAGEMENT RECRUITERS OF BRIDGEWATER
1170 Route 22 East, Bridgewater NJ 08807. 908/725-2595. **Fax:** 908/725-0439. **Contact:** Jennifer Lebron, Project Coordinator. **Description:** A full-service retainer and contingency executive search firm. Company pays fee. **Specializes in the areas of:** Banking; Finance; Insurance; Sales; Transportation. **Positions commonly filled include:** Accountant/Auditor; Bank Officer/Manager; Buyer; Claim Rep.; Credit Manager; Customer Service Rep.; Financial Analyst; Health Services Manager; Insurance Agent/Broker; Manufacturer's/Wholesaler's Sales Rep.; Underwriter/Assistant Underwriter. **Corporate headquarters location:** Cleveland OH. **Other U.S. locations:** Nationwide. **Average salary range of placements:** More than $50,000. **Number of placements per year:** 100 - 199.

MANAGEMENT RECRUITERS OF HADDONFIELD
19 Tanner Street, Haddonfield NJ 08033. 609/428-2233. **Contact:** Manager. **Description:** An executive search firm. **Specializes in the areas of:** High-Tech; Sales.

MANAGEMENT RECRUITERS OF MEDFORD
520 Stokes Road, Suite B6, Medford NJ 08055. 609/654-9109. **Fax:** 609/654-9166. **Contact:** Norman Talbot, President. **E-mail address:** mrinet@recom.com. **World Wide Web address:** http://www.recom.com/~mrinet. **Description:** An executive search firm. Company pays fee. **Specializes in the areas of:** Architecture/Construction; Biotechnology; Chemical; Electronics; Engineering; Food Industry; General Management; Industrial; Manufacturing; Paper; Petrochemical; Pharmaceutical; Sales; Technical. **Positions commonly filled include:** Aerospace Engineer; Biological Scientist; Biomedical Engineer; Chemical Engineer; Chemist; Civil Engineer; Draftsperson; Electrical/Electronics Engineer; Industrial Engineer; Manufacturing Engineer; Mechanical Engineer; Metallurgical Engineer; Quality Control Supervisor; Safety Engineer; Software Engineer; Systems Analyst. **Corporate headquarters location:** Cleveland OH. **Other U.S. locations:** Nationwide. **Average salary range of placements:** More than $50,000. **Number of placements per year:** 50 - 99.

MANAGEMENT RECRUITERS OF ORANGE COUNTY
16 Birch Run Avenue, Denville NJ 07834. 914/477-9509. **Fax:** 914/477-3016. **Contact:** Carolyn Chermak, President. **Description:** An executive search firm that also operates as a temporary agency. Company pays fee. **Specializes in the areas of:** Administration; Architecture/Construction; Biology; Computer Science/Software; Engineering; Food Industry; General Management; Industrial; Legal; Manufacturing; Nonprofit; Retail; Sales; Transportation. **Corporate headquarters location:** Cleveland OH. **Other U.S. locations:** Nationwide. **Average salary range of placements:** More than $50,000. **Number of placements per year:** 1 - 49.

MANAGEMENT RECRUITERS OF PASSAIC COUNTY
750 Hamburg Turnpike, Pompton Lakes NJ 07442. 973/831-7778. **Contact:** David Zawicki, Manager. **Description:** An executive search firm. **Specializes in the areas of:** Accounting/Auditing; Administration; Advertising; Architecture/Construction; Banking; Communications; Computer Science/Software; Construction; Electrical; Engineering; Finance; Food Industry; General Management; Health/Medical; Personnel/Labor Relations; Procurement; Publishing; Real Estate; Retail; Sales; Technical; Textiles; Transportation.

MANAGEMENT RECRUITERS OF SPARTA
191 Woodport Road, Suite 201, Sparta NJ 07871. 973/729-1888. **Toll-free phone:** 800/875-1896. **Fax:** 973/729-1620. **Contact:** Lance Incitti, President. **E-mail address:** recruiter@retailplacement.com. **World Wide Web address:** http://www.retailplacement.com. **Description:** An executive search firm specializing in all areas of retail management. Company pays fee. **Specializes in the areas of:** Accounting/Auditing; Finance; Retail. **Positions commonly filled include:** Auditor; Buyer; Controller; Financial Analyst; Human Resources Manager; Management Analyst/Consultant; Operations Manager. **Corporate headquarters location:** Cleveland OH. **Other U.S. locations:** Nationwide. **Average salary range of placements:** $30,000 - $50,000. **Number of placements per year:** 50 - 99.

NEIL MASON EXECUTIVE SEARCH
301 North Harrison Street, Suite 179, Princeton NJ 08540. 609/895-1400. **Contact:** Manager. **Description:** An executive search firm that provides placements in direct marketing.

McDERMOTT RESOURCES INC.
74 South Powder Mill Road, Morris Plains NJ 07950. 973/285-0066. **Fax:** 973/285-5463. **Contact:** Maureen McDermott, President. **Description:** A contingency search firm. Company pays fee. **Specializes in the areas of:** Banking; Secretarial. **Positions commonly filled include:** Accountant/Auditor; Bank Officer/Manager; Credit Manager; Financial Analyst; Human Resources Specialist. **Number of placements per year:** 50 - 99.

RICHARD MEYERS & ASSOCIATES, INC.
15 James Street, Florham Park NJ 07932. 973/765-9000. **Fax:** 973/765-9009. **Contact:** Richard Meyers, President. **Description:** An executive search firm. Company pays fee. **Specializes in the areas of:** Insurance; Risk Management. **Positions commonly filled include:** Insurance Agent/Broker; Underwriter/Assistant Underwriter. **Number of placements per year:** 100 - 199.

MIDDLEBROOK ASSOCIATES
6 Commerce Drive, Cranford NJ 07016. 908/709-0707. **Fax:** 908/272-6297. **Contact:** Rita Richards, Manager of Scientific Recruiting. **Description:** An executive search firm that also operates as a temporary and permanent employment agency. Company pays fee. **Specializes in the areas of:** Biology; Engineering; Food Industry; Technical. **Positions commonly filled include:** Biochemist; Biological Scientist; Biomedical Engineer; Chemical Engineer; Chemist; Design Engineer; Environmental Engineer; Food Scientist/Technologist; Industrial Engineer; Pharmacist; Science Technologist. **Number of placements per year:** 1 - 49.

NORMYLE/ERSTLING HEALTH SEARCH GROUP
350 West Passaic Street, Rochelle Park NJ 07662. 201/843-6009. **Fax:** 201/843-2060. **Contact:** Charles D. Kreps, Managing Partner. **Description:** An executive search firm. Company pays fee. **Specializes in the areas of:** Administration; Health/Medical; Insurance; Manufacturing; Sales. **Positions commonly filled include:** Biochemist; Biological Scientist; Biomedical Engineer; Computer Programmer; Customer Service Rep.; Dietician/Nutritionist; Health Services Manager; Insurance Agent/Broker; Manufacturer's/Wholesaler's Sales Rep.; MIS Specialist; Pharmacist; Registered Nurse; Respiratory Therapist; Services Sales Rep.; Systems Analyst. **Average salary range of placements:** More than $50,000. **Number of placements per year:** 100 - 199.

ORION CONSULTING, INC.
115 Route 46 West, Building B, Suite 13, Mountain Lakes NJ 07046. 973/402-8866. **Fax:** 973/402-9258. **Contact:** James Dromsky, President. **E-mail address:** oci@planet.net. **Description:** An executive search firm. **Specializes in the areas of:** Accounting/Auditing; Administration; Advertising; Banking; Chemical; Communications; Design; Engineering; Finance; Food Industry; General Management; Health/Medical; Industrial; Insurance; Legal; Manufacturing; Military; Operations Management; Personnel/Labor Relations; Pharmaceutical; Procurement; Sales; Technical; Transportation. **Number of placements per year:** 50 - 99.

PR MANAGEMENT CONSULTANTS
601 Ewing Street, Suite C5, Princeton NJ 08540. 609/921-6565. **Contact:** Jerry Koenig, President. **Description:** An executive search firm. Company pays fee. **Specializes in the areas of:** Engineering; General Management; Sales. **Positions commonly filled include:** Biochemist; Biomedical Engineer; Chemical Engineer; Design Engineer; Mechanical Engineer; Software Engineer; Statistician. **Average salary range of placements:** More than $50,000. **Number of placements per year:** 1 - 49.

PACE-SETTERS EXECUTIVE SEARCH
1033 Clifton Avenue, Clifton NJ 07013. 973/773-5757. **Fax:** 973/773-6201. **Contact:** Ken Rose, President. **Description:** An executive search firm. Company pays fee. **Specializes in the areas of:** Fashion. **Average salary range of placements:** More than $50,000.

FLORENCE PAPE LEGAL SEARCH, INC.
1208 Washington Street, Hoboken NJ 07030. 201/798-0200. **Fax:** 201/798-9088. **Contact:** Florence Pape, President. **Description:** An executive search firm operating on a contingency basis. Company pays fee. **Specializes in the areas of:** Legal. **Positions commonly filled include:** Attorney. **Average salary range of placements:** More than $50,000. **Number of placements per year:** 1 - 49.

RICK PASCAL & ASSOCIATES INC.
P.O. Box 543, Fair Lawn NJ 07410. 201/791-9541. **Fax:** 201/791-1861. **Contact:** Rick Pascal, CPC, President. **Description:** An executive search firm. **Specializes in the areas of:** Design; Packaging. **Positions commonly filled include:** Designer; Packaging Engineer; Packaging/Processing Worker.

PENNINGTON CONSULTING GROUP
65 South Main Street, Building B, Pennington NJ 08534. 609/737-8500. **Fax:** 609/737-8576. **Contact:** Robert B. White, President. **Description:** An executive search firm that operates on a contingency basis. Company pays fee. **Specializes in the areas of:** Wireless Communications. **Positions commonly filled include:** Software Engineer; Telecommunications Manager. **Other U.S. locations:** Richmond VA. **Average salary range of placements:** More than $50,000. **Number of placements per year:** 1 - 49.

THE PENNMORE GROUP
25 Chestnut Street, Suite 107, Haddonfield NJ 08033. 609/354-1414. **Fax:** 609/354-7660. **Contact:** Anthony Trasatti, President. **Description:** An executive search firm. Company pays fee. **Specializes in the areas of:** Accounting/Auditing; Banking; Finance; Insurance; Personnel/Labor Relations. **Positions commonly filled include:** Accountant/Auditor; Bank Officer/Manager; Financial Analyst; Human Resources Manager; Securities Sales Representative. **Average salary range of placements:** More than $50,000. **Number of placements per year:** 1 - 49.

PERSONNEL ASSOCIATES INC.
239 U.S. Highway 22, Green Brook NJ 08812-1916. 732/968-8866. **Fax:** 732/968-9437. **Contact:** Thomas C. Wood, President. **Description:** An executive search firm operating on a contingency basis. Company pays fee. **Specializes in the areas of:** Administration; Computer Science/Software. **Positions commonly filled include:** Computer Programmer; Internet Services Manager; MIS Specialist; Systems Analyst. **Other U.S. locations:** Nationwide. **Number of placements per year:** 50 - 99.

PETRUZZI ASSOCIATES
P.O. Box 141, Scotch Plains NJ 07076. 908/754-1940. **Contact:** Manager. **Description:** An executive search firm. **Specializes in the areas of:** Chemical; Health/Medical.

PHILADELPHIA SEARCH GROUP, INC.
One Cherry Hill, Suite 510, Cherry Hill NJ 08002. 609/667-2300. **Contact:** Manager. **Description:** An executive search firm that operates on a contingency basis. **Specializes in the areas of:** Health/Medical; Sales. **Positions commonly filled include:** Sales Manager; Sales Representative. **Average salary range of placements:** More than $50,000. **Number of placements per year:** 50 - 99.

PHOENIX BIOSEARCH, INC.
P.O. Box 6157, West Caldwell NJ 07006. 973/812-2666. **Fax:** 973/812-2727. **Contact:** Lee Stephenson, President. **Description:** An executive search firm operating on both retained and contingency bases. Company pays fee. **Specializes in the areas of:** Biology. **Positions commonly filled include:** Biochemist; Biological Scientist; Marketing Manager. **Average salary range of placements:** More than $50,000. **Number of placements per year:** 1 - 49.

PRINCETON EXECUTIVE SEARCH
2667 Nottingham Way, Hamilton NJ 08619. 609/584-1100. **Fax:** 609/584-1141. **Contact:** Andrew B. Barkocy, CPC, President. **Description:** An executive search firm. Company pays fee. **Specializes in the areas of:** Accounting/Auditing; Administration; Banking; Computer Science/Software; Engineering; Film Production; Personnel/Labor Relations. **Positions commonly filled include:** Accountant/Auditor; Aerospace Engineer; Agricultural Engineer; Bank Officer/Manager; Biomedical Engineer; Budget Analyst; Chemical Engineer; Civil Engineer; Credit Manager; Electrical/Electronics Engineer; Financial Analyst; General Manager; Human Resources Manager; Industrial Engineer; Mechanical Engineer; Nuclear Engineer; Petroleum Engineer; Purchasing Agent/Manager; Software Engineer; Systems Analyst. **Number of placements per year:** 1 - 49.

RAMMING & ASSOCIATES, INC.
3 Thackery Lane, Cherry Hill NJ 08003-1925. 609/428-7172. **Fax:** 609/428-7173. **Contact:** George Ramming, Owner. **E-mail address:** ramming@erols.com. **Description:** An executive search firm. Company pays fee. **Specializes in the areas of:** Engineering; General Management; Health/Medical; Manufacturing. **Positions commonly filled include:** Chemical Engineer; Design Engineer; Electrical/Electronics Engineer; General Manager; Mechanical Engineer; Software Engineer; Telecommunications Manager. **Average salary range of placements:** More than $50,000. **Number of placements per year:** 1 - 49.

RETAIL CONNECTION INC.
271 U.S. Highway 46, Suite D-105, Fairfield NJ 07004. 973/882-6662. **Toll-free phone:** 800/770-4945. **Fax:** 973/575-5858. **Contact:** Carole Thaller, President. **Description:** An executive search firm that operates on a contingency basis and also functions as a permanent employment agency. Company pays fee. **Specializes in the areas of:** Retail. **Positions commonly filled include:** Chief Financial Officer; Sales Manager. **Number of placements per year:** 50 - 99.

JEFF RICH ASSOCIATES
67 Walnut Avenue, Suite 303, Clark NJ 07066. 732/574-3888. **Contact:** Manager. **Description:** An executive search firm. **Specializes in the areas of:** Accounting/Auditing; Finance.

JAMES F. ROBINSON PROFESSIONAL RECRUITER
231 South White Horse Pike, Audubon NJ 08106. 609/547-5800. **Contact:** James F. Robinson, Owner. **Description:** An executive search firm. Company pays fee. **Specializes in the areas of:** Legal. **Positions commonly filled include:** Attorney.

ROCHESTER SYSTEMS INC.
227 East Bergen Place, Red Bank NJ 07701. 732/747-7474. **Fax:** 732/747-7055. **Contact:** Peter Gotch, Account Executive. **Description:** An executive search firm. Company pays fee. **Specializes in the areas of:** Accounting/Auditing; Computer Science/Software; Logistics; Manufacturing; MIS/EDP. **Positions commonly filled include:** Computer Programmer; Financial Analyst; Industrial Production Manager; Management Analyst/Consultant; MIS Manager; Operations/Production Manager; Software Engineer; Systems Analyst. **Number of placements per year:** 50 - 99.

GENE ROGERS ASSOCIATES, INC.
P.O. Box 454, Metuchen NJ 08840. 908/754-5621. **Contact:** Diane Markowitz, Manager. **Description:** An executive search firm. **Specializes in the areas of:** Banking; Investment. **Average salary range of placements:** More than $50,000.

THE RUSSELL GROUP INC.
23 North Avenue East, Cranford NJ 07016. 908/709-1188. **Fax:** 908/709-0959. **Contact:** William Russell, President. **Description:** An executive search firm. Company pays fee. **Specializes in the areas of:** Sales. **Average salary range of placements:** More than $50,000. **Number of placements per year:** 100 - 199.

ANTHONY RYAN ASSOCIATES
140 Route 17 North, Suite 305, Paramus NJ 07652. 201/967-7000. **Contact:** Marnie Livak, Manager. **Description:** An executive search firm. **Specializes in the areas of:** Computer Hardware/Software.

RYLAN FORBES CONSULTING GROUP
379 Thornall Street, 7th Floor, Edison NJ 08837. 732/205-1900. **Fax:** 732/205-1901. **Contact:** Joe Stauffer, Vice President. **Description:** An executive search firm that also operates as a temporary and permanent employment agency. **Specializes in the areas of:** Accounting/Auditing; Finance; Manufacturing; Retail. **Positions commonly filled include:** Accountant; Budget Analyst; Financial Analyst. **Number of placements per year:** 50 - 99.

R.S. SADOW ASSOCIATES
24 Heather Drive, Somerset NJ 08873. 732/545-4550. **Fax:** 732/545-0797. **Contact:** Ray Sadow, President. **Description:** An executive search firm operating on a contingency basis. Company pays fee. **Specializes in the areas of:** Accounting/Auditing; Administration; Banking; Computer Science/Software; Engineering; Finance; Industrial; Manufacturing; Publishing; Scientific; Technical. **Positions commonly filled include:** Accountant/Auditor; Aerospace Engineer; Agricultural Engineer; Bank Officer/Manager; Biological Scientist; Biomedical Engineer; Budget Analyst; Ceramics Engineer; Chemical Engineer; Chemist; Civil Engineer; Clerical Supervisor; Computer Programmer; Controller; Credit Manager; Customer Service Rep.; Draftsperson; Editor; Electrical/Electronics Engineer; Financial Analyst; Industrial Engineer; Industrial Production Manager; Materials Engineer; Mechanical Engineer; Purchasing Agent/Manager; Quality Control Supervisor; Software Engineer; Structural Engineer; Systems Analyst; Technical Writer/Editor. **Average salary range of placements:** More than $50,000. **Number of placements per year:** 1 - 49.

SALES CONSULTANTS
2 Hudson Place, Hoboken NJ 07030. **Fax:** 201/659-5009. **Contact:** Rick Sinay, Manager. **Description:** An executive search firm that also operates as a temporary agency. Company pays fee. **Specializes in the areas of:** Advertising; Food Industry; General Management; Manufacturing; Sales. **Positions commonly filled include:** Biochemist; Biological Scientist; Biomedical Engineer; Chemical Engineer; Chemist; Food Scientist/Technologist; Mechanical Engineer. **Average salary range of placements:** More than $50,000. **Number of placements per year:** 100 - 199.

SALES CONSULTANTS OF MORRIS COUNTY
364 Parsippany Road, Parsippany NJ 07054. 973/887-3838. **Fax:** 973/887-2304. **Contact:** Ernest Bivona, Office Manager. **E-mail address:** sci.manager @mrinet.com. **Description:** An executive search firm operating on a contingency basis. **Specializes in the areas of:** Computer Science/ Software; Engineering; Finance; Food Industry; General Management; Health/Medical; Industrial; Insurance; Publishing; Sales; Technical. **Positions commonly filled include:** Biological Scientist; Biomedical Engineer; Chemical Engineer; Civil Engineer; Mechanical Engineer; Metallurgical Engineer; Sales Rep.; Software Engineer; Telecommunications Manager. **Number of placements per year:** 50 - 99.

SALES CONSULTANTS OF OCEAN, INC.
2516 Highway 35, Manasquan NJ 08736. 732/223-0300. **Fax:** 732/223-0450. **Contact:** Mark Daly, Manager. **Description:** An executive search firm. Company pays fee. **Specializes in the areas of:** Advertising; Publishing; Sales. **Average salary range of placements:** More than $50,000. **Number of placements per year:** 100 - 199.

SALES CONSULTANTS OF SPARTA
376 Route 15, Suite 200, Sparta NJ 07871. 973/579-5555. **Fax:** 973/579-2220. **Contact:** Harvey Bass, Manager. **Description:** An executive search firm. **Specializes in the areas of:** Accounting/Auditing; Administration; Advertising; Architecture/Construction; Banking; Communications; Computer Science/Software; Design; Electrical; Engineering; Finance; Food Industry; General Management; Health/Medical; Industrial; Insurance; Legal; Manufacturing; Operations Management; Procurement; Publishing; Real Estate; Retail; Sales; Technical; Textiles; Transportation.

SALES CONSULTANTS, INC.
800 Kings Highway North, Cherry Hill NJ 08034. 609/779-9100. **Fax:** 609/779-9193. **Contact:** General Manager. **Description:** An executive search firm. Company pays fee. **Specializes in the areas of:** Food Industry; General Management; Industrial; Information Technology; Manufacturing; Publishing; Retail; Sales. **Positions commonly filled include:** Buyer; Customer Service Representative; Financial Analyst; General Manager; Insurance Agent/Broker; Management Trainee; Market Research Analyst; Purchasing Agent/Manager; Restaurant/Food Service Manager; Telecommunications Manager; Travel Agent. **Number of placements per year:** 100 - 199.

SANFORD ROSE ASSOCIATES
12 Minneakoning Road, Suite 4, Flemington NJ 08822-5729. 908/788-1788. **Fax:** 908/788-7847. **Contact:** Manager. **World Wide Web address:** http://www.sanfordrose.com. **Description:** An executive search firm. **Specializes in the areas of:** Engineering; Manufacturing. **Other U.S. locations:** Nationwide.

ROBERT SCOTT ASSOCIATES
P.O. Box 486, Rancocas NJ 08073-0486. 609/835-2224. **Fax:** 609/835-1933. **Contact:** Bob Scott, President. **Description:** An executive search firm. Company pays fee. **Specializes in the areas of:** Chemical; Engineering; Industrial; Manufacturing; Paper; Personnel/Labor Relations; Scientific; Technical. **Positions commonly filled include:** Biological Scientist; Biomedical Engineer; Ceramics Engineer; Chemical Engineer; Chemist; Civil Engineer; Electrical/Electronics Engineer; Human Resources Manager; Industrial Engineer; Manufacturing Engineer; Mechanical Engineer; Metallurgical Engineer; Operations Manager. **Average salary range of placements:** More than $50,000.

SEARCH ASSOCIATES
18 Bank Street, Summit NJ 07901. 908/277-6818. **Contact:** President. **Description:** An executive search firm. Company pays fee. **Positions commonly filled include:** Accountant/Auditor; Administrative Manager; Attorney; Bank Officer/Manager; Budget Analyst; Buyer; Credit Manager; Customer Service Rep.; Economist; Editor; Engineer; Financial Analyst; General Manager; Hotel Manager; Human Resources Manager; Industrial Production Manager; Management Analyst/Consultant; Manufacturer's/Wholesaler's Sales Rep.; Operations/Production Manager; Property and Real Estate Manager; Public Relations Specialist; Purchasing Agent/Manager; Quality Control Supervisor; Restaurant/Food Service Manager; Securities Sales Rep.; Technical Writer/Editor; Transportation/Traffic Specialist; Wholesale and Retail Buyer. **Number of placements per year:** 1 - 49.

SEARCH CONSULTANTS, INC.
One East Ridgewood Avenue, Paramus NJ 07653-0402. 201/444-1770. **Contact:** Walter Perog, Executive Recruiter. **Description:** An executive search firm. Company pays fee. **Specializes in the areas of:** Personnel/Labor Relations. **Positions commonly filled include:** Human Resources Specialist. **Average salary

range of placements: More than $50,000. **Number of placements per year:** 1 - 49.

SEARCH EDP INC.
150 River Road, Building C, Suite 3, Montville NJ 07045. 973/335-6600. **Contact:** Manager. **Description:** An executive search firm. **Specializes in the areas of:** Data Processing.

SKUPPSEARCH, INC.
580 Sylvan Avenue, Englewood Cliffs NJ 07632. 201/894-1824. **Fax:** 201/894-1324. **Contact:** Holly Skupp, President. **Description:** An executive search firm. Company pays fee. **Specializes in the areas of:** Banking; Brokerage; Computer Science/Software; Finance; Insurance. **Positions commonly filled include:** Editor; Multimedia Designer; Technical Writer/Editor; Webmaster. **Average salary range of placements:** $30,000 - $50,000. **Number of placements per year:** 1 - 49.

SNELLING PERSONNEL SERVICES
142 Highway 35, Eatontown NJ 07724. 732/389-0300. **Fax:** 732/542-2509. **Contact:** Frank Wyckoff, Owner/President. **Description:** An executive search firm that also operates as a temporary agency. Company pays fee. **Positions commonly filled include:** Administrative Manager; Claim Rep.; Clerical Supervisor; Computer Programmer; Design Engineer; Draftsperson; Financial Analyst; Health Services Manager; Hotel Manager; Human Resources Manager; Industrial Engineer; Industrial Production Manager; Management Trainee; Paralegal; Pharmacist; Software Engineer; Systems Analyst; Telecommunications Manager; Typist/Word Processor. **Average salary range of placements:** $20,000 - $29,999. **Number of placements per year:** 1000+.

PHYLLIS SOLOMON EXECUTIVE SEARCH
120 Sylvan Avenue, Englewood Cliffs NJ 07632. 201/947-8600. **Contact:** Phyllis Solomon, President. **Description:** An executive search firm. **Specializes in the areas of:** Pharmaceutical. **Positions commonly filled include:** Account Representative; Marketing Manager; Product Manager.

SOURCE SERVICES CORPORATION/SOURCE EDP
5 Independence Way, Princeton NJ 08540. 609/452-7277. **Fax:** 609/520-1742. **Contact:** Manager. **Description:** An executive search firm. **Specializes in the areas of:** Computer Hardware/Software; Information Technology.
Other area locations:

- One Gatehall Drive, Suite 250, Parsippany NJ 07054. 973/267-3222. (Accounting/Auditing; Computer Hardware/Software; Information Technology)
- 100 Woodbridge Center Drive, Suite 101, Woodbridge NJ 07095. 732/283-9510. (Computer Hardware/Software; Finance; Information Technology)

STELTON GROUP INC.
904 Oak Tree Road, Suite A, South Plainfield NJ 07080. 908/757-9888. **Contact:** Manager. **Description:** An executive search firm. **Specializes in the areas of:** Manufacturing; Telecommunications.

SUMMIT GROUP, INC.
143 Lakeside Boulevard, Landing NJ 07850. 973/398-2700. **Fax:** 973/398-0403. **Contact:** Gary Pezzuti, General Partner. **Description:** An executive search firm. Company pays fee. **Specializes in the areas of:** Engineering; Food Industry; Health/Medical; Industrial; Manufacturing; Materials; Transportation. **Positions commonly filled include:** Buyer; Industrial Engineer; Industrial Production Manager; Manufacturing Engineer; Marketing Specialist; Mechanical Engineer; Operations/Production Manager; Production Manager; Purchasing Agent/Manager; Quality Control Supervisor; Transportation/Traffic Specialist; Vice President. **Average salary range of placements:** More than $50,000. **Number of placements per year:** 50 - 99.

TATE & ASSOCIATES
1020 Springfield Avenue, Suite 201, Westfield NJ 07090. 908/232-2443. **Contact:** Manager. **Description:** An executive search firm.

TECHNOLOGY SYSTEMS, INC.
27 East Main Street, Little Falls NJ 07424. 973/256-1772. **Fax:** 973/812-1761. **Contact:** John Beddes, President. **Description:** An executive search firm that also operates as an employment agency. Company pays fee. **Specializes in the areas of:** Engineering. **Positions commonly filled include:** Design Engineer; Electrical/Electronics Engineer; Manufacturing Engineer; Mechanical Engineer; Sales Engineer; Software Engineer. **Corporate headquarters location:** This Location. **Average salary range of placements:** More than $50,000. **Number of placements per year:** 1 - 49.

TENEK CORPORATION
525 Milltown Road, North Brunswick NJ 08902. 732/248-1600. **Fax:** 732/248-1665. **Contact:** Peter Scocchi, Vice President. **Description:** An executive search firm. Company pays fee. **Specializes in the areas of:** Administration; Computer Science/Software; Engineering; Government; Industrial; Manufacturing; Secretarial; Technical; Telecommunications. **Positions commonly filled include:** Biomedical Engineer; Chemical Engineer; Civil Engineer; Electrical/Electronics Engineer; Industrial Designer; Mechanical Engineer; Software Engineer; Structural Engineer. **Number of placements per year:** 50 - 99.

ALLEN THOMAS ASSOCIATES
518 Prospect Avenue, Little Silver NJ 07739. 732/219-5353. **Fax:** 732/219-5808. **Contact:** Tom Benoit, President. **E-mail address:** recruit@allenthomas.com. **Description:** A contingency search firm. **Specializes in the areas of:** Health/Medical. **Positions commonly filled include:** Pharmacist; Physician; Sales Manager. **Average salary range of placements:** More than $50,000.

TOPAZ ATTORNEY SEARCH
383 Northfield Avenue, West Orange NJ 07052. 973/669-7300. **Fax:** 973/669-9811. **Contact:** Stewart Michaels, Chairman. **E-mail address:** topazlegal@aol.com. **Description:** An executive search firm operating on both retained and contingency bases. **Specializes in the areas of:** Legal. **Positions commonly filled include:** Attorney. **Average salary range of placements:** More than $50,000. **Number of placements per year:** 100 - 199.

WORLCO COMPUTER RESOURCES, INC.
901 Route 38, Cherry Hill NJ 08002. 609/665-4700. **Fax:** 609/665-8142. **Contact:** Bob Hughes, Managing Partner. **Description:** An executive search firm. Company pays fee. **Specializes in the areas of:** Administration; Computer Hardware/Software; Sales. **Positions commonly filled include:** Computer Programmer; Internet Services Manager; Marketing Specialist; MIS Specialist; Sales Rep.; Systems Analyst; Technical Writer/Editor; Telecommunications Manager. **Number of placements per year:** 100 - 199.

WORLD HEALTH RESOURCES, INC.
P.O. Box 499, Paterson NJ 07513-0499. 973/881-1777. **Contact:** Manager. **Description:** An executive search firm. **Specializes in the areas of:** Health/Medical.

ZWICKER ASSOCIATES
579 Franklin Turnpike, Suite 9, Ridgewood NJ 07450. 201/567-8734. **Contact:** Manager. **Description:** An executive search firm. **Specializes in the areas of:** Food Industry; Market Research.

PERMANENT EMPLOYMENT AGENCIES

A CHOICE NANNY
637 Wyckoff Avenue, Wyckoff NJ 07481-1442. 201/891-2273. **Fax:** 201/891-1722. **Contact:** Sue Vigil, General Manager. **Description:** A permanent employment agency that refers nannies to potential employers. Company pays fee. **Specializes in the areas of:** Child Care, In-Home; Nannies. **Positions commonly filled include:** Nanny. **Average salary range of placements:** Less than $25,000. **Number of placements per year:** 100 - 199.
Other U.S. locations:
- 248 Columbia Turnpike, Building One, Florham Park NJ 07932. 973/593-9090.
- 27 Mountain Boulevard, Suite 9-B, Warren NJ 07059. 908/754-9090.

A+ PERSONNEL
1017 Broadway, Bayonne NJ 07002. 201/437-5594. **Fax:** 201/437-2914. **Contact:** Jill G. Rowland, Vice President. **Description:** A permanent employment agency. Company pays fee. **Specializes in the areas of:** Accounting/Auditing; Administration; Computer Science/Software; Finance; Legal; Manufacturing; Personnel/Labor Relations; Secretarial. **Positions commonly filled include:** Accountant/Auditor; Advertising Clerk; Bank Officer/Manager; Brokerage Clerk; Budget Analyst; Buyer; Chemical Engineer; Civil Engineer; Claim Rep.; Clerical Supervisor; Computer Programmer; Credit Manager; Customer Service Rep.; Financial Analyst; Human Resources Manager; Industrial Engineer; Industrial Production Manager; Insurance Agent/Broker; Management Analyst/Consultant; Management Trainee; Mechanical Engineer; Operations/Production Manager; Paralegal; Public Relations Specialist; Purchasing Agent/Manager; Quality Control Supervisor; Securities Sales Rep.; Software Engineer; Systems Analyst; Travel Agent; Underwriter/Assistant Underwriter; Wholesale/Retail Buyer. **Number of placements per year:** 50 - 99.

ABC NATIONWIDE EMPLOYMENT
241 Main Street, Hackensack NJ 07601. 201/487-5515. **Fax:** 201/487-5591. **Contact:** Recruiter. **Description:** A permanent employment agency. Company pays fee. **Specializes in the areas of:** Engineering; Finance; Legal; Manufacturing; Personnel/Labor Relations; Secretarial. **Positions commonly filled include:** Accountant/Auditor; Civil Engineer; Clerical Supervisor; Credit Manager; Customer Service Rep.; Electrical/Electronics Engineer; Human Resources Manager; Industrial Engineer; Mechanical Engineer; Purchasing Agent/Manager.

ADVANCED PERSONNEL SERVICE
1341 Hamburg Turnpike, Suite 1, Wayne NJ 07470-4042. 973/694-0303. **Fax:** 973/696-3291. **Contact:** Daniel C. Kees, Vice President. **Description:** A permanent employment agency that also provides temporary placements. Company pays fee. **Specializes in the areas of:** Accounting/Auditing; Administration; Advertising; Banking; Economics; Finance; Food Industry; General Management; Industrial; Insurance; Legal; Manufacturing; Personnel/Labor Relations; Sales; Secretarial. **Positions commonly filled include:** Accountant/Auditor; Administrative Manager; Advertising Clerk; Bank Officer/Manager; Branch Manager; Budget Analyst; Claim Rep.; Clerical Supervisor; Credit Manager; Customer Service Rep.; Economist; Financial Analyst; Human Resources Specialist; Insurance Agent/Broker; Management Trainee; Manufacturer's/Wholesaler's Sales Rep.; Operations/Production Manager; Public Relations Specialist; Purchasing Agent/Manager; Securities Sales Rep.; Services Sales Rep.; Technical Writer/Editor; Telecommunications Manager; Transportation/Traffic Specialist; Travel Agent; Typist/Word Processor; Underwriter/Assistant Underwriter. **Benefits available to temporary workers:** Bonus Award/Plan; Paid Holidays; Paid Vacation. **Number of placements per year:** 200 - 499.

RAYMOND ALEXANDER ASSOCIATES
420 Minnisink Road, Totowa NJ 07512-1806. **Contact:** Ray Jezierski, Recruiting Manager. **Description:** A permanent employment agency. Company pays fee. **Specializes in the areas of:** Accounting/Auditing; Finance. **Positions commonly filled include:** Accountant/Auditor; Financial Analyst. **Average salary range of placements:** $30,000 - $50,000. **Number of placements per year:** 100 - 199.

ALLEN ASSOCIATES, INC.
33 Wood Avenue South, Suite 600, Iselin NJ 08830. 732/549-7555. **Fax:** 732/549-7550. **Contact:** Amy Regan, President. **Description:** A permanent employment agency. Company pays fee. **Specializes in the areas of:** Finance; Office Support; Personnel/Labor Relations; Secretarial. **Positions commonly filled include:** Accountant/Auditor; Administrative Manager; Clerical Supervisor; Credit Manager; Customer Service Rep.; Human Resources Specialist; Management Trainee; Secretary; Transportation/Traffic Specialist; Typist/Word Processor. **Average salary range of placements:** $20,000 - $40,000. **Number of placements per year:** 50 - 99.

ALLIANCE CONSULTANTS
4 Holiday Drive, Hopatcong NJ 07843-1449. 973/398-1776. **Contact:** Rose-ellen Horan, President. **Description:** A permanent employment agency. Company pays fee. **Specializes in the areas of:** Administration; General Management; Personnel/Labor Relations; Sales; Secretarial. **Positions commonly filled include:** Accountant/Auditor; Administrative Manager; Claim Rep.; Clerical Supervisor; Computer Programmer; General Manager; Human Resources Specialist; Insurance Agent/Broker; Manufacturer's/Wholesaler's Sales Rep.; Paralegal; Typist/Word Processor. **Average salary range of placements:** $30,000 - $50,000. **Number of placements per year:** 1 - 49.

ANDREW PERSONNEL SERVICES
P.O. Box 790, Chester NJ 07930. 908/879-2995. **Fax:** 908/879-8482. **Contact:** Manager. **Description:** A permanent employment agency. Company pays fee. **Specializes in the areas of:** Accounting/Auditing; Administration; Computer Science/Software; Engineering; Finance; Industrial; Insurance; Legal; Retail; Sales; Secretarial; Technical. **Positions commonly filled include:** Bank Officer/Manager; Blue-Collar Worker Supervisor; Chemical Engineer; Claim Rep.; Clerical Supervisor; Computer Programmer; Credit Manager; Customer Service Rep.; Design Engineer; Draftsperson; Environmental Engineer; Human Resources Specialist; Industrial Engineer; Industrial Production Manager; Internet Services Manager; Manufacturer's/Wholesaler's Sales Rep.; Mechanical Engineer; Multimedia Designer; Operations/Production Manager; Paralegal; Purchasing Agent/Manager; Services Sales Rep.; Software Engineer; Structural Engineer; Systems Analyst;

Technical Writer/Editor; Telecommunications Manager; Travel Agent; Typist/Word Processor. **Benefits available to temporary workers:** Medical Insurance. **Other area locations:** Clinton NJ; Little Falls NJ; Parsippany NJ. **Average salary range of placements:** $20,000 - $29,999.

ARDEN ASSOCIATES
1605 John Street, Fort Lee NJ 07024. 201/346-0414. **Contact:** Manager. **Description:** A permanent employment agency. **Specializes in the areas of:** Office Support.

BAI PERSONNEL SOLUTIONS INC.
One Independence Way, Princeton NJ 08540. 609/734-9631. **Fax:** 609/734-9619. **Contact:** Leigh Clayton, President. **Description:** A permanent employment agency that also offers contract services. Company pays fee. **Specializes in the areas of:** Accounting/Auditing; Administration; Banking; Computer Hardware/Software; Finance; Insurance; Legal; Personnel/Labor Relations; Sales; Secretarial. **Positions commonly filled include:** Accountant/Auditor; Brokerage Clerk; Budget Analyst; Claim Rep.; Clerical Supervisor; Computer Programmer; Credit Manager; Customer Service Rep.; Financial Analyst; Human Resources Specialist; Management Analyst/Consultant; MIS Specialist; Operations/Production Manager; Paralegal; Reporter; Services Sales Rep.; Technical Writer/Editor; Telecommunications Manager; Typist/Word Processor. **Other U.S. locations:** Albany NY; Schenectady NY. **Number of placements per year:** 100 - 199.

BERMAN & LARSON
140 Route 17 North, Suite 204, Paramus NJ 07652. 201/262-9200. **Toll-free phone:** 800/640-0126. **Fax:** 201/262-7060. **Contact:** Bob Larson, CPC, President. **E-mail address:** jobsbl@cybernex.com. **World Wide Web address:** http://www.jobsbl.com. **Description:** A permanent employment agency focusing on the placement of information systems professionals. Company pays fee. **Specializes in the areas of:** Computer Science/Software. **Positions commonly filled include:** Computer Programmer; Internet Services Manager; MIS Specialist; Software Engineer; Systems Analyst; Technical Writer/Editor. **Benefits available to temporary workers:** 401(k); Medical Insurance. **Number of placements per year:** 200 - 499.

CPS TECHNICAL PLACEMENTS
10 North Gaston Avenue, Somerville NJ 08876. 908/704-1770. **Fax:** 908/704-1554. **Contact:** Robert Fisher, Technical Employment Specialist. **Description:** A permanent employment agency that also provides temporary placements. Company pays fee. **Specializes in the areas of:** Biology; Engineering; Food Industry; Pharmaceutical. **Positions commonly filled include:** Biochemist; Biological Scientist; Biomedical Engineer; Chemical Engineer; Chemist; Clinical Lab Technician; Computer Programmer; Electrician; Food Scientist/Technologist; MIS Specialist; Pharmacist; Quality Control Supervisor; Technical Writer/Editor. **Number of placements per year:** 50 - 99.

CAPITOL SEARCH
215 East Ridgewood Avenue, Ridgewood NJ 07450. 201/444-6666. **Fax:** 201/444-4121. **Contact:** Bob Sanders, Owner. **Description:** A permanent employment agency. Company pays fee. **Specializes in the areas of:** Child Care, In-Home; Domestic Help; Eldercare, In-Home; Nannies. **Positions commonly filled include:** Computer Graphics Specialist; Domestic Help. **Number of placements per year:** 100 - 199.

CAREER CENTER, INC.
P.O. Box 1036, Hackensack NJ 07601. 201/342-1777. **Toll-free phone:** 800/227-3379. **Fax:** 201/342-1776. **Contact:** Sandra Franzino, CIS, Vice President. **Description:** A permanent employment agency that also provides temporary placements. Company pays fee. **Specializes in the areas of:** Accounting/Auditing; Administration; Advertising; Banking; Clerical; Communications; Computer Science/Software; Engineering; Fashion; Finance; Insurance; Manufacturing; Personnel/Labor Relations; Sales; Technical. **Positions commonly filled include:** Accountant/Auditor; Administrative Manager; Bank Officer/Manager; Customer Service Rep.; Data Entry Clerk; Draftsperson; EDP Specialist; Electrical/Electronics Engineer; Financial Analyst; Human Resources Manager; Industrial Designer; Industrial Engineer; Legal Secretary; Marketing Specialist; Mechanical Engineer; Medical Secretary; MIS Specialist; Operations/Production Manager; Purchasing Agent/Manager; Quality Control Supervisor; Receptionist; Sales Rep.; Secretary; Stenographer; Systems Analyst; Technician; Typist/Word Processor; Underwriter/Assistant Underwriter. **Benefits available to temporary workers:** 401(k); Medical Insurance; Paid Holidays; Paid Vacation. **Number of placements per year:** 1000+.

CAREER GROUP
515 Route 70, Brick NJ 08723. 732/477-0975. **Contact:** Manager. **Description:** A permanent employment agency. **Specializes in the areas of:** Office Support; Technical.

CAREERS FIRST, INC.
305 U.S. Route 130, Cinnaminson NJ 08077-3398. 609/786-0004. **Contact:** Gail Duncan, President. **Description:** A permanent employment agency. **Specializes in the areas of:** Administration; Computer Hardware/Software; Technical.

CAREERS USA
533 North Evergreen Avenue, Woodbury NJ 08096. 609/384-1600. **Fax:** 609/384-1310. **Contact:** Carla Janoff, President/Owner. **Description:** A permanent employment agency. Company pays fee. **Specializes in the areas of:** Accounting/Auditing; Administration; Computer Science/Software; General Management; Industrial; Manufacturing; Personnel/Labor Relations; Secretarial; Technical. **Positions commonly filled include:** Administrative Manager; Blue-Collar Worker Supervisor; Claim Rep.; Clerical Supervisor; Customer Service Rep.; Draftsperson; Editor; Financial Analyst; Human Resources Specialist; Industrial Production Manager; MIS Specialist; Operations/Production Manager; Paralegal; Purchasing Agent/Manager; Quality Control Supervisor; Typist/Word Processor. **Benefits available to temporary workers:** Paid Holidays; Paid Vacation. **Average salary range of placements:** $20,000 - $29,999.

CASTLE CAREERS INC.
141 South Avenue, Fanwood NJ 07023. 908/322-9140. **Contact:** Manager. **Description:** A permanent employment agency. **Specializes in the areas of:** Office Support.

CENTRAL TECHNICAL SERVICE INC.
389 Main Street, Hackensack NJ 07601. 201/342-0055. **Contact:** Manager. **Description:** A permanent employment agency. **Specializes in the areas of:** Engineering; Technical.

CITIZENS EMPLOYMENT SERVICES, INC.
One Magnolia Avenue, Montvale NJ 07645. 201/391-5144. **Fax:** 201/391-4477. **Contact:** Elaine Larfier, Manager. **Description:** A permanent employment agency. Company pays fee. **Specializes in the areas of:** Banking; Clerical; Computer Science/Software; Industrial; Insurance; Manufacturing; Retail; Sales. **Positions commonly filled include:** Accountant/

Auditor; Actuary; Bank Officer/Manager; Bookkeeper; Chemical Engineer; Claim Rep.; Computer Operator; Computer Programmer; Credit Manager; Customer Service Rep.; Data Entry Clerk; Draftsperson; EDP Specialist; Electrical/Electronics Engineer; Industrial Production Manager; Insurance Agent/Broker; Legal Secretary; Mechanical Engineer; Operations/ Production Manager; Purchasing Agent/Manager; Quality Control Supervisor; Sales Rep.; Secretary; Stenographer; Systems Analyst; Technician; Travel Agent; Typist/Word Processor; Underwriter/Assistant Underwriter. **Other area locations:** Parsippany NJ. **Average salary range of placements:** $30,000 - $50,000. **Number of placements per year:** 1000+.

GLENN DAVIS ASSOCIATES
124 Morris Turnpike, Randolph NJ 07869-2976. 973/895-4242. **Contact:** Manager. **Description:** A permanent employment agency. **Specializes in the areas of:** Computer Science/Software. **Positions commonly filled include:** MIS Specialist. **Number of placements per year:** 50 - 99.

EXECUTIVE SOFTWARE PLUS
24 Lyons Place, Westwood NJ 07675. 201/666-5484. **Fax:** 201/664-0693. **Contact:** Claire Monte, Vice President. **E-mail address:** exsoft@aol.com. **Description:** A permanent employment agency. **Specializes in the areas of:** Computer Science/ Software. **Positions commonly filled include:** Computer Programmer; Systems Analyst.

EXPRESS PERSONNEL SERVICES
2569 State Route 10, Morris Plains NJ 07950. 973/898-1001. **Fax:** 973/898-1005. **Contact:** Marianne Kemp, Personnel Supervisor. **Description:** A full-service staffing firm engaged in permanent placement, executive recruiting, and temporary placement. **Specializes in the areas of:** Accounting/ Auditing; Administration; Advertising; Computer Hardware/Software; Engineering; General Management; Industrial; Legal; Manufacturing; Publishing; Sales; Secretarial; Technical. **Positions commonly filled include:** Accountant/Auditor; Administrative Manager; Advertising Clerk; Blue-Collar Worker Supervisor; Claim Rep.; Clerical Supervisor; Computer Programmer; Customer Service Rep.; Design Engineer; Designer; Draftsperson; Editor; Electrical/Electronics Engineer; Electrician; General Manager; Human Resources Specialist; Management Trainee; Manufacturer's/ Wholesaler's Sales Rep.; MIS Specialist; Paralegal; Quality Control Supervisor; Software Engineer; Typist/Word Processor. **Benefits available to temporary workers:** Medical Insurance; Paid Vacation. **Corporate headquarters location:** Oklahoma City OK. **Average salary range of placements:** $20,000 - $29,999. **Number of placements per year:** 500 - 999.

G.A. AGENCY
524 South Avenue East, Cranford NJ 07016-3209. 908/272-2080. **Fax:** 908/272-2962. **Contact:** Mrs. Randy Ring, Manager. **Description:** A permanent employment agency. **Specializes in the areas of:** Education. **Positions commonly filled include:** Education Administrator; Teacher/Professor. **Other U.S. locations:** Nationwide. **Average salary range of placements:** $30,000 - $50,000. **Number of placements per year:** 200 - 499.

HALLMARK PERSONNEL INC.
140 North State Route 17, Suite 302, Paramus NJ 07652. 201/261-9010. **Contact:** Manager. **Description:** A permanent employment agency.

HORIZON GRAPHICS PERSONNEL
110 Cornelia Street, Boonton NJ 07005. 973/263-2126. **Fax:** 973/263-4601. **Contact:** John DeSalvo, Vice President. **Description:** A permanent employment agency. Company pays fee. **Specializes in the areas of:** Advertising; Art/Design; Publishing. **Positions commonly filled include:** Desktop Publishing Specialist; Editor; Graphic Artist; Proofreader; Technical Writer/ Editor; Writer. **Number of placements per year:** 100 - 199.

HUGHES & PODESLA PERSONNEL INC.
281 East Main Street, Somerville NJ 08876. 908/231-0880. **Contact:** Paul Podesla, President. **Description:** A permanent employment agency. Company pays fee. **Specializes in the areas of:** Accounting/Auditing; Engineering; Finance; General Management; Industrial; Manufacturing; Personnel/ Labor Relations; Sales; Technical. **Positions commonly filled include:** Accountant/Auditor; Biomedical Engineer; Budget Analyst; Buyer; Credit Manager; Customer Service Rep.; Design Engineer; Draftsperson; Electrical/Electronics Engineer; Financial Analyst; General Manager; Human Resources Manager; Industrial Engineer; Industrial Production Manager; Mechanical Engineer; Operations Manager; Purchasing Agent/Manager; Quality Control Supervisor; Transportation/Traffic Specialist. **Number of placements per year:** 1 - 49.

HUNT, LTD.
1050 Wall Street West, Suite 330, Lyndhurst NJ 07071. 201/438-8200. **Contact:** President. **Description:** A permanent employment agency. Company pays fee. **Specializes in the areas of:** Food Industry; Health/Medical; Manufacturing; Transportation. **Positions commonly filled include:** Customer Service Rep.; Distribution Manager; Warehouse Manager. **Number of placements per year:** 200 - 499.

IMPACT PERSONNEL, INC.
1901 North Olden Avenue, Suite 26A, Ewing NJ 08618. 609/406-1200. **Contact:** Manager. **Description:** A permanent employment agency. Company pays fee. **Specializes in the areas of:** Accounting/Auditing; Administration; Advertising; Banking; Computer Hardware/Software; Engineering; Fashion; Finance; Food Industry; General Management; Health/Medical; Industrial; Insurance; Legal; Manufacturing; Publishing; Retail; Sales; Secretarial; Technical. **Positions commonly filled include:** Accountant/Auditor; Administrative Assistant; Bookkeeper; Chemical Engineer; Claim Rep.; Clerk; Commercial Artist; Computer Programmer; Customer Service Rep.; Data Entry Clerk; Driver; Electrical/ Electronics Engineer; Factory Worker; Hotel Manager; Industrial Designer; Industrial Engineer; Legal Secretary; Light Industrial Worker; Mechanical Engineer; Medical Secretary; Quality Control Supervisor; Receptionist; Recruiter; Sales Rep.; Secretary; Software Engineer; Technician; Typist/ Word Processor. **Number of placements per year:** 500 - 999.

INFOSYSTEMS PLACEMENT SERVICES
17 Holmes Lane, Marlton NJ 08053-1911. 609/596-7770. **Fax:** 609/596-7772. **Contact:** Joe Dougherty, Owner. **E-mail address:** jadips@aol.com. **World Wide Web address:** http://www.infoplacement.com. **Description:** A permanent employment agency. Company pays fee. **Specializes in the areas of:** Administration; Computer Science/Software. **Positions commonly filled include:** Computer Operator; Computer Programmer; Database Manager; Internet Services Manager; MIS Specialist; Project Manager; Software Engineer; Systems Analyst; Systems Manager; Telecommunications Manager. **Average salary range of placements:** More than $50,000. **Number of placements per year:** 1 - 49.

JOULE PEOPLE PROVIDERS
2333 Whitehorse-Mercerville Road, Trenton NJ 08619. 609/588-5900. **Fax:** 609/588-9642. **Contact:** Rae Ann Powell, Manager. **Description:** A permanent employment agency. Company pays fee. **Specializes in the areas of:** Accounting/Auditing; Education; Engineering; Industrial; Legal; Manufacturing; Personnel/Labor Relations; Secretarial; Technical. **Positions commonly filled include:** Accountant/Auditor; Administrative Manager; Blue-Collar Worker Supervisor; Claim Rep.; Clerical Supervisor; Computer Programmer; Counselor; Customer Service Rep.; Human Resources Specialist; Management Trainee; Typist/Word Processor. **Benefits available to temporary workers:** Incentive Plan; Medical Insurance; Paid Holidays; Paid Vacation. **Corporate headquarters location:** Edison NJ. **Other U.S. locations:** Nationwide. **Average salary range of placements:** $20,000 - $29,999. **Number of placements per year:** 1000+.

JOSEPH KEYES ASSOCIATES
P.O. Box 745, Paramus NJ 07653-0745. 201/261-7400. **Fax:** 201/261-4836. **Contact:** Ed Michaels, Vice President. **Description:** A permanent employment agency that also provides temporary placement and career/outplacement counseling. Company pays fee. **Specializes in the areas of:** Accounting/Auditing; Engineering; Finance; Industrial; Manufacturing; Publishing. **Positions commonly filled include:** Accountant/Auditor; Administrative Manager; Blue-Collar Worker Supervisor; Broadcast Technician; Budget Analyst; Buyer; Ceramics Engineer; Claim Rep.; Clerical Supervisor; Credit Manager; Customer Service Rep.; Design Engineer; Designer; Draftsperson; Electrical/Electronics Engineer; Environmental Engineer; Financial Analyst; Human Resources Specialist; Industrial Engineer; Industrial Production Manager; Materials Engineer; Mechanical Engineer; Purchasing Agent/Manager; Quality Control Supervisor; Services Sales Rep.; Software Engineer; Technical Writer/Editor; Transportation/Traffic Specialist. **Average salary range of placements:** $30,000 - $50,000. **Number of placements per year:** 50 - 99.

MAYFAIR SERVICES
372 Buffalo Avenue, Paterson NJ 07503. 973/742-0990. **Fax:** 973/742-0991. **Contact:** Mary Costello, Owner. **Description:** A permanent employment agency that also offers contract services. **Specializes in the areas of:** Administration; Art/Design; Biology; Computer Hardware/Software; Engineering; General Management; Health/Medical; Industrial; Manufacturing; Personnel/Labor Relations; Publishing; Technical; Transportation. **Positions commonly filled include:** Aerospace Engineer; Agricultural Engineer; Architect; Biochemist; Biological Scientist; Biomedical Engineer; Blue-Collar Worker Supervisor; Buyer; Chemical Engineer; Chemist; Civil Engineer; Clinical Lab Technician; Customer Service Rep.; Design Engineer; Designer; Draftsperson; Electrical/Electronics Engineer; Electrician; Environmental Engineer; General Manager; Health Services Manager; Human Resources Specialist; Industrial Engineer; Industrial Production Manager; Library Technician; Management Trainee; Mechanical Engineer; Medical Records Technician; MIS Specialist; Multimedia Designer; Nuclear Medicine Technologist; Occupational Therapist; Operations/Production Manager; Pharmacist; Quality Control Supervisor; Science Technologist; Software Engineer; Structural Engineer; Typist/Word Processor; Veterinarian. **Average salary range of placements:** $20,000 - $29,999. **Number of placements per year:** 200 - 499.

MINI CONGLOMERATE SERVICE
1616 Pacific Avenue, Atlantic City NJ 08401-6939. 609/348-2299. **Contact:** Tom Murphy, President. **Description:** A permanent employment agency. **Specializes in the areas of:** Advertising; Broadcasting; Entertainment; General Management; Sales. **Positions commonly filled include:** Management Trainee; Travel Agent. **Average salary range of placements:** Less than $20,000. **Number of placements per year:** 1 - 49.

NANNIES PLUS
520 Speedwell Avenue, Suite 114, Morris Plains NJ 07950-2132. **Toll-free phone:** 800/752-0078. **Fax:** 973/285-5055. **Contact:** Margery Arbel, Consultant. **E-mail address:** joy@nanniesplus.com. **Description:** A permanent employment agency that provides live-in child care professionals. **Specializes in the areas of:** Child Care, In-Home. **Positions commonly filled include:** Nanny. **Average salary range of placements:** Less than $20,000. **Number of placements per year:** 200 - 499.

NEIGHBORHOOD NANNIES
5 North Haddon Avenue, Haddonfield NJ 08033. 609/795-5833. **Fax:** 609/216-0600. **Contact:** Celia Sarajian, Executive Director. **Description:** A permanent employment agency that also provides career/outplacement counseling. **Specializes in the areas of:** Child Care, In-Home; Eldercare, In-Home; Nannies. **Positions commonly filled include:** Nanny. **Number of placements per year:** 50 - 99.

NORRELL SERVICES
197 U.S. Highway 18 South, Suite 110, East Brunswick NJ 08816. 732/828-9111. **Fax:** 732/828-7766. **Contact:** Corrie Kirklen, Office Manager. **Description:** A permanent employment agency. **Specializes in the areas of:** Secretarial; Technical. **Positions commonly filled include:** Computer Programmer. **Number of placements per year:** 200 - 499.

OFFICEMATES5 OF ENGLEWOOD CLIFFS, INC.
DAYSTAR TEMPORARY SERVICES
560 Sylvan Avenue, Englewood Cliffs NJ 07632. 201/871-2203. **Fax:** 201/871-1116. **Contact:** Alice Eckstein, President. **Description:** A permanent employment agency. DayStar Temporary Services (also at this location) provides temporary placements. Company pays fee. **Specializes in the areas of:** Accounting/Auditing; Administration; Advertising; Banking; Computer Science/Software; Economics; Finance; General Management; Insurance; Legal; Personnel/Labor Relations; Publishing; Sales; Secretarial; Transportation. **Positions commonly filled include:** Accountant/Auditor; Administrative Manager; Advertising Clerk; Bank Officer/Manager; Branch Manager; Brokerage Clerk; Budget Analyst; Buyer; Claim Representative; Clerical Supervisor; Computer Programmer; Cost Estimator; Credit Manager; Customer Service Representative; Financial Analyst; General Manager; Hotel Manager; Human Resources Specialist; Human Service Worker; Management Analyst/Consultant; Market Research Analyst; MIS Specialist; Paralegal; Public Relations Specialist; Purchasing Agent/Manager; Quality Control Supervisor; Securities Sales Representative; Services Sales Representative; Systems Analyst; Typist/Word Processor; Underwriter/Assistant Underwriter; Video Production Coordinator. **Number of placements per year:** 50 - 99.

OMNE STAFFING SERVICES
355 Route 22 East, Green Brook NJ 08812. 732/271-0002. **Contact:** Manager. **Description:** A permanent employment agency providing placements in a wide range of fields.

PARK AVENUE PERSONNEL
41 Park Avenue, Rutherford NJ 07070-1713. 201/939-1911. **Fax:** 201/939-3555. **Contact:** Mary

Falzarano, President/Owner. **Description:** A full-service employment agency. Company pays fee. **Specializes in the areas of:** Accounting/Auditing; Banking; Finance; Personnel/Labor Relations; Sales; Secretarial. **Positions commonly filled include:** Accountant/Auditor; Administrative Manager; Clerical Supervisor; Financial Analyst; Human Resources Manager. **Average salary range of placements:** $30,000 - $50,000. **Number of placements per year:** 1 - 49.

THE PERSONNEL GROUP
ARTHUR JAMES & ASSOCIATES INC.
P.O. Box 4582, Warren NJ 07059. 908/754-6000. **Contact:** Manager. **Description:** A permanent employment agency with several subsidiaries including Arthur James & Associates, which specializes in placing personnel in the field of solid waste management.

PERSONNEL PLUS/TEMPS PLUS
500 State Route 17 South, Hasbrouck Heights NJ 07604-3121. 201/288-7800. **Fax:** 201/288-7995. **Contact:** Judi Stewart, Placement Consultant. **Description:** A permanent employment agency. Company pays fee. **Specializes in the areas of:** Accounting/Auditing; Clerical; Marketing; Personnel/Labor Relations; Sales. **Positions commonly filled include:** Account Representative; Accountant/Auditor; Administrative Assistant; Administrative Manager; Advertising Clerk; Clerical Supervisor; Controller; Credit Manager; Customer Service Representative; Financial Analyst; Human Resources Manager; Human Resources Specialist; Paralegal; Purchasing Agent/Manager; Sales Executive; Sales Manager; Sales Representative; Secretary; Services Sales Representative; Transportation/Traffic Specialist; Typist/Word Processor. **Average salary range of placements:** $30,000 - $50,000. **Number of placements per year:** 200 - 499.

POMERANTZ PERSONNEL
1375 Plainfield Avenue, Watchung NJ 07060. 908/757-5300. **Toll-free phone:** 800/754-7000. **Fax:** 908/757-0144. **Contact:** Keith Grade, Corporate Director. **World Wide Web address:** http://www.pomerantzstaffing.com. **Description:** A permanent employment agency. Company pays fee. **Specializes in the areas of:** Accounting/Auditing; Administration; Banking; Computer Hardware/Software; Food Industry; General Management; Health/Medical; Industrial; Light Industrial; Personnel/Labor Relations; Retail; Sales; Secretarial. **Corporate headquarters location:** This Location. **Other U.S. locations:** Nationwide. **Number of placements per year:** 200 - 499.

PREMIER PERSONNEL GROUP, INC.
10 Woodbridge Center Drive, Woodbridge NJ 07095-1106. 732/750-5600. **Fax:** 732/750-9787. **Contact:** Robert C. Walsh, Senior Recruiter. **Description:** A permanent employment agency. **Specializes in the areas of:** Accounting/Auditing; Advertising; Banking; Finance; Legal; Marketing; Personnel/Labor Relations; Sales; Secretarial. **Positions commonly filled include:** Account Representative; Accountant; Administrative Assistant; Claim Representative; Computer Operator; Database Manager; Human Resources Manager; Sales Engineer; Sales Representative; Secretary. **Corporate headquarters location:** This Location. **Average salary range of placements:** $20,000 - $29,999. **Number of placements per year:** 200 - 499.

QUALITY DOMESTICS, INC.
484 Bloomfield Avenue, 2nd Floor, Suite 7, Montclair NJ 07042-3417. 973/509-7376. **Contact:** Lewis Ross, President. **Description:** A permanent employment agency focusing on the placement of home health care professionals. **Average salary range of placements:** Less than $20,000. **Number of placements per year:** 100 - 199.

RSVP SERVICES
P.O. Box 8369, Cherry Hill NJ 08002-0369. 609/667-4488. **Contact:** Howard Levin, Director. **E-mail address:** hl@rsvjobs.com. **Description:** A permanent employment agency. **Specializes in the areas of:** Administration; Computer Hardware/Software; Electrical; Electronics.

READY PERSONNEL/READY TEMPS
Harborside Financial Center, 145 Plaza 2, Jersey City NJ 07311. 201/434-1800. **Fax:** 201/434-0900. **Contact:** Denise Arthur, Owner. **Description:** A permanent employment agency. **Specializes in the areas of:** Accounting/Auditing; Finance.

RECRUITMENT ALTERNATIVES, INC.
York House East, P.O. Box 554, Moorestown NJ 08057. 609/273-1066. **Contact:** Thomas J. Jaskel, Senior Vice President. **Description:** A permanent employment agency. **Specializes in the areas of:** Personnel/Labor Relations. **Positions commonly filled include:** Human Resources Manager; Recruiter. **Number of placements per year:** 1 - 49.

S-H-S OF CHERRY HILL
929 North Kings Highway, Cherry Hill NJ 08034. 609/779-9030. **Fax:** 609/779-0898. **Contact:** Account Manager. **Description:** A permanent employment agency. Company pays fee. **Specializes in the areas of:** Accounting/Auditing; Administration; Engineering; Human Resources; Insurance; Manufacturing; Office Support. **Positions commonly filled include:** Accountant/Auditor; Biomedical Engineer; Chemical Engineer; Chemist; Credit Manager; Electrical/Electronics Engineer; Financial Analyst; Human Resources Manager; Mechanical Engineer; Petroleum Engineer; Physical Therapist; Underwriter/Assistant Underwriter.

SJ NURSES
850 Hamilton Avenue, Trenton NJ 08629. 609/396-7100. **Toll-free phone:** 800/727-2476. **Fax:** 609/396-7559. **Contact:** Vice President of Operations. **E-mail address:** sjpoblete@aol.com. **Description:** A permanent employment agency focusing on home health care placements. **Specializes in the areas of:** Health/Medical. **Positions commonly filled include:** Licensed Practical Nurse; Occupational Therapist; Physical Therapist; Registered Nurse; Respiratory Therapist; Speech-Language Pathologist.

SCIENTIFIC SEARCH, INC.
560 Fellowship Road, Suite 309, Mount Laurel NJ 08054. 609/866-0200. **Fax:** 609/722-5307. **Contact:** Robert I. Greensberg, President. **Description:** A permanent employment agency. Company pays fee. **Specializes in the areas of:** Computer Science/Software; Health/Medical. **Positions commonly filled include:** Computer Programmer; Health Services Manager; Nuclear Medicine Technologist; Occupational Therapist; Physical Therapist; Physician; Registered Nurse; Respiratory Therapist; Systems Analyst. **Number of placements per year:** 50 - 99.

SELECTIVE PERSONNEL
288 Summerhill Road, East Brunswick NJ 08816. 609/497-2900. **Contact:** Manager. **Description:** A permanent employment agency. **Specializes in the areas of:** Accounting/Auditing; Administration; Banking; Clerical; Computer Hardware/Software; Engineering; Finance; Health/Medical; Insurance; Legal; Manufacturing; Personnel/Labor Relations; Sales; Technical.

ARLINE SIMPSON ASSOCIATES, INC.
114 Essex Street, Rochelle Park NJ 07662. 201/843-1414. **Toll-free phone:** 800/843-6483. **Fax:** 201/843-6483. **Contact:** Arline Simpson, President. **Description:** A permanent employment agency that also offers some executive search services. Company pays fee. **Specializes in the areas of:** Accounting/Auditing; Fashion; Legal; Manufacturing; Personnel/Labor Relations; Publishing; Retail; Secretarial; Technical. **Positions commonly filled include:** Accountant/Auditor; Administrative Assistant; Bookkeeper; Buyer; Chemist; Computer Programmer; Credit Manager; Customer Service Representative; Designer; Draftsperson; Food Scientist/Technologist; Industrial Engineer; Legal Secretary; Manufacturer's/Wholesaler's Sales Rep.; Manufacturing Engineer; Mechanical Engineer; MIS Specialist; Paralegal; Receptionist; Sales Representative; Securities Sales Representative; Systems Analyst; Typist/Word Processor. **Average salary range of placements:** $20,000 - $29,999. **Number of placements per year:** 200 - 499.

SNELLING PERSONNEL SERVICES
5425 Route 70, Pennsauken NJ 08109. 609/662-5424. **Contact:** Chris Deegler, Owner/Manager. **Description:** A permanent employment agency that also offers some temporary placements. **Specializes in the areas of:** Accounting/Auditing; Banking; Clerical; Finance; Food Industry; Health/Medical; Personnel/Labor Relations; Sales. **Corporate headquarters location:** Dallas TX. **Other U.S. locations:** Nationwide.

SOURCE ONE PERSONNEL
133 Franklin Corner Road, Lawrenceville NJ 08648. 609/895-0895. **Fax:** 609/895-0574. **Contact:** Toni Baroncelli, Vice President of the Administrative Division. **Description:** A permanent employment agency. Company pays fee. **Specializes in the areas of:** Accounting/Auditing; Retail; Sales. **Positions commonly filled include:** Accountant/Auditor; Budget Analyst; Computer Programmer; Customer Service Representative; Internet Services Manager; MIS Specialist; Paralegal; Services Sales Representative; Software Engineer; Typist/Word Processor. **Benefits available to temporary workers:** Paid Holidays; Paid Vacation. **Average salary range of placements:** $20,000 - $29,999. **Number of placements per year:** 200 - 499.

SOURCE SERVICES CORPORATION
15 Essex Road, Paramus NJ 07652. 201/843-2020. **Fax:** 201/843-7705. **Contact:** Jackie Finestone, Branch Manager. **Description:** A permanent employment agency. Company pays fee. **Specializes in the areas of:** Accounting/Auditing; Administration; Banking; Computer Science/Software; Engineering; Finance; Health/Medical; Legal; Manufacturing. **Positions commonly filled include:** Accountant/Auditor; Attorney; Budget Analyst; Computer Programmer; Credit Manager; Financial Analyst; Licensed Practical Nurse; MIS Specialist; Registered Nurse; Software Engineer. **Benefits available to temporary workers:** Profit Sharing. **Corporate headquarters location:** Dallas TX. **Other U.S. locations:** Nationwide. **Number of placements per year:** 1000+.

STAFFING SERVICES GROUP
15 Bleeker Street, Millburn NJ 07041. 201/379-4900. **Toll-free phone:** 800/321-6663. **Contact:** Office Manager. **Description:** A permanent employment agency placing personnel in most major industries. The agency also provides some temporary placements.

ULTIMATE SOLUTIONS, INC.
151 West Passaic Street, Rochelle Park NJ 07662. 201/909-3717. **Fax:** 201/587-0772. **Contact:** Caryn S. Reiman, Manager/Owner. **E-mail address:** jobs@ultimatesolutions.com. **World Wide Web address:** http://www.ultimatesolutions.com. **Description:** A permanent employment agency that also provides some temporary placements. Company pays fee. **Specializes in the areas of:** Computer Science/Software; High-Tech; Scientific; Technical. **Positions commonly filled include:** Computer Programmer; Database Manager; MIS Specialist; Systems Analyst; Systems Manager; Telecommunications Manager. **Corporate headquarters location:** This Location. **Average salary range of placements:** More than $50,000. **Number of placements per year:** 200 - 499.

DON WALDRON & ASSOCIATES
220 North Centre Street, Merchantville NJ 08109. 609/663-5151. **Contact:** Manager. **Description:** A permanent employment agency. **Specializes in the areas of:** Sales.

WINTERS & ROSS
442 Main Street, Fort Lee NJ 07024-2860. 201/947-8400. **Fax:** 201/947-1035. **Contact:** Marilyn Winters, Vice President. **Description:** A permanent employment agency focusing on the placement of office support personnel. **NOTE:** Bilingual positions are offered. Company pays fee. **Specializes in the areas of:** Accounting/Auditing; Clerical; Finance; Legal; Personnel/Labor Relations; Secretarial. **Positions commonly filled include:** Accountant/Auditor; Administrative Assistant; Bookkeeper; Clerical Supervisor; Computer Programmer; Credit Manager; Customer Service Representative; Data Entry Clerk; EDP Specialist; Financial Analyst; Human Resources Specialist; Legal Secretary; Management Trainee; Receptionist; Secretary; Stenographer; Typist/Word Processor. **Average salary range of placements:** $20,000 - $29,999. **Number of placements per year:** 100 - 199.

CLAIRE WRIGHT ASSOCIATION
1280 U.S. Highway 46, Parsippany NJ 07054-4911. 973/402-8400. **Fax:** 973/402-8519. **Contact:** K. Kelley, Counselor. **Description:** A permanent employment agency. Company pays fee. **Specializes in the areas of:** Accounting/Auditing; Administration; Advertising; Computer Hardware/Software; Engineering; Finance; Insurance; Legal; Manufacturing; Sales; Technical. **Positions commonly filled include:** Accountant/Auditor; Advertising Clerk; Chemical Engineer; Claim Representative; Computer Programmer; Draftsperson; Electrical/Electronics Engineer; Environmental Engineer; Financial Analyst; Human Resources Specialist; Industrial Engineer; Insurance Agent/Broker; Internet Services Manager; Market Research Analyst; Mechanical Engineer; Metallurgical Engineer; MIS Specialist; Nuclear Engineer; Paralegal; Property and Real Estate Manager; Purchasing Agent/Manager; Securities Sales Representative; Software Engineer; Technical Writer/Editor; Telecommunications Manager; Typist/Word Processor; Underwriter/Assistant Underwriter. **Average salary range of placements:** $30,000 - $50,000. **Number of placements per year:** 1 - 49.

YOURS IN TRAVEL PERSONNEL AGENCY, INC.
301 Route 17 North, Suite 800, Rutherford NJ 07070. 201/438-3500. **Contact:** Robyn Hering, Vice President. **Description:** A permanent employment agency. Company pays fee. **Specializes in the areas of:** Travel. **Positions commonly filled include:** Travel Agent.

TEMPORARY EMPLOYMENT AGENCIES

AMERICAN STAFFING RESOURCES
1432 Brunswick Avenue, Lawrenceville NJ 08638-3317. 609/392-1400. **Toll-free phone:** 800/AMSTAF-9. **Fax:** 609/393-7612. **Contact:** Sarah Crossley, Branch Supervisor. **Description:** A temporary agency. Company pays fee. **Specializes in the areas of:** Accounting/Auditing; Administration; Industrial; Light Industrial; Secretarial; Technical. **Positions commonly filled include:** Accountant/Auditor; Administrative Manager; Civil Engineer; Claim Representative; Clerical Supervisor; Management Trainee; Market Research Analyst; Paralegal; Typist/Word Processor. **Benefits available to temporary workers:** Paid Holidays; Paid Vacation. **Corporate headquarters location:** Feasterville PA. **Number of placements per year:** 200 - 499.

ANGELORD INC.
930 Stuyvesant Avenue, Union NJ 07083-6940. 908/687-5442. **Fax:** 908/688-5482. **Contact:** Bella Guariella, President. **Description:** A temporary agency. **Specializes in the areas of:** Sales; Secretarial. **Positions commonly filled include:** Accountant/Auditor; Services Sales Representative; Typist/Word Processor. **Average salary range of placements:** $20,000 - $29,999. **Number of placements per year:** 50 - 99.

ARC MEDICAL AND PROFESSIONAL PERSONNEL
36 State Route 10, Suite D, East Hanover NJ 07936. 973/428-0101. **Fax:** 973/428-8257. **Contact:** Roslyn Durkin, Assistant Director. **Description:** A temporary employment agency that also provides permanent placements. Company pays fee. **Specializes in the areas of:** Health/Medical; Pharmaceutical. **Positions commonly filled include:** Biochemist; Biological Scientist; Chemist; Clinical Lab Technician; Medical Records Technician; Pharmacist; Physician; Registered Nurse; Scientist; Typist/Word Processor. **Number of placements per year:** 1 - 49.

DUNHILL TEMPORARY SYSTEMS
105 College Road East, Princeton NJ 08540. 609/452-1222. **Fax:** 609/452-9222. **Contact:** David Campasano, Branch Manager. **Description:** A temporary agency. Company pays fee. **Specializes in the areas of:** Administration; Computer Science/Software; Industrial; Personnel/Labor Relations; Sales; Secretarial. **Positions commonly filled include:** Blue-Collar Worker Supervisor; Brokerage Clerk; Electrical/Electronics Engineer; Paralegal; Services Sales Representative. **Other U.S. locations:** Woodbury NY. **Average salary range of placements:** $20,000 - $29,999. **Number of placements per year:** 1000+.

ENRICHED LIVING
18 Davenport Street, Somerville NJ 08876. 908/707-9779. **Fax:** 908/707-9809. **Contact:** Tracy Posada, Nursing Coordinator. **Description:** A temporary agency. **Specializes in the areas of:** Health/Medical. **Positions commonly filled include:** Dietician/Nutritionist; Licensed Practical Nurse; Physical Therapist; Registered Nurse; Social Worker. **Number of placements per year:** 1 - 49.

ITC TEMPS INC.
232 Boulevard, Suite 8, Hasbrouck Heights NJ 07604. 201/462-0264. **Fax:** 201/462-0282. **Contact:** Manager. **Description:** A temporary agency that also offers contract services. **Specializes in the areas of:** Personnel/Labor Relations; Secretarial. **Positions commonly filled include:** Customer Service Representative; Human Resources Specialist; Typist/Word Processor. **Benefits available to temporary workers:** Bonus Award/Plan; Medical Insurance; Paid Vacation. **Average salary range of placements:** $30,000 - $50,000. **Number of placements per year:** 1 - 49.

INTEGRO STAFFING SERVICES
One Gatehall Drive, Parsippany NJ 07054. 973/267-6363. **Fax:** 973/267-5128. **Contact:** Manager. **Description:** A temporary employment agency. **Specializes in the areas of:** Accounting/Auditing; Banking; Biology; Computer Science/Software; Finance; Legal; Secretarial; Technical. **Positions commonly filled include:** Accountant/Auditor; Administrative Manager; Biochemist; Biological Scientist; Brokerage Clerk; Chemical Engineer; Chemist; Clinical Lab Technician; Computer Programmer; Paralegal; Typist/Word Processor. **Benefits available to temporary workers:** Bonus Award/Plan; Paid Holidays; Paid Vacation. **Other area locations:** Iselin NJ; Lawrenceville NJ; Mount Laurel NJ; Rutherford NJ. **Number of placements per year:** 1000+.

JOULE TEMPORARIES
1235 Route 1 South, Edison NJ 08837. 732/906-0906. **Contact:** Manager. **Description:** A temporary agency. **Specializes in the areas of:** Administration; Chemical; Engineering. **Positions commonly filled include:** Branch Manager; Chemical Engineer; Chemist; Civil Engineer; Designer; Draftsperson; Electrical/Electronics Engineer; Electrician; Industrial Engineer; Mechanical Engineer; Services Sales Representative; Stationary Engineer. **Number of placements per year:** 200 - 499.

KAYE PERSONNEL INC.
1868 Route 70 East, Cherry Hill NJ 08003. 609/489-1200. **Fax:** 609/489-1010. **Contact:** Carolyn Kaye, Staffing Coordinator. **Description:** A temporary agency. Company pays fee. **Specializes in the areas of:** Industrial; Manufacturing; Personnel/Labor Relations; Publishing; Secretarial; Technical. **Positions commonly filled include:** Customer Service Representative; Secretary; Typist/Word Processor. **Other U.S. locations:** Nationwide. **Number of placements per year:** 1000+.

KELLY SCIENTIFIC RESOURCES
242 Old New Brunswick Road, Suite 140, Piscataway NJ 08854. 732/981-1399. **Fax:** 732/981-1377. **Contact:** Branch Manager. **World Wide Web address:** http://www.kellyscientific.com. **Description:** A temporary agency for scientific professionals. **Specializes in the areas of:** Biomedical; Biotechnology; Chemical; Environmental; Food Industry; Petrochemical; Pharmaceutical. **Corporate headquarters location:** Troy MI.

KELLY SCIENTIFIC RESOURCES
140 Route 17 North, Suite 271, Paramus NJ 07652. 201/599-5959. **Fax:** 201/599-8470. **Contact:** Branch Manager. **World Wide Web address:** http://www.kellyscientific.com. **Description:** A temporary agency for scientific professionals. **Specializes in the areas of:** Biomedical; Biotechnology; Chemical; Environmental; Food Industry; Petrochemical; Pharmaceutical. **Corporate headquarters location:** Troy MI.

KELLY SERVICES, INC.
222 Ridgedale Avenue, Cedar Knolls NJ 07927. 973/540-1800. **Fax:** 973/540-1257. **Contact:** Branch Manager. **Description:** A temporary agency. **Specializes in the areas of:** Accounting/Auditing; Advertising; Engineering; Finance; Secretarial. **Positions commonly filled include:** Biochemist; Biological Scientist; Biomedical Engineer; Blue-Collar Worker Supervisor; Chemical Engineer; Chemist; Civil

Engineer; Claim Representative; Clerical Supervisor; Clinical Lab Technician; Computer Programmer; Customer Service Representative; Human Resources Specialist; Industrial Engineer; MIS Specialist; Multimedia Designer; Paralegal; Pharmacist; Purchasing Agent/Manager; Quality Assurance Engineer; Software Engineer; Typist/Word Processor. **Benefits available to temporary workers:** Paid Holidays; Paid Vacation. **Corporate headquarters location:** Troy MI. **Number of placements per year:** 1000+.

KELLY SERVICES, INC.
313 Courtyard, Somerville NJ 08876. 908/526-6225. **Fax:** 908/526-1625. **Contact:** Tammy Tsang, Office Manager. **Description:** A temporary agency. Company pays fee. **Specializes in the areas of:** Accounting/Auditing; Administration; Engineering; Finance; Secretarial. **Positions commonly filled include:** Biochemist; Biological Scientist; Biomedical Engineer; Chemical Engineer; Chemist; Civil Engineer; Claim Representative; Clerical Supervisor; Clinical Lab Technician; Computer Programmer; Human Resources Specialist; Industrial Production Manager; Mechanical Engineer; MIS Specialist; Multimedia Designer; Paralegal; Purchasing Agent/Manager; Quality Assurance Engineer; Software Engineer; Typist/Word Processor. **Benefits available to temporary workers:** Paid Holidays; Paid Vacation. **Corporate headquarters location:** Troy MI. **Number of placements per year:** 1000+.

LAB SUPPORT INC.
475 Market Street, 1st Floor, Elmwood Park NJ 07407. 201/794-8077. **Contact:** Manager. **Description:** A temporary agency. **Specializes in the areas of:** Biology; Food Industry; Health/Medical; Manufacturing; Technical. **Positions commonly filled include:** Biochemist; Biological Scientist; Chemist; Food Scientist/Technologist; Metallurgical Engineer; Science Technologist. **Benefits available to temporary workers:** 401(k); Medical Insurance; Paid Holidays; Paid Vacation. **Other U.S. locations:** Nationwide. **Average salary range of placements:** $30,000 - $50,000. **Number of placements per year:** 200 - 499.

MANPOWER TECHNICAL SERVICES
51 Haddonfield Road, Suite 325, Cherry Hill NJ 08002. 609/665-8177. **Fax:** 609/665-8249. **Contact:** Lisa Christensen, Area Manager. **Description:** A temporary agency. Founded in 1948. **Specializes in the areas of:** Accounting/Auditing; Administration; Biology; Computer Hardware/Software; Engineering; Finance; Manufacturing; Technical. **Positions commonly filled include:** Accountant/Auditor; Actuary; Aerospace Engineer; Biochemist; Biological Scientist; Buyer; Chemical Engineer; Chemist; Civil Engineer; Clinical Lab Technician; Computer Programmer; Credit Manager; Design Engineer; Designer; Dietician/Nutritionist; Draftsperson; Economist; Electrical/Electronics Engineer; Environmental Engineer; Industrial Engineer; Internet Services Manager; Mechanical Engineer; Multimedia Designer; Purchasing Agent/Manager; Quality Control Supervisor; Science Technologist; Software Engineer; Structural Engineer; Technical Writer/Editor. **Benefits available to temporary workers:** 401(k); Dental Insurance; Life Insurance; Medical Insurance; Paid Holidays; Paid Vacation. **Corporate headquarters location:** Milwaukee WI. **Average salary range of placements:** $30,000 - $50,000. **Number of placements per year:** 50 - 99.

OLSTEN STAFFING SERVICES
2 Worlds Fair Drive, Somerset NJ 08873-1369. 732/563-1660. **Fax:** 732/563-1665. **Contact:** Nicole Ambrosio, Customer Service Manager. **Description:** A temporary agency. Company pays fee. **Specializes in the areas of:** Accounting/Auditing; Sales. **Positions commonly filled include:** Accountant/Auditor; Advertising Clerk; Biochemist; Biological Scientist; Blue-Collar Worker Supervisor; Brokerage Clerk; Budget Analyst; Chemist; Clinical Lab Technician; Computer Programmer; Customer Service Rep.; Industrial Production Manager; Operations/Production Manager; Paralegal; Systems Analyst; Technical Writer/Editor; Typist/Word Processor. **Benefits available to temporary workers:** Medical Insurance; Paid Vacation. **Corporate headquarters location:** Melville NY. **Other U.S. locations:** Nationwide. **Average salary range of placements:** $20,000 - $29,999. **Number of placements per year:** 1000+.

OMNE STAFFING SERVICES, INC.
11 Bleeker Street, Milburn NJ 07041. 973/379-4900. **Fax:** 973/379-9119. **Contact:** Barry M. Sinins, President. **Description:** A temporary agency. **Specializes in the areas of:** Administration; Computer Science/Software; Engineering; Industrial; Manufacturing. **Positions commonly filled include:** Blue-Collar Worker Supervisor; Chemical Engineer; Civil Engineer; Clerical Supervisor; Computer Programmer; Customer Service Rep.; Design Engineer; Designer; Draftsperson; Electrical/Electronics Engineer; Electrician; Industrial Engineer; Mechanical Engineer; MIS Specialist; Software Engineer; Structural Engineer; Technical Writer/Editor. **Benefits available to temporary workers:** 401(k); Medical Insurance; Paid Holidays; Paid Vacation. **Other U.S. locations:** CA; DC; FL; PA; TX. **Average salary range of placements:** $20,000 - $29,999. **Number of placements per year:** 1000+.

PAT'S SECRETARIAL SERVICE
777 Walnut Avenue, Cranford NJ 07016-3300. 908/276-6366. **Contact:** Recruiter. **Description:** A temporary agency. **Specializes in the areas of:** Engineering; Legal; Secretarial. **Positions commonly filled include:** Clerical Supervisor; Clinical Lab Technician; Typist/Word Processor.

PROFESSIONAL ROSTER
1000 Herrontown Road, Suite 5, Princeton NJ 08540-7702. 609/921-9561. **Fax:** 609/921-9572. **Contact:** Director. **World Wide Web address:** http://www.princetonol.com/proster. **Description:** A temporary agency. **Specializes in the areas of:** Administration; Communications; Computer Hardware/Software; Finance; Sales; Technical.

PROTOCALL BUSINESS STAFFING SERVICES
426 High Street, Burlington NJ 08016-4502. 609/387-0300. **Fax:** 609/779-7471. **Contact:** Vince Moore, Regional Recruitment Coordinator. **Description:** A temporary employment agency. **Specializes in the areas of:** Accounting/Auditing; Computer Science/Software; Health/Medical; Industrial; Manufacturing; Secretarial. **Positions commonly filled include:** Accountant/Auditor; Claim Rep.; Clinical Lab Technician; Computer Programmer; Customer Service Rep.; Electrical/Electronics Engineer; Human Service Worker; Licensed Practical Nurse; Management Trainee; Medical Records Technician; MIS Specialist; Physical Therapist; Purchasing Agent/Manager; Quality Control Supervisor; Registered Nurse; Respiratory Therapist; Systems Analyst; Typist/Word Processor; Underwriter/Assistant Underwriter. **Corporate headquarters location:** Voorhees NJ. **Average salary range of placements:** $20,000 - $29,000. **Number of placements per year:** 1000+.

REMEDY INTELLIGENT STAFFING
1930 Route 70 East, Executive Mews, Suite W111, Cherry Hill NJ 08003. 609/751-1900. **Toll-free phone:** 888/751-1900. **Fax:** 609/751-1361. **Contact:** Tom Jenkins, President. **Description:** A temporary agency. **Specializes in the areas of:** Administration; Banking;

Finance; Secretarial. **Positions commonly filled include:** Clerical Supervisor; Customer Service Rep.; Human Resources Specialist; Management Trainee; Services Sales Rep.; Typist/Word Processor. **Benefits available to temporary workers:** Medical Insurance. **Other U.S. locations:** Nationwide. **Average salary range of placements:** $20,000 - $29,999. **Number of placements per year:** 500 - 999.

SNELLING PERSONNEL SERVICES
47 River Road, Summit NJ 07901. 908/273-6500. **Fax:** 908/273-4379. **Contact:** Marilyn Richards, Vice President. **Description:** A temporary agency that also provides permanent employment. Company pays fee. **Specializes in the areas of:** Administration; Clerical; Finance; Legal; Personnel/Labor Relations; Sales; Secretarial. **Positions commonly filled include:** Administrative Manager; Brokerage Clerk; Claim Representative; Clerical Supervisor; Customer Service Representative; Dental Assistant/Dental Hygienist; Human Resources Specialist; Management Trainee; Medical Records Technician; MIS Specialist; Paralegal; Receptionist; Securities Sales Representative; Services Sales Representative; Transportation/Traffic Specialist; Typist/Word Processor. **Benefits available to temporary workers:** 401(k); Paid Holidays. **Average salary range of placements:** $20,000 - $29,999. **Number of placements per year:** 500 - 999.

SUPPORTIVE CARE, INC.
383 North Kings Highway, Suite 213, Cherry Hill NJ 08034. 609/482-6630. **Fax:** 609/482-6632. **Contact:** Debbie Kramer, Manager. **Description:** A temporary employment agency. **Specializes in the areas of:** Health/Medical. **Positions commonly filled include:** Certified Nursing Aide; Home Health Aide; Licensed Practical Nurse; Registered Nurse. **Average salary range of placements:** Less than $20,000. **Number of placements per year:** 1 - 49.

TRS STAFFING SOLUTIONS, INC.
P.O. Box 566, Marlton NJ 08053. 609/985-9721. **Toll-free phone:** 800/535-8374. **Fax:** 609/985-6772. **Contact:** Joanne Becmer, Staffing Consultant. **Description:** A temporary agency. Company pays fee. **Specializes in the areas of:** Administration; Computer Science/Software; Engineering; Manufacturing; Personnel/Labor Relations; Secretarial; Technical. **Positions commonly filled include:** Architect; Chemical Engineer; Chemist; Civil Engineer; Clerical Supervisor; Computer Programmer; Construction and Building Inspector; Cost Estimator; Draftsperson; Electrical/Electronics Engineer; Environmental Engineer; Internet Services Manager; Mechanical Engineer; Metallurgical Engineer; Mining Engineer; MIS Specialist; Multimedia Designer; Petroleum Engineer; Software Engineer; Structural Engineer; Surveyor; Systems Analyst; Telecommunications Manager. **Benefits available to temporary workers:** 401(k); Medical Insurance.

TEMPORARY CLAIM PROFESSIONAL
8004 Lincoln Drive West, Suite D, Marlton NJ 08053-3213. 609/988-0099. **Contact:** Patricia Winstein, Manager. **Description:** A temporary agency. Company pays fee. **Specializes in the areas of:** Insurance. **Positions commonly filled include:** Adjuster; Claim Rep.; Underwriter/Assistant Underwriter. **Benefits available to temporary workers:** Bonus Award/Plan; Medical Insurance. **Other U.S. locations:** Bel Air MD. **Average salary range of placements:** $30,000 - $50,000. **Number of placements per year:** 50 - 99.

TEMPORARY EXCELLENCE INC.
205 Robin Road, Suite 200, Paramus NJ 07652. 201/599-1010. **Fax:** 201/599-1122. **Contact:** Lupita Cunningham, President. **Description:** A temporary agency. Company pays fee. **Specializes in the areas of:** Accounting/Auditing; Fashion; Finance; Health/Medical; Personnel/Labor Relations; Retail; Sales; Secretarial. **Positions commonly filled include:** Accountant/Auditor; Clerical Supervisor; Credit Manager; Customer Service Rep.; Human Resources Specialist; Typist/Word Processor. **Benefits available to temporary workers:** Medical Insurance; Paid Vacation. **Average salary range of placements:** $30,000 - $50,000. **Number of placements per year:** 1000+.

TEMPS PLUS
500 Route 17 South, Hasbrouck Heights NJ 07604. 201/288-7800. **Fax:** 201/288-7995. **Contact:** Amy Ellman, Placement Consultant. **Description:** A temporary agency. Company pays fee. **Specializes in the areas of:** Accounting/Auditing; Advertising; Finance; Personnel/Labor Relations; Sales; Secretarial; Transportation. **Positions commonly filled include:** Accountant/Auditor; Administrative Manager; Advertising Clerk; Clerical Supervisor; Credit Manager; Customer Service Representative; Financial Analyst; Human Resources Specialist; Management Trainee; Paralegal; Purchasing Agent/Manager; Transportation/Traffic Specialist; Typist/Word Processor. **Benefits available to temporary workers:** Bonus Award/Plan; Paid Holidays; Paid Vacation. **Other U.S. locations:** Nationwide.

UNITEMP TEMPORARY PERSONNEL
95 Route 17 South, Paramus NJ 07652. 201/845-7444. **Fax:** 201/845-7451. **Contact:** Molly Kissel, Vice President. **Description:** A temporary agency. Company pays fee. **Specializes in the areas of:** Accounting/Auditing; Administration; Health/Medical; Insurance; Legal; Office Support; Personnel/Labor Relations; Secretarial. **Positions commonly filled include:** Claim Representative; Customer Service Representative; Editor; Library Technician; Mathematician; Medical Records Technician; Paralegal; Typist/Word Processor. **Benefits available to temporary workers:** Paid Vacation. **Other area locations:** Secaucus NJ; Woodcliff Lake NJ. **Number of placements per year:** 1000+.

WINSTON STAFFING SERVICES
301 Route 17 North, Rutherford NJ 07070. 201/460-9200. **Toll-free phone:** 800/4WINSTON. **Contact:** Michael A. Gallo, Vice President. **E-mail address:** info@winston-data.com. **World Wide Web address:** http://www.winston-data.com. **Description:** A temporary agency. **Specializes in the areas of:** Accounting/Auditing; Advertising; Banking; Computer Science/Software; Fashion; Finance; General Management; Health/Medical; Legal; Personnel/Labor Relations; Sales; Secretarial. **Positions commonly filled include:** Accountant/Auditor; Administrator; Advertising Clerk; Attorney; Blue-Collar Worker Supervisor; Brokerage Clerk; Budget Analyst; Buyer; Claim Rep.; Clerical Supervisor; Clinical Lab Technician; Computer Programmer; Counselor; Credit Manager; Customer Service Rep.; Dental Assistant/Dental Hygienist; Dietician/Nutritionist; EEG Technologist; EKG Technician; Emergency Medical Technician; Health Services Manager; Human Resources Specialist; Licensed Practical Nurse; Management Trainee; Manufacturer's/Wholesaler's Sales Rep.; Market Research Analyst; Medical Records Technician; MIS Specialist; Multimedia Designer; Occupational Therapist; Paralegal; Pharmacist; Physical Therapist; Physician; Public Relations Specialist; Purchasing Agent/Manager; Quality Control Supervisor; Radiological Technologist; Recreational Therapist; Registered Nurse; Respiratory Therapist; Securities Sales Rep.; Software Engineer; Statistician; Systems Analyst; Telecommunications Manager; Typist/Word Processor. **Benefits available to temporary workers:** Paid Vacation. **Number of placements per year:** 1000+.

CONTRACT SERVICES FIRMS

CDI CORPORATION
899 Mountain Avenue, Springfield NJ 07081. 973/379-9790. **Contact:** Manager. **World Wide Web address:** http://www.cdicorp.com. **Description:** A contract services firm. **Specializes in the areas of:** Technical. **Corporate headquarters location:** Philadelphia PA. **Other U.S. locations:** Nationwide. **International locations:** Worldwide.

JOULE INDUSTRIAL CONTRACTORS
429 East Broad Street, Gibbstown NJ 08027. 609/423-7500. **Toll-free phone:** 800/445-6853. **Fax:** 609/423-3209. **Contact:** Ken Leipert, Recruiter. **Description:** A contract services firm. **Specializes in the areas of:** Food Industry; Light Industrial. **Positions commonly filled include:** Millwright; Pipe Fitter; Welder. **Benefits available to temporary workers:** 401(k); Dental Insurance; Life Insurance; Medical Insurance. **Corporate headquarters location:** Edison NJ. **Average salary range of placements:** $20,000 - $29,999. **Number of placements per year:** 100 - 199.

ROTATOR SERVICES INC.
575 Cranbury Road, East Brunswick NJ 08816. 732/238-6050. **Fax:** 732/238-2152. **Contact:** Dan Klein, Technical Specialist. **Description:** A contract services firm. **Specializes in the areas of:** Administration; Architecture/Construction; Computer Science/Software; Engineering; Secretarial; Technical. **Positions commonly filled include:** Architect; Biochemist; Biological Scientist; Biomedical Engineer; Chemical Engineer; Chemist; Civil Engineer; Clinical Lab Technician; Computer Programmer; Cost Estimator; Design Engineer; Designer; Draftsperson; Electrical/Electronics Engineer; Environmental Engineer; Industrial Engineer; Landscape Architect; Mechanical Engineer; Mining Engineer; MIS Specialist; Nuclear Engineer; Pharmacist; Quality Control Supervisor; Structural Engineer; Systems Analyst; Technical Writer/Editor; Telecommunications Manager. **Benefits available to temporary workers:** 401(k); Medical Insurance. **Average salary range of placements:** $30,000 - $50,000. **Number of placements per year:** 500 - 999.

SHARP TECHNICAL SERVICES, INC.
P.O. Box 323, Mount Royal NJ 08061. 609/853-5752. **Fax:** 609/853-0780. **Contact:** Personnel. **E-mail address:** stsl@voicenet.com. **Description:** A contract engineering and technical support firm. **Specializes in the areas of:** Design; Engineering. **Positions commonly filled include:** Biochemist; Buyer; Chemical Engineer; Civil Engineer; Computer Programmer; Construction and Building Inspector; Cost Estimator; Design Engineer; Designer; Draftsperson; Electrical/Electronics Engineer; Environmental Engineer; Industrial Engineer; Mechanical Engineer; MIS Specialist; Purchasing Agent/Manager; Software Engineer; Structural Engineer; Systems Analyst; Technical Writer/Editor; Telecommunications Manager. **Benefits available to temporary workers:** 401(k); Credit Union; Medical Insurance; Paid Holidays; Paid Vacation. **Other area locations:** Eatontown NJ. **Average salary range of placements:** $30,000 - $50,000. **Number of placements per year:** 200 - 499.

YOH SCIENTIFIC
30 Columbia Turnpike, Florham Park NJ 07932. 973/377-8634. **Contact:** Manager. **Description:** A contract services firm. **Specializes in the areas of:** Chemical; Pharmaceutical. **Other U.S. locations:** Nationwide.

YOH SCIENTIFIC
5 Independence Way, 1st Floor, Princeton NJ 08540. 609/514-1210. **Contact:** Manager. **Description:** A contract services firm. **Specializes in the areas of:** Pharmaceutical; Scientific. **Other U.S. locations:** Nationwide.

CAREER/OUTPLACEMENT COUNSELING FIRMS

A PROFESSIONAL EDGE
248 Columbia Turnpike, Florham Park NJ 07932-1210. 973/966-6963x14. **Fax:** 973/966-6539. **Contact:** Martin P. Murphy, Executive Vice President. **Description:** A Professional Edge is a career/outplacement counseling firm. Company pays fee. **Specializes in the areas of:** Accounting/Auditing; Administration; Advertising; Banking; Computer Science/Software; Economics; Fashion; Finance; General Management; Insurance; Personnel/Labor Relations; Retail; Sales; Secretarial; Technical. **Positions commonly filled include:** Accountant/Auditor; Administrative Manager; Bank Officer/Manager; Branch Manager; Brokerage Clerk; Computer Programmer; Counselor; Customer Service Representative; Financial Analyst; Human Resources Specialist; Insurance Agent/Broker; Management Analyst/Consultant; Management Trainee; MIS Specialist; Operations/Production Manager; Public Relations Specialist; Securities Sales Representative; Services Sales Representative; Software Engineer; Systems Analyst; Telecommunications Manager; Typist/Word Processor. **Average salary range of placements:** $20,000 - $100,000. **Number of placements per year:** 200 - 499.

AARON CAREER SERVICES
520 Main Street, Suite 302, Fort Lee NJ 07024. 201/592-0593. **Contact:** Manager. **E-mail address:** careerw@aol.com. **Description:** A full-service resume writing and preparation service that also offers executive recruiting and career counseling.

CAREER RESUME ADVANTAGE INC.
959 Route 46 East, Suite 101, Parsippany NJ 07054-3409. 973/402-8777. **Toll-free phone:** 800/RESUME911. **Fax:** 973/402-8777. **Contact:** John Thorn, President. **E-mail address:** john@resume911.com. **World Wide Web address:** http://www.resume911.com. **Description:** A resume writing and career counseling service. **Other area locations:** Hackensack NJ.

PERMIAN INTERNATIONAL, INC.
227 Route 206, Flanders NJ 07836-9114. 973/927-7373. **Fax:** 973/927-7172. **Contact:** Don Marletta, President. **Description:** A career/outplacement counseling service. **Number of placements per year:** 1 - 49.

NEW MEXICO

EXECUTIVE SEARCH FIRMS

CULVER GROUP
P.O. Box 3645, Albuquerque NM 87110. 505/255-8973. **Contact:** Manager. **Description:** An executive search firm. **Specializes in the areas of:** Health/Medical.

EXECUTIVE SEARCH
7901-B Mountain Road Northeast, Albuquerque NM 87110. 505/268-3100. **Fax:** 505/268-3572. **Contact:** Peter Dunlap, Manager. **Description:** An executive search firm.

ROBERT HALF INTERNATIONAL/ACCOUNTEMPS
2155 Louisiana Boulevard NE, Suite 6500, Albuquerque NM 87110. 505/884-4557. **Contact:** Manager. **World Wide Web address:** http://www.roberthalf.com. **Description:** An executive search firm. Accountemps (also at this location) provides temporary placements. **Specializes in the areas of:** Accounting/Auditing. **Corporate headquarters location:** Menlo Park CA. **Other U.S. locations:** Nationwide.

MANAGEMENT RECRUITERS INTERNATIONAL
2500 Louisiana Boulevard NE, Suite 506, Albuquerque NM 87110. 505/875-0920. **Contact:** Manager. **Description:** An executive search firm.

MANAGEMENT RESOURCE CONSULTING
11200 Montgomery Boulevard NE, Suite 8, Albuquerque NM 87111-2677. 505/275-1234. **Fax:** 505/275-1235. **Contact:** Robert Schultz, President. **Description:** An executive search firm focusing on human resource management and mining management primarily in base metals, as well as industrial minerals and coal. Company pays fee. **Specializes in the areas of:** Human Resources; Mining. **Positions commonly filled include:** Human Resources Specialist; Mining Engineer. **Average salary range of placements:** More than $50,000. **Number of placements per year:** 50 - 99.

NEW MEXICO HEALTH RESOURCES, INC.
300 San Mateo Boulevard NE, Suite 905, Albuquerque NM 87108. 505/260-0993. **Toll-free phone:** 800/288-6930. **Fax:** 505/260-1919. **Contact:** Office Manager. **E-mail address:** nmhealth@nmhr.org. **World Wide Web address:** http://www.nmhr.org/nmhealth. **Description:** A nonprofit executive search firm with an emphasis on recruitment and retention of health professionals for designated rural and underserved populations in New Mexico. **Specializes in the areas of:** Health/Medical; Nonprofit. **Positions commonly filled include:** Dental Assistant/Dental Hygienist; Dentist; Emergency Medical Technician; Nurse Practitioner; Occupational Therapist; Physical Therapist; Physician; Physician Assistant; Recreational Therapist; Registered Nurse; Respiratory Therapist. **Average salary range of placements:** More than $50,000. **Number of placements per year:** 1 - 49.

MARCIA OWEN ASSOCIATES
660 Granada Street, Santa Fe NM 87501. 505/983-7775. **Contact:** Manager. **Description:** An executive search firm. **Specializes in the areas of:** Administration.

ROADRUNNER PERSONNEL, INC.
4015 Carlisle Boulevard NE, Suite C, Albuquerque NM 87107. 505/881-1994. **Fax:** 505/881-8749. **Contact:** Research Director. **E-mail address:** exec-recruiter@compuserve.com. **Description:** An executive search firm operating on a contingency basis. Company pays fee. **Specializes in the areas of:** Marketing; Sales. **Positions commonly filled include:** Account Manager; Account Rep.; Marketing Manager; Marketing Specialist; Sales Engineer; Sales Executive; Sales Rep. **Average salary range of placements:** More than $50,000. **Number of placements per year:** 50 - 99.

SNELLING EXECUTIVE SEARCH
2601 Wyoming Boulevard NE, Suite 106, Albuquerque NM 87112-1031. 505/293-7800. **Fax:** 505/298-7408. **Contact:** Sue Lane, Manager. **E-mail address:** snelling@sandia.net. **Description:** An executive search firm. Company pays fee. **Specializes in the areas of:** Accounting/Auditing; Computer Science/Software; Engineering; Finance; General Management; Health/Medical; Marketing; Retail; Sales; Secretarial. **Positions commonly filled include:** Accountant/Auditor; Adjuster; Administrative Manager; Advertising Clerk; Architect; Bank Officer/Manager; Buyer; Clerical Supervisor; Computer Programmer; Credit Manager; Customer Service Rep.; Dental Assistant/Dental Hygienist; Design Engineer; Draftsperson; Electrical/Electronics Engineer; General Manager; Hotel Manager; Human Resources Manager; Landscape Architect; Management Trainee; Mechanical Engineer; Metallurgical Engineer; MIS Specialist; Occupational Therapist; Operations/Production Manager; Paralegal; Physician; Purchasing Agent/Manager; Registered Nurse; Respiratory Therapist; Services Sales Rep.; Software Engineer; Systems Analyst; Telecommunications Manager; Typist/Word Processor; Underwriter/Assistant Underwriter. **Corporate headquarters location:** Dallas TX. **International locations:** Worldwide. **Average salary range of placements:** $30,000 - $50,000. **Number of placements per year:** 50 - 99.

PERMANENT EMPLOYMENT AGENCIES

ALBUQUERQUE PERSONNEL, INC.
6011 Osuna Road NE, Suite B, Albuquerque NM 87109. 505/888-3555. **Fax:** 505/883-9022. **Contact:** Manager. **Description:** A permanent employment agency. **Specializes in the areas of:** Accounting/Auditing; Administration; Advertising; Architecture/Construction; Banking; Broadcasting; Computer Science/Software; Engineering; Finance; Food Industry; General Management; Health/Medical; Industrial; Legal; Manufacturing; Personnel/Labor Relations; Publishing; Retail; Sales; Secretarial; Technical; Transportation. **Positions commonly filled include:** Accountant/Auditor; Adjuster; Administrative Manager; Advertising Clerk; Bank Officer/Manager; Blue-Collar Worker Supervisor; Budget Analyst; Buyer; Civil Engineer; Claim Rep.; Clerical Supervisor; Computer Programmer; Construction and Building Inspector; Construction Contractor; Cost Estimator; Counselor; Credit Manager; Customer Service Rep.; Dental Assistant/Dental Hygienist; Designer; Draftsperson; Economist; Electrician; Emergency Medical Technician; Financial Analyst; General Manager; Health Services Manager; Hotel Manager; Human Resources Manager; Industrial Engineer; Industrial Production Manager; Insurance Agent/Broker; Management Analyst/Consultant; Management Trainee; Manufacturer's/Wholesaler's Sales Rep.; Mechanical Engineer; Operations/Production Manager; Paralegal; Property and Real Estate Manager; Public Relations Specialist; Purchasing Agent/Manager;

Quality Control Supervisor; Radio/TV Announcer/Broadcaster; Real Estate Agent; Restaurant/Food Service Manager; Services Sales Rep.; Software Engineer; Systems Analyst; Technical Writer/Editor; Transportation/Traffic Specialist; Travel Agent; Urban/Regional Planner; Veterinarian; Wholesale and Retail Buyer. **Number of placements per year:** 50 - 99.

EXCEL OF ALBUQUERQUE, INC.
1700 Louisiana Boulevard NE, Suite 210, Albuquerque NM 87110-7014. 505/262-1871. **Fax:** 505/268-4954. **Contact:** Office Manager. **Description:** A permanent employment agency. **Specializes in the areas of:** Accounting/Auditing; Construction; Environmental; Health/Medical.

SANDERSON EMPLOYMENT SERVICE INC.
500 Chama Boulevard NE, Albuquerque NM 87108. 505/265-8827. **Fax:** 505/268-5536. **Contact:** Bill Sanderson, President. **Description:** A permanent employment agency. Company pays fee. **Specializes in the areas of:** Accounting/Auditing; Clerical; Computer Hardware/Software; Engineering; Sales; Secretarial; Technical. **Positions commonly filled include:** Accountant/Auditor; Aerospace Engineer; Bookkeeper; Civil Engineer; Computer Programmer; Data Entry Clerk; EDP Specialist; Electrical/Electronics Engineer; Legal Secretary; Mechanical Engineer; Medical Secretary; Physicist; Receptionist; Sales Representative; Secretary; Stenographer; Systems Analyst; Typist/Word Processor. **Number of placements per year:** 100 - 199.

TRAMBLEY THE RECRUITER
5325 Wyoming Boulevard NE, Suite 8, Albuquerque NM 87109. 505/821-5440. **Fax:** 505/821-8509. **Contact:** J. Brian Trambley, CPC. **Description:** A permanent employment agency. Company pays fee. **Specializes in the areas of:** Heavy Equipment; Industrial; Technical. **Positions commonly filled include:** Agricultural Engineer; Design Engineer; Designer; Electrical/Electronics Engineer; Industrial Engineer; Mechanical Engineer; Metallurgical Engineer; Quality Control Supervisor; Software Engineer; Structural Engineer. **Number of placements per year:** 50 - 99.

TEMPORARY EMPLOYMENT AGENCIES

MANPOWER, INC.
580 North Telshor, Las Cruces NM 88011. 505/522-6028. **Contact:** Branch Manager. **Description:** A temporary agency. Company pays fee. **Specializes in the areas of:** Industrial; Office Support; Technical; Telecommunications; Word Processing. **Positions commonly filled include:** Accountant/Auditor; Accounting Clerk; Administrative Assistant; Assembly Worker; Biological Scientist; Bookkeeper; CADD Operator; Chemist; Computer Operator; Customer Service Manager; Desktop Publishing Specialist; Electrician; Inspector/Tester/Grader; Inventory Control Specialist; Machine Operator; Material Control Specialist; Order Clerk; Packaging/Processing Worker; Painter; Project Engineer; Proofreader; Receptionist; Records Manager; Research Assistant; Secretary; Software Engineer; Stenographer; Stock Clerk; Systems Analyst; Technical Writer/Editor; Technician; Telemarketer; Test Operator; Transcriptionist; Typist/Word Processor; Welder. **Benefits available to temporary workers:** Life Insurance; Medical Insurance; Paid Holidays; Paid Vacation. **Number of placements per year:** 1000+.

SANTA FE SERVICES
142 Lincoln Avenue, #205, Santa Fe NM 87501. 505/984-8511. **Fax:** 505/986-8122. **Contact:** Don Woodin, President. **Description:** A temporary employment agency that also provides permanent placements. Founded in 1981. Company pays fee. **Specializes in the areas of:** Accounting/Auditing; Advertising; General Management; Legal; Secretarial. **Positions commonly filled include:** Accountant/Auditor; Administrative Manager; Bank Officer/Manager; Clerical Supervisor; General Manager; Hotel Manager; Management Trainee; Operations/Production Manager; Paralegal; Property and Real Estate Manager; Purchasing Agent/Manager; Typist/Word Processor. **Average salary range of placements:** $20,000 - $29,999. **Number of placements per year:** 100 - 199.

SCIENTEMPS, INC.
457 Washington Street SE, Albuquerque NM 87108. 505/268-0074. **Fax:** 505/268-9326. **Contact:** Judi Richardson, President. **E-mail address:** scitemps@flash.net. **World Wide Web address:** http://www.flash.net/~scitemps. **Description:** A temporary agency. Scientemps provides laboratory and technical temporary, temp-to-perm, and permanent positions. Founded in 1991. Company pays fee. **Specializes in the areas of:** Biology; Computer Science/Software; Engineering; Food Industry; Health/Medical; Technical. **Positions commonly filled include:** Biological Scientist; Biomedical Engineer; Chemist; Clinical Lab Technician; Design Engineer; Designer; Draftsperson; Electrical/Electronics Engineer; Environmental Engineer; Food Scientist/Technologist; Geologist/Geophysicist; Mechanical Engineer; Metallurgical Engineer; Science Technologist. **Benefits available to temporary workers:** Medical Insurance; Paid Holidays. **Number of placements per year:** 100 - 199.

CONTRACT SERVICES FIRMS

BUTLER SERVICE GROUP
2201 San Pedro Boulevard NE, Building 3, Suite 230, Albuquerque NM 87110. 505/883-2700. **Fax:** 505/883-8333. **Contact:** Steve Garcia, Senior Recruiter. **Description:** A contract technical services firm that is a division of Butler International. Company pays fee. **Specializes in the areas of:** Computer Science/Software; Engineering; Environmental; Manufacturing; Technical. **Positions commonly filled include:** Biological Scientist; Budget Analyst; Chemist; Computer Programmer; Design Engineer; Designer; Draftsperson; Electrical/Electronics Engineer; Environmental Engineer; Librarian; Library Technician; Mechanical Engineer; MIS Specialist; Nuclear Engineer; Software Engineer; Structural Engineer; Systems Analyst. **Benefits available to temporary workers:** 401(k); Medical Insurance; Paid Holidays. **Corporate headquarters location:** Montvale NJ. **International locations:** Worldwide. **Average salary range of placements:** $30,000 - $50,000. **Number of placements per year:** 100 - 199.

CDI CORPORATION (MIDWEST)
2730 San Pedro Drive NE, Suite H, Albuquerque NM 87110. 505/888-4544. **Toll-free phone:** 800/975-6564. **Fax:** 505/888-3233. **Contact:** Shawn Murphy, Technical Manager. **E-mail address:** sgmurphy@cdicorp.com. **World Wide Web address:** http://www.cdicorp.com. **Description:** A contract services firm. Founded in 1945. Company pays fee.

Specializes in the areas of: Administration; Art/Design; Biology; Computer Science/Software; Engineering; Finance; General Management; Health/Medical; Industrial; Manufacturing; Personnel/Labor Relations; Publishing; Secretarial; Technical; Transportation. **Positions commonly filled include:** Accountant/Auditor; Aerospace Engineer; Agricultural Engineer; Architect; Biological Scientist; Biomedical Engineer; Blue-Collar Worker Supervisor; Budget Analyst; Buyer; Chemical Engineer; Chemist; Civil Engineer; Clerical Supervisor; Clinical Lab Technician; Computer Programmer; Construction Contractor; Cost Estimator; Customer Service Representative; Design Engineer; Designer; Draftsperson; Editor; Electrical/Electronics Engineer; Environmental Engineer; Financial Analyst; Food Scientist/ Technologist; General Manager; Geographer; Geologist/Geophysicist; Human Resources Manager; Human Service Worker; Industrial Engineer; Industrial Production Manager; Internet Services Manager; Landscape Architect; Librarian; Library Technician; Management Analyst/Consultant; Market Research Analyst; Mathematician; Mechanical Engineer; Medical Records Technician; Metallurgical Engineer; Mining Engineer; MIS Specialist; Multimedia Designer; Nuclear Engineer; Nuclear Medicine Technologist; Operations/Production Manager; Petroleum Engineer; Physical Therapist; Physicist; Public Relations Specialist; Quality Control Supervisor; Radiological Technologist; Science Technologist; Software Engineer; Stationary Engineer; Statistician; Strategic Relations Manager; Structural Engineer; Surveyor; Systems Analyst; Technical Writer/Editor; Telecommunications Manager; Transportation/Traffic Specialist; Typist/Word Processor; Urban/Regional Planner; Video Production Coordinator. **Corporate headquarters location:** Philadelphia PA. **Other U.S. locations:** Nationwide. **International locations:** Worldwide. **Average salary range of placements:** $50,000 - $80,000. **Number of placements per year:** 1000+.

COMFORCE TECHNICAL SERVICES, INC.
6400 Uptown Boulevard, Suite 460W, Albuquerque NM 87110. 505/889-3535. **Fax:** 505/889-3331. **Description:** A contract services firm. **Specializes in the areas of:** Technical.

NEW YORK

EXECUTIVE SEARCH FIRMS

A&A STAFFING HEALTH CARE
175 Main Street, White Plains NY 10601. 914/428-1515. **Contact:** Manager. **Description:** An executive search firm for home health care professionals. **Specializes in the areas of:** Health/Medical.

AJC SEARCH
119 North Park Avenue, Rockville Centre NY 11570. 516/766-1699. **Fax:** 516/766-3889. **Contact:** Jay Cohen, Principal. **Description:** An executive search firm. Company pays fee. **Specializes in the areas of:** Accounting/Auditing; Computer Science/Software; Economics; Finance; Health/Medical; Insurance; Legal; Sales. **Positions commonly filled include:** Accountant/Auditor; Actuary; Attorney; Computer Programmer; Consultant; Dental Assistant/Hygienist; Dentist; Dietician/Nutritionist; Financial Analyst; Insurance Agent/Broker; Mathematician; Paralegal; Pharmacist; Physical Therapist; Physician; Registered Nurse; Securities Sales Rep.; Statistician; Systems Analyst; Underwriter/Assistant Underwriter. **Average salary range of placements:** More than $50,000. **Number of placements per year:** 1 - 49.

APA SEARCH
721 West Boston Post Road, Mamaroneck NY 10601. 914/698-2800. **Contact:** Howard Kesten, President. **Description:** An executive search firm. **Specializes in the areas of:** Automotive; General Management; Manufacturing; Retail; Sales; Transportation. **Positions commonly filled include:** Manufacturing Engineer; Marketing Specialist; Purchasing Agent/Manager; Sales Representative; Technical Writer/Editor.

AZR INC.
245 Fifth Avenue, New York NY 10016. 212/545-7842. **Contact:** Richard Silverman, President. **Description:** An executive search firm. **Specializes in the areas of:** Computer Science/Software. **Positions commonly filled include:** Computer Programmer; Internet Services Manager; MIS Specialist; Multimedia Designer; Software Engineer; Systems Analyst; Technical Writer/Editor; Telecommunications Manager. **Average salary range of placements:** More than $50,000. **Number of placements per year:** 50 - 99.

ACCOUNTANTS CHOICE PERSONNEL
Charles Lindbergh Boulevard, Suite 400, Uniondale NY 11553. 212/643-4400. **Contact:** Manager. **Description:** An executive search firm. **Specializes in the areas of:** Accounting/Auditing.

ACCOUNTANTS EXECUTIVE SEARCH
ACCOUNTANTS ON CALL
535 Fifth Avenue, Suite 1200, New York NY 10017. 212/682-5900. **Contact:** Manager. **Description:** An executive search firm. Accountants on Call (also at this location) is a temporary agency. **Specializes in the areas of:** Accounting/Auditing; Finance.
Other area locations:
- 500 North Broadway, Suite 237, Jericho NY 11753. 516/935-0050.

ADEPT TECH RECRUITING
219 Glendale Road, Scarsdale NY 10583. 914/725-8583. **Contact:** Fred Press, President. **Description:** An executive search firm. Company pays fee. **Specializes in the areas of:** Administration; Computer Science/Software; Finance; Health/Medical; Information Systems. **Average salary range of placements:** $30,000 - $50,000. **Number of placements per year:** 1 - 49.

ADVICE PERSONNEL
230 Park Avenue, Suite 903, New York NY 10169-0005. 212/682-4400. **Fax:** 212/697-0343. **Contact:** Alan Schwartz, Principals. **Description:** An executive search firm operating on a contingency basis. Company pays fee. **Specializes in the areas of:** Accounting/Auditing; Finance; Secretarial; Tax. **Positions commonly filled include:** Accountant/Auditor; Budget Analyst; Chief Financial Officer; Controller; Credit Manager; Customer Service Rep.; Finance Director; Financial Analyst; Secretary; Typist/Word Processor. **Average salary range of placements:** More than $50,000. **Number of placements per year:** 500 - 999.

ADVISORS' SEARCH GROUP
370 Lexington Avenue, New York NY 10017. 212/557-7533. **Contact:** Manager. **Description:** An executive search firm. **Specializes in the areas of:** Investment.

ALFUS GROUP
353 Lexington Avenue, New York NY 10016-0941. 212/599-1000. **Fax:** 212/599-1523. **Contact:** Phillip Alfus, President. **E-mail address:** phatag@aol.com. **World Wide Web address:** http://www.quikpage.com/a/alfus. **Description:** A retained executive search firm focusing on the leisure and hospitality industries. Company pays fee. **Specializes in the areas of:** Food Industry; Hotel/Restaurant; Personnel/Labor Relations; Sales. **Positions commonly filled include:** Chief Financial Officer; Food Scientist/Technologist; Hotel Manager; Human Resources Specialist; Marketing Manager; Restaurant/Food Service Manager; Sales Executive; Vice President. **Corporate headquarters location:** This location. **Other U.S. locations:** San Francisco CA. **International locations:** Rome, Italy **Average salary range of placements:** More than $50,000. **Number of placements per year:** 50 - 99.

ALITE ASSOCIATES, INC.
150 Broadway, New York NY 10038. 212/822-4300. **Contact:** Maria Alite, President. **Description:** A full-service contingency executive search firm focusing on the banking and brokerage industries. **Specializes in the areas of:** Accounting/Auditing; Banking; Computer Science/Software; Finance. **Positions commonly filled include:** Telecommunications Manager.

FRANKLIN ALLEN CONSULTANTS LTD.
401 Franklin Avenue, Suite 102, Garden City NY 11530-5943. 516/248-4511. **Fax:** 516/294-6646. **Contact:** Howard Roher/Allen Kupchi, Recruiters. **E-mail address:** frnklnalln@aol.com. **Description:** An executive search firm. Company pays fee. **Specializes in the areas of:** Accounting/Auditing; Administration; Banking; Computer Science/Software; Finance; Food Industry; General Management; Health/Medical; Marketing; MIS/EDP; Personnel/Labor Relations; Retail; Sales; Scientific; Technical. **Positions commonly filled include:** Accountant/Auditor; Biochemist; Biological Scientist; Cable TV Installer; Chief Financial Officer; Controller; EEG Technologist; EKG Technician; Finance Director; Financial Analyst; General Manager; Human Resources Manager; Industrial Engineer; Marketing Manager; MIS Specialist; Occupational Therapist; Physical Therapist; Physician; Purchasing Agent/Manager; Quality Control Supervisor; Respiratory Therapist; Sales Executive; Sales Manager; Speech-Language Pathologist; Statistician; Surgical Technician; Systems Analyst; Vice President. **Average salary range of placements:** $30,000 - $50,000. **Number of placements per year:** 50 - 99.

ALPHA HEALTH SERVICES CORPORATION
200 East 82nd Street, New York NY 10028. 212/517-8110. **Contact:** Fred Press, Director. **Description:** An executive search firm that places nurses and other health care professionals. Founded in 1981. **Specializes in the areas of:** Administration; Computer Science/Software; Finance; Health/Medical; Insurance. **Positions commonly filled include:** Assistant Manager; Blue-Collar Worker Supervisor; Certified Nursing Aide; Claim Rep.; Clerical Supervisor; Clinical Lab Technician; Computer Programmer; Dietician/Nutritionist; EKG Technician; Emergency Medical Technician; Internet Services Manager; Licensed Practical Nurse; Medical Records Technician; MIS Specialist; Multimedia Designer; Occupational Therapist; Physical Therapist; Radiological Technologist; Registered Nurse; Respiratory Therapist; Software Engineer; Speech-Language Pathologist; Systems Analyst; Systems Manager; Telecommunications Manager; Webmaster. **Average salary range of placements:** $30,000 - $50,000. **Number of placements per year:** 1 - 49.

AMERICAN MEDICAL PERSONNEL SERVICES, INC.
521 Erie Boulevard West, Suite 1, Syracuse NY 13204. **Toll-free phone:** 800/724-2443. **Fax:** 800/321-8449. **Contact:** Joseph F. Papa, President. **E-mail address:** papajoe@servtech.com. **World Wide Web address:** http://www.nap.resourcecenter.com/americanmed. **Description:** An executive search firm that also operates as a temporary agency. Company pays fee. **Specializes in the areas of:** Health/Medical. **Positions commonly filled include:** Medical Records Technician; Nuclear Medicine Technologist; Occupational Therapist; Pharmacist; Physical Therapist; Physician; Registered Nurse; Respiratory Therapist; Speech-Language Pathologist; Surgical Technician.

AMES O'NEILL ASSOCIATES INC.
330 Venderbilt Motor Parkway, Hauppauge NY 11788. 516/582-4800. **Fax:** 516/234-6094. **Contact:** George C. Ames, President. **Description:** An executive search firm. Company pays fee. **Specializes in the areas of:** Computer Science/Software; Engineering; Marketing; Sales. **Positions commonly filled include:** Aerospace Engineer; Biomedical Engineer; Chemical Engineer; Computer Programmer; Electrical/Electronics Engineer; Industrial Engineer; Mechanical Engineer; Metallurgical Engineer; Software Engineer; Systems Analyst; Technical Writer/Editor. **Average salary range of placements:** More than $50,000. **Number of placements per year:** 1 - 49.

ASTER SEARCH GROUP
555 Madison Avenue, Suite 2300, New York NY 10022. 212/888-6182. **Contact:** Manager. **Description:** An executive search firm. **Specializes in the areas of:** Health/Medical.

AUDIT DATA SEARCH LTD.
535 Broadhollow Road, Melville NY 11747. 516/454-6666. **Fax:** 516/454-1595. **Contact:** Jack Rose, President. **Description:** An executive search firm. **Specializes in the areas of:** Information Systems. **Positions commonly filled include:** Information Systems Auditor. **Number of placements per year:** 50 - 99.

AVALON HEALTH GROUP
245 East 54th Street, Suite 3T, New York NY 10022. 212/758-3786. **Fax:** 212/758-5304. **Contact:** Manager. **Description:** An executive search firm for high-end positions in the health care field. **Specializes in the areas of:** Health/Medical.

BACAL & ASSOCIATES
10 East 39th Street, New York NY 10016. 212/953-7200. **Contact:** Dorothy Bacal. **Description:** An executive search firm. **Specializes in the areas of:** Legal. **Positions commonly filled include:** Attorney.

BADER RESEARCH CORPORATION
6 East 45th Street, Room 1601, New York NY 10017-2414. 212/682-4750. **Contact:** Manager. **Description:** An executive search firm. **NOTE:** Attorneys must have a minimum of two years post-law school legal experience. Company pays fee. **Specializes in the areas of:** Legal. **Positions commonly filled include:** Attorney. **Average salary range of placements:** More than $50,000.

BARTL & EVINS
333 North Broadway, Jericho NY 11753-2007. 516/433-3333. **Fax:** 516/433-2692. **Contact:** Frank Bartl, Vice President. **E-mail address:** bartl@ibm.net. **World Wide Web address:** http://www.bartl.evins.com. **Description:** An executive search firm operating on both retainer and contingency bases and focusing on the placement of financial services professionals. Fidelity Investment Services (also at this location) is the parent company of Bartl & Evins. **Specializes in the areas of:** Accounting/Auditing; Administration; Finance. **Positions commonly filled include:** Accountant/Auditor; Financial Analyst; General Manager; Systems Analyst. **Average salary range of placements:** More than $50,000. **Number of placements per year:** 200 - 499.

BASELINE RECRUITERS NETWORK
230 Park Avenue, New York NY 10169. 212/697-7575. **Contact:** Manager. **Description:** An executive search firm that places professionals in the legal field. Company pays fee. **Specializes in the areas of:** Legal. **Positions commonly filled include:** Attorney; Paralegal. **Average salary range of placements:** $30,000 - $50,000. **Number of placements per year:** 50 - 99.

NEAIL BEHRINGER CONSULTANTS, INC.
24 East 38th Street, Suite 4B, New York NY 10016. 212/689-7555. **Fax:** 212/689-6868. **Contact:** Neail Behringer, President. **Description:** An executive search firm operating on a retainer basis. **Specializes in the areas of:** Fashion; Health/Medical; Retail. **Positions commonly filled include:** Buyer; Designer; Manufacturer's/Wholesaler's Sales Rep.; Quality Control Supervisor; Registered Nurse. **Other U.S. locations:** Nationwide. **Average salary range of placements:** More than $50,000. **Number of placements per year:** 1 - 49.

BEISHLINE EXECUTIVE SEARCH
451 Evergreen Drive, Tonawanda NY 14150. 716/694-5154. **Fax:** 716/694-8462. **Contact:** John R. Beishline, President. **Description:** An executive search firm. Company pays fee. **Specializes in the areas of:** Architecture/Construction; Engineering; Food Industry; General Management; Industrial; Personnel/Labor Relations; Sales. **Positions commonly filled include:** Aerospace Engineer; Agricultural Scientist; Architect; Biomedical Engineer; Buyer; Chemical Engineer; Chemist; Civil Engineer; Construction Contractor; Designer; Draftsperson; Electrical/Electronics Engineer; Food Scientist/Technologist; Geologist/Geophysicist; Human Resources Manager; Industrial Engineer; Industrial Production Manager; Mechanical Engineer; Metallurgical Engineer; Mining Engineer; Nuclear Engineer; Purchasing Agent/Manager; Quality Control Supervisor; Services Sales Representative; Structural Engineer. **Number of placements per year:** 1 - 49.

ROSA BENNETT ENTERPRISES INC.
235 North Main Street, Spring Valley NY 10977. 914/425-4727. **Fax:** 914/425-7193. **Contact:** Rosa Bennett, President. **Description:** An executive search firm. **Positions commonly filled include:** Computer Programmer; Human Resources Specialist; Systems

Analyst; Technical Writer/Editor; Telecommunications Manager. **Other area locations:** New York NY.

BENSON ASSOCIATES
280 Madison Avenue, New York NY 10016. 212/683-5962. **Fax:** 212/679-2724. **Contact:** Irwin Cohen, Partner. **Description:** An executive search firm. Company pays fee. **Specializes in the areas of:** Accounting/Auditing; Advertising; Broadcasting; Finance; Sales. **Positions commonly filled include:** Financial Analyst; Human Resources Manager. **Average salary range of placements:** $30,000 - $50,000. **Number of placements per year:** 50 - 99.

BERKEL ASSOCIATES, INC.
477 Madison Avenue, Suite 707, New York NY 10022-4503. 212/826-3000. **Fax:** 212/826-3006. **Contact:** Carol Bernstein, President. **Description:** A contingency search firm. **Specializes in the areas of:** Administration; Computer Science/Software; Legal; Personnel/Labor Relations; Secretarial. **Positions commonly filled include:** Accountant/Auditor; Administrative Manager; Attorney; Clerical Supervisor; Computer Programmer; Counselor; Human Resources Specialist; Internet Services Manager; Legal Secretary; Library Technician; MIS Specialist; Paralegal; Typist/Word Processor.

MICHAEL BLITZER ASSOCIATES INC.
120 East 56th Street, New York NY 10022. 212/935-9177. **Contact:** Michael Blitzer, Owner. **Description:** An executive search firm. **Specializes in the areas of:** High-Tech.

BORNHOLDT SHIVAS & FRIENDS
400 East 87th Street, Basement Suite, New York NY 10128-6533. 212/557-5252. **Fax:** 212/557-5704. **Contact:** John Bornholdt, President. **E-mail address:** bsandf@aol.com. **World Wide Web address:** http://members.aol.com/bsandf. **Description:** An executive search firm. Founded in 1982. Company pays fee. **Specializes in the areas of:** Advertising; Art/Design; Food Industry; General Management; Manufacturing; Personnel/Labor Relations; Publishing; Retail; Sales. **Positions commonly filled include:** Administrative Manager; Advertising Account Executive; Advertising Clerk; Branch Manager; Budget Analyst; Computer Programmer; Customer Service Rep.; Designer; Economist; Editor; Electrical/Electronics Engineer; Financial Analyst; Food Scientist/Technologist; General Manager; Human Resources Manager; Management Analyst/Consultant; Management Trainee; Manufacturer's/Wholesaler's Sales Rep.; Market Research Analyst; Operations/Production Manager; Paralegal; Physical Therapist; Public Relations Specialist; Services Sales Rep.; Statistician; Systems Analyst; Technical Writer/Editor. **Number of placements per year:** 100 - 199.

BOS BUSINESS CONSULTANTS
4211 North Buffalo Street, Orchard Park NY 14127. 716/662-0800. **Fax:** 716/662-0623. **Contact:** John Bos, Owner. **E-mail address:** bosbc@aol.com. **World Wide Web address:** http://www.members.aol.com/bosbc/bosbc.html. **Description:** An executive search firm that focuses on the placement of personnel in the engineering, marketing, computer, and scientific fields. Bos Business Consultants operates on both contingency and retainer bases. Company pays fee. **Specializes in the areas of:** Computer Science/Software; Engineering; Industrial; Manufacturing. **Positions commonly filled include:** Aerospace Engineer; Biomedical Engineer; Chemical Engineer; Computer Programmer; Design Engineer; Designer; Electrical/Electronics Engineer; Financial Analyst; Food Scientist/Technologist; Human Resources Manager; Industrial Engineer; Mechanical Engineer; MIS Specialist; Operations/Production Manager; Quality Control Supervisor; Software Engineer; Systems Analyst. **Average salary range of placements:** More than $50,000. **Number of placements per year:** 1 - 49.

BRANTHOVER ASSOCIATES
51 East 42nd Street, Suite 500, New York NY 10017. 212/949-9400. **Fax:** 212/949-5905. **Contact:** Jeanne Branthover, President. **E-mail address:** branthover@aol.com. **Description:** An executive search firm. **Specializes in the areas of:** Accounting/Auditing; Administration; Advertising; Banking; Computer Science/Software; Finance; General Management; Manufacturing; Personnel/Labor Relations; Publishing; Sales. **Positions commonly filled include:** Accountant/Auditor; Bank Officer/Manager; Budget Analyst; Computer Programmer; Credit Manager; Customer Service Representative; Financial Analyst; General Manager; Human Resources Manager; Systems Analyst. **Number of placements per year:** 50 - 99.

BRUCKS CONSULTANTS
4 Tobey Village Office Park, Pittsford NY 14534. 716/248-9090. **Contact:** Manager. **Description:** An executive search firm. **Specializes in the areas of:** Engineering.

BRUML ASSOCIATES INC.
306 Birchwood Park Drive, Jericho NY 11753-2307. 516/822-7940. **Contact:** Michael Bruml, Owner. **Description:** An executive search firm operating on a contingency basis. Company pays fee. **Specializes in the areas of:** Computer Science/Software; Engineering; Technical. **Positions commonly filled include:** Biomedical Engineer; Computer Engineer; Design Engineer; Electrical/Electronics Engineer; Software Engineer. **Average salary range of placements:** $30,000 - $50,000. **Number of placements per year:** 1 - 49.

BURNS PERSONNEL
3300 Monroe Avenue, Rochester NY 14618. 716/385-6300. **Contact:** Jackie Tedesco, President. **World Wide Web address:** http://www.burnspersonnel.com. **Description:** An executive search firm that also provides temporary placement. Company pays fee. **Specializes in the areas of:** Computer Science/Software; Engineering; Industrial; Manufacturing; Personnel/Labor Relations; Secretarial; Technical. **Positions commonly filled include:** Biochemist; Biological Scientist; Biomedical Engineer; Chemical Engineer; Chemist; Computer Programmer; Draftsperson; EKG Technician; Electrical/Electronics Engineer; Emergency Medical Technician; Human Resources Specialist; Industrial Engineer; Materials Engineer; Mechanical Engineer; MIS Specialist; Software Engineer; Systems Analyst; Typist/Word Processor. **Average salary range of placements:** $20,000 - $29,999. **Number of placements per year:** 500 - 999.

CFI RESOURCES INC.
7 Clover Drive, Great Neck NY 11021-1817. 516/466-1221. **Fax:** 516/487-1774. **Contact:** Leo Cohen, Principal Partner. **E-mail address:** cfires@specctata.com. **World Wide Web address:** http://www.cfires.com. **Description:** An executive search firm providing nationwide placement in sales, marketing, engineering, and applications professions for the electronics industry. Company pays fee. **Specializes in the areas of:** Engineering; Marketing; Sales; Scientific; Technical. **Positions commonly filled include:** Computer Programmer; Design Engineer; EDP Specialist; Electrical/Electronics Engineer; General Manager; Mechanical Engineer; MIS Specialist; Software Engineer. **Other U.S. locations:** Nationwide. **Average salary range of placements:** More than $50,000. **Number of placements per year:** 50 - 99.

CK RESOURCES
420 Lexington Street, Suite 2024, New York NY 10169-0005. 212/986-5929. **Fax:** 212/986-3718. **Contact:** Cindy Karp, CEO. **E-mail address:** cksearch@escape.com. **Description:** An executive search firm. Company pays fee. **Specializes in the areas of:** Accounting/Auditing; Banking; Finance; Personnel/Labor Relations. **Positions commonly filled include:** Financial Analyst; Human Resources Manager; Purchasing Agent/Manager; Telecommunications Manager. **Average salary range of placements:** $30,000 - $50,000.

CT GROUP
264 North Elm Street, North Massapequa NY 11758-2525. 516/797-3642. **Fax:** 516/795-4350. **Contact:** Camille T. Coppola, Managing Director. **Description:** An executive search firm. Company pays fee. **Specializes in the areas of:** Health/Medical; Insurance. **Positions commonly filled include:** Health Services Manager; Home Health Aide; Nurse; Pharmacist; Registered Nurse; Services Sales Representative. **Number of placements per year:** 50 - 99.

J.P. CANON ASSOCIATES
225 Broadway, Suite 3602, New York NY 10007. 212/233-3131. **Fax:** 212/233-0457. **Contact:** James E. Rohan, Senior Partner. **E-mail address:** headhunter@iname.com. **World Wide Web address:** http://www.jpcanon.com. **Description:** An executive search firm operating on a contingency basis. The firm focuses on placement in the materials management, logistics, purchasing, and systems professions. Company pays fee. **Positions commonly filled include:** Buyer; Consultant; Customer Service Rep.; Database Manager; Industrial Engineer; Industrial Production Manager; Logistics Manager; Management Analyst/Consultant; Materials Manager; Operations Manager; Purchasing Agent/Manager; Systems Analyst; Systems Manager; Transportation/Traffic Specialist; Vice President. **Average salary range of placements:** More than $50,000. **Number of placements per year:** 100 - 199.

CANTOR CONCERN
330 West 58th Street, Suite 216, New York NY 10019-1827. 212/333-3000. **Fax:** 212/245-1012. **Contact:** Marie Raperto, President. **E-mail address:** 102255,1127@compuserve.com. **World Wide Web address:** http://www.cantorconcern.com. **Description:** A retained executive search firm focusing on public relations, corporate communications, and investor relations. Company pays fee. **Specializes in the areas of:** Public Relations. **Positions commonly filled include:** Editor; Public Relations Specialist; Vice President. **Average salary range of placements:** More than $50,000. **Number of placements per year:** 50 - 99.

CARE GIVERS
1900 Genesee Street, Utica NY 13502. 315/797-7050. **Contact:** Manager. **Description:** An executive search firm that places nurses for in-home health care. **Specializes in the areas of:** Health/Medical.

CARTER/MACKAY OF GREAT NECK
111 Great Neck Road, Great Neck NY 11021. 516/829-9250. **Fax:** 516/829-6787. **Contact:** Manager. **Description:** An executive search firm. **Specializes in the areas of:** Sales. **Other U.S. locations:** Framingham MA; Cary NJ; Hasbrouck Heights NJ.

CASALE MANAGEMENT SERVICES, INC.
550 Old Country Road, Hicksville NY 11803. 516/942-8600. **Contact:** Frank Casale, President. **Description:** An executive search firm that also operates as a temporary agency. Company pays fee. **Specializes in the areas of:** MIS/EDP. **Positions commonly filled include:** Computer Programmer; MIS Specialist; Multimedia Designer; Systems Analyst; Technical Writer/Editor; Telecommunications Manager. **Average salary range of placements:** More than $50,000. **Number of placements per year:** 50 - 99.

CASTLEREA ASSOCIATES
188 East Post Road, Suite 401, White Plains NY 10601. 914/946-1383. **Fax:** 914/946-2019. **Contact:** Frank DeLigio, President. **Description:** An executive search firm serving the staffing and consulting industries. Company pays fee. **Specializes in the areas of:** Consulting; General Management. **Positions commonly filled include:** Account Manager; Account Rep.; Chief Financial Officer; Consultant; Controller; Customer Service Rep.; Management Analyst/Consultant; Marketing Manager; Operations Manager; Sales Executive; Sales Rep.; Vice President of Marketing. **Average salary range of placements:** More than $50,000. **Number of placements per year:** 1 - 49.

CAVAN SYSTEMS, LTD.
10 Cuttermill Road, Suite 403A, Great Neck NY 11021. 516/487-7777. **Fax:** 516/487-7857. **Contact:** Chris O'Brien, President. **Description:** An executive search firm. Company pays fee. **Specializes in the areas of:** Computer Science/Software; Information Systems; Multimedia. **Positions commonly filled include:** Communications Engineer; Computer Programmer; Internet Services Manager; Media Specialist; MIS Specialist; Network Engineer; Online Content Specialist; Software Engineer; Systems Analyst; Systems Manager; Telecommunications Analyst; Webmaster. **Average salary range of placements:** More than $50,000. **Number of placements per year:** 50 - 99.

CHRISS CAREER LIMITED
220 White Plains Road, Tarrytown NY 10591. 914/631-3334. **Contact:** Judy Chriss, President. **Description:** An executive search firm that operates on a contingency basis. Company pays fee. **Specializes in the areas of:** Health/Medical; Personnel/Labor Relations; Sales; Secretarial. **Positions commonly filled include:** Human Resources Manager; Physical Therapist; Registered Nurse. **Average salary range of placements:** $30,000 - $50,000. **Number of placements per year:** 100 - 199.

TOBY CLARK ASSOCIATES, INC.
405 East 54th Street, Suite 6C, New York NY 10022-5123. 212/752-5670. **Contact:** Mrs. Toby Clark, President. **Description:** An executive search firm. Company pays fee. **Specializes in the areas of:** Communications; Marketing; Public Relations. **Positions commonly filled include:** Advertising Account Executive; Marketing Manager; Public Relations Manager. **Average salary range of placements:** More than $50,000.

COLTON PARTNERSHIP
63 Wall Street, Suite 2901, New York NY 10005. 212/248-9700. **Fax:** 212/509-1633. **Contact:** Scott Colton, President. **E-mail address:** citi63i@aol.com. **World Wide Web address:** http://www.colt.nexel.com. **Description:** A retainer search firm. Company pays fee. **Specializes in the areas of:** Computer Science/Software; Engineering; General Management; Insurance; Investment; Manufacturing; Personnel/Labor Relations; Technical. **Positions commonly filled include:** Bank Officer/Manager; Computer Programmer; Design Engineer; Designer; Electrical/Electronics Engineer; Financial Analyst; Human Resources Manager; Internet Services Manager; Management Analyst/Consultant; MIS Specialist; Multimedia Designer; Quality Control Supervisor; Science Technologist; Securities Sales Rep.; Software

Engineer. **Other U.S. locations:** Nationwide. **Number of placements per year:** 1 - 49.

COLUMBIA CONSULTING GROUP
230 Park Avenue, Suite 456, New York NY 10169. 212/983-2525. **Contact:** Manager. **Description:** A generalist executive search firm.

COMPASS SEARCH
P.O. Box 734, Schenectady NY 12301-0734. 518/383-1600. **Contact:** Manager. **Description:** An executive recruiting firm. **Specializes in the areas of:** Construction. **Positions commonly filled include:** Controller; Estimator; President; Project Manager; Supervisor; Vice President.

COMPU-TECH PERSONNEL AGENCY
775 Park Avenue, Suite 118, Huntington NY 11743. 516/673-6944. **Contact:** Freda Frankel, President. **Description:** An executive search firm operating on a contingency basis. **Specializes in the areas of:** Accounting/Auditing; Administration; Computer Science/Software; Finance. **Positions commonly filled include:** Accountant/Auditor; Budget Analyst; Computer Programmer; Credit Manager; Financial Analyst; Systems Analyst. **Average salary range of placements:** $30,000 - $50,000. **Number of placements per year:** 50 - 99.

COMPUTECH CAREER SEARCH
P.O. Box 642, Mount Vision NY 13810. 607/433-5272. **Contact:** Manager. **Description:** An executive search firm. **Specializes in the areas of:** Business Services; Engineering; Information Technology.

COMPUTER PEOPLE
1231 Delaware Avenue, Buffalo NY 14209. 716/883-0771. **Contact:** Manager. **Description:** An executive search firm. **Specializes in the areas of:** Computer Programming; Computer Science/Software.

COMPUTER PLACEMENTS UNLIMITED, INC.
102 Palo Alto Drive, Plainview NY 11803. 516/933-7707. **Contact:** Manager. **Description:** An executive search firm. **Specializes in the areas of:** Computer Science/Software; Data Processing; Information Technology.

COMPUTER RESOURCES CORPORATION
25 West 43rd Street, Suite 1502, New York NY 10036. 212/575-0817. **Contact:** Manager. **Description:** An executive search firm. **Specializes in the areas of:** Computer Science/Software; Information Systems; Information Technology.

CONFIDENTIAL SEARCH INC.
226 East 68th Street, New York NY 10021-6001. 212/734-0584. **Fax:** 212/734-0584. **Contact:** Melvin Cantor, Owner. **Description:** An executive search firm operating on a contingency basis. **Specializes in the areas of:** Accounting/Auditing; Banking; Finance. **Positions commonly filled include:** Accountant/Auditor; Bank Officer/Manager; Branch Manager; Brokerage Clerk; Financial Analyst; Market Research Analyst; Securities Sales Representative. **Average salary range of placements:** More than $50,000. **Number of placements per year:** 1 - 49.

CONSORTIUM
1156 Avenue of the Americas, 4th Floor, New York NY 10036. 212/221-1544. **Contact:** Alexander C. Valcic, Recruiter. **Description:** An executive search and contract services firm. **Specializes in the areas of:** Accounting/Auditing; Administration; Banking; Computer Hardware/Software; Engineering; Finance; Health/Medical; Legal; Personnel/Labor Relations; Technical. **Positions commonly filled include:** Accountant/Auditor; Aerospace Engineer; Aircraft Mechanic/Engine Specialist; Attorney; Bank Officer/Manager; Chemical Engineer; Computer Programmer; Design Engineer; Designer; Electrical/Electronics Engineer; Emergency Medical Technician; Financial Analyst; Health Services Manager; Human Resources Manager; Human Service Worker; Management Analyst/Consultant; MIS Specialist; Multimedia Designer; Occupational Therapist; Physical Therapist; Physician; Registered Nurse; Respiratory Therapist; Securities Sales Rep.; Software Engineer; Speech-Language Pathologist; Systems Analyst; Technical Writer/Editor; Telecommunications Manager. **Other U.S. locations:** Nationwide. **Average salary range of placements:** More than $50,000. **Number of placements per year:** 100 - 199.

CONSPECTUS INC.
222 Purchase Street, Rye NY 10580-2101. 914/698-8300. **Contact:** Eric Stieglitz, Managing Director. **Description:** An executive search firm operating on both retainer and contingency bases. Company pays fee. **Specializes in the areas of:** Banking; Finance. **Positions commonly filled include:** Economist; Financial Analyst; Securities Sales Rep. **Average salary range of placements:** More than $50,000.

CONSULTING PARTNERS OF AMERICA
2255 Glades Road, Suite 324A, Melville NY 11747-4402. 516/293-3555. **Fax:** 516/420-1979. **Contact:** Jack Wishna, CPC, President. **Description:** An executive search firm operating on both retained and contingency bases. Consulting Partners of America also provides consulting services for mergers and acquisitions and strategic growth programs for the public accounting community. Company pays fee. **Specializes in the areas of:** Accounting/Auditing. **Positions commonly filled include:** Auditor; Budget Analyst. **Corporate headquarters location:** Boca Raton FL. **Other area locations:** New York NY. **Average salary range of placements:** More than $50,000. **Number of placements per year:** 500 - 999.

THE CORNELL GROUP
68 North Plank Road, Suite 202, Newburgh NY 12550. 914/565-8905. **Fax:** 914/565-5688. **Contact:** Alan Guarino, President. **Description:** An executive search firm. Company pays fee. **Specializes in the areas of:** Accounting/Auditing; Banking; Finance. **Positions commonly filled include:** Bank Officer/Manager; Financial Analyst; Securities Sales Rep. **Number of placements per year:** 50 - 99.

CORPORATE CAREERS, INC./R.J. ASSOCIATES
188 East Post Road, White Plains NY 10601. 914/946-2003. **Fax:** 914/946-2019. **Contact:** Richard Birnbaum, President. **E-mail address:** rjassociates@msn.com. **Description:** An executive search firm. Company pays fee. **Specializes in the areas of:** Accounting/Auditing; Computer Science/Software; Economics; Engineering; Finance; Food Industry; General Management; Industrial; Manufacturing; Personnel/Labor Relations; Publishing; Sales; Technical. **Positions commonly filled include:** Accountant/Auditor; Biochemist; Biological Scientist; Biomedical Engineer; Budget Analyst; Chemical Engineer; Chemist; Civil Engineer; Clinical Lab Technician; Computer Programmer; Credit Manager; Customer Service Rep.; Design Engineer; Designer; Draftsperson; Electrical/Electronics Engineer; Environmental Engineer; Financial Analyst; Food Scientist/Technologist; Human Resources Specialist; Industrial Engineer; Industrial Production Manager; Management Analyst/Consultant; Market Research Analyst; Mechanical Engineer; MIS Specialist; Multimedia Designer; Operations Manager; Public Relations Specialist; Purchasing Agent/Manager; Quality Control Supervisor; Software Engineer; Strategic Relations Manager; Structural Engineer;

Systems Analyst; Telecommunications Manager; Transportation/Traffic Specialist; Typist/Word Processor. **Benefits available to temporary workers:** 401(k); Paid Holidays; Paid Vacation. **Average salary range of placements:** More than $50,000. **Number of placements per year:** 200 - 499.

CORPORATE MOVES, INC.
P.O. Box 1638, Williamsville NY 14231-1638. 716/633-0234. **Fax:** 716/626-9147. **Contact:** Office Manager. **E-mail address:** corpmoves@aol.com. **Description:** An executive search firm. Company pays fee. **Specializes in the areas of:** Health/Medical; Industrial; Marketing; Sales. **Positions commonly filled include:** Account Manager; Account Rep.; Management Analyst/Consultant; Manufacturer's/Wholesaler's Sales Rep.; Marketing Manager; Marketing Specialist; Product Manager; Sales and Marketing Manager; Sales Engineer; Sales Executive; Sales Manager; Sales Rep.; Services Sales Rep.; Vice President of Marketing and Sales. **Average salary range of placements:** More than $50,000. **Number of placements per year:** 50 - 99.

CORPORATE SEARCH INC.
6800 Jericho Turnpike, Suite 203W, Syosett NY 11791-4401. 516/496-3200. **Fax:** 516/496-3165. **Contact:** Claire Zukerman, President. **E-mail address:** clairez@corporatesearch.com. **World Wide Web address:** http://www.corporatesearch.com. **Description:** A contingency search firm. Company pays fee. **Specializes in the areas of:** Accounting/Auditing; Finance; Manufacturing; Personnel/Labor Relations; Sales; Secretarial; Tax. **Positions commonly filled include:** Accountant/Auditor; Administrative Manager; Budget Analyst; Buyer; Credit Manager; Customer Service Rep.; Financial Analyst; Human Resources Specialist; Management Trainee; Paralegal; Purchasing Agent/Manager; Services Sales Rep.; Transportation/Traffic Specialist; Typist/Word Processor. **Number of placements per year:** 100 - 199.

COWIN ASSOCIATES
One Old Country Road, Carle Place NY 11514-1801. 516/741-3020. **Fax:** 516/741-4953. **Contact:** David M. Cowin, President. **E-mail address:** cowinone@aol.com. **Description:** An executive search firm operating on both retained and contingency bases that focuses on the placement of high-level professionals in the aerospace and related high-technology industries. Company pays fee. **Specializes in the areas of:** Aerospace; Engineering. **Positions commonly filled include:** Aerospace Engineer; Design Engineer; Electrical/Electronics Engineer; Mechanical Engineer; MIS Specialist; Systems Analyst; Telecommunications Manager. **Average salary range of placements:** More than $50,000. **Number of placements per year:** 50 - 99.

CRISPI, WAGNER & COMPANY, INC.
420 Lexington Avenue, Suite 400, New York NY 10170. 212/687-2340. **Contact:** Nicholas Crispi, President. **Description:** An executive search firm. **Specializes in the areas of:** Finance. **Number of placements per year:** 1 - 49.

CROMWELL PARTNERS INC.
441 Lexington Avenue, New York NY 10017. 212/953-3220. **Contact:** Manager. **Description:** An executive search firm. **Specializes in the areas of:** Finance.

FRANK CUOMO & ASSOCIATES INC.
111 Brook Street, Scarsdale NY 10583. 914/723-8001. **Contact:** Frank Cuomo, President. **Description:** An executive search firm that focuses on placement in sales, marketing, engineering, manufacturing, and management professions. The firm operates on both contingency and retainer bases. Company pays fee. **Specializes in the areas of:** Engineering; General Management; Industrial; Manufacturing; Sales. **Positions commonly filled include:** Chemical Engineer; Chemist; Civil Engineer; Construction Contractor; Cost Estimator; Design Engineer; Electrical/Electronics Engineer; Environmental Engineer; General Manager; Industrial Engineer; Industrial Production Manager; Manufacturer's/Wholesaler's Sales Rep.; Market Research Analyst; Mechanical Engineer; Metallurgical Engineer; Petroleum Engineer; Product Manager; Services Sales Rep.; Structural Engineer. **Average salary range of placements:** More than $50,000.

D&L ASSOCIATES, INC.
505 5th Avenue, Suite 302, New York NY 10017. 212/687-7111. **Fax:** 212/687-0541. **Contact:** David Werner, CEO. **E-mail address:** dlinc@msn.com. **Description:** An executive search firm focusing on the information systems field and all areas of accounting and finance. D&L Associates' clients consist primarily of *Fortune* 500 companies. The firm operates on a contingency basis. Founded in 1993. Company pays fee. **Specializes in the areas of:** Accounting/Auditing; Administration; Computer Science/Software; Finance. **Positions commonly filled include:** Accountant/Auditor; Bank Officer/Manager; Branch Manager; Brokerage Clerk; Budget Analyst; Computer Programmer; Credit Manager; Financial Analyst; Management Analyst/Consultant; MIS Specialist; Software Engineer; Systems Analyst. **Average salary range of placements:** More than $50,000. **Number of placements per year:** 500 - 999.

DAPEXS CONSULTANTS INC.
5320 West Genesee Street, Camillus NY 13031-2203. 315/484-9300. **Fax:** 315/484-9330. **Contact:** Peter J. Leofsky, President. **E-mail address:** dapexs@servtech.com. **World Wide Web address:** http://www.servtech.com/public/dapexs. **Description:** An executive search firm that focuses on the placement of computer professionals and accounting/financial executives. Dapexs Consultants Inc. operates on both retainer and contingency bases. Company pays fee. **Specializes in the areas of:** Administration; Computer Science/Software. **Positions commonly filled include:** Computer Programmer; Internet Services Manager; Management Analyst/Consultant; MIS Specialist; Software Engineer; Systems Analyst; Technical Writer/Editor; Telecommunications Manager.

THE DARTMOUTH GROUP
1200 Broadway, Suite 7D, New York NY 10001. 212/689-2713. **Fax:** 212/532-6519. **Contact:** Paul D. Storfer, Senior Associate. **Description:** A retained search firm focusing on the cosmetic, pharmaceutical, and packaging industries in upper-middle and middle management. **Specializes in the areas of:** Engineering; Manufacturing; Sales; Technical. **Positions commonly filled include:** General Manager; Manufacturer's/Wholesaler's Sales Rep.; Quality Control Supervisor.

DATACOM PLACEMENTS INC.
309 Syosset Woodbury Road, Woodbury NY 11797. 516/496-9893. **Contact:** Manager. **Description:** An executive search firm. **Specializes in the areas of:** Computer Programming.

DATAMARK ASSOCIATES INC.
145 West 45th Street, New York NY 10036. 212/354-7800. **Contact:** Manager. **Description:** An executive search firm. **Specializes in the areas of:** Data Processing.

BERT DAVIS EXECUTIVE SEARCH
425 Madison Avenue, Suite 14A, New York NY 10017. 212/838-4000. **Contact:** Office Manager.

Description: An executive search firm. **Specializes in the areas of:** Publishing.

CAROLYN DAVIS ASSOCIATES INC.
701 Westchester Avenue, White Plains NY 10604. 914/682-7040. **Fax:** 914/682-8361. **Contact:** Carolyn Davis, President. **Description:** An executive search firm. Company pays fee. **Specializes in the areas of:** Insurance. **Positions commonly filled include:** Actuary; Claim Representative; Insurance Agent/Broker; Underwriter/Assistant Underwriter. **Number of placements per year:** 1 - 49.

DENISON GROUP
122 East 42nd Street, 46th Floor, New York NY 10168. 212/949-6594. **Contact:** Office Manager. **Description:** An executive search firm.

THE DEVELOPMENT RESOURCE GROUP
104 East 40th Street, Suite 304, New York NY 10016. 212/983-1600. **Fax:** 212/983-1687. **Contact:** David Cheng, Associate. **Description:** An executive search and consulting firm that works exclusively with nonprofit organizations. **Specializes in the areas of:** Nonprofit. **Positions commonly filled include:** Chief Executive Officer; Director of Development; President. **Other U.S. locations:** Washington DC. **Average salary range of placements:** More than $50,000. **Number of placements per year:** 50 - 99.

SETH DIAMOND ASSOCIATES INC.
45 West 45th Street, Suite 801, New York NY 10036. 212/944-6190. **Fax:** 212/944-6197. **Contact:** Seth Diamond, CPC, President. **E-mail address:** sdiam85572@aol.com. **Description:** An executive search firm. Company pays fee. **Specializes in the areas of:** Accounting/Auditing; Administration; Advertising; Architecture/Construction; Banking; Computer Science/Software; Fashion; Finance; General Management; Health/Medical; Legal; Manufacturing; Marketing; MIS/EDP; Personnel/Labor Relations; Publishing; Retail; Sales; Secretarial. **Positions commonly filled include:** Accountant/ Auditor; Administrative Assistant; Administrative Manager; Advertising Account Executive; Advertising Clerk; Bank Officer/Manager; Budget Analyst; Buyer; Chief Financial Officer; Clerical Supervisor; Computer Animator; Computer Programmer; Controller; Credit Manager; Customer Service Rep.; Economist; Editor; Editorial Assistant; Finance Director; Financial Analyst; Human Resources Manager; Internet Services Manager; Market Research Analyst; Marketing Manager; Marketing Specialist; Online Content Specialist; Paralegal; Sales Executive; Sales Manager; Sales Rep.; Software Engineer; Statistician; Systems Analyst; Systems Manager; Technical Writer/Editor; Telecommunications Manager; Typist/Word Processor. **Average salary range of placements:** $30,000 - $50,000. **Number of placements per year:** 200 - 499.

DIXON HEALTHCARE EMPLOYMENT
2807 Church Avenue, Brooklyn NY 11226. 718/941-3222. **Contact:** Manager. **Description:** An executive search firm for health care professionals. **Specializes in the areas of:** Health/Medical.

DONAHUE & MOORE ASSOCIATES LTD.
295 Madison Avenue, New York NY 10017. 212/683-8255. **Contact:** Manager. **Description:** An executive search firm. **Specializes in the areas of:** Data Processing.

DRUMMOND ASSOCIATES, INC.
50 Broadway, Suite 1201, New York NY 10004. 212/248-1120. **Contact:** Chester Fienberg, President. **Description:** An executive search firm. **Specializes in the areas of:** Banking; Finance. **Number of placements per year:** 1 - 49.

DURHAM MEDICAL STAFFING
P.O. Box 478, Depew NY 14043. 716/681-7402. **Fax:** 716/681-7408. **Contact:** Manager. **Description:** An executive search firm that places physicians and nurse practitioners. **Specializes in the areas of:** Health/Medical.

DYMANEX SEARCH INC.
P.O. Drawer 800, Hamburg NY 14075. 716/648-7800. **Contact:** Manager. **Description:** An executive search firm. **Specializes in the areas of:** Engineering; Manufacturing; Technical.

ETC SEARCH, INC.
226 East 54th Street, Suite 308, New York NY 10022. 212/371-3880. **Fax:** 212/754-4877. **Contact:** Marlene Eskenazie, Managing Director. **Description:** An executive search firm. Company pays fee. **Specializes in the areas of:** Administration; Computer Science/Software; Information Technology. **Positions commonly filled include:** Computer Programmer; Database Manager; Network Engineer; Software Engineer; Systems Analyst. **Number of placements per year:** 50 - 99.

KRIS EDWARDS AGENCY INC.
405 Lexington Avenue, New York NY 10174-0002. 212/986-9400. **Fax:** 212/986-6868. **Contact:** Ms. Kris Edwards, President. **Description:** An executive search firm operating on a contingency basis. Clients include various *Fortune* 500 companies. Company pays fee. **Specializes in the areas of:** Advertising; Art/Design; Publishing. **Positions commonly filled include:** Designer; Graphic Designer; Multimedia Designer. **Number of placements per year:** 200 - 499.

EFCO CONSULTANTS, INC.
P.O. Box 1486, Quogue NY 11959. 516/829-9200. **Fax:** 516/466-4509. **Contact:** Norman Fells, President. **Description:** An executive search firm that focuses on MIS sales, marketing, and management placements. Efco Consultants operates on both retainer and contingency bases. Company pays fee. **Specializes in the areas of:** Computer Science/Software; Sales. **Positions commonly filled include:** Management Analyst/Consultant; MIS Specialist; Software Engineer; Systems Analyst. **Average salary range of placements:** More than $50,000. **Number of placements per year:** 50 - 99.

ELLIOT ASSOCIATES INC.
104 South Broadway, Tarrytown NY 10591. 914/631-4904. **Fax:** 914/631-6481. **Contact:** Bernadette Madden, Vice President of Administration. **Description:** An executive search firm operating on a retainer basis. Company pays fee. **Specializes in the areas of:** Food Industry; General Management; Retail. **Positions commonly filled include:** Food Scientist/ Technologist; Hotel Manager; Human Resources Specialist. **Other U.S. locations:** Nationwide. **Average salary range of placements:** More than $50,000. **Number of placements per year:** 200 - 499.

DAVID M. ELLNER ASSOCIATES
Two Penn Plaza, New York NY 10121. 212/279-0665. **Fax:** 516/883-7494. **Contact:** David Ellner, CEO. **Description:** An executive search firm. Company pays fee. **Specializes in the areas of:** Computer Science/Software. **Positions commonly filled include:** Computer Programmer; Electrical/Electronics Engineer; Systems Analyst. **Average salary range of placements:** More than $50,000.

THE EMPLOYMENT STORE/TES TECHNICAL
333 Andrews Street, Rochester NY 14604. 716/232-5402. **Fax:** 716/232-2147. **Contact:** Brian Klingenberger, Technical Recruiter. **E-mail address:** inquiry @employmentstore.com. **World Wide Web address:**

http://www.employmentstore.com. **Description:** An executive search firm that also provides temporary and contract placements. TES Technical focuses on the placement of technical professionals nationwide. Company pays fee. **Specializes in the areas of:** Computer Science/Software; Engineering; Finance; General Management; Health/Medical; Marketing; Sales; Scientific; Secretarial; Technical. **Positions commonly filled include:** Aerospace Engineer; Biomedical Engineer; Ceramics Engineer; Chemical Engineer; Civil Engineer; Clerical Supervisor; Computer Programmer; Credit Manager; Customer Service Rep.; Design Engineer; Draftsperson; Electrical/Electronics Engineer; Environmental Engineer; Industrial Engineer; Industrial Production Manager; Internet Services Manager; Mechanical Engineer; Medical Records Technician; MIS Specialist; Paralegal; Quality Control Supervisor; Services Sales Rep.; Software Engineer; Structural Engineer; Systems Analyst; Technical Writer/Editor; Typist/Word Processor. **Benefits available to temporary workers:** Paid Holidays; Paid Vacation. **Average salary range of placements:** $30,000 - $50,000. **Number of placements per year:** 50 - 99.

EQUATE EXECUTIVE SEARCH
12 West 37th Street, 7th Floor, New York NY 10018. 212/736-0606. **Contact:** Manager. **Description:** An executive search firm. **Specializes in the areas of:** Computer Science/Software.

ERIC ROBERT ASSOCIATES
350 7th Avenue, New York NY 10001-5013. 212/695-5900. **Fax:** 212/695-5809. **Contact:** Eric Silverman, President. **E-mail address:** ericrob@nyc.pipeline.com. **Description:** An executive search firm that provides placements in all areas of information technology. Clients include *Fortune* 1000 companies. Company pays fee. **Specializes in the areas of:** Computer Science/Software. **Positions commonly filled include:** Computer Programmer; Internet Services Manager; MIS Specialist; Technical Writer/Editor; Telecommunications Manager. **Average salary range of placements:** More than $50,000. **Number of placements per year:** 100 - 199.

ETHAN ALLEN MEDICAL SEARCH
404 Troy Schenectady Road, Latham NY 12110-3217. 518/785-7555. **Fax:** 518/785-8034. **Contact:** M. James Roarke, President. **Description:** An executive search firm that operates on both contingency and retainer bases. Company pays fee. **Specializes in the areas of:** Health/Medical. **Positions commonly filled include:** Occupational Therapist; Physical Therapist; Speech-Language Pathologist. **Average salary range of placements:** $30,000 - $50,000. **Number of placements per year:** 50 - 99.

EXECU-SEARCH GROUP
675 Third Avenue, New York NY 10017. 212/922-1001. **Fax:** 212/922-0033. **Contact:** Manager. **Description:** An executive search firm specializing in accounting, auditing, and finance job placements.

EXECUTIVE & TECHNICAL RECRUITERS, INC.
180 Oser Avenue, Suite 0400, Hauppauge NY 11788. 516/952-1300. **Fax:** 516/952-1248. **Contact:** Manager. **Description:** An executive search firm focusing on the placement of high-end, technical computer professionals. **Specializes in the areas of:** Computer Programming; Computer Science/Software. **Positions commonly filled include:** Computer Programmer; Systems Analyst.

EXECUTIVE CONNECTIONS, INC.
575 North Street, White Plains NY 10605. 914/949-1923. **Toll-free phone:** 800/969-3932. **Fax:** 914/949-5324. **Contact:** Bob Friscia, President. **Description:** An executive search firm. **Positions commonly filled include:** Account Manager; Applications Engineer; Chemist; Marketing Manager; Marketing Specialist; Operations Manager; Sales Engineer; Sales Executive; Sales Manager.

EXECUTIVE DIRECTIONS INC.
2 Penn Plaza, Suite 1185, New York NY 10121-1185. 212/594-5775. **Fax:** 212/594-4183. **Contact:** Gus Oakes, CPC, President. **Description:** An executive search firm. **Specializes in the areas of:** Administration; Computer Science/Software. **Positions commonly filled include:** Computer Programmer; Management Analyst/Consultant; Systems Analyst. **Number of placements per year:** 100 - 199.

EXECUTIVE EXCHANGE
450 7th Avenue, Room 955, New York NY 10123. 212/736-2350. **Contact:** Manager. **Description:** An executive search firm. **Specializes in the areas of:** Telecommunications.

EXECUTIVE IMAGE
330 Third Avenue, Suite 11G, New York NY 10010. 212/532-8565. **Contact:** Manager. **Description:** An executive search firm. **Specializes in the areas of:** Accounting/Auditing; Finance.

EXECUTIVE LINK
15 Penn Plaza, OF-2, New York NY 10001. 212/760-0176. **Contact:** Manager. **Description:** An executive search firm. **Specializes in the areas of:** Hotel/Restaurant.

EXECUTIVE PLACEMENT CORPORATION
1172 Sibley Tower, Rochester NY 14604. 716/454-1424. **Contact:** Manager. **Description:** An executive search firm.

EXECUTIVE RESOURCES LTD.
200 East 66th Street, New York NY 10021. 212/593-2819. **Contact:** Manager. **Description:** An executive search firm. **Specializes in the areas of:** Banking; Finance. **Positions commonly filled include:** Branch Manager; Broker; Financial Analyst.

EXECUTIVE SEARCH ASSOCIATES
300 Hempstead Turnpike, West Hempstead NY 11552. 516/292-9700. **Contact:** Manager. **Description:** An executive search firm. **Specializes in the areas of:** Information Technology.

EXECUTIVE SEARCH CONSULTANTS
350 Fifth Avenue, Suite 5501, New York NY 10118. 212/330-1900. **Contact:** Manager. **Description:** An executive search firm. **Specializes in the areas of:** Consumer Sales/Marketing; Direct Marketing; Finance.

EXECUTIVE SEARCH GROUP INC.
116 West 32nd Street, New York NY 10011. 212/594-1448. **Contact:** Manager. **Description:** An executive search firm.
Other area locations:
- 3811 Saries Court, Seaford NY 11783.

EXECUTIVE SEARCH INC.
48 Headquarters Plaza, Marstown NY 07960. 212/604-0700. **Contact:** Manager. **Description:** An executive search firm that also provides temporary placements.

EXECUTIVE SYSTEMS
1 Ten Plaza, New York NY 10119. 212/967-0505. **Contact:** Manager. **Description:** An executive search firm.

EXEK RECRUITERS LTD.
35 Flatt Road, Rochester NY 14623. 716/292-0550. **Contact:** Manager. **Description:** An executive search firm. **Specializes in the areas of:** Engineering.

FABIAN ASSOCIATES, INC.
521 Fifth Avenue, Suite 1700, New York NY 10175. 212/697-9460. **Fax:** 212/697-9488. **Contact:** Jeanne Fabian, President. **Description:** An executive search firm. **Specializes in the areas of:** Accounting/Auditing; Administration; Banking; Finance; Food Industry; Health/Medical; Manufacturing. **Positions commonly filled include:** Accountant/Auditor; EDP Specialist; MIS Specialist. **Number of placements per year:** 1 - 49.

FAIRFIELD INTERNATIONAL RESOURCES
Trump Tower, 725 Fifth Avenue, New York NY 10022-2519. 212/838-0220. **Fax:** 212/838-3456. **Contact:** Fashion Director. **World Wide Web address:** http://www.fairfieldinternational.com. **Description:** A retained executive search firm that fills positions exclusively in retail, apparel manufacturing, and cosmetics. **Specializes in the areas of:** Apparel; Retail. **Positions commonly filled include:** Associate Buyer; Buyer; Designer; Merchandiser; Production Manager; Public Relations Specialist.

FANNING PERSONNEL
507 Fifth Avenue, Suite 800, New York NY 10017-4906. 212/867-1725. **Fax:** 212/867-1338. **Contact:** Dave Cowen, President. **E-mail address:** resume@fanning.com. **World Wide Web address:** http://www.fanning.com. **Description:** A contingency search firm. Company pays fee. **Specializes in the areas of:** Administration; Banking; Broadcasting; Computer Science/Software; Entertainment; Fashion; Finance; Personnel/Labor Relations; Secretarial. **Positions commonly filled include:** Computer Programmer; Human Resources Specialist; Internet Services Manager; MIS Specialist; Systems Analyst; Typist/Word Processor. **Average salary range of placements:** $30,000 - $50,000. **Number of placements per year:** 100 - 199.

FEDERAL PLACEMENT SERVICES
35 Park Avenue, Suite 6M, Suffern NY 10901. 914/357-4577. **Fax:** 914/357-5945. **Contact:** Joan Bialkin, President. **E-mail address:** fepl@aol.com. **Description:** An executive search firm operating on a contingency basis. Company pays fee. **Specializes in the areas of:** Banking. **Positions commonly filled include:** Accountant/Auditor; Bank Officer/Manager; Branch Manager; Budget Analyst; Credit Manager; Financial Analyst; Human Resources Specialist; Property and Real Estate Manager. **Average salary range of placements:** More than $50,000. **Number of placements per year:** 1 - 49.

C.R. FLETCHER ASSOCIATES
108 East Washington Street, Syracuse NY 13202-1618. 315/471-1000. **Fax:** 315/471-6500. **Contact:** Carol R. Fletcher, President. **Description:** A nationwide executive search firm that operates on both retainer and contingency bases. **Specializes in the areas of:** Accounting/Auditing; Administration; Finance; Personnel/Labor Relations; Sales. **Positions commonly filled include:** Accountant/Auditor; Budget Analyst; Computer Programmer; Financial Analyst; Human Resources Manager; Manufacturer's/Wholesaler's Sales Rep.; MIS Specialist; Pharmacist; Physical Therapist; Recreational Therapist; Services Sales Rep.; Systems Analyst; Telecommunications Manager. **Average salary range of placements:** More than $50,000. **Number of placements per year:** 50 - 99.

FOCUS AND FOCUS CAPITAL MARKETS
71 Vanderbilt Avenue, Suite 200, New York NY 10017. 212/986-3344. **Fax:** 212/986-3370. **Contact:** Scott Gerson, President. **E-mail address:** scott3@juno.com. **World Wide Web address:** http://www.focuscapital.com. **Description:** An executive search firm that provides investment placements including derivative trading and trading technology positions. Company pays fee. **Specializes in the areas of:** Computer Science/Software. **Positions commonly filled include:** Computer Programmer; Data Entry Clerk; Database Manager; Economist; EDP Specialist; Management Analyst/Consultant; MIS Specialist; Multimedia Designer; Software Engineer; Systems Analyst; Systems Manager. **Average salary range of placements:** More than $50,000. **Number of placements per year:** 100 - 199.

FOLEY PROCTOR YOSKOWITZ
24 East 39th Street, New York NY 10016. 212/928-1110. **Contact:** Manager. **Description:** An executive search firm. **Specializes in the areas of:** Health/Medical; Physician Executive. **Other U.S. locations:** Morristown NJ.

FORRAY ASSOCIATES, INC.
950 3rd Avenue, New York NY 10022. 212/279-0404. **Contact:** Manager. **Description:** An executive search firm. **Specializes in the areas of:** Finance; Marketing; Sales.

F-O-R-T-U-N-E PERSONNEL CONSULTANTS
1155 Avenue of the Americas, 15th Floor, New York NY 10036. **Toll-free phone:** 800/886-7839. **Fax:** 212/302-2422. **Contact:** Manager. **Description:** This location houses administrative offices only. Overall, F-O-R-T-U-N-E Personnel Consultants is an executive search firm. **Corporate headquarters location:** This Location.
Other area locations:

- 505 Fifth Avenue, Suite 1100, New York NY 10017. 212/557-1000. (Administration; Biotechnology; Consumer Products; Engineering; Logistics; Materials; Pharmaceutical; Purchasing; Quality Assurance)

F-O-R-T-U-N-E PERSONNEL CONSULTANTS OF ROCKLAND COUNTY, INC.
71 East Eckerson Road, Suite A, Spring Valley NY 10977-3014. 914/426-3200. **Fax:** 914/426-3814. **Contact:** Mark Axelrod, President. **E-mail address:** fpcrock@frontiernet.net. **Description:** A middle-management and executive-level search firm. Company pays fee. **Specializes in the areas of:** Engineering; Manufacturing. **Positions commonly filled include:** Manufacturing Manager; Mechanical Engineer; Metallurgical Engineer; Quality Assurance Engineer; Quality Control Supervisor. **Other U.S. locations:** Nationwide. **Average salary range of placements:** More than $50,000. **Number of placements per year:** 1 - 49.

FRANKLIN SEARCH RESOURCES, INC.
225 West 34th Street, Suite 806, New York NY 10122. 212/465-0600. **Fax:** 212/268-0336. **Contact:** Peter Franklin, CPC, President. **E-mail address:** franklin-search@erols.com. **Description:** An executive search firm operating on both retainer and contingency bases. Company pays fee. **Specializes in the areas of:** Accounting/Auditing; Finance. **Positions commonly filled include:** Accountant/Auditor; Controller; Finance Director; Financial Analyst. **Average salary range of placements:** More than $50,000. **Number of placements per year:** 50 - 99.

FRONTRUNNER SEARCH, LTD.
P.O. Box 349, Baldwin NY 11510-0349. 516/223-5627. **Fax:** 516/867-6681. **Contact:** Daniel J. Ahrens, President. **Description:** An executive search firm. **NOTE:** The company accepts applications from experienced banking personnel only. Company pays

fee. **Specializes in the areas of:** Banking; Mortgage. **Number of placements per year:** 50 - 99.

THE FRY GROUP INC.
369 Lexington Avenue, New York NY 10017. 212/557-0011. **Contact:** John Fry, President. **Description:** An executive search firm operating on both retainer and contingency bases that focuses on placing public relations and corporate communications personnel. Company pays fee. **Specializes in the areas of:** Advertising; Communications; Public Relations. **Positions commonly filled include:** Public Relations Specialist. **Other U.S. locations:** Nationwide. **Average salary range of placements:** More than $50,000. **Number of placements per year:** 50 - 99.

RONNIE GALE PERSONNEL CORPORATION
11821 Queens Boulevard, Flushing NY 11375. 718/261-1111. **Fax:** 718/261-9748. **Contact:** Gail Landres, President. **Description:** An executive search firm. **Specializes in the areas of:** Accounting/Auditing; Administration; Sales; Secretarial. **Positions commonly filled include:** Accountant/Auditor; Administrative Assistant; Administrative Manager; Advertising Clerk; Clerical Supervisor; Computer Programmer; Credit Manager; Customer Service Rep.; Secretary; Systems Analyst; Typist/Word Processor. **Average salary range of placements:** $25,000 - $60,000. **Number of placements per year:** 200 - 499.

GATEWAY SEARCH INC.
1120 Avenue of the Americas, 4th Floor, New York NY 10036. 212/626-6714. **Contact:** Manager. **Description:** An executive search firm that focuses on technical placements. **Specializes in the areas of:** Computer Hardware/Software.

GENESIS EMPLOYMENT CONSULTANTS
507 Fifth Avenue, 3rd Floor, New York NY 10017. 212/406-9500. **Fax:** 212/732-1348. **Contact:** Michael W. Huffman, President. **Description:** An executive search firm operating on a contingency basis. Company pays fee. **Specializes in the areas of:** Administration; Advertising; Banking; Broadcasting; Finance; Legal; Personnel/Labor Relations; Secretarial. **Positions commonly filled include:** Accountant/Auditor; Administrative Assistant; Advertising Clerk; Brokerage Clerk; Clerical Supervisor; Customer Service Rep.; Desktop Publishing Specialist; Library Technician; Paralegal; Secretary; Travel Agent; Typist/Word Processor. **Average salary range of placements:** $30,000 - $50,000. **Number of placements per year:** 500 - 999.

GILBERT & VAN CAMPEN INTERNATIONAL
420 Lexington Avenue, New York NY 10170. 212/661-2122. **Contact:** Manager. **Description:** An executive search firm that places high-level executives.

GLOBAL RECRUITING INC.
87 George Road, Old Chatham NY 12136. **Contact:** Manager. **Description:** An executive search firm offering placement services for positions with manufacturers, suppliers, and consultants in the chemical and paper industries.

THE GOLDMAN GROUP, INC.
40 East 34th Street, Suite 1105, New York NY 10016. 212/685-9311. **Fax:** 212/532-2740. **Contact:** Elaine Goldman, President. **Description:** An executive search firm operating on a retainer basis. **Specializes in the areas of:** Communications; Investor Relations; Public Affairs; Public Relations. **Positions commonly filled include:** Marketing Specialist; Public Relations Specialist. **Average salary range of placements:** More than $50,000.

GRUEN RESOURCES, INC.
323 Clocktower Commons, Brewster NY 10509. 914/279-8827. **Fax:** 914/279-8845. **Contact:** Connie Gruen, President. **E-mail address:** cmgruen@aol.com. **Description:** An executive search firm that recruits commercial real estate and financial services personnel. The firm operates on both retainer and contingency bases. **Specializes in the areas of:** Banking; Computer Science/Software; Finance. **Positions commonly filled include:** Financial Analyst; Management Analyst/Consultant; MIS Specialist; Property and Real Estate Manager. **Average salary range of placements:** More than $50,000. **Number of placements per year:** 1 - 49.

HBC GROUP
370 Lexington Avenue, Room 2200, New York NY 10017-6503. 212/661-8300. **Contact:** Norman Gershgorn, President. **Description:** An executive search firm that also offers contract services and career counseling. Company pays fee. **Specializes in the areas of:** Accounting/Auditing; Banking. **Positions commonly filled include:** Bank Officer/Manager; Financial Analyst; Financial Consultant; Financial Manager. **Average salary range of placements:** More than $50,000. **Number of placements per year:** 50 - 99.

THE HAAS ASSOCIATES, INC.
443 West 24th Street, New York NY 10011. 212/741-2457. **Contact:** Margaret Haas, President. **E-mail address:** mhaas@pipeline.com. **Description:** An executive search firm. Company pays fee. **Specializes in the areas of:** Banking; Computer Science/Software; Engineering; Finance; Industrial; Manufacturing. **Average salary range of placements:** More than $50,000. **Number of placements per year:** 1 - 49.

STEPHEN M. HAAS LEGAL INC.
60 East 42nd Street, Room 1501, New York NY 10165-1599. 212/661-5555. **Fax:** 212/972-1279. **Contact:** Marilyn Wallberg, President. **Description:** An executive search firm operating on a contingency basis. Company pays fee. **Specializes in the areas of:** Legal. **Positions commonly filled include:** Attorney. **Number of placements per year:** 1 - 49.

ROBERT HALF INTERNATIONAL/ACCOUNTEMPS
One Marine Midland Center, Suite 3560, Buffalo NY 14203. 716/833-5322. **Contact:** Manager. **Description:** An executive search firm. Accountemps (also at this location) provides temporary placements. **Corporate headquarters location:** Menlo Park CA. **Other U.S. locations:** Nationwide.

ROBERT HALF INTERNATIONAL INFORMATION SYSTEMS DIVISION
565 Fifth Avenue, 30th Floor, New York NY 10017. 212/290-2700. **Fax:** 212/290-8100. **Contact:** Director. **Description:** An executive search firm. Company pays fee. **Specializes in the areas of:** Accounting/Auditing; Administration; Advertising; Architecture/Construction; Banking; Broadcasting; Computer Science/Software; Engineering; Finance; General Management; Industrial; Insurance; Legal; Manufacturing; Nonprofit; Personnel/Labor Relations; Sales; Technical. **Positions commonly filled include:** Computer Programmer; Financial Analyst; Management; Science Technologist; Software Engineer; Statistician; Systems Analyst; Technical Writer/Editor. **Corporate headquarters location:** Menlo Park CA. **International locations:** Worldwide. **Number of placements per year:** 200 - 499.

THE HAMPTON GROUP
33 Flying Point Road, Suite 207, Southampton NY 11968. 516/287-3330. **Fax:** 516/287-5610. **Contact:** Belle Lareau, Partner. **Description:** An executive search firm that focuses on placing middle and senior

management professionals. Company pays fee. **Specializes in the areas of:** Biology; Biotechnology; Health/Medical; Pharmaceutical. **Positions commonly filled include:** Biological Scientist; Biomedical Engineer; Chemist; Pharmacist; Surgical Technician. **Other U.S. locations:** Nationwide. **Average salary range of placements:** More than $50,000. **Number of placements per year:** 1 - 49.

HART-MERRELL PERSONNEL
P.O. Box 92340, Rochester NY 14692. 716/359-3060. **Fax:** 716/359-2295. **Contact:** George W. Merrell, President. **E-mail address:** careers@hart-merrell.com. **Description:** An executive search firm. Founded in 1980. Company pays fee. **Specializes in the areas of:** Accounting/Auditing; Computer Science/Software; Engineering; Finance; Industrial; Manufacturing; Publishing; Sales; Secretarial; Technical. **Positions commonly filled include:** Accountant/Auditor; Biomedical Engineer; Blue-Collar Worker Supervisor; Buyer; Chemical Engineer; Computer Programmer; Construction and Building Inspector; Construction Contractor; Cost Estimator; Credit Manager; Design Engineer; Designer; Draftsperson; Electrical/Electronics Engineer; Electrician; Financial Analyst; Human Resources Specialist; Industrial Engineer; Industrial Production Manager; Manufacturer's/Wholesaler's Sales Rep.; Mechanical Engineer; MIS Specialist; Paralegal; Purchasing Agent/Manager; Quality Control Supervisor; Services Sales Rep.; Software Engineer; Stationary Engineer; Structural Engineer; Systems Analyst; Typist/Word Processor. **Average salary range of placements:** $30,000 - $50,000. **Number of placements per year:** 100 - 199.

HAWKES-PEERS & COMPANY, INC.
224 Fifth Avenue, 6th Floor, New York NY 10001. 212/593-3131. **Contact:** Ted King, President. **Description:** An executive search firm. **Specializes in the areas of:** Banking; Sales. **Number of placements per year:** 100 - 199.

HEALTHCARE RECRUITERS OF NEW YORK
445 Electronics Parkway, Building 2, Suite 208, Liverpool NY 13088. 315/453-4080. **Fax:** 315/453-9525. **Contact:** Dean McNitt, President. **Description:** An executive search firm. Company pays fee. **Specializes in the areas of:** Health/Medical. **Positions commonly filled include:** Biological Scientist; Biomedical Engineer; Chemical Engineer; Chemist; Clinical Lab Technician; Computer Programmer; Dental Assistant/Hygienist; Dentist; Dietician/Nutritionist; EKG Technician. **Corporate headquarters location:** Dallas TX. **Number of placements per year:** 100 - 199.

HEALTHSEARCH GROUP
109 Croton Avenue, Ossining NY 10562. 914/941-6107. **Fax:** 914/941-1748. **Contact:** Alan Gordon, President. **Description:** An executive search firm operating on both retainer and contingency bases. Company pays fee. **Specializes in the areas of:** Health/Medical; Nonprofit; Personnel/Labor Relations. **Positions commonly filled include:** Branch Manager; Clinical Lab Technician; Dietician/Nutritionist; EEG Technologist; EKG Technician; Food Scientist/Technologist; Health Services Manager; Human Resources Specialist; Medical Records Technician; Nuclear Medicine Technologist; Occupational Therapist; Pharmacist; Physical Therapist; Physician; Psychologist; Radiological Technologist; Recreational Therapist; Registered Nurse; Respiratory Therapist; Social Worker; Speech-Language Pathologist. **Other U.S. locations:** Nationwide. **Average salary range of placements:** More than $50,000. **Number of placements per year:** 500 - 999.

F.P. HEALY & COMPANY INC.
230 Park Avenue, Suite 232, New York NY 10169-0083. **Toll-free phone:** 800/374-3259. **Fax:** 212/661-0383. **Contact:** Frank P. Healy, President. **Description:** A retained executive search firm. Company pays fee. **Specializes in the areas of:** Administration; Banking; Computer Science/Software; Engineering; General Management; Manufacturing; Sales. **Positions commonly filled include:** Accountant/Auditor; Actuary; Aerospace Engineer; Electrical/Electronics Engineer; General Manager; Science Technologist; Software Engineer; Systems Analyst. **Average salary range of placements:** More than $50,000. **Number of placements per year:** 100 - 199.

HELLER INFORMATION SERVICES
2 West 45th Street, New York NY 10036. 212/819-1919. **Fax:** 212/819-9196. **Contact:** Charles Heller, President. **E-mail address:** cheller@msn.com. **World Wide Web address:** http://www.hellerandassociates.com. **Description:** An executive search firm. Company pays fee. **Specializes in the areas of:** Library Services. **Positions commonly filled include:** Librarian; Library Technician. **Number of placements per year:** 200 - 499.

STANLEY HERZ & CO.
Mill Pond Office Complex, Suite 103, Somers NY 10589. 914/277-7500. **Fax:** 914/277-7749. **Contact:** Stanley Herz, Principal. **World Wide Web address:** http://www.stanleyherz.com. **Description:** An executive search firm operating on a retainer basis. Company pays fee. **Specializes in the areas of:** General Management. **Average salary range of placements:** More than $50,000. **Number of placements per year:** 1 - 49.

HESSEL ASSOCIATES
420 Lexington Avenue, Suite 300, New York NY 10170-0399. 212/297-6105. **Fax:** 212/682-1029. **Contact:** Jeffrey Hessel, President. **Description:** An executive search firm operating on both retainer and contingency bases. **Specializes in the areas of:** Accounting/Auditing; Banking; Computer Science/Software; Consulting; Finance. **Average salary range of placements:** More than $50,000.

RUTH HIRSCH ASSOCIATES
400 Madison Avenue, Suite 1507, New York NY 10017. 212/396-0200. **Contact:** Office Manager. **Description:** An executive search firm. **Specializes in the areas of:** Advertising; Architecture/Construction; Art/Design; Engineering.

HORIZON EXECUTIVE SEARCH GROUP
2001 Marcus Avenue, Suite East 240, Lake Success NY 11042. 516/358-4141. **Fax:** 516/358-7133. **Contact:** Manager. **Description:** An executive search firm. **Specializes in the areas of:** Banking; Computer Science/Software.

HOSPITALITY ASSOCIATES
12 West 37th Street, New York NY 10018. 212/697-7855. **Contact:** P. Jason King, President. **Description:** An executive search firm. Company pays fee. **Specializes in the areas of:** Food Industry; Hotel/Restaurant; Personnel/Labor Relations. **Positions commonly filled include:** Hotel Manager; Sales Rep. **Number of placements per year:** 500 - 999.

HOSPITALITY INTERNATIONAL
P.O. Box 5008, Cortland NY 13045. 607/756-8550. **Fax:** 607/756-8620. **Contact:** Susan Stafford, Vice President. **Description:** An executive search firm. **Specializes in the areas of:** Hotel/Restaurant.

HOWARD-SLOAN-KOLLER GROUP
353 Lexington Avenue, New York NY 10023. 212/661-5250. **Contact:** Manager. **Description:** An

executive search firm. **Specializes in the areas of:** Publishing.

HOWE-LEWIS INTERNATIONAL
521 Fifth Avenue, 36th Floor, New York NY 10175-3699. 212/697-5000. **Contact:** Heather Altman, Director of Research. **Description:** An executive search firm that operates on a retainer basis. **Specializes in the areas of:** Health/Medical; Nonprofit. **Positions commonly filled include:** Education Administrator; Health Services Manager; Human Resources Manager; Physician. **Average salary range of placements:** More than $50,000. **Number of placements per year:** 1 - 49.

ARNOLD HUBERMAN ASSOCIATES, INC.
51 East 25th Street, Suite 501, New York NY 10010. 212/545-9033. **Contact:** Manager. **Description:** An executive search firm. **Specializes in the areas of:** Public Relations.

HUDSON SEARCH CONSULTANTS INC.
271 Madison Avenue, Suite 1103, New York NY 10016. 212/949-9111. **Contact:** Manager. **Description:** An executive search firm that provides placements in the finance industry.

HUNTER PLACEMENT INC.
656 Elmwood Avenue, Buffalo NY 14222. 716/884-9242. **Contact:** Gina Collora, President. **Description:** An executive search firm operating on a contingency basis. Company pays fee. **Specializes in the areas of:** Accounting/Auditing; Administration; Finance; Health/Medical; Legal; Personnel/Labor Relations; Secretarial. **Positions commonly filled include:** Accountant/Auditor; Administrative Manager; Attorney; Budget Analyst; Buyer; Claim Rep.; Clerical Supervisor; Construction Contractor; Credit Manager; Customer Service Rep.; Financial Analyst; Health Services Manager; Human Resources Manager; Licensed Practical Nurse; Medical Records Technician; Operations/Production Manager; Paralegal; Strategic Relations Manager; Typist/Word Processor. **Number of placements per year:** 100 - 199.

HUNTINGTON PERSONNEL CONSULTANTS, INC.
P.O. Box 1077, Huntington NY 11743-0640. 516/549-8888. **Fax:** 516/549-3012. **Contact:** Jeannette A. Henry, CPC, President. **E-mail address:** jahenry@i-2000.com. **Description:** An executive search firm. Company pays fee. **Specializes in the areas of:** Administration; Business Systems Analysis; Computer Operations; Computer Programming; Consulting; Data Communications; Data Security; Information Technology; Network Administration; Software Development; Software Documentation; Software Engineering; Software Quality Assurance; Software Training; Systems Administration; Systems Design; Systems Programming; Technical Writing; Telecommunications; Telephone Technical Support. **Positions commonly filled include:** Computer Programmer; Software Engineer; Systems Analyst; Technical Writer/Editor.

INFORMATION SYSTEMS SEARCH
747 Third Avenue, 31st Floor, New York NY 10017. 212/319-3700. **Contact:** Manager. **Description:** An executive search firm that focuses on the placement of PC and LAN support professionals. **Specializes in the areas of:** Computer Hardware/Software; Technical.

INTERNATIONAL MEDICAL PLACEMENT
100 Sylvan Parkway, Suite 200, Amherst NY 14228. 716/689-6000. **Contact:** Manager. **Description:** An executive search firm that places physicians. **Specializes in the areas of:** Health/Medical.

INTERSPACE INTERACTIVE INC.
50 East 42nd Street, Suite 2400, New York NY 10017. 212/867-6661. **Fax:** 212/867-6682. **Contact:** Bill Ellis, President. **Description:** An executive search firm. Company pays fee. **Specializes in the areas of:** Accounting/Auditing; Computer Science/Software; Engineering; Finance; General Management; Personnel/Labor Relations; Sales. **Positions commonly filled include:** Accountant/Auditor; Manufacturer's/Wholesaler's Sales Rep.; Marketing Specialist; Public Relations Specialist; Services Sales Rep.; Software Engineer; Systems Analyst. **Number of placements per year:** 100 - 199.

ANN ISRAEL & ASSOCIATES
730 5th Avenue, Suite 900, New York NY 10019. 212/333-8730. **Contact:** Manager. **Description:** An executive search firm. **Specializes in the areas of:** Legal.

IVANA LEGAL SERVICES, INC.
420 Lexington Avenue, Suite 2545, New York NY 10170. 212/286-9560. **Fax:** 212/490-2074. **Contact:** Jennifer Sirras, President. **Description:** An executive search firm. **Specializes in the areas of:** Finance; Legal; Personnel/Labor Relations. **Positions commonly filled include:** Paralegal; Typist/Word Processor. **Average salary range of placements:** $30,000 - $50,000. **Number of placements per year:** 1 - 49.

R.I. JAMES INC.
325 Riverside Drive, New York NY 10025-4156. 212/662-0203. **Fax:** 212/864-9602. **Contact:** Rhoda Isaacs, President. **Description:** An executive search firm operating on both retainer and contingency bases. Company pays fee. **Specializes in the areas of:** Logistics; Transportation. **Positions commonly filled include:** Industrial Engineer; Management Analyst/Consultant; Operations/Production Manager; Transportation/Traffic Specialist. **Average salary range of placements:** More than $50,000. **Number of placements per year:** 1 - 49.

JOSEPH ASSOCIATES INC.
229 Main Street, Huntington NY 11743-6955. 516/351-5805. **Fax:** 516/421-4123. **Contact:** Joe Nakelski, President. **E-mail address:** joeassoc@aol.com. **World Wide Web address:** http://www.josephassociates.com. **Description:** An executive search firm operating on both retainer and contingency bases. The firm also offers consulting services to client companies. **Specializes in the areas of:** Administration; Computer Hardware/Software. **Positions commonly filled include:** Computer Programmer; Database Manager; Economist; Human Resources Manager; Internet Services Manager; MIS Specialist; Software Engineer; Statistician; Systems Analyst; Systems Manager; Technical Writer/Editor; Telecommunications Manager; Webmaster. **Benefits available to temporary workers:** Disability Coverage; Medical Insurance; Workers Compensation Plan. **Corporate headquarters location:** This Location. **Other U.S. locations:** Nationwide. **Average salary range of placements:** More than $50,000. **Number of placements per year:** 50 - 99.

KPA GROUP, INC.
150 Broadway, Suite 1900, New York NY 10038. 212/964-3640. **Toll-free phone:** 800/BANK-TEMP. **Fax:** 212/964-6959. **Contact:** Len Adams, President. **E-mail address:** lenadams@pipeline.com. **Description:** An executive search firm. **Specializes in the areas of:** Accounting/Auditing; Administration; Banking; Finance; Marketing; MIS/EDP; Personnel/Labor Relations; Sales; Secretarial. **Positions commonly filled include:** Accountant/Auditor; Bank Officer/Manager; Branch Manager; Brokerage Clerk. **Average salary**

range of placements: $30,000 - $50,000. **Number of placements per year:** 200 - 499.

IRENE KANE PERSONNEL
27 West Neck Road, Huntington NY 11743. 516/351-1800. **Fax:** 516/351-1626. **Contact:** Ellen West, Owner/Manager. **Description:** An executive search firm operating on a contingency basis. Company pays fee. **Specializes in the areas of:** Computer Science/Software; Engineering. **Positions commonly filled include:** Aerospace Engineer; Computer Programmer; Design Engineer; Electrical/Electronics Engineer; MIS Specialist; Software Engineer; Systems Analyst; Technical Writer/Editor. **Average salary range of placements:** $30,000 - $50,000. **Number of placements per year:** 50 - 99.

KAUFMAN ASSOCIATES LTD.
450 7th Avenue, 9th Floor, New York NY 10123. 212/643-0625. **Fax:** 212/643-8598. **Contact:** Eugene A. Kaufman, CPC, President. **Description:** An executive search firm. Company pays fee. **Specializes in the areas of:** Apparel; Fashion; Home Furnishings. **Positions commonly filled include:** Designer; Merchandiser.

THE KAY GROUP OF FIFTH AVENUE
350 Fifth Avenue, Suite 2205, New York NY 10118. 212/947-4646. **Fax:** 212/947-3472. **Contact:** Joseph H. Kay, President. **Description:** A contingency search firm. Company pays fee. **Specializes in the areas of:** Accounting/Auditing; Administration; Advertising; Communications; Food Industry; General Management; Health/Medical; Industrial Sales and Marketing; Personnel/Labor Relations. **Average salary range of placements:** More than $50,000. **Number of placements per year:** 50 - 99.

KENSINGTON GROUP, INC.
One Maiden Lane, 10th Floor, New York NY 10038-4015. 212/227-0099. **Contact:** Ken DeMott, President. **Description:** An executive search firm. Company pays fee. **Specializes in the areas of:** Banking; Brokerage. **Positions commonly filled include:** Accountant/Auditor; Bank Officer/Manager; Credit Manager; Financial Analyst; Human Resources Manager; Securities Sales Rep.; Technical Writer/Editor. **Average salary range of placements:** More than $50,000. **Number of placements per year:** 1 - 49.

KINGSBURY WAX BOVA
230 Park Avenue, Suite 1000, New York NY 10169. 212/297-0300. **Contact:** Manager. **Description:** A retained executive search firm. **Specializes in the areas of:** Finance.

FRED KOFFLER ASSOCIATES
942 Greenfield Road, Woodmere NY 11598. 516/569-6582. **Contact:** Fred Koffler, President. **Description:** An executive search firm operating on a retainer basis. Company pays fee. **Specializes in the areas of:** Accounting/Auditing; Engineering; Finance; General Management; Industrial; Legal; Manufacturing; Personnel/Labor Relations; Publishing; Sales; Technical. **Positions commonly filled include:** Attorney; Biological Scientist; Biomedical Engineer; Chemical Engineer; Design Engineer; Designer; Electrical/Electronics Engineer; Environmental Engineer; Financial Analyst; Human Resources Specialist; Industrial Engineer; Industrial Production Manager; Management Analyst/Consultant; Market Research Analyst; Mechanical Engineer; MIS Specialist; Public Relations Specialist; Purchasing Agent/Manager; Quality Control Supervisor; Software Engineer; Structural Engineer; Systems Analyst; Technical Writer/Editor; Telecommunications Manager. **Average salary range of placements:** More than $50,000. **Number of placements per year:** 1 - 49.

KOLTNOW & COMPANY
1120 6th Avenue, Suite 4000, New York NY 10036. 212/626-6606. **Fax:** 212/626-6607. **Contact:** Emily Koltnow, President. **Description:** An executive search firm. Company pays fee. **Specializes in the areas of:** Fashion. **Positions commonly filled include:** Designer; Sales Manager. **Number of placements per year:** 1 - 49.

KORN/FERRY INTERNATIONAL
237 Park Avenue, 11th Floor, New York NY 10017. 212/687-1834. **Contact:** Manager. **Description:** An executive search firm that places upper-level managers in a variety of industries. **Corporate headquarters location:** Los Angeles CA. **International locations:** Worldwide. **Average salary range of placements:** More than $50,000.

KRAMER EXECUTIVE RESOURCES
110 East 59th Street, Suite 251, New York NY 10022. 212/832-1122. **Contact:** Manager. **Description:** An executive search firm. **Specializes in the areas of:** Accounting/Auditing; Finance.

EVIE KREISLER & ASSOCIATES
1460 Broadway, New York NY 10036-7306. 212/921-8999. **Contact:** Kathy Gross, Vice President. **Description:** An executive search firm operating on both retainer and contingency bases. Company pays fee. **Specializes in the areas of:** Retail. **Positions commonly filled include:** Buyer; Human Resources Manager; MIS Specialist; Operations/Production Manager; Quality Control Supervisor. **Corporate headquarters location:** Los Angeles CA. **Average salary range of placements:** More than $50,000.

LAKE ASSOCIATES
453 Kinns Road, Clifton Park NY 12065. 518/877-3071. **Fax:** 518/877-3072. **Contact:** Ernest Steinmann, Director. **Description:** An executive and technical search firm focusing on electronics, pharmaceuticals, and biotech industries. Company pays fee. **Specializes in the areas of:** Accounting/Auditing; Administration; Biology; Computer Science/Software; Engineering; Finance; Industrial; Manufacturing; Personnel/Labor Relations; Sales; Technical. **Positions commonly filled include:** Aerospace Engineer; Biochemist; Biological Scientist; Chemical Engineer; Chemist; Electrical/Electronics Engineer; Environmental Engineer; Food Scientist/Technologist; Industrial Engineer; Mechanical Engineer; MIS Specialist; Operations/Production Manager; Pharmacist; Purchasing Agent/Manager; Quality Control Supervisor; Science Technologist; Software Engineer; Structural Engineer; Technical Writer/Editor; Telecommunications Manager. **Average salary range of placements:** More than $50,000. **Number of placements per year:** 1 - 49.

LAMALIE AMROP INTERNATIONAL
200 Park Avenue, Suite 3100, New York NY 10166. 212/953-7900. **Contact:** Manager. **Description:** A generalist executive search firm.

DAVID LAWRENCE ASSOCIATES
60 East 42nd Street, New York NY 11710. 212/883-1100. **Fax:** 212/883-0838. **Contact:** Larry Rheingold, President. **Description:** An executive search firm. **Specializes in the areas of:** Computer Hardware/Software. **Positions commonly filled include:** Computer Programmer; MIS Specialist; Software Engineer; Technician.

LAWRENCE EXECUTIVE SEARCH
32 Reni Road, Manhasset NY 11030-1223. 516/627-5361. **Fax:** 516/627-5536. **Contact:** Lawrence Kamisher, President. **E-mail address:** lkamisher@aol.com. **Description:** An executive search firm that operates on a retainer basis. Company pays fee.

Specializes in the areas of: Advertising; Art/Design; Computer Science/Software; Marketing; Publishing; Sales. **Positions commonly filled include:** Account Manager; Account Rep.; Advertising Account Executive; Computer Programmer; Consultant; Controller; Customer Service Rep.; Graphic Artist; Graphic Designer; Market Research Analyst; Marketing Manager; Marketing Specialist; MIS Specialist; Sales Executive; Sales Manager; Sales Rep.; Software Engineer; Telecommunications Manager. **Average salary range of placements:** More than $50,000. **Number of placements per year:** 1 - 49.

MICHAEL JOHN LAWRENCE & ASSOCIATES, INC.
31 East John Street, Hicksville NY 11801. 516/938-3636. **Contact:** Manager. **Description:** A retainer and contingency executive search firm. The firm also provides career/outplacement services. Company pays fee. **Specializes in the areas of:** Accounting/Auditing; Administration; Advertising; Banking; Education; Engineering; Finance; Food Industry; General Management; Health/Medical; Industrial; Insurance; Legal; Manufacturing; Personnel/Labor Relations; Retail; Sales. **Positions commonly filled include:** Accountant/Auditor; Actuary; Adjuster; Administrative Manager; Attorney; Bank Officer/Manager; Chemical Engineer; Civil Engineer; Claim Rep.; Counselor; Education Administrator; Environmental Engineer; Financial Analyst; General Manager; Health Services Manager; Human Resources Specialist; Industrial Engineer; Insurance Agent/Broker; Licensed Practical Nurse; Management Analyst/Consultant; Mechanical Engineer; MIS Specialist; Occupational Therapist; Operations/Production Manager; Paralegal; Physician; Property and Real Estate Manager; Psychologist; Public Relations Specialist; Quality Control Supervisor; Registered Nurse; Restaurant/Food Service Manager; Securities Sales Rep.; Services Sales Rep.; Social Worker; Software Engineer; Strategic Relations Manager; Telecommunications Manager; Typist/Word Processor; Underwriter/Assistant Underwriter; Urban/Regional Planner. **Average salary range of placements:** More than $50,000. **Number of placements per year:** 1 - 49.

LEGAL SEARCH LTD.
35 East 35th Avenue, New York NY 10016. 212/725-1704. **Contact:** Manager. **Description:** An executive search firm. **Specializes in the areas of:** Legal.

WILLIAM K. LONG ASSOCIATES INC.
11 John Street, Room 300, New York NY 10038-4009. 212/571-0960. **Fax:** 212/732-0540. **Contact:** Maureen Cahill, President. **Description:** An executive search firm operating on both retainer and contingency bases. Company pays fee. **Specializes in the areas of:** Insurance. **Average salary range of placements:** More than $50,000. **Number of placements per year:** 1 - 49.

M.B. INC.
505 Fifth Avenue, 9th Floor, New York NY 10017. 212/661-4937. **Fax:** 212/661-4937. **Contact:** Alan Levine, President. **E-mail address:** info@mbincexec.com. **Description:** An executive search firm that specializes in senior-level marketing, sales, financial, and general management executive placements on both permanent and temporary bases nationwide. Company pays fee. **Specializes in the areas of:** Finance; General Management; Sales. **Positions commonly filled include:** Vice President of Marketing and Sales. **Average salary range of placements:** More than $75,000.

THE MVP GROUP
150 Broadway, 21st Floor, New York NY 10038. 212/571-1830. **Fax:** 212/393-1048. **Contact:** Charlie Otersen, Vice President. **Description:** An executive search firm. **Specializes in the areas of:** Administration; Banking; Computer Science/Software; Finance; Personnel/Labor Relations. **Positions commonly filled include:** Accountant/Auditor; Financial Analyst; Human Resources Manager; Securities Sales Representative. **Other U.S. locations:** Boston MA. **Number of placements per year:** 500 - 999.

MACINNIS, WARD & ASSOCIATES, INC.
551 Fifth Avenue, Suite 3300, New York NY 10176. 212/808-8080. **Fax:** 212/808-8088. **Contact:** Mary A. Ward, President. **Description:** An executive search firm. Company pays fee. **Specializes in the areas of:** Banking; Real Estate. **Positions commonly filled include:** Accountant/Auditor; Attorney; Bank Officer/Manager; Budget Analyst; Civil Engineer; Construction Contractor; Economist; Electrical/Electronics Engineer; Financial Analyst; General Manager; Management Analyst/Consultant; Mechanical Engineer; Operations/Production Manager; Property and Real Estate Manager; Purchasing Agent/Manager; Real Estate Agent; Structural Engineer; Underwriter/Assistant Underwriter. **Number of placements per year:** 100 - 199.

IVAN A. MACK ASSOCIATES, INC.
420 Lexington Avenue, Suite 300, New York NY 10170. 212/297-6123. **Fax:** 212/682-8479. **Contact:** Ivan Mack, President. **Description:** An executive search firm operating on a contingency basis. Company pays fee. **Specializes in the areas of:** Accounting/Auditing; Finance. **Positions commonly filled include:** Accountant/Auditor; Bookkeeper; Legal Secretary; Secretary. **Average salary range of placements:** More than $50,000. **Number of placements per year:** 100 - 199.

MAGILL ASSOCIATES, INC.
3601 Hempstead Turnpike, Levittown NY 11756. 516/579-4100. **Fax:** 516/579-4998. **Contact:** Joel Hamroff, President. **World Wide Web address:** http://www.magillstaff.com. **Description:** An executive search firm. Company pays fee. **Specializes in the areas of:** Accounting/Auditing; Administration; Banking; Computer Science/Software; Finance; Legal; Personnel/Labor Relations; Sales; Secretarial; Technical. **Positions commonly filled include:** Accountant/Auditor; Bank Officer/Manager; Chemist; Claim Rep.; Clerical Supervisor; Clinical Lab Technician; Computer Programmer; Credit Manager; Customer Service Rep.; Financial Analyst; Human Resources Specialist; MIS Specialist; Paralegal; Software Engineer; Systems Analyst; Typist/Word Processor. **Average salary range of placements:** $30,000 - $100,000. **Number of placements per year:** 200 - 499.

MAGNA SEARCH INC.
2848 Lindale Street, Wantagh NY 11793. 516/679-3330. **Contact:** Manager. **Description:** An executive search firm that provides placements in heating, air conditioning, and refrigeration industries.

MANAGEMENT RECRUITERS INTERNATIONAL
P.O. Box 386, Stone Ridge NY 12484. 914/339-1300. **Contact:** Manager. **Description:** An executive search firm. **Specializes in the areas of:** Chemical; Sales.
Other area locations:
- 435 New Karner Road, Suite 201, Albany NY 12205. 518/464-1461. (Marketing)
- 118 North Bedford Road, Suite 103, Mount Kisco NY 10549. 914/241-2788. (Food Industry; Publishing)
- 16 West Main Street, Rochester NY 14614. 716/454-2440. (Data Processing; Engineering; Sales)

MANAGEMENT RECRUITERS OF GRAMERCY
200 Park Avenue South, Suite 1510, New York NY 10003. 212/505-5530. **Fax:** 212/505-6240. **Contact:** Steve Schwartz, Owner/Manager. **Description:** An executive search firm operating on both retainer and contingency bases. **Specializes in the areas of:** Advertising; Health/Medical; Market Research; Publishing; Sales; Sales Promotion. **Positions commonly filled include:** Market Research Analyst; Services Sales Representative; Technical Writer/Editor. **Average salary range of placements:** More than $50,000. **Number of placements per year:** 1 - 49.

MANAGEMENT RECRUITERS OF MADRID
P.O. Box 218, Madrid NY 13660-0218. 315/322-0222. **Fax:** 315/322-0220. **Contact:** Nicole Scott, Owner/Manager. **E-mail address:** mrslc@northweb.com. **World Wide Web address:** http://www.mrinet.com. **Description:** An executive search firm operating on both retainer and contingency bases. Company pays fee. **Positions commonly filled include:** Hotel Manager; Human Resources Manager; Pharmacist; Physician. **Corporate headquarters location:** Cleveland OH. **Other U.S. locations:** Nationwide. **Average salary range of placements:** More than $50,000. **Number of placements per year:** 1 - 49.

MANAGEMENT RECRUITERS OF NASSAU INC.
77 North Centre Avenue, Suite 211, Rockville Centre NY 11570. 516/536-3111. **Contact:** Thomas Wielder, Executive Vice President. **Description:** An executive search firm. Company pays fee. **Specializes in the areas of:** Banking; Engineering; Finance; General Management; Manufacturing; Sales; Technical. **Positions commonly filled include:** Accountant/Auditor; Bank Officer/Manager; Chemical Engineer; Environmental Engineer; Financial Analyst; Financial Services Sales Rep.; Mechanical Engineer; Securities Sales Rep.; Structural Engineer. **Corporate headquarters location:** Cleveland OH. **International locations:** Worldwide. **Average salary range of placements:** More than $50,000.

MANAGEMENT RECRUITERS OF SUFFOLK
225 Main Street, Suite 204, Northport NY 11768. 516/261-0400. **Contact:** Manager. **Description:** An executive search firm. **Specializes in the areas of:** Industrial.

MANAGEMENT RECRUITERS OF UTICA/ROME
1721 Black River Boulevard, Executive Building, Suite 205, Rome NY 13440-2425. 315/339-6342. **Fax:** 315/339-6415. **Contact:** Robert Mosca, Vice President. **Description:** An executive search firm focusing on the placement of technical and health care professionals. Company pays fee. **Specializes in the areas of:** Engineering; Health/Medical; Manufacturing; Sales. **Positions commonly filled include:** Customer Service Rep.; Design Engineer; Electrical/Electronics Engineer; Mechanical Engineer; Occupational Therapist; Operations/Production Manager; Pharmacist; Physical Therapist; Physician; Purchasing Agent/Manager; Quality Control Supervisor; Registered Nurse; Speech-Language Pathologist. **Corporate headquarters location:** Cleveland OH. **Other U.S. locations:** Nationwide. **Number of placements per year:** 1 - 49.

MANAGEMENT RECRUITERS OF WOODBURY COMPUSEARCH
100 Crossways Park West, Suite 208, Woodbury NY 11797. 516/364-9290. **Fax:** 516/364-4478. **Contact:** Bill Jose, Manager. **Description:** An executive search firm. **Specializes in the areas of:** Accounting/Auditing; Administration; Architecture/Construction; Banking; Communications; Computer Science/Software; Electrical; Engineering; Finance; Food Industry; General Management; Health/Medical; Industrial; Insurance; Legal; Manufacturing; Personnel/Labor Relations; Procurement; Publishing; Real Estate; Retail; Sales; Technical; Textiles; Transportation.

MAR-EL EMPLOYMENT AGENCY
3000 Hempstead Turnpike, Levittown NY 11756. 516/579-7777. **Fax:** 516/579-7765. **Contact:** Scott Harvey, Executive Recruiter. **Description:** An executive search firm that focuses on accounting, finance, bookkeeping, and office support placements. The firm operates on a contingency basis. Company pays fee. **Specializes in the areas of:** Accounting/Auditing; Secretarial; Technical. **Positions commonly filled include:** Accountant/Auditor; Administrative Worker/Clerk; Bookkeeper; Data Entry Clerk; Legal Secretary; Medical Secretary; Receptionist; Secretary; Technician; Typist/Word Processor. **Other area locations:** Farmingdale NY. **Average salary range of placements:** $30,000 - $50,000. **Number of placements per year:** 50 - 99.

MARCUS & ASSOCIATES
501 Fifth Avenue, Suite 2014, New York NY 10017-3610. 212/856-9888. **Contact:** Ellen Marcus, President. **Description:** A professional recruiting firm that operates on a contingency basis. **Specializes in the areas of:** Accounting/Auditing; Finance; Personnel/Labor Relations. **Positions commonly filled include:** Accountant/Auditor; Budget Analyst; Financial Analyst; Human Resources Manager. **Number of placements per year:** 100 - 199.

MARSHALL CONSULTANTS, INC.
360 East 65th Street, New York NY 10021. 212/628-8400. **Contact:** Manager. **Description:** An executive search firm. **Specializes in the areas of:** Communications.

MARSHALL-ALAN ASSOCIATES, INC.
5 West 37th Street, 8th Floor, New York NY 10018. 212/382-2440. **Fax:** 212/764-5411. **Contact:** Alan Massarsky, President. **Description:** An executive search firm. Company pays fee. **Specializes in the areas of:** Food Industry. **Positions commonly filled include:** Caterer; Chef/Cook/Kitchen Worker; Food and Beverage Service Worker; Hotel Manager; Restaurant/Food Service Manager. **Number of placements per year:** 200 - 499.

MAXWELL GROUP
10 East 42nd Street, Suite 2226, New York NY 10165. 212/867-4646. **Contact:** Manager. **Description:** An executive search firm. **Specializes in the areas of:** Banking; Finance.

McLAUGHLIN RESOURCES
2 West 45th Street, New York NY 10036. 212/764-2120. **Fax:** 212/869-0281. **Contact:** Brian McLaughlin, President. **Description:** An executive search firm that also operates as a temporary agency. **Specializes in the areas of:** Accounting/Auditing; Finance; Health/Medical; Insurance. **Positions commonly filled include:** Accountant/Auditor; Controller; Financial Analyst; Management Trainee; Mathematician; Mechanical Engineer; Physicist. **Average salary range of placements:** More than $50,000. **Number of placements per year:** 50 - 99.

THE MELVILLE GROUP, INC.
734 Walt Whitman Road, Suite 202, Melville NY 11747. 516/421-5560. **Fax:** 516/427-2016. **Contact:** Ginny Pepper, President. **Description:** A nationwide recruitment firm focusing on banking and health care. Company pays fee. **Specializes in the areas of:** Banking; Health/Medical. **Positions commonly filled include:** Bank Officer/Manager; Health Services Manager; Licensed Practical Nurse; Registered Nurse; Social Worker.

MENTORTECH
462 Seventh Avenue, 4th Floor, New York NY 10018. 212/736-5870x212. **Fax:** 212/736-9046. **Contact:** Joe Sabrin, Executive Vice President. **Description:** An executive search firm. Company pays fee. **Specializes in the areas of:** Administration; Computer Science/Software; Personnel/Labor Relations; Sales. **Positions commonly filled include:** Human Resources Specialist; Internet Services Manager; MIS Specialist; Multimedia Designer; Services Sales Representative; Software Engineer; Technical Writer/Editor; Telecommunications Manager. **Number of placements per year:** 50 - 99.

METROPOLITAN PERSONNEL SYSTEMS
METROPOLITAN NURSING SERVICES
49 Court Street, Binghamton NY 13901. 607/722-1666. **Fax:** 607/722-0449. **Contact:** Jim Ivan, Technical Division Manager. **Description:** An executive search firm. Company pays fee. **Specializes in the areas of:** Accounting/Auditing; Administration; Computer Science/Software; Education; Engineering; Food Industry; General Management; Health/Medical; Industrial; Manufacturing; Personnel/Labor Relations; Retail; Sales; Secretarial; Technical; Transportation. **Positions commonly filled include:** Accountant/Auditor; Administrative Manager; Advertising Clerk; Aerospace Engineer; Agricultural Engineer; Biochemist; Biomedical Engineer; Budget Analyst; Buyer; Chemical Engineer; Civil Engineer; Claim Rep.; Clerical Supervisor; Clinical Lab Technician; Computer Programmer; Counselor; Credit Manager; Customer Service Rep.; Dental Assistant/Hygienist; Design Engineer; Dietician/Nutritionist; Draftsperson; Education Administrator; EEG Technologist; EKG Technician; Electrical/Electronics Engineer; Electrician; Environmental Engineer; Financial Analyst; Food Scientist/Technologist; General Manager; Health Services Manager; Human Resources Specialist; Human Service Worker; Industrial Engineer; Industrial Production Manager; Licensed Practical Nurse; Management Analyst/Consultant; Management Trainee; Manufacturer's/Wholesaler's Sales Rep.; Market Research Analyst; Mechanical Engineer; Medical Records Technician; MIS Specialist; Multimedia Designer; Occupational Therapist; Paralegal; Physical Therapist; Preschool Worker; Public Relations Specialist; Purchasing Agent/Manager; Quality Control Supervisor; Registered Nurse; Respiratory Therapist; Restaurant/Food Service Manager; Social Worker; Software Engineer; Speech-Language Pathologist; Strategic Relations Manager; Structural Engineer; Surgical Technician; Systems Analyst; Teacher/Professor; Technical Writer/Editor; Telecommunications Manager; Typist/Word Processor; Video Production Coordinator. **Benefits available to temporary workers:** 401(k); Life Insurance; Paid Holidays; Paid Vacation. **Other area locations:** Cortland NY; Elmira NY; Ithaca NY; Syracuse NY. **Average salary range of placements:** $30,000 - $50,000. **Number of placements per year:** 1000+.

MICKLER ASSOCIATES INC.
39 Clarendon Place, Buffalo NY 14209-0118. 716/881-2222. **Contact:** Gary R. Mickler, President. **Description:** An executive search firm operating on both retainer and contingency bases. Mickler Associates focuses on sales and marketing with an emphasis on food and consumer products. **Specializes in the areas of:** Engineering; Food Industry; Manufacturing; Sales. **Positions commonly filled include:** Buyer; Chemical Engineer; Chemist; Electrical/Electronics Engineer; Food Scientist/Technologist; Manufacturer's/Wholesaler's Sales Rep.; Market Research Analyst; Operations/Production Manager; Purchasing Agent/Manager; Quality Control Supervisor; Restaurant/Food Service Manager. **Number of placements per year:** 1 - 49.

HERBERT MINES ASSOCIATES
375 Park Avenue, Suite 301, New York NY 10152. 212/355-0909. **Contact:** Manager. **Description:** An executive search firm. **Specializes in the areas of:** Retail.

THE MITCHELL GROUP
8 Archer Lane, Scarsdale NY 10583-7704. **Toll-free phone:** 800/648-2435. **Contact:** Ken Mitchell, Proprietor. **Description:** An executive search firm operating on both retainer and contingency bases. Company pays fee. **Specializes in the areas of:** Insurance. **Positions commonly filled include:** Actuary. **Number of placements per year:** 1 - 49.

MOLLOY PARTNERS
340 Broadway, Sarasota Springs NY 12866. 518/581-2532. **Contact:** Manager. **Description:** An executive search firm. **Specializes in the areas of:** High-Tech.

NATEK CORPORATION
9 Maple Avenue, Saratoga NY 12866. 518/583-0456. **Fax:** 518/583-0558. **Contact:** Mark Dillon, President. **E-mail address:** natek96@aol.com. **World Wide Web address:** http://www.natek.com. **Description:** An executive search firm operating on both retainer and contingency bases. Company pays fee. **Specializes in the areas of:** Engineering; Marketing; Sales; Scientific; Technical. **Positions commonly filled include:** Applications Engineer; Chemical Engineer; Design Engineer; Electrical/Electronics Engineer; Industrial Engineer; Manufacturing Engineer; Sales Executive; Sales Manager; Sales Rep. **Corporate headquarters location:** Saratoga NY. **Other U.S. locations:** Nationwide. **Average salary range of placements:** More than $50,000. **Number of placements per year:** 50 - 99.

NATIONAL ENGINEERING SEARCH
3700 East Avenue, Rochester NY 14625. 716/248-3160. **Contact:** Manager. **Description:** An executive search firm that places hardware and software engineers.

NEAL MANAGEMENT, INC.
152 Madison Avenue, Suite 605, New York NY 10016. 212/686-1686. **Fax:** 212/686-1590. **Contact:** Peter Tannenbaum, President. **Description:** An executive search firm. Company pays fee. **Specializes in the areas of:** Accounting/Auditing; Banking; Finance. **Positions commonly filled include:** Accountant/Auditor; Bank Officer/Manager; Computer Programmer; Credit Manager; Economist; Systems Analyst. **Number of placements per year:** 1 - 49.

NOBLE & ASSOCIATES
420 Madison Avenue, New York NY 10017. 212/838-7020. **Fax:** 212/838-7344. **Contact:** Donald Noble, Principal. **Description:** An executive search firm that operates on both retainer and contingency bases. Company pays fee. **Specializes in the areas of:** Advertising; Personnel/Labor Relations; Retail; Sales. **Positions commonly filled include:** General Manager; Human Resources Manager; Public Relations Specialist. **Other U.S. locations:** San Francisco CA. **Average salary range of placements:** More than $50,000. **Number of placements per year:** 50 - 99.

OPTIMAL RESOURCES
18 East 48th Street, New York NY 10017. 212/486-7713. **Fax:** 212/486-8042. **Contact:** Frank J. Marzi, Vice President. **World Wide Web address:** http://www.nyctemps.com. **Description:** A search firm operating on a contingency basis. The firm also provides temporary placements. Company pays fee. **Specializes in the areas of:** Administration; Advertising; Banking; Computer Science/Software;

Fashion; Finance; Personnel/Labor Relations; Sales; Secretarial. **Positions commonly filled include:** Brokerage Clerk; Financial Analyst; Human Resources Specialist; Management Trainee; Paralegal; Public Relations Specialist; Securities Sales Rep. **Average salary range of placements:** $30,000 - $50,000. **Number of placements per year:** 200 - 499.

PRC HEALTH PROFESSIONAL PLACEMENT AND RECRUITMENT
P.O. Box 102, Manlius NY 13104-0102. 315/682-7015. **Contact:** William P. Colangelo, President. **Description:** A contingency search firm. **Positions commonly filled include:** Occupational Therapist; Pharmacist; Physical Therapist; Speech-Language Pathologist. **Average salary range of placements:** $30,000 - $50,000. **Number of placements per year:** 50 - 99.

LYNNE PALMER EXECUTIVE RECRUITMENT, INC.
342 Madison Avenue, Suite 1430, New York NY 10173. 212/883-0203. **Fax:** 212/883-0149. **Contact:** Elena Bourgoin, Recruiter. **E-mail address:** lynnepalmer@worldnet.att.net. **Description:** An executive search firm operating on both retainer and contingency bases. Company pays fee. **Specializes in the areas of:** Publishing.

ARTHUR PANN ASSOCIATES
701 Westchester Avenue, Suite A1, White Plains NY 10604. 914/686-0700. **Fax:** 914/946-2019. **Contact:** Art Pann, CPC, President. **Description:** An executive search firm operating on both retained and contingency bases. Company pays fee. **Specializes in the areas of:** Accounting/Auditing; Administration; Engineering. **Positions commonly filled include:** Applications Engineer; Architect; Chief Financial Officer; Computer Programmer; Controller; Database Manager; Design Engineer; Finance Director; Financial Analyst; Human Resources Manager; Manufacturing Engineer; Multimedia Designer; Software Engineer; Systems Analyst; Systems Manager; Telecommunications Manager; Webmaster. **Average salary range of placements:** More than $50,000. **Number of placements per year:** 50 - 99.

PARKER CLARK EXECUTIVE RECRUITMENT
370 Lexington Avenue, New York NY 10017. 212/983-5950. **Contact:** Manager. **Description:** An executive search firm. **Specializes in the areas of:** Accounting/Auditing; Finance.

THE PARKS GROUP INC.
230 Park Avenue, Suite 450, New York NY 10169. 212/286-0777. **Fax:** 212/286-1973. **Contact:** Marie Parks, CPC, President. **E-mail address:** marie@gaparks.com. **World Wide Web address:** http://www.gaparks.com. **Description:** An executive search firm operating on a contingency basis. Company pays fee. **Specializes in the areas of:** Finance; Legal; Personnel/Labor Relations; Secretarial. **Positions commonly filled include:** Accountant/Auditor; Attorney; Human Resources Manager; Legal Secretary; MIS Specialist; Paralegal; Typist/Word Processor. **Other U.S. locations:** Nationwide. **Average salary range of placements:** $40,000 - $75,000. **Number of placements per year:** 100 - 199.

PATHWAY EXECUTIVE SEARCH, INC.
60 East 42nd Street, Lincoln Building, Suite 405, New York NY 10165. 212/557-2650. **Fax:** 212/682-1743. **Contact:** Jay Berger, President. **Description:** An executive search firm. Company pays fee. **Specializes in the areas of:** Banking; Computer Science/Software; Finance; Technical. **Positions commonly filled include:** Computer Programmer; Management Analyst/Consultant; Securities Sales Rep.; Software Engineer; Systems Analyst. **Number of placements per year:** 50 - 99.

PAXTON RESOURCES INC.
50 Main Street, Suite 1000, White Plains NY 10606-1920. 914/682-2088. **Fax:** 914/682-2192. **Contact:** Barbara Paxton, President. **Description:** An executive search firm operating on a contingency basis. Company pays fee. **Specializes in the areas of:** Human Resources. **Positions commonly filled include:** Human Resources Manager; Public Relations Specialist; Training Specialist. **Average salary range of placements:** More than $50,000. **Number of placements per year:** 1 - 49.

PEAK SEARCH INC.
25 West 31st Street, Suite A, New York NY 10001. 212/947-6600. **Fax:** 212/947-6780. **Contact:** Richard Eichenberg, President. **Description:** An executive search firm that provides permanent and temporary placement. **Specializes in the areas of:** Accounting/Auditing; Banking; Legal. **Positions commonly filled include:** Accountant/Auditor; Attorney; Bank Officer/Manager; Brokerage Clerk; Budget Analyst; Credit Manager; Financial Analyst. **Number of placements per year:** 200 - 499.

PERSONNEL ASSOCIATES INC.
731 James Street, Suite 209, Syracuse NY 13203. 315/422-0070. **Fax:** 315/474-7293. **Contact:** Peter J. Baskin, CPC, President. **E-mail address:** pbaskin@ix.netcom.com. **Description:** An executive search firm operating on both retainer and contingency bases. **Specializes in the areas of:** Insurance. **Number of placements per year:** 1 - 49.

PERSONNEL CONSULTING ASSOCIATES
7600 Jericho Turnpike, Woodbury NY 11797. 212/269-8508. **Contact:** Joseph Slater, President. **Description:** An executive search firm. **Specializes in the areas of:** Banking; Finance; Investment; Personnel/Labor Relations.

PERSONNEL SERVICES CENTER
10 East 39th Street, Room 527, New York NY 10016. 212/447-9173. **Fax:** 212/684-3650. **Contact:** Michael R. Morano, Ph.D., President. **Description:** An executive search firm that also provides career/outplacement counseling. Company pays fee. **Specializes in the areas of:** Accounting/Auditing; Administration; General Management; Retail; Sales; Secretarial. **Positions commonly filled include:** Account Manager; Accountant/Auditor; Administrative Assistant; Administrative Manager; Advertising Executive; Advertising Clerk; Applications Engineer; Clerical Supervisor; Financial Analyst; Management Analyst/Consultant; Management Trainee; Operations Manager; Production Manager; Sales Engineer; Sales Executive; Sales Rep.; Secretary; Social Worker; Systems Analyst; Systems Manager; Vice President. **Other U.S. locations:** Nationwide. **Average salary range of placements:** More than $50,000. **Number of placements per year:** 1 - 49.

PHARMACEUTICAL RECRUITERS INC.
271 Madison Avenue, Suite 1200, New York NY 10016. 212/557-5627. **Fax:** 212/557-5866. **Contact:** Manager. **Description:** An executive search firm. **Specializes in the areas of:** Pharmaceutical.

PHOENIX SEARCH GROUP
350 Fifth Avenue, Suite 2714, New York NY 10118. 212/564-3456. **Contact:** Office Manager. **Description:** An executive search firm. **Specializes in the areas of:** Computer Hardware/Software; Information Technology.

PHYSICIAN INTERNATIONAL INC.
4 Vermont Street, Buffalo NY 14213. 716/884-3700. **Fax:** 716/884-4241. **Contact:** Patricia Fatta, Vice President. **Description:** An executive search firm. Company pays fee. **Specializes in the areas of:** Health/Medical. **Positions commonly filled include:** Licensed Practical Nurse; Physical Therapist; Physician; Registered Nurse. **Number of placements per year:** 500 - 999.

THE PINNACLE GROUP
130 Water Street, Suite 4F, New York NY 10005. 212/968-1200. **Contact:** Manager. **Description:** An executive search firm. **Specializes in the areas of:** Finance.

P.G. PRAGER SEARCH ASSOCIATES, LTD.
1461 Franklin Avenue, Garden City NY 11530. 516/294-4400. **Fax:** 516/294-4443. **Contact:** Paul Gershon Prager, President. **Description:** A contingency search firm. Company pays fee. **Specializes in the areas of:** Accounting/Auditing; Administration; Banking; Computer Science/Software; Finance; Insurance; Legal; Personnel/Labor Relations; Sales; Secretarial. **Positions commonly filled include:** Accountant/Auditor; Attorney; Bank Officer/Manager; Budget Analyst; Buyer; Credit Manager; Customer Service Rep.; Human Resources Manager; Industrial Production Manager; Insurance Agent/Broker; Management Analyst/Consultant; Manufacturer's/Wholesaler's Sales Rep.; Paralegal; Public Relations Specialist; Purchasing Agent/Manager; Quality Control Supervisor; Systems Analyst; Underwriter/Assistant Underwriter. **Average salary range of placements:** More than $50,000. **Number of placements per year:** 1 - 49.

PRO SEARCH ASSOCIATES, INC.
15 North Mill Street, Nyack NY 10960-3015. 914/353-2260. **Fax:** 914/353-2366. **Contact:** Edwin Kahn, Principal. **Description:** An executive search firm operating on both retainer and contingency bases. Company pays fee. **Specializes in the areas of:** Administration; Computer Science/Software; Finance. **Positions commonly filled include:** Computer Programmer; Financial Analyst; Internet Services Manager; Systems Analyst; Telecommunications Manager. **Average salary range of placements:** More than $50,000. **Number of placements per year:** 1 - 49.

PROFESSIONAL PLACEMENT ASSOCIATES INC.
14 Rye Ridge Plaza, Rye Brook NY 10573. 914/251-1000. **Fax:** 914/251-1055. **Contact:** Laura J. Schacter, President. **Description:** An executive search firm. Company pays fee. **Specializes in the areas of:** Health/Medical. **Positions commonly filled include:** Biomedical Engineer; Dental Assistant/Dental Hygienist; Dietician/Nutritionist; EKG Technician; Health Services Manager; Human Resources Manager; Medical Records Technician; Nuclear Medicine Technologist; Occupational Therapist; Pharmacist; Physical Therapist; Physician; Respiratory Therapist; Social Worker; Speech-Language Pathologist. **Number of placements per year:** 100 - 199.

PROFESSIONAL SUPPORT INC.
501 John James Audubon Parkway, Amherst NY 14228-1143. 716/688-0235. **Toll-free phone:** 800/444-6760. **Fax:** 716/688-0239. **Contact:** Greg Eastmer, Vice President. **Description:** An executive search firm. Company pays fee. **Specializes in the areas of:** Accounting/Auditing; Administration; Personnel/Labor Relations. **Positions commonly filled include:** Accountant/Auditor; Computer Programmer; Financial Analyst; Human Resources Manager; Management Analyst/Consultant; MIS Specialist; Quality Control Supervisor; Software Engineer; Systems Analyst. **Benefits available to temporary workers:** 401(k); Life Insurance; Medical Insurance; Paid Holidays; Paid Vacation; Sick Days. **Other area locations:** Rochester NY. **Other U.S. locations:** Cleveland OH. **Average salary range of placements:** $30,000 - $50,000. **Number of placements per year:** 100 - 199.

PROMOTION RECRUITERS, INC.
11 Rectory Lane, Scarsdale NY 10583. 914/723-2657. **Contact:** Manager. **Description:** An executive search firm. **Specializes in the areas of:** Broadcasting.

PRYOR PERSONNEL AGENCY, INC.
147 Old Country Road, Hicksville NY 11801-4007. 516/935-0100. **Fax:** 516/931-7842. **Contact:** Patricia Pryor Bonica, President. **E-mail address:** ppryor1575@aol.com. **World Wide Web address:** http://www.pryor.com. **Description:** An executive search firm operating on both retainer and contingency bases. Company pays fee. **Specializes in the areas of:** Insurance. **Positions commonly filled include:** Accountant/Auditor; Actuary; Adjuster; Claim Rep.; Financial Analyst; Human Resources Manager; Insurance Agent/Broker; Systems Analyst; Underwriter/Assistant Underwriter. **Average salary range of placements:** More than $50,000. **Number of placements per year:** 500 - 999.

QUEST ORGANIZATION
11 Penn Plaza, Suite 935, New York NY 10001. 212/971-0033. **Fax:** 212/971-6256. **Contact:** Michael F. Rosenblatt, President. **E-mail address:** questorg@aol.com. **Description:** An executive search firm. Company pays fee. **Specializes in the areas of:** Accounting/Auditing; Administration; Banking; Fashion; Finance; Personnel/Labor Relations. **Positions commonly filled include:** Accountant/Auditor; Budget Analyst; Chief Financial Officer; Consultant; Controller; EDP Specialist; Finance Director; Financial Analyst; Fund Manager; Human Resources Manager; Management Analyst/Consultant; Market Research Analyst. **Average salary range of placements:** More than $50,000. **Other U.S. locations:** Washington DC; Philadelphia PA. **Number of placements per year:** 100 - 199.

ROI ASSOCIATES INC.
48 South Service Road, Suite 100, Melville NY 11747. 516/465-2065. **Fax:** 516/516-2067. **Contact:** Peter Portanoua, Partner. **E-mail address:** pportanoua@compuserve.com. **Description:** An executive search firm. Company pays fee. **Specializes in the areas of:** Distribution; Finance; General Management; Manufacturing; Materials. **Positions commonly filled include:** General Manager; Operations/Production Manager; Purchasing Agent/Manager. **Number of placements per year:** 1 - 49.

RAND THOMPSON CONSULTANTS
261 Madison Avenue, 27th Floor, New York NY 10016. 212/972-0090. **Fax:** 212/370-0047. **Contact:** John Kelly, President. **Description:** An executive search firm. Company pays fee. **Specializes in the areas of:** Accounting/Auditing; Administration; Banking; Finance; General Management; Insurance; Legal; Personnel/Labor Relations. **Positions commonly filled include:** Accountant/Auditor; Administrative Manager; Attorney; Bank Officer/Manager; Budget Analyst; Credit Manager; Financial Analyst; Human Resources Manager; Insurance Agent/Broker; Purchasing Agent/Manager; Sales Engineer; Systems Analyst. **Number of placements per year:** 100 - 199.

RECRUITMENT GROUP
P.O. Box 410, Williamsville NY 14231. 716/631-8960. **Contact:** Manager. **Description:** An executive search firm. **Specializes in the areas of:** Engineering; Sales.

REDSTONE AFFILIATES
50 Main Street, White Plains NY 10606. 914/945-0735. **Contact:** Manager. **Description:** An executive search firm. **Specializes in the areas of:** Banking; Finance; Investment.

REDWOOD/CASEY INC.
152 Madison Avenue, 22nd Floor, New York NY 10016. 212/843-8585. **Fax:** 212/843-9043. **Contact:** Ms. Walenberg. **E-mail address:** redwood@redwoodpartners.com. **World Wide Web address:** http://www.redwoodpartners.com. **Description:** An executive search firm. Company pays fee. **Specializes in the areas of:** Advertising; Sales. **Positions commonly filled include:** Account Manager; Computer Animator; Computer Programmer; Consultant; Graphic Artist; Graphic Designer; Management Analyst/Consultant; Market Research Analyst; Marketing Specialist; Online Content Specialist; Sales Executive; Sales Rep.; Vice President of Marketing. **Average salary range of placements:** More than $50,000. **Number of placements per year:** 100 - 199.

DANIEL F. REILLY AND ASSOCIATES INC.
481 Main Street, New Rochelle NY 10801. 914/636-6542. **Fax:** 914/636-0221. **Contact:** Daniel Reilly, President. **E-mail address:** dfreilly@aol.com. **World Wide Web address:** http://www.amsquare.com/america/dfreilly.html. **Description:** An executive search firm. Company pays fee. **Specializes in the areas of:** Software Development. **Positions commonly filled include:** Software Engineer; Technical Writer/Editor. **Average salary range of placements:** More than $50,000. **Number of placements per year:** 50 - 99.

RESOURCE SERVICES, INC.
20 Crossways Park North, 3rd Floor, Woodbury NY 11797. 516/496-4100. **Fax:** 516/496-4110. **Contact:** Joseph Trainor, President. **Description:** An executive search firm operating on a contingency basis and focusing on the placement of data processing and telecommunications professionals. **Specializes in the areas of:** Computer Science/Software. **Positions commonly filled include:** MIS Specialist. **Average salary range of placements:** More than $50,000. **Number of placements per year:** 200 - 499.

RESPONSE STAFFING SERVICES CAREER ADVISORS, INC.
23 East 39th Street, New York NY 10016. 212/983-8870. **Fax:** 212/983-9492. **Contact:** Allen Gutterman, President. **Description:** An executive search firm operating on both retainer and contingency bases. Company pays fee. **Specializes in the areas of:** Accounting/Auditing; Architecture/Construction; Banking; Computer Hardware/Software; Finance; Health/Medical; Insurance; Secretarial. **Positions commonly filled include:** Accountant; Actuary; Bank Officer/Manager; Biological Scientist; Biomedical Engineer; Brokerage Clerk; Claim Rep.; Clinical Lab Technician; Computer Programmer; Construction and Building Inspector; Credit Manager; Customer Service Rep.; EEG Technologist; EKG Technician; Emergency Medical Technician; Financial Analyst; Health Services Manager; Insurance Agent/Broker; Licensed Practical Nurse; Medical Records Technician; Nuclear Medicine Technologist; Occupational Therapist; Paralegal; Pharmacist; Physical Therapist; Physician; Property and Real Estate Manager; Recreational Therapist; Registered Nurse; Respiratory Therapist; Securities Sales Rep.; Software Engineer; Surgical Technician; Systems Analyst; Underwriter/Assistant Underwriter. **Average salary range of placements:** $30,000 - $50,000. **Number of placements per year:** 200 - 499.

RETAIL RECRUITERS INC.
225 West 34th Street, Suite 1316, New York NY 10122. 212/714-0313. **Contact:** Office Manager. **Description:** An executive search firm. **Specializes in the areas of:** Retail.

E.J. RHODES EXECUTIVE SEARCH
555 5th Avenue, 5th Floor, New York NY 10017. 212/983-2000. **Fax:** 212/983-8333. **Contact:** Manager. **Description:** An executive search firm. **Specializes in the areas of:** Banking; Finance; Real Estate.

RITECH MANAGEMENT INC.
2 Pennsylvania Plaza, Suite 1500, New York NY 10121. 212/268-7778. **Contact:** Ben Michaels, President. **Description:** An executive search firm operating on a contingency basis. The firm focuses on the placement of PC, LAN, and WAN systems engineers in full-time, salaried positions as well as long-term consulting assignments at client sites. **Positions commonly filled include:** Computer Programmer; Internet Services Manager; Multimedia Designer; Software Engineer; Systems Analyst; Telecommunications Manager. **Average salary range of placements:** More than $50,000. **Number of placements per year:** 50 - 99.

RITTA PROFESSIONAL SEARCH, INC.
6 Automation Lane, Albany NY 12205-1604. 518/458-7340. **Fax:** 518/458-7017. **Contact:** Arthur E. Hansen, President. **Description:** An executive search firm that focuses on the placement of research and development engineers and scientists in various electrical, mechanical, materials, and electronic fields. Founded in 1974. **Specializes in the areas of:** Computer Science/Software; Engineering. **Positions commonly filled include:** Aerospace Engineer; Computer Programmer; Design Engineer; Electrical/Electronics Engineer; Environmental Engineer; Mechanical Engineer; Software Engineer; Systems Analyst; Telecommunications Manager. **Average salary range of placements:** More than $50,000.

ROBERTS EXECUTIVE RECRUITMENT
Colonial Square, Route 822, Brewster NY 10509. 914/279-5575. **Fax:** 914/278-7174. **Contact:** Bob Roberts, President. **Description:** An executive search firm operating on a contingency basis. The firm focuses on placement in chemical process industries such as pulp and paper and the conversion of non-woven textiles. Company pays fee. **Specializes in the areas of:** Engineering; Technical. **Positions commonly filled include:** Chemical Engineer; Chemist; Mining Engineer. **Number of placements per year:** 50 - 99.

BOB ROSS EXECUTIVE SEARCH CORPORATION
150 West 51st Street, Suite 1811, New York NY 10019. 212/969-9030. **Fax:** 212/969-9067. **Contact:** Bob Ross, President. **E-mail address:** bobross7@ix.netcom.com. **Description:** An executive search firm operating on both retainer and contingency bases. Company pays fee. **Specializes in the areas of:** Computer Operations; Software Quality Assurance. **Positions commonly filled include:** Computer Operator; Computer Programmer. **Other U.S. locations:** Nationwide. **Average salary range of placements:** More than $50,000. **Number of placements per year:** 200 - 499.

ROTH YOUNG OF LONG ISLAND
333 North Broadway, Suite 2001, Jericho NY 11753. 516/822-6000. **Fax:** 516/822-6018. **Contact:** George T. Jung, President. **Description:** An executive search firm. Company pays fee. **Specializes in the areas of:** Accounting/Auditing; Finance; Food Industry; Hotel/Restaurant; Human Resources; Retail; Sales. **Positions commonly filled include:** Accountant/Auditor; Bank Officer/Manager; Buyer; Computer Programmer; Credit Manager; Dietician/Nutritionist; Financial Analyst; Food Scientist/Technologist; Health Services Manager;

Human Resources Manager; Manufacturer's/ Wholesaler's Sales Rep.; Occupational Therapist; Physical Therapist; Registered Nurse; Restaurant/Food Service Manager; Store Manager; Systems Analyst. **Number of placements per year:** 200 - 499.

RUSSELL REYNOLDS ASSOCIATES, INC.
200 Park Avenue, 23rd Floor, New York NY 10166. 212/351-2000. **Contact:** Manager. **Description:** A generalist executive search firm.

RYAN SEARCH ASSOCIATES
35 East 35th Street, New York NY 10019. 212/683-3220. **Contact:** Manager. **Description:** An executive search firm. **Specializes in the areas of:** Legal.

SDC COMPUTER SERVICE
290 Elwood Davis Road, Suite 106, Liverpool NY 13008. 315/457-6560. **Contact:** Manager. **Description:** An executive search firm that focuses on placing computer programmers. **Specializes in the areas of:** Computer Science/ Software.

S.W. MANAGEMENT
170 Broadway, Suite 909, New York NY 10038. 212/962-6310. **Fax:** 212/962-7733. **Contact:** Shirley Whelan, President. **Description:** An executive search firm. Company pays fee. **Specializes in the areas of:** Accounting/Auditing; Administration; Banking; Economics; Finance; Insurance; Legal; Personnel/Labor Relations; Secretarial. **Positions commonly filled include:** Accountant/Auditor; Administrative Assistant; Assistant Manager; Bank Officer/Manager; Budget Analyst; Claim Rep.; Clerical Supervisor; Computer Programmer; Credit Manager; Customer Service Rep.; Financial Analyst; Human Resources Manager; Insurance Agent/Broker; Librarian; Management Trainee; MIS Specialist; Purchasing Agent/Manager; Secretary; Systems Analyst; Typist/Word Processor; Underwriter/Assistant Underwriter. **Number of placements per year:** 200 - 499.

ST. LAWRENCE INTERNATIONAL, INC.
6432 Baird Avenue, Syracuse NY 13206-1045. 315/428-8517. **Contact:** Kathi Rodgers, President. **Description:** An executive search firm. **Specializes in the areas of:** Finance; Manufacturing; Sales. **Positions commonly filled include:** Financial Analyst; Human Resources Manager; Industrial Engineer; Mechanical Engineer; Nuclear Engineer.

SALES CAREERS
1320 Bolten Road, Pelham NY 10803. 914/632-8800. **Fax:** 914/632-9355. **Contact:** John Donahoe, President. **Description:** An executive search firm that recruits on a contingency basis. Company pays fee. **Specializes in the areas of:** Sales. **Positions commonly filled include:** Sales Manager; Sales Representative. **Average salary range of placements:** More than $50,000. **Number of placements per year:** 100 - 199.

SALES CONSULTANTS OF WESTCHESTER
9 Skyline Drive, Hawthorne NY 10532. 914/592-1290. **Fax:** 914/592-1258. **Contact:** Bob Penney, Manager. **Description:** An executive search firm. **Specializes in the areas of:** Communications; Computer Science/Software; Food Industry; General Management; Health/Medical; Publishing; Sales; Telecommunications. **Positions commonly filled include:** Marketing Manager; Sales Engineer; Sales Executive; Sales Manager; Sales Representative; Telecommunications Manager. **Average salary range of placements:** More than $50,000. **Number of placements per year:** 100 - 199.

SALES SEARCH, LTD./EXECUTIVE RESUME SERVICE
48 Burd Street, Suite 202, Nyack NY 10960. 914/353-2040. **Fax:** 914/353-2633. **Contact:** John Ratcliff, CPC, President. **Description:** An executive search firm. Executive Resume Service provides resume writing services. **Specializes in the areas of:** Engineering; Industrial; Light Industrial; Marketing; Sales; Scientific; Technical. **Positions commonly filled include:** Account Manager; Account Rep.; Applications Engineer; Branch Manager; Chemical Engineer; Customer Service Rep.; Electrical/Electronics Engineer; Management Trainee; Marketing Manager; Metallurgical Engineer; Sales Engineer; Sales Executive; Sales Manager; Sales Rep. **Average salary range of placements:** $30,000 - $50,000. **Number of placements per year:** 1 - 49.

SAXON MORSE ASSOCIATES
P.O. Box 177, Pomona NY 10970-0177. 201/886-0300. **Contact:** Stan Case, Recruiter. **Description:** An executive search firm operating on both retainer and contingency bases. Company pays fee. **Specializes in the areas of:** Personnel/Labor Relations; Sales. **Positions commonly filled include:** Accountant/ Auditor; Electrical/Electronics Engineer; Health Services Manager. **Average salary range of placements:** More than $50,000. **Number of placements per year:** 50 - 99.

SEARCH MASTERS INC.
60 East 42nd Street, Suite 453, New York NY 10165. 212/867-9494. **Contact:** Manager. **Description:** An executive search firm. **Specializes in the areas of:** Accounting/Auditing.

SEARCHAMERICA INC.
86 Kathleen Drive, Syosset NY 11791. 516/921-3120. **Contact:** Jonathan S. Messer, Chairman and CEO. **Description:** An executive search firm operating on both retainer and contingency bases. Company pays fee. **Specializes in the areas of:** Administration; Banking; Economics; Finance; General Management; Legal; Personnel/Labor Relations; Sales. **Positions commonly filled include:** Accountant/Auditor; Administrative Manager; Attorney; Bank Officer/ Manager; Budget Analyst; Economist; Financial Analyst; Human Resources Manager; Management Analyst/Consultant; Paralegal; Public Relations Specialist; Securities Sales Rep.; Strategic Relations Manager; Systems Analyst; Technical Writer/Editor; Telecommunications Manager. **International locations:** Worldwide. **Average salary range of placements:** More than $50,000. **Number of placements per year:** 50 - 99.

SETFORD-SHAW-NAJARIAN ASSOCIATES
115 Broadway, 20th Floor, New York NY 10006. 212/962-1500. **Fax:** 212/962-1543. **Contact:** Matt Malvese, Consultant. **E-mail address:** tisny@tisny.com. **World Wide Web address:** http://www.tisny.com. **Description:** An executive search firm. **Specializes in the areas of:** Data Processing. **Positions commonly filled include:** Computer Programmer; Financial Analyst; Software Engineer; Systems Analyst. **Number of placements per year:** 200 - 499.

SHARP PLACEMENT PROFESSIONALS
55 Post Avenue, Suite 202, Westbury NY 11590. 516/876-9222. **Fax:** 516/876-9080. **Contact:** Donald Levine, CPC, President. **E-mail address:** don@sharpsearch.com. **World Wide Web address:** http://www.sharpsearch.com. **Description:** An executive search firm. Company pays fee. **Specializes in the areas of:** Computer Science/Software; Engineering; Personnel/Labor Relations; Sales; Technical. **Positions commonly filled include:** Account Manager; Chief Financial Officer; Computer Programmer; Database Manager; Design Engineer; Financial Consultant; Human Resources Manager; Internet Services Manager; Management Analyst/ Consultant; Manufacturing Engineer; Marketing Manager; Multimedia Designer; Online Content

Specialist; Operations Manager; Public Relations Specialist; Sales Engineer; Sales Rep.; Software Engineer; Systems Analyst; Systems Manager; Telecommunications Manager; Webmaster. **Benefits available to temporary workers:** Medical Insurance. **Corporate headquarters location:** Westbury NY. **Other U.S. locations:** Nationwide. **Average salary range of placements:** More than $50,000. **Number of placements per year:** 1 - 49.

MARINA SIRRAS & ASSOCIATES
420 Lexington Avenue, Suite 2546, New York NY 10170. 212/490-0333. **Fax:** 212/490-2074. **Contact:** Marina Sirras, Principal. **Description:** An executive search firm. Company pays fee. **Specializes in the areas of:** Legal. **Positions commonly filled include:** Attorney; Paralegal.

SMYTH ASSOCIATES
220 East 42nd Street, 28th Floor, New York NY 10017. 212/682-9300. **Contact:** Office Manager. **Description:** An executive search firm that focuses on placements in the finance industry.

SNELLING PERSONNEL SERVICES
1717 Central Avenue, Albany NY 12205-4756. 518/869-9575. **Fax:** 518/869-9256. **Contact:** Ms. Kristi Nastars, President. **Description:** A contingency search firm. Founded in 1951. Company pays fee. **Specializes in the areas of:** Accounting/Auditing; Administration; Engineering; Finance; Sales; Secretarial; Technical. **Positions commonly filled include:** Accountant; Bank Officer/Manager; Chemical Engineer; Computer Programmer; Electrical/Electronics Engineer; Environmental Engineer; Financial Analyst; Industrial Engineer; Mechanical Engineer; MIS Specialist; Software Engineer; Systems Analyst; Technical Writer/Editor. **Corporate headquarters location:** Dallas TX. **Other U.S. locations:** Nationwide. **Average salary range of placements:** $30,000 - $50,000. **Number of placements per year:** 50 - 99.

SOURCE FINANCE
2 Penn Plaza, Suite 1176, New York NY 10121-1199. 212/868-5100. **Fax:** 212/868-5115. **Contact:** Phillip D. Bank, C.P.A., Managing Partner. **World Wide Web address:** http://www.experienceondemand.com. **Description:** An executive search firm operating on a contingency basis as one division of Source Services Corporation. Company pays fee. **Specializes in the areas of:** Accounting/Auditing; Banking; Finance. **Positions commonly filled include:** Accountant/Auditor; Bank Officer/Manager; Credit Manager; Financial Analyst; Management Analyst/Consultant. **Benefits available to temporary workers:** Stock Purchase. **Average salary range of placements:** More than $50,000. **Number of placements per year:** 100 - 199.

SOURCE SERVICES CORPORATION
925 Westchester Avenue, Suite 309, White Plains NY 10604. 914/428-9100. **Fax:** 914/428-9438. **Contact:** Manager. **Description:** An executive search firm. The divisions at this location include Source Consulting, Source EDP, and Source Finance. **Specializes in the areas of:** Computer Hardware/Software; Finance; Information Technology. **Corporate headquarters location:** Dallas TX. **Other U.S. locations:** Nationwide.

SPECTOR EXECUTIVE SEARCH
4 Marlin Lane, Port Washington NY 11050. 516/944-8500. **Contact:** Manager. **Description:** An executive search firm that provides placements in the legal industry.

MITCHELL SPITZ EXECUTIVE SEARCH
75 Lexington Avenue, Suite 410, New York NY 10022. 212/572-8313. **Contact:** Office Manager. **Description:** An executive search firm that focuses on the placement of investment bankers.

TOBY SPITZ ASSOCIATES INC.
110 East 59th Street, 6th Floor, New York NY 10022. 212/909-0480. **Fax:** 212/909-0479. **Contact:** Manager. **Description:** An executive search firm that provides legal industry placements.

SPORN GROUP INC.
56 Pine Street, 6th Floor, New York NY 10005. 212/344-5050. **Contact:** David Sporn, President. **Description:** An executive search firm. Company pays fee. **Specializes in the areas of:** Accounting/Auditing; Finance; Legal; Personnel/Labor Relations; Sales. **Positions commonly filled include:** Accountant/Auditor; Attorney; Computer Programmer; Financial Analyst; Human Resources Manager; Management Analyst/Consultant; Systems Analyst. **Number of placements per year:** 50 - 99.

SPRING ASSOCIATES, INC.
10 East 23rd Street, New York NY 10010. 212/753-8080. **Contact:** Manager. **Description:** An executive search firm. **Specializes in the areas of:** Public Relations.

STAFFING SERVICES
660 White Plains Road, Suite 400, Tarrytown NY 10591. 914/332-6660. **Fax:** 914/332-5178. **Contact:** Debra Pohl, Professional Recruiter. **Description:** An executive search firm operating on both retainer and contingency bases. **Specializes in the areas of:** Banking; Finance; General Management; Legal; Manufacturing; Personnel/Labor Relations; Pharmaceutical; Real Estate; Sales. **Positions commonly filled include:** Accountant/Auditor; Actuary; Administrative Manager; Bank Officer/Manager; Biological Scientist; Budget Analyst; Chemist; Computer Programmer; Credit Manager; Customer Service Rep.; Financial Analyst; General Manager; Human Resources Manager; Market Research Analyst; MIS Specialist; Paralegal; Pharmacist; Property and Real Estate Manager; Public Relations Specialist; Quality Assurance Engineer; Systems Analyst; Technical Writer/Editor; Underwriter/Assistant Underwriter. **Number of placements per year:** 50 - 99.

STAFKINGS HEALTH CARE SYSTEMS
P.O. Box 1015, Binghamton NY 13902. 607/772-8080. **Contact:** Manager. **Description:** An executive search firm focusing on the placement of home health aides, CNAs, LPNs, and some RNs. Positions typically begin as temporary and may become permanent. **Specializes in the areas of:** Health/Medical. **Corporate headquarters location:** This Location.
Other area locations:

- Genesee Mall, Auburn NY 13021. 315/252-3441.
- East Towne Mall, 116 Baldwin Street, Elmira NY 14901. 607/734-3646.

STENTIFORD & BERARDI ASSOCIATES
1140 6th Avenue, 9th Floor, New York NY 10036. 212/382-1616. **Contact:** Manager. **Description:** An executive search firm. **Specializes in the areas of:** Publishing.

STRATEGIC RECRUITING
501 Fifth Avenue, Suite 1715, New York NY 10017. 212/922-1650. **Fax:** 212/922-1654. **Contact:** Gary Platt, President and Owner. **E-mail address:** stratrecru@aol.com. **Description:** An executive search firm operating on a contingency basis. Company pays fee. **Specializes in the areas of:** Administration; Computer Science/Software; Information Technology; Public Relations; Secretarial. **Positions commonly filled include:** Administrative Assistant; Chief Financial Officer; Controller; Human Resources Manager; MIS

Specialist; Public Relations Specialist; Secretary; Systems Analyst. **Average salary range of placements:** $30,000 - $50,000. **Number of placements per year:** 200 - 499.

SYNERGY PARTNERS INC.
275 Madison Avenue, 21st Floor, New York NY 10016. 212/922-2800. **Fax:** 212/922-2807. **Contact:** Marcy Becker, Principal. **Description:** An executive search firm operating on a contingency basis. Company pays fee. **Specializes in the areas of:** Accounting/Auditing; Banking; Finance. **Positions commonly filled include:** Accountant/Auditor; Budget Analyst; Financial Analyst. **Average salary range of placements:** More than $50,000. **Number of placements per year:** 100 - 199.

TAD HEALTH SERVICES
30 North Union Street, Suite 102, Rochester NY 14607. 716/454-5511. **Contact:** Office Manager. **Description:** An executive search firm offering placements for health care professionals in positions such as LPNs, CNAs, RNs, and medical technicians. **Specializes in the areas of:** Health/Medical.

TAYLOR JORDAN ASSOCIATES, INC.
108-18 Queens Boulevard, Forest Hills NY 11375. 718/793-4400. **Contact:** Mr. Pace Langsam, Director of Marketing. **Description:** An executive search firm operating on a contingency basis. Company pays fee. **Specializes in the areas of:** Accounting/Auditing; Computer Science/Software; General Management; Manufacturing. **Positions commonly filled include:** Accountant/Auditor; Human Resources Manager; Industrial Engineer; Industrial Production Manager; MIS Specialist. **Average salary range of placements:** More than $50,000.

TAYLOR SEARCH ASSOCIATES
550 Cross Keys Office Park, New York NY 14450. 716/425-4500. **Contact:** Manager. **Description:** An executive search firm. **Specializes in the areas of:** Sales.

TECH OPTIONS, INC.
P.O. Box 386, Lenox Hill Station NY 10021. 212/988-3067. **Contact:** Martha Kellner, President. **Description:** An executive search and consulting firm focusing on placements of client/server and computer systems experts. The clientele are primarily financial firms in the New York metropolitan area. Company pays fee. **Specializes in the areas of:** Computer Science/Software; Finance. **Positions commonly filled include:** Computer Programmer; MIS Specialist; Software Engineer; Systems Analyst. **Other U.S. locations:** Montclair NJ. **Average salary range of placements:** More than $50,000. **Number of placements per year:** 1 - 49.

TECHNO-TRAC SYSTEMS, INC.
251 Central Park West, New York NY 10024. 212/769-TRAC. **Fax:** 212/873-1596. **Contact:** Mort Trachtenberg, President. **E-mail address:** technomt@bigfoot.com. **Description:** An executive search firm. Company pays fee. **Specializes in the areas of:** Administration; Banking; Computer Science/Software. **Positions commonly filled include:** Budget Analyst; Computer Programmer; Database Manager; Financial Analyst; Management Analyst/Consultant; MIS Specialist; Software Engineer; Systems Analyst; Systems Manager. **Average salary range of placements:** More than $50,000. **Number of placements per year:** 1 - 49.

TELEMARKETING RECRUITERS
114 East 32nd Street, New York NY 10016. 212/213-1818. **Contact:** Manager. **Description:** An executive search firm. **Specializes in the areas of:** Direct Marketing; Telemarketing.

TELEQUEST COMMUNICATIONS
2 Executive Boulevard, Suite 201, Suffern NY 10901. 914/357-2212. **Fax:** 914/357-7826. **Contact:** Tom Bartchak, President. **Description:** A contingency executive search firm that operates on permanent and contract bases. Areas of concentration include voice, data, LAN, WAN, and international and trading floor support. **Specializes in the areas of:** Telecommunications. **Positions commonly filled include:** Telecommunications Analyst/Manager. **Number of placements per year:** 1 - 49.

PHILLIP THOMAS PERSONNEL, INC.
535 Fifth Avenue, Suite 606, New York NY 10017. 212/867-0860. **Fax:** 212/490-0315. **Contact:** Tina Carberry, President. **Description:** A contingency search firm that also provides temporary placements. Company pays fee. **Specializes in the areas of:** Accounting/Auditing; Banking; Finance. **Positions commonly filled include:** Accountant/Auditor; Administrative Assistant; Human Resources Specialist; MIS Specialist; Portfolio Securities Specialist; Securities Sales Rep. **Average salary range of placements:** $30,000 - $50,000. **Number of placements per year:** 50 - 99.

THORSEN ASSOCIATES, INC.
2020 Grand Avenue, Baldwin NY 11510. 516/868-6500. **Fax:** 516/868-7842. **Contact:** Peter T. Thorsen, President. **E-mail address:** thorsen@concentric.net. **Description:** An executive search firm. Company pays fee. **Specializes in the areas of:** Engineering; Industrial; Manufacturing. **Positions commonly filled include:** Blue-Collar Worker Supervisor; Chemical Engineer; Chemist; Design Engineer; Draftsperson; Electrical/Electronics Engineer; Industrial Engineer; Industrial Production Manager; Materials Engineer; Mechanical Engineer; Purchasing Agent/Manager; Quality Control Supervisor. **Average salary range of placements:** More than $50,000. **Number of placements per year:** 1 - 49.

TODD ARRO, INC.
P.O. Box 172, Kenmore NY 14217-0172. 716/871-0993. **Contact:** Joseph Todaro, President. **Description:** A contingency search firm. Company pays fee. **Specializes in the areas of:** Engineering; Health/Medical; Industrial; Sales. **Positions commonly filled include:** Chemical Engineer; Electrical/Electronics Engineer; Manufacturer's/Wholesaler's Sales Rep.; Mechanical Engineer; Services Sales Rep. **Number of placements per year:** 1 - 49.

E.G. TODD PHYSICIAN SEARCH
One Byram Brook Place, Armonk NY 10504. 914/273-5666. **Contact:** Manager. **Description:** An executive search firm that places physicians. **Specializes in the areas of:** Health/Medical.

TRAYNOR CONFIDENTIAL LTD.
P.O. Box 189, Pittsford NY 14534. 716/387-0383. **Fax:** 716/387-0384. **Contact:** Tom Traynor, President. **Description:** An executive search firm operating on a contingency basis. Company pays fee. **Specializes in the areas of:** Accounting/Auditing; Administration; Architecture/Construction; Computer Science/Software; Finance. **Positions commonly filled include:** Accountant/Auditor; Architect; Civil Engineer; Computer Programmer; Construction and Building Inspector; Construction Contractor; Financial Analyst; Internet Services Manager; Landscape Architect; Market Research Analyst; MIS Specialist; Property and Real Estate Manager; Software Engineer. **Average salary range of placements:** $30,000 - $50,000. **Number of placements per year:** 1 - 49.

TREBOR, WELDON, LAWRENCE, LEVINE
355 Lexington Avenue, 11th Floor, New York NY 10017. 212/867-0066. **Fax:** 212/867-2784. **Contact:** Lawrence Levine, Partner. **Description:** A retainer search firm focusing on marketing services, marketing research, and promotion marketing disciplines. Company pays fee. **Specializes in the areas of:** Advertising; Food Industry; Sales. **Positions commonly filled include:** Market Research Analyst. **Other U.S. locations:** Dobbs Ferry NY. **Average salary range of placements:** More than $50,000.

KAREN TRIPI ASSOCIATES
60 East 42nd Street, Suite 2140, New York NY 10165. 212/972-5258. **Contact:** Office Manager. **Description:** An executive search firm. **Specializes in the areas of:** Direct Marketing.

VENTURE RESOURCES
11 Penn Plaza, Suite 1001, New York NY 10001. 212/273-7700. **Fax:** 212/273-7777. **Contact:** Corry Prohens, President. **World Wide Web address:** http://www.venre.com. **Description:** An executive search firm operating on both retained and contingency bases. **Specializes in the areas of:** Banking; Computer Science/Software; Finance; MIS/EDP; Technical. **Positions commonly filled include:** Computer Programmer; Database Manager; Financial Analyst; Internet Services Manager; MIS Specialist; Online Content Specialist; Operations/Production Manager; Systems Analyst/Manager. **Average salary range of placements:** More than $50,000. **Number of placements per year:** 100 - 199.

VINTAGE RESOURCES, INC.
11 East 44th Street, Suite 708, New York NY 10017. 212/867-1001. **Fax:** 212/490-9277. **Contact:** Perry Fishman, Vice President. **Description:** An executive search firm that operates on a contingency basis. Company pays fee. **Specializes in the areas of:** Advertising; Direct Marketing; Marketing; Sales. **Positions commonly filled include:** Account Manager; Advertising Executive; Advertising Clerk; Database Manager; Marketing Specialist; Production Manager. **Average salary range of placements:** $30,000 - $50,000. **Number of placements per year:** 200 - 499.

WALLACE LAW REGISTRY
11 East 44th Street, 3rd Floor, New York NY 10017. 212/984-1132. **Fax:** 212/972-3519. **Contact:** Sharon Elliot, Esq., Placement Director. **Description:** An executive search firm operating on a contingency basis. The firm also provides some temporary placements. Company pays fee. **Specializes in the areas of:** Legal. **Positions commonly filled include:** Attorney. **Other U.S. locations:** Nationwide. **Average salary range of placements:** More than $50,000. **Number of placements per year:** 500 - 999.

CHARLES WANNER ASSOCIATES LTD.
60 East 42nd Street, Room 1401, New York NY 10165. 212/557-2000. **Contact:** Manager. **Description:** An executive search firm operating on both retainer and contingency bases. Company pays fee. **Specializes in the areas of:** Accounting/Auditing; Administration; Banking; Finance; General Management; Legal; Technical. **Positions commonly filled include:** Accountant; Bank Officer/Manager; Computer Programmer; Credit Manager; Financial Analyst; Management Analyst/Consultant; MIS Specialist; Paralegal; Systems Analyst. **Average salary range of placements:** More than $50,000. **Number of placements per year:** 50 - 99.

WAYNE GROUP LTD.
84 Williams Street, New York NY 10038. 212/668-1414. **Contact:** Manager. **Description:** An executive search firm. **Specializes in the areas of:** Technical.

WEBER MANAGEMENT CONSULTANTS
205 East Main Street, Suite 2-3A, Huntington NY 11743. 516/673-4700. **Fax:** 516/673-4885. **Contact:** Ronald Weber, President. **Description:** An executive search firm. Company pays fee. **Specializes in the areas of:** Administration; Engineering; Food Industry; General Management; Industrial; Manufacturing; Marketing; Personnel/Labor Relations; Sales. **Positions commonly filled include:** Human Resources Manager; Industrial Production Manager; Management Analyst/Consultant; Purchasing Agent/Manager. **Number of placements per year:** 50 - 99.

WEHN ASSOCIATES, INC.
71 Vanderbilt Avenue, New York NY 10017. 212/675-3224. **Fax:** 212/986-4245. **Contact:** President. **Description:** An executive search firm. **Specializes in the areas of:** Administration; Computer Science/Software. **Positions commonly filled include:** Architect; Computer Programmer; Designer; Software Engineer; Systems Analyst; Technical Writer/Editor. **Number of placements per year:** 50 - 99.

WERBIN ASSOCIATES EXECUTIVE SEARCH, INC.
140 Riverside Drive, 10 N, New York NY 10024. 212/799-6111. **Contact:** Susan Werbin, President. **Description:** An executive search firm. Werbin Associates focuses on placing data processing professionals, both technical and managerial. The firm also places quantitative researchers and analysts for investment modeling, decision systems, and market research. Founded in 1978. Company pays fee. **Specializes in the areas of:** Accounting/Auditing; Administration; Advertising; Banking; Computer Science/Software; Economics; Finance; Insurance; Manufacturing. **Positions commonly filled include:** Computer Programmer; Economist; Electrical/Electronics Engineer; Financial Analyst; Management Analyst/Consultant; Researcher; Science Technologist; Software Engineer; Systems Analyst; Technical Writer/Editor. **Average salary range of placements:** More than $50,000. **Number of placements per year:** 1 - 49.

WESTFIELD ASSOCIATES, INC.
One North Broadway, White Plains NY 10601. 914/761-4333. **Fax:** 914/761-4341. **Contact:** Manager. **Description:** An executive search firm. Company pays fee. **Specializes in the areas of:** Accounting/Auditing; Personnel/Labor Relations; Secretarial. **Positions commonly filled include:** Accountant/Auditor; Credit Manager; Customer Service Rep.; Human Resources Manager; Paralegal; Purchasing Agent/Manager; Systems Analyst. **Number of placements per year:** 100 - 199.

WINSTON RESOURCES
1400 Old Country Road, Suite 303, Westbury NY 11590. 516/333-3222. **Fax:** 516/333-5099. **Contact:** Bryan Amante, Account Executive. **Description:** An executive search firm. Company pays fee. **Specializes in the areas of:** Accounting/Auditing; Administration; Banking; Computer Science/Software; Finance; General Management; Health/Medical; Personnel/Labor Relations. **Positions commonly filled include:** Accountant; Clinical Lab Technician; Computer Programmer; Financial Analyst; Internet Services Manager; Licensed Practical Nurse; Management Analyst/Consultant; MIS Specialist; Occupational Therapist; Radiological Technologist; Registered Nurse; Speech-Language Pathologist; Systems Analyst. **Corporate headquarters location:** New York NY. **Average salary range of placements:** $30,000 - $50,000. **Number of placements per year:** 200 - 499.

S.R. WOLMAN ASSOCIATES, INC.
133 East 35th Street, New York NY 10007. 212/685-2692. **Fax:** 212/889-4379. **Contact:** Steve Wolman,

President. **Description:** An executive search firm. Company pays fee. **Specializes in the areas of:** Advertising; Art/Design; Fashion; Finance; General Management; Marketing; Retail; Sales. **Positions commonly filled include:** Buyer; Customer Service Rep.; Designer; Human Resources Manager; Internet Services Manager; Management Analyst/Consultant; Manufacturer's/Wholesaler's Sales Rep.; Market Research Analyst; Multimedia Designer; Operations/Production Manager; Quality Control Supervisor; Services Sales Rep.; Telecommunications Manager; Video Production Coordinator. **Average salary range of placements:** More than $50,000. **Number of placements per year:** 50 - 99.

PERMANENT EMPLOYMENT AGENCIES

AARP FOUNDATION SENIOR COMMUNITY SERVICE EMPLOYMENT PROGRAM
331 Main Mall, Suite 103, Poughkeepsie NY 12601. 914/485-8030. **Fax:** 914/485-8031. **Contact:** Joseph F. Dirac, Project Director. **E-mail address:** scjdirac@aol.com. **Description:** A permanent employment agency. **Specializes in the areas of:** Education; Food Industry; Industrial; Personnel/Labor Relations; Secretarial. **Positions commonly filled include:** Accountant/Auditor; Administrative Manager; Clerical Supervisor; Library Technician; Teacher/Professor. **Number of placements per year:** 1 - 49.

ATS RELIANCE, INC.
250 Mill Street, Suite 310, Rochester NY 14614-1026. 716/777-4090. **Fax:** 716/777-4058. **Contact:** Chris Bell, Manager. **Description:** An employment agency that provides permanent and temporary technical personnel. Founded in 1984. **Specializes in the areas of:** Computer Science/Software; Engineering; Industrial; Manufacturing; Technical. **Positions commonly filled include:** Aerospace Engineer; Agricultural Engineer; Biochemist; Biological Scientist; Civil Engineer; Computer Programmer; Design Engineer; Draftsperson; Electrical/Electronics Engineer; Environmental Engineer; Industrial Engineer; Internet Services Manager; Materials Engineer; Mechanical Engineer; MIS Specialist; Quality Control Supervisor; Software Engineer; Structural Engineer; Systems Analyst; Technical Writer/Editor; Urban/Regional Planner.

ACCOUNTING & COMPUTER PERSONNEL
200 Salina Meadows Parkway, Suite 180, Syracuse NY 13212. 315/457-8000. **Fax:** 315/457-0029. **Contact:** William E. Winnewisser, President. **Description:** A permanent employment agency focusing on the placement of accounting and computer personnel. Company pays fee. **Specializes in the areas of:** Accounting/Auditing; Administration; Advertising; Architecture/Construction; Art/Design; Banking; Biology; Broadcasting; Computer Science/Software; Economics; Engineering; Finance; Food Industry; General Management; Health/Medical; Industrial; Insurance; Legal; Manufacturing; Nonprofit; Personnel/Labor Relations; Publishing; Retail; Sales; Technical. **Positions commonly filled include:** Accountant/Auditor; Bank Officer/Manager; Budget Analyst; Computer Programmer; Cost Estimator; Credit Manager; Financial Analyst; Software Engineer; Systems Analyst; Technical Writer/Editor. **Number of placements per year:** 50 - 99.

ACCUSTAFF INC.
466 Main Street, New Rochelle NY 10801. 914/654-9400. **Fax:** 914/654-9480. **Contact:** Patricia Longo, CPC, Manager. **World Wide Web address:** http://www.accustaff.com. **Description:** A permanent employment agency that focuses on administrative support and also provides temporary placements. **Specializes in the areas of:** Accounting/Auditing; Administration; General Management; Light Industrial; Personnel/Labor Relations; Sales; Secretarial. **Positions commonly filled include:** Account Manager; Account Rep.; Administrative Assistant; Administrative Manager; Clerical Supervisor; Credit Manager; Customer Service Rep.; Database Manager; Human Resources Manager; Marketing Manager; Sales Executive; Sales Manager; Typist/Word Processor. **Average salary range of placements:** $20,000 - $29,999. **Number of placements per year:** 100 - 199.

ADAM PERSONNEL, INC.
11 East 44th Street, New York NY 10017. 212/557-9150. **Fax:** 212/557-9348. **Contact:** Jill Barry, Vice President. **Description:** A permanent and temporary employment agency. Company pays fee. **Specializes in the areas of:** Accounting/Auditing; Banking; Fashion; Legal; Nonprofit; Secretarial. **Positions commonly filled include:** Administrative Assistant; Clerical Supervisor; Controller; Credit Manager; Customer Service Representative; Editorial Assistant; Financial Analyst; Management Trainee; Secretary. **Corporate headquarters location:** This Location. **Average salary range of placements:** $20,000 - $29,999. **Number of placements per year:** 200 - 499.

ADELE POSTON NURSES REGISTRY
16 East 79th Street, New York NY 10021-0150. 212/879-7474. **Fax:** 212/988-7191. **Contact:** Mr. Jerry Bohne, Director. **Description:** A permanent employment agency that places qualified nurses and home health care professionals. Company pays fee. **Specializes in the areas of:** Domestic Help; Health/Medical; Nannies; Secretarial. **Positions commonly filled include:** EEG Technologist; Health Services Manager; Licensed Practical Nurse; Occupational Therapist; Physical Therapist; Physician; Recreational Therapist; Registered Nurse; Respiratory Therapist; Speech-Language Pathologist. **Average salary range of placements:** $30,000 - $50,000. **Number of placements per year:** 500 - 999.

ALL HOME SERVICES AGENCY, LTD.
2121 Broadway, New York NY 10023. 212/799-9360. **Contact:** Nedra J. Kleinman, President. **Description:** A permanent employment agency. Company pays fee. **Specializes in the areas of:** Domestic Help; Eldercare, In-Home; Health/Medical. **Positions commonly filled include:** Chauffeur; Chef/Cook/Kitchen Worker; Housekeeper; Nanny; Nursing Aide. **Number of placements per year:** 200 - 499.

THE ALOE GROUP
170 East Post Road, White Plains NY 10601. 914/761-8900. **Contact:** Edward Aloe, President. **Description:** A permanent employment agency that places residential mortgage loan originators nationwide. **Specializes in the areas of:** Mortgage.

AMESGROUP
928 Broadway, Suite 1101A, New York NY 10010-6008. 212/475-5900. **Fax:** 212/674-2401. **Contact:** Max Sabrin, Director. **E-mail address:** amesgroup@aol.com. **World Wide Web address:** http://www.quikpage.com/a/amesgroup. **Description:** A permanent employment agency. Company pays fee. **Specializes in the areas of:** Administration; Banking; Computer Science/Software; Finance; Health/Medical; Insurance; Printing; Publishing; Sales; Scientific; Secretarial; Technical. **Positions commonly filled include:** Accountant/Auditor; Administrative Assistant; Bookkeeper; Computer Programmer; Customer Service Rep.; EDP Specialist; Legal Secretary; Marketing

Specialist; MIS Specialist; Public Relations Specialist; Secretary; Software Engineer; Systems Analyst; Technical Writer/Editor; Typist/Word Processor. **Corporate headquarters location:** This Location. **Average salary range of placements:** More than $50,000. **Number of placements per year:** 1 - 49.

AMHERST PERSONNEL GROUP, INC.
550 West Old Country Road, Hicksville NY 11801. 516/433-7610. **Fax:** 516/433-7848. **Contact:** Recruiter. **Description:** A permanent employment agency. **Specializes in the areas of:** Retail; Sales.

ANALYTIC RECRUITING INC.
12 East 41st Street, 9th Floor, New York NY 10017. 212/545-8511. **Fax:** 212/545-8520. **Contact:** Rita Raz, Principal. **Description:** A permanent employment agency. Company pays fee. **Specializes in the areas of:** Administration; Banking; Computer Science/Software; Economics; Finance; Sales. **Positions commonly filled include:** Computer Programmer; Economist; Financial Analyst; Management Analyst/Consultant; Mathematician; Statistician; Systems Analyst. **Number of placements per year:** 100 - 199.

ANTES ASSOCIATES
80 Ridgeview Drive, Pleasantville NY 10570. 914/773-1400. **Fax:** 914/773-0114. **Contact:** Barbara Antes, President. **Description:** A permanent employment agency. **Specializes in the areas of:** Health/Medical. **Positions commonly filled include:** Dietician/Nutritionist; Pharmacist; Registered Nurse; Social Worker. **Corporate headquarters location:** This Location. **Other U.S. locations:** CT; NJ. **Average salary range of placements:** More than $30,000. **Number of placements per year:** 1 - 49.

APRIL TECHNICAL RECRUITING
P.O. Box 40303, Rochester NY 14604-0803. 716/325-5220. **Fax:** 716/546-4870. **Contact:** Ron Schumaker, Technical Recruiter. **Description:** A permanent employment agency. Company pays fee. **Specializes in the areas of:** Administration; Computer Science/Software; Engineering; Manufacturing; Technical. **Positions commonly filled include:** Accountant/Auditor; Chemical Engineer; Civil Engineer; Computer Programmer; Design Engineer; Draftsperson; Electrical/Electronics Engineer; Environmental Engineer; Industrial Engineer; Industrial Production Manager; Mechanical Engineer; MIS Specialist; Quality Control Supervisor; Software Engineer; Structural Engineer; Systems Analyst. **Average salary range of placements:** $30,000 - $50,000.

ARROW EMPLOYMENT AGENCY, INC.
150 Route 110, Melville NY 11747. 516/271-3700. **Contact:** Don Becker, President. **Description:** A permanent employment agency. Company pays fee. **NOTE:** Applicants should include minimum salary requirement and maximum commuting distance with resumes. **Specializes in the areas of:** Computer Science/Software; Engineering; Industrial; Manufacturing; Secretarial; Technical. **Positions commonly filled include:** Bookkeeper; Chemist; Clerk; Computer Programmer; Customer Service Rep.; Data Entry Clerk; Draftsperson; Factory Worker; Industrial Engineer; Legal Secretary; Manufacturing Engineer; Mechanical Engineer; Medical Secretary; Operations/Production Manager; Quality Control Supervisor; Receptionist; Sales Executive; Secretary; Software Engineer; Systems Analyst; Technician. **Number of placements per year:** 50 - 99.

ARROW EMPLOYMENT AGENCY, INC.
320 North Broadway, Hicksville NY 11801-2910. 516/931-4200. **Fax:** 516/931-4298. **Contact:** Norman Shapp, Operations Manager. **Description:** A permanent employment agency. Company pays fee. **Specializes in the areas of:** Industrial; Sales; Technical. **Positions commonly filled include:** Accountant/Auditor; Aerospace Engineer; Biomedical Engineer; Budget Analyst; Chemical Engineer; Computer Programmer; Editor; Electrical/Electronics Engineer; Health Services Manager; Human Resources Manager; Industrial Engineer; Management Analyst/Consultant; Paralegal; Public Relations Specialist; Restaurant/Food Service Manager; Telecommunications Manager. **Average salary range of placements:** $30,000 - $50,000. **Number of placements per year:** 200 - 499.

ASHER PERSONNEL CONSULTANTS
507 Fifth Avenue, 3rd Floor, New York NY 10017-4906. 212/972-5627. **Contact:** David Glickman, President. **Description:** A full-service permanent employment agency. Founded in 1985. **Specializes in the areas of:** Accounting/Auditing; Advertising; Banking; Consumer Package Goods; Cosmetics; Fashion; Finance; Insurance; Legal; Personnel/Labor Relations; Retail; Sales; Secretarial. **Positions commonly filled include:** Accountant/Auditor; Administrative Assistant; Advertising Clerk; Budget Analyst; Buyer; Clerical Supervisor; Credit Manager; Financial Analyst; Human Resources Specialist; Paralegal; Typist/Word Processor. **Average salary range of placements:** $30,000 - $60,000.

AUTO CAREERS
P.O. Box 3004, Schenectady NY 12303-3004. 518/356-0804. **Fax:** 518/356-5091. **Contact:** Tom Anderson, President. **World Wide Web address:** http://www.ttomo313.com. **Description:** A permanent employment agency. Company pays fee. **Specializes in the areas of:** Accounting/Auditing; Automotive; Finance; General Management; Sales; Secretarial; Technical. **Positions commonly filled include:** Automotive Mechanic. **Average salary range of placements:** $30,000 - $50,000. **Number of placements per year:** 100 - 199.

BARKSDALE HOME CARE SERVICES CORPORATION
327 Fifth Avenue, Pelham NY 10803. 914/738-5600. **Fax:** 914/738-0658. **Contact:** Rosa K. Barksdale, CEO. **Description:** A permanent employment agency providing licensed home health care. **Specializes in the areas of:** Health/Medical. **Positions commonly filled include:** Home Health Aide; Licensed Practical Nurse; Registered Nurse. **Average salary range of placements:** Less than $20,000.

BEAVER PERSONNEL, INC.
265 West 14th Street, Suite 1103, New York NY 10011-7103. 212/243-5540. **Fax:** 212/243-1266. **Contact:** John Klein, Manager. **Description:** An employment agency that focuses on placing permanent and temporary professionals. Company pays fee. **Specializes in the areas of:** Printing. **Positions commonly filled include:** Cost Estimator; Customer Service Rep.; Desktop Publishing Specialist; Operations/Production Manager; Press Operator; Purchasing Agent/Manager.

BEST DOMESTIC SERVICES AGENCY, INC.
30 East 42nd Street, Suite 1517, New York NY 10016. 212/685-0351. **Fax:** 212/685-2067. **Contact:** Deborah Dickenson, Manager. **Description:** A permanent employment agency. Company pays fee. **Specializes in the areas of:** Domestic Help; Nannies. **Positions commonly filled include:** Housekeeper; Nanny. **Number of placements per year:** 200 - 499.

BEVAN RESOURCES
50 Main Street, Suite 1000, White Plains NY 10606. 914/682-2060. **Fax:** 914/682-2194. **Contact:** Cathy Bevan, President. **Description:** A permanent employment agency. Company pays fee. **Specializes**

in the areas of: Accounting/Auditing; Administration; Legal; Office Support; Personnel/Labor Relations; Secretarial. **Positions commonly filled include:** Accountant/Auditor; Administrative Manager; Clerical Supervisor; Customer Service Rep.; Human Resources Manager; Management Trainee; Secretary. **Number of placements per year:** 1 - 49.

BEVLIN PERSONNEL INC.
110 Mamaroneck Avenue, White Plains NY 10601. 914/683-0880. **Fax:** 914/683-8625. **Contact:** Beverly Borwick, President. **Description:** A permanent employment agency with clients ranging from *Fortune* 500 corporations to small firms. Company pays fee. **Specializes in the areas of:** Accounting/Auditing; Finance; Personnel/Labor Relations; Secretarial. **Positions commonly filled include:** Accountant; Administrative Assistant; Brokerage Clerk; Clerical Supervisor; Human Resources Manager; Marketing Specialist. **Number of placements per year:** 200 - 499.

BONFIELD EMPLOYMENT AGENCY
16 East 79th Street, Suite 4G, New York NY 10021. 212/288-1010. **Fax:** 212/988-7191. **Contact:** Angela Kapikian, Manager. **Description:** A permanent employment agency. Company pays fee. **Specializes in the areas of:** Domestic Help; Secretarial. **Positions commonly filled include:** Caterer; Domestic Help; Driver; Waitstaff. **Number of placements per year:** 200 - 499.

THE BRITISH CONNECTION
120 East 56th Street, New York NY 10022-3607. 212/223-2510. **Fax:** 212/755-3238. **Contact:** Sally Dwek, President. **E-mail address:** britishconn@aol.com. **Description:** A permanent employment agency that focuses on placing experienced personal assistants, administrative assistants, secretaries, and receptionists. Company pays fee. **Specializes in the areas of:** Secretarial. **Positions commonly filled include:** Administrative Assistant. **Average salary range of placements:** $30,000 - $50,000. **Number of placements per year:** 50 - 99.

E.E. BROOKE INC.
420 Lexington Avenue, Suite 2560, New York NY 10170-2599. 212/687-8400. **Fax:** 212/687-0118. **Contact:** John Kerr, President. **Description:** A permanent employment agency. Founded in 1923. Company pays fee. **Specializes in the areas of:** Accounting/Auditing; Administration; Finance; General Management; Personnel/Labor Relations; Publishing. **Positions commonly filled include:** Accountant/Auditor; Budget Analyst; Credit Manager; Customer Service Rep.; Editor; Financial Analyst; General Manager; Human Resources Manager; Management Trainee; MIS Specialist; Purchasing Agent/Manager; Services Sales Rep.; Systems Analyst; Technical Writer/Editor; Transportation/Traffic Specialist; Typist/Word Processor. **Number of placements per year:** 500 - 999.

BROOKVILLE STAFFING SERVICES, INC.
555 Broad Hollow Road, Suite 102, Melville NY 11747. 516/694-6161. **Toll-free phone:** 800/474-8465. **Fax:** 516/694-1388. **Contact:** Andrew Fishman, President. **E-mail address:** brookmis@aol.com. **World Wide Web address:** http://www.brookvillestaffing.com. **Description:** A permanent employment agency. Company pays fee. **Specializes in the areas of:** Accounting/Auditing; Administration; Computer Science/Software; Finance; Legal; MIS/EDP; Personnel/Labor Relations; Secretarial. **Positions commonly filled include:** Accountant/Auditor; Administrative Assistant; Budget Analyst; Chief Financial Officer; Controller; Customer Service Rep.; Financial Analyst; Human Resources Manager; Management Analyst/Consultant; Software Engineer; Systems Analyst; Systems Manager; Typist/Word Processor. **Average salary range of placements:** More than $50,000. **Number of placements per year:** 100 - 199.

C.C. BURKE LIMITED
60 East 42nd Street, Suite 911, New York NY 10165-0999. 212/286-0092. **Fax:** 212/286-0396. **Contact:** Charlene Burke, President. **E-mail address:** burkecc@aol.com. **Description:** A permanent employment agency. Company pays fee. **Specializes in the areas of:** Accounting/Auditing; Advertising; Art/Design; Computer Science/Software; Marketing; Sales. **Positions commonly filled include:** Account Manager; Account Rep.; Accountant/Auditor; Administrative Manager; Advertising Executive; Computer Programmer; Database Manager; Graphic Artist; Graphic Designer; Human Resources Manager; Internet Services Manager; Management Trainee; Market Research Analyst; Marketing Manager; Marketing Specialist; MIS Specialist; Online Content Specialist; Production Manager; Public Relations Specialist; Purchasing Agent/Manager; Sales Engineer; Sales Executive; Systems Analyst; Technical Writer/Editor; Telecommunications Manager; Webmaster. **Average salary range of placements:** $30,000 - $50,000. **Number of placements per year:** 50 - 99.

CAREER BLAZERS PERSONNEL SERVICE
445 Broadhollow Road, Suite 19, Melville NY 11747. 516/756-2400. **Fax:** 516/756-2426. **Contact:** Barbara Gebhardt, President. **World Wide Web address:** http://www.cblazers.com. **Description:** A full-service permanent employment agency that also provides temporary placements and computer training. The agency focuses on office support placements. Founded in 1949. Company pays fee. **Specializes in the areas of:** Accounting/Auditing; Advertising; Banking; Broadcasting; Legal; Personnel/Labor Relations; Sales; Secretarial. **Positions commonly filled include:** Accountant/Auditor; Customer Service Rep.; Human Resources Manager; Management Trainee; Paralegal; Quality Control Supervisor; Typist/Word Processor. **Corporate headquarters location:** New York NY. **Other U.S. locations:** Nationwide. **Average salary range of placements:** $20,000 - $29,999. **Number of placements per year:** 500 - 999.

CAREER BLAZERS PERSONNEL SERVICE
590 Fifth Avenue, New York NY 10036. 212/719-3232. **Contact:** Office Manager. **World Wide Web address:** http://www.cblazers.com. **Description:** A permanent employment agency. Company pays fee. **Positions commonly filled include:** Accountant/Auditor; Administrative Assistant; Advertising Clerk; Bookkeeper; Clerk; Commercial Artist; Credit Manager; Customer Service Rep.; Data Entry Clerk; Driver; Factory Worker; Human Resources Manager; Legal Secretary; Medical Secretary; Public Relations Specialist; Receptionist; Sales Rep.; Technical Writer/Editor. **Corporate headquarters location:** This Location. **Number of placements per year:** 1000+.

CAREER BLAZERS PERSONNEL SERVICE
202 Mamaroneck Avenue, White Plains NY 10601. 914/949-1166. **Contact:** Robert Miller, President. **World Wide Web address:** http://www.cblazers.com. **Description:** A permanent employment agency. Company pays fee. **Specializes in the areas of:** Accounting/Auditing; Banking; Finance; Legal; Sales; Secretarial. **Positions commonly filled include:** Accountant/Auditor; Administrative Assistant; Bookkeeper; Clerk; Credit Manager; Customer Service Representative; Data Entry Clerk; Human Resources Manager; Legal Secretary; Medical Secretary; Receptionist; Sales Representative; Stenographer; Typist/Word Processor. **Corporate headquarters location:** This Location: **Other U.S. locations:** Nationwide. **Number of placements per year:** 1000+.

CAREER CONCEPTS, INC.
25 West 43rd Street, Suite 708, New York NY 10036. 212/790-2600. **Fax:** 212/869-5598. **Contact:** Steven A. Sandler, President. **Description:** A permanent employment agency that also conducts executive searches on a contingency basis. Company pays fee. **Specializes in the areas of:** Accounting/Auditing; Banking; Brokerage; Finance; Personnel/Labor Relations. **Positions commonly filled include:** Accountant/Auditor; Bank Officer/Manager; Budget Analyst; Chief Financial Officer; Controller; Finance Director; Financial Analyst; Human Resources Manager; Operations Manager. **Corporate headquarters location:** This Location. **Average salary range of placements:** $30,000 - $50,000. **Number of placements per year:** 200 - 499.

CARLILE PERSONNEL AGENCY INC.
3 Ellinwood Court, Suite 202, New Hartford NY 13413. 315/736-3083. **Fax:** 315/736-5340. **Contact:** Doug Manning, Recruiter. **Description:** A permanent employment agency. Company pays fee. **Specializes in the areas of:** Accounting/Auditing; Administration; Computer Science/Software; Engineering; Finance; Industrial; Manufacturing; Personnel/Labor Relations; Sales; Technical. **Positions commonly filled include:** Accountant/Auditor; Chemical Engineer; Civil Engineer; Computer Programmer; Designer; Draftsperson; Electrical/Electronics Engineer; Human Resources Manager; Industrial Engineer; Industrial Production Manager; Management Analyst/Consultant; Manufacturer's/Wholesaler's Sales Rep.; Mechanical Engineer; Operations/Production Manager; Purchasing Agent/Manager; Quality Control Supervisor; Software Engineer; Structural Engineer; Systems Analyst. **Number of placements per year:** 1 - 49.

CONCORDE SEARCH
One North Broadway, White Plains NY 10601. 914/428-0700. **Fax:** 914/428-4865. **Contact:** Richard Greenwald, President. **Description:** A permanent employment agency. **Specializes in the areas of:** Accounting/Auditing; Finance; Personnel/Labor Relations; Sales. **Positions commonly filled include:** Accountant/Auditor; Bank Officer/Manager; Brokerage Clerk; Computer Programmer; Customer Service Rep.; Financial Analyst; Mathematician; Securities Sales Rep.; Underwriter/Assistant Underwriter.

MARILYN COOPER PERSONNEL
17 Battery Place, Suite 2046, New York NY 10004. 212/968-0550. **Contact:** Marilyn Cooper, President. **Description:** A permanent employment agency. **Specializes in the areas of:** Accounting/Auditing; Sales; Transportation. **Positions commonly filled include:** Accountant/Auditor; Transportation/Traffic Specialist.

CROSS STAFFING
150 Broadway, Suite 902, New York NY 10038. 212/227-6705. **Contact:** James Zamparelli, President. **Description:** A permanent employment agency. Company pays fee. **Specializes in the areas of:** Banking; Brokerage; Clerical. **Positions commonly filled include:** Administrative Assistant; Bookkeeper; Brokerage Clerk; Data Entry Clerk; Receptionist; Secretary; Stenographer; Typist/Word Processor. **Number of placements per year:** 1000+.

MAGGI DOLAN PLACEMENT, INC.
5360 Genesee Street, Bowmansville NY 14026-1044. 716/683-5360. **Toll-free phone:** 800/246-6372. **Fax:** 716/683-0203. **Contact:** Maggi Dolan, President. **Description:** A full-service employment agency providing both permanent and temporary placements. Company pays fee. **Specializes in the areas of:** Advertising; Art/Design; Health/Medical; Insurance; Legal; Publishing; Secretarial; Technical. **Positions commonly filled include:** Advertising Clerk; Architect; Chemist; Claim Rep.; Customer Service Rep.; Dental Assistant/Hygienist; Design Engineer; Designer; Draftsperson; Editor; EEG Technologist; EKG Technician; Emergency Medical Technician; Medical Records Technician; Multimedia Designer; Nuclear Medicine Technologist; Paralegal; Physical Therapist; Physician; Public Relations Specialist; Radiological Technologist; Registered Nurse; Surgical Technician; Technical Writer/Editor; Typist/Word Processor; Video Production Coordinator. **Average salary range of placements:** $30,000 - $50,000. **Number of placements per year:** 200 - 499.

ES VEE EDP PLACEMENT AGENCY
421 7th Avenue, Room 1205, New York NY 10001. 212/947-7730. **Fax:** 212/629-4192. **Contact:** Steven Vanchel, General Manager. **Description:** A permanent employment agency. Company pays fee. **Positions commonly filled include:** Computer Programmer; Software Engineer; Systems Analyst. **Average salary range of placements:** $30,000 - $80,000.

EDEN PERSONNEL, INC.
280 Madison Avenue, New York NY 10016. 212/685-8600. **Contact:** Randie Rice, Office Manager. **Description:** A permanent employment agency. Company pays fee. **Specializes in the areas of:** Accounting/Auditing; Administration; Advertising; Computer Hardware/Software; Fashion; Finance; Food Industry; Health/Medical; Industrial; Legal; Nonprofit; Personnel/Labor Relations; Retail; Secretarial. **Positions commonly filled include:** Administrative Assistant; Clerk; Data Entry Clerk; Legal Secretary; Light Industrial Worker; Medical Secretary; Nurse; Receptionist; Secretary; Typist/Word Processor.

IRWIN EDWARDS RECRUITERS INC.
510 Broadhollow Road, Melville NY 11747. 516/454-4850. **Fax:** 516/454-4925. **Contact:** Manager. **Description:** A permanent employment agency. Company pays fee. **Specializes in the areas of:** Banking; Insurance; Secretarial. **Positions commonly filled include:** Accountant/Auditor; Actuary; Bank Officer/Manager; Claim Rep.; Credit Manager; Underwriter/Assistant Underwriter. **Number of placements per year:** 100 - 199.

EMPLOYMENT RECRUITERS AGENCY
11821 Queens Boulevard, Suite 609, Forest Hills NY 11375. 718/263-2300. **Fax:** 718/263-9668. **Contact:** Brian Moran, President. **Description:** A permanent employment agency. Company pays fee. **Specializes in the areas of:** Accounting/Auditing; Administration; Advertising; Architecture/Construction; Banking; Computer Science/Software; Fashion; Finance; General Management; Health/Medical; Insurance; Legal; Manufacturing; Personnel/Labor Relations; Secretarial. **Positions commonly filled include:** Accountant/Auditor; Administrative Manager; Clerical Supervisor; Credit Manager; Customer Service Rep.; Financial Analyst; General Manager; Human Resources Manager; Management Analyst/Consultant; Management Trainee; Paralegal. **Number of placements per year:** 200 - 499.

EXECUTIVE CORPORATE STAFFING
30 East 42nd Street, New York NY 10017. 212/972-0350. **Contact:** Manager. **Description:** A permanent employment agency that also provides temporary placements.

FILCRO PERSONNEL
275 Madison Avenue, New York NY 10016. 212/599-0909. **Fax:** 212/599-1024. **Contact:** Jana Evans, Manager of Recruitment. **Description:** A permanent employment agency. Company pays fee. **Specializes in the areas of:** Communications; Finance;

Legal; Secretarial; Word Processing. **Positions commonly filled include:** Administrative Assistant; Paralegal; Secretary; Typist/Word Processor. **Number of placements per year:** 200 - 499.

FINEST EMPLOYMENT AGENCY
50 East 42nd Street, Room 1305, New York NY 10017-5405. **Contact:** Richard Friedman, President. **Description:** A permanent and temporary agency that focuses on the placement of legal and medical office support personnel. Company pays fee. **Specializes in the areas of:** Health/Medical; Legal; Secretarial. **Positions commonly filled include:** Customer Service Rep.; Dental Assistant/Hygienist; Health Services Manager; Legal Secretary; Medical Secretary; Paralegal; Typist/Word Processor. **Average salary range of placements:** $30,000 - $50,000. **Number of placements per year:** 200 - 499.

FIRST CHOICE RECRUITERS
40 Rector Street, New York NY 10006. 212/406-1866. **Contact:** Manager. **Description:** A permanent employment agency that also offers some executive placements. **Specializes in the areas of:** Finance; Legal.

FRIEDMAN EMPLOYMENT AGENCY, INC.
45 West 34th Street, New York NY 10001. 212/695-4750. **Fax:** 212/239-4942. **Contact:** George Friedman, President. **Description:** A permanent employment agency. Company pays fee. **Specializes in the areas of:** Legal; Secretarial. **Positions commonly filled include:** Accountant; Administrative Assistant; Attorney; Paralegal; Secretary; Typist/Word Processor. **Number of placements per year:** 1000+.

GRAPHICS FOR HIRE, INC.
62 Bowman Avenue, Rye Brook NY 10573-2818. 914/937-9646. **Fax:** 914/937-0558. **Contact:** Patricia Simone, Creative Placement Director. **Description:** A permanent employment agency that focuses on placing experienced computer graphics professionals, designers, art directors, copywriters, proofreaders, and creative directors. Company pays fee. **Specializes in the areas of:** Advertising; Art/Design; Publishing. **Positions commonly filled include:** Art Director; Designer; Graphic Designer; Multimedia Designer. **Number of placements per year:** 1 - 49.

GROUP AGENCY, INC.
1419 Avenue J, Brooklyn NY 11230. 718/258-9202. **Fax:** 718/258-9200. **Contact:** Counselor. **Description:** A permanent employment agency. **Specializes in the areas of:** Light Industrial; Office Support. **Positions commonly filled include:** Accountant/Auditor; Administrative Assistant; Bookkeeper; Clerk; Commercial Artist; Credit Manager; Customer Service Rep.; Data Entry Clerk; Draftsperson; Driver; Factory Worker; Human Resources Manager; Legal Secretary; Medical Secretary; Receptionist; Sales Rep.; Secretary; Stenographer; Typist/Word Processor. **Number of placements per year:** 500 - 999.

HAMPSHIRE ASSOCIATES, INC.
71 West 23rd Street, Suite 509, New York NY 10010-4102. 212/924-3999. **Contact:** Charles A. Winston, President. **Description:** A permanent employment agency. Company pays fee. **Specializes in the areas of:** Electronics; Engineering; Technical. **Positions commonly filled include:** Aerospace Engineer; Biomedical Engineer; Electrical/Electronics Engineer; Industrial Engineer; Manufacturing Engineer; Marketing Specialist; Mechanical Engineer; Software Engineer; Systems Analyst. **Average salary range of placements:** More than $50,000. **Number of placements per year:** 100 - 199.

HARBROWE, INC.
222 Mamaroneck Avenue, White Plains NY 10605. 914/949-6400. **Fax:** 914/949-6924. **Contact:** Valerie Gehn, Vice President. **Description:** A permanent employment agency. Company pays fee. **Specializes in the areas of:** Accounting/Auditing; Industrial Sales and Marketing; Medical Sales and Marketing; Office Support; Sales; Secretarial. **Positions commonly filled include:** Accountant; Administrative Assistant; Buyer; Claim Rep.; Clerical Supervisor; Computer Operator; Computer Programmer; Controller; Credit Manager; Human Resources Manager; Paralegal; Purchasing Agent/Manager; Sales Engineer; Sales Executive; Sales Manager; Sales Rep.; Secretary; Typist/Word Processor; Underwriter/Assistant Underwriter. **Average salary range of placements:** $30,000 - $50,000. **Number of placements per year:** 100 - 199.

HEALTHPRO PLACEMENT SERVICE
33 Park Drive, Putnam Valley NY 10579. 914/528-5300. **Fax:** 914/528-5303. **Contact:** Recruiter. **Description:** A permanent employment agency. **Specializes in the areas of:** Health/Medical. **Positions commonly filled include:** Dental Assistant/Dental Hygienist; Dental Lab Technician; Dentist; Licensed Practical Nurse; Respiratory Therapist.

HERON HOME & HEALTH CARE AGENCY
168-30 89th Avenue, Jamaica NY 11432. 516/292-6200. **Contact:** Director. **Description:** A permanent employment agency and contract services firm. **Specializes in the areas of:** Health/Medical. **Positions commonly filled include:** Licensed Practical Nurse; Occupational Therapist; Physical Therapist; Registered Nurse; Respiratory Therapist; Social Worker; Speech-Language Pathologist. **Other U.S. locations:** Queens NY. **Average salary range of placements:** $30,000 - $50,000. **Number of placements per year:** 1 - 49.

HUNTER MAC & ASSOCIATES
139 Fulton Street, New York NY 10038. 212/267-2790. **Fax:** 212/962-2339. **Contact:** Patrick McKeown, Vice President. **Description:** A permanent employment agency. Company pays fee. **Specializes in the areas of:** Accounting/Auditing; Administration; Banking; Computer Science/Software; Finance; Insurance; Personnel/Labor Relations; Secretarial. **Positions commonly filled include:** Accountant/Auditor; Administrative Manager; Brokerage Clerk; Computer Programmer; Financial Analyst; Human Resources Manager; Management Trainee; Securities Sales Rep.; Systems Analyst. **Number of placements per year:** 200 - 499.

IDEAL PERSONNEL
333 North Broadway, Suite 4133, Jericho NY 11753. 516/433-3333. **Fax:** 516/433-2692. **Contact:** Nancy Young, Manager/Vice President. **Description:** A permanent employment agency. **Specializes in the areas of:** Secretarial. **Positions commonly filled include:** Typist/Word Processor. **Average salary range of placements:** $20,000 - $29,999. **Number of placements per year:** 200 - 499.

INFORMATION SYSTEMS STAFFING, INC.
5730 Commons Park Drive, East Syracuse NY 13057. 315/449-1838. **Toll-free phone:** 800/466-1939. **Fax:** 315/449-1939. **Contact:** Manager. **E-mail address:** office@issi-syr.com. **World Wide Web address:** http://www.issi-syr.com. **Description:** A permanent employment agency focusing on the placement of contract and permanent computer professionals in central New York. Company pays fee. **Specializes in the areas of:** Administration; Computer Science/Software; MIS/EDP. **Positions commonly filled include:** Computer Programmer; Database Manager; MIS Specialist; Software Engineer; Systems Analyst; Systems Manager; Vice President. **Average salary**

range of placements: $30,000 - $50,000. **Number of placements per year:** 50 - 99.

INNOVATIONS ASSOCIATES
627 Field Street, Johnson City NY 13790-1057. 607/798-9376. **Fax:** 607/797-3485. **Contact:** Gene P. George, Director of Personnel Services. **Description:** A permanent employment agency. Company pays fee. **Specializes in the areas of:** Accounting/Auditing; Administration; Advertising; Art/Design; Computer Science/Software; Engineering; Sales. **Positions commonly filled include:** Accountant/Auditor; Advertising Clerk; Civil Engineer; Clerical Supervisor; Computer Programmer; Customer Service Rep.; Draftsperson; Electrical/Electronics Engineer; Industrial Engineer; Market Research Analyst; Mechanical Engineer; MIS Specialist; Multimedia Designer; Public Relations Specialist; Quality Control Supervisor; Software Engineer; Structural Engineer; Surveyor; Systems Analyst; Technical Writer/Editor; Telecommunications Manager. **Benefits available to temporary workers:** 401(k); Medical Insurance.

ISLAND SEARCH GROUP INC.
20 Crossways Park North, Woodbury NY 11797. 516/677-0015. **Fax:** 516/677-6099. **Contact:** Illene Glasser, President. **Description:** A full-service employment agency that also provides temporary placements. Founded in 1991. Company pays fee. **Specializes in the areas of:** Accounting/Auditing; Banking; Legal; Personnel/Labor Relations; Retail; Sales; Secretarial. **Positions commonly filled include:** Accountant/Auditor; Advertising Clerk; Bank Officer/Manager; Budget Analyst; Clerical Supervisor; Credit Manager; Customer Service Rep.; Financial Analyst; Human Resources Specialist; Management Trainee; Market Research Analyst; Paralegal; Typist/Word Processor. **Benefits available to temporary workers:** Paid Holidays; Paid Vacation. **Average salary range of placements:** $20,000 - $29,999. **Number of placements per year:** 200 - 499.

JDC ASSOCIATES
330 Vanderbilt-Motor Parkway, Suite 101, Hauppauge NY 11788. 516/231-8581. **Fax:** 516/231-8011. **Contact:** Lori Boyle, President. **Description:** An employment agency. Company pays fee. **Specializes in the areas of:** Accounting/Auditing; Computer Science/Software; Health/Medical; Sales; Secretarial. **Positions commonly filled include:** Accountant/Auditor; Administrative Assistant; Clerical Supervisor; Computer Programmer; Customer Service Rep.; Pharmacist; Physical Therapist; Sales Rep.; Secretary.

J.K. STAFFING LTD.
56 Harrison Street, Suite 405, New Rochelle NY 10801-6555. 914/633-7810. **Fax:** 914/633-7864. **Contact:** Janet Brown, Receptionist. **Description:** A permanent employment agency that places nursing and home health care professionals. Company pays fee. **Positions commonly filled include:** Dietician/Nutritionist; Licensed Practical Nurse; Registered Nurse. **Number of placements per year:** 1000+.

JOSEF GROUP PERSONNEL
P.O. Box 14464, Albany NY 12212. 518/386-0890. **Fax:** 518/869-9950. **Contact:** Manager. **Description:** An employment agency focusing on permanent placements. Founded in 1992. Company pays fee. **Specializes in the areas of:** Health/Medical; Legal; Secretarial. **Positions commonly filled include:** Attorney; Dental Assistant/Dental Hygienist; Dietician/Nutritionist; EEG Technologist; EKG Technician; Emergency Medical Technician; Licensed Practical Nurse; Paralegal; Physical Therapist; Physician; Recreational Therapist; Registered Nurse; Respiratory Therapist; Typist/Word Processor. **Average salary range of placements:** $20,000 - $29,999. **Number of placements per year:** 100 - 199.

JUST ONE BREAK, INC.
120 Wall Street, 20th Floor, New York NY 10005. 212/785-7300. **Contact:** Recruiter. **Description:** A nonprofit permanent employment agency for people with disabilities. **Specializes in the areas of:** Accounting/Auditing; Administration; Banking; Broadcasting; Computer Science/Software; Disabled Applicants; Finance; Food Industry; Nonprofit; Personnel/Labor Relations; Retail; Sales; Technical. **Positions commonly filled include:** Accountant; Administrative Assistant; Bank Officer/Manager; Clerical Supervisor; Counselor; Customer Service Manager; Database Manager; Graphic Artist; Management Trainee; MIS Specialist; Operations Manager; Paralegal; Sales Rep.; Secretary; Social Worker; Systems Analyst; Systems Manager; Telecommunications Manager. **Number of placements per year:** 200 - 499.

KLK PERSONNEL
507 Fifth Avenue, Suite 900, New York NY 10017. 212/986-9200. **Fax:** 212/986-0197. **Contact:** President. **Description:** A permanent employment agency. **Specializes in the areas of:** Accounting/Auditing; Administration; Advertising; Banking; Broadcasting; Fashion; Finance; Insurance; Legal; Personnel/Labor Relations. **Positions commonly filled include:** Accountant/Auditor; Administrative Assistant; Bookkeeper; Buyer; Computer Programmer; Customer Service Rep.; Data Entry Clerk; Legal Secretary; MIS Specialist; Purchasing Agent/Manager; Sales Rep.; Secretary; Systems Analyst; Typist/Word Processor. **Number of placements per year:** 500 - 999.

LISA KALUS & ASSOCIATES
26 Broadway, Suite 400, New York NY 10004-1701. 212/837-7889. **Contact:** Lisa Kalus, President. **Description:** A permanent employment agency that places managerial-level personnel. Company pays fee. **Specializes in the areas of:** Architecture/Construction; Engineering. **Positions commonly filled include:** Civil Engineer; Construction Contractor; Cost Estimator; Electrical/Electronics Engineer; Mechanical Engineer; Structural Engineer. **Average salary range of placements:** More than $50,000. **Number of placements per year:** 50 - 99.

KTECH SYSTEMS GROUP, INC.
One Silicon Alley Plaza, 90 William Street, Suite 302, New York NY 10038. 212/344-1444. **Toll-free phone:** 888/355-3133. **Fax:** 212/324-1451. **Contact:** Dick Lewis, CEO. **E-mail address:** info@ktechsys.com. **World Wide Web address:** http://www.ktechsys.com. **Description:** A permanent employment agency and contract services firm. Company pays fee. **Specializes in the areas of:** Administration; Computer Science/Software; Finance; Information Systems; Technical. **Positions commonly filled include:** Applications Engineer; Computer Programmer; Database Manager; Internet Services Manager; MIS Specialist; Software Engineer; Systems Analyst; Systems Manager; Technical Writer/Editor; Telecommunications Manager; Webmaster. **Benefits available to temporary workers:** Medical Insurance. **Average salary range of placements:** More than $50,000. **Number of placements per year:** 500 - 999.

TINA LANE PERSONNEL, INC.
317 Madison Avenue, Suite 605, New York NY 10017. 212/682-1333. **Fax:** 212/682-1499. **Contact:** Helene G. Cohen, Executive Vice President. **Description:** A permanent employment agency. Company pays fee. **Specializes in the areas of:** Accounting/Auditing; Banking; Consumer Products; Finance; Real Estate. **Positions commonly filled**

include: Accountant; Administrative Assistant; Computer Programmer; Financial Analyst; Human Resources Specialist; Property and Real Estate Manager; Systems Analyst; Typist/Word Processor. **Average salary range of placements:** $30,000 - $80,000. **Number of placements per year:** 200 - 499.

JOSEPH T. MALONEY AND ASSOCIATES, INC.
51 East 42nd Street, Suite 1508, New York NY 10017. 212/377-0100. **Contact:** Betty Lopez, Manager. **Description:** A permanent employment agency. Company pays fee. **Specializes in the areas of:** Accounting/Auditing; Banking; Clerical; Finance; Insurance; Legal; Personnel/Labor Relations; Sales. **Positions commonly filled include:** Accountant/Auditor; Administrative Assistant; Attorney; Bank Officer/Manager; Bookkeeper; Brokerage Clerk; Claim Rep.; Clerk; Computer Programmer; Customer Service Rep.; Data Entry Clerk; Economist; EDP Specialist; Financial Analyst; Human Resources Manager; Legal Secretary; Marketing Specialist; MIS Specialist; Office Manager; Receptionist; Sales Rep.; Secretary; Stenographer; Typist/Word Processor. **Number of placements per year:** 500 - 999.

LYNN MARSHALL PERSONNEL AGENCY, INC.
91-31 Queens Boulevard, Rego Park NY 11373. 718/446-5200. **Fax:** 718/446-5202. **Contact:** Lynn Marshall, Owner/President. **Description:** A permanent employment agency. Company pays fee. **Specializes in the areas of:** Accounting/Auditing; Legal; Secretarial. **Positions commonly filled include:** Administrative Assistant; Bookkeeper; Clerical Supervisor; Computer Programmer; Credit Manager; Customer Service Rep.; Human Resources Manager; Management Trainee; Services Sales Rep.; Systems Analyst; Typist/Word Processor. **Number of placements per year:** 50 - 99.

MEDICAL STAFFERS
292 Madison Avenue, 17th Floor, New York NY 10017. 212/213-5632. **Fax:** 212/213-5660. **Contact:** Executive Director. **Description:** A permanent employment agency. Company pays fee. **Specializes in the areas of:** Health/Medical. **Positions commonly filled include:** Chemist; Clinical Lab Technician; Dental Assistant/Hygienist; Dentist; Dietician/Nutritionist; EEG Technologist; EKG Technician; Licensed Practical Nurse; Medical Records Technician; Nuclear Medicine Technologist; Nurse; Occupational Therapist; Pharmacist; Physical Therapist; Physician; Physician Assistant; Recreational Therapist; Registered Nurse; Respiratory Therapist; Social Worker; Speech-Language Pathologist; Surgical Technician. **Number of placements per year:** 200 - 499.

MEDSTAFF SERVICES
16 East 40th Street, New York NY 10016-0113. 212/576-1192. **Fax:** 212/576-1574. **Contact:** Manager. **Description:** A permanent employment agency. **Specializes in the areas of:** Health/Medical; Insurance; Nonprofit; Personnel/Labor Relations; Secretarial. **Positions commonly filled include:** Claim Rep.; Clerical Supervisor; Clinical Lab Technician; Customer Service Rep.; Dental Assistant/Hygienist; EEG Technologist; EKG Technician; Emergency Medical Technician; Health Services Manager; Medical Records Technician; Pharmacist; Physical Therapist; Physician; Radiological Technologist; Registered Nurse; Science Technologist; Social Worker; Typist/Word Processor. **Number of placements per year:** 1000+.

METRO SUPPORT GROUP
370 Lexington Avenue, Suite 1508, New York NY 10017. 212/818-1177. **Fax:** 212/818-0291. **Contact:** Renee Chandler, President. **Description:** A permanent employment agency. Metro Support Group's clients include brokerage firms, banks, advertising agencies, entertainment corporations, and legal firms. Company pays fee. **Specializes in the areas of:** Communications; Personnel/Labor Relations; Secretarial. **Positions commonly filled include:** Administrative Assistant; Advertising Clerk; Brokerage Clerk; Clerical Supervisor; Human Resources Manager; Secretary. **Average salary range of placements:** $30,000 - $50,000. **Number of placements per year:** 200 - 499.

MILAZZO ASSOCIATES, INC.
17 Battery Place, Suite 2632, New York NY 10004. 212/344-2334. **Fax:** 212/344-1910. **Contact:** Peter Milazzo, President. **Description:** A permanent employment agency. **Specializes in the areas of:** Accounting/Auditing; Administration; Banking; Computer Science/Software; Economics; Finance; Legal; Personnel/Labor Relations; Sales; Secretarial; Technical. **Positions commonly filled include:** Accountant/Auditor; Administrative Manager; Bank Officer/Manager; Brokerage Clerk; Credit Manager; Customer Service Rep.; Economist; Financial Analyst; Human Resources Manager; Management Analyst/Consultant; Operations/Production Manager; Paralegal; Public Relations Specialist; Purchasing Agent/Manager; Securities Sales Rep.; Services Sales Rep.; Strategic Relations Manager; Systems Analyst; Technical Writer/Editor; Telecommunications Manager; Typist/Word Processor. **Other U.S. locations:** Nationwide. **Number of placements per year:** 50 - 99.

NATIONAL EMPLOYMENT DATABASE, INC.
50 Broad Street, New York NY 10004. 212/269-1994. **Fax:** 212/269-1995. **Contact:** Raphael D. Bloom, President. **E-mail address:** nedjobsrus@aol.com. **World Wide Web address:** http://www.occ.com/ned1. **Description:** A database employment service. Company pays fee. **Specializes in the areas of:** Accounting/Auditing; Administration; Banking; Computer Science/Software; Finance; Legal; Publishing; Secretarial. **Positions commonly filled include:** Accountant/Auditor; Administrative Manager; Brokerage Clerk; Computer Programmer; Economist; Electrical/Electronics Engineer; Human Resources Manager; Management Trainee; Operations/Production Manager; Paralegal; Software Engineer; Systems Analyst. **Other U.S. locations:** Nationwide. **Average salary range of placements:** $30,000 - $50,000. **Number of placements per year:** 500 - 999.

NATIONWIDE PERSONNEL GROUP
474 Elmwood Avenue, Suite 201, Buffalo NY 14222. 716/881-2144. **Fax:** 716/881-0711. **Contact:** Mark Gademsky, C.P.C./President. **E-mail address:** gademsky@localnet.com. **Description:** A permanent employment agency. Company pays fee. **Specializes in the areas of:** Administration; Computer Science/Software; Engineering. **Positions commonly filled include:** Computer Programmer; Design Engineer; Electrical/Electronics Engineer; Internet Services Manager; Mathematician; Mechanical Engineer; MIS Specialist; Software Engineer; Systems Analyst; Telecommunications Manager. **Average salary range of placements:** $35,000 - $120,000. **Number of placements per year:** 50 - 99.

THE NEW YORK NANNY CENTER, INC.
31 South Bayles Avenue, Port Washington NY 11050. 516/767-5136. **Fax:** 516/767-5166. **Contact:** Carol Solomon, Director. **Description:** A permanent employment agency. **Specializes in the areas of:** Child Care, In-Home. **Positions commonly filled include:** Nanny. **Number of placements per year:** 100 - 199.

NEW YORK-NEW YORK PERSONNEL
170 Broadway, Suite 906, New York NY 10038. 212/267-3500. **Fax:** 212/791-3746. **Contact:** Personnel. **Description:** A permanent employment agency. Company pays fee. **Specializes in the areas**

of: Banking; Finance; Insurance; Legal; Secretarial. **Positions commonly filled include:** Administrative Assistant; Computer Operator; Legal Secretary; Paralegal; Secretary; Typist/Word Processor; Underwriter/Assistant Underwriter. **Corporate headquarters location:** This Location. **Average salary range of placements:** $30,000 - $50,000.

NOAH ASSOCIATES
P.O. Box 606, Amawalk NY 10501. 914/737-1819. **Fax:** 914/737-1853. **Contact:** Norman Houle, President. **Description:** A permanent employment agency. Company pays fee. **Specializes in the areas of:** Accounting/Auditing; Administration; Biology; Computer Science/Software; Engineering; Finance; General Management; Industrial; Manufacturing; Personnel/Labor Relations; Sales; Technical; Transportation. **Positions commonly filled include:** Accountant/Auditor; Aerospace Engineer; Biological Scientist; Biomedical Engineer; Buyer; Ceramics Engineer; Chemical Engineer; Chemist; Civil Engineer; Compliance Analyst; Computer Programmer; Customer Service Rep.; Electrical/Electronics Engineer; Human Resources Manager; Industrial Designer; Industrial Engineer; Manufacturing Engineer; Marketing Specialist; Mechanical Engineer; MIS Specialist; Purchasing Agent/Manager; Quality Control Supervisor; Sales Rep.; Software Engineer; Systems Analyst. **Number of placements per year:** 1 - 49.

NORRELL STAFFING SERVICES
420 Lexington Avenue, Suite 2516, New York NY 10017. 212/697-5240. **Fax:** 212/557-0034. **Contact:** Kathy Lally, Recruiter. **Description:** A permanent employment agency. Company pays fee. **Specializes in the areas of:** Accounting/Auditing; Administration; Computer Science/Software; Finance; Personnel/Labor Relations; Sales; Secretarial; Technical. **Positions commonly filled include:** Accountant/Auditor; Customer Service Representative; Financial Analyst; Human Resources Manager; Paralegal; Services Sales Representative; Typist/Word Processor. **Benefits available to temporary workers:** Dental Insurance; Medical Insurance; Paid Holidays; Paid Vacation; Stock Purchase. **Corporate headquarters location:** Atlanta GA. **Other U.S. locations:** Nationwide. **Average salary range of placements:** $30,000 - $50,000. **Number of placements per year:** 1000+.

NORRIS EMPLOYMENT CONSULTANTS
P.O. Box 2460, Liverpool NY 13089-2460. 315/695-4999. **Fax:** 315/695-4030. **Contact:** Donald W. Norris Jr., President. **Description:** A permanent employment agency. Company pays fee. **Specializes in the areas of:** Engineering; Manufacturing; Personnel/Labor Relations. **Positions commonly filled include:** Electrical/Electronics Engineer; General Manager; Human Resources Manager; Industrial Engineer; Industrial Production Manager; Mechanical Engineer. **Number of placements per year:** 1 - 49.

K.A. NOWACK CAREER SPECIALISTS
170 Broadway, New York NY 10038. 212/732-1919. **Fax:** 212/233-1040. **Contact:** Kathleen Nowack, President. **Description:** A permanent employment agency. **Specializes in the areas of:** Accounting/Auditing; Art/Design; Banking; Economics; Finance; Insurance; Legal; Personnel/Labor Relations; Sales; Secretarial; Technical. **Positions commonly filled include:** Accountant/Auditor; Aerospace Engineer; Budget Analyst; Claim Representative; Computer Programmer; Customer Service Rep.; Financial Analyst; Management Trainee; Operations/Production Manager; Paralegal; Securities Sales Rep.; Telecommunications Manager; Typist/Word Processor; Underwriter/Assistant Underwriter. **Number of placements per year:** 50 - 99.

OTEC.COM
24 West 40th Street, 11th Floor, New York NY 10018-3904. 212/768-0600. **Fax:** 212/768-8309. **Contact:** Kelly Michaelian, Office Manager. **E-mail address:** jobs@otec.com. **World Wide Web address:** http://www.otec.com. **Description:** A permanent employment agency that also offers contract services. Company pays fee. **Specializes in the areas of:** Administration; Banking; Computer Science/Software; Engineering; Finance; Network Administration. **Positions commonly filled include:** Applications Engineer; Chief Financial Officer; Computer Animator; Computer Programmer; Database Manager; Design Engineer; Graphic Artist; Graphic Designer; Human Resources Manager; Internet Services Manager; Management Analyst/Consultant; MIS Specialist; Multimedia Designer; Online Content Specialist; Software Engineer; Systems Analyst; Systems Manager; Technical Writer/Editor; Telecommunications Manager; Video Production Coordinator; Webmaster. **Benefits available to temporary workers:** Medical Insurance. **Corporate headquarters location:** This Location. **Other U.S. locations:** Burlingame CA. **Average salary range of placements:** More than $50,000. **Number of placements per year:** 100 - 199.

PARSONS, ANDERSON AND GEE, INC.
642 Kreag Road, Pittsford NY 14534-3705. 716/586-8679. **Fax:** 716/586-0247. **Contact:** Art Fandel, General Manager. **Description:** A permanent employment agency. Company pays fee. **Specializes in the areas of:** Accounting/Auditing; Administration; Computer Science/Software; Engineering; Finance; Food Industry; General Management; Industrial; Insurance; Manufacturing; Personnel/Labor Relations; Publishing; Sales; Technical. **Positions commonly filled include:** Accountant/Auditor; Biomedical Engineer; Buyer; Chemical Engineer; Computer Programmer; Designer; Electrical/Electronics Engineer; Human Resources Manager; Industrial Engineer; Industrial Production Manager; Manufacturer's/Wholesaler's Sales Rep.; Mechanical Engineer; Purchasing Agent/Manager; Quality Control Supervisor; Securities Sales Rep.; Software Engineer; Stationary Engineer; Structural Engineer; Systems Analyst; Technical Writer/Editor. **Number of placements per year:** 1 - 49.

PHOENIX EMPLOYMENT AGENCY
205 West 14th Street, New York NY 10011-7114. 212/255-3436. **Fax:** 212/255-8308. **Contact:** Steve Blecher, Owner. **Description:** A permanent employment agency. Company pays fee. **Specializes in the areas of:** Food Industry; Industrial; Manufacturing. **Positions commonly filled include:** Blue-Collar Worker Supervisor; Electrician; Electronics Technician; Industrial Production Manager; Operations/Production Manager; Restaurant/Food Service Manager; Warehouse Manager. **Number of placements per year:** 100 - 199.

POSTON PERSONNEL
16 East 79th Street, Suite G4, New York NY 10021. 212/535-4116. **Fax:** 212/988-7080. **Contact:** Jerry Bohne, Owner. **Description:** A permanent employment agency. Company pays fee. **Positions commonly filled include:** Administrative Assistant; Bookkeeper; Clerk; Commercial Artist; Customer Service Rep.; Human Resources Manager; Legal Secretary; Marketing Specialist; Medical Secretary; Receptionist; Sales Rep.; Secretary; Stenographer; Technical Writer/Editor. **Number of placements per year:** 50 - 99.

PRESTIGE PERSONNEL
32-30 58th Street, Woodside NY 11377. 718/721-2200. **Contact:** Office Manager. **Description:** A permanent employment agency. **Positions commonly filled include:** Bookkeeper; Legal Secretary; Real Estate Agent. **Number of placements per year:** 500 - 999.

QUALITY CARE ASSOCIATES
51 Purchase Street, Rye NY 10580. 914/967-8254. **Fax:** 914/967-1854. **Contact:** Sue Felder, Owner. **E-mail address:** quality@newdirection.com. **Description:** A permanent employment agency focusing on the placement of in-home child care providers. **Positions commonly filled include:** Child Care Director. **Corporate headquarters location:** Westchester NY. **Average salary range of placements:** $20,000 - $29,999. **Number of placements per year:** 50 - 99.

QUALITY HEALTHCARE STAFFING INC.
1359 Coney Island Avenue, Brooklyn NY 11230. 718/338-8500. **Fax:** 718/338-8838. **Contact:** Malca Fass, Administrator. **Description:** A permanent employment agency. **Specializes in the areas of:** Health/Medical. **Positions commonly filled include:** Licensed Practical Nurse; Registered Nurse. **Number of placements per year:** 100 - 199.

QUANTUM PERSONNEL AGENCY INC.
17 East 45th Street, New York NY 10017. 212/286-0111. **Fax:** 212/808-5279. **Contact:** Office Manager. **Description:** A permanent employment agency. **Specializes in the areas of:** Computer Science/Software. **Positions commonly filled include:** Computer Programmer; Systems Analyst. **Number of placements per year:** 500 - 999.

REM RESOURCES, INC.
507 Fifth Avenue, Suite 1106, New York NY 10017. 212/661-0090. **Fax:** 212/661-0107. **Contact:** Gabrielle Rem, President. **E-mail address:** reminc1 @aol.com. **Description:** A full-service employment agency that provides both permanent and temporary placements. **Specializes in the areas of:** Accounting/Auditing; Administration; Advertising; Broadcasting; Computer Science/Software; Fashion; Finance; Insurance; Legal; Nonprofit; Personnel/Labor Relations; Publishing; Sales; Secretarial. **Positions commonly filled include:** Accountant/Auditor; Administrative Assistant; Brokerage Clerk; Budget Analyst; Business Analyst; Computer Programmer; Customer Service Rep.; Database Manager; Editorial Assistant; Executive Assistant; Finance Director; Financial Analyst; Fund Manager; Health Services Manager; Human Resources Manager; Internet Specialist; Market Research Analyst; Office Manager; Operations/Production Manager; Purchasing Agent/ Manager; Receptionist; Systems Analyst. **Other U.S. locations:** Nationwide. **Number of placements per year:** 200 - 499.

REPUBLIC EMPLOYMENT AGENCY
181 Broadway, New York NY 10007. 212/964-0640. **Fax:** 212/267-0032. **Contact:** Tony Freddo, Office Manager. **Description:** A permanent employment agency that also provides some temporary placements. Company pays fee. **Specializes in the areas of:** Health/Medical; Secretarial. **Positions commonly filled include:** Dental Assistant/Dental Hygienist; Dentist; Health Services Manager; Medical Records Technician; Registered Nurse. **Average salary range of placements:** $20,000 - $29,999. **Number of placements per year:** 200 - 499.

RIBOLOW ASSOCIATES
230 Park Avenue, Suite 222, New York NY 10169. 212/808-0580. **Fax:** 212/573-6050. **Contact:** Adele Ribolow, President. **E-mail address:** http://www.zqlm53a.prodigy.com. **World Wide Web address:** simonoz@prodigy.com. **Description:** A permanent employment agency that also provides some temporary placements. Company pays fee. **Specializes in the areas of:** Advertising; Nonprofit; Public Relations; Publishing; Secretarial. **Positions commonly filled include:** Editor; Editorial Assistant; Managing Editor; Market Research Analyst; Production Manager; Public Relations Specialist; Sales Executive; Secretary. **Corporate headquarters location:** This Location. **Number of placements per year:** 100 - 199.

BETH RICHMAN ASSOCIATES
535 Fifth Avenue, New York NY 10017-3610. 212/986-5169. **Fax:** 212/490-0315. **Contact:** Beth Richman, President. **Description:** A full-service permanent employment agency that places support and professional personnel primarily in the Wall Street community. Company pays fee. **Specializes in the areas of:** Accounting/Auditing; Banking; Computer Science/Software; Finance; Sales; Secretarial. **Positions commonly filled include:** Accountant/ Auditor; Bank Officer/Manager; Computer Programmer; Customer Service Rep.; Financial Analyst; Human Resources Manager; Insurance Agent/ Broker; MIS Specialist; Public Relations Specialist; Technical Writer/Editor; Typist/Word Processor. **Average salary range of placements:** $30,000 - $50,000. **Number of placements per year:** 50 - 99.

FRAN ROGERS PERSONNEL
One Huntington Quadrangle, Suite 2S09, Melville NY 11747. 516/752-8888. **Contact:** Fran Rogers, President. **Description:** A permanent employment agency. Company pays fee. **Specializes in the areas of:** Accounting/Auditing; Administration; Banking; Computer Science/Software; Engineering; Finance; Technical. **Positions commonly filled include:** Accountant/Auditor; Administrative Assistant; Bookkeeper; EDP Specialist; Electrical/Electronics Engineer; Financial Analyst; MIS Specialist; Receptionist; Systems Analyst; Typist/Word Processor. **Number of placements per year:** 200 - 499.

ALEXANDER ROSS ASSOCIATES, INC.
21 East 40th Street, Suite 1802, New York NY 10016. 212/889-9333. **Contact:** Ben Lichtenstein, President. **Description:** A permanent employment agency. **Specializes in the areas of:** Change Management; Human Resources; Organization Development. **Number of placements per year:** 1 - 49.

SALES RECRUITERS INTERNATIONAL LTD.
660 White Plains Road, 5th Floor, Tarrytown NY 10591. 914/631-0090. **Fax:** 914/631-1089. **Contact:** Richard J. Harris, President. **Description:** A permanent employment agency. Company pays fee. **Specializes in the areas of:** Sales; Secretarial. **Positions commonly filled include:** Manufacturer's/Wholesaler's Sales Rep.; Services Sales Rep. **Number of placements per year:** 50 - 99.

SENIOR RESOURCES
60 East 42nd Street, Suite 731, New York NY 10165. 212/986-8017. **Contact:** Thomas S. Lyons, Vice President. **Description:** A permanent employment agency. **Positions commonly filled include:** Bookkeeper; Clerk; Customer Service Rep.; Data Entry Clerk; Receptionist; Typist/Word Processor. **Number of placements per year:** 100 - 199.

SIGMA STAFFING
535 Broad Hollow Road, Melville NY 11747. 516/694-7707. **Contact:** Thea Linker, President. **Description:** A permanent employment agency that also provides some temporary placements. Company pays fee. **Specializes in the areas of:** Accounting/Auditing; Administration; Computer Science/Software; Finance; Technical. **Positions commonly filled include:** Accountant/Auditor; Bookkeeper; Computer Programmer; EDP Specialist; Financial Analyst; MIS Specialist; Systems Analyst. **Number of placements per year:** 50 - 99.

SLOAN PERSONNEL, INC.
317 Madison Avenue, 21st Floor, New York NY 10017. 212/949-7200. **Fax:** 212/949-8599. **Contact:** Office Manager. **Description:** A permanent employment agency. **Specializes in the areas of:** Clerical; Office Support; Secretarial. **Positions commonly filled include:** Administrative Assistant; Bookkeeper; Clerk; Customer Service Rep.; Data Entry Clerk; Legal Secretary; Medical Secretary; Receptionist; Typist/Word Processor. **Number of placements per year:** 200 - 499.

STAFF BY MANNING, LTD.
38 East 57th Street, New York NY 10022-2512. 212/753-8080. **Fax:** 212/753-8079. **Contact:** Recruiter. **Description:** A permanent employment agency. Company pays fee. **Specializes in the areas of:** Administration; Operations Management; Personnel/Labor Relations; Secretarial. **Positions commonly filled include:** Administrative Assistant; Administrative Manager; Clerical Supervisor; Office Manager. **Number of placements per year:** 1 - 49.

STAMM PERSONNEL AGENCY INC.
27 Whitehall Street, New York NY 10004. 212/509-6600. **Fax:** 212/509-3773. **Contact:** Ted Sommermann, Executive Recruiter. **Description:** A permanent employment agency. Company pays fee. **Specializes in the areas of:** Administration; Computer Science/Software; Consulting; Finance; Investment; Sales; Secretarial. **Positions commonly filled include:** Accountant/Auditor; Attorney; Brokerage Clerk; Computer Programmer; Customer Service Rep.; Economist; Editor; Financial Analyst; Securities Sales Rep.; Systems Analyst; Technical Writer/Editor. **Number of placements per year:** 100 - 199.

TALENT TREE STAFFING SERVICES
One Water Street, 3rd Floor, White Plains NY 10601-1009. **Contact:** Staffing Consultant. **Description:** An employment agency that provides both permanent and temporary placements. **Specializes in the areas of:** Clerical; Light Industrial; Word Processing. **Positions commonly filled include:** Blue-Collar Worker Supervisor; Customer Service Rep.; Typist/Word Processor. **Benefits available to temporary workers:** 401(k); Dental Insurance; Vision Plan. **Corporate headquarters location:** Houston TX. **Number of placements per year:** 1000+.

TAX NETWORK RESOURCES, INC.
19 Hanover Place, Hicksville NY 11801. 212/983-3030. **Contact:** Mike Marino, President. **Description:** A permanent employment agency. Founded in 1990. **Specializes in the areas of:** Accounting/Auditing; Tax. **Positions commonly filled include:** Accountant/Auditor; Tax Specialist. **Number of placements per year:** 1 - 49.

HILLARY TAYLOR PERSONNEL
2 John Street, 2nd Floor, New York NY 10038. 212/619-8200. **Fax:** 212/385-0454. **Contact:** Hillary Taylor, President. **Description:** A permanent employment agency. Company pays fee. **Specializes in the areas of:** Accounting/Auditing; Advertising; Banking; Fashion; Finance; Legal; Secretarial. **Positions commonly filled include:** Accountant; Administrative Assistant; Customer Service Rep.; Financial Analyst; Paralegal; Secretary; Typist/Word Processor. **Average salary range of placements:** $30,000 - $50,000. **Number of placements per year:** 50 - 99.

TEMPO SERVICES, INC.
1400 Old Country Road, Suite 211, Westbury NY 11590. 516/333-2323. **Contact:** Office Manager. **Description:** A permanent employment agency that also offers some temporary placements. Company pays fee. **Positions commonly filled include:** Accountant/Auditor; Bookkeeper; Clerk; Computer Programmer; Credit Manager; Data Entry Clerk; Draftsperson; EDP Specialist; Financial Analyst; Legal Secretary; Marketing Specialist; Medical Secretary; Nurse; Purchasing Agent/Manager; Receptionist; Secretary; Stenographer; Systems Analyst; Typist/Word Processor. **Corporate headquarters location:** Woodbury NY. **Number of placements per year:** 1000+.

TEMPO SERVICES, INC.
287 Northern Boulevard, Great Neck NY 11021. 516/466-4664. **Fax:** 516/466-7001. **Contact:** Lisa J. Felner, Branch Manager. **Description:** A permanent employment agency. **Specializes in the areas of:** Accounting/Auditing; Banking; Personnel/Labor Relations; Sales; Secretarial. **Positions commonly filled include:** Administrative Manager; Customer Service Rep.; General Manager; Human Resources Manager; Market Research Analyst; Typist/Word Processor. **Benefits available to temporary workers:** 401(k); Paid Vacation; Referral Bonus Plan. **Corporate headquarters location:** Woodbury NY. **Average salary range of placements:** $20,000 - $29,999. **Number of placements per year:** 1000+.

TYLER SEARCH CONSULTANTS
42 West 38th Street, 12th Floor, New York NY 10018. 212/719-2200. **Fax:** 212/719-2898. **Contact:** William P. Conroy, President. **E-mail address:** tylersc@ibm.net. **Description:** A permanent employment agency. **Specializes in the areas of:** Banking; Brokerage; Communications; Finance; Import/Export; Transportation. **Positions commonly filled include:** Account Manager; Controller; Credit Analyst; Credit Manager; Financial Analyst; Logistics Manager; Marketing Specialist; Operations Manager; Sales Manager; Systems Specialist; Vice President.

UNITED PERSONNEL AGENCY, INC.
51 East 42nd Street, Suite 1410, New York NY 10017. 212/490-2197. **Fax:** 212/338-9677. **Contact:** Michael P. Williams, President. **E-mail address:** upagency@ix.netcom.com. **Description:** A permanent and temporary employment agency. Company pays fee. **Specializes in the areas of:** Accounting/Auditing; Advertising; Banking; Broadcasting; Computer Science/Software; Legal; Nonprofit; Personnel/Labor Relations; Publishing; Secretarial; Word Processing. **Positions commonly filled include:** Accountant/Auditor; Budget Analyst; Claim Rep.; Paralegal; Software Engineer; Systems Analyst. **Number of placements per year:** 1000+.

VANCE PERSONNEL
505 Fifth Avenue, New York NY 10017. 212/661-8860. **Contact:** Larry Stevens, President. **Description:** A permanent employment agency. Company pays fee. **Specializes in the areas of:** Brokerage; Finance; Secretarial. **Positions commonly filled include:** Accountant/Auditor; Advertising Clerk; Bookkeeper; Clerk; Credit Manager; Customer Service Rep.; Data Entry Clerk; Human Resources Manager; Legal Secretary; Medical Secretary; Public Relations Specialist; Receptionist; Secretary; Stenographer; Typist/Word Processor. **Number of placements per year:** 200 - 499.

DON WALDRON & ASSOCIATES
450 Seventh Avenue, Suite 507A, New York NY 10123. 212/239-9110. **Fax:** 212/239-9114. **Contact:** Don Waldron, President. **Description:** A permanent employment agency. **Specializes in the areas of:** Advertising.

WEHINGER SERVICES
375 North Broadway, Jericho NY 11753. 516/938-7944. **Fax:** 516/938-3625. **Contact:** Chuck Copt,

Vice President. **Description:** A permanent employment agency. Company pays fee. **Specializes in the areas of:** Banking; Insurance; Retail. **Positions commonly filled include:** Actuary; Adjuster; Bank Officer/ Manager; Claim Rep.; Customer Service Rep.; Insurance Agent/Broker; Management Trainee; Underwriter/Assistant Underwriter; Wholesale/Retail Buyer. **Number of placements per year:** 100 - 199.

WESTCHESTER EMPLOYMENT AGENCY
109 Croton Avenue, Ossining NY 10562. 914/941-8150. **Fax:** 914/941-1748. **Contact:** Alan Gordon, President. **Description:** A permanent employment agency. Founded in 1962. Company pays fee. **Specializes in the areas of:** Accounting/Auditing; Administration; Engineering; Finance; General Management; Industrial; Insurance; Legal; Manufacturing; Personnel/Labor Relations; Retail; Sales; Technical. **Positions commonly filled include:** Accountant/Auditor; Administrative Manager; Bookkeeper; Claim Rep.; Clerk; Customer Service Rep.; Data Entry Clerk; Marketing Specialist; Medical Secretary; Operations/Production Manager; Public Relations Specialist; Purchasing Agent/Manager; Software Engineer; Technical Writer/Editor. **Number of placements per year:** 200 - 499.

WOODBURY PERSONNEL
375 North Broadway, Suite 105, Jericho NY 11753-2008. 516/938-7910. **Toll-free phone:** 800/641-0060. **Fax:** 516/938-7370. **Contact:** Chuck Copt, President. **Description:** A permanent employment agency. Company pays fee. **Specializes in the areas of:** Banking; Insurance; Legal; Personnel/Labor Relations; Retail. **Positions commonly filled include:** Accountant/Auditor; Adjuster; Attorney; Branch Manager; Insurance Agent/Broker; Management Trainee; Paralegal; Underwriter/Assistant Underwriter. **Average salary range of placements:** $30,000 - $50,000. **Number of placements per year:** 200 - 499.

YOURS IN TRAVEL PERSONNEL AGENCY, INC.
12 West 37th Street, New York NY 10018. 212/697-7855. **Contact:** Jason King, President. **World Wide Web address:** http://www.yoursintravel.com. **Description:** A permanent employment agency providing placements from entry-level to senior executives. Founded in 1972. Company pays fee. **NOTE:** All inquiries, applications, and resumes must be sent to this location. Applications can be sent to the company Website. **Specializes in the areas of:** Hotel/Restaurant; Tourism; Transportation; Travel. **Positions commonly filled include:** Travel Agent. **Corporate headquarters location:** This Location. **Other U.S. locations:** Nationwide.

TEMPORARY EMPLOYMENT AGENCIES

AM & PM TEMPS
619 Roanoke Avenue, Riverhead NY 11901-2727. 516/369-5980. **Toll-free phone:** 800/424-5059. **Contact:** Kathy Smith, Staffing Specialist. **E-mail address:** amptemps@juno.com. **Description:** A temporary agency that also provides permanent placement. Company pays fee. **Specializes in the areas of:** Computer Science/Software; General Management; Light Industrial; Manufacturing; Retail; Sales; Secretarial. **Positions commonly filled include:** Accountant/Auditor; Administrative Manager; EKG Technician; General Manager; Manufacturer's/ Wholesaler's Sales Rep.; Paralegal. **Number of placements per year:** 50 - 99.

AADAMS PERSONNEL AGENCY
3915 Main Street, Suite 301, Flushing NY 11354. 718/359-0800. **Contact:** Manager. **Description:** A temporary agency. **Specializes in the areas of:** Sales; Secretarial. **Positions commonly filled include:** Accountant/Auditor; Architect; Buyer; Chemical Engineer; Chemist; Civil Engineer; Clerical Supervisor; Clinical Lab Technician; Electrical/Electronics Engineer; Financial Analyst; General Manager; Human Resources Specialist; Industrial Engineer; MIS Specialist; Physical Therapist; Recreational Therapist; Systems Analyst. **Average salary range of placements:** $20,000 - $29,999. **Number of placements per year:** 50 - 99.

ACCUSTAFF INC.
425 Broadhollow Road, Suite 116, Melville NY 11747. 516/293-7050. **Fax:** 516/293-7057. **Contact:** Marketing/Sales Department. **Description:** A temporary agency that also provides some permanent placements. **Specializes in the areas of:** Office Support; Telemarketing. **Positions commonly filled include:** Accountant/Auditor; Bookkeeper; Claim Rep.; Clerk; Customer Service Rep.; Data Entry Clerk; Legal Secretary; Medical Secretary; MIS Specialist; Quality Control Supervisor; Receptionist; Secretary; Typist/Word Processor. **Benefits available to temporary workers:** 401(k). **Corporate headquarters location:** Woodbury NY. **Other U.S. locations:** Nationwide. **Number of placements per year:** 1000+.

ACCUSTAFF INC.
1975 Hempstead Turnpike, East Meadow NY 11554. 516/227-2700. **Fax:** 516/227-0544. **Contact:** Ms. Star Aponte, Branch Manager. **Description:** A temporary agency that also provides temp-to-hire and permanent staffing. Company pays fee. **Specializes in the areas of:** Banking; Publishing; Secretarial. **Positions commonly filled include:** Customer Service Rep.; Typist/Word Processor. **Benefits available to temporary workers:** Paid Holidays; Paid Vacation; Referral Bonus Plan. **Number of placements per year:** 500 - 999.

ADECCO
551 Fifth Avenue, Suite 501, New York NY 10017. 212/682-3438. **Contact:** Office Supervisor. **Description:** A temporary agency that also provides some permanent placements. Company pays fee. **Specializes in the areas of:** Accounting/Auditing; Advertising; Banking; Broadcasting; Clerical; Communications; Fashion; Finance; Food Industry; Insurance; Nonprofit; Personnel/Labor Relations; Public Relations; Publishing; Retail; Textiles. **Positions commonly filled include:** Accountant/Auditor; Administrative Assistant; Assistant Manager; Bookkeeper; Clerk; Customer Service Rep.; Data Entry Clerk; EDP Specialist; Legal Secretary; Medical Secretary; Receptionist; Stenographer; Typist/Word Processor. **Number of placements per year:** 1000+.

ADECCO
500 Old Country Road, Suite 110, Garden City NY 11530-1921. 516/741-4944. **Fax:** 516/741-5094. **Contact:** Office Manager. **Description:** A temporary agency that also provides temp-to-hire and some permanent placements. **Specializes in the areas of:** Accounting/Auditing; Administration; Advertising; Banking; Finance; Insurance; Manufacturing; Personnel/Labor Relations; Retail; Sales; Secretarial. **Positions commonly filled include:** Administrative Manager; Brokerage Clerk; Budget Analyst; Claim Rep.; Clerical Supervisor; Clinical Lab Technician; Computer Programmer; Credit Manager; Customer

Service Rep.; Financial Analyst; General Manager; Health Services Manager; Human Resources Specialist; Industrial Engineer; Industrial Production Manager; Internet Services Manager; Management Trainee; Market Research Analyst; Medical Records Technician; Systems Analyst; Telecommunications Manager; Typist/Word Processor; Underwriter/ Assistant Underwriter. **Benefits available to temporary workers:** Medical Insurance; Paid Holidays; Paid Vacation. **Corporate headquarters location:** Redwood City CA. **Other U.S. locations:** Nationwide. **Average salary range of placements:** $20,000 - $39,999. **Number of placements per year:** 50 - 99.

BESTEMP TEMPORARY SERVICES, INC.
49 South Main Street, Gloversville NY 12078. 518/725-1459. **Fax:** 518/725-1473. **Contact:** Mr. Jody Eschler, President. **Description:** A temporary agency. **Specializes in the areas of:** Industrial; Manufacturing; Sales; Secretarial. **Positions commonly filled include:** Blue-Collar Worker Supervisor; Customer Service Rep.; Manufacturer's/Wholesaler's Sales Rep.; Typist/Word Processor. **Benefits available to temporary workers:** Paid Holidays; Paid Vacation. **Other area locations:** Albany NY. **Average salary range of placements:** Less than $20,000. **Number of placements per year:** 200 - 499.

CGR STAFFING SERVICES
8 West 40th Street, 8th Floor, New York NY 10018. 212/764-3434. **Fax:** 212/997-5072. **Contact:** Office Manager. **Description:** A temporary agency that also provides some permanent placements. Company pays fee. **Specializes in the areas of:** Advertising; Art/ Design; Publishing; Sales; Technical. **Positions commonly filled include:** Administrative Manager; Broadcast Technician; Computer Programmer; Customer Service Rep.; Designer; Internet Services Manager; MIS Specialist; Multimedia Designer; Technical Writer; Typist/Word Processor. **Corporate headquarters location:** Stamford CT. **Average salary range of placements:** $30,000 - $50,000.

CAREER OBJECTIVES PERSONNEL
103 South Bedford Road, Suite 207, Mount Kisco NY 10549. 914/666-8318. **Fax:** 914/666-0296. **Contact:** Lynn Robins, President. **Description:** A temporary employment agency that also provides permanent placement of office personnel. Company pays fee. **Specializes in the areas of:** Accounting/Auditing; Administration; Computer Science/Software; Insurance; Legal; Nonprofit; Personnel/Labor Relations; Publishing; Secretarial. **Positions commonly filled include:** Accountant/Auditor; Administrative Manager; Advertising Clerk; Brokerage Clerk; Clerical Supervisor; Computer Programmer; Credit Manager; Customer Service Rep.; Financial Analyst; Human Resources Manager; Paralegal; Public Relations Specialist; Purchasing Agent/Manager; Quality Control Supervisor; Typist/Word Processor. **Average salary range of placements:** $20,000 - $29,999. **Number of placements per year:** 200 - 499.

COMPUTER GRAPHIC RESOURCES
8 West 40th Street, 8th Floor, New York NY 10018. 212/764-3434. **Contact:** Office Manager. **Description:** A temporary employment agency that also provides some temp-to-perm and permanent placements. **Specializes in the areas of:** Computer Graphics. **Positions commonly filled include:** Graphic Artist.

DENTAFORCE DENTAL PLACEMENTS
3097 Steinway Street, Long Island City NY 11103-3820. 718/728-5454. **Contact:** Recruiter. **Description:** A temporary employment agency that also provides some permanent placements. **Specializes in the areas of:** Health/Medical. **Positions commonly filled include:** Dental Assistant/Dental Hygienist; Dentist. **Average salary range of placements:** $20,000 - $29,999. **Number of placements per year:** 500 - 999.

DENTAL PLACEMENT PLUS
76 East Main Street, Suite 4, Huntington NY 11743. 516/423-8888. **Contact:** Linda Stewart, President. **Description:** A temporary and permanent employment agency. Company pays fee. **Specializes in the areas of:** Health/Medical; Personnel/Labor Relations. **Positions commonly filled include:** Dental Assistant/ Dental Hygienist; Dentist. **Average salary range of placements:** $20,000 - $29,999. **Number of placements per year:** 1 - 49.

DUNHILL STAFFING SYSTEMS OF BUFFALO
584 Delaware Avenue, Buffalo NY 14202-1207. 716/885-0245. **Contact:** Lynne J. Breen, Manager. **E-mail address:** dunbuf@aol.com. **World Wide Web address:** http://www.dunhillstaff.com. **Description:** A temporary agency. **Specializes in the areas of:** Accounting/Auditing; Administration; Health/Medical; Legal; Secretarial. **Positions commonly filled include:** Account Manager; Accountant; Administrative Assistant; Clerical Supervisor; Human Resources Manager; Marketing Specialist; Medical Records Technician; Paralegal; Secretary; Typist/Word Processor. **Corporate headquarters location:** Hauppauge NY. **Average salary range of placements:** $30,000 - $50,000. **Number of placements per year:** 100 - 199.

EUROMONDE, INC.
370 Lexington Avenue, Suite 1003, New York NY 10017. 212/661-5577. **Fax:** 212/661-5841. **Contact:** Manager. **Description:** A temporary agency focusing on the placement of bilingual personnel, particularly in secretarial and administrative support areas. The agency also provides some permanent placements. Company pays fee. **Specializes in the areas of:** Administration; Advertising; Banking; Fashion; Finance; Insurance; Nonprofit; Personnel/Labor Relations; Publishing; Secretarial. **Positions commonly filled include:** Accountant/Auditor; Administrative Manager; Bank Officer/Manager; Computer Programmer; Customer Service Rep.; Financial Analyst; Human Resources Specialist; MIS Specialist; Operations/Production Manager; Transportation/Traffic Specialist; Typist/ Word Processor. **Other U.S. locations:** CT; NJ.

EXTRA HELP EMPLOYMENT SERVICE
478 Delaware Avenue, Buffalo NY 14202. 716/885-1004. **Contact:** Judy Millard, Branch Manager. **Description:** A temporary agency that also offers some temp-to-hire and permanent placements. Company pays fee. **Specializes in the areas of:** Accounting/Auditing; Administration; Advertising; Banking; Computer Science/Software; Design; Engineering; Industrial; Manufacturing; Personnel/ Labor Relations; Publishing; Sales; Secretarial; Technical. **Positions commonly filled include:** Accountant/Auditor; Bank Officer/Manager; Chemical Engineer; Civil Engineer; Computer Programmer; Customer Service Rep.; Design Engineer; Designer; Draftsperson; Electrical/Electronics Engineer; Electrician; Environmental Engineer; Financial Analyst; General Manager; Human Resources Manager; Industrial Engineer; Materials Engineer; Mechanical Engineer; Medical Records Technician; Operations/ Production Manager; Quality Control Supervisor; Services Sales Rep.; Software Engineer; Structural Engineer; Systems Analyst; Typist/Word Processor. **Corporate headquarters location:** Rochester NY.

EXTRA HELP EMPLOYMENT SERVICE
950 New Loudon Road, Latham NY 12110. 518/782-1200. **Fax:** 518/782-1273. **Contact:** Karen Becker, Manager. **Description:** A temporary agency that also provides permanent placement. Company pays fee. **Specializes in the areas of:** Accounting/Auditing; Computer Science/Software; Engineering; General Management; Industrial; Legal. **Positions commonly filled include:** Administrative Manager; Clerical Supervisor; Computer Programmer; Customer Service Rep.; Draftsperson; General Manager; Industrial Engineer; Insurance Agent/Broker; Manufacturer's/Wholesaler's Sales Rep.; Mechanical Engineer; Paralegal. **Corporate headquarters location:** Rochester NY. **Average salary range of placements:** $30,000 - $50,000. **Number of placements per year:** 500 - 999.

FIFTH AVENUE EMPLOYMENT SERVICES
320 Fifth Avenue, Brooklyn NY 11215. 718/369-4028. **Contact:** Wale Oyekoya, Manager. **Description:** A temporary agency that also provides permanent placement. **Specializes in the areas of:** Accounting/Auditing; Administration; Banking; Computer Science/Software; Health/Medical; Industrial; Manufacturing; Personnel/Labor Relations; Secretarial. **Positions commonly filled include:** Accountant/Auditor; Bank Officer/Manager; Blue-Collar Worker Supervisor; Budget Analyst; Civil Engineer; Clerical Supervisor; Clinical Lab Technician; Computer Programmer; Customer Service Rep.; Dental Assistant/Hygienist; Electrician; Human Resources Specialist; Licensed Practical Nurse; Management Trainee; Manufacturer's/Wholesaler's Sales Rep.; Medical Records Technician; Physical Therapist; Preschool Worker; Registered Nurse; Restaurant/Food Service Manager; Social Worker; Systems Analyst; Teacher/Professor; Typist/Word Processor. **Average salary range of placements:** $20,000 - $29,999. **Number of placements per year:** 200 - 499.

FORUM TEMPORARY SERVICES
342 Madison Avenue, Suite 404, New York NY 10017. 212/687-7200. **Contact:** Mary Beth Schmid, Placement Counselor. **Description:** A temporary agency. Company pays fee. **Specializes in the areas of:** Accounting/Auditing; Administration; Banking; Finance; Legal; Personnel/Labor Relations; Secretarial; Word Processing. **Positions commonly filled include:** Accountant/Auditor; Brokerage Clerk; Budget Analyst; Credit Manager; Customer Service Rep.; Desktop Publishing Specialist; Financial Analyst; Human Resources Specialist; Paralegal; Records Manager; Securities Sales Rep.; Services Sales Rep.; Typist/Word Processor. **Benefits available to temporary workers:** Paid Holidays. **Number of placements per year:** 1000+.

FREELANCE ADVANCERS, INC.
420 Lexington Avenue, Suite 2007, New York NY 10070. 212/661-0900. **Fax:** 212/661-1883. **Contact:** Manager. **Description:** A temporary agency focusing on desktop publishing and multimedia talent including graphic designers, Web designers, art directors, illustrators, proofreaders, and production/trafficking personnel. **Specializes in the areas of:** Advertising; Art/Design; Publishing. **Positions commonly filled include:** Designer; Graphic Designer; Multimedia Designer. **Average salary range of placements:** $30,000 - $50,000. **Number of placements per year:** 50 - 99.

GRAPHIC TECHNIQUES, INC.
268 Central Avenue, Albany NY 12206. 518/449-3066. **Fax:** 518/463-6747. **Contact:** Richard L. Koza, General Manager. **E-mail address:** rlk@empireone.com. **Description:** A temporary agency. **Specializes in the areas of:** Administration; Architecture/Construction; Engineering; Industrial; Manufacturing; Secretarial; Technical. **Positions commonly filled include:** Ceramics Engineer; Chemical Engineer; Chemist; Civil Engineer; Computer Programmer; Customer Service Rep.; Design Engineer; Designer; Draftsperson; Electrical/Electronics Engineer; Environmental Engineer; Industrial Engineer; Materials Engineer; Mechanical Engineer; Paralegal; Software Engineer; Structural Engineer; Systems Analyst; Typist/Word Processor. **Benefits available to temporary workers:** Paid Holidays; Paid Vacation. **Number of placements per year:** 100 - 199.

H&H TEMPORARY SERVICES
342 Madison Avenue, New York NY 10173-0002. 212/370-4020. **Contact:** SueAnn Haeslop, President. **Description:** A temporary agency. Company pays fee. **Specializes in the areas of:** Accounting/Auditing; Banking; Finance; Personnel/Labor Relations; Secretarial. **Positions commonly filled include:** Accountant/Auditor; Brokerage Clerk; Financial Analyst; Human Resources Manager; Management Trainee; Typist/Word Processor. **Average salary range of placements:** $30,000 - $50,000. **Number of placements per year:** 100 - 199.

HEADWAY CORPORATE STAFFING SERVICES
317 Madison Avenue, 3rd Floor, New York NY 10017. 212/849-8500. **Contact:** Diane Cohen, Vice President. **Description:** A temporary agency. Company pays fee. **Specializes in the areas of:** Accounting/Auditing; Administration; Advertising; Computer Science/Software; Finance; Personnel/Labor Relations; Secretarial. **Positions commonly filled include:** Accountant/Auditor; Administrative Manager; Customer Service Representative; Financial Analyst; Human Resources Manager; Internet Services Manager; Systems Analyst; Typist/Word Processor. **Average salary range of placements:** $30,000 - $50,000. **Number of placements per year:** 500 - 999.

HOT BEAR/DE BELLA PRODUCTIONS AND EDITORIAL TEMPS
303 East 83rd Street, Suite 25D, New York NY 10028. 212/988-8189. **Fax:** 212/988-8189. **Contact:** Rosalynd Carol Friedman, Copywriter/President. **Description:** A temporary agency. **Specializes in the areas of:** Advertising; Art/Design; Publishing. **Positions commonly filled include:** Copy Editor; Editor; Proofreader; Writer. **Average salary range of placements:** $30,000 - $65,000. **Number of placements per year:** 1 - 49.

INSURANCE OVERLOAD SYSTEMS
35 Pinelawn Road, Suite 114E, Melville NY 11747. **Toll-free phone:** 800/221-5430. **Contact:** Laura Merrill, Branch Manager. **Description:** A temporary agency. **Specializes in the areas of:** Insurance. **Positions commonly filled include:** Adjuster; Claim Rep.; Underwriter/Assistant Underwriter. **Corporate headquarters location:** Dallas TX. **Number of placements per year:** 100 - 199.

INTERIM PERSONNEL
259 Monroe Avenue, Rochester NY 14607. 716/454-3200. **Fax:** 716/454-6258. **Contact:** Jody McGuinn, Manager/Owner. **Description:** A temporary agency that also provides temp-to-hire and permanent placements. **Specializes in the areas of:** Computer Science/Software; Industrial; Secretarial. **Positions commonly filled include:** Accountant/Auditor; Clerical Supervisor; Credit Manager; Customer Service Rep.; Industrial Production Manager; Typist/Word Processor. **Benefits available to temporary workers:** Paid Holidays; Paid Vacation.

KELLY SERVICES, INC.
7-11 South Broadway, Suite 408, White Plains NY 10601-3531. 914/761-5885. **Fax:** 914/761-5443.

Contact: Nancy Doyle, Office Manager. **Description:** A temporary agency. **Specializes in the areas of:** Accounting/Auditing; Administration; Secretarial. **Positions commonly filled include:** Accountant/Auditor; Administrative Manager; Customer Service Rep.; Typist/Word Processor. **Benefits available to temporary workers:** Paid Holidays; Paid Vacation. **Corporate headquarters location:** Troy MI. **Other U.S. locations:** Nationwide. **Number of placements per year:** 1000+.

KELLY SERVICES, INC.
125 Wolf Road, Suite 403, Albany NY 12205. 518/393-0262. **Fax:** 518/393-0266. **Contact:** Ginger Newton, Senior Staffing Coordinator. **Description:** A temporary agency. Founded in 1946. Company pays fee. **Specializes in the areas of:** Light Industrial; Manufacturing; Personnel/Labor Relations; Sales; Secretarial; Technical. **Positions commonly filled include:** Accountant/Auditor; Blue-Collar Worker Supervisor; Chemical Engineer; Claim Rep.; Clerical Supervisor; Computer Programmer; Customer Service Rep.; Draftsperson; Electrical/Electronics Engineer; Human Resources Specialist; Management Trainee; Mechanical Engineer; Systems Analyst; Technical Writer/Editor; Typist/Word Processor. **Benefits available to temporary workers:** Medical Insurance; Paid Holidays; Paid Vacation. **Corporate headquarters location:** Troy MI. **Average salary range of placements:** Less than $20,000. **Number of placements per year:** 500 - 999.

LAB SUPPORT INC.
One Water Street, White Plains NY 10601-1009. **Toll-free phone:** 800/995-7378. **Contact:** Recruiter. **Description:** A temporary agency that focuses on the placement of professionals in industrial laboratories. Company pays fee. **Specializes in the areas of:** Biology; Food Industry; Industrial; Manufacturing; Personnel/Labor Relations; Technical. **Positions commonly filled include:** Biochemist; Biological Scientist; Chemical Engineer; Chemist; Food Scientist/Technologist; Science Technologist. **Benefits available to temporary workers:** Medical Insurance; Paid Holidays; Paid Vacation. **Corporate headquarters location:** Calabasas CA. **Average salary range of placements:** $30,000 - $50,000. **Number of placements per year:** 200 - 499.

MANPOWER TECHNICAL SERVICES
100 Jericho Quadrangle, Suite 208, Jericho NY 11753. 516/681-6640. **Contact:** Karen George, Technical Manager. **Description:** A temporary agency. Company pays fee. **Specializes in the areas of:** Administration; Computer Science/Software; Engineering; Manufacturing; Technical. **Positions commonly filled include:** Accountant/Auditor; Aerospace Engineer; Broadcast Technician; Buyer; Computer Programmer; Design Engineer; Designer; Draftsperson; Electrical/Electronics Engineer; Electrician; Industrial Engineer; Mechanical Engineer; MIS Specialist; Operations/Production Manager; Purchasing Agent/Manager; Quality Control Supervisor; Software Engineer; Systems Analyst; Technical Writer/Editor; Telecommunications Manager. **Benefits available to temporary workers:** Medical Insurance; Paid Holidays; Paid Vacation. **Corporate headquarters location:** Milwaukee WI. **Other U.S. locations:** Nationwide. **Average salary range of placements:** $30,000 - $50,000. **Number of placements per year:** 1 - 49.

MANPOWER TEMPORARY SERVICES
720 Fifth Avenue, 10th Floor, New York NY 10019. 212/307-1008. **Contact:** Office Manager. **Description:** A temporary agency. **Specializes in the areas of:** Banking; Clerical; Fashion; Nonprofit; Publishing. **Positions commonly filled include:** Bookkeeper; Clerk; Data Entry Clerk; Receptionist; Secretary; Typist/Word Processor. **Corporate headquarters location:** Milwaukee WI. **Other U.S. locations:** Nationwide. **Number of placements per year:** 1000+.

MANPOWER TEMPORARY SERVICES
161 Avenue of the Americas, 14th Floor, New York NY 10013. 212/366-6005. **Contact:** Branch Manager. **Description:** A temporary agency. Company pays fee. **Specializes in the areas of:** Clerical; Data Processing; Industrial; Professional; Technical; Telecommunications; Word Processing. **Positions commonly filled include:** Accountant/Auditor; Accounting Clerk; Administrative Assistant; Biological Scientist; Bookkeeper; Chemist; Customer Service Manager; Designer; Desktop Publishing Specialist; Electrician; Inventory Control Specialist; Library Technician; Materials Engineer; Order Clerk; Painter; Project Engineer; Proofreader; Receptionist; Secretary; Software Engineer; Stenographer; Systems Analyst; Technical Writer/Editor; Telemarketer; Transcriptionist; Typesetter; Welder. **Corporate headquarters location:** Milwaukee WI. **Other U.S. locations:** Nationwide. **Number of placements per year:** 1000+.

MANPOWER TEMPORARY SERVICES
5 Penn Plaza, New York NY 10001-1810. 212/563-7080. **Fax:** 212/562-8393. **Contact:** Karl Muhlbauer, Technical Recruiter. **Description:** A temporary agency that also provides contract services. **Specializes in the areas of:** Computer Science/Software; Engineering; Technical. **Positions commonly filled include:** Computer Programmer; Design Engineer; Industrial Engineer; Mechanical Engineer; Systems Analyst; Technical Writer/Editor; Telecommunications Manager. **Benefits available to temporary workers:** Life Insurance; Medical Insurance; Paid Vacation; Referral Bonus Plan; Stock Purchase. **Corporate headquarters location:** Milwaukee WI. **Other U.S. locations:** Nationwide. **Average salary range of placements:** More than $50,000. **Number of placements per year:** 200 - 499.

MANPOWER TEMPORARY SERVICES
350 Motor Parkway, Hauppauge NY 11788-5101. 516/434-1405. **Contact:** Branch Manager. **Description:** A temporary agency. **Specializes in the areas of:** Accounting/Auditing; Banking; Industrial; Secretarial; Telemarketing; Word Processing. **Positions commonly filled include:** Accountant/Auditor; Administrative Assistant; Clerk; Telemarketer; Typist/Word Processor. **Corporate headquarters location:** Milwaukee WI. **Other U.S. locations:** Nationwide. **Benefits available to temporary workers:** Medical Insurance; Paid Holidays; Paid Vacation.

MANPOWER TEMPORARY SERVICES
Route 26 North, Lowville NY 13367. 315/376-6899. **Contact:** Diane McDade, Branch Supervisor. **Description:** A temporary agency that focuses on technical, industrial, and clerical placements. Company pays fee. **Specializes in the areas of:** Accounting/Auditing; Banking; Computer Science/Software; Industrial; Manufacturing; Personnel/Labor Relations; Sales; Secretarial; Technical. **Positions commonly filled include:** Automotive Mechanic; Blue-Collar Worker Supervisor; Customer Service Rep.; Mechanical Engineer; Paralegal; Typist/Word Processor. **Benefits available to temporary workers:** Life Insurance; Medical Insurance; Paid Holidays; Paid Vacation. **Corporate headquarters location:** Milwaukee WI. **Number of placements per year:** 100 - 199.

MANPOWER TEMPORARY SERVICES
5790 Widewaters Parkway, Dewitt NY 13214. 315/446-1000. **Contact:** Branch Manager. **Description:** A temporary agency. Company pays fee. **Specializes in the areas of:** Light Industrial; Office

Support; Technical; Telemarketing; Word Processing. **Positions commonly filled include:** Accountant/Auditor; Accounting Clerk; Administrative Assistant; Assembler; Biological Scientist; Bookkeeper; Chemist; Customer Service Rep.; Designer; Desktop Publishing Specialist; Electrician; Inventory Control Specialist; Painter; Project Engineer; Receptionist; Records Manager; Research Assistant; Secretary; Software Engineer; Systems Analyst; Technical Writer/Editor; Technician; Telemarketer; Typist/Word Processor; Welder. **Benefits available to temporary workers:** Life Insurance; Medical Insurance; Paid Holidays; Paid Vacation. **Number of placements per year:** 1000+.

MANPOWER TEMPORARY SERVICES
125 Park Avenue, 10th Floor, New York NY 10017. 212/557-9110. **Fax:** 212/557-9111. **Contact:** Angelina Lovatto, Branch Supervisor. **Description:** A temporary agency. **Specializes in the areas of:** Administration; Banking; Finance; Legal; Personnel/Labor Relations; Secretarial. **Positions commonly filled include:** Computer Programmer; Customer Service Rep.; Systems Analyst; Technical Writer/Editor; Typist/Word Processor. **Corporate headquarters location:** Milwaukee WI. **Other U.S. locations:** Nationwide. **Number of placements per year:** 50 - 99.

MED-SCRIBE, INC.
215 Alexander Street, Rochester NY 14607. 716/262-3668. **Fax:** 716/262-3694. **Contact:** Bobbie Reif, Administrator. **E-mail address:** medjobs@medscribe.com. **Description:** A temporary and permanent employment agency. Company pays fee. **Specializes in the areas of:** Health/Medical. **Positions commonly filled include:** Health Services Manager; Medical Records Technician; Secretary. **Benefits available to temporary workers:** Medical Insurance; Paid Holidays. **Average salary range of placements:** Less than $20,000. **Number of placements per year:** 1 - 49.

METRO RESOURCES OF ROCHESTER INC.
1825 Buffalo Road, Rochester NY 14624-1501. 716/426-8060. **Fax:** 716/426-7720. **Contact:** James Pisaturo, President. **Description:** A temporary agency. **Specializes in the areas of:** Accounting/Auditing; Banking; Computer Science/Software; Engineering; Industrial; Manufacturing; Personnel/Labor Relations; Secretarial; Technical. **Positions commonly filled include:** Accountant/Auditor; Administrative Manager; Advertising Clerk; Architect; Blue-Collar Worker Supervisor; Buyer; Chemical Engineer; Civil Engineer; Claim Rep.; Clerical Supervisor; Clinical Lab Technician; Computer Programmer; Credit Manager; Customer Service Rep,; Design Engineer; Designer; Draftsperson; Editor; Electrical/Electronics Engineer; Electrician; Environmental Engineer; Financial Analyst; Human Resources Manager; Human Service Worker; Industrial Engineer; Industrial Production Manager; Management Trainee; Mechanical Engineer; Multimedia Designer; Services Sales Rep.; Software Engineer; Statistician; Structural Engineer; Surveyor; Systems Analyst; Technical Writer/Editor; Typist/Word Processor. **Benefits available to temporary workers:** Paid Holidays; Paid Vacation. **Average salary range of placements:** $20,000 - $29,999.

MORGAN-MURRAY PERSONNEL/M&M TOP TEMPS
1461 Lakeland Avenue, Bohemia NY 11716. 516/567-7474. **Fax:** 516/567-9483. **Contact:** Barbara Murray, President. **Description:** A temporary agency that also provides permanent placement. **Specializes in the areas of:** Accounting/Auditing; Advertising; Art/Design; Banking; Broadcasting; Economics; Engineering; Finance; Food Industry; General Management; Health/Medical; Industrial; Insurance; Legal; Manufacturing; Personnel/Labor Relations; Retail; Sales; Secretarial; Technical. **Positions commonly filled include:** Accountant/Auditor; Adjuster; Administrative Manager; Advertising Clerk; Bank Officer/Manager; Biochemist; Blue-Collar Worker Supervisor; Buyer; Chemical Engineer; Chemist; Claim Rep.; Clerical Supervisor; Credit Manager; Customer Service Rep.; Draftsperson; Environmental Engineer; Human Resources Specialist; Industrial Production Manager; Insurance Agent/Broker; Management Trainee; Paralegal; Property and Real Estate Manager; Purchasing Agent/ Manager; Quality Control Supervisor; Restaurant/Food Service Manager; Telecommunications Manager; Typist/Word Processor. **Number of placements per year:** 50 - 99.

OLSTEN STAFFING SERVICES
275 Broad Hollow Road, Melville NY 11747. 516/752-8851. **Toll-free phone:** 800/WORK-NOW. **Fax:** 516/752-8853. **Contact:** Manager. **World Wide Web address:** http://www.worknow.com. **Description:** A temporary agency. Founded in 1950. **Specializes in the areas of:** Accounting/Auditing; Banking; Finance; Industrial; Legal; Technical. **Positions commonly filled include:** Accountant/Auditor; Attorney; Customer Service Rep.; Draftsperson; Financial Analyst; Paralegal; Typist/Word Processor. **Benefits available to temporary workers:** Bonus Award/Plan. **Other U.S. locations:** Nationwide. **Number of placements per year:** 1000+.

OLSTEN STAFFING SERVICES
183 East Main Street, Suite 110, Rochester NY 14604-1617. 716/232-4070. **Fax:** 716/232-6926. **Contact:** Diane Knipper, Recruiter. **Description:** A temporary agency. Founded in 1950. **Specializes in the areas of:** Accounting/Auditing; Administration; Banking; Engineering; Finance; Industrial; Legal; Light Industrial; Manufacturing; Marketing; Personnel/Labor Relations; Publishing; Retail; Sales; Secretarial. **Positions commonly filled include:** Administrative Assistant; Administrative Manager; Bank Officer/Manager; Blue-Collar Worker Supervisor; Brokerage Clerk; Budget Analyst; Buyer; Civil Engineer; Claim Rep.; Clerical Supervisor; Clinical Lab Technician; Computer Programmer; Construction and Building Inspector; Customer Service Rep.; Design Engineer; Designer; Draftsperson; Electrical/Electronics Engineer; Financial Analyst; Human Resources Specialist; Human Service Worker; Industrial Engineer; Industrial Production Manager; Internet Services Manager; Management Trainee; Market Research Analyst; Medical Records Technician; MIS Specialist; Operations/Production Manager; Paralegal; Restaurant/Food Service Manager; Sales Rep.; Secretary; Software Engineer; Strategic Relations Manager; Systems Analyst; Technical Writer/Editor; Telecommunications Manager; Typist/Word Processor; Underwriter/Assistant Underwriter. **Benefits available to temporary workers:** Daycare Assistance; Medical Insurance; Paid Holidays; Paid Vacation. **Corporate headquarters location:** Melville NY. **Other U.S. locations:** Nationwide.

PAYWISE INC.
310 Madison Avenue, New York NY 10017-6002. 212/953-1287. **Contact:** Manager. **Description:** A temporary employment agency. Company pays fee. **Specializes in the areas of:** Accounting/Auditing; Banking; Computer Science/Software; Finance; General Management; Secretarial. **Positions commonly filled include:** Accountant/Auditor; Administrative Manager; Blue-Collar Worker Supervisor; Brokerage Clerk; Claim Rep.; Clerical Supervisor; Computer Programmer; Credit Manager; Customer Service Rep.; Management Trainee; MIS Specialist; Services Sales Rep.; Systems Analyst; Typist/Word Processor. **Average salary range of placements:** $20,000 - $29,999. **Number of placements per year:** 500 - 999.

PILOT TEMPORARIES INC.
2670 Millersport Highway, Getzville NY 14068. 716/639-8230. **Contact:** President. **Description:** A temporary agency. Company pays fee. **Specializes in the areas of:** Architecture/Construction. **Positions commonly filled include:** Automotive Mechanic; Construction Contractor; Electrician. **Average salary range of placements:** $20,000 - $29,999. **Number of placements per year:** 500 - 999.

PREFERRED PROFESSIONALS
777 Third Avenue, New York NY 10017. 212/688-6347. **Contact:** Michael Druhot, General Manager. **Description:** A temporary agency. **Specializes in the areas of:** Advertising; Secretarial. **Positions commonly filled include:** Accountant/Auditor; Advertising Clerk; Receptionist; Typist/Word Processor. **Other U.S. locations:** Nationwide. **Number of placements per year:** 1000+.

REMEDY INTELLIGENT STAFFING
570 Taxter Road, Elmsford NY 10523. 914/592-5444. **Fax:** 914/592-2737. **Contact:** Manager. **Description:** A temporary agency. **Specializes in the areas of:** Accounting/Auditing; Architecture/Construction; Banking; Finance; Food Industry; Health/Medical; Industrial; Legal; Manufacturing; Personnel/Labor Relations; Publishing; Secretarial. **Positions commonly filled include:** Customer Service Rep. **Benefits available to temporary workers:** Dental Insurance; Life Insurance; Medical Insurance. **Corporate headquarters location:** San Juan Capistrano CA. **Other U.S. locations:** Nationwide. **Average salary range of placements:** $20,000 - $29,999. **Number of placements per year:** 500 - 999.

REP TEMPS, INC.
100 Park Avenue, New York NY 10017. 212/818-8955. **Fax:** 212/818-8956. **Contact:** Tracey Norton, Director of Recruiting. **Description:** A temporary agency. Company pays fee. **Specializes in the areas of:** Advertising; Broadcasting; Personnel/Labor Relations; Sales. **Corporate headquarters location:** Chicago IL. **Other U.S. locations:** Nationwide.

SHARP NURSES INC.
215 Park Avenue South, Suite 1304, New York NY 10003. 212/780-0044. **Fax:** 212/780-0046. **Contact:** Ms. Ruth Rama Witt, Vice President/General Manager. **Description:** A temporary agency that provides nursing placements to institutional clients only. **Specializes in the areas of:** Health/Medical. **Positions commonly filled include:** Certified Nursing Aide; Home Health Aide; Licensed Practical Nurse; Registered Nurse. **Corporate headquarters location:** Los Angeles CA. **Other U.S. locations:** Nationwide. **Number of placements per year:** 1000+.

SPECIAL COUNSEL
20 West 55th Street, 2nd Floor, New York NY 10019. 212/245-5599. **Fax:** 212/245-6010. **Contact:** Manager. **World Wide Web address:** http://www.specialcounsel.com. **Description:** A temporary and permanent employment agency. **Specializes in the areas of:** Legal.

STAFF MANAGERS
499 Jericho Turnpike, Mineola NY 11501. 516/294-7214. **Fax:** 516/294-1431. **Contact:** Ruth Stuart, President. **Description:** A temporary agency that also provides permanent placements. Company pays fee. **Specializes in the areas of:** Accounting/Auditing; Administration; Banking; Computer Science/Software; Engineering; Finance; General Management; Industrial; Insurance; Manufacturing; Personnel/Labor Relations; Sales; Secretarial; Technical. **Positions commonly filled include:** Accountant/Auditor; Adjuster; Aerospace Engineer; Bank Officer/Manager; Blue-Collar Worker Supervisor; Buyer; Chemical Engineer; Claim Rep.; Clerical Supervisor; Computer Programmer; Credit Manager; Customer Service Rep.; Design Engineer; Draftsperson; Electrical/Electronics Engineer; Environmental Engineer; Financial Analyst; Human Resources Specialist; Industrial Engineer; Insurance Agent/Broker; Internet Services Manager; Management Trainee; MIS Specialist; Operations/Production Manager; Purchasing Agent/Manager; Quality Control Supervisor; Software Engineer; Systems Analyst; Technical Writer/Editor; Telecommunications Manager; Typist/Word Processor. **Benefits available to temporary workers:** Bonus Award/Plan; Medical Insurance; Paid Holidays. **Number of placements per year:** 100 - 199.

STAFKINGS PERSONNEL SYSTEMS
222 South Fulton Street, Ithaca NY 14850-3306. 607/273-5335. **Fax:** 607/273-1054. **Contact:** Branch Manager. **Description:** A temporary agency. Company pays fee. **Specializes in the areas of:** Food Industry; Health/Medical; Industrial. **Positions commonly filled include:** Accountant/Auditor; Clerical Supervisor; Clinical Lab Technician; Customer Service Rep.; Food Scientist/Technologist; Human Resources Specialist; Licensed Practical Nurse; Medical Records Technician; MIS Specialist; Registered Nurse; Systems Analyst; Travel Agent; Typist/Word Processor. **Corporate headquarters location:** Binghamton NY. **Average salary range of placements:** Less than $20,000.

SWING SHIFT
One Horatio Street, New York NY 10014-1618. 212/206-1222. **Fax:** 212/727-9754. **Contact:** Harriet Livathinos, President. **Description:** A temporary agency focusing on the placement of office support and desktop publishing production personnel. Backgrounds sought include graphics, page layout, and presentation software. Company pays fee. **Specializes in the areas of:** Advertising; Computer Science/Software; Secretarial. **Positions commonly filled include:** Desktop Publishing Specialist; Paralegal; Typist/Word Processor. **Average salary range of placements:** $20,000 - $29,999. **Number of placements per year:** 1 - 49.

TAC STAFFING SERVICES
505 Fifth Avenue, Suite 1000, New York NY 10017. 212/687-5213. **Contact:** Manager. **Description:** A temporary agency. **Specializes in the areas of:** Clerical; Data Processing; Office Support. **Other U.S. locations:** Nationwide.

TEMP FORCE OF NEW YORK
180 Broadway, Suite 1101, New York NY 10038. 212/267-TEMP. **Fax:** 212/267-8412. **Contact:** Cynthia Peck, Office Manager. **Description:** A temporary employment agency. **Specializes in the areas of:** Accounting/Auditing; Advertising; Banking; Finance; Health/Medical; Insurance; Legal; Publishing; Secretarial. **Positions commonly filled include:** Accountant/Auditor; Bookkeeper; Clerk; Computer Programmer; Customer Service Rep.; Data Entry Clerk; Desktop Publishing Specialist; Driver; Legal Secretary; Medical Secretary; Paralegal; Purchasing Agent/Manager; Receptionist; Secretary; Stenographer; Typist/Word Processor. **Benefits available to temporary workers:** 401(k); Medical Insurance; Paid Vacation. **Corporate headquarters location:** Woodbury NY. **Other U.S. locations:** Nationwide. **Average salary range of placements:** $30,000 - $50,000. **Number of placements per year:** 1000+.

TEMPORARY RESOURCE CENTER
18 East 48th Street, 19th Floor, New York NY 10017. 212/486-7884. **Toll-free phone:** 888/693-8367. **Fax:** 212/486-8042. **Contact:** Andrew Greenberg, President. **Description:** A temporary

agency. **Specializes in the areas of:** Accounting/Auditing; Banking; Finance; Personnel/ Labor Relations; Secretarial. **Positions commonly filled include:** Advertising Clerk; Brokerage Clerk; Computer Programmer; Customer Service Rep.; Financial Analyst; Human Resources Specialist; Internet Services Manager; Systems Analyst; Typist/Word Processor.

TEMPOSITIONS, INC.
420 Lexington Avenue, Suite 2100, New York NY 10170. 212/490-7400. **Fax:** 212/867-1759. **Contact:** Anne Marie Karash, Director of Operations. **Description:** A temporary agency. Company pays fee. **Specializes in the areas of:** Advertising; Communications; Computer Science/Software; Legal; Office Support; Personnel/Labor Relations; Secretarial. **Positions commonly filled include:** Accountant/Auditor; Administrative Assistant; Customer Service Rep.; Data Entry Clerk; Desktop Publishing Specialist; Licensed Practical Nurse; MIS Specialist; Paralegal; Registered Nurse; Secretary; Social Worker; Technician; Telemarketer; Therapist; Typist/Word Processor. **Benefits available to temporary workers:** Daycare Assistance; Paid Holidays; Paid Vacation; Referral Bonus Plan. **Other area locations:** Melville NY; White Plains NY. **Other U.S. locations:** San Francisco CA. **Average salary range of placements:** $20,000 - $29,999. **Number of placements per year:** 1000+.

UNIQUE SUPPORT SERVICES, INC.
160 Broadway, Suite 801, New York NY 10038. 212/406-0062. **Toll-free phone:** 800/232-4303. **Fax:** 212/406-5882. **Contact:** Lance W. Payton, Professional Staffing Manager. **World Wide Web address:** http://www.infohouse.com/unique. **Description:** A temporary agency that also provides permanent placement. Company pays fee. **Specializes in the areas of:** Computer Science/Software; General Management; Secretarial. **Positions commonly filled include:** Typist/Word Processor. **Other U.S. locations:** Washington DC; Morristown NJ; Newark NJ; Wyomissing PA. **Average salary range of placements:** $20,000 - $29,999. **Number of placements per year:** 200 - 499.

VANTAGE STAFFING SERVICES
180 East Post Road, White Plains NY 10601. 914/761-1120. **Fax:** 914/997-8319. **Contact:** Kathy O'Connor, President. **Description:** A temporary agency that also provides permanent placement. Company pays fee. **Specializes in the areas of:** Accounting/Auditing; Banking; Finance; Legal; Personnel/Labor Relations; Secretarial. **Positions commonly filled include:** Accountant/Auditor; Administrative Manager; Bank Officer/Manager; Brokerage Clerk; Clerical Supervisor; Credit Manager; Customer Service Rep.; Financial Analyst; Human Resources Specialist; Paralegal; Typist/Word Processor. **Benefits available to temporary workers:** Dental Insurance; Paid Holidays; Paid Vacation. **Other area locations:** Stamford CT. **Average salary range of placements:** $30,000 - $50,000. **Number of placements per year:** 100 - 199.

WESTERN STAFF SERVICES
7525 Morgan Road, Liverpool NY 13090-3938. 315/453-5533. **Fax:** 315/453-3958. **Contact:** Michele Washburn, Office Manager. **World Wide Web address:** http://www.beatemp.com. **Description:** A temporary employment agency that also provides permanent placements. Company pays fee. **Specializes in the areas of:** Accounting/Auditing; Administration; General Management; Industrial; Personnel/Labor Relations; Secretarial. **Positions commonly filled include:** Administrative Manager; Blue-Collar Worker Supervisor; Claim Rep.; Clerical Supervisor; Customer Service Rep.; Electrical/Electronics Engineer; Human Resources Specialist; Industrial Production Manager; Purchasing Agent/Manager; Quality Control Supervisor; Services Sales Rep.; Typist/Word Processor. **Benefits available to temporary workers:** 401(k); Paid Holidays; Paid Vacation. **Corporate headquarters location:** Walnut Creek CA. **Other U.S. locations:** Nationwide. **Number of placements per year:** 1000+.

WESTERN STAFF SERVICES
3 Ellinwood Court, Suite 202, New Hartford NY 13413. 315/736-3884. **Fax:** 315/736-5340. **Contact:** Jack Altdoerffer, Vice President of Marketing. **Description:** A temporary employment agency. The company also provides permanent placements. Company pays fee. **Specializes in the areas of:** Banking; Broadcasting; Engineering; Finance; Food Industry; General Management; Industrial; Personnel/Labor Relations; Retail; Sales; Secretarial; Technical. **Positions commonly filled include:** Accountant/Auditor; Administrative Manager; Bank Officer/Manager; Blue-Collar Worker Supervisor; Claim Rep.; Clerical Supervisor; Computer Programmer; Design Engineer; Designer; Electrical/Electronics Engineer; Electrician; Human Resources Specialist; Human Service Worker; Industrial Engineer; Management Trainee; Services Sales Rep.; Technical Writer/Editor; Telecommunications Manager; Transportation/Traffic Specialist; Typist/Word Processor. **Other U.S. locations:** Nationwide.

CONTRACT SERVICES FIRMS

ACCREDITED CARE, INC.
106 West Third Street, Suite 707, Jamestown NY 14701. 716/484-7101. **Contact:** Patricia Bova, Manager. **Description:** A licensed home health care agency that provides contract personnel to care for patients in their homes and in local medical facilities. Founded in 1979. **Specializes in the areas of:** Health/Medical. **Positions commonly filled include:** Administrative Manager; Blue-Collar Worker Supervisor; Clerical Supervisor; Dietician/Nutritionist; Health Services Manager; Home Health Aide; Human Resources Specialist; Human Service Worker; Licensed Practical Nurse; Management Trainee; Occupational Therapist; Physical Therapist; Registered Nurse; Social Worker; Speech-Language Pathologist.

CDI CORPORATION
1811 Route 52, Suite G, Hopewell Junction NY 12533. 518/464-9700. **Contact:** Manager. **World Wide Web address:** http://www.cdicorp.com. **Description:** A contract services firm. **Specializes in the areas of:** Technical.

CDI CORPORATION (NORTHEAST)
2060 Fairport Nine Mile Point Road, Suite 400, Penfield NY 14526. 716/377-3310. **Toll-free phone:** 800/207-3140. **Fax:** 716/377-5225. **Contact:** Beverly Haynes, Branch Manager. **E-mail address:** cdicorp@aol.com. **World Wide Web address:** http://www.cdicorp.com. **Description:** A contract services firm focusing on the placement of supplemental engineering, technical, and information services personnel. Company pays fee. **Specializes in the areas of:** Advertising; Computer Science/Software; Engineering; Manufacturing; Technical. **Positions commonly filled include:** Buyer; Chemist; Computer Programmer; Customer Service Rep.; Design Engineer; Designer; Draftsperson; Electrical/Electronics Engineer; Financial Analyst; Industrial Engineer; Industrial Production Manager; Mechanical

Engineer; MIS Specialist; Purchasing Agent/Manager; Quality Control Supervisor; Software Engineer; Systems Analyst; Technical Writer/Editor; Telecommunications Manager. **Corporate headquarters location:** Philadelphia PA. **Other U.S. locations:** Nationwide. **International locations:** Worldwide. **Number of placements per year:** 200 - 499.

COMFORCE CORPORATION
2001 Marcus Avenue, Suite N216, New Hyde Park NY 11042-1011. 516/352-3200. **Fax:** 516/352-3362. **Contact:** Advertising Account Manager. **E-mail address:** contact@comforce.com. **World Wide Web address:** http://www.comforce.com. **Description:** A telecommunications and computer support contract labor corporation. Company pays fee. **Specializes in the areas of:** Computer Science/Software; Telecommunications. **Positions commonly filled include:** Computer Programmer; Electrical/Electronics Engineer; MIS Specialist; Software Engineer; Systems Analyst; Telecommunications Manager. **Benefits available to temporary workers:** Medical Insurance; Paid Holidays; Paid Vacation. **Average salary range of placements:** $30,000 - $50,000. **Number of placements per year:** 500 - 999.

COMFORCE INFORMATION TECHNOLOGIES, INC.
5788 Widewaters Parkway, DeWitt NY 13214. 315/445-5550. **Fax:** 315/445-5551. **Contact:** Manager. **Description:** A contract services firm. **Specializes in the areas of:** Computer Science/Software.

COMFORCE TELECOM, INC.
37 East Main Street, Elmsford NY 10523. 914/592-7240. **Fax:** 914/592-7246. **Contact:** Manager. **Description:** A contract services firm. **Specializes in the areas of:** Telecommunications.

COMPFORCE
6780 Pittsford-Palmyra Road, Fairport NY 14450. 716/223-2300. **Toll-free phone:** 800/724-1223. **Fax:** 716/223-3484. **Contact:** Janet Longtin, Recruiter. **Description:** A contract services firm that also provides direct and temporary-to-direct placements. **Specializes in the areas of:** Computer Science/Software. **Positions commonly filled include:** Computer Programmer; Software Engineer; Systems Analyst; Technical Writer/Editor. **Benefits available to temporary workers:** 401(k); Life Insurance; Medical Insurance; Paid Holidays; Paid Vacation; Referral Bonus Plan. **Other area locations:** Syracuse NY. **Average salary range of placements:** More than $50,000. **Number of placements per year:** 50 - 99.

CONTRACT SPECIALTIES GROUP
755 Waverly Avenue, Suite 305, Holtsville NY 11742. 516/475-7900. **Contact:** Manager. **Description:** A contract services firm. Company pays fee. **Specializes in the areas of:** Engineering; Manufacturing. **Positions commonly filled include:** Aerospace Engineer; Architect; Buyer; Civil Engineer; Computer Programmer; Construction and Building Inspector; Cost Estimator; Design Engineer; Designer; Draftsperson; Electrical/Electronics Engineer; Industrial Engineer; Industrial Production Manager; Mechanical Engineer; Software Engineer; Structural Engineer; Systems Analyst; Technical Writer/Editor. **Benefits available to temporary workers:** Paid Holidays; Paid Vacation. **Other U.S. locations:** Nationwide. **Average salary range of placements:** $30,000 - $50,000. **Number of placements per year:** 50 - 99.

EDP CONTRACT SERVICES, INC.
2 Penn Plaza, Suite 1190, New York NY 10121. 212/947-6033. **Contact:** Douglas Heppner, Manager. **Description:** A contract services firm. Company pays fee. **Specializes in the areas of:** Accounting/Auditing; Banking; Computer Science/Software; Engineering; Finance; Insurance; Manufacturing; MIS/EDP; Nonprofit; Personnel/Labor Relations; Publishing; Technical. **Positions commonly filled include:** Computer Operator; EDP Specialist; MIS Specialist; Systems Analyst; Technical Writer/Editor. **Number of placements per year:** 1000+.

ELITE TECHNICAL SERVICES, INC.
900 Wheeler Road, Suite 290, Hauppauge NY 11788. 516/366-2345. **Toll-free phone:** 800/ELITE-50. **Contact:** Manager. **E-mail address:** elite500@aol.com. **Description:** A contract services firm. **Positions commonly filled include:** Electrical/Electronics Engineer; Software Engineer.

PLATINUM IT CONSULTING
535 Fifth Avenue, Suite 1004, New York NY 10017. 212/661-8355. **Fax:** 212/687-4347. **Contact:** Rick Vigilis, Recruiter. **E-mail address:** platinum@haven.ios.com. **Description:** A contract services firm. **Specializes in the areas of:** Computer Science/Software. **Positions commonly filled include:** Computer Operator; Computer Programmer; Database Manager; Internet Services Manager; MIS Specialist; Project Manager; Systems Analyst; Technical Writer/Editor. **Benefits available to temporary workers:** Medical Insurance. **Other U.S. locations:** Madison NJ.

PROVISION TECHNOLOGIES
21 Penn Plaza, Suite 701, New York NY 10001. 212/695-6611. **Fax:** 212/695-6192. **Contact:** Manager. **World Wide Web address:** http://www.careerbase.com. **Description:** A contract services and consulting firm. **Specializes in the areas of:** Computer Science/Software; Information Technology.
Other area locations:
- 1001 James Street, Syracuse NY 13203. 315/422-2480.

PROVISION TECHNOLOGIES
TAD TECHNICAL SERVICES
51 Symphony Circle, Buffalo NY 14201. 716/884-0106. **Fax:** 716/884-1927. **Contact:** Manager. **World Wide Web address:** http://www.careerbase.com. **Description:** A contract services and consulting firm. **Specializes in the areas of:** Computer Science/Software; Information Technology.
Other area locations:
- 1040B University Avenue, Rochester NY 14607. 716/242-5320.

SUPERIOR CONCEPTS
21 Front Street, Schenectady NY 12305-1301. 518/393-4425. **Fax:** 518/370-0103. **Contact:** Gayle C. Belden, President/Program Director. **Description:** A contract services firm that also provides some permanent placements. Superior Concepts focuses on providing placements in the Middle East. **Specializes in the areas of:** Accounting/Auditing; Administration; Architecture/Construction; Banking; Computer Science/Software; Education; Engineering; Finance; Food Industry; Health/Medical; Industrial; Manufacturing; Personnel/Labor Relations; Sales; Technical. **Positions commonly filled include:** Accountant/Auditor; Administrative Manager; Aerospace Engineer; Architect; Attorney; Bank Officer/Manager; Biomedical Engineer; Chemical Engineer; Computer Programmer; Construction and Building Inspector; Dental Assistant/Hygienist; Design Engineer; Education Administrator; EEG Technologist; Electrical/Electronics Engineer; Financial Analyst; Food Scientist/Technologist; Health Services Manager; Human Resources Specialist; Industrial Engineer; Internet Services Manager; Landscape Architect; Manufacturer's/Wholesaler's Sales Rep.; Market Research Analyst; Mechanical Engineer; MIS Specialist; Multimedia Designer; Occupational

Therapist; Operations/Production Manager; Petroleum Engineer; Pharmacist; Physician; Property and Real Estate Manager; Quality Control Supervisor; Registered Nurse; Restaurant/Food Service Manager; Securities Sales Rep.; Software Engineer; Stationary Engineer; Structural Engineer; Systems Analyst; Technical Writer/Editor; Telecommunications Manager; Transportation/Traffic Specialist; Urban/Regional Planner. **Number of placements per year:** 50 - 99.

TAD RESOURCES
120 Finn Court, Farmingdale NY 11735-1107. 516/694-8800. **Fax:** 516/694-8804. **Contact:** Christina Sepe, Branch Manager. **Description:** A contract services firm. **Specializes in the areas of:** Computer Science/Software; Engineering; Industrial; Manufacturing; Transportation. **Positions commonly filled include:** Aerospace Engineer; Biomedical Engineer; Buyer; Ceramics Engineer; Chemical Engineer; Civil Engineer; Computer Programmer; Construction and Building Inspector; Construction Contractor; Cost Estimator; Design Engineer; Designer; Draftsperson; Electrical/Electronics Engineer; Environmental Engineer; Industrial Engineer; Materials Engineer; Mechanical Engineer; MIS Specialist; Nuclear Engineer; Operations/Production Manager; Purchasing Agent/Manager; Quality Control Supervisor; Software Engineer; Structural Engineer; Systems Analyst; Technical Writer/Editor; Telecommunications Manager. **Corporate headquarters location:** Cambridge MA. **Average salary range of placements:** More than $50,000. **Number of placements per year:** 50 - 99.

VOLT SERVICES GROUP
1221 Avenue of the Americas, 47th Floor, New York NY 10020. 212/719-7841. **Toll-free phone:** 800/367-8658. **Fax:** 212/719-7850. **Contact:** Joseph Musacchio, Vice President of Professional Services. **World Wide Web address:** http://www.volteast.com. **Description:** A contract services firm. **Specializes in the areas of:** Banking; Broadcasting; Computer Science/Software; Engineering; Industrial; Insurance. **Positions commonly filled include:** Account Manager; Account Representative; Administrative Assistant; Architect; Buyer; Computer Animator; Computer Operator; Computer Programmer; Database Manager; Design Engineer; Human Resources Manager; Manufacturing Engineer; MIS Specialist; Project Manager; Purchasing Agent/Manager; Software Engineer; Stationary Engineer; Systems Analyst; Technical Writer/Editor; Telecommunications Manager. **Benefits available to temporary workers:** Medical Insurance; Paid Holidays; Paid Vacation. **Corporate headquarters location:** This Location. **Other U.S. locations:** Nationwide. **International locations:** Worldwide. **Average salary range of placements:** More than $50,000. **Number of placements per year:** 1000+.

H.L. YOH COMPANY
301 Exchange Boulevard, Rochester NY 14608. 716/454-5400. **Fax:** 716/454-2105. **Contact:** Johnna Ufret, Technical Recruiter. **E-mail address:** yohit@vivanet.com. **Description:** A contract services firm. Founded in 1942. Company pays fee. **Specializes in the areas of:** Administration; Art/Design; Computer Science/Software; Engineering; Industrial; Manufacturing; Technical. **Positions commonly filled include:** Accountant/Auditor; Aerospace Engineer; Agricultural Engineer; Aircraft Mechanic/Engine Specialist; Biological Scientist; Biomedical Engineer; Blue-Collar Worker Supervisor; Chemical Engineer; Chemist; Civil Engineer; Clinical Lab Technician; Computer Programmer; Customer Service Representative; Design Engineer; Designer; Draftsperson; Electrical/Electronics Engineer; Environmental Engineer; Human Resources Manager; Industrial Engineer; Industrial Production Manager; Internet Services Manager; Management Analyst/ Consultant; Mechanical Engineer; Metallurgical Engineer; MIS Specialist; Operations/Production Manager; Quality Control Supervisor; Software Engineer; Stationary Engineer; Structural Engineer; Systems Analyst; Technical Writer/Editor; Telecommunications Manager. **Benefits available to temporary workers:** Paid Holidays; Paid Vacation. **Corporate headquarters location:** Radnor PA. **Other U.S. locations:** Nationwide. **Average salary range of placements:** $30,000 - $50,000. **Number of placements per year:** 100 - 199.

CAREER/OUTPLACEMENT COUNSELING FIRMS

ACG INTERNATIONAL
60 East 42nd Street, New York NY 10016. 212/883-1010. **Contact:** Barry Mann, General Manager. **Description:** A career/outplacement counseling firm. **Number of placements per year:** 1 - 49.

MERRILL ADAMS ASSOCIATES
30 Rockefeller Plaza, Suite 2835, New York NY 10112. 212/332-7888. **Fax:** 212/332-7887. **Contact:** Arthur Schill, Executive Vice President. **Description:** A career/outplacement counseling firm. **Specializes in the areas of:** Accounting/Auditing; Administration; Advertising; Banking; Computer Science/Software; Economics; Education; Engineering; Finance; Food Industry; General Management; Health/Medical; Industrial; Insurance; Legal; Manufacturing; Personnel/Labor Relations; Publishing; Retail; Sales; Technical. **Positions commonly filled include:** Accountant/Auditor; Administrative Manager; Aerospace Engineer; Architect; Attorney; Bank Officer/Manager; Biochemist; Biological Scientist; Branch Manager; Broadcast Technician; Budget Analyst; Buyer; Chemical Engineer; Chemist; Chief Executive Officer; Chief Financial Officer; Civil Engineer; Computer Programmer; Construction Contractor; Credit Manager; Customer Service Rep.; Design Engineer; Designer; Dietician/Nutritionist; Draftsperson; Economist; Editor; Education Administrator; Electrical/Electronics Engineer; Environmental Engineer; Financial Analyst; Food Scientist/Technologist; General Manager; Health Services Manager; Hotel Manager; Human Resources Specialist; Industrial Engineer; Industrial Production Manager; Insurance Agent/Broker; Internet Services Manager; Librarian; Management Analyst/Consultant; Management Trainee; Manufacturer's/Wholesaler's Sales Rep.; Market Research Analyst; Mathematician; Mechanical Engineer; Medical Records Technician; MIS Specialist; Multimedia Designer; Occupational Therapist; Operations/Production Manager; Petroleum Engineer; Pharmacist; Physician; Property and Real Estate Manager; Psychologist; Public Relations Specialist; Quality Control Supervisor; Real Estate Agent; Recreational Therapist; Restaurant/Food Service Manager; Services Sales Rep.; Social Worker; Software Engineer; Strategic Relations Manager; Structural Engineer; Systems Analyst; Technical Writer/Editor; Telecommunications Manager; Underwriter/Assistant Underwriter; Vice President. **Corporate headquarters location:** Parsippany NJ. **Other area locations:** Princeton NJ. **Number of placements per year:** 1 - 49.

AMERICAN BUSINESS CONSULTANTS
990 Woodbury Road, Highland Mills NY 10930. 914/344-1521. **Fax:** 914/344-1531. **Contact:** William

Neal, President. **E-mail address:** wcneal@warwick.net. **Description:** A career/outplacement counseling firm. Company pays fee. **Specializes in the areas of:** General Management; Industrial; Manufacturing. **Positions commonly filled include:** Chemical Engineer; Electrical/Electronics Engineer; General Manager; Human Resources Manager; Industrial Engineer; Industrial Production Manager; Mechanical Engineer; Purchasing Agent/Manager; Quality Control Supervisor. **Other U.S. locations:** Nationwide. **Number of placements per year:** 200 - 499.

CAREER & FAMILY DYNAMICS
100 Park Avenue, 16th Floor, New York NY 10017. 212/880-2607. **Fax:** 212/880-6499. **Contact:** Terre B. Schmidt, CSW, President. **Description:** A career/outplacement counseling firm.

CAREER DEVELOPMENT SERVICES
706 East Avenue, Rochester NY 14607-2105. 716/244-0750. **Fax:** 716/244-7115. **Contact:** Deborah Nicholas, Manager of Public Relations. **E-mail address:** cardev1@frontiernet.net. **World Wide Web address:** http://www.careerdev.org. **Description:** A career/outplacement counseling firm providing career planning services for a variety of professions and occupations. Career Development Services offers corporate training, in-house career resource library services, career coaching, employee career centers, and national client services. Founded in 1975. **Positions commonly filled include:** Administrative Assistant; Chemical Engineer; Chemist; Commercial Artist; Customer Service Rep; Draftsperson; EDP Specialist; Factory Worker; Manufacturing Engineer; Marketing Specialist; Medical Secretary; Nurse; Public Relations Specialist; Receptionist; Secretary; Software Engineer; Technical Writer/Editor. **Number of placements per year:** 200 - 499.

THE LLOYD COMPANY
445 Broadhollow Road, Suite 120, Melville NY 11747. 516/777-7600. **Fax:** 516/777-7626. **Contact:** Manager. **Description:** A career/outplacement counseling service that also offers temporary placement. Company pays fee. **Specializes in the areas of:** Art/Design; Banking; Biology; Brokerage; Computer Science/Software; Food Industry; Health/Medical; Mortgage; Publishing; Real Estate; Sales. **Positions commonly filled include:** Bank Officer/Manager; Biological Scientist; Computer Programmer; Credit Manager; Hotel Manager; Medical Records Technician; Occupational Therapist; Physical Therapist; Physician; Property and Real Estate Manager; Restaurant/Food Service Manager; Systems Analyst. **Number of placements per year:** 200 - 499.

RLS CAREER CENTER
3049 East Genesee Street, Syracuse NY 13224. 315/446-0566. **Fax:** 315/446-5869. **Contact:** Jerridith Wilson, Executive Director. **Description:** A career counseling firm. RLS Career Center is a community-based, nonprofit educational institution providing individuals, businesses, and organizations with career development services. The center offers a variety of education and career planning services, including outplacement and training. Founded in 1974.

NORTH CAROLINA

EXECUTIVE SEARCH FIRMS

A FIRST RESOURCE
P.O. Box 15451, Winston-Salem NC 27113. 336/784-5898. **Fax:** 336/784-6702. **Contact:** Karen L. Siburt, CPC, President. **Description:** An executive search firm focusing on the placement of manufacturing management including plant management, shift supervisors, and engineers. A First Resource also specializes in computer professional placement. Company pays fee. **Number of placements per year:** 50 - 99.

ATS HEALTH SERVICES
601 South Kings Drive, Suite HH, Charlotte NC 28204. 704/342-2710. **Contact:** Office Manager. **Description:** An executive search firm that places health care personnel including CNAs and LPNs. **Specializes in the areas of:** Health/Medical.

ACCOUNTANTS EXECUTIVE SEARCH
ACCOUNTANTS ON CALL
227 West Trade Street, Suite 1908, Charlotte NC 28202. 704/376-0006. **Fax:** 704/376-4787. **Contact:** Manager. **World Wide Web address:** http://www.aocnet.com. **Description:** An executive search firm. Accountants On Call (also at this location) is a temporary agency. **Specializes in the areas of:** Accounting/Auditing; Banking; Finance; Manufacturing.

ACCOUNTANTS EXECUTIVE SEARCH
ACCOUNTANTS ON CALL
5540 Center View Drive, Suite 208, Raleigh NC 27606. 919/859-5550. **Contact:** Office Manager. **Description:** An executive search firm. Accountants On Call (also at this location) is a temporary agency. **Specializes in the areas of:** Accounting/Auditing; Finance.

ACCOUNTANTS EXECUTIVE SEARCH
ACCOUNTANTS ON CALL
1801 Stanley Road, Suite 206, Greensboro NC 27407. 336/292-3800. **Contact:** Office Manager. **Description:** An executive search firm. Accountants On Call (also at this location) is a temporary agency. **Specializes in the areas of:** Accounting/Auditing; Finance.

ACCURATE STAFFING CONSULTANTS, INC.
1328-D Starbrook Drive, Charlotte NC 28210. 704/554-9675. **Fax:** 704/554-5914. **Contact:** Catherine Wall, President. **Description:** An executive search firm. Company pays fee. **Specializes in the areas of:** Accounting/Auditing; Administration; Banking; Computer Science/Software; Engineering; Industrial; Manufacturing; Personnel/Labor Relations; Secretarial; Technical. **Average salary range of placements:** $30,000 - $50,000. **Number of placements per year:** 50 - 99.

ADKINS & ASSOCIATES
P.O. Box 16062, Greensboro NC 27416. 336/378-1261. **Contact:** Manager. **Description:** An executive search firm. **Specializes in the areas of:** Textiles.

ADVANCED PERSONNEL RESOURCES
P.O. Box 4923, Greensboro NC 27404-4923. 910/272-7720. **Contact:** Diane Z. Gaines, President. **Description:** An executive search firm. Company pays fee. **Specializes in the areas of:** Accounting/Auditing; Administration; Computer Science/Software; Finance; General Management; Insurance; Legal; Manufacturing; Personnel/Labor Relations; Publishing; Sales; Secretarial.

ALPHA OMEGA EXECUTIVE SEARCH
7522 LaSater Road, Clemmons NC 27012. 910/778-1271. **Fax:** 910/778-1274. **Contact:** Tracy Barnes, President. **Description:** An executive search firm operating on both retained and contingency bases. Company pays fee. **Specializes in the areas of:** Accounting/Auditing; Engineering; Industrial; Personnel/Labor Relations; Technical. **Positions commonly filled include:** Accountant; Applications Engineer; Budget Analyst; Buyer; Chief Financial Officer; Controller; Cost Estimator; Design Engineer; Draftsperson; Electrical/Electronics Engineer; Electrician; Environmental Engineer; Finance Director; Financial Analyst; Graphic Designer; Human Resources Manager; Industrial Engineer; Industrial Production Manager; Manufacturing Engineer; Mechanical Engineer; Metallurgical Engineer; MIS Specialist; Operations Manager; Production Manager; Project Manager; Purchasing Agent/Manager; Quality Control Supervisor; Sales Engineer; Sales Executive; Software Engineer; Technical Writer/Editor. **Average salary range of placements:** More than $50,000. **Number of placements per year:** 1 - 49.

AMCELL ASSOCIATES
5970 Fairview Road, Suite 512, Charlotte NC 28210. 704/643-1247. **Contact:** Manager. **Description:** An executive search firm. **Specializes in the areas of:** Banking; Finance; Manufacturing; Paper; Pharmaceutical; Publishing; Textiles.

AMERICAN QUALITY STAFFING, INC.
189 Wind Chime Court, Suite 104, Raleigh NC 27615. 919/676-8232. **Fax:** 919/676-8298. **Contact:** Nancy Callihan, President. **Description:** An executive search firm operating on a contingency basis. Company pays fee. **Specializes in the areas of:** Engineering; Technical. **Positions commonly filled include:** Draftsperson; Electrical/Electronics Engineer; MIS Specialist; Software Engineer. **Other U.S. locations:** Nationwide. **Average salary range of placements:** $30,000 - $50,000. **Number of placements per year:** 100 - 199.

AMERIPRO SEARCH, INC.
20468-A Chartwell Centre Drive, Cornelius NC 28031. 704/896-8991. **Fax:** 704/896-8855. **Contact:** Elaine C. Brauninger, President. **E-mail address:** ameripro@1stfamily.com. **Description:** An executive search firm. Company pays fee. **Specializes in the areas of:** Accounting/Auditing; Administration; Computer Science/Software; Data Processing; Engineering; Finance; General Management; Industrial; Manufacturing; MIS/EDP; Personnel/Labor Relations; Sales; Technical. **Positions commonly filled include:** Accountant/Auditor; Administrative Manager; Advertising Clerk; Aerospace Engineer; Biochemist; Biological Scientist; Branch Manager; Designer; Engineer; Financial Analyst; General Manager; Industrial Production Manager; Internet Services Manager; MIS Specialist; Operations Research Analyst; Science Technologist; Scientist; Software Engineer; Technical Writer/Editor; Telecommunications Manager. **Average salary range of placements:** More than $50,000. **Number of placements per year:** 100 - 199.

AMOS & ASSOCIATES
633-B Chapel Hill Road, Burlington NC 27215. 336/222-0231. **Fax:** 336/222-1214. **Contact:** Diane Amos, President. **E-mail address:** famsamos@netpath.net. **World Wide Web address:** http://www.amosassociates.com. **Description:** An executive search firm. Company pays fee. **Specializes in the

areas of: Computer Science/Software. **Positions commonly filled include:** Computer Programmer; MIS Specialist; Operations Manager; Software Engineer; Systems Analyst; Systems Manager. **Average salary range of placements:** More than $50,000. **Number of placements per year:** 50 - 99.

ANDERSON & ASSOCIATES
112 South Tryon Street, Suite 800, Charlotte NC 28284. 704/347-0090. **Contact:** Manager. **Description:** An executive search firm.

ANDOS ASSOCIATES INC.
1805 Vincennes Place, Wilmington NC 28405. 910/256-8116. **Contact:** Manager. **Description:** An executive search firm. **Specializes in the areas of:** Biotechnology; Health/Medical; Pharmaceutical.

ANDREWS & ASSOCIATES, INC.
6100 Fairview Road, Suite 1420, Charlotte NC 28210. 704/556-0088. **Contact:** Dwight L. Andrews, Principal. **Description:** An executive search firm. Company pays fee. **Specializes in the areas of:** Accounting/Auditing; Administration; Finance. **Positions commonly filled include:** Accountant/Auditor; Bookkeeper. **Number of placements per year:** 1 - 49.

ARJAY & ASSOCIATES
875 Walnut Street, Cary NC 27511. 919/469-5540. **Contact:** Manger. **Description:** An executive search firm. **Specializes in the areas of:** Engineering; Technical.

ATCHISON & ASSOCIATES, INC.
612 Pasteur Drive, Suite 209, Greensboro NC 27403. 336/855-5943. **Contact:** Bill Atchison, President. **Description:** An executive search firm operating on both retainer and contingency bases. Company pays fee. **Specializes in the areas of:** Accounting/Auditing; Engineering; Industrial; Manufacturing; Technical. **Positions commonly filled include:** Accountant/Auditor; Chemical Engineer; Chemist; Credit Manager; Electrical/Electronics Engineer; Environmental Engineer; Financial Analyst; Industrial Engineer; Manufacturing Engineer; Mechanical Engineer; Metallurgical Engineer; Operations/Production Manager; Purchasing Agent/Manager; Quality Control Supervisor; Software Engineer. **Average salary range of placements:** $30,000 - $50,000. **Number of placements per year:** 1 - 49.

AYERS & ASSOCIATES, INC.
P.O. Box 16065, Greensboro NC 27416. 336/378-1761. **Fax:** 336/275-8232. **Contact:** Dick Ayers, Account Manager. **E-mail address:** dicka11034@aol.com. **Description:** An executive search firm operating on a contingency basis. Company pays fee. **Specializes in the areas of:** Engineering; General Management; Industrial; Manufacturing; Personnel/Labor Relations; Textiles. **Positions commonly filled include:** Accountant/Auditor; Buyer; Chemical Engineer; Chemist; Credit Manager; Electrical/Electronics Engineer; Industrial Engineer; Industrial Production Manager; Management Analyst/Consultant; Management Trainee; Mechanical Engineer; Operations/Production Manager; Quality Control Supervisor; Systems Analyst; Textile Manager; Transportation/Traffic Specialist. **Average salary range of placements:** $30,000 - $75,000. **Number of placements per year:** 1 - 49.

BANK SEARCH
P.O. Box 491, Ayden NC 28513. 919/355-8282. **Contact:** David Melvin, Owner. **Description:** An executive search firm. Company pays fee. **Specializes in the areas of:** Banking. **Positions commonly filled include:** Bank Officer/Manager; Branch Manager. **Average salary range of placements:** $30,000 - $50,000. **Number of placements per year:** 1 - 49.

JIM BEATTY & ASSOCIATES
6525 Morrison Boulevard, Suite 121, Charlotte NC 28211. **Contact:** Manager. **Description:** An executive search firm. Company pays fee. **Positions commonly filled include:** Bank Officer/Manager; Construction Contractor; Education Administrator; Health Services Manager; Human Resources Specialist; Internet Services Manager; MIS Specialist; Physician; Property and Real Estate Manager; Quality Control Supervisor; Securities Sales Representative; Software Engineer.

BENNETT ALLEN & ASSOCIATES
7422 Carmel Executive Park Drive, Charlotte NC 28226. 704/541-5891. **Contact:** Ben Liebstein, President. **Description:** An executive search firm. Company pays fee. **Specializes in the areas of:** Engineering. **Positions commonly filled include:** Aerospace Engineer; Agricultural Engineer; Electrical/Electronics Engineer; Mechanical Engineer; Mining Engineer; Structural Engineer.

BULLINGTON ASSOCIATES
3700 National Drive, Suite 214, Raleigh NC 27612. 919/781-1350. **Fax:** 919/781-5947. **Contact:** Hal Keyser, Manager. **Description:** An executive search firm. Company pays fee. **Specializes in the areas of:** Sales. **Number of placements per year:** 1 - 49.

CAREER SEARCH INC.
P.O. Box 97007, Raleigh NC 27624. 919/878-7900. **Fax:** 919/878-1865. **Contact:** Ron Burton, President. **Description:** An executive search firm. Company pays fee. **Specializes in the areas of:** Engineering; General Management; Manufacturing; Materials; Personnel/Labor Relations; Purchasing. **Positions commonly filled include:** Buyer; Chemical Engineer; Electrical/Electronics Engineer; Environmental Engineer; General Manager; Human Resources Specialist; Industrial Engineer; Industrial Production Manager; Materials Engineer; Mechanical Engineer;Purchasing Agent/Manager; Quality Control Supervisor. **Average salary range of placements:** More than $50,000. **Number of placements per year:** 1 - 49.

CARTER/MACKAY OF CARY
2000 Regency Parkway, Suite 460, Cary NC 27511. 919/380-1200. **Fax:** 919/380-1267. **Contact:** Manager. **Description:** An executive search firm. **Specializes in the areas of:** Sales. **Other U.S. locations:** Framingham MA; Hasbrouck Heights NJ; Great Neck NY.

CHRISTOPHER GROUP
P.O. Box 20664, Raleigh NC 27619. 919/833-5650. **Fax:** 919/833-5625. **Contact:** Manager. **Description:** A contingency executive search firm. Specializes exclusively in the placement of experienced real estate and mortgage professionals with financial institutions, corporate real estate entities, developers, valuation/consulting firms, and brokerage/management organizations. Founded in 1985. Company pays fee. **Specializes in the areas of:** Banking; Finance. **Positions commonly filled include:** Bank Officer/Manager; Real Estate Agent; Underwriter/Assistant Underwriter. **Average salary range of placements:** More than $50,000. **Number of placements per year:** 1 - 49.

CLARKS & ASSOCIATES
1400-D Millgate Drive, Winston-Salem NC 27103. 336/765-7377. **Contact:** Manager. **Description:** An executive search firm.

SL COLLINS ASSOCIATES
P.O. Box 472181, Charlotte NC 28247-2181. 704/365-9889. **Fax:** 704/365-9890. **Contact:** Steve

Collins, President/Owner. **E-mail address:** collins@slcollins.com. **World Wide Web address:** http://www.slcollins.com. **Description:** An executive search firm. Company pays fee. **Specializes in the areas of:** Biotechnology; Pharmaceutical. **Positions commonly filled include:** Biological Scientist; Chemical Engineer; Chemist; Industrial Engineer; Manufacturing Engineer; Operations Manager; Production Manager; Project Manager. **Number of placements per year:** 50 - 99.

DAVIS TECHNICAL SEARCH CONSULTANTS
249 Normandy Road, Mooresville NC 28115. 704/664-7279. **Contact:** Manager. **Description:** An executive search firm. **Specializes in the areas of:** Manufacturing.

DUNHILL PROFESSIONAL SEARCH
975 Walnut Street, Suite 260, Cary NC 27511. 919/460-9988. **Contact:** Manager. **Description:** An executive search firm. **Corporate headquarters location:** Woodbury NY. **Other U.S. locations:** Nationwide.

EASTERN SEARCH GROUP
P.O. Box 4655, Wilmington NC 28406. 910/799-7700. **Fax:** 910/392-6266. **Contact:** Fred Wells, President. **Description:** An executive search firm. Company pays fee. **Specializes in the areas of:** Computer Science/Software; Engineering; Industrial; Scientific; Technical. **Positions commonly filled include:** Chemical Engineer; Computer Programmer; Electrical/Electronics Engineer; Industrial Engineer; Mechanical Engineer; MIS Specialist; Production Manager; Quality Control Supervisor; Software Engineer; Statistician; Systems Analyst. **Average salary range of placements:** More than $50,000. **Number of placements per year:** 50 - 99.

BRUCE EDWARDS & ASSOCIATES INC.
1000 Park 40 Plaza, Suite 290, Durham NC 27713. 919/544-9911. **Contact:** Manager. **Description:** An executive search firm.

ELIN VAR
3200 Beechleaf Court, Raleigh NC 27604. 919/878-4454. **Contact:** Manager. **Description:** An executive search firm. **Specializes in the areas of:** Accounting/Auditing; Finance.

PHIL ELLIS ASSOCIATES, INC.
2030 Eastwood Road, Wilmington NC 28403. 910/256-9810. **Fax:** 910/256-9887. **Contact:** Phil Ellis, President. **Description:** An executive search firm operating on both retainer and contingency bases. Company pays fee. **Specializes in the areas of:** Biology; Manufacturing; Pharmaceutical; Technical. **Positions commonly filled include:** Biochemist; Biological Scientist; Biomedical Engineer; Chemical Engineer; Chemist; Electrical/Electronics Engineer; Environmental Engineer; General Manager; Industrial Engineer; Industrial Production Manager; Mechanical Engineer; Metallurgical Engineer; Operations/Production Manager; Pharmacist; Quality Control Supervisor; Science Technologist. **Average salary range of placements:** More than $50,000. **Number of placements per year:** 50 - 99.

ENVIRONMENTAL RECRUITING SERVICES (ERS)
21514 GulfStar Court, Cornelius NC 28031. 704/896-3336. **Fax:** 704/896-3337. **Contact:** Brian MacLamroc, President. **Description:** An executive search firm operating on both retainer and contingency bases. **Specializes in the areas of:** Civil Engineering; Environmental. **Positions commonly filled:** Chemical Engineer; Civil Engineer; Construction Contractor; Cost Estimator; Structural Engineer; Transportation & Traffic Specialist. **Average salary range of placements:** More than $50,000. **Number of placements per year:** 50 - 99.

EXECUTIVE CONNECTIONS
P.O. Box 1853, Lexington NC 27293. 910/249-0031. **Fax:** 910/249-0036. **Contact:** Manager. **Description:** An executive search firm specializing in engineering, manufacturing, human resources, and information technology.

EXECUTIVE RECRUITMENT SPECIALISTS, INC.
6407 Idlewild Road, Building 1, Suite 103, Charlotte NC 28212. 704/536-8830. **Fax:** 704/536-8893. **Contact:** Eric Sklut, President. **Description:** An executive search firm. Company pays fee. **Specializes in the areas of:** Computer Science/Software; Engineering; Finance; General Management; Government; Health/Medical; Manufacturing. **Positions commonly filled include:** Accountant/Auditor; Biomedical Engineer; Electrical/Electronics Engineer; General Manager; Health Services Manager; Licensed Practical Nurse; Mechanical Engineer; Medical Records Technician; Nuclear Medicine Technologist; Occupational Therapist; Physical Therapist; Quality Control Supervisor; Radiological Technologist; Recreational Therapist; Registered Nurse; Respiratory Therapist; Software Engineer; Speech-Language Pathologist. **Number of placements per year:** 50 - 99.

C.D. FAYLING ASSOCIATES, INC.
P.O. Box 2011, Pinehurst NC 28374. 910/295-4901. **Contact:** Manager. **Description:** An executive search firm. Company pays fee. **Specializes in the areas of:** Accounting/Auditing; Engineering; General Management; Manufacturing; Personnel/Labor Relations; Sales. **Positions commonly filled include:** Accountant/Auditor; Attorney; Branch Manager; Buyer; Customer Service Representative; Design Engineer; Electrical/Electronics Engineer; General Manager; Human Resources Specialist; Industrial Engineer; Industrial Production Manager; Purchasing Agent/Manager; Quality Control Supervisor. **Average salary range of placements:** More than $50,000. **Number of placements per year:** 1 - 49.

F-O-R-T-U-N-E PERSONNEL CONSULTANTS
P.O. Box 460, Pineville NC 28134. 704/889-1100. **Fax:** 704/889-1109. **Contact:** Manager. **Description:** An executive search firm. **Specializes in the areas of:** Biotechnology; Medical Technology; Pharmaceutical. **Corporate headquarters location:** New York NY. **Other U.S. locations:** Nationwide.

F-O-R-T-U-N-E PERSONNEL CONSULTANTS
Pomona Executive Center, 304B Pomona Drive, Greensboro NC 27407. 336/852-4455. **Fax:** 336/852-3429. **Contact:** Manager. **Description:** An executive search firm. **Specializes in the areas of:** Engineering; Logistics; Manufacturing; Materials; Transportation. **Corporate headquarters location:** New York NY. **Other U.S. locations:** Nationwide.

THE FURNITURE AGENCY INC.
P.O. Box 53, High Point NC 27261. 336/841-3221. **Toll-free phone:** 800/833-3261. **Fax:** 336/841-5651. **Contact:** Brady Stern, President. **E-mail address:** furniturea@aol.com. **Description:** An executive search firm that focuses on the placement of personnel in the furniture industry. Company pays fee. **Specializes in the areas of:** Design; Engineering; Industrial; Manufacturing. **Positions commonly filled include:** Engineer; General Manager; Plant Manager; Superintendent. **Average salary range of placements:** More than $50,000.

GLOVIER & ASSOCIATES
4732 Lebanon Road, Charlotte NC 28227. 704/545-0877. **Contact:** Jim Glovier, Owner. **Description:** An

executive search firm. Company pays fee. **Specializes in the areas of:** Engineering; General Management; Manufacturing; Sales. **Positions commonly filled include:** Accountant/Auditor; Chemist; Cost Estimator; Credit Manager; Designer; Draftsperson; Environmental Engineer; Forester/Conservation Scientist; General Manager; Industrial Engineer; Mechanical Engineer; Operations/Production Manager; Quality Control Supervisor. **Average salary range of placements:** More than $50,000. **Number of placements per year:** 1 - 49.

STEWART GREENE & COMPANY/THE TRIAD
P.O. Box 625, Pleasant Garden NC 27313. 910/674-5345. **Physical address:** 5504 Stonebridge Road, Pleasant Garden NC. **Fax:** 910/674-5937. **Contact:** Bill Greene, President. **Description:** An executive search firm focusing on the furniture industry. Company pays fee. **Specializes in the areas of:** Architecture/Construction; Engineering; General Management; Manufacturing; Sales. **Positions commonly filled include:** Buyer; Credit Manager; Design Engineer; Designer; Engineer; General Manager; Human Resources Specialist; Industrial Designer; Industrial Production Manager; Mechanical Engineer; Purchasing Agent/Manager; Quality Control Supervisor. **Number of placements per year:** 50 - 99.

ROBERT HALF INTERNATIONAL
300 North Greene Street, Suite 275, Greensboro NC 27401. 336/274-4253. **Fax:** 336/273-2882. **Contact:** Placement Manager. **Description:** An executive search firm. Company pays fee. **Specializes in the areas of:** Accounting/Auditing; Administration; Banking; Computer Hardware/Software; Finance. **Positions commonly filled include:** Accountant/Auditor; Bookkeeper; Clerk; Computer Operator; Computer Programmer; CPA; Credit Manager; Data Entry Clerk; EDP Specialist; Software Engineer; Systems Analyst. **Corporate headquarters location:** Menlo Park CA. **Other U.S. locations:** Nationwide. **International locations:** Worldwide.

ROBERT HALF INTERNATIONAL ACCOUNTEMPS
3605 Glenwood Road, Suite 390, Raleigh NC 27612. 919/682-3944. **Contact:** Manager. **Description:** An executive search firm. Accountemps (also at this location) provides temporary placements. **Corporate headquarters location:** Menlo Park CA. **Other U.S. locations:** Nationwide. **International locations:** Worldwide.

ROBERT HALF INTERNATIONAL ACCOUNTEMPS
201 South College Street, Suite 2010, Charlotte NC 28244. 704/548-8447. **Contact:** Manager. **Description:** An executive search firm. Accountemps (also at this location) provides temporary placements. **Corporate headquarters location:** Menlo Park CA. **Other U.S. locations:** Nationwide. **International locations:** Worldwide.

ROBERT HALF INTERNATIONAL ACCOUNTEMPS
6101 Carnegie Boulevard, Suite 460, Charlotte NC 28209. 704/553-7100. **Contact:** Manager. **Description:** An executive search firm. Accountemps (also at this location) provides temporary placements. **Corporate headquarters location:** Menlo Park CA. **Other U.S. locations:** Nationwide. **International locations:** Worldwide.

HALLMARK RECRUITERS
194 Wood Duck Loop, Mooresville NC 28115. 704/664-9800. **Fax:** 704/664-8393. **Contact:** Linda Beckham, Personnel. **Description:** An executive search firm. **Specializes in the areas of:** Manufacturing. **Positions commonly filled include:** Biochemist; Chemical Engineer; Chemist; Hotel Manager; Materials Engineer; Purchasing Agent/Manager; Quality Control Supervisor. **Average salary range of placements:** More than $50,000. **Number of placements per year:** 100 - 199.

HIGHLANDER SEARCH
210 West Friendly Avenue, Greensboro NC 27401. 336/333-9886. **Contact:** Jeffrey Penley, CPC, President. **Description:** An executive search firm. Company pays fee. **Specializes in the areas of:** Accounting/Auditing; Engineering; Manufacturing. **Positions commonly filled include:** Controller. **Average salary range of placements:** More than $50,000. **Number of placements per year:** 1 - 49.

HUNKLER MEDICAL ASSOCIATES
6701 Carmel Road, Suite 204, Charlotte NC 28226. 704/542-6691. **Contact:** Manager. **Description:** An executive search firm. **Specializes in the areas of:** Medical Sales and Marketing.

INFORMATION SYSTEMS PROFESSIONALS, INC.
5904 Castlebrook Drive, Raleigh NC 27604. 919/954-9100. **Toll-free phone:** 800/951-9100. **Fax:** 919/954-1947. **Contact:** Bradley Moses, Principal. **E-mail address:** ispros@nando.net. **World Wide Web address:** http://www.citysearch.com/rdulispros. **Description:** An executive search firm. **Specializes in the areas of:** Computer Science/Software; Scientific; Technical. **Positions commonly filled include:** Computer Animator; Computer Operator; Computer Programmer; Database Manager; Electrical/Electronics Engineer; Internet Services Manager; Management Analyst/ Consultant; Operations Manager; Project Manager; Software Engineer; Systems Analyst; Systems Manager; Technical Writer/Editor; Telecommunications Manager; Webmaster. **Average salary range of placements:** More than $50,000. **Number of placements per year:** 1 - 49.

INSURANCE PROFESSIONAL SEARCH
6869 Fairview Road, Suite 200, Charlotte NC 28210. 704/362-5638. **Contact:** Susan Belton, Owner. **Description:** An executive search firm. Company pays fee. **Specializes in the areas of:** Insurance. **Positions commonly filled include:** Accountant/Auditor; Actuary; Adjuster; Claim Rep.; Collector; Insurance Agent; Investigator; Underwriter/Assistant Underwriter. **Average salary range of placements:** More than $50,000. **Number of placements per year:** 1 - 49.

S.N. JONES & ASSOCIATES
424 Woodbyne Avenue, Henderson NC 28739. 704/692-3546. **Fax:** 704/692-2268. **Contact:** Sandra Jones, Principal. **Description:** An executive search firm. Company pays fee. **Specializes in the areas of:** Accounting/Auditing; Health/Medical. **Positions commonly filled include:** Health Services Manager; Medical Records Technician; Physical Therapist; Registered Nurse. **Average salary range of placements:** $30,000 - $50,000. **Number of placements per year:** 1 - 49.

KILGO & COMPANY
8318 Pineville-Matthews Road, Suite 708, Charlotte NC 28226. 704/544-0342. **Fax:** 704/542-6353. **Contact:** Don Kilgo, Owner. **Description:** An executive search firm for experienced technical personnel. Company pays fee. **Specializes in the areas of:** Computer Science/ Software. **Positions commonly filled include:** Sales Representative; Sales Manager. **Number of placements per year:** 1 - 49.

LaVALLEE & ASSOCIATES
4176 Sulgrave Court, Winston-Salem NC 27104. 336/760-1911. **Contact:** Michael J. Lavallee,

Managing Partner. **Description:** An executive search firm. Company pays fee. **Positions commonly filled include:** Computer Programmer; Systems Analyst. **Number of placements per year:** 1 - 49.

LEGAL PLACEMENT SPECIALISTS
606 Wade Avenue, Suite 100, Raleigh NC 27605. 919/829-2550. **Contact:** Manager. **Description:** An executive search firm that places lawyers. **Specializes in the areas of:** Legal.

LINDEN GROUP INC.
6408 Honegger Drive, Suite B, Charlotte NC 28211. 704/367-0309. **Contact:** Manager. **Description:** An executive search firm. **Specializes in the areas of:** Automotive; Food Industry.

MSB ASSOCIATES
115 South Fawn Forest Lane, Pittsboro NC 27312. 919/542-6868. **Contact:** Michael Bovelsky, Owner. **E-mail address:** bovelsky@aol.com. **Description:** An executive search firm. Company pays fee. **Specializes in the areas of:** Manufacturing. **Positions commonly filled include:** Data Processor; Design Engineer; Financial Manager; General Manager; Industrial Engineer; Industrial Production Manager; Manufacturer's/Wholesaler's Sales Rep.; Manufacturing Engineer; Marketing Specialist; Materials Engineer; Materials Manager; Metallurgical Engineer; Plant Manager; Quality Control Supervisor; Sales and Marketing Manager. **Number of placements per year:** 1 - 49.

MANAGEMENT RECRUITERS INTERNATIONAL
5701 Westpark Drive, Suite 110, Charlotte NC 28217. 704/525-9270. **Fax:** 704/527-0070. **Contact:** John Lewis, General Manager. **Description:** An executive search firm. Company pays fee. **Specializes in the areas of:** Art/Design; Computer Science/Software; Engineering; Finance; Food Industry; General Management; Health/Medical; Industrial; Insurance; Manufacturing; Personnel/Labor Relations; Publishing; Sales; Technical; Transportation. **Positions commonly filled include:** Administrative Manager; Bank Officer/Manager; Biomedical Engineer; Branch Manager; Buyer; Chemical Engineer; Chiropractor; Computer Programmer; Construction Contractor; Customer Service Representative; Dentist; Designer; EEG Technologist; EKG Technician; Financial Analyst; General Manager; Health Services Manager; Industrial Engineer; Industrial Production Manager; Management Analyst/Consultant; Manufacturer's/ Wholesaler's Sales Rep.; Occupational Therapist; Operations/Production Manager; Pharmacist; Physical Therapist; Physician; Purchasing Agent/Manager; Quality Control Supervisor; Recreational Therapist; Registered Nurse; Respiratory Therapist; Securities Sales Representative; Software Engineer; Surveyor; Systems Analyst; Transportation/Traffic Specialist; Underwriter/Assistant Underwriter; Veterinarian. **Corporate headquarters location:** Cleveland OH. **Other U.S. locations:** Nationwide. **International locations:** Worldwide. **Number of placements per year:** 200 - 499.

MANAGEMENT RECRUITERS INTERNATIONAL
53 Arlington Street, Asheville NC 28801. 704/258-9646. **Fax:** 704/252-0866. **Contact:** Paul Rumson, President. **Description:** An executive search firm operating on both retainer and contingency bases. Company pays fee. **Specializes in the areas of:** Computer Science/Software; Engineering; Industrial; Manufacturing. **Positions commonly filled include:** Chemical Engineer; Chemist; Computer Programmer; Designer; Draftsperson; Electrical/Electronics Engineer; Hotel Manager; Industrial Engineer; Industrial Production Manager; Materials Engineer; Mechanical Engineer; Mining Engineer; Purchasing Agent/ Manager; Quality Control Supervisor; Restaurant/Food Service Manager; Software Engineer; Structural Engineer. **Corporate headquarters location:** Cleveland OH. **Other U.S. locations:** Nationwide. **International locations:** Worldwide. **Average salary range of placements:** More than $50,000. **Number of placements per year:** 1 - 49.

MANAGEMENT RECRUITERS INTERNATIONAL
P.O. Box 629, Cedar Mountain NC 28718. 704/884-4118. **Fax:** 704/884-3512. **Contact:** Frank Schoff, President. **Description:** An executive search firm. **Specializes in the areas of:** Accounting/Auditing; Administration; Advertising; Architecture/ Construction; Banking; Communications; Computer Hardware/Software; Design; Electrical; Engineering; Food Industry; General Management; Health/Medical; Insurance; Legal; Manufacturing; Operations Management; Personnel/Labor Relations; Procurement; Publishing; Retail; Sales; Technical; Textiles; Transportation. **Corporate headquarters location:** Cleveland OH. **Other U.S. locations:** Nationwide. **International locations:** Worldwide.

MANAGEMENT RECRUITERS INTERNATIONAL
835 Highland Avenue SE, Hickory NC 28602. 704/324-2020. **Contact:** Manager. **Description:** An executive search firm. **Specializes in the areas of:** Accounting/Auditing; Administration; Advertising; Architecture/Construction; Banking; Communications; Computer Hardware/Software; Design; Electrical; Engineering; Food Industry; General Management; Health/Medical; Insurance; Legal; Manufacturing; Operations Management; Personnel/Labor Relations; Procurement; Publishing; Technical; Textiles; Transportation. **Corporate headquarters location:** Cleveland OH. **Other U.S. locations:** Nationwide. **International locations:** Worldwide.

MANAGEMENT RECRUITERS INTERNATIONAL
120 North Franklin, Building J, P.O. Box 1186, Rocky Mount NC 27802-1186. 919/442-8000. **Fax:** 919/442-9000. **Contact:** Bob Manning, Manager. **E-mail address:** mri@web-point.com. **Description:** An executive search firm. **Specializes in the areas of:** Accounting/Auditing; Administration; Advertising; Architecture/Construction; Banking; Communications; Computer Hardware/Software; Design; Electrical; Engineering; Food Industry; General Management; Health/Medical; Insurance; Legal; Manufacturing; Operations Management; Personnel/Labor Relations; Procurement; Publishing; Retail; Sales; Technical; Textiles; Transportation. **Corporate headquarters location:** Cleveland OH. **Other U.S. locations:** Nationwide. **International locations:** Worldwide.

MANAGEMENT RECRUITERS INTERNATIONAL
P.O. Box 395, Cove City NC 28523. 919/633-1900. **Fax:** 919/633-3121. **Contact:** Fred Eatman, Owner/Manager. **Description:** An executive search firm operating on a retainer basis. The firm also provides career/outplacement counseling. Company pays fee. **Specializes in the areas of:** Engineering; Food Industry; General Management; Manufacturing. **Positions commonly filled include:** Accountant/Auditor; Agricultural Engineer; Biomedical Engineer; Blue-Collar Worker Supervisor; Ceramics Engineer; Chemical Engineer; Civil Engineer; Electrical/Electronics Engineer; Environmental Engineer; General Manager; Human Resources Specialist; Industrial Engineer; Industrial Production Manager; Manufacturing Engineer; Materials Engineer; Mechanical Engineer; Purchasing Agent/Manager; Telecommunications Manager. **Corporate headquarters location:** Cleveland OH. **Other U.S. locations:** Nationwide. **International locations:** Worldwide. **Average salary range of placements:** $30,000 - $50,000. **Number of placements per year:** 50 - 99.

MANAGEMENT RECRUITERS INTERNATIONAL
P.O. Box 2902, Matthews NC 28106. 704/841-8850. **Contact:** Manager. **Description:** An executive search firm. **Specializes in the areas of:** High-Tech; Packaging; Sales. **Corporate headquarters location:** Cleveland OH. **Other U.S. locations:** Nationwide. **International locations:** Worldwide.

MANAGEMENT RECRUITERS INTERNATIONAL
19501 Highway 73 West, Suite 20, Cornelius NC 28031. 704/896-1916. **Contact:** Manager. **Description:** An executive search firm. **Specializes in the areas of:** Data Processing. **Corporate headquarters location:** Cleveland OH. **Other U.S. locations:** Nationwide. **International locations:** Worldwide.

MANAGEMENT RECRUITERS INTERNATIONAL
111 NW Railroad Street, Enfield NC 27823. 919/445-4251. **Contact:** Manager. **Description:** An executive search firm. **Specializes in the areas of:** Paper; Plastics. **Corporate headquarters location:** Cleveland OH. **Other U.S. locations:** Nationwide. **International locations:** Worldwide.

MANAGEMENT RECRUITERS INTERNATIONAL
211 South Center Street, Suite 305, Statesville NC 28677. 704/871-9890. **Fax:** 704/873-2143. **Contact:** Manager. **Description:** An executive search firm. **Specializes in the areas of:** Health/Medical; Textiles. **Corporate headquarters location:** Cleveland OH. **Other U.S. locations:** Nationwide. **International locations:** Worldwide.

MANAGEMENT RECRUITERS INTERNATIONAL SALES CONSULTANTS
107 Edinburgh South, Suite 210, Cary NC 27511. 919/460-9595. **Fax:** 919/460-0642. **Contact:** Rose Hays, Manager. **Description:** An executive search firm. Company pays fee. **Specializes in the areas of:** Administration; Advertising; Banking; Communications; Computer Hardware/Software; Computer Science/Software; Design; Electrical; Engineering; General Management; Health/Medical; Industrial; Insurance; Legal; Manufacturing; Marketing; Operations Management; Publishing; Sales; Scientific; Technical; Textiles; Transportation. **Positions commonly filled include:** Account Representative; Aerospace Engineer; Branch Manager; Chemical Engineer; Claim Representative; Consultant; Design Engineer; Electrical/Electronics Engineer; General Manager; Marketing Manager; Marketing Specialist; Mechanical Engineer; Sales Engineer; Sales Executive; Sales Manager; Sales Representative; Software Engineer; Systems Analyst; Telecommunications Manager; Vice President of Marketing and Sales. **Corporate headquarters location:** Cleveland OH. **Other U.S. locations:** Nationwide. **International locations:** Worldwide. **Average salary range of placements:** More than $50,000. **Number of placements per year:** 100 - 199.

MANAGEMENT RECRUITERS OF BURLINGTON
336 Holly Hill Lane, Burlington NC 27215. 336/584-1444. **Fax:** 336/584-9754. **Contact:** Dick Pike, Owner. **E-mail address:** burlnc!manager@mrinet.com. **Description:** An executive search firm. Company pays fee. **Specializes in the areas of:** Engineering; Industrial; Manufacturing; Publishing; Sales; Technical. **Positions commonly filled include:** Chemical Engineer; Chemist; Design Engineer; Industrial Engineer; Industrial Production Manager; Manufacturer's/Wholesaler's Sales Rep.; Mechanical Engineer; Quality Control Supervisor; Science Technologist. **Corporate headquarters location:** Cleveland OH. **Other U.S. locations:** Nationwide. **International locations:** Worldwide. **Average salary range of placements:** More than $50,000. **Number of placements per year:** 1 - 49.

MANAGEMENT RECRUITERS OF DURHAM
5102 Chapel Hill/Durham Boulevard, Durham NC 27707. 919/489-6521. **Contact:** Steve Kanauss, Manager. **Description:** An executive search firm. **Specializes in the areas of:** Accounting/Auditing; Administration; Advertising; Architecture/Construction; Banking; Communications; Computer Hardware/Software; Design; Electrical; Engineering; Food Industry; General Management; Health/Medical; Insurance; Legal; Manufacturing; Operations Management; Personnel/Labor Relations; Procurement; Publishing; Retail; Sales; Technical; Textiles; Transportation. **Corporate headquarters location:** Cleveland OH. **Other U.S. locations:** Nationwide. **International locations:** Worldwide.

MANAGEMENT RECRUITERS OF FAYETTEVILLE
951 South McPherson Church Road, Suite 105, Fayetteville NC 28303. 910/483-2555. **Fax:** 910/483-6524. **Contact:** John Semmes, Manager. **E-mail address:** mrifaync@worldnet.att.net. **World Wide Web address:** http://www.home.att.net/~mrifaync/. **Description:** An executive search firm. **Specializes in the areas of:** Engineering; General Management; Scientific; Technical. **Positions commonly filled include:** Applications Engineer; Design Engineer; Electrical/Electronics Engineer; Human Resources Manager; Industrial Engineer; Manufacturing Engineer; Mechanical Engineer; Operations Manager; Production Manager; Project Manager; Quality Control Supervisor. **Corporate headquarters location:** Cleveland OH. **Other U.S. locations:** Nationwide. **International locations:** Worldwide. **Average salary range of placements:** $30,000 - $50,000. **Number of placements per year:** 50 - 99.

MANAGEMENT RECRUITERS OF GREENSBORO
324 West Wendover Avenue, Suite 230, Greensboro NC 27408. 336/378-1818. **Fax:** 336/378-0129. **Contact:** Manager. **Description:** An executive search firm that also offers contract services and career counseling. Company pays fee. **Specializes in the areas of:** Apparel; Engineering; General Management; Pharmaceutical; Textiles. **Positions commonly filled include:** Accountant/Auditor; Biochemist; Biological Scientist; Biomedical Engineer; Buyer; Chemical Engineer; Chemist; Civil Engineer; Computer Programmer; Design Engineer; Designer; Electrical/Electronics Engineer; Environmental Engineer; Financial Analyst; Food Scientist/Technologist; General Manager; Industrial Engineer; Industrial Production Manager; Management Analyst/Consultant; Market Research Analyst; Mechanical Engineer; Metallurgical Engineer; MIS Specialist; Purchasing Agent/Manager; Quality Control Supervisor; Services Sales Representative; Statistician; Telecommunications Manager. **Corporate headquarters location:** Cleveland OH. **Other U.S. locations:** Nationwide. **International locations:** Worldwide. **Average salary range of placements:** More than $50,000. **Number of placements per year:** 100 - 199.

MANAGEMENT RECRUITERS OF HIGH POINT
110 Scott Road, High Point NC 27262. 336/869-1200. **Fax:** 336/869-1566. **Contact:** Manager. **Description:** An executive search firm. **Specializes in the areas of:** Agriculture; Information Systems. **Corporate headquarters location:** Cleveland OH. **Other U.S. locations:** Nationwide. **International locations:** Worldwide.

MANAGEMENT RECRUITERS OF KANNAPOLIS
305 South Main Street, Kannapolis NC 28081. 704/938-6144. **Toll-free phone:** 800/868-6177. **Fax:** 704/938-3480. **Contact:** Tom Whitley, President. **Description:** An executive search firm operating on a contingency basis. Company pays fee. **Specializes in the areas of:** Computer Science/Software; Information

Systems. **Positions commonly filled include:** Computer Programmer; Database Manager; MIS Specialist; Software Engineer; Systems Analyst; Systems Manager; Telecommunications Manager. **Corporate headquarters location:** Cleveland OH. **Other U.S. locations:** Nationwide. **International locations:** Worldwide. **Number of placements per year:** 50 - 99.

MANAGEMENT RECRUITERS OF KINSTON
P.O. Box 219, Kinston NC 28502. 919/527-9191. **Fax:** 919/527-3625. **Contact:** William Thomas, President/Owner. **E-mail address:** mrkinston@esn.net. **World Wide Web address:** http://www.esn.net/mrkinston. **Description:** An executive search firm. Company pays fee. **Specializes in the areas of:** Engineering; Food Industry; General Management; Health/Medical; Industrial; Light Industrial; Manufacturing; Paper; Scientific; Technical. **Positions commonly filled include:** Electrical/Electronics Engineer; Industrial Engineer; Mechanical Engineer; Nuclear Medicine Technologist; Occupational Therapist; Physician; Quality Control Supervisor; Radiological Technologist. **Corporate headquarters location:** Cleveland OH. **Other U.S. locations:** Nationwide. **International locations:** Worldwide. **Average salary range of placements:** More than $50,000. **Number of placements per year:** 100 - 199.

MANAGEMENT RECRUITERS OF LOUISBURG
P.O. Box 8, Louisburg NC 27549. 919/496-2153. **Fax:** 919/496-1417. **Contact:** Darrell Perry, Owner. **Description:** An executive search firm. Company pays fee. **Specializes in the areas of:** Administration; Engineering. **Positions commonly filled include:** Chemical Engineer; Design Engineer; Electrical/Electronics Engineer; Environmental Engineer; Industrial Engineer; Mechanical Engineer; Quality Control Supervisor; Transportation/Traffic Specialist. **Corporate headquarters location:** Cleveland OH. **Other U.S. locations:** Nationwide. **International locations:** Worldwide. **Average salary range of placements:** More than $50,000. **Number of placements per year:** 50 - 99.

MANAGEMENT RECRUITERS OF RALEIGH
INTER EXEC
5509 Creedmoor Road, Suite 206, Raleigh NC 27612-2812. 919/781-0400. **Contact:** Phillip Stanley, Office Manager. **E-mail address:** mrraleigh@horizons.net. **World Wide Web address:** http://www.mrinet.com. **Description:** An executive search firm. Inter Exec (also at this location) is also an executive search firm. Company pays fee. **Specializes in the areas of:** Accounting/Auditing; Administration; Communications; Computer Hardware/Software; Design; Electrical; Electronics; Engineering; Food Industry; General Management; Health/Medical; Human Resources; Insurance; Manufacturing; Operations Management; Personnel/Labor Relations; Petrochemical; Pharmaceutical; Procurement; Publishing; Retail; Sales; Technical; Textiles; Transportation. **Corporate headquarters location:** Cleveland OH. **Other U.S. locations:** Nationwide. **International locations:** Worldwide. **Average salary range of placements:** More than $50,000. **Number of placements per year:** 100 - 199.

MANAGEMENT RECRUITERS OF WINSTON-SALEM
P.O. Box 17054, Winston-Salem NC 27116-7054. 336/723-0484. **Contact:** Mike Jones, Manager. **Description:** An executive search firm. **Specializes in the areas of:** Accounting/Auditing; Administration; Advertising; Architecture/Construction; Banking; Communications; Computer Hardware/Software; Design; Electrical; Engineering; Food Industry; General Management; Health/Medical; Insurance; Legal; Manufacturing; Operations Management; Personnel/Labor Relations; Procurement; Publishing; Retail; Sales; Technical; Textiles; Transportation. **Corporate headquarters location:** Cleveland OH. **Other U.S. locations:** Nationwide. **International locations:** Worldwide.

MARK III PERSONNEL INC.
4801 East Independence Boulevard, Suite 604, Charlotte NC 28212. 704/535-5883. **Contact:** Mr. Lindsay Allen, President. **Description:** An executive search firm. Company pays fee. **Specializes in the areas of:** Engineering; Environmental; Personnel/Labor Relations; Technical. **Positions commonly filled include:** Chemical Engineer; Chemist; Electrical/Electronics Engineer; Environmental Engineer; Logistics Manager; Materials Engineer; Mechanical Engineer. **Average salary range of placements:** More than $50,000. **Number of placements per year:** 1 - 49.

MEDICAL PROFESSIONALS
P.O. Box 837, Wrightsville Beach NC 28480. 910/256-8115. **Fax:** 910/256-6961. **Contact:** Donna Paap, President. **E-mail address:** donna@medpro-search.com. **World Wide Web address:** http://www.medpro-search.com. **Description:** An executive search firm. **Specializes in the areas of:** Health/Medical. **Positions commonly filled include:** Nurse Practitioner; Physician; Physician Assistant. **Average salary range of placements:** More than $50,000. **Number of placements per year:** 1 - 49.

MERRICK & MOORE
P.O. Box 8816, Asheville NC 28814. 704/258-1831. **Contact:** M.B. Parker, President. **Description:** A retained executive search firm. Company pays fee. **Specializes in the areas of:** Banking; Engineering; Health/Medical; Manufacturing; Technical. **Positions commonly filled include:** Accountant/Auditor; Aerospace Engineer; Attorney; Bank Officer/Manager; Biological Scientist; Chemist; EDP Specialist; Electrical/Electronics Engineer; Financial Analyst; Health Services Worker; Industrial Engineer; Mechanical Engineer; Systems Analyst. **Number of placements per year:** 1 - 49.

METALS & WOOD AGENCY
P.O. Box 5354, High Point NC 27262. 336/869-3867. **Contact:** Gerald Lloyd, President. **Description:** An executive search firm that focuses on the wood and metal furniture manufacturing industries. Company pays fee. **Specializes in the areas of:** Engineering; General Management; Industrial; Manufacturing. **Positions commonly filled include:** Buyer; Chief Executive Officer; Chief Financial Officer; Environmental Engineer; General Manager; Industrial Engineer; Industrial Production Manager; Management Analyst/Consultant; Mechanical Engineer; MIS Specialist; Purchasing Agent/Manager; Vice President. **Average salary range of placements:** $45,000 - $150,000.

MOFFITT INTERNATIONAL, INC.
Park Terrace Center, Suite 1316A, Asheville NC 28806. 704/251-4550. **Fax:** 704/251-4555. **Contact:** Tim Moffitt, President. **E-mail address:** moffit@aol.com. **World Wide Web address:** http://www.mii.com. **Description:** An executive search firm operating on a retainer basis. Company pays fee. **Specializes in the areas of:** Accounting/Auditing; Administration; Architecture/Construction; Banking; Computer Science/Software; Engineering; General Management; Health/Medical; Legal; Marketing; Personnel/Labor Relations; Pharmaceutical; Sales; Scientific; Technical. **Positions commonly filled include:** Accountant; Architect; Attorney; Auditor; Bank Officer/Manager; Branch Manager; Budget Analyst; Chief Financial Officer; Civil Engineer; Computer Operator; Construction Contractor;

Controller; Cost Estimator; Database Manager; Design Engineer; Draftsperson; Electrical/Electronics Engineer; Environmental Engineer; Finance Director; Financial Analyst; Fund Manager; Human Resources Manager; Internet Services Manager; Management Analyst/Consultant; Marketing Manager; Marketing Specialist; Mechanical Engineer; MIS Specialist; Operations Manager; Physical Therapist; Physician; Project Manager; Sales Engineer; Sales Executive; Sales Manager; Sales Representative; Software Engineer; Statistician; Systems Analyst; Systems Manager; Technical Writer/Editor; Telecommunications Manager; Transportation/Traffic Specialist. **Corporate headquarters location:** This Location. **Other U.S. locations:** Nationwide. **International locations:** Worldwide. **Average salary range of placements:** More than $50,000. **Number of placements per year:** 500 - 999.

MORGAN GROUP
P.O. Box 470488, Charlotte NC 28247. 704/541-0040. **Fax:** 704/541-0810. **Contact:** John Chaplin, President. **E-mail address:** jchapbud@ix.netcom.com. **Description:** An executive search firm. Company pays fee. **Specializes in the areas of:** Computer Hardware/Software; Engineering. **Positions commonly filled include:** Electrical/Electronics Engineer; Environmental Engineer; General Manager; Industrial Engineer; Quality Control Supervisor; Software Engineer. **Average salary range of placements:** More than $50,000. **Number of placements per year:** 50 - 99.

NAGEL EXECUTIVE SEARCH INC.
2505 South 17th Street, Wilmington NC 28401. 910/392-0797. **Contact:** Manager. **Description:** An executive search firm that provides placements in the apparel industry.

NATIONAL SERVICES, INC.
P.O. Box 6505, Raleigh NC 27628-6505. 919/787-8000. **Contact:** Bill Poole, President. **Description:** An executive search firm. **Specializes in the areas of:** Accounting/Auditing; Computer Hardware/Software; Engineering; General Management; Manufacturing; Personnel/Labor Relations; Technical. **Number of placements per year:** 1 - 49.

NATIONWIDE RECRUITERS
7523 Little Avenue, Suite 213, Charlotte NC 28226. 704/541-2595. **Contact:** Manager. **Description:** An executive search firm. **Specializes in the areas of:** Packaging; Paper; Publishing.

ODYSSEY GROUP, INC.
5111 Nations Crossing Road, Suite 150, Charlotte NC 28217. 704/525-2502. **Toll-free phone:** 888/525-2520. **Fax:** 704/525-2540. **Contact:** Brian E. Smith, President. **E-mail address:** odysseyxls@aol.com. **World Wide Web address:** http://www.therapy-jobs.com. **Description:** An executive search firm. Company pays fee. **Specializes in the areas of:** Health/Medical. **Positions commonly filled include:** Occupational Therapist; Physical Therapist; Speech-Language Pathologist; Vice President. **Average salary range of placements:** More than $50,000. **Number of placements per year:** 50 - 99.

PARENICA & COMPANY
19250 Stableford Lane, Cornelius NC 28031. 704/896-0060. **Fax:** 704/896-0240. **Contact:** James Parenica, President. **Description:** An executive search firm. Company pays fee. **Specializes in the areas of:** Banking; Computer Science/Software; General Management; Personnel/Labor Relations. **Positions commonly filled include:** General Manager; Human Resources Specialist; MIS Specialist. **Average salary range of placements:** More than $50,000. **Number of placements per year:** 1 - 49.

THE PERKINS GROUP
7621 Little Avenue, Suite 216, Charlotte NC 28226. 704/543-1111. **Fax:** 704/543-0945. **Contact:** R. Patrick Perkins, President. **E-mail address:** perk@vnet.net. **World Wide Web address:** http://www.perkinsgroup.com. **Description:** An executive search firm. Company pays fee. **Specializes in the areas of:** Accounting/Auditing; Engineering; Finance; Industrial; Manufacturing; Marketing; Personnel/Labor Relations; Sales. **Positions commonly filled include:** Accountant/Auditor; Chemical Engineer; Chief Financial Officer; Controller; Credit Manager; Design Engineer; EDP Specialist; Electrical/Electronics Engineer; Financial Analyst; General Manager; Human Resources Manager; Industrial Engineer; Industrial Production Manager; Manufacturing Engineer; Marketing Manager; Mechanical Engineer; Metallurgical Engineer; MIS Specialist; Operations Manager; Product Manager; Purchasing Agent/Manager; Sales Engineer; Sales Executive; Sales Manager. **Average salary range of placements:** More than $50,000. **Number of placements per year:** 100 - 199.

ROBISON & ASSOCIATES
128 South Tryon Street, Suite 1350, Charlotte NC 28202. 704/376-0059. **Contact:** Manager. **Description:** An executive search firm.

SAIN-WADE CORPORATION
400 West Market Street, Suite 208, Greensboro NC 27401. 336/274-3336. **Contact:** Mary Sain-Wade, President. **Description:** An executive search firm operating on a contingency basis. Company pays fee. **Positions commonly filled include:** Accountant/Auditor; Industrial Engineer; Industrial Production Manager; Manufacturing Engineer; Registered Nurse; Respiratory Therapist. **Other U.S. locations:** Nationwide. **Average salary range of placements:** More than $50,000. **Number of placements per year:** 1 - 49.

SALES CONSULTANTS OF CONCORD, INC.
254 Church Street, Concord NC 28025. 704/786-0700. **Fax:** 704/782-1356. **Contact:** Anna Lee Pearson, President. **Description:** An executive search firm. Company pays fee. **Specializes in the areas of:** Computer Science/Software; General Management; Health/Medical; Sales; Technical; Telecommunications. **Positions commonly filled include:** Branch Manager; Customer Service Rep.; Economist; Electrical/Electronics Engineer; General Manager; Health Services Manager; Management Analyst/Consultant; Manufacturer's/Wholesaler's Sales Rep.; Marketing Manager; Physical Therapist; Physician; Product Manager; Psychologist; Sales Manager; Services Sales Rep.; Software Engineer. **Number of placements per year:** 1 - 49.

SALES CONSULTANTS OF HIGH POINT
2411 Penny Road, Suite 101, High Point NC 27265. 336/883-4433. **Contact:** Manager. **Description:** An executive search firm. **Specializes in the areas of:** Accounting/Auditing; Administration; Advertising; Architecture/Construction; Banking; Communications; Computer Hardware/Software; Design; Electrical; Engineering; Food Industry; General Management; Health/Medical; Insurance; Legal; Manufacturing; Operations Management; Personnel/Labor Relations; Procurement; Publishing; Retail; Sales; Technical; Textiles; Transportation.

SANFORD ROSE ASSOCIATES
3405-H West Wendover Avenue, Greensboro NC 27407. 336/852-3003. **Fax:** 336/852-3039. **Contact:**

Manager. **World Wide Web address:** http://www.sanfordrose.com. **Description:** An executive search firm. **Specializes in the areas of:** Publishing.

SANFORD ROSE ASSOCIATES
Main Street Square, Suite 202J, Graham NC 27253. 910/229-1800. **Fax:** 910/229-1844. **Contact:** Manager. **World Wide Web address:** http://www.sanfordrose.com. **Description:** An executive search firm. **Specializes in the areas of:** Engineering; Manufacturing.

SANFORD ROSE ASSOCIATES
3816-21 South New Hope Road, Gastonia NC 28056. **Toll-free phone:** 800/373-0790. **Fax:** 704/824-0995. **Contact:** Manager. **World Wide Web address:** http://www.sanfordrose.com. **Description:** An executive search firm for the steel fabrication industry. **Specializes in the areas of:** General Management; Sales.

SANFORD ROSE ASSOCIATES OF CHARLOTTE
P.O. Box 13490, Charlotte NC 28270. 704/366-0730. **Toll-free phone:** 800/272-8760. **Fax:** 704/365-0620. **Contact:** James L. Downs, CEO. **E-mail address:** jdownssra@aol.com. **World Wide Web address:** http://www.sra-charlotte.com. **Description:** An executive search firm operating on a contingency basis. Sanford Rose Associates of Charlotte also provides some contract services. Company pays fee. **Specializes in the areas of:** Administration; Computer Science/Software. **Positions commonly filled include:** Account Manager; Account Representative; Computer Operator; Computer Programmer; Database Manager; General Manager; Human Resources Manager; Internet Services Manager; Management Analyst/Consultant; MIS Specialist; Online Content Specialist; Operations Manager; Sales Executive; Sales Manager; Software Engineer; Systems Analyst; Systems Manager; Technical Writer/Editor; Telecommunications Manager. **Average salary range of placements:** More than $50,000. **Number of placements per year:** 50 - 99.

SEARCH CONSULTANTS WORLDWIDE INC.
8929 Saint Croix Lane, Charlotte NC 28277. 704/814-0977. **Contact:** Gordon Graybeil, Managing Principal. **Description:** An executive search firm operating on a contingency basis. Company pays fee. **Specializes in the areas of:** Engineering; General Management; Industrial. **Positions commonly filled include:** Electrical/Electronics Engineer; Environmental Engineer; Geologist/Geophysicist; Industrial Engineer; Mechanical Engineer. **Number of placements per year:** 1 - 49.

SICKENBERGER ASSOCIATES
612 Pasteur Drive, Greensboro NC 27403. 336/852-4220. **Contact:** Manager. **Description:** An executive search firm. **Specializes in the areas of:** Engineering; Fashion; Sales.

SNELLING SEARCH
P.O. Box 932, Bethel NC 27812. 919/758-0541. **Fax:** 919/758-0184. **Contact:** Ted Keel, Owner/Manager. **E-mail address:** recruit@interpath.com. **Description:** An executive search firm. Company pays fee. **Specializes in the areas of:** Accounting/Auditing; Banking; Computer Science/Software; Food Industry; Hotel/Restaurant; Industrial; Textiles. **Positions commonly filled include:** Accountant/Auditor; Applications Engineer; Bank Officer/Manager; Branch Manager; Chemical Engineer; Chief Financial Officer; Computer Programmer; Controller; Database Manager; Finance Director; Financial Analyst; General Manager; Hotel Manager; Human Resources Manager; Industrial Production Manager; Manufacturing Engineer; MIS Specialist; Operations Engineer; Operations/Production Manager; Production Manager; Quality Control Supervisor; Restaurant/Food Service Manager; Sales Engineer; Sales Representative; Secretary; Software Engineer; Systems Analyst; Systems Manager. **Corporate headquarters location:** Dallas TX. **Other U.S. locations:** Nationwide. **Average salary range of placements:** More than $50,000. **Number of placements per year:** 1 - 49.

SNELLING SEARCH
5838 Faringdon Place, Suite 1, Raleigh NC 27609. 919/876-0660. **Fax:** 919/876-0355. **Contact:** Robert J. Helfenbein, Owner/Manager. **Description:** An executive search firm operating on a contingency basis. Founded in 1951. Company pays fee. **Specializes in the areas of:** Accounting/Auditing; Administration; Computer Science/Software; Engineering; Health/Medical; Industrial; Legal; Manufacturing; Sales; Secretarial. **Positions commonly filled include:** Accountant/Auditor; Administrative Manager; Branch Manager; Clerical Supervisor; Computer Programmer; Customer Service Representative; Design Engineer; Electrical/Electronics Engineer; Health Services Manager; Industrial Engineer; Internet Services Manager; Manufacturer's/Wholesaler's Sales Rep.; Mechanical Engineer; Medical Records Technician; MIS Specialist; Occupational Therapist; Paralegal; Physical Therapist; Registered Nurse; Restaurant/Food Service Manager; Services Sales Representative; Software Engineer; Typist/Word Processor. **Corporate headquarters location:** Dallas TX. **Other U.S. locations:** Nationwide. **Average salary range of placements:** $30,000 - $50,000. **Number of placements per year:** 50 - 99.

SOURCE SERVICES CORPORATION
100 North Tryon Street, Charlotte NC 28202-4000. 704/333-8311. **Toll-free phone:** 800/334-3617. **Contact:** Manager. **Description:** An executive search firm that also provides some temporary placements. The divisions at this location include Source Consulting, Source EDP, Source Finance, and Accountant Source Temps. Company pays fee. **Specializes in the areas of:** Accounting/Auditing; Administration; Banking; Computer Science/Software; Finance; Technical. **Positions commonly filled include:** Accountant/Auditor; Bank Officer/Manager; Branch Manager; Budget Analyst; Computer Programmer; Credit Manager; Financial Analyst; Human Resources Specialist; MIS Manager; Systems Analyst; Technical Writer/Editor. **Average salary range of placements:** More than $50,000. **Number of placements per year:** 100 - 199.

SPARKS PERSONNEL SERVICES
1400 Battleground Avenue, Suite 132, Greensboro NC 27408. 336/272-1333. **Fax:** 336/272-9397. **Contact:** Chris Sparks, Vice President. **Description:** An executive search firm. Company pays fee. **Specializes in the areas of:** Accounting/Auditing; Administration; Advertising; Banking; Computer Science/Software; Engineering; Finance; General Management; Industrial; Manufacturing; Personnel/Labor Relations; Sales; Secretarial; Textiles. **Positions commonly filled include:** Accountant/Auditor; Bank Officer/Manager; Blue-Collar Worker Supervisor; Branch Manager; Buyer; Claim Representative; Computer Programmer; Credit Manager; Customer Service Representative; Electrical/Electronics Engineer; Financial Analyst; General Manager; Human Resources Specialist; Industrial Engineer; Industrial Production Manager; Insurance Agent/Broker; Management Analyst/Consultant; Management Trainee; Mechanical Engineer; MIS Specialist; Purchasing Agent/Manager; Securities Sales Representative; Software Engineer; Systems Analyst; Travel Agent. **Other area locations:** Charlotte NC; Raleigh NC; Wilmington NC. **Average salary range of placements:** $30,000 - $50,000. **Number of placements per year:** 50 - 99.

SPORTS GROUP INTERNATIONAL
804 Salem Woods Drive, Suite 103, Raleigh NC 27615. 919/846-1860. **Fax:** 919/848-0236. **Contact:** Lesley White, Manager. **Description:** An executive search firm operating on a retainer basis. Company pays fee. **Specializes in the areas of:** Sales. **Positions commonly filled include:** Sales/Marketing Manager. **Average salary range of placements:** More than $50,000. **Number of placements per year:** 1 - 49.

STAFF ACCOUNTANTS
2915 Providence Road, Suite 418, Charlotte NC 28211. 704/364-2996. **Fax:** 704/364-1766. **Contact:** Phillip B. Goldberg, President. **Description:** An executive search firm. Company pays fee. **Specializes in the areas of:** Accounting/Auditing. **Positions commonly filled include:** Accountant/Auditor; Tax Specialist. **Average salary range of placements:** $30,000 - $50,000. **Number of placements per year:** 1 - 49.

SUMMIT OCCUPATIONAL STAFFING
523 Summit Street, Winston-Salem NC 27101. 336/777-1978. **Toll-free phone:** 800/568-2575. **Fax:** 336/777-0706. **Contact:** James L. Salkeld, National Placement Director. **Description:** An executive search firm, that operates on a contingency basis, with a division that provides temp-to-perm and temporary placements. Company pays fee. **Specializes in the areas of:** Health/Medical; Legal; Nonprofit; Personnel/Labor Relations; Secretarial. **Positions commonly filled include:** Administrative Assistant; Administrative Manager; Biomedical Engineer; Certified Nursing Aide; Chief Financial Officer; Clerical Supervisor; Clinical Lab Technician; Counselor; Credit Manager; Customer Service Representative; Emergency Medical Technician; Finance Director; General Manager; Human Resources Manager; Licensed Practical Nurse; Medical Records Technician; Nuclear Medicine Technologist; Occupational Therapist; Paralegal; Pharmacist; Physical Therapist; Physician; Psychologist; Purchasing Agent/Manager; Radiological Technologist; Registered Nurse; Respiratory Therapist; Secretary; Speech-Language Pathologist; Surgical Technician; Typist/Word Processor. **Benefits available to temporary workers:** Workers Compensation Plan. **Average salary range of placements:** $30,000 - $50,000. **Number of placements per year:** 50 - 99.

TECHNICAL ASSOCIATES
347 North Caswell Road, Charlotte NC 28204. 704/333-9011. **Contact:** Ron Kretel, Manager. **Description:** An executive search firm. **Specializes in the areas of:** Engineering.

WADDY R. THOMSON ASSOCIATES
233 South Sharon Amity Road, Suite 106, Charlotte NC 28211. 704/366-1956. **Fax:** 704/366-8480. **Contact:** Waddy Thomson, Principal. **E-mail address:** wthomson@bigfoot.com. **Description:** An executive search firm operating on a contingency basis. Company pays fee. **Specializes in the areas of:** Food Industry; Industrial; Insurance; Manufacturing; Retail; Transportation. **Positions commonly filled include:** Environmental Engineer; Environmental Scientist; Safety Engineer. **Average salary range of placements:** More than $50,000. **Number of placements per year:** 1 - 49.

RANDY WALLEY ASSOCIATES
P.O. Box 2701, High Point NC 27261. 336/885-0644. **Contact:** Manager. **Description:** An executive search firm. **Specializes in the areas of:** Apparel.

DAVID WEINFELD GROUP
6512 Six Forks Road, Suite 603B, Raleigh NC 27615. 919/676-7828. **Fax:** 919/676-7399. **Contact:** David Weinfeld, President. **Description:** An executive search firm. Company pays fee. **Specializes in the areas of:** Computer Science/Software; Engineering; Information Technology; Sales; Telecommunications. **Positions commonly filled include:** Computer Programmer; Design Engineer; Electrical/Electronics Engineer; Management Analyst/Consultant; Marketing Manager; Services Sales Rep.; Software Engineer; Systems Analyst; Telecommunications Manager. **Average salary range of placements:** More than $50,000. **Number of placements per year:** 50 - 99.

JOHN R. WILLIAMS & ASSOCIATES
2102 North Elm Street, Suite H, Greensboro NC 27408. 336/279-8800. **Contact:** John R. Williams, President and Owner. **Description:** An executive search firm. Company pays fee. **Specializes in the areas of:** Accounting/Auditing; Banking; Engineering; General Management; Industrial; Manufacturing; Personnel/Labor Relations. **Positions commonly filled include:** Attorney; Bank Officer; Chemical Engineer; Civil Engineer; Controller; Electrical/Electronics Engineer; Environmental Engineer; Human Resources Manager; Industrial Engineer; Industrial Production Manager; Mechanical Engineer; Quality Control Supervisor. **Number of placements per year:** 1 - 49.

WILSON PERSONNEL INC.
134 Montford Avenue, Asheville NC 28801. 704/258-3900. **Fax:** 704/258-3902. **Contact:** Ken Schapira, Executive Vice President. **Description:** An executive search firm operating on a contingency basis. Company pays fee. **Specializes in the areas of:** Engineering; Management; Manufacturing; Technical.

PERMANENT EMPLOYMENT AGENCIES

A-1 STAFFING & PERSONNEL, INC.
25 Heritage Place, Asheville NC 28806. 704/252-0708. **Toll-free phone:** 800/645-0708. **Fax:** 704/252-0788. **Contact:** Jean Calloway, Manager. **E-mail address:** a1janice@aol.com. **Description:** A permanent employment agency. Company pays half the fee. **Specializes in the areas of:** Accounting/Auditing; Administration; Finance; Food Industry; General Management; Industrial; Insurance; Legal; Manufacturing; Nonprofit; Personnel/Labor Relations; Publishing; Retail; Sales; Secretarial; Technical; Transportation. **Positions commonly filled include:** Accountant/Auditor; Adjuster; Administrative Manager; Advertising Clerk; Automotive Mechanic; Bank Officer/Manager; Blue-Collar Worker Supervisor; Branch Manager; Broadcast Technician; Buyer; Chemical Engineer; Clerical Supervisor; Clinical Lab Technician; Collector; Computer Programmer; Counselor; Credit Manager; Customer Service Representative; Editor; Electrical/Electronics Engineer; Electrician; Food Scientist/Technologist; General Manager; Hotel Manager; Human Resources Manager; Human Service Worker; Industrial Engineer; Industrial Production Manager; Investigator; Landscape Architect; Management Analyst/Consultant; Management Trainee; Manufacturer's/Wholesaler's Sales Rep.; Mechanical Engineer; MIS Specialist; Operations/Production Manager; Paralegal; Property and Real Estate Manager; Public Relations Specialist; Purchasing Agent/Manager; Quality Control Supervisor; Restaurant/Food Service Manager; Securities Sales Representative; Services Sales Representative; Technical Writer/Editor; Travel Agent; Typist/Word Processor; Wholesale and Retail Buyer. **Benefits available to temporary workers:** Paid Vacation. **Average salary range of placements:**

$20,000 - $29,999. **Number of placements per year:** 100 - 199.

ALEXIUS PERSONNEL ASSOCIATES INC.
3708 Wrightsville Avenue #24, Wilmington NC 28403. 910/799-6700. **Contact:** Manager. **Description:** An employment agency providing temporary and permanent professional placements.

ANDERSON & DANIEL PERSONNEL
P.O. Box 5157, Wilmington NC 28403. 910/799-8500. **Physical address:** 4900 Randall Parkway, Suite F, Wilmington NC 28403. **Fax:** 910/791-0706. **Contact:** Elma B. Daniel, President. **Description:** An employment agency offering permanent, temporary, and temp-to-perm placements. Company pays fee. **Specializes in the areas of:** Accounting/Auditing; Administration; Computer Science/Software; Engineering; Legal; Personnel/Labor Relations; Secretarial; Technical; Transportation. **Positions commonly filled include:** Accountant/Auditor; Bank Officer/Manager; Blue-Collar Worker Supervisor; Buyer; Ceramics Engineer; Chemical Engineer; Chemist; Civil Engineer; Clerical Supervisor; Clinical Lab Technician; Computer Programmer; Cost Estimator; Credit Manager; Dental Assistant/Dental Hygienist; Design Engineer; Draftsperson; Electrical/Electronics Engineer; Environmental Engineer; Financial Analyst; Human Resources Specialist; Industrial Engineer; Industrial Production Manager; Licensed Practical Nurse; Management Trainee; Materials Engineer; Mechanical Engineer; Medical Records Technician; Metallurgical Engineer; MIS Specialist; Operations/Production Manager; Property and Real Estate Manager; Purchasing Agent/Manager; Quality Control Supervisor; Registered Nurse; Software Engineer; Statistician; Structural Engineer; Systems Analyst; Technical Writer/Editor; Typist/Word Processor. **Corporate headquarters location:** This Location. **Average salary range of placements:** $20,000 - $29,999. **Number of placements per year:** 100 - 199.

APPLE RESOURCES INC.
P.O. Box 52221, Durham NC 27717. **Contact:** Personnel. **Description:** A permanent employment agency. Company pays fee. **Specializes in the areas of:** Engineering; Manufacturing; Personnel/Labor Relations; Technical. **Positions commonly filled include:** Accountant/Auditor; Design Engineer; Financial Analyst; General Manager; Industrial Engineer; Industrial Production Manager; Mechanical Engineer; Purchasing Agent/Manager; Quality Control Supervisor. **Number of placements per year:** 1 - 49.

ASSOCIATES EMPLOYMENT INC.
3200 Park Road, Suite 226, Charlotte NC 28209. 704/525-4344. **Contact:** Manager. **Description:** A permanent placement agency. **Specializes in the areas of:** Legal.

CALDWELL PERSONNEL SERVICES
214 South Center Street, Taylorsville NC 28681. 704/632-4995. **Fax:** 704/635-1264. **Contact:** Cara Kelso, Office Manager. **Description:** A permanent employment agency. Company pays fee. **Specializes in the areas of:** Industrial; Light Industrial; Secretarial. **Positions commonly filled include:** Accountant; Blue-Collar Worker Supervisor; Clerical Supervisor; Computer Operator; Customer Service Representative; Electrician; Paralegal; Sales Representative; Secretary. **Benefits available to temporary workers:** Medical Insurance. **Corporate headquarters location:** Lenoir NC. **Other area locations:** Hickory NC; Morganton NC; North Wilkesboro NC; Statesville NC. **Average salary range of placements:** Less than $20,000. **Number of placements per year:** 100 - 199.

CAREER STAFFING
800 Clanton Road, Suite W, Charlotte NC 28217. 704/525-8400. **Fax:** 704/525-8682. **Contact:** Jim Chambers, President. **Description:** A permanent employment agency. Company pays fee. **Specializes in the areas of:** Light Industrial; Secretarial. **Positions commonly filled include:** Administrative Assistant; Administrative Manager; Assistant Manager; Blue-Collar Worker Supervisor; Clerical Supervisor; Human Resources Manager; Secretary; Typist/Word Processor. **Benefits available to temporary workers:** Medical Insurance; Paid Holidays; Paid Vacation. **Corporate headquarters location:** This location. **Other area locations:** Gaitonia NC; Statesville NC. **Average salary range of placements:** $20,000 - $29,999. **Number of placements per year:** 200 - 499.

CAREERS UNLIMITED
1911 Hillandale Road, Suite 1210, Durham NC 27705. 919/383-2575. **Fax:** 919/383-5706. **Contact:** Angela Coleman, Branch Manager. **E-mail address:** snelling_durham@compuserve.com. **World Wide Web address:** http://www.snelling.com/durham. **Description:** A permanent employment agency. **Specializes in the areas of:** Accounting/Auditing; Clerical; Light Industrial; Secretarial. **Positions commonly filled include:** Administrative Assistant; Customer Service Representative; Medical Records Technician; Paralegal; Quality Control Supervisor; Sales Representative; Secretary; Typist/Word Processor; Underwriter/Assistant Underwriter. **Number of placements per year:** 1000+.

CORPORATE STAFFING CONSULTANTS, INC.
P.O. Box 221739, Charlotte NC 28222. 704/366-1800. **Toll-free phone:** 800/809-1818. **Fax:** 704/366-0070. **Contact:** Alan W. Madsen, CPC, President. **Description:** A permanent employment agency. **Specializes in the areas of:** Administration; Banking; Engineering; Industrial; Insurance; Personnel/Labor Relations; Secretarial; Technical. **Other U.S. locations:** Nationwide.

CREATIVE STAFFING SERVICE
9107-B South Tryon Street, Charlotte NC 28273. 704/583-4600. **Contact:** Manager. **Description:** A permanent employment agency that also provides temporary placements.

CREATIVE STAFFING SERVICE
P.O. Box 35226, Charlotte NC 28235. 704/529-0111. **Contact:** Manager. **Description:** A permanent employment agency that also provides temporary placements.

DATAMASTERS
P.O. Box 14548, Greensboro NC 27415-4548. **Toll-free phone:** 800/DATA-MASTERS. **Fax:** 336/373-1501. **Contact:** Manager. **E-mail address:** email@datamasters.com. **World Wide Web address:** http://www.datamasters.com/dm. **Description:** A permanent employment agency. Company pays fee. **Specializes in the areas of:** Computer Science/Software. **Positions commonly filled include:** Computer Programmer; Science Technologist; Systems Analyst. **Average salary range of placements:** $30,000 - $100,000. **Number of placements per year:** 100 - 199.

DURHAM JOB SERVICE OFFICE
1105 South Briggs Avenue, Durham NC 27703. 919/560-6880. **Contact:** Manager. **Description:** A permanent employment agency. **Positions commonly filled include:** Accountant/Auditor; Actuary; Administrative Assistant; Advertising Clerk; Aerospace Engineer; Agricultural Engineer; Architect; Attorney; Bank Officer/Manager; Biological Scientist; Biomedical Engineer; Bookkeeper; Buyer; Ceramics Engineer;

Chemical Engineer; Chemist; Civil Engineer; Claim Representative; Clerk; Commercial Artist; Computer Operator; Computer Programmer; Construction Trade Worker; Credit Manager; Customer Service Representative; Data Entry Clerk; Dietician/Nutritionist; Draftsperson; Driver; Economist; EDP Specialist; Electrical/Electronics Engineer; Factory Worker; Financial Analyst; Food Scientist/Technologist; General Manager; Hotel Manager; Human Resources Manager; Industrial Designer; Industrial Engineer; Insurance Agent/Broker; Legal Secretary; Light Industrial Worker; Marketing Specialist; Mechanical Engineer; Medical Secretary; Metallurgical Engineer; Mining Engineer; MIS Specialist; Nurse; Operations/Production Manager; Petroleum Engineer; Physicist; Public Relations Specialist; Purchasing Agent/Manager; Quality Control Supervisor; Receptionist; Reporter; Sales Representative; Secretary; Statistician; Stenographer; Systems Analyst; Technical Writer/Editor; Technician; Typist/Word Processor; Underwriter/Assistant Underwriter. **Number of placements per year:** 1000+.

ELITE PERSONNEL AND JOB FORCE
P.O. Box 52029, Durham NC 27717-2029. 919/493-1449. **Contact:** Ms. Lise Gussow, President. **Description:** A permanent employment agency. **Specializes in the areas of:** Office Support.

EXECUTIVE STAFFING SERVICES, INC.
4101 Lake Boone Trail, Suite 112, Raleigh NC 27607-7506. 919/783-6695. **Recorded jobline:** 919/990-2455. **Contact:** Brenda Savage, Recruiting Specialist. **Description:** A permanent employment agency. Company pays fee. **Specializes in the areas of:** Accounting/Auditing; Art/Design; Computer Science/Software; Electronics; Engineering; Industrial; Manufacturing; Personnel/Labor Relations; Sales; Secretarial; Technical. **Positions commonly filled include:** Administrative Manager; Advertising Clerk; Buyer; Computer Programmer; Customer Service Representative; Designer; Draftsperson; Electrical/Electronics Engineer; Human Resources Specialist; Medical Records Technician; Purchasing Agent/Manager; Quality Control Supervisor; Technical Writer/Editor; Telecommunications Manager; Typist/Word Processor. **Benefits available to temporary workers:** Medical Insurance; Paid Holidays; Paid Vacation. **Corporate headquarters location:** Cary NC. **Other area locations:** Greensboro NC; Winston-Salem NC. **Other U.S. locations:** Columbia SC. **Number of placements per year:** 1000+.

F-O-R-T-U-N-E PERSONNEL CONSULTANTS OF RALEIGH, INC.
P.O. Box 98388, Raleigh NC 27624-8388. 919/848-9929. **Fax:** 919/848-9666. **Contact:** Rick Deckelbaum, Vice President. **Description:** A permanent employment agency. Company pays fee. **Specializes in the areas of:** Accounting/Auditing; Banking; Computer Science/Software; Engineering; Finance; Food Industry; Manufacturing; Personnel/Labor Relations. **Positions commonly filled include:** Accountant/Auditor; Aerospace Engineer; Biomedical Engineer; Ceramics Engineer; Chemical Engineer; Chemist; Civil Engineer; Computer Programmer; Electrical/Electronics Engineer; Financial Analyst; General Manager; Human Resources Manager; Industrial Engineer; Materials Engineer; Mechanical Engineer; Metallurgical Engineer; Petroleum Engineer; Software Engineer; Statistician; Systems Analyst. **Number of placements per year:** 200 - 499.

FRIDAY STAFFING
1944 Hendersonville Road, Asheville NC 28803. 704/684-1788. **Contact:** Manager. **Description:** A permanent employment agency. **Positions commonly filled include:** Accountant/Auditor; Administrative Assistant; Bookkeeper; Customer Service Representative; Data Entry Clerk; Draftsperson; Factory Worker; Light Industrial Worker; Medical Secretary; Receptionist; Secretary; Typist/Word Processor.

FRIDAY STAFFING
227 Duncan Hill Road, Hendersonville NC 28792. 704/697-1507. **Contact:** Manager. **Description:** A permanent employment agency. **Positions commonly filled include:** Accountant/Auditor; Administrative Assistant; Bookkeeper; Customer Service Representative; Data Entry Clerk; Draftsperson; Factory Worker; Light Industrial Worker; Medical Secretary; Receptionist; Secretary; Typist/Word Processor.

GRAHAM & ASSOCIATES
2100-J West Cornwallis Drive, Greensboro NC 27408. 336/288-9330. **Contact:** Gary Graham, CPC, President. **Description:** A permanent employment agency. Company pays fee. **Specializes in the areas of:** Accounting/Auditing; Banking; Clerical; Computer Hardware/Software; Engineering; Legal; Manufacturing; MIS/EDP; Personnel/Labor Relations; Technical. **Positions commonly filled include:** Accountant/Auditor; Administrative Assistant; Aerospace Engineer; Agricultural Engineer; Attorney; Bank Officer/Manager; Bookkeeper; Buyer; Ceramics Engineer; Chemical Engineer; Chemist; Civil Engineer; Clerk; Computer Operator; Computer Programmer; Credit Manager; Customer Service Representative; Data Entry Clerk; Draftsperson; Economist; EDP Specialist; Electrical/Electronics Engineer; Factory Worker; Financial Analyst; General Manager; Human Resources Manager; Industrial Designer; Industrial Engineer; Legal Secretary; Light Industrial Worker; Marketing Specialist; Mechanical Engineer; Medical Secretary; Metallurgical Engineer; Mining Engineer; Operations/Production Manager; Petroleum Engineer; Physicist; Purchasing Agent/Manager; Quality Control Supervisor; Receptionist; Secretary; Stenographer; Systems Analyst; Technical Writer/Editor; Technician; Typist/Word Processor. **Number of placements per year:** 200 - 499.

GRANITE PERSONNEL SERVICE
4 Park Avenue, Granite Falls NC 28630. 704/396-2369. **Contact:** President. **Description:** A permanent employment agency. **Specializes in the areas of:** Administration; Clerical; Sales; Technical. **Number of placements per year:** 50 - 99.

GREER PERSONNEL
5500 McNeely Drive, Suite 102, Raleigh NC 27612. 919/571-0051. **Fax:** 919/571-7450. **Contact:** Deborah G. Greer, President/Owner. **Description:** A permanent employment agency. **Specializes in the areas of:** Accounting/Auditing; Bookkeeping; Clerical; Engineering; Finance; Legal; Office Support.

THE JOBS MARKET, INC.
902 Greensboro Road, High Point NC 27260. 336/889-3777. **Fax:** 336/889-7795. **Contact:** David Phillips, President. **E-mail address:** jobsmkt@spyder.net. **World Wide Web address:** http://www.spyder.net/impress. **Description:** A full-service employment agency that also publishes a newspaper of employment opportunities. Company pays fee. **Number of placements per year:** 1 - 49.

THE JOBS MARKET, INC.
237 Main Street SW, Lenoir NC 28645-5418. 704/758-9519. **Contact:** Manager. **Description:** A permanent employment agency. **Specializes in the areas of:** Architecture/Construction; General Management; Industrial; Manufacturing; Personnel/Labor Relations; Sales; Secretarial; Transportation.

Positions commonly filled include: Architect; Automotive Mechanic; Blue-Collar Worker Supervisor; Claim Representative; Clerical Supervisor; Computer Programmer; Construction Contractor; Customer Service Representative; Dental Assistant/Dental Hygienist; Dietician/Nutritionist; Electrician; Forester/Conservation Scientist; General Manager; Health Services Manager; Industrial Production Manager; Landscape Architect; Management Trainee; Manufacturer's/Wholesaler's Sales Rep.; Operations/Production Manager; Paralegal; Pharmacist; Preschool Worker; Public Relations Specialist; Restaurant/Food Service Manager; Securities Sales Representative; Structural Engineer; Surveyor; Typist/Word Processor. **Corporate headquarters location:** Highpoint NC. **Average salary range of placements:** $20,000 - $29,999. **Number of placements per year:** 500 - 999.

JOBS OF FAYETTEVILLE
5489 Yadkin Road, Fayetteville NC 28303-3165. 910/864-0073. **Fax:** 910/864-6118. **Contact:** Owner. **Description:** A permanent employment agency. **Specializes in the areas of:** Accounting/Auditing; Art/Design; Banking; Biology; Broadcasting; Education; Finance; Food Industry; Health/Medical; Industrial; Insurance; Manufacturing; Retail; Sales; Secretarial; Transportation. **Average salary range of placements:** Less than $20,000. **Number of placements per year:** 500 - 999.

LEARNING HOW OPPORTUNITY PLUS
P.O. Box 35481, Charlotte NC 28235. 704/376-4735. **Contact:** Dallas R. Bolan, Director. **Description:** A permanent employment agency and career/outplacement counseling firm that focuses on the placement of physically disabled workers. Company pays fee. **Average salary range of placements:** $20,000 - $29,999. **Number of placements per year:** 200 - 499.

LEGAL PERSONNEL SERVICE
3724 National Drive, Suite 121, Raleigh NC 27612. 919/787-0049. **Contact:** Manager. **Description:** A permanent and temporary employment agency that places paralegals and legal secretaries. **Specializes in the areas of:** Legal.

MTS, INC.
7621 Little Avenue, Suite 210, Charlotte NC 28226. 704/544-0800. **Toll-free phone:** 800/206-5960. **Fax:** 704/544-1998. **Contact:** Linda Thurman, Manager of Technical Recruiting. **E-mail address:** lindat@mtss.com. **World Wide Web address:** http://www.freeyellow.com/member/mts/index.html. **Description:** A permanent employment agency. **Specializes in the areas of:** Administration; Architecture/Construction; Banking; Computer Science/Software; Education; Engineering; Finance; Food Industry; General Management; Industrial; Printing; Publishing; Scientific; Technical; Transportation. **Positions commonly filled include:** Applications Engineer; Architect; Chemical Engineer; Civil Engineer; Computer Operator; Computer Programmer; Consultant; Database Manager; Design Engineer; Draftsperson; Electrical/Electronics Engineer; Graphic Artist; Graphic Designer; Industrial Engineer; Industrial Production Manager; Management Analyst/Consultant; Manufacturing Engineer; Mechanical Engineer; MIS Specialist; Operations Manager; Production Manager; Project Manager; Quality Control Supervisor; Systems Analyst; Systems Manager; Technical Writer/Editor; Telecommunications Manager; Transportation/Traffic Specialist; Webmaster. **Benefits available to temporary workers:** 401(k); IRA; Medical Insurance; Paid Holidays; Paid Vacation; Vision Plan. **Corporate headquarters location:** Fayetteville NC. **Average salary range of placements:** $30,000 - $50,000. **Number of placements per year:** 200 - 499.

MEGA FORCE
16 East Rowan Street, Suite 300, Raleigh NC 27609. 919/571-0001. **Fax:** 919/571-0530. **Contact:** Manager. **Description:** A permanent employment agency. Company pays fee. **Specializes in the areas of:** Clerical; Office Support.

MYERS & ASSOCIATES
13420 Reese Boulevard West, Huntersville NC 28078. 704/875-8300. **Fax:** 704/875-8891. **Contact:** Joseph N. Myers, Sr., President. **Description:** A permanent employment agency. Company pays fee. **Specializes in the areas of:** Administration; Engineering; Health/Medical; Industrial; Manufacturing. **Positions commonly filled include:** Accountant/Auditor; Buyer; Chemical Engineer; Computer Programmer; Electrical/Electronics Engineer; Industrial Engineer; Mechanical Engineer; Metallurgical Engineer; Occupational Therapist; Physical Therapist; Respiratory Therapist; Software Engineer; Systems Analyst. **Number of placements per year:** 1 - 49.

NEASE PERSONNEL SERVICES
105 Oakmont Drive, Suite A, Greenville NC 27858. 919/756-5820. **Fax:** 919/756-0697. **Contact:** Lori D. Nease, CPC, President. **Description:** A permanent employment agency.

NORTH CAROLINA SEARCH
5970 Fairview Road, Charlotte NC 28210. 704/553-0050. **Contact:** Manager. **Description:** A permanent and temporary employment agency. **Specializes in the areas of:** Office Support.

PRO STAFF ACCOUNTING SERVICES
212 South Tryon Street, Suite 410, Charlotte NC 28281. 704/370-0075. **Fax:** 704/376-4885. **Contact:** Susan J. Dewar, Staffing Manager. **E-mail address:** careers@prostaff-carolinas.com. **World Wide Web address:** http://www.prostaff-carolinas.com. **Description:** A permanent employment agency. Founded in 1982. **Specializes in the areas of:** Accounting/Auditing; Administration; Banking; Finance. **Positions commonly filled include:** Accountant/Auditor; Bank Officer/Manager; Branch Manager; Budget Analyst; Credit Analyst; Financial Analyst. **Benefits available to temporary workers:** 401(k); Direct Deposit; Medical Insurance; Paid Holidays; Paid Vacation; Referral Bonus Plan; Scholarship Program. **Corporate headquarters location:** Minneapolis MN. **Number of placements per year:** 500 - 999.

PRO STAFF PERSONNEL SERVICES
212 South Tryon Street, UCB Building, Suite 1300, Charlotte NC 28281. 704/376-8367. **Fax:** 704/376-8355. **Contact:** Vicki Sweginnis, Staffing Manager. **E-mail address:** careers@prostaff-carolinas.com. **World Wide Web address:** http://www.prostaff-carolinas.com. **Description:** A permanent employment agency. Founded in 1982. **Specializes in the areas of:** Administration; Banking; Secretarial. **Positions commonly filled include:** Accountant/Auditor; Administrative Manager; Bank Officer/Manager; Customer Service Representative; Typist/Word Processor. **Benefits available to temporary workers:** 401(k); Direct Deposit; Paid Holidays; Paid Vacation; Referral Bonus Plan. **Corporate headquarters location:** Minneapolis MN. **Number of placements per year:** 1000+.

PROFESSIONAL PERSONNEL ASSOCIATES INC.
7520 East Independence Boulevard, Suite 160, Charlotte NC 28227. 704/532-2599. **Fax:** 704/536-8192. **Contact:** Gregory Whitt, President/Owner. **Description:** A permanent employment agency that also provides contract services. **Specializes in the areas of:** Computer Science/Software; Engineering;

Industrial; Manufacturing; Personnel/Labor Relations. **Positions commonly filled include:** Aerospace Engineer; Buyer; Chemical Engineer; Chemist; Civil Engineer; Computer Programmer; Design Engineer; Designer; Electrical/Electronics Engineer; Environmental Engineer; Human Resources Specialist; Industrial Engineer; Industrial Production Manager; Mechanical Engineer; Metallurgical Engineer; MIS Specialist; Nuclear Engineer; Purchasing Agent/Manager; Quality Control Supervisor; Software Engineer; Structural Engineer. **Average salary range of placements:** $30,000 - $50,000. **Number of placements per year:** 50 - 99.

REP & ASSOCIATES
P.O. Box 55, Washington NC 27889. 919/946-6643. **Contact:** Richard Phelan, Recruiter. **Description:** A permanent employment agency. Company pays fee. **Specializes in the areas of:** Computer Science/Software. **Positions commonly filled include:** MIS Specialist; Systems Analyst; Systems Manager. **Average salary range of placements:** More than $50,000.

REMEDY INTELLIGENT STAFFING
4421 Stuart Andrew Boulevard, Suite 102, Charlotte NC 28217. 704/521-9818. **Fax:** 704/525-7736. **Contact:** Staffing Coordinator. **Description:** A permanent employment agency. **Specializes in the areas of:** Sales; Secretarial. **Positions commonly filled include:** Accountant/Auditor; Administrative Manager; Clerical Supervisor; Customer Service Representative; Human Resources Specialist; Industrial Production Manager; Management Trainee; MIS Specialist; Operations/Production Manager; Paralegal; Services Sales Representative; Typist/Word Processor. **Benefits available to temporary workers:** 401(k); Daycare Assistance; Dental Insurance; Medical Insurance; Paid Holidays. **Corporate headquarters location:** San Juan Capistrano CA. **Other U.S. locations:** Nationwide. **Average salary range of placements:** $20,000 - $29,999. **Number of placements per year:** 1000+.

DON RICHARD ASSOCIATES OF CHARLOTTE
2650 One First Union Center, 301 South College Street, Charlotte NC 28202. 704/377-6447. **Fax:** 704/377-2410. **Contact:** Edward K. Turner, President. **Description:** A permanent employment agency. **Specializes in the areas of:** Accounting/Auditing; Banking; Finance.

SUMMIT COMPUTER SERVICES INC.
7516 East Independence Boulevard, Charlotte NC 28227-9405. 704/568-8095. **Fax:** 704/568-8098. **Contact:** Robert A. Moeller, Recruiter. **Description:** A permanent employment agency that also offers contract technical services. Company pays fee. **Specializes in the areas of:** Computer Science/Software. **Positions commonly filled include:** Computer Scientist; Software Engineer; Technical Writer/Editor. **Average salary range of placements:** $30,000 - $50,000. **Number of placements per year:** 50 - 99.

TALENT TREE STAFFING SERVICES
5821 Fairview Road, Suite 315, Charlotte NC 28209. 704/553-1111. **Toll-free phone:** 800/737-2154. **Fax:** 704/554-0524. **Contact:** Zina Lyons, Senior Staffing Consultant. **Description:** An employment agency that provides both permanent and temporary placements. Company pays fee. **Specializes in the areas of:** Banking; Health/Medical; Industrial; Manufacturing; Personnel/Labor Relations; Secretarial. **Positions commonly filled include:** Administrative Manager; Blue-Collar Worker Supervisor; Customer Service Representative; Human Resources Specialist; Management Trainee; Medical Records Technician; Operations/Production Manager; Paralegal; Quality Control Supervisor; Securities Sales Representative; Typist/Word Processor. **Benefits available to temporary workers:** 401(k); Dental Insurance; Medical Insurance. **Corporate headquarters location:** Houston TX. **Other U.S. locations:** Nationwide. **Average salary range of placements:** $20,000 - $29,999. **Number of placements per year:** 1000+.

THE UNDERWOOD GROUP
ACCREDITED PERSONNEL
2840 Plaza Place, Suite 211, Raleigh NC 27612. 919/782-3024. **Fax:** 919/783-0492. **Contact:** Holly McWilliams, Manager. **E-mail address:** tug@underwoodgroup.com. **Description:** A permanent employment agency that also provides contract services. Company pays fee. **Specializes in the areas of:** Administration; Computer Science/Software; Data Processing; Engineering. **Positions commonly filled include:** Computer Programmer; Database Manager; Design Engineer; Electrical/Electronics Engineer; MIS Specialist; Software Engineer; Systems Analyst. **Benefits available to temporary workers:** 401(k); Dental Insurance; Medical Insurance; Reimbursement Accounts. **Average salary range of placements:** $30,000 - $50,000. **Number of placements per year:** 1 - 49.

WOODS-HOYLE, INC.
P.O. Box 9902, Greensboro NC 27429. 336/273-4557. **Fax:** 336/275-4945. **Contact:** Anne Marie Woods, President. **E-mail address:** amwoods@netmcr. **World Wide Web address:** http://www.woodshoyle.com. **Description:** A permanent employment agency. Company pays fee. **Specializes in the areas of:** Computer Science/Software. **Positions commonly filled include:** Computer Programmer; Database Manager; MIS Specialist; Systems Analyst; Systems Manager; Telecommunications Manager. **Average salary range of placements:** $30,000 - $50,000. **Number of placements per year:** 50 - 99.

YOUNGBLOOD STAFFING
115 West Main Street, Whiteville NC 28472. 910/640-2341. **Toll-free phone:** 800/892-4344. **Fax:** 910/640-2126. **Contact:** Jacqueline S. Jacobs, Staffing Specialist. **Description:** A permanent employment agency. **Specializes in the areas of:** Industrial; Secretarial. **Positions commonly filled include:** Administrative Manager; Automotive Mechanic; Clerical Supervisor; Customer Service Representative; Human Resources Specialist; Quality Control Supervisor; Services Sales Representative; Typist/Word Processor. **Other area locations:** Elizabethtown NC; Wilmington NC. **Average salary range of placements:** Less than $20,000. **Number of placements per year:** 500 - 999.

YOUNGBLOOD STAFFING
4024 Oleander Drive, Suite A, Wilmington NC 28403-6814. 910/799-0103. **Fax:** 910/791-1503. **Contact:** Traci A. Roberts, Operations Manager. **Description:** A permanent employment agency. **Specializes in the areas of:** Accounting/Auditing; Administration; Banking; Finance; General Management; Industrial; Manufacturing; Personnel/Labor Relations; Sales; Secretarial. **Positions commonly filled include:** Accountant/Auditor; Administrative Manager; Advertising Clerk; Bank Officer/Manager; Blue-Collar Worker Supervisor; Branch Manager; Brokerage Clerk; Chemical Engineer; Claim Representative; Clerical Supervisor; Clinical Lab Technician; Computer Programmer; Credit Manager; Customer Service Representative; Electrical/Electronics Engineer; Financial Analyst; Food Scientist/Technologist; General Manager; Human Resources Specialist; Industrial Production Manager; Management Analyst/Consultant; Management Trainee; Manufacturer's/Wholesaler's Sales Rep.; Medical

Records Technician; Operations/Production Manager; Paralegal; Property and Real Estate Manager; Purchasing Agent/Manager; Quality Control Supervisor; Services Sales Representative; Technical Writer/Editor; Typist/Word Processor; Underwriter/ Assistant Underwriter. **Other area locations:** Elizabethtown NC; Whiteville NC. **Average salary range of placements:** Less than $20,000. **Number of placements per year:** 1000+.

TEMPORARY EMPLOYMENT AGENCIES

ACCUSTAFF INCORPORATED
9211 North Tryon Street, Suite 10A, Charlotte NC 28262. **Contact:** Recruiter. **Description:** A temporary agency that also provides permanent placement. **Specializes in the areas of:** Industrial; Retail; Sales; Secretarial. **Positions commonly filled include:** Blue-Collar Worker Supervisor; Claim Rep.; Clerical Supervisor; Computer Programmer; Construction Contractor; Electrician; Human Resources Specialist; Management Trainee; Manufacturer's/Wholesaler's Sales Rep.; MIS Specialist; Operations/Production Manager. **Benefits available to temporary workers:** Medical Insurance; Paid Vacation; Referral Bonus Plan. **Corporate headquarters location:** Jacksonville FL. **Other U.S. locations:** Nationwide. **Average salary range of placements:** Less than $20,000. **Number of placements per year:** 1000+.

ACTION STAFFMASTERS
805 Spring Forest Road, Suite 800, Raleigh NC 27609. 919/783-9009. **Fax:** 919/783-0008. **Contact:** Branch Manager. **Description:** A temporary agency. **Specializes in the areas of:** Manufacturing; Secretarial. **Positions commonly filled include:** Electrician; Purchasing Agent/Manager. **Benefits available to temporary workers:** Paid Holidays. **Average salary range of placements:** Less than $20,000. **Number of placements per year:** 1000+.

ACTION TECHNICAL STAFFING
214A East Arlington Boulevard, Greenville NC 27858. 919/353-1000. **Fax:** 919/237-3720. **Contact:** Jackie Schultz, Technical Manager. **Description:** A temporary agency. **Specializes in the areas of:** Accounting/ Auditing; Administration; Computer Science/Software; Engineering; Industrial; Manufacturing; Personnel/ Labor Relations; Secretarial; Technical. **Positions commonly filled include:** Accountant/Auditor; Administrative Manager; Aerospace Engineer; Agricultural Engineer; Aircraft Mechanic/Engine Specialist; Bank Officer/Manager; Blue-Collar Worker Supervisor; Buyer; Chemical Engineer; Chemist; Draftsperson; Electrical/Electronics Engineer; Financial Analyst; Human Resources Specialist; Industrial Engineer; Industrial Production Manager; MIS Specialist; Paralegal; Pharmacist; Purchasing Agent/ Manager; Quality Control Supervisor; Securities Sales Rep.; Surveyor; Technical Writer/Editor; Telecommunications Manager; Typist/Word Processor. **Benefits available to temporary workers:** 401(k); Paid Vacation. **Average salary range of placements:** $30,000 - $50,000. **Number of placements per year:** 50 - 99.

COASTAL TEMPORARY SERVICES, INC.
P.O. Box 1860, Whiteville NC 28472-1860. 910/642-4443. **Contact:** Estalene Marlowe, Marketing Representative. **Description:** A temporary agency. **Specializes in the areas of:** Accounting/Auditing; Manufacturing; Personnel/Labor Relations; Retail; Secretarial. **Positions commonly filled include:** Accountant/Auditor; Construction Contractor; Customer Service Representative; Electrician. **Other area locations:** Elizabethtown NC; Havelock NC; New Bern NC; Ocean Isle Beach NC.

DP PROS INC.
P.O. Box 2229, Burlington NC 27216-2229. 336/222-8030. **Contact:** Manager. **Description:** A temporary agency. Company pays fee. **Specializes in the areas of:** MIS/EDP. **Positions commonly filled include:** Computer Programmer; Systems Analyst. **Number of placements per year:** 1 - 49.

EXPRESS PERSONNEL SERVICES
1100 South Mint Street, Suite 104, Charlotte NC 28203. 704/347-5077. **Contact:** Terance O. Bott, Owner. **Description:** A temporary agency that also provides permanent placements. **Specializes in the areas of:** Architecture/Construction; Engineering; Sales; Secretarial; Technical. **Positions commonly filled include:** Architect; Civil Engineer; Computer Programmer; Draftsperson; Services Sales Representative; Software Engineer; Systems Analyst; Typist/Word Processor. **Benefits available to temporary workers:** Computer Training; Medical Insurance; Paid Holidays; Paid Vacation. **Average salary range of placements:** $20,000 - $29,999. **Number of placements per year:** 1 - 49.

FIVE STAR STAFFING, INC.
5404 Hillsboro Street, Raleigh NC 27606. 919/854-4488. **Contact:** Elizabeth Hotaling, Marketing Representative. **Description:** A temporary agency. **Specializes in the areas of:** Accounting/Auditing; Finance; Personnel/Labor Relations; Secretarial. **Positions commonly filled include:** Accountant/Auditor; Clerical Supervisor; Financial Analyst; Human Resources Specialist; Typist/Word Processor.

FORBES TEMPORARY STAFFING
6401 Carmel Road, Suite 107, Charlotte NC 28226. 704/542-0312. **Contact:** Frieda Smith, President. **Description:** A temporary employment agency. **Specializes in the areas of:** Apparel; Computer Hardware/Software; Food Industry; Health/Medical; Hotel/Restaurant; Office Support; Technical; Textiles.

INTERIM PERSONNEL, INC.
4300 Six Forks Road, Suite 100, Raleigh NC 27609. 919/420-0026. **Contact:** Manager. **Description:** A temporary agency. **Specializes in the areas of:** Banking; Clerical. **Positions commonly filled include:** Administrative Worker/Clerk; Construction Trade Worker; Data Entry Clerk; Draftsperson; Driver; Factory Worker; Legal Secretary; Light Industrial Worker; Marketing Specialist; Medical Secretary; Nurse; Purchasing Agent/Manager; Quality Control Supervisor; Receptionist; Secretary; Statistician; Stenographer; Technical Writer/Editor; Technician; Typist/Word Processor; Underwriter/Assistant Underwriter. **Corporate headquarters location:** Fort Lauderdale FL. **Other U.S. locations:** Nationwide. **Number of placements per year:** 200 - 499.

INTERIM PERSONNEL, INC.
4101-C Stuart Andrews Boulevard, Charlotte NC 28217. 704/529-1534. **Toll-free phone:** 800/900-JOBS. **Fax:** 704/529-0187. **Contact:** Manager. **Description:** A temporary agency. Company pays fee. **Specializes in the areas of:** Banking; Industrial; Light Industrial; Manufacturing; Personnel/Labor Relations; Secretarial; Technical; Transportation. **Positions commonly filled include:** Blue-Collar Worker Supervisor; Branch Manager; Claim Representative; Clerical Supervisor; Customer Service Representative; Draftsperson; Electrician; Human Resources Specialist;

Operations/Production Manager; Quality Control Supervisor; Typist/Word Processor. **Corporate headquarters location:** Fort Lauderdale FL. **Other U.S. locations:** Nationwide. **Average salary range of placements:** $20,000 - $29,999. **Number of placements per year:** 1000+.

KELLY SERVICES, INC.
620 Green Valley Road, Suite 206, Greensboro NC 27408. 336/292-4371. **Fax:** 336/852-6822. **Contact:** District Manager. **Description:** A temporary agency. **Specializes in the areas of:** Accounting/Auditing; Administration; Advertising; Banking; Computer Science/Software; Engineering; Finance; General Management; Industrial; Insurance; Legal; Manufacturing; Personnel/Labor Relations; Publishing; Sales; Secretarial; Technical. **Positions commonly filled include:** Accountant/Auditor; Administrative Assistant; Bookkeeper; Clerk; Computer Operator; Computer Programmer; Customer Service Representative; Data Entry Clerk; Designer; Human Resources Manager; Insurance Agent/Broker; Legal Secretary; Light Industrial Worker; Marketing Specialist; MIS Specialist; Purchasing Agent/Manager; Receptionist; Records Manager; Secretary; Technical Writer/Editor; Typist/Word Processor. **Number of placements per year:** 1000+.

KELLY SERVICES, INC.
2701 Coltsgate Road, Suite 102, Charlotte NC 28211. 704/364-4790. **Fax:** 704/364-6616. **Contact:** Office Manager. **Description:** A temporary agency. **Specializes in the areas of:** Accounting/Auditing; Administration; Advertising; Banking; Computer Science/Software; Engineering; Finance; General Management; Industrial; Insurance; Legal; Manufacturing; Personnel/Labor Relations; Publishing; Sales; Secretarial; Technical. **Positions commonly filled include:** Accountant/Auditor; Administrative Assistant; Bookkeeper; Clerk; Computer Operator; Computer Programmer; Customer Service Representative; Data Entry Clerk; Designer; Human Resources Manager; Insurance Agent/Broker; Legal Secretary; Light Industrial Worker; Marketing Specialist; MIS Specialist; Purchasing Agent/Manager; Receptionist; Records Manager; Secretary; Technical Writer/Editor; Typist/Word Processor. **Number of placements per year:** 1000+.

KEY TEMPORARIES, INC.
4600 Park Road, Suite 100, Charlotte NC 28209. 704/643-0911. **Toll-free phone:** 800/444-3094. **Fax:** 704/643-0913. **Contact:** Branch Manager. **Description:** A temporary agency. Company pays fee. **Specializes in the areas of:** Accounting/Auditing; Banking; Computer Science/Software; Finance; Health/Medical; Insurance; Legal; Personnel/Labor Relations; Sales; Secretarial; Technical. **Positions commonly filled include:** Accountant/Auditor; Administrative Manager; Claim Representative; Computer Programmer; Customer Service Representative; Human Resources Specialist; Medical Records Technician; Paralegal; Services Sales Representative. **Average salary range of placements:** $20,000 - $29,999.

MANPOWER, INC.
351 Walnut Street, Waynesville NC 28786-3219. 704/452-1494. **Fax:** 704/452-7392. **Contact:** Traci Burrell, Branch Manager. **Description:** A temporary agency. Company pays fee. **Specializes in the areas of:** Finance; Manufacturing; Sales; Secretarial. **Positions commonly filled include:** Claim Representative; Credit Manager; Customer Service Representative; Financial Analyst; Paralegal; Services Sales Representative; Typist/Word Processor. **Benefits available to temporary workers:** 401(k); Paid Holidays; Paid Vacation; Stock Option. **Corporate headquarters location:** Milwaukee WI. **Other U.S. locations:** Nationwide. **Average salary range of placements:** $20,000 - $29,999. **Number of placements per year:** 50 - 99.

MANPOWER, INC.
5033-E South Boulevard, Charlotte NC 28217. 704/522-9288. **Contact:** Branch Manager. **Description:** A temporary agency. Company pays fee. **Specializes in the areas of:** Data Processing; Light Industrial; Office Support. **Corporate headquarters location:** Milwaukee WI. **Other U.S. locations:** Nationwide. **Number of placements per year:** 1000+.

McCAIN EMPLOYMENT AGENCY
P.O. Box 252, Kinston NC 28502-2522. 919/527-8367. **Fax:** 919/527-0250. **Contact:** Patricia McCain, President. **Description:** A temporary agency that also provides permanent placements. Company pays fee. **Specializes in the areas of:** Accounting/Auditing; Banking; Finance; Industrial; Manufacturing; Personnel/Labor Relations; Sales; Secretarial. **Positions commonly filled include:** Accountant/Auditor; Administrative Manager; Blue-Collar Worker Supervisor; Claim Representative; Computer Programmer; Counselor; Customer Service Representative; Electrician; General Manager; Industrial Production Manager; Management Trainee; Manufacturer's/Wholesaler's Sales Rep.; Medical Records Technician; Paralegal; Purchasing Agent/Manager; Quality Control Supervisor; Typist/Word Processor; Video Production Coordinator. **Benefits available to temporary workers:** Medical Insurance; Paid Holidays; Paid Vacation; Vision Insurance. **Average salary range of placements:** Less than $20,000. **Number of placements per year:** 500 - 999.

MEBANE TEMPORARY SERVICES
P.O. Box 248, Mebane NC 27302. 919/563-1115. **Contact:** Nancy H. Berry, Partner. **Description:** A temporary agency. **Specializes in the areas of:** Clerical; Construction; Food Industry; Manufacturing; Sales; Secretarial; Technical. **Positions commonly filled include:** Administrative Assistant; Bookkeeper; Claim Representative; Clerk; Computer Programmer; Construction Trade Worker; Credit Manager; Customer Service Representative; Data Entry Clerk; Draftsperson; Driver; EDP Specialist; Factory Worker; Hotel Manager; Legal Secretary; Light Industrial Worker; Marketing Specialist; Medical Secretary; Public Relations Specialist; Purchasing Agent/Manager; Receptionist; Sales Representative; Secretary; Typist/Word Processor.

NORRELL SERVICES
700 Blue Ridge Road, Suite 107, Raleigh NC 27606. 919/834-2069. **Contact:** Manager. **Description:** A temporary agency operating a light industrial division and a clerical division. **Specializes in the areas of:** Administration; Light Industrial; Office Support; Secretarial. **Positions commonly filled include:** Administrative Assistant; Assembler; Customer Service Representative; Telemarketer; Typist/Word Processor; Warehouse/Distribution Worker. **Benefits available to temporary workers:** Dental Insurance; Medical Insurance; Vision Insurance. **Corporate headquarters location:** Atlanta GA. **Other U.S. locations:** Nationwide.

OFFICE SPECIALISTS
1100 Crescent Green, Suite 120, Cary NC 27511-4587. 919/233-8383. **Contact:** Office Manager. **Description:** A temporary agency. Company pays fee. **Specializes in the areas of:** Chemical; Computer Science/Software; Pharmaceutical; Secretarial. **Positions commonly filled include:** Customer Service Representative; Data Entry Clerk; Typist/Word

Processor. **Benefits available to temporary workers:** Medical Insurance; Paid Vacation. **Corporate headquarters location:** Peabody MA. **Average salary range of placements:** Less than $20,000. **Number of placements per year:** 1000+.

OLSTEN STAFFING SERVICES
2301 West Meadowview Road, The Henderson Building, Suite 100, Greensboro NC 27407. 336/852-0500. **Contact:** Meridith Loy, Customer Service Representative. **Description:** A temporary agency. **Specializes in the areas of:** Clerical; Manufacturing. **Positions commonly filled include:** Accountant/Auditor; Administrative Assistant; Bank Officer/Manager; Bookkeeper; Clerk; Computer Operator; Computer Programmer; Construction Trade Worker; Customer Service Representative; Data Entry Clerk; Draftsperson; Driver; EDP Specialist; Factory Worker; General Manager; Human Resources Manager; Legal Secretary; Light Industrial Worker; Medical Secretary; MIS Specialist; Operations/Production Manager; Public Relations Specialist; Purchasing Agent/Manager; Quality Control Supervisor; Receptionist; Sales Representative; Secretary; Stenographer; Systems Analyst; Technician; Typist/Word Processor. **Corporate headquarters location:** Melville NY. **Other U.S. locations:** Nationwide. **Number of placements per year:** 1000+.

OLSTEN STAFFING SERVICES
P.O. Box 12877, Research Triangle Park NC 27709. 919/549-8383. **Fax:** 919/541-2059. **Contact:** Cynthia S. Heath, Vice President. **Description:** A temporary agency. Founded in 1950. **Specializes in the areas of:** Accounting/Auditing; Administration; Advertising; Banking; Computer Science/Software; Data Processing; Economics; Engineering; Finance; General Management; Industrial; Insurance; Legal; Manufacturing; Nonprofit; Personnel/Labor Relations; Publishing; Sales; Secretarial; Technical; Transportation. **Positions commonly filled include:** Accountant/Auditor; Administrative Manager; Advertising Clerk; Attorney; Blue-Collar Worker Supervisor; Budget Analyst; Buyer; Chemical Engineer; Chemist; Claim Representative; Clerical Supervisor; Clinical Lab Technician; Customer Service Representative; Design Engineer; Designer; Draftsperson; Electrical/Electronics Engineer; Human Resources Specialist; Industrial Engineer; Industrial Production Manager; Librarian; Mechanical Engineer; Medical Records Technician; Paralegal; Purchasing Agent/Manager; Quality Control Supervisor; Reporter; Software Engineer; Statistician; Structural Engineer; Technical Writer/Editor; Typist/Word Processor. **Benefits available to temporary workers:** 401(k); Medical Insurance; Paid Vacation. **Corporate headquarters location:** Melville NY. **Other U.S. locations:** Nationwide. **Average salary range of placements:** $16,000 - $29,999. **Number of placements per year:** 1000+.

PERSONNEL SERVICES UNLIMITED, INC.
824 South DeKalb Street, Shelby NC 28150. 704/484-0344. **Contact:** Tim Blackwell, Vice President. **Description:** A temporary agency. **Specializes in the areas of:** Clerical; Insurance; Legal; Manufacturing. **Positions commonly filled include:** Administrative Assistant; Bookkeeper; Clerk; Computer Operator; Customer Service Representative; Data Entry Clerk; Factory Worker; Legal Secretary; Light Industrial Worker; Receptionist; Secretary; Typist/Word Processor.

QUALITY PLUS TEMPORARIES, INC.
5200 Park Road, Suite 131, Charlotte NC 28209. 704/522-7587. **Contact:** Marjorie M. Rich, Owner. **Description:** A temporary agency. **Specializes in the areas of:** Health/Medical. **Positions commonly filled include:** Health Services Worker; Nurse. **Number of placements per year:** 1000+.

QUALITY TEMPORARY SERVICES
934 Durham Road, Suite E, Wake Forest NC 27587-9033. 919/556-1201. **Fax:** 919/556-1447. **Contact:** Cindy Hammond, Assistant Manager. **Description:** A temporary and temp-to-perm agency. **Specializes in the areas of:** Accounting/Auditing; Industrial; Manufacturing; Personnel/Labor Relations; Secretarial; Technical. **Positions commonly filled include:** Accountant/Auditor; Biochemist; Chemist; Computer Programmer; Credit Manager; Customer Service Representative; Electrician; Human Resources Specialist; Mechanical Engineer; Medical Records Technician; Purchasing Agent/Manager; Quality Control Supervisor; Typist/Word Processor. **Benefits available to temporary workers:** Paid Holidays; Paid Vacation. **Corporate headquarters location:** Flint MI. **Other area locations:** Rocky Mount NC; Tarboro NC. **Other U.S. locations:** SC. **Number of placements per year:** 200 - 499.

QUALITY TEMPORARY SERVICES
3031 Zebulon Road, Rocky Mount NC 27804. 919/443-4001. **Fax:** 919/443-3831. **Contact:** Crystal Harding, Manager. **Description:** A temporary agency. Company pays fee. **Specializes in the areas of:** Administration; Industrial; Manufacturing; Personnel/Labor Relations; Retail; Sales; Secretarial; Technical. **Positions commonly filled include:** Accountant/Auditor; Administrative Manager; Blue-Collar Worker Supervisor; Claim Representative; Clerical Supervisor; Customer Service Representative; Electrician; Human Resources Specialist; Landscape Architect; Management Trainee; Manufacturer's/Wholesaler's Sales Rep.; Medical Records Technician; MIS Specialist; Operations/Production Manager; Paralegal; Quality Control Supervisor; Services Sales Representative; Typist/Word Processor. **Benefits available to temporary workers:** Medical Insurance; Paid Holidays; Paid Vacation. **Corporate headquarters location:** Flint MI. **Other area locations:** Tarboro NC; Wake Forest NC. **Other U.S. locations:** SC. **Number of placements per year:** 100 - 199.

SPECIAL COUNSEL
5600 77 Center Drive, Suite 170, Charlotte NC 28217. 704/529-5590. **Fax:** 704/529-5639. **Contact:** Manager. **World Wide Web address:** http://www.specialcounsel.com. **Description:** A temporary and permanent employment agency. **Specializes in the areas of:** Legal.

STAFFMARK
323 South Chestnut Street, Henderson NC 27536. 919/438-3888. **Toll-free phone:** 800/211-1169. **Fax:** 919/438-2619. **Contact:** Office Manager. **Description:** A temporary and temp-to-perm agency. Company pays fee. **Specializes in the areas of:** General Labor; Personnel/Labor Relations; Secretarial; Technical. **Positions commonly filled include:** Advertising Clerk; Blue-Collar Worker Supervisor; Customer Service Representative; Draftsperson; Human Resources Specialist; Human Service Worker; Management Trainee; Paralegal; Preschool Worker; Public Relations Specialist; Reporter. **Benefits available to temporary workers:** Paid Holidays; Paid Vacation. **Average salary range of placements:** Less than $20,000. **Number of placements per year:** 1000+.

TEMPORARY STAFFING SYSTEMS
P.O. Box 2789, Gastonia NC 28053. 704/854-5011. **Fax:** 704/854-5009. **Contact:** Randy Vincent, Vice President of Operations. **Description:** A temporary agency that also offers contract services. Company pays fee. **Specializes in the areas of:** Industrial;

Manufacturing; Secretarial. **Positions commonly filled include:** Administrative Assistant; Blue-Collar Worker Supervisor; Branch Manager; Chemical Engineer; Clerical Supervisor; Clerk; Computer Programmer; Customer Service Representative; Draftsperson; Electrician; Engineer; Factory Worker; General Manager; Human Resources Specialist; Industrial Designer; Industrial Production Manager; Light Industrial Worker; Management Trainee; Mechanical Engineer; Metallurgical Engineer; MIS Specialist; Secretary; Typist/Word Processor. **Benefits available to temporary workers:** Bonus Award/Plan; Medical Insurance. **Other area locations:** Charlotte NC; Hendersonville NC; Hickory NC; Lenoir NC; Lincolnton NC; Mount Holly NC; Shelby NC. **Number of placements per year:** 200 - 499.

WILL/STAFF PERSONNEL SERVICES
202 East Woodlawn Road, Charlotte NC 28217. 704/529-6222. **Fax:** 704/525-4790. **Contact:** Katherine McKinnish, Technical Recruiter. **Description:** A temporary agency. Company pays fee. **Specializes in the areas of:** Engineering; Secretarial. **Positions commonly filled include:** Accountant/Auditor; Administrative Manager; Automotive Mechanic; Bank Officer/Manager; Branch Manager; Buyer; Clerical Supervisor; Computer Programmer; Cost Estimator; Dental Assistant/Dental Hygienist; Draftsperson; Electrician; Industrial Engineer; Industrial Production Manager; Mechanical Engineer; MIS Specialist; Paralegal; Purchasing Agent/Manager; Restaurant/Food Service Manager; Systems Analyst; Typist/Word Processor. **Benefits available to temporary workers:** Medical Insurance; Paid Vacation. **Corporate headquarters location:** Greenville SC. **Other U.S. locations:** Atlanta GA; Columbia SC; Spartanburg SC. **Average salary range of placements:** $20,000 - $29,999. **Number of placements per year:** 100 - 199.

WINSTON TEMPORARY STAFFING
185 Charlois Boulevard, Winston-Salem NC 27103-1521. 336/760-9300. **Fax:** 336/765-0630. **Contact:** Manager. **Description:** A temporary agency. **Specializes in the areas of:** Food Industry; Industrial; Manufacturing. **Positions commonly filled include:** Blue-Collar Worker Supervisor; Electrician; Quality Control Supervisor; Restaurant/Food Service Manager. **Benefits available to temporary workers:** Dental Insurance; Medical Insurance. **Average salary range of placements:** Less than $20,000. **Number of placements per year:** 200 - 499.

CONTRACT SERVICES FIRMS

CDI CORPORATION
8001 Aerial Center Parkway, Suite 100, Morrisville NC 27560. 919/481-9043. **Fax:** 919/467-7653. **Contact:** Manager. **World Wide Web address:** http://www.cdicorp.com. **Description:** A contract services firm. **Specializes in the areas of:** Computer Science/Software. **Corporate headquarters location:** Philadelphia PA. **Other U.S. locations:** Nationwide. **International locations:** Worldwide.

CDI CORPORATION
2730 East W.T. Harris Boulevard, Suite 101, Charlotte NC 28213. 704/599-0083. **Contact:** Manager. **World Wide Web address:** http://www.cdicorp.com. **Description:** A contract services firm. **Specializes in the areas of:** Engineering; Technical. **Corporate headquarters location:** Philadelphia PA. **Other U.S. locations:** Nationwide. **International locations:** Worldwide.

COMFORCE TECHNICAL SERVICES, INC.
2221 Edge Lake Drive, Suite 160, Charlotte NC 28217. 704/357-3030. **Fax:** 704/357-3134. **Contact:** Colleen LeGrand, Office Manager. **Description:** A contract services firm. **Specializes in the areas of:** Administration; Banking; Computer Science/Software; Finance; Information Technology; Technical. **Positions commonly filled include:** Bank Officer/Manager; Computer Programmer; Human Service Worker; Internet Services Manager; Management Analyst/Consultant; MIS Specialist; Software Engineer; Systems Analyst; Technical Writer/Editor; Telecommunications Manager. **Average salary range of placements:** $30,000 - $50,000. **Number of placements per year:** 200 - 499.

COMFORCE TELECOM, INC.
5410 Highway 55, Suite AJ, Durham NC 27713. 919/484-1147. **Fax:** 919/484-1227. **Contact:** Manager. **Description:** A contract services firm. **Specializes in the areas of:** Telecommunications.

EMPLOYMENT CONSULTANTS INC.
4401 Colwick Road, Suite 406, Charlotte NC 28211. 704/365-8294. **Fax:** 704/365-2581. **Contact:** Brad Phillips, Managerial Consultant. **Description:** A contract services firm. **Specializes in the areas of:** Administration; Advertising; Architecture/Construction; Art/Design; Banking; Biology; Broadcasting; Computer Science/Software; Education; Engineering; Fashion; Finance; Food Industry; General Management; Industrial; Manufacturing; Personnel/Labor Relations; Retail; Sales; Secretarial; Technical; Transportation. **Positions commonly filled include:** Accountant/Auditor; Adjuster; Aerospace Engineer; Architect; Attorney; Bank Officer/Manager; Broadcast Technician; Buyer; Chemical Engineer; Chemist; Civil Engineer; Claim Representative; Clerical Supervisor; Clinical Lab Technician; Computer Programmer; Construction Contractor; Credit Manager; Customer Service Representative; Design Engineer; Designer; Draftsperson; Editor; Education Administrator; EKG Technician; Electrician; Emergency Medical Technician; Environmental Engineer; Financial Aid Officer; Financial Analyst; Food Scientist/Technologist; Forester/Conservation Scientist; General Manager; Geographer; Geologist/Geophysicist; Health Services Manager; Hotel Manager; Human Resources Manager; Human Service Worker; Industrial Designer; Industrial Engineer; Insurance Agent/Broker; Internet Services Manager; Landscape Architect; Library Technician; Light Industrial Worker; Management Analyst/Consultant; Mechanical Engineer; Medical Records Technician; Metallurgical Engineer; MIS Specialist; Nuclear Engineer; Occupational Therapist; Parking Attendant; Reporter; Restaurant/Food Service Manager; Science Technologist; Software Engineer; Stationary Engineer; Structural Engineer; Technical Writer/Editor; Underwriter/Assistant Underwriter. **Average salary range of placements:** $30,000 - $50,000. **Number of placements per year:** 1000+.

MKR PERSONNEL SOLUTIONS INC.
P.O. Box 52071, Raleigh NC 27612. 919/783-6571. **Physical address:** 5540 McNeely Drive, Suite 303, Raleigh NC. **Toll-free phone:** 800/489-6571. **Fax:** 919/783-0207. **Contact:** Mike Kidwell, President. **E-mail address:** mkidwell@nando.net. **Description:** A contract services firm. Company pays fee. **Specializes in the areas of:** Administration; Computer Science/Software. **Positions commonly filled include:** MIS Specialist; Software Engineer; Systems Analyst; Telecommunications Manager. **Benefits available to temporary workers:** Medical Insurance; Paid Vacation. **Average salary range of placements:** More than $50,000.

PCS - PERSONAL COMMUNICATIONS SERVICE
P.O. Box 12311, Research Triangle Park NC 27709. 919/544-4575. **Toll-free phone:** 800/937-7270. **Fax:** 919/544-3725. **Contact:** Barbara Hibbert, Technical Staffing Manager. **Description:** A contract services firm. **Specializes in the areas of:** Art/Design; Computer Science/Software; Publishing; Technical. **Positions commonly filled include:** Civil Engineer; Computer Programmer; Customer Service Representative; Design Engineer; Designer; Editor; Environmental Engineer; Internet Services Manager; Market Research Analyst; MIS Specialist; Multimedia Designer; Software Engineer; Systems Analyst; Technical Writer/Editor; Telecommunications Manager. **Other U.S. locations:** CA; CO; GA; MA; NJ; NY; OH; TX. **Average salary range of placements:** $30,000 - $50,000.

PROVISION TECHNOLOGIES
5925 Carnegie Boulevard, Suite 500, Charlotte NC 28209. 704/571-3822. **Fax:** 704/571-3823. **Contact:** Manager. **World Wide Web address:** http://www.careerbase.com. **Description:** A contract services firm. **Specializes in the areas of:** Computer Science/Software; Information Technology. **Corporate headquarters location:** Cambridge MA.

PROVISION TECHNOLOGIES
4813 Emperor Boulevard, Suite 120, Durham NC 27703. 919/941-5520. **Fax:** 919/941-5281. **Contact:** Manager. **World Wide Web address:** http://www.careerbase.com. **Description:** A contract services firm. **Specializes in the areas of:** Computer Science/Software; Information Technology. **Corporate headquarters location:** Cambridge MA.

SENC TECHNICAL SERVICES INC.
3142 Wrightsville Avenue, Wilmington NC 28403-4112. 910/251-1925. **Fax:** 910/251-0225. **Contact:** Recruiter. **Description:** A contract services firm. **Specializes in the areas of:** Engineering; Technical. **Positions commonly filled include:** Architect; Biochemist; Biological Scientist; Chemical Engineer; Chemist; Civil Engineer; Clinical Lab Technician; Computer Programmer; Construction and Building Inspector; Cost Estimator; Design Engineer; Designer; Draftsperson; Electrical/Electronics Engineer; Electrician; Environmental Engineer; Financial Analyst; Industrial Engineer; Industrial Production Manager; Mechanical Engineer; MIS Specialist; Quality Control Supervisor; Software Engineer; Structural Engineer; Surveyor; Systems Analyst; Technical Writer/Editor. **Average salary range of placements:** $20,000 - $29,999. **Number of placements per year:** 100 - 199.

SNELLING PERSONNEL SERVICES
Executive Park, Suite 205, Asheville NC 28801-2427. 704/252-0610. **Fax:** 704/252-7467. **Contact:** Larry R. Davis, Manager. **E-mail address:** snelling@ioa.com. **World Wide Web address:** http://www.snelling.com/asheville. **Description:** A contract services firm that also provides temporary and permanent placements. Company pays fee. **Specializes in the areas of:** Accounting/Auditing; Administration; Computer Science/Software; Engineering; Industrial; Manufacturing; Sales; Secretarial; Technical. **Positions commonly filled include:** Accountant/Auditor; Biomedical Engineer; Blue-Collar Worker Supervisor; Chemical Engineer; Chemist; Civil Engineer; Clerical Supervisor; Computer Programmer; Customer Service Representative; Design Engineer; Designer; Draftsperson; Electrical/Electronics Engineer; Financial Analyst; Industrial Engineer; Industrial Production Manager; Management Trainee; Manufacturer's/Wholesaler's Sales Rep.; Mechanical Engineer; MIS Specialist; Quality Control Supervisor; Restaurant/Food Service Manager; Services Sales Representative; Software Engineer; Structural Engineer; Surveyor; Systems Analyst; Technical Writer/Editor; Typist/Word Processor. **Benefits available to temporary workers:** 401(k); Medical Insurance; Paid Holidays; Paid Vacation. **Average salary range of placements:** $30,000 - $50,000. **Number of placements per year:** 1000+.

VOLT TECHNICAL SERVICES
400 Blue Ridge Road, Suite 105, Raleigh NC 27612. 919/782-7440. **Toll-free phone:** 800/595-8658. **Fax:** 919/782-5549. **Contact:** Manager. **E-mail address:** voltral@ral.mindspring.com. **Description:** A contract services firm. Company pays fee. **Specializes in the areas of:** Computer Programming; Engineering; Manufacturing; Technical. **Positions commonly filled include:** Biological Scientist; Biomedical Engineer; Ceramics Engineer; Chemical Engineer; Civil Engineer; Clinical Lab Technician; Computer Programmer; Design Engineer; Designer; Draftsperson; Electrical/Electronics Engineer; Environmental Engineer; Materials Engineer; Mechanical Engineer; Metallurgical Engineer; MIS Specialist; Multimedia Designer; Nuclear Engineer; Operations/Production Manager; Petroleum Engineer; Software Engineer; Structural Engineer; Systems Analyst; Technical Writer/Editor; Telecommunications Manager. **Corporate headquarters location:** New York NY. **Other U.S. locations:** Nationwide. **Number of placements per year:** 100 - 199.

H.L. YOH COMPANY
717 South Torrence, Suite 300, Charlotte NC 28204. 704/332-1020. **Contact:** Manager. **Description:** A contract services firm. **Specializes in the areas of:** Engineering; High-Tech.

H.L. YOH COMPANY
16 East Rowan Street, Suite 525, Raleigh NC 27609. 919/781-1380. **Contact:** Manager. **Description:** A contract services firm that places people in contract, temporary, and permanent positions. **Specializes in the areas of:** Computer Science/Software; Engineering; Information Technology; Scientific.

CAREER/OUTPLACEMENT COUNSELING FIRMS

CPRESUMES, INC.
1727-8B Sardis Road North, Charlotte NC 28270. 704/849-2333. **Fax:** 704/849-2322. **Contact:** Vasant K. Patel, Senior Consultant. **Description:** A professional resume writing and job search consulting firm.

KING CAREER CONSULTING
2915 Providence Road, Suite 300, Charlotte NC 28211-2750. 704/366-1685. **Fax:** 704/364-9678. **Contact:** Jerry King, President. **Description:** A career/outplacement counseling firm. **Specializes in the areas of:** Executives; General Management. **Number of placements per year:** 50 - 99.

NORTH DAKOTA

EXECUTIVE SEARCH FIRMS

CAREER CONNECTION
1621 South University Drive, Suite 215, Fargo ND 58103. 701/232-4614. **Fax:** 701/241-9822. **Contact:** Twila Deahl, Recruiter. **Description:** An executive search firm operating on a contingency basis. Company pays fee. **Specializes in the areas of:** Administration; Computer Science/Software; Engineering; Industrial; Manufacturing; Personnel/Labor Relations; Technical. **Positions commonly filled include:** Accountant/Auditor; Agricultural Engineer; Civil Engineer; Computer Programmer; Design Engineer; Designer; Draftsperson; Electrical/Electronics Engineer; Environmental Engineer; Manufacturer's/Wholesaler's Sales Rep.; Mechanical Engineer; MIS Specialist; Operations/Production Manager; Purchasing Agent/Manager; Quality Control Supervisor; Services Sales Representative; Software Engineer; Structural Engineer; Surveyor; Systems Analyst; Technical Writer/Editor; Telecommunications Manager. **Average salary range of placements:** $30,000 - $50,000. **Number of placements per year:** 100 - 199.

DUNHILL EXECUTIVE SEARCH
PROFESSIONAL MANAGEMENT ASSOCIATION
109 1/2 Broadway, Fargo ND 58102. 701/235-3719. **Toll-free phone:** 800/473-2512. **Fax:** 701/235-7092. **Contact:** Albert Raney, President. **E-mail address:** dsfargo@rrnet.com. **Description:** An executive search firm. Company pays fee. **Specializes in the areas of:** Accounting/Auditing; Computer Science/Software; Engineering; Health/Medical. **Corporate headquarters location:** New York NY. **Average salary range of placements:** More than $50,000. **Number of placements per year:** 1 - 49.

PERSONNEL SERVICES, INC.
401 South Main Street, Minot ND 58701. 701/852-2038. **Toll-free phone:** 800/774-2038. **Fax:** 701/852-8614. **Contact:** Manager. **E-mail address:** psi@minot.ndak.net. **World Wide Web address:** http://www.profilesndakota.com. **Description:** An executive search firm that also provides permanent and temporary placements. The firm also provides contract services and offers career/outplacement counseling. **Specializes in the areas of:** Accounting/Auditing; Administration; Advertising; Banking; Computer Science/Software; Finance; General Management; Personnel/Labor Relations; Retail; Sales; Secretarial. **Positions commonly filled include:** Accountant/Auditor; Administrative Manager; Advertising Clerk; Architect; Bank Officer/Manager; Branch Manager; Broadcast Technician; Budget Analyst; Claim Representative; Computer Programmer; Construction and Building Inspector; Customer Service Representative; Dental Assistant/Dental Hygienist; Editor; Financial Analyst; General Manager; Health Services Manager; Hotel Manager; Human Resources Manager; Human Service Worker; Management Analyst/Consultant; Management Trainee; Manufacturer's/Wholesaler's Sales Rep.; Market Research Analyst; MIS Specialist; Multimedia Designer; Public Relations Specialist; Purchasing Agent/Manager; Radio/TV Announcer/Broadcaster; Reporter; Restaurant/Food Service Manager; Securities Sales Representative; Services Sales Representative; Surveyor; Technical Writer/Editor. **Average salary range of placements:** $20,000 - $29,999. **Number of placements per year:** 100 - 199.

PERMANENT EMPLOYMENT AGENCIES

HUMAN RESOURCES, INC. (HRI)
518 Northern Pacific Avenue, Fargo ND 58102. 701/237-9495. **Contact:** Manager. **Description:** An employment agency that provides both permanent and temporary placements. **Specializes in the areas of:** Accounting/Auditing; Administration; Engineering; General Management; Personnel/Labor Relations; Sales.

INTERIM PERSONNEL
1450 25th Street South, Fargo ND 58103. 701/298-8300. **Contact:** Manager. **Description:** A full-service employment agency that provides permanent and temporary placement. **Specializes in the areas of:** Clerical; Light Industrial.

SNELLING PERSONNEL SERVICES
609 1/2 First Avenue North, Fargo ND 58103. 701/237-0600. **Contact:** Manager. **Description:** A permanent employment agency. Snelling Personnel Services focuses primarily on placement of management and sales professionals. **Other U.S. locations:** Nationwide.

TEMPORARY EMPLOYMENT AGENCIES

DENTAL FILL-INS
P.O. Box 504, Wahpeton ND 58074-0504. 701/642-8376. **Contact:** Manager. **Description:** A temporary employment agency focusing on the placement of dental personnel. The agency also provides contract services. Founded in 1989. **Specializes in the areas of:** Health/Medical; Personnel/Labor Relations. **Positions commonly filled include:** Dental Assistant/Dental Hygienist; Dentist. **Average salary range of placements:** $30,000 - $50,000. **Number of placements per year:** 100 - 199.

OLSTEN STAFFING SERVICES
KRAMER & ASSOCIATES
EXPRESSWAY PERSONNEL
P.O. Box 105, Bismarck ND 58502-0105. 701/222-0071. **Fax:** 701/222-8481. **Contact:** Al Kramer, President. **Description:** A temporary employment agency. Expressway Personnel (also at this location) offers permanent placements. Full benefits are available. Founded in 1950. **Specializes in the areas of:** Accounting/Auditing; Administration; Advertising; Architecture/Construction; Art/Design; Banking; Computer Science/Software; Economics; Education; Engineering; Fashion; Finance; Food Industry; General Management; Industrial; Insurance; Legal; Manufacturing; Nonprofit; Personnel/Labor Relations; Publishing; Retail; Sales; Secretarial; Technical; Transportation. **Positions commonly filled include:** Accountant/Auditor; Adjuster; Administrative Manager; Advertising Clerk; Agricultural Engineer; Architect; Attorney; Bank Officer/Manager; Biochemist; Blue-Collar Worker Supervisor; Branch Manager; Broadcast Technician; Brokerage Clerk; Budget Analyst; Buyer; Civil Engineer; Claim Representative; Clerical Supervisor; Clinical Lab

Technician; Computer Programmer; Construction and Building Inspector; Construction Contractor; Cost Estimator; Counselor; Credit Manager; Customer Service Representative; Dental Assistant/Dental Hygienist; Design Engineer; Designer; Dietician/Nutritionist; Draftsperson; Economist; Editor; Education Administrator; Electrical/Electronics Engineer; Electrician; Emergency Medical Technician; Environmental Engineer; Financial Analyst; General Manager; Health Services Manager; Human Resources Specialist; Industrial Engineer; Librarian; Licensed Practical Nurse; Management Analyst/Consultant; Management Trainee; Manufacturer's/Wholesaler's Sales Rep.; Market Research Analyst; Mechanical Engineer; Medical Records Technician; Mining Engineer; Occupational Therapist; Paralegal; Public Relations Specialist; Quality Control Supervisor; Real Estate Agent; Restaurant/Food Service Manager; Services Sales Representative; Software Engineer; Systems Analyst; Teacher/Professor; Technical Writer/Editor; Telecommunications Manager; Typist/ Word Processor; Underwriter/Assistant Underwriter. **International locations:** Worldwide. **Number of placements per year:** 1000+.

CAREER/OUTPLACEMENT COUNSELING FIRMS

GREEN THUMB, INC.
2206 East Broadway, Bismarck ND 58501. 701/258-8879. **Fax:** 701/258-8874. **Contact:** Project Director. **Description:** A career/outplacement counseling firm that also serves as an employment agency. Green Thumb is best known for operating the Senior Community Service Program (SCSEP), authorized by the Older Americans Act under a grant from the U.S. Department of Labor. **Specializes in the areas of:** Education; Nonprofit; Personnel/Labor Relations; Retail. **Corporate headquarters location:** Arlington VA. **Positions commonly filled include:** Clerk; Daycare Worker; Typist/Word Processor. **Number of placements per year:** 200 - 499.

OHIO

EXECUTIVE SEARCH FIRMS

ACCOUNTANTS EXECUTIVE SEARCH
ACCOUNTANTS ON CALL
250 East Fifth Street, Suite 1630, Cincinnati OH 45202. 513/381-4545. **Fax:** 513/381-4672. **Contact:** Joseph Vitale, Branch Manager. **E-mail address:** jsvitale@mindspring.com. **World Wide Web address:** http://www.aocnet.com. **Description:** An executive search firm. Accountants On Call is a temporary employment agency. Company pays fee. **Specializes in the areas of:** Accounting/Auditing; Finance. **Positions commonly filled include:** Accountant/Auditor; Chief Financial Officer; Controller; Finance Director; Financial Analyst. **Benefits available to temporary workers:** Medical Insurance; Paid Vacation. **Corporate headquarters location:** Saddlebrook NJ. **Other U.S. locations:** Nationwide. **Average salary range of placements:** $30,000 - $50,000.

ACCOUNTANTS EXECUTIVE SEARCH
ACCOUNTANTS ON CALL
700 Ackerman Road, Suite 390, Columbus OH 43202. 614/267-7200. **Fax:** 614/267-7595. **Contact:** Frank Bishop, President. **E-mail address:** fbishop@aoc-aes.com. **Description:** An executive search firm operating on both retained and contingency bases. Accountants on Call places clients in temporary positions. Company pays fee. **Specializes in the areas of:** Accounting/Auditing; Administration; Banking; Computer Science/Software; Finance. **Positions commonly filled include:** Accountant/Auditor; Budget Analyst; Computer Programmer; Credit Manager; Financial Analyst; Internet Services Manager; Management Analyst/Consultant; MIS Specialist; Systems Analyst; Telecommunications Manager. **Corporate headquarters location:** Saddlebrook NJ. **Other U.S. locations:** Nationwide. **Number of placements per year:** 200 - 499.

ACCOUNTANTS EXECUTIVE SEARCH
ACCOUNTANTS ON CALL
Rockside Square 2, 6133 Rockside Road, Suite 206, Independence OH 44131. 216/328-0888. **Contact:** Manager. **Description:** An executive search firm. Accountants on Call is a temporary agency. **Specializes in the areas of:** Accounting/Auditing; Finance. **Corporate headquarters location:** Saddlebrook NJ. **Other U.S. locations:** Nationwide.

ACCOUNTANTS SELECT
P.O. Box 16366, Cleveland OH 44116. 440/333-5122. **Contact:** Manager. **Description:** An executive search firm. **Specializes in the areas of:** Accounting/Auditing; Finance.

ADVANCEMENT RECRUITING SERVICES
P.O. Box 209, Avon OH 44011-0209. 440/937-9910. **Fax:** 440/937-6098. **Contact:** Rudy Socha, President. **Description:** An executive search firm. Company pays fee. **Specializes in the areas of:** Administration; Engineering; Health/Medical; Manufacturing; Personnel/Labor Relations. **Positions commonly filled include:** Biomedical Engineer; Ceramics Engineer; Chemical Engineer; Chemist; Computer Programmer; Design Engineer; Electrical/Electronics Engineer; Environmental Engineer; Human Resources Specialist; Industrial Engineer; Materials Engineer; Mechanical Engineer; Metallurgical Engineer; MIS Specialist; Physician; Purchasing Agent/Manager; Quality Control Supervisor; Software Engineer; Systems Analyst. **Number of placements per year:** 50 - 99.

AEROSOURCE/PROGRESSIVE SEARCH CONCEPTS
26300 Euclid Avenue, Euclid OH 44132. 216/731-3001. **Fax:** 216/731-3002. **Contact:** David Linke, President. **Description:** An executive search firm that recruits for the aerospace and aviation industries, filling positions such as aerospace engineer, aircraft mechanic, and repair engineers. Progressive Search Concepts is non-specialized, filling a wide range of positions in many industries. Company pays fee. **Number of placements per year:** 1 - 49.

ALLTECH RESOURCES, INC.
6000 Lombardo Center, Suite 310, Cleveland OH 44131. 216/642-5689. **Fax:** 216/642-9419. **Contact:** Sandy Pawlowski, Resource Manager. **E-mail address:** alltech@coil.com. **World Wide Web address:** http://www.alltech-inc.com. **Description:** An executive search firm that also provides contract placements. **Specializes in the areas of:** Administration; Computer Science/Software; Technical. **Positions commonly filled include:** Computer Programmer; Management Analyst/Consultant; MIS Specialist; Science Technologist; Software Engineer; Systems Analyst; Technical Writer/Editor; Telecommunications Manager. **Benefits available to temporary workers:** Dental Insurance; Medical Insurance; Paid Holidays; Paid Vacation. **Corporate headquarters location:** Chicago IL. **Average salary range of placements:** More than $50,000. **Number of placements per year:** 200 - 499.

DAVE ARNOLD & ASSOCIATES, INC.
P.O. Box 182, Aurora OH 44202-0182. 440/543-8551. **Fax:** 440/543-8551. **Contact:** Dave Arnold, President. **E-mail address:** arnold@now-online.com. **World Wide Web address:** http://www.now-online.com/daajobs. **Description:** An executive search firm operating on both retainer and contingency bases. Company pays fee. **Specializes in the areas of:** Chemical; Industrial; Manufacturing; Publishing; Sales; Technical. **Positions commonly filled include:** Biological Scientist; Biomedical Engineer; Ceramics Engineer; Chemical Engineer; Chemist; Civil Engineer; Industrial Engineer; Manufacturing Engineer; Marketing Specialist; Mechanical Engineer; Sales Rep. **Number of placements per year:** 50 - 99.

AUTOMOTIVE CAREERS
77 West Elmwood Drive, Suite 205, Centerville OH 45459. 937/438-8090. **Fax:** 937/433-1758. **Contact:** Dan Ankney, President. **Description:** An executive search firm. **Specializes in the areas of:** Automotive Retailing.

AUTOMOTIVE PERSONNEL
14805 Detroit Avenue, Cleveland OH 44107. 216/226-7958. **Fax:** 216/226-7541. **Contact:** Donald Jasensky, President. **Description:** An executive search firm operating on both retainer and contingency bases. **Specializes in the areas of:** Finance; Insurance. **Positions commonly filled include:** Adjuster; Bank Officer/Manager; Financial Analyst; Securities Sales Rep. **Number of placements per year:** 50 - 99.

BALDWIN & ASSOCIATES
3975 Erie Avenue, Cincinnati OH 45208. 513/272-2400. **Contact:** W. Keith Baldwin, President. **World Wide Web address:** http://www.baldwin-assoc.com. **Description:** An executive search firm. Company pays fee. **Specializes in the areas of:** Engineering; Manufacturing; Technical. **Positions commonly filled include:** Aerospace Engineer; Bank Officer/Manager; Biomedical Engineer; Ceramics Engineer; Civil Engineer; Electrical/Electronics Engineer; Industrial Engineer; Marketing Specialist; Mechanical Engineer; Metallurgical Engineer; Purchasing Agent/Manager; Quality Control Supervisor; Systems Analyst. **Number of placements per year:** 50 - 99.

J.W. BARLEYCORN & ASSOCIATES
1614 Lancaster Avenue, Reynoldsburg OH 43068. 614/861-4400. **Contact:** Manager. **Description:** An executive search firm.

BASON ASSOCIATES INC.
11311 Cornell Park Drive, Suite 200, Cincinnati OH 45242. 513/469-9881. **Contact:** Office Manager. **Description:** A search firm that places executives in a variety of industries both locally and worldwide.

BENKE & ASSOCIATES
956 Hanna Building, Cleveland OH 44115. 216/771-6822. **Contact:** Manager. **Description:** An executive search firm. **Specializes in the areas of:** Accounting/Auditing; Banking; Information Systems.

BOWDEN & COMPANY
5000 Rockside Road, Cleveland OH 44131. 216/447-1800. **Contact:** Manager. **Description:** A generalist executive search firm.

J.W. BRANDENBURG & ASSOCIATES
1362 Snowmass Road, Columbus OH 43235. 614/785-9630. **Contact:** Manager. **Description:** An executive search firm.

J.B. BROWN & ASSOCIATES
Terminal Tower, Cleveland OH 44113. 216/696-2525. **Fax:** 216/696-5825. **Contact:** Jeffrey B. Brown, President. **Description:** An executive search firm that also offers contract services. Company pays fee. **Specializes in the areas of:** Accounting/Auditing; Administration; Advertising; Banking; Computer Science/Software; Engineering; Finance; Insurance; Manufacturing; Personnel/Labor Relations; Sales. **Positions commonly filled include:** Accountant/Auditor; Actuary; Attorney; Bank Officer/Manager; Budget Analyst; Buyer; Chemical Engineer; Computer Programmer; Credit Manager; Design Engineer; Designer; Electrical/Electronics Engineer; Environmental Engineer; Financial Analyst; General Manager; Human Resources Specialist; Industrial Engineer; Industrial Production Manager; Insurance Agent/Broker; Management Trainee; Market Research Analyst; Mechanical Engineer; MIS Specialist; Pharmacist; Purchasing Agent/Manager; Software Engineer; Structural Engineer; Telecommunications Manager; Underwriter/Assistant Underwriter. **Average salary range of placements:** $30,000 - $50,000. **Number of placements per year:** 200 - 499.

BUCKMAN-ENOCHS & ASSOCIATES INC.
1625 Bethel Road, Suite 202, Columbus OH 43220. 614/457-7807. **Contact:** Manager. **Description:** An executive search firm. **Specializes in the areas of:** Sales.

BURKS GROUP
23811 Chagrin Boulevard, Suite 280, Beachwood OH 44122. 216/595-8765. **Fax:** 216/595-8770. **Contact:** Manager. **E-mail address:** earliburks@worldnet.att.net. **World Wide Web address:** http://www.burks-group.com. **Description:** An executive search firm. Clients include BMW, Diebold, General Motors, Loctite, Mahanna, and Onstar. Company pays fee. **Specializes in the areas of:** Accounting/Auditing; Automotive; Computer Science/Software; Engineering; Finance; General Management; Industrial; Manufacturing; MIS/EDP; Personnel/Labor Relations. **Positions commonly filled include:** Accountant/Auditor; Computer Programmer; Design Engineer; Electrical/Electronics Engineer; Financial Analyst; Human Resources Manager; Industrial Engineer; Mechanical Engineer; MIS Manager; Purchasing Agent/Manager; Quality Control Supervisor; Software Engineer; Systems Analyst; Systems Engineer. **Average salary range of placements:** More than $80,000. **Number of placements per year:** 1 - 49.

CAREER ENTERPRISES
5 East Main Street, Hudson OH 44236. 216/656-1700. **Fax:** 216/656-1234. **Contact:** Stuart Taylor, President. **World Wide Web address:** http://www.careerenterprises.com. **Description:** An executive search firm. **Specializes in the areas of:** Information Systems; Scientific; Technical. **Positions commonly filled include:** Database Manager; General Manager; Internet Services Manager; Project Manager; Software Engineer; Telecommunications Manager; Webmaster. **Average salary range of placements:** More than $50,000. **Number of placements per year:** 50 - 99.

CAREER RECRUITERS
5500 Laurent Drive, Suite 115, Cleveland OH 44129. 440/888-9431. **Contact:** Manager. **Description:** An executive search firm that also provides permanent and temporary placements. **Specializes in the areas of:** Engineering; MIS/EDP.

CAREER SPECIALISTS INC.
P.O. Box 371, Delphos OH 45833. 419/695-1234x1244. **Contact:** Jerry Backus, Recruiter. **Description:** An executive search firm. Company pays fee. **Specializes in the areas of:** Accounting/Auditing; Engineering; General Management; Manufacturing; Personnel/Labor Relations. **Positions commonly filled include:** Accountant/Auditor; Buyer; Ceramics Engineer; Chemical Engineer; Chemist; Computer Programmer; Customer Service Rep.; Draftsperson; Electrical/Electronics Engineer; Industrial Designer; Industrial Engineer; Manufacturing Engineer; Mechanical Engineer; Operations Manager; Purchasing Agent/Manager; Quality Control Supervisor; Software Engineer; Technical Illustrator; Technical Writer/Editor. **Number of placements per year:** 50 - 99.

CASCADE GROUP
136 East Main Street, Kent OH 44240. 330/677-1118. **Contact:** Manager. **Description:** An executive search firm.

CENTRAL EXECUTIVE SEARCH, INC.
6151 Wilson Mills Road., Highland Heights OH 44143. 440/461-5400. **Contact:** Office Manager. **Description:** An executive search firm. **Specializes in the areas of:** Packaging; Paper.

CHILD & ELDER CARE INSIGHTS, INC.
19111 Detroit Road, Suite 104, Rocky River OH 44116. 440/356-2900. **Contact:** Elisabeth A. Bryenton, President. **Description:** An executive search firm. Company pays fee. **Specializes in the areas of:** Child Care, In-Home; Eldercare, In-Home. **Positions commonly filled include:** Nanny; Preschool Worker.

CHOICE PERSONNEL/LaGRANGE & ASSOCIATES
432 Walnut Street, Suite 208, Cincinnati OH 45202-3909. 513/333-2500. **Fax:** 513/333-2504. **Contact:** Robert LaGrange, President. **Description:** Choice Personnel is an executive search firm that operates on a contingency basis. LaGrange & Associates is an executive search firm that operates on a contingency basis and specializes in the hospitality field. Company pays fee. **Specializes in the areas of:** Food Industry; Insurance; Printing; Retail; Sales; Transportation. **Positions commonly filled include:** Human Resources Specialist; Management Trainee. **Other U.S. locations:** Nationwide. **Average salary range of placements:** $30,000 - $50,000. **Number of placements per year:** 100 - 199.

E. CHRISTIAN & ASSOCIATES
P.O. Box 664, Hudson OH 44236-0664. 330/656-0480. **Contact:** Manager. **Description:** An executive

search firm that operates primarily on a contingency basis for large consulting and group insurance companies. **Specializes in the areas of:** Insurance; Personnel/Labor Relations. **Positions commonly filled include:** Account Manager; Actuary; Underwriter/Assistant Underwriter.

COMBINED RESOURCES INC.
25300 Lorain Road, Suite 2C, North Olmsted OH 44070. 440/716-2244. **Contact:** Gil Sherman, President. **Description:** An executive search firm. Company pays fee. **Specializes in the areas of:** Administration; Advertising; Art/Design; Computer Science/Software; Economics; Engineering; General Management; Industrial; Manufacturing; Personnel/Labor Relations; Retail; Sales. **Positions commonly filled include:** Administrative Manager; Computer Programmer; Credit Manager; Customer Service Rep.; Designer; Economist; Electrical/Electronics Engineer; Financial Analyst; Human Resources Manager; Industrial Engineer; Management Analyst/Consultant; Manufacturer's/Wholesaler's Sales Rep.; Mechanical Engineer; Operations/Production Manager; Purchasing Agent/Manager; Services Sales Rep.; Software Engineer; Systems Analyst; Transportation Specialist; Wholesale/Retail Buyer.

COMPUTER & TECHNICAL ASSOCIATES
200 Westview Towers, 21010 Center Ridge Road, Suite 200, Rocky River OH 44116. **Toll-free phone:** 800/752-3674. **Contact:** Dean Flood, Manager. **World Wide Web address:** http://www.comptechnet.com. **Description:** An executive search firm concentrating on computer disciplines. Company pays fee. **Specializes in the areas of:** Administration; Computer Science/Software; Engineering. **Positions commonly filled include:** Computer Programmer; Electrical/Electronics Engineer; Software Engineer; Systems Analyst; Technical Writer/Editor; Telecommunications Manager. **Average salary range of placements:** More than $50,000. **Number of placements per year:** 100 - 199.

CONTINENTAL SEARCH CONSULTANTS
P.O. Box 14, Pickerington OH 43147. 614/868-8100. **Contact:** Roosevelt Tabb, Principal. **Description:** An executive search firm. Company pays fee. **Specializes in the areas of:** Computer Science/Software; Engineering; Food Industry; General Management; Industrial; Manufacturing; Personnel/Labor Relations; Sales. **Positions commonly filled include:** Chemical Engineer; Computer Programmer; Electrical/Electronics Engineer; Environmental Engineer; General Manager; Human Service Worker; Industrial Engineer; Industrial Production Manager; Internet Services Manager; Materials Engineer; Mechanical Engineer; Metallurgical Engineer; Purchasing Agent/Manager; Quality Control Supervisor; Restaurant/Food Service Manager; Software Engineer; Systems Analyst. **Average salary range of placements:** More than $50,000. **Number of placements per year:** 1 - 49.

CORNERSTONE RECRUITERS INC.
24200 Chagrin Boulevard, Beachwood OH 44122. 216/591-1744. **Contact:** Manager. **Description:** An executive search firm. **Specializes in the areas of:** Engineering.

CORPORATE RESEARCH
3540 Secor Road, Suite 300, Toledo OH 43606. 419/535-1941. **Contact:** Manager. **Description:** An executive search firm.

J.D. COTTER SEARCH, INC.
2999 East Dublin-Granville Road, Suite 301, Columbus OH 43231. 614/895-2065. **Fax:** 614/895-3071. **Contact:** Joseph Cotter, Manager. **Description:** An executive search firm. Company pays fee. **Specializes in the areas of:** Accounting/Auditing; Administration; Engineering; Food Industry; General Management; Manufacturing; Personnel/Labor Relations; Sales. **Positions commonly filled include:** Accountant/Auditor; Biomedical Engineer; Budget Analyst; Buyer; Chemical Engineer; Chemist; Civil Engineer; Credit Manager; Electrical/Electronics Engineer; Financial Analyst; General Manager; Human Resources Manager; Industrial Engineer; Management Analyst/Consultant; Mechanical Engineer; Purchasing Agent/Manager; Quality Control Supervisor; Software Engineer; Structural Engineer; Systems Analyst; Transportation/Traffic Specialist. **Average salary range of placements:** More than $50,000. **Number of placements per year:** 200 - 499.

CROSS-JORDAN CORPORATION
4986 Gateway Drive, Suite B, Medina OH 44256. 330/723-7203. **Fax:** 330/722-7436. **Contact:** Norman M. Ferris, President. **Description:** An executive search firm operating on both retainer and contingency bases. Cross-Jordan Corporation is a member of the Nationwide Interchange Service (NIS), one of the world's largest independent recruiter networks. Company pays fee. **Specializes in the areas of:** Engineering; General Management; Technical. **Positions commonly filled include:** Buyer; Chemical Engineer; Draftsperson; Electrical/Electronics Engineer; Industrial Engineer; Industrial Production Manager; Mechanical Engineer; Operations/Production Manager; Purchasing Agent/Manager; Quality Control Supervisor; Software Engineer; Structural Engineer; Technical Writer/Editor; Telecommunications Manager. **Number of placements per year:** 1 - 49.

DATA BANK CORPORATION
635 West 7th Street, Suite 100, Cincinnati OH 45203-1546. 513/241-9955. **Toll-free phone:** 800/733-0020. **Fax:** 513/333-6364. **Contact:** Wayne Ivey, President. **E-mail address:** jobs@databankcorp.com. **World Wide Web address:** http://www.databankcorp.com. **Description:** An executive search firm. Data Bank is an information systems recruiter that places experienced professionals, mid-level managers, and executives. Company pays fee. **Specializes in the areas of:** Administration; Computer Science/Software; Information Systems. **Positions commonly filled include:** Computer Programmer; Internet Services Manager; Management Analyst/Consultant; MIS Specialist; Software Engineer; Systems Analyst; Technical Writer/Editor; Telecommunications Manager. **Number of placements per year:** 100 - 199.

DEFFET GROUP INC.
7801 Marysville Road, Ostrander OH 43061. 614/666-7600. **Fax:** 614/666-7610. **Contact:** Daniel Deffet, Managing Partner. **Description:** An executive search firm. Company pays fee. **Specializes in the areas of:** Health/Medical. **Positions commonly filled include:** Health Services Manager; Physical Therapist; Respiratory Therapist; Speech-Language Pathologist. **Number of placements per year:** 50 - 99.

DELTA MEDICAL SEARCH ASSOCIATES
615 Rome Hilliard Road, Columbus OH 43228. 614/878-0550. **Contact:** Marilyn Wallace, President. **Description:** An executive search firm. The firm focuses on the placement of health care professionals in clinical and management positions. **Specializes in the areas of:** Health/Medical. **Positions commonly filled include:** Administrator; Physician; Registered Nurse. **Average salary range of placements:** More than $50,000. **Number of placements per year:** 1 - 49.

PETE DELUKE & ASSOCIATES
113 North Ohio Avenue, Suite 204, Sidney OH 45365. 937/497-1515. **Contact:** Office Manager. **Description:** An executive search firm. **Specializes in**

the areas of: Engineering; Human Resources. **Positions commonly filled include:** Engineer; Human Resources Manager.

DILLARD EXECUTIVE SEARCH
1617 Hawthorne Park, Columbus OH 43203. 614/252-5848. **Contact:** Manager. **Description:** An executive search firm. **Specializes in the areas of:** Administration; Human Resources.

DRAYTON & ASSOCIATES
120 West Fifth Street, Suite 501, Cincinnati OH 45202. 513/621-4018. **Fax:** 513/345-2402. **Contact:** Brad Drayton, President. **Description:** An executive search firm. Company pays fee. **Specializes in the areas of:** Accounting/Auditing; Advertising; Banking; Engineering; Fashion; Finance; General Management; Personnel/Labor Relations; Sales. **Positions commonly filled include:** Accountant/Auditor; Bank Officer/ Manager; Biomedical Engineer; Budget Analyst; Buyer; Chemical Engineer; Civil Engineer; Credit Manager; Designer; Economist; Electrical/Electronics Engineer; Financial Analyst; Human Resources Manager; Industrial Engineer; Industrial Production Manager; Insurance Agent/Broker; Management Analyst/ Consultant; Manufacturer's/Wholesaler's Sales Rep.; Mechanical Engineer; Operations/Production Manager; Purchasing Agent/Manager; Quality Control Supervisor; Services Sales Rep.; Software Engineer; Stationary Engineer; Structural Engineer; Underwriter/ Assistant Underwriter. **Average salary range of placements:** $30,000 - $50,000. **Number of placements per year:** 50 - 99.

B.P. DRISCOL & ASSOCIATES, INC.
75 Windrush Drive, Moreland Hills OH 44022. 440/247-8568. **Contact:** Barbara Driscol, President. **Description:** A retained executive search firm. **Specializes in the areas of:** Health/Medical. **Positions commonly filled include:** Physician. **Average salary range of placements:** More than $50,000. **Number of placements per year:** 1 - 49.

DUNHILL PROFESSIONAL SEARCH OF COLUMBUS
1166 Goodale Boulevard, Suite 200, Columbus OH 43212. 614/421-0111. **Contact:** John Salzman, Owner. **Description:** An executive search firm. **Specializes in the areas of:** Computer Hardware/Software; Sales.

ELITE RESOURCES GROUP
71 Baker Boulevard, Akron OH 44333. 330/867-9412. **Fax:** 330/867-0468. **Contact:** Gary Suhay, President. **Description:** An executive search firm operating on a retainer basis. Company pays fee. **Specializes in the areas of:** Engineering; General Management; Industrial; Technical; Transportation. **Positions commonly filled include:** Buyer; Chemical Engineer; Chemist; Design Engineer; Designer; Electrical/Electronics Engineer; Environmental Engineer; Industrial Engineer; Industrial Production Manager; Mechanical Engineer; Metallurgical Engineer; Statistician; Transportation/Traffic Specialist. **Average salary range of placements:** More than $50,000. **Number of placements per year:** 1 - 49.

EMPLOYMENT SOLUTIONS GROUP INC.
7801 Laurel Avenue, Cincinnati OH 45243. 513/561-4040. **Fax:** 513/561-4095. **Contact:** Christopher Albrecht, President. **E-mail address:** esgretsrch@aol.com. **Description:** An executive search firm. Company pays fee. **Specializes in the areas of:** Architecture/Construction; Design; Retail. **Positions commonly filled include:** Architect; Buyer; General Manager; Project Manager. **Average salary range of placements:** More than $50,000. **Number of placements per year:** 1 - 49.

EXECUTECH
500 South Depeyster Street, Kent OH 44240. 330/677-0010. **Fax:** 330/677-0148. **Contact:** Mark Seaholts, President. **Description:** An executive search firm that also provides contract services. Company pays fee. **Specializes in the areas of:** Accounting/Auditing; Administration; Engineering; General Management; Industrial; Manufacturing; Personnel/Labor Relations; Publishing; Sales; Technical. **Positions commonly filled include:** Administrative Manager; Chemical Engineer; Chemist; Design Engineer; Electrical/Electronics Engineer; General Manager; Human Resources Specialist; Industrial Engineer; Industrial Production Manager; Mechanical Engineer; MIS Specialist; Operations/ Production Manager; Physician. **Other U.S. locations:** Tampa FL; Raleigh NC. **Average salary range of placements:** More than $50,000. **Number of placements per year:** 50 - 99.

EXECUTECH CONSULTANTS, INC.
P.O. Box 29385, Cincinnati OH 45229. 513/281-6416. **Fax:** 513/281-6674. **Contact:** Howard Bond, Publisher. **Description:** An executive search firm. **Specializes in the areas of:** Accounting/Auditing; Advertising; Broadcasting; Computer Science/ Software; Economics; Education; Engineering; Finance; Food Industry; General Management; Manufacturing; Personnel/Labor Relations; Publishing; Sales. **Positions commonly filled include:** Accountant; Advertising Clerk; Bank Officer/Manager; Economist; Editor; Management Analyst/Consultant; Management Trainee; Manufacturer's/Wholesaler's Sales Rep.

EXECUTIVE CONNECTION
8221 Brecksville Road, Building 3, Suite 2, Brecksville OH 44141. 440/838-5657. **Fax:** 440/838-5668. **Contact:** Mr. S.P. Brandvold, President. **E-mail address:** econnect@staffing.net. **Description:** An executive search firm that focuses on placing management and technical personnel with manufacturing clients. Company pays fee. **Specializes in the areas of:** Engineering; Food Industry; General Management; Industrial; Manufacturing. **Positions commonly filled include:** Buyer; Chemical Engineer; Chemist; Design Engineer; Designer; Electrical/ Electronics Engineer; Environmental Engineer; Industrial Engineer; Manufacturing Engineer; Mechanical Engineer; Operations/Production Manager; Purchasing Agent/Manager; Quality Control Supervisor; Technician. **Average salary range of placements:** More than $50,000. **Number of placements per year:** 1 - 49.

EXECUTIVE CONNECTIONS
5890 Sawmill Road, Dublin OH 43107. 614/760-1833. **Contact:** Manager. **Description:** An executive search firm specializing in sales, computers, finance, and management positions.

EXECUTIVE DIRECTIONS
4919 Spruce Hill Drive NW, Canton OH 44718. 330/499-1001. **Contact:** R. Glenn Richards, Vice President. **Description:** An executive search firm. Company pays fee. **Specializes in the areas of:** Automotive; Engineering; General Management; Packaging; Publishing; Sales; Technical. **Positions commonly filled include:** Biological Scientist; Chemical Engineer; Chemist; Human Resources Manager; Industrial Production Manager; Mechanical Engineer; Operations Manager; Purchasing Agent/Manager; Quality Control Supervisor. **Number of placements per year:** 1 - 49.

EXECUTIVE RECRUITMENT & CONSULTING INC.
24300 Chagrin Boulevard, Suite 301A, Beachwood OH 44122. 216/378-0100. **Contact:** Manager. **Description:** An executive search firm.

EXECUTIVE RESOURCES, INC.
P.O. Box 32, Dayton OH 45401. 937/274-4500. **Contact:** Manager. **Description:** An executive search firm offering a wide range of placements in such fields as food and drug procurement, sales, retail management, and data processing.

EXECUTIVE SEARCH LTD.
4830 Interstate Drive, Cincinnati OH 45246. 513/874-6901. **Contact:** Jim Cimino, Vice President. **E-mail address:** execsrch@concentric.net. **World Wide Web address:** http://www.executivesearch.com. **Description:** An executive search firm operating on both retainer and contingency bases. Company pays fee. **Specializes in the areas of:** Accounting/Auditing; Administration; Computer Science/Software; Engineering; Finance; General Management; Industrial; Manufacturing; Personnel/Labor Relations; Sales; Technical. **Positions commonly filled include:** Accountant/Auditor; Biomedical Engineer; Budget Analyst; Buyer; Chemical Engineer; Chemist; Civil Engineer; Computer Programmer; Design Engineer; Designer; Electrical/Electronics Engineer; Environmental Engineer; Financial Analyst; Health Services Manager; Human Resources Specialist; Industrial Engineer; Industrial Production Manager; Manufacturer's/Wholesaler's Sales Rep.; Mechanical Engineer; MIS Specialist; Pharmacist; Physical Therapist; Physician; Purchasing Agent/Manager; Quality Control Supervisor; Respiratory Therapist; Software Engineer; Structural Engineer; Systems Analyst; Transportation/Traffic Specialist. **Average salary range of placements:** More than $50,000. **Number of placements per year:** 200 - 499.

F.L.A.G.
625 East County Line Road, Springfield OH 45502. 937/342-0200. **Fax:** 937/342-0201. **Contact:** Tom Warren, Manager. **Description:** An executive search firm focusing on the placement of technical and sales professionals nationwide in the following industries: fuel, lubricants, and greases. The firm operates on both retainer and contingency bases. Company pays fee. **Specializes in the areas of:** Industrial; Sales; Technical. **Positions commonly filled include:** Chemist. **Average salary range of placements:** More than $50,000. **Number of placements per year:** 1 - 49.

FENZEL MILAR ASSOCIATES
602 Quincy Street, Ironton OH 45638. 740/532-6409. **Fax:** 740/533-0813. **Contact:** John Milar, Owner. **Description:** An executive search firm operating on a contingency basis. Company pays fee. **Specializes in the areas of:** Administration; Computer Science/Software; Engineering; Manufacturing. **Positions commonly filled include:** Chemical Engineer; Electrical/Electronics Engineer; Industrial Engineer; Materials Engineer; Mechanical Engineer; MIS Specialist; Software Engineer; Systems Analyst. **Average salary range of placements:** $30,000 - $60,000. **Number of placements per year:** 1 - 49.

FITZPATRICK & ASSOCIATES
62187 Sorrento Avenue NW, Canton OH 44718. 330/497-8994. **Contact:** Manager. **Description:** An executive search firm.

FLOWERS & ASSOCIATES
ASSOCIATED TEMPORARIES
1446 South Reynolds Road, Maumee OH 43537-1634. 419/893-4816. **Fax:** 419/891-0779. **Contact:** William J. Ross, President. **Description:** An executive search firm that also offers career/outplacement counseling. Associated Temporaries is a temporary placement agency. Company pays fee. **Specializes in the areas of:** Accounting/Auditing; Computer Science/Software; Engineering; Finance; General Management; Industrial; Manufacturing; Technical; Transportation. **Positions commonly filled include:** Accountant/Auditor; Blue-Collar Worker Supervisor; Buyer; Ceramics Engineer; Chemical Engineer; Chemist; Civil Engineer; Clerical Supervisor; Clinical Lab Technician; Computer Programmer; Customer Service Rep.; Design Engineer; Designer; Draftsperson; Electrical/Electronics Engineer; Environmental Engineer; Financial Analyst; Human Resources Specialist; Industrial Engineer; Industrial Production Manager; Management Analyst/Consultant; Management Trainee; Materials Engineer; Mechanical Engineer; MIS Specialist; Operations/Production Manager; Purchasing Agent/Manager; Quality Control Supervisor; Services Sales Rep.; Software Engineer; Structural Engineer; Systems Analyst; Transportation/Traffic Specialist; Typist/Word Processor. **Benefits available to temporary workers:** Paid Holidays; Paid Vacation. **Number of placements per year:** 50 - 99.

F-O-R-T-U-N-E PERSONNEL CONSULTANTS
8170 Corporate Park Drive, Suite 304, Cincinnati OH 45242. 513/891-6996. **Fax:** 513/891-7382. **Contact:** James Boule, President. **Description:** An executive search firm. Company pays fee. **Specializes in the areas of:** Engineering; Food Industry; General Management; Manufacturing; Publishing; Sales. **Corporate headquarters location:** New York NY. **Other U.S. locations:** Nationwide.

FREDERICK-LEHMANN & ASSOCIATES
TEMPORARILY YOURS/TEMP FORCE
7750 Reynolds Road, Mentor OH 44060. 440/951-6306. **Contact:** Manager. **Description:** An executive search firm that places personnel in a variety of industries. Temporarily Yours places personnel in clerical and industrial positions. Tech Force is a third division that provides technical and computer industry placements. **Specializes in the areas of:** Computer Science/Software; Industrial; Technical.

FRISTOE & CARLTON
77 Milford Drive, Hudson OH 44236. 330/655-3535. **Fax:** 330/655-3585. **Contact:** Jack Fristoe, President. **Description:** An executive search firm. Company pays fee. **Specializes in the areas of:** Advertising; Sales. **Positions commonly filled include:** Advertising Clerk; Public Relations Specialist. **Number of placements per year:** 1 - 49.

GAMMILL GROUP
8425 Pulsar Place, Columbus OH 43240. 614/848-7726. **Contact:** Manager. **Description:** An executive search firm. **Specializes in the areas of:** Information Technology.

GAYHART & ASSOCIATES
1250 Old River Road, 2nd Floor, Cleveland OH 44113. 216/861-7010. **Contact:** Richard F. Albertini, President. **Description:** An executive search firm. Company pays fee. **Specializes in the areas of:** Architecture/Construction; Computer Science/Software; Engineering; General Management; Industrial; Manufacturing; Personnel/Labor Relations; Technical. **Positions commonly filled include:** Aerospace Engineer; Architect; Biological Scientist; Biomedical Engineer; Ceramics Engineer; Chemical Engineer; Chemist; Civil Engineer; Computer Programmer; Construction and Building Inspector; Construction Contractor; Cost Estimator; Designer; Draftsperson; Electrical/Electronics Engineer; Food Scientist/Technologist; General Manager; Industrial Engineer; Landscape Architect; Materials Engineer; Mechanical Engineer; Metallurgical Engineer; Mining Engineer; Nuclear Engineer; Petroleum Engineer; Quality Control Supervisor; Software Engineer; Stationary Engineer; Structural Engineer; Systems Analyst; Technical Writer/Editor. **Number of placements per year:** 100 - 199.

H.L. GOEHRING & ASSOCIATES, INC.
3200 Wrenford Street, Dayton OH 45409-1250. 937/294-8854. **Fax:** 937/294-4699. **Contact:** Hal Goehring, President. **Description:** An executive search firm. Company pays fee. **Specializes in the areas of:** Engineering; General Management; Industrial; Manufacturing; Personnel/Labor Relations; Publishing; Sales. **Positions commonly filled include:** Buyer; Electrical/Electronics Engineer; Financial Analyst; General Manager; Human Resources Manager; Industrial Engineer; Mechanical Engineer; Purchasing Agent/Manager; Quality Control Supervisor. **Average salary range of placements:** More than $50,000. **Number of placements per year:** 1 - 49.

R. GREEN & ASSOCIATES
One South St. Clair Street, Toledo OH 43602. 419/249-2800. **Fax:** 419/249-2803. **Contact:** Manager. **Description:** An executive search firm. **Specializes in the areas of:** Automotive; Consumer Products; Manufacturing.

GRIFFITHS & ASSOCIATES
P.O. Box 678, Northfield OH 44067. 330/467-3131. **Fax:** 330/468-1845. **Contact:** Bob Griffiths, President. **Description:** An executive search firm. Company pays fee. **Specializes in the areas of:** Accounting/Auditing; Engineering; Food Industry; General Management; Industrial; Manufacturing; Personnel/Labor Relations; Sales; Technical. **Positions commonly filled include:** Accountant/Auditor; Aerospace Engineer; Biological Scientist; Biomedical Engineer; Buyer; Ceramics Engineer; Chemical Engineer; Chemist; Electrical/Electronics Engineer; Environmental Engineer; Industrial Designer; Industrial Engineer; Manufacturing Engineer; Marketing Specialist; Mechanical Engineer; Operations/Production Manager; Purchasing Agent/Manager; Quality Control Supervisor; Software Engineer. **Number of placements per year:** 1 - 49.

GEORGE GUM & ASSOCIATES
24400 Highland Road, Suite 30, Cleveland OH 44143. 216/531-1888. **Contact:** Office Manager. **Description:** An executive search firm. **Specializes in the areas of:** Retail.

GUTHOFF & ASSOCIATES
659-A Park Meadow Road, Westerville OH 43081. 614/794-9950. **Contact:** Manager. **Description:** An executive search firm. **Specializes in the areas of:** Banking; Engineering; Human Resources; Manufacturing; Telecommunications.

H.J.C. INC.
3731 Edinburgh Drive, Uniontown OH 44685. 216/653-3325. **Fax:** 216/650-4801. **Contact:** Harry Cummings, Director. **E-mail address:** hjcrecruit@aol.com. **Description:** An executive search firm. Company pays fee. **Specializes in the areas of:** Accounting/Auditing; Administration; Chemical; Engineering; Food Industry; General Management; Industrial; Legal; Manufacturing; Personnel/Labor Relations; Rubber; Sales; Technical; Transportation. **Average salary range of placements:** More than $50,000. **Number of placements per year:** 1 - 49.

RUSS HADICK & ASSOCIATES
7100 Corporate Way, Suite B, Centerville OH 45459. 937/439-7700. **Fax:** 937/439-7705. **Contact:** Russ Hadick, President. **E-mail address:** rhassoc@rcinet.com. **World Wide Web address:** http://www.rharecruiters.com. **Description:** An executive search firm. Company pays fee. **Specializes in the areas of:** Accounting/Auditing; Administration; Computer Hardware/Software; Engineering; Finance; Manufacturing; Personnel/Labor Relations; Technical. **Positions commonly filled include:** Accountant/Auditor; Aerospace Engineer; Attorney; Buyer; Chemical Engineer; Chemist; Civil Engineer; Computer Programmer; Credit Manager; Draftsperson; Economist; EDP Specialist; Electrical/Electronics Engineer; Financial Analyst; Human Resources Manager; Industrial Engineer; Marketing Specialist; Mechanical Engineer; MIS Specialist; Purchasing Agent/Manager; Quality Control Supervisor; Sales Rep.; Systems Analyst; Technical Writer/Editor; Technician. **Number of placements per year:** 50 - 99.

HAHN AND ASSOCIATES
7026 Corporate Way, Suite 212, Dayton OH 45459. 937/436-3141. **Fax:** 937/436-3252. **Contact:** Kenneth Hahn, Owner. **Description:** An executive search firm operating on a contingency basis. **Specializes in the areas of:** Administration; Engineering; General Management; Materials; Personnel/Labor Relations.

ROBERT HALF INTERNATIONAL/ACCOUNTEMPS
140 East Town Street, Suite 1150, Columbus OH 43215. 614/221-9300. **Contact:** Manager. **Description:** An executive search firm. Accountemps (also at this location) provides temporary placements. **Corporate headquarters location:** Menlo Park CA. **International locations:** Worldwide.

HAMMANN & ASSOCIATES
3540 Blue Rock Road, Cincinnati OH 45239. 513/385-2528. **Fax:** 513/741-2692. **Contact:** Ed Hammann, Owner. **E-mail address:** ehamman@cssweb.com. **Description:** An executive search firm operating on a contingency basis. Company pays fee. **Specializes in the areas of:** Administration; Computer Science/Software. **Positions commonly filled include:** Computer Programmer; Database Manager; Internet Services Manager; Management Analyst/Consultant; MIS Specialist; Multimedia Designer; Project Manager; Software Engineer; Systems Analyst; Systems Manager; Technical Writer/Editor; Telecommunications Manager; Webmaster. **Average salary range of placements:** $30,000 - $50,000. **Number of placements per year:** 1 - 49.

HEALTH CARE ADVANTAGE
3373 Wilkinson Drive, Fairlawn OH 44333. 330/666-0552. **Fax:** 330/666-8122. **Contact:** Lucy J. Randles, President. **E-mail address:** hcalucy@aol.com. **Description:** An executive search firm focusing exclusively on health care systems. Client employers include academic institutions, research and development organizations, hospitals, clinics, nursing homes, managed care companies, and medical supply companies. Company pays fee. **Specializes in the areas of:** Biology; Health/Medical; Technical. **Positions commonly filled include:** Biological Scientist; Biomedical Engineer; Chemical Engineer; Chemist; Clinical Lab Technician; Dental Lab Technician; Dietician/Nutritionist; EEG Technologist; EKG Technician; Emergency Medical Technician; Environmental Engineer; Food Scientist/Technologist; Health Services Manager; Human Resources Manager; Human Service Worker; Medical Records Technician; MIS Specialist; Nuclear Medicine Technologist; Occupational Therapist; Pharmacist; Physical Therapist; Radiological Technologist; Recreational Therapist; Registered Nurse; Respiratory Therapist; Social Worker; Speech-Language Pathologist; Surgical Technician; Technical Writer/Editor. **Average salary range of placements:** $30,000 - $50,000. **Number of placements per year:** 1 - 49.

HEALTHCARE RECRUITERS INTERNATIONAL
4015 Executive Park Drive, Suite 115, Cincinnati OH 45241. 513/554-4445. **Fax:** 513/554-4449. **Contact:** Manager. **Description:** An executive search firm dedicated exclusively to the health care industry. The firm also offers career and outplacement counseling.

Company pays fee. **Specializes in the areas of:** Health/Medical. **Positions commonly filled include:** Attorney; Biomedical Engineer; Computer Programmer; Dental Assistant/Dental Hygienist; Dentist; Dietician/Nutritionist; Economist; Electrical/Electronics Engineer; Financial Analyst; General Manager; Health Services Manager; Human Resources Specialist; Management Analyst/Consultant; Market Research Analyst; MIS Specialist; Occupational Therapist; Operations/Production Manager; Pharmacist; Physical Therapist; Physician; Psychologist; Recreational Therapist; Registered Nurse; Respiratory Therapist; Services Sales Rep.; Social Worker; Sociologist; Software Engineer; Speech-Language Pathologist; Surgical Technician; Systems Analyst; Veterinarian. **Average salary range of placements:** More than $50,000. **Number of placements per year:** 1 - 49.

J.D. HERSEY & ASSOCIATES
1695 Old Henderson Road, Columbus OH 43220. 614/459-4555. **Fax:** 614/459-4544. **Contact:** Jeff Hersey, President. **E-mail address:** jdhersey@earthlink.net. **World Wide Web address:** http://www.jdhersey.com. **Description:** An executive search firm. Company pays fee. **Specializes in the areas of:** Architecture/Construction; Computer Science/Software; Retail; Sales. **Positions commonly filled include:** Buyer; Computer Programmer; Construction Contractor; Cost Estimator; Manufacturer's/Wholesaler's Sales Rep.; Systems Analyst. **Average salary range of placements:** More than $50,000. **Number of placements per year:** 50 - 99.

HIGGINS & ASSOCIATES
P.O. Box 375, Kent OH 44240. 330/673-2245. **Contact:** Manager. **Description:** A generalist executive search firm.

W.A. HILL & ASSOCIATES
632 Vine Street, Suite 800, Cincinnati OH 45202. 513/241-1255. **Contact:** Manager. **Description:** An executive search firm. **Specializes in the areas of:** Information Systems.

HITE EXECUTIVE SEARCH
HITE MANAGEMENT CONSULTANTS, INC.
P.O. Box 43217, Cleveland OH 44143-0217. 440/461-1600. **Contact:** William A. Hite, III, President. **World Wide Web address:** http://www.hite-mgmt.com. **Description:** An executive search firm operating on a retained basis. **Specializes in the areas of:** Accounting/Auditing; Administration; Advertising; Architecture/Construction; Banking; Computer Hardware/Software; Engineering; Finance; General Management; Health/Medical; Legal; Manufacturing; Nonprofit; Personnel/Labor Relations; Sales; Technical. **Corporate headquarters location:** This Location. **Other U.S. locations:** Nationwide. **Average salary range of placements:** More than $50,000. **Number of placements per year:** 50 - 99.

HUMAN RESOURCE RECRUITERS
P.O. Box 18007, Cleveland Heights OH 44118-0007. 216/932-1592. **Fax:** 216/932-1594. **Contact:** John Goldthwaite, President. **Description:** An executive search firm operating on a contingency basis. Company pays fee. **Specializes in the areas of:** Manufacturing; Personnel/Labor Relations. **Positions commonly filled include:** Human Resources Specialist. **Number of placements per year:** 1 - 49.

R.W. HUNT GROUP
10999 Reed Hartman Highway, Suite 333, Cincinnati OH 45242. 513/821-4121. **Fax:** 513/821-4117. **Contact:** Rick Ramsay, President. **E-mail address:** rwhunt@aol.com. **Description:** A contingency and retained search firm. Company pays fee. **Positions commonly filled include:** Chemical Engineer; Design Engineer; Designer; Electrical/Electronics Engineer; Environmental Engineer; Industrial Engineer; Industrial Production Manager; Mechanical Engineer; Metallurgical Engineer; Operations/Production Manager; Quality Control Supervisor; Software Engineer; Stationary Engineer. **Average salary range of placements:** $30,000 - $50,000. **Number of placements per year:** 1 - 49.

ITS TECHNICAL STAFFING
INTERCONNECT TECHNICAL SERVICES, INC.
313 Jefferson Avenue, Toledo OH 43604. 419/259-3656. **Fax:** 419/255-0519. **Contact:** Roger Radelhoff, President. **Description:** An executive search firm operating on a contingency basis. The firm also offers permanent employment consulting services. **Specializes in the areas of:** Computer Science/Software; Engineering; Industrial; Manufacturing; Personnel/Labor Relations; Technical. **Positions commonly filled include:** Chemical Engineer; Civil Engineer; Computer Programmer; Construction and Building Inspector; Construction Contractor; Cost Estimator; Design Engineer; Designer; Draftsperson; Electrical/Electronics Engineer; Electrician; Environmental Engineer; Human Resources Specialist; Industrial Engineer; Industrial Production Manager; Mechanical Engineer; Software Engineer; Strategic Relations Manager; Structural Engineer; Surveyor; Technical Writer/Editor. **Other U.S. locations:** Fort Wayne IN; Flint MI; Cleveland OH; Columbus OH. **Average salary range of placements:** $30,000 - $50,000. **Number of placements per year:** 100 - 199.

ICON MANAGEMENT GROUP
621 West Broad Street, Suite 2-D, Pataskala OH 43062. 740/927-4404. **Fax:** 740/927-0392. **Contact:** Robert Bremer, President. **Description:** An executive search firm. Company pays fee. **Specializes in the areas of:** Administration; Computer Science/Software; Engineering; Industrial; Manufacturing; Personnel/Labor Relations. **Positions commonly filled include:** Aerospace Engineer; Agricultural Engineer; Biomedical Engineer; Ceramics Engineer; Chemical Engineer; Chemist; Civil Engineer; Computer Programmer; Designer; Electrical/Electronics Engineer; Human Resources Manager; Industrial Engineer; Industrial Production Manager; Manufacturer's/Wholesaler's Sales Rep.; Materials Engineer; Mechanical Engineer; Operations/Production Manager; Purchasing Agent/Manager; Quality Control Supervisor; Software Engineer; Structural Engineer; Systems Analyst. **Number of placements per year:** 50 - 99.

INSURANCE RECRUITING SPECIALISTS
6100 Channingway Boulevard, Suite 506, Columbus OH 43232. 614/864-2324. **Contact:** Manager. **Description:** An executive search firm. **Specializes in the areas of:** Insurance.

INTERCONNECT TECHNICAL SERVICES
125 Dillmont Drive, Columbus OH 43235. 614/841-7799. **Contact:** Manager. **Description:** An executive search firm. **Specializes in the areas of:** Computer Science/Software; Engineering; Information Systems; Technical.

INTERIM EXECUTIVE RECRUITING
1760 Manley Road, Maumee OH 43537. 419/893-2400. **Fax:** 419/893-2491. **Contact:** Jeff DePerro, President. **Description:** An executive search firm. **Positions commonly filled include:** Accountant; Auditor; Computer Programmer; Designer; Draftsperson; Employment Interviewer; Engineer; Financial Manager; Human Resources Manager; Industrial Production Manager; Machinist; Millwright; Purchasing Agent/Manager; Quality Control Supervisor; Systems Analyst; Tool and Die Maker; Welder. **Number of placements per year:** 500 - 999.

IVES & ASSOCIATES, INC.
471 East Broad Street, Suite 2010, Columbus OH 43215. 614/228-0202. **Contact:** Phyllis E. Ives, President. **Description:** An executive search firm. **Specializes in the areas of:** Accounting/Auditing; Advertising; Communications; Distribution; Food Industry; General Management; Legal; Manufacturing; Operations Management; Personnel/Labor Relations; Sales; Transportation.

JAEGER INTERNATIONAL INC.
4889 Sinclair Road, Suite 112, Columbus OH 43229. 614/885-0364. **Fax:** 614/885-0415. **Contact:** Ted Langley, President. **E-mail address:** ilcook2@aol.com. **World Wide Web address:** http://www.jaegerint.com. **Description:** An executive search firm focusing on technical, professional, and managerial placements. Company pays fee. **Specializes in the areas of:** Automotive; Computer Science/Software; Engineering; Industrial; Manufacturing; Telecommunications. **Positions commonly filled include:** Chemical Engineer; Computer Programmer; Design Engineer; Electrical/Electronics Engineer; Environmental Engineer; Industrial Engineer; Manufacturing Engineer; Mechanical Engineer; Quality Control Supervisor; Software Engineer. **Average salary range of placements:** More then $50,000. **Number of placements per year:** 1 - 49.

J. JOSEPH & ASSOCIATES
3809 Darrow Road, Stow OH 44224. 330/688-2101. **Contact:** Manager. **Description:** An executive search firm. **Specializes in the areas of:** Medical Sales and Marketing; Sales.

KBK MANAGEMENT ASSOCIATES
5500 Market Street, Suite 92, Youngstown OH 44512. 330/788-6508. **Toll-free phone:** 800/875-6546. **Fax:** 330/788-0645. **Contact:** Joanne Malys, Recruiting Specialist. **E-mail address:** jamalys@aol.com. **Description:** An executive search firm. Company pays fee. **Positions commonly filled include:** Accountant/Auditor; Actuary; Blue-Collar Worker Supervisor; Buyer; Chemist; Computer Programmer; Cost Estimator; Draftsperson; Engineer; Financial Analyst; Geologist/Geophysicist; Human Resources Manager; Mathematician; Purchasing Agent/Manager; Quality Control Supervisor; Statistician; Systems Analyst. **Number of placements per year:** 50 - 99.

RICHARD KADER & ASSOCIATES
7850 Freeway Circle, Berea OH 44017. 216/891-1700. **Contact:** Richard Kader. **Description:** An executive search firm. **Specializes in the areas of:** Sales.

KAISER NATIONWIDE
P.O. Box 41297, Dayton OH 45441-0297. 937/885-4105. **Fax:** 937/885-5310. **Contact:** Herman Kaiser, President. **E-mail address:** rakaiser@erinet.com. **World Wide Web address:** http://www.jobpoint.com/jpc. **Description:** An executive search firm. Company pays fee. **Specializes in the areas of:** Administration; Engineering; General Management; Health/Medical; Manufacturing; Technical; Transportation. **Positions commonly filled include:** Biomedical Engineer; Chemical Engineer; Design Engineer; Electrical/Electronics Engineer; Environmental Engineer; General Manager; Industrial Engineer; Mechanical Engineer; MIS Specialist; Quality Control Supervisor; Software Engineer; Structural Engineer; Systems Analyst. **Average salary range of placements:** More than $50,000. **Number of placements per year:** 50 - 99.

A.T. KEARNEY EXECUTIVE SEARCH
1200 Bank One Center, 600 Superior Avenue East, Cleveland OH 44114. 216/241-6880. **Contact:** David Lauderback, Managing Director. **Description:** An executive search firm operating on a retainer basis. **Specializes in the areas of:** Finance; High-Tech; Industrial; Nonprofit. **Corporate headquarters location:** Chicago IL. **International locations:** Worldwide.

LAMALIE AMROP INTERNATIONAL
127 Public Square, Key Tower, Suite 4110, Cleveland OH 44114. 216/694-3000. **Contact:** Manager. **Description:** A generalist executive search firm. **Other U.S. locations:** Nationwide.

LAUGHLIN & ASSOCIATES
260 Northland Boulevard, Suite 114, Cincinnati OH 45246. 513/772-1082. **Contact:** Office Manager. **Description:** An executive search firm. **Specializes in the areas of:** Sales.

LEITH & ASSOCIATES
24500 Center Ridge Road, Suite 325, Westlake OH 44145. 216/808-1130. **Contact:** Office Manager. **Description:** An executive search firm. **Specializes in the areas of:** Sales.

LOPRESTI & ASSOCIATES
12 Westerville Square, Suite 216, Westerville OH 43081. 614/794-9494. **Contact:** Office Manager. **Description:** An executive search firm. **Specializes in the areas of:** Banking; Finance.

MANAGEMENT RECRUITERS INTERNATIONAL
3450 West Central Avenue, Suite 360, Toledo OH 43606. 419/537-1100. **Fax:** 419/537-8730. **Contact:** Branch Manager. **Description:** An executive search firm. Company pays fee. **Specializes in the areas of:** Computer Science/Software; Engineering; General Management; Industrial; Manufacturing; Personnel/Labor Relations; Sales. **Positions commonly filled include:** Chemical Engineer; Computer Programmer; Electrical/Electronics Engineer; General Manager; Human Resources Manager; Industrial Engineer; Mechanical Engineer; Metallurgical Engineer; Operations/Production Manager; Purchasing Agent/Manager; Quality Control Supervisor; Systems Analyst. **Number of placements per year:** 50 - 99.

MANAGEMENT RECRUITERS INTERNATIONAL
1900 East Dublin-Granville Road, Suite 110B, Columbus OH 43229. 614/794-3200. **Fax:** 614/794-3233. **Contact:** Dick Stoltz, Business Manager. **E-mail address:** columbus!manager@mrinet.com. **Description:** An executive search firm. Company pays fee. **Specializes in the areas of:** Administration; Architecture/Construction; Computer Science/Software; Engineering; Food Industry; General Management; Industrial; Manufacturing; Personnel/Labor Relations; Transportation. **Positions commonly filled include:** Agricultural Engineer; Biochemist; Buyer; Chemical Engineer; Computer Programmer; Construction Manager; Cost Estimator; Credit Manager; Customer Service Rep.; Electrical/Electronics Engineer; Environmental Engineer; Food Scientist/Technologist; Human Resources Specialist; Industrial Engineer; Internet Services Manager; Metallurgical Engineer; MIS Specialist; Multimedia Designer; Operations/Production Manager; Purchasing Agent/Manager; Quality Control Supervisor; Software Engineer; Systems Analyst; Telecommunications Manager. **Number of placements per year:** 200 - 499.

MANAGEMENT RECRUITERS INTERNATIONAL
8090 Market Street, Suite 2, Youngstown OH 44512. 330/726-6656. **Fax:** 330/726-0199. **Contact:** Donald A. Somers, President. **Description:** An executive search firm operating on both retained and contingency bases. Company pays fee. **Positions commonly filled include:** Bank Officer/Manager; Computer Programmer; MIS Specialist; Software Engineer; Systems Analyst; Technical Writer/Editor;

Telecommunications Manager. **Average salary range of placements:** More than $50,000. **Number of placements per year:** 100 - 199.

MANAGEMENT RECRUITERS INTERNATIONAL
20600 Chagrin Boulevard, Suite 703, Cleveland OH 44122. 216/561-6776. **Fax:** 216/561-2393. **Contact:** Manager. **Description:** An executive search firm. Company pays fee. **Specializes in the areas of:** Finance; Food Industry; Health/Medical; Industrial; Insurance; Manufacturing; Personnel/Labor Relations; Publishing; Sales. **Positions commonly filled include:** Actuary; Administrative Manager; Branch Manager; General Manager; Health Services Manager; Human Resources Manager; Manufacturer's/Wholesaler's Sales Rep.; Occupational Therapist; Operations/ Production Manager; Physical Therapist; Physician; Purchasing Agent/Manager; Telecommunications Manager. **Average salary range of placements:** More than $50,000. **Number of placements per year:** 200 - 499.

MANAGEMENT RECRUITERS OF AKRON
1900 West Market Street, Akron OH 44313-6927. 330/867-2900. **Contact:** Tom Gerst, Manager. **Description:** An executive search firm. **Specializes in the areas of:** Plastics; Professional.

MANAGEMENT RECRUITERS OF CINCINNATI
36 East 4th Street, Suite 800, Cincinnati OH 45202. 513/651-5500. **Fax:** 513/651-3298. **Contact:** Joe McCullough, Co-Owner/Manager. **Description:** An executive search firm. **Specializes in the areas of:** Accounting/Auditing; Administration; Advertising; Architecture/Construction; Banking; Communications; Computer Hardware/Software; Construction; Design; Electrical; Engineering; Finance; Food Industry; General Management; Health/Medical; Industrial; Insurance; Legal; Manufacturing; Operations Management; Personnel/Labor Relations; Procurement; Publishing; Real Estate; Retail; Sales; Technical; Textiles; Transportation.

MANAGEMENT RECRUITERS OF CLEVELAND
812 Huron Road East, Suite 760, Cleveland OH 44115. 216/436-2436. **Fax:** 216/436-2441. **Contact:** Gary Gardiner, President. **E-mail address:** 76351.2662@compuserve.com. **Description:** An executive search firm. Company pays fee. **Specializes in the areas of:** Heating, Air Conditioning, and Refrigeration. **Positions commonly filled include:** Applications Engineer; Construction Contractor; Environmental Engineer; Industrial Engineer; Sales Executive; Sales Manager; Sales Rep. **Average salary range of placements:** $30,000 - $50,000. **Number of placements per year:** 50 - 99.

MANAGEMENT RECRUITERS OF CLEVELAND (DOWNTOWN)
7530 Lucerne Drive, Suite 303, Cleveland OH 44130. 440/243-5151. **Fax:** 440/243-4868. **Contact:** Jeff DiPaolo, Manager. **Description:** An executive search firm. Company pays fee. **Specializes in the areas of:** Accounting/Auditing; Administration; Architecture/ Construction; Biology; Communications; Data Processing; Engineering; Industrial; Legal; Manufacturing; Operations Management; Personnel/ Labor Relations; Sales. **Positions commonly filled include:** Aerospace Engineer; Architect; Attorney; Biochemist; Biomedical Engineer; Chemical Engineer; Design Engineer; Draftsperson; Electrical/Electronics Engineer; Environmental Engineer; Human Resources Specialist; Industrial Engineer; Internet Services Manager; Mechanical Engineer; MIS Specialist; Operations/Production Manager; Paralegal; Quality Control Supervisor; Software Engineer; Structural Engineer; Technical Writer/Editor; Telecommunications Manager. **Number of placements per year:** 100 - 199.

MANAGEMENT RECRUITERS OF CLEVELAND (LAKE)
Euclid Office Plaza, 26250 Euclid Avenue, Suite 811, Cleveland OH 44132-3674. 216/261-7696. **Fax:** 216/261-7699. **Contact:** Terry Wesley, Manager. **Description:** An executive search firm. **Specializes in the areas of:** Accounting/Auditing; Administration; Advertising; Architecture/Construction; Banking; Communications; Computer Hardware/Software; Construction; Electrical; Engineering; Finance; Food Industry; General Management; Health/Medical; Industrial; Insurance; Legal; Manufacturing; Operations Management; Procurement; Publishing; Real Estate; Retail; Sales; Technical; Textiles; Transportation.

MANAGEMENT RECRUITERS OF CLEVELAND (NORTHEAST)
8039 Broadmoor Road, Suite 20, Mentor OH 44060. 440/946-2355. **Contact:** General Manager. **Description:** An executive search firm. **Specializes in the areas of:** Banking.

MANAGEMENT RECRUITERS OF CLEVELAND (SOUTH)
9700 Rockside Road, Suite 100, Cleveland OH 44125-6264. 216/642-5788. **Fax:** 216/642-5933. **Contact:** Paul Montigny, Owner. **Description:** An executive search firm. **Specializes in the areas of:** Accounting/Auditing; Administration; Advertising; Architecture/Construction; Banking; Communications; Computer Hardware/Software; Construction; Design; Electrical; Engineering; Finance; Food Industry; General Management; Health/Medical; Legal; Manufacturing; Operations Management; Personnel/ Labor Relations; Procurement; Publishing; Real Estate; Retail; Sales; Technical; Textiles; Transportation.

MANAGEMENT RECRUITERS OF CLEVELAND (SOUTHWEST)
P.O. Box 178, Brunswick OH 44212-0178. 330/273-4300. **Fax:** 330/273-2862. **Contact:** Bob Boal, Manager. **Description:** An executive search firm. **Specializes in the areas of:** Accounting/Auditing; Administration; Advertising; Architecture/Construction; Banking; Communications; Computer Hardware/ Software; Construction; Design; Electrical; Engineering; Finance; Food Industry; General Management; Health/Medical; Industrial; Insurance; Legal; Manufacturing; Operations Management; Personnel/Labor Relations; Procurement; Publishing; Real Estate; Retail; Sales; Technical; Textiles; Transportation.

MANAGEMENT RECRUITERS OF COLUMBUS (WEST)
800 East Broad Street, Columbus OH 43205. 614/252-6200. **Contact:** Cheryl Clossman, Office Manager. **Description:** An executive search firm. **Specializes in the areas of:** Accounting/Auditing; Administration; Advertising; Architecture/Construction; Banking; Communications; Computer Hardware/ Software; Construction; Design; Electrical; Engineering; Finance; Food Industry; General Management; Health/Medical; Industrial; Insurance; Legal; Manufacturing; Operations Management; Personnel/Labor Relations; Procurement; Publishing; Real Estate; Retail; Sales; Technical; Textiles; Transportation.

MANAGEMENT RECRUITERS OF DAYTON
333 West First Street, Suite 304, Dayton OH 45402-1831. 937/228-8271. **Fax:** 937/228-2620. **Contact:** Manager. **Description:** An executive search firm. **Specializes in the areas of:** Accounting/Auditing; Administration; Advertising; Architecture/Construction; Banking; Communications; Computer Hardware/ Software; Construction; Design; Electrical; Engineering; Finance; Food Industry; General Management; Health/Medical; Industrial; Insurance; Legal; Manufacturing; Operations Management; Personnel/Labor Relations; Procurement; Publishing;

Real Estate; Retail; Sales; Technical; Textiles; Transportation.

MANAGEMENT RECRUITERS OF NORTH CANTON
P.O. Box 2970, North Canton OH 44720. 330/497-0122. **Fax:** 330/497-9730. **Contact:** Roger Bascom, Manager. **E-mail address:** mrnc@compuserve.com. **World Wide Web address:** http://www.mrnc.com. **Description:** An executive search firm. Company pays fee. **Specializes in the areas of:** Administration; Computer Hardware/Software; Information Technology; Manufacturing; Packaging; Publishing. **Positions commonly filled include:** Computer Programmer; Design Engineer; Designer; General Manager; Mechanical Engineer; MIS Specialist; Operations/Production Manager; Quality Control Supervisor; Systems Analyst. **Average salary range of placements:** $30,000 - $50,000.

MANAGEMENT RECRUITERS OF SOLON
P.O. Box 39361, Solon OH 44139. 440/248-7300. **Contact:** Kim Barnett, Manager. **Description:** An executive search firm. **Specializes in the areas of:** Accounting/Auditing; Administration; Advertising; Architecture/Construction; Banking; Communications; Computer Hardware/Software; Construction; Design; Electrical; Engineering; Finance; Food Industry; General Management; Health/Medical; Industrial; Insurance; Legal; Manufacturing; Operations Management; Personnel/Labor Relations; Procurement; Publishing; Real Estate; Retail; Sales; Technical; Textiles; Transportation.

BENNY MARTINEZ EXECUTIVE SEARCH
1215 Rosedale, Maumee OH 43537. 419/893-2933. **Contact:** Manager. **Description:** An executive search firm that concentrates on placing sales and marketing executives with companies that produce consumer packaged goods. **Specializes in the areas of:** Consumer Package Goods.

MARVEL CONSULTANTS INC.
28601 Chagrin Boulevard, Suite 470, Cleveland OH 44122. 216/292-2855. **Fax:** 216/292-7207. **Contact:** Marvin B. Basil, President. **Description:** An executive search firm. Company pays fee. **Specializes in the areas of:** Accounting/Auditing; Biology; Computer Science/Software; Engineering; Finance; General Management; Health/Medical; Industrial; Legal; Marketing; Personnel/Labor Relations; Sales; Transportation. **Positions commonly filled include:** Accountant/Auditor; Biological Scientist; Blue-Collar Worker Supervisor; Budget Analyst; Buyer; Chemist; Computer Programmer; Credit Manager; Customer Service Rep.; Designer; Draftsperson; Engineer; Financial Analyst; Human Resources Manager; Management Analyst/Consultant; Manufacturer's/Wholesaler's Sales Rep.; Occupational Therapist; Operations/Production Manager; Physical Therapist; Physician; Purchasing Agent/Manager; Quality Control Supervisor; Services Sales Rep.; Systems Analyst.

MESSINA MANAGEMENT SYSTEMS
4770 Duke Drive, Suite 140, Mason OH 45040. 513/398-3331. **Fax:** 513/398-0496. **Contact:** Vincent Messina, President. **Description:** An executive search firm that also operates as a temporary agency. Company pays fee. **Specializes in the areas of:** Accounting/Auditing; Administration; Computer Science/Software; Engineering; Finance; Industrial; Manufacturing; Sales; Scientific; Secretarial. **Average salary range of placements:** $30,000 - $50,000. **Number of placements per year:** 100 - 199.

MIAMI PROFESSIONAL SEARCH
1341 Stratford Drive, Piqua OH 45356. 937/778-9797. **Fax:** 937/773-2142. **Contact:** Lloyd E. Shoemaker, Owner. **Description:** An executive search firm. Company pays fee. **Specializes in the areas of:** Accounting/Auditing; Banking; Engineering; Finance; General Management; Industrial; Manufacturing; Personnel/Labor Relations; Sales. **Positions commonly filled include:** Accountant/Auditor; Bank Officer/Manager; Budget Analyst; Buyer; Chemical Engineer; Computer Programmer; Credit Manager; Draftsperson; Electrical/Electronics Engineer; Financial Analyst; Human Resources Manager; Industrial Engineer; Management Trainee; Mechanical Engineer; Operations/Production Manager; Purchasing Agent/Manager; Quality Control Supervisor; Systems Analyst; Telecommunications Manager; Transportation/Traffic Specialist. **Average salary range of placements:** $30,000 - $50,000. **Number of placements per year:** 1 - 49.

MIDLAND CONSULTANTS
4311 Ridge Road, Brooklyn OH 44144. 216/398-9330. **Fax:** 216/398-0879. **Contact:** David Sgro, President. **E-mail address:** midland@bright.net. **Description:** An executive search firm. **Specializes in the areas of:** Administration; Biology; Computer Science/Software; Engineering; General Management; Industrial; Manufacturing; Plastics; Publishing; Rubber; Sales. **Positions commonly filled include:** Bank Officer/Manager; Biochemist; Biological Scientist; Chemist; Computer Programmer; Design Engineer; Designer; Draftsperson; Electrical/Electronics Engineer; Environmental Engineer; Human Resources Specialist; Industrial Engineer; Mechanical Engineer; MIS Manager; Operations/Production Manager; Software Engineer; Systems Analyst. **Average salary range of placements:** $30,000 - $50,000. **Number of placements per year:** 100 - 199.

MILLION & ASSOCIATES
441 Vine Street, Suite 1831, Cincinnati OH 45202. 513/579-8770. **Contact:** Ken Million, President. **Description:** An executive search firm operating on a retainer basis for manufacturing, banking, medical, and service industries. **Average salary range of placements:** More than $50,000.

MINORITY EXECUTIVE SEARCH
P.O. Box 18063, Cleveland OH 44118. 216/932-2022. **Fax:** 216/932-7988. **Contact:** Eral Burks, Managing Director. **Description:** An executive search firm focusing on job placements for women and minorities. **Specializes in the areas of:** Accounting/Auditing; Banking; Engineering; Finance; Legal; Manufacturing; Personnel/Labor Relations; Sales; Technical; Transportation. **Positions commonly filled include:** Accountant/Auditor; Bank Officer/Manager; Biomedical Engineer; Chemical Engineer; Chemist; Computer Programmer; Credit Manager; Customer Service Rep.; Design Engineer; Electrical/Electronics Engineer; Environmental Engineer; Financial Analyst; Human Resources Specialist; Industrial Engineer; Mechanical Engineer; MIS Specialist; Operations/Production Manager; Public Relations Specialist; Purchasing Agent/Manager; Services Sales Rep.; Software Engineer; Systems Analyst; Technical Writer/Editor; Telecommunications Manager. **Average salary range of placements:** More than $50,000. **Number of placements per year:** 200 - 499.

CLAYTON MOYER ASSOCIATES
1631 Professional Plaza, Columbus OH 43220. 614/442-8200. **Contact:** Manager. **Description:** An executive search firm. **Specializes in the areas of:** Software Development.

MYERS & ASSOCIATES
4571 Stephen Circle, Canton OH 44718. 330/494-3274. **Fax:** 330/489-0790. **Contact:** George Myers, President. **Description:** An executive search firm operating on a contingency basis. Company pays fee.

Specializes in the areas of: Computer Science/Software; Engineering; Manufacturing. **Positions commonly filled include:** Accountant/Auditor; Attorney; Computer Programmer; Design Engineer; Designer; Draftsperson; Electrical/Electronics Engineer; Electrician; Industrial Engineer; Industrial Production Manager; Mechanical Engineer; Systems Analyst. **Average salary range of placements:** Less than $20,000. **Number of placements per year:** 1 - 49.

NATIONAL REGISTER
2700 East Dublin-Granville Road, Columbus OH 43231. 614/890-1200. **Fax:** 614/890-1259. **Contact:** Dave Molnar, President. **Description:** An executive search firm. Company pays fee. **Specializes in the areas of:** Sales. **Positions commonly filled include:** Account Manager; Sales Manager; Sales Rep. **Number of placements per year:** 200 - 499.

NATIONAL REGISTER OF AKRON, INC.
3050 Ridgewood Road, Akron OH 44333. 330/665-3720. **Fax:** 330/665-3780. **Contact:** Michael Hamilton, CPC, Manager. **Description:** An executive search firm operating on both retainer and contingency bases. Company pays fee. **Specializes in the areas of:** Sales; Transportation. **Positions commonly filled include:** Manufacturer's/Wholesaler's Sales Rep.; Sales Engineer; Sales Executive; Sales Manager; Sales Rep.; Transportation/Traffic Specialist. **Average salary range of placements:** $30,000 - $50,000. **Number of placements per year:** 100 - 199.

NATIONAL REGISTER OF TOLEDO
8245-B Farnsworth Road, Waterville OH 43566. 419/878-9810. **Fax:** 419/878-9402. **Contact:** Randy Seidletz, General Manager. **Description:** An executive search firm operating on both retained and contingency bases. Company pays fee. **Specializes in the areas of:** Sales; Transportation. **Positions commonly filled include:** Account Rep.; Branch Manager; Customer Service Rep.; Distribution Manager; Marketing Manager; Marketing Specialist; Operations Manager; Sales Engineer; Sales Executive; Sales Rep.; Transportation/Traffic Specialist. **Average salary range of placements:** $30,000 - $50,000. **Number of placements per year:** 100 - 199.

NEWCOMB-DESMOND & ASSOCIATES
73 Powhatton Drive, Milford OH 45150. 513/831-9522. **Fax:** 513/831-9557. **Contact:** Michael J. Desmond, Chief Operating Officer. **E-mail address:** mdesmond@fuse.net. **Description:** An executive search firm that also operates as a temporary agency and contract services firm. Founded in 1979. Company pays fee. **Specializes in the areas of:** Computer Science/Software; Engineering; Industrial; Insurance; Manufacturing; Personnel/Labor Relations. **Positions commonly filled include:** Accountant/Auditor; Administrative Manager; Advertising Clerk; Aerospace Engineer; Bank Officer/Manager; Biochemist; Biological Scientist; Biomedical Engineer; Chemical Engineer; Chemist; Computer Programmer; Customer Service Representative; Design Engineer; Designer; Draftsperson; Electrical/Electronics Engineer; Electrician; Environmental Engineer; Human Resources Specialist; Human Service Worker; Industrial Engineer; Management Analyst/Consultant; Manufacturer's/Wholesaler's Sales Rep.; Market Research Analyst; Mechanical Engineer; MIS Specialist; Operations/Production Manager; Purchasing Agent/Manager; Quality Control Supervisor; Services Sales Representative; Software Engineer; Stationary Engineer; Structural Engineer; Systems Analyst; Technical Writer/Editor; Telecommunications Manager. **Benefits available to temporary workers:** Paid Holidays; Paid Vacation. **Average salary range of placements:** $30,000 - $50,000. **Number of placements per year:** 200 - 499.

NORTH AMERICAN PERSONNEL
83 North Miller Road, Suite 102, Akron OH 44333. 330/869-0056. **Fax:** 330/869-0978. **Contact:** Harvey Lipton, President. **Description:** An executive search firm. Company pays fee. **Specializes in the areas of:** Engineering; Food Industry; General Management; Industrial; Manufacturing; Sales; Technical. **Positions commonly filled include:** Accountant/Auditor; Chemical Engineer; Chemist; Design Engineer; Engineer; Environmental Engineer; Financial Manager; General Manager; Human Resources Manager; Operations/Production Manager; Science Technologist. **Average salary range of placements:** More than $50,000. **Number of placements per year:** 50 - 99.

NORTH PEAK GROUP
812 Huron Road, Suite 315, Cleveland OH 44115. 216/621-1070. **Fax:** 216/621-0825. **Contact:** Matthew Bruns, President. **E-mail address:** mbruns6108@aol.com. **Description:** An executive search firm. Company pays fee. **Specializes in the areas of:** Computer Science/Software; Environmental; MIS/EDP. **Positions commonly filled include:** Biochemist; Computer Programmer; Environmental Engineer; MIS Specialist; Restaurant/Food Service Manager; Software Engineer; Telecommunications Manager. **Average salary range of placements:** More than $50,000. **Number of placements per year:** 50 - 99.

NORTHCOAST PERSONNEL
1250 Old River Road, Cleveland OH 44113. 216/861-2200. **Contact:** Recruiter. **Description:** An executive search firm. Company pays fee. **Specializes in the areas of:** Administration; Engineering; Industrial; Manufacturing. **Positions commonly filled include:** Accountant; Architect; Buyer; Chemical Engineer; Civil Engineer; Computer Programmer; Cost Estimator; Design Engineer; Designer; Draftsperson; Electrical/Electronics Engineer; Environmental Engineer; Industrial Engineer; Industrial Production Manager; Mechanical Engineer; Structural Engineer; Systems Analyst. **Number of placements per year:** 100 - 199.

O'BRIEN & ROOF COMPANY
6812 Caine Road, Columbus OH 43235. 614/766-8500. **Fax:** 614/766-8505. **Contact:** Lindy O'Brien, President. **Description:** An executive search firm. Company pays fee. **Specializes in the areas of:** Accounting/Auditing; Architecture/Construction; Finance; Food Industry; General Management; Hotel/Restaurant; Personnel/Labor Relations; Retail; Sales. **Positions commonly filled include:** Accountant/Auditor; Architect; Attorney; Civil Engineer; Construction Contractor; Cost Estimator; Designer; Financial Analyst; Food Scientist/Technologist; General Manager; Mechanical Engineer; MIS Specialist; Restaurant/Food Service Manager. **Average salary range of placements:** $30,000 - $50,000. **Number of placements per year:** 50 - 99.

OLSTEN FINANCIAL STAFFING
Ohio Savings Plaza, 1801 East Ninth Street, Suite 1040, Cleveland OH 44114. 216/241-7100. **Fax:** 216/241-7170. **Contact:** Matt McDonough, Market Manager. **Description:** An executive search firm that also provides temporary and temp-to-hire financial placements. Company pays fee. **Specializes in the areas of:** Accounting/Auditing; Banking; Finance. **Positions commonly filled include:** Account Manager; Accountant; Auditor; Budget Analyst; Chief Financial Officer; Controller; Credit Manager; Financial Analyst. **Corporate headquarters location:** Melville NY. **Average salary range of placements:** $20,000 - $29,999. **Number of placements per year:** 500 - 999.

OLSTEN PROFESSIONAL STAFFING SERVICES
3515 Michigan Avenue, Cincinnati OH 45208. 513/321-4313. **Fax:** 513/533-6757. **Contact:**

Manager. **E-mail address:** olsten@megalinx.net. **Description:** An executive search firm operating on a contingency basis. The firm also provides contract placements. Company pays fee. **Specializes in the areas of:** Accounting/Auditing; Administration; Art/Design; Banking; Computer Science/Software; Engineering; Finance; General Management; Manufacturing; Personnel/Labor Relations; Publishing; Sales; Technical. **Positions commonly filled include:** Accountant/Auditor; Bank Officer/Manager; Budget Analyst; Ceramics Engineer; Chemical Engineer; Civil Engineer; Claim Rep.; Clinical Lab Technician; Computer Programmer; Customer Service Rep.; Draftsperson; Electrical/Electronics Engineer; Environmental Engineer; Financial Analyst; Human Resources Specialist; Industrial Engineer; Internet Services Manager; Manufacturer's/Wholesaler's Sales Rep.; Market Research Analyst; Mechanical Engineer; MIS Specialist; Operations/Production Manager; Quality Control Supervisor; Securities Sales Rep.; Services Sales Rep.; Software Engineer; Structural Engineer; Surveyor; Systems Analyst; Technical Writer/Editor; Telecommunications Manager; Typist/Word Processor. **Benefits available to temporary workers:** Bonus Award/Plan; Medical Insurance; Paid Vacation. **Average salary range of placements:** $30,000 - $125,000.

PARAGON RECRUITING OFFICIALS
2000 Henderson Road, Columbus OH 43220. 614/442-8900. **Contact:** Vince Procopio, President. **Description:** An executive search firm focusing on data processing professions. **Specializes in the areas of:** Computer Science/Software. **Positions commonly filled include:** Computer Programmer; MIS Specialist; Systems Analyst. **Number of placements per year:** 1 - 49.

PATTERSON PERSONNEL
P.O. Box 101, Millersburg OH 44654. 330/674-4040. **Fax:** 330/674-3765. **Contact:** Manager. **Description:** An executive search firm focusing on technical and production management placements. Company pays fee. **Specializes in the areas of:** Engineering. **Positions commonly filled include:** Ceramics Engineer; Chemical Engineer; Chemist; Electrical/Electronics Engineer; Industrial Engineer; Manufacturing Engineer; Marketing Specialist; Materials Engineer; Mechanical Engineer; Operations/Production Manager; Plant Engineer; Quality Control Supervisor; Sales Representative. **Average salary range of placements:** More than $50,000. **Number of placements per year:** 50 - 99.

PERSONALIZED PLACEMENT
6641 Suffield Road, Cleveland OH 44124. 440/449-3380. **Fax:** 440/449-3381. **Contact:** Ronald Kemelhar, Employment Specialist. **Description:** An executive search firm that focuses on the placement of sales, sales management, and marketing personnel in the automotive, industrial, and institutional markets. Company pays fee. **Specializes in the areas of:** Automotive; Health/Medical; Light Industrial; Marketing; Sales; Scientific; Technical. **Positions commonly filled include:** Account Manager; Account Rep.; Applications Engineer; Branch Manager; Chemical Engineer; Civil Engineer; Environmental Engineer; Industrial Engineer; Management Trainee; Mechanical Engineer; Metallurgical Engineer; Sales Engineer; Sales Executive; Sales Manager; Sales Representative; Software Engineer; Vice President of Sales. **Average salary range of placements:** $30,000 - $50,000. **Number of placements per year:** 1 - 49.

K.J. PHILLIPS ASSOCIATES
10671 Tech Woods Circle, Cincinnati OH 45242. 513/733-5562. **Contact:** Manager. **Description:** An executive search firm. **Specializes in the areas of:** Information Systems.

PLACEMENT SERVICES LIMITED, INC.
753 West Waterloo Road, Akron OH 44314. 330/762-3838. **Toll-free phone:** 800/860-2252. **Contact:** Manager. **Description:** An executive search firm operating on a retainer basis. The firm also provides temporary and contract placements. **Specializes in the areas of:** Computer Science/Software; Engineering; Food Industry; Health/Medical; Industrial; Manufacturing; Personnel/Labor Relations. **Positions commonly filled include:** Blue-Collar Worker Supervisor; Chemical Engineer; Chemist; Civil Engineer; Computer Programmer; Designer; Electrical/Electronics Engineer; Human Resources Manager; Industrial Engineer; Mechanical Engineer; Purchasing Agent/Manager; Software Engineer; Structural Engineer; Systems Analyst. **Average salary range of placements:** $30,000 - $50,000. **Number of placements per year:** 100 - 199.

PREMIUM SEARCH
1166 Goodale Boulevard, Columbus OH 43212. 614/299-8120. **Contact:** Manager. **Description:** An executive search firm. **Specializes in the areas of:** Insurance.

THE PROFESSIONAL CONSULTANTS, INC.
290 Churchill Road, Youngstown OH 44505. 330/759-8700. **Contact:** Sherry Burns, Vice President. **Description:** An executive search firm. Company pays fee. **Specializes in the areas of:** Accounting/Auditing; Engineering; Industrial; Manufacturing. **Positions commonly filled include:** Accountant/Auditor; Ceramics Engineer; Design Engineer; Electrical/Electronics Engineer; Materials Engineer; Mechanical Engineer; Metallurgical Engineer; Quality Control Supervisor; Software Engineer. **Average salary range of placements:** $30,000 - $50,000. **Number of placements per year:** 50 - 99.

PROVIDENCE PERSONNEL CONSULTANTS
2404 Fourth Street, Suite 1, Cuyahoga Falls OH 44221-2659. 330/929-6431. **Toll-free phone:** 800/968-5717. **Fax:** 330/929-4335. **Contact:** Donna Early, President. **E-mail address:** ppcconsult@aol.com. **Description:** An executive search firm operating on a contingency basis. Providence Personnel Consultants also provides career and outplacement counseling services. Company pays fee. **Specializes in the areas of:** Accounting/Auditing; Administration; Advertising; Banking; Construction; Engineering; Finance; Health/Medical; Industrial; Management; Manufacturing; Personnel/Labor Relations; Professional; Sales; Technical; Transportation. **Positions commonly filled include:** Account Manager; Account Rep.; Accountant/Auditor; Administrative Assistant; Administrative Manager; Advertising Executive; Advertising Clerk; Aerospace Engineer; Applications Engineer; Bank Officer/Manager; Blue-Collar Worker Supervisor; Budget Analyst; Buyer; Ceramics Engineer; Chemical Engineer; Chemist; Chief Financial Officer; Civil Engineer; Clerical Supervisor; Computer Programmer; Controller; Cost Estimator; Credit Manager; Customer Service Rep.; Database Manager; Design Engineer; Draftsperson; Electrical/Electronics Engineer; Environmental Engineer; Finance Director; Financial Analyst; Food Scientist/Technologist; Graphic Artist; Graphic Designer; Human Resources Manager; Industrial Engineer; Industrial Production Manager; Internet Services Manager; Manufacturing Engineer; Market Research Analyst; Marketing Manager; Marketing Specialist; Mechanical Engineer; Medical Records Technician; MIS Specialist; Operations/Production Manager; Paralegal; Pharmacist; Physical Therapist; Purchasing Agent/Manager; Quality Control Supervisor; Registered Nurse; Sales Engineer; Sales Rep.; Secretary; Software Engineer; Systems Analyst; Systems Manager; Typist/Word Processor. **Corporate**

headquarters location: This Location. **Average salary range of placements:** More than $50,000. **Number of placements per year:** 200 - 499.

QUALITY PLUS
9930 Johnny Cake Ridge Road, Suite 2C, Mentor OH 44060. 440/350-1666. **Fax:** 440/354-4111. **Contact:** Manager. **Description:** An executive search firm operating on a contingency basis. Company pays fee. **Specializes in the areas of:** Accounting/Auditing; Engineering; General Management; Manufacturing; Personnel/Labor Relations; Secretarial; Technical; Transportation. **Positions commonly filled include:** Accountant/Auditor; Buyer; Cost Estimator; Design Engineer; Designer; Draftsperson; Electrical/Electronics Engineer; Industrial Engineer; Purchasing Agent/Manager; Quality Control Supervisor. **Number of placements per year:** 200 - 499.

QUALITY SOURCE, INC.
14650 Detroit Avenue, Suite 325, Cleveland OH 44107-4210. 216/529-9911. **Fax:** 216/529-0062. **Contact:** Debra L. Stitt, CPC, President. **Description:** An executive search firm that also operates as an employment agency. Company pays fee. **Specializes in the areas of:** Legal; Personnel/Labor Relations; Secretarial. **Positions commonly filled include:** Administrative Manager; Clerical Supervisor; Customer Service Rep.; Human Resources Specialist; Librarian; Paralegal. **Number of placements per year:** 50 - 99.

QUESTCOR COMPANY
P.O. Box 212, Dublin OH 43017-0212. 614/761-2920. **Fax:** 614/761-2556. **Contact:** Joyce Bushong, Recruiter. **Description:** An executive search firm operating on a retainer basis. Company pays fee. **Specializes in the areas of:** Engineering; Food Industry; General Management; Manufacturing; Personnel/Labor Relations; Sales; Technical. **Positions commonly filled include:** Biochemist; Biological Scientist; Biomedical Engineer; Buyer; Ceramics Engineer; Chemical Engineer; Chemist; Civil Engineer; Design Engineer; Electrical/Electronics Engineer; Environmental Engineer; Forester/Conservation Scientist; Human Resources Specialist; Industrial Engineer; Market Research Analyst; Materials Engineer; Mechanical Engineer; Telecommunications Manager. **Average salary range of placements:** More than $50,000. **Number of placements per year:** 1 - 49.

QUESTRY ASSOCIATES
5001 Mayfield Road, Suite 115, Cleveland OH 44124. 216/381-4799. **Contact:** Manager. **Description:** A generalist executive search firm.

BILL REBER & ASSOCIATES, INC.
P.O. Box 690, Dayton OH 45459. 937/433-5400. **Physical address:** 77 West Elmwood Drive, Suite 205, Dayton OH. **Fax:** 937/433-1758. **Contact:** Bill Reber, CPC, President. **Description:** An executive search firm. **Specializes in the areas of:** Accounting/Auditing; Engineering; Manufacturing; Materials; Personnel/Labor Relations; Sales. **Positions commonly filled include:** Human Resources Manager; Inventory Control Specialist; Materials Engineer; Planner; Purchasing Agent/Manager; Quality Control Supervisor; Safety Engineer.

RECRUITING SERVICES INC.
2367 Auburn Avenue, Cincinnati OH 45219. **Contact:** Mr. Joe Ganim, Vice President. **E-mail address:** jganim@rsijobs.com. **Description:** An executive search firm and employment agency operating on a contingency basis. **Positions commonly filled include:** Computer Programmer; Design Engineer; Software Engineer; Systems Analyst. **Number of placements per year:** 100 - 199.

RECRUITMASTERS OF CINCINNATI
5237 Traverse Court, West Chester OH 45069-5587. 513/860-1717. **Fax:** 513/860-1717. **Contact:** Frank J. Watson, President. **Description:** An executive search firm operating on a contingency basis. **Specializes in the areas of:** Computer Science/Software; Personnel/Labor Relations; Sales. **Positions commonly filled include:** Accountant/Auditor; Computer Programmer; Sales Rep.; Systems Analyst. **Average salary range of placements:** $30,000 - $50,000. **Number of placements per year:** 1 - 49.

W.R. RENNER & ASSOCIATES
2710 Beckett Street, Lebanon OH 45036. 513/777-7000. **Fax:** 513/777-4942. **Contact:** Bill Renner, Owner. **Description:** An executive search firm that recruits engineering and computer professionals for the manufacturing and service industries. Company pays fee. **Specializes in the areas of:** Accounting/Auditing; Computer Science/Software; Engineering; General Management; Industrial; Manufacturing; Technical. **Positions commonly filled include:** Accountant/Auditor; Administrative Manager; Aerospace Engineer; Chemical Engineer; Chemist; Civil Engineer; Computer Programmer; Cost Estimator; Design Engineer; Designer; Electrical/Electronics Engineer; Environmental Engineer; Financial Analyst; Industrial Engineer; Industrial Production Manager; Mechanical Engineer; MIS Specialist; Purchasing Agent/Manager; Quality Control Supervisor; Software Engineer; Structural Engineer; Systems Analyst; Telecommunications Manager. **Average salary range of placements:** $30,000 - $80,000. **Number of placements per year:** 1 - 49.

RESOURCE TECHNE GROUP
9991 Walnutridge Court, Cincinnati OH 45242. 513/793-3121. **Fax:** 513/793-3132. **Contact:** Cathy Landers, Manager. **Description:** An executive search firm. Company pays fee. **Specializes in the areas of:** Engineering; Industrial; Manufacturing; Personnel/Labor Relations. **Positions commonly filled include:** Chemical Engineer; Chemist; Design Engineer; Electrical/Electronics Engineer; Human Resources Specialist; Materials Engineer; Mechanical Engineer; MIS Specialist; Software Engineer; Systems Analyst. **Average salary range of placements:** $30,000 - $50,000.

REVERE ASSOCIATES
P.O. Box 498, Bath OH 44210. 330/666-6442. **Contact:** Manager. **Description:** An executive search firm. **Specializes in the areas of:** Industrial.

RICH & ASSOCIATES
5432 Mayfield Road, Suite 204, Lyndhurst OH 44124. 440/449-2279. **Contact:** Manager. **Description:** An executive search firm. **Specializes in the areas of:** Data Processing; Information Systems; MIS/EDP.

SJR & ASSOCIATES
24300 Chagrin Boulevard, Cleveland OH 44122. 216/831-5228. **Fax:** 216/751-5665. **Contact:** Scott Riffle, CPC, Owner. **Description:** An executive search firm operating on a contingency basis. Company pays fee. **Specializes in the areas of:** Engineering; Manufacturing. **Positions commonly filled include:** Buyer; Ceramics Engineer; Chemical Engineer; Design Engineer; Electrical/Electronics Engineer; General Manager; Industrial Engineer; Materials Engineer; Mechanical Engineer; Metallurgical Engineer; Operations/Production Manager; Purchasing Agent/Manager; Quality Control Supervisor. **Average salary range of placements:** More than $50,000. **Number of placements per year:** 50 - 99.

SACHS ASSOCIATES
509 Liberty Drive, Suite B, Huron OH 44839. 419/433-3837. **Contact:** Scott Sachs, President. **Description:** An executive search firm. Company pays fee. **Specializes in the areas of:** Information Technology. **Positions commonly filled include:** Aerospace Engineer; Computer Programmer; Design Engineer; Electrical/Electronics Engineer; Internet Services Manager; Management Analyst/Consultant; MIS Specialist; Software Engineer; Systems Analyst. **Number of placements per year:** 1 - 49.

SALES CONSULTANTS OF CINCINNATI
11311 Cornell Park Drive, Suite 404, Cincinnati OH 45242. 513/247-0707. **Fax:** 513/247-2575. **Contact:** Brittany Buckman, Office Coordinator. **Description:** An executive search firm. **Specializes in the areas of:** Accounting/Auditing; Administration; Advertising; Architecture/Construction; Banking; Communications; Computer Hardware/Software; Construction; Design; Electrical; Engineering; Finance; Food Industry; General Management; Health/Medical; Industrial; Insurance; Legal; Manufacturing; Operations Management; Personnel/Labor Relations; Procurement; Publishing; Real Estate; Retail; Sales; Technical; Textiles; Transportation.

SANFORD ROSE ASSOCIATES
4450 Belden Village Street NW, Suite 209, Canton OH 44718. 330/649-9100. **Fax:** 330/649-9101. **Contact:** Manager. **World Wide Web address:** http://www.sanfordrose.com. **Description:** An executive search firm. **Specializes in the areas of:** Engineering; General Management; Sales.
Other area locations:
- 3040 West Market Street, Fairlawn OH 44333. 330/865-4545.
- P.O. Box 6093, Hudson OH 44236. 330/653-3325. (Engineering)

SANFORD ROSE ASSOCIATES OF CLEVELAND
26250 Euclid Avenue, Suite 211, Cleveland OH 44132. 216/731-0005. **Contact:** Ralph Orkin, Owner. **World Wide Web address:** http://www.sanfordrose.com. **Description:** A contingency search firm. Company pays fee. **Specializes in the areas of:** Administration; Computer Science/Software. **Positions commonly filled include:** Computer Programmer; MIS Specialist; Software Engineer; Systems Analyst. **Average salary range of placements:** $30,000 - $50,000. **Number of placements per year:** 1 - 49.

SANFORD ROSE ASSOCIATES OF COLUMBUS
2586 Tiller Lane, Columbus OH 43229. 614/523-1663. **Contact:** Bill Earhart, Owner/President. **World Wide Web address:** http://www.sanfordrose.com. **Description:** An executive search firm. Company pays fee. **Specializes in the areas of:** Administration; Computer Science/Software; Engineering; Manufacturing. **Positions commonly filled include:** Computer Programmer; Mechanical Engineer; MIS Specialist; Software Engineer; Systems Analyst; Telecommunications Manager. **Average salary range of placements:** More than $50,000. **Number of placements per year:** 1 - 49.

SANFORD ROSE ASSOCIATES OF LIMA
114 1/2 North West Street, Suite 204, Lima OH 45801. 419/227-5740. **Fax:** 419/227-6004. **Contact:** Tom Dautenhahn, Owner. **World Wide Web address:** http://www.sanfordrose.com. **Description:** An executive search firm. Company pays fee. **Specializes in the areas of:** Engineering; Manufacturing. **Positions commonly filled include:** Electrical/Electronics Engineer; Industrial Engineer; Manufacturing Engineer; Mechanical Engineer; Metallurgical Engineer; Quality Control Supervisor. **Number of placements per year:** 1 - 49.

SANFORD ROSE ASSOCIATES OF YOUNGSTOWN
545 North Broad Street, Suite 2, Canfield OH 44406-9204. 330/533-9270. **Fax:** 330/533-9272. **Contact:** Richard H. Ellison, CPC, President. **E-mail address:** ellisor@aol.com. **World Wide Web address:** http://www.sanfordrose.com. **Description:** An executive search firm. Founded in 1970. Company pays fee. **Specializes in the areas of:** Administration; Computer Science/Software. **Positions commonly filled include:** Computer Programmer; Internet Services Manager; MIS Specialist; Multimedia Designer; Software Engineer; Systems Analyst; Telecommunications Manager. **Average salary range of placements:** More than $50,000. **Number of placements per year:** 50 - 99.

SEARCH TECHNOLOGY
P.O. Box 48, Powell OH 43065. 614/761-3383. **Fax:** 614/761-0122. **Contact:** Dennis T. Caron, Principal. **E-mail address:** dcaron1@aol.com. **Description:** An executive search firm. Company pays fee. **NOTE:** The firm requires that candidates have two or more years experience related to large-scale process industries and a degree in engineering. **Specializes in the areas of:** Engineering; Manufacturing. **Positions commonly filled include:** Chemical Engineer; Controls Engineer; Electrical/Electronics Engineer; Instrument Engineer; Process Engineer; Software Engineer. **Average salary range of placements:** More than $50,000. **Number of placements per year:** 1 - 49.

SEARCHMARK MEDICAL
4 Triangle Park Drive, Cincinnati OH 45246. 513/772-7720. **Contact:** Manager. **Description:** An executive search firm that focuses on sales, marketing, and management positions in the health care industry. **Specializes in the areas of:** Health/Medical. **Corporate headquarters location:** This Location.
Other area locations:
- 7050 Engle Road, Suite 100, Cleveland OH 44130. 440/816-7600.

SELECTIVE SEARCH
659 Park Meadow Road, Westerville OH 43081. 614/899-0575. **Contact:** Manager. **Description:** An executive search firm. **Specializes in the areas of:** Plastics; Rubber.

SELL & ASSOCIATES
503 South Front Street, Suite 210, Columbus OH 43215. 614/221-8199. **Contact:** Mark Sell, Manager. **Description:** An executive search firm.

SHAFER JONES ASSOCIATES
P.O. Box 405, Troy OH 45373-0405. 937/335-1885. **Fax:** 937/335-2237. **Contact:** Paul Jones, Owner. **Description:** An executive search firm operating on a contingency basis. Founded in 1992. Company pays fee. **Specializes in the areas of:** Accounting/Auditing; Computer Science/Software; Engineering; Finance; Health/Medical; Manufacturing; Personnel/Labor Relations. **Positions commonly filled include:** Accountant; Buyer; Computer Programmer; Design Engineer; Electrical/Electronics Engineer; Financial Analyst; Human Resources Specialist; Mechanical Engineer; MIS Specialist; Pharmacist; Purchasing Agent/Manager; Quality Control Supervisor; Software Engineer; Technical Writer/ Editor. **Average salary range of placements:** More than $50,000.

SNELLING PERSONNEL SERVICES
3460 South Dixie Drive, Suite 200, Dayton OH 45439. 937/297-2300. **Fax:** 937/297-2305. **Contact:** Doug Wales, President. **E-mail address:** snelling@erinet.com. **World Wide Web address:** http://www.snelling.com/dayton. **Description:** An executive search firm that also provides contract services. Company pays fee. **Specializes in the areas of:** Administration;

Advertising; Engineering; Finance; Food Industry; General Management; Health/Medical; Industrial; Manufacturing; Personnel/Labor Relations; Sales; Technical. **Positions commonly filled include:** Claim Rep.; Clinical Lab Technician; Computer Programmer; Customer Service Rep.; Electrical/Electronics Engineer; Environmental Engineer; Human Resources Specialist; Industrial Engineer; Manufacturer's/Wholesaler's Sales Rep.; MIS Specialist; Operations/Production Manager; Registered Nurse; Respiratory Therapist; Restaurant/Food Service Manager; Services Sales Rep.; Software Engineer; Surgical Technician; Systems Analyst; Technical Writer/Editor; Telecommunications Manager. **Number of placements per year:** 100 - 199.

CHARLES V. SNIDER & ASSOCIATES INC.
6929 West 130th Street, Suite 401, Cleveland OH 44130. 216/884-1656. **Contact:** Office Manager. **Description:** An executive search firm. **Specializes in the areas of:** Legal.

SOURCE SERVICES CORPORATION
525 Vine Street, Suite 2250, Cincinnati OH 45202. 513/651-4044. **Fax:** 513/651-3512. **Contact:** Greg Johnson, Managing Director. **E-mail address:** ssccio@sourcesvc.com. **Description:** An executive search firm operating on a contingency basis. **Specializes in the areas of:** Computer Science/Software; Consulting; Finance. **Positions commonly filled include:** Accountant/Auditor; Aerospace Engineer; Agricultural Engineer; Bank Officer/Manager; Biomedical Engineer; Budget Analyst; Chemical Engineer; Civil Engineer; Clerical Supervisor; Computer Programmer; Cost Estimator; Credit Manager; Customer Service Rep.; Design Engineer; Economist; Electrical/Electronics Engineer; Environmental Engineer; Financial Analyst; Industrial Engineer; Internet Services Manager; Licensed Practical Nurse; Management Analyst/Consultant; Market Research Analyst; Mechanical Engineer; MIS Specialist; Operations/Production Manager; Paralegal; Purchasing Agent/Manager; Quality Control Supervisor; Registered Nurse; Software Engineer; Strategic Relations Manager; Structural Engineer; Systems Analyst; Transportation/Traffic Specialist. **Corporate headquarters location:** Dallas TX. **Average salary range of placements:** $30,000 - $50,000. **Number of placements per year:** 200 - 499.
Other area locations:
- 1105 Schrock Road, Suite 510, Columbus OH 43229. 614/846-3311. (Accounting/Auditing; Computer Hardware/Software; Finance; Information Technology)
- One South Main Street, Suite 1440, Dayton OH 45402. 937/461-4660. (Accounting/Auditing; Computer Hardware/Software; Finance; Information Technology; Manufacturing)
- 3 Summit Park Drive, Suite 550, Independence OH 44131. 216/328-5900. (Accounting/Auditing; Computer Hardware/Software; Finance; Information Technology)

SPEER & ASSOCIATES
9624 Cincinnati Columbus Road, Suite 312, Cincinnati OH 45241. 513/777-0200. **Contact:** Manager. **Description:** An executive search firm. **Specializes in the areas of:** Transportation.

STEPHENS ASSOCIATES LTD.
P.O. Box 151114, Columbus OH 43215. 614/469-9990. **Physical address:** 480 South 3rd Street, Columbus OH. **Contact:** Manager. **Description:** An executive search firm.

STERLING PERSONNEL RESOURCES
1129 West Miamisburg Centerville Road, Suite 307, Dayton OH 45449. 937/384-0190. **Contact:** Manager. **Description:** An executive search firm. **Specializes in the areas of:** Accounting/Auditing; Administration; Engineering; Information Systems; Manufacturing.

R.L. STEVENS & ASSOCIATES
5005 Rockside Road, Suite 900, Independence OH 44131. 216/642-1933. **Contact:** Office Manager. **Description:** An executive search firm that places professionals in white-collar positions.

SUCCESS PERSONNEL
350 East Broad Street, Suite 150, Columbus OH 43215. 614/221-5125. **Contact:** Office Manager. **Description:** An executive search firm.

SUTTON ASSOCIATES
1200 Stephens Road, Sidney OH 45365. 937/497-1700. **Contact:** Tom Sutton. **Description:** A retained executive search firm that places middle to upper-level managers.

TABB & ASSOCIATES
1460 West Lane Avenue, Suite 250, Columbus OH 43221. 614/486-8888. **Fax:** 614/486-3950. **Contact:** Roosevelt Tabb, President. **E-mail address:** tabros@sprintmail.com. **Description:** An executive search firm. **Specializes in the areas of:** Computer Science/Software; Engineering; Food Industry; General Management; Industrial; Insurance; Light Industrial; Marketing; Sales; Scientific; Technical. **Positions commonly filled include:** Applications Engineer; Auditor; Chemical Engineer; Chief Financial Officer; Computer Programmer; Controller; Database Manager; Finance Director; Financial Analyst; Human Resources Manager; Manufacturing Engineer; Marketing Manager; Mechanical Engineer; Metallurgical Engineer; MIS Specialist; Operations Manager; Project Manager; Quality Control Supervisor; Sales Engineer; Sales Executive; Sales Manager; Software Engineer; Systems Analyst; Systems Manager. **Average salary range of placements:** More than $50,000. **Number of placements per year:** 1 - 49.

TALENT RESEARCH CORPORATION
P.O. Box 36214, Cincinnati OH 45236. 513/242-4100. **Fax:** 513/641-0204. **Contact:** Robert Wick, President. **Description:** An executive search firm operating on a contingency basis. Founded in 1962. Company pays fee. **Specializes in the areas of:** Engineering; Manufacturing; Technical. **Positions commonly filled include:** Aerospace Engineer; Agricultural Engineer; Ceramics Engineer; Chemical Engineer; Computer Programmer; Design Engineer; Electrical/Electronics Engineer; Industrial Engineer; Materials Engineer; Mechanical Engineer; MIS Specialist; Petroleum Engineer; Quality Control Supervisor; Software Engineer; Systems Analyst. **Average salary range of placements:** $30,000 - $50,000. **Number of placements per year:** 50 - 99.

TECHNICAL RECRUITING SERVICES
6100 Channingway Boulevard, Suite 506, Columbus OH 43232. 614/864-2270. **Fax:** 614/864-3994. **Contact:** Nick Lang, President. **Description:** An executive search firm. Company pays fee. **Specializes in the areas of:** Engineering; General Management; Industrial; Manufacturing; Technical. **Positions commonly filled include:** Electrical/Electronics Engineer; Industrial Engineer; Manufacturer's/Wholesaler's Sales Rep.; Mechanical Engineer. **Number of placements per year:** 50 - 99.

TECHNICAL SEARCH ASSOCIATES
20325 Center Ridge Road, Suite 622, Rocky River OH 44116. 440/356-0880. **Fax:** 440/356-9036. **Contact:** John Brunshwig, Director. **Description:** An executive search firm. **Specializes in the areas of:** Engineering;

Manufacturing. **Positions commonly filled include:** Aerospace Engineer; Electrical/Electronics Engineer; Mechanical Engineer; Software Engineer; Structural Engineer. **Number of placements per year:** 1 - 49.

TEKNON EMPLOYMENT RESOURCES, INC.
17 South St. Clair Street, Suite 300, Dayton OH 45402. 937/222-5300. **Fax:** 937/222-6311. **Contact:** Bill Gaffney, Vice President of Recruiting. **E-mail address:** 102152.735@compuserve.com. **Description:** An executive search firm. Company pays fee. **Specializes in the areas of:** Computer Science/Software; Data Communications; Telecommunications. **Positions commonly filled include:** Branch Manager; Computer Programmer; General Manager; Sales and Marketing Rep.; Software Engineer; Systems Analyst; Telecommunications Manager. **Average salary range of placements:** More than $50,000. **Number of placements per year:** 50 - 99.

THOMAS-SCHADE & ASSOCIATES
6243 Colebrook Road, Cleveland OH 44120. 440/887-0090. **Contact:** Danielle Schade, Partner. **Description:** An executive search firm. Company pays fee. **Specializes in the areas of:** Computer Science/Software; Engineering; Fire Protection Engineering; Manufacturing; Sales; Security. **Positions commonly filled include:** Branch Manager; Computer Programmer; Construction Contractor; Electrical/Electronics Engineer; General Manager; Librarian; Library Technician; MIS Manager; Services Sales Representative; Software Engineer; Systems Analyst. **Average salary range of placements:** More than $50,000. **Number of placements per year:** 50 - 99.

FRED C. TIPPEL AND ASSOCIATES
105 Shawnee Drive, Marietta OH 45750. 740/374-3288. **Fax:** 740/374-3294. **Contact:** Fred C. Tippel, Owner/Director. **Description:** An executive search firm operating on both contingency and retainer bases. Company pays fee. **Specializes in the areas of:** Engineering; General Management; Manufacturing. **Positions commonly filled include:** Chemical Engineer; Chemist; Design Engineer; Electrical/Electronics Engineer; Environmental Engineer; General Manager; Industrial Engineer; Operations/Production Manager. **Number of placements per year:** 1 - 49.

TULLY WOODMANSEE & ASSOCIATES
7720 Rivers Edge Drive, Suite 101, Columbus OH 43235. 614/844-5480. **Contact:** Manager. **Description:** A generalist executive search firm for upper-level professionals. **Average salary range of placements:** More than $50,000.

TUPA SLACK & ASSOCIATES
24803 Detroit Road, Westlake OH 44145. 216/835-2848. **Contact:** Manager. **Description:** A generalist executive search firm.

J.P. WALTON & ASSOCIATES
9601 Dorothy Avenue, Cleveland OH 44125. 216/883-4141. **Fax:** 216/883-5717. **Contact:** Patrick Walton, Owner. **Description:** An executive search firm that focuses on the corrugated containers and folding carton industries. **Specializes in the areas of:** Accounting/Auditing; Administration; Art/Design; Engineering; General Management; Industrial; Manufacturing; Sales. **Positions commonly filled include:** Accountant/Auditor; Administrative Manager; Blue-Collar Worker Supervisor; Computer Programmer; Customer Service Rep.; General Manager; Industrial Engineer; Industrial Production Manager; Management Trainee; Manufacturer's/Wholesaler's Sales Rep.; Mechanical Engineer; MIS Specialist; Purchasing Agent/Manager; Quality Control Supervisor; Services Sales Rep.; Systems Analyst. **Number of placements per year:** 1 - 49.

R. WEGESIN & ASSOCIATES
P.O. Box 721, Dublin OH 43017. 614/798-0431. **Contact:** Manager. **Description:** An executive search firm. **Specializes in the areas of:** Manufacturing.

WEIPER RECRUITING SERVICES
1672 McCabe Lane, Cincinnati OH 45255-3095. 513/232-4300. **Contact:** Dave Weiper, Recruiter. **E-mail address:** coec@cin.ix.net. **World Wide Web address:** http://www.occ.com/wrs. **Description:** An executive search firm operating on a contingency basis. Company pays fee. **Specializes in the areas of:** Computer Science/Software. **Positions commonly filled include:** Computer Programmer; Internet Services Manager; Systems Analyst. **Average salary range of placements:** $30,000 - $50,000. **Number of placements per year:** 50 - 99.

WORLD SEARCH
4130 Linden Avenue, Claypool Building, Suite 125, Dayton OH 45432. 937/254-9071. **Fax:** 937/254-0229. **Contact:** Manager. **Description:** An executive search firm and employment agency. **Specializes in the areas of:** Engineering.

PERMANENT EMPLOYMENT AGENCIES

ADECCO
801-B West 8th Street, Suite 516, Cincinnati OH 45203. 513/381-1188. **Fax:** 513/381-1287. **Contact:** Sharon L. Blake, Branch Manager. **Description:** A permanent employment agency that also provides temporary placements. Company pays fee. **Specializes in the areas of:** Administration; Advertising; Banking; Data Processing; Finance; General Management; Insurance; Legal; Manufacturing; Nonprofit; Personnel/Labor Relations; Sales; Secretarial; Transportation. **Positions commonly filled include:** Accountant/Auditor; Administrative Assistant; Administrative Manager; Advertising Clerk; Bank Officer/Manager; Brokerage Clerk; Budget Analyst; Claim Rep.; Clerical Supervisor; Cost Estimator; Counselor; Credit Manager; Customer Service Rep.; Data Entry Clerk; Health Services Manager; Human Resources Specialist; Management Trainee; Market Research Analyst; Operations/Production Manager; Paralegal; Public Relations Specialist; Purchasing Agent/Manager; Quality Control Supervisor; Secretary; Strategic Relations Manager; Telecommunications Manager; Transportation/Traffic Specialist; Typist/Word Processor; Underwriter/Assistant Underwriter. **Benefits available to temporary workers:** Medical Insurance; Paid Holidays; Paid Vacation; Referral Bonus Plan. **Other U.S. locations:** Nationwide.

ADVANCEMENT L.L.C.
32200 Solon Road, Solon OH 44139-3535. 440/248-8550. **Fax:** 440/248-0740. **Contact:** Patrick Gallagher, Account Executive. **Description:** A permanent employment agency. **Specializes in the areas of:** Computer Science/Software; Engineering; Scientific; Technical. **Positions commonly filled include:** Architect; Biomedical Engineer; Ceramics Engineer; Civil Engineer; Design Engineer; Designer; Draftsperson; Electrical/Electronics Engineer; Industrial Engineer; Materials Engineer; Mechanical Engineer; Metallurgical Engineer; Nuclear Engineer; Software Engineer; Structural Engineer; Technical Writer/Editor; Typist/Word Processor. **Benefits available to temporary workers:** Dental Insurance; Life Insurance; Medical Insurance; Paid Holidays; Paid Vacation;

Vision Insurance. **Average salary range of placements:** More than $50,000. **Number of placements per year:** 200 - 499.

AMERICAN BUSINESS PERSONNEL SERVICES, INC.
11499 Chester Road, Suite 2610, Cincinnati OH 45246. 513/772-1200. **Fax:** 513/326-2278. **Contact:** Manager. **Description:** A permanent employment agency. Company pays fee. **Specializes in the areas of:** Computer Hardware/Software; Computer Programming; Computer Science/Software; Engineering. **Positions commonly filled include:** Computer Programmer; Engineer; Systems Analyst; Technical Support Representative. **Average salary range of placements:** $30,000 - $50,000. **Number of placements per year:** 1000+.

BELCAN TECHNICAL SERVICES
2494 Technical Drive, Miamisburg OH 45342. 937/859-8880. **Contact:** Manager. **Description:** A permanent employment agency. **Specializes in the areas of:** Computer Science/Software; Engineering.

RICHARD L. BENCIN & ASSOCIATES
8553 Timber Trail, Cleveland OH 44141. 216/526-6726. **Contact:** Richard Bencin. **Description:** A permanent employment agency that places personnel in call centers. **Specializes in the areas of:** Direct Marketing; Telemarketing.

N.L. BENKE & ASSOCIATES, INC.
1422 Euclid Avenue, Suite 956, Cleveland OH 44115. 216/771-6822. **Contact:** Norman L. Benke, President. **Description:** A permanent employment agency. Company pays fee. **Specializes in the areas of:** Accounting/Auditing; Banking; Computer Science/Software; Finance; Insurance; Personnel/Labor Relations. **Positions commonly filled include:** Accountant/Auditor; Adjuster; Administrative Manager; Attorney; Bank Officer/Manager; Budget Analyst; Buyer; Clerical Supervisor; Computer Programmer; Credit Manager; Customer Service Rep.; Economist; Financial Analyst; Human Resources Manager; Management Analyst/Consultant; Management Trainee; Purchasing Agent/Manager; Quality Control Supervisor; Securities Sales Rep.; Software Engineer; Systems Analyst; Underwriter/Assistant Underwriter. **Number of placements per year:** 200 - 499.

BRADLEY-PIERCE PERSONNEL
1392 Warren Road, Cleveland OH 44107. 216/521-0032. **Fax:** 216/521-0032. **Contact:** Recruiter. **Description:** A permanent employment agency. **Specializes in the areas of:** Accounting/Auditing; Banking; Engineering; Finance; Manufacturing; Personnel/Labor Relations. **Positions commonly filled include:** Accountant/Auditor; Administrative Manager; Bank Officer/Manager; Chemical Engineer; Chemist; Credit Manager; Customer Service Rep.; Electrical/Electronics Engineer; Human Resources Specialist; Industrial Engineer; Management Trainee; Manufacturer's/Wholesaler's Sales Rep.; Mechanical Engineer.

CBS PERSONNEL SERVICES
435 Elm Street, Suite 700, Cincinnati OH 45202. 513/651-1111. **Fax:** 513/651-3052. **Contact:** Manager. **Description:** A full-service employment agency offering permanent, temporary, and contract placements. The agency also provides career/outplacement counseling. Company pays fee. **Specializes in the areas of:** Accounting/Auditing; Administration; Banking; Bookkeeping; Clerical; Computer Science/Software; Engineering; Finance; General Management; Health/Medical; Industrial; Manufacturing; Personnel/Labor Relations; Retail; Sales; Secretarial; Technical; Transportation. **Positions commonly filled include:** Accountant/Auditor; Actuary; Adjuster; Administrative Manager; Advertising Clerk; Bank Officer/Manager; Blue-Collar Worker Supervisor; Budget Analyst; Chemical Engineer; Civil Engineer; Claim Rep.; Clerical Supervisor; Clinical Lab Technician; Computer Programmer; Counselor; Credit Manager; Customer Service Rep.; Dental Assistant/Hygienist; Design Engineer; Designer; Dietician/Nutritionist; Draftsperson; Economist; EEG Technologist; EKG Technician; Electrical/Electronics Engineer; Emergency Medical Technician; Financial Analyst; Food Scientist/Technologist; Health Services Manager; Human Resources Specialist; Industrial Engineer; Internet Services Manager; Licensed Practical Nurse; Management Analyst/Consultant; Management Trainee; Manufacturer's/Wholesaler's Sales Rep.; Market Research Analyst; Mechanical Engineer; Medical Records Technician; MIS Specialist; Multimedia Designer; Occupational Therapist; Operations/Production Manager; Physical Therapist; Public Relations Specialist; Purchasing Agent/Manager; Quality Control Supervisor; Radiological Technologist; Recreational Therapist; Registered Nurse; Respiratory Therapist; Science Technologist; Securities Sales Rep.; Services Sales Rep.; Software Engineer; Strategic Relations Manager; Structural Engineer; Surgical Technician; Systems Analyst; Technical Writer/Editor; Telecommunications Manager; Typist/Word Processor. **Benefits available to temporary workers:** Medical Insurance.
Other area locations:

- 130 West Second Street, Suite 1910, Dayton OH 45402. 937/222-2525. (Clerical; Computer Science/Software; Finance; Office Support)

CAREER CONNECTIONS, INC.
35 Elliott Street, Athens OH 45701. 740/594-4941. **Fax:** 740/592-6289. **Contact:** Valerie Kinnard, General Manager. **E-mail address:** careerconnections@compuserve.com. **Description:** A permanent employment agency. Company pays fee. **Specializes in the areas of:** Administration; General Management; Industrial; Light Industrial; Manufacturing; Secretarial. **Positions commonly filled include:** Automotive Mechanic; Computer Programmer; Customer Service Rep.; Paralegal; Social Worker; Technical Writer/Editor. **Average salary range of placements:** Less than $20,000. **Number of placements per year:** 200 - 499.

CHAMPION PERSONNEL SYSTEM, INC.
CHAMPION OFFICE STAFFING
668 Euclid Avenue, Suite 300A, Cleveland OH 44114. 216/781-5900. **Fax:** 216/781-8786. **Contact:** Robert Schepens, President. **E-mail address:** hdhntr1@aol.com. **Description:** A permanent employment agency that also provides temporary placement. Company pays fee. **Specializes in the areas of:** Accounting/Auditing; Administration; Advertising; Bookkeeping; Broadcasting; Clerical; Finance; Health/Medical; Personnel/Labor Relations; Publishing; Secretarial; Word Processing. **Positions commonly filled include:** Accountant/Auditor; Bookkeeper; Budget Analyst; Clerical Supervisor; Credit Manager; Customer Service Rep.; Financial Analyst; Human Resources Specialist; Office Manager; Tax Specialist; Typist/Word Processor. **Benefits available to temporary workers:** Bonus Award/Plan; Paid Vacation. **Other area locations:** Beachwood OH. **Number of placements per year:** 1000+.

CLOPTON'S PLACEMENT SERVICE
23241 Shurmer Drive, Cleveland OH 44128-4927. 216/292-4830. **Fax:** 216/292-4830. **Contact:** Fred Clopton, President. **Description:** A permanent employment agency. **Specializes in the areas of:** Computer Science/Software; Engineering; Technical. **Positions commonly filled include:** Biomedical Engineer; Electrical/Electronics Engineer; Mechanical

Engineer; Quality Control Supervisor; Software Engineer; Systems Analyst; Technical Writer/Editor. **Number of placements per year:** 1 - 49.

CORELL ASSOCIATES
5017 Cooper Road, Cincinnati OH 45242. 513/793-9808. **Fax:** 513/793-9304. **Contact:** Ed Corell, Owner. **Description:** A permanent employment agency. Company pays fee. **Specializes in the areas of:** Accounting/Auditing; Engineering; Industrial; Manufacturing; Technical. **Positions commonly filled include:** Accountant/Auditor; Actuary; Adjuster; Aerospace Engineer; Agricultural Engineer; Biological Scientist; Biomedical Engineer; Blue-Collar Worker Supervisor; Buyer; Ceramics Engineer; Chemical Engineer; Chemist; Civil Engineer; Collector; Computer Programmer; Designer; Draftsperson; Electrical/Electronics Engineer; Financial Analyst; Human Resources Manager; Industrial Engineer; Industrial Production Manager; Management Trainee; Materials Engineer; Mechanical Engineer; Metallurgical Engineer; Mining Engineer; Petroleum Engineer; Purchasing Agent/Manager; Quality Control Supervisor; Science Technologist; Software Engineer; Structural Engineer; Systems Analyst;. **Number of placements per year:** 1 - 49.

CORPORATE DIRECTIONS GROUP
26777 Lorain Road, Suite 602, Cleveland OH 44070-3200. 440/734-1360. **Fax:** 440/734-1939. **Contact:** Leslee Basgaitis, Senior Partner. **Description:** A permanent employment agency. Company pays fee. **Specializes in the areas of:** Sales. **Number of placements per year:** 50 - 99.

DANKOWSKI AND ASSOCIATES, INC.
P.O. Box 39478, North Ridgeville OH 44039. 440/327-8717. **Contact:** Thomas A. Dankowski, Owner. **Description:** A permanent employment agency. **Specializes in the areas of:** Personnel/Labor Relations. **Positions commonly filled include:** Human Resources Manager.

ALAN N. DAUM & ASSOCIATES
6233 Riverside Drive, Dublin OH 43017. 614/793-1200. **Contact:** Alan N. Daum, President. **E-mail address:** aldaum@aol.com. **Description:** A permanent employment agency. Company pays fee. **Specializes in the areas of:** Computer Hardware/Software; Engineering; Food Industry; Manufacturing; Technical. **Positions commonly filled include:** Computer Programmer; Electrical/Electronics Engineer; Software Engineer. **Number of placements per year:** 1 - 49.

TONIA DEAL CONSULTANTS
77 Milford Corporation Center, Hudson OH 44236. 216/655-3610. **Fax:** 216/655-3629. **Contact:** Brian DiFeo, Recruiting Manager. **E-mail address:** tdc@gwis.com. **Description:** A permanent employment agency and executive search firm. Company pays fee. **Specializes in the areas of:** Engineering; General Management; Purchasing; Technical; Transportation. **Positions commonly filled include:** Buyer; Chemical Engineer; Chemist; Cost Estimator; Industrial Engineer; Industrial Production Manager; Mechanical Engineer; Purchasing Agent/Manager; Quality Control Supervisor; Transportation/Traffic Specialist. **Number of placements per year:** 1 - 49.

DENTAL PERSONNEL PLACEMENT SERVICE
5597 Valencia Park Boulevard, Hilliard OH 43026-8795. 614/529-8367. **Contact:** Tracy Brown, Owner. **E-mail address:** tbrown@netset.com. **Description:** A permanent employment agency that also provides temporary placement for dental assistants, dentists, hygienists, and front desk personnel. Company pays fee. **Average salary range of placements:** $30,000 - $50,000. **Number of placements per year:** 200 - 499.

DOWNING & DOWNING
7757 Auburn Road, Unit 9, Concord OH 44077. 440/357-1996. **Contact:** Gus Downing, Owner. **Description:** A permanent employment agency. **Specializes in the areas of:** Security. **Positions commonly filled include:** Investigator; Loss Prevention Specialist; Security Manager.

EASTERN PERSONNEL SERVICES INC.
326 West 4th Street, Cincinnati OH 45202. 513/421-4666. **Contact:** Manager. **Description:** A permanent employment agency that also provides temporary and contract placements. Company pays fee. **Specializes in the areas of:** Accounting/Auditing; Administration; Advertising; Architecture/Construction; Art/Design; Banking; Computer Science/Software; Education; Engineering; Finance; Food Industry; General Management; Health/Medical; Industrial; Insurance; Legal; Manufacturing; Nonprofit; Personnel/Labor Relations; Publishing; Retail; Sales; Secretarial; Technical; Transportation. **Positions commonly filled include:** Accountant/Auditor; Administrative Manager; Advertising Clerk; Architect; Bank Officer/Manager; Civil Engineer; Claim Rep.; Clerical Supervisor; Clinical Lab Technician; Computer Programmer; Construction and Building Inspector; Construction Contractor; Counselor; Credit Manager; Customer Service Rep.; Dental Assistant/Hygienist; Dentist; Design Engineer; Designer; Dietician/Nutritionist; Draftsperson; Editor; Education Administrator; Electrical/Electronics Engineer; Electrician; Emergency Medical Technician; Environmental Engineer; Financial Analyst; Health Services Manager; Human Resources Specialist; Human Service Worker; Industrial Engineer; Landscape Architect; Licensed Practical Nurse; Management Analyst/Consultant; Management Trainee; Manufacturer's/Wholesaler's Sales Rep.; Market Research Analyst; Mechanical Engineer; Medical Records Technician; MIS Specialist; Multimedia Designer; Occupational Therapist; Operations/Production Manager; Paralegal; Petroleum Engineer; Physical Therapist; Preschool Worker; Property and Real Estate Manager; Public Relations Specialist; Purchasing Agent/Manager; Quality Control Supervisor; Registered Nurse; Restaurant/Food Service Manager; Securities Sales Rep.; Social Worker; Software Engineer; Structural Engineer; Surveyor; Systems Analyst; Teacher/Professor; Technical Writer/Editor; Telecommunications Manager; Transportation/Traffic Specialist; Typist/Word Processor; Underwriter/Assistant Underwriter; Urban/Regional Planner; Video Production Coordinator. **Average salary range of placements:** $20,000 - $29,999. **Number of placements per year:** 200 - 499.

ELITE PERSONNEL AGENCY
940 Terminal Tower, Cleveland OH 44113. 216/771-7810. **Fax:** 216/348-7085. **Contact:** Recruiter. **Description:** A permanent employment agency. Company pays fee. **Specializes in the areas of:** Legal; Secretarial. **Average salary range of placements:** $20,000 - $29,999. **Number of placements per year:** 100 - 199.

ENTERPRISE SEARCH ASSOCIATES
77 West Elmwood Drive, Dayton OH 45459. 937/438-8774. **Contact:** Jeff Linck, Owner. **Description:** A permanent employment agency. Company pays fee. **Specializes in the areas of:** Administration; Computer Hardware/Software. **Positions commonly filled include:** Computer Programmer; EDP Specialist; MIS Specialist; Software Engineer; Systems Analyst.

EXACT PERSONNEL SPECIALISTS
Terminal Tower, Suite 820, Cleveland OH 44113. 216/736-4800. **Fax:** 216/696-5825. **Contact:** Linda Stevens, CPC, Executive Director. **Description:** A full-

service employment agency. Company pays fee. **Specializes in the areas of:** Accounting/Auditing; Legal; Secretarial. **Positions commonly filled include:** Administrative Assistant; Attorney; Executive Assistant; Human Resources Specialist; Legal Secretary; Management Trainee; Paralegal; Typist/ Word Processor. **Average salary range of placements:** $20,000 - $29,999. **Number of placements per year:** 200 - 499.

FWC RECRUITERS
P.O. Box 441193, Cleveland OH 44141. 216/351-3930. **Contact:** Manager. **Description:** A permanent employment agency that also offers contract services. **Specializes in the areas of:** Software Development.

FUNCTIONAL TECHNICAL SERVICES
4300 West Streetsboro Road, Ridgeville OH 44286. 216/659-2434. **Contact:** Owner. **Description:** A permanent employment agency. Company pays fee. **Specializes in the areas of:** Engineering; Manufacturing; Technical. **Positions commonly filled include:** Draftsperson; Electrical/Electronics Engineer; Factory Worker; Light Industrial Worker; Mechanical Engineer. **Number of placements per year:** 1 - 49.

GRADUATE CONSULTANTS
16600 Sprague Road, Suite 380, Middleburg Heights OH 44130. 440/891-6800. **Contact:** Bob Satullo, Owner. **Description:** A permanent employment agency focusing on the recruitment of recent college graduates. **Specializes in the areas of:** Banking; Finance; Food Industry; Retail. **Positions commonly filled include:** Bank Officer/Manager; Branch Manager; Claim Rep.; Management Trainee; Restaurant/Food Service Manager. **Average salary range of placements:** $20,000 - $29,999. **Number of placements per year:** 100 - 199.

GRAPHIC ARTS EMPLOYMENT SERVICE, INC.
2430 Central Parkway, Cincinnati OH 45214. 606/331-6567. **Fax:** 606/331-6568. **Contact:** James P. Carlin, President. **E-mail address:** gaes@ngtech.com. **World Wide Web address:** http://www.ngtech.com/gaes. **Description:** A permanent employment agency. Company pays fee. **Specializes in the areas of:** Packaging; Publishing. **Positions commonly filled include:** Cost Estimator; Customer Service Rep.; Electrical/Electronics Engineer; General Manager; Operations/Production Manager; Printing Press Operator; Quality Control Supervisor; Sales Rep. **Average salary range of placements:** $30,000 - $90,000. **Number of placements per year:** 1 - 49.

T. GROOMS & ASSOCIATES
P.O. Box 15342, Columbus OH 43215. 614/258-6712. **Contact:** Manager. **Description:** A permanent employment agency. **Specializes in the areas of:** Government. **Positions commonly filled include:** Corrections Officer; Firefighter; Police/Law Enforcement Officer.

DONALD A. HECKAMAN & ASSOCIATES INC.
23210 Chagrin Boulevard, Beachwood OH 44122. 216/591-1400. **Contact:** Manager. **Description:** A permanent employment agency that places personnel from entry-level up to mid-management.

T.J. HUGHES ASSOCIATES
16490 Heather Lane, Suite 102, Middleburg Heights OH 44130. 440/891-9151. **Contact:** Manager. **Description:** A permanent employment agency. **Specializes in the areas of:** Clerical.

RICHARD JOHNS CAREER CONSULTANTS
26949 Chagrin Boulevard, Suite 202, Cleveland OH 44122. 216/464-2912. **Fax:** 216/464-0927. **Contact:** Richard Johns, CPC, President. **Description:** A permanent employment agency. **Specializes in the areas of:** Accounting/Auditing; Banking; Film Production; Hotel/Restaurant; Retail.

ANNE JONES STAFFING, INC.
571 High Street, Worthington OH 43085-4132. 614/848-6033. **Toll-free phone:** 800/WIL-WORK. **Fax:** 614/848-6016. **Contact:** Sheila A. Jones, President. **Description:** A permanent employment agency that also provides temporary placements. Company pays fee. **Specializes in the areas of:** Health/Medical; Industrial; Secretarial. **Positions commonly filled include:** Administrative Assistant; Bookkeeper; Clerk; Customer Service Rep.; Dietician/ Nutritionist; Medical Secretary; Nurse; Office Manager; Receptionist; Secretary; Typist/Word Processor.

LAINE'S S.M.G.
P.O. Box 997, Shaker Heights OH 44120. 216/991-4125. **Contact:** Eunice Glenn, Owner. **Description:** A permanent employment agency that provides computerized job searches. The company also offers resume services. **Specializes in the areas of:** Accounting/Auditing; Architecture/Construction; Art/ Design; Banking; Education; Engineering; Fashion; Food Industry; General Management; Health/Medical; Industrial; Insurance; Legal; Manufacturing; Personnel/ Labor Relations; Publishing; Retail; Sales; Secretarial; Transportation. **Number of placements per year:** 1 - 49.

LEGAL STAFF CONSULTANTS
1336 Woodman Drive, Dayton OH 45432. 937/258-8757. **Fax:** 937/258-0865. **Contact:** Roy Wells, Manager. **Description:** A permanent employment agency. Company pays fee. **Specializes in the areas of:** Legal. **Positions commonly filled include:** Attorney; Legal Secretary; Paralegal. **Average salary range of placements:** $20,000 - $29,999. **Number of placements per year:** 100 - 199.

R.E. LOWE ASSOCIATES, INC.
8080 Ravines Edge Court, Worthington OH 43235. 614/436-6650. **Fax:** 614/436-2789. **Contact:** Dave Deringer, Recruiter. **Description:** A permanent employment agency. **Specializes in the areas of:** Accounting/Auditing; Computer Science/Software; Engineering; Finance; Health/Medical; Insurance. **Positions commonly filled include:** Accountant/ Auditor; Budget Analyst; Chemical Engineer; Claim Representative; Consultant; Credit Manager; Data Analyst; EDP Specialist; Electrical/Electronics Engineer; Environmental Engineer; Financial Analyst; Industrial Engineer; Manufacturing Engineer; Nurse; Packaging Engineer; Physician; Tax Specialist; Underwriter/Assistant Underwriter; Water/Wastewater Engineer. **Number of placements per year:** 200 - 499.

MEDICAL STAFF CONSULTANTS
1336 Woodman Drive, Dayton OH 45432. 937/258-0318. **Fax:** 937/258-0865. **Contact:** Chris Hucke, Manager. **Description:** A permanent employment agency. Company pays fee. **Specializes in the areas of:** Health/Medical. **Positions commonly filled include:** Claim Representative; Clinical Lab Technician; Dental Assistant/Dental Hygienist; Dentist; Dietician/ Nutritionist; EEG Technologist; EKG Technician; Emergency Medical Technician; Health Services Manager; Licensed Practical Nurse; Medical Assistant; Medical Records Technician; Medical Secretary; Occupational Therapist; Pharmacist; Physical Therapist; Physician; Psychologist; Radiological Technologist; Receptionist; Recreational Therapist; Registered Nurse; Respiratory Therapist; Social Worker; Sociologist; Speech-Language Pathologist; Surgical Technician. **Average salary range of placements:** $20,000 - $29,999. **Number of placements per year:** 200 - 499.

MEDSEARCH STAFFING SERVICES INC.
7271 Engle Road, Suite 115, Middleburg Heights OH 44130. 440/243-6363. **Contact:** Ralph E. Steeber, CPC, President. **E-mail address:** rsteeber@medstaffing.com. **World Wide Web address:** http://www.medstaffing.com. **Description:** A permanent employment agency. Company pays fee. **Specializes in the areas of:** Health/Medical. **Positions commonly filled include:** Marketing Specialist; Medical Secretary; Occupational Therapist; Pharmacist; Physical Therapist; Physician; Psychologist; Respiratory Therapist; Sales Manager; Sales Rep.; Surgical Technician. **Number of placements per year:** 100 - 199.

NATIONAL CORPORATE SERVICES, INC.
240 West Elmwood Drive, Suite 2010, Dayton OH 45459. 937/435-3100. **Fax:** 937/436-0802. **Contact:** Tammy Osborn, Division Manager. **E-mail address:** ncs452@aol.com. **Description:** A permanent employment agency. Company pays fee. **Specializes in the areas of:** Convenience Stores. **Positions commonly filled include:** Accountant/Auditor; Buyer; District Manager; General Manager; Marketing Manager; Supervisor. **Number of placements per year:** 100 - 199.

OHIO BUREAU OF EMPLOYMENT SERVICES
P.O. Box 398, Marysville OH 43040-0398. 937/644-9195. **Fax:** 937/642-1129. **Contact:** Jo Ann Lee, Manager. **Description:** A permanent employment agency and state unemployment office. **Positions commonly filled include:** Administrative Assistant; Bookkeeper; Clerk; Construction Trade Worker; Customer Service Rep.; Data Entry Clerk; Electrical/Electronics Engineer; Legal Secretary; Mechanical Engineer; Medical Secretary; Purchasing Agent/Manager; Quality Control Supervisor; Receptionist; Secretary; Typist/Word Processor. **Number of placements per year:** 500 - 999.

OPRANDI STAFFING
15 West Locust Street, Newark OH 43055. 740/345-9783. **Contact:** Manager. **Description:** A permanent employment agency that also offers temporary placements.

JERRY PAUL ASSOCIATES
1662 State Road, Cuyahoga Falls OH 44223. 330/923-2345. **Contact:** Jerry Paul, President. **Description:** A permanent employment agency. **Specializes in the areas of:** Administration; Banking; Computer Hardware/Software; Hotel/Restaurant; Sales. **Positions commonly filled include:** Hotel Manager; Restaurant/Food Service Manager; Sales Rep. **Number of placements per year:** 50 - 99.

PROFESSIONAL DOMESTIC SERVICES
6660 Doubletree Avenue, Columbus OH 43229. **Contact:** Recruiter. **Description:** A permanent employment agency that places household professionals including butlers, chefs, personal assistants, nannies, and household managers. **Positions commonly filled include:** Chef/Cook/Kitchen Worker; Nanny; Teacher/Professor. **Average salary range of placements:** $30,000 - $50,000.

PROFESSIONAL EMPLOYMENT SERVICES
6957A Promway Avenue NW, North Canton OH 44720. 330/966-2277. **Fax:** 330/966-2419. **Contact:** Audrey H. Stull, Vice President/Owner. **Description:** A permanent employment agency. Founded in 1992. Company pays fee. **Specializes in the areas of:** Health/Medical; Industrial; Legal; Manufacturing; Marketing; Non-Specialized; Sales; Scientific; Technical. **Positions commonly filled include:** Accountant/Auditor; Blue-Collar Worker Supervisor; Clinical Lab Technician; Computer Programmer; Dental Assistant/Hygienist; Draftsperson; Industrial Production Manager; Management Trainee; Typist/Word Processor. **Benefits available to temporary workers:** Paid Holidays; Paid Vacation. **Corporate headquarters location:** Akron OH. **Other area locations:** Barberton OH; Streetsboro OH. **Number of placements per year:** 1000+.

PROFESSIONAL RESTAFFING OF OHIO, INC.
373 North Washington Street, Tiffin OH 44883-1361. 419/447-3465. **Contact:** Recruiter. **Description:** A permanent employment agency. Company pays fee. **Specializes in the areas of:** Accounting/Auditing; Engineering; Food Industry; Industrial; Manufacturing; Personnel/Labor Relations; Sales; Secretarial. **Positions commonly filled include:** Accountant/Auditor; Administrative Manager; Blue-Collar Worker Supervisor; Clerical Supervisor; Computer Programmer; Customer Service Rep.; Design Engineer; Draftsperson; Occupational Therapist; Paralegal; Physical Therapist; Services Sales Rep.; Systems Analyst; Typist/Word Processor. **Benefits available to temporary workers:** Paid Vacation. **Number of placements per year:** 200 - 499.

QUALITY ASSOCIATES INC.
4921 Para Drive, Cincinnati OH 45237. 513/242-4477. **Contact:** Manager. **Description:** A permanent placement agency.

REED RECRUITING INC.
P.O. Box 3262, Cuyahoga Falls OH 44223. 330/825-4500. **Fax:** 330/825-7442. **Contact:** Denise Szabo, Medical Recruiter. **Description:** A permanent employment agency. **Specializes in the areas of:** Health/Medical. **Positions commonly filled include:** Dentist; Physician; Psychologist; Registered Nurse; Social Worker.

RENTECH VENTURES, INC.
P.O. Box 23159, Chagrin Falls OH 44023. 440/548-8311. **Fax:** 440/548-8306. **Contact:** Rose Renovich, President. **Description:** A professional permanent employment agency that also provides career testing and counseling. The agency's primary focus is on educators. **Specializes in the areas of:** Education; Engineering; General Management; Industrial; Legal; Manufacturing; Nonprofit; Personnel/Labor Relations; Technical.

THE RESERVES NETWORK
2525 Maple Avenue, Zanesville OH 43702-2674. 740/453-0326. **Contact:** Manager. **Description:** A permanent employment agency. Company pays fee. **Specializes in the areas of:** Manufacturing; Mining. **Positions commonly filled include:** Accountant/Auditor; Bookkeeper; Buyer; Ceramics Engineer; Chemical Engineer; Chemist; Civil Engineer; Clerk; Computer Programmer; Data Entry Clerk; Draftsperson; EDP Specialist; Electrical/Electronics Engineer; Industrial Engineer; Legal Secretary; Mechanical Engineer; Medical Secretary; Metallurgical Engineer; Office Manager; Operations/Production Manager; Purchasing Agent/Manager; Quality Control Supervisor; Receptionist; Sales Rep.; Secretary; Stenographer; Systems Analyst; Technical Writer/Editor; Technician; Typist/Word Processor. **Number of placements per year:** 50 - 99.

SELECTIVE SEARCH ASSOCIATES
1206 North Main Street, Suite 112, North Canton OH 44720. 330/494-5584. **Fax:** 330/494-8911. **Contact:** Michael E. Ziarko, President. **Description:** A permanent employment agency. Company pays fee. **Specializes in the areas of:** Computer Science/Software; Engineering. **Positions commonly filled include:** Computer Programmer; Electrical/Electronics Engineer; Mechanical Engineer; Nuclear Engineer; Software

Engineer; Systems Analyst. **Number of placements per year:** 1 - 49.

TALENT TREE STAFFING SERVICES
6500 Poe Avenue, Dayton OH 45414. **Contact:** Recruiter. **Description:** A permanent employment agency. **Specializes in the areas of:** Retail; Sales; Secretarial. **Positions commonly filled include:** Computer Programmer; Construction Contractor; Electrician; Human Resources Specialist; Management Trainee; MIS Specialist; Services Sales Rep.; Software Engineer; Systems Analyst; Technical Writer/Editor; Typist/Word Processor. **Benefits available to temporary workers:** 401(k); Medical Insurance; Paid Vacation; Stock Option. **Corporate headquarters location:** Houston TX.

TALENT TREE STAFFING SERVICES
3540 Secor Road, Suite 303, Toledo OH 43606. 419/535-9911. **Fax:** 419/535-8415. **Contact:** April Reinhart, General Manager. **Description:** A permanent employment agency that also provides temporary placements. Company pays fee. **Specializes in the areas of:** Administration; Computer Science/Software; Food Industry; General Management; Industrial; Legal; Manufacturing; Secretarial. **Positions commonly filled include:** Accountant/Auditor; Administrative Manager; Blue-Collar Worker Supervisor; Customer Service Rep.; Draftsperson; Human Resources Specialist; Industrial Engineer; Management Trainee; Mechanical Engineer; Operations/Production Manager; Public Relations Specialist; Quality Control Supervisor; Restaurant/Food Service Manager; Services Sales Rep.; Software Engineer; Telecommunications Manager; Typist/Word Processor. **Benefits available to temporary workers:** 401(k); Dental Insurance; Medical Insurance; Paid Holidays; Paid Vacation. **Corporate headquarters location:** Houston TX. **Other U.S. locations:** Nationwide. **Number of placements per year:** 1 - 49.

TEAM AMERICA
110 East Wilson Bridge Road, Worthington OH 43085. 614/848-3995. **Toll-free phone:** 800/962-2758. **Fax:** 614/848-8702. **Recorded jobline:** 614/848-6008x4. **Contact:** Tish Scheck, Placement Coordinator. **Description:** A permanent employment agency. **Specializes in the areas of:** Publishing; Sales; Secretarial. **Positions commonly filled include:** Customer Service Rep.; Electrician; Landscape Architect; Warehouse/Distribution Worker. **Corporate headquarters location:** This Location. **Other U.S. locations:** Cleveland OH; Dayton OH.

TECH/AID OF OHIO
34950 Chardon Road, Suite 101, Willoughby Hills OH 44094. 216/749-3060. **Contact:** Manager. **Description:** A permanent employment agency. Company pays fee. **Specializes in the areas of:** Accounting/Auditing; Banking; Computer Hardware/Software; Engineering; Finance; Insurance; Manufacturing; MIS/EDP; Nonprofit; Personnel/Labor Relations; Publishing; Technical. **Positions commonly filled include:** Computer Operator; Computer Programmer; EDP Specialist; MIS Specialist; Systems Analyst; Technical Writer/Editor. **Number of placements per year:** 1000+.

TECHNICAL/MANAGEMENT RESOURCES
310 Lorraine Drive, Pickerington OH 43147. 614/837-8888. **Fax:** 614/837-9718. **Contact:** Gordon S. Mead, President. **E-mail address:** techmgmtr@sprintmail.com. **Description:** A permanent employment agency. Company pays fee. **Specializes in the areas of:** Engineering; Industrial. **Positions commonly filled include:** Electrical/Electronics Engineer; General Manager; Industrial Engineer; Manufacturing Engineer; Mechanical Engineer; Operations Manager; Production Manager. **Average salary range of placements:** More than $50,000. **Number of placements per year:** 1 - 49.

VECTOR TECHNICAL
7911 Enterprise Drive, 2nd Floor, Mentor OH 44060. 440/946-8800. **Fax:** 440/946-8808. **Contact:** Timothy Bleich, Vice President. **E-mail address:** vectortech@ncweb.com. **World Wide Web address:** http://www.vectortechnicalinc.com. **Description:** A permanent employment agency. Company pays fee. **Specializes in the areas of:** Biology; Computer Science/Software; Engineering; Industrial; Manufacturing; Technical. **Positions commonly filled include:** Aerospace Engineer; Agricultural Engineer; Architect; Biological Scientist; Biomedical Engineer; Blue-Collar Worker Supervisor; Ceramics Engineer; Chemical Engineer; Chemist; Civil Engineer; Computer Programmer; Cost Estimator; Designer; Draftsperson; Electrical/Electronics Engineer; Electrician; Industrial Engineer; Industrial Production Manager; Materials Engineer; Mechanical Engineer; Metallurgical Engineer; Mining Engineer; Nuclear Engineer; Operations/Production Manager; Software Engineer; Stationary Engineer; Structural Engineer; Systems Analyst. **Number of placements per year:** 100 - 199.

WARNER & ASSOCIATES, INC.
101 East College Avenue, Westerville OH 43081. 614/891-9003. **Fax:** 614/890-8405. **Contact:** Tom Warner, President. **Description:** A permanent employment agency. **Specializes in the areas of:** Engineering; Manufacturing; Materials. **Positions commonly filled include:** Chemical Engineer; Civil Engineer; Electrical/Electronics Engineer; Environmental Engineer; Industrial Engineer; Inventory Control Specialist; Manufacturing Engineer; Mechanical Engineer; Packaging Engineer; Plant Manager; Purchasing Agent/Manager; Quality Control Supervisor; Water/Wastewater Engineer.

TEMPORARY EMPLOYMENT AGENCIES

ACCUSTAFF
1014 Vine Street, Suite 1650, Cincinnati OH 45202-1141. 513/241-4222. **Fax:** 513/241-5294. **Contact:** Manager. **Description:** A temporary placement agency. Company pays fee. **Specializes in the areas of:** Administration; Banking; Computer Science/Software; Industrial; Legal; Manufacturing; Personnel/Labor Relations; Publishing; Secretarial. **Positions commonly filled include:** Attorney; Bank Officer/Manager; Blue-Collar Worker Supervisor; Claim Rep.; Clerical Supervisor; Computer Programmer; Credit Manager; Customer Service Rep.; Dietician/Nutritionist; Draftsperson; Editor; Financial Analyst; General Manager; Human Resources Specialist; Human Service Worker; Management Trainee; Manufacturer's/Wholesaler's Sales Rep.; MIS Specialist; Operations/Production Manager; Paralegal; Pharmacist; Property and Real Estate Manager; Public Relations Manager; Purchasing Agent/Manager; Quality Control Supervisor; Restaurant/Food Service Manager; Services Sales Rep.; Systems Analyst; Typist/Word Processor; Underwriter/Assistant Underwriter. **Average salary range of placements:** $20,000 - $29,999. **Number of placements per year:** 1 - 49.

ADECCO
3655 Soldano Boulevard, Columbus OH 43228. 614/279-6614. **Contact:** Monica Polly, Manager. **Description:** A temporary agency. Company pays fee. **Specializes in the areas of:** Clerical; Construction; Food Industry; Personnel/Labor Relations. **Positions commonly filled include:** Computer Operator;

Computer Programmer; Construction Trade Worker; Data Entry Clerk; Draftsperson; Driver; Factory Worker; Food Scientist/Technologist; Food Service Manager; Light Industrial Worker; Office Manager; Operations/Production Manager; Quality Control Supervisor; Receptionist; Typist/Word Processor. **Number of placements per year:** 500 - 999.

ALL STAR PERSONNEL, INC.
21625 Chagrin Road, Suite 260, Beachwood OH 44122. 216/991-7827. **Fax:** 216/991-3704. **Contact:** Joyce Goodman, CPC, President. **Description:** A temporary agency that also provides permanent placements. Company pays fee. **Specializes in the areas of:** Administration; Computer Science/Software; Secretarial. **Positions commonly filled include:** Computer Programmer; MIS Specialist; Securities Sales Rep.; Systems Analyst; Typist/Word Processor. **Number of placements per year:** 50 - 99.

BELCAN STAFFING SERVICES
425 Walnut Street, Suite 200, Cincinnati OH 45202. 513/241-8367. **Contact:** Mary Beth Puthoff, Area Recruiter. **E-mail address:** mbp@belrs.belcan.com. **Description:** A temporary agency that provides short-term, long-term, and temp-to-hire positions. The agency focuses on office clerical and light industrial placements. Company pays fee. **Specializes in the areas of:** Clerical; Data Processing; General Labor; Health/Medical; Professional; Secretarial; Word Processing. **Positions commonly filled include:** Accountant/Auditor; Blue-Collar Worker Supervisor; Claim Rep.; Credit Manager; Customer Service Rep.; Financial Analyst; Health Services Manager; Human Resources Specialist; Management Trainee; Medical Records Technician; Services Sales Rep. **Benefits available to temporary workers:** 401(k); Medical Insurance; Paid Holidays; Paid Vacation; Referral Bonus Plan. **Other U.S. locations:** Florence KY; Raleigh NC; Fairfield OH; Kenwood OH. **Average salary range of placements:** Less than $20,000. **Number of placements per year:** 1000+.

CROWN TEMPORARY SERVICES OF CINCINNATI
230 Northland Boulevard, Suite 300, Cincinnati OH 45246. 513/772-7242. **Contact:** Dick Diana, Manager. **Description:** A temporary agency. Company pays fee. **Specializes in the areas of:** Accounting/Auditing; Banking; Clerical; Engineering; Finance; Insurance; Legal; Manufacturing; Personnel/Labor Relations. **Positions commonly filled include:** Accountant/Auditor; Administrative Assistant; Advertising Clerk; Bookkeeper; Claim Representative; Clerk; Computer Operator; Computer Programmer; Construction Trade Worker. **Number of placements per year:** 1000+.

CROWN TEMPORARY SERVICES OF CINCINNATI
7796 Montgomery Road, Cincinnati OH 45236. 513/793-0444. **Contact:** Manager. **Description:** A temporary agency. Company pays fee. **Specializes in the areas of:** Accounting/Auditing; Banking; Clerical; Engineering; Finance; Insurance; Legal; Manufacturing; Personnel/Labor Relations. **Positions commonly filled include:** Accountant/Auditor; Administrative Assistant; Advertising Clerk; Bookkeeper; Claim Rep.; Clerk; Computer Programmer; Construction Trade Worker; Customer Service Rep.; Data Entry Clerk; Legal Secretary; Light Industrial Worker; Marketing Specialist; Medical Secretary; Office Manager; Receptionist; Sales Rep.; Secretary; Typist/Word Processor. **Number of placements per year:** 1000+.

CUSTOM STAFFING, INC.
712 West North Street, Lima OH 45801. 419/221-3097. **Toll-free phone:** 800/860-3072. **Fax:** 419/221-2564. **Contact:** D. Roche Simmons, Manager. **Description:** A temporary agency. **Specializes in the areas of:** Accounting/Auditing; Industrial; Manufacturing; Secretarial; Technical. **Positions commonly filled include:** Accountant/Auditor; Blue-Collar Worker Supervisor; Broadcast Technician; Clerical Supervisor; Clinical Lab Technician; Computer Programmer; Customer Service Rep.; Draftsperson; Electrician; Landscape Architect; Licensed Practical Nurse; Medical Records Technician; Registered Nurse. **Other U.S. locations:** Columbus OH; Findlay OH; Marysville OH. **Average salary range of placements:** Less than $20,000. **Number of placements per year:** 200 - 499.

DELTA DESIGN DRAFTING INC.
12019 County Road 8, Delta OH 43515. 419/822-3686. **Fax:** 419/822-3686. **Contact:** Mike Gormley, President. **World Wide Web address:** http://www.bright.net/~deltadd/. **Description:** A temporary agency that also offers permanent placement and contract services. Company pays fee. **Specializes in the areas of:** Architecture/Construction; Engineering; Food Industry; Industrial; Manufacturing; Secretarial; Technical. **Positions commonly filled include:** Architect; Chemical Engineer; Clerical Supervisor; Construction and Building Inspector; Cost Estimator; Design Engineer; Draftsperson; Electrical/Electronics Engineer; Environmental Engineer; Human Resources Specialist; Industrial Engineer; Mechanical Engineer; Petroleum Engineer; Quality Control Supervisor; Software Engineer; Structural Engineer; Technical Writer/Editor; Typist/Word Processor. **Benefits available to temporary workers:** Life Insurance; Medical Insurance; Paid Holidays; Paid Vacation. **Average salary range of placements:** $30,000 - $50,000. **Number of placements per year:** 1 - 49.

EXTRA HELP TEMPORARY SERVICE
120 West 2nd Street, Suite 1010, Dayton OH 45402. 937/224-1452. **Contact:** Paul L. Sacksteder, President. **Description:** A temporary agency. Company pays fee. **Specializes in the areas of:** Clerical; Construction; Legal; Manufacturing. **Positions commonly filled include:** Administrative Assistant; Advertising Clerk; Bookkeeper; Claim Rep.; Clerk; Construction Trade Worker; Customer Service Rep.; Data Entry Clerk; Draftsperson; Factory Worker; Legal Secretary; Light Industrial Worker; Medical Secretary; Office Manager; Receptionist; Secretary; Stenographer; Typist/Word Processor. **Number of placements per year:** 500 - 999.

R.L. GIRTON ASSOCIATES INC.
1557 Briarwood Way, Uniontown OH 44685. 330/896-3616. **Contact:** Manager. **Description:** A temporary agency. **Specializes in the areas of:** Plastics; Rubber. **Positions commonly filled include:** Facilities Engineer.

INTERIM PERSONNEL
6924 Spring Valley Drive, Suite 240, Holland OH 43528. 419/865-3017. **Contact:** Manager. **Description:** A temporary agency that also provides permanent placements. Company pays fee. **Specializes in the areas of:** Engineering; Industrial; Manufacturing; Personnel/Labor Relations; Technical. **Positions commonly filled include:** Blue-Collar Worker Supervisor; Bookkeeper; Chemical Engineer; Clerk; Computer Programmer; Credit Manager; Customer Service Rep.; Data Entry Clerk; Design Engineer; Draftsperson; Electrical/Electronics Engineer; Human Resources Specialist; Industrial Engineer; Legal Secretary; Light Industrial Worker; Mechanical Engineer; Medical Secretary; MIS Specialist; Office Manager; Paralegal; Purchasing Agent/Manager; Quality Control Supervisor; Receptionist; Science Technologist; Secretary; Systems Analyst; Technician; Typist/Word Processor. **Benefits available to temporary workers:** Medical Insurance; Paid Holidays;

Paid Vacation. **Corporate headquarters location:** Fort Lauderdale FL. **Other U.S. locations:** Nationwide. **Number of placements per year:** 1000+.

JOB EXPRESS
6660 North High Street, Worthington OH 43085. 614/759-4696. **Toll-free phone:** 800/759-4696. **Fax:** 614/759-4660. **Contact:** Cindy Skalican, Principal. **Description:** A temporary agency that also provides permanent placements and contract services. Job Express offers career counseling, resume services, and a resume database on the Internet. Company pays fee. **Specializes in the areas of:** Administration; Office Support; Retail; Sales; Secretarial; Transportation. **Positions commonly filled include:** Accountant/Auditor; Blue-Collar Worker Supervisor; Clerical Supervisor; Customer Service Rep; Electrical/Electronics Engineer; Electrician; Human Resources Specialist; Manufacturer's/Wholesaler's Sales Rep.; Restaurant/Food Service Manager; Transportation/Traffic Specialist; Typist/Word Processor. **Benefits available to temporary workers:** Medical Insurance; Paid Holidays; Paid Vacation. **Average salary range of placements:** $20,000 - $29,999. **Number of placements per year:** 200 - 499.

KELLY SERVICES, INC.
6430 East Main Street, Reynoldsburg OH 43068. 614/221-6775. **Fax:** 614/224-9169. **Contact:** Cherie Nelson, District Manager. **Description:** A temporary agency. Kelly Services also provides permanent placement in the areas of office services, marketing, technical, light industrial, and outsourcing. Company pays fee. **Specializes in the areas of:** Accounting/Auditing; Banking; Computer Science/Software; Finance; Industrial; Insurance; Legal; Manufacturing; Personnel/Labor Relations; Secretarial. **Positions commonly filled include:** Accountant/Auditor; Administrative Manager; Blue-Collar Worker Supervisor; Claim Rep.; Clerical Supervisor; Clinical Lab Technician; Computer Programmer; Credit Manager; Draftsperson; Human Resources Specialist; Paralegal; Typist/Word Processor; Underwriter/Assistant Underwriter. **Benefits available to temporary workers:** Medical Insurance; Paid Holidays; Paid Vacation. **Corporate headquarters location:** Troy MI. **Other U.S. locations:** Nationwide. **Average salary range of placements:** Less than $20,000. **Number of placements per year:** 500 - 999.

MANPOWER TEMPORARY SERVICES
1275 North Fairfield Road, Dayton OH 45432-2633. 937/426-2668. **Fax:** 937/426-1762. **Contact:** Branch Manager. **Description:** A temporary agency. Company pays fee. **Specializes in the areas of:** Industrial; Sales; Secretarial. **Positions commonly filled include:** Claim Rep.; Clerical Supervisor; Customer Service Rep.; Paralegal; Property and Real Estate Manager; Public Relations Specialist; Purchasing Agent/Manager; Services Sales Rep.; Typist/Word Processor. **Average salary range of placements:** Less than $20,000. **Number of placements per year:** 200 - 499.

MANPOWER TEMPORARY SERVICES
70 Fairway Drive, Unit 3, Wilmington OH 45177. 937/382-4900. **Fax:** 937/383-1414. **Contact:** Branch Manager. **Description:** A temporary agency. Founded in 1948. **Specializes in the areas of:** Clerical; Computer Science/Software; Industrial; Manufacturing; Personnel/Labor Relations; Secretarial; Technical. **Positions commonly filled include:** Accountant/Auditor; Customer Service Representative. **Benefits available to temporary workers:** 401(k); Medical Insurance; Paid Holidays; Paid Vacation; Stock Purchase. **Corporate headquarters location:** Milwaukee WI. **Average salary range of placements:** Less than $20,000.

MANPOWER TEMPORARY SERVICES
One Cleveland Center, 1375 East 9th Street, Cleveland OH 44114-1724. 216/771-5474. **Contact:** Branch Manager. **Description:** A temporary agency. Company pays fee. **Specializes in the areas of:** Data Processing; Light Industrial; Office Support; Professional; Technical; Telemarketing; Word Processing. **Positions commonly filled include:** Accountant/Auditor; Accounting Clerk; Administrative Assistant; Biological Scientist; Bookkeeper; Chemist; Customer Service Rep.; Designer; Desktop Publishing Specialist; Electrician; Inspector/Tester/Grader; Inventory Control Specialist; Material Control Specialist; Packaging/Processing Worker; Painter; Proofreader; Receptionist; Records Manager; Research Assistant; Secretary; Software Engineer; Stock Clerk; Systems Analyst; Technical Writer/Editor; Technician; Telemarketer; Typist/Word Processor. **Benefits available to temporary workers:** Life Insurance; Medical Insurance; Paid Holidays; Paid Vacation. **Number of placements per year:** 1000+.

MANPOWER TEMPORARY SERVICES
3 Centennial Plaza, Suite 101, 895 Central Avenue, Cincinnati OH 45202-1961. 513/621-7250. **Contact:** Branch Manager. **Description:** A temporary agency. Company pays fee. **Specializes in the areas of:** Data Processing; Light Industrial; Office Support; Professional; Technical; Telemarketing; Word Processing. **Positions commonly filled include:** Accountant/Auditor; Accounting Clerk; Administrative Assistant; Assembler; Biological Scientist; Bookkeeper; Chemist; Customer Service Rep.; Designer; Desktop Publishing Specialist; Electrician; Inspector/Tester/Grader; Inventory Control Specialist; Material Control Specialist; Order Clerk; Packaging/Processing Worker; Painter; Proofreader; Receptionist; Records Manager; Research Assistant; Secretary; Software Engineer; Systems Analyst; Technical Writer/Editor; Technician; Telemarketer; Typist/Word Processor; Welder. **Benefits available to temporary workers:** Life Insurance; Medical Insurance; Paid Holidays; Paid Vacation. **Number of placements per year:** 1000+.

NESCO SERVICE COMPANY
1115 Lyons Road, Dayton OH 45458-1856. 937/435-2700. **Fax:** 937/435-2716. **Contact:** Duane Golden, District Manager. **Description:** A temporary agency. **Specializes in the areas of:** Industrial; Manufacturing. **Positions commonly filled include:** Draftsperson; Industrial Production Manager; Mechanical Engineer. **Benefits available to temporary workers:** 401(k); Medical Insurance; Paid Vacation. **Number of placements per year:** 500 - 999.

NORRELL SERVICES, INC.
5151 Monroe Street, Suite 110, Toledo OH 43623. 419/842-0111. **Contact:** Branch Manager. **Description:** A temporary agency. **Specializes in the areas of:** Banking; Clerical; Personnel/Labor Relations. **Positions commonly filled include:** Accountant/Auditor; Bookkeeper; Clerk; Computer Programmer; Data Entry Clerk; General Manager; Legal Secretary; Light Industrial Worker; Receptionist; Secretary; Stenographer; Typist/Word Processor. **Number of placements per year:** 1000+.

NORTH CENTRAL PERSONNEL POOL, INC.
713 South Main Street, Mansfield OH 44907. 419/756-9449. **Fax:** 419/756-4550. **Contact:** Jennifer Smith, Recruiter. **Description:** A temporary agency. Company pays fee. **Specializes in the areas of:** Health/Medical. **Positions commonly filled include:** Certified Nursing Aide; Nurse. **Corporate headquarters location:** New York NY. **Average salary range of placements:** $20,000 - $29,999. **Number of placements per year:** 1 - 49.

OLSTEN STAFFING SERVICES
2052 Front Street, Cuyahoga Falls OH 44221. 330/922-8367. **Contact:** Branch Manager. **Description:** A temporary agency. Company pays fee. **Specializes in the areas of:** Clerical; Manufacturing. **Positions commonly filled include:** Bookkeeper; Clerk; Computer Operator; Customer Service Rep.; Data Entry Clerk; Draftsperson; Driver; Human Resources Manager; Legal Secretary; Light Industrial Worker; Medical Secretary; Nurse; Office Manager; Public Relations Specialist; Receptionist; Secretary; Statistician; Stenographer; Typist/Word Processor. **Number of placements per year:** 1000+.

OLSTEN STAFFING SERVICES
3409 South Boulevard, Columbus OH 43204-1213. 614/276-4200. **Contact:** Branch Manager. **Description:** A temporary agency. **Specializes in the areas of:** Administration; Industrial; Manufacturing; Retail. **Benefits available to temporary workers:** Medical Insurance; Paid Vacation. **Average salary range of placements:** Less than $20,000. **Number of placements per year:** 1000+.

PALMER TEMPS
THE PALMER GROUP
4302 Roosevelt Boulevard, Middletown OH 45044-6625. 513/422-1126. **Toll-free phone:** 800/860-8367. **Fax:** 513/422-1503. **Contact:** Manager. **E-mail address:** palmer@palmergrp.com. **World Wide Web address:** http://www.palmergrp.com. **Description:** A temporary agency that also offers permanent employment and career outplacement counseling. **Specializes in the areas of:** Accounting/Auditing; Computer Science/Software; Insurance; Personnel/Labor Relations; Sales; Secretarial. **Positions commonly filled include:** Accountant/Auditor; Advertising Clerk; Credit Manager; Draftsperson; Human Resources Specialist; Technical Writer/Editor; Typist/Word Processor. **Benefits available to temporary workers:** Medical Insurance; Paid Holidays; Paid Vacation. **Average salary range of placements:** $20,000 - $29,999. **Number of placements per year:** 1000+.

PHARMACY RELIEF NETWORK
P.O. Box 659, Lima OH 45802-0659. 419/222-7070. **Toll-free phone:** 888/727-2007. **Fax:** 419/222-3665. **Contact:** Helen Hooks, Operations Coordinator. **Description:** A temporary agency that also provides permanent placements. The agency places medical professionals in hospital, retail, and institutional settings. Company pays fee. **Specializes in the areas of:** Health/Medical. **Positions commonly filled include:** Dental Assistant/Dental Hygienist; Licensed Practical Nurse; Pharmacist; Pharmacy Technician; Registered Nurse. **Average salary range of placements:** More than $50,000. **Number of placements per year:** 200 - 499.

SANKER & ASSOCIATES
7522 Redcoat Drive, Indian Springs OH 45011. 513/887-8000. **Fax:** 513/887-2226. **Contact:** Patricia Sanker, President. **Description:** A temporary agency that focuses on the placement of graphic designers and desktop publishers. Company pays fee. **Specializes in the areas of:** Advertising; Art/Design; Publishing. **Positions commonly filled include:** Designer; Desktop Publishing Specialist; Graphic Designer; Technical Writer/Editor. **Corporate headquarters location:** Cincinnati OH. **Average salary range of placements:** $20,000 - $29,999. **Number of placements per year:** 1 - 49.

SPECIAL COUNSEL
1000 Terminal Tower Building, 50 Public Square, Cleveland OH 44113. 216/622-2100. **Fax:** 216/622-2110. **Contact:** Manager. **World Wide Web address:** http://www.specialcounsel.com. **Description:** A temporary and permanent employment agency. **Specializes in the areas of:** Legal.

TANDEM STAFFING
787 North Main Street, Akron OH 44310. 330/253-0088. **Fax:** 330/253-9818. **Contact:** Howard W. Ryder, President. **Description:** A temporary agency. **Specializes in the areas of:** Light Industrial; Manufacturing. **Positions commonly filled include:** Blue-Collar Worker Supervisor; Industrial Production Manager. **Average salary range of placements:** $20,000 - $29,999. **Number of placements per year:** 100 - 199.

THE TARGET HUMAN RESOURCE COMPANIES, INC.
14650 Detroit Avenue, Suite 430, Cleveland OH 44107. **Toll-free phone:** 800/244-1779. **Fax:** 216/226-5708. **Contact:** Jacquie Julius, Customer Service Manager. **E-mail address:** tthrc@aol.com. **World Wide Web address:** http://www.realpages.com/target. **Description:** A temporary agency. The firm also provides permanent placements and human resource consulting. Founded in 1987. Company pays fee. **Specializes in the areas of:** Accounting/Auditing; Food Industry; Industrial; Manufacturing; Personnel/Labor Relations; Sales; Secretarial; Technical. **Positions commonly filled include:** Accountant/Auditor; Automotive Mechanic; Blue-Collar Worker Supervisor; Customer Service Rep.; Electrician; Human Resources Specialist; Industrial Production Manager; Quality Control Supervisor; Restaurant/Food Service Manager; Services Sales Rep.; Typist/Word Processor. **Benefits available to temporary workers:** Bonus Award/Plan; Life Insurance; Medical Insurance. **Corporate headquarters location:** This Location. **Other area locations:** Brunswick OH; Columbus OH; Elyria OH. **Average salary range of placements:** $20,000 - $29,999. **Number of placements per year:** 500 - 999.

TECHPRO MEDICAL SERVICE
1516 Old Beech Court, Dayton OH 45458. 937/885-3944. **Contact:** Manager. **Description:** A temporary agency. **Specializes in the areas of:** Health/Medical.

TEMPORARILY YOURS PLACEMENT
5035 Mayfield Road, Lyndhurst OH 44124-2603. **Contact:** Recruiter. **Description:** A temporary agency. Company pays fee. **Specializes in the areas of:** Accounting/Auditing; Food Industry; Health/Medical; Industrial; Personnel/Labor Relations; Publishing; Retail; Sales; Secretarial; Technical. **Positions commonly filled include:** Blue-Collar Worker Supervisor; Clerical Supervisor; Counselor; Electrician; Human Resources Specialist; Landscape Architect; Paralegal; Services Sales Representative; Typist/Word Processor. **Benefits available to temporary workers:** Paid Vacation. **Corporate headquarters location:** Mentor OH. **Other U.S. locations:** Warrensville Heights OH. **Average salary range of placements:** Less than $20,000. **Number of placements per year:** 200 - 499.

CONTRACT SERVICES FIRMS

ALLIANCE TECHNICAL SERVICES
5045 North Main Street, Suite 330, Dayton OH 45415-3637. 937/277-6117. **Fax:** 937/277-1979. **Contact:** Ken Overholser, Regional Manager. **Description:** A contract services firm focusing on technical fields. **Specializes in the areas of:** Computer Science/Software; Engineering; Industrial; Manufacturing; Technical. **Positions commonly filled include:** Ceramics Engineer; Civil Engineer; Clinical Lab Technician; Computer Programmer; Design Engineer;

Designer; Draftsperson; Electrical/Electronics Engineer; Electrician; Industrial Engineer; Industrial Production Manager; Materials Engineer; Mechanical Engineer; Operations/Production Manager; Quality Control Supervisor; Software Engineer; Structural Engineer; Systems Analyst; Technical Writer/Editor. **Corporate headquarters location:** Alliance OH. **Other U.S. locations:** Bingham Farms MI; Columbus OH; Warren OH; Greenville SC. **Average salary range of placements:** $30,000 - $50,000.

BELCAN TECHNICAL SERVICES
11591 Goldcoast Drive, Cincinnati OH 45249. **Toll-free phone:** 800/945-1900. **Fax:** 513/489-0830. **Contact:** John Kennedy, Recruiter. **Description:** A contract services firm. **Specializes in the areas of:** Computer Science/Software; Engineering; Industrial; Manufacturing. **Positions commonly filled include:** Accountant/Auditor; Aerospace Engineer; Agricultural Engineer; Architect; Biological Scientist; Biomedical Engineer; Buyer; Chemical Engineer; Chemist; Civil Engineer; Clinical Lab Technician; Computer Programmer; Construction Contractor; Cost Estimator; Designer; Draftsperson; Editor; Electrical/Electronics Engineer; Financial Analyst; Food Scientist/ Technologist; Geographer; Health Services Manager; Human Resources Manager; Industrial Engineer; Industrial Production Manager; Mechanical Engineer; Purchasing Agent/Manager; Quality Control Supervisor; Radiological Technologist; Software Engineer; Stationary Engineer; Structural Engineer; Surveyor; Systems Analyst; Technical Writer/Editor; Wholesale and Retail Buyer. **Number of placements per year:** 1000+.

CONTRACT SOLUTIONS, INC.
655 Eden Park Drive, Suite 790, Cincinnati OH 45202. 513/621-2230. **Contact:** Manager. **Description:** A contract services firm that also provides some permanent placements. **Specializes in the areas of:** Information Systems; Information Technology.

DLD TECHNICAL SERVICES
24050 Commerce Park, Suite 203, Cleveland OH 44122. 216/360-9595. **Fax:** 216/360-9599. **Contact:** Albert Cohen, President. **Description:** A contract technical services company. **Specializes in the areas of:** Computer Science/Software; Engineering; Industrial; Technical. **Positions commonly filled include:** Aerospace Engineer; Buyer; Ceramics Engineer; Chemical Engineer; Civil Engineer; Computer Programmer; Design Engineer; Designer; Draftsperson; Electrical/Electronics Engineer; Industrial Engineer; Materials Engineer; Mechanical Engineer; Metallurgical Engineer; Nuclear Engineer; Purchasing Agent/ Manager; Quality Control Supervisor; Radiological Technologist; Software Engineer; Structural Engineer; Systems Analyst; Technical Writer/Editor. **Benefits available to temporary workers:** Paid Holidays; Paid Vacation. **Average salary range of placements:** More than $50,000. **Number of placements per year:** 50 - 99.

FLEX-TECH PROFESSIONAL SERVICES
413 Columbus Avenue, Suite 300, Sandusky OH 44870. 419/625-3974. **Fax:** 419/625-7417. **Contact:** Cecil Weatherspoon, President. **Description:** A contract services firm. **Specializes in the areas of:** Banking; Computer Hardware/Software; Engineering; General Management; Industrial; Manufacturing; Personnel/Labor Relations; Sales. **Positions commonly filled include:** Administrative Assistant; Aerospace Engineer; Architect; Biological Scientist; Budget Analyst; Buyer; Ceramics Engineer; Chemical Engineer; Chemist; Computer Programmer; Customer Service Rep.; Draftsperson; EDP Specialist; Electrical/ Electronics Engineer; Industrial Designer; Industrial Engineer; Manufacturing Engineer; Marketing Specialist; Mechanical Engineer; MIS Specialist; Operations/Production Manager; Purchasing Agent/Manager; Quality Control Supervisor; Secretary; Software Engineer; Systems Analyst; Technical Writer/Editor. **Benefits available to temporary workers:** Bonus Award/Plan; Paid Vacation. **Other U.S. locations:** Phoenix AZ; Detroit MI; Cleveland OH. **Average salary range of placements:** $30,000 - $50,000. **Number of placements per year:** 100 - 199.

GLOBAL RESOURCES GROUP
6047 Frantz Road, Suite 106, Dublin OH 43017. **Contact:** Peadar Lynch, President/CEO. **Description:** A contract services firm focusing on the placement of human resources personnel. **Specializes in the areas of:** Engineering; Health/Medical; Industrial; Manufacturing; Personnel/Labor Relations; Technical. **Positions commonly filled include:** Accountant/ Auditor; Administrative Manager; Attorney; Blue-Collar Worker Supervisor; Buyer; Chemical Engineer; Clerical Supervisor; Computer Programmer; Design Engineer; Designer; Draftsperson; Electrical/Electronics Engineer; Environmental Engineer; Financial Analyst; Human Resources Specialist; Industrial Engineer; Internet Services Manager; Licensed Practical Nurse; Management Analyst/Consultant; Mechanical Engineer; MIS Specialist; Operations/Production Manager; Paralegal; Purchasing Agent/Manager; Quality Control Supervisor; Registered Nurse; Science Technologist; Software Engineer; Systems Analyst.

NORTH AMERICAN TECHNICAL SERVICES
3951 Erie Street, Suite 214, Willoughby OH 44094. 440/975-0400. **Toll-free phone:** 800/330-9680. **Fax:** 440/975-1211. **Contact:** Recruiter. **Description:** A contract services firm. **Specializes in the areas of:** Engineering; Sales; Transportation. **Positions commonly filled include:** Ceramics Engineer; Chemical Engineer; Civil Engineer; Design Engineer; Draftsperson; Electrical/Electronics Engineer; Environmental Engineer; Industrial Engineer; Materials Engineer; Mechanical Engineer; Operations/Production Manager; Petroleum Engineer; Software Engineer; Structural Engineer; Technical Writer/Editor.

NORTH STAR RESOURCES
29170 Euclid Avenue, Wickliffe OH 44092-2473. 440/944-8484. **Toll-free phone:** 800/875-9562. **Fax:** 440/944-8909. **Contact:** Joyce McLean, President. **Description:** A contract services firm that also provides permanent placements. Company pays fee. **Specializes in the areas of:** Architecture/Construction; Chemical; Computer Science/Software; Electronics; Engineering; Manufacturing; Technical. **Positions commonly filled include:** Aerospace Engineer; Architect; Buyer; Ceramics Engineer; Chemical Engineer; Chemist; Civil Engineer; Computer Programmer; Cost Estimator; Design Engineer; Designer; Draftsperson; Electrical/Electronics Engineer; Environmental Engineer; Industrial Engineer; Materials Engineer; Mechanical Engineer; MIS Specialist; Operations/Production Manager; Purchasing Agent/ Manager; Quality Control Supervisor; Software Engineer; Structural Engineer; Surveyor; Systems Analyst; Technical Writer/Editor. **Benefits available to temporary workers:** Paid Holidays. **Average salary range of placements:** $30,000 - $50,000. **Number of placements per year:** 1 - 49.

PAK/TEEM CONTRACT SERVICES
11500 Rockfield Court, Cincinnati OH 45241-1919. 513/772-1515. **Fax:** 513/772-6381. **Contact:** Denise DeMoss, General Manager. **E-mail address:** ptsvcs@ cinti.net. **Description:** A contract services firm that provides technical placement. **Specializes in the areas of:** Engineering; Light Industrial. **Positions commonly filled include:** Blue-Collar Worker Supervisor; Ceramics Engineer; Chemical Engineer; Civil Engineer;

Construction Contractor; Cost Estimator; Design Engineer; Designer; Draftsperson; Electrical/Electronics Engineer; Electrician; Environmental Engineer; Industrial Engineer; Materials Engineer; Mechanical Engineer; Metallurgical Engineer; Structural Engineer; Technical Writer/Editor. **Benefits available to temporary workers:** Credit Union; Dental Insurance; Medical Insurance; Paid Holidays; Paid Vacation. **Average salary range of placements:** $30,000 - $50,000. **Number of placements per year:** 1 - 49.

PROFESSIONAL STAFF MANAGEMENT
7 West 7th Street, Suite 1990, Cincinnati OH 45202. 513/721-7880. **Fax:** 513/721-5315. **Contact:** Manager. **Description:** A contract services firm.

PROVISION TECHNOLOGIES
260 Northland Boulevard, Suite 204, Cincinnati OH 45246. 513/772-8231. **Fax:** 513/772-4313. **Contact:** Manager. **World Wide Web address:** http://www.careerbase.com. **Description:** A contract services and consulting firm. **Specializes in the areas of:** Computer Science/Software; Information Technology.
Other area locations:
- 3250 West Market Street, Suite 306A, Akron OH 44333. 330/836-0395.
- A contract services and consulting firm.

RDS, INC.
P.O. Box 24389, Dayton OH 45424-0389. 937/236-8602. **Toll-free phone:** 800/876-8602. **Fax:** 937/237-3835. **Contact:** Beth Tschirhart, In-Client Services Manager. **E-mail address:** rapiddsgn@aol.com. **Description:** A contract services firm. RDS focuses on engineering and design services and project engineering management services. Founded in 1946. **Specializes in the areas of:** Design; Engineering; Industrial; Manufacturing; Technical. **Positions commonly filled include:** Ceramics Engineer; Chemical Engineer; Design Engineer; Designer; Draftsperson; Electrical/Electronics Engineer; Industrial Engineer; Industrial Production Manager; Materials Engineer; Mechanical Engineer; Operations/Production Manager; Quality Control Supervisor; Technical Writer/Editor. **Benefits available to temporary workers:** Medical Insurance; Paid Holidays; Paid Vacation. **Other U.S. locations:** Nationwide. **Average salary range of placements:** $30,000 - $50,000. **Number of placements per year:** 200 - 499.

S&P SOLUTIONS
35000 Chardon Road, Suite 200, Willoughby Hills OH 44094. 440/646-9111. **Toll-free phone:** 800/978-9113. **Fax:** 440/646-1429. **Contact:** Suzanne Nebe, Recruiter. **E-mail address:** recruiting @sps-solutions.com. **World Wide Web address:** http://www.sps-solutions.com. **Description:** A contract services firm. Company pays fee. **Specializes in the areas of:** Computer Science/Software; Scientific; Technical. **Positions commonly filled include:** Computer Programmer; Consultant; Database Manager; MIS Specialist; Software Engineer; Systems Analyst. **Number of placements per year:** 100 - 199.

TAD TECHNICAL SERVICES
6555 Busch Boulevard, Suite 230, Columbus OH 43229. **Toll-free phone:** 800/260-8007. **Fax:** 614/431-1614. **Contact:** Lou Trupo, Jr., Branch Manager. **World Wide Web address:** http://www.tadgroup@aol.com. **Description:** A contract services firm. Company pays fee. **Specializes in the areas of:** Administration; Architecture/Construction; Automotive; Computer Hardware/Software; Engineering; Food Industry; Health/Medical; Industrial; Light Industrial; Manufacturing; Publishing; Technical; Transportation. **Positions commonly filled include:** Account Rep.; Administrative Assistant; Administrative Manager; Applications Engineer; Architect; Assistant Manager; Biochemist; Biomedical Engineer; Buyer; Chemical Engineer; Clerical Supervisor; Computer Programmer; Customer Service Rep.; Design Engineer; Draftsperson; Electrical/Electronics Engineer; Electrician; Food Scientist/Technologist; Geologist/Geophysicist; Human Resources Specialist; Management Analyst/Consultant; Manufacturing Engineer; Mechanical Engineer; Medical Records Technician; MIS Specialist; Operations/Production Manager; Quality Control Supervisor; Sales Engineer; Secretary; Surgical Technician; Systems Analyst; Systems Manager; Telecommunications Manager; Transportation/Traffic Specialist; Typist/Word Processor. **Benefits available to temporary workers:** 401(k); Dental Insurance; Medical Insurance; Paid Holidays; Paid Vacation. **Corporate headquarters location:** Cambridge MA. **Number of placements per year:** 1000+.

TEAMWORK U.S.A.
27801 Euclid Avenue, Suite 550, Euclid OH 44132. 216/261-5151. **Fax:** 216/261-7248. **Contact:** Michael Freshwater, General Manager. **Description:** A contract services firm. Company pays fee. **Specializes in the areas of:** Computer Science/Software; Engineering; Industrial; Manufacturing; Personnel/Labor Relations; Technical. **Positions commonly filled include:** Administrative Manager; Aerospace Engineer; Agricultural Engineer; Biomedical Engineer; Blue-Collar Worker Supervisor; Budget Analyst; Buyer; Ceramics Engineer; Chemical Engineer; Chemist; Civil Engineer; Clinical Lab Technician; Computer Programmer; Construction and Building Inspector; Construction Contractor; Cost Estimator; Customer Service Rep.; Design Engineer; Designer; Draftsperson; EEG Technologist; EKG Technician; Electrical/Electronics Engineer; Electrician; Environmental Engineer; Human Resources Specialist; Human Service Worker; Industrial Engineer; Industrial Production Manager; Materials Engineer; Mechanical Engineer; Nuclear Medicine Technologist; Petroleum Engineer; Public Relations Specialist; Services Sales Rep.; Software Engineer; Structural Engineer; Systems Analyst. **Average salary range of placements:** $20,000 - $29,999. **Number of placements per year:** 200 - 499.

TRADESMAN INTERNATIONAL
1549 Boettler Road, Unit D, Uniontown OH 44685-7766. 330/896-0420. **Toll-free phone:** 800/896-4062. **Fax:** 330/896-1183. **Contact:** David Briggs, Recruiter. **Description:** A contract services firm focusing on skilled labor. **Specializes in the areas of:** Construction; Industrial; Manufacturing; Personnel/Labor Relations. **Positions commonly filled include:** Blue-Collar Worker Supervisor; Construction Contractor; Electrician. **Corporate headquarters location:** Solon OH. **Other U.S. locations:** Indianapolis IN; Louisville KY; Baltimore MD; Cincinnati OH; Cleveland OH; Columbus OH. **Average salary range of placements:** $20,000 - $29,999. **Number of placements per year:** 1000+.

H.L. YOH COMPANY
11311 Cornell Park Drive, Suite 402, Cincinnati OH 45242. 513/469-6202. **Toll-free phone:** 800/696-6488. **Fax:** 513/469-6205. **Contact:** Mike Brogan, Account Representative. **E-mail address:** yohcinci@concentric.net. **World Wide Web address:** http://www.hlyoh.com. **Description:** A contract services firm. Company pays fee. **Specializes in the areas of:** Computer Operations; Computer Programming; Electrical; Engineering. **Positions commonly filled include:** Computer Programmer; Computer Support Technician; Electrical/Electronics Engineer; Mechanical Engineer; Software Engineer. **Other U.S. locations:** Nationwide. **Average salary range of placements:** $30,000 - $50,000. **Number of placements per year:** 100 - 199.

CAREER/OUTPLACEMENT COUNSELING FIRMS

A BETTER RESUME
409 Red Haw Road, Dayton OH 45405. 937/278-3242. **Fax:** 937/278-4625. **Contact:** Stephen Coleman, President. **E-mail address:** steveco85@aol.com. **Description:** A resume writing service.

ALLEN & ASSOCIATES
25825 Science Park Drive, Suite 260, Beachwood OH 44122. 216/765-8220. **Toll-free phone:** 800/562-7911. **Fax:** 216/765-8309. **Contact:** Manager. **World Wide Web address:** http://www.allenandassociates.com. **Description:** A career/outplacement counseling firm. **Corporate headquarters location:** Maitland FL.

BOARDMAN RESUME & SECRETARIAL SERVICE
6714 Market Street, Youngstown OH 44512. 330/726-8889. **Contact:** Mary L. Baxter, Director. **Description:** A career/outplacement counseling firm.

40 PLUS OF CENTRAL OHIO
1100 King Avenue, Columbus OH 43212. 614/297-0040. **Contact:** President. **Description:** A career/outplacement counseling firm.

JOB TRAINING PARTNERSHIP
300 Market Avenue North, Canton OH 44702. 330/455-7121. **Contact:** Industrial Training Coordinator. **Description:** A career/outplacement counseling service. **Specializes in the areas of:** Nonprofit. **Positions commonly filled include:** Case Manager. **Number of placements per year:** 1 - 49.

MORAN & ASSOCIATES
126 West John Street, Maumee OH 43537. 419/893-9707. **Fax:** 419/893-7348. **Contact:** Weston and Karen Moran, Owners. **Description:** A resume writing and counseling service.

DAVID G. ROBERTS GROUP
29525 Chagrin Boulevard, Suite 214, Cleveland OH 44122-5404. 216/595-8200. **Fax:** 216/595-8208. **Contact:** David G. Roberts, Human Resources. **Description:** A career/outplacement counseling firm.

OKLAHOMA

EXECUTIVE SEARCH FIRMS

AMERI RESOURCE
2525 Northwest Expressway, Suite 532, Oklahoma City OK 73112. 405/842-5900. **Toll-free phone:** 800/583-7823. **Fax:** 405/843-9879. **Contact:** Manager. **Description:** An executive search firm. Company pays fee. **Specializes in the areas of:** Administration; Banking; Computer Science/Software; Engineering; Finance; Food Industry; General Management; Health/Medical; Industrial; Manufacturing; Personnel/Labor Relations; Publishing; Secretarial; Technical. **Positions commonly filled include:** Accountant/Auditor; Actuary; Administrative Manager; Aerospace Engineer; Agricultural Engineer; Architect; Bank Officer/Manager; Blue-Collar Worker Supervisor; Civil Engineer; Clerical Supervisor; Computer Programmer; Construction and Building Inspector; Construction Contractor; Cost Estimator; Credit Manager; Customer Service Rep.; Dental Assistant/Hygienist; Design Engineer; Designer; Draftsperson; Electrical/Electronics Engineer; Electrician; Financial Analyst; Human Resources Specialist; Industrial Engineer; Internet Services Manager; Licensed Practical Nurse; Management Analyst/Consultant; Management Trainee; Manufacturer's/Wholesaler's Sales Rep.; Market Research Analyst; Mechanical Engineer; MIS Specialist; Multimedia Designer; Nuclear Engineer; Operations/Production Manager; Petroleum Engineer; Purchasing Agent/Manager; Quality Control Supervisor; Software Engineer; Structural Engineer; Systems Analyst; Technical Writer/Editor; Typist/Word Processor. **Other area locations:** Tulsa OK. **Number of placements per year:** 1000+.

ANDREWS & ASSOCIATES INC.
4500 South Garnett Road, Suite 205, Tulsa OK 74146. 918/664-3537. **Fax:** 918/628-1601. **Contact:** Jeffrey L. Andrews, President. **E-mail address:** jandrews@iamerica.net. **Description:** An executive search firm. Company pays fee. **Specializes in the areas of:** Accounting/Auditing. **Positions commonly filled include:** Tax Specialist.

BANCSEARCH, INC.
P.O. Box 700516, Tulsa OK 74170-0516. 918/496-9477. **Fax:** 918/494-2003. **Contact:** Don Cunningham, President. **E-mail address:** bancsearch@aol.com. **World Wide Web address:** http://www.bancsearch.com. **Description:** An executive search firm. Company pays fee. **Specializes in the areas of:** Banking; Finance. **Positions commonly filled include:** Bank Officer/Manager; Credit Manager; Financial Analyst; Mortgage Banker; Trust Officer. **Average salary range of placements:** More than $50,000. **Number of placements per year:** 1 - 49.

BANKER PERSONNEL SERVICE
2211 Westpark Drive, Norman OK 73069. 405/364-4322. **Contact:** Manager. **Description:** An executive search firm. **Specializes in the areas of:** Banking.

BELT JOY REED & ASSOCIATES
P.O. Box 18446, Oklahoma City OK 73154. 405/842-6336. **Fax:** 405/842-6357. **Contact:** Manager. **Description:** An executive search firm. **Specializes in the areas of:** Health/Medical.

DUNHILL PERSONNEL OF NORTHEAST TULSA, INC.
10159 East 11th Street, Suite 370, Tulsa OK 74128-3054. 918/832-8857. **Toll-free phone:** 800/466-8857. **Fax:** 918/832-8859. **Contact:** Joy M. Porrello, President. **Description:** An executive search firm. Company pays fee. **Specializes in the areas of:** Banking; Credit and Collection. **Average salary range of placements:** More than $50,000. **Number of placements per year:** 1 - 49.

EXECUTIVE RESOURCES GROUP, INC.
2601 West Wilshire Boulevard, Oklahoma City OK 73116. 405/843-8344. **Fax:** 405/879-0393. **Contact:** George Orr, President. **Description:** An executive search firm. Company pays fee. **Specializes in the areas of:** Engineering; Manufacturing. **Positions commonly filled include:** Biomedical Engineer; Chemical Engineer; Civil Engineer; Electrical/Electronics Engineer; Industrial Engineer; Manufacturing Engineer; Mechanical Engineer; Purchasing Agent/Manager; Quality Control Supervisor; Software Engineer. **Number of placements per year:** 1 - 49.

EXPRESS PERSONNEL SERVICES
7321 Southwestern, Oklahoma City OK 73139. 405/634-6600. **Contact:** P.J. Jackson, Regional Manager. **Description:** An executive search firm. Company pays fee. **Specializes in the areas of:** Accounting/Auditing; Computer Science/Software; Engineering; Health/Medical; Industrial; Legal. **Positions commonly filled include:** Accountant/Auditor; Administrative Manager; Advertising Clerk; Blue-Collar Worker Supervisor; Clerical Supervisor; Computer Programmer; Customer Service Rep.; Draftsperson; Human Resources Specialist; Industrial Production Manager; Registered Nurse; Typist/Word Processor. **Other U.S. locations:** Nationwide. **Average salary range of placements:** Less than $20,000.

EXPRESS PERSONNEL SERVICES
6300 NW Expressway, Oklahoma City OK 73132. 405/840-5000. **Fax:** 405/720-9390. **Contact:** Harvey H. H. Homsey, Research & Development Manager. **Description:** An executive search firm. **Specializes in the areas of:** Accounting/Auditing; Advertising; Computer Science/Software; Food Industry; General Management; Industrial; Insurance; Legal; Manufacturing; Personnel/Labor Relations; Publishing; Sales; Secretarial; Technical. **Positions commonly filled include:** Administrative Manager; Advertising Clerk; Architect; Blue-Collar Worker Supervisor; Claim Rep.; Computer Programmer; Customer Service Rep.; Dental Assistant/Hygienist; Designer; Dietician/Nutritionist; Draftsperson; Editor; Education Administrator; EEG Technologist; EKG Technician; Electrical/Electronics Engineer; Electrician; Emergency Medical Technician; Food Scientist/Technologist; Human Resources Specialist; Human Service Worker; Manufacturer's/Wholesaler's Sales Rep.; Market Research Analyst; Medical Records Technician; Multimedia Designer; Paralegal; Public Relations Specialist; Quality Control Supervisor; Restaurant/Food Service Manager; Services Sales Rep.; Software Engineer; Systems Analyst; Technical Writer/Editor. **Average salary range of placements:** $30,000 - $50,000. **Number of placements per year:** 1000+.

JAMES FARRIS ASSOCIATES
410 North Classen, Suite E, Oklahoma City OK 73118. 405/848-0535. **Contact:** Manager. **Description:** An executive search firm.

FOOD MANUFACTURING CONSULTANTS
5929 North May Avenue, Suite 506, Oklahoma City OK 73112. 405/840-3632. **Contact:** Larry Toth, President. **Description:** An executive search firm operating on both retainer and contingency bases. Company pays fee. **Specializes in the areas of:** Food Industry; Manufacturing; Sales. **Positions commonly filled include:** Food Scientist/Technologist; Industrial

Engineer; Manufacturer's/Wholesaler's Sales Rep.; Operations/Production Manager; Quality Control Supervisor. **Average salary range of placements:** More than $50,000. **Number of placements per year:** 100 - 199.

ROBERT HALF INTERNATIONAL
211 North Robinson, Suite 310, Oklahoma City OK 73102. 405/236-0880. **Fax:** 405/232-9230. **Contact:** Branch Manager. **E-mail address:** rhicokc@aol.com. **World Wide Web address:** http://www.rhic.rhalf. **Description:** An executive search firm operating on a contingency basis. Company pays fee. **Specializes in the areas of:** Accounting/Auditing; Administration; Banking; Finance; Secretarial. **Positions commonly filled include:** Accountant/Auditor; Bank Officer/Manager; Computer Programmer; Credit Manager; Customer Service Rep.; Financial Analyst; Human Resources Specialist; Management Analyst/Consultant; MIS Specialist; Purchasing Agent/Manager; Systems Analyst; Typist/Word Processor; Underwriter/Assistant Underwriter. **Corporate headquarters location:** Menlo Park CA. **Other U.S. locations:** Nationwide. **International locations:** Worldwide. **Average salary range of placements:** $20,000 - $29,999. **Number of placements per year:** 500 - 999.

ROBERT HALF INTERNATIONAL/ACCOUNTEMPS
6120 South Yale Street, Suite 420, Tulsa OK 74136. 918/493-3393. **Contact:** Manager. **World Wide Web address:** http://www.roberthalf.com. **Description:** An executive search firm. Accountemps (also at this location) provides temporary placements in the accounting industry. **NOTE:** Accountemps can be reached at 918/585-1700. **Specializes in the areas of:** Accounting/Auditing; Finance. **Corporate headquarters location:** Menlo Park CA. **Other U.S. locations:** Nationwide. **International locations:** Worldwide.

HEALTHCARE RESOURCES GROUP
3945 SE 15th Street, Oklahoma City OK 73115. 405/677-7872. **Contact:** Manager. **Description:** An executive search firm. **Specializes in the areas of:** Health/Medical.

HIGH TECH RESOURCES
6120 South Yale Street, Suite 100, Tulsa OK 74136. 918/481-8822. **Contact:** Manager. **Description:** An executive search firm. **Specializes in the areas of:** High-Tech.

IRON MOUNTAIN SEARCH, INC.
60599 East 100th Road, Miami OK 74354. **Toll-free phone:** 800/542-8066. **Contact:** Manager. **Description:** An executive search firm. **Specializes in the areas of:** Computer Programming.

MANAGEMENT RECRUITERS INTERNATIONAL
5801 East 41st Street, Suite 440, Tulsa OK 74135. 918/663-6744. **Contact:** Manager. **Description:** An executive search firm. **Specializes in the areas of:** Administration; Engineering; Sales.

MANAGEMENT RECRUITERS OF OKLAHOMA CITY
3441 West Memorial Road, Suite 4, Oklahoma City OK 73134. 405/752-8848. **Fax:** 405/752-8783. **Contact:** Gary Roy, Manager. **Description:** An executive search firm. **Specializes in the areas of:** Accounting/Auditing; Administration; Advertising; Architecture/Construction; Banking; Communications; Computer Hardware/Software; Finance; Food Industry; General Management; Health/Medical; Insurance; Legal; Manufacturing; Publishing; Real Estate; Retail; Sales; Technical; Textiles; Transportation.

MANAGEMENT SEARCH, INC.
6051 North Brookline, Suite 125, Oklahoma City OK 73112. 405/842-3173. **Contact:** David Orwig, President. **Description:** An executive search firm. Company pays fee. **Specializes in the areas of:** Agri-Business; Sales; Technical. **Positions commonly filled include:** Agricultural Engineer; Agricultural Scientist; Biological Scientist; Veterinarian. **Number of placements per year:** 1 - 49.

MIDWEST FINANCIAL SERVICES COMPANY
4335 Quail Ridge, Suite 100, Enid OK 73703. 580/234-2211. **Fax:** 580/234-7711. **Contact:** Paul G. Krienke, President. **E-mail address:** pgk@fullnet.net. **Description:** An executive search firm operating on a contingency basis. Company pays fee. **Specializes in the areas of:** Banking. **Positions commonly filled include:** Bank Officer/Manager; Branch Manager; Financial Analyst. **Average salary range of placements:** $30,000 - $50,000. **Number of placements per year:** 1 - 49.

NATIONAL RECRUITERS
P.O. Box 2090, Ardmore OK 73402. **Toll-free phone:** 800/598-0255. **Contact:** Manager. **Description:** An executive search firm. **Specializes in the areas of:** Software Development; Telecommunications.

TERRY NEESE PERSONNEL AGENCY
2709 West I-44 Service Road, Oklahoma City OK 73112. 405/942-8551. **Fax:** 405/942-2840. **Contact:** Brenda Wampler, Executive Assistant. **E-mail address:** okearl@worldnet.att.net. **Description:** An executive search firm operating on a contingency basis. Company pays fee. **Specializes in the areas of:** Accounting/Auditing; Administration; Banking; Computer Science/Software; Engineering; Finance; General Management; Health/Medical; Legal; Light Industrial; Personnel/Labor Relations; Sales; Secretarial. **Positions commonly filled include:** Accountant/Auditor; Administrative Manager; Advertising Clerk; Bank Officer/Manager; Blue-Collar Worker Supervisor; Brokerage Clerk; Budget Analyst; Chemical Engineer; Computer Programmer; Credit Manager; Customer Service Rep.; Data Entry Clerk; Dental Assistant/Hygienist; Draftsperson; Electrical/Electronics Engineer; Emergency Medical Technician; Human Resources Manager; Internet Services Manager; Management Analyst/Consultant; Management Trainee; Manufacturer's/Wholesaler's Sales Rep.; Medical Records Technician; Paralegal; Public Relations Specialist; Receptionist; Registered Nurse; Sales Rep.; Secretary; Stenographer; Systems Analyst; Technical Writer/Editor; Typist/Word Processor. **Benefits available to temporary workers:** Life Insurance; Medical Insurance; Paid Vacation; Sick Days. **Number of placements per year:** 200 - 499.

PROFESSIONAL RESOURCES GROUP
7030 South Yale Street, Suite 300, Tulsa OK 74136. 918/481-0088. **Contact:** Manager. **Description:** An executive search firm.

PROSPECTIVE PERSONNEL SERVICE, INC.
P.O. Box 27253, Tulsa OK 74149. 918/425-1700. **Contact:** Linda Kinney, President. **E-mail address:** bankrcrtr@aol.com. **Description:** An executive search firm operating on a contingency basis. Founded in 1981. Company pays fee. **Specializes in the areas of:** Banking. **Positions commonly filled include:** Auditor; Bank Officer/Manager. **Number of placements per year:** 1 - 49.

REALITY GROUP
P.O. Box 2675, Broken Arrow OK 74013. 918/492-2922. **Fax:** 918/492-2929. **Contact:** Larry C. Nobles, President. **Description:** An executive search firm. Company pays fee. **Specializes in the areas of:** Chemical; Engineering. **Positions commonly filled include:** Chemical Engineer; Environmental Engineer; Mechanical Engineer; Safety Engineer.

SALES CONSULTANTS
6525 North Meridian Avenue, Suite 212, Oklahoma City OK 73116. 405/721-6400. **Contact:** Manager. **Description:** An executive search firm. **Specializes in the areas of:** Sales.

SALES RECRUITERS INC.
6803 South Western, Suite 305, Oklahoma City OK 73139. 405/848-1536. **Fax:** 405/636-1561. **Contact:** J.R. Rimele, President. **World Wide Web address:** http://www.telepath.com/salesrec. **Description:** An executive search firm. Company pays fee. **Specializes in the areas of:** Health/Medical; Sales. **Positions commonly filled include:** Account Rep.; Marketing Manager; Safety Engineer; Sales Manager; Sales Rep. **Average salary range of placements:** $30,000 - $50,000. **Number of placements per year:** 1 - 49.

SUMNER-RAY TECHNICAL RESOURCES
4775 South Harvard Avenue, Suite D, Tulsa OK 74135. 918/742-9760. **Fax:** 918/742-9816. **Contact:** Carl Gist, President. **Description:** An executive search firm that also provides temporary and contract placements. Sumner-Ray Technical Resources is a division of StaffMark. Company pays fee. **Specializes in the areas of:** Engineering; Manufacturing; Personnel/Labor Relations. **Positions commonly filled include:** Aerospace Engineer; Agricultural Engineer; Ceramics Engineer; Chemical Engineer; Civil Engineer; Computer Programmer; Design Engineer; Designer; Draftsperson; Electrical/Electronics Engineer; Human Resources Specialist; Industrial Engineer; Industrial Production Manager; Mechanical Engineer; Purchasing Agent/Manager; Quality Control Supervisor; Structural Engineer; Systems Analyst; Technical Writer/Editor. **Number of placements per year:** 50 - 99.

U.S. GAS SEARCH
5215 East 71st Street, Suite 1500, Tulsa OK 74136. 918/492-6668. **Fax:** 918/492-6674. **Contact:** Keith Louderback, President. **E-mail address:** usgassearch@webzone.net. **Description:** An executive search firm focusing on the placement of marketing, supply, trading, transportation, and risk management professionals in the natural gas industry pays fee. **Specializes in the areas of:** Oil and Gas. **Positions commonly filled include:** Marketing Manager; Marketing Specialist. **Average salary range of placements:** More than $50,000. **Number of placements per year:** 1 - 49.

VILLAREAL & ASSOCIATES
427 South Boston Avenue, Suite 215, Tulsa OK 74103. 918/584-0808. **Fax:** 918/584-6281. **Contact:** Morey Villareal, President. **Description:** An executive search firm operating on a retainer basis. Company pays fee. **Positions commonly filled include:** MIS Specialist; Software Engineer. **Average salary range of placements:** More than $50,000. **Number of placements per year:** 1 - 49.

JOHN WYLIE ASSOCIATES, INC.
1727 East 71st Street, Tulsa OK 74136. 918/496-2100. **Contact:** John L. Wylie, President. **Description:** An executive search firm. **Specializes in the areas of:** Computer Hardware/Software; Engineering; Manufacturing; Technical. **Number of placements per year:** 1 - 49.

PERMANENT EMPLOYMENT AGENCIES

AC PERSONNEL SERVICES, INC.
P.O. Box 271052, Oklahoma City OK 73137. 405/728-3503. **Fax:** 405/682-0666. **Contact:** Delores Lantz, President. **Description:** A permanent employment agency. Company pays fee. **Positions commonly filled include:** Computer Programmer; General Manager; Management Trainee; Services Sales Representative; Systems Analyst. **Number of placements per year:** 100 - 199.

DEMARGE EMPLOYMENT
3608 NW 58th Street, Oklahoma City OK 73112-4409. **Contact:** Administrator. **Description:** A permanent employment agency. Company pays fee. **Specializes in the areas of:** Child Care, In-Home; Nannies. **Positions commonly filled include:** Nanny. **Average salary range of placements:** Less than $20,000. **Number of placements per year:** 1 - 49.

MANPOWER TECHNICAL SERVICES
5727 South Lewis, Suite 575, Tulsa OK 74105. 918/712-8700. **Contact:** Manager. **Description:** A permanent employment agency. **Positions commonly filled include:** Buyer; Computer Programmer; Designer; Draftsperson; Editor; Engineer; Purchasing Agent/Manager; Systems Analyst; Technical Writer/Editor; Technician. **Other U.S. locations:** Nationwide.

LLOYD RICHARDS PERSONNEL SERVICE
507 South Main Street, Suite 502, Tulsa OK 74103. 918/582-5251. **Fax:** 918/582-5250. **Contact:** Lloyd Richards, CPC. **Description:** A permanent employment agency. **Specializes in the areas of:** Accounting/Auditing; Bookkeeping; Chemical; Clerical; Computer Science/Software; Engineering; Finance; Health/Medical; Legal; Manufacturing; Retail; Sales.

SOONER PLACEMENT SERVICE
4001 North Classen Boulevard, Suite 210, Oklahoma City OK 73118. 405/528-2501. **Fax:** 405/524-8046. **Contact:** Louis Borgman, Owner. **Description:** A permanent employment agency. Company pays fee. **Specializes in the areas of:** Accounting/Auditing; Engineering; Legal; Oil and Gas; Sales; Secretarial. **Positions commonly filled include:** Accountant/Auditor; Paralegal; Petroleum Engineer. **Number of placements per year:** 50 - 99.

TEMPORARY EMPLOYMENT AGENCIES

CHEROKEE TEMPS, INC.
427 North Meridian Avenue, Oklahoma City OK 73107. **Contact:** Manager. **Description:** A temporary agency. Company pays fee. **Specializes in the areas of:** Administration; Industrial; Manufacturing; Personnel/Labor Relations; Sales; Secretarial. **Positions commonly filled include:** Automotive Mechanic; Clerical Supervisor; Construction Contractor; Customer Service Rep.; Management Trainee; Manufacturer's/Wholesaler's Sales Rep.; Medical Records Technician; Typist/Word Processor. **Benefits available to temporary workers:** 401(k); Dental Insurance; Medical Insurance. **Corporate headquarters location:** Muskegee OK.

DOW PERSONNEL INC.
4833 South Sheridan Road, Suite 418, Tulsa OK 74145. 918/664-6811. **Fax:** 918/664-6811. **Contact:** Paul McKinney, President. **Description:** A temporary agency. **Specializes in the areas of:** Light Industrial; Nonprofit; Secretarial. **Positions commonly filled include:** Customer Service Rep.; Management Trainee;

Secretary; Typist/Word Processor. **Average salary range of placements:** Less than $20,000. **Number of placements per year:** 1 - 49.

INTERIM PERSONNEL
100 City Plaza West, 5310 East 31st Street, Tulsa OK 74135. 918/664-4445. **Fax:** 918/664-4501. **Contact:** Tim Terhune, President. **E-mail address:** tterhune@swbell.net. **World Wide Web address:** http://www.interim.com. **Description:** A temporary agency. Company pays fee. **Specializes in the areas of:** Accounting/Auditing; Personnel/Labor Relations; Secretarial. **Positions commonly filled include:** Accountant/Auditor; Administrative Manager; Advertising Clerk; Branch Manager; Budget Analyst; Claim Rep.; Clerical Supervisor; Credit Manager; Financial Analyst; Human Resources Specialist; Management Trainee; Market Research Analyst; Technical Writer/Editor; Typist/Word Processor. **Benefits available to temporary workers:** Bonus Award/Plan; Medical Insurance; Paid Holidays; Paid Vacation. **Corporate headquarters location:** Fort Lauderdale FL. **Other U.S. locations:** Nationwide. **Average salary range of placements:** $20,000 - $29,999. **Number of placements per year:** 500 - 999.

KEY TEMPORARY PERSONNEL
5272 South Lewis Avenue, Tulsa OK 74105. 918/747-0000. **Fax:** 918/747-0140. **Recorded jobline:** 918/748-3333. **Contact:** Recruiting and Training Specialist. **E-mail address:** keyjobs@ionet.net. **World Wide Web address:** http://www.keyjobs.com. **Description:** A temporary agency. Company pays fee. **Specializes in the areas of:** Administration; Advertising; Banking; Engineering; Finance; Health/Medical; Industrial; Legal; Light Industrial; Manufacturing; Personnel/Labor Relations; Secretarial; Technical. **Positions commonly filled include:** Accountant/Auditor; Administrative Manager; Advertising Clerk; Attorney; Blue-Collar Worker Supervisor; Chemical Engineer; Chemist; Clerical Supervisor; Computer Programmer; Cost Estimator; Credit Manager; Customer Service Rep.; Design Engineer; Designer; Draftsperson; Electrical/Electronics Engineer; Financial Analyst; Health Services Manager; Human Resources Specialist; Industrial Engineer; Mechanical Engineer; Medical Records Technician; MIS Specialist; Paralegal; Quality Control Supervisor; Systems Analyst; Technical Writer/Editor; Typist/Word Processor. **Benefits available to temporary workers:** 401(k); Medical Insurance; Paid Vacation; Performance Bonus; Referral Bonus Plan. **Average salary range of placements:** $20,000 - $29,999. **Number of placements per year:** 1000+.

MANPOWER TEMPORARY SERVICES
3030 Northwest Expressway, Suite 702, Oklahoma City OK 73112. 405/942-5111. **Contact:** Dave Keith, Regional Vice President. **Description:** A temporary agency. **Specializes in the areas of:** Accounting/Auditing; Banking; Clerical; Computer Hardware/Software; Construction; Finance; Insurance; Legal; Manufacturing. **Positions commonly filled include:** Accountant/Auditor; Administrative Assistant; Bookkeeper; Clerk; Computer Programmer; Construction Trade Worker; Data Entry Clerk; Draftsperson; EDP Specialist; Factory Worker; Legal Secretary; Light Industrial Worker; Medical Secretary; Receptionist; Secretary; Stenographer; Systems Analyst; Technician; Typist/Word Processor. **Number of placements per year:** 1000+.

STAFFMARK
4775 South Harvard Avenue, Tulsa OK 74635. 918/744-8367. **Fax:** 918/744-1232. **Contact:** Carolyn Powers, Division Manager. **Description:** A temporary agency that also offers temp-to-hire opportunities. Company pays fee. **Specializes in the areas of:** General Labor; Industrial; Manufacturing. **Positions commonly filled include:** Aircraft Mechanic/Engine Specialist; Automotive Mechanic; Blue-Collar Worker Supervisor; Construction and Building Inspector; Cost Estimator; Draftsperson; Electrician; General Manager; Industrial Production Manager; Machinist. **Benefits available to temporary workers:** 401(k); Medical Insurance; Paid Holidays; Paid Vacation. **Corporate headquarters location:** Fayetteville AR. **Average salary range of placements:** Less than $20,000. **Number of placements per year:** 500 - 999.

STAFFMARK
116 West 8th Street, Bristow OK 74010. **Contact:** Recruiter. **Description:** A temporary agency that also provides contract services. Company pays fee. **Specializes in the areas of:** Industrial; Manufacturing; Secretarial. **Positions commonly filled include:** Claim Rep.; Clerical Supervisor; Customer Service Rep.; Typist/Word Processor. **Benefits available to temporary workers:** 401(k); Medical Insurance; Paid Holidays; Paid Vacation. **Corporate headquarters location:** Fayetteville AR. **Average salary range of placements:** Less than $20,000. **Number of placements per year:** 200 - 499.

STAFFMARK
6349 South Memorial Avenue, Tulsa OK 74133-2390. 918/252-9696. **Fax:** 918/252-2170. **Contact:** Jane Nazerman, Branch Manager. **Description:** A temporary and temp-to-hire agency. Company pays fee. **Specializes in the areas of:** Accounting/Auditing; Administration; Advertising; Banking; Finance; Insurance; Legal; Personnel/Labor Relations; Publishing; Sales; Secretarial. **Positions commonly filled include:** Administrative Manager; Advertising Clerk; Brokerage Clerk; Claim Rep.; Clerical Supervisor; Computer Programmer; Credit Manager; Customer Service Rep.; Human Resources Specialist; Paralegal; Systems Analyst; Typist/Word Processor. **Benefits available to temporary workers:** 401(k); Medical Insurance; Paid Holidays; Paid Vacation. **Corporate headquarters location:** Fayetteville AR. **Number of placements per year:** 1000+.

STAFFMARK MEDICAL STAFFING
2140 South Harvard, Tulsa OK 74114. 918/743-5900. **Contact:** Manager. **Description:** A temporary and temp-to-hire agency. **Specializes in the areas of:** Health/Medical. **Positions commonly filled include:** Claim Rep.; Dental Assistant/Dental Hygienist; EEG Technologist; EKG Technician; Emergency Medical Technician; Licensed Practical Nurse; Medical Records Technician; Radiological Technologist; Registered Nurse; Surgical Technician; Typist/Word Processor. **Benefits available to temporary workers:** 401(k); Medical Insurance; Paid Holidays; Paid Vacation. **Number of placements per year:** 1000+.

CAREER/OUTPLACEMENT COUNSELING FIRMS

EXECU TRAIN
3817 Northwest Expressway, Suite 100, Oklahoma City OK 73112-1465. 405/942-4494. **Contact:** Manager. **Description:** A training agency providing computer courses including night, semester-long, and one-week classes.

PAB PERSONNEL AGENCY, INC.
121 South Santa Fe, Suite A, Norman OK 73069. 405/329-1933. **Contact:** Manager. **Description:** A career/outplacement counseling service.

OREGON

EXECUTIVE SEARCH FIRMS

ACCOUNTANTS EXECUTIVE SEARCH
ACCOUNTANTS ON CALL
222 SW Columbia Street, Suite 1115, Portland OR 97201. 503/228-0300. **Contact:** Manager. **Description:** An executive search firm. Accountants On Call (also at this location) is a temporary agency. **Specializes in the areas of:** Accounting/Auditing; Finance.

ACCOUNTANTS NORTHWEST
522 SW 5th Avenue, Suite 625, Portland OR 97204. 503/242-3528. **Contact:** Manager. **Description:** An executive search firm. **Specializes in the areas of:** Accounting/Auditing.

AUGUSTON & ASSOCIATES
510 SW 3rd Avenue, Suite 204, Portland OR 97204. 503/299-6298. **Contact:** Manager. **Description:** An executive search firm. **Specializes in the areas of:** Health/Medical.

THE BRENTWOOD GROUP LIMITED
9 Monroe Parkway, Suite 230, Lake Oswego OR 97035. 503/697-8136. **Fax:** 503/697-8161. **Contact:** Manager. **E-mail address:** brentwood@transport.com. **Description:** An executive search firm that operates on a retained basis. Company pays fee. **Specializes in the areas of:** Computer Science/Software; High-Tech; Insurance. **Positions commonly filled include:** Adjuster; Chief Executive Officer; Claim Representative; Underwriter/Assistant Underwriter. **Average salary range of placements:** More than $50,000. **Number of placements per year:** 50 - 99.

D. BROWN & ASSOCIATES, INC.
610 SW Alder Street, Suite 1111, Portland OR 97205. 503/224-6860. **Fax:** 503/241-8855. **Contact:** Manager. **Description:** An executive search firm. Founded in 1968. Company pays fee. **Specializes in the areas of:** Accounting/Auditing; Computer Science/Software; Information Systems, Health/ Medical. **Positions commonly filled include:** Accountant/Auditor; MIS Specialist; Physician; Systems Analyst. **Average salary range of placements:** More than $50,000. **Number of placements per year:** 50 - 99.

COMPUTER RECRUITERS
CREATIVE DATA CORPORATION
Denney Square, 6700 SW 105th Avenue, Beaverton OR 97008. 503/643-2464. **Fax:** 503/646-1118. **Contact:** Manager. **Description:** An executive search firm. Creative Data Corporation (also at this location) provides contract placements. **Specializes in the areas of:** Computer Hardware/Software; Information Systems.

CORPORATE BUILDERS, INC.
812 SW Washington Street, Suite 660, Portland OR 97205-3218. 503/223-4344. **Fax:** 503/221-7778. **Contact:** William C. Meysing, CEO. **Description:** An executive search firm. Founded in 1981. Company pays fee. **Specializes in the areas of:** Architecture/Construction; Engineering. **Positions commonly filled include:** Civil Engineer; Construction Contractor; Cost Estimator; Design Engineer; Electrical/Electronics Engineer; Environmental Engineer; Mechanical Engineer; Mining Engineer; Structural Engineer.

EDP MARKETS INC.
EDP CONSULTANTS
4000 SE International Way, Suite F203, Portland OR 97222. 503/654-9600. **Contact:** Manager. **E-mail address:** jobs@edpmarkets. **World Wide Web address:** http://www.edpmarkets.com. **Description:** An executive search firm and permanent placement agency. EDP Consultants (also at this location) provides contract services. **Specializes in the areas of:** High-Tech.

EXECUTIVES WORLDWIDE, INC.
P.O. Box 145, Suite 400, Bend OR 97709-0145. 541/385-5405. **Fax:** 541/385-5407. **Contact:** C. Ray Gould, President. **World Wide Web address:** http://www.eworldwide.com. **Description:** An executive search firm operating on both retained and contingency bases. **Specializes in the areas of:** High-Tech; Legal. **Positions commonly filled include:** Attorney; Biological Scientist; Biomedical Engineer; Chemical Engineer; Chemist; Civil Engineer; Computer Programmer; Construction Contractor; Design Engineer; Electrical/Electronics Engineer; Environmental Engineer; Geotechnical Engineer; Human Resources Manager; Industrial Engineer; Industrial Production Manager; Mechanical Engineer; Nuclear Engineer; Operations/Production Manager; Paralegal; Pharmacist; Systems Analyst. **Number of placements per year:** 50 - 99.

EXPRESS PERSONNEL SERVICES
621 SW Morrison Street, Suite 500, Portland OR 97205-3808. 503/224-5500. **Fax:** 503/242-1527. **Contact:** Brandon W. Byars, Recruiting Coordinator. **Description:** An executive search firm that also provides contract placements and temporary clerical and light industrial placements. Company pays fee. **Specializes in the areas of:** Accounting/Auditing; Administration; Banking; Computer Science/Software; Engineering; Finance; Food Industry; General Management; Industrial; Insurance; Manufacturing; Nonprofit; Personnel/Labor Relations; Sales; Secretarial; Technical. **Positions commonly filled include:** Accountant/Auditor; Administrative Manager; Advertising Clerk; Automotive Mechanic; Bank Officer/Manager; Blue-Collar Worker Supervisor; Branch Manager; Buyer; Chemical Engineer; Clerical Supervisor; Computer Programmer; Credit Manager; Customer Service Representative; Design Engineer; Draftsperson; Electrical/Electronics Engineer; Electrician; Environmental Engineer; Financial Analyst; Food Scientist/Technologist; General Manager; Human Resources Specialist; Industrial Engineer; Internet Services Manager; Management Analyst/Consultant; Manufacturer's/Wholesaler's Sales Rep.; Market Research Analyst; Mechanical Engineer; MIS Specialist; Operations/Production Manager; Purchasing Agent/Manager; Quality Control Supervisor; Science Technologist; Securities Sales Representative; Software Engineer; Systems Analyst; Technical Writer/Editor; Typist/Word Processor. **Benefits available to temporary workers:** 401(k); Medical Insurance; Paid Holidays; Paid Vacation; Referral Bonus Plan. **Corporate headquarters location:** Oklahoma City OK. **Other U.S. locations:** Nationwide. **Average salary range of placements:** $30,000 - $50,000. **Number of placements per year:** 500 - 999.

GLOBAL RECRUITMENT SERVICES, INC.
P.O. Box 82592, Portland OR 97282. 503/230-2521. **Contact:** Recruiter. **Description:** An executive search firm that focuses on energy and environmental opportunities. Company pays fee. **Positions commonly filled include:** Environmental Engineer; Utilities Director. **Average salary range of placements:** More than $50,000. **Number of placements per year:** 1 - 49.

HACKENSCHMIDT, WEAVER & FOX, INC.
13747 SW Farmington Road, Beaverton OR 97005-2603. 503/644-7744. **Fax:** 503/644-8730. **Contact:** Bob Weaver, Senior Recruiter. **Description:** An executive search firm operating on both retained and contingency bases. Founded in 1980. Company pays fee. **Specializes in the areas of:** Computer Science/Software; Engineering; General Management; Industrial; Personnel/Labor Relations. **Positions commonly filled include:** Applications Engineer; Chemical Engineer; Chemist; Chief Financial Officer; Computer Programmer; Controller; Design Engineer; General Manager; Human Resources Manager; Industrial Engineer; Industrial Production Manager; Manufacturing Engineer; Mechanical Engineer; Metallurgical Engineer; Production Manager; Project Manager; Purchasing Agent/Manager; Quality Control Supervisor; Sales Engineer; Software Engineer; Systems Analyst; Systems Manager. **Average salary range of placements:** More than $50,000. **Number of placements per year:** 1 - 49.

ROBERT HALF INTERNATIONAL ACCOUNTEMPS
222 SW Columbia, Suite 800, Portland OR 97201. 503/222-9778. **Fax:** 503/243-1027. **Contact:** Manager. **World Wide Web address:** http://www.roberthalf.com. **Description:** An executive search firm. Accountemps (also at this location) provides temporary accounting placements. **Specializes in the areas of:** Accounting/Auditing; Finance. **Corporate headquarters location:** Menlo Park CA. **International locations:** Worldwide.

DON HARRIS INC.
7110 SW Fir Loop, Suite 250, Tigard OR 97223. 503/684-6639. **Contact:** Manager. **Description:** An executive search firm. **Specializes in the areas of:** Data Processing.

MANAGEMENT RECRUITERS INTERNATIONAL OFFICEMATES5 OF PORTLAND
2020 Lloyd Center, Portland OR 97232-1376. 503/287-8701. **Contact:** Manager. **Description:** An executive search firm. OfficeMates5 (also at this location) provides permanent office placements. **Specializes in the areas of:** Accounting/Auditing; Administration; Advertising; Architecture/Construction; Banking; Communications; Computer Hardware/Software; Design; Electrical; Engineering; Food Industry; General Management; Health/Medical; Insurance; Legal; Manufacturing; Operations Management; Personnel/Labor Relations; Procurement; Publishing; Retail; Sales; Technical; Textiles; Transportation.

MANAGEMENT SOLUTIONS
One SW Columbia Street, Suite 1100, Portland OR 97258-2013. 503/222-6600. **Fax:** 503/228-3310. **Contact:** Manager. **Description:** An executive search firm. **Specializes in the areas of:** High-Tech.

NATIONWIDE PERSONNEL RECRUITING & CONSULTING INC. (NPRC)
20834 SW Martinazzi Avenue, Tualatin OR 97062-9327. 503/692-4925. **Fax:** 503/692-6764. **Contact:** Barbara Bodle, President. **Description:** An executive search firm. Company pays fee. **Specializes in the areas of:** Architecture/Construction; Computer Science/Software; Engineering; General Management; Industrial; Manufacturing; Sales; Technical. **Positions commonly filled include:** Ceramics Engineer; Chemical Engineer; Civil Engineer; Design Engineer; Electrical/Electronics Engineer; Environmental Engineer; Financial Analyst; General Manager; Industrial Engineer; Industrial Production Manager; Manufacturer's/Wholesaler's Sales Rep.; Mechanical Engineer; MIS Specialist; Nuclear Engineer; Operations/Production Manager; Quality Control Supervisor; Services Sales Representative; Software Engineer; Stationary Engineer; Structural Engineer. **Average salary range of placements:** More than $50,000. **Number of placements per year:** 100 - 199.

NORTHWEST LEGAL SEARCH
2701 NW Baughn, Suite 450, Portland OR 97210. 503/224-9601. **Contact:** Manager. **Description:** An executive search firm. **Specializes in the areas of:** Legal.

PACIFIC COAST RECRUITERS
P.O. Box 7080, Eugene OR 97401. 541/345-6866. **Fax:** 541/345-0547. **Contact:** David Watson, Executive Director. **E-mail address:** dlbw@aol.com. **Description:** An executive search firm operating on both retained and contingency bases that specializes in all facets of the property/casualty insurance market including underwriting, claims, loss control, risk management, sales and marketing, and worker's compensation. Founded in 1984. **Specializes in the areas of:** Insurance. **Positions commonly filled include:** Adjuster; Claim Representative; Underwriter/Assistant Underwriter. **Average salary range of placements:** More than $50,000. **Number of placements per year:** 1 - 49.

ROTH YOUNG EXECUTIVE RECRUITERS
7931 NE Halsey Street, Suite 314, Portland OR 97213. 503/255-1655. **Contact:** Office Manager. **Description:** An executive search firm. **Specializes in the areas of:** Health/Medical.

SANFORD ROSE ASSOCIATES
10200 SW Eastridge Street, Suite 200, Portland OR 97225. 503/297-9191. **Fax:** 503/297-3528. **Contact:** Jack D. Stiles, Director. **World Wide Web address:** http://www.sanfordrose.com. **Description:** An executive search firm. **Specializes in the areas of:** Engineering; Food Industry; Personnel/Labor Relations. **Positions commonly filled include:** Electrical/Electronics Engineer; Food Scientist/Technologist; Purchasing Agent/Manager; Software Engineer.

SEARCH NORTH AMERICA
620 SW 5th Avenue, Suite 925, Portland OR 97204. 503/222-6461. **Contact:** Manager. **Description:** An executive search firm. **Specializes in the areas of:** Paper.

SEARCH NORTHWEST ASSOCIATES (SNA)
10117 SE Sunnyside Road, Suite F-727, Clackamas OR 97015. 503/654-1487. **Fax:** 503/654-9110. **Contact:** Douglas L. Jansen, CPC, President. **Description:** An executive search firm focusing on the foundry, metal fabrication, chemical, and high-tech industries. Founded in 1977. Company pays fee. **Specializes in the areas of:** Computer Science/Software; Engineering; General Management; Manufacturing. **Positions commonly filled include:** Biomedical Engineer; Ceramics Engineer; Chemical Engineer; Civil Engineer; Electrical/Electronics Engineer; Environmental Engineer; General Manager; Industrial Engineer; Materials Engineer; Mechanical Engineer; Metallurgical Engineer; Mining Engineer; Petroleum Engineer; Purchasing Agent/Manager; Quality Control Supervisor; Software Engineer. **Average salary range of placements:** More than $50,000. **Number of placements per year:** 100 - 199.

WOLF ENVIRONMENTAL GROUP
25 NW 23rd Place, Suite 6-116, Portland OR 97210. 503/241-0881. **Fax:** 503/241-0976. **Contact:** Judy Stockton, Owner. **E-mail address:** judywolf@aol.com. **Description:** An executive search firm operating on a contingency basis. Founded in 1991. Company pays fee. **Specializes in the areas of:** Engineering;

Environmental. **Positions commonly filled include:** Agricultural Engineer; Biological Scientist; Chemical Engineer; Chemist; Civil Engineer; Environmental Engineer; Environmental Scientist; Industrial Engineer; Structural Engineer; Surveyor; Technical Writer/Editor. **Average salary range of placements:** More than $50,000. **Number of placements per year:** 1 - 49.

WOODWORTH INTERNATIONAL GROUP
620 SW Fifth Avenue, Suite 1225, Portland OR 97204-1426. 503/225-5000. **Fax:** 503/225-5005. **Contact:** Gail Woodworth, President. **Description:** An executive search firm operating on a retained basis. The firm also provides management consulting services to companies. Company pays fee. **Specializes in the areas of:** Architecture/Construction; Computer Science/Software; Engineering; Finance; General Management; Health/Medical; Insurance; Manufacturing; Personnel/Labor Relations; Retail; Sales; Transportation. **Positions commonly filled include:** Accountant/Auditor; Administrative Manager; Aerospace Engineer; Bank Officer/Manager; Biomedical Engineer; Branch Manager; Budget Analyst; Buyer; Chemical Engineer; Chemist; Civil Engineer; Computer Programmer; Credit Manager; Customer Service Representative; Design Engineer; Designer; Editor; Electrical/Electronics Engineer; Environmental Engineer; Financial Analyst; General Manager; Human Resources Manager; Industrial Engineer; Industrial Production Manager; Internet Services Manager; Management Analyst/Consultant; Mechanical Engineer; Metallurgical Engineer; MIS Specialist; Multimedia Designer; Nuclear Engineer; Nuclear Medicine Technologist; Operations/Production Manager; Physician; Property and Real Estate Manager; Purchasing Agent/Manager; Quality Control Supervisor; Software Engineer; Structural Engineer; Systems Analyst; Technical Writer/Editor; Telecommunications Manager; Transportation/Traffic Specialist; Video Producer. **Average salary range of placements:** More than $50,000. **Number of placements per year:** 200 - 499.

PERMANENT EMPLOYMENT AGENCIES

API EMPLOYMENT AGENCY
5022 Commercial Street SE, Salem OR 97302. 503/585-9572. **Fax:** 503/364-3722. **Contact:** Recruiter. **Description:** A permanent employment agency. **Specializes in the areas of:** Automotive; Computer Science/Software; Industrial; Manufacturing. **Positions commonly filled include:** Accountant/Auditor; Automotive Mechanic; Clerical Supervisor; Customer Service Representative; Electrical/Electronics Engineer; General Manager. **Average salary range of placements:** $30,000 - $50,000. **Number of placements per year:** 50 - 99.

ADAMS & ASSOCIATES PERSONNEL, INC.
121 SW Morrison Street, Suite 430, Portland OR 97204. 503/224-5870. **Contact:** Office Manager. **Description:** A permanent employment agency. Company pays fee. **Specializes in the areas of:** Clerical. **Positions commonly filled include:** Administrative Assistant; Advertising Clerk; Bookkeeper; Claim Representative; Clerk; Computer Operator; Customer Service Representative; Data Entry Clerk; Legal Secretary; Medical Secretary; Public Relations Specialist; Purchasing Agent/Manager; Receptionist; Sales Representative; Secretary; Stenographer; Typist/Word Processor. **Number of placements per year:** 500 - 999.

ADVANCE PERSONNEL SERVICES
441 Union Street NE, Salem OR 97301. 503/581-8906. **Contact:** Phil Lackaff, Manager. **Description:** A permanent employment agency. Company pays fee. **Positions commonly filled include:** Accountant/Auditor; Administrative Assistant; Bank Officer/Manager; Bookkeeper; Buyer; Claim Representative; Clerk; Commercial Artist; Computer Operator; Computer Programmer; Credit Manager; Customer Service Representative; Data Entry Clerk; Draftsperson; Driver; General Manager; Human Resources Manager; Legal Secretary; Purchasing Agent/Manager; Receptionist; Sales Representative; Secretary; Stenographer; Typist/Word Processor; Underwriter/Assistant Underwriter. **Number of placements per year:** 200 - 499.

AUNTIE FAY DOMESTIC AGENCY
10725 SW Barbur Boulevard, Suite 60, Portland OR 97219. 503/293-6252. **Contact:** Loyce Swayze, Owner. **Description:** A permanent employment agency that also provides some temporary placements. Company pays fee. **Specializes in the areas of:** Child Care, In-Home; Eldercare, In-Home; Health/Medical. **Positions commonly filled include:** Certified Nursing Aide; Cook; Domestic Help; Housekeeper; Licensed Practical Nurse; Nanny; Preschool Worker; Registered Nurse.

FIRST CHOICE PERSONNEL
11330 SW Ambiance Place, Tigard OR 97223. 503/620-0717. **Fax:** 503/244-1544. **Contact:** Randall B. Carrier, CPC, President. **Description:** A permanent employment agency. Company pays fee. **Specializes in the areas of:** Computer Science/Software. **Positions commonly filled include:** Computer Programmer; Software Engineer; Systems Analyst. **Number of placements per year:** 1 - 49.

JOBWORKS AGENCY INC.
1100 East Marina Way, Suite 221, Hood River OR 97031. 541/386-4407. **Contact:** Manager. **Description:** A permanent employment agency that also provides some temporary placements.

JOBWORKS AGENCY INC.
405 West 4th Street, The Dalles OR 97058. 541/296-4455. **Contact:** Manager. **Description:** A permanent employment agency that also provides some temporary placements.

LEGAL NORTHWEST
522 SE 5th Avenue, Suite 625, Portland OR 97204. 503/242-2514. **Contact:** Manager. **Description:** A permanent employment agency that also provides temporary placements. **Specializes in the areas of:** Legal.

OFFICE CAREERS INC.
dba CORPORATE CAREERS INC.
1001 SW 5th Avenue, Suite 1210, Portland OR 97204-1128. 503/242-2323. **Fax:** 503/242-1129. **Contact:** Susan Johnson, President. **Description:** A permanent employment agency. Founded in 1972. Company pays fee. **Specializes in the areas of:** Accounting/Auditing; Administration; General Management; Personnel/Labor Relations; Sales; Secretarial. **Positions commonly filled include:** Accountant/Auditor; Administrative Manager; Advertising Clerk; Clerical Supervisor; Customer Service Representative; Financial Analyst; Human Resources Manager; Human Service Worker; Paralegal; Public Relations Specialist; Services Sales Representative; Typist/Word Processor.

OREGON STATE EMPLOYMENT DEPARTMENT
P.O. Box 10, Newport OR 97365. 541/265-8891. **Fax:** 541/265-5975. **Recorded jobline:** 541/265-

8100x1211. **Contact:** Steve Corwin, Employment Specialist. **World Wide Web address:** http://www.emp.state.or.us. **Description:** A state operated employment agency that provides job placement and career services. **Corporate headquarters location:** Salem OR. **Average salary range of placements:** $20,000 - $29,999. **Number of placements per year:** 1000+.

NANCY L. SALUN EMPLOYMENT AGENCY
1717 Avalon Street, Klamath Falls OR 97603. 541/882-5872. **Fax:** 541/882-5468. **Contact:** Manager. **Description:** A permanent employment agency. **Positions commonly filled include:** Accountant/Auditor; Administrative Manager; Advertising Clerk; Automotive Mechanic; Bank Officer/Manager; Blue-Collar Worker Supervisor; Branch Manager; Claim Representative; Clerical Supervisor; Computer Programmer; Construction and Building Inspector; Credit Manager; Draftsperson; Forester/Conservation Scientist; General Manager; Health Services Manager; Hotel Manager; Industrial Production Manager; Insurance Agent/Broker; Landscape Architect; Licensed Practical Nurse; Manufacturer's/Wholesaler's Sales Rep.; Market Research Analyst; Medical Records Technician; Occupational Therapist; Physical Therapist; Preschool Worker; Property and Real Estate Manager; Radiological Technologist; Real Estate Agent; Registered Nurse; Securities Sales Representative; Services Sales Representative; Social Worker; Stationary Engineer; Surveyor; Systems Analyst; Telecommunications Manager; Transportation/Traffic Specialist; Typist/Word Processor; Veterinarian.

SNELLING PERSONNEL SERVICES
10300 SW Greenburg Road, Suite 560, Portland OR 97223-5418. 503/244-4774. **Fax:** 503/244-7029. **Contact:** Recruiter. **Description:** A permanent employment agency. Company pays fee. **Specializes in the areas of:** General Management; Sales. **Positions commonly filled include:** Advertising Clerk; Aerospace Engineer; Bank Officer/Manager; Branch Manager; Brokerage Clerk; Buyer; Civil Engineer; Clerical Supervisor; Computer Programmer; Construction Contractor; Credit Manager; Customer Service Representative; Draftsperson; Electrical/Electronics Engineer; General Manager; Human Resources Manager; Management Trainee; Mechanical Engineer; MIS Specialist; Paralegal; Restaurant/Food Service Manager; Services Sales Representative; Software Engineer; Structural Engineer; Systems Analyst; Typist/Word Processor. **Benefits available to temporary workers:** 401(k); Bonus Award/Plan; Paid Holidays; Paid Vacation. **Corporate headquarters location:** Dallas TX. **Other U.S. locations:** Nationwide. **Average salary range of placements:** $30,000 - $50,000. **Number of placements per year:** 50 - 99.

SOURCE SERVICES CORPORATION
10220 SW Greenburg Road, Suite 625, Portland OR 97223. 503/768-4546. **Contact:** Office Manager. **Description:** A permanent placement agency operating several divisions. **Specializes in the areas of:** Computer Hardware/Software; Finance. **Corporate headquarters location:** Dallas TX. **Other U.S. locations:** Nationwide.

TALENT TREE STAFFING SERVICE
700 NE Multnomah, Suite 1125, Portland OR 97232. 503/233-9121. **Fax:** 503/233-9398. **Contact:** Manager. **World Wide Web address:** http://www.ttree.com. **Description:** A permanent employment agency that also provides temporary placements. Founded in 1976. Company pays fee. **Specializes in the areas of:** Administration; Banking; Personnel/Labor Relations; Secretarial. **Positions commonly filled include:** Administrative Manager; Branch Manager; Clerical Supervisor; Customer Service Representative; Human Resources Specialist; Market Research Analyst; Typist/Word Processor. **Benefits available to temporary workers:** Bonus Award/Plan; Dental Insurance; Medical Insurance; Paid Vacation. **Corporate headquarters location:** Houston TX. **Other U.S. locations:** Nationwide. **Average salary range of placements:** $20,000 - $29,999.

TALENT TREE STAFFING SERVICES
8625 SW Cascade Avenue, Suite 601, Beaverton OR 97005. 503/626-0393. **Fax:** 503/626-0173. **Contact:** Amy Schultz, Senior Staffing Consultant. **E-mail address:** aeschult@ttree.com. **World Wide Web address:** http://www.ttree.com. **Description:** A permanent employment agency that also provides temporary placements. Founded in 1976. **Specializes in the areas of:** Accounting/Auditing; Administration; Banking; Computer Science/Software; Finance; Health/Medical; Manufacturing; Personnel/Labor Relations; Retail; Sales; Secretarial; Technical. **Positions commonly filled include:** Accountant/Auditor; Administrative Manager; Bank Officer/Manager; Branch Manager; Claim Representative; Clerical Supervisor; Customer Service Representative; Human Resources Specialist; Operations/Production Manager; Public Relations Specialist; Purchasing Agent/Manager; Quality Control Supervisor; Services Sales Representative. **Benefits available to temporary workers:** Bonus Award/Plan; Dental Insurance; Medical Insurance; Referral Bonus Plan. **Corporate headquarters location:** Houston TX. **Other U.S. locations:** Nationwide. **Number of placements per year:** 1000+.

TRIAD TECHNOLOGY GROUP
10200 SW Greenburg Road, Suite 350, Portland OR 97223. 503/293-9545. **Fax:** 503/293-9546. **Contact:** Bruno Amicci, President. **E-mail address:** triadjob@triadtechnology.com. **World Wide Web address:** http://www.triadtechnology.com. **Description:** A permanent employment agency that also provides some contract placements. Company pays fee. **Specializes in the areas of:** Administration; Engineering; Information Technology. **Positions commonly filled include:** Computer Programmer; Database Manager; Internet Services Manager; MIS Specialist; Project Manager; Software Engineer; Systems Analyst; Systems Manager; Technical Writer/Editor; Telecommunications Manager. **Average salary range of placements:** More than $50,000. **Number of placements per year:** 50 - 99.

TEMPORARY EMPLOYMENT AGENCIES

ABLE TEMPORARY SERVICE
12950 SW Pacific Highway, Suite 1A, Tigard OR 97223-5061. 503/684-8389. **Contact:** Branch Manager. **Description:** A temporary agency. **Specializes in the areas of:** Construction; Industrial; Sales; Secretarial. **Positions commonly filled include:** Customer Service Representative. **Corporate headquarters location:** Medford OR. **Number of placements per year:** 1 - 49.

ABLE TEMPORARY SERVICE
1611 Bay Shore Drive, Coos Bay OR 97420. 541/756-6126. **Fax:** 541/756-6312. **Contact:** Joanna Warner, Branch Manager. **Description:** A temporary agency. Company pays fee. **Specializes in the areas of:** Accounting/Auditing; Advertising; Agriculture; Computer Science/Software; Electronics; Finance; Food Industry; Health/Medical; Industrial; Manufacturing; Retail; Sales; Secretarial. **Positions**

commonly filled include: Advertising Clerk; Agricultural Engineer; Claim Representative; Clerical Supervisor; Construction and Building Inspector; Customer Service Representative; Dental Assistant/Dental Hygienist; Emergency Medical Technician; Human Resources Specialist; Insurance Agent/Broker; Internet Services Manager; Licensed Practical Nurse; Management Trainee; Medical Records Technician; Operations/Production Manager; Registered Nurse; Restaurant/Food Service Manager; Services Sales Representative; Typist/Word Processor. **Corporate headquarters location:** Medford OR. **Average salary range of placements:** Less than $20,000. **Number of placements per year:** 200 - 499.

ADAMS TEMPORARIES
7567 SW Mohawk Street, Tualatin OR 97062. 503/692-6106. **Contact:** Manager. **Description:** A temporary agency. **Specializes in the areas of:** Administration; Clerical; Light Industrial; Office Support; Telemarketing.

BARRETT BUSINESS SERVICES, INC.
2401 NE Cornell Road, Hillsboro OR 97124. 503/648-5053. **Contact:** Branch Manager. **Description:** A temporary agency. Founded in 1951. **Specializes in the areas of:** Architecture/Construction; Engineering; Industrial; Personnel/Labor Relations; Secretarial. **Positions commonly filled include:** Blue-Collar Worker Supervisor; Civil Engineer; Clerical Supervisor; Computer Programmer; Construction and Building Inspector; Construction Contractor; Cost Estimator; Customer Service Representative; Design Engineer; Designer; Draftsperson; Electrical/Electronics Engineer; Electrician; Human Resources Specialist; Industrial Engineer; Industrial Production Manager; Mechanical Engineer; Purchasing Agent/Manager; Quality Control Supervisor; Software Engineer; Structural Engineer; Systems Analyst; Typist/Word Processor. **Benefits available to temporary workers:** Medical Insurance; Paid Holidays; Paid Vacation. **Corporate headquarters location:** Portland OR. **Average salary range of placements:** $20,000 - $29,999. **Number of placements per year:** 1000+.

BARRETT BUSINESS SERVICES, INC.
8700 SW Elligsen Road, Suite 2, Wilsonville OR 97070. 503/685-5042. **Contact:** Manager. **Description:** A temporary agency. **Specializes in the areas of:** Transportation. **Positions commonly filled include:** Truck Driver. **Corporate headquarters location:** Portland OR.

BROOKS TEMPORARY SERVICE
1130 NE Alberta Street, Portland OR 97211. 503/284-7930. **Toll-free phone:** 800/540-7930. **Fax:** 503/284-7977. **Contact:** Margaret Brooks, Vice President of Employment Services. **E-mail address:** sbrooks@sbrooks.com. **World Wide Web address:** http://www.sbrooks.com. **Description:** A temporary agency. Founded in 1981.

CREATIVE ASSETS
222 SW Yamhill, Portland OR 97204. **Contact:** Manager. **World Wide Web address:** http://www.creativeassets.com. **Description:** A temporary agency. **Specializes in the areas of:** Digital Arts; Graphic Arts. **Other U.S. locations:** San Francisco CA; Seattle WA.

EMPLOYMENT TRENDS, LLC
4800 SW Griffith Drive, Suite 104, Beaverton OR 97005. 503/350-2300. **Fax:** 503/644-7087. **Contact:** Recruiter. **World Wide Web address:** http://www.employmenttrends.com. **Description:** A temporary agency. Founded in 1993. **Specializes in the areas of:** Banking; Insurance; Light Industrial; Personnel/Labor Relations; Secretarial. **Positions commonly filled include:** Blue-Collar Worker Supervisor; Claim Representative; Clerical Supervisor; Customer Service Representative; Human Resources Specialist; Management Trainee; Typist/Word Processor. **Benefits available to temporary workers:** Bonus Award/Plan; Paid Holidays. **Other area locations:** Portland OR. **Average salary range of placements:** Less than $20,000. **Number of placements per year:** 1000+.

HIRE GROUND
516 SE Morrison, Suite 910, Portland OR 97214-2327. 503/236-1159. **Contact:** Staffing Coordinator. **Description:** A temporary agency. Company pays fee. **Specializes in the areas of:** Banking. **Positions commonly filled include:** Bank Teller; Customer Service Representative; Receptionist; Typist/Word Processor. **Average salary range of placements:** Less than $20,000. **Number of placements per year:** 1 - 49.

IMPACT STAFFING
10220 SW Greenberg Road, Suite 540, Portland OR 97223. 503/526-0241. **Toll-free phone:** 800/445-9039. **Fax:** 503/641-3947. **Contact:** Manager. **E-mail address:** donnella@pde.com. **Description:** A temporary agency. **Specializes in the areas of:** Computer Science/Software; Engineering; Industrial; Manufacturing; Technical. **Positions commonly filled include:** Aerospace Engineer; Agricultural Engineer; Aircraft Mechanic/Engine Specialist; Biochemist; Biological Scientist; Biomedical Engineer; Chemical Engineer; Chemist; Civil Engineer; Clinical Lab Technician; Computer Programmer; Construction and Building Inspector; Construction Contractor; Design Engineer; Designer; Draftsperson; Electrical/Electronics Engineer; Electrician; Environmental Engineer; Geologist/Geophysicist; Industrial Engineer; Industrial Production Manager; Internet Services Manager; Metallurgical Engineer; Mining Engineer; MIS Specialist; Multimedia Designer; Nuclear Engineer; Nuclear Medicine Technologist; Quality Control Supervisor; Science Technologist; Software Engineer; Structural Engineer; Systems Analyst; Technical Writer/Editor; Telecommunications Manager; Video Production Coordinator. **Benefits available to temporary workers:** 401(k); Dental Insurance; Medical Insurance; Paid Holidays; Paid Vacation; Vision Plan. **Other U.S. locations:** San Diego CA; Seattle WA. **Number of placements per year:** 200 - 499.

KELLY SERVICES, INC.
111 NE 3rd Street, McMinnville OR 97128. 503/434-4337. **Fax:** 503/472-0969. **Contact:** Recruiter/Trainer. **Description:** A temporary agency. Founded in 1946. Company pays fee. **Specializes in the areas of:** Accounting/Auditing; Administration; Data Processing; Industrial; Manufacturing; Personnel/Labor Relations; Sales; Secretarial; Technical. **Positions commonly filled include:** Accountant/Auditor; Clerical Supervisor; Customer Service Representative; Typist/Word Processor. **Benefits available to temporary workers:** Paid Holidays; Paid Vacation. **Corporate headquarters location:** Troy MI. **Average salary range of placements:** $20,000 - $29,999. **Number of placements per year:** 500 - 999.

KELLY SERVICES, INC.
8285 SW Nimbus Avenue, Suite 130, Beaverton OR 97008. 503/643-1614. **Fax:** 503/641-9086. **Contact:** Recruiter/Trainer. **Description:** A temporary agency. Founded in 1946. Company pays fee. **Specializes in the areas of:** Administration; Industrial; Light Industrial; Manufacturing; Personnel/Labor Relations; Sales; Secretarial; Technical. **Positions commonly filled include:** Accountant/Auditor; Clerical Supervisor; Customer Service Representative; Typist/Word Processor. **Benefits available to temporary workers:**

Paid Holidays; Paid Vacation. **Corporate headquarters location:** Troy MI. **Average salary range of placements:** $20,000 - $29,999. **Number of placements per year:** 500 - 999.

KELLY SERVICES, INC.
5250 NE Elam Young Parkway, Hillsboro OR 97124. 503/648-2757. **Fax:** 503/640-9575. **Contact:** Recruiter/Trainer. **Description:** A temporary agency. Founded in 1946. Company pays fee. **Specializes in the areas of:** Administration; Industrial; Light Industrial; Manufacturing; Personnel/Labor Relations; Sales; Secretarial; Technical. **Positions commonly filled include:** Accountant/Auditor; Clerical Supervisor; Customer Service Representative; Typist/Word Processor. **Benefits available to temporary workers:** Paid Holidays; Paid Vacation. **Corporate headquarters location:** Troy MI. **Average salary range of placements:** $20,000 - $29,999. **Number of placements per year:** 500 - 999.

KELLY SERVICES, INC.
456 State Street, Suite 100, Salem OR 97301. 503/364-3591. **Fax:** 503/588-1965. **Contact:** Recruiter/Trainer. **Description:** A temporary agency. Founded in 1946. Company pays fee. **Specializes in the areas of:** Administration; Industrial; Light Industrial; Manufacturing; Personnel/Labor Relations; Sales; Secretarial; Technical. **Positions commonly filled include:** Accountant/Auditor; Clerical Supervisor; Customer Service Representative; Typist/Word Processor. **Benefits available to temporary workers:** Paid Holidays; Paid Vacation. **Corporate headquarters location:** Troy MI. **Average salary range of placements:** $20,000 - $29,999. **Number of placements per year:** 500 - 999.

KELLY SERVICES, INC.
1823 14th Avenue SE, Albany OR 97321. 541/967-8858. **Fax:** 541/967-7152. **Contact:** Recruiter/Trainer. **Description:** A temporary agency. Founded in 1946. Company pays fee. **Specializes in the areas of:** Administration; Industrial; Light Industrial; Manufacturing; Personnel/Labor Relations; Sales; Secretarial; Technical. **Positions commonly filled include:** Accountant/Auditor; Clerical Supervisor; Customer Service Representative; Typist/Word Processor. **Benefits available to temporary workers:** Paid Holidays; Paid Vacation. **Corporate headquarters location:** Troy MI. **Average salary range of placements:** $20,000 - $29,999. **Number of placements per year:** 500 - 999.

KELLY SERVICES, INC.
700 NE Multnomah, Suite 350, Portland OR 97232-4103. 503/230-2221. **Contact:** Recruiter/Trainer. **Description:** A temporary agency. Founded in 1946. Company pays fee. **Specializes in the areas of:** Administration; Industrial; Light Industrial; Manufacturing; Personnel/Labor Relations; Sales; Secretarial; Technical. **Positions commonly filled include:** Accountant/Auditor; Clerical Supervisor; Customer Service Representative; Human Service Worker; Typist/Word Processor. **Benefits available to temporary workers:** Paid Holidays; Paid Vacation. **Corporate headquarters location:** Troy MI. **Average salary range of placements:** $20,000 - $29,999. **Number of placements per year:** 500 - 999.

MANPOWER TEMPORARY SERVICES
1000 Broadway, Suite 1550, Portland OR 97205-3067. 503/226-6281. **Contact:** Branch Manager. **Description:** A temporary agency. Company pays fee. **Specializes in the areas of:** Data Processing; Industrial; Office Support; Technical; Word Processing. **Positions commonly filled include:** Accountant/Auditor; Accounting Clerk; Administrative Assistant; Assembly Worker; Biological Scientist; Bookkeeper; Chemist; Computer Operator; Customer Service Representative; Desktop Publishing Specialist; Electrician; Inspector/Tester/Grader; Inventory Control Specialist; Machine Operator; Packaging/Processing Worker; Painter; Project Engineer; Proofreader; Receptionist; Research Assistant; Secretary; Software Engineer; Stenographer; Systems Analyst; Technical Writer/Editor; Technician; Typist/Word Processor; Welder. **Benefits available to temporary workers:** Life Insurance; Medical Insurance; Paid Holidays; Paid Vacation. **Number of placements per year:** 1000+.

NORTHWEST TEMPORARY & STAFFING SERVICES
522 SW 5th Avenue, Suite 825, Portland OR 97204. 503/242-0611. **Fax:** 503/274-7895. **Contact:** Amy Floersch, Recruiter. **Description:** A temporary agency. Founded in 1985. **Specializes in the areas of:** Accounting/Auditing; Engineering; Health/Medical; Industrial; Legal; Secretarial; Technical. **Positions commonly filled include:** Accountant/Auditor; Claim Representative; Clerical Supervisor; Computer Programmer; Customer Service Representative; Design Engineer; Draftsperson; Electrical/Electronics Engineer; Financial Analyst; Medical Records Technician; Paralegal; Systems Analyst; Typist/Word Processor. **Benefits available to temporary workers:** 401(k); Medical Insurance; Paid Holidays; Paid Vacation. **Corporate headquarters location:** This Location. **Other area locations:** Bellevue WA; Kent WA; Lynnwood WA; Seattle WA. **Number of placements per year:** 1000+.

PRO TEM PROFESSIONAL TEMPORARY SERVICES
1001 SW 5th Avenue, Suite 1225, Portland OR 97204. 503/228-1177. **Contact:** Office Manager. **Description:** A temporary agency. Company pays fee. **Specializes in the areas of:** Personnel/Labor Relations. **Positions commonly filled include:** Accountant/Auditor; Clerk; Computer Operator; Computer Programmer; Data Entry Clerk; Draftsperson; Electrical/Electronics Engineer; Financial Analyst; Legal Secretary; Receptionist; Secretary; Stenographer; Systems Analyst; Technical Writer/Editor; Technician; Typist/Word Processor. **Number of placements per year:** 1000+.

QUEST TEMPORARY SERVICES
P.O. Box 518, Wilsonville OR 97070. 503/682-9292. **Fax:** 503/682-4912. **Contact:** B.J. Shrock, Owner. **Description:** A temporary agency that also provides career/outplacement counseling. Founded in 1995. Company pays fee. **Specializes in the areas of:** Industrial; Manufacturing; Personnel/Labor Relations; Publishing; Secretarial. **Positions commonly filled include:** Administrative Manager; Blue-Collar Worker Supervisor; Clerical Supervisor; Computer Programmer; Credit Manager; Customer Service Representative; Draftsperson; Human Resources Specialist; Industrial Production Manager; Management Trainee; Medical Records Technician; Operations/Production Manager; Paralegal; Purchasing Agent/Manager; Quality Control Supervisor; Technical Writer/Editor; Typist/Word Processor; Underwriter/Assistant Underwriter. **Benefits available to temporary workers:** Paid Holidays; Paid Vacation. **Average salary range of placements:** Less than $20,000. **Number of placements per year:** 1000+.

SAINT VINCENT DE PAUL EMPLOYMENT
546 High Street NE, Salem OR 97301. 503/375-2030. **Fax:** 503/375-2050. **Contact:** Manager. **Description:** Saint Vincent De Paul Employment is a temporary agency that focuses on placing people with disabilities. **Specializes in the areas of:** Administration; Clerical; Industrial; Nonprofit; Secretarial. **Positions commonly filled include:** Accountant/Auditor; Architect; Clerical Supervisor; Customer Service Representative. **Benefits available to temporary**

workers: Medical Insurance; Paid Vacation; Retirement Plan. **Corporate headquarters location:** Portland OR. **Other area locations:** Corvallis OR. **Average salary range of placements:** Less than $20,000. **Number of placements per year:** 200 - 499.

SOUTHERN OREGON TEMPORARY
720 East Jackson Street, Medford OR 97504. 541/779-4433. **Contact:** Branch Manager. **Description:** A temporary agency. Founded in 1969. **Specializes in the areas of:** Accounting/Auditing; Administration; Banking; Computer Science/Software; Education; Finance; General Management; Personnel/Labor Relations; Retail; Sales; Technical. **Positions commonly filled include:** Accountant/ Auditor; Actuary; Adjuster; Advertising Clerk; Aerospace Engineer; Agricultural Engineer; Bank Officer/Manager; Biochemist; Blue-Collar Worker Supervisor; Buyer; Chemical Engineer; Computer Operator; Computer Programmer; Customer Service Representative; Draftsperson; Economist; Financial Analyst; General Manager; Human Resources Specialist; Industrial Engineer; Management Trainee; Mechanical Engineer; MIS Specialist; Operations/ Production Manager; Property and Real Estate Manager; Quality Control Supervisor; Recreational Therapist; Respiratory Therapist; Restaurant/Food Service Manager; Software Engineer; Structural Engineer; Systems Analyst; Technical Writer/Editor; Telecommunications Manager; Typist/Word Processor; Underwriter/Assistant Underwriter; Video Production Coordinator. **Number of placements per year:** 100 - 199.

SUMMIT STAFFING
149 SW Third Avenue, Suite 100, Hillsboro OR 97123. 503/640-4288. **Fax:** 503/693-1850. **Contact:** Manager. **Description:** A temporary agency. Founded in 1994. Company pays fee. **Specializes in the areas of:** Engineering. **Positions commonly filled include:** Civil Engineer; Design Engineer; Designer; Draftsperson; Structural Engineer; Surveyor. **Benefits available to temporary workers:** Medical Insurance; Paid Holidays; Paid Vacation. **Average salary range of placements:** $20,000 - $29,999.

UNIFORCE STAFFING SERVICES
10121 SE Sunnyside Road, Suite 235, Clackamas OR 97015-9749. 503/652-2543. **Fax:** 503/659-0257. **Contact:** Lisa Poppleton, Manager. **E-mail address:** uniforc3@ix.netcom.com. **Description:** A temporary agency. **Specializes in the areas of:** Accounting/ Auditing; Light Industrial; Printing; Publishing; Retail; Secretarial. **Positions commonly filled include:** Administrative Manager; Biological Scientist; Biomedical Engineer; Chemical Engineer; Chemist; Civil Engineer; Computer Programmer; Customer Service Representative; Design Engineer; Designer; Draftsperson; Electrical/Electronics Engineer; Environmental Engineer; Food Scientist/Technologist; Industrial Engineer; Mechanical Engineer; Metallurgical Engineer; MIS Specialist; Software Engineer; Stationary Engineer; Structural Engineer; Systems Analyst; Technical Writer/Editor. **Benefits available to temporary workers:** 401(k); Dental Insurance; Health Club Discount; Medical Insurance; Vision Plan. **Corporate headquarters location:** New York NY. **Number of placements per year:** 1000+.

CONTRACT SERVICES FIRMS

CDI CORPORATION
15250 NW Greenbriar Parkway, Beaverton OR 97006. 503/693-6587. **Contact:** Manager. **World Wide Web address:** http://www.cdicorp.com. **Description:** A contract services firm. **Specializes in the areas of:** Engineering; Technical. **Corporate headquarters location:** Philadelphia PA. **Other U.S. locations:** Nationwide. **International locations:** Worldwide.

RESOURCE TECHNOLOGY GROUP
10300 SW Greenburg Road, Portland OR 97223. 503/293-6933. **Contact:** Manager. **Description:** A contract services firm. **Specializes in the areas of:** High-Tech.

UNIFORCE TECHNICAL SERVICES
7320 SW Hunziker Road, Suite 104, Tigard OR 97223. 503/968-1311. **Fax:** 503/968-1088. **Contact:** Donna Schultz, Vice President. **E-mail address:** uniforc3@ix.netcom.com. **Description:** A contract services firm. Company pays fee. **Specializes in the areas of:** Computer Science/Software; Engineering; Industrial; Scientific; Technical. **Positions commonly filled include:** Accountant/Auditor; Administrative Assistant; Aerospace Engineer; Agricultural Engineer; Architect; Bank Officer/Manager; Biomedical Engineer; Bookkeeper; Ceramics Engineer; Civil Engineer; Claim Representative; Clerk; Commercial Artist; Computer Programmer; Construction Trade Worker; Customer Service Representative; Data Entry Clerk; Draftsperson; Driver; EDP Specialist; Electrical/ Electronics Engineer; Factory Worker; General Manager; Hotel Manager; Industrial Designer; Industrial Engineer; Legal Secretary; Light Industrial Worker; Marketing Specialist; Mechanical Engineer; Medical Secretary; Metallurgical Engineer; Mining Engineer; Petroleum Engineer; Public Relations Specialist; Purchasing Agent/Manager; Receptionist; Secretary; Stenographer; Systems Analyst; Technical Writer/Editor; Technician; Typist/Word Processor. **Corporate headquarters location:** New York NY. **Number of placements per year:** 1000+.

VOLT TECHNICAL SERVICES
6443 SW Beaverton Hillsdale Highway, Suite 425, Portland OR 97221. 503/292-7525. **Contact:** Manager. **Description:** A contract services firm. **Specializes in the areas of:** Technical.

CAREER/OUTPLACEMENT COUNSELING FIRMS

BERNARD HALDANE & ASSOCIATES
1221 SW Wamhill, Portland OR 97205. 503/295-5926. **Contact:** Manager. **Description:** A career/ outplacement consulting firm.

PENNSYLVANIA

EXECUTIVE SEARCH FIRMS

ACS & ASSOCIATES
2835 82nd Avenue SE, Mercer Island PA 98040. 206/236-0766. **Contact:** Manager. **Description:** An executive search firm. **Specializes in the areas of:** Sales.

ACCOUNTANTS EXECUTIVE SEARCH
2005 Market Street, Suite 520, Philadelphia PA 19103. 215/568-5600. **Contact:** Mark S. Libes, President. **Description:** An executive search firm. **Specializes in the areas of:** Accounting/Auditing; Banking; Finance.

J.N. ADAMS & ASSOCIATES INC.
301 South Allen Street, Suite 103A, State College PA 16801. 814/234-0670. **Fax:** 814/234-4361. **Contact:** Eric M. Berg, President. **World Wide Web address:** http://www.state-college.com/jnadams. **Description:** An executive search firm. Company pays fee. **Specializes in the areas of:** Engineering; Manufacturing; Quality Assurance. **Positions commonly filled include:** Chemical Engineer; Design Engineer; Mechanical Engineer; Metallurgical Engineer; Quality Control Supervisor; Statistician. **Average salary range of placements:** More than $50,000. **Number of placements per year:** 50 - 99.

ADVANCE RECRUITING SERVICES
1250 Wall Avenue, Clairton PA 15025. 412/233-8808. **Fax:** 412/233-8814. **Contact:** Joe Giansante, Owner. **Description:** An executive search firm that also offers contract services and temporary placements. Company pays fee. **Specializes in the areas of:** Computer Science/Software; Sales; Telephone Technical Support. **Positions commonly filled include:** MIS Specialist; Multimedia Designer; Services Sales Representative; Software Engineer; Technical Writer/Editor; Telecommunications Manager; Video Production Coordinator. **Benefits available to temporary workers:** Medical Insurance. **Average salary range of placements:** $30,000 - $50,000. **Number of placements per year:** 1 - 49.

ADVANCED TECHNOLOGY RESOURCES
239 4th Avenue, Suite 212, Pittsburgh PA 15222. 412/281-9930. **Contact:** Bernie Flynn, Principal. **E-mail address:** bflynn@atrinc.com. **World Wide Web address:** http://www.industry.net/advanced.tech. **Description:** An executive search firm operating on both retainer and contingency bases. Advanced Technology Resources also offers contract services. Company pays fee. **NOTE:** Interested applicants should send resumes to 350 Saxonburg Road, Butler PA 16002-3621. **Specializes in the areas of:** Administration; Computer Science/Software; Engineering; Manufacturing; Sales; Technical. **Positions commonly filled include:** Computer Programmer; Electrical/Electronics Engineer; Financial Analyst; Internet Services Manager; Management Analyst/Consultant; Software Engineer; Statistician; Systems Analyst; Technical Writer/Editor. **Average salary range of placements:** More than $50,000. **Number of placements per year:** 100 - 199.

ADVANCED TECHNOLOGY RESOURCES
350 Saxonbury Road, Butler PA 16002-3621. 412/282-3333. **Fax:** 412/282-3345. **Contact:** Bernie Flynn, Principal. **E-mail address:** bflynn@atrinc.com. **World Wide Web address:** http://www.industry.net/advanced.tech. **Description:** An executive search firm. **Specializes in the areas of:** Engineering; Information Technology; Software; Telecommunications. **Other area locations:** Pittsburgh PA.

ADVENT ASSOCIATES
350 Carogin Drive, State College PA 16803. 814/235-1401. **Contact:** Howie Schultz, President. **Description:** An executive search firm. **Specializes in the areas of:** Physician Executive.

GLEN ALAN & ASSOCIATES INC.
5421 Downs Run, Suite B, Pipersville PA 18947-1155. 215/766-0376. **Contact:** Glenn Marad, President. **Description:** An executive search firm. Company pays fee. **Specializes in the areas of:** Retail; Sales. **Number of placements per year:** 200 - 499.

ALEXANDER PERSONNEL ASSOCIATES
One Oxford Valley, Suite 702, Langhorne PA 19047. 215/757-4935. **Contact:** Joyce Beck, CPC, Manager. **Description:** An executive search firm operating on a contingency basis. Company pays fee. **Specializes in the areas of:** Accounting/Auditing; Engineering; General Management; Industrial; Manufacturing; Office Support; Sales; Secretarial; Technical.

AMATO & ASSOCIATES INSURANCE RECRUITERS
1313 Medford Road, Suite 100, Wynnewood PA 19096-2418. 610/642-9696. **Fax:** 610/642-9797. **Contact:** Ms. Bobbi Amato, President. **Description:** An executive search firm operating on both retained and contingency bases. Company pays fee. **Specializes in the areas of:** Insurance. **Positions commonly filled include:** Account Representative; Branch Manager; Insurance Agent/Broker; Loss Prevention Specialist; Underwriter/Assistant Underwriter. **Average salary range of placements:** More than $50,000. **Number of placements per year:** 1 - 49.

AMERICAN SEARCH ASSOCIATES
3801 Kings Arms Lane, York PA 17402-5125. 717/757-2033. **Fax:** 717/757-2422. **Contact:** Bill Willson, President. **Description:** American Search Associates is a nationwide executive search firm operating on both retainer and contingency bases. Company pays fee. **Specializes in the areas of:** Accounting/Auditing; Engineering; Food Industry; General Management; Industrial; Manufacturing; Personnel/Labor Relations; Publishing. **Positions commonly filled include:** Accountant/Auditor; Aerospace Engineer; Architect; Attorney; Biological Scientist; Buyer; Chemical Engineer; Chemist; Civil Engineer; Computer Programmer; Customer Service Representative; Design Engineer; Designer; Draftsperson; Electrical/Electronics Engineer; Electrician; Environmental Engineer; General Manager; Human Resources Manager; Industrial Engineer; Industrial Production Manager; Manufacturer's/Wholesaler's Sales Rep.; Materials Engineer; Mechanical Engineer; Mining Engineer; MIS Specialist; Nuclear Engineer; Operations/Production Manager; Petroleum Engineer; Purchasing Agent/Manager; Quality Control Supervisor; Services Sales Representative; Software Engineer; Stationary Engineer; Structural Engineer; Systems Analyst. **Average salary range of placements:** $30,000 - $50,000. **Number of placements per year:** 50 - 99.

ANDRE GROUP, INC.
500 North Gulph Road, Suite 210, King of Prussia PA 19406. 610/337-0600. **Fax:** 610/337-1333. **Contact:** Richard Andre, President. **Description:** An executive search firm. Company pays fee. **Specializes in the areas of:** Human Resources. **Average salary range of placements:** More than $50,000. **Number of placements per year:** 200 - 499.

ASHLEY SEARCH CONSULTANTS
3070 Bristol Pike, Suite 221, Bensalem PA 19020-5364. 215/245-5200. **Fax:** 215/245-5779. **Contact:** Craig Belnick, President. **E-mail address:** ashleysc@erols.com. **Description:** An executive search firm operating on a contingency basis. Company pays fee. **Specializes in the areas of:** Accounting/Auditing; Administration; Engineering; Fashion; General Management; Personnel/Labor Relations; Retail. **Positions commonly filled include:** Accountant/Auditor; Chief Financial Officer; Computer Programmer; Controller; Design Engineer; Finance Director; Human Resources Manager; Management Trainee; MIS Specialist; Purchasing Agent/Manager; Software Engineer; Systems Analyst; Systems Manager. **Average salary range of placements:** $30,000 - $50,000. **Number of placements per year:** 50 - 99.

ATOMIC PERSONNEL, INC.
P.O. Box 11244, Philadelphia PA 19027-0244. 215/885-4223. **Fax:** 215/885-4225. **Contact:** Arthur L. Krasnow, President. **Description:** An executive search firm operating on a contingency basis. Company pays fee. **Specializes in the areas of:** Construction; Engineering; Food Industry; Industrial; Marketing; Sales; Scientific; Technical. **Positions commonly filled include:** Biological Scientist; Biomedical Engineer; Ceramics Engineer; Chemical Engineer; Civil Engineer; Controls Engineer; Electrical/Electronics Engineer; Industrial Engineer; Manufacturing Engineer; Mechanical Engineer; Metallurgical Engineer; Quality Control Supervisor; Safety Engineer; Sales Representative.

BARR ASSOCIATES
93 South Westend Boulevard, Suite 105B, Quakertown PA 18951. 215/538-9411. **Fax:** 215/538-9466. **Contact:** Mr. Charly Barr, Owner/Director. **E-mail address:** barr@pipeline.com. **Description:** A technical recruitment firm focusing on the high-technology electronics and semiconductor industries. **Specializes in the areas of:** Engineering. **Positions commonly filled include:** Design Engineer; Electrical/Electronics Engineer; Human Resources Manager; Market Research Analyst; Operations/Production Manager; Quality Control Supervisor; Software Engineer; Technical Writer/Editor; Telecommunications Manager. **Number of placements per year:** 50 - 99.

BARTON PERSONNEL SYSTEMS, INC.
121 North Cedar Crest Boulevard, Allentown PA 18104-4664. 610/439-8751. **Fax:** 610/439-1207. **Contact:** Malcolm Singerman, Manager. **Description:** An executive search firm operating on a retainer basis. Company pays fee. **Specializes in the areas of:** Accounting/Auditing; Engineering; Finance; Health/Medical; Information Technology; Sales. **Positions commonly filled include:** Accountant/Auditor; Buyer; Computer Programmer; Electrical/Electronics Engineer; Human Resources Manager; Management Analyst/Consultant; MIS Specialist; Physical Therapist; Software Engineer; Systems Analyst. **Average salary range of placements:** More than $50,000. **Number of placements per year:** 200 - 499.

BASILONE-OLIVER EXECUTIVE SEARCH
2987 Babcock Boulevard, Pittsburgh PA 15237. 412/931-9501. **Fax:** 412/931-9741. **Contact:** Larry S. Basilone, Partner/Owner. **Description:** An executive search firm operating on a contingency basis. Company pays fee. **Specializes in the areas of:** Accounting/Auditing; Banking; Computer Science/Software; Economics; Finance; Industrial; Manufacturing; Personnel/Labor Relations; Retail. **Positions commonly filled include:** Accountant/Auditor; Chief Financial Officer; Controller; Financial Analyst; Human Resources Manager; Manufacturing Manager; Market Research Analyst; President; Statistician. **Other U.S. locations:** Nationwide. **Average salary range of placements:** More than $50,000. **Number of placements per year:** 50 - 99.

BENDER & ASSOCIATES
Penn Center West, Building 3, Suite 221, Pittsburgh PA 15276. 412/787-8550. **Contact:** Manager. **Description:** An executive search firm. **Specializes in the areas of:** Computer Hardware/Software; Engineering.

T.W. BORIS ASSOCIATION
375 Warner Road, Wayne PA 19087. 610/687-8165. **Fax:** 610/687-5830. **Contact:** Theodore Boris, President. **World Wide Web address:** http://www.quikpage.com/t/twba. **Description:** An executive search firm operating on both retained and contingency bases. Company pays fee. **Specializes in the areas of:** Administration; Computer Science/Software; Engineering; Information Technology; Sales; Technical. **Average salary range of placements:** More than $50,000. **Number of placements per year:** 50 - 99.

BRACKIN & SAYERS ASSOCIATES
1000 McKnight Park Drive, Pittsburgh PA 15227. 412/367-4644. **Contact:** Manager. **Description:** An executive search firm. **Specializes in the areas of:** Accounting/Auditing; Finance; Human Resources; Manufacturing; Materials; Public Relations.

CMIS
24 Hagerty Boulevard, Suite 9, West Chester PA 19382. 610/430-0013. **Fax:** 610/696-5430. **Contact:** Peter DiNicola, President. **E-mail address:** cmis@erols.com. **Description:** An executive search firm. Company pays fee. **Specializes in the areas of:** Computer Science/Software; Sales. **Positions commonly filled include:** Computer Programmer; Software Engineer; Systems Analyst; Telecommunications Manager. **Average salary range of placements:** More than $50,000. **Number of placements per year:** 1 - 49.

CALIBER ASSOCIATES
125 Strafford Avenue, Suite 112, Wayne PA 19087. 610/971-1880. **Fax:** 610/971-1887. **Contact:** Steven P. Hochberg, President. **Description:** An executive search firm. Company pays fee. **Specializes in the areas of:** Biology; Food Industry; General Management; Health/Medical. **Positions commonly filled include:** Biological Scientist; Chemist; Health Services Manager; Pharmacist. **Number of placements per year:** 1 - 49.

CAREER CONCEPTS STAFFING SERVICES
4504 Peach Street, Erie PA 16509. 814/868-2333. **Fax:** 814/868-3238. **Contact:** Joseph A. DiGiorgio, Vice President. **Description:** An executive search firm. Company pays fee. **Specializes in the areas of:** Accounting/Auditing; Administration; Computer Science/Software; Engineering; Finance; Food Industry; General Management; Industrial; Manufacturing; Personnel/Labor Relations; Plastics; Sales; Technical. **Positions commonly filled include:** Accountant/Auditor; Aerospace Engineer; Agricultural Engineer; Biological Scientist; Biomedical Engineer; Buyer; Chemical Engineer; Chemist; Civil Engineer; Electrical/Electronics Engineer; General Manager; Health Services Manager; Human Resources Manager; Industrial Engineer; Industrial Production Manager; Mechanical Engineer; Purchasing Agent/Manager; Quality Control Supervisor; Science Technologist; Technical Writer/Editor. **Number of placements per year:** 50 - 99.

CAREER QUEST CONFIDENTIAL, INC.
355 5th Avenue, Park Building, Suite 1021, Pittsburgh PA 15222. 412/471-9577. **Fax:** 412/471-9580. **Contact:** Thomas Geibel, President. **E-mail address:** careerqst@aol.com. **Description:** An executive recruiting firm. Company pays fee. **Specializes in the areas of:** Administration; Computer Science/Software; Engineering; Finance; Health/Medical; Legal; Manufacturing; Secretarial; Technical. **Positions commonly filled include:** Accountant/Auditor; Brokerage Clerk; Chemical Engineer; Civil Engineer; Clerical Supervisor; Computer Programmer; Credit Manager; Dental Assistant/Dental Hygienist; Design Engineer; Designer; Draftsperson; Electrical/Electronics Engineer; Environmental Engineer; Financial Analyst; General Manager; Human Resources Manager; Industrial Engineer; Industrial Production Manager; Legal Secretary; Mechanical Engineer; Medical Records Technician; Metallurgical Engineer; Mining Engineer; Nuclear Engineer; Operations/Production Manager; Paralegal; Petroleum Engineer; Registered Nurse; Software Engineer; Stationary Engineer; Structural Engineer; Surveyor; Systems Analyst; Technical Writer/Editor; Typist/Word Processor. **Average salary range of placements:** $20,000 - $29,999. **Number of placements per year:** 1 - 49.

A.D. CHECK & ASSOCIATES, INC.
204 South Franklin, Wilkes-Barre PA 18701. 717/829-5066. **Contact:** Manager. **Description:** An executive search firm. **Specializes in the areas of:** Manufacturing.

RICHARD CHRISTINE ASSOCIATES
Front & Orange Streets, Media PA 19063. 610/565-3310. **Fax:** 610/565-5492. **Contact:** Richard Christine, Owner. **Description:** An executive search firm. Company pays fee. **Specializes in the areas of:** Engineering; Manufacturing; Sales; Technical. **Positions commonly filled include:** Chemical Engineer; Electrical/Electronics Engineer; Industrial Engineer; Mechanical Engineer. **Number of placements per year:** 1 - 49.

CHURCHILL & AFFILIATES
1200 Bustleton Pike, Suite 3, Feasterville PA 19053-4118. 215/364-8070. **Fax:** 215/322-4391. **Contact:** Harvey Wasserman, President. **E-mail address:** hjwsearch@aol.com. **Description:** An executive search firm operating on a retainer basis. Company pays fee. **Specializes in the areas of:** Sales. **Positions commonly filled include:** Internet Services Manager; Market Research Analyst; Multimedia Designer; Public Relations Specialist; Strategic Relations Manager. **Average salary range of placements:** More than $50,000. **Number of placements per year:** 50 - 99.

JOSEPH CONAHAN EXECUTIVE RECRUITERS
251 South 24th Street, 3rd Floor, Philadelphia PA 19103. 215/545-3337. **Contact:** Office Manager. **Description:** An executive search firm. **Specializes in the areas of:** Accounting/Auditing; Finance.

CONSEARCH
911 Poplar Street, Erie PA 16502. 814/459-5588. **Fax:** 814/459-5582. **Contact:** Jim Lyons, President/Owner. **Description:** An executive search firm. Company pays fee. **Specializes in the areas of:** Engineering; Manufacturing. **Positions commonly filled include:** Accountant/Auditor; Aerospace Engineer; Bank Officer/Manager; Buyer; Ceramics Engineer; Computer Programmer; Electrical/Electronics Engineer; Financial Analyst; General Manager; Human Resources Manager; Industrial Engineer; Industrial Production Manager; Materials Engineer; Mechanical Engineer; Metallurgical Engineer; Occupational Therapist; Operations/Production Manager; Purchasing Agent/Manager; Quality Control Supervisor; Software Engineer; Systems Analyst. **Number of placements per year:** 1 - 49.

CORPORATE MANAGEMENT SERVICES
P.O. Box 16271, Pittsburgh PA 15220. 412/279-1180. **Contact:** Manager. **Description:** An executive search firm. **Specializes in the areas of:** Engineering; Manufacturing.

COURTRIGHT & ASSOCIATES
P.O. Box 503, Clarks Summit PA 18411. 717/586-0735. **Contact:** Robert Courtright, President. **Description:** An executive search firm. Company pays fee. **Specializes in the areas of:** Biotechnology. **Average salary range of placements:** More than $50,000. **Number of placements per year:** 1 - 49.

DPSI MEDICAL
612 West 29th Street, Erie PA 16508. 814/868-0961. **Contact:** Ron Spero, CPC, President/Owner. **Description:** An executive search firm operating on both retainer and contingency bases. Company pays fee. **Specializes in the areas of:** Health/Medical. **Positions commonly filled include:** Physical Therapist; Physician.

P. ROBERT DANN
1601 Market Street, Suite 600, Philadelphia PA 19103. 215/563-8008. **Fax:** 215/563-4456. **Contact:** Robert Schneiderman, President. **Description:** An executive search firm. Company pays fee. **Specializes in the areas of:** Accounting/Auditing; Administration; General Management; Health/Medical; Legal. **Positions commonly filled include:** Accountant/Auditor; Attorney; Branch Manager; Computer Programmer; Customer Service Representative; Dietician/Nutritionist; General Manager; Health Services Manager; Hotel Manager; Human Resources Manager; MIS Specialist; Occupational Therapist; Paralegal; Physical Therapist; Physician; Restaurant/Food Service Manager; Securities Sales Representative; Services Sales Representative; Systems Analyst; Travel Agent. **Average salary range of placements:** $20,000 - $29,999. **Number of placements per year:** 200 - 499.

DELTA PROSEARCH
P.O. Box 267, Delta PA 17314. 717/456-7172. **Toll-free phone:** 800/753-6693. **Contact:** John Banister, President. **Description:** An executive search firm. Company pays fee. **Specializes in the areas of:** Health/Medical; Pharmaceutical. **Positions commonly filled include:** Medical Technologist; Pharmacist; Physical Therapist. **Number of placements per year:** 1 - 49.

ROBERT J. DEPAUL & ASSOCIATES INC.
71 McMurray Road, Brookside Office Park, Suite 208, Pittsburgh PA 15241. 412/561-0417. **Contact:** David J. Shopf, Placement Counselor. **Description:** An executive search firm focusing on information management. The firm offers permanent and temporary placements, contracting, and management consulting. Consulting services include third generation programming languages (COBOL, CICS, C); database design (IMS, Oracle, Rdb, DB2); PC support & training services; microcomputer based languages (DBase, Clipper, Paradox); and networking & client server technology (Novell). Company pays fee. **Specializes in the areas of:** Administration; Banking; Computer Science/Software; Health/Medical; Retail. **Positions commonly filled include:** Computer Programmer; Network Engineer; Systems Analyst; Technical Writer/Editor; Telecommunications Manager. **Benefits available to temporary workers:** Dental Insurance; Medical Insurance. **Average salary range of placements:** $30,000 - $50,000.

DIVERSIFIED SEARCH, INC.
2005 Market Street, Suite 3300, Philadelphia PA 19103. 215/732-6666. **Contact:** Leslie Mazza, Manager. **Description:** An executive search firm.

DUNHILL PROFESSIONAL SEARCH
801 West Street Road, Feasterville PA 19053. 215/357-6591. **Fax:** 215/953-1612. **Contact:** Dave Bontempo, CPC, Vice President. **Description:** An executive search firm. Company pays fee. **Specializes in the areas of:** Accounting/Auditing; Finance; Information Systems; Sales; Secretarial. **Positions commonly filled include:** Accountant/Auditor; Customer Service Representative; EDP Specialist; Financial Analyst; Typist/Word Processor. **Number of placements per year:** 100 - 199.

DUNN ASSOCIATES
229 Limberline Drive, Greensburg PA 15601. 412/832-9822. **Fax:** 412/832-9836. **Contact:** Margaret Dunn, President. **Description:** An executive search firm operating on a retainer basis. Company pays fee. **Specializes in the areas of:** Accounting/Auditing; Administration; Engineering; Finance; General Management; Home Furnishings; Industrial; Manufacturing; Personnel/Labor Relations; Sales. **Positions commonly filled include:** Human Resources Manager; Manufacturing Engineer; Manufacturing Manager; Plant Manager; Vice President. **Average salary range of placements:** More than $50,000. **Number of placements per year:** 1 - 49.

EDEN AND ASSOCIATES, INC.
794 North Valley Road, Paoli PA 19301. 610/889-9993. **Fax:** 610/889-9660. **Contact:** Brooks D. Eden, President. **Description:** An executive search firm. Company pays fee. **Specializes in the areas of:** Food Industry; Retail. **Positions commonly filled include:** Accountant/Auditor; Architect; Buyer; Draftsperson; General Manager; Human Resources Manager; Industrial Engineer; Market Research Analyst; MIS Specialist; Pharmacist; Systems Analyst; Transportation/Traffic Specialist. **Average salary range of placements:** More than $50,000. **Number of placements per year:** 100 - 199.

EXECU-SEARCH
4232 Northern Heights, Commerce Building, Suite 201, Monroeville PA 15146. 412/374-9904. **Contact:** Recruiter. **Description:** An executive search firm specializing in sales, marketing, management, and administrative positions.

EXECUTIVE AVAIL-A-SEARCH
2938 Columbia Avenue, Suite 1502, Lancaster PA 17603. 717/291-1871. **Contact:** Anthony Spinelli, President. **Description:** An executive search firm. **Specializes in the areas of:** Accounting/Auditing; Administration; Clerical; Engineering; Finance; Legal; Manufacturing; Sales; Technical.

EXECUTIVE CAREER RESOURCE GROUP
1235 West Lakes Drive, Berwyn PA 19312. 610/640-2020. **Contact:** Manager. **Description:** An executive search firm.

FINANCIAL SEARCH GROUP
1100 Bank Tower, Fourth Avenue at Wood Street, Pittsburgh PA 15222. 412/288-0505. **Contact:** Manager. **Description:** An executive search firm. **Specializes in the areas of:** Finance.

HOWARD FISCHER ASSOCIATES, INC.
1800 Kennedy Boulevard, 7th Floor, Philadelphia PA 19103. 215/568-8363. **Contact:** Office Manager. **Description:** An executive search firm.

FOCUS PERSONNEL ASSOCIATES, INC.
900 Jonnet Building, Jonnet Plaza, Suite 900, Monroeville PA 15146. 412/856-4166. **Contact:** Manager. **Description:** An executive search firm. **Specializes in the areas of:** Finance; Food Industry; Retail; Sales.

FOCUS PERSONNEL ASSOCIATES, INC.
550 Pinetown Road, Suite 230, Fort Washington PA 19034. 215/654-7000. **Fax:** 215/654-7925. **Contact:** Gail C. Welkes, President. **Description:** An executive search firm. Company pays fee. **Specializes in the areas of:** Sales. **Positions commonly filled include:** Account Manager; Account Representative; Branch Manager; Management Trainee; Manufacturer's/Wholesaler's Sales Rep.; Sales Engineer; Sales Executive; Sales Manager; Sales Representative; Services Sales Representative. **Average salary range of placements:** $30,000 - $100,000. **Number of placements per year:** 100 - 199.

F-O-R-T-U-N-E GROUP INTERNATIONAL
1410 West Street Road, Warminster PA 18974. 215/675-3100. **Fax:** 215/675-3080. **Contact:** Michael G. Strand, President. **World Wide Web address:** http://www.fortunegroup.com. **Description:** An executive search firm. **Specializes in the areas of:** Architecture/Construction; Computer Hardware/Software; Health/Medical; Marketing; Sales; Scientific; Technical. **Positions commonly filled include:** Architect; Attorney; Biomedical Engineer; Buyer; Chemical Engineer; Civil Engineer; Database Manager; Design Engineer; Electrical/Electronics Engineer; Environmental Engineer; Manufacturing Engineer; Marketing Manager; Mechanical Engineer; MIS Specialist; Operations Manager; Physician; Production Manager; Project Manager; Purchasing Agent/Manager; Quality Control Supervisor; Sales Engineer; Sales Executive; Software Engineer; Statistician; Telecommunications Manager. **Corporate headquarters location:** New York NY. **Other U.S. locations:** Nationwide. **Average salary range of placements:** $80,000 - $250,000.

F-O-R-T-U-N-E PERSONNEL CONSULTANTS
3644 Route 378, Bethlehem PA 18018. 610/866-1300. **Contact:** Manager. **Description:** An executive search firm. **Specializes in the areas of:** Computer Science/Software; Manufacturing. **Corporate headquarters location:** New York NY. **Other U.S. locations:** Nationwide.

F-O-R-T-U-N-E PERSONNEL CONSULTANTS OF PHILADELPHIA
1528 Walnut Street, Suite 1625, Philadelphia PA 19102. 215/546-9490. **Contact:** Manager. **Description:** An executive search firm. **Corporate headquarters location:** New York NY. **Other U.S. locations:** Nationwide.

FOX-MORRIS ASSOCIATES
One Gateway Center, 18th Floor, Pittsburgh PA 15222. 412/232-0410. **Fax:** 412/232-3055. **Contact:** Murray S. Leety, Branch Manager. **Description:** An executive search firm operating on both retainer and contingency bases. The firm also offers career/outplacement services. Company pays fee. **Specializes in the areas of:** Accounting/Auditing; Engineering; Finance; General Management; Industrial; Manufacturing; Personnel/Labor Relations; Technical. **Positions commonly filled include:** Chemical Engineer; Chemist; Civil Engineer; Computer Programmer; Design Engineer; Electrical/Electronics Engineer; Environmental Engineer; Financial Analyst; General Manager; Human Resources Specialist; Industrial Engineer; Industrial Production Manager; Mechanical Engineer; Metallurgical Engineer; MIS Specialist; Property and Real Estate Manager; Purchasing

Agent/Manager; Software Engineer; Systems Analyst; Transportation/Traffic Specialist. **Corporate headquarters location:** Philadelphia PA. **Other U.S. locations:** Nationwide. **Average salary range of placements:** More than $50,000. **Number of placements per year:** 50 - 99.

FOX-MORRIS ASSOCIATES
1617 JFK Boulevard, Suite 1850, Philadelphia PA 19103. 215/561-6300. **Contact:** Manager. **Description:** An executive search firm. **Specializes in the areas of:** Banking; Engineering; Finance; Human Resources; Information Systems. **Corporate headquarters location:** This location. **Other area locations:** Pittsburgh PA. **Other U.S. locations:** Nationwide.

THE GMW GROUP, INC.
900 5th Avenue, Pittsburgh PA 15219. 412/281-6057. **Contact:** Shelley Millen, President. **Description:** An executive search firm that also offers career/outplacement services. Company pays fee. **Specializes in the areas of:** Engineering; Sales. **Positions commonly filled include:** Chemical Engineer; Civil Engineer; Computer Programmer; Customer Service Representative; Human Resources Manager; Mechanical Engineer; Metallurgical Engineer; Mining Engineer; MIS Specialist; Public Relations Specialist; Securities Sales Representative; Services Sales Representative; Software Engineer; Systems Analyst; Telecommunications Manager. **Average salary range of placements:** More than $50,000. **Number of placements per year:** 100 - 199.

GATEWAY RESOURCES INC.
21 Yost Boulevard, Suite 302, Pittsburgh PA 15221. 412/824-9470. **Contact:** Manager. **Description:** An executive search firm. **Specializes in the areas of:** Computer Hardware/Software; Engineering.

J.H. GLASS & ASSOCIATES
P.O. Box 1015, Bala-Cynwyd PA 19004. 215/877-0101. **Contact:** J.H. Glass, President. **Description:** An executive search firm. Company pays fee. **Specializes in the areas of:** Computer Science/Software; Engineering; General Management; Manufacturing; Sales; Technical. **Positions commonly filled include:** Accountant/Auditor; Computer Programmer; Design Engineer; Engineer; General Manager; Industrial Production Manager; Internet Services Manager; Management Analyst/Consultant; Manufacturer's/Wholesaler's Sales Rep.; MIS Specialist; Multimedia Designer; Operations/Production Manager; Physical Therapist; Purchasing Agent/Manager; Quality Control Supervisor; Systems Analyst. **Average salary range of placements:** More than $50,000. **Number of placements per year:** 200 - 499.

ROBERT HALF INTERNATIONAL ACCOUNTEMPS
2000 Market Street, 18th Floor, Philadelphia PA 19103. 215/568-4580. **Fax:** 215/564-1968. **Contact:** Manager. **Description:** An executive search firm. **Corporate headquarters location:** Menlo Park CA. **International locations:** Worldwide.

ROBERT HALF INTERNATIONAL ACCOUNTEMPS
120 Fifth Avenue, Suite 2690, Pittsburgh PA 15222. 412/471-5946. **Contact:** Manager. **Description:** An executive search firm. **Specializes in the areas of:** Accounting/Auditing; Finance. **Corporate headquarters location:** Menlo Park CA. **International locations:** Worldwide.

GARRICK HALL & ASSOCIATES
260 South Broad Street, Suite 1600, Philadelphia PA 19102-5021. 215/546-0030. **Fax:** 215/546-4920. **Contact:** William J. Yamarick, President. **Description:** An executive search firm. Company pays fee. **Specializes in the areas of:** Computer Science/Software; Health/Medical; Industrial; Manufacturing; Sales. **Positions commonly filled include:** Management Trainee; Services Sales Representative. **Number of placements per year:** 100 - 199.

HAMSON GINN ASSOCIATES
724 West Lancaster Avenue, One Devon Square, Suite 206, Wayne PA 19087. 610/293-9110. **Contact:** Manager. **Description:** An executive search firm. **Specializes in the areas of:** Computer Hardware/Software.

THE HASTINGS GROUP
P.O. Box 36, Palm PA 18070-0036. 215/541-0303. **Fax:** 215/541-0305. **Contact:** Frank Hastings, President/Owner. **Description:** An executive search firm. Company pays fee. **Specializes in the areas of:** Accounting/Auditing; Administration; Banking; Economics; Engineering; Finance; Food Industry; General Management; Health/Medical; Industrial; Manufacturing; Personnel/Labor Relations; Sales. **Positions commonly filled include:** Accountant/Auditor; Administrative Manager; Attorney; Bank Officer/Manager; Branch Manager; Budget Analyst; Buyer; Clerical Supervisor; Cost Estimator; Credit Manager; Customer Service Representative; Economist; Facilities Engineer; Food Scientist/Technologist; General Manager; Health Services Manager; Human Resources Specialist; Industrial Engineer; Industrial Production Manager; Management Analyst/Consultant; Market Research Analyst; Mechanical Engineer; Medical Records Technician; MIS Specialist; Occupational Therapist; Operations/Production Manager; Paralegal; Pharmacist; Physical Therapist; Purchasing Agent/Manager; Quality Control Supervisor; Registered Nurse; Respiratory Therapist; Services Sales Representative; Statistician; Systems Analyst; Telecommunications Manager. **Average salary range of placements:** More than $50,000. **Number of placements per year:** 50 - 99.

HAYES ASSOCIATES
522 Lanfair Road, Elkins Park PA 19027. 215/735-3079. **Contact:** Manager. **Description:** An executive search firm. **Specializes in the areas of:** Computer Science/Software.

HEALTHCARE RECRUITERS INTERNATIONAL
8150 Perry Highway, Suite 332, Pittsburgh PA 15237. 412/369-5330. **Contact:** Manager. **Description:** An executive search firm. **Specializes in the areas of:** Health/Medical.

HUMAN RESOURCE SOLUTIONS
506 Park Road North, Wyamissing PA 19610. 610/371-9505. **Fax:** 610/373-8618. **Contact:** Thomas N. Dondore, President. **E-mail address:** tomhrs@aol.com. **Description:** An executive search firm. Human Resource Solutions offers human resource consulting, executive and management search, training and development, contract recruiting, and electronic staff sourcing. Company pays fee. **Specializes in the areas of:** Accounting/Auditing; Administration; Banking; Computer Science/Software; Engineering; Fashion; Finance; Food Industry; General Management; Industrial; Insurance; Manufacturing; Personnel/Labor Relations; Retail; Sales; Technical. **Positions commonly filled include:** Accountant/Auditor; Administrative Manager; Aerospace Engineer; Agricultural Engineer; Attorney; Bank Officer/Manager; Biological Scientist; Biomedical Engineer; Branch Manager; Budget Analyst; Buyer; Chemical Engineer; Chemist; Civil Engineer; Computer Programmer; Credit Manager; Design Engineer; Designer; Economist;

Editor; Electrical/Electronics Engineer; Environmental Engineer; Financial Analyst; General Manager; Health Services Manager; Human Resources Manager; Industrial Engineer; Industrial Production Manager; Management Analyst/Consultant; Management Trainee; Manufacturer's/Wholesaler's Sales Rep.; Market Research Analyst; Materials Engineer; Mechanical Engineer; MIS Specialist; Multimedia Designer; Nuclear Engineer; Petroleum Engineer; Purchasing Agent/Manager; Quality Control Supervisor; Science Technologist; Securities Sales Representative; Services Sales Representative; Software Engineer; Stationary Engineer; Strategic Relations Manager; Structural Engineer; Systems Analyst; Telecommunications Manager; Transportation/Traffic Specialist.

INTERACTIVE SEARCH
2949 West Germantown Pike, Moorestown PA 19403. 610/630-3670. **Fax:** 610/630-3678. **Contact:** Manager. **Description:** An executive search firm operating on both retainer and contingency bases. Company pays fee. **Specializes in the areas of:** Chemical; Engineering; Health/Medical; Information Systems.

INTERCONTINENTAL EXECUTIVE GROUP
P.O. Box 766, Richboro PA 18954. 215/957-9012. **Contact:** Manager. **Description:** An executive search firm.

J-RAND SEARCH
P.O. Box B, Bethlehem PA 18015. 610/867-4649. **Fax:** 610/867-9750. **Contact:** Michael P. Watts, President. **Description:** An executive search firm. Company pays fee. **Specializes in the areas of:** Accounting/Auditing; Administration; Banking; Biology; Computer Science/Software; Engineering; Finance; Food Industry; General Management; Health/Medical; Industrial; Manufacturing; Personnel/Labor Relations; Technical; Transportation. **Positions commonly filled include:** Accountant/Auditor; Aerospace Engineer; Agricultural Engineer; Biological Scientist; Biomedical Engineer; Ceramics Engineer; Chemical Engineer; Chemist; Civil Engineer; Computer Programmer; Cost Estimator; Designer; Electrical/Electronics Engineer; Financial Analyst; Food Scientist/Technologist; General Manager; Industrial Engineer; Industrial Production Manager; Materials Engineer; Mechanical Engineer; Metallurgical Engineer; Meteorologist; Mining Engineer; Operations/Production Manager; Petroleum Engineer; Pharmacist; Physician; Purchasing Agent/Manager; Quality Control Supervisor; Software Engineer; Stationary Engineer; Statistician; Structural Engineer; Systems Analyst. **Number of placements per year:** 50 - 99.

JK RESOURCES
1056 Jeter Avenue, Bethlehem PA 18015-2552. 610/867-5997. **Fax:** 610/867-5946. **Contact:** Jane Kauffman, Owner. **Description:** An executive search firm that focuses on placement of safety, industrial hygiene, and environmental professionals nationwide. Company pays fee. **Specializes in the areas of:** Engineering; Industrial; Insurance; Manufacturing; Personnel/Labor Relations; Technical. **Positions commonly filled include:** Chemical Engineer; Civil Engineer; Environmental Engineer; Human Resources Manager. **Number of placements per year:** 1 - 49.

NANCY JACKSON INC.
343 North Washington Avenue, Scranton PA 18503. 717/346-8711. **Fax:** 717/346-9940. **Contact:** Nancy Jackson, President. **Description:** An executive search firm operating on a contingency basis. Company pays fee. **Specializes in the areas of:** Accounting/Auditing; Administration; Banking; Computer Science/Software; Engineering; Finance; General Management; Health/Medical; Manufacturing; Personnel/Labor Relations; Publishing; Sales; Secretarial. **Positions commonly filled include:** Accountant/Auditor; Administrative Manager; Bank Officer/Manager; Biomedical Engineer; Buyer; Ceramics Engineer; Chemical Engineer; Chemist; Civil Engineer; Claim Representative; Clerical Supervisor; Computer Programmer; Credit Manager; Customer Service Representative; Dental Assistant/Dental Hygienist; Draftsperson; Economist; Electrical/Electronics Engineer; Financial Analyst; General Manager; Health Services Manager; Human Resources Manager; Industrial Engineer; Industrial Production Manager; Management Analyst/Consultant; Materials Engineer; Mechanical Engineer; Metallurgical Engineer; Occupational Therapist; Operations/Production Manager; Paralegal; Physical Therapist; Public Relations Specialist; Purchasing Agent/Manager; Quality Control Supervisor; Software Engineer. **Number of placements per year:** 100 - 199.

JEFFERSON-ROSS ASSOCIATES, INC.
2 Penn Center, Suite 312, Philadelphia PA 19102. 215/564-5322. **Fax:** 215/587-0766. **Contact:** Craig Zander, Vice President of Operations. **Description:** An executive search firm. Company pays fee. **Specializes in the areas of:** Accounting/Auditing; Administration; Banking; Computer Science/Software; Finance; General Management; Health/Medical; Insurance; Marketing; Sales. **Positions commonly filled include:** Account Manager; Administrative Manager; Branch Manager; Computer Operator; Computer Programmer; Consultant; Controller; Credit Manager; Database Manager; Finance Director; General Manager; Human Resources Manager; Information Systems Consultant; Insurance Agent/Broker; Market Research Analyst; Marketing Manager; Marketing Specialist; MIS Specialist; Operations Manager; Project Manager; Sales Executive; Sales Manager; Sales Representative; Software Engineer; Systems Manager; Telecommunications Manager. **Average salary range of placements:** More than $50,000. **Number of placements per year:** 100 - 199.

CLIFTON JOHNSON ASSOCIATES INC.
One Monroeville Center, Suite 450, Monroeville PA 15146. 412/856-8000. **Fax:** 412/856-8026. **Contact:** Clifton Johnson, President. **E-mail address:** clifton@nb.net. **Description:** An executive search firm. The firm's clients include *Fortune* 500 companies. The firm belongs to the Nationwide Interchange Service Network, one of the largest computerized networks of professional recruiters. Founded in 1969. **Specializes in the areas of:** Computer Science/Software; Engineering; Industrial; Manufacturing. **Positions commonly filled include:** Aerospace Engineer; Chemical Engineer; Civil Engineer; Computer Programmer; Design Engineer; Electrical/Electronics Engineer; Environmental Engineer; Food Scientist/Technologist; Geologist/Geophysicist; Industrial Engineer; Industrial Production Manager; Mechanical Engineer; Metallurgical Engineer; Mining Engineer; Petroleum Engineer; Quality Control Supervisor; Software Engineer; Structural Engineer; Systems Analyst; Telecommunications Manager. **Average salary range of placements:** $30,000 - $50,000.

KATRON EXECUTIVE SEARCH
1000 Conshohocken Road, Suite 304, Conshohocken PA 19428. 610/941-5359. **Contact:** Manager. **Description:** An executive search firm. **Specializes in the areas of:** Engineering.

BLAIR KERSHAW ASSOCIATES, INC.
1983 West Eighth Street, Box 302, Erie PA 16505. 814/454-5872. **Fax:** 814/452-4598. **Contact:** Blair Kershaw, President. **Description:** An executive search

firm operating on both contingency and retainer bases. **Specializes in the areas of:** Accounting/Auditing; Engineering; Manufacturing; Technical. **Positions commonly filled include:** Accountant/Auditor; Chemical Engineer; Chemist; Design Engineer; Electrical/Electronics Engineer; Food Scientist/ Technologist; General Manager; Mechanical Engineer; Physical Therapist. **Average salary range of placements:** More than $50,000.

KRAYBILL ASSOCIATES
104 Alleyne Drive, Pittsburgh PA 15215. 412/288-0825. **Contact:** Manager. **Description:** An executive search firm. **Specializes in the areas of:** Legal.

LAWRENCE PERSONNEL
1000 Valley Forge Circle, Suite 110, King of Prussia PA 19406-1111. 610/783-5400. **Fax:** 610/783-6008. **Contact:** Larry Goldberg, CPC, General Manager. **Description:** An executive search firm operating on both retained and contingency bases. Company pays fee. **Specializes in the areas of:** Computer Science/Software; Data Communications; Engineering; Telecommunications. **Positions commonly filled include:** Broadcast Technician; Designer; Electrical/Electronics Engineer; Internet Services Manager; Mechanical Engineer; MIS Specialist; Software Engineer; Systems Analyst; Technical Writer/Editor; Telecommunications Manager. **Number of placements per year:** 1 - 49.

J. WRIGHT LEONARD
1500 Walnut Street, Suite 506, Philadelphia PA 19102. 215/732-6677. **Contact:** Manager. **Description:** An executive search firm.

PAT LIPTON & ASSOCIATES
5927 Howe Street, Pittsburgh PA 15232. 412/661-3361. **Contact:** Manager. **Description:** An executive search firm. **Specializes in the areas of:** Advertising; Food Industry. **Other U.S. locations:** Nationwide.

ROBERT LOHRKE ASSOCIATES
307 Investment Building, 239 4th Avenue, Pittsburgh PA 15222. 412/261-2601. **Contact:** Manager. **Description:** An executive search firm. **Specializes in the areas of:** Engineering; Technical.

M.K. AND ASSOCIATES
422 North Main Street, Suite 2A, Butler PA 16001. 412/285-7474. **Fax:** 412/285-8339. **Contact:** Jerry McMahon, Recruiter. **Description:** An executive search firm operating on a contingency basis. Company pays fee. **Specializes in the areas of:** Food Industry. **Positions commonly filled include:** Chemical Engineer; Food Scientist/Technologist; Mechanical Engineer; Operations/Production Manager; Quality Control Supervisor; Science Technologist.

MANAGEMENT RECRUITERS INTERNATIONAL
115 Hidden Valley Road, McMurray PA 15317. 412/942-4100. **Fax:** 412/942-4111. **Contact:** Manager. **Description:** An executive search firm operating on both retainer and contingency bases. Company pays fee. **Specializes in the areas of:** Chemical; Engineering. **Positions commonly filled include:** Chemical Engineer; Chemist. **Corporate headquarters location:** Cleveland OH. **Other U.S. locations:** Nationwide.

MANAGEMENT RECRUITERS INTERNATIONAL
129 Willowbrook Lane, West Chester PA 19382-5571. 610/436-6556. **Fax:** 610/436-6545. **Contact:** Robert Meitz, President. **Description:** An executive search firm operating on both retained and contingency bases. **Specializes in the areas of:** Chemical; Engineering; Food Industry; Petrochemical. **Positions commonly filled include:** Accountant/ Auditor; Biological Scientist; Chemist; Engineer; Financial Analyst; Food Scientist/Technologist; General Manager. **Corporate headquarters location:** Cleveland OH. **Other U.S. locations:** Nationwide. **Average salary range of placements:** More than $50,000. **Number of placements per year:** 1 - 49.

MANAGEMENT RECRUITERS INTERNATIONAL
64 East Uwchlan Avenue, Suite 272, Exton PA 19341. 610/331-6651. **Contact:** Manager. **Description:** An executive search firm. **Specializes in the areas of:** Accounting/Auditing; Biology; Engineering; Health/Medical; Industrial; Insurance; Manufacturing; Sales; Technical. **Positions commonly filled include:** Accountant/Auditor; Biological Scientist; Biomedical Engineer; Chemical Engineer; Chemist; Civil Engineer; Computer Programmer; Electrical/ Electronics Engineer; Environmental Engineer; Health Services Manager; Mechanical Engineer; MIS Specialist; Systems Analyst; Underwriter/Assistant Underwriter. **Corporate headquarters location:** Cleveland OH. **Other U.S. locations:** Nationwide. **Number of placements per year:** 100 - 199.

MANAGEMENT RECRUITERS INTERNATIONAL
2 Chatham Center, Suite 1570, Pittsburgh PA 15219. 412/566-2100. **Fax:** 412/566-2229. **Contact:** Manager. **Description:** An executive search firm. **Specializes in the areas of:** Computer Hardware/Software; Information Technology; Telecommunications. **Corporate headquarters location:** Cleveland OH. **Other U.S. locations:** Nationwide.

MANAGEMENT RECRUITERS INTERNATIONAL
1035 Voyce Road, Suite 120, Upper St. Clair PA 15241. 412/257-9585. **Contact:** Manager. **Description:** An executive search firm. **Specializes in the areas of:** Engineering; Information Technology; Manufacturing. **Corporate headquarters location:** Cleveland OH. **Other U.S. locations:** Nationwide.

MANAGEMENT RECRUITERS INTERNATIONAL
3925 Reed Boulevard, Suite 200, Murrysville PA 15668. 412/325-4011. **Contact:** Manager. **Description:** An executive search firm. **Specializes in the areas of:** Chemical; Health/Medical. **Corporate headquarters location:** Cleveland OH. **Other U.S. locations:** Nationwide.

MANAGEMENT RECRUITERS INTERNATIONAL
300 Weyman Plaza, Suite 200, Pittsburgh PA 15236. 412/885-5222. **Contact:** Manager. **Description:** An executive search firm. **Specializes in the areas of:** Information Systems. **Corporate headquarters location:** Cleveland OH. **Other U.S. locations:** Nationwide.

MANAGEMENT RECRUITERS OF BUCKS COUNTY, INC. COMPUSEARCH
678 Louis Drive, Warminster PA 18974. 215/675-6440. **Contact:** Michael Mashack, Manager. **Description:** An executive search firm. Company pays fee. **Specializes in the areas of:** Construction; Health/Medical; Real Estate. **Positions commonly filled include:** Administrator; Estimator; Information Systems Consultant; Leasing Specialist/Consultant; Nurse; Project Manager; Property and Real Estate Manager. **Corporate headquarters location:** Cleveland OH. **Other U.S. locations:** Nationwide.

MANAGEMENT RECRUITERS OF DELAWARE COUNTY, INC./COMPUSEARCH
7 Saint Alban Circle, Newtown Square PA 19073. 610/356-8360. **Fax:** 610/356-8731. **Contact:** Sandy Bishop, Manager. **Description:** An executive search firm. **Specializes in the areas of:** Accounting/Auditing; Administration; Advertising; Architecture/ Construction; Banking; Communications; Computer Hardware/Software; Design; Electrical; Engineering;

Finance; Food Industry; General Management; Health/Medical; Insurance; Legal; Manufacturing; Operations Management; Personnel/Labor Relations; Procurement; Publishing; Retail; Sales; Technical; Textiles; Transportation. **Corporate headquarters location:** Cleveland OH. **Other U.S. locations:** Nationwide.

MANAGEMENT RECRUITERS OF LEHIGH VALLEY, INC. COMPUSEARCH
1414 Millard Street, Suite 102, Bethlehem PA 18018. 610/974-9770. **Fax:** 610/974-9775. **Contact:** Fred Meyer, Manager. **Description:** An executive search firm. **Specializes in the areas of:** Accounting/Auditing; Administration; Advertising; Architecture/Construction; Banking; Communications; Computer Hardware/Software; Design; Electrical; Engineering; Finance; Food Industry; General Management; Health/Medical; Insurance; Legal; Manufacturing; Operations Management; Personnel/Labor Relations; Procurement; Publishing; Retail; Sales; Technical; Textiles; Transportation. **Corporate headquarters location:** Cleveland OH. **Other U.S. locations:** Nationwide.

MANAGEMENT RECRUITERS OF MANAYUNK/ CHESTNUT HILL, INC. COMPUSEARCH
161 Leverington Avenue, Suite 102, Philadelphia PA 19127. 215/482-6881. **Fax:** 215/482-7518. **Contact:** Recruiter. **Description:** An executive search firm. Company pays fee. **Specializes in the areas of:** Biology; Biotechnology; Computer Science/Software; Legal; Pharmaceutical; Technical. **Positions commonly filled include:** Attorney; Biological Scientist; Clinical Lab Technician; Computer Programmer; Science Technologist; Systems Analyst. **Corporate headquarters location:** Cleveland OH. **Other U.S. locations:** Nationwide. **Number of placements per year:** 50 - 99.

MANAGEMENT RECRUITERS OF PHILADELPHIA, INC. COMPUSEARCH
325 Chestnut Street, Chestnut Place, Suite 1106, Philadelphia PA 19106. 215/829-1900. **Contact:** Manager. **Description:** An executive search firm. **Specializes in the areas of:** Accounting/Auditing; Administration; Advertising; Architecture/Construction; Banking; Communications; Computer Hardware/Software; Design; Electrical; Engineering; Finance; Food Industry; General Management; Health/Medical; Insurance; Legal; Manufacturing; Operations Management; Personnel/Labor Relations; Procurement; Publishing; Retail; Sales; Technical; Textiles; Transportation. **Corporate headquarters location:** Cleveland OH. **Other U.S. locations:** Nationwide.

GEORGE R. MARTIN EXECUTIVE SEARCH
P.O. Box 673, Doylestown PA 18901. 215/348-8146. **Contact:** George R. Martin, Owner/Manager. **Description:** An executive search firm. **Specializes in the areas of:** Chemical; Engineering; Manufacturing; Personnel/Labor Relations; Pharmaceutical; Plastics; Sales; Technical.

K. MAXIN & ASSOCIATES
Allegheny Center, Building 10, Suite 421, Pittsburgh PA 15212. 412/322-2595. **Toll-free phone:** 800/867-8447. **Fax:** 412/322-7027. **Contact:** Keith A. Maxin, President. **Description:** An executive search firm operating on a retainer basis. Company pays fee. **Specializes in the areas of:** Construction; Real Estate. **Positions commonly filled include:** Branch Manager; Construction and Building Inspector; Cost Estimator; Electrical/Electronics Engineer; General Manager; Human Resources Manager; Mechanical Engineer; Property and Real Estate Manager; Purchasing Agent/Manager. **Average salary range of placements:** More than $50,000. **Number of placements per year:** 1 - 49.

ROBERT McCLURE LTD.
P.O. Box 497, Beaver PA 15009. 412/775-1525. **Fax:** 412/775-9633. **Contact:** Manager. **Description:** An executive search firm operating on both retainer and contingency bases. Company pays fee. **Specializes in the areas of:** Computer Science/Software; Engineering; Industrial; Manufacturing; Personnel/Labor Relations; Sales; Technical. **Positions commonly filled include:** Civil Engineer; Computer Programmer; Cost Estimator; Design Engineer; Electrical/Electronics Engineer; Environmental Engineer; Geologist/Geophysicist; Human Resources Specialist; Industrial Engineer; Industrial Production Manager; Mechanical Engineer; Metallurgical Engineer; MIS Specialist; Multimedia Designer; Quality Control Supervisor; Software Engineer; Structural Engineer; Systems Analyst; Technical Writer/Editor. **Other U.S. locations:** Nationwide.

McNICHOL & ASSOCIATES
620 Chestnut Street, Suite 1031, Philadelphia PA 19106. 215/922-4142. **Contact:** Manager. **Description:** An executive search firm. **Specializes in the areas of:** Architecture/Construction; Engineering.

MEDICAL CONNECTION
P.O. Box 57175, Philadelphia PA 19111-7175. 215/663-1705. **Fax:** 215/663-1706. **Contact:** Paul R. Stevens, CPC, President. **E-mail address:** stevens025@aol.com. **Description:** An executive search firm that focuses on placing medical imaging and biomedical repair technicians/engineers and medical equipment sales personnel. Company pays fee. **Positions commonly filled include:** Biomedical Engineer. **Average salary range of placements:** $30,000 - $50,000. **Number of placements per year:** 50 - 99.

B. PAUL MICKEY & ASSOCIATES
1001 Liberty Avenue, Suite 500, Pittsburgh PA 15222. 412/261-5858. **Fax:** 412/471-0263. **Contact:** B. Paul Mickey, President/Owner. **Description:** An executive search firm operating on a retainer basis. **Specializes in the areas of:** Engineering; General Management; Industrial; Manufacturing. **Positions commonly filled include:** Chemical Engineer; Electrical/Electronics Engineer; Mechanical Engineer; Metallurgical Engineer. **Average salary range of placements:** More than $50,000. **Number of placements per year:** 1 - 49.

ROY MORRIS ASSOCIATES
4550 McKnight Road, Suite 205, Pittsburgh PA 15237. 412/931-0353. **Contact:** Manager. **Description:** An executive search firm. **Specializes in the areas of:** Manufacturing.

THE MORRIS GROUP
919 Conestoga Road, Bryn Mawr PA 19010-0188. 610/520-0100. **Fax:** 610/520-0814. **Contact:** Peter J. Mays, Manager of Sales Recruitment. **Description:** An executive search firm operating on a contingency basis. Company pays fee. **Specializes in the areas of:** Accounting/Auditing; Architecture/Construction; Finance; General Management; Industrial; Insurance; Manufacturing; Personnel/Labor Relations; Sales; Technical. **Positions commonly filled include:** Budget Analyst; Chemical Engineer; Civil Engineer; Design Engineer; Financial Analyst; Human Resources Manager; Insurance Agent/Broker; Manufacturer's/Wholesaler's Sales Rep.; Market Research Analyst; Securities Sales Rep.; Services Sales Rep.; Strategic Relations Manager; Underwriter/Assistant Underwriter. **Number of placements per year:** 200 - 499.

JOHN MORROW & ASSOCIATES
819 Cypress Street, Irwin PA 15642. 412/864-9512. **Fax:** 412/864-9654. **Contact:** John Morrow, Owner. **Description:** An executive search firm operating on a retainer basis for real estate and construction owners, developers, and asset managers. Company pays fee. **Specializes in the areas of:** Architecture/Construction; Engineering; Finance. **Positions commonly filled include:** Construction Contractor; Financial Analyst; General Manager; Landscape Architect; Management Analyst/Consultant; Market Research Analyst; Property and Real Estate Manager; Stationary Engineer. **Corporate headquarters location:** Pittsburgh PA. **Average salary range of placements:** More than $50,000. **Number of placements per year:** 1 - 49.

ORION DELTA GROUP LTD.
1200 Reedsdale, Pittsburgh PA 15233. 412/231-2414. **Contact:** Manager. **Description:** An executive search firm. **Specializes in the areas of:** Health/Medical.

LaMONTE OWENS, INC.
P.O. Box 27742, Philadelphia PA 19118. 215/248-0500. **Physical address:** 805 East Willow Grove Avenue, Philadelphia PA. **Fax:** 215/233-3737. **Contact:** LaMonte Owens, President/Owner. **Description:** An executive search firm. **Specializes in the areas of:** Accounting/Auditing; Administration; Architecture/Construction; Banking; Biology; Computer Science/Software; Engineering; Finance; Health/Medical; Personnel/Labor Relations; Sales; Technical. **Positions commonly filled include:** Accountant/Auditor; Administrative Manager; Aerospace Engineer; Architect; Bank Officer/Manager; Biological Scientist; Biomedical Engineer; Branch Manager; Budget Analyst; Buyer; Ceramics Engineer; Chemical Engineer; Chemist; Civil Engineer; Clerical Supervisor; Computer Programmer; Credit Manager; Economist; Electrical/Electronics Engineer; Financial Analyst; Health Services Manager; Human Resources Manager; Industrial Engineer; Management Analyst/Consultant; Materials Engineer; Mechanical Engineer; Metallurgical Engineer; Nuclear Engineer; Purchasing Agent/Manager; Registered Nurse; Securities Sales Rep.; Software Engineer; Statistician; Systems Analyst. **Number of placements per year:** 1 - 49.

PENN ASSOCIATES
2 Penn Center, Suite 200, Philadelphia PA 19102. 215/854-6336. **Contact:** Joseph A. Dickerson, Principal. **Description:** An executive search firm. Company pays fee. **Specializes in the areas of:** Personnel/Labor Relations. **Positions commonly filled include:** Human Resources Manager; Management Analyst/Consultant; Psychologist. **Average salary range of placements:** More than $50,000. **Number of placements per year:** 1 - 49.

PENN SEARCH
997 Old Eagle School Road, Suite 202, Wayne PA 19087. 610/964-8820. **Fax:** 610/964-8916. **Contact:** Charlie DiGiovanni, President. **E-mail address:** pennsear@erols.com. **Description:** An executive search firm and permanent employment agency. Company pays fee. **Specializes in the areas of:** Accounting/Auditing; Finance. **Positions commonly filled include:** Accountant; Auditor; Budget Analyst; Chief Financial Officer; Controller; Credit Manager; Finance Director; Financial Analyst; Management Analyst/Consultant. **Average salary range of placements:** More than $50,000.

PERSONNEL RESOURCES ORGANIZATION
121 South Broad Street, Suite 1030, Philadelphia PA 19107. 215/735-7500. **Fax:** 215/735-5426. **Contact:** Larry Cesare, President. **Description:** A legal search firm focusing on the placement of partners and associate-level attorneys. Company pays fee. **Specializes in the areas of:** Legal. **Positions commonly filled include:** Attorney. **Average salary range of placements:** More than $50,000.

PRESTIGE PERSONNEL
1150 1st Avenue, King of Prussia PA 19406-1316. 610/768-4030. **Fax:** 610/768-4034. **Contact:** Chris Hooven, Owner. **Description:** An executive search firm. Company pays fee. **Specializes in the areas of:** Engineering; Manufacturing; Technical. **Positions commonly filled include:** Chemical Engineer; Design Engineer; Designer; Industrial Engineer; Mechanical Engineer; Metallurgical Engineer; Mining Engineer; Operations/Production Manager; Quality Control Supervisor; Software Engineer. **Average salary range of placements:** $30,000 - $50,000.

PROBE TECHNOLOGY
P.O. Box 60521, King of Prussia PA 19406. 610/337-8544. **Fax:** 610/337-8068. **Contact:** Tom Belletieri, Owner. **Description:** An executive search firm focusing on placements in high-tech industries with an emphasis on CEOs, vice presidents, directors, and managers in sales, manufacturing, operations, and research and development. Company pays fee. **Specializes in the areas of:** Biology; Engineering; General Management; Health/Medical; Industrial; Manufacturing; Sales; Technical. **Positions commonly filled include:** Biomedical Engineer; Buyer; Ceramics Engineer; Chemical Engineer; Electrical/Electronics Engineer; General Manager; Industrial Engineer; Industrial Production Manager; Materials Engineer; Mechanical Engineer; Metallurgical Engineer; Purchasing Agent/Manager; Quality Control Supervisor; Services Sales Representative. **Average salary range of placements:** More than $50,000. **Number of placements per year:** 1 - 49.

PROFESSIONAL RECRUITERS INC.
P.O. Box 4, Bala-Cynwyd PA 19004. 610/667-9355. **Contact:** Manager. **Description:** An executive search firm.

PROSEARCH, INC.
400 Baldwin Road, Pittsburgh PA 15205. 412/276-4200. **Contact:** Manager. **Description:** An executive search firm. **Specializes in the areas of:** Engineering; Finance; Human Resources.

QUESTOR CONSULTANTS, INC.
2515 North Broad Street, Colmar PA 18915. 215/997-9262. **Fax:** 215/997-9226. **Contact:** Sal Bevivino, President. **Description:** An executive search firm. Company pays fee. **Specializes in the areas of:** Insurance; Legal. **Positions commonly filled include:** Adjuster; Attorney; Claim Representative; Underwriter/Assistant Underwriter. **Average salary range of placements:** More than $50,000. **Number of placements per year:** 1 - 49.

R.H.A. EXECUTIVE PERSONNEL SERVICES
33 West Lancaster Avenue, Ardmore PA 19003. 610/642-3092x33. **Contact:** Marisela R. Allen, Vice President. **E-mail address:** 76100.2747@compuserve.com. **World Wide Web address:** http://www.ourworld.compuserve.com/homepages/jallenenterprises. **Description:** An executive search firm operating on a retained basis. R.H.A. Executive Personnel Services also offers career/outplacement counseling. Company pays fee. **Specializes in the areas of:** Food Industry; General Management; Legal; Manufacturing; Personnel/Labor Relations; Retail; Sales; Secretarial; Technical; Transportation. **Positions commonly filled include:** Administrative Manager; Agricultural Engineer; Attorney; Automotive Mechanic; Biological Scientist; Blue-Collar Worker Supervisor; Budget Analyst; Buyer; Chemist; Claim

Representative; Clerical Supervisor; Clinical Lab Technician; Electrician; Food Scientist/Technologist; Health Services Manager; Hotel Manager; Human Resources Manager; Market Research Analyst; Public Relations Specialist; Purchasing Agent/Manager; Quality Control Supervisor; Restaurant/Food Service Manager; Systems Analyst; Typist/Word Processor. **Number of placements per year:** 100 - 199.

ALAN RAEBURN CONSULTANTS
5471 Pocusset Street, Pittsburgh PA 15217. 412/422-6110. **Fax:** 412/422-6112. **Contact:** Recruiter. **E-mail address:** alraeburn@aol.com. **Description:** An executive search firm operating on a retainer basis. Founded in 1988. Company pays fee. **Specializes in the areas of:** Accounting/Auditing; Administration; Engineering; Finance; General Management; Industrial; Manufacturing; Personnel/Labor Relations; Sales. **Positions commonly filled include:** Branch Manager; Buyer; Design Engineer; General Manager; Human Resources Manager; Industrial Engineer; Industrial Production Manager; Manufacturer's/Wholesaler's Sales Rep.; Operations/Production Manager; Systems Analyst. **Other U.S. locations:** New York NY. **Average salary range of placements:** More than $50,000. **Number of placements per year:** 1 - 49.

REESE ASSOCIATES
10475 Perry Highway, Wexford PA 1509Q. 412/935-8644. **Contact:** Manager. **Description:** An executive search firm. **Specializes in the areas of:** Manufacturing.

RICE COHEN INTERNATIONAL
301 Oxford Valley Road, Suite 1506-A, Yardley PA 19067. 215/321-4100. **Fax:** 215/321-6370. **Contact:** Gene Rice, Managing Partner. **World Wide Web address:** http://www.rci-intl.com. **Description:** An executive search firm operating on both retained and contingency bases. Company pays fee. **Specializes in the areas of:** Accounting/Auditing; Administration; Advertising; Architecture/Construction; Banking; Communications; Computer Hardware/Software; Design; Electrical; Engineering; Finance; Food Industry; General Management; Health/Medical; Insurance; Legal; Manufacturing; Operations Management; Personnel/Labor Relations; Procurement; Publishing; Retail; Sales; Technical; Textiles; Transportation. **Average salary range of placements:** More than $50,000. **Number of placements per year:** 200 - 499.

THE RICHARDS GROUP
1608 Walnut Street, Suite 1702, Philadelphia PA 19103. 215/735-9450. **Fax:** 215/735-9430. **Contact:** Larry Winitsky, President. **Description:** An executive search firm. Founded in 1984. Company pays fee. **Specializes in the areas of:** Accounting/Auditing; Administration; Advertising; Banking; Computer Science/Software; Finance; General Management; Health/Medical; Insurance; Nonprofit; Personnel/Labor Relations; Retail; Sales; Secretarial. **Positions commonly filled include:** Accountant/Auditor; Actuary; Administrative Manager; Bank Officer/Manager; Branch Manager; Brokerage Clerk; Buyer; Claim Representative; Clerical Supervisor; Computer Programmer; Credit Manager; Customer Service Representative; Dietician/Nutritionist; EEG Technologist; EKG Technician; Financial Analyst; General Manager; Health Services Manager; Human Resources Manager; Insurance Agent/Broker; Management Trainee; Manufacturer's/Wholesaler's Sales Rep.; Market Research Analyst; Medical Records Technician; Occupational Therapist; Operations/Production Manager; Recreational Therapist; Registered Nurse; Respiratory Therapist; Services Sales Representative; Systems Analyst; Technical Writer/Editor; Telecommunications Manager; Transportation/Traffic Specialist; Typist/Word Processor; Underwriter/Assistant Underwriter.

RITTENHOUSE RECRUITERS, INC.
708 Lake Side Drive, Southampton PA 18966. 215/322-6533. **Fax:** 215/322-6551. **Contact:** Sheldon Dennis, CPC, President. **Description:** An executive search firm operating on a contingency basis. Founded in 1988. Company pays fee. **Specializes in the areas of:** Health/Medical; Insurance. **Positions commonly filled include:** Accountant/Auditor; Adjuster; Administrative Manager; Attorney; Branch Manager; Budget Analyst; Claim Representative; Clerical Supervisor; Customer Service Representative; Financial Analyst; General Manager; Health Services Manager; Human Resources Manager; Licensed Practical Nurse; Management Analyst/Consultant; Paralegal; Physical Therapist; Physician; Registered Nurse; Underwriter/Assistant Underwriter. **Number of placements per year:** 50 - 99.

JASON ROBERTS ASSOCIATES INC.
200 Monument Road, Bala-Cynwyd PA 19004. 610/667-1440. **Fax:** 610/667-1573. **Contact:** Robert Kirschner, President. **Description:** An executive search firm operating on both retainer and contingency bases. The firm exclusively provides placements in the field of SAP (System-Application-Program) and technology resources. Company pays fee. **Average salary range of placements:** $30,000 - $50,000. **Number of placements per year:** 100 - 199.

ROBIN JEFFREY ASSOCIATES
128 Miflin Street, Philadelphia PA 19148. 215/755-5030. **Contact:** Manager. **Description:** An executive search firm.

ROMAC INTERNATIONAL
2100 Wharton Street, Suite 710, Pittsburgh PA 15203. 412/481-6015. **Contact:** Manager. **Description:** An executive search firm. **Specializes in the areas of:** Accounting/Auditing; Finance. **Other U.S. locations:** Nationwide.

ROMAC INTERNATIONAL
4 Glenhardie Corporate Center, 1255 Drummers Lane, Suite 103, Wayne PA 19087. 610/989-3680. **Contact:** Manager. **Description:** An executive search firm that also operates a temporary placement division. **Specializes in the areas of:** Accounting/Auditing; Finance; Human Resources; Information Technology.

ROTH YOUNG PERSONNEL SERVICES
3087 Carson Street, Murrysville PA 15668. 412/733-5900. **Contact:** Manager. **Description:** An executive search firm. **Specializes in the areas of:** Health/Medical; Hotel/Restaurant; Retail.

S-H-S INTERNATIONAL
P.O. Box 1204, Wilkes-Barre PA 18703-1204. 717/825-3411. **Fax:** 717/825-7790. **Contact:** Chris Hackett, Search Consultant. **E-mail address:** prg@mail.microserve.net. **World Wide Web address:** http://www.shsint.com. **Description:** An executive search firm. Founded in 1968. Company pays fee. **Specializes in the areas of:** Accounting/Auditing; Banking; Computer Science/Software; Engineering; Finance; Personnel/Labor Relations; Publishing. **Positions commonly filled include:** Accountant/Auditor; Aerospace Engineer; Biological Scientist; Budget Analyst; Ceramics Engineer; Chemical Engineer; Chemist; Civil Engineer; Clinical Lab Technician; Computer Programmer; Credit Manager; Designer; Draftsperson; Editor; Financial Analyst; Human Resources Manager; Industrial Engineer; Landscape Architect; Materials Engineer; Mechanical

Engineer; Medical Records Technician; Metallurgical Engineer; Occupational Therapist; Physical Therapist; Purchasing Agent/Manager; Software Engineer; Systems Analyst; Technical Writer/Editor. **Average salary range of placements:** $30,000 - $50,000. **Number of placements per year:** 50 - 99.

SHS ASSOCIATES, INC.
P.O. Box 230, Media PA 19063-0230. 610/566-0600. **Fax:** 610/566-0636. **Contact:** Skip W. Schneider, Managing Partner. **Description:** A contingency executive search firm, providing mid- to senior-level placements. Founded in 1964. Company pays fee. **Specializes in the areas of:** Accounting/Auditing; Finance; Personnel/Labor Relations. **Positions commonly filled include:** Chief Financial Officer; Controller; Finance Director; Human Resources Manager. **Corporate headquarters location:** This Location. **Other U.S. locations:** Nationwide. **Average salary range of placements:** More than $50,000. **Number of placements per year:** 1 - 49.

SHS OF ALLENTOWN
1401 North Cedar Crest Boulevard, Suite 56, Allentown PA 18104-2307. 610/437-5551. **Fax:** 610/437-1027. **Contact:** David Mostow, President. **Description:** An executive search firm that specializes in the placement of professionals in the minerals processing, battery, explosives, and chemical industries. **Positions commonly filled include:** Chemist; Construction Contractor; Designer; Engineer; General Manager; Mining Engineer; Operations/Production Manager; Quality Control Supervisor. **Average salary range of placements:** More than $50,000. **Number of placements per year:** 50 - 99.

SALES CONSULTANTS OF NEWTOWN
301 South State Street, Newtown PA 18940. 215/579-2450. **Fax:** 215/579-2458. **Contact:** Jim Plappert, Owner. **E-mail address:** jplappert@scnewtown.com. **World Wide Web address:** http://www.scnewtown.com. **Description:** An executive search firm focusing on the placement of management personnel in the life, health, and pension insurance industries. Founded in 1989. Company pays fee. **Specializes in the areas of:** Insurance; Sales. **Positions commonly filled include:** Account Manager; Account Representative; Customer Service Representative; Insurance Agent/Broker; Marketing Manager; Sales Representative; Underwriter/Assistant Underwriter. **Number of placements per year:** 50 - 99.

SANFORD ROSE ASSOCIATES
3500 Brooktree Center, Suite 220, Wexford PA 15090. 412/934-2261. **Contact:** Manager. **World Wide Web address:** http://www.sanfordrose.com. **Description:** An executive search firm. **Specializes in the areas of:** Finance; Manufacturing.

SANFORD ROSE ASSOCIATES
130 Almshouse Road, Suite 107A, Richboro PA 18954. 215/953-7433. **Fax:** 215/953-7449. **Contact:** Manager. **World Wide Web address:** http://www.sanfordrose.com. **Description:** An executive search firm. **Specializes in the areas of:** MIS/EDP; Technical.

SANFORD ROSE ASSOCIATES
P.O. Box 1017, Buckingham PA 18912. 215/794-5570. **Fax:** 215/794-5672. **Contact:** Manager. **World Wide Web address:** http://www.sanfordrose.com. **Description:** An executive search firm. **Specializes in the areas of:** Engineering; Manufacturing; Marketing.

SNELLING PERSONNEL SERVICES
111 Presidential Boulevard, Bala-Cynwyd PA 19004. 610/667-4222. **Fax:** 610/667-4963. **Contact:** Office Manager. **Description:** An executive search firm. **Specializes in the areas of:** Engineering; Finance; General Management; Sales.

SOURCE SERVICES CORPORATION
Foster Plaza, Building 6, 681 Andersen Drive, Pittsburgh PA 15220. 412/928-9800. **Contact:** Manager. **Description:** An executive search firm. **Specializes in the areas of:** Accounting/Auditing; Information Systems.

SOURCE SERVICES CORPORATION
1760 Market Street, 12th Floor, Philadelphia PA 19103. 215/665-1717. **Fax:** 215/665-2894. **Contact:** Manager. **Description:** An executive search firm. The divisions at this location include Source EDP, Source Finance, and Accountant Source Temps. **Specializes in the areas of:** Accounting/Auditing; Computer Hardware/Software; Finance; Information Technology.

SPECTRUM CONSULTANTS, INC.
RETAIL RECRUITERS
111 Presidential Boulevard, Suite 211, Bala-Cynwyd PA 19004-1008. 610/667-6565. **Fax:** 610/667-5323. **Contact:** Shirlee Berman, President. **Description:** An executive search firm. Founded in 1978. Company pays fee. **Specializes in the areas of:** Accounting/Auditing; Administration; Advertising; Architecture/Construction; Food Industry; Health/Medical; Manufacturing; Marketing; Personnel/Labor Relations; Retail; Sales. **Positions commonly filled include:** Accountant; Advertising Account Executive; Assistant Manager; Auditor; Buyer; Chief Financial Officer; Consultant; Controller; Designer; Dietician/Nutritionist; Finance Director; Financial Analyst; Graphic Artist; Graphic Designer; Human Resources Manager; Industrial Engineer; Management Analyst/Consultant; Market Research Analyst; Marketing Manager; MIS Specialist; Occupational Therapist; Operations Manager; Pharmacist; Physical Therapist; Production Manager; Project Manager; Quality Control Supervisor; Registered Nurse; Respiratory Therapist; Sales Executive; Sales Manager; Speech-Language Pathologist; Systems Analyst; Systems Manager; Telecommunications Manager; Transportation/Traffic Specialist. **Average salary range of placements:** More than $50,000. **Number of placements per year:** 100 - 199.

KENN SPINRAD INC.
P.O. Box 4095, Reading PA 19606. 610/779-0944. **Fax:** 610/779-8338. **Contact:** Manager. **World Wide Web address:** http://www-elecsp.com/kspin/kspin.htm. **Description:** An executive search firm operating on both retainer and contingency bases. Company pays fee. **Specializes in the areas of:** Engineering; Fashion; Industrial; Textiles. **Positions commonly filled include:** Buyer; Chemical Engineer; Chemist; Chief Financial Officer; Computer Programmer; Industrial Engineer; Industrial Production Manager; Manufacturing Engineer; Market Research Analyst; Mechanical Engineer; Metallurgical Engineer; Operations/Production Manager; Purchasing Agent/Manager; Quality Control Supervisor; Software Engineer; Systems Analyst. **Average salary range of placements:** More than $50,000. **Number of placements per year:** 100 - 199.

STAFFING ALLIANCE
P.O. Box 3165, Westchester PA 19381. 610/430-7430. **Fax:** 215/887-6322. **Contact:** Jeannine Jubeck, Vice President. **World Wide Web address:** http://www.staffalliance.com. **Description:** An executive search firm for the staffing industry. **Specializes in the areas of:** Personnel/Labor Relations.

DANIEL STERN & ASSOCIATES
211 North Whitfield Street, Pittsburgh PA 15206. 412/363-9700. **Contact:** Manager. **Description:** An

executive search firm. **Specializes in the areas of:** Health/Medical.

STEWART ASSOCIATES
245 Butler Avenue, Lancaster PA 17601. 717/299-9242. **Fax:** 717/299-4879. **Contact:** Walter S. Poyck, Owner. **Description:** An executive search firm operating on a contingency basis. Company pays fee. **Specializes in the areas of:** Engineering. **Positions commonly filled include:** Account Representative; Biological Scientist; Buyer; Chemical Engineer; Chemist; Controller; Design Engineer; Draftsperson; Engineer; Environmental Engineer; General Manager; Human Resources Manager; Industrial Production Manager; Mechanical Engineer; Metallurgical Engineer; Public Relations Specialist; Quality Control Supervisor; Sales Engineer; Technical Writer/Editor; Telecommunications Manager. **Number of placements per year:** 1 - 49.

SPENCER STUART AND ASSOCIATES
2005 Market Street, Suite 2350, Philadelphia PA 19103. 215/563-0010. **Contact:** Manager. **Description:** An executive search firm.

SUBER & McAULEY TECHNICAL SEARCH
One Parkway Center, Suite 200, Pittsburgh PA 15220. 412/922-3336. **Fax:** 412/922-5716. **Contact:** John C. Suber, Partner/Recruiter. **E-mail address:** smts@aol.com. **Description:** An executive search firm operating on both contingency and retainer bases for engineering and manufacturing-based industries such as engineered materials, computer hardware and software, plastics, metal working, and power electronics. Suber & McAuley provides search services to *Fortune* 500 companies, several member companies of the Pittsburgh High Technology Council, and many other small to medium-sized companies. Founded in 1991. Company pays fee. **Specializes in the areas of:** Engineering; Manufacturing; Technical. **Positions commonly filled include:** Chemical Engineer; Design Engineer; Electrical/Electronics Engineer; Industrial Engineer; Industrial Production Manager; Market Research Analyst; Mechanical Engineer; Metallurgical Engineer; Purchasing Agent/Manager; Quality Control Supervisor; Science Technologist; Software Engineer; Telecommunications Manager; Video Production Coordinator. **Average salary range of placements:** More than $50,000. **Number of placements per year:** 100 - 199.

SUBURBAN PLACEMENT SERVICE
21 North York Road, Willow Grove PA 19090-3420. 215/657-6262. **Fax:** 215/657-6431. **Contact:** Ed Fort, Manager. **Description:** An executive search firm. Founded in 1971. Company pays fee. **Specializes in the areas of:** Computer Science/Software. **Positions commonly filled include:** Aerospace Engineer; Computer Programmer; Customer Service Rep.; Electrical/Electronics Engineer; MIS Specialist; Software Engineer; Systems Analyst; Telecommunications Analyst. **Number of placements per year:** 50 - 99.

SYSTEMS PERSONNEL INC.
115 West State Street, Media PA 19063. 610/565-8880. **Fax:** 610/565-1482. **Contact:** Gerald B. Reynolds, Partner. **Description:** An executive search firm. Founded in 1974. Company pays fee. **Specializes in the areas of:** Administration; MIS/EDP; Technical. **Positions commonly filled include:** Computer Programmer; MIS Specialist; Software Engineer; Statistician; Systems Analyst; Telecommunications Manager. **Number of placements per year:** 100 - 199.

TARGET SEARCH INC.
Station Square One, Suite 204, Paoli PA 19301-1314. 610/889-2000. **Fax:** 610/889-2424. **Contact:** Manager. **Description:** An executive search firm. Founded in 1992. Company pays fee. **Specializes in the areas of:** Food Industry. **Positions commonly filled include:** Branch Manager; Dietician/Nutritionist; General Manager; Hotel Manager; Restaurant/Food Service Manager. **Average salary range of placements:** More than $50,000. **Number of placements per year:** 50 - 99.

TERRY TAYLOR & ASSOCIATES
459 Bechman Street, Springdale PA 15144. 412/274-5627. **Fax:** 412/274-5627. **Contact:** Terry Taylor, Principal. **Description:** An executive search firm working on both retainer and contingency bases. Founded in 1975. Company pays fee. **Specializes in the areas of:** Administration; Consulting; Finance; Health/Medical; Human Resources; Information Systems; Information Technology; Telecommunications. **Positions commonly filled include:** Accountant/Auditor; Economist; Financial Analyst; Internet Services Manager; Management Analyst/Consultant; Mathematician; Securities Sales Representative; Systems Analyst; Telecommunications Manager. **Average salary range of placements:** More than $50,000. **Number of placements per year:** 1 - 49.

TECHNICAL PERSONNEL
P.O. Box 101050, Pittsburgh PA 15237. 412/367-4311. **Contact:** Manager. **Description:** An executive search firm. **Specializes in the areas of:** Technical.

TELL/COM RECRUITERS
306 Corporate Drive East, Langhorne PA 19047. 215/860-4100. **Fax:** 215/968-6680. **Contact:** Dennis F. Young, President. **E-mail address:** dennyyoung@aol.com. **Description:** An executive search firm that specializes in placing sales, management, and engineering professionals within the telecommunications industry. Founded in 1983. Company pays fee. **Specializes in the areas of:** Sales. **Positions commonly filled include:** Telecommunications Manager. **Number of placements per year:** 200 - 499.

TEMPLETON & ASSOCIATES
1518 Walnut Street, Suite 1008, Philadelphia PA 19106. 215/772-0555. **Contact:** Manager. **Description:** An executive search firm. **Specializing in the areas of:** Legal.

TOWER CONSULTANTS, LTD.
621B Swedesford Road, Swedesford Corporate Center, Malvern PA 19355. 610/722-9300. **Contact:** Donna DeHart, Vice President. **E-mail address:** towercons@aol.com. **Description:** An executive search firm operating on a retained basis. Founded in 1988. Company pays fee. **Specializes in the areas of:** Personnel/Labor Relations. **Positions commonly filled include:** Human Resources Manager. **Number of placements per year:** 50 - 99.

W.G. TUCKER & ASSOCIATES
2908 McKelvey Road, Suite 2, Pittsburgh PA 15221-4569. 412/244-9309. **Fax:** 412/244-9195. **Contact:** Weida G. Tucker, President. **E-mail address:** tuckerwg@ix.netcom.com. **Description:** An executive search firm operating on a retainer basis. Company pays fee. **Specializes in the areas of:** Accounting/Auditing; Administration; Banking; General Management; Marketing; Personnel/Labor Relations; Sales; Transportation. **Positions commonly filled include:** Accountant/Auditor; Actuary; Aerospace Engineer; Attorney; Bank Officer/Manager; Biological Scientist; Biomedical Engineer; Branch Manager; Budget Analyst; Buyer; Ceramics Engineer; Chemical Engineer; Chemist; Civil Engineer; Claim Representative; Clinical Lab Technician; Computer

Programmer; Cost Estimator; Credit Manager; Customer Service Representative; Dietician/ Nutritionist; Draftsperson; Editor; Education Administrator; Electrical/Electronics Engineer; Financial Analyst; Food Scientist/Technologist; General Manager; Geologist/Geophysicist; Health Services Manager; Human Resources Manager; Industrial Engineer; Insurance Agent/Broker; Library Technician; Management Analyst/Consultant; Management Trainee; Materials Engineer; Mechanical Engineer; Metallurgical Engineer; Mining Engineer; Nuclear Engineer; Occupational Therapist; Paralegal; Petroleum Engineer; Pharmacist; Physical Therapist; Physician; Public Relations Specialist; Purchasing Agent/ Manager; Quality Control Supervisor; Restaurant/Food Service Manager; Science Technologist; Services Sales Representative; Software Engineer; Structural Engineer; Systems Analyst; Technical Writer/Editor; Underwriter/Assistant Underwriter; Urban/Regional Planner.

WHITTLESEY & ASSOCIATES, INC.
300 South High Street, West Chester PA 19382. 610/436-6500. **Fax:** 610/344-0018. **Contact:** Toni J. Ritchey, Director. **Description:** An executive search firm operating on a retainer basis. Company pays fee. **Specializes in the areas of:** Engineering; Food Industry; General Management; Health/Medical; Industrial; Light Industrial; Personnel/Labor Relations; Sales; Technical. **Positions commonly filled include:** Account Manager; Chemical Engineer; Controller; Electrical/Electronics Engineer; General Manager; Human Resources Manager; Industrial Engineer; Manufacturer's/ Wholesaler's Sales Rep.; Marketing Manager; Production Manager; Project Manager; Sales Executive; Sales Manager. **Average salary range of placements:** More than $50,000. **Number of placements per year:** 1 - 49.

WITTHAUER ASSOCIATES LTD.
P.O. Box 40, Chalfont PA 18914. 215/822-6411. **Contact:** Manager. **Description:** An executive search firm. **Specializes in the areas of:** Computer Hardware/Software; Technical.

YORKTOWNE PERSONNEL
103 East Market Street, York PA 17401. 717/843-0079. **Fax:** 717/843-5792. **Contact:** Roger M. Geiger, President. **Description:** An executive search firm operating on both retainer and contingency bases. Company pays fee. **Specializes in the areas of:** Accounting/Auditing; Engineering; Food Industry; General Management; Industrial; Personnel/Labor Relations; Technical. **Positions commonly filled include:** Account Manager; Accountant/Auditor; Budget Analyst; Buyer; Chemical Engineer; Chief Financial Officer; Civil Engineer; Controller; Credit Manager; Design Engineer; Electrical/Electronics Engineer; Environmental Engineer; Financial Analyst; Human Resources Manager; Industrial Designer; Industrial Engineer; Industrial Production Manager; Manufacturing Engineer; Mechanical Engineer; Metallurgical Engineer; Operations/Productic Manager; Production Manager; Purchasing Age Manager; Quality Control Supervisor; Sales Engin Software Engineer; Transportation/Traffic Speci **Number of placements per year:** 50 - 99.

PERMANENT EMPLOYMENT AGENCIES

ACSYS RESOURCES
1700 Market Street, Suite 3110, Philadelphia PA 19103. 215/568-6810. **Contact:** Manager. **Description:** A permanent employment agency. **Specializes in the areas of:** Accounting/Auditing; Consulting; Finance; Sales.

ACTION PERSONNEL SERVICES
1622 Main Street, Dickson City PA 18519. 717/383-0243. **Fax:** 717/383-2565. **Contact:** Nick Swatkowski, President. **Description:** A permanent employment agency. Company pays fee. **Specializes in the areas of:** Accounting/Auditing; Engineering; General Management; Industrial; Manufacturing; Personnel/Labor Relations. **Positions commonly filled include:** Accountant/Auditor; Buyer; Ceramics Engineer; Chemical Engineer; Civil Engineer; Computer Programmer; Draftsperson; Electrical/Electronics Engineer; Industrial Engineer; Industrial Production Manager; Manufacturing Engineer; Materials Engineer; Mechanical Engineer; Metallurgical Engineer; Occupational Therapist; Petroleum Engineer; Physical Therapist; Sales Executive; Sales Manager; Software Engineer; Systems Analyst; Telecommunications Manager. **Number of placements per year:** 1 - 49.

ADVANCE PERSONNEL
P.O. Box 8383, Reading PA 19603. 610/374-4089. **Contact:** Manager. **Description:** A permanent employment agency. Company pays fee. **Positions commonly filled include:** Administrative Assistant; Bookkeeper; Claim Representative; Clerk; Customer Service Representative; Data Entry Clerk; Legal Secretary; Medical Secretary; Receptionist; Secretary; Stenographer; Typist/Word Processor. **Number of placements per year:** 200 - 499.

ALL STAFFING INC.
100 West Ridge Street, P.O. Box 219, Lansford PA 18232. 717/645-8883. **Physical address:** 100 West Ridge Street, Lansford PA. **Fax:** 717/6 **Contact:** Stan Costello, Jr., President. **Des** permanent employment agency. Compan **Specializes in the areas of:** Accounti Administration; Advertising; Comput Software; Finance; Health/Medical Manufacturing; Personnel/Labor Rela Sales; Secretarial. **Positions commonl** Accountant/Auditor; Computer Prog Assistant/Dental Hygienist; Dental Dentist; Draftsperson; Economist; E EKG Technician; Financial Analyst; Health Services Manager; Human R Insurance Agent/Broker; Man Manufacturer's/Wholesaler's Sa Records Technician; Nuclear M Occupational Therapist; P Therapist; Physician; Phy Radiological Technologist; Respiratory Therapist; Servic Surgical Technician; Systems Retail Buyer. **Number of plac**

ASAP STAFFING
P.O. Box 425, Springho 9520. **Fax:** 215/542-95 President. **Description:** agency. **Specializes** Accounting/Auditing; Biology; Computer Finance; Health/Medi Manufacturing; Per Secretarial; Techni **include:** Accounta Agricultural Engine Biological Scient Analyst; Buyer Engineer; Che Programmer; C Entry Clerk; Dentis

Electrical/Electronics Engineer; Emergency Medical Technician; Financial Analyst; Health Services Manager; Industrial Engineer; Industrial Production Manager; Licensed Practical Nurse; Materials Engineer; Mathematician; Mechanical Engineer; Medical Records Technician; Metallurgical Engineer; Mining Engineer; Nuclear Engineer; Nuclear Medicine Technologist; Occupational Therapist; Paralegal; Petroleum Engineer; Pharmacist; Physical Therapist; Physician; Physicist; Psychologist; Purchasing Agent/Manager; Quality Control Supervisor; Radiological Technologist; Recreational Therapist; Registered Nurse; Science Technologist; Software Engineer; Stationary Engineer; Statistician; Structural Engineer; Systems Analyst; Veterinarian. **Number of placements per year:** 50 - 99.

BECKER TEMPORARY SERVICES, INC.
One Bala Plaza, Suite LL36, Bala-Cynwyd PA 19004. 610/667-3010. **Fax:** 610/667-4209. **Contact:** Harvey A. Becker, President. **Description:** A permanent employment agency that also provides temporary placements. Company pays fee. **Specializes in the areas of:** Insurance; Legal; Sales; Secretarial. **Positions commonly filled include:** Customer Service Representative; Typist/Word Processor. **Other area locations:** King of Prussia PA; Philadelphia PA. **Average salary range of placements:** $30,000 - $50,000. **Number of placements per year:** 100 - 199.

BRADLEY PROFESSIONAL SERVICES
440 East Swedesford Road, Suite 1070, Wayne PA 19087. 610/254-9995. **Fax:** 610/971-9480. **Contact:** Manager. **Description:** A permanent employment agency. Company pays fee. **Specializes in the areas of:** Accounting/Auditing; Biology; Computer Science/Software; Engineering; Health/Medical; Personnel/Labor Relations; Technical. **Positions commonly filled include:** Accountant/Auditor; Aerospace Engineer; Agricultural Scientist; Architect; Biological Scientist; Biomedical Engineer; Buyer; Ceramics Engineer; Chemical Engineer; Chemist; Civil Engineer; Clinical Lab Technician; Computer rogrammer; Designer; Draftsperson; Electrical/ lectronics Engineer; Human Resources Manager; dustrial Engineer; Management Analyst/Consultant; aterials Engineer; Mechanical Engineer; Metallurgical gineer; Mining Engineer; Nuclear Engineer; troleum Engineer; Pharmacist; Physician; Science hnologist; Software Engineer; Stationary Engineer; tistician; Structural Engineer; Systems Analyst; hnical Writer/Editor. **Number of placements per** : 100 - 199.

EERS USA
JFK Boulevard, Philadelphia PA 19103. 61-3800. **Contact:** Manager. **Description:** A nent employment agency.

RD ASSOCIATES INC.
orporate Drive East, Langhorne PA 19047. 8-1980. **Fax:** 215/860-4109. **Contact:** Cliff Owner. **World Wide Web address:** ww.ipd.com/eoffice/215-968-1980.html. **ion:** A permanent employment agency. pays fee. **Specializes in the areas of:** Hardware/Software; Information gy. **Positions commonly filled include:** Programmer; MIS Specialist; Systems **umber of placements per year:** 1 - 49.

R PROFESSIONALS UNLIMITED
night Road, Suite 302, Pittsburgh PA /367-4191. **Fax:** 412/367-1152. **Contact:** Manager. **Description:** A permanent agency. **Specializes in the areas of:** omputer Science/Software. **Positions filled include:** Bank Officer/Manager; ogrammer; Human Resources Manager; Software Engineer; Systems Analyst. **Number of placements per year:** 100 - 199.

J. CROYLE AND ASSOCIATES, INC.
3244 USX Tower, 32nd Floor, Pittsburgh PA 15219. 412/281-4080. **Fax:** 412/281-8308. **Contact:** Joan Croyle, President. **Description:** A permanent employment agency that focuses on entry-level to mid-management positions as well as administrative, secretarial, and clerical support positions. **Specializes in the areas of:** Fashion; Finance; Food Industry; General Management; Legal; Retail; Secretarial. **Positions commonly filled include:** Clerical Supervisor; Customer Service Representative; Hotel Manager; Management Trainee; Restaurant/Food Service Manager; Services Sales Representative; Typist/Word Processor. **Average salary range of placements:** $20,000 - $29,999. **Number of placements per year:** 100 - 199.

DENTAL POWER OF DELAWARE VALLEY, INC.
1528 Walnut Street, Suite 1802, Philadelphia PA 19102. 215/735-6929. **Contact:** Manager. **Description:** A permanent employment agency for dental professionals. **Specializes in the areas of:** Health/Medical.

DiCENZO PERSONNEL SPECIALISTS
428 Forbes Avenue, Suite 110, Pittsburgh PA 15219. 412/281-6207. **Fax:** 412/281-9326. **Contact:** Carmela DiCenzo, Owner. **Description:** A permanent employment agency. Company pays fee. **Specializes in the areas of:** Accounting/Auditing; Administration; Computer Science/Software; Engineering; Finance; Food Industry; General Management; Industrial; Manufacturing; Personnel/Labor Relations; Sales; Secretarial; Technical. **Positions commonly filled include:** Accountant/Auditor; Adjuster; Administrative Manager; Aerospace Engineer; Agricultural Engineer; Bank Officer/Manager; Biological Scientist; Biomedical Engineer; Blue-Collar Worker Supervisor; Branch Manager; Budget Analyst; Buyer; Chemical Engineer; Chemist; Civil Engineer; Claim Rep.; Computer Programmer; Credit Manager; Customer Service Rep.; Draftsperson; Economist; Electrical/Electronics Engineer; Electrician; Financial Analyst; General Manager; Industrial Engineer; Industrial Production Manager; Management Analyst/Consultant; Mechanical Engineer; Metallurgical Engineer; Mining Engineer; Nuclear Engineer; Paralegal; Petroleum Engineer; Public Relations Specialist; Purchasing Agent/Manager; Quality Control Supervisor; Services Sales Rep.; Software Engineer; Stationary Engineer; Structural Engineer; Technical Writer/Editor.

DOUGHERTY & ASSOCIATES, INC.
1730 Walton Road, Suite 304, Blue Bell PA 19422. 610/825-2131. **Contact:** George J. Dougherty, President. **Description:** A permanent employment agency.

EMPLOYMENT CORPORATION OF AMERICA (E.C.A.)
2250 Hickory Road, Plymouth Meeting PA 19462. 610/941-0800. **Fax:** 610/941-0810. **Contact:** Recruiter. **Description:** A permanent employment agency focusing on placements with *Fortune* 500 companies. Company pays fee. **Specializes in the areas of:** Sales. **Average salary range of placements:** $30,000 - $50,000.

EXPRESS PERSONNEL SERVICE
260 South Broad Street, 14th Floor, Philadelphia PA 19102. 215/893-1200. **Contact:** Office Manager. **Description:** A permanent employment agency.

FINANCIAL INDUSTRY STAFFING COMPANY
1717 Swede Road, Blue Bell PA 19422. 610/277-4997. **Fax:** 610/277-0220. **Contact:** Manager.

Description: A permanent employment agency. Founded in 1986. Company pays fee. **Specializes in the areas of:** Accounting/Auditing; Administration; Banking; Computer Science/Software; Finance; General Management. **Positions commonly filled include:** Accountant/Auditor; Actuary; Adjuster; Bank Officer/Manager; Branch Manager; Brokerage Clerk; Budget Analyst; Claim Rep.; Clerical Supervisor; Computer Programmer; Cost Estimator; Credit Manager; Customer Service Rep.; Economist; Financial Analyst; General Manager; Human Resources Specialist; Management Analyst/Consultant; Management Trainee; Manufacturer's/Wholesaler's Sales Rep.; Market Research Analyst; MIS Specialist; Operations/Production Manager; Purchasing Agent/Manager; Quality Control Supervisor; Securities Sales Rep.; Services Sales Rep.; Systems Analyst; Technical Writer/Editor; Telecommunications Manager; Typist/Word Processor; Underwriter/Assistant Underwriter. **Benefits available to temporary workers:** Life Insurance; Medical Insurance; Referral Bonus Plan. **Corporate headquarters location:** Boston MA. **Number of placements per year:** 200 - 499.

GENERAL EMPLOYMENT & TRIAD PERSONNEL
1617 JFK Boulevard, Suite 930, Philadelphia PA 19103. 215/569-3226. **Fax:** 215/569-8164. **Contact:** Bill Gouldey, Manager. **Description:** A permanent employment agency. **Specializes in the areas of:** Administration; Computer Science/Software. **Positions commonly filled include:** Computer Programmer; Internet Services Manager; MIS Specialist; Systems Analyst; Telecommunications Manager.

JERRY GOLDBERG & ASSOCIATES INC.
1404 East Market Street, York PA 17403. 717/843-0041. **Fax:** 717/843-8883. **Contact:** Jerry Goldberg, President. **Description:** A permanent employment agency. Company pays fee. **Specializes in the areas of:** Engineering; Environmental; Industrial; Manufacturing; Personnel/Labor Relations; Safety; Technical. **Positions commonly filled include:** Accountant/Auditor; Agricultural Engineer; Biomedical Engineer; Buyer; Chemical Engineer; Computer Programmer; Designer; Electrical/Electronics Engineer; Financial Analyst; Human Resources Manager; Industrial Engineer; Industrial Production Manager; Mechanical Engineer; Operations/Production Manager; Purchasing Agent/Manager; Quality Control Supervisor; Software Engineer; Structural Engineer; Systems Analyst.

MERRILL GRUMER ASSOCIATES, INC.
1500 Walnut Street, Suite 307, Philadelphia PA 19102. 215/875-8100. **Fax:** 215/875-8200. **Contact:** Merrill Grumer, President. **Description:** A permanent employment agency. Company pays fee. **Specializes in the areas of:** Administration; Legal; MIS/EDP; Secretarial. **Positions commonly filled include:** Administrative Assistant; Administrative Manager; Branch Manager; Clerical Supervisor; Controller; Database Manager; Finance Director; Human Resources Manager; Librarian; Marketing Manager; MIS Specialist; Operations Manager; Paralegal; Secretary; Systems Manager; Typist/Word Processor. **Average salary range of placements:** $30,000 - $50,000. **Number of placements per year:** 50 - 99.

HALLMARK PERSONNEL INC.
ABLE TEMPS
1845 Market Street, Camp Hill PA 17011. 717/761-8111. **Fax:** 717/761-8862. **Contact:** Deborah Abel, Vice President of Marketing. **Description:** A permanent placement agency. Able Temps (also at this location) provides temporary placement. Company pays fee. **Specializes in the areas of:** General Management; Health/Medical; Legal; Sales; Secretarial. **Positions commonly filled include:** Accountant/Auditor; Administrative Manager; Bank Officer/Manager; Branch Manager; Brokerage Clerk; Budget Analyst; Claim Rep.; Credit Manager; Customer Service Rep.; General Manager; Hotel Manager; Human Resources Specialist; Insurance Agent/Broker; Management Trainee; Manufacturer's/Wholesaler's Sales Rep.; Market Research Analyst; Medical Records Technician; Paralegal; Purchasing Agent/Manager; Quality Control Supervisor; Securities Sales Rep.; Services Sales Rep.; Technical Writer/Editor; Typist/Word Processor; Underwriter/Assistant Underwriter. **Average salary range of placements:** $20,000 - $29,999. **Number of placements per year:** 100 - 199.

HI-Q PERSONNEL SERVICES
5415 North Fifth Street, Philadelphia PA 19120. 215/924-1985. **Contact:** Manager. **Description:** A permanent employment agency that also provides temporary placements.

HOSKINS HAINS ASSOCIATES
3835 Walnut Street, Harrisburg PA 17109. 717/657-8444. **Fax:** 717/657-8459. **Contact:** Patricia Hoskins, Owner. **Description:** A permanent employment agency that also conducts executive searches. Company pays fee. **Specializes in the areas of:** Accounting/Auditing; Clerical; Computer Hardware/Software; Engineering; Finance; Manufacturing; Personnel/Labor Relations. **Positions commonly filled include:** Accountant/Auditor; Budget Analyst; Chemical Engineer; Chief Financial Officer; Computer Animator; Computer Operator; Computer Programmer; Controller; Data Entry Clerk; Database Manager; Design Engineer; Draftsperson; EDP Specialist; Electrical/Electronics Engineer; Financial Analyst; Human Resources Manager; Industrial Engineer; Mechanical Engineer; Metallurgical Engineer; MIS Specialist; Purchasing Agent/Manager; Quality Control Supervisor; Receptionist; Sales Representative; Secretary; Statistician; Systems Analyst; Technical Writer/Editor; Typist/Word Processor. **Average salary range of placements:** $30,000 - $50,000. **Number of placements per year:** 50 - 99.

HOSPITALITY SERVICES
Dublin Hall, Suite 411, 1777 Sentry Parkway West, Blue Bell PA 19422. 215/643-9040. **Fax:** 215/643-9043. **Contact:** Ron Miles, Partner. **Description:** A permanent employment agency. **Specializes in the areas of:** Food Industry; General Management; Personnel/Labor Relations. **Positions commonly filled include:** Accountant/Auditor; Construction Contractor; Dietician/Nutritionist; Food Scientist/Technologist; Hotel Manager; Restaurant/Food Service Manager. **Number of placements per year:** 50 - 99.

INTERIM LEGAL PROFESSIONALS, INC.
1617 JFK Boulevard, Suite 1020, Philadelphia PA 19103. 215/568-5899. **Fax:** 215/568-5810. **Contact:** Don Jeffries, Managing Director. **Description:** A permanent employment agency. Company pays fee. **Specializes in the areas of:** Legal. **Positions commonly filled include:** Attorney; Legal Secretary; Paralegal. **Average salary range of placements:** $30,000 - $50,000. **Number of placements per year:** 100 - 199.

JJH
3412 Progress Drive, Suite C, Bensalem PA 19020. 215/633-9331. **Contact:** Manager. **Description:** A permanent employment agency that focuses on naval architectural placements. **Number of placements per year:** 50 - 99.

JEWISH EMPLOYMENT AND VOCATIONAL SERVICE
1845 Walnut Street, 7th Floor, Philadelphia PA 19103. 215/854-1800. **Contact:** Office Manager. **Description:** A permanent employment agency.

KATHY KARR PERSONNEL, INC.
2512 West Main Street, Jeffersonville PA 19403. 610/630-0760. **Fax:** 610/630-9155. **Contact:** Kathy Karr, President. **Description:** A permanent employment agency. Company pays fee. **Specializes in the areas of:** Accounting/Auditing; Administration; Architecture/Construction; Banking; Clerical; Engineering; Finance; General Management; Industrial; Legal; Manufacturing; Sales; Secretarial; Transportation. **Positions commonly filled include:** Accountant/Auditor; Administrative Manager; Advertising Clerk; Aerospace Engineer; Agricultural Engineer; Architect; Bank Officer/Manager; Biochemist; Biological Scientist; Biomedical Engineer; Blue-Collar Worker Supervisor; Branch Manager; Brokerage Clerk; Budget Analyst; Buyer; Ceramics Engineer; Chemical Engineer; Chemist; Civil Engineer; Claim Representative; Clerical Supervisor; Computer Programmer; Construction and Building Inspector; Construction Contractor; Cost Estimator; Credit Manager; Customer Service Representative; Dental Assistant/Dental Hygienist; Design Engineer; Designer; Draftsperson; Economist; Editor; Electrical/Electronics Engineer; Electrician; Environmental Engineer; Financial Analyst; General Manager; Health Services Manager; Human Resources Specialist; Industrial Engineer; Industrial Production Manager; Landscape Architect; Library Technician; Management Analyst/Consultant; Management Trainee; Manufacturer's/Wholesaler's Sales Rep.; Market Research Analyst; Materials Engineer; Mathematician; Mechanical Engineer; Metallurgical Engineer; MIS Specialist; Operations/Production Manager; Paralegal; Property and Real Estate Manager; Public Relations Specialist; Purchasing Agent/Manager; Quality Control Supervisor; Services Sales Representative; Software Engineer; Strategic Relations Manager; Systems Analyst; Technical Writer/Editor; Telecommunications Manager; Travel Agent; Typist/Word Processor; Underwriter/Assistant Underwriter. **Number of placements per year:** 200 - 499.

EVERETT KELLEY ASSOCIATES, INC.
1601 Market Street, Suite 325, Philadelphia PA 19103. 215/981-0800. **Contact:** Office Manager. **Description:** A permanent employment agency.

LAW SKIL
429 Forbes Avenue, Suite 1200, Pittsburgh PA 15219. 412/471-7944. **Fax:** 412/471-1922. **Contact:** Joan Csaszar, President. **Description:** A permanent employment agency that also provides temporary placements. Company pays fee. **Specializes in the areas of:** Legal. **Positions commonly filled include:** Attorney; Paralegal; Secretary; Typist/Word Processor. **Benefits available to temporary workers:** Paid Vacation. **Number of placements per year:** 200 - 499.

LONDON PERSONNEL SERVICES
3 Garrett Road, Upper Darby PA 19082. 610/734-3223. **Fax:** 610/734-3226. **Contact:** Manager. **Description:** A permanent employment agency. **Specializes in the areas of:** Administration; Industrial; Light Industrial; MIS/EDP; Scientific; Secretarial; Technical. **Positions commonly filled include:** Administrative Assistant; Blue-Collar Worker Supervisor; Secretary; Typist/Word Processor; Warehouse/Distribution Worker. **Average salary range of placements:** Less than $20,000. **Number of placements per year:** 1000+.

MAIN LINE PERSONNEL SERVICE
100 Presidential Boulevard, Suite 200, Bala-Cynwyd PA 19004. 610/667-1820. **Fax:** 610/668-5000. **Contact:** Bart Marshall, Vice President. **Description:** A permanent employment agency. Company pays fee. **Specializes in the areas of:** Computer Science/Software; Engineering; Personnel/Labor Relations; Technical. **Positions commonly filled include:** Aerospace Engineer; Agricultural Scientist; Biological Scientist; Biomedical Engineer; Ceramics Engineer; Chemical Engineer; Civil Engineer; Computer Programmer; Electrical/Electronics Engineer; Geologist/Geophysicist; Human Resources Manager; Industrial Engineer; Materials Engineer; Mechanical Engineer; Metallurgical Engineer; Mining Engineer; Nuclear Engineer; Petroleum Engineer; Software Engineer; Stationary Engineer; Structural Engineer; Systems Analyst. **Number of placements per year:** 1000+.

MARK JOSEPH ASSOCIATES
1521 Cedar Cliff Drive, Camp Hill PA 17011. 717/975-3505. **Fax:** 717/975-3565. **Contact:** Gina Ripple, Manager. **Description:** A permanent employment agency. **Specializes in the areas of:** Accounting/Auditing; Finance.

J. McMANUS ASSOCIATES
237 West Lancaster Avenue, Devon PA 19333-1592. 610/688-2006. **Fax:** 610/688-2007. **Contact:** Jeanne McManus, Owner. **Description:** A permanent employment agency. Company pays fee. **Specializes in the areas of:** Administration; Computer Science/Software; Insurance; Legal; Secretarial. **Positions commonly filled include:** Computer Programmer; Customer Service Representative; MIS Specialist; Systems Analyst; Typist/Word Processor; Underwriter/Assistant Underwriter. **Average salary range of placements:** $20,000 - $29,999. **Number of placements per year:** 1 - 49.

MEDICAL PERSONNEL POOL
PERSONNEL POOL
1800 Linglestown Road, Suite 301, Harrisburg PA 17110. 717/233-2444. **Contact:** Manager. **Description:** A permanent employment agency that also provides temporary placements. Personnel Pool (also at this location) provides permanent and temporary clerical and industrial placements. **Specializes in the areas of:** Health/Medical.

T. R. MUMFORD ASSOCIATES
215 Rear Kenrick Avenue, Denora PA 15033. 412/655-7550. **Contact:** Manager. **Description:** A permanent employment agency. **Specializes in the areas of:** Secretarial.

NATIONAL COMPUTERIZED EMPLOYMENT
2014 West 8th Street, Erie PA 16505. 814/454-3874. **Fax:** 814/454-8097. **Contact:** Joseph W. Beck, President. **Description:** A permanent employment agency. Company pays fee. **Specializes in the areas of:** Engineering; Industrial; Plastics. **Positions commonly filled include:** Chemical Engineer; Electrical/Electronics Engineer; Mechanical Engineer; Metallurgical Engineer; Operations/Production Manager; Quality Control Supervisor; Software Engineer; Systems Analyst. **Benefits available to temporary workers:** Medical Insurance; Paid Holidays; Paid Vacation. **Number of placements per year:** 50 - 99.

NORCON ASSOCIATES, INC.
P.O. Box 405, Newtown Square PA 19073-0405. 610/359-1707. **Contact:** Manager. **Description:** A permanent employment agency. **Specializes in the areas of:** Technical.

NORTHEAST AGRI EMPLOYMENT SERVICE
P.O. Box 233, Roaring Spring PA 16673. 814/224-4542. **Fax:** 814/224-4542. **Contact:** Russell F. Brown, Owner. **Description:** A permanent employment agency that focuses on agricultural industries including seed, feed, fertilizer, finance, and equipment companies in the northeastern United States.

Company pays fee. **Specializes in the areas of:** Agri-Business; Sales. **Positions commonly filled include:** Agricultural Scientist; Dietician/Nutritionist; Sales Manager. **Average salary range of placements:** $30,000 - $50,000. **Number of placements per year:** 50 - 99.

OLSTEN STAFFING SERVICES
1617 JFK Boulevard, Suite 420, Philadelphia PA 19103. 215/568-7795. **Toll-free phone:** 800/WORK-NOW. **Fax:** 215/569-3174. **Contact:** Manager. **Description:** A permanent employment agency that also provides temporary placements. Company pays fee. **Corporate headquarters location:** Melville NY. **Other U.S. locations:** Nationwide. **Average salary range of placements:** $20,000 - $29,999. **Number of placements per year:** 1000+.

PRN CONSULTANTS
941 Durham Road, Langhorne PA 19047. 215/750-6161. **Contact:** Placement Recruiter. **Description:** A permanent employment agency. **Specializes in the areas of:** Health/Medical.

PAL EMPLOYMENT
1239 Vine Street, Philadelphia PA 19107. 215/569-2277. **Contact:** Manager. **Description:** A permanent employment agency.

THE PHILADELPHIA NANNY NETWORK
225 South 15th Street, Suite 1507, Philadelphia PA 19102. 215/546-3002. **Toll-free phone:** 800/765-6269. **Fax:** 215/546-9644. **Contact:** Executive Director. **Description:** A permanent nanny placement and referral service operating throughout Connecticut, Delaware, New Jersey, New York, and Pennsylvania. **Specializes in the areas of:** Education. **Number of placements per year:** 100 - 199.

PHYSICIAN BILLING SOLUTIONS, INC. (PBSI)
1265 Drummers Lane, Suite 207, Wayne PA 19087-1570. 610/341-0902. **Fax:** 610/341-0907. **Contact:** Manager. **E-mail address:** pbsi@worldnet.att.net. **Description:** A permanent employment agency that also provides temporary placements. **Specializes in the areas of:** Health/Medical; Insurance. **Positions commonly filled include:** Collector; Customer Service Representative; Financial Analyst; Medical Records Technician. **Benefits available to temporary workers:** Medical Insurance. **Corporate headquarters location:** This Location. **Other area locations:** Pittsburgh PA. **Other U.S. locations:** Baltimore MD. **Average salary range of placements:** $20,000 - $29,999. **Number of placements per year:** 100 - 199.

PITTSBURGH PLACEMENT SERVICE
356 Locust Avenue, Washington PA 15301. 412/225-8100. **Toll-free phone:** 888/809-2133. **Fax:** 412/225-8827. **Contact:** Jerome T. Cypher, President. **Description:** A permanent employment agency. Company pays fee. **Specializes in the areas of:** Food Industry. **Positions commonly filled include:** Hotel Manager; Human Resources Specialist; Management Trainee; Restaurant/Food Service Manager. **Average salary range of placements:** $20,000 - $29,999. **Number of placements per year:** 200 - 499.

POWERS PERSONNEL
1530 Chestnut Street, Suite 310, Philadelphia PA 19102. 215/563-5520. **Contact:** Jean Powers, President. **Description:** A permanent employment agency that also provides temporary placements. **Specializes in the areas of:** Clerical; Legal; Secretarial.

Q-SOURCE
2950 Felton Road, Suite 102, Norristown PA 19401. 610/278-7993. **Fax:** 610/278-7985. **Contact:** John Quigley, President. **Description:** A permanent employment agency. Company pays fee. **Specializes in the areas of:** Administration; Computer Science/Software; Engineering; Industrial; Manufacturing; Technical. **Positions commonly filled include:** Ceramics Engineer; Chemical Engineer; Chemist; Computer Programmer; Design Engineer; Electrical/Electronics Engineer; Food Scientist/Technologist; Management Analyst/Consultant; Materials Engineer; Mechanical Engineer; Metallurgical Engineer; MIS Specialist; Quality Control Supervisor; Software Engineer; Structural Engineer; Systems Analyst. **Number of placements per year:** 1 - 49.

QUEST SYSTEMS, INC.
1150 1st Avenue, Suite 255, King of Prussia PA 19406. 610/265-8100. **Toll-free phone:** 800/368-2900. **Fax:** 610/265-6974. **Contact:** Charles Lagana, Manager. **E-mail address:** questsyst@aol.com. **World Wide Web address:** http://www.questsyst.com. **Description:** A permanent employment agency. Company pays fee. **Specializes in the areas of:** Administration; Computer Science/Software. **Positions commonly filled include:** Computer Programmer; Electrical/Electronics Engineer; Financial Analyst; MIS Specialist; Multimedia Designer; Software Engineer; Systems Analyst; Technical Writer/Editor; Telecommunications Manager. **Corporate headquarters location:** Bethesda MD. **Other U.S. locations:** Atlanta GA; Baltimore MD. **Average salary range of placements:** More than $50,000. **Number of placements per year:** 200 - 499.

S-H-S INTERNATIONAL
101 East Lancaster Avenue, Wayne PA 19087. 610/687-6104. **Fax:** 610/687-6102. **Contact:** Paul Reitman, General Manager. **Description:** A permanent employment agency. Company pays fee. **Specializes in the areas of:** Accounting/Auditing; Banking; Computer Science/Software; Engineering; Finance; Insurance; Legal; Sales; Secretarial; Technical. **Positions commonly filled include:** Accountant/Auditor; Actuary; Adjuster; Administrative Manager; Architect; Attorney; Bank Officer/Manager; Biochemist; Biological Scientist; Biomedical Engineer; Branch Manager; Buyer; Chemical Engineer; Chemist; Civil Engineer; Claim Representative; Clerical Supervisor; Computer Programmer; Customer Service Representative; Dental Assistant/Dental Hygienist; Design Engineer; Draftsperson; Editor; EKG Technician; Electrical/Electronics Engineer; Emergency Medical Technician; Environmental Engineer; Financial Analyst; Food Scientist/Technologist; Industrial Engineer; Insurance Agent/Broker; Internet Services Manager; Management Analyst/Consultant; Management Trainee; Market Research Analyst; Mechanical Engineer; Medical Records Technician; Metallurgical Engineer; MIS Specialist; Multimedia Designer; Nuclear Engineer; Occupational Therapist; Operations/Production Manager; Paralegal; Pharmacist; Physical Therapist; Physician; Purchasing Agent/Manager; Quality Control Supervisor; Radiological Technologist; Registered Nurse; Respiratory Therapist; Science Technologist; Securities Sales Representative; Services Sales Representative; Software Engineer; Statistician; Structural Engineer; Technical Writer/Editor; Telecommunications Manager; Travel Agent; Typist/Word Processor; Underwriter/Assistant Underwriter. **Number of placements per year:** 50 - 99.

TOM SAWCHAK ACTION OF PENNSYLVANIA
1622 Main Street, Dickson City PA 18447. 717/383-0241. **Contact:** Tom Sawchak, Owner. **Description:** A permanent employment agency. Company pays fee. **Specializes in the areas of:** Clerical; Engineering; Insurance; Manufacturing; Sales. **Positions commonly filled include:** Applications Engineer; Chemical

Engineer; Chief Financial Officer; Civil Engineer; Manufacturing Engineer; Mechanical Engineer; Operations Manager; Sales Engineer; Sales Executive. **Number of placements per year:** 1 - 49.

ELAYNE SCOTT ASSOCIATES
1601 Market Street, Philadelphia PA 19103. 215/561-0088. **Contact:** Manager. **Description:** A permanent legal placement firm. **Specializes in the areas of:** Legal.

SELECT PERSONNEL, INC.
3070 Bristol Pike, Building 2, Suite 205, Bensalem PA 19020. 215/245-4800. **Fax:** 215/245-4990. **Contact:** Marjorie Stilwell, President. **E-mail address:** selectpersonnel@jobnet.com. **Description:** A permanent employment agency. Company pays fee. **Specializes in the areas of:** Administration; Computer Hardware/Software; Electronics; Engineering; Industrial; Manufacturing; Personnel/Labor Relations; Sales. **Positions commonly filled include:** Accountant/ Auditor; Aerospace Engineer; Architect; Biological Scientist; Bookkeeper; Buyer; Ceramics Engineer; Chemical Engineer; Chemist; Civil Engineer; Computer Programmer; Customer Service Rep.; Electrical/ Electronics Engineer; Industrial Engineer; Manufacturing Engineer; Marketing Specialist; Mechanical Engineer; Metallurgical Engineer; MIS Specialist; Operations/Production Manager; Purchasing Agent/Manager; Quality Control Supervisor; Sales Rep.; Software Engineer; Systems Analyst; Technical Illustrator; Technical Writer/Editor; Technician. **Number of placements per year:** 200 - 499.

SINGMASTER PERSONNEL SERVICES
P.O. Box 708, Devon PA 19333. 610/687-4970. **Physical address:** 406 Devon State Road, Devon PA. **Fax:** 610/687-4927. **Contact:** Alan Singmaster, Owner. **Description:** A permanent employment agency that focuses on placing management and engineering professionals in heavy manufacturing positions. Founded in 1980. Company pays fee. **Specializes in the areas of:** Engineering; General Management; Manufacturing; Metals. **Positions commonly filled include:** Ceramics Engineer; Design Engineer; Electrical/Electronics Engineer; Mechanical Engineer; Metallurgical Engineer; Purchasing Agent/Manager; Quality Control Supervisor. **Average salary range of placements:** More than $50,000. **Number of placements per year:** 1 - 49.

SOURCE EDP
150 South Warner Road, Suite 238, King of Prussia PA 19406. 610/341-1960. **Contact:** Manager. **Description:** A permanent employment agency. **Specializes in the areas of:** Administration; Computer Hardware/Software; Technical.

STRAUSS PERSONNEL SERVICE
239 Fourth Avenue, Suite 1105, Pittsburgh PA 15222. 412/281-8235. **Toll-free phone:** 888/457-4777. **Fax:** 412/281-9417. **Contact:** T. Jeff McGraw, Owner. **Description:** A permanent placement agency. Founded in 1952. Company pays fee. **Specializes in the areas of:** Accounting/Auditing; Banking; Finance; Sales; Secretarial. **Positions commonly filled include:** Accountant/Auditor; Administrative Assistant; Bank Officer/Manager; Branch Manager; Budget Analyst; Chief Financial Officer; Controller; Customer Service Rep.; Financial Analyst; Internet Services Manager; Management Analyst/Consultant; Paralegal; Sales Executive; Sales Manager; Sales Rep.; Secretary; Typist/Word Processor. **Number of placements per year:** 50 - 99.

STROHL SYSTEMS
500 North Gulph Road, Suite 500, King of Prussia PA 19406. 610/768-4120. **Contact:** Myles L. Strohl, President. **Description:** A permanent employment agency. **Specializes in the areas of:** Administration.

STRONGIN TECHNICAL ENTERPRISES OF PENNSYLVANIA, INC.
958 Town Center, New Britain PA 18901. 215/230-8530. **Contact:** Kenneth Strongin, President. **Description:** A permanent employment agency. Founded in 1993. Company pays fee. **Specializes in the areas of:** Architecture/Construction; Engineering; Manufacturing; Technical. **Positions commonly filled include:** Chemical Engineer; Chemist; Civil Engineer; Draftsperson; Electrical/Electronics Engineer; Environmental Engineer; Industrial Engineer; Mechanical Engineer; Pharmacist. **Average salary range of placements:** $30,000 - $50,000. **Number of placements per year:** 50 - 99.

TOD SERVICES INC.
332 Fifth Avenue, Warner Center, 6th Floor, Pittsburgh PA 15222. 412/391-7500. **Fax:** 412/391-9488. **Contact:** Manager. **Description:** A permanent employment agency. **Specializes in the areas of:** Legal. **Positions commonly filled include:** Accountant/ Auditor; Administrative Manager; Advertising Clerk; Branch Manager; Budget Analyst; Buyer; Claim Rep.; Clerical Supervisor; Computer Programmer; Cost Estimator; Credit Manager; Customer Service Rep.; Financial Analyst; Management Trainee; Paralegal; Purchasing Agent/Manager; Services Sales Rep.; Statistician; Systems Analyst; Technical Writer/Editor. **Number of placements per year:** 500 - 999.

TRIANGLE ASSOCIATES INTERNATIONAL
P.O. Box 506, Warrington PA 18976. 215/343-3702. **Fax:** 215/343-3703. **Contact:** Mr. S.R. Ostroff, President. **Description:** A permanent employment agency. Company pays fee. **Specializes in the areas of:** Chemical; Engineering; Pharmaceutical; Plastics. **Positions commonly filled include:** Ceramics Engineer; Chemical Engineer; Chemist; Electrical/Electronics Engineer; Materials Engineer; Mechanical Engineer; Metallurgical Engineer.

UNITED EMPLOYMENT
44 North 15th Street, Allentown PA 18102. 610/437-5040. **Fax:** 610/437-9650. **Contact:** Michael Stauffer, Manager. **Description:** A permanent employment agency. Company pays fee. **Specializes in the areas of:** Economics; Engineering; Food Industry; Industrial; Manufacturing; Personnel/Labor Relations; Sales. **Positions commonly filled include:** Agricultural Engineer; Biological Scientist; Chemical Engineer; Chemist; Civil Engineer; Construction Contractor; Cost Estimator; Design Engineer; Draftsperson; Environmental Engineer; General Manager; Geologist/ Geophysicist; Human Resources Manager; Industrial Engineer; Mechanical Engineer; Metallurgical Engineer; Nuclear Engineer; Physicist; Science Technologist; Structural Engineer. **Number of placements per year:** 100 - 199.

VOGUE PERSONNEL INC.
One Penn Center, Suburban Station, Suite 352, Philadelphia PA 19103. 215/564-0720. **Fax:** 215/564-0722. **Contact:** Ronald Sacks, President. **Description:** A permanent employment agency. Company pays fee. **Specializes in the areas of:** Accounting/Auditing; Administration; Advertising; Banking; Health/Medical; Insurance; Legal; Personnel/ Labor Relations; Secretarial. **Positions commonly filled include:** Accountant/Auditor; Advertising Clerk; Clerical Supervisor; Customer Service Rep.; Human Resources Manager; Management Trainee; Medical Records Technician; Paralegal; Public Relations Specialist; Secretary. **Average salary range of placements:** $30,000 - $50,000. **Number of placements per year:** 50 - 99.

YOUR OTHER HANDS, INC.
714-B South Colorado Street, Philadelphia PA 19146. 215/790-0990. **Fax:** 215/546-5237. **Contact:** Suzette Trimmer, Owner. **Description:** A permanent employment agency. Company pays fee. **Specializes in the areas of:** Child Care, In-Home; Nannies. **Positions commonly filled include:** Preschool Worker. **Number of placements per year:** 100 - 199.

TEMPORARY EMPLOYMENT AGENCIES

ACCOUNTANTS ON CALL
437 Grant Street, Suite 1615, Pittsburgh PA 15219. 412/391-0900. **Contact:** Manager. **Description:** A temporary agency. **Specializes in the areas of:** Accounting/Auditing; Finance.

ADECCO
150 South Warner Road, Suite 132, King of Prussia PA 19406. 610/341-9050. **Fax:** 610/341-9057. **Contact:** Manager. **Description:** A temporary agency. Company pays fee. **Specializes in the areas of:** Accounting/Auditing; Administration; Clerical; General Management; Personnel/Labor Relations; Sales; Secretarial. **Positions commonly filled include:** Accountant/Auditor; Adjuster; Administrative Manager; Branch Manager; Claim Representative; Clerical Supervisor; Clinical Lab Technician; Collector; Counselor; Customer Service Representative; General Manager; Human Resources Manager; Investigator; Management Trainee; Manufacturer's/Wholesaler's Sales Rep.; Medical Records Technician; Public Relations Specialist; Quality Control Supervisor; Securities Sales Representative; Services Sales Representative. **Number of placements per year:** 100 - 199.

ALLEGHENY PERSONNEL SERVICES
200 Commerce Drive, Suite 210, Coraopolis PA 15108. 412/264-7733. **Fax:** 412/264-8883. **Contact:** Ron Alvarado, Branch Manager. **Description:** A temporary agency that also provides permanent placement. Company pays fee. **Specializes in the areas of:** Accounting/Auditing; Administration; Banking; Finance; General Management; Health/Medical; Industrial; Insurance; Legal; Personnel/Labor Relations; Sales; Secretarial. **Positions commonly filled include:** Accountant/Auditor; Administrative Manager; Customer Service Representative; Typist/Word Processor. **Benefits available to temporary workers:** Computer Training; Medical Insurance; Paid Vacation; Referral Bonus Plan. **Corporate headquarters location:** Pittsburgh PA. **Other U.S. locations:** Monroeville PA; North Hills PA.

AMERICAN STAFFING RESOURCES
P.O. Box 285, Feasterville PA 19053. 215/364-3838. **Toll-free phone:** 800/AMSTAFF. **Fax:** 215/364-5381. **Contact:** Carolyn Anderson, Vice President of Operations. **Description:** A temporary agency that also provides permanent placements. Company pays fee. **Specializes in the areas of:** Accounting/Auditing; Finance; Light Industrial; Marketing; Sales; Scientific; Technical.

CAPITAL AREA TEMPORARY SERVICES
P.O. Box 32, Lemoyne PA 17043. 717/761-0133. **Contact:** Paul V. Gaughan, President. **Description:** A temporary agency. **Specializes in the areas of:** Clerical; Manufacturing. **Positions commonly filled include:** Administrative Worker/Clerk; Bookkeeper; Clerk; Factory Worker; Legal Secretary; Light Industrial Worker; Receptionist; Secretary; Stenographer; Typist/Word Processor.

CHARLY'S TEMPORARY SERVICES
2 Poplar Street, P.O. Box 747, Conshohocken PA 19428. 610/834-7608. **Fax:** 610/834-7665. **Contact:** Barbara Bass, Director of Recruitment. **Description:** A temporary agency that also provides some permanent placements. **Specializes in the areas of:** Accounting/Auditing; Administration; Advertising; Banking; Computer Science/Software; Engineering; Food Industry; Health/Medical; Sales; Secretarial. **Positions commonly filled include:** Administrative Manager; Advertising Clerk; Clerical Supervisor; Clinical Lab Technician; Credit Manager; Customer Service Representative; Financial Analyst; General Manager; Hotel Manager; Human Service Worker; Market Research Analyst; Medical Records Technician; Paralegal; Preschool Worker; Restaurant/Food Service Manager; Typist/Word Processor. **Number of placements per year:** 1 - 49.

CORESTAFF INC.
P.O. Box 15444, Philadelphia PA 19149-0444. 215/864-0500. **Physical address:** Sterling Commerce Center, Suite 303, 1819 JFK Boulevard, Philadelphia PA 19103. **Toll-free phone:** 800/564-1755. **Fax:** 215/563-6329. **Contact:** Joan Valk, Manager. **Description:** A temporary agency. Company pays fee. **Specializes in the areas of:** Accounting/Auditing; Finance; Food Industry; General Management; Industrial; Insurance; Manufacturing; Nonprofit; Personnel/Labor Relations; Publishing; Retail; Sales; Secretarial; Technical; Transportation. **Positions commonly filled include:** Accountant; Administrative Assistant; Administrative Manager; Advertising Clerk; Applications Engineer; Architect; Auditor; Biochemist; Biological Scientist; Biomedical Engineer; Blue-Collar Worker Supervisor; Branch Manager; Clerical Supervisor; Clinical Lab Technician; Computer Operator; Computer Programmer; Construction Contractor; Customer Service Representative; Draftsperson; Editor; Electrician; General Manager; Hotel Manager; Human Resources Specialist; Human Service Worker; Management Trainee; Manufacturer's/Wholesaler's Sales Rep.; Market Research Analyst; Operations/Production Manager; Paralegal; Public Relations Specialist; Purchasing Agent/Manager; Restaurant/Food Service Manager; Services Sales Representative; Typist/Word Processor. **Benefits available to temporary workers:** Medical Insurance; Paid Holidays; Paid Vacation. **Corporate headquarters location:** This Location. **Other U.S. locations:** NJ. **Average salary range of placements:** $30,000 - $50,000. **Number of placements per year:** 1000+.

EDP/TEMPS OF PENNSYLVANIA
401 City Line Avenue, Suite 915, Bala-Cynwyd PA 19004. 610/667-2990. **Contact:** Manager. **Description:** A temporary agency. **Specializes in the areas of:** Accounting/Auditing; Administration; Banking; Computer Hardware/Software; Engineering; Finance; Insurance; Manufacturing; Nonprofit; Personnel/Labor Relations; Publishing; Technical.

HOBBIE TEMPORARY PERSONNEL
1015 York Road, Suite 113, Willow Grove PA 19090. 215/658-0100. **Contact:** Shelly Smith, Staffing Specialist. **Description:** A temporary agency that also provides some permanent placements. Company pays fee. **Specializes in the areas of:** Industrial; Secretarial; Technical. **Positions commonly filled include:** Customer Service Representative; Industrial Engineer; Receptionist; Typist/Word Processor. **Corporate headquarters location:** Allentown PA. **Other area locations:** Landsdale PA; Quakertown PA. **Average salary range of placements:** Less than $20,000. **Number of placements per year:** 500 - 999.

HUMAN ASSETS INC.
4 Park Plaza, Wyomissing PA 19610. 610/375-2773. **Fax:** 610/375-2884. **Contact:** Kerry S. Seward, President. **Description:** A temporary agency. Company pays fee. **Specializes in the areas of:** Manufacturing; Sales; Technical. **Positions commonly filled include:** Typist/Word Processor. **Average salary range of placements:** Less than $20,000. **Number of placements per year:** 50 - 99.

INTERIM PERSONNEL
108 West Lancaster Avenue, Shillington PA 19607-1858. 610/777-1555. **Fax:** 610/777-9494. **Contact:** General Manager. **World Wide Web address:** http://www.interim.com. **Description:** A temporary agency that also provides some permanent placements. Company pays fee. **Specializes in the areas of:** Administration; Industrial; Manufacturing; Sales; Secretarial; Technical. **Positions commonly filled include:** Administrative Manager; Aircraft Mechanic/Engine Specialist; Automotive Mechanic; Blue-Collar Worker Supervisor; Claim Representative; Clerical Supervisor; Computer Programmer; Customer Service Representative; Draftsperson; Management Trainee; Operations/Production Manager; Quality Control Supervisor; Services Sales Representative; Travel Agent; Typist/Word Processor. **Benefits available to temporary workers:** Dental Insurance; Medical Insurance; Paid Vacation; Referral Bonus Plan. **Corporate headquarters location:** Fort Lauderdale FL. **Other U.S. locations:** Nationwide. **Average salary range of placements:** $20,000 - $29,999.

INTERIM PERSONNEL OF LEHIGH VALLEY PA, INC.
1045 South Cedar Crest Boulevard, Allentown PA 18103-5443. 610/432-7500. **Fax:** 610/435-3114. **Contact:** Tina I. Durman Hamilton, President/Owner. **World Wide Web address:** http://www.interim.com. **Description:** A temporary agency that also provides some permanent placements. Company pays fee. **Specializes in the areas of:** Computer Science/Software; Industrial; Light Industrial; Marketing; Sales; Scientific; Secretarial; Technical. **Positions commonly filled include:** Account Representative; Administrative Assistant; Administrative Manager; Advertising Clerk; Applications Engineer; Blue-Collar Worker Supervisor; Claim Representative; Clerical Supervisor; Computer Operator; Computer Programmer; Construction Contractor; Customer Service Representative; Database Manager; Electrical/Electronics Engineer; Food Scientist/Technologist; Industrial Engineer; Sales Executive; Sales Representative; Secretary; Typist/Word Processor. **Benefits available to temporary workers:** Bonus Award/Plan; Dental Insurance; Medical Insurance; Paid Vacation; Prescription Drugs; Scholarship Program; Vision Insurance. **Corporate headquarters location:** Fort Lauderdale FL. **Other U.S. locations:** Nationwide. **Average salary range of placements:** $20,000 - $29,999. **Number of placements per year:** 500 - 999.

KELLY SERVICES, INC.
101 Chesley Drive, Media PA 19063. 610/565-7030. **Fax:** 610/892-9308. **Contact:** Catherine W. Corcoran, Branch Manager. **Description:** A temporary agency. **Specializes in the areas of:** Secretarial; Technical. **Positions commonly filled include:** Attorney; Computer Programmer; Systems Analyst; Typist/Word Processor. **Corporate headquarters location:** Troy MI. **Other U.S. locations:** Nationwide. **Average salary range of placements:** $20,000 - $29,999. **Number of placements per year:** 1000+.

KEYNOTE SYSTEMS INC.
345 4th Avenue, Pittsburgh PA 15222. 412/261-0187. **Contact:** Manager. **Description:** A temporary agency. **Specializes in the areas of:** Computer Science/Software; Government; Health/Medical. **Positions commonly filled include:** Claim Representative; Computer Operator; Customer Service Representative; Data Entry Clerk; Human Service Worker; Licensed Practical Nurse; Medical Records Technician; Registered Nurse; Systems Analyst. **Benefits available to temporary workers:** Bonus Award/Plan; Paid Vacation. **Average salary range of placements:** $30,000 - $50,000. **Number of placements per year:** 50 - 99.

KEYSTAFF
350 South Main Street, Suite 213A, Doylestown PA 18901. 215/340-9971. **Fax:** 215/348-9386. **Contact:** Kathleen Mulloy, Manager. **Description:** A temporary and permanent employment agency. Company pays fee. **Specializes in the areas of:** Accounting/Auditing; Banking; Engineering; Finance; Insurance; Legal; Manufacturing; Nonprofit; Secretarial. **Positions commonly filled include:** Bank Officer/Manager; Customer Service Representative; Financial Analyst; Typist/Word Processor. **Benefits available to temporary workers:** Paid Holidays; Paid Vacation.

LAB SUPPORT INC.
Foster Plaza, Building 5, Suite 300, Pittsburgh PA 15220. 412/364-6240. **Contact:** Manager. **Description:** A temporary placement agency. **Specializes in the areas of:** Biology; Chemical; Technical. **Corporate headquarters location:** Calabasas CA. **Other U.S. locations:** Nationwide.

MARSETTA LANE TEMPORARY SERVICES, INC.
355 Fifth Avenue, Suite 1104, Pittsburgh PA 15222-2407. 412/261-6076. **Contact:** Placement Coordinator. **Description:** A temporary agency that also provides permanent placements. **Specializes in the areas of:** Accounting/Auditing; Office Support; Secretarial; Word Processing. **Positions commonly filled include:** Accountant/Auditor; Customer Service Representative; Data Entry Clerk; Legal Secretary; Medical Secretary; Receptionist; Secretary; Typist/Word Processor. **Number of placements per year:** 1000+.

LEAFSTONE INC.
1617 JFK Boulevard, Suite 1650, Philadelphia PA 19103. 215/568-5533. **Fax:** 215/568-5580. **Contact:** Sharie Slusser, Resource Manager. **Description:** A temporary agency. **Specializes in the areas of:** Finance; Legal; Office Support; Secretarial. **Positions commonly filled include:** Accountant; Administrative Assistant; Claim Representative; Clerical Supervisor; Computer Operator; Customer Service Representative; Typist/Word Processor. **Benefits available to temporary workers:** 401(k); Dental Insurance; Life Insurance; Medical Insurance. **Corporate headquarters location:** Jericho NY. **Other U.S. locations:** Nationwide. **International locations:** London, England; India. **Average salary range of placements:** $20,000 - $29,999.

LEGAL SEARCH
1515 Market Street, Philadelphia PA 19103. 215/568-7191. **Fax:** 215/568-7194. **Contact:** Mark Rocco, President. **Description:** A temporary and permanent employment agency. Company pays fee. **Specializes in the areas of:** Legal; Secretarial. **Positions commonly filled include:** Legal Secretary; Paralegal. **Average salary range of placements:** $20,000 - $29,999. **Number of placements per year:** 200 - 499.

MANPOWER TEMPORARY SERVICES
Westin William Penn Hotel, 555 Grant Street, Suite 300, Pittsburgh PA 15219. 412/434-6507. **Contact:** Branch Manager. **Description:** A temporary agency. Company pays fee. **Specializes in the areas of:**

Industrial; Office Support; Technical; Telecommunications; Word Processing. **Positions commonly filled include:** Accountant/Auditor; Accounting Clerk; Administrative Assistant; Assembly Worker; Biological Scientist; Bookkeeper; CADD Operator; Chemist; Computer Operator; Customer Service Representative; Desktop Publishing Specialist; Electrician; Inspector/Tester/Grader; Inventory Control Specialist; Machine Operator; Material Control Specialist; Order Clerk; Packaging/Processing Worker; Painter; Project Engineer; Proofreader; Receptionist; Records Manager; Research Assistant; Secretary; Software Engineer; Stenographer; Stock Clerk; Systems Analyst; Technical Writer/Editor; Telemarketer; Test Operator; Transcriptionist; Typist/Word Processor; Welder. **Benefits available to temporary workers:** Computer Training; Life Insurance; Medical Insurance; Paid Holidays; Paid Vacation. **Number of placements per year:** 1000+.

MANPOWER TEMPORARY SERVICES
10 Penn Center, Suite 615, 1801 Market Street, Philadelphia PA 19103. 215/568-4050. **Fax:** 215/568-4050. **Contact:** Branch Manager. **Description:** A temporary agency. Company pays fee. **Specializes in the areas of:** Data Processing; Light Industrial; Office Support; Professional; Technical; Telemarketing; Word Processing. **Positions commonly filled include:** Accountant/Auditor; Accounting Clerk; Administrative Assistant; Assembler; Biological Scientist; Bookkeeper; Chemist; Computer Operator; Customer Service Representative; Designer; Desktop Publishing Specialist; Electrician; Inspector/Tester/Grader; Inventory Control Specialist; Machine Operator; Material Control Specialist; Order Clerk; Packaging/Processing Worker; Painter; Project Engineer; Proofreader; Receptionist; Research Assistant; Secretary; Software Engineer; Systems Analyst; Technical Writer/Editor; Technician; Telemarketer; Typist/Word Processor; Welder. **Benefits available to temporary workers:** Computer Training; Life Insurance; Medical Insurance; Paid Holidays; Paid Vacation. **Number of placements per year:** 1000+.

METROPOLITAN PERSONNEL, INC.
P.O. Box 641, Valley Forge PA 19482. 610/933-4000. **Fax:** 610/687-4670. **Contact:** Lawrence J. LaBoon, President. **Description:** A temporary agency that also provides permanent placements. Company pays fee. **Specializes in the areas of:** Accounting/Auditing; Administration; Computer Science/Software; General Management; Light Industrial; Marketing; Personnel/Labor Relations; Sales; Secretarial. **Positions commonly filled include:** Technical Writer/Editor; Typist/Word Processor. **Average salary range of placements:** $20,000 - $29,999. **Number of placements per year:** 100 - 199.

NORRELL SERVICES
100 Hightower Boulevard, Suite 301, Pittsburgh PA 15205. 412/788-4970. **Fax:** 412/788-4974. **Contact:** Deborah E. Beswarick, Customer Service Manager. **Description:** A temporary agency that also offers temp-to-hire, outsourcing, and project management services. Founded in 1960. Company pays fee. **Specializes in the areas of:** Industrial; Light Industrial; Secretarial; Technical. **Positions commonly filled include:** Accounting Clerk; Administrative Assistant; Advertising Clerk; Customer Service Representative; Receptionist; Secretary; Services Sales Representative; Typist/Word Processor. **Benefits available to temporary workers:** 401(k); Dental Insurance; Medical Insurance; Stock Purchase; Vision Plan. **Corporate headquarters location:** Atlanta GA. **Other U.S. locations:** Nationwide. **International locations:** Canada. **Average salary range of placements:** Less than $20,000. **Number of placements per year:** 100 - 199.

NORRELL SERVICES
610 Freedom Business Center Drive, Suite 104, King Of Prussia PA 19406. 610/265-3600. **Contact:** Kelly McGinley, Customer Service Manager. **Description:** A temporary agency. **Specializes in the areas of:** Accounting/Auditing; Personnel/Labor Relations; Secretarial. **Positions commonly filled include:** Accountant/Auditor; Customer Service Representative; Typist/Word Processor. **Benefits available to temporary workers:** Medical Insurance; Paid Holidays; Paid Vacation. **Corporate headquarters location:** Atlanta GA. **Other U.S. locations:** Nationwide. **Average salary range of placements:** $20,000 - $29,999. **Number of placements per year:** 500 - 999.

OFFICETEAM
630 Freedom Business Center, King of Prussia PA 19406. 610/337-5848. **Toll-free phone:** 800/804-8367. **Fax:** 610/337-7308. **Contact:** Dawn Hornibrook, Division Director. **Description:** A temporary agency. **Specializes in the areas of:** Administration; Personnel/Labor Relations. **Positions commonly filled include:** Administrative Manager; Advertising Clerk; Clerical Supervisor; Customer Service Representative; Typist/Word Processor.

OLSTEN STAFFING SERVICES
1503 North Cedarcrest Boulevard, Suite 318, Allentown PA 18104. 610/435-0553. **Contact:** Manager. **Description:** A temporary agency. **Specializes in the areas of:** Accounting/Auditing; Advertising; Architecture/Construction; Banking; Clerical; Computer Hardware/Software; Finance; Insurance; Legal; Manufacturing; Personnel/Labor Relations; Sales. **Corporate headquarters location:** Melville NY.

OLSTEN STAFFING SERVICES
4720 Carlisle Pike, Suite 300, Mechanicsburg PA 17005. 717/731-6100. **Contact:** Branch Manager. **Description:** A temporary agency. **Specializes in the areas of:** Accounting/Auditing; Advertising; Architecture/Construction; Clerical; Computer Hardware/Software; Design; Food Industry; Insurance; Legal; Manufacturing; Nonprofit; Publishing; Sales; Secretarial; Technical. **Positions commonly filled include:** Accountant/Auditor; Administrative Assistant; Bookkeeper; Claim Representative; Computer Programmer; Customer Service Representative; Data Entry Clerk; Designer; Draftsperson; EDP Specialist; Factory Worker; Financial Analyst; Insurance Agent/Broker; Legal Secretary; Light Industrial Worker; Mechanical Engineer; Medical Secretary; Purchasing Agent/Manager; Receptionist; Records Manager; Sales Representative; Secretary; Statistician; Stenographer; Systems Analyst; Technical Writer/Editor; Technician; Typist/Word Processor. **Corporate headquarters location:** Melville NY. **Number of placements per year:** 1000+.

OLSTEN STAFFING SERVICES
4 Gateway Center, Suite 205, Pittsburgh PA 15222. 412/261-7200. **Fax:** 412/261-5647. **Contact:** Cindy Cheran, Branch Manager. **Description:** A temporary agency. **Specializes in the areas of:** Accounting/Auditing; Engineering; Office Support; Secretarial. **Positions commonly filled include:** Administrative Assistant; Attorney; Secretary. **Benefits available to temporary workers:** Medical Insurance; Paid Holidays; Paid Vacation. **Corporate headquarters location:** Melville NY. **Average salary range of placements:** $20,000 - $29,999. **Number of placements per year:** 1000+.

OLSTEN STAFFING SERVICES
1023 East Baltimore Pike, Suite 220, Media PA 19063-5126. 610/565-7510. **Fax:** 610/565-7516. **Contact:** Pauline McDaniel, Branch Manager. **Description:** A temporary agency. Company pays fee. **Specializes in the areas of:** Administration; Industrial; Legal; Manufacturing; Personnel/Labor Relations; Secretarial; Technical. **Positions commonly filled include:** Claim Rep.; Computer Programmer; Customer Service Rep.; Electrical/Electronics Engineer; Human Resources Specialist; MIS Specialist; Paralegal; Services Sales Rep.; Typist/Word Processor. **Benefits available to temporary workers:** Bonus Award/Plan; Paid Vacation. **Corporate headquarters location:** Melville NY.

OLSTEN STAFFING SERVICES
403 West Lincoln Highway, Suite 108, Exton PA 19341. 610/363-5999. **Fax:** 610/363-0346. **Contact:** Jackie McCullough, Recruiter. **Description:** A temporary agency. **Specializes in the areas of:** Accounting/Auditing; Data Processing; Industrial; Light Industrial; Personnel/Labor Relations; Technical. **Positions commonly filled include:** Accountant/ Auditor; Buyer; Clerical Supervisor; Computer Programmer; Customer Service Representative; Design Engineer; Electrical/Electronics Engineer; Human Resources Specialist; Industrial Engineer; MIS Specialist; Quality Control Supervisor; Software Engineer; Systems Analyst. **Benefits available to temporary workers:** Medical Insurance. **Corporate headquarters location:** Melville NY. **Average salary range of placements:** $20,000 - $29,999. **Number of placements per year:** 1000+.

PANCOAST TEMPORARY SERVICES, INC.
100 5th Avenue, Suite 609, Pittsburgh PA 15222. 412/261-4820. **Contact:** Ann Pancoast, President. **Description:** A temporary agency. **Specializes in the areas of:** Accounting/Auditing; Administration; Banking; Computer Science/Software; Finance; Insurance; Nonprofit; Personnel/Labor Relations; Sales; Secretarial. **Positions commonly filled include:** Accountant/Auditor; Actuary; Administrative Manager; Bank Officer/Manager; Blue-Collar Worker Supervisor; Branch Manager; Brokerage Clerk; Budget Analyst; Buyer; Claim Representative; Customer Service Representative; Financial Analyst; General Manager; Human Resources Manager; Librarian; Library Technician; Services Sales Representative; Technical Writer/Editor; Telecommunications Manager; Typist/ Word Processor; Underwriter/Assistant Underwriter. **Benefits available to temporary workers:** Paid Vacation; Referral Bonus Plan. **Number of placements per year:** 1000+.

PLACERS, INC.
311 East Street Road, Feasterville PA 19053. 215/364-5627. **Fax:** 215/364-5638. **Contact:** Lisa Spain, Regional Operations Manager. **Description:** A temporary agency that also provides some permanent placements. Company pays fee. **Specializes in the areas of:** Manufacturing; Secretarial. **Positions commonly filled include:** Customer Service Representative; Human Resources Specialist; Operations/Production Manager; Typist/Word Processor. **Benefits available to temporary workers:** Bonus Award/Plan; Paid Holidays; Paid Vacation. **Average salary range of placements:** $30,000 - $50,000. **Number of placements per year:** 1 - 49.

PRATT PERSONNEL SERVICES (EAST)
7434 Frankford Avenue, Philadelphia PA 19136-3826. 215/537-1212. **Fax:** 215/537-1223. **Contact:** Sherry Myshko, Branch Manager. **Description:** A temporary agency. Company pays fee. **Specializes in the areas of:** Accounting/Auditing; Clerical; Engineering; Light Industrial; Manufacturing; Publishing; Secretarial. **Positions commonly filled include:** Accountant/Auditor; Blue-Collar Worker Supervisor; Chemical Engineer; Chemist; Customer Service Rep.; Electrical/Electronics Engineer; Industrial Engineer; Mechanical Engineer; Purchasing Agent/ Manager; Structural Engineer; Typist/Word Processor. **Average salary range of placements:** Less than $20,000. **Number of placements per year:** 200 - 499.

PRATT PERSONNEL SERVICES (WEST)
222 South Easton Road, Suite 222, Glenside PA 19082. 215/542-8367. **Fax:** 215/572-7828. **Contact:** Manager. **Description:** A temporary agency. **Specializes in the areas of:** Accounting/Auditing; Clerical; Light Industrial; Manufacturing; Publishing; Secretarial. **Positions commonly filled include:** Blue-Collar Worker Supervisor; Claim Rep.; Customer Service Rep.; Typist/Word Processor. **Average salary range of placements:** Less than $20,000. **Number of placements per year:** 500 - 999.

PROTOCALL BUSINESS STAFFING
400 Market Street, Suite 810, Philadelphia PA 19106. 215/592-7111. **Contact:** Susan L. Hansen, Branch Manager. **Description:** A temporary agency. Company pays fee. **Specializes in the areas of:** Business Services; Health/Medical; Industrial; Manufacturing; Personnel/Labor Relations. **Positions commonly filled include:** Accountant/Auditor; Administrative Assistant; Administrative Manager; Administrative Worker/Clerk; Bookkeeper; Clerk; Computer Operator; Computer Programmer; Customer Service Rep.; Data Entry Clerk; Draftsperson; Driver; EDP Specialist; Factory Worker; Health Services Worker; Legal Secretary; Light Industrial Worker; Medical Records Technician; Medical Secretary; Nurse; Receptionist; Sales Rep.; Secretary; Stenographer; Technician; Typist/Word Processor. **Corporate headquarters location:** Voorhees NJ. **Other U.S. locations:** DE. **Number of placements per year:** 1000+.

SNELLING PERSONNEL SERVICES
160 North Point Boulevard, Suite 101, Lancaster PA 17601. 717/560-1110. **Contact:** Tim Crouser, Partner. **Description:** A temporary agency. Company pays fee. **Specializes in the areas of:** Hotel/Restaurant; Marketing; Sales. **Positions commonly filled include:** Administrative Manager; Administrative Worker/Clerk; Bookkeeper; Claim Rep.; Clerical Supervisor; Clerk; Computer Programmer; Credit Manager; Customer Service Rep.; Data Entry Clerk; Draftsperson; Factory Worker; Hotel Manager; Human Resources Specialist; Legal Secretary; Light Industrial Worker; MIS Specialist; Paralegal; Receptionist; Restaurant/Food Service Manager; Secretary; Services Sales Representative; Travel Agent; Typist/Word Processor. **Benefits available to temporary workers:** 401(k); Medical Insurance; Paid Holidays; Paid Vacation. **Average salary range of placements:** $20,000 - $29,999. **Number of placements per year:** 1 - 49.

SPECIAL COUNSEL
1617 JFK Boulevard, Suite 810, Philadelphia PA 19103. 215/569-0999. **Fax:** 215/529-0299. **Contact:** Manager. **World Wide Web address:** http://www.specialcounsel.com. **Description:** A temporary and permanent employment agency. **Specializes in the areas of:** Legal.

TRC STAFFING SERVICES
582 Middletown Boulevard, Suite B-22, Langhorne PA 19047. 215/752-3502. **Fax:** 215/752-3501. **Contact:** Manager. **Description:** A temporary agency. **Specializes in the areas of:** Accounting/Auditing; Administration; Advertising; Architecture/ Construction; Computer Science/Software; Food Industry; General Management; Health/Medical; Industrial; Insurance; Legal; Manufacturing;

Personnel/Labor Relations; Sales; Secretarial. **Positions commonly filled include:** Accountant/Auditor; Administrative Manager; Claim Rep.; Clerical Supervisor; Computer Programmer; Credit Manager; Customer Service Rep.; Human Resources Specialist; Landscape Architect; MIS Specialist; Paralegal; Typist/Word Processor; Underwriter/Assistant Underwriter. **Benefits available to temporary workers:** Medical Insurance; Paid Holidays; Paid Vacation. **Average salary range of placements:** Less than $20,000. **Number of placements per year:** 1000+.

TAC STAFFING SERVICES, INC.
Radnor Corporate Center, Building 1, Suite 290, Radnor PA 19087. 610/225-0565. **Contact:** Office Manager. **World Wide Web address:** http://www.tacstaffing.com. **Description:** A temporary agency. **Specializes in the areas of:** Accounting/Auditing; Advertising; Banking; Clerical; Education; Finance; Health/Medical; Insurance; Legal; Manufacturing; Nonprofit; Personnel/Labor Relations; Publishing; Sales; Transportation. **Corporate headquarters location:** Newton Upper Falls MA. **Other U.S. locations:** Nationwide. **International locations:** Worldwide.

TAC STAFFING SERVICES, INC.
1617 JFK Boulevard, Suite 326, Philadelphia PA 19103. 215/568-4466. **Fax:** 215/568-3096. **Contact:** Branch Manager. **World Wide Web address:** http://www.tacstaffing.com. **Description:** A temporary agency. **Specializes in the areas of:** Accounting/Auditing; Advertising; Banking; Clerical; Education; Finance; Health/Medical; Insurance; Legal; Nonprofit; Personnel/Labor Relations; Publishing; Sales; Secretarial; Transportation. **Positions commonly filled include:** Administrative Assistant; Clerical Supervisor; Customer Service Rep.; Daycare Worker; Medical Records Technician; Secretary. **Benefits available to temporary workers:** Medical Insurance; Paid Vacation. **Corporate headquarters location:** Newton Upper Falls MA. **Other U.S. locations:** Nationwide. **International locations:** Worldwide. **Average salary range of placements:** $20,000 - $29,999. **Number of placements per year:** 500 - 999.

TAD TECHNICAL SERVICES
1150 1st Avenue, Suite 400, King of Prussia PA 19406. 610/962-9990. **Fax:** 610/962-9988. **Contact:** Sonya Mendelovich, Branch Manager. **E-mail address:** tad1inpa@aol.com. **Description:** A temporary agency. **Specializes in the areas of:** Administration; Biology; Computer Science/Software; Engineering; Technical. **Positions commonly filled include:** Aerospace Engineer; Aircraft Mechanic/Engine Specialist; Architect; Biochemist; Biological Scientist; Biomedical Engineer; Buyer; Chemical Engineer; Chemist; Civil Engineer; Clinical Lab Technician; Computer Programmer; Cost Estimator; Design Engineer; Designer; Draftsperson; Editor; Electrical/Electronics Engineer; Electrician; Environmental Engineer; Food Scientist/Technologist; Industrial Engineer; Mechanical Engineer; Metallurgical Engineer; MIS Specialist; Multimedia Designer; Operations/Production Manager; Pharmacist; Purchasing Agent/Manager; Quality Control Supervisor; Science Technologist; Software Engineer; Structural Engineer; Systems Analyst; Technical Writer/Editor; Technician. **Benefits available to temporary workers:** 401(k); Life Insurance; Medical Insurance; Paid Holidays; Paid Vacation. **International locations:** Worldwide. **Average salary range of placements:** $30,000 - $50,000. **Number of placements per year:** 500 - 999.

TANDEM PERSONNEL, INC.
677 West Dekalb Pike, King of Prussia PA 19406. 610/768-0700. **Fax:** 610/768-9243. **Contact:** Manager. **Description:** A temporary agency. **Specializes in the areas of:** Accounting/Auditing; Administration; Sales; Secretarial; Technical. **Positions commonly filled include:** Accountant/Auditor; Advertising Clerk; Biochemist; Biological Scientist; Biomedical Engineer; Chemical Engineer; Chemist; Clinical Lab Technician; Computer Programmer; Customer Service Representative; Human Resources Specialist; Librarian; Library Technician; Pharmacist; Systems Analyst; Travel Agent; Typist/Word Processor. **Benefits available to temporary workers:** Medical Insurance; Paid Holidays; Paid Vacation. **Number of placements per year:** 1000+.

TODAYS TEMPORARY
1255 Drummers Lane, Gilenhardie Four, Suite 101, Wayne PA 19087-1565. **Contact:** Martha A. Dalton, Branch Manager. **World Wide Web address:** http://www.todays.com. **Description:** A temporary agency. **Specializes in the areas of:** Marketing; Sales; Secretarial. **Positions commonly filled include:** Administrative Assistant; Claim Representative; Customer Service Representative; Data Entry Clerk; Human Resources Manager; Marketing Manager; Receptionist; Sales Representative; Secretary; Switchboard Operator; Telemarketer; Typist/Word Processor. **Benefits available to temporary workers:** Computer Training; Life Insurance; Medical Insurance; Paid Holidays; Paid Vacation; Prescription Drugs; Vision Insurance. **Corporate headquarters location:** Dallas TX. **Other U.S. locations:** Nationwide. **Average salary range of placements:** $20,000 - $29,999. **Number of placements per year:** 100 - 199.

TOPS TEMPORARIES INC.
10 Duff Road, Suite 206, Pittsburgh PA 15235. 412/243-8677. **Fax:** 412/243-8577. **Contact:** J. David Cepicka, Sales Manager. **Description:** A temporary agency. Founded in 1987. **Specializes in the areas of:** Engineering; Secretarial. **Positions commonly filled include:** Accountant/Auditor; Aerospace Engineer; Architect; Buyer; Chemical Engineer; Civil Engineer; Computer Programmer; Design Engineer; Designer; Draftsperson; Electrical/Electronics Engineer; Industrial Engineer; Mechanical Engineer; Metallurgical Engineer; Nuclear Engineer; Purchasing Agent/Manager; Quality Control Supervisor; Software Engineer; Technical Writer; Typist. **Benefits available to temporary workers:** Paid Holidays; Paid Vacation. **Corporate headquarters location:** This Location. **Other area locations:** Murrysville PA; New Stanton PA; Warrendale PA. **Average salary range of placements:** Less than $20,000. **Number of placements per year:** 1000+.

UNI TEMP TEMPORARY SERVICE
1709 East Chocolate Avenue, Hershey PA 17033. 717/533-8367. **Contact:** Gery Huffman, Office Manager. **Description:** A temporary agency that also offers career/outplacement counseling. Company pays fee. **Specializes in the areas of:** Accounting/Auditing; Administration; Advertising; Finance; Food Industry; Health/Medical; Industrial; Insurance; Legal; Manufacturing; Publishing; Secretarial; Technical. **Positions commonly filled include:** Accountant/Auditor; Administrative Manager; Advertising Clerk; Automotive Mechanic; Buyer; Claim Representative; Clerical Supervisor; Clinical Lab Technician; Computer Programmer; Credit Manager; Customer Service Representative; Draftsperson; Electrician; Manufacturer's/Wholesaler's Sales Rep.; Medical Records Technician; MIS Specialist; Paralegal; Purchasing Agent/Manager; Quality Control Supervisor; Systems Analyst; Typist/Word Processor. **Benefits available to temporary workers:** Medical Insurance; Paid Holidays; Paid Vacation. **Corporate headquarters location:** Lebanon PA. **Average salary range of placements:** $20,000 - $29,999. **Number of placements per year:** 1 - 49.

UNIFORCE TEMPORARY SERVICES
Rural Route 1, Box 381-K, Hazleton PA 18201. 717/454-2455. **Fax:** 717/454-2687. **Contact:** Dorothy Minnig, Accounts Manager. **Description:** A temporary agency. Company pays fee. **Specializes in the areas of:** Accounting/Auditing; Administration; Banking; Finance; General Management; Health/Medical; Legal; Manufacturing; Personnel/Labor Relations; Publishing; Sales; Secretarial. **Positions commonly filled include:** Accountant/Auditor; Biochemist; Blue-Collar Worker Supervisor; Buyer; Clerical Supervisor; Computer Programmer; Customer Service Rep.; Financial Analyst; General Manager; Human Resources Specialist; Market Research Analyst; Medical Records Technician; MIS Specialist; Operations/Production Manager; Paralegal; Purchasing Agent/Manager; Quality Control Supervisor; Services Sales Representative; Systems Analyst; Technical Writer/Editor; Typist/Word Processor. **Corporate headquarters location:** New Hyde Park NY. **Other area locations:** Bloomsburg PA; Scranton PA; Wilkes-Barre PA. **Average salary range of placements:** Less than $20,000. **Number of placements per year:** 1000+.

UNITED HEALTH & HUMAN SERVICES
2901 Cheltenham Avenue, 2nd Floor, Philadelphia PA 19150. 215/881-6820. **Contact:** Gregory Bockman, Human Resources Manager. **Description:** A temporary agency that focuses on placements in the field of mental health/mental retardation. **Specializes in the areas of:** Health/Medical; Nonprofit. **Positions commonly filled include:** Counselor; Human Service Worker; Psychologist; Recreational Therapist; Social Worker; Sociologist. **Benefits available to temporary workers:** Medical Insurance.

UNITED TECHNICAL ASSOCIATES, INC.
1259 South Cedarcrest Boulevard, Suite 225, Allentown PA 18103. 610/434-6446. **Contact:** John F. Pavlick, Manager. **Description:** A temporary agency. **Specializes in the areas of:** Administration; Clerical; Computer Hardware/Software; Construction; Engineering; Food Industry; Manufacturing; Technical. **Corporate headquarters location:** Reading PA. **Other U.S. locations:** Nationwide.

UNITED TECHNICAL ASSOCIATES, INC.
5500 Allentown Boulevard, Harrisburg PA 17112. 717/657-3106. **Contact:** Manager. **Description:** A temporary agency. **Specializes in the areas of:** Administration; Clerical; Computer Hardware/Software; Construction; Engineering; Food Industry; Manufacturing; Technical. **Positions commonly filled include:** Accountant/Auditor; Administrative Assistant; Administrative Worker/Clerk; Aerospace Engineer; Biological Scientist; Biomedical Engineer; Bookkeeper; Ceramics Engineer; Chemical Engineer; Chemist; Civil Engineer; Clerk; Computer Programmer; Data Entry Clerk; Designer; Draftsperson; EDP Specialist; Electrical/Electronics Engineer; Factory Worker; Industrial Engineer; Legal Secretary; Light Industrial Worker; Mechanical Engineer; Medical Secretary; Metallurgical Engineer; Mining Engineer; Petroleum Engineer; Physicist; Quality Control Supervisor; Receptionist; Secretary; Statistician; Stenographer; Systems Analyst; Technical Writer/Editor; Technician; Typist/Word Processor. **Corporate headquarters location:** Reading PA. **Other U.S. locations:** Nationwide. **Number of placements per year:** 500 - 999.

UNITED TECHNICAL ASSOCIATES, INC.
50 Stevens Avenue, Reading PA 19609. 610/678-5882. **Contact:** Manager. **Description:** A temporary agency. **Specializes in the areas of:** Technical. **Corporate headquarters location:** This Location. **Other U.S. locations:** Nationwide.

VIRTUAL WORKPLACE, INC.
400 Penn Center Boulevard, Suite 600, Pittsburgh PA 15235. 412/829-9552. **Toll-free phone:** 800/999-2VWI. **Contact:** Recruiter. **E-mail address:** vwi@crouse.com. **Description:** A temporary and permanent staffing agency catering to environmental consulting firms, remediation contractors, and industrial clients. Virtual Workplace, Inc. (VWI) is affiliated with Crouse Enterprises, Inc., an environmental engineering, consulting, and remediation group. VWI's main areas of activity include staffing for geotechnical investigation and remediation, and civil and environmental engineering and consulting. VWI's ISO division is among the few groups in the country that provides a full scope of consulting services in the ISO 9000, QA 9000, and the initial introduction of a new 14000 series of certifications for design and production industries. Founded in 1994. Company pays fee. **Specializes in the areas of:** Architecture/Construction; Biology; Engineering; Environmental; Industrial; Technical. **Positions commonly filled include:** Chemical Engineer; Chemist; Civil Engineer; Construction and Building Inspector; Cost Estimator; Design Engineer; Designer; Draftsperson; Environmental Engineer; Forester/Conservation Scientist; Geologist/Geophysicist; Industrial Engineer; Mechanical Engineer; Metallurgical Engineer; Mining Engineer; Petroleum Engineer. **Benefits available to temporary workers:** 401(k); Medical Insurance; Paid Holidays; Paid Vacation. **Corporate headquarters location:** This location. **Other U.S. locations:** Anchorage AK. **Average salary range of placements:** $20,000 - $29,999. **Number of placements per year:** 50 - 99.

VISIONS TEMPORARY SERVICE
232 High Street, Pottstown PA 19464-0178. 610/327-8900. **Contact:** Renee Thomas, Office Manager. **Description:** A temporary agency. **Specializes in the areas of:** Banking; Secretarial; Transportation. **Positions commonly filled include:** Accountant/Auditor; Bank Officer/Manager; Buyer; Customer Service Representative; Typist/Word Processor. **Other U.S. locations:** DC; DE; FL; NJ; NY.

WILLIFORD AND ASSOCIATES
WILLIFORD LEGAL PERSONNEL
1616 Walnut Street, Suite 2008, Philadelphia PA 19103. 215/893-1121. **Fax:** 215/893-1149. **Contact:** Darece Williford, Principal. **Description:** A temporary and permanent employment agency. Williford and Associates also offers resume services and a legal secretarial training program. **Specializes in the areas of:** Legal; Secretarial. **Positions commonly filled include:** Administrative Assistant; Clerical Supervisor; Computer Operator; Customer Service Representative; Legal Secretary; Paralegal; Secretary; Typist/Word Processor. **Benefits available to temporary workers:** Bonus Award/Plan; Medical Insurance. **Average salary range of placements:** $20,000 - $29,999. **Number of placements per year:** 200 - 499.

CONTRACT SERVICES FIRMS

AA STAFFING SOLUTIONS, INC.
333 Union Street, Allentown PA 18102. 610/770-8880. **Fax:** 610/770-8882. **Contact:** Chris Oncidi, Owner. **Description:** A contract services firm. Company pays fee. **Specializes in the areas of:** Computer Science/Software; Engineering; Industrial; Manufacturing; Personnel/Labor Relations; Secretarial; Technical. **Positions commonly filled include:** Blue-Collar Worker Supervisor; Claim Representative; Clerical Supervisor; Computer Programmer;

Construction and Building Inspector; Construction Contractor; Cost Estimator; Customer Service Representative; Draftsperson; Electrical/Electronics Engineer; Electrician; General Manager; Geographer; Industrial Engineer; Landscape Architect; MIS Specialist; Quality Control Supervisor; Services Sales Representative; Software Engineer; Surveyor; Systems Analyst; Technical Writer/Editor; Typist/Word Processor. **Benefits available to temporary workers:** Medical Insurance; Paid Holidays; Paid Vacation. **Average salary range of placements:** $20,000 - $29,999. **Number of placements per year:** 500 - 999.

ALTERNATIVE STAFFING, INC.
208 Bursca Drive, Suite 800, P.O. Box 394, Bridgeville PA 15017. 412/221-4541. **Fax:** 412/221-2193. **Contact:** Victor W. Paolicelli, President. **Description:** A contract services firm that focuses on placing human resource management personnel. **Specializes in the areas of:** Personnel/Labor Relations. **Benefits available to temporary workers:** Credit Union; Dental Insurance; Medical Insurance.

CDI CORPORATION
1717 Arch Street, 35th Floor, Philadelphia PA 19103. 215/569-2200. **Fax:** 215/569-1750. **Contact:** Recruiter. **Description:** A contract services firm that focuses on technical placements in the aerospace, electronics, industrial, marine, power, and transportation industries. **Specializes in the areas of:** Design; Engineering; Technical. **Positions commonly filled include:** Assembly Worker; Buyer; Data Processor; Designer; Engineer; Inspector/Tester/Grader; Machinist; Software Engineer; Systems Analyst; Technical Illustrator; Technical Writer/Editor; Technician. **Corporate headquarters location:** This Location. **Other U.S. locations:** Nationwide. **International locations:** Worldwide.

CDI CORPORATION (CENTRAL)
8 Parkway, Suite 320, Pittsburgh PA 15220. 412/922-5660. **Fax:** 412/922-5703. **Contact:** Heather Duncan, Marketing Account Manager. **World Wide Web address:** http://www.cdicorp.com. **Description:** A contract services firm. **Specializes in the areas of:** Administration; Computer Science/Software; Engineering. **Positions commonly filled include:** Computer Programmer; Design Engineer; Draftsperson; Electrical/Electronics Engineer; Mechanical Engineer; Nuclear Engineer; Software Engineer; Systems Analyst; Technical Writer/Editor. **Corporate headquarters location:** Philadelphia PA. **Other U.S. locations:** Nationwide. **International locations:** Worldwide.

H-TECH INC.
P.O. Box 436, Bridgeville PA 15017. 412/221-5920. **Fax:** 412/221-2193. **Contact:** Richard R. Hall, Recruiter. **Description:** A contract services firm. Founded in 1983. **Specializes in the areas of:** Engineering. **Positions commonly filled include:** Chemical Engineer; Design Engineer; Designer; Draftsperson; Electrical/Electronics Engineer; Mechanical Engineer. **Benefits available to temporary workers:** 401(k); Medical Insurance; Paid Holidays; Paid Vacation. **Average salary range of placements:** $30,000 - $50,000. **Number of placements per year:** 50 - 99.

IMC INTERNATIONAL, INC.
200 James Place, Monroeville PA 15146. 412/372-7808. **Fax:** 412/372-1314. **Contact:** E. Niles Morgan, President. **Description:** A contract services firm. **Specializes in the areas of:** Computer Science/Software; Engineering; General Management; Industrial; Personnel/Labor Relations; Technical; Transportation. **Positions commonly filled include:** Buyer; Chemical Engineer; Civil Engineer; Construction and Building Inspector; Construction Contractor; Cost Estimator; Design Engineer; Designer; Draftsperson; Electrical/Electronics Engineer; Electrician; Emergency Medical Technician; Environmental Engineer; Human Resources Manager; Industrial Engineer; Mechanical Engineer; Metallurgical Engineer; Mining Engineer; MIS Specialist; Nuclear Engineer; Petroleum Engineer; Purchasing Agent/Manager; Quality Control Supervisor; Services Sales Representative; Software Engineer; Structural Engineer; Surveyor; Technical Writer/Editor; Telecommunications Manager; Transportation/Traffic Specialist. **Average salary range of placements:** $30,000 - $50,000. **Number of placements per year:** 500 - 999.

PROFESSIONAL RESOURCE GROUP, INC.
4076 South Market Street, Suite E, Mechanicsburg PA 17055. 717/790-0707. **Fax:** 717/697-5576. **Contact:** Anthony Zelko, General Manager. **Description:** A contract services firm that focuses on the placement of skilled MIS professionals. Company pays fee. **Specializes in the areas of:** Computer Programming; Computer Science/Software. **Positions commonly filled include:** Computer Programmer; Software Engineer; Systems Analyst; Technical Writer/Editor; Telecommunications Manager. **Average salary range of placements:** $30,000 - $50,000. **Number of placements per year:** 1 - 49.

PROVISION TECHNOLOGIES
503 Martindale Street, 6th Floor, Pittsburgh PA 15212. 412/322-8360. **Toll-free phone:** 888/393-0339. **Fax:** 412/322-8361. **Contact:** Manager. **World Wide Web address:** http://www.careerbase.com. **Description:** A contract services and consulting firm. **Specializes in the areas of:** Computer Science/Software; Information Technology. **Corporate headquarters location:** Cambridge MA. **Other U.S. locations:** Nationwide.

PROVISION TECHNOLOGIES
900 East 8th Avenue, Suite 300, King of Prussia PA 19406. 610/238-0940. **Contact:** Manager. **World Wide Web address:** http://www.careerbase.com. **Description:** A contract services and consulting firm. **Specializes in the areas of:** Computer Science/Software; Information Technology. **Corporate headquarters location:** Cambridge MA. **Other U.S. locations:** Nationwide.

RHI CONSULTING
ACCOUNTEMPS
630 Freedom Business Center, King of Prussia PA 19406. 610/337-3650. **Toll-free phone:** 800/803-8367. **Fax:** 610/357-7038. **Contact:** Jacqueline K. Lloyd, Division Director. **E-mail address:** rhickop@aol.com. **World Wide Web address:** http://www.rhic.com. **Description:** A contract services firm. Company pays fee. **Specializes in the areas of:** Computer Science/Software; Information Technology. **Positions commonly filled include:** Accountant/Auditor; Computer Programmer; Credit Manager; Financial Analyst; MIS Specialist; Systems Analyst; Technical Writer/Editor. **Benefits available to temporary workers:** Medical Insurance; Paid Holidays; Paid Vacation; Referral Bonus Plan. **Corporate headquarters location:** Menlo Park CA. **Other U.S. locations:** Nationwide. **Number of placements per year:** 200 - 499.

TECH/AID OF PENNSYLVANIA
630 West Germantown Pike, Suite 361, Plymouth Meeting PA 19462. 610/834-7340. **Toll-free phone:** 800/642-6881. **Fax:** 610/834-7531. **Contact:** Mark Bondi, Technical Recruiter. **E-mail address:** plymouthmtg@techaid.com. **World Wide Web address:** http://www.techaid.com. **Description:** A contract services firm. Company pays fee. **Specializes**

in the areas of: Computer Science/Software; Engineering; Scientific; Technical. **Average salary range of placements:** $30,000 - $50,000. **Number of placements per year:** 1000+.

H.L. YOH COMPANY
1818 Market Street, 20th Floor, Philadelphia PA 19103. 215/656-2650. **Contact:** Manager. **Description:** A contract services firm. **Specializes in the areas of:** Engineering; Information Technology.

CAREER/OUTPLACEMENT COUNSELING FIRMS

R. DAVENPORT & ASSOCIATES
1910 Cochran, Manor Oaks 2, Suite 844, Pittsburgh PA 15220. 412/561-4003. **Contact:** Manager. **Description:** A career management and counseling firm.

EXECUTIVE MARKETING SERVICES
500 North Gulph Road, Suite 501, King of Prussia PA 19406-2816. 610/265-1714. **Fax:** 610/992-9701. **Contact:** Audrey Robinson, Manager. **Description:** A career development and marketing firm. **Specializes in the areas of:** General Management; Sales. **Number of placements per year:** 200 - 499.

BERNARD HALDANE & ASSOCIATES
2 PNC Plaza, Suite 2580, Pittsburgh PA 15222. 412/263-5627. **Contact:** Manager. **Description:** A career/outplacement counseling firm.

RHODE ISLAND

EXECUTIVE SEARCH FIRMS

ACCOUNTING RESOURCES INC.
155 Westminster Street, Suite 1250, Providence RI 02903. 401/272-1200. **Fax:** 401/272-1201. **Contact:** Richard Carriere, CPA/CPC. **Description:** An executive search firm. Company pays fee. **Specializes in the areas of:** Accounting/Auditing; Finance. **Positions commonly filled include:** Accountant/Auditor; Bank Officer/Manager; Budget Analyst; Computer Programmer; Cost Estimator; Credit Manager; Financial Analyst; Human Resources Manager; MIS Specialist; Systems Analyst. **Average salary range of placements:** $30,000 - $50,000. **Number of placements per year:** 100 - 199.

BEDFORD GROUP
154 Quicksand Pond Road, Little Compton RI 02837. 401/635-4646. **Contact:** Manager. **Description:** An executive search firm providing worldwide placements in electronics, telecommunications, medical devices, and health communication. The firm operates on a retainer basis. **Average salary range of placements:** $70,000+.

CAREER CONSULTANTS
3 Regency Plaza, Providence RI 02903. 401/273-8910. **Contact:** Manager. **Description:** An executive search firm. **Specializes in the areas of:** Sales.

CENTRAL EMPLOYMENT AGENCY
1246 Chalkstone Avenue, Providence RI 02908. 401/273-9150. **Contact:** Manager. **Description:** An executive search firm that also provides temp-to-perm placements. **Specializes in the areas of:** Light Industrial.

CREATIVE INPUT, INC.
P.O. Box 1725, East Greenwich RI 02818. 401/885-3254. **Contact:** Richard Brien, Manager. **Description:** An executive search firm. **Specializes in the areas of:** Textiles.

DALEY & ASSOCIATES INC.
P.O. Box 41088, Providence RI 02940. 401/725-1390. **Contact:** Manager. **Description:** An executive search firm specializing in insurance, MIS, engineering, and accounting.

DORRA SEARCH INC.
One Richmond Square, Providence RI 02906. 401/453-1555. **Fax:** 401/453-1566. **Contact:** Bethany Gold, Managing Director. **Description:** An executive search firm. Company pays fee. **Specializes in the areas of:** Accounting/Auditing; Administration; Computer Science/Software. **Positions commonly filled include:** Accountant/Auditor; Computer Programmer; MIS Specialist; Systems Analyst. **Average salary range of placements:** More than $50,000. **Number of placements per year:** 1 - 49.

EXECUTIVE'S SILENT PARTNER
400 Reservoir Avenue, Providence RI 02907. 401/461-5170. **Contact:** Manager. **Description:** An executive search firm. **Specializes in the areas of:** Manufacturing.

FURLONG PROFESSIONAL SERVICES
227 James Trail, West Kingston RI 02892. 401/539-9011. **Fax:** 401/539-7482. **Contact:** Manager. **Description:** An executive search firm. **Specializes in the areas of:** Information Systems.

GREENE PERSONNEL CONSULTANTS
1925 Broad Street, Cranston RI 02905. 401/461-9700. **Contact:** Manager. **Description:** An executive search firm specializing in marketing, advertising, PR, consumer goods an services, and financial services.

ROBERT HALF INTERNATIONAL/ACCOUNTEMPS
198 Dyer Street, Providence RI 02903. 401/274-9265. **Contact:** Manager. **World Wide Web address:** http://www.roberthalf.com. **Description:** An executive search firm. Accountemps (also at this location) provides temporary accounting placements. OfficeTeam (also at this location) provides temporary placements in office support. **NOTE:** OfficeTeam can be reached at 401/274-8700. **Corporate headquarters location:** Menlo Park CA. **International locations:** Worldwide.

HEALTH CARE EXECUTIVE SEARCH
48 Lake Drive, North Kingstown RI 02852. 401/884-2649. **Contact:** Manager. **Description:** An executive search firm that focuses on placing manufacturers in health care companies.

HIGHLAND EMPLOYMENT AGENCY
368 Cranston Street, Providence RI 02907. 401/751-5520. **Fax:** 401/751-4999. **Contact:** Manager. **Description:** An executive search firm.

KENNEDY PERSONNEL SERVICES
438 East Main Road, Middletown RI 02842. 401/846-2190. **Contact:** Manager. **Description:** An executive search firm. **Specializes in the areas of:** Office Support.

ALBERT G. LEE & ASSOCIATES
106 Greenwood Avenue, Rumford RI 02916. 401/434-7614. **Contact:** Albert G. Lee, CEO. **Description:** An executive search firm. Company pays fee. **Specializes in the areas of:** Accounting/Auditing; Administration; Advertising; Biology; Engineering; Finance; Food Industry; General Management; Health/Medical; Industrial; Legal; Manufacturing; Personnel/Labor Relations; Retail; Sales; Technical. **Positions commonly filled include:** Accountant/Auditor; Advertising Account Executive; Bank Officer/Manager; Biological Scientist; Computer Programmer; Computer Scientist; Design Engineer; Human Resources Manager; Manufacturing Engineer; Sales/Marketing Manager. **Average salary range of placements:** More than $50,000. **Number of placements per year:** 1 - 49.

LOFLIN GROUP INC.
1445 Wampanoag Trail, Suite 115, East Providence RI 02915. 401/433-3200. **Contact:** Kevin Loflin, President. **Description:** An executive search firm operating on a contingency basis. Company pays fee. **Positions commonly filled include:** Accountant/Auditor; Computer Programmer; Financial Analyst; Systems Analyst. **Average salary range of placements:** More than $50,000. **Number of placements per year:** 50 - 99.

LYBROOK ASSOCIATES, INC.
P.O. Box 572, Newport RI 02840. 401/683-6990. **Contact:** Manager. **Description:** An executive search firm. **Specializes in the areas of:** Chemistry.

MANAGEMENT RECRUITERS INTERNATIONAL
101 Dyer Street, Providence RI 02903. 401/274-2810. **Contact:** Manager. **Description:** An executive search firm. **Specializes in the areas of:** Accounting/Auditing; Administration; Advertising; Architecture/Construction; Banking; Communications; Computer Hardware/Software; Design; Electrical; Engineering; Food Industry; General Management; Health/Medical; Insurance; Legal; Manufacturing;

Operations Management; Personnel/Labor Relations; Procurement; Publishing; Retail; Sales; Technical; Textiles; Transportation.

MANAGEMENT SEARCH INC.
One State Street, Suite 501, Providence RI 02908. 401/273-5511. **Contact:** Manager. **Description:** An executive search firm.

NUGENT ASSOCIATES
960 Reservoir Avenue, Cranston RI 02910. 401/944-1414. **Contact:** Manager. **Description:** An executive search firm. **Specializes in the areas of:** Technical.

PKS ASSOCIATES, INC.
P.O. Box 5021, Greene RI 02827. 401/397-6154. **Fax:** 401/397-6722. **Contact:** Paul Spremulli, Operations Manager. **Description:** An executive search firm operating on a contingency basis. Company pays fee. **Specializes in the areas of:** Computer Science/Software; Engineering; General Management; Industrial; Manufacturing; Personnel/Labor Relations; Technical. **Positions commonly filled include:** Accountant/Auditor; Attorney; Blue-Collar Worker Supervisor; Computer Programmer; Dental Assistant/Hygienist; Dentist; Design Engineer; Designer; Draftsperson; Electrical/Electronics Engineer; Environmental Engineer; Human Resources Specialist; Industrial Engineer; Licensed Practical Nurse; Mechanical Engineer; MIS Specialist; Occupational Therapist; Operations/Production Manager; Physical Therapist; Quality Control Supervisor; Recreational Therapist; Registered Nurse; Respiratory Therapist; Software Engineer; Structural Engineer; Systems Analyst. **Corporate headquarters location:** This Location. **Other area locations:** Warwick RI. **Average salary range of placements:** \$30,000 - \$50,000. **Number of placements per year:** 200 - 499.

ALAN PRICE ASSOCIATES, INC.
300 Front Street, Suite 507, Pawtucket RI 02860. 401/728-8499. **Contact:** Manager. **Description:** An executive search firm. **Specializes in the areas of:** High-Tech.

PRO SEARCH, INC.
3960 Post Road, Warwick RI 02886. 401/885-9595. **Contact:** Manager. **Description:** An executive search firm. **Specializes in the areas of:** Banking; Sales; Telecommunications.

SALES CONSULTANTS OF RHODE ISLAND
349 Centerville Road, Warwick RI 02886-4324. 401/737-3200. **Contact:** Peter C. Cotton, Owner/President. **E-mail address:** slscnsltnt@aol.com. **World Wide Web address:** http://www.mrinet.com. **Description:** An executive search firm operating on both retained and contingency bases. Company pays fee. **Specializes in the areas of:** Marketing; Sales. **Average salary range of placements:** More than \$50,000. **Number of placements per year:** 1 - 49.

SCHATTLE & DUQUETTE
1130 Kenrod Road, North Kingstown RI 02852. 401/739-0500. **Contact:** Manager. **Description:** An executive search firm providing placements in middle management, MIS, and sales.

SEARCH PERSONNEL, INC.
773 Victory Highway, West Greenwich RI 02817. 401/392-1250. **Contact:** Manager. **Description:** An executive search firm.

SPECTRUM BUSINESS ASSOCIATES LTD.
P.O. Box 95, Newport RI 02840. 401/849-6560. **Contact:** Manager. **Description:** An executive search firm. **Specializes in the areas of:** Maritime.

STORTI ASSOCIATES
4042 Post Road, Unit #8, Warwick RI 02886. 401/885-3100. **Fax:** 401/885-3107. **Contact:** Michael Storti, President. **Description:** An executive search firm. Company pays fee. **Specializes in the areas of:** Accounting/Auditing; Administration; Affirmative Action; Banking; Computer Hardware/Software; Engineering; Finance; Health/Medical; Manufacturing; Sales. **Positions commonly filled include:** Accountant/Auditor; Biochemist; Biological Scientist; Biomedical Engineer; Ceramics Engineer; Chemical Engineer; Chemist; Computer Programmer; EDP Specialist; Electrical/Electronics Engineer; Marketing Specialist; Mechanical Engineer; MIS Specialist; Purchasing Agent/Manager; Quality Control Supervisor; Sales Rep.; Software Engineer; Systems Analyst.

SULLIVAN & COGLIANO
100 Jefferson Boulevard, Warwick RI 02888. 401/463-3811. **Contact:** Manager. **Description:** An executive search firm. **Specializes in the areas of:** Construction; Engineering; Health/Medical; Information Technology; Logistics; Marketing; Sales; Transportation.

SYLVESTRO ASSOCIATES
5586 Post Road, Suite 208, East Greenwich RI 02818. 401/885-0855. **Contact:** Manager. **Description:** An executive search firm.

TAD STAFFING SERVICE/TECHNICAL DIVISION
10 Orm Street, Providence RI 02904. 401/273-2300. **Contact:** Manager. **Description:** An executive search firm. The Technical Division specializes in technical placements. **Specializes in the areas of:** Administration.

WESTMINTER GROUP
40 Westminster Street, Providence RI 02903. 401/273-9300. **Contact:** Manager. **Description:** An executive search firm.

PERMANENT EMPLOYMENT AGENCIES

AQUIDNECK EMPLOYMENT SERVICE
170 Aquidneck Avenue, Middletown RI 02842-7600. **Contact:** Kenneth Quirk, Recruiter. **Description:** A permanent employment agency that also provides temporary placements. Company pays fee. **Specializes in the areas of:** Banking; Legal; Manufacturing; Sales; Secretarial. **Positions commonly filled include:** Customer Service Representative; Typist/Word Processor. **Average salary range of placements:** Less than \$20,000.

THE BARRETT GROUP
1130 Tenrod Road, Building E, Suite 302, North Kingstown RI 02852. 401/295-2333. **Fax:** 401/294-3654. **Contact:** Kevin Tetler, Vice President. **Description:** A permanent employment agency that also provides career/outplacement counseling. Founded in 1989. **Number of placements per year:** 200 - 499.

CAREERS UNLIMITED
560 Jefferson Boulevard, Suite 205, Warwick RI 02886. 401/736-8880. **Contact:** Arlette Dumais, President. **Description:** A permanent employment agency. Company pays fee. **Specializes in the areas of:** Insurance. **Positions commonly filled include:** Claim Representative; Insurance Agent/Broker; Underwriter/Assistant Underwriter. **Number of placements per year:** 100 - 199.

CASS & COMPANY
One Richmond Square, Providence RI 02906. 401/453-2277. **Contact:** Manager. **Description:** A permanent placement agency. **Specializes in the areas of:** Nannies.

COLONY PERSONNEL ASSOCIATES INC.
2845 Post Road, Warwick RI 02886-3145. 401/739-0670. **Fax:** 401/738-5523. **Contact:** Elaine Atturio, President. **E-mail address:** colony_jobs@ids.net. **Description:** A permanent employment agency that also offers contract services. Founded in 1989. Company pays fee. **Specializes in the areas of:** Accounting/Auditing; Administration; Engineering; Finance; General Management; Manufacturing; Retail; Sales; Secretarial; Technical. **Positions commonly filled include:** Accountant/Auditor; Adjuster; Administrative Manager; Bank Officer/Manager; Blue-Collar Worker Supervisor; Chemical Engineer; Chemist; Civil Engineer; Claim Rep.; Clerical Supervisor; Computer Programmer; Cost Estimator; Credit Manager; Customer Service Rep.; Design Engineer; Designer; Electrical/Electronics Engineer; Electrician; Environmental Engineer; Health Services Manager; Industrial Engineer; Management Analyst/Consultant; Management Trainee; Manufacturer's/Wholesaler's Sales Rep.; Mechanical Engineer; MIS Specialist; Purchasing Agent/Manager; Quality Control Supervisor; Software Engineer; Statistician; Structural Engineer; Systems Analyst; Typist/Word Processor. **Number of placements per year:** 100 - 199.

EMPLOY EASE
P.O. Box 346, Albion RI 02802. 401/723-1600. **Contact:** Manager. **Description:** A permanent employment agency. **Specializes in the areas of:** Human Resources.

JOB CONNECTION LTD.
189 Governor Street, Providence RI 02906-3124. 401/274-4450. **Fax:** 401/274-4451. **Contact:** Laurie Robinson, Human Resources Coordinator. **E-mail address:** jobconnection@compuserve.com. **Description:** A permanent employment agency. Founded in 1986. Company pays fee. **Specializes in the areas of:** Human Services. **Positions commonly filled include:** Counselor; Human Service Worker; Occupational Therapist; Physical Therapist; Registered Nurse; Social Worker; Speech-Language Pathologist; Teacher/Professor. **Other U.S. locations:** Natick MA. **Average salary range of placements:** $20,000 - $29,999. **Number of placements per year:** 50 - 99.

JOB LINK
674 Elmwood Avenue, Providence RI 02907. 401/941-3240. **Fax:** 401/941-3255. **Contact:** Roland Snead, Office Recruiter. **Description:** A permanent employment agency. **Number of placements per year:** 200 - 499.

JOHNSON & TREGAR ASSOCIATES
76 Westminster Street, Suite 321, Providence RI 02903. 401/831-5550. **Fax:** 401/831-5558. **Contact:** Jack Tregar, Partner. **Description:** A permanent employment agency. Company pays fee. **Specializes in the areas of:** Engineering; General Management; Industrial; Manufacturing; Personnel/ Labor Relations. **Positions commonly filled include:** Biological Scientist; Biomedical Engineer; Buyer; Chemical Engineer; Chemist; Design Engineer; Electrical/Electronics Engineer; Environmental Engineer; Human Resources Specialist; Industrial Engineer; Mechanical Engineer; Metallurgical Engineer; Operations/Production Manager; Purchasing Agent/Manager; Quality Control Supervisor; Software Engineer; Stationary Engineer; Statistician; Transportation/Traffic Specialist.

NEW ENGLAND CONSULTANTS, INC.
156 Centerville Road, Warwick RI 02886. 401/732-4650. **Fax:** 401/732-4654. **Contact:** Mary Shaw, President. **Description:** A permanent employment agency. Company pays fee. **Specializes in the areas of:** Computer Hardware/Software; Engineering; Manufacturing; Technical. **Positions commonly filled include:** Computer Programmer; EDP Specialist; Electrical/Electronics Engineer; Industrial Designer; Industrial Engineer; Manufacturing Engineer; Mechanical Engineer; MIS Specialist; Operations/Production Manager; Quality Control Supervisor; Sales Representative; Software Engineer; Systems Analyst. **Number of placements per year:** 1 - 49.

OCCUPATIONS UNLIMITED, INC.
560 Jefferson Boulevard, Warwick RI 02886. 401/732-9377. **Toll-free phone:** 800/575-9675. **Fax:** 401/732-9666. **Contact:** Manny Rivas, Employment Counselor. **E-mail address:** occunlmtd@aol.com. **Description:** A permanent employment agency. Founded in 1992. **Specializes in the areas of:** Personnel/Labor Relations; Secretarial; Technical. **Positions commonly filled include:** Administrative Manager; Blue-Collar Worker Supervisor; Claim Rep.; Clerical Supervisor; Computer Programmer; Customer Service Rep.; Electrical/Electronics Engineer; Financial Analyst; Human Resources Specialist; Industrial Engineer; Mechanical Engineer; MIS Specialist; Operations/Production Manager; Purchasing Agent/Manager; Transportation/Traffic Specialist. **Average salary range of placements:** $20,000 - $29,999. **Number of placements per year:** 1000+.

OFFICE SPECIALISTS
235 Promenade Street, Suite 419, Providence RI 02908. 401/831-1234. **Contact:** Manager. **Description:** A permanent employment agency. **Specializes in the areas of:** Office Support.

PERSONNEL PEOPLE, INC.
203 Turkshead Building, Providence RI 02903. 401/273-2500. **Contact:** Manager. **Description:** A permanent employment agency that also provides temporary placements. **Specializes in the areas of:** Administration; Office Support.

PROJECTS WITH INDUSTRY
40 Fountain Street, 2nd Floor, Providence RI 02903. 401/861-4460. **Contact:** Manager. **Description:** A federally funded employment agency that provides placements for people with physical and mental disabilities. **Other area locations:** Wakefield RI.

SUMMIT TECHNICAL SERVICES
355 Centerville Road, Warwick RI 02886. 401/738-9097. **Contact:** Manager. **Description:** A permanent employment agency. **Specializes in the areas of:** Engineering.

TEMPORARY EMPLOYMENT AGENCIES

ABLE PERSONNEL RESOURCE INC.
389 Main Street, Pawtucket RI 02860. 401/728-2234. **Toll-free phone:** 888/247-9281. **Contact:** Manager. **Description:** A temporary employment agency. **Specializes in the areas of:** Manufacturing.

CAPITOL PERSONNEL INC.
850 Waterman Avenue, East Providence RI 02914. 401/438-6067. **Contact:** Manager. **Description:** A temporary agency that also provides some permanent placements. **Specializes in the areas of:** Manufacturing.

KELLY SERVICES, INC.
70 Jefferson Boulevard, Warwick RI 02888. 401/467-2100. **Toll-free phone:** 800/848-9154. **Fax:** 401/467-3530. **Contact:** Paul Bordonaro, Branch Manager. **World Wide Web address:** http://www.kellyservices.com. **Description:** A temporary agency. Company pays fee. **Specializes in the areas of:** Accounting/Auditing; Administration; Clerical; Computer Science/Software; Engineering; Finance; General Management; Health/Medical; Industrial; Manufacturing; Personnel/Labor Relations; Sales; Secretarial; Technical. **Positions commonly filled include:** Accountant/Auditor; Biomedical Engineer; Blue-Collar Worker Supervisor; Buyer; Claim Rep.; Clerical Supervisor; Clerk; Clinical Lab Technician; Computer Programmer; Customer Service Rep.; Data Entry Clerk; Design Engineer; Draftsperson; Electrical/Electronics Engineer; Financial Analyst; Food Scientist/Technologist; Human Resources Specialist; Legal Secretary; Management Trainee; Mechanical Engineer; Medical Records Technician; Medical Secretary; MIS Specialist; Purchasing Agent/Manager; Quality Control Supervisor; Sales Rep.; Secretary; Software Engineer; Stenographer; Systems Analyst; Typist/Word Processor. **Benefits available to temporary workers:** 401(k); Medical Insurance; Paid Holidays; Paid Vacation. **Corporate headquarters location:** Troy MI. **Other U.S. locations:** Nationwide. **Average salary range of placements:** $30,000 - $50,000. **Number of placements per year:** 500 - 999.

NORRELL SERVICES
855 Waterman Avenue, East Providence RI 02914. 401/434-0851. **Contact:** Maria Doherty, Manager. **Description:** A temporary agency that also provides permanent placements. **Specializes in the areas of:** Accounting/Auditing; Administration; Banking; Computer Science/Software; Economics; Engineering; Finance; Food Industry; General Management; Industrial; Insurance; Legal; Manufacturing; Nonprofit; Personnel/Labor Relations; Publishing; Retail; Sales; Secretarial; Technical; Transportation. **Positions commonly filled include:** Accountant/Auditor; Administrative Manager; Aerospace Engineer; Bank Officer/Manager; Biomedical Engineer; Budget Analyst; Chemical Engineer; Chemist; Civil Engineer; Claim Rep.; Clerical Supervisor; Computer Programmer; Cost Estimator; Credit Manager; Customer Service Rep.; Design Engineer; Designer; Dietician/Nutritionist; Draftsperson; Electrical/Electronics Engineer; Environmental Engineer; Financial Analyst; Food Scientist/Technologist; Human Resources Specialist; Industrial Engineer; Management Analyst/Consultant; Management Trainee; Market Research Analyst; Mechanical Engineer; MIS Specialist; Operations/Production Manager; Paralegal; Public Relations Specialist; Purchasing Agent/Manager; Quality Control Supervisor; Restaurant/Food Service Manager; Services Sales Rep.; Software Engineer; Strategic Relations Manager; Structural Engineer; Systems Analyst; Technical Writer/Editor; Telecommunications Manager; Typist/Word Processor. **Benefits available to temporary workers:** 401(k); Medical Insurance; Paid Holidays; Paid Vacation. **Corporate headquarters location:** Atlanta GA. **Other U.S. locations:** Nationwide. **Average salary range of placements:** $20,000 - $29,999. **Number of placements per year:** 50 - 99.

ON LINE TEMP INC./ON LINE STAFF INC.
One Richmond Square, Providence RI 02906. 401/274-1500. **Fax:** 401/274-1803. **Contact:** Susan Reid, Owner. **Description:** A temporary agency that provides some permanent placements. Company pays fee. **Specializes in the areas of:** Computer Science/Software; Engineering; Personnel/Labor Relations; Technical. **Positions commonly filled include:** Biochemist; Biological Scientist; Chemist; Computer Programmer; Design Engineer; Designer; Draftsperson; Editor; Engineer; Internet Services Manager; Mathematician; MIS Specialist; Multimedia Designer; Science Technologist; Systems Analyst; Technical Writer/Editor; Telecommunications Manager. **Number of placements per year:** 100 - 199.

PRO STAFF PERSONNEL SERVICES
115 Cedar Street, Providence RI 02903. 401/351-0720. **Contact:** Manager. **Description:** A temporary agency that also offers some permanent positions. **Specializes in the areas of:** Administration; Clerical; Light Industrial.

SPECTRA TEMPS/TRACEY ASSOCIATES
260 West Exchange Street, Providence RI 02903-1000. 401/521-4400. **Fax:** 401/541-3992. **Contact:** Kerry Tracey, President. **Description:** A temporary agency. The company also offers permanent placement and some management level searches. Founded in 1985. Company pays fee. **Specializes in the areas of:** Accounting/Auditing; Legal; Personnel/Labor Relations; Secretarial. **Positions commonly filled include:** Clerical Supervisor; Human Resources Specialist; Paralegal; Typist/Word Processor. **Benefits available to temporary workers:** Paid Vacation. **Average salary range of placements:** $20,000 - $29,999. **Number of placements per year:** 1 - 49.

TAC STAFFING SERVICES
55 Dorrance Street, Providence RI 02903. 401/272-5410. **Fax:** 401/272-9138. **Contact:** Office Manager. **Description:** A temporary agency. Company pays fee. **Specializes in the areas of:** Accounting/Auditing; Advertising; Banking; Clerical; Education; Health/Medical; Insurance; Legal; Manufacturing; Nonprofit; Personnel/Labor Relations; Publishing; Sales; Transportation. **Positions commonly filled include:** Administrative Worker/Clerk; Bookkeeper; Data Entry Clerk; Legal Secretary; Light Industrial Worker; Medical Secretary; Receptionist; Secretary; Typist/Word Processor. **Number of placements per year:** 1000+. **Corporate headquarters location:** Newton MA. **Other U.S. locations:** Nationwide.

CONTRACT SERVICES FIRMS

TECH/AID OF RHODE ISLAND
240 Chestnut Street, Warwick RI 02888. 401/467-7560. **Fax:** 401/461-4880. **Contact:** Kevin Garvey, Manager. **Description:** A contract services firm. Company pays fee. **Specializes in the areas of:** Architecture/Construction; Cable TV; Computer Hardware/Software; Engineering; Manufacturing; Technical. **Positions commonly filled include:** Aerospace Engineer; Architect; Ceramics Engineer; Chemical Engineer; Civil Engineer; Draftsperson; Electrical/Electronics Engineer; Estimator; Factory Worker; Industrial Designer; Industrial Engineer; Mechanical Engineer; Metallurgical Engineer; Mining Engineer; Operations/Production Manager; Petroleum Engineer; Purchasing Agent/ Manager; Quality Control Supervisor; Technical Writer/Editor; Technician. **Number of placements per year:** 1000+.

UNIFIED MANAGEMENT CORPORATION
1420 Mineral Spring Avenue, North Providence RI 02904. 401/354-8600. **Contact:** Office Manager. **Description:** A contract services firm that specializes in payroll and worker's compensation. **Specializes in the areas of:** Payroll.

SOUTH CAROLINA

EXECUTIVE SEARCH FIRMS

ATLANTIC RECRUITERS
P.O. Box 4787, Spartanburg SC 29305. 864/573-7800. **Contact:** Manager. **Description:** An executive search firm. **Specializes in the areas of:** Automotive; Metals; Paper; Plastics; Technical.

BOCK & ASSOCIATES
2375 East Main Street, Suite A105, Spartanburg SC 29307. 864/579-7396. **Contact:** Kevin Bock, Owner/President. **Description:** An executive search firm that provides placement for professionals who work with polymer-based materials used primarily in the manufacturing of medical devices. Company pays fee. **Specializes in the areas of:** Engineering; Industrial; Manufacturing; Personnel/Labor Relations; Technical. **Positions commonly filled include:** Biological Scientist; Biomedical Engineer; Chemical Engineer; Chemist; Human Resources Manager; Mechanical Engineer. **Average salary range of placements:** More than $50,000. **Number of placements per year:** 1 - 49.

COLUMBIA HEALTH CARE SERVICE
530 Howell Road, Suite 203, Greenville SC 29615. 864/322-7122. **Contact:** Manager. **Description:** An executive search firm that provides medical placements including medical receptionists, medical assistants, health insurance personnel, nurses, and LPNs. **NOTE:** The first 90 days are spent under the employ of Columbia Health Care, after which workers may become full-time employees of the client company with benefits. Please contact Columbia Health Care Service for more details. **Specializes in the areas of:** Health/Medical.

COLUMBIA HEALTH CARE SERVICE
P.O. Box 8363, Columbia SC 29202. 803/782-2000. **Contact:** Manager. **Description:** This location houses the corporate offices. Columbia Health Care Service is an executive search firm focusing on the placement of medical receptionists, medical assistants, nurses, LPNs, and some health insurance personnel. This location also houses the company's legal staffing branch. **Specializes in the areas of:** Health/Medical.

COLUMBIA LEGAL PROFESSIONALS
COLUMBIA STAFFING
P.O. Box 8386, Columbia SC 29202. 803/790-1200. **Contact:** Manager. **Description:** An executive search firm. Columbia Staffing (also at this location) provides temporary placements. **Specializes in the areas of:** Legal.

CONTEMPORARY MANAGEMENT SERVICES
P.O. Box 24131, Greenville SC 29616. 864/244-7070. **Fax:** 864/244-1111. **Contact:** Manager. **Description:** An executive search firm. **Specializes in the areas of:** Engineering; Manufacturing.

CORPORATE SOLUTIONS
P.O. Box 1974, Simpsonville SC 29681-1974. 864/297-5888. **Contact:** Manager. **Description:** An executive search firm. **NOTE:** The firm prefers to receive resumes by fax. Please call for number. **Specializes in the areas of:** Engineering; Finance; Information Systems; Manufacturing.

DUNHILL PROFESSIONAL SEARCH
6 Village Square, 231 Hampton Street, Greenwood SC 29646. 864/229-5251. **Contact:** Hal Freese, President. **Description:** An executive search firm. **Specializes in the areas of:** Accounting/Auditing; Computer Hardware/Software; Engineering; Manufacturing.

DUNHILL STAFFING
96 Villa Road, Greenville SC 29615. 864/242-9870. **Fax:** 864/271-7181. **Contact:** Duke Haynie, President. **Description:** An executive search firm operating on both retained and contingency bases. Company pays fee. **Specializes in the areas of:** Human Resources. **Positions commonly filled include:** Human Resources Manager. **Other U.S. locations:** Nationwide. **Average salary range of placements:** More than $50,000. **Number of placements per year:** 1 - 49.

EASTERN PERSONNEL SERVICES
960 Morrisson Drive, Charleston SC 29403. 803/863-9111. **Fax:** 803/863-0710. **Contact:** Paul Day, President. **Description:** An executive search firm operating on a contingency basis. The firm also operates as a temporary agency, contract services firm, and career/outplacement counseling agency. Company pays fee. **Specializes in the areas of:** Administration; Computer Science/Software; General Management; Insurance; Legal; Personnel/Labor Relations; Sales; Secretarial. **Positions commonly filled include:** Accountant/Auditor; Administrative Manager; Advertising Clerk; Architect; Attorney; Bank Officer/Manager; Buyer; Claim Rep.; Clerical Supervisor; Credit Manager; Customer Service Rep.; Designer; Draftsperson; Electrical/Electronics Engineer; Electrician; Financial Analyst; Human Resources Specialist; Human Service Worker; Industrial Engineer; Industrial Production Manager; Landscape Architect; Management Analyst/Consultant; Manufacturer's/Wholesaler's Sales Rep.; Market Research Analyst; Medical Records Technician; MIS Specialist; Operations/Production Manager; Property and Real Estate Manager; Purchasing Agent/Manager; Quality Control Supervisor; Services Sales Rep.; Systems Analyst; Typist/Word Processor; Underwriter/Assistant Underwriter. **Benefits available to temporary workers:** Medical Insurance; Paid Vacation. **Other U.S. locations:** Savannah GA. **Average salary range of placements:** $20,000 - $29,999. **Number of placements per year:** 500 - 999.

EDMONDS PERSONNEL INC.
P.O. Box 26313, Greenville SC 29616. 864/288-4848. **Fax:** 864/288-2114. **Contact:** Dave Edmonds, Owner. **E-mail address:** edmonds@teleplex.net. **World Wide Web address:** http://www.teleplex.net/edmonds. **Description:** An executive search firm. Company pays fee. **Specializes in the areas of:** Engineering; Manufacturing; Transportation. **Positions commonly filled include:** Aerospace Engineer; Buyer; Design Engineer; Designer; Electrical/Electronics Engineer; Electrician; Human Resources Specialist; Industrial Engineer; Industrial Production Manager; Mechanical Engineer; Metallurgical Engineer; Quality Control Supervisor; Science Technologist; Technical Writer/Editor; Telecommunications Manager. **Average salary range of placements:** $30,000 - $50,000. **Number of placements per year:** 1 - 49.

ENGINEER & TECHNICAL RECRUITING
P.O. Box 40895, Charleston SC 29423-0895. 803/552-3177. **Contact:** John Fernandez, Manager. **Description:** An executive search firm. **Specializes in the areas of:** Engineering; Technical. **Positions commonly filled include:** Chemist; Engineer.

ENGINEERING PERSONNEL NETWORK
P.O. Box 1426, Irmo SC 29063. 803/781-2087. **Fax:** 843/732-7986. **Contact:** Manager. **Description:** An executive search firm. **Specializes in the areas of:** Engineering; Environmental; Industrial; Public Administration.

EVERS PERSONNEL SEARCH
1345 Garner Lane, Suite 103A, Columbia SC 29210. 803/772-0451. **Fax:** 803/798-3004. **Contact:** Jim Evers, Owner. **Description:** An executive search firm. Founded in 1991. **Specializes in the areas of:** Sales. **Positions commonly filled include:** Branch Manager; Manufacturer's/Wholesaler's Sales Rep.; Sales Representative. **Average salary range of placements:** $30,000 - $50,000. **Number of placements per year:** 50 - 99.

EXECUTIVE PLACEMENT
P.O. Box 5663, Hilton Head Island SC 29938. 843/785-2705. **Contact:** Manager. **Description:** An executive search firm.

FINANCIAL SEARCH ASSOCIATES
312 Wilton Street, Greenville SC 29609. 864/370-9872. **Contact:** Manager. **Description:** An executive search firm. **Specializes in the areas of:** Accounting/Auditing; Finance.

FORD & ASSOCIATES
P.O. Box 3648, Myrtle Beach SC 29578-3648. 843/497-5350. **Fax:** 843/497-5351. **Contact:** Travis Ford, President. **Description:** An executive search and contract services firm operating on a contingency basis. The firm focuses on placing management and technical staff in the textile, automobile OEM, chemical, and plastics industries in the Southeast. Company pays fee. **Specializes in the areas of:** Accounting/Auditing; Chemical Engineering; Data Processing; Engineering; Industrial; Logistics; Manufacturing; Personnel/Labor Relations; Quality Assurance. **Positions commonly filled include:** Accountant/Auditor; Chemical Engineer; Computer Programmer; Environmental Engineer; Human Resources Manager; Industrial Engineer; Industrial Production Manager; Manufacturing Engineer; Mechanical Engineer; Operations/Production Manager; Quality Assurance Engineer. **Number of placements per year:** 50 - 99.

F-O-R-T-U-N-E PERSONNEL CONSULTANTS
25 Woods Lake Road, Suite 410, Greenville SC 29607. 864/241-7700. **Fax:** 864/241-7704. **Contact:** Recruiter. **E-mail address:** fortunegrev@mindspring.com. **Description:** An executive search firm. **Specializes in the areas of:** Health/Medical; Manufacturing. **Positions commonly filled include:** Biochemist; Biological Scientist; Biomedical Engineer; Chemical Engineer; Chemist; Clinical Lab Technician; Design Engineer; Environmental Engineer; Industrial Engineer; Industrial Production Manager; Mechanical Engineer; MIS Specialist; Operations/Production Manager; Pharmacist; Quality Control Supervisor; Veterinarian. **Corporate headquarters location:** New York NY. **Other U.S. locations:** Nationwide. **Average salary range of placements:** More than $50,000. **Number of placements per year:** 1 - 49.
Other area locations:
- 100 Miracle Mile Drive, Suite F, Anderson SC 29621. 864/226-5322. (Biotechnology; Health/Medical; Pharmaceutical)
- 410 Mill Street, Mount Pleasant SC 29464. 803/884-0505.

F-O-R-T-U-N-E PERSONNEL CONSULTANTS OF COLUMBIA
108 Columbia Northeast Drive, Columbia SC 29223. 803/788-8877. **Fax:** 803/788-1509. **Contact:** Jill Felts, Vice President. **E-mail address:** fortune@conterra.com. **World Wide Web address:** http://www.conterra.com/fortune. **Description:** An executive search firm. The company recruits and places middle and upper management personnel in manufacturing industries. Founded in 1980. Company pays fee. **Specializes in the areas of:** Accounting/Auditing; Administration; Engineering; Finance; General Management; Industrial; Manufacturing; Quality Assurance; Sales; Technical; Transportation. **Positions commonly filled include:** Account Manager; Accountant/Auditor; Buyer; Chief Financial Officer; Controller; Design Engineer; Electrical/Electronics Engineer; Finance Director; Financial Analyst; General Manager; Human Resources Manager; Industrial Engineer; Industrial Production Manager; Management Analyst/Consultant; Manufacturer's/Wholesaler's Sales Rep.; Manufacturing Engineer; Marketing Manager; Mechanical Engineer; Metallurgical Engineer; Operations/Production Manager; Purchasing Agent/Manager; Quality Control Supervisor; Sales Engineer; Software Engineer; Systems Manager; Transportation/Traffic Specialist. **Corporate headquarters location:** New York NY. **Other U.S. locations:** Nationwide. **Average salary range of placements:** More than $50,000. **Number of placements per year:** 200 - 499.

THOMAS GLOVER & ASSOCIATES INC.
200 East Main Street, Spartanburg SC 29306. 864/585-9890. **Contact:** Manager. **Description:** An executive search firm. **Specializes in the areas of:** Computer Science/Software.

ROBERT HALF INTERNATIONAL/ACCOUNTEMPS
75 Beattie Place, Suite 930, Greenville SC 29601. 864/232-4253. **Contact:** Manager. **Description:** An executive search firm. Accountemps (also at this location) provides temporary placements. **Corporate headquarters location:** Menlo Park CA.

HEALTH CARE SEARCH ASSOCIATES
P.O. Box 17334, Greenville SC 29606-8334. 864/242-1999. **Fax:** 864/271-1426. **Contact:** David Gahan, Owner/Manager. **Description:** An executive search firm. Company pays fee. **Specializes in the areas of:** Health/Medical. **Positions commonly filled include:** Medical Records Technician; Nuclear Medicine Technologist; Radiological Technologist; Registered Nurse; Speech-Language Pathologist. **Number of placements per year:** 1 - 49.

KERSEY & ASSOCIATES INC.
600 Oak Forest Road, Spartanburg SC 29301. 864/574-6724. **Contact:** Manager. **Description:** An executive search firm. **Specializes in the areas of:** Information Technology.

MANAGEMENT RECRUITERS INTERNATIONAL
113 Court Street, Pickens SC 29671. 864/878-1113. **Contact:** Manager. **Description:** An executive search firm. **Specializes in the areas of:** Manufacturing. **Corporate headquarters location:** Cleveland OH. **Other U.S. locations:** Nationwide. **International locations:** Worldwide.
Other area locations:
- P.O. Box 639, Travelers Rest SC 29690-0639. 864/834-0643. (Manufacturing)

MANAGEMENT RECRUITERS OF AIKEN
P.O. Box 730, Aiken SC 29802-0730. 843/648-1361. **Contact:** Michael Hardwick, Manager. **Description:** An executive search firm. Company pays fee. **Specializes in the areas of:** Apparel; Computer Hardware/Software; Electronics; Health/Medical; Medical Software; Metals; Plastics; Textiles. **Corporate headquarters location:** Cleveland OH. **Other U.S. locations:** Nationwide. **International locations:** Worldwide. **Number of placements per year:** 500 - 999.

MANAGEMENT RECRUITERS OF ANDERSON
P.O. Box 2874, Anderson SC 29622. 864/225-1258. **Fax:** 864/225-2332. **Contact:** Rod Pagan, Owner. **Description:** An executive search firm. Company pays fee. **Specializes in the areas of:** Automotive; Computer

Science/Software; Data Processing; Health/Medical; Pharmaceutical. **Positions commonly filled include:** Accountant/Auditor; Biological Scientist; Biomedical Engineer; Buyer; Chemical Engineer; Chemist; Computer Programmer; Electrical/Electronics Engineer; General Manager; Human Resources Manager; Industrial Engineer; Mechanical Engineer; Purchasing Agent/Manager; Systems Analyst. **Corporate headquarters location:** Cleveland OH. **Other U.S. locations:** Nationwide. **International locations:** Worldwide. **Number of placements per year:** 50 - 99.

MANAGEMENT RECRUITERS OF COLUMBIA
P.O. Box 50785, Columbia SC 29250. 843/254-1334. **Fax:** 843/254-1527. **Contact:** Bob Keen, Manager. **Description:** An executive search firm. **Specializes in the areas of:** Accounting/Auditing; Administration; Advertising; Architecture/Construction; Banking; Communications; Computer Hardware/Software; Design; Electrical; Engineering; Food Industry; General Management; Health/Medical; Insurance; Legal; Manufacturing; Operations Management; Personnel/Labor Relations; Procurement; Publishing; Retail; Sales; Technical; Textiles; Transportation. **Corporate headquarters location:** Cleveland OH. **Other U.S. locations:** Nationwide. **International locations:** Worldwide.

MANAGEMENT RECRUITERS OF FLORENCE
P.O. Box 5320, Florence SC 29502-5320. 843/664-1112. **Contact:** Al Feimster, Manager. **Description:** An executive search firm. **Specializes in the areas of:** Manufacturing. **Corporate headquarters location:** Cleveland OH. **Other U.S. locations:** Nationwide. **International locations:** Worldwide.

MANAGEMENT RECRUITERS OF ORANGEBURG
2037 Saint Matthews Road, Orangeburg SC 29118. 803/531-4101. **Fax:** 803/536-3714. **Contact:** Virginia Rucker, Administrative Manager. **World Wide Web address:** http://www.oburg.net/mri/index.html. **Description:** An executive search firm. Company pays fee. **Specializes in the areas of:** Computer Science/Software; Engineering; Industrial; Personnel/Labor Relations; Scientific; Technical. **Positions commonly filled include:** Applications Engineer; Auditor; Chemical Engineer; Computer Programmer; Electrical/Electronics Engineer; General Manager; Human Resources Manager; Industrial Engineer; Industrial Production Manager; Manufacturing Engineer; Marketing Manager; Mechanical Engineer; Metallurgical Engineer; MIS Specialist; Operations Manager; Production Manager; Project Manager; Purchasing Agent/Manager; Quality Control Supervisor; Sales Engineer; Software Engineer; Systems Analyst; Systems Manager; Transportation/Traffic Specialist. **Corporate headquarters location:** Cleveland OH. **Other U.S. locations:** Nationwide. **International locations:** Worldwide. **Average salary range of placements:** $30,000 - $50,000. **Number of placements per year:** 50 - 99.

MANAGEMENT RECRUITERS OF ROCK HILL
1925 Ebenezer Road, Rock Hill SC 29732. 803/324-5181. **Fax:** 803/324-3431. **Contact:** Herman Smith, Manager. **Description:** An executive search firm. **Specializes in the areas of:** Accounting/Auditing; Administration; Advertising; Architecture/Construction; Banking; Communications; Computer Hardware/Software; Design; Electrical; Engineering; Food Industry; General Management; Health/Medical; Insurance; Legal; Manufacturing; Operations Management; Personnel/Labor Relations; Procurement; Publishing; Retail; Sales; Technical; Textiles; Transportation. **Corporate headquarters location:** Cleveland OH. **Other U.S. locations:** Nationwide. **International locations:** Worldwide.

McCORMICK ASSOCIATES
304 Pine Bark Road, Anderson SC 29625. 864/225-1468. **Contact:** Manager. **Description:** An executive search firm.

MILLER & ASSOCIATES
1852 Wallace School Road, Suite E, Charleston SC 29407-4887. 843/571-6630. **Fax:** 803/571-0230. **Contact:** Al E. Miller Jr., Owner/Manager. **Description:** An executive search firm. Company pays fee. **Specializes in the areas of:** Accounting/Auditing; Administration; Computer Science/Software; Engineering; Finance; Industrial; Manufacturing; Personnel/Labor Relations; Sales; Technical. **Positions commonly filled include:** Accountant/Auditor; Ceramics Engineer; Civil Engineer; Design Engineer; Designer; Draftsperson; Electrical/Electronics Engineer; Environmental Engineer; Financial Analyst; General Manager; Human Resources Specialist; Industrial Engineer; Industrial Production Manager; Manufacturing Engineer; Materials Engineer; Mechanical Engineer; Metallurgical Engineer; MIS Specialist; Purchasing Agent/Manager; Quality Control Supervisor; Software Engineer; Systems Analyst. **Average salary range of placements:** More than $50,000. **Number of placements per year:** 1 - 49.

NATIONWIDE PHYSICIAN RECRUITERS
6569 East Shore Road, Columbia SC 29206. **Toll-free phone:** 800/533-6799. **Fax:** 803/787-6441. **Contact:** Jerry Roberts, Physician Recruiter. **Description:** An executive search firm operating on a contingency basis. Founded in 1984. **Positions commonly filled include:** Physician. **Average salary range of placements:** More than $50,000. **Number of placements per year:** 1 - 49.

PALACE PERSONNEL SERVICES
1900 Broad River Road, Columbia SC 29210. 843/798-3533. **Fax:** 843/750-3113. **Contact:** Dick Powlas, President. **Description:** An executive search firm that also operates as a permanent and temporary employment agency. Founded in 1984. Company pays fee. **Specializes in the areas of:** Engineering; Manufacturing; Secretarial. **Positions commonly filled include:** Accountant/Auditor; Blue-Collar Worker Supervisor; Branch Manager; Buyer; Chemist; Civil Engineer; Clerical Supervisor; Computer Programmer; Customer Service Representative; Design Engineer; Designer; Draftsperson; Electrician; Environmental Engineer; General Manager; Human Resources Specialist; Industrial Engineer; Industrial Production Manager; Manufacturer's/Wholesaler's Sales Rep.; Mechanical Engineer; MIS Specialist; Software Engineer. **Benefits available to temporary workers:** Medical Insurance; Paid Holidays; Paid Vacation. **Average salary range of placements:** $30,000 - $50,000. **Number of placements per year:** 100 - 199.

PENN HILL ASSOCIATES
P.O. Box 1367, Pawleys Island SC 29585. 803/237-8988. **Fax:** 803/237-9220. **Contact:** Conrad L. Kohler, CPC. **Description:** An executive search firm. **Specializes in the areas of:** Consumer Finance.

THE PERSONNEL NETWORK, INC.
P.O. Box 1426, Irmo SC 29063. 843/781-2087. **Fax:** 843/732-7986. **Contact:** Chuck Larsen, President. **Description:** An executive search firm that focuses on engineering, industrial, environmental, medical, and public administration professions. Founded in 1987. Company pays fee. **Specializes in the areas of:** Administration; Engineering; Food Industry; General Management; Health/Medical; Industrial; Manufacturing; Personnel/Labor Relations; Sales. **Positions commonly filled include:** Accountant/Auditor; Administrative Manager; Biomedical Engineer; Blue-Collar Worker Supervisor; Buyer; Ceramics

Engineer; Chemical Engineer; Civil Engineer; Construction Contractor; Design Engineer; Electrical/ Electronics Engineer; Environmental Engineer; General Manager; Geologist/Geophysicist; Hotel Manager; Industrial Engineer; Industrial Production Manager; Materials Engineer; Mechanical Engineer; Metallurgical Engineer; Operations/Production Manager; Physical Therapist; Physician; Purchasing Agent/Manager; Quality Control Supervisor; Registered Nurse; Restaurant/Food Service Manager; Structural Engineer. **Average salary range of placements:** $30,000 - $50,000.

PHILLIPS RESOURCE GROUP
330 Pelham Road, Greenville SC 29615. 864/271-6350. **Fax:** 864/271-8499. **Contact:** Mr. A.M. Hicks, President. **E-mail address:** jbostic@globalvision.net. **World Wide Web address:** http://www.globalvision.net/phillips. **Description:** An executive search firm. Company pays fee. **Specializes in the areas of:** Administration; Engineering; Manufacturing; Personnel/Labor Relations; Sales; Technical. **Positions commonly filled include:** Accountant/Auditor; Chemical Engineer; Chemist; Computer Programmer; EDP Specialist; Electrical/Electronics Engineer; Industrial Engineer; Manufacturing Engineer; Marketing Specialist; Mechanical Engineer; Metallurgical Engineer; MIS Specialist. **Corporate headquarters location:** This Location. **Other area locations:** Charleston SC; Charlotte NC. **Average salary range of placements:** More than $50,000. **Number of placements per year:** 50 - 99.

PHYSICIANS UNLIMITED
900 East North Street, Suite 200, Greenville SC 29601. 864/370-2336. **Contact:** Manager. **Description:** An executive search firm that places physicians. **Specializes in the areas of:** Health/Medical.

SALES CONSULTANTS
MANAGEMENT RECRUITERS OF GREENVILLE
330 Pelham Road, Suite 109B, Greenville SC 29615. 864/370-1341. **Contact:** Dick Brennecke, President. **Description:** An executive search firm. **Specializes in the areas of:** Communications; Computer Hardware/ Software; General Management; Health/Medical; Industrial; Manufacturing; Marketing; Printing; Publishing; Sales; Textiles. **Positions commonly filled include:** Account Manager; Account Rep.; Chemical Engineer; Chemist; Electrical/Electronics Engineer; Manufacturer's/Wholesaler's Sales Rep.; Marketing Manager; Mechanical Engineer; Sales Engineer; Sales Executive; Sales Manager; Sales Representative; Services Sales Representative. **Corporate headquarters location:** Cleveland OH. **Other U.S. locations:** Nationwide. **International locations:** Worldwide. **Average salary range of placements:** $30,000 - $50,000. **Number of placements per year:** 50 - 99.

SANFORD ROSE ASSOCIATES
4458 Augusta Road, Building One, Suite C, Lexington SC 29072. 803/957-7300. **Fax:** 803/957-7380. **Contact:** Manager. **World Wide Web address:** http://www.sanfordrose.com. **Description:** An executive search firm. **Specializes in the areas of:** General Management; Medical Sales and Marketing. **Corporate headquarters location:** Akron OH. **Other U.S. locations:** Nationwide. **International locations:** Singapore.

SEARCH AND RECRUIT INTERNATIONAL
2501 Northforest Drive, North Charleston SC 29420. 803/572-4040. **Fax:** 803/572-4045. **Contact:** Les Callahan, Southeast Regional Manager. **Description:** An executive search firm operating on both retained and contingency bases. Company pays fee. **Specializes in the areas of:** Computer Science/Software; Engineering; Food Industry; Health/Medical; Industrial; Scientific; Technical. **Positions commonly filled include:** Accountant/ Auditor; Biological Scientist; Biomedical Engineer; Ceramics Engineer; Chemical Engineer; Civil Engineer; Computer Programmer; Electrical/Electronics Engineer; Electrician; Financial Analyst; Geologist/Geophysicist; Industrial Engineer; Industrial Production Manager; Materials Engineer; Mechanical Engineer; Medical Records Technician; Metallurgical Engineer; Nuclear Engineer; Nuclear Medicine Technologist; Occupational Therapist; Operations/Production Manager; Pharmacist; Physical Therapist; Physician; Quality Control Supervisor; Respiratory Therapist; Software Engineer; Speech-Language Pathologist; Stationary Engineer; Structural Engineer; Systems Analyst. **Average salary range of placements:** $30,000 - $50,000. **Number of placements per year:** 100 - 199.

JOHN SHELL ASSOCIATES, INC.
P.O. Box 23291, Columbia SC 29224. 803/788-6619. **Physical address:** 115 Atrium Way, Suite 122, Columbia SC. **Fax:** 803/788-1758. **Contact:** John C. Shell III, CPA, President. **E-mail address:** shellacc@aol.com. **Description:** An executive search firm that provides temporary and permanent placement for accounting and financial professionals. Company pays fee. **Specializes in the areas of:** Accounting/Auditing; Finance. **Positions commonly filled include:** Accountant/Auditor; Credit Manager; Financial Analyst. **Average salary range of placements:** $30,000 - $50,000. **Number of placements per year:** 50 - 99.

SOUTHERN RECRUITERS & CONSULTANTS, INC.
P.O. Box 2745, Aiken SC 29802-2745. 843/648-7834. **Fax:** 843/642-2770. **Contact:** Ray Fehrenbach, President. **World Wide Web address:** http://www.southernrecruiters.com. **Description:** An executive search firm. Company pays fee. **Specializes in the areas of:** Accounting/Auditing; Administration; Computer Science/Software; Engineering; General Management; Health/Medical; Manufacturing; MIS/ EDP; Personnel/Labor Relations; Technical. **Positions commonly filled include:** Accountant/Auditor; Bank Officer/Manager; Biochemist; Biomedical Engineer; Buyer; Civil Engineer; Computer Programmer; Design Engineer; Designer; Draftsperson; Electrical/Electronics Engineer; Environmental Engineer; General Manager; Human Resources Manager; Industrial Engineer; Mechanical Engineer; Metallurgical Engineer; MIS Specialist; Purchasing Agent/Manager; Quality Control Supervisor; Software Engineer; Structural Engineer; Systems Analyst. **Average salary range of placements:** $30,000 - $50,000. **Number of placements per year:** 100 - 199.

PERMANENT EMPLOYMENT AGENCIES

ACCUSTAFF
1755 St. Julian Place, Columbia SC 29204. 843/765-0820. **Contact:** Manager. **Description:** A permanent employment agency.

AUTOMOTIVE CAREER PLACEMENT COUNSELORS
6 Craftsman Court, Suite D, Greer SC 29650. 864/877-0359. **Toll-free phone:** 800/467-ACPC. **Fax:** 864/877-1210. **Contact:** David Freeborn, President. **E-mail address:** dlf4kfa@aol.com. **Description:** A

permanent employment agency. **Specializes in the areas of:** Automotive. **Number of placements per year:** 100 - 199.

COMPANION EMPLOYMENT SERVICES
P.O. Box 869, Columbia SC 29205. 803/771-6454. **Physical address:** 2511 Devine Street, Columbia SC. **Fax:** 803/765-1431. **Contact:** Personnel Consultant. **Description:** A permanent employment agency. **Specializes in the areas of:** Computer Science/Software; Data Processing.

CRAIN SEARCH
P.O. Box 17606, Greenville SC 29606. 864/271-4555. **Contact:** Manager. **Description:** A permanent placement agency.

DUNHILL PERSONNEL OF ST. ANDREWS
Interstate Center, 16 Berryhill Road, Suite 120, Columbia SC 29210. 803/772-6751. **Fax:** 803/798-0874. **Contact:** Manager. **Description:** A permanent employment agency. Company pays fee. **Specializes in the areas of:** Engineering; Industrial; Manufacturing; Sales; Textiles. **Positions commonly filled include:** Accountant/Auditor; Aerospace Engineer; Computer Programmer; Electrical/Electronics Engineer; Human Resources Manager; Industrial Engineer; Manufacturer's/Wholesaler's Sales Rep.; Materials Engineer; Mechanical Engineer; Meteorologist; Operations/Production Manager; Quality Control Supervisor; Software Engineer; Systems Analyst. **Number of placements per year:** 50 - 99.

EMPLOYMENT STAFFING
122 Trinity Street, Abbeville SC 29620-2130. **Contact:** Manager. **Description:** A permanent employment agency. **Corporate headquarters location:** Shelby NC. **Other U.S. locations:** Marion NC; Columbia SC. **Average salary range of placements:** $20,000 - $29,999. **Number of placements per year:** 1000+.

HARVEY PERSONNEL, INC.
P.O. Box 1931, Spartanburg SC 29304. 864/582-5616. **Fax:** 864/582-3588. **Contact:** Howard L. Harvey, CPC, President. **Description:** A permanent employment agency. Company pays fee. **Specializes in the areas of:** Accounting/Auditing; Administration; Computer Hardware/Software; Engineering; General Management; Industrial; Manufacturing; Personnel/Labor Relations; Technical. **Positions commonly filled include:** Accountant/Auditor; Biological Scientist; Biomedical Engineer; Buyer; Ceramics Engineer; Chemical Engineer; Chemist; Civil Engineer; EDP Specialist; Electrical/Electronics Engineer; Industrial Engineer; Manufacturing Engineer; Manufacturing Manager; Mechanical Engineer; Metallurgical Engineer; MIS Specialist; Operations/Production Manager; Plastics Engineer; Purchasing Agent/Manager; Quality Control Supervisor; Software Engineer; Systems Analyst. **Number of placements per year:** 1 - 49.

PRL & ASSOCIATES, INC.
P.O. Box 340, Lexington SC 29071. 803/957-3222. **Contact:** Perrin R. Love, President. **Description:** A permanent employment agency focusing on placement and consulting services for human resource professionals. Company pays fee. **Specializes in the areas of:** Accounting/Auditing; Administration; Banking; Computer Science/Software; Engineering; Finance; General Management; Manufacturing; Personnel/Labor Relations. **Positions commonly filled include:** Accountant/Auditor; Administrative Manager; Bank Officer/Manager; Biomedical Engineer; Branch Manager; Buyer; Chemical Engineer; Civil Engineer; Computer Programmer; Electrical/Electronics Engineer; Environmental Engineer; Financial Analyst; General Manager; Human Resources Manager; Industrial Engineer; Mechanical Engineer; Metallurgical Engineer; MIS Specialist; Operations/Production Manager; Purchasing Agent/Manager; Quality Control Supervisor; Software Engineer; Systems Analyst. **Average salary range of placements:** $30,000 - $50,000. **Number of placements per year:** 1 - 49.

PHELPS PERSONNEL
P.O. Box 4177, Greenville SC 29608. 864/232-8139. **Fax:** 864/271-1426. **Contact:** Ronald A. Phelps, President. **Description:** A permanent employment agency. Founded in 1976. Company pays fee. **Specializes in the areas of:** Engineering; Manufacturing. **Positions commonly filled include:** Design Engineer; Electrical/Electronics Engineer; Industrial Engineer; Manufacturing Engineer; Mechanical Engineer; Quality Assurance Engineer. **Average salary range of placements:** $30,000 - $50,000. **Number of placements per year:** 1 - 49.

SNELLING PERSONNEL
2704 East North Street, Greenville SC 29615-1715. 864/268-9300. **Fax:** 864/268-7676. **Contact:** Sharon Hill, Manager. **Description:** A permanent employment agency that also provides temporary placements. **Specializes in the areas of:** Accounting/Auditing; Administration; Engineering; Industrial; Light Industrial; Manufacturing; Secretarial; Transportation. **Positions commonly filled include:** Accountant/Auditor; Buyer; Credit Manager; Customer Service Representative; Design Engineer; Electrical/Electronics Engineer; Industrial Engineer; Mechanical Engineer. **Benefits available to temporary workers:** Bonus Award/Plan; Paid Holidays. **Corporate headquarters location:** Dallas TX. **Other U.S. locations:** Nationwide. **Number of placements per year:** 100 - 199.

SNELLING PERSONNEL SERVICES
P.O. Box 1800, Lexington SC 29071. 803/359-7644. **Physical address:** 114 Haygood Avenue, Lexington SC. **Fax:** 803/359-3008. **Contact:** Gina A. McCuen, CPC, Owner. **Description:** A permanent employment agency that also provides temporary and temp-to-hire placements. Company pays fee. **Specializes in the areas of:** Accounting/Auditing; Administration; Computer Science/Software; Finance. **Positions commonly filled include:** Accountant/Auditor; Administrative Assistant; Administrative Manager; Advertising Clerk; Architect; Bank Officer/Manager; Biological Scientist; Bookkeeper; Branch Manager; Buyer; Chemical Engineer; Chemist; Civil Engineer; Claim Representative; Clerk; Commercial Artist; Computer Operator; Computer Programmer; Credit Manager; Customer Service Representative; Data Entry Clerk; Dietician/Nutritionist; Draftsperson; Driver; EDP Specialist; Electrical/Electronics Engineer; Factory Worker; Financial Analyst; Human Resources Manager; Industrial Engineer; Insurance Agent/Broker; Legal Secretary; Light Industrial Worker; Management Trainee; Marketing Specialist; Mechanical Engineer; Medical Secretary; Metallurgical Engineer; MIS Specialist; Nurse; Public Relations Specialist; Quality Control Supervisor; Receptionist; Reporter; Sales Representative; Secretary; Software Engineer; Stenographer; Systems Analyst; Technician; Typist/Word Processor. **Corporate headquarters location:** Dallas TX. **Other U.S. locations:** Nationwide. **Average salary range of placements:** $20,000 - $29,999. **Number of placements per year:** 200 - 499.

SOUTHERN PERSONNEL
989 Knox Abbott Drive, Casey SC 29023. 843/791-4131. **Contact:** Manager. **Description:** A permanent placement agency.

THE STROMAN COMPANY
P.O. Box 701, Mauldin SC 29662. 864/297-4387. **Fax:** 864/297-7182. **Contact:** Michael Stroman,

President. **E-mail address:** mstroman@mindspring.com. **Description:** A permanent employment agency. Company pays fee. **Specializes in the areas of:** Apparel; Engineering; Fashion; Finance; General Management; Industrial. **Positions commonly filled include:** Chemical Engineer; Civil Engineer; Computer Programmer; Design Engineer; Designer; Electrical/Electronics Engineer; Environmental Engineer; Human Resources Specialist; Industrial Engineer; Mechanical Engineer; Public Relations Specialist; Software Engineer. **Average salary range of placements:** More than $50,000. **Number of placements per year:** 100 - 199.

TRS (TOTAL RECRUITING SERVICES)
P.O. Box 26147, Greenville SC 29616. 864/297-3110. **Contact:** Manager. **Description:** A permanent employment agency that also offers some temporary and executive placements. **Specializes in the areas of:** Administration; Clerical; Engineering; Technical.

TALENT TREE STAFFING SERVICES
25 Woods Lake Road, Suite 222, Greenville SC 29607. 864/233-4301. **Contact:** Branch Manager. **Description:** A permanent employment agency that also provides temporary placements. **Positions commonly filled include:** Administrative Worker/Clerk; Clerk; Computer Operator; Construction Trade Worker; Data Entry Clerk; Driver; Factory Worker; Light Industrial Worker; Receptionist; Typist/Word Processor. **Number of placements per year:** 1000+.

TEMPORARY EMPLOYMENT AGENCIES

ACCEL TEMPORARY SERVICES
P.O. Box 10422, Greenville SC 29603. 864/271-8638. **Contact:** Manager. **Description:** A temporary agency. Company pays fee. **Specializes in the areas of:** Computer Hardware/Software; Engineering; Manufacturing; Personnel/Labor Relations; Technical. **Positions commonly filled include:** Aerospace Engineer; Biological Scientist; Biomedical Engineer; Ceramics Engineer; Chemical Engineer; Chemist; Civil Engineer; Draftsperson; Electrical/Electronics Engineer; Human Resources Manager; Industrial Designer; Industrial Engineer; Mechanical Engineer; Metallurgical Engineer; Quality Control Supervisor; Statistician; Technician. **Number of placements per year:** 50 - 99.

CAROLINA PERSONNEL SERVICES
600 Columbia Avenue, Lexington SC 29072. 803/356-7004. **Contact:** Manager. **Description:** A temporary agency that also offers some permanent placements and executive search services. **Specializes in the areas of:** Accounting/Auditing; Clerical; Light Industrial; Secretarial. **Positions commonly filled include:** Secretary.

CHARLES FOSTER STAFFING, INC.
7301 Rivers Avenue, Suite 240, North Charleston SC 29406-4650. 803/572-8100. **Fax:** 803/572-3574. **Contact:** Dottie Karst, President. **E-mail address:** cfstaff@ix.netcom.com. **Description:** A temporary agency that also provides permanent placements. Company pays fee. **Specializes in the areas of:** Sales; Secretarial; Technical. **Positions commonly filled include:** Accountant/Auditor; Administrative Manager; Advertising Clerk; Attorney; Bank Officer/Manager; Biochemist; Biological Scientist; Biomedical Engineer; Branch Manager; Budget Analyst; Buyer; Chemical Engineer; Civil Engineer; Clerical Supervisor; Clinical Lab Technician; Computer Programmer; Cost Estimator; Credit Manager; Customer Service Representative; Design Engineer; Designer; Draftsperson; Electrical/Electronics Engineer; Environmental Engineer; Financial Analyst; General Manager; Health Services Manager; Human Resources Specialist; Industrial Engineer; Manufacturer's/Wholesaler's Sales Rep.; Market Research Analyst; MIS Specialist; Paralegal; Purchasing Agent/Manager; Quality Control Supervisor; Services Sales Representative; Software Engineer; Systems Analyst; Technical Writer/Editor; Typist/Word Processor. **Benefits available to temporary workers:** Paid Holidays; Paid Vacation. **Average salary range of placements:** $30,000 - $50,000. **Number of placements per year:** 50 - 99.

HEALTH FORCE
P.O. Box 3548, Columbia SC 29230. 843/779-4555. **Contact:** Manager. **Description:** A temporary agency. **Specializes in the areas of:** Health/Medical.

JERMAN PERSONNEL SERVICES, INC.
455 St. Andrews Road, Suite C4, Columbia SC 29210. 843/798-0556. **Fax:** 803/731-7771. **Contact:** Tony Cashion, Vice President. **Description:** A temporary agency that also provides permanent placements. Company pays fee. **Specializes in the areas of:** Banking; Legal; Publishing; Sales; Secretarial. **Positions commonly filled include:** Customer Service Representative; Electrician; Manufacturer's/Wholesaler's Sales Rep.; Medical Records Technician; Paralegal; Typist/Word Processor.

PINDRUM STAFFING SERVICE INC.
P.O. Box 17296, Greenville SC 29606. 864/675-6024. **Fax:** 864/675-6119. **Contact:** Jonathan Pinson, General Manager. **Description:** A temporary agency. Company pays fee. **Specializes in the areas of:** Computer Science/Software; Finance; Health/Medical; Manufacturing; Personnel/Labor Relations; Secretarial; Technical. **Positions commonly filled include:** Administrative Manager; Automotive Mechanic; Blue-Collar Worker Supervisor; Budget Analyst; Buyer; Claim Representative; Clerical Supervisor; Computer Programmer; Customer Service Representative; Dental Assistant/Dental Hygienist; Design Engineer; Human Resources Specialist; Purchasing Agent/Manager; Quality Control Supervisor; Restaurant/Food Service Manager; Technical Writer/Editor; Typist/Word Processor. **Benefits available to temporary workers:** Bonus Award/Plan; Medical Insurance; Paid Holidays; Paid Vacation. **Number of placements per year:** 200 - 499.

ROPER SERVICES
P.O. Box 21009, Columbia SC 29221. 843/798-8500. **Physical address:** 220 Executive Center Drive, Columbia SC. **Contact:** Manager. **Description:** A temporary agency. Company pays fee. **Specializes in the areas of:** Clerical; Construction; Manufacturing; Sales; Secretarial. **Positions commonly filled include:** Bookkeeper; Ceramics Engineer; Civil Engineer; Clerk; Construction Trade Worker; Data Entry Clerk; Draftsperson; Electrical/Electronics Engineer; Factory Worker; Human Resources Manager; Industrial Designer; Industrial Engineer; Legal Secretary; Light Industrial Worker; Mechanical Engineer; Medical Secretary; Receptionist; Secretary; Stenographer; Telemarketer; Typist/Word Processor. **Number of placements per year:** 1000+.

SMITH TEMPS/SMITH PERSONNEL, INC.
P.O. Box 5815, Hilton Head Island SC 29938. 843/785-4604. **Fax:** 843/785-4639. **Contact:** Joni Tarr, Manager. **E-mail address:** smthper@sprynet.com. **Description:** A temporary agency. Smith Temps is a division of Smith Personnel, Inc., which handles permanent placement. Company pays fee. **Specializes in the areas of:** Accounting/Auditing; Administration;

Architecture/Construction; Computer Science/ Software; Food Industry; General Management; Insurance; Legal; Marketing; Sales; Secretarial. **Positions commonly filled include:** Accountant/ Auditor; Brokerage Clerk; Clerical Supervisor; Customer Service Rep.; General Manager; Hotel Manager; Human Resources Specialist; Landscape Architect; Management Trainee; Medical Records Technician; Paralegal; Property and Real Estate Manager; Purchasing Agent/Manager; Restaurant/Food Service Manager; Typist/Word Processor.

STAFFING SOLUTIONS
2000 Centerpoint Drive, Suite 2245, Columbia SC 29210. 843/798-1700. **Contact:** Anne Stewart, Branch Manager. **Description:** A temporary agency that also provides permanent placements. The agency focuses on office and clerical work, light industrial, and health services. Company pays fee. **Specializes in the areas of:** Accounting/Auditing; Health/Medical; Industrial; Sales; Secretarial. **Positions commonly filled include:** Administrative Manager; Claim Representative; Clerical Supervisor; Customer Service Representative; EKG Technician; Licensed Practical Nurse; Management Trainee; Registered Nurse. **Corporate headquarters location:** Dallas TX. **Average salary range of placements:** Less than $20,000. **Number of placements per year:** 1000+.

STAFFMARK
P.O. Box 2952, Spartanburg SC 29304. 864/585-6562. **Fax:** 864/573-5047. **Contact:** Kathy Chandler, General Manager. **Description:** A temporary agency that also offers permanent and contract placements. Company pays fee. **Specializes in the areas of:** Industrial; Manufacturing; Secretarial; Technical. **Positions commonly filled include:** Administrative Assistant; Blue-Collar Worker Supervisor; Bookkeeper; Clerical Supervisor; Clerk; Computer Programmer; Construction Trade Worker; Customer Service Representative; Data Entry Clerk; Draftsperson; Electrical/Electronics Engineer; Environmental Engineer; Factory Worker; General Manager; Human Resources Specialist; Industrial Engineer; Industrial Production Manager; Legal Secretary; Light Industrial Worker; Operations/Production Manager; Paralegal; Purchasing Agent/Manager; Receptionist; Restaurant/ Food Service Manager; Secretary; Software Engineer; Stenographer; Surveyor; Transportation/Traffic Specialist; Typist/Word Processor. **Benefits available to temporary workers:** Medical Insurance; Paid Holidays; Paid Vacation. **Average salary range of placements:** Less than $20,000. **Number of placements per year:** 200 - 499.

TECHNICAL SOUTH INC.
100 Executive Center Drive, Greenville SC 29615. 864/288-8105. **Contact:** Manager. **Description:** A temporary employment agency. **Specializes in the areas of:** Engineering; Industrial; Manufacturing. **Positions commonly filled include:** Buyer; Ceramics Engineer; Chemical Engineer; Civil Engineer; Computer Programmer; Construction Contractor; Cost Estimator; Design Engineer; Designer; Draftsperson; Electrical/ Electronics Engineer; Environmental Engineer; Industrial Engineer; Materials Engineer; Mechanical Engineer; Metallurgical Engineer; Purchasing Agent/Manager; Software Engineer; Structural Engineer; Surveyor; Technical Writer/Editor.

TRANSWORLD SERVICES GROUP
123 West Antrim Drive, Greenville SC 29607. 864/458-7181. **Contact:** Manager. **Description:** A temporary agency. Company pays fee. **Specializes in the areas of:** Accounting/Auditing; Secretarial. **Positions commonly filled include:** Bank Officer/Manager; Branch Manager; Human Resources Specialist; Industrial Engineer; Technical Writer/Editor; Typist/Word Processor. **Benefits available to temporary workers:** Bonus Award/Plan; Medical Insurance; Paid Vacation. **Other area locations:** Greenville SC. **Average salary range of placements:** $20,000 - $29,999. **Number of placements per year:** 200 - 499.

CONTRACT SERVICES FIRMS

AIDE INC. DESIGN SERVICES
P.O. Box 6226, Greenville SC 29606. 864/244-6123. **Toll-free phone:** 800/968-8971. **Fax:** 864/322-1040. **Contact:** Ed Bamford, Recruiting Manager. **E-mail address:** recruit@aide.com. **World Wide Web address:** http://www.aide.com. **Description:** A contract services firm. Company pays fee. **Specializes in the areas of:** Computer Science/Software; Engineering; Manufacturing. **Positions commonly filled include:** Architect; Ceramics Engineer; Chemical Engineer; Civil Engineer; Computer Programmer; Design Engineer; Designer; Draftsperson; Electrical/Electronics Engineer; Environmental Engineer; Industrial Engineer; Materials Engineer; Mechanical Engineer; Metallurgical Engineer; MIS Specialist; Software Engineer; Structural Engineer; Systems Analyst. **Benefits available to temporary workers:** 401(k); Dental Insurance; Life Insurance; Medical Insurance; Paid Holidays; Paid Vacation. **Number of placements per year:** 200 - 499.

CDI CORPORATION
150 Executive Center Drive, Suite 19, Greenville SC 29615. 864/676-9150. **Contact:** Manager. **World Wide Web address:** http://www.cdicorp.com. **Description:** A contract services firm. **Specializes in the areas of:** Engineering; Technical. **Corporate headquarters location:** Philadelphia PA. **Other U.S. locations:** Nationwide. **International locations:** Worldwide.

CDI INFORMATION SERVICES
1517 Gregg Street, Columbia SC 29201. 843/988-0012. **Fax:** 843/988-0096. **Contact:** Manager. **World Wide Web address:** http://www.cdicorp.com. **Description:** A contract services firm. **Specializes in the areas of:** Computer Science/Software. **Corporate headquarters location:** Philadelphia PA. **Other U.S. locations:** Nationwide. **International locations:** Worldwide.

COMFORCE TECHNICAL SERVICES, INC.
P.O. Box 221, Greenville SC 29615. 864/987-9625. **Fax:** 864/987-9621. **Contact:** Manager. **Description:** A contract services firm. **Specializes in the areas of:** Process Technology.

SOUTH DAKOTA

EXECUTIVE SEARCH FIRMS

MANAGEMENT RECRUITERS INTERNATIONAL
2600 South Minnesota Avenue, Suite 202, Sioux Falls SD 57105. 605/334-9291. **Fax:** 605/334-9826. **Contact:** Manager. **Description:** An executive search firm. **Specializes in the areas of:** Banking; Computer Science/Software; Engineering.

REGENCY RECRUITING, INC.
P.O. Box 77, North Sioux City SD 57049. 605/232-3205. **Fax:** 605/232-3159. **Contact:** Brad Moore, CPC, President. **E-mail address:** rgncyrctg@aol.com. **Description:** An executive search firm focusing on the placement of computer and computer management personnel in the Midwest. Company pays fee. **Specializes in the areas of:** Computer Science/Software. **Positions commonly filled include:** Computer Programmer; Management Analyst/Consultant; MIS Specialist; Systems Analyst. **Number of placements per year:** 50 - 99.

STAFF SEARCH
312 9th Avenue SE, Suite B, Watertown SD 57201. 605/882-3406. **Fax:** 605/882-4490. **Contact:** Manager. **Description:** An executive search firm that focuses on the placement of computer professionals. **Specializes in the areas of:** Computer Science/Software.

PERMANENT EMPLOYMENT AGENCIES

CAREERS UNLIMITED
P.O. Box 89132, Sioux Falls SD 57105. 605/336-9800. **Fax:** 605/336-9890. **Contact:** Carol Dane, Owner/Manager. **Description:** A full-service employment agency handling permanent, temporary, and temp-to-hire positions, as well as contract work. Careers Unlimited also networks with several executive search firms. Founded in 1986. Company pays fee. **Specializes in the areas of:** Accounting/Auditing; Banking; Finance; Food Industry; General Management; Sales. **Positions commonly filled include:** Accountant/Auditor; Administrative Manager; Bank Officer/Manager; Blue-Collar Worker Supervisor; Branch Manager; Claim Representative; Clerical Supervisor; Computer Programmer; Cost Estimator; Credit Manager; Customer Service Representative; Draftsperson; Electrical/Electronics Engineer; Financial Analyst; General Manager; Health Services Manager; Hotel Manager; Industrial Engineer; Management Trainee; Manufacturer's/Wholesaler's Sales Rep.; Mechanical Engineer; Medical Records Technician; MIS Specialist; Paralegal; Public Relations Specialist; Purchasing Agent/Manager; Restaurant/Food Service Manager; Services Sales Representative; Software Engineer; Telecommunications Manager; Typist/Word Processor; Underwriter/Assistant Underwriter. **Average salary range of placements:** $20,000 - $29,999. **Number of placements per year:** 50 - 99.

SNELLING PERSONNEL SERVICES
2720 West 12th Street, Suite 200, Sioux Falls SD 57104. 605/334-1434. **Contact:** Staffing Specialist. **Description:** A permanent employment agency. **Specializes in the areas of:** Accounting/Auditing; Banking; Engineering; Hotel/Restaurant; Sales; Secretarial. **Other U.S. locations:** Nationwide.

WESTERN PLAINS HEALTH CONSORTIUM
522 7th Street, Suite 202, Rapid City SD 57701. **Toll-free phone:** 800/248-5111. **Fax:** 605/394-6737. **Contact:** Recruitment Coordinator. **Description:** A permanent employment agency. **Specializes in the areas of:** Health/Medical. **Positions commonly filled include:** Clinical Lab Technician; Licensed Practical Nurse; Occupational Therapist; Physical Therapist; Radiological Technologist; Registered Nurse. **Number of placements per year:** 1 - 49.

TEMPORARY EMPLOYMENT AGENCIES

AVAILABILITY EMPLOYMENT INC.
2701 South Minnesota Avenue, Suite 6, Sioux Falls SD 57105. 605/336-0353. **Contact:** Recruiting. **Description:** A temporary agency that also offers permanent placements. **Specializes in the areas of:** Administration; Computer Programming.

OLSTEN STAFFING SERVICES
209 East St. Joseph, Rapid City SD 57701. 605/348-8010. **Contact:** Carole Conrad, Owner. **Description:** A temporary agency. **Specializes in the areas of:** Accounting/Auditing; Banking; Clerical; Insurance; Sales. **Positions commonly filled include:** Accountant/Auditor; Administrative Worker/Clerk; Claim Representative; Clerk; Computer Operator; Construction Trade Worker; Credit Manager; Customer Service Representative; Data Processor; Insurance Agent/Broker; Marketing Specialist; Nurse; Public Relations Specialist; Receptionist; Sales Representative; Secretary; Stenographer; Typist/Word Processor.

CAREER/OUTPLACEMENT COUNSELING FIRMS

CAREER PLANNING CENTER
421 South Main Street, Aberdeen SD 57401-4324. 605/626-2298. **Fax:** 605/626-3154. **Contact:** Jeff Mitchell, Director. **Description:** A career/outplacement counseling firm. Founded in 1985. **Positions commonly filled include:** Accountant/Auditor; Automotive Mechanic; Blue-Collar Worker Supervisor; Clinical Lab Technician; Counselor; Electrician; Emergency Medical Technician; General Manager; Human Service Worker; Management Trainee; Preschool Worker; Services Sales Representative; Social Worker; Typist/Word Processor. **Average salary range of placements:** Less than $20,000. **Number of placements per year:** 100 - 199.

TENNESSEE

EXECUTIVE SEARCH FIRMS

ACCOUNTANTS & BOOKKEEPERS
310 Walnut Bend Road, Cordova TN 38018-7283. 901/755-6444. **Contact:** Diane Shipp, Office Manager. **Description:** An executive search firm. **NOTE:** All resumes should be sent to P.O. Box 38304, Memphis TN 38183. **Specializes in the areas of:** Accounting/Auditing; Bookkeeping.

ADVANCED COMPUTER CAREERS
5115 Maryland Way, Brentwood TN 37027. 615/377-0776. **Contact:** Manager. **Description:** An executive search firm. **Specializes in the areas of:** Computer Science/Software.

ANDERSON McINTYRE PERSONNEL SERVICES
6148 Lee Highway, Suite 100, Chattanooga TN 37421. 423/894-9571. **Fax:** 423/892-7413. **Contact:** Maureen McIntyre, Owner. **Description:** An executive search firm. The firm is also a full-service employment agency offering career counseling and contract services. **Specializes in the areas of:** Administration; Advertising; Architecture/Construction; Computer Science/Software; Finance; General Management; Health/Medical; Legal; Manufacturing; Sales; Secretarial. **Positions commonly filled include:** Accountant/Auditor; Administrative Manager; Advertising Clerk; Branch Manager; Claim Representative; Clerical Supervisor; Computer Programmer; Credit Manager; Draftsperson; Management Trainee; Medical Records Technician; Paralegal; Physical Therapist; Physician; Systems Analyst; Travel Agent; Typist/Word Processor. **Average salary range of placements:** $30,000 - $50,000. **Number of placements per year:** 100 - 199.

AUSTIN-ALLEN COMPANY
8127 Walnut Grove Road, Cordova TN 38018. 901/756-0900. **Fax:** 901/756-0933. **Contact:** Mr. C.A. Cupp, General Manager. **Description:** An executive search firm operating on a contingency basis. Company pays fee. **Specializes in the areas of:** Accounting/Auditing; Engineering; Personnel/Labor Relations. **Positions commonly filled include:** Accountant/Auditor; Chemical Engineer; Electrical/Electronics Engineer; Human Resources Manager; Industrial Engineer; Industrial Production Manager; Manufacturing Engineer; Materials Engineer; Mechanical Engineer; Metallurgical Engineer; Purchasing Agent/Manager; Quality Control Supervisor. **Number of placements per year:** 100 - 199.

BAKER & BAKER EMPLOYMENT SERVICE
1191 West Main Street, Hendersonville TN 37075. **Contact:** Owner. **Description:** An executive search firm operating on a contingency basis. Company pays fee. **Specializes in the areas of:** Engineering; Industrial; Manufacturing. **Positions commonly filled include:** Accountant/Auditor; Ceramics Engineer; Chemical Engineer; Civil Engineer; Design Engineer; Electrical/Electronics Engineer; Environmental Engineer; Human Resources Specialist; Industrial Engineer; Management Trainee; Materials Engineer; Mechanical Engineer; Metallurgical Engineer; Occupational Therapist; Physical Therapist; Quality Control Supervisor; Technical Writer/Editor. **Average salary range of placements:** $30,000 - $50,000. **Number of placements per year:** 50 - 99.

B.K. BARNES & ASSOCIATES
475 Metroplex Drive, Building 400, Suite 405, Nashville TN 37211-3143. 615/832-9935. **Contact:** Mr. B.K. Barnes, President. **Description:** An executive search firm. Company pays fee. **Specializes in the areas of:** Accounting/Auditing; Administration; Banking; Engineering; Finance; General Management; Health/Medical; Manufacturing; Secretarial. **Positions commonly filled include:** Accountant/Auditor; Actuary; Bank Officer/Manager; Ceramics Engineer; Computer Programmer; Credit Manager; Electrical/Electronics Engineer; Financial Analyst; General Manager; Human Resources Manager; Industrial Engineer; Materials Engineer; Mechanical Engineer; Metallurgical Engineer; Pharmacist; Physician; Restaurant/Food Service Manager; Systems Analyst. **Number of placements per year:** 100 - 199.

BISSONETTE & ASSOCIATES
1233 Courtfield Road, Knoxville TN 37922. 423/691-2700. **Fax:** 423/694-6282. **Contact:** William T. Bissonette Sr., President. **Description:** An executive search firm. Company pays fee. **Specializes in the areas of:** Sales. **Positions commonly filled include:** Sales Rep. **Number of placements per year:** 1 - 49.

CARROLL & ASSOCIATES
4646 Poplar Avenue, Suite 418, Memphis TN 38117. 901/683-1332. **Contact:** Manager. **Description:** An executive search firm. **Specializes in the areas of:** Accounting/Auditing; Administration.

COOK ASSOCIATES INTERNATIONAL, INC.
P.O. Box 962, Brentwood TN 37027. 615/373-8264. **Fax:** 615/371-8215. **Contact:** Stephen G. Cook, General Manager. **E-mail address:** cai@bellsouth.net. **Description:** An executive search firm operating on both retainer and contingency bases. **Specializes in the areas of:** Accounting/Auditing; Administration; Computer Science/Software; Engineering; Health/Medical; Industrial; Insurance; Legal; Manufacturing; Personnel/Labor Relations; Publishing. **Positions commonly filled include:** Accountant/Auditor; Actuary; Attorney; Biomedical Engineer; Budget Analyst; Buyer; Chemical Engineer; Computer Programmer; Cost Estimator; Design Engineer; Dietician/Nutritionist; Electrical/Electronics Engineer; Electrician; Environmental Engineer; Financial Analyst; General Manager; Health Services Manager; Hotel Manager; Human Resources Specialist; Industrial Engineer; Mechanical Engineer; MIS Specialist; Occupational Therapist; Paralegal; Physical Therapist; Quality Control Supervisor; Registered Nurse; Software Engineer; Stationary Engineer; Systems Analyst. **Corporate headquarters location:** This Location. **Other U.S. locations:** Hopkinsville KY; Greenville SC. **Number of placements per year:** 100 - 199.

CRAIG SERVICES
P.O. Box 1202, Morristown TN 37816. 423/587-3189. **Contact:** Manager. **Description:** An executive search firm.

F-O-R-T-U-N-E PERSONNEL CONSULTANTS
2700 South Roan Street, Suite 206, Johnson City TN 37601. 423/926-1124. **Fax:** 423/926-1123. **Contact:** Walter E. Engel, President/CEO. **Description:** An executive search firm. Company pays fee. **Specializes in the areas of:** Accounting/Auditing; Engineering; Finance; General Management; Industrial; Manufacturing; Personnel/Labor Relations; Technical. **Positions commonly filled include:** Accountant/Auditor; Biomedical Engineer; Budget Analyst; Buyer; Ceramics Engineer; Chemical Engineer; Cost Estimator; Credit Manager; Customer Service Representative; Design Engineer; Financial Analyst; General Manager; Human Resources Specialist; Industrial Engineer; Industrial Production Manager; Materials Engineer; Mechanical Engineer; Metallurgical Engineer; Operations/Production Manager; Petroleum

Engineer; Purchasing Agent/Manager; Quality Control Supervisor; Software Engineer; Systems Analyst. **Corporate headquarters location:** New York NY. **Other U.S. locations:** Nationwide. **Average salary range of placements:** More than $50,000. **Number of placements per year:** 1 - 49.

F-O-R-T-U-N-E PERSONNEL CONSULTANTS
5726 Marlin Road, Franklin Building, Suite 212, Chattanooga TN 37411. 423/855-0444. **Fax:** 423/892-0083. **Contact:** Brenda Dickson, President. **Description:** An executive search firm operating on both retainer and contingency bases. Company pays fee. **Specializes in the areas of:** Accounting/Auditing; Administration; Engineering; Manufacturing; Personnel/Labor Relations. **Positions commonly filled include:** Accountant/Auditor; Buyer; Chemical Engineer; Chemist; Civil Engineer; Computer Programmer; Design Engineer; Electrical/Electronics Engineer; Environmental Engineer; Financial Analyst; General Manager; Human Resources Specialist; Industrial Engineer; Industrial Production Manager; Mechanical Engineer; Metallurgical Engineer; Purchasing Agent/Manager; Quality Control Supervisor; Systems Analyst; Transportation/Traffic Specialist. **Corporate headquarters location:** New York NY. **Other U.S. locations:** Nationwide. **Average salary range of placements:** $30,000 - $50,000. **Number of placements per year:** 1 - 49.

F-O-R-T-U-N-E PERSONNEL CONSULTANTS OF NASHVILLE
125 Belle Forest Circle, Suite 205, Nashville TN 37221. 615/662-9110. **Fax:** 615/662-9140. **Contact:** Tom Oglesby, President. **Description:** An executive search firm. Company pays fee. **Specializes in the areas of:** Manufacturing. **Positions commonly filled include:** Design Engineer; Electrical/Electronics Engineer; General Manager; Human Resources Manager; Industrial Engineer; Mechanical Engineer; Purchasing Agent/Manager; Quality Control Supervisor.

GROS EXECUTIVE SEARCH INC.
155 Franklin Road, Suite 181, Brentwood TN 37027. 615/661-4568. **Contact:** Manager. **Description:** An executive search firm. **Specializes in the areas of:** Plastics.

ROBERT HALF INTERNATIONAL/ACCOUNTEMPS
1111 Northshore Drive, Suite N525, Knoxville TN 37919. 423/588-6500. **Contact:** Manager. **World Wide Web address:** http://www.roberthalf.com. **Description:** An executive search firm. Accountemps (also at this location) provides temporary placements. **Specializes in the areas of:** Accounting/Auditing. **Corporate headquarters location:** Menlo Park CA. **Other area locations:**

- 6750 Poplar Avenue, Suite 701, Memphis TN 38138. 901/753-7600.

HAMILTON RYKER COMPANY
P.O Box 1068, Martin TN 38237. 901/587-3161. **Toll-free phone:** 800/644-9449. **Fax:** 901/588-0810. **Contact:** Professional Staffing Manager. **Description:** An executive search firm operating on both retainer and contingency bases. Company pays fee. **Specializes in the areas of:** Accounting/Auditing; Administration; Architecture/Construction; Computer Science/Software; Engineering; General Management; Industrial; Manufacturing; Personnel/Labor Relations; Technical. **Positions commonly filled include:** Accountant/Auditor; Architect; Budget Analyst; Buyer; Chemical Engineer; Civil Engineer; Computer Programmer; Cost Estimator; Credit Manager; Design Engineer; Designer; Draftsperson; Electrical/Electronics Engineer; Environmental Engineer; Financial Analyst; General Manager; Human Resources Specialist; Industrial Engineer; Industrial Production Manager; Management Analyst/Consultant; Management Trainee; Market Research Analyst; Mechanical Engineer; Metallurgical Engineer; Mining Engineer; MIS Specialist; Operations/Production Manager; Purchasing Agent/Manager; Quality Control Supervisor; Software Engineer; Structural Engineer; Systems Analyst. **Corporate headquarters location:** This Location. **Other area locations:** Memphis TN; Nashville TN.

HEALTHCARE RECRUITERS INTERNATIONAL
185 South Center Street, Suite 200, Collierville TN 38017. 901/853-0900. **Fax:** 901/853-6500. **Contact:** Manager. **Description:** An executive search firm. **Specializes in the areas of:** Health/Medical.

HELFER EXECUTIVE CONSULTANTS
P.O. Box 50239, Nashville TN 37205-0239. 615/356-2777. **Contact:** Manager. **Description:** A generalist executive search firm operating on a retainer basis.

HESTER & ASSOCIATES
100 Cherokee Boulevard, Suite 2108, Chattanooga TN 37405. 423/265-0148. **Fax:** 423/265-6418. **Contact:** Mike Schoonover, President. **E-mail address:** mschoon500@aol.com. **Description:** An executive search firm operating on a retainer basis. The firm concentrates on industrial/manufacturing environments. Founded in 1984. Company pays fee. **Specializes in the areas of:** Computer Science/Software; Engineering; Finance; General Management; Industrial; Manufacturing; Personnel/Labor Relations; Sales; Technical. **Positions commonly filled include:** Aerospace Engineer; Chemical Engineer; Computer Programmer; Credit Manager; Design Engineer; Engineer; General Manager; Human Resources Manager; Industrial Production Manager; Purchasing Agent/Manager; Quality Control Supervisor; Systems Analyst; Telecommunications Manager. **Average salary range of placements:** More than $50,000. **Number of placements per year:** 50 - 99.

RANDALL HOWARD & ASSOCIATES, INC.
P.O. Box 382397, Memphis TN 38183-2397. 901/754-3333. **Fax:** 901/758-5578. **Contact:** Randall C. Howard, CPC, President. **Description:** An executive search firm for senior management. Company pays fee. **Average salary range of placements:** More than $50,000. **Number of placements per year:** 1 - 49.

INFORMATION SYSTEMS GROUP, INC.
5100 Poplar Avenue, 27th Floor, Memphis TN 38137. 901/821-7493. **Contact:** Harold Lepman, President. **Description:** An executive search firm. Company pays fee. **Specializes in the areas of:** Computer Science/Software. **Positions commonly filled include:** Computer Programmer; Systems Analyst. **Number of placements per year:** 1 - 49.

J&D RESOURCES (JDR)
6555 Quince Road, Suite 425, Memphis TN 38119. 901/753-0500. **Fax:** 901/753-0550. **Contact:** Jill T. Herrin, President. **Description:** An executive search firm. J&D Resources (JDR) provides permanent and contract information systems positions. Founded in 1987. Company pays fee. **Specializes in the areas of:** Administration; Computer Science/Software. **Positions commonly filled include:** Computer Programmer; MIS Specialist; Software Engineer; Systems Analyst. **Average salary range of placements:** $30,000 - $50,000. **Number of placements per year:** 50 - 99.

KOERNER & ASSOCIATES, INC.
P.O. Box 2126, Brentwood TN 37024. 615/371-6162. **Contact:** Pam L. Koerner, President. **Description:** An executive search firm that handles attorney placement at all levels and for all practice areas, including corporate in-house, management, and

financial institutions. Services include consulting and mergers. Founded in 1989. **Specializes in the areas of:** Legal. **Positions commonly filled include:** Attorney. **Average salary range of placements:** More than $50,000. **Number of placements per year:** 1 - 49.

MANAGEMENT RECRUITERS INTERNATIONAL
5495 Winchester Road, Suite 5, Memphis TN 38115. 901/794-3130. **Fax:** 901/794-5671. **Contact:** Wally Watson, General Manager. **Description:** An executive search firm for logistics management and warehouse/distribution management. Company pays fee. **Specializes in the areas of:** Accounting/Auditing; Engineering; Finance; General Management; Industrial; Logistics; Manufacturing; Personnel/Labor Relations; Sales. **Positions commonly filled include:** Accountant/ Auditor; Chemical Engineer; Electrical/Electronics Engineer; Financial Analyst; General Manager; Human Resources Manager; Industrial Engineer; Mechanical Engineer; Operations/Production Manager; Quality Control Supervisor; Transportation/Traffic Specialist. **Number of placements per year:** 1 - 49.

MANAGEMENT RECRUITERS INTERNATIONAL SALES CONSULTANTS OF CHATTANOOGA
7010 Lee Highway, Suite 216, Chattanooga TN 37421. 423/894-5500. **Fax:** 423/894-1177. **Contact:** Bill Cooper, General Manager. **Description:** An executive search firm operating on a contingency basis. Sales Consultants is a division of Management Recruiters International. A third division, CompuSearch, also has an office based at this location. Founded in 1980. Company pays fee. **Specializes in the areas of:** Administration; Computer Science/Software; Engineering; General Management; Manufacturing; Sales; Technical. **Positions commonly filled include:** Chemical Engineer; Chemist; Computer Programmer; Design Engineer; Environmental Engineer; General Manager; Industrial Engineer; Information Systems Consultant; Internet Services Manager; Manufacturer's/Wholesaler's Sales Rep.; Mechanical Engineer; MIS Specialist; Quality Control Supervisor; Services Sales Rep.; Software Engineer; Systems Analyst. **Corporate headquarters location:** Cleveland OH. **Other U.S. locations:** Nationwide. **Average salary range of placements:** $30,000 - $50,000. **Number of placements per year:** 100 - 199.

MANAGEMENT RECRUITERS OF CHATTANOOGA (NORTH)
5211 Highway 153, Suite H, Hixson TN 37343. 423/877-4040. **Fax:** 423/877-4466. **Contact:** Mr. C.E. Ensminger, President. **Description:** An executive search firm operating on a contingency basis. Company pays fee. **Specializes in the areas of:** Accounting/Auditing; Administration; Computer Science/Software; Engineering; Finance; Industrial; Manufacturing; Personnel/Labor Relations; Sales. **Positions commonly filled include:** Accountant/ Auditor; Branch Manager; Budget Analyst; Buyer; Ceramics Engineer; Chemical Engineer; Chemist; Computer Programmer; Design Engineer; Draftsperson; Financial Analyst; General Manager; Human Resources Specialist; Industrial Engineer; Materials Engineer; Mechanical Engineer; Metallurgical Engineer; MIS Specialist; Operations/Production Manager; Purchasing Agent/Manager; Quality Control Supervisor; Software Engineer; Telecommunications Manager. **Other U.S. locations:** Nationwide. **Average salary range of placements:** $30,000 - $90,000. **Number of placements per year:** 100 - 199.

MANAGEMENT RECRUITERS OF FRANKLIN
236 Public Square, Suite 201, Franklin TN 37064-2520. 615/791-4391. **Fax:** 615/791-4769. **Contact:** Roger H. Marriott, President. **Description:** An executive search firm operating on a contingency basis. Founded in 1989. Company pays fee. **Specializes in the areas of:** Printing; Publishing. **Positions commonly filled include:** Cost Estimator; Customer Service Rep.; General Manager; Operations/ Production Manager; Purchasing Agent/Manager; Quality Control Supervisor; Sales Executive; Sales Manager; Sales Rep.; Systems Manager; Transportation/Traffic Specialist; Vice President of Sales. **Corporate headquarters location:** Cleveland OH. **Other U.S. locations:** Nationwide. **Average salary range of placements:** More than $50,000. **Number of placements per year:** 1 - 49.

MANAGEMENT RECRUITERS OF KNOXVILLE
9050B Executive Park Drive, Suite 16, Knoxville TN 37923. 423/694-1628. **Contact:** Manager. **Description:** An executive search firm. **Specializes in the areas of:** Accounting/Auditing; Administration; Advertising; Architecture/Construction; Banking; Communications; Computer Hardware/Software; Finance; Food Industry; General Management; Health/ Medical; Insurance; Legal; Manufacturing; Personnel/ Labor Relations; Publishing; Retail; Technical; Textiles; Transportation.

MANAGEMENT RECRUITERS OF LENOIR CITY
530 Highway 321 North, Suite 303, Lenoir City TN 37771. 423/986-3000. **Contact:** Mr. R.S. Strobo, Manager. **Description:** An executive search firm operating on a contingency basis. **Specializes in the areas of:** Engineering; Industrial; Light Industrial; Manufacturing. **Positions commonly filled include:** Applications Engineer; Design Engineer; Electrical/ Electronics Engineer; Industrial Engineer; Industrial Production Manager; Manufacturing Engineer; Mechanical Engineer; Quality Control Supervisor; Sales Engineer.

W.R. McLEOD & ASSOCIATES
201 Thompson Lane, Suite 8A, Nashville TN 37211. 615/333-2969. **Fax:** 615/331-3139. **Contact:** Manager. **Description:** An executive search firm. The firm focuses on the placement of salespeople and managers in the restaurant, printing and publishing, and food industries; and also places office, computer, and auto dealership personnel. Company pays fee. **Specializes in the areas of:** Computer Science/ Software; Food Industry; General Management; Health/Medical; Publishing; Retail; Sales; Secretarial. **Positions commonly filled include:** Computer Programmer; General Manager; Hotel Manager; Management Analyst/Consultant; Management Trainee; Restaurant/Food Service Manager; Services Sales Rep.; Systems Analyst. **Average salary range of placements:** $30,000 - $50,000. **Number of placements per year:** 100 - 199.

MEDICAL & DENTAL RESOURCES
1916 Patterson Street, Nashville TN 37203. 615/329-2033. **Contact:** Manager. **Description:** An executive search firm. **Specializes in the areas of:** Dental; Health/Medical.

MEMPHIS LEGAL PERSONNEL SERVICE
40 South Mid America Mall, Suite 1050, Memphis TN 38103. 901/527-3573. **Contact:** Manager. **Description:** An executive search firm. **Specializes in the areas of:** Legal.

THE MORGAN GROUP
P.O. Box 121153, Nashville TN 37212. 615/297-5272. **Fax:** 615/297-6945. **Contact:** E. Allen Morgan, Managing Partner. **Description:** An executive search firm. Founded in 1978. Company pays fee. **Specializes in the areas of:** Accounting/Auditing; Administration; Finance; General Management; Industrial; Manufacturing. **Positions commonly filled include:** Accountant/Auditor; Bank Officer/Manager; Budget Analyst; Cost Estimator; Financial Analyst; Financial

Services Sales Rep.; General Manager; Management Analyst/Consultant; Systems Analyst. **Average salary range of placements:** $30,000 - $50,000. **Number of placements per year:** 1 - 49.

PERSONNEL LINK
3935 Summer Avenue, Suite 3, Memphis TN 38122. 901/327-9182. **Fax:** 901/324-7603. **Contact:** Mrs. Leonell Klank, Recruiter. **Description:** An executive search firm operating on a contingency basis. Founded in 1993. Company pays fee. **Specializes in the areas of:** Accounting/Auditing; Advertising; Engineering; Food Industry; Health/Medical; Insurance; Legal; Manufacturing; Personnel/Labor Relations; Sales; Secretarial; Transportation. **Positions commonly filled include:** Accountant/Auditor; Adjuster; Administrative Manager; Advertising Clerk; Biological Scientist; Blue-Collar Worker Supervisor; Brokerage Clerk; Budget Analyst; Chemist; Chiropractor; Claim Rep.; Clerical Supervisor; Clinical Lab Technician; Computer Programmer; Counselor; Credit Manager; Customer Service Rep.; Dental Assistant/Hygienist; Dental Lab Technician; Draftsperson; EEG Technologist; EKG Technician; Electrician; Engineer; Financial Analyst; Food Scientist/Technologist; Health Services Manager; Hotel Manager; Human Resources Manager; Human Service Worker; Industrial Production Manager; Insurance Agent/Broker; Landscape Architect; Librarian; Licensed Practical Nurse; Management Trainee; Manufacturer's/Wholesaler's Sales Rep.; Medical Records Technician; Paralegal; Physical Therapist; Property and Real Estate Manager; Public Relations Specialist; Purchasing Agent/Manager; Quality Control Supervisor; Radiological Technologist; Recreational Therapist; Reporter; Respiratory Therapist; Restaurant/Food Service Manager; Securities Sales Rep.; Services Sales Rep.; Social Worker; Surgical Technician; Surveyor; Systems Analyst; Transportation/Traffic Specialist; Travel Agent; Underwriter/Assistant Underwriter; Water Transportation Specialist; Wholesale and Retail Buyer. **Average salary range of placements:** $20,000 - $29,999. **Number of placements per year:** 100 - 199.

PHYSICIAN PLACEMENT SERVICE OF AMERICA
906 Loggers Run Trail, Franklin TN 37069. 615/662-5435. **Toll-free phone:** 800/359-7421. **Contact:** Dennis Bottomley, Executive Director. **E-mail address:** ppsadb@aol.com. **World Wide Web address:** http://www.physician-placement.com. **Description:** An executive search firm. Founded in 1989. Company pays fee. **Specializes in the areas of:** Health/Medical. **Positions commonly filled include:** Physician. **Corporate headquarters location:** This Location. **Other U.S. locations:** Escondido CA; Acworth GA. **Average salary range of placements:** More than $50,000. **Number of placements per year:** 1 - 49.

PITTMAN GROUP
P.O. Box 1244, Collierville TN 38027. 901/854-6828. **Contact:** Manager. **Description:** An executive search firm. **Specializes in the areas of:** Information Systems.

QUEST INTERNATIONAL
123 Lake Haven Lane, Hendersonville TN 37075. 615/824-8900. **Fax:** 615/264-3333. **Contact:** Bill Griffin, President. **Description:** An executive search firm operating on a contingency basis. Company pays fee. **Specializes in the areas of:** Food Industry; Hotel/Restaurant. **Positions commonly filled include:** General Manager; Hotel Manager; Human Resources Specialist; Restaurant/Food Service Manager. **Corporate headquarters location:** Nashville TN. **Number of placements per year:** 1 - 49.

SALES CONSULTANTS
P.O. Box 38328, Memphis TN 38183. 901/751-1995. **Fax:** 901/751-9903. **Contact:** Wayne Williams, Managing Principal. **E-mail address:** info@saleshunter.com. **World Wide Web address:** http://www.saleshunter.com. **Description:** An executive search firm operating on a contingency basis. Company pays fee. **Specializes in the areas of:** Sales. **Positions commonly filled include:** Account Manager; Account Rep.; Sales Engineer; Sales Executive; Sales Manager; Sales Rep. **Average salary range of placements:** More than $50,000. **Number of placements per year:** 50 - 99.

SALES CONSULTANTS OF NASHVILLE
7003 Chadwick Drive, Suite 331, Brentwood TN 37023. 615/373-1111. **Contact:** Branch Manager. **Description:** An executive search firm. **Specializes in the areas of:** Accounting/Auditing; Administration; Advertising; Architecture/Construction; Banking; Communications; Computer Hardware/Software; Electrical; Engineering; Finance; Food Industry; General Management; Health/Medical; Insurance; Legal; Manufacturing; Operations Management; Personnel/Labor Relations; Publishing; Retail; Sales; Technical; Textiles; Transportation.

SNELLING PERSONNEL SERVICES
6100 Building, 5721 Marlin Road, Suite 3300, Chattanooga TN 37411. 423/894-1500. **Toll-free phone:** 800/891-1505. **Fax:** 423/894-1507. **Contact:** John C. Parham, Manager. **Description:** An executive search firm operating on a contingency basis. Company pays fee. **Specializes in the areas of:** Accounting/Auditing; Administration; Banking; Computer Science/Software; Engineering; Finance; General Management; Health/Medical; Industrial; Insurance; Manufacturing; Personnel/Labor Relations. **Positions commonly filled include:** Accountant/Auditor; Architect; Bank Officer/Manager; Chemical Engineer; Chemist; Civil Engineer; Computer Programmer; Credit Manager; Customer Service Rep.; Design Engineer; Designer; Draftsperson; Education Administrator; Electrical/Electronics Engineer; Environmental Engineer; Human Resources Specialist; Industrial Engineer; Management Analyst/Consultant; Management Trainee; Manufacturer's/Wholesaler's Sales Rep.; Mechanical Engineer; MIS Specialist; Operations/Production Manager; Physician; Purchasing Agent/Manager; Quality Control Supervisor; Restaurant/Food Service Manager; Software Engineer; Structural Engineer; Systems Analyst; Technical Writer/Editor; Telecommunications Manager; Typist/Word Processor; Underwriter/Assistant Underwriter. **Corporate headquarters location:** Dallas TX. **Other U.S. locations:** Nationwide. **Average salary range of placements:** $30,000 - $50,000. **Number of placements per year:** 50 - 99.

SOFTWARE RESOURCE CONSULTANTS INC.
P.O. Box 38118, Memphis TN 38183. 901/759-7225. **Fax:** 901/759-1721. **Contact:** P. Sheth. **E-mail address:** src1@bellsouth.net. **Description:** An executive search firm operating on a contingency basis. The firm focuses on the placement of entry- to senior-level professionals on a contract and permanent basis. **Specializes in the areas of:** Computer Science/Software; Engineering; Information Technology; Technical; Telecommunications; Wireless Communications. **Positions commonly filled include:** Computer Programmer; Database Manager; Design Engineer; Development Manager; Project Manager; Software Engineer; Systems Analyst; Systems Manager; Telecommunications Manager. **Other U.S. locations:** Washington DC. **Average salary range of placements:** More than $50,000. **Number of placements per year:** 1 - 49.

STEWART & ASSOCIATES INC.
P.O. Box 6004, Kingsport TN 37663. 423/239-7995. **Contact:** Manager. **Description:** A generalist executive search firm.

TECHNICAL RESOURCE ASSOCIATES
P.O. Box 1269, Hendersonville TN 37077. 615/824-1444. **Fax:** 615/824-7696. **Contact:** Richard D. Holtz, President. **Description:** An executive search firm operating on a contingency basis. The firm focuses on high-tech, advanced materials industries as well as environmental, safety, and health industries. Founded in 1978. Company pays fee. **Specializes in the areas of:** Engineering; General Management; Industrial; Manufacturing; Sales; Technical. **Positions commonly filled include:** Aerospace Engineer; Biomedical Engineer; Ceramics Engineer; Chemical Engineer; Chemist; Civil Engineer; Design Engineer; Electrical/Electronics Engineer; Environmental Engineer; General Manager; Industrial Engineer; Industrial Production Manager; Materials Engineer; Mechanical Engineer; Metallurgical Engineer; Operations/Production Manager; Quality Control Supervisor; Science Technologist; Statistician; Structural Engineer. **Number of placements per year:** 1 - 49.

PERMANENT EMPLOYMENT AGENCIES

AAA EMPLOYMENT
5700 Building, Suite 102, East Gate Center, Chattanooga TN 37411. 423/855-0583. **Contact:** Manager. **Description:** A permanent employment agency that provides placements in a wide range of industries.

ADVANTAGE PERSONNEL INC.
5312 Rynggold Road, Suite 202, P.O. Box 9878, Chattanooga TN 37412. 423/499-9397. **Contact:** Manager. **Description:** A permanent placement agency.

CAREER PROFESSIONALS, INC. (CPI)
P.O. Box 1216, Morristown TN 37816. 423/587-4363. **Contact:** Jim Beelaert, President. **Description:** A permanent employment agency. **Specializes in the areas of:** Engineering; Food Industry; Publishing. **Positions commonly filled include:** Accountant/Auditor; Electrical/Electronics Engineer; Financial Analyst; Human Resources Manager; Industrial Engineer; Mechanical Engineer; Metallurgical Engineer; Statistician. **Number of placements per year:** 1 - 49.

CORNERSTONE EMPLOYMENT SERVICES
702 Inverness Avenue, Nashville TN 37204. 615/297-0298. **Contact:** Manager. **Description:** A permanent employment agency. **Specializes in the areas of:** Retail. **Positions commonly filled include:** Retail Manager.

DUNHILL OF MEMPHIS, INC.
5120 Stage Road, Suite 2, Memphis TN 38134. 901/386-2500. **Contact:** Mike Rhodes, Manager. **Description:** A permanent employment agency. **Specializes in the areas of:** Distribution; Engineering; Manufacturing.

EAGLE SYSTEMS
6060 Primarcy Parkway, Memphis TN 38119. 901/685-3704. **Contact:** Manager. **Description:** A permanent employment agency. **Specializes in the areas of:** Computer Programming; Computer Science/Software.

ENGINEER ONE, INC.
P.O. Box 23037, Knoxville TN 37933. 423/675-1221. **Toll-free phone:** 800/251-9847. **Fax:** 423/675-1230. **Contact:** Manager. **Description:** A permanent employment agency that focuses primarily on the placement of engineers and professionals in the chemical processing, electrical/electronic, and mechanical manufacturing industries. Company pays fee. **Specializes in the areas of:** Computer Science/Software; Engineering; Food Industry; Industrial; Manufacturing; Sales; Technical. **Positions commonly filled include:** Aerospace Engineer; Agricultural Engineer; Biochemist; Ceramics Engineer; Chemical Engineer; Civil Engineer; Computer Programmer; Electrical/Electronics Engineer; General Manager; Geologist/Geophysicist; Industrial Engineer; Mechanical Engineer; MIS Specialist; Nuclear Engineer; Operations/Production Manager; Petroleum Engineer; Purchasing Agent/Manager; Quality Control Supervisor; Software Engineer; Structural Engineer; Systems Engineer. **Other U.S. locations:** TX. **Average salary range of placements:** More than $50,000. **Number of placements per year:** 100 - 199.

EXPRESS PERSONNEL SERVICES, INC.
8807 Kingston Pike, Knoxville TN 37923. 423/531-1720. **Fax:** 423/531-3267. **Contact:** Celia Spinner, Owner. **Description:** A permanent employment agency. Company pays fee. **Specializes in the areas of:** Computer Science/Software; Engineering; General Management; Industrial; Manufacturing; Personnel/Labor Relations; Sales; Technical; Transportation. **Positions commonly filled include:** Administrative Manager; Biomedical Engineer; Branch Manager; Chemical Engineer; Clerical Supervisor; Computer Programmer; Construction Contractor; Customer Service Representative; Electrical/Electronics Engineer; Emergency Medical Technician; General Manager; Human Resources Manager; Industrial Engineer; Industrial Production Manager; Management Analyst/Consultant; Mechanical Engineer; Metallurgical Engineer; Operations/Production Manager; Purchasing Agent/Manager; Quality Control Supervisor; Sociologist; Software Engineer; Systems Analyst; Technical Writer/Editor; Transportation/Traffic Specialist. **Number of placements per year:** 1 - 49.

MADISON PERSONNEL
1864 Poplar Crest Cove, Memphis TN 38119. 901/761-2660. **Fax:** 901/761-3339. **Contact:** David White, Owner/Manager. **Description:** A permanent employment agency. Company pays fee. **Specializes in the areas of:** Accounting/Auditing; Clerical; Computer Science/Software; Engineering; Manufacturing. **Positions commonly filled include:** Accountant/Auditor; Administrative Assistant; Bookkeeper; Chemical Engineer; Credit Manager; Design Engineer; Electrical/Electronics Engineer; Financial Analyst; Industrial Engineer; Legal Secretary; Mechanical Engineer; Medical Secretary; Quality Control Supervisor; Receptionist; Secretary; Stenographer; Systems Analyst. **Average salary range of placements:** More than $50,000. **Number of placements per year:** 50 - 99.

MANAGEMENT RECRUITERS OF MURFREESBORO
P.O. Box 4094, Murfreesboro TN 37133-4094. **Contact:** Manager. **Description:** A permanent employment agency that also provides some temporary placement services. **Specializes in the areas of:** Japanese Bilingual.

PIERCY EMPLOYMENT SERVICES
386-D Carriage House Drive, Jackson TN 38305. 901/664-4400. **Contact:** Bea Long, Placement Consultant. **Description:** A permanent employment agency. **Specializes in the areas of:** Administration; Clerical; Data Processing; Industrial; Secretarial; Technical. **Number of placements per year:** 1 - 49.

POPLAR EMPLOYMENT SERVICE
5575 Poplar Avenue, Memphis TN 38119. 901/761-2596. **Contact:** Yvonne McGuire, Office Manager.

Description: A full-service employment agency. **Specializes in the areas of:** Accounting/Auditing; Health/Medical; Personnel/Labor Relations; Secretarial. **Positions commonly filled include:** Accountant/Auditor; Administrative Manager; Claim Representative; Clerical Supervisor; Customer Service Representative; Dental Assistant/Dental Hygienist; Design Engineer; Health Services Manager; Human Resources Specialist; Human Service Worker; Licensed Practical Nurse; Management Trainee; Medical Technologist; Paralegal; Physical Therapist; Radiological Technologist. **Average salary range of placements:** $20,000 - $29,999. **Number of placements per year:** 50 - 99.

RASMUSSEN & ASSOCIATES, INC.
P.O. Box 5037, Kingsport TN 37663. 423/239-6664. **Fax:** 423/239-4832. **Contact:** W.L. (Bill) Rasmussen, President. **Description:** A permanent employment agency that also provides executive searches on a contingency basis. **Specializes in the areas of:** Accounting/Auditing; Engineering; Finance; General Management; Manufacturing; Personnel/Labor Relations; Publishing. **Positions commonly filled include:** Accountant/Auditor; Budget Analyst; Buyer; Chemist; Designer; Electrical/Electronics Engineer; Financial Analyst; General Manager; Human Resources Manager; Industrial Engineer; Mechanical Engineer; Metallurgical Engineer; Nuclear Engineer; Purchasing Agent/Manager; Quality Control Supervisor; Software Engineer. **Number of placements per year:** 1 - 49.

RESOURCE PERSONNEL SERVICES
P.O. Box 101339, Nashville TN 37224. 615/366-0300. **Contact:** Manager. **Description:** A permanent employment agency that focuses on the placement of truck drivers. **Specializes in the areas of:** Transportation.

SHILOH CAREERS INTERNATIONAL, INC.
P.O. Box 831, Brentwood TN 37024-0831. 615/373-3090. **Fax:** 615/373-3480. **Contact:** Mary Ann Webber, President. **E-mail address:** mawd@ mindspring.com. **Description:** A permanent employment agency that provides property and casualty insurance placements. **Specializes in the areas of:** Insurance. **Number of placements per year:** 1 - 49.

STAFFING SOLUTIONS
1801 Downtown West Boulevard, Knoxville TN 37919. 423/690-2311. **Contact:** Manager. **Description:** A permanent employment agency. **Specializes in the areas of:** Accounting/Auditing; Banking; Computer Science/Software; Finance; Office Support; Technical. **Positions commonly filled include:** Accountant/Auditor; Administrative Assistant; Computer Operator; Computer Programmer; Data Entry Clerk; Engineer; Industrial Designer.

TENNESSEE JOB SERVICE
909 Eighth Avenue North, Nashville TN 37245-3700. **Fax:** 615/741-6106. **Contact:** Personnel Director. **Description:** A permanent employment agency. **Positions commonly filled include:** Accountant/Auditor; Administrative Manager; Architect; Attorney; Biological Scientist; Branch Manager; Budget Analyst; Buyer; Chemist; Computer Programmer; Construction Contractor; Counselor; Dentist; Designer; Dietician/Nutritionist; Draftsperson; Economist; Editor; Education Administrator; Engineer; Financial Analyst; Forester/Conservation Scientist; General Manager; Geographer; Geologist/Geophysicist; Health Services Manager; Hotel Manager; Human Resources Manager; Librarian; Management Analyst/Consultant; Manufacturer's/Wholesaler's Sales Rep.; Mathematician; Meteorologist; Nuclear Medicine Technologist; Paralegal; Pharmacist; Physical Therapist; Physician; Physicist; Public Relations Specialist; Purchasing Agent/Manager; Radiological Technologist; Recreational Therapist; Registered Nurse; Reporter; Respiratory Therapist; Restaurant/Food Service Manager; Science Technologist; Social Worker; Sociologist; Statistician; Systems Analyst; Teacher/Professor; Technical Writer/Editor; Underwriter/Assistant Underwriter; Veterinarian.

TEMPORARY EMPLOYMENT AGENCIES

A-1 STAFFING & PERSONNEL
10368 Wallace Alley Street, Suite 18, Kingsport TN 37663. 423/279-0788. **Fax:** 423/279-0575. **Contact:** Janice Wininger, Operations Director. **E-mail address:** a-1beth@aol.com. **Description:** A full-service staffing firm providing temporary, temp-to-perm, and permanent placements. **Specializes in the areas of:** Administration; Computer Science/Software; Engineering; Finance; Food Industry; General Management; Health/Medical; Insurance; Legal; Personnel/Labor Relations; Printing; Retail; Sales; Secretarial; Technical. **Corporate headquarters location:** This Location. **Other U.S. locations:** NC. **Average salary range of placements:** $20,000 - $29,999. **Number of placements per year:** 100 - 199.

ACCOUNTANTS ON CALL
1101 Kermit Drive, Suite 600, Nashville TN 37217-5110. 615/399-0200. **Fax:** 615/399-2285. **Contact:** Milton Ellis, President. **World Wide Web address:** http://www.aocnet.com. **Description:** A temporary agency that also provides permanent placements and executive searches on a contingency basis. Company pays fee. **Specializes in the areas of:** Accounting/Auditing; Finance. **Positions commonly filled include:** Accountant/Auditor; Actuary; Chief Financial Officer; Controller; Cost Estimator; Credit Manager; Finance Director; Financial Analyst. **Benefits available to temporary workers:** Paid Vacation. **Other U.S. locations:** Nationwide. **Average salary range of placements:** $20,000 - $29,999. **Number of placements per year:** 1000+.

ACCOUNTING SOLUTIONS
115 Suburban Road, Knoxville TN 37923. 423/690-0055. **Contact:** Manager. **Description:** A temporary agency that provides temporary and permanent accounting placements. Company pays fee. **Specializes in the areas of:** Accounting/Auditing; Finance. **Positions commonly filled include:** Accountant/Auditor; Budget Analyst; Credit Manager. **Average salary range of placements:** $20,000 - $29,999. **Number of placements per year:** 50 - 99.

ANGEL MEDICAL PERSONNEL POOL
1326 Eighth Avenue North, Nashville TN 37208. 615/726-0308. **Contact:** Manager. **Description:** A temporary placement agency. **Specializes in the areas of:** Health/Medical.

ARVIE PERSONNEL SERVICES
1719 West End Avenue, Suite 116W, Nashville TN 37203. 615/321-9577. **Fax:** 615/321-4949. **Contact:** Janice Threalkill-Sawyers, President. **Description:** A temporary agency. Company pays fee. **Specializes in the areas of:** Personnel/Labor Relations; Secretarial. **Positions commonly filled include:** Accountant/Auditor; Landscape Architect. **Number of placements per year:** 200 - 499.

D.S.A.
4515 Poplar Avenue, Suite 327, Memphis TN 38117. 901/685-7373. **Contact:** Manager. **Description:** A temporary agency. Company pays fee. **Specializes in the areas of:** Clerical; Dental. **Average salary range of placements:** $20,000 - $29,999. **Number of placements per year:** 100 - 199.

GATEWAY GROUP PERSONNEL
1770 Kirby Parkway, Suite 216, Memphis TN 38138-7405. 901/756-6050. **Fax:** 901/756-8445. **Contact:** Darlene Murphy, President. **Description:** A temporary placement firm operating on a contingency basis. Gateway Group focuses on accounting, banking, and administrative support personnel, and also provides permanent placements. Company pays fee. **Specializes in the areas of:** Accounting/Auditing; Administration; Banking; Finance; General Management; Personnel/Labor Relations; Secretarial. **Positions commonly filled include:** Accountant/Auditor; Actuary; Attorney; Bank Officer/Manager; Branch Manager; Brokerage Clerk; Budget Analyst; Clerical Supervisor; Credit Manager; Customer Service Representative; Financial Analyst; General Manager; Human Resources Specialist; Strategic Relations Manager; Typist/Word Processor. **Benefits available to temporary workers:** Dental Insurance; Medical Insurance. **Number of placements per year:** 200 - 499.

HEALTH STAFF
5100 Poplar Avenue, Suite 117, Memphis TN 38137. 901/761-4878. **Contact:** Manager. **Description:** A temporary and temp-to-perm agency. **Specializes in the areas of:** Health/Medical; Pharmaceutical.

KELLY SERVICES, INC.
404 BNA Drive, Suite 200, Nashville TN 37217. 615/367-1964. **Contact:** Manager. **Description:** A temporary service that also provides temp-to-perm placements. Company pays fee. **Specializes in the areas of:** Accounting/Auditing; Administration; Banking; Broadcasting; Computer Science/Software; Engineering; Finance; General Management; Health/Medical; Industrial; Insurance; Manufacturing; Office Support; Personnel/Labor Relations; Publishing; Sales; Secretarial. **Positions commonly filled include:** Accountant/Auditor; Administrative Manager; Blue-Collar Worker Supervisor; Claim Representative; Clerical Supervisor; Clinical Lab Technician; Computer Programmer; Customer Service Representative; Financial Analyst; General Manager; Human Resources Specialist; Industrial Production Manager; Management Trainee; Market Research Analyst; Medical Records Technician; MIS Specialist; Services Sales Representative; Systems Analyst; Typist/Word Processor. **Benefits available to temporary workers:** Medical Insurance; Paid Holidays; Paid Vacation. **Corporate headquarters location:** Troy MI. **Other U.S. locations:** Nationwide. **Average salary range of placements:** $20,000 - $29,999. **Number of placements per year:** 1000+.

MANPOWER TEMPORARY SERVICES
121 Henslee Drive, Suite H, Dickson TN 37055. 615/446-4483. **Fax:** 615/446-4881. **Contact:** Sherry Bear, Branch Manager. **Description:** A temporary agency. **Specializes in the areas of:** Accounting/Auditing; Administration; Computer Science/Software; Engineering; Food Industry; General Management; Health/Medical; Legal; Manufacturing; Personnel/Labor Relations; Secretarial. **Positions commonly filled include:** Accountant/Auditor; Adjuster; Advertising Clerk; Blue-Collar Worker Supervisor; Branch Manager; Customer Service Representative; Draftsperson; Electrician; Health Services Manager; Human Resources Specialist; Industrial Engineer; Insurance Agent/Broker; Landscape Architect; Management Analyst/Consultant; Management Trainee; Manufacturer's/Wholesaler's Sales Rep.; Mechanical Engineer; Medical Records Technician; Metallurgical Engineer; Multimedia Designer; Paralegal; Public Relations Specialist; Purchasing Agent/Manager; Quality Control Supervisor; Reporter; Securities Sales Representative; Software Engineer; Typist/Word Processor. **Benefits available to temporary workers:** Life Insurance; Medical Insurance; Paid Holidays; Paid Vacation; Referral Bonus Plan; Stock Purchase. **Corporate headquarters location:** Milwaukee WI. **Other U.S. locations:** Nationwide. **Number of placements per year:** 500 - 999.

MANPOWER, INC.
1365 Flowering Dogwood Lane, Suite E, Dyersburg TN 38024. 901/285-3124. **Fax:** 901/286-5548. **Contact:** Lana Wood, Branch Manager. **Description:** A temporary agency. Manpower also has divisions specializing in technical and professional placements for full-time, permanent jobs. **Specializes in the areas of:** Accounting/Auditing; Computer Science/Software; Engineering; Industrial; Manufacturing; Personnel/Labor Relations; Sales; Secretarial; Technical. **Positions commonly filled include:** Accountant/Auditor; Administrative Manager; Architect; Bank Officer/Manager; Blue-Collar Worker Supervisor; Budget Analyst; Claim Rep.; Clerical Supervisor; Computer Programmer; Credit Manager; Customer Service Rep.; Draftsperson; Electrical/Electronics Engineer; Electrician; General Manager; Hotel Manager; Human Resources Specialist; Industrial Engineer; Library Technician; Mechanical Engineer; Medical Records Technician; MIS Specialist; Public Relations Specialist; Purchasing Agent/Manager; Securities Sales Representative; Services Sales Rep.; Typist/Word Processor. **Benefits available to temporary workers:** Paid Holidays; Paid Vacation. **Corporate headquarters location:** Milwaukee WI. **Other U.S. locations:** Nationwide. **Number of placements per year:** 200 - 499.

MANPOWER, INC.
1801 West End Avenue, Suite 100, Nashville TN 37203. 615/327-9922. **Contact:** Branch Manager. **Description:** A temporary agency. Company pays fee. **Specializes in the areas of:** Data Processing; Light Industrial; Office Support; Professional; Technical; Telemarketing; Word Processing. **Positions commonly filled include:** Accountant/Auditor; Accounting Clerk; Administrative Assistant; Biological Scientist; Bookkeeper; Chemist; Computer Operator; Customer Service Representative; Designer; Desktop Publishing Specialist; Electrician; Inspector/Tester/Grader; Machine Operator; Material Control Specialist; Order Clerk; Packaging/Processing Worker; Painter; Project Engineer; Proofreader; Receptionist; Research Assistant; Secretary; Software Engineer; Systems Analyst; Technical Writer/Editor; Telemarketer; Typist/Word Processor; Welder. **Benefits available to temporary workers:** Life Insurance; Medical Insurance; Paid Holidays; Paid Vacation. **Corporate headquarters location:** Milwaukee WI. **Other U.S. locations:** Nationwide. **Number of placements per year:** 1000+.

MEGA FORCE
Wedgewood Office Park, P.O. Box 3686, Cleveland TN 37312. 423/476-8583. **Physical address:** 442 Inman Street, Cleveland TN 37311. **Fax:** 423/472-3839. **Contact:** Rhonda Bolton, Office Manager. **Description:** A temporary agency providing professional staffing. Mega Force provides technical staffing, direct search and placement services, and career transition services. **Specializes in the areas of:** Accounting/Auditing; Computer Science/Software; Customer Service; Data Processing; Design; Engineering; General Labor; Light Industrial;

Secretarial; Technical; Telemarketing; Word Processing. **Benefits available to temporary workers:** 401(k); Medical Insurance; Paid Vacation; Referral Bonus Plan. **Corporate headquarters location:** Fayetteville NC. **Other U.S. locations:** GA; SC. **Average salary range of placements:** Less than $20,000. **Number of placements per year:** 500 - 999.

NORRELL SERVICES
1770 Kirby Parkway, Suite 330, Memphis TN 38138. 901/751-0501. **Contact:** Branch Manager. **Description:** A temporary agency. Company pays fee. **Specializes in the areas of:** Banking; Clerical; Finance; Insurance; Secretarial. **Positions commonly filled include:** Administrative Assistant; Customer Service Rep.; Data Entry Clerk; Receptionist; Secretary; Stenographer. **Corporate headquarters location:** Atlanta GA. **Other U.S. locations:** Nationwide. **International locations:** Canada. **Number of placements per year:** 1000+.

OLSTEN STAFFING SERVICES
162-D Marketplace Boulevard, Knoxville TN 37922. 423/539-0200. **Toll-free phone:** 800/WORK-NOW. **Fax:** 423/539-0522. **Contact:** Larry Marion, Branch Manager. **Description:** A temporary agency. Company pays fee. **Specializes in the areas of:** Accounting/Auditing; Administration; Engineering; General Management; Industrial; Legal; Manufacturing; Personnel/Labor Relations; Secretarial; Technical. **Positions commonly filled include:** Accountant/Auditor; Actuary; Administrative Assistant; Administrative Manager; Biomedical Engineer; Blue-Collar Worker Supervisor; Bookkeeper; Branch Manager; Broadcast Technician; Budget Analyst; Ceramics Engineer; Chemical Engineer; Civil Engineer; Claim Representative; Clerical Supervisor; Clerk; Computer Programmer; Customer Service Representative; Design Engineer; Draftsperson; Electrical/Electronics Engineer; Environmental Engineer; Factory Worker; General Manager; Human Resources Specialist; Industrial Engineer; Industrial Production Manager; Internet Services Manager; Legal Secretary; Light Industrial Worker; Manufacturer's/Wholesaler's Sales Rep.; Market Research Analyst; Materials Engineer; Mechanical Engineer; Medical Secretary; Metallurgical Engineer; MIS Specialist; Paralegal; Quality Control Supervisor; Receptionist; Secretary; Software Engineer; Stenographer; Structural Engineer; Systems Analyst; Technical Writer/Editor; Typist/Word Processor. **Benefits available to temporary workers:** Life Insurance; Medical Insurance; Paid Vacation. **Corporate headquarters location:** Melville NY. **Other U.S. locations:** Nationwide. **Number of placements per year:** 1000+.

PHARM TEMP PHARMACY PERSONNEL
OPTI TEMP/DEN TEMP
4515 Poplar Avenue, Suite 327, Memphis TN 38117. 901/685-7373. **Contact:** Wally Gardner, President/CEO. **Description:** A temporary agency providing temporary and permanent placement of pharmacy personnel. Opti Temp, also at this location, focuses on placing optical personnel, while Den Temp places dental personnel. Company pays fee. **Specializes in the areas of:** Health/Medical; Pharmaceutical; Sales; Secretarial. **Positions commonly filled include:** Clinical Lab Technician; Customer Service Representative; Dental Assistant/Dental Hygienist; Dentist; Health Services Manager; Medical Records Technician; Pharmacist; Pharmacy Technician. **Average salary range of placements:** $20,000 - $29,999. **Number of placements per year:** 100 - 199.

SPECIAL COUNSEL
6401 Poplar Avenue, Suite 555, Memphis TN 38119. 901/762-0111. **Fax:** 901/762-0176. **Contact:** Manager. **World Wide Web address:** http://www.specialcounsel.com. **Description:** A temporary and permanent employment agency. **Specializes in the areas of:** Legal.

SPECIAL COUNSEL
AMICUS LEGAL STAFFING INC.
1900 Church Street, Suite 425, Nashville TN 37203. 615/320-7700. **Contact:** Manager. **World Wide Web address:** http://www.specialcounsel.com. **Description:** A temporary agency that also provides some permanent placements. **Specializes in the areas of:** Legal.

TEMP STAFF
919 East College Street, Pulaski TN 38478-4432. 931/762-0803. **Fax:** 931/762-0851. **Contact:** Tammy Kachur or Keith Sanders. **Description:** A temporary employment agency. Temp Staff focuses on industrial labor and also places craftsmen and clerical personnel. Company pays fee. **Specializes in the areas of:** Banking; Construction; Engineering; Food Industry; Industrial; Manufacturing; Secretarial. **Positions commonly filled include:** Electrician; Licensed Practical Nurse; Typist/Word Processor. **Average salary range of placements:** Less than $20,000. **Number of placements per year:** 200 - 499.

UNIFORCE SERVICES
302 Wesley Street, Suite 2, Johnson City TN 37601. 423/283-7774. **Contact:** Beth Begley, Account Manager. **Description:** A national temporary staffing firm. Company pays fee. **Specializes in the areas of:** Technical. **Positions commonly filled include:** Biochemist; Biological Scientist; Ceramics Engineer; Chemist; Food Scientist/Technologist; Materials Engineer; Metallurgical Engineer; Science Technologist. **Benefits available to temporary workers:** 401(k); Medical Insurance; Paid Vacation. **Corporate headquarters location:** New Hyde Park NY. **Other U.S. locations:** Nationwide. **Average salary range of placements:** $20,000 - $29,999. **Number of placements per year:** 100 - 199.

CONTRACT SERVICES FIRMS

AMERICAN TECHNICAL ASSOCIATES, INC.
P.O. Box 10844, Knoxville TN 37939-0844. 423/588-5751. **Fax:** 423/554-4138. **Contact:** Brian White, Vice President. **E-mail address:** atatemps@aol.com. **Description:** A contract services firm. Company pays fee. **Specializes in the areas of:** Computer Science/Software; Engineering; Industrial; Technical. **Positions commonly filled include:** Accountant; Architect; Biochemist; Biological Scientist; Biomedical Engineer; Ceramics Engineer; Chemical Engineer; Chemist; Civil Engineer; Computer Programmer; Cost Estimator; Design Engineer; Designer; Draftsperson; Electrical/Electronics Engineer; Electrician; Environmental Engineer; Materials Engineer; Mechanical Engineer; Metallurgical Engineer; MIS Specialist; Software Engineer; Structural Engineer; Systems Analyst; Technical Writer/Editor; Typist/Word Processor. **Benefits available to temporary workers:** 401(k); Paid Holidays; Paid Vacation. **Corporate headquarters location:** This Location. **Average salary range of placements:** More than $50,000. **Number of placements per year:** 200 - 499.

CDI CORPORATION
1905 American Way, Kingsport TN 37660. 423/578-4100. **Fax:** 423/578-4311. **Contact:** Manager. **World**

Wide Web address: http://www.cdicorp.com. Description: A contract services firm. Specializes in the areas of: Technical. Corporate headquarters location: Philadelphia PA. Other U.S. locations: Nationwide. International locations: Worldwide.

CDI INFORMATION SYSTEMS
Union Square, Suite 610, Chattanooga TN 37402. 423/266-9720. **Fax:** 423/266-9737. **Contact:** Manager. **Description:** A contract services firm. **Specializes in the areas of:** Technical. **Corporate headquarters location:** Philadelphia PA. **Other U.S. locations:** Nationwide. **International locations:** Worldwide.

C.J. STAFFING SERVICES
7010 Lee Highway, Suite 214, Chattanooga TN 37421. 423/899-0866. **Toll-free phone:** 800/264-5519. **Fax:** 423/894-3819. **Contact:** Manager. **Description:** A contract services firm. This is the personnel placement division of C.J. Enterprises, Inc., which provides consulting, administrative management, and technical services. **Specializes in the areas of:** Health/Medical; Personnel/Labor Relations. **Positions commonly filled include:** Blue-Collar Worker Supervisor; Customer Service Representative; Draftsperson; Human Resources Specialist; Management Analyst/Consultant; Management Trainee; Pharmacist; Physician; Radio/TV Announcer/Broadcaster; Registered Nurse; Systems Analyst. **Benefits available to temporary workers:** 401(k); Paid Holidays; Paid Vacation. **Number of placements per year:** 200 - 499.

CENTRAL TECHNICAL SERVICE INC.
5909 Shelby Oaks Drive, Memphis TN 38134. 901/385-1127. **Contact:** Manager. **Description:** A contract services firm. **Specializes in the areas of:** Technical.

ROBERT HALF INTERNATIONAL
402 BNA Drive, Suite 410, Nashville TN 37217. 615/360-8065. **Fax:** 615/360-2030. **Contact:** Kevin Cullen, Recruiting Manager. **E-mail address:** rhicbna@aol.com. **Description:** A contract services firm. This location also conducts executive searches and houses three divisions: Financial, Information Systems, and OfficeTeam. Founded in 1948. Company pays fee. **Specializes in the areas of:** Administration; Computer Science/Software. **Positions commonly filled include:** Computer Programmer; Internet Services Manager; MIS Specialist; Multimedia Designer; Operations/Production Manager; Software Engineer; Systems Analyst; Technical Writer/Editor; Telecommunications Manager. **Corporate headquarters location:** Menlo Park CA. **Other U.S. locations:** Nationwide. **Average salary range of placements:** $30,000 - $50,000. **Number of placements per year:** 1 - 49.

UNLIMITED STAFFING SOLUTIONS, INC.
1161 Murfreesboro Road, Suite 521, Nashville TN 37217. 615/366-0721. **Fax:** 615/366-0759. **Contact:** Barbara Thomas, Manager. **E-mail address:** ussinc@mindspring.com. **World Wide Web address:** http://www.unlimitedstaffing.com. **Description:** A contract services firm. **Specializes in the areas of:** Accounting/Auditing; Administration; Banking; Clerical; Engineering; Industrial; Light Industrial; Printing; Secretarial. **Benefits available to temporary workers:** 401(k); Dental Insurance; Life Insurance; Medical Insurance; Paid Holidays; Paid Vacation. **Corporate headquarters location:** Bloomfield Hills TN. **Average salary range of placements:** $30,000 - $50,000. **Number of placements per year:** 100 - 199.

ROBERT WALKER ASSOCIATES
P.O. Box 166, Old Hickory TN 37138-0166. **Contact:** President. **Description:** A contract services firm. Company pays fee. **Specializes in the areas of:** Accounting/Auditing; Engineering; Industrial; Manufacturing; Personnel/Labor Relations. **Positions commonly filled include:** Accountant/Auditor; Blue-Collar Worker Supervisor; Buyer; Ceramics Engineer; Chemical Engineer; Chemist; Civil Engineer; Computer Programmer; Cost Estimator; Design Engineer; Draftsperson; Electrical/Electronics Engineer; Environmental Engineer; Financial Analyst; General Manager; Human Resources Specialist; Industrial Production Manager; Materials Engineer; Mechanical Engineer; MIS Specialist; Operations/Production Manager; Purchasing Agent/Manager; Quality Control Supervisor; Systems Analyst. **Average salary range of placements:** $30,000 - $50,000. **Number of placements per year:** 1 - 49.

CAREER/OUTPLACEMENT COUNSELING FIRMS

BRADEN RESUME & SECRETARIAL
108 La Plaza Drive, Hendersonville TN 37075. 615/822-3317. **Fax:** 615/826-9611. **Contact:** Carolyn S. Braden, CPRW, Owner. **E-mail address:** bradenres@aol.com. **Description:** A career/outplacement counseling firm that provides writing, editing, design, and typesetting of professional job search materials for entry-level to senior management candidates.

CD RESUME SERVICE/CAREERPRO
325 Plus Park Boulevard, Suite 210, Nashville TN 37217. 615/399-3858. **Contact:** Danitza Grimes, Owner. **Description:** A career/outplacement counseling firm that helps clients identify their marketable skills and qualifications, focus on the unadvertised job market, and plan a self-marketing strategy. Founded in 1958.

COCHRAN ADVERTISING RESUME SERVICE
1430 Madison Street, Clarksville TN 37040. 931/551-[illegible]074. **Contact:** Jim Watson, Writer. **Description:** A resume writing service that focuses on developing resumes to highlight skills and experience. Cochran Advertising Resume Service utilizes in-depth interviews to identify job skills and ascertain goals and objectives. The company is professionally certified to create resumes, and its resume package includes data on interview preparation and an ongoing resume updating service.

MS. SECRETARY
131 Third Avenue North, Suite 101, Franklin TN 37064. 615/794-3223. **Contact:** Marilyn McAdams, Owner. **Description:** A resume writing service.

PENCIL FOUNDATION
421 Great Circle Road, Suite 100, Nashville TN 37228. 615/242-3167. **Fax:** 615/254-6748. **Contact:** Program Director. **Description:** A career/outplacement counseling service. PENCIL (Public Education and Nashville Citizens Involved in Leadership) provides skills training. **Number of placements per year:** 200 - 499.

TEXAS

EXECUTIVE SEARCH FIRMS

ABA EXECUTIVE SEARCH
P.O. Box 35806, Houston TX 77235. 713/661-9909. **Contact:** Allan Butler, Owner. **Description:** An executive search firm. **Specializes in the areas of:** General Management; Oil and Gas; Sales.

ABACUS MANAGEMENT SERVICE
5215 North O'Connor Boulevard, Suite 200, Irving TX 75039. 972/868-9169. **Contact:** Manager. **Description:** Abacus Management Service is an executive search firm.

ACCOUNTANTS EXECUTIVE SEARCH
ACCOUNTANTS ON CALL
2828 Routh, Suite 690, Dallas TX 75201. 214/979-9001. **Fax:** 214/969-0046. **Contact:** Branch Manager. **Description:** An executive search firm operating on a contingency basis. Accountants On Call (also at this location) is a temporary agency. Company pays fee. **Specializes in the areas of:** Accounting/Auditing; Finance. **Positions commonly filled include:** Accountant; Chief Financial Officer; Controller; Credit Manager; Finance Director; Financial Analyst. **Corporate headquarters location:** Saddle Brook NJ. **Average salary range of placements:** $30,000 - $50,000.
Other area locations:
- 5550 LBJ Freeway, Suite 310, Dallas TX 75240. 972/980-4184.
- 1990 Post Oak Boulevard, Suite 720, Houston TX 77056. 713/961-5603.

ACCOUNTANTS EXECUTIVE SEARCH
ACCOUNTANTS ON CALL
1200 Summit Avenue, Suite 306, Fort Worth TX 76102. 817/870-1800. **Fax:** 817/870-1890. **Contact:** Mark Wegesin, Branch Manager. **Description:** An executive search firm operating on a contingency basis. Accountants On Call (also at this location) is a temporary agency. Founded in 1979. Company pays fee. **Specializes in the areas of:** Accounting/Auditing; Finance. **Positions commonly filled include:** Accountant/Auditor; Credit Manager; Financial Analyst. **Corporate headquarters location:** Saddle Brook NJ. **Number of placements per year:** 1000+.

ACCOUNTING CONTRACTORS INC.
1100 Centennial Boulevard, Richardson TX 75231. 972/889-3321. **Contact:** Manager. **Description:** An executive search firm that also provides contract placements. **Specializes in the areas of:** Accounting/Auditing.

ACCUSEARCH
5959 Gateway West, Suite 601, El Paso TX 79925. 915/778-9312. **Fax:** 915/778-9314. **Contact:** Manager. **Description:** An executive search firm. **Specializes in the areas of:** Manufacturing.

ACKERMAN JOHNSON INC.
333 North Sam Houston Parkway East, Suite 1210, Houston TX 77060-2417. 281/999-8879. **Fax:** 281/999-7570. **Contact:** Frederick W. Stang, President. **E-mail address:** ajhoust@ackermanjohnsn.com. **Description:** An executive search firm. Founded in 1981. Company pays fee. **Specializes in the areas of:** Advertising; Computer Science/Software; Engineering; Food Industry; General Management; Industrial; Manufacturing; Personnel/Labor Relations; Sales. **Positions commonly filled include:** Aerospace Engineer; Biochemist; Branch Manager; Chemical Engineer; Chemist; Civil Engineer; Computer Programmer; Customer Service Rep.; Design Engineer; Electrical/Electronics Engineer; Environmental Engineer; General Manager; Industrial Engineer; Management Analyst/Consultant; Management Trainee; Manufacturer's/Wholesaler's Sales Rep. Mechanical Engineer; Petroleum Engineer; Public Relations Specialist; Restaurant/Food Service Manager; Services Sales Rep.; Software Engineer; Stationary Engineer; Structural Engineer; Systems Analyst; Telecommunications Manager. **Average salary range of placements:** More than $50,000. **Number of placements per year:** 100 - 199.

ACTION RECRUITING SERVICES
5373 West Alabama, Suite 318, Houston TX 77056. 713/629-9740. **Contact:** M. Ken Smith III, President. **Description:** An executive search firm that provides placements in restaurants. Company pays fee. **Specializes in the areas of:** Food Industry. **Positions commonly filled include:** Restaurant/Food Service Manager. **Average salary range of placements:** $30,000 - $50,000. **Number of placements per year:** 100 - 199.

AGRI-LC
131 Degan Street, Lewisville TX 75057. 972/221-7568. **Fax:** 972/221-1409. **Contact:** Lawrence W Keeley, Owner/Manager. **Description:** An executive search firm focusing on the recruitment of personnel in all segments of agriculture. Founded in 1969. Company pays fee. **Specializes in the areas of:** Accounting/Auditing; Administration; Advertising; Biology; Engineering; Finance; Food Industry; General Management; Manufacturing; Personnel/Labor Relations; Sales. **Positions commonly filled include:** Accountant/Auditor; Administrative Manager; Agricultural Engineer; Bank Officer/Manager; Biochemist; Biological Scientist; Blue-Collar Worker Supervisor; Branch Manager; Budget Analyst; Buyer; Chemical Engineer; Chemist; Civil Engineer; Computer Programmer; Construction Contractor; Credit Manager; Customer Service Representative; Design Engineer; Editor; Environmental Engineer; Financial Analyst; Food Scientist/Technologist; Forester/Conservation Scientist; General Manager; Human Resources Specialist; Industrial Engineer; Landscape Architect; Licensed Practical Nurse; Management Trainee; Mechanical Engineer; MIS Specialist; Purchasing Agent/Manager; Quality Control Supervisor; Restaurant/Food Service Manager; Systems Analyst; Transportation/Traffic Specialist; Underwriter/Assistant Underwriter; Veterinarian. **Corporate headquarters location:** Kansas City KS. **Average salary range of placements:** $30,000 - $50,000. **Number of placements per year:** 1 - 49.

ALBRECHT & ASSOCIATES EXECUTIVE SEARCH
10700 Richmond Avenue, Suite 217, Houston TX 77042. 713/784-7444. **Fax:** 713/784-5049. **Contact:** Franke M. Albrecht, President. **E-mail address:** albrecht@aol.net. **Description:** An executive search firm operating on both retainer and contingency bases. Company pays fee. **Specializes in the areas of:** Administration; Biology; Computer Science/Software Engineering; Health/Medical; Technical. **Positions commonly filled include:** Biochemist; Biological Scientist; Biomedical Engineer; Chemical Engineer; Chemist; Civil Engineer; Clinical Lab Technician; Geologist/Geophysicist; Management Analyst/Consultant; Mechanical Engineer; MIS Specialist; Operations/Production Manager; Petroleum Engineer; Pharmacist; Structural Engineer; Systems Analyst. **Corporate headquarters location:** Cleveland OH. **Average salary range of placements:** More than $50,000. **Number of placements per year:** 100 - 199.

ALPHA RESOURCES GROUP
1916 Brabent Drive, Plano TX 75025. 214/692-1616. **Contact:** Manager. **Description:** An executive search firm. **Specializes in the areas of:** Hotel/Restaurant.

PETER W. AMBLER COMPANY
14651 Dallas Parkway, Suite 402, Dallas TX 75240. 972/404-8712. **Contact:** Manager. **Description:** A generalist, retained executive search firm.

AMERI SEARCH
P.O. Box 427, Rockwall TX 75087. 972/722-8033. **Toll-free phone:** 800/226-0534. **Fax:** 972/722-0633. **Contact:** John Scott, Owner. **Description:** An executive search firm. Company pays fee. **Specializes in the areas of:** Food Industry. **Positions commonly filled include:** Agricultural Engineer; Biochemist; Biological Scientist; Design Engineer; Electrical/Electronics Engineer; Environmental Engineer; Food Scientist/Technologist; General Manager; Human Resources Specialist; Industrial Engineer; Industrial Production Manager; Mechanical Engineer; Public Relations Manager; Purchasing Agent/Manager; Quality Control Supervisor; Stationary Engineer; Transportation/Traffic Specialist; Veterinarian. **Average salary range of placements:** $30,000 - $50,000. **Number of placements per year:** 1 - 49.

AMERICAN RESOURCES
4420 FM 1960 West, Suite 206, Houston TX 77068. 281/444-6515. **Contact:** Manager. **Description:** An executive search firm. **Specializes in the areas of:** Computer Hardware/Software; Electronics; Engineering; Manufacturing; Sales; Transportation.

ANDREWS-CARTER PERSONNEL SERVICE
P.O. Box 835956, Richardson TX 75083. 972/239-9484. **Fax:** 972/239-3753. **Contact:** Leann Andrews, Owner. **Description:** An executive search firm operating on both retainer and contingency bases. Company pays fee. **Specializes in the areas of:** Food Industry; Health/Medical; Sales. **Positions commonly filled include:** Loan Officer; Restaurant/Food Service Manager; Sales Representative. **Number of placements per year:** 1 - 49.

APEX COMPUTER PLACEMENTS INC.
616 North Bell Avenue, Denton TX 76201. 940/565-0658. **Contact:** Manager. **Description:** An executive search firm. **Specializes in the areas of:** Computer Hardware/Software.

AREND & ASSOCIATES
P.O. Box 821311, Houston TX 77282-1311. 713/827-7800. **Contact:** Manager. **Description:** An executive search firm that places personnel in a wide range of industries.

ATWOOD PROFESSIONAL SEARCH
P.O. Box 58411, Houston TX 77258. 281/333-1061. **Contact:** Dan Atwood, President. **Description:** An executive search firm. **Specializes in the areas of:** Engineering; Oil and Gas.

AUDIT PROFESSIONALS INTERNATIONAL
3312 Woodford Drive, Suite 400, Arlington TX 76013. 817/277-0888. **Contact:** Keith Malcolm, CPA, Vice President. **E-mail address:** hedman@onramp.net. **Description:** An executive search firm that also provides contract services. Founded in 1987. Company pays fee. **Specializes in the areas of:** Accounting/Auditing; Administration; Finance; Information Systems. **Positions commonly filled include:** Accountant/Auditor; Actuary; Internet Services Manager; Telecommunications Manager. **Average salary range of placements:** More than $50,000. **Number of placements per year:** 50 - 99.

MARILYN AUSTIN & ASSOCIATES
11999 Katy Freeway, Suite 150, Houston TX 77079. 281/493-5706. **Fax:** 281/597-5354. **Contact:** Marilyn Austin, Owner. **Description:** An executive search firm. **Specializes in the areas of:** Banking; Finance; Health/Medical.

AUSTIN GROUP
11511 Katy Freeway, Suite 290, Houston TX 77079. 281/497-8595. **Fax:** 281/597-0099. **Contact:** Manager. **Description:** An executive search firm. **Specializes in the areas of:** Accounting/Auditing; Chemical; Economics; Electronics; Engineering; Tax.

BALDWIN & COMPANY
5858 Westheimer, Suite 403, Houston TX 77057. 713/977-2300. **Contact:** Manager. **Description:** An executive search firm. **Specializes in the areas of:** Accounting/Auditing; Finance.

R. GAINES BATY ASSOCIATES, INC.
12750 Merritt Drive, Suite 990, Lockbox 199, Dallas TX 75251. 972/386-7900. **Fax:** 972/387-2224. **Contact:** R. Gaines Baty, President. **E-mail address:** rgba@rgba.com. **Description:** A worldwide executive search firm for MIS management and information technology consulting positions, as well as bilingual accounting and auditing positions. Company pays fee. **Specializes in the areas of:** Computer Science/Software; Finance; MIS/EDP. **Positions commonly filled include:** Accountant/Auditor; Management Analyst/Consultant; MIS Specialist; Systems Analyst; Telecommunications Manager. **Average salary range of placements:** More than $50,000. **Number of placements per year:** 1 - 49.

BENCHMARK PROFESSIONALS
P.O. Box 1212, Leander TX 78646-1212. 512/259-5666. **Fax:** 512/259-5670. **Contact:** Mr. J.B. Pearson, Owner. **Description:** An executive search firm. **Specializes in the areas of:** Engineering; Health/Medical; Manufacturing; Technical. **Positions commonly filled include:** Biological Scientist; Biomedical Engineer; Chemical Engineer; Chemist; Electrical/Electronics Engineer; General Manager; Health Services Manager; Industrial Engineer; Mechanical Engineer; Operations/Production Manager; Physician; Quality Control Supervisor; Registered Nurse.

BEST/WORLD ASSOCIATES
505 West Abram Street, 3rd Floor, Arlington TX 76010. 817/861-0000. **Toll-free phone:** 800/749-2846. **Fax:** 817/459-2378. **Contact:** G. Tim Best, President. **Description:** An executive search firm operating on a retainer basis. Company pays fee. **Specializes in the areas of:** Banking; Computer Science/Software; Engineering; Finance; Food Industry; Manufacturing; Personnel/Labor Relations; Sales. **Positions commonly filled include:** Accountant/Auditor; Chemical Engineer; Economist; Electrical/Electronics Engineer; Environmental Engineer; Financial Analyst; Food Scientist/Technologist; Human Resources Specialist; Management Analyst/Consultant; Market Research Analyst; Mechanical Engineer; MIS Specialist; Software Engineer; Statistician; Systems Analyst. **Corporate headquarters location:** This Location. **Other U.S. locations:** Phoenix AZ; Torrance CA; Orlando FL; Piscataway NJ. **Average salary range of placements:** More than $50,000. **Number of placements per year:** 50 - 99.

BILSON & HAZEN INTERNATIONAL
1231 Greenway Drive, Suite 390, Irving TX 75034. 972/753-1193. **Fax:** 972/753-0969. **Contact:** Frederick Sagoe, President. **Description:** An executive search firm that also offers temporary and contract services. Company pays fee. **Specializes in the areas**

of: Computer Science/Software; Personnel/Labor Relations; Sales. **Positions commonly filled include:** Administrative Manager; Branch Manager; Claim Rep.; Computer Programmer; Design Engineer; Electrical/ Electronics Engineer; Human Resources Specialist; Manufacturer's/Wholesaler's Sales Rep.; Market Research Analyst; MIS Specialist; Software Engineer; Technical Writer/Editor; Telecommunications Manager. **Benefits available to temporary workers:** Dental Insurance; Medical Insurance. **Average salary range of placements:** More than $50,000. **Number of placements per year:** 50 - 99.

BIOSOURCE INTERNATIONAL
1878 Hilltop Drive, Suite 100, Lewisville TX 75067-2114. 972/317-7060. **Fax:** 972/317-0500. **Contact:** Ric J. Favors, Principal. **E-mail address:** biosource@why.net. **World Wide Web address:** http://www.why.net/users/biosource/index.html. **Description:** An executive search firm. Company pays fee. **Specializes in the areas of:** Biotechnology; Health/Medical; Pharmaceutical; Scientific; Technical. **Positions commonly filled include:** Biochemist; Biological Scientist; Biomedical Engineer; Chemical Engineer; Chemist; Chief Executive Officer; Compliance Analyst; Computer Programmer; Electrical/Electronics Engineer; General Manager; Management Analyst/Consultant; Mechanical Engineer; MIS Specialist; Multimedia Designer; Physician; President; Production Manager; Quality Assurance Engineer; Quality Control Supervisor; Science Technologist; Software Engineer; Statistician; Systems Analyst; Technical Writer/Editor. **Corporate headquarters location:** This Location. **Other U.S. locations:** Carlsbad CA; Sarasota FL; Greensboro NC. **Average salary range of placements:** More than $50,000. **Number of placements per year:** 1 - 49.

MARTIN BIRNBACH & ASSOCIATES
15150 Preston Road, Suite 300, Dallas TX 75248. 972/490-5627. **Contact:** Manager. **Description:** An executive search firm. **Specializes in the areas of:** Sales.

HOWARD C. BLOOM EXECUTIVE SEARCH
INTERIM LEGAL PROFESSIONALS
5000 Quorum Drive, Suite 770, Dallas TX 75240. 972/385-6455. **Fax:** 972/385-1006. **Contact:** Howard Bloom, President. **Description:** An executive search firm. Interim Legal Professionals (also at this location) provides permanent legal placements. Company pays fee. **Specializes in the areas of:** Legal. **Positions commonly filled include:** Attorney. **Number of placements per year:** 1 - 49.

BOLES & ASSOCIATES
1750 North Collins Boulevard, Suite 200, Richardson TX 75080. **Fax:** 972/480-9886. **Contact:** Terry C. Boles, Managing Partner. **E-mail address:** bolesassoc@aol.com. **Description:** A retained executive search firm. Founded in 1989. **Specializes in the areas of:** Administration; Engineering; General Management; Human Resources; Sales. **Positions commonly filled include:** Telecommunications Manager. **Average salary range of placements:** More than $50,000. **Number of placements per year:** 1 - 49.

BOND & ASSOCIATES
8509 Fair Haven Court, Fort Worth TX 76176. 817/236-3549. **Contact:** Manager. **Description:** An executive search firm. **Specializes in the areas of:** Engineering; Health/Medical; Information Technology.

BORREL PERSONNEL
P.O. Box 31900-386, Houston TX 77231-1900. 713/541-1328. **Contact:** Manager. **Description:** An executive search firm. **Specializes in the areas of:** Accounting/Auditing; Finance; Health/Medical; Real Estate; Software Development.

BRIDGE PERSONNEL
8350 North Central Expressway, Suite M1226, Dallas TX 75206. 214/692-8273. **Fax:** 214/369-6070. **Contact:** Jim Peeler, CPA, Owner. **Description:** An executive search firm operating on both retainer and contingency bases. Company pays fee. **Specializes in the areas of:** Accounting/Auditing; Administration; Computer Science/Software; Finance; Information Systems. **Positions commonly filled include:** Accountant/Auditor; Computer Programmer; Financial Analyst; Software Engineer; Systems Analyst; Telecommunications Manager.

BROOKLEA & ASSOCIATES, INC.
12200 Ford Road, Suite 108, Farmers Branch TX 75234. 972/484-9400. **Fax:** 972/484-9400. **Contact:** Recruiter. **Description:** An executive search firm operating on a contingency basis. Company pays fee. **Specializes in the areas of:** Accounting/Auditing; Architecture/Construction; Art/Design; Finance; Health/Medical; Sales; Secretarial. **Positions commonly filled include:** Accountant/Auditor; Architect; Draftsperson; Emergency Medical Technician; Health Services Manager; Landscape Architect; Licensed Practical Nurse; Medical Records Technician; Occupational Therapist; Physical Therapist; Physician; Recreational Therapist; Registered Nurse; Respiratory Therapist; Services Sales Rep.; Surgical Technician; Surveyor; Veterinarian. **Number of placements per year:** 100 - 199.

BROWNSON & ASSOCIATES
5599 San Felipe, Suite 610, Houston TX 77056. 713/626-4790. **Contact:** Manager. **Description:** An executive search firm.

D. BRUSH & ASSOCIATES
9099 Katy Freeway, Houston TX 77024. 713/935-9777. **Fax:** 713/935-0165. **Contact:** Ms. D. Brush, Owner. **Description:** An executive search firm. **Specializes in the areas of:** Computer Hardware/Software.

BUCKLEY GROUP
15851 Dallas Parkway, Dallas TX 75248. 972/490-1722. **Contact:** Manager. **Description:** An executive search firm that places sales and marketing professionals in high-technology companies. **Specializes in the areas of:** Marketing; Sales.

BUNDY-STEWART ASSOCIATES, INC.
13601 Preston Road, Suite 107W, Dallas TX 75240. 972/458-0626. **Fax:** 972/661-2670. **Contact:** Carolyn Stewart, Owner. **Description:** An executive search firm operating on a contingency basis. **Specializes in the areas of:** Accounting/Auditing; Administration; Computer Science/Software; Engineering; Industrial; Insurance; Manufacturing; Personnel/Labor Relations; Real Estate; Sales; Telecommunications. **Positions commonly filled include:** Accountant/Auditor; Attorney; Buyer; Computer Programmer; Credit Manager; Customer Service Rep.; Design Engineer; Draftsperson; Electrical/Electronics Engineer; Human Resources Specialist; Industrial Engineer; Industrial Production Manager; Market Research Analyst; Mechanical Engineer; MIS Specialist; Purchasing Agent/Manager; Quality Control Supervisor; Securities Sales Rep.; Software Engineer; Systems Analyst; Telecommunications Manager.

BURGESON HOSPITALITY SEARCH
13300 Old Blanco Road, San Antonio TX 78248. **Fax:** 210/492-9921. **Contact:** Tom Burgeson, President. **Description:** An executive search firm. Founded in 1979. Company pays fee. **Positions commonly filled include:** Hotel Manager. **Number of placements per year:** 50 - 99.

C.G. & COMPANY
5050 East University, Suite 9B, Odessa TX 79762. 915/362-7681. **Fax:** 915/362-3578. **Contact:** Cathy George, CPC, Owner. **Description:** An executive search firm operating on both retainer and contingency bases. **Specializes in the areas of:** Computer Science/Software; Engineering; Manufacturing; Technical. **Positions commonly filled include:** Accountant/Auditor; Administrative Manager; Advertising Clerk; Aerospace Engineer; Agricultural Engineer; Architect; Attorney; Bank Officer/Manager; Blue-Collar Worker Supervisor; Brokerage Clerk; Budget Analyst; Buyer; Chemical Engineer; Chemist; Civil Engineer; Clerical Supervisor; Computer Programmer; Construction Contractor; Cost Estimator; Counselor; Credit Manager; Customer Service Rep.; Design Engineer; Designer; Draftsperson; Electrical/Electronics Engineer; Electrician; Environmental Engineer; Financial Analyst; Geologist/Geophysicist; Human Resources Specialist; Industrial Engineer; Industrial Production Manager; Management Analyst/Consultant; Management Trainee; Manufacturer's/Wholesaler's Sales Rep.; Market Research Analyst; Mechanical Engineer; Medical Records Technician; Metallurgical Engineer; Mining Engineer; MIS Specialist; Multimedia Designer; Occupational Therapist; Paralegal; Petroleum Engineer; Physical Therapist; Physician; Public Relations Specialist; Purchasing Agent/Manager; Quality Control Supervisor; Radio/TV Announcer/Broadcaster; Radiological Technologist; Recreational Therapist; Registered Nurse; Respiratory Therapist; Restaurant/Food Service Manager; Securities Sales Rep.; Services Sales Rep.; Software Engineer; Speech-Language Pathologist; Systems Analyst; Technical Writer/Editor; Telecommunications Manager; Travel Agent; Typist/Word Processor. **Average salary range of placements:** More than $50,000. **Number of placements per year:** 100 - 199.

CAD TECHNOLOGY, INC.
1111 Wilcrest Green, Suite 450, Houston TX 77042. 713/785-2411. **Fax:** 713/785-1625. **Contact:** Jeani DeSisto, Staffing Coordinator. **Description:** An executive search firm operating on a contingency basis. Company pays fee. **Specializes in the areas of:** Architecture/Construction; Computer Science/Software; Engineering. **Positions commonly filled include:** Architect; Buyer; Chemical Engineer; Civil Engineer; Computer Programmer; Construction and Building Inspector; Cost Estimator; Design Engineer; Designer; Draftsperson; Electrical/Electronics Engineer; Environmental Engineer; Geologist/Geophysicist; Industrial Engineer; Mechanical Engineer; Mining Engineer; MIS Specialist; Operations/Production Manager; Petroleum Engineer; Quality Control Supervisor; Software Engineer; Structural Engineer; Systems Analyst; Technical Writer/Editor; Telecommunications Manager; Transportation/Traffic Specialist. **Number of placements per year:** 100 - 199.

CARPENTER & ASSOCIATES
8333 Douglas Avenue, Suite 875, Dallas TX 75225. 214/691-6585. **Fax:** 214/691-6838. **Contact:** Elsie Carpenter, President. **Description:** An executive search firm. Founded in 1981. Company pays fee. **Specializes in the areas of:** Advertising; Fashion; Personnel/Labor Relations; Retail. **Positions commonly filled include:** Buyer; Retail Manager; Retail Merchandiser. **Number of placements per year:** 1 - 49.

CHAMPION PERSONNEL SERVICE
8326 Wind Willow Drive, Houston TX 77040. 713/937-6160. **Fax:** 713/896-0543. **Contact:** Dee Jones, Consultant. **Description:** An executive search firm operating on a contingency basis. Company pays fee. **Specializes in the areas of:** Construction; Engineering; Manufacturing. **Positions commonly filled include:** Biological Scientist; Biomedical Engineer; Chemical Engineer; Civil Engineer; Computer Programmer; Construction Contractor; Cost Estimator; Electrical/Electronics Engineer; Environmental Engineer; Human Resources Specialist; Industrial Engineer; Industrial Production Manager; Licensed Practical Nurse; Materials Engineer; Mechanical Engineer; Metallurgical Engineer; Nuclear Engineer; Purchasing Agent/Manager; Quality Control Supervisor; Registered Nurse; Software Engineer; Structural Engineer; Systems Analyst.

CHERBONNIER GROUP
3050 Post Oak Boulevard, Houston TX 77056-6527. **Contact:** L.M. Cherbonnier, President. **Description:** An executive search firm operating on a retainer basis. Founded in 1969. Company pays fee. **Specializes in the areas of:** Accounting/Auditing; Administration; Architecture/Construction; Banking; Computer Science/Software; Engineering; Finance; General Management; Health/Medical; Legal; Personnel/Labor Relations. **Positions commonly filled include:** Attorney; Biomedical Engineer; Chemical Engineer; Chemist; Civil Engineer; Design Engineer; Electrical/Electronics Engineer; Environmental Engineer; General Manager; Geologist/Geophysicist; Mechanical Engineer; MIS Specialist; Occupational Therapist; Operations/Production Manager; Petroleum Engineer; Physician; Software Engineer; Telecommunications Manager. **Corporate headquarters location:** This Location. **Other U.S. locations:** Jackson MS; Seattle WA. **Number of placements per year:** 1 - 49.

JOSEPH CHRIS PARTNERS
900 Rockmead Drive, Suite 101, Humble TX 77339. 281/359-0060. **Contact:** Manager. **Description:** An executive search firm. **Specializes in the areas of:** Construction; Real Estate.

COMPUTER MANAGEMENT SEARCH
12801 North Central Expressway, Suite 1170, Dallas TX 75243. 972/458-0090. **Contact:** Manager. **Description:** An executive search firm. **Specializes in the areas of:** Computer Hardware/Software; Computer Programming; Computer Science/Software.

COMPUTER PROFESSIONALS UNLIMITED
13612 Midway Road, Suite 333, Dallas TX 75244. 972/233-1773. **Fax:** 972/233-9619. **Contact:** V.J. Zapotocky, Owner/President. **E-mail address:** zipzap@onramp.net. **Description:** An executive search firm that also provides contract services. Founded in 1978. Company pays fee. **Specializes in the areas of:** Computer Science/Software; Engineering; Information Technology. **Positions commonly filled include:** Computer Programmer; Electrical/Electronics Engineer; Internet Services Manager; MIS Specialist; Software Engineer; Systems Analyst; Technical Writer/Editor; Telecommunications Manager. **Average salary range of placements:** More than $50,000. **Number of placements per year:** 50 - 99.

COMPUTER TECHNOLOGY SEARCH
5599 San Felipe, Suite 800, Houston TX 77056. 713/785-2005. **Fax:** 713/785-5179. **Contact:** Karl F. Decker, Manager. **Description:** An executive search firm operating on a contingency basis. Company pays fee. **Specializes in the areas of:** Computer Science/Software. **Positions commonly filled include:** Computer Programmer; Internet Services Manager; MIS Specialist; Multimedia Designer; Software Engineer; Statistician; Systems Analyst; Technical Writer/Editor; Telecommunications Manager. **Corporate headquarters location:** Dallas TX. **Other U.S. locations:** Los Angeles CA; Atlanta GA; Chicago IL; Kansas City KS. **Number of placements per year:** 100 - 199.

CORPORATE SEARCH ASSOCIATES
4180 North Mesa, Suite 107, El Paso TX 79902. 915/534-2583. **Contact:** Manager. **Description:** An executive search firm.

CORPORATE SEARCH INC.
3028 Lubbock Avenue, Fort Worth TX 76109. 817/926-0320. **Toll-free phone:** 800/429-1763. **Fax:** 817/926-1610. **Contact:** John S. Gramentine, President. **Description:** An executive search firm. Company pays fee. **Specializes in the areas of:** Computer Science/Software; Food Industry; Personnel/Labor Relations; Retail; Sales. **Positions commonly filled include:** Branch Manager; General Manager; Human Resources Specialist; Management Trainee; Public Relations Specialist; Services Sales Representative; Software Engineer; Systems Analyst; Telecommunications Manager. **Average salary range of placements:** More than $50,000. **Number of placements per year:** 200 - 499.

CRAIG AFFILIATES, INC.
901 Waterfall Way, Suite 107, Richardson TX 75080. 972/644-3264. **Fax:** 972/644-4065. **Contact:** Edward C. Nemec, President. **Description:** An executive search firm. **Specializes in the areas of:** Food Industry. **Positions commonly filled include:** Branch Manager; Buyer; General Manager. **Number of placements per year:** 50 - 99.

DDR, INC.
8111 LBJ Freeway, Suite 1155, Dallas TX 75251. 972/783-9981. **Contact:** Account Executive. **E-mail address:** ddrdal@gte.net. **Description:** An executive search firm. **Specializes in the areas of:** Technical. **Positions commonly filled include:** Computer Animator; Computer Operator; Computer Programmer; Database Manager; Financial Analyst; Hardware Engineer; Operations Manager; Project Manager; Software Engineer; Systems Analyst; Technical Writer/Editor. **Benefits available to temporary workers:** Dental Insurance; Life Insurance; Medical Insurance.

DFM & ASSOCIATES
4201 Spring Valley Road, Suite 1400, Dallas TX 75244. 972/776-3536. **Contact:** Denise M. Frost, President. **Description:** An executive search firm. Company pays fee. **Specializes in the areas of:** Legal; Secretarial. **Positions commonly filled include:** Accountant/Auditor; Clerical Supervisor; Customer Service Representative; Paralegal. **Number of placements per year:** 50 - 99.

DKS & ASSOCIATES
P.O. Box 5491, Katy TX 77491. 281/395-6300. **Contact:** Manager. **Description:** An executive search firm. **Specializes in the areas of:** Food Industry.

DAHER & ASSOCIATES/INSURANCE SEARCH SPECIALISTS
5311 Kirby Drive, Suite 200, Houston TX 77005. 713/520-8261. **Fax:** 713/520-0526. **Contact:** Liz Daher, President. **Description:** An executive search firm operating on a contingency basis. Founded in 1989. Company pays fee. **Specializes in the areas of:** Insurance. **Positions commonly filled include:** Accountant/Auditor; Actuary; Adjuster; Claim Rep.; Insurance Agent/Broker; Underwriter/Assistant Underwriter. **Number of placements per year:** 200 - 499.

DAMON & ASSOCIATES, INC.
7515 Greenville Avenue, Suite 900, Dallas TX 75231. 214/696-6990. **Fax:** 214/696-6993. **Contact:** Dick Damon, President. **Description:** An executive search firm. As a member of the First Interview Recruiting Network, the company provides the opportunity to interview in over 100 major markets in the U.S. and Canada. Founded in 1978. Company pays fee. **Specializes in the areas of:** Sales. **Average salary range of placements:** $30,000 - $50,000. **Number of placements per year:** 50 - 99.

THE DANBROOK GROUP
4100 Spring Valley Road, Suite 700-LB #2, Dallas TX 75244. 972/392-0057. **Contact:** Anne Kennedy, Senior Partner. **Description:** An executive search firm operating on a contingency basis. Company pays fee. **Specializes in the areas of:** Accounting/Auditing; Banking; Finance; General Management; Insurance. **Positions commonly filled include:** Accountant/Auditor; Adjuster; Bookkeeper; Chief Financial Officer; Claim Rep.; Credit Manager; Customer Service Rep.; Finance Director; Financial Analyst; Insurance Agent/Broker; Sales Rep.; Underwriter/Assistant Underwriter. **Average salary range of placements:** More than $50,000. **Number of placements per year:** 100 - 199.

JOHN DAVIDSON & ASSOCIATES
3198 Royal Lane, Suite 100, Dallas TX 75229. 214/352-7800. **Contact:** Manager. **Description:** A generalist executive search firm.

DENSON & ASSOCIATES
3100 Weslayan, Suite 300, Houston TX 77027. 713/993-9191. **Contact:** Manager. **Description:** An executive search firm. **Specializes in the areas of:** Oil and Gas. **Positions commonly filled include:** Petroleum Engineer.

DENTON-LEWIS ASSOCIATES
4242 Lively Lane, Suite 100, Dallas TX 75220. 214/358-5597. **Fax:** 214/358-5684. **Contact:** Hank Denton, Principal Consultant. **Description:** An executive search firm. Founded in 1980. Company pays fee. **Specializes in the areas of:** Banking; Finance; Insurance; Personnel/Labor Relations. **Positions commonly filled include:** Marketing Specialist.

DILWORTH & WOOLRIDGE INC.
5555 Morningside Drive, Suite 206, Houston TX 77005. 713/521-2800. **Contact:** Manager. **Description:** An executive search firm. **Specializes in the areas of:** Legal.

DIVERSIFIED ENGINEERING SEARCH
5599 San Felipe Road, Suite 850, Houston TX 77056. 713/629-5800. **Contact:** Manager. **Description:** An executive search firm. **Specializes in the areas of:** Engineering.

C. MICHAEL DIXON ASSOCIATES, INC.
P.O. Box 293371, Lewisville TX 75029. 972/317-0608. **Fax:** 972/317-0349. **Contact:** Mike Dixon, President. **E-mail address:** cmdixon@flash.net. **Description:** C. Michael Dixon Associates is an executive search firm. Founded in 1988. Company pays fee. **Specializes in the areas of:** Chemical; Engineering; Manufacturing; Petrochemical; Technical. **Positions commonly filled include:** Chemical Engineer; Electrical/Electronics Engineer; Industrial Engineer; Mechanical Engineer; Systems Analyst. **Average salary range of placements:** More than $50,000. **Number of placements per year:** 1 - 49.

JOHN A. DOMINO & ASSOCIATES
2121 East Broadway Street, Suite F, Pearland TX 77581. 281/485-2595. **Contact:** Manager. **Description:** An executive search firm. **Specializes in the areas of:** Health/Medical.

DUNHILL PROFESSIONAL SEARCH
P.O. Box 3114, McAllen TX 78502. 956/687-9531. **Contact:** Lloyd Steele, President. **Description:** An executive search firm operating on a contingency basis. Company pays fee. **Specializes in the areas of:**

Engineering; Food Industry; Industrial; Manufacturing; Technical. **Positions commonly filled include:** Biomedical Engineer; Chemical Engineer; Electrical/Electronics Engineer; Food Scientist/Technologist; Industrial Engineer; Industrial Production Manager; Mechanical Engineer; Quality Control Supervisor. **Corporate headquarters location:** Hauppauge NY. **Other U.S. locations:** Nationwide. **Average salary range of placements:** $30,000 - $50,000. **Number of placements per year:** 1 - 49.

DUNHILL PROFESSIONAL SEARCH
10303 Northwest Freeway, Suite 520, Houston TX 77092. 713/956-1146. **Fax:** 713/688-7544. **Contact:** Harry Coates, Manager. **Description:** An executive search firm operating on a contingency basis. **Specializes in the areas of:** Accounting/Auditing; Banking; Finance; Food Industry; General Management; Health/Medical; Manufacturing; Personnel/Labor Relations; Publishing; Sales. **Positions commonly filled include:** Accountant/Auditor; Bank Officer/Manager; Buyer; Chemical Engineer; Civil Engineer; Cost Estimator; Credit Manager; Customer Service Rep.; Economist; EEG Technologist; EKG Technician; General Manager; Health Services Manager; Hotel Manager; Human Resources Specialist; Human Service Worker; Industrial Production Manager; Manufacturer's/Wholesaler's Sales Rep.; Market Research Analyst; Medical Records Technician; Occupational Therapist; Pharmacist; Purchasing Agent/Manager; Quality Control Supervisor; Recreational Therapist; Registered Nurse; Services Sales Rep. **Corporate headquarters location:** Hauppauge NY. **Other U.S. locations:** Nationwide. **Average salary range of placements:** $30,000 - $50,000. **Number of placements per year:** 1 - 49.

EAI HEALTHCARE STAFFING
3120 SW Freeway, Suite 215, Houston TX 77098. 281/445-9001. **Contact:** Manager. **Description:** An executive search firm. **Specializes in the areas of:** Health/Medical.

EDP COMPUTER SERVICES
4600 Post Oak Place, Suite 203, Houston TX 77027. 713/960-1717. **Contact:** Manager. **Description:** An executive search firm. **Specializes in the areas of:** Computer Science/Software; Information Systems; Information Technology.

EISSLER & ASSOCIATES
1610 Woodstead Court, Suite 230, The Woodlands TX 77380. 281/367-1052. **Contact:** Manager. **Description:** An executive search firm. **Specializes in the areas of:** Plastics; Sales; Telecommunications.

ELLIOT ASSOCIATES INC.
505 Powell Street, Austin TX 78703. 512/472-4484. **Contact:** Manager. **Description:** An executive search firm. **Specializes in the areas of:** Hotel/Restaurant.

THE ELSWORTH GROUP
12910 Queens Forest, San Antonio TX 78230. 210/493-7211. **Contact:** Manager. **Description:** An executive search firm. Company pays fee. **Specializes in the areas of:** Computer Science/Software; Engineering; General Management; Industrial; Manufacturing; Sales; Technical; Transportation. **Positions commonly filled include:** Aerospace Engineer; Biomedical Engineer; Chemical Engineer; Civil Engineer; Computer Programmer; Cost Estimator; Designer; Draftsperson; Electrical/Electronics Engineer; General Manager; Industrial Engineer; Management Analyst/Consultant; Manufacturer's/Wholesaler's Sales Rep.; Mechanical Engineer; Metallurgical Engineer; Nuclear Engineer; Operations/Production Manager; Petroleum Engineer; Physicist; Production Manager; Purchasing Agent/Manager; Quality Control Supervisor; Software Engineer; Structural Engineer; Systems Analyst; Technical Writer/Editor. **Number of placements per year:** 1 - 49.

EMPLOYEE SOURCES
One Pinedale Street, Houston TX 77006. **Fax:** 713/520-7518. **Contact:** Manager. **Description:** An executive search firm operating on both retainer and contingency bases. Company pays fee. **Specializes in the areas of:** Accounting/Auditing; Administration; Engineering; Finance; Insurance; Personnel/Labor Relations; Sales. **Positions commonly filled include:** Accountant/Auditor; Budget Analyst; Electrical/Electronics Engineer; Environmental Engineer; Financial Analyst; Human Resources Specialist; Industrial Engineer; Mechanical Engineer; MIS Specialist; Purchasing Agent/Manager; Securities Sales Rep.; Services Sales Rep.; Software Engineer. **Average salary range of placements:** $30,000 - $50,000. **Number of placements per year:** 1 - 49.

THE ENERGISTS
10260 Westheimer, Suite 300, Houston TX 77042. 713/781-6881. **Fax:** 713/781-2998. **Contact:** Alex Preston, President. **Description:** An executive search firm with a primary focus on placing upper-level professionals. Company pays fee. **Specializes in the areas of:** Engineering; Oil and Gas. **Positions commonly filled include:** Geologist/Geophysicist; Petroleum Engineer. **Number of placements per year:** 50 - 99.

EXECU STAFF
P.O. Box 533601, Harlingen TX 78553. 956/504-9379. **Contact:** Manager. **Description:** An executive search firm.

EXECUTEAM
5858 Westheimer, Suite 303, Houston TX 77057. 713/952-6760. **Contact:** Laura Bowen, Staffing Coordinator. **Description:** An executive search firm. **Specializes in the areas of:** Accounting/Auditing; Clerical; Executives; Legal; Office Support; Secretarial.

THE EXECUTIVE CONSULTING GROUP
701 North Post Oak Road, Suite 610, Houston TX 77024. 713/686-9500. **Fax:** 713/686-9599. **Contact:** David L. Gandin, Partner. **Description:** An executive search firm operating on a contingency basis. Company pays fee. **Specializes in the areas of:** Banking; Finance. **Positions commonly filled include:** Accountant/Auditor; Bank Officer/Manager; Budget Analyst; Financial Analyst; Management Analyst/Consultant.

EXECUTIVE RESTAURANT SEARCH
PINNACLE SEARCH GROUP
2925 LBJ Freeway, Suite 253, Dallas TX 75234. 972/484-8600. **Contact:** Manager. **Description:** An executive search firm specializing in all levels of restaurant management. Pinnacle Search Group (also at this location) is the agency's food sales division. **Specializes in the areas of:** Restaurant.

EXECUTIVE SEARCH CONSULTANTS
3030 North Josey Lane, Suite 101-117, Carrollton TX 75007. 972/394-4131. **Contact:** Manager. **Description:** An executive search firm. **Specializes in the areas of:** Accounting/Auditing; Sales.

EXECUTIVE SEARCH INTERNATIONAL
1700 Alma Drive, Suite 370, Plano TX 75075. 972/424-4714. **Contact:** Manager. **Description:** An executive search firm.

EXECUTIVE SEARCH PERSONNEL
14999 Preston Road, Box D212-308, Dallas TX 75230. 972/386-6633. **Fax:** 972/386-9933. **Contact:**

Manager. **Description:** An executive search firm. Company pays fee. **Specializes in the areas of:** Accounting/Auditing; Administration; Banking; Finance; Food Industry; General Management; Health/Medical; Industrial; Insurance; Manufacturing; Nonprofit; Personnel/Labor Relations; Retail; Sales; Technical. **Positions commonly filled include:** Accountant/Auditor; Attorney; Buyer; Financial Analyst; General Manager; Human Resources Manager; Management Analyst/Consultant; Manufacturer's/Wholesaler's Sales Rep.; Securities Sales Rep.; Services Sales Rep.; Underwriter/Assistant Underwriter. **Number of placements per year:** 1 - 49.

EXECUTIVE SOURCE INTERNATIONAL
16500 San Pedro Avenue, Suite 295, San Antonio TX 78232. 210/494-0103. **Contact:** Warren Cook, Owner. **Description:** An executive search firm operating on both retainer and contingency bases. The firm focuses on the placement of professionals in pharmaceutical and biotechnology firms. **Positions commonly filled include:** Chemical Engineer; Civil Engineer; Electrical/Electronics Engineer; Environmental Engineer; Industrial Engineer; Mechanical Engineer; Operations/Production Manager. **Average salary range of placements:** More than $50,000. **Number of placements per year:** 1 - 49.

OTIS FAULKNER & ASSOCIATES INC.
2628 Windsor Place, Plano TX 75075. 972/423-1712. **Contact:** Manager. **Description:** An executive search firm. **Specializes in the areas of:** Medical Sales and Marketing; Sales.

CLAIRE FONTAINE & ASSOCIATES
701 Brazos, Suite 495, Austin TX 78701. 512/320-1400. **Contact:** Manager. **Description:** An executive search firm. **Specializes in the areas of:** Administration; Clerical.

FOOD PRO RECRUITERS
14526 Jones Maltsberger, Suite 210, San Antonio TX 78247. 210/494-9272. **Contact:** Rick King, Manager. **Description:** An executive search firm. **Specializes in the areas of:** Food Industry; Pharmaceutical.

F-O-R-T-U-N-E PERSONNEL CONSULTANTS
5403 Everhart Road, Suite 54, Corpus Christi TX 78411-4843. 512/852-3836. **Fax:** 512/852-3837. **Contact:** Personnel. **Description:** An executive search firm operating on a contingency basis. Company pays fee. **Specializes in the areas of:** Engineering; Manufacturing. **Positions commonly filled include:** Aerospace Engineer; Chemical Engineer; Chemist; Design Engineer; Electrical/Electronics Engineer; Mechanical Engineer. **Corporate headquarters location:** New York NY. **Other U.S. locations:** Nationwide. **Average salary range of placements:** $30,000 - $50,000. **Number of placements per year:** 1 - 49.

F-O-R-T-U-N-E PERSONNEL CONSULTANTS/SAN ANTONIO
10924 Vance Jackson Road, Suite 303, San Antonio TX 78230. 210/690-9797. **Fax:** 210/696-6909. **Contact:** Jim Morrisey, CPC, President. **E-mail address:** fortunesat@fortunesat.com. **World Wide Web address:** http://www.fortunesat.com. **Description:** An executive search firm operating on both contingency and retainer bases. Founded in 1980. Company pays fee. **Specializes in the areas of:** Engineering; Industrial; Manufacturing. **Positions commonly filled include:** Design Engineer; Electrical/Electronics Engineer; Industrial Engineer; Mechanical Engineer; Software Engineer. **Corporate headquarters location:** New York NY. **Other U.S. locations:** Nationwide. **Average salary range of placements:** More than $50,000. **Number of placements per year:** 50 - 99.

FOX-MORRIS ASSOCIATES
5400 LBJ Freeway, Suite 1445, Dallas TX 75240. 972/404-8044. **Contact:** Manager. **Description:** An executive search firm that places upper-level managers. **Specializes in the areas of:** Human Resources; Sales.

GILLHAM & ASSOCIATES
3400 Carlisle Street, Suite 100, Dallas TX 75204. **Contact:** Rick Gillham, President. **Description:** An executive search firm operating on a retainer basis. Founded in 1982. **Specializes in the areas of:** Real Estate. **Positions commonly filled include:** Accountant/Auditor; Construction/Building Inspector; Construction Contractor; Financial Analyst; Hotel Manager; Management Analyst/Consultant; Market Research Analyst; Property and Real Estate Manager. **Average salary range of placements:** More than $50,000. **Number of placements per year:** 50 - 99.

ABEL M. GONZALEZ & ASSOCIATES
P.O. Box 681845, San Antonio TX 78268. 210/695-5555. **Fax:** 210/695-8955. **Contact:** Abel Gonzalez, General Manager. **E-mail address:** abel695555@webtv.net. **Description:** An executive search firm operating on both retainer and contingency bases. Founded in 1978. Company pays fee. **Specializes in the areas of:** Advertising; Banking; Food Industry; General Management; Industrial; Manufacturing; Personnel/Labor Relations; Sales. **Positions commonly filled include:** Account Manager; Account Rep.; Accountant; Advertising Executive; Auditor; Bank Officer/Manager; Branch Manager; Chemical Engineer; Chemist; Civil Engineer; Computer Programmer; Environmental Engineer; Finance Director; Financial Analyst; Food Scientist/Technologist; General Manager; Human Resources Manager; Industrial Engineer; Industrial Production Manager; Manufacturing Engineer; Marketing Manager; Mechanical Engineer; Operations/Production Manager; Public Relations Specialist; Sales Engineer; Sales Executive; Sales Rep.; Systems Analyst; Transportation/Traffic Specialist; Vice President. **Corporate headquarters location:** This Location. **Average salary range of placements:** More than $50,000. **Number of placements per year:** 1 - 49.

GRIFFIN ANDERSON & ASSOCIATES
1631 Dorchester Drive, Suite 104-A, Plano TX 75075. 972/612-0188. **Contact:** Manager. **Description:** An executive search firm. **Specializes in the areas of:** Sales.

H+M RECRUITERS
P.O. Box 121747, Arlington TX 76012. 817/261-6565. **Fax:** 817/461-6565. **Contact:** Bruce Powers, Ph.D., Partner. **Description:** An executive search firm operating on a contingency basis. Founded in 1986. Company pays fee. **Specializes in the areas of:** Chemical; Engineering; Industrial; Manufacturing; Plastics; Rubber; Technical. **Positions commonly filled include:** Biochemist; Chemical Engineer; Chemist; Design Engineer; Industrial Engineer; Mechanical Engineer. **Average salary range of placements:** More than $50,000. **Number of placements per year:** 1 - 49.

H.P.R. HEALTH STAFF
2201 North Collins Street, Suite 260, Arlington TX 76011. 817/261-3355. **Fax:** 817/543-3155. **Contact:** Vera E. Harris, CPC, Owner. **E-mail address:** vharris@1america.net. **Description:** An executive search firm operating on a contingency basis. Company pays fee. **Specializes in the areas of:** Health/Medical. **Positions commonly filled include:** Chief Financial Officer; Clinical Lab Technician; Controller; Dental Assistant/Dental Hygienist; Dentist; Dietician/Nutritionist; EEG Technologist; EKG Technician; Environmental Engineer; Health Services Manager; Human Resources

Manager; Licensed Practical Nurse; Medical Records Technician; Nuclear Medicine Technologist; Occupational Therapist; Pharmacist; Physical Therapist; Physician; Psychologist; Radiological Technologist; Registered Nurse; Respiratory Therapist; Speech-Language Pathologist; Surgical Technician. **Average salary range of placements:** $30,000 - $50,000.

ROBERT HALF INTERNATIONAL/ACCOUNTEMPS
1280 Hawkins Boulevard, El Paso TX 79925. 915/593-6699. **Contact:** Manager. **Description:** An executive search firm. Accountemps (also at this location) provides temporary placements. **Corporate headquarters location:** Menlo Park CA. **Other U.S. locations:** Nationwide.

HARAGAN ASSOCIATES
8350 Meadow Road, Suite 262, Dallas TX 75231. 214/363-3634. **Fax:** 214/363-3652. **Contact:** Mr. Pat W. Haragan, Principal/Owner. **Description:** An executive search firm operating on a retainer basis. Haragan Associates focuses exclusively on the health care industry including pharmaceuticals, medical devices, biotechnology, diagnostics, medical equipment, and services. **Specializes in the areas of:** Biology; General Management; Health/Medical; Manufacturing; Sales; Technical. **Positions commonly filled include:** Biochemist; Biological Scientist; Biomedical Engineer; Chemist; Clinical Lab Technician; Food Scientist/Technologist; Health Services Manager; Human Resources Specialist; Nuclear Medicine Technologist; Occupational Therapist; Pharmacist; Physical Therapist; Physician; Quality Control Supervisor; Registered Nurse; Veterinarian. **Average salary range of placements:** More than $50,000. **Number of placements per year:** 1 - 49.

DARLENE HAY & ASSOCIATES
2400 Augusta Drive, Houston TX 77057. 713/789-0486. **Contact:** Darlene Hay, Owner. **Description:** An executive search firm.

HEALTH NETWORK USA
13154 Coit Road, Suite 202, Dallas TX 75240. **Toll-free phone:** 800/872-0212. **Fax:** 972/918-9997. **Contact:** David J. Elliott, President. **E-mail address:** hninfo@hnusa.com. **Description:** An executive search firm. **Specializes in the areas of:** Health/Medical. **Positions commonly filled include:** Clinical Lab Technician; Dental Assistant/Hygienist; Dental Lab Technician; Dentist; Dietician/Nutritionist; EEG Technologist; EKG Technician; Health Services Manager; Human Resources Manager; Licensed Practical Nurse; Medical Records Technician; Nuclear Medicine Technologist; Occupational Therapist; Pharmacist; Physical Therapist; Physician; Psychologist; Public Relations Specialist; Purchasing Agent/Manager; Radiological Technologist; Recreational Therapist; Registered Nurse; Respiratory Therapist; Social Worker; Speech-Language Pathologist; Surgical Technician. **Number of placements per year:** 50 - 99.

HEALTH PROFESSIONALS OF AMERICA
P.O. Box 34829, Houston TX 77234. 281/481-9923. **Fax:** 281/481-9922. **Contact:** Joseph Balesky, CEO. **Description:** An executive search firm operating on a contingency basis. Founded in 1980. Company pays fee. **Specializes in the areas of:** Health/Medical. **Positions commonly filled include:** Accountant/Auditor; Biomedical Engineer; Claim Rep.; Clerical Supervisor; Clinical Lab Technician; Computer Programmer; Dietician/Nutritionist; Education Administrator; EEG Technologist; EKG Technician; Financial Analyst; Health Services Manager; Licensed Practical Nurse; Medical Records Technician; MIS Specialist; Nuclear Medicine Technologist; Occupational Therapist; Pharmacist; Physical Therapist; Physician; Psychologist; Public Relations Specialist; Registered Nurse; Respiratory Therapist; Restaurant/Food Service Manager; Speech-Language Pathologist; Surgical Technician; Systems Analyst; Typist/Word Processor. **Average salary range of placements:** More than $50,000. **Number of placements per year:** 1 - 49.

HEALTHCARE RECRUITERS INTERNATIONAL
4100 Spring Valley Road, Suite 800, Dallas TX 75244. 972/851-5470. **Contact:** Jim Wimberly, President. **Description:** An executive search firm. Company pays fee. **Specializes in the areas of:** Health/Medical; Sales; Technical. **Positions commonly filled include:** Biomedical Engineer; General Manager; Marketing Specialist; Sales Rep.; Technician. **Number of placements per year:** 1 - 49.

HEALTHCARE RECRUITERS OF HOUSTON, INC.
9301 Southwest Freeway, Suite 650, Houston TX 77074. 713/771-7344. **Fax:** 713/771-5326. **Contact:** James Tipton, President. **Description:** An executive search firm. Company pays fee. **Specializes in the areas of:** Health/Medical; Sales. **Positions commonly filled include:** Biological Scientist; Chemist; Dentist; Dietician/Nutritionist; General Manager; Health Services Manager; Licensed Practical Nurse; Medical Records Technician; Occupational Therapist; Pharmacist; Physical Therapist; Physician; Registered Nurse; Respiratory Therapist; Social Worker; Veterinarian. **Number of placements per year:** 100 - 199.

HEDMAN & ASSOCIATES
3312 Woodford, Suite 200-400, Arlington TX 76013. 817/277-0888. **Contact:** Kent R. Hedman, Owner. **Description:** An executive search firm operating two divisions. One specializes in financial areas, and the other provides general placements. **Specializes in the areas of:** Accounting/Auditing; Finance.

HEIDRICK & STRUGGLES INC.
2200 Ross Avenue, Suite 4700-E, Dallas TX 75201. 214/220-2130. **Contact:** Manager. **Description:** An executive search firm.

HERNDON & ASSOCIATES
5100 Westheimer Road, Suite 200, Houston TX 77056. 713/968-6577. **Contact:** Manager. **Description:** An executive search firm. **Specializes in the areas of:** Finance; Legal; Technical.

KEN HERST HOTEL EXECUTIVE SEARCH
6750 West Loop South, Suite 940, Bellaire TX 77401. 713/660-0008. **Fax:** 713/660-0009. **Contact:** Ken Herst, Owner. **Description:** An executive search firm for the hotel, resort, conference center, motel, and private club industries. The firm fills middle- and upper-management positions. Company pays fee. **Specializes in the areas of:** Hotel/Restaurant. **Positions commonly filled include:** Accountant/Auditor; General Manager; Hotel Manager; Human Resources Manager; Property and Real Estate Manager. **Average salary range of placements:** $30,000 - $50,000. **Number of placements per year:** 1 - 49.

HORN & ASSOCIATES
P.O. Box 151944, Arlington TX 76015. 817/465-3463. **Contact:** Brian Horn, Owner. **Description:** An executive search firm. **Specializes in the areas of:** Health/Medical.

HOUSTON CREATIVE CONNECTIONS
701 North Post Oak Road, Suite 675, Houston TX 77024. 713/957-2393. **Toll-free phone:** 800/361-6152. **Fax:** 713/957-4014. **Contact:** Kirk Hoebeck, Personnel/Sales Manager. **E-mail address:** kirk@houstoncreative.com. **World Wide Web address:**

http://www.houstoncreative.com. **Description:** An executive search firm that also provides temporary, temp-to-perm, permanent, and contract placements. Founded in 1985. Company pays fee. **Specializes in the areas of:** Advertising; Art/Design; Engineering; Printing; Publishing; Technical. **Positions commonly filled include:** Advertising Clerk; Civil Engineer; Design Engineer; Designer; Draftsperson; Editor; Environmental Engineer; Human Resources Specialist; Internet Services Manager; Landscape Architect; Market Research Analyst; Mechanical Engineer; Multimedia Designer; Public Relations Specialist; Radio/TV Announcer/Broadcaster; Reporter; Structural Engineer; Technical Writer/Editor; Typist/Word Processor; Video Production Coordinator. **Corporate headquarters location:** This Location. **Average salary range of placements:** $30,000 - $50,000. **Number of placements per year:** 50 - 99.

HOUTZ-STRAWN ASSOCIATES
11402 Bee Caves Road West, Austin TX 78733. 512/263-1131. **Contact:** Manager. **Description:** An executive search firm. **Specializes in the areas of:** Biotechnology; Pharmaceutical.

THE HUMAN ELEMENT OF BUSINESS, INC.
307 Texas Avenue, El Paso TX 79901. 915/542-1562. **Fax:** 915/534-7730. **Contact:** Kim Miller, Human Resources Manager. **Description:** An executive search firm operating on both retainer and contingency bases. Company pays fee. **Specializes in the areas of:** Accounting/Auditing; Administration; Banking; Engineering; Finance; Food Industry; General Management; Industrial; Manufacturing; Personnel/Labor Relations; Retail. **Positions commonly filled include:** Accountant/Auditor; Administrative Manager; Bank Officer/Manager; Buyer; Civil Engineer; Credit Manager; Environmental Engineer; Financial Analyst; General Manager; Human Resources Specialist; Industrial Engineer; Industrial Production Manager; Licensed Practical Nurse; Mechanical Engineer; Operations/Production Manager; Purchasing Agent/Manager; Registered Nurse. **Other area locations:** Austin TX. **Number of placements per year:** 1 - 49.

HUNTER & MICHAELS
7502 Greenville Avenue, Suite 500, Dallas TX 75231. 214/750-4666. **Contact:** Manager. **Description:** An executive search firm. **Specializes in the areas of:** Sales.

HYMAN & ASSOCIATES
719 Sawdust Road, Suite 217, Spring TX 77380. 281/292-1969. **Contact:** Manager. **Description:** An executive search firm. **Specializes in the areas of:** Human Resources; Operations Management; Sales.

INNOVATIVE STAFF SEARCH
425 Solidad Street, Suite 200, San Antonio TX 78205. 210/472-1636. **Contact:** Manager. **Description:** An executive search firm that focuses on the health care field. Company pays fee. **Specializes in the areas of:** Health/Medical. **Positions commonly filled include:** Nurse Practitioner; Pharmacist; Physical Therapist; Physician; Physician Assistant. **Average salary range of placements:** More than $50,000. **Number of placements per year:** 100 - 199.

INSIDE TRACK
504 Hilltop Drive, Weatherford TX 76086. 817/599-7094. **Fax:** 817/596-0807. **Contact:** Matthew DiLorenzo, Senior Technical Recruiter. **Description:** An executive search firm. Founded in 1989. Company pays fee. **Specializes in the areas of:** Administration; Computer Science/Software; Engineering; High-Tech; Industrial; Manufacturing; Sales; Telecommunications. **Positions commonly filled include:** Computer Programmer; Design Engineer; Electrical/Electronics Engineer; General Manager; Marketing Manager; Materials Engineer; Mechanical Engineer; MIS Specialist; Operations Manager; Quality Control Supervisor; Sales Manager; Software Engineer; Systems Analyst; Telecommunications Manager. **Average salary range of placements:** More than $50,000. **Number of placements per year:** 1 - 49.

INSURANCE SEARCH
P.O. Box 7354, The Woodlands TX 77387. 281/367-0137. **Fax:** 281/367-3842. **Contact:** Bert Dionne, President. **Description:** An executive search firm for insurance companies, brokers, and risk management companies. Founded in 1979. Company pays fee. **Specializes in the areas of:** Insurance. **Positions commonly filled include:** Accountant/Auditor; Actuary; Administrative Manager; Attorney; Claim Representative; Computer Programmer; Construction and Building Inspector; Insurance Agent/Broker; Sales Representative; Systems Analyst; Underwriter/Assistant Underwriter. **Average salary range of placements:** $30,000 - $50,000. **Number of placements per year:** 100 - 199.

INTRATECH RESOURCE GROUP, INC.
6565 West Loop South, Suite 540, Bellaire TX 77401. 713/669-1733. **Fax:** 713/667-5507. **Contact:** James B. Lewis, President. **Description:** Intratech Resource Group is an executive search firm. Company pays fee. **Specializes in the areas of:** Computer Science/Software. **Positions commonly filled include:** Computer Programmer; Management Analyst/Consultant; Software Engineer; Systems Analyst. **Number of placements per year:** 50 - 99.

J.D. & ASSOCIATES
700 Highlander Boulevard, Suite 110, Arlington TX 76015. 817/467-7714. **Contact:** Manager. **Description:** An executive search firm that places personnel in a variety of industries.

JP & ASSOCIATES
4144 North Central Expressway, Suite 680, Dallas TX 75204. 214/827-4585. **Contact:** Manager. **Description:** An executive search firm. **Specializes in the areas of:** Computer Hardware/Software; High-Tech.

KAHN RICHARDS & ASSOCIATES
6223 Richmond, Suite 103, Houston TX 77057. 713/781-1181. **Contact:** Manager. **Description:** An executive search firm. **Specializes in the areas of:** Computer Science/Software.

KAWA STIEWIG & EDWARDS INC. (KS&E)
12800 Hillcrest Road, Suite 232, Dallas TX 75230. 972/385-7757. **Contact:** Manager. **Description:** An executive search firm. KS&E also operates a temporary service that places personnel in a wide variety of industries. **Specializes in the areas of:** Automotive.

A.T. KEARNEY EXECUTIVE SEARCH
500 North Akard, Suite 4170, Dallas TX 75201. 214/969-0010. **Contact:** Manager. **Description:** An executive search firm.
Other area locations:
- Penzoil Place, Suite 2250, 711 Louisiana, Houston TX 77002. 713/222-1276.

KENZER CORPORATION
3030 LBJ Freeway, Suite 1430, Dallas TX 75234. 972/620-7776. **Fax:** 972/243-7570. **Contact:** Melinda Sumurdy, Vice President. **Description:** An executive search firm operating on a retainer basis. Founded in 1973. Company pays fee. **Specializes in the areas of:** Fashion; Food Industry; General Management; Retail; Sales. **Positions commonly filled include:**

Accountant/Auditor; Branch Manager; Financial Analyst; Hotel Manager; Human Resources Specialist; Management Trainee; Manufacturer's/Wholesaler's Sales Rep.; Operations/Production Manager; Public Relations Specialist; Restaurant/Food Service Manager; Services Sales Rep. **Corporate headquarters location:** New York NY. **Average salary range of placements:** More than $50,000. **Number of placements per year:** 200 - 499.

KEY PEOPLE INC.
P.O. Box 24773, Forth Worth TX 76124-1773. 817/457-6108. **Contact:** Don (Petro) Petrusaitis, President. **Description:** An executive search firm operating on a contingency basis. The company focuses on the graphic arts industry. Company pays fee. **Specializes in the areas of:** Publishing. **Positions commonly filled include:** Administrative Manager; Blue-Collar Worker Supervisor; Buyer; Chemist; Clerical Supervisor; Computer Programmer; Customer Service Rep.; Electrical/Electronics Engineer; General Manager; Human Resources Specialist; Industrial Engineer; Industrial Production Manager; Management Trainee; Mechanical Engineer; MIS Specialist; Quality Control Supervisor; Transportation Specialist. **Average salary range of placements:** More than $50,000.

KORN/FERRY INTERNATIONAL
500 North Akard Street, 3232 Lincoln Plaza, Dallas TX 75201. 214/954-1834. **Contact:** Manager. **Description:** An executive search firm that places upper-level managers in a variety of industries. **Corporate headquarters location:** Los Angeles CA. **International locations:** Worldwide. **Average salary range of placements:** More than $50,000.
Other area locations:
- 1100 Louisiana, Suite 2850, Houston TX 77002. 713/651-1834.

EVIE KREISLER & ASSOCIATES
2720 Stemmons Freeway, Suite 812, Dallas TX 75207. 214/631-8994. **Contact:** Manager. **Description:** An executive search firm. **Specializes in the areas of:** Distribution; Manufacturing; Retail.

KRESSENBERG ASSOCIATES
8111 LBJ Freeway, Suite 665, Dallas TX 75251. 972/234-1491. **Contact:** Manager. **Description:** An executive search firm.

KRISTAN INTERNATIONAL EXECUTIVE SEARCH
12 Greenway Plaza, Suite 1100, Houston TX 77046. 713/961-3040. **Fax:** 713/961-3626. **Contact:** Robert P. Kristan, President. **World Wide Web address:** http://www.kristan.com. **Description:** An executive search firm operating on a retainer basis. Company pays fee. **Specializes in the areas of:** Architecture/Construction; Computer Science/Software; General Management; Home Furnishings; Sales. **Positions commonly filled include:** Account Manager; Architect; General Manager; Human Resources Specialist; Manufacturing Engineer; Marketing Manager; Sales Executive; Sales Manager; Vice President of Sales. **Corporate headquarters location:** This Location. **Average salary range of placements:** More than $50,000. **Number of placements per year:** 500 - 999.

LAMALIE AMROP INTERNATIONAL
1601 Elm Street, Suite 4150, Dallas TX 75201. 214/754-0019. **Contact:** Manager. **Description:** A generalist executive search firm.
Other area locations:
- 1301 McKinney Street, Suite 3130, Houston TX 77010. 713/739-8602.

LEA RANDOLPH & ASSOCIATES
10210 North Central Expressway, Suite 216, Dallas TX 75231. 214/987-4415. **Fax:** 214/369-9548. **Contact:** Manager. **Description:** An executive search firm. **Specializes in the areas of:** Health/Medical.

LEGAL NETWORK
600 North Pearl Street, Dallas TX 75201. 214/777-6400. **Contact:** Manager. **Description:** An executive search firm. **Specializes in the areas of:** Legal.

LEHMAN & McLESKY
98 San Jacinto Boulevard, Suite 440, Austin TX 78701. 512/478-1131. **Contact:** Manager. **Description:** An executive search firm that places personnel in a variety of industries.

GEORGE LEHMAN ASSOCIATES INC.
P.O. Box 90881, Houston TX 77290. 281/443-0044. **Contact:** George Lehman, Owner. **Description:** An executive search firm. **Specializes in the areas of:** Accounting/Auditing; Finance. **Positions commonly filled include:** Accountant.

LOEWENSTEIN & ASSOCIATES
5847 San Felipe Street, Suite 1250, Houston TX 77057-3009. 713/952-1840. **Toll-free phone:** 800/486-0152. **Fax:** 713/952-4534. **Contact:** Jessica Cooper, Recruiter. **E-mail address:** loewenst@worldnet.att.net. **Description:** An executive search firm. The firm focuses on the recruitment of technical sales, marketing, consulting, engineering, and management professionals. Company pays fee. **Specializes in the areas of:** Computer Science/Software; Engineering; Industrial; Sales; Technical. **Positions commonly filled include:** Chemical Engineer; Computer Programmer; Industrial Engineer; Mechanical Engineer; MIS Specialist; Services Sales Representative; Software Engineer; Systems Analyst. **Average salary range of placements:** More than $50,000. **Number of placements per year:** 1 - 49.

M.H. LOGAN & ASSOCIATES
5641 Yale Boulevard, Suite 102, Dallas TX 75206. 214/706-0558. **Contact:** Manager. **Description:** An executive search firm that places most levels of professionals within the restaurant management industry. **Specializes in the areas of:** Restaurant.

LUCAS FINANCIAL STAFFING
12655 North Central Expressway, Suite 730, Dallas TX 75243. 972/490-0011. **Fax:** 972/991-4144. **Contact:** Andrea Jennings, Regional Manager. **Description:** An executive search firm operating on both retained and contingency bases. Lucas Financial Staffing also provides some contract placements. Company pays fee. **Specializes in the areas of:** Accounting/Auditing; Finance. **Positions commonly filled include:** Accountant/Auditor; Budget Analyst; Chief Financial Officer; Controller; Credit Manager; EDP Specialist; Finance Director; Financial Analyst; Systems Analyst. **Benefits available to temporary workers:** 401(k); Medical Insurance; Paid Vacation. **Corporate headquarters location:** Atlanta GA. **Average salary range of placements:** $30,000 - $50,000. **Number of placements per year:** 200 - 499.

LUSK & ASSOCIATES PERSONNEL SERVICE INC.
P.O. Box 7500-331, Dallas TX 75209-0500. 214/528-9966. **Fax:** 214/528-2002. **Contact:** B.J. Alessio, President. **E-mail address:** dallasjob@aol.com. **Description:** An executive search firm operating on both retained and contingency bases. Company pays fee. **Specializes in the areas of:** Accounting/Auditing; Administration; Finance; General Management; Personnel/Labor Relations; Sales; Secretarial. **Positions commonly filled include:** Accountant; Administrative Assistant; Administrative Manager; Chief Financial Officer; Controller; Customer Service Representative; Finance Director; Human Resources Manager; Marketing Manager; Marketing Specialist; Multimedia

Designer; Purchasing Agent/Manager; Secretary. **Average salary range of placements:** $30,000 - $50,000. **Number of placements per year:** 1 - 49.

MH EXECUTIVE SEARCH GROUP
P.O. Box 868068, Plano TX 75086. 972/578-1511. **Contact:** Manager. **Description:** An executive search firm. **Specializes in the areas of:** Packaging.

MANAGEMENT RECRUITERS INTERNATIONAL
2200 Space Park Drive, Suite 420, Houston TX 77058. 281/335-0363. **Fax:** 281/335-0362. **Contact:** Len Bird, President. **Description:** An executive search firm. Company pays fee. **Specializes in the areas of:** Engineering; Health/Medical; Manufacturing. **Positions commonly filled include:** Accountant/Auditor; Agricultural Engineer; Biomedical Engineer; Ceramics Engineer; Chemical Engineer; Chemist; Civil Engineer; Electrical/Electronics Engineer; Financial Analyst; Industrial Production Manager; Materials Engineer; Mechanical Engineer; Metallurgical Engineer; Mining Engineer; Occupational Therapist; Operations/ Production Manager; Petroleum Engineer; Physical Therapist; Software Engineer. **Corporate headquarters location:** Cleveland OH. **Other U.S. locations:** Nationwide. **Number of placements per year:** 50 - 99.

MANAGEMENT RECRUITERS INTERNATIONAL
317 South Friendswood Drive, Friendswood TX 77546. 281/996-0008. **Contact:** Louis Belview, Owner. **Description:** An executive search firm operating on a contingency basis. Company pays fee. **Specializes in the areas of:** Engineering; Food Industry; Health/Medical; Industrial; Manufacturing. **Positions commonly filled include:** Chemical Engineer; Chemist; Civil Engineer; Electrical/Electronics Engineer; Environmental Engineer; Food Scientist/Technologist; General Manager; Health Services Manager; Human Resources Manager; Industrial Engineer; Industrial Production Manager; Materials Engineer; Mechanical Engineer; Medical Records Technician; Metallurgical Engineer; Occupational Therapist; Operations/ Production Manager; Petroleum Engineer; Pharmacist; Physical Therapist; Physician; Physicist; Psychologist; Recreational Therapist; Registered Nurse; Respiratory Therapist; Social Worker; Speech-Language Pathologist; Surgical Technician. **Corporate headquarters location:** Cleveland OH. **Other U.S. locations:** Nationwide. **Average salary range of placements:** More than $50,000. **Number of placements per year:** 1 - 49.

MANAGEMENT RECRUITERS INTERNATIONAL
15150 Preston Road, Dallas TX 75248. 972/991-4500. **Contact:** George Buntrock, General Manager. **Description:** An executive search firm. Company pays fee. **Specializes in the areas of:** Accounting/Auditing; Administration; Computer Science/Software; Engineering; Food Industry; General Management; Health/Medical; Paper; Retail; Technical. **Positions commonly filled include:** Ceramics Engineer; Chemical Engineer; Computer Programmer; Customer Service Representative; Electrical/Electronics Engineer; General Manager; Health Services Manager; Industrial Engineer; Industrial Production Manager; Materials Engineer; Mechanical Engineer; Metallurgical Engineer; Operations/Production Manager; Pharmacist; Physical Therapist; Purchasing Agent/Manager; Quality Control Supervisor; Registered Nurse; Software Engineer; Speech-Language Pathologist; Systems Analyst; Transportation/Traffic Specialist. **Corporate headquarters location:** Cleveland OH. **Other U.S. locations:** Nationwide. **Number of placements per year:** 1 - 49.

MANAGEMENT RECRUITERS INTERNATIONAL
1360 Post Oak Boulevard, Suite 2110, Houston TX 77056. 713/850-9850. **Fax:** 713/850-1429. **Contact:** Rich Bolls, Manager. **Description:** An executive search firm. **Specializes in the areas of:** Accounting/Auditing; Administration; Advertising; Architecture/ Construction; Banking; Communications; Computer Hardware/Software; Construction; Design; Electrical; Engineering; Finance; Food Industry; General Management; Health/Medical; Industrial; Insurance; Legal; Manufacturing; Personnel/Labor Relations; Procurement; Publishing; Retail; Sales; Technical; Textiles; Transportation.

MANAGEMENT RECRUITERS INTERNATIONAL
1009 West Randol Mill Road, Suite 209, Arlington TX 76012. 817/469-6161. **Contact:** Bob Stoessel, Manager. **Description:** An executive search firm. **Specializes in the areas of:** Accounting/Auditing; Administration; Advertising; Architecture/ Construction; Banking; Communications; Computer Hardware/Software; Design; Electrical; Engineering; Finance; Food Industry; General Management; Health/Medical; Insurance; Legal; Manufacturing; Operations Management; Personnel/Labor Relations; Procurement; Publishing; Retail; Sales; Technical; Textiles; Transportation.

MANAGEMENT RECRUITERS INTERNATIONAL
1250 Capital of Texas Highway, Building 3, Suite 650, Austin TX 78746. 512/327-8292. **Contact:** Manager. **Description:** An executive search firm. **Specializes in the areas of:** Advertising; Biotechnology; Health/Medical; High-Tech; Pharmaceutical.

MANAGEMENT RECRUITERS INTERNATIONAL
7550 Interstate Highway West, Suite 1230, San Antonio TX 78229. 210/525-1800. **Contact:** Manager. **Description:** An executive search firm. **Specializes in the areas of:** Food Industry; Manufacturing.

MANAGEMENT RECRUITERS INTERNATIONAL
10707 Corporate Drive, Stafford TX 77477. 281/240-0220. **Contact:** Manager. **Description:** An executive search firm that provides placements in the lumber industry.

MANAGEMENT RECRUITERS INTERNATIONAL
1660 South Stemmons, Suite 460, Lewisville TX 75067. 972/434-9612. **Contact:** Manager. **Description:** An executive search firm. **Specializes in the areas of:** Plastics; Sales.

MANAGEMENT RECRUITERS INTERNATIONAL
8700 Crownhill, Suite 701, San Antonio TX 78209. 210/829-8666. **Contact:** Manager. **Description:** An executive search firm. **Specializes in the areas of:** Food Industry; Manufacturing.

MANAGEMENT RECRUITERS INTERNATIONAL
4703 81st Place, Lubbock TX 79424. 806/749-2345. **Contact:** Manager. **Description:** An executive search firm. **Specializes in the areas of:** Engineering; Health/Medical; Marketing.

MANAGEMENT RECRUITERS INTERNATIONAL
494 South Seguin, New Braunfels TX 78130. 830/629-6290. **Contact:** Manager. **Description:** An executive search firm. **Specializes in the areas of:** Insurance.

MANAGEMENT RECRUITERS OF CHAMPIONS
3934 FM 1960 West, Suite 105, Houston TX 77068-3546. 281/580-6020. **Fax:** 281/580-6029. **Contact:** Gary Akin, President. **E-mail address:** mrichamp@swbell.net. **World Wide Web address:** http://www.mrichampions.com. **Description:** An executive search firm operating on both retained and contingency bases in two major areas: benefits administration/consulting

and engineering design. Company pays fee. **Specializes in the areas of:** Engineering; Food Industry; Health/Medical; Manufacturing. **Positions commonly filled include:** Account Rep.; Administrative Manager; Applications Engineer; Design Engineer; Electrical/Electronics Engineer; Manufacturing Engineer; Mechanical Engineer; Operations Manager; Production Manager; Project Manager; Sales Engineer; Sales Rep. **Corporate headquarters location:** Cleveland OH. **Other U.S. locations:** Nationwide. **Average salary range of placements:** $30,000 - $50,000. **Number of placements per year:** 1 - 49.

MANAGEMENT RECRUITERS OF DALLAS
13101 Preston Road, Suite 560, Dallas TX 75240. 972/788-1515. **Fax:** 972/701-8242. **Contact:** Robert S. Lineback, General Manager. **Description:** An executive search firm operating on both retainer and contingency bases. Company pays fee. **Specializes in the areas of:** Accounting/Auditing; Administration; Advertising; Architecture/Construction; Banking; Communications; Computer Hardware/Software; Design; Electrical; Engineering; Finance; Food Industry; General Management; Health/Medical; Insurance; Legal; Manufacturing; Operations Management; Personnel/Labor Relations; Procurement; Publishing; Retail; Sales; Technical; Transportation. **Positions commonly filled include:** Accountant/Auditor; Actuary; Administrative Manager; Aerospace Engineer; Agricultural Engineer; Bank Officer/Manager; Biochemist; Biological Scientist; Biomedical Engineer; Branch Manager; Chemical Engineer; Chemist; Civil Engineer; Clinical Lab Technician; Computer Programmer; Design Engineer; Designer; Dietician/Nutritionist; EEG Technologist; EKG Technician; Electrical/Electronics Engineer; Emergency Medical Technician; Environmental Engineer; Financial Analyst; Food Scientist/Technologist; General Manager; Health Services Manager; Human Resources Specialist; Industrial Engineer; Licensed Practical Nurse; Management Analyst/Consultant; Management Trainee; Manufacturer's/Wholesaler's Sales Rep.; Mechanical Engineer; Medical Records Technician; Metallurgical Engineer; Mining Engineer; MIS Specialist; Multimedia Designer; Nuclear Engineer; Nuclear Medicine Technologist; Occupational Therapist; Operations/Production Manager; Petroleum Engineer; Pharmacist; Physical Therapist; Physician; Physicist; Purchasing Agent/Manager; Quality Control Supervisor; Radiological Technologist; Registered Nurse; Respiratory Therapist; Restaurant/Food Service Manager; Science Technologist; Securities Sales Rep.; Services Sales Rep.; Software Engineer; Structural Engineer; Surgical Technician; Systems Analyst; Telecommunications Manager; Transportation/Traffic Specialist; Underwriter/Assistant Underwriter. **Corporate headquarters location:** Cleveland OH. **Other U.S. locations:** Nationwide. **Average salary range of placements:** More than $50,000. **Number of placements per year:** 200 - 499.

MANAGEMENT RECRUITERS OF LBJ PARK/DALLAS
3003 LBJ Freeway, Suite 220E, Dallas TX 75234. 972/488-1133. **Fax:** 972/488-1099. **Contact:** Ray Vlasek, General Manager. **E-mail address:** mrdfw@airmail.net. **Description:** An executive search firm. Founded in 1960. Company pays fee. **Specializes in the areas of:** Engineering; Manufacturing; Software Engineering; Telecommunications. **Positions commonly filled include:** Computer Programmer; Electrical/Electronics Engineer; Mechanical Engineer; MIS Specialist; Software Engineer. **Corporate headquarters location:** Cleveland OH. **Other U.S. locations:** Nationwide. **Number of placements per year:** 50 - 99.

MANAGEMENT RECRUITERS OF ROUND ROCK
301 Hesters Crossing Road, Suite 110, Round Rock TX 78681. 512/310-1918. **Fax:** 512/310-8318. **Contact:** Matthew Powers, Account Executive. **Description:** An executive search firm operating on both retainer and contingency bases. Company pays fee. **Specializes in the areas of:** Engineering; Industrial; Manufacturing. **Positions commonly filled include:** Chemical Engineer; Design Engineer; Electrical/Electronics Engineer; Industrial Engineer; Mechanical Engineer; Metallurgical Engineer. **Corporate headquarters location:** Cleveland OH. **Other U.S. locations:** Nationwide. **Average salary range of placements:** $30,000 - $50,000. **Number of placements per year:** 100 - 199.

RAY MARBURGER & ASSOCIATES INC.
9800 Northwest Freeway, Suite 505, Houston TX 77092. 713/683-8798. **Contact:** Ray Marburger, Senior Consultant. **Description:** An executive search firm that operates on a contingency basis. Founded in 1980. Company pays fee. **Specializes in the areas of:** Accounting/Auditing. **Positions commonly filled include:** Accountant/Auditor; Financial Analyst; Systems Analyst. **Average salary range of placements:** $30,000 - $50,000. **Number of placements per year:** 50 - 99.

McDUFFY-EDWARDS
3117 Medina Drive, Garland TX 75041. 972/864-1174. **Fax:** 972/864-8559. **Contact:** Tom Edwards, Partner. **E-mail address:** tom@mcduffy-edwards.com. **World Wide Web address:** http://www.mcduffy-edwards.com. **Description:** An executive search firm that also provides consulting services and seminars. Founded in 1980. Company pays fee. **Specializes in the areas of:** Computer Science/Software; Marketing; Sales; Scientific; Technical. **Positions commonly filled include:** Account Manager; Account Representative; Customer Service Representative; General Manager; Internet Services Manager; Management Analyst/Consultant; Market Research Analyst; Marketing Manager; Marketing Specialist; Operations Manager; Project Manager; Sales Engineer; Sales Executive; Sales Manager; Sales Representative; Software Engineer; Systems Analyst; Systems Manager; Telecommunications Manager; Vice President of Marketing and Sales. **Average salary range of placements:** More than $50,000. **Number of placements per year:** 50 - 99.

McKINLEY•AREND INTERNATIONAL
3200 Southwest Freeway, Suite 3300, Houston TX 77027-7526. 713/623-6400. **Fax:** 713/975-0022. **Contact:** Jim McKinley, Managing Director. **Description:** An executive search firm operating on a retainer basis. Company pays fee. **Specializes in the areas of:** Chemical; Energy; Engineering; Finance; Food Industry; General Management; Industrial; Legal; Manufacturing; Nonprofit; Personnel/Labor Relations; Sales; Technical; Transportation. **Positions commonly filled include:** Accountant/Auditor; Biological Scientist; Biomedical Engineer; Board of Directors; Ceramics Engineer; Chemist; Civil Engineer; Electrical/Electronics Engineer; Industrial Engineer; Manufacturing Engineer; Mechanical Engineer; Metallurgical Engineer; Operations/Production Manager; Public Relations Specialist; Quality Control Supervisor; Senior Manager. **Number of placements per year:** 50 - 99.

MEDICAL SEARCH SOLUTIONS
15905 Bent Tree Forest Circle, Suite 1065, Dallas TX 75248. 972/490-3778. **Fax:** 972/934-2246. **Contact:** Penny Peters, CPC, Medical Recruiting Specialist. **Description:** An executive search firm. Company pays fee. **Specializes in the areas of:** Health/Medical. **Positions commonly filled include:** Administrative Assistant; Administrative Manager; Assistant Manager; Clinical Lab Technician; Controller; Dietician/Nutritionist; EEG Technologist; EKG Technician;

Emergency Medical Technician; Finance Director; Financial Analyst; Health Services Manager; Licensed Practical Nurse; Medical Assistant; Medical Records Technician; Nurse Practitioner; Occupational Therapist; Office Manager; Operations Manager; Pharmacist; Physical Therapist; Physician; Physician Assistant; Radiological Technologist; Recreational Therapist; Registered Nurse; Respiratory Therapist; Speech-Language Pathologist; Surgical Technician. **Average salary range of placements:** $30,000 - $50,000. **Number of placements per year:** 50 - 99.

METRO CAREERS, INC.
6001 Savoy, Suite 505, Houston TX 77036. 713/978-6508. **Contact:** Glynn W. Hopkins, Jr., Owner/CEO. **Description:** An executive search firm operating on a contingency basis. Company pays fee. **Specializes in the areas of:** Accounting/Auditing; Administration; Architecture/Construction; Engineering; Finance; General Management; Manufacturing; Personnel/Labor Relations; Sales; Technical. **Positions commonly filled include:** Blue-Collar Worker Supervisor; Budget Analyst; Buyer; Chemical Engineer; Chemist; Civil Engineer; Clerical Supervisor; Construction and Building Inspector; Construction Contractor; Cost Estimator; Credit Manager; Customer Service Representative; Design Engineer; Designer; Draftsperson; Electrical/Electronics Engineer; Environmental Engineer; Financial Analyst; Human Resources Specialist; Human Service Worker; Industrial Engineer; Industrial Production Manager; Management Analyst/Consultant; Manufacturer's/ Wholesaler's Sales Rep.; Mechanical Engineer; Metallurgical Engineer; Petroleum Engineer; Services Sales Representative; Technical Writer/Editor; Telecommunications Manager. **Average salary range of placements:** $30,000 - $50,000. **Number of placements per year:** 100 - 199.

MICHAEL JAMES & ASSOCIATES
191-A West Main Street, Lewisville TX 75057. 972/221-2400. **Contact:** Manager. **Description:** An executive search firm for the semiconductor industry. **Specializes in the areas of:** Electronics.

W. ROBERT MICHAELS & COMPANY
5065 Westheimer Road, Suite 830, Houston TX 77056. 713/965-9175. **Contact:** Office Manager. **Description:** An executive search firm. **Specializes in the areas of:** Construction; Engineering.

MOORE & MOORE ASSOCIATES
P.O. Box 797772, Dallas TX 75379. 972/248-4441. **Contact:** Manager. **Description:** An executive search firm. **Specializes in the areas of:** Medical Sales and Marketing. **Positions commonly filled include:** Sales Manager.

NATIONAL HUMAN RESOURCE GROUP
609 Capital Ridge Road, Austin TX 78746. 512/328-4448. **Fax:** 512/328-1696. **Contact:** Vicki Volick, President. **E-mail address:** nbrg@zilker.net. **Description:** An executive search firm operating on both retainer and contingency bases. National Human Resource Group also offers technical consulting and contract services. Company pays fee. **Specializes in the areas of:** Computer Science/Software. **Positions commonly filled include:** Computer Programmer; MIS Specialist; Multimedia Designer; Systems Analyst. **Average salary range of placements:** More than $50,000. **Number of placements per year:** 1 - 49.

NATIONWIDE MEDICAL PLACEMENT
11407 Meadow Lake Drive, Houston TX 77077. 281/496-0160. **Contact:** Manager. **Description:** An executive search firm. **Specializes in the areas of:** Health/Medical.

NOLL HUMAN RESOURCE SERVICES
5720 LBJ Freeway, Suite 610, Dallas TX 75240. 972/392-2900. **Toll-free phone:** 800/536-7600. **Fax:** 972/934-3600. **Contact:** Perry Smith, Manager. **E-mail address:** 103266.2233@compuserve.com. **World Wide Web address:** http://www.aol.nollinc.com. **Description:** An executive search firm operating on both retained and contingency bases. Company pays fee. **Specializes in the areas of:** Logistics; Sales; Transportation. **Positions commonly filled include:** Database Manager; Environmental Engineer; Industrial Engineer; Manufacturing Engineer; Marketing Manager; MIS Specialist; Physician; Registered Nurse; Sales Engineer; Sales Executive; Sales Manager; Sales Representative; Software Engineer; Systems Analyst; Systems Manager; Telecommunications Manager; Transportation/Traffic Specialist. **Corporate headquarters location:** Omaha NE. **Average salary range of placements:** More than $50,000. **Number of placements per year:** 50 - 99.

ODELL & ASSOCIATES INC.
12700 Park Central Place, Suite 1404, Dallas TX 75251. 972/458-7900. **Fax:** 972/233-1215. **Contact:** Bob Dralle, Executive Vice President. **Description:** An executive search firm. Company pays fee. **Specializes in the areas of:** Accounting/Auditing; Data Processing; Engineering; Finance; Health/Medical; Legal. **Positions commonly filled include:** Accountant/Auditor; Actuary; Attorney; Computer Programmer; Financial Analyst; Medical Records Technician; Occupational Therapist; Registered Nurse; Respiratory Therapist; Systems Analyst. **Number of placements per year:** 100 - 199.

THE DUNCAN O'DELL GROUP
P.O. Box 1161, La Porte TX 77572. 281/470-1881. **Fax:** 281/470-1880. **Contact:** Jim Hall, Senior Partner. **Description:** A national search firm that focuses on the placement of manufacturing professionals with three or more years experience. Company pays fee. **Specializes in the areas of:** Manufacturing; Personnel/Labor Relations. **Positions commonly filled include:** Buyer; Design Engineer; Electrical/Electronics Engineer; Mechanical Engineer; Metallurgical Engineer. **Average salary range of placements:** More than $50,000. **Number of placements per year:** 50 - 99.

OPPORTUNITY UNLIMITED PERSONNEL CONSULTANTS
2720 West Mockingbird Lane, Dallas TX 75235. 214/357-9196. **Toll-free phone:** 800/969-0888. **Fax:** 214/357-0140. **Contact:** John T. Kearley, President. **E-mail address:** oui@onramp.net. **Description:** An executive search firm operating on a contingency basis. Founded in 1959. Company pays fee. **Specializes in the areas of:** Aerospace; Communications; Computer Science/Software; Data Processing; Engineering; Personnel/Labor Relations; Technical. **Positions commonly filled include:** Aerospace Engineer; Biomedical Engineer; Computer Programmer; Design Engineer; Electrical/Electronics Engineer; Mechanical Engineer; Multimedia Designer; Software Engineer; Systems Analyst; Telecommunications Manager. **Number of placements per year:** 100 - 199.

MERLE W. OWENS & ASSOCIATES
301 Commerce Street, Suite 1205, Fort Worth TX 76102. 817/335-1776. **Contact:** Manager. **Description:** A generalist executive search firm with clients in most major industries.

THE PAILIN GROUP
8500 North Stemmons Freeway, Suite 6070, LB #55, Dallas TX 75247-3832. 214/630-1703. **Fax:** 214/630-1704. **Contact:** David L. Pailin, Sr., Senior Partner. **E-mail address:** palingrouppsc@compuserve.com. **Description:** A retained executive

search firm. Founded in 1989. Company pays fee. **Specializes in the areas of:** Accounting/Auditing; Administration; Advertising; Banking; Computer Science/Software; Economics; Engineering; Environmental; Finance; Food Industry; General Management; Health/Medical; Industrial; Insurance; Legal; Manufacturing; Nonprofit; Personnel/Labor Relations; Retail; Sales; Transportation. **Positions commonly filled include:** Accountant/Auditor; Administrative Manager; Aerospace Engineer; Architect; Attorney; Bank Officer/Manager; Budget Analyst; Ceramics Engineer; Civil Engineer; Computer Programmer; Construction Contractor; Cost Estimator; Credit Manager; Customer Service Representative; Design Engineer; Environmental Engineer; Financial Analyst; General Manager; Health Services Manager; Human Service Worker; Industrial Engineer; Materials Engineer; Mechanical Engineer; Metallurgical Engineer; Mining Engineer; MIS Specialist; Nuclear Engineer; Petroleum Engineer; Pharmacist; Physician; Quality Control Supervisor; Securities Sales Representative; Services Sales Representative; Software Engineer; Statistician; Systems Analyst; Technical Writer/Editor; Telecommunications Manager. **Corporate headquarters location:** This Location. **Other U.S. locations:** Philadelphia PA. **Average salary range of placements:** More than $50,000. **Number of placements per year:** 100 - 199.

PAN AMERICAN SEARCH
600 Sunland Park, Building 2, Suite 200, El Paso TX 79912. 915/833-9991. **Contact:** Manager. **Description:** An executive search firm. **Specializes in the areas of:** Engineering; Manufacturing.

PATE RESOURCES GROUP
595 Orleans Street, Suite 707, Beaumont TX 77701. 409/833-4514. **Toll-free phone:** 800/669-4514. **Fax:** 409/833-4646. **Contact:** W.L. Pate Jr., CPC, CTS, President. **E-mail address:** pateresgrp@aol.com. **Description:** An executive search firm operating on both retainer and contingency bases. Pate Resources Group also offers career/outplacement counseling and contract, permanent, and temporary placements. Founded in 1989. Company pays fee. **Specializes in the areas of:** Accounting/Auditing; Administration; Computer Science/Software; Engineering; Finance; Food Industry; General Management; Health/Medical; Industrial; Personnel/Labor Relations; Sales; Secretarial; Technical. **Positions commonly filled include:** Account Manager; Account Representative; Accountant/Auditor; Administrative Assistant; Administrative Manager; Biochemist; Biological Scientist; Biomedical Engineer; Chemical Engineer; Chemist; Chief Financial Officer; Civil Engineer; Clinical Lab Technician; Computer Programmer; Construction Contractor; Controller; Credit Manager; Customer Service Representative; Design Engineer; Electrical/Electronics Engineer; Environmental Engineer; Finance Director; Financial Analyst; Food Scientist/Technologist; General Manager; Graphic Artist; Graphic Designer; Hotel Manager; Human Resources Manager; Industrial Engineer; Internet Services Manager; Management Analyst/Consultant; Manufacturing Engineer; Market Research Analyst; Marketing Manager; Mechanical Engineer; Metallurgical Engineer; MIS Specialist; Nuclear Engineer; Occupational Therapist; Operations/Production Manager; Paralegal; Petroleum Engineer; Pharmacist; Physical Therapist; Physician; Project Manager; Public Relations Specialist; Purchasing Agent/Manager; Quality Control Supervisor; Registered Nurse; Respiratory Therapist; Sales Engineer; Sales Executive; Sales Manager; Sales Representative; Secretary; Software Engineer; Speech-Language Pathologist; Strategic Relations Manager; Structural Engineer; Systems Analyst; Systems Manager; Telecommunications Manager; Transportation/Traffic Specialist; Underwriter/Assistant Underwriter. **Average salary range of placements:** More than $50,000. **Number of placements per year:** 50 - 99.

PATTERSON & ASSOCIATES
3109 Knox Street, Suite 535, Dallas TX 75205. 214/749-1935. **Contact:** Joel Patterson, President. **Description:** An executive search firm. Company pays fee. **Specializes in the areas of:** Sales. **Positions commonly filled include:** Management Trainee; Manufacturer's/Wholesaler's Sales Rep.; Sales Rep. **Number of placements per year:** 100 - 199.

PEDLEY STRINGER & ASSOCIATES
7719 Wood Hollow, Suite 216, Austin TX 78731. 512/418-8848. **Fax:** 512/418-1236. **Contact:** Manager. **Description:** An executive search firm for the semiconductor industry. **Specializes in the areas of:** Electronics.

PEOPLE SOURCE
9200 Old Katy Road, Houston TX 77055. 713/935-3300. **Contact:** William Sonne, CEO/Owner. **Description:** An executive search firm. Company pays fee. **Specializes in the areas of:** Information Technology; Scientific.

THE PERSONNEL OFFICE
24127 Boerne Stage Road, San Antonio TX 78255-9517. 210/698-0300. **Fax:** 210/698-3299. **Contact:** F. Carl Hensley, President & CEO. **Description:** An executive search firm operating on both retainer and contingency bases. The firm also offers contract and temporary placements. Company pays fee. **Specializes in the areas of:** Administration; Computer Science/Software; Engineering; Sales. **Positions commonly filled include:** Accountant/Auditor; Computer Programmer; Customer Service Representative; Database Manager; Design Engineer; Electrical/Electronics Engineer; Environmental Engineer; General Manager; Health Services Manager; Human Resources Manager; Industrial Engineer; Manufacturer's/Wholesaler's Sales Rep.; Manufacturing Engineer; MIS Specialist; Software Engineer; Systems Analyst; Systems Manager; Telecommunications Manager. **Average salary range of placements:** $30,000 - $74,000. **Number of placements per year:** 1000+.

RICK PETERSON & ASSOCIATES
333 North Sam Houston Parkway East, Houston TX 77060. 281/591-7777. **Contact:** Rick Peterson, President. **Description:** An executive search firm. **Specializes in the areas of:** Finance.

PHOENIX STAFFING
P.O. Box 791891, San Antonio TX 78279. 210/377-3628. **Fax:** 210/820-0138. **Contact:** Clarke Mosley, Area Manager. **E-mail address:** jcmosley@aol.com. **Description:** An executive search firm. Phoenix Staffing also offers temporary placements, contract services, and career/outplacement counseling. Founded in 1984. Company pays fee. **Specializes in the areas of:** Accounting/Auditing; Administration; Computer Science/Software; Food Industry; General Management; Industrial; Light Industrial; Manufacturing; Personnel/Labor Relations; Sales; Secretarial. **Positions commonly filled include:** Accountant/Auditor; Administrative Manager; Bank Officer/Manager; Chemical Engineer; Computer Programmer; Customer Service Representative; Financial Analyst; Human Resources Specialist; Mechanical Engineer; MIS Specialist; Occupational Therapist; Property and Real Estate Manager; Purchasing Agent/Manager; Restaurant/Food Service Manager; Securities Sales Representative; Software Engineer; Systems Analyst; Telecommunications

Manager. **Corporate headquarters location:** Houston TX. **Other area locations:** Austin TX; Laredo TX. **Other U.S. locations:** San Diego CA. **Average salary range of placements:** $30,000 - $50,000. **Number of placements per year:** 1 - 49.

PIPER-MORGAN PERSONNEL
3355 West Alabama Street, Suite 1120, Houston TX 77098. 713/840-9922. **Contact:** Manager. **Description:** An executive search firm. **Specializes in the areas of:** Oil and Gas.

PRACTICE DYNAMICS
11222 Richmond Avenue, Suite 125, Houston TX 77082. 281/531-0911. **Contact:** Manager. **Description:** An executive search firm. **Specializes in the areas of:** Health/Medical. **Positions commonly filled include:** Physician; Registered Nurse.

PREMIER HEALTH STAFF
1905 Central Drive, Suite 200, Bedford TX 76021. 817/540-4067. **Toll-free phone:** 800/224-4488. **Fax:** 817/540-0680. **Contact:** Mike Mayeux, Vice President of Rehab Search. **E-mail address:** shiloh@onramp.net. **Description:** An executive search firm that also provides temporary and contract services. Company pays fee. **Specializes in the areas of:** Health/Medical. **Positions commonly filled include:** Physical Therapist; Speech-Language Pathologist. **Average salary range of placements:** More than $50,000. **Number of placements per year:** 50 - 99.

PRENG & ASSOCIATES, INC.
2925 Briar Park, Suite 1111, Houston TX 77042. 713/266-2600. **Contact:** David Preng, President. **Description:** An executive search firm. **Specializes in the areas of:** Chemical; Engineering; Manufacturing; Petrochemical; Pharmaceutical.

PRESCOTT LEGAL SEARCH
3900 Essex Lane, Suite 200, Houston TX 77027. 713/439-0911. **Contact:** Manager. **Description:** An executive search firm. **Specializes in the areas of:** Legal. **Positions commonly filled include:** Attorney.

PRIORITY SEARCH
4110 Rio Bravo, Suite 215, El Paso TX 79902. 915/534-4457. **Contact:** Manager. **Description:** An executive search firm. **Specializes in the areas of:** Manufacturing.

PRITCHARD & ASSOCIATES
4800 Sugar Grove Boulevard, Suite 290, Stafford TX 77477. 281/240-2212. **Contact:** Manager. **Description:** An executive search firm. **Specializes in the areas of:** Computer Hardware/Software.

PROFESSIONAL EXECUTIVE RECRUITERS
1701 Gateway Boulevard, Suite 419, Richardson TX 75080. 972/235-3984. **Contact:** Manager. **Description:** An executive search firm. **Specializes in the areas of:** Construction.

PROTHERO & ASSOCIATES INC.
555 Republic Drive, Suite 200, Plano TX 75074. 972/516-4266. **Contact:** Manager. **Description:** An executive search firm.

PROVIDENT RESOURCES GROUP
13355 Noel Road, Richardson TX 75080. 972/702-7980. **Contact:** Vickie Thompson, Office Manager. **Description:** An executive search firm. Company pays fee. **Specializes in the areas of:** Construction; Real Estate. **Positions commonly filled include:** Construction Contractor; Construction Manager; Cost Estimator; Customer Service Representative; Operations/Production Manager; Purchasing Agent/Manager. **Average salary range of placements:** More than $50,000. **Number of placements per year.** 1 - 49.

QUALITY INFORMATION SERVICE (QIS)
P.O. Box 1559, Whitney TX 76692. 254/694-6319. **Fax:** 254/694-6434. **Contact:** Betty Schatz, Senior Account Manager. **Description:** An executive search firm. Company pays fee. **Specializes in the areas of:** Computer Science/Software. **Positions commonly filled include:** Computer Programmer; Database Manager; Electrical/Electronics Engineer; MIS Specialist; Software Engineer; Systems Analyst; Technical Writer/Editor. **Number of placements per year:** 50 - 99.

R&R PERSONNEL SPECIALISTS
409 South White Oak Road, Suite A, White Oak TX 75693. 903/759-4299. **Toll-free phone:** 800/575-1608. **Fax:** 903/759-4496. **Contact:** Rodney Lemons, CEO. **Description:** An executive search firm operating on both retainer and contingency bases. Founded in 1994. Company pays fee. **Specializes in the areas of:** Personnel/Labor Relations; Retail; Secretarial. **Positions commonly filled include:** Accountant/Auditor; Administrative Manager; Advertising Clerk; Agricultural Engineer; Aircraft Mechanic/Engine Specialist; Attorney; Automotive Mechanic; Blue-Collar Worker Supervisor; Branch Manager; Buyer; Claim Representative; Clerical Supervisor; Computer Programmer; Construction Contractor; Cost Estimator; Counselor; Credit Manager; Customer Service Representative; Dental Assistant/Dental Hygienist; Designer; Draftsperson; Education Administrator; EEG Technologist; EKG Technician; Electrical/Electronics Engineer; Electrician; Emergency Medical Technician; Financial Analyst; General Manager; Hotel Manager; Human Resources Specialist; Human Service Worker; Industrial Engineer; Industrial Production Manager; Insurance Agent/Broker; Licensed Practical Nurse; Management Trainee; Manufacturer's/Wholesaler's Sales Rep.; Mechanical Engineer; Medical Records Technician; Mining Engineer; Operations/Production Manager; Paralegal; Pharmacist; Physical Therapist; Physician; Physicist; Psychologist; Public Relations Specialist; Purchasing Agent/Manager; Quality Control Supervisor; Registered Nurse; Respiratory Therapist; Restaurant/Food Service Manager; Securities Sales Representative; Services Sales Representative; Surgical Technician; Systems Analyst; Teacher/Professor; Technical Writer/Editor; Telecommunications Manager; Travel Agent; Typist/Word Processor.

RECRUITING ASSOCIATES
P.O. Box 8473, Amarillo TX 79114. 806/353-9548. **Fax:** 806/353-9540. **Contact:** Mike Rokey, CPC, Owner/Manager. **E-mail address:** mikedr@arn.net. **Description:** An executive search firm operating on a contingency basis. Founded in 1978. Company pays fee. **Specializes in the areas of:** Computer Science/Software; Engineering. **Positions commonly filled include:** Accountant/Auditor; Applications Engineer; Computer Operator; Computer Programmer; Database Manager; Design Engineer; Electrical/Electronics Engineer; Mechanical Engineer; MIS Specialist; Software Engineer; Systems Analyst; Technical Writer/Editor. **Benefits available to temporary workers:** 401(k); Medical Insurance. **Average salary range of placements:** $30,000 - $50,000. **Number of placements per year:** 1 - 49.

REDSTONE & ASSOCIATES
20715 Towne Vue Court, Humble TX 77538. 281/446-5625. **Contact:** Randy Redstone, Owner. **Description:** A retained search firm. Company pays fee. **Specializes in the areas of:** Construction; Engineering; Manufacturing; Sales. **Positions commonly filled include:** Accountant/Auditor;

Chemical Engineer; Construction Contractor; Cost Estimator; Metallurgical Engineer; Quality Control Supervisor. **International locations:** Worldwide. **Average salary range of placements:** More than $50,000. **Number of placements per year:** 1 - 49.

RESTAURANT RECRUITERS OF AMERICA, INC.
3701 Kirby, Suite 814, Houston TX 77098. 713/529-0123. **Fax:** 713/523-5830. **Contact:** Bill Troff, Search Consultant. **Description:** A full-service executive search firm operating on a contingency basis. **Specializes in the areas of:** Restaurants. **Positions commonly filled include:** Restaurant/Food Service Manager; Vice President of Operations. **Corporate headquarters location:** This Location. **Average salary range of placements:** $30,000 - $50,000. **Number of placements per year:** 100 - 199.

RICCIONE & ASSOCIATES
16415 Addison Road, Suite 404, Dallas TX 75248. 972/380-6432. **Fax:** 972/407-0659. **Contact:** Nick Riccione, President. **E-mail address:** hitec@riccione.com. **World Wide Web address:** http://www.riccione.com. **Description:** An executive search and contract services firm operating on a contingency basis. Company pays fee. **Specializes in the areas of:** Computer Science/Software; Engineering; High-Tech. **Positions commonly filled include:** Computer Programmer; Software Engineer; Systems Analyst. **Average salary range of placements:** More than $50,000. **Number of placements per year:** 50 - 99.

BART ROBERSON & COMPANY, INC.
11777 Katy Freeway, Suite 375, Houston TX 77079. 281/493-5466. **Fax:** 281/493-2363. **Contact:** Bart Roberson, Owner. **Description:** An executive search firm operating on both retainer and contingency bases. Company pays fee. **Specializes in the areas of:** Accounting/Auditing; Economics; Engineering; Finance; Food Industry; Industrial; Manufacturing; Personnel/Labor Relations; Sales; Technical. **Positions commonly filled include:** Accountant/Auditor; Biochemist; Budget Analyst; Buyer; Chemical Engineer; Chemist; Civil Engineer; Cost Estimator; Credit Manager; Design Engineer; Economist; Electrical/Electronics Engineer; Environmental Engineer; Financial Analyst; Geologist/Geophysicist; Health Services Manager; Human Resources Specialist; Industrial Engineer; Management Analyst/Consultant; Mechanical Engineer; Metallurgical Engineer; Mining Engineer; Petroleum Engineer; Purchasing Agent/Manager; Quality Control Supervisor; Strategic Relations Manager; Structural Engineer; Systems Analyst. **Average salary range of placements:** More than $50,000. **Number of placements per year:** 200 - 499.

THE RODDY GROUP
99 North Post Oak Lane, Suite 4207, Houston TX 77024. 713/681-7686. **Contact:** Manager. **Description:** An executive search firm that provides placement in the energy industry.

ROMAC INTERNATIONAL
12770 Coit Road, Suite 128, Dallas TX 75251. 972/934-2111. **Contact:** Manager. **Description:** An executive search firm. **Specializes in the areas of:** Accounting/Auditing; Finance; Information Technology.

ROTH YOUNG PERSONNEL SERVICES
11999 Katy Freeway, Suite 490, Houston TX 77079. 281/368-8550. **Fax:** 281/368-8560. **Contact:** Rob Gladstone, Executive Vice President. **Description:** An executive search firm operating on both retainer and contingency bases. Founded in 1964. **Specializes in the areas of:** Advertising; Finance; Food Industry; Manufacturing; Personnel/Labor Relations; Retail; Sales; Transportation. **Positions commonly filled include:** Buyer; Computer Programmer; General Manager; Hotel Manager; Human Resources Specialist; Industrial Engineer; Manufacturer's/Wholesaler's Sales Rep.; Operations/Production Manager; Purchasing Agent/Manager; Restaurant/Food Service Manager; Systems Analyst; Transportation/Traffic Specialist. **Average salary range of placements:** More than $50,000. **Number of placements per year:** 50 - 99.

ROTH YOUNG PERSONNEL SERVICES/DALLAS
5344 Alpha Road, Dallas TX 75240. 972/233-5000. **Fax:** 972/233-8213. **Contact:** Ben Dickerson, Recruiter. **Description:** An executive search firm operating on both retainer and contingency bases. Company pays fee. **Specializes in the areas of:** Engineering; Food Industry; General Management; Industrial; Light Industrial; Personnel/Labor Relations; Sales; Transportation. **Positions commonly filled include:** Account Manager; Account Representative; Applications Engineer; Biological Scientist; Buyer; Chemical Engineer; Chief Financial Officer; Controller; Design Engineer; Electrical/Electronics Engineer; Food Scientist/Technologist; General Manager; Human Resources Manager; Industrial Engineer; Industrial Production Manager; Manufacturing Engineer; Market Research Analyst; Marketing Manager; Mechanical Engineer; Operations Manager; Production Manager; Project Manager; Purchasing Agent/Manager; Quality Control Supervisor; Sales Executive; Sales Manager; Sales Representative. **Corporate headquarters location:** New York NY. **Other U.S. locations:** Nationwide. **Average salary range of placements:** $30,000 - $50,000. **Number of placements per year:** 1 - 49.

ROTTMAN GROUP INC.
1425 Greenway Drive, Suite 565, Irving TX 75038. 972/518-1330. **Contact:** Manager. **Description:** An executive search firm. **Specializes in the areas of:** Health/Medical.

RUSSELL REYNOLDS ASSOCIATES, INC.
2001 Ross Avenue, Suite 1900, Dallas TX 75201. 214/220-2033. **Contact:** Manager. **Description:** An executive search firm. **Specializes in the areas of:** Banking; Chemical; Health/Medical; Technical.

RUSSELL REYNOLDS ASSOCIATES, INC.
1000 Louisiana Street, Suite 4800, Houston TX 77002. 713/658-1776. **Contact:** Manager. **Description:** A generalist executive search firm.

SAI EXECUTIVE SEARCH (SLOAN ASSOCIATES INC.)
P.O. Box 220418, El Paso TX 79913. 915/585-1005. **Contact:** Manager. **Description:** An executive search firm that focuses on the placement of physicians. **Specializes in the areas of:** Health/Medical.

SABER CONSULTANTS
5300 Hollister, Suite 100, Houston TX 77040. 713/462-6900. **Fax:** 713/462-8600. **Contact:** Manager. **Description:** An executive search firm. Company pays fee. **Specializes in the areas of:** Architecture/Construction. **Positions commonly filled include:** Construction Contractor; Cost Estimator. **Number of placements per year:** 50 - 99.

SALES CONSULTANTS OF HOUSTON
5075 Westheimer, Suite 790, Houston TX 77056. 713/627-0809. **Fax:** 713/622-7285. **Contact:** Jim DeForest, General Manager. **Description:** An executive search firm. **Specializes in the areas of:** Accounting/Auditing; Administration; Advertising; Architecture/Construction; Banking; Communications; Computer Hardware/Software; Construction; Design; Electrical; Engineering; Finance; Food Industry;

General Management; Health/Medical; Industrial; Insurance; Legal; Manufacturing; Operations Management; Personnel/Labor Relations; Procurement; Publishing; Retail; Sales; Technical; Textiles; Transportation.

SALES RECRUITERS OF HOUSTON
340 North Sam Houston Parkway East, Suite 263, Houston TX 77060. 281/447-0309. **Contact:** Sam Stitt, Executive Recruiter. **Description:** An executive search firm operating on a contingency basis. Company pays fee. **Specializes in the areas of:** Sales. **Average salary range of placements:** $30,000 - $50,000. **Number of placements per year:** 50 - 99.

SALINAS & ASSOCIATES PERSONNEL SERVICE
1700 Commerce Street, Suite 1660, Dallas TX 75201. 214/747-7878. **Fax:** 214/747-7877. **Contact:** Gerry Salinas, Owner/Recruiter. **E-mail address:** ger@flash.net. **Description:** An executive search firm operating on both retainer and contingency bases. Salinas & Associates also offers contract services and career/outplacement counseling. Company pays fee. **Specializes in the areas of:** Accounting/Auditing; Advertising; Banking; Computer Hardware/Software; Fashion; Finance; Personnel/Labor Relations; Sales. **Positions commonly filled include:** Account Manager; Account Representative; Accountant; Administrative Assistant; Administrative Manager; Advertising Account Executive; Advertising Clerk; Auditor; Bank Officer/Manager; Budget Analyst; Buyer; Chemist; Claim Representative; Controller; Counselor; Credit Manager; Customer Service Representative; Database Manager; Human Resources Manager; Market Research Analyst; Marketing Manager; Marketing Specialist; Sales Engineer; Sales Executive; Sales Manager; Secretary. **Corporate headquarters location:** This Location. **Other U.S. locations:** Nationwide. **Average salary range of placements:** Less than $20,000. **Number of placements per year:** 50 - 99.

SANFORD ROSE ASSOCIATES
4210 Spicewood Springs Road, Suite 211, Austin TX 78759. 512/418-8444. **Fax:** 512/418-8441. **Contact:** Manager. **World Wide Web address:** http://www.sanfordrose.com. **Description:** An executive search firm. **Specializes in the areas of:** Electronics; Manufacturing.

DAVID SCHREIBER & ASSOCIATES
1000 FM 1960 West, Suite 207, Houston TX 77090. 281/893-8282. **Contact:** Manager. **Description:** An executive search firm. **Specializes in the areas of:** Finance.

R.L. SCOTT ASSOCIATES
307 West 7th Street, Suite 1800, Fort Worth TX 76102. 817/877-3622. **Fax:** 817/332-3947. **Contact:** Randall Scott, President. **Description:** An executive search firm focusing on placement in psychiatric, rehabilitation, and rural medical/surgical hospitals. Founded in 1988. Company pays fee. **Specializes in the areas of:** Health/Medical. **Positions commonly filled include:** Accountant/Auditor; Counselor; Medical Records Technician; Physical Therapist; Recreational Therapist; Registered Nurse; Respiratory Therapist; Social Worker; Speech-Language Pathologist. **Average salary range of placements:** More than $50,000. **Number of placements per year:** 50 - 99.

SEARCH COM, INC.
12680 Hillcrest Road, Dallas TX 75230. 972/490-0300. **Contact:** Susan Abrahamson, President. **Description:** An executive search firm. Founded in 1986. Company pays fee. **Specializes in the areas of:** Advertising; Art/Design; Publishing; Sales. **Positions commonly filled include:** Designer; Editor; Market Research Analyst; Multimedia Designer; Public Relations Specialist; Technical Writer/Editor. **Average salary range of placements:** More than $50,000. **Number of placements per year:** 1 - 49.

SEARCH CONSULTANTS, INC.
4545 Post Oak Place, Suite 208, Houston TX 77027. 713/622-9188. **Contact:** Manager. **World Wide Web address:** http://www.searchconsultants.com. **Description:** An executive search firm.

SEARCH CONSULTANTS, INC.
P.O. Box 58345, Houston TX 77258. 281/474-7422. **Contact:** Manager. **World Wide Web address:** http://www.searchconsultants.com. **Description:** An executive search firm that places technical staff in a wide range of industries.

THE SEARCH GROUP RECRUITING FIRM
P.O. Box 926193, Houston TX 77292. 713/681-2300. **Contact:** Manager. **Description:** An executive search firm.

SEARCH NETWORK INTERNATIONAL
12801 North Central Expressway, Suite 115, Dallas TX 75243. 972/980-4991. **Fax:** 972/980-8917. **Contact:** Manager. **E-mail address:** resumes@snint.com. **World Wide Web address:** http://www.snint.com. **Description:** An executive search firm operating on a contingency basis. Founded in 1976. Company pays fee. **Specializes in the areas of:** Accounting/Auditing; Computer Science/Software; Engineering; Food Industry; Industrial; Manufacturing. **Positions commonly filled include:** Accountant/Auditor; Aerospace Engineer; Architect; Biochemist; Biomedical Engineer; Buyer; Chemical Engineer; Chemist; Civil Engineer; Computer Programmer; Cost Estimator; Design Engineer; Designer; Draftsperson; Environmental Engineer; Financial Analyst; Food Scientist/Technologist; Geologist/Geophysicist; Industrial Engineer; Industrial Production Manager; Internet Services Manager; Mathematician; Mechanical Engineer; Metallurgical Engineer; Mining Engineer; MIS Specialist; Multimedia Designer; Operations/Production Manager; Petroleum Engineer; Public Relations Specialist; Purchasing Agent/Manager; Quality Control Supervisor; Software Engineer; Statistician; Structural Engineer; Systems Analyst; Telecommunications Manager. **Number of placements per year:** 500 - 999.

SEARCHAMERICA INC.
5908 Meadowcreek Drive, Dallas TX 75248. 972/233-3302. **Fax:** 972/233-1518. **Contact:** Harvey Weiner, President. **E-mail address:** searchamerica@aol.com. **Description:** An executive search firm focusing on the hospitality field. Industries covered include private country, city, and yacht club management, and corporate management for the hotel, restaurant, and club fields. SearchAmerica also provides consultation services to boards of directors. Founded in 1974. **Specializes in the areas of:** Consulting; General Management; Hotel/Restaurant; Personnel/Labor Relations. **Average salary range of placements:** More than $50,000. **Number of placements per year:** 50 - 99.

SELECT STAFF
8200 Nashville Avenue, Suite C109, Lubbock TX 79423. 806/794-5511. **Fax:** 806/794-5869. **Contact:** Manager. **Description:** An executive search firm operating on a contingency basis. Company pays fee. **Specializes in the areas of:** Accounting/Auditing; Administration; Food Industry; General Management; Personnel/Labor Relations; Retail; Sales; Secretarial. **Positions commonly filled include:** Accountant/Auditor; Adjuster; Administrative Manager; Advertising Clerk; Architect; Attorney; Bank Officer/Manager; Blue-Collar Worker Supervisor;

Branch Manager; Brokerage Clerk; Buyer; Chemical Engineer; Civil Engineer; Claim Representative; Clerical Supervisor; Counselor; Credit Manager; Customer Service Representative; Dental Assistant/Dental Hygienist; Draftsperson; Electrical/Electronics Engineer; Electrician; Environmental Engineer; General Manager; Health Services Manager; Hotel Manager; Human Resources Specialist; Human Service Worker; Industrial Engineer; Landscape Architect; Licensed Practical Nurse; Manufacturer's/Wholesaler's Sales Rep.; MIS Specialist; Operations/Production Manager; Paralegal; Pharmacist; Property and Real Estate Manager; Public Relations Specialist; Purchasing Agent/Manager; Quality Control Supervisor; Restaurant/Food Service Manager; Securities Sales Representative; Social Worker; Systems Analyst; Technical Writer/Editor; Telecommunications Manager; Transportation/Traffic Specialist; Underwriter/ Assistant Underwriter. **Average salary range of placements:** $20,000 - $29,999. **Number of placements per year:** 500 - 999.

MARVIN L. SILCOTT & ASSOCIATES, INC.
7557 Rambler Road, Suite 1336, Dallas TX 75231. 214/369-7802. **Fax:** 214/369-7875. **Contact:** Marvin L. Silcott, President. **Description:** An executive search firm focusing on retained searches for general counsels, chief patent counsels, and other top legal positions. Founded in 1973. Company pays fee. **Specializes in the areas of:** Legal. **Positions commonly filled include:** Attorney. **Average salary range of placements:** More than $50,000. **Number of placements per year:** 50 - 99.

SNELLING PERSONNEL SERVICES
146 American Bank Plaza, Corpus Christi TX 78475. 512/883-7903. **Contact:** Ms. Jean Cole, Owner/Manager. **Description:** An executive search firm. Company pays fee. **Specializes in the areas of:** Accounting/Auditing; Architecture/Construction; Engineering; Industrial; Legal; Manufacturing; Personnel/Labor Relations; Sales; Secretarial. **Positions commonly filled include:** Architect; Chemical Engineer; Civil Engineer; Clerical Supervisor; Computer Programmer; Cost Estimator; Customer Service Representative; Dental Assistant/Dental Hygienist; Draftsperson; Electrical/Electronics Engineer; Human Resources Manager; Industrial Engineer; Industrial Production Manager; Management Trainee; Mechanical Engineer; Metallurgical Engineer; Paralegal; Services Sales Representative; Structural Engineer; Surgical Technician; Systems Analyst; Technical Writer/Editor. **Other U.S. locations:** Nationwide. **Number of placements per year:** 50 - 99.

SNELLING PERSONNEL SERVICES
12770 Coit Road, Suite 250, Dallas TX 75251. 972/701-8080. **Contact:** Don Lummus, Owner. **Description:** An executive search firm. **Specializes in the areas of:** Accounting/Auditing; Engineering; Food Industry; Health/Medical; Insurance; Legal; Manufacturing; Sales. **Other U.S. locations:** Nationwide. **Number of placements per year:** 200 - 499.

SNELLING PERSONNEL SERVICES
5151 Belt Line Road, Suite 365, Dallas TX 75240. 972/934-9030. **Fax:** 972/934-3639. **Contact:** Sam D. Bingham, CPC, Owner. **Description:** An executive search firm operating on a contingency basis. Company pays fee. **Specializes in the areas of:** Accounting/Auditing; Biology; Computer Science/ Software; Engineering; Food Industry; Industrial; Manufacturing; Sales; Secretarial; Technical. **Positions commonly filled include:** Accountant/Auditor; Chemical Engineer; Chemist; Computer Programmer; Credit Manager; Customer Service Representative; Electrical/Electronics Engineer; Environmental Engineer; Food Scientist/Technologist; Industrial Engineer; Industrial Production Manager; Mechanical Engineer; Metallurgical Engineer; Mining Engineer; Nuclear Engineer; Operations/Production Manager; Petroleum Engineer; Services Sales Representative; Software Engineer; Systems Analyst. **Other U.S. locations:** Nationwide. **Average salary range of placements:** $30,000 - $50,000. **Number of placements per year:** 100 - 199.

SOLUTIONS
RR 3, Box 204B, Leander TX 78641. 512/219-0224. **Fax:** 512/918-2805. **Contact:** Karen Beall, Owner. **Description:** An executive search firm operating on both retainer and contingency bases. Company pays fee. **Specializes in the areas of:** Health/Medical; Sales. **Positions commonly filled include:** Administrative Manager; Biomedical Engineer; Claim Representative; Customer Service Representative; Dietician/ Nutritionist; Emergency Medical Technician; Health Services Manager; Nuclear Medicine Technologist; Occupational Therapist; Operations/Production Manager; Pharmacist; Physical Therapist; Physician; Psychologist; Public Relations Specialist; Quality Control Supervisor; Radiological Technologist; Recreational Therapist; Registered Nurse; Respiratory Therapist; Social Worker; Speech-Language Pathologist. **Number of placements per year:** 1 - 49.

SOURCE SERVICES CORPORATION
5429 LBJ Freeway, Suite 275, Dallas TX 75240. 972/387-1600. **Contact:** Manager. **Description:** An executive search firm. The divisions at this location include Source EDP, Source Engineering, and Source Finance. **Specializes in the areas of:** Accounting/Auditing; Computer Hardware/Software; Engineering; Finance.

SOURCE SERVICES CORPORATION
8701 North Mopac, Suite 455, Austin TX 78759. 512/345-7473. **Fax:** 512/345-7736. **Contact:** Manager. **Description:** An executive search firm. The divisions at this location include Source EDP and Source Finance. **Specializes in the areas of:** Computer Hardware/Software; Finance; Information Technology.

SOURCE SERVICES CORPORATION
520 Post Oak Boulevard, Suite 700, Houston TX 77027. 713/439-1077. **Fax:** 713/439-1167. **Contact:** Manager. **Description:** An executive search firm. The divisions at this location include Source Consulting, Source EDP, Source Finance, Source Legal, and Accountant Source Temps. **Specializes in the areas of:** Accounting/Auditing; Computer Hardware/Software; Finance; Information Technology; Legal.

SPRADLEY LEGAL SEARCH
3131 McKinney Street, Suite 490, Dallas TX 75204. 214/969-5900. **Contact:** Manager. **Description:** An executive search firm. **Specializes in the areas of:** Legal.

STAFF EXTENSION INC.
13612 Midway, Suite 103, Dallas TX 75244. 972/991-4737. **Fax:** 972/991-5325. **Contact:** Jack R. Williams, President. **E-mail address:** staffing@ staffext.com. **World Wide Web address:** http://www. staffext.com. **Description:** An executive search firm that also operates as a temporary agency and contract services firm. Founded in 1990. Company pays fee. **Specializes in the areas of:** Accounting/Auditing; Administration; Computer Science/Software; Engineering; Finance; General Management; Health/ Medical; Manufacturing; Personnel/Labor Relations; Sales; Technical. **Corporate headquarters location:** This Location. **Other U.S. locations:** Denver CO; Houston TX. **Number of placements per year:** 50 - 99.

R.A. STONE & ASSOCIATES
5495 Belt Line Road, Suite 153, Dallas TX 75240. 972/233-0483. **Contact:** Manager. **Description:** An executive search firm. **Specializes in the areas of:** Broadcasting; Health/Medical.

STRATEGIC OUTSOURCING CORPORATION
100 North Central Expressway, Suite 1000, Richardson TX 75080. 972/437-2220. **Fax:** 972/437-2310. **Contact:** Brandt Hamby, Recruiting Manager. **E-mail address:** 50C@why.net. **Description:** An executive search firm operating on a retainer basis. Company pays fee. **Specializes in the areas of:** Computer Science/Software; Engineering; General Management; Publishing; Sales; Technical. **Positions commonly filled include:** Branch Manager; Computer Programmer; General Manager; Software Engineer; Strategic Relations Manager; Systems Analyst. **Corporate headquarters location:** Dallas TX. **Average salary range of placements:** More than $50,000. **Number of placements per year:** 1 - 49.

TGA COMPANY
P.O. Box 331121, Fort Worth TX 76163. 817/370-0865. **Fax:** 817/292-6451. **Contact:** Tom Green, President. **Description:** An executive search firm. Company pays fee. **Specializes in the areas of:** Accounting/Auditing; Computer Science/Software; Finance; Information Systems; Technical. **Positions commonly filled include:** Accountant/Auditor; Chief Financial Officer; Controller; Credit Manager; Financial Analyst; MIS Specialist; Software Engineer; Systems Analyst. **Average salary range of placements:** More than $50,000. **Number of placements per year:** 50 - 99.

TNS PARTNERS, INC.
8140 Walnut Hill Lane, Suite 301, Dallas TX 75231. 972/991-3555. **Contact:** Manager. **Description:** A generalist executive search firm.

TRS
P.O. Box 405, Sugar Land TX 77478. 281/263-3560. **Contact:** Manager. **Description:** An executive search firm. **Specializes in the areas of:** Engineering.

THE TALON GROUP
16801 Addison Road, Suite 255, Dallas TX 75248. 972/931-8223. **Fax:** 972/931-8063. **Contact:** Robert A. Piper, President. **E-mail address:** talongrp@gte.net. **Description:** An executive search firm operating on a retainer basis. Company pays fee. **Specializes in the areas of:** Construction; Housing; Manufacturing; Real Estate. **Positions commonly filled include:** Architect; Chief Financial Officer; Civil Engineer; Construction Superintendent; Controller; Cost Estimator; General Manager; Marketing Manager; MIS Specialist; Operations Manager; Production Manager; Project Manager; Purchasing Agent/Manager; Sales Manager; Vice President. **Average salary range of placements:** More than $50,000. **Number of placements per year:** 50 - 99.

BETTY TANNER PROFESSIONAL EMPLOYMENT SERVICE, INC.
5539 North Mesa Street, El Paso TX 79912. 915/587-5166. **Fax:** 915/587-5191. **Contact:** Bruce Tanner, General Manager. **Description:** An executive search firm operating on both retainer and contingency bases. The firm also provides career/outplacement counseling. Founded in 1988. Company pays fee. **Specializes in the areas of:** Accounting/Auditing; Computer Science/Software; Engineering; Finance; Health/Medical; Industrial; Manufacturing; Personnel/Labor Relations. **Positions commonly filled include:** Accountant/Auditor; Biomedical Engineer; Budget Analyst; Buyer; Ceramics Engineer; Chemical Engineer; Computer Programmer; Designer; Electrical/Electronics Engineer; Financial Analyst; General Manager; Human Resources Manager; Industrial Engineer; Industrial Production Manager; Manufacturer's/Wholesaler's Sales Rep.; Materials Engineer; Mechanical Engineer; Metallurgical Engineer; Operations/Production Manager; Physical Therapist; Purchasing Agent/Manager; Quality Control Supervisor; Software Engineer; Systems Analyst; Transportation/Traffic Specialist. **Average salary range of placements:** More than $50,000. **Number of placements per year:** 50 - 99.

TECH-NET
14785 Preston Road, Dallas TX 75240-7876. 972/934-3000. **Contact:** Chris Cole, Owner. **Description:** An executive search firm that focuses on the placement of engineers in sales positions, particularly those positions which utilize UNIX-based design tools. Founded in 1989. Company pays fee. **Specializes in the areas of:** Computer Science/Software; Engineering; Sales; Technical. **Positions commonly filled include:** Aerospace Engineer; Design Engineer; Electrical/Electronics Engineer; Mechanical Engineer; MIS Specialist; Software Engineer; Technical Representative. **Average salary range of placements:** More than $50,000. **Number of placements per year:** 1 - 49.

TECHFIND
5959 Gateway West, Suite 601, El Paso TX 79925. 915/775-1176. **Contact:** Manager. **Description:** An executive search firm.

TECHNICAL STAFFING SOLUTIONS
16775 Addison Road, Suite 240, Dallas TX 75248. 972/788-1771. **Fax:** 972/788-0661. **Contact:** Don Fink, Office Manager. **Description:** An executive search and contract services firm. Founded in 1989. Company pays fee. **Specializes in the areas of:** Accounting/Auditing; Chemical; Engineering; Information Systems; Manufacturing; Oil and Gas; Technical. **Positions commonly filled include:** Accountant/Auditor; Administrative Worker/Clerk; Chemical Engineer; Chemist; Computer Programmer; Design Engineer; Electrical/Electronics Engineer; Environmental Engineer; Financial Analyst; Mechanical Engineer; Software Engineer. **Average salary range of placements:** More than $50,000. **Number of placements per year:** 100 - 199.

TEXAS PERSONNEL
985 Interstate 10 North, Beaumont TX 77706. 409/892-5000. **Fax:** 409/892-5068. **Contact:** Cliff Heubel, Owner. **Description:** An executive search firm that operates on a contingency basis. Founded in 1992. Company pays fee. **Specializes in the areas of:** Banking; Computer Science/Software; Insurance; Sales; Secretarial. **Positions commonly filled include:** Accountant/Auditor; Automotive Mechanic; Bank Officer/Manager; Computer Programmer; Dental Assistant/Dental Hygienist; Manufacturer's/Wholesaler's Sales Rep.; MIS Specialist; Services Sales Representative; Systems Analyst; Typist/Word Processor. **Number of placements per year:** 100 - 199.

TOTAL PERSONNEL INC.
P.O. Box 28975, Dallas TX 75228. 214/327-1165. **Fax:** 214/328-3061. **Contact:** Sherry Phillips, President. **Description:** An executive search firm operating on both retainer and contingency bases. Company pays fee. **Specializes in the areas of:** Administration; Computer Science/Software; Data Processing. **Positions commonly filled include:** Computer Programmer; Education Administrator; Software Engineer; Systems Analyst; Teacher/Professor; Technical Writer/Editor; Telecommunications Manager. **Average salary range**

of placements: More than $50,000. **Number of placements per year:** 1 - 49.

CRAIG TROTMAN & ASSOCIATES
3109 Carlisle Street, Suite 206A, Dallas TX 75204. 214/954-1919. **Contact:** Manager. **Description:** An executive search firm. **Specializes in the areas of:** Consumer Package Goods.

THE URBAN PLACEMENT SERVICE
602 Sawyer Street, Suite 460, Houston TX 77007. 713/880-2211. **Fax:** 713/880-5577. **Contact:** Willie S. Bright, Owner/Manager. **E-mail address:** urbanplacment@msn.com. **Description:** An executive search firm. Founded in 1971. **Specializes in the areas of:** Accounting/Auditing; Administration; Computer Science/Software; Engineering; Finance; Food Industry; Industrial; Manufacturing; Personnel/Labor Relations; Technical. **Positions commonly filled include:** Accountant/Auditor; Brokerage Clerk; Budget Analyst; Buyer; Chemical Engineer; Chemist; Civil Engineer; Computer Programmer; Cost Estimator; Design Engineer; Draftsperson; EDP Specialist; Electrical/Electronics Engineer; Financial Analyst; Human Resources Manager; Industrial Engineer; Marketing Specialist; Mechanical Engineer; MIS Specialist; Operations/Production Manager; Petroleum Engineer; Purchasing Agent/Manager; Quality Control Supervisor; Sales Representative; Secretary; Systems Analyst; Technical Writer/Editor; Typist/Word Processor. **Average salary range of placements:** $30,000 - $50,000. **Number of placements per year:** 1 - 49.

VALPERS INC.
8303 Southwest Freeway, Suite 750, Houston TX 77074. 713/771-9420. **Fax:** 713/771-7924. **Contact:** Donald R. Caffee, President. **Description:** An executive search firm and employment agency focusing on the placement of professionals in the industrial valve and fluid flow industries. Valpers also provides contract services on both retainer and contingency bases. Founded in 1981. Company pays fee. **Specializes in the areas of:** Engineering; General Management; Industrial; Manufacturing; Sales; Technical. **Positions commonly filled include:** Customer Service Representative; Design Engineer; Electrical/Electronics Engineer; General Manager; Human Resources Specialist; Industrial Production Manager; Manufacturer's/Wholesaler's Sales Rep.; Market Research Analyst; Materials Engineer; Mechanical Engineer; Metallurgical Engineer; Nuclear Engineer; Operations/Production Manager; Quality Control Supervisor. **Average salary range of placements:** More than $50,000. **Number of placements per year:** 1 - 49.

DICK VAN VLIET & ASSOCIATES
2401 Fountain View Drive, Suite 322, Houston TX 77057. 713/952-0371. **Contact:** Dick Van Vliet, President. **Description:** An executive search firm operating on a contingency basis. Founded in 1985. Company pays fee. **Specializes in the areas of:** Accounting/Auditing; Administration; Computer Science/Software; Finance; Sales. **Positions commonly filled include:** Accountant/Auditor; Budget Analyst; Credit Manager; Financial Analyst; Human Resources Specialist; MIS Specialist; Systems Analyst. **Average salary range of placements:** $30,000 - $100,000. **Number of placements per year:** 50 - 99.

VICK & ASSOCIATES
RECRUITERS ONLINE NETWORK
3325 Landershire Lane, Suite 1001, Plano TX 75023-6218. 972/612-8425. **Fax:** 972/612-1924. **Contact:** Bill Vick, Owner. **World Wide Web address:** http://www.ipa.com. **Description:** An executive search firm. Company pays fee. **Specializes in the areas of:** Computer Science/Software; General Management; Sales; Technical. **Positions commonly filled include:** Regional Manager; Sales Manager. **Number of placements per year:** 50 - 99.

DARRYL VINCENT AND ASSOCIATES
12651 Briar Forest, Suite 165, Houston TX 77077. 281/497-5240. **Fax:** 281/497-7945. **Contact:** Darryl Vincent, Owner. **E-mail address:** dvincent02@sprynet.com. **World Wide Web address:** http://home.sprynet.com/sprynet/dvincent02/index.html. **Description:** An executive search firm that places sales and marketing managers in the consumer package goods industry. **Specializes in the areas of:** Packaging; Sales. **Average salary range of placements:** More than $50,000. **Number of placements per year:** 50 - 99.

DENIS P. WALSH & ASSOCIATES, INC.
5402 Bent Bough, Houston TX 77088. 281/931-9121. **Fax:** 281/820-4285. **Contact:** Denis P. Walsh, Jr., President. **Description:** An executive search firm operating on a contingency basis. The firm provides staffing for the refining/petrochemical and environmental industries. Company pays fee. **Specializes in the areas of:** Engineering. **Positions commonly filled include:** Chemical Engineer; Construction Contractor; Cost Estimator; Electrical/Electronics Engineer; Environmental Engineer; Mechanical Engineer. **Number of placements per year:** 1 - 49.

WARD HOWELL INTERNATIONAL, INC.
7502 Greenville Avenue, Suite 500, Dallas TX 75231. 214/749-0099. **Contact:** Manager. **Description:** An executive search firm.

WATKINS & ASSOCIATES
7322 SW Freeway, Suite 620, Houston TX 77074. 713/777-5261. **Contact:** Manager. **Description:** An executive search firm operating on both retainer and contingency bases. **Specializes in the areas of:** Accounting/Auditing; Manufacturing; Oil and Gas; Petrochemical; Sales.

ROBERT WESSON & ASSOCIATES
14800 Quorum Drive, Suite 440, Dallas TX 75240. 972/239-8613. **Contact:** Bob McDermid, Partner. **Description:** An executive search firm. Company pays fee. **Specializes in the areas of:** Food Industry; Sales. **Positions commonly filled include:** Accountant/Auditor; Architect; Human Resources Manager; Management Trainee; Purchasing Agent/Manager; Restaurant/Food Service Manager. **Number of placements per year:** 100 - 199.

WHEELER, MOORE & ELAM COMPANY
14800 Quorum Drive, Suite 200, Dallas TX 75240. 972/386-8806. **Contact:** Dr. Mark Moore, President. **Description:** An executive search firm operating on a retainer basis with clients nationwide. The company also provides career/outplacement counseling services. Founded in 1984. Company pays fee. **Specializes in the areas of:** Accounting/Auditing; Administration; Engineering; Finance; General Management; Legal; Manufacturing; Personnel/Labor Relations; Sales; Technical. **Average salary range of placements:** More than $50,000. **Number of placements per year:** 1 - 49.

THE WHITAKER COMPANIES
820 Gessner, Suite 1400, Houston TX 77024. 713/465-1500. **Fax:** 713/932-2525. **Contact:** Bruce Whitaker, CPC, President/Owner. **E-mail address:** bruce@whitakercos.com. **World Wide Web address:** http://www.whitakercos.com. **Description:** An executive search and contract services firm operating five divisions. **Specializes in the areas of:** Accounting/Auditing; Administration; Computer

Science/Software; Engineering; Finance; Health/Medical; Legal; MIS/EDP. **Positions commonly filled include:** Accountant; Attorney; Bank Officer/Manager; Chemical Engineer; Chemist; Chief Financial Officer; Civil Engineer; Database Manager; Electrical/Electronics Engineer; Environmental Engineer; Finance Director; Financial Analyst; Geologist/Geophysicist; Intellectual Property Lawyer; Mechanical Engineer; MIS Specialist; Physician; Software Engineer; Systems Analyst; Systems Manager; Technical Writer/Editor. **Benefits available to temporary workers:** 401(k); Dental Insurance; Medical Insurance; Paid Holidays. **Corporate headquarters location:** This Location. **Other area locations:** Austin TX; Dallas TX. **Other U.S. locations:** Vincennes IN. **Average salary range of placements:** More than $50,000. **Number of placements per year:** 100 - 199.

WILLIAMS COMPANY
8080 North Central Expressway, Suite 100, Dallas TX 75206. 214/891-6340. **Contact:** Manager. **Description:** An executive search firm. **Specializes in the areas of:** Retail.

THE WILSON GROUP
418 Peoples Street, Corpus Christi TX 78413. 512/883-3535. **Contact:** Manager. **Description:** An executive search firm that also provides permanent and temporary placements.

WINDSOR CONSULTANTS INC.
13201 Northwest Freeway, Suite 704, Houston TX 77040-6025. 713/460-0586. **Fax:** 713/460-0945. **Contact:** Dan Narsh, President. **Description:** A contingency and retained executive search firm. Company pays fee. **Specializes in the areas of:** Food Industry; Health/Medical; Legal; Sales. **Positions commonly filled include:** Attorney; Management Trainee; Manufacturer's/Wholesaler's Sales Rep.; Medical Records Technician; Registered Nurse; Restaurant/Food Service Manager. **Corporate headquarters location:** This Location. **Other U.S. locations:** Washington DC; Chicago IL; New York NY. **Average salary range of placements:** More than $50,000. **Number of placements per year:** 100 - 199.

WITT/KIEFFER, FORD, HADELMAN & LLOYD
2 Lincoln Center, 5420 LBJ Freeway, Suite 460, Dallas TX 75240. 972/490-1370. **Contact:** Manager. **Description:** An executive search firm for upper-level professionals. **Specializes in the areas of:** Health/Medical.

JOHN W. WORSHAM & ASSOCIATES INC.
5851 San Felipe, Suite 770, Houston TX 77057. 713/266-3235. **Contact:** Manager. **Description:** An executive search firm. **Specializes in the areas of:** Banking.

THE WRIGHT GROUP
9217 Frenchman's Way, Dallas TX 75220. 214/351-1115. **Contact:** Jay J. Wright, President. **Description:** An executive search firm. Founded in 1985. Company pays fee. **Specializes in the areas of:** Marketing. **Positions commonly filled include:** Market Research Analyst. **Number of placements per year:** 1 - 49.

R.S. WYATT ASSOCIATES, INC.
501 Saint James Court, Southlake TX 76092. 817/421-8726. **Fax:** 817/421-1374. **Contact:** Robert S. Wyatt, Ph.D., Principal. **E-mail address:** rswassoc@aol.com. **Description:** An executive search and consulting firm operating on a retainer basis. The company provides services to the retail sector and firms that support retail organizations. Company pays fee. **Specializes in the areas of:** Consulting; General Management; Personnel/Labor Relations; Retail. **Positions commonly filled include:** Accountant/Auditor; Branch Manager; Buyer; Computer Programmer; Credit Manager; Customer Service Representative; Design Engineer; General Manager; Human Resources Specialist; Industrial Engineer; Management Analyst/Consultant; Public Relations Specialist; Software Engineer; Systems Analyst; Transportation/Traffic Specialist. **Average salary range of placements:** More than $50,000. **Number of placements per year:** 1 - 49.

WYMAN & ASSOCIATES, INC.
P.O. Box 13253, Arlington TX 76094. 817/572-5212. **Fax:** 817/483-5550. **Contact:** David Wyman, President. **E-mail address:** wyman@arlington.net. **Description:** An executive search firm operating on both retainer and contingency bases. Company pays fee. **Specializes in the areas of:** Computer Science/Software; General Management; Personnel/Labor Relations; Restaurant. **Positions commonly filled include:** Attorney; Claim Representative; Computer Programmer; Dietician/ Nutritionist; EEG Technologist; EKG Technician; Food Scientist/Technologist; Health Services Manager; Hotel Manager; Human Resources Specialist; Insurance Agent/Broker; Internet Services Manager; Licensed Practical Nurse; Market Research Analyst; MIS Specialist; Multimedia Designer; Occupational Therapist; Physical Therapist; Registered Nurse; Respiratory Therapist; Restaurant/Food Service Manager; Software Engineer; Surgical Technician; Systems Analyst; Telecommunications Manager; Underwriter/Assistant Underwriter. **Average salary range of placements:** $30,000 - $50,000. **Number of placements per year:** 1 - 49.

PERMANENT EMPLOYMENT AGENCIES

AARP SENIOR COMMUNITY SERVICE EMPLOYMENT PROGRAM
2301 North Akard Street, Suite 111, Dallas TX 75201. 214/954-0442. **Contact:** Arnold Parra, Project Director. **Description:** A permanent placement agency for people aged 55 and over. **Positions commonly filled include:** Accountant/ Auditor; Administrative Manager; Blue-Collar Worker Supervisor; Branch Manager; Clerical Supervisor; Credit Manager; General Manager; Human Service Worker; Petroleum Engineer; Restaurant/Food Service Manager; Teacher/Professor. **Other U.S. locations:** Nationwide. **Number of placements per year:** 1 - 49.

ABILENE EMPLOYMENT SERVICE
1290 South Willis Street, Suite 111, Abilene TX 79605. 915/698-0451. **Fax:** 915/690-1242. **Contact:** Vi Ballard, Owner. **Description:** A permanent employment agency. **Specializes in the areas of:** Accounting/Auditing; Banking; Computer Science/Software; General Management; Health/Medical; Insurance; Legal; Manufacturing; Retail; Secretarial; Transportation. **Positions commonly filled include:** Accountant/Auditor; Administrative Manager; Advertising Clerk; Aircraft Mechanic/Engine Specialist; Automotive Mechanic; Bank Officer/Manager; Blue-Collar Worker Supervisor; Branch Manager; Buyer; Clerical Supervisor; Computer Programmer; Cost Estimator; Counselor; Customer Service Representative; Electrician; General Manager; Human Service Worker; Landscape Architect; Medical Records Technician; Operations/Production Manager; Physical Therapist; Property and Real Estate Manager; Quality Control Supervisor; Real Estate Agent; Restaurant/Food Service Manager; Securities Sales Representative; Software Engineer; Systems Analyst;

Travel Agent; Typist/Word Processor. **Average salary range of placements:** $20,000 - $29,999. **Number of placements per year:** 1 - 49.

ABILITIES UNLIMITED PERSONNEL
P.O. Box 90991, Houston TX 77290. 281/999-6300. **Contact:** Manager. **Description:** A permanent employment agency.

ACCOUNTING ACTION PERSONNEL
3010 LBJ Freeway, Suite 710, Dallas TX 75234. 972/241-1543. **Contact:** Cheryl Bieke, Office Manager. **Description:** Accounting Action Personnel is a permanent employment agency. Company pays fee. **Specializes in the areas of:** Accounting/Auditing; Administration; Finance. **Positions commonly filled include:** Accountant/Auditor; Administrative Assistant; Bookkeeper; Clerk; Credit Manager; Data Entry Clerk; Receptionist; Secretary; Typist/Word Processor.

ADSTAFF MANAGEMENT & PERSONNEL CONSULTANTS, INC.
6200 Savoy Drive, Suite 300, Houston TX 77036. 713/782-8838. **Fax:** 713/782-6909. **Contact:** Beverlyn Hunter, Office Manager. **Description:** A full-service employment agency providing permanent and temporary placements. **Specializes in the areas of:** Accounting/Auditing; Secretarial. **Positions commonly filled include:** Accountant/Auditor; Blue-Collar Worker Supervisor; Buyer; Claim Representative; Clinical Lab Technician; Computer Programmer; Customer Service Representative; Dental Assistant/Dental Hygienist; Financial Analyst; Licensed Practical Nurse; Management Trainee; Medical Records Technician; MIS Specialist; Occupational Therapist; Physical Therapist; Quality Control Supervisor; Registered Nurse; Systems Analyst; Typist/Word Processor. **Other area locations:** Austin TX. **Number of placements per year:** 1 - 49.

AUSTIN INSURANCE RECRUITERS
1000 West Bank, 5A-110, Austin TX 78746. 512/329-8815. **Contact:** Manager. **Description:** A permanent employment agency. **Specializes in the areas of:** Insurance.

AUSTIN MEDICAL PERSONNEL
1010 West Rosedale Street, Fort Worth TX 76104. 817/335-2433. **Contact:** Manager. **Description:** A permanent placement agency. **Specializes in the areas of:** Health/Medical.

AWARE AFFILIATES PERSONNEL SERVICE
P.O. Box 470183, Fort Worth TX 76147. 817/870-2591. **Fax:** 817/870-2590. **Contact:** Mike Keeton, President. **Description:** A permanent employment agency. **Specializes in the areas of:** Accounting/Auditing; Administration; Advertising; Finance; General Management; Health/Medical; Insurance; Legal; Manufacturing; Nonprofit; Personnel/Labor Relations; Publishing; Retail; Sales; Secretarial; Technical; Transportation. **Positions commonly filled include:** Accountant/Auditor; Adjuster; Administrative Manager; Advertising Clerk; Blue-Collar Worker Supervisor; Branch Manager; Claim Representative; Clerical Supervisor; Computer Programmer; Cost Estimator; Counselor; Credit Manager; Customer Service Representative; Editor; Financial Analyst; General Manager; Health Services Manager; Hotel Manager; Human Resources Specialist; Insurance Agent/Broker; Library Technician; Management Trainee; Manufacturer's/Wholesaler's Sales Rep.; Operations/Production Manager; Paralegal; Property and Real Estate Manager; Purchasing Agent/Manager; Quality Control Supervisor; Securities Sales Representative; Services Sales Representative; Transportation/Traffic Specialist; Travel Agent; Typist/Word Processor; Underwriter/Assistant Underwriter. **Average salary range of placements:** $20,000 - $29,999. **Number of placements per year:** 200 - 499.

B.G. PERSONNEL SERVICES
P.O. Box 803026, Dallas TX 75380. 972/960-7741. **Contact:** Manager. **Description:** A permanent employment agency. **Specializes in the areas of:** Real Estate.

BABICH & ASSOCIATES, INC.
6060 North Central Expressway, Suite 544, Dallas TX 75206. 214/361-5735. **Contact:** Anthony Beshara, President. **Description:** A permanent employment agency. Company pays fee. **Specializes in the areas of:** Accounting/Auditing; Administration; Clerical; Computer Hardware/Software; Engineering; Finance; Manufacturing; Sales; Technical. **Positions commonly filled include:** Accountant/Auditor; Administrative Assistant; Agricultural Engineer; Bookkeeper; Ceramics Engineer; Civil Engineer; Computer Programmer; Customer Service Representative; Data Entry Clerk; EDP Specialist; Electrical/Electronics Engineer; Financial Analyst; General Manager; Human Resources Manager; Industrial Engineer; Mechanical Engineer; Medical Secretary; Metallurgical Engineer; Receptionist; Secretary; Systems Analyst; Typist/Word Processor. **Number of placements per year:** 500 - 999.

BABICH & ASSOCIATES, INC.
One Summit Avenue, Suite 602, Fort Worth TX 76102. 817/336-7261. **Contact:** Anthony Beshara, President. **Description:** A permanent employment agency. Company pays fee. **Specializes in the areas of:** Accounting/Auditing; Administration; Clerical; Computer Hardware/Software; Engineering; Manufacturing; Sales; Technical. **Positions commonly filled include:** Accountant/Auditor; Administrative Assistant; Agricultural Engineer; Bookkeeper; Ceramics Engineer; Civil Engineer; Computer Programmer; Customer Service Representative; Data Entry Clerk; EDP Specialist; Electrical/Electronics Engineer; Financial Analyst; General Manager; Human Resources Manager; Industrial Engineer; Mechanical Engineer; Medical Secretary; Metallurgical Engineer; Receptionist; Sales Representative; Secretary; Stenographer; Systems Analyst; Typist/Word Processor. **Number of placements per year:** 500 - 999.

BEST PERSONNEL
6575 West Loop South, Suite 480, Houston TX 77401. 713/623-6466. **Contact:** Office Manager. **Description:** A permanent employment agency.

BESTSTAFF SERVICES, INC.
3730 Kirby Street, Suite 320, Houston TX 77098. 713/527-8233. **Fax:** 713/527-0813. **Contact:** David Harris, CEO. **Description:** A full-service employment agency that provides permanent, temporary, and contract placements. **Specializes in the areas of:** Advertising; Banking; Engineering; Personnel/Labor Relations; Sales; Secretarial; Technical. **Positions commonly filled include:** Accountant/Auditor; Administrative Manager; Advertising Clerk; Aerospace Engineer; Bank Officer/Manager; Budget Analyst; Chemical Engineer; Civil Engineer; Claim Representative; Computer Programmer; Design Engineer; Electrical/Electronics Engineer; General Manager; Human Resources Specialist; Industrial Engineer; Internet Services Manager; Management Analyst/Consultant; Mechanical Engineer; Property and Real Estate Manager; Quality Control Supervisor; Restaurant/Food Service Manager; Securities Sales Representative; Software Engineer; Structural Engineer; Systems Analyst; Technical Writer/Editor;

Typist/Word Processor. **Benefits available to temporary workers:** Paid Holidays; Paid Vacation; Referral Bonus Plan. **Average salary range of placements:** $30,000 - $50,000. **Number of placements per year:** 100 - 199.

BORDER PROFESSIONAL RECRUITERS
5901 McPherson, Suite 5A, Laredo TX 78041. 956/727-4296. **Contact:** Manager. **Description:** A permanent employment agency that also offers temporary placements. **Specializes in the areas of:** Clerical; Industrial.

BOTT & ASSOCIATES
P.O. Box 42405, Houston TX 77242-2405. 713/782-9814. **Fax:** 713/782-9817. **Contact:** K.W. Bott, President. **Description:** A permanent employment agency. Company pays fee. **Specializes in the areas of:** Engineering. **Positions commonly filled include:** Ceramics Engineer; Chemical Engineer; Civil Engineer; Design Engineer; Environmental Engineer; Industrial Engineer; Manufacturing Engineer; Materials Engineer; Mechanical Engineer; Metallurgical Engineer; Petroleum Engineer; Production Manager; Project Manager; Sales Engineer; Structural Engineer. **Average salary range of placements:** $30,000 - $50,000. **Number of placements per year:** 100 - 199.

BRAINPOWER PERSONNEL AGENCY
4210 50th Street, Suite A, Lubbock TX 79413-3810. 806/795-0644. **Fax:** 806/795-0645. **Contact:** Phil Crenshaw, CPC, Owner. **Description:** A permanent employment agency. **Specializes in the areas of:** Accounting/Auditing; Administration; Computer Science/Software; Data Processing; Engineering; Finance; Health/Medical; Sales; Secretarial. **Positions commonly filled include:** Accountant/Auditor; Computer Programmer; Customer Service Representative; Electrical/Electronics Engineer; MIS Specialist; Social Worker; Software Engineer. **Average salary range of placements:** $20,000 - $29,999. **Number of placements per year:** 1 - 49.

BROWN & KEENE PERSONNEL
14160 Dallas Parkway, Suite 450, Dallas TX 75240. 972/701-9292. **Contact:** Manager. **Description:** A permanent employment agency. **Specializes in the areas of:** Administration.

BRUCO, INC.
P.O. Box 1214, Pasadena TX 77501. 713/473-9251. **Fax:** 713/473-2456. **Contact:** Stella Walters, Manager. **Description:** A permanent employment agency. **Specializes in the areas of:** Accounting/Auditing; Clerical; Finance.

BULLOCK PERSONNEL, INC.
1020 NE Loop 410, Suite 530, San Antonio TX 78209. 210/828-7301. **Fax:** 210/828-8711. **Contact:** Recruiter. **Description:** A permanent employment agency. **Specializes in the areas of:** Accounting/Auditing; Administration; Finance; General Management; Legal; Personnel/Labor Relations; Retail; Sales; Secretarial. **Positions commonly filled include:** Accountant/Auditor; Administrative Manager; Bank Officer/Manager; Clerical Supervisor; Computer Programmer; Customer Service Representative; General Manager; Human Resources Specialist; Purchasing Agent/Manager.

BURNETT'S STAFFING, INC.
Burnett Building, 2710 Avenue E East, Arlington TX 76011. 817/649-7000. **Contact:** Paul W. Burnett, President. **Description:** A permanent employment agency. Company pays fee. **Specializes in the areas of:** Administration; MIS/EDP; Secretarial. **Positions commonly filled include:** Accountant/Auditor; Administrative Assistant; Administrative Manager; Advertising Clerk; Bookkeeper; Claim Representative; Clerical Supervisor; Computer Operator; Controller; Credit Manager; Customer Service Representative; Data Entry Clerk; Human Resources Manager; Marketing Specialist; Receptionist; Secretary; Typist/Word Processor; Webmaster. **Benefits available to temporary workers:** Medical Insurance; Paid Holidays; Paid Vacation; Profit Sharing. **Average salary range of placements:** $20,000 - $29,999.

BURNETT'S STAFFING, INC.
1200 Walnut Hill Lane, Suite 1000, Irving TX 75038. 972/580-3333. **Fax:** 972/580-7711. **Contact:** Manager. **Description:** A permanent, temp-to-hire, and temporary employment agency. **Specializes in the areas of:** Administration; Clerical; Secretarial.

CONTINENTAL PERSONNEL SERVICE
6671 Southwest Freeway, Suite 101, Houston TX 77074. 713/771-7181. **Fax:** 713/771-4444. **Contact:** Richard Quinn, Owner. **Description:** A permanent employment agency. **Specializes in the areas of:** Engineering; Health/Medical; Manufacturing; Quantitative Marketing. **Positions commonly filled include:** Chemical Engineer; Civil Engineer; Dentist; Electrical/Electronics Engineer; Environmental Engineer; Factory Worker; Industrial Engineer; Manufacturing Engineer; Mechanical Engineer; Medical Records Technician; Nuclear Engineer; Nurse; Packaging Engineer; Physician; Plant Manager; Quality Control Supervisor; Safety Specialist; Supervisor; Technician; Water/Wastewater Engineer.

CONTINENTAL PERSONNEL SERVICE
8700 North Stemmons Freeway, Suite 109, Dallas TX 75247-3715. 214/630-8912. **Contact:** Charles K. Cash, Owner. **Description:** A full-service employment agency. **Specializes in the areas of:** Accounting/Auditing; Administration; Banking; Computer Science/Software; Engineering; Finance; General Management; Insurance; Personnel/Labor Relations; Sales; Secretarial. **Positions commonly filled include:** Accountant/Auditor; Administrative Manager; Aerospace Engineer; Agricultural Engineer; Bank Officer/Manager; Blue-Collar Worker Supervisor; Branch Manager; Brokerage Clerk; Ceramics Engineer; Chemical Engineer; Claim Rep.; Clerical Supervisor; Computer Programmer; Construction Contractor; Credit Manager; Customer Service Rep.; Design Engineer; Draftsperson; Electrical/Electronics Engineer; Financial Analyst; General Manager; Health Services Manager; Hotel Manager; Human Resources Specialist; Insurance Agent/Broker; Management Trainee; Manufacturer's/Wholesaler's Sales Rep.; Materials Engineer; Mechanical Engineer; Medical Records Technician; Metallurgical Engineer; Mining Engineer; MIS Specialist; Nuclear Engineer; Operations/Production Manager; Paralegal; Petroleum Engineer; Property and Real Estate Manager; Purchasing Agent/Manager; Quality Control Supervisor; Restaurant/Food Service Manager; Securities Sales Rep.; Services Sales Rep.; Software Engineer; Structural Engineer; Systems Analyst; Technical Writer/Editor; Telecommunications Manager; Transportation/Traffic Specialist; Typist/Word Processor; Underwriter/Assistant Underwriter. **Average salary range of placements:** $20,000 - $29,999. **Number of placements per year:** 200 - 499.

DH&A (DONICE HALL & ASSOCIATES)
1519 West Clay, Houston TX 77019. 713/942-7744. **Contact:** Manager. **Description:** A permanent employment agency. **Specializes in the areas of:** Accounting/Auditing; Banking.

DALLAS EMPLOYMENT SERVICE, INC.
750 North St. Paul Street, Suite 1180, Dallas TX 75201. 214/954-0700. **Toll-free phone:** 800/954-

1666. **Fax:** 214/754-0148. **Contact:** Christina Orlando, System Administrator. **World Wide Web address:** http://www.des-inc.com/des. **Description:** A permanent employment agency. Company pays fee. **Specializes in the areas of:** Accounting/Auditing; Administration; Fashion; Finance; Industrial; Legal; Manufacturing; Personnel/Labor Relations; Sales; Secretarial. **Positions commonly filled include:** Administrative Manager; Advertising Clerk; Branch Manager; Brokerage Clerk; Clerical Supervisor; Credit Manager; Customer Service Representative; General Manager; Internet Services Manager; Management Trainee; Paralegal; Services Sales Representative; Travel Agent; Typist/Word Processor. **Number of placements per year:** 200 - 499.

DATAPRO PERSONNEL CONSULTANTS
13355 Noel Road, Suite 2001, Dallas TX 75240. 972/661-8600. **Fax:** 972/661-1309. **Contact:** Jack Kallison, Owner. **Description:** A permanent employment agency. Company pays fee. **Specializes in the areas of:** Computer Programming; Computer Science/Software. **Positions commonly filled include:** Computer Programmer; EDP Specialist; Project Manager; Software Engineer; Systems Analyst; Technical Writer/Editor.

DAY STAR SERVICES
6750 West Loop South, Suite 140, Bellaire TX 77401. 713/664-1000. **Contact:** Manager. **Description:** A permanent and temporary employment agency. **Specializes in the areas of:** Administration; Clerical; Office Support.

DENTAL RESOURCE MANAGEMENT
P.O. Box 17513, Austin TX 78760. 512/462-2959. **Fax:** 512/462-0104. **Contact:** Kathy Waid, Owner. **Description:** A permanent employment agency. Founded in 1986. Company pays fee. **Specializes in the areas of:** Dental. **Positions commonly filled include:** Dental Assistant/Dental Hygienist. **Average salary range of placements:** $20,000 - $29,999.

DR. PERSONNEL OF SAN ANTONIO
8535 Wurzbach Road, Suite 101, San Antonio TX 78229. 210/699-0325. **Fax:** 210/614-2071. **Contact:** Manager. **Description:** A permanent employment agency focusing on placement of medical and dental support staff. Founded in 1980. Company pays fee. **Specializes in the areas of:** Health/Medical. **Positions commonly filled include:** Clinical Lab Technician; Dental Assistant/Dental Hygienist; EEG Technologist; EKG Technician; Health Services Manager; Medical Records Technician; Physical Therapist; Registered Nurse. **Average salary range of placements:** $20,000 - $29,999. **Number of placements per year:** 50 - 99.

DONOVAN & WATKINS
1360 Post Oak Boulevard, Suite 100, Houston TX 77056. 713/968-1700. **Contact:** Manager. **Description:** A permanent employment agency that also provides temporary placements. **Specializes in the areas of:** Accounting/Auditing; Administration; Legal.

DUNHILL OF ARLINGTON
1301 South Bowen Road, Suite 370, Arlington TX 76013. 817/265-2291. **Fax:** 817/265-2294. **Contact:** Jon Molkentine, Director. **Description:** A permanent employment agency. **Specializes in the areas of:** Accounting/Auditing; Health/Medical. **Positions commonly filled include:** Accountant/Auditor; Human Resources Manager; Physical Therapist. **Number of placements per year:** 50 - 99.

E&A PERSONNEL SERVICES
1616 San Pedro Avenue, San Antonio TX 78212-3613. 210/733-7575. **Fax:** 210/734-8941. **Contact:** Manager. **E-mail address:** ea-impex@+xdirect.net. **World Wide Web address:** http://www.resumes-us.com. **Description:** A permanent employment agency focusing on professional placements for ex-military personnel. Founded in 1992. Company pays fee. **Specializes in the areas of:** Administration; Computer Science/Software; Personnel/Labor Relations. **Positions commonly filled include:** Administrative Manager; Bank Officer/Manager; Branch Manager; Computer Programmer; Design Engineer; Electrician; General Manager; Hotel Manager; Human Resources Manager; Industrial Production Manager; Management Analyst/Consultant; MIS Specialist; Operations/Production Manager; Restaurant/Food Service Manager; Statistician; Systems Analyst; Technical Writer/Editor; Underwriter/Assistant Underwriter. **Average salary range of placements:** $30,000 - $50,000. **Number of placements per year:** 100 - 199.

EVINS PERSONNEL CONSULTANTS
3115 Southwest Boulevard, San Angelo TX 76904-5772. 915/944-2571. **Fax:** 915/942-1878. **Contact:** Gayle Marecek, Owner/Manager. **E-mail address:** evinsper@wcc.net. **Description:** A permanent employment agency. **Positions commonly filled include:** Accountant/Auditor; Administrative Manager; Bank Officer/Manager; Branch Manager; Clerical Supervisor; Computer Programmer; Cost Estimator; Credit Manager; Customer Service Rep.; Dental Assistant/Dental Hygienist; Draftsperson; Electrical/Electronics Engineer; General Manager; Human Resources Manager; Licensed Practical Nurse; Medical Records Technician; Paralegal; Property/Real Estate Manager; Public Relations Specialist; Purchasing Agent/Manager; Quality Control Supervisor; Radio/TV Announcer/Broadcaster; Registered Nurse; Systems Analyst; Typist/Word Processor; Underwriter/Assistant Underwriter. **Average salary range of placements:** $20,000 - $29,999.

EVINS PERSONNEL CONSULTANTS
2013 West Anderson Lane, Austin TX 78757. 512/454-9561. **Fax:** 512/483-9191. **Contact:** Manager. **Description:** A permanent employment agency. Company pays fee. **Positions commonly filled include:** Accountant/Auditor; Computer Programmer; Customer Service Rep.; Human Resources Manager; Registered Nurse; Typist/Word Processor. **Average salary range of placements:** $20,000 - $29,999. **Number of placements per year:** 500 - 999.

EVINS PERSONNEL CONSULTANTS OF KILLEEN, INC.
206 West Avenue B, Killeen TX 76541. 254/526-4161. **Fax:** 254/634-6913. **Contact:** Michelle G. Sweeney, Owner. **Description:** A permanent employment agency. **Specializes in the areas of:** Accounting/Auditing; Advertising; Banking; Finance; Food Industry; General Management; Health/Medical; Insurance; Legal; Publishing; Retail; Sales; Technical; Transportation. **Positions commonly filled include:** Accountant/Auditor; Automotive Mechanic; Branch Manager; Clerical Supervisor; Computer Programmer; Credit Manager; Dental Assistant/Dental Hygienist; General Manager; Management Trainee; Medical Records Technician; Occupational Therapist; Physical Therapist; Registered Nurse; Restaurant/Food Service Manager; Social Worker; Surveyor; Travel Agent. **Number of placements per year:** 1 - 49.

EVINS PERSONNEL CONSULTANTS
209 South Leggett, Abilene TX 79605. 915/677-9153. **Contact:** Manager. **Description:** A permanent employment agency that also provides some temporary placements.

EXPRESS PERSONNEL SERVICES
P.O. Box 8136, Waco TX 76714-8136. 254/776-3300. **Contact:** J.G. Scofield, Owner. **Description:** A

permanent and temporary employment agency. Company pays fee. **Specializes in the areas of:** Accounting/Auditing; Administration; Architecture/Construction; Banking; Clerical; Computer Hardware/Software; Engineering; Finance; Food Industry; Health/Medical; Insurance; Legal; Manufacturing; Physician Executive; Sales; Secretarial.

EXPRESS PERSONNEL SERVICES
3701 South Cooper Street, Suite 250, Arlington TX 76015. 817/468-9118. **Fax:** 817/468-9211. **Contact:** Gary Gibson, Owner/Manager. **Description:** A permanent and temporary employment agency operating on a contingency basis. Company pays fee. **Specializes in the areas of:** Accounting/Auditing; Banking; Computer Science/Software; Finance; General Management; Health/Medical; Industrial; Insurance; Personnel/Labor Relations; Publishing; Sales; Secretarial. **Positions commonly filled include:** Accountant/Auditor; Administrative Manager; Advertising Clerk; Bank Officer/Manager; Blue-Collar Worker Supervisor; Branch Manager; Clerical Supervisor; Cost Estimator; Customer Service Representative; General Manager; Human Resources Specialist; Industrial Production Manager; Management Trainee; Paralegal; Public Relations Specialist; Quality Control Supervisor; Technical Writer/Editor; Typist/Word Processor. **Benefits available to temporary workers:** Medical Insurance; Paid Holidays; Paid Vacation. **Other U.S. locations:** Nationwide. **Average salary range of placements:** $30,000 - $50,000. **Number of placements per year:** 1 - 49.

FELDT PERSONNEL
7211 Regency Square Boulevard, Suite 201, Houston TX 77036. 713/781-6562. **Fax:** 713/781-9868. **Contact:** Marcia Feldt, President. **Description:** Feldt Personnel is a permanent employment agency. **Specializes in the areas of:** Accounting/Auditing; Finance.

FINANCIAL PROFESSIONALS
4100 Spring Valley Road, Suite 307, Dallas TX 75244. 972/991-8999. **Toll-free phone:** 800/856-5599. **Fax:** 972/702-0776. **Contact:** Kathleen Knight, Vice President of Operations. **E-mail address:** ffsw039@prodigy.com. **Description:** A permanent employment agency that also provides temporary placements. Company pays fee. **Specializes in the areas of:** Banking; Finance. **Positions commonly filled include:** Accountant; Administrative Assistant; Auditor; Bank Officer/Manager; Branch Manager; Chief Financial Officer; Controller; Credit Manager; Customer Service Representative; Finance Director; Financial Analyst; Human Resources Manager; Operations Manager. **Benefits available to temporary workers:** Medical Insurance; Paid Holidays; Paid Vacation. **Corporate headquarters location:** This Location. **Other area locations:** Fort Worth TX; Houston TX. **Average salary range of placements:** $20,000 - $29,999. **Number of placements per year:** 1 - 49.

GIBSON ARNOLD & ASSOCIATES
550 Westscott, Suite 560, Houston TX 77007. 713/869-3600. **Contact:** Manager. **Description:** A permanent employment agency. **Specializes in the areas of:** Legal.

GULCO INTERNATIONAL RECRUITING SERVICES
15710 JFK Boulevard, Suite 110, Houston TX 77032. 281/590-9001. **Fax:** 281/590-1503. **Contact:** Rodney Gullo, President. **E-mail address:** gulcointl@worldnet.att.net. **Description:** A permanent employment agency. Company pays fee. **Specializes in the areas of:** Engineering; Finance; Health/Medical; Manufacturing; Personnel/Labor Relations. **Positions commonly filled include:** Accountant/Auditor; Buyer; Chemical Engineer; Civil Engineer; Computer Programmer; Cost Estimator; Designer; Electrical/Electronics Engineer; Financial Analyst; Geologist/Geophysicist; Health Services Manager; Human Resources Manager; Licensed Practical Nurse; Materials Engineer; Mechanical Engineer; Mergers/Acquisitions Specialist; Mining Engineer; Nuclear Engineer; Occupational Therapist; Operations/Production Manager; Petroleum Engineer; Physical Therapist; Physician; Purchasing Agent/Manager; Quality Control Supervisor; Registered Nurse; Respiratory Therapist; Science Technologist; Software Engineer; Stationary Engineer; Structural Engineer; Surgical Technician; Systems Analyst; Technical Writer/Editor. **Average salary range of placements:** More than $50,000. **Number of placements per year:** 50 - 99.

ROBERT HALF INTERNATIONAL
1300 Post Oak Boulevard, Suite 350, Houston TX 77056. 713/623-4700. **Recorded jobline:** 713/993-2504. **Fax:** 713/623-6782. **Contact:** Manager. **E-mail address:** rhishou@aol.com. **Description:** An executive search firm. Company pays fee. **Specializes in the areas of:** Accounting/Auditing; Administration; Banking; Computer Science/Software; Finance; Secretarial. **Positions commonly filled include:** Accountant/Auditor; Bank Officer/Manager; Budget Analyst; Clerical Supervisor; Computer Programmer; Credit Manager; Customer Service Rep.; Financial Analyst; Internet Services Manager; Management Analyst/Consultant; Market Research Analyst; MIS Specialist; Systems Analyst; Typist/Word Processor. **Benefits available to temporary workers:** Holiday Bonus; Medical Insurance; Paid Vacation; Vision Plan. **Corporate headquarters location:** Menlo Park CA. **Other U.S. locations:** Nationwide. **Average salary range of placements:** $30,000 - $50,000. **Number of placements per year:** 500 - 999.

HEALTHCARE STAFF RESOURCES, INC.
1445 MacArthur Drive, Suite 100, Carrollton TX 75007. 972/323-3388. **Toll-free phone:** 800/284-0429. **Fax:** 972/446-1920. **Contact:** Barb Greene, Human Resources Manager. **Description:** A permanent employment agency that also provides temporary placements. Company pays fee. **Specializes in the areas of:** Health/Medical. **Positions commonly filled include:** Occupational Therapist; Physical Therapist. **Benefits available to temporary workers:** 401(k); Dental Insurance; Life Insurance; Medical Insurance; Vision Plan. **Corporate headquarters location:** Albuquerque NM. **Average salary range of placements:** More than $50,000. **Number of placements per year:** 100 - 199.

INFO TEC INC.
14275 Midway Road, Suite 140, Dallas TX 75244-3620. 972/661-8400. **Fax:** 972/490-5964. **Contact:** Kim Pinney, Vice President. **E-mail address:** infotec95@aol.com. **Description:** A permanent employment agency and consulting company offering permanent, contract, and contract-to-hire placements in both hardware and software positions. Company pays fee. **Specializes in the areas of:** Computer Science/Software. **Positions commonly filled include:** Computer Programmer; Management Analyst/Consultant; MIS Specialist; Systems Analyst; Technical Writer/Editor. **Benefits available to temporary workers:** Dental Insurance; Medical Insurance. **Average salary range of placements:** $30,000 - $50,000. **Number of placements per year:** 50 - 99.

JOB MARKET PERSONNEL AGENCY
2806 34th Street, Lubbock TX 79410. 806/797-8383. **Contact:** Ginger Hale, Owner. **Description:** A

permanent employment agency. **Specializes in the areas of:** Retail; Sales; Secretarial; Technical; Transportation. **Positions commonly filled include:** Accountant/Auditor; Adjuster; Administrative Manager; Advertising Clerk; Agricultural Engineer; Automotive Mechanic; Bank Officer/Manager; Civil Engineer; Computer Programmer; Customer Service Representative; Design Engineer; EKG Technician; Environmental Engineer; Financial Analyst; General Manager; Industrial Production Manager; Management Analyst/Consultant; Mechanical Engineer; MIS Specialist; Property and Real Estate Manager; Quality Control Supervisor; Registered Nurse; Services Sales Representative; Software Engineer; Telecommunications Manager; Transportation/Traffic Specialist; Typist/Word Processor. **Number of placements per year:** 1 - 49.

JOB SERVICES, INC.
6404 Callaghan Road, San Antonio TX 78229. 210/344-3444. **Contact:** Ike Kelly, President. **Description:** A permanent employment agency. Company pays fee. **Specializes in the areas of:** Industrial; Manufacturing. **Positions commonly filled include:** Accountant/Auditor; Adjuster; Administrative Manager; Advertising Clerk; Automotive Mechanic; Bank Officer/Manager; Blue-Collar Worker Supervisor; Branch Manager; Buyer; Claim Representative; Clerical Supervisor; Clinical Lab Technician; Collector; Computer Programmer; Construction Contractor; Cost Estimator; Customer Service Representative; Dental Assistant/Dental Hygienist; Dental Lab Technician; Draftsperson; Electrician; Emergency Medical Technician; General Manager; Hotel Manager; Industrial Engineer; Investigator; Licensed Practical Nurse; Management Trainee; Manufacturer's/Wholesaler's Sales Rep.; Mechanical Engineer; Medical Records Technician; Paralegal; Physical Therapist; Preschool Worker; Property and Real Estate Manager; Public Relations Specialist; Purchasing Agent/Manager; Quality Control Supervisor; Real Estate Agent; Respiratory Therapist; Restaurant/Food Service Manager; Securities Sales Representative; Services Sales Representative; Systems Analyst; Travel Agent; Wholesale and Retail Buyer. **Number of placements per year:** 100 - 199.

JOBS, ETC., INC.
3201 Old Houston Road, Huntsville TX 77340. 409/295-5627. **Contact:** Paula Ohendalski, Owner. **Description:** A permanent employment agency. **Positions commonly filled include:** Accountant/Auditor; Administrative Manager; Advertising Clerk; Bank Officer/Manager; Blue-Collar Worker Supervisor; Branch Manager; Budget Analyst; Buyer; Claim Representative; Clerical Supervisor; Computer Programmer; Construction Contractor; Customer Service Representative; Dental Assistant/Dental Hygienist; Design Engineer; Draftsperson; Editor; Electrician; Emergency Medical Technician; General Manager; Health Services Manager; Hotel Manager; Human Resources Specialist; Human Service Worker; Industrial Production Manager; Landscape Architect; Licensed Practical Nurse; Occupational Therapist; Paralegal; Public Relations Specialist; Purchasing Agent/Manager; Quality Control Supervisor; Radio/TV Announcer/Broadcaster; Real Estate Agent; Registered Nurse; Respiratory Therapist; Restaurant/Food Service Manager; Software Engineer; Systems Analyst; Typist/Word Processor; Video Production Coordinator. **Average salary range of placements:** Less than $20,000. **Number of placements per year:** 500 - 999.

KEY PEOPLE, INC.
520 Post Oak Boulevard, Suite 830, Houston TX 77027. 713/877-1427. **Fax:** 713/877-1826. **Contact:** Betty Thompson, President. **Description:** A permanent employment agency. Founded in 1981. Company pays fee. **Specializes in the areas of:** Accounting/Auditing; Computer Science/Software; Secretarial. **Positions commonly filled include:** Accountant/Auditor; Administrative Assistant; Bookkeeper; Clerk; Computer Programmer; EDP Specialist; Systems Analyst. **Benefits available to temporary workers:** Paid Holidays; Paid Vacation. **Average salary range of placements:** $30,000 - $50,000. **Number of placements per year:** 1 - 49.

KINDRICK & LUTHER
2200 Post Oak Boulevard, Suite 360, Houston TX 77056. 713/629-5559. **Contact:** Manager. **Description:** A permanent employment agency that also provides temporary placements. **Specializes in the areas of:** Accounting/Auditing.

LDS EMPLOYMENT CENTER
16333 Hafer Road, Houston TX 77090. 281/580-2564. **Contact:** Manager. **Description:** A permanent employment agency that also provides some temporary placements. LDS places people in a wide range of industries.

LRJ STAFFING SERVICES
301 West Central Drive, Suite 200, Temple TX 76501. 254/742-1981. **Toll-free phone:** 800/581-1850. **Fax:** 254/774-9675. **Contact:** David Kyle, Branch Manager. **Description:** A full-service, minority-owned employment agency. Company pays fee. **Specializes in the areas of:** Computer Science/Software; Engineering; Industrial; Light Industrial; Manufacturing; Personnel/Labor Relations; Publishing; Technical. **Positions commonly filled include:** Blue-Collar Worker Supervisor; Computer Programmer; Customer Service Representative; Industrial Engineer; Industrial Production Manager; Services Sales Representative; Systems Analyst; Typist/Word Processor. **Benefits available to temporary workers:** Paid Holidays; Sick Days. **Corporate headquarters location:** Austin TX. **Other area locations:** Dallas TX; San Antonio TX. **Average salary range of placements:** $20,000 - $29,999. **Number of placements per year:** 50 - 99.

LEGEND MARINE, INC.
9894 Bissonnet Street, Suite 860, Houston TX 77036-8246. 713/776-1000. **Fax:** 713/776-1058. **Contact:** Dean Clark, Recruiter. **Description:** A permanent employment agency that focuses on the offshore placement of marine personnel. **Specializes in the areas of:** Maritime. **Average salary range of placements:** $20,000 - $29,999. **Number of placements per year:** 100 - 199.

THE LUKENS GROUP
5300 Memorial Drive, Suite 270, Houston TX 77007. 713/864-5588. **Contact:** Manager. **Description:** A permanent employment agency that also provides temporary and executive placements. **Specializes in the areas of:** Accounting/Auditing; Finance.

MARQUESS & ASSOCIATES
15441 Knoll Trail Drive, Suite 280, Dallas TX 75248. 972/490-5288. **Fax:** 972/490-5004. **Contact:** Terri Marquess, Owner. **Description:** A permanent employment agency. Company pays fee. **Specializes in the areas of:** Retail; Sales; Secretarial; Technical. **Positions commonly filled include:** Accountant/Auditor; Administrative Manager; Advertising Clerk; Buyer; Clerical Supervisor; Computer Programmer; Credit Manager; Customer Service Representative; Electrical/Electronics Engineer; Financial Analyst; General Manager; Human Service Worker; Industrial Engineer; Management Trainee; Mechanical Engineer; MIS Specialist; Services Sales Representative; Software Engineer; Systems Analyst; Technical Writer/Editor; Telecommunications Manager.

Average salary range of placements: $20,000 - $29,999. **Number of placements per year:** 50 - 99.

MEDTEX STAFFING
2100 Highway 360, Suite 404, Grand Prairie TX 75050. 972/647-2047. **Fax:** 972/660-6870. **Contact:** Office Manager. **Description:** A permanent employment agency. **Specializes in the areas of:** Health/Medical. **Positions commonly filled include:** Nurse.

MORNINGSIDE NANNIES
2370 Rice Boulevard, Suite 111, Houston TX 77005. 713/526-3989. **Contact:** Patricia Cascio, Owner. **Description:** A permanent employment agency providing live-in, live-out, and part-time child care positions in the Houston area. **NOTE:** Applicants must have training in child development or references relating to child care work experience. **Specializes in the areas of:** Child Care, In-Home. **Positions commonly filled include:** Nanny. **Number of placements per year:** 100 - 199.

OFICINA DE EMPLEOS, INC.
5415 Maple Avenue, Suite 112A, Dallas TX 75235-7429. 214/634-0500. **Fax:** 214/634-1001. **Contact:** Robert Wingfield, Jr., Owner. **Description:** A permanent employment agency that places documented workers, primarily from Mexico, with companies that need laborers in construction and landscaping. Company pays fee. **Specializes in the areas of:** General Labor. **Number of placements per year:** 500 - 999.

O'KEEFE & ASSOCIATES
3420 Executive Center Drive, Suite 114, Austin TX 78731. 512/343-1134. **Fax:** 512/343-0142. **Contact:** Recruiter. **Description:** A permanent employment agency. Company pays fee. **Specializes in the areas of:** Administration; Computer Hardware/Software; Engineering. **Positions commonly filled include:** Computer Programmer; Electrical/Electronics Engineer; Software Engineer; Systems Analyst. **Number of placements per year:** 50 - 99.

OMNI CONSORTIUM, INC.
1035 Dairy-Ashforth Road, Suite 350, Houston TX 77079. 281/589-6550. **Contact:** Alvin Tolentino, Vice President. **Description:** A permanent employment agency. **Specializes in the areas of:** Education; Health/Medical. **Positions commonly filled include:** Physical Therapist; Teacher/Professor. **Number of placements per year:** 100 - 199.

P&P PERSONNEL SERVICE
604 North Gray, Killeen TX 76541-4847. 254/526-9962. **Contact:** Gordon Plumlee, Owner. **Description:** A permanent employment agency. **Specializes in the areas of:** Accounting/Auditing; Banking; Computer Science/Software; Finance; General Management; Insurance; Legal; Secretarial. **Positions commonly filled include:** Accountant/Auditor; Claim Representative; Clerical Supervisor; Dental Assistant/Hygienist; Insurance Agent/Broker; Licensed Practical Nurse; Management Trainee; Medical Records Technician; Paralegal; Registered Nurse; Social Worker. **Number of placements per year:** 50 - 99.

PARKER WORTHINGTON
The Madison Building, 15851 Dallas Parkway, Suite 500, Dallas TX 75248. 972/980-1744. **Contact:** Susan W. Parker, President. **Description:** A permanent employment agency.

PERRY PERSONNEL SERVICES INC.
16000 Stuebner Airline Road, Spring TX 77379. 281/251-6369. **Contact:** Manager. **Description:** A permanent employment agency.

THE PERSONNEL CONNECTION
16479 North Dallas Parkway, Suite 110, Dallas TX 75248. 972/713-9900. **Contact:** Placement Officer. **Description:** A permanent employment agency. **Specializes in the areas of:** Administration; Office Support. **Positions commonly filled include:** Clerk; Receptionist; Secretary; Typist/Word Processor.

PERSONNEL CONSULTANTS INC. (PCI)
4620 Fairmont Parkway, Suite 106, Pasadena TX 77504. 281/998-8060. **Fax:** 281/998-7794. **Contact:** Judy Hausler, President. **Description:** A permanent employment agency. Company pays fee. **Positions commonly filled include:** Accountant/Auditor; Blue-Collar Worker Supervisor; Buyer; Chemist; Claim Representative; Clerical Supervisor; Clinical Lab Technician; Computer Programmer; Construction and Building Inspector; Construction Contractor; Cost Estimator; Credit Manager; Customer Service Representative; Draftsperson; EEG Technologist; EKG Technician; Emergency Medical Technician; Engineer; Financial Analyst; General Manager; Geologist/Geophysicist; Health Services Manager; Human Service Worker; Industrial Production Manager; Insurance Agent/Broker; Licensed Practical Nurse; Manufacturer's/Wholesaler's Sales Rep.; Medical Records Technician; Paralegal; Physical Therapist; Physician; Property and Real Estate Manager; Purchasing Agent/Manager; Registered Nurse; Respiratory Therapist; Services Sales Representative; Surgical Technician; Systems Analyst; Technical Writer/Editor; Wholesale and Retail Buyer. **Number of placements per year:** 50 - 99.

PERSONNEL ONE, INC.
5400 LBJ Freeway, Suite 120, Dallas TX 75240. 972/982-8500. **Recorded jobline:** 214/982-8510. **Fax:** 972/982-8505. **Contact:** Christine McNunn, Branch Manager. **Description:** A permanent employment agency that also provides temporary placements. Company pays fee. **Specializes in the areas of:** Accounting/Auditing; Administration; Computer Science/Software; Engineering; General Management; Personnel/Labor Relations; Secretarial. **Positions commonly filled include:** Administrative Manager; Claim Representative; Clerical Supervisor; Counselor; Credit Manager; Customer Service Representative; Electrical/Electronics Engineer; Financial Analyst. **Benefits available to temporary workers:** Paid Holidays; Paid Vacation. **Corporate headquarters location:** Coral Gables FL. **Other U.S. locations:** FL; NJ. **Average salary range of placements:** $20,000 - $29,999. **Number of placements per year:** 1 - 49.

PLACEMENTS UNLIMITED
932 North Valley Mills Drive, Waco TX 76710. 254/741-0526. **Fax:** 254/741-0529. **Contact:** Ginger Sharp, President. **Description:** A permanent employment agency. Company pays fee. **Specializes in the areas of:** Banking; Industrial; Manufacturing; Secretarial. **Positions commonly filled include:** Accountant/Auditor; Aircraft Mechanic/Engine Specialist; Automotive Mechanic; Blue-Collar Worker Supervisor; Buyer; Clerical Supervisor; Customer Service Representative; MIS Specialist; Purchasing Agent/Manager; Technical Writer/Editor; Typist/Word Processor. **Average salary range of placements:** Less than $20,000. **Number of placements per year:** 100 - 199.

PROFESSIONAL CONCEPTS PERSONNEL
4692 East University Boulevard, Suite 101, Odessa TX 79762. 915/362-9214. **Contact:** Ms. Ruby Bruns, Owner. **Description:** A permanent employment agency. **Positions commonly filled include:** Blue-Collar Worker Supervisor; Branch Manager; Broadcast Technician; Claim Representative; Clerical Supervisor; Clinical Lab Technician; Computer Programmer;

Construction and Building Inspector; Cost Estimator; Counselor; Credit Manager; Customer Service Representative; Dental Assistant/Dental Hygienist; Dental Lab Technician; Designer; Draftsperson; EEG Technologist; EKG Technician; Electrician; Emergency Medical Technician; General Manager; Health Services Manager; Human Resources Manager; Licensed Practical Nurse; Management Analyst/Consultant; Management Trainee; Manufacturer's/Wholesaler's Sales Rep.; Medical Records Technician; Occupational Therapist; Paralegal; Physical Therapist; Property and Real Estate Manager; Purchasing Agent/Manager; Recreational Therapist; Respiratory Therapist; Services Sales Representative; Social Worker; Surveyor; Systems Analyst; Travel Agent. **Number of placements per year:** 50 - 99.

PROFESSIONS TODAY
2811 South Loop 289, Suite 20, Lubbock TX 79423. 806/745-8595. **Fax:** 806/748-0571. **Contact:** Gebrell Ward, Owner. **Description:** A permanent employment agency. Company pays fee. **Specializes in the areas of:** Accounting/Auditing; Administration; Computer Hardware/Software; Engineering; General Management; Health/Medical; Industrial; Sales; Secretarial. **Positions commonly filled include:** Accountant/Auditor; Administrative Assistant; Bookkeeper; Clerk; Computer Programmer; Customer Service Representative; Data Entry Clerk; Legal Secretary; Marketing Specialist; Medical Secretary; Receptionist; Sales Representative; Secretary; Typist/Word Processor. **Number of placements per year:** 100 - 199.

QUEST PERSONNEL RESOURCES, INC.
50 Briar Hollow Lane, Suite 510 East, Houston TX 77027-9306. 713/961-0605. **Toll-free phone:** 800/846-6081. **Fax:** 713/961-1857. **Contact:** Cristina M. Tolpo, Branch Manager. **Description:** A permanent employment agency that also provides temporary placements. Company pays fee. **Specializes in the areas of:** Legal; Secretarial. **Positions commonly filled include:** Accountant/Auditor; Accounting Clerk; Administrative Assistant; Clerical Supervisor; Customer Service Representative; Data Entry Clerk; Human Resources Manager; Paralegal; Receptionist; Typist/Word Processor. **Benefits available to temporary workers:** Paid Vacation. **Other area locations:** Dallas TX. **Average salary range of placements:** $30,000 - $50,000. **Number of placements per year:** 100 - 199.

REMEDY INTELLIGENT STAFFING
8310 North Capital of Texas Highway, Suite 195, Austin TX 78731. 512/502-9000. **Fax:** 512/502-9305. **Contact:** Joe Kilpatrick, Owner. **Description:** A permanent employment agency. Company pays fee. **Specializes in the areas of:** Accounting/Auditing; Administration; Advertising; Computer Science/Software; Engineering; Industrial; Personnel/Labor Relations; Publishing; Retail; Sales; Secretarial; Technical. **Positions commonly filled include:** Accountant/Auditor; Administrative Manager; Advertising Clerk; Bank Officer/Manager; Branch Manager; Brokerage Clerk; Budget Analyst; Claim Representative; Clerical Supervisor; Computer Programmer; Cost Estimator; Credit Manager; Customer Service Representative; Design Engineer; Draftsperson; Electrical/Electronics Engineer; Environmental Engineer; Financial Analyst; General Manager; Human Resources Specialist; Insurance Agent/Broker; Management Analyst/Consultant; Market Research Analyst; MIS Specialist; Multimedia Designer; Paralegal; Property and Real Estate Manager; Purchasing Agent/Manager; Quality Control Supervisor; Real Estate Agent; Services Sales Representative; Software Engineer; Systems Analyst; Technical Writer/Editor; Telecommunications Manager; Travel Agent. **Benefits available to temporary workers:** 401(k); Dental Insurance; Medical Insurance; Paid Holidays; Paid Vacation. **Corporate headquarters location:** Mission Viejo CA. **Other U.S. locations:** Nationwide. **Average salary range of placements:** $30,000 - $50,000. **Number of placements per year:** 1000+.

REMEDY INTELLIGENT STAFFING
4225 Wingren Drive, Suite 115, Irving TX 75062. 972/650-2005. **Fax:** 972/650-1521. **Contact:** Manager. **Description:** A permanent employment agency. Company pays fee. **Specializes in the areas of:** Secretarial. **Positions commonly filled include:** Accountant/Auditor; Clerical Supervisor; Customer Service Representative; Management Trainee. **Benefits available to temporary workers:** Medical Insurance; Paid Holidays. **Corporate headquarters location:** Mission Viejo CA. **Other U.S. locations:** Nationwide. **Average salary range of placements:** $20,000 - $29,999. **Number of placements per year:** 100 - 199.

RESOURCE RECRUITERS INC.
4100 Spring Valley Road, Suite 800, Dallas TX 75244. 972/851-5408. **Contact:** Ms. Terez Scribner, President. **Description:** A permanent employment agency. Company pays fee. **Specializes in the areas of:** Accounting/Auditing; Finance; Food Industry; Insurance; Legal; Manufacturing; Personnel/Labor Relations; Sales; Secretarial. **Positions commonly filled include:** Accountant/Auditor; Advertising Clerk; Clerical Supervisor; Collector; Credit Manager; Customer Service Representative; Human Resources Manager; Management Trainee; Manufacturer's/Wholesaler's Sales Rep.; Restaurant/Food Service Manager; Services Sales Representative; Typist/Word Processor; Underwriter/Assistant Underwriter. **Number of placements per year:** 50 - 99.

R.A. RODRIGUEZ & ASSOCIATES
10935 Ben Crenshaw, Suite 210, El Paso TX 79935. 915/598-5028. **Contact:** Manager. **Description:** A permanent employment agency. **Specializes in the areas of:** Manufacturing.

SAY AHHH MEDICAL OFFICE SERVICES
2203 Eighth Avenue, Fort Worth TX 76110. 817/927-2924. **Contact:** Manager. **Description:** A permanent employment agency that also offers temporary placements. **Specializes in the areas of:** Health/Medical.

SEEGERS ESTES & ASSOCIATES, INC.
14405 Walters Road, Suite 350, Houston TX 77014-1320. 281/587-8765. **Fax:** 281/587-8778. **Contact:** Recruiter. **Description:** A permanent employment agency focusing on engineering and technical placement in the chemical process refining industry. Company pays fee. **Specializes in the areas of:** Engineering. **Positions commonly filled include:** Chemical Engineer; Electrical/Electronics Engineer; Mechanical Engineer. **Average salary range of placements:** More than $50,000. **Number of placements per year:** 1 - 49.

SNELLING PERSONNEL SERVICES
1169 East 42nd Street, Odessa TX 79762. 915/367-7066. **Fax:** 915/550-7066. **Contact:** Jane Williams, Owner. **Description:** A permanent employment agency. Company pays fee. **Specializes in the areas of:** Accounting/Auditing; Engineering; General Management; Industrial; Sales; Secretarial; Technical. **Positions commonly filled include:** Accountant/Auditor; Blue-Collar Worker Supervisor; Customer Service Representative; Services Sales Representative; Typist/Word Processor. **Other U.S. locations:** Nationwide. **Average salary range of

placements: $30,000 - $50,000. **Number of placements per year:** 50 - 99.

SNELLING PERSONNEL SERVICES
1925 East Beltline, Suite 403, Carrollton TX 75006. 972/242-8575. **Fax:** 972/242-7186. **Contact:** Manager. **Description:** A permanent employment agency. Company pays fee. **Specializes in the areas of:** Accounting/Auditing; Administration; General Management; Industrial; Legal; Personnel/Labor Relations; Sales; Secretarial. **Positions commonly filled include:** Accountant/Auditor; Administrative Assistant; Bookkeeper; Claim Representative; Clerk; Credit Manager; Customer Service Representative; Data Entry Clerk; Executive Assistant; Factory Worker; Legal Secretary; Light Industrial Worker; Marketing Specialist; Medical Secretary; Receptionist; Sales Representative; Secretary; Typist/Word Processor. **Other U.S. locations:** Nationwide. **Number of placements per year:** 50 - 99.

SNELLING PERSONNEL SERVICES OF LONGVIEW
1800 Northwest Loop 281, Suite 205, Longview TX 75604. 903/297-2223. **Contact:** Carmen Jones, Owner. **Description:** A permanent employment agency. **Other U.S. locations:** Nationwide.

STAFF FINDERS
ABACUS ACCOUNTING PERSONNEL
3040 Post Oak Boulevard, Houston TX 77056. 713/850-9131. **Contact:** Manager. **Description:** A permanent employment agency that also provides some temporary placements. Abacus Accounting Personnel (also at this location) provides on temporary and permanent accounting positions. **Specializes in the areas of:** Accounting/Auditing; Secretarial.

STAFF FINDERS
ABACUS ACCOUNTING PERSONNEL
515 West Greens Road, Houston TX 77067. 281/875-5700. **Contact:** Manager. **Description:** A permanent employment agency that also provides temporary placements. Abacus Accounting Personnel (also at this location) provides on temporary and permanent accounting positions. **Specializes in the areas of:** Accounting/Auditing; Secretarial.

STEELE & ASSOCIATES
9525 Katy Freeway, Suite 109, Houston TX 77024. 713/461-5823. **Contact:** Manager. **Description:** A permanent employment agency. **Specializes in the areas of:** Administration; Clerical; Insurance.

STEHOUWER & ASSOCIATES
2939 Mossrock, San Antonio TX 78230-5118. 210/349-4995. **Fax:** 210/349-4996. **Contact:** Personnel. **E-mail address:** ronsteh@connect.com. **Description:** A permanent employment agency that also provides organizational design consulting and psychological profiling. **Specializes in the areas of:** Administration; Art/Design; Computer Science/Software; Engineering; Technical. **Positions commonly filled include:** Aerospace Engineer; Chemical Engineer; Chemist; Civil Engineer; Computer Programmer; Design Engineer; Mechanical Engineer; MIS Specialist; Software Engineer; Structural Engineer; Systems Analyst. **Average salary range of placements:** More than $50,000.

SUMMIT SEARCH SPECIALISTS
14825 St. Mary's Lane, Suite 275, Houston TX 77079. 281/497-5840. **Fax:** 281/497-5841. **Contact:** David Bunce, Owner. **Description:** A permanent employment agency. **Specializes in the areas of:** Insurance. **Positions commonly filled include:** Accountant; Actuary; Claim Representative; Insurance Agent/Broker; Loss Prevention Specialist; Underwriter/Assistant Underwriter.

TSP PERSONNEL SERVICES, INC.
2246 Lamar Boulevard, Paris TX 75460. 903/785-0034. **Fax:** 903/784-0864. **Contact:** Kelley Ferguson, Owner/Manager. **Description:** A permanent employment agency that also provides temporary placements. Company pays fee. **Specializes in the areas of:** Accounting/Auditing; Industrial; Light Industrial; Retail; Sales; Secretarial. **Positions commonly filled include:** Bank Officer/Manager; Clerical Supervisor; Electrician; Secretary. **Corporate headquarters location:** This Location. **Average salary range of placements:** $20,000 - $29,999. **Number of placements per year:** 200 - 499.

TARRANT COUNTY EMPLOYMENT NETWORK
1400 Circle Drive, Suite 100, Fort Worth TX 76119. 817/531-5670. **Fax:** 817/531-5677. **Contact:** Betty Johnson, Program Coordinator. **Description:** A permanent employment agency that also provides career counseling services. **Specializes in the areas of:** Accounting/Auditing; Administration; Computer Science/Software; Education; Finance; Food Industry; General Management; Health/Medical; Industrial; Manufacturing; Personnel/Labor Relations; Retail; Sales; Secretarial; Transportation. **Positions commonly filled include:** Accountant/Auditor; Administrative Manager; Automotive Mechanic; Biomedical Engineer; Blue-Collar Worker Supervisor; Budget Analyst; Claim Rep.; Clerical Supervisor; Clinical Lab Technician; Computer Programmer; Construction and Building Inspector; Counselor; Credit Manager; Customer Service Rep.; Dental Assistant/Dental Hygienist; Draftsperson; Education Administrator; EEG Technologist; EKG Technician; Electrical/Electronics Engineer; Electrician; General Manager; Health Services Manager; Human Resources Specialist; Insurance Agent/Broker; Librarian; Medical Records Technician; MIS Specialist; Operations/Production Manager; Property and Real Estate Manager; Purchasing Agent/Manager; Radiological Technologist; Restaurant/Food Service Manager; Securities Sales Rep.; Systems Analyst; Teacher/Professor; Travel Agent; Typist/Word Processor. **Average salary range of placements:** $20,000 - $29,999. **Number of placements per year:** 200 - 499.

THOMAS OFFICE PERSONNEL SERVICE (TOPS)
3909 Flintridge Drive, Irving TX 75038. 972/252-2660. **Contact:** Margaret Thomas, Co-Founder. **Description:** A permanent employment agency. Company pays fee. **Specializes in the areas of:** Accounting/Auditing; Administration; General Management; Insurance; Manufacturing; Personnel/Labor Relations; Publishing; Secretarial. **Positions commonly filled include:** Accountant/Auditor; Branch Manager; Clerical Supervisor; Customer Service Representative; General Manager; Human Resources Specialist; Paralegal; Secretary; Typist/Word Processor. **Average salary range of placements:** $20,000 - $35,000. **Number of placements per year:** 1 - 49.

TODAYS LEGAL STAFFING
700 Pearl Street, Suite 350, Dallas TX 75201. 214/754-0700. **Toll-free phone:** 800/693-1514. **Contact:** Karen Gilmore, Branch Manager. **World Wide Web address:** http://www.todays.com. **Description:** A permanent employment agency. Company pays fee. **Specializes in the areas of:** Legal; Secretarial. **Positions commonly filled include:** Attorney; Paralegal; Typist/Word Processor. **Other U.S. locations:** Nationwide. **Average salary range of placements:** $30,000 - $50,000. **Number of placements per year:** 200 - 499.

TRAVEL SEARCH NETWORK
12860 Hillcrest Road, Suite 112, Dallas TX 75230-1519. 972/458-1145. **Fax:** 972/490-4790. **Contact:**

Gina Tedesco, Vice President of Operations. **Description:** A permanent and temporary employment agency. Company pays fee. **Specializes in the areas of:** Travel. **Positions commonly filled include:** Travel Agent. **Other area locations:** Houston TX. **Average salary range of placements:** $30,000 - $50,000. **Number of placements per year:** 200 - 499.

TRAVEL SEARCH NETWORK
4615 Post Oak Place, Suite 140, Houston TX 77027. 713/624-7177. **Contact:** Manager. **Description:** A permanent and temporary employment agency. **Specializes in the areas of:** Travel. **Other area locations:** Dallas TX.

VINSON AND ASSOCIATES
4100 McEwen, Suite 180, Dallas TX 75244. 972/980-8800. **Contact:** Fred Vinson, Manager. **Description:** A permanent employment agency that also provides temporary placements. **Specializes in the areas of:** Accounting/Auditing; Banking; Clerical; Finance; Insurance; Legal; Manufacturing; Sales.

WESTLAKE NANNIES
P.O. Box 161133, Austin TX 78716. 512/328-0996. **Fax:** 512/328-1290. **Contact:** Karen Long, Owner. **Description:** A nanny placement agency. Founded in 1994. **Average salary range of placements:** Less than $20,000. **Number of placements per year:** 100 - 199.

TEMPORARY EMPLOYMENT AGENCIES

A-1 PERSONNEL
5800 Corporate Drive, Suite B1, Houston TX 77036-2319. 713/773-2900. **Fax:** 713/773-4325. **Contact:** Sandy Radcliffe, Personnel Representative. **Description:** A-1 Personnel is a temporary agency. Company pays fee. **Specializes in the areas of:** Accounting/Auditing; Industrial; Light Industrial; Personnel/Labor Relations; Secretarial. **Positions commonly filled include:** Accountant/Auditor; Clerical Supervisor; Customer Service Rep.; General Manager; Systems Analyst; Typist/Word Processor. **Average salary range of placements:** $20,000 - $29,999. **Number of placements per year:** 200 - 499.

ABC TEMPS INC.
3109 Carlisle Street, Suite 208, Dallas TX 75204. 214/754-7052. **Fax:** 214/954-1525. **Contact:** Patti Perry, Regional Manager. **Description:** A temporary agency. Company pays fee. **Specializes in the areas of:** Accounting/Auditing; Manufacturing; Personnel/Labor Relations; Secretarial. **Positions commonly filled include:** Blue-Collar Worker Supervisor; Credit Manager; Customer Service Representative; Human Resources Specialist; Typist/Word Processor. **Benefits available to temporary workers:** Credit Union; Paid Holidays; Paid Vacation. **Corporate headquarters location:** This Location. **Other area locations:** Fort Worth TX. **Average salary range of placements:** Less than $20,000. **Number of placements per year:** 200 - 499.

ACCLAIM SERVICES, INC.
5445 La Sierra, Suite 317, Dallas TX 75231. 214/750-1818. **Fax:** 214/750-4403. **Contact:** Manager. **Description:** A temporary agency. Company pays fee. **Specializes in the areas of:** Computer Science/Software. **Positions commonly filled include:** Management Analyst/Consultant; Software Engineer; Systems Analyst; Technical Writer/Editor; Telecommunications Manager. **Average salary range of placements:** More than $50,000. **Number of placements per year:** 50 - 99.

ACTION PERSONNEL INC.
P.O. Drawer 3309, Texas City TX 77591-3309. **Contact:** President. **Description:** A temporary agency. **Specializes in the areas of:** Accounting/Auditing; Administration; Banking; Computer Science/Software; Finance; General Management; Health/Medical; Industrial; Legal; Personnel/Labor Relations; Sales; Secretarial. **Positions commonly filled include:** Accountant/Auditor; Administrative Manager; Advertising Clerk; Bank Officer/Manager; Claim Representative; Clerical Supervisor; Computer Programmer; Credit Manager; Customer Service Representative; Draftsperson; Medical Records Technician; Paralegal; Public Relations Specialist; Purchasing Agent/Manager; Systems Analyst; Travel Agent; Typist/Word Processor.

ADD-A-TEMP
WOODLANDS EXECUTIVE EMPLOYMENT
25025 North I-45, Suite 300, The Woodlands TX 77380. 281/367-3700. **Contact:** Jill Silman, President. **Description:** Add-A-Temp is a temporary agency and Woodlands Executive Employment is an executive search firm. Company pays fee. **Specializes in the areas of:** Accounting/Auditing; Administration; Clerical; Computer Hardware/Software; Finance; Technical. **Positions commonly filled include:** Accountant/Auditor; Administrative Assistant; Bank Officer/Manager; Bookkeeper; Clerk; Computer Operator; Computer Programmer; Data Entry Clerk; Draftsperson; EDP Specialist; Electrical/Electronics Engineer; Financial Analyst; General Manager; Human Resources Manager; Legal Secretary; Light Industrial Worker; Medical Secretary; MIS Specialist; Receptionist; Secretary; Stenographer; Systems Analyst; Technical Writer/Editor; Technician; Typist/Word Processor. **Number of placements per year:** 50 - 99.

ADECCO
5151 Flynn Parkway, Suite 103, Corpus Christi TX 78411-4318. 512/814-2342. **Fax:** 512/814-2346. **Contact:** Patty Hale, Office Supervisor. **Description:** A temporary agency. Company pays fee. **Specializes in the areas of:** Banking; Health/Medical; Industrial; Manufacturing; Secretarial. **Positions commonly filled include:** Clerical Supervisor; Computer Programmer; Customer Service Representative; Medical Records Technician; Typist/Word Processor. **Benefits available to temporary workers:** Paid Holidays; Paid Vacation; Referral Bonus Plan. **Corporate headquarters location:** Redwood City CA. **Other U.S. locations:** Nationwide. **International locations:** Worldwide. **Average salary range of placements:** $20,000 - $29,999. **Number of placements per year:** 500 - 999.

ADECCO
13201 Northwest Freeway, Suite 700, Houston TX 77040. 713/690-9500. **Fax:** 713/690-6465. **Contact:** Holly Rodriguez, Branch Manager. **Description:** A temporary agency. Company pays fee. **Specializes in the areas of:** Administration; Engineering; Light Industrial; Manufacturing; Personnel/Labor Relations; Technical. **Positions commonly filled include:** Accountant/Auditor; Blue-Collar Worker Supervisor; Buyer; Chemical Engineer; Civil Engineer; Computer Programmer; Customer Service Rep.; Design Engineer; Designer; Draftsperson; Electrical/Electronics Engineer; Financial Analyst; Human Resources Specialist; Industrial Engineer; Mechanical Engineer; MIS Specialist; Multimedia Designer; Paralegal; Petroleum Engineer; Purchasing Agent/Manager; Quality Control Supervisor; Software Engineer; Structural Engineer; Surveyor; Systems Analyst; Technical Writer/Editor; Telecommunications Manager. **Benefits available to temporary workers:** 401(k); Dental Insurance; Medical Insurance; Paid Holidays; Paid Vacation; Tuition

Insurance; Paid Holidays; Paid Vacation; Tuition Assistance. **Corporate headquarters location:** Redwood City CA. **Other U.S. locations:** Nationwide. **International locations:** Worldwide. **Average salary range of placements:** $30,000 - $50,000. **Number of placements per year:** 1000+.

ALLIANCE LEGAL STAFFING
1845 Woodall Rogers, Suite 1200, Dallas TX 75201. 214/954-8096. **Fax:** 214/954-1290. **Contact:** Manager. **Description:** A temporary agency. Company pays fee. **Specializes in the areas of:** Legal. **Positions commonly filled include:** Attorney; Paralegal. **Benefits available to temporary workers:** Paid Holidays; Paid Vacation. **Number of placements per year:** 200 - 499.

ATTORNEY RESOURCES, INC.
750 North St. Paul, Suite 540, Dallas TX 75201. 214/922-8050. **Toll-free phone:** 800/324-4828. **Fax:** 214/871-3041. **Contact:** Jennifer Colby, Manager. **E-mail address:** ari@airmail.net. **World Wide Web address:** http://www.cpgs.com/attorney.resource. **Description:** A temporary agency that also provides permanent placements in law firms. Company pays fee. **Specializes in the areas of:** Administration; Legal; Secretarial. **Positions commonly filled include:** Attorney; Legal Secretary; Paralegal. **Benefits available to temporary workers:** Paid Holidays; Paid Vacation; Referral Bonus Plan. **Corporate headquarters location:** This Location. **Other area locations:** Austin TX; Fort Worth TX. **Other U.S. locations:** Tulsa OK. **Number of placements per year:** 100 - 199.

ANN BEST ELITE TEMPORARIES
1501 North Amburn Road, Texas City TX 77591. 409/933-0095. **Fax:** 409/933-0269. **Contact:** Ann Best, President/Owner. **Description:** A temporary agency. Company pays fee. **Specializes in the areas of:** Accounting/Auditing; Administration; Construction; General Management; Legal; Personnel/Labor Relations; Secretarial. **Positions commonly filled include:** Accountant/Auditor; Administrative Manager; Blue-Collar Worker Supervisor; Chemical Engineer; Civil Engineer; Clerical Supervisor; Computer Programmer; Construction and Building Inspector; Construction Contractor; Dental Assistant/Dental Hygienist; Electrical/Electronics Engineer; Electrician; General Manager; Human Resources Manager; Human Service Worker; Paralegal; Purchasing Agent/Manager; Recreational Therapist; Systems Analyst; Typist/Word Processor. **Average salary range of placements:** $20,000 - $29,999. **Number of placements per year:** 1 - 49.

BURNETT PERSONNEL SERVICES
9800 Richmond Avenue, Suite 800, Houston TX 77042. 713/977-4777. **Fax:** 713/977-7533. **Contact:** Sue Burnett, President. **E-mail address:** sue@houston.burnettps.com. **World Wide Web address:** http://www.burnettps.com. **Description:** A temporary agency that also provides permanent placements. Company pays fee. **Specializes in the areas of:** Accounting/Auditing; Clerical; Computer Science/Software; Legal; Secretarial. **Positions commonly filled include:** Accountant/Auditor; Administrative Assistant; Computer Programmer; Customer Service Representative; Data Entry Clerk; Human Resources Specialist; Legal Secretary; MIS Specialist; Office Manager; Paralegal; Secretary; Systems Analyst; Typist/Word Processor. **Corporate headquarters location:** This Location. **Other area locations:** Austin TX; El Paso TX. **Average salary range of placements:** $20,000 - $29,999. **Number of placements per year:** 500 - 999.

CDI TELECOMMUNICATIONS
2425 North Central Expressway, Suite 101, Richardson TX 75080. 972/480-8333. **Contact:** Branch Manager. **World Wide Web address:** http://www.cdicorp.com. **Description:** A temporary agency. **Specializes in the areas of:** Telecommunications. **Corporate headquarters location:** Philadelphia PA. **Other U.S. locations:** Nationwide. **International locations:** Worldwide. **Number of placements per year:** 1000+.

CLAYTON PERSONNEL SERVICES
480 Sam Houston Parkway East, Suite 140, Houston TX 77060. 281/999-3080. **Fax:** 281/931-5115. **Contact:** Teresa Moratto, Office Manager. **Description:** A temporary and temp-to-hire agency. Company pays fee. **Specializes in the areas of:** Accounting/Auditing; Secretarial. **Positions commonly filled include:** Account Representative; Accountant; Administrative Manager; Buyer; Customer Service Representative; Typist/Word Processor. **Benefits available to temporary workers:** Dental Insurance; Medical Insurance; Paid Vacation; Referral Bonus Plan. **Average salary range of placements:** $20,000 - $29,999. **Number of placements per year:** 1 - 49.

CO-COUNSEL
1221 Lamar, Suite 1210, Houston TX 77010. 713/650-8195. **Fax:** 713/650-6748. **Contact:** Operations Supervisor. **Description:** A temporary agency that provides staff for litigation support projects. Founded in 1988. **Specializes in the areas of:** Legal. **Positions commonly filled include:** Attorney; Legal Assistant; Legal Secretary; Librarian; Paralegal. **Benefits available to temporary workers:** Paid Holidays; Paid Vacation.

CO-COUNSEL
600 North Pearl Street, Suite 430, Dallas TX 75201. 214/720-3939. **Fax:** 214/720-0555. **Contact:** Staffing Coordinator. **Description:** A temporary agency. **Specializes in the areas of:** Legal. **Positions commonly filled include:** Attorney; Paralegal. **Average salary range of placements:** $30,000 - $50,000.

COLVIN RESOURCES GROUP
4141 Blue Lake Center, Dallas TX 75244-5132. 972/788-5114. **Fax:** 972/490-5015. **Contact:** Sheila Bridges, Senior Account Executive. **Description:** A temporary and permanent placement agency. Company pays fee. **Specializes in the areas of:** Accounting/Auditing; Architecture/Construction; Banking; Finance; General Management; Health/Medical; Personnel/Labor Relations; Secretarial. **Positions commonly filled include:** Accountant/Auditor; Budget Analyst; Credit Manager; Financial Analyst; Human Resources Specialist; Property and Real Estate Manager; Typist/Word Processor. **Average salary range of placements:** $30,000 - $50,000. **Number of placements per year:** 200 - 499.

COMPUTEMP INC.
5177 Richmond Avenue, Suite 580, Houston TX 77056-6736. 713/623-8355. **Fax:** 713/623-8357. **Contact:** Branch Manager. **World Wide Web address:** http://www.computemp.com. **Description:** A temporary agency. Company pays fee. **Specializes in the areas of:** Computer Science/Software; Technical. **Positions commonly filled include:** Computer Programmer; MIS Specialist; Software Engineer; Systems Analyst; Technical Writer/Editor; Telecommunications Manager. **Benefits available to temporary workers:** 401(k); Bonus Award/Plan; Medical Insurance. **Corporate headquarters location:** Boca Raton FL. **Other U.S. locations:** Nationwide. **Average salary range of placements:** $30,000 - $50,000. **Number of placements per year:** 100 - 199.

COMPUTEMP INC.
12870 Hillcrest Road, Suite 226, Dallas TX 75230. 972/661-1064. **Fax:** 972/661-9143. **Contact:** Linda

Farris, Manager. **E-mail address:** dallas@computemp.com. **World Wide Web address:** http://www.computemp.com. **Description:** A temporary agency. Founded in 1984. Company pays fee. **Specializes in the areas of:** Computer Science/Software; Data Processing; Information Technology; Personnel/Labor Relations; Technical. **Positions commonly filled include:** Computer Operator; Computer Programmer; Internet Services Manager; Library Technician; MIS Specialist; Multimedia Designer; Software Engineer; Systems Analyst; Technical Writer/Editor; Telecommunications Manager. **Benefits available to temporary workers:** 401(k); Medical Insurance; Paid Vacation. **Corporate headquarters location:** Boca Raton FL. **Other U.S. locations:** Nationwide. **Average salary range of placements:** $30,000 - $50,000. **Number of placements per year:** 200 - 499.

CONTRACT DESIGN PERSONNEL
2225 East Randol Mill Road, Suite 223, Arlington TX 76011. 817/640-6119. **Fax:** 817/640-6256. **Contact:** Stan Baker, Director of Recruiting Operations. **Description:** A temporary agency that also offers some permanent placements. Company pays fee. **Specializes in the areas of:** Engineering; High-Tech; Multimedia; Technical. **Positions commonly filled include:** Aerospace Engineer; Architect; Chemical Engineer; Civil Engineer; Computer Programmer; Design Engineer; Designer; Draftsperson; Electrical/Electronics Engineer; Environmental Engineer; Industrial Engineer; Mechanical Engineer; Metallurgical Engineer; Mining Engineer; Multimedia Designer; Nuclear Engineer; Petroleum Engineer; Software Engineer; Structural Engineer; Systems Analyst; Technical Writer/Editor. **Benefits available to temporary workers:** Paid Holidays. **Number of placements per year:** 100 - 199.

CORBETT PERSONNEL SERVICES
South Gessner, Suite 315, Houston TX 77063. 713/974-3800. **Contact:** Manager. **Description:** A temporary, temp-to-perm, and permanent employment agency. **Specializes in the areas of:** Administration; Clerical; Office Support. **Positions commonly filled include:** Administrative Assistant; Bookkeeper; Receptionist.

CREATIVE STAFFING SERVICES
1533 North Lee Trevino Drive, Suite 200, El Paso TX 79936. 915/591-5111. **Fax:** 915/593-7482. **Contact:** Justin R. Hill, Account Executive. **E-mail address:** crestafser@aol.com. **Description:** A temporary and permanent employment agency. Company pays fee. **Specializes in the areas of:** Accounting/Auditing; Computer Science/Software; General Management; Industrial; Light Industrial; Nonprofit; Personnel/Labor Relations; Printing; Retail; Sales; Secretarial; Technical; Transportation. **Positions commonly filled include:** Accountant/Auditor; Blue-Collar Worker Supervisor; Budget Analyst; Buyer; Clerical Supervisor; Computer Programmer; Customer Service Rep.; Human Resources Specialist; Landscape Architect; Manufacturer's/Wholesaler's Sales Rep.; Multimedia Designer; Operations/Production Manager; Paralegal; Preschool Worker; Purchasing Agent/Manager; Quality Control Supervisor; Services Sales Rep.; Systems Analyst; Technical Writer/Editor; Typist/Word Processor; Video Production Coordinator. **Benefits available to temporary workers:** Medical Insurance; Paid Holidays; Paid Vacation. **Corporate headquarters location:** This Location. **Average salary range of placements:** $30,000 - $50,000. **Number of placements per year:** 1 - 49.

CREDIT UNION EMPLOYMENT RESOURCES, INC.
1001 West Loop South, Suite 216, Houston TX 77027. 713/961-4567. **Toll-free phone:** 800/344-8285. **Fax:** 713/961-4569. **Contact:** Manager. **Description:** A temporary and permanent staffing agency that provides placement in credit unions. Company pays fee. **Specializes in the areas of:** Accounting/Auditing; Banking. **Positions commonly filled include:** Accountant/Auditor; Bank Officer/Manager; Credit Manager; Customer Service Representative; Human Resources Specialist; Internet Services Manager; MIS Specialist; Securities Sales Representative. **Average salary range of placements:** $20,000 - $29,999. **Number of placements per year:** 200 - 499.

GAIL DARLING STAFFING
GAIL DARLING'S PROFESSIONAL DESK
25 Butterfield Trail, El Paso TX 79902. 915/532-5605. **Fax:** 915/544-8826. **Contact:** Phyllis Caves, Account Manager. **Description:** A temporary agency. Gail Darling's Professional Desk (also at this location) provides permanent placement and some executive searches. Founded in 1986. Company pays fee. **Specializes in the areas of:** Accounting/Auditing; Administration; Architecture/Construction; Banking; Computer Science/Software; Engineering; Finance; General Management; Industrial; Insurance; Legal; Manufacturing; Personnel/Labor Relations; Publishing; Retail; Secretarial. **Positions commonly filled include:** Accountant/Auditor; Bank Officer/Manager; Budget Analyst; Buyer; Chemical Engineer; Civil Engineer; Clerk; Computer Programmer; Credit Manager; Customer Service Representative; Economist; Editor; Environmental Engineer; Financial Analyst; General Manager; Human Resources Manager; Industrial Engineer; Industrial Production Manager; Internet Services Manager; Management Analyst/Consultant; Market Research Analyst; Mechanical Engineer; Metallurgical Engineer; Mining Engineer; MIS Specialist; Nuclear Engineer; Operations/Production Manager; Paralegal; Petroleum Engineer; Property and Real Estate Manager; Public Relations Specialist; Purchasing Agent/Manager; Securities Sales Representative; Strategic Relations Manager; Structural Engineer; Surveyor; Systems Analyst; Technical Writer/Editor; Telecommunications Manager; Typist/Word Processor. **Average salary range of placements:** $20,000 - $29,999.

DEPENDABLE DENTAL STAFFING
18601 LBJ Freeway, Mesquite TX 75150-5600. **Fax:** 972/681-9657. **Contact:** Karen Houston, Vice President. **Description:** A temporary agency. **Specializes in the areas of:** Health/Medical. **Positions commonly filled include:** Dental Assistant/Dental Hygienist; Dentist. **Other area locations:** Arlington TX. **Average salary range of placements:** $30,000 - $50,000. **Number of placements per year:** 200 - 499.

DIVERSIFIED TEMPS
12801 North Central Expressway, Suite 210, Dallas TX 75243. 972/980-4398. **Fax:** 972/934-0151. **Contact:** Manager. **E-mail address:** ew821@aol.com. **Description:** A temporary agency. Company pays fee. **Specializes in the areas of:** Accounting/Auditing; Administration; Computer Science/Software; Personnel/Labor Relations; Sales; Secretarial. **Positions commonly filled include:** Accountant/Auditor; Adjuster; Administrative Manager; Budget Analyst; Claim Representative; Clerical Supervisor; Computer Programmer; Customer Service Representative; Draftsperson; Financial Analyst; General Manager; Human Resources Specialist; Management Trainee; Medical Records Technician; MIS Specialist; Purchasing Agent/Manager; Quality Control Supervisor; Services Sales Representative; Social Worker; Software Engineer; Telecommunications Manager; Typist/Word Processor. **Benefits available to temporary workers:** Dental Insurance; Medical Insurance. **Average salary range of placements:**

$20,000 - $29,999. **Number of placements per year:** 1000+.

DRIVING FORCE, INC.
2030 Las Vegas Trail, Fort Worth TX 76108. 817/246-7113. **Contact:** G. Wayne Brown, Sr., President. **Description:** A temporary agency. **Specializes in the areas of:** Transportation. **Positions commonly filled include:** Driver. **Benefits available to temporary workers:** Credit Union; Dental Insurance; Life Insurance; Medical Insurance. **Other area locations:** Abilene TX; Austin TX; Dallas TX; Houston TX; San Antonio TX. **Average salary range of placements:** $30,000 - $50,000. **Number of placements per year:** 1 - 49.

ESPRIT TEMPORARY SERVICES
P.O. Box 35443, Dallas TX 75235. 214/631-3832. **Fax:** 214/638-2908. **Contact:** John Wilson, Recruiter. **Description:** A temporary agency. **Specializes in the areas of:** Administration; Customer Service; General Labor; Secretarial. **Positions commonly filled include:** Administrative Assistant; Administrative Manager; Blue-Collar Worker Supervisor; Computer Operator; Electrician; Human Resources Manager; Industrial Production Manager; Paralegal; Typist/Word Processor. **Benefits available to temporary workers:** Dental Insurance; Medical Insurance; Paid Vacation. **Average salary range of placements:** $30,000 - $50,000. **Number of placements per year:** 200 - 499.

FIRSTWORD STAFFING SERVICES
10000 North Central Expressway, Suite 118, Dallas TX 75231. 214/360-0020. **Fax:** 214/360-9206. **Contact:** Mary Burke, Corporate Services Manager. **Description:** A temporary agency. Company pays fee. **Specializes in the areas of:** Computer Science/Software; Personnel/Labor Relations; Secretarial; Technical. **Positions commonly filled include:** Claim Representative; Clerical Supervisor; Computer Programmer; Cost Estimator; Customer Service Representative; Electronics Technician; Paralegal; Typist/Word Processor. **Benefits available to temporary workers:** Dental Insurance; Medical Insurance; Paid Holidays; Paid Vacation; Referral Bonus Plan. **Corporate headquarters location:** Charlotte NC. **Average salary range of placements:** $20,000 - $29,999.

HEALTH CARE TEMP
8926 Sherbourne Street, Suite D, Houston TX 77016. 713/631-7106. **Contact:** Manager. **Description:** A temporary agency that also provides some permanent placements. **Specializes in the areas of:** Health/Medical. **Positions commonly filled include:** Licensed Vocational Nurse; Registered Nurse.

IMPRIMIS STAFFING SOLUTIONS
5550 LBJ Freeway, Suite 150, Dallas TX 75240. 972/419-1631. **Recorded jobline:** 972/419-1733. **Fax:** 972/419-1970. **Contact:** Meg Graham, Recruiter. **World Wide Web address:** http://www.imprimis-group.com. **Description:** A temporary agency that also offers some permanent placements. **Specializes in the areas of:** Accounting/Auditing; Administration; Clerical; Computer Science/Software; Finance; Insurance; Legal; Nonprofit; Personnel/Labor Relations; Secretarial. **Positions commonly filled include:** Human Resources Specialist; Typist/Word Processor. **Benefits available to temporary workers:** 401(k); Medical Insurance; Paid Holidays; Paid Vacation. **Other area locations:** Fort Worth TX. **Average salary range of placements:** $20,000 - $29,999. **Number of placements per year:** 1000+.

INSURANCE TEMPORARY SERVICES, INC.
2777 Stemmons Freeway, LB26, Dallas TX 75207. 214/638-7777. **Fax:** 214/634-8500. **Contact:** Susie Lowry, President. **Description:** A temporary agency. **Specializes in the areas of:** Insurance. **Positions commonly filled include:** Adjuster; Claim Representative; Customer Service Representative; Typist/Word Processor.

INTERIM PERSONNEL
85 Interstate 10 North, Suite 101, Beaumont TX 77707. 409/832-9444. **Fax:** 409/832-8440. **Contact:** Manager. **Description:** A temporary agency that also provides permanent placements. **Specializes in the areas of:** Banking; Industrial; Retail; Secretarial. **Benefits available to temporary workers:** Medical Insurance; Paid Holidays; Paid Vacation. **Average salary range of placements:** Less than $20,000. **Number of placements per year:** 1000+.

INTERSEARCH ASSOCIATES, INC.
5100 Westheimer Road, Suite 370, Houston TX 77056-5507. 713/960-0444. **Fax:** 713/460-1411. **Contact:** Ivonne Dominguez, Office Manager. **Description:** A temporary agency that also provides some permanent placements. Company pays fee. **Specializes in the areas of:** Accounting/Auditing; Banking; Finance; Mortgage; Personnel/Labor Relations. **Positions commonly filled include:** Accountant/Auditor; Bank Officer/Manager; Claim Representative; Computer Programmer; Customer Service Representative; Human Resources Specialist; Management Trainee; MIS Specialist; Systems Analyst. **Benefits available to temporary workers:** Paid Holidays; Paid Vacation. **Average salary range of placements:** $30,000 - $50,000. **Number of placements per year:** 200 - 499.

KADCO CONTRACT DESIGN CORPORATION
3100 Wilcrest Drive, Suite 230, Houston TX 77042. 713/780-2424. **Contact:** Jacqueline Kyle, President. **Description:** A temporary agency that also offers contract services. **Specializes in the areas of:** Engineering. **Positions commonly filled include:** Architect; Buyer; Chemical Engineer; Chemist; Civil Engineer; Construction and Building Inspector; Cost Estimator; Design Engineer; Designer; Draftsperson; Electrical/Electronics Engineer; Environmental Engineer; Mechanical Engineer; Metallurgical Engineer; Petroleum Engineer; Purchasing Agent/Manager; Quality Control Supervisor; Radiological Technologist; Structural Engineer. **Benefits available to temporary workers:** 401(k); Medical Insurance; Paid Vacation. **Average salary range of placements:** More than $50,000. **Number of placements per year:** 100 - 199.

KELLY SCIENTIFIC RESOURCES
2323 North Central Expressway, Suite 155, Richardson TX 75080. 972/234-8175. **Fax:** 972/690-4825. **Contact:** Branch Manager. **World Wide Web address:** http://www.kellyscientific.com. **Description:** A temporary agency for scientific professionals. **Specializes in the areas of:** Biomedical; Biotechnology; Chemical; Environmental; Food Industry; Petrochemical; Pharmaceutical. **Other U.S. locations:** Nationwide.

KELLY SCIENTIFIC RESOURCES
13831 Northwest Freeway, Suite 640, Houston TX 77040. 713/690-2155. **Contact:** Branch Manager. **World Wide Web address:** http://www.kellyscientific.com. **Description:** A temporary agency for scientific professionals. **Specializes in the areas of:** Biomedical; Biotechnology; Chemical; Environmental; Petrochemical. **Other U.S. locations:** Nationwide.

KELLY SERVICES, INC.
1800 Teague Drive, Suite 100, Sherman TX 75090 903/893-7777. **Contact:** Branch Manager. **Description:** A temporary agency. **Specializes in the areas of:** Accounting/Auditing; Banking; Clerical;

Computer Hardware/Software; Engineering; Finance; Food Industry; Health/Medical; Legal; Manufacturing; Secretarial; Technical; Transportation.

KELLY SERVICES, INC.
1616 South Kentucky, Building D, Suite 110, Amarillo TX 79102. 806/355-9696. **Fax:** 806/359-0308. **Contact:** Branch Manager. **Description:** A temporary agency. Founded in 1946. Company pays fee. **Specializes in the areas of:** Accounting/Auditing; Administration; Finance; Insurance; Secretarial. **Positions commonly filled include:** Administrative Assistant; Marketing Specialist; Secretary; Typist/ Word Processor. **Benefits available to temporary workers:** Medical Insurance; Paid Holidays; Paid Vacation. **Other U.S. locations:** Nationwide. **Average salary range of placements:** $20,000 - $29,999. **Number of placements per year:** 500 - 999.

LINK STAFFING SERVICES
1800 Bering Drive, Suite 801, Houston TX 77054. 713/784-4400. **Toll-free phone:** 800/848-5465. **Fax:** 713/784-4454. **Contact:** Ted Long, Vice President. **Description:** A temporary agency. **Specializes in the areas of:** Food Industry; General Management; Industrial; Manufacturing. **Positions commonly filled include:** Automotive Mechanic; Blue-Collar Worker Supervisor; Construction and Building Inspector; Draftsperson; Electrician; Industrial Production Manager. **Benefits available to temporary workers:** Dental Insurance; Medical Insurance. **Average salary range of placements:** $30,000 - $50,000. **Number of placements per year:** 1000+.

MANPOWER TEMPORARY SERVICES
8303 North Mopac Expressway, Austin TX 78759. 512/343-2141. **Contact:** Branch Manager. **World Wide Web address:** http://www.manpower.com. **Description:** A temporary agency. Company pays fee. **Specializes in the areas of:** Data Processing; Industrial; Office Support; Professional; Technical; Word Processing. **Positions commonly filled include:** Accountant/Auditor; Accounting Clerk; Administrative Assistant; Assembly Worker; Biological Scientist; Bookkeeper; Chemist; Computer Operator; Customer Service Representative; Desktop Publishing Specialist; Electrician; Inspector/Tester/Grader; Machine Operator; Packaging/Processing Worker; Painter; Project Engineer; Proofreader; Receptionist; Research Assistant; Secretary; Software Engineer; Stenographer; Systems Analyst; Technical Writer/Editor; Typist/Word Processor; Welder. **Benefits available to temporary workers:** Life Insurance; Medical Insurance; Paid Holidays; Paid Vacation. **Number of placements per year:** 1000+.

MANPOWER TEMPORARY SERVICES
5402 South Staples Street, Suite 103, Corpus Christi TX 78411. 512/991-1196. **Fax:** 512/992-4454. **Contact:** GeeGee Ross, Branch Supervisor. **World Wide Web address:** http://www.manpower.com. **Description:** A temporary agency. **Specializes in the areas of:** Accounting/Auditing; Banking; Computer Science/Software; Engineering; Industrial; Manufacturing; Personnel/Labor Relations; Secretarial; Technical. **Positions commonly filled include:** Accountant/Auditor; Administrative Manager; Advertising Clerk; Architect; Biochemist; Biological Scientist; Biomedical Engineer; Blue-Collar Worker Supervisor; Branch Manager; Brokerage Clerk; Buyer; Chemical Engineer; Chemist; Civil Engineer; Claim Representative; Clerical Supervisor; Computer Programmer; Customer Service Rep.; Design Engineer; Draftsperson; Electrical/Electronics Engineer; Electrician; Environmental Engineer; Geologist/ Geophysicist; Human Resources Specialist; Human Service Worker; Industrial Engineer; Industrial Production Manager; Librarian; Mechanical Engineer; MIS Specialist; Purchasing Agent/Manager; Quality Control Supervisor; Social Worker; Software Engineer; Statistician; Structural Engineer; Surveyor; Technical Writer/Editor; Telecommunications Manager; Typist/ Word Processor. **Number of placements per year:** 1000+.

MANPOWER, INC.
12225 Greenville Avenue, Suite 495, Dallas TX 75243. 972/699-9337. **Contact:** W.H. Wilson, Area Manager. **World Wide Web address:** http://www.manpower.com. **Description:** A temporary agency. Company pays fee. **Specializes in the areas of:** Data Processing; Light Industrial; Office Support; Technical; Travel. **Benefits available to temporary workers:** Life Insurance; Medical Insurance; Paid Holidays; Paid Vacation. **Number of placements per year:** 1000+.

MANPOWER, INC.
440 Louisiana, Suite 470, Houston TX 77002. 713/228-3131. **Contact:** Branch Manager. **World Wide Web address:** http://www.manpower.com. **Description:** A temporary agency. Company pays fee. **Specializes in the areas of:** Light Industrial; Office Support; Telemarketing; Word Processing. **Positions commonly filled include:** Accountant/Auditor; Accounting Clerk; Administrative Assistant; Assembler; Biological Scientist; Bookkeeper; Chemist; Computer Operator; Customer Service Representative; Designer; Desktop Publishing Specialist; Electrician; Inventory Control Specialist; Machine Operator; Materials Manager; Packaging/Processing Worker; Proofreader; Receptionist; Research Assistant; Secretary; Systems Analyst; Technical Writer/Editor; Typist/Word Processor. **Benefits available to temporary workers:** Life Insurance; Medical Insurance; Paid Holidays; Paid Vacation. **Number of placements per year:** 1000+.

CURTIS McINTOSH ASSOCIATES
P.O. Box 884, Fort Worth TX 76101. 817/335-7724. **Contact:** Manager. **Description:** A temporary agency. **Specializes in the areas of:** Transportation. **Positions commonly filled include:** Truck Driver.

NURSES TODAY, INC.
4230 LBJ Freeway, Suite 110, Dallas TX 75244. 972/233-9966. **Fax:** 972/233-5354. **Contact:** Anita Porco, CEO. **Description:** A temporary agency. Nurses Today is also a home health care agency and provider of case management services. **Specializes in the areas of:** Health/Medical; Industrial. **Positions commonly filled include:** Certified Nursing Aide; Licensed Practical Nurse; Registered Nurse. **Average salary range of placements:** $30,000 - $50,000.

OLSTEN STAFFING SERVICES
40 Northeast Loop 410, Suite 545, San Antonio TX 78216-5827. 210/349-9911. **Fax:** 210/349-5702. **Contact:** Faye Ripper, Personnel Recruiter. **Description:** A temporary agency. Founded in 1950. Company pays fee. **Specializes in the areas of:** Accounting/Auditing; Administration; Computer Science/Software; Engineering; Industrial; Legal; Manufacturing; Personnel/Labor Relations; Secretarial; Technical. **Positions commonly filled include:** Accounting Clerk; Clerical Supervisor; Computer Scientist; Customer Service Representative; Human Resources Manager; Sales Representative; Typist/Word Processor. **Benefits available to temporary workers:** Medical Insurance. **Corporate headquarters location:** Melville NY. **Other U.S. locations:** Nationwide. **International locations:** United Kingdom. **Number of placements per year:** 1000+.

OLSTEN STAFFING SERVICES
1445 MacArthur Drive, Suite 236, Carrollton TX 75007. 972/245-5700. **Fax:** 972/446-1020. **Contact:**

Branch Manager. **Description:** A temporary agency. **Specializes in the areas of:** Accounting/Auditing; Administration; Banking; Computer Science/Software; Engineering; Finance; General Management; Health/Medical; Industrial; Insurance; Legal; Manufacturing; Personnel/Labor Relations; Secretarial; Technical. **Positions commonly filled include:** Accountant/Auditor; Administrative Manager; Blue-Collar Worker Supervisor; Chemical Engineer; Clerical Supervisor; Clinical Lab Technician; Computer Programmer; Credit Manager; Customer Service Representative; Human Resources Specialist; Mechanical Engineer; Medical Records Technician; Paralegal; Quality Control Supervisor; Registered Nurse; Respiratory Therapist; Software Engineer; Technical Writer/Editor; Typist/Word Processor. **Benefits available to temporary workers:** Daycare Assistance; Medical Insurance; Paid Vacation. **Corporate headquarters location:** Melville NY. **Other U.S. locations:** Nationwide. **International locations:** United Kingdom. **Average salary range of placements:** $20,000 - $29,999. **Number of placements per year:** 1000+.

OLSTEN STAFFING SERVICES
9400 North Central Avenue, Suite 112, Dallas TX 75231. 214/373-7400. **Fax:** 214/739-4649. **Contact:** Sorya Doeung, Office Automation Specialist. **Description:** A temporary agency. **Specializes in the areas of:** Accounting/Auditing; Industrial; Light Industrial; Sales; Secretarial. **Positions commonly filled include:** Administrative Assistant; Secretary; Typist/Word Processor. **Benefits available to temporary workers:** Medical Insurance; Paid Vacation. **Corporate headquarters location:** Melville NY. **Other U.S. locations:** Nationwide. **International locations:** United Kingdom. **Average salary range of placements:** $20,000 - $29,999. **Number of placements per year:** 1000+.

OLSTEN STAFFING SERVICES
275 West Campbell, Suite 117, Richardson TX 75080. 972/669-8900. **Fax:** 972/669-2254. **Contact:** Melissa Reisberg, Customer Service Manager. **E-mail address:** choff.olsten@intur.net. **Description:** A temporary agency. Company pays fee. **Specializes in the areas of:** Personnel/Labor Relations. **Positions commonly filled include:** Customer Service Representative; Typist/Word Processor. **Corporate headquarters location:** Melville NY. **Other U.S. locations:** Nationwide. **International locations:** United Kingdom. **Average salary range of placements:** Less than $20,000.

PRIORITY PERSONNEL, INC.
312 West Hopkins Street, San Marcos TX 78666. 512/392-2323. **Fax:** 512/396-2366. **Contact:** Placement. **Description:** A temporary agency. Founded in 1994. Company pays fee. **Specializes in the areas of:** Accounting/Auditing; Administration; Industrial; Manufacturing; Secretarial. **Positions commonly filled include:** Automotive Mechanic; Blue-Collar Worker Supervisor; Clerical Supervisor; Electrician; Landscape Architect; Management Trainee; Mechanical Engineer; Quality Control Supervisor; Services Sales Representative; Typist/Word Processor. **Average salary range of placements:** Less than $20,000. **Number of placements per year:** 1000+.

PRO STAFF PERSONNEL SERVICES
14755 Preston Road, Dallas TX 75240. 972/239-8800. **Toll-free phone:** 800/938-9675. **Fax:** 972/239-4600. **Contact:** Katherine Tolsch, Branch Manager. **Description:** A temporary agency that also provides permanent placements. Company pays fee. **Specializes in the areas of:** Accounting/Auditing; Advertising; Computer Science/Software; Engineering; Finance; Light Industrial; Manufacturing; Sales; Secretarial; Technical. **Positions commonly filled include:** Accountant/Auditor; Administrative Manager; Advertising Clerk; Bank Officer/Manager; Blue-Collar Worker Supervisor; Branch Manager; Brokerage Clerk; Budget Analyst; Claim Representative; Clerical Supervisor; Computer Programmer; Cost Estimator; Design Engineer; Electrical/Electronics Engineer; Financial Analyst; General Manager; Human Resources Specialist; Industrial Engineer; Industrial Production Manager; Management Analyst/Consultant; Management Trainee; Manufacturer's/Wholesaler's Sales Rep.; Market Research Analyst; Mechanical Engineer; MIS Specialist; Operations/Production Manager; Purchasing Agent/Manager; Quality Control Supervisor; Services Sales Representative; Software Engineer; Systems Analyst; Technical Writer/Editor; Typist/Word Processor; Underwriter/Assistant Underwriter. **Benefits available to temporary workers:** 401(k); Medical Insurance; Paid Holidays; Paid Vacation. **Corporate headquarters location:** Minneapolis MN. **Other U.S. locations:** Nationwide. **Average salary range of placements:** $20,000 - $29,999. **Number of placements per year:** 1000+.

PRO STAFF PERSONNEL SERVICES
122 West Carpenter Freeway, Suite 515, Irving TX 75039. 972/650-1500. **Recorded jobline:** 972/712-6528. **Fax:** 972/650-0857. **Contact:** Manager. **Description:** A temporary agency. **Specializes in the areas of:** Accounting/Auditing; Administration; Art/Design; Secretarial; Technical. **Positions commonly filled include:** Customer Service Representative; Light Industrial Worker; Receptionist; Typist/Word Processor. **Benefits available to temporary workers:** 401(k); Medical Insurance. **Corporate headquarters location:** Minneapolis MN. **Other U.S. locations:** Nationwide. **Average salary range of placements:** Less than $20,000. **Number of placements per year:** 1000+.

RESPIRATORY STAFFING SPECIALIST INC.
310 East Interstate 30, Suite 290, Garland TX 75043. 972/226-5421. **Toll-free phone:** 800/758-3275. **Fax:** 972/226-0323. **Contact:** Carla DeWitt, President. **Description:** A temporary agency. **Specializes in the areas of:** Health/Medical. **Positions commonly filled include:** Respiratory Therapist. **Average salary range of placements:** $20,000 - $29,999. **Number of placements per year:** 1 - 49.

RESTAURANT SERVERS, INC.
10530 Shady Trail, Dallas TX 75220. 214/350-1166. **Fax:** 214/350-0454. **Contact:** Carol Fisher, Owner. **Description:** A temporary agency that also provides contract services for event management and food protection management. **Specializes in the areas of:** Food Industry. **Positions commonly filled include:** Blue-Collar Worker Supervisor; Education Administrator; Management Trainee; Registered Nurse; Restaurant/Food Service Manager; Teacher/Professor. **Average salary range of placements:** Less than $20,000. **Number of placements per year:** 200 - 499.

SOS STAFFING SERVICES
1327 Empire Central, Suite 130, Dallas TX 75247. 214/638-0766. **Contact:** Manager. **Description:** A temporary agency that also provides permanent placements. Company pays fee. **Specializes in the areas of:** Administration; Industrial; Manufacturing; Personnel/Labor Relations; Secretarial. **Positions commonly filled include:** Accountant/Auditor; Automotive Mechanic; Blue-Collar Worker Supervisor; Buyer; Claim Representative; Clerical Supervisor; Computer Programmer; Cost Estimator; Credit Manager; Customer Service Representative; Design Engineer; Draftsperson; Hotel Manager; Human Service Worker; Landscape Architect; Mechanical Engineer; Operations/Production Manager; Purchasing

Agent/Manager; Restaurant/Food Service Manager; Telecommunications Manager; Travel Agent; Typist/Word Processor. **Benefits available to temporary workers:** Paid Holidays; Paid Vacation. **Number of placements per year:** 100 - 199.

ANNE SADOVSKY & COMPANY
7557 Rambler Road, Suite 1454, Dallas TX 75231. 214/692-9300. **Fax:** 214/692-9823. **Contact:** Manager. **Description:** A temporary agency. Company pays fee. **Specializes in the areas of:** Housing; Sales. **Average salary range of placements:** $20,000 - $29,999. **Number of placements per year:** 1000+.

SPECIAL COUNSEL
AMICUS LEGAL STAFFING INC.
901 Main Street, Suite 2830, Dallas TX 75202. 972/934-9111. **Contact:** Manager. **Description:** A temporary agency that also provides some permanent placements and executive searches. **Specializes in the areas of:** Legal.

SUBURBAN SERVICES
4801 Woodway Drive, Suite 260, Houston TX 77056. 713/626-9440. **Fax:** 713/626-9442. **Contact:** Manager. **Description:** A temporary and permanent staffing service. Company pays fee. **Specializes in the areas of:** Administration; Computer Hardware/Software; Industrial; Insurance; Legal; Personnel/Labor Relations; Secretarial. **Positions commonly filled include:** Accountant/Auditor; Bookkeeper; Clerk; Computer Operator; Computer Programmer; Credit Manager; Customer Service Representative; Data Entry Clerk; EDP Specialist; Factory Worker; Legal Secretary; Light Industrial Worker; Marketing Specialist; Medical Secretary; MIS Specialist; Public Relations Specialist; Purchasing Agent/Manager; Receptionist; Sales Representative; Secretary; Software Engineer; Systems Analyst; Technician; Typist/Word Processor. **Number of placements per year:** 100 - 199.

TRC STAFFING SERVICES INC.
1300 Summit Avenue, Suite 634, Fort Worth TX 76102. 817/335-1550. **Contact:** Amy Haines, Operations Manager. **E-mail address:** trc@onramp.net. **Description:** A temporary and temp-to-perm employment agency. Founded in 1990. Company pays fee. **Specializes in the areas of:** Clerical; Industrial; Manufacturing; Secretarial; Technical. **Positions commonly filled include:** Accountant/Auditor; Buyer; Chemist; Claim Representative; Computer Programmer; Customer Service Representative; Paralegal; Systems Analyst; Technical Writer/Editor. **Benefits available to temporary workers:** Medical Insurance; Paid Holidays; Paid Vacation. **Corporate headquarters location:** Atlanta GA. **Number of placements per year:** 1000+.

TEMP 2000 TEMPORARY SERVICES, INC.
14114 North Dallas Parkway, Suite 420, Dallas TX 75240. 972/385-0060. **Contact:** Elizabeth Taylor, Operations Manager. **Description:** A temporary agency. **Specializes in the areas of:** Accounting/Auditing; Legal; Personnel/Labor Relations; Secretarial; Technical. **Positions commonly filled include:** Accountant/Auditor; Clerical Supervisor; Computer Programmer; Customer Service Representative; Human Resources Specialist; MIS Specialist; Paralegal; Systems Analyst; Typist/Word Processor. **Benefits available to temporary workers:** Paid Vacation. **Average salary range of placements:** $20,000 - $29,999. **Number of placements per year:** 100 - 199.

TEMPORARY HELP SERVICE INC.
P.O. Box 53021, Lubbock TX 79453. 806/799-3159. **Fax:** 806/799-0183. **Contact:** John Arland, President. **Description:** A temporary agency. **Specializes in the areas of:** Legal; Manufacturing. **Positions commonly filled include:** Clerical Supervisor.

TEMPORARY RESOURCES, INC.
P.O. Box 3024, Midland TX 79702-3024. 915/684-0527. **Fax:** 915/684-0836. **Contact:** Patricia de Little, President. **Description:** A temporary agency. Company pays fee. **Specializes in the areas of:** Personnel/Labor Relations; Secretarial. **Positions commonly filled include:** Accountant/Auditor; Administrative Manager; Advertising Clerk; Bank Officer/Manager; Branch Manager; Brokerage Clerk; Buyer; Claim Representative; Clerical Supervisor; Customer Service Representative; Draftsperson; General Manager; Health Services Manager; Internet Services Manager; Management Trainee; Manufacturer's/Wholesaler's Sales Rep.; Market Research Analyst; Medical Records Technician; Paralegal; Petroleum Engineer; Quality Control Supervisor; Radio/TV Announcer/Broadcaster; Reporter; Securities Sales Representative; Services Sales Representative; Travel Agent; Typist/Word Processor; Underwriter/Assistant Underwriter. **Benefits available to temporary workers:** Bonus Award/Plan; Medical Insurance; Paid Vacation. **Average salary range of placements:** Less than $20,000. **Number of placements per year:** 1000+.

TODAYS TEMPORARY
4100 Alpha Road, Suite 215, Dallas TX 75244-4332. 972/788-4435. **Contact:** Kristen Prather, Operations Manager. **World Wide Web address:** http://www.todays.com. **Description:** A temporary staffing agency. Company pays fee. **Specializes in the areas of:** Accounting/Auditing; Computer Science/Software; Legal; Personnel/Labor Relations; Sales. **Positions commonly filled include:** Clerical Supervisor; Financial Analyst; Human Resources Specialist; Human Service Worker. **Benefits available to temporary workers:** Paid Holidays; Paid Vacation. **Corporate headquarters location:** 18111 Preston Road, Suite 700, Dallas TX 75252. **Number of placements per year:** 1000+.

TODAYS TEMPORARY
18111 Preston Road, Suite 700, Dallas TX 75252. 972/380-9380. **Fax:** 972/713-4196. **Contact:** Rhonda Page, Communications Manager. **World Wide Web address:** http://www.todays.com. **Description:** A temporary agency. **Specializes in the areas of:** Accounting/Auditing; Banking; Legal; Secretarial. **Positions commonly filled include:** Accountant/Auditor; Administrative Manager; Advertising Clerk; Attorney; Brokerage Clerk; Claim Representative; Computer Programmer; Customer Service Representative; Paralegal; Typist/Word Processor. **Benefits available to temporary workers:** 401(k); Paid Holidays; Paid Vacation. **Corporate headquarters location:** This Location. **Average salary range of placements:** Less than $20,000. **Number of placements per year:** 1000+.

TODAYS TEMPORARY
1900 West Loop South, Suite 110, Houston TX 77027. 713/621-9880. **Fax:** 713/621-9923. **Contact:** Michelle Donahue, Operations Manager. **Description:** A temporary agency. Company pays fee. **Specializes in the areas of:** Administration; Computer Science/Software; Personnel/Labor Relations; Sales; Secretarial. **Positions commonly filled include:** Accountant/Auditor; Administrative Manager; Buyer; Credit Manager; Customer Service Representative; Human Resources Specialist; Services Sales Representative; Typist/Word Processor. **Benefits available to temporary workers:** Paid Holidays; Paid Vacation. **Corporate headquarters location:** Dallas TX. **Average salary range of placements:** Less than $20,000. **Number of placements per year:** 200 - 499.

TOTAL TEMPORARY SERVICES
2901 North 10th Street, Suite P, McAllen TX 78501. 956/631-8367. **Fax:** 956/630-4502. **Contact:** Supervisor. **Description:** A temporary agency. Company pays fee. **Specializes in the areas of:** Accounting/Auditing; Banking; Health/Medical; Industrial; Insurance; Legal; Manufacturing; Retail; Sales; Secretarial; Technical. **Positions commonly filled include:** Accountant/Auditor; Claim Representative; Clerical Supervisor; Customer Service Representative; Electrician; Environmental Engineer; Paralegal; Quality Control Supervisor; Real Estate Agent; Surveyor; Typist/Word Processor. **Corporate headquarters location:** This Location. **Other area locations:** Brownsville TX; Harlinger TX. **Average salary range of placements:** Less than $20,000. **Number of placements per year:** 1000+.

VOLT TEMPORARY SERVICES OF DALLAS
9330 LBJ Freeway, Suite 1060, Dallas TX 75243-9946. 972/690-8358. **Contact:** Office Manager. **Description:** A temporary agency. **Specializes in the areas of:** Clerical; Computer Hardware/Software; Engineering; Manufacturing; Personnel/Labor Relations; Technical.

WESTERN TEMPORARY SERVICE
323 Las Colinas Boulevard East, Irving TX 75039-5556. 972/831-8833. **Fax:** 972/831-8856. **Contact:** Staffing Coordinator. **Description:** A temporary agency. **Specializes in the areas of:** Industrial; Personnel/Labor Relations; Sales; Secretarial; Technical. **Positions commonly filled include:** Blue-Collar Worker Supervisor; Customer Service Rep.; Human Resources Specialist; Management Trainee; Services Sales Rep. **Benefits available to temporary workers:** 401(k); Medical Insurance; Paid Holidays; Paid Vacation. **Corporate headquarters location:** Walnut Creek CA. **Number of placements per year:** 1000+.

CONTRACT SERVICES FIRMS

ABACUS TECHNICAL SERVICE
1701 North Collins Boulevard, Richardson TX 75080. 972/644-4105. **Contact:** Manager. **Description:** A contract services firm. **Specializes in the areas of:** Technical. **Positions commonly filled include:** Computer Programmer.

ALTERNATIVE RESOURCES CORPORATION
1800 West Loop South, Suite 1660, Houston TX 77027. 713/871-9900. **Fax:** 713/871-9038. **Contact:** Manager. **World Wide Web address:** http://www.alrc.com. **Description:** A contract services firm that focuses on information technology services. **Specializes in the areas of:** Technical. **Positions commonly filled include:** MIS Specialist; Technical Writer/Editor.

ALTERNATIVE RESOURCES CORPORATION
15770 North Dallas Parkway, Suite 400, Dallas TX 75248. 972/934-0505. **Contact:** Manager. **World Wide Web address:** http://www.alrc.com. **Description:** A contract services firm.

ARCHITECTURAL CAREER NETWORK
9225 Katy Freeway, Suite 412, Houston TX 77024. 713/464-3838. **Contact:** Keith Lakin, Manager. **Description:** A contract services firm. Client companies include architectural and related engineering and construction firms. Company pays fee. **Specializes in the areas of:** Architecture/Construction; Engineering. **Positions commonly filled include:** Architect; Construction Contractor; Designer; Draftsperson; Interior Designer; Landscape Architect.

B&M AIR & SPACE DIVISION
2925 LBJ Freeway, Suite 278, Dallas TX 75234. 972/241-8408. **Fax:** 972/241-4363. **Contact:** Miguel Zurite, Division Manager. **World Wide Web address:** http://www.bm@net.com. **Description:** A contract services firm. **Specializes in the areas of:** Aerospace; Computer Science/Software; Engineering; Industrial; Personnel/Labor Relations; Scientific; Technical. **Positions commonly filled include:** Aerospace Engineer; Aircraft Mechanic/Engine Specialist; Biomedical Engineer; Chemical Engineer; Chemist; Civil Engineer; Clinical Lab Technician; Computer Programmer; Design Engineer; Designer; Draftsperson; Electrical/Electronics Engineer; Electrician; Environmental Engineer; Human Resources Specialist; Industrial Engineer; Librarian; Management Analyst/Consultant; Mechanical Engineer; Metallurgical Engineer; MIS Specialist; Nuclear Engineer; Petroleum Engineer; Science Technologist; Software Engineer; Structural Engineer; Systems Analyst. **Benefits available to temporary workers:** 401(k); Medical Insurance; Paid Holidays; Paid Vacation. **Average salary range of placements:** More than $50,000. **Number of placements per year:** 1000+.

BELCAN TECHNICAL SERVICES
11482 Luna Road, Suite 100, Dallas TX 75234. 972/401-3636. **Toll-free phone:** 800/288-8418. **Fax:** 972/401-3388. **Contact:** Steven Roth, Team Leader. **E-mail address:** sroth@tech.belcan.com. **World Wide Web address:** http://www.belcan.com. **Description:** A contract services firm. Company pays fee. **Specializes in the areas of:** Administration; Engineering. **Positions commonly filled include:** Aerospace Engineer; Applications Engineer; Buyer; Chemical Engineer; Civil Engineer; Computer Animator; Computer Operator; Computer Programmer; Cost Estimator; Database Manager; Design Engineer; Designer; Draftsperson; Electrical/Electronics Engineer; Environmental Engineer; Graphic Artist; Graphic Designer; Human Resources Specialist; Industrial Engineer; Mechanical Engineer; MIS Specialist; Multimedia Designer; Project Manager; Quality Control Supervisor; Software Engineer; Structural Engineer; Systems Analyst; Systems Manager; Technical Writer/Editor; Telecommunications Manager. **Benefits available to temporary workers:** 401(k); Medical Insurance; Paid Holidays; Paid Vacation. **Corporate headquarters location:** Cincinnati OH. **Other U.S. locations:** Nationwide. **Average salary range of placements:** More than $50,000. **Number of placements per year:** 200 - 499.

BUTLER INTERNATIONAL
914 Royal Lane, Irving TX 76039. 817/355-9655. **Contact:** Manager. **Description:** A contract services firm. Company pays fee. **Specializes in the areas of:** Aerospace; Computer Science/Software; Engineering; Food Industry; Industrial; Manufacturing; Personnel/Labor Relations; Technical. **Positions commonly filled include:** Aircraft Mechanic/Engine Specialist; Budget Analyst; Buyer; Chemical Engineer; Chemist; Civil Engineer; Clinical Lab Technician; Computer Programmer; Cost Estimator; Customer Service Representative; Design Engineer; Designer; Draftsperson; Editor; Electrician; Environmental Engineer; Industrial Engineer; Mechanical Engineer; MIS Specialist; Petroleum Engineer; Software Engineer; Structural Engineer; Systems Analyst; Technical Writer/Editor; Telecommunications Manager. **Benefits available to temporary workers:** Paid Holidays; Paid Vacation. **Corporate headquarters**

location: Montvale NJ. **Number of placements per year:** 200 - 499.

CDI CORPORATION
P.O. Box 14422, Austin TX 78761. 512/837-1073. **Fax:** 512/832-9568. **Contact:** Manager. **World Wide Web address:** http://www.cdicorp.com. **Description:** A contract services firm. **Specializes in the areas of:** Engineering; Technical. **Corporate headquarters location:** Philadelphia PA. **Other U.S. locations:** Nationwide. **International locations:** Worldwide.

CDI CORPORATION
1810 Laurel Avenue, Beaumont TX 77701. 409/835-5290. **Contact:** Manager. **World Wide Web address:** http://www.cdicorp.com. **Description:** A contract services firm. **Specializes in the areas of:** Engineering; Technical. **Corporate headquarters location:** Philadelphia PA. **Other U.S. locations:** Nationwide. **International locations:** Worldwide.

CAREER PARTNERS
P.O. Box 167101, Irving TX 75016-7101. 972/518-0104. **Fax:** 972/518-0287. **Contact:** Cliff Taylor, Owner/Manager. **Description:** A contract services firm. **Specializes in the areas of:** Information Systems. **Positions commonly filled include:** Computer Programmer; MIS Specialist; Software Engineer; Systems Analyst; Telecommunications Manager. **Average salary range of placements:** More than $50,000. **Number of placements per year:** 50 - 99.

CARLTECH
24 Greenway Plaza, Suite 1204, Houston TX 77046. 713/629-5700. **Toll-free phone:** 800/324-5050. **Fax:** 713/629-4209. **Contact:** Sales Manager. **E-mail address:** carltech@firstnethou.com. **Description:** A contract services firm. **Specializes in the areas of:** Computer Science/Software; Engineering; Technical. **Positions commonly filled include:** Chemical Engineer; Civil Engineer; Computer Programmer; Design Engineer; Designer; Draftsperson; Electrical/Electronics Engineer; Environmental Engineer; Mechanical Engineer; MIS Specialist; Software Engineer; Structural Engineer; Systems Analyst. **Benefits available to temporary workers:** 401(k); Paid Vacation. **Average salary range of placements:** $30,000 - $50,000. **Number of placements per year:** 100 - 199.

CERTIFIED PERSONNEL SERVICE INC.
P.O. Box 1677, Pasadena TX 77501. 713/477-0321. **Toll-free phone:** 800/234-8054. **Fax:** 713/477-2194. **Contact:** Tom Warren, President. **Description:** A contract services firm. Founded in 1974. Company pays fee. **Specializes in the areas of:** Accounting/Auditing; Architecture/Construction; Computer Science/Software; Engineering; Industrial; Manufacturing; Personnel/Labor Relations; Secretarial. **Positions commonly filled include:** Accountant/Auditor; Chemical Engineer; Chemist; Civil Engineer; Computer Programmer; Construction and Building Inspector; Construction Contractor; Cost Estimator; Counselor; Design Engineer; Designer; Draftsperson; Electrical/Electronics Engineer; Electrician; Human Resources Specialist; Mechanical Engineer; Purchasing Agent/Manager; Software Engineer; Stationary Engineer; Systems Analyst; Technical Writer/Editor. **Benefits available to temporary workers:** 401(k); Medical Insurance; Paid Holidays; Paid Vacation. **Average salary range of placements:** $30,000 - $50,000. **Number of placements per year:** 1000+.

COMFORCE INFORMATION TECHNOLOGIES, INC.
5055 Keller Springs, Suite 550, Dallas TX 75248. 972/248-8555. **Fax:** 972/248-3181. **Contact:** Manager. **Description:** A contract services firm. **Specializes in the areas of:** Computer Science/Software.

CORECOM
9430 Research Boulevard, Building 1, Suite 120, Austin TX 78759. 512/343-1747. **Fax:** 512/343-6677. **Contact:** Manager. **Description:** A contract services firm. **Specializes in the areas of:** Computer Science/Software; Engineering; Health/Medical; Publishing; Technical. **Positions commonly filled include:** Public Relations Specialist; Technical Writer/Editor. **Benefits available to temporary workers:** Dental Insurance; Medical Insurance. **Average salary range of placements:** $30,000 - $50,000. **Number of placements per year:** 50 - 99.

DSI STAFF CONNXIONS
P.O. Box 2665, Houston TX 77252-2665. **Contact:** Manager. **Description:** A staff leasing agency. **Specializes in the areas of:** Payroll.

DESIGN QUEST INC.
P.O. Box 6555, Tyler TX 75711. 903/561-6241. **Fax:** 903/534-9170. **Contact:** Louis Adams, Recruiter. **Description:** A contract services firm that provides technical engineering support to companies. **Specializes in the areas of:** Engineering; Personnel/Labor Relations. **Positions commonly filled include:** Chemical Engineer; Civil Engineer; Design Engineer; Designer; Draftsperson; Electrical/Electronics Engineer; Industrial Engineer; Mechanical Engineer; Petroleum Engineer; Structural Engineer. **Average salary range of placements:** More than $50,000. **Number of placements per year:** 100 - 199.

EDP STAFFING SERVICES
4500 Fuller Drive, Suite 405, Irving TX 75038. 972/650-8384. **Contact:** Manager. **Description:** A contract services firm. **Specializes in the areas of:** Computer Hardware/Software; Technical.

FOCUS POINT, INC.
13201 Northwest Freeway, Suite 520, Houston TX 77040-6008. 713/939-7644. **Fax:** 713/939-7355. **Contact:** Randy Williams, Branch Manager. **Description:** A contract services firm that places technical personnel. Company pays fee. **Specializes in the areas of:** Computer Science/Software; Engineering; Industrial; Manufacturing; Technical. **Positions commonly filled include:** Aerospace Engineer; Architect; Biomedical Engineer; Branch Manager; Buyer; Ceramics Engineer; Chemical Engineer; Chemist; Civil Engineer; Computer Programmer; Construction Contractor; Cost Estimator; Design Engineer; Designer; Draftsperson; Electrical/Electronics Engineer; Environmental Engineer; General Manager; Geologist/Geophysicist; Human Resources Specialist; Industrial Engineer; Industrial Production Manager; Internet Services Manager; Materials Engineer; Mechanical Engineer; Metallurgical Engineer; Mining Engineer; MIS Specialist; Multimedia Designer; Nuclear Engineer; Petroleum Engineer; Purchasing Agent/Manager; Quality Control Supervisor; Science Technologist; Software Engineer; Structural Engineer; Surveyor; Systems Analyst; Technical Writer/Editor; Telecommunications Manager. **Benefits available to temporary workers:** Paid Holidays. **Corporate headquarters location:** Dallas TX. **Average salary range of placements:** $30,000 - $50,000. **Number of placements per year:** 100 - 199.

HEALTHCARE PROVIDERS
9100 Southwest Freeway, Houston TX 77074. 713/778-0114. **Contact:** Manager. **Description:** Provides contract placements in hospitals. **Specializes in the areas of:** Health/Medical. **Positions commonly filled include:** Respiratory Therapist.

L.K. JORDAN & ASSOCIATES
321 Texan Trail, Suite 100, Corpus Christi TX 78411. 512/814-9700. **Contact:** Recruiter. **Description:** A contract services firm. Company pays fee. **Specializes in the areas of:** Accounting/Auditing; Administration; Engineering; Industrial; Secretarial. **Positions commonly filled include:** Accountant/Auditor; Administrative Manager; Branch Manager; Chemical Engineer; Civil Engineer; Clerical Supervisor; Computer Programmer; Design Engineer; Financial Analyst; Human Resources Specialist; Mechanical Engineer; MIS Specialist; Pharmacist; Purchasing Agent/Manager; Registered Nurse; Services Sales Representative; Software Engineer; Structural Engineer; Systems Analyst; Typist/Word Processor. **Average salary range of placements:** $30,000 - $50,000. **Number of placements per year:** 100 - 199.

PROFESSIONAL SEARCH CONSULTANTS
3050 Post Oak Boulevard, Suite 1615, Houston TX 77056. 713/960-9215. **Fax:** 713/960-1172. **Contact:** L. Malek, Manager. **Description:** A contract services firm. **Specializes in the areas of:** Accounting/Auditing; Computer Science/Software; Engineering; Finance; General Management; Health/Medical; Information Technology; Manufacturing; Personnel/Labor Relations; Sales; Technical. **Positions commonly filled include:** Accountant/Auditor; Attorney; Budget Analyst; Chemical Engineer; Computer Programmer; Construction Contractor; Cost Estimator; Design Engineer; EEG Technologist; EKG Technician; Electrical/Electronics Engineer; Environmental Engineer; Financial Analyst; General Manager; Geologist/Geophysicist; Human Resources Specialist; Industrial Engineer; Industrial Production Manager; Market Research Analyst; Materials Engineer; Mechanical Engineer; Metallurgical Engineer; MIS Specialist; Multimedia Designer; Occupational Therapist; Operations/Production Manager; Petroleum Engineer; Physician; Recreational Therapist; Registered Nurse; Software Engineer; Structural Engineer; Systems Analyst; Telecommunications Manager. **Average salary range of placements:** More than $50,000. **Number of placements per year:** 50 - 99.

PROVISION TECHNOLOGIES
5930 LBJ Freeway, Suite 301, Dallas TX 75240. 972/503-8500. **Fax:** 800/277-2037. **Contact:** Manager. **E-mail address:** information@provisiondallas.com. **World Wide Web address:** http://www.provisiondallas.com. **Description:** A contract services and consulting firm that also provides some permanent placements. **Specializes in the areas of:** Computer Science/Software; Information Technology.

PROVISION TECHNOLOGIES
6101 Balcones Drive, Suite 202, Austin TX 78731. 512/458-2577. **Fax:** 512/452-7401. **Contact:** Manager. **World Wide Web address:** http://www.careerbase.com. **Description:** A contract services and consulting firm. **Specializes in the areas of:** Computer Science/Software; Information Technology.

PROVISION TECHNOLOGIES
2620 Fountain View, Suite 318, Houston TX 77057. 713/706-3282. **Fax:** 713/789-8517. **Contact:** Manager. **World Wide Web address:** http://www.careerbase.com. **Description:** A contract services and consulting firm. **Specializes in the areas of:** Computer Science/Software; Information Technology.

REHABWORKS
9535 Forest Lane, Suite 114, Dallas TX 75243. 972/480-8034. **Contact:** Manager. **Description:** One of two contract rehabilitation companies owned by Horizon Healthcare Corporation. Together, Community Rehabilitation Center and RehabWorks provide occupational, speech, and physical therapy services to patients in nursing homes and geriatric units at hospitals through 276 contracts, covering approximately 31,000 beds. **Specializes in the areas of:** Health/Medical.

RESOURCE STAFFING
1360 Post Oak Road, Suite 745, Houston TX 77056. 713/621-9895. **Fax:** 713/621-8832. **Contact:** Lisa Kay Smith, Staffing Manager. **E-mail address:** staffing@onramp.net. **World Wide Web address:** http://www.onramp.net/~staffing. **Description:** A contract services firm. Founded in 1988. Company pays fee. **Specializes in the areas of:** Accounting/Auditing; Administration; Banking; Computer Science/Software; Finance; Legal; Personnel/Labor Relations; Sales; Secretarial. **Positions commonly filled include:** Accountant/Auditor; Computer Programmer; Credit Manager; Customer Service Representative; Human Resources Specialist; Internet Services Manager; MIS Specialist; Multimedia Designer; Software Engineer; Systems Analyst; Technical Writer/Editor; Typist/Word Processor. **Benefits available to temporary workers:** Paid Holidays; Referral Bonus Plan. **Other area locations:** Dallas TX. **Average salary range of placements:** $20,000 - $29,999. **Number of placements per year:** 1 - 49.

ROBERT SHIELDS & ASSOCIATES
P.O. Box 890723, Houston TX 77289-0723. 281/488-7961. **Toll-free phone:** 800/423-5383. **Fax:** 281/486-1496. **Contact:** Manager. **E-mail address:** itjobs@aol.com. **Description:** A contract services firm. Company pays fee. **Specializes in the areas of:** Computer Science/Software; Engineering. **Positions commonly filled include:** Chemical Engineer; Computer Programmer; MIS Specialist; Software Engineer; Systems Analyst. **Average salary range of placements:** More than $50,000. **Number of placements per year:** 100 - 199.

TAD TECHNICAL SERVICES
4300 Alpha Road, Suite 100, Dallas TX 75244. 972/980-0510. **Contact:** Manager. **Description:** A contract services firm. **Specializes in the areas of:** Administration; Aerospace; Clerical; Computer Hardware/Software; Engineering; Manufacturing; Technical. **Corporate headquarters location:** Cambridge MA. **Other U.S. locations:** Nationwide. **International locations:** Canada; England.

TAD TECHNICAL SERVICES
4160 SW H.K. Dodgen Loop, Temple TX 76504. 254/773-3366. **Fax:** 254/773-4555. **Contact:** Branch Manager. **Description:** A contract services firm. **Specializes in the areas of:** Accounting/Auditing; Computer Science/Software; Engineering; Health/Medical; Industrial; Manufacturing; Personnel/Labor Relations; Secretarial. **Positions commonly filled include:** Accountant/Auditor; Aerospace Engineer; Architect; Blue-Collar Worker Supervisor; Budget Analyst; Chemical Engineer; Chemist; Civil Engineer; Clerical Supervisor; Clinical Lab Technician; Computer Programmer; Customer Service Representative; Design Engineer; Designer; Draftsperson; Editor; Electrical/Electronics Engineer; Electrician; Environmental Engineer; Financial Analyst; Human Resources Specialist; Industrial Engineer; Industrial Production Manager; Internet Services Manager; Licensed Practical Nurse; Manufacturer's/Wholesaler's Sales Rep.; Market Research Analyst; Mathematician; Mechanical Engineer; Medical Records Technician; Metallurgical Engineer; MIS Specialist; Multimedia Designer; Occupational Therapist; Operations/Production Manager; Public Relations Specialist; Purchasing Agent/Manager; Quality Control Supervisor; Registered Nurse; Services Sales Representative; Software Engineer; Structural

Engineer; Systems Analyst; Technical Writer/Editor; Telecommunications Manager. **Benefits available to temporary workers:** 401(k); Medical Insurance; Paid Holidays. **Corporate headquarters location:** Cambridge MA. **Other U.S. locations:** Nationwide. **International locations:** Canada; England. **Average salary range of placements:** $20,000 - $29,999. **Number of placements per year:** 200 - 499.

TAD TECHNICAL SERVICES
901 North McDonald Street, Suite 405, McKinney TX 75069. 972/542-6175. **Fax:** 972/758-2116. **Contact:** K. Carter, Recruiter. **E-mail address:** clawson1@airmail.net. **World Wide Web address:** http://www.webz.airmail.net/tadtech1. **Description:** A contract services firm that also provides temporary placements. **Specializes in the areas of:** Accounting/Auditing; Administration; Art/Design; Computer Science/Software; Engineering; General Management; Industrial; Light Industrial; Sales; Secretarial; Technical. **Positions commonly filled include:** Chemical Engineer; Chemist; Civil Engineer; Computer Programmer; Design Engineer; Designer; Draftsperson; Electrical/Electronics Engineer; Industrial Engineer; Industrial Production Manager; Mechanical Engineer; MIS Specialist; Software Engineer; Systems Analyst; Technical Writer/Editor; Telecommunications Manager. **Benefits available to temporary workers:** 401(k); Dental Insurance; Medical Insurance; Paid Holidays; Paid Vacation; Vision Insurance. **Corporate headquarters location:** Cambridge MA. **Other U.S. locations:** Nationwide. **International locations:** Canada; England. **Average salary range of placements:** More than $50,000. **Number of placements per year:** 1000+.

TECHNICAL CAREERS
12750 Merit Drive, Suite 1430, Dallas TX 75251. 972/991-9424. **Fax:** 972/851-0651. **Contact:** Cary Tobolka, President. **E-mail address:** rng@connect.net. **World Wide Web address:** http://www.technicalcareers.com. **Description:** A contract services firm operating on both retainer and contingency bases. Founded in 1978. **Specializes in the areas of:** Computer Science/Software; Engineering; Industrial; Manufacturing; Personnel/Labor Relations; Technical. **Positions commonly filled include:** Aerospace Engineer; Agricultural Engineer; Chemical Engineer; Civil Engineer; Computer Programmer; Design Engineer; Designer; Electrical/Electronics Engineer; Environmental Engineer; Human Resources Specialist; Industrial Engineer; Industrial Production Manager; Internet Services Manager; Management Analyst/Consultant; Manufacturer's/Wholesaler's Sales Rep.; Mechanical Engineer; Metallurgical Engineer; MIS Specialist; Multimedia Designer; Nuclear Engineer; Purchasing Agent/Manager; Quality Control Supervisor; Science Technologist; Software Engineer; Structural Engineer; Systems Analyst; Telecommunications Manager. **Benefits available to temporary workers:** Dental Insurance; Life Insurance; Medical Insurance; Retirement Plan. **Corporate headquarters location:** This Location. **Other area locations:** Addison TX. **Other U.S. locations:** San Diego CA. **Average salary range of placements:** More than $50,000. **Number of placements per year:** 100 - 199.

TECHNICAL CAREERS
15851 Dallas Parkway, Suite 960, Dallas TX 75248. 972/789-5313. **Contact:** Manager. **Description:** A contract services firm. **Corporate headquarters location:** 12750 Merit Drive, Suite 1430, Dallas TX 75251. **Other U.S. locations:** San Diego CA.

TECHSYSTEMS
12710 Research Boulevard, Suite 205, Austin TX 78759. 512/331-4009. **Fax:** 512/331-6299. **Contact:** Technical Recruiter. **Description:** A contract services firm. Company pays fee. **Specializes in the areas of:** Computer Science/Software; Engineering; Industrial; Manufacturing; Personnel/Labor Relations; Publishing. **Positions commonly filled include:** Administrative Manager; Aerospace Engineer; Agricultural Engineer; Aircraft Mechanic/Engine Specialist; Biochemist; Biological Scientist; Biomedical Engineer; Buyer; Chemical Engineer; Chemist; Civil Engineer; Clinical Lab Technician; Computer Programmer; Design Engineer; Designer; Draftsperson; Editor; EKG Technician; Electrical/Electronics Engineer; Electrician; Environmental Engineer; Geographer; Geologist/Geophysicist; Human Service Worker; Industrial Engineer; Internet Services Manager; Market Research Analyst; Mechanical Engineer; Petroleum Engineer; Preschool Worker; Psychologist; Software Engineer; Stationary Engineer; Structural Engineer; Systems Analyst. **Corporate headquarters location:** Baltimore MD. **Other U.S. locations:** Nationwide. **Number of placements per year:** 1000+.

TRIPLEX COMPUTER CORPORATION
P.O. Box 1949, Sugar Land TX 77487-1949. 281/240-6263. **Contact:** Manager. **Description:** A contract services firm that also provides permanent placements. **Specializes in the areas of:** Computer Science/Software.

UNIVERSAL REHABILITATION SERVICES, INC.
P.O. Box 691689, Houston TX 77269-1689. 281/820-9462. **Fax:** 281/820-0769. **Contact:** Ron McCreight, Executive Director. **Description:** A contract services firm that provides personnel to health care facilities and home health agencies. **Positions commonly filled include:** Occupational Therapist; Physical Therapist; Social Worker; Speech-Language Pathologist. **Average salary range of placements:** More than $50,000. **Number of placements per year:** 100 - 199.

VOLT TECHNICAL SERVICES
1800 St. James Place, Suite 204, Houston TX 77056-4109. 713/626-8658. **Fax:** 713/626-8660. **Contact:** Russell Moores, Branch Manager. **E-mail address:** voltexas@ix.netcom.com. **Description:** A contract services firm. Founded in 1951. **Specializes in the areas of:** Engineering; Industrial; Manufacturing; Technical. **Positions commonly filled include:** Chemical Engineer; Chemist; Civil Engineer; Clinical Lab Technician; Computer Programmer; Construction Contractor; Cost Estimator; Design Engineer; Designer; Draftsperson; Electrical/Electronics Engineer; Environmental Engineer; Geologist/Geophysicist; Industrial Engineer; Internet Services Manager; Mechanical Engineer; Mining Engineer; MIS Specialist; Petroleum Engineer; Software Engineer; Structural Engineer; Systems Analyst; Technical Writer/Editor. **Benefits available to temporary workers:** 401(k); Medical Insurance; Paid Holidays; Paid Vacation. **Corporate headquarters location:** New York NY. **Other U.S. locations:** Nationwide. **Number of placements per year:** 100 - 199.

VOLT TECHNICAL SERVICES
275 West Campbell Road, Suite 211, Richardson TX 75080. 972/669-0458. **Toll-free phone:** 800/531-7426. **Fax:** 972/669-9749. **Contact:** Katherine Lockwood, Regional Manager. **E-mail address:** lockwood@gte.net. **Description:** A contract services firm. **Specializes in the areas of:** Computer Science/Software; Engineering; Technical. **Positions commonly filled include:** Administrative Manager; Aerospace Engineer; Aircraft Mechanic/Engine Specialist; Biochemist; Biomedical Engineer; Budget Analyst; Buyer; Chemical Engineer; Chemist; Civil Engineer; Computer Programmer; Design Engineer; Designer; Draftsperson; Electrical/Electronics Engineer;

Electrician; Environmental Engineer; Human Resources Specialist; Industrial Engineer; Industrial Production Manager; Software Engineer; Statistician; Strategic Relations Manager; Systems Analyst; Technical Writer/Editor; Telecommunications Manager. **Corporate headquarters location:** New York NY. **Other U.S. locations:** Nationwide. **Average salary range of placements:** $30,000 - $50,000. **Number of placements per year:** 500 - 999.

H.L. YOH COMPANY
3730 Kirby Drive, Suite 810, Houston TX 77098. 713/661-1100. **Fax:** 713/661-9507. **Contact:** David Baio, Manager. **Description:** A contract services firm. **Specializes in the areas of:** Administration; Architecture/Construction; Computer Hardware/ Software; Engineering; Manufacturing; Personnel/ Labor Relations; Technical. **Positions commonly filled include:** Aerospace Engineer; Architect; Buyer; Chemical Engineer; Chemist; Civil Engineer; Commercial Artist; Computer Operator; Computer Programmer; Data Entry Clerk; Draftsperson; Driver; Editor; EDP Specialist; Electrical/Electronics Engineer; Human Resources Manager; Industrial Designer; Industrial Engineer; Manufacturing Engineer; Mechanical Engineer; Metallurgical Engineer; MIS Specialist; Operations/Production Manager; Purchasing Agent/Manager; Quality Control Supervisor; Reporter; Software Engineer; Systems Analyst; Technical Illustrator; Technical Writer/Editor; Technician; Typist/Word Processor. **Number of placements per year:** 200 - 499.

H.L. YOH COMPANY
13601 Preston Road, Suite 1020E, Dallas TX 75240. 972/239-9875. **Contact:** Manager. **Description:** A contract services firm. **Specializes in the areas of:** Architecture/Construction; Computer Hardware/ Software; Engineering; Manufacturing; Technical.

H.L. YOH COMPANY
7800 Shoal Creek Boulevard, Suite 129 South, Austin TX 78757. 512/302-3373. **Contact:** Manager. **Description:** A contract services firm. **Specializes in the areas of:** High-Tech.

CAREER/OUTPLACEMENT COUNSELING FIRMS

ALLEN & ASSOCIATES
4099 McEwen, Suite 150, Dallas TX 75244. 972/385-7112. **Toll-free phone:** 800/562-7214. **Fax:** 972/788-2131. **Contact:** Manager. **World Wide Web address:** http://www.allenandassociates.com. **Description:** A career/outplacement counseling firm. **Corporate headquarters location:** Maitland FL. **Other U.S. locations:** Nationwide.

ALLEN & ASSOCIATES
5444 Westhierner Boulevard, Suite 1967, Houston TX 77056. 713/960-9603. **Toll-free phone:** 800/562-7567. **Fax:** 713/960-9796. **Contact:** Manager. **World Wide Web address:** http://www.allenandassociates.com. **Description:** A career/outplacement counseling service. **Corporate headquarters location:** Maitland FL. **Other U.S. locations:** Nationwide.

FAIRCHILD BARKLEY & ASSOCIATES
15770 Dallas Parkway, Dallas TX 75248. 972/387-4800. **Fax:** 972/386-5210. **Contact:** R.J. Porter, President. **Description:** A career/outplacement counseling service. Company pays fee. **Positions commonly filled include:** Accountant/Auditor; Administrative Manager; Aerospace Engineer; Agricultural Engineer; Architect; Bank Officer/ Manager; Biochemist; Biomedical Engineer; Branch Manager; Budget Analyst; Chemical Engineer; Civil Engineer; Claim Representative; Clerical Supervisor; Computer Programmer; Cost Estimator; Credit Manager; Customer Service Representative; Design Engineer; Economist; Environmental Engineer; Industrial Engineer; Management Analyst/Consultant; MIS Specialist; Operations/Production Manager; Petroleum Engineer; Public Relations Specialist; Restaurant/Food Service Manager; Services Sales Representative; Structural Engineer; Systems Analyst; Telecommunications Manager. **Average salary range of placements:** More than $50,000. **Number of placements per year:** 100 - 199.

SER-JOBS FOR PROGRESS, INC.
1817 East 6th Street, Austin TX 78702. 512/473-8966. **Contact:** Operations Manager. **Description:** A career/outplacement counseling firm that provides employment and resume assistance. Founded in 1972. **Specializes in the areas of:** Education; Nonprofit. **Positions commonly filled include:** Counselor; Customer Service Representative; Management Trainee; MIS Specialist; Services Sales Representative; Typist/Word Processor. **Other area locations:** Dallas TX. **International locations:** Puerto Rico. **Average salary range of placements:** $20,000 - $29,999. **Number of placements per year:** 100 - 199.

UTAH

EXECUTIVE SEARCH FIRMS

ACCOUNTSTAFF
3098 South Highland Drive, Highland Park Plaza, Suite 260, Salt Lake City UT 84106. 801/463-7700. **Contact:** Manager. **Description:** An executive search firm. **Specializes in the areas of:** Accounting/Auditing.

APOGEE ASSOCIATES
2565 East Rockhampton Road, Sandy UT 84092. 801/576-1790. **Contact:** Manager. **Description:** An executive search firm. **Specializes in the areas of:** Computer Hardware/Software.

CDI INFORMATION SERVICES
5500 West Amelia Earhart Drive, Salt Lake City UT 84116. 801/521-8621. **Toll-free phone:** 800/536-8624. **Fax:** 801/521-8611. **Contact:** John Axelsen, Manager. **World Wide Web address:** http://www.cdicorp.com. **Description:** An executive search firm operating on both retained and contingency bases. Company pays fee. **Specializes in the areas of:** Computer Science/Software; Engineering; Finance. **Positions commonly filled include:** Computer Operator; Computer Programmer; Database Manager; Internet Services Manager; MIS Specialist; Online Content Specialist; Software Engineer; Systems Analyst; Systems Manager; Technical Writer/Editor; Telecommunications Manager. **Benefits available to temporary workers:** 401(k); Dental Insurance; Medical Insurance; Paid Vacation. **Corporate headquarters location:** Philadelphia PA. **Other U.S. locations:** Nationwide. **International locations:** Worldwide.

DENTAL PERSONNEL
2469 East Fort Union Boulevard, Suite 100-1, Midvale UT 84121. 801/942-2992. **Contact:** Manager. **Description:** An executive search firm. **Specializes in the areas of:** Dental.

F-O-R-T-U-N-E PERSONNEL CONSULTANTS
1536 North Woodland Park Drive, Suite 200, Salt Lake City UT 84041. 801/775-0444. **Fax:** 801/775-0447. **Contact:** Manager. **Description:** An executive search firm. **Specializes in the areas of:** Engineering. **Corporate headquarters location:** New York NY. **Other U.S. locations:** Nationwide.

ROBERT HALF INTERNATIONAL
50 West Broadway, Suite 500, Salt Lake City UT 84101. 801/364-5500. **Fax:** 801/364-3585. **Contact:** Recruiter. **World Wide Web address:** http://www.rhii.com. **Description:** An executive search firm. **Specializes in the areas of:** Accounting/Auditing; Administration; Finance; Secretarial. **Positions commonly filled include:** Account Manager; Administrative Assistant; Administrative Manager; Auditor; Bank Officer/Manager; Controller; Cost Estimator; Credit Manager; Customer Service Representative; Finance Director; Financial Analyst; Secretary; Typist/Word Processor. **Benefits available to temporary workers:** Dental Insurance; Medical Insurance; Paid Holidays; Paid Vacation; Vision Insurance. **Corporate headquarters location:** Menlo Park CA. **Other U.S. locations:** Nationwide. **International locations:** Worldwide. **Average salary range of placements:** $30,000 - $50,000. **Number of placements per year:** 50 - 99.

ROBERT HALF INTERNATIONAL ACCOUNTEMPS
7090 South Union Park Avenue, Suite 240, Midvale UT 84047. 801/569-9400. **Contact:** Manager. **World Wide Web address:** http://www.roberthalf.com. **Description:** An executive search firm. Accountemps (also at this location) provides temporary placements. **Specializes in the areas of:** Accounting/Auditing. **Corporate headquarters location:** Menlo Park CA. **Other U.S. locations:** Nationwide.

MANAGEMENT RECRUITERS INTERNATIONAL
6600 South 1100 East, Suite 520, Salt Lake City UT 84121. 801/264-9800. **Fax:** 801/264-9807. **Contact:** Recruiter. **E-mail address:** jobsusa@mrislc.com. **World Wide Web address:** http://www.mrislc.com. **Description:** An executive search firm operating on both retained and contingency bases. Company pays fee. **Specializes in the areas of:** Accounting/Auditing; Administration; Banking; Biology; Computer Science/Software; Engineering; Finance; General Management; Health/Medical; Industrial; Sales; Technical. **Corporate headquarters location:** Cleveland OH. **Other U.S. locations:** Nationwide.

MANAGEMENT RECRUITERS OF OGDEN
533 26th Street, Suite 203, Ogden UT 84401-2459. 801/621-1777. **Fax:** 801/621-1788. **Contact:** Jerry Manning, Manager. **Description:** An executive search firm operating on a contingency basis. Management Recruiters focuses on placing technical professionals in general manufacturing areas as well as HVAC, major appliances, and printing industries. Founded in 1994. Company pays fee. **Specializes in the areas of:** Engineering; General Management; Industrial; Manufacturing; Publishing. **Positions commonly filled include:** Aerospace Engineer; Design Engineer; Designer; Draftsperson; Electrical/Electronics Engineer; Environmental Engineer; Human Resources Manager; Industrial Engineer; Management Analyst/Consultant; Materials Engineer; Mechanical Engineer; Quality Control Supervisor; Statistician; Structural Engineer. **Corporate headquarters location:** Cleveland OH. **Other U.S. locations:** Nationwide. **Average salary range of placements:** $30,000 - $50,000. **Number of placements per year:** 1 - 49.

MANAGEMENT RECRUITERS OF PROVO
2230 North University Parkway, Building 11-I, Provo UT 84604-1509. 801/375-0777. **Fax:** 801/375-5757. **Contact:** Larry J. Massung, General Manager. **E-mail address:** gen_mgr@recruitr.com. **Description:** An executive search firm. Founded in 1994. Company pays fee. **Specializes in the areas of:** Automation/Robotics; Computer Science/Software; Engineering; Finance; General Management; Information Technology; Manufacturing; Technical. **Positions commonly filled include:** Computer Programmer; Controller; Design Engineer; Electrical/Electronics Engineer; Financial Analyst; General Manager; Industrial Engineer; Market Research Analyst; Mechanical Engineer; MIS Specialist; Operations/Production Manager; Quality Control Supervisor; Software Engineer; Systems Analyst. **Corporate headquarters location:** Cleveland OH. **International locations:** Worldwide. **Average salary range of placements:** More than $50,000. **Number of placements per year:** 50 - 99.

PRINCE, PERELSON & ASSOCIATES
19 East 200 South, Suite 1000, Salt Lake City UT 84111. 801/532-1000. **Contact:** Manager. **Description:** An executive search firm. **Specializes in the areas of:** Engineering; Manufacturing.

PROFESSIONAL RECRUITERS TEMPORARY RESOURCES
220 East 3900 South, Suite 9, Salt Lake City UT 84107. 801/268-9940. **Contact:** Lora Lea Mock, Owner. **Description:** An executive search firm. Temporary Resources (also at this location) provides

temporary placements. **Specializes in the areas of:** Accounting/Auditing; Administration; Computer Hardware/Software; Electrical; Engineering; General Management; Manufacturing; Medical Sales and Marketing; Technical. **Number of placements per year:** 500 - 999.

STM ASSOCIATES
230 South 500 East, Suite 500, Salt Lake City UT 84102. 801/531-6500. **Fax:** 801/531-6062. **Contact:** Recruiter. **Description:** An executive search firm.

SANFORD ROSE ASSOCIATES
8941 Upper Lando Lane, Park City UT 84098. 435/647-9755. **Fax:** 435/647-9069. **Contact:** Recruiter. **World Wide Web address:** http://www.sanfordrose.com. **Description:** An executive search firm. **Other U.S. locations:** Nationwide.

SOURCE SERVICES CORPORATION
505 East 200 South, Suite 300, Salt Lake City UT 84102. 801/328-0011. **Fax:** 801/363-3574. **Contact:** Manager. **Description:** An executive search firm. The divisions at this location include Source Consulting, Source EDP, Source Finance, and Accountant Source Temps. **Specializes in the areas of:** Accounting/Auditing; Computer Hardware/Software; Finance; Information Technology.

TROUT & ASSOCIATES, INC.
15 Gatehouse Lane, Sandy UT 84092-4846. 801/576-1547. **Fax:** 801/576-1541. **Contact:** Thomas L. Trout, President. **Description:** An executive search firm operating on a retainer basis. Trout & Associates also provides outplacement and career counseling for client companies and individuals. Founded in 1973. Company pays fee. **Specializes in the areas of:** Accounting/Auditing; Computer Science/Software; Engineering; Finance; Health/Medical; Manufacturing; Technical. **Positions commonly filled include:** Accountant/Auditor; Aerospace Engineer; Chemical Engineer; Computer Programmer; Design Engineer; Financial Analyst; General Manager; Materials Engineer; Mechanical Engineer; MIS Specialist; Software Engineer; Systems Analyst. **International locations:** Worldwide. **Average salary range of placements:** More than $50,000. **Number of placements per year:** 1 - 49.

PERMANENT EMPLOYMENT AGENCIES

DEECO INTERNATIONAL
P.O. Box 57033, Salt Lake City UT 84157. 801/261-3326. **Fax:** 801/261-3955. **Contact:** Dee McBride, Manager. **Description:** A permanent employment agency. Company pays fee. **Specializes in the areas of:** Computer Science/Software; Health/Medical; Sales; Technical. **Positions commonly filled include:** Biomedical Engineer; Design Engineer; Software Engineer. **Average salary range of placements:** More than $50,000.

EXPRESS PERSONNEL SERVICES
56 East 7800 South, Midvale UT 84047. 801/255-1441. **Fax:** 801/255-1488. **Contact:** Recruiter. **Description:** A permanent agency that also provides temporary placements. **Other U.S. locations:** Nationwide.

FRANKLIN-NEWBERY ENGINEERING
655 East 4500 South, Suite 102, Murray UT 84107. 801/261-3282. **Contact:** Manager. **Description:** A permanent placement agency. **Specializes in the areas of:** Technical.

THE NANNY CONNECTION
1231 South 425 West, Bountiful UT 84010. 801/295-6496. **Contact:** Linda Farrer, Director. **E-mail address:** nannyconnect@unidial.com. **Description:** A permanent employment agency. **Specializes in the areas of:** Nannies. **Number of placements per year:** 100 - 199.

SNELLING PERSONNEL SERVICES
1030 West 4500 South, Suite 202, Salt Lake City UT 84123. 801/268-8444. **Fax:** 801/268-8796. **Contact:** Recruiter. **Description:** A permanent employment agency that also provides temporary placements. **Corporate headquarters location:** Dallas TX. **Other U.S. locations:** Nationwide.

STAFFING LOGIC
545 East 4500 South, Building E, Suite 165, Murray UT 84107. 801/263-1113. **Fax:** 801/263-1191. **Contact:** Manager. **Description:** An employment agency. Staffing Logic provides both permanent (70 percent) and temporary (30 percent) placement. The company interviews, screens, tests, and counsels individuals before placement and focuses highly on out-of-state orientation and assistance. Company pays fee. **Specializes in the areas of:** Accounting/Auditing; Engineering; Legal; Manufacturing; Personnel/Labor Relations; Secretarial. **Positions commonly filled include:** Accountant/Auditor; Blue-Collar Worker Supervisor; Civil Engineer; Claim Rep.; Clerical Supervisor; Clinical Lab Technician; Computer Programmer; Credit Manager; Customer Service Rep.; Draftsperson; Human Resources Manager; Industrial Engineer; Industrial Production Manager; Management Trainee; Materials Engineer; Paralegal; Purchasing Agent/Manager; Quality Control Supervisor; Sales Rep. **Average salary range of placements:** $20,000 - $29,999. **Number of placements per year:** 100 - 199.

YOUR JOB CONNECTION
1399 South 700 East, Salt Lake City UT 84105. 801/486-0583. **Contact:** Manager. **Description:** A permanent placement agency. **Specializes in the areas of:** Clerical; Office Support.

TEMPORARY EMPLOYMENT AGENCIES

INTERMOUNTAIN STAFFING RESOURCES
P.O. Box 65157, Salt Lake City UT 84165. 801/467-6565. **Fax:** 801/467-5090. **Contact:** Mark Holland, President. **Description:** A temporary agency that also provides permanent placements. Company pays fee. **Specializes in the areas of:** Accounting/Auditing; Engineering; Finance; Personnel/Labor Relations; Secretarial; Technical. **Positions commonly filled include:** Accountant/Auditor; Administrative Manager; Aerospace Engineer; Blue-Collar Worker Supervisor; Branch Manager; Budget Analyst; Claim Representative; Clerical Supervisor; Computer Programmer; Credit Manager; Customer Service Representative; Design Engineer; Draftsperson; Electrical/Electronics Engineer; Electrician; General Manager; Human Resources Manager; Industrial Production Manager; Management Trainee; Mechanical Engineer; Operations/Production Manager;

Purchasing Agent/Manager; Services Sales Representative; Structural Engineer; Systems Analyst. **Benefits available to temporary workers:** 401(k); Cafeteria; Paid Holidays; Paid Vacation. **Corporate headquarters location:** This Location. **Other U.S. locations:** Phoenix AZ; Denver CO; Boise ID; Las Vegas NV. **Average salary range of placements:** $30,000 - $50,000. **Number of placements per year:** 1000+.

MANPOWER TECHNICAL SERVICES
1106 East 6600 South, Suite 200, Salt Lake City UT 84121. 801/264-1198. **Fax:** 801/262-9598. **Contact:** Manager. **E-mail address:** techjobs@utah-inter.net. **Description:** A temporary agency. Manpower focuses on the computer field (programmers, network technicians, etc.) and engineering professions (designers and drafters). Company pays fee. **Specializes in the areas of:** Computer Science/Software; Engineering; Manufacturing. **Positions commonly filled include:** Aerospace Engineer; Biomedical Engineer; Civil Engineer; Computer Programmer; Design Engineer; Designer; Draftsperson; Electrical/Electronics Engineer; Environmental Engineer; Industrial Engineer; Quality Control Supervisor; Software Engineer; Structural Engineer; Surveyor; Systems Analyst; Technical Writer/Editor; Telecommunications Manager; Transportation/Traffic Specialist. **Benefits available to temporary workers:** Medical Insurance; Paid Holidays; Paid Vacation. **Corporate headquarters location:** Milwaukee WI. **Other U.S. locations:** Nationwide. **Average salary range of placements:** $30,000 - $50,000. **Number of placements per year:** 200 - 499.

OLSTEN STAFFING SERVICES
5434 South 1900 West, Suite 6, Roy UT 84067. 801/825-0500. **Fax:** 801/825-0555. **Contact:** Kevin Fullmer, Account Representative. **Description:** A temporary agency that also offers permanent placement. Company pays fee. **Specializes in the areas of:** Accounting/Auditing; Engineering; Industrial; Manufacturing; Personnel/Labor Relations; Secretarial; Technical. **Positions commonly filled include:** Accountant/Auditor; Administrative Manager; Aerospace Engineer; Blue-Collar Worker Supervisor; Buyer; Clerical Supervisor; Counselor; Customer Service Representative; Draftsperson; Electrical/Electronics Engineer; General Manager; Human Resources Manager; Industrial Engineer; Industrial Production Manager; Management Trainee; Manufacturer's/Wholesaler's Sales Rep.; Mechanical Engineer; Purchasing Agent/Manager; Quality Control Supervisor; Restaurant/Food Service Manager; Securities Sales Representative; Services Sales Representative; Structural Engineer; Systems Analyst. **Benefits available to temporary workers:** Medical Insurance; Paid Vacation; Referral Bonus Plan. **Corporate headquarters location:** Melville NY. **Average salary range of placements:** Less than $20,000. **Number of placements per year:** 1000+.

PEAK TEMPORARY SERVICES
575 East 4500 South, Suite B210, Murray UT 84107-2973. 801/264-1212. **Fax:** 801/264-1277. **Contact:** Manager. **Description:** A temporary agency that also offers temp-to-hire placements. Company pays fee. **Specializes in the areas of:** Manufacturing. **Positions commonly filled include:** Blue-Collar Worker Supervisor; Design Engineer; Draftsperson; Electrical/Electronics Engineer; Industrial Engineer; Industrial Production Manager; Manufacturer's/Wholesaler's Sales Rep.; Materials Engineer; Mechanical Engineer; MIS Specialist; Operations/Production Manager; Purchasing Agent/Manager; Quality Control Supervisor. **Average salary range of placements:** $20,000 - $29,999. **Number of placements per year:** 200 - 499.

SYSTEMS WEST
136 South Main Street, Suite A-300, Salt Lake City UT 84101. 801/364-7900. **Fax:** 801/364-9700. **Contact:** Kari Cahoon, Recruiter. **Description:** A temporary agency. **Specializes in the areas of:** Computer Science/Software; Legal. **Positions commonly filled include:** Attorney; Computer Programmer; Systems Analyst. **Number of placements per year:** 100 - 199.

CONTRACT SERVICES FIRMS

CDI CORPORATION
P.O. Box 22030, Salt Lake City UT 84122. **Toll-free phone:** 800/536-8624. **Fax:** 801/521-8611. **Contact:** Steve Simonson, Recruiter. **E-mail address:** cdieng@bitcorp.com. **World Wide Web address:** http://www.cdicorp.com. **Description:** A contract services firm for a variety of industries. Founded in 1950. Company pays fee. **Positions commonly filled include:** Civil Engineer; Computer Programmer; Draftsperson; Materials Engineer; MIS Specialist; Software Engineer; Structural Engineer; Systems Analyst; Technical Writer/Editor. **Corporate headquarters location:** Philadelphia PA. **Other U.S. locations:** Nationwide. **Average salary range of placements:** $30,000 - $50,000. **Number of placements per year:** 500 - 999.

EMPLOYEE LEASING AND MANAGEMENT
302 West 5400 South, Suite 108, Salt Lake City UT 84107. **Contact:** Manager. **Description:** A contract services firm. Founded in 1988. **Positions commonly filled include:** Typist/Word Processor.

SOFTWARE ENGINEERING SOLUTIONS
165 SW Temple Street, Salt Lake City UT 84101. 801/539-0130. **Contact:** Manager. **Description:** A contract services firm. **Specializes in the areas of:** Computer Programming; Engineering.

VOLT SERVICES GROUP
1100 East 6600 South, Suite 260, Salt Lake City UT 84121. 801/264-9970. **Fax:** 801/264-8632. **Contact:** Jessica Gillert, Branch Manager. **E-mail address:** djohnsto@ix.netcom.com. **World Wide Web address:** http://www.volt.com. **Description:** A contract services firm. The agency focuses on placing high-level computer professionals. **Specializes in the areas of:** Engineering. **Positions commonly filled include:** Computer Programmer; Draftsperson; Editor; Electrical/Electronics Engineer; Electrician; Mechanical Engineer; MIS Specialist; Systems Analyst; Technical Writer/Editor. **Corporate headquarters location:** Orange CA. **Other U.S. locations:** Nationwide. **Average salary range of placements:** $30,000 - $50,000. **Number of placements per year:** 200 - 499.

VERMONT

EXECUTIVE SEARCH FIRMS

AAA SEARCH ASSOCIATES
156 College Street, Burlington VT 05403. 802/865-9191. **Contact:** Manager. **Description:** An executive search firm. **Specializes in the areas of:** Wire and Cable.

DUNHILL SEARCH OF VERMONT
P.O. Box 204, Warren VT 05674. 802/496-0115. **Contact:** Manager. **Description:** An executive search firm. **Corporate headquarters location:** Hauppauge NY. **Other U.S. locations:** Nationwide.

ECKLER PERSONNEL NETWORK (EPN)
P.O. Box 549, Woodstock VT 05091. **Toll-free phone:** 800/522-1605. **Contact:** G.K. Eckler, President. **E-mail address:** epn@sover.net. **Description:** An executive search firm operating on both retainer and contingency bases. The firm focuses on business software fields including information technology services and software product support and development. Company pays fee. **Specializes in the areas of:** Administration; Computer Science/Software. **Positions commonly filled include:** Computer Programmer; Internet Services Manager; MIS Specialist; Multimedia Designer; Software Engineer; Systems Analyst. **Average salary range of placements:** $30,000 - $50,000. **Number of placements per year:** 50 - 99.

MANAGEMENT RECRUITERS OF BURLINGTON
187 St. Paul Street, Suite 4, Burlington VT 05401. 802/865-0541. **Contact:** Michael O'Connor, Recruiting. **Description:** An executive search firm focusing on finance, banking, and computer industries. **Specializes in the areas of:** Banking; Computer Programming; Finance; Investment.

MARKETSEARCH ASSOCIATES
P.O. Box 462, Williston VT 05495. 802/434-2460. **Contact:** Manager. **Description:** An executive search firm. **Specializes in the areas of:** Sales.

CANDIS PERRAULT ASSOCIATES INC.
5 Covington Lane, Shelburne VT 05482. 802/985-1017. **Contact:** Manager. **Description:** An executive search firm. **Specializes in the areas of:** Finance.

JAY TRACEY ASSOCIATES
P.O. Box 30, Plymouth VT 05034. 802/672-3000. **Contact:** Manager. **Description:** An executive search firm. **Specializes in the areas of:** Factory Automation; Industrial.

VOLL ASSOCIATES
14 Heritage Lane, Shelburne VT 05482. 802/985-8605. **Contact:** Manager. **Description:** An executive search firm. **Specializes in the areas of:** Finance; Insurance.

PERMANENT EMPLOYMENT AGENCIES

DEPARTMENT OF EMPLOYMENT AND TRAINING
25 Main Street, Springfield VT 05156. 802/885-2167. **Contact:** Manager. **Description:** A permanent employment agency. **Positions commonly filled include:** Accountant/Auditor; Administrative Assistant; Bank Officer/Manager; Bookkeeper; Civil Engineer; Clerk; Computer Operator; Computer Programmer; Construction Trade Worker; Data Entry Clerk; Draftsperson; Driver; Electrical/Electronics Engineer; Factory Worker; Hotel Manager; Human Resources Manager; Industrial Designer; Industrial Engineer; Insurance Agent/Broker; Legal Secretary; Light Industrial Worker; Mechanical Engineer; Medical Secretary; Nurse; Purchasing Agent/Manager; Quality Control Supervisor; Receptionist; Sales Representative; Secretary; Typist/Word Processor. **Number of placements per year:** 500 - 999.

TAD RESOURCES
100 Dorset Street, Suite 14, South Burlington VT 05403. 802/658-5007. **Contact:** Manager. **Description:** A permanent and temporary staffing service. TAD Resources also operates a technical division at this location. **Specializes in the areas of:** Administration; Clerical; Personnel/Labor Relations.

TECHNICAL CONNECTION
P.O. Box 1402, Burlington VT 05402. 802/658-8324. **Contact:** Christopher Johnson, Director. **E-mail address:** vtjobs@aol.com. **World Wide Web address:** http://members.aol.com/vtjobs. **Description:** A permanent employment agency. The agency focuses on technical fields including computers, mechanical engineering, and surveying. **Specializes in the areas of:** Computer Science/Software; Engineering.

TEMPORARY EMPLOYMENT AGENCIES

ADECCO
407 Main Street, Bennington VT 05201. 802/442-9956. **Fax:** 802/442-3011. **Contact:** Branch Manager. **Description:** A temporary agency. Adecco also provides temp-to-hire placements and some permanent placements. **Specializes in the areas of:** Manufacturing; Office Support.

GFI PRO STAFFING
P.O. Box 8144, Brattleboro VT 05304. 802/257-1146. **Contact:** Beth Butler, Recruiter. **Description:** A temporary agency that focuses on office placements. **Specializes in the areas of:** Data Processing; Office Support.

HARMON PERSONNEL SERVICES
50 Elliott Street, Brattleboro VT 05301. 802/254-8639. **Contact:** Manager. **Description:** A temporary agency focusing on clerical placements. **Specializes in the areas of:** Clerical; Data Processing; Industrial; Office Support.

THE PERSONNEL CONNECTION
272 South Main Street, Rutland VT 05701. 802/773-3737. **Fax:** 802/773-3424. **Contact:** Manager. **Description:** A temporary agency that also provides temp-to-perm placements. **Specializes in the areas of:** Administration; General Labor; Office Support.

PERSONNEL DEPARTMENT INC.
1234 Williston Road, South Burlington VT 05403-5720. 802/865-4243. **Contact:** Office Manager. **World Wide Web address:** http://www.together.net/~vtjobs. **Description:** A temporary agency. **Specializes in the areas of:** Accounting/Auditing; Computer Science/Software; Engineering; Finance; Industrial;

Manufacturing; Personnel/Labor Relations; Secretarial; Technical. **Positions commonly filled include:** Accountant/ Auditor; Administrative Manager; Aerospace Engineer; Architect; Blue-Collar Worker Supervisor; Chemical Engineer; Civil Engineer; Claim Representative; Clerical Supervisor; Computer Programmer; Construction Contractor; Cost Estimator; Credit Manager; Customer Service Representative; Design Engineer; Designer; Draftsperson; Electrical/Electronics Engineer; Electrician; Environmental Engineer; Financial Analyst; Human Resources Specialist; Industrial Engineer; Industrial Production Manager; Insurance Agent/Broker; Internet Services Manager; Mechanical Engineer; MIS Specialist; Multimedia Designer; Nuclear Engineer; Petroleum Engineer; Quality Control Supervisor; Science Technologist; Software Engineer; Structural Engineer; Surveyor; Systems Analyst; Technical Writer/Editor; Telecommunications Manager; Transportation/Traffic Specialist; Typist/Word Processor. **Benefits available to temporary workers:** Medical Insurance; Paid Holidays; Paid Vacation. **Corporate headquarters location:** This Location. **Other area locations:** St. Albans VT. **Number of placements per year:** 1000+.

TRIAD TEMPORARY SERVICES, INC.
P.O. Box 789, Williston VT 05495. 802/864-8255. **Physical address:** 19 Commerce Street, Williston VT. **Toll-free phone:** 800/894-8455. **Fax:** 802/864-0046. **Contact:** Stan Grandfield, President. **Description:** A temporary agency. Founded in 1986. **Specializes in the areas of:** Banking; Computer Science/Software; Food Industry; Industrial; Retail; Sales; Secretarial. **Positions commonly filled include:** Accountant/ Auditor; Administrative Manager; Architect; Attorney; Civil Engineer; Claim Representative; Clerical Supervisor; Computer Programmer; Customer Service Representative; Designer; Electrical/Electronics Engineer; Hotel Manager; Human Resources Specialist; Human Service Worker; Industrial Engineer; Management Trainee; Mechanical Engineer; MIS Specialist; Operations/Production Manager; Purchasing Agent/Manager; Restaurant/Food Service Manager; Services Sales Representative; Software Engineer; Systems Analyst; Technical Writer/Editor; Transportation/Traffic Specialist; Typist/Word Processor. **Benefits available to temporary workers:** Paid Holidays; Paid Vacation. **Average salary range of placements:** Less than $20,000. **Number of placements per year:** 1000+.

WESTERN STAFF SERVICES
P.O. Box 1550, Burlington VT 05402-1550. 802/862-4282. **Fax:** 802/862-4555. **Contact:** Branch Manager. **Description:** A temporary agency that also provides permanent placements. **Specializes in the areas of:** Clerical; Light Industrial; Office Support; Secretarial; Technical.

VIRGINIA

EXECUTIVE SEARCH FIRMS

A LA CARTE INTERNATIONAL
3330 Pacific Avenue, Suite 500, Virginia Beach VA 23451-2983. 757/425-6111. **Fax:** 757/425-8507. **Contact:** Manager. **Description:** An executive search firm. **Specializes in the areas of:** Food Industry. **Other U.S. locations:** CA.

AARON-JONES INC.
2010 Corporate Ridge, McLean VA 22102. 703/734-0014. **Contact:** Manager. **Description:** An executive search firm that places personnel in a wide range of industries.

ABILITY RESOURCES, INC.
716 Church Street, Alexandria VA 22314. 703/548-6400. **Contact:** Noel L. Ruppert, President. **Description:** An executive search firm. Company pays fee. **Specializes in the areas of:** Accounting/Auditing; Defense Industry; Economics; Engineering; Finance; General Management; Nonprofit; Technical. **Positions commonly filled include:** Accountant/Auditor; Economist; Engineer; Financial Analyst; General Manager; Management Analyst/Consultant; Mathematician; Operations/Production Manager; Statistician; Systems Analyst. **Number of placements per year:** 1 - 49.

ACCENT PERSONNEL INC.
4907 Fitzhugh Avenue, Richmond VA 23230. 804/359-9416. **Contact:** Manager. **Description:** An executive search firm.

ACCOUNTANTS EXECUTIVE SEARCH
ACCOUNTANTS ON CALL
701 East Franklin Street, Suite 1408, Richmond VA 23219. 804/225-0200. **Fax:** 804/225-0217. **Contact:** Manager. **Description:** An executive search firm. Accountants On Call (also at this location) is a temp-to-perm agency focusing on entry-level positions. **Specializes in the areas of:** Accounting/Auditing; Banking; Finance.

ACTION RECRUITERS INC.
Timbrook Square Shopping Center, 8800 Timberlake Road, Lynchburg VA 24502. 804/237-0908. **Contact:** Manager. **Description:** An executive search firm that places professionals in a wide range of industries.

ADAMS SOURCES
P.O. Box 70634, Richmond VA 23255. 804/282-5674. **Toll-free phone:** 800/927-6716. **Fax:** 804/282-5675. **Contact:** Zack Adams, Recruiter. **Description:** An executive search firm that focuses on accounting, banking, and retirement planning. Company pays fee. **Specializes in the areas of:** Accounting/Auditing; Administration; Advertising; Banking; Engineering; Personnel/Labor Relations. **Positions commonly filled include:** Accountant/Auditor; Advertising Account Executive; Bank Officer/Manager; Controller; Design Engineer; Electrician; Human Resources Manager; Management Analyst/Consultant; Manufacturing Engineer; MIS Specialist; Sales Executive; Sales Manager; Sales Representative; Systems Analyst. **Average salary range of placements:** $30,000 - $50,000. **Number of placements per year:** 1 - 49.

ALLIANCE GROUP
P.O. Box 935, Lexington VA 24450. 540/261-2260. **Contact:** Reed Ferguson, Principal. **Description:** An executive search firm. Company pays fee. **Specializes in the areas of:** Engineering. **Positions commonly filled include:** Chemical Engineer; Civil Engineer; Environmental Engineer; Geologist/Geophysicist; Materials Engineer; Mechanical Engineer; Structural Engineer. **Average salary range of placements:** More than $50,000. **Number of placements per year:** 1 - 49.

BARNES & ASSOCIATES RETAIL SEARCH
P.O. Box 36556, Richmond VA 23235. 804/379-8264. **Fax:** 804/379-8379. **Contact:** William Barnes, President. **Description:** An executive search firm. Company pays fee. **Specializes in the areas of:** Fashion; General Management; Personnel/Labor Relations; Retail. **Positions commonly filled include:** Branch Manager; Buyer; General Manager; Human Resources Specialist; Management Trainee; MIS Specialist; Operations/Production Manager; Purchasing Agent/Manager; Transportation/Traffic Specialist. **Average salary range of placements:** More than $50,000. **Number of placements per year:** 1 - 49.

BENT ASSOCIATES
412 NationsBank Building, Harrisonburg VA 22801. 540/433-5300. **Fax:** 540/433-5717. **Contact:** Judith Bent, President/Owner. **Description:** An executive search firm operating on a retainer basis. The firm also provides career/outplacement counseling. Company pays fee. **Specializes in the areas of:** General Management; Industrial; Sales; Secretarial. **Positions commonly filled include:** Accountant/Auditor; Administrative Manager; Claim Rep.; Computer Programmer; Construction Contractor; Credit Manager; Customer Service Rep.; Electrical/Electronics Engineer; Environmental Engineer; Industrial Engineer; MIS Specialist; Operations/Production Manager; Paralegal; Purchasing Agent/Manager; Quality Control Supervisor; Transportation/Traffic Specialist. **Average salary range of placements:** $30,000 - $50,000. **Number of placements per year:** 1 - 49.

THE BEST AGENCY
2905 Lamkin Way, Charlottesville VA 22901. 804/978-7748. **Fax:** 804/978-7387. **Contact:** James N. Best, President. **Description:** An executive search firm that places senior management in the hotel industry. Company pays fee. **Positions commonly filled include:** Accountant/Auditor; Hotel Manager. **Average salary range of placements:** More than $50,000. **Number of placements per year:** 1 - 49.

BRAULT & ASSOCIATES LTD.
11703 Bowman Green Drive, Reston VA 20190. 703/471-0920. **Contact:** Manager. **Description:** An executive search firm. **Specializes in the areas of:** High-Tech.

CAREER MARKET CONSULTANTS
1092 Lastin Road, Virginia Beach VA 23451. 757/428-8888. **Contact:** Manager. **Description:** An executive search firm. **Specializes in the areas of:** Hotel/Restaurant; Technical.

CAREER REGISTRY
1600 East Little Creek Road, Suite 322, Norfolk VA 23518-4136. 757/480-2757. **Contact:** Office Manager. **Description:** An executive search firm operating on both contingency and retainer bases. **Specializes in the areas of:** Engineering; Manufacturing. **Positions commonly filled include:** Accountant/Auditor; Biomedical Engineer; Chemical Engineer; Computer Programmer; Electrical/Electronics Engineer; Electrician; Environmental Engineer; Industrial Engineer; Mechanical Engineer; Software Engineer; Systems Analyst.

CERTIFIED PLACEMENT ASSOCIATES INC.
2807 East Purham Road, Suite 105, Richmond VA 23294. 804/270-1770. **Contact:** Office Manager.

Description: An executive search firm. **Specializes in the areas of:** Technical.

CONTEC SEARCH, INC.
5803 Stone Ridge Drive, Centerville VA 20120. 703/968-0477. **Fax:** 703/968-0064. **Contact:** Brian Canatsey, President. **World Wide Web address:** http://www.mnsinc.com/contec. **Description:** Contec Search is an executive search firm operating on a contingency basis. Company pays fee. **Specializes in the areas of:** Computer Science/Software; Finance; Health/Medical; Manufacturing. **Positions commonly filled include:** Computer Programmer; Database Manager; Financial Analyst; Systems Analyst; Systems Manager. **Average salary range of placements:** More than $50,000. **Number of placements per year:** 50 - 99.

CORPORATE CONNECTION LTD.
7202 Glen Forest Drive, Richmond VA 23226-3778. 804/288-8844. **Contact:** President. **Description:** A full-service executive recruiting firm. **Specializes in the areas of:** Accounting/Auditing; Administration; Banking; Computer Science/Software; Engineering; Finance; General Management; Industrial; Insurance; Legal; Manufacturing; Nonprofit; Personnel/Labor Relations; Publishing; Retail; Sales; Secretarial; Technical. **Positions commonly filled include:** Accountant/Auditor; Adjuster; Administrative Manager; Advertising Clerk; Aerospace Engineer; Agricultural Engineer; Bank Officer/Manager; Biological Scientist; Biomedical Engineer; Blue-Collar Worker Supervisor; Brokerage Clerk; Budget Analyst; Chemical Engineer; Chemist; Civil Engineer; Claim Rep.; Clerical Supervisor; Clinical Lab Technician; Computer Programmer; Cost Estimator; Credit Manager; Customer Service Rep.; Design Engineer; Designer; Draftsperson; Electrical/Electronics Engineer; Environmental Engineer; Financial Analyst; Human Resources Manager; Industrial Engineer; Industrial Production Manager; Insurance Agent/Broker; Librarian; Library Technician; Management Analyst/ Consultant; Management Trainee; Manufacturer's/ Wholesaler's Sales Rep.; Market Research Analyst; Mechanical Engineer; Medical Records Technician; Metallurgical Engineer; Mining Engineer; Property and Real Estate Manager; Public Relations Specialist; Purchasing Agent/Manager; Quality Control Supervisor; Restaurant/Food Service Manager; Securities Sales Rep.; Services Sales Rep.; Software Engineer; Strategic Relations Manager; Structural Engineer; Systems Analyst; Transportation/Traffic Specialist; Typist/Word Processor; Underwriter/ Assistant Underwriter; Urban/Regional Planner. **Average salary range of placements:** $30,000 - $50,000. **Number of placements per year:** 200 - 499.

CURRAN ASSOCIATES
P.O. Box 420, Occoquan VA 22125. **Physical address:** 312 Poplar Alley, Occoquan VA. **Toll-free phone:** 800/497-0497. **Fax:** 703/497-4652. **Contact:** David Curran, President. **Description:** An executive search firm that also provides career/outplacement counseling. Company pays fee. **Specializes in the areas of:** Food Industry. **Positions commonly filled include:** Assistant Manager; General Manager; Management Trainee; Operations Manager; Production Manager; Restaurant/Food Service Manager; Sales Executive; Sales Representative. **Average salary range of placements:** $30,000 - $50,000. **Number of placements per year:** 50 - 99.

BETH DAISEY ASSOCIATES
1800 Diagonal Road, Suite 600, Alexandria VA 22314. 703/751-2328. **Contact:** Office Manager. **Description:** An executive search firm. **Specializes in the areas of:** Travel.

CAROL DAY AND ASSOCIATES
2105 Electric Road SW, Roanoke VA 24018. 540/989-2831. **Fax:** 540/989-5910. **Contact:** Carol Day, Owner. **Description:** An executive search firm. **Specializes in the areas of:** Accounting/Auditing; Administration; Computer Science/Software; Engineering; Health/Medical; Manufacturing; Retail; Sales; Secretarial. **Positions commonly filled include:** Accountant/Auditor; Buyer; Chemical Engineer; Civil Engineer; Clerical Supervisor; Computer Programmer; Customer Service Rep.; Electrical/Electronics Engineer; Industrial Engineer; Management Trainee; Mechanical Engineer; MIS Specialist; Paralegal; Quality Control Supervisor; Software Engineer. **Average salary range of placements:** $30,000 - $50,000. **Number of placements per year:** 50 - 99.

DONMAC ASSOCIATES
P.O. Box 2541, Reston VA 20195. 703/620-2866. **Fax:** 703/620-2867. **Contact:** Connie Andersen, President. **Description:** An executive search firm. Company pays fee. **Specializes in the areas of:** Computer Science/Software; Data Processing; Engineering. **Positions commonly filled include:** Computer Programmer; Electrical/Electronics Engineer; Software Engineer; Systems Analyst. **Number of placements per year:** 50 - 99.

DUNHILL PROFESSIONAL SEARCH
8100 Three Chopt Road, Suite 133, Richmond VA 23229-4833. 804/282-2216. **Contact:** P. Frank Lassiter, President. **Description:** An executive search firm operating on both retainer and contingency bases. Company pays fee. **Specializes in the areas of:** Banking; Engineering. **Positions commonly filled include:** Bank Officer/Manager; Chemical Engineer; Design Engineer; Industrial Engineer; Mechanical Engineer; Securities Sales Representative; Trust Officer. **Average salary range of placements:** $30,000 - $50,000. **Number of placements per year:** 1 - 49.

DURILL & ASSOCIATES
7200 Glen Forest Drive, Suite 306, Richmond VA 23226. 804/282-0595. **Contact:** Office Manager. **Description:** An executive search firm. **Specializes in the areas of:** Finance.

EFFECTIVE STAFFING INC.
209 Elden Street, Suite 208, Herndon VA 20170-4815. 703/742-9300. **Fax:** 703/742-9747. **Contact:** Mike Millard, President. **Description:** An executive search firm operating on a contingency basis. The firm also provides temporary and contract services. Company pays fee. **Specializes in the areas of:** Accounting/Auditing; Administration; Banking; Computer Science/Software; Finance; General Management; Legal; Personnel/Labor Relations; Publishing; Sales; Secretarial; Technical. **Positions commonly filled include:** Accountant/Auditor; Administrative Manager; Bank Officer/Manager; Broadcast Technician; Budget Analyst; Computer Programmer; Counselor; Customer Service Rep.; Design Engineer; Economist; Education Administrator; Financial Analyst; General Manager; Health Services Manager; Human Resources Specialist; Human Service Worker; Management Analyst/Consultant; Market Research Analyst; Medical Records Technician; MIS Specialist; Multimedia Designer; Occupational Therapist; Operations/Production Manager; Paralegal; Physical Therapist; Quality Control Supervisor; Registered Nurse; Services Sales Rep.; Technical Writer/Editor; Telecommunications Manager. **Average salary range of placements:** More than $50,000. **Number of placements per year:** 1 - 49.

ENGINEERING & MIS GUILD
8260 Greensboro Drive, Suite 200, McLean VA 22102. 703/761-4023. **Fax:** 703/761-4024. **Contact:**

William J. Joyce, Principal. **E-mail address:** resumes@guildcorp.com. **World Wide Web address:** http://www.guildhome.com. **Description:** An executive search firm operating on both retainer and contingency bases. Company pays fee. **Specializes in the areas of:** Administration; Computer Science/Software; Engineering. **Positions commonly filled include:** Computer Programmer; Customer Service Representative; Design Engineer; Electrical/Electronics Engineer; Internet Services Manager; Management Analyst/Consultant; MIS Specialist; Software Engineer; Telecommunications Manager. **Average salary range of placements:** More than $50,000. **Number of placements per year:** 200 - 499.

EXECUTIVE RECRUITERS OF FAIRFAX
1907 Clarks Glen Place, Vienna VA 22182. 703/556-9580. **Contact:** Joe Segal, President. **Description:** An executive search firm. Company pays fee. **Specializes in the areas of:** Food Industry; Hotel/Restaurant. **Positions commonly filled include:** Hotel Manager; Restaurant/Food Service Manager. **Number of placements per year:** 50 - 99.

EXECUTIVE SALES SEARCH
8232 Ammonett Drive, Richmond VA 23235. 804/560-7327. **Fax:** 804/560-7564. **Contact:** David W. Bell, President. **E-mail address:** salesone1@aol.com. **Description:** An executive search firm that operates on a contingency basis and also acts as a contract services firm. Company pays fee. **Specializes in the areas of:** Sales. **Positions commonly filled include:** Account Manager; Account Representative; Advertising Account Executive; Branch Manager; General Manager; Management Analyst/Consultant; Manufacturer's/Wholesaler's Sales Rep.; Marketing Manager; Marketing Specialist; Sales Engineer; Sales Executive; Sales Manager; Sales Representative. **Average salary range of placements:** More than $50,000. **Number of placements per year:** 100 - 199.

EXECUTIVE TRANSITIONS INTERNATIONAL
1655 North Fort Myers Drive, Suite 1150, Arlington VA 22209. 703/243-3838. **Contact:** Manager. **Description:** An executive search firm.

FGI
1595 Spring Hill Road, Vienna VA 22182. 703/847-0010. **Contact:** Manager. **Description:** An executive search firm. **Specializes in the areas of:** Aerospace; Defense Industry; High-Tech; Telecommunications.

F-O-R-T-U-N-E PERSONNEL CONSULTANTS
112 West Main Street, Suite 1, Berryville VA 22611. 540/955-0500. **Fax:** 540/955-0518. **Contact:** Manager. **Description:** An executive search firm. **Specializes in the areas of:** Banking; Engineering; Finance; Logistics; Materials; Purchasing. **Corporate headquarters location:** New York NY. **Other U.S. locations:** Nationwide.

THE GEMINI GROUP
9749 Ashworth Drive, Richmond VA 23236. 804/276-3091. **Fax:** 804/320-2880. **Contact:** Mr. Terry Lee Stacy, M.A., President. **E-mail address:** doctoriobl@aol.com. **Description:** An executive search firm that also offers career/outplacement counseling. **Specializes in the areas of:** General Management; Health/Medical. **Positions commonly filled include:** Accountant/Auditor; Administrative Manager; Buyer; Chemist; Claim Rep.; Computer Programmer; Customer Service Rep.; Editor; Financial Analyst; General Manager; Human Resources Specialist; Industrial Production Manager; Logistics Support Worker; Manufacturer's/Wholesaler's Sales Rep.; Property and Real Estate Manager; Purchasing Agent/Manager; Quality Control Supervisor; Restaurant/Food Service Manager. **Other U.S. locations:** DC; MD; NC. **Average salary range of placements:** More than $50,000. **Number of placements per year:** 200 - 499.

GLASSMAN ASSOCIATES INC.
6603 Anthony Crest Square, McLean VA 22101. 703/442-8866. **Contact:** Manager. **Description:** An executive search firm.

GRAHAM ASSOCIATES
P.O. Box 7345, Roanoke VA 24019. 540/362-8851. **Contact:** Bill Graham, Manager. **Description:** An executive search firm. **Specializes in the areas of:** Engineering.

B.H. GRINER & ASSOCIATES
450 Maple Avenue East, Suite 302, Vienna VA 22180. 703/242-9804. **Contact:** Manager. **Description:** An executive search firm that places personnel in a variety of industries.

HALBRECHT & COMPANY, INC.
10195 Main Street, Suite L, Fairfax VA 22031. 703/359-2880. **Contact:** Thomas J. Maltby, Director. **Description:** An executive search firm operating on both retainer and contingency bases. Company pays fee. **Specializes in the areas of:** Administration; Computer Science/Software; Technical. **Positions commonly filled include:** Actuary; Computer Programmer; EDP Specialist; Electrical/Electronics Engineer; Internet Services Manager; Management Analyst/Consultant; Mathematician; Software Engineer; Statistician; Systems Analyst. **Other U.S. locations:** Greenwich CT. **Number of placements per year:** 50 - 99.

ROBERT HALF INTERNATIONAL/ACCOUNTEMPS
1100 Wilson Boulevard, Suite 900, Arlington VA 22209. 703/243-3600. **Contact:** Manager. **Description:** An executive search firm. Accountemps (also at this location) provides temporary placements. Company pays fee. **Specializes in the areas of:** Accounting/Auditing. **Positions commonly filled include:** Accountant/Auditor; Bookkeeper; Data Entry Clerk; EDP Specialist; Financial Analyst. **Corporate headquarters location:** Menlo Park CA. **Number of placements per year:** 200 - 499.
Other area locations:
- 4101 Cox Road, Suite 300, Glen Allen VA 23060. 804/965-9600.

HASLOWE PERSONNEL
5622 Columbia Pike, Bailey's Crossroads VA 22041. 703/820-0020. **Contact:** Manager. **Description:** An executive search firm. **Specializes in the areas of:** Finance; Retail; Sales.

HERB GRETZ ASSOCIATES
1206 Laskin Road, Suite 201, Virginia Beach VA 23451. 757/422-8952. **Contact:** Manager. **Description:** An executive search firm. **Specializes in the areas of:** Medical Sales and Marketing.

INFORMATION SPECIALISTS CO., INC. (INSPEC)
P.O. Box 55313, Virginia Beach VA 23455. 757/460-7790. **Fax:** 757/460-7886. **Contact:** Hugo E. Schluter, CPC, Senior Vice President. **Description:** An executive search firm. Company pays fee. **Specializes in the areas of:** Computer Science/Software; Engineering; Industrial; Marketing; Sales. **Positions commonly filled include:** Biomedical Engineer; Chemical Engineer; Chemist; Civil Engineer; Computer Programmer; Design Engineer; Electrical/Electronics Engineer; Geologist/Geophysicist; Industrial Engineer; Mechanical Engineer; Metallurgical Engineer; Sales Engineer; Sales Manager; Software Engineer; Technical Writer/Editor; Telecommunications Manager. **Average salary range of placements:** More than $50,000. **Number of placements per year:** 1 - 49.

JEFFREY IRVING ASSOCIATES
216 South Payne Street, Alexandria VA 22314. 703/836-7770. **Contact:** Manager. **Description:** An executive search firm that places personnel in a variety of industries.

A.T. KEARNEY EXECUTIVE SEARCH
225 Reinekers Lane, Alexandria VA 23214. 703/739-4624. **Contact:** Manager. **Description:** An executive search firm. **Corporate headquarters location:** Chicago IL. **Other U.S. locations:** Nationwide. **International locations:** Worldwide.

KOGEN PERSONNEL
127 Danville Avenue, Colonial Heights VA 23805. 804/526-0870. **Fax:** 804/526-0869. **Contact:** Manager. **Description:** Kogen Personnel is an executive search firm that also provides temporary placements. **Specializes in the areas of:** Computer Science/Software; Engineering; Food Industry; General Management; Retail; Sales; Technical. **Positions commonly filled include:** Accountant/Auditor; Administrative Manager; Attorney; Bank Officer/ Manager; Biological Scientist; Blue-Collar Worker Supervisor; Branch Manager; Buyer; Chemist; Claim Rep.; Clerical Supervisor; Computer Programmer; Construction and Building Inspector; Counselor; Credit Manager; Customer Service Representative; Draftsperson; Economist; Education Administrator; Electrical/Electronics Engineer; Electrician; Financial Analyst; Food Scientist/Technologist; General Manager; Health Services Manager; Hotel Manager; Human Resources Manager; Industrial Engineer; Industrial Production Manager; Insurance Agent/ Broker; Landscape Architect; Librarian; Library Technician; Licensed Practical Nurse; Management Analyst/Consultant; Management Trainee; Manufacturer's/Wholesaler's Sales Rep.; Mechanical Engineer; Medical Records Technician; Paralegal; Pharmacist; Physical Therapist; Physician; Property and Real Estate Manager; Public Relations Specialist; Purchasing Agent/Manager; Quality Control Supervisor; Radio/TV Announcer/Broadcaster; Radiological Technologist; Real Estate Agent; Recreational Therapist; Registered Nurse; Reporter; Respiratory Therapist; Restaurant/Food Service Manager; Science Technologist; Securities Sales Rep.; Services Sales Rep.; Social Worker; Sociologist; Software Engineer; Surveyor; Systems Analyst; Teacher/Professor; Technical Writer/Editor; Telecommunications Manager; Transportation/Traffic Specialist; Travel Agent; Typist/Word Processor; Underwriter/Assistant Underwriter; Veterinarian. **Average salary range of placements:** $20,000 - $29,999. **Number of placements per year:** 100 - 199.

LEE STAFFING RESOURCES
703 Thimble Shoals Boulevard, Suite B-1, Newport News VA 23606. 757/873-0792. **Fax:** 757/873-0087. **Contact:** Kristin Gerczak, Recruiter. **Description:** An executive search firm operating on both retainer and contingency bases. Company pays fee. **Specializes in the areas of:** Accounting/Auditing; Administration; Advertising; Art/Design; Engineering; Finance; Food Industry; General Management; Industrial; Legal; Manufacturing; Personnel/Labor Relations; Retail; Sales; Secretarial; Technical. **Positions commonly filled include:** Accountant/ Auditor; Actuary; Adjuster; Administrative Manager; Aerospace Engineer; Agricultural Engineer; Aircraft Mechanic/Engine Specialist; Attorney; Bank Officer/ Manager; Biochemist; Biological Scientist; Biomedical Engineer; Blue-Collar Worker Supervisor; Branch Manager; Buyer; Chemical Engineer; Chemist; Civil Engineer; Clerical Supervisor; Clinical Lab Technician; Computer Programmer; Construction and Building Inspector; Construction Contractor; Cost Estimator; Counselor; Credit Manager; Customer Service Rep.; Design Engineer; Designer; Draftsperson; Economist; Electrical/Electronics Engineer; Electrician; Environmental Engineer; Financial Analyst; Food Scientist/Technologist; General Manager; Health Services Manager; Hotel Manager; Human Resources Specialist; Human Service Worker; Industrial Engineer; Industrial Production Manager; Insurance Agent/ Broker; Internet Services Manager; Management Analyst/Consultant; Management Trainee; Manufacturer's/Wholesaler's Sales Rep.; Market Research Analyst; Mechanical Engineer; Metallurgical Engineer; Mining Engineer; MIS Specialist; Multimedia Designer; Paralegal; Petroleum Engineer; Property and Real Estate Manager; Public Relations Specialist; Purchasing Agent/Manager; Quality Control Supervisor; Real Estate Agent; Restaurant/Food Service Manager; Services Sales Rep.; Software Engineer; Stationary Engineer; Statistician; Strategic Relations Manager; Structural Engineer; Surveyor; Systems Analyst; Technical Writer/Editor; Telecommunications Manager; Typist/Word Processor; Underwriter/Assistant Underwriter. **Number of placements per year:** 1000+.
Other area locations:

- 2010 Old Greenbriar Road, Suite B, Chesapeake VA 23320. 757/420-8011.

CAROL MADEN GROUP RECRUITING
2019 Cunningham Drive, Suite 218, Hampton VA 23666. 757/827-9010. **Contact:** Manager. **Description:** An executive search firm. **Specializes in the areas of:** Computer Science/Software; Engineering; Technical.

MANAGEMENT RECRUITERS INTERNATIONAL
2 East Church Street, Martinsville VA 24112. 540/638-2000. **Fax:** 540/638-2008. **Contact:** John Matthews, Manager. **Description:** An executive search firm operating on a contingency basis. The firm focuses on manufacturing industries. Company pays fee. **Specializes in the areas of:** Engineering; Home Furnishings; Industrial; Manufacturing; Personnel/ Labor Relations; Sales. **Positions commonly filled include:** Accountant/Auditor; Blue-Collar Worker Supervisor; General Manager; Industrial Engineer; Plant Manager; Quality Control Supervisor. **Average salary range of placements:** $30,000 - $50,000. **Number of placements per year:** 1 - 49.
Other area locations:

- 5001A Lee Highway, Suite 102, Arlington VA 22207. 703/276-1135. (Human Resources; Information Systems; Sales; Telecommunications)
- 2511 Memorial Avenue, Suite 202, Lynchburg VA 24501. 804/528-1611. (Accounting/Auditing; Engineering; Finance)
- 45571 Shepherd Drive, Suite 101A, Sterling VA 20164. 703/430-3700. (Engineering; Health/Medical)

MANAGEMENT RECRUITERS OF McLEAN
6849 Old Dominion Drive, Suite 225, McLean VA 22101. 703/442-4842. **Contact:** Howard Reitkopp, Manager. **Description:** An executive search firm. **Specializes in the areas of:** Accounting/Auditing; Administration; Advertising; Architecture/ Construction; Banking; Communications; Computer Hardware/Software; Design; Electrical; Engineering; Finance; Food Industry; General Management; Health/ Medical; Insurance; Legal; Manufacturing; Operations Management; Personnel/Labor Relations; Procurement; Publishing; Retail; Sales; Technical; Textiles; Transportation.

MANAGEMENT RECRUITERS OF ROANOKE
1960 Electric Road, Suite B, Roanoke VA 24018. 540/989-1676. **Contact:** Paul Sharp, Manager. **Description:** An executive search firm. **Specializes in the areas of:** Accounting/Auditing; Administration;

Advertising; Architecture/Construction; Banking; Communications; Computer Hardware/Software; Design; Electrical; Engineering; Finance; Food Industry; General Management; Health/Medical; Insurance; Legal; Manufacturing; Operations Management; Personnel/Labor Relations; Procurement; Publishing; Retail; Sales; Technical; Textiles; Transportation.

THE McCORMICK GROUP
4024 Plank Road, Fredericksburg VA 22409. 540/786-9777. **Fax:** 540/786-9355. **Contact:** William J. McCormick, President. **Description:** An executive search and consulting firm. Company pays fee. **Specializes in the areas of:** Biology; Computer Science/Software; Engineering; Health/Medical; Insurance; Legal; Personnel/Labor Relations; Retail; Sales; Technical. **Positions commonly filled include:** Accountant/Auditor; Architect; Attorney; Biological Scientist; Civil Engineer; Computer Programmer; Cost Estimator; Design Engineer; Designer; Editor; EEG Technologist; Electrical/Electronics Engineer; Environmental Engineer; Financial Analyst; Health Services Manager; Human Resources Specialist; Licensed Practical Nurse; Management Analyst/ Consultant; MIS Specialist; Multimedia Designer; Physical Therapist; Physician; Public Relations Specialist; Services Sales Representative; Software Engineer; Systems Analyst; Technical Writer/Editor. **Corporate headquarters location:** This Location. **Other area locations:** Arlington VA. **Other U.S. locations:** Jacksonville FL; Boston MA; Kansas City MO. **Average salary range of placements:** More than $50,000. **Number of placements per year:** 1 - 49.

THE McCORMICK GROUP
1400 Wilson Boulevard, Arlington VA 22209. 703/841-1700. **Contact:** Manager. **Description:** An executive search firm placing personnel in a wide range of industries. **Other area locations:** Fredericksburg VA.

MID-ATLANTIC SEARCH
4714 Woodglenn Court, Virginia Beach VA 23462. 757/456-2244. **Fax:** 757/456-0220. **Contact:** Jerry Kiehne, President. **Description:** An executive search firm. Company pays fee. **Specializes in the areas of:** Engineering; Manufacturing. **Positions commonly filled include:** Chemical Engineer; Chemist; Civil Engineer; Electrical/Electronics Engineer; Industrial Engineer; Materials Engineer; Mechanical Engineer; Nuclear Engineer; Structural Engineer. **Number of placements per year:** 1 - 49.

MILLION & ASSOCIATES
1301 April Way, Herndon VA 20170. 703/742-0874. **Fax:** 703/742-9479. **Contact:** Wendy Million, President/Owner. **Description:** An executive search firm operating on both retainer and contingency bases that focuses on mortgage banking. Company pays fee. **Specializes in the areas of:** Mortgage. **Positions commonly filled include:** Mortgage Banker; Mortgage Originator. **Average salary range of placements:** $30,000 - $50,000. **Number of placements per year:** 100 - 199.

NETWORK COMPANIES
1595 Spring Hill Road, Suite 220, Vienna VA 22182. 703/790-1100. **Fax:** 703/790-1123. **Contact:** Ron Sall, Director. **Description:** An executive search firm focusing on accounting, finance, and information technology placements. The firm also provides temporary and contract services. Founded in 1985. Company pays fee. **Specializes in the areas of:** Accounting/Auditing; Computer Science/Software; Finance; Personnel/Labor Relations; Sales; Technical. **Positions commonly filled include:** Accountant/ Auditor; Budget Analyst; Computer Programmer; Customer Service Representative; Financial Analyst; General Manager; Human Resources Specialist; Management Analyst/Consultant; MIS Specialist; Services Sales Representative; Software Engineer; Systems Analyst; Technical Writer/Editor; Telecommunications Manager; Typist/Word Processor. **Average salary range of placements:** More than $50,000. **Number of placements per year:** 500 - 999.

NORRELL STAFFING SERVICES
10208 West Broad Street, Glen Allen VA 23060. 804/346-3500. **Contact:** Heike Smith, Area Services Manager. **Description:** An executive search firm that also offers temporary and contract services. Company pays fee. **Specializes in the areas of:** Accounting/Auditing; Administration; Advertising; Banking; Computer Hardware/Software; Engineering; Finance; Food Industry; General Management; Manufacturing; Personnel/Labor Relations; Sales; Secretarial; Technical. **Positions commonly filled include:** Accountant/Auditor; Administrative Manager; Architect; Biological Scientist; Biomedical Engineer; Blue-Collar Worker Supervisor; Branch Manager; Budget Analyst; Buyer; Chemical Engineer; Chemist; Civil Engineer; Claim Representative; Clerical Supervisor; Clinical Lab Technician; Computer Programmer; Cost Estimator; Customer Service Representative; Design Engineer; Designer; Draftsperson; Editor; Electrical/Electronics Engineer; Electrician; Environmental Engineer; Financial Analyst; General Manager; Human Resources Manager; Human Service Worker; Industrial Engineer; Industrial Production Manager; Internet Services Manager; Management Trainee; Mechanical Engineer; Medical Records Technician; Metallurgical Engineer; MIS Specialist; Multimedia Designer; Operations/Production Manager; Paralegal; Purchasing Agent/Manager; Quality Control Supervisor; Restaurant/Food Service Manager; Services Sales Representative; Software Engineer; Statistician; Structural Engineer; Systems Analyst; Typist/Word Processor. **Benefits available to temporary workers:** 401(k); Dental Insurance; Medical Insurance; Paid Holidays; Paid Vacation. **Corporate headquarters location:** Atlanta GA. **Average salary range of placements:** $20,000 - $29,999. **Number of placements per year:** 1000+.

NORRELL STAFFING SERVICES
1109 Eden Way North, Chesapeake VA 23320-2765. 757/436-3446. **Fax:** 757/436-4080. **Contact:** Manager. **Description:** An executive search firm. **Specializes in the areas of:** Administration; Clerical; Light Industrial; Technical.

OERTH ASSOCIATES, INC.
601 King Street, Suite 405, Alexandria VA 22314. 703/739-1348. **Fax:** 703/739-1349. **Contact:** Lorraine C. Oerth, President. **Description:** An executive search firm. Company pays fee. **Specializes in the areas of:** Construction; Real Estate. **Positions commonly filled include:** Construction Manager; Estimator; Property and Real Estate Manager; Superintendent. **Number of placements per year:** 100 - 199.

PLACEMENT PROFESSIONALS INC.
P.O. Box 29772, Richmond VA 23242. 804/741-1246. **Contact:** Manager. **Description:** An executive search firm. Company pays fee. **Specializes in the areas of:** Accounting/Auditing; Advertising; Banking; Computer Hardware/Software; Economics; Engineering; Finance; Health/Medical; Insurance; Legal; Manufacturing; Personnel/Labor Relations; Sales; Technical. **Positions commonly filled include:** Accountant/Auditor; Aerospace Engineer; Agricultural Engineer; Attorney; Bank Officer/Manager; Biological Scientist; Biomedical Engineer; Budget Analyst; Buyer; Chemical Engineer; Civil Engineer; Computer

Programmer; Controller; Credit Manager; Economist; Electrical/Electronics Engineer; Financial Analyst; Human Resources Manager; Industrial Engineer; Mechanical Engineer; Metallurgical Engineer; Nuclear Engineer; Occupational Therapist; Petroleum Engineer; Pharmacist; Physical Therapist; Public Relations Specialist; Purchasing Agent/Manager; Registered Nurse; Software Engineer; Speech-Language Pathologist; Stationary Engineer; Structural Engineer; Systems Analyst; Technical Writer/Editor; Underwriter/Assistant Underwriter; Wholesale and Retail Buyer.

PROFESSIONAL CAREER CONSULTANTS
319 William Street, Fredericksburg VA 22401. 540/371-8608. **Fax:** 540/371-0764. **Contact:** Christine Garber, General Manager. **World Wide Web address:** http://www.members.com/execrutr. **Description:** An executive search firm. **Specializes in the areas of:** Insurance. **Positions commonly filled include:** Account Representative; Accountant; Adjuster; Administrative Assistant; Chief Financial Officer; Claim Representative; Consultant; Controller; Customer Service Representative; Finance Director; Human Resources Manager; Industrial Engineer; Insurance Agent/Broker; Marketing Manager; Marketing Specialist; Operations Manager; Paralegal; Sales Executive; Sales Manager; Sales Representative; Statistician; Underwriter/Assistant Underwriter. **Average salary range of placements:** $30,000 - $50,000. **Number of placements per year:** 1 - 49.

PROFESSIONAL SEARCH PERSONNEL
4900 Leesburg Pike, Suite 402, Alexandria VA 22302-1103. 703/671-0010. **Contact:** Chuck Cherel, Owner/Manager. **Description:** An executive search firm operating on both retainer and contingency bases. Company pays fee. **Specializes in the areas of:** Accounting/Auditing; Administration; Architecture/Construction; Banking; Biology; Computer Hardware/Software; Engineering; Finance; Health/Medical; Industrial; Personnel/Labor Relations; Technical. **Positions commonly filled include:** Accountant/Auditor; Actuary; Aerospace Engineer; Architect; Bank Officer/Manager; Biological Scientist; Biomedical Engineer; Buyer; Chemical Engineer; Chemist; Computer Programmer; Cost Estimator; Credit Manager; Design Engineer; Designer; Draftsperson; Electrical/Electronics Engineer; Environmental Engineer; Financial Analyst; Geologist/Geophysicist; Human Resources Manager; Industrial Engineer; Internet Services Manager; Manufacturer's/Wholesaler's Sales Rep.; Mechanical Engineer; Metallurgical Engineer; MIS Specialist; Nuclear Engineer; Occupational Therapist; Petroleum Engineer; Physical Therapist; Quality Control Supervisor; Respiratory Therapist; Securities Sales Representative; Software Engineer; Systems Analyst. **Average salary range of placements:** More than $50,000. **Number of placements per year:** 50 - 99.

RECRUITING RESOURCES INC.
13813 Village Mill Drive, Midlothian VA 23113. 804/794-1813. **Contact:** Manager. **Description:** An executive search firm. **Specializes in the areas of:** Computer Programming; Sales; Technical.

RELIANCE STAFFING SERVICES
751-E Thimble Shoals Boulevard, Newport News VA 23606. 757/873-6644. **Fax:** 757/873-2341. **Contact:** Heather Walker, Recruiter. **Description:** An executive search firm. Company pays fee. **Positions commonly filled include:** Accountant/Auditor; Advertising Clerk; Blue-Collar Worker Supervisor; Computer Programmer; Design Engineer; Designer; Draftsperson; Electrical/Electronics Engineer; Electrician; Human Resources Specialist; Industrial Engineer; Paralegal; Purchasing Agent/Manager; Software Engineer; Structural Engineer; Systems Analyst; Technical Writer/Editor; Typist/Word Processor. **Corporate headquarters location:** Chesapeake VA. **Other area locations:** Suffolk VA; Virginia Beach VA. **Number of placements per year:** 500 - 999.

DON RICHARD ASSOCIATES
8300 Greensboro Drive, Suite 720, McLean VA 22102. 703/827-5990. **Contact:** Manager. **Description:** An executive search firm that places accounting and financial personnel in both permanent and temporary positions. **Specializes in the areas of:** Accounting/Auditing; Bookkeeping; Finance. **Corporate headquarters location:** Richmond VA.

DON RICHARD ASSOCIATES
4701 Columbus Street, Suite 102, Virginia Beach VA 23462. 757/518-8600. **Contact:** Manager. **Description:** An executive search firm. **Specializes in the areas of:** Accounting/Auditing; Office Support. **Corporate headquarters location:** Richmond VA.

DON RICHARD ASSOCIATES OF RICHMOND
7275 Glen Forest Drive, Suite 200, Richmond VA 23226-3772. 804/282-6300. **Fax:** 804/282-6792. **Recorded jobline:** 804/282-1177. **Contact:** Mike Beck, MIS Director. **E-mail address:** dranet@i2020.net. **World Wide Web address:** http://www.donrichard.com. **Description:** An executive search firm. Founded in 1978. Company pays fee. **Specializes in the areas of:** Accounting/Auditing; Administration; Computer Science/Software; Finance; Information Systems; Secretarial. **Positions commonly filled include:** Accountant/Auditor; Administrative Manager; Budget Analyst; Clerical Supervisor; Computer Programmer; Credit Manager; Design Engineer; Financial Analyst; Internet Services Manager; Management Analyst/Consultant; MIS Specialist; Multimedia Designer; Operations/Production Manager; Quality Control Supervisor; Services Sales Rep.; Software Engineer; Systems Analyst; Technical Writer/Editor; Telecommunications Manager; Typist/Word Processor. **Corporate headquarters location:** This Location. **Other area locations:** Norfolk VA. **Other U.S. locations:** Washington DC; Tampa FL; Atlanta GA; Charlotte NC. **Average salary range of placements:** $30,000 - $50,000. **Number of placements per year:** 50 - 99.

SEARCH & RECRUIT INTERNATIONAL
4455 South Boulevard, Virginia Beach VA 23452. 757/490-3151. **Toll-free phone:** 800/880-JOBS. **Fax:** 757/497-6503. **Contact:** General Manager. **E-mail address:** contact@searchandrecruit.com. **World Wide Web address:** http://www.searchandrecruit.com. **Description:** An executive search firm. **Specializes in the areas of:** Engineering; Food Industry; Industrial; Manufacturing; Publishing. **Positions commonly filled include:** Chemical Engineer; Computer Programmer; Design Engineer; Draftsperson; Electrical/Electronics Engineer; Electrician; Environmental Engineer; General Manager; Mechanical Engineer; MIS Specialist; Quality Control Supervisor; Software Engineer; Technical Writer/Editor; Telecommunications Manager. **Other U.S. locations:** Charleston SC. **Average salary range of placements:** $30,000 - $50,000. **Number of placements per year:** 200 - 499.

SEARCH CONSULTANTS, INC.
2002 Langdon Road, Suite 28, Roanoke VA 24015. 540/776-3114. **Contact:** Manager. **Description:** An executive search firm. **Specializes in the areas of:** Health/Medical.

SOUDER & ASSOCIATES
P.O. Box 71, Bridgewater VA 22812. 540/828-2365. **Fax:** 540/828-2851. **Contact:** E.G. Souder, President. **Description:** A national executive search firm. Founded in 1997. Company pays fee. **Specializes in the areas**

of: Engineering; Food Industry; Manufacturing; Personnel/Labor Relations; Sales. **Positions commonly filled include:** Buyer; Ceramics Engineer; Chemical Engineer; Design Engineer; Electrical/Electronics Engineer; Environmental Engineer; Food Scientist/Technologist; General Manager; Human Resources Specialist; Industrial Engineer; Industrial Production Manager; Management Trainee; Materials Engineer; Mechanical Engineer; Metallurgical Engineer; MIS Specialist; Restaurant/Food Service Manager. **Average salary range of placements:** More than $50,000. **Number of placements per year:** 50 - 99.

SOURCE SERVICES CORPORATION
8045 Leesburg Pike, Suite 200, Vienna VA 22182. 703/790-5610. **Fax:** 703/790-1331. **Contact:** Manager. **Description:** An executive search firm. The divisions at this location include Source EDP, Source Engineering, Source Finance, Source Healthcare Staffing, and Accountant Source Temps. **Specializes in the areas of:** Accounting/Auditing; Computer Hardware/Software; Engineering; Finance; Health/Medical; Information Technology.

STRATEGIC SEARCH, INC.
5206 Markel Road, Suite 302, Richmond VA 23230. 804/285-6100. **Fax:** 804/285-6182. **Contact:** Dorrie Steinberg, President. **Description:** An executive search firm. Company pays fee. **Specializes in the areas of:** Computer Science/Software; Manufacturing; Personnel/Labor Relations; Technical. **Positions commonly filled include:** Computer Programmer; Human Resources Specialist; MIS Specialist; Purchasing Agent/Manager; Software Engineer; Systems Analyst; Technical Writer/Editor; Telecommunications Manager. **Other U.S. locations:** Yorktown PA. **Average salary range of placements:** $30,000 - $50,000. **Number of placements per year:** 50 - 99.

BILLIE SUMMERS & ASSOCIATES
10024 Purcell Road, Richmond VA 23228. 804/262-6800. **Contact:** Manager. **Description:** An executive search firm. **Specializes in the areas of:** Sales.

THE TALLEY GROUP
P.O. Box 2918, Staunton VA 24402-2918. 540/248-7009. **Fax:** 540/248-7046. **Contact:** John Burkhill, President. **E-mail address:** talley@cfw.com. **World Wide Web address:** http://www.talley-group.com. **Description:** A national executive search firm operating on both a retainer and contingency basis. Company pays fee. **Specializes in the areas of:** Accounting/Auditing; Banking; Computer Science/Software; Engineering; Finance; Food Industry; Human Resources; Industrial; Information Systems; Light Industrial; Manufacturing; Personnel/Labor Relations; Printing; Publishing; Retail; Sales; Scientific; Technical. **Positions commonly filled include:** Accountant; Auditor; Chemical Engineer; Chief Financial Officer; Computer Programmer; Controller; Cost Estimator; Database Manager; Design Engineer; Draftsperson; Electrical/Electronics Engineer; Environmental Engineer; Financial Analyst; Food Scientist/Technologist; Human Resources Manager; Industrial Engineer; Industrial Production Manager; Management Trainee; Manufacturing Engineer; Marketing Manager; Mechanical Engineer; Metallurgical Engineer; MIS Specialist; Operations/Production Manager; Project Manager; Purchasing Agent/Manager; Quality Control Supervisor; Sales Engineer; Sales Manager; Software Engineer; Systems Analyst; Systems Manager. **Number of placements per year:** 1 - 49.

TASK FORCE OF VIRGINIA, INC.
969 Waverly Village Road, Fredericksburg VA 22407. 540/785-6666. **Contact:** Bart D. Mix, President. **Description:** An executive search firm operating on a contingency basis. The firm also offers temporary placements. Company pays fee. **Specializes in the areas of:** Accounting/Auditing; Administration; General Labor; General Management; Industrial; Manufacturing; Secretarial. **Positions commonly filled include:** Accountant/Auditor; Blue-Collar Worker Supervisor; Branch Manager; Budget Analyst; Buyer; Claim Representative; Computer Programmer; Customer Service Representative; Dental Assistant/Dental Hygienist; Draftsperson; Education Administrator; Electrician; Financial Analyst; General Manager; Health Services Manager; Human Resources Specialist; Industrial Production Manager; Internet Services Manager; Management Trainee; Manufacturer's/Wholesaler's Sales Rep.; MIS Specialist; Operations/Production Manager; Paralegal; Physical Therapist; Public Relations Specialist; Quality Control Supervisor; Services Sales Representative; Software Engineer; Systems Analyst; Telecommunications Manager. **Benefits available to temporary workers:** Paid Holidays; Paid Vacation. **Average salary range of placements:** $30,000 - $50,000. **Number of placements per year:** 1 - 49.

U.S. SEARCH
712 West Broad Street, Suite 3, Falls Church VA 22046. 703/448-1900. **Fax:** 703/448-1907. **Contact:** Arnie Hiller, President. **E-mail address:** ahsearch@aol.com. **Description:** An executive search firm operating on both retainer and contingency bases that focuses on the composite materials, plastics, specialty chemicals, packaging, and plastics/rubber processing equipment industries. Company pays fee. **Specializes in the areas of:** Engineering; General Management; Manufacturing; Sales; Technical. **Positions commonly filled include:** Account Manager; Account Representative; Chemist; Manufacturing Engineer; Marketing Analyst; Marketing Specialist; Materials Engineer; Sales Engineer; Sales Executive; Sales Manager; Sales Representative; Vice President of Marketing. **Average salary range of placements:** More than $50,000. **Number of placements per year:** 1 - 49.

LAWRENCE VEBER ASSOCIATES
507 Tozewell Avenue, Cape Charles VA 23310. 757/331-4676. **Fax:** 757/331-4676. **Contact:** Larry Veber, President. **Description:** An executive search firm operating on both contingency and retainer bases. Company pays fee. **Specializes in the areas of:** Food Industry; Health/Medical; Retail. **Positions commonly filled include:** Computer Programmer; MIS Specialist; Physical Therapist; Physician; Systems Analyst. **Average salary range of placements:** More than $50,000. **Number of placements per year:** 1 - 49.

VIRGINIA EMPLOYMENT REFERRAL SERVICE
23 Old Street, Petersburg VA 23803. 804/733-4771. **Contact:** Bill Auchmoody, Vice President. **E-mail address:** varefr19@mail.us.net. **Description:** An executive search firm. Company pays fee. **Specializes in the areas of:** Accounting/Auditing; Administration; Advertising; Banking; Engineering; Food Industry; General Management; Manufacturing; Personnel/Labor Relations; Sales; Secretarial; Technical. **Positions commonly filled include:** Accountant/Auditor; Bank Officer/Manager; Blue-Collar Worker Supervisor; Branch Manager; Civil Engineer; Computer Programmer; Electrical/Electronics Engineer; Financial Analyst; General Manager; Industrial Engineer; Management Trainee; Manufacturer's/Wholesaler's Sales Rep.; Mechanical Engineer; MIS Specialist; Operations/Production Manager; Purchasing Agent/Manager; Restaurant/Food Service Manager; Services Sales Rep.; Telecommunications Manager. **Average salary range of placements:** $30,000 - $50,000. **Number of placements per year:** 100 - 199.

WAYNE ASSOCIATES INC.
2628 Barrett Street, Virginia Beach VA 23452-7404. 757/340-0555. **Fax:** 757/340-0555. **Contact:** Robert Cozzens, Owner. **E-mail address:** wai@infi.net. **Description:** An executive search firm operating on both retainer and contingency bases. Company pays fee. **Specializes in the areas of:** Engineering; Manufacturing; Sales. **Positions commonly filled include:** Biological Scientist; Chemical Engineer; Chemist; Design Engineer; Draftsperson; Mechanical Engineer. **Average salary range of placements:** $30,000 - $50,000.

BILL YOUNG & ASSOCIATES
8381 Old Courthouse Road, Suite 300, Vienna VA 22182. 703/573-0200. **Fax:** 703/573-3612. **Contact:** Angela C. Berkman, Resource Center Manager. **E-mail address:** applicant@billyoung.com. **World Wide Web address:** http://www.billyoung.com. **Description:** An executive search firm focusing on the placement of technical and computer personnel. Company pays fee. **Specializes in the areas of:** Administration; Computer Science/Software; Telecommunications. **Positions commonly filled include:** Computer Programmer; Human Resources Specialist; Internet Services Manager; Management Analyst/Consultant; Multimedia Designer; Operations/Production Manager; Software Engineer; Systems Analyst; Technical Writer/Editor; Telecommunications Manager. **Average salary range of placements:** More than $50,000. **Number of placements per year:** 50 - 99.

PERMANENT EMPLOYMENT AGENCIES

A CHOICE NANNY
1911 Fort Myers Drive, Arlington VA 22209. 703/525-2229. **Contact:** Manager. **Description:** A permanent employment agency. **Specializes in the areas of:** Nannies. **Other U.S. locations:** FL; MD; NJ.

A PLUS PERSONNEL
5339 Virginia Beach Boulevard, Suite 201, Virginia Beach VA 23462. 757/518-9290. **Contact:** Manager. **Description:** A permanent employment agency. **Specializes in the areas of:** Office Support.

ACCESS ENTERPRISES INC.
1608 Spring Hill Road, Suite 210, Vienna VA 22182. 703/442-9004. **Contact:** Manager. **Description:** A permanent employment agency. **Specializes in the areas of:** Accounting/Auditing; Data Processing; Engineering; Secretarial.

ACCU TECH
3601 West Hundred Road, Suite 102, Chester VA 23831. 804/768-9564. **Contact:** Manager. **Description:** A permanent employment agency that also provides temporary placements. **Specializes in the areas of:** Technical.

NANCY ALLEN ASSOCIATES, INC.
1730 North Lynn Street, Suite #603, Rosslyn VA 22209. 703/247-4222. **Fax:** 703/247-4181. **Contact:** Polly Frye, Manager. **E-mail address:** naa@ix.netcom.com. **Description:** A permanent employment agency. **Specializes in the areas of:** Administration; Legal; MIS/EDP; Nonprofit; Office Support; Personnel/Labor Relations; Secretarial. **Positions commonly filled include:** Administrative Assistant; Administrative Manager; Bank Officer/Manager; Clerical Supervisor; Editorial Assistant; Graphic Artist; Librarian; MIS Specialist; Paralegal. **Average salary range of placements:** $20,000 - $29,999. **Number of placements per year:** 100 - 199.

ALPHA OMEGA RESOURCES INC.
Briarwood Business Center, Suite 14, Route 221, Forest VA 24551. 804/385-8640. **Fax:** 804/385-0192. **Contact:** Ben Livesay, President. **Description:** A permanent employment agency. Company pays fee. **Specializes in the areas of:** Accounting/Auditing; Administration; Computer Science/Software; Engineering; Finance; Food Industry; General Management; Health/Medical; Industrial; Insurance; Manufacturing; Personnel/Labor Relations; Publishing; Sales; Secretarial; Technical; Transportation. **Positions commonly filled include:** Accountant/Auditor; Administrative Manager; Architect; Attorney; Branch Manager; Buyer; Computer Programmer; Customer Service Representative; Design Engineer; Electrical/Electronics Engineer; Environmental Engineer; General Manager; Human Resources Specialist; Industrial Engineer; Industrial Production Manager; Insurance Agent/Broker; Internet Services Manager; Manufacturer's/Wholesaler's Sales Rep.; Mechanical Engineer; MIS Specialist; Operations/Production Manager; Paralegal; Physician; Public Relations Specialist; Quality Control Supervisor; Services Sales Representative; Software Engineer; Typist/Word Processor. **Benefits available to temporary workers:** Medical Insurance; Paid Holidays; Paid Vacation. **Number of placements per year:** 1000+.

AMERICAN TECHNICAL RESOURCES
1651 Old Meadow Road, Suite 105, McLean VA 22102-4308. 703/917-7800. **Contact:** Manager of Technical Recruiting. **Description:** A permanent employment agency. Company pays fee. **Specializes in the areas of:** Administration; Computer Hardware/Software; Defense Industry; Engineering; Military; Technical. **Positions commonly filled include:** Account Representative; Computer Operator; Computer Programmer; Computer Scientist; Customer Service Representative; Database Manager; Electrical/Electronics Engineer; MIS Specialist; Operations/Production Manager; Software Engineer; Systems Analyst; Technical Writer/Editor. **Number of placements per year:** 200 - 499.

ARCADIA EURE PROFESSIONAL STAFFING
2115 Executive Drive, Suite 3B, Hampton VA 23666. 757/827-5633. **Contact:** Manager. **Description:** A permanent employment agency. **Specializes in the areas of:** Health/Medical. **Positions commonly filled include:** Certified Nursing Aide; Licensed Practical Nurse; Registered Nurse.

ARDELLE ASSOCIATES
AA TEMPS
7002 Little River Turnpike, Suite N, Annandale VA 22003. 703/642-9125. **Contact:** Manager. **Description:** A permanent employment agency. AA Temps (also at this location) is the temporary division. **Specializes in the areas of:** Accounting/Auditing; Bookkeeping; Data Processing; Office Support.

ATLANTIC RESOURCE GROUP
5511 Staples Mill Road, Suite 100, Richmond VA 23228. 804/262-4400. **Contact:** Manager. **Description:** A permanent employment agency that places information technology professionals with at least 18 months experience. **Specializes in the areas of:** Information Technology.

AUSTIN ASSOCIATES MEDICAL PERSONNEL
1760 Reston Parkway #300, Reston VA 20190. 703/736-0500. **Contact:** Manager. **Description:** A permanent placement agency. **Specializes in the areas of:** Health/Medical.

CAREER DEVELOPMENT
108 North Payne Street, Alexandria VA 22314. 703/548-3400. **Contact:** Manager. **Description:** A permanent placement agency for junior military officers. **Specializes in the areas of:** Military.

CORE PERSONNEL
8201 Greensboro Drive, Suite 100, McLean VA 22102. 703/556-9610. **Contact:** Harvey Silver, President. **Description:** A permanent employment agency. Company pays fee. **Specializes in the areas of:** Computer Hardware/Software. **Positions commonly filled include:** Administrative Assistant; Clerk; Computer Programmer; Customer Service Representative; EDP Specialist; Legal Secretary; Medical Secretary; Receptionist; Sales Representative; Secretary; Stenographer; Systems Analyst; Typist/Word Processor.

CURZON STAFFING
1434 Duke Street, Alexandria VA 22314. 703/836-4403. **Contact:** Manager. **Description:** An employment agency that provides both permanent and temporary placements. **Specializes in the areas of:** Accounting/Auditing; Data Processing; Secretarial.

DOW PERSONNEL
281 Independence Boulevard, Suite 309, Virginia Beach VA 23462. 757/499-7065. **Fax:** 757/499-7068. **Contact:** Constance V. Wiseman, Manager. **E-mail address:** rrogers@virgo.massolant.navy.mil. **Description:** A permanent employment agency. **Specializes in the areas of:** Accounting/Auditing; Banking; Economics; Finance; Food Industry; General Management; Insurance; Manufacturing; Retail; Sales; Secretarial. **Positions commonly filled include:** Account Manager; Administrative Manager; Bank Officer/Manager; Branch Manager; Broadcast Technician; Claim Representative; Clerical Supervisor; Computer Programmer; Credit Manager; Customer Service Representative; Electrician; Financial Analyst; General Manager; Human Resources Specialist; Insurance Agent/Broker; Management Trainee; Medical Records Technician; Public Relations Specialist; Restaurant/Food Service Manager; Services Sales Representative. **Average salary range of placements:** $20,000 - $29,999. **Number of placements per year:** 100 - 199.

HATCH MARKETING SYSTEMS
3900 Waterside Court, Virginia Beach VA 23452-2114. 757/498-7372. **Fax:** 757/498-0312. **Contact:** Larry Hatch, President. **Description:** A permanent employment agency and consulting firm. **Specializes in the areas of:** Administration; Computer Science/Software; Engineering; General Management; Industrial; Sales. **Positions commonly filled include:** Chemical Engineer; Civil Engineer; Computer Programmer; Draftsperson; Electrical/Electronics Engineer; Environmental Engineer; General Manager; Industrial Engineer; Industrial Production Manager; Manufacturing Engineer; Production Manager; Project Manager; Sales Engineer; Sales Manager; Software Engineer. **Average salary range of placements:** $30,000 - $50,000. **Number of placements per year:** 1 - 49.

HISPANIC COMMITTEE OF VIRGINIA
5827 Columbia Pike, 2nd Floor, Falls Church VA 22041. 703/671-5666. **Fax:** 703/671-2325. **Contact:** Lubin Hernandez Palomino, Job Developer. **E-mail address:** elcomite@aol.com. **Description:** A private, nonprofit permanent employment agency. The Hispanic Committee of Virginia has been serving the Hispanic population since 1967. **Specializes in the areas of:** Education; Food Industry; Retail; Sales; Secretarial. **Positions commonly filled include:** Accountant/Auditor; Administrative Manager; Advertising Clerk; Automotive Mechanic; Blue-Collar Worker Supervisor; Claim Representative; Clerical Supervisor; Construction and Building Inspector; Design Engineer; Designer; Editor; Education Administrator; Electrician; Emergency Medical Technician; Financial Analyst; Food Scientist/Technologist; Health Services Manager; Hotel Manager; Human Resources Specialist; Human Service Worker; Landscape Architect; Management Trainee; Manufacturer's/Wholesaler's Sales Rep.; Paralegal; Preschool Worker; Property and Real Estate Manager; Psychologist; Public Relations Specialist; Purchasing Agent/Manager; Radio/TV Announcer/Broadcaster; Real Estate Agent; Registered Nurse; Reporter; Restaurant/Food Service Manager; Services Sales Representative; Social Worker; Teacher/Professor; Travel Agent; Typist/Word Processor. **Average salary range of placements:** $20,000 - $29,999. **Number of placements per year:** 200 - 499.

CAROL McNEW EMPLOYMENT SERVICE
300 Moore Street, Bristol VA 24201. 540/466-3318. **Fax:** 540/466-6894. **Contact:** Carol McNew, Owner. **Description:** A permanent employment agency. Company pays fee. **Specializes in the areas of:** Accounting/Auditing; Banking; Computer Science/Software; Fashion; Finance; General Management; Health/Medical; Legal; Personnel/Labor Relations; Publishing; Retail; Sales; Secretarial. **Positions commonly filled include:** Accountant/Auditor; Administrative Assistant; Bank Officer/Manager; Bookkeeper; Clerk; Computer Operator; Computer Programmer; Credit Manager; Customer Service Representative; Data Entry Clerk; Factory Worker; General Manager; Insurance Agent/Broker; Medical Secretary; Nurse; Operations/Production Manager; Purchasing Agent/Manager; Quality Control Supervisor; Receptionist; Sales Representative; Secretary; Stenographer; Typist/Word Processor. **Number of placements per year:** 200 - 499.

SUSAN MILLER & ASSOCIATES, INC.
4216 Evergreen Lane, Annandale VA 22003. 703/642-1901. **Contact:** Manager. **Description:** A permanent employment agency. Company pays fee. **Specializes in the areas of:** Accounting/Auditing; Office Support; Secretarial. **Positions commonly filled include:** Administrative Assistant; Executive Assistant; Legal Secretary; Office Manager; Receptionist.

NANNY DIMENSIONS
10560 Main Street, Suite 111, Fairfax VA 22030-7182. 703/691-0334. **Fax:** 703/691-3954. **Contact:** Recruiter. **Description:** A permanent employment agency that focuses on nanny placement. **Specializes in the areas of:** Child Care, In-Home; Eldercare, In-Home. **Positions commonly filled include:** Nanny. **Benefits available to temporary workers:** Dental Insurance; Medical Insurance. **Average salary range of placements:** Less than $20,000. **Number of placements per year:** 100 - 199.

NANNY FACTOR
5975 New England Woods Drive, Burke VA 22015-2911. 703/323-7945. **Toll-free phone:** 800/232-6269. **Fax:** 703/764-1350. **Contact:** Leslie Smith, Director. **Description:** A permanent employment agency that places full-time, live-in nannies with families in the metropolitan Washington DC area. Company pays fee. **Specializes in the areas of:** Nannies. **Average salary range of placements:** $20,000 - $29,999. **Number of placements per year:** 100 - 199.

NATIONAL RECRUITERS
One Columbus Center, Suite 600, Virginia Beach VA 23462. 757/490-7821. **Fax:** 757/427-1616. **Contact:** Lydia McHenry, President. **Description:** A permanent

employment agency. National Recruiters focuses on the placement of sales and management personnel as well as computer programmers. The agency also provides career/outplacement counseling. Company pays fee. **Specializes in the areas of:** Fashion; Finance; Food Industry; Retail; Sales. **Positions commonly filled include:** Adjuster; Branch Manager; Computer Programmer; Credit Manager; General Manager; Management Trainee; Manufacturer's/Wholesaler's Sales Rep.; Pharmacist; Restaurant/Food Service Manager; Securities Sales Representative. **Average salary range of placements:** $20,000 - $29,999.

OFFICETEAM
1100 Wilson Boulevard, Suite 900, Arlington VA 22209. 703/528-1010. **Contact:** Manager. **Description:** A permanent employment agency that also offers some temporary placements. **Specializes in the areas of:** Accounting/Auditing; Bookkeeping; Finance.

PAE PLACEMENT
1601 North Kent Street, Suite 900, Arlington VA 22209. 703/243-6464. **Fax:** 703/243-5607. **Contact:** Manager. **Description:** A permanent employment agency. **Specializes in the areas of:** Bilingual; International Executives.

PAUL-TITTLE ASSOCIATES, INC.
1485 Chain Bridge Road, Suite 304, McLean VA 22101-4501. 703/442-0500. **Fax:** 703/893-3871. **Contact:** Manager. **E-mail address:** pta@paul-tittle.com. **Description:** A permanent employment agency. **Specializes in the areas of:** Computer Science/Software; Electronics; Engineering; Sales; Telecommunications.

POTOMAC PERSONNEL
1640 King Street, Suite A, Alexandria VA 22314. 703/549-5055. **Contact:** Shonna Meadows, Branch Manager. **Description:** A permanent employment agency. Company pays fee. **Specializes in the areas of:** Clerical; Personnel/Labor Relations. **Positions commonly filled include:** Administrative Assistant; Bookkeeper; Clerk; Computer Operator; Data Entry Clerk; Legal Secretary; Medical Secretary; Receptionist; Secretary; Stenographer; Typist/Word Processor.

SELECT STAFFING SERVICES
P.O. Box 12189, Norfolk VA 23502-1289. 757/461-1582. **Fax:** 757/461-2835. **Contact:** Jeanie Hurrell, Manager. **Description:** A permanent employment agency that also provides temporary staffing. Select Staffing Services focuses on administrative, clerical, and technical job assignments. Founded in 1960. **Specializes in the areas of:** Accounting/Auditing; Administration; Computer Science/Software; Industrial; Legal; Personnel/Labor Relations; Sales; Secretarial. **Positions commonly filled include:** Accountant/Auditor; Claim Representative; Clerical Supervisor; Credit Manager; Customer Service Representative; Draftsperson; Human Resources Manager; MIS Specialist; Paralegal; Typist/Word Processor. **Benefits available to temporary workers:** 401(k); Life Insurance; Paid Holidays; Paid Vacation. **Corporate headquarters location:** Reston VA. **Average salary range of placements:** $20,000 - $29,999. **Number of placements per year:** 1000+.

SENIOR EMPLOYMENT RESOURCES (SER)
4201 John Marr Drive, Suite 236, Annandale VA 22003. 703/750-1936. **Fax:** 703/750-0269. **Contact:** Executive Director. **Description:** A permanent employment agency that places individuals who are over the age of 50. **Positions commonly filled include:** Accountant/Auditor; Administrative Assistant; Architect; Bookkeeper; Clerk; Computer Programmer; Credit Manager; Customer Service Representative; Data Entry Clerk; Draftsperson; Executive Assistant; Industrial Designer; Industrial Engineer; Legal Secretary; Medical Secretary; Public Relations Specialist; Purchasing Agent/Manager; Receptionist; Sales Representative; Typist/Word Processor. **Number of placements per year:** 200 - 499.

HELEN R. SKINNER ASSOCIATES INC.
8237 Idlywood Road, Vienna VA 22182. 703/847-0091. **Contact:** Manager. **Description:** A permanent employment agency. **Specializes in the areas of:** High-Tech.

SNELLING PERSONNEL SERVICES
45 West Boscawen Street, Winchester VA 22601-4750. 540/667-1911. **Fax:** 540/667-0505. **Contact:** Manager. **Description:** A permanent employment agency that also provides temporary placements. **Specializes in the areas of:** Accounting/Auditing; Administration; Art/Design; Banking; Education; Engineering; Food Industry; Health/Medical; Legal; Manufacturing; Personnel/Labor Relations; Publishing; Retail; Sales; Secretarial; Technical. **Positions commonly filled include:** Accountant/Auditor; Administrative Manager; Aerospace Engineer; Attorney; Bank Officer/Manager; Branch Manager; Buyer; Ceramics Engineer; Chemical Engineer; Civil Engineer; Computer Programmer; Electrical/Electronics Engineer; Health Services Manager; Hotel Manager; Human Resources Manager; Industrial Engineer; Industrial Production Manager; Library Technician; Management Trainee; Manufacturer's/Wholesaler's Sales Rep.; Materials Engineer; Mechanical Engineer; Metallurgical Engineer; Occupational Therapist; Paralegal; Purchasing Agent/Manager; Registered Nurse; Respiratory Therapist; Services Sales Representative; Systems Analyst; Teacher/Professor; Typist/Word Processor; Wholesale and Retail Buyer. **Number of placements per year:** 100 - 199.

SNELLING PERSONNEL SERVICES
8614 Westwood Center Drive, Suite 640, Vienna VA 22182. 703/448-0050. **Fax:** 703/448-3770. **Contact:** Manager. **Description:** A permanent employment agency. Snelling Personnel Services also provides temporary and contract services. Company pays fee. **Specializes in the areas of:** Administration; Banking; Computer Science/Software; Engineering; Finance; General Management; Health/Medical; Legal; Sales; Secretarial; Technical. **Positions commonly filled include:** Administrative Assistant; Bookkeeper; Clerk; Computer Programmer; Customer Service Representative; MIS Specialist; Physical Therapist; Sales Representative; Systems Analyst. **Corporate headquarters location:** Dallas TX. **Other U.S. locations:** Nationwide. **Number of placements per year:** 1000+.

SNELLING PERSONNEL SERVICES
2817 North Parham Road, Suite 5A, Richmond VA 23294-4409. 804/965-9500. **Fax:** 804/965-9533. **Contact:** Manager. **Description:** A permanent employment agency. Company pays fee. **Specializes in the areas of:** Advertising; Finance; Industrial; Legal; Personnel/Labor Relations; Sales. **Positions commonly filled include:** Accountant/Auditor; Clerical Supervisor; Customer Service Representative; Paralegal; Services Sales Representative; Typist/Word Processor. **Benefits available to temporary workers:** Medical Insurance; Paid Holidays. **Corporate headquarters location:** Dallas TX. **Other U.S. locations:** Nationwide. **Average salary range of placements:** Less than $20,000. **Number of placements per year:** 200 - 499.

TECHNICAL SEARCH CORPORATION
804 Moorefield Park Drive, Suite 103, Richmond VA 23236. 804/323-3000. **Fax:** 804/330-9378. **Contact:**

Mr. W.J. Kymmell, President. **Description:** A permanent employment agency. **Specializes in the areas of:** Computer Science/Software. **Positions commonly filled include:** Computer Programmer; Software Engineer; Systems Analyst. **Number of placements per year:** 50 - 99.

VIP PERSONNEL, INC.
668 Ridge Drive, Valentine VA 23887. 804/577-2411. **Contact:** Manager. **Description:** A permanent employment agency. **Specializes in the areas of:** Data Processing.

WANNAMAKER ASSOCIATES INC.
P.O. Box 5699, Richmond VA 23220. 804/358-0091. **Contact:** Bill Wannamaker, President. **Description:** A permanent employment agency. Company pays fee. **Specializes in the areas of:** Engineering; Manufacturing; Personnel/Labor Relations; Technical. **Positions commonly filled include:** Aerospace Engineer; Ceramics Engineer; Chemical Engineer; Draftsperson; Electrical/Electronics Engineer; Industrial Designer; Industrial Engineer; Machinist; Manufacturing Engineer; Mechanical Engineer; Metallurgical Engineer; Operations/Production Manager; Packaging Engineer; Quality Control Supervisor; Software Engineer. **Number of placements per year:** 50 - 99.

WISDOM & WILLIAMS
205 South Whiting Street, Alexandria VA 22304. 703/823-6660. **Contact:** Susan Miller, Recruiter. **Description:** A permanent employment agency. Company pays fee. **Specializes in the areas of:** Health/Medical; Legal; Nonprofit. **Positions commonly filled include:** Administrative Assistant; Clerk; Receptionist; Secretary; Typist/Word Processor. **Number of placements per year:** 50 - 99.

TEMPORARY EMPLOYMENT AGENCIES

ACCOUNTANTS ON CALL
8000 Towers Crescent Drive, Suite 825, Vienna VA 22182-2700. **Contact:** Recruiter. **Description:** A temporary agency. **Specializes in the areas of:** Accounting/Auditing; Finance. **Positions commonly filled include:** Accountant/Auditor; Budget Analyst; Credit Manager; Financial Analyst. **Corporate headquarters location:** Saddlebrook NJ. **Other U.S. locations:** Nationwide.

ACCOUNTING ASSETS INC.
8330 Boone Boulevard, Suite 800, Vienna VA 22182. 703/883-2123. **Contact:** Manager. **Description:** A temporary agency that also provides permanent placements. **Specializes in the areas of:** Accounting/Auditing; Bookkeeping.

ADVANTAGE STAFFING
620 Herndon Parkway, Suite 110, Herndon VA 20170. 703/904-9092. **Contact:** Manager. **Description:** A temporary agency. **Specializes in the areas of:** Health/Medical; Information Technology; Nonprofit; Secretarial. **Positions commonly filled include:** Customer Service Representative; Editor; Internet Services Manager; Multimedia Designer; Paralegal; Technical Writer/Editor; Typist/Word Processor. **Benefits available to temporary workers:** Medical Insurance; Paid Holidays; Paid Vacation; Profit Sharing. **Corporate headquarters location:** Stamford CT. **Other U.S. locations:** DC; MD; NY; PA. **Average salary range of placements:** $30,000 - $50,000. **Number of placements per year:** 1000+.

COMPUTEMP OF WASHINGTON, D.C.
12120 Sunset Hills Drive, Suite 120, Reston VA 20190. 703/481-3334. **Fax:** 703/481-3335. **Contact:** Mark W. Stein, President. **E-mail address:** computemp@aol.com. **World Wide Web address:** http://www.sunstudios.com/computemp. **Description:** A temporary agency. **Specializes in the areas of:** Administration; Computer Science/Software. **Positions commonly filled include:** MIS Specialist; Software Engineer. **Corporate headquarters location:** Boca Raton FL. **Average salary range of placements:** $30,000 - $50,000. **Number of placements per year:** 100 - 199.

EDP
2095 Chain Bridge Road, Vienna VA 22182-3794. 703/893-2400. **Contact:** Manager. **Description:** A temporary agency. Company pays fee. **Specializes in the areas of:** Accounting/Auditing; Administration; Banking; Computer Hardware/Software; Engineering; Finance; Insurance; Manufacturing; Nonprofit; Personnel/Labor Relations; Publishing; Technical. **Positions commonly filled include:** Computer Operator; Computer Programmer; EDP Specialist; MIS Specialist; Systems Analyst; Technical Writer/Editor. **Number of placements per year:** 1000+.

EXPRESS PERSONNEL SERVICES
2155 Electric Road, Suite B, Roanoke VA 24018. 540/776-8729. **Fax:** 540/776-5437. **Contact:** Hartley R. Gaston, Owner. **Description:** A temporary agency. **Specializes in the areas of:** Administration; Computer Science/Software; Manufacturing; Personnel/Labor Relations; Secretarial. **Positions commonly filled include:** Accountant/Auditor; Administrative Manager; Blue-Collar Worker Supervisor; Branch Manager; Claim Representative; Clerical Supervisor; Computer Programmer; Credit Manager; Customer Service Representative; Draftsperson; General Manager; Human Resources Manager; Human Service Worker; Industrial Engineer; Industrial Production Manager; Management Analyst/Consultant; Management Trainee; Market Research Analyst; Operations/Production Manager; Paralegal; Property and Real Estate Manager; Public Relations Specialist; Purchasing Agent/Manager; Quality Control Supervisor; Restaurant/Food Service Manager; Software Engineer; Systems Analyst; Typist/Word Processor; Underwriter/Assistant Underwriter. **Corporate headquarters location:** Oklahoma City OK. **Average salary range of placements:** $20,000 - $29,999.

KELLY SERVICES, INC.
3232 Riverside Drive, Danville VA 24541. 804/791-1597. **Contact:** A. Fulcher, Supervisor. **Description:** A temporary agency. Company pays fee. **Specializes in the areas of:** Computer Science/Software; Secretarial. **Positions commonly filled include:** Administrative Assistant; Marketing Specialist; Secretary; Typist/Word Processor. **Corporate headquarters location:** Troy MI. **Average salary range of placements:** Less than $20,000. **Number of placements per year:** 200 - 499.

LEAFSTONE, INC.
225 Reinekers Lane, Suite 240, Alexandria VA 22314-2875. 703/518-2300. **Fax:** 703/518-2305. **Contact:** Branch Manager. **E-mail address:** leafstoneva@microsoft.com. **World Wide Web address:** http://www.leafnet.com. **Description:** A temporary agency. Company pays fee. **Specializes in the areas of:** Finance; Nonprofit; Secretarial. **Positions commonly filled include:** Administrative Assistant; Administrative Manager; Advertising Clerk; Computer Operator; Customer Service Representative; Database Manager; Graphic Artist; Secretary; Technical Writer/Editor; Typist/Word Processor. **Benefits**

available to temporary workers: Credit Union; Direct Deposit; Medical Insurance; Paid Vacation. **Corporate headquarters location:** Jericho NY. **Average salary range of placements:** $20,000 - $29,999. **Number of placements per year:** 50 - 99.

MANPOWER TEMPORARY SERVICES
8280 Greensboro Drive, Suite 450, McLean VA 22102. 703/821-0101. **Contact:** Recruitment. **Description:** A temporary agency. Company pays fee. **Specializes in the areas of:** Clerical; Personnel/Labor Relations; Word Processing. **Positions commonly filled include:** Administrative Assistant; Bookkeeper; Clerk; Customer Service Representative; Data Entry Clerk; Legal Secretary; Secretary; Stenographer; Technical Writer/Editor; Typist/Word Processor. **Corporate headquarters location:** Milwaukee WI. **Number of placements per year:** 1000+.

MANPOWER TEMPORARY SERVICES
2300 Fall Hill Avenue, Fredericksburg VA 22401. 540/373-7801. **Fax:** 540/373-8106. **Contact:** Manager. **Description:** A temporary agency. **Specializes in the areas of:** Industrial; Insurance; Manufacturing; Sales; Secretarial. **Positions commonly filled include:** Claim Representative; Clerical Supervisor; Customer Service Representative; Industrial Engineer; Insurance Agent/Broker. **Benefits available to temporary workers:** Medical Insurance; Paid Holidays; Paid Vacation. **Corporate headquarters location:** Milwaukee WI. **Other U.S. locations:** Nationwide. **Average salary range of placements:** $20,000 - $29,999. **Number of placements per year:** 1000+.

MANPOWER TEMPORARY SERVICES
1051 East Cary, Suite 102, Richmond VA 23219. 804/780-1800. **Contact:** Branch Manager. **Description:** A temporary agency. Company pays fee. **Specializes in the areas of:** Office Support; Technical; Word Processing. **Positions commonly filled include:** Accountant/Auditor; Accounting Clerk; Administrative Assistant; Assembler; Biological Scientist; Bookkeeper; Chemist; Computer Programmer; Customer Service Representative; Designer; Desktop Publishing Specialist; Electrician; Inspector/Tester/Grader; Inventory Control Specialist; Machine Operator; Packaging/Processing Worker; Painter; Proofreader; Receptionist; Research Assistant; Secretary; Systems Analyst; Technical Writer/Editor; Telemarketer; Typist/Word Processor. **Corporate headquarters location:** Milwaukee WI. **Other U.S. locations:** Nationwide. **Number of placements per year:** 1000+.

NORTHERN VIRGINIA TEMPORARIES, INC.
7700 Leesburg Pike, Suite 218, Falls Church VA 22043. 703/761-4357. **Fax:** 703/556-0494. **Contact:** Larry Gwensberg, President. **Description:** A temporary agency that also provides permanent placements, executive searches, contract services, and career/outplacement counseling. Company pays fee. **Specializes in the areas of:** Sales; Secretarial. **Positions commonly filled include:** Sales Executive; Sales Representative; Secretary; Technical Writer/Editor. **Average salary range of placements:** $30,000 - $50,000.

OLSTEN STAFFING SERVICES
12350 Jefferson Avenue, Newport News VA 23602. 757/881-9760. **Toll-free phone:** 800/967-5669. **Contact:** Manager. **Description:** A temporary agency. **Specializes in the areas of:** Accounting/Auditing; Computer Science/Software; General Management; Industrial; Legal; Manufacturing; Personnel/Labor Relations; Secretarial; Technical. **Positions commonly filled include:** Accountant/Auditor; Administrative Manager; Advertising Clerk; Blue-Collar Worker Supervisor; Branch Manager; Buyer; Counselor; Credit Manager; Customer Service Representative; General Manager; Human Resources Specialist; Human Service Worker; Library Technician; Paralegal; Purchasing Agent/Manager. **Benefits available to temporary workers:** Paid Vacation. **Average salary range of placements:** Less than $20,000. **Number of placements per year:** 500 - 999.

PDS TEMPORARY SERVICE, INC.
309 Aragona Boulevard, Suite 112, Virginia Beach VA 23462. 757/499-1987. **Fax:** 757/499-8297. **Contact:** Trish Luchau, General Manager. **Description:** A temporary agency. **Specializes in the areas of:** Industrial; Manufacturing; Secretarial. **Positions commonly filled include:** Electrician; Typist/Word Processor. **Number of placements per year:** 1000+.

PRINTING PROFESSIONALS INC.
630 North Washington Street, Alexandria VA 22314. 703/549-5627. **Contact:** Manager. **Description:** A temporary agency that also provides permanent placements. **Specializes in the areas of:** Publishing.

REMEDY INTELLIGENT STAFFING
144 Business Park Drive, Suite 104, Virginia Beach VA 23462-6527. 757/490-8367. **Fax:** 757/499-4713. **Contact:** Joseph A. Kennedy, President. **Description:** A temporary agency that focuses on office automation and administration. **Specializes in the areas of:** Accounting/Auditing; Administration; Banking; Computer Science/Software; Health/Medical; Legal; Personnel/Labor Relations; Secretarial; Technical. **Positions commonly filled include:** Accountant/Auditor; Administrative Manager; Claim Representative; Clerical Supervisor; Computer Programmer; Customer Service Representative; Education Administrator; Electrical/Electronics Engineer; Human Resources Specialist; Human Service Worker; Medical Records Technician; MIS Specialist; Paralegal; Systems Analyst; Telecommunications Manager; Typist/Word Processor. **Benefits available to temporary workers:** 401(k); Life Insurance; Medical Insurance. **Number of placements per year:** 500 - 999.

SELECTEMPS
1033 North Fairfax Street, Alexandria VA 22314. 703/684-9117. **Toll-free phone:** 800/966-3639. **Fax:** 703/836-6536. **Contact:** Manager. **Description:** A temporary agency. **Specializes in the areas of:** Administration; Computer Science/Software; General Management; Personnel/Labor Relations; Secretarial. **Positions commonly filled include:** Blue-Collar Worker Supervisor; Claim Representative; Computer Programmer; Credit Manager; Customer Service Representative; General Manager; Human Service Worker; Insurance Agent/Broker; Operations/Production Manager; Paralegal; Property and Real Estate Manager; Public Relations Specialist; Purchasing Agent/Manager; Systems Analyst; Typist/Word Processor; Underwriter/Assistant Underwriter. **Corporate headquarters location:** Reston VA. **Other U.S. locations:** GA; MD; SC. **Average salary range of placements:** $20,000 - $29,999. **Number of placements per year:** 1000+.

STAT TEMPS, INC.
506 Westwood Office Park, Fredericksburg VA 22401. 540/373-2200. **Fax:** 540/373-5386. **Contact:** Cindy Duffer Matern, Vice President. **Description:** A temporary agency that also offers permanent placements. Company pays fee. **Specializes in the areas of:** Accounting/Auditing; Computer Science/Software; Engineering; General Management; Industrial; Legal; Manufacturing; Personnel/Labor Relations; Secretarial. **Positions commonly filled include:** Accountant/Auditor; Blue-Collar Worker Supervisor; Budget Analyst; Civil Engineer; Clerical

Supervisor; Computer Programmer; Construction Contractor; Credit Manager; Customer Service Representative; Dental Assistant/Dental Hygienist; Draftsperson; Electrical/Electronics Engineer; Emergency Medical Technician; General Manager; Human Resources Specialist; Industrial Engineer; Industrial Production Manager; Mechanical Engineer; Operations/Production Manager; Paralegal; Public Relations Specialist; Systems Analyst. **Benefits available to temporary workers:** Medical Insurance. **Average salary range of placements:** $20,000 - $29,999. **Number of placements per year:** 200 - 499.

TAC STAFFING SERVICES
2095 Chain Bridge Road, Vienna VA 22182. 703/893-5260. **Contact:** Manager. **Description:** A temporary agency. Company pays fee. **Specializes in the areas of:** Accounting/Auditing; Advertising; Banking; Clerical; Education; Finance; Health/Medical; Insurance; Legal; Manufacturing; Nonprofit; Personnel/Labor Relations; Publishing; Sales; Transportation. **Positions commonly filled include:** Bookkeeper; Clerk; Data Entry Clerk; Driver; Factory Worker; Legal Secretary; Light Industrial Worker; Medical Secretary; Receptionist; Secretary; Typist/Word Processor. **Other U.S. locations:** Nationwide. **Number of placements per year:** 1000+.

TAC STAFFING SERVICES
11864-B Sunrise Valley Drive, Reston VA 22091. 703/758-0100. **Contact:** Manager. **Description:** A temporary agency. **Specializes in the areas of:** Administration; Customer Service; Data Processing; Word Processing. **Other U.S. locations:** Nationwide.

TEAM PLACEMENT SERVICE, INC.
5113 Leesburg Pike, Suite 510, Falls Church VA 22041. 703/820-8618. **Toll-free phone:** 800/495-6767. **Fax:** 703/820-3368. **Contact:** Betty Peebles, President. **E-mail address:** epeebles@teamplace.com. **Description:** A temporary agency that provides staff for the health care industry including medical, dental, and biotechnology companies; hospitals; private practice; and insurance companies. The agency also some permanent placements. Company pays fee. **Specializes in the areas of:** Health/Medical. **Positions commonly filled include:** Administrative Assistant; Administrative Manager; Biochemist; Biological Scientist; Chemist; Dental Assistant/Dental Hygienist; Dentist; EKG Technician; Licensed Practical Nurse; Pharmacist; Physical Therapist; Registered Nurse. **Benefits available to temporary workers:** 401(k); Medical Insurance; Paid Vacation. **Other U.S. locations:** Silver Spring MD. **Average salary range of placements:** $30,000 - $50,000. **Number of placements per year:** 200 - 499.

TECH/AID OF VIRGINIA
2095 Chain Bridge Road, Suite 300, Vienna VA 22182. 703/893-6444. **Contact:** Manager. **Description:** A temporary agency. Company pays fee. **Specializes in the areas of:** Architecture/Construction; Cable TV; Computer Hardware/Software; Engineering; Manufacturing; Technical. **Positions commonly filled include:** Aerospace Engineer; Architect; Buyer; Ceramics Engineer; Chemical Engineer; Civil Engineer; Draftsperson; Electrical/Electronics Engineer; Estimator; Industrial Designer; Industrial Engineer; Manufacturing Engineer; Mechanical Engineer; Metallurgical Engineer; Mining Engineer; Operations/Production Manager; Petroleum Engineer; Purchasing Agent/Manager; Quality Control Supervisor; Technical Writer/Editor; Technician. **Number of placements per year:** 1000+.

TEMPORARIES NOW
7700 Little River Turnpike, Suite 300, Annandale VA 22003-2406. 703/914-9100. **Contact:** Placement Coordinator. **Description:** A temporary agency. Company pays fee. **Specializes in the areas of:** Clerical; Office Support; Personnel/Labor Relations; Secretarial; Word Processing. **Positions commonly filled include:** Customer Service Representative; Human Resources Specialist; Marketing Specialist; Technical Writer/Editor; Typist/Word Processor. **Benefits available to temporary workers:** Credit Union; Dental Insurance; Medical Insurance; Paid Holidays; Paid Vacation; Vision Insurance. **Average salary range of placements:** $20,000 - $29,999. **Number of placements per year:** 1000+.

TEMPORARY SOLUTIONS
10328 Battleview Parkway, Manassas VA 20109. 703/361-2220. **Fax:** 703/368-2640. **Contact:** Tracy Margerum, Recruiter. **Description:** A temporary agency. **Specializes in the areas of:** Accounting/Auditing; Administration; Banking; General Management; Industrial; Manufacturing; Personnel/Labor Relations; Retail; Secretarial. **Positions commonly filled include:** Accountant/Auditor; Administrative Manager; Bank Officer/Manager; Blue-Collar Worker Supervisor; Clerical Supervisor; Computer Programmer; Customer Service Representative; Financial Analyst; General Manager; Human Resources Specialist; Human Service Worker; MIS Specialist; Paralegal; Property and Real Estate Manager; Public Relations Specialist; Services Sales Representative; Technical Writer/Editor; Typist/Word Processor. **Corporate headquarters location:** This Location. **Other area locations:** Leesburg VA; Tysons Corner VA; Woodbridge VA. **Other U.S. locations:** Charlotte NC. **Number of placements per year:** 1000+.

TEMPWORLD STAFFING SERVICES
1593 Spring Hill Road, Suite 110, Vienna VA 22182. 703/448-8000. **Fax:** 703/448-8060. **Contact:** Ann Knoke, Staffing Manager. **Description:** A temporary agency that focuses on office support positions. **Specializes in the areas of:** Accounting/Auditing; Computer Science/Software; Finance; Personnel/Labor Relations; Retail; Sales; Secretarial. **Positions commonly filled include:** Administrative Assistant; Administrative Manager; Blue-Collar Worker Supervisor; Branch Manager; Customer Service Representative; Graphic Artist; Graphic Designer; Human Resources Specialist; Multimedia Designer; Purchasing Agent/Manager; Services Sales Representative; Technical Writer/Editor; Typist/Word Processor. **Benefits available to temporary workers:** 401(k); Paid Vacation. **Corporate headquarters location:** Atlanta GA. **Other U.S. locations:** AL; DC; GA. **Average salary range of placements:** $20,000 - $29,999. **Number of placements per year:** 500 - 999.

TEMPWORLD STAFFING SERVICES
1801 Reston Parkway, Suite 102, Reston VA 20190. 703/435-7474. **Fax:** 703/437-7511. **Contact:** Chris Meurer, Branch Manager. **Description:** A temporary agency focusing on clerical/secretarial, office automation, light industrial, and light technical positions. **Specializes in the areas of:** Administration; Secretarial. **Positions commonly filled include:** Customer Service Representative. **Corporate headquarters location:** Atlanta GA. **Other U.S. locations:** AL; DC; GA. **Average salary range of placements:** $20,000 - $29,999. **Number of placements per year:** 500 - 999.

WESTERN STAFF SERVICES
475 East Main Street, Wytheville VA 24382. 540/223-1896. **Contact:** Manager. **Description:** A temporary agency that also offers some permanent placements. **Specializes in the areas of:** General Management; Industrial; Manufacturing.

CONTRACT SERVICES FIRMS

B&M ASSOCIATES
7700 Leesburg Pike, Suite 204, Falls Church VA 22043. 703/448-9675. **Contact:** Manager. **Description:** A contract services firm that focuses on technical placements. **Specializes in the areas of:** Computer Science/Software; Information Systems.

BSC
8150 Leesburg Pike, Suite 700, Vienna VA 22182. 703/821-3500. **Fax:** 703/761-6763. **Contact:** Mary Barr, President. **Description:** A contract services firm that also provides career outplacement counseling. **Specializes in the areas of:** Engineering; General Management. **Positions commonly filled include:** Accountant/Auditor; Actuary; Adjuster; Administrative Manager; Advertising Clerk; Aerospace Engineer; Agricultural Engineer; Aircraft Mechanic/Engine Specialist; Architect; Attorney; Bank Officer/Manager; Biochemist; Biological Scientist; Biomedical Engineer; Blue-Collar Worker Supervisor; Branch Manager; Broadcast Technician; Brokerage Clerk; Budget Analyst; Construction and Building Inspector; Construction Contractor; Cost Estimator; Draftsperson; Electrical/Electronics Engineer; MIS Specialist; Multimedia Designer; Telecommunications Manager; Transportation/Traffic Specialist.

BRADFORD COMPANY
531 West Main Street, Waynesboro VA 22980-4529. 540/949-6992. **Fax:** 540/949-6996. **Contact:** Patricia L. Cabe, Manager. **Description:** A contract services firm. Company pays fee. **Specializes in the areas of:** Clerical; Light Industrial; Production; Secretarial. **Positions commonly filled include:** Administrative Assistant; Computer Operator; Customer Service Representative; Design Engineer; Draftsperson; Electrician; Medical Records Technician; Production Worker; Secretary; Typist/Word Processor. **Corporate headquarters location:** This Location. **Average salary range of placements:** Less than $30,000. **Number of placements per year:** 100 - 199.

BUTLER SERVICE GROUP INC.
6707 Old Dominion Drive, Suite 305, McLean VA 22101. 703/883-3900. **Contact:** Manager. **Description:** A contract services firm.

CDI CORPORATION
14120 Parke Long Court, Suite 200, Chantilly VA 20151. 703/222-0700. **Fax:** 703/222-0704. **Contact:** Recruiter. **World Wide Web address:** http://www.cdicorp.com. **Description:** A contract services firm. Company pays fee. **Specializes in the areas of:** Computer Science/Software; Engineering; Technical. **Positions commonly filled include:** Aerospace Engineer; Architect; Biochemist; Biological Scientist; Biomedical Engineer; Buyer; Chemical Engineer; Chemist; Civil Engineer; Computer Programmer; Design Engineer; Draftsperson; Editor; Electrical/Electronics Engineer; Environmental Engineer; Geologist/Geophysicist; Industrial Engineer; Internet Services Manager; Mathematician; Mechanical Engineer; MIS Specialist; Multimedia Designer; Petroleum Engineer; Science Technologist; Software Engineer; Systems Analyst; Technical Writer/Editor; Telecommunications Manager. **Benefits available to temporary workers:** 401(k); Medical Insurance; Paid Holidays; Paid Vacation. **Corporate headquarters location:** Philadelphia PA. **Other U.S. locations:** Nationwide. **International locations:** Worldwide. **Average salary range of placements:** More than $50,000. **Number of placements per year:** 500 - 999.

CADWORKS, INC.
1506 Willow Lawn Drive, Richmond VA 23230. 804/288-2233. **Fax:** 804/285-8256. **Contact:** Joy Haliburton, Client Services Manager. **Description:** A contract services firm focusing on proofing and design support and information services. Company pays fee. **Specializes in the areas of:** Architecture/Construction; Computer Science/Software; Engineering; Personnel/Labor Relations; Technical. **Positions commonly filled include:** Chemical Engineer; Chemist; Civil Engineer; Design Engineer; Designer; Draftsperson; Electrician; Industrial Engineer; Materials Engineer; Mechanical Engineer; Multimedia Designer; Science Technologist; Software Engineer; Structural Engineer; Technical Writer/Editor. **Benefits available to temporary workers:** Medical Insurance. **Average salary range of placements:** $30,000 - $50,000. **Number of placements per year:** 50 - 99.

COMPUTER PROFESSIONALS INC. (CPI)
1427 West Main Street, Richmond VA 23220. 804/353-7600. **Fax:** 804/353-2445. **Contact:** Meredith Hickman, Technical Recruiter. **Description:** A contract services firm that focuses on placing information systems consultants nationwide. Company pays fee. **Specializes in the areas of:** Computer Science/Software. **Positions commonly filled include:** Computer Programmer; Internet Services Manager; MIS Specialist; Systems Analyst. **Corporate headquarters location:** Lake Wylie SC. **Other U.S. locations:** Phoenix AZ; Tampa FL; Atlanta GA; Charlotte NC; Dallas TX. **Average salary range of placements:** $30,000 - $50,000. **Number of placements per year:** 1 - 49.

DPS, INC.
751-K Thimble Shoals Boulevard, Newport News VA 23606-3563. 757/873-3371. **Toll-free phone:** 800/328-3371. **Fax:** 757/873-3670. **Contact:** Recruiter. **E-mail address:** dpsjobs@dpsjobs.com. **Description:** A contract services firm that focuses on the placement of health care professionals for work on government contracts. **Specializes in the areas of:** Health/Medical. **Positions commonly filled include:** Dental Assistant/Dental Hygienist; Dentist; Licensed Practical Nurse; Medical Records Technician; Pharmacist; Physical Therapist; Radiological Technologist; Registered Nurse; Respiratory Therapist.

H.R. DIRECTIONS
P.O. Box 712, Wytheville VA 24382. 540/228-8337. **Contact:** J.R. Bybee, Recruiter. **Description:** A contract services firm that focuses on human resources staffing. Company pays fee. **Specializes in the areas of:** Accounting/Auditing; Industrial; Manufacturing; Personnel/Labor Relations. **Positions commonly filled include:** Accountant/Auditor; Clerical Supervisor; Computer Programmer; Human Resources Specialist; Human Service Worker; Industrial Engineer; Mechanical Engineer; MIS Specialist; Purchasing Agent/Manager. **Average salary range of placements:** $20,000 - $29,999. **Number of placements per year:** 50 - 99.

IPC TECHNOLOGIES, INC.
7200 Glen Forest Drive, Richmond VA 23226. 804/285-9300. **Toll-free phone:** 800/296-4472. **Fax:** 804/673-9744. **Contact:** Stormy Hamlin, Manager of Personnel. **E-mail address:** stormy@ipctech.com. **World Wide Web address:** http://www.ipctech.com. **Description:** A contract services and consulting firm focusing on GUI application development and database design. **Specializes in the areas of:** Computer Science/Software. **Positions commonly filled include:** Computer Programmer; Financial Analyst; Internet Services Manager; MIS Specialist; Software Engineer; Technical Writer/Editor. **Average salary range of placements:** More than $50,000. **Number of placements per year:** 50 - 99.

A.J. MORELLI CONTRACTING, INC.
P.O. Box 5007, Richmond VA 23220-5007. 804/783-0021. **Contact:** Percy A. Smith, General Manager. **Description:** A contract services firm. **Specializes in the areas of:** Food Industry; Industrial; Manufacturing; Personnel/Labor Relations; Transportation. **Positions commonly filled include:** Construction Contractor; Construction Manager; Customer Service Rep.; Human Service Worker; Management Trainee. **Average salary range of placements:** Less than $20,000. **Number of placements per year:** 1 - 49.

PROCUREMENT SOLUTIONS INC.
1313 West Hills Lane, Reston VA 20190-3924. 703/742-9661. **Fax:** 703/742-9662. **Contact:** Chuck Bates, President. **E-mail address:** chuck@erols.com. **Description:** A contract services firm. Company pays fee. **Specializes in the areas of:** Administration; Architecture/Construction; Computer Science/Software; Engineering; Food Industry; Industrial; Manufacturing; Nonprofit; Publishing; Retail; Technical. **Positions commonly filled include:** Automotive Engineer; Buyer; Purchasing Agent/Manager. **Corporate headquarters location:** This Location. **Other U.S. locations:** Washington DC; Baltimore MD. **Average salary range of placements:** $30,000 - $50,000. **Number of placements per year:** 1 - 49.

STRATEGIC STAFFING, INC.
SSI TECHNICAL SERVICES DIVISION
127 South Peyton Street, Suite 200, Alexandria VA 22314. 703/739-8898. **Fax:** 703/739-8199. **Contact:** Luis E. Cornejo, Technical Recruiter. **E-mail address:** ssistaff@aol.com. **Description:** A contract services firm focusing on the placement of technical, professional, and administrative support personnel. in the areas of office automation, networking, and information processing. **Specializes in the areas of:** Administration; Computer Science/Software; Engineering; Network Administration; Systems Administration. **Positions commonly filled include:** Computer Programmer; MIS Specialist; Systems Analyst; Technical Writer/Editor; Telecommunications Manager. **Average salary range of placements:** $30,000 - $50,000. **Number of placements per year:** 50 - 99.

VANTAGE PERSONNEL, INC.
2300 Clarendon Boulevard, Suite 1109, Arlington VA 22201. 703/247-4100. **Fax:** 703/247-4102. **Contact:** Mary Ann Wilkinson, CPC, President. **E-mail address:** mandre4100@aol.com. **Description:** A contract services firm. **Specializes in the areas of:** Personnel/Labor Relations. **Positions commonly filled include:** Administrative Assistant; Consultant; Counselor; Human Resources Manager; Management Analyst/Consultant; Operations Manager; Project Manager. **Other U.S. locations:** Denver CO. **Average salary range of placements:** $30,000 - $50,000. **Number of placements per year:** 1 - 49.

H.L. YOH COMPANY
P.O. Box 36801, Richmond VA 23235. 804/560-2811. **Contact:** Manager. **Description:** A contract services firm. **Specializes in the areas of:** Information Technology. **Corporate headquarters location:** Philadelphia PA. **Other U.S. locations:** Nationwide. **International locations:** China.

CAREER/OUTPLACEMENT COUNSELING FIRMS

A BETTER RESUME
218 Light Road, Winchester VA 22603-2028. 703/888-3790. **Contact:** Michael Rutkaus, President. **Description:** A career/outplacement counseling agency. **Specializes in the areas of:** Accounting/Auditing; Administration; Banking; Computer Science/Software; Education; Engineering; Legal; Manufacturing; Personnel/Labor Relations; Publishing; Sales. **Positions commonly filled include:** Accountant/Auditor; Adjuster; Architect; Bank Officer/Manager; Buyer; Design Engineer; Draftsperson; Editor; Financial Analyst; Human Resources Specialist; Management Analyst/Consultant; Management Trainee; Paralegal; Psychologist; Radio/TV Announcer/Broadcaster; Registered Nurse; Reporter; Social Worker; Teacher/Professor; Technical Writer/Editor; Telecommunications Manager; Typist/Word Processor. **Average salary range of placements:** $30,000 - $50,000. **Number of placements per year:** 50 - 99.

A PRIVATE RESUME SERVICE
2728 Colonial Avenue, Roanoke VA 24015. 540/981-0209. **Contact:** Manager. **Description:** A resume writing service.

BW CUSTOM RESUMES
18 Clarke Road, Richmond VA 23226. 804/359-1065. **Fax:** 804/359-4150. **Contact:** Betty H. Williams, Certified Professional Resume Writer. **Description:** A resume writing and career/outplacement counseling firm.

ERICH NORD ASSOCIATES
6801 Whittier Avenue, McLean VA 22101. 703/556-9505. **Contact:** Joan Wikstrom, Principal. **Description:** A career/outplacement counseling firm.

RESUMES & MORE!
919B East Market Street, Charlottesville VA 22911. 804/296-1777. **Fax:** 804/296-1231. **Contact:** Ariel MacLean, Owner/Operator. **E-mail address:** resume@cfw.com. **Description:** A resume writing service and career/outplacement counseling firm. **Number of placements per year:** 100 - 199.

WASHINGTON

EXECUTIVE SEARCH FIRMS

ACCOUNTANTS EXECUTIVE SEARCH
ACCOUNTANTS ON CALL
601 Union Street, Suite 1625, Seattle WA 98101. 206/467-0700. **Contact:** Manager. **Description:** An executive search firm focusing on accounting and finance placements. Accountants On Call (also at this location) is a temporary agency. **Other U.S. locations:** Nationwide.

ACCOUNTING PARTNERS
500 108th Avenue NE, Suite 1640, Bellevue WA 98004. 425/450-1990. **Contact:** Manager. **Description:** An executive search firm. **Specializes in the areas of:** Accounting/Auditing; Finance.

ACCOUNTING QUEST
101 Stewart Street, Suite 1000, Seattle WA 98101. 206/441-5600. **Contact:** Manager. **Description:** An executive search firm. **Specializes in the areas of:** Accounting/Auditing.

ADAMS & ASSOCIATES
701 5th Avenue, Seattle WA 98104. 206/447-9200. **Contact:** Manager. **Description:** An executive search firm. **Specializes in the areas of:** Marketing; Sales.

ALMOND & ASSOCIATES
P.O. Box 6124, Federal Way WA 98063-6124. 206/952-5555. **Contact:** Manager. **Description:** An executive search firm that places upper-level managers in a variety of industries. Almond & Associates also provides temporary and permanent office support placements.

ROD ASHER ASSOCIATES
411 108th Avenue NE, Suite 2050, Bellevue WA 98004. 206/646-1030. **Contact:** Manager. **Description:** An executive search firm. **Specializes in the areas of:** Computer Hardware/Software.

BSP & ASSOCIATES
3626 East 15th Avenue, Spokane WA 99223-3607. 509/534-5208. **Toll-free phone:** 800/975-9000. **Fax:** 509/534-2764. **Contact:** Scott Price, President. **E-mail address:** bspscott@ieway.com. **Description:** An executive search firm that operates on both retainer and contingency bases. Company pays fee. **Specializes in the areas of:** Administration; Engineering; Health/Medical; Personnel/Labor Relations. **Positions commonly filled include:** Actuary; Civil Engineer; Cost Estimator; Dental Assistant/Dental Hygienist; Engineer; Health Services Manager; Information Specialist; Occupational Therapist; Pharmacist; Physical Therapist; Physician; Speech-Language Pathologist; Systems Analyst; Telecommunications Manager. **Number of placements per year:** 50 - 99.

BEHRENS AND COMPANY
P.O. Box 157, Easton WA 98925. 509/656-0284. **Fax:** 509/656-2298. **Contact:** Rick Behrens, President. **Description:** An executive search firm that operates on both retainer and contingency bases. Behrens and Company focuses on placements in the food and packaging machinery industries. Company pays fee. **Specializes in the areas of:** Engineering; Industrial; Manufacturing; Sales. **Positions commonly filled include:** Branch Manager; Design Engineer; Electrical/Electronics Engineer; General Manager; Industrial Production Manager; Manufacturer's/Wholesaler's Sales Rep.; Mechanical Engineer; Operations/Production Manager. **Average salary range of placements:** More than $50,000. **Number of placements per year:** 50 - 99.

BELL & ASSOCIATES
15812 SE 50th Street, Bellevue WA 98006. 425/641-3231. **Fax:** 425/641-3250. **Contact:** Manager. **Description:** An executive search firm. **Specializes in the areas of:** Medical Sales and Marketing.

BERKANA INTERNATIONAL
3417 Fremont Avenue North, Suite 225, Seattle WA 98103. 206/547-3226. **Fax:** 206/547-3843. **Contact:** Paul Allen, Vice President. **E-mail address:** berkana@headhunters.com. **World Wide Web address:** http://www.headhunters.com. **Description:** An executive search firm operating on a retained basis. Company pays fee. **Specializes in the areas of:** Computer Science/Software; High-Tech. **Positions commonly filled include:** Computer Programmer; Electrical/Electronics Engineer; General Manager; Internet Services Manager; Multimedia Designer; Software Engineer; Strategic Relations Manager; Technical Writer/Editor; Telecommunications Manager; Video Production Coordinator. **Average salary range of placements:** More than $50,000. **Number of placements per year:** 1 - 49.

BIXLER GROUP
11502 NE 34th Avenue, Suite D, Vancouver WA 98686. 360/574-7995. **Fax:** 360/576-0189. **Contact:** Manager. **E-mail address:** bixlergrp@worldaccessnet.com. **Description:** An executive search firm. **Specializes in the areas of:** Data Processing; Engineering; Software Development; Technical.

BLACK & DEERING
1605 116th Avenue NE, Suite 211, Bellevue WA 98004. 206/646-0905. **Contact:** Manager. **Description:** An executive search firm. **Specializes in the areas of:** Health/Medical.

THE CAREER CLINIC, INC.
9725 Third Avenue NE, Suite 509, Seattle WA 98115. 206/524-9831. **Fax:** 206/524-4125. **Contact:** Jane Ray Wilkinson, President. **E-mail address:** career@careerseanet.com. **Description:** An executive search firm operating on a contingency basis. The firm also provides temporary services and career/outplacement counseling. Founded in 1967. Company pays fee. **Specializes in the areas of:** Administration; Architecture/Construction; Banking; Computer Science/Software; Engineering; Food Industry; General Management; Industrial; Insurance; Legal; Manufacturing; Retail; Sales; Secretarial; Technical; Transportation. **Positions commonly filled include:** Accountant/Auditor; Actuary; Adjuster; Administrative Manager; Aircraft Mechanic/Engine Specialist; Attorney; Bank Officer/Manager; Budget Analyst; Chemical Engineer; Civil Engineer; Claim Representative; Computer Programmer; Construction Contractor; Cost Estimator; Credit Manager; Customer Service Representative; Design Engineer; Draftsperson; Economist; Editor; Electrical/Electronics Engineer; Environmental Engineer; Financial Analyst; General Manager; Health Services Manager; Hotel Manager; Human Resources Specialist; Industrial Engineer; Insurance Agent/Broker; Internet Services Manager; Landscape Architect; Management Analyst/Consultant; Manufacturer's/Wholesaler's Sales Rep.; Market Research Analyst; Mechanical Engineer; MIS Specialist; Occupational Therapist; Paralegal; Property and Real Estate Manager; Purchasing Agent/Manager; Quality Control Supervisor; Radio/TV Announcer/Broadcaster; Recreational Therapist; Restaurant/Food Service Manager; Securities Sales Representative; Software

Engineer; Stationary Engineer; Structural Engineer; Surgical Technician; Surveyor; Systems Analyst; Teacher/Professor; Technical Writer/Editor; Typist/Word Processor; Urban/Regional Planner. **Number of placements per year:** 50 - 99.

CAREER SPECIALISTS INC.
155 108th Avenue NE, Suite 200, Bellevue WA 98004. 425/455-0582. **Contact:** Manager. **Description:** An executive search firm.

CASTLE HILL ASSOCIATES
10900 NE Eighth Street, Suite 900, Bellevue WA 98004. 425/462-8220. **Contact:** Manager. **Description:** An executive search firm. **Specializes in the areas of:** Accounting/Auditing; Finance.

J.F. CHURCH ASSOCIATES
P.O. Box 6128, Bellevue WA 98008-0128. 425/644-3278. **Fax:** 425/747-1293. **Contact:** Jim Church, President. **E-mail address:** jfchurch@scn.org. **Description:** An executive search firm. Company pays fee. **Specializes in the areas of:** Computer Science/Software; Sales. **Number of placements per year:** 1 - 49.

COMPUTER GROUP INC.
777 108th Avenue NE, Suite 1550, Bellevue WA 98004. 425/455-3100. **Contact:** Manager. **Description:** An executive search firm. **Specializes in the areas of:** Computer Science/Software.

COMPUTER PERSONNEL
720 Olive Way, Suite 510, Seattle WA 98101. 206/340-2722. **Fax:** 206/340-8845. **Contact:** Ron Meints, President. **Description:** An executive search firm. **Specializes in the areas of:** Computer Science/Software. **Positions commonly filled include:** Computer Programmer; Software Engineer; Systems Analyst. **Other U.S. locations:** Minneapolis MN.

JUDITH CUSHMAN & ASSOCIATES
1125 12th Avenue NW, Suite B-1A, Issaquah WA 98027. 425/392-8660. **Fax:** 425/391-9190. **Recorded jobline:** 206/633-7381. **Contact:** Judith Cushman, President. **E-mail address:** jcushman@mcw.com. **Description:** An executive search firm that operates on a retainer basis. Clients include Oglivy Public Relations Group, Arthur Andersen & Co., Grumman Corporation, Pratt & Whitney, Rockwell International, Levi Strauss & Co., General Electric, RJR Nabisco, E.I. DuPont de Nemours & Co., Exxon Corporation, Chase Manhattan Bank, and PepsiCo. Founded in 1981. Company pays fee. **Positions commonly filled include:** Public Relations Specialist. **Average salary range of placements:** More than $50,000. **Number of placements per year:** 1 - 49.

DEVON JAMES ASSOCIATES
12356 Northup Way, Suite 118, Bellevue WA 98005. 425/885-3050. **Contact:** Manager. **Description:** An executive search firm. **Specializes in the areas of:** High-Tech.

KATHY EVANS EXECUTIVE SEARCH, INC.
HEALTHCARE SPECIALISTS INC.
400 108th Avenue NE, Suite 300, Bellevue WA 98004. 425/453-5548. **Contact:** Kathy Evans, President. **Description:** An executive search firm. Company pays fee. **Specializes in the areas of:** Health/Medical; Sales. **Positions commonly filled include:** Services Sales Representative. **Number of placements per year:** 1 - 49.

EXECUTIVE RECRUITERS
P.O. Box 1766, Bellevue WA 98009. 425/447-7404. **Contact:** Manager. **Description:** An executive search firm focusing on the placement of professionals in high-technology areas. **Specializes in the areas of:** Computer Hardware/Software; Computer Science/Software; Wireless Communications.

FIRST CHOICE SEARCH
P.O. Box 16574, Seattle WA 98116. 206/938-1944. **Contact:** Manager. **Description:** An executive search firm.

F-O-R-T-U-N-E PERSONNEL CONSULTANTS OF EAST SEATTLE
11661 S.E. First Street, Suite 202, Bellevue WA 98005. 425/450-9665. **Fax:** 425/450-0357. **Contact:** Daniel Chin, President. **Description:** An executive search firm operating on a contingency basis. The firm also offers temporary placements. Founded in 1995. Company pays fee. **Specializes in the areas of:** Engineering; Industrial; Manufacturing; Transportation. **Positions commonly filled include:** Agricultural Engineer; Design Engineer; Designer; Electrical/Electronics Engineer; Industrial Engineer; Industrial Production Manager; Mechanical Engineer; Quality Control Supervisor; Software Engineer; Structural Engineer. **Corporate headquarters location:** New York NY. **Other U.S. locations:** Nationwide. **Average salary range of placements:** $30,000 - $50,000. **Number of placements per year:** 1 - 49.

HRA INSURANCE STAFFING
11100 NE Eighth Street, Suite 600, Bellevue WA 98004. 425/451-4007. **Contact:** Cyndie Boe, General Manager. **Description:** An executive search firm that operates on both retainer and contingency bases. Company pays fee. **Specializes in the areas of:** Insurance. **Positions commonly filled include:** Adjuster; Branch Manager; Insurance Agent/Broker; Underwriter/Assistant Underwriter. **Number of placements per year:** 1 - 49.

ROBERT HALF INTERNATIONAL
ACCOUNTEMPS
601 Union Street, Suite 4300, Seattle WA 98101. 206/749-0960. **Contact:** Manager. **World Wide Web address:** http://www.roberthalf.com. **Description:** An executive search firm. Accountemps (also at this location) provides temporary accounting placements. **Specializes in the areas of:** Accounting/Auditing. **Corporate headquarters location:** Menlo Park CA. **Other U.S. locations:** Nationwide.

N.G. HAYES COMPANY
P.O. Box 184, Medina WA 98039. 425/453-1313. **Contact:** Nelia Hayes, President. **E-mail address:** nghayes@aol.com. **Description:** An executive search firm serving the Puget Sound area. Company pays fee. **Specializes in the areas of:** Computer Science/Software; Marketing; Sales. **Positions commonly filled include:** Computer Programmer; Software Engineer; Systems Analyst. **Number of placements per year:** 1 - 49.

HEADDEN & ASSOCIATES
777 108th Avenue NE, Suite 600, Bellevue WA 98004. 425/451-2427. **Contact:** Manager. **Description:** An executive search firm.

HEMBREE GALBRAITH & ASSOCIATES
40 Lake Bellevue, Suite 100, Bellevue WA 98005. 425/453-5235. **Contact:** Manager. **Description:** An executive search firm. **Specializes in the areas of:** Sales.

HOUSER, MARTIN, MORRIS & ASSOCIATES
P.O. Box 90015, Bellevue WA 98009. 425/453-2700. **Fax:** 425/453-8726. **Contact:** Bob Holert, President. **E-mail address:** recruitr@houser.com. **World Wide Web address:** http://www.houser.com. **Description:** An executive search firm operating on

both retained and contingency bases. Company pays fee. **Specializes in the areas of:** Accounting/Auditing; Administration; Computer Science/Software; Engineering; Finance; Legal; MIS/EDP; Personnel/Labor Relations; Sales. **Positions commonly filled include:** Attorney; Chief Financial Officer; Computer Operator; Computer Programmer; Controller; Electrical/ Electronics Engineer; Finance Director; General Manager; Human Resources Manager; Industrial Engineer; Insurance Agent/Broker; Intellectual Property Lawyer; Manufacturing Engineer; Marketing Manager; Mechanical Engineer; MIS Specialist; Operations Manager; Production Manager; Purchasing Agent/ Manager; Quality Control Supervisor; Sales Executive; Sales Manager; Sales Representative; Software Engineer; Systems Analyst; Systems Manager; Telecommunications Manager; Underwriter/Assistant Underwriter. **Average salary range of placements:** More than $50,000. **Number of placements per year:** 100 - 199.

HUMAN RESOURCES INC.
451 SW 10th Street, Suite 112, Renton WA 98055. 425/228-2289. **Toll-free phone:** 800/309-2289. **Fax:** 425/228-3513. **Contact:** Gary Jacobs, Owner. **E-mail address:** humrr@aol.com. **Description:** An executive search firm that also provides temporary and contract services. Founded in 1994. Company pays fee. **Specializes in the areas of:** Accounting/Auditing; General Management; Legal; Personnel/Labor Relations; Sales; Secretarial. **Positions commonly filled include:** Accountant/Auditor; Blue-Collar Worker Supervisor; Budget Analyst; Claim Representative; Computer Programmer; Counselor; Credit Manager; Customer Service Representative; Dental Assistant/Dental Hygienist; Education Administrator; General Manager; Hotel Manager; Insurance Agent/Broker; Internet Services Manager; Management Analyst/Consultant; Manufacturer's/ Wholesaler's Sales Rep.; Medical Records Technician; MIS Specialist; Operations/Production Manager; Paralegal; Property and Real Estate Manager; Public Relations Specialist; Quality Control Supervisor; Radio/TV Announcer/Broadcaster; Real Estate Agent; Reporter; Restaurant/Food Service Manager; Services Sales Representative; Teacher/Professor; Technical Writer/Editor; Telecommunications Manager; Transportation/Traffic Specialist; Travel Agent; Typist/ Word Processor; Underwriter/Assistant Underwriter. **Corporate headquarters location:** Bothell WA. **Other area locations:** Auburn WA; Mercer Island WA; Olympia WA; Tacoma WA. **Average salary range of placements:** $20,000 - $29,999. **Number of placements per year:** 200 - 499.

HURD SIEGEL & ASSOCIATES
1111 3rd Avenue, Suite 2880, Seattle WA 98101. 206/622-4282. **Contact:** Manager. **Description:** An executive search firm that places personnel in a variety of industries.

THE JOBS COMPANY
8900 East Sprague Avenue, Spokane WA 99212-2927. 509/928-3151. **Fax:** 509/928-3168. **Contact:** Mr. Hager, Manager. **Description:** An executive search firm. Founded in 1973. **Specializes in the areas of:** Accounting/Auditing; Administration; Computer Science/Software; Engineering; General Management; Health/Medical; Personnel/Labor Relations; Publishing; Retail; Sales; Secretarial; Technical. **Positions commonly filled include:** Accountant/Auditor; Adjuster; Administrative Manager; Advertising Clerk; Automotive Mechanic; Biological Scientist; Biomedical Engineer; Blue-Collar Worker Supervisor; Branch Manager; Broadcast Technician; Brokerage Clerk; Budget Analyst; Buyer; Chemist; Claim Representative; Clerical Supervisor; Clinical Lab Technician; Computer Programmer; Construction and Building Inspector; Construction Contractor; Cost Estimator; Counselor; Credit Manager; Dental Assistant/Dental Hygienist; Dental Lab Technician; Designer; Draftsperson; Editor; EEG Technologist; EKG Technician; Electrical/Electronics Engineer; Electrician; Emergency Medical Technician; Financial Analyst; Financial Services Sales Representative; General Manager; Health Services Manager; Hotel Manager; Human Resources Manager; Industrial Engineer; Industrial Production Manager; Licensed Practical Nurse; Management Trainee; Manufacturer's/ Wholesaler's Sales Rep.; Mechanical Engineer; Medical Records Technician; Metallurgical Engineer; Nuclear Medicine Technologist; Occupational Therapist; Paralegal; Purchasing Agent/Manager; Quality Control Supervisor; Registered Nurse; Reporter; Respiratory Therapist; Restaurant/Food Service Manager; Securities Sales Representative; Services Sales Representative; Software Engineer; Stationary Engineer; Structural Engineer; Surgical Technician; Systems Analyst; Technical Writer/Editor; Telecommunications Manager; Typist/Word Processor.

KIRKBRIDE ASSOCIATES INC.
915 118th Avenue SE, Suite 370, Bellevue WA 98005. 425/453-5256. **Contact:** Manager. **Description:** An executive search firm. **Specializes in the areas of:** Engineering; Sales.

KORN/FERRY INTERNATIONAL
600 University Street, Suite 3428, Seattle WA 98101. 206/447-1834. **Contact:** Manager. **Description:** An executive search firm that places upper-level managers in a variety of industries. **Corporate headquarters location:** Los Angeles CA. **International locations:** Worldwide. **Average salary range of placements:** More than $50,000.

KOSSUTH & ASSOCIATES
800 Bellevue Way NE, Suite 400, Bellevue WA 98004. 425/450-9050. **Fax:** 425/450-0513. **Contact:** Jane Kossuth, President. **Description:** An executive search firm. Company pays fee. **Specializes in the areas of:** Communications; Computer Science/ Software; General Management; Sales; Technical. **Positions commonly filled include:** Computer Programmer; General Manager; Public Relations Specialist; Software Engineer; Systems Analyst; Technical Writer/Editor. **Number of placements per year:** 50 - 99.

LAWRENCE & ASSOCIATES
1200 Fifth Avenue, Suite 1927, Seattle WA 98101. 206/621-1228. **Contact:** Manager. **Description:** An executive search firm. **Specializes in the areas of:** Accounting/Auditing; Finance.

MCE TECHNICAL SEARCH
4204 Meridian Street, Suite 101, Bellingham WA 98226. 360/671-5221. **Contact:** Manager. **Description:** An executive search firm. **Specializes in the areas of:** Technical.

MACROSEARCH
13353 Bel-Red Road, Suite 206, Bellevue WA 98005. 425/641-7252. **Fax:** 425/641-0969. **Contact:** Vickie Stovall, Manager. **Description:** An executive search firm. Company pays fee. **Specializes in the areas of:** Computer Science/Software. **Positions commonly filled include:** Computer Programmer; Software Engineer; Systems Analyst; Teacher/Professor; Technical Writer/Editor. **Number of placements per year:** 50 - 99.

MANAGEMENT RECRUITERS INTERNATIONAL
703 Broadway, Suite 695, Vancouver WA 98660. 360/695-4688. **Contact:** Manager. **Description:** An executive search firm. **Specializes in the areas of:**

High-Tech; Medical Sales and Marketing. **Corporate headquarters location:** Cleveland OH.

MANAGEMENT RECRUITERS INTERNATIONAL
North 4407 Division Street, Spokane WA 99207. 509/484-0084. **Contact:** Manager. **Description:** An executive search firm. **Specializes in the areas of:** Food Industry. **Corporate headquarters location:** Cleveland OH.

MANAGEMENT RECRUITERS INTERNATIONAL
316 West Boone Street, Suite 370, Spokane WA 99201. 509/324-3333. **Contact:** Manager. **Description:** An executive search firm. **Specializes in the areas of:** Banking; Computer Hardware/Software; Engineering; Finance; Health/Medical; Pharmaceutical. **Corporate headquarters location:** Cleveland OH.

MANAGEMENT RECRUITERS INTERNATIONAL
2633A Parkmont Lane SW, Olympia WA 98502. 360/357-9996. **Contact:** Manager. **Description:** An executive search firm. **Specializes in the areas of:** Engineering; Health/Medical. **Corporate headquarters location:** Cleveland OH.

MANAGEMENT RECRUITERS OF LYNNWOOD
19109 36th Avenue West, Suite 100, Lynnwood WA 98036. 425/778-1212. **Fax:** 425/778-7840. **Contact:** Bud Naff, Owner. **Description:** An executive search firm that operates on a contingency basis primarily in the environmental consulting and health care industries. Company pays fee. **Specializes in the areas of:** Engineering; Health/Medical; Technical. **Positions commonly filled include:** Biological Scientist; Biomedical Engineer; Chemical Engineer; Chemist; Civil Engineer; Clinical Lab Technician; Electrical/Electronics Engineer; Geologist/Geophysicist; Industrial Engineer; Licensed Practical Nurse; Mechanical Engineer; Medical Records Technician; Meteorologist; Mining Engineer; Nuclear Engineer; Occupational Therapist; Physical Therapist; Physician; Radiological Technologist; Registered Nurse; Transportation/Traffic Specialist. **Corporate headquarters location:** Cleveland OH. **Average salary range of placements:** More than $50,000. **Number of placements per year:** 50 - 99.

MANAGEMENT RECRUITERS OF MERCER ISLAND
9725 SE 36th Street, Suite 312, Mercer Island WA 98040-3896. 206/232-0204. **Fax:** 206/232-6172. **Contact:** James J. Dykeman, Manager. **E-mail address:** mercer!jjd@mrinet.com. **Description:** An executive search firm. **Specializes in the areas of:** Accounting/Auditing; Administration; Advertising; Architecture/Construction; Banking; Communications; Computer Science/Software; Design; Electrical; Engineering; Finance; Food Industry; General Management; Health/Medical; Insurance; Legal; Manufacturing; MIS/EDP; Operations Management; Personnel/Labor Relations; Procurement; Publishing; Retail; Sales; Technical; Textiles; Transportation. **Corporate headquarters location:** Cleveland OH. **Number of placements per year:** 100 - 199.

MANAGEMENT RECRUITERS OF NORTH TACOMA
535 Dock Street, Suite 111, Tacoma WA 98402. 253/572-7542. **Toll-free phone:** 800/779-1502. **Fax:** 253/572-7872. **Contact:** Bill Saylor, President/Manager. **E-mail address:** ntacom@ix. netcom.com. **Description:** An executive search firm operating on both retained and contingency bases. Company pays fee. **Specializes in the areas of:** Administration; Computer Science/Software. **Positions commonly filled include:** Applications Engineer; Computer Operator; Computer Programmer; Database Manager; Design Engineer; MIS Manager; MIS Specialist; Sales Engineer; Software Engineer; Systems Analyst; Systems Manager; Technical Writer/Editor. **Corporate headquarters location:** Cleveland OH. **Average salary range of placements:** More than $50,000. **Number of placements per year:** 1 - 49.

MANAGEMENT RECRUITERS OF SEATTLE
2510 Fairview Avenue East, Seattle WA 98102-3216. 206/328-0936. **Toll-free phone:** 800/237-6562. **Fax:** 206/328-3256. **Contact:** Dan Jilka, Manager/Co-Owner. **Description:** An executive search firm that operates on both retainer and contingency bases. **Specializes in the areas of:** Administration; Computer Science/Software; Engineering; Food Industry; General Management; Health/Medical; Manufacturing; Retail; Sales; Technical. **Positions commonly filled include:** Aerospace Engineer; Biochemist; Biological Scientist; Biomedical Engineer; Branch Manager; Chemical Engineer; Chemist; Civil Engineer; Computer Programmer; Design Engineer; Designer; Electrical/Electronics Engineer; Environmental Engineer; General Manager; Industrial Engineer; Management Analyst/Consultant; Manufacturer's/Wholesaler's Sales Rep.; Mechanical Engineer; MIS Specialist; Multimedia Designer; Operations/Production Manager; Quality Control Supervisor; Restaurant/Food Service Manager; Science Technologist; Services Sales Representative; Software Engineer; Structural Engineer; Systems Analyst; Telecommunications Manager. **Corporate headquarters location:** Cleveland OH. **Average salary range of placements:** More than $50,000. **Number of placements per year:** 1 - 49.

MANAGEMENT RECRUITERS OF TACOMA
2709 Jahn Avenue NW, Suite H-11, Gig Harbor WA 98335. 253/858-9991. **Contact:** Dennis Johnson, Manager. **Description:** An executive search firm. **Specializes in the areas of:** Accounting/Auditing; Administration; Advertising; Architecture/Construction; Banking; Communications; Computer Science/Software; Design; Electrical; Engineering; Finance; Food Industry; General Management; Health/Medical; Insurance; Legal; Manufacturing; Operations Management; Personnel/Labor Relations; Procurement; Publishing; Retail; Sales; Technical; Textiles; Transportation. **Corporate headquarters location:** Cleveland OH. **Number of placements per year:** 1 - 49.

MARITIME RECRUITERS
P.O. Box 260, Mercer Island WA 98040. 206/232-6041. **Contact:** Manager. **Description:** An executive search firm. **Specializes in the areas of:** Maritime.

JOHN MASON & ASSOCIATES
P.O. Box 3823, Bellevue WA 98009. 425/453-1608. **Fax:** 425/451-9214. **Contact:** John Mason, Manager. **E-mail address:** masonsail@aol.com. **Description:** An executive search firm that places mid- to senior-level management and provides human resources consulting for small to mid-size companies. **Specializes in the areas of:** Computer Science/Software; Engineering; Finance; General Management; Manufacturing; Personnel/Labor Relations; Technical. **Positions commonly filled include:** Computer Programmer; Credit Manager; Design Engineer; Electrical/Electronics Engineer; General Manager; Human Resources Manager; Manufacturer's/Wholesaler's Sales Rep.; Mechanical Engineer; MIS Specialist; Software Engineer; Structural Engineer; Systems Analyst; Telecommunications Manager. **Average salary range of placements:** More than $50,000. **Number of placements per year:** 50 - 99.

McINTIRE & CARR
P.O. Box 1176, Issaquah WA 98027. 425/391-9320. **Fax:** 425/391-9374. **Contact:** Merlin McIntire, Owner/Manager. **E-mail address:** mem@halycon.com. **Description:** An executive search firm. Company pays

fee. **Specializes in the areas of:** Sales. **Average salary range of placements:** More than $50,000. **Number of placements per year:** 50 - 99.

MILLER & MILLER EXECUTIVE SEARCH
P.O. Box 3088, Kirkland WA 98083. 206/822-3145. **Contact:** Manager. **Description:** An executive search firm. **NOTE:** Please call before sending a resume. **Specializes in the areas of:** Biomedical; Biotechnology.

MORGAN PALMER MORGAN & HILL
P.O. Box 13353, Burton WA 98013. 206/463-5721. **Contact:** Manager. **Description:** An executive search firm. **Specializes in the areas of:** Finance.

THE OLDANI GROUP
188 106th Avenue NE, Suite 420, Bellevue WA 98004. 425/451-3938. **Contact:** Manager. **Description:** An executive search firm.

OMEGA ATTORNEY PLACEMENT
401 Second Avenue South, Suite 630, Seattle WA 98104. 206/467-5547. **Contact:** Manager. **Description:** An executive search firm. **Specializes in the areas of:** Legal. **Positions commonly filled include:** Attorney.

PACIFIC LAW RECRUITERS
1424 Fourth Avenue, Suite 915, Seattle WA 98101. 206/625-0654. **Contact:** Manager. **Description:** An executive search firm. **Specializes in the areas of:** Legal.

PACIFIC PERSONNEL GROUP
2146 Westlake Avenue North, Seattle WA 98109. 206/284-5961. **Fax:** 206/284-5963. **Contact:** Marlaine Kirsch, Managing Principal. **World Wide Web address:** http://www.ilsi.com/pacific/personnel.html. **Description:** An executive search firm operating on a contingency basis. Company pays fee. **Specializes in the areas of:** Insurance. **Positions commonly filled include:** Account Representative; Accountant/Auditor; Adjuster; Claim Representative; Customer Service Representative; General Manager; Insurance Agent/Broker; Operations Manager; Sales Manager; Underwriter/Assistant Underwriter. **Average salary range of placements:** $30,000 - $50,000. **Number of placements per year:** 50 - 99.

PARFITT GROUP
1540 140th Avenue NE, Suite 201, Bellevue WA 98004. 425/646-6300. **Contact:** Manager. **Description:** An executive search firm. **Specializes in the areas of:** High-Tech.

PASSAGE & ASSOCIATES
1001 4th Avenue, Suite 3200, Seattle WA 98154. 206/622-3330. **Contact:** Manager. **Description:** An executive search firm that places personnel in a variety of industries.

PERSONNEL CONSULTANTS INC.
14042 NE Eighth Street, Suite 201, Bellevue WA 98007. 425/641-0657. **Contact:** Larry L. Dykes, Owner/President. **Description:** An executive search firm. Company pays fee. **Specializes in the areas of:** Insurance; Sales. **Positions commonly filled include:** Actuary; Adjuster; Claim Representative; Collector; Insurance Agent/Broker; Investigator; Securities Sales Representative; Underwriter/Assistant Underwriter. **Number of placements per year:** 1 - 49.

PERSONNEL UNLIMITED INC.
West 25 Nora, Spokane WA 99205. 509/326-8880. **Fax:** 509/326-0112. **Contact:** Gary P. Desgrosellier, President. **Description:** An executive search firm. Company pays fee. **Specializes in the areas of:** Accounting/Auditing; Administration; Clerical; Computer Science/Software; Engineering; Finance; Food Industry; General Management; Health/Medical; Insurance; Legal; Manufacturing; Personnel/Labor Relations; Sales; Secretarial. **Positions commonly filled include:** Accountant/Auditor; Adjuster; Administrative Worker/Clerk; Agricultural Engineer; Bank Officer/Manager; Bookkeeper; Buyer; Ceramics Engineer; Chemical Engineer; Civil Engineer; Claim Representative; Clerical Supervisor; Collector; Computer Operator; Computer Programmer; Credit Manager; Customer Service Representative; Data Entry Clerk; Draftsperson; EDP Specialist; Electrical/Electronics Engineer; Financial Analyst; Food Scientist/Technologist; General Manager; Health Services Manager; Hotel Manager; Industrial Engineer; Investigator; Legal Secretary; Management Trainee; Manufacturer's/Wholesaler's Sales Rep.; Marketing Specialist; Materials Engineer; Mechanical Engineer; Medical Records Technician; Medical Secretary; Metallurgical Engineer; MIS Specialist; Operations/Production Manager; Public Relations Specialist; Purchasing Agent/Manager; Quality Control Supervisor; Receptionist; Registered Nurse; Secretary; Services Sales Representative; Statistician; Stenographer; Structural Engineer; Systems Analyst; Technical Writer/Editor; Technician; Travel Agent; Typist/Word Processor; Underwriter/Assistant Underwriter. **Number of placements per year:** 500 - 999.

REFFETT & ASSOCIATES
777 108th Avenue NE, Suite 600, Bellevue WA 98004. 425/637-2993. **Contact:** Office Manager. **Description:** An executive search firm.

RIGEL COMPUTER RESOURCES
1611 116th Avenue NE, Bellevue WA 98004. 425/646-4990. **Fax:** 425/646-3058. **Contact:** Rita Ashley, President. **Description:** An executive search firm. Company pays fee. **Specializes in the areas of:** Computer Science/Software. **Average salary range of placements:** More than $50,000. **Number of placements per year:** 50 - 99.

ROTH YOUNG PERSONNEL SERVICES
P.O. Box 3307, Bellevue WA 98009. 425/455-2141. **Contact:** Manager. **Description:** An executive search firm. **Specializes in the areas of:** Manufacturing; Sales. **Corporate headquarters location:** New York NY. **Other U.S. locations:** Nationwide.

BARBARA RUHL & ASSOCIATES
15 Diamond S Ranch, Bellevue WA 98004. 425/453-7299. **Contact:** Manager. **Description:** An executive search firm. **Specializes in the areas of:** Finance; Mortgage.

SANDER ASSOCIATES
2011 Market Street, Kirkland WA 98033. 425/827-6446. **Fax:** 425/827-6162. **Contact:** Patti Jones, Owner. **Description:** An executive search firm that operates on both retainer and contingency bases. Company pays fee. **Specializes in the areas of:** Health/Medical. **Positions commonly filled include:** Health Services Manager; Medical Records Technician; Physician. **Number of placements per year:** 1 - 49.

SUSAN SCHOOS & ASSOCIATES
120 Lakeside Avenue, Suite 330, Seattle WA 98122. 206/324-4942. **Contact:** Manager. **Description:** An executive search firm. **Specializes in the areas of:** Construction; Engineering; Manufacturing.

SCHULTZ GROUP INC.
401 Parkplace Center, Kirkland WA 98003. 425/822-1726. **Contact:** Manager. **Description:** An executive search firm. **Specializes in the areas of:** Information Systems.

SEARCH WEST
2101 Fourth Avenue, Suite 2120, Seattle WA 98121. 425/728-4084. **Fax:** 425/728-4087. **Contact:** Manager. **Description:** An executive search firm. **Specializes in the areas of:** Computer Hardware/Software; Engineering; Finance; General Management; Health/Medical; High-Tech; Nonprofit.

SEATTLE RECRUITERS
1001 Fourth Avenue, Suite 3200, Seattle WA 98154. 206/467-6617. **Contact:** Manager. **Description:** An executive search firm. **Specializes in the areas of:** Legal.

SMALL BUSINESS SOLUTIONS INC.
4511 100th Street East, Tacoma WA 98446. 253/537-1040. **Fax:** 253/531-7323. **Contact:** President. **Description:** An executive search firm. Founded in 1986. **Specializes in the areas of:** Accounting/Auditing; Computer Science/Software. **Positions commonly filled include:** Accountant/Auditor. **Average salary range of placements:** \$20,000 - \$29,999. **Number of placements per year:** 1 - 49.

SNELLING PERSONNEL SERVICES
2101 Fourth Avenue, Suite 1330, Seattle WA 98121. 206/441-8895. **Fax:** 206/448-5373. **Contact:** Sue and Tom Truscott, Owners/Managers. **E-mail address:** snelling@serv.net. **World Wide Web address:** http://www.snelling.com/seattle. **Description:** An executive search firm operating on a contingency basis. Founded in 1966. Company pays fee. **Specializes in the areas of:** Accounting/Auditing; Administration; Computer Science/Software; Finance; Marketing; Sales; Secretarial. **Corporate headquarters location:** Dallas TX. **Average salary range of placements:** \$30,000 - \$50,000. **Number of placements per year:** 200 - 499.

SOURCE SERVICES CORPORATION
500 108th Avenue NE, Suite 1780, Bellevue WA 98004. 425/454-6400. **Fax:** 425/688-0154. **Contact:** Manager. **Description:** An executive search firm. The divisions at this location include Source Consulting, Source EDP, and Source Finance. **Specializes in the areas of:** Computer Hardware/Software; Finance; Information Technology.

SUSAN STONEBERG EXECUTIVE SEARCH
8350 164th Avenue NE, Suite 303, Redmond WA 98052. 425/882-4862. **Contact:** Manager. **Description:** An executive search firm that places sales representatives and sales managers.

STRAIN PERSONNEL SPECIALISTS
801 Pine Street, Suite 1900, Seattle WA 98101. 206/382-1588. **Fax:** 206/622-1572. **Contact:** Joe Strain, CPC, Partner. **E-mail address:** joestrain@msn.com. **Description:** An executive search firm operating on a retainer basis. Strain Personnel Specialists also offers contract services. Company pays fee. **Specializes in the areas of:** Administration; Computer Science/Software; Engineering; Manufacturing; Personnel/Labor Relations; Technical. **Positions commonly filled include:** Computer Programmer; Design Engineer; Human Resources Manager; Internet Services Manager; Mathematician; MIS Specialist; Multimedia Designer; Science Technologist; Software Engineer; Systems Analyst; Technical Writer/Editor; Telecommunications Manager. **Average salary range of placements:** More than \$50,000. **Number of placements per year:** 50 - 99.

TSA, INC.
10116 36th Avenue SW, Suite 200, Lakewood WA 98499. 253/588-1216. **Fax:** 253/588-2528. **Contact:** Frank Adams, President. **World Wide Web address:** http://www.aaa-mall.com. **Description:** An executive search firm operating on both retained and contingency bases. The firm focuses on the areas of high-energy physics and applied superconductivity including magnets, cryogenics, materials, thin film, and electronics. Company pays fee. **Specializes in the areas of:** Engineering; Scientific; Technical. **Positions commonly filled include:** Applications Engineer; Chemical Engineer; Design Engineer; Electrical/Electronics Engineer; General Manager; Industrial Engineer; Manufacturing Engineer; Mechanical Engineer; Metallurgical Engineer; Operations Manager; Project Manager; Quality Control Supervisor. **Average salary range of placements:** More than \$50,000. **Number of placements per year:** 1 - 49.

THOMPSON & ASSOCIATES
2448 76th Avenue SE, Suite 212, Mercer Island WA 98040. 206/236-0153. **Contact:** Manager. **Description:** An executive search firm. **Specializes in the areas of:** Computer Programming; High-Tech. **Positions commonly filled include:** Computer Programmer.

THE TRIAD GROUP
12505 Bellevue-Redmond Road, Suite 208, Bellevue WA 98005. 425/454-0282. **Contact:** Manager. **Description:** An executive search firm. **Specializes in the areas of:** Computer Science/Software.

WALDRON & COMPANY
101 Stewart Street, Suite 1200, Seattle WA 98101. 206/441-4144. **Contact:** Manager. **Description:** An executive search firm. **Specializes in the areas of:** Nonprofit.

THE WASHINGTON FIRM
2 Nickerson Street, Courtyard Suite, Seattle WA 98109. 206/284-4800. **Fax:** 206/284-8844. **Contact:** Al Battson, Principal. **Description:** An executive search firm operating on a retainer basis. Company pays fee. **Specializes in the areas of:** Administration; Computer Science/Software; General Management; Health/Medical; Nonprofit; Personnel/Labor Relations. **Positions commonly filled include:** Applications Engineer; Chief Financial Officer; Controller; Database Manager; Finance Director; Financial Analyst; General Manager; Human Resources Manager; Marketing Manager; MIS Specialist; Multimedia Designer; Online Content Specialist; Property and Real Estate Manager; Sales Executive; Sales Manager; Software Engineer; Structural Engineer; Systems Analyst; Technical Writer/Editor. **Average salary range of placements:** More than \$50,000. **Number of placements per year:** 100 - 199.

WHITTALL MANAGEMENT GROUP
720 South 333rd Street, Suite 102, Federal Way WA 98003. 253/874-0710. **Fax:** 253/952-2918. **Contact:** Geoff Whittall, Vice President. **Description:** An executive search firm that operates on both retainer and contingency bases. Company pays fee. **Specializes in the areas of:** Computer Science/Software; Engineering; Food Industry; General Management; Industrial; Manufacturing; Personnel/Labor Relations; Sales; Technical. **Positions commonly filled include:** Computer Programmer; Construction Contractor; Design Engineer; Electrical/Electronics Engineer; Electrician; Environmental Engineer; Forester/Conservation Scientist; General Manager; Human Resources Manager; Industrial Engineer; Industrial Production Manager; Mechanical Engineer; MIS Specialist; Operations/Production Manager; Quality Control Supervisor; Software Engineer; Structural Engineer; Systems Analyst. **Average salary range of placements:** More than \$50,000. **Number of placements per year:** 50 - 99.

WILLIAMS RECRUITING
16336 NE 81st Street, Redmond WA 98052. 425/869-7775. **Fax:** 425/869-1849. **Contact:** Gail Williams, President. **Description:** An executive search firm operating on both retainer and contingency bases. Company pays fee. **Specializes in the areas of:** Biology; Engineering; Health/Medical. **Positions commonly filled include:** Assistant Manager; Biochemist; Biological Scientist; Biomedical Engineer; Chemist; Database Manager; Design Engineer; Electrical/Electronics Engineer; General Manager; Marketing Manager; Mechanical Engineer; Operations/Production Manager; Physician; Quality Control Supervisor; Statistician. **Average salary range of placements:** More than $50,000. **Number of placements per year:** 50 - 99.

WINSEARCH
900 Washington Street, Suite 800, Vancouver WA 98660. 206/343-0222. **Contact:** Manager. **Description:** An executive search firm. **Specializes in the areas of:** Computer Science/Software.

PERMANENT EMPLOYMENT AGENCIES

A.S.A.P. EMPLOYMENT SERVICES
4181 Wheaton Way, Suite 1, Bremerton WA 98310. 360/479-4310. **Contact:** Ralph and Roberta I. Long, Owners. **Description:** A permanent employment agency that also provides temporary placements. Company pays fee. **Positions commonly filled include:** Accountant/Auditor; Administrative Worker/Clerk; Advertising Clerk; Bank Officer/Manager; Bookkeeper; Buyer; Civil Engineer; Claim Rep.; Computer Programmer; Credit Manager; Customer Service Rep.; Data Entry Clerk; Draftsperson; Editor; EDP Specialist; Electrical/ Electronics Engineer; General Manager; Hotel Manager; Industrial Engineer; Legal Secretary; Manufacturer's/Wholesaler's Sales Rep.; Mechanical Engineer; Medical Secretary; Nurse; Public Relations Specialist; Purchasing Agent/Manager; Quality Control Supervisor; Receptionist; Reporter; Secretary; Services Sales Rep.; Stenographer; Systems Analyst; Technical Writer/Editor; Technician. **Number of placements per year:** 200 - 499.

ABLE PERSONNEL AGENCY
NT Office Building, North 4407 Division, Suite 625, Spokane WA 99207. 509/487-2734. **Contact:** William (Jay) Kinzer, Owner/Manager. **Description:** A permanent employment agency. **Specializes in the areas of:** Accounting/Auditing; Clerical; Engineering; Finance; Sales. **Positions commonly filled include:** Accountant/Auditor; Administrative Worker/Clerk; Bookkeeper; Buyer; Claim Representative; Credit Manager; Customer Service Representative; Data Entry Clerk; Draftsperson; General Manager; Legal Secretary; Manufacturer's/Wholesaler's Sales Rep.; Marketing Specialist; Medical Secretary; Purchasing Agent/Manager; Receptionist; Secretary; Services Sales Representative; Stenographer; Typist/Word Processor. **Number of placements per year:** 1 - 49.

ASHFORD CLARK PERSONNEL
4215 198th Street SW, Suite 102, Lynnwood WA 98036. 425/827-6617. **Contact:** Manager. **Description:** A permanent employment agency.

ASPEN PERSONNEL SERVICES, INC.
115 North Washington Street, Suite 200, Spokane WA 99201. 509/624-4858. **Contact:** Manager. **Description:** A permanent employment agency that also provides temporary placements.

AUTO CAREERS OF WASHINGTON
1075 Bellevue Way NE, Suite 361, Bellevue WA 98004. 425/643-4349. **Fax:** 425/643-4297. **Contact:** Ron Rasmussen, President. **Description:** A permanent employment agency. Company pays fee. **Specializes in the areas of:** Automotive. **Positions commonly filled include:** Accountant/Auditor; Automotive Mechanic; Clerical Supervisor; Credit Manager; General Manager; Office Manager; Sales Manager; Service Manager. **Number of placements per year:** 1 - 49.

BUSINESS CAREERS
600 108th Avenue NE, Suite 246, Bellevue WA 98004. 206/447-7411. **Fax:** 425/462-5217. **Contact:** Manager. **Description:** A permanent placement agency. **Specializes in the areas of:** Accounting/Auditing; Office Support; Sales.

BUSINESS CAREERS
1001 Fourth Avenue, Suite 828, Seattle WA 98154. 206/447-7474. **Contact:** Manager. **Description:** A permanent placement agency. **Specializes in the areas of:** Accounting/Auditing; Office Support; Sales.

BUSINESS CAREERS
15 South Grady Way, Suite 333, Renton WA 98055. 206/447-7433. **Contact:** Manager. **Description:** A permanent placement agency. **Specializes in the areas of:** Accounting/Auditing; Office Support; Sales.

BUSINESS CAREERS
1019 Pacific Avenue, Suite 1716, Tacoma WA 98402. 253/383-1881. **Contact:** Manager. **Description:** A permanent placement agency. **Specializes in the areas of:** Accounting/Auditing; Office Support; Sales.

CMS (CONSTRUCTION MANAGEMENT SERVICES)
40 Lake Bellevue, Suite 100, Bellevue WA 98005. 425/868-2211. **Contact:** Mark Mannon, Owner. **Description:** A permanent employment agency focusing on the placement of construction management personnel. **Specializes in the areas of:** Construction. **Positions commonly filled include:** Civil Engineer; Construction and Building Inspector; Cost Estimator. **Average salary range of placements:** $30,000 - $50,000. **Number of placements per year:** 50 - 99.

CAREER SERVICES
677 George Washington Way, Richland WA 99352-4208. 509/946-0643. **Contact:** Bob and Jean B. McKee, Owners. **Description:** A permanent employment agency that also provides temporary placements. **Specializes in the areas of:** Accounting/Auditing; Industrial; Professional; Sales; Secretarial; Technical; Word Processing. **Number of placements per year:** 50 - 99.

HALL KINION ASSOCIATES
3001 112th Avenue NE, Suite 101, Bellevue WA 98004. 425/889-5003. **Toll-free phone:** 800/234-1136. **Fax:** 425/889-5985. **Contact:** Maureen Kerber, Manager. **E-mail address:** mbk@hallkinion.com. **World Wide Web address:** http://www.hallkinion.com. **Description:** A permanent employment agency. Company pays fee. **Specializes in the areas of:** Computer Hardware/Software; Computer Science/Software; Engineering; Sales; Scientific; Technical. **Positions commonly filled include:** Computer Animator; Computer Programmer; Database Manager; Design Engineer; Editor; Engineer; Graphic Artist; Multimedia Designer; Project Manager; Software Engineer; Systems Analyst; Systems Manager; Technical Writer/Editor; Vice President; Webmaster. **Benefits available to temporary workers:** Stock Option. **Corporate headquarters location:** San

Jose CA. **Average salary range of placements:** More than $50,000. **Number of placements per year:** 500 - 999.

HALLMARK SERVICES
1904 3rd Avenue, Suite 819, Seattle WA 98101. 206/587-5360. **Contact:** Delores Gohndrone, Manager. **Description:** A permanent employment agency. Company pays fee. **Specializes in the areas of:** Clerical; Legal. **Positions commonly filled include:** Administrative Worker/Clerk; Receptionist; Secretary; Stenographer; Typist/Word Processor. **Number of placements per year:** 1 - 49.

HOSPITALITY EMPLOYMENT SERVICE
12308 East Broadway Avenue, Spokane WA 99216. 509/922-1187. **Fax:** 509/922-4647. **Contact:** Frank Pierson, Owner. **Description:** A permanent employment agency. **Specializes in the areas of:** Food Industry. **Average salary range of placements:** Less than $20,000. **Number of placements per year:** 500 - 999.

HUMAN RESOURCES INC.
2 Auburn Way North, Suite 102, Auburn WA 98002. 253/804-3477. **Contact:** Manager. **Description:** A permanent employment agency that also provides some temporary placements. **Corporate headquarters location:** Bothell WA. **Other area locations:** Mercer Island WA; Olympia WA; Renton WA; Tacoma WA.

JOBS UNLIMITED
870 SW 136th Street, Seattle WA 98166. 206/243-8225. **Fax:** 206/244-2767. **Contact:** Donna Lenox, Manager. **Description:** A permanent employment agency. Company pays fee. **Specializes in the areas of:** Industrial; Light Industrial; Marketing; Sales; Transportation. **Positions commonly filled include:** Accountant/Auditor; Aerospace Engineer; Aircraft Mechanic/Engine Specialist; Automotive Mechanic; Blue-Collar Worker Supervisor; Construction and Building Inspector; Construction Contractor; Customer Service Representative; Draftsperson; Driver; Electrical/Electronics Engineer; Electrician; Industrial Engineer; Industrial Production Manager; Mechanical Engineer; Operations/Production Manager; Quality Control Supervisor; Secretary. **Number of placements per year:** 1000+.

NATIONAL ASIAN PACIFIC CENTER ON AGING
Melborne Tower, 1511 3rd Avenue, Suite 914, Seattle WA 98101. **Toll-free phone:** 800/336-2722. **Contact:** Manager. **Description:** A nonprofit, private organization that offers permanent job placements in conjunction with funding from the Older American Act.

NELSON, COULSON & ASSOCIATES INC.
14450 NE 29th Place, Suite 115, Bellevue WA 98007-3697. 425/883-6612. **Toll-free phone:** 888/883-6612. **Fax:** 425/883-6916. **Contact:** Julie Golich, Manager. **E-mail address:** ncainc@ncainc.com. **World Wide Web address:** http://www.ncainc.com. **Description:** A permanent employment agency. Company pays fee. **Specializes in the areas of:** Administration; Computer Science/Software; Engineering; MIS/EDP; Scientific; Technical. **Positions commonly filled include:** Administrative Assistant; Buyer; Civil Engineer; Computer Operator; Computer Programmer; Design Engineer; Draftsperson; Electrical/Electronics Engineer; Manufacturing Engineer; Mechanical Engineer; Systems Analyst; Technical Writer/Editor; Typist/Word Processor. **Benefits available to temporary workers:** 401(k); Dental Insurance; Health Club Discount; Medical Insurance; Paid Holidays. **Average salary range of placements:** $30,000 - $50,000. **Number of placements per year:** 200 - 499.

OLSTEN KIMBERLY QUALITY CARE
4020 South 56th Street, Suite 101, Tacoma WA 98409. 253/475-6862. **Contact:** Blanche Jones, Branch Manager. **Description:** A permanent employment agency. **Specializes in the areas of:** Health/Medical. **Positions commonly filled include:** Accountant/Auditor; Administrative Assistant; Bookkeeper; Data Entry Clerk; Dietician/Nutritionist; Medical Secretary; Nurse; Public Relations Specialist; Typist/Word Processor.

PENINSULA NANNY PLACEMENT
13819 Chambana Place NW, Silverdale WA 98383. 360/697-4300. **Contact:** Manager. **Description:** A permanent employment agency that places nannies in part-time and full-time positions. Company pays fee. **Positions commonly filled include:** Nanny. **Average salary range of placements:** Less than $20,000.

JACK PORTER & ASSOCIATES
24119 SE 18th Place, Issaquah WA 98029. 425/392-9252. **Fax:** 425/391-9107. **Contact:** Jack Porter, President. **Description:** A permanent employment agency. Company pays fee. **Specializes in the areas of:** Engineering; Manufacturing. **Positions commonly filled include:** Aerospace Engineer; Agricultural Engineer; Biochemist; Biological Scientist; Biomedical Engineer; Chemical Engineer; Chemist; Civil Engineer; Construction Contractor; Cost Estimator; Design Engineer; Electrical/Electronics Engineer; Environmental Engineer; Food Scientist/Technologist; General Manager; Geologist/Geophysicist; Industrial Engineer; Industrial Production Manager; Management Trainee; Manufacturer's/Wholesaler's Sales Rep.; Mathematician; Mechanical Engineer; Mining Engineer; MIS Specialist; Operations/Production Manager; Petroleum Engineer; Quality Control Supervisor; Science Technologist; Software Engineer; Stationary Engineer; Statistician; Structural Engineer; Systems Analyst; Telecommunications Manager. **Number of placements per year:** 1 - 49.

SKILLS RESOURCE TRAINING CENTER
1103 West Sylvester, Pasco WA 99301. 509/546-0462. **Contact:** Michael Elich, Director of Training. **E-mail address:** mlelich@aol.com. **Description:** A permanent employment agency that also provides labor training and leasing. Company pays fee. **Specializes in the areas of:** Food Industry; Industrial; Manufacturing. **Positions commonly filled include:** Blue-Collar Worker Supervisor; Human Resources Specialist; Industrial Production Manager; Operations/Production Manager. **Average salary range of placements:** Less than $20,000. **Number of placements per year:** 1000+.

STAFFING RESOURCES
1000 Second Avenue, Suite 1700, Seattle WA 98104. 206/583-2711. **Fax:** 206/583-2725. **Contact:** B. Joy Pieroon, CPC, CTS, Manager. **Description:** A permanent employment agency. Company pays fee. **Specializes in the areas of:** Accounting/Auditing; Administration; Legal; Light Industrial; Secretarial. **Positions commonly filled include:** Accountant/Auditor; Administrative Assistant; Advertising Clerk; Budget Analyst; Buyer; Claim Representative; Clerical Supervisor; Computer Operator; Controller; Cost Estimator; Credit Manager; Customer Service Representative; Editorial Assistant; Financial Analyst; Human Resources Manager; Librarian; Management Trainee; Marketing Specialist; Paralegal; Purchasing Agent/Manager; Sales Representative; Secretary; Typist/Word Processor. **Benefits available to temporary workers:** Medical Insurance; Paid Holidays; Paid Vacation; Transportation Pass. **Average salary range of placements:** $20,000 - $29,999. **Number of placements per year:** 500 - 999.

THOMAS COMPANY
15434 SE 167th Place, Renton WA 98058. 425/255-7637. **Contact:** Thomas J. Yankowski, Executive Director. **Description:** A permanent employment agency. Company pays fee. **Specializes in the areas of:** Banking; Computer Science/Software; Finance; Insurance; MIS/EDP; Sales. **Positions commonly filled include:** Accountant/Auditor; Actuary; Administrative Worker/Clerk; Advertising Account Executive; Attorney; Bookkeeper; Claim Representative; Computer Programmer; Customer Service Representative; Data Entry Clerk; Economist; EDP Specialist; Financial Analyst; General Manager; Human Resources Manager; Insurance Agent/Broker; Management Analyst/Consultant; Marketing Specialist; Statistician; Systems Analyst; Technical Writer/Editor; Technician; Underwriter/Assistant Underwriter. **Number of placements per year:** 50 - 99.

TEMPORARY EMPLOYMENT AGENCIES

BOSTWICK TEMPORARY SERVICE
1109 First Avenue, Suite 406, Seattle WA 98101. 206/340-1516. **Contact:** Karen Willis, General Manager. **Description:** A temporary agency. **Specializes in the areas of:** Accounting/Auditing; Banking; Insurance; Legal; Personnel/Labor Relations; Secretarial. **Positions commonly filled include:** Computer Programmer; Customer Service Representative; Human Resources Specialist; Human Service Worker; Paralegal; Systems Analyst; Typist/Word Processor. **Benefits available to temporary workers:** Medical Insurance; Paid Holidays; Paid Vacation. **Number of placements per year:** 1000+.

COMPREHENSIVE STAFFING RESOURCES INC.
dba TECHSTAFF
720 Olive Way, Suite 1510, Seattle WA 98101. 206/382-5555. **Fax:** 206/382-5556. **Contact:** Manager. **Description:** A temporary agency. Company pays fee. **Specializes in the areas of:** Administration; Architecture/Construction; Computer Science/Software; Engineering; Personnel/Labor Relations; Technical; Transportation. **Positions commonly filled include:** Architect; Civil Engineer; Computer Programmer; Construction and Building Inspector; Design Engineer; Designer; Draftsperson; Electrical/Electronics Engineer; Environmental Engineer; Forester/Conservation Scientist; Geologist/Geophysicist; Industrial Engineer; Internet Services Manager; Landscape Architect; Mechanical Engineer; MIS Specialist; Multimedia Designer; Software Engineer; Structural Engineer; Surveyor; Systems Analyst; Technical Writer/Editor; Urban/Regional Planner. **Benefits available to temporary workers:** 401(k); Paid Holidays; Referral Bonus Plan. **Average salary range of placements:** $30,000 - $50,000. **Number of placements per year:** 100 - 199.

CONMARKE USA INC.
18717 76th Avenue West, Suite I, Lynnwood WA 98037. 425/712-1948. **Toll-free phone:** 800/417-8168. **Contact:** Joyce Clendenning, President. **Description:** A temporary agency. Company pays fee. **Specializes in the areas of:** Engineering. **Positions commonly filled include:** Cost Estimator; Design Engineer; Designer; Draftsperson; Electrical/Electronics Engineer. **Benefits available to temporary workers:** 401(k). **Average salary range of placements:** $30,000 - $50,000. **Number of placements per year:** 50 - 99.

COOPER PERSONNEL
1411 Fourth Avenue, Suite 1327, Seattle WA 98101. 206/583-0722. **Fax:** 206/223-4093. **Contact:** Bonnie Cooper, CPC, Owner. **Description:** A temporary agency that also offers permanent placement. Company pays fee. **Specializes in the areas of:** Administration; Legal; Secretarial. **Positions commonly filled include:** Administrative Assistant; Clerical Supervisor; Computer Operator; Customer Service Representative; Database Manager; Legal Secretary; Paralegal; Purchasing Agent/Manager; Receptionist; Secretary; Typist/Word Processor. **Average salary range of placements:** $20,000 - $29,999. **Number of placements per year:** 200 - 499.

CREATIVE ASSETS
101 Yesler Way, Suite 200, Seattle WA 98104. 206/682-6005. **Fax:** 206/682-5030. **Contact:** Principal. **E-mail address:** info@creativeassets.com. **World Wide Web address:** http://www.creativeassets.com. **Description:** A temporary agency that also offers permanent placement and contract services. Company pays fee. **Specializes in the areas of:** Art/Design; Publishing. **Positions commonly filled include:** Designer; Internet Services Manager; Multimedia Designer; Technical Writer/Editor; Video Production Coordinator. **Benefits available to temporary workers:** Medical Insurance. **Other U.S. locations:** San Francisco CA; Portland OR. **Number of placements per year:** 500 - 999.

EXPRESS PERSONNEL SERVICES
222 South Washington Street, Spokane WA 99201. 509/747-6011. **Fax:** 509/747-8930. **Contact:** Manager. **Description:** A temporary agency that also provides some permanent placements. Company pays fee. **Specializes in the areas of:** Accounting/Auditing; Computer Science/Software; General Management; Insurance; Personnel/Labor Relations. **Positions commonly filled include:** Accountant/Auditor; Adjuster; Architect; Attorney; Blue-Collar Worker Supervisor; Branch Manager; Credit Manager; Designer; Draftsperson. **Corporate headquarters location:** Oklahoma City OK. **Other U.S. locations:** Nationwide. **Average salary range of placements:** $20,000 - $29,999. **Number of placements per year:** 1000+.

EXPRESS PERSONNEL SERVICES
230 North Mission Street, Wenatchee WA 98801. 509/662-5187. **Fax:** 509/662-5285. **Contact:** Gene Anderson, President. **Description:** A temporary agency. Company pays fee. **Specializes in the areas of:** Accounting/Auditing; Engineering; Food Industry; Health/Medical; Industrial; Manufacturing; Sales; Secretarial. **Positions commonly filled include:** Accountant/Auditor; Agricultural Engineer; Automotive Mechanic; Bank Officer/Manager; Branch Manager; Buyer; Chemist; Clerical Supervisor; Computer Programmer; Construction Contractor; Cost Estimator; Customer Service Representative; Dental Assistant/Dental Hygienist; Draftsperson; EEG Technologist; EKG Technician; Electrician; Emergency Medical Technician; Food Scientist/Technologist; General Manager; Industrial Production Manager; Insurance Agent/Broker; Licensed Practical Nurse; Management Trainee; Manufacturer's/Wholesaler's Sales Rep.; Mechanical Engineer; Medical Records Technician; Metallurgical Engineer; Occupational Therapist; Operations/Production Manager; Physical Therapist; Quality Control Supervisor; Recreational Therapist; Registered Nurse; Respiratory Therapist; Restaurant/Food Service Manager; Securities Sales Representative; Surgical Technician; Typist/Word Processor. **Benefits available to temporary workers:** Medical Insurance; Paid Holidays; Paid Vacation. **Other U.S. locations:** Nationwide. **Average salary range of placements:** $20,000 - $29,999. **Number of placements per year:** 1000+.

EXPRESS PERSONNEL SERVICES
4027 Hoyt Avenue, Everett WA 98201. 425/339-8400. **Contact:** Manager. **Description:** A temporary agency that also offers permanent placements and career/outplacement counseling. **Specializes in the areas of:** Accounting/Auditing; Advertising; Banking; Computer Science/Software; Insurance; Legal; Manufacturing; Personnel/Labor Relations; Publishing; Secretarial; Technical. **Positions commonly filled include:** Blue-Collar Worker Supervisor; Claim Representative; Clerical Supervisor; Credit Manager; Customer Service Representative; Human Resources Specialist; Public Relations Specialist; Purchasing Agent/Manager; Quality Control Supervisor; Software Engineer; Systems Analyst; Typist/Word Processor. **Benefits available to temporary workers:** Medical Insurance; Paid Holidays; Paid Vacation. **Other U.S. locations:** Nationwide. **Average salary range of placements:** Less than $20,000. **Number of placements per year:** 1000+.

GUIDANCE SERVICES INC.
1010 South 336th Street, Suite 122, Federal Way WA 98003. 253/838-2401. **Contact:** Manager. **Description:** A temporary agency. Company pays fee. **Specializes in the areas of:** Accounting/Auditing; Banking; Finance; Legal; Manufacturing; Personnel/Labor Relations; Secretarial. **Positions commonly filled include:** Accountant/Auditor; Administrative Manager; Attorney; Branch Manager; Claim Representative; Clerical Supervisor; Credit Manager; Customer Service Representative; Financial Analyst; General Manager; Health Services Manager; Human Resources Specialist; Medical Records Technician; Paralegal. **Other U.S. locations:** AZ; NY; OR; VA. **Number of placements per year:** 200 - 499.

JOB CENTER
P.O. Box 4717, Federal Way WA 98063. 253/661-1207. **Fax:** 253/952-6286. **Contact:** Louie Liu, Executive Director. **World Wide Web address:** http://www.ucom.com/nwcyber/fwjobctr. **Description:** A temporary agency that provides placement for disadvantaged jobseekers. **Specializes in the areas of:** Education; Light Industrial; Retail; Secretarial. **Positions commonly filled include:** Electrician; Secretary; Social Worker. **Average salary range of placements:** Less than $20,000. **Number of placements per year:** 50 - 99.

KELLY SERVICES, INC.
703 Broadway, Suite 102, Vancouver WA 98660. 360/699-5337. **Fax:** 360/737-0489. **Contact:** Recruiter/Trainer. **World Wide Web address:** http://www.kellyservices.com. **Description:** A temporary agency. Overall, Kelly Services has more than 1,100 offices in 12 countries. Founded in 1946. Company pays fee. **Specializes in the areas of:** Administration; Industrial; Light Industrial; Manufacturing; Personnel/Labor Relations; Sales; Secretarial; Technical. **Positions commonly filled include:** Accountant/Auditor; Clerical Supervisor; Customer Service Representative; Typist/Word Processor. **Benefits available to temporary workers:** Paid Holidays; Paid Vacation. **Corporate headquarters location:** Troy MI. **Average salary range of placements:** $20,000 - $29,999. **Number of placements per year:** 500 - 999.

KELLY SERVICES, INC.
16040 Christensen Road, Suite 205, Seattle WA 98188. 206/243-7409. **Toll-free phone:** 800/505-6200. **Contact:** Manager. **World Wide Web address:** http://www.kellyservices.com. **Description:** A temporary agency. Overall, Kelly Services has more than 1,100 offices in 12 countries. Company pays fee. **Specializes in the areas of:** Administration; Computer Science/Software; Insurance; Manufacturing; Personnel/Labor Relations; Secretarial; Technical. **Positions commonly filled include:** Accountant/Auditor; Administrative Manager; Blue-Collar Worker Supervisor; Claim Representative; Clerical Supervisor; Computer Programmer; Customer Service Representative; Draftsperson; Human Resources Specialist; Industrial Production Manager; MIS Specialist; Software Engineer; Systems Analyst; Technical Writer/Editor; Typist/Word Processor. **Benefits available to temporary workers:** Paid Holidays; Paid Vacation. **Corporate headquarters location:** Troy MI. **Average salary range of placements:** Less than $20,000. **Number of placements per year:** 1000+.

KELLY SERVICES, INC.
1735 Cedardale Road, Suite A400, Mount Vernon WA 98274. 360/424-4858. **Toll-free phone:** 800/505-6200. **Contact:** Manager. **World Wide Web address:** http://www.kellyservices.com. **Description:** A temporary agency that also offers contract services. Overall, Kelly Services has more than 1,100 offices in 12 countries. Company pays fee. **Specializes in the areas of:** Accounting/Auditing; Administration; Computer Science/Software; Finance; Food Industry; General Management; Industrial; Insurance; Personnel/Labor Relations; Retail; Secretarial; Technical. **Positions commonly filled include:** Accountant/Auditor; Administrative Manager; Blue-Collar Worker Supervisor; Claim Representative; Clerical Supervisor; Computer Programmer; Customer Service Representative; Electrician; Human Resources Specialist; Management Trainee; MIS Specialist; Restaurant/Food Service Manager; Software Engineer; Systems Analyst; Technical Writer/Editor; Typist/Word Processor. **Benefits available to temporary workers:** Paid Holidays; Paid Vacation. **Corporate headquarters location:** Troy MI. **Average salary range of placements:** Less than $20,000. **Number of placements per year:** 500 - 999.

LABOR READY, INC.
1222 Tacoma Avenue South, Tacoma WA 98402. 253/383-8909. **Contact:** Manager. **Description:** A temporary agency. **Specializes in the areas of:** Construction; Manufacturing.

MANPOWER TEMPORARY SERVICES
1420 Fifth Avenue, Suite 1750, Seattle WA 98101. 206/583-0880. **Contact:** Branch Manager. **Description:** A temporary agency. Company pays fee. **Specializes in the areas of:** Industrial; Office Support; Technical; Word Processing. **Positions commonly filled include:** Accountant/Auditor; Accounting Clerk; Administrative Manager; Assembler; Biological Scientist; Bookkeeper; Chemist; Computer Operator; Customer Service Representative; Designer; Desktop Publishing Specialist; Electrician; Inventory Control Specialist; Machine Operator; Materials Manager; Order Clerk; Packaging Manager; Records Manager; Research Assistant; Secretary; Software Engineer; Stenographer; Systems Analyst; Technical Writer/Editor; Telemarketer; Typist/Word Processor. **Benefits available to temporary workers:** Life Insurance; Medical Insurance; Paid Holidays; Paid Vacation. **Corporate headquarters location:** Milwaukee WI. **International locations:** Worldwide. **Number of placements per year:** 1000+.

MANPOWER TEMPORARY SERVICES
10049 Kitsap Mall Boulevard, Building 108, Silverdale WA 98383. 360/698-2592. **Fax:** 360/698-7369. **Contact:** Linda Patterson, Branch Manager. **World Wide Web address:** http://www.manpower.com. **Description:** A temporary agency. **Specializes in the areas of:** Accounting/Auditing; Administration; Computer Science/Software; Industrial; Insurance; Legal; Light Industrial; Personnel/Labor Relations;

Retail; Sales; Secretarial; Transportation. **Positions commonly filled include:** Accountant/Auditor; Administrative Assistant; Administrative Manager; Buyer; Clerical Supervisor; Customer Service Representative; Database Manager; Editorial Assistant; Human Resources Manager; Paralegal; Sales Executive; Sales Manager; Sales Representative; Secretary; Typist/Word Processor. **Benefits available to temporary workers:** Life Insurance; Medical Insurance; Paid Holidays; Paid Vacation; Stock Purchase. **Corporate headquarters location:** Milwaukee WI. **International locations:** Worldwide.

NORTHWEST TEMPORARY SERVICES, INC.
600 108th Avenue NE, Suite 239, Bellevue WA 98004. 425/453-2310. **Fax:** 425/457-9285. **Contact:** Manager. **Description:** A temporary agency. **Specializes in the areas of:** Accounting/Auditing; Administration; Computer Science/Software; Engineering; Industrial; Legal; Manufacturing; Technical. **Positions commonly filled include:** Accountant/Auditor; Administrative Manager; Aerospace Engineer; Agricultural Engineer; Architect; Blue-Collar Worker Supervisor; Buyer; Chemical Engineer; Civil Engineer; Claim Representative; Clerical Supervisor; Computer Programmer; Construction and Building Inspector; Cost Estimator; Customer Service Representative; Design Engineer; Designer; Draftsperson; Editor; Electrical/Electronics Engineer; Electrician; Environmental Engineer; Financial Analyst; Geologist/Geophysicist; Industrial Engineer; Industrial Production Manager; Internet Services Manager; Market Research Analyst; Mechanical Engineer; Metallurgical Engineer; Multimedia Designer; Operations/Production Manager; Physicist; Purchasing Agent/Manager; Quality Control Supervisor; Radiological Technologist; Software Engineer; Stationary Engineer; Structural Engineer; Surveyor; Systems Analyst; Technical Writer/Editor; Typist/Word Processor. **Benefits available to temporary workers:** 401(k); Paid Vacation. **Other U.S. locations:** Portland OR.

OLSTEN STAFFING SERVICES
19115 West Valley Highway, Building H, Suite 111, Kent WA 98032. 425/656-4199. **Contact:** Manager. **Description:** A temporary agency. Company pays fee. **Specializes in the areas of:** Administration; Computer Science/Software; Manufacturing; Personnel/Labor Relations; Secretarial. **Positions commonly filled include:** Administrative Manager; Claim Representative; Clerical Supervisor; Computer Programmer; Customer Service Representative; Human Resources Specialist; Industrial Production Manager; Management Trainee; Manufacturer's/Wholesaler's Sales Rep.; Medical Records Technician; MIS Specialist; Operations/Production Manager; Systems Analyst; Technical Writer/Editor; Typist/Word Processor. **Corporate headquarters location:** Melville NY. **International locations:** Worldwide. **Number of placements per year:** 1000+.

OLSTEN STAFFING SERVICES
601 Union Street, Suite 732, 2 Union Square, Seattle WA 98101. 206/441-2962. **Fax:** 206/441-3504. **Contact:** Personnel Supervisor. **Description:** A temporary agency. **Specializes in the areas of:** Administration; Industrial; Manufacturing; Personnel/Labor Relations; Secretarial. **Positions commonly filled include:** Blue-Collar Worker Supervisor; Customer Service Representative; Services Sales Representative; Typist/Word Processor. **Benefits available to temporary workers:** Paid Vacation; Referral Bonus Plan. **Corporate headquarters location:** Melville NY. **International locations:** Nationwide. **Number of placements per year:** 1000+.

RESOURCE MANAGEMENT INTERNATIONAL
515 116th Avenue NE, Bellevue WA 98004. 425/454-7787. **Contact:** Vice President. **Description:** A temporary agency. Company pays fee. **Specializes in the areas of:** Art/Design; Computer Science/Software; Engineering. **Positions commonly filled include:** Aerospace Engineer; Agricultural Engineer; Aircraft Mechanic/Engine Specialist; Architect; Buyer; Chemical Engineer; Chemist; Civil Engineer; Computer Programmer; Cost Estimator; Design Engineer; Designer; Draftsperson; Editor; Electrical/Electronics Engineer; Electrician; Environmental Engineer; Geologist/Geophysicist; Industrial Engineer; Industrial Production Manager; Mechanical Engineer; Metallurgical Engineer; Mining Engineer; Nuclear Medicine Technologist; Quality Control Supervisor; Software Engineer; Structural Engineer; Systems Analyst; Technical Writer/Editor; Telecommunications Manager; Typist/Word Processor. **Benefits available to temporary workers:** 401(k); Medical Insurance; Paid Holidays; Paid Vacation. **Average salary range of placements:** More than $50,000. **Number of placements per year:** 100 - 199.

WOODS & ASSOCIATES
1221 2nd Avenue, Suite 430, Seattle WA 98101. 206/623-2930. **Contact:** Manager. **Description:** A temporary agency that also provides permanent placements. **NOTE:** Please call for an appointment before sending a resume. **Specializes in the areas of:** Legal.

CONTRACT SERVICES FIRMS

CDI CORPORATION (WEST)
104 South Freya, Yellow Flag Building, Spokane WA 99202. 509/535-6852. **Fax:** 509/536-4333. **Contact:** Robin Lovejoy, Branch Manager. **World Wide Web address:** http://www.cdicorp.com. **Description:** A contract services firm. Company pays fee. **Specializes in the areas of:** Aerospace; Chemical; Communications; Computer Hardware/Software; Electronics; Manufacturing; Medical Technology; Mining; Paper; Transportation. **Positions commonly filled include:** Computer Programmer; Designer; Draftsperson; Engineer; Systems Analyst; Technical Illustrator; Technical Writer/Editor; Technician. **Corporate headquarters location:** Philadelphia PA. **Other U.S. locations:** Nationwide. **Average salary range of placements:** $30,000 - $50,000. **Number of placements per year:** 500 - 999.

CTS TECHNICAL SERVICES
11100 NE Eighth Street, Suite 510, Bellevue WA 98004. 425/451-0051. **Contact:** Manager. **Description:** A contract services firm. **Specializes in the areas of:** Aerospace; Computer Hardware/Software.

COMFORCE TECHNICAL SERVICES, INC.
P.O. Box 97003, Redmond WA 98073. 425/883-2233. **Toll-free phone:** 800/398-2432. **Fax:** 425/869-9898. **Contact:** Manager. **Description:** A contract services firm. **Specializes in the areas of:** High-Tech; Technical.

COMFORCE TECHNICAL SERVICES, INC.
4905 Pacific Highway East, Suite 2A, Tacoma WA 98424. 253/922-9119. **Fax:** 253/922-9274. **Contact:** Manager. **Description:** A contract services firm. **Specializes in the areas of:** Technical.

MINI-SYSTEMS ASSOCIATES
14535 Bel-Red Road, Suite 200, Bellevue WA 98007. 425/644-9500. **Toll-free phone:** 800/644-8225. **Fax:** 425/644-0200. **Contact:** Lanny Love, Recruiter. **E-mail address:** resumes@wa.mini-systems.com. **Description:** A contract services firm that also provides permanent placements. Clients include private industry and government organizations across the United States. Company pays fee. **Specializes in the areas of:** Computer Science/Software; Engineering; Manufacturing; Technical. **Positions commonly filled include:** Buyer; Civil Engineer; Computer Programmer; Construction Contractor; Cost Estimator; Design Engineer; Designer; Draftsperson; Purchasing Agent/Manager; Software Engineer; Structural Engineer; Systems Analyst; Technical Writer/Editor. **Corporate headquarters location:** Culver City CA. **Average salary range of placements:** More than $50,000. **Number of placements per year:** 100 - 199.

TWO 56, INC.
1001 290th Avenue SE, Issaquah WA 98024. 425/222-6849. **Fax:** 425/222-4769. **Contact:** Manager. **E-mail address:** 75112,1356@compuserve.com. **Description:** A contract services firm. **Specializes in the areas of:** Banking; Computer Science/Software; Education; Finance; Manufacturing; Retail; Technical. **Positions commonly filled include:** Computer Programmer. **Average salary range of placements:** More than $50,000. **Number of placements per year:** 1 - 49.

H.L. YOH COMPANY
705 Main Street, Suite 201, Vancouver WA 98660. 360/696-2644. **Contact:** Manager. **Description:** A contract services firm. **Specializes in the areas of:** Computer Hardware/Software; High-Tech.
Other area locations:
- 130 Andover Park East, Seattle WA 98188. 206/431-7932.

CAREER/OUTPLACEMENT COUNSELING FIRMS

40 PLUS OF PUGET SOUND
515 116th Avenue NE, Suite 110, Bellevue WA 98004. 425/450-0040. **Contact:** Office Manager. **Description:** A career/outplacement counseling firm.

PACIFIC ASSOCIATES
2200 Sixth Avenue, Suite 260, Seattle WA 98121. 206/728-8826. **Contact:** Manager. **Description:** A career/outplacement counseling firm that also offers training programs.

WEST VIRGINIA

EXECUTIVE SEARCH FIRMS

DUNHILL PROFESSIONAL SEARCH
P.O. Box 547, Charleston WV 25322. 304/340-4260. **Fax:** 304/340-4262. **Contact:** Manager. **Description:** An executive search firm. **Specializes in the areas of:** Engineering; Health/Medical; Sales.

MANAGEMENT RECRUITERS INTERNATIONAL
1587 Washington Street East, Charleston WV 25311. 304/344-5632. **Fax:** 304/344-5639. **Contact:** Manager. **Description:** An executive search firm. **Specializes in the areas of:** Chemical. **International locations:** Worldwide.

PERMANENT EMPLOYMENT AGENCIES

KEY PERSONNEL, INC.
1124 Fourth Avenue, Suite 300, Huntington WV 25701. 304/529-3377. **Contact:** Recruiter. **Description:** A full-service permanent employment agency. Founded in 1975. Company pays fee. **Specializes in the areas of:** Accounting/Auditing; Banking; Computer Science/Software; Engineering; Finance; Food Industry; General Management; Health/Medical; Industrial; Manufacturing; Personnel/Labor Relations; Sales; Technical; Transportation. **Positions commonly filled include:** Accountant/Auditor; Adjuster; Bank Officer/Manager; Branch Manager; Chemical Engineer; Claim Rep.; Cost Estimator; Credit Manager; Customer Service Rep.; Health Services Manager; Human Resources Specialist; Industrial Engineer; Manufacturer's/Wholesaler's Sales Rep.; Mechanical Engineer; MIS Specialist; Purchasing Agent/Manager; Quality Control Supervisor; Restaurant/Food Service Manager; Services Sales Rep.; Systems Analyst; Transportation/Traffic Specialist; Underwriter/Assistant Underwriter. **Average salary range of placements:** $30,000 - $50,000. **Number of placements per year:** 50 - 99.

ONSITE COMMERCIAL STAFFING
1430-1 Edwin Miller Boulevard, Martinsburg WV 25401. 304/267-7363. **Contact:** Recruiting. **Description:** A permanent employment agency that also provides temporary placements. Onsite Commercial Staffing focuses on technical and business fields. **Specializes in the areas of:** Computer Hardware/Software; Computer Programming; Environmental; Telecommunications.

QUANTUM RESOURCES
P.O. Box 1751, Parkersburg WV 26102. 304/428-8028. **Contact:** Cindy Miller, Technical Recruiter. **Description:** A permanent employment agency that also provides temporary placements. **Specializes in the areas of:** Clerical; Computer Hardware/Software; Engineering; Industrial.

RESOURCE PERSONNEL SERVICES
1403 Eighth Avenue, Huntington WV 25701. 304/523-3295. **Contact:** Manager. **Description:** A permanent employment agency that focuses on the placement of truck drivers. **Specializes in the areas of:** Transportation.

TEMPORARY EMPLOYMENT AGENCIES

EXTRA SUPPORT STAFFING
1217-A Garfield Avenue, Parkersburg WV 26101. 304/485-5200. **Fax:** 304/485-5212. **Contact:** Charlotte King, Manager. **Description:** A temporary agency that also provides permanent placements. Founded in 1988. Company pays fee. **Specializes in the areas of:** Accounting/Auditing; Banking; Finance; General Management; Industrial; Light Industrial; Manufacturing; Personnel/Labor Relations; Sales; Secretarial. **Positions commonly filled include:** Accountant; Administrative Manager; Advertising Clerk; Human Resources Specialist; Paralegal; Teacher/Professor; Typist/Word Processor. **Benefits available to temporary workers:** Paid Holidays; Paid Vacation. **Average salary range of placements:** Less than $20,000. **Number of placements per year:** 1000+.

KELLY SERVICES, INC.
611 Virginia Street East, Charleston WV 25301. 304/345-4840. **Fax:** 304/342-4734. **Contact:** Branch Manager. **Description:** A temporary agency. Kelly Services also has a technical division at this location. **Specializes in the areas of:** Clerical; Food Industry; General Labor; Light Industrial; Office Support; Technical. **Other U.S. locations:** Nationwide.

SNELLING PERSONNEL SERVICES
P.O. Box 4522, Charleston WV 25364. 304/344-0101. **Contact:** Recruiting. **Description:** A temporary employment agency that also provides permanent placements. **Specializes in the areas of:** Accounting/Auditing; Computer Hardware/Software; Sales.

CONTRACT SERVICES FIRMS

BELCAN TECHNICAL SERVICES
116 West Washington Street, Suite 3E, Charles Town WV 25414. 304/725-6691. **Fax:** 304/728-1189. **Contact:** Howard Myers, Manager. **Description:** A contract services firm. **Specializes in the areas of:** Construction; Engineering. **Positions commonly filled include:** Civil Engineer; Design Engineer; Draftsperson; Project Manager. **Benefits available to temporary workers:** 401(k); Medical Insurance; Paid Holidays; Paid Vacation. **Other U.S. locations:** IN; OH. **Average salary range of placements:** $30,000 - $50,000. **Number of placements per year:** 100 - 199.

CDI CORPORATION
405 Capitol Street, Suite 809, Charleston WV 25301. **Toll-free phone:** 800/527-2527. **Fax:** 304/345-3995. **Contact:** Manager. **World Wide Web address:** http://www.cdicorp.com. **Description:** A contract services firm. **Specializes in the areas of:** Computer Science/Software; Technical.

CDI ENGINEERING GROUP
400 Berry Run Road, Suite 2, Parkersburg WV 26101. 304/485-7550. **Contact:** Manager. **World Wide Web address:** http://www.cdicorp.com. **Description:** A contract services firm. **Specializes in the areas of:** Engineering.

WISCONSIN

EXECUTIVE SEARCH FIRMS

ACCOUNTANTS EXECUTIVE SEARCH
3333 North Mayfair Road, Suite 213, Milwaukee WI 53222. 414/278-0001. **Fax:** 414/771-2586. **Contact:** Manager. **Description:** An executive search firm.

ACTION SEARCH CONSULTANTS
3090 Hermans Road, New Franken WI 54229. 920/866-2342. **Fax:** 920/866-2855. **Contact:** Jim Rakun, President. **E-mail address:** jrakun@aol.com. **Description:** An executive search firm. Company pays fee. **Specializes in the areas of:** Engineering. **Positions commonly filled include:** Chemical Engineer; Electrical/Electronics Engineer; Human Resources Manager; Industrial Engineer; Industrial Production Manager; Manufacturing Engineer; Mechanical Engineer; Metallurgical Engineer; Operations Manager; Production Manager; Project Manager; Purchasing Agent/Manager; Quality Control Supervisor; Sales Engineer; Sales Executive; Sales Manager; Sales Representative; Software Engineer. **Corporate headquarters location:** Green Bay WI. **Number of placements per year:** 1 - 49.

CAREER RECRUITERS
16655 West Bluemond Road, Suite 235-C, Brookfield WI 53005. 414/784-0595. **Fax:** 414/797-0853. **Contact:** Don Schoberg, Owner. **E-mail address:** cr@execpc.com. **Description:** An executive search firm that focuses on permanent placement of MIS professionals. Company pays fee. **Specializes in the areas of:** Computer Science/Software. **Positions commonly filled include:** Computer Programmer; MIS Specialist; Software Engineer; Systems Analyst. **Average salary range of placements:** More than $50,000. **Number of placements per year:** 1 - 49.

CAREER RESOURCES
757 Sand Lake Road, Onalaska WI 54650. 608/783-6307. **Fax:** 608/783-6302. **Contact:** Chris M. Jansson, CPC, Owner. **Description:** An executive search firm. **Specializes in the areas of:** Accounting/Auditing; Administration; Computer Science/Software; Finance; Personnel/Labor Relations. **Positions commonly filled include:** Accountant/Auditor; Bank Officer/Manager; Computer Programmer; Financial Analyst; Human Resources Manager; MIS Manager; Systems Analyst.

CAREERTRAC EMPLOYMENT SERVICE
135 West Wells Street, Suite 518, Milwaukee WI 53203-1807. 414/224-8722. **Fax:** 414/224-7080. **Contact:** Cindy Johnson, President. **Description:** An executive search firm. Company pays fee. **Specializes in the areas of:** Accounting/Auditing; Administration; Banking; Finance; Legal; Personnel/Labor Relations; Sales. **Positions commonly filled include:** Accountant/Auditor; Administrative Manager; Attorney; Buyer; Clerical Supervisor; Credit Manager; Financial Manager; General Manager; Human Resources Manager; Insurance Agent/Broker; MIS Manager; Operations/Production Manager; Paralegal; Public Relations Specialist; Purchasing Agent/Manager; Quality Control Supervisor; Systems Analyst. **Average salary range of placements:** $20,000 - $29,999. **Number of placements per year:** 100 - 199.

CHAMBERS & ASSOCIATES
7505 Sheridan Road, Kenosha WI 53143. 414/654-8240. **Contact:** Office Manager. **Description:** An executive search firm.

CONSTRUCTION SEARCH SPECIALISTS
115 Fifth Avenue, Suite 407, La Crosse WI 54601. 608/784-4711. **Fax:** 608/784-4904. **Contact:** Tamara McClain, Vice President. **E-mail address:** css@centuryinter.net. **Description:** An executive search firm that operates on a contingency basis. Company pays fee. **Specializes in the areas of:** Architecture/Construction; Design; Engineering. **Positions commonly filled include:** Architect; Civil Engineer; Construction and Building Inspector; Construction Contractor; Cost Estimator; Design Engineer; Draftsperson; Electrical/Electronics Engineer; Electrician; Environmental Engineer; Industrial Engineer; Mechanical Engineer; Mining Engineer; Structural Engineer; Surveyor. **Average salary range of placements:** More than $50,000. **Number of placements per year:** 1 - 49.

CORPORATE SEARCH INC.
P.O. Box 1808, Waukesha WI 53187-1808. 414/542-6260. **Fax:** 414/542-1236. **Contact:** Joseph Cali, President. **E-mail address:** cali@staffing.net. **Description:** An executive search firm. Company pays fee. **Specializes in the areas of:** Engineering; Manufacturing. **Positions commonly filled include:** Buyer; Chemical Engineer; Design Engineer; Electrical/Electronics Engineer; Environmental Engineer; Human Resources Manager; Mechanical Engineer; Metallurgical Engineer; Purchasing Agent/Manager; Software Engineer; Structural Engineer. **Number of placements per year:** 50 - 99.

DATA PROCESSING SEARCH
West 62 North 244 Washington Avenue, Cedarburg WI 53012. 414/375-4644. **Fax:** 414/375-5506. **Contact:** Manager. **Description:** An executive search firm. **Specializes in the areas of:** Data Processing; Information Systems; Information Technology.

DIECK, MUELLER AND ASSOCIATES, INC.
1017 Orchard Drive, Seymour WI 54165-1652. 920/833-7600. **Fax:** 920/833-2488. **Contact:** Daniel W. Dieck, President. **E-mail address:** dmainc@execpc.com. **Description:** An executive search firm. Company pays fee. **Specializes in the areas of:** Engineering; Finance; General Management; Marketing; Personnel/Labor Relations; Publishing; Sales. **Positions commonly filled include:** Account Manager; Chief Financial Officer; Controller; Environmental Engineer; Finance Director; Financial Analyst; Human Resources Manager; Manufacturing Engineer; Marketing Manager; Marketing Specialist; MIS Specialist; Operations Manager; Production Manager; Public Relations Specialist; Purchasing Agent/Manager; Quality Control Supervisor; Sales Engineer; Sales Executive; Sales Manager; Vice President of Finance; Vice President of Marketing and Sales. **Average salary range of placements:** More then $50,000. **Number of placements per year:** 50 - 99.

DOMRES PROFESSIONAL SEARCH
P.O. Box 103, Coleman WI 54112. 920/897-4890. **Contact:** Terry A. Domres, Principal. **Description:** An executive search firm that focuses on placement in the pulp, paper, and related industries. Company pays fee. **Positions commonly filled include:** Accountant/Auditor; Blue-Collar Worker Supervisor; Chemical Engineer; Computer Programmer; Electrical/Electronics Engineer; Environmental Engineer; Health Services Manager; Human Resources Manager; Mechanical Engineer; MIS Manager; Paper; Purchasing Agent/Manager; Quality Control Supervisor. **Number of placements per year:** 1 - 49.

J.M. EAGLE PARTNERS
11514 North Port Washington Road, Suite 105, Mequon WI 53092. 414/241-1400. **Fax:** 414/241-

4745. **Contact:** Jerry Moses, President. **Description:** An executive search firm. Company pays fee. **Specializes in the areas of:** Computer Science/Software; Diagnostic Imaging; Engineering; Finance; General Management; Health/Medical; Manufacturing; Personnel/Labor Relations; Sales; Technical. **Number of placements per year:** 1000+.

ENGINEERING PLACEMENT SPECIALISTS
P.O. Box 85, Appleton WI 54912. 920/739-1135. **Contact:** Manager. **Description:** An executive search firm operating on a contingency basis. **Specializes in the areas of:** Engineering.

EXECUTIVE PLACEMENT SERVICE
CAREER CONNECTIONS INC.
2825 North Mayfair Road, Suite 110, Milwaukee WI 53222. 414/778-2200. **Contact:** Manager. **Description:** An executive search firm. Career Connections Inc. (also at this location) provides temp-to-perm placements. **Specializes in the areas of:** Engineering; Industrial; Manufacturing. **Positions commonly filled include:** Engineer.

EXECUTIVE RECRUITERS, INC.
813 Ondossagon Way, Madison WI 53719-3249. 608/833-4004. **Fax:** 608/833-4774. **Contact:** Manager. **E-mail address:** gobadger2@aol.com. **Description:** An executive search firm. Founded in 1979. **Specializes in the areas of:** Data Processing; Engineering; Manufacturing; Technical. **Positions commonly filled include:** Electrical/Electronics Engineer; Environmental Engineer; Industrial Engineer; Manufacturing Engineer; Materials Engineer; Mechanical Engineer; Metallurgical Engineer; Operations Manager; Software Engineer. **Average salary range of placements:** More than $50,000.

EXECUTIVE RESOURCE INC.
553 Industrial Drive, P.O. Box 356, Hartland WI 53029-0356. 414/369-2540. **Fax:** 414/369-2558. **Contact:** Duane Strong, President. **E-mail address:** executiveresources@ptnet.net. **Description:** An executive search firm. Company pays fee. **Specializes in the areas of:** Accounting/Auditing; Banking; Engineering; Finance; General Management; Industrial; Personnel/Labor Relations; Technical. **Positions commonly filled include:** Accountant/Auditor; Agricultural Engineer; Bank Officer/Manager; Buyer; Chemical Engineer; Chemist; Credit Manager; Design Engineer; Electrical/Electronics Engineer; Financial Analyst; General Manager; Human Resources Manager; Industrial Engineer; Industrial Production Manager; Mechanical Engineer; Metallurgical Engineer; Purchasing Agent/Manager; Quality Control Supervisor; Structural Engineer. **Average salary range of placements:** More than $50,000. **Number of placements per year:** 50 - 99.

THE EXUTEC GROUP
2801 International Lane, Suite 106, Madison WI 53704-3119. 608/244-1088. **Fax:** 608/244-1241. **Contact:** Managing Partner. **Description:** A retained executive search firm. **Specializes in the areas of:** Advertising; Architecture/Construction; Art/Design; Engineering; Finance; General Management; Health/Medical; Legal; Nonprofit; Personnel/Labor Relations; Sales. **Positions commonly filled include:** Actuary; Attorney; Bank Officer/Manager; Brokerage Clerk; Design Engineer; Designer; Education Administrator; General Manager; Health Services Manager; Hotel Manager; Human Resources Manager; Industrial Engineer; Insurance Agent/Broker; Mechanical Engineer; MIS Manager; Physician; Public Relations Specialist. **Average salary range of placements:** More than $50,000. **Number of placements per year:** 1 - 49.

FINANCIAL MANAGEMENT PERSONNEL
P.O. Box 215, Brookfield WI 53008. 414/784-9630. **Fax:** 414/569-1910. **Contact:** John Higgins, Owner. **Description:** An executive search firm. Company pays fee. **Specializes in the areas of:** Accounting/Auditing; Finance; Manufacturing. **Positions commonly filled include:** Accountant/Auditor; Budget Analyst; Credit Manager; Financial Analyst. **Number of placements per year:** 1 - 49.

FIRST SEARCH EXECUTIVE RECRUITMENT
P.O Box 6, Hubertus WI 53033. 414/628-9950. **Fax:** 414/628-9951. **Contact:** Kate Dwyer, Principal. **Description:** An executive search firm. Company pays fee. **Specializes in the areas of:** Engineering; Food Industry; Sales. **Positions commonly filled include:** Budget Analyst; Buyer; Chemical Engineer; Chemist; Economist; Environmental Engineer; Financial Analyst; Industrial Engineer; Management Trainee; Manufacturer's/Wholesaler's Sales Rep.; Mechanical Engineer; Services Sales Representative; Wholesale and Retail Buyer.

FLORES FINANCIAL SERVICES
314 Sage Street, Suite 100, Lake Geneva WI 53147-1931. 414/248-2771. **Fax:** 414/248-2562. **Contact:** Robert C. Flores, President. **E-mail address:** rflores007@aol.com. **Description:** An executive search firm that focuses on global financial institutions and investment banking. Company pays fee. **Specializes in the areas of:** Economics; Finance; General Management. **Positions commonly filled include:** Bank Officer/Manager; Economist; Financial Analyst. **Average salary range of placements:** More than $50,000. **Number of placements per year:** 50 - 99.

FOOD STAFF 2000
9875 South Franklin Drive, Franklin WI 53132. 414/421-2000. **Contact:** Chuck Nolan, President. **Description:** An executive search firm. Company pays fee. **Specializes in the areas of:** Engineering; Food Industry; Personnel/Labor Relations; Sales; Technical; Transportation. **Positions commonly filled include:** Accountant/Auditor; Agricultural Engineer; Biological Scientist; Buyer; Computer Programmer; Electrical/Electronics Engineer; Food Scientist/Technologist; General Manager; Human Resources Manager; Industrial Engineer; Mechanical Engineer; Operations/Production Manager; Purchasing Agent/Manager; Restaurant/Food Service Manager; Systems Analyst. **Number of placements per year:** 200 - 499.

HR INC.
1017 West Glen Oaks Lane, Mequon WI 53092-3371. 414/241-8588. **Fax:** 414/241-4690. **Contact:** Mr. Sunny Mehta, President. **E-mail address:** hrinc@tesla.net. **Description:** An executive search firm. Company pays fee. **Positions commonly filled include:** Buyer; Chemical Engineer; Chemist; Cost Estimator; Design Engineer; Electrical/Electronics Engineer; General Manager; Human Resources Manager; Industrial Engineer; Industrial Production Manager; Management Analyst/Consultant; Mechanical Engineer; MIS Manager; Operations/Production Manager; Purchasing Agent/Manager; Quality Control Supervisor. **Number of placements per year:** 50 - 99.

ROBERT HALF INTERNATIONAL
ACCOUNTEMPS
411 East Wisconsin Street, Suite 2150, Milwaukee WI 53202. 414/271-4253. **Contact:** Manager. **World Wide Web address:** http://www.roberthalf.com. **Description:** An executive search firm. Accountemps (also at this location) provides temporary placements. **Specializes in the areas of:** Accounting/Auditing. **Corporate headquarters location:** Menlo Park CA. **Other U.S. locations:** Nationwide.

HEALTHCARE RECRUITERS INTERNATIONAL
6441 Enterprise Lane, Suite 207, Madison WI 53719. 608/274-4475. **Contact:** Manager. **Description:** An executive search firm. **Specializes in the areas of:** Health/Medical.

HUNTER MIDWEST
11101 West Janesville Road, Hales Corners WI 53130-2530. 414/529-3930x3100. **Toll-free phone:** 800/236-3930. **Fax:** 414/529-0394. **Contact:** Michael Certalic, Office Manager. **E-mail address:** mcertalic@huntermidwest.com. **Description:** An executive search firm that focuses on placing IS professionals with AS400, PC, LAN, or UNIX backgrounds. The firm's client base consists of over 8,000 companies in the upper Midwest. Company pays fee. **NOTE:** A minimum of one year of experience is required. The firm does not place recent college graduates. **Specializes in the areas of:** Computer Science/Software; MIS/EDP; Network Administration; Systems Administration. **Positions commonly filled include:** Computer Programmer; Network Administrator. **Number of placements per year:** 50 - 99.

INTERNATIONAL SEARCH
P.O. Box 381, Green Bay WI 54305-0381. 920/437-8055. **Toll-free phone:** 800/276-8319. **Fax:** 920/437-0343. **Contact:** Michael Wingers, Owner. **Description:** An executive search firm. Company pays fee. **Specializes in the areas of:** Accounting/Auditing; Computer Science/Software. **Positions commonly filled include:** Accountant/Auditor; Computer Programmer; Systems Analyst; Systems Manager. **Average salary range of placements:** $30,000 - $50,000. **Number of placements per year:** 1 - 49.

KORDUS CONSULTING GROUP
1470 East Standish Place, Milwaukee WI 53217-1958. 414/228-7979. **Fax:** 414/228-1080. **Contact:** Ms. Lee Walther Kordus, President. **E-mail address:** kcginc@aol.com. **Description:** An executive search firm. Company pays fee. **Specializes in the areas of:** Advertising; Food Industry; Marketing; Public Relations. **Positions commonly filled include:** Account Manager; Advertising Account Executive; Graphic Artist; Graphic Designer; Market Research Analyst; Marketing Manager; Marketing Specialist; Product Manager; Public Relations Specialist. **Average salary range of placements:** More than $50,000. **Number of placements per year:** 1 - 49.

MANAGEMENT RECRUITERS (MILWAUKEE WEST)
13000 West Bluemound Road, Suite 310, Elm Grove WI 53122-2655. 414/797-7500. **Fax:** 414/797-7515. **Contact:** Peder Medtlie, Manager. **E-mail address:** mrmilw@aol.com. **Description:** An executive search firm. Company pays fee. **Specializes in the areas of:** Information Technology; MIS/EDP; Pharmaceutical. **Positions commonly filled include:** Auditor; Database Manager; Internet Services Manager; Quality Control Supervisor; Systems Analyst; Systems Manager. **Corporate headquarters location:** Cleveland OH. **Other U.S. locations:** Nationwide. **Average salary range of placements:** $30,000 - $50,000. **Number of placements per year:** 50 - 99.

MANAGEMENT RECRUITERS INTERNATIONAL
8338 Corporate Drive, Suite 300, Racine WI 53406. 414/886-8000. **Contact:** Manager. **Description:** An executive search firm. **Specializes in the areas of:** Banking; Plastics; Technical. **Corporate headquarters location:** Cleveland OH. **Other U.S. locations:** Nationwide.

MANAGEMENT RECRUITERS INTERNATIONAL
20 East Milwaukee Street, Suite 304, Janesville WI 53545. 608/752-2125. **Contact:** Office Manager. **Description:** An executive search firm. **Specializes in the areas of:** Health/Medical; Manufacturing. **Corporate headquarters location:** Cleveland OH. **Other U.S. locations:** Nationwide.

MANAGEMENT RECRUITERS INTERNATIONAL COMPUSEARCH OF WAUSAU
3205 Terrace Court, Suite 1A, Wausau WI 54401-4915. 715/842-1750. **Fax:** 715/842-1741. **Contact:** Laurie L. Prochnow, President. **Description:** An executive search firm focusing on the information systems industry. Company pays fee. **Specializes in the areas of:** Administration; Computer Science/Software; MIS/EDP. **Positions commonly filled include:** Chief Financial Officer; Computer Operator; Computer Programmer; Database Manager; MIS Specialist; Project Manager; Systems Analyst; Systems Manager; Telecommunications Manager; Webmaster. **Average salary range of placements:** More than $50,000. **Number of placements per year:** 1 - 49.

MANAGEMENT RECRUITERS OF APPLETON COMPUSEARCH
911 North Lynndale Drive, Appleton WI 54914. 920/731-5221. **Contact:** Russ Hanson, Manager. **Description:** An executive search firm. **Specializes in the areas of:** Accounting/Auditing; Administration; Architecture/Construction; Communications; Computer Hardware/Software; Electrical; Engineering; Finance; General Management; Manufacturing; Operations Management; Personnel/Labor Relations; Publishing; Technical; Textiles; Transportation. **Corporate headquarters location:** Cleveland OH. **Other U.S. locations:** Nationwide.

MANAGEMENT RECRUITERS OF GREEN BAY
444 South Adams Street, Green Bay WI 54301. 920/437-4353. **Contact:** Mr. Garland Ross, Manager. **Description:** An executive search firm. **Specializes in the areas of:** Accounting/Auditing; Administration; Advertising; Architecture/Construction; Banking; Communications; Computer Hardware/Software; Electrical; Engineering; Finance; Food Industry; General Management; Health/Medical; Insurance; Legal; Manufacturing; Operations Management; Personnel/Labor Relations; Publishing; Technical; Transportation. **Corporate headquarters location:** Cleveland OH. **Other U.S. locations:** Nationwide.

MANAGEMENT RECRUITERS OF MILWAUKEE SALES CONSULTANTS
601 East Henry Clay, Milwaukee WI 53217-5646. 414/963-2520. **Fax:** 414/963-2539. **Contact:** Tim Lawler, President. **E-mail address:** mr/sc@mri-execsearch.com. **World Wide Web address:** http://www.recruiters-jobs.com. **Description:** An executive search firm. Company pays fee. **Specializes in the areas of:** Accounting/Auditing; Administration; Architecture/Construction; Banking; Communications; Computer Hardware/Software; Electrical; Engineering; Finance; Food Industry; General Management; Health/Medical; Legal; Manufacturing; Operations Management; Personnel/Labor Relations; Publishing; Sales; Technical; Transportation. **Corporate headquarters location:** Cleveland OH. **Other U.S. locations:** Nationwide. **International locations:** Worldwide. **Average salary range of placements:** More than $50,000. **Number of placements per year:** 100 - 199.

MANAGEMENT RECRUITERS OF MILWAUKEE (SOUTH)
5307 South 92nd Street, Suite 125, Hales Corners WI 53130. 414/529-8020. **Contact:** Office Manager. **Description:** An executive search firm. **Specializes in the areas of:** Accounting/Auditing; Administration; Advertising; Architecture/Construction; Banking;

Communications; Computer Hardware/Software; Electrical; Engineering; Finance; Food Industry; General Management; Health/Medical; Insurance; Legal; Manufacturing; Operations Management; Personnel/Labor Relations; Publishing; Technical; Transportation. **Corporate headquarters location:** Cleveland OH. **Other U.S. locations:** Nationwide.

MANAGEMENT RECRUITERS OF STEVENS POINT INC.
1117-W County Road DB, Mosinee WI 54455. 715/341-4900. **Fax:** 715/341-4992. **Contact:** Brad Barick, President. **E-mail address:** mri@coredcs.com. **World Wide Web address:** http://www.mrinet.com. **Description:** An executive search firm that focuses on the placement of commercial insurance professionals. Management Recruiters operates on both retained and contingency bases and also offers some contract placements. Company pays fee. **Specializes in the areas of:** Computer Science/Software; Insurance; Safety. **Positions commonly filled include:** Claim Representative; Computer Programmer; Environmental Engineer; Insurance Agent/Broker; MIS Manager; Software Engineer; Systems Analyst; Underwriter/Assistant Underwriter. **Corporate headquarters location:** Cleveland OH. **Other U.S. locations:** Nationwide. **Number of placements per year:** 1 - 49.

MARBL CONSULTANTS
One Park Plaza, 11270 West Park Place, Suite 270, Milwaukee WI 53027. 414/359-5627. **Fax:** 414/359-5620. **Contact:** Allan Adzima, President. **E-mail address:** marblcons@aero.net (text only). **Description:** An executive search firm operating on both retained and contingency bases. Company pays fee. **Specializes in the areas of:** Administration; Computer Science/Software; Engineering; General Management; Logistics; Manufacturing; Materials; Personnel/Labor Relations; Purchasing; Technical. **Positions commonly filled include:** Ceramics Engineer; Computer Programmer; Electrical/Electronics Engineer; General Manager; Human Resources Manager; Industrial Engineer; Industrial Production Manager; Materials Engineer; Mechanical Engineer; Metallurgical Engineer; Operations/Production Manager; Purchasing Agent/Manager; Quality Control Supervisor; Software Engineer; Systems Analyst; Transportation/Traffic Specialist. **Average salary range of placements:** More than $50,000. **Number of placements per year:** 100 - 199.

MARKENT PERSONNEL
P.O. Box 328, Wisconsin Dells WI 53965. 608/253-9705. **Contact:** Tom Udulutch, Owner. **Description:** An executive search firm that primarily recruits engineers for upper Midwest clients. Markent Personnel also focuses on manufacturing, safety, environmental, and international sales/marketing placements. Company pays fee. **Specializes in the areas of:** Accounting/Auditing; Computer Science/Software; Engineering; Industrial; Manufacturing; Sales. **Positions commonly filled include:** Accountant/Auditor; Agricultural Engineer; Architect; Architectural Engineer; Buyer; Chemical Engineer; Chemist; Computer Programmer; Cost Estimator; Design Engineer; Draftsperson; Electrical/Electronics Engineer; Environmental Engineer; Industrial Engineer; Industrial Production Manager; Mathematician; Mechanical Engineer; Metallurgical Engineer; MIS Manager; Purchasing Agent/Manager; Quality Control Supervisor; Software Engineer; Structural Engineer; Surveyor; Systems Analyst; Technical Writer/Editor. **Other area locations:** Madison WI; Philips WI. **Average salary range of placements:** $40,000 - $70,000. **Number of placements per year:** 50 - 99.

DAVID NEIL & ASSOCIATES
P.O. Box 149, Milwaukee WI 53201. 414/964-4666. **Contact:** Manager. **Description:** An executive search firm. **Specializes in the areas of:** Finance; Manufacturing.

PATTERSON RESOURCES
700 Rayovac Drive, Suite 120, Madison WI 53711. 608/277-9400. **Contact:** Ellen Patterson, President. **Description:** An executive search firm that also offers career counseling and contract services. Company pays fee. **Positions commonly filled include:** Accountant/Auditor; Architect; Attorney; Bank Officer/Manager; Health Services Manager; Human Resources Manager; MIS Manager; Purchasing Agent/Manager; Quality Control Supervisor; Restaurant/Food Service Manager. **Number of placements per year:** 1 - 49.

PLACEMENT SOLUTIONS
W270 S3979 Heather Drive, Waukesha WI 53188. 414/542-2250. **Fax:** 414/542-7373. **Contact:** Mary Sue Short, President. **E-mail address:** msshort@execpc.com. **World Wide Web address:** http://www.execpc.com/placement-solns. **Description:** An executive search firm operating on a contingency basis. The firm focuses on the placement of accounting personnel. Company pays fee. **Specializes in the areas of:** Accounting/Auditing. **Positions commonly filled include:** Accountant; Auditor; Chief Financial Officer; Controller; Financial Analyst; Tax Specialist. **Other U.S. locations:** New York NY.

PRAIRIE ENGINEERING
P.O. Box 165, DeForest WI 53532-0165. 608/846-7600. **Fax:** 608/846-7601. **Contact:** Manager. **Description:** An executive search firm. Company pays fee. **Specializes in the areas of:** Computer Science/Software; Engineering. **Positions commonly filled include:** Computer Programmer; Software Engineer; Systems Analyst; Technical Writer/Editor. **Average salary range of placements:** $30,000 - $50,000. **Number of placements per year:** 1 - 49.

PROFESSIONAL RESOURCE SERVICES
1825 Lone Oak Circle West, Brookfield WI 53045-5017. 414/782-6901. **Toll-free phone:** 800/729-5746. **Fax:** 414/938-0681. **Contact:** Sandra DeChant, Principal. **World Wide Web address:** http://www.prs2000.com. **Description:** An executive search firm that focuses on information systems staffing. Company pays fee. **Specializes in the areas of:** Computer Science/Software; Information Systems. **Positions commonly filled include:** Computer Programmer; Software Engineer; Systems Analyst. **Average salary range of placements:** $30,000 - $50,000. **Number of placements per year:** 1 - 49.

QUIRK-CORPORON & ASSOCIATES, INC.
P.O. Box 93386, Milwaukee WI 53203-0386. 414/271-8711. **Fax:** 414/224-9472. **Contact:** Chuck Corporon, President. **Description:** An executive search firm. Company pays fee. **Specializes in the areas of:** Banking; Health/Medical; Insurance; Sales. **Positions commonly filled include:** Accountant/Auditor; Actuary; Adjuster; Claim Representative; Customer Service Representative; Health Services Manager; Insurance Agent/Broker; Physician; Registered Nurse. **Number of placements per year:** 1 - 49.

CHARLES C. RAY ASSOCIATES INC.
1200 West Sierra Lane, Mequon WI 53092. 414/241-4150. **Contact:** Charles Ray, Owner. **Description:** An executive search firm that exclusively places individuals with a background in medical devices. **Specializes in the areas of:** Medical Sales and Marketing.

RECRUITING RESOURCES INC.
123 South Sixth Avenue, West Bend WI 53059. 414/338-2370. **Contact:** Manager. **Description:** An

executive search firm. **Specializes in the areas of:** Food Industry; Sales.

ROPELLA & ASSOCIATES
1307 East Road 5, Edgerton WI 53534-8799. 608/884-9250. **Fax:** 608/884-9705. **Contact:** Patrick B. Ropella, President. **Description:** An executive search firm that recruits exclusively for the chemical industry. Company pays fee. **Specializes in the areas of:** Chemical. **Positions commonly filled include:** Chemist; General Manager; Marketing Manager; Sales Manager; Science Technologist. **Average salary range of placements:** More than $50,000. **Number of placements per year:** 1 - 49.

ROTH YOUNG EXECUTIVE RECRUITERS
5215 North Ironwood Road, Suite 201, Milwaukee WI 53217. 414/962-7684. **Contact:** Manager. **Description:** An executive search firm that provides placements in the food industry. **Corporate headquarters location:** New York NY. **Other U.S. locations:** Nationwide.

ROWBOTTOM & ASSOCIATES
7707 West Menomonie River Parkway, Milwaukee WI 53213-2632. 414/475-1974. **Fax:** 414/475-5038. **Contact:** Mark Rowbottom, Owner. **E-mail address:** robottom@execpc.com. **Description:** An executive search firm. Company pays fee. **Specializes in the areas of:** Computer Science/Software; Information Systems. **Positions commonly filled include:** Computer Programmer; Internet Services Manager; MIS Manager; Software Engineer; Systems Analyst; Telecommunications Manager. **Average salary range of placements:** $30,000 - $50,000. **Number of placements per year:** 100 - 199.

SALES SEARCH
8200 Brown Deer Road, Milwaukee WI 53223. 414/365-3651. **Contact:** Manager. **Description:** An executive search firm. **Specializes in the areas of:** Sales.

SALES SPECIALISTS, INC.
614 West Brown Deer Road, Suite 300, Milwaukee WI 53217. 414/228-8810. **Fax:** 414/228-8815. **Contact:** Jeff Berg, Vice President. **E-mail address:** brntrout@gnn.com. **Description:** An executive search firm that places sales, management, and technical support personnel. Company pays fee. **Specializes in the areas of:** Computer Science/Software; Food Industry; General Management; Health/Medical; Industrial; Sales. **Positions commonly filled include:** Branch Manager; Customer Service Representative; General Manager; Landscape Architect; Management Trainee; Manufacturer's/Wholesaler's Sales Rep.; Operations/Production Manager; Securities Sales Representative; Services Sales Representative; Software Engineer; Systems Analyst; Telecommunications Manager. **Average salary range of placements:** More than $50,000. **Number of placements per year:** 50 - 99.

SANFORD ROSE ASSOCIATES
222 East Main Street, Port Washington WI 53074. 414/268-1750. **Fax:** 414/268-1753. **Contact:** Manager. **World Wide Web address:** http://www.sanfordrose.com. **Description:** An executive search firm. **Specializes in the areas of:** Automotive; Engineering; General Management.

R.F. SCOTT & COMPANY
140 South Park Street, Port Washington WI 53074. 414/284-1700. **Fax:** 414/284-6220. **Contact:** Robert Scott, President. **Description:** An executive search firm. Company pays fee. **Positions commonly filled include:** Chemical Engineer; Chemist; Computer Programmer; Electrical/Electronics Engineer; Industrial Engineer; Mechanical Engineer; Metallurgical Engineer; Quality Control Supervisor; Statistician; Structural Engineer; Systems Analyst. **Average salary range of placements:** More than $50,000. **Number of placements per year:** 50 - 99.

SOURCE SERVICES CORPORATION
1233 North Mayfair Road, Suite 300, Milwaukee WI 53226. 414/774-6700. **Fax:** 414/774-8155. **Contact:** Manager. **Description:** An executive search firm. The divisions at this location include Source EDP, Source Finance, and Accountant Source Temps. **Specializes in the areas of:** Accounting/Auditing; Computer Hardware/Software; Finance; Information Technology.

STAFF DEVELOPMENT CORPORATION
4040 North Calhoun Road, Brookfield WI 53005-1336. 414/783-0020. **Fax:** 414/783-0029. **Contact:** Mary Agnello, President. **Description:** An executive search firm operating on a retainer basis. Founded in 1990. Company pays fee. **Specializes in the areas of:** Health/Medical. **Positions commonly filled include:** EEG Technologist; EKG Technician; Emergency Medical Technician; Health Services Manager; Licensed Practical Nurse; Occupational Therapist; Pharmacist; Physical Therapist; Physician; Registered Nurse; Respiratory Therapist; Social Worker. **Average salary range of placements:** More than $50,000. **Number of placements per year:** 100 - 199.

T.E.M. ASSOCIATES
P.O. Box 5243, DePere WI 54115. 920/339-8055. **Fax:** 920/339-6177. **Contact:** Terri E. McCracken, President. **Description:** An executive search firm operating on a contingency basis. T.E.M. Associates primarily places professionals in the pulp, paper, and converting industries. Founded in 1994. **Specializes in the areas of:** Engineering; Manufacturing; Sales. **Positions commonly filled include:** Design Engineer; Designer; Electrical/Electronics Engineer; Environmental Engineer; Industrial Engineer; Industrial Production Manager; Market Research Analyst; Mechanical Engineer; Operations/Production Manager; Purchasing Agent/Manager; Quality Control Supervisor. **Number of placements per year:** 1 - 49.

TECHTRONIX TECHNICAL EMPLOYMENT
5401 North 76th Street, Milwaukee WI 53218. 414/466-3100. **Fax:** 414/466-3598. **Contact:** Louis Beauchamp, Vice President. **Description:** An executive search firm. Company pays fee. **Specializes in the areas of:** Administration; Computer Science/Software; Engineering; Manufacturing; Technical. **Positions commonly filled include:** Aerospace Engineer; Biomedical Engineer; Chemical Engineer; Computer Programmer; Electrical/Electronics Engineer; Human Resources Manager; Industrial Engineer; Industrial Production Manager; Mechanical Engineer; Metallurgical Engineer; Quality Control Supervisor; Software Engineer; Systems Analyst. **Number of placements per year:** 50 - 99.

U.S. TECH FORCE INC.
485 South Military Road, Fond du Lac WI 54935. 920/922-5000. **Toll-free phone:** 800/230-0505. **Fax:** 920/922-0060. **Contact:** Ron Deabler, Manager. **Description:** An executive search firm operating on a contingency basis. The firm focuses on office support, skilled trades, and engineering placement. Founded in 1990. **Specializes in the areas of:** Architecture/Construction; Engineering; Industrial; Manufacturing; Publishing; Secretarial. **Positions commonly filled include:** Buyer; Design Engineer; Industrial Engineer; Industrial Production Manager; Mechanical Engineer; Metallurgical Engineer; Purchasing Agent/Manager; Quality Control Supervisor. **Corporate headquarters location:** This Location. **Other area locations:** Appleton WI. **Number of placements per year:** 100 - 199.

UNIVERSAL SEARCH
8633 West Greenfield Avenue, West Allen WI 53214. 414/771-5972. **Contact:** Manager. **Description:** An executive search firm. **Specializes in the areas of:** Engineering.

VALLEY RECRUITING
1408 West Third Avenue, Oshkosh WI 54901-5604. 920/235-3727. **Fax:** 920/233-8851. **Contact:** Cliff Robl, Owner. **Description:** An executive search firm focusing on machine design, machine controls design, and industrial and/or manufacturing engineering placement. The firm concentrates on paper converting and manufacturing, food processing equipment manufacturing, and process control designing and manufacturing. **Specializes in the areas of:** Engineering; Manufacturing; Technical. **Positions commonly filled include:** Electrical/Electronics Engineer; Industrial Production Manager; Mechanical Engineer. **Average salary range of placements:** $30,000 - $50,000. **Number of placements per year:** 1 - 49.

PERMANENT EMPLOYMENT AGENCIES

A.B.R.
1521 Metro Drive, Suite 204, Schofield WI 54476. 715/355-7711. **Fax:** 715/355-4486. **Contact:** Carol Howard, Account Manager. **Description:** A permanent employment agency that also provides temporary placements. Company pays fee. **Positions commonly filled include:** Accountant/Auditor; Advertising Clerk; Claim Representative; Clerical Supervisor; Customer Service Representative; Typist/Word Processor; Underwriter/Assistant Underwriter. **Average salary range of placements:** $20,000 - $29,999. **Number of placements per year:** 200 - 499.

ALLEN, WAYNE, AND COMPANY
322 East Michigan Avenue, 6th Floor, Milwaukee WI 53202. 414/273-1080. **Toll-free phone:** 888/403-3400. **Fax:** 414/273-1090. **Contact:** Manager. **Description:** A permanent employment agency. Company pays fee. **Specializes in the areas of:** Accounting/Auditing; Administration; Architecture/Construction; Banking; Computer Science/Software; Engineering; Finance; General Management; Industrial; Insurance; Legal; Manufacturing; Personnel/Labor Relations; Publishing; Sales; Transportation. **Positions commonly filled include:** Accountant/Auditor; Actuary; Agricultural Engineer; Architect; Attorney; Bank Officer/Manager; Biological Scientist; Biomedical Engineer; Branch Manager; Budget Analyst; Buyer; Chemical Engineer; Chemist; Civil Engineer; Claim Representative; Computer Programmer; Construction Contractor; Cost Estimator; Credit Manager; Customer Service Representative; Designer; Economist; Electrical/Electronics Engineer; Environmental Engineer; Financial Analyst; Food Scientist/Technologist; General Manager; Geologist/Geophysicist; Health Services Manager; Hotel Manager; Human Resources Manager; Industrial Engineer; Industrial Production Manager; Insurance Agent/Broker; Librarian; Management Analyst/Consultant; Management Trainee; Manufacturer's/Wholesaler's Sales Rep.; Mechanical Engineer; Metallurgical Engineer; Mining Engineer; Operations/Production Manager; Paralegal; Property and Real Estate Manager; Purchasing Agent/Manager; Quality Control Supervisor; Real Estate Agent; Science Technologist; Securities Sales Representative; Services Sales Representative; Software Engineer; Stationary Engineer; Statistician; Structural Engineer; Systems Analyst; Technical Writer/Editor; Transportation/Traffic Specialist; Underwriter/Assistant Underwriter. **Number of placements per year:** 1 - 49.

AMERICAN TECHNICAL SERVICES, INC.
16535 West Bluemound Road, Brookfield WI 53005-5936. 414/789-0505. **Contact:** Manager. **Description:** A full-service employment agency focusing on permanent and contract placements in the skilled trades and engineering, office/clerical, data processing, and desktop publishing industries. Founded in 1991. **Specializes in the areas of:** Engineering; Manufacturing; Publishing. **Positions commonly filled include:** Design Engineer; Designer; Draftsperson; Electrician; Industrial Engineer; Mechanical Engineer; Purchasing Agent/Manager; Structural Engineer; Technical Writer/Editor. **Number of placements per year:** 500 - 999.

ARGUS TECHNICAL SERVICES
2339 West Wisconsin Avenue, Appleton WI 54914. 920/731-7703. **Fax:** 920/731-1886. **Contact:** John LaFay, Branch Manager. **Description:** A permanent employment agency. Company pays fee. **Specializes in the areas of:** Architecture/Construction; Computer Science/Software; Engineering; Industrial; Manufacturing; Personnel/Labor Relations; Technical. **Positions commonly filled include:** Aerospace Engineer; Architect; Biomedical Engineer; Chemical Engineer; Civil Engineer; Computer Programmer; Designer; Draftsperson; Electrical/Electronics Engineer; Electrician; General Manager; Industrial Engineer; Landscape Architect; Mechanical Engineer; Metallurgical Engineer; Production Manager; Quality Control Supervisor; Software Engineer; Stationary Engineer; Structural Engineer; Surveyor; Technical Writer/Editor; Urban/Regional Planner.

ASSOCIATED SECRETARIAL
7635 West Bluemound Road, Milwaukee WI 53213-3500. 414/476-4333. **Fax:** 414/476-4330. **Contact:** Mary Scheele, Owner. **Description:** A permanent employment agency. Company pays fee. **Specializes in the areas of:** Office Support. **Average salary range of placements:** $20,000 - $29,999. **Number of placements per year:** 50 - 99.

AUSTRIA AUSTRIA AND ASSOCIATES
P.O. Box 17682, Milwaukee WI 53217. 414/247-1865. **Contact:** Roger Austria, President. **Description:** A permanent employment agency. Founded in 1983. **Specializes in the areas of:** Engineering; General Management; Health/Medical; Manufacturing; Personnel/Labor Relations; Technical. **Positions commonly filled include:** Accountant/Auditor; Administrative Manager; Aerospace Engineer; Agricultural Engineer; Bank Officer/Manager; Buyer; Ceramics Engineer; Chemical Engineer; Chemist; Civil Engineer; Design Engineer; Education Administrator; EEG Technologist; EKG Technician; Electrical/Electronics Engineer; Emergency Medical Technician; Environmental Engineer; Financial Analyst; Food Scientist/Technologist; Human Service Worker; Industrial Engineer; Industrial Production Manager; Licensed Practical Nurse; Management Analyst/Consultant; Management Trainee; Materials Engineer; Mathematician; Mechanical Engineer; Medical Records Technician; Metallurgical Engineer; Mining Engineer; Nuclear Engineer; Nuclear Medicine Technologist; Occupational Therapist; Pharmacist; Physical Therapist; Physician; Physicist; Psychologist; Public Relations Specialist; Purchasing Agent/Manager; Quality Control Supervisor; Recreational Therapist; Registered Nurse; Respiratory Therapist; Science Technologist; Social Worker; Sociologist; Statistician; Strategic Relations Manager; Structural Engineer; Surgical Technician; Technical

Writer/Editor; Telecommunications Manager; Transportation/Traffic Specialist; Travel Agent. **Average salary range of placements:** $30,000 - $50,000. **Number of placements per year:** 50 - 99.

CONCORD STAFF SOURCE INC.
735 North Water Street, Suite 185, Milwaukee WI 53202. 414/291-6180. **Fax:** 414/272-3852. **Contact:** Bradley Brin, President. **E-mail address:** at@execpc.com. **Description:** A permanent employment agency. **Specializes in the areas of:** Computer Science/Software; Health/Medical. **Positions commonly filled include:** Computer Programmer; MIS Specialist; Occupational Therapist; Pharmacist; Physician; Radiological Technologist; Registered Nurse; Respiratory Therapist; Software Engineer; Speech-Language Pathologist; Systems Analyst; Systems Manager. **Average salary range of placements:** More than $50,000. **Number of placements per year:** 100 - 199.

DUNHILL OF GREEN BAY
336 South Jefferson Street, Green Bay WI 54301. 920/432-2977. **Contact:** Office Manager. **Description:** A permanent employment agency. **Specializes in the areas of:** Data Processing; Engineering; Manufacturing; Sales. **Positions commonly filled include:** Engineer; Sales Representative; Typist/Word Processor.

DUNHILL STAFFING SERVICES
735 North Water Street, Suite 105, Milwaukee WI 53202. 414/298-2000. **Contact:** Manager. **Description:** A permanent employment agency that also provides temporary placements. **Specializes in the areas of:** Accounting/Auditing; Administration; Secretarial. **Positions commonly filled include:** Accountant/Auditor; Budget Analyst; Butcher; Clerical Supervisor; Computer Programmer; Credit Manager; Customer Service Representative; Financial Analyst; Human Resources Manager; Insurance Agent/Broker; MIS Specialist; Paralegal; Software Engineer; Systems Analyst; Typist/Word Processor; Underwriter/Assistant Underwriter. **Number of placements per year:** 200 - 499.

EAGLE TECHNOLOGY GROUP INC.
11575 Theo Trecker Way, West Allis WI 53214. 414/453-9545. **Toll-free phone:** 800/964-9675. **Fax:** 414/453-9720. **Contact:** Tom Lemmer, Vice President. **E-mail address:** info@eagletechnologygroup.com. **World Wide Web address:** http://www.eagletechnologygroup.com. **Description:** A permanent employment agency that also provides some contract placements. Founded in 1993. Company pays fee. **Specializes in the areas of:** Computer Science/Software; Engineering; Industrial; Manufacturing; Technical. **Positions commonly filled include:** Architect; Biomedical Engineer; Blue-Collar Worker Supervisor; Branch Manager; Ceramics Engineer; Chemical Engineer; Chemist; Civil Engineer; Clinical Lab Technician; Computer Animator; Computer Operator; Computer Programmer; Database Manager; Design Engineer; Designer; Draftsperson; Electrical/Electronics Engineer; Electrician; Environmental Engineer; Graphic Artist; Graphic Designer; Human Resources Manager; Industrial Engineer; Industrial Production Manager; Internet Services Manager; Management Analyst/Consultant; Manufacturing Engineer; Materials Engineer; Mechanical Engineer; Metallurgical Engineer; Mining Engineer; MIS Specialist; Multimedia Designer; Nuclear Engineer; Production Manager; Project Manager; Quality Control Supervisor; Sales Engineer; Software Engineer; Stationary Engineer; Structural Engineer; Systems Analyst; Systems Manager; Technical Writer/Editor; Telecommunications Manager; Webmaster. **Benefits available to temporary workers:** 401(k); Bonus Award/Plan; Dental Insurance; Disability Coverage; Life Insurance; Medical Insurance; Paid Holidays; Paid Vacation. **Corporate headquarters location:** This Location. **Other U.S. locations:** Nationwide. **Average salary range of placements:** More than $50,000. **Number of placements per year:** 1000+.

EMPLOYABILITY
136 West Grand Avenue, Suite 101, Beloit WI 53511-6259. 608/365-9090. **Fax:** 608/365-9062. **Contact:** Betty Holloway, Office Manager. **Description:** A permanent employment agency that also provides some temporary placements. Company pays fee. **Specializes in the areas of:** Industrial; Manufacturing; Secretarial; Technical. **Positions commonly filled include:** Blue-Collar Worker Supervisor; Butcher; Clerical Supervisor; Customer Service Representative; General Manager; Industrial Production Manager; Operations/Production Manager; Quality Control Supervisor; Services Sales Representative; Typist/Word Processor. **Benefits available to temporary workers:** Bonus Award/Plan; Paid Holidays. **Corporate headquarters location:** Rockford IL. **Other area locations:** Delavan WI; Janesville WI. **Other U.S. locations:** Oregon IL. **Average salary range of placements:** $20,000 - $29,999. **Number of placements per year:** 500 - 999.

EPIC SKILLED & INDUSTRIAL
10701 West North Avenue, Milwaukee WI 53226. 414/476-8050. **Fax:** 414/771-4848. **Contact:** Michelle Roso, Employment Specialist. **Description:** A permanent employment agency that also provides some temporary placements. Company pays fee. **Specializes in the areas of:** Industrial; Manufacturing. **Positions commonly filled include:** Automotive Mechanic; Blue-Collar Worker Supervisor; Electrician. **Benefits available to temporary workers:** Medical Insurance; Paid Vacation. **Average salary range of placements:** $20,000 - $29,999. **Number of placements per year:** 200 - 499.

FOOD & DRUG PROFESSIONALS INC.
420 East Lake Street, Horicon WI 53032. 920/485-4100. **Fax:** 920/485-2444. **Contact:** Carl Fausett, CPC, President. **Description:** A permanent employment agency. Company pays fee. **Specializes in the areas of:** Food Industry; Pharmaceutical. **Positions commonly filled include:** Agricultural Engineer; Chemical Engineer; Designer; Draftsperson; Electrical/Electronics Engineer; Food Scientist/Technologist; Industrial Engineer; Mechanical Engineer; Science Technologist. **Number of placements per year:** 50 - 99.

INDUSTRIAL CONSULTING ENGINEERS, INC.
4076 North 70th Street, Suite 112, Milwaukee WI 53216. 414/464-6729. **Contact:** Richard W. Heiden, President. **Description:** A permanent employment agency. Company pays fee. **Specializes in the areas of:** Design; Engineering. **Positions commonly filled include:** Chemical Engineer; Civil Engineer; Draftsperson; Electrical/Electronics Engineer; General Manager; Industrial Engineer; Mechanical Engineer; Purchasing Agent/Manager; Quality Control Supervisor; Technical Writer/Editor. **Number of placements per year:** 50 - 99.

LEGAL PLACEMENT SERVICES, INC.
PERSONNEL SPECIALISTS
161 West Wisconsin Avenue, Suite 3054, Milwaukee WI 53203. 414/276-6689. **Contact:** General Manager. **Description:** A permanent employment agency. Company pays fee. **Specializes in the areas**

of: Legal. **Positions commonly filled include:** Accountant/Auditor; Administrative Assistant; Aerospace Engineer; Agricultural Engineer; Attorney; Biomedical Engineer; Ceramics Engineer; Chemical Engineer; Civil Engineer; Computer Operator; Computer Programmer; Data Entry Clerk; Electrical/Electronics Engineer; Industrial Engineer; Legal Secretary; Mechanical Engineer; Medical Secretary; Metallurgical Engineer; Mining Engineer; Paralegal; Petroleum Engineer; Receptionist; Sales Representative; Secretary; Stenographer; Systems Analyst; Typist/Word Processor.

MACPROS, INC.
727 North Milwaukee Street, Milwaukee WI 53202. 414/271-7767. **Fax:** 414/271-7764. **Contact:** Office Manager. **Description:** A permanent employment agency that also provides some temporary placements. Company pays fee. **Specializes in the areas of:** Advertising; Art/Design; Publishing; Sales. **Positions commonly filled include:** Computer Graphics Specialist. **Number of placements per year:** 50 - 99.

N.E.W.
P.O. Box 2239, Green Bay WI 54306-2239. 920/431-4400. **Fax:** 920/431-4404. **Contact:** Blaise Krautkramer, President. **Description:** A permanent employment agency that also provides some temporary placements. Company pays fee. **Specializes in the areas of:** Industrial; Manufacturing; Publishing. **Positions commonly filled include:** Accountant/Auditor; Automotive Mechanic; Blue-Collar Worker Supervisor; Ceramics Engineer; Claim Representative; Clerical Supervisor; Computer Programmer; Construction and Building Inspector; Construction Contractor; Construction Manager; Cost Estimator; Customer Service Representative; Design Engineer; Designer; Draftsperson; Electrical/Electronics Engineer; Electrician; General Manager; Industrial Engineer; Industrial Production Manager; Materials Engineer; Mechanical Engineer; Metallurgical Engineer; Structural Engineer; Typist/Word Processor. **Benefits available to temporary workers:** Dental Insurance; Medical Insurance. **Average salary range of placements:** Less than $20,000. **Number of placements per year:** 1000+.

PLACEMENTS OF RACINE INC.
222 Main Street, Suite 101, Racine WI 53403. 414/637-9355. **Contact:** Office Manager. **Description:** A permanent employment agency that also provides some temporary placements. Company pays fee. **Specializes in the areas of:** Accounting/Auditing; Administration; Clerical; Computer Hardware/Software; Engineering; Finance; Manufacturing; Sales. **Positions commonly filled include:** Accountant/Auditor; Agricultural Engineer; Bookkeeper; Buyer; Computer Programmer; Credit Manager; Customer Service Representative; Draftsperson; EDP Specialist; Electrical/Electronics Engineer; Financial Analyst; Industrial Engineer; Legal Secretary; Marketing Specialist; Mechanical Engineer; Medical Secretary; Metallurgical Engineer; MIS Specialist; Purchasing Agent/Manager; Quality Control Supervisor; Receptionist; Sales Representative; Secretary; Stenographer; Systems Analyst; Technical Writer/Editor; Technician; Typist/Word Processor. **Number of placements per year:** 50 - 99.

PROFESSIONAL ENGINEERING PLACEMENTS INC.
11941 West Rawson Avenue, Franklin WI 53132. 414/427-1700. **Fax:** 414/427-8080. **Contact:** Patty Wiza, President. **E-mail address:** proeng33@aol.com. **World Wide Web address:** http://www.proengineer.com. **Description:** A permanent employment agency. Company pays fee. **Specializes in the areas of:** Computer Science/Software; Engineering; Industrial. **Positions commonly filled include:** Computer Programmer; Design Engineer; Draftsperson; Electrical/Electronics Engineer; Industrial Engineer; Manufacturing Engineer; Mechanical Engineer; Production Manager; Project Manager; Quality Control Supervisor; Sales Engineer; Software Engineer. **Average salary range of placements:** $30,000 - $50,000. **Number of placements per year:** 50 - 99.

SEEK INC.
1160 Opportunity Drive, P.O. Box 148, Grafton WI 53024-0148. 414/377-8888. **Fax:** 414/375-3124. **Contact:** Carol Schneider, CPC. **Description:** SEEK is one of the largest full-service staffing services in southeast Wisconsin offering full-time, part-time, temporary, and direct-hire placements. **Specializes in the areas of:** Accounting/Auditing; Bookkeeping; Engineering; Finance. **Corporate headquarters location:** This Location. **Other area locations:** Fond du Lac WI; Milwaukee WI; Oshkosh WI; Sheboygan WI; West Bend WI.

SEEK INC.
107 South Main Street, Fond du Lac WI 54935. 920/924-7886. **Toll-free phone:** 800/221-6407. **Fax:** 920/924-7896. **Contact:** Manager. **Description:** SEEK is one of the largest full-service staffing services in southeast Wisconsin offering full-time, part-time, temporary, and direct-hire placements. Founded in 1971. Company pays fee. **Specializes in the areas of:** Engineering; Industrial; Secretarial. **Positions commonly filled include:** Accountant/Auditor; Administrative Manager; Blue-Collar Worker Supervisor; Clerical Supervisor; Computer Programmer; Customer Service Representative; Electrical/Electronics Engineer; General Manager; Industrial Engineer; Industrial Production Manager; Mechanical Engineer; MIS Specialist; Multimedia Designer; Operations/Production Manager; Software Engineer; Systems Analyst; Typist/Word Processor. **Benefits available to temporary workers:** Bonus Award/Plan; Medical Insurance. **Corporate headquarters location:** Grafton WI. **Other area locations:** Milwaukee WI; Oshkosh WI; Sheboygan WI; West Bend WI. **Average salary range of placements:** $20,000 - $29,999. **Number of placements per year:** 200 - 499.

SHORE PERSONNEL
363 West Main Street, Waukesha WI 53186-4613. 414/544-6166. **Fax:** 414/544-1954. **Contact:** Scott Nissen, Owner. **Description:** A permanent employment agency that also offers temp-to-perm placements. **Specializes in the areas of:** Industrial. **Positions commonly filled include:** Accountant/Auditor; Automotive Mechanic; Blue-Collar Worker Supervisor; Human Resources Manager; Typist/Word Processor. **Corporate headquarters location:** Greenfield WI. **Average salary range of placements:** Less than $20,000.

TOM SLOAN & ASSOCIATES INC.
P.O. Box 50, Watertown WI 53094. 920/261-8890. **Fax:** 920/261-6357. **Contact:** Tom Sloan, President. **Description:** A permanent employment agency that also provides some temporary placements. Company pays fee. **Specializes in the areas of:** Engineering; Food Industry; General Management; Manufacturing; Sales; Technical. **Positions commonly filled include:** Branch Manager; Chemist; Electrical/Electronics Engineer; Food Scientist/ Technologist; General Manager; Industrial Engineer; Mechanical Engineer; Purchasing Agent/Manager; Quality Control Supervisor; Services Sales Rep. **Number of placements per year:** 100 - 199.

SUAVE COMPANY, LTD.
P.O. Box 337, Amherst WI 54406. 715/824-2502. **Fax:** 715/824-2192. **Contact:** Gordy Suave, President. **Description:** A permanent employment agency with an emphasis on the dairy industry. Company pays fee. **Specializes in the areas of:** Engineering; Food Industry; General Management. **Positions commonly filled include:** Agricultural Engineer; Biological Scientist; Buyer; Chemical Engineer; Chemist; Civil Engineer; Customer Service Representative; Electrical /Electronics Engineer; Food Scientist/Technologist; General Manager; Industrial Engineer; Mechanical Engineer; Operations/Production Manager; Purchasing Agent/Manager; Quality Control Supervisor; Science Technologist; Services Sales Representative; Stationary Engineer. **Average salary range of placements:** $30,000 - $50,000. **Number of placements per year:** 1 - 49.

TECHSTAFF
11270 West Park Place, Suite 111, Milwaukee WI 53224-3624. 414/359-4444. **Fax:** 414/359-4949. **Contact:** Eric Robidoux, Recruiter. **E-mail address:** recruiter@techstaff.com. **World Wide Web address:** http://www.techstaff.com. **Description:** A permanent employment agency. Company pays fee. **Specializes in the areas of:** Engineering; Manufacturing; Technical. **Positions commonly filled include:** Chemical Engineer; Civil Engineer; Computer Programmer; Draftsperson; Electrical/Electronics Engineer; Environmental Engineer; Industrial Engineer; Industrial Production Manager; Mechanical Engineer; MIS Specialist; Purchasing Agent/Manager; Quality Control Supervisor; Software Engineer; Structural Engineer; Systems Analyst; Technical Writer/Editor. **Benefits available to temporary workers:** 401(k); Dental Insurance; Medical Insurance; Paid Holidays; Paid Vacation. **Other U.S. locations:** CA; FL; IA; IL; MI. **Average salary range of placements:** $30,000 - $50,000. **Number of placements per year:** 200 - 499.

TEMTEC CORPORATION
3927 South Howell Avenue, Milwaukee WI 53207. 414/769-3620. **Fax:** 414/769-3620. **Contact:** Dan Salem, General Manager. **Description:** A permanent employment agency that also provides temporary placements.

WORK CONNECTION
1045 West Clairemont Avenue, Eau Claire WI 54701-6104. 715/836-9675. **Fax:** 715/836-7974. **Contact:** Angie Tjepkema, Human Resources. **Description:** An employment agency that provides 70 percent permanent and 30 percent temporary placements. Founded in 1986. Company pays fee. **Specializes in the areas of:** Accounting/Auditing; Banking; Personnel/Labor Relations; Publishing; Retail; Sales; Secretarial; Technical; Transportation. **Positions commonly filled include:** Accountant/Auditor; Administrative Manager; Biochemist; Blue-Collar Worker Supervisor; Chemical Engineer; Chemist; Clinical Lab Technician; Credit Manager; Customer Service Representative; Dental Assistant/Dental Hygienist; Dietician/Nutritionist; Electrical/Electronics Engineer; Electrician; Food Scientist/Technologist; Human Resources Manager; Management Trainee; Paralegal; Preschool Worker; Purchasing Agent/Manager; Quality Control Supervisor; Restaurant/Food Service Manager; Systems Analyst; Typist/Word Processor. **Benefits available to temporary workers:** Medical Insurance. **Corporate headquarters location:** Minneapolis MN. **Other U.S. locations:** Nationwide. **Number of placements per year:** 1000+.

TEMPORARY EMPLOYMENT AGENCIES

ADTEC STAFFING
4414 Regent Street, Madison WI 53705. 608/231-3210. **Contact:** Manager. **Description:** A temporary agency that also provides permanent placements. **Specializes in the areas of:** Clerical; Computer Hardware/Software; Light Industrial; Secretarial.

CROWN SERVICES
10625 West North Avenue, Milwaukee WI 53226. 414/475-7409. **Contact:** Office Manager. **Description:** A temporary agency. Company pays fee. **Specializes in the areas of:** Accounting/Auditing; Banking; Clerical; Engineering; Finance; Insurance; Legal; Manufacturing; Personnel/Labor Relations. **Positions commonly filled include:** Accountant/Auditor; Administrative Assistant; Advertising Clerk; Bookkeeper; Claim Representative; Computer Operator; Computer Programmer; Construction Trade Worker; Customer Service Representative; Data Entry Clerk; Driver; Factory Worker; Legal Secretary; Receptionist; Sales Representative; Secretary; Typist/Word Processor. **Number of placements per year:** 1000+.

CUSTOM CARE
2317 International Lane, Madison WI 53704. 608/244-4377. **Contact:** Director of Operations. **Description:** A temporary agency. Founded in 1992. Company pays fee. **Specializes in the areas of:** Health/Medical. **Positions commonly filled include:** Certified Nursing Aide; Dental Assistant/Dental Hygienist; Dietician/Nutritionist; Licensed Practical Nurse; Registered Nurse. **Benefits available to temporary workers:** Paid Holidays; Paid Vacation. **Average salary range of placements:** $20,000 - $29,999. **Number of placements per year:** 500 - 999.

ENVIROSTAFF, INC.
16800 West Greenfield Avenue, Suite 400, Brookfield WI 53005. 414/778-1601. **Contact:** Tony Houdyshell, Manager. **Description:** A temporary agency providing personnel to environmental consultants, laboratories, and remediation companies. Professional and technical employees are placed on both long- and short-term assignments. **Specializes in the areas of:** Biology; Engineering; Food Industry; Industrial; Manufacturing. **Positions commonly filled include:** Biochemist; Biological Scientist; Chemical Engineer; Chemist; Civil Engineer; Clinical Lab Technician; Construction and Building Inspector; Construction Engineer; Design Engineer; Designer; Environmental Engineer; Forester/Conservation Scientist; Geologist/ Geophysicist; Industrial Engineer; Metallurgical Engineer; Mining Engineer; Nuclear Engineer; Petroleum Engineer; Quality Control Supervisor; Science Technologist; Structural Engineer; Surveyor; Transportation/Traffic Specialist. **Corporate headquarters location:** Minneapolis MN. **Average salary range of placements:** $20,000 - $29,999. **Number of placements per year:** 200 - 499.

GREENFIELD REHABILITATION AGENCY
7517 West Coldspring Road, Milwaukee WI 53220-2814. **Toll-free phone:** 800/704-4724xx23. **Fax:** 414/327-5411. **Contact:** Joel South, Recruiter. **Description:** A temporary agency which also offers contract services. Greenfield Rehabilitation Agency provides contract services to skilled nursing facilities, as well as temporary rehabilitation services. Founded in 1966. **Specializes in the areas of:** Health/Medical. **Positions commonly filled include:** Occupational Therapist; Physical Therapist; Speech-Language Pathologist. **Benefits available to temporary workers:**

Education Assistance; Paid Vacation. **Corporate headquarters location:** Greenfield WI.

HATCH STAFFING SERVICES
Galleria West, 18900 West Bluemount Road, Brookfield WI 53045. 414/789-8384. **Contact:** Manager. **Description:** A temporary and temp-to-perm agency. **Specializes in the areas of:** Administration; Customer Service; Information Technology; Management; Sales.

IDI CORPORATION
2830 Ramada Way, Suite 204, Green Bay WI 54304. 920/499-9943. **Toll-free phone:** 800/333-1389. **Fax:** 920/499-9067. **Contact:** Sue Ann Pay, Technical Recruiter. **Description:** A temporary agency that also offers permanent placements. Founded in 1967. Company pays fee. **Specializes in the areas of:** Engineering; Manufacturing; Technical. **Positions commonly filled include:** Aerospace Engineer; Agricultural Engineer; Architect; Ceramics Engineer; Chemical Engineer; Civil Engineer; Computer Programmer; Construction Contractor; Construction Manager; Design Engineer; Designer; Draftsperson; Electrical/Electronics Engineer; Environmental Engineer; Industrial Engineer; Landscape Architect; Materials Engineer; Mechanical Engineer; Metallurgical Engineer; Mining Engineer; Software Engineer; Structural Engineer; Surveyor. **Benefits available to temporary workers:** 401(k); Life Insurance; Medical Insurance; Paid Holidays; Paid Vacation; Profit Sharing. **Corporate headquarters location:** Brookfield WI. **Other area locations:** Madison WI. **Number of placements per year:** 100 - 199.

INTERIM PERSONNEL
2405 South Green Bay Road, Racine WI 53406. 414/633-7725. **Fax:** 414/633-7783. **Contact:** Lori Krezinski, Branch Manager. **Description:** A nationwide temporary agency that also provides permanent placement. Founded in 1946. Company pays fee. **Specializes in the areas of:** Manufacturing; Personnel/Labor Relations; Sales; Secretarial. **Positions commonly filled include:** Customer Service Representative; Human Resources Manager; Quality Control Supervisor; Typist/Word Processor. **Average salary range of placements:** Less than $20,000. **Number of placements per year:** 500 - 999.

LANDMARK, THE STAFFING RESOURCE
2020 Riverside Drive, Green Bay WI 54301. 920/437-3130. **Fax:** 920/431-3433. **World Wide Web address:** http://www.lanmrk.com. **Contact:** Donna Frey, Staffing Supervisor. **Description:** A temporary agency that focuses on placing sales representatives, account specialists, and staffing supervisors. **Specializes in the areas of:** Accounting/Auditing; Banking; Secretarial. **Positions commonly filled include:** Accountant/Auditor; Bank Officer/Manager; Credit Manager; Customer Service Representative; Human Resources Manager; Services Sales Representative; Underwriter/Assistant Underwriter. **Benefits available to temporary workers:** 401(k); Medical Insurance; Paid Holidays; Profit Sharing. **Corporate headquarters location:** Appleton WI. **Other area locations:** Appleton WI; Neenah WI; Oshkosh WI.

LANDMARK, THE STAFFING RESOURCE
10 College Avenue, Appleton WI 54911. 920/731-3130. **Toll-free phone:** 800/750-2528. **Fax:** 920/731-4974. **Contact:** Marianne Wicks, Staffing Supervisor. **E-mail address:** landmark@lanmrk.com. **World Wide Web address:** http://www.lanmrk.com. **Description:** A temporary agency. Company pays fee. **Specializes in the areas of:** Accounting/Auditing; Insurance; Office Support; Personnel/Labor Relations; Secretarial. **Positions commonly filled include:** Account Representative; Accountant; Adjuster; Administrative Assistant; Auditor; Budget Analyst; Claim Representative; Clerical Supervisor; Computer Operator; Controller; Cost Estimator; Customer Service Representative; Database Manager; Editorial Assistant; Financial Analyst; Graphic Artist; Graphic Designer; Marketing Specialist; Paralegal; Purchasing Agent/Manager; Sales Representative; Secretary. **Benefits available to temporary workers:** 401(k); Dental Insurance; Medical Insurance; Paid Holidays; Paid Vacation; Profit Sharing. **Corporate headquarters location:** Appleton WI. **Other area locations:** Green Bay WI; Neenah WI; Oshkosh WI.

MANPOWER TEMPORARY SERVICES
2797 Prairie Avenue, Beloit WI 53511-2288. 608/362-1330. **Fax:** 608/362-0585. **Contact:** Andrea Garvey, Service Representative. **Description:** A temporary employment agency. Company pays fee. **Specializes in the areas of:** Data Processing; Industrial; Manufacturing; Personnel/Labor Relations; Secretarial. **Positions commonly filled include:** Typist/Word Processor. **Benefits available to temporary workers:** Life Insurance; Medical Insurance; Paid Holidays; Paid Vacation. **Corporate headquarters location:** Milwaukee WI. **Other U.S. locations:** Nationwide. **Average salary range of placements:** Less than $20,000. **Number of placements per year:** 100 - 199.

MEDTEAMS
725 American Avenue, Waukesha WI 53188. 414/544-2573. **Toll-free phone:** 800/326-2011x2573. **Fax:** 414/544-4943. **Contact:** Judith Haeberle, Executive Director. **Description:** A temporary agency. Founded in 1987. **Specializes in the areas of:** Health/Medical. **Positions commonly filled include:** Licensed Practical Nurse; Nuclear Medicine Technologist; Occupational Therapist; Physical Therapist; Registered Nurse; Speech-Language Pathologist.

NORRELL STAFFING SERVICES, INC.
2509 North Mayfair Road, Milwaukee WI 53226-1402. 414/476-2777. **Fax:** 414/476-5066. **Contact:** Linda Caulk, Area Manager. **Description:** A temporary agency that also provides permanent placements. **Specializes in the areas of:** Administration; Industrial; Secretarial. **Positions commonly filled include:** Administrative Manager; Clerical Supervisor. **Benefits available to temporary workers:** Dental Insurance; Medical Insurance; Paid Holidays; Paid Vacation; Vision Plan. **Corporate headquarters location:** Atlanta GA. **Other U.S. locations:** Nationwide.

OLSTEN STAFFING SERVICES
7500 Green Bay Road, Kenosha WI 53142. 414/697-5140. **Contact:** Branch Manager. **Description:** A temporary agency that focuses on the placement of office and production professionals. This location trains and tests individuals and custom-matches employees to employers in the Kenosha area and across southeast Wisconsin. Company pays fee. **Specializes in the areas of:** Accounting/Auditing; Administration; Banking; Engineering; Finance; General Management; Industrial; Manufacturing; Nonprofit; Personnel/Labor Relations. **Positions commonly filled include:** Accountant/Auditor; Bank Officer/Manager; Blue-Collar Worker Supervisor; Chemical Engineer; Chemist; Clinical Lab Technician; Computer Programmer; Draftsperson; Paralegal; Typist/Word Processor. **Benefits available to temporary workers:** Medical Insurance. **Corporate headquarters location:** Melville NY. **International locations:** Worldwide. **Average salary range of placements:** $20,000 - $29,999. **Number of placements per year:** 1000+.

OLSTEN STAFFING SERVICES
2147 Brackett Avenue, Eau Claire WI 54701-4632. 715/834-7555. **Fax:** 715/834-8041. **Contact:**

Katherine Wright, Branch Manager. **Description:** A temporary employment agency. Company pays fee. **Specializes in the areas of:** Accounting/Auditing; Administration; Computer Science/Software; Engineering; Finance; General Management; Industrial; Insurance; Legal; Light Industrial; Manufacturing; Personnel/Labor Relations; Publishing; Secretarial; Technical. **Positions commonly filled include:** Accountant/Auditor; Administrative Manager; Blue-Collar Worker Supervisor; Branch Manager; Claim Representative; Clerical Supervisor; Health Services Worker; Human Resources Manager; Management Trainee; Manufacturer's/Wholesaler's Sales Rep.; Operations/Production Manager; Transportation/Traffic Specialist; Typist/Word Processor. **Benefits available to temporary workers:** Medical Insurance; Paid Holidays; Paid Vacation. **Corporate headquarters location:** Melville NY. **International locations:** Worldwide. **Average salary range of placements:** $20,000 - $29,999. **Number of placements per year:** 500 - 999.

OLSTEN STAFFING SERVICES
1017 East Avenue South, La Crosse WI 54601. 608/782-1100. **Fax:** 608/782-7080. **Contact:** Jeanne Barr, Divisional Sales Manager. **Description:** A temporary agency that also provides permanent placements. **Specializes in the areas of:** Accounting/Auditing; Administration; Manufacturing; Publishing; Secretarial. **Positions commonly filled include:** Accountant/Auditor; Clerical Supervisor; Computer Programmer; Cost Estimator; Customer Service Representative; Market Research Analyst; Operations/Production Manager; Services Sales Representative; Typist/Word Processor. **Corporate headquarters location:** Melville NY. **International locations:** Worldwide. **Average salary range of placements:** Less than $20,000. **Number of placements per year:** 1000+.

SITE PERSONNEL SERVICES, INC.
TRAINOR/SALICK & ASSOCIATES, INC.
16550 West Lisbon Road, Milwaukee WI 53204. 414/783-5181. **Fax:** 414/783-7905. **Contact:** Arn Reger, Resource Manager. **E-mail address:** tsacsi@execpc.com. **World Wide Web address:** http://www.tsacsi.com. **Description:** A certified minority-owned personnel agency focusing on the staffing of temporary and permanent design/drafting, technical, and engineering positions. Trainor/Salick & Associates, Inc. (also at this location) is an executive search firm. **Specializes in the areas of:** Administration; Computer Science/Software; Engineering; Industrial; Light Industrial; Transportation. **Positions commonly filled include:** Agricultural Engineer; Computer Programmer; Design Engineer; Draftsperson; Electrical/Electronics Engineer; Environmental Engineer; Industrial Engineer; Mechanical Engineer; Software Engineer; Systems Analyst. **Benefits available to temporary workers:** Paid Holidays. **Corporate headquarters location:** This Location. **Other U.S. locations:** Boulder CO; Tampa FL; Minneapolis MN; Cincinnati OH. **Average salary range of placements:** $30,000 - $50,000. **Number of placements per year:** 200 - 499.

TEMPO EMPLOYMENT SERVICES, INC.
P.O. Box 347, Reedsberg WI 53959. 608/524-2003. **Contact:** Vicki Burnett, President. **E-mail address:** tempo@mwt.com. **Description:** A temporary employment agency that also provides permanent placements. Founded in 1980. Company pays fee. **Specializes in the areas of:** General Management; Industrial; Light Industrial; Secretarial. **Positions commonly filled include:** Account Representative; Administrative Assistant; Assistant Manager; Blue-Collar Worker Supervisor; Branch Manager; Civil Engineer; Clerical Supervisor; Computer Operator; Customer Service Representative; Draftsperson; General Manager; Human Resources Manager; Industrial Production Manager; Management Trainee; Manufacturing Engineer; MIS Specialist; Operations Manager; Production Manager; Quality Control Supervisor; Sales Representative; Secretary; Typist/Word Processor. **Benefits available to temporary workers:** Medical Insurance; Referral Bonus Plan. **Average salary range of placements:** $20,000 - $29,999. **Number of placements per year:** 500 - 999.

TEMPS PLUS STAFFING SERVICES, INC.
7001 West Greenfield Avenue, West Allis WI 53214. 414/475-7300. **Toll-free phone:** 800/969-1470. **Fax:** 414/475-9119. **Contact:** Jim Watters, Vice President. **E-mail address:** jim9116w@aol.com. **World Wide Web address:** http://www.tempsplusjobs.com. **Description:** A temporary agency that also provides full-service permanent placement. Founded in 1987. Company pays fee. **Specializes in the areas of:** Administration; Banking; Computer Science/Software; Secretarial; Technical. **Positions commonly filled include:** Administrative Assistant; Certified Nursing Aide; Claim Representative; Computer Operator; Computer Programmer; Licensed Practical Nurse; MIS Specialist; Registered Nurse; Typist/Word Processor. **Benefits available to temporary workers:** Bonus Award/Plan; Credit Union; Medical Insurance; Paid Vacation. **Corporate headquarters location:** This Location. **Other area locations:** Kenosha WI; Shorewood WI. **Other U.S. locations:** Minneapolis MN. **Average salary range of placements:** $20,000 - $29,999. **Number of placements per year:** 500 - 999.

CONTRACT SERVICES FIRMS

AEROTEK, INC.
400 South Executive Drive, Suite 201, Brookfield WI 53005-4215. **Toll-free phone:** 800/726-1899. **Fax:** 414/821-1933. **Contact:** Senior Recruiter. **Description:** A contract services firm. Company pays fee. **Specializes in the areas of:** Computer Science/Software; Engineering; Industrial; Technical; Telecommunications. **Positions commonly filled include:** Chemical Engineer; Civil Engineer; Computer Programmer; Design Engineer; Designer; Draftsperson; Electrical/Electronics Engineer; Electrician; Industrial Engineer; Mechanical Engineer; Metallurgical Engineer; Software Engineer; Structural Engineer; Systems Analyst; Technical Writer/Editor. **Benefits available to temporary workers:** 401(k); Medical Insurance. **Corporate headquarters location:** Baltimore MD. **Other U.S. locations:** Nationwide. **Average salary range of placements:** $30,000 - $50,000. **Number of placements per year:** 1000+.

INTERIM TECHNOLOGIES
440 Science Drive, Suite 102, Madison WI 53711. 608/233-8201. **Fax:** 608/233-8416. **Contact:** Kelly Fandow, Technical Specialist. **Description:** A contract services firm. Interim Technologies is a strategic partner of *Fortune* 1000 companies providing supplemental staffing solutions to support data center operations, telecommunications, help desks, client/server and applications development and maintenance, and advanced technology training. **Specializes in the areas of:** Computer Science/Software. **Positions commonly filled include:** Computer Programmer; Internet Services Manager; MIS Specialist; Software Engineer; Systems Analyst. **Corporate headquarters location:** Lyndhurst NJ. **Other**

U.S. locations: Nationwide. **Average salary range of placements:** $30,000 - $50,000. **Number of placements per year:** 100 - 199.

MIDWEST PARALEGAL SERVICES, INC.
740 North Plankinton Avenue, Suite 500, Milwaukee WI 53203-2403. 414/276-3007. **Contact:** Director. **Description:** A contract services firm that provides freelance paralegal placements in corporations and law firms. **Positions commonly filled include:** Paralegal.

NORTHERN TECHNICAL SERVICES
8899 North 60th Street, Milwaukee WI 53223. **Toll-free phone:** 800/686-2819. **Fax:** 414/362-8880. **Contact:** Peter Ryan, Sales Manager. **Description:** A contract services firm focusing on high-tech placements. Founded in 1975. Company pays fee. **Specializes in the areas of:** Computer Science/Software; Engineering; Information Systems; Personnel/Labor Relations. **Positions commonly filled include:** Aerospace Engineer; Agricultural Engineer; Architect; Ceramics Engineer; Chemical Engineer; Civil Engineer; Computer Programmer; Design Engineer; Designer; Draftsperson; Electrical/Electronics Engineer; Industrial Engineer; Industrial Production Manager; Landscape Architect; Materials Engineer; Mechanical Engineer; Metallurgical Engineer; Mining Engineer; MIS Specialist; Petroleum Engineer; Quality Control Supervisor; Software Engineer; Structural Engineer; Systems Analyst; Technical Writer/Editor; Transportation/Traffic Specialist. **Benefits available to temporary workers:** 401(k); Paid Holidays. **Corporate headquarters location:** This Location. **Other area locations:** Green Bay WI; Mosinee WI. **Average salary range of placements:** $30,000 - $50,000. **Number of placements per year:** 200 - 499.

NORTHERN TECHNICAL SERVICES
1595 Allouez Avenue, Green Bay WI 54311. 920/465-3933. **Contact:** Manager. **Description:** A contract services firm. **Specializes in the areas of:** Engineering; Information Systems. **Corporate headquarters location:** Milwaukee WI. **Other area locations:** Mosinee WI.

OLSTEN HEALTH SERVICES
392 Red Cedar Street, Suite 4, Menomonie WI 54751-2386. 715/235-8077. **Contact:** Office Manager. **Description:** A contract services firm that provides in-home health care placements.

POLLAK AND SKAN, INC.
205 Bishops Way, Brookfield WI 53005-6220. 414/784-3399. **Toll-free phone:** 800/472-9423. **Fax:** 414/784-1913. **Contact:** Technical Recruiter. **E-mail address:** psmil@pscts.com. **World Wide Web address:** http://www.pscts.com. **Description:** A contract services firm that focuses on technical placements. Founded in 1951. Company pays fee. **Specializes in the areas of:** Computer Science/Software; Engineering; Manufacturing; Technical. **Positions commonly filled include:** Aerospace Engineer; Agricultural Engineer; Architect; Biochemist; Biological Scientist; Biomedical Engineer; Buyer; Ceramics Engineer; Chemical Engineer; Chemist; Civil Engineer; Clinical Lab Technician; Computer Programmer; Construction Contractor; Construction Manager; Cost Estimator; Design Engineer; Designer; Draftsperson; Electrical/Electronics Engineer; Electrician; Environmental Engineer; Industrial Engineer; Internet Services Manager; Materials Engineer; Mechanical Engineer; Metallurgical Engineer; Mining Engineer; MIS Specialist; Multimedia Designer; Nuclear Engineer; Petroleum Engineer; Purchasing Agent/Manager; Quality Control Supervisor; Software Engineer; Structural Engineer; Systems Analyst; Technical Writer/Editor. **Benefits available to temporary workers:** 401(k); Bonus Award/Plan; Dental Insurance; Life Insurance; Medical Insurance; Paid Holidays. **Corporate headquarters location:** Elk Glove Village IL. **Other U.S. locations:** GA; FL; IN; MI; NC; SC; TX. **Average salary range of placements:** More than $50,000. **Number of placements per year:** 200 - 499.

TAD TECHNICAL SERVICES
111 East South River Street, Appleton WI 54915-1746. 920/739-1500. **Fax:** 920/739-5912. **Contact:** Ken Depperman, Branch Manager. **Description:** A contract services firm that focuses on contract engineering and software services. Company pays fee. **Specializes in the areas of:** Computer Science/Software; Engineering; Industrial; Manufacturing; Technical. **Positions commonly filled include:** Architect; Computer Programmer; Construction Contractor; Construction Manager; Design Engineer; Designer; Draftsperson; Electrical/Electronics Engineer; Industrial Engineer; Mechanical Engineer; MIS Specialist; Quality Control Supervisor; Software Engineer; Structural Engineer; Systems Analyst; Technical Illustrator; Technical Writer/Editor. **Benefits available to temporary workers:** 401(k); Bonus Award/Plan; Paid Holidays; Paid Vacation. **Corporate headquarters location:** Cambridge MA. **International locations:** Worldwide. **Average salary range of placements:** $30,000 - $50,000. **Number of placements per year:** 200 - 499.

TECHNOLOGY CONSULTING CORPORATION
N-16 W23233, Stone Ridge Drive, Waukesha WI 53188. 414/650-6500. **Fax:** 414/650-6530. **Contact:** Recruiting. **World Wide Web address:** http://www.tcc-usa.com. **Description:** A contract services firm that places high-tech professionals and computer consultants. **Specializes in the areas of:** Computer Hardware/Software; Technical. **Positions commonly filled include:** Applications Engineer; Internet Services Manager; MIS Specialist; Systems Analyst. **Other area locations:** Green Bay WI; Madison WI. **Other U.S. locations:** Chicago IL.

THE WATERSTONE GROUP, INC.
1025 West Glen Oaks Lane, Mequon WI 53092. 414/241-8315. **Toll-free phone:** 800/291-3837. **Fax:** 414/241-8349. **Contact:** Office Manager. **Description:** A technical contract services firm. Founded in 1994. Company pays fee. **Specializes in the areas of:** Computer Science/Software; Engineering; Manufacturing; Technical. **Positions commonly filled include:** Architect; Biological Scientist; Chemical Engineer; Civil Engineer; Computer Programmer; Cost Estimator; Design Engineer; Designer; Draftsperson; Electrical/Electronics Engineer; Environmental Engineer; Industrial Engineer; Landscape Architect; Mechanical Engineer; MIS Specialist; Operations/Production Manager; Purchasing Agent/Manager; Quality Control Supervisor; Software Engineer; Structural Engineer; Systems Analyst; Technical Writer/Editor. **Benefits available to temporary workers:** 401(k); Dental Insurance; Life Insurance; Medical Insurance. **Corporate headquarters location:** This Location. **Other area locations:** Green Bay WI. **Average salary range of placements:** $30,000 - $50,000. **Number of placements per year:** 200 - 499.

THE WATERSTONE GROUP, INC.
1345B North Road, Green Bay WI 54313. 920/494-7727. **Contact:** Manager. **Description:** A contract services firm. **Specializes in the areas of:** Technical. **Corporate headquarters location:** Mequon WI.

CAREER/OUTPLACEMENT COUNSELING FIRMS

AT YOUR SERVICE
111 South Pine Street, Burlington WI 53105. 414/763-8467. **Contact:** Carol Demarco, Owner. **Description:** A career/outplacement counseling firm.

EMPLOYMENT OPTIONS
2095 Winnebago Street, Madison WI 53704. 608/244-5181. **Contact:** Administrative Assistant. **Description:** A career/outplacement counseling firm. **Number of placements per year:** 50 - 99.

BERNARD HALDANE & ASSOCIATES
15800 West Bluemound Road, Suite 320, Brookfield WI 53005. 414/784-2266. **Contact:** Manager. **Description:** A career/outplacement counseling firm.

OVER 50 EMPLOYMENT SERVICES, INC.
10 South Baldwin, Madison WI 53703. 608/255-5585. **Fax:** 608/255-5781. **Contact:** Office Manager. **Description:** A career/outplacement counseling firm and permanent placement agency for Dane County residents over the age of 50. The agency provides testing, assessments, job placements, resume counseling, training in job interview skills, and transitional and follow-up counseling. **Positions commonly filled include:** Accountant/Auditor; Advertising Clerk; Blue-Collar Worker Supervisor; Buyer; Counselor; Food Scientist/Technologist; Forester/Conservation Scientist; Health Services Manager; Hotel Manager; Human Resources Manager; Insurance Agent/Broker; Librarian; Management Trainee; Manufacturer's/Wholesaler's Sales Rep.; Property and Real Estate Manager; Public Relations Specialist; Services Sales Representative; Social Worker; Technical Writer/Editor. **Number of placements per year:** 200 - 499.

SUMMIT CAREER SERVICES
12321 87th Street, Wisconsin Rapids WI 54494. 715/325-5888. **Toll-free phone:** 800/693-8072. **Contact:** Marie Keenen Manshein, Owner/President. **Description:** A resume writing and career/outplacement counseling firm. The firm also provides critiques, interview assistance, and job search advice. Summit Career Services also offers an online resume database and Internet services.

WYOMING

EXECUTIVE SEARCH FIRMS

JDO ASSOCIATES
1218 East Pershing Boulevard, Suite 1021, Cheyenne WY 82001. 307/634-0959. **Contact:** Manager. **Description:** An executive search firm. **Specializes in the areas of:** Construction; Defense Industry.

MANAGEMENT RECRUITERS OF CHEYENNE
1008 East 21st Street, Cheyenne WY 82001. 307/635-8731. **Fax:** 307/635-6653. **Contact:** Office Manager. **Description:** An executive search firm operating on a contingency basis. Founded in 1978. Company pays fee. **Specializes in the areas of:** Communications; Computer Hardware/Software; Design; Electrical; Engineering; Manufacturing. **Positions commonly filled include:** Design Engineer; Draftsperson; Electrical/Electronics Engineer; Industrial Engineer; Industrial Production Manager; Materials Engineer; Mechanical Engineer; Metallurgical Engineer; Quality Control Supervisor; Software Engineer. **Average salary range of placements:** More than $50,000. **Number of placements per year:** 50 - 99.

PERMANENT EMPLOYMENT AGENCIES

THE EMPLOYMENT PLACE
721 East Lincolnway, Cheyenne WY 82001. 307/632-0534. **Contact:** Recruiting. **E-mail address:** tep@juno.com. **Description:** A permanent employment agency. The Employment Place maintains two divisions: one for agricultural placements and one for general employment. **Specializes in the areas of:** Agriculture; Computer Hardware/Software; Food Industry; Office Support.

EMPLOYMENT RESOURCES
P.O. Box 1610, Riverton WY 82501. 307/856-9231. **Fax:** 307/856-3468. **Contact:** Office Manager. **Description:** A state-run permanent employment agency.

EMPLOYMENT RESOURCES
P.O. Box 1448, Gillette WY 82717. 307/682-9313. **Fax:** 307/686-2975. **Contact:** Manager. **Description:** A state-run permanent employment agency.

SENIOR COMMUNITY EMPLOYMENT SERVICE
22 West Works Street, Sheridan WY 82801. 307/674-4447. **Fax:** 307/674-4448. **Contact:** Harvey Finch, Project Director. **Description:** A permanent employment agency that also trains and assists people age 55 and older. **Positions commonly filled include:** Certified Nursing Aide; Clerical Supervisor; Computer Operator; Daycare Worker; Electrician; Secretary; Typist/Word Processor. **Average salary range of placements:** Less than $20,000. **Number of placements per year:** 1 - 49.

TEMPORARY EMPLOYMENT AGENCIES

EXPRESS TEMPORARY SERVICE
2205 East Pershing Boulevard, Cheyenne WY 82001. 307/634-1635. **Fax:** 307/638-0493. **Contact:** Manager. **Description:** A temporary agency that also provides permanent placements. **Specializes in the areas of:** Clerical; Light Industrial; Retail; Sales. **Other U.S. locations:** WA.

OLSTEN STAFFING SERVICES
1031 Elk Street, Rock Springs WY 82901. 307/362-1881. **Toll-free phone:** 800/WORK-NOW. **Fax:** 307/362-8554. **Contact:** Linda Cole, Branch Manager. **Description:** A temporary agency that also provides permanent placements. Founded in 1940. **Specializes in the areas of:** Accounting/Auditing; Computer Hardware/Software; Finance; Industrial; Legal; Manufacturing; Personnel/Labor Relations; Sales; Secretarial; Technical. **Positions commonly filled include:** Accountant/Auditor; Administrative Manager; Buyer; Clerical Supervisor; Customer Service Representative; Draftsperson; Industrial Production Manager; Medical Records Technician; MIS Specialist; Paralegal; Technical Writer/Editor; Telecommunications Manager; Typist/Word Processor. **Benefits available to temporary workers:** Medical Insurance; Paid Holidays; Paid Vacation. **Corporate headquarters location:** Melville NY. **Other U.S. locations:** Nationwide. **Average salary range of placements:** $20,000 - $29,999. **Number of placements per year:** 200 - 499.

INDEX BY SPECIALIZATION

ACCOUNTING/AUDITING

Alabama

A-1 Emp. Svc, *Perm. Emp Agcy*
Mary Cheek & Assoc., *Exec Srch*
Clark Persnnl Svc of Mobile, *Exec Srch*
Dunhill of So. Birmingham, *Exec Srch*
Employment Consltnts, *Perm. Emp Agcy*
FORTUNE Persnnl Consltnts, *Exec Srch*
Robert Half Intl/Accountemps, *Exec Srch*
Langford Srch, *Exec Srch*
Mgmt. Recrtrs Intl, *Exec Srch*
Perform Staff Svc, *Perm. Emp Agcy*
Placers, *Perm. Emp Agcy*
J.L. Small Assoc., *Exec Srch*
Talent Tree Staffng, *Perm. Emp Agcy*
VIP Persnnl, *Perm. Emp Agcy*
WorkForce, *Temp. Agcy*

Alaska

Olsten Staff Svcs, *Temp. Agcy*
Professional Bus. Svc, *Temp. Agcy*

Arizona

Accountnts Exec Srch/Accountnts On Call, *Exec Srch*
Accounting & Bookkeeping Persnnl, *Exec Srch*
AccuStaff, *Perm. Emp Agcy*
AccuStaff, *Temp. Agcy*
Aidan Grp, *Contract Svc*
Andrews, Stevens & Assoc., *Contract Svc*
Construction Secretaries, *Perm. Emp Agcy*
Devau Human Resrcs, *Temp. Agcy*
Fishel Human Resrcs Assoc., *Exec Srch*
Robert Half Intl/Accountemps, *Exec Srch*
J.R. Professional Srch, *Exec Srch*
Kerry's Referrals, *Temp. Agcy*
Mgmt. Recrtrs Intl, *Exec Srch*
Mgmt. Recrtrs of Scottsdale, *Exec Srch*
Priority Staffng, *Perm. Emp Agcy*
Retiree Skills, *Temp. Agcy*
Snelling Persnnl Svcs, *Perm. Emp Agcy*
Source Svcs Corp, *Exec Srch*
Spectra Intl, *Exec Srch*
Staff One Srch, *Exec Srch*
Stivers Temp. Persnnl, *Temp. Agcy*
Volt Tech. Svcs, *Contract Svc*

Arkansas

Dunhill Persnnl, *Exec Srch*
Executive Recrtrs Outplacement Consltnts, *Exec Srch*
Mgmt. Recrtrs of Little Rock, *Exec Srch*
Premier Staffng, *Temp. Agcy*
SEARK Bus. Svcs, *Temp. Agcy*
Snelling Srch, *Exec Srch*

California

A Perm. Success Emp. Svcs, *Perm. Emp Agcy*
AAFA (American Assn of Finance & Acctng), *Exec Srch*
ABA Staffng, *Exec Srch*
AGA Recruitng, *Exec Srch*
Abacus Staffing for Acctng, *Exec Srch*
Accountnts Exchange, *Temp. Agcy*
Accountnts Exec Srch, *Exec Srch*
Accountnts Express, *Temp. Agcy*
Accntnts, *Temp. Agcy*
Accountnts On Call, *Exec Srch*
Accounting Additions, *Exec Srch*
Accounting Advantage, *Exec Srch*
The Accounting Guild, *Temp. Agcy*
The Accounting Guild, *Perm. Emp Agcy*
Accounting Partners, *Perm. Emp Agcy*
AccuStaff, *Perm. Emp Agcy*
AccuStaff, *Exec Srch*
AccuStaff Co, *Temp. Agcy*
Active Srch & Plcmnt, *Exec Srch*
Advantage Persnnl, *Perm. Emp Agcy*
Affordable Exec Recrtrs, *Exec Srch*
Allied Srch, *Exec Srch*
Alpha-Net Consltng Grp, *Exec Srch*
Alternative Staffing Grp, *Exec Srch*
Ankenbrandt Grp, *Exec Srch*
Answers Unlimtd, *Temp. Agcy*
John Anthony & Assoc., *Exec Srch*
Apple One Emp. Svcs, *Perm. Emp Agcy*
Apropos Emp. Agcy, *Perm. Emp Agcy*
Assured Persnnl Svcs, *Perm. Emp Agcy*
Automotive Career Plcmnt, *Exec Srch*
Bay Resrcs, *Exec Srch*
Ed Bell Assoc., *Exec Srch*
Best Temp. Svc, *Temp. Agcy*
Billington & Assoc., *Exec Srch*
Blaine & Assoc., *Perm. Emp Agcy*
Blue, Garni & Co, *Exec Srch*
Bradford Staff, *Temp. Agcy*
BridgeGate Grp, *Exec Srch*
Business Syst. Staffing & Assoc., *Perm. Emp Agcy*
CT Persnnl Svcs, *Perm. Emp Agcy*
California Srch Agcy, *Exec Srch*
Candy Stripers Medical Persnnl, *Perm. Emp Agcy*
Career Advantage, *Exec Srch*
Career Images, *Temp. Agcy*
Carver Dooley Assoc., *Exec Srch*
Chaitin & Assoc., *Exec Srch*
Champagne Temp. Help, *Temp. Agcy*
Choice Persnnl, *Perm. Emp Agcy*
Coast Persnnl, *Temp. Agcy*
Collier-Young Agcy, *Temp. Agcy*
Colt Syst. Professional Persnnl Svcs, *Perm. Emp Agcy*
COMFORCE Tech. Svcs, *Contract Svc*
Corporate Solut'ns, *Perm. Emp Agcy*
Marlene Critchfield Co, *Perm. Emp Agcy*
Crossroads Staff Svc, *Temp. Agcy*
Culver Staffing Resrcs, *Exec Srch*
DBL Assoc., *Exec Srch*
Dependable Emp. Agency Netwrk, *Perm. Emp Agcy*
Desert Persnnl, *Perm. Emp Agcy*
The Dial Grp, *Perm. Emp Agcy*
Drake Office Overload, *Temp. Agcy*
EDP Contrct Svcs, *Contract Svc*
Eleventh Hour Staff Svcs, *Temp. Agcy*
Employment Devlpmnt Dept, *Perm. Emp Agcy*
Employment Svc Agcy, *Perm. Emp Agcy*
Executive Resource Syst., *Exec Srch*
Express Persnnl Svcs, *Temp. Agcy*
Curtis Farmer Persnnl, *Exec Srch*
Fastek Tech. Svcs, *Perm. Emp Agcy*
Finesse Persnnl Assoc., *Exec Srch*
40 Plus of So. CA, *Exec Srch*
Pat Franklyn Assoc., *Temp. Agcy*
Fresquez & Assoc., *Exec Srch*
Gajek Kyle & Assoc., *Exec Srch*
Goldstein & Assoc., *Temp. Agcy*
Gould Persnnl Svcs, *Perm. Emp Agcy*
Robert Half Intl, *Exec Srch*
Hall Kinion, *Contract Svc*
Herrerias & Assoc., *Exec Srch*
Interim Acctng Prof'ls, *Perm. Emp Agcy*
Interim Persnnl, *Temp. Agcy*
Intertec Persnnl, *Temp. Agcy*
Jackson Persnnl, *Perm. Emp Agcy*
Anita Johnson & Assoc., *Temp. Agcy*
Kelly Svcs, *Temp. Agcy*
Kelly Tech. Svcs, *Temp. Agcy*
Kenneth, George, & Assoc., *Exec Srch*
Klein & Assoc., *Temp. Agcy*
John Kurosky & Assoc., *Exec Srch*
Lander Intl, *Exec Srch*
Larsen, Whitney, Blecksmith, & Zilliacus, *Exec Srch*
Lending Persnnl Svcs, *Exec Srch*
LINK Bus. & Persnnl Svcs/LINK Career Ctr, *Temp. Agcy*
The London Agcy, *Exec Srch*
The London Agcy, *Temp. Agcy*
Mgmnt. Recrtrs of Burlingame/Sales Consltnts, *Exec Srch*
Mgmt. Recrtrs of Encino, *Exec Srch*
Mgmt. Recrtrs of Laguna Hills, *Exec Srch*
Mgmt. Recrtrs of Pleasanton, *Exec Srch*
Mgmt. Srch Intl, *Exec Srch*
Mgmt. Solut'ns, *Exec Srch*
Manpower, *Temp. Agcy*
Rich Maries Agcy, *Perm. Emp Agcy*
The Martin Agencies, *Perm. Emp Agcy*
Maverick Staff Svc, *Perm. Emp Agcy*
K.E. McCarthy & Assoc., *Exec Srch*
Sabine McManus & Assoc., *Exec Srch*
Medical Financial Svcs, *Contract Svc*
Mesa Intl, *Exec Srch*
Joseph Michaels, *Perm. Emp Agcy*
Murray Enterprises Staff Svcs, *Temp. Agcy*
Musick & Assoc., *Exec Srch*
J.A. Myrben & Assoc., *Exec Srch*
Nelson HR Solut'ns, *Perm. Emp Agcy*
Nesco Svc Co, *Perm. Emp Agcy*
Newport Strategic Srch, *Exec Srch*
Norrell Temp. Svcs of CA, *Temp. Agcy*
Officemates5/Daystar Temp. Svcs, *Perm. Emp Agcy*
Olsten Staff Svcs, *Temp. Agcy*
Omni Express Temps, *Temp. Agcy*
Onyx Persnnl Svcs, *Perm. Emp Agcy*
PN Financial Recruitng, *Exec Srch*
Pacific Srch Grp, *Exec Srch*
Parker & Lynch Exec Srch, *Exec Srch*
Pasona Pacific, *Temp. Agcy*
Personalized Placemnt Agcy, *Temp. Agcy*
Pips Persnnl Svcs, *Perm. Emp Agcy*
Premier Persnnl Svcs, *Temp. Agcy*
Presidio Persnnl, *Temp. Agcy*
PrideStaff, *Temp. Agcy*
Pro Staff Persnnl Svcs, *Perm. Emp Agcy*
Probus Exec Srch, *Exec Srch*
Professional Srch Assoc., *Exec Srch*
ProSearch & Assoc., *Exec Srch*
Questemps, *Temp. Agcy*
RJ Assoc., *Exec Srch*
Ed Rast & Co, *Exec Srch*
Raycor Srch, *Exec Srch*
Remedy Intelligent Staffng, *Temp. Agcy*
Riley-Cole Recrtmnt Specialists, *Exec Srch*
Ritter Assoc., *Exec Srch*
Romac Intl, *Exec Srch*
Rowland Assoc., *Exec Srch*
Royal Staff Svcs, *Exec Srch*
Russell Staffing Resrcs, *Perm. Emp Agcy*
Ryan, Miller & Assoc., *Exec Srch*
S.R. & Assoc., *Exec Srch*
San Diego Persnnl & Employment, *Temp. Agcy*
Santa Barbara Plcmnt, *Perm. Emp Agcy*
Schlatter & Assoc., *Exec Srch*
Search West, *Exec Srch*
Select Persnnl Svcs, *Temp. Agcy*
David Sharp & Assoc., *Perm. Emp Agcy*
Sharp Persnnl & Srch, *Exec Srch*
Singer Strouse, *Exec Srch*
Snelling Persnnl Svcs, *Perm. Emp Agcy*
Source Svcs Corp, *Contract Svc*
Spectrum Temp. Employees, *Temp. Agcy*
Steinbrun, Hughes & Assoc., *Exec Srch*
Stivers Temp. Persnnl of CA, *Temp. Agcy*
Strategic Staffng, *Temp. Agcy*
Sun Persnnl Svcs, *Temp. Agcy*
T.R. Emp. Agcy, *Perm. Emp Agcy*
TRC Staff Svcs, *Perm. Emp Agcy*
TAD Resrcs Intl, *Perm. Emp Agcy*
Talent Tree Staffng, *Perm. Emp Agcy*
Tax Exec Srch, *Exec Srch*
TechniSkills, *Temp. Agcy*
Teleforce Intl, *Exec Srch*
Telford, Adams, & Alexander, *Exec Srch*
Judy Thompson & Assoc., *Exec Srch*
Thor Temp. Svcs, *Temp. Agcy*
TOD Staffng, *Exec Srch*
Today Persnnl, *Perm. Emp Agcy*
Trans U.S., *Perm. Emp Agcy*
The Truman Agcy, Persnnl Specialists, *Perm. Emp Agcy*
Tustin Persnnl Svcs, *Perm. Emp Agcy*
Unisearch, *Exec Srch*
United Staff Solut'ns, *Exec Srch*
United/Corestaff Staff Svcs, *Perm. Emp Agcy*
Victor Valley Persnnl Agcy, *Perm. Emp Agcy*
Volt Accnt'g Specialists, *Perm. Emp Agcy*
Volt Temp. Svcs, *Temp. Agcy*
Walker & Torrente, *Exec Srch*
D.L. Weaver & Assoc., *Exec Srch*
Western Staff Svcs, *Temp. Agcy*
The Windsor Grp, *Perm. Emp Agcy*
Your People Prof'ls, *Perm. Emp Agcy*
Amy Zimmerman & Assoc., *Perm. Emp Agcy*

Colorado

Accountnts Choice Persnnl, *Exec Srch*
Accountnts Exec Srch, *Exec Srch*
The Accnt'g Guild, *Temp. Agcy*
Adecco, *Temp. Agcy*
Ahrnsbrak & Assoc., *Perm. Emp Agcy*
C.S. Barnes, *Perm. Emp Agcy*
The Bridge, *Exec Srch*
Career Forum, *Exec Srch*
Casey Svcs, *Exec Srch*
COREStaff Svcs, *Perm. Emp Agcy*
Creative Career Connections, *Career/Outplacemnt*
Eleventh Hour Staff Svcs, *Perm. Emp Agcy*
40 Plus of CO, *Career/Outplacemnt*
Goodwin Persnnl, *Perm. Emp Agcy*
Robert Half Intl/Accountemps, *Exec Srch*
Interim Persnnl Svcs of Denver, *Temp. Agcy*
JobSearch, *Temp. Agcy*
Kelly Svcs, *Temp. Agcy*
LD Placemnts, *Perm. Emp Agcy*
National Affirmative Action Career Netwrk, *Exec Srch*
Norrell Temp. Svcs, *Temp. Agcy*
Office Specialists, *Temp. Agcy*
On Call Tech. Svcs/StaffMark, *Temp. Agcy*
Placement Prof'ls, *Exec Srch*
Real Estate Persnnl, *Exec Srch*
Rocky Mountain Recrtrs, *Exec Srch*
SOS Staff Svcs, *Temp. Agcy*
Sales Consltnts, *Exec Srch*
Snelling Persnnl Svcs, *Exec Srch*
Source Svcs Corp, *Exec Srch*
Star Persnnl, *Exec Srch*
Stivers Temp. Persnnl, *Temp. Agcy*
Talent Tree Staffng, *Perm. Emp Agcy*
Todays Temporary, *Temp. Agcy*
WSI Persnnl, *Perm. Emp Agcy*

Connecticut

A&A Resume & Persnnl Svcs, *Perm. Emp Agcy*
Accountnts Exec Srch/Accountnts on Call, *Exec Srch*
Admiral Staff Svcs, *Temp. Agcy*

Blackwood Assoc., *Exec Srch*
Bohan & Bradstreet, *Perm. Emp Agcy*
Buxbaum/Rink Consltng, *Exec Srch*
Thomas Byrne Assoc., *Perm. Emp Agcy*
Charter Persnnl Svcs, *Exec Srch*
Corporate Staff Solut'ns, *Temp. Agcy*
Diversified Emp. Svcs, *Perm. Emp Agcy*
Diversity Recruitng Svcs, *Exec Srch*
Dunhill Srch Intl, *Perm. Emp Agcy*
EDP Contrct Svcs, *Contract Svc*
Employment Opport., *Perm. Emp Agcy*
Executive Register, *Perm. Emp Agcy*
Financial Careers, *Exec Srch*
Robert Half Intl/Accountemps, *Exec Srch*
Harbor Assoc., *Exec Srch*
High-Tech Recrtrs, *Exec Srch*
Hipp Waters Prof'l Srch, *Exec Srch*
Impact Persnnl, *Temp. Agcy*
Intertec Persnnl, *Temp. Agcy*
Jobsource, *Perm. Emp Agcy*
Mgmt. Recrtrs Intl, *Exec Srch*
Mgmt. Srch, *Exec Srch*
Manpower, *Temp. Agcy*
McIntyre Assoc., *Temp. Agcy*
The McKnight Grp, *Exec Srch*
National Staff Svcs, *Temp. Agcy*
Office Svcs of CT, *Perm. Emp Agcy*
PRH Mgmt., *Exec Srch*
Paramount Resrcs, *Perm. Emp Agcy*
Pascale & LaMorte, *Perm. Emp Agcy*
Q.S.I., *Perm. Emp Agcy*
Resource Assoc., *Perm. Emp Agcy*
Howard Smith Assoc., *Exec Srch*
Source Svcs Corp, *Exec Srch*
Velen Assoc., *Perm. Emp Agcy*
Western Staff Svcs, *Temp. Agcy*
Western Staff Svcs, *Perm. Emp Agcy*
The Westfield Grp, *Exec Srch*
Workforce One, *Perm. Emp Agcy*

Delaware

Caldwell Staff Svcs, *Perm. Emp Agcy*
J.B. Groner Exec Srch, *Exec Srch*
E.W. Hodges & Assoc., *Exec Srch*
Independent Nat'l Srch & Assoc., *Exec Srch*
The Placers, *Temp. Agcy*
The Placers, *Exec Srch*

District of Columbia

Accountnts Exec Srch/Accountnts on Call, *Exec Srch*
Admin. Assist./Hire Stndrd Staffng, *Perm. Emp Agcy*
Network Companies, *Exec Srch*
Norrell Svcs, *Temp. Agcy*
Potomac Persnnl, *Perm. Emp Agcy*
Don Richard Assoc. of Washington DC, *Exec Srch*
Source Svcs Corp, *Temp. Agcy*
Tangent Corp, *Exec Srch*
TempWorld Staff Svcs, *Temp. Agcy*
Woodside Emp. Consltnts, *Perm. Emp Agcy*

Florida

AAA Employment, *Perm. Emp Agcy*
Accountnts Exec Srch/Accountnts On Call, *Exec Srch*
Accountnts Express, *Perm. Emp Agcy*
AccuTech, *Contract Svc*
Active Prof'ls, *Exec Srch*
Adecco, *Temp. Agcy*
Alpha Persnnl/Alpha Temps, *Perm. Emp Agcy*
Ambiance Persnnl, *Exec Srch*
Availability, *Perm. Emp Agcy*
B&B Persnnl, *Perm. Emp Agcy*
Brickell Persnnl Consltnts, *Temp. Agcy*
Bryan & Assoc./Worknet, Etc., *Exec Srch*
Career Planners, *Perm. Emp Agcy*
Careers USA, *Temp. Agcy*
CareerXchange, *Temp. Agcy*
Carrier's Career Svc, *Career/Outplacemnt*
Custom Staffng, *Temp. Agcy*
DGA Persnnl Grp, *Exec Srch*
Steven Douglas Assoc., *Exec Srch*
Dunhill of Tampa, *Exec Srch*
Employers' Assistant, *Temp. Agcy*
En-Data Corp, *Perm. Emp Agcy*
Ethan Allen Persnnl Plcmnt, *Exec Srch*
Future Force Persnnl, *Temp. Agcy*
Michael Gimbel & Assoc., *Exec Srch*
Girl Friday Persnnl, *Temp. Agcy*
HR Prof'l Consltnts, *Exec Srch*
Robert Half Intl/Accountemps, *Exec Srch*
Hastings & Hastings Persnnl Consltnts, *Temp. Agcy*
Interim Accnt'g Prof'ls, *Exec Srch*
Interim Persnnl, *Temp. Agcy*
Koerner Grp, *Exec Srch*
R.H. Larsen & Assoc., *Exec Srch*
Mgmt. Recrtrs Intl, *Exec Srch*
Mgmt. Recrtrs of Miami, *Exec Srch*
Mgmt. Recrtrs of St. Petersburg, *Exec Srch*
Mgmt. Recrtrs of Tallahassee, *Exec Srch*
Mgmt. Recrtrs of Tampa, *Exec Srch*
Norrell Svcs, *Temp. Agcy*
Office Ours, *Temp. Agcy*
Office Specialists, *Temp. Agcy*
Olsten Prof'l Staffng, *Temp. Agcy*
Olsten Staff Svcs, *Temp. Agcy*
OMNIPartners, *Exec Srch*
O'Quin Persnnl, *Temp. Agcy*
PMC&L Assoc., *Perm. Emp Agcy*
Pearce & Assoc., *Exec Srch*
Persnnl Ctr, *Perm. Emp Agcy*
Persnnl One, *Perm. Emp Agcy*
Priority Srch, *Exec Srch*
Pro Staff Persnnl Svcs, *Temp. Agcy*
Profes. Staffing/Able Body Temp. Svcs, *Contract Svc*
Pulp & Paper Intl, *Exec Srch*
Linda Robins & Assoc., *Temp. Agcy*
Romac Intl, *Exec Srch*
The Ryan Charles Grp, *Exec Srch*
Sales Consltnts of Fort Lauderdale, *Exec Srch*
Sales Consltnts of Jacksonville, *Exec Srch*
Doug Sears & Assoc., *Exec Srch*
Secretaries Unlimtd, *Temp. Agcy*
Shaver Emp. Agcy, *Perm. Emp Agcy*
Source Svcs Corp, *Exec Srch*
Spalding's Emp. Svc, *Perm. Emp Agcy*
Staff Leasing Grp, *Contract Svc*
Staffing Svcs Grp, *Perm. Emp Agcy*
Aaron Stewart Persnnl, *Exec Srch*
The Stewart Srch Grp, *Exec Srch*
Systems Srch, *Exec Srch*
TRC Staff Svcs, *Temp. Agcy*
TempSolutions, *Temp. Agcy*
Todays Temporary, *Temp. Agcy*
Uniquest Intl, *Exec Srch*
Victoria & Assoc. Persnnl, *Perm. Emp Agcy*
Terry Weiss & Assoc./Legal & Tax Exec Srch, *Exec Srch*
Western Staff Svcs, *Temp. Agcy*

Georgia

A Hiring Alternative, *Exec Srch*
A-OK Persnnl, *Perm. Emp Agcy*
A-1 Svc Persnnl, *Perm. Emp Agcy*
AAA Employment, *Perm. Emp Agcy*
A.D. & Assoc. Exec Srch, *Exec Srch*
Access Persnnl Svcs, *Perm. Emp Agcy*
Accountnts & Bookkeepers Persnnl, *Exec Srch*
Accountnts Exec Srch/Accountnts On Call, *Exec Srch*
Accounting Resource Temps, *Temp. Agcy*
Michael Alexander Grp, *Exec Srch*
Ashley-Nolan Intl, *Exec Srch*
Augusta Staffing Assoc., *Perm. Emp Agcy*
Bell Oaks Co, *Exec Srch*
Boreham Intl, *Exec Srch*
Bradshaw & Assoc., *Exec Srch*
Caldwell Svcs, *Temp. Agcy*
Career Placemnt Assoc. Staffng, *Exec Srch*
Career Placemnts, *Perm. Emp Agcy*
Catalina Resrcs, *Perm. Emp Agcy*
Chase Finan. Staffng/Tyler Tech. Staffng, *Perm. Emp Agcy*
Corporate Srch Consltnts, *Exec Srch*
Dunhill Prof'l Srch, *Exec Srch*
Elite Staff Svcs, *Perm. Emp Agcy*
Express Persnnl Svcs, *Temp. Agcy*
Express Persnnl Svcs, *Perm. Emp Agcy*
Express Persnnl Svcs, *Exec Srch*
Fox-Morris Assoc., *Exec Srch*
Hall Mngmnt Grp, *Exec Srch*
ISC of Atlanta/Intl Career Continuation, *Exec Srch*
Jordan Temps, *Temp. Agcy*
Kelly Svcs, *Temp. Agcy*
Kenzer Corp of GA, *Exec Srch*
Lucas Financial Srch, *Exec Srch*
MA&A Grp, *Perm. Emp Agcy*
Mgmt. Recrtrs of Atlanta, *Exec Srch*
Manpower Temp. Svcs, *Temp. Agcy*
Office Specialists, *Temp. Agcy*
Officemates5/DayStar Temp. Svcs, *Perm. Emp Agcy*
Olsten Staff Svcs, *Temp. Agcy*
Persnnl Opport., *Exec Srch*
Priority 1 Staff Svcs, *Temp. Agcy*
Professional Medical, *Perm. Emp Agcy*
Quality Temp. Svc, *Temp. Agcy*
Randstad Staff Svcs, *Perm. Emp Agcy*
Don Richard Assoc., *Exec Srch*
Romac Intl, *Exec Srch*
Snelling Persnnl Svcs, *Perm. Emp Agcy*
Source Svcs Corp, *Exec Srch*
Southern Emp. Svc, *Perm. Emp Agcy*
Staffing Resrcs, *Perm. Emp Agcy*
Temporary Specialties, *Temp. Agcy*
Toar Consltnts, *Exec Srch*
Todays Temporary, *Temp. Agcy*
WPPS Software Staffng, *Perm. Emp Agcy*
Western Staff Svcs, *Temp. Agcy*

Hawaii

Altres Staffng, *Temp. Agcy*
Dunhill Prof'l Srch of Hawaii, *Exec Srch*
Ellis & Assoc., *Exec Srch*
Mgmt. Srch & Consltng, *Exec Srch*
Olsten Staff Svcs, *Temp. Agcy*
Select Staff Svcs, *Temp. Agcy*

Idaho

Horne/Brown Intl, *Exec Srch*
Ward-Hoffman & Assoc., *Exec Srch*

Illinois

A.B.A. Placemnts/A.B.A. Temps, *Perm. Emp Agcy*
ASI Persnnl, *Perm. Emp Agcy*
The Ability Grp, *Exec Srch*
B.J. Abrams & Assoc., *Exec Srch*
Account Pros, *Exec Srch*
Accountant Source Temps, *Temp. Agcy*
Accountnts Exec Srch/Accountnts On Call, *Exec Srch*
Accurate Persnnl, *Perm. Emp Agcy*
Adecco, *Temp. Agcy*
Affiliated Persnnl Consltnts, *Perm. Emp Agcy*
American Engineering Co, *Exec Srch*
Armstrong-Hamilton Assoc., *Exec Srch*
Availability, *Perm. Emp Agcy*
Banner Persnnl, *Perm. Emp Agcy*
Barrett Partners, *Exec Srch*
Bell Persnnl, *Perm. Emp Agcy*
Bevelle & Assoc., *Exec Srch*
Burling Grp Exec. Srch Firm
CFR Exec Srch, *Exec Srch*
Carson Mngmnt Assoc., *Contract Svc*
Casey Staff Svcs, *Perm. Emp Agcy*
Chicago Financial Srch, *Exec Srch*
D. Clesen Co, *Exec Srch*
Consltnts to Exec Mgmt., *Exec Srch*
DayStar Temp. Svcs, *Temp. Agcy*
Diener & Assoc., *Exec Srch*
Dunhill Staff Svcs of Chicago, *Perm. Emp Agcy*
Dynamic People, *Temp. Agcy*
Eastman & Assoc., *Exec Srch*
Elsko Exec Srch, *Exec Srch*
Executive Financial Consltnts, *Exec Srch*
Executive Placemnt Consltnts, *Exec Srch*
Executive Referral Svcs, *Exec Srch*
Express Persnnl Svcs, *Temp. Agcy*
Fellows Plcmnt, *Temp. Agcy*
Financial Srch Corp, *Exec Srch*
First Staffng, *Perm. Emp Agcy*
Furst Staff Svcs, *Temp. Agcy*
General Emp. Enterprises, *Perm. Emp Agcy*
Global Srch, *Exec Srch*
David Gomez & Assoc., *Exec Srch*
Robert Half Intl/Accountemps, *Exec Srch*
Human Resource Connection, *Perm. Emp Agcy*
Human Resource Technlgy, *Exec Srch*
IZS Exec Srch, *Exec Srch*
Illinois Veterans Leadership Program, *Career/Outplacemnt*
Insurance Nat'l Srch/E.J. Ashton & Assoc., *Exec Srch*
Interstaff, *Temp. Agcy*
Interviewing Consltnts, *Perm. Emp Agcy*
ITEX Exec Srch, *Exec Srch*
Johnson Persnnl Co, *Exec Srch*
Kunzer Assoc., *Exec Srch*
Arlene Leff & Assoc., *Exec Srch*
Lynco Mngmnt Persnnl, *Exec Srch*
Mack & Assoc., *Temp. Agcy*
Magnum Srch, *Exec Srch*
Mgmt. Recrtrs Intl, *Exec Srch*
Mgmt. Recrtrs of Des Plaines, *Exec Srch*
Mgmt. Recrtrs of Rockford, *Exec Srch*
Manpower Temp. Svcs, *Temp. Agcy*
Maramax Persnnl, *Perm. Emp Agcy*
Juan Menefee & Assoc., *Exec Srch*
Merit Persnnl, *Perm. Emp Agcy*
Michael David Assoc., *Perm. Emp Agcy*
The Murphy Grp, *Perm. Emp Agcy*
NJW & Assoc., *Temp. Agcy*
Nocek & Assoc., *Exec Srch*
Norrell Financial Staffng, *Exec Srch*
Norrell Svcs, *Temp. Agcy*
Office Ours, *Temp. Agcy*
Officemates5 of Wheeling, *Exec Srch*
Olsten Information Technlgy Staffng, *Perm. Emp Agcy*
Olsten Staff Svcs, *Temp. Agcy*
Opportunity Persnnl, *Perm. Emp Agcy*
PS, *Perm. Emp Agcy*
Persnnl Connection, *Perm. Emp Agcy*
Persnnl Placemnt Consltnts, *Perm. Emp Agcy*
Prestige Emp. Svcs, *Perm. Emp Agcy*
Pro Staff Persnnl Svcs, *Temp. Agcy*
Professional Research Svcs, *Exec Srch*
Profile Temp. Svc, *Temp. Agcy*
ProSearch Plus, *Exec Srch*
The Raleigh Warwick Grp, *Exec Srch*
Remedy Intelligent Staffng, *Temp. Agcy*
Right Svcs, *Temp. Agcy*
The Robinson Grp, *Exec Srch*
Romac Intl, *Exec Srch*
The Ryan Charles Grp, *Exec Srch*
Sales Consltnts/Mgmt. Recrtrs Intl, *Exec Srch*

Source Svcs Corp, *Contract Svc*
Source Svcs Corp, *Exec Srch*
Staff It Persnnl Svcs, *Temp. Agcy*
Jean Thorne, *Temp. Agcy*
Whitney & Assoc., *Perm. Emp Agcy*
Working Relationships, *Perm. Emp Agcy*

Mississippi

Andrus Assoc. dba Svc Specialists Ltd., *Perm. Emp Agcy*
Capitol Staff Solut'ns, *Perm. Emp Agcy*
Coats & Coats Persnnl, *Perm. Emp Agcy*
Dunhill Prof'l Srch of Jackson, *Exec Srch*
EPSCO Persnnl, *Temp. Agcy*
Mgmt. Recrtrs Intl, *Exec Srch*
Norrell Staff Svcs, *Temp. Agcy*
Opportunities Unlimtd, *Perm. Emp Agcy*
Persnnl Unlimtd, *Exec Srch*
Jim Woodson & Assoc., *Exec Srch*

Missouri

ABC Emp. Svc, *Perm. Emp Agcy*
Accountant Source Temps, *Temp. Agcy*
Accountnts Exec Srch/Accountnts On Call, *Exec Srch*
Accountemps, *Temp. Agcy*
Accounting Career Consltnts, *Exec Srch*
Advanced Careers of Kansas Cty, *Exec Srch*
L.P. Banning, *Perm. Emp Agcy*
Bestemps, *Perm. Emp Agcy*
Bottom Line Prof'l Svcs, *Contract Svc*
Burns Emp. Svc, *Exec Srch*
Business Persnnl Svcs, *Temp. Agcy*
Crown Svcs, *Temp. Agcy*
Deck & Decker Emp. Svc, *Perm. Emp Agcy*
Decker Persnnl, *Perm. Emp Agcy*
Employer Advantage, *Exec Srch*
ExecuSearch, *Exec Srch*
ExecuTemps, *Temp. Agcy*
FORTUNE Persnnl Consltnts, *Exec Srch*
Robert Half Intl, *Exec Srch*
Huey Enterprises, *Exec Srch*
JoDoc Enterprises, *Temp. Agcy*
Linde Grp, *Perm. Emp Agcy*
Mgmt. Recrtrs Intl, *Exec Srch*
Mgmt. Recrtrs of Kansas Cty, *Exec Srch*
Mgmt. Recrtrs of Springfield, *Exec Srch*
Mgmt. Recrtrs of St. Louis, *Exec Srch*
Manpower Temp. Svcs, *Temp. Agcy*
Officemates5 of St. Louis, *Exec Srch*
Olsten Staff Svcs, *Temp. Agcy*
Search Prof'ls, *Exec Srch*
Snelling Persnnl Svcs, *Perm. Emp Agcy*
Source Svcs Corp, *Exec Srch*
Western Tech. Svcs, *Contract Svc*

Montana

Express Persnnl, *Perm. Emp Agcy*

Nebraska

Accounting Resrcs, *Perm. Emp Agcy*
Adecco, *Temp. Agcy*
Choice Enterprises, *Exec Srch*
Compusearch of Lincoln, *Exec Srch*
Corporate Recrtrs, *Exec Srch*
Donna's Office Svc, *Contract Svc*
Eggers Co, *Perm. Emp Agcy*
Robert Half Intl/Accountemps, *Exec Srch*
Hansen Agri-Placement, *Perm. Emp Agcy*
Kelly Svcs, *Temp. Agcy*
Mgmt. Recrtrs of Omaha/Officemates5, *Exec Srch*

Nevada

Acumen Persnnl, *Perm. Emp Agcy*
Robert Half Intl/Accountemps/OfficeTeam, *Exec Srch*
Mgmt. Recrtrs of Reno, *Exec Srch*
Talent Tree Staffng, *Perm. Emp Agcy*

New Hampshire

Able 1 Staffng, *Exec Srch*
Advanced Recruitng & Consltng, *Exec Srch*
Allstaff Contrct Svcs, *Perm. Emp Agcy*
Arc-Profiles, *Exec Srch*
Barclay Persnnl Syst., *Exec Srch*
Career Connections, *Perm. Emp Agcy*
Central New Hampshire Emp. Svcs, *Perm. Emp Agcy*
Cheshire Emp. Svc, *Temp. Agcy*
Curtis Assoc., *Exec Srch*
Dubois & Co, *Exec Srch*
Key Persnnl, *Perm. Emp Agcy*
Mgmt. Recrtrs Intl of Bedford, *Exec Srch*
Manpower Temp. Svcs, *Temp. Agcy*
National Emp. Svc Corp, *Perm. Emp Agcy*
Professional Recrtrs, *Perm. Emp Agcy*
R.G.T. Assoc., *Exec Srch*
Resource Recruit./Contemp. Accntnts, *Perm. Emp Agcy*
Surge Resrcs, *Contract Svc*
TAC Staff Svcs, *Temp. Agcy*
Thomas & Kavanaugh, *Perm. Emp Agcy*
Western Staff Svcs, *Temp. Agcy*

New Jersey

A+ Persnnl, *Perm. Emp Agcy*
A Prof'l Edge, *Career/Outplacemnt*
Abbott Assoc., *Exec Srch*
Accountnts Exec Srch/Accountnts On Call, *Exec Srch*
Accountnts Prof'l Srch, *Exec Srch*
Advanced Persnnl, *Perm. Emp Agcy*
Raymond Alexander Assoc., *Perm. Emp Agcy*
American Staffing Resrcs, *Temp. Agcy*
Andrew Persnnl Svcs, *Perm. Emp Agcy*
The Ascher Grp, *Exec Srch*
BAI Persnnl Solut'ns, *Exec Srch*
Balcor Assoc., *Exec Srch*
Blake & Assoc. Exec Srch, *Exec Srch*
Broad Waverly & Assoc., *Exec Srch*
Career Ctr, *Perm. Emp Agcy*
Career Srch Assoc., *Exec Srch*
Careers USA, *Perm. Emp Agcy*
Careerworks, *Exec Srch*
Corporate One, *Exec Srch*
Clark Davis Assoc., *Exec Srch*
Dunhill Prof'l Srch, *Exec Srch*
Executive Netwrk, *Exec Srch*
Executive Srch, *Exec Srch*
Express Persnnl Svcs, *Perm. Emp Agcy*
Foster Assoc., *Exec Srch*
The Foster McKay Grp, *Exec Srch*
Gibson Martin Consltng, *Exec Srch*
Grant Franks & Assoc., *Exec Srch*
Robert Half Intl/Accountemps, *Exec Srch*
Holm Persnnl Consltnts, *Exec Srch*
Hreshko Consltng Grp, *Exec Srch*
Hughes & Podesla Persnnl, *Perm. Emp Agcy*
Impact Persnnl, *Perm. Emp Agcy*
Integro Staff Svcs, *Temp. Agcy*
Inter-Regional Exec Srch, *Exec Srch*
Joule People Providers, *Perm. Emp Agcy*
Kelly Svcs, *Temp. Agcy*
Key Employment, *Exec Srch*
Joseph Keyes Assoc., *Perm. Emp Agcy*
MJE Recrtrs, *Exec Srch*
Mgmt. Recrtrs of Passaic Cnty, *Exec Srch*
Mgmt. Recrtrs of Sparta, *Exec Srch*
Manpower Tech. Svcs, *Temp. Agcy*
Officemates5 of Englewood Cliffs/DayStar Temp. Svcs, *Perm. Emp Agcy*
Olsten Staff Svcs, *Temp. Agcy*
Orion Consltng, *Exec Srch*
Park Avenue Persnnl, *Perm. Emp Agcy*
The Pennmore Grp, *Exec Srch*
Persnnl Plus/Temps Plus, *Perm. Emp Agcy*
Pomerantz Persnnl, *Perm. Emp Agcy*
Premier Persnnl Grp, *Perm. Emp Agcy*
Princeton Exec Srch, *Exec Srch*
Protocall Bus. Staff Svcs, *Temp. Agcy*
Ready Persnnl/Ready Temps, *Perm. Emp Agcy*
Jeff Rich Assoc., *Exec Srch*
Rochester Syst., *Exec Srch*
Rylan Forbes Consltng Grp, *Exec Srch*
S-H-S of Cherry Hill, *Perm. Emp Agcy*
R.S. Sadow Assoc., *Exec Srch*
Sales Consltnts of Sparta, *Exec Srch*
Selective Persnnl, *Perm. Emp Agcy*
Arline Simpson Assoc., *Perm. Emp Agcy*
Snelling Persnnl Svcs, *Perm. Emp Agcy*
Source One Persnnl, *Perm. Emp Agcy*
Source Svcs Corp, *Perm. Emp Agcy*
Source Svcs Corp, *Exec Srch*
Temporary Excellence, *Temp. Agcy*
Temps Plus, *Temp. Agcy*
Unitemp Temp. Persnnl, *Temp. Agcy*
Winston Staff Svcs, *Temp. Agcy*
Winters & Ross, *Perm. Emp Agcy*
Claire Wright Assn, *Perm. Emp Agcy*

New Mexico

Albuquerque Persnnl, *Perm. Emp Agcy*
Excel of Albuquerque, *Perm. Emp Agcy*
Robert Half Intl/Accountemps, *Exec Srch*
Sanderson Emp. Svc, *Perm. Emp Agcy*
Santa Fe Svcs, *Temp. Agcy*
Snelling Persnnl Svcs, *Exec Srch*

New York

AJC Srch, *Exec Srch*
Accountnts Choice Persnnl, *Exec Srch*
Accountnts Exec Srch/Accountnts On Call, *Exec Srch*
Accounting & Computer Persnnl, *Perm. Emp Agcy*
AccuStaff, *Perm. Emp Agcy*
Adam Persnnl, *Perm. Emp Agcy*
Merrill Adams Assoc., *Career/Outplacemnt*
Adecco, *Temp. Agcy*
Advice Persnnl, *Exec Srch*
Alite Assoc., *Exec Srch*
Franklin Allen Consltnts, *Exec Srch*
Asher Persnnl Consltnts, *Perm. Emp Agcy*
Auto Careers, *Perm. Emp Agcy*
Bartl & Evins, *Exec Srch*
Benson Assoc., *Exec Srch*
Bevan Resrcs, *Perm. Emp Agcy*
Bevlin Persnnl, *Perm. Emp Agcy*
Branthover Assoc., *Exec Srch*
E.E. Brooke, *Perm. Emp Agcy*
Brookville Staff Svcs, *Perm. Emp Agcy*
C.C. Burke Limited, *Perm. Emp Agcy*
CK Resrcs, *Exec Srch*
Career Blazers Persnnl, *Perm. Emp Agcy*
Career Concepts, *Perm. Emp Agcy*
Career Objectives Persnnl, *Temp. Agcy*
Carlile Persnnl Agcy, *Perm. Emp Agcy*
Compu-Tech Persnnl Agcy, *Exec Srch*
Concorde Srch, *Perm. Emp Agcy*
Confidential Srch, *Exec Srch*
Consortium, *Exec Srch*
Consulting Partners of America, *Exec Srch*
Marilyn Cooper Persnnl, *Perm. Emp Agcy*
The Cornell Grp, *Exec Srch*
Corporate Careers/R.J. Assoc., *Exec Srch*
Corporate Srch, *Exec Srch*
D&L Assoc., *Exec Srch*
Seth Diamond Assoc., *Exec Srch*
Dunhill Staffing Syst. of Buffalo, *Temp. Agcy*
EDP Contrct Svcs, *Contract Svc*
Eden Persnnl, *Perm. Emp Agcy*
Employment Recrtrs Agcy, *Perm. Emp Agcy*
Executive Image, *Exec Srch*
Extra Help Emp. Svc, *Temp. Agcy*
Fabian Assoc., *Exec Srch*
Fifth Avenue Emp. Svcs, *Temp. Agcy*
C.R. Fletcher Assoc., *Exec Srch*
Forum Temp. Svcs, *Temp. Agcy*
Franklin Srch Resrcs, *Exec Srch*
Ronnie Gale Persnnl Corp, *Exec Srch*
H&H Temp. Svcs, *Temp. Agcy*
HBC Grp, *Exec Srch*
Robert Half Intl/Information Syst. Division, *Exec Srch*
Harbrowe, *Perm. Emp Agcy*
Hart-Merrell Persnnl, *Exec Srch*
Headway Corporate Staff Svcs, *Temp. Agcy*
Hessel Assoc., *Exec Srch*
Hunter Mac & Assoc., *Perm. Emp Agcy*
Hunter Plcmnt, *Exec Srch*
Innovations Assoc., *Perm. Emp Agcy*
Interspace Interactive, *Exec Srch*
Island Srch Grp, *Perm. Emp Agcy*
JDC Assoc., *Perm. Emp Agcy*
Just One Break, *Perm. Emp Agcy*
KLK Persnnl, *Perm. Emp Agcy*
KPA Grp, *Exec Srch*
The Kay Grp of Fifth Avenue, *Exec Srch*
Kelly Svcs, *Temp. Agcy*
Fred Koffler Assoc., *Exec Srch*
Kramer Exec Resrcs, *Exec Srch*
Lake Assoc., *Exec Srch*
Tina Lane Persnnl, *Perm. Emp Agcy*
Michael John Lawrence & Assoc., *Exec Srch*
Ivan Mack Assoc., *Exec Srch*
Magill Assoc., *Exec Srch*
Joseph Maloney & Assoc., *Perm. Emp Agcy*
Mgmt. Recrtrs of Woodbury/ CompuSrch, *Exec Srch*
Manpower Temp. Svcs, *Temp. Agcy*
Mar-El Emp. Agcy, *Exec Srch*
Marcus & Assoc., *Exec Srch*
Lynn Marshall Persnnl Agcy, *Perm. Emp Agcy*
McLaughlin Resrcs, *Exec Srch*
Metro Resrcs of Rochester, *Temp. Agcy*
Metro Persnnl/Metro Nursing Svcs, *Exec Srch*
Milazzo Assoc., *Perm. Emp Agcy*
Morgan-Murray Persnnl/M&M Top Temps, *Temp. Agcy*
National Emp. Database, *Perm. Emp Agcy*
Neal Mgmt., *Exec Srch*
Noah Assoc., *Perm. Emp Agcy*
Norrell Staff Svcs, *Perm. Emp Agcy*
K.A. Nowack Career Specialists, *Perm. Emp Agcy*
Olsten Staff Svcs, *Temp. Agcy*
Arthur Pann Assoc., *Exec Srch*
Parker Clark Exec Recrtmnt, *Exec Srch*
Parsons, Anderson & Gee, *Perm. Emp Agcy*
Paywise, *Temp. Agcy*
Peak Srch, *Exec Srch*
Persnnl Svcs Ctr, *Exec Srch*
P.G. Prager Srch Assoc., *Exec Srch*
Professional Support, *Exec Srch*
Quest Organization, *Exec Srch*
Rand Thompson Consltnts, *Exec Srch*
Rem Resrcs, *Perm. Emp Agcy*
Remedy Intelligent Staffng, *Temp. Agcy*
Response Staff Svcs/Career Advisors, *Exec Srch*
Beth Richman Assoc., *Perm. Emp Agcy*
Fran Rogers Persnnl, *Perm. Emp Agcy*
Roth Young of Long Islnd, *Exec Srch*
S.W. Mgmt., *Exec Srch*
Search Masters, *Exec Srch*
Sigma Staffng, *Perm. Emp Agcy*
Snelling Persnnl Svcs, *Exec Srch*
Source Finance, *Exec Srch*
Sporn Grp, *Exec Srch*
Staff Managers, *Temp. Agcy*

Superior Concepts, *Contract Svc*
Synergy Partners, *Exec Srch*
Tax Netwrk Resrcs, *Perm. Emp Agcy*
Hillary Taylor Persnnl, *Perm. Emp Agcy*
Taylor Jordan Assoc., *Exec Srch*
Temp Force of NY, *Temp. Agcy*
Tempo Svcs, *Perm. Emp Agcy*
Temporary Resource Ctr, *Temp. Agcy*
Phil Thomas Persnnl, *Exec Srch*
Traynor Confidential Exec. Srch Firm
United Persnnl Agcy, *Perm. Emp Agcy*
Vantage Staff Svcs, *Temp. Agcy*
Charles Wanner Assoc. Exec. Srch Firm
Werbin Assoc. Exec Srch, *Exec Srch*
Westchester Emp. Agcy, *Perm. Emp Agcy*
Western Staff Svcs, *Temp. Agcy*
Westfield Assoc., *Exec Srch*
Winston Resrcs, *Exec Srch*

North Carolina

A-1 Staffing & Persnnl, *Perm. Emp Agcy*
Accountnts Exec Srch, *Exec Srch*
Accurate Staff Consltnts, *Exec Srch*
Action Tech. Staffng, *Temp. Agcy*
Advanced Persnnl Resrcs, *Exec Srch*
Alpha Omega Exec Srch, *Exec Srch*
AmeriPro Srch, *Exec Srch*
Anderson & Daniel Persnnl, *Perm. Emp Agcy*
Andrews & Assoc., *Exec Srch*
Atchison & Assoc., *Exec Srch*
Careers Unlimtd, *Perm. Emp Agcy*
Coastal Temp. Svcs, *Temp. Agcy*
Elin Var, *Exec Srch*
Executive Staff Svcs, *Perm. Emp Agcy*
C.D. Fayling Assoc., *Exec Srch*
Five Star Staffng, *Temp. Agcy*
FORTUNE Persnnl Consltnts of Raleigh, *Perm. Emp Agcy*
Graham & Assoc., *Perm. Emp Agcy*
Greer Persnnl, *Perm. Emp Agcy*
Robert Half Intl, *Exec Srch*
Highlander Srch, *Exec Srch*
Jobs of Fayetteville, *Perm. Emp Agcy*
S.N. Jones & Assoc., *Exec Srch*
Kelly Svcs, *Temp. Agcy*
Key Temps, *Temp. Agcy*
Mgmt. Recrtrs Intl, *Exec Srch*
Mgmt. Recrtrs of Durham, *Exec Srch*
Mgmt. Recrtrs of Raleigh/Inter Exec, *Exec Srch*
Mgmt. Recrtrs of Winston-Salem, *Exec Srch*
McCain Emp. Agcy, *Temp. Agcy*
Moffitt Intl, *Exec Srch*
National Svcs, *Exec Srch*
Olsten Staff Svcs, *Temp. Agcy*
The Perkin Grp, *Exec Srch*
Pro Staff Accnt'g Svcs, *Perm. Emp Agcy*
Quality Temp. Svcs, *Temp. Agcy*
Don Richard Assoc. of Charlotte, *Perm. Emp Agcy*
Sales Consltnts of High Point, *Exec Srch*
Snelling Persnnl Svcs, *Contract Svc*
Snelling Srch, *Exec Srch*
Source Svcs Corp, *Exec Srch*
Sparks Persnnl Svcs, *Exec Srch*
Staff Accntnts, *Exec Srch*
John Williams & Assoc., *Exec Srch*
Youngblood Staffng, *Perm. Emp Agcy*

North Dakota

Dunhill Exec Srch, *Exec Srch*
Human Resrcs, *Perm. Emp Agcy*
Olsten Staff Svcs/Kramer & Assoc./Expressway Persnnl, *Temp. Agcy*
Persnnl Svcs, *Exec Srch*

Ohio

Accountnts Exec Srch/Accountnts On Call, *Exec Srch*
Accountnts Select, *Exec Srch*
Benke & Assoc., *Exec Srch*
N.L. Benke & Assoc., *Perm. Emp Agcy*
Bradley-Pierce Persnnl, *Perm. Emp Agcy*
J.B. Brown & Assoc., *Exec Srch*
Burks Grp, *Exec Srch*
CBS Persnnl Svcs, *Perm. Emp Agcy*
Career Specialists, *Exec Srch*
Champion Persnnl, *Perm. Emp Agcy*
Corell Assoc., *Perm. Emp Agcy*
J.D. Cotter Srch, *Exec Srch*
Crown Temp. Svcs of Cincinnati, *Temp. Agcy*
Custom Staffng, *Temp. Agcy*
Drayton & Assoc., *Exec Srch*
Eastern Persnnl Svcs, *Perm. Emp Agcy*
Exact Persnnl Specialists, *Perm. Emp Agcy*
Executech, *Exec Srch*
Executech Consltnts, *Exec Srch*
Executive Srch Ltd., *Exec Srch*
Flowers & Assoc./Associated Temps, *Exec Srch*
Griffiths & Assoc., *Exec Srch*
H.J.C., *Exec Srch*
Russ Hadick & Assoc., *Exec Srch*
Hite Exec Srch/Hite Mngmnt Consltnts, *Exec Srch*
Ives & Assoc., *Exec Srch*
Rich Johns Career Consltnts, *Perm. Emp Agcy*
Kelly Svcs, *Temp. Agcy*
Laine's S.M.G., *Perm. Emp Agcy*
R.E. Lowe Assoc., *Perm. Emp Agcy*
Mgmt. Recrtrs of Cincinnati, *Exec Srch*
Mgmt. Recrtrs of Cleveland, *Exec Srch*
Mgmt. Recrtrs of Columbus, *Exec Srch*
Mgmt. Recrtrs of Dayton, *Exec Srch*
Mgmt. Recrtrs of Solon, *Exec Srch*
Marvel Consltnts, *Exec Srch*
Messina Mngmnt Syst., *Exec Srch*
Miami Prof'l Srch, *Exec Srch*
Minority Exec Srch, *Exec Srch*
O'Brien & Roof Co, *Exec Srch*
Olsten Financial Staffng, *Exec Srch*
Olsten Prof'l Staff Svcs, *Exec Srch*
Palmer Temps/The Palmer Grp, *Temp. Agcy*
The Prof'l Consltnts, *Exec Srch*
Professional Restaffing of OH, *Perm. Emp Agcy*
Providence Persnnl Consltnts, *Exec Srch*
Quality Plus, *Exec Srch*
Bill Reber & Assoc., *Exec Srch*
W.R. Renner & Assoc., *Exec Srch*
Sales Consltnts of Cincinnati, *Exec Srch*
Shafer Jones Assoc., *Exec Srch*
Source Svcs Corp, *Exec Srch*
Sterling Persnnl Resrcs, *Exec Srch*
The Target Human Resource Companies, *Temp. Agcy*
Tech/Aid of OH, *Perm. Emp Agcy*
Temporarily Yours Plcmnt, *Temp. Agcy*
J.P. Walton & Assoc., *Exec Srch*

Oklahoma

Andrews & Assoc., *Exec Srch*
Express Persnnl Svcs, *Exec Srch*
Robert Half Intl, *Exec Srch*
Interim Persnnl, *Temp. Agcy*
Mgmt. Recrtrs of Oklahoma Cty, *Exec Srch*
Manpower Temp. Svcs, *Temp. Agcy*
Terry Neese Persnnl Agcy, *Exec Srch*
Lloyd Richards Persnnl, *Perm. Emp Agcy*
Sooner Placemnt Svc, *Perm. Emp Agcy*
StaffMark, *Temp. Agcy*

Oregon

Able Temp. Svc, *Temp. Agcy*
Accountnts Exec Srch/Accountnts On Call, *Exec Srch*
Accountnts Nrthwest, *Exec Srch*
D. Brown & Assoc., *Exec Srch*
Express Persnnl Svcs, *Exec Srch*
Robert Half Intl/Accountemps, *Exec Srch*
Kelly Svcs, *Temp. Agcy*
Mgmt. Recrtrs/Officemates5 of Portland, *Exec Srch*
Northwest Temp. & Staff Svcs, *Temp. Agcy*
Office Careers, *Perm. Emp Agcy*
Southern Oregon Temporary, *Temp. Agcy*
Talent Tree Staffng, *Perm. Emp Agcy*
Uniforce Staffng Svcs, *Temp. Agcy*

Pennsylvania

Accountnts Exec Srch, *Exec Srch*
Accountnts On Call, *Temp. Agcy*
Acsys Resrcs, *Perm. Emp Agcy*
Action Persnnl Svcs, *Perm. Emp Agcy*
Adecco, *Temp. Agcy*
Alexander Persnnl Assoc., *Exec Srch*
All Staffng, *Perm. Emp Agcy*
Allegheny Persnnl Svcs, *Temp. Agcy*
American Srch Assoc., *Exec Srch*
American Staffing Resrcs, *Temp. Agcy*
ASAP Staffng, *Perm. Emp Agcy*
Ashley Srch Consltnts, *Exec Srch*
Barton Persnnl Syst., *Exec Srch*
Basilone-Oliver Exec Srch, *Exec Srch*
Brackin & Sayers Assoc., *Exec Srch*
Bradley Prof'l Svcs, *Perm. Emp Agcy*
Career Concepts Staff Svcs, *Exec Srch*
Charly's Temp. Svcs, *Temp. Agcy*
Joseph Conahan Exec Recrtrs, *Exec Srch*
COREStaff, *Temp. Agcy*
P. Robert Dann, *Exec Srch*
DiCenzo Persnnl Specialists, *Perm. Emp Agcy*
Dunhill Prof'l Srch, *Exec Srch*
Dunn Assoc., *Exec Srch*
EDP/Temps of PA, *Temp. Agcy*
Executive Avail-A-Search, *Exec Srch*
Financial Industry Staff Co, *Perm. Emp Agcy*
Fox-Morris Assoc., *Exec Srch*
Robert Half Intl/Accountemps, *Exec Srch*
The Hastings Grp, *Exec Srch*
Hoskins Hains Assoc., *Perm. Emp Agcy*
Human Resource Solut'ns, *Exec Srch*
J-Rand Srch, *Exec Srch*
Nancy Jackson, *Exec Srch*
Jefferson-Ross Assoc., *Exec Srch*
Kathy Karr Persnnl, *Perm. Emp Agcy*
Blair Kershaw Assoc., *Exec Srch*
Keystaff, *Temp. Agcy*
Marsetta Lane Temp. Svcs, *Temp. Agcy*
Mgmt. Recrtrs Intl, *Exec Srch*
Mgmt. Recrtrs of DE Cnty/CompuSrch, *Exec Srch*
Mgmt. Recrtrs of Lehigh Vly/CompuSrch, *Exec Srch*
Mgmt. Recrtrs of Philadelphia/ CompuSrch, *Exec Srch*
Mark Joseph Assoc., *Perm. Emp Agcy*
Metro Persnnl, *Temp. Agcy*
The Morris Grp, *Exec Srch*
Norrell Svcs, *Temp. Agcy*
Olsten Staff Svcs, *Temp. Agcy*
LaMonte Owens, *Exec Srch*
Pancoast Temp. Svcs, *Temp. Agcy*
Penn Srch, *Exec Srch*
Pratt Persnnl Svcs, *Temp. Agcy*
Pratt Persnnl Svcs, *Temp. Agcy*
Alan Raeburn Consltnts, *Exec Srch*
Rice Cohen Intl, *Exec Srch*
The Richards Grp, *Exec Srch*
Romac Intl, *Exec Srch*
S-H-S Intl, *Perm. Emp Agcy*
S-H-S Intl, *Exec Srch*
SHS Assoc., *Exec Srch*
Source Svcs Corp, *Exec Srch*
Source Svcs Corp, *Exec Srch*
Spectrum Consltnts/Retail Recrtrs, *Exec Srch*
Strauss Persnnl, *Perm. Emp Agcy*
TRC Staff Svcs, *Temp. Agcy*
TAC Staff Svcs, *Temp. Agcy*
Tandem Persnnl, *Temp. Agcy*
W.G. Tucker & Assoc., *Exec Srch*
Uni Temp Temp. Svc, *Temp. Agcy*
Uniforce Temp. Svcs, *Temp. Agcy*
Vogue Persnnl, *Perm. Emp Agcy*
Yorktowne Persnnl, *Exec Srch*

Rhode Island

Accounting Resrcs, *Exec Srch*
Colony Persnnl Assoc., *Perm. Emp Agcy*
Dorra Srch, *Exec Srch*
Kelly Svcs, *Temp. Agcy*
Albert Lee & Assoc., *Exec Srch*
Mgmt. Recrtrs Intl, *Exec Srch*
Norrell Svcs, *Temp. Agcy*
Spectra Temps/Tracey Assoc., *Temp. Agcy*
Storti Assoc., *Exec Srch*
TAC Staff Svcs, *Temp. Agcy*

South Carolina

Carolina Persnnl Svcs, *Temp. Agcy*
Dunhill Prof'l Srch, *Exec Srch*
Financial Srch Assoc., *Exec Srch*
Ford & Assoc., *Exec Srch*
FORTUNE Persnnl Consltnts of Columbia, *Exec Srch*
Harvey Persnnl, *Perm. Emp Agcy*
Mgmt. Recrtrs of Columbia, *Exec Srch*
Mgmt. Recrtrs of Rck Hill, *Exec Srch*
Miller & Assoc., *Exec Srch*
PRL & Assoc., *Perm. Emp Agcy*
John Shell Assoc., *Exec Srch*
Smith Temps/Smith Persnnl, *Temp. Agcy*
Snelling Persnnl Svcs, *Perm. Emp Agcy*
Southern Recrtrs & Consltnts, *Exec Srch*
Staffing Solut'ns, *Temp. Agcy*
Transworld Svcs Grp, *Temp. Agcy*

South Dakota

Careers Unlimtd, *Perm. Emp Agcy*
Olsten Staff Svcs, *Temp. Agcy*
Snelling Persnnl Svcs, *Perm. Emp Agcy*

Tennessee

Accountnts & Bookkeepers, *Exec Srch*
Accountnts On Call, *Temp. Agcy*
Accounting Solut'ns, *Temp. Agcy*
Austin-Allen Co, *Exec Srch*
B.K. Barnes & Assoc., *Exec Srch*
Carroll & Assoc., *Exec Srch*
Cook Assoc. Intl, *Exec Srch*
FORTUNE Persnnl Consltnts, *Exec Srch*
Gateway Grp Persnnl, *Temp. Agcy*
Robert Half Intl/Accountemps, *Exec Srch*
Hamilton Ryker Co, *Exec Srch*
Kelly Svcs, *Temp. Agcy*
Madison Persnnl, *Perm. Emp Agcy*
Mgmt. Recrtrs Intl, *Exec Srch*
Mgmt. Recrtrs of Chattanooga, *Exec Srch*
Mgmt. Recrtrs of Knoxville, *Exec Srch*
Manpower Temp. Svcs, *Temp. Agcy*
Manpower, *Temp. Agcy*
Mega Force, *Temp. Agcy*
The Morgan Grp, *Exec Srch*
Olsten Staff Svcs, *Temp. Agcy*
Persnnl Link, *Exec Srch*
Poplar Emp. Svc, *Perm. Emp Agcy*
Rasmussen & Assoc., *Perm. Emp Agcy*
Sales Consltnts of Nashville, *Exec Srch*
Snelling Persnnl Svcs, *Exec Srch*
Staffing Solut'ns, *Perm. Emp Agcy*

Unlimited Staff Solut'ns, *Contract Svc*
Rob Walker Assoc., *Contract Svc*

Texas

A-1 Persnnl, *Temp. Agcy*
ABC Temps, *Temp. Agcy*
Abilene Emp. Svc, *Perm. Emp Agcy*
Accountnts Exec Srch/Accountnts On Call, *Exec Srch*
Accounting Action Persnnl, *Perm. Emp Agcy*
Accounting Contractors, *Exec Srch*
Action Persnnl, *Temp. Agcy*
Add-A-Temp/Woodlands Exec Employment, *Temp. Agcy*
ADSTAFF Mngmnt & Persnnl Consltnts, *Perm. Emp Agcy*
Agri-LC, *Exec Srch*
Audit Prof'ls Intl, *Exec Srch*
Austin Grp, *Exec Srch*
Aware Affiliates Persnnl, *Perm. Emp Agcy*
Babich & Assoc., *Perm. Emp Agcy*
Baldwin & Co, *Exec Srch*
Ann Best Elite Temps, *Temp. Agcy*
Borrel Persnnl, *Exec Srch*
Brainpower Persnnl Agcy, *Perm. Emp Agcy*
Bridge Persnnl, *Exec Srch*
Brooklea & Assoc., *Exec Srch*
Bruco, *Perm. Emp Agcy*
Bullock Persnnl, *Perm. Emp Agcy*
Bundy-Stewart Assoc., *Exec Srch*
Burnett Persnnl Svcs, *Temp. Agcy*
Certified Persnnl, *Contract Svc*
Cherbonnier Grp, *Exec Srch*
Clayton Persnnl Svcs, *Temp. Agcy*
Colvin Resrcs Grp, *Temp. Agcy*
Continental Persnnl, *Perm. Emp Agcy*
Creative Staff Svcs, *Temp. Agcy*
Credit Union Emp. Resrcs, *Temp. Agcy*
DH&A (Donice Hall & Assoc.), *Perm. Emp Agcy*
Dallas Emp. Svc, *Perm. Emp Agcy*
The Danbrook Grp, *Exec Srch*
Gail Darling Staffing/Darling's Prof'l Desk, *Temp. Agcy*
Diversified Temps, *Temp. Agcy*
Donovan & Watkins, *Perm. Emp Agcy*
Dunhill of Arlington, *Perm. Emp Agcy*
Dunhill Prof'l Srch, *Exec Srch*
Employee Sources, *Exec Srch*
Evins Persnnl Consltnts of Killeen, *Perm. Emp Agcy*
Executeam, *Exec Srch*
Executive Srch Consltnts, *Exec Srch*
Executive Srch Persnnl, *Exec Srch*
Express Persnnl Svcs, *Perm. Emp Agcy*
Feldt Persnnl, *Perm. Emp Agcy*
Robert Half Intl, *Perm. Emp Agcy*
Hedman & Assoc., *Exec Srch*
The Human Element of Business, *Exec Srch*
Imprimis Staff Solut'ns, *Temp. Agcy*
InterSearch Assoc., *Temp. Agcy*
L.K. Jordan & Assoc., *Contract Svc*
Kelly Svcs, *Temp. Agcy*
Key People, *Perm. Emp Agcy*
Kindrick & Luther, *Perm. Emp Agcy*
George Lehman Assoc., *Exec Srch*
Lucas Financial Staffng, *Exec Srch*
The Lukens Grp, *Perm. Emp Agcy*
Lusk & Assoc. Persnnl, *Exec Srch*
Mgmt. Recrtrs Intl, *Exec Srch*
Mgmt. Recrtrs of Dallas, *Exec Srch*
Manpower Temp. Svcs, *Temp. Agcy*
Ray Marburger & Assoc., *Exec Srch*
Metro Careers, *Exec Srch*
Odell & Assoc., *Exec Srch*
Olsten Staff Svcs, *Temp. Agcy*
P&P Persnnl, *Perm. Emp Agcy*
The Pailin Grp, *Exec Srch*
Pate Resrcs Grp, *Exec Srch*
Persnnl One, *Perm. Emp Agcy*
Phoenix Staffng, *Exec Srch*
Priority Persnnl, *Temp. Agcy*
Pro Staff Persnnl Svcs, *Temp. Agcy*
Professional Srch Consltnts, *Contract Svc*
Professions Today, *Perm. Emp Agcy*
Remedy Intelligent Staffng, *Perm. Emp Agcy*
Resource Recrtrs, *Perm. Emp Agcy*
Resource Staffng, *Contract Svc*
Bart Roberson & Co, *Exec Srch*
Romac Intl, *Exec Srch*
Sales Consltnts of Houston, *Exec Srch*
Salinas & Assoc. Persnnl, *Exec Srch*
Search Netwrk Intl, *Exec Srch*
Select Staff, *Exec Srch*
Snelling Persnnl Svcs, *Perm. Emp Agcy*
Snelling Persnnl Svcs, *Exec Srch*
Source Svcs Corp, *Exec Srch*
Staff Extension, *Exec Srch*
Staff Finders/Abacus Accnt'g Persnnl, *Perm. Emp Agcy*
TGA Co, *Exec Srch*
TSP Persnnl Svcs, *Perm. Emp Agcy*
TAD Tech. Svcs, *Contract Svc*
Betty Tanner Prof'l Emp. Svc, *Exec Srch*
Tarrant Cnty Emp. Netwrk, *Perm. Emp Agcy*
Tech. Staff Solut'ns, *Exec Srch*
Temp 2000 Temp. Svcs, *Temp. Agcy*
Thomas Office Persnnl, *Perm. Emp Agcy*
Todays Temporary, *Temp. Agcy*
Total Temp. Svcs, *Temp. Agcy*
The Urban Placemnt Svc, *Exec Srch*
Dick Van Vliet & Assoc., *Exec Srch*
Vinson & Assoc., *Perm. Emp Agcy*
Watkins & Assoc., *Exec Srch*
Wheeler, Moore & Elam Co, *Exec Srch*
The Whitaker Companies, *Exec Srch*

Utah

AccountStaff, *Exec Srch*
Robert Half Intl, *Exec Srch*
Intermountain Staffing Resrcs, *Temp. Agcy*
Mgmt. Recrtrs Intl, *Exec Srch*
Olsten Staff Svcs, *Temp. Agcy*
Professional Recrtrs, *Exec Srch*
Source Svcs Corp, *Exec Srch*
Staffing Logic, *Perm. Emp Agcy*
Trout & Assoc., *Exec Srch*

Vermont

Persnnl Dept, *Temp. Agcy*

Virginia

A Better Resume, *Career/Outplacemnt*
Ability Resrcs, *Exec Srch*
Access Enterprises, *Perm. Emp Agcy*
Accountnts Exec Srch/Accountnts On Call, *Exec Srch*
Accountnts On Call, *Temp. Agcy*
Accounting Assests, *Temp. Agcy*
Adams Sources, *Exec Srch*
Alpha Omega Resrcs, *Perm. Emp Agcy*
Ardelle Assoc./AA Temps, *Perm. Emp Agcy*
Corporate Connection Exec. Srch Firm
Curzon Staffng, *Perm. Emp Agcy*
Carol Day & Assoc., *Exec Srch*
Dow Persnnl, *Perm. Emp Agcy*
EDP, *Temp. Agcy*
Effective Staffng, *Exec Srch*
H.R. Directions, *Contract Svc*
Robert Half Intl/Accountemps, *Exec Srch*
Lee Staffing Resrcs, *Exec Srch*
Mgmt. Recrtrs Intl, *Exec Srch*
Mgmt. Recrtrs of McLean, *Exec Srch*
Mgmt. Recrtrs of Roanoke, *Exec Srch*
Carol McNew Emp. Svc, *Perm. Emp Agcy*
Susan Miller & Assoc., *Perm. Emp Agcy*
Network Companies, *Exec Srch*
Norrell Staff Svcs, *Exec Srch*
OfficeTeam, *Perm. Emp Agcy*
Olsten Staff Svcs, *Temp. Agcy*
Placement Prof'ls, *Exec Srch*
Professional Srch Persnnl, *Exec Srch*
Remedy Intelligent Staffng, *Temp. Agcy*
Don Richard Assoc., *Exec Srch*
Select Staff Svcs, *Perm. Emp Agcy*
Snelling Persnnl Svcs, *Perm. Emp Agcy*
Source Svcs Corp, *Exec Srch*
STAT Temps, *Temp. Agcy*
TAC Staff Svcs, *Temp. Agcy*
The Talley Grp, *Exec Srch*
Task Force of VA, *Exec Srch*
Temporary Solut'ns, *Temp. Agcy*
TempWorld Staff Svcs, *Temp. Agcy*
Virginia Emp. Referral Svc, *Exec Srch*

Washington

Able Persnnl Agcy, *Perm. Emp Agcy*
Accounting Partners, *Exec Srch*
Accounting Quest, *Exec Srch*
Bostwick Temp. Svc, *Temp. Agcy*
Business Careers, *Perm. Emp Agcy*
Career Svcs, *Perm. Emp Agcy*
Castle Hill Assoc., *Exec Srch*
Express Persnnl Svcs, *Temp. Agcy*
Guidance Svcs, *Temp. Agcy*
Robert Half Intl/Accountemps, *Exec Srch*
Houser, Martin, Morris & Assoc., *Exec Srch*
Human Resrcs, *Exec Srch*
The Jobs Co, *Exec Srch*
Kelly Svcs, *Temp. Agcy*
Lawrence & Assoc., *Exec Srch*
Mgmt. Recrtrs of Mercer Islnd, *Exec Srch*
Mgmt. Recrtrs of Tacoma, *Exec Srch*
Manpower Temp. Svcs, *Temp. Agcy*
Northwest Temp. Svcs, *Temp. Agcy*
Persnnl Unlimtd, *Exec Srch*
Small Bus. Solut'ns, *Exec Srch*
Snelling Persnnl Svcs, *Exec Srch*
Staffing Resrcs, *Perm. Emp Agcy*

West Virginia

Extra Support Staffng, *Temp. Agcy*
Key Persnnl, *Perm. Emp Agcy*
Snelling Persnnl Svcs, *Temp. Agcy*

Wisconsin

Allen, Wayne, & Co, *Perm. Emp Agcy*
Career Resrcs, *Exec Srch*
Careertrac Emp. Svc, *Exec Srch*
Crown Svcs, *Temp. Agcy*
Dunhill Staff Svcs, *Perm. Emp Agcy*
Executive Resource, *Exec Srch*
Financial Mngmnt Persnnl, *Exec Srch*
Robert Half Intl/Accountemps, *Exec Srch*
Intl Srch, *Exec Srch*
Landmark, The Staffing Resource, *Temp. Agcy*
Mgmt. Recrtrs of Appleton/ CompuSrch, *Exec Srch*
Mgmt. Recrtrs of Green Bay, *Exec Srch*
Mgmt. Recrtrs of Milwaukee/Sales Consltnts, *Exec Srch*
Mgmt. Recrtrs of Milwaukee, *Exec Srch*
Markent Persnnl, *Exec Srch*
Olsten Staff Svcs, *Temp. Agcy*
Placement Solut'ns, *Exec Srch*
Placements of Racine, *Perm. Emp Agcy*
SEEK, *Perm. Emp Agcy*
Source Svcs Corp, *Exec Srch*
Work Connection, *Perm. Emp Agcy*

Wyoming

Olsten Staff Svcs, *Temp. Agcy*

ADMINISTRATION

Alabama

A-1 Emp. Svc, *Perm. Emp Agcy*
Assoc. Persnnl, *Exec Srch*
Dunhill of So. Birmingham, *Exec Srch*
Employment Consltnts, *Perm. Emp Agcy*
FORTUNE Persnnl Consltnts, *Exec Srch*
Mgmt. Recrtrs Intl, *Exec Srch*
J.L. Small Assoc., *Exec Srch*
VIP Persnnl, *Perm. Emp Agcy*
WorkForce, *Temp. Agcy*

Alaska

Alaska Exec Srch, *Exec Srch*
Elite Emp. Svc, *Temp. Agcy*

Arizona

AccuStaff, *Perm. Emp Agcy*
Aidan Grp, *Contract Svc*
Andrews, Stevens & Assoc., *Contract Svc*
CDI Corp, *Contract Svc*
Construction Secretaries, *Perm. Emp Agcy*
Devau Human Resrcs, *Temp. Agcy*
Fishel Human Resrcs Assoc., *Exec Srch*
Kerry's Referrals, *Temp. Agcy*
Mgmt. Recrtrs of Scottsdale, *Exec Srch*
Personalized Mngmnt Assoc., *Exec Srch*
Priority Staffng, *Perm. Emp Agcy*
Snelling Persnnl Svcs, *Perm. Emp Agcy*
Spectra Intl, *Exec Srch*
Stivers Temp. Persnnl, *Temp. Agcy*

Arkansas

Dunhill Persnnl, *Exec Srch*
Mgmt. Recrtrs of Little Rock, *Exec Srch*
Snelling Srch, *Exec Srch*
Turnage Emp. Svc Grp, *Exec Srch*

California

A Perm. Success Emp. Svcs, *Perm. Emp Agcy*
ABA Staffng, *Exec Srch*
A.S.A.P. Emp. Svc, *Perm. Emp Agcy*
Access Tech. Staffng, *Contract Svc*
The Accnt'g Guild, *Perm. Emp Agcy*
AccuStaff, *Exec Srch*
AccuStaff Co, *Temp. Agcy*
Act 1 Persnnl Svcs, *Perm. Emp Agcy*
Admin. Exec Srch, *Exec Srch*
Advantage Persnnl, *Perm. Emp Agcy*
Allied Srch, *Exec Srch*
Alpha-Net Consltng Grp, *Exec Srch*
Alternative Staffing Grp, *Exec Srch*
Ankenbrandt Grp, *Exec Srch*
Answers Unlimtd, *Temp. Agcy*
John Anthony & Assoc., *Exec Srch*
Apple One Emp. Svcs, *Perm. Emp Agcy*
Apropos Emp. Agcy, *Perm. Emp Agcy*
Arrowstaff Svcs, *Perm. Emp Agcy*
Associated Software Consltnts, *Exec Srch*
The Badger Grp, *Exec Srch*
Ed Bell Assoc., *Exec Srch*
Harvey Bell & Assoc., *Exec Srch*
Blaine & Assoc., *Perm. Emp Agcy*
Bradford Staff, *Temp. Agcy*
Business Syst. Staffing & Assoc., *Perm. Emp Agcy*
CDI Corp, *Temp. Agcy*
CN Assoc., *Exec Srch*
CT Persnnl Svcs, *Perm. Emp Agcy*
California Srch Agcy, *Exec Srch*
Candy Stripers Medical Persnnl, *Perm. Emp Agcy*
Career Advantage, *Exec Srch*
Career Quest, *Contract Svc*

Colorado

Connecticut

Delaware

District of Columbia

Florida

Georgia

Hawaii

Idaho
Horne/Brown Intl, *Exec Srch*
Ward-Hoffman & Assoc., *Exec Srch*

Illinois
A.B.A. Placemnts/A.B.A. Temps, *Perm. Emp Agcy*
The Ability Grp, *Exec Srch*
Adecco, *Temp. Agcy*
Advantage Persnnl, *Perm. Emp Agcy*
Assured Staffng, *Temp. Agcy*
Availability, *Perm. Emp Agcy*
Barry Persnnl Resrcs, *Perm. Emp Agcy*
Bell Persnnl, *Perm. Emp Agcy*
CES, *Exec Srch*
Carson Mngmnt Assoc., *Contract Svc*
CompuPro, *Exec Srch*
Computer Futures Exchange, *Exec Srch*
DayStar Temp. Svcs, *Temp. Agcy*
Dunhill Prof'l Srch of Rolling Meadows, *Exec Srch*
Dynamic Srch Syst., *Exec Srch*
The Esquire Staffing Grp, *Perm. Emp Agcy*
Eve Recrtrs *Perm. Emp Agcy*
Express Persnnl Svcs, *Temp. Agcy*
Fellows Plcmnt, *Temp. Agcy*
General Emp. Enterprises, *Perm. Emp Agcy*
Girman Grp, *Exec Srch*
David Gomez & Assoc., *Exec Srch*
Human Resource Connection, *Perm. Emp Agcy*
Human Resource Technlgy, *Exec Srch*
The Hunter Resource Grp, *Exec Srch*
Illinois Veterans Leadership Program, *Career/Outplacemnt*
Innovative Syst. Grp, *Exec Srch*
Insurance Nat'l Srch/E.J. Ashton & Assoc., *Exec Srch*
Interstaff, *Temp. Agcy*
Jender & Co, *Contract Svc*
Samuel Kroll & Assoc., *Exec Srch*
Kunzer Assoc., *Exec Srch*
Arlene Leff & Assoc., *Exec Srch*
Lynco Mngmnt Persnnl, *Exec Srch*
MBP Persnnl, *Exec Srch*
Magnum Srch, *Exec Srch*
Mgmt. Recrtrs Intl, *Exec Srch*
Mgmt. Recrtrs of Des Plaines, *Exec Srch*
Mgmt. Recrtrs of Rockford, *Exec Srch*
Maramax Persnnl, *Perm. Emp Agcy*
The Murphy Grp, *Perm. Emp Agcy*
NJW & Assoc., *Temp. Agcy*
National Srch, *Exec Srch*
Norrell Svcs, *Temp. Agcy*
Office Ours, *Temp. Agcy*
Officemates5 of Wheeling, *Exec Srch*
OfficeTeam, *Perm. Emp Agcy*
Olsten Staff Svcs, *Temp. Agcy*
Omega Tech. Corp, *Exec Srch*
PS, *Perm. Emp Agcy*
Persnnl Connection, *Perm. Emp Agcy*
Pro Staff Persnnl Svcs, *Temp. Agcy*
Professional Placemnt Svcs, *Exec Srch*
ProSearch Plus, *Exec Srch*
The Raleigh Warwick Grp, *Exec Srch*
Redell Srch, *Exec Srch*
Remedy Intelligent Staffng, *Temp. Agcy*
Right Svcs, *Temp. Agcy*
The Ryan Charles Grp, *Exec Srch*
Sales Consltnts/Mgmt. Recrtrs Intl, *Exec Srch*
Sales Consltnts of Chicago, *Exec Srch*
Sales Consltnts of Oak Brk, *Exec Srch*
Snelling Persnnl Svcs, *Temp. Agcy*
Snelling Srch, *Exec Srch*
Snyder Staffng, *Temp. Agcy*
TDF Corp, *Contract Svc*
Roy Talman & Assoc., *Exec Srch*
Technical Recruitng Consltnts, *Exec Srch*
Temporary Assoc., *Temp. Agcy*
Webb Emp. Svc, *Perm. Emp Agcy*
West Persnnl, *Perm. Emp Agcy*
Working World, *Temp. Agcy*
World Emp. Svc, *Perm. Emp Agcy*

Indiana
Adecco, *Temp. Agcy*
Canis Major/HR Quest, *Exec Srch*
The Consltng Forum, *Exec Srch*
Corporate Staff Resrcs, *Temp. Agcy*
Execusearch, *Exec Srch*
Hobart Emp. Agcy, *Perm. Emp Agcy*
Interim Persnnl, *Temp. Agcy*
Job Placemnt Svc, *Perm. Emp Agcy*
Mac Staffng, *Temp. Agcy*
Mgmt. Recrtrs Intl, *Exec Srch*
Mgmt. Recrtrs of Evansville, *Exec Srch*
Mgmt. Recrtrs of Indianapolis, *Exec Srch*
Mgmt. Recrtrs of Richmond/Staff Solut'ns, *Exec Srch*
National Corporate Consltnts/Advantage Svcs, *Exec Srch*
Oakwood Intl, *Exec Srch*
Officemates5 of Indianapolis, *Exec Srch*
Persnnl Recrtrs, *Exec Srch*
QCI Tech. Staffng, *Contract Svc*
Quiring Assoc. HR Consltng Grp, *Exec Srch*
The Registry, *Perm. Emp Agcy*
TAD Tech. Svcs, *Contract Svc*
H.L. Yoh Co, *Contract Svc*

Iowa
Burton Placemnt Svcs, *Exec Srch*
Byrnes & Rupkey, *Exec Srch*
CSI Employment, *Exec Srch*
Career Srch Assoc., *Exec Srch*
Executive Srch Assoc., *Exec Srch*
Helping Hands Temp. Svc, *Temp. Agcy*
Kelly Svcs, *Temp. Agcy*
Mgmt. Recrtrs Intl, *Exec Srch*
McGladrey Srch Grp, *Exec Srch*
Salem Mngmnt dba Rudy Salem Staff Svcs, *Temp. Agcy*
Staff Mgmt., *Contract Svc*
Nate Viall & Assoc., *Perm. Emp Agcy*

Kansas
Alternative Staffing & Persnnl, *Temp. Agcy*
Business Specialists, *Perm. Emp Agcy*
Dunhill Persnnl, *Exec Srch*
Eleventh Hour Staff Svcs, *Temp. Agcy*
Mgmt. Recrtrs of Overlnd Prk, *Exec Srch*
Morgan Hunter Corp Srch, *Perm. Emp Agcy*

Kentucky
Angel Grp Intl, *Exec Srch*
Manpower, *Temp. Agcy*
Karen Marshall Assoc., *Exec Srch*
OfficeTeam, *Temp. Agcy*
Precision Staffng, *Perm. Emp Agcy*
Snelling Persnnl Svcs, *Exec Srch*
Source Svcs Corp, *Exec Srch*

Louisiana
Ascent Consltng Grp, *Temp. Agcy*
Mgmt. Recrtrs of Baton Rouge, *Exec Srch*
Mgmt. Recrtrs-Metairie/Sales Consltnts, *Exec Srch*
Snelling Persnnl Svcs, *Exec Srch*
Talley & Assoc./Talley Temps, *Exec Srch*
Western Staff Svcs, *Temp. Agcy*

Maine
Accomplished Prof'ls, *Temp. Agcy*
Career Mngmnt Assoc., *Exec Srch*
Executive Srch of N.E., *Exec Srch*

Maryland
Admin Persnnl Svcs, *Perm. Emp Agcy*
Capitol Staff Solut'ns, *Temp. Agcy*
Contemporaries, *Temp. Agcy*
Employer Employee Exchange, *Exec Srch*
Futures, *Exec Srch*
L.S. Gross & Assoc., *Exec Srch*
Interim Persnnl, *Temp. Agcy*
JDG Assoc. Limited, *Exec Srch*
J.R. Assoc., *Perm. Emp Agcy*
Mgmt. Recrtrs of Annapolis, *Exec Srch*
Mgmt. Recrtrs-Baltimore/Sales Consltnts, *Exec Srch*
Mgmt. Recrtrs-Bethesda/CompuSearch, *Exec Srch*
Mgmt. Recrtrs of Frederick, *Exec Srch*
Merit Emp. Agcy, *Perm. Emp Agcy*
Micro Temps, *Temp. Agcy*
Onsite Commercial Staffng, *Perm. Emp Agcy*
Quest Syst., *Perm. Emp Agcy*
Sales Consltnts of Prince Georges Cnty, *Exec Srch*
TAD Staff Svcs, *Temp. Agcy*
Temps & Co, *Temp. Agcy*
Virtual Staff Svcs, *Perm. Emp Agcy*
White Ridgely Assoc., *Career/Outplacemnt*
Winston Srch, *Exec Srch*

Massachusetts
ABA Persnnl, *Temp. Agcy*
Abbot Persnnl Consltng Svcs, *Perm. Emp Agcy*
Ability Srch of N.E., *Perm. Emp Agcy*
Adecco, *Temp. Agcy*
Bradford Barnes Assoc., *Exec Srch*
C.R.W. & Assoc., *Perm. Emp Agcy*
Campbell Assoc., *Exec Srch*
Ciak Assoc., *Exec Srch*
Cleary Consltnts, *Perm. Emp Agcy*
Corporate Staff Solut'ns, *Temp. Agcy*
Derby Assoc., *Perm. Emp Agcy*
Discovery Persnnl, *Perm. Emp Agcy*
Diversity Srch Specialists, *Exec Srch*
Dunhill Staffing Syst., *Temp. Agcy*
EF Tech. Resrcs, *Perm. Emp Agcy*
Ford & Ford Exec Srch, *Exec Srch*
Harvest Persnnl, *Exec Srch*
I.T. Resrcs, *Perm. Emp Agcy*
John Leonard Persnnl Assoc., *Perm. Emp Agcy*
Logix, *Exec Srch*
Lynx, *Contract Svc*
Mgmt. Recrtrs Intl, *Exec Srch*
Mgmt. Recrtrs Intl of Braintree, *Exec Srch*
Mgmt. Recrtrs Intl of Springfield, *Exec Srch*
Mgmt. Recrtrs Intl of Westboro, *Exec Srch*
F.L. Mannix & Co, *Exec Srch*
Manpower, *Temp. Agcy*
McDevitt Assoc., *Exec Srch*
Morency Assoc., *Exec Srch*
Need Persnnl Plcmnt, *Temp. Agcy*
New Boston Select Staffng, *Temp. Agcy*
New England Persnnl, *Perm. Emp Agcy*
New England Srch, *Exec Srch*
Norrell Staff Svcs, *Contract Svc*
OfficeTeam, *Temp. Agcy*
Olsten Prof'l Accnt'g Svcs, *Exec Srch*
Olsten Staff Svcs, *Temp. Agcy*
Phillips & Assoc., *Exec Srch*
Pro Staff, *Temp. Agcy*
ProSearch, *Exec Srch*
J.E. Ranta Assoc., *Exec Srch*
Reardon Assoc., *Perm. Emp Agcy*
Routhier Placemnt Specialists, *Perm. Emp Agcy*
Sales Consltnts of Cape Cod, *Exec Srch*
Sales Consltnts of Plymouth Cnty, *Exec Srch*
Sales Consltnts of Wellesley, *Exec Srch*
George Sandel Assoc., *Perm. Emp Agcy*
Snelling Persnnl Svcs, *Perm. Emp Agcy*
Stone Consltng Grp & Legal Srch Specialists, *Exec Srch*
Tech Resource, *Contract Svc*
Timely Solut'ns, *Perm. Emp Agcy*
Total Tech. Svcs, *Perm. Emp Agcy*
Tricor Assoc., *Temp. Agcy*
Volt Svcs Grp, *Temp. Agcy*
S.B. Webster & Assoc., *Exec Srch*
WIND Job Ctr, *Career/Outplacemnt*
The Work Place, *Career/Outplacemnt*
Wright Assoc., *Exec Srch*

Michigan
AJM Prof'l Svcs, *Exec Srch*
Accountemps/Officeteam, *Temp. Agcy*
Advance Employment, *Exec Srch*
Advanced Resrcs of MI, *Contract Svc*
Advanced Tech. Resrcs, *Exec Srch*
The Aucon Co, *Exec Srch*
Beacon Svcs, *Exec Srch*
Career Quest, *Perm. Emp Agcy*
CIBER, *Contract Svc*
Corporate Staff Resrcs, *Perm. Emp Agcy*
Dynamic People, *Temp. Agcy*
Executive Mngmnt Srch, *Exec Srch*
Executive Recrtrs Intl, *Exec Srch*
GRS, *Exec Srch*
Joseph Goldring & Assoc., *Exec Srch*
Robert Half Intl, *Exec Srch*
The Hallman Grp, *Exec Srch*
Healthcare Recrtrs Intl, *Exec Srch*
Harvey Hohauser & Assoc., *Exec Srch*
Job Fair Netwrk of MI, *Perm. Emp Agcy*
Kelly Tech. Svcs, *Contract Svc*
Key Persnnl, *Perm. Emp Agcy*
David Lindemer Assoc., *Exec Srch*
Mgmt. Recrtrs of Battle Creek, *Exec Srch*
Mgmt. Recrtrs of Bingham Farms, *Exec Srch*
Mgmt. Recrtrs of Dearborn, *Exec Srch*
Mgmt. Recrtrs of Flint, *Exec Srch*
Mgmt. Recrtrs of Kalamazoo, *Exec Srch*
Mgmt. Recrtrs of Lansing, *Exec Srch*
Mgmt. Recrtrs of Livonia, *Exec Srch*
Mgmt. Recrtrs of Muskegon, *Exec Srch*
Mgmt. Recrtrs of Rochester, *Exec Srch*
Manpower Tech. Svcs, *Contract Svc*
Michigan Srch Plus, *Exec Srch*
Office Staffing Recruitng, *Exec Srch*
Open Page Srch Svcs, *Exec Srch*
Preferred Emp. Planning, *Perm. Emp Agcy*
Professional Career Srch, *Exec Srch*
Professional Persnnl Consltnts Intl, *Exec Srch*
Professional Resource Assoc., *Contract Svc*
ProSearch, *Exec Srch*
RHI Consltng, *Contract Svc*
Sales Consltnts of Detroit, *Exec Srch*
Source EDP, *Perm. Emp Agcy*
Trillium Staffng, *Temp. Agcy*
Unlimited Staff Solut'ns, *Contract Svc*
Wise Persnnl Svcs, *Perm. Emp Agcy*
Your Preference Referral Netwrk, *Perm. Emp Agcy*

Minnesota
Add On Staff Solut'ns, *Temp. Agcy*
Computer Employment, *Exec Srch*
Diversified Employment, *Perm. Emp Agcy*
EHS & Assoc., *Exec Srch*
Ells Persnnl Syst., *Exec Srch*
Firstaff, *Perm. Emp Agcy*
T.H. Hunter, *Exec Srch*
Mgmt. Recrtrs-Minneapolis/Sales Consltnts, *Exec Srch*
Manpower Tech. Svcs, *Perm. Emp Agcy*
NER (National Engineering Resrcs), *Exec Srch*
North American Recrtrs, *Exec Srch*
Sathe & Assoc. Exec Srch, *Exec Srch*
Systems Srch, *Exec Srch*

Mgmt. Recrtrs Intl, *Exec Srch*
Mgmt. Recrtrs of Cincinnati, *Exec Srch*
Mgmt. Recrtrs of Cleveland, *Exec Srch*
Mgmt. Recrtrs of Columbus, *Exec Srch*
Mgmt. Recrtrs of Dayton, *Exec Srch*
Mgmt. Recrtrs of No. Canton, *Exec Srch*
Mgmt. Recrtrs of Solon, *Exec Srch*
Messina Mngmnt Syst., *Exec Srch*
Midland Consltnts, *Exec Srch*
Northcoast Persnnl, *Exec Srch*
Olsten Prof'l Staff Svcs, *Exec Srch*
Olsten Staff Svcs, *Temp. Agcy*
Jerry Paul Assoc., *Perm. Emp Agcy*
Providence Persnnl Consltnts, *Exec Srch*
Sales Consltnts of Cincinnati, *Exec Srch*
Sanford Rose Assoc. of Cleveland, *Exec Srch*
Sanford Rose Assoc. of Columbus, *Exec Srch*
Sanford Rose Assoc. of Youngstown, *Exec Srch*
Snelling Persnnl Svcs, *Exec Srch*
Sterling Persnnl Resrcs, *Exec Srch*
TAD Tech. Svcs, *Contract Svc*
Talent Tree Staffng, *Perm. Emp Agcy*
J.P. Walton & Assoc., *Exec Srch*

Oklahoma

Ameri Resource, *Exec Srch*
Cherokee Temps, *Temp. Agcy*
Robert Half Intl, *Exec Srch*
Key Temp. Persnnl, *Temp. Agcy*
Mgmt. Recrtrs Intl, *Exec Srch*
Mgmt. Recrtrs of Oklahoma Cty, *Exec Srch*
Terry Neese Persnnl Agcy, *Exec Srch*
StaffMark, *Temp. Agcy*

Oregon

Adams Temps, *Temp. Agcy*
Express Persnnl Svcs, *Exec Srch*
Kelly Svcs, *Temp. Agcy*
Mgmt. Recrtrs/Officemates5 of Portland, *Exec Srch*
Office Careers, *Perm. Emp Agcy*
Saint Vincent De Paul Employment, *Temp. Agcy*
Southern Oregon Temporary, *Temp. Agcy*
Talent Tree Staffng, *Perm. Emp Agcy*
Triad Technlgy Grp, *Perm. Emp Agcy*

Pennsylvania

Adecco, *Temp. Agcy*
Advanced Technlgy Resrcs, *Exec Srch*
All Staffng, *Perm. Emp Agcy*
Allegheny Persnnl Svcs, *Temp. Agcy*
ASAP Staffng, *Perm. Emp Agcy*
Ashley Srch Consltnts, *Exec Srch*
T.W. Boris Assn, *Exec Srch*
CDI Corp, *Contract Svc*
Career Concepts Staff Svcs, *Exec Srch*
Career Quest Confidential, *Exec Srch*
Charly's Temp. Svcs, *Temp. Agcy*
P. Robert Dann, *Exec Srch*
Rob DePaul & Assoc., *Exec Srch*
DiCenzo Persnnl Specialists, *Perm. Emp Agcy*
Dunn Assoc., *Exec Srch*
EDP/Temps of PA, *Temp. Agcy*
Executive Avail-A-Search, *Exec Srch*
Financial Industry Staff Co, *Perm. Emp Agcy*
General Emp. & Triad Persnnl, *Perm. Emp Agcy*
Merrill Grumer Assoc., *Perm. Emp Agcy*
The Hastings Grp, *Exec Srch*
Human Resource Solut'ns, *Exec Srch*
Interim Persnnl, *Temp. Agcy*
J-Rand Srch, *Exec Srch*
Nancy Jackson, *Exec Srch*
Jefferson-Ross Assoc., *Exec Srch*
Kathy Karr Persnnl, *Perm. Emp Agcy*
London Persnnl Svcs, *Perm. Emp Agcy*
Mgmt. Recrtrs of DE Cnty/CompuSrch, *Exec Srch*
Mgmt. Recrtrs of Lehigh Vly/CompuSrch, *Exec Srch*
Mgmt. Recrtrs of Philadelphia/ CompuSrch, *Exec Srch*
J. McManus Assoc., *Perm. Emp Agcy*
Metro Persnnl, *Temp. Agcy*
OfficeTeam, *Temp. Agcy*
Olsten Staff Svcs, *Temp. Agcy*
LaMonte Owens, *Exec Srch*
Pancoast Temp. Svcs, *Temp. Agcy*
Q-Source, *Perm. Emp Agcy*
Quest Syst., *Perm. Emp Agcy*
Alan Raeburn Consltnts, *Exec Srch*
Rice Cohen Intl, *Exec Srch*
The Richards Grp, *Exec Srch*
Select Persnnl, *Perm. Emp Agcy*
Source EDP, *Perm. Emp Agcy*
Spectrum Consltnts/Retail Recrtrs, *Exec Srch*
Strohl Syst., *Perm. Emp Agcy*
Systems Persnnl, *Exec Srch*
TRC Staff Svcs, *Temp. Agcy*
TAD Tech. Svcs, *Temp. Agcy*
Tandem Persnnl, *Temp. Agcy*
Terry Taylor & Assoc., *Exec Srch*
W.G. Tucker & Assoc., *Exec Srch*
Uni Temp Temp. Svc, *Temp. Agcy*
Uniforce Temp. Svcs, *Temp. Agcy*
United Tech. Assoc., *Temp. Agcy*
Vogue Persnnl, *Perm. Emp Agcy*

Rhode Island

Colony Persnnl Assoc., *Perm. Emp Agcy*
Dorra Srch, *Exec Srch*
Kelly Svcs, *Temp. Agcy*
Albert Lee & Assoc., *Exec Srch*
Mgmt. Recrtrs Intl, *Exec Srch*
Norrell Svcs, *Temp. Agcy*
Persnnl People, *Perm. Emp Agcy*
Pro Staff Persnnl Svcs, *Temp. Agcy*
Storti Assoc., *Exec Srch*
Tad Staff Svc/Tad Staff Svc/Technical Division, *Exec Srch*

South Carolina

Eastern Persnnl Svcs, *Exec Srch*
FORTUNE Persnnl Consltnts of Columbia, *Exec Srch*
Harvey Persnnl, *Perm. Emp Agcy*
Mgmt. Recrtrs of Columbia, *Exec Srch*
Mgmt. Recrtrs of Rck Hill, *Exec Srch*
Miller & Assoc., *Exec Srch*
PRL & Assoc., *Perm. Emp Agcy*
The Persnnl Netwrk, *Exec Srch*
Phillips Resource Grp, *Exec Srch*
Smith Temps/Smith Persnnl, *Temp. Agcy*
Snelling Persnnl Svcs, *Perm. Emp Agcy*
Southern Recrtrs & Consltnts, *Exec Srch*
TRS (Total Recruitng Svcs), *Perm. Emp Agcy*

South Dakota

Availability Employment, *Temp. Agcy*

Tennessee

A-1 Staffing & Persnnl, *Temp. Agcy*
Anderson McIntyre Persnnl Svcs, *Exec Srch*
B.K. Barnes & Assoc., *Exec Srch*
Carroll & Assoc., *Exec Srch*
Cook Assoc. Intl, *Exec Srch*
FORTUNE Persnnl Consltnts, *Exec Srch*
Gateway Grp Persnnl, *Temp. Agcy*
Robert Half Intl, *Contract Svc*
Hamilton Ryker Co, *Exec Srch*
J&D Resrcs, *Exec Srch*
Kelly Svcs, *Temp. Agcy*
Mgmt. Recrtrs/Sales Consltnts-Chattanooga, *Exec Srch*
Mgmt. Recrtrs of Chattanooga, *Exec Srch*
Mgmt. Recrtrs of Knoxville, *Exec Srch*
Manpower Temp. Svcs, *Temp. Agcy*
The Morgan Grp, *Exec Srch*
Olsten Staff Svcs, *Temp. Agcy*
Piercy Emp. Svcs, *Perm. Emp Agcy*
Sales Consltnts of Nashville, *Exec Srch*
Snelling Persnnl Svcs, *Exec Srch*
Unlimited Staff Solut'ns, *Contract Svc*

Texas

Accounting Action Persnnl, *Perm. Emp Agcy*
Action Persnnl, *Temp. Agcy*
Add-A-Temp/Woodlands Exec Employment, *Temp. Agcy*
Adecco, *Temp. Agcy*
Agri-LC, *Exec Srch*
Albrecht & Assoc. Exec Srch, *Exec Srch*
Attorney Resrcs, *Temp. Agcy*
Audit Prof'ls Intl, *Exec Srch*
Aware Affiliates Persnnl, *Perm. Emp Agcy*
Babich & Assoc., *Perm. Emp Agcy*
Belcan Tech. Svcs, *Contract Svc*
Ann Best Elite Temps, *Temp. Agcy*
Boles & Assoc., *Exec Srch*
Brainpower Persnnl Agcy, *Perm. Emp Agcy*
Bridge Persnnl, *Exec Srch*
Brown & Keene Persnnl, *Perm. Emp Agcy*
Bullock Persnnl, *Perm. Emp Agcy*
Bundy-Stewart Assoc., *Exec Srch*
Burnett's Staffng, *Perm. Emp Agcy*
Cherbonnier Grp, *Exec Srch*
Continental Persnnl, *Perm. Emp Agcy*
Corbett Persnnl Svcs, *Temp. Agcy*
Dallas Emp. Svc, *Perm. Emp Agcy*
Gail Darling Staffing/Darling's Prof'l Desk, *Temp. Agcy*
Day Star Svcs, *Perm. Emp Agcy*
Diversified Temps, *Temp. Agcy*
Donovan & Watkins, *Perm. Emp Agcy*
E&A Persnnl Svcs, *Perm. Emp Agcy*
Employee Sources, *Exec Srch*
Esprit Temp. Svcs, *Temp. Agcy*
Executive Srch Persnnl, *Exec Srch*
Express Persnnl Svcs, *Perm. Emp Agcy*
Claire Fontaine & Assoc., *Exec Srch*
Robert Half Intl, *Perm. Emp Agcy*
The Human Element of Business, *Exec Srch*
Imprimis Staff Solut'ns, *Temp. Agcy*
Inside Track, *Exec Srch*
L.K. Jordan & Assoc., *Contract Svc*
Kelly Svcs, *Temp. Agcy*
Lusk & Assoc. Persnnl, *Exec Srch*
Mgmt. Recrtrs Intl, *Exec Srch*
Mgmt. Recrtrs of Dallas, *Exec Srch*
Metro Careers, *Exec Srch*
O'Keefe & Assoc., *Perm. Emp Agcy*
Olsten Staff Svcs, *Temp. Agcy*
The Pailin Grp, *Exec Srch*
Pate Resrcs Grp, *Exec Srch*
The Persnnl Connection, *Perm. Emp Agcy*
The Persnnl Office, *Exec Srch*
Persnnl One, *Perm. Emp Agcy*
Phoenix Staffng, *Exec Srch*
Priority Persnnl, *Temp. Agcy*
Pro Staff Persnnl Svcs, *Temp. Agcy*
Professions Today, *Perm. Emp Agcy*
Remedy Intelligent Staffng, *Perm. Emp Agcy*
Resource Staffng, *Contract Svc*
SOS Staff Svcs, *Temp. Agcy*
Sales Consltnts of Houston, *Exec Srch*
Select Staff, *Exec Srch*
Snelling Persnnl Svcs, *Perm. Emp Agcy*
Staff Extension, *Exec Srch*
Steele & Assoc., *Perm. Emp Agcy*
Stehouwer & Assoc., *Perm. Emp Agcy*
Suburban Svcs, *Temp. Agcy*
TAD Tech. Svcs, *Contract Svc*
Tarrant Cnty Emp. Netwrk, *Perm. Emp Agcy*
Thomas Office Persnnl, *Perm. Emp Agcy*
Todays Temporary, *Temp. Agcy*
Total Persnnl, *Exec Srch*
The Urban Placemnt Svc, *Exec Srch*
Dick Van Vliet & Assoc., *Exec Srch*
Wheeler, Moore & Elam Co, *Exec Srch*
The Whitaker Companies, *Exec Srch*
H.L. Yoh Co, *Contract Svc*

Utah

Robert Half Intl, *Exec Srch*
Mgmt. Recrtrs Intl, *Exec Srch*
Professional Recrtrs, *Exec Srch*

Vermont

Eckler Persnnl Netwrk, *Exec Srch*
The Persnnl Connection, *Temp. Agcy*
TAD Resrcs, *Perm. Emp Agcy*

Virginia

A Better Resume, *Career/Outplacemnt*
Adams Sources, *Exec Srch*
Nancy Allen Assoc., *Perm. Emp Agcy*
Alpha Omega Resrcs, *Perm. Emp Agcy*
American Tech. Resrcs, *Perm. Emp Agcy*
Computemp of Washington, D.C., *Temp. Agcy*
Corporate Connection Exec. Srch Firm
Carol Day & Assoc., *Exec Srch*
EDP, *Temp. Agcy*
Effective Staffng, *Exec Srch*
Engineering & MIS Guild, *Exec Srch*
Express Persnnl Svcs, *Temp. Agcy*
Halbrecht & Co, *Exec Srch*
HATCH Mrktng Syst., *Perm. Emp Agcy*
Lee Staffing Resrcs, *Exec Srch*
Mgmt. Recrtrs of McLean, *Exec Srch*
Mgmt. Recrtrs of Roanoke, *Exec Srch*
Norrell Staff Svcs, *Exec Srch*
Procurement Solut'ns, *Contract Svc*
Professional Srch Persnnl, *Exec Srch*
Remedy Intelligent Staffng, *Temp. Agcy*
Don Richard Assoc. of Richmond, *Exec Srch*
Select Staff Svcs, *Perm. Emp Agcy*
Selectemps, *Temp. Agcy*
Snelling Persnnl Svcs, *Perm. Emp Agcy*
Strategic Staffing/SSI Tech. Svcs Division, *Contract Svc*
TAC Staff Svcs, *Temp. Agcy*
Task Force of VA, *Exec Srch*
Temporary Solut'ns, *Temp. Agcy*
TempWorld Staff Svcs, *Temp. Agcy*
Virginia Emp. Referral Svc, *Exec Srch*
Bill Young & Assoc., *Exec Srch*

Washington

BSP & Assoc., *Exec Srch*
The Career Clinic, *Exec Srch*
Comprehensive Staff Resrcs dba Techstaff, *Temp. Agcy*
Cooper Persnnl, *Temp. Agcy*
Houser, Martin, Morris & Assoc., *Exec Srch*
The Jobs Co, *Exec Srch*
Kelly Svcs, *Temp. Agcy*
Mgmt. Recrtrs of Mercer Islnd, *Exec Srch*
Mgmt. Recrtrs of No. Tacoma, *Exec Srch*
Mgmt. Recrtrs of Seattle, *Exec Srch*
Mgmt. Recrtrs of Tacoma, *Exec Srch*
Manpower Temp. Svcs, *Temp. Agcy*
Nelson, Coulson & Assoc., *Perm. Emp Agcy*
Northwest Temp. Svcs, *Temp. Agcy*
Olsten Staff Svcs, *Temp. Agcy*
Persnnl Unlimtd, *Exec Srch*
Snelling Persnnl Svcs, *Exec Srch*
Staffing Resrcs, *Perm. Emp Agcy*

New Jersey
A Prof'l Edge, *Career/Outplacemnt*
Advanced Persnnl, *Perm. Emp Agcy*
Blake & Assoc. Exec Srch, *Exec Srch*
Career Ctr, *Perm. Emp Agcy*
Career Srch Assoc., *Exec Srch*
Express Persnnl Svcs, *Perm. Emp Agcy*
Horizon Graphics Persnnl, *Perm. Emp Agcy*
Impact Persnnl, *Perm. Emp Agcy*
Kelly Svcs, *Temp. Agcy*
Key Employment, *Exec Srch*
Mgmt. Recrtrs of Passaic Cnty, *Exec Srch*
Mini Conglomerate Svc, *Perm. Emp Agcy*
Officemates5 of Englewood Cliffs/DayStar Temp. Svcs, *Perm. Emp Agcy*
Orion Consltng, *Exec Srch*
Premier Persnnl Grp, *Perm. Emp Agcy*
Sales Consltnts, *Exec Srch*
Sales Consltnts of Ocean, *Exec Srch*
Sales Consltnts of Sparta, *Exec Srch*
Temps Plus, *Temp. Agcy*
Winston Staff Svcs, *Temp. Agcy*
Claire Wright Assn, *Perm. Emp Agcy*

New Mexico
Albuquerque Persnnl, *Perm. Emp Agcy*
Santa Fe Svcs, *Temp. Agcy*

New York
Accounting & Computer Persnnl, *Perm. Emp Agcy*
Merrill Adams Assoc., *Career/Outplacemnt*
Adecco, *Temp. Agcy*
Asher Persnnl Consltnts, *Perm. Emp Agcy*
Benson Assoc., *Exec Srch*
Bornholdt Shivas & Friends, *Exec Srch*
Branthover Assoc., *Exec Srch*
C.C. Burke Limited, *Perm. Emp Agcy*
CDI Corp, *Contract Svc*
CGR Staff Svcs, *Temp. Agcy*
Career Blazers Persnnl, *Perm. Emp Agcy*
Seth Diamond Assoc., *Exec Srch*
Maggi Dolan Plcmnt, *Perm. Emp Agcy*
Eden Persnnl, *Perm. Emp Agcy*
Kris Edwards Agcy, *Exec Srch*
Employment Recrtrs Agcy, *Perm. Emp Agcy*
Euromonde, *Temp. Agcy*
Extra Help Emp. Svc, *Temp. Agcy*
Freelance Advancers, *Temp. Agcy*
The Fry Grp, *Exec Srch*
Genesis Emp. Consltnts, *Exec Srch*
Graphics For Hire, *Perm. Emp Agcy*
Robert Half Intl/Information Syst. Division, *Exec Srch*
Headway Corporate Staff Svcs, *Temp. Agcy*
Ruth Hirsch Assoc., *Exec Srch*
Hot Bear/De Bella Prodctns & Editor'l Temps, *Temp. Agcy*
Innovations Assoc., *Perm. Emp Agcy*
KLK Persnnl, *Perm. Emp Agcy*
The Kay Grp of Fifth Avenue, *Exec Srch*
Lawrence Exec Srch, *Exec Srch*
Michael John Lawrence & Assoc., *Exec Srch*
Mgmt. Recrtrs of Gramercy, *Exec Srch*
Morgan-Murray Persnnl/M&M Top Temps, *Temp. Agcy*
Noble & Assoc., *Exec Srch*
Optimal Resrcs, *Exec Srch*
Preferred Prof'ls, *Temp. Agcy*
Redwood/Casey, *Exec Srch*
Rem Resrcs, *Perm. Emp Agcy*
Rep Temps, *Temp. Agcy*
Ribolow Assoc., *Perm. Emp Agcy*
Swing Shift, *Temp. Agcy*
Hillary Taylor Persnnl, *Perm. Emp Agcy*
Temp Force of NY, *Temp. Agcy*
TemPositions, *Temp. Agcy*
Trebor, Weldon, Lawrence, Levine, *Exec Srch*
United Persnnl Agcy, *Perm. Emp Agcy*
Vintage Resrcs, *Exec Srch*
Don Waldron & Assoc., *Perm. Emp Agcy*
Werbin Assoc. Exec Srch, *Exec Srch*
S.R. Wolman Assoc., *Exec Srch*

North Carolina
Employment Consltnts, *Contract Svc*
Kelly Svcs, *Temp. Agcy*
Mgmt. Recrtrs Intl, *Exec Srch*
Mgmt. Recrtrs of Durham, *Exec Srch*
Mgmt. Recrtrs of Winston-Salem, *Exec Srch*
Olsten Staff Svcs, *Temp. Agcy*
Sales Consltnts of High Point, *Exec Srch*
Sparks Persnnl Svcs, *Exec Srch*

North Dakota
Olsten Staff Svcs/Kramer & Assoc./Expressway Persnnl, *Temp. Agcy*
Persnnl Svcs, *Exec Srch*

Ohio
Adecco, *Perm. Emp Agcy*
J.B. Brown & Assoc., *Exec Srch*
Champion Persnnl, *Perm. Emp Agcy*
Combined Resrcs, *Exec Srch*
Drayton & Assoc., *Exec Srch*
Eastern Persnnl Svcs, *Perm. Emp Agcy*
Executech Consltnts, *Exec Srch*
Fristoe & Carlton, *Exec Srch*
Hite Exec Srch/Hite Mngmnt Consltnts, *Exec Srch*
Ives & Assoc., *Exec Srch*
Mgmt. Recrtrs of Cincinnati, *Exec Srch*
Mgmt. Recrtrs of Cleveland, *Exec Srch*
Mgmt. Recrtrs of Columbus, *Exec Srch*
Mgmt. Recrtrs of Dayton, *Exec Srch*
Mgmt. Recrtrs of Solon, *Exec Srch*
Providence Persnnl Consltnts, *Exec Srch*
Sales Consltnts of Cincinnati, *Exec Srch*
Sanker & Assoc., *Temp. Agcy*
Snelling Persnnl Svcs, *Exec Srch*

Oklahoma
Express Persnnl Svcs, *Exec Srch*
Key Temp. Persnnl, *Temp. Agcy*
Mgmt. Recrtrs of Oklahoma Cty, *Exec Srch*
StaffMark, *Temp. Agcy*

Oregon
Able Temp. Svc, *Temp. Agcy*
Mgmt. Recrtrs/Officemates5 of Portland, *Exec Srch*

Pennsylvania
All Staffng, *Perm. Emp Agcy*
Charly's Temp. Svcs, *Temp. Agcy*
Pat Lipton & Assoc., *Exec Srch*
Mgmt. Recrtrs of DE Cnty/CompuSrch, *Exec Srch*
Mgmt. Recrtrs of Lehigh Vly/CompuSrch, *Exec Srch*
Mgmt. Recrtrs of Philadelphia/ CompuSrch, *Exec Srch*
Olsten Staff Svcs, *Temp. Agcy*
Rice Cohen Intl, *Exec Srch*
The Richards Grp, *Exec Srch*
Spectrum Consltnts/Retail Recrtrs, *Exec Srch*
TRC Staff Svcs, *Temp. Agcy*
TAC Staff Svcs, *Temp. Agcy*
Uni Temp Temp. Svc, *Temp. Agcy*
Vogue Persnnl, *Perm. Emp Agcy*

Rhode Island
Albert Lee & Assoc., *Exec Srch*
Mgmt. Recrtrs Intl, *Exec Srch*
TAC Staff Svcs, *Temp. Agcy*

South Carolina
Mgmt. Recrtrs of Columbia, *Exec Srch*
Mgmt. Recrtrs of Rck Hill, *Exec Srch*

Tennessee
Anderson McIntyre Persnnl Svcs, *Exec Srch*
Mgmt. Recrtrs of Knoxville, *Exec Srch*
Persnnl Link, *Exec Srch*
Sales Consltnts of Nashville, *Exec Srch*

Texas
Ackerman Johnson, *Exec Srch*
Agri-LC, *Exec Srch*
Aware Affiliates Persnnl, *Perm. Emp Agcy*
BestStaff Svcs, *Perm. Emp Agcy*
Carpenter & Assoc., *Exec Srch*
Evins Persnnl Consltnts of Killeen, *Perm. Emp Agcy*
Abel Gonzalez & Assoc., *Exec Srch*
Houston Creative Connections, *Exec Srch*
Mgmt. Recrtrs Intl, *Exec Srch*
Mgmt. Recrtrs of Dallas, *Exec Srch*
The Pailin Grp, *Exec Srch*
Pro Staff Persnnl Svcs, *Temp. Agcy*
Remedy Intelligent Staffng, *Perm. Emp Agcy*
Roth Young Persnnl Svcs, *Exec Srch*
Sales Consltnts of Houston, *Exec Srch*
Salinas & Assoc. Persnnl, *Exec Srch*
Search Com, *Exec Srch*

Virginia
Adams Sources, *Exec Srch*
Lee Staffing Resrcs, *Exec Srch*
Mgmt. Recrtrs of McLean, *Exec Srch*
Mgmt. Recrtrs of Roanoke, *Exec Srch*
Norrell Staff Svcs, *Exec Srch*
Placement Prof'ls, *Exec Srch*
Snelling Persnnl Svcs, *Perm. Emp Agcy*
TAC Staff Svcs, *Temp. Agcy*
Virginia Emp. Referral Svc, *Exec Srch*

Washington
Express Persnnl Svcs, *Temp. Agcy*
Mgmt. Recrtrs of Mercer Islnd, *Exec Srch*
Mgmt. Recrtrs of Tacoma, *Exec Srch*

Wisconsin
The Exutec Grp, *Exec Srch*
Kordus Consltng Grp, *Exec Srch*
MacPros, *Perm. Emp Agcy*
Mgmt. Recrtrs of Green Bay, *Exec Srch*
Mgmt. Recrtrs of Milwaukee, *Exec Srch*

AEROSPACE

Arizona
Electronic Power Source, *Exec Srch*

Maryland
Wallach Assoc., *Exec Srch*

New Jersey
Dynamic Recrtrs, *Exec Srch*

New York
Cowin Assoc., *Exec Srch*

Texas
B&M Air & Space Division, *Contract Svc*
Butler Intl, *Contract Svc*
Opportunity Unlimtd Persnnl Consltnts, *Exec Srch*
TAD Tech. Svcs, *Contract Svc*

Virginia
FGI, *Exec Srch*

Washington
CDI Corp, *Contract Svc*
CTS Tech. Svcs, *Contract Svc*

AGRI-BUSINESS

California
Agri Srch Intl, *Exec Srch*
Valley Wide Employment, *Exec Srch*

Georgia
Agri-Assoc., *Exec Srch*
Agri-Persnnl, *Exec Srch*

Illinois
Agra Placemnts Exec. Srch Firm

Indiana
Agra Placemnts, *Perm. Emp Agcy*

Iowa
Agra Placemnts Exec. Srch Firm

Minnesota
Youth Emp. Project, *Perm. Emp Agcy*

Nebraska
Dunhill Prof'l Srch, *Exec Srch*

Oklahoma
Mgmt. Srch, *Exec Srch*

Pennsylvania
Northeast Agri Emp. Svc, *Perm. Emp Agcy*

AGRICULTURE

Arizona
Mgmt. Recrtrs Intl, *Exec Srch*

Illinois
Agra Placemnts Exec. Srch Firm

Kansas
Mgmt. Recrtrs of Topeka, *Exec Srch*

Minnesota
Agro Quality Srch, *Perm. Emp Agcy*

Missouri
Agri-Assoc., *Exec Srch*
Agri-Tech Persnnl, *Exec Srch*

Nebraska
Sales Consltnts of Omaha, *Exec Srch*

North Carolina
Mgmt. Recrtrs of High Point, *Exec Srch*

Oregon
Able Temp. Svc, *Temp. Agcy*

Wyoming
The Emp. Place, *Perm. Emp Agcy*

APPAREL

Alabama
General Persnnl Corp, *Perm. Emp Agcy*

California
American Magna Srch, *Exec Srch*

Colorado
Lee Mgmt. Grp, *Perm. Emp Agcy*

The Jobs Market, *Perm. Emp Agcy*
MTS, *Perm. Emp Agcy*
Mgmt. Recrtrs Intl, *Exec Srch*
Mgmt. Recrtrs of Durham, *Exec Srch*
Mgmt. Recrtrs of Winston-Salem, *Exec Srch*
Moffitt Intl, *Exec Srch*
Sales Consltnts of High Point, *Exec Srch*

North Dakota
Olsten Staff Svcs/Kramer & Assoc./Expressway Persnnl, *Temp. Agcy*

Ohio
Delta Design Drafting, *Temp. Agcy*
Eastern Persnnl Svcs, *Perm. Emp Agcy*
Employment Solut'ns Grp, *Exec Srch*
Gayhart & Assoc., *Exec Srch*
J.D. Hersey & Assoc., *Exec Srch*
Hite Exec Srch/Hite Mngmnt Consltnts, *Exec Srch*
Laine's S.M.G., *Perm. Emp Agcy*
Mgmt. Recrtrs Intl, *Exec Srch*
Mgmt. Recrtrs of Cincinnati, *Exec Srch*
Mgmt. Recrtrs of Cleveland, *Exec Srch*
Mgmt. Recrtrs of Columbus, *Exec Srch*
Mgmt. Recrtrs of Dayton, *Exec Srch*
Mgmt. Recrtrs of Solon, *Exec Srch*
North Star Resrcs, *Contract Svc*
O'Brien & Roof Co, *Exec Srch*
Sales Consltnts of Cincinnati, *Exec Srch*
TAD Tech. Svcs, *Contract Svc*

Oklahoma
Mgmt. Recrtrs of Oklahoma Cty, *Exec Srch*

Oregon
Barrett Bus. Svcs, *Temp. Agcy*
Corporate Builders, *Exec Srch*
Mgmt. Recrtrs/Officemates5 of Portland, *Exec Srch*
NPRC/Nationwde Persnnl Recruitng & Consltng, *Exec Srch*
Woodworth Intl Grp, *Exec Srch*

Pennsylvania
FORTUNE Grp Intl, *Exec Srch*
Kathy Karr Persnnl, *Perm. Emp Agcy*
Mgmt. Recrtrs of DE Cnty/CompuSrch, *Exec Srch*
Mgmt. Recrtrs of Lehigh Vly/CompuSrch, *Exec Srch*
Mgmt. Recrtrs of Philadelphia/ CompuSrch, *Exec Srch*
McNichol & Assoc., *Exec Srch*
The Morris Grp, *Exec Srch*
John Morrow & Assoc., *Exec Srch*
Olsten Staff Svcs, *Temp. Agcy*
LaMonte Owens, *Exec Srch*
Rice Cohen Intl, *Exec Srch*
Spectrum Consltnts/Retail Recrtrs, *Exec Srch*
Strongin Tech. Enterprises of PA, *Perm. Emp Agcy*
TRC Staff Svcs, *Temp. Agcy*
Virtual Workplace, *Temp. Agcy*

Rhode Island
Mgmt. Recrtrs Intl, *Exec Srch*
Tech/Aid of RI, *Contract Svc*

South Carolina
Mgmt. Recrtrs of Columbia, *Exec Srch*
Mgmt. Recrtrs of Rck Hill, *Exec Srch*
Smith Temps/Smith Persnnl, *Temp. Agcy*

Tennessee
Anderson McIntyre Persnnl Svcs, *Exec Srch*
Hamilton Ryker Co, *Exec Srch*
Mgmt. Recrtrs of Knoxville, *Exec Srch*
Sales Consltnts of Nashville, *Exec Srch*

Texas
Architectural Career Netwrk, *Contract Svc*
Brooklea & Assoc., *Exec Srch*
CAD Technlgy, *Exec Srch*
Certified Persnnl, *Contract Svc*
Cherbonnier Grp, *Exec Srch*
Colvin Resrcs Grp, *Temp. Agcy*
Gail Darling Staffing/Darling's Prof'l Desk, *Temp. Agcy*
Express Persnnl Svcs, *Perm. Emp Agcy*
Kristan Intl Exec Srch, *Exec Srch*
Mgmt. Recrtrs Intl, *Exec Srch*
Mgmt. Recrtrs of Dallas, *Exec Srch*
Metro Careers, *Exec Srch*
Saber Consltnts, *Exec Srch*
Sales Consltnts of Houston, *Exec Srch*
Snelling Persnnl Svcs, *Exec Srch*
H.L. Yoh Co, *Contract Svc*

Virginia
Cadworks, *Contract Svc*
Mgmt. Recrtrs of McLean, *Exec Srch*
Mgmt. Recrtrs of Roanoke, *Exec Srch*
Procurement Solut'ns, *Contract Svc*
Professional Srch Persnnl, *Exec Srch*
Tech/Aid of VA, *Temp. Agcy*

Washington
The Career Clinic, *Exec Srch*
Comprehensive Staff Resrcs dba Techstaff, *Temp. Agcy*
Mgmt. Recrtrs of Mercer Islnd, *Exec Srch*
Mgmt. Recrtrs of Tacoma, *Exec Srch*

Wisconsin
Allen, Wayne, & Co, *Perm. Emp Agcy*
Argus Tech. Svcs, *Perm. Emp Agcy*
Construction Srch Specialists, *Exec Srch*
The Exutec Grp, *Exec Srch*
Mgmt. Recrtrs of Appleton/ CompuSrch, *Exec Srch*
Mgmt. Recrtrs of Green Bay, *Exec Srch*
Mgmt. Recrtrs of Milwaukee/Sales Consltnts, *Exec Srch*
Mgmt. Recrtrs of Milwaukee, *Exec Srch*
U.S. Tech Force, *Exec Srch*

ART/DESIGN

Arizona
Adecco, *Temp. Agcy*
Taylor Design Recruitng, *Temp. Agcy*
Volt Tech. Svcs, *Contract Svc*

California
A.S.A.P. Emp. Svc, *Perm. Emp Agcy*
Answers Unlimtd, *Temp. Agcy*
ArtLinks, *Perm. Emp Agcy*
CDI Corp, *Temp. Agcy*
Employment Devlpmnt Dept, *Perm. Emp Agcy*
Fastek Tech. Svcs, *Perm. Emp Agcy*
40 Plus of So. CA, *Exec Srch*
Goldstein & Assoc., *Temp. Agcy*
Larkin Assoc., *Exec Srch*
MacTemps, *Temp. Agcy*
Maverick Staff Svc, *Perm. Emp Agcy*
Professional Recrtrs, *Exec Srch*
Santa Barbara Plcmnt, *Perm. Emp Agcy*
Technical Aid Corp, *Temp. Agcy*

Colorado
Office Specialists, *Temp. Agcy*

Connecticut
Admiral Staff Svcs, *Temp. Agcy*
CGR Staff Svcs, *Temp. Agcy*
Julian Assoc., *Perm. Emp Agcy*

District of Columbia
Access: Networking in the Public Interest, *Career/Outplacemnt*
Graphic Mac, *Temp. Agcy*
Portfolio, *Perm. Emp Agcy*
Potomac Persnnl, *Perm. Emp Agcy*

Florida
AAA Employment, *Perm. Emp Agcy*
Mgmt. Recrtrs Intl, *Exec Srch*
Temp-Art, *Temp. Agcy*
TempSolutions, *Temp. Agcy*

Georgia
Ad Options, *Perm. Emp Agcy*
Adecco Tech. Svcs, *Contract Svc*
Comprehensive Srch Grp, *Exec Srch*
Evie Kreisler & Assoc., *Exec Srch*
MacTemps, *Temp. Agcy*

Illinois
Bloom, Gross & Assoc., *Exec Srch*
Carson Mngmnt Assoc., *Contract Svc*
The Eastwood Grp, *Exec Srch*
David Gomez & Assoc., *Exec Srch*
Interstaff, *Temp. Agcy*
Kunzer Assoc., *Exec Srch*
MacIntyre Emp. Svc, *Perm. Emp Agcy*
Mgmt. Recrtrs of Elgin, *Exec Srch*
ProSearch Plus, *Exec Srch*

Indiana
Mac Staffng, *Temp. Agcy*

Kansas
Temtech, *Contract Svc*

Louisiana
Keenan Staffng, *Temp. Agcy*

Maryland
TAD Staff Svcs, *Temp. Agcy*

Massachusetts
Advance Persnnl, *Perm. Emp Agcy*
Alden & Clark, *Temp. Agcy*
Cyr Assoc., *Exec Srch*
Derby Assoc., *Perm. Emp Agcy*
Ford & Ford Exec Srch, *Exec Srch*
L.J. Gonzer Assoc., *Exec Srch*
Master Srch, *Perm. Emp Agcy*
Need Persnnl Plcmnt, *Temp. Agcy*
Stone & Youngblood, *Exec Srch*
Summit Tech. Svcs, *Temp. Agcy*

Michigan
AE Emp. Svcs, *Perm. Emp Agcy*
Advanced Tech. Resrcs, *Exec Srch*
Allied Tech. Svc, *Contract Svc*
Career Quest, *Perm. Emp Agcy*
Dynamic Persnnl, *Contract Svc*
Graphic Arts Mrktng Assoc., *Exec Srch*
Kelly Tech. Svcs, *Contract Svc*
Key Persnnl, *Perm. Emp Agcy*
Technical Prof'l Svc, *Perm. Emp Agcy*
Your Preference Referral Netwrk, *Perm. Emp Agcy*

Minnesota
Diversified Employment, *Perm. Emp Agcy*
EHS & Assoc., *Exec Srch*
Graphic Staffng, *Temp. Agcy*
Resource Srch, *Exec Srch*

New Hampshire
Allstaff Contrct Svcs, *Perm. Emp Agcy*
Sales Consltnts, *Exec Srch*
Surge Resrcs, *Contract Svc*

New Jersey
Blake & Assoc. Exec Srch, *Exec Srch*
Horizon Graphics Persnnl, *Perm. Emp Agcy*
Mayfair Svcs, *Perm. Emp Agcy*

New Mexico
CDI Corp, *Contract Svc*

New York
Accounting & Computer Persnnl, *Perm. Emp Agcy*
Bornholdt Shivas & Friends, *Exec Srch*
C.C. Burke Limited, *Perm. Emp Agcy*
CGR Staff Svcs, *Temp. Agcy*
Maggi Dolan Plcmnt, *Perm. Emp Agcy*
Kris Edwards Agcy, *Exec Srch*
Freelance Advancers, *Temp. Agcy*
Graphics For Hire, *Perm. Emp Agcy*
Ruth Hirsch Assoc., *Exec Srch*
Hot Bear/De Bella Prodctns & Editor'l Temps, *Temp. Agcy*
Innovations Assoc., *Perm. Emp Agcy*
Lawrence Exec Srch, *Exec Srch*
The Lloyd Co, *Career/Outplacemnt*
Morgan-Murray Persnnl/M&M Top Temps, *Temp. Agcy*
K.A. Nowack Career Specialists, *Perm. Emp Agcy*
S.R. Wolman Assoc., *Exec Srch*
H.L. Yoh Co, *Contract Svc*

North Carolina
Employment Consltnts, *Contract Svc*
Executive Staff Svcs, *Perm. Emp Agcy*
Jobs of Fayetteville, *Perm. Emp Agcy*
Mgmt. Recrtrs Intl, *Exec Srch*
PCS - Personal Communications Svc, *Contract Svc*

North Dakota
Olsten Staff Svcs/Kramer & Assoc./Exprswy Persnnl, *Temp. Agcy*

Ohio
Combined Resrcs, *Exec Srch*
Eastern Persnnl Svcs, *Perm. Emp Agcy*
Laine's S.M.G., *Perm. Emp Agcy*
Olsten Prof'l Staff Svcs, *Exec Srch*
Sanker & Assoc., *Temp. Agcy*
J.P. Walton & Assoc., *Exec Srch*

Texas
Brooklea & Assoc., *Exec Srch*
Houston Creative Connections, *Exec Srch*
Pro Staff Persnnl Svcs, *Temp. Agcy*
Search Com, *Exec Srch*
Stehouwer & Assoc., *Perm. Emp Agcy*
TAD Tech. Svcs, *Contract Svc*

Virginia
Lee Staffing Resrcs, *Exec Srch*
Snelling Persnnl Svcs, *Perm. Emp Agcy*

Washington
Creative Assets, *Temp. Agcy*
Resource Mngmnt Intl, *Temp. Agcy*

Wisconsin
The Exutec Grp, *Exec Srch*
MacPros, *Perm. Emp Agcy*

AUTOMOTIVE

Arizona
Clifford & Assoc., *Perm. Emp Agcy*
Dealer Connection, *Perm. Emp Agcy*

California

Action Plus Employer Svcs, *Perm. Emp Agcy*
Automotive Career Plcmnt, *Exec Srch*

Colorado

Woodmoor Grp, *Exec Srch*

Illinois

FORTUNE Persnnl Consltnts, *Exec Srch*
Sanford Rose Assoc., *Exec Srch*
Ray White Assoc., *Exec Srch*

Indiana

Continental Design Co, *Contract Svc*

Iowa

Quality Recrtrs, *Exec Srch*

Maryland

Auto Careers, *Exec Srch*

Massachusetts

Rob Davidson Assoc./Exec. & Prof. Resume Svc, *Exec Srch*
Mgmt. Developers, *Exec Srch*

Michigan

Alliance Industries, *Exec Srch*
Assoc., *Exec Srch*
Executech Resource Consltnts, *Perm. Emp Agcy*
Executive Recrtrs Intl, *Exec Srch*
GAM Exec Srch, *Exec Srch*
Kelly Scientific Resrcs, *Temp. Agcy*
Ludot Persnnl, *Perm. Emp Agcy*
Mgmt. Recrtrs Intl, *Exec Srch*
Modern Engineering, *Contract Svc*
Sales Consltnts of Lansing, *Exec Srch*
Duane Wilson Assoc., *Exec Srch*
H.L. Yoh Co, *Contract Svc*

Missouri

American Automotive Persnnl Consltnts, *Exec Srch*

New York

APA Srch, *Exec Srch*
Auto Careers, *Perm. Emp Agcy*

North Carolina

Linden Grp, *Exec Srch*

Ohio

Burks Grp, *Exec Srch*
Executive Directions, *Exec Srch*
R. Green & Assoc., *Exec Srch*
Jaeger Intl, *Exec Srch*
Personalized Plcmnt, *Exec Srch*
TAD Tech. Svcs, *Contract Svc*

Oregon

API Emp. Agcy, *Perm. Emp Agcy*

South Carolina

Atlantic Recrtrs, *Exec Srch*
Automotive Career Placemnt Counselors, *Perm. Emp Agcy*
Mgmt. Recrtrs of Anderson, *Exec Srch*

Texas

Kawa Stiewig & Edwards, *Exec Srch*

Washington

Auto Careers of Washington, *Perm. Emp Agcy*

Wisconsin

Sanford Rose Assoc., *Exec Srch*

BANKING

Alabama

A-1 Emp. Svc, *Perm. Emp Agcy*
Dunhill of So. Birmingham, *Exec Srch*
Mgmt. Recrtrs Intl, *Exec Srch*
Mgmt. Recrtrs Intl, *Exec Srch*
Perform Staff Svc, *Perm. Emp Agcy*
Talent Tree Staffng, *Perm. Emp Agcy*
VIP Persnnl, *Perm. Emp Agcy*

Alaska

Alaska Exec Srch, *Exec Srch*

Arizona

AccuStaff, *Perm. Emp Agcy*
Accustaff, *Temp. Agcy*
Aidan Grp, *Contract Svc*
Fishel Human Resrcs Assoc., *Exec Srch*
Beth Isabelle & Assoc., *Exec Srch*
Kerry's Referrals, *Temp. Agcy*
Mgmt. Recrtrs of Scottsdale, *Exec Srch*
Priority Staffng, *Perm. Emp Agcy*
Stivers Temp. Persnnl, *Temp. Agcy*

Arkansas

Mgmt. Recrtrs of Little Rock, *Exec Srch*
Premier Staffng, *Temp. Agcy*
Snelling Srch, *Exec Srch*
Spencer Careers, *Exec Srch*

California

AAFA (American Assn of Finance & Acctng), *Exec Srch*
ABA Staffng, *Exec Srch*
A.S.A.P. Emp. Svc, *Perm. Emp Agcy*
Accountnts Exec Srch/Accountnts On Call, *Exec Srch*
The Accnt'g Guild, *Temp. Agcy*
Affordable Exec Recrtrs, *Exec Srch*
Allard Assoc., *Exec Srch*
Allied Srch, *Exec Srch*
Alpha-Net Consltng Grp, *Exec Srch*
Alternative Staffing Grp, *Exec Srch*
Apple One Emp. Svcs, *Perm. Emp Agcy*
Apropos Emp. Agcy, *Perm. Emp Agcy*
Bay Resrcs, *Exec Srch*
Harvey Bell & Assoc., *Exec Srch*
Best Temp. Svc, *Temp. Agcy*
Blackhawk Advantage, *Exec Srch*
Blue, Garni & Co, *Exec Srch*
Brook-Blair Exec. Srch Firm
C.R. Assoc., *Exec Srch*
California Job Connection, *Perm. Emp Agcy*
Career Advantage, *Exec Srch*
Wayne Chamberlain & Assoc., *Exec Srch*
Champagne Temp. Help, *Temp. Agcy*
Choice Persnnl, *Perm. Emp Agcy*
Coast To Coast Exec Srch, *Exec Srch*
Collier-Young Agcy, *Temp. Agcy*
Dependable Emp. Agency Netwrk, *Perm. Emp Agcy*
The Dial Grp, *Perm. Emp Agcy*
Dunhill Prof'l Srch of San Francisco, *Exec Srch*
EDP Contrct Svcs, *Contract Svc*
Eleventh Hour Staff Svcs, *Temp. Agcy*
Emco Persnnl, *Perm. Emp Agcy*
Employment Devlpmnt Dept, *Perm. Emp Agcy*
Ethos Consltng, *Exec Srch*
Gavin Forbes & Assoc., *Exec Srch*
40 Plus of So. CA, *Exec Srch*
Goldstein & Assoc., *Temp. Agcy*
Gould Persnnl Svcs, *Perm. Emp Agcy*
Robert Half Intl, *Exec Srch*
Herrerias & Assoc., *Exec Srch*
Hochman & Assoc., *Exec Srch*
Interim Accnt'g Prof'ls, *Perm. Emp Agcy*
Intertec Design, *Perm. Emp Agcy*
Kelly Svcs, *Temp. Agcy*
Kenneth, George, & Assoc., *Exec Srch*
Klein & Assoc., *Temp. Agcy*
Larsen, Whitney, Blecksmith, & Zilliacus, *Exec Srch*
Lending Persnnl Svcs, *Exec Srch*
Lifter & Assoc., *Exec Srch*
The London Agcy, *Exec Srch*
The London Agcy, *Temp. Agcy*
Mgmt. Recrtrs Intl, *Exec Srch*
Mgmt. Recrtrs of Burlingame/Sales Consltnts, *Exec Srch*
Mgmt. Recrtrs of Encino, *Exec Srch*
Mgmt. Recrtrs of Pleasanton, *Exec Srch*
Mgmt. Recrtrs of San Francisco, *Exec Srch*
Mgmt. Srch Intl, *Exec Srch*
Manpower, *Temp. Agcy*
Maverick Staff Svc, *Perm. Emp Agcy*
K.E. McCarthy & Assoc., *Exec Srch*
Ed Meister Exec Srch, *Exec Srch*
Mesa Intl, *Exec Srch*
Musick & Assoc., *Exec Srch*
Nations Staff Solut'ns/Assoc. Resource Intl, *Exec Srch*
Nelson HR Solut'ns, *Perm. Emp Agcy*
Norrell Temp. Svcs of CA, *Temp. Agcy*
Olsten Staff Svcs, *Temp. Agcy*
On Assignment, *Temp. Agcy*
Online Prof'l Srch, *Exec Srch*
Pacific Srch Grp, *Exec Srch*
Pro Staff Persnnl Svcs, *Perm. Emp Agcy*
Remedy Intelligent Staffng, *Temp. Agcy*
Renoir Staff Svcs, *Perm. Emp Agcy*
Rich Rigler & Assoc., *Exec Srch*
Rowland Assoc., *Exec Srch*
Russell Staffing Resrcs, *Perm. Emp Agcy*
Ryan, Miller & Assoc., *Exec Srch*
Santa Barbara Plcmnt, *Perm. Emp Agcy*
Search West, *Exec Srch*
Search West of Ontario, *Exec Srch*
The September Grp, *Exec Srch*
David Sharp & Assoc., *Perm. Emp Agcy*
Sharp Persnnl & Srch, *Exec Srch*
Steinbrun, Hughes & Assoc., *Exec Srch*
Stivers Temp. Persnnl of CA, *Temp. Agcy*
TRC Staff Svcs, *Perm. Emp Agcy*
Talent Tree Staffng, *Perm. Emp Agcy*
Technical Directions, *Perm. Emp Agcy*
Telford, Adams, & Alexander, *Exec Srch*
Thor Temp. Svcs, *Temp. Agcy*
TOD Staffng, *Exec Srch*
Today Persnnl, *Perm. Emp Agcy*
Trans U.S., *Perm. Emp Agcy*
Truex Assoc., *Exec Srch*
United Staff Solut'ns, *Exec Srch*
Victor Valley Persnnl Agcy, *Perm. Emp Agcy*
Volt Temp. Svcs, *Temp. Agcy*
Walker & Torrente, *Exec Srch*
Western Staff Svcs of Walnut Crk/Westrn Medical, *Temp. Agcy*
The Windsor Grp, *Perm. Emp Agcy*

Colorado

Accountnts Choice Persnnl, *Exec Srch*
Adecco, *Temp. Agcy*
Ahrnsbrak & Assoc., *Perm. Emp Agcy*
BankTemps, *Temp. Agcy*
The Buxton Grp Limited, *Exec Srch*
Casey Svcs, *Exec Srch*
Dunhill Persnnl of Fort Collins, *Exec Srch*
Eleventh Hour Staff Svcs, *Perm. Emp Agcy*
Executive Srch Placemnts, *Exec Srch*
40 Plus of CO, *Career/Outplacemnt*
Interim Persnnl Svcs of Denver, *Temp. Agcy*
JobSearch, *Temp. Agcy*
Kelly Svcs, *Temp. Agcy*
Mgmt. Recrtrs of Boulder, *Exec Srch*
Manpower Intl, *Temp. Agcy*
National Affirmative Action Career Netwrk, *Exec Srch*
SOS Staff Svcs, *Temp. Agcy*
Sales Consltnts, *Exec Srch*
Talent Tree Staffng, *Perm. Emp Agcy*
Todays Temporary, *Temp. Agcy*

Connecticut

A&A Resume & Persnnl Svcs, *Perm. Emp Agcy*
Admiral Staff Svcs, *Temp. Agcy*
Bankers Srch, *Exec Srch*
Blackwood Assoc., *Exec Srch*
EDP Contrct Svcs, *Contract Svc*
Employment Opport., *Perm. Emp Agcy*
Financial Careers, *Exec Srch*
Financial Exec Srch, *Exec Srch*
Higbee Assoc., *Exec Srch*
Mgmt. Recrtrs Intl, *Exec Srch*
Office Svcs of CT, *Perm. Emp Agcy*
Siger & Assoc., *Exec Srch*
Howard Smith Assoc., *Exec Srch*
Source Svcs Corp, *Exec Srch*
Western Staff Svcs, *Temp. Agcy*
Western Staff Svcs, *Perm. Emp Agcy*

Delaware

Caldwell Staff Svcs, *Perm. Emp Agcy*
J.B. Groner Exec Srch, *Exec Srch*
E.W. Hodges & Assoc., *Exec Srch*
Horizons Resrcs, *Perm. Emp Agcy*
The Placers, *Temp. Agcy*
The Placers, *Exec Srch*

District of Columbia

Norrell Svcs, *Temp. Agcy*
Potomac Persnnl, *Perm. Emp Agcy*
Don Richard Assoc. of Washington DC, *Exec Srch*

Florida

AAA Employment, *Perm. Emp Agcy*
Accountnts Exec Srch/Accountnts On Call, *Exec Srch*
AccuTech, *Contract Svc*
Adecco, *Temp. Agcy*
Alpha Persnnl/Alpha Temps, *Perm. Emp Agcy*
Availability, *Perm. Emp Agcy*
Benson & Assoc., *Exec Srch*
Brickell Persnnl Consltnts, *Temp. Agcy*
Bryan & Assoc./Worknet, Etc., *Exec Srch*
Career Planners, *Perm. Emp Agcy*
Carrier's Career Svc, *Career/Outplacemnt*
Corporate Srch Consltnts, *Exec Srch*
DGA Persnnl Grp, *Exec Srch*
Steven Douglas Assoc., *Exec Srch*
Employers' Assistant, *Temp. Agcy*
Ethan Allen Persnnl Plcmnt, *Exec Srch*
Farwell Grp, *Exec Srch*
First Emp. Consltnts, *Exec Srch*
Five Star Temporary, *Temp. Agcy*
Future Force Persnnl, *Temp. Agcy*
Michael Gimbel & Assoc., *Exec Srch*
Girl Friday Persnnl, *Temp. Agcy*
Hastings & Hastings Persnnl Consltnts, *Temp. Agcy*
Kelly Svcs, *Temp. Agcy*
Koerner Grp, *Exec Srch*
R.H. Larsen & Assoc., *Exec Srch*
Mgmt. Recrtrs Intl, *Exec Srch*
Mgmt. Recrtrs of St. Petersburg, *Exec Srch*
Mgmt. Recrtrs of Tallahassee, *Exec Srch*
Mgmt. Recrtrs of Tampa, *Exec Srch*
Olsten Staff Svcs, *Temp. Agcy*
Persnnl One, *Perm. Emp Agcy*
Profes. Staffing/Able Body Temp. Svcs, *Contract Svc*
Linda Robins & Assoc., *Temp. Agcy*
Gene Rogers Assoc., *Exec Srch*

Romac Intl, *Exec Srch*
Sales Consltnts of Fort Lauderdale, *Exec Srch*
Sales Consltnts of Jacksonville, *Exec Srch*
Doug Sears & Assoc., *Exec Srch*
Shaver Emp. Agcy, *Perm. Emp Agcy*
Snelling Persnnl Svcs, *Temp. Agcy*
Spalding's Emp. Svc, *Perm. Emp Agcy*
Aaron Stewart Persnnl, *Exec Srch*
Transworld COREstaff, *Temp. Agcy*
Scott Watson & Assoc., *Perm. Emp Agcy*

Georgia

A-1 Svc Persnnl, *Perm. Emp Agcy*
Access Persnnl Svcs, *Perm. Emp Agcy*
Michael Alexander Grp, *Exec Srch*
Ashley-Nolan Intl, *Exec Srch*
Bell Oaks Co, *Exec Srch*
Catalina Resrcs, *Perm. Emp Agcy*
Chase Finan. Staffng/Tyler Tech. Staffng, *Perm. Emp Agcy*
Durham Staffng, *Perm. Emp Agcy*
Elite Staff Svcs, *Perm. Emp Agcy*
Executive Force, *Exec Srch*
Express Persnnl Svcs, *Perm. Emp Agcy*
Express Persnnl Svcs, *Exec Srch*
ISC of Atlanta/Intl Career Continuation, *Exec Srch*
Kenzer Corp of GA, *Exec Srch*
MA&A Grp, *Perm. Emp Agcy*
MSI Intl, *Exec Srch*
Mgmt. Recrtrs of Atlanta, *Exec Srch*
Manpower Temp. Svcs, *Temp. Agcy*
Jim Nixon & Assoc., *Exec Srch*
Norrell Corp, *Temp. Agcy*
Office Specialists, *Temp. Agcy*
Olsten Staff Svcs, *Temp. Agcy*
Priority 1 Staff Svcs, *Temp. Agcy*
Randstad Staff Svcs, *Perm. Emp Agcy*
Sanford Rose Assoc., *Exec Srch*
Southern Emp. Svc, *Perm. Emp Agcy*
TRC Staff Svcs, *Temp. Agcy*
Toar Consltnts, *Exec Srch*
Todays Temporary, *Temp. Agcy*
WPPS Software Staffng, *Perm. Emp Agcy*
Workman & Assoc., *Exec Srch*

Hawaii

Altres Staffng, *Temp. Agcy*
Dunhill Prof'l Srch of Hawaii, *Exec Srch*
Ellis & Assoc., *Exec Srch*
The Resume Place, *Career/Outplacemnt*

Idaho

FORTUNE Persnnl Consltnts, *Exec Srch*
Horne/Brown Intl, *Exec Srch*

Illinois

A.B.A. Placemnts/A.B.A. Temps, *Perm. Emp Agcy*
ASI Persnnl, *Perm. Emp Agcy*
Account Pros, *Exec Srch*
Accountnts Exec Srch/Accountnts On Call, *Exec Srch*
Accurate Persnnl, *Perm. Emp Agcy*
Adecco, *Temp. Agcy*
Armstrong-Hamilton Assoc., *Exec Srch*
Availability, *Perm. Emp Agcy*
Bankers Grp, *Exec Srch*
Barrett Partners, *Exec Srch*
Bell Persnnl, *Perm. Emp Agcy*
Bevelle & Assoc., *Exec Srch*
Casey Staff Svcs, *Perm. Emp Agcy*
Chicago Financial Srch, *Exec Srch*
Cogan & Assoc., *Exec Srch*
Computer Futures Exchange, *Exec Srch*
Consltnts to Exec Mngmnt Co Exec. Srch Firm
Contemporary Svcs, *Exec Srch*
Cook Assoc., *Exec Srch*
Crown Persnnl, *Perm. Emp Agcy*
Davis Temps, *Temp. Agcy*
DayStar Temp. Svcs, *Temp. Agcy*
Diener & Assoc., *Exec Srch*
Dunhill Staff Svcs of Chicago, *Perm. Emp Agcy*
The Eastwood Grp, *Exec Srch*
The Esquire Staffing Grp, *Perm. Emp Agcy*
Fellows Plcmnt, *Temp. Agcy*
Financial Srch Corp, *Exec Srch*
First Staffng, *Perm. Emp Agcy*
Gnodde Assoc., *Exec Srch*
David Gomez & Assoc., *Exec Srch*
Greystone Assoc., *Exec Srch*
HKA Mortgage Staffing & Training, *Perm. Emp Agcy*
Robert Half Intl/Accountemps, *Exec Srch*
Human Resource Connection, *Perm. Emp Agcy*
Interstaff, *Temp. Agcy*
Interviewing Consltnts, *Perm. Emp Agcy*
Kennedy & Co, *Exec Srch*
Kingsley Emp. Svc, *Perm. Emp Agcy*
Kunzer Assoc., *Exec Srch*
Lynco Mngmnt Persnnl, *Exec Srch*
MBP Persnnl, *Exec Srch*
Mack & Assoc., *Temp. Agcy*
Macro Resrcs, *Exec Srch*
Mgmt. Recrtrs Intl, *Exec Srch*
Mgmt. Recrtrs of Des Plaines, *Exec Srch*
Mgmt. Recrtrs of Rockford, *Exec Srch*
Manning & Assoc., *Exec Srch*
Manpower Temp. Svcs, *Temp. Agcy*
Maramax Persnnl, *Perm. Emp Agcy*
Merit Persnnl, *Perm. Emp Agcy*
The Murphy Grp, *Perm. Emp Agcy*
Norrell Financial Staffng, *Exec Srch*
Norrell HR Svcs, *Perm. Emp Agcy*
Officemates5 of Wheeling, *Exec Srch*
Olsten Information Technlgy Staffng, *Perm. Emp Agcy*
Persnnl Connection, *Perm. Emp Agcy*
Persnnl Placemnt Consltnts, *Perm. Emp Agcy*
Professional Research Svcs, *Exec Srch*
Profile Temp. Svc, *Temp. Agcy*
ProSearch Plus, *Exec Srch*
The Raleigh Warwick Grp, *Exec Srch*
Remedy Intelligent Staffng, *Temp. Agcy*
Right Svcs, *Temp. Agcy*
Romac Intl, *Exec Srch*
Sales Consltnts/Mgmt. Recrtrs Intl, *Exec Srch*
Sales Consltnts of Chicago, *Exec Srch*
Sales Consltnts of Oak Brk, *Exec Srch*
Smith Hanley Assoc., *Exec Srch*
Staffing Consltnts, *Perm. Emp Agcy*
Stivers Temp. Persnnl, *Temp. Agcy*
Roy Talman & Assoc., *Exec Srch*
Temporary Assoc., *Temp. Agcy*
K. David Umlauf Exec Srch Consltnts, *Exec Srch*
World Emp. Svc, *Perm. Emp Agcy*

Indiana

Bill Caldwell Emp. Svc, *Perm. Emp Agcy*
Crowe, Chizek & Co, *Perm. Emp Agcy*
Crown Temp. Svcs of Indianapolis, *Temp. Agcy*
Execusearch, *Exec Srch*
Hobart Emp. Agcy, *Perm. Emp Agcy*
Life Emp. Svc, *Perm. Emp Agcy*
Mgmt. Recrtrs Intl, *Exec Srch*
Mgmt. Recrtrs of Evansville, *Exec Srch*
Mgmt. Recrtrs of Indianapolis, *Exec Srch*
Mgmt. Recrtrs of Richmond/Staff Solut'ns, *Exec Srch*
Morley Grp, *Exec Srch*
National Corporate Consltnts/Advantage Svcs, *Exec Srch*
Officemates5 of Indianapolis, *Exec Srch*
Officemates5 of Indianapolis, *Exec Srch*
Perry Persnnl Plus, *Perm. Emp Agcy*
Quiring Assoc. HR Consltng Grp, *Exec Srch*
Rush Temps, *Temp. Agcy*

Iowa

Burton Placemnt Svcs, *Exec Srch*
Byrnes & Rupkey, *Exec Srch*
Helping Hands Temp. Svc, *Temp. Agcy*
The Human Resource Grp, *Exec Srch*
Mgmt. Recrtrs Intl, *Exec Srch*
McGladrey Srch Grp, *Exec Srch*
Persnnl, *Exec Srch*
Pratt-Younglove, *Perm. Emp Agcy*
Sedona Staff Svcs, *Exec Srch*

Kansas

Bossler-Hix Financial Careers, *Perm. Emp Agcy*
Business Specialists, *Perm. Emp Agcy*
Century, *Exec Srch*
Dunhill of Wichita, *Perm. Emp Agcy*
Eleventh Hour Staff Svcs, *Temp. Agcy*
Mgmt. Recrtrs of Overlnd Prk, *Exec Srch*
Smith Brown & Jones, *Exec Srch*

Kentucky

Angel Grp Intl, *Exec Srch*
Belcan Staff Svcs, *Perm. Emp Agcy*
C.M. Mngmnt Svcs, *Perm. Emp Agcy*
Engineering & Exec Srch, *Exec Srch*
Persnnl Solut'ns, *Perm. Emp Agcy*
Precision Staffng, *Perm. Emp Agcy*
Sharrow & Assoc., *Exec Srch*

Louisiana

Keenan Staffng, *Temp. Agcy*
Mgmt. Recrtrs of Baton Rouge, *Exec Srch*
Mgmt. Recrtrs-Metairie/Sales Consltnts, *Exec Srch*
Snelling Persnnl Svcs, *Exec Srch*
Talley & Assoc./Talley Temps, *Exec Srch*

Maine

Accomplished Prof'ls, *Temp. Agcy*
Career Mngmnt Assoc., *Exec Srch*
Executive Srch of N.E., *Exec Srch*

Maryland

Accountnts Exec Srch/Accountnts On Call, *Exec Srch*
Admin Persnnl Svcs, *Perm. Emp Agcy*
Atlas Persnnl Agcy, *Perm. Emp Agcy*
Dunhill of Rockville, *Perm. Emp Agcy*
Excel Temp. Svcs, *Temp. Agcy*
Futures, *Exec Srch*
The Hanover Grp, *Exec Srch*
Mgmt. Recrtrs of Annapolis, *Exec Srch*
Mgmt. Recrtrs-Baltimore/Sales Consltnts, *Exec Srch*
Mgmt. Recrtrs-Bethesda/CompuSearch, *Exec Srch*
Mgmt. Recrtrs of Frederick, *Exec Srch*
Onsite Commercial Staffng, *Perm. Emp Agcy*
Sales Consltnts of Prince Georges Cnty, *Exec Srch*
TAC Staff Svcs, *Temp. Agcy*
TAD Staff Svcs, *Temp. Agcy*
White Ridgely Assoc., *Career/Outplacemnt*

Massachusetts

Accountemps, *Temp. Agcy*
Adecco, *Temp. Agcy*
Anthony Michael & Co, *Exec Srch*
Arthur-Blair Assoc., *Perm. Emp Agcy*
Attorney Special Assignment Plcmnt, *Temp. Agcy*
Campbell Assoc., *Exec Srch*
Cleary Consltnts, *Perm. Emp Agcy*
The Client Server Grp, *Exec Srch*
Computer Security Plcmnt, *Exec Srch*
Davis Companies, *Temp. Agcy*
Derby Assoc., *Perm. Emp Agcy*
Discovery Persnnl, *Perm. Emp Agcy*
Eastwood Persnnl Assoc., *Exec Srch*
Greene & Co, *Exec Srch*
Harvest Persnnl, *Exec Srch*
JNB Assoc., *Exec Srch*
Johnson & Hill Staff Svc, *Temp. Agcy*
Judge Tech. Svcs, *Exec Srch*
Kingston-Dwight Assoc., *Perm. Emp Agcy*
L&L Temps, *Temp. Agcy*
Lane Emp. Svc, *Perm. Emp Agcy*
John Leonard Persnnl Assoc., *Perm. Emp Agcy*
Mgmt. Recrtrs Intl, *Exec Srch*
Mgmt. Recrtrs Intl of Braintree, *Exec Srch*
Mgmt. Recrtrs Intl of Springfield, *Exec Srch*
Mgmt. Recrtrs Intl of Westboro, *Exec Srch*
Manpower Temp. Svcs, *Temp. Agcy*
New Boston Select Grp, *Exec Srch*
Olsten Prof'l Accnt'g Svcs, *Exec Srch*
Resrcs Objectives, *Exec Srch*
Sales Consltnts of Cape Cod, *Exec Srch*
Sales Consltnts of Plymouth Cnty, *Exec Srch*
Sales Consltnts of Wellesley, *Exec Srch*
Scott-Wayne Assoc., *Perm. Emp Agcy*
Selectemps, *Temp. Agcy*
Spectra Prof'l Srch/Spectra Temps, *Perm. Emp Agcy*
Straube Assoc., *Exec Srch*
Technical Persnnl Svcs, *Perm. Emp Agcy*
WIND Job Ctr, *Career/Outplacemnt*

Michigan

Accountnts One, *Perm. Emp Agcy*
Accountemps/Officeteam, *Temp. Agcy*
Advance Employment, *Exec Srch*
The Advantage Grp, *Exec Srch*
Benford Assoc., *Exec Srch*
Career Quest, *Perm. Emp Agcy*
ExecuQuest, *Exec Srch*
Express Persnnl Svcs, *Temp. Agcy*
Robert Half Intl, *Exec Srch*
Harvey Hohauser & Assoc., *Exec Srch*
William Howard Agcy, *Perm. Emp Agcy*
Henry Labus Persnnl, *Perm. Emp Agcy*
Mgmt. Recrtrs Intl, *Exec Srch*
Mgmt. Recrtrs of Bingham Farms, *Exec Srch*
Mgmt. Recrtrs of Dearborn, *Exec Srch*
Mgmt. Recrtrs of Grand Rapids, *Exec Srch*
Mgmt. Recrtrs of Kalamazoo, *Exec Srch*
Mgmt. Recrtrs of Lansing, *Exec Srch*
Mgmt. Recrtrs of Muskegon, *Exec Srch*
Mgmt. Recrtrs of Rochester, *Exec Srch*
Office Staffing Recruitng, *Exec Srch*
Olsten Prof'l Accnt'g Svcs, *Temp. Agcy*
ProSearch, *Exec Srch*
Sales Consltnts of Detroit, *Exec Srch*
TEA, *Perm. Emp Agcy*
Trillium Staffng, *Temp. Agcy*
Wing Tips & Pumps, *Exec Srch*

Minnesota

Abby Blu, *Temp. Agcy*
Add On Staff Solut'ns, *Temp. Agcy*
Ells Persnnl Syst., *Exec Srch*
Employment Advisors, *Perm. Emp Agcy*
T.H. Hunter, *Exec Srch*
Mgmt. Recrtrs-Minneapolis/Sales Consltnts, *Exec Srch*
Thomas Moore, *Temp. Agcy*
Sathe & Assoc. Exec Srch, *Exec Srch*
Jean Thorne, *Temp. Agcy*
Ultimate Srch Unlimtd/Temps Unlimtd, *Perm. Emp Agcy*
West Emp. Solut'ns, *Perm. Emp Agcy*

Mississippi

Andrus Assoc. dba Svc Specialists Ltd., *Perm. Emp Agcy*
EPSCO Persnnl, *Temp. Agcy*

Missouri

Burns Emp. Svc, *Exec Srch*
Business Persnnl Svcs, *Temp. Agcy*
Crown Svcs, *Temp. Agcy*
Deck & Decker Emp. Svc, *Perm. Emp Agcy*
Employer Advantage, *Exec Srch*
Charles Luntz & Assoc., *Exec Srch*
Mgmt. Recrtrs Intl, *Exec Srch*
Mgmt. Recrtrs of Kansas Cty, *Exec Srch*
Mgmt. Recrtrs of Springfield, *Exec Srch*
Mgmt. Recrtrs of St. Louis, *Exec Srch*
Manpower Temp. Svcs, *Temp. Agcy*
National Physician Placemnt Svcs, *Exec Srch*
Officemates5 of St. Louis, *Exec Srch*
Sanford Rose Assoc., *Exec Srch*
Snelling Persnnl Svcs, *Perm. Emp Agcy*

Montana

Express Persnnl, *Perm. Emp Agcy*

Nebraska

Adams, *Exec Srch*
Compusearch of Lincoln, *Exec Srch*
Corporate Recrtrs, *Exec Srch*
Dunhill Prof'l Srch, *Exec Srch*
Eggers Co, *Perm. Emp Agcy*
Kelly Svcs, *Temp. Agcy*
Mgmt. Recrtrs of Omaha/Officemates5, *Exec Srch*
Noll HR Svcs, *Exec Srch*
Sales Consltnts of Omaha, *Exec Srch*

Nevada

Talent Tree Staffng, *Perm. Emp Agcy*

New Hampshire

Able 1 Staffng, *Exec Srch*
Arc-Profiles, *Exec Srch*
Central New Hampshire Emp. Svcs, *Perm. Emp Agcy*
Cheshire Emp. Svc, *Temp. Agcy*
Dubois & Co, *Exec Srch*
Mgmt. Recrtrs Intl of Bedford, *Exec Srch*
Manpower Temp. Svcs, *Temp. Agcy*
National Emp. Svc Corp, *Perm. Emp Agcy*
Professional Recrtrs, *Perm. Emp Agcy*
R.G.T. Assoc., *Exec Srch*
Resource Recruitng//Contemp. Accntnts, *Perm. Emp Agcy*
Sales Consltnts of Nashua-Manchester, *Exec Srch*
TAC Staff Svcs, *Temp. Agcy*
Thomas & Kavanaugh, *Perm. Emp Agcy*

New Jersey

A Prof'l Edge, *Career/Outplacemnt*
Accountnts Exec Srch/Accountnts On Call, *Exec Srch*
Advanced Persnnl, *Perm. Emp Agcy*
David Allen Assoc., *Exec Srch*
BAI Persnnl Solut'ns, *Exec Srch*
Blake & Assoc. Exec Srch, *Exec Srch*
Bonifield Assoc., *Exec Srch*
Career Ctr, *Perm. Emp Agcy*
Citizens Emp. Svcs, *Perm. Emp Agcy*
Cox Darrow & Owens, *Exec Srch*
D'Andrea Assoc., *Exec Srch*
Dunhill Prof'l Srch, *Exec Srch*
Executive Srch, *Exec Srch*
Hreshko Consltng Grp, *Exec Srch*
Impact Persnnl, *Perm. Emp Agcy*
Integro Staff Svcs, *Temp. Agcy*
MJE Recrtrs, *Exec Srch*
Mgmt. Recrtrs of Bridgewater, *Exec Srch*
Mgmt. Recrtrs of Passaic Cnty, *Exec Srch*
McDermott Resrcs, *Exec Srch*
Officemates5 of Englewood Cliffs/DayStar Temp. Svcs, *Perm. Emp Agcy*
Orion Consltng, *Exec Srch*
Park Avenue Persnnl, *Perm. Emp Agcy*
The Pennmore Grp, *Exec Srch*
Pomerantz Persnnl, *Perm. Emp Agcy*
Premier Persnnl Grp, *Perm. Emp Agcy*
Princeton Exec Srch, *Exec Srch*
Remedy Intelligent Staffng, *Temp. Agcy*
Gene Rogers Assoc., *Exec Srch*
R.S. Sadow Assoc., *Exec Srch*
Sales Consltnts of Sparta, *Exec Srch*
Selective Persnnl, *Perm. Emp Agcy*
SkuppSearch, *Exec Srch*
Snelling Persnnl Svcs, *Perm. Emp Agcy*
Source Svcs Corp, *Perm. Emp Agcy*
Winston Staff Svcs, *Temp. Agcy*

New Mexico

Albuquerque Persnnl, *Perm. Emp Agcy*

New York

Accounting & Computer Persnnl, *Perm. Emp Agcy*
AccuStaff, *Temp. Agcy*
Adam Persnnl, *Perm. Emp Agcy*
Merrill Adams Assoc., *Career/Outplacemnt*
Adecco, *Temp. Agcy*
Alite Assoc., *Exec Srch*
Franklin Allen Consltnts Exec. Srch Firm
AMESgroup, *Perm. Emp Agcy*
Analytic Recruitng, *Perm. Emp Agcy*
Asher Persnnl Consltnts, *Perm. Emp Agcy*
Branthover Assoc., *Exec Srch*
CK Resrcs, *Exec Srch*
Career Blazers Persnnl, *Perm. Emp Agcy*
Career Concepts, *Perm. Emp Agcy*
Confidential Srch, *Exec Srch*
Consortium, *Exec Srch*
Conspectus, *Exec Srch*
The Cornell Grp, *Exec Srch*
Cross Staffng, *Perm. Emp Agcy*
Seth Diamond Assoc., *Exec Srch*
Drummond Assoc., *Exec Srch*
EDP Contrct Svcs, *Contract Svc*
Irwin Edwards Recrtrs, *Perm. Emp Agcy*
Employment Recrtrs Agcy, *Perm. Emp Agcy*
Euromonde, *Temp. Agcy*
Executive Resrcs Exec. Srch Firm
Extra Help Emp. Svc, *Temp. Agcy*
Fabian Assoc., *Exec Srch*
Fanning Persnnl, *Exec Srch*
Federal Placemnt Svcs, *Exec Srch*
Fifth Avenue Emp. Svcs, *Temp. Agcy*
Forum Temp. Svcs, *Temp. Agcy*
Frontrunner Srch, *Exec Srch*
Genesis Emp. Consltnts, *Exec Srch*
Gruen Resrcs, *Exec Srch*
H&H Temp. Svcs, *Temp. Agcy*
HBC Grp, *Exec Srch*
The Haas Assoc., *Exec Srch*
Robert Half Intl/Information Syst. Division, *Exec Srch*
Hawkes-Peers & Co, *Exec Srch*
F.P. Healy & Co, *Exec Srch*
Hessel Assoc., *Exec Srch*
Horizon Exec Srch Grp, *Exec Srch*
Hunter Mac & Assoc., *Perm. Emp Agcy*
Island Srch Grp, *Perm. Emp Agcy*
Just One Break, *Perm. Emp Agcy*
KLK Persnnl, *Perm. Emp Agcy*
KPA Grp, *Exec Srch*
Kensington Grp, *Exec Srch*
Tina Lane Persnnl, *Perm. Emp Agcy*
Michael John Lawrence & Assoc., *Exec Srch*
The Lloyd Co, *Career/Outplacemnt*
The MVP Grp, *Exec Srch*
MacInnis, Ward & Assoc., *Exec Srch*
Magill Assoc., *Exec Srch*
Joseph Maloney & Assoc., *Perm. Emp Agcy*
Mgmt. Recrtrs of Nassau, *Exec Srch*
Mgmt. Recrtrs of Woodbury/ CompuSrch, *Exec Srch*
Manpower Temp. Svcs, *Temp. Agcy*
Maxwell Grp, *Exec Srch*
The Melville Grp, *Exec Srch*
Metro Resrcs of Rochester, *Temp. Agcy*
Milazzo Assoc., *Perm. Emp Agcy*
Morgan-Murray Persnnl/M&M Top Temps, *Temp. Agcy*
National Emp. Database, *Perm. Emp Agcy*
Neal Mgmt., *Exec Srch*
New York-New York Persnnl, *Perm. Emp Agcy*
K.A. Nowack Career Specialists, *Perm. Emp Agcy*
Olsten Staff Svcs, *Temp. Agcy*
Optimal Resrcs, *Exec Srch*
OTEC.COM, *Perm. Emp Agcy*
Pathway Exec Srch, *Exec Srch*
Paywise, *Temp. Agcy*
Peak Srch, *Exec Srch*
Persnnl Consltng Assoc., *Exec Srch*
P.G. Prager Srch Assoc., *Exec Srch*
Quest Organization, *Exec Srch*
Rand Thompson Consltnts, *Exec Srch*
Redstone Affiliates, *Exec Srch*
Remedy Intelligent Staffng, *Temp. Agcy*
Response Staff Svcs/Career Advisors, *Exec Srch*
E.J. Rhodes Exec Srch, *Exec Srch*
Beth Richman Assoc., *Perm. Emp Agcy*
Fran Rogers Persnnl, *Perm. Emp Agcy*
S.W. Mgmt., *Exec Srch*
SearchAmerica, *Exec Srch*
Source Finance, *Exec Srch*
Staff Managers, *Temp. Agcy*
Staffing Svcs, *Exec Srch*
Superior Concepts, *Contract Svc*
Synergy Partners, *Exec Srch*
Hillary Taylor Persnnl, *Perm. Emp Agcy*
Techno-Trac Syst., *Exec Srch*
Temp Force of NY, *Temp. Agcy*
Tempo Svcs, *Perm. Emp Agcy*
Temporary Resource Ctr, *Temp. Agcy*
Phil Thomas Persnnl, *Exec Srch*
Tyler Srch Consltnts, *Perm. Emp Agcy*
United Persnnl Agcy, *Perm. Emp Agcy*
Vantage Staff Svcs, *Temp. Agcy*
Venture Resrcs, *Exec Srch*
Volt Svcs Grp, *Contract Svc*
Charles Wanner Assoc. Exec. Srch Firm
Wehinger Svcs, *Perm. Emp Agcy*
Werbin Assoc. Exec Srch, *Exec Srch*
Western Staff Svcs, *Temp. Agcy*
Winston Resrcs, *Exec Srch*
Woodbury Persnnl, *Perm. Emp Agcy*

North Carolina

Accountnts Exec Srch, *Exec Srch*
Accurate Staff Consltnts, *Exec Srch*
Amcell Assoc., *Exec Srch*
Bank Srch, *Exec Srch*
Christopher Grp, *Exec Srch*
COMFORCE Tech. Svcs, *Contract Svc*
Corporate Staff Consltnts, *Perm. Emp Agcy*
Employment Consltnts, *Contract Svc*
FORTUNE Persnnl Consltnts of Raleigh, *Perm. Emp Agcy*
Graham & Assoc., *Perm. Emp Agcy*
Robert Half Intl, *Exec Srch*
Interim Persnnl, *Temp. Agcy*
Jobs of Fayetteville, *Perm. Emp Agcy*
Kelly Svcs, *Temp. Agcy*
Key Temps, *Temp. Agcy*
MTS, *Perm. Emp Agcy*
Mgmt. Recrtrs Intl, *Exec Srch*
Mgmt. Recrtrs of Durham, *Exec Srch*
Mgmt. Recrtrs of Winston-Salem, *Exec Srch*
McCain Emp. Agcy, *Temp. Agcy*
Merrick & Moore, *Exec Srch*
Moffitt Intl, *Exec Srch*
Olsten Staff Svcs, *Temp. Agcy*
Parenica & Co, *Exec Srch*
Pro Staff Accnt'g Svcs, *Perm. Emp Agcy*
Pro Staff Persnnl Svcs, *Perm. Emp Agcy*
Don Richard Assoc. of Charlotte, *Perm. Emp Agcy*
Sales Consltnts of High Point, *Exec Srch*
Snelling Srch, *Exec Srch*
Source Svcs Corp, *Exec Srch*
Sparks Persnnl Svcs, *Exec Srch*
Talent Tree Staffng, *Perm. Emp Agcy*
John Williams & Assoc., *Exec Srch*
Youngblood Staffng, *Perm. Emp Agcy*

North Dakota

Olsten Staff Svcs/Kramer & Assoc./Expressway Persnnl, *Temp. Agcy*
Persnnl Svcs, *Exec Srch*

Ohio

Accountnts Exec Srch/Accountnts on Call, *Exec Srch*
AccuStaff, *Temp. Agcy*
Adecco, *Perm. Emp Agcy*
Benke & Assoc., *Exec Srch*
N.L. Benke & Assoc., *Perm. Emp Agcy*
Bradley-Pierce Persnnl, *Perm. Emp Agcy*
J.B. Brown & Assoc., *Exec Srch*
CBS Persnnl Svcs, *Perm. Emp Agcy*
Crown Temp. Svcs of Cincinnati, *Temp. Agcy*
Drayton & Assoc., *Exec Srch*
Eastern Persnnl Svcs, *Perm. Emp Agcy*
Flex-Tech Prof'l Svcs, *Contract Svc*
Graduate Consltnts, *Perm. Emp Agcy*
Guthoff & Assoc., *Exec Srch*
Hite Exec Srch/Hite Mngmnt Consltnts, *Exec Srch*
Rich Johns Career Consltnts, *Perm. Emp Agcy*
Kelly Svcs, *Temp. Agcy*
Laine's S.M.G., *Perm. Emp Agcy*
Lopresti & Assoc., *Exec Srch*
Mgmt. Recrtrs of Cincinnati, *Exec Srch*
Mgmt. Recrtrs of Cleveland, *Exec Srch*
Mgmt. Recrtrs of Columbus, *Exec Srch*
Mgmt. Recrtrs of Dayton, *Exec Srch*
Mgmt. Recrtrs of Solon, *Exec Srch*
Miami Prof'l Srch, *Exec Srch*
Minority Exec Srch, *Exec Srch*
Norrell Svcs, *Temp. Agcy*
Olsten Financial Staffng, *Exec Srch*
Olsten Prof'l Staff Svcs, *Exec Srch*
Jerry Paul Assoc., *Perm. Emp Agcy*
Providence Persnnl Consltnts, *Exec Srch*
Sales Consltnts of Cincinnati, *Exec Srch*
Tech/Aid of OH, *Perm. Emp Agcy*

Oklahoma

Ameri Resource, *Exec Srch*
BancSearch, *Exec Srch*
Banker Persnnl, *Exec Srch*
Dunhill Persnnl of Nrtheast Tulsa, *Exec Srch*
Robert Half Intl, *Exec Srch*
Key Temp. Persnnl, *Temp. Agcy*
Mgmt. Recrtrs of Oklahoma Cty, *Exec Srch*
Manpower Temp. Svcs, *Temp. Agcy*
Midwest Financial Svcs Co, *Exec Srch*
Terry Neese Persnnl Agcy, *Exec Srch*
Prospective Persnnl, *Exec Srch*
StaffMark, *Temp. Agcy*

Oregon

Employment Trends, *Temp. Agcy*
Express Persnnl Svcs, *Exec Srch*
Hire Ground, *Temp. Agcy*
Mgmt. Recrtrs/Officemates5 of Portland, *Exec Srch*

Southern Oregon Temporary, *Temp. Agcy*
Talent Tree Staffng, *Perm. Emp Agcy*

Pennsylvania

Accountnts Exec Srch, *Exec Srch*
Allegheny Persnnl Svcs, *Temp. Agcy*
ASAP Staffng, *Perm. Emp Agcy*
Basilone-Oliver Exec Srch, *Exec Srch*
Charly's Temp. Svcs, *Temp. Agcy*
Computer Prof'ls Unlimtd, *Perm. Emp Agcy*
Rob DePaul & Assoc., *Exec Srch*
EDP/Temps of PA, *Temp. Agcy*
Financial Industry Staff Co, *Perm. Emp Agcy*
Fox-Morris Assoc., *Exec Srch*
The Hastings Grp, *Exec Srch*
Human Resource Solut'ns, *Exec Srch*
J-Rand Srch, *Exec Srch*
Nancy Jackson, *Exec Srch*
Jefferson-Ross Assoc., *Exec Srch*
Kathy Karr Persnnl, *Perm. Emp Agcy*
Keystaff, *Temp. Agcy*
Mgmt. Recrtrs of DE Cnty/CompuSrch, *Exec Srch*
Mgmt. Recrtrs of Lehigh Vly/CompuSrch, *Exec Srch*
Mgmt. Recrtrs of Philadelphia/ CompuSrch, *Exec Srch*
Olsten Staff Svcs, *Temp. Agcy*
LaMonte Owens, *Exec Srch*
Pancoast Temp. Svcs, *Temp. Agcy*
Rice Cohen Intl, *Exec Srch*
The Richards Grp, *Exec Srch*
S-H-S Intl, *Perm. Emp Agcy*
S-H-S Intl, *Exec Srch*
Strauss Persnnl, *Perm. Emp Agcy*
TAC Staff Svcs, *Temp. Agcy*
W.G. Tucker & Assoc., *Exec Srch*
Uniforce Temp. Svcs, *Temp. Agcy*
Visions Temp. Svc, *Temp. Agcy*
Vogue Persnnl, *Perm. Emp Agcy*

Rhode Island

Aquidneck Emp. Svc, *Perm. Emp Agcy*
Mgmt. Recrtrs Intl, *Exec Srch*
Norrell Svcs, *Temp. Agcy*
Pro Srch, *Exec Srch*
Storti Assoc., *Exec Srch*
TAC Staff Svcs, *Temp. Agcy*

South Carolina

Jerman Persnnl Svcs, *Temp. Agcy*
Mgmt. Recrtrs of Columbia, *Exec Srch*
Mgmt. Recrtrs of Rck Hill, *Exec Srch*
PRL & Assoc., *Perm. Emp Agcy*

South Dakota

Careers Unlimtd, *Perm. Emp Agcy*
Mgmt. Recrtrs Intl, *Exec Srch*
Olsten Staff Svcs, *Temp. Agcy*
Snelling Persnnl Svcs, *Perm. Emp Agcy*

Tennessee

B.K. Barnes & Assoc., *Exec Srch*
Gateway Grp Persnnl, *Temp. Agcy*
Kelly Svcs, *Temp. Agcy*
Mgmt. Recrtrs of Knoxville, *Exec Srch*
Norrell Svcs, *Temp. Agcy*
Sales Consltnts of Nashville, *Exec Srch*
Snelling Persnnl Svcs, *Exec Srch*
Staffing Solut'ns, *Perm. Emp Agcy*
Temp Staff, *Temp. Agcy*
Unlimited Staff Solut'ns, *Contract Svc*

Texas

Abilene Emp. Svc, *Perm. Emp Agcy*
Action Persnnl, *Temp. Agcy*
Adecco, *Temp. Agcy*
Marilyn Austin & Assoc., *Exec Srch*
Best/World Assoc., *Exec Srch*
BestStaff Svcs, *Perm. Emp Agcy*
Cherbonnier Grp, *Exec Srch*
Colvin Resrcs Grp, *Temp. Agcy*
Continental Persnnl, *Perm. Emp Agcy*
Credit Union Emp. Resrcs, *Temp. Agcy*
DH&A (Donice Hall & Assoc.), *Perm. Emp Agcy*
The Danbrook Grp, *Exec Srch*
Gail Darling Staffing/Darling's Prof'l Desk, *Temp. Agcy*
Denton-Lewis Assoc., *Exec Srch*
Dunhill Prof'l Srch, *Exec Srch*
Evins Persnnl Consltnts of Killeen, *Perm. Emp Agcy*
The Exec Consltng Grp, *Exec Srch*
Executive Srch Persnnl, *Exec Srch*
Express Persnnl Svcs, *Perm. Emp Agcy*
Financial Prof'ls, *Perm. Emp Agcy*
Abel Gonzalez & Assoc., *Exec Srch*
Robert Half Intl, *Perm. Emp Agcy*
The Human Element of Business, *Exec Srch*
Interim Persnnl, *Temp. Agcy*
InterSearch Assoc., *Temp. Agcy*
Kelly Svcs, *Temp. Agcy*
Mgmt. Recrtrs Intl, *Exec Srch*
Mgmt. Recrtrs of Dallas, *Exec Srch*
Manpower Temp. Svcs, *Temp. Agcy*
Olsten Staff Svcs, *Temp. Agcy*
P&P Persnnl, *Perm. Emp Agcy*
The Pailin Grp, *Exec Srch*
Placements Unlimtd, *Perm. Emp Agcy*
Resource Staffng, *Contract Svc*
Russell Reynolds Assoc., *Exec Srch*
Sales Consltnts of Houston, *Exec Srch*
Salinas & Assoc. Persnnl, *Exec Srch*
Texas Persnnl, *Exec Srch*
Todays Temporary, *Temp. Agcy*
Total Temp. Svcs, *Temp. Agcy*
Vinson & Assoc., *Perm. Emp Agcy*
John Worsham & Assoc., *Exec Srch*

Utah

Mgmt. Recrtrs Intl, *Exec Srch*

Vermont

Mgmt. Recrtrs of Burlington, *Exec Srch*
Triad Temp. Svcs, *Temp. Agcy*

Virginia

A Better Resume, *Career/Outplacemnt*
Accountnts Exec Srch/Accountnts On Call, *Exec Srch*
Adams Sources, *Exec Srch*
Corporate Connection Exec. Srch Firm
Dow Persnnl, *Perm. Emp Agcy*
Dunhill Prof'l Srch, *Exec Srch*
EDP, *Temp. Agcy*
Effective Staffng, *Exec Srch*
FORTUNE Persnnl Consltnts, *Exec Srch*
Mgmt. Recrtrs of McLean, *Exec Srch*
Mgmt. Recrtrs of Roanoke, *Exec Srch*
Carol McNew Emp. Svc, *Perm. Emp Agcy*
Norrell Staff Svcs, *Exec Srch*
Placement Prof'ls, *Exec Srch*
Professional Srch Persnnl, *Exec Srch*
Remedy Intelligent Staffng, *Temp. Agcy*
Snelling Persnnl Svcs, *Perm. Emp Agcy*
TAC Staff Svcs, *Temp. Agcy*
The Talley Grp, *Exec Srch*
Temporary Solut'ns, *Temp. Agcy*
Virginia Emp. Referral Svc, *Exec Srch*

Washington

Bostwick Temp. Svc, *Temp. Agcy*
The Career Clinic, *Exec Srch*
Express Persnnl Svcs, *Temp. Agcy*
Guidance Svcs, *Temp. Agcy*
Mgmt. Recrtrs Intl, *Exec Srch*
Mgmt. Recrtrs of Mercer Islnd, *Exec Srch*
Mgmt. Recrtrs of Tacoma, *Exec Srch*
Thomas Co, *Perm. Emp Agcy*
Two 56, *Contract Svc*

West Virginia

Extra Support Staffng, *Temp. Agcy*
Key Persnnl, *Perm. Emp Agcy*

Wisconsin

Allen, Wayne, & Co, *Perm. Emp Agcy*
Careertrac Emp. Svc, *Exec Srch*
Crown Svcs, *Temp. Agcy*
Executive Resource, *Exec Srch*
Landmark, The Staffing Resource, *Temp. Agcy*
Mgmt. Recrtrs Intl, *Exec Srch*
Mgmt. Recrtrs of Green Bay, *Exec Srch*
Mgmt. Recrtrs of Milwaukee, *Exec Srch*
Olsten Staff Svcs, *Temp. Agcy*
Quirk-Corporon & Assoc., *Exec Srch*
Temps Plus Staff Svcs, *Perm. Emp Agcy*
Work Connection, *Perm. Emp Agcy*

BIOLOGY

California

Apropos Emp. Agcy, *Perm. Emp Agcy*
Assist Tech. Svc, *Contract Svc*
Biosource Tech. Svc, *Contract Svc*
CDI Corp, *Temp. Agcy*
California Srch Agcy, *Exec Srch*
Employment Devlpmnt Dept, *Perm. Emp Agcy*
Fastek Tech. Svcs, *Perm. Emp Agcy*
FORTUNE Persnnl Consltnts of Beverly Hills, *Exec Srch*
40 Plus of So. CA, *Exec Srch*
Kelly Tech. Svcs, *Temp. Agcy*
John Kurosky & Assoc., *Exec Srch*
Lab Support, *Temp. Agcy*
Mgmt. Recrtrs of Laguna Hills, *Exec Srch*
Med Quest, *Exec Srch*
Med-Exec Intl, *Exec Srch*
Medical Exec Recrtrs, *Exec Srch*
Mini-Systems Assoc., *Exec Srch*
National Srch Assoc., *Exec Srch*
Ed Rast & Co, *Exec Srch*
Sage Technolog's, *Exec Srch*
Santa Barbara Plcmnt, *Perm. Emp Agcy*
Technical Aid Corp, *Temp. Agcy*
TechniQuest, *Exec Srch*
Unisearch, *Exec Srch*
United Staff Solut'ns, *Exec Srch*

Colorado

Health Technlgy, *Exec Srch*
Lab Support, *Temp. Agcy*

Connecticut

Charter Persnnl Svcs, *Exec Srch*
Lab Support, *Temp. Agcy*
Mgmt. Recrtrs Intl, *Exec Srch*

Delaware

E.W. Hodges & Assoc., *Exec Srch*

Florida

AAA Employment, *Perm. Emp Agcy*
AccuTech, *Contract Svc*
Mgmt. Recrtrs of Coral Gables, *Exec Srch*
Mgmt. Recrtrs of Plant Cty, *Exec Srch*
Mankuta Gallagher & Assoc., *Exec Srch*

Georgia

Elite Staff Svcs, *Perm. Emp Agcy*
ISC of Atlanta/Intl Career Continuation, *Exec Srch*
Mgmt. Recrtrs Intl, *Exec Srch*

Illinois

Illinois Veterans Leadership Program, *Career/Outplacemnt*
Mgmt. Recrtrs of Albion, *Exec Srch*
Pelichem Assoc., *Exec Srch*
The Raleigh Warwick Grp, *Exec Srch*
Voigt Assoc., *Exec Srch*

Kansas

Smith Brown & Jones, *Exec Srch*

Louisiana

Talley & Assoc./Talley Temps, *Exec Srch*

Maine

John Jay & Co, *Exec Srch*

Maryland

L.S. Gross & Assoc., *Exec Srch*
TAD Staff Svcs, *Temp. Agcy*

Massachusetts

Ability Srch of N.E., *Perm. Emp Agcy*
Cyr Assoc., *Exec Srch*
The Environmental Careers Organization, *Contract Svc*
Harvest Persnnl, *Exec Srch*
Human Resource Consltnts, *Perm. Emp Agcy*
Lab Support, *Temp. Agcy*
Logix, *Exec Srch*
Master Srch, *Perm. Emp Agcy*
Need Persnnl Plcmnt, *Temp. Agcy*
Selectemps, *Temp. Agcy*
Stone Consltng Grp & Legal Srch Specialists, *Exec Srch*
Winfield Assoc., *Exec Srch*

Michigan

Executive Mngmnt Srch, *Exec Srch*
Healthcare Recrtrs Intl, *Exec Srch*
Intertec Design, *Contract Svc*
Kelly Tech. Svcs, *Contract Svc*
Professional Advancement Institute, *Exec Srch*

Minnesota

Agri-Business Svcs, *Exec Srch*
T.H. Hunter, *Exec Srch*
Laboratory Resrcs, *Contract Svc*
Northland Emp. Svcs, *Exec Srch*

Missouri

ABC Emp. Svc, *Perm. Emp Agcy*
Bottom Line Prof'l Svcs, *Contract Svc*
Burns Emp. Svc, *Exec Srch*
Jim Crumpley & Assoc., *Exec Srch*
Jackson Emp. Agcy, *Perm. Emp Agcy*
J.D. Ruhmann & Assoc., *Exec Srch*
Western Tech. Svcs, *Contract Svc*

Montana

FORTUNE Persnnl Consltnts, *Exec Srch*

New Hampshire

Allstaff Contrct Svcs, *Perm. Emp Agcy*
Dubois & Co, *Exec Srch*
Sales Consltnts of Nashua-Manchester, *Exec Srch*

New Jersey

Gary Bell Assoc., *Exec Srch*
Blake & Assoc. Exec Srch, *Exec Srch*
CPS Tech. Placemnts, *Perm. Emp Agcy*
Integro Staff Svcs, *Temp. Agcy*
The Keller Grp/Careers, *Exec Srch*
Lab Support, *Temp. Agcy*

Illinois
SHS, *Exec Srch*
Search Source, *Exec Srch*

Kansas
Network of Excellence, *Exec Srch*

Massachusetts
F.L. Mannix & Co, *Exec Srch*
Selectemps, *Temp. Agcy*
Stone & Youngblood, *Exec Srch*

Michigan
Graphic Arts Mrktng Assoc., *Exec Srch*

Mississippi
Recruitment & Training of MS, *Perm. Emp Agcy*

Missouri
Jay Alexandr & Assoc. dba Kirdonn Grp, *Perm. Emp Agcy*

New Jersey
T.J. Koellhoffer & Assoc., *Exec Srch*
Mini Conglomerate Svc, *Perm. Emp Agcy*

New Mexico
Albuquerque Persnnl, *Perm. Emp Agcy*

New York
Accounting & Computer Persnnl, *Perm. Emp Agcy*
Adecco, *Temp. Agcy*
Benson Assoc., *Exec Srch*
Career Blazers Persnnl, *Perm. Emp Agcy*
Fanning Persnnl, *Exec Srch*
Genesis Emp. Consltnts, *Exec Srch*
Robert Half Intl/Information Syst. Division, *Exec Srch*
Just One Break, *Perm. Emp Agcy*
KLK Persnnl, *Perm. Emp Agcy*
Morgan-Murray Persnnl/M&M Top Temps, *Temp. Agcy*
Promotion Recrtrs, *Exec Srch*
Rem Resrcs, *Perm. Emp Agcy*
Rep Temps, *Temp. Agcy*
United Persnnl Agcy, *Perm. Emp Agcy*
Volt Svcs Grp, *Contract Svc*
Western Staff Svcs, *Temp. Agcy*

North Carolina
Employment Consltnts, *Contract Svc*
Jobs of Fayetteville, *Perm. Emp Agcy*

Ohio
Champion Persnnl, *Perm. Emp Agcy*
Executech Consltnts, *Exec Srch*

Tennessee
Kelly Svcs, *Temp. Agcy*

Texas
R.A. Stone & Assoc., *Exec Srch*

BROKERAGE

Florida
Benson & Assoc., *Exec Srch*

Illinois
Chicago Financial Srch, *Exec Srch*
J.R. Scott & Assoc., *Exec Srch*
T.I. Vincent & Assoc., *Exec Srch*

New Jersey
SkuppSearch, *Exec Srch*

New York
Career Concepts, *Perm. Emp Agcy*
Cross Staffng, *Perm. Emp Agcy*
Kensington Grp, *Exec Srch*
The Lloyd Co, *Career/Outplacemnt*
Tyler Srch Consltnts, *Perm. Emp Agcy*
Vance Persnnl, *Perm. Emp Agcy*

CHEMICAL

Alabama
Hughes & Assoc., *Exec Srch*
Mgmt. Recrtrs Intl, *Exec Srch*

Arizona
Volt Tech. Svcs, *Contract Svc*

Arkansas
Mgmt. Recrtrs of Little Rock, *Exec Srch*

California
Kelly Scientific Resrcs, *Temp. Agcy*
Mgmt. Recrtrs of Encino, *Exec Srch*

Colorado
The Bridge, *Exec Srch*
Kelly Scientific Resrcs, *Temp. Agcy*
Mgmt. Recrtrs Intl, *Exec Srch*
Woodmoor Grp, *Exec Srch*

Delaware
The Franklin Co, *Exec Srch*

Florida
Gallin Assoc., *Exec Srch*
The Mac Grp, *Exec Srch*
Mgmt. Recrtrs Intl, *Exec Srch*
Mgmt. Recrtrs of Plant Cty, *Exec Srch*
Mgmt. Recrtrs of St. Petersburg, *Exec Srch*
Mgmt. Recrtrs of Tallahassee, *Exec Srch*
Mgmt. Recrtrs of Tampa, *Exec Srch*
Sales Consltnts of Fort Lauderdale, *Exec Srch*
Sales Consltnts of Jacksonville, *Exec Srch*
The Witt Grp, *Exec Srch*

Georgia
Bradshaw & Assoc., *Exec Srch*
FORTUNE Persnnl Consltnts of Atlanta, *Exec Srch*
Kelly Scientific Resrcs, *Temp. Agcy*
Mgmt. Recrtrs of Atlanta, *Exec Srch*
Mgmt. Recrtrs of Savannah, *Exec Srch*

Idaho
Mgmt. Recrtrs of Boise, *Exec Srch*

Illinois
Corporate Environment, *Exec Srch*
Hanover Crown & Assoc., *Exec Srch*
Kelly Scientific Resrcs, *Temp. Agcy*
Mgmt. Recrtrs of Rockford, *Exec Srch*
Officemates5 of Wheeling, *Exec Srch*
Sales Consltnts/Mgmt. Recrtrs Intl, *Exec Srch*
Sales Consltnts of Oak Brk, *Exec Srch*
Twin Oaks Technical, *Exec Srch*

Indiana
Agra Placemnts, *Perm. Emp Agcy*
Execusearch, *Exec Srch*
Mgmt. Recrtrs of Evansville, *Exec Srch*
Mgmt. Recrtrs of Indianapolis, *Exec Srch*
Mgmt. Recrtrs of Richmond/Staff Solut'ns, *Exec Srch*
National Corporate Consltnts/Advantage Svcs, *Exec Srch*
Officemates5 of Indianapolis, *Exec Srch*

Iowa
Agra Placemnts Exec. Srch Firm
Mgmt. Recrtrs Intl, *Exec Srch*

Kansas
Mgmt. Recrtrs of Overlnd Prk, *Exec Srch*

Kentucky
Angel Grp Intl, *Exec Srch*

Louisiana
Dunhill of Baton Rouge, *Exec Srch*
Mgmt. Recrtrs of Baton Rouge, *Exec Srch*
Mgmt. Recrtrs-Metairie/Sales Consltnts, *Exec Srch*

Maryland
Kelly Scientific Resrcs, *Temp. Agcy*
Mgmt. Recrtrs of Annapolis, *Exec Srch*
Mgmt. Recrtrs-Baltimore/Sales Consltnts, *Exec Srch*
Mgmt. Recrtrs of Frederick, *Exec Srch*
Sales Consltnts of Prince Georges Cnty, *Exec Srch*

Massachusetts
Lab Support, *Temp. Agcy*

Michigan
Durham Assoc., *Exec Srch*
Kelly Scientific Resrcs, *Temp. Agcy*
Mgmt. Recrtrs of Bingham Farms, *Exec Srch*
Mgmt. Recrtrs of Dearborn, *Exec Srch*
Mgmt. Recrtrs of Flint, *Exec Srch*
Mgmt. Recrtrs of Grand Rapids, *Exec Srch*
Mgmt. Recrtrs of Kalamazoo, *Exec Srch*
Mgmt. Recrtrs of Lansing, *Exec Srch*
Mgmt. Recrtrs of Muskegon, *Exec Srch*
Mgmt. Recrtrs of Rochester, *Exec Srch*
Sales Consltnts of Detroit, *Exec Srch*
Sales Consltnts of Lansing, *Exec Srch*
Sales Executives, *Perm. Emp Agcy*
Gene Wagner Assoc., *Exec Srch*

Minnesota
Kelly Scientific Resrcs, *Temp. Agcy*
Mgmt. Recrtrs-Minneapolis/Sales Consltnts, *Exec Srch*

Missouri
Kelly Scientific Resrcs, *Temp. Agcy*
Mgmt. Recrtrs of Kansas Cty, *Exec Srch*
Mgmt. Recrtrs of Springfield, *Exec Srch*
Mgmt. Recrtrs of St. Louis, *Exec Srch*
Officemates5 of St. Louis, *Exec Srch*

Nebraska
Compusearch of Lincoln, *Exec Srch*
Mgmt. Recrtrs of Omaha/Officemates5, *Exec Srch*

New Jersey
Gary Bell Assoc., *Exec Srch*
Joule Temps, *Temp. Agcy*
Kelly Scientific Resrcs, *Temp. Agcy*
Mgmt. Recrtrs of Medford, *Exec Srch*
Orion Consltng, *Exec Srch*
Petruzzi Assoc., *Exec Srch*
Rob Scott Assoc., *Exec Srch*
Yoh Scientific, *Contract Svc*

New York
Mgmt. Recrtrs Intl, *Exec Srch*

North Carolina
Office Specialists, *Temp. Agcy*

Ohio
Dave Arnold & Assoc., *Exec Srch*
H.J.C., *Exec Srch*
North Star Resrcs, *Contract Svc*

Oklahoma
Reality Grp, *Exec Srch*
Lloyd Richards Persnnl, *Perm. Emp Agcy*

Pennsylvania
Interactive Srch, *Exec Srch*
Lab Support, *Temp. Agcy*
Mgmt. Recrtrs Intl, *Exec Srch*
George Martin Exec Srch, *Exec Srch*
Triangle Assoc. Intl, *Perm. Emp Agcy*

Texas
Austin Grp, *Exec Srch*
C. Michael Dixon Assoc., *Exec Srch*
H+M Recrtrs, *Exec Srch*
Kelly Scientific Resrcs, *Temp. Agcy*
McKinley•Arend Intl, *Exec Srch*
Preng & Assoc., *Exec Srch*
Russell Reynolds Assoc., *Exec Srch*
Tech. Staff Solut'ns, *Exec Srch*

Washington
CDI Corp, *Contract Svc*

West Virginia
Mgmt. Recrtrs Intl, *Exec Srch*

Wisconsin
Ropella & Assoc., *Exec Srch*

CHILD CARE, IN-HOME

California
Mothers-in-Deed/Town End Nannies, *Perm. Emp Agcy*

Maine
Portland Nannies, *Perm. Emp Agcy*

Maryland
A Choice Nanny, *Contract Svc*

Massachusetts
American Nanny Co, *Perm. Emp Agcy*
The Original Nanny Svc, *Perm. Emp Agcy*
Parents in a Pinch, *Perm. Emp Agcy*
Yankee Sitters Nanny Agcy, *Perm. Emp Agcy*

Michigan
Nanny Attachment Svc, *Perm. Emp Agcy*
The Nanny Netwrk, *Perm. Emp Agcy*

Minnesota
Youth Emp. Project, *Perm. Emp Agcy*

Missouri
TLC CareGivers, *Perm. Emp Agcy*

Montana
Nannies Preferred, *Perm. Emp Agcy*

Nevada
Kids Care Connection, *Perm. Emp Agcy*
Nanny Placemnt Agcy, *Perm. Emp Agcy*

New Jersey
A Choice Nanny, *Perm. Emp Agcy*
Capitol Srch, *Perm. Emp Agcy*
Nannies Plus, *Perm. Emp Agcy*
Neighborhood Nannies, *Perm. Emp Agcy*

New York
The New York Nanny Ctr, *Perm. Emp Agcy*

Ohio
Child & Elder Care Insights, *Exec Srch*

Oklahoma
DeMarge Employment, *Perm. Emp Agcy*

Oregon
Auntie Fay Domestic Agcy, *Perm. Emp Agcy*

Pennsylvania
Your Other Hands, *Perm. Emp Agcy*

Texas
Morningside Nannies, *Perm. Emp Agcy*

Virginia
Nanny Dimensions, *Perm. Emp Agcy*

CLERICAL

Alaska
Alaska Exec Srch, *Exec Srch*
Elite Emp. Svc, *Temp. Agcy*
Manpower Temp. Svc, *Temp. Agcy*

Arizona
Adecco, *Temp. Agcy*
Kerry's Referrals, *Temp. Agcy*
Norrell Temp. Svcs, *Temp. Agcy*

California
Act 1 Persnnl Svcs, *Perm. Emp Agcy*
Apple One Emp. Svcs, *Perm. Emp Agcy*
Assured Persnnl Svcs, *Perm. Emp Agcy*
CT Persnnl Svcs, *Perm. Emp Agcy*
Career Images, *Temp. Agcy*
Colt Syst. Prof'l Persnnl Svcs, *Perm. Emp Agcy*
COMFORCE Tech. Svcs, *Contract Svc*
The Dial Grp, *Perm. Emp Agcy*
Drake Office Overload, *Temp. Agcy*
Full Svc Temps, *Temp. Agcy*
Interim Industrial Staffng, *Temp. Agcy*
Interim Persnnl, *Temp. Agcy*
Kelly Svcs, *Temp. Agcy*
Manpower, *Temp. Agcy*
Rich Maries Agcy, *Perm. Emp Agcy*
McCall Staff Svcs, *Perm. Emp Agcy*
Norrell Temp. Svcs of CA, *Temp. Agcy*
O'Brien Emp. Svcs, *Temp. Agcy*
Olsten Staff Svcs, *Temp. Agcy*
Pips Persnnl Svcs, *Perm. Emp Agcy*
Prestige Persnnl, *Perm. Emp Agcy*
PrideStaff, *Temp. Agcy*
Remedy Intelligent Staffng, *Temp. Agcy*
Snelling Persnnl Svcs, *Perm. Emp Agcy*
Stivers Temp. Persnnl of CA, *Temp. Agcy*
TAC Staff Svcs, *Temp. Agcy*
Thor Temp. Svcs, *Temp. Agcy*
Tustin Persnnl Svcs, *Perm. Emp Agcy*
WGI Solut'ns, *Exec Srch*
Western Staff Svcs of Walnut Crk/Westrn Medical, *Temp. Agcy*
Wollborg-Michelson Persnnl, *Perm. Emp Agcy*

Colorado
Absolute Emp. Svcs, *Perm. Emp Agcy*
Adecco, *Temp. Agcy*
Aspen Persnnl Svcs, *Perm. Emp Agcy*
Eagle Valley Temps, *Temp. Agcy*
Goodwin Persnnl, *Perm. Emp Agcy*
Kelly Svcs, *Perm. Emp Agcy*
SOS Staff Svcs, *Temp. Agcy*
Senior Skills, *Temp. Agcy*
Terry Persnnl, *Perm. Emp Agcy*

Connecticut
Charter Persnnl Svcs, *Perm. Emp Agcy*
Employment Opport., *Perm. Emp Agcy*
Manpower, *Temp. Agcy*
The McKnight Grp, *Exec Srch*
National Staff Svcs, *Temp. Agcy*
Western Staff Svcs, *Perm. Emp Agcy*

Delaware
Sussex Emp. Svcs, *Perm. Emp Agcy*

District of Columbia
Snelling Persnnl, *Perm. Emp Agcy*

Florida
AccuStaff, *Temp. Agcy*
AccuStaff, *Perm. Emp Agcy*
Availability, *Perm. Emp Agcy*
DGA Persnnl Grp, *Exec Srch*
Girl Friday Persnnl, *Temp. Agcy*
Hallmark Persnnl, *Perm. Emp Agcy*
Impact Persnnl, *Perm. Emp Agcy*
Kelly Svcs, *Temp. Agcy*
Manpower Temp. Svcs, *Temp. Agcy*
Office Ours, *Temp. Agcy*
Office Specialists, *Temp. Agcy*
PMC&L Assoc., *Perm. Emp Agcy*

Georgia
Access Persnnl Svcs, *Perm. Emp Agcy*
Kelly Svcs, *Temp. Agcy*
Norrell Corp, *Temp. Agcy*

Idaho
Volt Tech. Svcs, *Contract Svc*
Western Staff Svcs, *Temp. Agcy*

Illinois
Able's Pool of Temps, *Temp. Agcy*
Availability, *Perm. Emp Agcy*
Banner Persnnl, *Perm. Emp Agcy*
The Esquire Staffing Grp, *Perm. Emp Agcy*
Fellows Plcmnt, *Temp. Agcy*
First Staffng, *Perm. Emp Agcy*
Interviewing Consltnts, *Perm. Emp Agcy*
Michael David Assoc., *Perm. Emp Agcy*
The Murphy Grp, *Perm. Emp Agcy*
Office Ours, *Temp. Agcy*
Opportunity Persnnl, *Perm. Emp Agcy*
Paige Persnnl, *Perm. Emp Agcy*
SER Bus. And Tech. Institute, *Perm. Emp Agcy*
Snelling Persnnl Svcs, *Temp. Agcy*
Snyder Staffng, *Temp. Agcy*
Stivers Temp. Persnnl, *Temp. Agcy*
Talent Tree of Illinois, *Perm. Emp Agcy*

Indiana
Adecco, *Perm. Emp Agcy*
Crown Temp. Svcs of Indianapolis, *Temp. Agcy*
Data Access, *Perm. Emp Agcy*
Pat Day Persnnl, *Perm. Emp Agcy*
Employment Plus, *Temp. Agcy*
Express Persnnl, *Temp. Agcy*
Flexible Persnnl, *Temp. Agcy*
Hunter-Lawyer Persnnl, *Perm. Emp Agcy*
Morley Grp, *Exec Srch*
Norrell Staff Svcs of Evansville, *Temp. Agcy*
Pyramids Persnnl, *Perm. Emp Agcy*
The Registry, *Perm. Emp Agcy*

Iowa
Cambridge Staffng, *Perm. Emp Agcy*
Persnnl, *Exec Srch*
Sedona Staff Svcs, *Exec Srch*

Kansas
Manpower, *Temp. Agcy*
Uniforce Staff Svcs, *Temp. Agcy*

Kentucky
C.M. Mngmnt Svcs, *Perm. Emp Agcy*
Precision Staffng, *Temp. Agcy*
Precision Staffng, *Perm. Emp Agcy*
Temporary Prof'ls, *Temp. Agcy*

Louisiana
Interim Persnnl, *Temp. Agcy*
Manpower, *Temp. Agcy*
Professional Temps, *Temp. Agcy*
Western Staff Svcs, *Temp. Agcy*

Maryland
Admin Persnnl Svcs, *Perm. Emp Agcy*
Careers III, *Perm. Emp Agcy*
Dunhill of Rockville, *Perm. Emp Agcy*
TAC Staff Svcs, *Temp. Agcy*

Massachusetts
Abbot Persnnl Consltng Svcs, *Perm. Emp Agcy*
Kelly Svcs, *Temp. Agcy*
Lane Emp. Svc, *Perm. Emp Agcy*
Manpower Temp. Svcs, *Temp. Agcy*
Molari, *Temp. Agcy*
New Boston Select Staffng, *Temp. Agcy*
New Perspectives Persnnl, *Temp. Agcy*
Office Specialists, *Temp. Agcy*
TAD Staff Svcs, *Temp. Agcy*

Michigan
Beacon Svcs, *Temp. Agcy*
Davis-Smith Medical Emp. Svc, *Perm. Emp Agcy*
Diversified Recrtrs, *Perm. Emp Agcy*
Entech Svcs, *Temp. Agcy*
Grosse Pointe Employment, *Perm. Emp Agcy*
Manpower, *Temp. Agcy*

Minnesota
Alternative Staffng, *Perm. Emp Agcy*
Award Temp. Svcs, *Temp. Agcy*
Ells Persnnl Syst., *Exec Srch*
NER (National Engineering Resrcs), *Exec Srch*

Mississippi
Capitol Staff Solut'ns, *Perm. Emp Agcy*
Opportunities Unlimtd, *Perm. Emp Agcy*

Missouri
Crown Svcs, *Temp. Agcy*
LandAJob, *Perm. Emp Agcy*
B. Loehr Temps, *Temp. Agcy*
Olsten Staff Svcs, *Temp. Agcy*

Montana
Express Persnnl, *Perm. Emp Agcy*
Kelly Svcs, *Temp. Agcy*
Manpower Temp. Svcs, *Temp. Agcy*

Nebraska
Ameri Srch, *Perm. Emp Agcy*
Donna's Office Svc, *Contract Svc*
Kelly Svcs, *Temp. Agcy*
Odyssey Grp, *Exec Srch*

Nevada
Manpower Temp. Svcs, *Temp. Agcy*
Matrix Grp, *Exec Srch*
Nevada Bus. Svcs, *Career/Outplacemnt*

New Hampshire
Able 1 Staffng, *Exec Srch*
Allstaff Contrct Svcs, *Perm. Emp Agcy*
Kelly Svcs, *Temp. Agcy*
R.G.T. Assoc., *Exec Srch*
TAC Staff Svcs, *Temp. Agcy*

New Jersey
Career Ctr, *Perm. Emp Agcy*
Citizens Emp. Svcs, *Perm. Emp Agcy*
Persnnl Plus/Temps Plus, *Perm. Emp Agcy*
Selective Persnnl, *Perm. Emp Agcy*
Snelling Persnnl Svcs, *Temp. Agcy*
Snelling Persnnl Svcs, *Perm. Emp Agcy*
Winters & Ross, *Perm. Emp Agcy*

New Mexico
Sanderson Emp. Svc, *Perm. Emp Agcy*

New York
Adecco, *Temp. Agcy*
Cross Staffng, *Perm. Emp Agcy*
Joseph Maloney & Assoc., *Perm. Emp Agcy*
Manpower Temp. Svcs, *Temp. Agcy*
Sloan Persnnl, *Perm. Emp Agcy*
TAC Staff Svcs, *Temp. Agcy*
Talent Tree Staffng, *Perm. Emp Agcy*

North Carolina
Careers Unlimtd, *Perm. Emp Agcy*
Graham & Assoc., *Perm. Emp Agcy*
Granite Persnnl, *Perm. Emp Agcy*
Greer Persnnl, *Perm. Emp Agcy*
Interim Persnnl, *Temp. Agcy*
Mebane Temp. Svcs, *Temp. Agcy*
Mega Force, *Perm. Emp Agcy*
Olsten Staff Svcs, *Temp. Agcy*
Persnnl Svcs Unlimtd, *Temp. Agcy*

North Dakota
Interim Persnnl, *Perm. Emp Agcy*

Ohio
Adecco, *Temp. Agcy*
Belcan Staff Svcs, *Temp. Agcy*
CBS Persnnl Svcs, *Perm. Emp Agcy*
Champion Persnnl, *Perm. Emp Agcy*
Crown Temp. Svcs of Cincinnati, *Temp. Agcy*
Extra Help Temp. Svc, *Temp. Agcy*
T.J. Hughes Assoc., *Perm. Emp Agcy*
Manpower Temp. Svcs, *Temp. Agcy*
Norrell Svcs, *Temp. Agcy*
Olsten Staff Svcs, *Temp. Agcy*

Oklahoma
Manpower Temp. Svcs, *Temp. Agcy*
Lloyd Richards Persnnl, *Perm. Emp Agcy*

Oregon
Adams & Assoc. Persnnl, *Perm. Emp Agcy*
Adams Temps, *Temp. Agcy*
Saint Vincent De Paul Employment, *Temp. Agcy*

Pennsylvania
Adecco, *Temp. Agcy*
Capital Area Temp. Svcs, *Temp. Agcy*
Executive Avail-A-Search, *Exec Srch*
Hoskins Hains Assoc., *Perm. Emp Agcy*
Kathy Karr Persnnl, *Perm. Emp Agcy*
Olsten Staff Svcs, *Temp. Agcy*
Powers Persnnl, *Perm. Emp Agcy*
Pratt Persnnl Svcs, *Temp. Agcy*

Tom Sawchak Action of PA, *Perm. Emp Agcy*
TAC Staff Svcs, *Temp. Agcy*
United Tech. Assoc., *Temp. Agcy*

Rhode Island
Kelly Svcs, *Temp. Agcy*
Pro Staff Persnnl Svcs, *Temp. Agcy*
TAC Staff Svcs, *Temp. Agcy*

South Carolina
Carolina Persnnl Svcs, *Temp. Agcy*
Roper Svcs, *Temp. Agcy*
TRS (Total Recruitng Svcs), *Perm. Emp Agcy*

South Dakota
Olsten Staff Svcs, *Temp. Agcy*

Tennessee
D.S.A., *Temp. Agcy*
Madison Persnnl, *Perm. Emp Agcy*
Norrell Svcs, *Temp. Agcy*
Piercy Emp. Svcs, *Perm. Emp Agcy*
Unlimited Staff Solut'ns, *Contract Svc*

Texas
Add-A-Temp/Woodlands Exec Employment, *Temp. Agcy*
Babich & Assoc., *Perm. Emp Agcy*
Border Prof'l Recrtrs, *Perm. Emp Agcy*
Bruco, *Perm. Emp Agcy*
Burnett Persnnl Svcs, *Temp. Agcy*
Burnett's Staffng, *Perm. Emp Agcy*
Corbett Persnnl Svcs, *Temp. Agcy*
Day Star Svcs, *Perm. Emp Agcy*
Executeam, *Exec Srch*
Express Persnnl Svcs, *Perm. Emp Agcy*
Claire Fontaine & Assoc., *Exec Srch*
Imprimis Staff Solut'ns, *Temp. Agcy*
Kelly Svcs, *Temp. Agcy*
Steele & Assoc., *Perm. Emp Agcy*
TRC Staff Svcs, *Temp. Agcy*
TAD Tech. Svcs, *Contract Svc*
Vinson & Assoc., *Perm. Emp Agcy*
Volt Temp. Svcs of Dallas, *Temp. Agcy*

Utah
Your Job Connection, *Perm. Emp Agcy*

Vermont
Harmon Persnnl Svcs, *Temp. Agcy*
TAD Resrcs, *Perm. Emp Agcy*
Western Staff Svcs, *Temp. Agcy*

Virginia
Bradford Co, *Contract Svc*
Manpower Temp. Svcs, *Temp. Agcy*
Norrell Staff Svcs, *Exec Srch*
Potomac Persnnl, *Perm. Emp Agcy*
TAC Staff Svcs, *Temp. Agcy*
Temps Now, *Temp. Agcy*

Washington
Able Persnnl Agcy, *Perm. Emp Agcy*
Hallmark Svcs, *Perm. Emp Agcy*
Persnnl Unlimtd, *Exec Srch*

West Virginia
Kelly Svcs, *Temp. Agcy*
Quantum Resrcs, *Perm. Emp Agcy*

Wisconsin
ADTEC Staffng, *Temp. Agcy*
Crown Svcs, *Temp. Agcy*
Placements of Racine, *Perm. Emp Agcy*

Wyoming
Express Temp. Svc, *Temp. Agcy*

COMMUNICATIONS

Alabama
Mgmt. Recrtrs Intl, *Exec Srch*

Arizona
Mgmt. Recrtrs of Scottsdale, *Exec Srch*

Arkansas
Mgmt. Recrtrs of Little Rock, *Exec Srch*

California
Business Syst. Staffing & Assoc., *Perm. Emp Agcy*
Davidson & Assoc., *Exec Srch*
Mgmt. Recrtrs of Burlingame/Sales Consltnts, *Exec Srch*
Mgmt. Recrtrs of Encino, *Exec Srch*
Mgmt. Recrtrs of Pleasanton, *Exec Srch*
Mesa Intl, *Exec Srch*

Colorado
Sales Consltnts, *Exec Srch*

Connecticut
Mgmt. Recrtrs Intl, *Exec Srch*

District of Columbia
Travaille Exec Srch, *Exec Srch*

Florida
Mgmt. Recrtrs of St. Petersburg, *Exec Srch*
Mgmt. Recrtrs of Tallahassee, *Exec Srch*
Mgmt. Recrtrs of Tampa, *Exec Srch*
Media Mgmt. Resrcs, *Exec Srch*
Sales Consltnts of Fort Lauderdale, *Exec Srch*
Sales Consltnts of Jacksonville, *Exec Srch*

Georgia
Mgmt. Recrtrs of Atlanta, *Exec Srch*
Steve Wyman & Assoc., *Exec Srch*

Illinois
Mgmt. Recrtrs of Des Plaines, *Exec Srch*
Mgmt. Recrtrs of Rockford, *Exec Srch*
Officemates5 of Wheeling, *Exec Srch*
Pahlman, Murphy & Attridge, *Exec Srch*
Sales Consltnts/Mgmt. Recrtrs Intl, *Exec Srch*
Sales Consltnts of Oak Brk, *Exec Srch*

Indiana
Execusearch, *Exec Srch*
Mgmt. Recrtrs of Evansville, *Exec Srch*
Mgmt. Recrtrs of Indianapolis, *Exec Srch*
Mgmt. Recrtrs of Richmond/Staff Solut'ns, *Exec Srch*
Officemates5 of Indianapolis, *Exec Srch*

Iowa
Mgmt. Recrtrs Intl, *Exec Srch*

Kansas
Mgmt. Recrtrs of Overlnd Prk, *Exec Srch*

Kentucky
Angel Grp Intl, *Exec Srch*
Engineering & Exec Srch, *Exec Srch*

Louisiana
Mgmt. Recrtrs of Baton Rouge, *Exec Srch*
Mgmt. Recrtrs-Metairie/Sales Consltnts, *Exec Srch*

Maryland
Adecco, *Temp. Agcy*
Mgmt. Recrtrs of Annapolis, *Exec Srch*
Mgmt. Recrtrs-Baltimore/Sales Consltnts, *Exec Srch*
Mgmt. Recrtrs-Bethesda/CompuSearch, *Exec Srch*
Mgmt. Recrtrs of Frederick, *Exec Srch*
Sales Consltnts of Prince Georges Cnty, *Exec Srch*

Massachusetts
Chaloner Assoc., *Exec Srch*
Franklin Intl Srch, *Exec Srch*
Mgmt. Recrtrs Intl, *Exec Srch*
Mgmt. Recrtrs Intl of Braintree, *Exec Srch*
Mgmt. Recrtrs Intl of Springfield, *Exec Srch*
Mgmt. Recrtrs Intl of Westboro, *Exec Srch*
Micro-Comm Exec Srch, *Exec Srch*
Sales Consltnts of Cape Cod, *Exec Srch*
Sales Consltnts of Plymouth Cnty, *Exec Srch*
Sales Consltnts of Wellesley, *Exec Srch*
United Prof'l Plcmnt, *Exec Srch*
The Ward Grp, *Exec Srch*

Michigan
Mgmt. Recrtrs of Bingham Farms, *Exec Srch*
Mgmt. Recrtrs of Dearborn, *Exec Srch*
Mgmt. Recrtrs of Flint, *Exec Srch*
Mgmt. Recrtrs of Kalamazoo, *Exec Srch*
Mgmt. Recrtrs of Lansing, *Exec Srch*
Mgmt. Recrtrs of Muskegon, *Exec Srch*
Mgmt. Recrtrs of Rochester, *Exec Srch*
Sales Consltnts of Detroit, *Exec Srch*
Sales Consltnts of Farmington Hills, *Exec Srch*

Minnesota
Mgmt. Recrtrs-Minneapolis/Sales Consltnts, *Exec Srch*

Missouri
Mgmt. Recrtrs of Kansas Cty, *Exec Srch*
Mgmt. Recrtrs of Springfield, *Exec Srch*
Mgmt. Recrtrs of St. Louis, *Exec Srch*
Officemates5 of St. Louis, *Exec Srch*

Nebraska
Compusearch of Lincoln, *Exec Srch*
Mgmt. Recrtrs of Omaha/Officemates5, *Exec Srch*

New Hampshire
Access Consltng, *Perm. Emp Agcy*
Barros Assoc., *Perm. Emp Agcy*
Mgmt. Recrtrs Intl of Bedford, *Exec Srch*

New Jersey
Career Ctr, *Perm. Emp Agcy*
Mgmt. Recrtrs of Passaic Cnty, *Exec Srch*
Orion Consltng, *Exec Srch*
Professional Roster, *Temp. Agcy*
Sales Consltnts of Sparta, *Exec Srch*

New York
Adecco, *Temp. Agcy*
Toby Clark Assoc., *Exec Srch*
Filcro Persnnl, *Perm. Emp Agcy*
The Fry Grp, *Exec Srch*
The Goldman Grp, *Exec Srch*
The Kay Grp of Fifth Avenue, *Exec Srch*
Mgmt. Recrtrs of Woodbury/ CompuSrch, *Exec Srch*
Marshall Consltnts, *Exec Srch*
Metro Support Grp, *Perm. Emp Agcy*
Sales Consltnts of Westchester, *Exec Srch*
TemPositions, *Temp. Agcy*
Tyler Srch Consltnts, *Perm. Emp Agcy*

North Carolina
Mgmt. Recrtrs Intl, *Exec Srch*
Mgmt. Recrtrs of Durham, *Exec Srch*
Mgmt. Recrtrs of Raleigh/Inter Exec, *Exec Srch*
Mgmt. Recrtrs of Winston-Salem, *Exec Srch*
Sales Consltnts of High Point, *Exec Srch*

Ohio
Ives & Assoc., *Exec Srch*
Mgmt. Recrtrs of Cincinnati, *Exec Srch*
Mgmt. Recrtrs of Cleveland, *Exec Srch*
Mgmt. Recrtrs of Columbus, *Exec Srch*
Mgmt. Recrtrs of Dayton, *Exec Srch*
Mgmt. Recrtrs of Solon, *Exec Srch*
Sales Consltnts of Cincinnati, *Exec Srch*

Oklahoma
Mgmt. Recrtrs of Oklahoma Cty, *Exec Srch*

Oregon
Mgmt. Recrtrs/Officemates5 of Portland, *Exec Srch*

Pennsylvania
Mgmt. Recrtrs of DE Cnty/CompuSrch, *Exec Srch*
Mgmt. Recrtrs of Lehigh Vly/CompuSrch, *Exec Srch*
Mgmt. Recrtrs of Philadelphia/ CompuSrch, *Exec Srch*
Rice Cohen Intl, *Exec Srch*

Rhode Island
Mgmt. Recrtrs Intl, *Exec Srch*

South Carolina
Mgmt. Recrtrs of Columbia, *Exec Srch*
Mgmt. Recrtrs of Rck Hill, *Exec Srch*
Sales Consltnts/Mgmt. Recrtrs of Greenville, *Exec Srch*

Tennessee
Mgmt. Recrtrs of Knoxville, *Exec Srch*
Sales Consltnts of Nashville, *Exec Srch*

Texas
Mgmt. Recrtrs Intl, *Exec Srch*
Mgmt. Recrtrs of Dallas, *Exec Srch*
Opportunity Unlimtd Persnnl Consltnts, *Exec Srch*
Sales Consltnts of Houston, *Exec Srch*

Virginia
Mgmt. Recrtrs of McLean, *Exec Srch*
Mgmt. Recrtrs of Roanoke, *Exec Srch*

Washington
CDI Corp, *Contract Svc*
Kossuth & Assoc., *Exec Srch*
Mgmt. Recrtrs of Mercer Islnd, *Exec Srch*
Mgmt. Recrtrs of Tacoma, *Exec Srch*

Wisconsin
Mgmt. Recrtrs of Appleton/ CompuSrch, *Exec Srch*
Mgmt. Recrtrs of Green Bay, *Exec Srch*
Mgmt. Recrtrs of Milwaukee, *Exec Srch*

Wyoming
Mgmt. Recrtrs of Cheyenne, *Exec Srch*

COMPUTER HARDWARE/SOFTWARE

Alabama
A-1 Emp. Svc, *Perm. Emp Agcy*
Mgmt. Recrtrs Intl, *Exec Srch*
Perform Staff Svc, *Perm. Emp Agcy*

Arizona
Erickson & Assoc., *Perm. Emp Agcy*
Hunter Tech. Svcs, *Perm. Emp Agcy*
Mgmt. Recrtrs of Scottsdale, *Exec Srch*
Source Svcs Corp, *Exec Srch*

Tech/Aid of Arizona, *Perm. Emp Agcy*
Tele-Solution Srch, *Exec Srch*

Arkansas
Mgmt. Recrtrs of Little Rock, *Exec Srch*
StaffMark, *Temp. Agcy*

California
AW Data Processing Persnnl, *Perm. Emp Agcy*
AWS, *Exec Srch*
Addleman & Jenkins Assoc., *Exec Srch*
Alexander & Co, *Exec Srch*
Alternative Staffing Grp, *Exec Srch*
Amarx Srch, *Exec Srch*
Apple One Emp. Svcs, *Perm. Emp Agcy*
Associated Software Consltnts, *Exec Srch*
Barnes & Assoc., *Exec Srch*
Deborah Bishop & Assoc., *Exec Srch*
Bryson Myers Co, *Exec Srch*
The Computer Resrcs Grp, *Perm. Emp Agcy*
Culver Persnnl Svcs, *Exec Srch*
Data Careers Persnnl Svcs & Srch Grp, *Perm. Emp Agcy*
Data Syst. Srch Consltnts, *Perm. Emp Agcy*
Dunhill Prof'l Srch of San Francisco, *Exec Srch*
DuVall & Assoc., *Exec Srch*
EDP Contrct Svcs, *Contract Svc*
Executive Directions, *Exec Srch*
Executive Resource Syst., *Exec Srch*
Finesse Persnnl Assoc., *Exec Srch*
FORTUNE Persnnl Consltnts, *Exec Srch*
Charles Fralick Assoc., *Exec Srch*
Full Svc Temps, *Temp. Agcy*
The Goodman Grp, *Exec Srch*
Great 400 Grp Intl, *Perm. Emp Agcy*
Robert Half Intl, *Exec Srch*
Hutton Barnes & Assoc., *Exec Srch*
Innovative Srch Assoc., *Exec Srch*
Cindy Jackson Srch, *Exec Srch*
Aaron Jensen Assoc., *Exec Srch*
Kelly Svcs, *Temp. Agcy*
Kelly Tech. Svcs, *Temp. Agcy*
The London Agcy, *Temp. Agcy*
MIS Srch, *Exec Srch*
MS Data Svc Corp, *Perm. Emp Agcy*
Mgmt. Recrtrs of Burlingame/Sales Consltnts, *Exec Srch*
Mgmt. Recrtrs of Encino, *Exec Srch*
Mgmt. Recrtrs of Pleasanton, *Exec Srch*
Mgmt. Recrtrs of San Francisco, *Exec Srch*
Rich Maries Agcy, *Perm. Emp Agcy*
J.M. Meredith & Assoc., *Exec Srch*
Mesa Intl, *Exec Srch*
Micro Temps Syst. & Programming, *Temp. Agcy*
James Moore & Assoc., *Exec Srch*
Optimum Exec Srch, *Exec Srch*
Protocol Srch & Selection, *Exec Srch*
RGA Assoc., *Exec Srch*
Remedy Intelligent Staffng, *Temp. Agcy*
Larry Rosenthal & Assoc., *Exec Srch*
Rowland Assoc., *Exec Srch*
Royal Staff Svcs, *Exec Srch*
SMC Grp, *Exec Srch*
Penni Safford & Assoc., *Exec Srch*
Search West, *Exec Srch*
Source Svcs Corp, *Exec Srch*
Splaine & Assoc., *Exec Srch*
Fred Stuart Persnnl Svcs, *Perm. Emp Agcy*
Sunday & Assoc., *Perm. Emp Agcy*
Systems Careers, *Exec Srch*
TRC Staff Svcs, *Perm. Emp Agcy*
Tech/Aid of CA, *Temp. Agcy*
Technical Directions, *Perm. Emp Agcy*
Thor Temp. Svcs, *Temp. Agcy*
Trend Westrn Tech. Corp, *Temp. Agcy*
Larry Wade & Assoc., *Exec Srch*
D.L. Weaver & Assoc., *Exec Srch*
Wendell Assoc., *Exec Srch*
Western Staff Svcs of Walnut Crk/Westrn Medical, *Temp. Agcy*
Zeiger Tech. Careers, *Perm. Emp Agcy*

Colorado
The Ardent Grp, *Exec Srch*
Daniels & Patterson Corp Srch, *Exec Srch*
EDP Recruitng Svcs, *Exec Srch*
40 Plus of CO, *Career/Outplacemnt*
Premier Consltng, *Exec Srch*
SOS Staff Svcs, *Temp. Agcy*
Sales Consltnts, *Exec Srch*
Source Svcs Corp, *Exec Srch*
J.Q. Turner & Assoc., *Exec Srch*
H.L. Yoh Co, *Contract Svc*

Connecticut
Baldwin Assoc., *Exec Srch*
Development Syst., *Exec Srch*
Emmons Assoc., *Exec Srch*
McIntyre Assoc., *Exec Srch*
Source Svcs Corp, *Exec Srch*
Wallace Assoc., *Exec Srch*

Delaware
Proview Resrcs, *Exec Srch*
H.L. Yoh Co, *Contract Svc*

Florida
Active Prof'ls, *Exec Srch*
DGA Persnnl Grp, *Exec Srch*
Decision Consltnts, *Perm. Emp Agcy*
Bob Graham & Assoc., *Exec Srch*
Innotech Global Resrcs, *Exec Srch*
Mgmt. Recrtrs of St. Petersburg, *Exec Srch*
Mgmt. Recrtrs of Tallahassee, *Exec Srch*
Mgmt. Recrtrs of Tampa, *Exec Srch*
The Persnnl Institute, *Exec Srch*
Romac Intl, *Exec Srch*
Sales Consltnts of Fort Lauderdale, *Exec Srch*
Sales Consltnts of Jacksonville, *Exec Srch*
Sales Consltnts of Sarasota, *Exec Srch*
Source Svcs Corp, *Exec Srch*

Georgia
Augusta Staffing Assoc., *Perm. Emp Agcy*
The Bowers Grp, *Exec Srch*
Bradshaw & Assoc., *Exec Srch*
Data Mngmnt & Staff Recrtrs, *Exec Srch*
Dunhill Prof'l Srch, *Exec Srch*
Fox-Morris Assoc., *Exec Srch*
Mgmt. Recrtrs of Atlanta, *Exec Srch*
Manpower Temp. Svcs, *Temp. Agcy*
Persnnl Opport., *Exec Srch*
Quest Syst., *Perm. Emp Agcy*
Randstad Staff Svcs, *Perm. Emp Agcy*
Rita Corp, *Exec Srch*
Source Svcs Corp, *Exec Srch*
Southeastern Data Grp, *Exec Srch*
Southern Emp. Svc, *Perm. Emp Agcy*
H.L. Yoh Co, *Contract Svc*

Hawaii
Select Staff Svcs, *Temp. Agcy*

Idaho
Western Staff Svcs, *Temp. Agcy*

Illinois
Availability, *Perm. Emp Agcy*
William Blender & Assoc., *Exec Srch*
Executive Srch Netwrk, *Exec Srch*
General Emp. Enterprises/Triad Persnnl, *Perm. Emp Agcy*
Girman Grp, *Exec Srch*
Mgmt. Recrtrs Intl, *Exec Srch*
Nationwide Computer Srch, *Exec Srch*
Network Srch, *Exec Srch*
Quantum Prof'l Srch/Quantum Staff Svcs, *Exec Srch*
Sales Consltnts of Chicago, *Exec Srch*
Source Svcs Corp, *Exec Srch*
Stone Enterprises, *Exec Srch*
Wills & Co, *Perm. Emp Agcy*

Indiana
CompuSrch, *Exec Srch*
Execusearch, *Exec Srch*
Mgmt. Recrtrs of Evansville, *Exec Srch*
Mgmt. Recrtrs of Indianapolis, *Exec Srch*
Mgmt. Recrtrs of Richmond/Staff Solut'ns, *Exec Srch*
National Corporate Consltnts/Advantage Svcs, *Exec Srch*
Officemates5 of Indianapolis, *Exec Srch*
Pollak & Skan, *Contract Svc*
Source Svcs Corp, *Exec Srch*
H.L. Yoh Co, *Contract Svc*

Iowa
Executive Resrcs, *Perm. Emp Agcy*
Mgmt. Recrtrs Intl, *Exec Srch*
Persnnl, *Exec Srch*

Kansas
Dunhill of Wichita, *Perm. Emp Agcy*
Dunhill Persnnl, *Exec Srch*
Mgmt. Recrtrs of Overlnd Prk, *Exec Srch*
Manpower, *Temp. Agcy*
Source Svcs Corp, *Exec Srch*

Kentucky
Access Computer Careers, *Perm. Emp Agcy*
Angel Grp Intl, *Exec Srch*
C.M. Mngmnt Svcs, *Perm. Emp Agcy*
Computer Career Consltnts, *Perm. Emp Agcy*
Houck Career Consltnts, *Perm. Emp Agcy*
Snelling Persnnl Svcs, *Exec Srch*

Louisiana
Mgmt. Recrtrs of Baton Rouge, *Exec Srch*
Mgmt. Recrtrs-Metairie/Sales Consltnts, *Exec Srch*
Snelling Persnnl Svcs, *Exec Srch*

Maine
CompuSource, *Exec Srch*

Maryland
Admin Persnnl Svcs, *Perm. Emp Agcy*
Career Netwrk Svc, *Perm. Emp Agcy*
Columbia Consltng, *Exec Srch*
Comtex, *Exec Srch*
A.G. Fishkin & Assoc., *Exec Srch*
Futures, *Exec Srch*
J.R. Assoc., *Perm. Emp Agcy*
Mgmt. Recrtrs of Annapolis, *Exec Srch*
Mgmt. Recrtrs-Baltimore/Sales Consltnts, *Exec Srch*
Mgmt. Recrtrs-Bethesda/CompuSearch, *Exec Srch*
Mgmt. Recrtrs of Frederick, *Exec Srch*
Mgmt. Recrtrs of Washington, D.C., *Exec Srch*
Sales Consltnts of Baltimore Cty, *Exec Srch*
Sales Consltnts of Columbia, *Exec Srch*
Sales Consltnts of Prince Georges Cnty, *Exec Srch*
Search Consltnts, *Exec Srch*
Source Svcs Corp, *Exec Srch*
Tech/Aid of MD, *Temp. Agcy*
Technical Prof'l Srch Grp, *Perm. Emp Agcy*
Tri-Serv, *Perm. Emp Agcy*

Massachusetts
Additional Tech. Support Svcs, *Perm. Emp Agcy*
Advance Persnnl, *Perm. Emp Agcy*
Blaney Exec Srch, *Exec Srch*
Brentwood Persnnl, *Perm. Emp Agcy*
Contrct Solut'ns, *Contract Svc*
Editorial Svcs of N.E., *Temp. Agcy*
Enginuity Srch, *Exec Srch*
General Computer Resrcs, *Temp. Agcy*
Interactive Software Plcmnt, *Exec Srch*
Lake & Manning, *Exec Srch*
Lane Emp. Svc, *Perm. Emp Agcy*
John Leonard Persnnl Assoc., *Perm. Emp Agcy*
The Littleton Grp, *Exec Srch*
Mgmt. Recrtrs Intl, *Exec Srch*
Mgmt. Recrtrs Intl of Braintree, *Exec Srch*
Mgmt. Recrtrs Intl of Springfield, *Exec Srch*
Mgmt. Recrtrs Intl of Westboro, *Exec Srch*
Morency Assoc., *Exec Srch*
New Boston Select Grp, *Exec Srch*
New Dimensions in Technlgy, *Exec Srch*
E.S. Rando Assoc., *Perm. Emp Agcy*
Louis Rudzinsky Assoc., *Exec Srch*
Sales Consltnts of Cape Cod, *Exec Srch*
Sales Consltnts of Plymouth Cnty, *Exec Srch*
Sales Consltnts of Wellesley, *Exec Srch*
Source EDP, *Perm. Emp Agcy*
Source Svcs Corp, *Exec Srch*
TAD Staff Svcs, *Temp. Agcy*
Tech/Aid, *Contract Svc*
Tesmer Allen Assoc., *Perm. Emp Agcy*
H.L. Yoh Co, *Contract Svc*

Michigan
Career Srch, *Exec Srch*
Clark & Hartman Prof'l Srch, *Perm. Emp Agcy*
Joe Giles & Assoc., *Perm. Emp Agcy*
William Howard Agcy, *Perm. Emp Agcy*
Ludot Persnnl, *Perm. Emp Agcy*
Mgmt. Recrtrs of Bingham Farms, *Exec Srch*
Mgmt. Recrtrs of Dearborn, *Exec Srch*
Mgmt. Recrtrs of Flint, *Exec Srch*
Mgmt. Recrtrs of Kalamazoo, *Exec Srch*
Mgmt. Recrtrs of Lansing, *Exec Srch*
Mgmt. Recrtrs of Muskegon, *Exec Srch*
Mgmt. Recrtrs of Rochester, *Exec Srch*
Sales Consltnts of Detroit, *Exec Srch*
Sales Consltnts of Farmington Hills, *Exec Srch*
Sales Executives, *Perm. Emp Agcy*
Software Svcs Corp, *Contract Svc*
Technical Aid Corp, *Contract Svc*

Minnesota
Alternative Staffng, *Perm. Emp Agcy*
Mgmt. Recrtrs-Minneapolis/Sales Consltnts, *Exec Srch*
NER (National Engineering Resrcs), *Exec Srch*
Pioneer Srch, *Exec Srch*
Source Svcs Corp, *Exec Srch*
Twin Cty Srch, *Exec Srch*

Mississippi
Dunhill Prof'l Srch of Jackson, *Exec Srch*
Opportunities Unlimtd, *Perm. Emp Agcy*

Missouri
Mgmt. Recrtrs of Kansas Cty, *Exec Srch*
Mgmt. Recrtrs of Springfield, *Exec Srch*
Mgmt. Recrtrs of St. Louis, *Exec Srch*
Officemates5 of St. Louis, *Exec Srch*
Raiche & Assoc., *Exec Srch*
Snelling Persnnl Svcs, *Perm. Emp Agcy*

Nebraska
Compusearch of Lincoln, *Exec Srch*
Mgmt. Recrtrs of Omaha/Officemates5, *Exec Srch*
Reliable Nat'l Persnnl Consltnts, *Exec Srch*

Nevada
Acumen Persnnl, *Perm. Emp Agcy*
Mgmt. Recrtrs of Reno, *Exec Srch*
Manpower Temp. Svcs, *Temp. Agcy*

New Hampshire
Able 1 Staffng, *Exec Srch*
Mgmt. Recrtrs Intl of Bedford, *Exec Srch*
R.G.T. Assoc., *Exec Srch*
Tech/Aid of NH, *Perm. Emp Agcy*
Technical Directions, *Perm. Emp Agcy*

New Jersey
Alta Assoc., *Exec Srch*
BAI Persnnl Solut'ns, *Exec Srch*
Capstone Assoc., *Exec Srch*
Careers First, *Perm. Emp Agcy*
Carter/MacKay Persnnl, *Exec Srch*
Express Persnnl Svcs, *Perm. Emp Agcy*
Impact Persnnl, *Perm. Emp Agcy*
Paul Kull & Co, *Exec Srch*
Mgmt. Recrtrs Intl, *Exec Srch*
Manpower Tech. Svcs, *Temp. Agcy*
Mayfair Svcs, *Perm. Emp Agcy*
Pomerantz Persnnl, *Perm. Emp Agcy*
Professional Roster, *Temp. Agcy*
RSVP Svcs, *Perm. Emp Agcy*
Anthony Ryan Assoc., *Exec Srch*
Selective Persnnl, *Perm. Emp Agcy*
Source Svcs Corp, *Exec Srch*
Worlco Computer Resrcs, *Exec Srch*
Claire Wright Assn, *Perm. Emp Agcy*

New Mexico
Sanderson Emp. Svc, *Perm. Emp Agcy*

New York
Consortium, *Exec Srch*
Eden Persnnl, *Perm. Emp Agcy*
Gateway Srch, *Exec Srch*
Information Syst. Srch, *Exec Srch*
Joseph Assoc., *Exec Srch*
David Lawrence Assoc., *Exec Srch*
Phoenix Srch Grp, *Exec Srch*
Response Staff Svcs/Career Advisors, *Exec Srch*
Source Svcs Corp, *Exec Srch*

North Carolina
Forbes Temp. Staffng, *Temp. Agcy*
Graham & Assoc., *Perm. Emp Agcy*
Robert Half Intl, *Exec Srch*
Mgmt. Recrtrs Intl, *Exec Srch*
Mgmt. Recrtrs of Durham, *Exec Srch*
Mgmt. Recrtrs of Raleigh/Inter Exec, *Exec Srch*
Mgmt. Recrtrs of Winston-Salem, *Exec Srch*
Morgan Grp, *Exec Srch*
National Svcs, *Exec Srch*
Sales Consltnts of High Point, *Exec Srch*

Ohio
American Bus. Persnnl Svcs, *Perm. Emp Agcy*
Alan Daum & Assoc., *Perm. Emp Agcy*
Dunhill Prof'l Srch of Columbus, *Exec Srch*
Enterprise Srch Assoc., *Perm. Emp Agcy*
Flex-Tech Prof'l Svcs, *Contract Svc*
Russ Hadick & Assoc., *Exec Srch*
Hite Exec Srch/Hite Mngmnt Consltnts, *Exec Srch*
Mgmt. Recrtrs of Cincinnati, *Exec Srch*
Mgmt. Recrtrs of Cleveland, *Exec Srch*
Mgmt. Recrtrs of Columbus, *Exec Srch*
Mgmt. Recrtrs of Dayton, *Exec Srch*
Mgmt. Recrtrs of No. Canton, *Exec Srch*
Mgmt. Recrtrs of Solon, *Exec Srch*
Jerry Paul Assoc., *Perm. Emp Agcy*
Sales Consltnts of Cincinnati, *Exec Srch*
Source Svcs Corp, *Exec Srch*
TAD Tech. Svcs, *Contract Svc*
Tech/Aid of OH, *Perm. Emp Agcy*

Oklahoma
Mgmt. Recrtrs of Oklahoma Cty, *Exec Srch*
Manpower Temp. Svcs, *Temp. Agcy*
John Wylie Assoc., *Exec Srch*

Oregon
Computer Recrtrs/Creative Data Corp, *Exec Srch*
Mgmt. Recrtrs/Officemates5 of Portland, *Exec Srch*
Source Svcs Corp, *Perm. Emp Agcy*

Pennsylvania
Bender & Assoc., *Exec Srch*
Clifford Assoc., *Perm. Emp Agcy*
EDP/Temps of PA, *Temp. Agcy*
FORTUNE Grp Intl, *Exec Srch*
Gateway Resrcs, *Exec Srch*
Hamson Ginn Assoc., *Exec Srch*
Hoskins Hains Assoc., *Perm. Emp Agcy*
Mgmt. Recrtrs Intl, *Exec Srch*
Mgmt. Recrtrs of DE Cnty/CompuSrch, *Exec Srch*
Mgmt. Recrtrs of Lehigh Vly/CompuSrch, *Exec Srch*
Mgmt. Recrtrs of Philadelphia/ CompuSrch, *Exec Srch*
Olsten Staff Svcs, *Temp. Agcy*
Rice Cohen Intl, *Exec Srch*
Select Persnnl, *Perm. Emp Agcy*
Source EDP, *Perm. Emp Agcy*
Source Svcs Corp, *Exec Srch*
United Tech. Assoc., *Temp. Agcy*
Witthauer Assoc. Exec. Srch Firm

Rhode Island
Mgmt. Recrtrs Intl, *Exec Srch*
New England Consltnts, *Perm. Emp Agcy*
Storti Assoc., *Exec Srch*
Tech/Aid of RI, *Contract Svc*

South Carolina
Accel Temp. Svcs, *Temp. Agcy*
Dunhill Prof'l Srch, *Exec Srch*
Harvey Persnnl, *Perm. Emp Agcy*
Mgmt. Recrtrs of Aiken, *Exec Srch*
Mgmt. Recrtrs of Columbia, *Exec Srch*
Mgmt. Recrtrs of Rck Hill, *Exec Srch*
Sales Consltnts/Mgmt. Recrtrs of Greenville, *Exec Srch*

Tennessee
Mgmt. Recrtrs of Knoxville, *Exec Srch*
Sales Consltnts of Nashville, *Exec Srch*

Texas
Add-A-Temp/Woodlands Exec Employment, *Temp. Agcy*
American Resrcs, *Exec Srch*
Apex Computer Placemnts, *Exec Srch*
Babich & Assoc., *Perm. Emp Agcy*
D. Brush & Assoc., *Exec Srch*
Computer Mngmnt Srch, *Exec Srch*
EDP Staff Svcs, *Contract Svc*
Express Persnnl Svcs, *Perm. Emp Agcy*
JP & Assoc., *Exec Srch*
Kelly Svcs, *Temp. Agcy*
Mgmt. Recrtrs Intl, *Exec Srch*
Mgmt. Recrtrs of Dallas, *Exec Srch*
O'Keefe & Assoc., *Perm. Emp Agcy*
Pritchard & Assoc., *Exec Srch*
Professions Today, *Perm. Emp Agcy*
Sales Consltnts of Houston, *Exec Srch*
Salinas & Assoc. Persnnl, *Exec Srch*
Source Svcs Corp, *Exec Srch*
Suburban Svcs, *Temp. Agcy*
TAD Tech. Svcs, *Contract Svc*
Volt Temp. Svcs of Dallas, *Temp. Agcy*
H.L. Yoh Co, *Contract Svc*

Utah
Apogee Assoc., *Exec Srch*
Professional Recrtrs, *Exec Srch*
Source Svcs Corp, *Exec Srch*

Virginia
American Tech. Resrcs, *Perm. Emp Agcy*
Core Persnnl, *Perm. Emp Agcy*
EDP, *Temp. Agcy*
Mgmt. Recrtrs of McLean, *Exec Srch*
Mgmt. Recrtrs of Roanoke, *Exec Srch*
Norrell Staff Svcs, *Exec Srch*
Placement Prof'ls, *Exec Srch*
Professional Srch Persnnl, *Exec Srch*
Source Svcs Corp, *Exec Srch*
Tech/Aid of VA, *Temp. Agcy*

Washington
Rod Asher Assoc., *Exec Srch*
CDI Corp, *Contract Svc*
CTS Tech. Svcs, *Contract Svc*
Executive Recrtrs, *Exec Srch*
Hall Kinion Assoc., *Perm. Emp Agcy*
Mgmt. Recrtrs Intl, *Exec Srch*
Search West, *Exec Srch*
Source Svcs Corp, *Exec Srch*
H.L. Yoh Co, *Contract Svc*

West Virginia
Onsite Commercial Staffng, *Perm. Emp Agcy*
Quantum Resrcs, *Perm. Emp Agcy*
Snelling Persnnl Svcs, *Temp. Agcy*

Wisconsin
ADTEC Staffng, *Temp. Agcy*
Mgmt. Recrtrs of Appleton/ CompuSrch, *Exec Srch*
Mgmt. Recrtrs of Green Bay, *Exec Srch*
Mgmt. Recrtrs of Milwaukee, *Exec Srch*
Placements of Racine, *Perm. Emp Agcy*
Source Svcs Corp, *Exec Srch*
Technology Consltng Corp, *Contract Svc*

Wyoming
The Emp. Place, *Perm. Emp Agcy*
Mgmt. Recrtrs of Cheyenne, *Exec Srch*
Olsten Staff Svcs, *Temp. Agcy*

COMPUTER OPERATIONS

California
Justus Persnnl Svcs, *Perm. Emp Agcy*

Colorado
J.Q. Turner & Assoc., *Exec Srch*

Maine
CompuSource, *Exec Srch*

Maryland
Computer Mgmt., *Exec Srch*
Technical Prof'l Srch Grp, *Perm. Emp Agcy*

Massachusetts
Computer Express Intl, *Contract Svc*
Rostie & Assoc., *Exec Srch*

New Hampshire
Access Consltng, *Perm. Emp Agcy*

New York
Huntington Persnnl Consltnts, *Exec Srch*
Bob Ross Exec Srch Corp, *Exec Srch*

Ohio
H.L. Yoh Co, *Contract Svc*

COMPUTER PROGRAMMING

Arkansas
Executive Recrtrs Outplacement Consltnts, *Exec Srch*

California
Computer Prof'ls Unlimtd, *Exec Srch*
Corporate Resrcs, *Exec Srch*
Data Graph Exec Srch, *Exec Srch*
Ethos Consltng, *Exec Srch*

Connecticut
Atlantic Srch Grp, *Exec Srch*
Datapath Srch Corp, *Exec Srch*
Infonet Resrcs, *Exec Srch*
MRG Srch & Plcmnt, *Exec Srch*
Mgmt. Solut'ns, *Perm. Emp Agcy*
New England Persnnl, *Perm. Emp Agcy*

Georgia
Compaid Consltng Svcs, *Contract Svc*
Computer Srch Assoc., *Exec Srch*

Idaho
Volt Tech. Svcs, *Contract Svc*

Illinois
Grice Holdener & Assoc., *Exec Srch*
Mgmt. Recrtrs Intl, *Exec Srch*

Indiana
Mgmt. Recrtrs Intl, *Exec Srch*
McNerney & Assoc., *Exec Srch*

Maine
CompuSource, *Exec Srch*

Maryland
Computer Temps, *Temp. Agcy*
Technical Prof'l Srch Grp, *Perm. Emp Agcy*
Technical Software Solut'ns, *Temp. Agcy*

Massachusetts
Henry Elliott & Co, *Exec Srch*
General Computer Resrcs, *Temp. Agcy*

Michigan
Executech Resource Consltnts, *Perm. Emp Agcy*

New Jersey
Mgmt. Recrtrs Intl, *Exec Srch*

New York
Computer People, *Exec Srch*
Datacom Placemnts, *Exec Srch*
Executive & Tech. Recrtrs, *Exec Srch*
Huntington Persnnl Consltnts, *Exec Srch*

North Carolina
Volt Tech. Svcs, *Contract Svc*

Ohio
American Bus. Persnnl Svcs, *Perm. Emp Agcy*
H.L. Yoh Co, *Contract Svc*

Oklahoma
Iron Mountain Srch, *Exec Srch*

Pennsylvania
Professional Resource Grp, *Contract Svc*

South Dakota
Availability Employment, *Temp. Agcy*

Tennessee
Eagle Syst., *Perm. Emp Agcy*

Texas
Computer Mngmnt Srch, *Exec Srch*
Datapro Persnnl Consltnts, *Perm. Emp Agcy*

Utah
Software Engineering Solut'ns, *Contract Svc*

Vermont
Mgmt. Recrtrs of Burlington, *Exec Srch*

Virginia
Recruiting Resrcs, *Exec Srch*

Washington
Thompson & Assoc., *Exec Srch*

West Virginia
Onsite Commercial Staffng, *Perm. Emp Agcy*

COMPUTER SCIENCE/SOFTWARE

Alabama
Aerotek, *Perm. Emp Agcy*
Assoc. Persnnl, *Exec Srch*
Breen Persnnl, *Exec Srch*
Clark Persnnl Svc of Mobile, *Exec Srch*
Dunhill of So. Birmingham, *Exec Srch*
Employment Consltnts, *Perm. Emp Agcy*
FORTUNE Persnnl Consltnts, *Exec Srch*
Information Technlgy Svcs, *Exec Srch*
National Labor Line, *Exec Srch*
Seatec, *Contract Svc*
Snelling Persnnl Svcs, *Perm. Emp Agcy*
Snelling Srch, *Exec Srch*
VIP Persnnl, *Perm. Emp Agcy*

Arizona
Adecco, *Contract Svc*
Adecco, *Temp. Agcy*
Aztech Recrtmnt Co, *Exec Srch*
CDI Corp, *Contract Svc*
Computech Corp, *Exec Srch*
Paul Dicken Assoc., *Contract Svc*
Electronic Power Source, *Exec Srch*
General Emp. Enterprises, *Perm. Emp Agcy*
Kerry's Referrals, *Temp. Agcy*
Mgmt. Recrtrs Intl, *Exec Srch*
McEvoy & Johnson Assoc., *Exec Srch*
MEDA Tech. Svcs, *Contract Svc*
PDS Tech. Svc, *Contract Svc*
Priority Staffng, *Perm. Emp Agcy*
Professional Srch, *Exec Srch*
ProVision Technolog's, *Contract Svc*
Sales Consltnts, *Exec Srch*
SearchAmerica, *Exec Srch*
Snelling Persnnl Svcs, *Perm. Emp Agcy*
Spectra Intl, *Exec Srch*
Stivers Temp. Persnnl, *Temp. Agcy*
TSS Consltng, *Exec Srch*
Dean Vesling & Assoc., *Contract Svc*
Volt Tech. Svcs, *Contract Svc*
H.L. Yoh Co, *Contract Svc*

Arkansas
Intl Srch, *Exec Srch*
Spencer Careers, *Exec Srch*
Turnage Emp. Svc Grp, *Exec Srch*

California
A Perm. Success Emp. Svcs, *Perm. Emp Agcy*
ABA Staffng, *Exec Srch*
Access Tech. Staffng, *Contract Svc*
ACCESS Technlgy, *Exec Srch*
AccuStaff, *Perm. Emp Agcy*
AccuStaff Co, *Temp. Agcy*
Advanced Technlgy Consltnts, *Exec Srch*
Advantage Persnnl, *Perm. Emp Agcy*
Affordable Exec Recrtrs, *Exec Srch*
Allied Srch, *Exec Srch*
Alpha-Net Consltng Grp, *Exec Srch*
American Technical, *Temp. Agcy*
Amtec Engineering Corp, *Perm. Emp Agcy*
Ankenbrandt Grp, *Exec Srch*
Answers Unlimtd, *Temp. Agcy*
John Anthony & Assoc., *Exec Srch*
Apple One Emp. Svcs, *Perm. Emp Agcy*
Apropos Emp. Agcy, *Perm. Emp Agcy*
AROSE Recruitng Co, *Temp. Agcy*
Arrowstaff Svcs, *Perm. Emp Agcy*
B&M Assoc., *Contract Svc*
Robert Beech West, *Exec Srch*
Ed Bell Assoc., *Exec Srch*
Harvey Bell & Assoc., *Exec Srch*
Blaine & Assoc., *Perm. Emp Agcy*
Blue, Garni & Co, *Exec Srch*
Bozich & Cruz, *Exec Srch*
Brown Venture Assoc., *Exec Srch*
Bullis & Co, *Exec Srch*
Business Syst. Staffing & Assoc., *Perm. Emp Agcy*
CDI Corp, *Temp. Agcy*
CN Assoc., *Exec Srch*
CT Persnnl Svcs, *Perm. Emp Agcy*
California Job Connection, *Perm. Emp Agcy*
California Srch Agcy, *Exec Srch*
Career Quest, *Contract Svc*
Choice Persnnl, *Perm. Emp Agcy*
Coast To Coast Exec Srch, *Exec Srch*
Computer Netwrk Resrcs, *Exec Srch*
Computer Prof'ls Unlimtd, *Exec Srch*
Corporate Dynamix, *Exec Srch*
Corporate Srch, *Exec Srch*
Crossroads Staff Svc, *Temp. Agcy*
Culver Persnnl Svcs, *Perm. Emp Agcy*
Culver Staffing Resrcs, *Exec Srch*
Daley Consltng & Srch, *Exec Srch*
Data Center Persnnl, *Exec Srch*
Data Graph Exec Srch, *Exec Srch*
Dependable Emp. Agency Netwrk, *Perm. Emp Agcy*
Drake Office Overload, *Temp. Agcy*
Drummer Persnnl, *Exec Srch*
Dunhill Prof'l Srch, *Exec Srch*
Dynamic Synergy Corp, *Exec Srch*
EDP Contrct Svcs, *Contract Svc*
Eagle Srch Assoc., *Exec Srch*
Eastridge Infotech, *Perm. Emp Agcy*
Employment Devlpmnt Dept, *Perm. Emp Agcy*
Excel Tech. Svcs, *Exec Srch*
Executive Dynamics, *Exec Srch*
Executive Srch Consltnts, *Exec Srch*
Curtis Farmer Persnnl, *Exec Srch*
Fastek Tech. Svcs, *Perm. Emp Agcy*
Fay Tech Svcs, *Perm. Emp Agcy*
Fisher & Assoc., *Exec Srch*
40 Plus of So. CA, *Exec Srch*
Pat Franklyn Assoc., *Temp. Agcy*
GCO Exec Srch, *Exec Srch*
GM Assoc., *Exec Srch*
GPL Engineering, *Perm. Emp Agcy*
Dianne Gauger & Assoc., *Exec Srch*
General Emp. Enterprises, *Perm. Emp Agcy*
Goldstein & Assoc., *Temp. Agcy*
Gorelick & Assoc., *Exec Srch*
Gould Persnnl Svcs, *Perm. Emp Agcy*
Grant & Assoc., *Exec Srch*
Hire Ground, *Exec Srch*
Impact, *Exec Srch*
Intellex Persnnl Svcs, *Exec Srch*
IntelliSource Computer Careers, *Exec Srch*
Interim Persnnl, *Temp. Agcy*
Intl Staff Consltnts, *Exec Srch*
Alan Israel Exec Srch, *Exec Srch*
Jackson Persnnl, *Perm. Emp Agcy*
Kabl Ability Netwrk, *Exec Srch*
Kelly Svcs, *Temp. Agcy*
Klein & Assoc., *Temp. Agcy*
Klenin Grp, *Exec Srch*
John Kurosky & Assoc., *Exec Srch*
Lander Intl, *Exec Srch*
Larkin Assoc., *Exec Srch*
Larsen, Whitney, Blecksmith, & Zilliacus, *Exec Srch*
Lending Persnnl Svcs, *Exec Srch*
Lifter & Assoc., *Exec Srch*
LINK Bus. & Persnnl Svcs/LINK Career Ctr, *Temp. Agcy*
The London Agcy, *Exec Srch*
MacTemps, *Temp. Agcy*
Malibu Grp, *Exec Srch*
Mgmt. Recrtrs of Laguna Hills, *Exec Srch*
Mgmt. Recrtrs-Oakland/Sales Consltnts, *Exec Srch*
Mgmt. Recrtrs of Orange, *Exec Srch*
Mgmt. Solut'ns, *Exec Srch*
Manpower, *Temp. Agcy*
The Martin Agencies, *Perm. Emp Agcy*
Mason Concepts, *Exec Srch*
Master Srch, *Exec Srch*
Mata & Assoc., *Exec Srch*
Maverick Staff Svc, *Perm. Emp Agcy*
K.E. McCarthy & Assoc., *Exec Srch*
McCoy Limited, *Exec Srch*
Medical Exec Recrtrs, *Exec Srch*
Micro Temps Syst. & Programming, *Temp. Agcy*
Micro Track Temp. Svcs, *Temp. Agcy*
Milestone Prof'l Staffng, *Exec Srch*
MindSource Software Engineers, *Contract Svc*
Mini-Systems Assoc., *Exec Srch*
Multax Syst., *Perm. Emp Agcy*
Murray Enterprises Staff Svcs, *Temp. Agcy*
NCC Exec Srch, *Exec Srch*
National Resrcs, *Exec Srch*
National Srch Assoc., *Exec Srch*
Nations Staff Solut'ns/Assoc. Resource Intl, *Exec Srch*
Nelson HR Solut'ns, *Perm. Emp Agcy*
Net Workers, *Contract Svc*
New Venture Development, *Exec Srch*
Newport Strategic Srch, *Exec Srch*
Norrell Temp. Svcs of CA, *Temp. Agcy*
Bren Norris Assoc., *Contract Svc*
Omni Express Temps, *Temp. Agcy*
Omni Srch Exec. Srch Firm
Online Prof'l Srch, *Exec Srch*
PC Persnnl, *Exec Srch*
Pacific Srch Grp, *Exec Srch*
Pasona Pacific, *Temp. Agcy*
Peden & Assoc., *Exec Srch*
PeopleWare Tech. Resrcs, *Contract Svc*
Presidio Persnnl, *Temp. Agcy*
Pro Staff Persnnl Svcs, *Perm. Emp Agcy*
Profiles Exec Srch, *Exec Srch*
ProSearch & Assoc., *Exec Srch*
ProVision Technolog's, *Contract Svc*
Quest Worldwide Exec Srch, *Exec Srch*
Raphael Recrtmnt, *Exec Srch*
Ed Rast & Co, *Exec Srch*
Raycor Srch, *Exec Srch*
Reliance Staff Svcs, *Perm. Emp Agcy*
Renoir Staff Svcs, *Perm. Emp Agcy*
Ritter Assoc., *Exec Srch*
Russell Staffing Resrcs, *Perm. Emp Agcy*
SAI (Sloan Assoc.), *Exec Srch*
S.R. & Assoc., *Exec Srch*
Sales Consltnts of Sacramento, *Exec Srch*
Sanford Rose Assoc., *Exec Srch*
Santa Barbara Plcmnt, *Perm. Emp Agcy*
Sharf, Woodward & Assoc., *Perm. Emp Agcy*
David Sharp & Assoc., *Perm. Emp Agcy*
Sharp Persnnl & Srch, *Exec Srch*
Sierra Technlgy, *Contract Svc*
Smartsource Inc., *Contract Svc*
Source Engineering, *Perm. Emp Agcy*
Source Svcs Corp, *Contract Svc*
Spectrawest, *Exec Srch*
Adele Steinmetz, *Exec Srch*
Strategic Staffng, *Temp. Agcy*
Sun Persnnl Svcs, *Temp. Agcy*
System One, *Perm. Emp Agcy*
Systematics Agcy, *Perm. Emp Agcy*
Systems Research Grp, *Exec Srch*
TLC Staffng, *Temp. Agcy*
TRC Staff Svcs, *Perm. Emp Agcy*
TAD Resrcs Intl, *Perm. Emp Agcy*
TAD Tech. Svcs, *Contract Svc*
Talent Tree Staffng, *Perm. Emp Agcy*
Tech Srch, *Perm. Emp Agcy*
TechKnowledge, *Exec Srch*
Technical Srch Consltnts, *Exec Srch*
TechniSkills, *Temp. Agcy*
Technology Locator, *Contract Svc*
Teleforce Intl, *Exec Srch*
Telford, Adams, & Alexander, *Exec Srch*
TOD Staffng, *Exec Srch*
Today Persnnl, *Perm. Emp Agcy*
Trattner Netwrk, *Perm. Emp Agcy*
Trendtec, *Temp. Agcy*
Triple-J Svcs, *Exec Srch*
Unisearch, *Exec Srch*
United Staff Solut'ns, *Exec Srch*
United/Corestaff Staff Svcs, *Perm. Emp Agcy*
Volt Tech. Svcs, *Contract Svc*
Volt Temp. Svcs, *Temp. Agcy*
Western Staff Svcs, *Temp. Agcy*
Western Tech. Resrcs, *Exec Srch*

Colorado
Ahrnsbrak & Assoc., *Perm. Emp Agcy*
The Bridge, *Exec Srch*
Career Forum, *Exec Srch*
Career Mrktng Assoc., *Exec Srch*
Carlson, Bentley Assoc., *Exec Srch*
Casey Svcs, *Exec Srch*
Daniels & Patterson Corp Srch, *Exec Srch*
Dunhill Persnnl of Denver, *Exec Srch*
Eleventh Hour Staff Svcs, *Perm. Emp Agcy*
Enscicon Corp, *Perm. Emp Agcy*
FORTUNE Persnnl Consltnts, *Exec Srch*
GeoSearch, *Exec Srch*
Hallmark Persnnl Syst., *Exec Srch*
Health Technlgy, *Exec Srch*
Healthcare Recrtrs of The Rockies, *Exec Srch*
I.J. & Assoc., *Exec Srch*
Integrity Netwrk, *Exec Srch*
Interim Persnnl Svcs of Denver, *Temp. Agcy*
JobSearch, *Temp. Agcy*
Kelly Svcs, *Temp. Agcy*
Kelly Tech. Svcs, *Temp. Agcy*
Manpower Intl, *Temp. Agcy*
Miller Denver, *Exec Srch*
Office Specialists, *Temp. Agcy*
On Call Tech. Svcs/StaffMark, *Temp. Agcy*
Pendleton Resrcs, *Exec Srch*
Pinnacle Source, *Exec Srch*
Professional Srch & Plcmnt, *Exec Srch*
Snelling Persnnl Svcs, *Exec Srch*

Star Persnnl, *Exec Srch*
Talent Tree Staffng, *Perm. Emp Agcy*
Technical Aid Corp, *Temp. Agcy*
Todays Temporary, *Temp. Agcy*
Triad Consltnts, *Exec Srch*
J.Q. Turner & Assoc., *Exec Srch*
Welzig, Lowe & Assoc., *Exec Srch*

Connecticut

A&A Resume & Persnnl Svcs, *Perm. Emp Agcy*
Abraham & London, *Exec Srch*
BA Staffng, *Perm. Emp Agcy*
Bohan & Bradstreet, *Perm. Emp Agcy*
Charter Persnnl Svcs, *Exec Srch*
Chaves & Assoc., *Exec Srch*
Corporate Staff Solut'ns, *Temp. Agcy*
Data Pros, *Perm. Emp Agcy*
Data Trends, *Exec Srch*
Diversity Recruitng Svcs, *Exec Srch*
EDP Contrct Svcs, *Contract Svc*
Employment Opport., *Perm. Emp Agcy*
Executive Register, *Perm. Emp Agcy*
Hallmark Totaltech, *Perm. Emp Agcy*
Hipp Waters Prof'l Srch, *Exec Srch*
Hire Logic, *Temp. Agcy*
J.G. Hood Assoc., *Perm. Emp Agcy*
Infonet Resrcs, *Exec Srch*
Intertec Persnnl, *Temp. Agcy*
W.R. Lawry, *Perm. Emp Agcy*
Lutz Assoc., *Exec Srch*
Mgmt. Recrtrs Intl, *Exec Srch*
Maxwell-Marcus Staff Consltnts, *Exec Srch*
McIntyre Assoc., *Temp. Agcy*
McLaughlin Persnnl, *Temp. Agcy*
PRH Mgmt., *Exec Srch*
Pascale & LaMorte, *Perm. Emp Agcy*
Ed Pospesil & Co, *Exec Srch*
ProVision Technolog's, *Contract Svc*
Q.S.I., *Perm. Emp Agcy*
Resource Assoc., *Perm. Emp Agcy*
Siger & Assoc., *Exec Srch*
Source Svcs Corp, *Exec Srch*
Super Syst., *Perm. Emp Agcy*
TAD Tech. Svcs, *Contract Svc*
Tech/Aid of CT, *Temp. Agcy*
Technical Srch, *Exec Srch*
Western Staff Svcs, *Perm. Emp Agcy*
Workforce One, *Perm. Emp Agcy*

Delaware

J.B. Groner Exec Srch, *Exec Srch*

District of Columbia

C Assoc., *Exec Srch*
Full Svc Staffing & Technlgy, *Exec Srch*
Norrell Svcs, *Temp. Agcy*
Don Richard Assoc. of Washington DC, *Exec Srch*

Florida

AAA Employment, *Perm. Emp Agcy*
Academy Design & Tech. Svcs, *Contract Svc*
AccuTech, *Contract Svc*
Alpha Persnnl/Alpha Temps, *Perm. Emp Agcy*
American Exec Srch, *Exec Srch*
Arcus Staffing Resrcs, *Contract Svc*
Availability, *Perm. Emp Agcy*
B2D Tech. Svcs, *Contract Svc*
Bales-Waugh Grp/Bales Sales Recrtrs, *Exec Srch*
Belmont Training & Employment, *Perm. Emp Agcy*
Brickell Persnnl Consltnts, *Temp. Agcy*
Bryan & Assoc./Worknet, Etc., *Exec Srch*
Capital Data, *Exec Srch*
Career Concepts, *Exec Srch*
Career Planners, *Perm. Emp Agcy*
Central Florida Computer Placemnts, *Exec Srch*
Colli Assoc. of Tampa, *Exec Srch*
Computemp, *Temp. Agcy*
Computer Express Intl, *Contract Svc*
Computer Plus Staff Solut'ns, *Temp. Agcy*
Criterion Exec Srch, *Exec Srch*
Donbar Svc Corp, *Temp. Agcy*
En-Data Corp, *Perm. Emp Agcy*
Ethan Allen Persnnl Plcmnt, *Exec Srch*
Executive Directions, *Perm. Emp Agcy*
Future Force Persnnl, *Temp. Agcy*
Gallin Assoc., *Exec Srch*
Michael Gimbel & Assoc., *Exec Srch*
Girl Friday Persnnl, *Temp. Agcy*
HR Prof'l Consltnts, *Exec Srch*
Hastings & Hastings Persnnl Consltnts, *Temp. Agcy*
Keys Emp. Agcy, *Exec Srch*
Koerner Grp, *Exec Srch*
R.H. Larsen & Assoc., *Exec Srch*
Mgmt. Recrtrs Intl, *Exec Srch*
Mgmt. Recrtrs of Indialantic, *Exec Srch*
Mgmt. Recrtrs of Miami, *Exec Srch*
Mankuta Gallagher & Assoc., *Exec Srch*
Norrell Tech. Svcs, *Exec Srch*
Olsten Prof'l Staffng, *Temp. Agcy*
Olsten Staff Svcs, *Temp. Agcy*
OMNIPartners, *Exec Srch*
O'Quin Persnnl, *Temp. Agcy*
Persnnl One, *Perm. Emp Agcy*
Profes. Staffing/Able Body Temp. Svcs, *Contract Svc*
Jack Richman & Assoc., *Exec Srch*
Doug Sears & Assoc., *Exec Srch*
Shaver Emp. Agcy, *Perm. Emp Agcy*
Snelling Persnnl, *Exec Srch*
Staffing Solut'ns by Persnnl One, *Perm. Emp Agcy*
Aaron Stewart Persnnl, *Exec Srch*
Sun Solut'ns, *Contract Svc*
System One Tech. Staffng, *Exec Srch*
TRC Staff Svcs, *Temp. Agcy*
TechStaff, *Contract Svc*
Temporary Solut'ns, *Temp. Agcy*
TempSolutions, *Temp. Agcy*
Western Staff Svcs, *Temp. Agcy*

Georgia

Adecco Tech. Svcs, *Contract Svc*
Arjay & Assoc., *Exec Srch*
Ashley-Nolan Intl, *Exec Srch*
Boreham Intl, *Exec Srch*
Catalina Resrcs, *Perm. Emp Agcy*
Coast to Coast Tech. Svcs, *Temp. Agcy*
Commonwealth Consltnts, *Exec Srch*
Comprehensive Computer Consltng, *Contract Svc*
Comprehensive Srch Grp, *Exec Srch*
Computer Srch Assoc., *Exec Srch*
Computer Technlgy Srch, *Exec Srch*
Corporate Srch Consltnts, *Exec Srch*
Elite Staff Svcs, *Perm. Emp Agcy*
Executive Force, *Exec Srch*
Express Persnnl Svcs, *Perm. Emp Agcy*
Express Persnnl Svcs, *Exec Srch*
Hall Mngmnt Grp, *Exec Srch*
Howie & Assoc., *Exec Srch*
JES Srch Firm, *Perm. Emp Agcy*
Jordan Temps, *Temp. Agcy*
Leader Institute, *Exec Srch*
MA&A Grp, *Perm. Emp Agcy*
MIS Srch, *Exec Srch*
MacTemps, *Temp. Agcy*
Mgmt. Recrtrs Intl, *Exec Srch*
Mgmt. Recrtrs of Columbus, *Exec Srch*
Mgmt. Recrtrs of Marietta, *Exec Srch*
Mission Corps Intl/Helping Hands Temp. Svc, *Temp. Agcy*
NEIS, *Exec Srch*
Olsten Tech. Svcs, *Perm. Emp Agcy*
Pinnacle Consltng Grp, *Exec Srch*
Priority 1 Staff Svcs, *Temp. Agcy*
Randstad Staff Svcs, *Perm. Emp Agcy*
Sales Opport., *Exec Srch*
Sanford Rose Assoc., *Exec Srch*
Snelling Persnnl Svcs, *Exec Srch*
Software Srch, *Exec Srch*
Software Tech. Svcs, *Contract Svc*
Taurion Corp, *Exec Srch*
Tech Resource Grp, *Exec Srch*
Tennant & Assoc., *Exec Srch*
Toar Consltnts, *Exec Srch*
Todays Temporary, *Temp. Agcy*
WPPS Software Staffng, *Perm. Emp Agcy*
Western Staff Svcs, *Temp. Agcy*
Western Tech. Svcs, *Temp. Agcy*

Hawaii

Altres Staffng, *Temp. Agcy*
Dunhill Prof'l Srch of Hawaii, *Exec Srch*
Ellis & Assoc., *Exec Srch*
Mgmt. Recrtrs Intl, *Exec Srch*
Maresca & Assoc., *Exec Srch*
The Resume Place, *Career/Outplacemnt*
Sales Consltnts of Honolulu, *Exec Srch*

Idaho

Ward-Hoffman & Assoc., *Exec Srch*

Illinois

The Ability Grp, *Exec Srch*
Ablest Staffng, *Perm. Emp Agcy*
Accord, *Exec Srch*
Adecco, *Temp. Agcy*
Advanced Resrcs/Advanced Clinical, *Contract Svc*
Affiliated Persnnl Consltnts, *Perm. Emp Agcy*
Alternative Resrcs Corp, *Contract Svc*
American Engineering Co, *Exec Srch*
B.D.G. Software Netwrk, *Exec Srch*
Bell Persnnl, *Perm. Emp Agcy*
Britannia, *Exec Srch*
Business Syst. of America, *Exec Srch*
CES, *Exec Srch*
C.R.T., *Exec Srch*
Carson Mngmnt Assoc., *Contract Svc*
Cemco Syst., *Exec Srch*
Chicago Financial Srch, *Exec Srch*
CompuPro, *Exec Srch*
Computemp, *Temp. Agcy*
Computer Futures Exchange, *Exec Srch*
Computer Srch Grp, *Exec Srch*
Corporate Consltnts, *Exec Srch*
Data Interaction, *Exec Srch*
Dataquest, *Exec Srch*
DayStar Temp. Svcs, *Temp. Agcy*
Dunhill Prof'l Srch of Rolling Meadows, *Exec Srch*
Dunhill Staff Svcs of Chicago, *Perm. Emp Agcy*
Dynamic Srch Syst., *Exec Srch*
EDP/Temps & Contrct Svcs, *Temp. Agcy*
Executive Concepts, *Exec Srch*
Executive Srch Intl, *Exec Srch*
Express Persnnl Svcs, *Temp. Agcy*
First Srch, *Exec Srch*
First Staffng, *Perm. Emp Agcy*
General Emp. Enterprises, *Perm. Emp Agcy*
David Gomez & Assoc., *Exec Srch*
Elizabeth Howe & Assoc., *Exec Srch*
Human Resource Technlgy, *Exec Srch*
The Hunter Resource Grp, *Exec Srch*
Illinois Veterans Leadership Program, *Career/Outplacemnt*
Insurance Nat'l Srch/E.J. Ashton & Assoc., *Exec Srch*
Interviewing Consltnts, *Perm. Emp Agcy*
Jender & Co, *Contract Svc*
Johnson Persnnl Co, *Exec Srch*
Jerry Jung Co., *Exec Srch*
Samuel Kroll & Assoc., *Exec Srch*
Kunzer Assoc., *Exec Srch*
Arlene Leff & Assoc., *Exec Srch*
Lynco Mngmnt Persnnl, *Exec Srch*
Macro Resrcs, *Exec Srch*
Mgmt. Recrtrs of Des Plaines, *Exec Srch*
Mgmt. Recrtrs of Rockford, *Exec Srch*
Maramax Persnnl, *Perm. Emp Agcy*
Paul May & Assoc., *Exec Srch*
M.W. McDonald & Assoc., *Exec Srch*
Michael David Assoc., *Perm. Emp Agcy*
Mullins & Assoc., *Perm. Emp Agcy*
The Murphy Grp, *Perm. Emp Agcy*
National Srch, *Exec Srch*
Network Resource Grp, *Perm. Emp Agcy*
Nu-Way Srch, *Exec Srch*
Officemates5 of Wheeling, *Exec Srch*
Olsten Information Technlgy Staffng, *Perm. Emp Agcy*
Olsten Staff Svcs, *Temp. Agcy*
Omega Tech. Corp, *Exec Srch*
Omni One, *Perm. Emp Agcy*
Opportunity Persnnl, *Perm. Emp Agcy*
PS, *Perm. Emp Agcy*
Persnnl Connection, *Perm. Emp Agcy*
Pollak & Skan, *Contract Svc*
Professional Placemnt Svcs, *Exec Srch*
Professional Srch Center Limited, *Exec Srch*
ProVision Technolog's, *Contract Svc*
Redell Srch, *Exec Srch*
Remedy Intelligent Staffng, *Temp. Agcy*
Responsive Srch, *Exec Srch*
Right Svcs, *Temp. Agcy*
Sales Consltnts/Mgmt. Recrtrs Intl, *Exec Srch*
Sales Consltnts of Oak Brk, *Exec Srch*
Search Dynamics, *Exec Srch*
Sevcor Intl, *Exec Srch*
Shannonwood Staffers, *Temp. Agcy*
Smith Scott & Assoc., *Exec Srch*
Snelling Srch, *Exec Srch*
Synergistics Assoc. Exec. Srch Firm
Systems One, *Exec Srch*
TDF Corp, *Contract Svc*
TSC Mngmnt Svcs, *Exec Srch*
Roy Talman & Assoc., *Exec Srch*
Technical Recruitng Consltnts, *Exec Srch*
Walsh & Co, *Perm. Emp Agcy*
Webb Emp. Svc, *Perm. Emp Agcy*
Wilson-Douglas-Jordan, *Exec Srch*
Working World, *Temp. Agcy*
World Emp. Svc, *Perm. Emp Agcy*

Indiana

Alpha Rae Persnnl, *Perm. Emp Agcy*
Bill Caldwell Emp. Svc, *Perm. Emp Agcy*
Canis Major/HR Quest, *Exec Srch*
Career Consltnts, *Perm. Emp Agcy*
Careers Unlimtd, *Exec Srch*
The Consltng Forum, *Exec Srch*
Corporate Staff Resrcs, *Temp. Agcy*
Dunhill Staffing Syst., *Temp. Agcy*
Employment Recrtrs, *Perm. Emp Agcy*
Executec Persnnl Svcs, *Exec Srch*
Job Placemnt Svc, *Perm. Emp Agcy*
Kendall & Davis, *Perm. Emp Agcy*
Mac Staffng, *Temp. Agcy*
The Mallard Grp, *Exec Srch*
Mgmt. Recrtrs Intl, *Exec Srch*
Mgmt. Svcs, *Exec Srch*
Manpower Tech. Svcs, *Temp. Agcy*
Mays & Assoc., *Perm. Emp Agcy*
Oakwood Intl, *Exec Srch*
QCI Tech. Staffng, *Contract Svc*
Quiring Assoc. HR Consltng Grp, *Exec Srch*

Outsource II, *Temp. Agcy*
Professional Recrtrs, *Perm. Emp Agcy*
Professions, *Exec Srch*
ProVision Technolog's, *Contract Svc*
The Regency Grp, *Exec Srch*

New Hampshire
Access Consltng, *Perm. Emp Agcy*
Allstaff Contrct Svcs, *Perm. Emp Agcy*
Barros Assoc., *Perm. Emp Agcy*
Central New Hampshire Emp. Svcs, *Perm. Emp Agcy*
Chaucer Grp, *Exec Srch*
Cheshire Emp. Svc, *Temp. Agcy*
Contact Recrtrs, *Temp. Agcy*
Contrct Solut'ns, *Contract Svc*
The Cushing Grp, *Contract Svc*
Dubois & Co, *Exec Srch*
Enterprise Technolog's, *Exec Srch*
Exeter 2100, *Perm. Emp Agcy*
Hart, Hawkins & Co, *Exec Srch*
Kenda Syst., *Perm. Emp Agcy*
Key Persnnl, *Perm. Emp Agcy*
Lloyd Persnnl Consltnts, *Exec Srch*
National Emp. Svc Corp, *Perm. Emp Agcy*
Preferred Resrcs Grp, *Exec Srch*
Professional Recrtrs, *Perm. Emp Agcy*
Resource Recruitng/Contemp. Accntnts, *Perm. Emp Agcy*
Sales Consltnts of Nashua-Manchester, *Exec Srch*
Software Netwrks, *Perm. Emp Agcy*
Surge Resrcs, *Contract Svc*

New Jersey
A+ Persnnl, *Perm. Emp Agcy*
A Prof'l Edge, *Career/Outplacemnt*
Access Syst., *Exec Srch*
Adel-Lawrence Assoc., *Exec Srch*
Andrew Persnnl Svcs, *Perm. Emp Agcy*
Berman & Larson, *Perm. Emp Agcy*
Blake & Assoc. Exec Srch, *Exec Srch*
Career Ctr, *Perm. Emp Agcy*
Careers USA, *Perm. Emp Agcy*
Carter McKenzie, *Exec Srch*
Carter/MacKay Persnnl, *Exec Srch*
L. Cavaliere & Assoc., *Exec Srch*
Churchill & Harriman, *Exec Srch*
Citizens Emp. Svcs, *Perm. Emp Agcy*
Data Hunters, *Exec Srch*
The Datafinders Grp, *Exec Srch*
Glenn Davis Assoc., *Perm. Emp Agcy*
Dreier Consltng, *Exec Srch*
Dunhill Temp. Syst., *Temp. Agcy*
Executive Netwrk, *Exec Srch*
Executive Software Plus, *Perm. Emp Agcy*
Gibson Martin Consltng, *Exec Srch*
Holm Persnnl Consltnts, *Exec Srch*
Hreshko Consltng Grp, *Exec Srch*
InfoSystems Placemnt Svcs, *Perm. Emp Agcy*
Integro Staff Svcs, *Temp. Agcy*
J.M. Joseph Assoc., *Exec Srch*
T.J. Koellhoffer & Assoc., *Exec Srch*
L&K Assoc., *Exec Srch*
Lancaster Assoc./The Swan Grp, *Exec Srch*
Jon Lawrence Assoc., *Exec Srch*
MIS Srch, *Exec Srch*
Mgmt. Recrtrs of Bay Head, *Exec Srch*
Mgmt. Recrtrs of Orange Cnty, *Exec Srch*
Mgmt. Recrtrs of Passaic Cnty, *Exec Srch*
Officemates5 of Englewood Cliffs/DayStar Temp. Svcs, *Perm. Emp Agcy*
OMNE Staff Svcs, *Temp. Agcy*
Persnnl Assoc., *Exec Srch*
Princeton Exec Srch, *Exec Srch*
Protocall Bus. Staff Svcs, *Temp. Agcy*
Rochester Syst., *Exec Srch*
Rotator Svcs, *Contract Svc*
R.S. Sadow Assoc., *Exec Srch*
Sales Consltnts of Morris Cnty, *Exec Srch*
Sales Consltnts of Sparta, *Exec Srch*
Scientific Srch, *Perm. Emp Agcy*
SkuppSearch, *Exec Srch*
Source Svcs Corp, *Perm. Emp Agcy*
TRS Staff Solut'ns, *Temp. Agcy*
Tenek Corp, *Exec Srch*
Ultimate Solut'ns, *Perm. Emp Agcy*
Winston Staff Svcs, *Temp. Agcy*

New Mexico
Albuquerque Persnnl, *Perm. Emp Agcy*
Butler Svc Grp, *Contract Svc*
CDI Corp, *Contract Svc*
Scientemps, *Temp. Agcy*
Snelling Persnnl Svcs, *Exec Srch*

New York
AJC Srch, *Exec Srch*
AM & PM Temps, *Temp. Agcy*
ATS Reliance, *Perm. Emp Agcy*
AZR, *Exec Srch*
Accounting & Computer Persnnl, *Perm. Emp Agcy*
Merrill Adams Assoc., *Career/Outplacemnt*
Adept Tech Recruitng, *Exec Srch*
Alite Assoc., *Exec Srch*
Franklin Allen Consltnts Exec. Srch Firm
Alpha Health Svcs Corp, *Exec Srch*
Ames O'Neill Assoc., *Exec Srch*
AMESgroup, *Perm. Emp Agcy*
Analytic Recruitng, *Perm. Emp Agcy*
April Tech. Recruitng, *Perm. Emp Agcy*
Arrow Emp. Agcy, *Perm. Emp Agcy*
Berkel Assoc., *Exec Srch*
Bos Bus. Consltnts, *Exec Srch*
Branthover Assoc., *Exec Srch*
Brookville Staff Svcs, *Perm. Emp Agcy*
Bruml Assoc., *Exec Srch*
C.C. Burke Limited, *Perm. Emp Agcy*
Burns Persnnl, *Exec Srch*
CDI Corp, *Contract Svc*
Career Objectives Persnnl, *Temp. Agcy*
Carlile Persnnl Agcy, *Perm. Emp Agcy*
Cavan Syst., *Exec Srch*
Colton Partnership, *Exec Srch*
COMFORCE Corp, *Contract Svc*
COMFORCE Information Technolog's, *Contract Svc*
Compu-Tech Persnnl Agcy, *Exec Srch*
Computer People, *Exec Srch*
Computer Placemnts Unlimtd, *Exec Srch*
Computer Resrcs Corp, *Exec Srch*
Corporate Careers/R.J. Assoc., *Exec Srch*
D&L Assoc., *Exec Srch*
Dapexs Consltnts, *Exec Srch*
Seth Diamond Assoc., *Exec Srch*
EDP Contrct Svcs, *Contract Svc*
ETC Srch, *Exec Srch*
Efco Consltnts, *Exec Srch*
David Ellner Assoc., *Exec Srch*
Employment Recrtrs Agcy, *Perm. Emp Agcy*
The Emp. Store/TES Technical, *Exec Srch*
Equate Exec Srch, *Exec Srch*
Eric Robert Assoc., *Exec Srch*
Executive & Tech. Recrtrs, *Exec Srch*
Executive Directions, *Exec Srch*
Extra Help Emp. Svc, *Temp. Agcy*
Fanning Persnnl, *Exec Srch*
Fifth Avenue Emp. Svcs, *Temp. Agcy*
Focus & Focus Capital Markets, *Exec Srch*
Gruen Resrcs, *Exec Srch*
The Haas Assoc., *Exec Srch*
Robert Half Intl/Information Syst. Division, *Exec Srch*
Hart-Merrell Persnnl, *Exec Srch*
Headway Corporate Staff Svcs, *Temp. Agcy*
F.P. Healy & Co, *Exec Srch*
Hessel Assoc., *Exec Srch*
Horizon Exec Srch Grp, *Exec Srch*
Hunter Mac & Assoc., *Perm. Emp Agcy*
Information Syst. Staffng, *Perm. Emp Agcy*
Innovations Assoc., *Perm. Emp Agcy*
Interim Persnnl, *Temp. Agcy*
Interspace Interactive, *Exec Srch*
JDC Assoc., *Perm. Emp Agcy*
Just One Break, *Perm. Emp Agcy*
Irene Kane Persnnl, *Exec Srch*
Ktech Syst. Grp, *Perm. Emp Agcy*
Lake Assoc., *Exec Srch*
Lawrence Exec Srch, *Exec Srch*
The Lloyd Co, *Career/Outplacemnt*
The MVP Grp, *Exec Srch*
Magill Assoc., *Exec Srch*
Mgmt. Recrtrs of Woodbury/ CompuSrch, *Exec Srch*
Manpower Temp. Svcs, *Temp. Agcy*
Mentortech, *Exec Srch*
Metro Resrcs of Rochester, *Temp. Agcy*
Metro Persnnl/Metro Nursing Svcs, *Exec Srch*
Milazzo Assoc., *Perm. Emp Agcy*
National Emp. Database, *Perm. Emp Agcy*
Nationwide Persnnl Grp, *Perm. Emp Agcy*
Noah Assoc., *Perm. Emp Agcy*
Norrell Staff Svcs, *Perm. Emp Agcy*
Optimal Resrcs, *Exec Srch*
OTEC.COM, *Perm. Emp Agcy*
Parsons, Anderson & Gee, *Perm. Emp Agcy*
Pathway Exec Srch, *Exec Srch*
Paywise, *Temp. Agcy*
Platinum IT Consltng, *Contract Svc*
P.G. Prager Srch Assoc., *Exec Srch*
Pro Srch Assoc., *Exec Srch*
ProVision Technolog's, *Contract Svc*
ProVision Technolog's/TAD Tech. Svcs, *Contract Svc*
Quantum Persnnl Agcy, *Perm. Emp Agcy*
Rem Resrcs, *Perm. Emp Agcy*
Resource Svcs, *Exec Srch*
Beth Richman Assoc., *Perm. Emp Agcy*
Ritta Prof'l Srch, *Exec Srch*
Fran Rogers Persnnl, *Perm. Emp Agcy*
SDC Computer Svc, *Exec Srch*
Sales Consltnts of Westchester, *Exec Srch*
Sharp Placemnt Prof'ls, *Exec Srch*
Sigma Staffng, *Perm. Emp Agcy*
Staff Managers, *Temp. Agcy*
Stamm Persnnl Agcy, *Perm. Emp Agcy*
Strategic Recruitng, *Exec Srch*
Superior Concepts, *Contract Svc*
Swing Shift, *Temp. Agcy*
TAD Resrcs, *Contract Svc*
Taylor Jordan Assoc., *Exec Srch*
Tech Options, *Exec Srch*
Techno-Trac Syst., *Exec Srch*
TemPositions, *Temp. Agcy*
Traynor Confidential Exec. Srch Firm
Unique Support Svcs, *Temp. Agcy*
United Persnnl Agcy, *Perm. Emp Agcy*
Venture Resrcs, *Exec Srch*
Volt Svcs Grp, *Contract Svc*
Wehn Assoc., *Exec Srch*
Werbin Assoc. Exec Srch, *Exec Srch*
Winston Resrcs, *Exec Srch*
H.L. Yoh Co, *Contract Svc*

North Carolina
Accurate Staff Consltnts, *Exec Srch*
Action Tech. Staffng, *Temp. Agcy*
Advanced Persnnl Resrcs, *Exec Srch*
AmeriPro Srch, *Exec Srch*
Amos & Assoc., *Exec Srch*
Anderson & Daniel Persnnl, *Perm. Emp Agcy*
CDI Corp, *Contract Svc*
COMFORCE Tech. Svcs, *Contract Svc*
DataMasters, *Perm. Emp Agcy*
Eastern Srch Grp, *Exec Srch*
Employment Consltnts, *Contract Svc*
Executive Recrtmnt Specialists, *Exec Srch*
Executive Staff Svcs, *Perm. Emp Agcy*
FORTUNE Persnnl Consltnts of Raleigh, *Perm. Emp Agcy*
Information Syst. Prof'ls, *Exec Srch*
Kelly Svcs, *Temp. Agcy*
Key Temps, *Temp. Agcy*
Kilgo & Co, *Exec Srch*
MKR Persnnl Solut'ns, *Contract Svc*
MTS, *Perm. Emp Agcy*
Mgmt. Recrtrs Intl, *Exec Srch*
Mgmt. Recrtrs of Kannapolis, *Exec Srch*
Moffitt Intl, *Exec Srch*
Office Specialists, *Temp. Agcy*
Olsten Staff Svcs, *Temp. Agcy*
PCS - Personal Communications Svc, *Contract Svc*
Parenica & Co, *Exec Srch*
Professional Persnnl Assoc., *Perm. Emp Agcy*
ProVision Technolog's, *Contract Svc*
REP & Assoc., *Perm. Emp Agcy*
Sales Consltnts of Concord, *Exec Srch*
Sanford Rose Assoc. of Charlotte, *Exec Srch*
Snelling Persnnl Svcs, *Contract Svc*
Snelling Srch, *Exec Srch*
Source Svcs Corp, *Exec Srch*
Sparks Persnnl Svcs, *Exec Srch*
Summit Computer Svcs, *Perm. Emp Agcy*
The Underwood Grp, *Perm. Emp Agcy*
David Weinfeld Grp, *Exec Srch*
Woods-Hoyle, *Perm. Emp Agcy*
H.L. Yoh Co, *Contract Svc*

North Dakota
Career Connection, *Exec Srch*
Dunhill Exec Srch, *Exec Srch*
Olsten Staff Svcs/Kramer & Assoc./Expressway Persnnl, *Temp. Agcy*
Persnnl Svcs, *Exec Srch*

Ohio
Accountnts Exec Srch/Accountnts on Call, *Exec Srch*
AccuStaff, *Temp. Agcy*
Advancement L.L.C., *Perm. Emp Agcy*
All Star Persnnl, *Temp. Agcy*
Alliance Tech. Svcs, *Contract Svc*
AllTech Resrcs, *Exec Srch*
American Bus. Persnnl Svcs, *Perm. Emp Agcy*
Belcan Tech. Svcs, *Contract Svc*
Belcan Tech. Svcs, *Perm. Emp Agcy*
N.L. Benke & Assoc., *Perm. Emp Agcy*
J.B. Brown & Assoc., *Exec Srch*
Burks Grp, *Exec Srch*
CBS Persnnl Svcs, *Perm. Emp Agcy*
Clopton's Placemnt Svc, *Perm. Emp Agcy*
Combined Resrcs, *Exec Srch*
Computer & Tech. Assoc., *Exec Srch*
Continental Srch Consltnts, *Exec Srch*
DLD Tech. Svcs, *Contract Svc*
Data Bank Corp, *Exec Srch*
Eastern Persnnl Svcs, *Perm. Emp Agcy*
Executech Consltnts, *Exec Srch*
Executive Srch Exec. Srch Firm
Fenzel Milar Assoc., *Exec Srch*
Flowers & Assoc./Associated Temps, *Exec Srch*
Frederick-Lehmann & Assoc./Temporarily Yours, *Exec Srch*
Gayhart & Assoc., *Exec Srch*
Hammann & Assoc., *Exec Srch*
J.D. Hersey & Assoc., *Exec Srch*

ITS Tech. Staffing/Interconnect Tech. Svcs, *Exec Srch*
Icon Mngmnt Grp, *Exec Srch*
Interconnect Tech. Svcs, *Exec Srch*
Jaeger Intl, *Exec Srch*
Kelly Svcs, *Temp. Agcy*
R.E. Lowe Assoc., *Perm. Emp Agcy*
Mgmt. Recrtrs Intl, *Exec Srch*
Manpower Temp. Svcs, *Temp. Agcy*
Marvel Consltnts, *Exec Srch*
Messina Mngmnt Syst., *Exec Srch*
Midland Consltnts, *Exec Srch*
Myers & Assoc., *Exec Srch*
Newcomb-Desmond & Assoc., *Exec Srch*
North Peak Grp, *Exec Srch*
North Star Resrcs, *Contract Svc*
Olsten Prof'l Staff Svcs, *Exec Srch*
Palmer Temps/The Palmer Grp, *Temp. Agcy*
Paragon Recruitng Officials, *Exec Srch*
Placement Svcs Limited, *Exec Srch*
ProVision Technolog's, *Contract Svc*
RecruitMasters of Cincinnati, *Exec Srch*
W.R. Renner & Assoc., *Exec Srch*
S&P Solut'ns, *Contract Svc*
Sanford Rose Assoc. of Cleveland, *Exec Srch*
Sanford Rose Assoc. of Columbus, *Exec Srch*
Sanford Rose Assoc. of Youngstown, *Exec Srch*
Selective Srch Assoc., *Perm. Emp Agcy*
Shafer Jones Assoc., *Exec Srch*
Source Svcs Corp, *Exec Srch*
Tabb & Assoc., *Exec Srch*
Talent Tree Staffng, *Perm. Emp Agcy*
Teamwork U.S.A., *Contract Svc*
Teknon Emp. Resrcs, *Exec Srch*
Thomas-Schade & Assoc., *Exec Srch*
Vector Technical, *Perm. Emp Agcy*
Weiper Recruitng Svcs, *Exec Srch*

Oklahoma

Ameri Resource, *Exec Srch*
Express Persnnl Svcs, *Exec Srch*
Terry Neese Persnnl Agcy, *Exec Srch*
Lloyd Richards Persnnl, *Perm. Emp Agcy*

Oregon

API Emp. Agcy, *Perm. Emp Agcy*
Able Temp. Svc, *Temp. Agcy*
The Brentwood Grp Limited, *Exec Srch*
D. Brown & Assoc., *Exec Srch*
Express Persnnl Svcs, *Exec Srch*
First Choice Persnnl, *Perm. Emp Agcy*
Hackenschmidt, Weaver & Fox, *Exec Srch*
Impact Staffng, *Temp. Agcy*
NPRC/Nationwde Persnnl Recruitng & Consltng, *Exec Srch*
Search Nrthwest Assoc., *Exec Srch*
Southern Oregon Temporary, *Temp. Agcy*
Talent Tree Staffng, *Perm. Emp Agcy*
Uniforce Tech. Svcs, *Contract Svc*
Woodworth Intl Grp, *Exec Srch*

Pennsylvania

AA Staff Solut'ns, *Contract Svc*
Advance Recruitng Svcs, *Exec Srch*
Advanced Technlgy Resrcs, *Exec Srch*
All Staffng, *Perm. Emp Agcy*
ASAP Staffng, *Perm. Emp Agcy*
Basilone-Oliver Exec Srch, *Exec Srch*
T.W. Boris Assn, *Exec Srch*
Bradley Prof'l Svcs, *Perm. Emp Agcy*
CDI Corp, *Contract Svc*
CMIS, *Exec Srch*
Career Concepts Staff Svcs, *Exec Srch*
Career Quest Confidential, *Exec Srch*
Charly's Temp. Svcs, *Temp. Agcy*
Computer Prof'ls Unlimtd, *Perm. Emp Agcy*
Rob DePaul & Assoc., *Exec Srch*
DiCenzo Persnnl Specialists, *Perm. Emp Agcy*
Financial Industry Staff Co, *Perm. Emp Agcy*
FORTUNE Persnnl Consltnts, *Exec Srch*
General Emp. & Triad Persnnl, *Perm. Emp Agcy*
J.H. Glass & Assoc., *Exec Srch*
Garrick Hall & Assoc., *Exec Srch*
Hayes Assoc., *Exec Srch*
Human Resource Solut'ns, *Exec Srch*
IMC Intl, *Contract Svc*
Interim Persnnl of Lehigh Valley PA, *Temp. Agcy*
J-Rand Srch, *Exec Srch*
Nancy Jackson, *Exec Srch*
Jefferson-Ross Assoc., *Exec Srch*
Clifton Johnson Assoc., *Exec Srch*
Keynote Syst., *Temp. Agcy*
Lawrence Persnnl, *Exec Srch*
Main Line Persnnl, *Perm. Emp Agcy*
Mgmt. Recrtrs of Manayunk/Chestnut Hill/CompuSrch, *Exec Srch*
Rob McClure Exec. Srch Firm
J. McManus Assoc., *Perm. Emp Agcy*
Metro Persnnl, *Temp. Agcy*
LaMonte Owens, *Exec Srch*
Pancoast Temp. Svcs, *Temp. Agcy*
Professional Resource Grp, *Contract Svc*
ProVision Technolog's, *Contract Svc*
Q-Source, *Perm. Emp Agcy*
Quest Syst., *Perm. Emp Agcy*
RHI Consltng/Accountemps, *Contract Svc*
The Richards Grp, *Exec Srch*
S-H-S Intl, *Perm. Emp Agcy*
S-H-S Intl, *Exec Srch*
Suburban Placemnt Svc, *Exec Srch*
TRC Staff Svcs, *Temp. Agcy*
TAD Tech. Svcs, *Temp. Agcy*
Tech/Aid of PA, *Contract Svc*

Rhode Island

Dorra Srch, *Exec Srch*
Kelly Svcs, *Temp. Agcy*
Norrell Svcs, *Temp. Agcy*
On Line Temp/On Line Staff, *Temp. Agcy*
PKS Assoc., *Exec Srch*

South Carolina

Aide Design Svcs, *Contract Svc*
CDI Information Svcs, *Contract Svc*
Companion Emp. Svcs, *Perm. Emp Agcy*
Eastern Persnnl Svcs, *Exec Srch*
Thomas Glover & Assoc., *Exec Srch*
Mgmt. Recrtrs of Anderson, *Exec Srch*
Mgmt. Recrtrs of Orangeburg, *Exec Srch*
Miller & Assoc., *Exec Srch*
PRL & Assoc., *Perm. Emp Agcy*
Pindrum Staff Svc, *Temp. Agcy*
Search & Recruit Intl, *Exec Srch*
Smith Temps/Smith Persnnl, *Temp. Agcy*
Snelling Persnnl Svcs, *Perm. Emp Agcy*
Southern Recrtrs & Consltnts, *Exec Srch*

South Dakota

Mgmt. Recrtrs Intl, *Exec Srch*
Regency Recruitng, *Exec Srch*
Staff Srch, *Exec Srch*

Tennessee

A-1 Staffing & Persnnl, *Temp. Agcy*
Advanced Computer Careers, *Exec Srch*
American Tech. Assoc., *Contract Svc*
Anderson McIntyre Persnnl Svcs, *Exec Srch*
Cook Assoc. Intl, *Exec Srch*
Eagle Syst., *Perm. Emp Agcy*
Engineer One, *Perm. Emp Agcy*
Express Persnnl Svcs, *Perm. Emp Agcy*
Robert Half Intl, *Contract Svc*
Hamilton Ryker Co, *Exec Srch*
Hester & Assoc., *Exec Srch*
Information Syst. Grp, *Exec Srch*
J&D Resrcs, *Exec Srch*
Kelly Svcs, *Temp. Agcy*
Madison Persnnl, *Perm. Emp Agcy*
Mgmt. Recrtrs/Sales Consltnts-Chattanooga, *Exec Srch*
Mgmt. Recrtrs of Chattanooga, *Exec Srch*
Manpower, *Temp. Agcy*
W.R. McLeod & Assoc., *Exec Srch*
Mega Force, *Temp. Agcy*
Snelling Persnnl Svcs, *Exec Srch*
Software Resource Consltnts, *Exec Srch*
Staffing Solut'ns, *Perm. Emp Agcy*

Texas

Abilene Emp. Svc, *Perm. Emp Agcy*
Acclaim Svcs, *Temp. Agcy*
Ackerman Johnson, *Exec Srch*
Action Persnnl, *Temp. Agcy*
Albrecht & Assoc. Exec Srch, *Exec Srch*
B&M Air & Space Division, *Contract Svc*
R. Gaines Baty Assoc., *Exec Srch*
Best/World Assoc., *Exec Srch*
Bilson & Hazen Intl, *Exec Srch*
Brainpower Persnnl Agcy, *Perm. Emp Agcy*
Bridge Persnnl, *Exec Srch*
Bundy-Stewart Assoc., *Exec Srch*
Burnett Persnnl Svcs, *Temp. Agcy*
Butler Intl, *Contract Svc*
C.G. & Co, *Exec Srch*
CAD Technlgy, *Exec Srch*
CarlTech, *Contract Svc*
Certified Persnnl, *Contract Svc*
Cherbonnier Grp, *Exec Srch*
COMFORCE Information Technolog's, *Contract Svc*
Computemp, *Temp. Agcy*
Computer Mngmnt Srch, *Exec Srch*
Computer Prof'ls Unlimtd, *Exec Srch*
Computer Technlgy Srch, *Exec Srch*
Continental Persnnl, *Perm. Emp Agcy*
CoreCom, *Contract Svc*
Corporate Srch, *Exec Srch*
Creative Staff Svcs, *Temp. Agcy*
Gail Darling Staffing/Darling's Prof'l Desk, *Temp. Agcy*
Datapro Persnnl Consltnts, *Perm. Emp Agcy*
Diversified Temps, *Temp. Agcy*
E&A Persnnl Svcs, *Perm. Emp Agcy*
EDP Computer Svcs, *Exec Srch*
The Elsworth Grp, *Exec Srch*
Express Persnnl Svcs, *Perm. Emp Agcy*
FirstWord Staff Svcs, *Temp. Agcy*
Focus Point, *Contract Svc*
Robert Half Intl, *Perm. Emp Agcy*
Imprimis Staff Solut'ns, *Temp. Agcy*
Info Tec, *Perm. Emp Agcy*
Inside Track, *Exec Srch*
Intratech Resource Grp, *Exec Srch*
Kahn Richards & Assoc., *Exec Srch*
Key People, *Perm. Emp Agcy*
Kristan Intl Exec Srch, *Exec Srch*
LRJ Staff Svcs, *Perm. Emp Agcy*
Loewenstein & Assoc., *Exec Srch*
Mgmt. Recrtrs Intl, *Exec Srch*
Manpower Temp. Svcs, *Temp. Agcy*
McDuffy-Edwards, *Exec Srch*
National HR Grp, *Exec Srch*
Olsten Staff Svcs, *Temp. Agcy*
Opportunity Unlimtd Persnnl Consltnts, *Exec Srch*
P&P Persnnl, *Perm. Emp Agcy*
The Pailin Grp, *Exec Srch*
Pate Resrcs Grp, *Exec Srch*
The Persnnl Office, *Exec Srch*
Persnnl One, *Perm. Emp Agcy*
Phoenix Staffng, *Exec Srch*
Pro Staff Persnnl Svcs, *Temp. Agcy*
Professional Srch Consltnts, *Contract Svc*
ProVision Technolog's, *Contract Svc*
Quality Information Svc, *Exec Srch*
Recruiting Assoc., *Exec Srch*
Remedy Intelligent Staffng, *Perm. Emp Agcy*
Resource Staffng, *Contract Svc*
Riccione & Assoc., *Exec Srch*
Search Netwrk Intl, *Exec Srch*
Rob Shields & Assoc., *Contract Svc*
Snelling Persnnl Svcs, *Exec Srch*
Staff Extension, *Exec Srch*
Stehouwer & Assoc., *Perm. Emp Agcy*
Strategic Outsourcing Corp, *Exec Srch*
TGA Co, *Exec Srch*
TAD Tech. Svcs, *Contract Svc*
Betty Tanner Prof'l Emp. Svc, *Exec Srch*
Tarrant Cnty Emp. Netwrk, *Perm. Emp Agcy*
Tech-Net, *Exec Srch*
Technical Careers, *Contract Svc*
TechSystems, *Contract Svc*
Texas Persnnl, *Exec Srch*
Todays Temporary, *Temp. Agcy*
Total Persnnl, *Exec Srch*
Triplex Computer Corp, *Contract Svc*
The Urban Placemnt Svc, *Exec Srch*
Dick Van Vliet & Assoc., *Exec Srch*
Vick & Assoc./Recruiters Online Netwrk, *Exec Srch*
Volt Tech. Svcs, *Contract Svc*
The Whitaker Companies, *Exec Srch*
Wyman & Assoc., *Exec Srch*

Utah

CDI Information Svcs, *Exec Srch*
Deeco Intl, *Perm. Emp Agcy*
Mgmt. Recrtrs Intl, *Exec Srch*
Mgmt. Recrtrs of Provo, *Exec Srch*
Manpower Tech. Svcs, *Temp. Agcy*
Systems West, *Temp. Agcy*
Trout & Assoc., *Exec Srch*

Vermont

Eckler Persnnl Netwrk, *Exec Srch*
Persnnl Dept, *Temp. Agcy*
Technical Connection, *Perm. Emp Agcy*
Triad Temp. Svcs, *Temp. Agcy*

Virginia

A Better Resume, *Career/Outplacemnt*
Alpha Omega Resrcs, *Perm. Emp Agcy*
B&M Assoc., *Contract Svc*
CDI Corp, *Contract Svc*
Cadworks, *Contract Svc*
Computemp of Washington, D.C., *Temp. Agcy*
Computer Prof'ls, *Contract Svc*
Contec Srch, *Exec Srch*
Corporate Connection Exec. Srch Firm
Carol Day & Assoc., *Exec Srch*
Donmac Assoc., *Exec Srch*
Effective Staffng, *Exec Srch*
Engineering & MIS Guild, *Exec Srch*
Express Persnnl Svcs, *Temp. Agcy*
Halbrecht & Co, *Exec Srch*
HATCH Mrktng Syst., *Perm. Emp Agcy*
IPC Technolog's, *Contract Svc*
Information Specialists Co, *Exec Srch*
Kelly Svcs, *Temp. Agcy*
Kogen Persnnl, *Exec Srch*
Carol Maden Grp Recruitng, *Exec Srch*
The McCormick Grp, *Exec Srch*

Carol McNew Emp. Svc, *Perm. Emp Agcy*
Network Companies, *Exec Srch*
Olsten Staff Svcs, *Temp. Agcy*
Paul-Tittle Assoc., *Perm. Emp Agcy*
Procurement Solut'ns, *Contract Svc*
Remedy Intelligent Staffng, *Temp. Agcy*
Don Richard Assoc. of Richmond, *Exec Srch*
Select Staff Svcs, *Perm. Emp Agcy*
Selectemps, *Temp. Agcy*
Snelling Persnnl Svcs, *Perm. Emp Agcy*
STAT Temps, *Temp. Agcy*
Strategic Srch, *Exec Srch*
Strategic Staffing/SSI Tech. Svcs Division, *Contract Svc*
The Talley Grp, *Exec Srch*
Technical Srch Corp, *Perm. Emp Agcy*
TempWorld Staff Svcs, *Temp. Agcy*
Bill Young & Assoc., *Exec Srch*

Washington

Berkana Intl, *Exec Srch*
The Career Clinic, *Exec Srch*
J.F. Church Assoc., *Exec Srch*
Comprehensive Staff Resrcs dba Techstaff, *Temp. Agcy*
Computer Grp, *Exec Srch*
Computer Persnnl, *Exec Srch*
Executive Recrtrs, *Exec Srch*
Express Persnnl Svcs, *Temp. Agcy*
Hall Kinion Assoc., *Perm. Emp Agcy*
N.G. Hayes Co, *Exec Srch*
Houser, Martin, Morris & Assoc., *Exec Srch*
The Jobs Co, *Exec Srch*
Kelly Svcs, *Temp. Agcy*
Kossuth & Assoc., *Exec Srch*
Macrosearch, *Exec Srch*
Mgmt. Recrtrs of Mercer Islnd, *Exec Srch*
Mgmt. Recrtrs of No. Tacoma, *Exec Srch*
Mgmt. Recrtrs of Seattle, *Exec Srch*
Mgmt. Recrtrs of Tacoma, *Exec Srch*
Manpower Temp. Svcs, *Temp. Agcy*
John Mason & Assoc., *Exec Srch*
Mini-Systems Assoc., *Contract Svc*
Nelson, Coulson & Assoc., *Perm. Emp Agcy*
Northwest Temp. Svcs, *Temp. Agcy*
Olsten Staff Svcs, *Temp. Agcy*
Persnnl Unlimtd, *Exec Srch*
Resource Mngmnt Intl, *Temp. Agcy*
Rigel Computer Resrcs, *Exec Srch*
Small Bus. Solut'ns, *Exec Srch*
Snelling Persnnl Svcs, *Exec Srch*
Strain Persnnl Specialists, *Exec Srch*
Thomas Co, *Perm. Emp Agcy*
The Triad Grp, *Exec Srch*
Two 56, *Contract Svc*
The Washington Firm, *Exec Srch*
Whittall Mngmnt Grp, *Exec Srch*
WinSearch, *Exec Srch*

West Virginia

CDI Corp, *Contract Svc*
Key Persnnl, *Perm. Emp Agcy*

Wisconsin

Aerotek, *Contract Svc*
Allen, Wayne, & Co, *Perm. Emp Agcy*
Argus Tech. Svcs, *Perm. Emp Agcy*
Career Recrtrs, *Exec Srch*
Career Resrcs, *Exec Srch*
Concord Staff Source, *Perm. Emp Agcy*
J.M. Eagle Partners, *Exec Srch*
Eagle Technlgy Grp, *Perm. Emp Agcy*
Hunter Midwest, *Exec Srch*
Interim Technolog's, *Contract Svc*
Intl Srch, *Exec Srch*
Mgmt. Recrtrs/CompuSrch of Wausau, *Exec Srch*
Mgmt. Recrtrs of Stevens Point, *Exec Srch*
MARBL Consltnts, *Exec Srch*
Markent Persnnl, *Exec Srch*
Northern Tech. Svcs, *Perm. Emp Agcy*
Olsten Staff Svcs, *Temp. Agcy*
Pollak & Skan, *Contract Svc*
Prairie Engineering, *Exec Srch*
Professional Engineering Placemnts, *Perm. Emp Agcy*
Professional Resource Svcs, *Exec Srch*
Rowbottom & Assoc., *Exec Srch*
Sales Specialists, *Exec Srch*
Site Persnnl Svcs/Trainor/Salick & Assoc., *Temp. Agcy*
TAD Tech. Svcs, *Contract Svc*
Techtronix Tech. Employment, *Exec Srch*
Temps Plus Staff Svcs, *Perm. Emp Agcy*
The Waterstone Grp, *Contract Svc*

CONSTRUCTION

Arizona

Crown Tech. Svc, *Contract Svc*
Norrell Temp. Svcs, *Temp. Agcy*
Tech/Aid of Arizona, *Perm. Emp Agcy*

California

C-E Srch, *Exec Srch*
Contractors Labor Pool, *Temp. Agcy*
Douglas Dorflinger & Assoc., *Exec Srch*
Filipinos For Affirmative Action, *Perm. Emp Agcy*
Griffith & Assoc., *Exec Srch*
Interim Industrial Staffng, *Temp. Agcy*
K&C Assoc., *Exec Srch*
Mgmt. Recrtrs of Burlingame/Sales Consltnts, *Exec Srch*
Mgmt. Recrtrs of Encino, *Exec Srch*
Mgmt. Recrtrs of Pleasanton, *Exec Srch*
Mgmt. Recrtrs of San Francisco, *Exec Srch*
Mesa Intl, *Exec Srch*
Search West of Ontario, *Exec Srch*
Thor Temp. Svcs, *Temp. Agcy*

Colorado

Chuck's Contrct Labor Svc, *Contract Svc*
Eagle Valley Temps, *Temp. Agcy*
Mgmt. West, *Exec Srch*
Pendleton Resrcs, *Exec Srch*
Sales Consltnts, *Exec Srch*
Terry Persnnl, *Perm. Emp Agcy*
York & Assoc., *Exec Srch*

Connecticut

Mgmt. Recrtrs Intl, *Exec Srch*
Tech/Aid of CT, *Temp. Agcy*

Delaware

Hornberger Mngmnt Co, *Exec Srch*

Florida

All Trades Staffng, *Contract Svc*
Mgmt. Recrtrs of St. Petersburg, *Exec Srch*
Mgmt. Recrtrs of Tallahassee, *Exec Srch*
Mgmt. Recrtrs of Tampa, *Exec Srch*
Sage Consltnts, *Exec Srch*
Sales Consltnts of Fort Lauderdale, *Exec Srch*
Sales Consltnts of Jacksonville, *Exec Srch*
Specialized Srch Assoc., *Exec Srch*
Workers of Florida, *Temp. Agcy*

Georgia

Mgmt. Recrtrs of Atlanta, *Exec Srch*

Indiana

Execusearch, *Exec Srch*
Mgmt. Recrtrs of Evansville, *Exec Srch*
Mgmt. Recrtrs of Indianapolis, *Exec Srch*
Mgmt. Recrtrs of Richmond/Staff Solut'ns, *Exec Srch*
Officemates5 of Indianapolis, *Exec Srch*

Kansas

Manpower, *Temp. Agcy*

Kentucky

Temporary Prof'ls, *Temp. Agcy*

Maryland

Telesec Staff Svcs, *Temp. Agcy*

Massachusetts

Apollo Design Svc, *Contract Svc*
Berkshire Srch Assoc., *Exec Srch*
Construction Directory, *Perm. Emp Agcy*
Executive Srch Nrtheast, *Exec Srch*
Mgmt. Recrtrs Intl, *Exec Srch*
Mgmt. Recrtrs Intl of Braintree, *Exec Srch*
Mgmt. Recrtrs Intl of Westboro, *Exec Srch*
Sales Consltnts of Cape Cod, *Exec Srch*
Sales Consltnts of Wellesley, *Exec Srch*
Tech/Aid, *Contract Svc*

Michigan

Continental Srch Assoc., *Exec Srch*
William Howard Agcy, *Perm. Emp Agcy*

Minnesota

LaBree & Assoc., *Exec Srch*
Mgmt. Recrtrs-Minneapolis/Sales Consltnts, *Exec Srch*

Nevada

Labor Finders, *Temp. Agcy*
Mgmt. Recrtrs Intl, *Exec Srch*
Manpower Temp. Svcs, *Temp. Agcy*

New Hampshire

Mgmt. Recrtrs Intl of Bedford, *Exec Srch*
Tech/Aid of NH, *Perm. Emp Agcy*

New Jersey

Mgmt. Recrtrs of Passaic Cnty, *Exec Srch*

New Mexico

Excel of Albuquerque, *Perm. Emp Agcy*

New York

Compass Srch, *Exec Srch*

North Carolina

Mebane Temp. Svcs, *Temp. Agcy*

Ohio

Adecco, *Temp. Agcy*
Extra Help Temp. Svc, *Temp. Agcy*
Mgmt. Recrtrs of Cincinnati, *Exec Srch*
Mgmt. Recrtrs of Cleveland, *Exec Srch*
Mgmt. Recrtrs of Columbus, *Exec Srch*
Mgmt. Recrtrs of Dayton, *Exec Srch*
Mgmt. Recrtrs of Solon, *Exec Srch*
Providence Persnnl Consltnts, *Exec Srch*
Sales Consltnts of Cincinnati, *Exec Srch*
Tradesman Intl, *Contract Svc*

Oklahoma

Manpower Temp. Svcs, *Temp. Agcy*

Oregon

Able Temp. Svc, *Temp. Agcy*

Pennsylvania

Atomic Persnnl, *Exec Srch*
Mgmt. Recrtrs of Bucks Cnty/CompuSrch, *Exec Srch*
K. Maxin & Assoc., *Exec Srch*
United Tech. Assoc., *Temp. Agcy*

Rhode Island

Sullivan & Cogliano, *Exec Srch*

South Carolina

Roper Svcs, *Temp. Agcy*

Tennessee

Temp Staff, *Temp. Agcy*

Texas

Ann Best Elite Temps, *Temp. Agcy*
Champion Persnnl, *Exec Srch*
Joseph Chris Partners, *Exec Srch*
Mgmt. Recrtrs Intl, *Exec Srch*
W. Robert Michaels & Co, *Exec Srch*
Professional Exec Recrtrs, *Exec Srch*
Provident Resrcs Grp, *Exec Srch*
Redstone & Assoc., *Exec Srch*
Sales Consltnts of Houston, *Exec Srch*
The Talon Grp, *Exec Srch*

Virginia

Oerth Assoc., *Exec Srch*

Washington

CMS (Construction Mngmnt Svcs), *Perm. Emp Agcy*
Labor Ready, *Temp. Agcy*
Susan Schoos & Assoc., *Exec Srch*

West Virginia

Belcan Tech. Svcs, *Contract Svc*

Wyoming

JDO Assoc., *Exec Srch*

CONSULTING

California

BridgeGate Grp, *Exec Srch*
Lifter & Assoc., *Exec Srch*

Colorado

Goodwin Persnnl, *Perm. Emp Agcy*

Connecticut

Siger & Assoc., *Exec Srch*

Florida

Michael Gimbel & Assoc., *Exec Srch*

Illinois

Banner Persnnl, *Perm. Emp Agcy*
The Robinson Grp, *Exec Srch*

Massachusetts

New Dimensions in Technlgy, *Exec Srch*

Minnesota

Bright Srch/Professional Staffng, *Exec Srch*
Flatley Tech. Svcs, *Temp. Agcy*

Missouri

HDB Inc., *Perm. Emp Agcy*

New Hampshire

BeneTemps, *Temp. Agcy*

New Jersey

Foster Assoc., *Exec Srch*

New York

Castlerea Assoc., *Exec Srch*

Washington
Bixler Grp, *Exec Srch*

Wisconsin
Data Processing Srch, *Exec Srch*
Dunhill of Green Bay, *Perm. Emp Agcy*
Executive Recrtrs, *Exec Srch*
Manpower Temp. Svcs, *Temp. Agcy*

DESIGN

Alabama
Mgmt. Recrtrs Intl, *Exec Srch*

Arkansas
Mgmt. Recrtrs of Little Rock, *Exec Srch*

California
Corporate Srch, *Exec Srch*
Full Svc Temps, *Temp. Agcy*
Tech/Aid of CA, *Temp. Agcy*

Colorado
Sales Consltnts, *Exec Srch*

Florida
B2D Tech. Svcs, *Contract Svc*
DGA Persnnl Grp, *Exec Srch*
Mgmt. Recrtrs of Tallahassee, *Exec Srch*
Mgmt. Recrtrs of Tampa, *Exec Srch*
Sales Consltnts of Fort Lauderdale, *Exec Srch*
Sales Consltnts of Jacksonville, *Exec Srch*

Georgia
Claremont-Branan, *Perm. Emp Agcy*

Illinois
Gifford Assoc., *Exec Srch*
Mgmt. Recrtrs of Des Plaines, *Exec Srch*
Mgmt. Recrtrs of Rockford, *Exec Srch*
Sales Consltnts/Mgmt. Recrtrs Intl, *Exec Srch*
Sales Consltnts of Oak Brk, *Exec Srch*

Indiana
Continental Design Co, *Contract Svc*
Mid West Persnnl, *Perm. Emp Agcy*

Iowa
Mgmt. Recrtrs/CompuSrch, *Exec Srch*

Kansas
Mgmt. Recrtrs of Overlnd Prk, *Exec Srch*

Kentucky
Angel Grp Intl, *Exec Srch*

Louisiana
Mgmt. Recrtrs-Baton Rouge/Sales Consltnts, *Exec Srch*
Mgmt. Recrtrs-Metairie/Sales Consltnts, *Exec Srch*

Maryland
Mgmt. Recrtrs of Annapolis, *Exec Srch*
Mgmt. Recrtrs-Baltimore/Sales Consltnts, *Exec Srch*
Mgmt. Recrtrs-Bethesda/CompuSearch, *Exec Srch*
Mgmt. Recrtrs of Frederick, *Exec Srch*
Mgmt. Recrtrs of Washington, D.C., *Exec Srch*
Sales Consltnts of Prince Georges Cnty, *Exec Srch*

Massachusetts
Apollo Design Svc, *Contract Svc*
Berkshire Srch Assoc., *Exec Srch*
CDI Corp, *Contract Svc*

Michigan
Barman Staff Solut'ns/Barman Persnnl, *Perm. Emp Agcy*
Design & Engineering Svc, *Temp. Agcy*
William Howard Agcy, *Perm. Emp Agcy*
Mgmt. Recrtrs of Bingham Farms, *Exec Srch*
Mgmt. Recrtrs of Dearborn, *Exec Srch*
Mgmt. Recrtrs of Flint, *Exec Srch*
Mgmt. Recrtrs of Kalamazoo, *Exec Srch*
Mgmt. Recrtrs of Lansing, *Exec Srch*
Mgmt. Recrtrs of Muskegon, *Exec Srch*
Mgmt. Recrtrs of Rochester, *Exec Srch*
Resource Technolog's Corp, *Perm. Emp Agcy*
Sales Consltnts of Detroit, *Exec Srch*
Sales Consltnts of Farmington Hills, *Exec Srch*

Minnesota
Design Persnnl Resrcs, *Temp. Agcy*
Mgmt. Recrtrs-Minneapolis/Sales Consltnts, *Exec Srch*

Missouri
Mgmt. Recrtrs of Kansas Cty, *Exec Srch*
Mgmt. Recrtrs of Springfield, *Exec Srch*
Mgmt. Recrtrs of St. Louis, *Exec Srch*
Officemates5 of St. Louis, *Exec Srch*

Nebraska
Compusearch of Lincoln, *Exec Srch*
Mgmt. Recrtrs of Omaha/Officemates5, *Exec Srch*

New Hampshire
Technical Emp. Svcs, *Contract Svc*

New Jersey
Orion Consltng, *Exec Srch*
Rick Pascal & Assoc., *Exec Srch*
Sales Consltnts of Sparta, *Exec Srch*
Sharp Tech. Svcs, *Contract Svc*

New York
Extra Help Emp. Svc, *Temp. Agcy*

North Carolina
The Furniture Agcy, *Exec Srch*
Mgmt. Recrtrs/Sales Consltnts, *Exec Srch*
Mgmt. Recrtrs of Durham, *Exec Srch*
Mgmt. Recrtrs of Raleigh/Inter Exec, *Exec Srch*
Mgmt. Recrtrs of Winston-Salem, *Exec Srch*
Sales Consltnts of High Point, *Exec Srch*

Ohio
Employment Solut'ns Grp, *Exec Srch*
Mgmt. Recrtrs of Cincinnati, *Exec Srch*
Mgmt. Recrtrs of Cleveland, *Exec Srch*
Mgmt. Recrtrs of Cleveland, *Exec Srch*
Mgmt. Recrtrs of Columbus, *Exec Srch*
Mgmt. Recrtrs of Dayton, *Exec Srch*
Mgmt. Recrtrs of Solon, *Exec Srch*
RDS, *Contract Svc*
Sales Consltnts of Cincinnati, *Exec Srch*

Oregon
Mgmt. Recrtrs/Officemates5 of Portland, *Exec Srch*

Pennsylvania
CDI Corp, *Contract Svc*
Mgmt. Recrtrs of DE Cnty/CompuSrch, *Exec Srch*
Mgmt. Recrtrs of Lehigh Vly/CompuSrch, *Exec Srch*
Mgmt. Recrtrs of Philadelphia/ CompuSrch, *Exec Srch*
Olsten Staff Svcs, *Temp. Agcy*
Rice Cohen Intl, *Exec Srch*

Rhode Island
Mgmt. Recrtrs Intl, *Exec Srch*

South Carolina
Mgmt. Recrtrs of Columbia, *Exec Srch*
Mgmt. Recrtrs of Rck Hill, *Exec Srch*

Tennessee
Mega Force, *Temp. Agcy*

Texas
Mgmt. Recrtrs Intl, *Exec Srch*
Mgmt. Recrtrs of Dallas, *Exec Srch*
Sales Consltnts of Houston, *Exec Srch*

Virginia
Mgmt. Recrtrs of McLean, *Exec Srch*
Mgmt. Recrtrs of Roanoke, *Exec Srch*

Washington
Mgmt. Recrtrs of Mercer Islnd, *Exec Srch*
Mgmt. Recrtrs of Tacoma, *Exec Srch*

Wisconsin
Construction Srch Specialists, *Exec Srch*
Industrial Consltng Engineers, *Perm. Emp Agcy*

Wyoming
Mgmt. Recrtrs of Cheyenne, *Exec Srch*

DIRECT MARKETING

California
Bristol Assoc., *Exec Srch*

Illinois
Advantage Persnnl, *Perm. Emp Agcy*
Carpenter Assoc., *Exec Srch*
Ridenour & Assoc., *Exec Srch*

Michigan
C.A. Moore & Assoc., *Exec Srch*

New York
Executive Srch Consltnts, *Exec Srch*
Telemarketing Recrtrs, *Exec Srch*
Karen Tripi Assoc., *Exec Srch*
Vintage Resrcs, *Exec Srch*

Ohio
Rich Bencin & Assoc., *Perm. Emp Agcy*

DISTRIBUTION

Alaska
Olsten Staff Svcs, *Temp. Agcy*

California
Bridgecreek Persnnl, *Exec Srch*
Dominguez Metz & Assoc., *Exec Srch*

Colorado
JFI (Jobs For Industry), *Perm. Emp Agcy*

Georgia
Durham Staffng, *Perm. Emp Agcy*

Illinois
Sanford Rose Assoc., *Exec Srch*
Stone Enterprises, *Exec Srch*
Strand Assoc., *Perm. Emp Agcy*

Mississippi
Norrell Staff Svcs, *Temp. Agcy*

New Jersey
Career Srch Assoc., *Exec Srch*

New York
ROI Assoc., *Exec Srch*

Ohio
Ives & Assoc., *Exec Srch*

Tennessee
Dunhill of Memphis, *Perm. Emp Agcy*

Texas
Evie Kreisler & Assoc., *Exec Srch*

DOMESTIC HELP

California
Andrew & Potter, *Perm. Emp Agcy*
Yolanda's Agcy, *Perm. Emp Agcy*

Florida
Nannies 'N More, *Perm. Emp Agcy*

Georgia
Smith Agcy, *Perm. Emp Agcy*

Michigan
Grosse Pointe Employment, *Perm. Emp Agcy*

Montana
Heartland Nannies & Companions/Heartland Caregivers, *Contract Svc*

New Jersey
Capitol Srch, *Perm. Emp Agcy*

New York
Adele Poston Nurses Registry, *Perm. Emp Agcy*
All Home Svcs Agcy, *Perm. Emp Agcy*
Best Domestic Svcs Agcy, *Perm. Emp Agcy*
Bonfield Emp. Agcy, *Perm. Emp Agcy*

ECONOMICS

Arizona
Andrews, Stevens & Assoc., *Contract Svc*

California
CDI Corp, *Temp. Agcy*
Fay Tech Svcs, *Perm. Emp Agcy*
40 Plus of So. CA, *Exec Srch*
Gould Persnnl Svcs, *Perm. Emp Agcy*
Klein & Assoc., *Temp. Agcy*
Pasona Pacific, *Temp. Agcy*
Royal Staff Svcs, *Exec Srch*
David Sharp & Assoc., *Perm. Emp Agcy*
Tax Exec Srch, *Exec Srch*
Walker & Torrente, *Exec Srch*

Colorado
JobSearch, *Temp. Agcy*

Connecticut
The Westfield Grp, *Exec Srch*

Delaware
J.B. Groner Exec Srch, *Exec Srch*

Florida
Bryan & Assoc./Worknet, Etc., *Exec Srch*
Hastings & Hastings Persnnl Consltnts, *Temp. Agcy*

Georgia
Elite Staff Svcs, *Perm. Emp Agcy*
Express Persnnl Svcs, *Exec Srch*

Illinois
Accurate Recruitng, *Perm. Emp Agcy*
Computer Futures Exchange, *Exec Srch*
Interstaff, *Temp. Agcy*

Louisiana
Clertech Grp, *Exec Srch*

Maryland
JDG Assoc. Limited, *Exec Srch*

Massachusetts
Need Persnnl Plcmnt, *Temp. Agcy*
Olsten Prof'l Accnt'g Svcs, *Exec Srch*

Michigan
Career Quest, *Perm. Emp Agcy*

Minnesota
T.H. Hunter, *Exec Srch*
McGladrey & Pullen, *Exec Srch*

New Hampshire
National Emp. Svc Corp, *Perm. Emp Agcy*
Surge Resrcs, *Contract Svc*

New Jersey
A Prof'l Edge, *Career/Outplacemnt*
Advanced Persnnl, *Perm. Emp Agcy*
Blake & Assoc. Exec Srch, *Exec Srch*
Officemates5 of Englewood Cliffs/DayStar Temp. Svcs, *Perm. Emp Agcy*

New York
AJC Srch, *Exec Srch*
Accounting & Computer Persnnl, *Perm. Emp Agcy*
Merrill Adams Assoc., *Career/Outplacemnt*
Analytic Recruitng, *Perm. Emp Agcy*
Corporate Careers/R.J. Assoc., *Exec Srch*
Milazzo Assoc., *Perm. Emp Agcy*
Morgan-Murray Persnnl/M&M Top Temps, *Temp. Agcy*
K.A. Nowack Career Specialists, *Perm. Emp Agcy*
S.W. Mgmt., *Exec Srch*
SearchAmerica, *Exec Srch*
Werbin Assoc. Exec Srch, *Exec Srch*

North Carolina
Olsten Staff Svcs, *Temp. Agcy*

North Dakota
Olsten Staff Svcs/Kramer & Assoc./Expressway Persnnl, *Temp. Agcy*

Ohio
Combined Resrcs, *Exec Srch*
Executech Consltnts, *Exec Srch*

Pennsylvania
Basilone-Oliver Exec Srch, *Exec Srch*
The Hastings Grp, *Exec Srch*
United Employment, *Perm. Emp Agcy*

Rhode Island
Norrell Svcs, *Temp. Agcy*

Texas
Austin Grp, *Exec Srch*
The Pailin Grp, *Exec Srch*
Bart Roberson & Co, *Exec Srch*

Virginia
Ability Resrcs, *Exec Srch*
Dow Persnnl, *Perm. Emp Agcy*
Placement Prof'ls, *Exec Srch*

Wisconsin
Flores Financial Svcs, *Exec Srch*

EDUCATION

California
Harvey Bell & Assoc., *Exec Srch*
Dependable Emp. Agency Netwrk, *Perm. Emp Agcy*
Employment Devlpmnt Dept, *Perm. Emp Agcy*
Integrated Community Svcs, *Perm. Emp Agcy*
MacNaughton Assoc., *Exec Srch*
TRC Staff Svcs, *Perm. Emp Agcy*
Trans U.S., *Perm. Emp Agcy*
UAW Labor Emp. & Training Corp, *Perm. Emp Agcy*
United Staff Solut'ns, *Exec Srch*
Volt Temp. Svcs, *Temp. Agcy*
Your People Prof'ls, *Perm. Emp Agcy*

Colorado
40 Plus of CO, *Career/Outplacemnt*
JobSearch, *Temp. Agcy*
Kelly Svcs, *Temp. Agcy*

Connecticut
Admiral Staff Svcs, *Temp. Agcy*

District of Columbia
Access: Networking in the Public Interest, *Career/Outplacemnt*
Potomac Persnnl, *Perm. Emp Agcy*

Florida
Belmont Training & Employment, *Perm. Emp Agcy*
Employers' Assistant, *Temp. Agcy*
Zanco Persnnl Resrcs, *Perm. Emp Agcy*

Georgia
Elite Staff Svcs, *Perm. Emp Agcy*
Mission Corps Intl/Helping Hands Temp. Svc, *Temp. Agcy*
Peachtree Mngmnt & Consltng, *Temp. Agcy*
Randstad Staff Svcs, *Perm. Emp Agcy*

Idaho
Magic Valley Rehabilitation Svcs, *Career/Outplacemnt*

Illinois
CES, *Exec Srch*
SER Bus. & Tech. Institute, *Perm. Emp Agcy*

Iowa
Helping Hands Temp. Svc, *Temp. Agcy*

Kansas
Network of Excellence, *Exec Srch*

Maine
At Work Persnnl, *Temp. Agcy*

Maryland
American Svc Technlgy, *Contract Svc*
Sales Consltnts of Baltimore Cty, *Exec Srch*
TAC Staff Svcs, *Temp. Agcy*
TAD Staff Svcs, *Temp. Agcy*

Massachusetts
Auerbach Assoc., *Exec Srch*
Brattle Temps, *Temp. Agcy*
Carney, Sandoe & Assoc., *Exec Srch*
Editorial Svcs of N.E., *Temp. Agcy*
Educational Mngmnt Netwrk, *Exec Srch*
Gilvar & Assoc., *Exec Srch*
In Srch of Nanny, *Perm. Emp Agcy*
Johnson & Hill Staff Svc, *Temp. Agcy*
TAC Staff Svcs, *Temp. Agcy*

Michigan
William Howard Agcy, *Perm. Emp Agcy*
Michigan Indian Emp. & Training Svcs, *Perm. Emp Agcy*

Mississippi
Mississippi State Emp. Svcs, *Perm. Emp Agcy*
Recruitment & Training of MS, *Perm. Emp Agcy*

Missouri
Burns Emp. Svc, *Exec Srch*
Business Persnnl Svcs, *Temp. Agcy*
Educational Placemnt Svc, *Perm. Emp Agcy*
Employer Advantage, *Exec Srch*

Nevada
Nevada Bus. Svcs, *Career/Outplacemnt*
Talent Tree Staffng, *Perm. Emp Agcy*

New Hampshire
Allstaff Contrct Svcs, *Perm. Emp Agcy*
Surge Resrcs, *Contract Svc*

New Jersey
G.A. Agcy, *Perm. Emp Agcy*
Joule People Providers, *Perm. Emp Agcy*

New York
AARP Foundation Senior Community Svc/Employment Program, *Perm. Emp Agcy*
Michael John Lawrence & Assoc., *Exec Srch*
Merrill Adams Assoc., *Career/Outplacemnt*
Metro Persnnl/Metro Nursing Svcs, *Exec Srch*
Superior Concepts, *Contract Svc*

North Carolina
Employment Consltnts, *Contract Svc*
Jobs of Fayetteville, *Perm. Emp Agcy*
MTS, *Perm. Emp Agcy*

North Dakota
Green Thumb, *Career/Outplacemnt*
Olsten Staff Svcs/Kramer & Assoc./Expressway Persnnl, *Temp. Agcy*

Ohio
Eastern Persnnl Svcs, *Perm. Emp Agcy*
Executech Consltnts, *Exec Srch*

Laine's S.M.G., *Perm. Emp Agcy*
Rentech Ventures, *Perm. Emp Agcy*

Oregon
Southern Oregon Temporary, *Temp. Agcy*

Pennsylvania
The Philadelphia Nanny Netwrk, *Perm. Emp Agcy*
TAC Staff Svcs, *Temp. Agcy*

Rhode Island
TAC Staff Svcs, *Temp. Agcy*

Texas
OMNI Consortium, *Perm. Emp Agcy*
Ser-Jobs for Progress, *Career/Outplacemnt*
Tarrant Cnty Emp. Netwrk, *Perm. Emp Agcy*

Virginia
A Better Resume, *Career/Outplacemnt*
Hispanic Committee of VA, *Perm. Emp Agcy*
Snelling Persnnl Svcs, *Perm. Emp Agcy*
TAC Staff Svcs, *Temp. Agcy*

Washington
Job Ctr, *Temp. Agcy*
Two 56, *Contract Svc*

ELDERCARE, IN-HOME

Massachusetts
Arbor Assoc., *Temp. Agcy*

Montana
Heartland Nannies & Companions/Heartland Caregivers, *Contract Svc*

New Jersey
Capitol Srch, *Perm. Emp Agcy*
Neighborhood Nannies, *Perm. Emp Agcy*

New York
All Home Svcs Agcy, *Perm. Emp Agcy*

Ohio
Child & Elder Care Insights, *Exec Srch*

Oregon
Auntie Fay Domestic Agcy, *Perm. Emp Agcy*

Virginia
Nanny Dimensions, *Perm. Emp Agcy*

ELECTRICAL

Alabama
Mgmt. Recrtrs Intl, *Exec Srch*

Arizona
Mgmt. Recrtrs of Scottsdale, *Exec Srch*

Arkansas
Mgmt. Recrtrs of Little Rock, *Exec Srch*

California
GPL Engineering, *Perm. Emp Agcy*
Mgmt. Recrtrs of Burlingame/Sales Consltnts, *Exec Srch*
Mgmt. Recrtrs of Encino, *Exec Srch*
Mgmt. Recrtrs of Pleasanton, *Exec Srch*
Mesa Intl, *Exec Srch*

Colorado
Dunhill Persnnl of Fort Collins, *Exec Srch*
Mgmt. Recrtrs of Colorado Springs, *Exec Srch*
Sales Consltnts, *Exec Srch*

Connecticut
Mgmt. Recrtrs Intl, *Exec Srch*
Matrix Srch, *Perm. Emp Agcy*

Florida
Mgmt. Recrtrs of St. Petersburg, *Exec Srch*
Mgmt. Recrtrs of Tallahassee, *Exec Srch*
Mgmt. Recrtrs of Tampa, *Exec Srch*
Sales Consltnts of Fort Lauderdale, *Exec Srch*
Sales Consltnts of Jacksonville, *Exec Srch*

Georgia
Mgmt. Recrtrs of Atlanta, *Exec Srch*

Illinois
Mgmt. Recrtrs of Des Plaines, *Exec Srch*
Mgmt. Recrtrs of Rockford, *Exec Srch*
Officemates5 of Wheeling, *Exec Srch*
Sales Consltnts/Mgmt. Recrtrs Intl, *Exec Srch*

Indiana
Execusearch, *Exec Srch*
Mgmt. Recrtrs of Evansville, *Exec Srch*

Mgmt. Recrtrs of Indianapolis, *Exec Srch*
Mgmt. Recrtrs of Richmond/Staff Solut'ns, *Exec Srch*
Officemates5 of Indianapolis, *Exec Srch*

Iowa
Mgmt. Recrtrs/CompuSrch, *Exec Srch*

Kansas
Mgmt. Recrtrs of Overlnd Prk, *Exec Srch*

Kentucky
Angel Grp Intl, *Exec Srch*

Louisiana
Clertech Grp, *Exec Srch*
Mgmt. Recrtrs-Baton Rouge/Sales Consltnts, *Exec Srch*
Mgmt. Recrtrs-Metairie/Sales Consltnts, *Exec Srch*

Maryland
Mgmt. Recrtrs of Annapolis, *Exec Srch*
Mgmt. Recrtrs-Baltimore/Sales Consltnts, *Exec Srch*
Mgmt. Recrtrs-Bethesda/CompuSearch, *Exec Srch*
Mgmt. Recrtrs of Frederick, *Exec Srch*
Sales Consltnts of Prince Georges Cnty, *Exec Srch*

Massachusetts
Brady Emp. Svc, *Perm. Emp Agcy*
Mgmt. Recrtrs Intl of Braintree, *Exec Srch*
Mgmt. Recrtrs Intl of Springfield, *Exec Srch*
Mgmt. Recrtrs Intl of Westboro, *Exec Srch*
Sales Consltnts of Cape Cod, *Exec Srch*
Sales Consltnts of Plymouth Cnty, *Exec Srch*
Sales Consltnts of Wellesley, *Exec Srch*

Michigan
Mgmt. Recrtrs of Bingham Farms, *Exec Srch*
Mgmt. Recrtrs of Dearborn, *Exec Srch*
Mgmt. Recrtrs of Flint, *Exec Srch*
Mgmt. Recrtrs of Kalamazoo, *Exec Srch*
Mgmt. Recrtrs of Lansing, *Exec Srch*
Mgmt. Recrtrs of Muskegon, *Exec Srch*
Mgmt. Recrtrs of Rochester, *Exec Srch*
Sales Consltnts of Detroit, *Exec Srch*
Sales Consltnts of Farmington Hills, *Exec Srch*
Sales Consltnts of Lansing, *Exec Srch*

Minnesota
Mgmt. Recrtrs-Minneapolis/Sales Consltnts, *Exec Srch*

Missouri
Mgmt. Recrtrs of Kansas Cty, *Exec Srch*
Mgmt. Recrtrs of Springfield, *Exec Srch*
Mgmt. Recrtrs of St. Louis, *Exec Srch*
Officemates5 of St. Louis, *Exec Srch*

Nebraska
Compusearch of Lincoln, *Exec Srch*
Mgmt. Recrtrs of Omaha/Officemates5, *Exec Srch*

New Hampshire
Mgmt. Recrtrs Intl of Bedford, *Exec Srch*

New Jersey
Brookdale Srch Assoc., *Exec Srch*
Dow-Tech, *Exec Srch*
Mgmt. Recrtrs of Bay Head, *Exec Srch*
Mgmt. Recrtrs of Passaic Cnty, *Exec Srch*
RSVP Svcs, *Perm. Emp Agcy*
Sales Consltnts of Sparta, *Exec Srch*

New York
Mgmt. Recrtrs of Woodbury/ CompuSrch, *Exec Srch*

North Carolina
Mgmt. Recrtrs/Sales Consltnts, *Exec Srch*
Mgmt. Recrtrs of Durham, *Exec Srch*
Mgmt. Recrtrs of Raleigh/Inter Exec, *Exec Srch*
Mgmt. Recrtrs of Winston-Salem, *Exec Srch*
Sales Consltnts of High Point, *Exec Srch*

Ohio
Mgmt. Recrtrs of Cincinnati, *Exec Srch*
Mgmt. Recrtrs of Cleveland, *Exec Srch*
Mgmt. Recrtrs of Columbus, *Exec Srch*
Mgmt. Recrtrs of Dayton, *Exec Srch*
Mgmt. Recrtrs of Solon, *Exec Srch*
Sales Consltnts of Cincinnati, *Exec Srch*
H.L. Yoh Co, *Contract Svc*

Oregon
Mgmt. Recrtrs/Officemates5 of Portland, *Exec Srch*

Pennsylvania
Mgmt. Recrtrs of DE Cnty/CompuSrch, *Exec Srch*
Mgmt. Recrtrs of Lehigh Vly/CompuSrch, *Exec Srch*
Mgmt. Recrtrs of Philadelphia/ CompuSrch, *Exec Srch*
Rice Cohen Intl, *Exec Srch*

Rhode Island
Mgmt. Recrtrs Intl, *Exec Srch*

South Carolina
Mgmt. Recrtrs of Columbia, *Exec Srch*
Mgmt. Recrtrs of Rck Hill, *Exec Srch*

Tennessee
Sales Consltnts of Nashville, *Exec Srch*

Texas
Mgmt. Recrtrs Intl, *Exec Srch*
Mgmt. Recrtrs of Dallas, *Exec Srch*
Sales Consltnts of Houston, *Exec Srch*

Utah
Professional Recrtrs, *Exec Srch*

Virginia
Mgmt. Recrtrs of McLean, *Exec Srch*
Mgmt. Recrtrs of Roanoke, *Exec Srch*

Washington
Mgmt. Recrtrs of Mercer Islnd, *Exec Srch*
Mgmt. Recrtrs of Tacoma, *Exec Srch*

Wisconsin
Mgmt. Recrtrs of Appleton/ CompuSrch, *Exec Srch*
Mgmt. Recrtrs of Green Bay, *Exec Srch*
Mgmt. Recrtrs of Milwaukee/Sales Consltnts, *Exec Srch*

Wyoming
Mgmt. Recrtrs of Cheyenne, *Exec Srch*

ELECTRONICS

Arizona
Circuit Technlgy Srch, *Exec Srch*
Holdan & Assoc., *Exec Srch*

California
Thomas Beck, *Exec Srch*
Brown Venture Assoc., *Exec Srch*
California Srch Consltnts, *Exec Srch*
COMFORCE Tech. Svcs, *Contract Svc*
Dunhill Prof'l Srch of San Francisco, *Exec Srch*
Cindy Jackson Srch, *Exec Srch*
New Venture Development, *Exec Srch*
Sanford Rose Assoc., *Exec Srch*
Splaine & Assoc., *Exec Srch*
Technical Srch Consltnts, *Exec Srch*

Connecticut
Corporate Staff Solut'ns, *Temp. Agcy*
Matrix Srch, *Perm. Emp Agcy*
Workforce One, *Perm. Emp Agcy*

Florida
Sage Consltnts, *Exec Srch*

Illinois
Sellers & Assoc., *Exec Srch*

Indiana
The Bennett Grp, *Exec Srch*
FORTUNE Persnnl Consltnts, *Exec Srch*

Maryland
Wallach Assoc., *Exec Srch*

Massachusetts
Rob Davidson Assoc./Exec. & Prof. Resume Svc, *Exec Srch*
Bruce Rafey Assoc., *Exec Srch*
Selectemps, *Temp. Agcy*

Missouri
Dunhill Persnnl System of Missouri, *Exec Srch*

New Hampshire
Sprout/Standish, *Exec Srch*

New Jersey
Brookdale Srch Assoc., *Exec Srch*
Dow-Tech, *Exec Srch*
Garrett Grp, *Exec Srch*
Mgmt. Recrtrs of Bay Head, *Exec Srch*
Mgmt. Recrtrs of Medford, *Exec Srch*
RSVP Svcs, *Perm. Emp Agcy*

New York
Hampshire Assoc., *Perm. Emp Agcy*

North Carolina
Executive Staff Svcs, *Perm. Emp Agcy*
Mgmt. Recrtrs of Raleigh/Inter Exec, *Exec Srch*

Ohio
North Star Resrcs, *Contract Svc*

Oregon
Able Temp. Svc, *Temp. Agcy*

Pennsylvania
Select Persnnl, *Perm. Emp Agcy*

South Carolina
Mgmt. Recrtrs of Aiken, *Exec Srch*

Texas
American Resrcs, *Exec Srch*
Austin Grp, *Exec Srch*
Michael James & Assoc., *Exec Srch*
Pedley Stringer & Assoc., *Exec Srch*
Sanford Rose Assoc., *Exec Srch*

Virginia
Paul-Tittle Assoc., *Perm. Emp Agcy*

Washington
CDI Corp, *Contract Svc*

ENGINEERING

Alabama
Aerotek, *Perm. Emp Agcy*
Assoc. Persnnl, *Exec Srch*
Breen Persnnl, *Exec Srch*
Mary Cheek & Assoc., *Exec Srch*
Clark Persnnl Svc of Mobile, *Exec Srch*
Employment Consltnts, *Perm. Emp Agcy*
FORTUNE Persnnl Consltnts, *Exec Srch*
Mgmt. Recrtrs Intl, *Exec Srch*
National Labor Line, *Exec Srch*
Placers, *Perm. Emp Agcy*
Seatec, *Contract Svc*
J.L. Small Assoc., *Exec Srch*
Snelling Persnnl Svcs, *Perm. Emp Agcy*
Snelling Srch/Snelling Persnnl Svcs, *Exec Srch*
Weldtek Testing Laboratory, *Career/Outplacemnt*
WorkForce, *Temp. Agcy*

Alaska
Olsten Staff Svcs, *Temp. Agcy*
Professional Bus. Svc, *Temp. Agcy*

Arizona
Adecco, *Contract Svc*
Adecco, *Temp. Agcy*
Aztech Recrtmnt Co, *Exec Srch*
CDI Corp, *Contract Svc*
C.S. Assoc., *Exec Srch*
Circuit Technlgy Srch, *Exec Srch*
Paul Dicken Assoc., *Contract Svc*
The Dorfman Grp, *Exec Srch*
Electronic Power Source, *Exec Srch*
Erickson & Assoc., *Perm. Emp Agcy*
General Emp. Enterprises, *Perm. Emp Agcy*
J.R. Prof'l Srch, *Exec Srch*
Mgmt. Recrtrs Intl, *Exec Srch*
Mgmt. Recrtrs of Scottsdale, *Exec Srch*
MEDA Tech. Svcs, *Contract Svc*
PDS Tech. Svc, *Contract Svc*
Priority Staffng, *Perm. Emp Agcy*
Professional Exec Research Consltng, *Exec Srch*
Retiree Skills, *Temp. Agcy*
SearchAmerica, *Exec Srch*
Snelling Persnnl Svcs, *Perm. Emp Agcy*
Spectra Intl, *Exec Srch*
Stivers Temp. Persnnl, *Temp. Agcy*
TSS Consltng, *Exec Srch*
Tech/Aid of Arizona, *Perm. Emp Agcy*
Tele-Solution Srch, *Exec Srch*
Volt Tech. Svcs, *Contract Svc*

Arkansas
Dunhill Persnnl, *Exec Srch*
Executive Recrtrs Outplacement Consltnts, *Exec Srch*
Intl Srch, *Exec Srch*
Mgmt. Recrtrs of Little Rock, *Exec Srch*
Morris & Assoc., *Exec Srch*
Snelling Srch, *Exec Srch*
Turnage Emp. Svc Grp, *Exec Srch*
Utopia, *Exec Srch*

California
AM Engineering, *Perm. Emp Agcy*
A.S.A.P. Emp. Svc, *Perm. Emp Agcy*
ACCESS Technlgy, *Exec Srch*
AccuStaff, *Exec Srch*
AccuStaff Co, *Temp. Agcy*
Advanced Technlgy Consltnts, *Exec Srch*
Affordable Exec Recrtrs, *Exec Srch*
Alfano Temp. Persnnl, *Temp. Agcy*
Alpha-Net Consltng Grp, *Exec Srch*
American Technical, *Temp. Agcy*
Amtec Engineering Corp, *Perm. Emp Agcy*
John Anthony & Assoc., *Exec Srch*
Apple One Emp. Svcs, *Perm. Emp Agcy*

Arrowstaff Svcs, *Perm. Emp Agcy*
Assist Tech. Svc, *Contract Svc*
B&M Assoc., *Contract Svc*
Thomas Beck, *Exec Srch*
Harvey Bell & Assoc., *Exec Srch*
Best Temp. Svc, *Temp. Agcy*
Blue, Garni & Co, *Exec Srch*
Brandenburg Smith & Assoc., *Exec Srch*
James Brandon & Assoc., *Exec Srch*
Bryson Myers Co, *Exec Srch*
Bullis & Co, *Exec Srch*
Business Syst. Staffing & Assoc., *Perm. Emp Agcy*
CDI Corp, *Temp. Agcy*
CN Assoc., *Exec Srch*
CT Persnnl Svcs, *Perm. Emp Agcy*
California Srch Agcy, *Exec Srch*
California Srch Consltnts, *Exec Srch*
Career Advantage, *Exec Srch*
Wayne Chamberlain & Assoc., *Exec Srch*
Coast Persnnl, *Temp. Agcy*
Consultant Svcs, *Exec Srch*
Corporate Srch, *Exec Srch*
Corporate Technlgy, *Exec Srch*
Crossroads Staff Svc, *Temp. Agcy*
Culver Persnnl Svcs, *Perm. Emp Agcy*
Culver Persnnl Svcs, *Exec Srch*
Data Careers Persnnl Svcs & Srch Grp, *Perm. Emp Agcy*
Drake Office Overload, *Temp. Agcy*
Dunhill Prof'l Srch, *Exec Srch*
EDP Contrct Svcs, *Contract Svc*
Eleventh Hour Staff Svcs, *Temp. Agcy*
Employment Devlpmnt Dept, *Perm. Emp Agcy*
Engineering Tech. Svc, *Temp. Agcy*
Executive Directions, *Exec Srch*
Executive Resource Syst., *Exec Srch*
Executive Srch Consltnts, *Exec Srch*
Curtis Farmer Persnnl, *Exec Srch*
Fastek Tech. Svcs, *Perm. Emp Agcy*
Fay Tech Svcs, *Perm. Emp Agcy*
Fisher & Assoc., *Exec Srch*
Fisher Persnnl Mngmnt Svcs, *Exec Srch*
FORTUNE Persnnl Consltnts, *Exec Srch*
40 Plus of So. CA, *Exec Srch*
Fresquez & Assoc., *Exec Srch*
GM Assoc., *Exec Srch*
GPL Engineering, *Perm. Emp Agcy*
Garnett Emp. Svcs, *Temp. Agcy*
Dianne Gauger & Assoc., *Exec Srch*
Global Srch, *Exec Srch*
The Goodman Grp, *Exec Srch*
Grant & Assoc., *Exec Srch*
Great 400 Grp Intl, *Perm. Emp Agcy*
Griffith & Assoc., *Exec Srch*
Harley Assoc., *Exec Srch*
Healthcare Exec Recrtrs, *Exec Srch*
Holland McFadzean & Assoc., *Exec Srch*
Impact, *Exec Srch*
Independent Resource System, *Exec Srch*
Industrial Svcs Co, *Temp. Agcy*
IntelliSource Computer Careers, *Exec Srch*
Interim Persnnl, *Temp. Agcy*
Intl Srch Consltnts, *Perm. Emp Agcy*
Intl Staff Consltnts, *Exec Srch*
Interstate Recrtrs, *Exec Srch*
JPM Intl, *Exec Srch*
Jerome & Co, *Exec Srch*
K&C Assoc., *Exec Srch*
Kelly Svcs, *Temp. Agcy*
Kelly Tech. Svcs, *Temp. Agcy*
Klein & Assoc., *Temp. Agcy*
Kuhn Med-Tech, *Exec Srch*
John Kurosky & Assoc., *Exec Srch*
Larsen, Whitney, Blecksmith, & Zilliacus, *Exec Srch*
The London Agcy, *Temp. Agcy*
MK Tech. Svc, *Temp. Agcy*
Malibu Grp, *Exec Srch*
Mgmt. Recrtrs of Burlingame/Sales Consltnts, *Exec Srch*
Mgmt. Recrtrs of Encino, *Exec Srch*
Mgmt. Recrtrs of Laguna Hills, *Exec Srch*
Mgmt. Recrtrs-Oakland/Sales Consltnts, *Exec Srch*
Mgmt. Recrtrs of Pleasanton, *Exec Srch*
Mgmt. Recrtrs of Redlands, *Exec Srch*
Mgmt. Recrtrs of San Francisco, *Exec Srch*
Mgmt. Solut'ns, *Exec Srch*
Manpower, *Temp. Agcy*
Markar Assoc., *Exec Srch*
Master Srch, *Exec Srch*
Maverick Staff Svc, *Perm. Emp Agcy*
McCoy Limited, *Exec Srch*
Med Quest, *Exec Srch*
Mesa Intl, *Exec Srch*
Milestone Prof'l Staffng, *Exec Srch*
Mini-Systems Assoc., *Exec Srch*
Monroe Persnnl Svcs, *Perm. Emp Agcy*
Morgen Design, *Contract Svc*
Multax Syst., *Perm. Emp Agcy*
Multisearch Recrtrs, *Exec Srch*
Murray Enterprises Staff Svcs, *Temp. Agcy*
?CC Exec Srch, *Exec Srch*
Nelson HR Solut'ns, *Perm. Emp Agcy*
Net Workers, *Contract Svc*
New Venture Development, *Exec Srch*
Nyborg-Dow Assoc., *Exec Srch*
Omni Express Temps, *Temp. Agcy*
Princeton Corporate Consltnts, *Exec Srch*
Pro Found, *Perm. Emp Agcy*
Pro Staff Persnnl Svcs, *Perm. Emp Agcy*
Professional Recrtrs, *Exec Srch*
Professional Srch, *Exec Srch*
Questemps, *Temp. Agcy*
Raphael Recrtmnt, *Exec Srch*
Remedy Intelligent Staffng, *Temp. Agcy*
Resource Perspectives, *Exec Srch*
Richmar Assoc., *Temp. Agcy*
Rich Rigler & Assoc., *Exec Srch*
Riley-Cole Recrtmnt Specialists, *Exec Srch*
Ritter Assoc., *Exec Srch*
Larry Rosenthal & Assoc., *Exec Srch*
Rowland Assoc., *Exec Srch*
Royal Staff Svcs, *Exec Srch*
Sales Consltnts of Modesto, *Exec Srch*
Sales Consltnts of Sacramento, *Exec Srch*
Sanford Rose Assoc., *Exec Srch*
Santa Barbara Plcmnt, *Perm. Emp Agcy*
Sarver & Carruth Assoc., *Exec Srch*
The Srch Grp, *Exec Srch*
The Srch Netwrk, *Exec Srch*
Search West, *Exec Srch*
Sierra Technlgy, *Contract Svc*
Source Engineering, *Perm. Emp Agcy*
Source Svcs Corp, *Exec Srch*
Southwest Srch Assoc., *Exec Srch*
Spectrawest, *Exec Srch*
Adele Steinmetz, *Exec Srch*
Sun Persnnl Svcs, *Temp. Agcy*
System One, *Perm. Emp Agcy*
Systems Research Grp, *Exec Srch*
TAD Data Svcs, *Perm. Emp Agcy*
TLC Staffng, *Temp. Agcy*
T.R. Emp. Agcy, *Perm. Emp Agcy*
TRC Staff Svcs, *Perm. Emp Agcy*
TAD Resrcs Intl, *Perm. Emp Agcy*
TAD Tech. Svcs, *Contract Svc*
Tech/Aid of CA, *Temp. Agcy*
Technical Aid Corp, *Temp. Agcy*
Technical Srch Consltnts, *Exec Srch*
TechniQuest, *Exec Srch*
TechniSkills, *Temp. Agcy*
Technology Locator, *Contract Svc*
TechSource, *Contract Svc*
Teleforce Intl, *Exec Srch*
Trattner Netwrk, *Perm. Emp Agcy*
Trend Westrn Tech. Corp, *Temp. Agcy*
Trendtec, *Temp. Agcy*
Triple-J Svcs, *Exec Srch*
The Truman Agcy, Persnnl Specialists, *Perm. Emp Agcy*
Tustin Persnnl Svcs, *Perm. Emp Agcy*
Unisearch, *Exec Srch*
United Staff Solut'ns, *Exec Srch*
United/Corestaff Staff Svcs, *Perm. Emp Agcy*
Victor Valley Persnnl Agcy, *Perm. Emp Agcy*
Volt Tech. Svcs, *Contract Svc*
Volt Temp. Svcs, *Temp. Agcy*
Western Staff Svcs, *Temp. Agcy*
Western Tech. Resrcs, *Exec Srch*
S.R. Wilson, *Exec Srch*
Your People Prof'ls, *Perm. Emp Agcy*
Don Zee Assoc., *Exec Srch*

Colorado

Ahrnsbrak & Assoc., *Perm. Emp Agcy*
The Bridge, *Exec Srch*
CDI Corp, *Contract Svc*
Career Forum, *Exec Srch*
Career Mrktng Assoc., *Exec Srch*
Clockwise Partners, *Exec Srch*
Dunhill Persnnl of Boulder, *Exec Srch*
Dunhill Persnnl of Fort Collins, *Exec Srch*
Enscicon Corp, *Perm. Emp Agcy*
FORTUNE Persnnl Consltnts, *Exec Srch*
40 Plus of CO, *Career/Outplacemnt*
GeoSearch, *Exec Srch*
Gimble & Nicol Exec Srch, *Exec Srch*
Hallmark Persnnl Syst., *Exec Srch*
Health Technlgy, *Exec Srch*
JobSearch, *Temp. Agcy*
Kelly Svcs, *Temp. Agcy*
Kelly Tech. Svcs, *Temp. Agcy*
Mgmt. Recrtrs of Boulder, *Exec Srch*
Mgmt. Recrtrs of Colorado Springs, *Exec Srch*
Manpower Intl, *Temp. Agcy*
Martinez & Hromada Assoc., *Contract Svc*
Miller Denver, *Exec Srch*
National Affirmative Action Career Netwrk, *Exec Srch*
Olsten Staff Svcs, *Temp. Agcy*
On Call Tech. Svcs/StaffMark, *Temp. Agcy*
Pendleton Resrcs, *Exec Srch*
Real Estate Persnnl, *Exec Srch*
SOS Staff Svcs, *Temp. Agcy*
Sales Consltnts, *Exec Srch*
Snelling Persnnl Svcs, *Exec Srch*
Star Persnnl, *Exec Srch*
Talent Tree Staffng, *Perm. Emp Agcy*
Technical Aid Corp, *Temp. Agcy*
Technical Recrtrs of Colorado Springs, *Exec Srch*
Todays Temporary, *Temp. Agcy*
J.Q. Turner & Assoc., *Exec Srch*
Welzig, Lowe & Assoc., *Exec Srch*
Woodmoor Grp, *Exec Srch*
H.L. Yoh Co, *Contract Svc*

Connecticut

A&A Resume & Persnnl Svcs, *Perm. Emp Agcy*
Admiral Staff Svcs, *Temp. Agcy*
Availability of Hartford, *Perm. Emp Agcy*
Blackwood Assoc., *Exec Srch*
Bohan & Bradstreet, *Perm. Emp Agcy*
Cahill Assoc., *Exec Srch*
Charter Persnnl Svcs, *Exec Srch*
Cheney Assoc., *Exec Srch*
Cupples Consltng Svcs, *Exec Srch*
Data Pros, *Perm. Emp Agcy*
Diversified Emp. Svcs, *Perm. Emp Agcy*
Diversity Recruitng Svcs, *Exec Srch*
Dunhill Srch Intl, *Perm. Emp Agcy*
EDP Contrct Svcs, *Contract Svc*
Employment Opport., *Perm. Emp Agcy*
Engineering Resource Recrtrs, *Exec Srch*
Executive Register, *Perm. Emp Agcy*
Fox Ridge Svcs, *Temp. Agcy*
Friedman Assoc., *Exec Srch*
Hallmark Totaltech, *Perm. Emp Agcy*
High-Tech Recrtrs, *Exec Srch*
Hire Logic, *Temp. Agcy*
J.G. Hood Assoc., *Perm. Emp Agcy*
Human Resource Consltnts Exec. Srch Firm
Industrial Recrtrs Assn, *Perm. Emp Agcy*
JAT, *Perm. Emp Agcy*
Jobshop, *Perm. Emp Agcy*
W.R. Lawry, *Perm. Emp Agcy*
Lineal Recruitng Svcs, *Perm. Emp Agcy*
Lutz Assoc., *Exec Srch*
MJF Assoc., *Exec Srch*
Mgmt. Recrtrs Intl, *Exec Srch*
Mgmt. Srch, *Exec Srch*
Matrix Srch, *Perm. Emp Agcy*
Maxwell-Marcus Staff Consltnts, *Exec Srch*
New England Persnnl, *Perm. Emp Agcy*
Office Svcs of CT, *Perm. Emp Agcy*
PRH Mgmt., *Exec Srch*
Barry Persky & Co., *Exec Srch*
Quality Control Recrtrs, *Exec Srch*
Russo Assoc., *Exec Srch*
Source Svcs Corp, *Exec Srch*
Stewart Assoc., *Exec Srch*
Strategic Srch, *Exec Srch*
Super Syst., *Perm. Emp Agcy*
TAD Tech. Svcs, *Contract Svc*
Tech/Aid of CT, *Temp. Agcy*
Technical Srch, *Exec Srch*
Tech. Staff Solut'ns, *Temp. Agcy*
Wallace Assoc., *Exec Srch*
Western Staff Svcs, *Temp. Agcy*
Western Staff Svcs, *Perm. Emp Agcy*

Delaware

FORTUNE Persnnl Consltnts, *Exec Srch*
J.B. Groner Exec Srch, *Exec Srch*
E.W. Hodges & Assoc., *Exec Srch*
Independent Nat'l Srch & Assoc., *Exec Srch*
H.L. Yoh Co, *Contract Svc*

District of Columbia

Norrell Svcs, *Temp. Agcy*

Florida

AAA Employment, *Perm. Emp Agcy*
Academy Design & Tech. Svcs, *Contract Svc*
AccuTech, *Contract Svc*
Active Prof'ls, *Exec Srch*
Advanced R&D, *Contract Svc*
American Exec Srch, *Exec Srch*
Atlantic Prof'l Recrtrs, *Exec Srch*
Availability, *Perm. Emp Agcy*
B2D Tech. Svcs, *Contract Svc*
The Brand Co, *Exec Srch*
CDI Corp, *Contract Svc*
Cantrell & Assoc., *Exec Srch*
Career Planners, *Perm. Emp Agcy*
Colli Assoc. of Tampa, *Exec Srch*
Criterion Exec Srch, *Exec Srch*
DGA Persnnl Grp, *Exec Srch*
Donbar Svc Corp, *Temp. Agcy*
Ethan Allen Persnnl Plcmnt, *Exec Srch*
First Emp. Consltnts, *Exec Srch*
FORTUNE Persnnl Consltnts, *Exec Srch*
GCA/Gulf Coast Assoc., *Exec Srch*

Gallin Assoc., *Exec Srch*
Bob Graham & Assoc., *Exec Srch*
HR Prof'l Consltnts, *Exec Srch*
Janus Career Svc, *Perm. Emp Agcy*
Just Mngmnt Svcs, *Exec Srch*
Koerner Grp, *Exec Srch*
The Mac Grp, *Exec Srch*
Mgmt. Recrtrs of Bonita Springs, *Exec Srch*
Mgmt. Recrtrs of Coral Gables, *Exec Srch*
Mgmt. Recrtrs of Indialantic, *Exec Srch*
Mgmt. Recrtrs of Jacksonville, *Exec Srch*
Mgmt. Recrtrs of Lake Cnty, *Exec Srch*
Mgmt. Recrtrs of Miami, *Exec Srch*
Mgmt. Recrtrs of Pensacola, *Exec Srch*
Mgmt. Recrtrs of St. Petersburg, *Exec Srch*
Mgmt. Recrtrs of Tallahassee, *Exec Srch*
Mgmt. Recrtrs of Tampa, *Exec Srch*
Mankuta Gallagher & Assoc., *Exec Srch*
Manpower Tech. Svcs, *Perm. Emp Agcy*
Manpower Temp. Svcs, *Temp. Agcy*
Norrell Tech. Svcs, *Exec Srch*
Olsten Staff Svcs, *Temp. Agcy*
OMNIPartners, *Exec Srch*
O'Quin Persnnl, *Temp. Agcy*
PMC&L Assoc., *Perm. Emp Agcy*
The Persnnl Institute, *Exec Srch*
Persnnl One, *Perm. Emp Agcy*
Priority Srch, *Exec Srch*
Profes. Staffing/Able Body Temp. Svcs, *Contract Svc*
Pulp & Paper Intl, *Exec Srch*
Jack Richman & Assoc., *Exec Srch*
Roth Young of Tampa, *Exec Srch*
The Ryan Charles Grp, *Exec Srch*
Sales Consltnts of Fort Lauderdale, *Exec Srch*
Sales Consltnts of Jacksonville, *Exec Srch*
Sales Consltnts of Sarasota, *Exec Srch*
Search Enterprises South, *Exec Srch*
Doug Sears & Assoc., *Exec Srch*
Snelling Persnnl, *Exec Srch*
Source Svcs Corp, *Exec Srch*
Specialized Srch Assoc., *Exec Srch*
The Stewart Srch Grp, *Exec Srch*
Summit Exec Srch Consltnts, *Exec Srch*
System One Tech. Staffng, *Exec Srch*
TRC Staff Svcs, *Temp. Agcy*
TechStaff, *Contract Svc*

Georgia

A.D. & Assoc. Exec Srch, *Exec Srch*
Adecco Tech. Svcs, *Contract Svc*
Anderson Industrial Assoc., *Exec Srch*
Arjay & Assoc., *Exec Srch*
Ashley-Nolan Intl, *Exec Srch*
Atlanta Tech. Support, *Contract Svc*
Augusta Staffing Assoc., *Perm. Emp Agcy*
Bell Oaks Co, *Exec Srch*
Broward-Dobbs, *Exec Srch*
Business Prof'l Grp, *Perm. Emp Agcy*
Career Placemnts, *Perm. Emp Agcy*
Claremont-Branan, *Perm. Emp Agcy*
Coast to Coast Tech. Svcs, *Temp. Agcy*
Corporate Srch Consltnts, *Exec Srch*
Dunhill Prof'l Srch, *Exec Srch*
Elite Staff Svcs, *Perm. Emp Agcy*
Express Persnnl Svcs, *Perm. Emp Agcy*
Express Persnnl Svcs, *Exec Srch*
FORTUNE Persnnl Consltnts of Atlanta, *Exec Srch*
Fox-Morris Assoc., *Exec Srch*
The HR Grp, *Exec Srch*
Hall Mngmnt Grp, *Exec Srch*
Hines Recruitng Assn, *Exec Srch*
ISC of Atlanta/Intl Career Continuation, *Exec Srch*
Job Shop, *Exec Srch*
Jordan Temps, *Temp. Agcy*
Evie Kreisler & Assoc., *Exec Srch*
MAU, *Perm. Emp Agcy*
MSI Intl, *Exec Srch*
Mgmt. Recrtrs of Atlanta, *Exec Srch*
Mgmt. Recrtrs of Atlanta, *Exec Srch*
Mgmt. Recrtrs of Columbus, *Exec Srch*
Mgmt. Recrtrs of Marietta, *Exec Srch*
Mgmt. Recrtrs of Savannah, *Exec Srch*
Medical Srch, *Exec Srch*
Millard & Assoc., *Exec Srch*
NEIS, *Exec Srch*
Olsten Staff Svcs, *Temp. Agcy*
Olsten Tech. Svcs, *Perm. Emp Agcy*
Persnnl Opport., *Exec Srch*
Pro-Tech, *Exec Srch*
Randstad Staff Svcs, *Perm. Emp Agcy*
Sanford Rose Assoc., *Exec Srch*
SearchAmerica, *Exec Srch*
Snelling Persnnl Svcs, *Exec Srch*
TRC Staff Svcs, *Temp. Agcy*
Team One Partners, *Exec Srch*
Technical Assoc., *Contract Svc*
Toar Consltnts, *Exec Srch*
Western Tech. Svcs, *Temp. Agcy*
H.L. Yoh Co, *Contract Svc*

Hawaii

Dunhill Prof'l Srch of Hawaii, *Exec Srch*
Ellis & Assoc., *Exec Srch*

Idaho

Finney & Assoc., *Exec Srch*
Horne/Brown Intl, *Exec Srch*
Volt Tech. Svcs, *Contract Svc*
Ward-Hoffman & Assoc., *Exec Srch*

Illinois

The Ability Grp, *Exec Srch*
B.J. Abrams & Assoc., *Exec Srch*
Accord, *Exec Srch*
Advanced Tech. Srch, *Exec Srch*
American Contrct Svcs, *Contract Svc*
American Engineering Co, *Exec Srch*
American Tech. Srch, *Exec Srch*
Availability, *Perm. Emp Agcy*
B-W & Assoc., *Perm. Emp Agcy*
Banner Persnnl, *Perm. Emp Agcy*
Bevelle & Assoc., *Exec Srch*
Britannia, *Exec Srch*
Burton Placemnt Svcs, *Exec Srch*
CDI Corp, *Contract Svc*
Carson Mngmnt Assoc., *Contract Svc*
Carter Assoc., *Exec Srch*
Cast Metals Persnnl, *Exec Srch*
Corporate Environment, *Exec Srch*
Crown Persnnl, *Perm. Emp Agcy*
Cumberland Grp, *Exec Srch*
Ned Dickey & Assoc./Dickey Staff Solut'ns, *Exec Srch*
Diener & Assoc., *Exec Srch*
Dunhill Prof'l Srch of Rolling Meadows, *Exec Srch*
Effective Srch, *Exec Srch*
Ellington & Assoc., *Exec Srch*
Engineering Mngmnt Staff Recruitng, *Exec Srch*
Executive Srch Intl, *Exec Srch*
Executive Srch Netwrk, *Exec Srch*
Express Persnnl Svcs, *Temp. Agcy*
First Srch, *Exec Srch*
First Staffng, *Perm. Emp Agcy*
General Emp. Enterprises, *Perm. Emp Agcy*
The Glenwood Grp, *Exec Srch*
Hanover Crown & Assoc., *Exec Srch*
Healthcare Recrtrs Intl, *Exec Srch*
E.A. Hoover & Assoc., *Exec Srch*
Hufford Assoc., *Exec Srch*
Human Resource Technlgy, *Exec Srch*
Interviewing Consltnts, *Perm. Emp Agcy*
J.C.G. Limited, *Perm. Emp Agcy*
Jender & Co, *Contract Svc*
Johnson Persnnl Co, *Exec Srch*
Jerry Jung Co., *Exec Srch*
Kunzer Assoc., *Exec Srch*
Arlene Leff & Assoc., *Exec Srch*
Lynco Mngmnt Persnnl, *Exec Srch*
Macro Resrcs, *Exec Srch*
Magnum Srch, *Exec Srch*
Mgmt. Recrtrs of Albion, *Exec Srch*
Mgmt. Recrtrs of Des Plaines, *Exec Srch*
Mgmt. Recrtrs of Elgin, *Exec Srch*
Mgmt. Recrtrs of Rockford, *Exec Srch*
Mgmt. Recrtrs of Springfield, *Exec Srch*
Mgmt. Support Svcs, *Exec Srch*
Manpower Temp. Svcs, *Temp. Agcy*
Manufacturing Resrcs, *Exec Srch*
Marsteller Wilcox Assoc., *Exec Srch*
Mathey Svcs, *Exec Srch*
McCullum Assoc., *Temp. Agcy*
M.W. McDonald & Assoc., *Exec Srch*
Juan Menefee & Assoc., *Exec Srch*
Michael David Assoc., *Perm. Emp Agcy*
R. Michaels & Assoc., *Exec Srch*
Midwest Consltng Corp, *Exec Srch*
Mullins & Assoc., *Perm. Emp Agcy*
The Murphy Grp, *Perm. Emp Agcy*
National Srch, *Exec Srch*
John O'Connor & Assoc., *Exec Srch*
Officemates5 of Wheeling, *Exec Srch*
Omega Tech. Corp, *Exec Srch*
Omni One, *Perm. Emp Agcy*
Omni Srch Exec. Srch Firm
Pelichem Assoc., *Exec Srch*
Pollak & Skan, *Contract Svc*
PolyTechnical Consltnts, *Exec Srch*
Prestige Emp. Svcs, *Perm. Emp Agcy*
Professional Research Svcs, *Exec Srch*
The Raleigh Warwick Grp, *Exec Srch*
The Ryan Charles Grp, *Exec Srch*
Sales Consltnts/Mgmt. Recrtrs Intl, *Exec Srch*
Sanford Rose Assoc., *Exec Srch*
Search Dynamics, *Exec Srch*
Search Enterprises, *Exec Srch*
Select Srch, *Exec Srch*
Selectability, *Perm. Emp Agcy*
Sellers & Assoc., *Exec Srch*
Snelling Persnnl Svcs, *Exec Srch*
Snelling Srch, *Exec Srch*
Stivers Temp. Persnnl, *Temp. Agcy*
Stone Enterprises, *Exec Srch*
Strand Assoc., *Perm. Emp Agcy*
Systems Research, *Perm. Emp Agcy*
TDF Corp, *Contract Svc*
TSC Mngmnt Svcs, *Exec Srch*
Roy Talman & Assoc., *Exec Srch*
Technical Netwrk Srch, *Exec Srch*
Technical Recruitng Consltnts, *Exec Srch*
Technical Srch, *Exec Srch*
Web/Pack Tech, *Perm. Emp Agcy*
World Emp. Svc, *Perm. Emp Agcy*
Xagas & Assoc., *Exec Srch*
H.L. Yoh Co, *Contract Svc*

Indiana

ACA Calumet, *Contract Svc*
ACA Kokomo, *Contract Svc*
Alpha Rae Persnnl, *Perm. Emp Agcy*
Angola Persnnl Svcs, *Perm. Emp Agcy*
Belcan Tech. Svcs, *Contract Svc*
The Bennett Grp, *Exec Srch*
CMS Mngmnt Svcs, *Contract Svc*
Bill Caldwell Emp. Svc, *Perm. Emp Agcy*
Canis Major/HR Quest, *Exec Srch*
Career Consltnts, *Perm. Emp Agcy*
Careers Unlimtd, *Exec Srch*
Century Persnnl, *Perm. Emp Agcy*
Chevigny Persnnl Agcy, *Exec Srch*
Continental Design Co, *Contract Svc*
Corporate Staff Resrcs, *Temp. Agcy*
Crown Temp. Svcs of Indianapolis, *Temp. Agcy*
Data Access, *Perm. Emp Agcy*
Dunhill of Brown Cnty, *Exec Srch*
Dunhill Prof'l Srch, *Exec Srch*
Employment Mart, *Perm. Emp Agcy*
Employment Recrtrs, *Perm. Emp Agcy*
Execusearch, *Exec Srch*
Executec Persnnl Svcs, *Exec Srch*
Great Lakes Srch, *Exec Srch*
The Hart Line, *Exec Srch*
Hobart Emp. Agcy, *Perm. Emp Agcy*
Job Placemnt Svc, *Perm. Emp Agcy*
Johnson Brown Assoc., *Exec Srch*
Krise Prof'l Persnnl Svcs, *Perm. Emp Agcy*
Lange & Assoc., *Exec Srch*
The Mallard Grp, *Exec Srch*
Mgmt. Recrtrs of Evansville, *Exec Srch*
Mgmt. Recrtrs of Indianapolis, *Exec Srch*
Mgmt. Recrtrs of Richmond/Staff Solut'ns, *Exec Srch*
Mgmt. Svcs, *Exec Srch*
Manpower Tech. Svcs, *Temp. Agcy*
Mays & Assoc., *Perm. Emp Agcy*
McNerney & Assoc., *Exec Srch*
Mid West Persnnl, *Perm. Emp Agcy*
Miller Persnnl Consltnts, *Exec Srch*
Monte Denbo Assoc., *Exec Srch*
Morley Grp, *Exec Srch*
National Corporate Consltnts/Advantage Svcs, *Exec Srch*
Oakwood Intl, *Exec Srch*
Officemates5 of Indianapolis, *Exec Srch*
Officemates5 of Indianapolis, *Exec Srch*
Persnnl Plus, *Exec Srch*
Persnnl Recrtrs, *Exec Srch*
Pollak & Skan, *Contract Svc*
QCI Tech. Staffng, *Contract Svc*
Quality Srch, *Perm. Emp Agcy*
Quiring Assoc. HR Consltng Grp, *Exec Srch*
Rush Temps, *Temp. Agcy*
TAD Tech. Svcs, *Contract Svc*
Technetics Corp, *Contract Svc*
Technical Srch & Recrtrs, *Exec Srch*
Try Temps, *Temp. Agcy*
Wimmer Temps & Direct Plcmnt, *Temp. Agcy*
H.L. Yoh Co, *Contract Svc*

Iowa

Agra Placemnts Exec. Srch Firm
Brei & Assoc., *Perm. Emp Agcy*
Burton Placemnt Svcs, *Exec Srch*
Byrnes & Rupkey, *Exec Srch*
CDI Corp, *Contract Svc*
CSI Employment, *Exec Srch*
Cambridge Staffng, *Perm. Emp Agcy*
Career Srch Assoc., *Exec Srch*
City & Nat'l Employment/Recruiting Co, *Perm. Emp Agcy*
Drake-Brennan dba Snelling Persnnl, *Exec Srch*
Executive Engineering Srch, *Exec Srch*
Executive Srch Assoc., *Exec Srch*
Helping Hands Temp. Svc, *Temp. Agcy*
The Human Resource Grp, *Exec Srch*
Mgmt. Recrtrs/CompuSrch, *Exec Srch*
Manpower Tech. Svcs, *Contract Svc*
McGladrey Srch Grp, *Exec Srch*
Mid-States Tech. Staff Svcs, *Temp. Agcy*
Premier Srch Grp, *Exec Srch*
Salem Mngmnt dba Rudy Salem Staff Svcs, *Temp. Agcy*
Staff Mgmt., *Contract Svc*

Staffing Edge, *Perm. Emp Agcy*
TAD Tech. Svcs, *Contract Svc*
TechStaff, *Temp. Agcy*
Tucker Persnnl Consltnts, *Exec Srch*

Kansas

Business Specialists, *Perm. Emp Agcy*
CDI Corp, *Contract Svc*
Dunhill of Wichita, *Perm. Emp Agcy*
Eleventh Hour Staff Svcs, *Temp. Agcy*
Flaming & Assoc., *Perm. Emp Agcy*
Foster Design Co, *Contract Svc*
Mgmt. Recrtrs of Overlnd Prk, *Exec Srch*
Mgmt. Recrtrs of Topeka, *Exec Srch*
J.T. Nelson & Assoc., *Perm. Emp Agcy*
Network of Excellence, *Exec Srch*
Parr & Assoc., *Perm. Emp Agcy*
Smith Brown & Jones, *Exec Srch*
Stoneburner Assoc., *Exec Srch*
Technical Job Svc, *Perm. Emp Agcy*
Temtech, *Contract Svc*
Wyatt & Assoc., *Contract Svc*

Kentucky

Angel Grp Intl, *Exec Srch*
C.M. Mngmnt Svcs, *Perm. Emp Agcy*
J.E.M. & Assoc., *Temp. Agcy*
Kolok Enterprises, *Exec Srch*
Kovac Berrins AG, *Exec Srch*
Mgmt. Recrtrs Intl, *Exec Srch*
Mgmt. Recrtrs of Richmond, *Exec Srch*
Manpower, *Temp. Agcy*
Neessen Prof'l Srch, *Exec Srch*
Persnnl Solut'ns, *Perm. Emp Agcy*
Professional Srch, *Exec Srch*
Sanford Rose Assoc., *Exec Srch*
Sharrow & Assoc., *Exec Srch*
Snelling Persnnl Svcs, *Exec Srch*
TLI Tech. Staffng, *Perm. Emp Agcy*

Louisiana

Accounting Persnnl Consltnts/STAT Resrcs, *Perm. Emp Agcy*
Astro Exec. Srch Firm, *Exec Srch*
CDI Engineering, *Contract Svc*
Clertech Grp, *Exec Srch*
Delta Persnnl, *Perm. Emp Agcy*
Dunhill of Baton Rouge, *Exec Srch*
Dunhill Persnnl System of LA, *Exec Srch*
Interim Persnnl, *Temp. Agcy*
Mgmt. Recrtrs-Baton Rouge/Sales Consltnts, *Exec Srch*
Mgmt. Recrtrs-Metairie/Sales Consltnts, *Exec Srch*
River Region Persnnl, *Exec Srch*
Snelling Persnnl Svcs, *Exec Srch*
Talley & Assoc./Talley Temps, *Exec Srch*
Technical & Prof'l Sources, *Exec Srch*
Universal Persnnl, *Contract Svc*

Maine

Career Mngmnt Assoc., *Exec Srch*
Global Engineers, *Contract Svc*
Goodrich Consltng, *Exec Srch*
John Jay & Co, *Exec Srch*
National Recrtrs of ME, *Exec Srch*
Paper Industry Recrtmnt, *Perm. Emp Agcy*
The Porter Hamel Grp, *Exec Srch*

Maryland

D.W. Baird & Assoc., *Exec Srch*
Cemcon Intl, *Perm. Emp Agcy*
Cross Country Consltnts/Fallstaff Srch, *Exec Srch*
Echelon Svc Co, *Contract Svc*
Employer Employee Exchange, *Exec Srch*
FORTUNE Persnnl Consltnts, *Exec Srch*
Futures, *Exec Srch*
L.S. Gross & Assoc., *Exec Srch*
JDG Assoc. Limited, *Exec Srch*
J.R. Assoc., *Perm. Emp Agcy*
Mgmt. Recrtrs of Annapolis, *Exec Srch*
Mgmt. Recrtrs-Baltimore/Sales Consltnts, *Exec Srch*
Mgmt. Recrtrs-Bethesda/CompuSearch, *Exec Srch*
Mgmt. Recrtrs of Frederick, *Exec Srch*
Micro Temps, *Temp. Agcy*
Onsite Commercial Staffng, *Perm. Emp Agcy*
Sales Consltnts of Columbia, *Exec Srch*
Sales Consltnts of Prince Georges Cnty, *Exec Srch*
Sanford Rose Assoc., *Exec Srch*
TCM Enterprises, *Exec Srch*
TAD Staff Svcs, *Temp. Agcy*
Tech/Aid of MD, *Temp. Agcy*
Technical Prof'l Srch Grp, *Perm. Emp Agcy*
Technical Talent Locators, *Perm. Emp Agcy*
Telesec Staff Svcs, *Temp. Agcy*
Tri-Serv, *Perm. Emp Agcy*
Vey Mark Assoc., *Exec Srch*
Virtual Staff Svcs, *Perm. Emp Agcy*
Winston Srch, *Exec Srch*

Massachusetts

Abbott's of Boston, *Exec Srch*
Ability Srch of N.E., *Perm. Emp Agcy*
Additional Tech. Support Svcs, *Perm. Emp Agcy*
Advance Persnnl, *Perm. Emp Agcy*
Ansara, Bickford, & Fiske, *Exec Srch*
Apollo Design Svc, *Contract Svc*
Applied Resrcs, *Exec Srch*
Architechs, *Exec Srch*
B&M Assoc., *Contract Svc*
Berkshire Srch Assoc., *Exec Srch*
Brady Emp. Svc, *Perm. Emp Agcy*
Brentwood Persnnl, *Perm. Emp Agcy*
CDI Corp, *Contract Svc*
Construction Directory, *Perm. Emp Agcy*
Cyr Assoc., *Exec Srch*
Rob Davidson Assoc./Exec. & Prof. Resume Svc, *Exec Srch*
Derby Assoc., *Perm. Emp Agcy*
Digital Arts Grp, *Contract Svc*
Diversity Assoc., *Exec Srch*
Diversity Srch Specialists, *Exec Srch*
Dunhill Staffing Syst., *Temp. Agcy*
Engineering Mngmnt Support, *Temp. Agcy*
Enginuity Srch, *Exec Srch*
The Environmental Careers Organization, *Contract Svc*
FORTUNE Persnnl Consltnts of Topsfield, *Exec Srch*
Gilreath Weatherby, *Exec Srch*
L.J. Gonzer Assoc., *Exec Srch*
A. Greenstein & Co, *Exec Srch*
HM Assoc., *Exec Srch*
Harbor Consltng Corp, *Exec Srch*
Harvest Persnnl, *Exec Srch*
Human Resource Consltnts, *Perm. Emp Agcy*
Hunter Assoc., *Perm. Emp Agcy*
Judge Tech. Svcs, *Exec Srch*
Lake & Manning, *Exec Srch*
Lane Emp. Svc, *Perm. Emp Agcy*
John Leonard Persnnl Assoc., *Perm. Emp Agcy*
The Littleton Grp, *Exec Srch*
Locke Assoc., *Exec Srch*
Logix, *Exec Srch*
Mgmt. Recrtrs Intl of Braintree, *Exec Srch*
Mgmt. Recrtrs Intl of Springfield, *Exec Srch*
Mgmt. Recrtrs Intl of Westboro, *Exec Srch*
Mgmt. Srch, *Exec Srch*
F.L. Mannix & Co, *Exec Srch*
Marlette Persnnl Srch, *Exec Srch*
Master Srch, *Perm. Emp Agcy*
McDevitt Assoc., *Exec Srch*
Micro Tech Consltnts, *Temp. Agcy*
Micro Tech Prof'ls, *Temp. Agcy*
Morgan & Assoc., *Exec Srch*
National Engineering Svc, *Contract Svc*
Nationwide Bus. Svc, *Perm. Emp Agcy*
Need Persnnl Plcmnt, *Temp. Agcy*
New Boston Select Grp, *Exec Srch*
New Dimensions in Technlgy, *Exec Srch*
New England Recrtrs, *Exec Srch*
New England Srch, *Exec Srch*
Paladin Persnnl Consltnts, *Exec Srch*
D.P. Parker & Assoc., *Exec Srch*
Norman Powers Assoc., *Exec Srch*
Propos Assoc., *Perm. Emp Agcy*
Louis Rudzinsky Assoc., *Exec Srch*
Sales Consltnts of Cape Cod, *Exec Srch*
Sales Consltnts of Plymouth Cnty, *Exec Srch*
Sales Consltnts of Wellesley, *Exec Srch*
George Sandel Assoc., *Perm. Emp Agcy*
Selected Executives, *Exec Srch*
Source Svcs Corp, *Exec Srch*
Stone Consltng Grp & Legal Srch Specialists, *Exec Srch*
Straube Assoc., *Exec Srch*
Summit Tech. Svcs, *Temp. Agcy*
TAD Staff Svcs, *Temp. Agcy*
Tech/Aid, *Contract Svc*
Technical Persnnl Svcs, *Perm. Emp Agcy*
Tesmer Allen Assoc., *Perm. Emp Agcy*
Total Tech. Svcs, *Perm. Emp Agcy*
United Prof'l Plcmnt, *Exec Srch*
Van/Grace Assoc., *Exec Srch*
Vanguard Exec Svcs, *Exec Srch*
WIND Job Ctr, *Career/Outplacemnt*
Winfield Assoc., *Exec Srch*
H.L. Yoh Co, *Contract Svc*

Michigan

AE Emp. Svcs, *Perm. Emp Agcy*
Acro Svc Corp, *Contract Svc*
Action Mngmnt Corp, *Perm. Emp Agcy*
Advance Assoc., *Exec Srch*
Advance Employment, *Exec Srch*
Advance Persnnl of MI, *Exec Srch*
Advanced Tech. Resrcs, *Exec Srch*
Allegheny Srch Assoc., *Exec Srch*
Allied Tech. Svc, *Contract Svc*
Argus & Assoc., *Contract Svc*
Assoc., *Exec Srch*
The Aucon Co, *Exec Srch*
Barman Staff Solut'ns/Barman Persnnl, *Perm. Emp Agcy*
Beacon Svcs, *Exec Srch*
Benford Assoc., *Exec Srch*
Bryant Bureau, *Exec Srch*
CDI Corp, *Contract Svc*
Career Assoc., *Contract Svc*
Carmac Exec Recruitng, *Exec Srch*
Case & Co, *Exec Srch*
Continental Srch Assoc., *Exec Srch*
Contrct Prof'ls, *Perm. Emp Agcy*
Corporate Bus. Svcs Exec. Srch Firm
Corporate Staff Resrcs, *Perm. Emp Agcy*
Davidson, Laird & Assoc., *Exec Srch*
Design & Engineering Svc, *Temp. Agcy*
Devlan, *Perm. Emp Agcy*
Dickson Assoc., *Exec Srch*
Diversified Recrtrs, *Perm. Emp Agcy*
Dynamic Persnnl, *Contract Svc*
Gene Ellefson & Assoc., *Exec Srch*
Engineering Prof'ls, *Perm. Emp Agcy*
Exec-Tech Corp, *Exec Srch*
ExecuSearch of Southwst MI, *Perm. Emp Agcy*
Executive & Tech. Persnnl, *Exec Srch*
Executive Mngmnt Srch, *Exec Srch*
Executive Recrtrs Intl, *Exec Srch*
Express Persnnl Svcs, *Temp. Agcy*
FORTUNE Persnnl Consltnts of Troy, *Exec Srch*
David Franklin Assoc., *Exec Srch*
GBL Assoc., *Exec Srch*
GRS, *Exec Srch*
Giacomin Grp, *Exec Srch*
Joe Giles & Assoc., *Perm. Emp Agcy*
Joseph Goldring & Assoc., *Exec Srch*
The Hallman Grp, *Exec Srch*
Healthcare Recrtrs Intl, *Exec Srch*
Harvey Hohauser & Assoc., *Exec Srch*
William Howard Agcy, *Perm. Emp Agcy*
IBA Srch Consltnts, *Exec Srch*
Intertec Design, *Contract Svc*
Job Fair Netwrk of MI, *Perm. Emp Agcy*
Kelly Tech. Svcs, *Contract Svc*
Key Persnnl, *Perm. Emp Agcy*
Ludot Persnnl, *Perm. Emp Agcy*
Mgmt. Recrtrs of Battle Creek, *Exec Srch*
Mgmt. Recrtrs of Bingham Farms, *Exec Srch*
Mgmt. Recrtrs of Dearborn, *Exec Srch*
Mgmt. Recrtrs of Flint, *Exec Srch*
Mgmt. Recrtrs of Kalamazoo, *Exec Srch*
Mgmt. Recrtrs of Lansing, *Exec Srch*
Mgmt. Recrtrs of Livonia, *Exec Srch*
Mgmt. Recrtrs of Muskegon, *Exec Srch*
Mgmt. Recrtrs of Rochester, *Exec Srch*
Mgmt. Recrtrs of Southeast MI, *Exec Srch*
Manpower Tech. Svcs, *Contract Svc*
METROSTAFF, *Exec Srch*
Michigan Srch Plus, *Exec Srch*
Darnell Mitchell & Assoc., *Exec Srch*
Nationwide Career Netwrk, *Perm. Emp Agcy*
Office Staffing Recruitng, *Exec Srch*
Parr Srch, *Exec Srch*
Preferred Emp. Planning, *Perm. Emp Agcy*
Professional Advancement Institute, *Exec Srch*
Professional Persnnl Consltnts Intl, *Exec Srch*
Professional Resource Assoc., *Contract Svc*
RC Engineering & Mngmnt Svcs, *Contract Svc*
Resource Technolog's Corp, *Perm. Emp Agcy*
Roth Young Persnnl Svcs of Detroit, *Exec Srch*
Sales Consltnts of Auburn Hills, *Exec Srch*
Sales Consltnts of Detroit, *Exec Srch*
Sales Consltnts of Farmington Hills, *Exec Srch*
Sales Consltnts of Lansing, *Exec Srch*
Sanford Rose Assoc., *Exec Srch*
Selective Recruitng Assoc., *Exec Srch*
Sharrow & Assoc., *Exec Srch*
Snelling Persnnl Svcs, *Perm. Emp Agcy*
Software Svcs Corp, *Contract Svc*
Source Svcs Corp, *Perm. Emp Agcy*
Source Technlgy, *Exec Srch*
Sygnetics, *Temp. Agcy*
TAD Tech. Svcs, *Contract Svc*
Technical Aid Corp, *Contract Svc*
Technical Prof'l Svc, *Perm. Emp Agcy*
Temporary Tech. Svcs, *Temp. Agcy*
Thomas & Assoc. of MI, *Exec Srch*
Trillium Staffng, *Temp. Agcy*
Troy Tech Svcs, *Exec Srch*
Unlimited Staff Solut'ns, *Contract Svc*
Venture Mngmnt & Staffng, *Exec Srch*
Weliver & Assoc., *Exec Srch*
Henry Welker & Assoc., *Perm. Emp Agcy*
Wing Tips & Pumps, *Exec Srch*
Wise Persnnl Svcs, *Perm. Emp Agcy*
Wood Persnnl Svcs/Wood Temp. Staffng, *Perm. Emp Agcy*
Jim Woodson & Assoc., *Exec Srch*
Workforce, *Temp. Agcy*

Minnesota

Agri-Business Svcs, *Exec Srch*
Answer Persnnl, *Temp. Agcy*
Bradley & Assoc., *Exec Srch*
Bright Srch/Professional Staffng, *Exec Srch*
CDI Corp, *Contract Svc*
Charles Dahl & Assoc., *Exec Srch*
Dietrich & Assoc., *Exec Srch*
Diversified Employment, *Perm. Emp Agcy*
Ells Persnnl Syst., *Exec Srch*
Execu-Tech Srch, *Exec Srch*
Flatley Tech. Svcs, *Temp. Agcy*
Roger Gilmer & Assoc., *Exec Srch*
HR Svcs of Plymouth, *Exec Srch*
T.H. Hunter, *Exec Srch*
Jackley Srch Consltnts, *Exec Srch*
Lynn Temporary, *Temp. Agcy*
Mgmt. Recrtrs-Minneapolis/Sales Consltnts, *Exec Srch*
Manpower Tech. Svcs, *Perm. Emp Agcy*
Lee Marsh & Assoc., *Exec Srch*
NER (National Engineering Resrcs), *Exec Srch*
North American Recrtrs, *Exec Srch*
Northland Emp. Svcs, *Exec Srch*
Nycor Srch, *Exec Srch*
Persnnl Assist. Corp, *Exec Srch*
Pioneer Srch, *Exec Srch*
Precision Design, *Contract Svc*
Programming Alternatives of MN, *Exec Srch*
Regency Recrtrs, *Exec Srch*
Resource Srch, *Exec Srch*
Sathe & Assoc. Exec Srch, *Exec Srch*
Search Specialists, *Exec Srch*
Searchtek, *Exec Srch*
Staff Connection, *Exec Srch*
Sysdyne Corp, *Contract Svc*
Technical Resrcs, *Perm. Emp Agcy*
Ultimate Srch Unlimtd/Temps Unlimtd, *Perm. Emp Agcy*
Work Place Solut'ns, *Contract Svc*
H.L. Yoh Co, *Contract Svc*

Mississippi

Andrus Assoc. dba Svc Specialists, *Perm. Emp Agcy*
Coats & Coats Persnnl, *Perm. Emp Agcy*
Dunhill Prof'l Srch of Jackson, *Exec Srch*
EPSCO Persnnl, *Temp. Agcy*
Impact Persnnl Svcs, *Exec Srch*
Mgmt. Recrtrs Intl, *Exec Srch*
Opportunities Unlimtd, *Perm. Emp Agcy*
Persnnl Unlimtd, *Exec Srch*
Tatum Persnnl, *Perm. Emp Agcy*
Jim Woodson & Assoc., *Exec Srch*

Missouri

ABC Emp. Svc, *Perm. Emp Agcy*
Advanced Careers of Kansas Cty, *Exec Srch*
Agri-Tech Persnnl, *Exec Srch*
Austin Nichols Tech. Temps, *Temp. Agcy*
L.P. Banning, *Perm. Emp Agcy*
Bottom Line Prof'l Svcs, *Contract Svc*
Ken Brown & Co, *Exec Srch*
Burns Emp. Svc, *Exec Srch*
Business Persnnl Svcs, *Temp. Agcy*
CDI Corp, *Contract Svc*
The Christiansen Grp, *Exec Srch*
COMFORCE Tech. Svcs, *Contract Svc*
Crider & Assoc., *Perm. Emp Agcy*
Crown Svcs, *Temp. Agcy*
Jim Crumpley & Assoc., *Exec Srch*
Debbon Recruitng Grp, *Exec Srch*
Deck & Decker Emp. Svc, *Perm. Emp Agcy*
Decker Persnnl, *Perm. Emp Agcy*
Design Alternatives, *Perm. Emp Agcy*
Dunhill Persnnl System of Missouri, *Exec Srch*
Employer Advantage, *Exec Srch*
Executive Recrtrs, *Exec Srch*
FORTUNE Persnnl Consltnts, *Exec Srch*
Haskell Assoc., *Exec Srch*
J.M. Grp, *Exec Srch*
JRL Exec Recrtrs, *Exec Srch*
Jackson Emp. Agcy, *Perm. Emp Agcy*
JoDoc Enterprises, *Temp. Agcy*
Mgmt. Recrtrs of Kansas Cty, *Exec Srch*
Mgmt. Recrtrs of Springfield, *Exec Srch*
Mgmt. Recrtrs of St. Louis, *Exec Srch*
Mgmt. Recrtrs of St. Louis, *Exec Srch*
Manpower Temp. Svcs, *Temp. Agcy*
J. Miles Persnnl Svcs, *Exec Srch*
Officemates5 of St. Louis, *Exec Srch*
Oldfield Grp, *Exec Srch*
Sales Recrtrs, *Exec Srch*
Gordon Smith & Assoc., *Exec Srch*
Snelling Persnnl Svcs, *Perm. Emp Agcy*
Team Intl, *Contract Svc*
Technical Resrcs Intl, *Exec Srch*
Western Tech. Svcs, *Contract Svc*
H.L. Yoh Co, *Contract Svc*

Montana

Express Persnnl, *Perm. Emp Agcy*
FORTUNE Persnnl Consltnts, *Exec Srch*
W.R. Knapp & Assoc., *Exec Srch*
Labor Contracting Staff Svcs, *Perm. Emp Agcy*

Nebraska

Choice Enterprises, *Exec Srch*
Compusearch of Lincoln, *Exec Srch*
Express Persnnl, *Exec Srch*
Hahn Tech. Staffng, *Exec Srch*
Hansen Agri-Placement, *Perm. Emp Agcy*
Mgmt. Recrtrs of Omaha/Officemates5, *Exec Srch*
Don Pariset Assoc., *Exec Srch*
Professional Recrtrs, *Perm. Emp Agcy*

Nevada

Mgmt. Recrtrs Intl, *Exec Srch*
Mgmt. Recrtrs of Reno, *Exec Srch*
Manpower Temp. Svcs, *Temp. Agcy*
Matrix Grp, *Exec Srch*
Talent Tree Staffng, *Perm. Emp Agcy*

New Hampshire

Able 1 Staffng, *Exec Srch*
Access Consltng, *Perm. Emp Agcy*
Affordable Solut'ns, *Contract Svc*
Allstaff Contrct Svcs, *Perm. Emp Agcy*
Barclay Persnnl Syst., *Exec Srch*
Barrett & Co, *Exec Srch*
CDI Corp, *Contract Svc*
Central New Hampshire Emp. Svcs, *Perm. Emp Agcy*
Chaucer Grp, *Perm. Emp Agcy*
Chaucer Grp, *Exec Srch*
Cheshire Emp. Svc, *Temp. Agcy*
Contact Recrtrs, *Temp. Agcy*
Contrct Solut'ns, *Contract Svc*
Dubois & Co, *Exec Srch*
Enterprise Technolog's, *Exec Srch*
High Tech Opport., *Exec Srch*
Mgmt. Recrtrs Intl of Bedford, *Exec Srch*
National Emp. Svc Corp, *Perm. Emp Agcy*
Preferred Resrcs Grp, *Exec Srch*
R.G.T. Assoc., *Exec Srch*
Sales Consltnts of Nashua-Manchester, *Exec Srch*
Source Svcs Corp/Source Engineering, *Exec Srch*
Surge Resrcs, *Contract Svc*
Tech/Aid of NH, *Perm. Emp Agcy*
Technical Directions, *Perm. Emp Agcy*
Technical Emp. Svcs, *Contract Svc*
Technical Needs, *Exec Srch*
Tri-State Prof'ls, *Temp. Agcy*

New Jersey

ABC Nationwide Employment, *Perm. Emp Agcy*
Adel-Lawrence Assoc., *Exec Srch*
Andrew Persnnl Svcs, *Perm. Emp Agcy*
R.P. Barone Assoc., *Exec Srch*
Gary Bell Assoc., *Exec Srch*
Blake & Assoc. Exec Srch, *Exec Srch*
CPS Tech. Placemnts, *Perm. Emp Agcy*
Career Ctr, *Perm. Emp Agcy*
Career Srch Assoc., *Exec Srch*
Careerworks, *Exec Srch*
Central Tech. Svc, *Perm. Emp Agcy*
Cox Darrow & Owens, *Exec Srch*
Clark Davis Assoc., *Exec Srch*
M.T. Donaldson Assoc., *Exec Srch*
Dreier Consltng, *Exec Srch*
Electronic Srch, *Exec Srch*
Express Persnnl Svcs, *Perm. Emp Agcy*
FORTUNE Persnnl Consltnts of Menlo Prk, *Exec Srch*
Garrett Grp, *Exec Srch*
Grant Franks & Assoc., *Exec Srch*
Harris Exec Srch, *Exec Srch*
Hughes & Podesla Persnnl, *Perm. Emp Agcy*
Impact Persnnl, *Perm. Emp Agcy*
Inter-Regional Exec Srch, *Exec Srch*
J.M. Joseph Assoc., *Exec Srch*
Joule People Providers, *Perm. Emp Agcy*
Joule Temps, *Temp. Agcy*
Kelly Svcs, *Temp. Agcy*
Key Employment, *Exec Srch*
Joseph Keyes Assoc., *Perm. Emp Agcy*
T.J. Koellhoffer & Assoc., *Exec Srch*
Paul Kull & Co, *Exec Srch*
Mgmt. Recrtrs of Bay Head, *Exec Srch*
Mgmt. Recrtrs of Medford, *Exec Srch*
Mgmt. Recrtrs of Orange Cnty, *Exec Srch*
Mgmt. Recrtrs of Passaic Cnty, *Exec Srch*
Manpower Tech. Svcs, *Temp. Agcy*
Mayfair Svcs, *Perm. Emp Agcy*
Middlebrook Assoc., *Exec Srch*
OMNE Staff Svcs, *Temp. Agcy*
Orion Consltng, *Exec Srch*
PR Mngmnt Consltnts, *Exec Srch*
Pat's Secretarial Svc, *Temp. Agcy*
Princeton Exec Srch, *Exec Srch*
Ramming & Assoc., *Exec Srch*
Rotator Svcs, *Contract Svc*
S-H-S of Cherry Hill, *Perm. Emp Agcy*
R.S. Sadow Assoc., *Exec Srch*
Sales Consltnts of Morris Cnty, *Exec Srch*
Sales Consltnts of Sparta, *Exec Srch*
Sanford Rose Assoc., *Exec Srch*
Rob Scott Assoc., *Exec Srch*
Selective Persnnl, *Perm. Emp Agcy*
Sharp Tech. Svcs, *Contract Svc*
Source Svcs Corp, *Perm. Emp Agcy*
Summit Grp, *Exec Srch*
TRS Staff Solut'ns, *Temp. Agcy*
Technology Syst., *Exec Srch*
Tenek Corp, *Exec Srch*
Claire Wright Assn, *Perm. Emp Agcy*

New Mexico

Albuquerque Persnnl, *Perm. Emp Agcy*
Butler Svc Grp, *Contract Svc*
CDI Corp, *Contract Svc*
Sanderson Emp. Svc, *Perm. Emp Agcy*
Scientemps, *Temp. Agcy*
Snelling Persnnl Svcs, *Exec Srch*

New York

ATS Reliance, *Perm. Emp Agcy*
Accounting & Computer Persnnl, *Perm. Emp Agcy*
Merrill Adams Assoc., *Career/Outplacemnt*
Ames O'Neill Assoc., *Exec Srch*
April Tech. Recruitng, *Perm. Emp Agcy*
Arrow Emp. Agcy, *Perm. Emp Agcy*
Beishline Exec Srch, *Exec Srch*
Bos Bus. Consltnts, *Exec Srch*
Brucks Consltnts, *Exec Srch*
Bruml Assoc., *Exec Srch*
Burns Persnnl, *Exec Srch*
CDI Corp, *Contract Svc*
CFI Resrcs, *Exec Srch*
Carlile Persnnl Agcy, *Perm. Emp Agcy*
Colton Partnership, *Exec Srch*
Computech Career Srch, *Exec Srch*
Consortium, *Exec Srch*
Contrct Specialties Grp, *Contract Svc*
Corporate Careers/R.J. Assoc., *Exec Srch*
Cowin Assoc., *Exec Srch*
Frank Cuomo & Assoc., *Exec Srch*
The Dartmouth Grp, *Exec Srch*
Dymanex Srch, *Exec Srch*
EDP Contrct Svcs, *Contract Svc*
The Emp. Store/TES Technical, *Exec Srch*
Exek Recrtrs Exec. Srch Firm
Extra Help Emp. Svc, *Temp. Agcy*
FORTUNE Persnnl Consltnts, *Exec Srch*
Graphic Techniques, *Temp. Agcy*
The Haas Assoc., *Exec Srch*
Robert Half Intl/Information Syst. Division, *Exec Srch*
Hampshire Assoc., *Perm. Emp Agcy*
Hart-Merrell Persnnl, *Exec Srch*
F.P. Healy & Co, *Exec Srch*
Ruth Hirsch Assoc., *Exec Srch*
Innovations Assoc., *Perm. Emp Agcy*
Interspace Interactive, *Exec Srch*
Lisa Kalus & Assoc., *Perm. Emp Agcy*
Irene Kane Persnnl, *Exec Srch*
Fred Koffler Assoc., *Exec Srch*
Lake Assoc., *Exec Srch*
Michael John Lawrence & Assoc., *Exec Srch*
Mgmt. Recrtrs of Nassau, *Exec Srch*
Mgmt. Recrtrs of Utica/Rome, *Exec Srch*
Mgmt. Recrtrs of Woodbury/ CompuSrch, *Exec Srch*
Manpower Tech. Svcs, *Temp. Agcy*
Manpower Temp. Svcs, *Temp. Agcy*
Metro Resrcs of Rochester, *Temp. Agcy*
Metro Persnnl/Metro Nursing Svcs, *Exec Srch*
Mickler Assoc., *Exec Srch*
Morgan-Murray Persnnl/M&M Top Temps, *Temp. Agcy*
Natek Corp, *Exec Srch*
Nationwide Persnnl Grp, *Perm. Emp Agcy*
Noah Assoc., *Perm. Emp Agcy*
Norris Emp. Consltnts, *Perm. Emp Agcy*
Olsten Staff Svcs, *Temp. Agcy*
OTEC.COM, *Perm. Emp Agcy*
Arthur Pann Assoc., *Exec Srch*
Parsons, Anderson & Gee, *Perm. Emp Agcy*
Recruitment Grp, *Exec Srch*
Ritta Prof'l Srch, *Exec Srch*
Roberts Exec Recrtmnt, *Exec Srch*
Fran Rogers Persnnl, *Perm. Emp Agcy*
Sales Srch, Ltd./Executive Resume Svc, *Exec Srch*
Sharp Placemnt Prof'ls, *Exec Srch*
Snelling Persnnl Svcs, *Exec Srch*
Staff Managers, *Temp. Agcy*
Superior Concepts, *Contract Svc*
TAD Resrcs, *Contract Svc*
Thorsen Assoc., *Exec Srch*
Todd Arro, *Exec Srch*
Volt Svcs Grp, *Contract Svc*
Weber Mngmnt Consltnts, *Exec Srch*
Westchester Emp. Agcy, *Perm. Emp Agcy*
Western Staff Svcs, *Temp. Agcy*
H.L. Yoh Co, *Contract Svc*

North Carolina

Accurate Staff Consltnts, *Exec Srch*
Action Tech. Staffng, *Temp. Agcy*
Alpha Omega Exec Srch, *Exec Srch*
American Quality Staffng, *Exec Srch*
AmeriPro Srch, *Exec Srch*
Anderson & Daniel Persnnl, *Perm. Emp Agcy*
Apple Resrcs, *Perm. Emp Agcy*
Arjay & Assoc., *Exec Srch*
Atchison & Assoc., *Exec Srch*
Ayers & Assoc., *Exec Srch*
Bennett Allen & Assoc., *Exec Srch*
CDI Corp, *Contract Svc*
Career Srch, *Exec Srch*
Corporate Staff Consltnts, *Perm. Emp Agcy*
Eastern Srch Grp, *Exec Srch*
Employment Consltnts, *Contract Svc*
Executive Recrtmnt Specialists, *Exec Srch*
Executive Staff Svcs, *Perm. Emp Agcy*
Express Persnnl Svcs, *Temp. Agcy*
C.D. Fayling Assoc., *Exec Srch*
FORTUNE Persnnl Consltnts of Raleigh, *Perm. Emp Agcy*
FORTUNE Persnnl Consltnts, *Exec Srch*
The Furniture Agcy, *Exec Srch*
Glovier & Assoc., *Exec Srch*
Graham & Assoc., *Perm. Emp Agcy*
Stew Greene & Co/The Triad, *Exec Srch*
Greer Persnnl, *Perm. Emp Agcy*
Highlander Srch, *Exec Srch*
Kelly Svcs, *Temp. Agcy*
MTS, *Perm. Emp Agcy*
Mgmt. Recrtrs/Sales Consltnts, *Exec Srch*
Mgmt. Recrtrs of Burlington, *Exec Srch*
Mgmt. Recrtrs of Durham, *Exec Srch*
Mgmt. Recrtrs of Fayetteville, *Exec Srch*
Mgmt. Recrtrs of Greensboro, *Exec Srch*
Mgmt. Recrtrs of Kinston, *Exec Srch*
Mgmt. Recrtrs of Louisburg, *Exec Srch*
Mgmt. Recrtrs of Raleigh/Inter Exec, *Exec Srch*
Mgmt. Recrtrs of Winston-Salem, *Exec Srch*
Mark III Persnnl, *Exec Srch*
Merrick & Moore, *Exec Srch*
Metals & Wood Agcy, *Exec Srch*
Moffitt Intl, *Exec Srch*
Morgan Grp, *Exec Srch*
Myers & Assoc., *Perm. Emp Agcy*
National Svcs, *Exec Srch*
Olsten Staff Svcs, *Temp. Agcy*
The Perkin Grp, *Exec Srch*
Professional Persnnl Assoc., *Perm. Emp Agcy*
SENC Tech. Svcs, *Contract Svc*
Sales Consltnts of High Point, *Exec Srch*
Sanford Rose Assoc., *Exec Srch*
Search Consltnts Worldwide, *Exec Srch*
Sickenberger Assoc., *Exec Srch*
Snelling Persnnl Svcs, *Contract Svc*
Snelling Srch, *Exec Srch*
Sparks Persnnl Svcs, *Exec Srch*
Technical Assoc., *Exec Srch*
The Underwood Grp, *Perm. Emp Agcy*
Volt Tech. Svcs, *Contract Svc*
David Weinfeld Grp, *Exec Srch*
Will/Staff Persnnl Svcs, *Temp. Agcy*
John Williams & Assoc., *Exec Srch*
Wilson Persnnl, *Exec Srch*
H.L. Yoh Co, *Contract Svc*

North Dakota

Career Connection, *Exec Srch*
Dunhill Exec Srch, *Exec Srch*
Human Resrcs, *Perm. Emp Agcy*
Olsten Staff Svcs/Kramer & Assoc./Expressway Persnnl, *Temp. Agcy*

Ohio

Advancement L.L.C., *Perm. Emp Agcy*
Advancement Recruitng Svcs, *Exec Srch*
Alliance Tech. Svcs, *Contract Svc*
American Bus. Persnnl Svcs, *Perm. Emp Agcy*
Baldwin & Assoc., *Exec Srch*
Belcan Tech. Svcs, *Contract Svc*
Belcan Tech. Svcs, *Perm. Emp Agcy*
Bradley-Pierce Persnnl, *Perm. Emp Agcy*
J.B. Brown & Assoc., *Exec Srch*
Burks Grp, *Exec Srch*
CBS Persnnl Svcs, *Perm. Emp Agcy*
Career Recrtrs, *Exec Srch*
Career Specialists, *Exec Srch*
Clopton's Placemnt Svc, *Perm. Emp Agcy*
Combined Resrcs, *Exec Srch*
Computer & Tech. Assoc., *Exec Srch*
Continental Srch Consltnts, *Exec Srch*
Corell Assoc., *Perm. Emp Agcy*
Cornerstone Recrtrs, *Exec Srch*
J.D. Cotter Srch, *Exec Srch*
Cross-Jordan Corp, *Exec Srch*
Crown Temp. Svcs of Cincinnati, *Temp. Agcy*
DLD Tech. Svcs, *Contract Svc*
Alan Daum & Assoc., *Perm. Emp Agcy*
Tonia Deal Consltnts, *Perm. Emp Agcy*
Delta Design Drafting, *Temp. Agcy*
Pete DeLuke & Assoc., *Exec Srch*
Drayton & Assoc., *Exec Srch*
Eastern Persnnl Svcs, *Perm. Emp Agcy*
Elite Resrcs Grp, *Exec Srch*
Executech, *Exec Srch*
Executech Consltnts, *Exec Srch*
Executive Connection, *Exec Srch*
Executive Directions, *Exec Srch*
Executive Srch Ltd., *Exec Srch*
Fenzel Milar Assoc., *Exec Srch*
Flex-Tech Prof'l Svcs, *Contract Svc*
Flowers & Assoc./Associated Temps, *Exec Srch*
FORTUNE Persnnl Consltnts, *Exec Srch*
Functional Tech. Svcs, *Perm. Emp Agcy*
Gayhart & Assoc., *Exec Srch*
Global Resrcs Grp, *Contract Svc*
H.L. Goehring & Assoc., *Exec Srch*
Griffiths & Assoc., *Exec Srch*
Guthoff & Assoc., *Exec Srch*
H.J.C., *Exec Srch*
Russ Hadick & Assoc., *Exec Srch*
Hahn & Assoc., *Exec Srch*
Hite Exec Srch/Hite Mngmnt Consltnts, *Exec Srch*
ITS Tech. Staffing/Interconnect Tech. Svcs, *Exec Srch*
Icon Mngmnt Grp, *Exec Srch*
Interconnect Tech. Svcs, *Exec Srch*
Interim Persnnl, *Temp. Agcy*
Jaeger Intl, *Exec Srch*
Kaiser Nationwide, *Exec Srch*
Laine's S.M.G., *Perm. Emp Agcy*
R.E. Lowe Assoc., *Perm. Emp Agcy*
Mgmt. Recrtrs of Cincinnati, *Exec Srch*
Mgmt. Recrtrs of Cleveland, *Exec Srch*
Mgmt. Recrtrs of Cleveland, *Exec Srch*
Mgmt. Recrtrs of Cleveland, *Exec Srch*
Mgmt. Recrtrs of Cleveland, *Exec Srch*
Mgmt. Recrtrs of Columbus, *Exec Srch*
Mgmt. Recrtrs of Dayton, *Exec Srch*
Mgmt. Recrtrs of Solon, *Exec Srch*
Marvel Consltnts, *Exec Srch*
Messina Mngmnt Syst., *Exec Srch*
Miami Prof'l Srch, *Exec Srch*
Midland Consltnts, *Exec Srch*
Minority Exec Srch, *Exec Srch*
Myers & Assoc., *Exec Srch*
Newcomb-Desmond & Assoc., *Exec Srch*
North American Persnnl, *Exec Srch*
North American Tech. Svcs, *Contract Svc*
North Star Resrcs, *Contract Svc*
Northcoast Persnnl, *Exec Srch*
Olsten Prof'l Staff Svcs, *Exec Srch*
Pak/Teem Contrct Svcs, *Contract Svc*
Patterson Persnnl, *Exec Srch*
Placement Svcs Limited, *Exec Srch*
The Prof'l Consltnts, *Exec Srch*
Professional Restaffing of OH, *Perm. Emp Agcy*
Providence Persnnl Consltnts, *Exec Srch*
Quality Plus, *Exec Srch*
Questcor Co, *Exec Srch*
RDS, *Contract Svc*
Bill Reber & Assoc., *Exec Srch*
W.R. Renner & Assoc., *Exec Srch*
Rentech Ventures, *Perm. Emp Agcy*
Resource Techne Grp, *Exec Srch*
SJR & Assoc., *Exec Srch*
Sales Consltnts of Cincinnati, *Exec Srch*
Sanford Rose Assoc., *Exec Srch*
Sanford Rose Assoc. of Columbus, *Exec Srch*
Sanford Rose Assoc. of Lima, *Exec Srch*
Search Technlgy, *Exec Srch*
Selective Srch Assoc., *Perm. Emp Agcy*
Shafer Jones Assoc., *Exec Srch*
Snelling Persnnl Svcs, *Exec Srch*
Sterling Persnnl Resrcs, *Exec Srch*
Tabb & Assoc., *Exec Srch*
TAD Tech. Svcs, *Contract Svc*
Talent Research Corp, *Exec Srch*
Teamwork U.S.A., *Contract Svc*
Tech/Aid of OH, *Perm. Emp Agcy*
Technical Recruitng Svcs, *Exec Srch*
Technical Srch Assoc., *Exec Srch*
Technical/Mgmt. Resrcs, *Perm. Emp Agcy*
Thomas-Schade & Assoc., *Exec Srch*
Fred Tippel & Assoc., *Exec Srch*
Vector Technical, *Perm. Emp Agcy*
J.P. Walton & Assoc., *Exec Srch*
Warner & Assoc., *Perm. Emp Agcy*
World Srch, *Exec Srch*
H.L. Yoh Co, *Contract Svc*

Oklahoma

Ameri Resource, *Exec Srch*
Executive Resrcs Grp, *Exec Srch*
Express Persnnl Svcs, *Exec Srch*
Key Temp. Persnnl, *Temp. Agcy*
Mgmt. Recrtrs Intl, *Exec Srch*
Terry Neese Persnnl Agcy, *Exec Srch*
Reality Grp, *Exec Srch*
Lloyd Richards Persnnl, *Perm. Emp Agcy*
Sooner Placemnt Svc, *Perm. Emp Agcy*
Sumner-Ray Tech. Resrcs, *Exec Srch*
John Wylie Assoc., *Exec Srch*

Oregon

Barrett Bus. Svcs, *Temp. Agcy*
CDI Corp, *Contract Svc*
Corporate Builders, *Exec Srch*
Express Persnnl Svcs, *Exec Srch*
Hackenschmidt, Weaver & Fox, *Exec Srch*
Impact Staffng, *Temp. Agcy*
Mgmt. Recrtrs/Officemates5 of Portland, *Exec Srch*
NPRC/Nationwde Persnnl Recruitng & Consltng, *Exec Srch*
Northwest Temp. & Staff Svcs, *Temp. Agcy*
Sanford Rose Assoc., *Exec Srch*
Search Nrthwest Assoc., *Exec Srch*
Summit Staffng, *Temp. Agcy*
Triad Technlgy Grp, *Perm. Emp Agcy*
Uniforce Tech. Svcs, *Contract Svc*
Wolf Environmental Grp, *Exec Srch*
Woodworth Intl Grp, *Exec Srch*

Pennsylvania

AA Staff Solut'ns, *Contract Svc*
Action Persnnl Svcs, *Perm. Emp Agcy*
J.N. Adams & Assoc., *Exec Srch*
Advanced Technlgy Resrcs, *Exec Srch*
Alexander Persnnl Assoc., *Exec Srch*
American Srch Assoc., *Exec Srch*
ASAP Staffng, *Perm. Emp Agcy*
Ashley Srch Consltnts, *Exec Srch*
Atomic Persnnl, *Exec Srch*
Barr Assoc., *Exec Srch*
Barton Persnnl Syst., *Exec Srch*
Bender & Assoc., *Exec Srch*
T.W. Boris Assn, *Exec Srch*
Bradley Prof'l Svcs, *Perm. Emp Agcy*
CDI Corp, *Contract Svc*
Career Concepts Staff Svcs, *Exec Srch*
Career Quest Confidential, *Exec Srch*
Charly's Temp. Svcs, *Temp. Agcy*
Rich Christine Assoc., *Exec Srch*
Consearch, *Exec Srch*
Corporate Mngmnt Svcs, *Exec Srch*
DiCenzo Persnnl Specialists, *Perm. Emp Agcy*
Dunn Assoc., *Exec Srch*
EDP/Temps of PA, *Temp. Agcy*
Executive Avail-A-Search, *Exec Srch*
Fox-Morris Assoc., *Exec Srch*
The GMW Grp, *Exec Srch*
Gateway Resrcs, *Exec Srch*
J.H. Glass & Assoc., *Exec Srch*
Jerry Goldberg & Assoc., *Perm. Emp Agcy*
H-Tech, *Contract Svc*
The Hastings Grp, *Exec Srch*
Hoskins Hains Assoc., *Perm. Emp Agcy*
Human Resource Solut'ns, *Exec Srch*
IMC Intl, *Contract Svc*
Interactive Srch, *Exec Srch*
J-Rand Srch, *Exec Srch*
JK Resrcs, *Exec Srch*
Nancy Jackson, *Exec Srch*
Clifton Johnson Assoc., *Exec Srch*
Kathy Karr Persnnl, *Perm. Emp Agcy*
Katron Exec Srch, *Exec Srch*
Blair Kershaw Assoc., *Exec Srch*
Keystaff, *Temp. Agcy*
Lawrence Persnnl, *Exec Srch*
Rob Lohrke Assoc., *Exec Srch*
Main Line Persnnl, *Perm. Emp Agcy*
Mgmt. Recrtrs of DE Cnty/CompuSrch, *Exec Srch*
Mgmt. Recrtrs of Lehigh Vly/CompuSrch, *Exec Srch*
Mgmt. Recrtrs of Philadelphia/ CompuSrch, *Exec Srch*
George Martin Exec Srch, *Exec Srch*
Rob McClure Ltd., *Exec Srch*
McNichol & Assoc., *Exec Srch*
B. Paul Mickey & Assoc., *Exec Srch*
John Morrow & Assoc., *Exec Srch*
National Computerized Employment, *Perm. Emp Agcy*
Olsten Staff Svcs, *Temp. Agcy*
LaMonte Owens, *Exec Srch*
Pratt Persnnl Svcs, *Temp. Agcy*
Prestige Persnnl, *Exec Srch*
Probe Technlgy, *Exec Srch*
ProSearch, *Exec Srch*
Q-Source, *Perm. Emp Agcy*
Alan Raeburn Consltnts, *Exec Srch*
Rice Cohen Intl, *Exec Srch*
S-H-S Intl, *Perm. Emp Agcy*
S-H-S Intl, *Exec Srch*
Sanford Rose Assoc., *Exec Srch*
Tom Sawchak Action of PA, *Perm. Emp Agcy*
Select Persnnl, *Perm. Emp Agcy*
Singmaster Persnnl Svcs, *Perm. Emp Agcy*
Snelling Persnnl Svcs, *Exec Srch*
Kenn Spinrad, *Exec Srch*

Stewart Assoc., *Exec Srch*
Strongin Tech. Enterprises of PA, *Perm. Emp Agcy*
Suber & McAuley Tech. Srch, *Exec Srch*
TAD Tech. Svcs, *Temp. Agcy*
Tech/Aid of PA, *Contract Svc*
Tops Temps, *Temp. Agcy*
Triangle Assoc. Intl, *Perm. Emp Agcy*
United Employment, *Perm. Emp Agcy*
United Tech. Assoc., *Temp. Agcy*
Virtual Workplace, *Temp. Agcy*
Whittlesey & Assoc., *Exec Srch*
H.L. Yoh Co, *Contract Svc*
Yorktowne Persnnl, *Exec Srch*

Rhode Island

Alan Price Assoc., *Exec Srch*
Colony Persnnl Assoc., *Perm. Emp Agcy*
Johnson & Tregar Assoc., *Perm. Emp Agcy*
Kelly Svcs, *Temp. Agcy*
Albert Lee & Assoc., *Exec Srch*
Mgmt. Recrtrs Intl, *Exec Srch*
New England Consltnts, *Perm. Emp Agcy*
Norrell Svcs, *Temp. Agcy*
On Line Temp/On Line Staff, *Temp. Agcy*
PKS Assoc., *Exec Srch*
Storti Assoc., *Exec Srch*
Sullivan & Cogliano, *Exec Srch*
Summit Tech. Svcs, *Perm. Emp Agcy*
Tech/Aid of RI, *Contract Svc*

South Carolina

Accel Temp. Svcs, *Temp. Agcy*
Aide Design Svcs, *Contract Svc*
Bock & Assoc., *Exec Srch*
CDI Corp, *Contract Svc*
Contemporary Mngmnt Svcs, *Exec Srch*
Corporate Solut'ns, *Exec Srch*
Dunhill Persnnl of St. Andrews, *Perm. Emp Agcy*
Dunhill Prof'l Srch, *Exec Srch*
Edmonds Persnnl, *Exec Srch*
Engineer & Tech. Recruitng, *Exec Srch*
Engineering Persnnl Netwrk, *Exec Srch*
Ford & Assoc., *Exec Srch*
FORTUNE Persnnl Consltnts of Columbia, *Exec Srch*
Harvey Persnnl, *Perm. Emp Agcy*
Mgmt. Recrtrs of Columbia, *Exec Srch*
Mgmt. Recrtrs of Orangeburg, *Exec Srch*
Mgmt. Recrtrs of Rck Hill, *Exec Srch*
Miller & Assoc., *Exec Srch*
PRL & Assoc., *Perm. Emp Agcy*
Palace Persnnl Svcs, *Exec Srch*
The Persnnl Netwrk, *Exec Srch*
Phelps Persnnl, *Perm. Emp Agcy*
Phillips Resource Grp, *Exec Srch*
Search & Recruit Intl, *Exec Srch*
Snelling Persnnl, *Perm. Emp Agcy*
Southern Recrtrs & Consltnts, *Exec Srch*
The Stroman Co, *Perm. Emp Agcy*
TRS (Total Recruitng Svcs), *Perm. Emp Agcy*
Technical South, *Temp. Agcy*

South Dakota

Mgmt. Recrtrs Intl, *Exec Srch*
Snelling Persnnl Svcs, *Perm. Emp Agcy*

Tennessee

A-1 Staffing & Persnnl, *Temp. Agcy*
American Tech. Assoc., *Contract Svc*
Austin-Allen Co, *Exec Srch*
Baker & Baker Emp. Svc, *Exec Srch*
B.K. Barnes & Assoc., *Exec Srch*
Career Prof'ls, *Perm. Emp Agcy*
Cook Assoc. Intl, *Exec Srch*
Dunhill of Memphis, *Perm. Emp Agcy*
Engineer One, *Perm. Emp Agcy*
Express Persnnl Svcs, *Perm. Emp Agcy*
FORTUNE Persnnl Consltnts, *Exec Srch*
Hamilton Ryker Co, *Exec Srch*
Hester & Assoc., *Exec Srch*
Kelly Svcs, *Temp. Agcy*
Madison Persnnl, *Perm. Emp Agcy*
Mgmt. Recrtrs/Sales Consltnts-Chattanooga, *Exec Srch*
Mgmt. Recrtrs of Chattanooga, *Exec Srch*
Mgmt. Recrtrs of Lenoir Cty, *Exec Srch*
Manpower, *Temp. Agcy*
Mega Force, *Temp. Agcy*
Olsten Staff Svcs, *Temp. Agcy*
Persnnl Link, *Exec Srch*
Rasmussen & Assoc., *Perm. Emp Agcy*
Sales Consltnts of Nashville, *Exec Srch*
Snelling Persnnl Svcs, *Exec Srch*
Software Resource Consltnts, *Exec Srch*
Technical Resource Assoc., *Exec Srch*
Temp Staff, *Temp. Agcy*
Unlimited Staff Solut'ns, *Contract Svc*
Rob Walker Assoc., *Contract Svc*

Texas

Ackerman Johnson, *Exec Srch*
Adecco, *Temp. Agcy*
Agri-LC, *Exec Srch*
Albrecht & Assoc. Exec Srch, *Exec Srch*
American Resrcs, *Exec Srch*
Architectural Career Netwrk, *Contract Svc*
Atwood Prof'l Srch, *Exec Srch*
Austin Grp, *Exec Srch*
B&M Air & Space Division, *Contract Svc*
Babich & Assoc., *Perm. Emp Agcy*
Belcan Tech. Svcs, *Contract Svc*
Benchmark Prof'ls, *Exec Srch*
Best/World Assoc., *Exec Srch*
BestStaff Svcs, *Perm. Emp Agcy*
Boles & Assoc., *Exec Srch*
Bond & Assoc., *Exec Srch*
Bott & Assoc., *Perm. Emp Agcy*
Brainpower Persnnl Agcy, *Perm. Emp Agcy*
Bundy-Stewart Assoc., *Exec Srch*
Butler Intl, *Contract Svc*
CDI Corp, *Contract Svc*
C.G. & Co, *Exec Srch*
CAD Technlgy, *Exec Srch*
CarlTech, *Contract Svc*
Certified Persnnl, *Contract Svc*
Champion Persnnl, *Exec Srch*
Cherbonnier Grp, *Exec Srch*
Computer Prof'ls Unlimtd, *Exec Srch*
Continental Persnnl, *Perm. Emp Agcy*
Contrct Design Persnnl, *Temp. Agcy*
CoreCom, *Contract Svc*
Gail Darling Staffing/Darling's Prof'l Desk, *Temp. Agcy*
Design Quest, *Contract Svc*
Diversified Engineering Srch, *Exec Srch*
C. Michael Dixon Assoc., *Exec Srch*
Dunhill Prof'l Srch, *Exec Srch*
The Elsworth Grp, *Exec Srch*
Employee Sources, *Exec Srch*
The Energists, *Exec Srch*
Express Persnnl Svcs, *Perm. Emp Agcy*
Focus Point, *Contract Svc*
FORTUNE Persnnl Consltnts/San Antonio, *Exec Srch*
Gulco Intl Recruitng Svcs, *Perm. Emp Agcy*
H+M Recrtrs, *Exec Srch*
Houston Creative Connections, *Exec Srch*
The Human Element of Business, *Exec Srch*
Inside Track, *Exec Srch*
L.K. Jordan & Assoc., *Contract Svc*
KADCO Contrct Design Corp, *Temp. Agcy*
Kelly Svcs, *Temp. Agcy*
LRJ Staff Svcs, *Perm. Emp Agcy*
Loewenstein & Assoc., *Exec Srch*
Mgmt. Recrtrs Intl, *Exec Srch*
Mgmt. Recrtrs of Champions, *Exec Srch*
Mgmt. Recrtrs of Dallas, *Exec Srch*
Mgmt. Recrtrs of LBJ Prk/Dallas, *Exec Srch*
Mgmt. Recrtrs of Round Rock, *Exec Srch*
Manpower Temp. Svcs, *Temp. Agcy*
McKinley•Arend Intl, *Exec Srch*
Metro Careers, *Exec Srch*
W. Robert Michaels & Co, *Exec Srch*
Odell & Assoc., *Exec Srch*
O'Keefe & Assoc., *Perm. Emp Agcy*
Olsten Staff Svcs, *Temp. Agcy*
Opportunity Unlimtd Persnnl Consltnts, *Exec Srch*
The Pailin Grp, *Exec Srch*
Pan American Srch, *Exec Srch*
Pate Resrcs Grp, *Exec Srch*
The Persnnl Office, *Exec Srch*
Persnnl One, *Perm. Emp Agcy*
Preng & Assoc., *Exec Srch*
Pro Staff Persnnl Svcs, *Temp. Agcy*
Professional Srch Consltnts, *Contract Svc*
Professions Today, *Perm. Emp Agcy*
Recruiting Assoc., *Exec Srch*
Redstone & Assoc., *Exec Srch*
Remedy Intelligent Staffng, *Perm. Emp Agcy*
Riccione & Assoc., *Exec Srch*
Bart Roberson & Co, *Exec Srch*
Roth Young Persnnl Svcs/Dallas, *Exec Srch*
Sales Consltnts of Houston, *Exec Srch*
Search Netwrk Intl, *Exec Srch*
Seegers Estes & Assoc., *Perm. Emp Agcy*
Rob Shields & Assoc., *Contract Svc*
Snelling Persnnl Svcs, *Perm. Emp Agcy*
Snelling Persnnl Svcs, *Exec Srch*
Source Svcs Corp, *Exec Srch*
Staff Extension, *Exec Srch*
Stehouwer & Assoc., *Perm. Emp Agcy*
Strategic Outsourcing Corp, *Exec Srch*
TRS, *Exec Srch*
TAD Tech. Svcs, *Contract Svc*
Betty Tanner Prof'l Emp. Svc, *Exec Srch*
Tech-Net, *Exec Srch*
Technical Careers, *Contract Svc*
Tech. Staff Solut'ns, *Exec Srch*
TechSystems, *Contract Svc*
The Urban Placemnt Svc, *Exec Srch*
Valpers, *Exec Srch*
Volt Tech. Svcs, *Contract Svc*
Volt Temp. Svcs of Dallas, *Temp. Agcy*
Denis Walsh & Assoc., *Exec Srch*
Wheeler, Moore & Elam Co, *Exec Srch*
The Whitaker Companies, *Exec Srch*
H.L. Yoh Co, *Contract Svc*

Utah

CDI Information Svcs, *Exec Srch*
FORTUNE Persnnl Consltnts, *Exec Srch*
Intermountain Staffing Resrcs, *Temp. Agcy*
Mgmt. Recrtrs of Ogden, *Exec Srch*
Mgmt. Recrtrs of Provo, *Exec Srch*
Manpower Tech. Svcs, *Temp. Agcy*
Olsten Staff Svcs, *Temp. Agcy*
Prince, Perelson & Assoc., *Exec Srch*
Professional Recrtrs, *Exec Srch*
Software Engineering Solut'ns, *Contract Svc*
Staffing Logic, *Perm. Emp Agcy*
Trout & Assoc., *Exec Srch*
Volt Svcs Grp, *Contract Svc*

Vermont

Persnnl Dept, *Temp. Agcy*
Technical Connection, *Perm. Emp Agcy*

Virginia

A Better Resume, *Career/Outplacemnt*
Ability Resrcs, *Exec Srch*
Access Enterprises, *Perm. Emp Agcy*
Adams Sources, *Exec Srch*
Alliance Grp, *Exec Srch*
Alpha Omega Resrcs, *Perm. Emp Agcy*
American Tech. Resrcs, *Perm. Emp Agcy*
BSC, *Contract Svc*
CDI Corp, *Contract Svc*
Cadworks, *Contract Svc*
Career Registry, *Exec Srch*
Corporate Connection Exec. Srch Firm
Carol Day & Assoc., *Exec Srch*
Donmac Assoc., *Exec Srch*
Dunhill Prof'l Srch, *Exec Srch*
EDP, *Temp. Agcy*
Engineering & MIS Guild, *Exec Srch*
FORTUNE Persnnl Consltnts, *Exec Srch*
Graham Assoc., *Exec Srch*
HATCH Mrktng Syst., *Perm. Emp Agcy*
Information Specialists Co, *Exec Srch*
Kogen Persnnl, *Exec Srch*
Lee Staffing Resrcs, *Exec Srch*
Carol Maden Grp Recruitng, *Exec Srch*
Mgmt. Recrtrs Intl, *Exec Srch*
Mgmt. Recrtrs of McLean, *Exec Srch*
Mgmt. Recrtrs of Roanoke, *Exec Srch*
The McCormick Grp, *Exec Srch*
Mid-Atlantic Srch, *Exec Srch*
Norrell Staff Svcs, *Exec Srch*
Paul-Tittle Assoc., *Perm. Emp Agcy*
Placement Prof'ls, *Exec Srch*
Procurement Solut'ns, *Contract Svc*
Professional Srch Persnnl, *Exec Srch*
Search & Recruit Intl, *Exec Srch*
Snelling Persnnl Svcs, *Perm. Emp Agcy*
Souder & Assoc., *Exec Srch*
Source Svcs Corp, *Exec Srch*
STAT Temps, *Temp. Agcy*
Strategic Staffing/SSI Tech. Svcs Division, *Contract Svc*
The Talley Grp, *Exec Srch*
Tech/Aid of VA, *Temp. Agcy*
U.S. Srch, *Exec Srch*
Virginia Emp. Referral Svc, *Exec Srch*
Wannamaker Assoc., *Perm. Emp Agcy*
Wayne Assoc., *Exec Srch*

Washington

Able Persnnl Agcy, *Perm. Emp Agcy*
BSP & Assoc., *Exec Srch*
Behrens & Co, *Exec Srch*
Bixler Grp, *Exec Srch*
The Career Clinic, *Exec Srch*
Comprehensive Staff Resrcs dba Techstaff, *Temp. Agcy*
Conmarke USA, *Temp. Agcy*
Express Persnnl Svcs, *Temp. Agcy*
FORTUNE Persnnl Consltnts of E. Seattle, *Exec Srch*
Hall Kinion Assoc., *Perm. Emp Agcy*
Houser, Martin, Morris & Assoc., *Exec Srch*
The Jobs Co, *Exec Srch*
Kirkbride Assoc., *Exec Srch*
Mgmt. Recrtrs Intl, *Exec Srch*
Mgmt. Recrtrs of Lynwood, *Exec Srch*
Mgmt. Recrtrs of Mercer Islnd, *Exec Srch*
Mgmt. Recrtrs of Seattle, *Exec Srch*
Mgmt. Recrtrs of Tacoma, *Exec Srch*
John Mason & Assoc., *Exec Srch*
Mini-Systems Assoc., *Contract Svc*
Nelson, Coulson & Assoc., *Perm. Emp Agcy*
Northwest Temp. Svcs, *Temp. Agcy*
Persnnl Unlimtd, *Exec Srch*
Jack Porter & Assoc., *Perm. Emp Agcy*
Resource Mngmnt Intl, *Temp. Agcy*

Susan Schoos & Assoc., *Exec Srch*
Search West, *Exec Srch*
Strain Persnnl Specialists, *Exec Srch*
TSA, *Exec Srch*
Whittall Mngmnt Grp, *Exec Srch*
Williams Recruitng, *Exec Srch*

West Virginia
Belcan Tech. Svcs, *Contract Svc*
CDI Engineering Grp, *Contract Svc*
Dunhill Prof'l Srch, *Exec Srch*
Key Persnnl, *Perm. Emp Agcy*
Quantum Resrcs, *Perm. Emp Agcy*

Wisconsin
Action Srch Consltnts, *Exec Srch*
Aerotek, *Contract Svc*
Allen, Wayne, & Co, *Perm. Emp Agcy*
American Tech. Svcs, *Perm. Emp Agcy*
Argus Tech. Svcs, *Perm. Emp Agcy*
Austria Austria & Assoc., *Perm. Emp Agcy*
Construction Srch Specialists, *Exec Srch*
Corporate Srch, *Exec Srch*
Crown Svcs, *Temp. Agcy*
Dieck, Mueller & Assoc., *Exec Srch*
Dunhill of Green Bay, *Perm. Emp Agcy*
J.M. Eagle Partners, *Exec Srch*
Eagle Technlgy Grp, *Perm. Emp Agcy*
Engineering Placemnt Specialists, *Exec Srch*
EnviroStaff, *Temp. Agcy*
Executive Placemnt Svc/Career Connections, *Exec Srch*
Executive Recrtrs, *Exec Srch*
Executive Resource, *Exec Srch*
The Exutec Grp, *Exec Srch*
First Srch Exec Recrtmnt, *Exec Srch*
Food Staff 2000, *Exec Srch*
IDI Corp, *Temp. Agcy*
Industrial Consltng Engineers, *Perm. Emp Agcy*
Mgmt. Recrtrs of Appleton/ CompuSrch, *Exec Srch*
Mgmt. Recrtrs of Green Bay, *Exec Srch*
Mgmt. Recrtrs of Milwaukee/Sales Consltnts, *Exec Srch*
Mgmt. Recrtrs of Milwaukee, *Exec Srch*
MARBL Consltnts, *Exec Srch*
Markent Persnnl, *Exec Srch*
Northern Tech. Svcs, *Perm. Emp Agcy*
Olsten Staff Svcs, *Temp. Agcy*
Placements of Racine, *Perm. Emp Agcy*
Pollak & Skan, *Contract Svc*
Prairie Engineering, *Exec Srch*
Professional Engineering Placemnts, *Perm. Emp Agcy*
Sanford Rose Assoc., *Exec Srch*
SEEK, *Perm. Emp Agcy*
Site Persnnl Svcs/Trainor/Salick & Assoc., *Temp. Agcy*
Tom Sloan & Assoc., *Perm. Emp Agcy*
Suave Co, *Perm. Emp Agcy*
T.E.M. Assoc., *Exec Srch*
TAD Tech. Svcs, *Contract Svc*
Techstaff, *Perm. Emp Agcy*
Techtronix Tech. Employment, *Exec Srch*
U.S. Tech Force, *Exec Srch*
Universal Srch, *Exec Srch*
Valley Recruitng, *Exec Srch*
The Waterstone Grp, *Contract Svc*

Wyoming
Mgmt. Recrtrs of Cheyenne, *Exec Srch*

ENTERTAINMENT

Arizona
J.R. Prof'l Srch, *Exec Srch*

California
Business Syst. Staffing & Assoc., *Perm. Emp Agcy*
Executive Temps, *Temp. Agcy*
Justus Persnnl Svcs, *Perm. Emp Agcy*

New Jersey
Mini Conglomerate Svc, *Perm. Emp Agcy*

New York
Fanning Persnnl, *Exec Srch*

ENVIRONMENTAL

California
JPM Intl, *Exec Srch*
Kelly Scientific Resrcs, *Temp. Agcy*
Mgmt. Recrtrs Intl, *Exec Srch*
McCormack & Assoc., *Exec Srch*

Colorado
The Bridge, *Exec Srch*
Kelly Scientific Resrcs, *Temp. Agcy*

Connecticut
Mgmt. Srch, *Exec Srch*

District of Columbia
Access: Networking in the Public Interest, *Career/Outplacemnt*

Florida
Environmental Health & Safety Srch Assoc., *Exec Srch*

Georgia
Kelly Scientific Resrcs, *Temp. Agcy*
Mgmt. Recrtrs of Savannah, *Exec Srch*

Illinois
Corporate Environment, *Exec Srch*

Maryland
Kelly Scientific Resrcs, *Temp. Agcy*

Massachusetts
Michael Anthony Assoc., *Exec Srch*
Rob Davidson Assoc./Exec. & Prof. Resume Svc, *Exec Srch*
Derek Assoc., *Exec Srch*
Executive Srch Nrtheast, *Exec Srch*
Locke Assoc., *Exec Srch*

Michigan
Executive Recrtrs Intl, *Exec Srch*
Kelly Scientific Resrcs, *Temp. Agcy*

Minnesota
EnviroStaff, *Temp. Agcy*

Missouri
EnviroStaff, *Temp. Agcy*
Kelly Scientific Resrcs, *Temp. Agcy*

New Jersey
R.W. Apple & Assoc., *Exec Srch*
Gary Bell Assoc., *Exec Srch*
Kelly Scientific Resrcs, *Temp. Agcy*

New Mexico
Butler Svc Grp, *Contract Svc*
Excel of Albuquerque, *Perm. Emp Agcy*

North Carolina
Environmental Recruitng Svcs, *Exec Srch*
Mark III Persnnl, *Exec Srch*

Ohio
North Peak Grp, *Exec Srch*

Oregon
Wolf Environmental Grp, *Exec Srch*

Pennsylvania
Jerry Goldberg & Assoc., *Perm. Emp Agcy*
Virtual Workplace, *Temp. Agcy*

South Carolina
Engineering Persnnl Netwrk, *Exec Srch*

Texas
Kelly Scientific Resrcs, *Temp. Agcy*
The Pailin Grp, *Exec Srch*

West Virginia
Onsite Commercial Staffng, *Perm. Emp Agcy*

FASHION

Arizona
Personalized Mngmnt Assoc., *Exec Srch*

California
American Magna Srch, *Exec Srch*
Apple One Emp. Svcs, *Perm. Emp Agcy*
Business Syst. Staffing & Assoc., *Perm. Emp Agcy*
Malibu Grp, *Exec Srch*
Pro Staff Persnnl Svcs, *Perm. Emp Agcy*
Riley-Cole Recrtmnt Specialists, *Exec Srch*
Scott-Thaler Assoc., *Exec Srch*
Seitchik, Corwin & Seitchik, *Exec Srch*

Colorado
40 Plus of CO, *Career/Outplacemnt*

Florida
Just Mngmnt Svcs, *Exec Srch*
Retail Exec Srch, *Exec Srch*

Georgia
Kenzer Corp of GA, *Exec Srch*
Evie Kreisler & Assoc., *Exec Srch*
Mgmt. Recrtrs of Marietta, *Exec Srch*

Hawaii
Ellis & Assoc., *Exec Srch*

Illinois
Executive Referral Svcs, *Exec Srch*
Arlene Leff & Assoc., *Exec Srch*

Indiana
Life Emp. Svc, *Perm. Emp Agcy*

Iowa
Helping Hands Temp. Svc, *Temp. Agcy*

Louisiana
Talley & Assoc./Talley Temps, *Exec Srch*

Maryland
Futures, *Exec Srch*
Sales Consltnts of Baltimore Cty, *Exec Srch*

Massachusetts
Adecco, *Temp. Agcy*
Cyr Assoc., *Exec Srch*
Derby Assoc., *Perm. Emp Agcy*
Ford & Ford Exec Srch, *Exec Srch*
Manpower Temp. Svcs, *Temp. Agcy*
SearchNet, *Exec Srch*

Minnesota
Roth Young Exec Recrtrs, *Exec Srch*

Nebraska
Rose Crum Assoc., *Exec Srch*

Nevada
Charm Unlimtd, *Perm. Emp Agcy*

New Hampshire
Clayman Mngmnt Svc, *Exec Srch*
Sales Consltnts, *Exec Srch*

New Jersey
A Prof'l Edge, *Career/Outplacemnt*
Career Ctr, *Perm. Emp Agcy*
Career Mngmnt Intl, *Exec Srch*
Impact Persnnl, *Perm. Emp Agcy*
Pace-Setters Exec Srch, *Exec Srch*
Arline Simpson Assoc., *Perm. Emp Agcy*
Temporary Excellence, *Temp. Agcy*
Winston Staff Svcs, *Temp. Agcy*

New York
Adam Persnnl, *Perm. Emp Agcy*
Adecco, *Temp. Agcy*
Asher Persnnl Consltnts, *Perm. Emp Agcy*
Neail Behringer Consltnts, *Exec Srch*
Seth Diamond Assoc., *Exec Srch*
Eden Persnnl, *Perm. Emp Agcy*
Employment Recrtrs Agcy, *Perm. Emp Agcy*
Euromonde, *Temp. Agcy*
Fanning Persnnl, *Exec Srch*
KLK Persnnl, *Perm. Emp Agcy*
Kaufman Assoc. Exec. Srch Firm
Koltnow & Co, *Exec Srch*
Manpower Temp. Svcs, *Temp. Agcy*
Optimal Resrcs, *Exec Srch*
Quest Organization, *Exec Srch*
Rem Resrcs, *Perm. Emp Agcy*
Hillary Taylor Persnnl, *Perm. Emp Agcy*
Winston Resrcs, *Exec Srch*
S.R. Wolman Assoc., *Exec Srch*

North Carolina
Employment Consltnts, *Contract Svc*
Sickenberger Assoc., *Exec Srch*

North Dakota
Olsten Staff Svcs/Kramer & Assoc./Expressway Persnnl, *Temp. Agcy*

Ohio
Drayton & Assoc., *Exec Srch*
Laine's S.M.G., *Perm. Emp Agcy*

Pennsylvania
Ashley Srch Consltnts, *Exec Srch*
J. Croyle & Assoc., *Perm. Emp Agcy*
Human Resource Solut'ns, *Exec Srch*
Kenn Spinrad, *Exec Srch*

South Carolina
The Stroman Co, *Perm. Emp Agcy*

Texas
Carpenter & Assoc., *Exec Srch*
Dallas Emp. Svc, *Perm. Emp Agcy*
Kenzer Corp, *Exec Srch*
Salinas & Assoc. Persnnl, *Exec Srch*

Virginia
Barnes & Assoc. Retail Srch, *Exec Srch*

Carol McNew Emp. Svc, *Perm. Emp Agcy*
National Recrtrs, *Perm. Emp Agcy*

FINANCE

Alabama

A-1 Emp. Svc, *Perm. Emp Agcy*
Dunhill of So. Birmingham, *Exec Srch*
Employment Consltnts, *Perm. Emp Agcy*
FORTUNE Persnnl Consltnts, *Exec Srch*
Langford Srch, *Exec Srch*
Snelling Srch/Snelling Persnnl Svcs, *Exec Srch*
VIP Persnnl, *Perm. Emp Agcy*

Alaska

Olsten Staff Svcs, *Temp. Agcy*

Arizona

Accountnts Exec Srch/Accountnts On Call, *Exec Srch*
Accounting & Bookkeeping Persnnl, *Exec Srch*
AccuStaff, *Perm. Emp Agcy*
Aidan Grp, *Contract Svc*
Clifford & Assoc., *Perm. Emp Agcy*
Mgmt. Recrtrs of Scottsdale, *Exec Srch*
Priority Staffng, *Perm. Emp Agcy*
Spectra Intl, *Exec Srch*
Stivers Temp. Persnnl, *Temp. Agcy*

Arkansas

Dunhill Persnnl, *Exec Srch*
Executive Recrtrs Outplacement Consltnts, *Exec Srch*
Snelling Srch, *Exec Srch*

California

A Perm. Success Emp. Svcs, *Perm. Emp Agcy*
ABA Staffng, *Exec Srch*
AGA Recruitng, *Exec Srch*
Abacus Staffing for Acctng, *Exec Srch*
Accountnts Exec Srch, *Exec Srch*
Accntnts, *Temp. Agcy*
Accountnts On Call, *Exec Srch*
Accounting Additions, *Exec Srch*
Accounting Advantage, *Exec Srch*
The Accnt'g Guild, *Temp. Agcy*
AccuStaff, *Perm. Emp Agcy*
AccuStaff Co, *Temp. Agcy*
Active Srch & Plcmnt, *Exec Srch*
Affordable Exec Recrtrs, *Exec Srch*
Allied Srch, *Exec Srch*
Alpha-Net Consltng Grp, *Exec Srch*
Alternative Staffing Grp, *Exec Srch*
Answers Unlimtd, *Temp. Agcy*
John Anthony & Assoc., *Exec Srch*
Apple One Emp. Svcs, *Perm. Emp Agcy*
Apropos Emp. Agcy, *Perm. Emp Agcy*
Automotive Career Plcmnt, *Exec Srch*
Bay Resrcs, *Exec Srch*
Ed Bell Assoc., *Exec Srch*
Harvey Bell & Assoc., *Exec Srch*
Best Temp. Svc, *Temp. Agcy*
Billington & Assoc., *Exec Srch*
Blaine & Assoc., *Perm. Emp Agcy*
Blue, Garni & Co, *Exec Srch*
BridgeGate Grp, *Exec Srch*
Bullis & Co, *Exec Srch*
C.R. Assoc., *Exec Srch*
Career Advantage, *Exec Srch*
Carver Dooley Assoc., *Exec Srch*
Chaitin & Assoc., *Exec Srch*
Champagne Temp. Help, *Temp. Agcy*
Choice Persnnl, *Perm. Emp Agcy*
Collier-Young Agcy, *Temp. Agcy*
Colt Syst. Prof'l Persnnl Svcs, *Perm. Emp Agcy*
Corporate Solut'ns, *Perm. Emp Agcy*
Crossroads Staff Svc, *Temp. Agcy*
Culver Persnnl Svcs, *Perm. Emp Agcy*
Culver Persnnl Svcs/The Culver Grp, *Exec Srch*
DBL Assoc., *Exec Srch*
Data Careers Persnnl Svcs & Srch Grp, *Perm. Emp Agcy*
Demery Assoc., *Exec Srch*
Dependable Emp. Agency Netwrk, *Perm. Emp Agcy*
The Dial Grp, *Perm. Emp Agcy*
Rob Dingman Co, *Exec Srch*
EDP Contrct Svcs, *Contract Svc*
Eleventh Hour Staff Svcs, *Temp. Agcy*
Emco Persnnl, *Perm. Emp Agcy*
Employment Devlpmnt Dept, *Perm. Emp Agcy*
Ethos Consltng, *Exec Srch*
Executive Resource Syst., *Exec Srch*
Express Persnnl Svcs, *Temp. Agcy*
Curtis Farmer Persnnl, *Exec Srch*
Fay Tech Svcs, *Perm. Emp Agcy*
40 Plus of So. CA, *Exec Srch*
Fresquez & Assoc., *Exec Srch*
Gajek Kyle & Assoc., *Exec Srch*
Gould Persnnl Svcs, *Perm. Emp Agcy*
Robert Half Intl, *Exec Srch*
Herrerias & Assoc., *Exec Srch*
Holland McFadzean & Assoc., *Exec Srch*
Interim Accnt'g Prof'ls, *Perm. Emp Agcy*
Justus Persnnl Svcs, *Perm. Emp Agcy*
Kearney Boyle & Assoc., *Exec Srch*
Kelly Svcs, *Temp. Agcy*
Kelly Tech. Svcs, *Temp. Agcy*
Kizer Ashlyn Exec Srch, *Exec Srch*
Klein & Assoc., *Temp. Agcy*
John Kurosky & Assoc., *Exec Srch*
Marvin Laba & Assoc., *Exec Srch*
Larsen, Whitney, Blecksmith, & Zilliacus, *Exec Srch*
Lending Persnnl Svcs, *Exec Srch*
Lifter & Assoc., *Exec Srch*
The London Agcy, *Exec Srch*
The London Agcy, *Temp. Agcy*
Mahoney & Brewer Assoc., *Exec Srch*
Malibu Grp, *Exec Srch*
Mgmt. Recrtrs of Burlingame/Sales Consltnts, *Exec Srch*
Mgmt. Recrtrs of Encino, *Exec Srch*
Mgmt. Recrtrs of Laguna Hills, *Exec Srch*
Mgmt. Recrtrs-Oakland/Sales Consltnts, *Exec Srch*
Mgmt. Recrtrs of Pleasanton, *Exec Srch*
Mgmt. Recrtrs of Redlands, *Exec Srch*
Mgmt. Srch Intl, *Exec Srch*
Mgmt. Solut'ns, *Exec Srch*
Manpower, *Temp. Agcy*
Maverick Staff Svc, *Perm. Emp Agcy*
K.E. McCarthy & Assoc., *Exec Srch*
Sabine McManus & Assoc., *Exec Srch*
Mesa Intl, *Exec Srch*
Joseph Michaels, *Perm. Emp Agcy*
Musick & Assoc., *Exec Srch*
J.A. Myrben & Assoc., *Exec Srch*
NCC Exec Srch, *Exec Srch*
Nations Staff Solut'ns/Assoc. Resource Intl, *Exec Srch*
Nelson HR Solut'ns, *Perm. Emp Agcy*
Newport Strategic Srch, *Exec Srch*
O'Crowley & O''Toole Exec Srch, *Exec Srch*
Olsten Staff Svcs, *Temp. Agcy*
Omni Express Temps, *Temp. Agcy*
On Assignment, *Temp. Agcy*
Onyx Persnnl Svcs, *Perm. Emp Agcy*
PN Financial Recruitng, *Exec Srch*
Pacific Srch Grp, *Exec Srch*
Parker & Lynch Exec Srch, *Exec Srch*
Pips Persnnl Svcs, *Perm. Emp Agcy*
Pro Staff Persnnl Svcs, *Perm. Emp Agcy*
Probus Exec Srch, *Exec Srch*
Professional Srch Assoc., *Exec Srch*
ProFile Persnnl, *Perm. Emp Agcy*
Questemps, *Temp. Agcy*
RJ Assoc., *Exec Srch*
Ed Rast & Co, *Exec Srch*
Remedy Intelligent Staffng, *Temp. Agcy*
Riley-Cole Recrtmnt Specialists, *Exec Srch*
Ritter Assoc., *Exec Srch*
Romac Intl, *Exec Srch*
Rowland Assoc., *Exec Srch*
Royal Staff Svcs, *Exec Srch*
Russell Staffing Resrcs, *Perm. Emp Agcy*
Ryan, Miller & Assoc., *Exec Srch*
Santa Barbara Plcmnt, *Perm. Emp Agcy*
Schlatter & Assoc., *Exec Srch*
Search West, *Exec Srch*
The September Grp, *Exec Srch*
David Sharp & Assoc., *Perm. Emp Agcy*
Sharp Persnnl & Srch, *Exec Srch*
Charles Skorina & Co, *Exec Srch*
Source Svcs Corp, *Contract Svc*
M.H. Springer & Assoc., *Exec Srch*
Steinbrun, Hughes & Assoc., *Exec Srch*
Stivers Temp. Persnnl of CA, *Temp. Agcy*
TRC Staff Svcs, *Perm. Emp Agcy*
Talent Tree Staffng, *Perm. Emp Agcy*
Tax Exec Srch, *Exec Srch*
Technical Directions, *Perm. Emp Agcy*
Teleforce Intl, *Exec Srch*
Telford, Adams, & Alexander, *Exec Srch*
Judy Thompson & Assoc., *Exec Srch*
Thor Temp. Svcs, *Temp. Agcy*
TOD Staffng, *Exec Srch*
Today Persnnl, *Perm. Emp Agcy*
Truex Assoc., *Exec Srch*
The Truman Agcy, Persnnl Specialists, *Perm. Emp Agcy*
Tustin Persnnl Svcs, *Perm. Emp Agcy*
UAW Labor Emp. & Training Corp, *Perm. Emp Agcy*
United Staff Solut'ns, *Exec Srch*
United/Corestaff Staff Svcs, *Perm. Emp Agcy*
Victor Valley Persnnl Agcy, *Perm. Emp Agcy*
Volt Temp. Svcs, *Temp. Agcy*
Walker & Torrente, *Exec Srch*
D.L. Weaver & Assoc., *Exec Srch*
Western Staff Svcs, *Temp. Agcy*
WestPacific Nat'l Srch, *Exec Srch*
William-Johns Co, *Exec Srch*
Worldwide Exec Srch, *Exec Srch*
Your People Prof'ls, *Perm. Emp Agcy*

Colorado

Accountnts Choice Persnnl, *Exec Srch*
Accountnts Exec Srch, *Exec Srch*
The Accnt'g Guild, *Temp. Agcy*
Adecco, *Temp. Agcy*
Ahrnsbrak & Assoc., *Perm. Emp Agcy*
C.S. Barnes, *Perm. Emp Agcy*
The Buxton Grp Limited, *Exec Srch*
Casey Svcs, *Exec Srch*
Eleventh Hour Staff Svcs, *Perm. Emp Agcy*
40 Plus of CO, *Career/Outplacemnt*
JobSearch, *Temp. Agcy*
Kelly Svcs, *Temp. Agcy*
Mgmt. Recrtrs of Colorado Springs, *Exec Srch*
Manpower Intl, *Temp. Agcy*
National Affirmative Action Career Netwrk, *Exec Srch*
Norrell Temp. Svcs, *Temp. Agcy*
On Call Tech. Svcs/StaffMark, *Temp. Agcy*
Rocky Mountain Recrtrs, *Exec Srch*
SOS Staff Svcs, *Temp. Agcy*
Sales Consltnts, *Exec Srch*
Snelling Persnnl Svcs, *Exec Srch*
Source Svcs Corp, *Exec Srch*
Star Persnnl, *Exec Srch*
Talent Tree Staffng, *Perm. Emp Agcy*
Todays Temporary, *Temp. Agcy*
Woodmoor Grp, *Exec Srch*

Connecticut

A&A Resume & Persnnl Svcs, *Perm. Emp Agcy*
Ryan Abbott Srch Assoc., *Exec Srch*
Achieva Grp, *Exec Srch*
Admiral Staff Svcs, *Temp. Agcy*
Advanced Plcmnt, *Temp. Agcy*
Bohan & Bradstreet, *Perm. Emp Agcy*
Buxbaum/Rink Consltng, *Exec Srch*
Thomas Byrne Assoc., *Perm. Emp Agcy*
Corporate Staff Solut'ns, *Temp. Agcy*
Diversity Recruitng Svcs, *Exec Srch*
Dunhill Srch Intl, *Perm. Emp Agcy*
EDP Contrct Svcs, *Contract Svc*
Financial Careers, *Exec Srch*
Harbor Assoc., *Exec Srch*
High-Tech Recrtrs, *Exec Srch*
Hipp Waters Prof'l Srch, *Exec Srch*
Impact Persnnl, *Temp. Agcy*
Intertec Persnnl, *Temp. Agcy*
Mgmt. Recrtrs Intl, *Exec Srch*
McIntyre Assoc., *Temp. Agcy*
The McKnight Grp, *Exec Srch*
Merry Emp. Grp, *Perm. Emp Agcy*
Office Svcs of CT, *Perm. Emp Agcy*
PRH Mgmt., *Exec Srch*
Paramount Resrcs, *Perm. Emp Agcy*
Pascale & LaMorte, *Perm. Emp Agcy*
Barry Persky & Co., *Exec Srch*
Q.S.I., *Perm. Emp Agcy*
Resource Assoc., *Perm. Emp Agcy*
Siger & Assoc., *Exec Srch*
Howard Smith Assoc., *Exec Srch*
Source Svcs Corp, *Exec Srch*
Strategic Executives, *Exec Srch*
Strategic Srch, *Exec Srch*
Velen Assoc., *Perm. Emp Agcy*
Western Staff Svcs, *Temp. Agcy*
Western Staff Svcs, *Perm. Emp Agcy*
The Westfield Grp, *Exec Srch*
Workforce One, *Perm. Emp Agcy*
Bob Wright Recruitng, *Exec Srch*

Delaware

Caldwell Staff Svcs, *Perm. Emp Agcy*
Discovery Staffng, *Exec Srch*
J.B. Groner Exec Srch, *Exec Srch*
E.W. Hodges & Assoc., *Exec Srch*
Independent Nat'l Srch & Assoc., *Exec Srch*
The Placers, *Exec Srch*

District of Columbia

Accountnts Exec Srch/Accountnts on Call, *Exec Srch*
Career Blazers Persnnl, *Perm. Emp Agcy*
Network Companies, *Exec Srch*
Norrell Svcs, *Temp. Agcy*
Don Richard Assoc. of Washington DC, *Exec Srch*
Source Svcs Corp, *Temp. Agcy*
Tangent Corp, *Exec Srch*

Florida

AAA Employment, *Perm. Emp Agcy*
Accountnts Exec Srch/Accountnts On Call, *Exec Srch*
Accountnts Express, *Perm. Emp Agcy*
AccuTech, *Contract Svc*
Active Prof'ls, *Exec Srch*
Availability, *Perm. Emp Agcy*
B&B Persnnl, *Perm. Emp Agcy*
Brickell Persnnl Consltnts, *Temp. Agcy*
Bryan & Assoc./Worknet, Etc., *Exec Srch*
Career Planners, *Perm. Emp Agcy*
Carrier's Career Svc, *Career/Outplacemnt*
Corporate Srch Consltnts, *Exec Srch*
DGA Persnnl Grp, *Exec Srch*

Steven Douglas Assoc., *Exec Srch*
Ethan Allen Persnnl Plcmnt, *Exec Srch*
Farwell Grp, *Exec Srch*
First Emp. Consltnts, *Exec Srch*
Michael Gimbel & Assoc., *Exec Srch*
Girl Friday Persnnl, *Temp. Agcy*
Robert Half Intl/Accountemps, *Exec Srch*
Hastings & Hastings Persnnl Consltnts, *Temp. Agcy*
Janus Career Svc, *Perm. Emp Agcy*
Kay Hancock Apfel Exec Srch, *Exec Srch*
Koerner Grp, *Exec Srch*
R.H. Larsen & Assoc., *Exec Srch*
Mgmt. Recrtrs of Miami, *Exec Srch*
Mgmt. Recrtrs of St. Petersburg, *Exec Srch*
Mgmt. Recrtrs of Tallahassee, *Exec Srch*
Mgmt. Recrtrs of Tampa, *Exec Srch*
Office Specialists, *Temp. Agcy*
Olsten Staff Svcs, *Temp. Agcy*
OMNIPartners, *Exec Srch*
Persnnl Ctr, *Perm. Emp Agcy*
Priority Srch, *Exec Srch*
Profes. Staffing/Able Body Temp. Svcs, *Contract Svc*
Linda Robins & Assoc., *Temp. Agcy*
Robinson & Assoc., *Exec Srch*
Romac Intl, *Exec Srch*
The Ryan Charles Grp, *Exec Srch*
Sales Consltnts of Fort Lauderdale, *Exec Srch*
Sales Consltnts of Jacksonville, *Exec Srch*
Doug Sears & Assoc., *Exec Srch*
Skeegan & Assoc., *Exec Srch*
Source Svcs Corp, *Exec Srch*
Spalding's Emp. Svc, *Perm. Emp Agcy*
Aaron Stewart Persnnl, *Exec Srch*
The Stewart Srch Grp, *Exec Srch*
Sun Persnnl West, *Exec Srch*
Suncoast Grp, *Perm. Emp Agcy*
Todays Temporary, *Temp. Agcy*
Uniquest Intl, *Exec Srch*

Georgia

A-OK Persnnl, *Perm. Emp Agcy*
A-1 Svc Persnnl, *Perm. Emp Agcy*
AAA Employment, *Perm. Emp Agcy*
A.D. & Assoc. Exec Srch, *Exec Srch*
Accountnts & Bookkeepers Persnnl, *Exec Srch*
Accountnts Exec Srch/Accountnts On Call, *Exec Srch*
Michael Alexander Grp, *Exec Srch*
Ashley-Nolan Intl, *Exec Srch*
Bell Oaks Co, *Exec Srch*
Bradshaw & Assoc., *Exec Srch*
Career Placemnt Assoc. Staffng, *Exec Srch*
Catalina Resrcs, *Perm. Emp Agcy*
Chase Finan. Staffng/Tyler Tech. Staffng, *Perm. Emp Agcy*
Corporate Srch Consltnts, *Exec Srch*
Dunhill Prof'l Srch, *Exec Srch*
Durham Staffng, *Perm. Emp Agcy*
Elite Staff Svcs, *Perm. Emp Agcy*
Executive Resource Grp, *Exec Srch*
Express Persnnl Svcs, *Perm. Emp Agcy*
Fox-Morris Assoc., *Exec Srch*
ISC of Atlanta/Intl Career Continuation, *Exec Srch*
Lucas Financial Srch, *Exec Srch*
MA&A Grp, *Perm. Emp Agcy*
Mahoney & Brewer Assoc., *Exec Srch*
Mgmt. Recrtrs Intl, *Exec Srch*
Mgmt. Recrtrs of Atlanta, *Exec Srch*
More Persnnl Svcs, *Perm. Emp Agcy*
NEIS, *Exec Srch*
Jim Nixon & Assoc., *Exec Srch*
Olsten Staff Svcs, *Temp. Agcy*
Perimeter Plcmnt, *Exec Srch*
Priority 1 Staff Svcs, *Temp. Agcy*
Randstad Staff Svcs, *Perm. Emp Agcy*
Don Richard Assoc., *Exec Srch*
Romac Intl, *Exec Srch*
Snelling Persnnl Svcs, *Perm. Emp Agcy*
Source Svcs Corp, *Exec Srch*
Southern Prof'l Recrtrs, *Exec Srch*
Toar Consltnts, *Exec Srch*
Todays Temporary, *Temp. Agcy*
WPPS Software Staffng, *Perm. Emp Agcy*
Western Staff Svcs, *Temp. Agcy*

Hawaii

Dunhill Prof'l Srch of Hawaii, *Exec Srch*
Ellis & Assoc., *Exec Srch*
Mgmt. Srch & Consltng, *Exec Srch*

Idaho

FORTUNE Persnnl Consltnts, *Exec Srch*
Horne/Brown Intl, *Exec Srch*

Illinois

Account Pros, *Exec Srch*
Accountant Source Temps, *Temp. Agcy*
Accountnts Exec Srch/Accountnts On Call, *Exec Srch*
Advanced Persnnl, *Perm. Emp Agcy*
American Engineering Co, *Exec Srch*
Armstrong-Hamilton Assoc., *Exec Srch*
Availability, *Perm. Emp Agcy*
Bankers Grp, *Exec Srch*
Banner Persnnl, *Perm. Emp Agcy*
Barrett Partners, *Exec Srch*
Bell Persnnl, *Perm. Emp Agcy*
Burling Grp Exec. Srch Firm
CFR Exec Srch, *Exec Srch*
Capital Svcs Grp, *Exec Srch*
Carson Mngmnt Assoc., *Contract Svc*
Casey Staff Svcs, *Perm. Emp Agcy*
Chicago Financial Srch, *Exec Srch*
D. Clesen Co, *Exec Srch*
Cogan & Assoc., *Exec Srch*
Computer Futures Exchange, *Exec Srch*
Consltnts to Exec Mngmnt Co Exec. Srch Firm
Contemporary Svcs, *Exec Srch*
Dunhill Staff Svcs of Chicago, *Perm. Emp Agcy*
Eastman & Assoc., *Exec Srch*
The Eastwood Grp, *Exec Srch*
Elsko Exec Srch, *Exec Srch*
The Esquire Staffing Grp, *Perm. Emp Agcy*
Executive Financial Consltnts, *Exec Srch*
Executive Options Exec. Srch Firm
Executive Placemnt Consltnts, *Exec Srch*
Executive Referral Svcs, *Exec Srch*
Express Persnnl Svcs, *Temp. Agcy*
Fellows Plcmnt, *Temp. Agcy*
Financial Srch Corp, *Exec Srch*
First Staffng, *Perm. Emp Agcy*
Global Srch, *Exec Srch*
Gnodde Assoc., *Exec Srch*
David Gomez & Assoc., *Exec Srch*
Greystone Assoc., *Exec Srch*
Robert Half Intl/Accountemps, *Exec Srch*
Elizabeth Howe & Assoc., *Exec Srch*
Human Resource Connection, *Perm. Emp Agcy*
Human Resource Technlgy, *Exec Srch*
IZS Exec Srch, *Exec Srch*
Illinois Veterans Leadership Program, *Career/Outplacemnt*
Insurance Nat'l Srch/E.J. Ashton & Assoc., *Exec Srch*
Interstaff, *Temp. Agcy*
ITEX Exec Srch, *Exec Srch*
Kennedy & Co, *Exec Srch*
Kenzer Corp, *Exec Srch*
Kingsley Emp. Svc, *Perm. Emp Agcy*
Kunzer Assoc., *Exec Srch*
Arlene Leff & Assoc., *Exec Srch*
Lynco Mngmnt Persnnl, *Exec Srch*
Lynco Mngmnt Persnnl, *Exec Srch*
Mack & Assoc., *Temp. Agcy*
Macro Resrcs, *Exec Srch*
Magnum Srch, *Exec Srch*
Mgmt. Recrtrs of Des Plaines, *Exec Srch*
Mgmt. Support Svcs, *Exec Srch*
Michael David Assoc., *Perm. Emp Agcy*
The Murphy Grp, *Perm. Emp Agcy*
National Srch, *Exec Srch*
Nocek & Assoc., *Exec Srch*
Norrell Financial Staffng, *Exec Srch*
Officemates5 of Wheeling, *Exec Srch*
Opportunity Persnnl, *Perm. Emp Agcy*
PS, *Perm. Emp Agcy*
Profile Temp. Svc, *Temp. Agcy*
ProSearch Plus, *Exec Srch*
The Raleigh Warwick Grp, *Exec Srch*
Remedy Intelligent Staffng, *Temp. Agcy*
Right Svcs, *Temp. Agcy*
Romac Intl, *Exec Srch*
The Ryan Charles Grp, *Exec Srch*
Sales Consltnts/Mgmt. Recrtrs Intl, *Exec Srch*
Sales Consltnts of Oak Brk, *Exec Srch*
Smith Hanley Assoc., *Exec Srch*
Snelling Persnnl Svcs, *Exec Srch*
Stivers Temp. Persnnl, *Temp. Agcy*
Strategic Resrcs Unlimtd, *Exec Srch*
Roy Talman & Assoc., *Exec Srch*
T.I. Vincent & Assoc., *Exec Srch*
Working World, *Temp. Agcy*
World Emp. Svc, *Perm. Emp Agcy*

Indiana

CMS Mngmnt Svcs, *Contract Svc*
Bill Caldwell Emp. Svc, *Perm. Emp Agcy*
Creative Financial Staffng, *Exec Srch*
Crowe, Chizek & Co, *Perm. Emp Agcy*
Crown Temp. Svcs of Indianapolis, *Temp. Agcy*
Execusearch, *Exec Srch*
Express Persnnl, *Temp. Agcy*
Flexible Accntnts, *Temp. Agcy*
Great Lakes Srch, *Exec Srch*
Hobart Emp. Agcy, *Perm. Emp Agcy*
Job Placemnt Svc, *Perm. Emp Agcy*
Life Emp. Svc, *Perm. Emp Agcy*
Mgmt. Recrtrs of Evansville, *Exec Srch*
Mgmt. Recrtrs of Indianapolis, *Exec Srch*
Mgmt. Recrtrs of Richmond/Staff Solut'ns, *Exec Srch*
Morley Grp, *Exec Srch*
National Corporate Consltnts/Advantage Svcs, *Exec Srch*
Officemates5 of Indianapolis, *Exec Srch*
Officemates5 of Indianapolis, *Exec Srch*
Quiring Assoc. HR Consltng Grp, *Exec Srch*
Rush Temps, *Temp. Agcy*
Sanford Rose Assoc., *Exec Srch*

Iowa

Burton Placemnt Svcs, *Exec Srch*
Byrnes & Rupkey, *Exec Srch*
Drake-Brennan dba Snelling Persnnl, *Exec Srch*
Executive Srch Assoc., *Exec Srch*
Helping Hands Temp. Svc, *Temp. Agcy*
The Human Resource Grp, *Exec Srch*
Persnnl, *Exec Srch*
Salem Mngmnt dba Rudy Salem Staff Svcs, *Temp. Agcy*
Staffing Edge, *Perm. Emp Agcy*

Kansas

Bowman & Marshall, *Perm. Emp Agcy*
Business Specialists, *Perm. Emp Agcy*
Dunhill Persnnl, *Exec Srch*
Eleventh Hour Staff Svcs, *Temp. Agcy*
Kaplan & Assoc., *Exec Srch*
Mgmt. Recrtrs of Topeka, *Exec Srch*
Midwest Srch Grp, *Exec Srch*
Morgan Hunter Corp Srch, *Perm. Emp Agcy*
Source Svcs Corp, *Exec Srch*
Western Staff Svcs, *Temp. Agcy*

Kentucky

Engineering & Exec Srch, *Exec Srch*
Persnnl Solut'ns, *Perm. Emp Agcy*
Sharrow & Assoc., *Exec Srch*

Louisiana

Ascent Consltng Grp, *Temp. Agcy*
Career Persnnl Consltnts, *Exec Srch*
Keenan Staffng, *Temp. Agcy*
Talley & Assoc./Talley Temps, *Exec Srch*

Maine

Accomplished Prof'ls, *Temp. Agcy*
At Work Persnnl, *Temp. Agcy*
Bonney Staffing & Training, *Perm. Emp Agcy*
Career Mngmnt Assoc., *Exec Srch*
Executive Srch of N.E., *Exec Srch*

Maryland

Accountnts Exec Srch/Accountnts On Call, *Exec Srch*
Admin Persnnl Svcs, *Perm. Emp Agcy*
Atlas Persnnl Agcy, *Perm. Emp Agcy*
Brandjes Assoc., *Exec Srch*
Caplan Assoc., *Exec Srch*
Computrade, *Exec Srch*
Cross Country Consltnts/Fallstaff Srch, *Exec Srch*
Dunhill of Rockville, *Perm. Emp Agcy*
Futures, *Exec Srch*
Grant/Morgan Assoc., *Exec Srch*
L.S. Gross & Assoc., *Exec Srch*
The Hanover Grp, *Exec Srch*
A.T. Kearney, *Exec Srch*
Mgmt. Recrtrs of Annapolis, *Exec Srch*
Mgmt. Recrtrs-Baltimore/Sales Consltnts, *Exec Srch*
Mgmt. Recrtrs-Bethesda/CompuSearch, *Exec Srch*
Mgmt. Recrtrs of Frederick, *Exec Srch*
Mgmt. Recrtrs of Washington, D.C., *Exec Srch*
Merit Emp. Agcy, *Perm. Emp Agcy*
Network Srch, *Exec Srch*
Don Richard Assoc., *Exec Srch*
Sales Consltnts of Prince Georges Cnty, *Exec Srch*
Source Svcs Corp, *Exec Srch*
Sudina Srch, *Exec Srch*
TAC Staff Svcs, *Temp. Agcy*
TAD Staff Svcs, *Temp. Agcy*
White Ridgely Assoc., *Career/Outplacemnt*
Winston Srch, *Exec Srch*

Massachusetts

Ability Srch of N.E., *Perm. Emp Agcy*
Account Pros, *Exec Srch*
Accountemps, *Temp. Agcy*
Anthony Michael & Co, *Exec Srch*
Arnold Assoc., *Exec Srch*
Arthur-Blair Assoc., *Perm. Emp Agcy*
Atlantic Srch Grp, *Exec Srch*
Attorney Special Assignment Plcmnt, *Temp. Agcy*
Baskind Consltng & Plcmnt, *Exec Srch*
Campbell Assoc., *Exec Srch*
Cleary Consltnts, *Perm. Emp Agcy*
Computer Security Plcmnt, *Exec Srch*
Corporate Staff Solut'ns, *Temp. Agcy*
Rob Davidson Assoc./Exec. & Prof. Resume Svc, *Exec Srch*
Davis Companies, *Temp. Agcy*
Derby Assoc., *Perm. Emp Agcy*
Douglas-Allen, *Exec Srch*
Editorial Svcs of N.E., *Temp. Agcy*
Excalibur Assoc., *Exec Srch*
Greene & Co, *Exec Srch*

Harvest Persnnl, *Exec Srch*
JNB Assoc., *Exec Srch*
Johnson & Hill Staff Svc, *Temp. Agcy*
Kennison & Assoc., *Temp. Agcy*
Kingston-Dwight Assoc., *Perm. Emp Agcy*
The Kinlin Co, *Exec Srch*
Lane Emp. Svc, *Perm. Emp Agcy*
John Leonard Persnnl Assoc., *Perm. Emp Agcy*
Lynx, *Contract Svc*
Mgmt. Recrtrs Intl of Braintree, *Exec Srch*
Mgmt. Recrtrs Intl of Springfield, *Exec Srch*
Mgmt. Recrtrs Intl of Westboro, *Exec Srch*
Mgmt. Srch, *Exec Srch*
Manpower Temp. Svcs, *Temp. Agcy*
Master Srch, *Perm. Emp Agcy*
McDevitt Assoc., *Exec Srch*
Morency Assoc., *Exec Srch*
New Boston Select Grp, *Exec Srch*
New Dimensions in Technlgy, *Exec Srch*
New England Srch, *Exec Srch*
Olsten Prof'l Accnt'g Svcs, *Exec Srch*
The Pickwick Grp, *Exec Srch*
Placement Co, *Perm. Emp Agcy*
Pro Staff, *Temp. Agcy*
Proquest, *Exec Srch*
J.E. Ranta Assoc., *Exec Srch*
Reardon Assoc., *Perm. Emp Agcy*
Robsham Assoc., *Exec Srch*
Romac Intl, *Perm. Emp Agcy*
Russell Reynolds Assoc., *Exec Srch*
Sales Consltnts of Cape Cod, *Exec Srch*
Sales Consltnts of Plymouth Cnty, *Exec Srch*
Sales Consltnts of Wellesley, *Exec Srch*
Scott-Wayne Assoc., *Perm. Emp Agcy*
Selected Executives, *Exec Srch*
Spectra Prof'l Srch/Spectra Temps, *Perm. Emp Agcy*
Stone & Youngblood, *Exec Srch*
Sullivan Assoc., *Exec Srch*
T.F.S. Human Resource Solut'ns, *Exec Srch*
TAD Staff Svcs, *Temp. Agcy*
WIND Job Ctr, *Career/Outplacemnt*
Xavier Assoc., *Exec Srch*

Michigan

Accent on Achievement, *Exec Srch*
Accountnts Exec Srch/Accountnts On Call, *Exec Srch*
Accountnts One, *Perm. Emp Agcy*
Accountemps/Officeteam, *Temp. Agcy*
The Advantage Grp, *Exec Srch*
Automotive Careers, *Exec Srch*
Career Quest, *Perm. Emp Agcy*
Dickson Assoc., *Exec Srch*
ExecuQuest, *Exec Srch*
GRS, *Exec Srch*
Joseph Goldring & Assoc., *Exec Srch*
Robert Half Intl, *Exec Srch*
Healthcare Recrtrs Intl, *Exec Srch*
Harvey Hohauser & Assoc., *Exec Srch*
Mgmt. Recrtrs of Battle Creek, *Exec Srch*
Mgmt. Recrtrs of Grand Rapids, *Exec Srch*
Mgmt. Recrtrs of Livonia, *Exec Srch*
Mgmt. Recrtrs of Rochester, *Exec Srch*
Manpower Tech. Svcs, *Contract Svc*
Michigan Srch Plus, *Exec Srch*
C.A. Moore & Assoc., *Exec Srch*
Nationwide Career Netwrk, *Perm. Emp Agcy*
Office Staffing Recruitng, *Exec Srch*
Olsten Prof'l Accnt'g Svcs, *Temp. Agcy*
Preferred Emp. Planning, *Perm. Emp Agcy*
Professional Persnnl Consltnts Intl, *Exec Srch*
ProSearch, *Exec Srch*
Sales Executives, *Perm. Emp Agcy*
Source Svcs Corp, *Perm. Emp Agcy*
Sterling Field Assoc., *Exec Srch*
Trillium Staffng, *Temp. Agcy*
Unlimited Staff Solut'ns, *Contract Svc*
Wing Tips & Pumps, *Exec Srch*

Minnesota

Accountnts Exchange, *Exec Srch*
Accountnts Exec Srch/Accountnts On Call, *Exec Srch*
Accountnts Placemnt Registry, *Exec Srch*
Add On Staff Solut'ns, *Temp. Agcy*
Advance Persnnl Resrcs, *Exec Srch*
Archambault Grp, *Exec Srch*
Charles Dahl & Assoc., *Exec Srch*
Ells Persnnl Syst., *Exec Srch*
Employment Advisors, *Perm. Emp Agcy*
Financial Staff Recrtrs, *Perm. Emp Agcy*
Hayden & Assoc., *Exec Srch*
Hayden Srch Grp, *Exec Srch*
T.H. Hunter, *Exec Srch*
LaBree & Assoc., *Exec Srch*
Mgmt. Recrtrs-Minneapolis/Sales Consltnts, *Exec Srch*
Manpower Tech. Svcs, *Perm. Emp Agcy*
C.A. Moore & Assoc., *Exec Srch*
Thomas Moore, *Temp. Agcy*
North American Recrtrs, *Exec Srch*
Professional Alternatives, *Perm. Emp Agcy*
Sathe & Assoc. Exec Srch, *Exec Srch*
Staff It Persnnl Svcs, *Temp. Agcy*
Ultimate Srch Unlimtd/Temps Unlimtd, *Perm. Emp Agcy*
West Emp. Solut'ns, *Perm. Emp Agcy*
Whitney & Assoc., *Perm. Emp Agcy*

Mississippi

Andrus Assoc. dba Svc Specialists Ltd., *Perm. Emp Agcy*
Opportunities Unlimtd, *Perm. Emp Agcy*

Missouri

ABC Emp. Svc, *Perm. Emp Agcy*
Accountant Source Temps, *Temp. Agcy*
Accountnts Exec Srch/Accountnts On Call, *Exec Srch*
Accountemps, *Temp. Agcy*
Accounting Career Consltnts, *Exec Srch*
Advanced Careers of Kansas Cty, *Exec Srch*
L.P. Banning, *Perm. Emp Agcy*
Bottom Line Prof'l Svcs, *Contract Svc*
Burns Emp. Svc, *Exec Srch*
Business Persnnl Svcs, *Temp. Agcy*
Deck & Decker Emp. Svc, *Perm. Emp Agcy*
Decker Persnnl, *Perm. Emp Agcy*
Employer Advantage, *Exec Srch*
ExecuSearch, *Exec Srch*
Jackson Emp. Agcy, *Perm. Emp Agcy*
Mgmt. Recrtrs of Kansas Cty, *Exec Srch*
Mgmt. Recrtrs of Springfield, *Exec Srch*
Mgmt. Recrtrs of St. Louis, *Exec Srch*
Mgmt. Recrtrs of St. Louis, *Exec Srch*
Manpower Temp. Svcs, *Temp. Agcy*
National Physician Placemnt Svcs, *Exec Srch*
Officemates5 of St. Louis, *Exec Srch*
Pinnacle Exec Grp, *Exec Srch*
Search Prof'ls, *Exec Srch*
Snelling Persnnl Svcs, *Perm. Emp Agcy*
Source Svcs Corp, *Exec Srch*

Nebraska

Choice Enterprises, *Exec Srch*
Express Persnnl, *Exec Srch*
Hansen Agri-Placement, *Perm. Emp Agcy*
Outsource II, *Temp. Agcy*
Reliable Nat'l Persnnl Consltnts, *Exec Srch*
Sales Consltnts of Omaha, *Exec Srch*

Nevada

Talent Tree Staffng, *Perm. Emp Agcy*

New Hampshire

Able 1 Staffng, *Exec Srch*
Advanced Recruitng & Consltng, *Exec Srch*
Allstaff Contrct Svcs, *Perm. Emp Agcy*
Arc-Profiles, *Exec Srch*
Central New Hampshire Emp. Svcs, *Perm. Emp Agcy*
Cheshire Emp. Svc, *Temp. Agcy*
Mgmt. Recrtrs Intl of Bedford, *Exec Srch*
National Emp. Svc Corp, *Perm. Emp Agcy*
R.G.T. Assoc., *Exec Srch*
Sales Consltnts of Nashua-Manchester, *Exec Srch*
STAT Srch, *Exec Srch*
Surge Resrcs, *Contract Svc*
TAC Staff Svcs, *Temp. Agcy*

New Jersey

A+ Persnnl, *Perm. Emp Agcy*
A Prof'l Edge, *Career/Outplacemnt*
ABC Nationwide Employment, *Perm. Emp Agcy*
Abbott Assoc., *Exec Srch*
Accountnts Exec Srch/Accountnts On Call, *Exec Srch*
Advanced Persnnl, *Perm. Emp Agcy*
Raymond Alexander Assoc., *Perm. Emp Agcy*
Allen Assoc., *Perm. Emp Agcy*
Anderson Wright Assoc., *Exec Srch*
Andrew Persnnl Svcs, *Perm. Emp Agcy*
The Ascher Grp, *Exec Srch*
BAI Persnnl Solut'ns, *Exec Srch*
Balcor Assoc., *Exec Srch*
Blake & Assoc. Exec Srch, *Exec Srch*
Career Ctr, *Perm. Emp Agcy*
Career Mngmnt Intl, *Exec Srch*
Career Srch Assoc., *Exec Srch*
Careerworks, *Exec Srch*
Corporate One, *Exec Srch*
Dunhill Prof'l Srch, *Exec Srch*
Executive Netwrk, *Exec Srch*
Executive Srch, *Exec Srch*
Foster Assoc., *Exec Srch*
The Foster McKay Grp, *Exec Srch*
Gibson Martin Consltng, *Exec Srch*
Hreshko Consltng Grp, *Exec Srch*
Hughes & Podesla Persnnl, *Perm. Emp Agcy*
Impact Persnnl, *Perm. Emp Agcy*
Integro Staff Svcs, *Temp. Agcy*
Inter-Regional Exec Srch, *Exec Srch*
Kelly Svcs, *Temp. Agcy*
Joseph Keyes Assoc., *Perm. Emp Agcy*
MJE Recrtrs, *Exec Srch*
Mgmt. Recrtrs of Bridgewater, *Exec Srch*
Mgmt. Recrtrs of Passaic Cnty, *Exec Srch*
Mgmt. Recrtrs of Sparta, *Exec Srch*
Manpower Tech. Svcs, *Temp. Agcy*
Officemates5 of Englewood Cliffs/DayStar Temp. Svcs, *Perm. Emp Agcy*
Orion Consltng, *Exec Srch*
Park Avenue Persnnl, *Perm. Emp Agcy*
The Pennmore Grp, *Exec Srch*
Premier Persnnl Grp, *Perm. Emp Agcy*
Professional Roster, *Temp. Agcy*
Ready Persnnl/Ready Temps, *Perm. Emp Agcy*
Remedy Intelligent Staffng, *Temp. Agcy*
Jeff Rich Assoc., *Exec Srch*
Rylan Forbes Consltng Grp, *Exec Srch*
R.S. Sadow Assoc., *Exec Srch*
Sales Consltnts of Morris Cnty, *Exec Srch*
Sales Consltnts of Sparta, *Exec Srch*
Selective Persnnl, *Perm. Emp Agcy*
SkuppSearch, *Exec Srch*
Snelling Persnnl Svcs, *Temp. Agcy*
Snelling Persnnl Svcs, *Perm. Emp Agcy*
Source Svcs Corp, *Perm. Emp Agcy*
Source Svcs Corp, *Exec Srch*
Temporary Excellence, *Temp. Agcy*
Temps Plus, *Temp. Agcy*
Winston Staff Svcs, *Temp. Agcy*
Winters & Ross, *Perm. Emp Agcy*
Claire Wright Assn, *Perm. Emp Agcy*

New Mexico

Albuquerque Persnnl, *Perm. Emp Agcy*
CDI Corp, *Contract Svc*
Snelling Persnnl Svcs, *Exec Srch*

New York

AJC Srch, *Exec Srch*
Accountnts Exec Srch/Accountnts On Call, *Exec Srch*
Accounting & Computer Persnnl, *Perm. Emp Agcy*
Merrill Adams Assoc., *Career/Outplacemnt*
Adecco, *Temp. Agcy*
Adept Tech Recruitng, *Exec Srch*
Advice Persnnl, *Exec Srch*
Alite Assoc., *Exec Srch*
Franklin Allen Consltnts Exec. Srch Firm
Alpha Health Svcs Corp, *Exec Srch*
AMESgroup, *Perm. Emp Agcy*
Analytic Recruitng, *Perm. Emp Agcy*
Asher Persnnl Consltnts, *Perm. Emp Agcy*
Auto Careers, *Perm. Emp Agcy*
Bartl & Evins, *Exec Srch*
Benson Assoc., *Exec Srch*
Bevlin Persnnl, *Perm. Emp Agcy*
Branthover Assoc., *Exec Srch*
E.E. Brooke, *Perm. Emp Agcy*
Brookville Staff Svcs, *Perm. Emp Agcy*
CK Resrcs, *Exec Srch*
Career Blazers Persnnl, *Perm. Emp Agcy*
Career Concepts, *Perm. Emp Agcy*
Carlile Persnnl Agcy, *Perm. Emp Agcy*
Compu-Tech Persnnl Agcy, *Exec Srch*
Concorde Srch, *Perm. Emp Agcy*
Confidential Srch, *Exec Srch*
Consortium, *Exec Srch*
Conspectus, *Exec Srch*
The Cornell Grp, *Exec Srch*
Corporate Careers/R.J. Assoc., *Exec Srch*
Corporate Srch, *Exec Srch*
Crispi, Wagner & Co, *Exec Srch*
Cromwell Partners, *Exec Srch*
D&L Assoc., *Exec Srch*
Seth Diamond Assoc., *Exec Srch*
Drummond Assoc., *Exec Srch*
EDP Contrct Svcs, *Contract Svc*
Eden Persnnl, *Perm. Emp Agcy*
Employment Recrtrs Agcy, *Perm. Emp Agcy*
The Emp. Store/TES Technical, *Exec Srch*
Euromonde, *Temp. Agcy*
Executive Image, *Exec Srch*
Executive Resrcs Ltd., *Exec Srch*
Executive Srch Consltnts, *Exec Srch*
Fabian Assoc., *Exec Srch*
Fanning Persnnl, *Exec Srch*
Filcro Persnnl, *Perm. Emp Agcy*
First Choice Recrtrs, *Perm. Emp Agcy*
C.R. Fletcher Assoc., *Exec Srch*
Forray Assoc., *Exec Srch*
Forum Temp. Svcs, *Temp. Agcy*
Franklin Srch Resrcs, *Exec Srch*
Genesis Emp. Consltnts, *Exec Srch*
Gruen Resrcs, *Exec Srch*
H&H Temp. Svcs, *Temp. Agcy*
The Haas Assoc., *Exec Srch*
Robert Half Intl/Information Syst. Division, *Exec Srch*
Hart-Merrell Persnnl, *Exec Srch*
Headway Corporate Staff Svcs, *Temp. Agcy*
Hessel Assoc., *Exec Srch*
Hunter Mac & Assoc., *Perm. Emp Agcy*
Hunter Plcmnt, *Exec Srch*
Interspace Interactive, *Exec Srch*

Ivana Legal Svcs, *Exec Srch*
Just One Break, *Perm. Emp Agcy*
KLK Persnnl, *Perm. Emp Agcy*
KPA Grp, *Exec Srch*
Kingsbury Wax Bova, *Exec Srch*
Fred Koffler Assoc., *Exec Srch*
Kramer Exec Resrcs, *Exec Srch*
Ktech Syst. Grp, *Perm. Emp Agcy*
Lake Assoc., *Exec Srch*
Tina Lane Persnnl, *Perm. Emp Agcy*
Michael John Lawrence & Assoc., *Exec Srch*
M.B., *Exec Srch*
The MVP Grp, *Exec Srch*
Ivan Mack Assoc., *Exec Srch*
Magill Assoc., *Exec Srch*
Joseph Maloney & Assoc., *Perm. Emp Agcy*
Mgmt. Recrtrs of Nassau, *Exec Srch*
Mgmt. Recrtrs of Woodbury/ CompuSrch, *Exec Srch*
Manpower Temp. Svcs, *Temp. Agcy*
Marcus & Assoc., *Exec Srch*
Maxwell Grp, *Exec Srch*
McLaughlin Resrcs, *Exec Srch*
Milazzo Assoc., *Perm. Emp Agcy*
Morgan-Murray Persnnl/M&M Top Temps, *Temp. Agcy*
National Emp. Database, *Perm. Emp Agcy*
Neal Mgmt., *Exec Srch*
New York-New York Persnnl, *Perm. Emp Agcy*
Noah Assoc., *Perm. Emp Agcy*
Norrell Staff Svcs, *Perm. Emp Agcy*
K.A. Nowack Career Specialists, *Perm. Emp Agcy*
Olsten Staff Svcs, *Temp. Agcy*
Optimal Resrcs, *Exec Srch*
OTEC.COM, *Perm. Emp Agcy*
Parker Clark Exec Recrtmnt, *Exec Srch*
The Parks Grp, *Exec Srch*
Parsons, Anderson & Gee, *Perm. Emp Agcy*
Pathway Exec Srch, *Exec Srch*
Paywise, *Temp. Agcy*
Persnnl Consltng Assoc., *Exec Srch*
The Pinnacle Grp, *Exec Srch*
P.G. Prager Srch Assoc., *Exec Srch*
Pro Srch Assoc., *Exec Srch*
Quest Organization, *Exec Srch*
ROI Assoc., *Exec Srch*
Rand Thompson Consltnts, *Exec Srch*
Redstone Affiliates, *Exec Srch*
Rem Resrcs, *Perm. Emp Agcy*
Remedy Intelligent Staffng, *Temp. Agcy*
Response Staff Svcs/Career Advisors, *Exec Srch*
E.J. Rhodes Exec Srch, *Exec Srch*
Beth Richman Assoc., *Perm. Emp Agcy*
Fran Rogers Persnnl, *Perm. Emp Agcy*
Roth Young of Long Islnd, *Exec Srch*
S.W. Mgmt., *Exec Srch*
St. Lawrence Intl, *Exec Srch*
SearchAmerica, *Exec Srch*
Sigma Staffng, *Perm. Emp Agcy*
Snelling Persnnl Svcs, *Exec Srch*
Source Finance, *Exec Srch*
Source Svcs Corp, *Exec Srch*
Sporn Grp, *Exec Srch*
Staff Managers, *Temp. Agcy*
Staffing Svcs, *Exec Srch*
Stamm Persnnl Agcy, *Perm. Emp Agcy*
Superior Concepts, *Contract Svc*
Synergy Partners, *Exec Srch*
Hillary Taylor Persnnl, *Perm. Emp Agcy*
Tech Options, *Exec Srch*
Temp Force of NY, *Temp. Agcy*
Temporary Resource Ctr, *Temp. Agcy*
Phil Thomas Persnnl, *Exec Srch*
Traynor Confidential Exec. Srch Firm
Tyler Srch Consltnts, *Perm. Emp Agcy*
Vance Persnnl, *Perm. Emp Agcy*
Vantage Staff Svcs, *Temp. Agcy*
Venture Resrcs, *Exec Srch*
Charles Wanner Assoc. Exec. Srch Firm
Werbin Assoc. Exec Srch, *Exec Srch*
Westchester Emp. Agcy, *Perm. Emp Agcy*
Western Staff Svcs, *Temp. Agcy*
Winston Resrcs, *Exec Srch*
S.R. Wolman Assoc., *Exec Srch*

North Carolina

A-1 Staffing & Persnnl, *Perm. Emp Agcy*
Accountnts Exec Srch/Accountnts On Call, *Exec Srch*
Amcell Assoc., *Exec Srch*
AmeriPro Srch, *Exec Srch*
Andrews & Assoc., *Exec Srch*
Christopher Grp, *Exec Srch*
COMFORCE Tech. Svcs, *Contract Svc*
Elin Var, *Exec Srch*
Employment Consltnts, *Contract Svc*
Executive Recrtmnt Specialists, *Exec Srch*
Five Star Staffng, *Temp. Agcy*
FORTUNE Persnnl Consltnts of Raleigh, *Perm. Emp Agcy*
Greer Persnnl, *Perm. Emp Agcy*
Robert Half Intl, *Exec Srch*
Jobs of Fayetteville, *Perm. Emp Agcy*
Kelly Svcs, *Temp. Agcy*
Key Temps, *Temp. Agcy*
MTS, *Perm. Emp Agcy*
Mgmt. Recrtrs Intl, *Exec Srch*
Manpower, *Temp. Agcy*
McCain Emp. Agcy, *Temp. Agcy*
Olsten Staff Svcs, *Temp. Agcy*
The Perkin Grp, *Exec Srch*
Pro Staff Accnt'g Svcs, *Perm. Emp Agcy*
Don Richard Assoc. of Charlotte, *Perm. Emp Agcy*
Source Svcs Corp, *Exec Srch*
Sparks Persnnl Svcs, *Exec Srch*
Youngblood Staffng, *Perm. Emp Agcy*

North Dakota

Olsten Staff Svcs/Kramer & Assoc./Expressway Persnnl, *Temp. Agcy*
Persnnl Svcs, *Exec Srch*

Ohio

Accountnts Exec Srch/Accountnts On Call, *Exec Srch*
Accountnts Select, *Exec Srch*
Adecco, *Perm. Emp Agcy*
Automotive Persnnl, *Exec Srch*
N.L. Benke & Assoc., *Perm. Emp Agcy*
Bradley-Pierce Persnnl, *Perm. Emp Agcy*
J.B. Brown & Assoc., *Exec Srch*
Burks Grp, *Exec Srch*
CBS Persnnl Svcs, *Perm. Emp Agcy*
Champion Persnnl, *Perm. Emp Agcy*
Crown Temp. Svcs of Cincinnati, *Temp. Agcy*
Drayton & Assoc., *Exec Srch*
Eastern Persnnl Svcs, *Perm. Emp Agcy*
Executech Consltnts, *Exec Srch*
Executive Srch Ltd., *Exec Srch*
Flowers & Assoc./Associated Temps, *Exec Srch*
Graduate Consltnts, *Perm. Emp Agcy*
Russ Hadick & Assoc., *Exec Srch*
Hite Exec Srch/Hite Mngmnt Consltnts, *Exec Srch*
A.T. Kearney Exec Srch, *Exec Srch*
Kelly Svcs, *Temp. Agcy*
Lopresti & Assoc., *Exec Srch*
R.E. Lowe Assoc., *Perm. Emp Agcy*
Mgmt. Recrtrs of Cincinnati, *Exec Srch*
Mgmt. Recrtrs of Cleveland, *Exec Srch*
Mgmt. Recrtrs of Cleveland, *Exec Srch*
Mgmt. Recrtrs of Cleveland, *Exec Srch*
Mgmt. Recrtrs of Columbus, *Exec Srch*
Mgmt. Recrtrs of Dayton, *Exec Srch*
Mgmt. Recrtrs of Solon, *Exec Srch*
Marvel Consltnts, *Exec Srch*
Messina Mngmnt Syst., *Exec Srch*
Miami Prof'l Srch, *Exec Srch*
Minority Exec Srch, *Exec Srch*
O'Brien & Roof Co, *Exec Srch*
Olsten Financial Staffng, *Exec Srch*
Olsten Prof'l Staff Svcs, *Exec Srch*
Providence Persnnl Consltnts, *Exec Srch*
Sales Consltnts of Cincinnati, *Exec Srch*
Shafer Jones Assoc., *Exec Srch*
Snelling Persnnl Svcs, *Exec Srch*
Source Svcs Corp, *Exec Srch*
Tech/Aid of OH, *Perm. Emp Agcy*

Oklahoma

Ameri Resource, *Exec Srch*
BancSearch, *Exec Srch*
Robert Half Intl/Accountemps, *Exec Srch*
Key Temp. Persnnl, *Temp. Agcy*
Mgmt. Recrtrs of Oklahoma Cty, *Exec Srch*
Manpower Temp. Svcs, *Temp. Agcy*
Terry Neese Persnnl Agcy, *Exec Srch*
Lloyd Richards Persnnl, *Perm. Emp Agcy*
StaffMark, *Temp. Agcy*

Oregon

Able Temp. Svc, *Temp. Agcy*
Accountnts Exec Srch/Accountnts On Call, *Exec Srch*
Express Persnnl Svcs, *Exec Srch*
Robert Half Intl/Accountemps, *Exec Srch*
Source Svcs Corp, *Perm. Emp Agcy*
Southern Oregon Temporary, *Temp. Agcy*
Talent Tree Staffng, *Perm. Emp Agcy*
Woodworth Intl Grp, *Exec Srch*

Pennsylvania

Accountnts Exec Srch, *Exec Srch*
Accountnts On Call, *Temp. Agcy*
Acsys Resrcs, *Perm. Emp Agcy*
All Staffng, *Perm. Emp Agcy*
Allegheny Persnnl Svcs, *Temp. Agcy*
American Staffing Resrcs, *Temp. Agcy*
ASAP Staffng, *Perm. Emp Agcy*
Barton Persnnl Syst., *Exec Srch*
Basilone-Oliver Exec Srch, *Exec Srch*
Brackin & Sayers Assoc., *Exec Srch*
Career Concepts Staff Svcs, *Exec Srch*
Career Quest Confidential, *Exec Srch*
Joseph Conahan Exec Recrtrs, *Exec Srch*
COREStaff, *Temp. Agcy*
J. Croyle & Assoc., *Perm. Emp Agcy*
DiCenzo Persnnl Specialists, *Perm. Emp Agcy*
Dunhill Prof'l Srch, *Exec Srch*
Dunn Assoc., *Exec Srch*
EDP/Temps of PA, *Temp. Agcy*
Executive Avail-A-Search, *Exec Srch*
Financial Industry Staff Co, *Perm. Emp Agcy*
Financial Srch Grp, *Exec Srch*
Focus Persnnl Assoc., *Exec Srch*
Fox-Morris Assoc., *Exec Srch*
Robert Half Intl/Accountemps, *Exec Srch*
The Hastings Grp, *Exec Srch*
Hoskins Hains Assoc., *Perm. Emp Agcy*
Human Resource Solut'ns, *Exec Srch*
J-Rand Srch, *Exec Srch*
Nancy Jackson, *Exec Srch*
Jefferson-Ross Assoc., *Exec Srch*
Kathy Karr Persnnl, *Perm. Emp Agcy*
Keystaff, *Temp. Agcy*
Leafstone, *Temp. Agcy*
Mgmt. Recrtrs of DE Cnty/CompuSrch, *Exec Srch*
Mgmt. Recrtrs of Lehigh Vly/CompuSrch, *Exec Srch*
Mgmt. Recrtrs of Philadelphia/ CompuSrch, *Exec Srch*
Mark Joseph Assoc., *Perm. Emp Agcy*
The Morris Grp, *Exec Srch*
John Morrow & Assoc., *Exec Srch*
Olsten Staff Svcs, *Temp. Agcy*
LaMonte Owens, *Exec Srch*
Pancoast Temp. Svcs, *Temp. Agcy*
Penn Srch, *Exec Srch*
ProSearch, *Exec Srch*
Alan Raeburn Consltnts, *Exec Srch*
Rice Cohen Intl, *Exec Srch*
The Richards Grp, *Exec Srch*
Romac Intl, *Exec Srch*
Romac Intl, *Exec Srch*
S-H-S Intl, *Perm. Emp Agcy*
S-H-S Intl, *Exec Srch*
SHS Assoc., *Exec Srch*
Sanford Rose Assoc., *Exec Srch*
Snelling Persnnl Svcs, *Exec Srch*
Source Svcs Corp, *Exec Srch*
Strauss Persnnl, *Perm. Emp Agcy*
TAC Staff Svcs, *Temp. Agcy*
Terry Taylor & Assoc., *Exec Srch*
Uni Temp Temp. Svc, *Temp. Agcy*
Uniforce Temp. Svcs, *Temp. Agcy*

Rhode Island

Accounting Resrcs, *Exec Srch*
Colony Persnnl Assoc., *Perm. Emp Agcy*
Kelly Svcs, *Temp. Agcy*
Albert Lee & Assoc., *Exec Srch*
Norrell Svcs, *Temp. Agcy*
Storti Assoc., *Exec Srch*

South Carolina

Corporate Solut'ns, *Exec Srch*
Financial Srch Assoc., *Exec Srch*
FORTUNE Persnnl Consltnts of Columbia, *Exec Srch*
Miller & Assoc., *Exec Srch*
PRL & Assoc., *Perm. Emp Agcy*
Pindrum Staff Svc, *Temp. Agcy*
John Shell Assoc., *Exec Srch*
Snelling Persnnl Svcs, *Perm. Emp Agcy*
The Stroman Co, *Perm. Emp Agcy*

South Dakota

Careers Unlimtd, *Perm. Emp Agcy*

Tennessee

A-1 Staffing & Persnnl, *Temp. Agcy*
Accountnts On Call, *Temp. Agcy*
Accounting Solut'ns, *Temp. Agcy*
Anderson McIntyre Persnnl Svcs, *Exec Srch*
B.K. Barnes & Assoc., *Exec Srch*
FORTUNE Persnnl Consltnts, *Exec Srch*
Gateway Grp Persnnl, *Temp. Agcy*
Hester & Assoc., *Exec Srch*
Kelly Svcs, *Temp. Agcy*
Mgmt. Recrtrs of Chattanooga, *Exec Srch*
Mgmt. Recrtrs of Knoxville, *Exec Srch*
The Morgan Grp, *Exec Srch*
Norrell Svcs, *Temp. Agcy*
Rasmussen & Assoc., *Perm. Emp Agcy*
Sales Consltnts of Nashville, *Exec Srch*
Snelling Persnnl Svcs, *Exec Srch*
Staffing Solut'ns, *Perm. Emp Agcy*

Texas

Accountnts Exec Srch/Accountnts On Call, *Exec Srch*
Accounting Action Persnnl, *Perm. Emp Agcy*
Action Persnnl, *Temp. Agcy*
Add-A-Temp/Woodlands Exec Employment, *Temp. Agcy*
Agri-LC, *Exec Srch*
Audit Prof'ls Intl, *Exec Srch*
Marilyn Austin & Assoc., *Exec Srch*
Aware Affiliates Persnnl, *Perm. Emp Agcy*

Babich & Assoc., *Perm. Emp Agcy*
Baldwin & Co, *Exec Srch*
R. Gaines Baty Assoc., *Exec Srch*
Best/World Assoc., *Exec Srch*
Borrel Persnnl, *Exec Srch*
Brainpower Persnnl Agcy, *Perm. Emp Agcy*
Bridge Persnnl, *Exec Srch*
Brooklea & Assoc., *Exec Srch*
Bruco, *Perm. Emp Agcy*
Bullock Persnnl, *Perm. Emp Agcy*
Cherbonnier Grp, *Exec Srch*
Colvin Resrcs Grp, *Temp. Agcy*
Continental Persnnl, *Perm. Emp Agcy*
Dallas Emp. Svc, *Perm. Emp Agcy*
The Danbrook Grp, *Exec Srch*
Gail Darling Staffing/Darling's Prof'l Desk, *Temp. Agcy*
Denton-Lewis Assoc., *Exec Srch*
Dunhill Prof'l Srch, *Exec Srch*
Employee Sources, *Exec Srch*
Evins Persnnl Consltnts of Killeen, *Perm. Emp Agcy*
The Exec Consltng Grp, *Exec Srch*
Executive Srch Persnnl, *Exec Srch*
Express Persnnl Svcs, *Perm. Emp Agcy*
Feldt Persnnl, *Perm. Emp Agcy*
Financial Prof'ls, *Perm. Emp Agcy*
Gulco Intl Recruitng Svcs, *Perm. Emp Agcy*
Robert Half Intl, *Perm. Emp Agcy*
Hedman & Assoc., *Exec Srch*
Herndon & Assoc., *Exec Srch*
The Human Element of Business, *Exec Srch*
Imprimis Staff Solut'ns, *Temp. Agcy*
InterSearch Assoc., *Temp. Agcy*
Kelly Svcs, *Temp. Agcy*
George Lehman Assoc., *Exec Srch*
Lucas Financial Staffng, *Exec Srch*
The Lukens Grp, *Perm. Emp Agcy*
Lusk & Assoc. Persnnl, *Exec Srch*
Mgmt. Recrtrs Intl, *Exec Srch*
Mgmt. Recrtrs of Dallas, *Exec Srch*
McKinley•Arend Intl, *Exec Srch*
Metro Careers, *Exec Srch*
Odell & Assoc., *Exec Srch*
Olsten Staff Svcs, *Temp. Agcy*
P&P Persnnl, *Perm. Emp Agcy*
The Pailin Grp, *Exec Srch*
Pate Resrcs Grp, *Exec Srch*
Rick Peterson & Assoc., *Exec Srch*
Pro Staff Persnnl Svcs, *Temp. Agcy*
Professional Srch Consltnts, *Contract Svc*
Resource Recrtrs, *Perm. Emp Agcy*
Resource Staffng, *Contract Svc*
Bart Roberson & Co, *Exec Srch*
Romac Intl, *Exec Srch*
Roth Young Persnnl Svcs, *Exec Srch*
Sales Consltnts of Houston, *Exec Srch*
Salinas & Assoc. Persnnl, *Exec Srch*
David Schreiber & Assoc., *Exec Srch*
Source Svcs Corp, *Exec Srch*
Staff Extension, *Exec Srch*
TGA Co, *Exec Srch*
Betty Tanner Prof'l Emp. Svc, *Exec Srch*
Tarrant Cnty Emp. Netwrk, *Perm. Emp Agcy*
The Urban Placemnt Svc, *Exec Srch*
Dick Van Vliet & Assoc., *Exec Srch*
Vinson & Assoc., *Perm. Emp Agcy*
Wheeler, Moore & Elam Co, *Exec Srch*
The Whitaker Companies, *Exec Srch*

Utah

CDI Information Svcs, *Exec Srch*
Robert Half Intl, *Exec Srch*
Intermountain Staffing Resrcs, *Temp. Agcy*
Mgmt. Recrtrs Intl, *Exec Srch*
Mgmt. Recrtrs of Provo, *Exec Srch*
Source Svcs Corp, *Exec Srch*
Trout & Assoc., *Exec Srch*

Vermont

Mgmt. Recrtrs of Burlington, *Exec Srch*
Candis Perrault Assoc., *Exec Srch*
Persnnl Dept, *Temp. Agcy*
Voll Assoc., *Exec Srch*

Virginia

Ability Resrcs, *Exec Srch*
Accountnts Exec Srch/Accountnts On Call, *Exec Srch*
Accountnts On Call, *Temp. Agcy*
Alpha Omega Resrcs, *Perm. Emp Agcy*
Contec Srch, *Exec Srch*
Corporate Connection Exec. Srch Firm
Dow Persnnl, *Perm. Emp Agcy*
Durill & Assoc., *Exec Srch*
EDP, *Temp. Agcy*
Effective Staffng, *Exec Srch*
FORTUNE Persnnl Consltnts, *Exec Srch*
Haslowe Persnnl, *Exec Srch*
Leafstone, *Temp. Agcy*
Lee Staffing Resrcs, *Exec Srch*
Mgmt. Recrtrs Intl, *Exec Srch*
Mgmt. Recrtrs of McLean, *Exec Srch*
Mgmt. Recrtrs of Roanoke, *Exec Srch*
Carol McNew Emp. Svc, *Perm. Emp Agcy*
National Recrtrs, *Perm. Emp Agcy*
Network Companies, *Exec Srch*
Norrell Staff Svcs, *Exec Srch*
OfficeTeam, *Perm. Emp Agcy*
Placement Prof'ls, *Exec Srch*
Professional Srch Persnnl, *Exec Srch*
Don Richard Assoc., *Exec Srch*
Snelling Persnnl Svcs, *Perm. Emp Agcy*
Source Svcs Corp, *Exec Srch*
TAC Staff Svcs, *Temp. Agcy*
The Talley Grp, *Exec Srch*
TempWorld Staff Svcs, *Temp. Agcy*

Washington

Able Persnnl Agcy, *Perm. Emp Agcy*
Accounting Partners, *Exec Srch*
Castle Hill Assoc., *Exec Srch*
Guidance Svcs, *Temp. Agcy*
Houser, Martin, Morris & Assoc., *Exec Srch*
Kelly Svcs, *Temp. Agcy*
Lawrence & Assoc., *Exec Srch*
Mgmt. Recrtrs Intl, *Exec Srch*
Mgmt. Recrtrs of Mercer Islnd, *Exec Srch*
Mgmt. Recrtrs of Tacoma, *Exec Srch*
John Mason & Assoc., *Exec Srch*
Morgan Palmer Morgan & Hill, *Exec Srch*
Persnnl Unlimtd, *Exec Srch*
Barbara Ruhl & Assoc., *Exec Srch*
Search West, *Exec Srch*
Snelling Persnnl Svcs, *Exec Srch*
Source Svcs Corp, *Exec Srch*
Thomas Co, *Perm. Emp Agcy*
Two 56, *Contract Svc*

West Virginia

Extra Support Staffng, *Temp. Agcy*
Key Persnnl, *Perm. Emp Agcy*

Wisconsin

Allen, Wayne, & Co, *Perm. Emp Agcy*
Career Resrcs, *Exec Srch*
Careertrac Emp. Svc, *Exec Srch*
Crown Svcs, *Temp. Agcy*
Dieck, Mueller & Assoc., *Exec Srch*
J.M. Eagle Partners, *Exec Srch*
Executive Resource, *Exec Srch*
The Exutec Grp, *Exec Srch*
Financial Mngmnt Persnnl, *Exec Srch*
Flores Financial Svcs, *Exec Srch*
Mgmt. Recrtrs of Appleton/ CompuSrch, *Exec Srch*
Mgmt. Recrtrs of Green Bay, *Exec Srch*
Mgmt. Recrtrs of Milwaukee/Sales Consltnts, *Exec Srch*
Mgmt. Recrtrs of Milwaukee, *Exec Srch*
David Neil & Assoc., *Exec Srch*
Olsten Staff Svcs, *Temp. Agcy*
Placements of Racine, *Perm. Emp Agcy*
SEEK, *Perm. Emp Agcy*
Source Svcs Corp, *Exec Srch*

Wyoming

Olsten Staff Svcs, *Temp. Agcy*

FOOD

Alabama

A-1 Emp. Svc, *Perm. Emp Agcy*
Labor Finders, *Temp. Agcy*
Mgmt. Recrtrs Intl, *Exec Srch*
WorkForce, *Temp. Agcy*

Arizona

Executemps, *Exec Srch*
Mgmt. Recrtrs of Scottsdale, *Exec Srch*
Personalized Mngmnt Assoc., *Exec Srch*
Professional Exec Research Consltng, *Exec Srch*
WSA Assoc., *Exec Srch*
Weinman & Assoc., *Exec Srch*

Arkansas

Dunhill Persnnl, *Exec Srch*
Mgmt. Recrtrs of Little Rock, *Exec Srch*

California

ABA Staffng, *Exec Srch*
AWS, *Exec Srch*
Alpha-Net Consltng Grp, *Exec Srch*
Apple One Emp. Svcs, *Perm. Emp Agcy*
Ballantyne Assoc., *Exec Srch*
Biosource Tech. Svc, *Contract Svc*
The Black Leopard, *Exec Srch*
Bristol Assoc., *Exec Srch*
California Srch Agcy, *Exec Srch*
Candy Stripers Medical Persnnl, *Perm. Emp Agcy*
Career Advantage, *Exec Srch*
Coast To Coast Exec Srch, *Exec Srch*
Collier-Young Agcy, *Temp. Agcy*
Consultant Svcs, *Exec Srch*
Marlene Critchfield Co, *Perm. Emp Agcy*
Crossroads Staff Svc, *Temp. Agcy*
Culver Persnnl Svcs, *Perm. Emp Agcy*
Culver Staffing Resrcs, *Exec Srch*
Dunhill Prof'l Srch of Oakland, *Exec Srch*
Employment Devlpmnt Dept, *Perm. Emp Agcy*
Employment Svc Agcy, *Perm. Emp Agcy*
Ethos Consltng, *Exec Srch*
Finesse Persnnl Assoc., *Exec Srch*
Fisher Persnnl Mngmnt Svcs, *Exec Srch*
40 Plus of So. CA, *Exec Srch*
Fresquez & Assoc., *Exec Srch*
Garnett Emp. Svcs, *Temp. Agcy*
Gorelick & Assoc., *Exec Srch*
Griffith & Assoc., *Exec Srch*
Hill & Assoc., *Exec Srch*
Hollander Horizon Intl, *Exec Srch*
Interim Industrial Staffng, *Temp. Agcy*
Interim Persnnl, *Temp. Agcy*
Kelly Scientific Resrcs, *Temp. Agcy*
Kelly Svcs, *Temp. Agcy*
John Kurosky & Assoc., *Exec Srch*
Lab Support, *Temp. Agcy*
Labor World, *Temp. Agcy*
Malibu Grp, *Exec Srch*
Mgmt. Recrtrs of Burlingame/Sales Consltnts, *Exec Srch*
Mgmt. Recrtrs of Clovis, *Exec Srch*
Mgmt. Recrtrs of Encino, *Exec Srch*
Mgmt. Recrtrs of Laguna Hills, *Exec Srch*
Mgmt. Recrtrs-Oakland/Sales Consltnts, *Exec Srch*
Mgmt. Recrtrs of Pleasanton, *Exec Srch*
Mgmt. Srch Intl, *Exec Srch*
Maverick Staff Svc, *Perm. Emp Agcy*
Mesa Intl, *Exec Srch*
Mixtec Grp, *Exec Srch*
M.O.R.E. Emp. Svcs, *Perm. Emp Agcy*
Musick & Assoc., *Exec Srch*
National Hospitality Recrtrs, *Exec Srch*
Nesco Svc Co, *Perm. Emp Agcy*
Pacific Srch Grp, *Exec Srch*
Professional Srch Assoc., *Exec Srch*
Resource Perspectives, *Exec Srch*
Riley-Cole Recrtmnt Specialists, *Exec Srch*
Risher Assoc., *Exec Srch*
Royal Staff Svcs, *Exec Srch*
Sales Consltnts of Modesto, *Exec Srch*
Avery Schlueter Exec Srch, *Exec Srch*
Search West, *Exec Srch*
Steinbrun, Hughes & Assoc., *Exec Srch*
Thor Temp. Svcs, *Temp. Agcy*
Triple-J Svcs, *Exec Srch*
Unisearch, *Exec Srch*
United Staff Solut'ns, *Exec Srch*
Your People Prof'ls, *Perm. Emp Agcy*

Colorado

Chuck's Contrct Labor Svc, *Contract Svc*
Dunhill Persnnl of Boulder, *Exec Srch*
Eleventh Hour Staff Svcs, *Perm. Emp Agcy*
Executives By Sterling, *Exec Srch*
40 Plus of CO, *Career/Outplacemnt*
Hallmark Persnnl Syst., *Exec Srch*
JobSearch, *Temp. Agcy*
Kelly Scientific Resrcs, *Temp. Agcy*
Mgmt. Recrtrs of Colorado Springs, *Exec Srch*
National Affirmative Action Career Netwrk, *Exec Srch*
SOS Staff Svcs, *Temp. Agcy*
Sales Consltnts, *Exec Srch*
TPM Staff Svc, *Temp. Agcy*
Woodmoor Grp, *Exec Srch*
The Woodstone Consltng Co, *Exec Srch*

Connecticut

Admiral Staff Svcs, *Temp. Agcy*
Diversity Recruitng Svcs, *Exec Srch*
Employment Opport., *Perm. Emp Agcy*
Harris Heery & Assoc., *Exec Srch*
Lab Support, *Temp. Agcy*
Mgmt. Recrtrs Intl, *Exec Srch*
Office Svcs of CT, *Perm. Emp Agcy*
Barry Persky & Co., *Exec Srch*
Quality Control Recrtrs, *Exec Srch*
Bob Wright Recruitng, *Exec Srch*
Yankee Hospitality Srch, *Exec Srch*

Delaware

Independent Nat'l Srch & Assoc., *Exec Srch*
The Placers, *Temp. Agcy*

Florida

AAA Employment, *Perm. Emp Agcy*
American Exec Srch, *Exec Srch*
B&B Persnnl, *Perm. Emp Agcy*
Belmont Training & Employment, *Perm. Emp Agcy*
Bryan & Assoc./Worknet, Etc., *Exec Srch*
Career Choice, *Exec Srch*
Five Star Temporary, *Temp. Agcy*
Future Force Persnnl, *Temp. Agcy*

Janus Career Svc, *Perm. Emp Agcy*
The Mac Grp, *Exec Srch*
Mgmt. Recrtrs of Lake Cnty, *Exec Srch*
Mgmt. Recrtrs of St. Petersburg, *Exec Srch*
Mgmt. Recrtrs of Tallahassee, *Exec Srch*
Mgmt. Recrtrs of Tampa, *Exec Srch*
McGuire Exec Srch, *Exec Srch*
Profes. Staffing/Able Body Temp. Svcs, *Contract Svc*
Roth Young of Tampa, *Exec Srch*
Sales Consltnts of Fort Lauderdale, *Exec Srch*
Sales Consltnts of Jacksonville, *Exec Srch*
Shaver Emp. Agcy, *Perm. Emp Agcy*
Staffing Svcs Grp, *Perm. Emp Agcy*
The Stewart Srch Grp, *Exec Srch*

Georgia

AAA Employment, *Perm. Emp Agcy*
Charles Bernard & Assoc., *Exec Srch*
Boreham Intl, *Exec Srch*
DSA (Dixie Srch Assoc.), *Exec Srch*
Dunhill Prof'l Srch, *Exec Srch*
Express Persnnl Svcs, *Exec Srch*
FORTUNE Persnnl Consltnts of Atlanta, *Exec Srch*
Kelly Scientific Resrcs, *Temp. Agcy*
Kenzer Corp of GA, *Exec Srch*
Mgmt. Recrtrs of Atlanta, *Exec Srch*
Mgmt. Recrtrs of Atlanta, *Exec Srch*
National Restaurant Srch, *Exec Srch*
Jim Nixon & Assoc., *Exec Srch*
Oliver Srch, *Exec Srch*
Peachtree Mngmnt & Consltng, *Temp. Agcy*
Personalized Mngmnt Assoc., *Exec Srch*
RIF (Resrcs in Food), *Exec Srch*
Ranger Svcs, *Temp. Agcy*
P.J. Reda & Assoc., *Exec Srch*
Whittaker & Assoc., *Exec Srch*

Hawaii

Dunhill Prof'l Srch of Hawaii, *Exec Srch*
Ellis & Assoc., *Exec Srch*
Olsten Staff Svcs, *Temp. Agcy*

Idaho

Horne/Brown Intl, *Exec Srch*
Mgmt. Recrtrs of Boise, *Exec Srch*
Ward-Hoffman & Assoc., *Exec Srch*

Illinois

A.B.A. Placemnts/A.B.A. Temps, *Perm. Emp Agcy*
American Contrct Svcs, *Contract Svc*
American Tech. Srch, *Exec Srch*
B-W & Assoc., *Perm. Emp Agcy*
Burling Grp Ltd., *Exec Srch*
Busch Emp. Agcy, *Perm. Emp Agcy*
Cook Assoc., *Exec Srch*
Corporate Environment, *Exec Srch*
Diener & Assoc., *Exec Srch*
Evergreene Partners, *Exec Srch*
Executive Referral Svcs, *Exec Srch*
Fellows Plcmnt, *Temp. Agcy*
Hanover Crown & Assoc., *Exec Srch*
Human Resource Technlgy, *Exec Srch*
Irwin & Wagner, *Exec Srch*
Kenzer Corp, *Exec Srch*
Kunzer Assoc., *Exec Srch*
Lynco Mngmnt Persnnl, *Exec Srch*
Mgmt. Recrtrs of Albion, *Exec Srch*
Mgmt. Recrtrs of Arlington Heights, *Exec Srch*
Mgmt. Recrtrs of Des Plaines, *Exec Srch*
Mgmt. Recrtrs of Mattoon, *Exec Srch*
Mgmt. Recrtrs of Rockford, *Exec Srch*
Manufacturing Resrcs, *Exec Srch*
Marsteller Wilcox Assoc., *Exec Srch*
Michael David Assoc., *Perm. Emp Agcy*
The Murphy Grp, *Perm. Emp Agcy*
National Srch, *Exec Srch*
Officemates5 of Wheeling, *Exec Srch*
ProSearch Plus, *Exec Srch*
Remedy Intelligent Staffng, *Temp. Agcy*
Ritt-Ritt & Assoc., *Exec Srch*
Sales Consltnts/Mgmt. Recrtrs Intl, *Exec Srch*
Sales Consltnts of Oak Brk, *Exec Srch*
Search Enterprises, *Exec Srch*
Ralph Smith & Assoc., *Exec Srch*
Smith Hanley Assoc., *Exec Srch*
Snelling Persnnl Svcs, *Temp. Agcy*
Strategic Resrcs Unlimtd, *Exec Srch*
Technical Srch, *Exec Srch*
Temporary Assoc., *Temp. Agcy*
VG & Assoc., *Perm. Emp Agcy*
Valentine & Assoc., *Exec Srch*
Michael Wayne Recrtrs, *Exec Srch*
Web/Pack Tech, *Perm. Emp Agcy*
World Emp. Svc, *Perm. Emp Agcy*
Xagas & Assoc., *Exec Srch*

Indiana

AccuStaff, *Temp. Agcy*
Career Consltnts, *Perm. Emp Agcy*
Execusearch, *Exec Srch*
Life Emp. Svc, *Perm. Emp Agcy*
Mgmt. Recrtrs of Evansville, *Exec Srch*
Mgmt. Recrtrs of Indianapolis, *Exec Srch*
Mgmt. Recrtrs of Richmond/Staff Solut'ns, *Exec Srch*
National Corporate Consltnts/Advantage Svcs, *Exec Srch*
Officemates5 of Indianapolis, *Exec Srch*
Quality Srch, *Perm. Emp Agcy*
Unique, *Exec Srch*

Iowa

Blanchard Svcs, *Temp. Agcy*
Executive Srch Assoc., *Exec Srch*
Helping Hands Temp. Svc, *Temp. Agcy*
Mgmt. Recrtrs/CompuSrch, *Exec Srch*
Persnnl, *Exec Srch*
Pratt-Younglove, *Perm. Emp Agcy*

Kansas

David Baehr & Assoc., *Exec Srch*
Business Specialists, *Perm. Emp Agcy*
Eleventh Hour Staff Svcs, *Temp. Agcy*
Mgmt. Recrtrs of Overlnd Prk, *Exec Srch*
Network of Excellence, *Exec Srch*
Smith Brown & Jones, *Exec Srch*
Stoneburner Assoc., *Exec Srch*
Temtech, *Contract Svc*

Kentucky

Angel Grp Intl, *Exec Srch*
Belcan Staff Svcs, *Perm. Emp Agcy*
C.M. Mngmnt Svcs, *Perm. Emp Agcy*
Engineering & Exec Srch, *Exec Srch*
Precision Staffng, *Perm. Emp Agcy*

Louisiana

Mgmt. Recrtrs-Baton Rouge/Sales Consltnts, *Exec Srch*
Mgmt. Recrtrs-Metairie/Sales Consltnts, *Exec Srch*
Talley & Assoc./Talley Temps, *Exec Srch*
Technical Resource Staff Svcs, *Temp. Agcy*
Western Staff Svcs, *Temp. Agcy*

Maine

At Work Persnnl, *Temp. Agcy*
The Porter Hamel Grp, *Exec Srch*

Maryland

Futures, *Exec Srch*
L.S. Gross & Assoc., *Exec Srch*
Interim Persnnl, *Temp. Agcy*
Kelly Scientific Resrcs, *Temp. Agcy*
Mgmt. Recrtrs of Annapolis, *Exec Srch*
Mgmt. Recrtrs-Baltimore/Sales Consltnts, *Exec Srch*
Mgmt. Recrtrs-Bethesda/CompuSearch, *Exec Srch*
Mgmt. Recrtrs of Frederick, *Exec Srch*
Sales Consltnts of Baltimore Cty, *Exec Srch*
Sales Consltnts of Prince Georges Cnty, *Exec Srch*
Sanford Rose Assoc., *Exec Srch*
TAD Staff Svcs, *Temp. Agcy*

Massachusetts

Beacon Srch Prof'ls, *Exec Srch*
Computer Security Plcmnt, *Exec Srch*
Cyr Assoc., *Exec Srch*
Futures, *Exec Srch*
H.R.I. Svcs, *Exec Srch*
Hospitality Exec Srch, *Exec Srch*
Lab Support, *Temp. Agcy*
Mgmt. Recrtrs Intl of Braintree, *Exec Srch*
Mgmt. Recrtrs Intl of Springfield, *Exec Srch*
Mgmt. Recrtrs Intl of Westboro, *Exec Srch*
Manpower Temp. Svcs, *Temp. Agcy*
New England Job Plcmnt, *Perm. Emp Agcy*
Recruiting Specialists, *Exec Srch*
Sales Consltnts of Cape Cod, *Exec Srch*
Sales Consltnts of Plymouth Cnty, *Exec Srch*
Sales Consltnts of Wellesley, *Exec Srch*
Stone & Youngblood, *Exec Srch*
TAD Staff Svcs, *Temp. Agcy*
United Prof'l Plcmnt, *Exec Srch*
The Work Place, *Career/Outplacemnt*

Michigan

Barman Staff Solut'ns/Barman Persnnl, *Perm. Emp Agcy*
Benford Assoc., *Exec Srch*
Corporate Bus. Svcs Exec. Srch Firm
Express Persnnl Svcs, *Temp. Agcy*
Harper Assoc., *Exec Srch*
William Howard Agcy, *Perm. Emp Agcy*
Kelly Scientific Resrcs, *Temp. Agcy*
Mgmt. Recrtrs of Bingham Farms, *Exec Srch*
Mgmt. Recrtrs of Dearborn, *Exec Srch*
Mgmt. Recrtrs of Flint, *Exec Srch*
Mgmt. Recrtrs of Kalamazoo, *Exec Srch*
Mgmt. Recrtrs of Lansing, *Exec Srch*
Mgmt. Recrtrs of Muskegon, *Exec Srch*
Preferred Emp. Planning, *Perm. Emp Agcy*
Roth Young Persnnl Svcs of Detroit, *Exec Srch*
Sales Consltnts of Detroit, *Exec Srch*
Trillium Staffng, *Temp. Agcy*

Minnesota

Agri-Business Svcs, *Exec Srch*
Answer Persnnl, *Temp. Agcy*
Bradley & Assoc., *Exec Srch*
EHS & Assoc., *Exec Srch*
Focus Exec Srch, *Exec Srch*
HR Svcs of Plymouth, *Exec Srch*
T.H. Hunter, *Exec Srch*
Kelly Scientific Resrcs, *Temp. Agcy*
Mgmt. Recrtrs-Minneapolis/Sales Consltnts, *Exec Srch*
Metro Hospitality Consltnts, *Exec Srch*
Resource Srch, *Exec Srch*
Roth Young Exec Recrtrs, *Exec Srch*
Sathe & Assoc. Exec Srch, *Exec Srch*
Technical Resrcs, *Perm. Emp Agcy*
Total Srch, *Exec Srch*
Ultimate Srch Unlimtd/Temps Unlimtd, *Perm. Emp Agcy*
West Emp. Solut'ns, *Perm. Emp Agcy*

Mississippi

Coats & Coats Persnnl, *Perm. Emp Agcy*
EPSCO Persnnl, *Temp. Agcy*
Mgmt. Recrtrs of Jackson, *Exec Srch*

Missouri

Agri-Tech Persnnl, *Exec Srch*
Jay Alexandr & Assoc. dba Kirdonn Grp, *Perm. Emp Agcy*
L.P. Banning, *Perm. Emp Agcy*
Ken Brown & Co, *Exec Srch*
Burns Emp. Svc, *Exec Srch*
Business Persnnl Svcs, *Temp. Agcy*
The Christiansen Grp, *Exec Srch*
Debbon Recruitng Grp, *Exec Srch*
Deck & Decker Emp. Svc, *Perm. Emp Agcy*
Decker Persnnl, *Perm. Emp Agcy*
Annie Gray Assoc., *Exec Srch*
JRL Exec Recrtrs, *Exec Srch*
Jackson Emp. Agcy, *Perm. Emp Agcy*
JoDoc Enterprises, *Temp. Agcy*
Kelly Scientific Resrcs, *Temp. Agcy*
Mgmt. Recrtrs of Kansas Cty, *Exec Srch*
Mgmt. Recrtrs of Springfield, *Exec Srch*
Mgmt. Recrtrs of St. Louis, *Exec Srch*
Mgmt. Recrtrs of St. Louis, *Exec Srch*
J. Miles Persnnl Svcs, *Exec Srch*
Officemates5 of St. Louis, *Exec Srch*
Snelling Persnnl Svcs, *Perm. Emp Agcy*
Toberson Grp, *Perm. Emp Agcy*
Western Tech. Svcs, *Contract Svc*

Nebraska

Compusearch of Lincoln, *Exec Srch*
Corporate Recrtrs, *Exec Srch*
Express Persnnl, *Exec Srch*
Hansen Agri-Placement, *Perm. Emp Agcy*
Mgmt. Recrtrs of Omaha/Officemates5, *Exec Srch*

Nevada

Labor Finders, *Temp. Agcy*

New Hampshire

Allstaff Contrct Svcs, *Perm. Emp Agcy*
Barclay Persnnl Syst., *Exec Srch*
Mgmt. Recrtrs Intl of Bedford, *Exec Srch*
Manpower Temp. Svcs, *Temp. Agcy*
National Emp. Svc Corp, *Perm. Emp Agcy*
Pelham Prof'l Grp, *Temp. Agcy*
Sales Consltnts, *Exec Srch*

New Jersey

Advance Positions, *Exec Srch*
Advanced Persnnl, *Perm. Emp Agcy*
David Allen Assoc., *Exec Srch*
Blake & Assoc. Exec Srch, *Exec Srch*
CPS Tech. Placemnts, *Perm. Emp Agcy*
Career Srch Assoc., *Exec Srch*
Corporate One, *Exec Srch*
Data Prof'ls Unlimtd, *Exec Srch*
M.T. Donaldson Assoc., *Exec Srch*
FORTUNE Persnnl Consltnts of Menlo Prk, *Exec Srch*
Lawrence Glaser Assoc., *Exec Srch*
Hunt, Ltd., *Perm. Emp Agcy*
Impact Persnnl, *Perm. Emp Agcy*
Insearch, *Exec Srch*
J.M. Joseph Assoc., *Exec Srch*
Joule Industrial Contractors, *Contract Svc*
The Keller Grp/Careers, *Exec Srch*
Kelly Scientific Resrcs, *Temp. Agcy*
Lab Support, *Temp. Agcy*
Mgmt. Catalysts, *Exec Srch*
Mgmt. Recrtrs of Medford, *Exec Srch*
Mgmt. Recrtrs of Orange Cnty, *Exec Srch*
Mgmt. Recrtrs of Passaic Cnty, *Exec Srch*
Middlebrook Assoc., *Exec Srch*
Orion Consltng, *Exec Srch*
Pomerantz Persnnl, *Perm. Emp Agcy*

Sales Consltnts, *Exec Srch*
Sales Consltnts of Morris Cnty, *Exec Srch*
Sales Consltnts of Sparta, *Exec Srch*
Snelling Persnnl Svcs, *Perm. Emp Agcy*
Summit Grp, *Exec Srch*
Zwicker Assoc., *Exec Srch*

New Mexico
Albuquerque Persnnl, *Perm. Emp Agcy*
Scientemps, *Temp. Agcy*

New York
AARP Foundation Senior Community Svc/Employment Program, *Perm. Emp Agcy*
Accounting & Computer Persnnl, *Perm. Emp Agcy*
Merrill Adams Assoc., *Career/Outplacemnt*
Adecco, *Temp. Agcy*
Alfus Grp, *Exec Srch*
Franklin Allen Consltnts Exec. Srch Firm
Beishline Exec Srch, *Exec Srch*
Bornholdt Shivas & Friends, *Exec Srch*
Corporate Careers/R.J. Assoc., *Exec Srch*
Eden Persnnl, *Perm. Emp Agcy*
Elliot Assoc., *Exec Srch*
Fabian Assoc., *Exec Srch*
Hospitality Assoc., *Exec Srch*
Just One Break, *Perm. Emp Agcy*
The Kay Grp of Fifth Avenue, *Exec Srch*
Lab Support, *Temp. Agcy*
Michael John Lawrence & Assoc., *Exec Srch*
The Lloyd Co, *Career/Outplacemnt*
Mgmt. Recrtrs of Woodbury/ CompuSrch, *Exec Srch*
Marshall-Alan Assoc., *Exec Srch*
Metro Persnnl/Metro Nursing Svcs, *Exec Srch*
Mickler Assoc., *Exec Srch*
Morgan-Murray Persnnl/M&M Top Temps, *Temp. Agcy*
Parsons, Anderson & Gee, *Perm. Emp Agcy*
Phoenix Emp. Agcy, *Perm. Emp Agcy*
Remedy Intelligent Staffng, *Temp. Agcy*
Roth Young of Long Islnd, *Exec Srch*
Sales Consltnts of Westchester, *Exec Srch*
Stafkings Persnnl Syst., *Temp. Agcy*
Superior Concepts, *Contract Svc*
Trebor, Weldon, Lawrence, Levine, *Exec Srch*
Weber Mngmnt Consltnts, *Exec Srch*
Western Staff Svcs, *Temp. Agcy*

North Carolina
A-1 Staffing & Persnnl, *Perm. Emp Agcy*
Employment Consltnts, *Contract Svc*
Forbes Temp. Staffng, *Temp. Agcy*
FORTUNE Persnnl Consltnts of Raleigh, *Perm. Emp Agcy*
Jobs of Fayetteville, *Perm. Emp Agcy*
Linden Grp, *Exec Srch*
MTS, *Perm. Emp Agcy*
Mgmt. Recrtrs Intl, *Exec Srch*
Mgmt. Recrtrs of Durham, *Exec Srch*
Mgmt. Recrtrs of Kinston, *Exec Srch*
Mgmt. Recrtrs of Raleigh/Inter Exec, *Exec Srch*
Mgmt. Recrtrs of Winston-Salem, *Exec Srch*
Mebane Temp. Svcs, *Temp. Agcy*
Sales Consltnts of High Point, *Exec Srch*
Snelling Srch, *Exec Srch*
Waddy Thomson Assoc., *Exec Srch*
Winston Temp. Staffng, *Temp. Agcy*

North Dakota
Olsten Staff Svcs/Kramer & Assoc./Expressway Persnnl, *Temp. Agcy*

Ohio
Adecco, *Temp. Agcy*
Choice Persnnl/LaGrange & Assoc., *Exec Srch*
Continental Srch Consltnts, *Exec Srch*
J.D. Cotter Srch, *Exec Srch*
Alan Daum & Assoc., *Perm. Emp Agcy*
Delta Design Drafting, *Temp. Agcy*
Eastern Persnnl Svcs, *Perm. Emp Agcy*
Executech Consltnts, *Exec Srch*
Executive Connection, *Exec Srch*
FORTUNE Persnnl Consltnts, *Exec Srch*
Graduate Consltnts, *Perm. Emp Agcy*
Griffiths & Assoc., *Exec Srch*
H.J.C., *Exec Srch*
Ives & Assoc., *Exec Srch*
Laine's S.M.G., *Perm. Emp Agcy*
Mgmt. Recrtrs of Cincinnati, *Exec Srch*
Mgmt. Recrtrs of Cleveland, *Exec Srch*
Mgmt. Recrtrs of Cleveland, *Exec Srch*
Mgmt. Recrtrs of Cleveland, *Exec Srch*
Mgmt. Recrtrs of Columbus, *Exec Srch*
Mgmt. Recrtrs of Dayton, *Exec Srch*
Mgmt. Recrtrs of Solon, *Exec Srch*
North American Persnnl, *Exec Srch*
O'Brien & Roof Co, *Exec Srch*
Placement Svcs Limited, *Exec Srch*
Professional Restaffing of OH, *Perm. Emp Agcy*
Questcor Co, *Exec Srch*
Sales Consltnts of Cincinnati, *Exec Srch*

Snelling Persnnl Svcs, *Exec Srch*
Tabb & Assoc., *Exec Srch*
TAD Tech. Svcs, *Contract Svc*
Talent Tree Staffng, *Perm. Emp Agcy*
The Target Human Resource Companies, *Temp. Agcy*
Temporarily Yours Plcmnt, *Temp. Agcy*

Oklahoma
Ameri Resource, *Exec Srch*
Express Persnnl Svcs, *Exec Srch*
Food Manufacturing Consltnts, *Exec Srch*
Mgmt. Recrtrs of Oklahoma Cty, *Exec Srch*

Oregon
Able Temp. Svc, *Temp. Agcy*
Express Persnnl Svcs, *Exec Srch*
Mgmt. Recrtrs/Officemates5 of Portland, *Exec Srch*
Sanford Rose Assoc., *Exec Srch*

Pennsylvania
American Srch Assoc., *Exec Srch*
Atomic Persnnl, *Exec Srch*
Caliber Assoc., *Exec Srch*
Career Concepts Staff Svcs, *Exec Srch*
Charly's Temp. Svcs, *Temp. Agcy*
COREStaff, *Temp. Agcy*
J. Croyle & Assoc., *Perm. Emp Agcy*
DiCenzo Persnnl Specialists, *Perm. Emp Agcy*
Eden & Assoc., *Exec Srch*
Focus Persnnl Assoc., *Exec Srch*
The Hastings Grp, *Exec Srch*
Hospitality Svcs, *Perm. Emp Agcy*
Human Resource Solut'ns, *Exec Srch*
J-Rand Srch, *Exec Srch*
Pat Lipton & Assoc., *Exec Srch*
M.K. & Assoc., *Exec Srch*
Mgmt. Recrtrs Intl, *Exec Srch*
Mgmt. Recrtrs of DE Cnty/CompuSrch, *Exec Srch*
Mgmt. Recrtrs of Lehigh Vly/CompuSrch, *Exec Srch*
Mgmt. Recrtrs of Philadelphia/ CompuSrch, *Exec Srch*
Olsten Staff Svcs, *Temp. Agcy*
Pittsburgh Placemnt Svc, *Perm. Emp Agcy*
R.H.A. Exec Persnnl Svcs, *Exec Srch*
Rice Cohen Intl, *Exec Srch*
Spectrum Consltnts/Retail Recrtrs, *Exec Srch*
TRC Staff Svcs, *Temp. Agcy*
Target Srch, *Exec Srch*
Uni Temp Temp. Svc, *Temp. Agcy*
United Employment, *Perm. Emp Agcy*
United Tech. Assoc., *Temp. Agcy*
Whittlesey & Assoc., *Exec Srch*
Yorktowne Persnnl, *Exec Srch*

Rhode Island
Albert Lee & Assoc., *Exec Srch*
Mgmt. Recrtrs Intl, *Exec Srch*
Norrell Svcs, *Temp. Agcy*

South Carolina
Mgmt. Recrtrs of Columbia, *Exec Srch*
Mgmt. Recrtrs of Rck Hill, *Exec Srch*
The Persnnl Netwrk, *Exec Srch*
Search & Recruit Intl, *Exec Srch*
Smith Temps/Smith Persnnl, *Temp. Agcy*

South Dakota
Careers Unlimtd, *Perm. Emp Agcy*

Tennessee
A-1 Staffing & Persnnl, *Temp. Agcy*
Career Prof'ls, *Perm. Emp Agcy*
Engineer One, *Perm. Emp Agcy*
Mgmt. Recrtrs of Knoxville, *Exec Srch*
Manpower Temp. Svcs, *Temp. Agcy*
W.R. McLeod & Assoc., *Exec Srch*
Persnnl Link, *Exec Srch*
Quest Intl, *Exec Srch*
Sales Consltnts of Nashville, *Exec Srch*
Temp Staff, *Temp. Agcy*

Texas
Ackerman Johnson, *Exec Srch*
ACTION Recruitng Svcs, *Exec Srch*
Agri-LC, *Exec Srch*
Ameri Srch, *Exec Srch*
Andrews-Carter Persnnl, *Exec Srch*
Best/World Assoc., *Exec Srch*
Butler Intl, *Contract Svc*
Corporate Srch, *Exec Srch*
Craig Affiliates, *Exec Srch*
DKS & Assoc., *Exec Srch*
Dunhill Prof'l Srch, *Exec Srch*
Evins Persnnl Consltnts of Killeen, *Perm. Emp Agcy*
Executive Srch Persnnl, *Exec Srch*
Express Persnnl Svcs, *Perm. Emp Agcy*
Food Pro Recrtrs, *Exec Srch*
Abel Gonzalez & Assoc., *Exec Srch*
The Human Element of Business, *Exec Srch*

Kelly Scientific Resrcs, *Temp. Agcy*
Kelly Svcs, *Temp. Agcy*
Kenzer Corp, *Exec Srch*
Link Staff Svcs, *Temp. Agcy*
Mgmt. Recrtrs Intl, *Exec Srch*
Mgmt. Recrtrs of Champions, *Exec Srch*
Mgmt. Recrtrs of Dallas, *Exec Srch*
McKinley•Arend Intl, *Exec Srch*
The Pailin Grp, *Exec Srch*
Pate Resrcs Grp, *Exec Srch*
Phoenix Staffng, *Exec Srch*
Resource Recrtrs, *Perm. Emp Agcy*
Restaurant Recrtrs of America, *Exec Srch*
Restaurant Servers, *Temp. Agcy*
Bart Roberson & Co, *Exec Srch*
Roth Young Persnnl Svcs, *Exec Srch*
Sales Consltnts of Houston, *Exec Srch*
Search Netwrk Intl, *Exec Srch*
Select Staff, *Exec Srch*
Snelling Persnnl Svcs, *Exec Srch*
Tarrant Cnty Emp. Netwrk, *Perm. Emp Agcy*
The Urban Placemnt Svc, *Exec Srch*
Rob Wesson & Assoc., *Exec Srch*
Windsor Consltnts, *Exec Srch*

Vermont
Triad Temp. Svcs, *Temp. Agcy*

Virginia
A La Carte Intl, *Exec Srch*
Alpha Omega Resrcs, *Perm. Emp Agcy*
Curran Assoc., *Exec Srch*
Dow Persnnl, *Perm. Emp Agcy*
Executive Recrtrs of Fairfax, *Exec Srch*
Hispanic Committee of VA, *Perm. Emp Agcy*
Kogen Persnnl, *Exec Srch*
Lee Staffing Resrcs, *Exec Srch*
Mgmt. Recrtrs of McLean, *Exec Srch*
Mgmt. Recrtrs of Roanoke, *Exec Srch*
A.J. Morelli Contracting, *Contract Svc*
National Recrtrs, *Perm. Emp Agcy*
Norrell Staff Svcs, *Exec Srch*
Procurement Solut'ns, *Contract Svc*
Search & Recruit Intl, *Exec Srch*
Snelling Persnnl Svcs, *Perm. Emp Agcy*
Souder & Assoc., *Exec Srch*
The Talley Grp, *Exec Srch*
Lawrence Veber Assoc., *Exec Srch*
Virginia Emp. Referral Svc, *Exec Srch*

Washington
The Career Clinic, *Exec Srch*
Express Persnnl Svcs, *Temp. Agcy*
Hospitality Emp. Svc, *Perm. Emp Agcy*
Kelly Svcs, *Temp. Agcy*
Mgmt. Recrtrs of Mercer Islnd, *Exec Srch*
Mgmt. Recrtrs of Seattle, *Exec Srch*
Mgmt. Recrtrs of Tacoma, *Exec Srch*
Persnnl Unlimtd, *Exec Srch*
Skills Resource Training Ctr, *Perm. Emp Agcy*
Whittall Mngmnt Grp, *Exec Srch*

West Virginia
Kelly Svcs, *Temp. Agcy*
Key Persnnl, *Perm. Emp Agcy*

Wisconsin
EnviroStaff, *Temp. Agcy*
First Srch Exec Recrtmnt, *Exec Srch*
Food & Drug Prof'ls, *Perm. Emp Agcy*
Food Staff 2000, *Exec Srch*
Kordus Consltng Grp, *Exec Srch*
Mgmt. Recrtrs of Green Bay, *Exec Srch*
Mgmt. Recrtrs of Milwaukee/Sales Consltnts, *Exec Srch*
Mgmt. Recrtrs of Milwaukee, *Exec Srch*
Recruiting Resrcs, *Exec Srch*
Sales Specialists, *Exec Srch*
Tom Sloan & Assoc., *Perm. Emp Agcy*
Suave Co, *Perm. Emp Agcy*

Wyoming
The Emp. Place, *Perm. Emp Agcy*

GENERAL LABOR

California
Labor World, *Temp. Agcy*
Wollborg-Michelson Persnnl, *Perm. Emp Agcy*

Colorado
Aspen Persnnl Svcs, *Perm. Emp Agcy*
Chuck's Contrct Labor Svc, *Contract Svc*

Florida
Profes. Staffing/Able Body Temp. Svcs, *Contract Svc*

Kansas
Eleventh Hour Staff Svcs, *Temp. Agcy*

Maryland

Adecco, *Temp. Agcy*

North Carolina

StaffMark, *Temp. Agcy*

Ohio

Belcan Staff Svcs, *Temp. Agcy*

Oklahoma

StaffMark, *Temp. Agcy*

Tennessee

Mega Force, *Temp. Agcy*

Texas

Esprit Temp. Svcs, *Temp. Agcy*
Oficina de Empleos, *Perm. Emp Agcy*

Vermont

The Persnnl Connection, *Temp. Agcy*

Virginia

Task Force of VA, *Exec Srch*

West Virginia

Kelly Svcs, *Temp. Agcy*

GENERAL MANAGEMENT

Alabama

A-1 Emp. Svc, *Perm. Emp Agcy*
FORTUNE Persnnl Consltnts, *Exec Srch*
Mgmt. Recrtrs Intl, *Exec Srch*
VIP Persnnl, *Perm. Emp Agcy*

Arizona

Aidan Grp, *Contract Svc*
Andrews, Stevens & Assoc., *Contract Svc*
Construction Secretaries, *Perm. Emp Agcy*
Dealer Connection, *Perm. Emp Agcy*
Fishel Human Resrcs Assoc., *Exec Srch*
Kerry's Referrals, *Temp. Agcy*
Mgmt. Recrtrs of Scottsdale, *Exec Srch*
Priority Staffng, *Perm. Emp Agcy*
Professional Exec Research Consltng, *Exec Srch*
Spectra Intl, *Exec Srch*

Arkansas

Intl Srch, *Exec Srch*
Mgmt. Recrtrs of Little Rock, *Exec Srch*
Premier Staffng, *Temp. Agcy*
Snelling Srch, *Exec Srch*
Turnage Emp. Svc Grp, *Exec Srch*
Utopia, *Exec Srch*

California

ABA Staffng, *Exec Srch*
A.S.A.P. Emp. Svc, *Perm. Emp Agcy*
Action Plus Employer Svcs, *Perm. Emp Agcy*
Affordable Exec Recrtrs, *Exec Srch*
Allied Srch, *Exec Srch*
Alpha-Net Consltng Grp, *Exec Srch*
Answers Unlimtd, *Temp. Agcy*
John Anthony & Assoc., *Exec Srch*
Apple One Emp. Svcs, *Perm. Emp Agcy*
Apropos Emp. Agcy, *Perm. Emp Agcy*
Ballantyne Assoc., *Exec Srch*
Harvey Bell & Assoc., *Exec Srch*
Bennett & Co Consltng Grp, *Exec Srch*
Best Temp. Svc, *Temp. Agcy*
Bialla & Assoc., *Exec Srch*
Blue, Garni & Co, *Exec Srch*
Bradford Staff, *Temp. Agcy*
Brooks Assoc., *Exec Srch*
Bullis & Co, *Exec Srch*
Business Syst. Staffing & Assoc., *Perm. Emp Agcy*
California Srch Agcy, *Exec Srch*
Candy Stripers Medical Persnnl, *Perm. Emp Agcy*
Career Quest, *Contract Svc*
Claimsearch/The Srch Grp, *Exec Srch*
Collier-Young Agcy, *Temp. Agcy*
Consultant Svcs, *Exec Srch*
Marlene Critchfield Co, *Perm. Emp Agcy*
Crossroads Staff Svc, *Temp. Agcy*
Culver Persnnl Svcs, *Perm. Emp Agcy*
Culver Persnnl Svcs/The Culver Grp, *Exec Srch*
Culver Staffing Resrcs, *Exec Srch*
Desert Persnnl, *Perm. Emp Agcy*
Rob Dingman Co, *Exec Srch*
Drake Office Overload, *Temp. Agcy*
Eleventh Hour Staff Svcs, *Temp. Agcy*
Employment Devlpmnt Dept, *Perm. Emp Agcy*
Ethos Consltng, *Exec Srch*
Express Persnnl Svcs, *Temp. Agcy*
Finesse Persnnl Assoc., *Exec Srch*
Fisher & Assoc., *Exec Srch*
Fisher Persnnl Mngmnt Svcs, *Exec Srch*
FORTUNE Persnnl Consltnts of Beverly Hills, *Exec Srch*
40 Plus of So. CA, *Exec Srch*
Fresquez & Assoc., *Exec Srch*
Garnett Emp. Svcs, *Temp. Agcy*
Dianne Gauger & Assoc., *Exec Srch*
Goldstein & Assoc., *Temp. Agcy*
Gorelick & Assoc., *Exec Srch*
Gould Persnnl Svcs, *Perm. Emp Agcy*
Grant & Assoc., *Exec Srch*
Herrerias & Assoc., *Exec Srch*
Interim Persnnl, *Temp. Agcy*
Jerome & Co, *Exec Srch*
K&C Assoc., *Exec Srch*
Kabl Ability Netwrk, *Exec Srch*
Kuhn Med-Tech, *Exec Srch*
John Kurosky & Assoc., *Exec Srch*
Lending Persnnl Svcs, *Exec Srch*
The London Agcy, *Exec Srch*
Mgmt. Recrtrs of Burlingame/Sales Consltnts, *Exec Srch*
Mgmt. Recrtrs of Encino, *Exec Srch*
Mgmt. Recrtrs of Laguna Hills, *Exec Srch*
Mgmt. Recrtrs-Oakland/Sales Consltnts, *Exec Srch*
Mgmt. Recrtrs of Pleasanton, *Exec Srch*
Mgmt. Recrtrs of Redlands, *Exec Srch*
Manpower, *Temp. Agcy*
Maverick Staff Svc, *Perm. Emp Agcy*
K.E. McCarthy & Assoc., *Exec Srch*
Mesa Intl, *Exec Srch*
Milestone Prof'l Staffng, *Exec Srch*
Musick & Assoc., *Exec Srch*
NCC Exec Srch, *Exec Srch*
Nelson HR Solut'ns, *Perm. Emp Agcy*
Nesco Svc Co, *Perm. Emp Agcy*
Norsell & Assoc., *Exec Srch*
Onyx Persnnl Svcs, *Perm. Emp Agcy*
Pacific Srch Grp, *Exec Srch*
Pasona Pacific, *Temp. Agcy*
Presidio Persnnl, *Temp. Agcy*
Pro Staff Persnnl Svcs, *Perm. Emp Agcy*
Professional Recrtrs, *Exec Srch*
Professional Srch Assoc., *Exec Srch*
ProFile Persnnl, *Perm. Emp Agcy*
Ed Rast & Co, *Exec Srch*
Remedy Intelligent Staffng, *Temp. Agcy*
Resource Perspectives, *Exec Srch*
Riley-Cole Recrtmnt Specialists, *Exec Srch*
Ritter Assoc., *Exec Srch*
Russell Staffing Resrcs, *Perm. Emp Agcy*
Santa Barbara Plcmnt, *Perm. Emp Agcy*
David Sharp & Assoc., *Perm. Emp Agcy*
Steinbrun, Hughes & Assoc., *Exec Srch*
Fred Stuart Persnnl Svcs, *Perm. Emp Agcy*
T.R. Emp. Agcy, *Perm. Emp Agcy*
TechKnowledgE, *Exec Srch*
Teleforce Intl, *Exec Srch*
Telford, Adams, & Alexander, *Exec Srch*
Today Persnnl, *Perm. Emp Agcy*
Truex Assoc., *Exec Srch*
The Truman Agcy, Persnnl Specialists, *Perm. Emp Agcy*
United Staff Solut'ns, *Exec Srch*
United/Corestaff Staff Svcs, *Perm. Emp Agcy*
Walker & Torrente, *Exec Srch*
Western Staff Svcs, *Temp. Agcy*
Wollborg-Michelson Persnnl, *Perm. Emp Agcy*
Your People Prof'ls, *Perm. Emp Agcy*
Zeiger Tech. Careers, *Perm. Emp Agcy*

Colorado

Ahrnsbrak & Assoc., *Perm. Emp Agcy*
Career Forum, *Exec Srch*
Casey Svcs, *Exec Srch*
Dunhill Persnnl of Boulder, *Exec Srch*
Eleventh Hour Staff Svcs, *Perm. Emp Agcy*
Executives By Sterling, *Exec Srch*
40 Plus of CO, *Career/Outplacemnt*
JobSearch, *Temp. Agcy*
Kelly Svcs, *Temp. Agcy*
Mgmt. Recrtrs of Colorado Springs, *Exec Srch*
On Call Tech. Svcs/StaffMark, *Temp. Agcy*
Real Estate Persnnl, *Exec Srch*
SOS Staff Svcs, *Temp. Agcy*
Sales Consltnts, *Exec Srch*
Star Persnnl, *Exec Srch*
Todays Temporary, *Temp. Agcy*
Julie West & Assoc., *Exec Srch*

Connecticut

Admiral Staff Svcs, *Temp. Agcy*
Advanced Plcmnt, *Temp. Agcy*
Bohan & Bradstreet, *Perm. Emp Agcy*
Buxbaum/Rink Consltng, *Exec Srch*
Cahill Assoc., *Exec Srch*
Charter Persnnl Svcs, *Perm. Emp Agcy*
Charter Persnnl Svcs, *Exec Srch*
Corporate Staff Solut'ns, *Temp. Agcy*
Cupples Consltng Svcs, *Exec Srch*
Diversity Recruitng Svcs, *Exec Srch*
Industrial Recrtrs Assn, *Perm. Emp Agcy*
W.R. Lawry, *Perm. Emp Agcy*
MJF Assoc., *Exec Srch*
Mgmt. Recrtrs Intl, *Exec Srch*
Maxwell-Marcus Staff Consltnts, *Exec Srch*
McIntyre Assoc., *Temp. Agcy*
Office Svcs of CT, *Perm. Emp Agcy*
PRH Mgmt., *Exec Srch*
Barry Persky & Co., *Exec Srch*
Wallace Assoc., *Exec Srch*
Western Staff Svcs, *Temp. Agcy*
Bob Wright Recruitng, *Exec Srch*

Delaware

FORTUNE Persnnl Consltnts, *Exec Srch*
J.B. Groner Exec Srch, *Exec Srch*
E.W. Hodges & Assoc., *Exec Srch*
Independent Nat'l Srch & Assoc., *Exec Srch*
The Placers, *Temp. Agcy*

District of Columbia

Career Blazers Persnnl, *Perm. Emp Agcy*
NRI Staffing Resrcs, *Temp. Agcy*
Network Companies, *Exec Srch*
Potomac Persnnl, *Perm. Emp Agcy*
Savoy Partners Exec. Srch Firm
Tangent Corp, *Exec Srch*

Florida

AAA Employment, *Perm. Emp Agcy*
AccuTech, *Contract Svc*
Active Prof'ls, *Exec Srch*
Adecco, *Temp. Agcy*
American Exec Srch, *Exec Srch*
American Recrtrs, *Exec Srch*
Availability, *Perm. Emp Agcy*
B&B Persnnl, *Perm. Emp Agcy*
Bales-Waugh Grp/Bales Sales Recrtrs, *Exec Srch*
Belmont Training & Employment, *Perm. Emp Agcy*
The Brand Co, *Exec Srch*
Bryan & Assoc./Worknet, Etc., *Exec Srch*
CareerXchange, *Temp. Agcy*
Carrier's Career Svc, *Career/Outplacemnt*
Employers' Assistant, *Temp. Agcy*
Ethan Allen Persnnl Plcmnt, *Exec Srch*
Five Star Temporary, *Temp. Agcy*
Girl Friday Persnnl, *Temp. Agcy*
Janus Career Svc, *Perm. Emp Agcy*
Just Mngmnt Svcs, *Exec Srch*
Koerner Grp, *Exec Srch*
R.H. Larsen & Assoc., *Exec Srch*
Mgmt. Recrtrs of Bonita Springs, *Exec Srch*
Mgmt. Recrtrs of Lake Cnty, *Exec Srch*
Mgmt. Recrtrs of St. Petersburg, *Exec Srch*
Mgmt. Recrtrs of Tallahassee, *Exec Srch*
Mgmt. Recrtrs of Tampa, *Exec Srch*
Manpower Temp. Svcs, *Temp. Agcy*
OMNIPartners, *Exec Srch*
PMC&L Assoc., *Perm. Emp Agcy*
Persnnl One, *Perm. Emp Agcy*
Profes. Staffing/Able Body Temp. Svcs, *Contract Svc*
The Ryan Charles Grp, *Exec Srch*
Sales Consltnts of Fort Lauderdale, *Exec Srch*
Sales Consltnts of Jacksonville, *Exec Srch*
Sanford Rose Assoc., *Exec Srch*
Doug Sears & Assoc., *Exec Srch*
Shaver Emp. Agcy, *Perm. Emp Agcy*
Spalding's Emp. Svc, *Perm. Emp Agcy*
Staffing Svcs Grp, *Perm. Emp Agcy*
The Stewart Srch Grp, *Exec Srch*
Sun Persnnl West, *Exec Srch*
Suncoast Grp, *Perm. Emp Agcy*
TRC Staff Svcs, *Temp. Agcy*

Georgia

AAA Employment, *Perm. Emp Agcy*
A.D. & Assoc. Exec Srch, *Exec Srch*
Accurate Medical Placemnt/The Accurate Grp, *Exec Srch*
Augusta Staffing Assoc., *Perm. Emp Agcy*
Bell Oaks Co, *Exec Srch*
Boreham Intl, *Exec Srch*
Corporate Srch Consltnts, *Exec Srch*
Elite Staff Svcs, *Perm. Emp Agcy*
Express Persnnl Svcs, *Perm. Emp Agcy*
Express Persnnl Svcs, *Exec Srch*
First Pro, *Temp. Agcy*
ISC of Atlanta/Intl Career Continuation, *Exec Srch*
Kenzer Corp of GA, *Exec Srch*
MSI Intl, *Exec Srch*
Bob Maddox Assoc., *Exec Srch*
Mgmt. Recrtrs/Sales Consltnts of Cobb Cnty, *Exec Srch*
Mgmt. Recrtrs of Atlanta, *Exec Srch*
Mgmt. Recrtrs of Atlanta, *Exec Srch*
Mgmt. Recrtrs of Marietta, *Exec Srch*
Manpower Temp. Svcs, *Temp. Agcy*
More Persnnl Svcs, *Perm. Emp Agcy*
NEIS, *Exec Srch*
Pinnacle Consltng Grp, *Exec Srch*
Professional Medical, *Perm. Emp Agcy*
RIF (Resrcs in Food), *Exec Srch*
Randstad Staff Svcs, *Perm. Emp Agcy*
P.J. Reda & Assoc., *Exec Srch*

Sanford Rose Assoc., *Exec Srch*
Southern Emp. Svc, *Perm. Emp Agcy*
Team One Partners, *Exec Srch*
Toar Consltnts, *Exec Srch*

Hawaii
Dunhill Prof'l Srch of Hawaii, *Exec Srch*
Ellis & Assoc., *Exec Srch*
Mgmt. Srch & Consltng, *Exec Srch*
Maresca & Assoc., *Exec Srch*
The Resume Place, *Career/Outplacemnt*

Idaho
Horne/Brown Intl, *Exec Srch*
Idaho Dept. of Employment/JobSvc, *Perm. Emp Agcy*
Ward-Hoffman & Assoc., *Exec Srch*

Illinois
ASI Persnnl, *Perm. Emp Agcy*
B.J. Abrams & Assoc., *Exec Srch*
American Tech. Srch, *Exec Srch*
Armstrong-Hamilton Assoc., *Exec Srch*
Banner Persnnl, *Perm. Emp Agcy*
Bevelle & Assoc., *Exec Srch*
Burling Grp Ltd., *Exec Srch*
Carson Mngmnt Assoc., *Contract Svc*
Cast Metals Persnnl, *Exec Srch*
Cook Assoc., *Exec Srch*
Corporate Environment, *Exec Srch*
Diener & Assoc., *Exec Srch*
Executive Referral Svcs, *Exec Srch*
Express Persnnl Svcs, *Temp. Agcy*
David Gomez & Assoc., *Exec Srch*
Human Resource Connection, *Perm. Emp Agcy*
Human Resource Technlgy, *Exec Srch*
The Hunter Resource Grp, *Exec Srch*
Illinois Veterans Leadership Program, *Career/Outplacemnt*
Interstaff, *Temp. Agcy*
Interviewing Consltnts, *Perm. Emp Agcy*
Irwin & Wagner, *Exec Srch*
Jender & Co, *Contract Svc*
Kunzer Assoc., *Exec Srch*
Arlene Leff & Assoc., *Exec Srch*
Lynco Mngmnt Persnnl, *Exec Srch*
Magnum Srch, *Exec Srch*
Mgmt. Recrtrs of Albion, *Exec Srch*
Mgmt. Recrtrs of Des Plaines, *Exec Srch*
Mgmt. Recrtrs of Rockford, *Exec Srch*
Mgmt. Support Svcs, *Exec Srch*
Marsteller Wilcox Assoc., *Exec Srch*
Mount Prospect Emp. Svc, *Perm. Emp Agcy*
The Murphy Grp, *Perm. Emp Agcy*
NJW & Assoc., *Temp. Agcy*
National Srch, *Exec Srch*
Officemates5 of Wheeling, *Exec Srch*
Pelichem Assoc., *Exec Srch*
Persnnl Connection, *Perm. Emp Agcy*
Persnnl Placemnt Consltnts, *Perm. Emp Agcy*
Professional Research Svcs, *Exec Srch*
RPh On The Go, USA, *Temp. Agcy*
Remedy Intelligent Staffng, *Temp. Agcy*
Retail Staffers, *Exec Srch*
Right Svcs, *Temp. Agcy*
Ritt-Ritt & Assoc., *Exec Srch*
The Robinson Grp, *Exec Srch*
The Ryan Charles Grp, *Exec Srch*
SHS, *Exec Srch*
Sales Consltnts/Mgmt. Recrtrs Intl, *Exec Srch*
Sales Consltnts of Oak Brk, *Exec Srch*
Select Staffng, *Perm. Emp Agcy*
Selectability, *Perm. Emp Agcy*
Ralph Smith & Assoc., *Exec Srch*
Strategic Resrcs Unlimtd, *Exec Srch*
Webb Emp. Svc, *Perm. Emp Agcy*
Working World, *Temp. Agcy*
World Emp. Svc, *Perm. Emp Agcy*

Indiana
Bill Caldwell Emp. Svc, *Perm. Emp Agcy*
Careers Unlimtd, *Exec Srch*
Corporate Staff Resrcs, *Temp. Agcy*
Employment Recrtrs, *Perm. Emp Agcy*
Execusearch, *Exec Srch*
Job Placemnt Svc, *Perm. Emp Agcy*
Lange & Assoc., *Exec Srch*
Life Emp. Svc, *Perm. Emp Agcy*
Mgmt. Recrtrs of Evansville, *Exec Srch*
Mgmt. Recrtrs of Indianapolis, *Exec Srch*
Mgmt. Recrtrs of Richmond/Staff Solut'ns, *Exec Srch*
Oakwood Intl, *Exec Srch*
Officemates5 of Indianapolis, *Exec Srch*
Perry Persnnl Plus, *Perm. Emp Agcy*
Quality Srch, *Perm. Emp Agcy*
Rush Temps, *Temp. Agcy*
Unique, *Exec Srch*
Wimmer Temps & Direct Plcmnt, *Temp. Agcy*

Iowa
Burton Placemnt Svcs, *Exec Srch*
Byrnes & Rupkey, *Exec Srch*
CSI Employment, *Exec Srch*
Executive Engineering Srch, *Exec Srch*
Executive Srch Assoc., *Exec Srch*
Helping Hands Temp. Svc, *Temp. Agcy*
The Human Resource Grp, *Exec Srch*
Mgmt. Recrtrs/CompuSrch, *Exec Srch*
McGladrey Srch Grp, *Exec Srch*
Persnnl, *Exec Srch*
Salem Mngmnt dba Rudy Salem Staff Svcs, *Temp. Agcy*
Sanford Rose Assoc., *Exec Srch*

Kansas
Business Specialists, *Perm. Emp Agcy*
Mgmt. Recrtrs of Overlnd Prk, *Exec Srch*
Network of Excellence, *Exec Srch*
Stoneburner Assoc., *Exec Srch*
Temtech, *Contract Svc*

Kentucky
Angel Grp Intl, *Exec Srch*
Belcan Staff Svcs, *Perm. Emp Agcy*
Kovac Berrins AG, *Exec Srch*
Mgmt. Recrtrs of Richmond, *Exec Srch*
Neessen Prof'l Srch, *Exec Srch*

Louisiana
Delta Persnnl, *Perm. Emp Agcy*
Mgmt. Recrtrs-Baton Rouge/Sales Consltnts, *Exec Srch*
Mgmt. Recrtrs-Metairie/Sales Consltnts, *Exec Srch*
Sanford Rose Assoc., *Exec Srch*
Talley & Assoc./Talley Temps, *Exec Srch*
Technical Resource Staff Svcs, *Temp. Agcy*

Maine
Accomplished Prof'ls, *Temp. Agcy*
ASK, *Temp. Agcy*
At Work Persnnl, *Temp. Agcy*
Career Mngmnt Assoc., *Exec Srch*
Executive Srch of N.E., *Exec Srch*
John Jay & Co, *Exec Srch*

Maryland
D.W. Baird & Assoc., *Exec Srch*
Futures, *Exec Srch*
L.S. Gross & Assoc., *Exec Srch*
Mgmt. Recrtrs of Annapolis, *Exec Srch*
Mgmt. Recrtrs-Baltimore/Sales Consltnts, *Exec Srch*
Mgmt. Recrtrs-Bethesda/CompuSearch, *Exec Srch*
Mgmt. Recrtrs of Frederick, *Exec Srch*
Tom McCall & Assoc., *Perm. Emp Agcy*
Sales Consltnts of Baltimore Cty, *Exec Srch*
Sales Consltnts of Prince Georges Cnty, *Exec Srch*
Sales Consltnts of Rockville, *Exec Srch*
TCM Enterprises, *Exec Srch*
TAD Staff Svcs, *Temp. Agcy*
Winston Srch, *Exec Srch*

Massachusetts
Ability Srch of N.E., *Perm. Emp Agcy*
Brady Emp. Svc, *Perm. Emp Agcy*
Cyr Assoc., *Exec Srch*
FORTUNE Persnnl Consltnts of Topsfield, *Exec Srch*
Gilreath Weatherby, *Exec Srch*
Harvest Persnnl, *Exec Srch*
Johnson & Hill Staff Svc, *Temp. Agcy*
Lake & Manning, *Exec Srch*
The Littleton Grp, *Exec Srch*
Mgmt. Recrtrs Intl of Braintree, *Exec Srch*
Mgmt. Recrtrs Intl of Springfield, *Exec Srch*
Mgmt. Recrtrs Intl of Westboro, *Exec Srch*
Master Srch, *Perm. Emp Agcy*
McDevitt Assoc., *Exec Srch*
Need Persnnl Plcmnt, *Temp. Agcy*
New Dimensions in Technlgy, *Exec Srch*
D.P. Parker & Assoc., *Exec Srch*
Pro Staff, *Temp. Agcy*
Quality Persnnl, *Perm. Emp Agcy*
Sales Consltnts of Cape Cod, *Exec Srch*
Sales Consltnts of Mansfield, *Exec Srch*
Sales Consltnts of Plymouth Cnty, *Exec Srch*
Sales Consltnts of Wellesley, *Exec Srch*
Stone & Youngblood, *Exec Srch*
Straube Assoc., *Exec Srch*
T.F.S. Human Resource Solut'ns, *Exec Srch*
Volt Svcs Grp, *Temp. Agcy*
S.B. Webster & Assoc., *Exec Srch*
WIND Job Ctr, *Career/Outplacemnt*

Michigan
Action Mngmnt Corp, *Perm. Emp Agcy*
Allied Tech. Svc, *Contract Svc*
Assoc., *Exec Srch*
The Aucon Co, *Exec Srch*
Beacon Svcs, *Exec Srch*
Career Quest, *Perm. Emp Agcy*
Case & Co, *Exec Srch*
Corporate Bus. Svcs Exec. Srch Firm
Corporate Staff Resrcs, *Perm. Emp Agcy*
ExecuQuest, *Exec Srch*
Executive & Tech. Persnnl, *Exec Srch*
Executive Mngmnt Srch, *Exec Srch*
Executive Recrtrs Intl, *Exec Srch*
Express Persnnl Svcs, *Temp. Agcy*
FORTUNE Persnnl Consltnts, *Exec Srch*
David Franklin Assoc., *Exec Srch*
GRS, *Exec Srch*
Giacomin Grp, *Exec Srch*
Joseph Goldring & Assoc., *Exec Srch*
Grosse Pointe Employment, *Perm. Emp Agcy*
Human Resrcs Emp. Svcs, *Perm. Emp Agcy*
Lambert Intl, *Exec Srch*
David Lindemer Assoc., *Exec Srch*
Mgmt. Recrtrs of Bingham Farms, *Exec Srch*
Mgmt. Recrtrs of Dearborn, *Exec Srch*
Mgmt. Recrtrs of Flint, *Exec Srch*
Mgmt. Recrtrs of Kalamazoo, *Exec Srch*
Mgmt. Recrtrs of Lansing, *Exec Srch*
Mgmt. Recrtrs of Livonia, *Exec Srch*
Mgmt. Recrtrs of Muskegon, *Exec Srch*
Mgmt. Recrtrs of Rochester, *Exec Srch*
Mgmt. Recrtrs of Southeast MI, *Exec Srch*
Michigan Srch Plus, *Exec Srch*
Office Staffing Recruitng, *Exec Srch*
Preferred Emp. Planning, *Perm. Emp Agcy*
Sales Consltnts of Farmington Hills, *Exec Srch*
Sales Consltnts of Lansing, *Exec Srch*
Sales Executives, *Perm. Emp Agcy*
Sanford Rose Assoc., *Exec Srch*
Source Technlgy, *Exec Srch*
Technical Prof'l Svc, *Perm. Emp Agcy*
Thomas & Assoc. of MI, *Exec Srch*
Trillium Staffng, *Temp. Agcy*
Venture Mngmnt & Staffng, *Exec Srch*
Henry Welker & Assoc., *Perm. Emp Agcy*
Workforce, *Temp. Agcy*
Your Preference Referral Netwrk, *Perm. Emp Agcy*

Minnesota
Abby Blu, *Temp. Agcy*
Advance Persnnl Resrcs, *Exec Srch*
Agri-Business Svcs, *Exec Srch*
Bright Srch/Professional Staffng, *Exec Srch*
Diversified Employment, *Perm. Emp Agcy*
Ells Persnnl Syst., *Exec Srch*
Employment Advisors, *Perm. Emp Agcy*
Heinze & Assoc., *Exec Srch*
Mgmt. Recrtrs-Minneapolis/Sales Consltnts, *Exec Srch*
McGladrey & Pullen, *Exec Srch*
North American Recrtrs, *Exec Srch*
Nycor Srch, *Exec Srch*
Professional Alternatives, *Perm. Emp Agcy*
Resource Srch, *Exec Srch*
Sathe & Assoc. Exec Srch, *Exec Srch*
Ultimate Srch Unlimtd/Temps Unlimtd, *Perm. Emp Agcy*
Working Relationships, *Perm. Emp Agcy*

Mississippi
Coats & Coats Persnnl, *Perm. Emp Agcy*
EPSCO Persnnl, *Temp. Agcy*
Impact Persnnl Svcs, *Exec Srch*
Recruitment & Training of MS, *Perm. Emp Agcy*

Missouri
ABC Emp. Svc, *Perm. Emp Agcy*
Advanced Careers of Kansas Cty, *Exec Srch*
L.P. Banning, *Perm. Emp Agcy*
Bottom Line Prof'l Svcs, *Contract Svc*
Burns Emp. Svc, *Exec Srch*
Business Persnnl Svcs, *Temp. Agcy*
Debbon Recruitng Grp, *Exec Srch*
Deck & Decker Emp. Svc, *Perm. Emp Agcy*
Decker Persnnl, *Perm. Emp Agcy*
Employer Advantage, *Exec Srch*
FORTUNE Persnnl Consltnts, *Exec Srch*
Haskell Assoc., *Exec Srch*
JRL Exec Recrtrs, *Exec Srch*
JoDoc Enterprises, *Temp. Agcy*
Charles Luntz & Assoc., *Exec Srch*
Mgmt. Recrtrs of Kansas Cty, *Exec Srch*
Mgmt. Recrtrs of Springfield, *Exec Srch*
Mgmt. Recrtrs of St. Louis, *Exec Srch*
Mgmt. Recrtrs of St. Louis, *Exec Srch*
Manpower Temp. Svcs, *Temp. Agcy*
Officemates5 of St. Louis, *Exec Srch*
Olsten Staff Svcs, *Temp. Agcy*
Snelling Persnnl Svcs, *Perm. Emp Agcy*

Nebraska
Business Professions, *Perm. Emp Agcy*
Compusearch of Lincoln, *Exec Srch*
Corporate Recrtrs, *Exec Srch*
Express Persnnl, *Exec Srch*
Hansen Agri-Placement, *Perm. Emp Agcy*
Mgmt. Recrtrs of Omaha/Officemates5, *Exec Srch*
Noll HR Svcs, *Exec Srch*
Outsource II, *Temp. Agcy*
Sharp Persnnl, *Temp. Agcy*

Nevada

Nevada Bus. Svcs, *Career/Outplacemnt*

New Hampshire

Allstaff Contrct Svcs, *Perm. Emp Agcy*
Barrett & Co, *Exec Srch*
Cheshire Emp. Svc, *Temp. Agcy*
Dubois & Co, *Exec Srch*
Mgmt. Recrtrs Intl of Bedford, *Exec Srch*
Manpower Temp. Svcs, *Temp. Agcy*
National Emp. Svc Corp, *Perm. Emp Agcy*
Preferred Resrcs Grp, *Exec Srch*
Sales Consltnts, *Exec Srch*
Surge Resrcs, *Contract Svc*

New Jersey

A Prof'l Edge, *Career/Outplacemnt*
Advance Positions, *Exec Srch*
Advanced Persnnl, *Perm. Emp Agcy*
David Allen Assoc., *Exec Srch*
Alliance Consltnts, *Perm. Emp Agcy*
Gary Bell Assoc., *Exec Srch*
Blake & Assoc. Exec Srch, *Exec Srch*
Career Mngmnt Intl, *Exec Srch*
Career Srch Assoc., *Exec Srch*
Careers USA, *Perm. Emp Agcy*
Careerworks, *Exec Srch*
D'Andrea Assoc., *Exec Srch*
Executive Srch, *Exec Srch*
Express Persnnl Svcs, *Perm. Emp Agcy*
FORTUNE Persnnl Consltnts, *Exec Srch*
Holm Persnnl Consltnts, *Exec Srch*
Hreshko Consltng Grp, *Exec Srch*
Hughes & Podesla Persnnl, *Perm. Emp Agcy*
Impact Persnnl, *Perm. Emp Agcy*
Paul Kull & Co, *Exec Srch*
Major Srch, *Exec Srch*
Mgmt. Recrtrs of Medford, *Exec Srch*
Mgmt. Recrtrs of Orange Cnty, *Exec Srch*
Mgmt. Recrtrs of Passaic Cnty, *Exec Srch*
Mayfair Svcs, *Perm. Emp Agcy*
Mini Conglomerate Svc, *Perm. Emp Agcy*
Officemates5 of Englewood Cliffs/DayStar Temp. Svcs, *Perm. Emp Agcy*
Orion Consltng, *Exec Srch*
PR Mngmnt Consltnts, *Exec Srch*
Pomerantz Persnnl, *Perm. Emp Agcy*
Ramming & Assoc., *Exec Srch*
Sales Consltnts of Morris Cnty, *Exec Srch*
Sales Consltnts of Sparta, *Exec Srch*
Winston Staff Svcs, *Temp. Agcy*

New Mexico

Albuquerque Persnnl, *Perm. Emp Agcy*
CDI Corp, *Contract Svc*
Santa Fe Svcs, *Temp. Agcy*
Snelling Persnnl Svcs, *Exec Srch*

New York

AM & PM Temps, *Temp. Agcy*
APA Srch, *Exec Srch*
Accounting & Computer Persnnl, *Perm. Emp Agcy*
AccuStaff, *Perm. Emp Agcy*
Merrill Adams Assoc., *Career/Outplacemnt*
Franklin Allen Consltnts Exec. Srch Firm
American Bus. Consltnts, *Career/Outplacemnt*
Auto Careers, *Perm. Emp Agcy*
Beishline Exec Srch, *Exec Srch*
Bornholdt Shivas & Friends, *Exec Srch*
Branthover Assoc., *Exec Srch*
E.E. Brooke, *Perm. Emp Agcy*
Castlerea Assoc., *Exec Srch*
Colton Partnership, *Exec Srch*
Corporate Careers/R.J. Assoc., *Exec Srch*
Frank Cuomo & Assoc., *Exec Srch*
Seth Diamond Assoc., *Exec Srch*
Elliot Assoc., *Exec Srch*
Employment Recrtrs Agcy, *Perm. Emp Agcy*
The Emp. Store/TES Technical, *Exec Srch*
Extra Help Emp. Svc, *Temp. Agcy*
Robert Half Intl/Information Syst. Division, *Exec Srch*
F.P. Healy & Co, *Exec Srch*
Stanley Herz & Co., *Exec Srch*
Interspace Interactive, *Exec Srch*
The Kay Grp of Fifth Avenue, *Exec Srch*
Fred Koffler Assoc., *Exec Srch*
Michael John Lawrence & Assoc., *Exec Srch*
M.B., *Exec Srch*
Mgmt. Recrtrs of Nassau, *Exec Srch*
Mgmt. Recrtrs of Woodbury/ CompuSrch, *Exec Srch*
Metro Persnnl/Metro Nursing Svcs, *Exec Srch*
Morgan-Murray Persnnl/M&M Top Temps, *Temp. Agcy*
Noah Assoc., *Perm. Emp Agcy*
Parsons, Anderson & Gee, *Perm. Emp Agcy*
Paywise, *Temp. Agcy*
Persnnl Svcs Ctr, *Exec Srch*
ROI Assoc., *Exec Srch*
Rand Thompson Consltnts, *Exec Srch*
Sales Consltnts of Westchester, *Exec Srch*
SearchAmerica, *Exec Srch*
Staff Managers, *Temp. Agcy*
Staffing Svcs, *Exec Srch*
Taylor Jordan Assoc., *Exec Srch*
Unique Support Svcs, *Temp. Agcy*
Charles Wanner Assoc. Exec. Srch Firm
Weber Mngmnt Consltnts, *Exec Srch*
Westchester Emp. Agcy, *Perm. Emp Agcy*
Western Staff Svcs, *Temp. Agcy*
Winston Resrcs, *Exec Srch*
S.R. Wolman Assoc., *Exec Srch*

North Carolina

A-1 Staffing & Persnnl, *Perm. Emp Agcy*
Advanced Persnnl Resrcs, *Exec Srch*
AmeriPro Srch, *Exec Srch*
Ayers & Assoc., *Exec Srch*
Career Srch, *Exec Srch*
Employment Consltnts, *Contract Svc*
Executive Recrtmnt Specialists, *Exec Srch*
C.D. Fayling Assoc., *Exec Srch*
Glovier & Assoc., *Exec Srch*
Stew Greene & Co/The Triad, *Exec Srch*
The Jobs Market, *Perm. Emp Agcy*
Kelly Svcs, *Temp. Agcy*
King Career Consltng, *Career/Outplacemnt*
MTS, *Perm. Emp Agcy*
Mgmt. Recrtrs/Sales Consltnts, *Exec Srch*
Mgmt. Recrtrs of Durham, *Exec Srch*
Mgmt. Recrtrs of Fayetteville, *Exec Srch*
Mgmt. Recrtrs of Greensboro, *Exec Srch*
Mgmt. Recrtrs of Kinston, *Exec Srch*
Mgmt. Recrtrs of Raleigh/Inter Exec, *Exec Srch*
Mgmt. Recrtrs of Winston-Salem, *Exec Srch*
Metals & Wood Agcy, *Exec Srch*
Moffitt Intl, *Exec Srch*
National Svcs, *Exec Srch*
Olsten Staff Svcs, *Temp. Agcy*
Parenica & Co, *Exec Srch*
Sales Consltnts of Concord, *Exec Srch*
Sales Consltnts of High Point, *Exec Srch*
Sanford Rose Assoc., *Exec Srch*
Search Consltnts Worldwide, *Exec Srch*
Sparks Persnnl Svcs, *Exec Srch*
John Williams & Assoc., *Exec Srch*
Youngblood Staffng, *Perm. Emp Agcy*

North Dakota

Human Resrcs, *Perm. Emp Agcy*
Olsten Staff Svcs/Kramer & Assoc./Expressway Persnnl, *Temp. Agcy*
Persnnl Svcs, *Exec Srch*

Ohio

Adecco, *Perm. Emp Agcy*
Burks Grp, *Exec Srch*
CBS Persnnl Svcs, *Perm. Emp Agcy*
Career Connections, *Perm. Emp Agcy*
Career Specialists, *Exec Srch*
Combined Resrcs, *Exec Srch*
Continental Srch Consltnts, *Exec Srch*
J.D. Cotter Srch, *Exec Srch*
Cross-Jordan Corp, *Exec Srch*
Tonia Deal Consltnts, *Perm. Emp Agcy*
Drayton & Assoc., *Exec Srch*
Eastern Persnnl Svcs, *Perm. Emp Agcy*
Elite Resrcs Grp, *Exec Srch*
Executech, *Exec Srch*
Executech Consltnts, *Exec Srch*
Executive Connection, *Exec Srch*
Executive Directions, *Exec Srch*
Executive Srch Ltd., *Exec Srch*
Flex-Tech Prof'l Svcs, *Contract Svc*
Flowers & Assoc./Associated Temps, *Exec Srch*
FORTUNE Persnnl Consltnts, *Exec Srch*
Gayhart & Assoc., *Exec Srch*
H.L. Goehring & Assoc., *Exec Srch*
Griffiths & Assoc., *Exec Srch*
H.J.C., *Exec Srch*
Hahn & Assoc., *Exec Srch*
Hite Exec Srch/Hite Mngmnt Consltnts, *Exec Srch*
Ives & Assoc., *Exec Srch*
Kaiser Nationwide, *Exec Srch*
Laine's S.M.G., *Perm. Emp Agcy*
Mgmt. Recrtrs of Cincinnati, *Exec Srch*
Mgmt. Recrtrs of Cleveland, *Exec Srch*
Mgmt. Recrtrs of Cleveland, *Exec Srch*
Mgmt. Recrtrs of Cleveland, *Exec Srch*
Mgmt. Recrtrs of Columbus, *Exec Srch*
Mgmt. Recrtrs of Dayton, *Exec Srch*
Mgmt. Recrtrs of Solon, *Exec Srch*
Marvel Consltnts, *Exec Srch*
Miami Prof'l Srch, *Exec Srch*
Midland Consltnts, *Exec Srch*
North American Persnnl, *Exec Srch*
O'Brien & Roof Co, *Exec Srch*
Olsten Prof'l Staff Svcs, *Exec Srch*
Quality Plus, *Exec Srch*
Questcor Co, *Exec Srch*
W.R. Renner & Assoc., *Exec Srch*
Rentech Ventures, *Perm. Emp Agcy*
Sales Consltnts of Cincinnati, *Exec Srch*
Sanford Rose Assoc., *Exec Srch*
Snelling Persnnl Svcs, *Exec Srch*
Tabb & Assoc., *Exec Srch*
Talent Tree Staffng, *Perm. Emp Agcy*
Technical Recruitng Svcs, *Exec Srch*
Fred Tippel & Assoc., *Exec Srch*
J.P. Walton & Assoc., *Exec Srch*

Oklahoma

Ameri Resource, *Exec Srch*
Express Persnnl Svcs, *Exec Srch*
Mgmt. Recrtrs of Oklahoma Cty, *Exec Srch*
Terry Neese Persnnl Agcy, *Exec Srch*

Oregon

Express Persnnl Svcs, *Exec Srch*
Hackenschmidt, Weaver & Fox, *Exec Srch*
Mgmt. Recrtrs/Officemates5 of Portland, *Exec Srch*
NPRC/Nationwde Persnnl Recruitng & Consltng, *Exec Srch*
Office Careers, *Perm. Emp Agcy*
Search Nrthwest Assoc., *Exec Srch*
Snelling Persnnl Svcs, *Perm. Emp Agcy*
Southern Oregon Temporary, *Temp. Agcy*
Woodworth Intl Grp, *Exec Srch*

Pennsylvania

Action Persnnl Svcs, *Perm. Emp Agcy*
Adecco, *Temp. Agcy*
Alexander Persnnl Assoc., *Exec Srch*
Allegheny Persnnl Svcs, *Temp. Agcy*
American Srch Assoc., *Exec Srch*
Ashley Srch Consltnts, *Exec Srch*
Caliber Assoc., *Exec Srch*
Career Concepts Staff Svcs, *Exec Srch*
COREStaff, *Temp. Agcy*
J. Croyle & Assoc., *Perm. Emp Agcy*
P. Robert Dann, *Exec Srch*
DiCenzo Persnnl Specialists, *Perm. Emp Agcy*
Dunn Assoc., *Exec Srch*
Executive Mrktng Svcs, *Career/Outplacemnt*
Financial Industry Staff Co, *Perm. Emp Agcy*
Fox-Morris Assoc., *Exec Srch*
J.H. Glass & Assoc., *Exec Srch*
Hallmark Persnnl/Able Temps, *Perm. Emp Agcy*
The Hastings Grp, *Exec Srch*
Hospitality Svcs, *Perm. Emp Agcy*
Human Resource Solut'ns, *Exec Srch*
IMC Intl, *Contract Svc*
J-Rand Srch, *Exec Srch*
Nancy Jackson, *Exec Srch*
Jefferson-Ross Assoc., *Exec Srch*
Kathy Karr Persnnl, *Perm. Emp Agcy*
Mgmt. Recrtrs of DE Cnty/CompuSrch, *Exec Srch*
Mgmt. Recrtrs of Lehigh Vly/CompuSrch, *Exec Srch*
Mgmt. Recrtrs of Philadelphia/ CompuSrch, *Exec Srch*
Metro Persnnl, *Temp. Agcy*
B. Paul Mickey & Assoc., *Exec Srch*
The Morris Grp, *Exec Srch*
Probe Technlgy, *Exec Srch*
R.H.A. Exec Persnnl Svcs, *Exec Srch*
Alan Raeburn Consltnts, *Exec Srch*
Rice Cohen Intl, *Exec Srch*
The Richards Grp, *Exec Srch*
Singmaster Persnnl Svcs, *Perm. Emp Agcy*
Snelling Persnnl Svcs, *Exec Srch*
TRC Staff Svcs, *Temp. Agcy*
W.G. Tucker & Assoc., *Exec Srch*
Uniforce Temp. Svcs, *Temp. Agcy*
Whittlesey & Assoc., *Exec Srch*
Yorktowne Persnnl, *Exec Srch*

Rhode Island

Colony Persnnl Assoc., *Perm. Emp Agcy*
Johnson & Tregar Assoc., *Perm. Emp Agcy*
Kelly Svcs, *Temp. Agcy*
Albert Lee & Assoc., *Exec Srch*
Mgmt. Recrtrs Intl, *Exec Srch*
Norrell Svcs, *Temp. Agcy*
PKS Assoc., *Exec Srch*

South Carolina

Eastern Persnnl Svcs, *Exec Srch*
FORTUNE Persnnl Consltnts of Columbia, *Exec Srch*
Harvey Persnnl, *Perm. Emp Agcy*
Mgmt. Recrtrs of Columbia, *Exec Srch*
Mgmt. Recrtrs of Rck Hill, *Exec Srch*
PRL & Assoc., *Perm. Emp Agcy*
The Persnnl Netwrk, *Exec Srch*
Sales Consltnts/Mgmt. Recrtrs of Greenville, *Exec Srch*
Sanford Rose Assoc., *Exec Srch*
Smith Temps/Smith Persnnl, *Temp. Agcy*
Southern Recrtrs & Consltnts, *Exec Srch*
The Stroman Co, *Perm. Emp Agcy*

South Dakota
Careers Unlimtd, *Perm. Emp Agcy*

Tennessee
A-1 Staffing & Persnnl, *Temp. Agcy*
Anderson McIntyre Persnnl Svcs, *Exec Srch*
B.K. Barnes & Assoc., *Exec Srch*
Express Persnnl Svcs, *Perm. Emp Agcy*
FORTUNE Persnnl Consltnts, *Exec Srch*
Gateway Grp Persnnl, *Temp. Agcy*
Hamilton Ryker Co, *Exec Srch*
Hester & Assoc., *Exec Srch*
Kelly Svcs, *Temp. Agcy*
Mgmt. Recrtrs/Sales Consltnts-Chattanooga, *Exec Srch*
Mgmt. Recrtrs of Knoxville, *Exec Srch*
Manpower Temp. Svcs, *Temp. Agcy*
W.R. McLeod & Assoc., *Exec Srch*
The Morgan Grp, *Exec Srch*
Olsten Staff Svcs, *Temp. Agcy*
Rasmussen & Assoc., *Perm. Emp Agcy*
Sales Consltnts of Nashville, *Exec Srch*
Snelling Persnnl Svcs, *Exec Srch*
Technical Resource Assoc., *Exec Srch*

Texas
ABA Exec Srch, *Exec Srch*
Abilene Emp. Svc, *Perm. Emp Agcy*
Ackerman Johnson, *Exec Srch*
Action Persnnl, *Temp. Agcy*
Agri-LC, *Exec Srch*
Aware Affiliates Persnnl, *Perm. Emp Agcy*
Ann Best Elite Temps, *Temp. Agcy*
Boles & Assoc., *Exec Srch*
Bullock Persnnl, *Perm. Emp Agcy*
Cherbonnier Grp, *Exec Srch*
Colvin Resrcs Grp, *Temp. Agcy*
Continental Persnnl, *Perm. Emp Agcy*
Creative Staff Svcs, *Temp. Agcy*
The Danbrook Grp, *Exec Srch*
Gail Darling Staffing/Darling's Prof'l Desk, *Temp. Agcy*
Dunhill Prof'l Srch, *Exec Srch*
The Elsworth Grp, *Exec Srch*
Evins Persnnl Consltnts of Killeen, *Perm. Emp Agcy*
Executive Srch Persnnl, *Exec Srch*
Express Persnnl Svcs, *Perm. Emp Agcy*
Abel Gonzalez & Assoc., *Exec Srch*
Haragan Assoc., *Exec Srch*
The Human Element of Business, *Exec Srch*
Kenzer Corp, *Exec Srch*
Kristan Intl Exec Srch, *Exec Srch*
Link Staff Svcs, *Temp. Agcy*
Lusk & Assoc. Persnnl, *Exec Srch*
Mgmt. Recrtrs Intl, *Exec Srch*
Mgmt. Recrtrs of Dallas, *Exec Srch*
McKinley•Arend Intl, *Exec Srch*
Metro Careers, *Exec Srch*
Olsten Staff Svcs, *Temp. Agcy*
P&P Persnnl, *Perm. Emp Agcy*
The Pailin Grp, *Exec Srch*
Pate Resrcs Grp, *Exec Srch*
Persnnl One, *Perm. Emp Agcy*
Phoenix Staffng, *Exec Srch*
Professional Srch Consltnts, *Contract Svc*
Professions Today, *Perm. Emp Agcy*
Roth Young Persnnl Svcs/Dallas, *Exec Srch*
Sales Consltnts of Houston, *Exec Srch*
SearchAmerica, *Exec Srch*
Select Staff, *Exec Srch*
Snelling Persnnl Svcs, *Perm. Emp Agcy*
Staff Extension, *Exec Srch*
Strategic Outsourcing Corp, *Exec Srch*
TAD Tech. Svcs, *Contract Svc*
Tarrant Cnty Emp. Netwrk, *Perm. Emp Agcy*
Thomas Office Persnnl, *Perm. Emp Agcy*
Valpers, *Exec Srch*
Vick & Assoc./Recruiters Online Netwrk, *Exec Srch*
Wheeler, Moore & Elam Co, *Exec Srch*
R.S. Wyatt Assoc., *Exec Srch*
Wyman & Assoc., *Exec Srch*

Utah
Mgmt. Recrtrs Intl, *Exec Srch*
Mgmt. Recrtrs of Ogden, *Exec Srch*
Mgmt. Recrtrs of Provo, *Exec Srch*
Professional Recrtrs, *Exec Srch*

Virginia
Ability Resrcs, *Exec Srch*
Alpha Omega Resrcs, *Perm. Emp Agcy*
BSC, *Contract Svc*
Barnes & Assoc. Retail Srch, *Exec Srch*
Bent Assoc., *Exec Srch*
Corporate Connection Exec. Srch Firm
Dow Persnnl, *Perm. Emp Agcy*
Effective Staffng, *Exec Srch*
The Gemini Grp, *Exec Srch*
HATCH Mrktng Syst., *Perm. Emp Agcy*
Kogen Persnnl, *Exec Srch*
Lee Staffing Resrcs, *Exec Srch*
Mgmt. Recrtrs of McLean, *Exec Srch*
Mgmt. Recrtrs of Roanoke, *Exec Srch*
Carol McNew Emp. Svc, *Perm. Emp Agcy*
Norrell Staff Svcs, *Exec Srch*
Olsten Staff Svcs, *Temp. Agcy*
Selectemps, *Temp. Agcy*
Snelling Persnnl Svcs, *Perm. Emp Agcy*
STAT Temps, *Temp. Agcy*
Task Force of VA, *Exec Srch*
Temporary Solut'ns, *Temp. Agcy*
U.S. Srch, *Exec Srch*
Virginia Emp. Referral Svc, *Exec Srch*
Western Staff Svcs, *Temp. Agcy*

Washington
The Career Clinic, *Exec Srch*
Express Persnnl Svcs, *Temp. Agcy*
Human Resrcs, *Exec Srch*
The Jobs Co, *Exec Srch*
Kelly Svcs, *Temp. Agcy*
Kossuth & Assoc., *Exec Srch*
Mgmt. Recrtrs of Mercer Islnd, *Exec Srch*
Mgmt. Recrtrs of Seattle, *Exec Srch*
Mgmt. Recrtrs of Tacoma, *Exec Srch*
John Mason & Assoc., *Exec Srch*
Persnnl Unlimtd, *Exec Srch*
Search West, *Exec Srch*
The Washington Firm, *Exec Srch*
Whittall Mngmnt Grp, *Exec Srch*

West Virginia
Extra Support Staffng, *Temp. Agcy*
Key Persnnl, *Perm. Emp Agcy*

Wisconsin
Allen, Wayne, & Co, *Perm. Emp Agcy*
Austria Austria & Assoc., *Perm. Emp Agcy*
Dieck, Mueller & Assoc., *Exec Srch*
J.M. Eagle Partners, *Exec Srch*
Executive Resource, *Exec Srch*
The Exutec Grp, *Exec Srch*
Flores Financial Svcs, *Exec Srch*
Mgmt. Recrtrs of Appleton/ CompuSrch, *Exec Srch*
Mgmt. Recrtrs of Green Bay, *Exec Srch*
Mgmt. Recrtrs of Milwaukee/Sales Consltnts, *Exec Srch*
Mgmt. Recrtrs of Milwaukee, *Exec Srch*
MARBL Consltnts, *Exec Srch*
Olsten Staff Svcs, *Temp. Agcy*
Sales Specialists, *Exec Srch*
Sanford Rose Assoc., *Exec Srch*
Tom Sloan & Assoc., *Perm. Emp Agcy*
Suave Co, *Perm. Emp Agcy*
Tempo Emp. Svcs, *Temp. Agcy*

GOVERNMENT

California
Hughes Perry & Assoc., *Exec Srch*
Justus Persnnl Svcs, *Perm. Emp Agcy*
Mahoney & Brewer Assoc., *Exec Srch*

Florida
Romac Intl, *Exec Srch*

Georgia
Mahoney & Brewer Assoc., *Exec Srch*

New Jersey
Tenek Corp, *Exec Srch*

North Carolina
Executive Recrtmnt Specialists, *Exec Srch*

Ohio
T. Grooms & Assoc., *Perm. Emp Agcy*

Pennsylvania
Keynote Syst., *Temp. Agcy*

HEALTH/MEDICAL

Alabama
A-1 Emp. Svc, *Perm. Emp Agcy*
Employment Consltnts, *Perm. Emp Agcy*
Healthcare Recrtrs of Alabama, *Exec Srch*
Mgmt. Recrtrs Intl, *Exec Srch*
Medex, *Temp. Agcy*
Snelling Persnnl Svcs, *Perm. Emp Agcy*
Snelling Srch, *Exec Srch*
VIP Persnnl, *Perm. Emp Agcy*

Alaska
Alaska Exec Srch, *Exec Srch*

Arizona
Arizona Medical Exchange, *Perm. Emp Agcy*
BJB Medical Assoc., *Exec Srch*
EAI Healthcare Staff Solut'ns, *Temp. Agcy*
Favorite Nurses, *Temp. Agcy*
Fusion Grp, *Exec Srch*
Human Resource Netwrk, *Perm. Emp Agcy*
Kelly Assisted Living Svcs, *Temp. Agcy*
Mgmt. Recrtrs of Scottsdale, *Exec Srch*
Pearson & Assoc., *Exec Srch*
Priority Staffng, *Perm. Emp Agcy*
Sales Consltnts, *Exec Srch*
Marjorie Starr & Assoc., *Exec Srch*
Stivers Temp. Persnnl, *Temp. Agcy*
Witt/Kieffer, Ford, Hadelman & Lloyd, *Exec Srch*

Arkansas
Mgmt. Recrtrs of Little Rock, *Exec Srch*
Search Assoc., *Exec Srch*
Turnage Emp. Svc Grp, *Exec Srch*

California
ABA Staffng, *Exec Srch*
ARI Intl, *Exec Srch*
Action Plus Employer Svcs, *Perm. Emp Agcy*
Allied Srch, *Exec Srch*
Apple One Emp. Svcs, *Perm. Emp Agcy*
Apropos Emp. Agcy, *Perm. Emp Agcy*
Armstrong & Assoc., *Contract Svc*
Assured Persnnl Svcs, *Perm. Emp Agcy*
Harvey Bell & Assoc., *Exec Srch*
Bristol Assoc., *Exec Srch*
Bryson Myers Co, *Exec Srch*
CRI Prof'l Srch, *Exec Srch*
Candy Stripers Medical Persnnl, *Perm. Emp Agcy*
Carlson & Assoc., *Exec Srch*
Coast To Coast Exec Srch, *Exec Srch*
Collier-Young Agcy, *Temp. Agcy*
Culver Persnnl Svcs, *Perm. Emp Agcy*
Culver Persnnl Svcs, *Exec Srch*
Culver Staffing Resrcs, *Exec Srch*
DEC & Assoc. Healthcare Persnnl, *Temp. Agcy*
DNA Medical Srch, *Exec Srch*
Dental Plus Medical, *Temp. Agcy*
Rob Dingman Co, *Exec Srch*
Drake Office Overload, *Temp. Agcy*
Dunhill Prof'l Srch of San Francisco, *Exec Srch*
Eaton & Assoc., *Exec Srch*
Edwards & Assoc., *Exec Srch*
Employment Devlpmnt Dept, *Perm. Emp Agcy*
Employment Svc Agcy, *Perm. Emp Agcy*
Ensearch Mngmnt Consltnts, *Exec Srch*
Ethos Consltng, *Exec Srch*
Executive Medical Srch, *Exec Srch*
Faithful Support Syst., *Temp. Agcy*
Filipinos For Affirmative Action, *Perm. Emp Agcy*
FORTUNE Persnnl Consltnts, *Exec Srch*
40 Plus of So. CA, *Exec Srch*
Garrison-Randall, *Exec Srch*
Goldstein & Assoc., *Temp. Agcy*
The Goodman Grp, *Exec Srch*
Gould Persnnl Svcs, *Perm. Emp Agcy*
Griffith & Assoc., *Exec Srch*
Healthcare Exec Recrtrs, *Exec Srch*
Healthcare Recrtrs Intl, *Exec Srch*
HealthCare Recrtrs of San Diego, *Exec Srch*
Bruce Henry Assoc., *Exec Srch*
Interim Industrial Staffng, *Temp. Agcy*
Interim Persnnl, *Temp. Agcy*
Interstate Recrtrs, *Exec Srch*
JPM Intl, *Exec Srch*
Roye Johnston & Assoc., *Exec Srch*
Justus Persnnl Svcs, *Perm. Emp Agcy*
Kelly Assisted Living Svcs, *Temp. Agcy*
Kelly Svcs, *Temp. Agcy*
Kenneth, George, & Assoc., *Exec Srch*
Kuhn Med-Tech, *Exec Srch*
John Kurosky & Assoc., *Exec Srch*
Lab Support, *Temp. Agcy*
Legal Resource People, *Temp. Agcy*
Leinow Assoc., *Exec Srch*
The London Agcy, *Exec Srch*
The London Agcy, *Temp. Agcy*
MacNaughton Assoc., *Exec Srch*
Judy Madrigal & Assoc., *Exec Srch*
Mahoney & Brewer Assoc., *Exec Srch*
Malibu Grp, *Exec Srch*
Mgmt. Recrtrs of Burlingame/Sales Consltnts, *Exec Srch*
Mgmt. Recrtrs of Encino, *Exec Srch*
Mgmt. Recrtrs-Oakland/Sales Consltnts, *Exec Srch*
Mgmt. Recrtrs of Orange, *Exec Srch*
Mgmt. Recrtrs of Pleasanton, *Exec Srch*
Mgmt. Srch Intl, *Exec Srch*
Rich Maries Agcy, *Perm. Emp Agcy*
Maverick Staff Svc, *Perm. Emp Agcy*
Sabine McManus & Assoc., *Exec Srch*
Med Quest, *Exec Srch*
Med-Exec Intl, *Exec Srch*
The Medical Center Agcy, *Perm. Emp Agcy*
Medical Exec Recrtrs, *Exec Srch*
Medical Financial Svcs, *Contract Svc*
Medical Staff Unlimtd, *Perm. Emp Agcy*
Mesa Intl, *Exec Srch*
Mixtec Grp, *Exec Srch*

Kelly Assisted Living Svcs, *Temp. Agcy*
Mgmt. Recrtrs of Overlnd Prk, *Exec Srch*
Mgmt. Recrtrs of Topeka, *Exec Srch*
Network of Excellence, *Exec Srch*
Parr & Assoc., *Perm. Emp Agcy*
Persnnl Mgmt. Resrcs, *Exec Srch*
Peterson Grp, *Exec Srch*
Preferred Medical Plcmnt, *Perm. Emp Agcy*
Sherriff & Assoc., *Exec Srch*
B.E. Smith Assoc., *Exec Srch*
Stoneburner Assoc., *Exec Srch*
Temtech, *Contract Svc*
Uniforce Staff Svcs, *Temp. Agcy*

Kentucky

Angel Grp Intl, *Exec Srch*
Belcan Staff Svcs, *Perm. Emp Agcy*
Engineering & Exec Srch, *Exec Srch*
First Choice Svcs, *Exec Srch*
Healthcare Recrtrs Intl, *Exec Srch*
Olsten Kimberly Quality Care, *Perm. Emp Agcy*
Precision Staffng, *Perm. Emp Agcy*

Louisiana

Healthcare Recrtrs Intl, *Exec Srch*
Keenan Staffng, *Temp. Agcy*
MSI Physician Recrtrs, *Exec Srch*
Mgmt. Recrtrs-Baton Rouge/Sales Consltnts, *Exec Srch*
Mgmt. Recrtrs-Metairie/Sales Consltnts, *Exec Srch*
Medforce Physician Svcs, *Perm. Emp Agcy*
Medi-Lend Nursing Svcs, *Perm. Emp Agcy*
Premier Staffng, *Temp. Agcy*
Shiell Persnnl, *Perm. Emp Agcy*
Snelling Persnnl Svcs, *Exec Srch*
Talley & Assoc./Talley Temps, *Exec Srch*
Western Staff Svcs, *Temp. Agcy*
X Techs, *Temp. Agcy*

Maine

At Work Persnnl, *Temp. Agcy*
Career Mngmnt Assoc., *Exec Srch*
John Jay & Co, *Exec Srch*
Lake Medical Assoc., *Exec Srch*
New England Home Health Care, *Contract Svc*

Maryland

Caplan Assoc., *Exec Srch*
Fallstaff Srch, *Exec Srch*
Futures, *Exec Srch*
L.S. Gross & Assoc., *Exec Srch*
Healthcare Recrtrs Intl, *Exec Srch*
Mgmt. Recrtrs of Annapolis, *Exec Srch*
Mgmt. Recrtrs-Baltimore/Sales Consltnts, *Exec Srch*
Mgmt. Recrtrs-Bethesda/CompuSearch, *Exec Srch*
Mgmt. Recrtrs of Frederick, *Exec Srch*
Mgmt. Recrtrs of Washington, D.C., *Exec Srch*
NRI Healthcare, *Temp. Agcy*
Sales Consltnts of Baltimore Cty, *Exec Srch*
Sales Consltnts of Prince Georges Cnty, *Exec Srch*
Sudina Srch, *Exec Srch*
TAC Staff Svcs, *Temp. Agcy*
TAD Staff Svcs, *Temp. Agcy*
Telesec Staff Svcs, *Temp. Agcy*
Universal Health Care Placemnts, *Exec Srch*
White Ridgely Assoc., *Career/Outplacemnt*
Witt/Kieffer, Ford, Hadelman & Lloyd, *Exec Srch*

Massachusetts

A.S.I. Temps, *Temp. Agcy*
Abbott's of Boston, *Exec Srch*
Michael Anthony Assoc., *Exec Srch*
Auerbach Assoc., *Exec Srch*
Nathan Barry & Assoc., *Exec Srch*
Bowdoin Grp, *Exec Srch*
Bradford Barnes Assoc., *Exec Srch*
Brattle Temps, *Temp. Agcy*
Breitner Clark & Hall, *Exec Srch*
CEC Assoc., *Exec Srch*
Cleary Consltnts, *Perm. Emp Agcy*
Rob Davidson Assoc./Exec. & Prof. Resume Svc, *Exec Srch*
DeLuca & Assoc., *Exec Srch*
Directions Medical Grp, *Exec Srch*
Dunhill Staffing Syst., *Temp. Agcy*
Editorial Svcs of N.E., *Temp. Agcy*
Fitzgerald Assoc., *Exec Srch*
FORTUNE Persnnl Consltnts, *Exec Srch*
Harvest Persnnl, *Exec Srch*
Healthcare Recrtrs Intl, *Exec Srch*
Hilton Assoc., *Perm. Emp Agcy*
Human Resource Consltnts, *Perm. Emp Agcy*
Human Svc Options, *Temp. Agcy*
Johnson & Hill Staff Svc, *Temp. Agcy*
L&L Temps, *Temp. Agcy*
John Leonard Persnnl Assoc., *Perm. Emp Agcy*
Mgmt. Recrtrs Intl of Braintree, *Exec Srch*
Mgmt. Recrtrs Intl of Springfield, *Exec Srch*
Mgmt. Recrtrs Intl of Westboro, *Exec Srch*
Manpower, *Temp. Agcy*
Medical Bureau, *Exec Srch*
Molari, *Temp. Agcy*
Navin Grp, *Exec Srch*
Northeast Srch, *Exec Srch*
P.A.R. Assoc., *Exec Srch*
Phillips & Assoc., *Exec Srch*
The Pickwick Grp, *Exec Srch*
Pro Staff, *Temp. Agcy*
E.S. Rando Assoc., *Perm. Emp Agcy*
Russell Reynolds Assoc., *Exec Srch*
Sales Consltnts of Cape Cod, *Exec Srch*
Sales Consltnts of Plymouth Cnty, *Exec Srch*
Sales Consltnts of Wellesley, *Exec Srch*
George Sandel Assoc., *Perm. Emp Agcy*
Stone & Youngblood, *Exec Srch*
Straube Assoc., *Exec Srch*
TAD Staff Svcs, *Temp. Agcy*
Travcorps, *Temp. Agcy*
Michael Ward Assoc., *Perm. Emp Agcy*
WIND Job Ctr, *Career/Outplacemnt*
Winfield Assoc., *Exec Srch*

Michigan

Action Sell Assoc., *Exec Srch*
AEGIS Grp, *Exec Srch*
Barman Staff Solut'ns/Barman Persnnl, *Perm. Emp Agcy*
Beacon Svcs, *Temp. Agcy*
Catalyst Health Care Grp, *Exec Srch*
Circlewood Srch Grp, *Exec Srch*
Dental Medical Svcs, *Temp. Agcy*
Devlan, *Perm. Emp Agcy*
Entech Svcs, *Temp. Agcy*
Executive Mngmnt Srch, *Exec Srch*
Express Persnnl Svcs, *Temp. Agcy*
FORTUNE Persnnl Consltnts of Troy, *Exec Srch*
Genesys Health Persnnl, *Exec Srch*
Joseph Goldring & Assoc., *Exec Srch*
Grosse Pointe Employment, *Perm. Emp Agcy*
Harper Assoc., *Exec Srch*
Health Care Prof'ls, *Perm. Emp Agcy*
Healthcare Recrtrs Intl, *Exec Srch*
William Howard Agcy, *Perm. Emp Agcy*
Kelly Assisted Living Svcs, *Temp. Agcy*
Mgmt. Recrtrs of Battle Creek, *Exec Srch*
Mgmt. Recrtrs of Bingham Farms, *Exec Srch*
Mgmt. Recrtrs of Dearborn, *Exec Srch*
Mgmt. Recrtrs of Flint, *Exec Srch*
Mgmt. Recrtrs of Grand Rapids, *Exec Srch*
Mgmt. Recrtrs of Kalamazoo, *Exec Srch*
Mgmt. Recrtrs of Lansing, *Exec Srch*
Mgmt. Recrtrs of Muskegon, *Exec Srch*
Mgmt. Recrtrs of Rochester, *Exec Srch*
MedMatch, *Exec Srch*
Medsearch, *Exec Srch*
METROSTAFF, *Exec Srch*
Nationwide Career Netwrk, *Perm. Emp Agcy*
Nustar Temp. Svcs, *Temp. Agcy*
Olsten Prof'l Accnt'g Svcs, *Temp. Agcy*
Premier Healthcare Recrtrs, *Exec Srch*
Professional Advancement Institute, *Exec Srch*
Professional Persnnl Consltnts Intl, *Exec Srch*
Rehabilitation Therapy Resrcs, *Exec Srch*
Roth Young Persnnl Svcs of Detroit, *Exec Srch*
Sales Consltnts of Auburn Hills, *Exec Srch*
Sales Consltnts of Detroit, *Exec Srch*
Sales Consltnts of Farmington Hills, *Exec Srch*
Sales Consltnts of Genesee, *Exec Srch*
Sales Executives, *Perm. Emp Agcy*
Sharrow & Assoc., *Exec Srch*
Snelling Persnnl Svcs, *Perm. Emp Agcy*
Sterling Field Assoc., *Exec Srch*
Venture Mngmnt & Staffng, *Exec Srch*
Wing Tips & Pumps, *Exec Srch*

Minnesota

Alternative Choice Health Svcs, *Exec Srch*
Bright Srch/Professional Staffng, *Exec Srch*
EHS & Assoc., *Exec Srch*
Ells Persnnl Syst., *Exec Srch*
Erspamer Assoc., *Exec Srch*
Fogarty & Assoc., *Exec Srch*
Health Persnnl Options Corp, *Perm. Emp Agcy*
Healthcare Recrtrs of MN, *Exec Srch*
Hilleren & Assoc., *Exec Srch*
T.H. Hunter, *Exec Srch*
Johnson Temps, *Temp. Agcy*
Mgmt. Recrtrs-Minneapolis/Sales Consltnts, *Exec Srch*
MedSearch Corp, *Exec Srch*
North American Recrtrs, *Exec Srch*
Resource Srch, *Exec Srch*
Roth Young Exec Recrtrs, *Exec Srch*
Ultimate Srch Unlimtd/Temps Unlimtd, *Perm. Emp Agcy*

Mississippi

Recruitment & Training of MS, *Perm. Emp Agcy*

Missouri

American Health Care, *Temp. Agcy*
Anderson Healthcare, *Exec Srch*
AnesTemps, *Temp. Agcy*
L.P. Banning, *Perm. Emp Agcy*
Business Persnnl Svcs, *Temp. Agcy*
Jim Crumpley & Assoc., *Exec Srch*
Deck & Decker Emp. Svc, *Perm. Emp Agcy*
Decker Persnnl, *Perm. Emp Agcy*
Employer Advantage, *Exec Srch*
Healthcare Recrtrs Intl, *Exec Srch*
Insurance Overload Syst., *Temp. Agcy*
Kelly Scientific Resrcs, *Temp. Agcy*
Kendall & Davis Co, *Contract Svc*
Kendallwood/Arcadia Health Care Svcs, *Temp. Agcy*
Kennison & Assoc., *Perm. Emp Agcy*
Mgmt. Recrtrs of Kansas Cty, *Exec Srch*
Mgmt. Recrtrs of Springfield, *Exec Srch*
Mgmt. Recrtrs of St. Louis, *Exec Srch*
Mgmt. Recrtrs of St. Louis, *Exec Srch*
Medical Resrcs & Assoc., *Exec Srch*
National Physician Placemnt Svcs, *Exec Srch*
Officemates5 of St. Louis, *Exec Srch*
Olsten Staff Svcs, *Temp. Agcy*
RehabCare Grp, *Contract Svc*
RehabWorks, *Contract Svc*
Toberson Grp, *Perm. Emp Agcy*

Montana

Express Persnnl, *Perm. Emp Agcy*
Finn's Employment, *Exec Srch*
Kelly Svcs, *Temp. Agcy*

Nebraska

Arcadia Health Care, *Perm. Emp Agcy*
Aureus Grp, *Exec Srch*
Choice Enterprises, *Exec Srch*
Compusearch of Lincoln, *Exec Srch*
Corporate Recrtrs, *Exec Srch*
Rose Crum Assoc., *Exec Srch*
Kelly Svcs, *Temp. Agcy*
Mgmt. Recrtrs of Omaha/Officemates5, *Exec Srch*
Noll HR Svcs, *Exec Srch*
Sales Consltnts of Omaha, *Exec Srch*

Nevada

Mgmt. Recrtrs of Reno, *Exec Srch*

New Hampshire

Able 1 Staffng, *Exec Srch*
Allstaff Contrct Svcs, *Perm. Emp Agcy*
Barrett & Co, *Exec Srch*
Career Profiles, *Exec Srch*
Central New Hampshire Emp. Svcs, *Perm. Emp Agcy*
Clayman Mngmnt Svc, *Exec Srch*
Dubois & Co, *Exec Srch*
Hillsborough Recrtrs, *Exec Srch*
Mgmt. Recrtrs Intl of Bedford, *Exec Srch*
Pamela Mulligan, *Exec Srch*
National Emp. Svc Corp, *Perm. Emp Agcy*
Sales Consltnts of Nashua-Manchester, *Exec Srch*
Spectrum Medical Srch, *Exec Srch*
STAT Srch, *Exec Srch*

New Jersey

Adel-Lawrence Assoc., *Exec Srch*
ARC Medical & Prof'l Persnnl, *Temp. Agcy*
Assurance Health Care Svcs, *Exec Srch*
Gary Bell Assoc., *Exec Srch*
Blake & Assoc. Exec Srch, *Exec Srch*
Carter/MacKay Persnnl, *Exec Srch*
M.T. Donaldson Assoc., *Exec Srch*
Drew Assoc. Intl, *Exec Srch*
Enriched Living, *Temp. Agcy*
Foley Proctor Yoskowitz, *Exec Srch*
Hadley Assoc., *Exec Srch*
Headhunters Exec Srch, *Exec Srch*
Healthcare Recrtrs Intl, *Exec Srch*
Huff Assoc., *Exec Srch*
Hunt, Ltd., *Perm. Emp Agcy*
Impact Persnnl, *Perm. Emp Agcy*
J.M. Joseph Assoc., *Exec Srch*
Lab Support, *Temp. Agcy*
Mgmt. Recrtrs of Passaic Cnty, *Exec Srch*
Mayfair Svcs, *Perm. Emp Agcy*
Normyle/Erstling Health Srch Grp, *Exec Srch*
Orion Consltng, *Exec Srch*
Petruzzi Assoc., *Exec Srch*
Philadelphia Srch Grp, *Exec Srch*
Pomerantz Persnnl, *Perm. Emp Agcy*
Protocall Bus. Staff Svcs, *Temp. Agcy*
Ramming & Assoc., *Exec Srch*
SJ Nurses, *Perm. Emp Agcy*
Sales Consltnts of Morris Cnty, *Exec Srch*
Sales Consltnts of Sparta, *Exec Srch*
Scientific Srch, *Perm. Emp Agcy*
Selective Persnnl, *Perm. Emp Agcy*
Snelling Persnnl Svcs, *Perm. Emp Agcy*
Source Svcs Corp, *Perm. Emp Agcy*
Summit Grp, *Exec Srch*
Supportive Care, *Temp. Agcy*
Temporary Excellence, *Temp. Agcy*

Allen Thomas Assoc., *Exec Srch*
Unitemp Temp. Persnnl, *Temp. Agcy*
Winston Staff Svcs, *Temp. Agcy*
World Health Resrcs, *Exec Srch*

New Mexico

Albuquerque Persnnl, *Perm. Emp Agcy*
CDI Corp, *Contract Svc*
Culver Grp, *Exec Srch*
Excel of Albuquerque, *Perm. Emp Agcy*
New Mexico Health Resrcs, *Exec Srch*
Scientemps, *Temp. Agcy*
Snelling Persnnl Svcs, *Exec Srch*

New York

A&A Staffing Health Care, *Exec Srch*
AJC Srch, *Exec Srch*
Accounting & Computer Persnnl, *Perm. Emp Agcy*
Accredited Care, *Contract Svc*
Merrill Adams Assoc., *Career/Outplacemnt*
Adele Poston Nurses Registry, *Perm. Emp Agcy*
Adept Tech Recruitng, *Exec Srch*
All Home Svcs Agcy, *Perm. Emp Agcy*
Franklin Allen Consltnts Exec. Srch Firm
Alpha Health Svcs Corp, *Exec Srch*
American Medical Persnnl Svcs, *Exec Srch*
AMESgroup, *Perm. Emp Agcy*
Antes Assoc., *Perm. Emp Agcy*
Aster Srch Grp, *Exec Srch*
Avalon Health Grp, *Exec Srch*
Barksdale Home Care Svcs Corp, *Perm. Emp Agcy*
Neail Behringer Consltnts, *Exec Srch*
CT Grp, *Exec Srch*
Care Givers, *Exec Srch*
Chriss Career Limited, *Exec Srch*
Consortium, *Exec Srch*
Corporate Moves, *Exec Srch*
Dentaforce Dental Placemnts, *Temp. Agcy*
Dental Placemnt Plus, *Temp. Agcy*
Seth Diamond Assoc., *Exec Srch*
Dixon Healthcare Employment, *Exec Srch*
Maggi Dolan Plcmnt, *Perm. Emp Agcy*
Dunhill Staffing Syst. of Buffalo, *Temp. Agcy*
Durham Medical Staffng, *Exec Srch*
Eden Persnnl, *Perm. Emp Agcy*
Employment Recrtrs Agcy, *Perm. Emp Agcy*
The Emp. Store/TES Technical, *Exec Srch*
Ethan Allen Medical Srch, *Exec Srch*
Fabian Assoc., *Exec Srch*
Fifth Avenue Emp. Svcs, *Temp. Agcy*
Finest Emp. Agcy, *Perm. Emp Agcy*
Foley Proctor Yoskowitz, *Exec Srch*
The Hampton Grp, *Exec Srch*
Healthcare Recrtrs of NY, *Exec Srch*
Healthpro Placemnt Svc, *Perm. Emp Agcy*
Healthsearch Grp, *Exec Srch*
Heron Home & Health Care Agcy, *Perm. Emp Agcy*
Howe-Lewis Intl, *Exec Srch*
Hunter Plcmnt, *Exec Srch*
Intl Medical Plcmnt, *Exec Srch*
JDC Assoc., *Perm. Emp Agcy*
Josef Grp Persnnl, *Perm. Emp Agcy*
The Kay Grp of Fifth Avenue, *Exec Srch*
Michael John Lawrence & Assoc., *Exec Srch*
The Lloyd Co, *Career/Outplacemnt*
Mgmt. Recrtrs of Gramercy, *Exec Srch*
Mgmt. Recrtrs of Utica/Rome, *Exec Srch*
Mgmt. Recrtrs of Woodbury/ CompuSrch, *Exec Srch*
McLaughlin Resrcs, *Exec Srch*
Med-Scribe, *Temp. Agcy*
Medical Staffers, *Perm. Emp Agcy*
Medstaff Svcs, *Perm. Emp Agcy*
The Melville Grp, *Exec Srch*
Metro Persnnl/Metro Nursing Svcs, *Exec Srch*
Morgan-Murray Persnnl/M&M Top Temps, *Temp. Agcy*
Physician Intl, *Exec Srch*
Professional Placemnt Assoc., *Exec Srch*
Quality Healthcare Staffng, *Perm. Emp Agcy*
Remedy Intelligent Staffng, *Temp. Agcy*
Republic Emp. Agcy, *Perm. Emp Agcy*
Response Staff Svcs/Career Advisors, *Exec Srch*
Sales Consltnts of Westchester, *Exec Srch*
Sharp Nurses, *Temp. Agcy*
Stafkings Health Care Syst., *Exec Srch*
Stafkings Persnnl Syst., *Temp. Agcy*
Superior Concepts, *Contract Svc*
Tad Health Svcs, *Exec Srch*
Temp Force of NY, *Temp. Agcy*
Todd Arro, *Exec Srch*
E.G. Todd Physician Srch, *Exec Srch*
Winston Resrcs, *Exec Srch*

North Carolina

ATS Health Svcs, *Exec Srch*
Andos Assoc., *Exec Srch*
Executive Recrtmnt Specialists, *Exec Srch*
Forbes Temp. Staffng, *Temp. Agcy*
Jobs of Fayetteville, *Perm. Emp Agcy*
S.N. Jones & Assoc., *Exec Srch*
Key Temps, *Temp. Agcy*
Mgmt. Recrtrs/Sales Consltnts, *Exec Srch*
Mgmt. Recrtrs of Durham, *Exec Srch*
Mgmt. Recrtrs of Kinston, *Exec Srch*
Mgmt. Recrtrs of Raleigh/Inter Exec, *Exec Srch*
Mgmt. Recrtrs of Winston-Salem, *Exec Srch*
Medical Prof'ls, *Exec Srch*
Merrick & Moore, *Exec Srch*
Moffitt Intl, *Exec Srch*
Myers & Assoc., *Perm. Emp Agcy*
Odyssey Grp, *Exec Srch*
Quality Plus Temps, *Temp. Agcy*
Sales Consltnts of Concord, *Exec Srch*
Sales Consltnts of High Point, *Exec Srch*
Snelling Srch, *Exec Srch*
Summit Occupational Staffng, *Exec Srch*
Talent Tree Staffng, *Perm. Emp Agcy*

North Dakota

Dental Fill-Ins, *Temp. Agcy*
Dunhill Exec Srch, *Exec Srch*

Ohio

Advancement Recruitng Svcs, *Exec Srch*
Belcan Staff Svcs, *Temp. Agcy*
CBS Persnnl Svcs, *Perm. Emp Agcy*
Champion Persnnl, *Perm. Emp Agcy*
Deffet Grp, *Exec Srch*
Delta Medical Srch Assoc., *Exec Srch*
B.P. Driscol & Assoc., *Exec Srch*
Eastern Persnnl Svcs, *Perm. Emp Agcy*
Global Resrcs Grp, *Contract Svc*
Health Care Advantage, *Exec Srch*
Healthcare Recrtrs Intl, *Exec Srch*
Hite Exec Srch/Hite Mngmnt Consltnts, *Exec Srch*
Anne Jones Staffng, *Perm. Emp Agcy*
Kaiser Nationwide, *Exec Srch*
Laine's S.M.G., *Perm. Emp Agcy*
R.E. Lowe Assoc., *Perm. Emp Agcy*
Mgmt. Recrtrs of Cincinnati, *Exec Srch*
Mgmt. Recrtrs of Cleveland, *Exec Srch*
Mgmt. Recrtrs of Cleveland, *Exec Srch*
Mgmt. Recrtrs of Cleveland, *Exec Srch*
Mgmt. Recrtrs of Columbus, *Exec Srch*
Mgmt. Recrtrs of Dayton, *Exec Srch*
Mgmt. Recrtrs of Solon, *Exec Srch*
Marvel Consltnts, *Exec Srch*
Medical Staff Consltnts, *Perm. Emp Agcy*
Medsearch Staff Svcs, *Perm. Emp Agcy*
North Central Persnnl Pool, *Temp. Agcy*
Personalized Plcmnt, *Exec Srch*
Pharmacy Relief Netwrk, *Temp. Agcy*
Placement Svcs Limited, *Exec Srch*
Professional Emp. Svcs, *Perm. Emp Agcy*
Providence Persnnl Consltnts, *Exec Srch*
Reed Recruitng, *Perm. Emp Agcy*
Sales Consltnts of Cincinnati, *Exec Srch*
Searchmark Medical, *Exec Srch*
Shafer Jones Assoc., *Exec Srch*
Snelling Persnnl Svcs, *Exec Srch*
TAD Tech. Svcs, *Contract Svc*
TechPro Medical Svc, *Temp. Agcy*
Temporarily Yours Plcmnt, *Temp. Agcy*

Oklahoma

Ameri Resource, *Exec Srch*
Belt Joy Reed & Assoc., *Exec Srch*
Express Persnnl Svcs, *Exec Srch*
Healthcare Resrcs Grp, *Exec Srch*
Key Temp. Persnnl, *Temp. Agcy*
Mgmt. Recrtrs of Oklahoma Cty, *Exec Srch*
Terry Neese Persnnl Agcy, *Exec Srch*
Lloyd Richards Persnnl, *Perm. Emp Agcy*
Sales Recrtrs, *Exec Srch*
StaffMark Medical Staffng, *Temp. Agcy*

Oregon

Able Temp. Svc, *Temp. Agcy*
Auguston & Assoc., *Exec Srch*
Auntie Fay Domestic Agcy, *Perm. Emp Agcy*
D. Brown & Assoc., *Exec Srch*
Mgmt. Recrtrs/Officemates5 of Portland, *Exec Srch*
Northwest Temp. & Staff Svcs, *Temp. Agcy*
Roth Young Exec Recrtrs, *Exec Srch*
Talent Tree Staffng, *Perm. Emp Agcy*
Woodworth Intl Grp, *Exec Srch*

Pennsylvania

All Staffng, *Perm. Emp Agcy*
Allegheny Persnnl Svcs, *Temp. Agcy*
ASAP Staffng, *Perm. Emp Agcy*
Barton Persnnl Syst., *Exec Srch*
Bradley Prof'l Svcs, *Perm. Emp Agcy*
Caliber Assoc., *Exec Srch*
Career Quest Confidential, *Exec Srch*
Charly's Temp. Svcs, *Temp. Agcy*
DPSI Medical, *Exec Srch*
P. Robert Dann, *Exec Srch*
Delta ProSearch, *Exec Srch*
Dental Power of Delaware Valley, *Perm. Emp Agcy*
Rob DePaul & Assoc., *Exec Srch*
FORTUNE Grp Intl, *Exec Srch*
Garrick Hall & Assoc., *Exec Srch*
Hallmark Persnnl/Able Temps, *Perm. Emp Agcy*
The Hastings Grp, *Exec Srch*
Healthcare Recrtrs Intl, *Exec Srch*
Interactive Srch, *Exec Srch*
J-Rand Srch, *Exec Srch*
Nancy Jackson, *Exec Srch*
Jefferson-Ross Assoc., *Exec Srch*
Keynote Syst., *Temp. Agcy*
Mgmt. Recrtrs of Bucks Cnty/CompuSrch, *Exec Srch*
Mgmt. Recrtrs of DE Cnty/CompuSrch, *Exec Srch*
Mgmt. Recrtrs of Lehigh Vly/CompuSrch, *Exec Srch*
Mgmt. Recrtrs of Philadelphia/ CompuSrch, *Exec Srch*
Medical Persnnl Pool/Persnnl Pool, *Perm. Emp Agcy*
Orion Delta Grp Exec. Srch Firm
LaMonte Owens, *Exec Srch*
PRN Consltnts, *Perm. Emp Agcy*
Physician Billing Solut'ns, *Perm. Emp Agcy*
Probe Technlgy, *Exec Srch*
Protocall Bus. Staffng, *Temp. Agcy*
Rice Cohen Intl, *Exec Srch*
The Richards Grp, *Exec Srch*
Rittenhouse Recrtrs, *Exec Srch*
Roth Young Persnnl Svcs, *Exec Srch*
Spectrum Consltnts/Retail Recrtrs, *Exec Srch*
Daniel Stern & Assoc., *Exec Srch*
TRC Staff Svcs, *Temp. Agcy*
TAC Staff Svcs, *Temp. Agcy*
Terry Taylor & Assoc., *Exec Srch*
Uni Temp Temp. Svc, *Temp. Agcy*
Uniforce Temp. Svcs, *Temp. Agcy*
United Health & Human Svcs, *Temp. Agcy*
Vogue Persnnl, *Perm. Emp Agcy*
Whittlesey & Assoc., *Exec Srch*

Rhode Island

Kelly Svcs, *Temp. Agcy*
Albert Lee & Assoc., *Exec Srch*
Mgmt. Recrtrs Intl, *Exec Srch*
Storti Assoc., *Exec Srch*
Sullivan & Cogliano, *Exec Srch*
TAC Staff Svcs, *Temp. Agcy*

South Carolina

Columbia Health Care Svc, *Exec Srch*
FORTUNE Persnnl Consltnts, *Exec Srch*
Health Care Srch Assoc., *Exec Srch*
Health Force, *Temp. Agcy*
Mgmt. Recrtrs of Aiken, *Exec Srch*
Mgmt. Recrtrs of Anderson, *Exec Srch*
Mgmt. Recrtrs of Columbia, *Exec Srch*
Mgmt. Recrtrs of Rck Hill, *Exec Srch*
The Persnnl Netwrk, *Exec Srch*
Physicians Unlimtd, *Exec Srch*
Pindrum Staff Svc, *Temp. Agcy*
Sales Consltnts/Mgmt. Recrtrs of Greenville, *Exec Srch*
Search & Recruit Intl, *Exec Srch*
Southern Recrtrs & Consltnts, *Exec Srch*
Staffing Solut'ns, *Temp. Agcy*

South Dakota

Western Plains Health Consortium, *Perm. Emp Agcy*

Tennessee

A-1 Staffing & Persnnl, *Temp. Agcy*
Anderson McIntyre Persnnl Svcs, *Exec Srch*
Angel Medical Persnnl Pool, *Temp. Agcy*
B.K. Barnes & Assoc., *Exec Srch*
C.J. Staff Svcs, *Contract Svc*
Cook Assoc. Intl, *Exec Srch*
Health Staff, *Temp. Agcy*
Healthcare Recrtrs Intl, *Exec Srch*
Kelly Svcs, *Temp. Agcy*
Mgmt. Recrtrs of Knoxville, *Exec Srch*
Manpower Temp. Svcs, *Temp. Agcy*
W.R. McLeod & Assoc., *Exec Srch*
Medical & Dental Resrcs, *Exec Srch*
Persnnl Link, *Exec Srch*
Pharm Temp Pharmacy Persnnl/Opti Temp/Den Temp, *Temp. Agcy*
Physician Placemnt Svc of America, *Exec Srch*
Poplar Emp. Svc, *Perm. Emp Agcy*
Sales Consltnts of Nashville, *Exec Srch*
Snelling Persnnl Svcs, *Exec Srch*

Texas

Abilene Emp. Svc, *Perm. Emp Agcy*
Action Persnnl, *Temp. Agcy*
Adecco, *Temp. Agcy*
Albrecht & Assoc. Exec Srch, *Exec Srch*
Andrews-Carter Persnnl, *Exec Srch*
Marilyn Austin & Assoc., *Exec Srch*
Austin Medical Persnnl, *Perm. Emp Agcy*
Aware Affiliates Persnnl, *Perm. Emp Agcy*
Benchmark Prof'ls, *Exec Srch*

BioSource Intl, *Exec Srch*
Bond & Assoc., *Exec Srch*
Borrel Persnnl, *Exec Srch*
Brainpower Persnnl Agcy, *Perm. Emp Agcy*
Brooklea & Assoc., *Exec Srch*
Cherbonnier Grp, *Exec Srch*
Colvin Resrcs Grp, *Temp. Agcy*
Continental Persnnl, *Perm. Emp Agcy*
CoreCom, *Contract Svc*
Dependable Dental Staffng, *Temp. Agcy*
Dr. Persnnl of San Antonio, *Perm. Emp Agcy*
John Domino & Assoc., *Exec Srch*
Dunhill of Arlington, *Perm. Emp Agcy*
Dunhill Prof'l Srch, *Exec Srch*
EAI Healthcare Staffng, *Exec Srch*
Evins Persnnl Consltnts of Killeen, *Perm. Emp Agcy*
Executive Srch Persnnl, *Exec Srch*
Express Persnnl Svcs, *Perm. Emp Agcy*
Gulco Intl Recruitng Svcs, *Perm. Emp Agcy*
H.P.R. Health Staff, *Exec Srch*
Haragan Assoc., *Exec Srch*
Health Care Temp, *Temp. Agcy*
Health Netwrk USA, *Exec Srch*
Health Prof'ls of America, *Exec Srch*
Healthcare Providers, *Contract Svc*
Healthcare Recrtrs Intl, *Exec Srch*
Healthcare Recrtrs of Houston, *Exec Srch*
Healthcare Staff Resrcs, *Perm. Emp Agcy*
Horn & Assoc., *Exec Srch*
Innovative Staff Srch, *Exec Srch*
Kelly Svcs, *Temp. Agcy*
Korn/Ferry Intl, *Exec Srch*
Lea Randolph & Assoc., *Exec Srch*
Mgmt. Recrtrs Intl, *Exec Srch*
Mgmt. Recrtrs of Champions, *Exec Srch*
Mgmt. Recrtrs of Dallas, *Exec Srch*
Medical Srch Solut'ns, *Exec Srch*
MedTex Staffng, *Perm. Emp Agcy*
Nationwide Medical Plcmnt, *Exec Srch*
Nurses Today, *Temp. Agcy*
Odell & Assoc., *Exec Srch*
Olsten Staff Svcs, *Temp. Agcy*
OMNI Consortium, *Perm. Emp Agcy*
The Pailin Grp, *Exec Srch*
Pate Resrcs Grp, *Exec Srch*
Practice Dynamics, *Exec Srch*
Premier Health Staff, *Exec Srch*
Professional Srch Consltnts, *Contract Svc*
Professions Today, *Perm. Emp Agcy*
RehabWorks, *Contract Svc*
Respiratory Staffing Specialist, *Temp. Agcy*
Rottman Grp, *Exec Srch*
Russell Reynolds Assoc., *Exec Srch*
SAI Exec Srch (Sloan Assoc.), *Exec Srch*
Sales Consltnts of Houston, *Exec Srch*
Say Ahhh Medical Office Svcs, *Perm. Emp Agcy*
R.L. Scott Assoc., *Exec Srch*
Snelling Persnnl Svcs, *Exec Srch*
Solutions, *Exec Srch*
Staff Extension, *Exec Srch*
R.A. Stone & Assoc., *Exec Srch*
TAD Tech. Svcs, *Contract Svc*
Betty Tanner Prof'l Emp. Svc, *Exec Srch*
Tarrant Cnty Emp. Netwrk, *Perm. Emp Agcy*
Total Temp. Svcs, *Temp. Agcy*
The Whitaker Companies, *Exec Srch*
Windsor Consltnts, *Exec Srch*
Witt/Kieffer, Ford, Hadelman & Lloyd, *Exec Srch*

Utah

Deeco Intl, *Perm. Emp Agcy*
Mgmt. Recrtrs Intl, *Exec Srch*
Trout & Assoc., *Exec Srch*

Virginia

Advantage Staffng, *Temp. Agcy*
Alpha Omega Resrcs, *Perm. Emp Agcy*
Arcadia Eure Prof'l Staffng, *Perm. Emp Agcy*
Austin Assoc. Medical Persnnl, *Perm. Emp Agcy*
Contec Srch, *Exec Srch*
DPS, *Contract Svc*
Carol Day & Assoc., *Exec Srch*
The Gemini Grp, *Exec Srch*
Mgmt. Recrtrs of McLean, *Exec Srch*
Mgmt. Recrtrs of Roanoke, *Exec Srch*
The McCormick Grp, *Exec Srch*
Carol McNew Emp. Svc, *Perm. Emp Agcy*
Placement Prof'ls, *Exec Srch*
Professional Srch Persnnl, *Exec Srch*
Remedy Intelligent Staffng, *Temp. Agcy*
Search Consltnts, *Exec Srch*
Snelling Persnnl Svcs, *Perm. Emp Agcy*
Source Svcs Corp, *Exec Srch*
TAC Staff Svcs, *Temp. Agcy*
Team Placemnt Svc, *Temp. Agcy*
Lawrence Veber Assoc., *Exec Srch*
Wisdom & Williams, *Perm. Emp Agcy*

Washington

BSP & Assoc., *Exec Srch*
Black & Deering, *Exec Srch*
Kathy Evans Exec Srch/Healthcare Specialists, *Exec Srch*
Express Persnnl Svcs, *Temp. Agcy*
The Jobs Co, *Exec Srch*
Mgmt. Recrtrs of Lynwood, *Exec Srch*
Mgmt. Recrtrs of Mercer Islnd, *Exec Srch*
Mgmt. Recrtrs of Seattle, *Exec Srch*
Mgmt. Recrtrs of Tacoma, *Exec Srch*
Olsten Kimberly Quality Care, *Perm. Emp Agcy*
Persnnl Unlimtd, *Exec Srch*
Sander Assoc., *Exec Srch*
Search West, *Exec Srch*
The Washington Firm, *Exec Srch*
Williams Recruitng, *Exec Srch*

West Virginia

Dunhill Prof'l Srch, *Exec Srch*
Key Persnnl, *Perm. Emp Agcy*

Wisconsin

Austria Austria & Assoc., *Perm. Emp Agcy*
Concord Staff Source, *Perm. Emp Agcy*
Custom Care, *Temp. Agcy*
J.M. Eagle Partners, *Exec Srch*
The Exutec Grp, *Exec Srch*
Greenfield Rehabilitation Agcy, *Temp. Agcy*
Healthcare Recrtrs Intl, *Exec Srch*
Mgmt. Recrtrs of Green Bay, *Exec Srch*
Mgmt. Recrtrs of Milwaukee/Sales Consltnts, *Exec Srch*
Mgmt. Recrtrs of Milwaukee, *Exec Srch*
Medteams, *Temp. Agcy*
Quirk-Corporon & Assoc., *Exec Srch*
Sales Specialists, *Exec Srch*
Staff Devlpmnt Corp, *Exec Srch*

HIGH-TECH

Arizona

Bartholdi & Co, *Exec Srch*
Corporate Dynamix, *Exec Srch*
Dean Vesling & Assoc., *Contract Svc*

California

The Badger Grp, *Exec Srch*
Deborah Bishop & Assoc., *Exec Srch*
Brandenburg Smith & Assoc., *Exec Srch*
Drummer Persnnl, *Exec Srch*
Fastek Tech. Svcs, *Perm. Emp Agcy*
Haley Assoc., *Exec Srch*
Heuristics Srch, *Exec Srch*
Fred Hood & Assoc., *Exec Srch*
Innovative Srch Assoc., *Exec Srch*
Job Link, *Exec Srch*
A.T. Kearney Exec Srch, *Exec Srch*
Barry Kleinman & Assoc., *Exec Srch*
Lefeber & Assoc., *Exec Srch*
Lloyd Ritter & Assoc., *Perm. Emp Agcy*
Maciejewski & Assoc., *Exec Srch*
Mahoney & Brewer Assoc., *Exec Srch*
Mgmt. Recrtrs Intl, *Exec Srch*
J.M. Meredith & Assoc., *Exec Srch*
Craig Miller Assoc., *Exec Srch*
Pinsker & Co, *Exec Srch*
Probus Exec Srch, *Exec Srch*
Sanford Rose Assoc., *Exec Srch*
Charles Skorina & Co, *Exec Srch*
R.J. Watkins & Co, *Exec Srch*
D.L. Weaver & Assoc., *Exec Srch*

Colorado

FORTUNE Persnnl Consltnts, *Exec Srch*
Young & Thulin, *Exec Srch*

Florida

Career Concepts, *Exec Srch*
Lasher Assoc., *Exec Srch*
Mgmt. Recrtrs Intl, *Exec Srch*

Georgia

Mahoney & Brewer Assoc., *Exec Srch*
Phoenix Partners, *Exec Srch*

Indiana

The Bennett Grp, *Exec Srch*

Kentucky

The Hindman Co, *Exec Srch*

Maryland

Career Netwrk Svc, *Perm. Emp Agcy*
Seek Intl, *Exec Srch*

Massachusetts

Blaney Exec Srch, *Exec Srch*
Bradford Barnes Assoc., *Exec Srch*
Fenwick Partners, *Exec Srch*
Gustin Partners Exec. Srch Firm
John Kennedy Assoc., *Exec Srch*
Professional Placemnt Consltng Grp, *Exec Srch*
Russell Reynolds Assoc., *Exec Srch*
Sullivan Assoc., *Exec Srch*
Xavier Assoc., *Exec Srch*

Minnesota

Jackley Srch Consltnts, *Exec Srch*
Professional Recrtrs, *Exec Srch*
Searchtek, *Exec Srch*

Missouri

H.L. Yoh Co, *Contract Svc*

New Hampshire

Shawn Alexander Assoc., *Exec Srch*
Bartholdi & Co, *Exec Srch*

New Jersey

Mgmt. Recrtrs of Haddonfield, *Exec Srch*

New York

Michael Blitzer Assoc., *Exec Srch*
Molloy Partners, *Exec Srch*

North Carolina

Mgmt. Recrtrs Intl, *Exec Srch*
H.L. Yoh Co, *Contract Svc*

Ohio

A.T. Kearney Exec Srch, *Exec Srch*

Oklahoma

High Tech Resrcs, *Exec Srch*

Oregon

The Brentwood Grp Limited, *Exec Srch*
EDP Markets/EDP Consltnts, *Exec Srch*
Executives Worldwide, *Exec Srch*
Mgmt. Solut'ns, *Exec Srch*
Resource Technlgy Grp, *Contract Svc*

Rhode Island

Alan Price Assoc., *Exec Srch*

Texas

Contrct Design Persnnl, *Temp. Agcy*
Inside Track, *Exec Srch*
JP & Assoc., *Exec Srch*
Mgmt. Recrtrs Intl, *Exec Srch*
Riccione & Assoc., *Exec Srch*
H.L. Yoh Co, *Contract Svc*

Virginia

Brault & Assoc. Exec. Srch Firm
FGI, *Exec Srch*
Helen Skinner Assoc., *Perm. Emp Agcy*

Washington

Berkana Intl, *Exec Srch*
COMFORCE Tech. Svcs, *Contract Svc*
Devon James Assoc., *Exec Srch*
Mgmt. Recrtrs Intl, *Exec Srch*
Parfitt Grp, *Exec Srch*
Search West, *Exec Srch*
Thompson & Assoc., *Exec Srch*
H.L. Yoh Co, *Contract Svc*

HOTEL/RESTAURANT

Arizona

The Bren Grp, *Exec Srch*
WSA Assoc., *Exec Srch*
Weinman & Assoc., *Exec Srch*

California

Bentley Price Assoc., *Exec Srch*
Bowman Assoc., *Exec Srch*
Bristol Assoc., *Exec Srch*
National Hospitality Recrtrs, *Exec Srch*
Peter Joseph Assoc., *Exec Srch*
Worldwide Exec Srch, *Exec Srch*

Colorado

Coast to Coast Exec Srch, *Exec Srch*
Executives By Sterling, *Exec Srch*

Connecticut

Yankee Hospitality Srch, *Exec Srch*

District of Columbia

Snelling Persnnl, *Perm. Emp Agcy*

Florida

Career Choice, *Exec Srch*
Executive Srch Intl, *Exec Srch*
McGuire Exec Srch, *Exec Srch*

'he Stewart Srch Grp, *Exec Srch*
Vorkers of Florida, *Temp. Agcy*

Georgia

SA (Dixie Srch Assoc.), *Exec Srch*
Elliot Assoc., *Exec Srch*
Omega Exec Srch, *Exec Srch*

Illinois

T.A. Davis & Assoc., *Exec Srch*
Executive Referral Svcs, *Exec Srch*
National Restaurant Srch, *Exec Srch*
Ritt-Ritt & Assoc., *Exec Srch*

Indiana

Dobias Grp, *Exec Srch*
J. Spahn & Assoc., *Exec Srch*

Maine

Jobs Unlimtd/Ideal Solut'ns, *Perm. Emp Agcy*

Maryland

HRM Srch Team, *Exec Srch*

Massachusetts

Beacon Srch Prof'ls, *Exec Srch*
New American Srch, *Exec Srch*
Partridge Assoc., *Exec Srch*
Search Intl, *Exec Srch*

Michigan

Lake Assoc., *Exec Srch*
Rooney Persnnl Co, *Exec Srch*

Minnesota

Brink Intl Assoc., *Exec Srch*
Eric Kercheval & Assoc., Exec Recrtrs, *Exec Srch*
Roth Young Exec Recrtrs, *Exec Srch*
Youth Emp. Project, *Perm. Emp Agcy*

Missouri

Decker Persnnl, *Perm. Emp Agcy*
Toberson Grp, *Perm. Emp Agcy*

New Jersey

Insearch, *Exec Srch*

New York

Alfus Grp, *Exec Srch*
Executive Link, *Exec Srch*
Hospitality Assoc., *Exec Srch*
Hospitality Intl, *Exec Srch*
Roth Young of Long Islnd, *Exec Srch*
Yours In Travel Persnnl Agcy, *Perm. Emp Agcy*

North Carolina

Forbes Temp. Staffng, *Temp. Agcy*
Snelling Srch, *Exec Srch*

Ohio

Rich Johns Career Consltnts, *Perm. Emp Agcy*
O'Brien & Roof Co, *Exec Srch*
Jerry Paul Assoc., *Perm. Emp Agcy*

Pennsylvania

Roth Young Persnnl Svcs, *Exec Srch*
Snelling Persnnl Svcs, *Temp. Agcy*

South Dakota

Snelling Persnnl Svcs, *Perm. Emp Agcy*

Tennessee

Quest Intl, *Exec Srch*

Texas

Alpha Resrcs Grp, *Exec Srch*
Elliot Assoc., *Exec Srch*
Ken Herst Hotel Exec Srch, *Exec Srch*
SearchAmerica, *Exec Srch*

Virginia

Career Market Consltnts, *Exec Srch*
Executive Recrtrs of Fairfax, *Exec Srch*

HUMAN RESOURCES

Arizona

Fishel Human Resrcs Assoc., *Exec Srch*
Rob Saxon & Assoc., *Exec Srch*

California

Bennett & Co Consltng Grp, *Exec Srch*
Rich Gast & Assoc., *Exec Srch*
Marvin Laba & Assoc., *Exec Srch*
MacNaughton Assoc., *Exec Srch*
Sanford Rose Assoc., *Exec Srch*
TLC Staffng, *Temp. Agcy*

Florida

Interim Accnt'g Prof'ls, *Exec Srch*

Georgia

R.A. Clark Consltng, *Exec Srch*

Illinois

Abbott Smith Assoc., *Exec Srch*
B.J. Abrams & Assoc., *Exec Srch*
Maramax Persnnl, *Perm. Emp Agcy*
Retail Staffers, *Exec Srch*

Indiana

Morley Grp, *Exec Srch*
Technical Srch & Recrtrs, *Exec Srch*

Iowa

Mgmt. Recrtrs Intl, *Exec Srch*
Premier Srch Grp, *Exec Srch*

Maryland

Brindisi Srch, *Exec Srch*

Massachusetts

Resource Mngmnt Intl, *Contract Svc*
Willmott & Assoc., *Exec Srch*

Michigan

Smith Prof'l Srch, *Exec Srch*
Weliver & Assoc., *Exec Srch*

Minnesota

George Konik Assoc. Inc, *Exec Srch*

New Jersey

Frank Allen & Assoc., *Exec Srch*
Balcor Assoc., *Exec Srch*
Dean-Wharton Assoc., *Exec Srch*
Fox-Morris Assoc., *Exec Srch*
Karras Persnnl, *Exec Srch*
Mgmt. Recrtrs Intl, *Exec Srch*
S-H-S of Cherry Hill, *Perm. Emp Agcy*

New Mexico

Mgmt. Resource Consltng, *Exec Srch*

New York

Paxton Resrcs, *Exec Srch*
Alexander Ross Assoc., *Perm. Emp Agcy*
Roth Young of Long Islnd, *Exec Srch*

Ohio

Pete DeLuke & Assoc., *Exec Srch*
Dillard Exec Srch, *Exec Srch*
Guthoff & Assoc., *Exec Srch*

Pennsylvania

Andre Grp, *Exec Srch*
Brackin & Sayers Assoc., *Exec Srch*
Fox-Morris Assoc., *Exec Srch*
ProSearch, *Exec Srch*
Romac Intl, *Exec Srch*
Terry Taylor & Assoc., *Exec Srch*

Rhode Island

Employ Ease, *Perm. Emp Agcy*

South Carolina

Dunhill Staffng, *Exec Srch*

Texas

Boles & Assoc., *Exec Srch*
Fox-Morris Assoc., *Exec Srch*
Hyman & Assoc., *Exec Srch*

Virginia

Mgmt. Recrtrs Intl, *Exec Srch*
The Talley Grp, *Exec Srch*

HUMAN SERVICES

District of Columbia

Access: Networking in the Public Interest, *Career/Outplacemnt*

Maine

Combined Resrcs, *Contract Svc*

Massachusetts

Arbor Assoc., *Temp. Agcy*
Human Svc Options, *Temp. Agcy*
Pro Staff, *Temp. Agcy*

Minnesota

Kaposia, *Perm. Emp Agcy*

Rhode Island

Job Connection, *Perm. Emp Agcy*

INDUSTRIAL

Alabama

A-1 Emp. Svc, *Perm. Emp Agcy*
Aerotek, *Perm. Emp Agcy*
Mary Cheek & Assoc., *Exec Srch*
Clark Persnnl Svc of Mobile, *Exec Srch*
Employment Consltnts, *Perm. Emp Agcy*
FORTUNE Persnnl Consltnts, *Exec Srch*
Labor Finders, *Temp. Agcy*
Manpower, *Temp. Agcy*
National Labor Line, *Exec Srch*
J.L. Small Assoc., *Exec Srch*
VIP Persnnl, *Perm. Emp Agcy*
Weldtek Testing Laboratory, *Career/Outplacemnt*
WorkForce, *Temp. Agcy*

Alaska

Manpower Temp. Svc, *Temp. Agcy*

Arizona

Adecco, *Contract Svc*
CDI Corp, *Contract Svc*
Devau Human Resrcs, *Temp. Agcy*
Manpower Intl, *Temp. Agcy*
Priority Staffng, *Perm. Emp Agcy*
Stivers Temp. Persnnl, *Temp. Agcy*

Arkansas

Intl Srch, *Exec Srch*
Turnage Emp. Svc Grp, *Exec Srch*
Utopia, *Exec Srch*

California

AccuStaff, *Exec Srch*
Alpha-Net Consltng Grp, *Exec Srch*
Apple One Emp. Svcs, *Perm. Emp Agcy*
Apropos Emp. Agcy, *Perm. Emp Agcy*
Arrowstaff Svcs, *Perm. Emp Agcy*
Best Temp. Svc, *Temp. Agcy*
Dan Bolen & Assoc., *Exec Srch*
CDI Corp, *Temp. Agcy*
California Job Connection, *Perm. Emp Agcy*
California Srch Agcy, *Exec Srch*
Career Quest, *Contract Svc*
Wayne Chamberlain & Assoc., *Exec Srch*
Crossroads Staff Svc, *Temp. Agcy*
Culver Persnnl Svcs, *Perm. Emp Agcy*
Drake Office Overload, *Temp. Agcy*
Dunhill Prof'l Srch, *Exec Srch*
Eleventh Hour Staff Svcs, *Temp. Agcy*
Employment Devlpmnt Dept, *Perm. Emp Agcy*
Employment Svc Agcy, *Perm. Emp Agcy*
Fisher Persnnl Mngmnt Svcs, *Exec Srch*
40 Plus of So. CA, *Exec Srch*
Dianne Gauger & Assoc., *Exec Srch*
Griffith & Assoc., *Exec Srch*
Industrial Svcs Co, *Temp. Agcy*
Interim Industrial Staffng, *Temp. Agcy*
Interim Persnnl, *Temp. Agcy*
Intl Staff Consltnts, *Exec Srch*
Intertec Persnnl, *Temp. Agcy*
JPM Intl, *Exec Srch*
Jerome & Co, *Exec Srch*
Kelly Svcs, *Temp. Agcy*
Klein & Assoc., *Temp. Agcy*
John Kurosky & Assoc., *Exec Srch*
Lab Support, *Temp. Agcy*
Labor World, *Temp. Agcy*
MK Tech. Svc, *Temp. Agcy*
Malibu Grp, *Exec Srch*
Mgmt. Recrtrs of Laguna Hills, *Exec Srch*
Mgmt. Recrtrs-Oakland/Sales Consltnts, *Exec Srch*
Manpower, *Temp. Agcy*
Maverick Staff Svc, *Perm. Emp Agcy*
Multisearch Recrtrs, *Exec Srch*
Murray Enterprises Staff Svcs, *Temp. Agcy*
Musick & Assoc., *Exec Srch*
Nelson HR Solut'ns, *Perm. Emp Agcy*
Norrell Temp. Svcs of CA, *Temp. Agcy*
Omni Express Temps, *Temp. Agcy*
Onyx Persnnl Svcs, *Perm. Emp Agcy*
Presidio Persnnl, *Temp. Agcy*
Pro Staff Persnnl Svcs, *Perm. Emp Agcy*
ProFile Persnnl, *Perm. Emp Agcy*
Questemps, *Temp. Agcy*
Remedy Intelligent Staffng, *Temp. Agcy*
Resource Persnnl Svcs, *Temp. Agcy*
Resource Perspectives, *Exec Srch*
Riley-Cole Recrtmnt Specialists, *Exec Srch*
Sales Consltnts of Modesto, *Exec Srch*
Sales Consltnts of Sacramento, *Exec Srch*
San Diego Persnnl & Employment, *Temp. Agcy*
Santa Barbara Plcmnt, *Perm. Emp Agcy*
Sierra Technlgy, *Contract Svc*
Spectrum Temp. Employees, *Temp. Agcy*
Sun Persnnl Svcs, *Temp. Agcy*
T.R. Emp. Agcy, *Perm. Emp Agcy*
TRC Staff Svcs, *Perm. Emp Agcy*

Technical Aid Corp, *Temp. Agcy*
Temps Unlimtd, *Temp. Agcy*
Trendtec, *Temp. Agcy*
United Staff Solut'ns, *Exec Srch*
United/Corestaff Staff Svcs, *Perm. Emp Agcy*
Victor Valley Persnnl Agcy, *Perm. Emp Agcy*
Volt Temp. Svcs, *Temp. Agcy*
WGI Solut'ns, *Exec Srch*
Western Staff Svcs, *Temp. Agcy*
Your People Prof'ls, *Perm. Emp Agcy*

Colorado

Aspen Persnnl Svcs, *Perm. Emp Agcy*
Career Forum, *Exec Srch*
Eagle Valley Temps, *Temp. Agcy*
Enscicon Corp, *Perm. Emp Agcy*
40 Plus of CO, *Career/Outplacemnt*
JobSearch, *Temp. Agcy*
Kelly Svcs, *Temp. Agcy*
Labor Ready, *Temp. Agcy*
Manpower Intl, *Temp. Agcy*
Mesa (Mgmt. Exec Svcs), *Exec Srch*
Olsten Staff Svcs, *Temp. Agcy*
On Call Tech. Svcs/StaffMark, *Temp. Agcy*
SOS Staff Svcs, *Temp. Agcy*
Star Persnnl, *Exec Srch*
Technical Aid Corp, *Temp. Agcy*
Todays Temporary, *Temp. Agcy*
J.Q. Turner & Assoc., *Exec Srch*
Western Staff Svcs, *Temp. Agcy*
Woodmoor Grp, *Exec Srch*

Connecticut

Admiral Staff Svcs, *Temp. Agcy*
Bohan & Bradstreet, *Perm. Emp Agcy*
CGS Staff Svcs, *Temp. Agcy*
Cahill Assoc., *Exec Srch*
Charter Persnnl Svcs, *Exec Srch*
Corporate Staff Solut'ns, *Temp. Agcy*
Hire Logic, *Temp. Agcy*
J.G. Hood Assoc., *Perm. Emp Agcy*
Human Resource Consltnts Exec. Srch Firm
Industrial Recrtrs Assn, *Perm. Emp Agcy*
Jobshop, *Perm. Emp Agcy*
Lutz Assoc., *Exec Srch*
MJF Assoc., *Exec Srch*
Mgmt. Recrtrs Intl, *Exec Srch*
Office Svcs of CT, *Perm. Emp Agcy*
Barry Persky & Co., *Exec Srch*
Quality Control Recrtrs, *Exec Srch*
Tech. Staff Solut'ns, *Temp. Agcy*
Western Staff Svcs, *Temp. Agcy*

Delaware

J.B. Groner Exec Srch, *Exec Srch*
E.W. Hodges & Assoc., *Exec Srch*
Independent Nat'l Srch & Assoc., *Exec Srch*
The Placers, *Temp. Agcy*

District of Columbia

Manpower, *Temp. Agcy*
Norrell Svcs, *Temp. Agcy*

Florida

AAA Employment, *Perm. Emp Agcy*
Academy Design & Tech. Svcs, *Contract Svc*
AccuTech, *Contract Svc*
Active Prof'ls, *Exec Srch*
Adecco, *Temp. Agcy*
All Trades Staffng, *Contract Svc*
American Exec Srch, *Exec Srch*
B&B Persnnl, *Perm. Emp Agcy*
The Brand Co, *Exec Srch*
Bryan & Assoc./Worknet, Etc., *Exec Srch*
Colli Assoc. of Tampa, *Exec Srch*
DGA Persnnl Grp, *Exec Srch*
Donbar Svc Corp, *Temp. Agcy*
Employers' Assistant, *Temp. Agcy*
Environmental Health & Safety Srch Assoc., *Exec Srch*
Ethan Allen Persnnl Plcmnt, *Exec Srch*
Five Star Temporary, *Temp. Agcy*
FORTUNE Persnnl Consltnts, *Exec Srch*
Girl Friday Persnnl, *Temp. Agcy*
Kelly Svcs, *Temp. Agcy*
Koerner Grp, *Exec Srch*
The Mac Grp, *Exec Srch*
Mgmt. Recrtrs of Jacksonville, *Exec Srch*
Mgmt. Recrtrs of Lake Cnty, *Exec Srch*
Mgmt. Recrtrs of Miami, *Exec Srch*
Mgmt. Recrtrs of Pensacola, *Exec Srch*
Mgmt. Recrtrs of St. Petersburg, *Exec Srch*
Mgmt. Recrtrs of Tallahassee, *Exec Srch*
Mgmt. Recrtrs of Tampa, *Exec Srch*
Manpower Temp. Svcs, *Temp. Agcy*
Norrell Svcs, *Temp. Agcy*
Norrell Tech. Svcs, *Exec Srch*
Priority Srch, *Exec Srch*
Profes. Staffing/Able Body Temp. Svcs, *Contract Svc*
The Reserves Netwrk, *Temp. Agcy*
The Ryan Charles Grp, *Exec Srch*
Sales Consltnts of Fort Lauderdale, *Exec Srch*
Sales Consltnts of Jacksonville, *Exec Srch*
Sales Consltnts of Sarasota, *Exec Srch*
Doug Sears & Assoc., *Exec Srch*
Staffing Svcs Grp, *Perm. Emp Agcy*
Summit Exec Srch Consltnts, *Exec Srch*
Sun Persnnl West, *Exec Srch*
Western Staff Svcs, *Temp. Agcy*

Georgia

Adecco Tech. Svcs, *Contract Svc*
All-Star Temp. & Emp. Svcs, *Temp. Agcy*
Anderson Industrial Assoc., *Exec Srch*
Arjay & Assoc., *Exec Srch*
Augusta Staffing Assoc., *Perm. Emp Agcy*
Comprehensive Srch Grp, *Exec Srch*
Corporate Srch Consltnts, *Exec Srch*
Elite Staff Svcs, *Perm. Emp Agcy*
Express Persnnl Svcs, *Perm. Emp Agcy*
Express Persnnl Svcs, *Exec Srch*
ISC of Atlanta/Intl Career Continuation, *Exec Srch*
Job Shop, *Exec Srch*
Kelly Svcs, *Temp. Agcy*
MSI Intl, *Exec Srch*
Mgmt. Recrtrs of Atlanta, *Exec Srch*
Mgmt. Recrtrs of Marietta, *Exec Srch*
Mgmt. Recrtrs of Savannah, *Exec Srch*
Norred & Assoc., *Perm. Emp Agcy*
Priority 1 Staff Svcs, *Temp. Agcy*
Quality Temp. Svc, *Temp. Agcy*
Randstad Staff Svcs, *Perm. Emp Agcy*
Ranger Svcs, *Temp. Agcy*
SearchAmerica, *Exec Srch*
Southern Emp. Svc, *Perm. Emp Agcy*
Team One Partners, *Exec Srch*
Todays Emp. Solut'ns, *Perm. Emp Agcy*
Western Staff Svcs, *Temp. Agcy*
Western Tech. Svcs, *Temp. Agcy*

Hawaii

Altres Staffng, *Temp. Agcy*
Dunhill Prof'l Srch of Hawaii, *Exec Srch*
Kelly Svcs, *Temp. Agcy*
Olsten Staff Svcs, *Temp. Agcy*

Idaho

Intermountain Staffing Resrcs, *Perm. Emp Agcy*
Western Staff Svcs, *Temp. Agcy*

Illinois

A.B.A. Placemnts/A.B.A. Temps, *Perm. Emp Agcy*
The Ability Grp, *Exec Srch*
Accurate Persnnl, *Perm. Emp Agcy*
AccuStaff Inc., *Temp. Agcy*
Adecco, *Temp. Agcy*
American Contrct Svcs, *Contract Svc*
American Tech. Srch, *Exec Srch*
Assured Staffng, *Temp. Agcy*
Banner Persnnl, *Perm. Emp Agcy*
Britannia, *Exec Srch*
Burling Grp Ltd., *Exec Srch*
Cook Assoc., *Exec Srch*
Corporate Environment, *Exec Srch*
Cumberland Grp, *Exec Srch*
Davis Temps, *Temp. Agcy*
Executive Srch Intl, *Exec Srch*
Express Persnnl Svcs, *Temp. Agcy*
Furst Staff Svcs, *Temp. Agcy*
Jender & Co, *Contract Svc*
Kunzer Assoc., *Exec Srch*
Arlene Leff & Assoc., *Exec Srch*
Lynco Mngmnt Persnnl, *Exec Srch*
Magnum Srch, *Exec Srch*
Mgmt. Recrtrs of Arlington Heights, *Exec Srch*
Mgmt. Recrtrs of Des Plaines, *Exec Srch*
Mgmt. Recrtrs of Rockford, *Exec Srch*
Mgmt. Support Svcs, *Exec Srch*
Manpower Temp. Svcs, *Temp. Agcy*
Manufacturing Resrcs, *Exec Srch*
Marsteller Wilcox Assoc., *Exec Srch*
Mathey Svcs, *Exec Srch*
National Srch, *Exec Srch*
Norrell Svcs, *Temp. Agcy*
Olsten Information Technlgy Staffng, *Perm. Emp Agcy*
Omega Tech. Corp, *Exec Srch*
Omni Srch Exec. Srch Firm
Pelichem Assoc., *Exec Srch*
Pollak & Skan, *Contract Svc*
Quantum Prof'l Srch/Quantum Staff Svcs, *Exec Srch*
The Raleigh Warwick Grp, *Exec Srch*
Remedy Intelligent Staffng, *Temp. Agcy*
Sales Consltnts/Mgmt. Recrtrs Intl, *Exec Srch*
Sales Consltnts of Oak Brk, *Exec Srch*
Ralph Smith & Assoc., *Exec Srch*
Snyder Staffng, *Temp. Agcy*
Staffing Consltnts, *Perm. Emp Agcy*
TSC Mngmnt Svcs, *Exec Srch*
Temporary Assoc., *Temp. Agcy*
Webb Emp. Svc, *Perm. Emp Agcy*
West Persnnl, *Perm. Emp Agcy*
Working World, *Temp. Agcy*
World Emp. Svc, *Perm. Emp Agcy*
Xagas & Assoc., *Exec Srch*

Indiana

AccuStaff, *Temp. Agcy*
Angola Persnnl Svcs, *Perm. Emp Agcy*
Bane & Assoc., *Perm. Emp Agcy*
Belcan Tech. Svcs, *Contract Svc*
Bill Caldwell Emp. Svc, *Perm. Emp Agcy*
Canis Major/HR Quest, *Exec Srch*
Career Consltnts, *Perm. Emp Agcy*
Careers Unlimtd, *Exec Srch*
Chevigny Persnnl Agcy, *Exec Srch*
Corporate Staff Resrcs, *Temp. Agcy*
Dunhill of Brown Cnty, *Exec Srch*
Dunhill Prof'l Srch, *Exec Srch*
Dunhill Staffing Syst., *Temp. Agcy*
Employment Recrtrs, *Perm. Emp Agcy*
Express Persnnl, *Temp. Agcy*
First Call Temp. Svcs, *Temp. Agcy*
Flexible Persnnl, *Temp. Agcy*
Hobart Emp. Agcy, *Perm. Emp Agcy*
Interim Persnnl, *Temp. Agcy*
Job Placemnt Svc, *Perm. Emp Agcy*
Johnson Brown Assoc., *Exec Srch*
Mgmt. Recrtrs Intl, *Exec Srch*
Norrell Staff Svcs, *Temp. Agcy*
Olsten Staff Svcs, *Temp. Agcy*
Perry Persnnl Plus, *Perm. Emp Agcy*
Persnnl Mgmt., *Temp. Agcy*
Quiring Assoc. HR Consltng Grp, *Exec Srch*
Rush Temps, *Temp. Agcy*
Star Staffng, *Temp. Agcy*
TRC Staff Svcs, *Temp. Agcy*
Technetics Corp, *Contract Svc*
Time Svcs, *Perm. Emp Agcy*
Try Temps, *Temp. Agcy*
Warrick Cnty Emp. & Training Ctr, *Career/Outplacemnt*
Wimmer Temps & Direct Plcmnt, *Temp. Agcy*

Iowa

Burton Placemnt Svcs, *Exec Srch*
Byrnes & Rupkey, *Exec Srch*
CSI Employment, *Exec Srch*
Helping Hands Temp. Svc, *Temp. Agcy*
Salem Mngmnt dba Rudy Salem Staff Svcs, *Temp. Agcy*
Staff Mgmt., *Contract Svc*

Kansas

Business Specialists, *Perm. Emp Agcy*
Foster Design Co, *Contract Svc*
Kansas Workforce, *Temp. Agcy*
Key Staffng, *Temp. Agcy*
Mgmt. Recrtrs of Topeka, *Exec Srch*
Manpower, *Temp. Agcy*
Network of Excellence, *Exec Srch*
Parr & Assoc., *Perm. Emp Agcy*
Stoneburner Assoc., *Exec Srch*
Western Staff Svcs, *Temp. Agcy*

Kentucky

Belcan Staff Svcs, *Perm. Emp Agcy*
The Exec Advantage, *Exec Srch*
Manpower, *Temp. Agcy*
Persnnl Solut'ns, *Perm. Emp Agcy*
Precision Staffng, *Temp. Agcy*
Precision Staffng, *Perm. Emp Agcy*
Staffing Alternatives, *Temp. Agcy*
TLI Tech. Staffng, *Perm. Emp Agcy*
Weller-Wooley & Assoc., *Exec Srch*

Louisiana

Career Persnnl Consltnts, *Exec Srch*
Interim Persnnl, *Temp. Agcy*
Manpower, *Temp. Agcy*
Olsten Persnnl/Briggs Legal Staffng, *Perm. Emp Agcy*
Technical & Prof'l Sources, *Exec Srch*
Technical Resource Staff Svcs, *Temp. Agcy*

Maine

At Work Persnnl, *Temp. Agcy*
Goodrich Consltng, *Exec Srch*
John Jay & Co, *Exec Srch*
National Recrtrs of ME, *Exec Srch*
Paper Industry Recrtmnt, *Perm. Emp Agcy*

Maryland

D.W. Baird & Assoc., *Exec Srch*
Echelon Svc Co, *Contract Svc*
L.S. Gross & Assoc., *Exec Srch*
Onsite Commercial Staffng, *Perm. Emp Agcy*
Sales Consltnts of Baltimore Cty, *Exec Srch*
TAD Staff Svcs, *Temp. Agcy*
Winston Srch, *Exec Srch*

Massachusetts

Abbott's of Boston, *Exec Srch*
Ability Srch of N.E., *Perm. Emp Agcy*
Brady Emp. Svc, *Perm. Emp Agcy*
Carter/MacKay of Framingham, *Exec Srch*
Corporate Staff Solut'ns, *Temp. Agcy*
Cyr Assoc., *Exec Srch*
Dunhill Staffing Syst., *Temp. Agcy*
Engineering Mngmnt Support, *Temp. Agcy*
Gilreath Weatherby, *Exec Srch*
L.J. Gonzer Assoc., *Exec Srch*
Interim Persnnl, *Temp. Agcy*
Johnson & Hill Staff Svc, *Temp. Agcy*
Kelly Svcs, *Temp. Agcy*
L&L Temps, *Temp. Agcy*
Mgmt. Recrtrs Intl, *Exec Srch*
Manpower, *Temp. Agcy*
Mass Temps, *Temp. Agcy*
Master Srch, *Perm. Emp Agcy*
Molari, *Temp. Agcy*
Need Persnnl Plcmnt, *Temp. Agcy*
New England Persnnl, *Perm. Emp Agcy*
Norrell Staff Svcs, *Contract Svc*
Pro Staff, *Temp. Agcy*
Russell Reynolds Assoc., *Exec Srch*
George Sandel Assoc., *Perm. Emp Agcy*
Selectemps, *Temp. Agcy*
Tech/Aid, *Contract Svc*
Technical Persnnl Svcs, *Perm. Emp Agcy*
Total Tech. Svcs, *Perm. Emp Agcy*
United Prof'l Plcmnt, *Exec Srch*
Volt Svcs Grp, *Temp. Agcy*

Michigan

Advance Employment, *Exec Srch*
Allied Tech. Svc, *Contract Svc*
Alternative Staff, *Temp. Agcy*
The Aucon Co, *Exec Srch*
Barman Staff Solut'ns/Barman Persnnl, *Perm. Emp Agcy*
Beacon Svcs, *Temp. Agcy*
Beacon Svcs, *Exec Srch*
Benford Assoc., *Exec Srch*
Career Assoc., *Contract Svc*
Dynamic Persnnl, *Contract Svc*
ExecuSearch of Southwst MI, *Perm. Emp Agcy*
Executive & Tech. Persnnl, *Exec Srch*
Executive Mngmnt Srch, *Exec Srch*
Executive Recrtrs Intl, *Exec Srch*
Express Persnnl Svcs, *Temp. Agcy*
Joseph Goldring & Assoc., *Exec Srch*
Steven Greene & Assoc., *Perm. Emp Agcy*
Human Resrcs Emp. Svcs, *Perm. Emp Agcy*
Interim Persnnl, *Temp. Agcy*
Job Fair Netwrk of MI, *Perm. Emp Agcy*
Kelly Tech. Svcs, *Contract Svc*
Key Persnnl, *Perm. Emp Agcy*
Mgmt. Recrtrs of Battle Creek, *Exec Srch*
Mgmt. Recrtrs of Flint, *Exec Srch*
Mgmt. Recrtrs of Livonia, *Exec Srch*
Mgmt. Recrtrs of Southeast MI, *Exec Srch*
METROSTAFF, *Exec Srch*
Michigan Srch Plus, *Exec Srch*
Office Staffing Recruitng, *Exec Srch*
Parr Srch, *Exec Srch*
Preferred Emp. Planning, *Perm. Emp Agcy*
Professional Resource Assoc., *Contract Svc*
Sales Consltnts of Auburn Hills, *Exec Srch*
Selective Recruitng Assoc., *Exec Srch*
Skill Tech Employment, *Perm. Emp Agcy*
Source Technlgy, *Exec Srch*
TAD Tech. Svcs, *Contract Svc*
Technical Prof'l Svc, *Perm. Emp Agcy*
Temporary Tech. Svcs, *Temp. Agcy*
Thomas & Assoc. of MI, *Exec Srch*
Trillium Staffng, *Temp. Agcy*
Venture Mngmnt & Staffng, *Exec Srch*
Wood Persnnl Svcs/Wood Temp. Staffng, *Perm. Emp Agcy*
Workforce, *Temp. Agcy*

Minnesota

A&B Persnnl, *Perm. Emp Agcy*
Advantage Persnnl, *Perm. Emp Agcy*
Answer Persnnl, *Temp. Agcy*
Award Temp. Svcs, *Temp. Agcy*
Bright Srch/Professional Staffng, *Exec Srch*
Diversified Employment, *Perm. Emp Agcy*
Express Persnnl Svcs, *Perm. Emp Agcy*
HR Svcs of Plymouth, *Exec Srch*
Mgmt. Recrtrs-Minneapolis/Sales Consltnts, *Exec Srch*
Manpower Tech. Svcs, *Perm. Emp Agcy*
Manpower Temp. Svcs, *Temp. Agcy*
NER (National Engineering Resrcs), *Exec Srch*
North American Recrtrs, *Exec Srch*
Nycor Srch, *Exec Srch*
Persnnl Assist. Corp, *Exec Srch*
Professional Recrtrs, *Exec Srch*
Programming Alternatives of MN, *Exec Srch*
Regency Recrtrs, *Exec Srch*
Resource Srch, *Exec Srch*
Sathe & Assoc. Exec Srch, *Exec Srch*
Technical Resrcs, *Perm. Emp Agcy*
Temp Force, *Temp. Agcy*
H.L. Yoh Co, *Contract Svc*

Mississippi

Andrus Assoc. dba Svc Specialists Ltd., *Perm. Emp Agcy*
Coats & Coats Persnnl, *Perm. Emp Agcy*
Columbus Persnnl, *Temp. Agcy*
EPSCO Persnnl, *Temp. Agcy*
Impact Persnnl Svcs, *Exec Srch*
Persnnl Unlimtd, *Exec Srch*

Missouri

ABC Emp. Svc, *Perm. Emp Agcy*
Jay Alexandr & Assoc. dba Kirdonn Grp, *Perm. Emp Agcy*
Bestemps, *Perm. Emp Agcy*
Burns Emp. Svc, *Exec Srch*
Business Persnnl Svcs, *Temp. Agcy*
The Christiansen Grp, *Exec Srch*
Crider & Assoc., *Perm. Emp Agcy*
Crown Svcs, *Temp. Agcy*
Deck & Decker Emp. Svc, *Perm. Emp Agcy*
Decker Persnnl, *Perm. Emp Agcy*
Dunhill Persnnl System of Missouri, *Exec Srch*
Employer Advantage, *Exec Srch*
FORTUNE Persnnl Consltnts, *Exec Srch*
Haskell Assoc., *Exec Srch*
JoDoc Enterprises, *Temp. Agcy*
B. Loehr Temps, *Temp. Agcy*
Mgmt. Recrtrs of Kansas Cty, *Exec Srch*
Mgmt. Recrtrs of Springfield, *Exec Srch*
Mgmt. Recrtrs of St. Louis, *Exec Srch*
Mgmt. Recrtrs of St. Louis, *Exec Srch*
Manpower Temp. Svcs, *Temp. Agcy*
J. Miles Persnnl Svcs, *Exec Srch*
National Physician Placemnt Svcs, *Exec Srch*
Officemates5 of St. Louis, *Exec Srch*
Olsten Staff Svcs, *Temp. Agcy*
Snelling Persnnl Svcs, *Perm. Emp Agcy*
Workforce, *Temp. Agcy*

Nebraska

Adecco, *Temp. Agcy*
Corporate Recrtrs, *Exec Srch*
Express Persnnl, *Exec Srch*
Kelly Svcs, *Temp. Agcy*
Sales Consltnts of Omaha, *Exec Srch*
Sharp Persnnl, *Temp. Agcy*

Nevada

Labor Finders, *Temp. Agcy*
Manpower Temp. Svcs, *Temp. Agcy*

New Hampshire

Affordable Solut'ns, *Contract Svc*
Barclay Persnnl Syst., *Exec Srch*
Chaucer Grp, *Perm. Emp Agcy*
Chaucer Grp, *Exec Srch*
Kelly Svcs, *Temp. Agcy*
Manpower Temp. Svcs, *Temp. Agcy*
National Emp. Svc Corp, *Perm. Emp Agcy*
Preferred Resrcs Grp, *Exec Srch*
Sales Consltnts of Nashua-Manchester, *Exec Srch*
Surge Resrcs, *Contract Svc*

New Jersey

Advanced Persnnl, *Perm. Emp Agcy*
American Staffing Resrcs, *Temp. Agcy*
Andrew Persnnl Svcs, *Perm. Emp Agcy*
Blake & Assoc. Exec Srch, *Exec Srch*
Career Srch Assoc., *Exec Srch*
Careers USA, *Perm. Emp Agcy*
Citizens Emp. Svcs, *Perm. Emp Agcy*
Cox Darrow & Owens, *Exec Srch*
M.T. Donaldson Assoc., *Exec Srch*
Dunhill Temp. Syst., *Temp. Agcy*
Dynamic Recrtrs, *Exec Srch*
Express Persnnl Svcs, *Perm. Emp Agcy*
Hughes & Podesla Persnnl, *Perm. Emp Agcy*
Impact Persnnl, *Perm. Emp Agcy*
Joule People Providers, *Perm. Emp Agcy*
Kaye Persnnl, *Temp. Agcy*
Joseph Keyes Assoc., *Perm. Emp Agcy*
Mgmt. Recrtrs of Bay Head, *Exec Srch*
Mgmt. Recrtrs of Medford, *Exec Srch*
Mgmt. Recrtrs of Orange Cnty, *Exec Srch*
Mayfair Svcs, *Perm. Emp Agcy*
OMNE Staff Svcs, *Temp. Agcy*
Orion Consltng, *Exec Srch*
Pomerantz Persnnl, *Perm. Emp Agcy*
Protocall Bus. Staff Svcs, *Temp. Agcy*
R.S. Sadow Assoc., *Exec Srch*
Sales Consltnts of Morris Cnty, *Exec Srch*
Sales Consltnts of Sparta, *Exec Srch*
Rob Scott Assoc., *Exec Srch*
Summit Grp, *Exec Srch*
Tenek Corp, *Exec Srch*

New Mexico

Albuquerque Persnnl, *Perm. Emp Agcy*
CDI Corp, *Contract Svc*
Manpower, *Temp. Agcy*
Trambley The Recruiter, *Perm. Emp Agcy*

New York

AARP Foundation Senior Community Svc/Employment Program, *Perm. Emp Agcy*
ATS Reliance, *Perm. Emp Agcy*
Accounting & Computer Persnnl, *Perm. Emp Agcy*
Merrill Adams Assoc., *Career/Outplacemnt*
American Bus. Consltnts, *Career/Outplacemnt*
Arrow Emp. Agcy, *Perm. Emp Agcy*
Beishline Exec Srch, *Exec Srch*
Bestemp Temp. Svcs, *Temp. Agcy*
Bos Bus. Consltnts, *Exec Srch*
Burns Persnnl, *Exec Srch*
Carlile Persnnl Agcy, *Perm. Emp Agcy*
Corporate Careers/R.J. Assoc., *Exec Srch*
Corporate Moves, *Exec Srch*
Frank Cuomo & Assoc., *Exec Srch*
Eden Persnnl, *Perm. Emp Agcy*
Extra Help Emp. Svc, *Temp. Agcy*
Fifth Avenue Emp. Svcs, *Temp. Agcy*
Graphic Techniques, *Temp. Agcy*
The Haas Assoc., *Exec Srch*
Robert Half Intl/Information Syst. Division, *Exec Srch*
Hart-Merrell Persnnl, *Exec Srch*
Interim Persnnl, *Temp. Agcy*
Fred Koffler Assoc., *Exec Srch*
Lab Support, *Temp. Agcy*
Lake Assoc., *Exec Srch*
Michael John Lawrence & Assoc., *Exec Srch*
Mgmt. Recrtrs of Suffolk, *Exec Srch*
Mgmt. Recrtrs of Woodbury/ CompuSrch, *Exec Srch*
Manpower Temp. Svcs, *Temp. Agcy*
Metro Resrcs of Rochester, *Temp. Agcy*
Metro Persnnl/Metro Nursing Svcs, *Exec Srch*
Morgan-Murray Persnnl/M&M Top Temps, *Temp. Agcy*
Noah Assoc., *Perm. Emp Agcy*
Olsten Staff Svcs, *Temp. Agcy*
Parsons, Anderson & Gee, *Perm. Emp Agcy*
Phoenix Emp. Agcy, *Perm. Emp Agcy*
Remedy Intelligent Staffng, *Temp. Agcy*
Sales Srch, Ltd./Executive Resume Svc, *Exec Srch*
Staff Managers, *Temp. Agcy*
Stafkings Persnnl Syst., *Temp. Agcy*
Superior Concepts, *Contract Svc*
TAD Resrcs, *Contract Svc*
Thorsen Assoc., *Exec Srch*
Todd Arro, *Exec Srch*
Volt Svcs Grp, *Contract Svc*
Weber Mngmnt Consltnts, *Exec Srch*
Westchester Emp. Agcy, *Perm. Emp Agcy*
Western Staff Svcs, *Temp. Agcy*
H.L. Yoh Co, *Contract Svc*

North Carolina

A-1 Staffing & Persnnl, *Perm. Emp Agcy*
Accurate Staff Consltnts, *Exec Srch*
AccuStaff Inc., *Temp. Agcy*
Action Tech. Staffng, *Temp. Agcy*
Alpha Omega Exec Srch, *Exec Srch*
AmeriPro Srch, *Exec Srch*
Atchison & Assoc., *Exec Srch*
Ayers & Assoc., *Exec Srch*
Caldwell Persnnl Svcs, *Perm. Emp Agcy*
Corporate Staff Consltnts, *Perm. Emp Agcy*
Eastern Srch Grp, *Exec Srch*
Employment Consltnts, *Contract Svc*
Executive Staff Svcs, *Perm. Emp Agcy*
The Furniture Agcy, *Exec Srch*
Interim Persnnl, *Temp. Agcy*
The Jobs Market, *Perm. Emp Agcy*
Jobs of Fayetteville, *Perm. Emp Agcy*
Kelly Svcs, *Temp. Agcy*
MTS, *Perm. Emp Agcy*
Mgmt. Recrtrs/Sales Consltnts, *Exec Srch*
Mgmt. Recrtrs of Burlington, *Exec Srch*
Mgmt. Recrtrs of Kinston, *Exec Srch*
McCain Emp. Agcy, *Temp. Agcy*
Metals & Wood Agcy, *Exec Srch*
Myers & Assoc., *Perm. Emp Agcy*
Olsten Staff Svcs, *Temp. Agcy*
The Perkin Grp, *Exec Srch*
Professional Persnnl Assoc., *Perm. Emp Agcy*
Quality Temp. Svcs, *Temp. Agcy*
Search Consltnts Worldwide, *Exec Srch*
Snelling Persnnl Svcs, *Contract Svc*
Snelling Srch, *Exec Srch*
Sparks Persnnl Svcs, *Exec Srch*
Talent Tree Staffng, *Perm. Emp Agcy*
Temporary Staffing Syst., *Temp. Agcy*
Waddy Thomson Assoc., *Exec Srch*
John Williams & Assoc., *Exec Srch*
Winston Temp. Staffng, *Temp. Agcy*
Youngblood Staffng, *Perm. Emp Agcy*

North Dakota

Career Connection, *Exec Srch*
Olsten Staff Svcs/Kramer & Assoc./Expressway Persnnl, *Temp. Agcy*

Ohio

AccuStaff, *Temp. Agcy*
Alliance Tech. Svcs, *Contract Svc*
Dave Arnold & Assoc., *Exec Srch*
Belcan Tech. Svcs, *Contract Svc*
Burks Grp, *Exec Srch*
CBS Persnnl Svcs, *Perm. Emp Agcy*
Career Connections, *Perm. Emp Agcy*
Combined Resrcs, *Exec Srch*
Continental Srch Consltnts, *Exec Srch*
Corell Assoc., *Perm. Emp Agcy*
Custom Staffng, *Temp. Agcy*
DLD Tech. Svcs, *Contract Svc*
Delta Design Drafting, *Temp. Agcy*
Eastern Persnnl Svcs, *Perm. Emp Agcy*
Elite Resrcs Grp, *Exec Srch*
Executech, *Exec Srch*
Executive Connection, *Exec Srch*
Executive Srch Ltd., *Exec Srch*
F.L.A.G., *Exec Srch*
Flex-Tech Prof'l Svcs, *Contract Svc*
Flowers & Assoc./Associated Temps, *Exec Srch*
Frederick-Lehmann & Assoc./Temporarily Yours, *Exec Srch*
Gayhart & Assoc., *Exec Srch*
Global Resrcs Grp, *Contract Svc*
H.L. Goehring & Assoc., *Exec Srch*
Griffiths & Assoc., *Exec Srch*
H.J.C., *Exec Srch*
ITS Tech. Staffing/Interconnect Tech. Svcs, *Exec Srch*
Icon Mngmnt Grp, *Exec Srch*
Interim Persnnl, *Temp. Agcy*
Jaeger Intl, *Exec Srch*
Anne Jones Staffng, *Perm. Emp Agcy*
A.T. Kearney Exec Srch, *Exec Srch*
Kelly Svcs, *Temp. Agcy*
Laine's S.M.G., *Perm. Emp Agcy*
Mgmt. Recrtrs of Cincinnati, *Exec Srch*
Mgmt. Recrtrs of Cleveland, *Exec Srch*
Mgmt. Recrtrs of Cleveland, *Exec Srch*
Mgmt. Recrtrs of Cleveland, *Exec Srch*
Mgmt. Recrtrs of Columbus, *Exec Srch*
Mgmt. Recrtrs of Dayton, *Exec Srch*
Mgmt. Recrtrs of Solon, *Exec Srch*
Manpower Temp. Svcs, *Temp. Agcy*
Marvel Consltnts, *Exec Srch*
Messina Mngmnt Syst., *Exec Srch*
Miami Prof'l Srch, *Exec Srch*
Midland Consltnts, *Exec Srch*
Nesco Svc Co, *Temp. Agcy*
Newcomb-Desmond & Assoc., *Exec Srch*
North American Persnnl, *Exec Srch*
Northcoast Persnnl, *Exec Srch*
Olsten Staff Svcs, *Temp. Agcy*
Placement Svcs Limited, *Exec Srch*
The Prof'l Consltnts, *Exec Srch*
Professional Emp. Svcs, *Perm. Emp Agcy*
Professional Restaffing of OH, *Perm. Emp Agcy*
Providence Persnnl Consltnts, *Exec Srch*
RDS, *Contract Svc*
W.R. Renner & Assoc., *Exec Srch*
Rentech Ventures, *Perm. Emp Agcy*
Resource Techne Grp, *Exec Srch*
Revere Assoc., *Exec Srch*
Sales Consltnts of Cincinnati, *Exec Srch*
Snelling Persnnl Svcs, *Exec Srch*
Tabb & Assoc., *Exec Srch*
TAD Tech. Svcs, *Contract Svc*
Talent Tree Staffng, *Perm. Emp Agcy*
The Target HR Companies, *Temp. Agcy*
Teamwork U.S.A., *Contract Svc*
Technical Recruitng Svcs, *Exec Srch*
Technical/Mgmt. Resrcs, *Exec Srch*
Temporarily Yours Plcmnt, *Temp. Agcy*
Tradesman Intl, *Contract Svc*
Vector Technical, *Perm. Emp Agcy*
J.P. Walton & Assoc., *Exec Srch*

Oklahoma

Ameri Resource, *Exec Srch*
Cherokee Temps, *Temp. Agcy*
Express Persnnl Svcs, *Exec Srch*
Key Temp. Persnnl, *Temp. Agcy*
StaffMark, *Temp. Agcy*

Oregon

API Emp. Agcy, *Perm. Emp Agcy*
Able Temp. Svc, *Temp. Agcy*
Barrett Bus. Svcs, *Temp. Agcy*
Express Persnnl Svcs, *Exec Srch*
Hackenschmidt, Weaver & Fox, *Exec Srch*
Impact Staffng, *Temp. Agcy*
Kelly Svcs, *Temp. Agcy*
Manpower Temp. Svcs, *Temp. Agcy*
NPRC/Nationwde Persnnl Recruitng & Consltng, *Exec Srch*
Northwest Temp. & Staff Svcs, *Temp. Agcy*
Quest Temp. Svcs, *Temp. Agcy*
Saint Vincent De Paul Employment, *Temp. Agcy*
Uniforce Tech. Svcs, *Contract Svc*

Pennsylvania

AA Staff Solut'ns, *Contract Svc*
Action Persnnl Svcs, *Perm. Emp Agcy*
Alexander Persnnl Assoc., *Exec Srch*
All Staffng, *Perm. Emp Agcy*
Allegheny Persnnl Svcs, *Temp. Agcy*
American Srch Assoc., *Exec Srch*
ASAP Staffng, *Perm. Emp Agcy*
Atomic Persnnl, *Exec Srch*
Basilone-Oliver Exec Srch, *Exec Srch*
Career Concepts Staff Svcs, *Exec Srch*
COREStaff, *Temp. Agcy*
DiCenzo Persnnl Specialists, *Perm. Emp Agcy*
Dunn Assoc., *Exec Srch*
Fox-Morris Assoc., *Exec Srch*
Jerry Goldberg & Assoc., *Perm. Emp Agcy*
Garrick Hall & Assoc., *Exec Srch*
The Hastings Grp, *Exec Srch*
Hobbie Temp. Persnnl, *Temp. Agcy*
Human Resource Solut'ns, *Exec Srch*
IMC Intl, *Contract Svc*
Interim Persnnl of Lehigh Valley PA, *Temp. Agcy*
J-Rand Srch, *Exec Srch*
JK Resrcs, *Exec Srch*
Clifton Johnson Assoc., *Exec Srch*
Kathy Karr Persnnl, *Perm. Emp Agcy*
London Persnnl Svcs, *Perm. Emp Agcy*
Mgmt. Recrtrs Intl, *Exec Srch*
Manpower Temp. Svcs, *Temp. Agcy*
Rob McClure Ltd., *Exec Srch*
B. Paul Mickey & Assoc., *Exec Srch*
The Morris Grp, *Exec Srch*
National Computerized Employment, *Perm. Emp Agcy*
Norrell Svcs, *Contract Svc*
Olsten Staff Svcs, *Temp. Agcy*
Probe Technlgy, *Exec Srch*
Protocall Bus. Staffng, *Temp. Agcy*
Q-Source, *Perm. Emp Agcy*
Alan Raeburn Consltnts, *Exec Srch*
Select Persnnl, *Perm. Emp Agcy*
Kenn Spinrad, *Exec Srch*
TRC Staff Svcs, *Temp. Agcy*
Uni Temp Temp. Svc, *Temp. Agcy*
United Employment, *Perm. Emp Agcy*
Virtual Workplace, *Temp. Agcy*
Whittlesey & Assoc., *Exec Srch*
Yorktowne Persnnl, *Exec Srch*

Rhode Island

Johnson & Tregar Assoc., *Perm. Emp Agcy*
Kelly Svcs, *Temp. Agcy*
Albert Lee & Assoc., *Exec Srch*
Norrell Svcs, *Temp. Agcy*
PKS Assoc., *Exec Srch*

South Carolina

Bock & Assoc., *Exec Srch*
Dunhill Persnnl of St. Andrews, *Perm. Emp Agcy*
Engineering Persnnl Netwrk, *Exec Srch*
Ford & Assoc., *Exec Srch*
FORTUNE Persnnl Consltnts of Columbia, *Exec Srch*
Harvey Persnnl, *Perm. Emp Agcy*
Mgmt. Recrtrs of Orangeburg, *Exec Srch*
Miller & Assoc., *Exec Srch*
The Persnnl Netwrk, *Exec Srch*
Sales Consltnts/Mgmt. Recrtrs of Greenville, *Exec Srch*
Search & Recruit Intl, *Exec Srch*
Snelling Persnnl, *Perm. Emp Agcy*
Staffing Solut'ns, *Temp. Agcy*
StaffMark, *Temp. Agcy*
The Stroman Co, *Perm. Emp Agcy*
Technical South, *Temp. Agcy*

Tennessee

American Tech. Assoc., *Contract Svc*
Baker & Baker Emp. Svc, *Exec Srch*
Cook Assoc. Intl, *Exec Srch*
Engineer One, *Perm. Emp Agcy*
Express Persnnl Svcs, *Perm. Emp Agcy*
FORTUNE Persnnl Consltnts, *Exec Srch*
Hamilton Ryker Co, *Exec Srch*
Hester & Assoc., *Exec Srch*
Kelly Svcs, *Temp. Agcy*
Mgmt. Recrtrs of Chattanooga, *Exec Srch*
Mgmt. Recrtrs of Lenoir Cty, *Exec Srch*
Manpower, *Temp. Agcy*
The Morgan Grp, *Exec Srch*
Olsten Staff Svcs, *Temp. Agcy*
Piercy Emp. Svcs, *Perm. Emp Agcy*
Snelling Persnnl Svcs, *Exec Srch*
Technical Resource Assoc., *Exec Srch*
Temp Staff, *Temp. Agcy*
Unlimited Staff Solut'ns, *Contract Svc*
Rob Walker Assoc., *Contract Svc*

Texas

A-1 Persnnl, *Temp. Agcy*
Ackerman Johnson, *Exec Srch*
Action Persnnl, *Temp. Agcy*
Adecco, *Temp. Agcy*
B&M Air & Space Division, *Contract Svc*
Border Prof'l Recrtrs, *Perm. Emp Agcy*
Bundy-Stewart Assoc., *Exec Srch*
Butler Intl, *Contract Svc*
Certified Persnnl, *Contract Svc*
Creative Staff Svcs, *Temp. Agcy*
Dallas Emp. Svc, *Perm. Emp Agcy*
Gail Darling Staffing/Darling's Prof'l Desk, *Temp. Agcy*
Dunhill Prof'l Srch, *Exec Srch*
The Elsworth Grp, *Exec Srch*
Executive Srch Persnnl, *Exec Srch*
Express Persnnl Svcs, *Perm. Emp Agcy*
Focus Point, *Contract Svc*
FORTUNE Persnnl Consltnts/San Antonio, *Exec Srch*
Abel Gonzalez & Assoc., *Exec Srch*
H+M Recrtrs, *Exec Srch*
The Human Element of Business, *Exec Srch*
Inside Track, *Exec Srch*
Interim Persnnl, *Temp. Agcy*
Job Svcs, *Perm. Emp Agcy*
L.K. Jordan & Assoc., *Contract Svc*
LRJ Staff Svcs, *Perm. Emp Agcy*
Link Staff Svcs, *Temp. Agcy*
Loewenstein & Assoc., *Exec Srch*
Mgmt. Recrtrs of Round Rock, *Exec Srch*
Manpower Temp. Svcs, *Temp. Agcy*
McKinley•Arend Intl, *Exec Srch*
Nurses Today, *Temp. Agcy*
Olsten Staff Svcs, *Temp. Agcy*
The Pailin Grp, *Exec Srch*
Pate Resrcs Grp, *Exec Srch*
Phoenix Staffng, *Exec Srch*
Placements Unlimtd, *Perm. Emp Agcy*
Priority Persnnl, *Temp. Agcy*
Professions Today, *Perm. Emp Agcy*
Remedy Intelligent Staffng, *Perm. Emp Agcy*
Bart Roberson & Co, *Exec Srch*
Roth Young Persnnl Svcs/Dallas, *Exec Srch*
SOS Staff Svcs, *Temp. Agcy*
Sales Consltnts of Houston, *Exec Srch*
Search Netwrk Intl, *Exec Srch*
Snelling Persnnl Svcs, *Perm. Emp Agcy*
Snelling Persnnl Svcs, *Exec Srch*
Suburban Svcs, *Temp. Agcy*
TRC Staff Svcs, *Temp. Agcy*
TSP Persnnl Svcs, *Perm. Emp Agcy*
TAD Tech. Svcs, *Contract Svc*
Betty Tanner Prof'l Emp. Svc, *Exec Srch*
Tarrant Cnty Emp. Netwrk, *Perm. Emp Agcy*
Technical Careers, *Contract Svc*
TechSystems, *Contract Svc*
Total Temp. Svcs, *Temp. Agcy*
The Urban Placemnt Svc, *Exec Srch*
Valpers, *Exec Srch*
Volt Tech. Svcs, *Contract Svc*
Western Temp. Svc, *Temp. Agcy*

Utah

Mgmt. Recrtrs of Ogden, *Exec Srch*
Olsten Staff Svcs, *Temp. Agcy*

Vermont

Harmon Persnnl Svcs, *Temp. Agcy*
Persnnl Dept, *Temp. Agcy*
Jay Tracey Assoc., *Exec Srch*
Triad Temp. Svcs, *Temp. Agcy*

Virginia

Alpha Omega Resrcs, *Perm. Emp Agcy*
Bent Assoc., *Exec Srch*
Corporate Connection Exec. Srch Firm
H.R. Directions, *Contract Svc*
HATCH Mrktng Syst., *Perm. Emp Agcy*
Information Specialists Co, *Exec Srch*
Lee Staffing Resrcs, *Exec Srch*
Mgmt. Recrtrs Intl, *Exec Srch*
Manpower Temp. Svcs, *Temp. Agcy*
A.J. Morelli Contracting, *Contract Svc*
Olsten Staff Svcs, *Temp. Agcy*
PDS Temp. Svc, *Temp. Agcy*
Procurement Solut'ns, *Contract Svc*
Professional Srch Persnnl, *Exec Srch*
Search & Recruit Intl, *Exec Srch*
Select Staff Svcs, *Perm. Emp Agcy*
Snelling Persnnl Svcs, *Perm. Emp Agcy*
STAT Temps, *Temp. Agcy*
The Talley Grp, *Exec Srch*
Task Force of VA, *Exec Srch*
Temporary Solut'ns, *Temp. Agcy*
Western Staff Svcs, *Temp. Agcy*

William Blender & Assoc., *Exec Srch*
Computer Srch Grp, *Exec Srch*
Data Interaction, *Exec Srch*
Hamilton Grey Exec Srch, *Contract Svc*
Pro Staff Persnnl Svcs, *Temp. Agcy*
Pro-Tech Srch, *Exec Srch*
Recruitment Netwrk, *Exec Srch*
Sanford Rose Assoc., *Exec Srch*
Smith Scott & Assoc., *Exec Srch*
Source Svcs Corp, *Exec Srch*

Indiana
Johnson Brown Assoc., *Exec Srch*
Source Svcs Corp, *Exec Srch*

Iowa
Mgmt. Recrtrs Intl, *Exec Srch*

Kansas
Search One, *Exec Srch*
Source Svcs Corp, *Exec Srch*

Kentucky
ProVision Technolog's, *Contract Svc*
Romac Intl, *Exec Srch*
Source Svcs Corp, *Exec Srch*

Louisiana
Dunhill Persnnl System of LA, *Exec Srch*

Maine
Great Moose Lake Corp, *Exec Srch*

Maryland
Columbia Consltng, *Exec Srch*
A.G. Fishkin & Assoc., *Exec Srch*
ProVision Technolog's/National Recruitng Ctr, *Contract Svc*

Massachusetts
Michael Anthony Assoc., *Exec Srch*
Delores George, CPC, *Exec Srch*
Gustin Partners Exec. Srch Firm
HM Assoc., *Exec Srch*
Judge Tech. Svcs, *Exec Srch*
New Dimensions in Technlgy, *Exec Srch*
ProVision Technolog's, *Contract Svc*
Setford-Shaw-Najarjan Assoc., *Exec Srch*
Source Svcs Corp, *Exec Srch*

Michigan
Mgmt. Recrtrs Intl, *Exec Srch*
Persnnl At Law, *Temp. Agcy*
ProVision Technolog's, *Contract Svc*
Technical Aid Corp, *Contract Svc*
Henry Welker & Assoc., *Perm. Emp Agcy*
H.L. Yoh Co, *Contract Svc*

Minnesota
Computemp, *Contract Svc*
Charles Dahl & Assoc., *Exec Srch*
ProVision Technolog's, *Contract Svc*
Source Svcs Corp, *Exec Srch*

Missouri
Bradford & Galt Consltng Svcs, *Perm. Emp Agcy*

Nebraska
ProVision Technolog's, *Contract Svc*

New Hampshire
Access Data Persnnl, *Exec Srch*
Contrct Solut'ns, *Contract Svc*
National Emp. Svc Corp, *Perm. Emp Agcy*

New Jersey
Corporate Information Srch, *Exec Srch*
Sales Consltnts, *Exec Srch*
Source Svcs Corp/Source EDP, *Exec Srch*

New York
Computech Career Srch, *Exec Srch*
Computer Placemnts Unlimtd, *Exec Srch*
Computer Resrcs Corp, *Exec Srch*
ETC Srch, *Exec Srch*
Executive Srch Assoc., *Exec Srch*
Huntington Persnnl Consltnts, *Exec Srch*
Phoenix Srch Grp, *Exec Srch*
ProVision Technolog's/TAD Tech. Svcs, *Contract Svc*
Source Svcs Corp, *Exec Srch*
Strategic Recruitng, *Exec Srch*

North Carolina
COMFORCE Tech. Svcs, *Contract Svc*
ProVision Technolog's, *Contract Svc*
David Weinfeld Grp, *Exec Srch*
H.L. Yoh Co, *Contract Svc*

Ohio
Contrct Solut'ns, *Contract Svc*
Gammill Grp, *Exec Srch*
Mgmt. Recrtrs of No. Canton, *Exec Srch*
ProVision Technolog's, *Contract Svc*
Sachs Assoc., *Exec Srch*
Source Svcs Corp, *Exec Srch*

Oregon
D. Brown & Assoc., *Exec Srch*
Triad Technlgy Grp, *Perm. Emp Agcy*

Pennsylvania
Advanced Technlgy Resrcs, *Exec Srch*
Barton Persnnl Syst., *Exec Srch*
T.W. Boris Assn, *Exec Srch*
Clifford Assoc., *Perm. Emp Agcy*
Mgmt. Recrtrs Intl, *Exec Srch*
ProVision Technolog's, *Contract Svc*
RHI Consltng/Accountemps, *Contract Svc*
Romac Intl, *Exec Srch*
Source Svcs Corp, *Exec Srch*
Terry Taylor & Assoc., *Exec Srch*
H.L. Yoh Co, *Contract Svc*

Rhode Island
Sullivan & Cogliano, *Exec Srch*

South Carolina
Kersey & Assoc., *Exec Srch*

Tennessee
Software Resource Consltnts, *Exec Srch*

Texas
Bond & Assoc., *Exec Srch*
Computemp, *Temp. Agcy*
Computer Prof'ls Unlimtd, *Exec Srch*
EDP Computer Svcs, *Exec Srch*
People Source, *Exec Srch*
Professional Srch Consltnts, *Contract Svc*
ProVision Technolog's, *Contract Svc*
Romac Intl, *Exec Srch*
Source Svcs Corp, *Exec Srch*

Utah
Mgmt. Recrtrs of Provo, *Exec Srch*
Source Svcs Corp, *Exec Srch*

Virginia
Advantage Staffng, *Temp. Agcy*
Atlantic Resource Grp, *Perm. Emp Agcy*
Source Svcs Corp, *Exec Srch*
H.L. Yoh Co, *Contract Svc*

Washington
Source Svcs Corp, *Exec Srch*

Wisconsin
Data Processing Srch, *Exec Srch*
Hatch Staff Svcs, *Temp. Agcy*
Mgmt. Recrtrs, *Exec Srch*
Source Svcs Corp, *Exec Srch*

INSURANCE

Alabama
A-1 Emp. Svc, *Perm. Emp Agcy*
Mgmt. Recrtrs Intl, *Exec Srch*
Manpower, *Temp. Agcy*
Placers, *Perm. Emp Agcy*
VIP Persnnl, *Perm. Emp Agcy*

Arizona
Insurance Support Svcs, *Temp. Agcy*
Kerry's Referrals, *Temp. Agcy*
Mgmt. Recrtrs of Scottsdale, *Exec Srch*
Priority Staffng, *Perm. Emp Agcy*
Stivers Temp. Persnnl, *Temp. Agcy*

Arkansas
Mgmt. Recrtrs of Little Rock, *Exec Srch*
Premier Staffng, *Temp. Agcy*
Snelling Srch, *Exec Srch*
Turnage Emp. Svc Grp, *Exec Srch*

California
ABA Staffng, *Exec Srch*
A.S.A.P. Emp. Svc, *Perm. Emp Agcy*
Amato & Assoc. of CA, *Exec Srch*
Answers Unlimtd, *Temp. Agcy*
John Anthony & Assoc., *Exec Srch*
Apropos Emp. Agcy, *Perm. Emp Agcy*
Harvey Bell & Assoc., *Exec Srch*
Best Temp. Svc, *Temp. Agcy*
Blackhawk Advantage, *Exec Srch*
Business Syst. Staffing & Assoc., *Perm. Emp Agcy*
CRI Prof'l Srch, *Exec Srch*
California Mngmnt Srch, *Exec Srch*
Candy Stripers Medical Persnnl, *Perm. Emp Agcy*
Champagne Temp. Help, *Temp. Agcy*
Chase Morgan & Assoc., *Exec Srch*
Choice Persnnl, *Perm. Emp Agcy*
Claimsearch/The Srch Grp, *Exec Srch*
Collier-Young Agcy, *Temp. Agcy*
Computer Netwrk Resrcs, *Exec Srch*
Crossroads Staff Svc, *Temp. Agcy*
Culver Persnnl Svcs, *Perm. Emp Agcy*
Culver Persnnl Svcs/The Culver Grp, *Exec Srch*
Culver Staffing Resrcs, *Exec Srch*
Daco Recruitng, *Exec Srch*
Dependable Emp. Agency Netwrk, *Perm. Emp Agcy*
EDP Contrct Svcs, *Contract Svc*
Eleventh Hour Staff Svcs, *Temp. Agcy*
Employment Devlpmnt Dept, *Perm. Emp Agcy*
Finesse Persnnl Assoc., *Exec Srch*
GM Mgmt., *Exec Srch*
Goldstein & Assoc., *Temp. Agcy*
The Goodman Grp, *Exec Srch*
Gould Persnnl Svcs, *Perm. Emp Agcy*
Insurance Srch Grp, *Exec Srch*
Interim Industrial Staffng, *Temp. Agcy*
JPM Intl, *Exec Srch*
Jackson Persnnl, *Perm. Emp Agcy*
Jatinen & Assoc., *Exec Srch*
Legal Resource People, *Temp. Agcy*
Lending Persnnl Svcs, *Exec Srch*
Lifter & Assoc., *Exec Srch*
The London Agcy, *Temp. Agcy*
Malibu Grp, *Exec Srch*
Mgmt. Recrtrs of Burlingame/Sales Consltnts, *Exec Srch*
Mgmt. Recrtrs of Encino, *Exec Srch*
Maverick Staff Svc, *Perm. Emp Agcy*
The Medical Center Agcy, *Perm. Emp Agcy*
Medical Staff Unlimtd, *Perm. Emp Agcy*
Mesa Intl, *Exec Srch*
Musick & Assoc., *Exec Srch*
Nations Staff Solut'ns/Assoc. Resource Intl, *Exec Srch*
O'Crowley & O''Toole Exec Srch, *Exec Srch*
Olsten Staff Svcs, *Temp. Agcy*
Onyx Persnnl Svcs, *Perm. Emp Agcy*
Pacific Recruitng Offices, *Exec Srch*
Pacific Srch Grp, *Exec Srch*
Pasona Pacific, *Temp. Agcy*
Presidio Persnnl, *Temp. Agcy*
Pro Staff Persnnl Svcs, *Perm. Emp Agcy*
Pryor & Assoc., *Perm. Emp Agcy*
Remedy Intelligent Staffng, *Temp. Agcy*
Rich Rigler & Assoc., *Exec Srch*
The Rogan Grp, *Exec Srch*
Russell Staffing Resrcs, *Perm. Emp Agcy*
Santa Barbara Plcmnt, *Perm. Emp Agcy*
Search West, *Exec Srch*
Search West of Ontario, *Exec Srch*
Sharp Persnnl & Srch, *Exec Srch*
Stivers Temp. Persnnl of CA, *Temp. Agcy*
Stone & Assoc., *Exec Srch*
TRC Staff Svcs, *Perm. Emp Agcy*
TAD Resrcs Intl, *Perm. Emp Agcy*
Telford, Adams, & Alexander, *Exec Srch*
Thor Temp. Svcs, *Temp. Agcy*
TOD Staffng, *Exec Srch*
Today Persnnl, *Perm. Emp Agcy*
Trans U.S., *Perm. Emp Agcy*
Truex Assoc., *Exec Srch*
Unisearch, *Exec Srch*
United Staff Solut'ns, *Exec Srch*
Victor Valley Persnnl Agcy, *Perm. Emp Agcy*
Volt Temp. Svcs, *Temp. Agcy*
Your People Prof'ls, *Perm. Emp Agcy*

Colorado
Adecco, *Temp. Agcy*
Ahrnsbrak & Assoc., *Perm. Emp Agcy*
Eleventh Hour Staff Svcs, *Perm. Emp Agcy*
40 Plus of CO, *Career/Outplacemnt*
JobSearch, *Temp. Agcy*
Manpower Intl, *Temp. Agcy*
Peak Ltd., *Exec Srch*
SOS Staff Svcs, *Temp. Agcy*
Sales Consltnts, *Exec Srch*
Stivers Temp. Persnnl, *Temp. Agcy*
Talent Tree Staffng, *Perm. Emp Agcy*

Connecticut
A&A Resume & Persnnl Svcs, *Perm. Emp Agcy*
Admiral Staff Svcs, *Temp. Agcy*
Andrews & Mahon, *Exec Srch*
Thomas Byrne Assoc., *Perm. Emp Agcy*
Clifford Garzone Assoc., *Exec Srch*
Corporate Staff Solut'ns, *Temp. Agcy*
Data Pros, *Perm. Emp Agcy*
EDP Contrct Svcs, *Contract Svc*
Hipp Waters Prof'l Srch, *Exec Srch*
Mgmt. Recrtrs Intl, *Exec Srch*
Office Svcs of CT, *Perm. Emp Agcy*
Howard Smith Assoc., *Exec Srch*
Strategic Srch, *Exec Srch*

Express Persnnl, *Exec Srch*
Mgmt. Recrtrs of Omaha/Officemates5, *Exec Srch*

Nevada

Mgmt. Recrtrs of Reno, *Exec Srch*
Talent Tree Staffng, *Perm. Emp Agcy*

New Hampshire

Able 1 Staffng, *Exec Srch*
Anthony Exec Srch, *Exec Srch*
Barclay Persnnl Syst., *Exec Srch*
Central New Hampshire Emp. Svcs, *Perm. Emp Agcy*
Mgmt. Recrtrs Intl of Bedford, *Exec Srch*
Manpower Temp. Svcs, *Temp. Agcy*
Sales Consltnts of Nashua-Manchester, *Exec Srch*
TAC Staff Svcs, *Temp. Agcy*

New Jersey

A Prof'l Edge, *Career/Outplacemnt*
Advanced Persnnl, *Perm. Emp Agcy*
Andrew Persnnl Svcs, *Perm. Emp Agcy*
BAI Persnnl Solut'ns, *Exec Srch*
Blake & Assoc. Exec Srch, *Exec Srch*
Bonifield Assoc., *Exec Srch*
Broad Waverly & Assoc., *Exec Srch*
Career Ctr, *Perm. Emp Agcy*
Citizens Emp. Svcs, *Perm. Emp Agcy*
Executive Netwrk, *Exec Srch*
Executive Srch, *Exec Srch*
FAB Assoc., *Exec Srch*
Hreshko Consltng Grp, *Exec Srch*
Impact Persnnl, *Perm. Emp Agcy*
Insearch, *Exec Srch*
Inter-Regional Exec Srch, *Exec Srch*
MJE Recrtrs, *Exec Srch*
Mgmt. Grp of America, *Exec Srch*
Mgmt. Recrtrs Intl, *Exec Srch*
Mgmt. Recrtrs of Bridgewater, *Exec Srch*
Rich Meyers & Assoc., *Exec Srch*
Normyle/Erstling Health Srch Grp, *Exec Srch*
Officemates5 of Englewood Cliffs/DayStar Temp. Svcs, *Perm. Emp Agcy*
Orion Consltng, *Exec Srch*
The Pennmore Grp, *Exec Srch*
S-H-S of Cherry Hill, *Perm. Emp Agcy*
Sales Consltnts of Morris Cnty, *Exec Srch*
Sales Consltnts of Sparta, *Exec Srch*
Selective Persnnl, *Perm. Emp Agcy*
SkuppSearch, *Exec Srch*
Temporary Claim Professional, *Temp. Agcy*
Unitemp Temp. Persnnl, *Temp. Agcy*
Claire Wright Assn, *Perm. Emp Agcy*

New York

AJC Srch, *Exec Srch*
Accounting & Computer Persnnl, *Perm. Emp Agcy*
Merrill Adams Assoc., *Career/Outplacemnt*
Adecco, *Temp. Agcy*
Alpha Health Svcs Corp, *Exec Srch*
AMESgroup, *Perm. Emp Agcy*
Asher Persnnl Consltnts, *Perm. Emp Agcy*
CT Grp, *Exec Srch*
Career Objectives Persnnl, *Temp. Agcy*
Colton Partnership, *Exec Srch*
Carolyn Davis Assoc., *Exec Srch*
Maggi Dolan Plcmnt, *Perm. Emp Agcy*
EDP Contrct Svcs, *Contract Svc*
Irwin Edwards Recrtrs, *Perm. Emp Agcy*
Employment Recrtrs Agcy, *Perm. Emp Agcy*
Euromonde, *Temp. Agcy*
Robert Half Intl/Information Syst. Division, *Exec Srch*
Hunter Mac & Assoc., *Perm. Emp Agcy*
Insurance Overload Syst., *Temp. Agcy*
KLK Persnnl, *Perm. Emp Agcy*
Michael John Lawrence & Assoc., *Exec Srch*
William Long Assoc., *Exec Srch*
Joseph Maloney & Assoc., *Perm. Emp Agcy*
Mgmt. Recrtrs of Woodbury/ CompuSrch, *Exec Srch*
McLaughlin Resrcs, *Exec Srch*
Medstaff Svcs, *Perm. Emp Agcy*
The Mitchell Grp, *Exec Srch*
Morgan-Murray Persnnl/M&M Top Temps, *Temp. Agcy*
New York-New York Persnnl, *Perm. Emp Agcy*
K.A. Nowack Career Specialists, *Perm. Emp Agcy*
Parsons, Anderson & Gee, *Perm. Emp Agcy*
Persnnl Assoc., *Exec Srch*
P.G. Prager Srch Assoc., *Exec Srch*
Pryor Persnnl Agcy, *Exec Srch*
Rand Thompson Consltnts, *Exec Srch*
Rem Resrcs, *Perm. Emp Agcy*
Response Staff Svcs/Career Advisors, *Exec Srch*
S.W. Mgmt., *Exec Srch*
Staff Managers, *Temp. Agcy*
Temp Force of NY, *Temp. Agcy*
Volt Svcs Grp, *Contract Svc*
Wehinger Svcs, *Perm. Emp Agcy*
Werbin Assoc. Exec Srch, *Exec Srch*
Westchester Emp. Agcy, *Perm. Emp Agcy*
Woodbury Persnnl, *Perm. Emp Agcy*

North Carolina

A-1 Staffing & Persnnl, *Perm. Emp Agcy*
Advanced Persnnl Resrcs, *Exec Srch*
Corporate Staff Consltnts, *Perm. Emp Agcy*
Insurance Prof'l Srch, *Exec Srch*
Jobs of Fayetteville, *Perm. Emp Agcy*
Kelly Svcs, *Temp. Agcy*
Key Temps, *Temp. Agcy*
Mgmt. Recrtrs/Sales Consltnts, *Exec Srch*
Mgmt. Recrtrs of Durham, *Exec Srch*
Mgmt. Recrtrs of Raleigh/Inter Exec, *Exec Srch*
Mgmt. Recrtrs of Winston-Salem, *Exec Srch*
Olsten Staff Svcs, *Temp. Agcy*
Persnnl Svcs Unlimtd, *Temp. Agcy*
Sales Consltnts of High Point, *Exec Srch*
Waddy Thomson Assoc., *Exec Srch*

North Dakota

Olsten Staff Svcs/Kramer & Assoc./Expressway Persnnl, *Temp. Agcy*

Ohio

Adecco, *Perm. Emp Agcy*
Automotive Persnnl, *Exec Srch*
N.L. Benke & Assoc., *Perm. Emp Agcy*
J.B. Brown & Assoc., *Exec Srch*
Choice Persnnl/LaGrange & Assoc., *Exec Srch*
E. Christian & Assoc., *Exec Srch*
Crown Temp. Svcs of Cincinnati, *Temp. Agcy*
Eastern Persnnl Svcs, *Perm. Emp Agcy*
Insurance Recruitng Specialists, *Exec Srch*
Kelly Svcs, *Temp. Agcy*
Laine's S.M.G., *Perm. Emp Agcy*
R.E. Lowe Assoc., *Perm. Emp Agcy*
Mgmt. Recrtrs of Cincinnati, *Exec Srch*
Mgmt. Recrtrs of Cleveland, *Exec Srch*
Mgmt. Recrtrs of Cleveland, *Exec Srch*
Mgmt. Recrtrs of Columbus, *Exec Srch*
Mgmt. Recrtrs of Dayton, *Exec Srch*
Mgmt. Recrtrs of Solon, *Exec Srch*
Newcomb-Desmond & Assoc., *Exec Srch*
Palmer Temps/The Palmer Grp, *Temp. Agcy*
Premium Srch, *Exec Srch*
Sales Consltnts of Cincinnati, *Exec Srch*
Tabb & Assoc., *Exec Srch*
Tech/Aid of OH, *Perm. Emp Agcy*

Oklahoma

Express Persnnl Svcs, *Exec Srch*
Mgmt. Recrtrs of Oklahoma Cty, *Exec Srch*
Manpower Temp. Svcs, *Temp. Agcy*
StaffMark, *Temp. Agcy*

Oregon

The Brentwood Grp Limited, *Exec Srch*
Employment Trends, *Temp. Agcy*
Express Persnnl Svcs, *Exec Srch*
Mgmt. Recrtrs/Officemates5 of Portland, *Exec Srch*
Pacific Coast Recrtrs, *Exec Srch*
Woodworth Intl Grp, *Exec Srch*

Pennsylvania

Allegheny Persnnl Svcs, *Temp. Agcy*
Amato & Assoc. Insurance Recrtrs, *Exec Srch*
ASAP Staffng, *Perm. Emp Agcy*
Becker Temp. Svcs, *Perm. Emp Agcy*
COREStaff, *Temp. Agcy*
EDP/Temps of PA, *Temp. Agcy*
Human Resource Solut'ns, *Exec Srch*
JK Resrcs, *Exec Srch*
Jefferson-Ross Assoc., *Exec Srch*
Keystaff, *Temp. Agcy*
Mgmt. Recrtrs of DE Cnty/CompuSrch, *Exec Srch*
Mgmt. Recrtrs of Lehigh Vly/CompuSrch, *Exec Srch*
Mgmt. Recrtrs of Philadelphia/ CompuSrch, *Exec Srch*
J. McManus Assoc., *Perm. Emp Agcy*
The Morris Grp, *Exec Srch*
Olsten Staff Svcs, *Temp. Agcy*
Pancoast Temp. Svcs, *Temp. Agcy*
Physician Billing Solut'ns, *Perm. Emp Agcy*
Questor Consltnts, *Exec Srch*
Rice Cohen Intl, *Exec Srch*
The Richards Grp, *Exec Srch*
Rittenhouse Recrtrs, *Exec Srch*
S-H-S Intl, *Perm. Emp Agcy*
Sales Consltnts of Newtown, *Exec Srch*
Tom Sawchak Action of PA, *Perm. Emp Agcy*
TRC Staff Svcs, *Temp. Agcy*
TAC Staff Svcs, *Temp. Agcy*
Uni Temp Temp. Svc, *Temp. Agcy*
Vogue Persnnl, *Perm. Emp Agcy*

Rhode Island

Careers Unlimtd, *Perm. Emp Agcy*
Mgmt. Recrtrs Intl, *Exec Srch*
Norrell Svcs, *Temp. Agcy*
TAC Staff Svcs, *Temp. Agcy*

South Carolina

Eastern Persnnl Svcs, *Exec Srch*
Mgmt. Recrtrs of Columbia, *Exec Srch*
Mgmt. Recrtrs of Rck Hill, *Exec Srch*
Smith Temps/Smith Persnnl, *Temp. Agcy*

South Dakota

Olsten Staff Svcs, *Temp. Agcy*

Tennessee

A-1 Staffing & Persnnl, *Temp. Agcy*
Cook Assoc. Intl, *Exec Srch*
Kelly Svcs, *Temp. Agcy*
Mgmt. Recrtrs of Knoxville, *Exec Srch*
Norrell Svcs, *Temp. Agcy*
Persnnl Link, *Exec Srch*
Sales Consltnts of Nashville, *Exec Srch*
Shiloh Careers Intl, *Perm. Emp Agcy*
Snelling Persnnl Svcs, *Exec Srch*

Texas

Abilene Emp. Svc, *Perm. Emp Agcy*
Austin Insurance Recrtrs, *Perm. Emp Agcy*
Aware Affiliates Persnnl, *Perm. Emp Agcy*
Bundy-Stewart Assoc., *Exec Srch*
Continental Persnnl, *Perm. Emp Agcy*
Daher & Assoc./Insurance Srch Specialists, *Exec Srch*
The Danbrook Grp, *Exec Srch*
Gail Darling Staffing/Darling's Prof'l Desk, *Temp. Agcy*
Denton-Lewis Assoc., *Exec Srch*
Employee Sources, *Exec Srch*
Evins Persnnl Consltnts of Killeen, *Perm. Emp Agcy*
Executive Srch Persnnl, *Exec Srch*
Express Persnnl Svcs, *Perm. Emp Agcy*
Imprimis Staff Solut'ns, *Temp. Agcy*
Insurance Srch, *Exec Srch*
Insurance Temp. Svcs, *Temp. Agcy*
Kelly Svcs, *Temp. Agcy*
Mgmt. Recrtrs Intl, *Exec Srch*
Mgmt. Recrtrs of Dallas, *Exec Srch*
Olsten Staff Svcs, *Temp. Agcy*
P&P Persnnl, *Perm. Emp Agcy*
The Pailin Grp, *Exec Srch*
Resource Recrtrs, *Perm. Emp Agcy*
Sales Consltnts of Houston, *Exec Srch*
Snelling Persnnl Svcs, *Exec Srch*
Steele & Assoc., *Perm. Emp Agcy*
Suburban Svcs, *Temp. Agcy*
Summit Srch Specialists, *Perm. Emp Agcy*
Texas Persnnl, *Exec Srch*
Thomas Office Persnnl, *Perm. Emp Agcy*
Total Temp. Svcs, *Temp. Agcy*
Vinson & Assoc., *Perm. Emp Agcy*

Vermont

Voll Assoc., *Exec Srch*

Virginia

Alpha Omega Resrcs, *Perm. Emp Agcy*
Corporate Connection Exec. Srch Firm
Dow Persnnl, *Perm. Emp Agcy*
EDP, *Temp. Agcy*
Mgmt. Recrtrs of McLean, *Exec Srch*
Mgmt. Recrtrs of Roanoke, *Exec Srch*
Manpower Temp. Svcs, *Temp. Agcy*
The McCormick Grp, *Exec Srch*
Placement Prof'ls, *Exec Srch*
Professional Career Consltnts, *Exec Srch*
TAC Staff Svcs, *Temp. Agcy*

Washington

Bostwick Temp. Svc, *Temp. Agcy*
The Career Clinic, *Exec Srch*
Express Persnnl Svcs, *Temp. Agcy*
HRA Insurance Staffng, *Exec Srch*
Kelly Svcs, *Temp. Agcy*
Mgmt. Recrtrs of Mercer Islnd, *Exec Srch*
Mgmt. Recrtrs of Tacoma, *Exec Srch*
Manpower Temp. Svcs, *Temp. Agcy*
Pacific Persnnl Grp, *Exec Srch*
Persnnl Consltnts, *Exec Srch*
Persnnl Unlimtd, *Exec Srch*
Thomas Co, *Perm. Emp Agcy*

Wisconsin

Allen, Wayne, & Co, *Perm. Emp Agcy*
Crown Svcs, *Temp. Agcy*
Landmark, The Staffing Resource, *Temp. Agcy*
Mgmt. Recrtrs of Green Bay, *Exec Srch*
Mgmt. Recrtrs of Milwaukee, *Exec Srch*
Mgmt. Recrtrs of Stevens Point, *Exec Srch*
Olsten Staff Svcs, *Temp. Agcy*
Quirk-Corporon & Assoc., *Exec Srch*

INVESTMENT

California

Ryan, Miller & Assoc., *Exec Srch*

Interstaff, *Temp. Agcy*
Law Corps Legal Staffng, *Temp. Agcy*
Major Hagen & Africa, *Exec Srch*
Mgmt. Recrtrs of Rockford, *Exec Srch*
Mgmt. Support Svcs, *Exec Srch*
Manpower Temp. Svcs, *Temp. Agcy*
Michael David Assoc., *Perm. Emp Agcy*
NJW & Assoc., *Temp. Agcy*
Officemates5 of Wheeling, *Exec Srch*
Olsten Information Technlgy Staffng, *Perm. Emp Agcy*
Olsten Staff Svcs, *Temp. Agcy*
Opportunity Persnnl, *Perm. Emp Agcy*
Persnnl Placemnt Consltnts, *Perm. Emp Agcy*
Vera Rast Partners, *Exec Srch*
Remedy Intelligent Staffng, *Temp. Agcy*
Right Svcs, *Temp. Agcy*
Keith Ross & Assoc., *Exec Srch*
Sales Consltnts/Mgmt. Recrtrs Intl, *Exec Srch*
Sales Consltnts of Oak Brk, *Exec Srch*
Seville Temp. Svcs, *Temp. Agcy*
Stivers Temp. Persnnl, *Temp. Agcy*
Templeton & Assoc., *Perm. Emp Agcy*
Verdin Assoc., *Exec Srch*
Anne Violante & Assoc., *Exec Srch*
Robert Whitfield & Assoc., *Exec Srch*
Philip Wieland & Assoc., *Exec Srch*
J. Williams & Assoc., *Exec Srch*
Working World, *Temp. Agcy*
World Emp. Svc, *Perm. Emp Agcy*

Indiana

Alpha Rae Persnnl, *Perm. Emp Agcy*
Bindley Assoc., *Exec Srch*
Crown Temp. Svcs of Indianapolis, *Temp. Agcy*
Execusearch, *Exec Srch*
Hobart Emp. Agcy, *Perm. Emp Agcy*
Job Placemnt Svc, *Perm. Emp Agcy*
Mgmt. Recrtrs of Evansville, *Exec Srch*
Mgmt. Recrtrs of Indianapolis, *Exec Srch*
Mgmt. Recrtrs of Richmond/Staff Solut'ns, *Exec Srch*
Officemates5 of Indianapolis, *Exec Srch*
Olsten Staff Svcs, *Temp. Agcy*
The Registry, *Perm. Emp Agcy*
Unique, *Exec Srch*

Iowa

Burton Placemnt Svcs, *Exec Srch*
Executive Srch Assoc., *Exec Srch*
Helping Hands Temp. Svc, *Temp. Agcy*
Mgmt. Recrtrs/CompuSrch, *Exec Srch*
Persnnl, *Exec Srch*

Kansas

Business Specialists, *Perm. Emp Agcy*
Eleventh Hour Staff Svcs, *Temp. Agcy*
Jag & Assoc. Attorney Srch, *Exec Srch*
Legal Srch Assoc., *Exec Srch*
LegalTEMPS of Kansas, *Contract Svc*
Mgmt. Recrtrs of Overlnd Prk, *Exec Srch*
Manpower, *Temp. Agcy*
Uniforce Staff Svcs, *Temp. Agcy*
Western Staff Svcs, *Temp. Agcy*
Wichita Bar Assn Legal Placemnt Svc, *Perm. Emp Agcy*

Kentucky

Angel Grp Intl, *Exec Srch*
Belcan Staff Svcs, *Perm. Emp Agcy*
The Legal Edge/The Prof'l Edge, *Temp. Agcy*
Precision Staffng, *Perm. Emp Agcy*
Professional Srch Consltnts, *Exec Srch*

Louisiana

Mgmt. Recrtrs-Baton Rouge/Sales Consltnts, *Exec Srch*
Mgmt. Recrtrs-Metairie/Sales Consltnts, *Exec Srch*
Olsten Persnnl/Briggs Legal Staffng, *Perm. Emp Agcy*
Special Counsel, *Temp. Agcy*
Talley & Assoc./Talley Temps, *Exec Srch*
Western Staff Svcs, *Temp. Agcy*

Maine

ASK, *Temp. Agcy*
At Work Persnnl, *Temp. Agcy*

Maryland

Futures, *Exec Srch*
L.S. Gross & Assoc., *Exec Srch*
Mgmt. Recrtrs of Annapolis, *Exec Srch*
Mgmt. Recrtrs-Baltimore/Sales Consltnts, *Exec Srch*
Mgmt. Recrtrs-Bethesda/CompuSearch, *Exec Srch*
Mgmt. Recrtrs of Frederick, *Exec Srch*
Sales Consltnts of Prince Georges Cnty, *Exec Srch*
Special Counsel, *Temp. Agcy*
TAC Staff Svcs, *Temp. Agcy*
TAD Staff Svcs, *Temp. Agcy*

Massachusetts

A.S.I. Temps, *Temp. Agcy*
Ability Srch of N.E., *Perm. Emp Agcy*
Attorney Special Assignment Plcmnt, *Temp. Agcy*
Bostonian Persnnl, *Perm. Emp Agcy*
The Center for Prof'l Devlpmnt in the Law, *Career/Outplacemnt*
Cleary Consltnts, *Perm. Emp Agcy*
Corporate Staff Solut'ns, *Temp. Agcy*
Diversity Srch Specialists, *Exec Srch*
Dunhill Staffing Syst., *Temp. Agcy*
Gillard Assoc., *Perm. Emp Agcy*
Harvest Persnnl, *Exec Srch*
Interim Persnnl, *Temp. Agcy*
Johnson & Hill Staff Svc, *Temp. Agcy*
Kennison & Assoc., *Temp. Agcy*
L&L Temps, *Temp. Agcy*
John Leonard Persnnl Assoc., *Perm. Emp Agcy*
Mgmt. Recrtrs Intl of Braintree, *Exec Srch*
Mgmt. Recrtrs Intl of Westboro, *Exec Srch*
Manpower, *Temp. Agcy*
New England Legal Srch, *Exec Srch*
New England Persnnl, *Perm. Emp Agcy*
Resrcs Objectives, *Exec Srch*
Routhier Placemnt Specialists, *Perm. Emp Agcy*
Sales Consltnts of Plymouth Cnty, *Exec Srch*
Sales Consltnts of Wellesley, *Exec Srch*
Selectemps, *Temp. Agcy*
Special Counsel, *Temp. Agcy*
Spectra Prof'l Srch/Spectra Temps, *Perm. Emp Agcy*
Volt Svcs Grp, *Temp. Agcy*
The Wallace Law Registry, *Temp. Agcy*

Michigan

Beacon Svcs, *Temp. Agcy*
Express Persnnl Svcs, *Temp. Agcy*
William Howard Agcy, *Perm. Emp Agcy*
Mgmt. Recrtrs of Bingham Farms, *Exec Srch*
Mgmt. Recrtrs of Flint, *Exec Srch*
Mgmt. Recrtrs of Kalamazoo, *Exec Srch*
Mgmt. Recrtrs of Lansing, *Exec Srch*
Mgmt. Recrtrs of Muskegon, *Exec Srch*
Mgmt. Recrtrs of Rochester, *Exec Srch*
C.A. Moore & Assoc., *Exec Srch*
Persnnl At Law, *Temp. Agcy*
Sales Consltnts of Detroit, *Exec Srch*
Sanford Rose Assoc., *Exec Srch*
Sharrow & Assoc., *Exec Srch*
Snelling Persnnl Svcs, *Perm. Emp Agcy*
T.M.S. Assoc., *Exec Srch*
Trillium Staffng, *Temp. Agcy*
Wing Tips & Pumps, *Exec Srch*

Minnesota

Abby Blu, *Temp. Agcy*
Alternative Staffng, *Perm. Emp Agcy*
Bright Srch/Professional Staffng, *Exec Srch*
Esquire Srch, *Exec Srch*
Firstaff, *Perm. Emp Agcy*
T.H. Hunter, *Exec Srch*
Interim Legal Prof'ls, *Temp. Agcy*
Howard Lieberman & Assoc., *Exec Srch*
Mgmt. Recrtrs-Minneapolis/Sales Consltnts, *Exec Srch*
Midwest Staff Svcs, *Temp. Agcy*
Ultimate Srch Unlimtd/Temps Unlimtd, *Perm. Emp Agcy*

Mississippi

Capitol Staff Solut'ns, *Perm. Emp Agcy*
EPSCO Persnnl, *Temp. Agcy*
Recruitment & Training of MS, *Perm. Emp Agcy*
Special Counsel, *Temp. Agcy*

Missouri

Aaron Consltng, *Exec Srch*
L.P. Banning, *Perm. Emp Agcy*
Bottom Line Prof'l Svcs, *Contract Svc*
Business Persnnl Svcs, *Temp. Agcy*
Crown Svcs, *Temp. Agcy*
Deck & Decker Emp. Svc, *Perm. Emp Agcy*
ExecuTemps, *Temp. Agcy*
Huey Enterprises, *Exec Srch*
JoDoc Enterprises, *Temp. Agcy*
Mgmt. Recrtrs of Kansas Cty, *Exec Srch*
Mgmt. Recrtrs of Springfield, *Exec Srch*
Mgmt. Recrtrs of St. Louis, *Exec Srch*
Mgmt. Recrtrs of St. Louis, *Exec Srch*
Manpower Temp. Svcs, *Temp. Agcy*
Officemates5 of St. Louis, *Exec Srch*
Olsten Staff Svcs, *Temp. Agcy*
Snelling Persnnl Svcs, *Perm. Emp Agcy*

Montana

Express Persnnl, *Perm. Emp Agcy*
Kelly Svcs, *Temp. Agcy*

Nebraska

Compusearch of Lincoln, *Exec Srch*
Corporate Recrtrs, *Exec Srch*
Donna's Office Svc, *Contract Svc*
Mgmt. Recrtrs of Omaha/Officemates5, *Exec Srch*

Nevada

Talent Tree Staffng, *Perm. Emp Agcy*

New Hampshire

Able 1 Staffng, *Exec Srch*
Allstaff Contrct Svcs, *Perm. Emp Agcy*
Barclay Persnnl Syst., *Exec Srch*
Career Connections, *Perm. Emp Agcy*
Central New Hampshire Emp. Svcs, *Perm. Emp Agcy*
Mgmt. Recrtrs Intl of Bedford, *Exec Srch*
Manpower Temp. Svcs, *Temp. Agcy*
Resource Recruitng/Contemp. Accntnts, *Perm. Emp Agcy*

New Jersey

A+ Persnnl, *Perm. Emp Agcy*
ABC Nationwide Employment, *Perm. Emp Agcy*
Advanced Persnnl, *Perm. Emp Agcy*
Andrew Persnnl Svcs, *Perm. Emp Agcy*
BAI Persnnl Solut'ns, *Exec Srch*
Blake & Assoc. Exec Srch, *Exec Srch*
Executive Srch, *Exec Srch*
Express Persnnl Svcs, *Perm. Emp Agcy*
Foster Assoc., *Exec Srch*
Impact Persnnl, *Perm. Emp Agcy*
Integro Staff Svcs, *Temp. Agcy*
Joule People Providers, *Perm. Emp Agcy*
L&K Assoc., *Exec Srch*
Law Pros Legal Placemnt Svcs, *Exec Srch*
Mgmt. Recrtrs of Orange Cnty, *Exec Srch*
Officemates5 of Englewood Cliffs/DayStar Temp. Svcs, *Perm. Emp Agcy*
Orion Consltng, *Exec Srch*
Florence Pape Legal Srch, *Exec Srch*
Pat's Secretarial Svc, *Temp. Agcy*
Premier Persnnl Grp, *Perm. Emp Agcy*
James Robinson Prof'l Recruiter, *Exec Srch*
Sales Consltnts of Sparta, *Exec Srch*
Selective Persnnl, *Perm. Emp Agcy*
Arline Simpson Assoc., *Perm. Emp Agcy*
Snelling Persnnl Svcs, *Temp. Agcy*
Source Svcs Corp, *Perm. Emp Agcy*
Topaz Attorney Srch, *Exec Srch*
Unitemp Temp. Persnnl, *Temp. Agcy*
Winston Staff Svcs, *Perm. Emp Agcy*
Winters & Ross, *Temp. Agcy*
Claire Wright Assn, *Perm. Emp Agcy*

New Mexico

Albuquerque Persnnl, *Perm. Emp Agcy*
Santa Fe Svcs, *Temp. Agcy*

New York

AJC Srch, *Exec Srch*
Accounting & Computer Persnnl, *Perm. Emp Agcy*
Adam Persnnl, *Perm. Emp Agcy*
Merrill Adams Assoc., *Career/Outplacemnt*
Asher Persnnl Consltnts, *Perm. Emp Agcy*
Bacal & Assoc., *Exec Srch*
Bader Research Corp, *Exec Srch*
Baseline Recrtrs Netwrk, *Exec Srch*
Berkel Assoc., *Exec Srch*
Bevan Resrcs, *Perm. Emp Agcy*
Brookville Staff Svcs, *Perm. Emp Agcy*
Career Blazers Persnnl, *Perm. Emp Agcy*
Career Objectives Persnnl, *Temp. Agcy*
Consortium, *Exec Srch*
Seth Diamond Assoc., *Exec Srch*
Maggi Dolan Plcmnt, *Perm. Emp Agcy*
Dunhill Staffing Syst. of Buffalo, *Temp. Agcy*
Eden Persnnl, *Perm. Emp Agcy*
Employment Recrtrs Agcy, *Perm. Emp Agcy*
Extra Help Emp. Svc, *Temp. Agcy*
Filcro Persnnl, *Perm. Emp Agcy*
Finest Emp. Agcy, *Perm. Emp Agcy*
First Choice Recrtrs, *Perm. Emp Agcy*
Forum Temp. Svcs, *Temp. Agcy*
Friedman Emp. Agcy, *Perm. Emp Agcy*
Genesis Emp. Consltnts, *Exec Srch*
Stephen Haas Legal, *Exec Srch*
Robert Half Intl/Information Syst. Division, *Exec Srch*
Hunter Plcmnt, *Exec Srch*
Island Srch Grp, *Perm. Emp Agcy*
Ann Israel & Assoc., *Exec Srch*
Ivana Legal Svcs, *Exec Srch*
Josef Grp Persnnl, *Perm. Emp Agcy*
KLK Persnnl, *Perm. Emp Agcy*
Fred Koffler Assoc., *Exec Srch*
Michael John Lawrence & Assoc., *Exec Srch*
Legal Srch Exec. Srch Firm
Magill Assoc., *Exec Srch*
Joseph Maloney & Assoc., *Perm. Emp Agcy*
Mgmt. Recrtrs of Woodbury/ CompuSrch, *Exec Srch*
Manpower Temp. Svcs, *Temp. Agcy*
Lynn Marshall Persnnl Agcy, *Perm. Emp Agcy*
Milazzo Assoc., *Perm. Emp Agcy*
Morgan-Murray Persnnl/M&M Top Temps, *Temp. Agcy*
National Emp. Database, *Perm. Emp Agcy*
New York-New York Persnnl, *Perm. Emp Agcy*
K.A. Nowack Career Specialists, *Perm. Emp Agcy*
Olsten Staff Svcs, *Temp. Agcy*
The Parks Grp, *Exec Srch*
Peak Srch, *Exec Srch*

P.G. Prager Srch Assoc., *Exec Srch*
Rand Thompson Consltnts, *Exec Srch*
Rem Resrcs, *Perm. Emp Agcy*
Remedy Intelligent Staffng, *Temp. Agcy*
Ryan Srch Assoc., *Exec Srch*
S.W. Mgmt., *Exec Srch*
SearchAmerica, *Exec Srch*
Marina Sirras & Assoc., *Exec Srch*
Special Counsel, *Temp. Agcy*
Sporn Grp, *Exec Srch*
Staffing Svcs, *Exec Srch*
Hillary Taylor Persnnl, *Perm. Emp Agcy*
Temp Force of NY, *Temp. Agcy*
TemPositions, *Temp. Agcy*
United Persnnl Agcy, *Perm. Emp Agcy*
Vantage Staff Svcs, *Temp. Agcy*
Wallace Law Registry, *Exec Srch*
Charles Wanner Assoc. Exec. Srch Firm
Westchester Emp. Agcy, *Perm. Emp Agcy*
Woodbury Persnnl, *Perm. Emp Agcy*

North Carolina

A-1 Staffing & Persnnl, *Perm. Emp Agcy*
Advanced Persnnl Resrcs, *Exec Srch*
Anderson & Daniel Persnnl, *Perm. Emp Agcy*
Assoc. Emp. Inc, *Perm. Emp Agcy*
Graham & Assoc., *Perm. Emp Agcy*
Greer Persnnl, *Perm. Emp Agcy*
Kelly Svcs, *Temp. Agcy*
Key Temps, *Temp. Agcy*
Legal Persnnl, *Perm. Emp Agcy*
Legal Placemnt Specialists, *Exec Srch*
Mgmt. Recrtrs/Sales Consltnts, *Exec Srch*
Mgmt. Recrtrs of Durham, *Exec Srch*
Mgmt. Recrtrs of Winston-Salem, *Exec Srch*
Moffitt Intl, *Exec Srch*
Olsten Staff Svcs, *Temp. Agcy*
Persnnl Svcs Unlimtd, *Temp. Agcy*
Sales Consltnts of High Point, *Exec Srch*
Snelling Srch, *Exec Srch*
Special Counsel, *Temp. Agcy*
Summit Occupational Staffng, *Exec Srch*

North Dakota

Olsten Staff Svc/Kramer & Assoc./Exprswy Persnnl, *Temp Agcy*

Ohio

AccuStaff, *Temp. Agcy*
Adecco, *Perm. Emp Agcy*
Crown Temp. Svcs of Cincinnati, *Temp. Agcy*
Eastern Persnnl Svcs, *Perm. Emp Agcy*
Elite Persnnl Agcy, *Perm. Emp Agcy*
Exact Persnnl Specialists, *Perm. Emp Agcy*
Extra Help Temp. Svc, *Temp. Agcy*
H.J.C., *Exec Srch*
Hite Exec Srch/Hite Mngmnt Consltnts, *Exec Srch*
ves & Assoc., *Exec Srch*
Kelly Svcs, *Temp. Agcy*
aine's S.M.G., *Perm. Emp Agcy*
egal Staff Consltnts, *Perm. Emp Agcy*
Mgmt. Recrtrs of Cincinnati, *Exec Srch*
Mgmt. Recrtrs of Cleveland, *Exec Srch*
Mgmt. Recrtrs of Cleveland, *Exec Srch*
Mgmt. Recrtrs of Cleveland, *Exec Srch*
Mgmt. Recrtrs of Cleveland, *Exec Srch*
Mgmt. Recrtrs of Columbus, *Exec Srch*
Mgmt. Recrtrs of Dayton, *Exec Srch*
Mgmt. Recrtrs of Solon, *Exec Srch*
Marvel Consltnts, *Exec Srch*
Minority Exec Srch, *Exec Srch*
rofessional Emp. Svcs, *Perm. Emp Agcy*
uality Source, *Exec Srch*
entech Ventures, *Perm. Emp Agcy*
ales Consltnts of Cincinnati, *Exec Srch*
harles Snider & Assoc., *Exec Srch*
pecial Counsel, *Temp. Agcy*
alent Tree Staffng, *Perm. Emp Agcy*

Oklahoma

xpress Persnnl Svcs, *Exec Srch*
ey Temp. Persnnl, *Temp. Agcy*
Mgmt. Recrtrs of Oklahoma Cty, *Exec Srch*
Manpower Temp. Svcs, *Temp. Agcy*
erry Neese Persnnl Agcy, *Exec Srch*
oyd Richards Persnnl, *Perm. Emp Agcy*
ooner Placemnt Svc, *Perm. Emp Agcy*
taffMark, *Temp. Agcy*

Oregon

xecutives Worldwide, *Exec Srch*
egal Nrthwest, *Perm. Emp Agcy*
gmt. Recrtrs/Officemates5 of Portland, *Exec Srch*
orthwest Legal Srch, *Exec Srch*
orthwest Temp. & Staff Svcs, *Temp. Agcy*

Pennsylvania

legheny Persnnl Svcs, *Temp. Agcy*
SAP Staffng, *Perm. Emp Agcy*
Becker Temp. Svcs, *Perm. Emp Agcy*
Career Quest Confidential, *Exec Srch*
J. Croyle & Assoc., *Perm. Emp Agcy*
P. Robert Dann, *Exec Srch*
Executive Avail-A-Search, *Exec Srch*
Merrill Grumer Assoc., *Perm. Emp Agcy*
Hallmark Persnnl/Able Temps, *Perm. Emp Agcy*
Interim Legal Prof'ls, *Perm. Emp Agcy*
Kathy Karr Persnnl, *Perm. Emp Agcy*
Keystaff, *Temp. Agcy*
Kraybill Assoc., *Exec Srch*
Law Skil, *Perm. Emp Agcy*
Leafstone, *Temp. Agcy*
Legal Srch, *Temp. Agcy*
Mgmt. Recrtrs of DE Cnty/CompuSrch, *Exec Srch*
Mgmt. Recrtrs of Lehigh Vly/CompuSrch, *Exec Srch*
Mgmt. Recrtrs of Manayunk/Chestnut Hill/CompuSrch, *Exec Srch*
Mgmt. Recrtrs of Philadelphia/ CompuSrch, *Exec Srch*
J. McManus Assoc., *Perm. Emp Agcy*
Olsten Staff Svcs, *Temp. Agcy*
Persnnl Resrcs Organization, *Exec Srch*
Powers Persnnl, *Perm. Emp Agcy*
Questor Consltnts, *Exec Srch*
R.H.A. Exec Persnnl Svcs, *Exec Srch*
Rice Cohen Intl, *Exec Srch*
S-H-S Intl, *Perm. Emp Agcy*
Elayne Scott Assoc., *Perm. Emp Agcy*
Special Counsel, *Temp. Agcy*
TRC Staff Svcs, *Temp. Agcy*
TAC Staff Svcs, *Temp. Agcy*
Templeton & Assoc., *Exec Srch*
TOD Svcs, *Perm. Emp Agcy*
Uni Temp Temp. Svc, *Temp. Agcy*
Uniforce Temp. Svcs, *Temp. Agcy*
Vogue Persnnl, *Perm. Emp Agcy*
Williford & Assoc./Williford Legal Persnnl, *Temp. Agcy*

Rhode Island

Aquidneck Emp. Svc, *Perm. Emp Agcy*
Albert Lee & Assoc., *Exec Srch*
Mgmt. Recrtrs Intl, *Exec Srch*
Norrell Svcs, *Temp. Agcy*
Spectra Temps/Tracey Assoc., *Temp. Agcy*
TAC Staff Svcs, *Temp. Agcy*

South Carolina

Columbia Legal Prof'ls/Columbia Staffng, *Exec Srch*
Eastern Persnnl Svcs, *Exec Srch*
Jerman Persnnl Svcs, *Temp. Agcy*
Mgmt. Recrtrs of Columbia, *Exec Srch*
Mgmt. Recrtrs of Rck Hill, *Exec Srch*
Smith Temps/Smith Persnnl, *Temp. Agcy*

Tennessee

A-1 Staffing & Persnnl, *Temp. Agcy*
Anderson McIntyre Persnnl Svcs, *Exec Srch*
Cook Assoc. Intl, *Exec Srch*
Koerner & Assoc., *Exec Srch*
Mgmt. Recrtrs of Knoxville, *Exec Srch*
Manpower Temp. Svcs, *Temp. Agcy*
Memphis Legal Persnnl, *Exec Srch*
Olsten Staff Svcs, *Temp. Agcy*
Persnnl Link, *Exec Srch*
Sales Consltnts of Nashville, *Exec Srch*
Special Counsel/Amicus Legal Staffng, *Temp. Agcy*

Texas

Abilene Emp. Svc, *Perm. Emp Agcy*
Action Persnnl, *Temp. Agcy*
Alliance Legal Staffng, *Temp. Agcy*
Attorney Resrcs, *Temp. Agcy*
Aware Affiliates Persnnl, *Perm. Emp Agcy*
Ann Best Elite Temps, *Temp. Agcy*
Howard Bloom Exec Srch/Interim Legal Prof'ls, *Exec Srch*
Bullock Persnnl, *Perm. Emp Agcy*
Burnett Persnnl Svcs, *Temp. Agcy*
Cherbonnier Grp, *Exec Srch*
Co-counsel, *Temp. Agcy*
DFM & Assoc., *Exec Srch*
Dallas Emp. Svc, *Perm. Emp Agcy*
Gail Darling Staffing/Darling's Prof'l Desk, *Temp. Agcy*
Dilworth & Woolridge, *Exec Srch*
Donovan & Watkins, *Perm. Emp Agcy*
Evins Persnnl Consltnts of Killeen, *Perm. Emp Agcy*
Executeam, *Exec Srch*
Express Persnnl Svcs, *Perm. Emp Agcy*
Gibson Arnold & Assoc., *Perm. Emp Agcy*
Herndon & Assoc., *Exec Srch*
Imprimis Staff Solut'ns, *Temp. Agcy*
Kelly Svcs, *Temp. Agcy*
Legal Netwrk, *Exec Srch*
Mgmt. Recrtrs Intl, *Exec Srch*
Mgmt. Recrtrs of Dallas, *Exec Srch*
McKinley•Arend Intl, *Exec Srch*
Odell & Assoc., *Exec Srch*
Olsten Staff Svcs, *Temp. Agcy*
P&P Persnnl, *Perm. Emp Agcy*
The Pailin Grp, *Exec Srch*
Prescott Legal Srch, *Exec Srch*
Quest Persnnl Resrcs, *Perm. Emp Agcy*
Resource Recrtrs, *Perm. Emp Agcy*
Resource Staffng, *Contract Svc*
Sales Consltnts of Houston, *Exec Srch*
Marvin Silcott & Assoc., *Exec Srch*
Snelling Persnnl Svcs, *Perm. Emp Agcy*
Snelling Persnnl Svcs, *Exec Srch*
Source Svcs Corp, *Exec Srch*
Special Counsel/Amicus Legal Staffng, *Temp. Agcy*
Spradley Legal Srch, *Exec Srch*
Suburban Svcs, *Temp. Agcy*
Temp 2000 Temp. Svcs, *Temp. Agcy*
Temporary Help Svc, *Temp. Agcy*
Todays Legal Staffng, *Perm. Emp Agcy*
Todays Temporary, *Temp. Agcy*
Total Temp. Svcs, *Temp. Agcy*
Vinson & Assoc., *Perm. Emp Agcy*
Wheeler, Moore & Elam Co, *Exec Srch*
The Whitaker Companies, *Exec Srch*
Windsor Consltnts, *Exec Srch*

Utah

Staffing Logic, *Perm. Emp Agcy*
Systems West, *Temp. Agcy*

Virginia

A Better Resume, *Career/Outplacemnt*
Nancy Allen Assoc., *Perm. Emp Agcy*
Corporate Connection Exec. Srch Firm
Effective Staffng, *Exec Srch*
Lee Staffing Resrcs, *Exec Srch*
Mgmt. Recrtrs of McLean, *Exec Srch*
Mgmt. Recrtrs of Roanoke, *Exec Srch*
The McCormick Grp, *Exec Srch*
Carol McNew Emp. Svc, *Perm. Emp Agcy*
Olsten Staff Svcs, *Temp. Agcy*
Placement Prof'ls, *Exec Srch*
Remedy Intelligent Staffng, *Temp. Agcy*
Select Staff Svcs, *Perm. Emp Agcy*
Snelling Persnnl Svcs, *Perm. Emp Agcy*
STAT Temps, *Temp. Agcy*
TAC Staff Svcs, *Temp. Agcy*
Wisdom & Williams, *Perm. Emp Agcy*

Washington

Bostwick Temp. Svc, *Temp. Agcy*
The Career Clinic, *Exec Srch*
Cooper Persnnl, *Temp. Agcy*
Express Persnnl Svcs, *Temp. Agcy*
Guidance Svcs, *Temp. Agcy*
Hallmark Svcs, *Perm. Emp Agcy*
Houser, Martin, Morris & Assoc., *Exec Srch*
Human Resrcs, *Exec Srch*
Mgmt. Recrtrs of Mercer Islnd, *Exec Srch*
Mgmt. Recrtrs of Tacoma, *Exec Srch*
Manpower Temp. Svcs, *Temp. Agcy*
Northwest Temp. Svcs, *Temp. Agcy*
Omega Attorney Plcmnt, *Exec Srch*
Pacific Law Recrtrs, *Exec Srch*
Persnnl Unlimtd, *Exec Srch*
Seattle Recrtrs, *Exec Srch*
Staffing Resrcs, *Perm. Emp Agcy*
Woods & Assoc., *Temp. Agcy*

Wisconsin

Allen, Wayne, & Co, *Perm. Emp Agcy*
Careertrac Emp. Svc, *Exec Srch*
Crown Svcs, *Temp. Agcy*
The Exutec Grp, *Exec Srch*
Legal Placemnt Svcs/Persnnl Specialists, *Perm. Emp Agcy*
Mgmt. Recrtrs of Green Bay, *Exec Srch*
Mgmt. Recrtrs of Milwaukee, *Exec Srch*
Olsten Staff Svcs, *Temp. Agcy*

Wyoming

Olsten Staff Svcs, *Temp. Agcy*

LIGHT INDUSTRIAL

Alaska

Manpower Temp. Svc, *Temp. Agcy*

Arizona

Electronic Power Source, *Exec Srch*

California

COMFORCE Tech. Svcs, *Contract Svc*
COMFORCE Tech. Svcs, *Perm. Emp Agcy*
Full Svc Temps, *Temp. Agcy*
Intertec Design, *Perm. Emp Agcy*
Kelly Svcs, *Temp. Agcy*
Klein & Assoc., *Temp. Agcy*
Nelson HR Solut'ns, *Perm. Emp Agcy*
PrideStaff, *Temp. Agcy*
Remedy Intelligent Staffng, *Temp. Agcy*
Santa Barbara Plcmnt, *Perm. Emp Agcy*
Adele Steinmetz, *Exec Srch*

TRC Staff Svcs, *Perm. Emp Agcy*
TAC Staff Svcs, *Temp. Agcy*
Today Persnnl, *Perm. Emp Agcy*
Victor Valley Persnnl Agcy, *Perm. Emp Agcy*

Colorado

Absolute Emp. Svcs, *Perm. Emp Agcy*
Goodwin Persnnl, *Perm. Emp Agcy*
Kelly Svcs, *Perm. Emp Agcy*
TPM Staff Svc, *Temp. Agcy*

Connecticut

Charter Persnnl Svcs, *Perm. Emp Agcy*
Talent Tree Staffng, *Perm. Emp Agcy*
United Persnnl Svcs, *Temp. Agcy*

Florida

AccuStaff, *Temp. Agcy*
Careers USA, *Temp. Agcy*
Kelly Svcs, *Temp. Agcy*
Manpower Temp. Svcs, *Temp. Agcy*
Olsten Staff Svcs, *Temp. Agcy*
Pro Staff Persnnl Svcs, *Temp. Agcy*
Workers of Florida, *Temp. Agcy*

Georgia

Express Persnnl Svcs, *Temp. Agcy*
Kelly Svcs, *Temp. Agcy*
Manpower Temp. Svcs, *Temp. Agcy*
Western Staff Svcs, *Temp. Agcy*

Hawaii

Altres Staffng, *Temp. Agcy*

Illinois

A.B.A. Placemnts/A.B.A. Temps, *Perm. Emp Agcy*
Adecco, *Temp. Agcy*
Quantum Prof'l Srch/Quantum Staff Svcs, *Exec Srch*
Staffing Consltnts, *Perm. Emp Agcy*

Indiana

Employment Plus, *Temp. Agcy*
Persnnl Mgmt., *Temp. Agcy*
Persnnl Partners, *Perm. Emp Agcy*
Pro Resrcs, *Perm. Emp Agcy*

Iowa

CSI Employment, *Exec Srch*
Kelly Svcs, *Temp. Agcy*
Salem Mngmnt dba Rudy Salem Staff Svcs, *Temp. Agcy*

Kentucky

Belcan Staff Svcs, *Perm. Emp Agcy*
Manpower, *Temp. Agcy*
Precision Staffng, *Perm. Emp Agcy*
Staffing Alternatives, *Temp. Agcy*

Louisiana

Professional Temps, *Temp. Agcy*
Western Staff Svcs, *Temp. Agcy*

Maryland

Adecco, *Temp. Agcy*
Interim Persnnl, *Temp. Agcy*

Massachusetts

ABA Persnnl, *Temp. Agcy*
Adecco, *Temp. Agcy*
L&L Temps, *Temp. Agcy*
Manpower Temp. Svcs, *Temp. Agcy*
New Boston Select Staffng, *Temp. Agcy*
Quality Persnnl, *Perm. Emp Agcy*
Selectemps, *Temp. Agcy*
Volt Svcs Grp, *Temp. Agcy*
The Work Place, *Career/Outplacemnt*

Michigan

Entech Svcs, *Temp. Agcy*
Mgmt. Recrtrs of Flint, *Exec Srch*
Manpower, *Temp. Agcy*

Minnesota

Add On Staff Solut'ns, *Temp. Agcy*
Advantage Persnnl, *Perm. Emp Agcy*
Award Temp. Svcs, *Temp. Agcy*

Mississippi

EPSCO Persnnl, *Temp. Agcy*

Missouri

Decker Persnnl, *Perm. Emp Agcy*
JoDoc Enterprises, *Temp. Agcy*
Manpower Temp. Svcs, *Temp. Agcy*

Montana

Kelly Svcs, *Temp. Agcy*
Manpower Temp. Svcs, *Temp. Agcy*

Nebraska

Sharp Persnnl, *Temp. Agcy*

New Hampshire

Allstaff Contrct Svcs, *Perm. Emp Agcy*
Manpower Temp. Svcs, *Temp. Agcy*
TAC Staff Svcs, *Temp. Agcy*

New Jersey

American Staffing Resrcs, *Temp. Agcy*
Broad Waverly & Assoc., *Exec Srch*
Joule Industrial Contractors, *Contract Svc*
Pomerantz Persnnl, *Perm. Emp Agcy*

New York

AM & PM Temps, *Temp. Agcy*
AccuStaff, *Perm. Emp Agcy*
Grp Agcy, *Perm. Emp Agcy*
Kelly Svcs, *Temp. Agcy*
Manpower Temp. Svcs, *Temp. Agcy*
Olsten Staff Svcs, *Temp. Agcy*
Sales Srch, Ltd./Executive Resume Svc, *Exec Srch*
Talent Tree Staffng, *Perm. Emp Agcy*

North Carolina

Caldwell Persnnl Svcs, *Perm. Emp Agcy*
Career Staffng, *Perm. Emp Agcy*
Careers Unlimtd, *Perm. Emp Agcy*
Interim Persnnl, *Temp. Agcy*
Mgmt. Recrtrs of Kinston, *Exec Srch*
Manpower, *Temp. Agcy*
Norrell Svcs, *Temp. Agcy*

North Dakota

Interim Persnnl, *Perm. Emp Agcy*

Ohio

Career Connections, *Perm. Emp Agcy*
Manpower Temp. Svcs, *Temp. Agcy*
Pak/Teem Contrct Svcs, *Contract Svc*
Personalized Plcmnt, *Exec Srch*
Tabb & Assoc., *Exec Srch*
TAD Tech. Svcs, *Contract Svc*
Tandem Staffng, *Temp. Agcy*

Oklahoma

Dow Persnnl, *Temp. Agcy*
Key Temp. Persnnl, *Temp. Agcy*
Terry Neese Persnnl Agcy, *Exec Srch*

Oregon

Adams Temps, *Temp. Agcy*
Employment Trends, *Temp. Agcy*
Kelly Svcs, *Temp. Agcy*
Uniforce Staff Svcs, *Temp. Agcy*

Pennsylvania

American Staffing Resrcs, *Temp. Agcy*
Interim Persnnl of Lehigh Valley PA, *Temp. Agcy*
London Persnnl Svcs, *Perm. Emp Agcy*
Manpower Temp. Svcs, *Temp. Agcy*
Metro Persnnl, *Temp. Agcy*
Norrell Svcs, *Contract Svc*
Olsten Staff Svcs, *Temp. Agcy*
Pratt Persnnl Svcs, *Temp. Agcy*
Whittlesey & Assoc., *Exec Srch*

Rhode Island

Central Emp. Agcy, *Exec Srch*
Pro Staff Persnnl Svcs, *Temp. Agcy*

South Carolina

Carolina Persnnl Svcs, *Temp. Agcy*
Snelling Persnnl, *Perm. Emp Agcy*

Tennessee

Mgmt. Recrtrs of Lenoir Cty, *Exec Srch*
Manpower, *Temp. Agcy*
Mega Force, *Temp. Agcy*
Unlimited Staff Solut'ns, *Contract Svc*

Texas

A-1 Persnnl, *Temp. Agcy*
Adecco, *Temp. Agcy*
Creative Staff Svcs, *Temp. Agcy*
LRJ Staff Svcs, *Perm. Emp Agcy*
Manpower, *Temp. Agcy*
Olsten Staff Svcs, *Temp. Agcy*
Phoenix Staffng, *Exec Srch*
Pro Staff Persnnl Svcs, *Temp. Agcy*
Roth Young Persnnl Svcs/Dallas, *Exec Srch*
TSP Persnnl Svcs, *Perm. Emp Agcy*
TAD Tech. Svcs, *Contract Svc*

Vermont

Western Staff Svcs, *Temp. Agcy*

Virginia

Bradford Co, *Contract Svc*
Norrell Staff Svcs, *Exec Srch*
The Talley Grp, *Exec Srch*

Washington

Job Ctr, *Temp. Agcy*
Jobs Unlimtd, *Perm. Emp Agcy*
Kelly Svcs, *Temp. Agcy*
Manpower Temp. Svcs, *Temp. Agcy*
Staffing Resrcs, *Perm. Emp Agcy*

West Virginia

Extra Support Staffng, *Temp. Agcy*
Kelly Svcs, *Temp. Agcy*

Wisconsin

ADTEC Staffng, *Temp. Agcy*
Olsten Staff Svcs, *Temp. Agcy*
Site Persnnl Svcs/Trainor/Salick & Assoc., *Temp. Agcy*
Tempo Emp. Svcs, *Temp. Agcy*

Wyoming

Express Temp. Svc, *Temp. Agcy*

LOGISTICS

Arizona

The Dorfman Grp, *Exec Srch*

California

Scott-Thaler Assoc., *Exec Srch*

Florida

Ambiance Persnnl, *Exec Srch*

Georgia

Mgmt. Recrtrs/Sales Consltnts of Cobb Cnty, *Exec Srch*
Mgmt. Recrtrs of Marietta, *Exec Srch*

Illinois

Armstrong-Hamilton Assoc., *Exec Srch*
Sanford Rose Assoc., *Exec Srch*

Michigan

Sanford Rose Assoc., *Exec Srch*

Minnesota

Fairfax Grp, *Exec Srch*

New Jersey

Advance Positions, *Exec Srch*
Rochester Syst., *Exec Srch*

New York

FORTUNE Persnnl Consltnts, *Exec Srch*
R.I. James, *Exec Srch*

North Carolina

FORTUNE Persnnl Consltnts, *Exec Srch*

Rhode Island

Sullivan & Cogliano, *Exec Srch*

South Carolina

Ford & Assoc., *Exec Srch*

Tennessee

Mgmt. Recrtrs Intl, *Exec Srch*

Texas

Noll HR Svcs, *Exec Srch*

Virginia

FORTUNE Persnnl Consltnts, *Exec Srch*

Wisconsin

MARBL Consltnts, *Exec Srch*

MANAGEMENT

California

AW Data Processing Persnnl, *Perm. Emp Agcy*
John Anthony & Assoc., *Exec Srch*
Paar & Assoc., *Exec Srch*

Indiana

Hunter-Lawyer Persnnl, *Perm. Emp Agcy*

Minnesota

Professional Recrtrs, *Exec Srch*

North Carolina

Wilson Persnnl, *Exec Srch*

Ohio

Providence Persnnl Consltnts, *Perm. Emp Agcy*

Wisconsin

Hatch Staff Svcs, *Temp. Agcy*

MANUFACTURING

Ethan Allen Persnnl Plcmnt, *Exec Srch*
First Emp. Consltnts, *Exec Srch*
Five Star Temporary, *Temp. Agcy*
FORTUNE Persnnl Consltnts of Jacksonville, *Exec Srch*
Future Force Persnnl, *Temp. Agcy*
GCA/Gulf Coast Assoc., *Exec Srch*
Girl Friday Persnnl, *Temp. Agcy*
Interim Persnnl, *Temp. Agcy*
Just Mngmnt Svcs, *Exec Srch*
Kelly Svcs, *Temp. Agcy*
Koerner Grp, *Exec Srch*
R.H. Larsen & Assoc., *Exec Srch*
The Mac Grp, *Exec Srch*
Mgmt. Recrtrs of Coral Gables, *Exec Srch*
Mgmt. Recrtrs of Indialantic, *Exec Srch*
Mgmt. Recrtrs of Lake Cnty, *Exec Srch*
Mgmt. Recrtrs of Miami, *Exec Srch*
Mgmt. Recrtrs of Pensacola, *Exec Srch*
Mgmt. Recrtrs of St. Petersburg, *Exec Srch*
Mgmt. Recrtrs of Tallahassee, *Exec Srch*
Mgmt. Recrtrs of Tampa, *Exec Srch*
Mankuta Gallagher & Assoc., *Exec Srch*
Norrell Tech. Svcs, *Exec Srch*
Olsten Staff Svcs, *Temp. Agcy*
O'Quin Persnnl, *Temp. Agcy*
Profes. Staffing/Able Body Temp. Svcs, *Contract Svc*
Progressive Persnnl, *Temp. Agcy*
Pulp & Paper Intl, *Exec Srch*
Linda Robins & Assoc., *Temp. Agcy*
The Ryan Charles Grp, *Exec Srch*
Sales Consltnts of Fort Lauderdale, *Exec Srch*
Sales Consltnts of Jacksonville, *Exec Srch*
Doug Sears & Assoc., *Exec Srch*
Shaver Emp. Agcy, *Perm. Emp Agcy*
Snelling Persnnl, *Exec Srch*
Staffing Svcs Grp, *Perm. Emp Agcy*
Summit Exec Srch Consltnts, *Exec Srch*
Sun Persnnl West, *Exec Srch*
System One Tech. Staffng, *Exec Srch*
TRC Staff Svcs, *Temp. Agcy*
TechStaff, *Contract Svc*
Transworld COREstaff, *Temp. Agcy*
Western Staff Svcs, *Temp. Agcy*

Georgia

A Hiring Alternative, *Exec Srch*
AAA Employment, *Perm. Emp Agcy*
Adecco Tech. Svcs, *Contract Svc*
Anderson Industrial Assoc., *Exec Srch*
Arjay & Assoc., *Exec Srch*
Ashley-Nolan Intl, *Exec Srch*
Augusta Staffing Assoc., *Perm. Emp Agcy*
Bell Oaks Co, *Exec Srch*
Caldwell Svcs, *Temp. Agcy*
Comprehensive Srch Grp, *Exec Srch*
Corporate Srch Consltnts, *Exec Srch*
Dunhill Prof'l Srch, *Exec Srch*
Durham Staffng, *Perm. Emp Agcy*
Elite Staff Svcs, *Perm. Emp Agcy*
Express Persnnl Svcs, *Perm. Emp Agcy*
Express Persnnl Svcs, *Exec Srch*
FORTUNE Persnnl Consltnts of Atlanta, *Exec Srch*
Fox-Morris Assoc., *Exec Srch*
Hall Mngmnt Grp, *Exec Srch*
Hines Recruitng Assn, *Exec Srch*
ISC of Atlanta/Intl Career Continuation, *Exec Srch*
Job Shop, *Exec Srch*
Kelly Svcs, *Temp. Agcy*
Kenzer Corp of GA, *Exec Srch*
Evie Kreisler & Assoc., *Exec Srch*
MAU, *Perm. Emp Agcy*
Mgmt. Recrtrs/Sales Consltnts of Cobb Cnty, *Exec Srch*
Mgmt. Recrtrs of Atlanta, *Exec Srch*
Mgmt. Recrtrs of Atlanta, *Exec Srch*
Mgmt. Recrtrs of Marietta, *Exec Srch*
Manpower Temp. Svcs, *Temp. Agcy*
Millard & Assoc., *Exec Srch*
Persnnl Opport., *Exec Srch*
Pro-Tech, *Exec Srch*
Quality Temp. Svc, *Temp. Agcy*
Randstad Staff Svcs, *Temp. Agcy*
Randstad Staff Svcs, *Perm. Emp Agcy*
Sanford Rose Assoc., *Exec Srch*
SearchAmerica, *Exec Srch*
Southern Emp. Svc, *Perm. Emp Agcy*
Team One Partners, *Exec Srch*
Temporary Specialties, *Temp. Agcy*
Toar Consltnts, *Exec Srch*
Western Tech. Svcs, *Temp. Agcy*
H.L. Yoh Co, *Contract Svc*

Hawaii

Dunhill Prof'l Srch of Hawaii, *Exec Srch*

Idaho

Horne/Brown Intl, *Exec Srch*
Idaho Dept. of Employment/JobSvc, *Perm. Emp Agcy*

Illinois

The Ability Grp, *Exec Srch*
Ablest Staffng, *Perm. Emp Agcy*
B.J. Abrams & Assoc., *Exec Srch*
Accord, *Exec Srch*
AccuStaff Inc., *Temp. Agcy*
Adecco, *Temp. Agcy*
Advanced Tech. Srch, *Exec Srch*
American Engineering Co, *Exec Srch*
American Tech. Srch, *Exec Srch*
Assured Staffng, *Temp. Agcy*
B-W & Assoc., *Perm. Emp Agcy*
Banner Persnnl, *Perm. Emp Agcy*
Britannia, *Exec Srch*
Burling Grp Ltd., *Exec Srch*
Carson Mngmnt Assoc., *Contract Svc*
Cast Metals Persnnl, *Exec Srch*
Cook Assoc., *Exec Srch*
Corporate Environment, Ltd., *Exec Srch*
Davis Temps, *Temp. Agcy*
Ned Dickey & Assoc./Dickey Staff Solut'ns, *Exec Srch*
Diener & Assoc., *Exec Srch*
Express Persnnl Svcs, *Temp. Agcy*
Fellows Plcmnt, *Temp. Agcy*
First Staffng, *Perm. Emp Agcy*
FORTUNE Persnnl Consltnts, *Exec Srch*
Furst Staff Svcs, *Temp. Agcy*
Girman Grp, *Exec Srch*
The Glenwood Grp, *Exec Srch*
David Gomez & Assoc., *Exec Srch*
Elizabeth Howe & Assoc., *Exec Srch*
Human Resource Connection, *Perm. Emp Agcy*
Human Resource Technlgy, *Exec Srch*
Illinois Veterans Leadership Program, *Career/Outplacemnt*
J.C.G. Limited, *Perm. Emp Agcy*
Jender & Co, *Contract Svc*
Johnson Persnnl Co, *Exec Srch*
Jerry Jung Co., *Exec Srch*
Kenzer Corp, *Exec Srch*
Evie Kreisler Assoc., *Exec Srch*
Kunzer Assoc., Ltd., *Exec Srch*
Lynco Mngmnt Persnnl, *Exec Srch*
Magnum Srch, *Exec Srch*
Mgmt. Recrtrs of Albion, *Exec Srch*
Mgmt. Recrtrs of Arlington Heights, *Exec Srch*
Mgmt. Recrtrs of Des Plaines, *Exec Srch*
Mgmt. Recrtrs of Elgin, *Exec Srch*
Mgmt. Recrtrs of Rockford, *Exec Srch*
Mgmt. Recrtrs of Springfield, *Exec Srch*
Mgmt. Recrtrs of St. Charles, *Exec Srch*
Manufacturing Resrcs, *Exec Srch*
Manufacturing Tech. Srch, *Exec Srch*
Marsteller Wilcox Assoc., *Exec Srch*
Mathey Svcs, *Exec Srch*
Michael David Assoc., *Perm. Emp Agcy*
R. Michaels & Assoc., *Exec Srch*
The Murphy Grp, *Perm. Emp Agcy*
New Directions, *Exec Srch*
Officemates5 of Wheeling, *Exec Srch*
Olsten Staff Svcs, *Temp. Agcy*
Omega Tech. Corp, *Exec Srch*
Omni Srch Exec. Srch Firm
Opportunity Persnnl, *Perm. Emp Agcy*
Pelichem Assoc., *Exec Srch*
Pollak & Skan, *Contract Svc*
Prestige Emp. Svcs, *Perm. Emp Agcy*
Professional Research Svcs, *Exec Srch*
Profile Temp. Svc, *Temp. Agcy*
The Raleigh Warwick Grp, *Exec Srch*
Remedy Intelligent Staffng, *Temp. Agcy*
Right Svcs, *Temp. Agcy*
The Robinson Grp, *Exec Srch*
Sales Consltnts/Mgmt. Recrtrs Intl, *Exec Srch*
Sales Consltnts of Oak Brk, *Exec Srch*
Search Dynamics, *Exec Srch*
Selectability, *Perm. Emp Agcy*
Sellers & Assoc., *Exec Srch*
Ralph Smith & Assoc., *Exec Srch*
Stivers Temp. Persnnl, *Temp. Agcy*
Stone Enterprises, *Exec Srch*
Systems Research, *Perm. Emp Agcy*
TSC Mngmnt Svcs, *Exec Srch*
Technical Netwrk Srch, *Exec Srch*
Technical Recruitng Consltnts, *Exec Srch*
Technical Srch, *Exec Srch*
Valentine & Assoc., *Exec Srch*
Vogrinc & Short, *Exec Srch*
Webb Emp. Svc, *Perm. Emp Agcy*
Working World, *Temp. Agcy*
World Emp. Svc, *Perm. Emp Agcy*
Xagas & Assoc., *Exec Srch*

Indiana

AccuStaff, *Temp. Agcy*
Alexander & Assoc., *Exec Srch*
Angola Persnnl Svcs, *Perm. Emp Agcy*
Bill Caldwell Emp. Svc, *Perm. Emp Agcy*
Canis Major/HR Quest, *Exec Srch*
Career Consltnts, *Perm. Emp Agcy*
Careers Unlimtd, *Exec Srch*
Chevigny Persnnl Agcy, *Exec Srch*
Continental Design Co, *Contract Svc*
Corporate Staff Resrcs, *Temp. Agcy*
Crowe, Chizek & Co, *Perm. Emp Agcy*
Crown Temp. Svcs of Indianapolis, *Temp. Agcy*
Dunhill of Brown Cnty, *Exec Srch*
Dunhill Prof'l Srch, *Exec Srch*
Dunhill Staffing Syst., *Temp. Agcy*
Employment Recrtrs, *Perm. Emp Agcy*
Execusearch, *Exec Srch*
Great Lakes Srch, *Exec Srch*
The Hart Line, *Exec Srch*
Job Placemnt Svc, *Perm. Emp Agcy*
Krise Prof'l Persnnl Svcs, *Perm. Emp Agcy*
Lange & Assoc., *Exec Srch*
The Mallard Grp, *Exec Srch*
Mgmt. Recrtrs of Evansville, *Exec Srch*
Mgmt. Recrtrs of Indianapolis, *Exec Srch*
Mgmt. Recrtrs of Richmond/Staff Solut'ns, *Exec Srch*
Mgmt. Svcs, *Exec Srch*
Mayhall Srch Grp, *Exec Srch*
Mays & Assoc., *Perm. Emp Agcy*
Mid West Persnnl, *Perm. Emp Agcy*
Miller Persnnl Consltnts, *Exec Srch*
Morley Grp, *Exec Srch*
National Corporate Consltnts/Advantage Svcs, *Exec Srch*
Norrell Staff Svcs, *Temp. Agcy*
Norrell Staff Svcs of Evansville, *Temp. Agcy*
Oakwood Intl, *Exec Srch*
Officemates5 of Indianapolis, *Exec Srch*
Officemates5 of Indianapolis, *Exec Srch*
Olsten Staff Svcs, *Temp. Agcy*
Perry Persnnl Plus, *Perm. Emp Agcy*
Quiring Assoc. HR Consltng Grp, *Exec Srch*
RDN Svcs, *Exec Srch*
Rush Temps, *Temp. Agcy*
Star Staffng, *Temp. Agcy*
TAD Tech. Svcs, *Contract Svc*
Technetics Corp, *Contract Svc*
Time Svcs, *Perm. Emp Agcy*
Warrick Cnty Emp. & Training Ctr, *Career/Outplacemnt*
Western Staff Svcs, *Temp. Agcy*
Wimmer Temps & Direct Plcmnt, *Temp. Agcy*

Iowa

Agra Placemnts Exec. Srch Firm
Blanchard Svcs, *Temp. Agcy*
Burton Placemnt Svcs, *Exec Srch*
Byrnes & Rupkey, *Exec Srch*
Cambridge Staffng, *Perm. Emp Agcy*
Executive Engineering Srch, *Exec Srch*
Executive Srch Assoc., *Exec Srch*
Helping Hands Temp. Svc, *Temp. Agcy*
Mgmt. Recrtrs/CompuSrch, *Exec Srch*
McGladrey Srch Grp, *Exec Srch*
Pratt-Younglove, *Perm. Emp Agcy*
Premier Srch Grp, *Exec Srch*
Salem Mngmnt dba Rudy Salem Staff Svcs, *Temp. Agcy*
Sedona Staff Svcs, *Exec Srch*
Staff Mgmt., *Contract Svc*
TechStaff, *Temp. Agcy*

Kansas

Business Specialists, *Perm. Emp Agcy*
Dunhill of Wichita, *Perm. Emp Agcy*
Eleventh Hour Staff Svcs, *Temp. Agcy*
Flaming & Assoc., *Perm. Emp Agcy*
Foster Design Co, *Contract Svc*
Kansas Workforce, *Temp. Agcy*
Key Staffng, *Temp. Agcy*
Mgmt. Recrtrs of Overlnd Prk, *Exec Srch*
Manpower, *Temp. Agcy*
J.T. Nelson & Assoc., *Perm. Emp Agcy*
Parr & Assoc., *Perm. Emp Agcy*
Smith Brown & Jones, *Exec Srch*
Stoneburner Assoc., *Exec Srch*
Temtech, *Contract Svc*

Kentucky

Angel Grp Intl, *Exec Srch*
C.M. Mngmnt Svcs, *Perm. Emp Agcy*
J.E.M. & Assoc., *Temp. Agcy*
Don Kestler & Assoc., *Exec Srch*
Kolok Enterprises, *Exec Srch*
Mgmt. Recrtrs of Richmond, *Exec Srch*
Neessen Prof'l Srch, *Exec Srch*
Persnnl Solut'ns, *Perm. Emp Agcy*
Precision Staffng, *Perm. Emp Agcy*
Professional Srch, *Exec Srch*
Snelling Persnnl Svcs, *Exec Srch*
Staffing Alternatives, *Temp. Agcy*
TLI Tech. Staffng, *Perm. Emp Agcy*
Weller-Wooley & Assoc., *Exec Srch*

Louisiana

Career Persnnl Consltnts, *Exec Srch*
Mgmt. Recrtrs Intl, *Exec Srch*

Mgmt. Recrtrs-Baton Rouge/Sales Consltnts, *Exec Srch*
Mgmt. Recrtrs-Metairie/Sales Consltnts, *Exec Srch*
Snelling Persnnl Svcs, *Exec Srch*
Talley & Assoc./Talley Temps, *Exec Srch*
Technical & Prof'l Sources, *Exec Srch*
Technical Resource Staff Svcs, *Temp. Agcy*

Maine

Accomplished Prof'ls, *Temp. Agcy*
At Work Persnnl, *Temp. Agcy*
Career Mngmnt Assoc., *Exec Srch*
Executive Srch of N.E., *Exec Srch*
Goodrich Consltng, *Exec Srch*
John Jay & Co, *Exec Srch*
National Recrtrs of ME, *Exec Srch*
Paper Industry Recrtmnt, *Perm. Emp Agcy*
The Porter Hamel Grp, *Exec Srch*

Maryland

D.W. Baird & Assoc., *Exec Srch*
Caplan Assoc., *Exec Srch*
Cemcon Intl, *Perm. Emp Agcy*
Echelon Svc Co, *Contract Svc*
FORTUNE Persnnl Consltnts, *Exec Srch*
Futures, *Exec Srch*
L.S. Gross & Assoc., *Exec Srch*
Mgmt. Recrtrs of Annapolis, *Exec Srch*
Mgmt. Recrtrs-Baltimore/Sales Consltnts, *Exec Srch*
Mgmt. Recrtrs-Bethesda/CompuSearch, *Exec Srch*
Mgmt. Recrtrs of Frederick, *Exec Srch*
Sales Consltnts of Baltimore Cty, *Exec Srch*
Sales Consltnts of Prince Georges Cnty, *Exec Srch*
TAC Staff Svcs, *Temp. Agcy*
TAD Staff Svcs, *Temp. Agcy*
Tech/Aid of MD, *Temp. Agcy*
Tri-Serv, *Perm. Emp Agcy*
Winston Srch, *Exec Srch*

Massachusetts

Abbott's of Boston, *Exec Srch*
Ability Srch of N.E., *Perm. Emp Agcy*
Additional Tech. Support Svcs, *Perm. Emp Agcy*
Apollo Design Svc, *Contract Svc*
Associated Career Netwrk, *Perm. Emp Agcy*
B&M Assoc., *Contract Svc*
Berkshire Srch Assoc., *Exec Srch*
Brady Emp. Svc, *Perm. Emp Agcy*
CDI Corp, *Contract Svc*
Corporate Staff Solut'ns, *Temp. Agcy*
Cyr Assoc., *Exec Srch*
Rob Davidson Assoc./Exec. & Prof. Resume Svc, *Exec Srch*
Diversity Assoc., *Exec Srch*
Dunhill Staffing Syst., *Temp. Agcy*
Engineering Mngmnt Support, *Temp. Agcy*
FORTUNE Persnnl Consltnts of Topsfield, *Exec Srch*
Gilreath Weatherby, *Exec Srch*
Hunter Assoc., *Perm. Emp Agcy*
Johnson & Hill Staff Svc, *Temp. Agcy*
L&L Temps, *Temp. Agcy*
Lab Support, *Temp. Agcy*
Lane Emp. Svc, *Perm. Emp Agcy*
The Littleton Grp, *Exec Srch*
Mgmt. Recrtrs Intl, *Exec Srch*
Mgmt. Recrtrs Intl of Braintree, *Exec Srch*
Manpower, *Temp. Agcy*
Mass Temps, *Temp. Agcy*
Master Srch, *Perm. Emp Agcy*
McDevitt Assoc., *Exec Srch*
Micro Tech Consltnts, *Temp. Agcy*
Morgan & Assoc., *Exec Srch*
Nationwide Bus. Svc, *Perm. Emp Agcy*
Need Persnnl Plcmnt, *Temp. Agcy*
New England Recrtrs, *Exec Srch*
New England Srch, *Exec Srch*
Norrell Staff Svcs, *Contract Svc*
Olsten Staff Svcs, *Temp. Agcy*
D.P. Parker & Assoc., *Exec Srch*
Norman Powers Assoc., *Exec Srch*
Pro Staff, *Temp. Agcy*
Reardon Assoc., *Perm. Emp Agcy*
Sales Consltnts of Plymouth Cnty, *Exec Srch*
Sales Consltnts of Wellesley, *Exec Srch*
George Sandel Assoc., *Perm. Emp Agcy*
Selected Executives, *Exec Srch*
Snelling Persnnl Svcs, *Perm. Emp Agcy*
Straube Assoc., *Exec Srch*
Sullivan Assoc., *Exec Srch*
Summit Tech. Svcs, *Temp. Agcy*
TAD Staff Svcs, *Temp. Agcy*
Tech/Aid, *Contract Svc*
Technical Persnnl Svcs, *Perm. Emp Agcy*
Total Tech. Svcs, *Perm. Emp Agcy*
United Prof'l Plcmnt, *Exec Srch*
Vanguard Exec Svcs, *Exec Srch*
S.B. Webster & Assoc., *Exec Srch*
WIND Job Ctr, *Career/Outplacemnt*
H.L. Yoh Co, *Contract Svc*

Michigan

Advance Assoc., *Exec Srch*
Advanced Tech. Resrcs, *Exec Srch*
Alternative Staff, *Temp. Agcy*
Assoc., *Exec Srch*
The Aucon Co, *Exec Srch*
Barman Staff Solut'ns/Barman Persnnl, *Perm. Emp Agcy*
Beacon Svcs, *Exec Srch*
Benford Assoc., *Exec Srch*
Career Assoc., *Contract Svc*
Career Quest, *Perm. Emp Agcy*
Carmac Exec Recruitng, *Exec Srch*
Case & Co, *Exec Srch*
Corporate Staff Resrcs, *Perm. Emp Agcy*
Davidson, Laird & Assoc., *Exec Srch*
Dynamic Persnnl, *Contract Svc*
Gene Ellefson & Assoc., *Exec Srch*
Elwell & Assoc., *Exec Srch*
Exec-Tech Corp, *Exec Srch*
ExecuQuest, *Exec Srch*
ExecuSearch of Southwst MI, *Perm. Emp Agcy*
Executive & Tech. Persnnl, *Exec Srch*
Executive Mngmnt Srch, *Exec Srch*
Executive Persnnl, *Exec Srch*
Executive Recrtrs Intl, *Exec Srch*
Express Persnnl Svcs, *Temp. Agcy*
FORTUNE Persnnl Consltnts of Troy, *Exec Srch*
David Franklin Assoc., *Exec Srch*
GRS, *Exec Srch*
Giacomin Grp, *Exec Srch*
Joseph Goldring & Assoc., *Exec Srch*
Steven Greene & Assoc., *Perm. Emp Agcy*
The Hallman Grp, *Exec Srch*
Healthcare Recrtrs Intl, *Exec Srch*
Harvey Hohauser & Assoc., *Exec Srch*
William Howard Agcy, *Perm. Emp Agcy*
Human Resrcs Emp. Svcs, *Perm. Emp Agcy*
IBA Srch Consltnts, *Exec Srch*
Interim Persnnl, *Temp. Agcy*
Job Fair Netwrk of MI, *Perm. Emp Agcy*
Kelly Tech. Svcs, *Contract Svc*
Key Persnnl, *Perm. Emp Agcy*
David Lindemer Assoc., *Exec Srch*
Ludot Persnnl, *Perm. Emp Agcy*
Mgmt. Recrtrs of Battle Creek, *Exec Srch*
Mgmt. Recrtrs of Bingham Farms, *Exec Srch*
Mgmt. Recrtrs of Dearborn, *Exec Srch*
Mgmt. Recrtrs of Flint, *Exec Srch*
Mgmt. Recrtrs of Kalamazoo, *Exec Srch*
Mgmt. Recrtrs of Lansing, *Exec Srch*
Mgmt. Recrtrs of Muskegon, *Exec Srch*
Mgmt. Recrtrs of Rochester, *Exec Srch*
Mgmt. Recrtrs of Southeast MI, *Exec Srch*
Manpower Tech. Svcs, *Contract Svc*
Michigan Srch Plus, *Exec Srch*
Nustar Temp. Svcs, *Temp. Agcy*
Office Staffing Recruitng, *Exec Srch*
Olsten Prof'l Accnt'g Svcs, *Temp. Agcy*
Parr Srch, *Exec Srch*
Preferred Emp. Planning, *Perm. Emp Agcy*
Professional Persnnl Consltnts Intl, *Exec Srch*
Professional Resource Assoc., *Contract Svc*
ProSearch, *Exec Srch*
Roth Young Persnnl Svcs of Detroit, *Exec Srch*
Sales Consltnts of Auburn Hills, *Exec Srch*
Sales Consltnts of Detroit, *Exec Srch*
Sales Consltnts of Farmington Hills, *Exec Srch*
Selective Recruitng Assoc., *Exec Srch*
Skill Tech Employment, *Perm. Emp Agcy*
Snelling Persnnl Svcs, *Perm. Emp Agcy*
Software Svcs Corp, *Contract Svc*
Source Svcs Corp, *Perm. Emp Agcy*
Sygnetics, *Temp. Agcy*
TEA, *Perm. Emp Agcy*
Technical Prof'l Svc, *Perm. Emp Agcy*
Temporary Tech. Svcs, *Temp. Agcy*
Thomas & Assoc. of MI, *Exec Srch*
Trillium Staffng, *Temp. Agcy*
Venture Mngmnt & Staffng, *Exec Srch*
Henry Welker & Assoc., *Perm. Emp Agcy*
Wing Tips & Pumps, *Exec Srch*
Wood Persnnl Svcs/Wood Temp. Staffng, *Perm. Emp Agcy*
Jim Woodson & Assoc., *Exec Srch*
Workforce, *Temp. Agcy*

Minnesota

A&B Persnnl, *Perm. Emp Agcy*
Abby Blu, *Temp. Agcy*
Advance Persnnl Resrcs, *Exec Srch*
Agri-Business Svcs, *Exec Srch*
Alternative Staffng, *Perm. Emp Agcy*
Answer Persnnl, *Temp. Agcy*
Bradley & Assoc., *Exec Srch*
Bright Srch/Professional Staffng, *Exec Srch*
Dietrich & Assoc., *Exec Srch*
Diversified Employment, *Perm. Emp Agcy*
Ells Persnnl Syst., *Exec Srch*
Express Persnnl Svcs, *Perm. Emp Agcy*
Fairfax Grp, *Exec Srch*
Flatley Tech. Svcs, *Temp. Agcy*
Roger Gilmer & Assoc., *Exec Srch*
HR Svcs of Plymouth, *Exec Srch*
T.H. Hunter, *Exec Srch*
Mgmt. Recrtrs-Minneapolis/Sales Consltnts, *Exec Srch*
Manpower Tech. Svcs, *Perm. Emp Agcy*
Brad Martin & Assoc., *Exec Srch*
Midwest Staff Svcs, *Temp. Agcy*
North American Recrtrs, *Exec Srch*
Nycor Srch, *Exec Srch*
Persnnl Assist. Corp, *Exec Srch*
Programming Alternatives of MN, *Exec Srch*
Regency Recrtrs, *Exec Srch*
Resource Srch, *Exec Srch*
Sathe & Assoc. Exec Srch, *Exec Srch*
Technical Resrcs, *Perm. Emp Agcy*
Work Place Solut'ns, *Contract Svc*

Mississippi

Andrus Assoc. dba Svc Specialists Ltd., *Perm. Emp Agcy*
Coats & Coats Persnnl, *Perm. Emp Agcy*
Columbus Persnnl, *Temp. Agcy*
EPSCO Persnnl, *Temp. Agcy*
Impact Persnnl Svcs, *Exec Srch*
Laborchex Companies, *Perm. Emp Agcy*
Norrell Staff Svcs, *Temp. Agcy*
Opportunities Unlimtd, *Perm. Emp Agcy*
Persnnl Unlimtd, *Exec Srch*
Recruitment & Training of MS, *Perm. Emp Agcy*
Tatum Persnnl, *Perm. Emp Agcy*
Jim Woodson & Assoc., *Exec Srch*

Missouri

ABC Emp. Svc, *Perm. Emp Agcy*
Adecco, *Temp. Agcy*
Advanced Careers of Kansas Cty, *Exec Srch*
Agri-Tech Persnnl, *Exec Srch*
Jay Alexandr & Assoc. dba Kirdonn Grp, *Perm. Emp Agcy*
American Automotive Persnnl Consltnts, *Exec Srch*
Austin Nichols Tech. Temps, *Temp. Agcy*
Ken Brown & Co, *Exec Srch*
Burns Emp. Svc, *Exec Srch*
Business Persnnl Svcs, *Temp. Agcy*
The Christiansen Grp, *Exec Srch*
Crider & Assoc., *Perm. Emp Agcy*
Crown Svcs, *Temp. Agcy*
Crown Svcs, *Temp. Agcy*
Deck & Decker Emp. Svc, *Perm. Emp Agcy*
Decker Persnnl, *Perm. Emp Agcy*
Employer Advantage, *Exec Srch*
Executive Recrtrs, *Exec Srch*
FORTUNE Persnnl Consltnts, *Exec Srch*
Gibson & Assoc., *Exec Srch*
Haskell Assoc., *Exec Srch*
JoDoc Enterprises, *Temp. Agcy*
J.B. Linde & Assoc., *Exec Srch*
Charles Luntz & Assoc., *Exec Srch*
Mgmt. Recrtrs of Kansas Cty, *Exec Srch*
Mgmt. Recrtrs of Springfield, *Exec Srch*
Mgmt. Recrtrs of St. Louis, *Exec Srch*
Mgmt. Recrtrs of St. Louis, *Exec Srch*
Manpower Temp. Svcs, *Temp. Agcy*
J. Miles Persnnl Svcs, *Exec Srch*
Norrell Svcs, *Temp. Agcy*
Officemates5 of St. Louis, *Exec Srch*
Olsten Staff Svcs, *Temp. Agcy*
Gordon Smith & Assoc., *Exec Srch*
Snelling Persnnl Svcs, *Perm. Emp Agcy*
Workforce, *Temp. Agcy*

Montana

Labor Contracting Staff Svcs, *Perm. Emp Agcy*

Nebraska

Choice Enterprises, *Exec Srch*
Compusearch of Lincoln, *Exec Srch*
Corporate Recrtrs, *Exec Srch*
Eggers Co, *Perm. Emp Agcy*
Express Persnnl, *Exec Srch*
Hahn Tech. Staffng, *Exec Srch*
Hansen Agri-Placement, *Perm. Emp Agcy*
Kelly Svcs, *Temp. Agcy*
Mgmt. Recrtrs of Omaha/Officemates5, *Exec Srch*
Professional Recrtrs, *Perm. Emp Agcy*
Sharp Persnnl, *Temp. Agcy*

Nevada

Mgmt. Recrtrs of Reno, *Exec Srch*
Talent Tree Staffng, *Perm. Emp Agcy*

New Hampshire

Affordable Solut'ns, *Contract Svc*
Central New Hampshire Emp. Svcs, *Perm. Emp Agcy*
Chaucer Grp, *Perm. Emp Agcy*
Chaucer Grp, *Exec Srch*
Cheshire Emp. Svc, *Temp. Agcy*
Dubois & Co, *Exec Srch*
Enterprise Technolog's, *Exec Srch*

Lloyd Persnnl Consltnts, *Exec Srch*
Mgmt. Recrtrs Intl of Bedford, *Exec Srch*
National Emp. Svc Corp, *Perm. Emp Agcy*
Pelham Prof'l Grp, *Temp. Agcy*
Preferred Resrcs Grp, *Exec Srch*
R.G.T. Assoc., *Exec Srch*
Resource Recruitng/Contemp. Accntnts, *Perm. Emp Agcy*
Surge Resrcs, *Contract Svc*
TAC Staff Svcs, *Temp. Agcy*
Tech/Aid of NH, *Perm. Emp Agcy*
Technical Needs, *Exec Srch*

New Jersey

A+ Persnnl, *Perm. Emp Agcy*
ABC Nationwide Employment, *Perm. Emp Agcy*
Advanced Persnnl, *Perm. Emp Agcy*
Balcor Assoc., *Exec Srch*
R.P. Barone Assoc., *Exec Srch*
Gary Bell Assoc., *Exec Srch*
Blake & Assoc. Exec Srch, *Exec Srch*
Brett Assoc., *Exec Srch*
Career Ctr, *Perm. Emp Agcy*
Career Srch Assoc., *Exec Srch*
Careers USA, *Perm. Emp Agcy*
Careerworks, *Exec Srch*
Citizens Emp. Svcs, *Perm. Emp Agcy*
Corporate One, *Exec Srch*
Cox Darrow & Owens, *Exec Srch*
M.T. Donaldson Assoc., *Exec Srch*
Dreier Consltng, *Exec Srch*
Express Persnnl Svcs, *Perm. Emp Agcy*
FORTUNE Persnnl Consltnts of Menlo Prk, *Exec Srch*
Grant Franks & Assoc., *Exec Srch*
Harris Exec Srch, *Exec Srch*
Hreshko Consltng Grp, *Exec Srch*
Huff Assoc., *Exec Srch*
Hughes & Podesla Persnnl, *Perm. Emp Agcy*
Hunt, Ltd., *Perm. Emp Agcy*
Impact Persnnl, *Perm. Emp Agcy*
J.M. Joseph Assoc., *Exec Srch*
Joule People Providers, *Perm. Emp Agcy*
Kaye Persnnl, *Temp. Agcy*
Joseph Keyes Assoc., *Perm. Emp Agcy*
T.J. Koellhoffer & Assoc., *Exec Srch*
Paul Kull & Co, *Exec Srch*
Lab Support, *Temp. Agcy*
Mgmt. Recrtrs of Bay Head, *Exec Srch*
Mgmt. Recrtrs of Medford, *Exec Srch*
Mgmt. Recrtrs of Orange Cnty, *Exec Srch*
Manpower Tech. Svcs, *Temp. Agcy*
Mayfair Svcs, *Perm. Emp Agcy*
Normyle/Erstling Health Srch Grp, *Exec Srch*
OMNE Staff Svcs, *Temp. Agcy*
Orion Consltng, *Exec Srch*
Protocall Bus. Staff Svcs, *Temp. Agcy*
Ramming & Assoc., *Exec Srch*
Rochester Syst., *Exec Srch*
Rylan Forbes Consltng Grp, *Exec Srch*
S-H-S of Cherry Hill, *Perm. Emp Agcy*
R.S. Sadow Assoc., *Exec Srch*
Sales Consltnts of Sparta, *Exec Srch*
Sales Consltnts, *Exec Srch*
Sanford Rose Assoc., *Exec Srch*
Rob Scott Assoc., *Exec Srch*
Selective Persnnl, *Perm. Emp Agcy*
Arline Simpson Assoc., *Perm. Emp Agcy*
Source Svcs Corp, *Perm. Emp Agcy*
Stelton Grp, *Exec Srch*
Summit Grp, *Exec Srch*
TRS Staff Solut'ns, *Temp. Agcy*
Tenek Corp, *Exec Srch*
Claire Wright Assn, *Perm. Emp Agcy*

New Mexico

Albuquerque Persnnl, *Perm. Emp Agcy*
Butler Svc Grp, *Contract Svc*
CDI Corp, *Contract Svc*

New York

AM & PM Temps, *Temp. Agcy*
APA Srch, *Exec Srch*
ATS Reliance, *Perm. Emp Agcy*
Accounting & Computer Persnnl, *Perm. Emp Agcy*
Merrill Adams Assoc., *Career/Outplacemnt*
Adecco, *Temp. Agcy*
American Bus. Consltnts, *Career/Outplacemnt*
April Tech. Recruitng, *Perm. Emp Agcy*
Arrow Emp. Agcy, *Perm. Emp Agcy*
Bestemp Temp. Svcs, *Temp. Agcy*
Bornholdt Shivas & Friends, *Exec Srch*
Bos Bus. Consltnts, *Exec Srch*
Branthover Assoc., *Exec Srch*
Burns Persnnl, *Exec Srch*
CDI Corp, *Contract Svc*
Carlile Persnnl Agcy, *Perm. Emp Agcy*
Colton Partnership, *Exec Srch*
Contrct Specialties Grp, *Contract Svc*
Corporate Careers/R.J. Assoc., *Exec Srch*
Corporate Srch, *Exec Srch*
Frank Cuomo & Assoc., *Exec Srch*
The Dartmouth Grp, *Exec Srch*
Seth Diamond Assoc., *Exec Srch*
Dymanex Srch, *Exec Srch*
EDP Contrct Svcs, *Contract Svc*
Employment Recrtrs Agcy, *Perm. Emp Agcy*
Extra Help Emp. Svc, *Temp. Agcy*
FORTUNE Persnnl Consltnts of Rockland Cnty, *Exec Srch*
Fabian Assoc., *Exec Srch*
Fifth Avenue Emp. Svcs, *Temp. Agcy*
Graphic Techniques, *Temp. Agcy*
The Haas Assoc., *Exec Srch*
Robert Half Intl/Information Syst. Division, *Exec Srch*
Hart-Merrell Persnnl, *Exec Srch*
F.P. Healy & Co, *Exec Srch*
Kelly Svcs, *Temp. Agcy*
Fred Koffler Assoc., *Exec Srch*
Lab Support, *Temp. Agcy*
Lake Assoc., *Exec Srch*
Michael John Lawrence & Assoc., *Exec Srch*
Mgmt. Recrtrs of Nassau, *Exec Srch*
Mgmt. Recrtrs of Utica/Rome, *Exec Srch*
Mgmt. Recrtrs of Woodbury/ CompuSrch, *Exec Srch*
Manpower Tech. Svcs, *Temp. Agcy*
Manpower Temp. Svcs, *Temp. Agcy*
Metro Resrcs of Rochester, *Temp. Agcy*
Metro Persnnl/Metro Nursing Svcs, *Exec Srch*
Mickler Assoc., *Exec Srch*
Morgan-Murray Persnnl/M&M Top Temps, *Temp. Agcy*
Noah Assoc., *Perm. Emp Agcy*
Norris Emp. Consltnts, *Perm. Emp Agcy*
Olsten Staff Svcs, *Temp. Agcy*
Parsons, Anderson & Gee, *Perm. Emp Agcy*
Phoenix Emp. Agcy, *Perm. Emp Agcy*
ROI Assoc., *Exec Srch*
Remedy Intelligent Staffng, *Temp. Agcy*
St. Lawrence Intl, *Exec Srch*
Staff Managers, *Temp. Agcy*
Staffing Svcs, *Exec Srch*
Superior Concepts, *Contract Svc*
TAD Resrcs, *Contract Svc*
Taylor Jordan Assoc., *Exec Srch*
Thorsen Assoc., *Exec Srch*
Weber Mngmnt Consltnts, *Exec Srch*
Werbin Assoc. Exec Srch, *Exec Srch*
Westchester Emp. Agcy, *Perm. Emp Agcy*
H.L. Yoh Co, *Contract Svc*

North Carolina

A-1 Staffing & Persnnl, *Perm. Emp Agcy*
Accountnts Exec Srch, *Exec Srch*
Accurate Staff Consltnts, *Exec Srch*
Action Staffmasters, *Temp. Agcy*
Action Tech. Staffng, *Temp. Agcy*
Advanced Persnnl Resrcs, *Exec Srch*
Amcell Assoc., *Exec Srch*
AmeriPro Srch, *Exec Srch*
Apple Resrcs, *Perm. Emp Agcy*
Atchison & Assoc., *Exec Srch*
Ayers & Assoc., *Exec Srch*
Career Srch, *Exec Srch*
Coastal Temp. Svcs, *Temp. Agcy*
Davis Tech. Srch Consltnts, *Exec Srch*
Phil Ellis Assoc., *Exec Srch*
Employment Consltnts, *Contract Svc*
Executive Recrtmnt Specialists, *Exec Srch*
Executive Staff Svcs, *Perm. Emp Agcy*
C.D. Fayling Assoc., *Exec Srch*
FORTUNE Persnnl Consltnts of Raleigh, *Perm. Emp Agcy*
FORTUNE Persnnl Consltnts, *Exec Srch*
The Furniture Agcy, *Exec Srch*
Glovier & Assoc., *Exec Srch*
Graham & Assoc., *Perm. Emp Agcy*
Stew Greene & Co/The Triad, *Exec Srch*
Hallmark Recrtrs, *Exec Srch*
Highlander Srch, *Exec Srch*
Interim Persnnl, *Temp. Agcy*
The Jobs Market, *Perm. Emp Agcy*
Jobs of Fayetteville, *Perm. Emp Agcy*
Kelly Svcs, *Temp. Agcy*
MSB Assoc., *Exec Srch*
Mgmt. Recrtrs/Sales Consltnts, *Exec Srch*
Mgmt. Recrtrs of Burlington, *Exec Srch*
Mgmt. Recrtrs of Durham, *Exec Srch*
Mgmt. Recrtrs of Kinston, *Exec Srch*
Mgmt. Recrtrs of Raleigh/Inter Exec, *Exec Srch*
Mgmt. Recrtrs of Winston-Salem, *Exec Srch*
Manpower, *Temp. Agcy*
McCain Emp. Agcy, *Temp. Agcy*
Mebane Temp. Svcs, *Temp. Agcy*
Merrick & Moore, *Exec Srch*
Metals & Wood Agcy, *Exec Srch*
Myers & Assoc., *Perm. Emp Agcy*
National Svcs, *Exec Srch*
Olsten Staff Svcs, *Temp. Agcy*
The Perkin Grp, *Exec Srch*
Persnnl Svcs Unlimtd, *Temp. Agcy*
Professional Persnnl Assoc., *Perm. Emp Agcy*
Quality Temp. Svcs, *Temp. Agcy*
Sales Consltnts of High Point, *Exec Srch*
Sanford Rose Assoc., *Exec Srch*
Snelling Persnnl Svcs, *Contract Svc*
Snelling Srch, *Exec Srch*
Sparks Persnnl Svcs, *Exec Srch*
Talent Tree Staffng, *Perm. Emp Agcy*
Temporary Staffing Syst., *Temp. Agcy*
Waddy Thomson Assoc., *Exec Srch*
Volt Tech. Svcs, *Contract Svc*
John Williams & Assoc., *Exec Srch*
Wilson Persnnl, *Exec Srch*
Winston Temp. Staffng, *Temp. Agcy*
Youngblood Staffng, *Perm. Emp Agcy*

North Dakota

Career Connection, *Exec Srch*
Olsten Staff Svcs/Kramer & Assoc./Expressway Persnnl, *Temp. Agcy*

Ohio

AccuStaff, *Temp. Agcy*
Adecco, *Perm. Emp Agcy*
Advancement Recruitng Svcs, *Exec Srch*
Alliance Tech. Svcs, *Contract Svc*
Dave Arnold & Assoc., *Exec Srch*
Baldwin & Assoc., *Exec Srch*
Belcan Tech. Svcs, *Contract Svc*
Bradley-Pierce Persnnl, *Perm. Emp Agcy*
J.B. Brown & Assoc., *Exec Srch*
Burks Grp, *Exec Srch*
CBS Persnnl Svcs, *Perm. Emp Agcy*
Career Connections, *Perm. Emp Agcy*
Career Specialists, *Exec Srch*
Combined Resrcs, *Exec Srch*
Continental Srch Consltnts, *Exec Srch*
Corell Assoc., *Perm. Emp Agcy*
J.D. Cotter Srch, *Exec Srch*
Crown Temp. Svcs of Cincinnati, *Temp. Agcy*
Custom Staffng, *Temp. Agcy*
Alan Daum & Assoc., *Perm. Emp Agcy*
Delta Design Drafting, *Temp. Agcy*
Eastern Persnnl Svcs, *Perm. Emp Agcy*
Executech, *Exec Srch*
Executech Consltnts, *Exec Srch*
Executive Connection, *Exec Srch*
Executive Srch Ltd., *Exec Srch*
Extra Help Temp. Svc, *Temp. Agcy*
Fenzel Milar Assoc., *Exec Srch*
Flex-Tech Prof'l Svcs, *Contract Svc*
Flowers & Assoc./Associated Temps, *Exec Srch*
FORTUNE Persnnl Consltnts, *Exec Srch*
Functional Tech. Svcs, *Perm. Emp Agcy*
Gayhart & Assoc., *Exec Srch*
Global Resrcs Grp, *Contract Svc*
H.L. Goehring & Assoc., *Exec Srch*
R. Green & Assoc., *Exec Srch*
Griffiths & Assoc., *Exec Srch*
Guthoff & Assoc., *Exec Srch*
H.J.C., *Exec Srch*
Russ Hadick & Assoc., *Exec Srch*
Hite Exec Srch/Hite Mngmnt Consltnts, *Exec Srch*
Human Resource Recrtrs, *Exec Srch*
ITS Tech. Staffing/Interconnect Tech. Svcs, *Exec Srch*
Icon Mngmnt Grp, *Exec Srch*
Interim Persnnl, *Temp. Agcy*
Ives & Assoc., *Exec Srch*
Jaeger Intl, *Exec Srch*
Kaiser Nationwide, *Exec Srch*
Kelly Svcs, *Temp. Agcy*
Laine's S.M.G., *Perm. Emp Agcy*
Mgmt. Recrtrs Intl, *Exec Srch*
Mgmt. Recrtrs of Cincinnati, *Exec Srch*
Mgmt. Recrtrs of Cleveland, *Exec Srch*
Mgmt. Recrtrs of Columbus, *Exec Srch*
Mgmt. Recrtrs of Dayton, *Exec Srch*
Mgmt. Recrtrs of No. Canton, *Exec Srch*
Mgmt. Recrtrs of Solon, *Exec Srch*
Manpower Temp. Svcs, *Temp. Agcy*
Messina Mngmnt Syst., *Exec Srch*
Miami Prof'l Srch, *Exec Srch*
Midland Consltnts, *Exec Srch*
Minority Exec Srch, *Exec Srch*
Myers & Assoc., *Exec Srch*
Nesco Svc Co, *Temp. Agcy*
Newcomb-Desmond & Assoc., *Exec Srch*
North American Persnnl, *Exec Srch*
North Star Resrcs, *Contract Svc*
Northcoast Persnnl, *Exec Srch*
Olsten Prof'l Staff Svcs, *Exec Srch*
Olsten Staff Svcs, *Temp. Agcy*
Placement Svcs Limited, *Exec Srch*
The Prof'l Consltnts, *Exec Srch*
Professional Emp. Svcs, *Perm. Emp Agcy*
Professional Restaffing of OH, *Perm. Emp Agcy*
Providence Persnnl Consltnts, *Exec Srch*
Quality Plus, *Exec Srch*
Questcor Co, *Exec Srch*
RDS, *Contract Svc*
Bill Reber & Assoc., *Exec Srch*

Utah

Mgmt. Recrtrs of Ogden, *Exec Srch*
Mgmt. Recrtrs of Provo, *Exec Srch*
Manpower Tech. Svcs, *Temp. Agcy*
Olsten Staff Svcs, *Temp. Agcy*
Peak Temp. Svcs, *Temp. Agcy*
Prince, Perelson & Assoc., *Exec Srch*
Professional Recrtrs, *Exec Srch*
Staffing Logic, *Perm. Emp Agcy*
Trout & Assoc., *Exec Srch*

Vermont

Adecco, *Temp. Agcy*
Persnnl Dept, *Temp. Agcy*

Virginia

A Better Resume, *Career/Outplacemnt*
Alpha Omega Resrcs, *Perm. Emp Agcy*
Career Registry, *Exec Srch*
Contec Srch, *Exec Srch*
Corporate Connection Exec. Srch Firm
Carol Day & Assoc., *Exec Srch*
Dow Persnnl, *Perm. Emp Agcy*
EDP, *Temp. Agcy*
Express Persnnl Svcs, *Temp. Agcy*
H.R. Directions, *Contract Svc*
Lee Staffing Resrcs, *Exec Srch*
Mgmt. Recrtrs of McLean, *Exec Srch*
Mgmt. Recrtrs of Roanoke, *Exec Srch*
Manpower Temp. Svcs, *Temp. Agcy*
Mid-Atlantic Srch, *Exec Srch*
A.J. Morelli Contracting, *Contract Svc*
Norrell Staff Svcs, *Exec Srch*
Olsten Staff Svcs, *Temp. Agcy*
PDS Temp. Svc, *Temp. Agcy*
Placement Prof'ls, *Exec Srch*
Procurement Solut'ns, *Contract Svc*
Search & Recruit Intl, *Exec Srch*
Snelling Persnnl Svcs, *Perm. Emp Agcy*
Souder & Assoc., *Exec Srch*
STAT Temps, *Temp. Agcy*
Strategic Srch, *Exec Srch*
TAC Staff Svcs, *Temp. Agcy*
The Talley Grp, *Exec Srch*
Task Force of VA, *Exec Srch*
Tech/Aid of VA, *Temp. Agcy*
Temporary Solut'ns, *Temp. Agcy*
U.S. Srch, *Exec Srch*
Virginia Emp. Referral Svc, *Exec Srch*
Wannamaker Assoc., *Perm. Emp Agcy*
Wayne Assoc., *Exec Srch*
Western Staff Svcs, *Temp. Agcy*

Washington

Behrens & Co, *Exec Srch*
CDI Corp, *Contract Svc*
The Career Clinic, *Exec Srch*
Express Persnnl Svcs, *Temp. Agcy*
FORTUNE Persnnl Consltnts of E. Seattle, *Exec Srch*
Guidance Svcs, *Temp. Agcy*
Kelly Svcs, *Temp. Agcy*
Labor Ready, *Temp. Agcy*
Mgmt. Recrtrs of Mercer Islnd, *Exec Srch*
Mgmt. Recrtrs of Seattle, *Exec Srch*
Mgmt. Recrtrs of Tacoma, *Exec Srch*
John Mason & Assoc., *Exec Srch*
Mini-Systems Assoc., *Contract Svc*
Northwest Temp. Svcs, *Temp. Agcy*
Olsten Staff Svcs, *Temp. Agcy*
Persnnl Unlimtd, *Exec Srch*
Jack Porter & Assoc., *Perm. Emp Agcy*
Roth Young Persnnl Svcs, *Exec Srch*
Susan Schoos & Assoc., *Exec Srch*
Skills Resource Training Ctr, *Perm. Emp Agcy*
Strain Persnnl Specialists, *Exec Srch*
Two 56, *Contract Svc*
Whittall Mngmnt Grp, *Exec Srch*

West Virginia

Extra Support Staffng, *Temp. Agcy*
Key Persnnl, *Perm. Emp Agcy*

Wisconsin

Allen, Wayne, & Co, *Perm. Emp Agcy*
American Tech. Svcs, *Perm. Emp Agcy*
Argus Tech. Svcs, *Perm. Emp Agcy*
Austria Austria & Assoc., *Perm. Emp Agcy*
Corporate Srch, *Exec Srch*
Crown Svcs, *Temp. Agcy*
Dunhill of Green Bay, *Perm. Emp Agcy*
J.M. Eagle Partners, *Exec Srch*
Eagle Technlgy Grp, *Perm. Emp Agcy*
Employability, *Perm. Emp Agcy*
EnviroStaff, *Temp. Agcy*
Epic Skilled & Industrial, *Perm. Emp Agcy*
Executive Placemnt Svc/Career Connections, *Exec Srch*
Executive Recrtrs, *Exec Srch*
Financial Mngmnt Persnnl, *Exec Srch*
IDI Corp, *Temp. Agcy*
Interim Persnnl, *Temp. Agcy*
Mgmt. Recrtrs Intl, *Exec Srch*
Mgmt. Recrtrs of Appleton/ CompuSrch, *Exec Srch*
Mgmt. Recrtrs of Green Bay, *Exec Srch*
Mgmt. Recrtrs of Milwaukee/Sales Consltnts, *Exec Srch*
Mgmt. Recrtrs of Milwaukee, *Exec Srch*
Manpower Temp. Svcs, *Temp. Agcy*
MARBL Consltnts, *Exec Srch*
Markent Persnnl, *Exec Srch*
N.E.W. Contracting Svcs, *Perm. Emp Agcy*
David Neil & Assoc., *Exec Srch*
Olsten Staff Svcs, *Temp. Agcy*
Placements of Racine, *Perm. Emp Agcy*
Pollak & Skan, *Contract Svc*
Tom Sloan & Assoc., *Perm. Emp Agcy*
T.E.M. Assoc., *Exec Srch*
TAD Tech. Svcs, *Contract Svc*
Techstaff, *Perm. Emp Agcy*
Techtronix Tech. Employment, *Exec Srch*
U.S. Tech Force, *Exec Srch*
Valley Recruitng, *Exec Srch*
The Waterstone Grp, *Contract Svc*

Wyoming

Mgmt. Recrtrs of Cheyenne, *Exec Srch*
Olsten Staff Svcs, *Temp. Agcy*

MARITIME

Alabama

Marine Jobs, *Perm. Emp Agcy*

Florida

CTI Grp, *Perm. Emp Agcy*
Passport Placemnt Svc, *Perm. Emp Agcy*

Louisiana

Rhema Emp. Agcy, *Exec Srch*

Rhode Island

Spectrum Bus. Assoc. Exec. Srch Firm

Texas

Legend Marine, *Perm. Emp Agcy*

Washington

Maritime Recrtrs, *Exec Srch*

MARKET RESEARCH

California

J. Carson & Assoc., *Exec Srch*

Illinois

Bloom, Gross & Assoc., *Exec Srch*
Pahlman, Murphy & Attridge, *Exec Srch*
Siegel Assoc., *Exec Srch*
Smith Hanley Assoc., *Exec Srch*

Maryland

Mgmt. Recrtrs of Washington, D.C., *Exec Srch*

Michigan

Graphic Arts Mrktng Assoc., *Exec Srch*

Missouri

Gruen & Assoc., *Exec Srch*

New Jersey

Zwicker Assoc., *Exec Srch*

New York

Mgmt. Recrtrs of Gramercy, *Exec Srch*

MARKETING

Alabama

Snelling Srch/Snelling Persnnl Svcs, *Exec Srch*

Alaska

Manpower Temp. Svc, *Temp. Agcy*
Olsten Staff Svcs, *Temp. Agcy*

California

Alexander & Co, *Exec Srch*
Bast & Assoc., *Exec Srch*
California Srch Agcy, *Exec Srch*
Decker & Assoc. Persnnl, *Perm. Emp Agcy*
Karsch/Card, *Exec Srch*
Kelly Svcs, *Temp. Agcy*
MarSearch Assoc., *Exec Srch*
New Venture Development, *Exec Srch*

Colorado

Ahrnsbrak & Assoc., *Perm. Emp Agcy*
Kelly Svcs, *Perm. Emp Agcy*

Connecticut

Strategic Executives, *Exec Srch*
Frank Wilkinson & Co, *Exec Srch*
Wittlan Grp, *Exec Srch*

Florida

AccuStaff, *Temp. Agcy*
Carrier's Career Svc, *Career/Outplacemnt*
Priority Srch, *Exec Srch*
Sanford Rose Assoc., *Exec Srch*
The Stewart Srch Grp, *Exec Srch*

Georgia

Ad Options, *Perm. Emp Agcy*
Dunhill Prof'l Srch, *Exec Srch*
Hire Intellect, *Temp. Agcy*

Illinois

Bloom, Gross & Assoc., *Exec Srch*
Executive Options Exec. Srch Firm
Hufford Assoc., *Exec Srch*
Pahlman, Murphy & Attridge, *Exec Srch*
Staffing Consltnts, *Perm. Emp Agcy*

Indiana

Mgmt. Recrtrs/Sales Consltnts, *Exec Srch*

Maryland

Placement Assoc., *Exec Srch*

Massachusetts

Career Success Intl, *Exec Srch*
Corporate Staff Solut'ns, *Temp. Agcy*
Dana Assoc., *Exec Srch*
New Dimensions in Technlgy, *Exec Srch*
Prestonwood Assoc., *Exec Srch*
Robsham Assoc., *Exec Srch*

Michigan

Graphic Arts Mrktng Assoc., *Exec Srch*

Minnesota

Professional Recrtrs, *Exec Srch*

New Hampshire

Barclay Persnnl Syst., *Exec Srch*
Career Connections, *Perm. Emp Agcy*
Chaucer Grp, *Exec Srch*
Manpower Temp. Svcs, *Temp. Agcy*
Sales Recrtrs, *Exec Srch*

New Jersey

Garrett Grp, *Exec Srch*
Persnnl Plus/Temps Plus, *Perm. Emp Agcy*
Premier Persnnl Grp, *Perm. Emp Agcy*

New Mexico

Roadrunner Persnnl, *Exec Srch*
Snelling Persnnl Svcs, *Exec Srch*

New York

Franklin Allen Consltnts Exec. Srch Firm
Ames O'Neill Assoc., *Exec Srch*
C.C. Burke Limited, *Perm. Emp Agcy*
CFI Resrcs, *Exec Srch*
Toby Clark Assoc., *Exec Srch*
Corporate Moves, *Exec Srch*
Seth Diamond Assoc., *Exec Srch*
The Emp. Store/TES Technical, *Exec Srch*
Forray Assoc., *Exec Srch*
KPA Grp, *Exec Srch*
Lawrence Exec Srch, *Exec Srch*
Mgmt. Recrtrs Intl, *Exec Srch*
Natek Corp, *Exec Srch*
Olsten Staff Svcs, *Temp. Agcy*
Sales Srch, Ltd./Executive Resume Svc, *Exec Srch*
Vintage Resrcs, *Exec Srch*
Weber Mngmnt Consltnts, *Exec Srch*
S.R. Wolman Assoc., *Exec Srch*

North Carolina

Mgmt. Recrtrs/Sales Consltnts, *Exec Srch*
Moffitt Intl, *Exec Srch*
The Perkin Grp, *Exec Srch*

Ohio

Marvel Consltnts, *Exec Srch*
Personalized Plcmnt, *Exec Srch*
Professional Emp. Svcs, *Perm. Emp Agcy*
Tabb & Assoc., *Exec Srch*

Pennsylvania

American Staffing Resrcs, *Temp. Agcy*
Atomic Persnnl, *Exec Srch*
FORTUNE Grp Intl, *Exec Srch*
Interim Persnnl of Lehigh Valley PA, *Temp. Agcy*
Jefferson-Ross Assoc., *Exec Srch*
Metro Persnnl, *Temp. Agcy*
Sanford Rose Assoc., *Exec Srch*
Snelling Persnnl Svcs, *Temp. Agcy*

Technical Prof'l Svc, *Perm. Emp Agcy*
Weliver & Assoc., *Exec Srch*

Minnesota
Ultimate Srch Unlimtd/Temps Unlimtd, *Perm. Emp Agcy*

Missouri
Olsten Staff Svcs, *Temp. Agcy*
Sanford Rose Assoc., *Exec Srch*

Nevada
Matrix Grp, *Exec Srch*

New Jersey
The Datafinders Grp, *Exec Srch*
Rochester Syst., *Exec Srch*

New York
Franklin Allen Consltnts Exec. Srch Firm
Brookville Staff Svcs, *Perm. Emp Agcy*
Casale Mngmnt Svcs, *Exec Srch*
Seth Diamond Assoc., *Exec Srch*
EDP Contrct Svcs, *Contract Svc*
Information Syst. Staffng, *Perm. Emp Agcy*
KPA Grp, *Exec Srch*
Venture Resrcs, *Exec Srch*

North Carolina
AmeriPro Srch, *Exec Srch*
DP Pros, *Temp. Agcy*
Graham & Assoc., *Perm. Emp Agcy*

Ohio
Burks Grp, *Exec Srch*
Career Recrtrs, *Exec Srch*
North Peak Grp, *Exec Srch*
Rich & Assoc., *Exec Srch*
Tech/Aid of OH, *Perm. Emp Agcy*

Pennsylvania
Merrill Grumer Assoc., *Perm. Emp Agcy*
London Persnnl Svcs, *Perm. Emp Agcy*
Sanford Rose Assoc., *Exec Srch*
Systems Persnnl, *Exec Srch*

South Carolina
Southern Recrtrs & Consltnts, *Exec Srch*

Texas
R. Gaines Baty Assoc., *Exec Srch*
Burnett's Staffng, *Exec Srch*
The Whitaker Companies, *Exec Srch*

Virginia
Nancy Allen Assoc., *Perm. Emp Agcy*

Washington
Houser, Martin, Morris & Assoc., *Exec Srch*
Mgmt. Recrtrs of Mercer Islnd, *Exec Srch*
Nelson, Coulson & Assoc., *Perm. Emp Agcy*
Thomas Co, *Perm. Emp Agcy*

Wisconsin
Hunter Midwest, *Exec Srch*
Mgmt. Recrtrs/CompuSrch of Wausau, *Exec Srch*
Mgmt. Recrtrs, *Exec Srch*

MORTGAGE

Illinois
Contemporary Svcs, *Exec Srch*
Uniforce Staff Svcs, *Temp. Agcy*

Maryland
Admin Persnnl Svcs, *Perm. Emp Agcy*

Massachusetts
Arthur-Blair Assoc., *Perm. Emp Agcy*

Nevada
Matrix Grp, *Exec Srch*

New Jersey
Cox Darrow & Owens, *Exec Srch*

New York
The Aloe Grp, *Perm. Emp Agcy*
Frontrunner Srch, *Exec Srch*
The Lloyd Co, *Career/Outplacemnt*

Texas
InterSearch Assoc., *Temp. Agcy*

Virginia
Million & Assoc., *Exec Srch*

Washington
Barbara Ruhl & Assoc., *Exec Srch*

MULTIMEDIA

California
Alexander & Co, *Exec Srch*
MacTemps, *Temp. Agcy*
Ed Rast & Co, *Exec Srch*

District of Columbia
Portfolio, *Perm. Emp Agcy*

Massachusetts
New Dimensions in Technlgy, *Exec Srch*
Pro Staff, *Temp. Agcy*

New Hampshire
Hart, Hawkins & Co, *Exec Srch*

New York
Cavan Syst., *Exec Srch*

Texas
Contrct Design Persnnl, *Temp. Agcy*

NANNIES

Colorado
ABC Nannies, *Perm. Emp Agcy*

Florida
A Choice Nanny, *Perm. Emp Agcy*
Nannies 'N More, *Perm. Emp Agcy*

Georgia
Smith Agcy, *Perm. Emp Agcy*

Maryland
A Choice Nanny, *Contract Svc*

Massachusetts
In Srch of Nanny, *Perm. Emp Agcy*
The Original Nanny Svc, *Perm. Emp Agcy*
Yankee Sitters Nanny Agcy, *Perm. Emp Agcy*

Michigan
Nanny Attachment Svc, *Perm. Emp Agcy*
The Nanny Netwrk, *Perm. Emp Agcy*

Montana
Heartland Nannies & Companions/Heartland Caregivers, *Contract Svc*

Nevada
Kids Care Connection, *Perm. Emp Agcy*
Nanny Placemnt Agcy, *Perm. Emp Agcy*

New Jersey
A Choice Nanny, *Perm. Emp Agcy*
Capitol Srch, *Perm. Emp Agcy*
Neighborhood Nannies, *Perm. Emp Agcy*

New York
Adele Poston Nurses Registry, *Perm. Emp Agcy*
Best Domestic Svcs Agcy, *Perm. Emp Agcy*

Oklahoma
DeMarge Employment, *Perm. Emp Agcy*

Pennsylvania
Your Other Hands, *Perm. Emp Agcy*

Rhode Island
Cass & Company, *Perm. Emp Agcy*

Utah
The Nanny Connection, *Perm. Emp Agcy*

Virginia
A Choice Nanny, *Perm. Emp Agcy*
Nanny Factor, *Perm. Emp Agcy*

NETWORK ADMINISTRATION

California
MindSource Software Engineers, *Contract Svc*
PC Persnnl, *Contract Svc*
PeopleWare Tech. Resrcs, *Contract Svc*
Smartsource Inc., *Contract Svc*

Massachusetts
New Dimensions in Technlgy, *Exec Srch*

New Hampshire
Barros Assoc., *Perm. Emp Agcy*
Professional Recrtrs, *Perm. Emp Agcy*

New York
Huntington Persnnl Consltnts, *Exec Srch*
OTEC.COM, *Perm. Emp Agcy*

Virginia
Strategic Staffing/SSI Tech. Svcs Division, *Contract Sv*

Wisconsin
Hunter Midwest, *Exec Srch*

Alabama
A-1 Emp. Svc, *Perm. Emp Agcy*
VIP Persnnl, *Perm. Emp Agcy*

Arizona
Stivers Temp. Persnnl, *Temp. Agcy*

California
ABA Staffng, *Exec Srch*
Answers Unlimtd, *Temp. Agcy*
Bennett & Co Consltng Grp, *Exec Srch*
Blue Moon Persnnl, *Temp. Agcy*
Business Syst. Staffing & Assoc., *Perm. Emp Agcy*
Champagne Temp. Help, *Temp. Agcy*
Culver Persnnl Svcs/The Culver Grp, *Exec Srch*
EDP Contrct Svcs, *Contract Svc*
Employment Devlpmnt Dept, *Perm. Emp Agcy*
40 Plus of So. CA, *Exec Srch*
Goldstein & Assoc., *Temp. Agcy*
Gould Persnnl Svcs, *Perm. Emp Agcy*
Integrated Community Svcs, *Perm. Emp Agcy*
Intertec Design, *Perm. Emp Agcy*
Justus Persnnl Svcs, *Perm. Emp Agcy*
Kabl Ability Netwrk, *Exec Srch*
Klein & Assoc., *Temp. Agcy*
Larsen, Whitney, Blecksmith, & Zilliacus, *Exec Srch*
The London Agcy, *Exec Srch*
The London Agcy, *Temp. Agcy*
MacNaughton Assoc., *Exec Srch*
Maverick Staff Svc, *Perm. Emp Agcy*
McCormack & Assoc., *Exec Srch*
Pacific Srch Grp, *Exec Srch*
Presidio Persnnl, *Temp. Agcy*
Pro Staff Persnnl Svcs, *Perm. Emp Agcy*
Ed Rast & Co, *Exec Srch*
Royal Staff Svcs, *Exec Srch*
Santa Barbara Plcmnt, *Perm. Emp Agcy*
TRC Staff Svcs, *Perm. Emp Agcy*
UAW Labor Emp. & Training Corp, *Perm. Emp Agcy*
Your People Prof'ls, *Perm. Emp Agcy*

Colorado
A to Z Bus. Svcs, *Perm. Emp Agcy*
40 Plus of CO, *Career/Outplacemnt*
JobSearch, *Temp. Agcy*
National Affirmative Action Career Netwrk, *Exec Srch*
Todays Temporary, *Temp. Agcy*

Connecticut
EDP Contrct Svcs, *Contract Svc*

Delaware
J.B. Groner Exec Srch, *Exec Srch*

District of Columbia
Access: Networking in the Public Interest, *Career/Outplacemnt*
Admin. Assist./Hire Standard Staffng, *Perm. Emp Agcy*
Best Temps, *Temp. Agcy*
K.M.S. Assoc., *Perm. Emp Agcy*
Morrison Assoc., *Exec Srch*
Potomac Persnnl, *Perm. Emp Agcy*
Sigman & Summerfield Assoc., *Perm. Emp Agcy*

Florida
AAA Employment, *Perm. Emp Agcy*
Alpha Persnnl/Alpha Temps, *Perm. Emp Agcy*
Aaron Stewart Persnnl, *Exec Srch*
TRC Staff Svcs, *Temp. Agcy*

Georgia
Elite Staff Svcs, *Perm. Emp Agcy*
Express Persnnl Svcs, *Exec Srch*
Bob Maddox Assoc., *Exec Srch*
Mission Corps Intl/Helping Hands Temp. Svc, *Temp. Ag*
Olsten Staff Svcs, *Temp. Agcy*
WPPS Software Staffng, *Perm. Emp Agcy*

Hawaii
Alu Like, *Career/Outplacemnt*
The Resume Place, *Career/Outplacemnt*

Idaho
Magic Valley Rehabilitation Svcs, *Career/Outplacemnt*

Illinois
AARP Foundation/Senior Community Svc Emp. Program, *Perm. Emp Agcy*
Able's Pool of Temps, *Temp. Agcy*
Interstaff, *Temp. Agcy*
Persnnl Placemnt Consltnts, *Perm. Emp Agcy*

OFFICE SUPPORT

S-H-S of Cherry Hill, *Perm. Emp Agcy*
Unitemp Temp. Persnnl, *Temp. Agcy*

New Mexico
Manpower, *Temp. Agcy*

New York
AccuStaff, *Temp. Agcy*
Bevan Resrcs, *Perm. Emp Agcy*
Grp Agcy, *Perm. Emp Agcy*
Harbrowe, *Perm. Emp Agcy*
Manpower Temp. Svcs, *Temp. Agcy*
Sloan Persnnl, *Perm. Emp Agcy*
TAC Staff Svcs, *Temp. Agcy*
TemPositions, *Temp. Agcy*

North Carolina
Elite Persnnl & Job Force, *Perm. Emp Agcy*
Forbes Temp. Staffng, *Temp. Agcy*
Greer Persnnl, *Perm. Emp Agcy*
Manpower, *Temp. Agcy*
Mega Force, *Perm. Emp Agcy*
Norrell Svcs, *Temp. Agcy*
North Carolina Srch, *Perm. Emp Agcy*

Ohio
CBS Persnnl Svcs, *Perm. Emp Agcy*
Job Express, *Temp. Agcy*
Manpower Temp. Svcs, *Temp. Agcy*

Oregon
Adams Temps, *Temp. Agcy*
Manpower Temp. Svcs, *Temp. Agcy*

Pennsylvania
Alexander Persnnl Assoc., *Exec Srch*
Marsetta Lane Temp. Svcs, *Temp. Agcy*
Leafstone, *Temp. Agcy*
Manpower Temp. Svcs, *Temp. Agcy*
Olsten Staff Svcs, *Temp. Agcy*

Rhode Island
Kennedy Personel Svcs, *Exec Srch*
Office Specialists, *Perm. Emp Agcy*

Tennessee
Kelly Svcs, *Temp. Agcy*
Manpower, *Temp. Agcy*
Staffing Solut'ns, *Perm. Emp Agcy*

Texas
Corbett Persnnl Svcs, *Temp. Agcy*
Day Star Svcs, *Perm. Emp Agcy*
Executeam, *Exec Srch*
Manpower, *Temp. Agcy*
The Persnnl Connection, *Perm. Emp Agcy*

Utah
Your Job Connection, *Perm. Emp Agcy*

Vermont
Adecco, *Temp. Agcy*
GFI Pro Staffng, *Temp. Agcy*
Harmon Persnnl Svcs, *Temp. Agcy*
The Persnnl Connection, *Temp. Agcy*
Western Staff Svcs, *Temp. Agcy*

Virginia
A Plus Persnnl, *Perm. Emp Agcy*
Nancy Allen Assoc., *Perm. Emp Agcy*
Ardelle Assoc./AA Temps, *Perm. Emp Agcy*
Manpower Temp. Svcs, *Temp. Agcy*
Susan Miller & Assoc., *Perm. Emp Agcy*
Don Richard Assoc., *Exec Srch*
Temps Now, *Temp. Agcy*

Washington
Business Careers, *Perm. Emp Agcy*
Manpower Temp. Svcs, *Temp. Agcy*

West Virginia
Kelly Svcs, *Temp. Agcy*

Wisconsin
Associated Secretarial, *Perm. Emp Agcy*
Landmark, The Staffing Resource, *Temp. Agcy*

Wyoming
The Emp. Place, *Perm. Emp Agcy*

OIL & GAS

California
Triple-J Svcs, *Exec Srch*

Colorado
Welzig, Lowe & Assoc., *Exec Srch*
Woodmoor Grp, *Exec Srch*

Minnesota
NER (National Engineering Resrcs), *Exec Srch*

Oklahoma
Sooner Placemnt Svc, *Perm. Emp Agcy*
U.S. Gas Srch, *Exec Srch*

Texas
ABA Exec Srch, *Exec Srch*
Atwood Prof'l Srch, *Exec Srch*
Denson & Assoc., *Exec Srch*
The Energists, *Exec Srch*
Korn/Ferry Intl, *Exec Srch*
Piper-Morgan Persnnl, *Exec Srch*
Tech. Staff Solut'ns, *Exec Srch*
Watkins & Assoc., *Exec Srch*

OPERATIONS MANAGEMENT

Alabama
Mgmt. Recrtrs Intl, *Exec Srch*

Arkansas
Mgmt. Recrtrs of Little Rock, *Exec Srch*

California
Marvin Laba & Assoc., *Exec Srch*
Mgmt. Recrtrs of Burlingame/Sales Consltnts, *Exec Srch*
Mgmt. Recrtrs of Encino, *Exec Srch*
Mgmt. Recrtrs of San Francisco, *Exec Srch*
Mesa Intl, *Exec Srch*
Professional Srch Assoc., *Exec Srch*

Colorado
Mgmt. Recrtrs of Colorado Springs, *Exec Srch*
Sales Consltnts, *Exec Srch*
The Woodstone Consltng Co, *Exec Srch*

Connecticut
Mgmt. Recrtrs Intl, *Exec Srch*

Florida
Mgmt. Recrtrs of St. Petersburg, *Exec Srch*
Mgmt. Recrtrs of Tallahassee, *Exec Srch*
Mgmt. Recrtrs of Tampa, *Exec Srch*
Sales Consltnts of Fort Lauderdale, *Exec Srch*
Sales Consltnts of Jacksonville, *Exec Srch*

Georgia
Mgmt. Recrtrs of Atlanta, *Exec Srch*

Illinois
Corporate Environment, *Exec Srch*
Mgmt. Recrtrs of Des Plaines, *Exec Srch*
Mgmt. Recrtrs of Rockford, *Exec Srch*
Officemates5 of Wheeling, *Exec Srch*
Sales Consltnts/Mgmt. Recrtrs Intl, *Exec Srch*
Sales Consltnts of Oak Brk, *Exec Srch*

Indiana
Mgmt. Recrtrs of Indianapolis, *Exec Srch*
Mgmt. Recrtrs of Richmond/Staff Solut'ns, *Exec Srch*

Iowa
Mgmt. Recrtrs Intl, *Exec Srch*

Kansas
Mgmt. Recrtrs of Overlnd Prk, *Exec Srch*

Kentucky
Angel Grp Intl, *Exec Srch*

Louisiana
Mgmt. Recrtrs of Baton Rouge, *Exec Srch*
Mgmt. Recrtrs-Metairie/Sales Consltnts, *Exec Srch*

Maryland
Mgmt. Recrtrs of Annapolis, *Exec Srch*
Mgmt. Recrtrs-Baltimore/Sales Consltnts, *Exec Srch*
Mgmt. Recrtrs-Bethesda/CompuSearch, *Exec Srch*
Mgmt. Recrtrs of Frederick, *Exec Srch*
Sales Consltnts of Prince Georges Cnty, *Exec Srch*

Massachusetts
Mgmt. Recrtrs Intl, *Exec Srch*
Mgmt. Recrtrs Intl of Braintree, *Exec Srch*
Sales Consltnts of Cape Cod, *Exec Srch*
Sales Consltnts of Mansfield, *Exec Srch*
Sales Consltnts of Plymouth Cnty, *Exec Srch*
Sales Consltnts of Wellesley, *Exec Srch*

Michigan
Christopher & Assoc., *Exec Srch*
Mgmt. Recrtrs of Bingham Farms, *Exec Srch*
Mgmt. Recrtrs of Dearborn, *Exec Srch*
Mgmt. Recrtrs of Flint, *Exec Srch*
Mgmt. Recrtrs of Kalamazoo, *Exec Srch*
Mgmt. Recrtrs of Lansing, *Exec Srch*
Mgmt. Recrtrs of Muskegon, *Exec Srch*
Mgmt. Recrtrs of Rochester, *Exec Srch*
Sales Consltnts of Detroit, *Exec Srch*
Sales Consltnts of Farmington Hills, *Exec Srch*

Minnesota
Mgmt. Recrtrs-Minneapolis/Sales Consltnts, *Exec Srch*

Missouri
Mgmt. Recrtrs of Kansas Cty, *Exec Srch*
Mgmt. Recrtrs of Springfield, *Exec Srch*
Mgmt. Recrtrs of St. Louis, *Exec Srch*
Officemates5 of St. Louis, *Exec Srch*

Nebraska
Compusearch of Lincoln, *Exec Srch*
Mgmt. Recrtrs of Omaha/Officemates5, *Exec Srch*

New Hampshire
Mgmt. Recrtrs Intl of Bedford, *Exec Srch*
Resource Recruitng/Contemp. Accntnts, *Perm. Emp Agcy*
Sales Consltnts of Nashua-Manchester, *Exec Srch*

New Jersey
Orion Consltng, *Exec Srch*
Sales Consltnts of Sparta, *Exec Srch*

New York
Staff By Manning, *Perm. Emp Agcy*

North Carolina
Mgmt. Recrtrs Intl, *Exec Srch*
Mgmt. Recrtrs of Durham, *Exec Srch*
Mgmt. Recrtrs of Raleigh/Inter Exec, *Exec Srch*
Mgmt. Recrtrs of Winston-Salem, *Exec Srch*
Sales Consltnts of High Point, *Exec Srch*

Ohio
Ives & Assoc., *Exec Srch*
Mgmt. Recrtrs of Cincinnati, *Exec Srch*
Mgmt. Recrtrs of Cleveland, *Exec Srch*
Mgmt. Recrtrs of Columbus, *Exec Srch*
Mgmt. Recrtrs of Dayton, *Exec Srch*
Mgmt. Recrtrs of Solon, *Exec Srch*
Sales Consltnts of Cincinnati, *Exec Srch*

Oregon
Mgmt. Recrtrs/Officemates5 of Portland, *Exec Srch*

Pennsylvania
Mgmt. Recrtrs of DE Cnty/CompuSrch, *Exec Srch*
Mgmt. Recrtrs of Lehigh Vly/CompuSrch, *Exec Srch*
Mgmt. Recrtrs of Philadelphia/ CompuSrch, *Exec Srch*
Rice Cohen Intl, *Exec Srch*

Rhode Island
Mgmt. Recrtrs Intl, *Exec Srch*

South Carolina
Mgmt. Recrtrs of Columbia, *Exec Srch*
Mgmt. Recrtrs of Rck Hill, *Exec Srch*

Tennessee
Sales Consltnts of Nashville, *Exec Srch*

Texas
Hyman & Assoc., *Exec Srch*
Mgmt. Recrtrs Intl, *Exec Srch*
Mgmt. Recrtrs of Dallas, *Exec Srch*
Sales Consltnts of Houston, *Exec Srch*

Virginia
Mgmt. Recrtrs of McLean, *Exec Srch*
Mgmt. Recrtrs of Roanoke, *Exec Srch*

Washington
Mgmt. Recrtrs of Mercer Islnd, *Exec Srch*
Mgmt. Recrtrs of Tacoma, *Exec Srch*

Wisconsin
Mgmt. Recrtrs of Appleton/ CompuSrch, *Exec Srch*
Mgmt. Recrtrs of Green Bay, *Exec Srch*
Mgmt. Recrtrs of Milwaukee, *Exec Srch*

PACKAGING

Arizona
The Dorfman Grp, *Exec Srch*

Connecticut
Wallace Assoc., *Exec Srch*

Florida
Mgmt. Recrtrs Intl, *Exec Srch*

Illinois
Caprio & Assoc., *Exec Srch*

Minnesota
G.J. Nienhaus & Assoc., *Exec Srch*

Barry Persky & Co., *Exec Srch*
Howard Smith Assoc., *Exec Srch*
Western Staff Svcs, *Temp. Agcy*
Western Staff Svcs, *Perm. Emp Agcy*
The Westfield Grp, *Exec Srch*
Workforce One, *Perm. Emp Agcy*

Delaware

J.B. Groner Exec Srch, *Exec Srch*
E.W. Hodges & Assoc., *Exec Srch*
Independent Nat'l Srch & Assoc., *Exec Srch*
The Placers, *Temp. Agcy*
The Placers, *Exec Srch*

District of Columbia

Best Temps, *Temp. Agcy*
Career Blazers Persnnl, *Perm. Emp Agcy*
K.M.S. Assoc., *Perm. Emp Agcy*
Network Companies, *Exec Srch*
Potomac Persnnl, *Perm. Emp Agcy*
Sigman & Summerfield Assoc., *Perm. Emp Agcy*
Tangent Corp, *Exec Srch*
Trifax Corp, *Perm. Emp Agcy*

Florida

AAA Employment, *Perm. Emp Agcy*
AccuStaff, *Temp. Agcy*
AccuTech, *Contract Svc*
Active Prof'ls, *Exec Srch*
The Addstaff Netwrk, *Perm. Emp Agcy*
Alpha Persnnl/Alpha Temps, *Perm. Emp Agcy*
Availability, *Perm. Emp Agcy*
B&B Persnnl, *Perm. Emp Agcy*
The Brand Co, *Exec Srch*
Bryan & Assoc./Worknet, Etc., *Exec Srch*
Career Planners, *Perm. Emp Agcy*
CareerXchange, *Temp. Agcy*
Carrier's Career Svc, *Career/Outplacemnt*
Computer Plus Staff Solut'ns, *Temp. Agcy*
DP Exec Srch, *Exec Srch*
Employers' Assistant, *Temp. Agcy*
Ethan Allen Persnnl Plcmnt, *Exec Srch*
Five Star Temporary, *Temp. Agcy*
Future Force Persnnl, *Temp. Agcy*
Gallin Assoc., *Exec Srch*
Girl Friday Persnnl, *Temp. Agcy*
HR Prof'l Consltnts, *Exec Srch*
Hastings & Hastings Persnnl Consltnts, *Temp. Agcy*
Janus Career Svc, *Perm. Emp Agcy*
Kelly Svcs, *Temp. Agcy*
Koerner Grp, *Exec Srch*
R.H. Larsen & Assoc., *Exec Srch*
Mgmt. Recrtrs of Miami, *Exec Srch*
Mgmt. Recrtrs of St. Petersburg, *Exec Srch*
Mgmt. Recrtrs of Tallahassee, *Exec Srch*
Mgmt. Recrtrs of Tampa, *Exec Srch*
Manpower Temp. Svcs, *Temp. Agcy*
NPF Assoc. Exec. Srch Firm
Norrell Tech. Svcs, *Exec Srch*
Olsten Staff Svcs, *Temp. Agcy*
Persnnl One, *Perm. Emp Agcy*
Pro Staff Persnnl Svcs, *Temp. Agcy*
Profes. Staffing/Able Body Temp. Svcs, *Contract Svc*
The Ryan Charles Grp, *Exec Srch*
Sales Consltnts of Fort Lauderdale, *Exec Srch*
Sales Consltnts of Jacksonville, *Exec Srch*
Search Enterprises South, *Exec Srch*
Doug Sears & Assoc., *Exec Srch*
Staffing Svcs Grp, *Perm. Emp Agcy*
Staffing Solut'ns by Persnnl One, *Perm. Emp Agcy*
Aaron Stewart Persnnl, *Exec Srch*
TRC Staff Svcs, *Temp. Agcy*
Temporary Solut'ns, *Temp. Agcy*
Todays Temporary, *Temp. Agcy*
Tower Consltnts, *Exec Srch*
Velkin Persnnl Svcs, *Perm. Emp Agcy*
Zanco Persnnl Resrcs, *Perm. Emp Agcy*

Georgia

A-1 Svc Persnnl, *Perm. Emp Agcy*
Accurate Medical Placemnt/The Accurate Grp, *Exec Srch*
Adecco Tech. Svcs, *Contract Svc*
Ashley-Nolan Intl, *Exec Srch*
Augusta Staffing Assoc., *Perm. Emp Agcy*
Boreham Intl, *Exec Srch*
Caldwell Svcs, *Temp. Agcy*
R.A. Clark Consltng, *Exec Srch*
Corporate Srch Consltnts, *Exec Srch*
Dunhill Prof'l Srch, *Exec Srch*
Dynamic People, *Temp. Agcy*
Elite Staff Svcs, *Perm. Emp Agcy*
Express Persnnl Svcs, *Perm. Emp Agcy*
Express Persnnl Svcs, *Exec Srch*
Fox-Morris Assoc., *Exec Srch*
The HR Grp, *Exec Srch*
Hall Mngmnt Grp, *Exec Srch*
ISC of Atlanta/Intl Career Continuation, *Exec Srch*
Job Shop, *Exec Srch*
Jordan Temps, *Temp. Agcy*
Kelly Svcs, *Temp. Agcy*
Kenzer Corp of GA, *Exec Srch*
Mgmt. Recrtrs of Atlanta, *Exec Srch*
Mgmt. Recrtrs of Marietta, *Exec Srch*
NEIS, *Exec Srch*
Olsten Staff Svcs, *Temp. Agcy*
Priority 1 Staff Svcs, *Temp. Agcy*
Randstad Staff Svcs, *Temp. Agcy*
Randstad Staff Svcs, *Perm. Emp Agcy*
Ranger Svcs, *Temp. Agcy*
P.J. Reda & Assoc., *Exec Srch*
SearchAmerica, *Exec Srch*
Southern Emp. Svc, *Perm. Emp Agcy*
Staffing Resrcs, *Perm. Emp Agcy*
TRC Staff Svcs, *Temp. Agcy*
Temp Resrcs, *Temp. Agcy*
Temporary Specialties, *Temp. Agcy*
Todays Emp. Solut'ns, *Perm. Emp Agcy*
Todays Temporary, *Temp. Agcy*
WPPS Software Staffng, *Perm. Emp Agcy*
Western Staff Svcs, *Temp. Agcy*
H.L. Yoh Co, *Contract Svc*

Hawaii

Ellis & Assoc., *Exec Srch*
Maresca & Assoc., *Exec Srch*
Olsten Staff Svcs, *Temp. Agcy*

Idaho

Horne/Brown Intl, *Exec Srch*
Intermountain Staffing Resrcs, *Perm. Emp Agcy*
Ward-Hoffman & Assoc., *Exec Srch*

Illinois

A.B.A. Placemnts/A.B.A. Temps, *Perm. Emp Agcy*
ASI Persnnl, *Perm. Emp Agcy*
The Ability Grp, *Exec Srch*
Accurate Recruitng, *Perm. Emp Agcy*
Adecco, *Temp. Agcy*
Affiliated Persnnl Consltnts, *Perm. Emp Agcy*
Armstrong-Hamilton Assoc., *Exec Srch*
Assured Staffng, *Temp. Agcy*
Banner Persnnl, *Perm. Emp Agcy*
Bevelle & Assoc., *Exec Srch*
Burling Grp Ltd., *Exec Srch*
Carson Mngmnt Assoc., *Contract Svc*
Ned Dickey & Assoc./Dickey Staff Solut'ns, *Exec Srch*
Dynamic People, *Temp. Agcy*
Eastman & Assoc., *Exec Srch*
Executive Referral Svcs, *Exec Srch*
Express Persnnl Svcs, *Temp. Agcy*
Fellows Plcmnt, *Temp. Agcy*
Furst Staff Svcs, *Temp. Agcy*
David Gomez & Assoc., *Exec Srch*
H/R Srch, *Perm. Emp Agcy*
Human Resource Connection, *Perm. Emp Agcy*
Human Resource Technlgy, *Exec Srch*
The Hunter Resource Grp, *Exec Srch*
Illinois Veterans Leadership Program, *Career/Outplacemnt*
Interim Persnnl, *Temp. Agcy*
Interstaff, *Temp. Agcy*
Irwin & Wagner, *Exec Srch*
Johnson Persnnl Co, *Exec Srch*
Kunzer Assoc., *Exec Srch*
Lynco Mngmnt Persnnl, *Exec Srch*
Mack & Assoc., *Temp. Agcy*
Magnum Srch, *Exec Srch*
Mgmt. Recrtrs Intl, *Exec Srch*
Mgmt. Recrtrs of Arlington Heights, *Exec Srch*
Mgmt. Recrtrs of Des Plaines, *Exec Srch*
Mgmt. Recrtrs of Rockford, *Exec Srch*
Mgmt. Recrtrs of St. Charles, *Exec Srch*
Mgmt. Support Svcs, *Exec Srch*
Manpower Temp. Svcs, *Temp. Agcy*
Marsteller Wilcox Assoc., *Exec Srch*
Medical Tech. Placemnts, *Temp. Agcy*
Juan Menefee & Assoc., *Exec Srch*
Merit Persnnl, *Perm. Emp Agcy*
Michael David Assoc., *Perm. Emp Agcy*
The Murphy Grp, *Perm. Emp Agcy*
NJW & Assoc., *Temp. Agcy*
National Srch, *Exec Srch*
Norrell Svcs, *Temp. Agcy*
Olsten Staff Svcs, *Temp. Agcy*
Omega Tech. Corp, *Exec Srch*
The Opport. Grp, *Perm. Emp Agcy*
Opportunity Persnnl, *Perm. Emp Agcy*
PS, *Perm. Emp Agcy*
Persnnl Connection, *Perm. Emp Agcy*
Persnnl Placemnt Consltnts, *Perm. Emp Agcy*
Professional Research Svcs, *Exec Srch*
ProSearch Plus, *Exec Srch*
The Raleigh Warwick Grp, *Exec Srch*
Remedy Intelligent Staffng, *Temp. Agcy*
Right Svcs, *Temp. Agcy*
Ritt-Ritt & Assoc., *Exec Srch*
Sales Consltnts/Mgmt. Recrtrs Intl, *Exec Srch*
Sales Consltnts of Oak Brk, *Exec Srch*
Search Centre, *Exec Srch*
Select Staffng, *Perm. Emp Agcy*
Seville Temp. Svcs, *Temp. Agcy*
Ralph Smith & Assoc., *Exec Srch*
Smith Scott & Assoc., *Exec Srch*
Snelling Srch, *Exec Srch*
Staffing Consltnts, *Perm. Emp Agcy*
Stivers Temp. Persnnl, *Temp. Agcy*
Strategic Resrcs Unlimtd, *Exec Srch*
Thirty Three Persnnl Ctr, *Perm. Emp Agcy*
West Persnnl, *Perm. Emp Agcy*
Working World, *Temp. Agcy*
World Emp. Svc, *Perm. Emp Agcy*

Indiana

Angola Persnnl Svcs, *Perm. Emp Agcy*
Canis Major/HR Quest, *Exec Srch*
Corporate Staff Resrcs, *Temp. Agcy*
Crown Temp. Svcs of Indianapolis, *Temp. Agcy*
Dunhill of Brown Cnty, *Exec Srch*
Execusearch, *Exec Srch*
Job Placemnt Svc, *Perm. Emp Agcy*
Johnson Brown Assoc., *Exec Srch*
Krise Prof'l Persnnl Svcs, *Perm. Emp Agcy*
Lange & Assoc., *Exec Srch*
Mgmt. Recrtrs of Evansville, *Exec Srch*
Mgmt. Recrtrs of Indianapolis, *Exec Srch*
Mgmt. Recrtrs of Richmond/Staff Solut'ns, *Exec Srch*
Mgmt. Svcs, *Exec Srch*
Norrell Staff Svcs, *Temp. Agcy*
Officemates5 of Indianapolis, *Exec Srch*
Olsten Staff Svcs, *Temp. Agcy*
Perry Persnnl Plus, *Perm. Emp Agcy*
Quiring Assoc. HR Consltng Grp, *Exec Srch*
RDN Svcs, *Exec Srch*
Rush Temps, *Temp. Agcy*
Unique, *Exec Srch*
Wimmer Temps & Direct Plcmnt, *Temp. Agcy*

Iowa

Burton Placemnt Svcs, *Exec Srch*
Byrnes & Rupkey, *Exec Srch*
CSI Employment, *Exec Srch*
Executive Srch Assoc., *Exec Srch*
Helping Hands Temp. Svc, *Temp. Agcy*
Kelly Svcs, *Temp. Agcy*
Mgmt. Recrtrs Intl, *Exec Srch*
McGladrey Srch Grp, *Exec Srch*
Salem Mngmnt dba Rudy Salem Staff Svcs, *Temp. Agcy*
Staff Mgmt., *Contract Svc*
Staffing Edge, *Perm. Emp Agcy*

Kansas

Business Specialists, *Perm. Emp Agcy*
Eleventh Hour Staff Svcs, *Temp. Agcy*
Mgmt. Recrtrs of Overlnd Prk, *Exec Srch*
Manpower, *Temp. Agcy*
Smith Brown & Jones, *Exec Srch*
Stoneburner Assoc., *Exec Srch*
Temtech, *Contract Svc*
Western Staff Svcs, *Temp. Agcy*

Kentucky

Angel Grp Intl, *Exec Srch*
J.E.M. & Assoc., *Temp. Agcy*
Neessen Prof'l Srch, *Exec Srch*
Precision Staffng, *Perm. Emp Agcy*
Professional Srch, *Exec Srch*

Louisiana

Career Persnnl Consltnts, *Exec Srch*
Keenan Staffng, *Temp. Agcy*
MDR & Assoc., *Exec Srch*
Mgmt. Recrtrs of Baton Rouge, *Exec Srch*
Mgmt. Recrtrs-Metairie/Sales Consltnts, *Exec Srch*
Norrell Staff Svcs, *Temp. Agcy*
Port Cty Enterprises, *Career/Outplacemnt*
River Region Persnnl, *Exec Srch*
Snelling Persnnl Svcs, *Exec Srch*
Talley & Assoc./Talley Temps, *Exec Srch*
Western Staff Svcs, *Temp. Agcy*

Maine

Accomplished Prof'ls, *Temp. Agcy*
Executive Srch of N.E., *Exec Srch*
Goodrich Consltng, *Exec Srch*
John Jay & Co, *Exec Srch*
The Porter Hamel Grp, *Exec Srch*

Maryland

Caplan Assoc., *Exec Srch*
Excel Temp. Svcs, *Temp. Agcy*
Futures, *Exec Srch*
L.S. Gross & Assoc., *Exec Srch*
Interim Persnnl, *Temp. Agcy*
Mgmt. Recrtrs of Annapolis, *Exec Srch*
Mgmt. Recrtrs-Baltimore/Sales Consltnts, *Exec Srch*
Mgmt. Recrtrs-Bethesda/CompuSearch, *Exec Srch*
Mgmt. Recrtrs of Frederick, *Exec Srch*
Sales Consltnts of Baltimore Cty, *Exec Srch*

Extra Help Emp. Svc, *Temp. Agcy*
Fanning Persnnl, *Exec Srch*
Fifth Avenue Emp. Svcs, *Temp. Agcy*
C.R. Fletcher Assoc., *Exec Srch*
Forum Temp. Svcs, *Temp. Agcy*
Genesis Emp. Consltnts, *Exec Srch*
H&H Temp. Svcs, *Temp. Agcy*
Robert Half Intl/Information Syst. Division, *Exec Srch*
Headway Corporate Staff Svcs, *Temp. Agcy*
Healthsearch Grp, *Exec Srch*
Hospitality Assoc., *Exec Srch*
Hunter Mac & Assoc., *Perm. Emp Agcy*
Hunter Plcmnt, *Exec Srch*
Interspace Interactive, *Exec Srch*
Island Srch Grp, *Perm. Emp Agcy*
Ivana Legal Svcs, *Exec Srch*
Just One Break, *Perm. Emp Agcy*
KLK Persnnl, *Perm. Emp Agcy*
KPA Grp, *Exec Srch*
The Kay Grp of Fifth Avenue, *Exec Srch*
Kelly Svcs, *Temp. Agcy*
Fred Koffler Assoc., *Exec Srch*
Lab Support, *Temp. Agcy*
Lake Assoc., *Exec Srch*
Michael John Lawrence & Assoc., *Exec Srch*
The MVP Grp, *Exec Srch*
Magill Assoc., *Exec Srch*
Joseph Maloney & Assoc., *Perm. Emp Agcy*
Mgmt. Recrtrs of Woodbury/ CompuSrch, *Exec Srch*
Manpower Temp. Svcs, *Temp. Agcy*
Marcus & Assoc., *Exec Srch*
Medstaff Svcs, *Perm. Emp Agcy*
Mentortech, *Exec Srch*
Metro Resrcs of Rochester, *Temp. Agcy*
Metro Support Grp, *Perm. Emp Agcy*
Metro Persnnl/Metro Nursing Svcs, *Exec Srch*
Milazzo Assoc., *Perm. Emp Agcy*
Morgan-Murray Persnnl/M&M Top Temps, *Temp. Agcy*
Noah Assoc., *Perm. Emp Agcy*
Noble & Assoc., *Exec Srch*
Norrell Staff Svcs, *Perm. Emp Agcy*
Norris Emp. Consltnts, *Perm. Emp Agcy*
K.A. Nowack Career Specialists, *Perm. Emp Agcy*
Olsten Staff Svcs, *Temp. Agcy*
Optimal Resrcs, *Exec Srch*
The Parks Grp, *Exec Srch*
Parsons, Anderson & Gee, *Perm. Emp Agcy*
Persnnl Consltng Assoc., *Exec Srch*
P.G. Prager Srch Assoc., *Exec Srch*
Professional Support, *Exec Srch*
Quest Organization, *Exec Srch*
Rand Thompson Consltnts, *Exec Srch*
Rem Resrcs, *Perm. Emp Agcy*
Remedy Intelligent Staffng, *Temp. Agcy*
Rep Temps, *Temp. Agcy*
S.W. Mgmt., *Exec Srch*
Saxon Morse Assoc., *Exec Srch*
SearchAmerica, *Exec Srch*
Sharp Placemnt Prof'ls, *Exec Srch*
Sporn Grp, *Exec Srch*
Staff By Manning, *Perm. Emp Agcy*
Staff Managers, *Temp. Agcy*
Staffing Svcs, *Exec Srch*
Superior Concepts, *Contract Svc*
Tempo Svcs, *Perm. Emp Agcy*
Temporary Resource Ctr, *Temp. Agcy*
TemPositions, *Temp. Agcy*
United Persnnl Agcy, *Perm. Emp Agcy*
Vantage Staff Svcs, *Temp. Agcy*
Weber Mngmnt Consltnts, *Exec Srch*
Westchester Emp. Agcy, *Perm. Emp Agcy*
Western Staff Svcs, *Temp. Agcy*
Westfield Assoc., *Exec Srch*
Winston Resrcs, *Exec Srch*
Woodbury Persnnl, *Perm. Emp Agcy*

North Carolina

A-1 Staffing & Persnnl, *Perm. Emp Agcy*
Accurate Staff Consltnts, *Exec Srch*
Action Tech. Staffng, *Temp. Agcy*
Advanced Persnnl Resrcs, *Exec Srch*
Alpha Omega Exec Srch, *Exec Srch*
AmeriPro Srch, *Exec Srch*
Anderson & Daniel Persnnl, *Perm. Emp Agcy*
Apple Resrcs, *Perm. Emp Agcy*
Ayers & Assoc., *Exec Srch*
Career Srch, *Exec Srch*
Coastal Temp. Svcs, *Temp. Agcy*
Corporate Staff Consltnts, *Perm. Emp Agcy*
Employment Consltnts, *Contract Svc*
Executive Staff Svcs, *Perm. Emp Agcy*
C.D. Fayling Assoc., *Exec Srch*
Five Star Staffng, *Temp. Agcy*
FORTUNE Persnnl Consltnts of Raleigh, *Perm. Emp Agcy*
Graham & Assoc., *Perm. Emp Agcy*
Interim Persnnl, *Temp. Agcy*
The Jobs Market, *Perm. Emp Agcy*
Kelly Svcs, *Temp. Agcy*
Key Temps, *Temp. Agcy*
Mgmt. Recrtrs Intl, *Exec Srch*
Mgmt. Recrtrs of Durham, *Exec Srch*
Mgmt. Recrtrs of Raleigh/Inter Exec, *Exec Srch*
Mgmt. Recrtrs of Winston-Salem, *Exec Srch*
Mark III Persnnl, *Exec Srch*
McCain Emp. Agcy, *Temp. Agcy*
Moffitt Intl, *Exec Srch*
National Svcs, *Exec Srch*
Olsten Staff Svcs, *Temp. Agcy*
Parenica & Co, *Exec Srch*
The Perkin Grp, *Exec Srch*
Professional Persnnl Assoc., *Perm. Emp Agcy*
Quality Temp. Svcs, *Temp. Agcy*
Sales Consltnts of High Point, *Exec Srch*
Sparks Persnnl Svcs, *Exec Srch*
StaffMark, *Temp. Agcy*
Summit Occupational Staffng, *Exec Srch*
Talent Tree Staffng, *Perm. Emp Agcy*
John Williams & Assoc., *Exec Srch*
Youngblood Staffng, *Perm. Emp Agcy*

North Dakota

Career Connection, *Exec Srch*
Dental Fill-Ins, *Temp. Agcy*
Green Thumb, *Career/Outplacemnt*
Human Resrcs, *Perm. Emp Agcy*
Olsten Staff Svcs/Kramer & Assoc./Expressway Persnnl, *Temp. Agcy*
Persnnl Svcs, *Exec Srch*

Ohio

AccuStaff, *Temp. Agcy*
Adecco, *Temp. Agcy*
Adecco, *Perm. Emp Agcy*
Advancement Recruitng Svcs, *Exec Srch*
N.L. Benke & Assoc., *Perm. Emp Agcy*
Bradley-Pierce Persnnl, *Perm. Emp Agcy*
J.B. Brown & Assoc., *Exec Srch*
Burks Grp, *Exec Srch*
CBS Persnnl Svcs, *Perm. Emp Agcy*
Career Specialists, *Exec Srch*
Champion Persnnl, *Perm. Emp Agcy*
E. Christian & Assoc., *Exec Srch*
Combined Resrcs, *Exec Srch*
Continental Srch Consltnts, *Exec Srch*
J.D. Cotter Srch, *Exec Srch*
Crown Temp. Svcs of Cincinnati, *Temp. Agcy*
Dankowski & Assoc., *Perm. Emp Agcy*
Drayton & Assoc., *Exec Srch*
Eastern Persnnl Svcs, *Perm. Emp Agcy*
Executech, *Exec Srch*
Executech Consltnts, *Exec Srch*
Executive Srch Ltd., *Exec Srch*
Flex-Tech Prof'l Svcs, *Contract Svc*
Gayhart & Assoc., *Exec Srch*
Global Resrcs Grp, *Contract Svc*
H.L. Goehring & Assoc., *Exec Srch*
Griffiths & Assoc., *Exec Srch*
H.J.C., *Exec Srch*
Russ Hadick & Assoc., *Exec Srch*
Hahn & Assoc., *Exec Srch*
Hite Exec Srch/Hite Mngmnt Consltnts, *Exec Srch*
Human Resource Recrtrs, *Exec Srch*
ITS Tech. Staffing/Interconnect Tech. Svcs, *Exec Srch*
Icon Mngmnt Grp, *Exec Srch*
Interim Persnnl, *Temp. Agcy*
Ives & Assoc., *Exec Srch*
Kelly Svcs, *Temp. Agcy*
Laine's S.M.G., *Perm. Emp Agcy*
Mgmt. Recrtrs Intl, *Exec Srch*
Mgmt. Recrtrs of Cincinnati, *Exec Srch*
Mgmt. Recrtrs of Cleveland, *Exec Srch*
Mgmt. Recrtrs of Columbus, *Exec Srch*
Mgmt. Recrtrs of Dayton, *Exec Srch*
Mgmt. Recrtrs of Solon, *Exec Srch*
Manpower Temp. Svcs, *Temp. Agcy*
Marvel Consltnts, *Exec Srch*
Miami Prof'l Srch, *Exec Srch*
Minority Exec Srch, *Exec Srch*
Newcomb-Desmond & Assoc., *Exec Srch*
Norrell Svcs, *Temp. Agcy*
O'Brien & Roof Co, *Exec Srch*
Olsten Prof'l Staff Svcs, *Exec Srch*
Palmer Temps/The Palmer Grp, *Temp. Agcy*
Placement Svcs Limited, *Exec Srch*
Professional Restaffing of OH, *Perm. Emp Agcy*
Providence Persnnl Consltnts, *Exec Srch*
Quality Plus, *Exec Srch*
Quality Source, *Exec Srch*
Questcor Co, *Exec Srch*
Bill Reber & Assoc., *Exec Srch*
RecruitMasters of Cincinnati, *Exec Srch*
Rentech Ventures, *Perm. Emp Agcy*
Resource Techne Grp, *Exec Srch*
Sales Consltnts of Cincinnati, *Exec Srch*
Shafer Jones Assoc., *Exec Srch*
Snelling Persnnl Svcs, *Exec Srch*
The Target Human Resource Companies, *Temp. Agcy*
Teamwork U.S.A., *Contract Svc*
Tech/Aid of OH, *Perm. Emp Agcy*
Temporarily Yours Plcmnt, *Temp. Agcy*
Tradesman Intl, *Contract Svc*

Oklahoma

Ameri Resource, *Exec Srch*
Cherokee Temps, *Temp. Agcy*
Express Persnnl Svcs, *Exec Srch*
Interim Persnnl, *Temp. Agcy*
Key Temp. Persnnl, *Temp. Agcy*
Terry Neese Persnnl Agcy, *Exec Srch*
StaffMark, *Temp. Agcy*
Sumner-Ray Tech. Resrcs, *Exec Srch*

Oregon

Barrett Bus. Svcs, *Temp. Agcy*
Employment Trends, *Temp. Agcy*
Express Persnnl Svcs, *Exec Srch*
Hackenschmidt, Weaver & Fox, *Exec Srch*
Kelly Svcs, *Temp. Agcy*
Mgmt. Recrtrs/Officemates5 of Portland, *Exec Srch*
Office Careers, *Perm. Emp Agcy*
Pro Tem Prof'l Temp. Svcs, *Temp. Agcy*
Quest Temp. Svcs, *Temp. Agcy*
Sanford Rose Assoc., *Exec Srch*
Southern Oregon Temporary, *Temp. Agcy*
Talent Tree Staffng, *Perm. Emp Agcy*
Woodworth Intl Grp, *Exec Srch*

Pennsylvania

AA Staff Solut'ns, *Contract Svc*
Action Persnnl Svcs, *Perm. Emp Agcy*
Adecco, *Temp. Agcy*
All Staffng, *Perm. Emp Agcy*
Allegheny Persnnl Svcs, *Temp. Agcy*
Alternative Staffng, *Contract Svc*
American Srch Assoc., *Exec Srch*
ASAP Staffng, *Perm. Emp Agcy*
Ashley Srch Consltnts, *Exec Srch*
Basilone-Oliver Exec Srch, *Exec Srch*
Bradley Prof'l Svcs, *Perm. Emp Agcy*
Career Concepts Staff Svcs, *Exec Srch*
COREStaff, *Temp. Agcy*
DiCenzo Persnnl Specialists, *Perm. Emp Agcy*
Dunn Assoc., *Exec Srch*
EDP/Temps of PA, *Temp. Agcy*
Fox-Morris Assoc., *Exec Srch*
Jerry Goldberg & Assoc., *Perm. Emp Agcy*
The Hastings Grp, *Exec Srch*
Hoskins Hains Assoc., *Perm. Emp Agcy*
Hospitality Svcs, *Perm. Emp Agcy*
Human Resource Solut'ns, *Exec Srch*
IMC Intl, *Contract Svc*
J-Rand Srch, *Exec Srch*
JK Resrcs, *Exec Srch*
Nancy Jackson, *Exec Srch*
Main Line Persnnl, *Perm. Emp Agcy*
Mgmt. Recrtrs of DE Cnty/CompuSrch, *Exec Srch*
Mgmt. Recrtrs of Lehigh Vly/CompuSrch, *Exec Srch*
Mgmt. Recrtrs of Philadelphia/ CompuSrch, *Exec Srch*
George Martin Exec Srch, *Exec Srch*
Rob McClure Ltd., *Exec Srch*
Metro Persnnl, *Temp. Agcy*
The Morris Grp, *Exec Srch*
Norrell Svcs, *Temp. Agcy*
OfficeTeam, *Temp. Agcy*
Olsten Staff Svcs, *Temp. Agcy*
LaMonte Owens, *Exec Srch*
Pancoast Temp. Svcs, *Temp. Agcy*
Penn Assoc., *Exec Srch*
Protocall Bus. Staffng, *Temp. Agcy*
R.H.A. Exec Persnnl Svcs, *Exec Srch*
Alan Raeburn Consltnts, *Exec Srch*
Rice Cohen Intl, *Exec Srch*
The Richards Grp, *Exec Srch*
S-H-S Intl, *Exec Srch*
SHS Assoc., *Exec Srch*
Select Persnnl, *Perm. Emp Agcy*
Spectrum Consltnts/Retail Recrtrs, *Exec Srch*
Staffing Alliance, *Exec Srch*
TRC Staff Svcs, *Temp. Agcy*
TAC Staff Svcs, *Temp. Agcy*
Tower Consltnts, *Exec Srch*
W.G. Tucker & Assoc., *Exec Srch*
Uniforce Temp. Svcs, *Temp. Agcy*
United Employment, *Perm. Emp Agcy*
Vogue Persnnl, *Perm. Emp Agcy*
Whittlesey & Assoc., *Exec Srch*
Yorktowne Persnnl, *Exec Srch*

Rhode Island

Johnson & Tregar Assoc., *Perm. Emp Agcy*
Kelly Svcs, *Temp. Agcy*
Albert Lee & Assoc., *Exec Srch*
Mgmt. Recrtrs Intl, *Exec Srch*
Norrell Svcs, *Temp. Agcy*
Occupations Unlimtd, *Perm. Emp Agcy*
On Line Temp/On Line Staff, *Temp. Agcy*
PKS Assoc., *Exec Srch*

Colorado
FORTUNE Persnnl Consltnts of Denver, *Exec Srch*
Mgmt. Recrtrs Intl, *Exec Srch*
Sales Consltnts, *Exec Srch*

Connecticut
Ryan Abbott Srch Assoc., *Exec Srch*
FORTUNE Persnnl Consltnts, *Exec Srch*
Mgmt. Recrtrs Intl, *Exec Srch*
C.A. McInnis & Assoc., *Exec Srch*
Yoh Scientific, *Contract Svc*

Delaware
The Franklin Co, *Exec Srch*

Florida
The Mac Grp, *Exec Srch*
Mgmt. Recrtrs of Plant Cty, *Exec Srch*
Mgmt. Recrtrs of St. Petersburg, *Exec Srch*
Mgmt. Recrtrs of Tallahassee, *Exec Srch*
Sage Consltnts, *Exec Srch*
Sales Consltnts of Jacksonville, *Exec Srch*
The Stewart Srch Grp, *Exec Srch*
Zackrison Assoc., *Exec Srch*

Georgia
FORTUNE Persnnl Consltnts of Atlanta, *Exec Srch*
Kelly Scientific Resrcs, *Temp. Agcy*
Mgmt. Recrtrs of Atlanta, *Exec Srch*

Illinois
Corporate Environment, *Exec Srch*
Executive Referral Svcs, *Exec Srch*
Kelly Scientific Resrcs, *Temp. Agcy*
Mgmt. Recrtrs of Des Plaines, *Exec Srch*
Mgmt. Recrtrs of Rockford, *Exec Srch*
Mgmt. Recrtrs of Springfield, *Exec Srch*
Officemates5 of Wheeling, *Exec Srch*
Sales Consltnts/Mgmt. Recrtrs Intl, *Exec Srch*
Sales Consltnts of Oak Brk, *Exec Srch*

Indiana
Execusearch, *Exec Srch*
Keith Hayes & Assoc., *Exec Srch*
Mgmt. Recrtrs of Evansville, *Exec Srch*
Mgmt. Recrtrs of Indianapolis, *Exec Srch*
Mgmt. Recrtrs of Richmond/Staff Solut'ns, *Exec Srch*
National Corporate Consltnts/Advantage Svcs, *Exec Srch*
Officemates5 of Indianapolis, *Exec Srch*

Kansas
The Chase Grp, *Exec Srch*

Louisiana
Shiell Persnnl, *Perm. Emp Agcy*

Maryland
Mgmt. Recrtrs of Annapolis, *Exec Srch*
Mgmt. Recrtrs-Baltimore/Sales Consltnts, *Exec Srch*
Mgmt. Recrtrs of Frederick, *Exec Srch*
Sales Consltnts of Prince Georges Cnty, *Exec Srch*

Massachusetts
Carter/MacKay of Framingham, *Exec Srch*
FORTUNE Persnnl Consltnts, *Exec Srch*
Mgmt. Recrtrs Intl, *Exec Srch*
Mgmt. Recrtrs Intl of Braintree, *Exec Srch*
Mgmt. Recrtrs Intl of Springfield, *Exec Srch*
Mgmt. Recrtrs Intl of Westboro, *Exec Srch*
Sales Consltnts of Cape Cod, *Exec Srch*
Sales Consltnts of Plymouth Cnty, *Exec Srch*
Sales Consltnts of Wellesley, *Exec Srch*
Scientific Resrcs, *Exec Srch*

Michigan
Devlan, *Perm. Emp Agcy*
Kelly Scientific Resrcs, *Temp. Agcy*
Sales Consltnts of Genesee, *Exec Srch*

Minnesota
Focus Exec Srch, *Exec Srch*
Kelly Scientific Resrcs, *Temp. Agcy*
Mgmt. Recrtrs-Minneapolis/Sales Consltnts, *Exec Srch*

Missouri
Jim Crumpley & Assoc., *Exec Srch*
Debbon Recruitng Grp, *Exec Srch*
Kelly Scientific Resrcs, *Temp. Agcy*
Mgmt. Recrtrs of Kansas Cty, *Exec Srch*
Mgmt. Recrtrs of Springfield, *Exec Srch*
Mgmt. Recrtrs of St. Louis, *Exec Srch*

Montana
FORTUNE Persnnl Consltnts, *Exec Srch*

New Hampshire
FORTUNE Persnnl Consltnts, *Exec Srch*

New Jersey
Anderson Wright Assoc., *Exec Srch*
Andos Assoc., *Exec Srch*
ARC Medical & Prof'l Persnnl, *Temp. Agcy*
Gary Bell Assoc., *Exec Srch*
Besen Assoc., *Exec Srch*
CPS Tech. Placemnts, *Perm. Emp Agcy*
Carter/MacKay Persnnl, *Exec Srch*
Dynamic Recrtrs, *Exec Srch*
Eagle Research, *Exec Srch*
FORTUNE Persnnl Consltnts, *Exec Srch*
The Keller Grp/Careers, *Exec Srch*
Kelly Scientific Resrcs, *Temp. Agcy*
Mgmt. Recrtrs of Medford, *Exec Srch*
Orion Consltng, *Exec Srch*
Phyllis Solomon Exec Srch, *Exec Srch*
Yoh Scientific, *Contract Svc*

New York
FORTUNE Persnnl Consltnts, *Exec Srch*
The Hampton Grp, *Exec Srch*
Pharmaceutical Recrtrs, *Exec Srch*
Staffing Svcs, *Exec Srch*

North Carolina
Amcell Assoc., *Exec Srch*
Andos Assoc., *Exec Srch*
SL Collins Assoc., *Exec Srch*
Phil Ellis Assoc., *Exec Srch*
FORTUNE Persnnl Consltnts, *Exec Srch*
Mgmt. Recrtrs of Greensboro, *Exec Srch*
Mgmt. Recrtrs of Raleigh/Inter Exec, *Exec Srch*
Moffitt Intl, *Exec Srch*
Office Specialists, *Temp. Agcy*

Pennsylvania
Delta ProSearch, *Exec Srch*
Mgmt. Recrtrs of Manayunk/Chestnut Hill/CompuSrch, *Exec Srch*
George Martin Exec Srch, *Exec Srch*
Triangle Assoc. Intl, *Perm. Emp Agcy*

South Carolina
FORTUNE Persnnl Consltnts, *Exec Srch*
Mgmt. Recrtrs of Anderson, *Exec Srch*

Tennessee
Health Staff, *Temp. Agcy*
Pharm Temp Pharmacy Persnnl/Opti Temp/Den Temp, *Temp. Agcy*

Texas
BioSource Intl, *Exec Srch*
Food Pro Recrtrs, *Exec Srch*
Houtz-Strawn Assoc., *Exec Srch*
Kelly Scientific Resrcs, *Temp. Agcy*
Mgmt. Recrtrs Intl, *Exec Srch*
Preng & Assoc., *Exec Srch*

Washington
Mgmt. Recrtrs Intl, *Exec Srch*

Wisconsin
Food & Drug Prof'ls, *Perm. Emp Agcy*
Mgmt. Recrtrs, *Exec Srch*

PLASTICS

California
Bridgecreek Persnnl, *Exec Srch*
J.H. Dugan & Assoc., *Exec Srch*
Eaton & Assoc., *Exec Srch*
Rich Rigler & Assoc., *Exec Srch*
Unisearch, *Exec Srch*

Florida
Mgmt. Recrtrs of Lake Cnty, *Exec Srch*

Georgia
FORTUNE Persnnl Consltnts of Atlanta, *Exec Srch*
Mgmt. Recrtrs of Savannah, *Exec Srch*
Pro-Tech, *Exec Srch*

Indiana
FORTUNE Persnnl Consltnts, *Exec Srch*
National Recruitng Svc, *Exec Srch*

Maryland
Mgmt. Recrtrs Intl, *Exec Srch*

Massachusetts
FORTUNE Persnnl Consltnts of Topsfield, *Exec Srch*
Master Srch, *Perm. Emp Agcy*
United Prof'l Plcmnt, *Exec Srch*

Michigan
Executech Resource Consltnts, *Perm. Emp Agcy*
Sales Consltnts of Lansing, *Exec Srch*
Sales Executives, *Perm. Emp Agcy*

Missouri
Allan-James Assoc., *Exec Srch*

New Jersey
Dynamic Recrtrs, *Exec Srch*

North Carolina
Mgmt. Recrtrs Intl, *Exec Srch*

Ohio
R.L. Girton Assoc., *Temp. Agcy*
Mgmt. Recrtrs of Akron, *Exec Srch*
Midland Consltnts, *Exec Srch*
Selective Srch, *Exec Srch*

Pennsylvania
Career Concepts Staff Svcs, *Exec Srch*
George Martin Exec Srch, *Exec Srch*
Triangle Assoc. Intl, *Perm. Emp Agcy*

South Carolina
Atlantic Recrtrs, *Exec Srch*
Mgmt. Recrtrs of Aiken, *Exec Srch*

Tennessee
Gros Exec Srch, *Exec Srch*

Texas
Eissler & Assoc., *Exec Srch*
H+M Recrtrs, *Exec Srch*
Mgmt. Recrtrs Intl, *Exec Srch*

Wisconsin
Mgmt. Recrtrs Intl, *Exec Srch*

PRINTING

California
Intertec Design, *Perm. Emp Agcy*
Monroe Persnnl Svcs, *Perm. Emp Agcy*
Victor Valley Persnnl Agcy, *Perm. Emp Agcy*

Colorado
Ahrnsbrak & Assoc., *Perm. Emp Agcy*

Connecticut
Bob Wright Recruitng, *Exec Srch*

District of Columbia
Graphic Mac, *Temp. Agcy*

Florida
Marathon Grp, *Exec Srch*

Illinois
A.B.A. Placemnts/A.B.A. Temps, *Perm. Emp Agcy*
Staffing Consltnts, *Perm. Emp Agcy*

Minnesota
Susan Lee & Assoc., *Exec Srch*

New York
AMESgroup, *Perm. Emp Agcy*
Beaver Persnnl, *Perm. Emp Agcy*

North Carolina
MTS, *Perm. Emp Agcy*

Ohio
Choice Persnnl/LaGrange & Assoc., *Exec Srch*

Oregon
Uniforce Staff Svcs, *Temp. Agcy*

South Carolina
Sales Consltnts/Mgmt. Recrtrs of Greenville, *Exec Srch*

Tennessee
A-1 Staffing & Persnnl, *Temp. Agcy*
Mgmt. Recrtrs of Franklin, *Exec Srch*
Unlimited Staff Solut'ns, *Contract Svc*

Texas
Creative Staff Svcs, *Temp. Agcy*
Houston Creative Connections, *Exec Srch*

Virginia
The Talley Grp, *Exec Srch*

PROCUREMENT

Alabama
Mgmt. Recrtrs Intl, *Exec Srch*

EDP Contrct Svcs, *Contract Svc*
Industrial Recrtrs Assn, *Perm. Emp Agcy*
Intertec Persnnl, *Temp. Agcy*
Mgmt. Recrtrs Intl, *Exec Srch*
Western Staff Svcs, *Perm. Emp Agcy*
Bob Wright Recruitng, *Exec Srch*

District of Columbia

Graphic Mac, *Temp. Agcy*
Potomac Persnnl, *Perm. Emp Agcy*

Florida

AAA Employment, *Perm. Emp Agcy*
Availability, *Perm. Emp Agcy*
Bryan & Assoc./Worknet, Etc., *Exec Srch*
Future Force Persnnl, *Temp. Agcy*
Mgmt. Recrtrs Intl, *Exec Srch*
Mgmt. Recrtrs of St. Petersburg, *Exec Srch*
Mgmt. Recrtrs of Tallahassee, *Exec Srch*
Mgmt. Recrtrs of Tampa, *Exec Srch*
Manpower Temp. Svcs, *Temp. Agcy*
Priority Srch, *Exec Srch*
Profes. Staffing/Able Body Temp. Svcs, *Contract Svc*
Sales Consltnts of Fort Lauderdale, *Exec Srch*
Sales Consltnts of Jacksonville, *Exec Srch*
Snelling Persnnl, *Exec Srch*
Aaron Stewart Persnnl, *Exec Srch*
TempSolutions, *Temp. Agcy*

Georgia

AAA Employment, *Perm. Emp Agcy*
Adecco Tech. Svcs, *Contract Svc*
Elite Staff Svcs, *Perm. Emp Agcy*
ISC of Atlanta/Intl Career Continuation, *Exec Srch*
Mgmt. Recrtrs of Atlanta, *Exec Srch*
NEIS, *Exec Srch*
Pinnacle Consltng Grp, *Exec Srch*
Randstad Staff Svcs, *Perm. Emp Agcy*
Ranger Svcs, *Temp. Agcy*
Staffing Resrcs, *Perm. Emp Agcy*
Temporary Specialties, *Temp. Agcy*
Toar Consltnts, *Exec Srch*
WPPS Software Staffng, *Perm. Emp Agcy*
Western Staff Svcs, *Temp. Agcy*

Hawaii

Sales Consltnts of Honolulu, *Exec Srch*

Illinois

B.J. Abrams & Assoc., *Exec Srch*
Accurate Recruitng, *Perm. Emp Agcy*
Burling Grp Ltd., *Exec Srch*
Caprio & Assoc., *Exec Srch*
Carson Mngmnt Assoc., *Contract Svc*
Cook Assoc., *Exec Srch*
David Gomez & Assoc., *Exec Srch*
Human Resource Technlgy, *Exec Srch*
Interstaff, *Temp. Agcy*
Kunzer Assoc., *Exec Srch*
Arlene Leff & Assoc., *Exec Srch*
Lynco Mngmnt Persnnl, *Exec Srch*
Lyons & Assoc., *Exec Srch*
Mgmt. Recrtrs of Elgin, *Exec Srch*
Mgmt. Recrtrs of Rockford, *Exec Srch*
McCullum Assoc., *Temp. Agcy*
The Murphy Grp, *Perm. Emp Agcy*
Officemates5 of Wheeling, *Exec Srch*
Remedy Intelligent Staffng, *Temp. Agcy*
Sales Consltnts/Mgmt. Recrtrs Intl, *Exec Srch*
Sales Consltnts of Oak Brk, *Exec Srch*
Sanford Rose Assoc., *Exec Srch*
Staffing Consltnts, *Perm. Emp Agcy*
VG & Assoc., *Perm. Emp Agcy*

Indiana

AccuStaff, *Temp. Agcy*
Execusearch, *Exec Srch*
Mac Staffng, *Temp. Agcy*
Mgmt. Recrtrs of Evansville, *Exec Srch*
Mgmt. Recrtrs of Indianapolis, *Exec Srch*
Mgmt. Recrtrs of Richmond/Staff Solut'ns, *Exec Srch*
Officemates5 of Indianapolis, *Exec Srch*
Unique, *Exec Srch*

Iowa

Burton Placemnt Svcs, *Exec Srch*
Helping Hands Temp. Svc, *Temp. Agcy*
Mgmt. Recrtrs Intl, *Exec Srch*

Kansas

Business Specialists, *Perm. Emp Agcy*
Key Staffng, *Temp. Agcy*
Mgmt. Recrtrs of Overlnd Prk, *Exec Srch*
Stoneburner Assoc., *Exec Srch*
Western Staff Svcs, *Temp. Agcy*

Kentucky

Angel Grp Intl, *Exec Srch*

Louisiana

Mgmt. Recrtrs of Baton Rouge, *Exec Srch*
Mgmt. Recrtrs-Metairie/Sales Consltnts, *Exec Srch*
Talley & Assoc./Talley Temps, *Exec Srch*

Maine

ASK, *Temp. Agcy*
Career Mngmnt Assoc., *Exec Srch*

Maryland

L.S. Gross & Assoc., *Exec Srch*
Mgmt. Recrtrs of Annapolis, *Exec Srch*
Mgmt. Recrtrs-Baltimore/Sales Consltnts, *Exec Srch*
Mgmt. Recrtrs-Bethesda/CompuSearch, *Exec Srch*
Mgmt. Recrtrs of Frederick, *Exec Srch*
Sales Consltnts of Baltimore Cty, *Exec Srch*
Sales Consltnts of Prince Georges Cnty, *Exec Srch*
TAC Staff Svcs, *Temp. Agcy*
TAD Staff Svcs, *Temp. Agcy*

Massachusetts

Ability Srch of N.E., *Perm. Emp Agcy*
Advance Persnnl, *Perm. Emp Agcy*
Alden & Clark, *Temp. Agcy*
Brattle Temps, *Temp. Agcy*
Clear Point Consltnts, *Exec Srch*
Editorial Svcs of N.E., *Temp. Agcy*
Ford & Ford Exec Srch, *Exec Srch*
Kingsbury Wax Bova, *Exec Srch*
Lake & Manning, *Exec Srch*
Mgmt. Recrtrs Intl, *Exec Srch*
Mgmt. Recrtrs Intl of Braintree, *Exec Srch*
Mgmt. Recrtrs Intl of Springfield, *Exec Srch*
Mass Temps, *Temp. Agcy*
Morency Assoc., *Exec Srch*
Need Persnnl Plcmnt, *Temp. Agcy*
Pro Staff, *Temp. Agcy*
Sales Consltnts of Cape Cod, *Exec Srch*
Sales Consltnts of Plymouth Cnty, *Exec Srch*
Sales Consltnts of Wellesley, *Exec Srch*
Selectemps, *Temp. Agcy*
Snelling Persnnl Svcs, *Perm. Emp Agcy*
Stone & Youngblood, *Exec Srch*
TAC Staff Svcs, *Temp. Agcy*
TAD Staff Svcs, *Temp. Agcy*
WIND Job Ctr, *Career/Outplacemnt*

Michigan

Advance Employment, *Exec Srch*
Calvert Assoc., *Perm. Emp Agcy*
Executive Recrtrs Intl, *Exec Srch*
Express Persnnl Svcs, *Temp. Agcy*
Graphic Arts Mrktng Assoc., *Exec Srch*
William Howard Agcy, *Perm. Emp Agcy*
Kelly Tech. Svcs, *Contract Svc*
John Lawrence Grp, *Exec Srch*
Mgmt. Recrtrs of Bingham Farms, *Exec Srch*
Mgmt. Recrtrs of Dearborn, *Exec Srch*
Mgmt. Recrtrs of Kalamazoo, *Exec Srch*
Mgmt. Recrtrs of Lansing, *Exec Srch*
Mgmt. Recrtrs of Muskegon, *Exec Srch*
Sales Consltnts of Detroit, *Exec Srch*
Snelling Persnnl Svcs, *Perm. Emp Agcy*
Trillium Staffng, *Temp. Agcy*
Unlimited Staff Solut'ns, *Contract Svc*
Workforce, *Temp. Agcy*

Minnesota

Advance Persnnl Resrcs, *Exec Srch*
Alternative Staffng, *Perm. Emp Agcy*
Diversified Employment, *Perm. Emp Agcy*
Ells Persnnl Syst., *Exec Srch*
Flatley Tech. Svcs, *Temp. Agcy*
Graphic Staffng, *Temp. Agcy*
T.H. Hunter, *Exec Srch*
Susan Lee & Assoc., *Exec Srch*
Lynn Temporary, *Temp. Agcy*
Mgmt. Recrtrs-Minneapolis/Sales Consltnts, *Exec Srch*
Manpower Tech. Svcs, *Perm. Emp Agcy*
NER (National Engineering Resrcs), *Exec Srch*
Total Srch, *Exec Srch*

Missouri

Jay Alexandr & Assoc. dba Kirdonn Grp, *Perm. Emp Agcy*
Business Persnnl Svcs, *Temp. Agcy*
Employer Advantage, *Exec Srch*
FORTUNE Persnnl Consltnts, *Exec Srch*
JRL Exec Recrtrs, *Exec Srch*
LandAJob, *Perm. Emp Agcy*
Charles Luntz & Assoc., *Exec Srch*
Mgmt. Recrtrs of Kansas Cty, *Exec Srch*
Mgmt. Recrtrs of Springfield, *Exec Srch*
Mgmt. Recrtrs of St. Louis, *Exec Srch*
Manpower Temp. Svcs, *Temp. Agcy*
National Physician Placemnt Svcs, *Exec Srch*
Officemates5 of St. Louis, *Exec Srch*

Nebraska

Compusearch of Lincoln, *Exec Srch*
Mgmt. Recrtrs of Omaha/Officemates5, *Exec Srch*
Sales Consltnts of Omaha, *Exec Srch*
Sharp Persnnl, *Temp. Agcy*

Nevada

Labor Finders, *Temp. Agcy*
Talent Tree Staffng, *Perm. Emp Agcy*

New Hampshire

Able 1 Staffng, *Exec Srch*
Career Profiles, *Exec Srch*
Cheshire Emp. Svc, *Temp. Agcy*
Dubois & Co, *Exec Srch*
Hart, Hawkins & Co, *Exec Srch*
Mgmt. Recrtrs Intl of Bedford, *Exec Srch*
Sprout/Standish, *Exec Srch*

New Jersey

Blake & Assoc. Exec Srch, *Exec Srch*
Express Persnnl Svcs, *Perm. Emp Agcy*
Horizon Graphics Persnnl, *Perm. Emp Agcy*
Impact Persnnl, *Perm. Emp Agcy*
Kaye Persnnl, *Temp. Agcy*
Joseph Keyes Assoc., *Perm. Emp Agcy*
Mgmt. Recrtrs of Passaic Cnty, *Exec Srch*
Mayfair Svcs, *Perm. Emp Agcy*
Officemates5 of Englewood Cliffs/DayStar Temp. Svcs, *Perm. Emp Agcy*
R.S. Sadow Assoc., *Exec Srch*
Sales Consltnts of Morris Cnty, *Exec Srch*
Sales Consltnts of Ocean, *Exec Srch*
Sales Consltnts of Sparta, *Exec Srch*
Sales Consltnts, *Exec Srch*
Arline Simpson Assoc., *Perm. Emp Agcy*

New Mexico

Albuquerque Persnnl, *Perm. Emp Agcy*
CDI Corp, *Contract Svc*

New York

Accounting & Computer Persnnl, *Perm. Emp Agcy*
AccuStaff, *Temp. Agcy*
Merrill Adams Assoc., *Career/Outplacemnt*
Adecco, *Temp. Agcy*
AMESgroup, *Perm. Emp Agcy*
Bornholdt Shivas & Friends, *Exec Srch*
Branthover Assoc., *Exec Srch*
E.E. Brooke, *Perm. Emp Agcy*
CGR Staff Svcs, *Temp. Agcy*
Career Objectives Persnnl, *Temp. Agcy*
Corporate Careers/R.J. Assoc., *Exec Srch*
Bert Davis Exec Srch, *Exec Srch*
Seth Diamond Assoc., *Exec Srch*
Maggi Dolan Plcmnt, *Perm. Emp Agcy*
EDP Contrct Svcs, *Contract Svc*
Kris Edwards Agcy, *Exec Srch*
Euromonde, *Temp. Agcy*
Extra Help Emp. Svc, *Temp. Agcy*
Freelance Advancers, *Temp. Agcy*
Graphics For Hire, *Perm. Emp Agcy*
Hart-Merrell Persnnl, *Exec Srch*
Hot Bear/De Bella Prodctns & Editor'l Temps, *Temp. Agcy*
Howard-Sloan-Koller Grp, *Exec Srch*
Fred Koffler Assoc., *Exec Srch*
Lawrence Exec Srch, *Exec Srch*
The Lloyd Co, *Career/Outplacemnt*
Mgmt. Recrtrs Intl, *Exec Srch*
Mgmt. Recrtrs of Gramercy, *Exec Srch*
Mgmt. Recrtrs of Woodbury/ CompuSrch, *Exec Srch*
Manpower Temp. Svcs, *Temp. Agcy*
National Emp. Database, *Perm. Emp Agcy*
Olsten Staff Svcs, *Temp. Agcy*
Lynne Palmer Exec Recrtmnt, *Exec Srch*
Parsons, Anderson & Gee, *Perm. Emp Agcy*
Rem Resrcs, *Perm. Emp Agcy*
Remedy Intelligent Staffng, *Temp. Agcy*
Ribolow Assoc., *Perm. Emp Agcy*
Sales Consltnts of Westchester, *Exec Srch*
Stentiford & Berardi Assoc., *Exec Srch*
Temp Force of NY, *Temp. Agcy*
United Persnnl Agcy, *Perm. Emp Agcy*

North Carolina

A-1 Staffing & Persnnl, *Perm. Emp Agcy*
Advanced Persnnl Resrcs, *Exec Srch*
Amcell Assoc., *Exec Srch*
Kelly Svcs, *Temp. Agcy*
MTS, *Perm. Emp Agcy*
Mgmt. Recrtrs Intl, *Exec Srch*
Mgmt. Recrtrs of Burlington, *Exec Srch*
Mgmt. Recrtrs of Durham, *Exec Srch*
Mgmt. Recrtrs of Raleigh/Inter Exec, *Exec Srch*
Mgmt. Recrtrs of Winston-Salem, *Exec Srch*
Nationwide Recrtrs, *Exec Srch*
Olsten Staff Svcs, *Temp. Agcy*
PCS - Personal Communications Svc, *Contract Svc*
Sales Consltnts of High Point, *Exec Srch*
Sanford Rose Assoc., *Exec Srch*

M.H. Logan & Assoc., *Exec Srch*
Wyman & Assoc., *Exec Srch*

RETAIL

Alabama

A-1 Emp. Svc, *Perm. Emp Agcy*
Labor Finders, *Temp. Agcy*
Mgmt. Recrtrs Intl, *Exec Srch*
Millman Srch Grp, *Exec Srch*
WorkForce, *Temp. Agcy*

Arizona

Clifford & Assoc., *Perm. Emp Agcy*
Dealer Connection, *Perm. Emp Agcy*
Devau Human Resrcs, *Temp. Agcy*
Personalized Mngmnt Assoc., *Exec Srch*
Spectra Intl, *Exec Srch*
Stivers Temp. Persnnl, *Temp. Agcy*

Arkansas

Mgmt. Recrtrs of Little Rock, *Exec Srch*

California

ABA Staffng, *Exec Srch*
Allard Assoc., *Exec Srch*
Allied Srch, *Exec Srch*
Best Temp. Svc, *Temp. Agcy*
Candy Stripers Medical Persnnl, *Perm. Emp Agcy*
Chaitin & Assoc., *Exec Srch*
Collier-Young Agcy, *Temp. Agcy*
Culver Persnnl Svcs, *Perm. Emp Agcy*
Culver Persnnl Svcs/The Culver Grp, *Exec Srch*
Dominguez Metz & Assoc., *Exec Srch*
Douglas Persnnl Assoc., *Exec Srch*
Employment Devlpmnt Dept, *Perm. Emp Agcy*
Ethos Consltng, *Exec Srch*
Executive Recrtrs, *Exec Srch*
Filipinos For Affirmative Action, *Perm. Emp Agcy*
Goldstein & Assoc., *Temp. Agcy*
Integrated Community Svcs, *Perm. Emp Agcy*
Interactive Srch Netwrk, *Exec Srch*
Intertec Design, *Perm. Emp Agcy*
Jobs Plus, *Perm. Emp Agcy*
Kenneth, George, & Assoc., *Exec Srch*
Evie Kreisler & Assoc., *Exec Srch*
Marvin Laba & Assoc., *Exec Srch*
The London Agcy, *Exec Srch*
Malibu Grp, *Exec Srch*
Mgmt. Recrtrs Intl, *Exec Srch*
Mgmt. Recrtrs of Burlingame/Sales Consltnts, *Exec Srch*
Mgmt. Recrtrs of Encino, *Exec Srch*
Mgmt. Recrtrs of Pleasanton, *Exec Srch*
Mgmt. Srch Intl, *Exec Srch*
Mesa Intl, *Exec Srch*
National Asian Pacific Center on Aging, *Perm. Emp Agcy*
Pacific Srch Grp, *Exec Srch*
Presidio Persnnl, *Temp. Agcy*
ProFile Persnnl, *Perm. Emp Agcy*
Ed Rast & Co, *Exec Srch*
Remedy Intelligent Staffng, *Temp. Agcy*
Riley-Cole Recrtmnt Specialists, *Exec Srch*
Scott-Thaler Assoc., *Exec Srch*
Select Persnnl Svcs, *Temp. Agcy*
Telford, Adams, & Alexander, *Exec Srch*
Thomas Staffng, *Temp. Agcy*
Trans U.S., *Perm. Emp Agcy*
United Staff Solut'ns, *Exec Srch*
United/Corestaff Staff Svcs, *Perm. Emp Agcy*
Victor Valley Persnnl Agcy, *Perm. Emp Agcy*
Volt Temp. Svcs, *Temp. Agcy*
Western Staff Svcs, *Temp. Agcy*
Worldwide Exec Srch, *Exec Srch*

Colorado

Creative Career Connections, *Career/Outplacemnt*
Eleventh Hour Staff Svcs, *Perm. Emp Agcy*
40 Plus of CO, *Career/Outplacemnt*
JobSearch, *Temp. Agcy*
Kelly Svcs, *Temp. Agcy*
Manpower Intl, *Temp. Agcy*
SOS Staff Svcs, *Temp. Agcy*
Sales Consltnts, *Exec Srch*
Star Persnnl, *Exec Srch*
TPM Staff Svc, *Temp. Agcy*

Connecticut

Development Syst., *Exec Srch*
Alice Groves Co., *Exec Srch*
Mgmt. Recrtrs Intl, *Exec Srch*
Retail Recrtrs, *Exec Srch*

Florida

AAA Employment, *Perm. Emp Agcy*
B&B Persnnl, *Perm. Emp Agcy*
Belmont Training & Employment, *Perm. Emp Agcy*
Bryan & Assoc./Worknet, Etc., *Exec Srch*
Carrier's Career Svc, *Career/Outplacemnt*
Crew Unlimtd, *Perm. Emp Agcy*
Employers' Assistant, *Temp. Agcy*
Five Star Temporary, *Temp. Agcy*
Future Force Persnnl, *Temp. Agcy*
Kelly Svcs, *Temp. Agcy*
Mgmt. Recrtrs of Tallahassee, *Exec Srch*
Mgmt. Recrtrs of Tampa, *Exec Srch*
OMNIPartners, *Exec Srch*
Profes. Staffing/Able Body Temp. Svcs, *Contract Svc*
Progressive Persnnl, *Temp. Agcy*
Retail Exec Srch, *Exec Srch*
Sales Consltnts of Coral Springs, *Exec Srch*
Sales Consltnts of Fort Lauderdale, *Exec Srch*
Sales Consltnts of Jacksonville, *Exec Srch*
Seniorstaff, *Temp. Agcy*
Shaver Emp. Agcy, *Perm. Emp Agcy*
Spalding's Emp. Svc, *Perm. Emp Agcy*
Staffing Svcs Grp, *Perm. Emp Agcy*
Suncoast Grp, *Perm. Emp Agcy*

Georgia

AAA Employment, *Perm. Emp Agcy*
Ashford Mngmnt Grp, *Exec Srch*
Augusta Staffing Assoc., *Perm. Emp Agcy*
Boreham Intl, *Exec Srch*
Comprehensive Srch Grp, *Exec Srch*
Elite Staff Svcs, *Perm. Emp Agcy*
Executive Placemnt Svcs, *Perm. Emp Agcy*
Express Persnnl Svcs, *Exec Srch*
Kenzer Corp of GA, *Exec Srch*
Evie Kreisler & Assoc., *Exec Srch*
Mgmt. Recrtrs of Atlanta, *Exec Srch*
Mission Corps Intl/Helping Hands Temp. Svc, *Temp. Agcy*
NEIS, *Exec Srch*
Jim Nixon & Assoc., *Exec Srch*
Olsten Staff Svcs, *Temp. Agcy*
Personalized Mngmnt Assoc., *Exec Srch*
Pinnacle Consltng Grp, *Exec Srch*
Randstad Staff Svcs, *Temp. Agcy*
Randstad Staff Svcs, *Perm. Emp Agcy*

Hawaii

Ellis & Assoc., *Exec Srch*
The Resume Place, *Career/Outplacemnt*

Idaho

Idaho Dept. of Employment/JobSvc, *Perm. Emp Agcy*

Illinois

A.B.A. Placemnts/A.B.A. Temps, *Perm. Emp Agcy*
Cook Assoc., *Exec Srch*
Davis Temps, *Temp. Agcy*
Eastman & Assoc., *Exec Srch*
The Esquire Staffing Grp, *Perm. Emp Agcy*
Executive Referral Svcs, *Exec Srch*
Express Persnnl Svcs, *Temp. Agcy*
Human Resource Connection, *Perm. Emp Agcy*
Kenzer Corp, *Exec Srch*
Evie Kreisler Assoc., *Exec Srch*
Kunzer Assoc., *Exec Srch*
Arlene Leff & Assoc., *Exec Srch*
Mgmt. Recrtrs of Rockford, *Exec Srch*
The Moran Grp, *Perm. Emp Agcy*
The Murphy Grp, *Perm. Emp Agcy*
Norrell HR Svcs, *Perm. Emp Agcy*
Officemates5 of Wheeling, *Exec Srch*
Professional Research Svcs, *Exec Srch*
ProSearch Plus, *Exec Srch*
Remedy Intelligent Staffng, *Temp. Agcy*
Retail Recrtrs, *Exec Srch*
Retail Staffers, *Exec Srch*
Sales Consltnts/Mgmt. Recrtrs Intl, *Exec Srch*
Staffing Consltnts, *Perm. Emp Agcy*
World Emp. Svc, *Perm. Emp Agcy*

Indiana

Bill Caldwell Emp. Svc, *Perm. Emp Agcy*
Pat Day Persnnl, *Perm. Emp Agcy*
Execusearch, *Exec Srch*
Job Placemnt Svc, *Perm. Emp Agcy*
Life Emp. Svc, *Perm. Emp Agcy*
Mgmt. Recrtrs of Evansville, *Exec Srch*
Mgmt. Recrtrs of Indianapolis, *Exec Srch*
Mgmt. Recrtrs of Richmond/Staff Solut'ns, *Exec Srch*
Officemates5 of Indianapolis, *Exec Srch*
Persnnl Mgmt., *Temp. Agcy*
Rush Temps, *Temp. Agcy*
Warrick Cnty Emp. & Training Ctr, *Career/Outplacemnt*

Iowa

Burton Placemnt Svcs, *Exec Srch*
Byrnes & Rupkey, *Exec Srch*
ZExecutive Srch Assoc., *Exec Srch*
Helping Hands Temp. Svc, *Temp. Agcy*
Mgmt. Recrtrs Intl, *Exec Srch*

Kansas

Business Specialists, *Perm. Emp Agcy*
Eleventh Hour Staff Svcs, *Temp. Agcy*
Key Staffng, *Temp. Agcy*
Mgmt. Recrtrs of Overlnd Prk, *Exec Srch*

Kentucky

Angel Grp Intl, *Exec Srch*

Louisiana

Mgmt. Recrtrs of Baton Rouge, *Exec Srch*
Mgmt. Recrtrs-Metairie/Sales Consltnts, *Exec Srch*
Talley & Assoc./Talley Temps, *Exec Srch*
Technical Resource Staff Svcs, *Temp. Agcy*

Maine

At Work Persnnl, *Temp. Agcy*
Career Mngmnt Assoc., *Exec Srch*
Tempo Emp. Svc, *Temp. Agcy*

Maryland

Adecco, *Temp. Agcy*
Caplan Assoc., *Exec Srch*
Executive Placemnt Assoc., *Exec Srch*
Futures, *Exec Srch*
Interim Persnnl, *Temp. Agcy*
Mgmt. Recrtrs of Annapolis, *Exec Srch*
Mgmt. Recrtrs-Baltimore/Sales Consltnts, *Exec Srch*
Mgmt. Recrtrs-Bethesda/CompuSearch, *Exec Srch*
Mgmt. Recrtrs of Frederick, *Exec Srch*
Placement Assoc., *Exec Srch*
Sales Consltnts of Baltimore Cty, *Exec Srch*
Sales Consltnts of Prince Georges Cnty, *Exec Srch*

Massachusetts

Adecco, *Temp. Agcy*
Nancy Atkins Assoc., *Exec Srch*
Ford & Ford Exec Srch, *Exec Srch*
Alan Levine Assoc., *Exec Srch*
Mgmt. Recrtrs Intl, *Exec Srch*
Mgmt. Recrtrs Intl of Braintree, *Exec Srch*
Mgmt. Recrtrs Intl of Westboro, *Exec Srch*
Mass Temps, *Temp. Agcy*
Pro Staff, *Temp. Agcy*
Recruiting Specialists, *Exec Srch*
The Retail Netwrk, *Exec Srch*
Sales Consltnts of Cape Cod, *Exec Srch*
Sales Consltnts of Plymouth Cnty, *Exec Srch*
Sales Consltnts of Wellesley, *Exec Srch*
Search Prof'ls, *Exec Srch*
SearchNet, *Exec Srch*
Stephen Sonis Assoc., *Exec Srch*
Stone & Youngblood, *Exec Srch*

Michigan

Automotive Careers, *Exec Srch*
Day Persnnl dba Dorothy Day Persnnl - MI, *Perm Emp Agcy*
Express Persnnl Svcs, *Temp. Agcy*
Mgmt. Recrtrs of Bingham Farms, *Exec Srch*
Mgmt. Recrtrs of Flint, *Exec Srch*
Mgmt. Recrtrs of Kalamazoo, *Exec Srch*
Mgmt. Recrtrs of Lansing, *Exec Srch*
Mgmt. Recrtrs of Muskegon, *Exec Srch*
Mgmt. Recrtrs of Rochester, *Exec Srch*
Preferred Emp. Planning, *Perm. Emp Agcy*
Rooney Persnnl Co, *Exec Srch*
Roth Young Persnnl Svcs of Detroit, *Exec Srch*
Sales Consltnts of Detroit, *Exec Srch*
Sales Consltnts of Farmington Hills, *Exec Srch*
Trillium Staffng, *Temp. Agcy*
Venture Mngmnt & Staffng, *Exec Srch*

Minnesota

Employment Advisors, *Perm. Emp Agcy*
T.H. Hunter, *Exec Srch*
Mgmt. Recrtrs-Minneapolis/Sales Consltnts, *Exec Srch*
Roth Young Exec Recrtrs, *Exec Srch*
Staff It Persnnl Svcs, *Temp. Agcy*
Total Srch, *Exec Srch*
West Emp. Solut'ns, *Perm. Emp Agcy*
Youth Emp. Project, *Perm. Emp Agcy*

Mississippi

Coats & Coats Persnnl, *Perm. Emp Agcy*
Recruitment & Training of MS, *Perm. Emp Agcy*

Missouri

Adecco, *Temp. Agcy*
American Automotive Persnnl Consltnts, *Exec Srch*
Deck & Decker Emp. Svc, *Perm. Emp Agcy*
Decker Persnnl, *Perm. Emp Agcy*
Annie Gray Assoc., *Exec Srch*
Huey Enterprises, *Exec Srch*
Huntress Real Estate Exec Srch, *Exec Srch*
JoDoc Enterprises, *Temp. Agcy*
Mgmt. Recrtrs of Kansas Cty, *Exec Srch*
Mgmt. Recrtrs of Springfield, *Exec Srch*
Mgmt. Recrtrs of St. Louis, *Exec Srch*
Manpower Temp. Svcs, *Temp. Agcy*
Snelling Persnnl Svcs, *Perm. Emp Agcy*
Toberson Grp, *Perm. Emp Agcy*

Apple One Emp. Svcs, *Perm. Emp Agcy*
Apropos Emp. Agcy, *Perm. Emp Agcy*
Automotive Career Plcmnt, *Exec Srch*
Ballantyne Assoc., *Exec Srch*
Barnes & Assoc., *Exec Srch*
Thomas Beck, *Exec Srch*
Rob Beech West, *Exec Srch*
Harvey Bell & Assoc., *Exec Srch*
Bennett & Co Consltng Grp, *Exec Srch*
Bialla & Assoc., *Exec Srch*
The Black Leopard, *Exec Srch*
BridgeGate Grp, *Exec Srch*
Brooks Assoc., *Exec Srch*
Business Syst. Staffing & Assoc., *Perm. Emp Agcy*
CN Assoc., *Exec Srch*
California Job Connection, *Perm. Emp Agcy*
California Srch Agcy, *Exec Srch*
Career Advantage, *Exec Srch*
Career Quest, *Contract Svc*
Chaitin & Assoc., *Exec Srch*
Champagne Temp. Help, *Temp. Agcy*
Coast To Coast Exec Srch, *Exec Srch*
Collier-Young Agcy, *Temp. Agcy*
Computer Netwrk Resrcs, *Exec Srch*
Consultant Svcs, *Exec Srch*
Corporate Dynamix, *Exec Srch*
Cory Assoc., *Exec Srch*
Cory Assoc. Agcy, *Exec Srch*
Marlene Critchfield Co, *Perm. Emp Agcy*
Culver Persnnl Svcs, *Perm. Emp Agcy*
Culver Persnnl Svcs, *Exec Srch*
Curphey & Malkin Assoc., *Exec Srch*
Decker & Assoc. Persnnl, *Perm. Emp Agcy*
Rob Dingman Co, *Exec Srch*
Drake Office Overload, *Temp. Agcy*
Drummer Persnnl, *Exec Srch*
Dunhill Prof'l Srch, *Exec Srch*
Dynamic Synergy Corp, *Exec Srch*
Eagle Srch Assoc., *Exec Srch*
Edwards & Assoc., *Exec Srch*
Eleventh Hour Staff Svcs, *Temp. Agcy*
Employment Devlpmnt Dept, *Perm. Emp Agcy*
Employment Svc Agcy, *Perm. Emp Agcy*
Ethos Consltng, *Exec Srch*
Executive Grp West, *Exec Srch*
Curtis Farmer Persnnl, *Exec Srch*
Fastek Tech. Svcs, *Perm. Emp Agcy*
Finesse Persnnl Assoc., *Exec Srch*
Fisher & Assoc., *Exec Srch*
Fisher Persnnl Mngmnt Svcs, *Exec Srch*
FORTUNE Persnnl Consltnts, *Exec Srch*
40 Plus of So. CA, *Exec Srch*
Fresquez & Assoc., *Exec Srch*
Garnett Emp. Svcs, *Temp. Agcy*
Dianne Gauger & Assoc., *Exec Srch*
Goldstein & Assoc., *Temp. Agcy*
The Goodman Grp, *Exec Srch*
Gorelick & Assoc., *Exec Srch*
Gould Persnnl Svcs, *Perm. Emp Agcy*
Grant & Assoc., *Exec Srch*
Hall Kinion, *Contract Svc*
Herrerias & Assoc., *Exec Srch*
Hill & Assoc., *Exec Srch*
Holland McFadzean & Assoc., *Exec Srch*
Independent Resource System, *Exec Srch*
Interim Industrial Staffng, *Temp. Agcy*
Interim Persnnl, *Temp. Agcy*
Intl Srch Consltnts, *Perm. Emp Agcy*
Intl Staff Consltnts, *Exec Srch*
Intertec Design, *Perm. Emp Agcy*
JAA Emp. Agcy, *Perm. Emp Agcy*
JPM Intl, *Exec Srch*
Cindy Jackson Srch, *Exec Srch*
Jackson Persnnl, *Perm. Emp Agcy*
K&C Assoc., *Exec Srch*
Kelly Svcs, *Temp. Agcy*
Klein & Assoc., *Temp. Agcy*
Klenin Grp, *Exec Srch*
Kuhn Med-Tech, *Exec Srch*
John Kurosky & Assoc., *Exec Srch*
Larkin Assoc., *Exec Srch*
Lending Persnnl Svcs, *Exec Srch*
The London Agcy, *Exec Srch*
Malibu Grp, *Exec Srch*
Mgmt. Recrtrs of Burlingame/Sales Consltnts, *Exec Srch*
Mgmt. Recrtrs of Encino, *Exec Srch*
Mgmt. Recrtrs of Laguna Hills, *Exec Srch*
Mgmt. Recrtrs-Oakland/Sales Consltnts, *Exec Srch*
Mgmt. Recrtrs of Orange, *Exec Srch*
Mgmt. Recrtrs of Pleasanton, *Exec Srch*
Mgmt. Recrtrs of Redlands, *Exec Srch*
Manpower, *Temp. Agcy*
The Martin Agencies, *Perm. Emp Agcy*
Master Consltnts Assoc., *Exec Srch*
Maverick Staff Svc, *Perm. Emp Agcy*
McCoy Limited, *Exec Srch*
Mesa Intl, *Exec Srch*
Milestone Prof'l Staffng, *Exec Srch*
Multisearch Recrtrs, *Exec Srch*
Murray Enterprises Staff Svcs, *Temp. Agcy*
Musick & Assoc., *Exec Srch*
Nelson HR Solut'ns, *Perm. Emp Agcy*
New Venture Development, *Exec Srch*
Norrell Temp. Svcs of CA, *Temp. Agcy*
Norsell & Assoc., *Exec Srch*
Officemates5/Daystar Temp. Svcs, *Perm. Emp Agcy*
Omni Express Temps, *Temp. Agcy*
Onyx Persnnl Svcs, *Perm. Emp Agcy*
Pacific Srch Grp, *Exec Srch*
Pasona Pacific, *Temp. Agcy*
Paster & Assoc., *Exec Srch*
Perkiss & Assoc., *Exec Srch*
Tom Pezman & Assoc., *Exec Srch*
Pips Persnnl Svcs, *Perm. Emp Agcy*
Premier Persnnl Svcs, *Temp. Agcy*
Presidio Persnnl, *Temp. Agcy*
Pro Found, *Perm. Emp Agcy*
Professional Recrtrs, *Exec Srch*
ProFile Persnnl, *Perm. Emp Agcy*
Progressive Srch & Consltng, *Exec Srch*
ProSearch & Assoc., *Exec Srch*
Ed Rast & Co, *Exec Srch*
Reliance Staff Svcs, *Perm. Emp Agcy*
Remedy Intelligent Staffng, *Temp. Agcy*
Resource Perspectives, *Exec Srch*
Ricci Lee Assoc., *Exec Srch*
Rob Riggs Assoc., *Exec Srch*
Rich Rigler & Assoc., *Exec Srch*
Riley-Cole Recrtmnt Specialists, *Exec Srch*
Ritter Assoc., *Exec Srch*
Royal Staff Svcs, *Exec Srch*
S.R. & Assoc., *Exec Srch*
Sales Consltnts, *Exec Srch*
Sales Consltnts of Modesto, *Exec Srch*
Sales Consltnts of Sacramento, *Exec Srch*
Sales Prof'ls Persnnl Svcs, *Exec Srch*
Santa Barbara Plcmnt, *Perm. Emp Agcy*
Search West, *Exec Srch*
Source Engineering, *Perm. Emp Agcy*
Spectrum Srch Assoc., *Exec Srch*
Steinbrun, Hughes & Assoc., *Exec Srch*
Adele Steinmetz, *Exec Srch*
Sun Persnnl Svcs, *Temp. Agcy*
Systems Research Grp, *Exec Srch*
TLC Staffng, *Temp. Agcy*
T.R. Emp. Agcy, *Perm. Emp Agcy*
TRC Staff Svcs, *Perm. Emp Agcy*
Talent Tree Staffng, *Perm. Emp Agcy*
Tax Exec Srch, *Exec Srch*
Teleforce Intl, *Exec Srch*
Telford, Adams, & Alexander, *Exec Srch*
Thomas Staffng, *Temp. Agcy*
TOD Staffng, *Exec Srch*
Today Persnnl, *Perm. Emp Agcy*
Truex Assoc., *Exec Srch*
The Truman Agcy, Persnnl Specialists, *Perm. Emp Agcy*
UAW Labor Emp. & Training Corp, *Perm. Emp Agcy*
Unisearch, *Exec Srch*
United Staff Solut'ns, *Exec Srch*
United/Corestaff Staff Svcs, *Perm. Emp Agcy*
Victor Valley Persnnl Agcy, *Perm. Emp Agcy*
Volt Temp. Svcs, *Temp. Agcy*
Wendell Assoc., *Exec Srch*
Western Staff Svcs, *Temp. Agcy*
Western Tech. Resrcs, *Exec Srch*
WestPacific Nat'l Srch, *Exec Srch*
William-Johns Co, *Exec Srch*
Winser Exec Srch, *Exec Srch*
Your People Prof'ls, *Perm. Emp Agcy*
Don Zee Assoc., *Exec Srch*
Amy Zimmerman & Assoc., *Perm. Emp Agcy*

Colorado

Absolute Emp. Svcs, *Perm. Emp Agcy*
Ahrnsbrak & Assoc., *Perm. Emp Agcy*
The Bridge, *Exec Srch*
Career Forum, *Exec Srch*
Casey Svcs, *Exec Srch*
Creative Career Connections, *Career/Outplacemnt*
Dunhill Persnnl of Fort Collins, *Exec Srch*
Eleventh Hour Staff Svcs, *Perm. Emp Agcy*
Executive Persnnl, *Exec Srch*
Executives By Sterling, *Exec Srch*
FORTUNE Persnnl Consltnts, *Exec Srch*
40 Plus of CO, *Career/Outplacemnt*
Health Technlgy, *Exec Srch*
Healthcare Recrtrs of The Rockies, *Exec Srch*
Integrity Netwrk, *Exec Srch*
JobSearch, *Temp. Agcy*
Kelly Svcs, *Temp. Agcy*
Mgmt. Recrtrs Intl, *Exec Srch*
Mgmt. Recrtrs of CO, *Exec Srch*
Mgmt. Recrtrs of Colorado Springs, *Exec Srch*
Manpower Intl, *Temp. Agcy*
Pinnacle Source, *Exec Srch*
Placement Prof'ls, *Exec Srch*
Real Estate Persnnl, *Exec Srch*
SOS Staff Svcs, *Temp. Agcy*
Sales Consltnts, *Exec Srch*
Scheer & Assoc., *Exec Srch*
Snelling Persnnl Svcs, *Exec Srch*
Star Persnnl, *Exec Srch*
Todays Temporary, *Temp. Agcy*
Triad Consltnts, *Exec Srch*
Julie West & Assoc., *Exec Srch*
Western Staff Svcs, *Temp. Agcy*
The Woodstone Consltng Co, *Exec Srch*

Connecticut

A&A Resume & Persnnl Svcs, *Perm. Emp Agcy*
Abraham & London, *Exec Srch*
Advanced Plcmnt, *Temp. Agcy*
Bohan & Bradstreet, *Perm. Emp Agcy*
Buxbaum/Rink Consltng, *Exec Srch*
CGR Staff Svcs, *Temp. Agcy*
Cahill Assoc., *Exec Srch*
Corporate Staff Solut'ns, *Temp. Agcy*
Cupples Consltng Svcs, *Exec Srch*
Diversified Emp. Svcs, *Perm. Emp Agcy*
Diversity Recruitng Svcs, *Exec Srch*
Dunhill Srch Intl, *Perm. Emp Agcy*
Employment Opport., *Perm. Emp Agcy*
Harris Heery & Assoc., *Exec Srch*
Hobson Assoc., *Exec Srch*
Impact Persnnl, *Temp. Agcy*
Industrial Recrtrs Assn, *Perm. Emp Agcy*
Intertec Persnnl, *Temp. Agcy*
Jobsource, *Perm. Emp Agcy*
Lineal Recruitng Svcs, *Perm. Emp Agcy*
MJF Assoc., *Exec Srch*
Mgmt. Recrtrs Intl, *Exec Srch*
Maxwell-Marcus Staff Consltnts, *Exec Srch*
McIntyre Assoc., *Temp. Agcy*
The McKnight Grp, *Exec Srch*
Office Svcs of CT, *Perm. Emp Agcy*
PRH Mgmt., *Exec Srch*
Barry Persky & Co., *Exec Srch*
Stewart Assoc., *Exec Srch*
Tucker Grp, *Exec Srch*
United Persnnl Svcs, *Temp. Agcy*
J.R. Vaughan & Assoc., *Perm. Emp Agcy*
Western Staff Svcs, *Perm. Emp Agcy*
Frank Wilkinson & Co, *Exec Srch*
Bob Wright Recruitng, *Exec Srch*

Delaware

Caldwell Staff Svcs, *Perm. Emp Agcy*
J.B. Groner Exec Srch, *Exec Srch*

District of Columbia

Admin. Assist./Hire Standard Staffng, *Perm. Emp Agcy*
Career Blazers Persnnl, *Perm. Emp Agcy*
Mee Derby & Co, *Exec Srch*
Savoy Partners Exec. Srch Firm
TempWorld Staff Svcs, *Temp. Agcy*

Florida

AAA Employment, *Perm. Emp Agcy*
AccuStaff, *Temp. Agcy*
Active Prof'ls, *Exec Srch*
Adecco, *Temp. Agcy*
Ambiance Persnnl, *Exec Srch*
American Exec Srch, *Exec Srch*
American Recrtrs, *Exec Srch*
B&B Persnnl, *Perm. Emp Agcy*
Bales-Waugh Grp/Bales Sales Recrtrs, *Exec Srch*
Belmont Training & Employment, *Perm. Emp Agcy*
Benson & Assoc., *Exec Srch*
The Brand Co, *Exec Srch*
Bryan & Assoc./Worknet, Etc., *Exec Srch*
Career Choice, *Exec Srch*
Career Planners, *Perm. Emp Agcy*
Carrier's Career Svc, *Career/Outplacemnt*
Crew Unlimtd, *Perm. Emp Agcy*
DGA Persnnl Grp, *Exec Srch*
Employers' Assistant, *Temp. Agcy*
Ethan Allen Persnnl Plcmnt, *Exec Srch*
Executive Sales Registry, *Exec Srch*
Five Star Temporary, *Temp. Agcy*
Future Force Persnnl, *Temp. Agcy*
Girl Friday Persnnl, *Temp. Agcy*
Ann Grogan & Assoc., *Exec Srch*
Hastings & Hastings Persnnl Consltnts, *Temp. Agcy*
Healthcare Recrtrs of Central Florida, *Exec Srch*
Interim Persnnl, *Temp. Agcy*
Janus Career Svc, *Perm. Emp Agcy*
Just Mngmnt Svcs, *Exec Srch*
Kelley & Keller Mngmnt Consltnts, *Exec Srch*
Kelly Svcs, *Temp. Agcy*
R.H. Larsen & Assoc., *Exec Srch*
Mgmt. Recrtrs Intl, *Exec Srch*
Mgmt. Recrtrs of Indialantic, *Exec Srch*
Mgmt. Recrtrs of Jacksonville, *Exec Srch*
Mgmt. Recrtrs of Lake Cnty, *Exec Srch*
Mgmt. Recrtrs of Miami, *Exec Srch*
Mgmt. Recrtrs of St. Petersburg, *Exec Srch*

Mgmt. Recrtrs of Tallahassee, *Exec Srch*
Mgmt. Recrtrs of Tampa, *Exec Srch*
Marathon Grp, *Exec Srch*
McGuire Exec Srch, *Exec Srch*
Norrell Svcs, *Temp. Agcy*
OMNIPartners, *Exec Srch*
OmniSearch, *Exec Srch*
O'Quin Persnnl, *Temp. Agcy*
Pearce & Assoc., *Exec Srch*
Perfect Srch, *Exec Srch*
Persnnl One, *Perm. Emp Agcy*
Priority Srch, *Exec Srch*
Profes. Staffing/Able Body Temp. Svcs, *Contract Svc*
R.M.H. Assoc., *Exec Srch*
Roth Young of Tampa, *Exec Srch*
The Ryan Charles Grp, *Exec Srch*
Sales Consltnts of Coral Springs, *Exec Srch*
Sales Consltnts of Fort Lauderdale, *Exec Srch*
Sales Consltnts of Jacksonville, *Exec Srch*
Sales Consltnts of Sarasota, *Exec Srch*
Search Masters Intl, *Exec Srch*
Doug Sears & Assoc., *Exec Srch*
Shaver Emp. Agcy, *Perm. Emp Agcy*
Snelling Persnnl Svcs, *Temp. Agcy*
Spalding's Emp. Svc, *Perm. Emp Agcy*
Specialized Srch Assoc., *Exec Srch*
Staff Leasing Grp, *Contract Svc*
Staffing Svcs Grp, *Perm. Emp Agcy*
Staffing Solut'ns by Persnnl One, *Perm. Emp Agcy*
The Stewart Srch Grp, *Exec Srch*
Sun Persnnl West, *Exec Srch*
Suncoast Grp, *Perm. Emp Agcy*

Georgia

A Hiring Alternative, *Exec Srch*
A-OK Persnnl, *Perm. Emp Agcy*
AAA Employment, *Perm. Emp Agcy*
A.D. & Assoc. Exec Srch, *Exec Srch*
Accurate Medical Placemnt/The Accurate Grp, *Exec Srch*
Ashley-Nolan Intl, *Exec Srch*
Charles Bernard & Assoc., *Exec Srch*
Boreham Intl, *Exec Srch*
Caldwell Svcs, *Temp. Agcy*
Career Placemnts, *Perm. Emp Agcy*
Catalina Resrcs, *Perm. Emp Agcy*
Commonwealth Consltnts, *Exec Srch*
Comprehensive Srch Grp, *Exec Srch*
Corporate Srch Consltnts, *Exec Srch*
Dunhill Prof'l Srch, *Exec Srch*
Elite Staff Svcs, *Perm. Emp Agcy*
Executive Force, *Exec Srch*
Express Persnnl Svcs, *Temp. Agcy*
Express Persnnl Svcs, *Perm. Emp Agcy*
Express Persnnl Svcs, *Exec Srch*
First Pro, *Temp. Agcy*
Fox-Morris Assoc., *Exec Srch*
ISC of Atlanta/Intl Career Continuation, *Exec Srch*
Kenzer Corp of GA, *Exec Srch*
Evie Kreisler & Assoc., *Exec Srch*
MSI Intl, *Exec Srch*
Mgmt. Recrtrs Intl, *Exec Srch*
Mgmt. Recrtrs of Atlanta, *Exec Srch*
Mgmt. Recrtrs of Marietta, *Exec Srch*
Mission Corps Intl/Helping Hands Temp. Svc, *Temp. Agcy*
More Persnnl Svcs, *Perm. Emp Agcy*
NEIS, *Exec Srch*
National Persnnl Recrtrs, *Exec Srch*
Olsten Staff Svcs, *Temp. Agcy*
Omni Recruitng, *Exec Srch*
Perimeter Plcmnt, *Exec Srch*
Personalized Mngmnt Assoc., *Exec Srch*
Persnnl Opport., *Exec Srch*
Pinnacle Consltng Grp, *Exec Srch*
Priority 1 Staff Svcs, *Temp. Agcy*
Professional Medical, *Perm. Emp Agcy*
Randstad Staff Svcs, *Perm. Emp Agcy*
Ranger Svcs, *Temp. Agcy*
Rowland, Mountain & Assoc., *Exec Srch*
Sales Opport., *Exec Srch*
Sanford Rose Assoc., *Exec Srch*
SearchAmerica, *Exec Srch*
Snelling Persnnl Svcs, *Exec Srch*
Sondra Srch, *Exec Srch*
Southern Emp. Svc, *Perm. Emp Agcy*
Staffing Resrcs, *Perm. Emp Agcy*
TRC Staff Svcs, *Temp. Agcy*
TempWorld Staff Svcs, *Temp. Agcy*
Todays Temporary, *Temp. Agcy*
WPPS Software Staffng, *Perm. Emp Agcy*
Western Staff Svcs, *Temp. Agcy*

Hawaii

Dunhill Prof'l Srch of Hawaii, *Exec Srch*
Ellis & Assoc., *Exec Srch*
Kelly Svcs, *Temp. Agcy*
The Resume Place, *Career/Outplacemnt*
Sales Consltnts of Honolulu, *Exec Srch*

Idaho

Horne/Brown Intl, *Exec Srch*
Idaho Dept. of Employment/JobSvc, *Perm. Emp Agcy*

Illinois

A.B.A. Placemnts/A.B.A. Temps, *Perm. Emp Agcy*
ASI Persnnl, *Perm. Emp Agcy*
Able's Pool of Temps, *Temp. Agcy*
B.J. Abrams & Assoc., *Exec Srch*
Accurate Recruitng, *Perm. Emp Agcy*
Adecco, *Temp. Agcy*
Advantage Persnnl, *Perm. Emp Agcy*
Affiliated Persnnl Consltnts, *Perm. Emp Agcy*
American Engineering Co, *Exec Srch*
Armstrong-Hamilton Assoc., *Exec Srch*
Availability, *Perm. Emp Agcy*
Banner Persnnl, *Perm. Emp Agcy*
Bell Persnnl, *Perm. Emp Agcy*
Britannia, *Exec Srch*
Brooke Chase Assoc., *Exec Srch*
Career Consltnts, *Exec Srch*
Carson Mngmnt Assoc., *Contract Svc*
Corporate Consltnts, *Exec Srch*
Corporate Environment, *Exec Srch*
Cumberland Grp, *Exec Srch*
DayStar Temp. Svcs, *Temp. Agcy*
Diener & Assoc., *Exec Srch*
Dunhill Prof'l Srch of Rolling Meadows, *Exec Srch*
Dunhill Staff Svcs of Chicago, *Perm. Emp Agcy*
Dynamic People, *Temp. Agcy*
Eastman & Assoc., *Exec Srch*
The Eastwood Grp, *Exec Srch*
The Esquire Staffing Grp, *Perm. Emp Agcy*
Executive Referral Svcs, *Exec Srch*
Executive Srch Intl, *Exec Srch*
Express Persnnl Svcs, *Temp. Agcy*
Fellows Plcmnt, *Temp. Agcy*
First Srch, *Exec Srch*
Girman Grp, *Exec Srch*
David Gomez & Assoc., *Exec Srch*
Healthcare Recrtrs Intl, *Exec Srch*
Elizabeth Howe & Assoc., *Exec Srch*
Human Resource Connection, *Perm. Emp Agcy*
Interstaff, *Temp. Agcy*
Interviewing Consltnts, *Perm. Emp Agcy*
Irwin & Wagner, *Exec Srch*
Kunzer Assoc., *Exec Srch*
Arlene Leff & Assoc., *Exec Srch*
Lomack Agcy, *Temp. Agcy*
Lynco Mngmnt Persnnl, *Exec Srch*
Lyons & Assoc., *Exec Srch*
MBP Persnnl, *Exec Srch*
Mack & Assoc., *Temp. Agcy*
Mgmt. Recrtrs of Arlington Heights, *Exec Srch*
Mgmt. Recrtrs of Rockford, *Exec Srch*
Mgmt. Recrtrs of St. Charles, *Exec Srch*
Mgmt. Support Svcs, *Exec Srch*
Maramax Persnnl, *Perm. Emp Agcy*
Rich Marks & Assoc., *Exec Srch*
Marsteller Wilcox Assoc., *Exec Srch*
Masters Assoc., *Exec Srch*
Paul May & Assoc., *Exec Srch*
M.W. McDonald & Assoc., *Exec Srch*
Juan Menefee & Assoc., *Exec Srch*
Michael David Assoc., *Perm. Emp Agcy*
Midwest Consltng Corp, *Exec Srch*
The Murphy Grp, *Perm. Emp Agcy*
NJW & Assoc., *Temp. Agcy*
National Srch, *Exec Srch*
Kenneth Nicholas & Assoc., *Exec Srch*
Norrell HR Svcs, *Perm. Emp Agcy*
Officemates5 of Wheeling, *Exec Srch*
Olsten Information Technlgy Staffng, *Perm. Emp Agcy*
Opportunity Persnnl, *Perm. Emp Agcy*
PS, *Perm. Emp Agcy*
Pelichem Assoc., *Exec Srch*
Persnnl Connection, *Perm. Emp Agcy*
Prestige Emp. Svcs, *Perm. Emp Agcy*
Professional Research Svcs, *Exec Srch*
ProSearch Plus, *Exec Srch*
Quantum Prof'l Srch/Quantum Staff Svcs, *Exec Srch*
The Raleigh Warwick Grp, *Exec Srch*
Recruitment Netwrk, *Exec Srch*
Remedy Intelligent Staffng, *Temp. Agcy*
Retail Staffers, *Exec Srch*
Right Svcs, *Temp. Agcy*
The Robinson Grp, *Exec Srch*
The Ryan Charles Grp, *Exec Srch*
SHS, *Exec Srch*
Sales Consltnts/Mgmt. Recrtrs Intl, *Exec Srch*
Sales Consltnts of Chicago, *Exec Srch*
Sales Consltnts of Oak Brk, *Exec Srch*
Sanford Rose Assoc., *Exec Srch*
Shannonwood Staffers, *Temp. Agcy*
Ralph Smith & Assoc., *Exec Srch*
Snelling Persnnl Svcs, *Temp. Agcy*
Snelling Persnnl Svcs, *Exec Srch*
Snelling Srch, *Exec Srch*
Staffing Consltnts, *Perm. Emp Agcy*
Staffing Team Intl, *Temp. Agcy*
Stern Prof'l Srch & Consltnts, *Exec Srch*
Strategic Resrcs Unlimtd, *Exec Srch*
Temporary Assoc., *Temp. Agcy*
VG & Assoc., *Perm. Emp Agcy*
Walsh & Co, *Perm. Emp Agcy*
Watters & Byrd, *Perm. Emp Agcy*
Web/Pack Tech, *Perm. Emp Agcy*
Webb Emp. Svc, *Perm. Emp Agcy*
West Persnnl, *Perm. Emp Agcy*
Working World, *Temp. Agcy*
World Emp. Svc, *Perm. Emp Agcy*

Indiana

ABS-AARON Bus. Syst., *Exec Srch*
AccuStaff, *Temp. Agcy*
Alpha Rae Persnnl, *Perm. Emp Agcy*
Bill Caldwell Emp. Svc, *Perm. Emp Agcy*
Corporate Staff Resrcs, *Temp. Agcy*
Pat Day Persnnl, *Perm. Emp Agcy*
Employment Recrtrs, *Perm. Emp Agcy*
Execusearch, *Exec Srch*
First Call Temp. Svcs, *Temp. Agcy*
Job Placemnt Svc, *Perm. Emp Agcy*
Johnson Brown Assoc., *Exec Srch*
Key Sales Persnnl, *Exec Srch*
Lange & Assoc., *Exec Srch*
Life Emp. Svc, *Perm. Emp Agcy*
The Mallard Grp, *Exec Srch*
Mgmt. Recrtrs Intl, *Exec Srch*
Mgmt. Recrtrs of Evansville, *Exec Srch*
Mgmt. Recrtrs of Indianapolis, *Exec Srch*
Mgmt. Recrtrs of Richmond/Staff Solut'ns, *Exec Srch*
Mgmt. Svcs, *Exec Srch*
Mayhall Srch Grp, *Exec Srch*
Oakwood Intl, *Exec Srch*
Officemates5 of Indianapolis, *Exec Srch*
Perry Persnnl Plus, *Perm. Emp Agcy*
Quiring Assoc. HR Consltng Grp, *Exec Srch*
Rush Temps, *Temp. Agcy*
Snelling & Snelling, *Perm. Emp Agcy*
Unique, *Exec Srch*
Warrick Cnty Emp. & Training Ctr, *Career/Outplacemnt*

Iowa

Bryant Bureau Sales Recrtrs, *Exec Srch*
Burton Placemnt Svcs, *Exec Srch*
Byrnes & Rupkey, *Exec Srch*
Cambridge Staffng, *Perm. Emp Agcy*
Drake-Brennan dba Snelling Persnnl, *Exec Srch*
Executive Resrcs, *Perm. Emp Agcy*
Executive Srch Assoc., *Exec Srch*
Helping Hands Temp. Svc, *Temp. Agcy*
Kelly Svcs, *Temp. Agcy*
Mgmt. Recrtrs Intl, *Exec Srch*
McGladrey Srch Grp, *Exec Srch*
Persnnl, *Exec Srch*
Salem Mngmnt dba Rudy Salem Staff Svcs, *Temp. Agcy*
Staffing Edge, *Perm. Emp Agcy*

Kansas

Business Specialists, *Perm. Emp Agcy*
Eleventh Hour Staff Svcs, *Temp. Agcy*
Key Staffng, *Temp. Agcy*
Mgmt. Recrtrs of Overlnd Prk, *Exec Srch*
Network of Excellence, *Exec Srch*
Parr & Assoc., *Perm. Emp Agcy*
Smith Brown & Jones, *Exec Srch*
Stoneburner Assoc., *Exec Srch*
Temtech, *Contract Svc*
Uniforce Staff Svcs, *Temp. Agcy*

Kentucky

Angel Grp Intl, *Exec Srch*
C.M. Mngmnt Svcs, *Perm. Emp Agcy*
The Exec Advantage, *Exec Srch*
Kovac Berrins AG, *Exec Srch*
Sharrow & Assoc., *Exec Srch*
Snelling Persnnl Svcs, *Exec Srch*

Louisiana

Ascent Consltng Grp, *Temp. Agcy*
Delta Persnnl, *Perm. Emp Agcy*
Keenan Staffng, *Temp. Agcy*
MDR & Assoc., *Exec Srch*
Mgmt. Recrtrs of Baton Rouge, *Exec Srch*
Mgmt. Recrtrs-Metairie/Sales Consltnts, *Exec Srch*
Shiell Persnnl, *Perm. Emp Agcy*
Snelling Persnnl Svcs, *Exec Srch*
Talley & Assoc./Talley Temps, *Exec Srch*
Technical & Prof'l Sources, *Exec Srch*

Maine

ASK, *Temp. Agcy*
At Work Persnnl, *Temp. Agcy*
Career Mngmnt Assoc., *Exec Srch*
Executive Srch of N.E., *Exec Srch*
Goodrich Consltng, *Exec Srch*
John Jay & Co, *Exec Srch*

National Recrtrs of ME, *Exec Srch*
Pro Srch, *Exec Srch*

Maryland

Adecco, *Temp. Agcy*
Admin Persnnl Svcs, *Perm. Emp Agcy*
Auto Careers, *Exec Srch*
D.W. Baird & Assoc., *Exec Srch*
Bear Trees Consltng, *Exec Srch*
Caplan Assoc., *Exec Srch*
Comprehensive Srch Grp, *Exec Srch*
Comtex, *Exec Srch*
Employer Employee Exchng, *Exec Srch*
Fallstaff Srch, *Exec Srch*
A.G. Fishkin & Assoc., *Exec Srch*
Futures, *Exec Srch*
J.R. Assoc., *Perm. Emp Agcy*
The Jonathan Ladd Co, *Perm. Emp Agcy*
Mgmt. Recrtrs of Annapolis, *Exec Srch*
Mgmt. Recrtrs-Baltimore/Sales Consltnts, *Exec Srch*
Mgmt. Recrtrs-Bethesda/CompuSearch, *Exec Srch*
Mgmt. Recrtrs of Frederick, *Exec Srch*
Tom McCall & Assoc., *Perm. Emp Agcy*
Porter Grp, *Exec Srch*
Sales Consltnts of Baltimore Cty, *Exec Srch*
Sales Consltnts of Columbia, *Exec Srch*
Sales Consltnts of Prince Georges Cnty, *Exec Srch*
Sales Consltnts of Rockville, *Exec Srch*
Seek Intl, *Exec Srch*
Sparks Persnnl Svcs, *Temp. Agcy*
TCM Enterprises, *Exec Srch*
TAC Staff Svcs, *Temp. Agcy*
TAD Staff Svcs, *Temp. Agcy*
White Ridgely Assoc., *Career/Outplacemnt*
Winston Srch, *Exec Srch*

Massachusetts

Ability Srch of N.E., *Perm. Emp Agcy*
Accurate Srch Consltnts, *Exec Srch*
Advance Persnnl, *Perm. Emp Agcy*
B&M Assoc., *Contract Svc*
Campbell Assoc., *Exec Srch*
Carter/MacKay of Framingham, *Exec Srch*
Centor Persnnl, *Perm. Emp Agcy*
Clayman & Co, *Exec Srch*
Cleary Consltnts, *Perm. Emp Agcy*
Coast To Coast Sales Recrtrs, *Exec Srch*
Corporate Staff Solut'ns, *Temp. Agcy*
Cyr Assoc., *Exec Srch*
Dana Assoc., *Exec Srch*
Rob Davidson Assoc./Exec. & Prof. Resume Svc, *Exec Srch*
Derby Assoc., *Perm. Emp Agcy*
Discovery Persnnl, *Perm. Emp Agcy*
Diversity Assoc., *Exec Srch*
Dunhill Staffing Syst., *Temp. Agcy*
Ford & Ford Exec Srch, *Exec Srch*
FORTUNE Persnnl Consltnts of Topsfield, *Exec Srch*
Futures, *Exec Srch*
Gilreath Weatherby, *Exec Srch*
A. Greenstein & Co, *Exec Srch*
H&G Assoc., *Exec Srch*
Hamblin Grp, *Exec Srch*
Hilton Assoc., *Perm. Emp Agcy*
Interim Persnnl, *Temp. Agcy*
Kelly Svcs, *Temp. Agcy*
Lake & Manning, *Exec Srch*
The Littleton Grp, *Exec Srch*
Mgmt. Recrtrs Intl, *Exec Srch*
Mgmt. Recrtrs Intl of Braintree, *Exec Srch*
Mgmt. Recrtrs Intl of Springfield, *Exec Srch*
Mgmt. Recrtrs Intl of Westboro, *Exec Srch*
Manpower, *Temp. Agcy*
McDevitt Assoc., *Exec Srch*
Morency Assoc., *Exec Srch*
Murphy Assoc., *Exec Srch*
Need Persnnl Plcmnt, *Temp. Agcy*
New Boston Select Staffng, *Perm. Emp Agcy*
New England Persnnl, *Perm. Emp Agcy*
New England Recrtrs, *Exec Srch*
Norrell Staff Svcs, *Contract Svc*
Paladin Persnnl Consltnts, *Exec Srch*
Phillips & Assoc., *Exec Srch*
Prestonwood Assoc., *Exec Srch*
Pro Staff, *Temp. Agcy*
Progressive Srch Assoc., *Exec Srch*
Resrcs Objectives, *Exec Srch*
Louis Rudzinsky Assoc., *Exec Srch*
Sales & Mrktng Srch, *Exec Srch*
Sales Consltnts of Cape Cod, *Exec Srch*
Sales Consltnts of Mansfield, *Exec Srch*
Sales Consltnts of Plymouth Cnty, *Exec Srch*
Sales Consltnts of Wellesley, *Exec Srch*
Sales Temps, *Temp. Agcy*
George Sandel Assoc., *Perm. Emp Agcy*
Selected Executives, *Exec Srch*
Selectemps, *Temp. Agcy*
Selective Office Staffng, *Perm. Emp Agcy*
Snelling Persnnl Svcs, *Perm. Emp Agcy*
Source EDP, *Perm. Emp Agcy*
Stone & Youngblood, *Exec Srch*
Straube Assoc., *Exec Srch*
Sullivan Assoc., *Exec Srch*
T.F.S. Human Resource Solut'ns, *Exec Srch*
The Tower Grp, *Exec Srch*
Tricor Assoc., *Temp. Agcy*
United Prof'l Plcmnt, *Exec Srch*
Unlimited Opport., *Temp. Agcy*
Volt Svcs Grp, *Temp. Agcy*
The Ward Grp, *Exec Srch*
WIND Job Ctr, *Career/Outplacemnt*

Michigan

Action Mngmnt Corp, *Perm. Emp Agcy*
Advance Employment, *Exec Srch*
Advanced Tech. Resrcs, *Exec Srch*
Allied Tech. Svc, *Contract Svc*
American Computer Svc, *Exec Srch*
Automotive Careers, *Exec Srch*
Braboy & Assoc., *Exec Srch*
Bryant Bureau, *Exec Srch*
Calvert Assoc., *Perm. Emp Agcy*
Career Quest, *Perm. Emp Agcy*
Carmac Exec Recruitng, *Exec Srch*
Corporate Bus. Svcs Exec. Srch Firm
Corporate Staff Resrcs, *Perm. Emp Agcy*
Day Persnnl dba Dorothy Day Persnnl - MI, Perm Emp Agcy
Gene Ellefson & Assoc., *Exec Srch*
Exec-Tech Corp, *Exec Srch*
Executech Resource Consltnts, *Perm. Emp Agcy*
Executive Mngmnt Srch, *Exec Srch*
Executive Recrtrs Intl, *Exec Srch*
Express Persnnl Svcs, *Temp. Agcy*
Giacomin Grp, *Exec Srch*
Joseph Goldring & Assoc., *Exec Srch*
Steven Greene & Assoc., *Perm. Emp Agcy*
Guidarelli Assoc., *Exec Srch*
Healthcare Recrtrs Intl, *Exec Srch*
William Howard Agcy, *Perm. Emp Agcy*
Human Resrcs Emp. Svcs, *Perm. Emp Agcy*
Kelly Svcs, *Temp. Agcy*
Lake Assoc., *Exec Srch*
Mgmt. Recrtrs Intl, *Exec Srch*
Mgmt. Recrtrs of Bingham Farms, *Exec Srch*
Mgmt. Recrtrs of Dearborn, *Exec Srch*
Mgmt. Recrtrs of Flint, *Exec Srch*
Mgmt. Recrtrs of Grand Rapids, *Exec Srch*
Mgmt. Recrtrs of Kalamazoo, *Exec Srch*
Mgmt. Recrtrs of Lansing, *Exec Srch*
Mgmt. Recrtrs of Livonia, *Exec Srch*
Mgmt. Recrtrs of Muskegon, *Exec Srch*
Mgmt. Recrtrs of Rochester, *Exec Srch*
Michigan Srch Plus, *Exec Srch*
Nationwide Career Netwrk, *Perm. Emp Agcy*
Office Staffing Recruitng, *Exec Srch*
Preferred Emp. Planning, *Perm. Emp Agcy*
Professional Career Srch, *Exec Srch*
Professional Persnnl Consltnts Intl, *Exec Srch*
Roth Young Persnnl Svcs of Detroit, *Exec Srch*
Sales Consltnts of Auburn Hills, *Exec Srch*
Sales Consltnts of Farmington Hills, *Exec Srch*
Sales Consltnts of Lansing, *Exec Srch*
Sales Executives, *Perm. Emp Agcy*
TRC Staff Svcs, *Temp. Agcy*
Thomas & Assoc. of MI, *Exec Srch*
Total Recrtmnt Svcs, *Exec Srch*
Trillium Staffng, *Temp. Agcy*
Venture Mngmnt & Staffng, *Exec Srch*
Henry Welker & Assoc., *Perm. Emp Agcy*
Wing Tips & Pumps, *Exec Srch*
Wise Persnnl Svcs, *Perm. Emp Agcy*
Workforce, *Temp. Agcy*

Minnesota

Add On Staff Solut'ns, *Temp. Agcy*
Advance Persnnl Resrcs, *Exec Srch*
Agri Consltnts, *Exec Srch*
Agri-Business Svcs, *Exec Srch*
Agro Quality Srch, *Perm. Emp Agcy*
Alternative Staffng, *Perm. Emp Agcy*
Bright Srch/Professional Staffng, *Exec Srch*
Diversified Employment, *Perm. Emp Agcy*
Ells Persnnl Syst., *Exec Srch*
Employment Advisors, *Perm. Emp Agcy*
Hayden & Assoc., *Exec Srch*
Healthcare Recrtrs of MN, *Exec Srch*
Hilleren & Assoc., *Exec Srch*
T.H. Hunter, *Exec Srch*
Mgmt. Recrtrs-Minneapolis/Sales Consltnts, *Exec Srch*
Mary Mayer, Ltd., *Exec Srch*
North American Recrtrs, *Exec Srch*
Professional Alternatives, *Perm. Emp Agcy*
Professional Recrtrs, *Exec Srch*
Resource Srch, *Exec Srch*
Roth Young Exec Recrtrs, *Exec Srch*
Sathe & Assoc. Exec Srch, *Exec Srch*
Search Specialists, *Exec Srch*
Ultimate Srch Unlimtd/Temps Unlimtd, *Perm. Emp Agcy*
West Emp. Solut'ns, *Perm. Emp Agcy*
Working Relationships, *Perm. Emp Agcy*

Mississippi

Andrus Assoc. dba Svc Specialists Ltd., *Perm. Emp Agcy*
Capitol Staff Solut'ns, *Perm. Emp Agcy*
Coats & Coats Persnnl, *Perm. Emp Agcy*
EPSCO Persnnl, *Temp. Agcy*
Recruitment & Training of MS, *Perm. Emp Agcy*
Tatum Persnnl, *Perm. Emp Agcy*

Missouri

ABC Emp. Svc, *Perm. Emp Agcy*
Adecco, *Temp. Agcy*
Advanced Careers of Kansas Cty, *Exec Srch*
Jay Alexandr & Assoc. dba Kirdonn Grp, *Perm. Emp Agcy*
American Automotive Persnnl Consltnts, *Exec Srch*
L.P. Banning, *Perm. Emp Agcy*
Burns Emp. Svc, *Exec Srch*
Business Persnnl Svcs, *Temp. Agcy*
Corporate Persnnl & Assoc., *Exec Srch*
Deck & Decker Emp. Svc, *Perm. Emp Agcy*
Decker Persnnl, *Perm. Emp Agcy*
Employer Advantage, *Exec Srch*
Healthcare Recrtrs Intl, *Exec Srch*
Huey Enterprises, *Exec Srch*
Charles Luntz & Assoc., *Exec Srch*
Mgmt. Recrtrs Intl, *Exec Srch*
Mgmt. Recrtrs of Kansas Cty, *Exec Srch*
Mgmt. Recrtrs of Springfield, *Exec Srch*
Mgmt. Recrtrs of St. Louis, *Exec Srch*
Manpower Temp. Svcs, *Temp. Agcy*
National Physician Placemnt Svcs, *Exec Srch*
Officemates5 of St. Louis, *Exec Srch*
Sales Recrtrs, *Exec Srch*
Snelling Persnnl Svcs, *Perm. Emp Agcy*
Toberson Grp, *Perm. Emp Agcy*

Montana

Express Persnnl, *Perm. Emp Agcy*
Kelly Svcs, *Temp. Agcy*
Labor Contracting Staff Svcs, *Perm. Emp Agcy*

Nebraska

Ameri Srch, *Perm. Emp Agcy*
Compusearch of Lincoln, *Exec Srch*
Corporate Recrtrs, *Exec Srch*
Rose Crum Assoc., *Exec Srch*
Eggers Co, *Perm. Emp Agcy*
Express Persnnl, *Exec Srch*
Hansen Agri-Placement, *Perm. Emp Agcy*
Kelly Svcs, *Temp. Agcy*
Mgmt. Recrtrs of Omaha/Officemates5, *Exec Srch*
Outsource II, *Temp. Agcy*
Recruiters Intl, *Exec Srch*
Sales Consltnts of Omaha, *Exec Srch*
Sharp Persnnl, *Temp. Agcy*

Nevada

Mgmt. Recrtrs of Reno, *Exec Srch*
Sales Staffing Specialists, *Perm. Emp Agcy*

New Hampshire

Able 1 Staffng, *Exec Srch*
Affordable Solut'ns, *Contract Svc*
Allstaff Contrct Svcs, *Perm. Emp Agcy*
Barclay Persnnl Syst., *Exec Srch*
Barrett & Co, *Exec Srch*
Career Connections, *Perm. Emp Agcy*
Career Profiles, *Exec Srch*
Central New Hampshire Emp. Svcs, *Perm. Emp Agcy*
Chaucer Grp, *Exec Srch*
Dubois & Co, *Exec Srch*
Kelly Svcs, *Temp. Agcy*
Lloyd Persnnl Consltnts, *Exec Srch*
Mgmt. Recrtrs Intl of Bedford, *Exec Srch*
Manpower Temp. Svcs, *Temp. Agcy*
National Emp. Svc Corp, *Perm. Emp Agcy*
R.G.T. Assoc., *Exec Srch*
Resource Recruitng/Contemp. Accntnts, *Perm. Emp Agcy*
Sales Consltnts, *Exec Srch*
Sales Consltnts of Nashua-Manchester, *Exec Srch*
Sales Recrtrs, *Exec Srch*
STAT Srch, *Exec Srch*
Surge Resrcs, *Contract Svc*
TAC Staff Svcs, *Temp. Agcy*
Technical Directions, *Perm. Emp Agcy*

New Jersey

A Prof'l Edge, *Career/Outplacemnt*
Access Syst., *Exec Srch*
Advanced Persnnl, *Perm. Emp Agcy*
Alliance Consltnts, *Perm. Emp Agcy*
Andrew Persnnl Svcs, *Perm. Emp Agcy*
Angelord, *Temp. Agcy*
BAI Persnnl Solut'ns, *Exec Srch*
Barclay Consltnts, *Exec Srch*
R.P. Barone Assoc., *Exec Srch*

Sales Consltnts of Cincinnati, *Exec Srch*
Sanford Rose Assoc., *Exec Srch*
Snelling Persnnl Svcs, *Exec Srch*
Tabb & Assoc., *Exec Srch*
Talent Tree Staffng, *Perm. Emp Agcy*
The Target HR Companies, *Temp. Agcy*
TEAM America, *Perm. Emp Agcy*
Temporarily Yours Plcmnt, *Temp. Agcy*
Thomas-Schade & Assoc., *Exec Srch*
J.P. Walton & Assoc., *Exec Srch*

Oklahoma

Cherokee Temps, *Temp. Agcy*
Express Persnnl Svcs, *Exec Srch*
Food Manufacturing Consltnts, *Exec Srch*
Mgmt. Recrtrs Intl, *Exec Srch*
Mgmt. Recrtrs of Oklahoma Cty, *Exec Srch*
Mgmt. Srch, *Exec Srch*
Terry Neese Persnnl Agcy, *Exec Srch*
Lloyd Richards Persnnl, *Perm. Emp Agcy*
Sales Consltnts, *Exec Srch*
Sales Recrtrs, *Exec Srch*
Sooner Placemnt Svc, *Perm. Emp Agcy*
StaffMark, *Temp. Agcy*

Oregon

Able Temp. Svc, *Temp. Agcy*
Express Persnnl Svcs, *Exec Srch*
Kelly Svcs, *Temp. Agcy*
Mgmt. Recrtrs/Officemates5 of Portland, *Exec Srch*
NPRC/Nationwde Persnnl Recruitng & Consltng, *Exec Srch*
Office Careers, *Perm. Emp Agcy*
Snelling Persnnl Svcs, *Perm. Emp Agcy*
Southern Oregon Temporary, *Temp. Agcy*
Talent Tree Staffng, *Perm. Emp Agcy*
Woodworth Intl Grp, *Exec Srch*

Pennsylvania

ACS & Assoc., *Exec Srch*
Acsys Resrcs, *Perm. Emp Agcy*
Adecco, *Temp. Agcy*
Advance Recruitng Svcs, *Exec Srch*
Advanced Technlgy Resrcs, *Exec Srch*
Glen Alan & Assoc., *Exec Srch*
Alexander Persnnl Assoc., *Exec Srch*
All Staffng, *Perm. Emp Agcy*
Allegheny Persnnl Svcs, *Temp. Agcy*
American Staffing Resrcs, *Temp. Agcy*
ASAP Staffng, *Perm. Emp Agcy*
Atomic Persnnl, *Exec Srch*
Barton Persnnl Syst., *Exec Srch*
Becker Temp. Svcs, *Perm. Emp Agcy*
T.W. Boris Assn, *Exec Srch*
CMIS, *Exec Srch*
Career Concepts Staff Svcs, *Exec Srch*
Charly's Temp. Svcs, *Temp. Agcy*
Rich Christine Assoc., *Exec Srch*
Churchill & Affiliates, *Exec Srch*
COREStaff, *Temp. Agcy*
DiCenzo Persnnl Specialists, *Perm. Emp Agcy*
Dunhill Prof'l Srch, *Exec Srch*
Dunn Assoc., *Exec Srch*
Employment Corp of America, *Perm. Emp Agcy*
Executive Avail-A-Search, *Exec Srch*
Executive Mrktng Svcs, *Career/Outplacemnt*
Focus Persnnl Assoc., *Exec Srch*
FORTUNE Grp Intl, *Exec Srch*
The GMW Grp, *Exec Srch*
J.H. Glass & Assoc., *Exec Srch*
Garrick Hall & Assoc., *Exec Srch*
Hallmark Persnnl/Able Temps, *Perm. Emp Agcy*
The Hastings Grp, *Exec Srch*
Human Assets, *Temp. Agcy*
Human Resource Solut'ns, *Exec Srch*
Interim Persnnl, *Temp. Agcy*
Nancy Jackson, *Exec Srch*
Jefferson-Ross Assoc., *Exec Srch*
Kathy Karr Persnnl, *Perm. Emp Agcy*
Mgmt. Recrtrs Intl, *Exec Srch*
Mgmt. Recrtrs of DE Cnty/CompuSrch, *Exec Srch*
Mgmt. Recrtrs of Lehigh Vly/CompuSrch, *Exec Srch*
Mgmt. Recrtrs of Philadelphia/ CompuSrch, *Exec Srch*
George Martin Exec Srch, *Exec Srch*
Rob McClure Ltd., *Exec Srch*
Metro Persnnl, *Temp. Agcy*
The Morris Grp, *Exec Srch*
Northeast Agri Emp. Svc, *Perm. Emp Agcy*
Olsten Staff Svcs, *Temp. Agcy*
LaMonte Owens, *Exec Srch*
Pancoast Temp. Svcs, *Temp. Agcy*
Probe Technlgy, *Exec Srch*
R.H.A. Exec Persnnl Svcs, *Exec Srch*
Alan Raeburn Consltnts, *Exec Srch*
Rice Cohen Intl, *Exec Srch*
The Richards Grp, *Exec Srch*
S-H-S Intl, *Perm. Emp Agcy*
Sales Consltnts of Newtown, *Exec Srch*
Tom Sawchak Action of PA, *Perm. Emp Agcy*
Select Persnnl, *Perm. Emp Agcy*
Snelling Persnnl Svcs, *Temp. Agcy*
Snelling Persnnl Svcs, *Exec Srch*
Spectrum Consltnts/Retail Recrtrs, *Exec Srch*
Strauss Persnnl, *Perm. Emp Agcy*
TRC Staff Svcs, *Temp. Agcy*
TAC Staff Svcs, *Temp. Agcy*
Tandem Persnnl, *Temp. Agcy*
Tell/Com Recrtrs, *Exec Srch*
Todays Temporary, *Temp. Agcy*
W.G. Tucker & Assoc., *Exec Srch*
Uniforce Temp. Svcs, *Temp. Agcy*
United Employment, *Perm. Emp Agcy*
Whittlesey & Assoc., *Exec Srch*

Rhode Island

Aquidneck Emp. Svc, *Perm. Emp Agcy*
Career Consltnts, *Exec Srch*
Colony Persnnl Assoc., *Perm. Emp Agcy*
Kelly Svcs, *Temp. Agcy*
Albert Lee & Assoc., *Exec Srch*
Mgmt. Recrtrs Intl, *Exec Srch*
Norrell Svcs, *Temp. Agcy*
Pro Srch, *Exec Srch*
Sales Consltnts of RI, *Exec Srch*
Storti Assoc., *Exec Srch*
Sullivan & Cogliano, *Exec Srch*
TAC Staff Svcs, *Temp. Agcy*

South Carolina

Dunhill Persnnl of St. Andrews, *Perm. Emp Agcy*
Eastern Persnnl Svcs, *Exec Srch*
Evers Persnnl Srch, *Exec Srch*
FORTUNE Persnnl Consltnts of Columbia, *Exec Srch*
Charles Foster Staffng, *Temp. Agcy*
Jerman Persnnl Svcs, *Temp. Agcy*
Mgmt. Recrtrs of Columbia, *Exec Srch*
Mgmt. Recrtrs of Rck Hill, *Exec Srch*
Miller & Assoc., *Exec Srch*
The Persnnl Netwrk, *Exec Srch*
Phillips Resource Grp, *Exec Srch*
Roper Svcs, *Temp. Agcy*
Sales Consltnts/Mgmt. Recrtrs of Greenville, *Exec Srch*
Smith Temps/Smith Persnnl, *Temp. Agcy*
Staffing Solut'ns, *Temp. Agcy*

South Dakota

Careers Unlimtd, *Perm. Emp Agcy*
Olsten Staff Svcs, *Temp. Agcy*
Snelling Persnnl Svcs, *Perm. Emp Agcy*

Tennessee

A-1 Staffing & Persnnl, *Temp. Agcy*
Anderson McIntyre Persnnl Svcs, *Exec Srch*
Bissonette & Assoc., *Exec Srch*
Engineer One, *Perm. Emp Agcy*
Express Persnnl Svcs, *Perm. Emp Agcy*
Hester & Assoc., *Exec Srch*
Kelly Svcs, *Temp. Agcy*
Mgmt. Recrtrs Intl, *Exec Srch*
Mgmt. Recrtrs of Chattanooga, *Exec Srch*
Manpower, *Temp. Agcy*
W.R. McLeod & Assoc., *Exec Srch*
Persnnl Link, *Exec Srch*
Pharm Temp Pharmacy Persnnl/Opti Temp/Den Temp, *Temp. Agcy*
Sales Consltnts, *Exec Srch*
Sales Consltnts of Nashville, *Exec Srch*
Technical Resource Assoc., *Exec Srch*

Texas

ABA Exec Srch, *Exec Srch*
Ackerman Johnson, *Exec Srch*
Action Persnnl, *Temp. Agcy*
Agri-LC, *Exec Srch*
American Resrcs, *Exec Srch*
Andrews-Carter Persnnl, *Exec Srch*
Aware Affiliates Persnnl, *Perm. Emp Agcy*
Babich & Assoc., *Perm. Emp Agcy*
Best/World Assoc., *Exec Srch*
BestStaff Svcs, *Perm. Emp Agcy*
Bilson & Hazen Intl, *Exec Srch*
Martin Birnbach & Assoc., *Exec Srch*
Boles & Assoc., *Exec Srch*
Brainpower Persnnl Agcy, *Perm. Emp Agcy*
Brooklea & Assoc., *Exec Srch*
Buckley Grp, *Exec Srch*
Bullock Persnnl, *Perm. Emp Agcy*
Bundy-Stewart Assoc., *Exec Srch*
Continental Persnnl, *Perm. Emp Agcy*
Corporate Srch, *Exec Srch*
Creative Staff Svcs, *Temp. Agcy*
Dallas Emp. Svc, *Perm. Emp Agcy*
Damon & Assoc., *Exec Srch*
Diversified Temps, *Temp. Agcy*
Dunhill Prof'l Srch, *Exec Srch*
Eissler & Assoc., *Exec Srch*
The Elsworth Grp, *Exec Srch*
Employee Sources, *Exec Srch*
Evins Persnnl Consltnts of Killeen, *Perm. Emp Agcy*
Executive Srch Consltnts, *Exec Srch*
Executive Srch Persnnl, *Exec Srch*
Express Persnnl Svcs, *Perm. Emp Agcy*
Otis Faulkner & Assoc., *Exec Srch*
Fox-Morris Assoc., *Exec Srch*
Abel Gonzalez & Assoc., *Exec Srch*
Griffin Anderson & Assoc., *Exec Srch*
Haragan Assoc., *Exec Srch*
Healthcare Recrtrs Intl, *Exec Srch*
Healthcare Recrtrs of Houston, *Exec Srch*
Hunter & Michaels, *Exec Srch*
Hyman & Assoc., *Exec Srch*
Inside Track, *Exec Srch*
Job Market Persnnl Agcy, *Perm. Emp Agcy*
Kenzer Corp, *Exec Srch*
Kristan Intl Exec Srch, *Exec Srch*
Loewenstein & Assoc., *Exec Srch*
Lusk & Assoc. Persnnl, *Exec Srch*
Mgmt. Recrtrs Intl, *Exec Srch*
Mgmt. Recrtrs of Dallas, *Exec Srch*
Marquess & Assoc., *Perm. Emp Agcy*
McDuffy-Edwards, *Exec Srch*
McKinley•Arend Intl, *Exec Srch*
Metro Careers, *Exec Srch*
Noll HR Svcs, *Exec Srch*
Olsten Staff Svcs, *Temp. Agcy*
The Pailin Grp, *Exec Srch*
Pate Resrcs Grp, *Exec Srch*
Patterson & Assoc., *Exec Srch*
The Persnnl Office, *Exec Srch*
Phoenix Staffng, *Exec Srch*
Pro Staff Persnnl Svcs, *Temp. Agcy*
Professional Srch Consltnts, *Contract Svc*
Professions Today, *Perm. Emp Agcy*
Redstone & Assoc., *Exec Srch*
Remedy Intelligent Staffng, *Perm. Emp Agcy*
Resource Recrtrs, *Perm. Emp Agcy*
Resource Staffng, *Contract Svc*
Bart Roberson & Co, *Exec Srch*
Roth Young Persnnl Svcs, *Exec Srch*
Anne Sadovsky & Co, *Temp. Agcy*
Sales Consltnts of Houston, *Exec Srch*
Sales Recrtrs of Houston, *Exec Srch*
Salinas & Assoc. Persnnl, *Exec Srch*
Search Com, *Exec Srch*
Select Staff, *Exec Srch*
Snelling Persnnl Svcs, *Perm. Emp Agcy*
Snelling Persnnl Svcs, *Exec Srch*
Solutions, *Exec Srch*
Staff Extension, *Exec Srch*
Strategic Outsourcing Corp, *Exec Srch*
TSP Persnnl Svcs, *Perm. Emp Agcy*
TAD Tech. Svcs, *Contract Svc*
Tarrant Cnty Emp. Netwrk, *Perm. Emp Agcy*
Tech-Net, *Exec Srch*
Texas Persnnl, *Exec Srch*
Todays Temporary, *Temp. Agcy*
Total Temp. Svcs, *Temp. Agcy*
Valpers, *Exec Srch*
Dick Van Vliet & Assoc., *Exec Srch*
Vick & Assoc./Recruiters Online Netwrk, *Exec Srch*
Darryl Vincent & Assoc., *Exec Srch*
Vinson & Assoc., *Perm. Emp Agcy*
Watkins & Assoc., *Exec Srch*
Rob Wesson & Assoc., *Exec Srch*
Western Temp. Svc, *Temp. Agcy*
Wheeler, Moore & Elam Co, *Exec Srch*
Windsor Consltnts, *Exec Srch*

Utah

Deeco Intl, *Perm. Emp Agcy*
Mgmt. Recrtrs Intl, *Exec Srch*

Vermont

Marketsearch Assoc., *Exec Srch*
Triad Temp. Svcs, *Temp. Agcy*

Virginia

A Better Resume, *Career/Outplacemnt*
Alpha Omega Resrcs, *Perm. Emp Agcy*
Bent Assoc., *Exec Srch*
Billie Summers & Assoc., *Exec Srch*
Corporate Connection Exec. Srch Firm
Carol Day & Assoc., *Exec Srch*
Dow Persnnl, *Perm. Emp Agcy*
Effective Staffng, *Exec Srch*
Executive Sales Srch, *Exec Srch*
Haslowe Persnnl, *Exec Srch*
HATCH Mrktng Syst., *Perm. Emp Agcy*
Hispanic Committee of VA, *Perm. Emp Agcy*
Information Specialists Co, *Exec Srch*
Kogen Persnnl, *Exec Srch*
Lee Staffing Resrcs, *Exec Srch*
Mgmt. Recrtrs Intl, *Exec Srch*
Mgmt. Recrtrs of McLean, *Exec Srch*
Mgmt. Recrtrs of Roanoke, *Exec Srch*
Manpower Temp. Svcs, *Temp. Agcy*
The McCormick Grp, *Exec Srch*

SCIENTIFIC

SECRETARIAL

Nesco Svc Co, *Perm. Emp Agcy*
Norrell Temp. Svcs of CA, *Temp. Agcy*
Officemates5/Daystar Temp. Svcs, *Perm. Emp Agcy*
Olsten Staff Svcs, *Temp. Agcy*
Onyx Persnnl Svcs, *Perm. Emp Agcy*
Pacific Srch Grp, *Exec Srch*
Personalized Placemnt Agcy, *Temp. Agcy*
Premier Persnnl Svcs, *Temp. Agcy*
Presidio Persnnl, *Temp. Agcy*
Prestige Persnnl, *Perm. Emp Agcy*
PrideStaff, *Temp. Agcy*
Pro Staff Persnnl Svcs, *Perm. Emp Agcy*
ProSearch & Assoc., *Exec Srch*
Quality Imaging Svcs, *Temp. Agcy*
Questemps, *Temp. Agcy*
Reliance Staff Svcs, *Perm. Emp Agcy*
Remedy Intelligent Staffng, *Temp. Agcy*
Resource Persnnl Svcs, *Temp. Agcy*
Royal Staff Svcs, *Exec Srch*
Russell Staffing Resrcs, *Perm. Emp Agcy*
San Diego Persnnl & Employment, *Temp. Agcy*
Santa Barbara Plcmnt, *Perm. Emp Agcy*
Select Persnnl Svcs, *Temp. Agcy*
David Sharp & Assoc., *Perm. Emp Agcy*
Sharp Persnnl & Srch, *Exec Srch*
Snelling Persnnl Svcs, *Perm. Emp Agcy*
Spectrum Temp. Employees, *Temp. Agcy*
Strategic Staffng, *Temp. Agcy*
Sun Persnnl Svcs, *Temp. Agcy*
TLC Staffng, *Temp. Agcy*
TRC Staff Svcs, *Perm. Emp Agcy*
TAC Staff Svcs, *Temp. Agcy*
TAD Resrcs Intl, *Perm. Emp Agcy*
Talent Tree Staffng, *Perm. Emp Agcy*
Temps Unlimtd, *Temp. Agcy*
Thomas Staffng, *Temp. Agcy*
Thor Temp. Svcs, *Temp. Agcy*
TOD Staffng, *Exec Srch*
Today Persnnl, *Perm. Emp Agcy*
Trans U.S., *Perm. Emp Agcy*
Truex Assoc., *Exec Srch*
The Truman Agcy, Persnnl Specialists, *Perm. Emp Agcy*
UAW Labor Emp. & Training Corp, *Perm. Emp Agcy*
United Persnnl, *Temp. Agcy*
United Staff Solut'ns, *Exec Srch*
United/Corestaff Staff Svcs, *Perm. Emp Agcy*
Victor Valley Persnnl Agcy, *Perm. Emp Agcy*
Volt Temp. Svcs, *Temp. Agcy*
Western Staff Svcs, *Temp. Agcy*
The Windsor Grp, *Perm. Emp Agcy*
Wollborg-Michelson Persnnl, *Perm. Emp Agcy*
Amy Zimmerman & Assoc., *Perm. Emp Agcy*

Colorado

A to Z Bus. Svcs, *Perm. Emp Agcy*
Absolute Emp. Svcs, *Perm. Emp Agcy*
Adecco, *Temp. Agcy*
Ahrnsbrak & Assoc., *Perm. Emp Agcy*
BankTemps, *Temp. Agcy*
Casey Svcs, *Exec Srch*
COREStaff Svcs, *Perm. Emp Agcy*
Creative Career Connections, *Career/Outplacemnt*
Eagle Valley Temps, *Temp. Agcy*
Eleventh Hour Staff Svcs, *Perm. Emp Agcy*
Executemps, *Temp. Agcy*
40 Plus of CO, *Career/Outplacemnt*
Interim Persnnl Svcs, *Temp. Agcy*
JobSearch, *Temp. Agcy*
Kelly Svcs, *Temp. Agcy*
Kelly Tech. Svcs, *Temp. Agcy*
LD Placemnts, *Perm. Emp Agcy*
Manpower Intl, *Temp. Agcy*
Norrell Temp. Svcs, *Temp. Agcy*
Office Specialists, *Temp. Agcy*
Olsten Staff Svcs, *Temp. Agcy*
SOS Staff Svcs, *Temp. Agcy*
Snelling Persnnl Svcs, *Exec Srch*
Stivers Temp. Persnnl, *Temp. Agcy*
TPM Staff Svc, *Temp. Agcy*
Talent Tree Staffng, *Perm. Emp Agcy*
Terry Persnnl, *Perm. Emp Agcy*
Todays Temporary, *Temp. Agcy*
Western Staff Svcs, *Temp. Agcy*

Connecticut

Admiral Staff Svcs, *Temp. Agcy*
Advanced Plcmnt, *Temp. Agcy*
CGS Staff Svcs, *Temp. Agcy*
Charter Persnnl Svcs, *Exec Srch*
Corporate Staff Solut'ns, *Temp. Agcy*
Diversified Emp. Svcs, *Perm. Emp Agcy*
Employment Opport., *Perm. Emp Agcy*
Impact Persnnl, *Temp. Agcy*
Intertec Persnnl, *Temp. Agcy*
Jobsource, *Perm. Emp Agcy*
Manpower, *Temp. Agcy*
McIntyre Assoc., *Temp. Agcy*
The McKnight Grp, *Exec Srch*
Office Svcs of CT, *Perm. Emp Agcy*
Paramount Resrcs, *Perm. Emp Agcy*
Western Staff Svcs, *Temp. Agcy*
Workforce One, *Perm. Emp Agcy*

Delaware

Caldwell Staff Svcs, *Perm. Emp Agcy*
Horizons Resrcs, *Perm. Emp Agcy*
The Placers, *Exec Srch*

District of Columbia

Admin. Assist./Hire Standard Staffng, *Perm. Emp Agcy*
Best Temps, *Temp. Agcy*
Career Blazers Persnnl, *Perm. Emp Agcy*
K.M.S. Assoc., *Perm. Emp Agcy*
Norrell Svcs, *Temp. Agcy*
Potomac Persnnl, *Perm. Emp Agcy*
Sigman & Summerfield Assoc., *Perm. Emp Agcy*
Tangent Corp, *Exec Srch*
Temporary Staffng, *Temp. Agcy*
TempWorld Staff Svcs, *Temp. Agcy*
Whitman Assoc., *Perm. Emp Agcy*

Florida

AAA Employment, *Perm. Emp Agcy*
AccuTech, *Contract Svc*
Active Prof'ls, *Exec Srch*
The Addstaff Netwrk, *Perm. Emp Agcy*
Adecco, *Temp. Agcy*
Alpha Persnnl/Alpha Temps, *Perm. Emp Agcy*
Ambiance Persnnl, *Exec Srch*
American Exec Srch, *Exec Srch*
Availability, *Perm. Emp Agcy*
B&B Persnnl, *Perm. Emp Agcy*
Belmont Training & Employment, *Perm. Emp Agcy*
Bryan & Assoc./Worknet, Etc., *Exec Srch*
Career Planners, *Perm. Emp Agcy*
Careers USA, *Temp. Agcy*
CareerXchange, *Temp. Agcy*
Carrier's Career Svc, *Career/Outplacemnt*
Central Florida Legal-Ease, *Perm. Emp Agcy*
Crew Unlimtd, *Perm. Emp Agcy*
Custom Staffng, *Temp. Agcy*
DGA Persnnl Grp, *Exec Srch*
Donbar Svc Corp, *Temp. Agcy*
Employers' Assistant, *Temp. Agcy*
Five Star Temporary, *Temp. Agcy*
Future Force Persnnl, *Temp. Agcy*
Girl Friday Persnnl, *Temp. Agcy*
HR Prof'l Consltnts, *Exec Srch*
Hastings & Hastings Persnnl Consltnts, *Temp. Agcy*
Interim Persnnl, *Temp. Agcy*
Kelly Svcs, *Temp. Agcy*
Norrell Svcs, *Temp. Agcy*
Office Ours, *Temp. Agcy*
Officemates5 Persnnl, *Perm. Emp Agcy*
Olsten Staff Svcs, *Temp. Agcy*
O'Quin Persnnl, *Temp. Agcy*
Persnnl One, *Perm. Emp Agcy*
Pro Staff Persnnl Svcs, *Temp. Agcy*
Profes. Staffing/Able Body Temp. Svcs, *Contract Svc*
Progressive Persnnl, *Temp. Agcy*
The Reserves Netwrk, *Temp. Agcy*
Linda Robins & Assoc., *Temp. Agcy*
Secretaries Unlimtd, *Temp. Agcy*
Seniorstaff, *Temp. Agcy*
Snelling Persnnl Svcs, *Temp. Agcy*
Spalding's Emp. Svc, *Perm. Emp Agcy*
Staffing Svcs Grp, *Perm. Emp Agcy*
Staffing Solut'ns by Persnnl One, *Perm. Emp Agcy*
Aaron Stewart Persnnl, *Exec Srch*
TRC Staff Svcs, *Temp. Agcy*
Todays Temporary, *Temp. Agcy*
Victoria & Assoc. Persnnl, *Perm. Emp Agcy*
Western Staff Svcs, *Temp. Agcy*

Georgia

A-OK Persnnl, *Perm. Emp Agcy*
A-1 Svc Persnnl, *Perm. Emp Agcy*
AAA Employment, *Perm. Emp Agcy*
Access Persnnl Svcs, *Perm. Emp Agcy*
Accurate Medical Placemnt/The Accurate Grp, *Exec Srch*
All-Star Temp. & Emp. Svcs, *Temp. Agcy*
Augusta Staffing Assoc., *Perm. Emp Agcy*
Boreham Intl, *Exec Srch*
Caldwell Svcs, *Temp. Agcy*
Cocounsel, *Perm. Emp Agcy*
Corporate Srch Consltnts, *Exec Srch*
Dynamic People, *Temp. Agcy*
Elite Staff Svcs, *Perm. Emp Agcy*
Express Persnnl Svcs, *Temp. Agcy*
Express Persnnl Svcs, *Exec Srch*
First Pro, *Temp. Agcy*
Kelly Svcs, *Temp. Agcy*
Manpower Temp. Svcs, *Temp. Agcy*
Jim Nixon & Assoc., *Exec Srch*
Norrell Svcs, *Temp. Agcy*
Office Specialists, *Temp. Agcy*
Officemates5/DayStar Temp. Svcs, *Perm. Emp Agcy*
Olsten Staff Svcs, *Temp. Agcy*
Pathfinders, *Perm. Emp Agcy*
Persnnl At Law, *Temp. Agcy*
Priority 1 Staff Svcs, *Temp. Agcy*
Quality Temp. Svc, *Temp. Agcy*
Randstad Staff Svcs, *Temp. Agcy*
Randstad Staff Svcs, *Perm. Emp Agcy*
Snelling Persnnl Svcs, *Exec Srch*
Southern Emp. Svc, *Perm. Emp Agcy*
Staffing Resrcs, *Perm. Emp Agcy*
TRC Staff Svcs, *Temp. Agcy*
Temporary Specialties, *Temp. Agcy*
TempWorld Staff Svcs, *Temp. Agcy*
Todays Temporary, *Temp. Agcy*
WPPS Software Staffng, *Perm. Emp Agcy*
Western Staff Svcs, *Temp. Agcy*

Hawaii

Altres Staffng, *Temp. Agcy*
Kelly Svcs, *Temp. Agcy*
Olsten Staff Svcs, *Temp. Agcy*

Illinois

A.B.A. Placemnts/A.B.A. Temps, *Perm. Emp Agcy*
ASI Persnnl, *Perm. Emp Agcy*
Accurate Persnnl, *Perm. Emp Agcy*
AccuStaff Inc., *Temp. Agcy*
Adecco, *Temp. Agcy*
Affiliated Persnnl Consltnts, *Perm. Emp Agcy*
American Engineering Co, *Exec Srch*
Assured Staffng, *Temp. Agcy*
Banner Persnnl, *Perm. Emp Agcy*
Bell Persnnl, *Perm. Emp Agcy*
Bevelle & Assoc., *Exec Srch*
Britannia, *Exec Srch*
Corporate Resrcs, Ltd./C.R. Temps, *Perm. Emp Agcy*
DayStar Temp. Svcs, *Temp. Agcy*
Dynamic People, *Temp. Agcy*
The Esquire Staffing Grp, *Perm. Emp Agcy*
Eve Recrtrs Ltd., *Perm. Emp Agcy*
Fellows Plcmnt, *Temp. Agcy*
First Staffng, *Perm. Emp Agcy*
Furst Staff Svcs, *Temp. Agcy*
David Gomez & Assoc., *Exec Srch*
H/R Srch, *Perm. Emp Agcy*
Human Resource Connection, *Perm. Emp Agcy*
Illinois Veterans Leadership Program, *Career/Outplacemnt*
Interstaff, *Temp. Agcy*
Interviewing Consltnts, *Perm. Emp Agcy*
Arlene Leff & Assoc., *Exec Srch*
Lomack Agcy, *Temp. Agcy*
MBP Persnnl, *Exec Srch*
MacIntyre Emp. Svc, *Perm. Emp Agcy*
Mack & Assoc., *Temp. Agcy*
Maramax Persnnl, *Perm. Emp Agcy*
McCullum Assoc., *Temp. Agcy*
Merit Persnnl, *Perm. Emp Agcy*
Mount Prospect Emp. Svc, *Perm. Emp Agcy*
The Murphy Grp, *Perm. Emp Agcy*
NJW & Assoc., *Temp. Agcy*
Norrell Svcs, *Temp. Agcy*
Office Ours, *Temp. Agcy*
OfficeTeam, *Perm. Emp Agcy*
The Opport. Grp, *Perm. Emp Agcy*
PS, *Perm. Emp Agcy*
Paige Persnnl, *Perm. Emp Agcy*
Persnnl Connection, *Perm. Emp Agcy*
Persnnl Placemnt Consltnts, *Perm. Emp Agcy*
Prestige Emp. Svcs, *Perm. Emp Agcy*
ProSearch Plus, *Exec Srch*
Quantum Prof'l Srch/Quantum Staff Svcs, *Exec Srch*
Remedy Intelligent Staffng, *Temp. Agcy*
Right Svcs, *Temp. Agcy*
SER Bus. And Tech. Institute, *Perm. Emp Agcy*
Select Staffng, *Perm. Emp Agcy*
Seville Temp. Svcs, *Temp. Agcy*
Shannonwood Staffers, *Temp. Agcy*
Snelling Persnnl Svcs, *Exec Srch*
Staffing Consltnts, *Perm. Emp Agcy*
Staffing Team Intl, *Temp. Agcy*
Tempfleet, *Temp. Agcy*
Temporary Assoc., *Temp. Agcy*
Walsh & Co, *Perm. Emp Agcy*
West Persnnl, *Perm. Emp Agcy*
Working World, *Temp. Agcy*

Indiana

AccuStaff, *Temp. Agcy*
Adecco, *Temp. Agcy*
Angola Persnnl Svcs, *Perm. Emp Agcy*
Dunhill Staffing Syst., *Temp. Agcy*
First Call Temp. Svcs, *Temp. Agcy*
Hunter-Lawyer Persnnl, *Perm. Emp Agcy*
Job Placemnt Svc, *Perm. Emp Agcy*
Kelly Svcs, *Temp. Agcy*
Life Emp. Svc, *Perm. Emp Agcy*
Norrell Staff Svcs, *Temp. Agcy*
Olsten Staff Svcs, *Temp. Agcy*
Perry Persnnl Plus, *Perm. Emp Agcy*
Persnnl Mgmt., *Temp. Agcy*

Snelling & Snelling, *Perm. Emp Agcy*
Star Staffng, *Temp. Agcy*
TRC Staff Svcs, *Temp. Agcy*
Time Svcs, *Perm. Emp Agcy*
Unique, *Exec Srch*
Warrick Cnty Emp. & Training Ctr, *Career/Outplacemnt*
Western Staff Svcs, *Temp. Agcy*

Iowa

Blanchard Svcs, *Temp. Agcy*
Burton Placemnt Svcs, *Exec Srch*
Byrnes & Rupkey, *Exec Srch*
CSI Employment, *Exec Srch*
Cambridge Staffng, *Perm. Emp Agcy*
Executive Srch Assoc., *Exec Srch*
Helping Hands Temp. Svc, *Temp. Agcy*
Kelly Svcs, *Temp. Agcy*
Persnnl, *Exec Srch*
Salem Mngmnt dba Rudy Salem Staff Svcs, *Temp. Agcy*
Sedona Staff Svcs, *Exec Srch*
Staff Mgmt., *Contract Svc*

Kansas

Alternative Staffing & Persnnl, *Temp. Agcy*
Business Specialists, *Perm. Emp Agcy*
Dunhill Persnnl, *Exec Srch*
Eleventh Hour Staff Svcs, *Temp. Agcy*
Kansas Workforce, *Temp. Agcy*
Key Staffng, *Temp. Agcy*
Morgan Hunter Corp Srch, *Perm. Emp Agcy*
Uniforce Staff Svcs, *Temp. Agcy*
Western Staff Svcs, *Temp. Agcy*
Wichita Bar Assn Legal Placemnt Svc, *Perm. Emp Agcy*

Kentucky

Belcan Staff Svcs, *Perm. Emp Agcy*
C.M. Mngmnt Svcs, *Perm. Emp Agcy*
Manpower, *Temp. Agcy*
OfficeTeam, *Temp. Agcy*
Precision Staffng, *Perm. Emp Agcy*

Louisiana

Keenan Staffng, *Temp. Agcy*
Olsten Persnnl/Briggs Legal Staffng, *Perm. Emp Agcy*
Talley & Assoc./Talley Temps, *Exec Srch*
Technical Resource Staff Svcs, *Temp. Agcy*
Western Staff Svcs, *Temp. Agcy*

Maine

Accomplished Prof'ls, *Temp. Agcy*
ASK, *Temp. Agcy*
At Work Persnnl, *Temp. Agcy*
Tempo Emp. Svc, *Temp. Agcy*

Maryland

Adecco, *Temp. Agcy*
Contemporaries, *Temp. Agcy*
Employer Employee Exchange, *Exec Srch*
Excel Temp. Svcs, *Temp. Agcy*
Marge Fox Persnnl Svcs, *Temp. Agcy*
Interim Persnnl, *Temp. Agcy*
Merit Emp. Agcy, *Perm. Emp Agcy*
Onsite Commercial Staffng, *Perm. Emp Agcy*
Sparks Persnnl Svcs, *Temp. Agcy*
TAD Staff Svcs, *Temp. Agcy*
Temps & Co, *Temp. Agcy*
Virtual Staff Svcs, *Perm. Emp Agcy*

Massachusetts

Ability Srch of N.E., *Perm. Emp Agcy*
Adecco, *Temp. Agcy*
Arthur-Blair Assoc., *Perm. Emp Agcy*
Brattle Temps, *Temp. Agcy*
Cleary Consltnts, *Perm. Emp Agcy*
Corporate Staff Solut'ns, *Temp. Agcy*
Discovery Persnnl, *Perm. Emp Agcy*
Dunhill Staffing Syst., *Temp. Agcy*
Franklin-Pierce Assoc., *Perm. Emp Agcy*
Harvest Persnnl, *Exec Srch*
Interim Persnnl, *Temp. Agcy*
Johnson & Hill Staff Svc, *Temp. Agcy*
Kelly Svcs, *Temp. Agcy*
Kennison & Assoc., *Temp. Agcy*
L&L Temps, *Temp. Agcy*
Lane Emp. Svc, *Perm. Emp Agcy*
John Leonard Persnnl Assoc., *Perm. Emp Agcy*
Manpower, *Temp. Agcy*
Mass Temps, *Temp. Agcy*
Need Persnnl Plcmnt, *Temp. Agcy*
New Boston Select Staffng, *Perm. Emp Agcy*
New England Persnnl, *Perm. Emp Agcy*
New Perspectives Persnnl, *Temp. Agcy*
Norrell Staff Svcs, *Contract Svc*
Office Specialists, *Temp. Agcy*
OfficeTeam, *Temp. Agcy*
Olsten Staff Svcs, *Temp. Agcy*
Pro Staff, *Temp. Agcy*
Propos Assoc., *Perm. Emp Agcy*
Quality Persnnl, *Perm. Emp Agcy*
Reardon Assoc., *Perm. Emp Agcy*
Routhier Placemnt Specialists, *Perm. Emp Agcy*
Selectemps, *Temp. Agcy*
Selective Office Staffng, *Perm. Emp Agcy*
The Skill Bureau, *Perm. Emp Agcy*
Snelling Persnnl Svcs, *Perm. Emp Agcy*
Spectra Prof'l Srch/Spectra Temps, *Perm. Emp Agcy*
TAC Staff Svcs, *Temp. Agcy*
TAD Staff Svcs, *Temp. Agcy*
Tech Resource, *Contract Svc*
Total Tech. Svcs, *Perm. Emp Agcy*
Tricor Assoc., *Temp. Agcy*
Unlimited Opport., *Temp. Agcy*
Volt Svcs Grp, *Temp. Agcy*
The Work Place, *Career/Outplacemnt*

Michigan

Accountemps/Officeteam, *Temp. Agcy*
Alternative Staff, *Temp. Agcy*
Career Quest, *Perm. Emp Agcy*
Davidson, Laird & Assoc., *Exec Srch*
Day Persnnl dba Dorothy Day Persnnl - MI, Perm Emp Agcy
Dynamic People, *Temp. Agcy*
Express Persnnl Svcs, *Temp. Agcy*
Grosse Pointe Employment, *Perm. Emp Agcy*
William Howard Agcy, *Perm. Emp Agcy*
Human Resrcs Emp. Svcs, *Perm. Emp Agcy*
Interim Persnnl, *Temp. Agcy*
Kelly Svcs, *Temp. Agcy*
METROSTAFF, *Exec Srch*
Michigan Srch Plus, *Exec Srch*
Nationwide Career Netwrk, *Perm. Emp Agcy*
Nustar Temp. Svcs, *Temp. Agcy*
Office Staffing Recruitng, *Exec Srch*
Permanent Staff Co, *Perm. Emp Agcy*
Persnnl At Law, *Temp. Agcy*
Preferred Emp. Planning, *Perm. Emp Agcy*
Professional Persnnl Consltnts Intl, *Exec Srch*
Snelling Persnnl Svcs, *Perm. Emp Agcy*
Sygnetics, *Temp. Agcy*
TRC Staff Svcs, *Temp. Agcy*
TEA, *Perm. Emp Agcy*
Total Employee Mgmt., *Temp. Agcy*
Trillium Staffng, *Temp. Agcy*
Unlimited Staff Solut'ns, *Contract Svc*
Venture Mngmnt & Staffng, *Exec Srch*
Workforce, *Temp. Agcy*
Your Preference Referral Netwrk, *Perm. Emp Agcy*

Minnesota

A&B Persnnl, *Perm. Emp Agcy*
Abby Blu, *Temp. Agcy*
Add On Staff Solut'ns, *Temp. Agcy*
Alternative Staffng, *Perm. Emp Agcy*
Diversified Employment, *Perm. Emp Agcy*
Ells Persnnl Syst., *Exec Srch*
Express Persnnl Svcs, *Perm. Emp Agcy*
Firstaff, *Perm. Emp Agcy*
Lynn Temporary, *Temp. Agcy*
Manpower Temp. Svcs, *Temp. Agcy*
Midwest Staff Svcs, *Temp. Agcy*
Secretary & Accnt'g Svc, *Perm. Emp Agcy*
Source Svcs Corp, *Contract Svc*
Staff It Persnnl Svcs, *Temp. Agcy*
Temp Force, *Temp. Agcy*
Jean Thorne, *Temp. Agcy*
Ultimate Srch Unlimtd/Temps Unlimtd, *Perm. Emp Agcy*
West Emp. Solut'ns, *Perm. Emp Agcy*
Working Relationships, *Perm. Emp Agcy*

Mississippi

Andrus Assoc. dba Svc Specialists Ltd., *Perm. Emp Agcy*
Capitol Staff Solut'ns, *Perm. Emp Agcy*
Coats & Coats Persnnl, *Perm. Emp Agcy*
Columbus Persnnl, *Temp. Agcy*
EPSCO Persnnl, *Temp. Agcy*
Laborchex Companies, *Perm. Emp Agcy*
Recruitment & Training of MS, *Perm. Emp Agcy*
Tatum Persnnl, *Perm. Emp Agcy*

Missouri

Accountant Source Temps, *Temp. Agcy*
Adecco, *Temp. Agcy*
L.P. Banning, *Perm. Emp Agcy*
Bestemps, *Perm. Emp Agcy*
Business Persnnl Svcs, *Temp. Agcy*
Deck & Decker Emp. Svc, *Perm. Emp Agcy*
Employer Advantage, *Exec Srch*
ExecuTemps, *Temp. Agcy*
JoDoc Enterprises, *Temp. Agcy*
LandAJob, *Perm. Emp Agcy*
Manpower Temp. Svcs, *Temp. Agcy*
National Physician Placemnt Svcs, *Exec Srch*
Norrell Svcs, *Temp. Agcy*
Olsten Staff Svcs, *Temp. Agcy*
Snelling Persnnl Svcs, *Temp. Agcy*
Snelling Persnnl Svcs, *Perm. Emp Agcy*
Workforce, *Temp. Agcy*

Montana

Express Persnnl, *Perm. Emp Agcy*
Kelly Svcs, *Temp. Agcy*

Nebraska

Adecco, *Temp. Agcy*
Choice Enterprises, *Exec Srch*
Corporate Recrtrs, *Exec Srch*
Donna's Office Svc, *Contract Svc*
Express Persnnl, *Exec Srch*
Kelly Svcs, *Temp. Agcy*
Noll HR Svcs, *Exec Srch*
Outsource II, *Temp. Agcy*
Sharp Persnnl, *Temp. Agcy*

Nevada

Manpower Temp. Svcs, *Temp. Agcy*
Nevada Bus. Svcs, *Career/Outplacemnt*
Talent Tree Staffng, *Perm. Emp Agcy*

New Hampshire

Able 1 Staffng, *Exec Srch*
Barclay Persnnl Syst., *Exec Srch*
Career Connections, *Perm. Emp Agcy*
Central New Hampshire Emp. Svcs, *Perm. Emp Agcy*
Cheshire Emp. Svc, *Temp. Agcy*
Key Persnnl, *Perm. Emp Agcy*
Manpower Temp. Svcs, *Temp. Agcy*
Pelham Prof'l Grp, *Temp. Agcy*
Resource Recruitng/Contemp. Accntnts, *Perm. Emp Agcy*
TAC Staff Svcs, *Temp. Agcy*
Western Staff Svcs, *Temp. Agcy*

New Jersey

A+ Persnnl, *Perm. Emp Agcy*
A Prof'l Edge, *Career/Outplacemnt*
ABC Nationwide Employment, *Perm. Emp Agcy*
Advanced Persnnl, *Perm. Emp Agcy*
Allen Assoc., *Perm. Emp Agcy*
Alliance Consltnts, *Perm. Emp Agcy*
American Staffing Resrcs, *Temp. Agcy*
Andrew Persnnl Svcs, *Perm. Emp Agcy*
Angelord, *Temp. Agcy*
The Ascher Grp, *Exec Srch*
BAI Persnnl Solut'ns, *Exec Srch*
Blake & Assoc. Exec Srch, *Exec Srch*
Careers USA, *Perm. Emp Agcy*
Dunhill Prof'l Srch, *Exec Srch*
Dunhill Temp. Syst., *Temp. Agcy*
Executive Netwrk, *Exec Srch*
Executive Srch, *Exec Srch*
Express Persnnl Svcs, *Perm. Emp Agcy*
Holm Persnnl Consltnts, *Exec Srch*
ITC Temps, *Temp. Agcy*
Impact Persnnl, *Perm. Emp Agcy*
Integro Staff Svcs, *Temp. Agcy*
Joule People Providers, *Perm. Emp Agcy*
Kaye Persnnl, *Temp. Agcy*
Kelly Svcs, *Temp. Agcy*
McDermott Resrcs, *Exec Srch*
Norrell Svcs, *Perm. Emp Agcy*
Officemates5 of Englewood Cliffs/DayStar Temp. Svcs, *Perm. Emp Agcy*
Park Avenue Persnnl, *Perm. Emp Agcy*
Pat's Secretarial Svc, *Temp. Agcy*
Pomerantz Persnnl, *Perm. Emp Agcy*
Premier Persnnl Grp, *Perm. Emp Agcy*
Protocall Bus. Staff Svcs, *Temp. Agcy*
Remedy Intelligent Staffng, *Temp. Agcy*
Rotator Svcs, *Contract Svc*
Arline Simpson Assoc., *Perm. Emp Agcy*
Snelling Persnnl Svcs, *Temp. Agcy*
TRS Staff Solut'ns, *Temp. Agcy*
Temporary Excellence, *Temp. Agcy*
Temps Plus, *Temp. Agcy*
Tenek Corp, *Exec Srch*
Unitemp Temp. Persnnl, *Temp. Agcy*
Winston Staff Svcs, *Temp. Agcy*
Winters & Ross, *Perm. Emp Agcy*

New Mexico

Albuquerque Persnnl, *Perm. Emp Agcy*
CDI Corp, *Contract Svc*
Sanderson Emp. Svc, *Perm. Emp Agcy*
Santa Fe Svcs, *Temp. Agcy*
Snelling Persnnl Svcs, *Exec Srch*

New York

AARP Foundation Senior Community Svc/Employment Program, *Perm. Emp Agcy*
AM & PM Temps, *Temp. Agcy*
Aadams Persnnl Agcy, *Temp. Agcy*
AccuStaff, *Temp. Agcy*
AccuStaff, *Perm. Emp Agcy*
Adam Persnnl, *Perm. Emp Agcy*
Adecco, *Temp. Agcy*
Adele Poston Nurses Registry, *Perm. Emp Agcy*
Advice Persnnl, *Exec Srch*
AMESgroup, *Perm. Emp Agcy*

Arrow Emp. Agcy, *Perm. Emp Agcy*
Asher Persnnl Consltnts, *Perm. Emp Agcy*
Auto Careers, *Perm. Emp Agcy*
Berkel Assoc., *Exec Srch*
Bestemp Temp. Svcs, *Temp. Agcy*
Bevan Resrcs, *Perm. Emp Agcy*
Bevlin Persnnl, *Perm. Emp Agcy*
Bonfield Emp. Agcy, *Perm. Emp Agcy*
The British Connection, *Perm. Emp Agcy*
Brookville Staff Svcs, *Perm. Emp Agcy*
Burns Persnnl, *Exec Srch*
Career Blazers Persnnl, *Perm. Emp Agcy*
Career Objectives Persnnl, *Temp. Agcy*
Chriss Career Limited, *Exec Srch*
Corporate Srch, *Exec Srch*
Seth Diamond Assoc., *Exec Srch*
Maggi Dolan Plcmnt, *Perm. Emp Agcy*
Dunhill Staffing Syst. of Buffalo, *Temp. Agcy*
Eden Persnnl, *Perm. Emp Agcy*
Irwin Edwards Recrtrs, *Perm. Emp Agcy*
Employment Recrtrs Agcy, *Perm. Emp Agcy*
The Emp. Store/TES Technical, *Exec Srch*
Euromonde, *Temp. Agcy*
Extra Help Emp. Svc, *Temp. Agcy*
Fanning Persnnl, *Exec Srch*
Fifth Avenue Emp. Svcs, *Temp. Agcy*
Filcro Persnnl, *Perm. Emp Agcy*
Finest Emp. Agcy, *Perm. Emp Agcy*
Forum Temp. Svcs, *Temp. Agcy*
Friedman Emp. Agcy, *Perm. Emp Agcy*
Ronnie Gale Persnnl Corp, *Exec Srch*
Genesis Emp. Consltnts, *Exec Srch*
Graphic Techniques, *Temp. Agcy*
H&H Temp. Svcs, *Temp. Agcy*
Harbrowe, *Perm. Emp Agcy*
Hart-Merrell Persnnl, *Exec Srch*
Headway Corporate Staff Svcs, *Temp. Agcy*
Hunter Mac & Assoc., *Perm. Emp Agcy*
Hunter Plcmnt, *Exec Srch*
Ideal Persnnl, *Perm. Emp Agcy*
Interim Persnnl, *Temp. Agcy*
Island Srch Grp, *Perm. Emp Agcy*
JDC Assoc., *Perm. Emp Agcy*
Josef Grp Persnnl, *Perm. Emp Agcy*
KPA Grp, *Exec Srch*
Kelly Svcs, *Temp. Agcy*
Magill Assoc., *Exec Srch*
Manpower Temp. Svcs, *Temp. Agcy*
Mar-El Emp. Agcy, *Exec Srch*
Lynn Marshall Persnnl Agcy, *Perm. Emp Agcy*
Medstaff Svcs, *Perm. Emp Agcy*
Metro Resrcs of Rochester, *Temp. Agcy*
Metro Support Grp, *Perm. Emp Agcy*
Metro Persnnl/Metro Nursing Svcs, *Exec Srch*
Milazzo Assoc., *Perm. Emp Agcy*
Morgan-Murray Persnnl/M&M Top Temps, *Temp. Agcy*
National Emp. Database, *Perm. Emp Agcy*
New York-New York Persnnl, *Perm. Emp Agcy*
Norrell Staff Svcs, *Perm. Emp Agcy*
K.A. Nowack Career Specialists, *Perm. Emp Agcy*
Olsten Staff Svcs, *Temp. Agcy*
Optimal Resrcs, *Exec Srch*
The Parks Grp, *Exec Srch*
Paywise, *Temp. Agcy*
Persnnl Svcs Ctr, *Exec Srch*
P.G. Prager Srch Assoc., *Exec Srch*
Preferred Prof'ls, *Temp. Agcy*
Rem Resrcs, *Perm. Emp Agcy*
Remedy Intelligent Staffng, *Temp. Agcy*
Republic Emp. Agcy, *Perm. Emp Agcy*
Response Staff Svcs/Career Advisors, *Exec Srch*
Ribolow Assoc., *Perm. Emp Agcy*
Beth Richman Assoc., *Perm. Emp Agcy*
S.W. Mgmt., *Exec Srch*
Sales Recrtrs Intl *Perm. Emp Agcy*
Sloan Persnnl, *Perm. Emp Agcy*
Snelling Persnnl Svcs, *Exec Srch*
Staff By Manning, *Perm. Emp Agcy*
Staff Managers, *Temp. Agcy*
Stamm Persnnl Agcy, *Perm. Emp Agcy*
Strategic Recruitng, *Exec Srch*
Swing Shift, *Temp. Agcy*
Hillary Taylor Persnnl, *Perm. Emp Agcy*
Temp Force of NY, *Temp. Agcy*
Tempo Svcs, *Perm. Emp Agcy*
Temporary Resource Ctr, *Temp. Agcy*
TemPositions, *Temp. Agcy*
Unique Support Svcs, *Temp. Agcy*
United Persnnl Agcy, *Perm. Emp Agcy*
Vance Persnnl, *Perm. Emp Agcy*
Vantage Staff Svcs, *Temp. Agcy*
Western Staff Svcs, *Temp. Agcy*
Westfield Assoc., *Exec Srch*

North Carolina

A-1 Staffing & Persnnl, *Perm. Emp Agcy*
Accurate Staff Consltnts, *Exec Srch*
AccuStaff Inc., *Temp. Agcy*
Action Staffmasters, *Temp. Agcy*
Action Tech. Staffng, *Temp. Agcy*
Advanced Persnnl Resrcs, *Exec Srch*
Anderson & Daniel Persnnl, *Perm. Emp Agcy*
Caldwell Persnnl Svcs, *Perm. Emp Agcy*
Career Staffng, *Perm. Emp Agcy*
Careers Unlimtd, *Perm. Emp Agcy*
Coastal Temp. Svcs, *Temp. Agcy*
Corporate Staff Consltnts, *Perm. Emp Agcy*
Employment Consltnts, *Contract Svc*
Executive Staff Svcs, *Perm. Emp Agcy*
Express Persnnl Svcs, *Temp. Agcy*
Five Star Staffng, *Temp. Agcy*
Interim Persnnl, *Temp. Agcy*
The Jobs Market, *Perm. Emp Agcy*
Jobs of Fayetteville, *Perm. Emp Agcy*
Kelly Svcs, *Temp. Agcy*
Key Temps, *Temp. Agcy*
Manpower, *Temp. Agcy*
McCain Emp. Agcy, *Temp. Agcy*
Mebane Temp. Svcs, *Temp. Agcy*
Norrell Svcs, *Temp. Agcy*
Office Specialists, *Temp. Agcy*
Olsten Staff Svcs, *Temp. Agcy*
Pro Staff Persnnl Svcs, *Perm. Emp Agcy*
Quality Temp. Svcs, *Temp. Agcy*
Remedy Intelligent Staffng, *Perm. Emp Agcy*
Snelling Persnnl Svcs, *Contract Svc*
Snelling Srch, *Exec Srch*
Sparks Persnnl Svcs, *Exec Srch*
StaffMark, *Temp. Agcy*
Summit Occupational Staffng, *Exec Srch*
Talent Tree Staffng, *Perm. Emp Agcy*
Temporary Staffing Syst., *Temp. Agcy*
Will/Staff Persnnl Svcs, *Temp. Agcy*
Youngblood Staffng, *Perm. Emp Agcy*

North Dakota

Olsten Staff Svcs/Kramer & Assoc./Expressway Persnnl, *Temp. Agcy*
Persnnl Svcs, *Exec Srch*

Ohio

AccuStaff, *Temp. Agcy*
Adecco, *Perm. Emp Agcy*
All Star Persnnl, *Temp. Agcy*
Belcan Staff Svcs, *Temp. Agcy*
CBS Persnnl Svcs, *Perm. Emp Agcy*
Career Connections, *Perm. Emp Agcy*
Champion Persnnl, *Perm. Emp Agcy*
Custom Staffng, *Temp. Agcy*
Delta Design Drafting, *Temp. Agcy*
Eastern Persnnl Svcs, *Perm. Emp Agcy*
Elite Persnnl Agcy, *Perm. Emp Agcy*
Exact Persnnl Specialists, *Perm. Emp Agcy*
Job Express, *Temp. Agcy*
Anne Jones Staffng, *Perm. Emp Agcy*
Kelly Svcs, *Temp. Agcy*
Laine's S.M.G., *Perm. Emp Agcy*
Manpower Temp. Svcs, *Temp. Agcy*
Messina Mngmnt Syst., *Exec Srch*
Palmer Temps/The Palmer Grp, *Temp. Agcy*
Professional Restaffing of OH, *Perm. Emp Agcy*
Quality Plus, *Exec Srch*
Quality Source, *Exec Srch*
Talent Tree Staffng, *Perm. Emp Agcy*
The Target HR Companies, *Temp. Agcy*
TEAM America, *Perm. Emp Agcy*
Temporarily Yours Plcmnt, *Temp. Agcy*

Oklahoma

Ameri Resource, *Exec Srch*
Cherokee Temps, *Temp. Agcy*
Dow Persnnl, *Temp. Agcy*
Express Persnnl Svcs, *Exec Srch*
Rob Half Intl, *Exec Srch*
Interim Persnnl, *Temp. Agcy*
Key Temp. Persnnl, *Temp. Agcy*
Terry Neese Persnnl Agcy, *Exec Srch*
Sooner Placemnt Svc, *Perm. Emp Agcy*
StaffMark, *Temp. Agcy*

Oregon

Able Temp. Svc, *Temp. Agcy*
Barrett Bus. Svcs, *Temp. Agcy*
Employment Trends, *Temp. Agcy*
Express Persnnl Svcs, *Exec Srch*
Kelly Svcs, *Temp. Agcy*
Northwest Temp. & Staff Svcs, *Temp. Agcy*
Office Careers, *Perm. Emp Agcy*
Quest Temp. Svcs, *Temp. Agcy*
Saint Vincent De Paul Employment, *Temp. Agcy*
Talent Tree Staffng, *Perm. Emp Agcy*
Uniforce Staff Svcs, *Temp. Agcy*

Pennsylvania

AA Staff Solut'ns, *Contract Svc*
Adecco, *Temp. Agcy*
Alexander Persnnl Assoc., *Exec Srch*
All Staffng, *Perm. Emp Agcy*
Allegheny Persnnl Svcs, *Temp. Agcy*
ASAP Staffng, *Perm. Emp Agcy*
Becker Temp. Svcs, *Perm. Emp Agcy*
Career Quest Confidential, *Exec Srch*
Charly's Temp. Svcs, *Temp. Agcy*
COREStaff, *Temp. Agcy*
J. Croyle & Assoc., *Perm. Emp Agcy*
DiCenzo Persnnl Specialists, *Perm. Emp Agcy*
Dunhill Prof'l Srch, *Exec Srch*
Merrill Grumer Assoc., *Perm. Emp Agcy*
Hallmark Persnnl/Able Temps, *Perm. Emp Agcy*
Hobbie Temp. Persnnl, *Temp. Agcy*
Interim Persnnl, *Temp. Agcy*
Nancy Jackson, *Exec Srch*
Kathy Karr Persnnl, *Perm. Emp Agcy*
Kelly Svcs, *Temp. Agcy*
Keystaff, *Temp. Agcy*
Marsetta Lane Temp. Svcs, *Temp. Agcy*
Leafstone, *Temp. Agcy*
Legal Srch, *Temp. Agcy*
London Persnnl Svcs, *Perm. Emp Agcy*
J. McManus Assoc., *Perm. Emp Agcy*
Metro Persnnl, *Temp. Agcy*
T R Mumford Assoc., *Perm. Emp Agcy*
Norrell Svcs, *Contract Svc*
Norrell Svcs, *Temp. Agcy*
Olsten Staff Svcs, *Temp. Agcy*
Pancoast Temp. Svcs, *Temp. Agcy*
Placers, *Temp. Agcy*
Powers Persnnl, *Perm. Emp Agcy*
Pratt Persnnl Svcs, *Temp. Agcy*
R.H.A. Exec Persnnl Svcs, *Exec Srch*
The Richards Grp, *Exec Srch*
S-H-S Intl, *Perm. Emp Agcy*
Strauss Persnnl, *Perm. Emp Agcy*
TRC Staff Svcs, *Temp. Agcy*
TAC Staff Svcs, *Temp. Agcy*
Tandem Persnnl, *Temp. Agcy*
Todays Temporary, *Temp. Agcy*
Tops Temps, *Temp. Agcy*
Uni Temp Temp. Svc, *Temp. Agcy*
Uniforce Temp. Svcs, *Temp. Agcy*
Visions Temp. Svc, *Temp. Agcy*
Vogue Persnnl, *Perm. Emp Agcy*
Williford & Assoc./Williford Legal Persnnl, *Temp. Agcy*

Rhode Island

Aquidneck Emp. Svc, *Perm. Emp Agcy*
Colony Persnnl Assoc., *Perm. Emp Agcy*
Kelly Svcs, *Temp. Agcy*
Norrell Svcs, *Temp. Agcy*
Occupations Unlimtd, *Perm. Emp Agcy*
Spectra Temps/Tracey Assoc., *Temp. Agcy*

South Carolina

Carolina Persnnl Svcs, *Temp. Agcy*
Eastern Persnnl Svcs, *Exec Srch*
Charles Foster Staffng, *Temp. Agcy*
Jerman Persnnl Svcs, *Temp. Agcy*
Palace Persnnl Svcs, *Exec Srch*
Pindrum Staff Svc, *Temp. Agcy*
Roper Svcs, *Temp. Agcy*
Smith Temps/Smith Persnnl, *Temp. Agcy*
Snelling Persnnl, *Perm. Emp Agcy*
Staffing Solut'ns, *Temp. Agcy*
StaffMark, *Temp. Agcy*
Transworld Svcs Grp, *Temp. Agcy*

South Dakota

Snelling Persnnl Svcs, *Perm. Emp Agcy*

Tennessee

A-1 Staffing & Persnnl, *Temp. Agcy*
Anderson McIntyre Persnnl Svcs, *Exec Srch*
Arvie Persnnl Svcs, *Temp. Agcy*
B.K. Barnes & Assoc., *Exec Srch*
Gateway Grp Persnnl, *Temp. Agcy*
Kelly Svcs, *Temp. Agcy*
Manpower, *Temp. Agcy*
W.R. McLeod & Assoc., *Exec Srch*
Mega Force, *Temp. Agcy*
Norrell Svcs, *Temp. Agcy*
Olsten Staff Svcs, *Temp. Agcy*
Persnnl Link, *Exec Srch*
Pharm Temp Pharmacy Persnnl/Opti Temp/Den Temp, *Temp. Agcy*
Piercy Emp. Svcs, *Perm. Emp Agcy*
Poplar Emp. Svc, *Perm. Emp Agcy*
Temp Staff, *Temp. Agcy*
Unlimited Staff Solut'ns, *Contract Svc*

Texas

A-1 Persnnl, *Temp. Agcy*
ABC Temps, *Temp. Agcy*
Abilene Emp. Svc, *Perm. Emp Agcy*
Action Persnnl, *Temp. Agcy*
Adecco, *Temp. Agcy*
ADSTAFF Mngmnt & Persnnl Consltnts, *Perm. Emp Agc*
Attorney Resrcs, *Temp. Agcy*

ware Affiliates Persnnl, *Perm. Emp Agcy*
nn Best Elite Temps, *Temp. Agcy*
estStaff Svcs, *Perm. Emp Agcy*
ainpower Persnnl Agcy, *Perm. Emp Agcy*
ooklea & Assoc., *Exec Srch*
illock Persnnl, *Perm. Emp Agcy*
urnett Persnnl Svcs, *Temp. Agcy*
urnett's Staffng, *Perm. Emp Agcy*
ertified Persnnl, *Contract Svc*
ayton Persnnl Svcs, *Temp. Agcy*
olvin Resrcs Grp, *Temp. Agcy*
ontinental Persnnl, *Perm. Emp Agcy*
eative Staff Svcs, *Temp. Agcy*
FM & Assoc., *Exec Srch*
allas Emp. Svc, *Perm. Emp Agcy*
ail Darling Staffing/Darling's Prof'l Desk, *Temp. Agcy*
versified Temps, *Temp. Agcy*
sprit Temp. Svcs, *Temp. Agcy*
ecuteam, *Exec Srch*
press Persnnl Svcs, *Perm. Emp Agcy*
rstWord Staff Svcs, *Temp. Agcy*
obert Half Intl, *Perm. Emp Agcy*
aprimis Staff Solut'ns, *Temp. Agcy*
terim Persnnl, *Temp. Agcy*
ob Market Persnnl Agcy, *Perm. Emp Agcy*
K. Jordan & Assoc., *Contract Svc*
elly Svcs, *Temp. Agcy*
ey People, *Perm. Emp Agcy*
ask & Assoc. Persnnl, *Exec Srch*
anpower Temp. Svcs, *Temp. Agcy*
arquess & Assoc., *Perm. Emp Agcy*
sten Staff Svcs, *Temp. Agcy*
&P Persnnl, *Perm. Emp Agcy*
ate Resrcs Grp, *Exec Srch*
ersnnl One, *Perm. Emp Agcy*
hoenix Staffng, *Exec Srch*
acements Unlimtd, *Perm. Emp Agcy*
iority Persnnl, *Temp. Agcy*
o Staff Persnnl Svcs, *Temp. Agcy*
ofessions Today, *Perm. Emp Agcy*
uest Persnnl Resrcs, *Perm. Emp Agcy*
&R Persnnl Specialists, *Exec Srch*
emedy Intelligent Staffng, *Perm. Emp Agcy*
esource Recrtrs, *Perm. Emp Agcy*
esource Staffng, *Contract Svc*
DS Staff Svcs, *Temp. Agcy*
elect Staff, *Exec Srch*
nelling Persnnl Svcs, *Perm. Emp Agcy*
nelling Persnnl Svcs, *Exec Srch*
aff Finders/Abacus Accnt'g Persnnl, *Perm. Emp Agcy*
uburban Svcs, *Temp. Agcy*
RC Staff Svcs, *Temp. Agcy*
SP Persnnl Svcs, *Perm. Emp Agcy*
AD Tech. Svcs, *Contract Svc*
arrant Cnty Emp. Netwrk, *Perm. Emp Agcy*
emp 2000 Temp. Svcs, *Temp. Agcy*
emporary Resrcs, *Temp. Agcy*
exas Persnnl, *Exec Srch*
homas Office Persnnl, *Perm. Emp Agcy*
odays Legal Staffng, *Perm. Emp Agcy*
odays Temporary, *Temp. Agcy*
otal Temp. Svcs, *Temp. Agcy*
estern Temp. Svc, *Temp. Agcy*

Utah
obert Half Intl, *Exec Srch*
termountain Staffing Resrcs, *Temp. Agcy*
sten Staff Svcs, *Temp. Agcy*
affing Logic, *Perm. Emp Agcy*

Vermont
ersnnl Dept, *Temp. Agcy*
iad Temp. Svcs, *Temp. Agcy*
estern Staff Svcs, *Temp. Agcy*

Virginia
cess Enterprises, *Perm. Emp Agcy*
dvantage Staffng, *Temp. Agcy*
ancy Allen Assoc., *Perm. Emp Agcy*
pha Omega Resrcs, *Perm. Emp Agcy*
nt Assoc., *Exec Srch*
adford Co, *Contract Svc*
rporate Connection Exec. Srch Firm
rzon Staffng, *Perm. Emp Agcy*
rol Day & Assoc., *Exec Srch*
w Persnnl, *Perm. Emp Agcy*
fective Staffng, *Exec Srch*
press Persnnl Svcs, *Temp. Agcy*
spanic Committee of VA, *Perm. Emp Agcy*
lly Svcs, *Temp. Agcy*
afstone, *Temp. Agcy*
e Staffing Resrcs, *Exec Srch*
anpower Temp. Svcs, *Temp. Agcy*
rol McNew Emp. Svc, *Perm. Emp Agcy*
san Miller & Assoc., *Perm. Emp Agcy*
rrell Staff Svcs, *Exec Srch*
rthern Virginia Temps, *Temp. Agcy*
sten Staff Svcs, *Temp. Agcy*
PDS Temp. Svc, *Temp. Agcy*
Remedy Intelligent Staffng, *Temp. Agcy*
Don Richard Assoc. of Richmond, *Exec Srch*
Select Staff Svcs, *Perm. Emp Agcy*
Selectemps, *Temp. Agcy*
Snelling Persnnl Svcs, *Perm. Emp Agcy*
STAT Temps, *Temp. Agcy*
Task Force of VA, *Exec Srch*
Temps Now, *Temp. Agcy*
Temporary Solut'ns, *Temp. Agcy*
TempWorld Staff Svcs, *Temp. Agcy*
Virginia Emp. Referral Svc, *Exec Srch*

Washington
Bostwick Temp. Svc, *Temp. Agcy*
The Career Clinic, *Exec Srch*
Career Svcs, *Perm. Emp Agcy*
Cooper Persnnl, *Temp. Agcy*
Express Persnnl Svcs, *Temp. Agcy*
Guidance Svcs, *Temp. Agcy*
Human Resrcs, *Exec Srch*
Job Ctr, *Temp. Agcy*
The Jobs Co, *Exec Srch*
Kelly Svcs, *Temp. Agcy*
Manpower Temp. Svcs, *Temp. Agcy*
Olsten Staff Svcs, *Temp. Agcy*
Persnnl Unlimtd, *Exec Srch*
Snelling Persnnl Svcs, *Exec Srch*
Staffing Resrcs, *Perm. Emp Agcy*

West Virginia
Extra Support Staffng, *Temp. Agcy*

Wisconsin
ADTEC Staffng, *Temp. Agcy*
Dunhill Staff Svcs, *Perm. Emp Agcy*
Employability, *Perm. Emp Agcy*
Interim Persnnl, *Temp. Agcy*
Landmark, The Staffing Resource, *Temp. Agcy*
Manpower Temp. Svcs, *Temp. Agcy*
Norrell Staff Svcs, *Temp. Agcy*
Olsten Staff Svcs, *Temp. Agcy*
SEEK, *Perm. Emp Agcy*
Tempo Emp. Svcs, *Temp. Agcy*
Temps Plus Staff Svcs, *Perm. Emp Agcy*
U.S. Tech Force, *Exec Srch*
Work Connection, *Perm. Emp Agcy*

Wyoming
Olsten Staff Svcs, *Temp. Agcy*

SOFTWARE DEVELOPMENT

California
Maciejewski & Assoc., *Exec Srch*

Massachusetts
Interactive Software Plcmnt, *Exec Srch*
Interactive Software Plcmnt, *Perm. Emp Agcy*

New Hampshire
Zymac/EDA Plus, *Exec Srch*

New York
Huntington Persnnl Consltnts, *Exec Srch*
Daniel Reilly & Assoc., *Exec Srch*

Ohio
FWC Recrtrs, *Perm. Emp Agcy*
Clayton Moyer Assoc., *Exec Srch*

Oklahoma
National Recrtrs, *Exec Srch*

Texas
Borrel Persnnl, *Exec Srch*

Washington
Bixler Grp, *Exec Srch*

SOFTWARE ENGINEERING

Arkansas
Executive Recrtrs Outplacement Consltnts, *Exec Srch*

California
Rich Beckstead & Assoc., *Exec Srch*
BridgeGate Grp, *Exec Srch*
Data Careers Persnnl Svcs & Srch Grp, *Perm. Emp Agcy*

Connecticut
The McKnight Grp, *Exec Srch*

Indiana
Alpha Rae Persnnl, *Perm. Emp Agcy*

Iowa
Staffing Edge, *Perm. Emp Agcy*

Massachusetts
Interactive Software Plcmnt, *Perm. Emp Agcy*
Lynx, *Contract Svc*
New Dimensions in Technlgy, *Exec Srch*
E.S. Rando Assoc., *Perm. Emp Agcy*

Minnesota
Custom Srch, *Exec Srch*

New York
Huntington Persnnl Consltnts, *Exec Srch*

Pennsylvania
Advanced Technlgy Resrcs, *Exec Srch*

Texas
Mgmt. Recrtrs of LBJ Prk/Dallas, *Exec Srch*

TAX

California
Accountnts Exec Srch, *Exec Srch*
Harrison & Hunt, *Exec Srch*
Singer Strouse, *Exec Srch*
Tax Exec Srch, *Exec Srch*

Florida
Terry Weiss & Assoc./Legal & Tax Exec Srch, *Exec Srch*

Georgia
Lucas Financial Srch, *Exec Srch*

Illinois
The Robinson Grp, *Exec Srch*

Minnesota
Whitney & Assoc., *Perm. Emp Agcy*

Missouri
Advantage Financial Grp, *Contract Svc*

New York
Advice Persnnl, *Exec Srch*
Corporate Srch, *Exec Srch*
Tax Netwrk Resrcs, *Perm. Emp Agcy*

Texas
Austin Grp, *Exec Srch*

TECHNICAL

Alabama
Mary Cheek & Assoc., *Exec Srch*
Dunhill of So. Birmingham, *Exec Srch*
Healthcare Recrtrs of Alabama, *Exec Srch*
Mgmt. Recrtrs Intl, *Exec Srch*
National Labor Line, *Exec Srch*
Seatec, *Contract Svc*

Alaska
Alaska Exec Srch, *Exec Srch*
Manpower Temp. Svc, *Temp. Agcy*
Olsten Staff Svcs, *Temp. Agcy*

Arizona
Adecco, *Contract Svc*
Aztech Recrtmnt Co, *Exec Srch*
CDI Corp, *Contract Svc*
Circuit Technlgy Srch, *Exec Srch*
COMFORCE Tech. Svcs, *Perm. Emp Agcy*
Datatech Svcs, *Contract Svc*
Devau Human Resrcs, *Temp. Agcy*
General Emp. Enterprises, *Perm. Emp Agcy*
J.R. Prof'l Srch, *Exec Srch*
Mgmt. Recrtrs of Scottsdale, *Exec Srch*
MEDA Tech. Svcs, *Contract Svc*
PDS Tech. Svc, *Contract Svc*
Priority Staffng, *Perm. Emp Agcy*
Professional Exec Research Consltng, *Exec Srch*
Snelling Persnnl Svcs, *Perm. Emp Agcy*
Spectra Intl, *Exec Srch*
Stivers Temp. Persnnl, *Temp. Agcy*
Taylor Design Recruitng, *Temp. Agcy*
Tech/Aid of Arizona, *Perm. Emp Agcy*

Arkansas
Mgmt. Recrtrs of Little Rock, *Exec Srch*
Morris & Assoc., *Exec Srch*
SEARK Bus. Svcs, *Temp. Agcy*
StaffMark, *Temp. Agcy*
Turnage Emp. Svc Grp, *Exec Srch*

California
ABA Staffng, *Exec Srch*
A.S.A.P. Emp. Svc, *Perm. Emp Agcy*
ACCESS Technlgy, *Exec Srch*
AccuStaff Co, *Temp. Agcy*
Alfano Temp. Persnnl, *Temp. Agcy*
Alpha-Net Consltng Grp, *Exec Srch*

Alternative Staffing Grp, *Exec Srch*
Amtec Engineering Corp, *Perm. Emp Agcy*
Ankenbrandt Grp, *Exec Srch*
Apple One Emp. Svcs, *Perm. Emp Agcy*
Apropos Emp. Agcy, *Perm. Emp Agcy*
B&M Assoc., *Contract Svc*
Biosource Tech. Svc, *Contract Svc*
Bradford Staff, *Temp. Agcy*
A.J. Brown & Assoc., *Exec Srch*
Bryson Myers Co, *Exec Srch*
CDI Corp, *Temp. Agcy*
CN Assoc., *Exec Srch*
CT Persnnl Svcs, *Perm. Emp Agcy*
California Srch Agcy, *Exec Srch*
Career Quest, *Contract Svc*
Centennial Assoc., *Contract Svc*
Chipton-Ross, *Temp. Agcy*
Coast Persnnl, *Temp. Agcy*
Coast To Coast Exec Srch, *Exec Srch*
Colt Syst. Prof'l Persnnl Svcs, *Perm. Emp Agcy*
COMFORCE Tech. Svcs, *Contract Svc*
COMFORCE Tech. Svcs, *Perm. Emp Agcy*
Complimate Tech. Staffng, *Temp. Agcy*
Corporate Srch, *Exec Srch*
Crossroads Staff Svc, *Temp. Agcy*
Culver Persnnl Svcs, *Exec Srch*
Curphey & Malkin Assoc., *Exec Srch*
D.P. Srch, *Exec Srch*
Daley Tech. Srch, *Exec Srch*
Drake Office Overload, *Temp. Agcy*
Dunhill Prof'l Srch, *Exec Srch*
EDP Contrct Svcs, *Contract Svc*
Eastridge Infotech, *Perm. Emp Agcy*
Employment Devlpmnt Dept, *Perm. Emp Agcy*
Engineering Tech. Svc, *Temp. Agcy*
Executive Srch Consltnts, *Exec Srch*
Curtis Farmer Persnnl, *Exec Srch*
Fastek Tech. Svcs, *Perm. Emp Agcy*
Fisher Persnnl Mngmnt Svcs, *Exec Srch*
FORTUNE Persnnl Consltnts, *Exec Srch*
40 Plus of So. CA, *Exec Srch*
Full Svc Temps, *Temp. Agcy*
Garnett Emp. Svcs, *Temp. Agcy*
Dianne Gauger & Assoc., *Exec Srch*
Grant & Assoc., *Exec Srch*
Great 400 Grp Intl, *Perm. Emp Agcy*
Harley Assoc., *Exec Srch*
Healthcare Exec Recrtrs, *Exec Srch*
Holland Exec Srch, *Exec Srch*
Hutton Barnes & Assoc., *Exec Srch*
Independent Resource System, *Exec Srch*
Integrated Community Svcs, *Perm. Emp Agcy*
Interim Persnnl, *Temp. Agcy*
Intl Srch Consltnts, *Perm. Emp Agcy*
Intl Staff Consltnts, *Exec Srch*
JPM Intl, *Exec Srch*
Jackson Persnnl, *Perm. Emp Agcy*
Job Link, *Exec Srch*
Kelly Svcs, *Temp. Agcy*
Kelly Tech. Svcs, *Temp. Agcy*
Klein & Assoc., *Temp. Agcy*
Kuhn Med-Tech, *Exec Srch*
John Kurosky & Assoc., *Exec Srch*
Lab Support, *Temp. Agcy*
Larkin Assoc., *Exec Srch*
MK Tech. Svc, *Temp. Agcy*
MS Data Svc Corp, *Perm. Emp Agcy*
Malibu Grp, *Exec Srch*
Mgmt. Recrtrs Intl, *Exec Srch*
Mgmt. Recrtrs of Burlingame/Sales Consltnts, *Exec Srch*
Mgmt. Recrtrs of Encino, *Exec Srch*
Mgmt. Recrtrs of Laguna Hills, *Exec Srch*
Mgmt. Recrtrs-Oakland/Sales Consltnts, *Exec Srch*
Mgmt. Recrtrs of Pleasanton, *Exec Srch*
Mgmt. Recrtrs of San Francisco, *Exec Srch*
Manpower, *Temp. Agcy*
Markar Assoc., *Exec Srch*
The Martin Agencies, *Perm. Emp Agcy*
Maverick Staff Svc, *Perm. Emp Agcy*
Mesa Intl, *Exec Srch*
Micro Temps Syst. & Programming, *Temp. Agcy*
Mini-Systems Assoc., *Exec Srch*
Multisearch Recrtrs, *Exec Srch*
Murray Enterprises Staff Svcs, *Temp. Agcy*
NCC Exec Srch, *Exec Srch*
National Asian Pacific Center on Aging, *Perm. Emp Agcy*
Nelson HR Solut'ns, *Perm. Emp Agcy*
Nelson Staff Solut'ns/Accountnts Plus, *Perm. Emp Agcy*
Net Workers, *Contract Svc*
Bren Norris Assoc., *Contract Svc*
Norsell & Assoc., *Exec Srch*
Omni Express Temps, *Temp. Agcy*
Douglas Owen Srch Consltnts, *Exec Srch*
Pasona Pacific, *Temp. Agcy*
PeopleWare Tech. Resrcs, *Contract Svc*
Personalized Placemnt Agcy, *Temp. Agcy*
Tom Pezman & Assoc., *Exec Srch*
Princeton Corporate Consltnts, *Exec Srch*
Pro Staff Persnnl Svcs, *Perm. Emp Agcy*
ProSearch & Assoc., *Exec Srch*
Quality Imaging Svcs, *Temp. Agcy*
Ed Rast & Co, *Exec Srch*
Reliance Staff Svcs, *Perm. Emp Agcy*
Resource Persnnl Svcs, *Temp. Agcy*
Resource Perspectives, *Exec Srch*
Richmar Assoc., *Temp. Agcy*
Riley-Cole Recrtmnt Specialists, *Exec Srch*
Robbins & Scott Exec Srch, *Exec Srch*
Rowland Assoc., *Exec Srch*
Royal Staff Svcs, *Exec Srch*
Sales Consltnts of Modesto, *Exec Srch*
Sales Consltnts of Sacramento, *Exec Srch*
Santa Barbara Plcmnt, *Perm. Emp Agcy*
Sarver & Carruth Assoc., *Exec Srch*
Search West, *Exec Srch*
David Sharp & Assoc., *Perm. Emp Agcy*
Sierra Technlgy, *Contract Svc*
Smartsource Inc., *Contract Svc*
Source Engineering, *Perm. Emp Agcy*
Adele Steinmetz, *Exec Srch*
Strategic Staffng, *Temp. Agcy*
Strategic Staffing Persnnl Solut'ns, *Temp. Agcy*
Sunday & Assoc., *Perm. Emp Agcy*
System One, *Perm. Emp Agcy*
Systems Research Grp, *Exec Srch*
TRC Staff Svcs, *Perm. Emp Agcy*
TAD Data Svcs, *Perm. Emp Agcy*
TAD Resrcs Intl, *Perm. Emp Agcy*
TAD Tech. Svcs, *Contract Svc*
Tax Exec Srch, *Exec Srch*
Technical Aid Corp, *Temp. Agcy*
Technical Directions, *Perm. Emp Agcy*
TechniSkills, *Temp. Agcy*
TechSource, *Contract Svc*
Techstaff West, *Exec Srch*
Thor Temp. Svcs, *Temp. Agcy*
Triple-J Svcs, *Exec Srch*
The Truman Agcy, Persnnl Specialists, *Perm. Emp Agcy*
Tustin Persnnl Svcs, *Perm. Emp Agcy*
UAW Labor Emp. & Training Corp, *Perm. Emp Agcy*
United Staff Solut'ns, *Exec Srch*
United/Corestaff Staff Svcs, *Perm. Emp Agcy*
Volt Tech. Svcs, *Contract Svc*
WGI Solut'ns, *Exec Srch*
Western Staff Svcs, *Temp. Agcy*
Western Tech. Resrcs, *Exec Srch*
Your People Prof'ls, *Perm. Emp Agcy*

Colorado

Adecco, *Temp. Agcy*
CDI Corp, *Contract Svc*
Career Forum, *Exec Srch*
Career Mrktng Assoc., *Exec Srch*
COREStaff Svcs, *Perm. Emp Agcy*
Dunhill Persnnl of Boulder, *Exec Srch*
Eleventh Hour Staff Svcs, *Perm. Emp Agcy*
Enscicon Corp, *Perm. Emp Agcy*
40 Plus of CO, *Career/Outplacemnt*
GeoSearch, *Exec Srch*
Goodwin Persnnl, *Perm. Emp Agcy*
Hallmark Persnnl Syst., *Exec Srch*
Health Technlgy, *Exec Srch*
Healthcare Recrtrs of The Rockies, *Exec Srch*
JobSearch, *Temp. Agcy*
Kelly Svcs, *Perm. Emp Agcy*
Lab Support, *Temp. Agcy*
Labor Ready, *Temp. Agcy*
Mgmt. Recrtrs of Colorado Springs, *Exec Srch*
Manpower Intl, *Temp. Agcy*
Martinez & Hromada Assoc., *Contract Svc*
Miller Denver, *Exec Srch*
National Exec Resrcs, *Exec Srch*
Olsten Staff Svcs, *Temp. Agcy*
On Call Tech. Svcs/StaffMark, *Temp. Agcy*
Pinnacle Source, *Exec Srch*
SOS Staff Svcs, *Temp. Agcy*
Sales Consltnts, *Exec Srch*
Snelling Persnnl Svcs, *Exec Srch*
Todays Temporary, *Temp. Agcy*
J.Q. Turner & Assoc., *Exec Srch*
Welzig, Lowe & Assoc., *Exec Srch*
Western Staff Svcs, *Temp. Agcy*
Woodmoor Grp, *Exec Srch*

Connecticut

A&A Resume & Persnnl Svcs, *Perm. Emp Agcy*
Admiral Staff Svcs, *Temp. Agcy*
Boehmer Tomasco & Alexander, *Exec Srch*
CGR Staff Svcs, *Temp. Agcy*
Cahill Assoc., *Exec Srch*
Charter Persnnl Svcs, *Perm. Emp Agcy*
Charter Persnnl Svcs, *Exec Srch*
Corporate Staff Solut'ns, *Temp. Agcy*
EDP Contrct Svcs, *Contract Svc*
Employment Opport., *Perm. Emp Agcy*
Fox Ridge Svcs, *Temp. Agcy*
Hallmark Totaltech, *Perm. Emp Agcy*
Higbee Assoc., *Exec Srch*
Hire Logic, *Temp. Agcy*
Human Resource Consltnts Exec. Srch Firm
Industrial Recrtrs Assn, *Perm. Emp Agcy*
JAT, Ltd., *Perm. Emp Agcy*
Jobshop, *Perm. Emp Agcy*
Lab Support, *Temp. Agcy*
W.R. Lawry, *Perm. Emp Agcy*
Lineal Recruitng Svcs, *Perm. Emp Agcy*
Lutz Assoc., *Exec Srch*
MJF Assoc., *Exec Srch*
Mgmt. Recrtrs Intl, *Exec Srch*
Matrix Srch, *Perm. Emp Agcy*
Maxwell-Marcus Staff Consltnts, *Exec Srch*
PRH Mgmt., *Exec Srch*
Barry Persky & Co., *Exec Srch*
Ed Pospesil & Co, *Exec Srch*
Reynolds Tech. Svcs, *Perm. Emp Agcy*
Russo Assoc., *Exec Srch*
Super Syst., *Perm. Emp Agcy*
TAD Tech. Svcs, *Contract Svc*
Tech/Aid of CT, *Temp. Agcy*
Tech. Staff Solut'ns, *Temp. Agcy*
Wallace Assoc., *Exec Srch*
Western Staff Svcs, *Temp. Agcy*
Western Staff Svcs, *Perm. Emp Agcy*
Workforce One, *Perm. Emp Agcy*

Delaware

FORTUNE Persnnl Consltnts, *Exec Srch*
J.B. Groner Exec Srch, *Exec Srch*
E.W. Hodges & Assoc., *Exec Srch*

District of Columbia

Abbtech Svcs, *Exec Srch*
Norrell Svcs, *Temp. Agcy*

Florida

AAA Employment, *Perm. Emp Agcy*
Academy Design & Tech. Svcs, *Contract Svc*
AccuTech, *Contract Svc*
Advanced R&D, *Contract Svc*
American Exec Srch, *Exec Srch*
B2D Tech. Svcs, *Contract Svc*
Bryan & Assoc./Worknet, Etc., *Exec Srch*
CDI Corp, *Contract Svc*
Capital Data, *Exec Srch*
Computemp, *Temp. Agcy*
Criterion Exec Srch, *Exec Srch*
DGA Persnnl Grp, *Exec Srch*
DP Exec Srch, *Exec Srch*
Dunhill Staff Svcs, *Exec Srch*
Ethan Allen Persnnl Plcmnt, *Exec Srch*
First Emp. Consltnts, *Exec Srch*
Five Star Temporary, *Temp. Agcy*
HR Prof'l Consltnts, *Exec Srch*
Kelly Svcs, *Temp. Agcy*
Mgmt. Recrtrs of St. Petersburg, *Exec Srch*
Mgmt. Recrtrs of Tallahassee, *Exec Srch*
Mgmt. Recrtrs of Tampa, *Exec Srch*
Manpower Tech. Svcs, *Perm. Emp Agcy*
Manpower Temp. Svcs, *Temp. Agcy*
Norrell Tech. Svcs, *Exec Srch*
Olsten Staff Svcs, *Temp. Agcy*
OMNIPartners, *Exec Srch*
The Persnnl Institute, *Exec Srch*
Persnnl One, *Perm. Emp Agcy*
Priority Srch, *Exec Srch*
Pro Staff Persnnl Svcs, *Temp. Agcy*
Profes. Staffing/Able Body Temp. Svcs, *Contract Svc*
Pulp & Paper Intl, *Exec Srch*
Sales Consltnts of Fort Lauderdale, *Exec Srch*
Sales Consltnts of Jacksonville, *Exec Srch*
Search Enterprises South, *Exec Srch*
Doug Sears & Assoc., *Exec Srch*
Staffing Svcs Grp, *Perm. Emp Agcy*
System One Tech. Staffng, *Exec Srch*
Technisource, *Exec Srch*
TechStaff, *Contract Svc*

Georgia

A.D. & Assoc. Exec Srch, *Exec Srch*
Adecco Tech. Svcs, *Contract Svc*
Anderson Industrial Assoc., *Exec Srch*
Ashley-Nolan Intl, *Exec Srch*
Atlanta Tech. Support, *Contract Svc*
Business Prof'l Grp, *Perm. Emp Agcy*
Caldwell Svcs, *Temp. Agcy*
Catalina Resrcs, *Perm. Emp Agcy*
Coast to Coast Tech. Svcs, *Temp. Agcy*
Comprehensive Computer Consltng, *Contract Svc*
Corporate Srch Consltnts, *Exec Srch*
Data Processing Svcs, *Exec Srch*
Dunhill Prof'l Srch, *Exec Srch*
Elite Staff Svcs, *Perm. Emp Agcy*
Express Persnnl Svcs, *Temp. Agcy*
Express Persnnl Svcs, *Perm. Emp Agcy*
Express Persnnl Svcs, *Exec Srch*
FORTUNE Persnnl Consltnts of Atlanta, *Exec Srch*

Hall Mngmnt Grp, *Exec Srch*
Job Shop, *Exec Srch*
Kelly Svcs, *Temp. Agcy*
MA&A Grp, *Perm. Emp Agcy*
MSI Intl, *Exec Srch*
Mgmt. Recrtrs Intl, *Exec Srch*
Mgmt. Recrtrs of Atlanta, *Exec Srch*
Manpower Temp. Svcs, *Temp. Agcy*
Millard & Assoc., *Exec Srch*
Office Specialists, *Temp. Agcy*
Olsten Staff Svcs, *Temp. Agcy*
Olsten Tech. Svcs, *Perm. Emp Agcy*
Randstad Staff Svcs, *Perm. Emp Agcy*
Sanford Rose Assoc., *Exec Srch*
SearchAmerica, *Exec Srch*
Software Tech. Svcs, *Contract Svc*
Technical Assoc., *Contract Svc*
Western Staff Svcs, *Temp. Agcy*
H.L. Yoh Co, *Contract Svc*

Hawaii

Altres Staffng, *Temp. Agcy*
Dunhill Prof'l Srch of Hawaii, *Exec Srch*
Ellis & Assoc., *Exec Srch*
Olsten Staff Svcs, *Temp. Agcy*

Idaho

Ward-Hoffman & Assoc., *Exec Srch*

Illinois

The Ability Grp, *Exec Srch*
Able's Pool of Temps, *Temp. Agcy*
Accord, *Exec Srch*
Adecco, *Temp. Agcy*
Advanced Tech. Srch, *Exec Srch*
Alternative Resrcs Corp, *Contract Svc*
American Contrct Svcs, *Contract Svc*
American Engineering Co, *Exec Srch*
American Tech. Srch, *Exec Srch*
Availability, *Perm. Emp Agcy*
Banner Persnnl, *Perm. Emp Agcy*
Britannia, *Exec Srch*
Burling Grp Exec. Srch Firm
Burton Placemnt Svcs, *Exec Srch*
CDI Corp, *Contract Svc*
Carson Mngmnt Assoc., *Contract Svc*
Computemp, *Temp. Agcy*
Corporate Environment, *Exec Srch*
Diener & Assoc., *Exec Srch*
Electronic Srch, *Exec Srch*
Executive Srch Netwrk, *Exec Srch*
Express Persnnl Svcs, *Temp. Agcy*
First Srch, *Exec Srch*
Furst Staff Svcs, *Temp. Agcy*
General Emp. Enterprises, *Perm. Emp Agcy*
Girman Grp, *Exec Srch*
HT Assoc., *Exec Srch*
Hufford Assoc., *Exec Srch*
Human Resource Technlgy, *Exec Srch*
Hunzer Assoc., *Exec Srch*
Lynco Mngmnt Persnnl, *Exec Srch*
MBP Persnnl, *Exec Srch*
Magnum Srch, *Exec Srch*
Mgmt. Recrtrs of Elgin, *Exec Srch*
Mgmt. Recrtrs of Rockford, *Exec Srch*
Mgmt. Recrtrs of Springfield, *Exec Srch*
Mgmt. Support Svcs, *Exec Srch*
Marsteller Wilcox Assoc., *Exec Srch*
Mathey Svcs, *Exec Srch*
M.W. McDonald & Assoc., *Exec Srch*
Medical Tech. Placemnts, *Temp. Agcy*
Michael David Assoc., *Perm. Emp Agcy*
. Michaels & Assoc., *Exec Srch*
The Murphy Grp, *Perm. Emp Agcy*
National Srch, *Exec Srch*
Officemates5 of Wheeling, *Exec Srch*
Omega Tech. Corp, *Exec Srch*
Omni One, *Perm. Emp Agcy*
Omni Srch Exec. Srch Firm
Pelichem Assoc., *Exec Srch*
Pollak & Skan, *Contract Svc*
Remedy Intelligent Staffng, *Temp. Agcy*
Sales Consltnts/Mgmt. Recrtrs Intl, *Exec Srch*
Sales Consltnts of Oak Brk, *Exec Srch*
Search Dynamics, *Exec Srch*
Search Enterprises, *Exec Srch*
Select Srch, *Exec Srch*
Selectability, *Perm. Emp Agcy*
Sevcor Intl, *Exec Srch*
Staffing Team Intl, *Temp. Agcy*
Systems Research, *Perm. Emp Agcy*
TSC Mngmnt Svcs, *Exec Srch*
Voigt Assoc., *Exec Srch*
Web/Pack Tech, *Perm. Emp Agcy*
Webb Emp. Svc, *Perm. Emp Agcy*
Working World, *Temp. Agcy*
World Emp. Svc, *Perm. Emp Agcy*
Zagas & Assoc., *Exec Srch*

Indiana

ACA Calumet, *Contract Svc*
ACA Kokomo, *Contract Svc*
AccuStaff, *Temp. Agcy*
Belcan Tech. Svcs, *Contract Svc*
Career Consltnts, *Perm. Emp Agcy*
Century Persnnl, *Perm. Emp Agcy*
Continental Design Co, *Contract Svc*
Corporate Staff Resrcs, *Temp. Agcy*
Dunhill of Brown Cnty, *Exec Srch*
Dunhill Prof'l Srch, *Exec Srch*
Dunhill Staffing Syst., *Temp. Agcy*
Employment Plus, *Temp. Agcy*
Execusearch, *Exec Srch*
Flexible Technicals, *Exec Srch*
Johnson Brown Assoc., *Exec Srch*
Kelly Svcs, *Temp. Agcy*
Mgmt. Recrtrs/Sales Consltnts, *Exec Srch*
Mgmt. Recrtrs of Evansville, *Exec Srch*
Mgmt. Recrtrs of Indianapolis, *Exec Srch*
Mgmt. Recrtrs of Richmond/Staff Solut'ns, *Exec Srch*
Manpower Tech. Svcs, *Temp. Agcy*
National Corporate Consltnts/Advantage Svcs, *Exec Srch*
Oakwood Intl, *Exec Srch*
Officemates5 of Indianapolis, *Exec Srch*
Persnnl Plus, *Exec Srch*
QCI Tech. Staffng, *Contract Svc*
Quality Srch, *Perm. Emp Agcy*
Quiring Assoc. HR Consltng Grp, *Exec Srch*
RDN Svcs, *Exec Srch*
Reliable Tech. Svcs, *Perm. Emp Agcy*
TRC Staff Svcs, *Temp. Agcy*
TAD Tech. Svcs, *Contract Svc*
Technetics Corp, *Contract Svc*
Try Temps, *Temp. Agcy*
Wimmer Temps & Direct Plcmnt, *Temp. Agcy*
H.L. Yoh Co, *Contract Svc*

Iowa

Burton Placemnt Svcs, *Exec Srch*
Byrnes & Rupkey, *Exec Srch*
CDI Corp, *Contract Svc*
Drake-Brennan dba Snelling Persnnl, *Exec Srch*
Mgmt. Recrtrs Intl, *Exec Srch*
Persnnl, *Exec Srch*
Premier Srch Grp, *Exec Srch*
Staff Mgmt., *Contract Svc*

Kansas

Business Specialists, *Perm. Emp Agcy*
CDI Corp, *Contract Svc*
Dunhill of Wichita, *Perm. Emp Agcy*
Eleventh Hour Staff Svcs, *Temp. Agcy*
Foster Design Co, *Contract Svc*
Mgmt. Recrtrs of Overlnd Prk, *Exec Srch*
Manpower, *Temp. Agcy*
J.T. Nelson & Assoc., *Perm. Emp Agcy*
Parr & Assoc., *Perm. Emp Agcy*
Stoneburner Assoc., *Exec Srch*
Temtech, *Contract Svc*
H.L. Yoh Co, *Contract Svc*

Kentucky

Angel Grp Intl, *Exec Srch*
C.M. Mngmnt Svcs, *Perm. Emp Agcy*
Manpower, *Temp. Agcy*
Precision Staffng, *Temp. Agcy*
Professional Srch, *Exec Srch*
Snelling Persnnl Svcs, *Exec Srch*
TLI Tech. Staffng, *Perm. Emp Agcy*
Versa-Tech Emp. Svcs, *Exec Srch*

Louisiana

Career Persnnl Consltnts, *Exec Srch*
Clertech Grp, *Exec Srch*
Dunhill of Baton Rouge, *Exec Srch*
Dunhill Persnnl System of LA, *Exec Srch*
Interim Persnnl, *Temp. Agcy*
Mgmt. Recrtrs of Baton Rouge, *Exec Srch*
Mgmt. Recrtrs-Metairie/Sales Consltnts, *Exec Srch*
Manpower, *Temp. Agcy*
Professional Temps, *Temp. Agcy*
Talley & Assoc./Talley Temps, *Exec Srch*
TECH 2000 Svcs & Staffng, *Temp. Agcy*
Universal Persnnl, *Contract Svc*
Western Staff Svcs, *Temp. Agcy*

Maine

Global Engineers, *Contract Svc*
John Jay & Co, *Exec Srch*
National Recrtrs of ME, *Exec Srch*
TAD Resrcs Intl, *Perm. Emp Agcy*
Technical Aid Corp, *Temp. Agcy*

Maryland

D.W. Baird & Assoc., *Exec Srch*
Bear Trees Consltng, *Exec Srch*
Capitol Staff Solut'ns, *Temp. Agcy*
Comtex, *Exec Srch*
DanSources Tech. Svcs, *Contract Svc*
Echelon Svc Co, *Contract Svc*
Employer Employee Exchange, *Exec Srch*
A.G. Fishkin & Assoc., *Exec Srch*
Futures, *Exec Srch*
J.R. Assoc., *Perm. Emp Agcy*
Ken Leiner Assoc., *Exec Srch*
Mgmt. Recrtrs of Annapolis, *Exec Srch*
Mgmt. Recrtrs-Baltimore/Sales Consltnts, *Exec Srch*
Mgmt. Recrtrs-Bethesda/CompuSearch, *Exec Srch*
Mgmt. Recrtrs of Frederick, *Exec Srch*
Micro Temps, *Temp. Agcy*
Sales Consltnts of Prince Georges Cnty, *Exec Srch*
TCM Enterprises, *Exec Srch*
TAD Staff Svcs, *Temp. Agcy*
Tech/Aid of MD, *Temp. Agcy*
Technical Software Solut'ns, *Temp. Agcy*
Technical Talent Locators, *Perm. Emp Agcy*
Tri-Serv, *Perm. Emp Agcy*
Virtual Staff Svcs, *Perm. Emp Agcy*

Massachusetts

Abbott's of Boston, *Exec Srch*
Ability Srch of N.E., *Perm. Emp Agcy*
Additional Tech. Support Svcs, *Perm. Emp Agcy*
Advance Persnnl, *Perm. Emp Agcy*
CDI Corp, *Contract Svc*
Clear Point Consltnts, *Exec Srch*
Corporate Growth Resrcs, *Exec Srch*
Cyr Assoc., *Exec Srch*
Digital Arts Grp, *Contract Svc*
Diversity Assoc., *Exec Srch*
Diversity Srch Specialists, *Exec Srch*
EF Tech. Resrcs, *Perm. Emp Agcy*
Engineering Mngmnt Support, *Temp. Agcy*
The Environmental Careers Organization, *Contract Svc*
L.J. Gonzer Assoc., *Exec Srch*
HM Assoc., *Exec Srch*
Harvest Persnnl, *Exec Srch*
Interim Technlgy, *Contract Svc*
Kelly Svcs, *Temp. Agcy*
Lake & Manning, *Exec Srch*
The Littleton Grp, *Exec Srch*
Logix, *Exec Srch*
Lynx, *Contract Svc*
Mgmt. Recrtrs Intl, *Exec Srch*
Mgmt. Recrtrs Intl of Braintree, *Exec Srch*
Mgmt. Recrtrs Intl of Springfield, *Exec Srch*
Mgmt. Recrtrs Intl of Westboro, *Exec Srch*
Manpower Temp. Svcs, *Temp. Agcy*
Master Srch, *Perm. Emp Agcy*
Micro-Comm Exec Srch, *Exec Srch*
Morency Assoc., *Exec Srch*
National Engineering Svc, *Contract Svc*
Nationwide Bus. Svc, *Perm. Emp Agcy*
Need Persnnl Plcmnt, *Temp. Agcy*
Norrell Staff Svcs, *Contract Svc*
Paladin Persnnl Consltnts, *Exec Srch*
Pro Staff, *Temp. Agcy*
Progressive Srch Assoc., *Exec Srch*
Propos Assoc., *Perm. Emp Agcy*
J.E. Ranta Assoc., *Exec Srch*
Louis Rudzinsky Assoc., *Exec Srch*
Sales Consltnts of Cape Cod, *Exec Srch*
Sales Consltnts of Mansfield, *Exec Srch*
Sales Consltnts of Plymouth Cnty, *Exec Srch*
Sales Consltnts of Wellesley, *Exec Srch*
George Sandel Assoc., *Perm. Emp Agcy*
Selectemps, *Temp. Agcy*
Stone Consltng Grp & Legal Srch Specialists, *Exec Srch*
Straube Assoc., *Exec Srch*
Tech Resource, *Contract Svc*
Tech/Aid, *Contract Svc*
Technical Persnnl Svcs, *Perm. Emp Agcy*
Total Tech. Svcs, *Perm. Emp Agcy*
WIND Job Ctr, *Career/Outplacemnt*
H.L. Yoh Co, *Contract Svc*

Michigan

Action Mngmnt Corp, *Perm. Emp Agcy*
Advance Assoc., *Exec Srch*
Allied Tech. Svc, *Contract Svc*
The Aucon Co, *Exec Srch*
CDI Corp, *Contract Svc*
Career Assoc., *Contract Svc*
Christopher & Assoc., *Exec Srch*
CIBER, *Contract Svc*
Corporate Staff Resrcs, *Perm. Emp Agcy*
Day Persnnl dba Dorothy Day Persnnl - MI, Perm Emp Agcy
Diversified Recrtrs, *Perm. Emp Agcy*
Entech Svcs, *Temp. Agcy*
Executive & Tech. Persnnl, *Exec Srch*
Executive Mngmnt Srch, *Exec Srch*
Executive Recrtrs Intl, *Exec Srch*
David Franklin Assoc., *Exec Srch*
GRS, *Exec Srch*
William Howard Agcy, *Perm. Emp Agcy*
IBA Srch Consltnts, *Exec Srch*

Job Fair Netwrk of MI, *Perm. Emp Agcy*
Kelly Tech. Svcs, *Contract Svc*
Lambert Intl, *Exec Srch*
Mgmt. Recrtrs Intl, *Exec Srch*
Mgmt. Recrtrs of Bingham Farms, *Exec Srch*
Mgmt. Recrtrs of Dearborn, *Exec Srch*
Mgmt. Recrtrs of Flint, *Exec Srch*
Mgmt. Recrtrs of Kalamazoo, *Exec Srch*
Mgmt. Recrtrs of Lansing, *Exec Srch*
Mgmt. Recrtrs of Muskegon, *Exec Srch*
Mgmt. Recrtrs of Rochester, *Exec Srch*
Mgmt. Recrtrs of Southeast MI, *Exec Srch*
Manpower Tech. Svcs, *Contract Svc*
Manpower, *Temp. Agcy*
Nationwide Career Netwrk, *Perm. Emp Agcy*
Preferred Emp. Planning, *Perm. Emp Agcy*
Professional Career Srch, *Exec Srch*
Professional Persnnl Consltnts Intl, *Exec Srch*
Professional Resource Assoc., *Contract Svc*
RHI Consltng, *Contract Svc*
Sales Consltnts of Detroit, *Exec Srch*
Sales Consltnts of Farmington Hills, *Exec Srch*
Sales Consltnts of Lansing, *Exec Srch*
Selective Recruitng Assoc., *Exec Srch*
Software Svcs Corp, *Contract Svc*
Source Technlgy, *Exec Srch*
TAD Tech. Svcs, *Contract Svc*
Technical Prof'l Svc, *Perm. Emp Agcy*
Temporary Tech. Svcs, *Temp. Agcy*
Trillium Staffng, *Temp. Agcy*
Unlimited Staff Solut'ns, *Contract Svc*
Venture Mngmnt & Staffng, *Exec Srch*
Duane Wilson Assoc., *Exec Srch*
Wing Tips & Pumps, *Exec Srch*
Wise Persnnl Svcs, *Perm. Emp Agcy*
H.L. Yoh Co, *Contract Svc*
Your Preference Referral Netwrk, *Perm. Emp Agcy*

Minnesota

Agri Consltnts, *Exec Srch*
Agri-Business Svcs, *Exec Srch*
Agro Quality Srch, *Perm. Emp Agcy*
Bright Srch/Professional Staffng, *Exec Srch*
CDI Corp, *Contract Svc*
Custom Srch, *Exec Srch*
Diversified Employment, *Perm. Emp Agcy*
Flatley Tech. Svcs, *Temp. Agcy*
George Konik Assoc. Inc, *Exec Srch*
T.H. Hunter, *Exec Srch*
Laboratory Resrcs, *Contract Svc*
Lynn Temporary, *Temp. Agcy*
Mgmt. Recrtrs Minneapolis/Sales Consltnts, *Exec Srch*
Manpower Tech. Svcs, *Perm. Emp Agcy*
Manpower Temp. Svcs, *Temp. Agcy*
Lee Marsh & Assoc., *Exec Srch*
NER (National Engineering Resrcs), *Exec Srch*
North American Recrtrs, *Exec Srch*
Northland Emp. Svcs, *Exec Srch*
Nycor Srch, *Exec Srch*
Persnnl Assist. Corp, *Exec Srch*
Programming Alternatives of MN, *Exec Srch*
Regency Recrtrs, *Exec Srch*
Staff Connection, *Exec Srch*
Technical Resrcs, *Perm. Emp Agcy*
Temp Force, *Temp. Agcy*
Twin Cty Srch, *Exec Srch*
H.L. Yoh Co, *Contract Svc*

Mississippi

Coats & Coats Persnnl, *Perm. Emp Agcy*
EPSCO Persnnl, *Temp. Agcy*
Opportunities Unlimtd, *Perm. Emp Agcy*
Recruitment & Training of MS, *Perm. Emp Agcy*

Missouri

ABC Emp. Svc, *Perm. Emp Agcy*
Advanced Careers of Kansas Cty, *Exec Srch*
Agri-Tech Persnnl, *Exec Srch*
L.P. Banning, *Perm. Emp Agcy*
Bottom Line Prof'l Svcs, *Contract Svc*
Burns Emp. Svc, *Exec Srch*
CDI Corp, *Contract Svc*
The Christiansen Grp, *Exec Srch*
COMFORCE Tech. Svcs, *Contract Svc*
Decker Persnnl, *Perm. Emp Agcy*
Design Alternatives, *Perm. Emp Agcy*
Employer Advantage, *Exec Srch*
JRL Exec Recrtrs, *Exec Srch*
B. Loehr Temps, *Temp. Agcy*
Charles Luntz & Assoc., *Exec Srch*
Mgmt. Recrtrs of Kansas Cty, *Exec Srch*
Mgmt. Recrtrs of Springfield, *Exec Srch*
Mgmt. Recrtrs of St. Louis, *Exec Srch*
Manpower Temp. Svcs, *Temp. Agcy*
Norrell Svcs, *Temp. Agcy*
Officemates5 of St. Louis, *Exec Srch*
Olsten Staff Svcs, *Temp. Agcy*
Pinnacle Exec Grp, *Exec Srch*
The River Bend Grp, *Exec Srch*
Gordon Smith & Assoc., *Exec Srch*
Snelling Persnnl Svcs, *Perm. Emp Agcy*
Source Svcs Corp, *Exec Srch*
Western Tech. Svcs, *Contract Svc*

Montana

W.R. Knapp & Assoc., *Exec Srch*
Manpower Temp. Svcs, *Temp. Agcy*

Nebraska

Adecco, *Temp. Agcy*
Compusearch of Lincoln, *Exec Srch*
Express Persnnl, *Exec Srch*
Mgmt. Recrtrs-Omaha/Officemates5, *Exec Srch*
Professional Persnnl, *Perm. Emp Agcy*
Sharp Persnnl, *Temp. Agcy*

Nevada

Manpower Temp. Svcs, *Temp. Agcy*

New Hampshire

Able 1 Staffng, *Exec Srch*
Access Consltng, *Perm. Emp Agcy*
Allstaff Contrct Svcs, *Perm. Emp Agcy*
Barclay Persnnl Syst., *Exec Srch*
CDI Corp, *Contract Svc*
Chaucer Grp, *Perm. Emp Agcy*
Chaucer Grp, *Exec Srch*
Contact Recrtrs, *Temp. Agcy*
Dubois & Co, *Exec Srch*
Enterprise Technolog's, *Exec Srch*
Kelly Svcs, *Temp. Agcy*
Key Persnnl, *Perm. Emp Agcy*
Lloyd Persnnl Consltnts, *Exec Srch*
Mgmt. Recrtrs Intl of Bedford, *Exec Srch*
Manpower Temp. Svcs, *Temp. Agcy*
Pelham Prof'l Grp, *Temp. Agcy*
Preferred Resrcs Grp, *Exec Srch*
Professional Recrtrs, *Perm. Emp Agcy*
R.G.T. Assoc., *Exec Srch*
Sales Consltnts of Nashua-Manchester, *Exec Srch*
Tech/Aid of NH, *Perm. Emp Agcy*
Technical Directions, *Perm. Emp Agcy*
Technical Needs, *Exec Srch*
Tri-State Prof'ls, *Temp. Agcy*

New Jersey

A Prof'l Edge, *Career/Outplacemnt*
Adel-Lawrence Assoc., *Exec Srch*
American Staffing Resrcs, *Temp. Agcy*
Andrew Persnnl Svcs, *Perm. Emp Agcy*
Broad Waverly & Assoc., *Exec Srch*
Brookdale Srch Assoc., *Exec Srch*
CDI Corp, *Contract Svc*
Career Ctr, *Perm. Emp Agcy*
Career Grp, *Perm. Emp Agcy*
Careers First, *Perm. Emp Agcy*
Careers USA, *Perm. Emp Agcy*
Carter/MacKay Persnnl, *Exec Srch*
Central Tech. Svc, *Perm. Emp Agcy*
Cox Darrow & Owens, *Exec Srch*
Executive Netwrk, *Exec Srch*
Express Persnnl Svcs, *Perm. Emp Agcy*
FORTUNE Persnnl Consltnts of Menlo Prk, *Exec Srch*
Huff Assoc., *Exec Srch*
Hughes & Podesla Persnnl, *Perm. Emp Agcy*
Impact Persnnl, *Perm. Emp Agcy*
Integro Staff Svcs, *Temp. Agcy*
J.M. Joseph Assoc., *Exec Srch*
Joule People Providers, *Perm. Emp Agcy*
Kaye Persnnl, *Temp. Agcy*
The Keller Grp/Careers, *Exec Srch*
Key Employment, *Exec Srch*
T.J. Koellhoffer & Assoc., *Exec Srch*
Paul Kull & Co, *Exec Srch*
L&K Assoc., *Exec Srch*
Lab Support, *Temp. Agcy*
Lancaster Assoc./The Swan Grp, *Exec Srch*
Mgmt. Catalysts, *Exec Srch*
Mgmt. Recrtrs of Bay Head, *Exec Srch*
Mgmt. Recrtrs of Medford, *Exec Srch*
Mgmt. Recrtrs of Passaic Cnty, *Exec Srch*
Manpower Tech. Svcs, *Temp. Agcy*
Mayfair Svcs, *Perm. Emp Agcy*
Middlebrook Assoc., *Exec Srch*
Norrell Svcs, *Perm. Emp Agcy*
Orion Consltng, *Exec Srch*
Professional Roster, *Temp. Agcy*
Rotator Svcs, *Contract Svc*
R.S. Sadow Assoc., *Exec Srch*
Sales Consltnts of Morris Cnty, *Exec Srch*
Sales Consltnts of Sparta, *Exec Srch*
Rob Scott Assoc., *Exec Srch*
Selective Persnnl, *Perm. Emp Agcy*
Arline Simpson Assoc., *Perm. Emp Agcy*
TRS Staff Solut'ns, *Temp. Agcy*
Tenek Corp, *Exec Srch*
Ultimate Solut'ns, *Perm. Emp Agcy*
Claire Wright Assn, *Perm. Emp Agcy*

New Mexico

Albuquerque Persnnl, *Perm. Emp Agcy*
Butler Svc Grp, *Contract Svc*
CDI Corp, *Contract Svc*
COMFORCE Tech. Svcs, *Contract Svc*
Manpower, *Temp. Agcy*
Sanderson Emp. Svc, *Perm. Emp Agcy*
Scientemps, *Temp. Agcy*
Trambley The Recruiter, *Perm. Emp Agcy*

New York

ATS Reliance, *Perm. Emp Agcy*
Accounting & Computer Persnnl, *Perm. Emp Agcy*
Merrill Adams Assoc., *Career/Outplacemnt*
Franklin Allen Consltnts Exec. Srch Firm
AMESgroup, *Perm. Emp Agcy*
April Tech. Recruitng, *Perm. Emp Agcy*
Arrow Emp. Agcy, *Perm. Emp Agcy*
Auto Careers, *Perm. Emp Agcy*
Bruml Assoc., *Exec Srch*
Burns Persnnl, *Exec Srch*
CDI Corp, *Contract Svc*
CFI Resrcs, *Exec Srch*
CGR Staff Svcs, *Temp. Agcy*
Carlile Persnnl Agcy, *Perm. Emp Agcy*
Colton Partnership, *Exec Srch*
Consortium, *Exec Srch*
Corporate Careers/R.J. Assoc., *Exec Srch*
The Dartmouth Grp, *Exec Srch*
Maggi Dolan Plcmnt, *Perm. Emp Agcy*
Dymanex Srch, *Exec Srch*
EDP Contrct Svcs, *Contract Svc*
The Emp. Store/TES Technical, *Exec Srch*
Extra Help Emp. Svc, *Temp. Agcy*
Graphic Techniques, *Temp. Agcy*
Robert Half Intl/Information Syst. Division, *Exec Srch*
Hampshire Assoc., *Perm. Emp Agcy*
Hart-Merrell Persnnl, *Exec Srch*
Information Syst. Srch, *Exec Srch*
Just One Break, *Perm. Emp Agcy*
Kelly Svcs, *Temp. Agcy*
Fred Koffler Assoc., *Exec Srch*
Ktech Syst. Grp, *Perm. Emp Agcy*
Lab Support, *Temp. Agcy*
Lake Assoc., *Exec Srch*
Magill Assoc., *Exec Srch*
Mgmt. Recrtrs of Nassau, *Exec Srch*
Mgmt. Recrtrs of Woodbury/ CompuSrch, *Exec Srch*
Manpower Tech. Svcs, *Temp. Agcy*
Manpower Temp. Svcs, *Temp. Agcy*
Mar-El Emp. Agcy, *Exec Srch*
Metro Resrcs of Rochester, *Temp. Agcy*
Metro Persnnl/Metro Nursing Svcs, *Exec Srch*
Milazzo Assoc., *Perm. Emp Agcy*
Morgan-Murray Persnnl/M&M Top Temps, *Temp. Agcy*
Natek Corp, *Exec Srch*
Noah Assoc., *Perm. Emp Agcy*
Norrell Staff Svcs, *Perm. Emp Agcy*
K.A. Nowack Career Specialists, *Perm. Emp Agcy*
Olsten Staff Svcs, *Temp. Agcy*
Parsons, Anderson & Gee, *Perm. Emp Agcy*
Pathway Exec Srch, *Exec Srch*
Roberts Exec Recrtmnt, *Exec Srch*
Fran Rogers Persnnl, *Perm. Emp Agcy*
Sales Srch, Ltd./Exec. Resume Svc, *Exec Srch*
Sharp Placemnt Prof'ls, *Exec Srch*
Sigma Staffng, *Perm. Emp Agcy*
Snelling Persnnl Svcs, *Exec Srch*
Staff Managers, *Temp. Agcy*
Superior Concepts, *Contract Svc*
Venture Resrcs, *Exec Srch*
Charles Wanner Assoc. Exec. Srch Firm
Wayne Grp Exec. Srch Firm
Westchester Emp. Agcy, *Perm. Emp Agcy*
Western Staff Svcs, *Temp. Agcy*
H.L. Yoh Co, *Contract Svc*

North Carolina

A-1 Staffing & Persnnl, *Perm. Emp Agcy*
Accurate Staff Consltnts, *Exec Srch*
Action Tech. Staffng, *Temp. Agcy*
Alpha Omega Exec Srch, *Exec Srch*
American Quality Staffng, *Exec Srch*
AmeriPro Srch, *Exec Srch*
Anderson & Daniel Persnnl, *Perm. Emp Agcy*
Apple Resrcs, *Perm. Emp Agcy*
Arjay & Assoc., *Exec Srch*
Atchison & Assoc., *Exec Srch*
CDI Corp, *Contract Svc*
COMFORCE Tech. Svcs, *Contract Svc*
Corporate Staff Consltnts, *Perm. Emp Agcy*
Eastern Srch Grp, *Exec Srch*
Phil Ellis Assoc., *Exec Srch*
Employment Consltnts, *Contract Svc*
Executive Staff Svcs, *Perm. Emp Agcy*
Express Persnnl Svcs, *Perm. Emp Agcy*
Forbes Temp. Staffng, *Temp. Agcy*
Graham & Assoc., *Perm. Emp Agcy*
Granite Persnnl, *Perm. Emp Agcy*

nformation Syst. Prof'ls, *Exec Srch*
nterim Persnnl, *Temp. Agcy*
<elly Svcs, *Temp. Agcy*
<ey Temps, *Temp. Agcy*
MTS, *Perm. Emp Agcy*
Mgmt. Recrtrs Intl, *Exec Srch*
Mgmt. Recrtrs of Burlington, *Exec Srch*
Mgmt. Recrtrs of Durham, *Exec Srch*
Mgmt. Recrtrs of Fayetteville, *Exec Srch*
Mgmt. Recrtrs of Kinston, *Exec Srch*
Mgmt. Recrtrs of Raleigh/Inter Exec, *Exec Srch*
Mgmt. Recrtrs of Winston-Salem, *Exec Srch*
Mark III Persnnl, *Exec Srch*
Mebane Temp. Svcs, *Temp. Agcy*
Merrick & Moore, *Exec Srch*
Moffitt Intl, *Exec Srch*
National Svcs, *Exec Srch*
Olsten Staff Svcs, *Temp. Agcy*
'CS - Personal Communications Svc, *Contract Svc*
Quality Temp. Svcs, *Temp. Agcy*
SENC Tech. Svcs, *Contract Svc*
Sales Consltnts of Concord, *Exec Srch*
Sales Consltnts of High Point, *Exec Srch*
Snelling Persnnl Svcs, *Contract Svc*
Source Svcs Corp, *Exec Srch*
StaffMark, *Temp. Agcy*
'olt Tech. Svcs, *Contract Svc*
Wilson Persnnl, *Exec Srch*

North Dakota

Career Connection, *Exec Srch*
Olsten Staff Svcs/Kramer & Assoc./Expressway Persnnl, *Temp. Agcy*

Ohio

Advancement L.L.C., *Perm. Emp Agcy*
Alliance Tech. Svcs, *Contract Svc*
AllTech Resrcs, *Exec Srch*
Dave Arnold & Assoc., *Exec Srch*
Baldwin & Assoc., *Exec Srch*
BBS Persnnl Svcs, *Perm. Emp Agcy*
Career Enterprises, *Exec Srch*
Clopton's Placemnt Svc, *Perm. Emp Agcy*
Corell Assoc., *Perm. Emp Agcy*
Cross-Jordan Corp, *Exec Srch*
Custom Staffng, *Temp. Agcy*
DLD Tech. Svcs, *Contract Svc*
Alan Daum & Assoc., *Perm. Emp Agcy*
Tonia Deal Consltnts, *Perm. Emp Agcy*
Delta Design Drafting, *Temp. Agcy*
Eastern Persnnl Svcs, *Perm. Emp Agcy*
Elite Resrcs Grp, *Exec Srch*
Executech, *Exec Srch*
Executive Directions, *Exec Srch*
Executive Srch Ltd., *Exec Srch*
F.L.A.G., *Exec Srch*
Flowers & Assoc./Associated Temps, *Exec Srch*
Frederick-Lehmann & Assoc./Temporarily Yours, *Exec Srch*
Functional Tech. Svcs, *Perm. Emp Agcy*
Gayhart & Assoc., *Exec Srch*
Global Resrcs Grp, *Contract Svc*
Griffiths & Assoc., *Exec Srch*
H.J.C., *Exec Srch*
Russ Hadick & Assoc., *Exec Srch*
Health Care Advantage, *Exec Srch*
Hite Exec Srch/Hite Mngmnt Consltnts, *Exec Srch*
ITS Tech. Staffing/Interconnect Tech. Svcs, *Exec Srch*
Interconnect Tech. Svcs, *Exec Srch*
Interim Persnnl, *Temp. Agcy*
Kaiser Nationwide, *Exec Srch*
Mgmt. Recrtrs of Cincinnati, *Exec Srch*
Mgmt. Recrtrs of Cleveland, *Exec Srch*
Mgmt. Recrtrs of Columbus, *Exec Srch*
Mgmt. Recrtrs of Dayton, *Exec Srch*
Mgmt. Recrtrs of Solon, *Exec Srch*
Manpower Temp. Svcs, *Temp. Agcy*
Minority Exec Srch, *Exec Srch*
North American Persnnl, *Exec Srch*
North Star Resrcs, *Contract Svc*
Olsten Prof'l Staff Svcs, *Exec Srch*
Personalized Plcmnt, *Exec Srch*
Professional Emp. Svcs, *Perm. Emp Agcy*
Providence Persnnl Consltnts, *Exec Srch*
Quality Plus, *Exec Srch*
Questcor Co, *Exec Srch*
RDS, *Contract Svc*
W.R. Renner & Assoc., *Exec Srch*
Sentech Ventures, *Perm. Emp Agcy*
S&P Solut'ns, *Contract Svc*
Sales Consltnts of Cincinnati, *Exec Srch*
Snelling Persnnl Svcs, *Exec Srch*
Tabb & Assoc., *Exec Srch*
TAD Tech. Svcs, *Contract Svc*
Talent Research Corp, *Exec Srch*
The Target HR Companies, *Temp. Agcy*
Teamwork U.S.A., *Contract Svc*
Tech/Aid of OH, *Perm. Emp Agcy*
Technical Recruitng Svcs, *Exec Srch*
Temporarily Yours Plcmnt, *Temp. Agcy*
Vector Technical, *Perm. Emp Agcy*

Oklahoma

Ameri Resource, *Exec Srch*
Express Persnnl Svcs, *Exec Srch*
Key Temp. Persnnl, *Temp. Agcy*
Mgmt. Recrtrs of Oklahoma Cty, *Exec Srch*
Mgmt. Srch, *Exec Srch*
John Wylie Assoc., *Exec Srch*

Oregon

CDI Corp, *Contract Svc*
Express Persnnl Svcs, *Exec Srch*
Impact Staffng, *Temp. Agcy*
Kelly Svcs, *Temp. Agcy*
Mgmt. Recrtrs/Officemates5 of Portland, *Exec Srch*
Manpower Temp. Svcs, *Temp. Agcy*
NPRC/Nationwde Persnnl Recruitng & Consltng, *Exec Srch*
Northwest Temp. & Staff Svcs, *Temp. Agcy*
Southern Oregon Temporary, *Temp. Agcy*
Talent Tree Staffng, *Perm. Emp Agcy*
Uniforce Tech. Svcs, *Contract Svc*
Volt Tech. Svcs, *Contract Svc*

Pennsylvania

AA Staff Solut'ns, *Contract Svc*
Advanced Technlgy Resrcs, *Exec Srch*
Alexander Persnnl Assoc., *Exec Srch*
American Staffing Resrcs, *Temp. Agcy*
ASAP Staffng, *Perm. Emp Agcy*
Atomic Persnnl, *Exec Srch*
T.W. Boris Assn, *Exec Srch*
Bradley Prof'l Svcs, *Perm. Emp Agcy*
CDI Corp, *Contract Svc*
Career Concepts Staff Svcs, *Exec Srch*
Career Quest Confidential, *Exec Srch*
Rich Christine Assoc., *Exec Srch*
COREStaff, *Temp. Agcy*
DiCenzo Persnnl Specialists, *Perm. Emp Agcy*
EDP/Temps of PA, *Temp. Agcy*
Executive Avail-A-Search, *Exec Srch*
FORTUNE Grp Intl, *Exec Srch*
Fox-Morris Assoc., *Exec Srch*
J.H. Glass & Assoc., *Exec Srch*
Jerry Goldberg & Assoc., *Perm. Emp Agcy*
Hobbie Temp. Persnnl, *Temp. Agcy*
Human Assets, *Temp. Agcy*
Human Resource Solut'ns, *Exec Srch*
IMC Intl, *Contract Svc*
Interim Persnnl, *Temp. Agcy*
J-Rand Srch, *Exec Srch*
JK Resrcs, *Exec Srch*
Kelly Svcs, *Temp. Agcy*
Blair Kershaw Assoc., *Exec Srch*
Lab Support, *Temp. Agcy*
Rob Lohrke Assoc., *Exec Srch*
London Persnnl Svcs, *Perm. Emp Agcy*
Main Line Persnnl, *Perm. Emp Agcy*
Mgmt. Recrtrs Intl, *Exec Srch*
Mgmt. Recrtrs of DE Cnty/CompuSrch, *Exec Srch*
Mgmt. Recrtrs of Lehigh Vly/CompuSrch, *Exec Srch*
Mgmt. Recrtrs of Manayunk/Chestnut Hill/CompuSrch, *Exec Srch*
Mgmt. Recrtrs of Philadelphia/ CompuSrch, *Exec Srch*
Manpower Temp. Svcs, *Temp. Agcy*
George Martin Exec Srch, *Exec Srch*
Rob McClure Ltd., *Exec Srch*
The Morris Grp, *Exec Srch*
Norcon Assoc., *Perm. Emp Agcy*
Norrell Svcs, *Contract Svc*
Olsten Staff Svcs, *Temp. Agcy*
LaMonte Owens, *Exec Srch*
Prestige Persnnl, *Exec Srch*
Probe Technlgy, *Exec Srch*
Q-Source, *Perm. Emp Agcy*
R.H.A. Exec Persnnl Svcs, *Exec Srch*
Rice Cohen Intl, *Exec Srch*
S-H-S Intl, *Perm. Emp Agcy*
Sanford Rose Assoc., *Exec Srch*
Source EDP, *Perm. Emp Agcy*
Strongin Tech. Enterprises of PA, *Perm. Emp Agcy*
Suber & McAuley Tech. Srch, *Exec Srch*
Systems Persnnl, *Exec Srch*
TAD Tech. Svcs, *Temp. Agcy*
Tandem Persnnl, *Temp. Agcy*
Tech/Aid of PA, *Contract Svc*
Technical Persnnl, *Exec Srch*
Uni Temp Temp. Svc, *Temp. Agcy*
United Tech. Assoc., *Temp. Agcy*
Virtual Workplace, *Temp. Agcy*
Whittlesey & Assoc., *Exec Srch*
Witthauer Assoc. Exec. Srch Firm
Yorktowne Persnnl, *Exec Srch*

Rhode Island

Colony Persnnl Assoc., *Perm. Emp Agcy*
Kelly Svcs, *Temp. Agcy*
Albert Lee & Assoc., *Exec Srch*
Mgmt. Recrtrs Intl, *Exec Srch*
New England Consltnts, *Perm. Emp Agcy*
Norrell Svcs, *Temp. Agcy*
Nugent Assoc., *Exec Srch*
Occupations Unlimtd, *Perm. Emp Agcy*
On Line Temp/On Line Staff, *Temp. Agcy*
PKS Assoc., *Exec Srch*
Tech/Aid of RI, *Contract Svc*

South Carolina

Accel Temp. Svcs, *Temp. Agcy*
Atlantic Recrtrs, *Exec Srch*
Bock & Assoc., *Exec Srch*
CDI Corp, *Contract Svc*
Engineer & Tech. Recruitng, *Exec Srch*
FORTUNE Persnnl Consltnts of Columbia, *Exec Srch*
Charles Foster Staffng, *Temp. Agcy*
Harvey Persnnl, *Perm. Emp Agcy*
Mgmt. Recrtrs of Columbia, *Exec Srch*
Mgmt. Recrtrs of Orangeburg, *Exec Srch*
Mgmt. Recrtrs of Rck Hill, *Exec Srch*
Miller & Assoc., *Exec Srch*
Phillips Resource Grp, *Exec Srch*
Pindrum Staff Svc, *Temp. Agcy*
Search & Recruit Intl, *Exec Srch*
Southern Recrtrs & Consltnts, *Exec Srch*
StaffMark, *Temp. Agcy*
TRS (Total Recruitng Svcs), *Perm. Emp Agcy*

Tennessee

A-1 Staffing & Persnnl, *Temp. Agcy*
American Tech. Assoc., *Contract Svc*
CDI Corp, *Contract Svc*
CDI Information Syst., *Contract Svc*
Central Tech. Svc, *Contract Svc*
Engineer One, *Perm. Emp Agcy*
Express Persnnl Svcs, *Perm. Emp Agcy*
FORTUNE Persnnl Consltnts, *Exec Srch*
Hamilton Ryker Co, *Exec Srch*
Hester & Assoc., *Exec Srch*
Mgmt. Recrtrs/Sales Consltnts-Chattanooga, *Exec Srch*
Mgmt. Recrtrs of Knoxville, *Exec Srch*
Manpower, *Temp. Agcy*
Mega Force, *Temp. Agcy*
Olsten Staff Svcs, *Temp. Agcy*
Piercy Emp. Svcs, *Perm. Emp Agcy*
Sales Consltnts of Nashville, *Exec Srch*
Software Resource Consltnts, *Exec Srch*
Staffing Solut'ns, *Perm. Emp Agcy*
Technical Resource Assoc., *Exec Srch*
Uniforce Svcs, *Temp. Agcy*

Texas

Abacus Tech. Svc, *Contract Svc*
Add-A-Temp/Woodlands Exec Employment, *Temp. Agcy*
Adecco, *Temp. Agcy*
Albrecht & Assoc. Exec Srch, *Exec Srch*
Alternative Resrcs Corp, *Contract Svc*
Aware Affiliates Persnnl, *Perm. Emp Agcy*
B&M Air & Space Division, *Contract Svc*
Babich & Assoc., *Perm. Emp Agcy*
Benchmark Prof'ls, *Exec Srch*
BestStaff Svcs, *Perm. Emp Agcy*
BioSource Intl, *Exec Srch*
Butler Intl, *Contract Svc*
CDI Corp, *Contract Svc*
C.G. & Co, *Exec Srch*
CarlTech, *Contract Svc*
Computemp, *Temp. Agcy*
Contrct Design Persnnl, *Temp. Agcy*
CoreCom, *Contract Svc*
Creative Staff Svcs, *Temp. Agcy*
DDR, *Exec Srch*
C. Michael Dixon Assoc., *Exec Srch*
Dunhill Prof'l Srch, *Exec Srch*
EDP Staff Svcs, *Contract Svc*
The Elsworth Grp, *Exec Srch*
Evins Persnnl Consltnts of Killeen, *Perm. Emp Agcy*
Executive Srch Persnnl, *Exec Srch*
FirstWord Staff Svcs, *Temp. Agcy*
Focus Point, *Contract Svc*
H+M Recrtrs, *Exec Srch*
Haragan Assoc., *Exec Srch*
Healthcare Recrtrs Intl, *Exec Srch*
Herndon & Assoc., *Exec Srch*
Houston Creative Connections, *Exec Srch*
Job Market Persnnl Agcy, *Perm. Emp Agcy*
Kelly Svcs, *Temp. Agcy*
LRJ Staff Svcs, *Perm. Emp Agcy*
Loewenstein & Assoc., *Exec Srch*
Mgmt. Recrtrs Intl, *Exec Srch*
Mgmt. Recrtrs of Dallas, *Exec Srch*
Manpower, *Temp. Agcy*
Marquess & Assoc., *Perm. Emp Agcy*
McDuffy-Edwards, *Exec Srch*
McKinley•Arend Intl, *Exec Srch*
Metro Careers, *Exec Srch*
Olsten Staff Svcs, *Temp. Agcy*

Opportunity Unlimtd Persnnl Consltnts, *Exec Srch*
Pate Resrcs Grp, *Exec Srch*
Pro Staff Persnnl Svcs, *Temp. Agcy*
Professional Srch Consltnts, *Contract Svc*
Remedy Intelligent Staffng, *Perm. Emp Agcy*
Bart Roberson & Co, *Exec Srch*
Russell Reynolds Assoc., *Exec Srch*
Sales Consltnts of Houston, *Exec Srch*
Snelling Persnnl Svcs, *Perm. Emp Agcy*
Snelling Persnnl Svcs, *Exec Srch*
Staff Extension, *Exec Srch*
Stehouwer & Assoc., *Perm. Emp Agcy*
Strategic Outsourcing Corp, *Exec Srch*
TGA Co, *Exec Srch*
TRC Staff Svcs, *Temp. Agcy*
TAD Tech. Svcs, *Contract Svc*
Tech-Net, *Exec Srch*
Technical Careers, *Contract Svc*
Tech. Staff Solut'ns, *Exec Srch*
Temp 2000 Temp. Svcs, *Temp. Agcy*
Total Temp. Svcs, *Temp. Agcy*
The Urban Placemnt Svc, *Exec Srch*
Valpers, *Exec Srch*
Vick & Assoc./Recruiters Online Netwrk, *Exec Srch*
Volt Tech. Svcs, *Contract Svc*
Volt Temp. Svcs of Dallas, *Temp. Agcy*
Western Temp. Svc, *Temp. Agcy*
Wheeler, Moore & Elam Co, *Exec Srch*
H.L. Yoh Co, *Contract Svc*

Utah

Deeco Intl, *Perm. Emp Agcy*
Franklin-Newbery Engineering, *Perm. Emp Agcy*
Intermountain Staffing Resrcs, *Temp. Agcy*
Mgmt. Recrtrs Intl, *Exec Srch*
Mgmt. Recrtrs of Provo, *Exec Srch*
Olsten Staff Svcs, *Temp. Agcy*
Professional Recrtrs, *Exec Srch*
Trout & Assoc., *Exec Srch*

Vermont

Persnnl Dept, *Temp. Agcy*
Western Staff Svcs, *Temp. Agcy*

Virginia

Ability Resrcs, *Exec Srch*
Accu Tech, *Perm. Emp Agcy*
Alpha Omega Resrcs, *Perm. Emp Agcy*
American Tech. Resrcs, *Perm. Emp Agcy*
CDI Corp, *Contract Svc*
Cadworks, *Contract Svc*
Career Market Consltnts, *Exec Srch*
Certified Placemnt Assoc., *Exec Srch*
Corporate Connection Exec. Srch Firm
EDP, *Temp. Agcy*
Effective Staffng, *Exec Srch*
Halbrecht & Co, *Exec Srch*
Kogen Persnnl, *Exec Srch*
Lee Staffing Resrcs, *Exec Srch*
Carol Maden Grp Recruitng, *Exec Srch*
Mgmt. Recrtrs of McLean, *Exec Srch*
Mgmt. Recrtrs of Roanoke, *Exec Srch*
Manpower Temp. Svcs, *Temp. Agcy*
The McCormick Grp, *Exec Srch*
Network Companies, *Exec Srch*
Norrell Staff Svcs, *Exec Srch*
Olsten Staff Svcs, *Temp. Agcy*
Placement Prof'ls, *Exec Srch*
Procurement Solut'ns, *Contract Svc*
Professional Srch Persnnl, *Exec Srch*
Recruiting Resrcs, *Exec Srch*
Remedy Intelligent Staffng, *Temp. Agcy*
Snelling Persnnl Svcs, *Perm. Emp Agcy*
Strategic Srch, *Exec Srch*
The Talley Grp, *Exec Srch*
Tech/Aid of VA, *Temp. Agcy*
U.S. Srch, *Exec Srch*
Virginia Emp. Referral Svc, *Exec Srch*
Wannamaker Assoc., *Perm. Emp Agcy*

Washington

Bixler Grp, *Exec Srch*
The Career Clinic, *Exec Srch*
Career Svcs, *Perm. Emp Agcy*
COMFORCE Tech. Svcs, *Contract Svc*
Comprehensive Staff Resrcs dba Techstaff, *Temp. Agcy*
Express Persnnl Svcs, *Temp. Agcy*
Hall Kinion Assoc., *Perm. Emp Agcy*
The Jobs Co, *Exec Srch*
Kelly Svcs, *Temp. Agcy*
Kossuth & Assoc., *Exec Srch*
MCE Tech. Srch, *Exec Srch*
Mgmt. Recrtrs of Lynwood, *Exec Srch*
Mgmt. Recrtrs of Mercer Islnd, *Exec Srch*
Mgmt. Recrtrs of Seattle, *Exec Srch*
Mgmt. Recrtrs of Tacoma, *Exec Srch*
Manpower Temp. Svcs, *Temp. Agcy*
John Mason & Assoc., *Exec Srch*
Mini-Systems Assoc., *Contract Svc*
Nelson, Coulson & Assoc., *Perm. Emp Agcy*
Northwest Temp. Svcs, *Temp. Agcy*
Strain Persnnl Specialists, *Exec Srch*
TSA, *Exec Srch*
Two 56, *Contract Svc*
Whittall Mngmnt Grp, *Exec Srch*

West Virginia

CDI Corp, *Contract Svc*
Kelly Svcs, *Temp. Agcy*
Key Persnnl, *Perm. Emp Agcy*

Wisconsin

Aerotek, *Contract Svc*
Argus Tech. Svcs, *Perm. Emp Agcy*
Austria Austria & Assoc., *Perm. Emp Agcy*
J.M. Eagle Partners, *Exec Srch*
Eagle Technlgy Grp, *Perm. Emp Agcy*
Employability, *Perm. Emp Agcy*
Executive Recrtrs, *Exec Srch*
Executive Resource, *Exec Srch*
Food Staff 2000, *Exec Srch*
IDI Corp, *Temp. Agcy*
Mgmt. Recrtrs Intl, *Exec Srch*
Mgmt. Recrtrs of Appleton/ CompuSrch, *Exec Srch*
Mgmt. Recrtrs of Green Bay, *Exec Srch*
Mgmt. Recrtrs of Milwaukee, *Exec Srch*
MARBL Consltnts, *Exec Srch*
Olsten Staff Svcs, *Temp. Agcy*
Pollak & Skan, *Contract Svc*
Tom Sloan & Assoc., *Perm. Emp Agcy*
TAD Tech. Svcs, *Contract Svc*
Technology Consltng Corp, *Contract Svc*
Techstaff, *Perm. Emp Agcy*
Techtronix Tech. Employment, *Exec Srch*
Temps Plus Staff Svcs, *Perm. Emp Agcy*
Valley Recruitng, *Exec Srch*
The Waterstone Grp, *Contract Svc*
Work Connection, *Perm. Emp Agcy*

Wyoming

Olsten Staff Svcs, *Temp. Agcy*

TELECOMMUNICATIONS

Arizona

Tele-Solution Srch, *Exec Srch*

California

John Anthony & Assoc., *Exec Srch*
Rich Beckstead & Assoc., *Exec Srch*
Gorelick & Assoc., *Exec Srch*
JPM Intl, *Exec Srch*
Kabl Ability Netwrk, *Exec Srch*
New Venture Development, *Exec Srch*
Newport Strategic Srch, *Exec Srch*
Tom Pezman & Assoc., *Exec Srch*
Smartsource Inc., *Contract Svc*
Spectrum Srch Assoc., *Exec Srch*
Teleforce Intl, *Exec Srch*
Unisearch, *Exec Srch*
Warren & Morris & Madison, *Exec Srch*

Colorado

Carlsen Resrcs, *Exec Srch*
Daniels & Patterson Corp Srch, *Exec Srch*
Mgmt. Recrtrs Intl, *Exec Srch*
J.Q. Turner & Assoc., *Exec Srch*

Connecticut

Baldwin Assoc., *Exec Srch*
Higbee Assoc., *Exec Srch*
McIntyre Assoc., *Exec Srch*

District of Columbia

Manpower, *Temp. Agcy*
Savoy Partners Exec. Srch Firm

Florida

All Trades Staffng, *Contract Svc*
COMFORCE Telecom, *Contract Svc*
Mgmt. Recrtrs Intl, *Exec Srch*
Media Mgmt. Resrcs, *Exec Srch*
Snelling Persnnl Svcs, *Temp. Agcy*
The Stewart Srch Grp, *Exec Srch*
System One Tech. Staffng, *Exec Srch*
Uniquest Intl, *Exec Srch*

Georgia

Atlanta Tech. Support, *Contract Svc*
COMFORCE Telecom, *Contract Svc*
Corporate Srch, *Exec Srch*
Delta Resource Grp, *Exec Srch*
Georgetown Discoveries, *Exec Srch*
Tennant & Assoc., *Exec Srch*

Illinois

Bonner & Stricklin & Assoc., *Exec Srch*
Bratland & Assoc., *Exec Srch*
COMFORCE Telecom, *Contract Svc*
Data Career Ctr, *Exec Srch*
First Srch, *Exec Srch*
Manpower Temp. Svcs, *Temp. Agcy*
SHS, *Exec Srch*
Sales Consltnts of Chicago, *Exec Srch*
Search Source, *Exec Srch*
Stone Enterprises, *Exec Srch*

Iowa

Executive Srch Assoc., *Exec Srch*

Maryland

A.G. Fishkin & Assoc., *Exec Srch*
Sales Consltnts of Columbia, *Exec Srch*
Sales Consltnts of Rockville, *Exec Srch*

Massachusetts

Bowdoin Grp, *Exec Srch*
Carter/MacKay of Framingham, *Exec Srch*
Franklin Intl Srch, *Exec Srch*
HM Assoc., *Exec Srch*
New Dimensions in Technlgy, *Exec Srch*
Professional Placemnt Consltng Grp, *Exec Srch*
L.A. Silver Assoc., *Exec Srch*

Michigan

Business-Trends, *Perm. Emp Agcy*
Sales Consltnts of Farmington Hills, *Exec Srch*

Minnesota

Add On HR Specialties, *Exec Srch*

Missouri

Executive Recrtrs, *Exec Srch*

Nebraska

The Regency Grp, *Exec Srch*
Sales Consltnts of Omaha, *Exec Srch*

New Hampshire

Pacific Srch Consltnts, *Exec Srch*

New Jersey

L&K Assoc., *Exec Srch*
Mgmt. Recrtrs Intl, *Exec Srch*
Stelton Grp, *Exec Srch*
Tenek Corp, *Exec Srch*

New Mexico

Manpower, *Temp. Agcy*

New York

COMFORCE Corp, *Contract Svc*
COMFORCE Telecom, *Contract Svc*
Executive Exchange, *Exec Srch*
Huntington Persnnl Consltnts, *Exec Srch*
Manpower Temp. Svcs, *Temp. Agcy*
Sales Consltnts of Westchester, *Exec Srch*
Telequest Communications, *Exec Srch*

North Carolina

COMFORCE Telecom, *Contract Svc*
Sales Consltnts of Concord, *Exec Srch*
David Weinfeld Grp, *Exec Srch*

Ohio

Guthoff & Assoc., *Exec Srch*
Jaeger Intl, *Exec Srch*
Teknon Emp. Resrcs, *Exec Srch*

Oklahoma

National Recrtrs, *Exec Srch*

Pennsylvania

Advanced Technlgy Resrcs, *Exec Srch*
Lawrence Persnnl, *Exec Srch*
Mgmt. Recrtrs Intl, *Exec Srch*
Manpower Temp. Svcs, *Temp. Agcy*
Terry Taylor & Assoc., *Exec Srch*

Rhode Island

Pro Srch, *Exec Srch*

Tennessee

Software Resource Consltnts, *Exec Srch*

Texas

Bundy-Stewart Assoc., *Exec Srch*
CDI Telecommunications, *Temp. Agcy*
Eissler & Assoc., *Exec Srch*
Inside Track, *Exec Srch*
Mgmt. Recrtrs of LBJ Prk/Dallas, *Exec Srch*

Virginia

FGI, *Exec Srch*
Mgmt. Recrtrs Intl, *Exec Srch*
Paul-Tittle Assoc., *Perm. Emp Agcy*
Bill Young & Assoc., *Exec Srch*

West Virginia

)nsite Commercial Staffng, *Perm. Emp Agcy*

Wisconsin

\erotek, *Contract Svc*

ELEMARKETING

Alaska

)lsten Staff Svcs, *Temp. Agcy*

California

Aanpower, *Temp. Agcy*

Florida

:areers USA, *Temp. Agcy*
:ustom Staffng, *Temp. Agcy*
Aanpower Temp. Svcs, *Temp. Agcy*

Georgia

Aanpower Temp. Svcs, *Temp. Agcy*

Massachusetts

Aanpower Temp. Svcs, *Temp. Agcy*

Michigan

Aanpower, *Temp. Agcy*

New York

ccuStaff, *Temp. Agcy*
Aanpower Temp. Svcs, *Temp. Agcy*
'elemarketing Recrtrs, *Exec Srch*

Ohio

ich Bencin & Assoc., *Perm. Emp Agcy*
Aanpower Temp. Svcs, *Temp. Agcy*

Oregon

dams Temps, *Temp. Agcy*

Pennsylvania

Aanpower Temp. Svcs, *Temp. Agcy*

Tennessee

Aanpower, *Temp. Agcy*
Aega Force, *Temp. Agcy*

Texas

Aanpower, *Temp. Agcy*

EXTILES

Alabama

eneral Persnnl Corp, *Perm. Emp Agcy*
Agmt. Recrtrs Intl, *Exec Srch*

Arizona

Agmt. Recrtrs of Scottsdale, *Exec Srch*

Arkansas

Agmt. Recrtrs of Little Rock, *Exec Srch*

California

Agmt. Recrtrs of Burlingame/Sales Consltnts, *Exec Srch*
Agmt. Recrtrs of Encino, *Exec Srch*
Agmt. Recrtrs of Pleasanton, *Exec Srch*
Aesa Intl, *Exec Srch*

Colorado

ee Mngmnt Grp, *Perm. Emp Agcy*
ales Consltnts, *Exec Srch*

Connecticut

Agmt. Recrtrs Intl, *Exec Srch*

Florida

gmt. Recrtrs of St. Petersburg, *Exec Srch*
gmt. Recrtrs of Tallahassee, *Exec Srch*
gmt. Recrtrs of Tampa, *Exec Srch*
ales Consltnts of Fort Lauderdale, *Exec Srch*
ales Consltnts of Jacksonville, *Exec Srch*

Georgia

xecutive Srch & Persnnl Svcs, *Exec Srch*
gmt. Recrtrs of Atlanta, *Exec Srch*

Illinois

gmt. Recrtrs of Rockford, *Exec Srch*
fficemates5 of Wheeling, *Exec Srch*
ales Consltnts/Mgmt. Recrtrs Intl, *Exec Srch*
ales Consltnts of Oak Brk, *Exec Srch*

Indiana

xecusearch, *Exec Srch*
Agmt. Recrtrs of Evansville, *Exec Srch*
Agmt. Recrtrs of Indianapolis, *Exec Srch*
Agmt. Recrtrs of Richmond/Staff Solut'ns, *Exec Srch*
fficemates5 of Indianapolis, *Exec Srch*

Iowa

Mgmt. Recrtrs Intl, *Exec Srch*

Kansas

Mgmt. Recrtrs of Overlnd Prk, *Exec Srch*
Network of Excellence, *Exec Srch*

Kentucky

Angel Grp Intl, *Exec Srch*

Louisiana

Mgmt. Recrtrs of Baton Rouge, *Exec Srch*
Mgmt. Recrtrs-Metairie/Sales Consltnts, *Exec Srch*

Maryland

Mgmt. Recrtrs of Annapolis, *Exec Srch*
Mgmt. Recrtrs-Baltimore/Sales Consltnts, *Exec Srch*
Mgmt. Recrtrs-Bethesda/CompuSearch, *Exec Srch*
Mgmt. Recrtrs of Frederick, *Exec Srch*
Sales Consltnts of Prince Georges Cnty, *Exec Srch*

Massachusetts

Cyr Assoc., *Exec Srch*
Mgmt. Recrtrs Intl of Braintree, *Exec Srch*
Mgmt. Recrtrs Intl of Springfield, *Exec Srch*
Mgmt. Recrtrs Intl of Westboro, *Exec Srch*
Sales Consltnts of Cape Cod, *Exec Srch*
Sales Consltnts of Plymouth Cnty, *Exec Srch*
Sales Consltnts of Wellesley, *Exec Srch*

Michigan

Mgmt. Recrtrs of Bingham Farms, *Exec Srch*
Mgmt. Recrtrs of Flint, *Exec Srch*
Mgmt. Recrtrs of Kalamazoo, *Exec Srch*
Mgmt. Recrtrs of Lansing, *Exec Srch*
Mgmt. Recrtrs of Muskegon, *Exec Srch*
Mgmt. Recrtrs of Rochester, *Exec Srch*
Sales Consltnts of Detroit, *Exec Srch*
Sales Consltnts of Farmington Hills, *Exec Srch*

Minnesota

Mgmt. Recrtrs-Minneapolis/Sales Consltnts, *Exec Srch*

Missouri

Mgmt. Recrtrs of Kansas Cty, *Exec Srch*
Mgmt. Recrtrs of Springfield, *Exec Srch*
Mgmt. Recrtrs of St. Louis, *Exec Srch*
Officemates5 of St. Louis, *Exec Srch*

Nebraska

Compusearch of Lincoln, *Exec Srch*
Mgmt. Recrtrs of Omaha/Officemates5, *Exec Srch*

New Jersey

Mgmt. Recrtrs of Passaic Cnty, *Exec Srch*
Sales Consltnts of Sparta, *Exec Srch*

New York

Adecco, *Temp. Agcy*
Mgmt. Recrtrs of Woodbury/ CompuSrch, *Exec Srch*

North Carolina

Adkins & Assoc., *Exec Srch*
Amcell Assoc., *Exec Srch*
Ayers & Assoc., *Exec Srch*
Forbes Temp. Staffng, *Temp. Agcy*
Mgmt. Recrtrs Intl, *Exec Srch*
Mgmt. Recrtrs of Durham, *Exec Srch*
Mgmt. Recrtrs of Greensboro, *Exec Srch*
Mgmt. Recrtrs of Raleigh/Inter Exec, *Exec Srch*
Mgmt. Recrtrs of Winston-Salem, *Exec Srch*
Sales Consltnts of High Point, *Exec Srch*
Snelling Srch, *Exec Srch*
Sparks Persnnl Svcs, *Exec Srch*

Ohio

Mgmt. Recrtrs of Cincinnati, *Exec Srch*
Mgmt. Recrtrs of Cleveland, *Exec Srch*
Mgmt. Recrtrs of Columbus, *Exec Srch*
Mgmt. Recrtrs of Dayton, *Exec Srch*
Mgmt. Recrtrs of Solon, *Exec Srch*
Sales Consltnts of Cincinnati, *Exec Srch*

Oklahoma

Mgmt. Recrtrs of Oklahoma Cty, *Exec Srch*

Oregon

Mgmt. Recrtrs/Officemates5 of Portland, *Exec Srch*

Pennsylvania

Mgmt. Recrtrs of DE Cnty/CompuSrch, *Exec Srch*
Mgmt. Recrtrs of Lehigh Vly/CompuSrch, *Exec Srch*
Mgmt. Recrtrs of Philadelphia/ CompuSrch, *Exec Srch*
Rice Cohen Intl, *Exec Srch*
Kenn Spinrad, *Exec Srch*

Rhode Island

Creative Input, *Exec Srch*
Mgmt. Recrtrs Intl, *Exec Srch*

South Carolina

Dunhill Persnnl of St. Andrews, *Perm. Emp Agcy*
Mgmt. Recrtrs of Aiken, *Exec Srch*
Mgmt. Recrtrs of Columbia, *Exec Srch*
Mgmt. Recrtrs of Rck Hill, *Exec Srch*
Sales Consltnts/Mgmt. Recrtrs of Greenville, *Exec Srch*

Tennessee

Mgmt. Recrtrs of Knoxville, *Exec Srch*
Sales Consltnts of Nashville, *Exec Srch*

Texas

Mgmt. Recrtrs Intl, *Exec Srch*
Sales Consltnts of Houston, *Exec Srch*

Virginia

Mgmt. Recrtrs of McLean, *Exec Srch*
Mgmt. Recrtrs of Roanoke, *Exec Srch*

Washington

Mgmt. Recrtrs of Mercer Islnd, *Exec Srch*
Mgmt. Recrtrs of Tacoma, *Exec Srch*

Wisconsin

Mgmt. Recrtrs of Appleton/ CompuSrch, *Exec Srch*

TRANSPORTATION

Alabama

A-1 Emp. Svc, *Perm. Emp Agcy*
Clark Persnnl Svc of Mobile, *Exec Srch*
Labor Finders, *Temp. Agcy*
Mgmt. Recrtrs Intl, *Exec Srch*

Arizona

The Bren Grp, *Exec Srch*
Clifford & Assoc., *Perm. Emp Agcy*
Dealer Connection, *Perm. Emp Agcy*
Mgmt. Recrtrs of Scottsdale, *Exec Srch*
Spectra Intl, *Exec Srch*

Arkansas

Mgmt. Recrtrs of Little Rock, *Exec Srch*

California

Alpha-Net Consltng Grp, *Exec Srch*
Apropos Emp. Agcy, *Perm. Emp Agcy*
Best Temp. Svc, *Temp. Agcy*
Blue, Garni & Co, *Exec Srch*
Business Syst. Staffing & Assoc., *Perm. Emp Agcy*
CDS Staff Svcs, *Contract Svc*
California Srch Agcy, *Exec Srch*
Culver Persnnl Svcs, *Perm. Emp Agcy*
Culver Persnnl Svcs, *Exec Srch*
Drake Office Overload, *Temp. Agcy*
Eleventh Hour Staff Svcs, *Temp. Agcy*
Employment Devlpmnt Dept, *Perm. Emp Agcy*
Ethos Consltng, *Exec Srch*
Fisher Persnnl Mngmnt Svcs, *Exec Srch*
40 Plus of So. CA, *Exec Srch*
Garnett Emp. Svcs, *Temp. Agcy*
Intl Staff Consltnts, *Exec Srch*
Labor World, *Temp. Agcy*
LeBlanc & Assoc., *Exec Srch*
Malibu Grp, *Exec Srch*
Mgmt. Recrtrs of Encino, *Exec Srch*
Mgmt. Recrtrs of Laguna Hills, *Exec Srch*
Mgmt. Recrtrs of Pleasanton, *Exec Srch*
Mgmt. Recrtrs of Redlands, *Exec Srch*
Maverick Staff Svc, *Perm. Emp Agcy*
Mesa Intl, *Exec Srch*
Mindseed Corp, *Exec Srch*
National Asian Pacific Center on Aging, *Perm. Emp Agcy*
ProFile Persnnl, *Perm. Emp Agcy*
Ed Rast & Co, *Exec Srch*
Scott-Thaler Assoc., *Exec Srch*
Thor Temp. Svcs, *Temp. Agcy*
The Truman Agcy, Persnnl Specialists, *Perm. Emp Agcy*
Western Staff Svcs, *Temp. Agcy*

Colorado

Eleventh Hour Staff Svcs, *Perm. Emp Agcy*
40 Plus of CO, *Career/Outplacemnt*
JobSearch, *Temp. Agcy*
Labor Ready, *Temp. Agcy*
SOS Staff Svcs, *Temp. Agcy*
Sales Consltnts, *Exec Srch*
Todays Temporary, *Temp. Agcy*
Woodmoor Grp, *Exec Srch*

Connecticut

Admiral Staff Svcs, *Temp. Agcy*
Mgmt. Recrtrs Intl, *Exec Srch*
Barry Persky & Co., *Exec Srch*

Florida

AAA Employment, *Perm. Emp Agcy*
Ambiance Persnnl, *Exec Srch*
B&B Persnnl, *Perm. Emp Agcy*

Bryan & Assoc./Worknet, Etc., *Exec Srch*
DGA Persnnl Grp, *Exec Srch*
FORTUNE Persnnl Consltnts, *Exec Srch*
Mgmt. Recrtrs of Lake Cnty, *Exec Srch*
Mgmt. Recrtrs of St. Petersburg, *Exec Srch*
Mgmt. Recrtrs of Tallahassee, *Exec Srch*
Mgmt. Recrtrs of Tampa, *Exec Srch*
OMNIPartners, *Exec Srch*
Profes. Staffing/Able Body Temp. Svcs, *Contract Svc*
Sales Consltnts of Fort Lauderdale, *Exec Srch*
Sales Consltnts of Jacksonville, *Exec Srch*

Georgia

A-OK Persnnl, *Perm. Emp Agcy*
All-Star Temp. & Emp. Svcs, *Temp. Agcy*
Boreham Intl, *Exec Srch*
Dunhill Prof'l Srch, *Exec Srch*
Elite Staff Svcs, *Perm. Emp Agcy*
Mgmt. Recrtrs/Sales Consltnts of Cobb Cnty, *Exec Srch*
Mgmt. Recrtrs of Atlanta, *Exec Srch*
Mgmt. Recrtrs of Marietta, *Exec Srch*
Millard & Assoc., *Exec Srch*
NEIS, *Exec Srch*
Randstad Staff Svcs, *Perm. Emp Agcy*

Hawaii

Ellis & Assoc., *Exec Srch*
Sales Consltnts of Honolulu, *Exec Srch*

Illinois

Bevelle & Assoc., *Exec Srch*
J.C.G. Limited, *Perm. Emp Agcy*
Mgmt. Recrtrs of Rockford, *Exec Srch*
John O'Connor & Assoc., *Exec Srch*
Officemates5 of Wheeling, *Exec Srch*
Sales Consltnts/Mgmt. Recrtrs Intl, *Exec Srch*
Sales Consltnts of Oak Brk, *Exec Srch*
Staffing Team Intl, *Temp. Agcy*
Stivers Temp. Persnnl, *Temp. Agcy*
Strand Assoc., *Perm. Emp Agcy*

Indiana

Execusearch, *Exec Srch*
Mgmt. Recrtrs of Evansville, *Exec Srch*
Mgmt. Recrtrs of Indianapolis, *Exec Srch*
Mgmt. Recrtrs of Richmond/Staff Solut'ns, *Exec Srch*
National Corporate Consltnts/Advantage Svcs, *Exec Srch*
Officemates5 of Indianapolis, *Exec Srch*
Persnnl Plus, *Exec Srch*
Rush Temps, *Temp. Agcy*
Warrick Cnty Emp. & Training Ctr, *Career/Outplacemnt*

Iowa

Mgmt. Recrtrs Intl, *Exec Srch*
Sanford Rose Assoc., *Exec Srch*

Kansas

Eleventh Hour Staff Svcs, *Temp. Agcy*
Mgmt. Recrtrs of Overlnd Prk, *Exec Srch*
Network of Excellence, *Exec Srch*
Smith Brown & Jones, *Exec Srch*

Kentucky

Angel Grp Intl, *Exec Srch*

Louisiana

Mgmt. Recrtrs of Baton Rouge, *Exec Srch*
Mgmt. Recrtrs-Metairie/Sales Consltnts, *Exec Srch*
Talley & Assoc./Talley Temps, *Exec Srch*

Maine

At Work Persnnl, *Temp. Agcy*

Maryland

American Svc Technlgy, *Contract Svc*
Futures, *Exec Srch*
Mgmt. Recrtrs of Annapolis, *Exec Srch*
Mgmt. Recrtrs-Baltimore/Sales Consltnts, *Exec Srch*
Mgmt. Recrtrs-Bethesda/CompuSearch, *Exec Srch*
Mgmt. Recrtrs of Frederick, *Exec Srch*
Sales Consltnts of Prince Georges Cnty, *Exec Srch*
TAC Staff Svcs, *Temp. Agcy*
TAD Staff Svcs, *Temp. Agcy*

Massachusetts

Cyr Assoc., *Exec Srch*
Derek Assoc., *Exec Srch*
Futures, *Exec Srch*
Mgmt. Recrtrs Intl, *Exec Srch*
Mgmt. Recrtrs Intl of Braintree, *Exec Srch*
Mgmt. Recrtrs Intl of Springfield, *Exec Srch*
Mgmt. Recrtrs Intl of Westboro, *Exec Srch*
Sales Consltnts of Cape Cod, *Exec Srch*
Sales Consltnts of Plymouth Cnty, *Exec Srch*
Sales Consltnts of Wellesley, *Exec Srch*

Michigan

Assoc., *Exec Srch*
Beacon Svcs, *Exec Srch*
Day Persnnl dba Dorothy Day Persnnl - MI, Perm Emp Agcy
Executive Mngmnt Srch, *Exec Srch*
Executive Recrtrs Intl, *Exec Srch*
William Howard Agcy, *Perm. Emp Agcy*
Job Fair Netwrk of MI, *Perm. Emp Agcy*
Mgmt. Recrtrs of Bingham Farms, *Exec Srch*
Mgmt. Recrtrs of Dearborn, *Exec Srch*
Mgmt. Recrtrs of Flint, *Exec Srch*
Mgmt. Recrtrs of Kalamazoo, *Exec Srch*
Mgmt. Recrtrs of Lansing, *Exec Srch*
Mgmt. Recrtrs of Muskegon, *Exec Srch*
Mgmt. Recrtrs of Rochester, *Exec Srch*
METROSTAFF, *Exec Srch*
Nustar Temp. Svcs, *Temp. Agcy*
Sales Consltnts of Detroit, *Exec Srch*
Sales Consltnts of Lansing, *Exec Srch*
Thomas & Assoc. of MI, *Exec Srch*
Unlimited Staff Solut'ns, *Contract Svc*

Minnesota

Advance Persnnl Resrcs, *Exec Srch*
Mgmt. Recrtrs-Minneapolis/Sales Consltnts, *Exec Srch*
West Emp. Solut'ns, *Perm. Emp Agcy*

Mississippi

Recruitment & Training of MS, *Perm. Emp Agcy*

Missouri

Agri-Tech Persnnl, *Exec Srch*
Business Persnnl Svcs, *Temp. Agcy*
The Christiansen Grp, *Exec Srch*
Employer Advantage, *Exec Srch*
JRL Exec Recrtrs, *Exec Srch*
Mgmt. Recrtrs Intl, *Exec Srch*
Mgmt. Recrtrs of Kansas Cty, *Exec Srch*
Mgmt. Recrtrs of Springfield, *Exec Srch*
Mgmt. Recrtrs of St. Louis, *Exec Srch*
Manpower Temp. Svcs, *Temp. Agcy*
J. Miles Persnnl Svcs, *Exec Srch*
Officemates5 of St. Louis, *Exec Srch*

Montana

W.R. Knapp & Assoc., *Exec Srch*

Nebraska

Compusearch of Lincoln, *Exec Srch*
Corporate Recrtrs, *Exec Srch*
Express Persnnl, *Exec Srch*
Mgmt. Recrtrs of Omaha/Officemates5, *Exec Srch*
Noll HR Svcs, *Exec Srch*
Sales Consltnts of Omaha, *Exec Srch*

Nevada

Mgmt. Recrtrs of Reno, *Exec Srch*

New Hampshire

Able 1 Staffng, *Exec Srch*
Mgmt. Recrtrs Intl of Bedford, *Exec Srch*
National Emp. Svc Corp, *Perm. Emp Agcy*
TAC Staff Svcs, *Temp. Agcy*

New Jersey

Advance Positions, *Exec Srch*
Career Srch Assoc., *Exec Srch*
Hunt, Ltd., *Perm. Emp Agcy*
Key Employment, *Exec Srch*
Mgmt. Recrtrs of Bridgewater, *Exec Srch*
Mgmt. Recrtrs of Orange Cnty, *Exec Srch*
Mgmt. Recrtrs of Passaic Cnty, *Exec Srch*
Mayfair Svcs, *Perm. Emp Agcy*
Officemates5 of Englewood Cliffs/DayStar Temp. Svcs, *Perm. Emp Agcy*
Orion Consltng, *Exec Srch*
Sales Consltnts of Sparta, *Exec Srch*
Summit Grp, *Exec Srch*
Temps Plus, *Temp. Agcy*

New Mexico

Albuquerque Persnnl, *Perm. Emp Agcy*
CDI Corp, *Contract Svc*

New York

APA Srch, *Exec Srch*
Marilyn Cooper Persnnl, *Perm. Emp Agcy*
R.I. James, *Exec Srch*
Mgmt. Recrtrs of Woodbury/ CompuSrch, *Exec Srch*
Metro Persnnl/Metro Nursing Svcs, *Exec Srch*
Noah Assoc., *Perm. Emp Agcy*
TAD Resrcs, *Contract Svc*
Tyler Srch Consltnts, *Perm. Emp Agcy*
Yours In Travel Persnnl Agcy, *Perm. Emp Agcy*

North Carolina

A-1 Staffing & Persnnl, *Perm. Emp Agcy*
Anderson & Daniel Persnnl, *Perm. Emp Agcy*
Employment Consltnts, *Contract Svc*
FORTUNE Persnnl Consltnts, *Exec Srch*
Interim Persnnl, *Temp. Agcy*
The Jobs Market, *Perm. Emp Agcy*
Jobs of Fayetteville, *Perm. Emp Agcy*
MTS, *Perm. Emp Agcy*
Mgmt. Recrtrs Intl, *Exec Srch*
Mgmt. Recrtrs of Durham, *Exec Srch*
Mgmt. Recrtrs of Raleigh/Inter Exec, *Exec Srch*
Mgmt. Recrtrs of Winston-Salem, *Exec Srch*
Olsten Staff Svcs, *Temp. Agcy*
Sales Consltnts of High Point, *Exec Srch*
Waddy Thomson Assoc., *Exec Srch*

North Dakota

Olsten Staff Svcs/Kramer & Assoc./Expressway Persnnl, *Temp. Agcy*

Ohio

Adecco, *Perm. Emp Agcy*
CBS Persnnl Svcs, *Perm. Emp Agcy*
Choice Persnnl/LaGrange & Assoc., *Exec Srch*
Tonia Deal Consltnts, *Perm. Emp Agcy*
Eastern Persnnl Svcs, *Perm. Emp Agcy*
Elite Resrcs Grp, *Exec Srch*
Flowers & Assoc./Associated Temps, *Exec Srch*
H.J.C., *Exec Srch*
Ives & Assoc., *Exec Srch*
Job Express, *Temp. Agcy*
Kaiser Nationwide, *Exec Srch*
Laine's S.M.G., *Perm. Emp Agcy*
Mgmt. Recrtrs Intl, *Exec Srch*
Mgmt. Recrtrs of Cincinnati, *Exec Srch*
Mgmt. Recrtrs of Cleveland, *Exec Srch*
Mgmt. Recrtrs of Columbus, *Exec Srch*
Mgmt. Recrtrs of Dayton, *Exec Srch*
Mgmt. Recrtrs of Solon, *Exec Srch*
Marvel Consltnts, *Exec Srch*
Minority Exec Srch, *Exec Srch*
National Register of Akron, *Exec Srch*
National Register of Toledo, *Exec Srch*
North American Tech. Svcs, *Contract Svc*
Providence Persnnl Consltnts, *Exec Srch*
Quality Plus, *Exec Srch*
Sales Consltnts of Cincinnati, *Exec Srch*
Speer & Assoc., *Exec Srch*
TAD Tech. Svcs, *Contract Svc*

Oklahoma

Mgmt. Recrtrs of Oklahoma Cty, *Exec Srch*

Oregon

Barrett Bus. Svcs, *Temp. Agcy*
Mgmt. Recrtrs/Officemates5 of Portland, *Exec Srch*
Woodworth Intl Grp, *Exec Srch*

Pennsylvania

COREStaff, *Temp. Agcy*
IMC Intl, *Contract Svc*
J-Rand Srch, *Exec Srch*
Kathy Karr Persnnl, *Perm. Emp Agcy*
Mgmt. Recrtrs of DE Cnty/CompuSrch, *Exec Srch*
Mgmt. Recrtrs of Lehigh Vly/CompuSrch, *Exec Srch*
Mgmt. Recrtrs of Philadelphia/ CompuSrch, *Exec Srch*
R.H.A. Exec Persnnl Svcs, *Exec Srch*
Rice Cohen Intl, *Exec Srch*
TAC Staff Svcs, *Temp. Agcy*
W.G. Tucker & Assoc., *Exec Srch*
Visions Temp. Svc, *Temp. Agcy*

Rhode Island

Mgmt. Recrtrs Intl, *Exec Srch*
Norrell Svcs, *Temp. Agcy*
Sullivan & Cogliano, *Exec Srch*
TAC Staff Svcs, *Temp. Agcy*

South Carolina

Edmonds Persnnl, *Exec Srch*
FORTUNE Persnnl Consltnts of Columbia, *Exec Srch*
Mgmt. Recrtrs of Columbia, *Exec Srch*
Mgmt. Recrtrs of Rck Hill, *Exec Srch*
Snelling Persnnl, *Perm. Emp Agcy*

Tennessee

Express Persnnl Svcs, *Perm. Emp Agcy*
Mgmt. Recrtrs of Knoxville, *Exec Srch*
Persnnl Link, *Exec Srch*
Resource Persnnl Svcs, *Perm. Emp Agcy*
Sales Consltnts of Nashville, *Exec Srch*

Texas

Abilene Emp. Svc, *Perm. Emp Agcy*
American Resrcs, *Exec Srch*
Aware Affiliates Persnnl, *Perm. Emp Agcy*
Creative Staff Svcs, *Temp. Agcy*
Driving Force, *Temp. Agcy*
The Elsworth Grp, *Exec Srch*
Evins Persnnl Consltnts of Killeen, *Perm. Emp Agcy*
Job Market Persnnl Agcy, *Perm. Emp Agcy*
Kelly Svcs, *Temp. Agcy*

ALPHABETICAL INDEX

A

B

E

F

G

I

J

N

O

P

Q

R

T

U

Other Adams Media Books

The Everything Get-A-Job Book

by Steven Graber

Managing Editor of the JobBank Series

The Everything Get-A-Job Book gives you the competitive edge, with a fun and non-intimidating approach to looking for your first job or just plain trying to find a better job. Jammed with tons of tips, strategies, and advice from the trenches, this comprehensive book will be indispensible to anyone hoping to land a great job. Find out how to:

- Find companies that are hiring without picking up the want ads
- Uncover valuable networking opportunities
- Search in-depth for job openings on the Internet
- Extensive information on writing cover letters and resumes—including what not to do
- Prepare for evil interview questions
- Dealing with head hunters and employment services
- Strategies to land multiple job offers
- Negotiate the best salary, bonus, and benefits package
- And much, much more!

Trade paperback, 1-58062-223-2, $12.95
8" x 9¼", 304 pages

Available Wherever Books Are Sold

If you cannot find these titles at your favorite retail outlet, you may order them directly from the publisher. BY PHONE: Call 1-800-872-5627. We accept Visa, Mastercard, and American Express. $4.95 will be added to your total order for shipping and handling. BY MAIL: Write out the full titles of the books you'd like to order and send payment, including $4.95 for shipping and handling, to: Adams Media Corporation, 260 Center Street, Holbrook, MA 02343. U.S.A. 30-day money-back guarantee. BY FAX: 800-872-5628. BY E-MAIL: jobbank@adamsonline.com.

Visit our exciting job and career site at http://www.careercity.com

Other Adams Media Books

The Adams Electronic Job Search Almanac 2000

Uncover thousands of jobs in minutes using your own computer! This comprehensive guide features hundreds of online resources available through commercial online services, the World Wide Web, newsgroups, and more. *The Adams Electronic Job Search Almanac 2000* also includes a selection of company joblines, advice on posting an electronic resume, and strategies for researching companies on the Internet. The book also features information on a variety of job-hunting software. 5½" x 8½", 312 pages, paperback, $10.95. ISBN: 1-58062-221-6, ISSN: 1099-016X

he JobBank Series

There are 35 *JobBank* books, each providing extensive, up-to-date nployment information on hundreds of the largest employers in each job arket. The #1 best-selling series of employment directories, the *JobBank* ries has been recommended as an excellent place to begin your job search the *New York Times*, the *Los Angeles Times*, the *Boston Globe*, and the *hicago Tribune*. *JobBank* books have been used by millions of people to nd jobs. Titles available:

The Atlanta JobBank • The Austin/San Antonio JobBank • The Boston JobBank • The Carolina JobBank • The Chicago JobBank • The Connecticut JobBank • The Dallas-Fort Worth JobBank • The Denver JobBank • The Detroit JobBank • he Florida JobBank • The Houston JobBank • The Indiana JobBank • The Las Vegas JobBank • The Los Angeles JobBank • The Minneapolis-St. Paul JobBank • The Missouri JobBank • The Northern New England JobBank • The New Jersey JobBank • The New Mexico JobBank • The Metropolitan New York JobBank • The Upstate New York JobBank • The Ohio JobBank • The ;reater Philadelphia JobBank • The Phoenix JobBank • The Pittsburgh JobBank • The Portland JobBank • The Salt Lake City JobBank • The San Francisco Bay Area JobBank • The Seattle JobBank • The Tennessee JobBank • The Virginia JobBank • The Metropolitan Washington DC obBank • The Wisconsin JobBank • The JobBank Guide to Computer & High-Tech Companies • The JobBank Guide to Health Care Companies

EACH JOBBANK BOOK IS 6" X 9¼", OVER 300 PAGES, PAPERBACK, $16.95.
For ISBNs and ISSNs, please visit http://www.careercity.com/booksoftware/jobbank.asp

JobBank List Service: If you are interested in variations of this information in electronic format for sales or job search mailings, please call 800-872-5627 x5304, or e-mail us at jobbank@adamsonline.com.

Available Wherever Books Are Sold

you cannot find these titles at your favorite retail outlet, you may order them directly from e publisher. BY PHONE: Call 1-800-872-5627. We accept Visa, Mastercard, and American xpress. $4.95 will be added to your total order for shipping and handling. BY MAIL: Write it the full titles of the books you'd like to order and send payment, including $4.95 for ipping and handling, to: Adams Media Corporation, 260 Center Street, Holbrook, MA 2343. U.S.A. 30-day money-back guarantee. BY FAX: 800-872-5628. BY E-MAIL: bbank@adamsonline.com. *Discounts available for standing orders.*

Visit our exciting job and career site at http://www.careercity.com

Other Adams Media Books

The Adams Cover Letter Almanac

The Adams Cover Letter Almanac is the most detailed cover letter resource in print, containing 600 cover letters used by real people to win real jobs. It features complete information on all types of letters, including networking, "cold," broadcast, and follow-up. In addition to advice on how to avoid fatal cover letter mistakes, the book includes strategies for people changing careers, relocating, recovering from layoff, and more. ISBN 1-55850-497-4. $5^{1}/_{2}$" x $8^{1}/_{2}$", 736 pages, paperback, $12.95.

The Adams Resume Almanac

This almanac features detailed information on resume development and layout, a review of the pros and cons of various formats, an exhaustive look at the strategies that will definitely get a resume noticed, and 600 sample resumes in dozens of career categories. *The Adams Resume Almanac* is the most comprehensive, thoroughly researched resume guide ever published. ISBN 1-55850-358-7. $5^{1}/_{2}$" x $8^{1}/_{2}$", 768 pages, paperback, $10.95.

The Adams Jobs Almanac

Updated annually, *The Adams Jobs Almanac* includes names and addresses of over 7,000 U.S. employers; information on which positions each company commonly fills; industry forecasts; geographical cross-references; employment prospects in all 50 states; and advice on preparing resumes and cover letters and standing out at interviews. $5^{1}/_{2}$" x $8^{1}/_{2}$", 952 pages, paperback, $16.95.

ISBN: 1-58062-220-8, ISSN: 1072-592X

Available Wherever Books Are Sold

If you cannot find these titles at your favorite retail outlet, you may order them directly from the publisher. BY PHONE: Call 1-800-872-5627. We accept Visa, Mastercard, and American Express. $4.95 will be added to your total order for shipping and handling. BY MAIL: Write out the full titles of the books you'd like to order and send payment, including $4.95 for shipping and handling, to: Adams Media Corporation, 260 Center Street, Holbrook, MA 02343. U.S.A. 30-day money-back guarantee. BY FAX: 800-872-5628. BY E-MAIL: jobbank@adamsonline.com. *Discounts available for standing orders.*

Visit our exciting job and career site at http://www.careercity.com

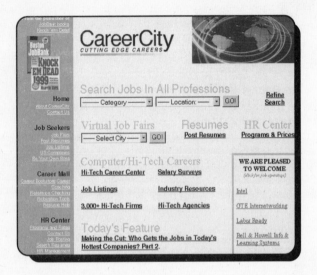